VARIETY
Film Reviews
1907-1980

A SIXTEEN-VOLUME SET,

Including an Index to Titles

Garland Publishing, Inc.
New York and London
1983

Contents

OF THE SIXTEEN-VOLUME SET

Film Reviews
1926–1929

VOLUME THREE

Garland Publishing, Inc.
New York and London
1983

Library of Congress Cataloging in Publication Data
Main entry under title:

Variety film reviews.
  Includes index.

  1. Moving-pictures—Reviews.   I. Daily variety.
PN1995.V34   1982   791.43′75   82-15691
ISBN 0-8240-5200-5 (v. 1)
ISBN 0-8240-5202-1 (v. 3)

Manufactured in the United States of America

Printed on acid-free,
250-year-life paper

User's Guide

The reviews in this collection are published in chronological order, by the date on which the review appeared. The date of each issue appears at the top of the column where the reviews for that issue begin. The reviews continue through that column and all following columns until a new date appears at the top of the page. Where blank spaces occur at the end of a column, this indicates the end of that particular week's reviews. An index to film titles, giving date of review, is published as the last volume in this set.

1926

"BEN-HUR"

A Metro-Goldwyn-Mayer production by special arrangement with A. L. Erlanger, Charles B. Dillingham and Florenz Ziegfeld, Jr. From the book by General Lew Wallace. Directed by Fred Niblo from the scenario of Carey Wilson. Adaptation by June Mathis. Titles by Katherine Hilliker and H. H. Caldwell. Musical score by David Mendoza and William Axt. Presented at the Cohan theatre, New York, Dec. 30. Running time 128 minutes.

Ben Hur	Ramon Navarro
Messala	Francis X. Bushman
Esther	May McAvoy
Mother of Hur	Claire McDowell
Tirzah	Kathleen Key
Iras	Carmel Myers
Simonides	Nigel de Brulier
Shiek Ilderim	Mitchell Lewis
San Ballat	Leo White
Arrius	Frank Currier
Balthasar	Charles Belcher
Madonna	Betty Bronson
Amrah	Dale Fuller
Joseph	Winter Hall

"Ben Hur" in film form has been years in coming to the screen; millions have been spent on it; one large film corporation as a result of its production was compelled to merge with another; actors and directors lost their reputations as a result of it; likewise others, also actors and directors, have made theirs. And it was well worth waiting all these years for!

Those who saw "Ben Hur" on the stage are the only ones that will realize what a really tremendous work has been accomplished through the screen production of the novel and play. Those who have through the years the play was the outstanding attraction on the road have been in the towns and smaller cities where it played, saw the mobs that gathered hours and hours prior to the opening of the doors to the gallery to get the cheaper seats that were unreserved, brought their own dinner in the form of sandwiches, so as to wait, will be the ones qualified to gather the tremendous sphere the present production of "Ben Hur" will have.

There will be no further reason for a future production of "Ben Hur" for the screen, unless there is some tremendous change in the art of visualization of the dramatic that is as yet unrealized. Then and only then, providing that there is some tremendous advancement in the art of direction and photography, will another "Ben Hur" be necessary. As the industry today stands, so does "Ben Hur" stand: the greatest achievement that has been accomplished on the screen for not only the screen itself, but for all motion picturedom.

The word "epic" has been applied to pictures time and again, but at the time that it was utilized there was no "Ben Hur," therefore you can scrap all the "epics" that have been shown prior to the arrival of "Ben Hur" and start a new book. This is the "epic" of motion picture achievement to date and don't let anybody tell you otherwise.

It isn't a picture! It's the Bible! And as does all literature as to fundamental plot come from the Bible, so does this picture above all pictures come from the same source.

"Ben Hur" is a picture that rises above spectacle, even though it is spectacle. When produced as a play the great Chariot Race scene was relied on to carry the play. On the screen it isn't the Chariot Race or the great battle scenes between the fleet of Rome and the pirate galleys of Golthar, which after all are the most tremendous scenes of this ilk that have ever been portrayed, that carry the great thrills. It is the tremendous heart throbs that one experiences leading to those scenes that make them great. It is the heart interest that has been inculcated into the silent presentation of Gen. Lew Wallace's tremendous play that make these scenes greater than any that have heretofore been photographed for projection.

It is the story of the oppression of the Jews, the birth of the Saviour, the progression of the Christus to the time of his crucifixion, the enslavement of the race from which Jesus himself sprang, and withal the tremendous love tale of the bond slave and a Prince of Jerusalem that holds an audience spell bound.

There is the kick and with it all a clutch at the throat that will bring tears to the eyes of the most blase and hardened, no matter be he Christian, Jew or Athiest. And the latter will possibly get the greatest kick of all out of this presentation. Surely there are none, no matter what their faith, creed or religious belief who can stand forth and say that there is a single moment or motif in this picture that gives offense.

In "Ben Hur" for all time the motion picture industry has an answer to the so-called reformer who cries that the industry is in the hands of the Jews. For never has the subject of the Christus been handled with greater delicacy, with greater reverence, or with greater splendor than in the handling of the scenes in which Jesus and the Virgin Mary are included. No matter whether it was in oils painted by those now immortal whose works now grace the greatest cathedrals of the world, or by sculptors whose works are the images at which we worship in our churches, those of us that are of the Faith, all that one will have to point to when accusations are made against the picture industry is the production of "Ben Hur" and say that those in control made it mattering not what their religion.

Their's was the money that financed this picture. Their's was the faith that placed more than $5,000,000 into its production. Their's was the faith that this story in which Christ, the Almighty, was so tremendous a figure that there was none other that could overshadow Him.

But aside from the biggest question of the picture, which naturally is the religious side, to return to the production itself: "Ben Hur" is the picture of pictures today. That isn't excepting "The Big Parade" or any other of the tremendous productions that have come forth in the entire life of the picture industry.

"Ben Hur" is a picture for all times. No matter what happens to others, "Ben Hur" will remain, as the Bible remains. There is a doubt in the writer's mind if "Ben Hur" will ever get to be shown in the picture theatres. It is a subject to remain in the legitimate theatre, the colleges, the schools and that ilk of community gatherings, but if it does eventually get to the picture houses, the prediction is made herewith that it will be more than three years before it does so. Those calendar periods of 1926, 1927, 1928 will have long rolled past before the regular picture theatres will get the production and that is something that one can have the greatest faith in that they ever had in anything.

"Ben Hur" will go down the ages of the picture industry to mark an epoch in its progress. An event that swung the tidal wave of humanity to the screen. The miracle picture that will convert the most skeptical.

In trying to describe the screen play itself one approaches a task that far more worthy fingers should try to pound out on a typewriter. To say that it is colossal, tremendous, terrific, magnificent, awe-inspiring, all means nothing. "Ben Hur" on the screen must be seen.

It immediately places Fred Niblo, who is given credit for the entire direction, in the class of the immortals among the directors of the screen. There always has been a question heretofore when a tremendous picture was turned out whether or not it equalled the things that D. W. Griffith has done in the past. This surpasses anything that Griffith ever did. Of course Niblo had the assistance of colors and the natural advance in technique, but when all is said and done, Fred Niblo today, after "Ben Hur," stands supreme among the modern directors.

The opening of the picture has scenes in old Jerusalem at the time of the exodus into Egypt, the passing of Joseph with Mary to his home, the appearance of the Star of Bethlehem and its guidance of the Three Wise Men to the scene of the Birth of the Saviour, and then with the passing of a score of years, a new era. The House of Hur, which has borne a long line of the Princes of the Blood, and Ben Hur, the youthful Prince, meets with his chum of years agone. The chum, Messala, has become a Roman officer, and would shun his companion of boyhood because the latter is a Jew. Yet he goes to his house and while there informs Ben Hur that he should forget he is a Jew. To which Ben Hur replies: "Forget that you are a Roman."

Thus starts the feud that finally culminates in the great chariot race at Antioch. But not before Ben Hur has suffered as a galley slave, with his mother and sister imprisoned beneath Jerusalem. Through all of the story the picturization carries a sustained interest that none can escape.

In detail there is too much in the picture to be conveyed in words. Suffice to say that there have been cheers at every performance since the day that the picture opened at the Cohan theatre in New York.

As to individual performance: first the Mary of Betty Bronson. It is without doubt the most tremendous individual score that any actress has ever made with but a single scene with a couple of close-ups. And in the color scenes she appears simply superb.

Then as to Ramon Novarro; he may never have appealed in former productions, but anyone who sees him in this picture will have to admit that he is without doubt a man's man and 100 per cent of that. Novarro is made for all time by his performance here.

Francis X. Bushman does a come-back in the role of the heavy (Messala) that makes him stand alone.

Don't let Bushy ever go back to the heroic stuff. He can land in that but if he will stick to heavies there is no doubt but with this background he will be the heavy of all times.

Nigel de Brulier gives a character performance as Simonides that is worthy of the greatest of artists, especially in the latter scenes of the picture. While as to Frank Currier as Arrius, all that it is necessary to say is "great," and he is all of that. If there ever was a true screen Roman, here is one, Mitchell Lewis as the great Sheik Ilderim carries himself well and scores to greatest advantage while watching the race scene.

Francis X. Bushman does a come-back in the role of the heavy (Messala) that makes him stand alone.

Don't let Bushy ever go back to the heroic stuff. He can land in that but if he will stick to heavies there is no doubt but with this background he will be the heavy of all times.

Nigel de Brulier gives a character performance as Simonides that is worthy of the greatest of artists, especially in the latter scenes of the picture. While as to Frank Currier as Arrius, all that it is necessary to say is "great," and he is all of that. If there ever was a true screen Roman, here is one, Mitchell Lewis as the great Sheik Ilderim carries himself well and scores to greatest advantage while watching the race scene.

As to the women, following Miss Bronson, May McAvoy in blond tresses as Esther deserves a full measure of credit for her performance. While Claire McDowell, as the Mother of Hur, and Kathleen Key, as his sister, both scored tremendously. But Carmel Myers, as the vampire Iras, looked a million dollars worth of woman and it is hard to understand how Ben Hur, even in the picture, could finally resist her.

There must have been considerable cutting in the final effort to get the picture down to the 12 reels as it is now at present, judging from the illustrations that appear in the booklet dispensed in the lobby. Both scenes and titles are missing. In some places the scenes are retained and other titles utilized, while in others the titles remained but are fitted to other scenes.

But in all it is a picture of pictures and certain to compel as wide-spread interest in the theatre as did the play in its time, only today the masses are greater and surely if there ever were a picture for the masses and classes alike, the young and the old, "Ben Hur" is it.

Fred.

"Ben-Hur's" force is its religion, and it's a tremendous force.

This Metro-Goldwyn picture could well have been called "The Birth of Religion" in a sub-title had its sponsors a desire to bring forth that side, which they have not. But it will speak for itself.

The chariot race, the slave rowers, three high, in the galleys; they are big and box office scenes, but religion here is the foremost and to the fore all of the time.

It must impress every sect, every faith, everybody. Degree of intelligence immaterial. For here is a picturized sermon embodying the spiritual that tells of the Beginning of Faith; tells everything to the eye that cannot miss the brain, and so emphatically, eloquently, artistically and picturesquely that it condenses into a pleasing sight all of the sermons of all of the clergy, ministers, rabbis and priests, within a single performance within a single theatre.

It might be ventured that Bob Ingersoll, atheist that he was, would have halted at this picture; he would have seen in "Ben-Hur" what no one could have told him or any other unbeliever. Not that those might reverse their belief, but this picture makes them believe in faith.

"Ben-Hur" as a lesson is a never-ending educator for good.

What matter the Chinese worship their idol or the barbarians the sun or the Gentiles Jesus or the Jews God? Those who worship, whether at altar or in pew, worship to their faith. Faith is humanity and humanity is the brotherhood of man—that's "Ben-Hur."

The church of any denomination or faith will get behind "Ben Hur." It's bigger than the book a Christian wrote; it's bigger than the play a Jew produced; it's the bigger lesson to teach the world, wide and far, what faith is, and as here adapted, directed and film-produced by Christians and Jews, bigger than all of the writings, all of the teachings and all of the missionaries.

"Ben-Hur" is the greatest single thing for religion, for the theatre, for the church, for the stage and screen, and for the masses, high and low, ever uttered.

Sime.

BIRTH OF A NATION

(3d REVIEW)

D. W. Griffith's picture first produced at the Liberty, New York, March 3, 1915. Based on Thomas Dixon's "The Clansman."

Currently at the Cameo, New York, week of Jan. 3. Running time, 134 mins.

Eleven years old next March and still a great picture.

The "Nation" was the first of the $2 pictures, and playing day and date with any of its modern sisters would still be considerable opposition on that basis. As showing at this house, or any theatre where it's playing on a "grind," the film is at a disadvantage because it never was and never will be a picture that can be walked in on. Besides which the musical score, still the greatest of all film instrumental accompaniments (and only rivaled by that turned out for "The Big Parade") needs a full orchestra to get it across. A pit group of 10 or 15 can't do it.

Shown as a "special," with a full orchestra, the backstage effects and missing the constant movement in the aisles to distract attention, there is yet a tremendous wallop to this Griffith release which all have strived for and not entirely obtained.

Two weeks after this film opened at the Liberty 11 years ago the picturization of the gathering of the clans and the mad galloping to a rescue pulled men out of their seats and made them yell. That was not witnessed just once, but several times. In Chicago, the first time it played there, two girls went into hysterics. At present there's a terrific kick to "The Big Parade" and they're yelling during the chariot race at "Ben-Hur," but it's doubtful if there has ever been or ever will be a picture that produced the succession of thrills this one did—and for so long a time after it was first shown—which may be, of course, because it was the first.

The "Nation" may be said to be something of a skeleton of its former self as showing at the Cameo. Despite the imposing running time of 134 minutes, it's been hacked and chopped for the deletion of valuable "bits." Some operator has spliced a strip of a battle scene upside down, and this print of the captions makes them hard to read.

No denying that the art of the camera has considerably advanced in the years since this one made its bow. That's obvious in some of the trick photography of the "Nation," although the double exposure battle stuff has a direct simile in some of "The Big Parade's" war shots, proving that exterior double photography as introduced by Bitzer is still the basis for such work.

Compare this Griffith 12-reeler to some of the present-day "specials" as to the money expended in the making and there's no comparison. The "Nation" is head and shoulders above them all under that specification despite that the buying power of the dollar has considerably lessened. The trade belief has always been that the "Nation" cost $100,000 or a little more to make, and then everybody in the film industry shook their heads upon learning Jeff McCarthy was going to try and "sell it" to the public at $2 the seat in '15.

That being so, look at the price list for some of the more recent big ones: "Ten Commandments," over $1,000,000; "Big Parade," $350,000; "Phantom of the Opera," $750,000; "Covered Wagon," $330,000, and "Ben-Hur," $5,000,000 (with few believing the latter figure possible). Looking at it from that angle, the "Nation" at $100,000 is still a world beater and will probably never be surpassed as regards production cost, while the resultant gross is now understood to be in excess of $4,000,000, with western territory, where it was sold on a state rights basis, not recorded.

It unquestionably rates with the modern films designated as legit house tenants. Two years ago when revived at the Apollo on 42d street with full equipment, "The Nation" was still the peer of them all, but now, with the advance made in producing these mammoth "specials," its technical deficiencies, in comparison, cannot be ignored. However, the manner in which Griffith told its story remains second to none.

Monday night in the Cameo it seemed that three out of five people had previously viewed it, judging from lobby remarks, and many declared themselves on the way it had been cut. The house was near capacity.

One slant on the "Nation" is that when it played at the Apollo those couple of years ago the Klan stuff had the house fighting itself because of the more or less rabid feeling over the K. K. K. at that time. Now, according to the way it was received at this house, it doesn't mean a thing so far as stirring up partial feeling on the matter is concerned.

The "Nation" is the grand old master. Jeff McCarthy handled it when it was new and is now supervising the only two pictures which may succeed to its past honors, "The Big Parade" and "Ben-Hur." What Griffith could do with Dixon's story on a bank roll and a remake assignment would be nobody's business. It would surely be handed down to posterity on that basis and its got a great chance now, simply on historical value if nothing else.

Jeff, you and I should tip our hats every time we pass a house where the "Nation" is billed. I do. *Skig.*

THE SEA BEAST

Produced by Warner Brothers, starring John Barrymore. Adapted by Bess Meredyth from the "Moby Dick" story by Herman Melville. Directed by Millard Webb. Previewed in Warners' projection room, New York, by invited group of newspaper people.

Ahab Ceeley....................John Barrymore
Esther Wiscasset...............Dolores Costello
Derek Ceeley...................George O'Hara
Flask..........................Mike Donlin
Queequeg.......................Sam Baker
Perth..........................George Burrell
Sea Captain....................Sam Allen
Stubbs.........................Frank Nelson
Mula...........................Mathilde Comont
Rev. Wiscasset.................James Barrows
Pip............................Vadim Uranoff
Fedallah.......................Sojin
Daggoo.........................Frank Hagney

For a reserved seat picture house "The Sea Beast" fits. Warner Brothers have chosen it for the Warner's on Broadway, opening January 15 as a twice daily performance picture theatre at $2 top. It is now playing Warner pictures under a grind policy at the usual admission.

A finely made picture and with a magnificent performance by John Barrymore, "The Sea Beast" firmly elevates itself above the regular program release while still not reaching the road show class. It's the type of film that lies within these two with "The Merry Widow" another (and also at $2 at the Embassy, with the Embassy a much smaller house than Warner's).

A gradual betterment in picture making and a demand for reserved seats in the larger city picture houses may bring about a string of reserved seats theatres for uncommon pictures that can not be exhibited for long runs in legit theatres. There may be from 12 to 16 cities in the United States capable of supporting the reserved seat theatre, giving the type of film it will play a run from four to eight weeks or longer. These cities will be far enough apart to be key towns for their territories, and if the distributor does not sell before showing, a reserved seat run is apt to increase the usual rental.

In "The Sea Beast" the Warners have a picture they can and do point to with much pride. It's picture making of the best, taking in land and sea, boats and whales. "Down to the Sea in Ships" was of whales but never a whale like "The Sea Beast." For this "Beast" was a notorious whale, a sharpshooting cuss of the ocean, with the records saying he had swam twice around the world on the underwater circuit.

Besides this whale when anyone went overboard while trying to catch him, would bite off a leg, the right leg, which was the kind of a sharpshooter he was, if a he. So many harpoons had fruitlessly landed in his skin that the whale if he would have remained still and out of the water long enough to have had his picture taken would have looked like a punchboard target.

And that's how John Barrymore lost a leg—the whale snipped it off, perfectly, after his villianous half-brother had viciously shoved John over the side of the boat John was trying to harpoon the whale from.

They got Mr. Barrymore back in the boat and at the finish of the picture Mr. Barrymore got the whale, once more while in the water. But he had to have a boat of his own and spend three years looking for the fish that grabbed his leg, before locating him.

Barrymore's expressions of suffering while having a tourniquet tied to his severed limb, and more so as they applied an antiseptic blazing iron to the raw flesh, are comparable to nothing that has been seen in a moving picture. While Mr. Barrymore's entire performance here, from method to make-up is worth a studious study, it's the kind of a performance that will interest those who believe in the physical person being necessarily present for conviction. "The Sea Beast" is very apt to draw from their seclusion that great class mass seldom seeing a moving picture.

A few tricks in the picture, but they will not be detected, for they are water scenes and required. A typhoon never has been better planted on the screen, while the whaling scenes with the harpooning are also a thrill. A love interest carries through and the story as adapted is exceptionally well done, possibly playing better than the book reads.

A general all around good performance and direction with photography attractive on many attractive scenes, on and off of the water.

This is a fine picture with drawing power, through itself and by virtue of the magic in the Barrymore name as well as his performance. This picture however without John Barrymore would have stood up—with him it's that much stronger, and a real result for a worthy effort by the Warners.

Sime.

A Kiss for Cinderella

Famous Players picture and Herbert Brenon production, featuring Betty Bronson, Tom Moore and Esther Ralston. Adapted from the play of the same title by J. M. Barrie. At the Rivoli, New York, as firm feature heading new regime of Balaban and Katz presentation program. Opening Dec. 25 for 10-day stay. Running time, 100 mins.

One of Barrie's whimsies that uses up too much footage in the telling. It perceptibly drags, for 100 minutes takes plenty of picture to hold a program house audience. At this theatre it amused, but would have been seen to much better advantage had 1,000 feet been chopped.

The punch is a comedy Cinderella ball wherein the house maid waif dreams her childlike obsession has come true. She pictures the characters confused with happenings from out of her dailyl life, herself being the central figure. The ball has been gorgeously done and mingled with the laughs is more than the usual splendor. But it's a long time in arriving and therein lies the fault.

In a London locale the action opens during the war with an air raid the initial attention demand. Tom Moore, as a policeman, investigates an unnecessary stream of light, finds the waif, becomes amazed at the girl's imaginative powers and furthers his quest until marriage is the final conclusion to be drawn.

Miss Bronson is splendid as the ultra imaginative waif, while Mr. Moore creditably balances her performance as the "Bobby." Other cast names were lost through the Rivoli having ceased to use programs, the cast insert on the screen being the only information.

The prestige of the Barrie name may explain the evident timidity in cutting expressed through the abundant footage. As it stands, it's a nice film but too fantastic in story to hold the masses. Besides which there's too much of it. *Skig.*

SOUL MATES

Elinor Glyn's story, "The Reason Why," adapted by Carey Wilson and directed by Jack Conway. Featuring Aileen Pringle and Edmund Lowe. A Metro-Goldwyn-Mayer production. At the Capitol, New York, week Jan. 3. Running time, 71 mins.

Velma..........................Aileen Pringle
Lord Tancred...................Edmund Lowe
Markrute.......................Phillips Smalley
Velma's Brother................Antonio D'Algy
Tancred's Mother...............Edythe Chapman
Velma's Maid...................Mary Hawes
Dolly..........................Katherine Bennett
Stevens........................Lucien Littlefield
Chauffeur......................Ned Sparks

It is noticeable that this production of an Elinor Glyn story is not made under the personal supervision of the author, as was the last one of her tales at the Capitol. That also was directed by Jack Conway. By making a comparison of the two it is easier to place the blame for the totally disconnected and exceedingly wishy-washy manner in which "The Only Thing" was produced.

This picture is much the usual Glyn twaddle, but that Elinor once discovered a tiger skin was more good on the floor than on a tiger's back undoubtedly gives her a standing with the flips and flaps of the Main Streets. When it is coupled, as it is in this case, with a title as fraught with possibilities as "Soul Mates" they will undoubtedly want to see the picture. But they are going to be disappointed, for there is about as much kick to this picture as there is to near-beer. The chances are that they'll go out and knock and the result will be little or nothing at the box office.

It is the old, old tale of a forced marriage with the bride rebelling, only different to the extent that in this case she did not marry to save the old homestead from foreclosure, but to assist a wealthy uncle in his social ambitions, even though he wasn't seen around in the picture after the marriage took place.

As a picture story this one is the bunk. Just material for a filler and that is about all that it will be looked upon as in the M. G. M. program. One couldn't expect the director to do any better with the material on hand. There were a couple of titles, however, by Joe Farnham that got laughs.

Aileen Pringle looked a bit tired and worn in the role of the bride, while Edmund Lowe looked as though he had stepped out of that column in the theatre programs headed "What the Well Dressed Man Will Wear," and counted on his clothes to carry him through the picture. Phillips Smalley possibly carried away the acting honors, while Ned Sparks, in a bit, ran second. If Katherine Bennett was the girl at the other table in the restaurant scene, then she topped the featured woman of the cast in the brief moment that she held the focus of the camera.

Don't bank on this one as a money-getter, other than what you can count on dragging in on the strength of the Elinor Glyn name, coupled with the title "Soul Mates."

Fred.

THAT ROYLE GIRL

Famous Players-Laskey release produced by D.W. Griffith as his for the firm. Based on story by Edwin Balmer. Scena 1st not credited on programs. Carol Dempster, W.C. Fields, James Kirkwood and Harrison Ford featured. At the Strand, New York, week Jan 10. Running time, 114 Minutes.

Joan Daisy Royle	Carol Dempster
Her Father	W.C. Fields
Calvin Clarke	James Kirkwood
Fred Ketlar	Harrison Ford
George Baretta	Paul Evert Jr.
Adele Ketlar	Marie Chambers
Cris Henchman	George Riges
Baretta's "Girl"	Florence Auri
Mrs. Clarke	Ida Waterman
Clarke's Fiancee	Alice Landley
Lola Neecon	Dorothea Love
Elman	Dore Davidson
Oliver	Frank Allward
Hofer	Bobby Watson

As "That Royle Girl" was run off at the Strand Sunday it went 114 minutes—a terribly long time to sit through any picture, no matter how good. The compensation for sitting through it all came near the end, when an old-fashioned cyclone scene was staged, better than usual. It is true, but still the old-fashioned, thrill-getting hokum which grew up with James A. Herne.

Aside from that and the performance by Carol Dempster, there's nothing to "That Royle Girl" worth saying much about.

It is just a long-winded film which gets all mixed up in the middle, starting out with a melting pot theme and then forgets all about it. The film also attempts one more explanation of the jazz-mad youngsters of this age. It is the poorest thing Griffith has turned out in a great many years—and one which can hardly be counted upon to stir up box office trade after the crowd drawn by his name has subsided.

Daisy Royle is the daughter of a crook. She meets Fred Ketlar, a jazz orchestra conductor, and falls in love with him. Ketlar's love for her is more or less physical.

Ketlar's wife is killed, actually by a gangster, but Ketlar is accused. In this way Daisy is implicated and meets Calvin Clarke, the district attorney. He falls in love with her, but struggles against showing it, and she finds in him the qualities she has always wanted.

So it works to the point where Daisy must prove to him that she is strictly on the level.

With a Chicago "Tribune" reporter Daisy disguises herself and sets out to trap the gangster who killed Mrs. Ketlar. She gets into a private party at a roadhouse and hears enough to get Ketlar released. As she is phoning a woman grabs her, thereby causing a ruckus, which makes Clarke think she was in danger. She was in plenty of danger, but after eluding everyone, a terrible cyclone came up and destroyed the adjacent buildings. Even after the gangsters had gotten her back and had cast her into a cellar, the storm continued with such fury that a flock of rafters fell on them and disposed of their villainy forever. Then came the district attorney and the clinch finish.

At least 30 minutes should be cut out of this picture before it is distributed generally, for neither the importance of the story nor the treatment it receives merits the extremely long running time.

In a vain effort to make a comedy, Griffith has dragged in W. C. Fields as the girl's father, but he doesn't belong in the picture, no matter how you look at it. He has nothing to do, and does it just like a man with nothing to do would do it. Harrison Ford as Ketlar is good, but James Kirkwood as the district attorney is off key.

With lots of running time lopped off and the whole thing recut in an effort to make the story tighter, "The Royle Girl" would qualify as a good program release, but even then the cyclone and melodramatic finish would be its actual redeeming features. *Sisk.*

MANNEQUIN

Paramount Production, presented by Adolph Zuckor and Jesse L. Lacky. From the Fanny Hurst Liberty prize story, adapted by Walter Woods, script by Frances Agnew. Featuring Alice Joyce, Warner Baxter, Dolores Costello and Zazu Pitts. Directed by James Cruze. At the Rivoli. New York, week Jan. 10. Running time, 04 minutes.

Selene Herrick	Alice Joyce
John Herrick	Warner Baxter
Joan Herrick	Dolores Costello
Annie Logan	Zazu Pitts
Martia Innesbrook	Walter Pidgeon
Terry Allen	Freeman Wood
Tote	Charlot Bird

This may be a $50,000 prize story, when the advertising angle is considered, but, as a straight story, had it appeared in any magazine and then been offered for pictures, it would have been handed the medal "old stuff." It even has a courtroom scene, and that is something almost passed out of pictures.

Fanny Hurst hasn't anything to be proud of in turning out this yarn. It is a wonder Jimmie Cruze managed to turn out a picture as interesting as it is with the material at hand. From a box-office standpoint "Mannequin" ranks as an average program attraction, and the exhibitor will have to judge whether or not the "Liberty" advertising splash is going to get any added money for him.

One thing "Mannequin" does do—it brings Dolores Costello to the screen in a role in which the girl has a chance to do something, and she may be the biggest bet that h[illegible] come along among the youn[illegible] eration of feminine screen players. She is a walloping hit in everything she does in this picture. Alice Joyce in a mother role also stands in the fore as an actress who should be praised, while Warner Baxter as the father handled his earlier scenes very well. But the character work contributed by Zazu Pitts is outstanding, next to little Miss Costello's contribution. Walter Pidgeon as the juvenile lead rather left something lacking in his conception of the role. Freeman Wood as the heavy overshadowed him completely.

"Mannequin" is the story of a half-wit nurse girl who steals the child of her employers and hides away with her in the slums, where the girl grows into lovely young womanhood. Her beauty obtains a position as model in New York's most exclusive shop. There she meets and falls in love with a young newspaperman, he in turn loving her. She advances the thought to him that, in the face of the many acquittals of good-looking women charged with murder, some big paper should advocate "sexless justice." He undertakes to wage the campaign.

In the face of it the girl, in trying to protect herself from the heavy, who has forced himself into her room, is charged with killing him, and thus becomes the first girl to face a jury on the "sexless justice" basis. But she is turned loose, just the same, and it is then discovered that she is the long-lost daughter of the judge who presided at her trial. Not much kick to that, is there?

But James Cruze has handled it in a way as to give the young girl every chance in the world to score, and she does just that. *Fred.*

"MIKE"

Metro-Goldwyn release written and directed by Marshall Neilan. A Neilan production. At the Capitol, New York, week Jan 10. Running time, 71 mins.

"Mike"	Sally O'Neill
Harlan	William Haines
Father	Charles Murray
Stinky	Ned Sparks
Tad	Ford Serling
Boy	Frankie Darro
Boy	Junior Coghlan
Girl	Muriel Frances Dana
Brush	Sam De Grasse

A rollicking sort of film held up by the comedy of Charles Murray and Ford Sterling. With Sally O'Neill and William Haines assigned to the love interest, the actual story is secondary to the antics of the aforementioned male duo. It's a railroad construction gang yarn in which the O'Hara family lives in a made over boxcar rigged up with many intricate appliances.

Laughs were plentifully sprinkled throughout the 74 minutes this feature consumed at the Sunday matinee and the house signed it off by an unmistakable mark of approval. However, were it not for Murray and Sterling the final verdict would be something else again.

Miss O'Neill caused some talk along "the street" through her performance in "Sally, Irene and Mary" but here reveals that she is not yet ready to accept the full responsibility of sustaining a feminine leading role. In this light vehicle she is cast in the title part, the somewhat tomboyish daughter of the construction gang's boss with two juvenile brothers and a sister to care for. When it's purely a matter of comedy Miss O'Neill seems at home, but in the more weighty moments there comes to view a lack of power which falls short of convincing.

On the other hand Murray, as the Irish gang boss, and Sterling, as his Dutch foreman, are all over the screen ably supported by laugh getting captions. Both are given plenty of footage to do a combined "stew" that continuously clicks and has the advantage of being "clean." As far as that goes the entire picture is above board, of the "innocent fun" type.

The kick Neilan has inserted comes with a train holdup after which a Marine Corps flying field is called upon to capture the auto fleeing bandits. For this passage Neilan has "shot" eight aeroplanes simultaneously taking off, in formation on the wing and for the final wallop eight parachute jumpers leaving the planes at the same time. It's pretty and effective, hence what matter if the human element is absent from the parachutes. It's a distant view so that all that can be seen are the white puff balls opening up for the descent. A neat idea which drew applause at this house.

The story is of a none too strong fabric weaved into the telling of "Mike's" l[illegible]ite of a sister saved from drowning in a canal by a vaseline haired wanderer (Mr. Haines). Having innocently served a prison term the traveller by request is up against it until the girl's father (Mr. Murray) takes him on as a member of his working crew. A flashback shows that prison was the result of the youth's having fallen asleep at his telegraph key after on duty for a stretch of 60 hours, without relief, and thereby causing a wreck on this same road.

In conjunction with the holdup, "Mike" flashes the news to the next telegraph station while the bandits lock both herself and the three youngsters in their boxcar and start it down grade on the main track. This leads to a train chase culminating in the rescue by means of the mammoth cup of a dredge being manipulated over to the boxcar so that Haines can pluck the brands from the burning, one by one as the wild boxcar and the rescuers on a flat workcar, race side by side. Enough of a thrill to hold.

Localed mostly out of doors this one should get off the "nut" early. It has been nicely photographed and capably titled but Murray and Sterling, two established screen comedians who here uphold their reputation, are the motive power which give this one its entertainment rating of okay. *Skig.*

THE WEDDING SONG

Cecile B. DeMille production directed by Alan Hale and released through P. D. C. Story by Ethel Watts Mumford. Leatrice Joy starred and Robert Ames, Rose Udami and Ethel Wales featured. At the Broadway, New York, Jan. 11. Running time, 65 minutes.

Hayes Hallam	Robert Ames
Old Themen	May Wells
George Pappadoulos	Jack Curtis
Ethea	Rose Rudami
Beatrice Glynn	Leatrice Joy
Paul Glynn, a crook	Charles Gerrard
"Mother," another crook	Ruby Lafayette
Madison Mellish	Casson Ferguson

One of the best program features flashed around New York in months.

Yet with all this value, it is shoved into a pop vaudeville house as the picture end of the bill. True, its title doesn't mean a lot and its star, Leatrice Joy, hasn't done a great deal in pictures lately, but that same Leatrice Joy just boosts her stock 500 per cent in this firm. And De Mille, comercially, will be the envy of the business if his unit keeps on turning out features this good.

That musn't be taken to mean that "The Wedding Song" is a big special. It isn't, but the entertainment value is solid all the way and the cast, photography, settings, story and scenario have been blended into what is an almost perfect entity. It may take some advertising and boosting to draw them in but it's a cinch they won't go out unsatisfied.

The hero, Hayes Hallam, is the owner of Vaimea Island, a pearl gathering spot in the Pacific. On his first trip to 'Frisco he is almost taken in a card game aboard ship when Paul Glynn, a crook exposes a card sharp who was putting the cards under the sheltering palms. Therefore, Glynn works in with Hallam and invites him as a family guest while in Frisco. His sister, Beatrice, is set to work on him, and things get to the point where she even marries him and brings the gang out to Vaimea isle as guests to make a big haul.

The plan is so well laid that a schooner has followed them to lie in wait for a getaway. But once married to Hallam, he trusts her so implicitly that she can't go through with the job. At last he finds out they're crooks and when he comes to the house to round them up he finds his wife with his pearls. Unfortunately, she was really innocent and had been trying to recover them from the rest of the gang. But he drove them all out into the rain and she had to come back and pull a bomb from under the house to prove that she had at last turned square.

It's a good picture story, the old stuff, perhaps, but done up brown in settings that are very colorful and filled with the atmosphere that they depict. Whoever photographed this did fine work and introduced something new to the business—the art of making men look as masculine as they should, instead of photographing them with that soft focus business which takes the beard off their chins.

The star, Miss Joy, gives a great performance and is sure of the every mood she is called upon to depict, while Robert Ames is a breezy hero, sufficiently ingenuous for the purposes of the story and then again, sufficiently strong to hold his own when things get tough. Everybody else all right, and if there is a discordant note in this one, it is hard to find.

But one thing. This picture doesn't claim to be anything else than a feature filled with entertainment. So this rave must not be misconstrued to the point where one thinks it is a $1,000,000 production. But for every dollar spent on it (and it is well put on) there is a dollar's worth of entertainment. *Sisk.*

WOMANHANDLED

Paramount production, presented by Adolph Zukor and Jesse L. Lasky, starring Richard Dix. From the story by Arthur Stringer, adapted by Luther Reed. Directed by Gregory La Cava. Running time, 70 minutes.

Bill Dana....................Richard Dix
Molly....................Esther Ralston
Aunt Abby....................Cora Williams
Gwen....................Olive Tell
The Kid....................Eli Nadel
Uncle Les....................Edmund Breese
Lucille....................Margaret Morris
The Butler....................Ivan Simpson
Pinky....................Edgar Nelson
Spike....................Tammany Young

"Womanhandled" is Richard Dix's answer to Gloria Swanson's "Manhandled." Both are by Arthur Stringer, and both appeared in the "Sat. Eve. Post," but where Gloria's picture was straight meller this one is a wow for laughs, and it gives Dix a chance to work like a house afire.

Incidentally it is Gregory La Cava's first production directed wholly by him, and it is safe to predict he is going a long way in making the pictures of the future. "Womanhandled" looks like a surefire box office bet anywhere, and where they like Dix it is going to knock the audiences for a row of water-towers.

Dix has the role of a wealthy New Yorker who gets his exercise and thrills by playing fast polo. He is a favorite with the ladies, and there have been any number of the ranks of the chorus to the society debs who have unsuccessfully set their caps for him. Then finally he meets a girl in Central Park, through rescuing her little cousin from drowning in the boat lake. She is the type that likes the big rough men from the West. She got that way reading Western novels and seeing westerns on the screen, so Dix as Bill Dana fits right into her scheme of things by doing a little lying and saying that the West is his meat.

He is so much in love that he even takes a rattler to Texas to the ranch of his Uncle Les. But the old place is changed. All the cowboys have gone to work in the movies and the old place isn't what it was. Cowboys there are, to be sure, but they are boys from New Joisey, and the Bowery, Noo Ywark, and they do their rounding up of the cattle in flivvers instead of on the backs of a bronc. Even the ranch house has steam heat, a bath, electric light and all the other modern conveniences. Therefore Bill decides that he is going back east, but just then a wire comes from his sweetie that she is on her way west to see the place for herself. That is where the fun begins. The ranch has to be transformed into the idea that she is carrying in her mind, and Bill proceeds to do it.

In the end, however, the girl gets wise to the plot and likewise to herself and all ends happily for both. The finish of the film, however, is a comedy wow in itself. A couple of bums sitting on a Central Park bench discussing the news of the day from a discarded paper that they have picked discover that Mr. and Mrs. Dana are going to be 'at home' at their Long Island place after the first of the month. To which one of the unkempt tramps remarks, "How very, very jolly," with which the picture fades out.

Dix is all over the lot in this one and does everything that his admirers want him to and, in addition, has a couple of comedy scenes that pull laughs. Esther Ralston looked like a million dollars in a couple of close-ups that La Cava shot of her, and played opposite to Dix in a manner that was most convincing. Little Eli Nadel as a precocious youngster was a howl and helped the comedy scenes along in great shape. Edmund Breese in the role of the western uncle contributed a corking performance. And last, and far from least, Tammany Young stuck over a couple of bits that planted him strong in the picture.

From a directorial standpoint La Cava didn't leave a thing wanting in the picture. He carried the story along at a pace that kept the audience either laughing or interested, and the weakest spot in the entire production was the cattle stampede when comparison is made with some of the big stampedes that have come along in the big westerns, but then this isn't a big western, it's a great comedy. *Fred.*

Lady Windermere's Fan

Ernst Lubitsch production from the play by Oscar Wilde. Adapted by Julien Josephson. Released by the Warner Bros. Running time, 79 minutes.

Lord Darlington....................Ronald Colman
Mrs. Erlynne....................Irene Rich
Lady Windermere....................May McAvoy
Lord Windermere....................Bert Lytell
Lord Augustus....................Edward Martindel
Duchess....................Helen Dunbar
Duchess....................Carrie Daumery
Duchess....................Billie Bennett

Judged from the standard of the usual product bearing the Warner Bros.' release marks this picture as far and away above the average of their product, but it is not as good a picture as one might have expected from Ernst Lubitsch. The trouble is not with the director, but with those who selected the story for him to direct. The tempo of this play is not that which Lubitsch can most effectively handle. Farce is his forte, and here they give him a comedy-drama which is in reality almost melodrama and expect him to be at his best. He is good, but far from at his best.

"Lady Windermere's Fan" is an English society drama. Beautifully cast in so far as the five leading players are concerned, well acted by them, and with clever touches of the director's art furnished by Lubitsch. The whole, however, finally evolves into nothing more nor less than a good program picture. It does not indicate that it will be a box office knockout at any stage of the game, although the first week of the New York engagement at Warner's will undoubtedly be big because of a combination of the holidays and the personal appearances of both Irene Rich and May McAvoy.

The story is that of a beautiful young wife who suspects her husband is carrying on an affair with another woman. Another man who is in love with her tips her off to look in hubby's check book and see if he hasn't been paying money to "the other woman." She does not know and never finds out that the "other woman" is in reality her mother, whom she has believed dead, mother having run off with a lover years before, but, returning broke, has decided to shake down her daughter's husband. When the crucial moment arrives and the daughter is about to repeat mother's mistake, the latter steps into the breach and at the risk of her future saves the day for the younger woman.

It is a different sort of a role for Miss Rich, that of the mother with a past. She has usually been a neglected wife and there seems no reason why on the strength of her performance in this production they should not go out and secure "Madam X" for her. She can play it and should mop up in the role. Ronald Colman as the heavy plays with a fine restraint and Miss McAvoy is most charming and effective as the young wife. Lytell is prone to overact at times, but in the majority of the scenes carries himself quite well.

Of the men, the one carrying the most conviction was Edward Martindel. Of the three gossipy old dowagers Helen Dunbar was the most effective.

Lubitsch in handling the scenes at the race track did most effective work, and the shots taken from the window in the apartment in which the wife sees her husband dismiss his own car and hail a taxi were also clever, as were the subsequent scenes with Miss McAvoy. Lubitsch had her use her hands in a manner that focused attention of the audience on them and they reflected most cleverly the emotions that the youthful actress was passing through. This was by far his best piece of direction in the picture. *Fred.*

Bluebeard's Seven Wives

Robert Kane production with Blanche Sweet, Lois Wilson and Ben Lyon featured. Story by Blanche Merrill and Paul Scofield. Directed by Alfred A. Santell. Released by First National. Running time, 72 minutes.

John Hart / Don Juan Hartes....................Ben Lyon
Mary Kelly....................Lois Wilson
Juliet....................Blanche Sweet
Gilda LaBray....................Dorothy Sebastion
Kathra Granni....................Diana Kane
Gindelheim....................Sam Hardy
Lem Lee....................Dick Bernard
P. Owers....................Andrew Mack
B. C. Duval....................Dan Pennell
Paris....................Wilfred Lytell

If this broad satire on pictures and picture folk is the type of material that we are to expect from the pen of Blanche Merrill then it looks as though Miss Merrill is pretty sure to score in filmdom as one of the authors who will be sought after. This is her first effort in writing for the silent drama, but without having ever been identified with the industry she has broadly satirized the whole in a manner that brought wow after wow of laughter from a Sunday audience at the Strand. The picture starts off like a house afire and only lets down somewhat at the finish, just when the audience wants the hero to turn with a twist and switch the tables on those who have directed his fate in the past.

Every angle of pictures is kidded. First the director with his army of "yes men"; then the sheik type of star, the press agent, the partners of the business of producing, the lovely leading lady and even the Pola Negri type of vamp.

The picture is a gag from start to finish, with the picture industry the butt of the joke.

John Hart works in a bank and is in love with the girl that browns the wheats in the window of a white front eatery. But love is a severe taskmaster and one cannot be in love and count nickels, dimes and dollars correctly. When the youth is found short at the bank he has to give up his savings and loses his job in the bargain.

Finally he takes a chance as an extra in a mob scene where they are shooting a picture and as the male lead fails to show, the director picks him and has him togged in the sta.'s costume. With the first scene the director discovers his protege has the divine spark and urges the owners to sign him immediately. Then the press agent comes in on the job and he immediately changes John Hart to Don Juan Hartez, the great Spanish lover. Plants him on an ocean liner and brings him to town.

It isn't long before Don Hartez mustaches and hair cuts are the craze and all the drug store cowboys are following the style. But the press agent hits on the brilliant idea of marrying and divorcing the star seven times in practically as many minutes, at least in the newspapers and thus the romance with the wheat browner is shattered. She still loves him and he is crazy about her, but picture business has forced them apart, until he in sheer desperation bolts the job, elopes with the hasher in a flivver coupe and the two finally settle down to a rube existence far away from the maddening crowds and the movies.

Ben Lyon handles his role here in corking style. The boy as the near-sighted begoggled stutterer is great. When he develops into Don Juan and "kisses 'em and then lets 'em drop" he's a scream. Lois Wilson is just too sweet in the ingenue lead and Blanche Sweet in the Juliet part with Lyon as Romeo went to the characterization as though she thoroughly enjoyed doing what was called for. Sam Hardy as the press agent slipped the snap and go into the role and just about hogged the comedy scenes of the picture. Dick Bernard and Andrew Mack were the producing partners and although Bernard injected some old fashioned horseplay he was in the main all that could be asked for while Mack delivered with a wallop. Dan Pennell, doing a burlesque De Mille, was a wow to the wise insiders.

In directing, Al. Santell carried the early part of the picture along at a tempo that was great and it was only the last few moments that lagged. *Fred.*

PEACOCK FEATHERS

Universal production, directed by Svend Gade and made from a story by E. Temple Bailey. Continuity by Gade and James O. Spearing. Jacqueline Logan featured. Running time, about 65 minutes.

Mimi LeBrun....................Jacqueline Logan
Mrs. LeBrun....................Helen Dunbar
Lionel Clark....................Youcca Troubetsky
Uncle George....................George Fawcett
Dr. Chandler....................Emmett King
Andy....................Ward Crane
Jimmy Chandler....................Cullen Landis

Svend Gade's last for Universal was "Siege," probably the best picture of program length U ever turned out, but the Swedish director has followed with a clap-trappy film of no especial importance.

The plot is of a poverty-stricken aristocrat, Mimi LeBrun, whose mother wants her to marry money. On the eve of her wedding she elopes with young Jimmy Chandler, who believes his Uncle George has left him a palatial home and ranch in California. Once they arrive there they find a tumbledown house surrounded by acres of land. Immediately the gal revolts.

In time she forgives her husband, for the deception was not intentional and things are going along okey when the jilted fiance heaves into view. For a few moments she thinks she will go back. Her husband isn't home. They sit down to talk. Presently the thin flame of a fire is seen on a snow-capped mountain, and she reads disaster to her husband. She shoves ex-sweetie aside, gets the ranch crew together and goes after him. He is found with a broken leg, and once more she decides to help him fight the battle that will make the ranch profitable. So the picture ends with the social butterfly determined to stick out the rough life of the ranch.

Not a convincing film, because neither Cullen Landis nor Jacqueline Logan put anything except day labor and mechanics into their work.

An unprogramed woman as the foreman's wife delivered a fine performance, while the director has inserted several touches which bolster up considerably. Some novelty in a fireworks display, but aside from that the film is set in the rut of mediocrity.

Of interest to lovers of good acting will be the appearance here of Prince Youcca Troubetsky, whose last work was in "Flower of the Night," with Pola Negri. He's stiff and cold. Although discarding the sideboards, he wears spats, carries a cane and has his hair plastered down. Ward Crane as the heavy gave good work, but his role was slight, while George Fawcett has the tiniest kind of a bit.

Maybe as a filler, but aside from that just another picture. *Sisk.*

INFATUATION

First National picture starring Corinne Griffith. Adapted from Somerset Maughm's play, "Caesar's Wife." Directed by Irving Cummings. Running time, 61 mins.

Violet Morgan....................Corinne Griffith
Sir Arthur Little....................Percy Marmont
Ronald Perry....................Malcolm McGregor
Osman Pasha....................Warner Oland
Lady Etheridge....................Clarissa Selwyn

Ronny's Sister..............Leola Lorraine
Pasha's Wife...............Claire du Bray

Not too interesting and being fairly actionless makes this just a so-so picture to be held up in those precincts where they believe Corinne Griffith to be the last word as a celluloid eyefull. A fair assortment of "names" should also aid in giving the film advance prestige, but it's actually a mild screen story without a kick.

It opens in Egypt in the midst of a rebellion. A flash-back informs that the battle is only a parlor story told in a London sitting room. Boosting the merits as a soldier of Sir Arthur Little (Percy Marmont) the tale fails to impress Violet Morgan (Miss Griffith) in his behalf but the dinner party brings these two together and the next flash is of them in Egypt as man and wife.

From there on it's the neglected wife seeking attention and getting it from the young attache (Malcolm McGregor). An attempt on Sir Arthur's life by a hidden marksman is frustrated by his wife whence the incident reveals to her that it is he whom she loves—and that puts this one away.

Cummings has extracted little action from the script mostly for the simple reason it isn't there. "Infatuation" unreels itself as one of those British parlor complexes switching to the Far East but still indoors. Miss Griffith looks good, as always, with no drastic demands made upon her to emote one way or the other. Mr. Marmont plays the "strong and silent soldier" and seems a bit miscast on a physique qualification. Mr. McGregor, as the youngster who becomes smitten with his superior's wife, has turned in as good a performance as the picture contains, the remaining characters being background.

The film may find an audience in England where they presumably dote on scripts pertaining to the foreign diplomatic service, but it's doubtful if the citizens of these states will perturb themselves about it. Minus the dialogue of the play it's something of a nicely produced dud, rating major house screening on the "names," but one of those pictures they'll never think of again after viewing it. *Skig.*

HANDS UP

Paramount (F. P.) Production, starring Raymond Griffith. From the story by Monty Brice. Adapted by Reginald Morris. Directed by Clarence Badger. At the Rivoli, New York, week Jan. 17. Running time, 61 minutes.

Confederate Spy..........Raymond Griffith
The Girl He Loves...........Marion Nixon
Other Girl He Loves...Virginia Lee Corbin
Mine Owner......................Mack Swain
Union General..............Montague Love
Abraham Lincoln............George Billings
Sitting Bull..................Noble Johnson
Brigham Young.........Charles K. French

Without doubt as good a screen burlesque of the Civil War as the "Battle of Too Soon" was a vaudeville comedy act. The picture is a succession of screams of laughter and Raymond Griffith just cuts another notch into his list of hits with "Hands-Up." There is a foreword on the film leader stating that certain liberties have been taken with historical facts which removes criticism through the use of the character of Abraham Lincoln. A clever touch in casting was registered here for they placed George Billings in the role of the president, the character he achieved fame in in "Abraham Lincoln" and the scenes in which he appears are shot with all seriousness.

As to the picture itself it isn't only a burlesque of the Civil War but of the wild and woolly west, Indians and all else in keeping with it.

The picture opens with a scene of a cabinet meeting in the White House with Lincoln glum and brooding, and his cabinet likewise. The Union without funds and little chance of raising any and the chances that they will have to let the South win the war. Pinkerton arrives. He has been on a secret mission for Lincoln and has learned that there is a tremendous gold strike in Nevada and that the owner of the mine is willing to finance the government. A Union officer is dispatched to bring the first shipment of gold East. It is to be a secret.

At the same time at the Confederate headquarters word has been recieved of what is happening and the army chief sends Raymond Griffith as his man to thwart the Union plans. Then the fun begins.

In the dash across the country, via wagon train, horseback and stage coach the two men meet. Griffith is captured as a spy and about to be executed. The way in which this gag is worked out brings laugh after laugh. Then the stage coach travel with Griffith seated with the two lovely daughters of the mine owner while their father and the Union officer are seated atop the vehicle. The attack by the Indians and the final rescue by the Confederate spy who shoots crap with Sitting Bull and wins his tribe from him, thus rescuing the mine owner and the two girls. Finally the scenes at the mine with the loading of the army truck with gold and the troubles in finally getting it started. Each one of these bits is worked out so as to obtain a maximum of laughs.

At the finish when peace is declared, the comedian has two girls on his hands. They are sisters, blonde and brunet. He loves 'em both. He's up against it for a moment until a stage coach drives up and out steps a bewhiskered individual who greets the girls, asks for their dad and then proceeds to introduce his wife, and his wife No. 2, and wife No. 3 and on and on, until a great light dawns on the hero of the story who takes the two girls, hops into the stage with them and the fade out shows the back of the stage coach disappearing with a sign on the back "To Salt Lake City."

Marion Nixon and Virginia Lee Corbin play the leads, opposite the star, with the former girl featured in the program and billing, although Miss Corbin registered better as to appearance and work before the camera. Mack Swain as the father of the girls contributes a great bit of western burlesque, while Montague Love does the Union officer with just enough swagger to make him laughable also.

However, it's a Griffith, and Griffith solely carries the picture.

Fred.

JUST SUPPOSE

First National release, produced by Inspiration Pictures, Inc. Richard Barthelmess starred in picturization of the stage play by A. E. Thomas. Directed by Kenneth Webb. At the Strand, New York, Jan. 17 week. Running time.. 71 minutes.

Prince Rupert of Koronia..............
Richard Barthelmess
Linda Lee Stafford...............Lois Moran
Count Anton Pechy (Toni)...Geoffrey Kerr
General Baron Karnaby.......Henry Vibart
The King......................George Spelvin
The Crown Prince...............Harry Short
Mrs. Stafford ....Bijou Fernandez
The King's Secretary....Prince Rokneddine

Richard Barthelmess is one of the really consistent stars in the picture world in that his vehicles generally strike a high level of entertainment value. "The Beautiful City," recently issued, was a bit slack, but preceding that he had turned out seven or eight humdingers in a row, and his stock was 'way above par.

Now, with Lois Moran as his right bower, Barthelmess has turned out "Just Suppose," and it takes rank as the best thing (from the public viewpoint) he has ever done. It is a sweet proposition, filled not only with sentiment but with a gentle whimsicality which both Mr. Barthelmess and Miss Moran express competently. The production is superb, ditto the direction, and the acting in every instance is of the best—and right here it is predicted that the week's receipts at the Strand (where a big revue is also on the bill) will reflect the merit of the show.

The story is that of a Prince who fell in love with an American girl On a mission here, he meets the sweet Linda Lee Stafford, and although he introduces himself as John Gregory she knew he was a prince. He visits at their house and remains overnight. With the arrival of morning comes General Karnaby, chief aide, with news that his brother in Europe has died and that he is now the Crown Prince, belonging to the state and no longer free to marry whom he would. Pathos and plenty of it, although it doesn't get maudlin.

Linda Lee hears of his new title with a breaking heart, the pain of which is reflected in as dainty a face as the projection machines have ever thrown to the screen. But the lovers part, and it is only several years later when she is summering in Austria that he dashes across the borders of his own Koronia to tell her that at last another heir has been born, and that he can with all honor renounce his rights to the throne.

That's a happy ending, something the play didn't have.

Barthelmess is great in every foot of film, and Miss Moran has not only the appearance of a girl who has been reared in a home and not in a studio, but her little face, while not the apex of beauty, is sweet and beatific. The girl is ideal for the part, and plays it so well that she shares the honors of the picture with Barthelmess. Geoffrey Kerr, who played the leading role on the stage, has a subsidiary part here, that of Toni, the Prince's confidential aide. Bijou Fernandez plays Linda Lee's mother, while Henry Vibart turns in a good piece of work as the gruff old general. Throughout it is all first rate, no shoddy anywhere, in either the production or the acting.

The continuity of "Just Suppose" is excellent, and any number of humorous incidents have been introduced which really belong. The production proper looks to have cost more than the usual Barthelmess films, but, then, the picture as a whole, is better than his usual releases (and the comment has already been made that they're usually fine), so the first runs should have no trouble turning in fine business When it gets to the daily changes its reputation will have been made.

Sisk.

VARIETEE

Berlin, Dec. 26.

"Varietee" is an Ufa film directed by E. A. Dupont, with Emil Jannings and Lya de Putti in the leading roles. It has been shown with good success at the Ufa Palast, and is a picture that will do very well in Germany and on the Continent.

For America it is a dubious proposition. You can sympathize with Mr. Laemmle's cutting department when trying to reshape it. The only way to get it over in America will be on Jannings' name.

The story concerns an acrobat who, attracted by a little Indian dancing girl, leaves wife and child to run away with her. They become members of a sensational acrobatic trio, the third partner of which is the conventional soft-soap movie villain. He seduces the girl. The acrobat finds it out and murders him. The last shot is in a prison years later. The deserted wife has succeeded in having her husband pardoned. He is free to begin a new life.

This rather banal story is told with a good deal of skill and much local color. Dupont has really done some splendid things, and there are moments that actually get you. The presentation of the vaudeville programs is most artistically done, somewhat in the modernistic manner of "Last Laugh."

But the film is much too long and often drags. The whole last revenge sequence, with Jannings continually glowering, is simply interminable. At least half an hour should come out. And not only that, the whole tone of the film is much too brutal for American taste. There is a frank lasciviousness and bestiality about it.

Jannings as the acrobat is splendid. He is a very great film actor, and will be even better when curbed. Lya de Putti does good and restrained work as the little oriental dancing girl. *Trask.*

THE SPLENDID ROAD

First National release, Frank Lloyd production, with Mr. Lloyd directing. Story by Virgie E. Roe. Featuring Anna Q. Nilsson, Lionel Barrymore and Robert Frazer. At Rialto, New York, week Jan. 11. Running time not caught—about 60 minutes.

Sandra Dehault............Anna Q. Nilsson
Stanton Halliday.............Robert Frazer
Dan Clehollis.............Lionel Barrymore
Banker John Grey..........Edwards Davis
Capt. Sutter.....................Roy Laidlow
Capt. Bashford............DeWitt Jennings
Capt. Lightfoot............Russell Simpson
Buck Lockwell.............George Bancroft
Satan's Sister............Gladys Brockwell
Angel Allie....................Pauline Garon
Lillian Grey...................Marceline Day
Hester Gephart...........Mary Jane Irving
Billy Gephart..................Mickey McBan
Dr. Bidwell.....................Edward Earle

Running a story for 55 minutes to build up to a big scene that flops with nothing much of anything, including action, before it in the mild melodramatic "Splendid Road" means the picture isn't there as a reliable first run for the big houses.

Enough acting and good enough acting by good-looking people and others, also a modicum of slapstick, consisting mostly of "falls." But neither or both can make up its deficiencies.

Though the first 15 minutes of the film were not seen, the last 45 tell that the first 15 make no difference in the general verdict.

It's about a girl named Sandra, who lived in California in a shack, taking care of a couple of kids she picked up somewhere. Looking for adventure, she ran into a divekeeper, besides a nice boy, and fell for the nice boy.

What the big scene meant to be was the overflow of the Sacramento River. At times it did look as though a couple of firemen were making quite a good job of flushing some studio street. The real flood looked like a small-time section of Niagara Falls caught from the sidelines. It's about the flattest big scene one could imagine.

Just what "The Splendid Road" was never did come out. According to the final caption it was the road to Oregon. There's a wallop for California back in '49, or even '69.

In production the picture is high grade and quite expensive. Anna Q. Nilsson gives a fetching performance as Sandra; Lionel Barrymore is doing a Frank Keenan western gambler that one could almost believe was Mr. Keenan himself, and Robert Frazer as the hero knocks out a couple of guys with one punch each, just to show the girl.

Of the others Pauline Garon makes her role of a honky tonk "entertainer" stand up. George Bancroft is the "falling" souse for the comedy. According to Mr. Bancroft that is the single way to get a laugh. Of the sizable remainder of the company they all did what had to be done, but none made it in any way exciting, nor did the director, Frank Lloyd, who must be held accountable for his flopping. This story would be vastly more interesting in book form than it now appears on the screen. *Sime.*

Arizona Sweepstakes

Universal production, starring Hoot Gibson. Directed by Clifford S. Smith. Story by Charles Locke. Running time, 57 minutes. At Loew's New York theatre one day, Jan. 12, as half a double bill.

Hoot Gibson stands second as a drawing card for Universal, according to Variety's story of a couple of weeks ago listing the stars of the different organizations for box-office values. That standing likely was determined on gross takings. If Gibson draws at all and it should ever be figured on the net he should lead the entire picture business, according to the cost of the "Arizona Sweepstakes" as it looks on the screen. Outside of the actors' salaries, it must have cost U a cup of coffee.

It's a funny picture, though, in a way, and with quite good comedy relief through introducing tough characters from the old Chinatown, San Francisco. Also three kidlets of one of the gangsters were laughmakers, from captions mostly.

Hoot as a cowboy from Ariz. visits Frisco, takes a sightseeing bus and becomes involved in a planted fight on the streets of Chinatown, put on to entertain the bus' customers. Hoot didn't know that until afterward. He was induced to remain in Chinatown and mix up similarly night for $10 daily.

This led to a fightingfest between two gangs. Hoot had to hide until leaving to ride the horse of his sweetheart's father, who owned the adjoining ranch to Bar Q, where Hoot was working for the villain of the picture.

At this juncture it sounded as though Kentucky had been moved to Arizona. But the race itself revealed roads, trails and hills Kentucky will never see. Hoot won the race, of course.

Hoot Gibson is said to be pretty strong in spots over the map. In those sections the comedy relief will save the picture. Otherwise his admirers will think he is loafing here. There isn't much wild west to the film.

Helen Lynch as his leading lady looked pleasing and didn't have to do anything else. Geo. Ovey gave an excellent performance as a crook, and Kate Price as mistress of the ranch's kitchen stuck in several laughs.

For those who like Gibson, an ordinary picture; for those who don't care, less; for U as a production, great. It could not have been made any cheaper if they had used a stereopticon. *Sime.*

The Unguarded Hour

First National picture produced by Earl Hudson. Directed by Lambert Hillyer with Milton Sills starred and Doris Kenyon featured. Story by Margarette Tuttle. Running time, 70 minutes.

A Yeggman	Jed Prouty
Another	Tammany Young
Russell Van Alstyne	Cornelius Keefe
Bryce Gilbert	Claude King
Countess Bianca	Dolores Cassinelli
Duke of Arona	Milton Sills

It seems almost any picture shoved into the Rialto has a curse on it. Of course, the house gets second runs occasionally from the Rivoli, but nine times out of ten, the pictures are shoved in the 42nd street house because they're not strong enough for the major of the F. P. Broadway duo. In this instance, the film is a First National product and maybe it is one that the Strand sidestepped—and wisely. For it is neither fish nor fowl—neither comedy nor drama and at its best, a machine made story badly produced.

An illustration comes at the beginning of the film, which shows an outside view of the Gilbert home. The shot which the camera took was a painted drop—somebody being too lazy to dig up a town house which would suit the purposes of the single shot.

The plot concerns Virginia Gilbert, harum-scarum daughter of Bryce Gilbert. At the opening she is holding a big dance in the family house—her guests being thugs and yeggmen for which she advertised. Her idea was that with such guests she would get a thrill. Then the next sequence shows her boy friend in the throes of an elopement, but papa walks in and this doesn't come about.

Then she goes to Italy, making the trip from Naples to a country estate in an aeroplane—of which many close-up shots are made. These shots are poorly done and a canvas background with its wrinkles shows up clearly. Her arrival at the country place is heralded by an accident—for the aeroplane bumps into and breaks off a high radio tower.

Her fall down is done for comedy and when the hero (Milton Sills) discovers her, she is caught in the fork of a tree. Sills is cast as an Italian Duke interested in radio.

In Italy there is a Count Stelio, naughty with the women. Before long he has one gal in trouble and tries to conquer Virginia. But she scraps and then in walks the Duke, who chases Stelio, only to find out a moment later that the gal in trouble has committed suicide. A letter which she leaves behind implicates Stelio and as the Duke advances to crush his bones, Stelio goes over a balcony and falls to his death on the pavement below. And then the film is ended with a comedy scene which follows directly after the two deaths.

Sills isn't fitted to this part by any stretch of the imagination. Miss Kenyon is excellent all the time and it probably isn't her fault that she is close-upped to death. Her role isn't especially logical but she makes it seem so. Claude King as her father is also good—which goes for Tammany Young. For comedy, incidentally, the director has Tammany duplicate the Harpo Marx comedy trick of dropping silverware from his sleeves and pockets.

"The Unguarded Hour" is set up as the antithesis of that "guarded" hour when girls resist going wrong. The title hasn't much to do with the picture, but then the picture hasn't much anyway. So it's 50-50. *Sisk.*

The Ancient Mariner

Fox production based on Samuel Taylor Coleridge's poem. Modern treatment by Eve Unsell. Story by Chester Barnett. Directed by Henry Bennett. Running time, 65 minutes.

Modern Sequence

Doris	Clara Bow
Victor Brant	Earle Williams
Joel Barlowe	Leslie Fenton
The Skipper	Nigel de Brulier

Ancient Mariner Sequence

The Mariner	Paul Panzer
Life in Death	Gladys Brockwell

Sea spirits, ice spirits, animals, the albatross, etc.

This film was designed as a Christmas proposition, and has the theme of charity running through it, the "Ancient Mariner" tale being utilized to illustrate the point of the modern sequence.

A man of the world tries to carry off an innocent country girl. To stop him, an old seaman tells him the story of the ancient mariner who shot the albatross, a bird which symbolized everything good. After he shot the bird, all the misfortunes of the world descended on him—he froze and then burned in the tropics—he saw visions of water and reached to find there was none. And only when he repented and was truly sorry did he get a break.

So in the modern sequence the villain was about to misuse the girl who had once saved his life and who had nursed him through blindness. But he heeded the seaman and in the end told the young boy who loved her that she was his.

The theme itself is old fashioned and poorly handled. The fantastic sequences, which illustrate the old poem, are good in spots, but the direction has been too loose, and the actors run wild. Some of the individual shots are good, but many are taken in miniature and show it plainly. At other times, painted sets were used for what should have been natural scenes and this cheapens the effect.

The one bright spot is a group of kids in several school room scenes. There are three or four who compare with the best of the juveniles in "Our Gang." Of the players Clara Bow does the best, while Earle Williams' attempt at a comeback is not altogether successful. For one thing, his mustache is unbecoming.

"The Ancient Mariner," at the Circle, a neighborhood house drawing an audience of working people, was jeered at several times. *Sisk.*

THE ENCHANTED HILL

Famous Players' production made from the story by Peter B. Kyne and directed by Irvin Willat. Jack Holt and Florence Vidor featured. At the Rialto, New York, Dec. 27. No programs available. Complete cast, therefore, is not set down. Running time, 68 minutes.

Lee Purdy	Jack Holt
Gail Ormsby	Florence Vidor
Shannon	Noah Beery
Todd	George Bancroft
Jasper Doak	Brandon Hurst

Another of the western series which Famous has made this year—and about on the same mediocre level as the rest. Here the old story of the good man who tried to protect a lady who had been told he was bad is related. The by-plot concerns his fight against certain villains who were trying to force him from his "enchanted hill" property by various threats. In the end he convinces the girl that he's as fine as they come and he routs the villains. Then, to make the honey taste sweeter, one of the bad boys tells him the real reason they were trying to make him give up his ranch was because a heavy coal vein ran through it.

Jack Holt is a modern ranch owner with flying machines and a machine gun instead of pistols. His performance is good, and Miss Vidor also does well, but Noah Beery as a vacillating bad man whose loyalty was measured by money, was most amusing, and George Bancroft was leery looking as another bad boy.

The direction is probably as good as the script deserved, for the whole story is pretty old stuff, and whatever draw it picks up will be due to the cast, which is good. Hardly first run material, but may be okeh for the daily changes. Its hackneyed plot won't make people talk, and, on the other hand, the even pace of the action won't make them walk out.

So it's an in-betweener. *Sisk.*

KEEP SMILING

Monte Banks production presented by Howard Estabrook. Story by Herman Raymaker and Clyde Bruckman. Directed by Akbert Austin and Gilbert W. Pratt. Running time, 59 minutes.

Monty	Monty Banks
James P. Ryan	Robert Edeson
Rose	Anne Cornwall
Gerald Deane	Stanhope Wheatcroft
A Double-Cross	Glen Cavender
Bardanni	Donald Morelli
Mother	Martha Franklin

One of those "built to order comedies" for a former two-reel comedian. The trouble with it is that they have stuck to two-reel methods in making a six-reel picture. Whoever is responsible for that must also be adjudged responsible for this picture not hitting a little better to the important money than it has.

Monty Banks shows nothing in the way of screen personality that should entitle him to get over in an ordinary picture, therefore if they want to get him across they will have to go after a type of story that is more potent than this one. On the screen the star also takes part credit for the story. Maybe that is what is the matter with the picture. There are, however, a number of good hearty big laughs in the picture for the audiences that frequent the smaller houses.

Banks is the type of screen comic that Dallas Welford was stage comedian when he first came to this country, and he should have the Welford type of material. Maybe they could dig up and adapt "Mr. Hopkinson" and possibly "30 Days in the Shade," both of which Welford did and which were funny. They would fit Banks and could be jazzed and gagged sufficiently to make them screen well.

This present one of his is so palpably an elaboration of what might have originally been a two-reeler that it creaks at the joints as far as the story is concerned and the last 20 minutes of it are given over entirely to a motor boat race filled with gag stuff.

The story deals with a boy who, because he was aboard a steamer that sank when he was a youngster, has a tremendous fear of the water. He sets as his object in life the invention of a lifesaving device that cannot fail. When he has perfected it he goes to present it to a millionaire ship-builder, is mistaken for a motor boat race driver, who is expected and forced into driving the speed boat of the millionaire. He does it, wins the race and the millionaire's daughter's hand.

Robert Edeson, as the millionaire, lends class to the picture. Anne Cornwall looked a little tired in the ingenue lead. Stanhope Wheatcroft, as the heavy, registered well enough. Banks pulled all the regulation falls and flops and what not that goes with the slapstick films, most of it unfunny. There was one touch of laughter in the dancing scene. In the race a couple of gags also brought laughs.

To fill in where there is a daily change of program it will get by if the audiences are not too particular. *Fred.*

BORROWED FINERY

Tiffany Production from the story by George Bronson Howard, directed by Oscar Apfel. All-star cast. Shown at the Stanley, New York, Jan. 18, one day. Running time, 70 minutes.

Sheila Conroy	Louise Lorraine
Channing Maynard	Ward Crane
Harlan	Lou Tellegen
Billy	Taylor Holmes
Mrs. Borden	Hedda Hopper
Maisie	Gertrude Astor
Mrs. Brown	Trixie Friganza

Little bit Potash and Perlmutter in spots, the two characters in the cloak and suit business decidedly remindful of Montague Glass' partners. But the picture is far better than the average feature one finds in the independent market. It has its laughs, some thrills and a bit of society action. For the average daily change house it will stand up with any of the program features that some of the big companies turn out.

A little model working "by cloaks and suits" borrows a gown to attend a millionaire's party. At the party she meets a crook who poses as a government agent and he enlists her as one of his assistants. He likewise secures an invitation to a country house over a week-end so that she will be able to obtain the necessary "evidence" that the wealthy widow, whose guest she is to be, smuggled a jewel of great price into the country.

In the end she and the crook are lined up and captured but the detective is in love with the girl, and she believing him a wealthy young man about town is likewise smitten. After the capture she makes her get away and later as she is about to take back her old modeling job the copper walks in on her and takes her to City Hall where a license is issued for their marriage.

There may not be so much kick in that but it is pretty cleverly handled in direction and the interest is fairly well sustained through the little more than an hour that the picture runs.

The cast looks strong enough to get some money at the box office. Lou Tellegen as the crook character handled himself with sufficient suggestion of mystery to get away with the heavy role. Ward Crane was the hero and just about got away with it. Taylor Holmes is a grouch hubby who is trying to keep a wife, two kids and a flat going on a bookkeepers salary and not getting away with it, playing the role with sufficient punch to make it register.

Trixie Friganza as a portly matron always telling about her operation, got what laughs there were in the picture. Working with a little short chap opposite her she wowed every time she hit the front of the lens. One cannot, however, hand Louise Lorraine anything as the lead in the picture. Gertrude Astor looked a whole lot better and could have handled the role to better advantage. *Fred.*

The Bashful Buccaneer

Rayart picture, made by Harry J. Brown. Reed Howes starred. Directed by Mr. Brown. Running time, 55 minutes.

Jerry Logan	Reed Howes
The Girl	Dorothy Dwan
Ship's Mate	Mitchell Lewis
Sailor	Bull Montana
Another Sailor	Gunboat Smith

Reed Howes was well known at one time as a male model for the Arrow collar advertisements. When he entered the movies with this as his sole claim to fame there was considerable pooh-poohing in wise circles. Rayart began using Howes as a stunt man, and right away his stock began to rise. Not only was he a fine stunt man, but he had good looks and was a passable actor.

If you look over most of the screen's stunt men you'll find that they're funny looking chaps with short, stocky legs, the neck of a bull and the general build of a circus strong man. Howes, on the other hand, is tall, muscular and yet not noticeably stocky, and if the camera isn't too deceptive, does his own stunts.

This latest of the series is a light affair which has him cast as a novelist whose latest book described a treasure hunt. Not long after he runs across two old sailors who tell him of a treasure island, and, fired with the spirit of adventure, they start out with a crew hired at one of the employment agencies. Of course, there's a girl on board, and there's also a parrot, this bird having the secret of the island's location. The parrot talks, giving the latitude and longitude, and then the crew of gorillas pull a mutiny.

Trouble, and plenty of it, which gives Howes a chance to climb all over the ship's rigging and fight in almost every spot. These high altitude fights are all great, while several others fought on deck are also good.

When the treasure island is approached the mutineers are in control of the ship, but the hero and his crowd escape in a rowboat and reach the island first. And from the top of a hill they see other men digging out a treasure chest. Looks like a real kick, but they are only motion picture actors playing scenes. Though this is somewhat of a let-down from what was expected, it provides for the happy ending, the rout of the villains and a slow fadeout.

Dorothy Dwan is a nice feminine lead, while Bull Montana, Gunboat Smith, Mitchell Lewis and several other tough-looking men provide the villainy, which is strictly elemental but good. So "The Bashful Buccaneer" frames up all around as a neat release of the popular-priced style.

And it shows that Howes is fast acquiring the reputation as the best stunt man in pictures. *Sisk.*

THE WINDING STAIR

William Fox production, written by A. E. W. Mason, directed by John Griffith Wray. Features Edmund Lowe and Alma Rubens. Running time, 63 minutes.

Marguerite	Alma Rubens
Paul	Edmund Lowe
Patras	Warner Oland
Gerard	Mahlon Hamilton
Mme. Muller	Emily Fitzroy
Onery	Chester Conklin
Andrea	Frank Leigh

One of those romantic melodramas with war as a background. It starts with the Morocco wars, with the French Foreign Legion battling nobly, and winds up in the trenches of the World War, where the hero vindicates himself for what is looked upon as a previous desertion from the ranks. From a box office angle the picture will make good in the daily change houses, where they like action and are not too strong on the details of story, and in addition there are three names the exhibitor can play up: Edmund Lowe, Alma Rubens and Mahlon Hamilton.

The cast does not do any extraordinary work anywhere. Lowe is prone to overact at times, Miss Rubens has nothing but her camera stare and Hamilton is rather stiff throughout.

Lowe as the hero is an officer in the Foreign Legion who falls in love with a dancing girl in one of those places that abound in Morocco (at least it would seem so from looking at the pictures that have scenes laid in that part of the world). He is ordered to the hills to quell an uprising among the natives, but discovers that this is only a ruse to draw the troops from the town.

When his superior officers won't listen, he deserts his own command and returns to the town to save his sweetheart and likewise the day for the Christians, who have been attacked by the natives.

For deserting he is cast out by his fellows and lives as a native until the World War starts, when he organizes his own command of natives and offers them to France under an assumed name. They are accepted. On Flanders field he performs such deeds of valor that his country again accepts him under his true name and restores his honors as well as his citizenship.

John Griffith Wray tried hard in the direction to get something into it that hadn't been done before, but even he could not find it, so he had to have Alma do a couple of parades in a clinging nightie. That helped some.

Chester Conklin, with some comedy stuff as the "sweet poppa" of the Madame of the dance hall, came in for a number of laughs through a couple of falls that he did over the place. *Fred.*

THE SCARLET SINNER

First National production supervised by Earl Hudson. Adapted from Gerald Beaumont story, "The Man Who Played Fidele." Directed by George Archinbaud, with Mary Astor and Lloyd Hughes featured. Running time, 70 minutes.

Fidele Tridon	Mary Astor
Philip Collett	Lloyd Hughes
Baron Kurt Badeau	Frank Morgan
Anton Tridon	Jed Prouty

This is a First National film, which in the ordinary event of things would have gone into the Strand, New York, for a week. As it is, the picture split honors at the New York with an independent release, "The Bashful Buccaneer," and came off a poor second. So maybe Joe Plunkett does the right thing by shelving a First National once in a while. For this one is mediocre throughout and wouldn't stand a chance in a first-run house.

The story concerns Fidele Tridon, whose father promised her in marriage when she was a child. When she reached womanhood Baron Kurt Badeau, to whom she had been trothed, came to claim his future wife. In those growing up years she fell in love with Philip Collett, a wealthy sportsman whose hobby was horses. That made the count angry, so he framed Collett into a duel and then faked a wound, the police being called in, etc., and things began to look bad for Collett.

Several reels of suspense and in the end, true love won. Matter of fact, the actual suspense was killed when the Baron framed the duel, for he revealed his villainous character at that time and didn't have a chance to crawl back into the shell behind his mask-like face.

The players are all good, but the direction is off key. In the tense scene which worked up to the duel, the Baron's valet is used for comedy relief and pulls one offensive gesture—thumbing his nose in the middle of a scene which should have been dramatic. Such stuff isn't strictly refined in any serious picture and this lays claim to being in that category.

Mary Astor and Lloyd Hughes are okeh as the lovers, but Frank Morgan, a corking legit player, walks away with acting honors as the baron. Jed Prouty kicks in a good performance as the girl's father, while minor characters do well. There's considerable race horse atmosphere in the film, and scenes shot on a race track near New Orleans furnished some excitement, but that's about as far as the meritorious portion of the picture goes.

"Scarlet Sinner" is well produced and on this item may be able to slide by in the daily changes. *Sisk.*

WAGES FOR WIVES

One of the William Fox Golden Series Productions. Based on "Chicken Feed," by Guy Bolton. Adapted by Kenneth B. Clarke. Directed by Frank Borzage. At Loew's Circle, New York, on double feature bill, one day, Jan. 18. Running time, 72 mins.

Nell Bailey	Jacqueline Logan
Danny Kester	Creighton Hale
Hughie Logan	Earle Foxe
Luella Logan	Za-Su Pitts
Jim Bailey	Claude Gillingwater
Chester Logan	David Butler
Annie Bailey	Margaret Seddon
Carol Bixby	Margaret Livingston
Mr. Tevis	Dan Mason
Judge McLean	Tom Ricketts

"Wages for Wives" is a picturization of the play "Chicken Feed," the basic plot of both may or may not have had their origination in the old Franklyn Ardell vaudeville sketch which had a wife going out on strike on her husband. However, the material at hand makes a corking picture for laugh purposes in the popular houses. The plot is interesting and carries behind it an idea that many a middle-class wife in a small town may relish and delight in taking her husband to, especially if he is the type of hubby in the picture. The cast is fairly strong in names and the picture looks strong enough to play any of the bigger neighborhood houses without the aid of a secondary feature, as was the case at Loew's Circle in New York.

The story is of a young girl about to be married, but who has watched the wedded life of both her older sister and her mother and noted the manner in which her father and her brother-in-law held out as far as money matters were concerned. Because of the object-lessons, she informs her husband-to-be that she will not go through with the ceremoney unless he will split his weekly salary 50-50 with her. When he refuses, egged on by his father-in-law and brother-in-law that were to be, the wife decides to call all bets off and, in addition, gets both her mother and sister to go on strike, taking them off on a vacation. A series of comedy situations develop from this, and in the end both sides are about willing to give up most anything providing that a return to normal home life can be arranged.

Jacqueline Logan as the ringleader walks away with things, while Za-Su Pitts as the sloppy sister was a laugh from start to finish. Margaret Seddon played the mother role to perfection.

The men, however, carried the picture along. Creighton Hale as the sappy bridegroom-to-be got laugh after laugh, while Earle Foxe in the role of the brother-in-law and David Butler as his brother were 100 per cent in the roles assigned them. Claude Gillingwater as the grouchy old man gave the type of finished performance that he is noted for. Dan Mason as the village gossip, little more than a bit, registered very well. *Fred.*

SWEET ADELINE

Chadwick Production, starring Charles Ray. Story and continuity by Charles E. Banks. Directed by Jerome Storm. At Loew's New York Jan. 14, one day. Running time, 63 minutes.

Ben Wilson	Charles Ray
Bill Wilson	Jack Clifford
Adeline Reynolds	Gertrude Olmstead
"Puffy"	Gertrude Short
Bates	Theodore Lorch
"Maw"	Ida Lewis

This follows "Some Punkins" in the group which I. E. Chadwick made for Ray. While it follows the cut-and-dried style of the pictures which made this young actor famous, it is also a bright and breezy light comedy-drama.

The story is that of the country boy whose big brother continually lords it over him. But the kid happens to be a member of the town quartet, and, with the aid of a prop violin in his bedroom, keeps the old tenor up to a good me-me-mee condition.

With ambitions to sing, he goes to Chicago and into a cafe, where the manager puts him on as a freak country kid trying to sing. He flops and everybody jeers. Backstage he grows resentful, so off comes the collar and up goes the courage. Then he steps once more before the curtains and sings "Sweet Adeline" so that everybody is stopped, and the impresarios present know one more great voice has been discovered.

Just a simple little story told in a simple manner and filled with those little incedents which Ray plays so bashfully and well. His performance is okeh, and Gertrude Olmstead is his nice leading woman. The other rural types are good.

Production, while not lavish, is adequate and of a sufficiently entertaining nature to be all right for the daily changes. *Sisk.*

When Husbands Flirt

Waldorf production made by C. B. C. Directed by William Wellman and produced by Harry Cohn. Dorothy Revier and Forrest Stanley featured. Running time, nearly 60 minutes.

Henry Gilbert.................Forrest Stanley
Charlotte Germaine...........Maud Wayne
Wilbur Belcher...............Thomas Rickets
Mrs. Belcher....................Ethel Wales
Mrs. Gilbert...................Dorothy Revier

A neat and unpretentious little comedy, made and released independently, which manages to pack a consistent flock of laughs and satisfy the audience.

The story concerns an old husband who is rather reckless and his lady love, Mrs. Germaine. In some way her card case got in the auto of his son-in-law and the wife saw it—immediately accusing (in her mind) her own husband of the "chasing."

Soe goes to see the Germaine woman, who calls up the old man, telling him that his wife has been to see her. Thus it goes—the old man's wife is advising her daughter to divorce her husband, while the young husband is trying to help the old boy.

Various devices are resorted to so that the conflicting characters will be brought together, and although the whole business is filled with hoak, it still gets over. Possibly its only fault is a tendency to prolong some of the action.

For stage purposes, if this hasn't been used before, there are the makings of a first class farce which would allow for plenty of spice, etc.

Dorothy Revier is the young wife, and good, but Edith Wales and Thomas Rickets, as Mr. and Mrs. Belcher, are the funniest.

Nice picture of the economical sort and suitable for the daily changes where they will take a good piece of entertainment, even if its cast isn't of starring quality. *Sisk.*

THE SKYROCKET

Associated Exhibitors, Inc., production, starring Peggy Hopkins Joyce. From the story by Adela Rogers St. Johns. Directed by Marshall Neilan. At the Colony, New York, week Jan. 24. Running time, 77 minutes.

Prologue

Rose Kimm...............Gladys Brockwell
Edward Kimm...............Charles West
Sharon Kimm............Muriel McCormac
Mickey.....................Junior Coughlan

In the Story

Sharon Kimm.........Peggy Hopkins Joyce
Mickey Reid........................Owen Moore
Lucia Morgan...............Gladys Hulette
Mildred Rideout.............Paulette Duval
Ruby Wright................Lilyan Tashman
William Dvorak.............Earle Williams
Sam Hertzfelt..............Bernard Randall
Stanley Craig....................Arnold Gregg
Peter Stanton.......................Benny Hall
Vladmir Strogin................Nick Dandau
Morris Pincus.................Sammy Cohen
Film Comedian.................Bull Montana
Comedy Director...............Eddie Dillon
Comedy Producer..................Hank Mann
Sharon's Secretary...........Joan Standing
Wardrobe Mistress........Eugenie Besserer

No question that Peggy Hopkins Joyce in "The Skyrocket" is going to be sure fire at the box office. If repeating in picture then Peggy will have to develop a little more picture talent along acting lines than displayed in this production.

At present, however, when Peggy comes before the camera she has two strikes called on her before lifting a bat. She looks good, even in the cheap little suit that she wears early in the picture, and when in real clothes she looks like a million dollars' worth from the beauty angle at least.

But Peggy has not quite grasped the trick of getting over on the screen. She photographs beautifully, but there is in the main a lack of expression and personality to get over her points.

From a publicity and box office angle, she should mop up at the box office for any exhibitor, and the smaller town the more certain they are of cashing, for the smaller towns never had a Peggy Joyce. This girl has obtained possibly more publicity than any other woman of her years, outside of screen stars, and she has not appeared in pictures heretofore. She has been on the stage, but only for a single season as a star, of a revue.

The story in which she debuts was picked with care, for it is an inside story of the rise of a picture star. It reveals the inner workings of innermost Hollywood. This, coupled with the Peggy Hopkins Joyce name, should make it a pipe.

Peggy is an extra girl trying to break into pictures. When she finally does get her chance she immediately becomes high-hatty as do so many of the overnight rich of filmdom. At the finish she flops with the weight of bankruptcy and topples from her highhorse, likewise true of a number of those stars once. Then she reveals her true self to her childhood sweetheart and is ready to begin all over again.

The idea of seeing Peggy fighting to protect her virtue from the director who made her on the screen and who threatens to unmake her should be enough to jam any house, and the chances are that it will go a long way toward doing so.

In lining up the supporting cast for the first picture for this star, a number of names have been secured, to carry her along. They weren't necessary. P. H. J. was all the name needed. But, on the other hand, the cast with her does corking work. The two kids in the prolog, Muriel McCormac and Junior Coughlan, do stand out for what they do. Then, in the story itself, Owen Moore as the lead was all that could be asked, while Earle Williams, as the heavy, was more than satisfactory. Paulette Duval, in a little more than a bit, registered with a resounding wow, while Gladys Hulette, playing in almost every scene with the star, seemed to steady her down to a certain extent. Sammy Cohen, in a comedy bit as an assistant director, hit a bulls-eye with what he had to do.

Don't forget when you get this one all that you have to do is to go out after it. Let them know that Peggy Joyce has come to town and they'll come to get a flash at her, and she's worth looking at, too!

Fred.

AMERICAN VENUS

Famous Players production from a story by Townsend Martin and produced to incorporate the last Atlantic City beauty contest. Adapted to the screen by Frederick Stowers and directed by Frank Tuttle. Esther Ralstons, Lawrence Gray, Ford Sterling and Fay Lanphier ("Miss America" featured. At the Rivoli, New York, week Jan. 24. Running time, 70 minutes.

Mary Gray....................Esther Ralston
Chip Armstrong............Lawrence Gray
Hugo Niles.......................Ford Sterling
Miss America..................Fay Lanphier
Miss Bayport...................Louise Brooks
Mrs. Hugo Niles..........Edna May Oliver
Horace Niles...........Kenneth MacKenna
John Gray..................William B. Mack
Sam Lorber...............George DeCarlton
The Artist............Wladislaw T. Benda
King Neptune.............Ernest Torrence
Neptune's Son, Triton..................
Douglas Fairbanks, Jr.

This is the long-heralded exploitation special of Famous Players—the picture to afford a million tieups for publicity and other purposes. Its chief tieup so far has been with the alleged expose of the New York "Graphic" of the last beauty contest in Atlantic City, in which, the "Graphic" charged, Fay Lanphier's selection was prearranged.

That has nothing to do with the picture.

Out in the sticks the beauty contest stuff may mean something, but on the merit of the film itself there are grave doubts. It is a milk and water story well done, but disappointing because of the generally weak yarn. The plot concerns two rival beauty cream factories out west. A son of one proprietor is engaged to marry the daughter of the other. This engagement is called off. A publicity man annexes himself to the minor plant and almost puts over the owner's daughter as "The American Venus." The plan was to have her endorse a cold cream and, on that basis, sell millions of jars, thus putting the other man out of business. But the girl's father became ill and she was called back home, going to Atlantic City the second time, but arriving too late for the final.

Her friend, "Miss Alabama," wins. Although the heroine has had an accident and is confined to her room, the winner endorses her father's cold cream gratis.

Some comedy because of Ford Sterling and Edna May Oliver. Sterling plays the wealthy cold cream magnate, and Miss Oliver is his wife—one of the type who hot-foots it behind the husband. Kenneth McKenna does a great job as their straight-laced son, but Lawrence Gray and Esther Ralston walk away with the real honors.

The pageant scenes are in color, some well done and some rather garish. The actual Atlantic City stuff wasn't much of a thrill. The producers tried to stress the undress angle by showing a series of supposedly thrilling "tableaux vivants." There was naked stuff in these and it may get censors sore in the more puritanical regions. As for the New York censors, they let anything and everything go through. It's different elsewhere, in several states.

Whether its exploitation values mean anything to the box office is for the exhibitors to judge. Aside from these values, whether they are legendary or real, the picture itself is an in-betweener, with a few laughs and no real dry spots, but on the other hand no really hilarious moments. Just lots of female flesh and silk bathing suit beauties, all dressed so that the maximum of sex appeal will be reflected on the screen.

It may give some of the old boys a kick, and then again it may not. *Sisk.*

NELL GWYN

Presented by British National Pictures, Ltd., starring Dorothy Gish. From the story of Marjorie Bowen. Scenario and direction by Herbert Wilcox. Special presentation at the Ritz Carlton Hotel Jan. 25. Running time, 82 minutes.

Nell Gwyn.......................Dorothy Gish
King Charles II..............Randle Ayrton
Lady Castlemaine.........Juliette Compton
Mrs. Gwyn................Sidney Fairbrother
Toby Clinker.........................Judd Green
Dickon.........................Edward Sorley

This English screen production of "Nell Gwyn" is going to lead a great many people to believe that they have discovered a new Dorothy Gish. But she is the same Dorothy Gish as always, but here at last has come a part that gives this consummate screen player a chance to really show what she can do. "Nell Gwyn" on the screen as played by Dorothy Gish is going to do as much to bring Miss Gish back as the presentation in this country did to bring Pola Negri to these shores and to make a screen star of her in the American sense of the word.

As for "Nell Gwyn" itself and as representative of the advancement of British photoplay production, it simply goes to prove that the English have grasped the idea of sexy stuff and proceeded to undress their players—or, at least, some of their women players—and if not to actually undress them, at least give the suggestion of undress. That Nell was the mistress of the king is not left to the imagination, even though it is not expressed in so many words in a sub-title; but the action conveys the story completely.

In the high spots (the de luxe houses) "Nell Gwyn" should get money, and a lot of it. The picture as it stands could go into any of the Broadway houses and go for two weeks, taking in the biggest house.

Just what its fate will be in the smaller houses is going to be something of a question, but the chances are that Dorothy Gish's name and her extraordinary performance here will bring it through a winner. True, it is a costume picture. One knows what the average exhibitor says about "those French Revolution pictures" (to the exhibitor anything in costume is French Revolution), but this one seems to have enough of that something in the sex line to overcome the costume handicap.

A pretty touch of sentiment about the presentation of the story. The little opening and closing shot of St. Martin's, London, with the tolling of the chimes, is most effective. The story takes Nell as an orange girl at the door of the Drury Lane, her gamin battle for existence amid poverty, her meeting with King Charles, her rise as his mistress and her unfailing loyalty to the people from whom she sprang and the monarch to whom she remained true, even in death.

All is told with a touch of comedy amid historic fact. The clash between Lady Castlemaine and Nell for the affections of the King is the principal theme. The bit with Nell on the stage of Old Drury, burlesquing in exaggerated costume the affections of Lady Castlemaine, is superbly handled.

As a matter of fact, there isn't a single fault to be found with the direction of the picture in any manner.

But it is to Dorothy Gish that the greatest tribute should be paid. Superb isn't the word that fits her performance; tremendous would possibly more actually convey the work she does. She is at once Gish, Pickford, Negri and Swanson in one. Incidentally, Juliette Compton as Lady Castlemaine is a bet that shouldn't be overlooked, for that girl looks like a million dollars, and she can troup. Both of the ladies are most generous in the display of their feminine charms. It is quite possible there may be a little censor trouble here and there in th.s country on some of the scenes.

Randle Ayrton in the role of the King registered emphatically. He is of the Holbrook Blinn type and rather suggests him, so finished is his work.

Sidney Fairbrother plays Nell's mother, a character part, while to the lot of Judd Green and Edward Sorley fall the two character roles of the old soldier and sailor.

To Herbert Wilcox and the British National Films, Ltd., it must be said that "Gwyn" is the first British picture this reviewer has seen, coming from the British Isles, that seems to have a chance in the best houses in America. "Nell Gwyn" not only has that chance, but should more than make good in those houses. *Fred.*

DANCE MADNESS

Metro-Goldwyn Mayer picture; Robert E. Leonard production, directed by Leonard. Features Claire Windsor and Conrad Nagel. Adapted from story by S. Jay Kaufman. Photographed by John Arnold and William Daniels. At Capitol, New York, week of Jan. 24. Running time, 74 minutes.
J.P. Smith .... Conrad Nagel
May Anderson .... Claire Windsor
Bud .... Douglas Gilmore
Valentina .... Hedda Hopper
Strokoff .... Mario Carillo

You wouldn't, or couldn't, call this one a new idea in screen narration, but the production behind it, Conrad Nagel's light comedy and the general studio treatment it has received make it a fit program leader.

It's frothy entertainment, and, while no one will ever pick it as among the best films of the year, it will amuse despite that the script keeps "telegraphing" its punches.

It's the young married couple thing with the wife doubling as her husband's flame of the moment to win him back. Constance Talmadge did a dual role in such a celluloid opus as this not so long ago, and Manhattanites are more or less familiar with Molnar's "The Guardsman," hence the novelty of the thing may be said to have its restrictions. But there's no dual role in "Dance Madness," and Nagel gives it a nice gait by means of excellent pantomiming.

Pictorially the film impresses. The interiors, and it's mostly indoors, are lavish, while Arnold and Williams have cranked to obtain good results.

Errors of makeup creep in every so often with the fault or laxity of the players in omitting to apply the chemicals to the nape of their necks proving eyesores, too obvious to be ignored. It detracts from the illusion on the screen.

And that's not to say that "Dance Madness" is the only offender in this respect. Film players, in general, seem loathe to place makeup on the back of their necks, mayhaps because they have no intention of turning their backs on the camera. But sometimes it happens. And the result is odious. In this instance the fault is with the minor roles.

The narration starts to get funny when the young couple (Miss Windsor and Mr. Nagel) are in Paris during their second wedded year. The bridegroom succumbs to the urge of his bachelor days and is smitten with the masked dancer in a show. The routine is not long in dawning on the wife. She pays a visit to the mysterious beauty, to find that the latter is the wife of her former ballet teacher. Thence the plot to frame the husband.

Nagel plays this writing for its full worth, and Leonard, the director, has given it momentum that builds as it progresses. It's as amusing as it is obvious, and for that achievement someone should get the credit. Therefore it looks like a split between the director and the male lead.

Because Nagel runs away with

the picture it is not to say that Miss Windsor is here incompetent. To the contrary; a nice, even performance is her contribution, besides which she wears an abundance of clothes that seem somewhat extreme in design at times and should either vehemently please or displease feminine viewers. The deduction is that the girls out front will keep looking, not an unimportant item.

The list of principals being small, their activities are as limited. The whole matter revolves around the newlyweds, the remaining members almost classifying as atmosphere.

Kaufman, in turning out this yarn, programed as an "original," has donated a well-knit story, and the captions have a tickle or two of their own. *Skig.*

THE YANKEE SENOR

William Fox production starring Tom Mix. From Katherine Fullerton Gerould's novel, "Conquistador," adapted by Eve Unsell. Directed by Emmett Flynn. At the Rialto, New York, week Jan. 24. Running time, 62 minutes.
Paul Wharton .... Tom Mix
Manuelita .... Olive Borden
Luke Martin .... Tom Kennedy
Juan Gutierrez .... Francis McDonald
Flora .... Margaret Livingston
Don Fernando Gutierrez .... Alec Francis
Doris Mayne .... Kathryn Hill
Abigail Mayne .... Martha Mattox

A Tom Mix starring picture that has been lifted above the average story and production Fox has given this star heretofore in the regular run of westerns. It is a class picture, made that way by just a little touch of Technicolor in the production. It is a shot showing a Mexican fiesta and in natural colors reveals the vari-colored garments of the players in amazing fashion.

Story is corking with sufficient suspense to make one wonder which girl the hero is finally going to grab off in the finish. From a box office angle the Tom Mix name is enough, but coupled with the snappy production this should be a top money getter.

With it all it is an action picture with the punch present right from the start. Emmett Flynn, who directed, and the star saw to that.

The action opens with Mix acting as the general manager and paymaster of a railroad construction gang. He is a soldier of fortune, his natural inclination being the Latin countries, because of his parentage. His mother was a high caste Mexican and his father a New Englander. Both are dead.

A letter from his mother's father has followed him across the world. When it reaches him, he is at the head of the railroad gang.

About this time a bunch of bandits arrive on the scene intent on copping the pay roll. Mix fools them as far as the money is concerned, but they wreck the camp.

He then seeks out his grandfather, who has adopted a foster child, and when the Yankee-Mex makes himself known he is taken to the old man's heart. He tells him his story of the bandit raid and how he fooled the gang. When he returns to get the money his foster uncle goes with him. The uncle is in reality the head of the bandit gang, and he plans to kill two birds with one stone. Mix is bound to a wild horse and is doing a male Mazeppa when Tony comes to his rescue and saves his life.

From then on it is nip and tuck between Mix and Unk. Money and women play the principal pawns between the two, finally winding up with a corking rough and tumble fight, with Mix the victor.

Olive Borden is opposite Mix. At first she is the betrothed of the Unk, but falls in love with the newcomer, and when he brings a girl from Boston on the scene, there is the deuce to pay. The Unk, foxy greaser, brings in a dancing dame to vamp the ridin' kid. She does her best to put over the little job for him and evidently because she

would like to do it, but when turned down she gives a corking imitation of the well known "hell hath no fury, etc." Margaret Livingston handles this role nicely.

Kathryn Hill, as the Back Bay lady, leaves much to be desired, although in the color stuff she looked fairly good. Tom Kennedy and Francis McDonald handle the heavy work, the latter getting his role over with atmospheric clarity.

A touch of comedy is added through the dragging in of a dirty story that is cleaned up and suggested. It's the old gag of "boys will do anything for a jack-knife," so they have the aunt of the Back Bay lady, an evident spinster, carrying a load of pocket knives into Mexico with her. Martha Mattox, in this role, gets a couple of touches over that implant the jack-knife gag.

In all, this is one of the best Mix westerns that has come along in some time. *Fred.*

FLAMING WATERS

Associated Arts Production released by F. B. O. From story by E. Lloyd Sheldon, adapted by Fred Myton, directed by Harmon Weight. Shown in projection room Jan. 22, 1926. Running time, 63 minutes.
Dan O'Neil .... Malcolm McGregor
Doris Laidlaw .... Pauline Garon
Mrs. O'Neil .... Mary Carr
Jasper Throne .... John Miljan
Midge .... Johnny Gough
Mrs. Rutherford .... Mayme Kelso

"Flaming Waters" is one of those good old fashioned melodramas that pulls at the heart strings and in the end has love and virtue triumphant, after the hero and shero have passed through all the trials and privations, pitfalls and whirlpools that villian can provide. This is frankly one of those pictures, but sufficiently well done to attract business in the average type of neighborhood house.

A couple of spots where the picture would have been better off for a little judicious cutting and undoubtedly the passing up of the tinting in the moonlight and fire scenes would have also helped, especially as in the spots where this effect was used it did not jibe. However, these are moderate defects that can and undoubtedly will be readily remedied.

The story is a tale of the sea and the oil fields. The hero (Malcolm McGregor) is the son of a woman who lost her husband at sea and her only thought is to make it possible for her boy to remain ashore. While he is on a voyage she invests in worthless oil stock. Her boy returns to find his mother dispossessed from the cottage he had provided for her and working as a washerwoman.

He hears the tale of the swindle and starts out to find the swindler. This leads them to the oil fields, where, after a succession of thrills, fights and a heavy rescue through the "flaming waters," he wins out, also winning the hand of the daughter of a big city capitalist.

The first thrill comes along in the second reel with a runaway automobile stage racing down the side of a mountain. Lot of kick to this. The second is a three-to-one fight, about a reel later, where, strange to say, the hero is not the victor. Additional fights later, and for the big wallop the rescue of his mother and his sweetheart from a building set amid a flow of burning oil.

Mr. McGregor handles the heroic role very well. Mary Carr, as his mother, won sympathy, but Pauline Garon looked far too sophisticated as the ingenue lead. The girl was positively hard-faced and utterly lacking in sympathy when most needed. John Miljan, as the heavy, delivered 100 per cent. He was the heavy of the old ten-twenty-thirty days, long cigaret holder, moustache and all. Johnny Gough in a character managed to score.

The picture is rather well directed in spots. While it does not look to

have cost a million to make, it certainly has some big stuff that will appeal to the fans. *Fred.*

BLUE BLOOD

I. E. Chadwick Production from the story by Frank Clark. Directed by Scott Dunlop. Starring George Walsh. Shown at the Stanley, N. Y. (25-cent grind house), one day, Jan. 21. Running time, 72 minutes.
Robert Chester .... George Walsh
Geraldine Hicks .... Cecille Evans
Percy Horton .... Philo McCullough
Delight Burns .... Joan Meredith
Leander Hicks .... Robert Boulder
Tim Reilly .... Harvey Clark
Amos Jenkins .... G. Howe Black
Charley Stevens .... Eugene Borden

An action melodrama with all the hoak in the world in it. It is a picture just about suited for the rind houses. Had it been a little more skilfully directed it would have stood up a little better, but the story and the direction just about pull every bit of action that there is in by the roots. The name of George Walsh, however, may pull some money, but other than that there is nothing in the picture to be counted on.

The entire production is shot in exteriors with the exception of a ballroom shot or two, so in that respect the cost was held down. It is the story of a chewing gum king who takes his daughter to a coast resort in California and meets there what he thinks is the malted milk king. He wants the latter to marry his daughter, but she is not so keen for him. In reality, he is a bootlegger. On the road, she meets a young scientist who is spending the summer hunting bugs and butterflies. She falls for him, and he rescues her from a couple of situations.

Mr. Walsh is the young scientist, and he combines all of his athletic activity in this production. At times George, with goggles, looks like a heavier edition of Harold Lloyd, although he doesn't give us the laughs that Harold does. At that it might not be a bad idea for Walsh to be starred in a series of athletic and sporting event comedies, where his well known prowess might be utilized to advantage.

The balance of the cast means virtually nothing. Cecille Evans, who plays opposite the star, looked good in a bathing suit, but that about let her out. Philo McCullough, as the heavy, over registered his villiany, and Robert Boulder, as the "popper," was a complete flop. A comedy character played by Harvey Clark, was also overdone, the direction relying on impossible horseplay in an effort to get it over, something that it failed to do.

Walsh, in providing thrills, did a little mountain climbing, swimming, some acrobatics on the sandy beach, took the heroine up in a flying machine, drove a motorcycle with a bathtub side car in which he had his negro servant packed for laugh purposes (here were a couple that did get over) and finally went on board a yacht and put up a fight with a couple of tough eggs to rescue the girl.

It's the hoak, but the kind that they want in the cheaper type of grind houses. *Fred.*

THE CHECKERED FLAG

Banner Productions picture, distributed through Apollo. Adapted by The Hattons from a story by John Mesereau. Featuring Elaine Hammerstein and Wallace MacDonald. Directed by John G. Adolphi. At Loew's New York theatre Jan. 19 as one-half double bill, single day. Running time not caught. Around 60 minutes.

Fair picture for the daily change houses, "The Checkered Flag," carrying some good names in its staff and playing cast.

Its story is heroic, of a mechanic who invents a carburetor and enters his own car with it in a race that also has the car of his prospective father-in-law entered.

Some villainy and the _river of the principal contender, Jack Reese, is spirited away, as in most race pictures, but here another channel has been gone into. The boy's fiancee drives the racing car for him, unknown to anyone—and winning.

The race is the main thing, and, of course, an insert, but wit the semblance well maintained. Audience is unaware who is driving the "27" car until the disclosure.

Miss Hammerstein looks well; Wallace MacDonald is a nice juvenile for it, while Lee Shumway and Lionel Bellmore also do good work.

A bit of comedy relief was nicely written by the Hattons (much better than they adapted th; story). This company could have handled anything given it, but not much was given to handle.

Anyway, not a bad picture, and stood out strongly at the New York.
Sime.

A Desperate Moment

Banner Productions picture, distributed through Apollo. Features Wanda Hawley and Theodor Von Eltz. Directed by Jack Dawn. At Loew's New York theatre, New York, one-half double bill, Jan. 19. Running time not caught. Around 55 minutes.

Seems a pity that such a picture as this should be turned out by anyone, especially an independent. How in the name of Heaven, , anything else, will the independents ever contrive to establish themselves if they make a picture like this, for any reason?

Off-hand and bluntly, after looking at this picture, one can only surmise that some one with a b...nk-roll turned up and they spilled the money, uselessly and foolishly, into "A Desperate Moment."

The Banner Productions can't be an amateur or a first timer, since on the same bill at Loew's New York they had another, "The Checkered Flag," and not a bad picture for the daily change houses.

It's not nice to tell exhibitors in print not to play "A Desperate Moment," but that is just what it amounts to. Any audience will either yawn over or kid it; none can like it—there's nothing to like in it.

Everything about the film is silly, from its story in the first place to the direction, with naught between excepting some fair acting, with Wanda Hawley in on that. Is this a return for Miss Hawley? Or a come-back? She's playing a daughter here, and fairly looks it, doing quite well otherwise, but Miss Hawley is too experienced a trouper not to have sensed that this one wasn't right.

There's some sea stuff, a fight with stowaways, poor fire aboard ship, landing on a desert island with canibals and other Robinson Crusoe stuff, merely nauseating in its implausibility, from any angle, even the cheapness of it all. But the inexpensiveness could easily be overlooked were there anything to sta...l up alongside of it.

While the picture isn't worth this space, it may be worth it to advise independents who are struggling and must do the best they can, with that end thoroughly understood, not to grab the first thing offered. Much more pleasant to favor independents when possible. A picture like this would frighten off the biggest moneyed chump who ever fell for picture making. It's of the vintage of 1915.

Not even for the hideaways, and the best it can hope for is $7.50 now and then in a one-night jerktown.
Sime.

THE RECKLESS LADY

Robert Kane production made for First National release. Story by Sir Phillip Gibbs, and scenario by Sada Cowan. Directed by Howard Higgin. At the Strand, New York, Jan. 24 week. Running time, 81 minutes.

Mrs. Fleming, the Reckless Lady...........Belle Bennett
Colonel Fleming...........James Kirkwood
Sylvia Fleming...........Lois Moran
Count Feodor...........Lowell Sherman
Ralph Hillier...........Ben Lyon
Sophie, the maid...........Marcia Harris
A Gendarme...........Charlie Murray

This one, although a corking good picture on its own account, looks like an effort to cash in on the "Stella Dallas" theme and the use of its two leading players, Belle Bennett and Lois Moran.

The leading strain is that of the careless mother who did wrong and who grew away from her child—an adorable little person whose life came close to being thrown away once she learned of her mother's reputation.

The girl had fallen in love with a fine and decent boy, Ralph Hillier. When discovering her mother had gambled for years just to support and educate her she called upon Count Feodor, a rather greasy looking Russian, and offered herself in marriage.

In the finale the mother is reunited to her husband (who left her when he found the count was his wife's lover). As the film closes the count is in the precarious predicament of a man hanging loosely onto vines trailing over a deep ravine.

There's a fine cast in this picture and it is also well directed. To make it stronger—the scenario is good most of the way, except that there is about 100 per cent. more kissing and hugging in the last reel than should be allowed.

Miss Moran as the daughter turns in another of those wistful performances, fast making her famous. Miss Bennett again plays her mother, just as she did in "Stella Dallas," and does a good job of it. There is a remarkable resemblance at times between Miss Bennett and Miss Moran and their coiffure in this picture add to the likeness. Ben Lyon is the young hero. Lyon is a static actor with a one-way expression. You either like him or you don't, but he seems established at the box office as a popular juvenile and his appearance here is justified. James Kirkwood, with white hair, etc., is the father, while Lowell Sherman can be counted upon to draw the shopgirl trade with his Russian count characterization. Sherman's features do not film well and his rather heavily lined face takes on a certain unpleasant grossness in pictures. Which probably explains the failure of those vehicles in which he has starred alone.

"The Reckless Lady" is a much better picture than those produced by the average First National units. That it represents a considerable outlay in salaries is apparent from the cast, while the physical end of the production has not been slighted.

Qualifies for the first runs as a good attraction. *Sisk.*

EIN WALZERTRAUM

Berlin, Dec. 28.

"A Waltz Dream," adapted from the libretto of Oskar Strauss's operetta by Robert Liebman and Norbert Falk. Directed by Ludwig Berger. An Ufa film. First shown at the Ufa Palast am Zoo.

So this is the great German film for which Germany has been waiting so long! Universally received by the press as a masterpiece. There can be no doubt that this picture will do very nicely on the Continent and will probably finish up by showing a profit for its producers.

But how do they have the nerve to take it seriously here? It simply drips the undiluted hokum—sentimental sob stuff mixed up with the sort of motivation typical of a musical comedy libretto. Beside it an ordinary Tom Mix release is a psychological character study of the first rank. And, furthermore, it is purely local in its appeal, demanding sympathy and delight in the Vienna waltz and the whole court and cafe life of Austria.

The story is so slight as hardly to bear recounting. It concerns a typical pre-war provincial princess who marries a young Viennese count much below her station. He feels himself in an inferior position and will not have anything to do with his wife, who is madly in love with him. He starts a flirtation with an attractive cafe violinist and plans to run off with her.

Unknown to both, she has been teaching the princess how to play a Vienna waltz and thus win back her husband. In the end it all comes out; the violinist plays the waltz, and the husband, believing it is his wife, falls at the princess's feet. The pore, pore little girl goes into the dark, dark night! Fade out! Need more be said?

Ludwig Berger's direction is not bad—even quite subtle at times. But it is not exceptional. At least ten men in America could have surpassed it. Willi Fritsch as the count is charmingly fresh, and Mady Christians characterizes the princess with a good deal of fidelity. (Who understands this type in America, however?) Julius Falkenstein plays a dried-up chancellor in the typically European manner. His comedy registers well here. Xenia Desvi is a type for the violinist, but there are limits to dumbness, even in film stars.

An "echt deutscher film"!
Trask.

THE BLACKBIRD

Metro-Goldwyn production, directed by Tod Browning from the screen play by Waldemar Young. Lon Chaney starred with Owen Moore and Renee Adoree featured. At the Capitol, New York, Jan. 31 week. Running time, 76 minutes.
The Blackbird } ....Lon Chaney
The Bishop of Limehouse }
"West End" Bertie...........Owen Moore
Fifi...........Renee Adoree
Polly...........Doris Lloyd
Ghost...........Andy McLennan
Red...........William Weston
A Sightseer...........Eric Mayne
Bertie's Man No. 1...........Sidney Bracy
Bertie's Man No. 2...........Ernie S. Adams

They're still playing up the fact that Lon Chaney can make himself more hideous and misshapen than anybody in pictures. In "The Blackbird" he plays a dual role, that of a crook and of his brother, a Limehouse missionary. Although the reverend fellow is crippled up plenty, the curse is taken off by one shot showing the crook throwing his arm and leg out of joint and then assuming the role of the man whom the world thought to be his brother. That's the basis of the story, for the crook falls in love with a music hall performer, while a flashier crook from the West End also goes for the same girl. It's a fight to the finish, and the girl comes to the Bishop to get advice. Naturally, he uses the old poison against the man who is really his rival and lets the girl know that the other man is a crook. It happened that she loved him a great deal, so when the Blackbird tried to plant a murder on her man the cops were tipped straight. In trying to hurry into his preacher outfit and escape John Law the crook fell, broke his back and died—without having his identity revealed to the world.

It's a good melodrama, excellently produced, and although it runs a little long for the bigger houses, the daily changes won't notice that.

Chaney handles his two parts well and Waldemar Young's scenario has been so constructed that the rather unique dual role is plausible at all times.

Renee Adoree, who smashed through to glory in "The Big Parade," hasn't a great deal to do here, and she is badly dressed in many scenes, but, at that, still makes an impression. Owen Moore, as "West End" Bertie, a clever crook, ranks with Chaney in so far as the acting goes, for Moore's role here is away from anything he's done in the past, and he handles every inch of the swagger with ease, distinction and force.

Tod Browning's direction is good, as always, while the atmosphere of the Limehouse section of London is planted within two minutes after the picture is on by the simple and effective device of showing the faces of six or seven bums.

"The Blackbird" is an okeh picture—good for the first runs and the smaller houses. What's more remarkable about it is that Chaney, who has recently had a great run of pictures (with a corresponding rise in fame), sticks to his more or less old line with outstanding success. And Metro has picked his stories so carefully that in the campaign to make him a real star, and not one of those phoney luminaries, it appears to have been eminently successful so far. *Sisk.*

Song and Dance Man

Famous Players picture and Herbert Brenon production. Adapted from the play of the same name by George M. Cohan. Directed by Brenon, with James Howe, photographer. At Rivoli, New York, week Jan. 31. Running time, 72 mins.
"Happy" Farrell...........Tom Moore
Leola Lane...........Bessie Love
Joseph Murdock...........Harrison Ford
Charles Nelson...........Norman Trevor
Fred Carroll...........'Bobby" Watson
Jane Rosemond...........Josephine Drake
Inspector Craig...........George Nash
Tom Crosby...........William Mack
Mrs. Lane...........Helen Lindroth

Ma Carroll..................Jane Jennings

Professionals, and especially vaudevillians, will poke holes in this one's continuity, but the lay people seem to like it. That was the impression at the Rivoli Sunday afternoon. It was a question as to how an audience would take to this accentuated stage story in screen form. Because they appear to like it on Broadway is no criterion that where the factory whistles blow it will be as acceptable. One depreciating angle with that viewpoint in mind is that what love interest this tale contains is secondary.

This picture is a celluloid simile to the play, "The Butter and Egg Man," current on Broadway. The latter show brought qualified reviews from the critics because they thought it was too "inside" for the public (even the producers were under that impression), but it's now in its 19th week.

"The Song and Dance Man," as a legitimate stage attraction, was believed to have more than an even chance so long as Cohan, himself, played it. The piece was never any sensation, but went along to neat grosses with Cohan the only draw. Now it has become a picture, and a nice one, as pictures go, but there's still that question protruding as to how interested the public will be in the psychology of a "small time" performer when that character is played by one who is short of Cohan's drawing power besides being involved in a script that is strictly limited as to interest in a love affair and also possesses a couple of anti-climaxes that detract.

The mental twist which brings the song and dance man back to New York, after he has made good as a business man, to again try to click as a comedian may entirely escape a lay audience. But just that peculiarity may catch the outside patron's fancy. If it does this picture is "in."

It's a cut back scenario telling a dual tale which concerns the title role and that of the girl who finally becomes a revue star and marries the artist pal of the producer.

Brenon, in directing, has taken manifold liberties with vaudeville as it is today. "Happy" Farrell (Tom Moore), the name part, obviously a pop house No. 2 act, jumps from the small time into the Palace, New York, and that's one fairytale right away for the N. V. A. lay-offs if they drop into the Rivoli this week.

Farrell also resides in a boarding house where "all the headliners stay"—and there's another one. Besides this, the girl (Bessie Love) is an immediate sensation as a Charleston dancer. Signed to a sliding scale contract that starts at $250 and bedecked in ermine after the opening performance she wanders into a room choked with flowers, despite she apparently hasn't been on speaking terms with a soul, not even an agent, other than her mother. That's three fairies in one.

These professional, or technical, lapses are plentiful. However, looking at it from the other angle, it shouldn't make such a difference. The heart interest in there, Moore blends into the requirements of his role and that goes double for Miss Love. Brenon has carried the ensemble depiction along for holding power, even if it doesn't grip as it should. But he has apparently brought his story to a close too fast. Twice the action could have been cut with the entire yarn told. Instead the footage continues, and that explains the anti-climaxes. If Brenon can plead not guilty then the scenarist must take the slap.

Norman Trevor is cast as the producer. Although extremely stilted and stiff in the early scenes, he warms up to favorably impress as a lens figure before the picture is entirely unwound. The major comedy punches, according to the Rivoli gathering, was the cross-firing by subtitle of the boarding house keeper (Josephine Drake) and the detective (George Nash). Jane Jennings made a submerged mother assignment stand out, as did "Bobby" Watson in playing Farrell's partner, who dies in the first half of the film as part of the cut-back sequence. Harrison Ford is rather colorless as the ultimate husband of the girl, but adequate and the remaining support of the personnel is par.

The scenes in front of the Palace are authentic enough, they having been "shot" in the wee hours some months ago, and the production views were gained over in the Earl Carroll theatre with the "Vanities" chorus obliging.

"The Song and Dance Man" is a tough one to say "yes" or "no" about. It's the exception to the rule, in that it should entertain major house gatherings, while there is a doubt as to its capabilities along such a line where the intelligence won't be able, in any way, to grasp the professional psychology of the leading character.

Incidentally, Brenon has included three of the theatrical sheets in the telling. When the action is in St. Joe, Mo., the "Billboard" is on display, mayhaps upholding the adage that Variety missed the mails again. When Farrell and the girl are looking for work, one carries a Variety and the other a "Billboard," giving that paper an edge; and when the girl has reached stardom the periodical revealed is "Theatre"—which may be the tipoff on how Brenon rates the trade press without giving the picture trade papers a tumble. Maybe Herbert has an assistant.

Skig.

THE RED KIMONA

Mrs. Wallace Reid production featuring Priscilla Bonner. Story by Adela Rogers St. John, adapted by Dorothy Arnzer. Directed by Walter Lang. At the Broadway, New York with 7 acts week Feb. 1. Running time, 59 minutes.

Well, here is one of those "inside of the white slave traffic" pictures that the exhibitors love to talk about. It has white slaving as its topic and a white slave as the heroine. As an excuse the story is handled with an allegorical introduction when Mrs. Wallace Reid enters the file room of a daily newspaper and opens one of 1917 files to a page on which is shown the story of "Gabrielle Darley," the name of the character in the production played by Priscilla Bonner. That this is a story based on fact is the excuse under which it is offered on the screen. After the picture Mrs. Reid is again shown, this time making a plea for this particular type of women who have been drawn into a life of shame through the false promises of man.

To those houses that care not what the result in the future and who like to go in for the rather lurid stuff this looks like a bet, but the majority of houses, especially the neighborhood theatres and the small-town houses want to lay off of this one.

It seems the day when "the line" can be shown in pictures is long since passed.

At the same time, before entering into the tale as related on the screen, it might be well to suggest a bit of judicious cutting in one scene. It is the one where the heroine is about to quit her prison cell after having been acquitted of murder. Just before going she points to a Red Cross poster touching the bottom line, which reads, "At the service of all mankind." That got a laugh from the Monday night audience at the Broadway, but possibly that audience is just a little too "wise." However, it would be just as well to cut that bit from the picture.

At the opening of the picture following the shot of Mrs. Reid, the heroine is shown in a "crib" supposedly in New Orleans. She is informed by the "girl next door" that her lover has left her flat and is on his way to Los Angeles to marry another girl. She follows, sees him in a jewelers purchasing a wedding ring, and shoots him dead.

At the trial her story comes out. It's the old tale of a small-town girl lured from home by the village sport, taken to the red light district and put to work. With her earnings he buys her a couple of diamond rings, but the idea of his using the money that has come to him through her shame to buy a wedding ring for another was too much. "He was her man, but he done her wrong," as the old "Frankie and Johnny" song runs.

The jury of 12 good men and true, native sons from Iowa and Nebraska who are Los' strongest boosters, turn her out a free woman. But she's broke. A society dame, publicity crazy, takes her up, just for the newspaper space. She keeps the girl at her home until the novelty wears off and then turns her loose, flat again.

As a last resort, after seeking a job and failing to connect (her story having been too well broadcast), she at last wires "the girl next door" in New Orleans, and gets the money to return to the "crib." She starts, but the society publicity hound's chauffeur has fallen in love with her, and he searches for her. The two keep crossing paths until she is at work in a hospital as a scrub woman and and he in the good old kahki ready to go overseas. He wants to marry her right there and then, but she says she will wait until he comes back, for that is her idea of bringing about her regeneration.

The picture as a picture is rather well directed and the detail for the most part is well carried out. As to the "crib" stuff itself, it's really not too rough, but still it is there, and it is a cinch that small-town mothers and fathers won't want their boys and girls, even though they may be nearing the voting age, to get a flash at this. Maybe some of those mothers and fathers wouldn't even understand the picture if they saw it, but the youngsters would soon tell 'em about it, and then some one would raise Hades.

Mrs. Reid or someone else may believe she is doing something for the fallen women in turning out a picture of this sort, but the chances are that she will do tremendous harm to the picture industry as a whole and to herself in particular because she sponsors it by permitting it to continue.

The cast is a good one, strong on names, even though for the most part they are in shots only for bits, but among those in the cast are Mary Carr, Tyrone Power, George Seigmann and others equally as well known.

And as a little side information, pictures such as this, although not so well made, which were the Germans' dream of quick money from the screen, set the German film industry back 10 years.

Fred.

MEMORY LANE

John M. Stahl production presented by Louis B. Mayer, released by First National. From an original by John M. Stahl and Benjamin Glazer. Featuring Eleanor Boardman and Conrad Nagel. At the Strand, New York, week Jan. 31. Running time 71 minutes.

Mary	Eleanor Boardman
Jimmie Holt	Conrad Nagel
Joe Field	William Haines
Mary's Father	John Steppling
Mary's Mother	Eugenia Ford
The Urchin	Frankie Darrow
Maids	Joan Standing Dot Farley

"Memory Lane" is decidedly an old fashioned type of feature production. It is old fashioned in its story and direction, and the only modern touch that there is about it is the cast that puts over as best it can a mediocre thought and story. The chances are that "Memory Lane" won't show up badly at the box office of the Strand this week because Vincent Lopez is at the house as an added attraction, but the picture isn't strong enough to get along without some box office aid at least as strong as this.

Those who viewed the picture on the first day started a thought as to whether or not there was a possibility that L. B. Mayer was just working out his First National contract as best he could and not paying any attention as to the type of picture that he was giving them to release.

The leader title describes the picture as "the old story; two boys and a girl." That's just it. A small town, two boys, both in love with the same girl. She is engaged to marry one. But the night before the wedding the other returns to the town after a year's absence and the next night he is in front of her house when the ceremony takes place, actually forced into the task of driving the car for the newlyweds to the station.

On the way the groom sees who is driving, there are some words, the groom is pushed out of the car and the bride is driven off by the man she didn't marry.

The car runs out of gas, the two sleep in the machine over night and the boy takes her back home the next morning. There the new hubby awaits her with open arms and they start on the deferred honeymoon.

A couple of years later, there having been happiness and a baby in the family in the meantime, the other boy again shows up, dressed like a flashy gambler, pulls a lot of hick stuff, and the husband, who asks him the why of the masquerade, seems surprised that he was unable to put it over. Confesses that he had to see her again and wanted to make sure of her happiness.

Then Daddy goes home and the wife convinces him that she never cared for the other guy at all.

That's a story!

If it is, so also are bedtime stories fit for adult consumption.

As to the cast, Eleanor Boardman, Conrad Nagel and William Haines take all the honors. The balance does not stand up any too strong. An exception is little Frankie Darrow, a kid actor who slips in a bit that stands out.

From a production standpoint the picture doesn't look as though it cost very much.

It won't do for a week stand and anyone that can pass it up in the day to day change houses might just as well do so unless Eleanor Boardman stands particularly strong at their box office. It was a shame to waste this girl in this picture.

Fred.

PHANTOM EXPRESS

Royal Pictures presents "The Phantom Express," with Ethel Shannon, David Butler, Frankie Darro, George Siegmann and William Rooker in cast. John G. Adolphi directed. Released via Banner Productions. Time of running, 58 minutes.

Outside the New York Theatre the billing made by the house had David Butler featured, the management evidently feeling Butler was entitled to it and that a name from the cast was necessary to make it look more like a real production. Butler plays the hero and does as well as he can with a role that didn't call for much acting until the few closing feet.

"The Phantom Express" is a story of railroads. It could have been quickly served up in a two-reeler.

Seems the express ran about 200 miles on a spur of track controlled by a small railway group that pinned its whole existence on that one run and its engineer, John Lane. George Siegmann as Hardy, towerman, looked with big eyes upon Lane's daughter who in turn loved young Jack Warner (Mr. Butler). Hardy was dead sore at heart when he found himself spurned by Norah Lane (Miss Shannon) and that the run he desired was filled by the girl's father.

So Hardy flicks a switch and wrecks the express. Apparently it didn't do much damage to the train as it was soon on the job although some passengers were killed and maimed for life. It was a head-on collision, with the engineer saved. All he lost was his reason and his job, and in this picture, others might have lost theirs, too, without a wreck.

Wasted a lot of celluloid on a commonplace story. Nothing new or novel to the film, and even the work of a little kiddie failed to lift it.

Just a picture.   *Mark.*

LURE OF THE WILD

Columbia production. Featuring Jane Novak, with Alan Roscoe, Richard Tucker, Pat Harmon, Mario Carilo, Billie Jeorn and the trained dog, Lightning, in the cast. Directed by Frank R. Strayer. Released by Apollo. Running time, 58 mins.

Although Jane Novak is featured and is a screen name bearing some weight, the outstanding star is Lightning, the dog.

With this dog in the cast, one naturally expects a story wherein a little child is a dominating figure, and sure enough.

A husband who absents himself much from his house starts on a trip, saying goodbye to his daughter and wife. He urges his boon male pal to keep Agnes company. The friend does.

So much so that when the husband returns unexpectedly and finds wifey being close-embraced by the friend, he slams him. Pushing his wife aside, he rushes upstairs, gets the child and speeds from the house in an auto. And the dog goes, too.

Some excellent shots of the outdoors. Several good dramatic scenes. Some play for comedy; some good and some ineffective.

One of the best climaxes was where the little girl was saved from going over the rapids by the dog.

The picture should do well in the neighborhoods where it is certain to have its biggest appeal. *Mark.*

BIG PAL

Royal production, starring William Russell. Directed by John G. Adolphi. From story by Jules Furthman. Distributed by Apollo Film Exchange. Running time, 62 minutes.
Dan Williams............William Russell
Helen Truscott........Julanne Johnston
Mary Williams.................Mary Carr
Johnny Williams...........Micky Bennett
Tim Williams..........Hayden Stevenson

For the want of a story the services of some players known in film circles just about go to waste. William Russell, the star of this picture, holding close to economic line, at times fades, while Micky Bennett, the freckle-faced kid, steps in and holds.

Number of things about the story loosely strung together. Russell as Dan Williams, who aspires to be a ring champ, is notified that his little pal, Johnny, his brother Tim's offspring, is held captive and that if he (Williams) doesn't stand for a knockout in the fifth that he will never see his stolen kin again.

To please Dan's mother who loves little Johnny, about the slangiest article that has hit the screen in moons, Dan, always a square mitter, decides to take a kay-o.

For once in many pictures the girl's father does not regard a fighter as too common.

Much play given to the ring fight.

This is quite well done and one place where the most money was spent on the film for "extras."

Through the work of young Bennett and his cronies the picture will get the most attention in the neighborhoods, where the kids will root long and loud for them.
                                Mark.

THE DESERT'S PRICE

Fox production starring Charles (Buck) Jones made from the story by William McLeod Raine. Directed by W. S. Van Dyke. Half of double bill at Loew's New York Jan. 29.
Nils McCann..............Buck Jones
Julia Starke..........Florence Gilbert
Her Younger Sister.........Pauline Garon
James Martin............Montague Love

A pretty good western, which has its star, Buck Jones, in civilian clothes most of the time, the sole western touch being a broadbrimmed hat. The plot concerns Nils McCann, whose father for years carried on a feud with the Starkes of the next ranch. Young McCann, home from college and ready to take over control of the ranch, finds the father of the Starkes has died and that a beautiful daughter, Julia, is the girl he'd give a couple of right arms for if he could be successful in the pursuit of his love for her. It so happened the McCann outfit had been blamed for a lot of dirty work which Jim Martin's gang of renegades had perpetrated, so obviously. McCann gets heroic and helps the girl out, eventually proving to them the ill-will they felt for his family should have been directed at the Martins.

The outdoor shots are excellent, some particularly well photographed. Jones gives a good performance and covers quite a lot of ground with his horseback riding and punches in a few faces with his fists. Florence Gilbert as the Starke girl is new to this reviewer and, if new to pictures, looks like a pretty miss who'll go a long way before long. Pauline Garon does her stock flapper act, this time different only in that the atmosphere is western. Montague Love as the meanest of the Martins is rough looking and convincing.

Okeh as one of the Jones series and an improvement over several of his recent releases.   *Sisk.*

RED HEELS

London, Jan. 16.

Films of stories connected with the stage, no matter what the country of their origin, are invariably miracles of imagination and ignorance. However, this Sasha-Stoll film's characters are very human.

A gamin of a girl who rises from cheap cabaret to revue, a worried but human manager, a backer who is merely a kind-hearted man-about-town, a jealous erstwhile star and a youth who marries the little actress. The old characters, perhaps, but cleaned and clad in the mental raiment of ordinary men and women. There is nothing exceptionally original in the story, which could easily lose some of its eight reels to great advantage.

The production of Michael Courtice is excellent. He doesn't mince matters nor does he go out to find nasty situations or emphasize suggestiveness. As a matter of fact, there are no such things in the picture. Lili Damita, his star, who gives a fine performance of the girl, strips consistently, but she wears her nakedness gracefully and without a sign of self-consciousness. She has ability which will raise her high in the profession without the need for audity.

The staging is good and realistic. Cabarets, theatres, backstage, houses of the mighty, fishing village settings and the like are all included. The storm scenes, which occupy much of the concluding footage, are the best seen in some time.

In no way is this a British picture, but it is notable that Eric Barclay stands out as a thoroughly uninteresting personality. He is self-conscious, awkward and without imagination, although having a part far above that of the average screen hero. The old theatre manager, the Vicomte and a host of other parts are admirably played by true artists, and, such being the case these days, their names are carefully withheld from screen billing.   *Gore.*

BEHIND THE FRONT

Famous Players, with Wallace Beery, Raymond Hatton and Mary Brian featured. Directed by Edward Sutherland. Adapted by Monty Brice from Hugh Wiley's "The Spoils of War," script by Ethel Doherty. At the Rivoli, New York, week Feb. 7, 1926. Running time, 61 minutes.
Riff Swanson.............Wallace Beery
Shorty McGee...........Raymond Hatton
Betty Bartlett-Cooper........Mary Brian
Percy Brown.............Richard Arlen
Capt. Bartlett-Cooper....Hayden Stevenson
Scottie ....Chester Conklin
Sergeant ....Tom Kennedy
Mrs. Bartlett-Cooper.....Frances Raymond
Mr. Bartlett-Cooper...Melbourne McDonald

Here's the great war with a laugh in it from start to finish. And what a combination to put the laughs over! Eddie Sutherland, who directed the production; Hugh Wiley, who wrote the original, and that pair of inimitable comics, Wallace Beery and Raymond Hatton. The former as the big Swede detective and the latter as a "dip" whom the "flattie" has been chasing, both of whom enlist because a classy girl asks them to, handing each one a photograph of herself unknown to the other, a trick whereby she has gained 25 recruits for her brother's volunteer company, and they all go off to the front firm in the belief that he is "her hero."

That's only the beginning, but with a start like that you can well imagine what happens once the crowds get over to France. And fast! Well, the laughs come so fast that before the first one has rolled off your lap there is another gurgling right down through your throat and a third on the way to follow it. From a box office standpoint this one looks as good as Chaplin's "Shoulder Arms" from a war comedy angle.

Broad burlesque of army etiquette right down the line from the highest to the lowest as far as the officers go, and then on into the non-com division to a last buck in the rear ranks.

The opening scenes show the troops going to camp. Swanson, a Swede "dick" (Beery), is said, to give you an example of the titles to have "water on the brain which freezes in winter so that everything slips his mind." He is marching with the troops, loses his way, and while trying to get straightened out has his watch lifted by Shorty the "dip" (Hatton).

As Shorty takes it on a run the copper follows, and both get into the home of the Bartlett-Coopers, where a recruiting drive is on and the daughter gets them both into the army. Shorty and Swanson mate up and become "buddies" in camp but they are the sloppiest couple of soldiers that ever slouched through the mud of Sunny France. That's another laugh. A sub-title announces "Sunny France," whereupon along comes a scene with it raining like Hades and the mud knee deep as the troops leave their train.

The adventures of Shorty and Swanson "behind the front" with the girls of France, and then at the front when they go over the top and get headed the wrong way are just one big laugh after another. The finish finds them back in the land of "free speech and speak-easies," and they slip the bridegroom of "their girl" a little present because he was the one who sent Brown's biscuits overseas to the troops. They also even things up with the hard-boiled sergeant that they had when they find him all togged out in new civvies.

Then for the blowoff the picture seems to finish where it started, for the copper asks his buddie the time, gets a peek as his own watch, and the chase is on again.

Beery and Hatton, together with Tom Kennedy, carry the picture. The latter is the hard-boiled sergeant, and how! He makes the role a masterpiece. Mary Brian as the girl has little to do, but does it very well. None of the others shine particularly, although Chester Conklin as "John Haig of the pre-war Scotch," is good for a laugh in a bit.

Beery and Hatton, however, together with the titles, make "Behind the Front" a wow for laughs and box offices. *Fred.*

What Happened to Jones

Wm. Seiter production, starring Reginald Denny. From the play by George Broadhurst, adapted by Mel Brown. A Universal-Jewel. Shown at the Colony, New York, week Feb. 7, 1926. Running time, 69 minutes.

Tom Jones..................Reginald Denny
Lucille Bigbee..................Marian Nixon
Mr. Bigbee..........Melbourne MacDowell
Mrs. Bigbee..............Frances Raymond
Ebenezer Goodly..............Otis Harlan
Mrs. Goodly..................Emily Fitzroy
Marjorie Goodly..........Margaret Quimby
Richard..............Ben Hendricks, Jr.
Henry Fuller..................William Austin
Minerva Starlight.............Nina Romano
Hilda...................................Zazu Pitts
The Bishop.........................John Elliott
Smith...............................Edward Cecil
Rector.......................Broderick O'Farrell

Corking screen comedy that just falls short of being another "Charley's Aunt." It is similar in type to the former to a certain extent. It plays fast and the good old fashioned hoak laughs are plentiful throughout the action.

One thing most noticeable is that Otis Harlan almost takes the picture away from the star.

For a box office bet, this one looks as though it was in, although the exhibitor will have to watch his step and not pay anything like "Charley's Aunt" prices for it, for it won't stand up as strong as that picture did at the box office.

The story in brief has to do with two men who are trying to dodge the complication that ensue after a poker game, which is raided by the police, from the hands of whom they escape by dodging into a woman's beauty parlor. They make a getaway later in women's attire after they have raised havoc and again caused the police to be called.

They are chased by the cops, and finally reach the home of the elder of the two where the wife is expected hubby to bring home his brother, a bishop. To cover himself, hubby has his gambling friend to pose as the bishop with the suit that belongs to the churchman.

From then on the fun speeds right along and fast.

Denny works hard and with the aid of considerable "mugging" gets his role over, but at all times he has a terrific time to take a scene away from Harlan, who is with him in practically everyone of the laugh producing moments. Marian Nixon plays the lead opposite, and gets away with it in good shape. But there is a girl in the cast by the name of Nina Romano who will bear watching. She is going to blossom as an ideal "vamp" type. Zazu Pitts stands out cleverly in a comedy role as a Swede servant girl who is always looking for a touch.

The picture is well worth playing anywhere, and with Denny's name to draw is certain to pull business and in addition please. *Fred.*

Grand Duchess and Waiter

Famous Players' production of the Alfred Savoir legit comedy. Directed by Malcolm St. Clair, with Adolphe Menjou starred and Florence Vidor featured. Reviewed at the Strand, New York, Feb. 7. Running time, 75 minutes.

Albert Belfort..............Adolphe Menjou
The Grand Duchess Zenia...Florence Vidor
The Grand Duke Peter.....Lawrence Grant
The Prince Paul...........Andre de Beranger
Prascovia, lady in waiting......Dot Farley
Henriette......................Barbara Pierce
Matard......................Brandon Hurst
Blake.....................William Courtright

Another good Menjou vehicle and, consequently, another step up the ladder for this comedian, whose screen vehicles all deal with his lady-killing abilities. Taken from the flop stage play, the premise has been slightly altered. The waiter here falls in love with a grand duchess is a rich Parisian who enters service to be near her. Menjou goes through the part like Sherman through Georgia.

The plot is slight, and unless its many comic incidents were so finely planted and executed, the picture might have become overly long and consequently tiresome. It is incident after incident, and every one funny. Thus when the clumsy waiter spills milk over the duchess, the laugh doesn't stop with that, for he tries to follow her and dry it off with a napkin, having no idea that grand duchesses are high and mighty people and not to be touched by the hand of a servant. There is also the moment when the maid falls hard for him; there is the episode where he is bidden to enter the lady's bathroom, where he is awakened by his own servant to get into the butler's uniform and begin his days of service for his adored lady.

A nice light comedy and likely to get good money wherever shown. Menjou must be building, for F-P has been furnishing him with good stories and not treating him like a stepchild. With Florence Vidor as the duchess and a fine cast supporting, the acting part moves well and swiftly. Mal St. Clair's direction is corking and his celebrated "light touch" is in evidence many times.

As a first-run this is a set-up. *Sisk.*

THREE FACES EAST

Rupert Julian Production presented by Cecil B. DeMille, released through Producers Distributing Corp. Jetta Goudal, Robert Ames, Henry Walthall and Clive Brook featured. From the play by Anthony Paul Kelly, adapted by C. Gardner Sullivan and Monte Katterjohn. Special showing at the Hotel Plaza, N. Y., Feb. 3, 1926. Running time, 86 minutes.

Miss Hawtree }
Fraulein Marks }.............Jetta Goudal
Frank Bennett....................Robert Ames
George Bennett...........Henry Walthall
Valdar..........................Clive Brook
Mrs. Bennett............Edythe Chapman
John Ames...............Clarence Burton
Firking...............................Ed Brady

"Three Faces East," the corking mystery play which Anthony Kelly wrote early in the war, has finally reached the screen. Yes, there are a couple of battle scenes in it, but in the main the screen version of the play sticks to the mystery story, although there are a number of spots where the love interest is brought to the foreground a little too mushily, but those are scenes that easily can be cut, and with that the action of the picture will gather considerable more speed, which is the thing that it needs.

A mystery play should be played with speed, especially this one, as any one who saw the play must know, and the long, draggy love scenes rather tend to slow up the entire story. At that, with almost an hour and a half of running time the picture could stand pruning. But it looks as though when this is accomplished it will be a corking mystery meller.

The cast is a strong one, but for the greater part cannot count too much on Jetta Goudal in the lead. She doesn't seem quite to fit and is the type of woman who will not get a bit of sympathy from the women in the audience, which fact was particularly noticeable at the Plaza, although they're a wise audience. Her supporting cast is excellent, especially Robert Ames, who has the juvenile lead. Clive Brook as the master spy gives a particularly masterful performance and is most convincing, while Henry B. Walthall shines in the picture. Miss Goudal is the only woman of note in the cast as far as the amount of work that is entrusted to those of the opposite sex, and she is not quite sufficient to carry a whole production alone. Her type of beauty, call it that if you will, does not stand up when it comes to an hour and 30 minute dose of it.

Of course, Rupert Julian had a chance to play Kaiser Wilhelm again and he didn't overlook that. He played it all over the lot.

The picture as a whole is just a program production and cannot be taken out of that classification unless the speed of the playing is heightened by cutting. *Fred.*

MOANA

Famous Players release of R. J. and F. H. Flaherty's super-travelog. At the Rialto, New York, week of Feb. 7. Running time, 69 minutes.

A magnified travel film that will play to many walkouts in a theatre and will mildly entertain those who linger. In either case it's an acute example of a picture that needs a strong show or presentation around it. It's interesting and has been well done, but there's no story, and a travelog is a travelog. Even "Grass" was that.

The Flahertys were responsible for "Nanook of the North." Here they have delved into the southern climes for their subject matter. A subtitle states that the men lingered with the Samoans for two years in order to win the confidence of the tribe and get the inside native stuff. "Nanook" created quite a stir, both in and out of picture circles. It doesn't seem likely that "Moana" will achieve similar results.

In regard to continuity, the film unwinds evenly in working up to the climax of "Moana," the youth of the film, gaining his manhood through undergoing the custom of a torturous tatooing siege. The Flahertys have pictured this so that closeups are seen of the boy with the perspiration pouring down his face amidst the wincing from the pain of the elaborate bone needle-work being pricked into his back and knee.

The action contains a couple of modified laughs and holds some exceptionally eye-filling rugged shore lines, with the surf pounding. The spearing of fish, the capture of a giant turtle in the water by two swimmers and the riding of the breakers by a home-made skiff provide the major "action" scenes.

A sidelight is that the majority of the young women screened are nude to the waist, while the men are simply covered by a waist cloth. At one point a girl picks up a live fish, somewhat larger than a minnow. As it squirms in her hand she bites the head off and continues to munch it while conversing with her boy friend.

Pictorially the film stands out and educationally it should be a treat; but when considered as major house fare there is a doubt. However, one guess is that it is particularly adaptable to double-feature houses. *Skig.*

The Midnight Express

Gerson production (Ind.), released through Jenyart. Directed by Oscar Apfel and made from the story by J.E. Natteford. Gaston Glass, Richard Holt and Wanda Hawley featured. At the Broadway, New York, shown in conjunction with the vaudeville bill week Feb. 7.

Hal Reynolds....................Richard Holt
Kate..............................Wanda Hawley
Matt Foster, her grandfather........Sam Allen
The Stranger......................Sam Glass

A hokey-pokey this one, with a cast that don't mean anything. Richard Holt, who plays now and then in the independents, is the hero, but Gaston Glass has the big part of the crook who reformed when he fell in love with the station master's granddaughter (Wanda Hawley). After her love had purified his dirty soul, the old station master recovered from his stroke of paralysis and laid on his blessing. The latter role was handled by Sam Allen, hitherto unknown to these eyes, but who made the rest of the cast look like amateurs.

The story is of a railroad system, and the owner's son works in the dispatcher's office. His parents are in a quandary about having him meet "the right kind of girl." Wanda is trotted in from the lonely station, which looks like the crossroads of a sand patch in the middle of Delaware, but which the subtitle describes as the nerve center of a great railroad system.

The excitement comes when the crook, trying his durndest to reform, outwits some robbers and loads a shipment of gold on a freight train.

The robbers jump the freight and uncouple the last few cars, setting them on a downgrade, where they will collide with the oncoming express and fast mail.

The girl is on one of the trains, and the crook who gets heroic blows up the bridge and runs the freight cars into a deep ravine, thereby saving many lives (subtitle) and making himself Big People around the folks who didn't like him so much before. The kick shows the cars tumbling. After they've tumbled a nice piece of toy track, by scale about 40 feet or so long, tumbles right in after them—which shows how it was all done, and not so carefully done at that.

The picture doesn't make the grade, even if its choo-choo trains do. Where there should have been excitement and acting there is often a series of ridiculous moments caused by the lamentations of Mr. Holt, who doesn't seem to interpret grief through any other method than by the wringing of the hands.

For the daily changes only, and how it got into the Broadway, unless given away, is a mystery. Otherwise it would have been half of a double bill in Loew's New York. *Sisk.*

LOVERS' ISLAND

Carries producing label of Associated Exhibitors. Actual producer Henri Diamant-Berger, who also directed. From the Smart Set story by T. Howard Kelly. Scenario by Arthur Hoerl. James Kirkwood and Hope Hampton co-starred. At the New York theatre, New York city, Feb. 5. Running time, 68 minutes.

Clemmy Dawson...............Hope Hampton
Jack Avery....................James Kirkwood
Capt. Joshua Dawson.........Louis Wolheim
Sam Johnson.......................Ivan Linow
Amanda Dawson.................Flora Finch
Julia Daw.....................Flora LaBreton
Randy Phelps....................Jack Raymond

This story has a corking plot. It enables its leading characters to carry along the theme in a gripping way. Its cast is exceptional.

One scene will make the tired business man sit up and glue his optics to the screen. This comes where Hope Hampton as the ward of the old sea captain goes to the famous island of love and romance, undresses and goes into the pool for a swim. Hot dog!

All roles handled excellently and Miss Hampton shows to unusual advantage. Mr. Kirkwood looked as though he needed a good barber and played rather seriously, but otherwise sustained his film rep as "opposite" the leading woman.

Some word is due Miss Le Breton. This is the young woman who ran out on Henry W. Savage as the result of a tilt over certain stage lines. She not only played effectively, but registers well in most of her main scenes. She's a blonde and wears her clothes well. Miss Finch showed that she had lost none of her old screen skill and made a little role stand up as part and parcel of the picture.

Mr. Wolheim was superb. He made his big dramatic climaxes as virile and impinging as possible. Ivan Linow, another physical giant and wrestler, deserves credit for his work. He acted well.

Looks one of the best program bets on A. E.'s list. *Mark.*

SHOOTIN' ROMANCE

Jack Hoxie "western," produced by Universal. Directed by Cliff Smith. Adapted from story by Ruth Comfort Mitchell. Shown at the New York, New York city, Feb. 5. Running time, 56 minutes.

Lightnin' Jack	Jack Hoxie
Donaldeen Travis	Olive Hasbrouck
Currier King	William A. Steele
Mrs. King	Carmen Phillips
Ricketts	Bob McKenzie
Mammy	Mattie Peters
Muriel Travis	Virginia Bradford

Some of these days somebody is going to slip Jack Hoxie a story that will run hell-bent for continuity and even fool the bunch around the Universal shop.

This one in some sections is A-1; in others, in distress. At best Hoxie, a big, strapping, wholesome type of western ranch foreman and a riding fool, seems cut out for the kind of roles he plays, yet the scenario writers should keep him doing the things that are somewhat in western reason.

A polo game is thrust in to extend the footage and perhaps to give the foreign salesman a good selling talk that might make that polo insertion a long-lost sport relative of the Prince of Wales.

It just about slowed up the plot but the next minute saw the polo pleasure seekers and ball chasers shooting men down. For a finale they have a pull for thrills with Hoxie quitting his mighty sweet acting hoss for a mid-air fight with the villain in a basket operated by cable. That made the film look foolish.

Leaving out the foozle there are some corking shots of western life. The picture got away to a bully start and introduced the girl in a way that was a credit to the director.

This girl is Olive Hasbrouck and she carried her role along to high credit. She has screen control, handles herself in her big scenes, and ingratiates herself on an audience as the story runs along.

That scene with the wild steer was as good as they make in films. That angle is modern and held both comedy and thrills.

The cast was adequate. Special mention must be made of Miss Phillips who made the villain's wife more than of secondary importance once she came into view.

As a "western" it will do, barring the awful finale. Photographically there is much to commend in this Hoxie "western." *Mark.*

MARE NOSTRUM

Metro-Goldwyn's adaptation of the Blasco Ibanez novel of the same name, featuring Alice Terry and Antonio Moreno. Directed by Rex Ingram. Scenario by Willis Goldbeck, with John F Seitz photographer. At the Criterion, New York, for a run at $2 top, opening Feb. 15. Running time, 115 minutes.

The Triton	Uni Apollor
Don Ferragut	Alex Nova
His son, Ulysses	Kada-abd-el-kader
Caragol	Hughie Mack

Freya Talberg	Alice Terry
Ulysses Ferragut	Antonio Moreno
Dona Cinta	Mlle. Kithnou
Esteban	Michael Brantford
Lepita	Rosita Ramirez
Toni	Frederick Mariott
Dr. Fedelmann	Mme. Paquerette
Count Kalendine	Fernand Mailly
Submarine Commander	Andre von Engelman

"Mare Nostrum" ("Our Sea") is a war picture. That cleans up any doubt as to the meaning of the title and the nature of the story. It's war stuff from a naval angle and not too potent in the telling at this day and date. As a $2 special-run picture it doesn't suffice, but as a program leader it can be cut to adequately meet such an assignment. There can be no doubt that of Metro-Goldwyn's quartet of "specials" now on Broadway this one is by far the weakest.

Ibanez, the author and a Spaniard, has taken the late upheaval of the world and woven a tale from his country's viewpoint. Spain was a neutral nation. The picture may interest them on the native soil of the writer, but there's been too much war stuff here and abroad, and what was left on these shores "The Big Parade" has used up. There's not a chance of "Mare Nostrum" ever being shown in Germany because of the manner in which is presented that country's submarine warfare. And the torpedoing of two ships (miniatures and in "slow" photography) is this film's kick.

"Mare Nostrum" was a book, so there is always a possibility it will draw the readers; but those viewing it with no memories and an open mind are liable to find in the story many uninteresting passages plus the handicap of not a single principal character either demanding or holding sympathy. Thus almost immediately the "love interest" is debatable, inasmuch as the woman in the case, Freya (Miss Terry) is a German spy, and the man, Ulysses (Mr. Moreno), a Spanish sea captain who deserts his home for her.

Freya dies before a firing squad (well pictured), and Ulysses meets his end at the hands of a German submarine, which he in turn sinks with a parting shot from a deck gun just before his ship takes its final plunge.

Previously his young son has been drowned as a result of another undersea attack, so it's one of those things where everybody dies. An offset to this melancholy finish is made through an underwater phantasy to show the "leads" alive as a climax.

That's the Ibanez novel as it shapes up in scenario form, and the construction isn't strong enough to sustain it by itself at $2 as a road sustain it by itself as a $2 road sibilities in limited capacity houses if the film is cut.

Ingram remained abroad a long time to make this one, and few will deny that he has turned out a picturesque gem. Barcelona, Pompeii, Naples, Marseilles—they're all there "in the flesh," and it's pretty work. But landscapes can't and don't make a picture which runs just five minutes short of two hours in actual reelage. Much can come out, and it may then project itself as a better vehicle. However, as it stands it must be taken and under such a stipulation its unquestionably draggy and inclined to establish a disinterested morale on the part of the viewers.

Ingram has allowed his sense of the dramatic to run rampant at times. The outcome is some heavily stressed scenes that seemed a throwback to the early screen war deportment of "the enemy" which drew snickers from this first night gathering. Besides which it's a greusome tale without a solid laugh during the entire telling. The submarine tangent of the picture holds, especially the views of the inner mechanics. And even if the sinkings are "models," the manner in which the action leading up to these tragedies has been woven possesses its points. But that's down in the last half hour and it's a long time arriving.

Miss Terry and Mr. Moreno give capable performances, despite their unsympathetic roles. Early "shots" of Miss Terry, supposedly reveling and gloating in the acquarium victories of a devil fish to gain its food, as an insight on her mentality, looked to be about the best piece of symbolism Ingram has turned in as well as marking Miss Terry's histrionic high mark. The tale is gruesome enough, but the director has further implied that atmosphere by lizards, snakes and other species of reptile. Moreno gives a standard performance all the way, and if you don't particularly care what becomes of him, still, you can't blame him for that.

A glance over the cast will reveal that the rest of the players are practically all foreigners, some being "types." Michael Brantford, a youngster, makes the part of Moreno's son stand out for full worth, while Mlle. Kithnou convinces as the deserted wife and mother who hates the sea because it is destroying her family. So prominent is she that what pathos there is in the picture is obtained by this girl, despite the story has her as a most plain and unattractive woman.

Mme. Parquerette plunges through the role of the masculine but feminine head of a branch of the spy system, and Fernand Mailly and Andre von Engelman are genuine enough as the German officers. Hughie Mack, an elephantine fat man, is evidently the "comedy relief" potion but does nothing. Uni Apollon impresses in the prolog to the main theme.

Ingram did plenty with another Ibanez story, "The Four Horsemen," but the combination is not as happy a one in this instance, although it's not entirely Ingram's fault. The story just doesn't seem to be there for American consumption. It may do for the Latin countries, especially in those localities which are seen on the screen, but the tale hints at being too localized and of too unsympathetic characters to establish itself as screen fare rating for a house unto itself over here.

Another thing is that Ingram has been away from these shores a long time. It wouldn't do him any harm to take a jaunt back here if for nothing else than to sit around, talk with the boys, and glance over what they're doing in picture work. Some of the footage here reveals that absence on Ingram's work. *Skig.*

DANCING MOTHERS

Famous Players production of the stage play by Edgar Selwyn and Elmund Goulding. Directed by Herbert Brenon and the screen play written by Forrest Halsey. Conway Tearle, Alice Joyce and Clara Bow featured. Reviewed at the Rivoli, New York, Feb. 14. Running time, 70 minutes.

Ethel Westcourt	Alice Joyce
Jerry Naughton	Conway Tearle
"Kittens" Westcourt	Clara Bow
Kenneth Cobb	Donald Keith
Mrs. Massarena	Dorothy Cumming
Irma	Elsie Lawson
Hugh Westcourt	Norman Trevor

F.-P. isn't quite sure whether the ending they're using on "Dancing Mothers," wherein the mother gets wise to herself and walks out on her selfish husband and daughter is the right one. So the Rivoli programs carry one of those coupons asking for an audience expression of opinion—the alternative ending probably being that the wife forgives them all and comes back to take up where she left off.

In plot this is the old one about the mother who put on her vamping clothes to get the man with whom her daughter was in love—to get him and throw him over, as a protective measure for the kid. But the mother, who had patiently sat by the fireside for years while her husband and daughter went the wild pace of the day, fell for the man who "threatened" her daughter and the ultimate view shows the mother preparing for an ocean voyage with him. As an excuse for her desertion of her rooster and chick, the plot harps heavily on the point that father and daughter thought only in terms of themselves and that their reason for wanting her to stay was to make their own easy lives easier.

"Dancing Mothers" is a well produced, beautifully played and generally good picture which has one bad feature—and that almost ruinous. It has an anti-climax which makes the concluding episodes seem long and weary. The point of the story is whether the mother really falls for the man she hoped to trick—or whether she resists him. It is quite clear that she falls, and after she does there is a flock of pleading, of subtitles and other choice bits of whatnot to delay the action, which will bring the whole thing to a finish. So for the regular audiences outside the bigger towns, the alternate happy ending and some heavy cutting on the last two reels would seem the solution of the problem.

Alice Joyce runs away with the film. As the mother she is beautiful and attractively gowned in every scene, while her affair is handled nicely by the director. Conway Tearle is okeh as the handsome lover, the only trouble with him is that his makeup worked itself into some creases on the neck.

Clara Bow is the flapper daughter and she appears to greater advantage than at any time since "Down to the Sea in Ships." Somebody has told her to quit trying to make everybody believe she's a great actress and just be herself, for the dark makeup on the eyes is out—the artificial emoting stuff is canned and her performance generally is the excellent result of an excellent director. Norman Trevor is good as the perplexed father, while Dorothy Cumming, as a friend of the wife, gives what she gives to any picture—a good performance.

"Dancing Mothers" should get over because the scenery, up to that anti-climax, is tight and well knit, and with a possible alternate ending, it would seem that a recutting of the film might turn the trick. *Sisk.*

PARTNERS AGAIN

Henry King production presented by Samuel Goldwyn; released by United Artists. From the play by Montagu Glass and Jules Eckert Goodman. Adapted by Frances Marion. Featuring George Sidney and Alexander Carr. Shown at the Mark Strand, New York, week Feb. 14, 1926. Running time, 61 minutes.

Abe Potash	George Sidney
Mawruss Perlmutter	Alexander Carr
Hattie Potash	Betty Jewel
Dan	Allan Forest
Schenckmann	Robert Schable
Rosie Potash	Lillian Elliott
Aviator	Earl Metcalf
Pazinsky	Lew Brice
Sammett	Gilbert Clayton
Mrs. Sammett	Anna Gilbert

Here is a screen comedy that combines a measure of thrills at the finish certain to keep the average audience on the edge of their seats and at the same time have them screaming with laughter. Incidentally, this is the combination of George Sidney and Alexander Carr in another of the series of "Potash and Perlmutter" stories, and George Sidney pretty much walks away with all the sympathy that there is in the picture. The "P. & P." stories themselves are too well known to need any synopsis of length. This one deals with the advent of the partners in the automotive industry and their operation of the Schenckmann Six agency.

The picture starts with a wow of a laugh when the partners take out a prospect with his wife to give them a demonstration of their car and finishes with a scream when the two partners try to escape the country via aeroplane to get away from a mob of creditors who have invested in the stock for a new motor that they are going to place on the market. That aeroplane stuff is about the best double trick stuff that has been shot in a long while.

George Sidney as Abe Potash, the good-hearted egg, who is even willing to help out his wife's relatives, scores heavily, while Alex Carr as his excitable partner is again in his old role. Betty Jewel as the ingenue lead carries off her scenes very well. Lillian Elliott as Mrs. Potash, however, stands out. Lew Brice, in for a couple of comedy bits as a good-for-nothing nephew, slips by the barrier with a trick mustache.

The titling held any number of laughs for a wise audience at the Strand Sunday, and a couple of pieces of business with Abe having a horse liniment rubdown at Rosie's hands was another laugh wow. But it is the stunts that he pulls while seemingly walking on the upper plane of a flying machine while it is high above the clouds that will make the audience howl loudest and longest. The final title after this terrific laugh scene seems flat, and therefore the picture seems to end abruptly, but it looks almost as though there was a laugh a second for the hour that the picture runs.

Henry King, who directed, is also responsible for "Stella Dallas." It would be hard to imagine that the two came from the hands of the same director, so different in tempo and style are the two productions, but they go to prove that King can make 'em cry with one and laugh with the other, and that is a pretty good indication that he is a director of parts. *Fred.*

THE AUCTION BLOCK

Metro-Goldwyn-Mayer picture and Hobart Henley production, featuring Eleanor Boardman and Charles Ray. Directed by Henley; adapted from Rex Beach's novel by Frederick and Fanny Hatton. At the Capitol, New York, week of Feb. 14. Running time, 72 minutes.
Bob Wharton..................Charles Ray
Lory Knight...........Eleanor Boardman
Bernice Lane.................Sally O'Neill
Carter Lane.................Ernest Gillen
Homer Lane.................Charles Clary
Robert Wharton, Sr........David Torrence
Mr. Knight.................James Corrigan
Edward Blake.............Forrest Seabury
Nat Slauson...................Ned Sparkes

A so-so comedy in which Charles Ray runs away with the honors. Co-featured is Eleanor Boardman, but it's doubtful if this picture will do that young woman any good. Screened in a light vein, the situation, roundly, is that Miss Boardman is limited to playing "straight" for Ray's frolicking. The film is transparent fare, never threatens to make a serious impression, and is just one of those things half the drop-ins expect to view when entering a cinema palace.

How close this celluloid adheres to the Beach novel of the same name cannot be stated. But one important item in the footage is a distinct resemblance of a "bit" character to Polly Moran. It's odds that it is Polly in the shoe-fitting scene. There's no program men-

tion of her, but that face—it must be Pol's.

Beyond that, this M.-G. effort concerns itself with Bob Wharton (Mr. Ray), who outbids everyone for a dance with Lorry Knight (Miss Boardman), the winner of a beauty contest. A hasty marriage breaks up when she sees numerous feminine photos in hubby's flat and realizes his wealthy dad is a good-natured financial source. Hence, back to mother, where the home folks are in ignorance of the marriage.

Wharton follows, is refused reconciliation, but puts the town into a turmoil through buying in on the local shoe store to give it his personal service as well as ideas. Financially, he makes good, although he can't make the grade with his wife. The bank president's daughter (Miss O'Neill) finally gets Wharton in a jam by intentionally breaking down her car, so that she and her idol have to stay out all night. The family demands a marriage, but the under-cover Mrs. Wharton wrings a confession from the flapper, and there's the happy finish.

It's a jaunt for Ray and he does extremely well. Doing a more or less wise-crackin' youngster under the Hatton adaptation, the subtitles are of more than ordinary assistance. Ray can take care of a number of these assignments to the benefit of both films and himself. On the other hand, the predicament of Miss Boardman puzzles. About a year ago this girl carried a neat quota of prestige along "the street" and was one of the outstanding "comers" in the feminine film contingent. At that time she was hitting the Capitol screen about once a month and building up a substantial following. However, since then Miss Boardman's prominence has dwindled. Her late pictures have not held the pace of the former vehicles and her performances have been so limited in scope that even her dressing has become affected. Always a good-looking girl, Miss Boardman hasn't appeared to her full advantage in this manner for some time. As her personal situation now stands, it will take a couple of corking releases to again approach the pace at which she was traveling about 12 months ago.

Sally O'Neill, as the flapper would-be vamp, is cast in a secondary role and reveals what she may possibly be—a future brilliant. The less responsibility this young lady carries right now in a picture, the more she stands out. She'll probably rise to shoulder a full burden some day, but not yet. Others in the cast are capable if not so important.

Henley, in directing, has given all the punch of the scenario to Ray, and the latter reaps accordingly. Other than that, the director has overseered creditably and evidently in the desired vein. Productionally, the picture is above board, and John Arnold has photographed nicely, albeit the lack of makeup behind the ears of some of the players is drastically prominent. *Skig.*

PLEASURE BUYERS

Produced by Warner Bros. From the novel by Arthur Somers Roche. Adapted by Hope Loring and Louis Lighton. Directed by Chet Withey, assisted by William McGann. Irene Rich and Clive Brook co-starred. At New York theatre, New York, Feb. 4. Running time, about 60 minutes.
Joan Wiswell...................Irene Rich
Tad Workman.................Clive Brook
Gene Cassenas............Gayne Whitman
Helen Ripley.................June Marlows
Burke.......................Heinie Conklin
Tommy Wiswell.............Don Alvarado
Kildare......................Edward Pell
Quintard....................Frank Campeau
General Ripley...............Winter Hall
Perry........................Frank Leigh

"The Pleasure Buyers" may have read like a million dollars. As a

picture it didn't turn out so fancy.

Picture pretty well staged and has capital photography. There are times that Chet Withey shows his master hand and the picture lives up to its title; yet the necessity of shuffling all the characters so that nearly everybody in the picture with the exception of the man that is killed is accused of murder makes too much mystery.

This took in the principal feminine character, splendidly enacted by Irene Rich. She got mixed up in the thing through a desire to shield her brother, Tommy.

It looked like a real picture the first part, but when the murder angle messed around, the bets were off and there was some doubt whether the picture would ever extricate itself. But the picture tripped long before the finish, despite some mighty hard work by Miss Rich.

One can see where it might run right in a novel, but on the screen it flopped. The popularity of the players, particularly Miss Rich, may create quite a demand for it. *Mark.*

DON'T

Metro-Goldwyn production from the story by Rupert Hughes. Directed by Alf Goulding. Sally O'Neil, John Patrick and Bert Roach featured. At Loew's New York, Feb. 13. Running time, 70 minutes.
Sally Moffatt...................Sally O'Neil
Ezra Moffatt.............DeWitt Jennings
Mrs. Moffatt.................Ethel Wales
Tom Carewe.................John Patrick
Uncle Nat.....................Bert Roach
Bertha Carewe.............Madeleine Field
Uncle Nat's adopted child......Helen Hoge

This is one of the few Metro's that wasn't shown at either the Capitol or Loew's State before going into the Loew vaudeville and picture houses around town. The first New York showing was given at the American (vaudeville and pictures) the last half last week, and it also showed at the New York Saturday. The reason is probably twofold. The suggestion here is that Sally O'Neil, recently featured and heavily exploited at the Capitol in "Mike," probably wasn't of the calibre to repeat so soon in either that house or the State, while the other reason (and the more logical) is that "Don't" is one of that type which critics pan in the first line houses, whereas the audiences in the smaller theatres will roar over its low comedy.

It isn't a bad picture, and although the story doesn't mean a great deal and its production hasn't cost much, it is funny in a loud and boisterous way. Thus when Sally Moffatt begins a flirtation in boarding school and continues it at home, much to the chagrin of a stern parent who had her future husband already picked, the real sweetheart is up against the necessity of proving himself to be the high man.

This opportunity presents itself when a gang of lunatics runs wild and kidnaps Sally, throwing the boy bound into the tonneau of a car and putting Sally on the front seat as the partner of the maniacal driver. Sally O'Neil and John Patrick are the lovers and do nicely, although Miss O'Neil's "cuteness" is overdone in many spots. A stew uncle is funnily played by Bert Roach, and his adopted child, a Belgian war orphan, is played by Helen Hoge, new to pictures, but so funny she makes Baby Peggy look like a question mark. This kid is a tiny proposition, and although roughly handled here, does many things for laughs, and justifies a good part in some future production. DeWitt Jennings and Ethel Wales are the parents and also grab laughs.

One mystery, however, is that a woman like Miss Wales, who has worked in a thousand films, is uncredited by a name line or similar mark of recognition while another

girl, who appears for a minute flash and has nothing to do with the plot, is given an introductory sub-title with her name. The reference is to Madeleine Field, as the boy's brother.

"Don't" isn't any feather in the cap of Rupert Hughes, but Metro has made it into a slapstick comedy which wears well and is certainly good stuff for the second runs and the neighborhoods. *Sisk.*

SEA HORSES

Famous-Players production made by Allan Dwan and directed by him. Adapted by Becky Gardiner from the novel by Francis Brett Young. Continuity by James Hamilton. Jack Holt, Florence Vidor, George Bancroft and William Powell featured. Reviewed at the Rivoli, New York, Feb. 22. Running time, 72 mins.

Captain George Glanville........Jack Holt
Helen Salvia..............Florence Vidor
Lorenzo Salvia............William Powell
Cochran..................George Bancroft
Bimbo-Bomba.....................Mack Swain
Senor Cordoza...........Frank Campeau
Harvey......................Allan Simpson
Marx........................George Nichols
Gina Salvia...............Little Mary Dow
Hendry..........................Dick LeReno
Cheadle.........................Frank Austin

An excellent melodrama which will be a whole lot better when the film is—if ever—re-edited to make the fore part run more quickly into the exciting last half. The title, too, is bad and means little or nothing. In its present usage "Sea Horses" refers to a dangerous reef mentioned twice in the film and shown for one brief moment in a sea storm staged in miniature—an F. P. economy measure.

The miniature scenes are excellent in several spots, but one, showing the vessel of the story anchored in the East African harbor of Panda, is so crude it would be out of place in a $10,000 independent production.

The bonus system for speedy production may be okeh but modern audiences read too much about movies not to spot these lamentably crude deceptions. On the other hand, the faked typhoon is so well handled audiences will accept and enthuse over it, although the model ship used in this lists so badly that it could never return to an even balance—as no ship minus a keel can go over to nearly 90 degrees and then come back. And this ship takes punishment in the miniature storm which is all out of proportion. To the public it may be all right, as the whole business is a melodrama and at this point things are pretty exciting anyway.

A Mrs. Silvia, deserted by her husband, is cast out by her in-laws and is against the necessity of retaining custody of her child when they make accusations against her character. A friend prevails upon the captain of a freighter going to Panda, in Portugese East Africa, to take her along, for the husband is there. On the way the captain falls in love with him. Arrived, they find the husband is a drunk living with a native woman, but the wife still makes an attempt to bring him around. He attacks her, however, and she flees, which brings the ship's crew to find the woman, while some of them locate her husband and in a good gun fight kill him.

Then comes the excitement. The native village, through its unscrupulous white rulers, attempts to hold the ship. One officer holds them back and kills off most until he is at last shot just as the woman and others reach the ship in safety. Then the storm, but a great wave washes the ship over the Sea Horses reef and out into the open water for safety and the long voyage home.

Jack Holt, Florence Vidor and George Bancroft, particularly Bancroft, take the acting honors. Dwan's direction is all right. Although the first of the film is laden with incidents to "set" the character of the ship's crew, it seems that this might readily be cut to shorten matters, as these men all "set" their own characters later in the crises which follow.

Becky Gardiner, one of the few women writers attached to the F.-P. staff, has made an excellent adaptation of the novel in that she has cleaved tightly to the main story and kept the mind so focused on the theme that what extraneous matter does appear is of little moment, as the spectator is wrapped in the impending romance between the captain and his passenger.

"Sea Horses" passes nicely and from the F.-P. point of view, probably better than that, as it looks to have been cheaply produced. As an item of interest to the trade, B. P. Schulberg and Hector Turnbull are listed as associate producers at the "West Coast Studio," a phrase which hasn't previously appeared on the F.-P. titles. *Sisk.*

The Cohens and Kellys

Universal-Jewel from the play, "Two Blocks Away," by Aaron Hoffman. Adapted by Harry Pollard, also director. At the Colony, N. Y., week of Feb. 21. Running time, 85 minutes.

Jacob Cohen......................George Sidney
Mrs. Cohen..........................Vera Gordon
Patrick Kelly.................Charlie Murray
Mrs. Kelly...........................Kate Pprice
Tim Kelly......................Jason Robards
Nannie Cohen...........................——

Anyone who ever saw "Two Blocks Away" would never recognize the play, except for one idea that is employed in the picture adaptation of that piece under the title of "The Cohens and the Kellys." It looks as though Universal thought that they could practically lift Anne Nichols' "Abie's Irish Rose," with "Two Blocks Away" as the excuse. The chances are that they won't—at least not without a fight on their hands—for the entire idea is the conflict between the races over the question of inter-marriage because of the love affairs between the son of the Kelly clan and the daughter of the Cohens. That was not part of "Two Blocks Away"; it is "Abie's Irish Rose" and it is "The Cohens and Kellys." At the early Sunday evening show several audible references to the similarity of the two were overheard in the audience.

There is no question as to "The Cohens and Kellys" as a box-office bet from a picture standpoint. It is as filled with laughs as "Abie's Irish Rose." It is funny as to action and it is funny as to titles, and both George Sidney and Charlie Murray are comedy wows. Vera Gordon supplies the necessary need of pathos as the wholesome Jewish mommer, while Kate Price is the comedy Irish mother.

The reviewer "caught" the Charles Dillingham production of "Two Blocks Away" in 1921, when it was produced at the Cohan theatre, New York. He has seen "Abie's Irish Rose." Sunday night he saw "The Cohens and Kellys." If Universal gets away with this, then anybody can come along and lift anything that they want from the stage and produce it as a picture and never pay a cent for it. That's just how much "The Cohens and Kellys" follows the original "Two Blocks Away."

In "Two Blocks Away" the central character was an old cobbler with an adopted daughter. In "The Cohens and Kellys" there have been a number of characters added until two factions have been built up. Cohen, the character corresponding to the old cobbler, had a wife, a daughter and a son. The Kellys consist of the father, mother and two sons. Likewise each family has a dog, and the picture starts with the feud between the two because of their racial differences. They are neighbors in the same building. Cohen runs a furnishing store and lives over it with his family. Kelly is a cop and his boy is likewise on the force.

The opening of the picture has Cohen receiving a letter from the credit association to the effect that he has to pay up. The Cohen dog and the Kelly dog start a fight in the hallway between the two apartments. First two young sons of about 10 or 12 years become involved, then the mothers of the two, and finally the fathers, while the daughter of the Cohens remains in the background, as does the older son of the Kellys, the two pantomiming a date for the back of the house.

Then comes a legacy to Cohen, and he moves "two blocks away." But before he gets away his daughter has married young Kelly, and when the baby arrives there is another quarrel between the Cohens and Kellys all over again. Cohen restricts his daughter to his home and refuses to let her husband or any of his clan see the baby. Finally the elder Kelly walks in with his brood and the girl decides to leave with her husband, the Cohens following her to the Kelly home, where a reconciliation is effected, Cohen and Kelly, with their arms about each other, declaring themselves partners.

There is no exact out-and-out lifting of "Abie" as to dialog or situations, but Harry Pollard, in adapting "Two Blocks Away" certainly has got about as close as he could to the Anne Nichols piece.

No matter what the outcome of a legal consideration, this film is a darn good laugh picture that will get a lot of dough. *Fred.*

TORRENT

Cosmopolitan production presented by Metro-Goldwyn-Mayer. From the novel by Blasco Ibanez, adapted by Dorothy Farnum. Featuring Greta Garbo and Ricardo Cortez. Directed by Monta Bell. At the Capitol, New York, week of Feb. 21. Running time, 68 min.

Don Rafael Brull............Ricardo Cortez
Leonora.........................Greta Garbo
Remedios.................Gertrude Olmstead
Pedro Boreno..............Edward Connelly
Cupido......................Lucien Littlefield
Dona Bernarda Brull........Martha Mattox
Dona Pepa.....................Lucy Beaumont
Don Andreas...................Tully Marshall
Don Mattias........................Mack Swain
Salvatti...............Arthur Edmund Carewe
Isabella.......................Lillian Leighton
King of Spain....................Marie Carille

Greta Garbo, making her American debut as a screen star, might just as well be hailed right here as the find of the year. This girl has everything with looks, acting ability and personality. When one is a Scandinavian and can put over a Latin characterization with sufficient power to make it most convincing, need there be any more said regarding her ability? She makes "Torrent" worth while. Louis Mayer can hand himself a few pats on the back for having brought this girl over from the other side. He certainly has something well worth while in her.

"Torrent" is a picturization of the Ibanez novel of the same name, and has been directed by Monta Bell. It is evident that the great scene of the rush of waters was counted on to carry the picture, but at this late date a bursting dam doesn't mean anything in a picture except as an incident. It is the story itself that carries here. The tale of the unrequited love of the little Spanish peasant girl, who develops into a great operatic star will hold because of its love twist.

The Ibanez name may pull some money, and while "Torrent" is well played and capably directed there is nothing about the picture that is going to make the public crazy about it. The money that it gets will have to be attracted, and possibly the angle of giving the public a chance to discover a new star of the future may be the point of attack.

Ricardo Cortez, in the earlier scenes, looks as handsome as ever, but also shows that he has possibilities as a character man in the closing action. There are other "names" in the cast, and although veterans they could not overshadow Greta Garbo. Hail this girl, for she'll get over. *Fred.*

MARRIED

Herman F. Jans production. Story by Marjorie Benton Cooke. Director uncredited. Features Owen Moore and Constance Bennett. At the Stanley, N. Y. (25c. daily change grind house), Feb. 17, 1926. Running time, 60 minutes.

Dennis Shawn....................Owen Moore
Marcia Livingston......Constance Bennett
Kate Pinto.............Evangeline Russell
Mme. DuPont......................Julia Hurley
Joe Pinto........................Nick Thomas
Chuck English...............Antrim Short

This feature is somewhat better than the average of the state right releases, at least as to the cast and the direction, although the story is typical of the state right field. It is laid out so that there are as many exterior scenes as possible. From the box office standpoint the picture will do well enough in the small grind houses, although in the bigger houses it fits for the average double feature bill.

The Owen Moore and Constance Bennett names coupled with the title "Married" should pull a little business.

The story is one of those combination society and lumber camp tales that the state right producers seem to eat up. The hero is the manager of lumber holdings of an estate, the sole surviving heir of which is a jazzy flapper. The lumber trust wants the tract. To compel its sale they try to purchase the adjoining tract, held by an aged woman. She refuses to sell, but demands the right to pick the husband of the flapper as well as the wife of the camp manager. Naturally she decides that the two are to wed each other.

They are married over the telephone, but the wise old lady, figuring that the kids might want to make it a marriage of convenience, includes a clause that unless they live together for three months she will dispose of her property to the trust.

Then the troubles begin. Neither wife nor husband cares to see the other. Finally the groom makes a call, deciding to go through with the provisions of the contract to save the property. The bride turns him down. He kidnaps her, taking her back to the lumber camp far from the jazz of Park avenue. There she eventually learns to love him, but not until there is a clash between her and a half-breed Indian girl for his affections.

Moore is the hero and just about as snappy a one as the fans could ask for, while Connie Bennett does well enough in her flapper moments, only to fall down when something a little more is called for in the later scenes of the picture.

Evangeline Russell steals the picture away from her whenever the two have a scene together, and altogether Miss Russell has far the best of it in the final analysis.

Why the director was not credited is something of a mystery, for he surely did the best he could with the material at hand. *Fred.*

Girl from Montmartre

First National release produced by Associated Holding Corporation (Sawyer-Lubin), with Lewis Stone featured. Was designed as starring vehicle for Barbara LaMarr, but star's death shifted billing. At the Rialto, New York, Feb. 21-week. Running time, 75 minutes.

Emilia.......................Barbara LaMarr
Jerome Hautrix..................Lewis Stone
Ewing..............................Robert Ellis
Rodney Brown..............William Eugene
Robert Hautrive..................E. L. Calvert
Lawrence Faneaux...........Mario Carrillo
Carmenata...................Mathilde Comont
Messager..........................Edward Piel
Don Angel.................Nicholas de Ruiz
Cab Driver.......................Bobby Mack

This picture was made before Barbara LaMarr's death and marked her return to West Coast production after having made a series in the east—most of them flops. The presenting company is here listed as Associate Holding Corporation, the new corporation formed by Sawyer and Lubin of the old Associated Pictures Corporation under which name they formerly produced. The new name, however, includes their activities in the construction of the Roxy theatre, New York.

Following Miss LaMarr's death her name was taken from all billing, and as projected at the Rialto the screen announcement had Lewis Stone as the sole name featured. The program mentions both as being featured, and certainly Miss La Marr has the important role. It is probably the first time a firm has taken the star's name off of any product following death, that statement being based on the Victor phonograph records of Caruso's voice, etc., which still hold their place and billing in the catalog.

In the case of John Bunny, Harold Lockwood and Olive Thomas—Their films were shown with their names attached for some time after their death, although the demand lessened sales value.

.n story this film is as slight as they make 'em. The idea is simply this: An aristocratic Englishman sees a cabaret dancer in a Parisian dive and comments on what he believes is her patrician birth and breeding. So when the war is over he goes down to Spain on a painting expedition and meets with the girl again. Thus the picture is a well contrived series of incidents to support the fragile plot. That it is well directed and well played by Stone makes it a fair first run and that it has been produced well and better than any of the LaMarr series in the recent past also gives it a chance in addition to whatever morbid interest may have been generated by the flood of heart interest stuff written by the picture critics since the star's death.

The prediction is that it will do but fairly, as Miss LaMarr while alive was never an outstanding drawing card. Stone's popularity may also be expected to help considerably.   *Bisk.*

OH! WHAT A NURSE

Warner Bros.' picture, starring Syd Chaplin. Based on an "original" and directed by Chas. F. ("Chuck") Reisner. At the Strand, N. Y., week of Feb. 21. Running time, 72 minutes.
Jerry Clark....................Syd Chaplin
June Harrison...........Patsy Ruth Miller
Clive Hurst.................Gayne Whitman
Capt. Ladye Kirby............Pat Hartigan
Mrs. Clark...................Edith Yorke
"Big Tim" Harrison........Dave Torrence
Eric Johnson..................Ed Kennedy
Mate.......................Raymond Wells
Editor....................Henry Barrowes

A follow-up for Syd Chaplin on his "Charley's Aunt," in that he again is doing a "dame." It's not another "Aunt," if there must be a comparison, but they laughed at the Strand and they'll laugh at it in other houses. The situations are "naturals." Chaplin probes them for full worth, and he is favored with excellent cast support for good measure.

Chaplin, equally as good a pantomimist as his brother Charlie, is swamped with opportunity when in skirts as regards displaying this art, and that he can do it has long been an acknowledged fact. How long he can continue to do these comedy female impersonations is something else again; but there's no doubt that this one can romp into any house and fulfill its mission despite the similar predecessor.

It's rather a wild yarn when all is said and done, drawing heavily on the imagination and the ingredient of coincidence to make the sequence plausible; but, on the other hand, it's one of those things where they sit there, laugh plenty and don't care about the story. The "gag" stuff jams it through.

As an outline, Chaplin opens as a cub reporter having to take over the lovesick column of his paper. A flighty girl (Miss Miller), who worships at the foot of this column, writes for advice, and the complications ensue through an uncle who would marry her off so as to gain the inheritance. Chaplin gets mixed up in a bootlegging ring as the false feminine leader and finishes as a

nurse protecting the girl on shipboard.

Reisner, directing, has crammed all kinds of action into the telling. There's nothing new about Reisner's connection with the Chaplin family, and that they should stick together is obvious. Both Syd and Charlie are in the habit of doing most of their own directing, but Reisner must have had a hand in it somewhere, and therefore a certain amount of credit is his due. If he had nothing directly to do with Syd's actions here, possibly he's responsible for the schooling of the support, and Mathew Betts, Dave Torrence and Ed Kennedy are of no little assistance. Patsy Ruth Miller is somewhat confined to the background, the love interest being more of an excuse than a paramount issue.

Chaplin is practically on the screen throughout the entire 72 minutes the picture runs. In spots his work actually sparkles, and it never ranges beneath the classification of "good."

They'll laugh and they'll like it, which means another money picture for Syd. At the end of the first regular matinee show on Washington's Birthday they were standing six deep downstairs, sitting in the aisles of the loges, the lobby was jammed and the box-office line was half-way to 47th street.   *Skig.*

THE OUTSIDER

Roland V. Lee production, presented by William Fox, starring Jacqueline Logan and Lou Tellegen. From the stage play by Dorothy Brandon. Shown at Loew's New York, New York, one day, Feb. 22, 1926. Running time, 63 minutes.
Leontine Sturdee....Jacqueline Logan
Anton Ragatsy...............Lou Tellegen
Basil Owen................Walter Pidgeon
Sir Jasper Sturdee..........Charles Lane
Pritchard..................Joan Standing
Shadow...................Gibson Gowland
Dr. Todd..................Crauford Kent

"The Outsider" is a sort of a "Miracle Man" picture, having as its principal character a faith healer, played by Lou Tellegen, while Jacqueline Logan has the role of the daughter of a famous London surgeon, severely injured while dancing at the Gypsy Camp of the healer, where she has gone to secure atmosphere for her next season's stage dances.

She has no faith in his power of healing her and returns home to London, but once there learns from her father and his eminent associates that there is no hope for her and she is doomed never to walk again. The faith healer returns, forces his way into her home and takes her away for almost a year, in which time he cures her of her affliction. She, in turn, falls in love with him. Finally it is her love that gives her the faith to walk, and the cure is complete. For the average daily change of bill house the picture is one that will get by nicely. It isn't a knockout, but a good program picture that should please the average audience.

Roland V. Lee directed the production. While the principal roles are carried by the two featured players, the supporting cast is sufficiently well balanced as to make the picture measure up fairly well with the regular run of program stuff.

The story opens with an interior of a theatre scene, switches to Budapest, where the dancer first meets with the gypsy healer and then finds its completion in London.

Of the supporting players Walter Pidgeon played the juvenile lead opposite Miss Logan, doing fairly well with the material in hand.

It is a straight dramatic story without any comedy relief of any

nature whatsoever, therefore a fairly strong comedy should be booked with it when played.   *Fred.*

LA BOHEME

King Vidor production presented by Metro-Goldwyn-Mayer, co-starring Lillian Gish and Jack Gilbert; suggested by Henry Murger's "The Latin Quarter," with story by Fred De Gresac, adapted by Ray Doyle and Harry Behn. At the Embassy, N. Y., for a run Feb. 24. Running time, 101 mins.
Mimi......................Lillian Gish
Rodolphe...................John Gilbert
Musette...................Renee Adoree
Colline.............Edward Everett Horton
Count Paul.....................Roy D'Arcy
Marcel...................Gino Corrado
Schaunard..............George Hassell
Alexis.......................David Mir
Bernard....................Gene Pouyet
Benoit.......................Karl Dane
Madame Benoit...........Mathilde Comont
Louise...................Catherine Vidor
Phemie..................Valentina Zimina
Theatre Manager...........Frank Currier

From now on everything that King Vidor directs will be compared with his "Big Parade." That will be a mistake, for a director, like an athlete, needs a change of pace occasionally, otherwise he goes stale. But the comparisons will be made nevertheless, just as everything that Griffith ever did or does calls for some comment regarding "The Birth of A Nation." Thus a great many people will say of "La Boheme," "Well, it's not a 'Big Parade'," but that won't be doing Vidor justice. Vidor has turned out a picture in "La Boheme" that is as good as any director could have done with a tragedy in costume on the screen. That he has a picture that won't stand up as a $2 attraction isn't Vidor's fault, it's the fault of the story.

On the other hand there is this to be said, the public is going to attend "La Boheme" because the musical fans know the opera and the picture fans will want to see Jack Gilbert and Lillian Gish. For these reasons the film will make good in the picture houses when it reaches there, which will not be a long time off.

It is possible that "La Boheme" will hold up for six or eight weeks at the little Embassy (600 capacity), but it is a cinch that it will not duplicate the tremendous draw that "The Merry Widow" was at this house.

Through the fact that the American representatives of Riccordi, the Milan music publisher who holds the rights to all of the Puccini works, would not permit of the utilization of that composer's score as an accompaniment to the picture, William Axt wrote an entirely original accompaniment, taking his theme numbers from the T. B. Harms catalog.

As a score it is great music but with 'La Boheme' the one chance that the picture has of getting over is with the Puccini music. If they can in any possible way arrange for that then they still have a chance of saving the day for the film. Without it they may just as well consider it was a waste of time for all concerned in making the picture.

The story of the love of Mimi and Rodolphe is too well known to need recounting here. Suffice to say that Vidor took the Fred De Gresac version of "Boheme" and made it into as corking a picture as one could with the material at hand.

However, as one views the picture you cannot help but think in the terms of Rodolphe the tenor, Marcel the baritone, Schaunard the basso, Mimi the soprano and Musette the contralto. And with that in mind, how could any picturization of a operatic plot be complete without the music that has become all too familiar in connection with the libretto?

The girls are going to go crazy over Jack Gilbert as Rodolphe, the lover, and the boys will like Mimi as played by Lillian Gish, although she gives a rather watered milk characterization. Then as to Roy D'Arcy as the Count, George Hassell as Schaunard and Karl Dane as

Benoit there isn't sufficient that can be said for their performances. They are types of the Latin Quarter and perfect as to the grand opera conception of those characters.

Incidentally, Henrik Sartov, cameraman, should receive a full meed of praise. There are several shadow shots that actually have the full stereoscopic values, excellent work.

The women folk of the cast, other than Miss Gish, include Renee Adoree as Musette, which character has been emasculated to a tremendous degree and it is almost too bad that Miss Adoree was assigned it, while Matilde Comont, in a character role, handled herself nicely. The other women mattered but little.

The pre-release houses, with de luxe showings, can stand for the picture for a week on the strength of the two stars and Vidor's name, but when it hits the little joints there is going to be a sore disappointment as to the matter of receipts. *Fred.*

LET'S GET MARRIED

Paramount Picture presented by Adolph Zukor and Jesse L. Lasky from the DuSouchet farce, "The Man From Mexico," with Richard Dix starred. Adapted by Luther Reed, directed by Gregory LaCava, script by J. Clarkson Miller. Shown at the Rivoli, N. Y., week March 1, 1926. Running time, 67 minutes.

Billy Dexter	Richard Dix
Mary Corbin	Lois Wilson
Jimmy	Nat Pendleton
Tommy	Douglas MacPherson
Slattery	"Gunboat" Smith
Billy's Father	Joseph Kilgour
Mary's Uncle	Tom Findlay
J. W. Smith	Edna Mae Oliver

Richard Dix looks as though he is on his way to cop the straight comedy honors of the screen. This latest of his productions, the second Gregory LaCava has directed, is an out and out wow for laughs for more than an hour. If you laughed at "Womanhandled" then you'll scream at "Let's Get Married." From a box office standpoint it is sure fire, for Dix has been growing in popularity every minute for the last year and more and this picture is going to add more to his popularity if such a thing is possible.

Imagine a modernized "Man From Mexico," which, in itself, was a howling success as a farce under that title and later as "Over the River," a musical comedy with Eddie Foy. Then imagine the same story set within the howling, whirling, jazzy atmosphere of today and depicted on the screen where the vision reaches so far beyond the limitations of the stage and you have "Let's Get Married."

Three former football stars celebrating the victory of their alma mater as they are about to enter a night club in the Roaring Forties a couple of "boys" from their rival temple of learning hand them the "razzberries" as they enter the club and the trio follow right in for an apology. Gee, it reminded one of a "football night at Jack's" and when the smoke of battle cleared, the night club was a wreck, the flying wedge of waiters scattered and the trio of "boys" were in the "pie wagon" on their way to station house.

The next morning Billy Dexter's dad asks his old pal the judge to give the youngster a warning and to threaten him with "30 days" the next time he gets in wrong with the cops. As a further discipline, father takes the nifty roadster away from him and forces him to use the electric that dad has been in the habit of driving. With that car he meets his fate when Mary Corbin (Lois Wilson) smacks into him from behind with her snappy sportster. This meeting leads to a love affair, and finally Billy (Richard Dix) informs dad that he is going to marry, so father sends him out to entertain a visiting hymn book buyer who is stopping at the Ritz, in order that the boy will get his first line on business and incidentally get enough to wed with and keep himself going.

Instead of a sanctimonious old egg with whiskers down to his midriff, J. W. Smith (Edna Mae Oliver), the hymn book buyer, proves to be a giddy old girl that would like to see the sights and the one place that she insists on seeing is the club which was the scene of Billy's football night escapade. She's the one that is responsible for the starting of a fight as a result of which Billy is again pinched and this time sent away for "30 days," escaping the day before his sentence expires, he is in fear that when caught he'll get an additional "sixer" so he prepares to marry the girl of his heart and flee the country. This takes up the final footage and is developed into a continuous laugh through the arm of the law trying to hand the bridegroom a pardon for the final day that he didn't serve.

Dix proves a wow from beginning to end, while Lois Wilson is charming and handles a car as though she would give heart failure to professional chauffeurs and taxi drivers alike. But Edna Mae Oliver pulls a laugh a second, while she is in front of the camera. She has a pan that is funny and she handles herself with the supreme knowledge that she knows all the tricks and delivers with them. "Gunboat" Smith as the copper (he is Dix's private sparring partner, incidentally), with that cauliled pan of his is another laugh. Bull Montana has nothing on the "Gooner" as Buckley used to call him, when it comes to looks or lack of 'em. Sidney Jarvis has a bit as the night club proprietor that he makes stand up, although he isn't programmed.

In directing the picture, LaCava (or is it Lee Cleaver or Mr. Meat Axe, or what?) shows that he has stepped right up with the foremost in the handling of feature productions for laughs and the combination of he and Dix is a most happy one, as is proven by the two pictures which they have worked out together as star and director. If anything should happen to bust this combination apart after so auspicious a start it would be a shame. *Fred.*

IRENE

First National's release of John McCormick's presentation starring Collene Moore. Adapted from the musical comedy of the same name and directed by Alfred E. Green. At Strand, New York, week of Feb 28. Running time, 83 mins.

Irene O'Dare	Colleen Moore
Donald Marshall	Lloyd Hughes
"Madame Lucy"	George K. Arthur
Pa O'Dare	Charles Murray
Ma O'Dare	Kate Price
Mrs. Warren Marshall	Ida Darling
Eleanor Hadley	Edward Earle
Bob Harrison	Lawrence Wheat
Helen Cheston	Maryon Aye
Jane Gilmour	Bess Flowers
Mrs. Cheston	Lydia Yeamans Titus
Mrs. Gilmour	Cora Macy

One more bullseye for Colleen Moore and a neat piece of work on the part of those concerned in the making. It follows the musical comedy script closely enough so that the story is easily recognized, while June Mathis, editorial director, has presumably modernized the "sides" so that the titling sparkles **in all reels. The picture afforded much amusement to a Sabbath matinee gathering at the Strand and gives every indication of being able to repeat that feat in either the larger or smaller houses.**

It entertains, it's clean, and other than the antics of Miss Moore there is the effeminate modiste characterization of George K. Arthur, as "Madame Lucy," a gem of its kind. Nothing fresh, vulgar or objectionable about the way Arthur plays it, just "sissified" and funny, so even the average lay mind will absorb it as desired. On the strength of it there's little doubt that Arthur runs only second to Miss Moore for personal honors.

This celluloid adaptation of a musical looks plenty of money. McCormick has seen fit to have had the fashion show done in natural color and as this must consume close to 1,000 feet, maybe more, it's quite a flash. The story breaks right into the "color" after which the plain black and white is brought back to finish. The fashion thing as done here, resembles a cabaret floor show backed by a stage setting with the costuming eccentrically designed in supposedly appropriate wear for the four seasons. Miss Moore, of course, leads what could be termed each "number" with the Irish mother breaking into the fur coat and negligee display to grab her daughter in the midst of the society function—whence the yarn is again picked up.

The story is in need of no retelling inasmuch as it's the basic formula of the poor girl who secures a chance to model clothes and eventually weds the wealthy son of an ultra family. Her difficulty in learning the "carriage" of a mannequin, the "jams" she gets in, the continuous battle between her and "Madame Lucy" and the sidelights of her lowly Irish family are all there and although it may read as a stock program, nevertheless Alfred Green, directing, has pieced it together to make a well-knit garment. No denying there is an abundance of "hoke" sprinkled throughout the action, while the general cast support for the star is an outstanding asset. Charles Murray and Kate Price play the Irish parents for every ounce that's there, Lloyd Hughes is a convincing juvenile, Ida Darling makes the aristocratic mother stand out and, as previously mentioned, Arthur is all over the place with his feminine gestures. Surprisingly, Eva Novak does just a "bit."

All kinds of opportunity for Miss Moore to clown in this rags to riches comedy and she cashes. No new angles to such a role for this girl and having previously proved her worth within such settings she again clicks, plus the production and work behind her. That's all it amounts to.

Green has lifted the diamond shaped iriging in and out idea from the show while the original score is used. According to the Strand audience there is an abundance of "Irene" enthusiasts around, for the melodies had many humming the lyrics. So much so, it became annoying if you happened to be sitting near one of 'em. However, that angle is certainly favorable to the picture as a financial prospect. As a musical "Irene" had a terrific vogue as a stage vehicle and this silent revival should catch that favoring breeze of a past squall.

Using up 85 minutes isn't as long as the cold figures would indicate. There's enough amusement to overlook the lengthy running time and while some trimming can be done, where the need is great, still this release can stand "as is" without suffering.

A good, wholesome comedy—and they'll like Miss Moore for it. *Skig.*

THE CAVE MAN

Warner Brothers production adapted to the screen by Daryl Zanuck from the original story of Gellett Burgess. Matt Moore and Marie Prevost featured. Directed by Lewis Milestone. At the Rialto, New York, Feb. 28. Running time, 75 minutes.

Mike Smagg	Matt Moore
Myra Gaylord	Marie Prevost
Brewster Bradford	John Patrick
Maid	Myrna Loy
Dolly Van Dam	Phyllis Haver
Mrs. Van Dam	Hedda Hopper

After Gellett Burgess wrote this one, which is pretty fancy entertainment of its kind, it was made into a stage play with Robert Edeson starred and was fairly successful. And from the looks of the picture, which has Matt Moore playing the coal-heaver who was tamed (for a little while) by a society girl, this will be most successful of all. First and most important is the story itself, but almost equal is Moore's performance, which is the best of the many good things he has turned in since his prominent position with Warner films. Miss Prevost is good to look at and has some nice moment, and another item of interest to the trade is the appearance of Myrna Loy, a newcomer in films, and although she plays a maid here, looks like one of the best vamp bets yet revealed. She is tall, has a provocative face, and one of those fancy-looking haircuts which is a lot of hohokus in itself but makes an impression.

The story here is about a bored society girl who turns half a hundred dollar bill loose with the instructions that the finder return it to her apartment and get the other half. And Mike Smagg, a tough tobacco-chewing coal-heaver, picks it up and busts into a Park avenue apartment house like a speed car taking a curve, upsetting a few elevator men and butlers. The girl grooms him for an appearance in society as an eccentric professor and he gets away with it, to the point where a girl is crazy to marry him. But he reveals his identity, is kicked out of society, and then gets so sore that he goes back for the girl who dragged him into society, puts her on his coal wagon and starts driving for the minister. It's a phoney ending but it's a punch at that, so why kick.

As stated before, Moore is great in this film. As the coal heaver he flashes a make-up that is perfect, and as the society boy he sticks comedy good for a quiet smile into every movement. Miss Prevost really plays straight for him, while the others don't matter much, but **one look at the cast is proof enough that there's no cheating in that direction.**

Okeh, this one, from the direction, production and scenario to the cast. The principal requirement of a comedy is that it shall produce laughs and give satisfaction.

This one qualifies just as strongly as a mamma's boy for a Y. M. C. A. job. *Sisk.*

Under Western Skies

Universal-Jewell production, with Norman Kerry starred. It's also labeled an Edward Sedgwick production. Edward Sedgwick directed. Edward Sedgwick wrote the story. Distributed by Universal Film Co. Shown at the New York theatre, New York, as part of double feature, Feb. 26. Running time, 57 minutes.

Bob Erskin	Norman Kerry
Ruth Baldwin	Anne Cornwall
Thomas Baldwin	Charles K. French
Beef Smith	Eddie Gribbon
Foreman Walsh	Harry Todd
R. J. Erskin	George Fawcett
Paul Stern	Ward Crane

Just what would have happened to "Under Western Skies" if the Pendleton (Ore.) Round-Up wasn't a mighty big part of its structure is beyond conjecture. Delete or eliminate that exciting outdoor "horse and cattle" play of the cowboys or cowhands and this picture wouldn't be worth much more than a couple of thin dimes.

This isn't taking away the hard, hard work that Mr. Kerry does as the hero, for he just about single-handed holds up the picture or what there is to it, barring its Pendleton feature and the comedy relief offered by Eddie Gribbon.

We must admit that Ward Crane makes a sleek-looking villain; seems the life of the picture heavy in the passing of years has agreed with Ward; he's seemingly bigger in avoirdupois and still as immac-

u'iate as ever. And credit must also go to Mr. Fawcett for his most excellent characterization of the rich old gink who was hellinbritches when it came to being a true sport on backing up a bet.

We recall Universal's photographing of the Calgary stampede for a Hoot Gibson picture. With U cameraing the Pendleton round-up the U just about grabs a monopoly on the biggest of the American western and Canadian rodeos.

There are some amazing "shots" of the broncho busting, the hog-tying of steers, bulldogging, and this bulldogging stuff just about raises 'em out of their seats the way those sharp and sure-flung lariats drop those steers in action; in fact, all the real thrills attendant upon this real man's play of the plains and ranches.

The rounding up of the wild horse—a part of the film proper—was well done, and Kerry's rough-riding and bronk work was also the real stuff.

The million dollar hurdle stuff was all to the English but rather lukewarm following the thrilling daredevilish work of the round-up boys, and Kerry in his film riding.

The story skids considerably and jumps a lot of traces, but the Pendleton round-up is there as a salvaging proposition that can't miss, especially in the family neighborhoods. *Mark.*

THE BLUE STREAK

A. Carlos presents Richard Talmadge in "The Blue Streak." A Richard Talmadge production. Story by James Bell Smith. Directed by Noel Smith. Distributed by Film Booking Offices. Shown at the New York theatre, New York, on double feature day, Feb. 26. Running time, about 60 minutes.

Richard Manley	Richard Talmadge
John Manley	Charles Clary
Inez Del Rio	Louise Lorraine
Jack Slade	Henry Hebert
Don Carlos	Charles Mailes

Dick Talmadge sure lives up to his billing in this title. He's every inch a blue streak, both with his fists and his legs and he is in there all the way making this picture a lively and thrilling celluloid play that, allowing for all its fistic overplay and faulty business stuff gives the exhibitor something to be thankful for these days.

Dick Talmadge is every bit a screen hero, having worked his way up the ladder through his apprenticeship as "double" for Douglas Fairbanks. He's some stunt man. On his performance in "The Blue Streak" he just about cops the title as the best in the business today. He was considered a corker when he did sensational stuff for Doug, and he is doing all the old tricks with a lot of new ones thrown in for good measure.

Talmadge has improved as a screen lead. He's not a bad-looking bird, and he sure flies when once in heroic action. His legs seem short and pudgy, yet they respond triphammer like when he swings them into play.

He just about licks a regiment of rough-looking "he men" in the Mexican episodes, where he goes to find out what's wrong with his father's mining shipments.

Of course there's villainy; doubledyed stuff, too, and through it all, over, above and under runs, rides and flies the intrepid Talmadge.

When Talmadge struck out for himself as a film star few of the wiseacres paid much attention to him. But he has kept coming, and with the right stories and the right direction he will be a real money card in any section of the universe. Film fans like plenty of action in their screen romances, and Talmadge is giving it to them triple-barreled.

His support is getting better and his story embellishment stronger. There were some bully scenes at times, but the story sidestepped, too, although Talmadge was given fighting to do and that prevented the story from getting lost entirely.

There were some genuinely amusing comedy "bits" and the scene on the dining car was as cleverly conceived as possible and great stuff for the family folks.

The neighborhood houses will find Talmadge worthy of respect; they will find him coming right along to the starring point where his name will cause both exhibitors and fans to rejoice that his film stunts are being filmed regularly.

The cast was good as a whole, the work of Miss Lorraine being splendid while that of Mr. Mailes was exceptionally characteristic.

The photography was A1. All things said and done, "The Blue Streak" is Richard Talmadge going like a house afire in daring stunts, fistic rough house and dynamic screen play. *Mark.*

The Gilded Butterfly

William Fox production. Story by Evelyn Campbell, directed by John Griffith Wray. Shown at Loew's Circle, N. Y., on double feature bill March 1, 1926. Running time, 70 minutes.

Linda Haverhill	Alma Rubens
Brian Anesty	Bert Lytell
John Converse	Huntley Gordon
Jim Haverhill	Frank Keenan
Courtney Roth	Herbert Rawlinson
Mrs. Ralston	Vera Lewis
Mr. Ralston	Arthur Hoyt
Colored Maid	Carolynne Snowden

Society drama with a moral. The moral is that a life of bluff leads to a sorrowful end. That's that as far as the story is concerned. The cast, however, has enough names in it to make the picture stand up anywhere in the daily change houses without an added feature to the bill, although at Loew's Circle it was shown on a double bill.

Alma Rubens plays the lead with Bert Lytell opposite. The heavy is Huntley Gordon, while Herbert Rawlinson and Frank Keenan play important roles in the early portion. Here are five names that should prove of value to the average box office and it gives the picture the aspect of an "all star" production.

The story is that of the daughter of a "bluffer" who has run through his own fortune and has borrowed from relatives and friends alike in his effort to keep up appearances. His final effort to wed his daughter to money ends in his death, for at the party he "throws" in the home of relatives in Washington, where he is staying under sufferance, his final instructions to his daughter are to keep up the bluff. His motto is "It matters not what you are but what you appear to be."

She begins her life on that theory with one of her father's old friends financing her with the idea that he'll be able to collect in the end. He tries to pin it on for a three-day party amid the Swiss Alps, but the hero steps in on the train as she is on her way to keep the rendezvous. The coincidence is that he is on his way to see the same man, and when he arrives at the hotel discovers the girl in the room. That makes it look like all bets are off, but instead she tells him if he will believe in her for just this once she'll pack and start directly for Washington and meet him there.

The final scenes are laid in Washington with the Mayflower Hotel as a background for some of the scenes. Here the heroine goes from bad to worse as far as debt is concerned, and finally is placed under arrest, although a good-hearted detective as one of his last tricks in life lets her have her freedom when he is smashed up in a taxi crash. That leaves things right for a happy ending.

There are a couple of corking thrills in the picture. The first is the avalanche of snow in the Alps which buries the train and the second is the taxi skidding into the side of a patrol wagon and in turn a fire truck crashing into both and wrecking them completely.

The picture for the average houses will fill the bill and pull some money on the strength of the names. *Fred.*

ONE OF THE BRAVEST

Gotham Production, presented by Samuel Sax, starring Ralph Lewis. Story by James J. Tynan, adapted by Henry McCarthy, directed by Frank O'Connor, supervised by Renaud Hoffman. At the Stanley, New York (25c. daily change grind), Feb. 27. Running time, 63 minutes.

John Kelly	Ralph Lewis
Patricia Kelly	Claire McDowell
Dan Kelly	Edward Hearn
Morris Levin	Sidney Franklin
Sarah Levin	Marion Mack
Satin Sanderson	Pat Somerset

One of those fire hero thrillers with an "Abie's Irish Rose" slant. It has as its heart interest the love affair between the daughter of a Hebrew shopkeeper and the son of the Irish fire chief. The "Cohens and the Kellys," which Universal turned out, has the same type of little shopkeeper, with an Irish cop and his son on the other side of the fence, but whereas the "C. and K." picture is built for straight comedy this one tends more to the out-and-out meller, with thrills and the comedy incidental.

It is a good picture of the independent type intended for the smaller neighborhood house. It has a couple of real kicks in it as far as the fire-fighting stuff is concerned.

Ralph Lewis as John Kelly is the captain of Engine 95, and his son Dan has just received his appointment. The youngster, while possessed of courage enough to tackle three stick-up men single handed, is a coward in face of fire. At his first blaze he develops a yellow streak, for which his father cannot forgive him.

The mother, knowing the fear that is in her boy's heart, sympathizes with him. She takes $1,100 of the receipts of the firemen's ball which her husband is holding and invests the money in phoney oil stock, in the hope that there will be a profit of a couple of hundred per cent in a week, so that the boy can quit the department and study law.

When dad discovers his loss he accuses the boy, figuring that a fellow that'd turn yellow at a fire would do anything, and the boy, to shield his mother, takes the blame.

The boy and Sarah Levin have fallen in love. To her he confides his predicament.She in turn persuades her father to advance the money to the boy so that the old chief can protect himself from disgrace.

In the end the boy proves his courage at a fire when he rescues his dad and at the same time captures the sure-thing stock salesman who fleeced his mother, the entire affair ending up with the betrothal of the Jewish girl and the Irish boy.

Mr. Lewis gives a corking account and Sidney Franklin plays opposite as the father of the girl. Edward Hearn is the boy and Marion Mack the girl. The former has the more difficult role, but handles it nicely. The honors for the best performance must go to Claire McDowell as the mother. Pat Somerset successfully plays the crook. *Fred.*

THE BLACK PIRATE

United Artists release starring Douglas Fairbanks. Story by Elton Thomas, with Albert Parker, director. Photographed in Technicolor by Henry Sharp. At the Selwyn, New York, for a run commencing March 8. Running time, 88 mins. Scale, $2 top.

Douglas Fairbanks
Billie Dove
Tempe Pigott
Donald Crisp
Sam de Grasse
Anders Randolf
Charles Stevens
John Wallace
Fred Becker
E. J. Ratcliffe

Fairbanks' initial feature "shot" completely in color and a picturesque picture shrewdly held down to 88 minutes, so that the eye strain doesn't become too trying. It's as great a boost for the Technicolor process as for Fairbanks and a sure-fire release for the regular program houses. Between the Fairbanks name and the color thing this one should be able to hold over in any of the major palaces.

It's doubtful if there is any real intent to attain a run at the Selwyn for "The Black Pirate," a non-official impression being that this weak-storied vehicle is just "in" the legit house for a showing. If a run does or not not develope it's okey either way—the "show" angle having been accomplished.

In the tale that it spins it's the weakest Fairbanks has ever had. More so than "The Thief of Bagdad" and certainly it is much less vital than "Don Q" in this respect. It's simply a matter of scores of pirates in color and the Fairbanks curriculum of "stunts." Beautiful stuff and made as easy as possible on the eyes by the costuming and backgrounds in subdued colors. There is a surprising lack of the glaring shades throughout, to which the program calls attention.

Fairbanks is up and down the screen with his acrobatics, the "punch" being his taking of a merchant vessel single handed as a pirate. In the title role it eventually evolves that he is a Duke, is responsible for capturing the pirate crew, upon which he has sworn vengeance for the death of his father, and the rescue of the Princess (Miss Dove), the only woman in the cast other than Tempe Pigott in a minor role.

The continuity has its lapses, there is more than a little that must be taken for granted, and the heroics are strictly of the screen. But it's easy to watch, there is a distinct appeal to the imagination, and it's Fairbanks. The youngsters should eat it up.

The action is fast and furious when Fairbanks goes out after the merchant vessel as a solo exploit. His best athletic bit is the manner in which he rips the sails by mounting to the cross arms, piercing the wide sail with his sword, grabbing the hilt and descending to the deck, his momentum retarded by the sword ripping the canvas as he comes down. A new angle on the swimming under water bit, as a hideaway getaway, is also inserted by the picturing of about 50 of Fairbanks' soldiers approaching the pirate ship through this method. A corking underwater effect. Previously he has "walked the plank" at the hands of the villain, but has had his bonds knifed by a sympathizer and has swum to shore to ride for his followers.

Mostly mob groupings. There are hundreds of men swarming all over the pirate ship. Also, the action opens up at a gait in that the pirates have just captured a vessel, tie its members to a mast and thence blow up the ship. Fairbanks and his father are the survivors of this, the parent dying upon reaching shore and his son proving himself a capable aspirant to the pirate crew at his own request by duelling the leader to death when a group come ashore to secretly bury the main portion of the treasure.

There is no dearth of action at any time, but the story impresses as little more than an excuse. Parker gets program credit for having directed and to this end has "shot" the mass ensembles advantageously although omitting the overhead shots so effective in "The Sea Beast." Adequate support is forthcoming from the surrounding principals although no one matters to any great extent outside of Fairbanks. However, Sharp's camera work is superb.

A feature of the initial showing was the doing away with the usual film announcements, the picture blasting right into the opening subtitle and on the program Mr. Fairbanks' name is modestly at the bottom of the cast.

It's no secret that Fairbanks has had a pirate picture in mind for some time. Even a program note mentions that it was his original purpose to do such a theme before "The Thief of Bagdad." That being the case and after viewing "The Black Pirate," with the thought of the money it must have cost and its "excuse" story, the long prevalent idea that Fairbanks should have done Sabatini's "Captain Blood" is but emphasized. The how and why of Fairbanks' passing up the picturization of that buccaneering piece of fiction, a Fairbanks "set-up" if there ever was one, comes very near being a tragedy of omission.

The 88 minutes the picture has been cut to is the tip-off that it's all ready to hop into a general release classification at any time with a guarantee of a quick turnover to the picture houses. And that is its field. Had it the "Captain Blood" story behind it and had that novel been made on the same scale as this, which meant a much higher production cost than "The Black Pirate," it could have remained a "special" for a couple of years and, perhaps, Fairbanks' greatest picture. But that's theorizing.

Getting down to facts is to say that Fairbanks is still "there" and this picture should get a lot of "dough." *Skig.*

THE FIRST YEAR

Fox Film production of the Frank Craven play with Matt Moore and Kathryn Perry. Adapted for the screen by Frances Marion and directed by Frank Borzage. At the Rialto, New York, March 7 week. Running time, about 75 minutes.

Tommy Tucker....................Matt Moore
Grace Livingston.............Kathryn Perry
Dick Loring....................John Patrick
Dr. Myron Livingston.......Frank Currier
Mr. Livingston................Frank Cooley
Mrs. Livingston............Virginia Madison
Mrs. Barstow........Margaret Livingston
Mr. Barstow.........J. Farrell McDonald
Hattie, the maid.......Carolynne Snowden

Nobody got very enthusiastic when Fox announced this one because the wise boys along the street all said that a picture containing the same subtleties as the play couldn't be made.

Their arguments at the time were very nice and very logical.

But nevertheless the picture has been made and it is okeh. As most people in the show business know, Frank Craven wrote this play on the premises that the first year of married life is the hardest, because both parties are adapting themselves to new conditions. Into it he told the story of Tommy Tucker and his bride and brought the whole thing to a roaring climax in the scene where a badly arranged dinner nearly spoiled a big real estate deal for her husband.

After that they split, but finally reunite after the bride's boyhood sweetheart has been disposed of.

It is a whale of a story in itself, for the characterization which Craven wrote of each person is accurate in almost every respect. Frances Marion's scenario grabs the needed spirit, while Frank Borzage's direction is not only good but fine in many spots—for there's no getting around the fact that both the scenarist and director had lots more to do with the making of this as a good picture than anyone else.

That they were handed a good play doesn't mean 10 cents' worth of itch powder. Lots of other people have been handed good plays and have turned out film botches.

Moreover, there is a corking cast. Matt Moore is better here than just a good actor; as the husband here he's immense. Kathryn Perry, virtually an unknown insofar as the great rank of filmgoers run, lifts herself 'way up the scale by her performance. And then comes the colored girl who plays the maid, Carolynne Snowden. Variety some time ago carried an Inside Stuff of Pictures story about her in which it was said that she scored so decisively further picture parts were planned for her. In an extremely difficult part she conveys the langour and general stupidity of the maid of whom Craven wrote. The others are corking too, that going for Farrell MacDonald and Frank Currier especially.

"The First Year" is a real comedy for the best screens, but it will probably need exploitation. And any press agent who forgets his press book long enough to do some real thinking to contrive a method to get the idea to the public will help his boss put this one over. Sounds like the bunk, a story like this, for the really big houses, but it isn't.

The trade will be tickled pink at this picture. *Sisk.*

Miss Brewster's Millions

Famous Players picture, starring Bebe Daniels. From "Brewster's Millions," by George Barr McCutcheon and the play by Winchell Smith. Adapted by Monty Brice, directed by Clarence Badger. At the Rivoli, New York, week March 7. Running time, 71 minutes.

Polly Brewster..................Bebe Daniels
Thos. B. Hancock, Jr........Warner Baxter
Ned Brewster..................Ford Sterling
Mr. Brent ....Andre de Beranger
Landlady ....Miss Beresford

Probably one of the best comedies Bebe Daniels has had in a long while. The picture starts with a laugh and keeps the audience in giggles to the finish. It is the George Barr McCutcheon story revamped to fit a girl instead of a young man. The manner in which the plot is worked out makes it not only acceptable with Miss Daniels in the role of the girl that has to spend a million in 30 days to get five, but proves to be highly amusing and entertaining.

From a box office standpoint the picture looks like surefire. It is just one gag after another and all with a laugh kick.

Miss Daniels as Polly Brewster is a $7.50 a day extra in pictures on the coast at the opening of the picture. At the studio she is a patsy, and they kick her around. She in her awkwardness falls over a wind machine, throws on the switch and practically blows every one out of the studio.

At her boarding house the landlady is waiting for her rent and Polly is trying to duck her, but instead of wanting the rent the landlady informs her that there is a young man waiting to see her. He is the attorney representing the estate of her late uncle, who has left her a million, but with the proviso that it is invested and she take $30 a week for expenses. That story breaks in the papers and her other uncle decides he'll make the tightwad uncle a laugh even in death, so he sends his attorney to her to insist that she spend the million in 30 days and he'll give her five.

From then on things move fast and furious and in the finish a wire comes with a flash that the $5,000,000 baby has gone broke, and the girl is about to be up against it again, then it is discovered that her picture investment has turned out a money maker and she is on easy street after all.

A lot of kick in the manner that Bebe Daniels handles the role of the spendthrift, but Ford Sterling as the representative of the $5,000,000 unk really carries off a lot of the comedy honors. Warner Baxter, playing opposite the star, also scores nicely. There is a girl vamp unprogramed who has a mint of looks and bats .400 in front of the camera.

The sets are corking. In one where Miss Daniels is shown in a spray bath there is a gasp from the audience when the water is shut off, for Bebe looks as though she is about to show everything. She fools 'em, for hidden by the spray was a cute bathing suit.

It's a cinch that 'Miss Brewster's Millions" is going to roll up a healthy box office return wherever it is shown. *Fred.*

BROKEN HEARTS

Jaffe Art Film production, presented by Louis N. Jaffe, featuring Maurice Schwartz and Lila Lee. From the play by Z. Libin, adapted by Frances Taylor Patterson, directed by Maurice Schwartz. At the Cameo, New York, week Feb. 28. Running time, 82 minutes.

Benjamin Rezanov.......Maurice Schwartz
Ruth Esterin...........................Lila Lee
Cantor Esterin............Wolf Goldfaden
Mama Esterin............Bina Abramowitz
Victor Kaplan................Isidor Cashier
Shprintze ....Anna Appel
Mr. Kruger............Charles Nathanson
Mrs. Kruger.......................Liza Silbert
Milton Kruger............Theodore Silbert
Miriam ....Miriam Elliss
Marriage Broker.........Morris Strassberg
Esther ....Henrietta Schnitzer
Benjamin's other............Betty Ferkauf
Mishka ....Louis Hyman
Captain of Cossacks.........Leonid Snegoff
David Adler.......................Julius Adler

There is but one single screen professional in this picture, Lila Lee. She makes the other players seem like the veriest of amateurs, even though they are recognized stage professionals of the Yiddish theatre. Maurice Schwartz is a producer of plays in Yiddish, and "Broken Hearts" is a production he presented on the stage.

For the picture he utilized his stage company for the cast, with the exception of Miss Lee. The picture may get a little money in strong Jewish neighborhoods where Schwartz is known to the populace, but for the out-and-out picture houses, where it will be shown on its merits, it hasn't a chance.

The story is a dreary tale, told in a halting fashion that wanders along through endless footage. The picture could be cut to decided advantage and about 15 minutes of the running time eliminated.

It is one of those tales of the emigrant from Russia who comes to America and makes good in a literary way. In Russia, where the story opens, the hero is compelled to flee for his life because of his writing He leaves a wife and his mother behind him.

Shortly after his arrival in New York the hero learns from a friend that his wife is dead, whereupon he meets and marries the daughter of the cantor of an East Side congregation, despite parental opposition by the girl's family, they having picked the dumbbell son of a wealthy cloak-and-suiter who made a lot of dough and left Hester street flat, moving to Riverside drive, where Sunday afternoon pinochle games are the particular diversion.

Atop of this comes a letter that says the wife in Russia is still alive, so the young people are parted, and the husband goes abroad to find his first wife, only to discover that she since has died in a hospital of the Soviet government, and likewise that the mother has passed beyond, leaving a note for both which explains the entire situation.

There is nothing left for the writer except to return to the States and look up his second wife. This he does, discovering her on Yom Kippur at the home of her parents, just as father and mother are about to leave to attend services. Naturally, there is the happy ending. To make it more intricate, the wife has had a baby.

So far as the cast is concerned, beyond Miss Lee, the actor Wold Goldfaden, who plays the father, is the only one that looks like a possibility for the screen in character in the future. No one, and Maurice Schwartz least of all, looks like anything for the screen. *Fred,*

THE PERFECT CLOWN

Chadwick Production, starring Larry Semon, directed by Fred Newmeyer. At the Stanley, New York (25c. grind), for one day, March 3. Running time, 70 mins.

Bert Larry.......................Larry Semon
Mrs. Mulligan.......................Kate Price
John Mulligan..................Oliver Hardy
The Girl.......................Dorothy Dwan
The Boss..........................Otis Harlan
The Porter.....................G. Howe Black

A mediocre slapstick program comedy, prolonged into a feature by boresome repetition. It has for a star a comedian of no little ability. Being well known, he should be a box-office attraction.

The story is replete with familiar and, by this time, threadbare bits. As no author is credited, it may have been pasted together.

The title, attractive, betrays nothing, and therefore is useful. A young bank clerk, unable to pay his board bill at Mrs. Mulligan's boarding house, is forced to stay out all night with a bag containing $10,000 entrusted to him by the boss. So is your old man, for that. To make the tale more aged, the bank clerk is in love with the boss' steno.

The repetitious action in a dark barn. The clerk and the office porter are there scared stiff through a whole night. They change clothes with two escaped convicts, not the same two as the others. That takes up the large part of the film's length and is boring.

G. Howe Black, whose name describes his color, as the porter did his best with widened eyes and white teeth. A cemetery at night was his worst nemesis. Semon's jack-in-the-box antics are always—good. Kate Price as Mrs. Mulligan was herself — considerable. Otis Harlan as the boss looked perturbed enough, while Dorothy Dwan, the girl, had nothing to do but look pretty. Being comely has its handicaps, often so her gestures were stiff. An unprogrammed prison warden with flat nose and vegetable ears was just horrid.

Having failed to do anything admirable in their attempt at making this poor pragram comedy a good feature, the sponsors have only to sit back while Semon's name draws in the kids and those kiddishly inclined—if it can.

THE BAT

Roland West's production of the mystery farce by Mary Roberts Rinehart and Avery Hopwood. Adapted and directed by Roland West and released through United Artists. At the Mark Strand, New York, week March 14. Running time, 91 minutes.

Gideon Bell	Andre de Beranger
Courtleigh Fleming	Charles Herzinger
Miss Cornelia Van Gorder	Emily Fitzroy
Lizzie Allen, the maid	Louise Fazenda
Richard Fleming	Arthur Houseman
Dr. Wells	Robert McKim
Brooks	Jack Pickford
Miss Dale Ogden	Jewel Carmen
Billy, the Jap butler	Sojin
Moletti	Tullio Carminati
Detective Anderson	Eddie Gribbon
The Unknown	Lee Shumway

This picture ran 91 minutes—a long time for anybody's film, but it was interesting every minute of the way. Its maker, Roland West, has made several other mystery films before "The Bat," and the story is that he paid heavy money for the film rights to this long-run legit show. On top of that he adapted and directed the film. Then cast it. And then had United Artists distribute it. And it is aces every minute.

The mystery, in case you didn't see the play, concerns the death of a bank president, the theft of $200,000, the disappearance of the young cashier and the mysterious criminal who, dressed like a bat, and whose sign was the shadow of a bat projected from the front of an electric flashlight. This mysterious criminal was behind a thousand suspicious actions but meantime, every member of the cast was suspected of having been the culprit. In the end a detective who assumed charge of the case and who had bossed the crowd around for several days, was caught and unmasked as the crook. A real finish and for the folks who hadn't seen the play, a kick.

There's not a star in the case but one man, an Italian actor named Tullio Carminati, gives a performance as the detective-crook that is one of the best things done by a newcomer to the screen. Carminati is apparently an experienced and excellent actor, but his playing as the detective immediately suggests that someone should feature him in a series of detective thrillers, for he suggests the bearing, the urbanity and the lightning mind one usually expects in master criminals.

Everybody else was okeh and Louise Fazenda drew her share of laughs with the hoke maid's part, while Eddie Gribbon was good for a giggle or so as the hick detective who knew not his intelligence from the lining of a coat pocket.

An excellent picture, "The Bat," and one which looks to have been made on an economical scale, aside from the heavy money for rights. But what the film costs is West's business alone and the exhibitor buying it can depend on real value, provided he caters to a clientele which appreciates this type of mystery thriller.

As first run stuff, it looks like a set-up for big money with the small houses to be as good. The only question is whether such a picture needs a star. And the only thing to do in a case like this is to check up on the big city showings and decide for yourself. *Sisk.*

MY OWN PAL

A. J. G. Blystone production, released by William Fox, starring Tom Mix. From the story, "The Gallant Guardsman," by Gerald Beaumont; adapted by Lillian Hayward. Shown at the Rialto, New York, week March 14, 1926. Runningtime, 62 minutes.

Tom O'Hara	Tom Mix
Alice Derring	Olive Borden
August Derring	Tom Santschi
The Clown	Jay Hunt
Jill	Virginia Marshall
Jud McIntyre	William Colvin
Mrs. Jud McIntyre	Hedda Nova
Mollie	Virginia Warwick
Sergeant McGuire	Tom McGuire
Trixie Tremaine	Helen Lynch
Baxter Barton	Bardson Bard
Slippery Sam	Jacques Rollens

Somewhat different action meller with Tom Mix as the star. While it gives Mix a chance to start with Tony in the wild and woolly on a Wyoming ranch, he winds up in metropolitan atmosphere as a mounted copper in Los Angeles.

But it's a picture that is action from the word go. It has cowboys, crooks, chorus girls and the circus all woven into the tale. With Mix, Tony and little Virginia Marshall as the three principals, it is surefire for the box office anywhere. It's a Mix, but a different Mix, and still one that Mix fans will love.

Tom and Tony are on a ranch in Wyoming, so the story goes, and Tom feels the urge to move on. There's something calling him in the city. He resigns and starts on the trail. He first runs into a one-ring circus and there finds Jill (Virginia Marshall), a little girl about eight, who is being mistreated by her father while the mother lies inside the tent dying.

Tom knocks the father for stake pins and then the mother asks him to take the youngster and rear it. Here's the first wow of the picture. Tom mounts Tony and rides off with the child's father and a part of the circus mob chasing him on horses. The star, riding alongside of a moving train, jumps Tony into the baggage car with the little girl in his arms. The way this is handled makes it appear as though the train was speeding right along when the horse and rider land in the car.

That's good for a hand anywhere, and on Broadway Sunday afternoon they didn't muff it. You get a wreath for thinking that one up, Tom, 'cause it's different.

Then the big city. Mix must have picked his spot because it looked as though he moved right into the middle of a chorus girls' boarding house. There was one flossy blonde with those come hither eyes that was right on his trail from the first minute he hit the place. A couple of bits here with the little girl "pal" dressed in cowgirl costume mimicking every move the star made was another laugh bit.

Tom meets the real girl, in this case Olive Borden, a good-looking brunet, who plays the daughter of the chief of the Los Angeles police. The first meeting was on the train, when she interceded for the cowboy and the girl and compelled the conductor to let them ride in the baggage car with Tony. The second meeting occurred in a park, where the girl is in a runaway carriage, and Tom and Tony rescue her. She fixes for him to come to the police riding tournament. Tom grabs off a job on the force on the strength of his horsemanship and daring.

Then, after he's on the job a while, he rounds up one of a band of crooks that has turned off a big jewelry job, chasing him on a motorcycle and lassooing the crook, who is driving a car, pulling a turnover of the car by running his motorcycle around a tree and snubbing his rope. That's another new one for the book of westerns.

Finally Tom rounds up the whole gang of crooks, after he had been suspended for neglect of duty. Incidentally, rescues the chief's daughter, kidnaped by the band. Meantime, he fixed it for the "come hither" chorus girl by wiring his former boss on the ranch to come on and grab a housekeeper for himself.

Tom handles the role of the cowboy-copper in great shape, and certainly looks as picturesque a figure in the uniform as he does in his regular cowboy costume, and boy, how he handled himself in a couple of fights. Olive Borden makes good as the lead, but in reality little Virginia Marshall is the leading lady of this picture. Jay Hunt has a bit as Joey in the circus scene and lands it, while Hedda Nova as the mother of the little girl puts over her bit. Tom McGuire [yes, he of Broadway] has turned "copper" at last and is playing a sergeant of police. Just wait till that 47th street mob gets wise to that. Even Con will slip him the go-by for that breach, for you can't even film "copper" on 47th street. Tom would have looked better in a fireman's hat, if you get that.

Helen Lynch handled the chorus girl and slipped her past the post, while Virginia Warwick was a gun-moll. Bardson Bard pulled the heavy, looked it, and gave the general impression that he was one tough guy.

The direction was nicely handled and there wasn't a minute that there wasn't something doing in the picture. In the final scenes there was a rip-snorter of a fight in a warehouse, and here Mix was made the hero of a couple of fast gags in the battle stuff that brought corking laughs from the audience.

It's a picture that'll get 'em, and get dough, too. *Fred.*

The Johnstown Flood

William Fox production, directed by Irving Cummins, with George O'Brien starred. Story by Edfrid Bingham and Robert Lord. At Loew's New York, New York, March 11. Running time, 65 minutes.

Tom O'Day	George O'Brien
Anna Burger	Janet Gaynor
Joe Burger	Paul Panzer
Mandel's Boy	George Harris
Gloria	Flo Gilbert
J. Hamilton	Paul Nicholson
The Lumber Camp Boss	Anders Randolph

Primarily, this is a thrill picture, with the Johnstown Flood, well reproduced, as the outstanding punch. Realizing that such a production item cannot occupy all the footage, the most interesting point is whether the story preceding the thrill stuff holds up or whether it is merely an excuse.

The answer to this is that the picture is good throughout, and, although probably not of the first-run type, because of its lack of big names, it is corking daily change material and probably better than that for certain theatres. The story of Johnstown, Pa., and its great flood of 1889, in which hundreds of lives were lost, is well told, and in production items several streets of the old town have been built to thoroughly establish the atmosphere. That some good research work was done is apparent, and much local color, such as the saloon and the music hall adjoining, has been introduced for comedy relief and serves well.

The love story concerns a young engineer and the ward of a lumber camp owner. The engineer warns the owner that if he continues to impound great quantities of water in the dam for the purpose of floating his logs, the dam will burst and flood the valley. Of course, he is pooh-poohed. One day the dam does begin to crack, and little Anna Burger, daughter of a workman, is atop it with her horse. In the village, the young engineer is marrying his sweetheart, so the kid mounts and gallops through the valley, warning people. And a mile or so behind her is the menacing flood, sweeping trees in its path and topped by thousands of logs, piling high upon every house carried away and striking many people. Finally the girl reaches the church, but not soon enough to warn the wedding party, for almost immediately the flood strikes and the subsequent scenes picture the devastation of the community at large and the separation of the husband and bride in particular. They are reunited and a happy finish winds up the picture.

George O'Brien is good, but Janet Gaynor, a newcomer and a corker, wins the lion's share of everything as the female Paul Revere. Florence Gilbert is pretty in all her scenes, while the others of the cast are excellent. In production, this film rates highly, for the flood scenes look on the level in most places and it is virtually impossible to spot the points where miniature stuff was used. That in itself makes a hit with the audience, and when caught it was apparently liked by everyone. *Sisk.*

THE UNTAMED LADY

Famous Players picture starring Gloria Swanson. Frank Tuttle production, directed by Tuttle, based on a Fanny Hurst story. George Webber, photographer. Adaptation by J. A. Creelman. At the Rivoli, New York, week March 14. Running time, 66 minutes.

St. Clair Van Tassel	Gloria Swanson
Larry Gastlen	Lawrence Gray
Uncle George	Joseph Smiley
Shorty	Charles Graham

Here's a picture whose title describes it and it's the only difference from many other of Gloria Swanson film opuses. As true as Heinz has 57 kinds, so has Miss Swanson done 27 of these things. **Fannie Hurst got $50,000 for turning out "Mannequin" in a magazine prize story contest but $1.50 top as the purchase price for this yarn and she'd still be on "velvet." It's a bad picture.**

Adaptation is credited to J. A. Creelman. If there is any blame for him, let him have it—good.

Miss Swanson here again does a spoiled, vain society miss who goes untamed until the strong willed young man comes along and only tones her down after she has drawn him into a chase which puts the youth in a hospital. That's the yarn in a nutshell. It's pretty awful—one of Miss Swanson's worst. She does nothing in the film other than to share a few closeups with Lawrence Gray, the hero, besides grabbing a few for herself of course.

Miss Swanson's cast name is "St. Clair Van Tassel." Although that string doesn't appear in a subtitle, it's on the house program and that's the direct tipoff on the picture as a whole.

Miss Swanson's exploits as the uncurbed "deb" run the usual gamut of events. She pouts, rages and frets. Also she is responsible for a yacht being caught in heavy tank weather and her mailed fist lover assigns her to the boiler room as punishment, and no one cares.

Tuttle has inserted nothing beyond that which the conventional rules require of such a story. Productionally the picture is adequate as to interiors, Miss Swanson's dressing, etc., but the action fails to hold and never grips. Then the comedy is never too strong although snickers are a reaction on one or two occasions.

Joseph Smiley as the wealthy and doting uncle is weak here, good there. Gray, as the ultimate husband, warms up as he goes along for a nice performance superior to the script. Miss Swanson has done this thing so often "The Untamed Lady" must have been something of a stage wait from her personal angle. The others are purely background.

Strictly mediocre stuff that won't help Miss Swanson a bit. *Skig.*

FASCINATING YOUTH

Sam Wood Production, presented by Famous Players. Story by Byron Morgan, adapted by Paul Schofield. Features the Paramount School Junior Stars of 1926. Shown at their graduation dinner Ritz-Carleton Hotel, March 2. Running time, 79 minutes.

Teddy Ward	Charles Rogers
Jeanne King	Ivy Harris
Ross Page	Jack Luden
Randy Furness	Robert Ward
Bobby Stearns	Claude Buchanan
Dotty Sinclair	Mona Palma
Lorraine Lane	Thelma Todd
Loris Lane	Josephine Dunn
Betty Kent	Thelda Kenvin
Mae Oliver	Jeanne Morgan

Mary Arnold	Dorothy Nourse
Johnnie	Irving Hartley
Frederick Maine	Greg Blackton
"Duke" Slade	Robert Andrews
Gregory	Charles Brokaw
Sally Lee	Iris Gray
John Ward	Ralph Lewis
Ward's Secretary	Joseph Burke
The Professor	James Bradbury, Sr.
The Sheriff	Harry Sweet
Deputy Sheriff	William Black

The following stars and directors appear as themselves: Richard Dix, Adolphe Menjou, Clara Bow, Lois Wilson, Percy Marmont, Chester Conklin, Thomas Meighan, Lila Lee, Lewis Milestone, Mal St. Clair.

Here is a picture that has exploitation values if any picture had them. It is the production destined to introduce to the public the 16 youthful graduates of the first Paramount School for Stars. They are known as the Junior Stars of 1926, and with the right type of selling to the public the picture should pull them in.

After that it is bound to interest and entertain. The box office appeal of the production will be big in the cities where the graduates hail from, but interest should be worked up easily in other localities, because of the general interest in pictures and the hope that every other girl and young fellow have that they might get the same sort of a chance.

Of course the fact that 10 stars of known value appear in the picture, not only for brief shots, but for bits that are rather important, is naturally going to help sell the public. But it is going to be up to exploitation to put the picture over. The exhibitor that passes it up, however, will be sorry when he sees the other fellow put it over, and it can be put over.

It is a story of youth from beginning to end. Youth in Greenwich Village and the urge to make good which lets a group of them into a lot of complications but finally brings them out victorious at the end.

The hero is Charles Rogers, who is the son of a wealthy hotel man (Ralph Lewis). Dad doesn't like the way the boy is killing his time over a uke in a village studio, and finally chases him on the job to manage one of his hotels at a winter resort, promising him if he makes good he can marry the girl he has picked for himself and not the one dad selected. Ivy Harris plays the heroine. She is a sketch artist and working in a picture studio "doing heads" of the stars. Then the boy gets the idea that he must advertise the winter sports at the hotel, and possibly get some picture stars on the job to attract the crowds. At the last minute, when it looks as though his scheme would flop, the girl jumps in and saves the day for him.

In addition to the love story is a lot of jazzy atmosphere and an ice boat race that hold the suspense right up to the last puff of wind.

Among the 16 new comers are a couple that look like surefire bets for the future on the screen. Among the boys those that stand out particularly are Charles Rogers, Jack Luden, Robert Ward and Irving Hartley. Ivy Harris heads the list of girls, but those that look like safe bets are Mona Palma, Thelma Todd and Josephine Dunn. The latter looks like a beauty prize winner off the screen, but didn't seem to hit just right before the camera.

In addition to the youngsters are about five professionals in addition to the stars who appear as themselves. Of these Ralph Lewis and James Bradbury, Sr., take the honors. The latter particularly good in a comedy character role that got lots of laughs. *Fred.*

STELLA MARIS

Universal-Jewel, starring Mary Philbin. From story by William J. Locke, adapted by Charles Brabin and Mary Alice Scully. Directed by Charles Brabin. Loew's New York, New York, on double-feature bill March 12. Running time, 69 minutes.

Stella Maris, Unity Blake	Mary Philbin
John Risca	Elliot Dexter
Louisa Risca	Gladys Brockwell
Walter Herold	Jason Robards
Sir Oliver Blount	Phillips Smalley
Lady Blount	Lillian Lawrence
Dr. Haynes	Robert Bolder

This production is one of those instances that goes toward proving something for the picture industry. It is simply this: Because a picture was a good picture eight years ago, it is no criterion that it would be a good picture today.

"Stella Maris," with Mary Pickford as the star, in 1918 was a great picture. Great because it proved something at that time, and that was that Miss Pickford could act and do something else besides play the sweet girl parts that called but for one trend of emotion. Possibly, had Mary Philbin had as great a vogue with the American film fans, there might be as much interest today in her undertaking a double role created on the screen by Miss Pickford.

But, unfortunately, Miss Philbin hasn't the vogue, which isn't her fault, but rather that of the producer to whom she is under contract, for, after a most auspicious start, she was permitted or assigned to a series of parts that did not give her sufficient scope for her talents, for she has talent and has proven it.

Had Mary Philbin been built up to her true screen worth and permitted to come along with "Stella Maris," it might have been another story. Incidentally, this "Stella Maris" is another story from the one that Miss Pickford did, and in the reviewer's humble opinion the current adaptation is far from having the values that the original did.

That, in a measure, may account for the flop which this picture is executing. It is doing exactly that; otherwise how can it be accounted that its first run on Broadway was in a daily change house on a double-feature bill. That speaks for itself.

This adaptation by Charles Brabin, who directed, and Mary Alice Scully deviates entirely from the thought that motivated the original, which tended to show the two sides of the world through the eyes of two girls in it, both played by the same actress.

To one was revealed all that was good and lovely; to the other, all wretched and sordid. But the Brabin - Scully version went at things hammer-and-tongs, and they just banged away at it through five reels and let it go at that. They told the story just about the way they wished let it go at that, and the result is a bobke.

There is one feature of the picture in this end, however, that does deserve notice and mention, and that is the photography contributed by Milton Moore, who handled double exposures in a manner that was a revelation.

Mary Philbin as Stella Maris looked and played the role beautifully. As Unity Blake, she was doing a Lon Chaney, which conception of the waif character was all wrong. Although Unity had a forbidding exterior, she was to have been as good of heart as Stella herself, but that was far from the impression achieved. Elliott Dexter's role, that of John Risca, in the original played by Conway Tearle, was entirely switched, for no good reason at all, and a juvenile lead added in Walter Herold, played by Jason Robards, who had little to do and didn't do that very well.

But Gladys Brockwell as the heavy! That's another story. After seeing this girl in this picture, one pauses to ask the why and wherefore of Pola Negri, Nita Naldi, et al. Miss Brockwell trouped around everyone else in the picture and looked like a million dollars, winning out in a role that didn't have a sympathetic moment in it. She should have a real chance.

"Stella Maris" may have been made by U. so as to have something that sounded like "Stella Dallas," but the exhibitor better use his nut, for the "Dallas" picture is a bit, while, "Maris" is far from that. *Fred.*

LADIES OF LEISURE

Columbia production presented by C. B. C., starring Elaine Hammerstein. Released in State Right market. Running time 61 minutes.

This picture just winds its way through an hour and as much footage as can pass through a projection machine in that time and gets nowhere.

Even the title, although about the best thing the picture can boast of, doesn't mean a thing in connection with the story itself. From the box office standpoint "Ladies of Leisure" looks to be a sure flop. Possibly the reason behind making it seems there was a chance to put over a plug for one of Irving Berlin's numbers.

Elaine Hammerstein plays the lead in the story and T. Roy Barnes is also in the cast. Miss Hammerstein is the companion to a society flapper, whose brother falls in love with her and proposes marriage but the girl decides that rather than have him learn of several events in her past life she will disappear.

Meantime the society flapper is pursuing Barnes who has the role of an eligible bachelor with the sole purpose of leading him to the altar. He in turn takes the former companion to his rooms after stopping her from jumping off a bridge. There he is confronted by the brother of the girl who is pursuing him who demands to know what he is doing with a companion in his rooms. At the precise moment to make things interesting little sister steps out of the bedroom instead of the heroine and calmly announces to her brother that she and the batch were married that afternoon. That cinches things for her and the poor batch has to go through a ceremony later to make good for the girl's lie.

It is difficult to determine who was the worst in the cast, they were all so bad. Barnes at one moment was doing comedy and the next would find him playing straight until it was impossible to figure what he was really trying to do. *Fred.*

Cowboy and Countess

William Fox western, starring Buck Jones. Story by Maxine Alton and Adele Buffington. Directed by R. William Neill. Running time, 60 minutes.

Jerry Whipple	Buck Jones
Countess Justina	Helen D'Algy
Nanette	Diana Miller
Edwin Irving Mansfield	Harvey Clark
Slim	Monte Collins, Jr.
Duke de Milos	Fletcher Norton
White Eagle	Himself

A lot of action in this western, which has Buck Jones as the star. At the same time it is a little different from the average western, as it takes the star to Europe at the head of a wild west show and mixes him up with the nobility. In addition to Jones, White Eagle, his horse, should come in for a large share of the praise that the picture deserves. For the average houses the picture will do nicely, and in the neighborhoods where they like westerns this one will surely please.

Jones, as Jerry Whipple, is a college-bred rancher who likes the West and the wild and woolly ways. Into the routine of the ranch a stranded theatrical manager eases his way, and suggests that the owner of the ranch and his collection of cowboys would be sure-fire money makers on a tour of Europe. But the rancher cannot see it until the Countes Justina comes into his life. The automobile in which she is touring goes off the road and falls down a mountainside, with Jerry rescuing the girl. She and her father, with the girl's traveling companion, spend the night at the home of the rancher, with the cowboy falling like a ton of lead for the girl.

The next morning he is ready to take the European trip and harkens to the pleadings of the busted manager. Then a steamer trip and finally the capitals of Europe, with the show a tremendous success, and at the moment when the villainous Duke is about to marry the Countess, who sends for the American, and he brings his whole show with him and rides off with the girl. That gives an excuse for a chase, a rough-and-tumble battle between the bandit henchmen of the Duke and the cowboys, and finally winds up with Jerry winning the Countess.

From an action standpoint there is nothing left out of this one. *Fred.*

Counsel for Defense

Associated Exhibitors' release, directed by Burton King, with Betty Compson and House Peters starred.

The tag title of this one bore the "Copyright, 1925," mark, which indicates it has been out and around for quite a few months. Moreover, the print reviewed was in deplorable condition with streaks running through it like Chinks through Shanghai.

The story is the old one about the crooked politicians who try to run the town and pick up a little graft money on the side. One of their little stunts is to railroad a famous typhoid specialist to jail and then take over the town water works and run them down so that they can be sold to the man they have picked—and thereby get a cut. But a typhoid epidemic breaks out, the old doctor's daughter gets on the local paper and does some of that fancy publishing which only newspapers can do in the movies, and after her father is released to care for the sick she and her boy friend, the editor, triumph over the whole crooked caboodle just on the eve of election.

The title is gained from the fact that the girl is a lawyer and pleads her father's case in court. But even that isn't much of a thrill, and this one is strictly for the honky tonkies. The players do well, but the various situations are of that maudlin variety which marked the films of the 1910 era. Betty Compson and Rockcliffe Fellows the heavy and Jay Hunt the old doctor.

Far below the recent A. E. standard, which has been good. *Sisk.*

THE BARRIER

Metro-Goldwyn release. Rex Beach's novel directed by George Hill. At the Capitol, N. Y., week March 21. Running time, 67 minutes.

Meade Durrell..............Norman Kerry
Gale....................Henry B. Walthall
Stark Bennett...........Lionel Barrymore
Necia......................Marceline Day
Sergeant Murphy............George Cooper
Alluna.......................Princess Neola
No Creek Lee...............Bert Woodruff
Poleon.......................Mario Carillo
First Mate...................Pat Harmon
Necia's Mother...............Shannon Day

Ten years ago Rex Beach, at the head of his own company, made a film version of his story, "The Barrier." This week at the Capitol, Metro-Goldwyn is presenting a remade version of the same story and remade with a couple of "kicks" in the filming that will make for box office surefire. The picture starts off with a terrific smash in a storm at sea that is one of the greatest scenes of its kind the camera has yet caught, and just before the final fade-out there is about 10 minutes of terrific suspense with an ice scene that in its way is just as good as the ice floe in Griffith's "Way Down East." With these two kicks, a story that carries melodramatic suspense and love interest, a couple of corking rough and tumble fights, all splendidly directed by George Hill, the M. G. M. combination can chalk up another winner to their credit.

The story, as far as the current adaptation goes, differs somewhat from the original screen version. In the former the character of "Poleon, the half-breed, was one of the outstanding figures, now, however, it proves to be just one of the minor roles.

The picture is well cast, and Norman Kerry makes a fine upstanding figure of the young army lieutenant in charge of the post in the far north. Marceline Day is featured in the billing, but does not stand out particularly. She is adequate for the role in a certain sense, but that is all. Henry B. Walthall, as Gale, gives about as fine a performance as one could ask, while Lionel Barrymore, as the heavy, troups about a million dollars' worth. George Cooper, in a comedy role, also scores, as does Bert Woodruff, doing a "sourdough."

It is the ice stuff, however, that will get to the audiences and make them talk about the picture. Whoever handled the photography and the matching up of the miniatures in this sequence certainly deserves a full measure of credit. A full rigged schooner is caught in an ice jam in the far north and the skipper, trying to make for sea, takes his vessel right into the jam, where it is finally crushed and sunk under a wall of falling ice.

This one is "in" as far as anything can be. *Fred.*

THE NEW KLONDIKE

Famous Players picture starring Tom Meighan and featuring Lila Lee. From a Ring Lardner story, adapted by T. J. Geraghty and directed by Lewis Milestone, Alvin Wyckoff, photographer. At the Rivoli, New York, week March 21. Running time, 77 mins.

Tom Kelly..................Thomas Meighan
Evelyn Lane...........................Lila Lee
"Bing" Allen......................Paul Kelly
Flamingo Applegate..........Hallie Manning
Morgan West......................Robert Craig
Owen......................George De Carleton
Joe Cooley......................J. W. Johnston
Bird Dog..........................Brenda Lane
Col. Dwyer......................Tefft Johnson

A combination Florida and baseball story. If it's not timely on one end the other angle may suffice. Not much above the average screen tale, with plenty of theatrical license taken on a big league team's training routine, but superior at least to the general run of scenarios with which Meighan has been afflicted lately.

Paul Kelly (from legit and brother to Gregory Kelly) well nigh runs away with the picture as a "busher" breaking into fast company. Kelly plays it four ways from the ace, and while he doesn't do much actual diamond work outside of taking a couple of swings at a ball, it's off the field that he clicks as the awkward but faithful friend.

Lardner wrote this Florida theme with his tongue in his cheek. Geraghty, the adapter, has lifted some of that satire to the screen. The laughs mainly center upon the real estate craze that hits the ball club. One action has the batter of a home run stopping to look over land maps with the different guardians of the sacks as he rounds the bases.

Meighan plays the star pitcher who is let out by the crooked manager and turns to real estate with himself the head of a company comprising his former fellow ball players.

"Cleaned" by the scheming bench director, the ball players have to go back to playing ball, but Meighan and his "busher" pal turn another deal that returns the money all around with a profit.

Meanwhile there is the girl (Lila Lee) whose grandmother is used as a dupe in the fraudulent land deal.

Not much for Meighan to do. As a ball player he doesn't even toss a ball, and the eventual fight is mirrored in the faces of the players standing outside a room. Meighan simply saunters through it, looking as good as ever, but not called upon for much other than the journey to "location."

Kelly's the one. If it's his first picture he has a great start. Miss Lee pars her male lead as to effort, while Hallie Manning, opposite Kelly as a maid, stamps the role to stand in relief. J. W. Johnston doesn't look like the manager of a ball club, but Robert Craig convinces as the shady realtor.

Milestone, directing, found time to get in a couple of aeroplane shots around Miami that may or may not mean anything with the slump the "blueprint state" is now undergoing being on, but it's pretty to look at and would have been prettier a week ago before the spring weather arrived.

Where they like Meighan they should pass this one. If they don't particularly dote on this star, then "The New Klondike" shapes as average major. Being a baseball picture you can at least call the count two-and-two. *Skig.*

DESERT GOLD

Famous Players production made on Coast under supervision of Hector Turnbull and B. P. Schulberg. Adapted by Lucien Hubbard from the story by Zane Grey and directed by George B. Seitz. Neil Hamilton, Shirley Mason, Robert Frazer and William Powell featured. At the Rialto, New York, March 21 week. Running time, about 70 minutes.

George Thorne..............Neil Hamilton
Mercedes Castanada..........Shirley Mason
Dick Gale....................Robert Frazer
"Snake" Landree.........William Powell
Don Sebastian...............Josef Swickard
Richard Stanton Gale, Sr.....George Irving
"One Round" Kelly..........Eddie Gribbon
Yaqui.......................Frank Lackteen
Sergeant....................Bernard Siegel
Goat-Herder.................Richard Howard
Verd..........................George Rigas
Half-wit......................Ralph Yearsley

For about two years Famous Players has been grinding out these Zane Grey's western stories, all substantially alike in theme, yet retold time and again with different characters. That they have proven unsuccessful in the big first runs is well known. Most have been made without benefit of a star cast. People long ago learned not to patronize a picture simply because it was an adaptation of a favorite book.

For the daily changes and other minor houses, the pictures probably fit well, because filled with action and good looking scenery, not to mention fairly popular players who are featured but not starred. This one is an excellent picture of its type but the cast is plainly weak in any presumed pulling power. Neither Neil Hamilton, William Powell, Robert Frazer nor Shirley Mason mean much in a box office sense, notwithstanding their individual work is good.

The story is about the daughter of a Mexican ranch owner and her love for Lieut. Thorne, of the U. S. Cavalry. "Snake" Landree, a villainous character, wrecks their ranch and tries to steal the girl, but the arrival of young Dick Gale from the east, a buddy of Lieut. Thorne's, gives the officer help in his struggle. When Gale rescues the girl in a hotel it immediately becomes a matter of escape. As Thorne is slightly hurt by a bullet he is left behind to round up his cavalrymen while Gale, the girl and a faithful Yaqui Indian follower hop to the desert. There the villains are within an inch of success when the Yaqui sacrifices himself by loosening rocks which pry up a huge boulder. Although it crushes him, it also starts a landslide which puts an end to Landree and his crew.

Then comes the "kick" in the story—a weak point for the picture.

The soldier has loved the girl and she has loved him. But with the arrival of Gale, she finds she loves him more, a silly thing inasmuch as she met him for but an instant whereas she had known Thorne, of exemplary character and outstanding bravery, for many months. But the windup is that Thorne realizes the girl loves his pal, so manlike he steps aside for the true lovers.

Well made, this picture, and well acted. Backgrounds good and the various minor parts stand up well. Hardly a first run, however, because the story has no novelty and the names but little pull of their own. *Sisk.*

TOO MUCH MONEY

First National picture, co-featuring Lewis Stone and Anna Q. Nilsson. Adapted from the play by Israel Zangwill. Directed by John Francis Dillon. Produced under supervision of Earl Hudson at the New York, one-half double bill, March 18, 1926. Running time, 83 minutes.

Robert Broadley..................Lewis Stone
Annabel Broadley............Anna Q. Nilsson
Stuart..........................Robert Cain
Duke Masters..................Derek Glynne
Rabinowitz......................Edward Elkas
Mrs. Rabinowitz..................Ann Brody

When Louis Stone's leading man days are over he may become a film comic, stooping at nothing the script calls for, even to taking a custard pie on the chin. Anyway, this is the summarization after watching Mr. Stone as Robert Broadley in this First National production. Here Stone is wallowing in a farcical rough-house "bit" in a delicatessen shop, where there is a run on herring at 5c. a dozen; later in a janitor's make-up, getting the worst of it in a scene with one of **the tenants, and finally beaned by his frau with a mirror when he is fighting the man who would steal his fortune and wife.**

The film seems a comedy proposition for Charles Chaplin, Buster Keaton, Harold Lloyd or one of the regularly established comics, but for Louis Stone it misses fire; it is too much low comedy for him to carry.

Miss Nilsson cops about all there is in this film, slow in starting and depended a great deal upon one funny situation; the dashing hero-husband of other big romantic films doing a slapstick scene in the delicatessen that would have been a set-up for some of the real screen funny boys.

The story calls for a big stretch of the imagination; a very rich man and his charming wife jump in a jiffy from the kind of luxuries one used to see in the DeMilles to extreme poverty with the pair in a kitchen washing dishes. In the poverty scenes there are some old camera stand-bys and captions.

There are some capitally staged "bits," but one must stop to pity the humorous plight the hero gets in. Too unnatural for results desired.

Just a commonplace story made more elastic by camera license.

Photographically there is nothing wrong with "Too Much Money." Its comedy may save it from falling from grace altogether. To play up Stone here as a low comedian doing slapstick might be the means of creating curiosity among his fans. That's the only chance the film has. *Mark.*

THE PART TIME WIFE

Labeled Gotham Production. Produced by Sam Sax. Alice Calhoun is starred. The scenario was adapted from the Snappy Stories novelette by Peggy Gaddis, adaptation by James J. Tynan and continuity by Henry McCarty. Directed by Henry McCarty; Glenn Belt, assistant director. Distributed by the Lumas Film Corp. (Sam Sax, president). At the New York theatre, New York, March 18, one-half double bill.

Doris Fuller....................Alice Calhoun
Kenneth Scott...................Robert Ellis
DeWitt Courtney............Freeman Wood
Ben Ellis........................Edwards Davis
Allen Keane......................Charles West
Nita Northrup....................Janice Peters
Toodles Thornton..........Patricia Palmer

There are times this picture looks immense; at others it fades fast into celluloid-killing stuff that slows the theme up considerably and renders a knockout to the impression that has obtained.

There are snatches and "bits" that help the film from doing a nose dive and there is quite a cast for this story.

Alice Calhoun just about hogs the picture, although there was a scene in which Janice Peters had the center. That was where Miss Peters, attired in bedtime negligee, was trying to force her physical charms upon the hero and the hero would have none of it, although at the time he was living a part-time life with his charming wife.

It is a movie story; a studio is used, and that made it cheaper on a lot of footage by having that sort of atmospheric locale. A writer and his wife seem pretty happy until the latter decides she must carve out her film-starring career. She **does, only to bring about some jealous climaxes when the screen lead makes real love to her.**

That vamping scene is a high light that shows that no respectable newspaper man is safe even in his own home, which is his palace, or words to that effect.

It's an independent film, the cast, more than anything else, apparently is biggest asset. *Mark.*

THE DEVIL'S CIRCUS

Metro-Goldwyn-Mayer picture starring Norma Shearer; featuring Charles E. Mack and Carmel Myers. Written and directed by Benjamin Christianson. At Capitol, New York, week March 28. Running time, 74 mins.

Mary	Norma Shearer
Carlstop	Charles Emmett Mack
Yonna	Carmel Myers
Lieberkind	John Miljan
Mrs. Petersen	Claire McDowell
Little Anita	Joyce Coad

Christianson's first picture on this side of the Atlantic and its story is undeniably foreign. Inasmuch as Christianson both wrote and directed this one it's to be assumed he about treated the subject as he saw fit, but "The Devil's Circus" is a study.

Its hero is a crook, the heroine is seduced by the villain, and the latter's femme eventually turns to the streets for a livelihood after he goes blind. It's foreign and it's different.

Being well done as to production there is no reason why American audiences should shun it if its tale is somewhat more potent than the usual prescription written by our scenario writers. That a better cast might have made this into a corking release will be realized upon the viewing. Although as it stands it fully rates a hearing in the first-line houses.

The story centers upon a one-ring circus, obviously Continental, but no word to imply as much. The only instances that the action is taking place in a foreign clime comprise a name stamped on a piano and a fleeting war glimpse which shows the hero, Carl (Mr. Mack) in a German uniform. And, maybaps, that's the initial American screen hero costumed in German gray.

Mary (Miss Shearer) comes to the city to join the circus and succeeds in securing a place in the ballet. Immediately desired by the lion tamer, Hugo (Mr. Miljan), she is eventually ravished by him while en route to a next stand after Carl, who has been looking after her, is sent to prison for a robbery which would have permitted them to marry.

The jealousy of Hugo's former love, Yonna (Miss Myers), leads the latter to disengage the pulley while Mary is working on a flying perch. She plunges into the cage of lions working beneath her as the "punch" of the circus and also the kick of the picture.

The action then takes two "shots" of the war and picks up the tale four years later with Mary, now a cripple, selling dolls on the streets. Eventually brought together, Mary tells Carl why she cannot wed him. He seeks Hugo for vengeance. But when he finally discovers him, Hugo is blind, with the jealous Yonna still clinging, albeit she has become a street walker.

Christianson has mixed a certain religious psychology into the telling through subtitles relating to Carl's and Mary's disbelief and belief in God, which morale they exchange as the hardships mount. That is, until Mary walks again at the finish of the picture, whence the affirmative side of the question is again accepted by Mary.

It may be that Christianson could not impart or draw from the players that which he desired in the way of characterization. Certainly Charles Emmett Mack has been seen to much better advantage than in this instance. A certain stiffness and unnaturalness about his performance here that never wears off. In the same vein is the "heavy" of Miljan, sometimes so stressed as to be melodramatic, although that seems to be the foreign vogue for villains.

Miss Shearer does not convince as the country girl become a circus aerialist. The four-year jump in the continuity which picks her up as a cripple shows her face as clear and as fresh as before the accident and the hardships of the war, a fault on somebody's part if realism were the objective. Of the more important members Miss Myers' playing impresses as the most genuine.

Productionally, nothing lavish other than a ballet which appears out of all proportion to a one-ring show. The flashes of Miss Shearer doing a casting act just below the ceiling and over the lion's cage is double photography well done by C. F. Reynolds. Beyond that Christianson has included a few things by suggestion, this taking in the seduction of Mary.

It's more weighty than the average screen fare over here, but that doesn't mean so much as the playing of the story somewhat offsets its strength. It won't do Christianson any harm, for they'll make allowances for his initial effort and this work should establish the fact that he knows what he's doing. It is more a matter of his getting the desired results from a U. S. cast.

The picture should be a delectable bit for the foreign market and can stand on its own in this country. But that it could have been a better film than it is is hardly deniable.

Skig.

The Dancer of Paris

Robert Kane production for First National release. Story by Michael Arlen. Directed by Alfred Santell, with Conway Tearle featured above Dorothy Mackaill, who plays the title part. At the Strand, New York, March 28 week. Running time, 76 minutes.

Noel Anson	Conway Tearle
Consuelo	Dorothy Mackaill
Sir Roy Martel	Robert Cain
Dr. Frank	Henry Vibart
Cortez	Paul Ellis
Mammy	Frances Miller Grant

The Arlen craze is almost over. And "The Dancer of Paris" may be counted upon to kill it in the movies before it gets a start, for this picture is a lurid 10c. flesh-tinted yarn of the sort servant girls love.

It has several direct attempts to introduce obscenity. As a matter of fact the screen hasn't yet seen a film which tries so hard to be nasty and thrilling as this one, but even those New York censors who don't mind what they let slip through cut a nice chunk of footage from that "big" scene wherein the girl dancer was having her clothes pulled from her by a queer mob of roues for whom she had done a "rising through the table" act.

It is all too obvious to be anything more than humorous to people who passed the fifth grade at school. Its chance' therefore, lies with the mugs who accept this sort of thing just as they accept the various "True Story" magazines and "autobiographies of modern courtesans.

In story it's about a gal who was vilely insulted and who, being sore as the deuce, yelled this sub-title:

"I detest all men. Curse them!"

So to haunt the man who insulted her she followed him everywhere, still remaining pure, of course, but putting up the appearance of being as wicked as the movies permit a lady to be.

In Paris a friend of the cad who "done" her dirt comes along and strikes up an acquaintanceship. He is convinced that she is not only the salt of the earth but the synthesis of all things beautiful. He courts and woos her plenty. His caddish friend does his worst to besmirch the girl's reputation and enlists the aid of her dancing partner.

This fellow drops her in a dance, but that doesn't kill her. To really sink her in the eyes of her hero she is framed to visit an expensive but vile joint in her meagre dancing costume, the pretext being a charity performance. She goes and her boy friend hears about it. He follows.

Once inside the place—where the ladies are naked when posing as statues, but modest enough to put shawls on afterward—she steps into an especially built elevator and is carried up through a table about which the guests are seated.

The arch-degenerate of the mob starts to introduce her, and the boys make a grab for her clothes, feeling in their Arlenish way that a lady shouldn't wear furs in a steam-heated room. But in comes the hero. He turns off the switch.

But the hero was too late. The censors of the grand old Empire State of New York had beaten him to it, for they sliced the scenes wherein the good gal lost everything but her purity and look of terror. Hero makes the rescue and has a nice time riding home in the taxi. At home they hear the dad is dying, but that on his lips is the ever recurrent name, "Consuelo," etc. He wants her to dance for him.

After being convinced her treatment has driven him mad she consents and dons two individual breastplates of the type used by the extra-attraction burlesque dancers, a loin cloth and a cloak to be used for dropping purposes. As the man dies she hooches or cooches. When through shaking it up the dying man utters his last sub-title, "I think I'll go to sleep." Many a coocher before has sent many a guy to sleep.

After that the gal asks the hero to take her back to America, where she was a good little child. Hero, obliging, falls over her almost nude body and contributes a great big kiss for purity's sake.

Conway Tearle, Dorothy Mackaill and Robert Cain are the principal actors in this. Tearle is the hero, Miss Mackaill doing as well as possible as the heroine, although her appearance here is detrimental to herself and a piece of miscasting by the producer. Cain is okeh as the villain.

It would be wrong to condemn "The Dancer of Paris" in totality. The director, Santell, has turned out a first rate job which at times almost but not quite mitigates the trashy story. His frequent close-ups of the various people reveal interesting studies, while the big scenes are lavishly put on and well handled.

This picture will be of little value in several sections where the censors are really strict. There it will probably be hacked beyond recognition. There's a chance that its attempt at filth will draw in some of the larger towns, but its booking should be a matter of judgment with the exhibitor. Ony one catering to a family or neighborhood clientele should screen it before exhibiting. The sub-titles make it very tiresome, as they constitute a great percentage of the footage. There are 113 sub-titles. First run houses playing it may expect a universal panning from the critics.

"The Dancer of Paris," whether it makes money or not, is that type of film which makes enemies for pictures as a whole. It in no way conforms to the recent Hays proclamation that the M. P. P. D. A. group is not making films which do not square with the proprieties of the churches of America.

Sisk.

The Gilded Highway

Warner Brothers release, made and directed by J Stewart Blackton. Adapted by Marion Constance from the novel, "A Little More," by W. B. Maxwell. Dorothy Devore and Johnny Harron featured. At Loew's New York Roof, March 26, as half of a double bill. Running time, over 80 minutes.

Jonathan Welby	Maclyn Arbuckle
Mrs. Welby	Florence Turner
Sarah	Mathilde Comont
Irene Quarts	Myrna Loy
Jack Welby	Johnny Harron
The Uncle of the Welbys	Sheldon Lewis
Primrose Welby	Dorothy Devore
Anabel Price	Andree Torneur
Hugo Blythe	Gardner James

Although Commodore J. Stewart Blackton was one of the pioneers in the movie business, his recent productions indicate that he still sticks to the old stories and directs them in the old way. This well-produced but nevertheless faulty film is but another example of the type of picture that Vitagraph used to make—until they made so many of them they sold out to Warners.

The story is of a happy though improvident middle class family. A rich uncle comes into their midst to spend his last days, and in his revengeful way leaves them an indefinite fortune. Immediately the family leaves off its humble living to dwell in a palace. The mother, who used to wash dishes, gets a lorgnette and uses it plenty; the father, who was once glad if his suits weren't shiny, takes to wearing the high hat and spats, while the children forget their old sweethearts to mingle and spend their money among the ultra set. And the parties given by them resemble parties such as were never given off a movie lot. But there comes the day of reckoning and the family is left without a dime. Boy and girl go to work, while mama and papa go to the poor-house. Like the characters in a Dickens' they sit huddled up, mourning their fate, but not stirring a hand to alleviate conditions.

The faithful family servant is running the old home as a boarding-house and takes them in. And the moral is that money isn't the only thing in life.

The scenario is the worst thing about the picture. It is as melodramatic in a silly way as anything produced recently. Maudlin sentiment loses its effect because the characters had behaved in the manner of damphools while they had money and the audience sympathy was not for them in poverty.

Too long, this picture, and unconvincing.

Maclyn Arbuckle is excellent as the father and Sheldon Lewis as the mean uncle also gives an actory but effective impersonation. Mathilde Comont as the maid has her comedy moment, but so many are forced by the director that her otherwise good work suffers.

For the daily changes this may slip by. As a first-run it is impossible, and that the Warners regard it accurately is indicated by the picture being one half of a double bill at the New York.

Sisk.

THE LADY FROM HELL

Associated Exhibitors' release, produced and directed by Stuart Paton, with Blanche Sweet starred. Adapted by J. Grubb Alexander from Norton S. Parker's story, "My Lord of the Double B." One half of a double bill at Loew's New York Roof, March 26. Running time, about 60 minutes.

Lady Margaret Darnley	Blanche Sweet
Sir Robin Carmichael	Roy Stewart
The Earl of Kennett	Ralph Lewis
Sir Hugh Stafford	Frank Elliott
The Hon. Charles Darnley	Edgar Norton
Billy Boy	Mickey Moore
Ruth King	Ruth Wallace

A moderately interesting romantic story, with the background attractively laid in the west of the United States and later in Scotland. The title is obtained from the appellation given the Scotch troops by the Germans during the World War, the Heinies being reported to have viewed kilted men with astonishment, noted their fighting prowess and straightway dubbed them "the ladies from hell." That at least serves as the explanation.

The romance is between Sir Robin Carmichael and Lady Margaret Darnley, receiving its climactic interest in Scotland when Sir Robin is arrested for a murder he is alleged to have committed in the west. But the windup has him proven guilty, for he is brought to this country for trial and execution. As he is about to get the rope hitched to his neck, a little boy rushes to the scafford and tells them that he shot the man, his father, because papa was beating mama with a bull-whip.

Previously Robin had been a cowpuncher in the west and circumstantial evidence was against him. In Scotland he and some cowboys whom he had brought over kidnaped Lady Margaret as she was about to be married to another man, brought her to his house and they were hitched. This being previous to the trial, she stuck close to him, despite an intense family opposition.

Both Miss Sweet and Mr. Stewart play their roles well, while the minor characters are all nicely chosen.

"The Lady from Hell" will serve as a satisfactory daily change program, and in localities where the star is strong, may be suitable for better use. *Sisk.*

The Other Woman's Story

Preferred Picture, produced by B. P. Schulberg, but now distributed in this territory by the Commonwealth Exchange. Robert Frazer, Mahlon Hamilton and Alice Calhoun featured. Story by Pearl Gaddis and directed by B. F. Stanley. At the Broadway, shown in conjunction with vaudeville. Running time, 63 minutes.

Mrs. Bennett Colby...........Alice Calhoun
Bennett Colby..............Robert Frazer
Miss Prentiss..........Helen Lee Worthing
Robert Marshall........Mahlon Hamilton
Mildred Van................Gertrude Short
The Judge..................David Torrence
The Prosecuting Attorney....Charles Clary

The finish has a woman charged with murder—plainly a first degree case. The state is New York and the penalty is the chair. Yet for quite a few minutes before the finale this plot ties tighter the bonds of evidence about her until it is plain she committed a crime which was almost pinned on her husband. And it is just as plain that her husband wants to get rid of her for another woman.

That's what is wrong with this picture.

No audience wants to see a woman sent to the chair, nor do they want to leave her, no matter how lying and despicable she might have been, in the shadow of an execution.

Robert Marshall was murdered. Bennett Colby was accused and convicted by a jury. New evidence. His "sweetheart" dug up a little prostie who knew the inside of the case and who told on Mrs. Colby. Tables turned. Colby released and his wife in custody.

In developing the story, the scenarist has been crude enough to use about 20 cut-backs, each a different version of what happened. By the time several witnesses had told what they knew and each a different story, the thread of the thing was too confused to ever be straightened. The director had a love for those cut-backs and he made them fade in and out as slowly as possible. Boresome.

Cast good in spots. Mahlon Hamilton the best. Helen Lee Worthing was nice as the other woman. Although she did her best to show them that blondes have sex appeal, she registered little in that line. Frazer was adequate as the accused man; Gertrude Short conventional as the prostie who gave the real solution, while Alice Calhoun as the real murderess was a total loss.

Not liked at the Broadway and not satisfactory for a house which takes pride in its clientele. Maybe okeh for the daily change grinds in the business districts of cities, but aside from that of little use to exhibitors. *Sisk.*

NORTH STAR

Five-reeler dramatic, featuring Strongheart, trained dog. Howard Estabrook production. Based on the novel by Rufus King. Adapted by Charles Horan. Directed by Paul Powell. Distributed by Associated Exhibitors. At the Stanley theatre, New York, March 29, 1926. Running time, 63 minutes.

Marcia Gale............Virginia Lee Corbin
Wilbur Gale...............Harold Austin
Noel Blake................Ken Maynard
Dick Robbins............Stuart Holmes
Archie West.................Clark Gable
Wayne Connor...........William Riley
Tramp.....................Syd Crossley
Tramp....................Jerry Mandi

As usual in productions featuring such trained dogs as Strongheart, the audience can wager heavy odds that there will be a scene where the canine star will be leaping at the villain's throat and tearing huge slices out of his clothes. In "North Star" there is no deviation from the expected.

However, one must attach especial praise in this picture, which has Strongheart pulling some of his sagacious and intelligent dog sense to the introduction of some comedy by-play that will go a long way in making this picture more popular in the neighborhoods where the dog stars have such loyal and unmistakable followers.

Two tattered knights of the road, ragged hoboes, are worked in most advantageously. Their scene in capturing Strongheart is very well done and a worthy asset in adding comedy, both novel and entertaining.

At best the big punch is the work of the dog. Strongheart adds another feather to his rep, that already has him working hard and keeping Jane Murfin's name in the credits—something that heretofore was passed up. Strongheart is cleverly trained, of that there is no doubt, and he does some of his splendid work in this film.

A love story. Not much of a one, to be sure, as the main theme is centered in a rich boy running away from a supposed murder, only to be blackmailed, until Strongheart chases the master mind over a precipice. That makes it easier for the silhouetted fadeout of the two hearts that are to beat as one "in the gloaming."

At the start is considerable background, some rich and stately interiors and exteriors to denote wealth; an auto is sent rolling down a high embankment into water, with Strongheart having a corking scene here, where he makes his escape from the tonneau.

Several fights between the main male characters, but the main encounter is between the villain and the dog.

Photography A1 and Strongheart most acceptable in all of his scenes.

A good picture of its kind; shows that real money is being spent to give the star dog some surroundings above the average.

The title is taken from the name of the dog that wins the main prize at a dog show. The characters by the human cast are, as a whole, pleasing. Miss Corbin is nice to look at, although with little to do in the feminine lead. The villain is Mr. Holmes, while the hero is Mr. Maynard. A good piece of acting was done by Mr. Austin, a handsome boy, who shows ability and may bear watching.

But the dog is the star, and readily shows his worth. *Mark.*

THE NEW CHAMPION

Produced by Columbia Pictures and released under the Perfection trademark. Story by Dorothy Howell and direction by Reaves Eason. William Fairbanks and Edith Roberts starred. At the New York as half of a double bill. Running time, 53 minutes.

A strictly small-time picture, not nearly so good as others made by the athletic William Fairbanks and fit only for the little houses where they change the program daily.

The story is about the brave blacksmith's helper who substitutes for Knockout Riley in a boxing match and wins not only the laurels but his sweetheart and $5,000—to pay for the operation which his mother has just undergone. Immediately the fight is over he hops into a car (bathrobe and all) and drives back to the old homestead where he finds his mother passing through a crisis. So with the title:

"I've won my fight, mother—now you must win yours," the picture goes to a fadeout.

Fairbanks and Miss Roberts are suitable but the scenario is jumpy and for long stretches the story wanders. To find another fault, a romance ripens between the boy's 16-year-old sister (played in the best manner of a river show-boat ingenue) and a tough old fighter of 40 or more.

This one probably cost $10,000 at the outside to produce. The exteriors used are meager and unpretentious, while everything else is taken outdoors. *Sisk.*

FOR HEAVEN'S SAKE

A Harold Lloyd production from the story by John Grey, Ted Wilde and Clyde Bruckman. Directed by Sam Taylor. Released by Paramount. At Rialto theatre, New York, for a run beginning April 4. Running time, 58 minutes.

The Uptown Boy.............Harold Lloyd
The Downtown Girl........Jobyna Ralston
The Roughneck................Noah Young
The Gangster................James Mason
The Optimist................Paul Wiegel

This is the first of the Harold Lloyd comedy features to be made by the comedian's own company for release through the Paramount organization. As a gag picture it is a perfect wow. And this despite the fact that in some quarters prior to its showing there were rumbles of doubt as to the strength of the feature. After seeing it there is no doubt but that it is a picture that is built to order for the exhibitor. It is full of laughs caused by action, with punch following punch in rapid succession, and the running time is just short of an hour, so that the theatre can get the turn over of the crowds. The first two days of the picture on Broadway at the Rialto found all house records shattered with an $8,150 day for Sunday (opening) and better than $7,000 for the second day, with the indications pointing to a $50,000 week with 1,900 seats. This will smash records there for all time.

That, in itself, is the answer to those who thought that the picture wasn't "there" before it arrived.

As to actual story, there is very little of that in the picture. Just a slender thread of a love tale on which to hang the gags. But it suffices to link things together and hold the laughs in place.

Lloyd portrays a young society boy who has more money than he knows what to do with. An example of his wealth is immediately registered when he buys a new car to match his trousers, and on wrecking it immediately walks into an auto salesroom, leaps into a car on the floor, writes out a check for nine "grand" and drives it out, only to have it wrecked a few minutes later after having helped the cops chase a gang of jewel thieves who shot the new machine full of holes. To cap the climax the car stalls on a railroad track, and as Lloyd is cranking it along comes a train and takes the car off the crank handle.

That's the uptown angle of the picture. The downtown end has Jobyna Ralston as the daughter of a mission worker in the slums. He has a little coffee cart from which he caters to the wants of the needy, his daughter assisting him. Along comes Lloyd and burns up the stand, giving the mission worker a check for $1,000 to repair the damage. But the missionary thinks it a contribution for the establishing of a mission. The result: Flaming headlines in the papers, "Millionaire Establishes Mission," which works up for another good gag and establishes a reason for the Lloyd to go back and see what it is all about.

Then the fun begins. Lloyd and the daughter of the mission worker meet. He falls and pulls a flock of laughs in a chase designed to round up business for the mission. This sequence had the Monday night audience rocking with laughter. The gangsters whom Lloyd had worked up to chase him into the Mission become his friends when he protects them from the coppers and finally the leader of the crowd, who has not been convinced, is knocked cold through a series of gags, he believing that the dude did the trick then also falls into line.

When Lloyd announces his engagement to wed the little mission worker, his society friends decide that they are going to take a hand in matters and kidnap the groom-to-be, with the reception committee of gangsters going after them to find out what it is all about. The final 14 minutes of the picture, with Lloyd and gangsters getting back to the mission by various means, the comedian trying to herd the committee of five drunks, is just that much solid laughter.

Lloyd, Miss Ralston and Noah Young carry the entire picture and the action is always in Lloyd's hands. The gags are so numerous that they have to be seen to be appreciated.

Sam Taylor directed, and has turned out a decidedly business-like picturization. Ralph Spence did the titles that fall naturally.

"For Heaven's Sake" may not stand up as "The Freshman" did to some people, but from an exhibitor's standpoint it is a better picture, for it has all the laughs that any audience could ask for and, in addition, has the advantage of running less than an hour in length. The Rialto has framed a show with the feature that needs but an hour and a half for a de luxe performance with a presentation. They are grinding 10 shows a day at the house from 10 a. m. to midnight.

Fred.

KIKI

First National release presented by Joseph M. Schenck with Norma Talmadge starred in Hans Kraly's adaptation of the Picard-Belasco play. Ronald Colman featured. Directed by Clarence Brown. At the Capitol, New York, April 4, week. Running time, 90 minutes.

Kiki	Norma Talmadge
Victor Renal	Ronald Colman
Paulette	Gertrude Astor
Baron Rapp	Marc MacDermott
Adolphe	George K. Arthur
Brule	William Orlamond
Joly	Erwin Connelly
Pierre	Frankie Darro
Pastryman	Mack Swain

When Jos. M. Schenck bought this picture from Belasco and paid about $75,000, Variety published the story, and it met with denials on all sides.

If $75,000 is really the price paid—it wasn't too much. "Kiki" has made a whale of a good comedy, not as well suited to Miss Talmadge as many other vehicles, but so filled with situations, slapstick and laughs that in its present excellent scenario form, there's not a chance of its flopping before a real audience.

Most peculiar of all is Miss Talmadge in the title part. She is not a comedienne and never has been; she is too large and too tall for the part. But with all these things against her here, she gives a creditable and amusing performance, which, if it isn't as subtle as it might have been, is about as effective as possible in its slapstick way. Miss Talmadge falls over couches, gets kicked out into the alley, kicks a valet around, does a little rolling over the floor and is a general roughneck.

The story, as almost anybody in a city of any size will remember, is of a Parisian gamin who falls in love with Victor Renal, a revue manager. She joins his show, ruins the opening night, but by her keen mind and various methods of trickery, so ingratiates herself into his affections that in the end he is only too glad to give up his old sweetheart and marry her.

And Kiki, despite her vicious temper and uncivilized ways, is as pure as snow and determined to keep herself so until the time when she marries. Thus, is the curse of the French play taken off, for in photoplay form, this is thoroughly in keeping with the requirements.

Ronald Colman, as the adored man, does well; ditto Marc McDermott as an old roue. Numerous smaller parts are well taken.

Aside from the work of Miss Talmadge, Clarence Brown, the director, is entitled to much credit, for his handling is apparent in many spots. Moreover, the scenario is unusually fine, while the physical end of the production is lavish, solid and handsome.

Thus, as a whole, "Kiki" is just one more good picture made by Joe Schenck with Norma Talmadge starred. If any other screen actress has held up so good a record in recent years as Miss Talmadge, it might be well to recall no other actress on the stage or screen has played such varied roles with unmistakable skill and ability.

"Kiki" is a box office setup and good for all over the country.

Sisk.

The Flaming Frontier

Universal Super-Production presented by Carl Laemmle. From the story by Edward Sedgwick, who also directed. Hoot Gibson, Dustin Farnum, Anne Cornwall, Kathleen Key featured. At the Colony, N. Y., for a run beginning April 4. Running time 101 minutes.

Bob Langdon	Hoot Gibson
Betty Stanwood	Anne Cornwall
Lieut. Col. Custer	Dustin Farnum
Sam Belden	Ward Crane
Lucretia Belden	Kathleen Key
"Jonesy"	Eddie Gribbon
"California Joe"	Harry Todd
Lawrence Stanwood	Harold Goodwin
Senator Stanwood	George Fawcett
Sitting Bull	Noble Johnson
Senator Harges	Charles K. French
Cyrus Penfield	William Steele
President Grant	Walter Rogers
Grant's Secretary	Ed Wilson
Rain-In-The-Face	Joe Bonoino

There are a flock of credits given for this picture on the program. It would have been more appropriate had the program stated who was actually to blame for having turned out this ordinary western with the idea that it could get over as a special. Universal undoubtedly is counting on the tremendous advertising expenditure that they are putting behind the picture to carry it over. But the truth must prevail. At best the picture only ranks as an ordinary western, not any better than the average Hoot Gibson that U is in the habit of turning out. How Universal or anyone else expects to get away with this one on Broadway at two-shows-a-day, with a $1 and $1.50 box office top scaled for the Colony theatre, is too much to figure. The chances are they won't be able to get past the barrier.

As a matter of fact it really seems regretable that a story abounding with so much red blooded historical fact should have been so terribly butchered. It is understood that U originally intended this picture to be a story of the founding and the early operation of the pony express. They started on the picture and then Famous beat them to the punch by issuing a program picture with the same theme and title. Then they let the picture rest and swung it around to Custer's Last Fight, spending, so the reports have it, some $400,000 on the production. It doesn't show that in the finished product, but the chances are that someone did burn up that amount.

The theme deals with the swindling of the Indians out of lands by the corrupt political Indian Ring that was in power in Washington during the administration of President Grant. This finally led to the uprising of the Sioux and other tribes and culminated in the massacre of Custer at the Little Big Horn and the Indian War that followed. There is a pretty love story of the pony express rider who, as Custer's protege, receives an appointment to West Point, entering the school at the same time that the son of Senator Stanwood does. The Senator obtained the rider appointment for Custer and the two boys become pals. The ring in order to discredit Senator Stanwood with President Grant plan to involve his son in a scandal at the Point, but his pal takes the blame and is dismissed from the academy just prior to the time that he was to have graduated. There has been a love affair between the Senator's daughter and the young westerner, but when he is before the head of the school and refuses to offer an explanation she believes the worst of him.

He returns west, becomes one of Custer's scouts, and is one of the few to escape death in the battle. The Senator's son, who is in Custer's command as an officer, makes a confession to his chief just before the fight and his story is included in the last dispatches of the Indian fighter. This clears the former pony rider and secures for him the commission in the army that he rightfully should have had and also permits of a happy ending.

In the matter of thrills, there is really but one in the picture, and that has been done so often that it lacked novelty. It was the burning of the dives that the representative of the Indian Ring was running just off the reservation. The gathering of the Indian tribes, the dances before the battle, the battle itself and all of the scenes in these sequences are so badly handled and directed that the least said about them the better. Suffice to say that Indian scenes had the same shot repeated again and again until they became tiresome. The battle stuff was awful.

Other things were just as bad. As an instance, Hoot Gibson at West Point was a nice blonde boy, but just as soon as got back on the plans he was possessed of long black hair. Things like that were noticeable throughout the picture. Gibson, by the way, failed to get over the wallop that he should have in this picture. He was much too jowly for a boy who is supposed to have lived the hardy life outdoors in the great west of early days.

Anne Cornwall, opposite Gibson, certainly made the most of the role and scored at every opportunity that presented itself. Dustin Farnum, as Custer, was all that could be asked, while George Fawcett was the good old trouper that he always is, and delivered a sterling performance. Ward Crane was convincing as the heavy, while Kathleen Key, as a vamp, managed herself nicely. Eddie Gribbon, in a comedy bit as a bootlegger, managed to slip over whatever laughs there were in the picture, and he was an honest relief. The balance of the cast was seemingly adequate.

"The Flaming Frontier" won't set fire to any boxoffice record. *Fred.*

THE BLIND GODDESS

Paramount picture, featuring Jack Holt, Ernest Torrence, Esther Ralston and Louise Dresser. From the novel by Arthur Train, adapted by Hope Loring and Louis D. Lighton. Script by Gertude Orr. At the Rivoli, N. Y., week April 4. Running time, 77 minutes.

Hugh Dillon	Jack Holt
"Big Bill" Devens	Ernest Torrence
Moira Devens	Esther Ralston
Mrs. Aileen Clayton	Louise Dresser
Tracy Redmond	Ward Crane
Henry Kelling	Richard Tucker
Taylor	Louis Payne
District Attorney	Charles Clary
Chief Detective	Erwin Connelly
Judge	Charles Lane

Here is a semi-society melodrama with a "Madame X" or "Stella Dallas" angle to it. As a picture it stands up as better than average program production, with a lot of suspense in the action. The story builds up perfectly on the screen, and when the wallop comes there is considerable kick. The cast is nicely balanced, and the picture looks as though it should stand up very well at the box office. There are four good names featured in Jack Holt, Ernest Torrence, Esther Ralston and Louise Dresser. The latter in a mother-who-has-sinned role makes it almost as fine a piece of work as Belle Bennett's Stella Dallas.

The tale revolves about a wealthy contractor who, through political power, has risen from a pick and shovel to the millionaire class. The role is in the hands of Ernest Torrence. Esther Ralston as his daughter has been reared by the father in the belief that her mother is dead. She is a headstrong flapper who has things pretty much her own way. The opening shot shows her driving a Hispano on a road that parallels the railroad and her dad with a number of companions are on the observation platform. An' boy how she drives that car! Just runs a flivver with a young lawyer (Jack Holt) off the road and steps away from a motor cop, who, when he finally does catch up with her, refuses to turn her in. She's Big Bill's daughter, and that's the reason.

The lawyer then butts in and insists on an arrest, but the copper laughs him out of it. He then turns to the girl and gives her a bawling out, recalling to her at the same time when they were kids and knew each other. The next day she gives her father the works to help the youngster along, with the result that he is appointed to the District Attorney's staff.

In the meantime the mother of the girl is still alive. A has-been prima donna with a cheap show, she manages to work her way from the coast to New York to see her daughter. The father forbids her seeing the child, and she gets a revolver to kill herself in her former husband's home in the event that her last appeal fails. The man, however, finally convinces her that it would be folly to have the daughter know that her mother is what she is, in the light of the belief he has built up in the girl's mind, and the mother sees the logic of the case. She leaves the revolver and takes herself off. Then the partner of the contractor appears with the information that the grand jury is conducting an investigation on one of their jobs, in which the partner has cheated. When Big Bill refuses to permit a bribing scheme, the partner shoots and kills him with the woman's revolver. A perfect case of circumstantial evidence is built up against the woman, who, remembering her promise to the dead man, refuses to reveal her identity.

Just as the jury is about to bring in its verdict a dictophone recording machine is brought in as evidence and the guilty man caught through the dying contractor having spoken the words naming his murderer, and the woman is freed. There is also a reconciliation between the girl and the young lawyer, who, knowing the woman's story, resigned his place in the public prosecutor's office to defend her, and thus became estranged from the girl he was to marry. For the final fadeout mother and daughter are left together.

The picture is perfectly played and the direction by Victor Fleming carries the story along at a pace that keeps the audience keyed up all the way.

Fred.

THE NIGHT CRY

Presented by the Warner Bros. with Rin-Tin-Tin as star. Story by Phil Klein and Edward Meagher. Directed by Herman Raymaker. At Warner's, N. Y., week April 3. Running time, 55 minutes.

"Rinty"	Rin-Tin-Tin
John Martin	John Harron
Mrs. Martin	June Marlowe
Miguel Hernandez	Gayne Whitman
Tony	Charles Conklin
Pedro	Don Alverez
Baby Martin	Mary Louise Miller

This is an out and out thrill picture with a dog star. It is a little different from the regular run of story in which Rin-Tin-Tin has been shown, but the story in a sense is somewhat similar to the original in which Strongheart, another dog star, appeared. The latter was accused of being a cattle killer and was finally exonerated. Rinty is marked a sheep killer and doomed, but likewise escapes paying the penalty when a condor is discovered to have been the culprit.

From an audience standpoint for the average neighborhood house the picture looks as though it would stand up for two or three days. For the de luxe presentation houses it is not sufficient in itself, and its Broadway punch may be laid to the fact that the dog star and his trainer are making personal appearances. This, with the fact that the police dog still has a tremendous vogue, will be responsible for good business at Warner's this week.

The scene of the story is laid in the western sheep country. "Rinty" is owned by John Martin, a sheep rancher, who together with his wife and child simply adore the dog. All of the sheepmen have been losing lambs from their flocks, and because Martin hasn't they believe his dog guilty of the raiding; it being an accepted fact that a sheep dog never raids his own flock. Martin is waited on but defends his dog and offers to lead the accusers to the flock to show them that the dog is on his job. But when they get to the herd the dog is missing. They search for him and find him near a slain lamb on a neighbor's ranch. The dog has been chasing the condor and just frightened him off into the night when the searchers come upon him. Immediately his death is decreed.

Martin takes the dog home to shoot him, but when the final moment comes cannot find it in his heart to go through. He hides the dog in his home and later balks a search of the house. This leads into a pretty comedy sequence. The next day the sheep ranchers find additional slain lambs and one of them decides to search Martin's home when only the wife and child are there. The final scenes are taken up with the man trying to kill the dog when he finds him in the house, the little child running forth and being picked up by the condor and carried off to its mountain top lair, the dog making its escape and, with the mother, climbing to the nest of the scavenger in time to rescue the babe.

For thrills the picture is better than the majority of dog star productions that have been shown, although Rin-Tin-Tin does not seem to get across on the screen with the appeal that the first of these dogs had.

John Harron and June Marlowe, featured with the dog, handle their roles nicely, but little Mary Louise, the baby, is about the best little actress in the picture. *Fred.*

THE CROWN OF LIES

Dimitri Buchowetski production starring Pola Negri, presented by Famous Players. Story by Ernest Vajda, adapted by Hope Loring and Louis D. Lighton. Shown at the Rivoli, New York, week March 27, 1926. Running time, 60 minutes.

Olga Kriga........................Pola Negri
Count Mirko.......................Noah Beery
John Knight.......................Robert Ames
Karl..............................Charles Post
Fritz.............................Arthur Hoyt
Vorski............................Mikhail Vavitch
Leading Lady......................Cissy Fitzgerald
Landlady..........................May Foster
Actress...........................Frankie Bailey

It is evident from the program billing for this picture that the original story that was shot for the screen was considerably edited before it was finally released. When all is said and done there is nothing to the Ernest Vajda tale but a little rewrite on "Such a Little Queen." There is a little thrill to the picture but it is so little that one really overlooks it. It does, however, give Pola a chance to act regally, and after all maybe that's what Pola wanted to do. Buchowetski who directed failed to show anything out of the ordinary in his handling of the story, taking it through sequence in a matter of fact manner, which naturally resulted in a matter of fact picture and that is all that this is.

The story is that of an emigrant girl from one of the Balkan states who has come to this country and found employment as a slavey in a theatrical boarding house. There she mimics the stalking legits who are the paying guests and is the object of the affections of a young flivver salesman who is also stopping there. He takes the slavey out to treat her to a cup of coffee and at the same time try and convince her that she should marry him and accompany him to Sylvania in the Balkans where he is to open an agency. Just at that minute in walks the man servant of Count Mirko who believes that she is the dead Queen of Sylvania, who was lost after the palace guards revolted and forced her to flee for her life. The girl resembles the late Queen so much that when she is brought to the Count he immediately decides that he will take her back to the country from which the nobles have been exiled and utilize the resemblance to compel the present ruler to restore their fortunes.

When the girl arrives in Sylvania, her strutting and mimicking of the queens of tragedy stand her in good stead for she really assumes a regal pose and the peasants believe truly she's the Queen, rise against the ruler, Vorski, and again place her on the throne. Through all this the flivver salesman is with her and when he wants to leave to return to the United States she begs him to again take her to that country, willingly giving up her throne and all the glamor and splendor of the palace for a flat in New York.

Pola Negri does fairly well in the earlier comedy moments and then during the tragedy that leads up to her coming on the throne is queenly enough, but she does all of the latter with a certain matter of factness that isn't at all imposing. Noah Beery as Count Mirko is by far the most accomplished player of the cast, while the mighty Charles Post certainly does fit the role assigned him. Robert Ames played the lead as though it were a boob character bit and in the later scenes managed to score although in the earlier portion of the picture he was unconvincing.

"The Crown of Lies" isn't one of those pictures that anyone is going to rave about and is classified as any ordinary program picture. *Fred.*

BRIDE OF THE STORM

J. Stuart Blackton production, starring Dolores Costello. Presented by Warner Bros. From the story, "Maryland, My Maryland," by James Francis Dwyer. Adapted by Marian Constanée. Shown at the Rialto, New York, week of March 27, 1926. Running time, 70 minutes.

Faith Fitzhugh.....................Dolores Costello
Dick Wayne.........................John Harron
Hans Kroom.........................Otto Mattieson
Piet Kroom.........................Sheldon Lewis
Jakob Kroom........................Tyrone Power
Mrs. Fitzhugh......................Julia Swayne Gordon
Faith (age 8)......................Evon Pelletier

Dolores Costella and three character impersonations given by Otto Mattieson, Sheldon Lewis and Tyrone Power are the outstanding features of this picture, which on the whole is just one of those program pictures of the type that Vitagraph turned out in the past that were designed for the neighborhood houses. That is all that this one is, and it has no place in the first-run houses. It is the last of the Vitagraph pictures that will play the Rialto, New York, under the agreement made some time ago under which a Federal Trade Commission action on the part of Vitagraph against Famous was discontinued. For last week there was a special Charleston contest staged at the theatre, which pulled the money.

The story of the picture itself is one of those "wave-the-American-flag" ideas. A mother and daughter start for the Far East on a steamer which is wrecked, and they are cast up on a lonely island where the light is in charge of the three generations of Krooms. The mother dies, the girl grows up without knowledge of her mother tongue, but there lingers in her mind the words and melody of "Maryland, My Maryland." Grandfather Kroom decides that the girl is Godsent, for no girl in her right mind would marry his idiot grandson. So he plans that when the girl grows up she and the boy will marry, and then the two elders of the family will claim the girl's fortune in America and divide it between them.

At that time the U. S. N. cable repair ship looms up, and the American boys come ashore. A young ensign hears the song of his native State being sung with a foreign accent, and his curiosity is aroused, but when he asks the Krooms as to the whereabouts of the singer they deny there is anyone else on the island. In the days that follow he meets the girl, the two fall in love, and finally he rescues her from the hands of the Kroom trio, all three of the latter losing their lives in the fight and the burning of the light that follows.

For out-and-out meller the picture isn't badly handled, but it is a cheap picture, lacking in class that would warrant it playing the pre-release theatres. In the neighborhood houses it should more than please, and the cast looks like good advertising value.

Dolores Costello looks like a million-dollar bet here, and even without "The Sea Beast" record behind her, she is the outstanding figure in this picture. Then comes the character trio, and finally Johnnie Harron, who plays the lead. Harron and Lewis put up about as corking a fight as has been seen in a long while, and they make it appear realistic enough for the average audience to want the hero really to win. Mattieson's work as the half-wit is as fine a piece of acting as has been screened in some time, while Tyrone Power as a typical "Capt. Hook" makes that role stand out tremendously. *Fred.*

CINDERELLA

UFA production, made in Germany, with Helga Thomas featured. Directed by Ludwig Berger, titled by Robert A. Sanborn and edited by Joseph R. Fleisler of the local UFA office. Presented here by the Film Associates, Inc., at the Klaw, April 4, at $1.65 top.

With the International Film Arts Guild already in operation to the extent of occupying the Cameo for a month with revivals of the best pictures made in the past, a new group devoted to the "artistic" in the new films comes to the fore. Called the Film Associates, Inc., they have presented two films, this being the second, on Sundays at the Klaw to slim audiences, a string quartet furnishing the musical accompaniment.

Their advisory board consists of Christian Brinton, occupation unknown; Sheldon Cheney, prominent in local art theatre movements; Jane Heap, who, with Friedrich Kiesler, helped organize the recent International Theatre Exposition; Lawrence Langner, a director of the Theatre Guild; Kenneth MacGowan, a director of the Greenwich Village Theatre, and Gilbert Seldes, the eminent "discoverer."

"Cinderella" is badly acted by actors who grimace and then act for dear life and no other reason.

Instead of being treated as a sweet little fantasy the German version of "Cinderella" is concerned with many kinds of magic other than that introduced into the original legend.

Here the prince is a stolid Teutonic looking fellow surrounded by stolid and funny looking courtiers, all of whom live in a funny looking palace which looks more like a prop set than those they used to build in the days when pictures were young. The big scene of the film is where the prince picks up the pretty girl's shoe and then sends him mob hunting for her through the royal gardens, roman candles spurting in every direction to supply the light.

Of the cast Helga Thomas is the heroine, and she looks like a blonde who might be corking in some other film. Here it's all a dead loss.

Attendance at the Klaw was slim for this one. Those in, people interested in the newer developments in pictures maybe, haw-hawed all the way through.

This one from UFA, called "Cinderella," is certainly the one instance where that old theme does a mile-deep flop for the simple reason it is a poor picture—artistically and commercially. *Sisk.*

THE FAR CRY

First National production starring Blanche Sweet. Adapted by Katherine Kavanaugh from Arthur Richman's stage play. Directed by Sylvano Balboni, under editorial supervision of June Mathis. Reviewed at Proctor's 58th St. theatre, April 5. Shown in conjunction with a vaude. bill. No Broadway first run. Running time, about 70 minutes.

Claire Marsh.......................Blanche Sweet
Dick Clayton.......................Jack Mulhall
Louise Marsh.......................Myrtle Stedman
Julian Marsh.......................Hobart Bosworth
Max Frasier........................Leo White
Helen Clayton......................Julia Swayne Gordon
Count Sturani......................John Sainpolis

This picture cost a barrel of somebody's money.

In the first place, the film rights cost $30,000. Secondly, the production is needlessly elaborate, a grand example of careless spending. The riot of big scenes, costumes and endless expensive interiors, capped by more than a reel of color stuff, makes $250,000 look like a moderate estimate. It is the first directorial effort of Sylvano Balboni, the husband of June Mathis, who until recently occupied a powerful and influential position with First National. Balboni was formerly a camera man.

With all its handicap of expense, "The Far Cry" is a good picture, but whether its rental value will be too high to let it mean profit to an exhibitor is an entirely different question. That it is a good picture doesn't mean that it is an exceptional draw, for the story is more or less prosaic as developed here. Utterly unlike the play, the picture is almost a spectacle at times, and where the play tried to portray the life of a decadent set of Americans in Europe, the picture goes to no such subtle lengths and merely lays out a story of a wealthy American heiress who marries a fortune hunter, divorces him after it is made clear that she left him before sundown on the day of their wedding (for purity's sake), and then engaged in a romance with a boyhood sweetheart whose opponent is a lecherous count. Thus the count and the young sweetheart contend for the girl's hand, and two guesses as to the winner.

Blanche Sweet, handling the lead in fine fashion, becomes more beautiful with every picture and in the color sequence she was something to grow enthusiastic over. Jack Mulhall did well opposite, while John Sainpolis, with his name changed to John St. Polis in the titles, is good as the Count. Hobart Bosworth, Myrtle Stedman, Eric Mayne, Mathilde Comont, Dorothy Revier and Julia Swayne Gordon fill the minor parts, completing an excellent and an expensive cast.

"The Far Cry" will pass muster as a first run feature, but it is impossible to neglect the unusual sum it must have cost. *Sisk.*

The Lawful Cheater

Produced by Benj. P. Schulberg. Written and directed by Frank O'Connor. Adapted by Adele Buffington. Clara Bow, featured player. Distributed by Commonwealth Co. Shown at the Stanley, New York, single feature, April 5, 1926. Running time, 57 minutes.

Molly Burns........................Clara Bow
Nooney..........................David Kirby
Richard Steele...............Raymond McKee
Roy Burns.....................Edward Hearn
Johnny Burns..................George Cooper
Tom Horan......................Fred Kelsey
Mrs. Perry Steele...........Gertrude Pedlar
"Graveyard" Lazardi................Jack Wise
"Silent" Sam Riley..........John T. Prince

Some years ago Bennie Schulberg was in the press department for Famous Players. He shifted jobs until the day came when he launched forth as an independent producer. Then came other days and Bennie is back with Famous, this time having a lot to say about future F-P subjects. Whether Bennie knows more letters than are in the "ABC's" of film economy, there are flashes in "The Lawful Cheater" that indicate Bennie Schulberg knows the ins and outs of feature production.

"The Lawful Cheater" didn't cost a lot of money, but on the whole flashes a pretty good expenditure. It's a modern story, deals with crooks and shows the inside of a prison with a girl prisoner gabbing from behind the screen to her sweetie.

It seemed a coincidence, but there was that picture which has a running fight between gunmen while the New York papers have been chockful of gang raids, murders and robberies. And there sat this girl behind the screen at a time, too, when the audience had just read in its evening papers that Gerald Chapman was to swing at midnight (Monday) for having failed to walk the straight and narrow.

In the hanging of Chapman there is supposed to be a moral. Bennie Schulberg's picture has a moral. There is no hanging to be sure, but a girl, caught innocently in a round up by the police goes to prison while every male member of the two gangs that caused the raid got away, i.e., from the cops, as several were bowled over in the exchange of bullets. The girl, realizing that her two brothers are going from bad to worse and that her sweetie, a rich woman's son, too, may turn to be a desperado, decides to save 'em.

With the prison chaplain she goes into the city and frames her brothers and lover. They believe she is tunneling to a bank. First they plan to be in at the death, but after trying honest living they turn straight and try to stop Molly, who at the finale falls with a bullet fired into her by that nemesis of city gangs, Tom Horan, head of a detective agency. She lives and marries her rich suitor. The stolen bonds were recovered by Molly and the real thief, Lazardi, forced to confess.

The picture jumps some high hurdles and slams the merry old imagination here and there, but withal the moral is impingly told in a way characteristic of film romances.

There are several corking scenes, showing that Mr. Schulberg knew his little old New York. There are moments of real city realism with the grim aftermath that one finds in the morning papers when men of stealth with guns roam at will the night before.

It was very easy for a confirmed bunch of bad boys and one a "chemist," an expert in counterfeiting, at that to finally go straight without any of them caught during their rounds.

There is one very nice feature to this picture. That's the work of Clara Bow as Molly Burns. She was in there acting all the time, keeping the film tempo up pronto and doing a "boy" impersonation that was wholly with'n premise.

Kelsey's work was excellent, and Jack Wise made a mean-acting Lazardi. Messrs. McKee, Hearn and Cooper carried their roles well. But atop it all was the work of Miss Bow, in fact she was never seen to better advantage.

As one watches some of the very good scenes the impression grows that Mr. Schulberg had a corking theme for something very big, but it petered out toward the close and fizzled like a leaky firecracker.

The story will be easily comprehended in all neighborhoods; preaches a pantomimic sermon that seems timely in these rabid days of "stick 'em up."

"The Lawful Cheater" adds a feather in Clara Bow's cap. The strength of the picture is in her acting and in the first part; after the girl goes to prison the story started to skid and careen aimlessly. They had builded well up to that point. It seemed all too easy the way the girl fooled her brothers and they supposed to be modern wise guys.

Mark.

KING OF THE TURF

F. B. O. production of the story by Louis Joseph Vance. Directed by James Hogan, with Patsy Ruth Miller and Kenneth Harlan featured. At Loew's New York Roof April 2, as half of double bill. Running time, 60 minutes.

Kate Fairfax................Patsy Ruth Miller
"Red" Kelly.....................David Kirby
"Soup" Conley.............William Franey
John Smith.................Kenneth Harlan

The hero's name is John Smith.

Even with such a disadvantage, this film is a good, interesting and well-made feature suitable for the smaller houses and those playing combination vaudeville bills.

Col. Fairfax, southerner with goatee, mint juleps, white columns on his front porch and lots of chivalry on his insides, is a race horse owner up to the time the local banker frames him on a theft, and the old Cunnel is taken to the jail house.

That he is innocent, his daughter persistently believes. While she is alone in the world, the son of the man who framed her dad comes courting. She turns him down like a pile driver dropping the weight. But he keeps coming around with threats, entreaties and mush words.

Finally, the old Cunnel gets out, bowed and a little older, but still filled to the brim with a love for humanity—this love being so pronounced that three real jail-birds, brought in for comic relief, come home with him, while a trusty in the jail, John Smith, is brought back to train his horses.

Meantime, the fellow who framed him has died and his son discovers that his father did wrong. So he goes to the Cunnel's daughter and tells her that if she'll marry him he'll make public his father's confession. But they outsmart the bad boy and put the comedy crooks into his safe. They rescue the written confession.

About this time the great race starts. The bad boy, peeved because the Cunnel's daughter has rejected him, tries to have the Cunnel's entry barred because the Cunnel is an ex-convict and therefore not a gentleman.

But the confession arrives in time, and who do you think married the girl? John Smith! No? Yes.

Cast is competent and production in general, while cheap in many spots, serves the purpose. Moderately interesting, too.

Sisk.

THE DANGER QUEST

Harry J. Brown production. Reed Howes starred. Story and continuity by Henry Roberts Symonds. Produced and directed by Harry J. Brown for Rayart release. Shown at the Stanley theatre, New York, March 31, as main feature. Running time, 57 minutes.

Rob Rollins.......................Reed Howes
Nan Colby.....................Ethel Shannon
Colonel Spiffy...............J. P. MacGowan
Spats Barrett.....................David Kirby
Roll Royce........................Billy Franey
Otto Shugars.....................Fred Kohler
Umhattan.........................George Reid
Inspector........................Rodney Keys

Another of the Reed Howes series from the Harry J. Brown producing shop. Howes, regarded as an out-and-out stunt man, continues to run, hop and jump his way through some of the stuff this handsome young man is fast becoming famous for in front of the film camera.

In this story, which has the African diamond mines as its main locale, Howes finds some new slants for his stuff, but the picture seems drawn out and becomes very commonplace in stretches.

Several thrills, but a number of the attempts to make a superman out of Howes fell wide of the mark. As an illustration, that scene where Howes turns back astride his horse and rides between two pursuers, also on horses, and upsets them as he does so, was a little too much for the imagination.

Howes at all times is pleasing in his work, having facial outlines and physical set-up that make him a typical lead in films. Once the Howes sponsors dig up some rip-snortin' stories and Howes continues to follow instructions, the independents will be getting just the sort of a flashy trip-hammer romantic bet they have been looking for since Hek was a pup.

"The Danger Quest" has a number of captions that were genuinely amusing, and it seemed a pity the pace wasn't maintained. The heavy was Fred Kohler, acceptable and hard working, but the best acting was done by J. P. MacGowan, as the wily, get-it-without-working gambler, who showed experience, skill and naturalness. Miss Shannon wasn't required to do a whole lot as the girl with whom the wall-scaling, high-fence-jumping, hut-crashing Howes, as Bob Rollins, falls in love, but she looked the part and was sweetly gracious.

The jungle native setting was most realistic, and one of the comedy strikes was made in the drum-beating bit, when the white man got dizzy and started to beat a jazz rhythm instead of the one-beat pat as done by the Zulu drummer.

Photographically, "The Danger Quest" measures up to snuff. Howes repeated some of his athletic tricks of previous films, and in the neighborhoods where Howes is building up a following the picture will rate high. Otherwise, just ordinary, and just a feature.

Mark.

THE LOVE TOY

Warner Brothers' classic. Lowell Sherman starred. Author anonymous. Scenario by Sonya Hovey. Directed by Erle C. Kenton. At the Stanley, New York, April 3. Running time, 65 minutes.

Peter Remsen................Lowell Sherman
The Bride.........................Jane Winton
King Lavoris....................Willard Louis
Prime Minister Albert....George Whitman
Queen Zita..................Ethel Grey Terry
Princess Patricia............Helene Costello
Lady-in-Waiting..............Maude George

On Broadway recently was shown a film wherein Lewis Stone took to slapstick comedy scenes, with custard pies supplanted by herring, which Mr. Stone flung into the outstretched arms of an army of delicatessen bargain hunters. Now comes a picture with Lowell Sherman doing daredevil stuff. However, "doubles" work much of the time. And it does not seem amiss to charge some of the gag writers out Golden Gate way with being pretty close readers of all the comedy writers employed by the newspapers.

This picture is an admixture of travesty, romance and whatnot, gauged on present day slang manufacture in the United States. The story takes place in one of those foreign countries where rich young Americans make googoo eyes at unmarried princesses, overthrow a couple of rebellious dynasties and lick bewhiskered throne contenders.

It is the same country that George Barr McCutcheon and Harold MacGrath have worked overtime in yesteryear. Lowell Sherman plays the young American who becomes the right bower to another American, a former bootlegger, now a king in one of those take-your-pick countries ruled only for novel and picture purposes. Before the local war is over Lowell is a hero and has copped the fair young princess.

There are some funny scenes; there is much that is stretched to the bursting point, and all the way there are slangy captions befitting stirring times within purple halls. The story almost loses itself at times, with Sherman taking a good rest and "doubles" working in some lively chases via auto and horse and outwitting a pursuing bevy of soldiers.

The main try is for broad, farcical comedy. It hits and it misses.

For a part that gives Sherman a chance to wear spic-and-span uniforms and has him far removed from the film seat of his usual villainy, it will suffice. But expecting an audience to believe Sherman goes through all that rough work in the open is beyond conjecture.

"The Love Toy" is a hodge-podge of slang titles, a sandwiching of outdoor slapbang comedy stuff and a two-ply yank at the imagination.

Mark.

THE BLACK GUARD

Jane Novak starred in Lee-Bradford production of Graham Cutts' story. Directed by Raymond Paito. At the Arena, New York, April 5. Running time, 55 minutes.

Michael Caviol, a young violinist, is hit on the head with a bottle he emptied of booze to balk his drunken grandmother in her attempt at getting more drunk. Grandma swings the bottle. From then on everything, including Michael, rests in a daze.

The bottle knocks out Michael, causing him to mount the heavens, where he swears to Mallol, the God of Music, to devote his love to nothing but his art. With the aid of another man's purse, Michael becomes, as he is next seen, Caviol, the master violinist. But Mike's oath to Mallol looks bad when Jane Novak, the Princess Maria Idourska, walks in. Being in love with both Maria and his fiddle, something must be done for Mike. So Maria marries, unwillingly, her cousin, Prince Paul, who, being a rake, is a prince in title only.

Maria and her cousin, ruling a province in Russia, are troubled with revolting subjects led by Levinski, Michael's old music teacher gone mad. Michael steps in as the people are about to break in the Idourska palace, succeeds in getting Maria to safety, stabs the naughty Prince Paul to death, and is in turn stabbed, but not to death, by Levinski. At this time it appears that the God Mallol is forgotten, everyone being interested in possessing Maria. An invalid from his wounds, Michael is found by the searching princess in Paris and the agony ends.

The story has possibilities but is woefully botched. Continuity is absent. The tale becomes interesting at times but verges toward the fanatic and is cut short by a change which takes place not only in the story but in the film. With three sets of titles, each in different style of lettering, this picture has evidently been handled by too many people. From appearances it has been made and remade.

Walter Pilla, as Michael, the musical genius, emotes too heavily. His acting often sways to femininity. Jane Novak also heaves too much. Being badly gowned throughout the film she is at a handicap as to appearance.

The mob scenes and interiors look like money, but the picture is bad all around.

THAT'S MY BABY

Douglas MacLean starred in Famous Players production of comedy, with book by G. J. Crone and Wade Boteler. Scenario by J. F. Poland. William Beaudine, director. At Rivoli (Publix), New York, week April 11. Running time, usual.

Alan Boyd	Douglas MacLean
Helen Raynor	Margaret Morris
John Raynor	Claude Gillingwater
Mrs. John Raynor	Eugenie Forde
Dave Barton	Wade Boteler
Schuyler Van Loon	Richard Tucker
Murphy	Fred Kelsey
The Baby	Harry Earles
Drug Clerk	William Orlamonde

In "That's My Baby" the credit for its undoubted hit should go to William Beaudine who directed the picture and J. F. Poland who scenarized it. Between those two any light comedian of personality could not have missed, although Douglas MacLean is something beyond just a screen comedian—he's an actor.

It's an accumulative humorous strip of film. In the opening sections the action is somewhat slow through planting the story. There it is that the captions keep up laughs. Some of them are peaches. When the fun grows faster captions are less noticeable.

Fun here is gotten in three ways—business (legitimate comedy), situations (gags) and stunts. MacLean gets as much from his legit comedy as from the rest. No nicer bit of picture fun anywhere than MacLean looking for the girl he fell in love with at first sight in a charity bazaar and told she is in Turkish costume, to find almost all of the girls are wearing the same Turkish costume.

Or the gag of MacLean being handed the baby, from which the picture derives its title, and the gagging ensuing from that. This leads into an extraordinary laughable bit of a fortune teller's tent coming down on top of its occupants.

Or the stunt of the airplane and parachute, also full of laughs, some yells. The plane and parachute bits are well worked for realism, with a tithe of a thrill.

This is not a continuous laugh as might be a gagging picture only. The story is nicely nursed along by its well-written continuity. That provides spaced rests, making the next laugh the better enjoyed and louder, instead of wondering what it will be, as happens with the gagging pictures. Here there is some interest in the unfolded tale. The combination is what makes Douglas MacLean a legitimate screen juvenile comedian.

In the parachute bit is a valuable aerial hint. MacLean in getting into the plane as a passenger is obliged to encase himself in a parachute strapped around his shoulders, to be released by a ring attached to a rope, if in danger. A caption says it is the regulation for passengers. There is no regulation nor ordinance to that effect, but there should be for aerial passengers in commercial planes. It's probably local option legislation, but the idea is fine.

"That's My Baby" should clean up. It's a most enjoyable comedy, for high or low, upstairs or down.

Harry Earles as "The Baby" is a personal success. He seems rather a midget for the work he must do, but looks like a two-year-old kid. Mr. Boteler plays a role; he helped write the story. Richard Tucker is the rival suitor, therefore the villain, and fairly. Through the business allotted him he would have done much better if taking it all in a lighter vein and not caring if he lost the girl, which he did.

Claude Gillingwater gave a handsome performance as the irascible banker, father of the girl, and the object of his wife's tirades. To many husbands and maybe wives the really funny bit of the picture will be Mrs. Raynor (Eugenie Forde) bawling out her husband over the phone and keeping it going long after he had hung up in his office.

And this for Sam Scribner: Sam, if you want to see yourself when you're "burning," see Gillingwater in this picture. *Sime.*

Last Days of Pompeii

London, April 1.

Made by Carmino Galleone for "W. & F.," this screen version of Bulwer Lytton's famous novel must take a high place among films. The production work is exceedingly fine and the interest is gradually piled up through Roman orgies and tragic games of amphitheatre to the eruption of Vesuvius, which blotted out Pompeii for all time.

No finer spectacular work has ever been done than is found in these final scenes, and the acting story keeps strictly to Lytton's work.

Acting honors go to the German player, Bernhardt Goetzke. Maria Corda is not convincing as the blind slave girl, but the Countess de Liguoro is excellent, and Victor Varconi is good. Many smaller parts are well played.

The whole feature speaks of a brilliant direction. *Gore.*

RED DICE

Cecil B. DeMille production, released through Producers' Distributing Corp. Directed by William K. Howard, with Rod LaRocque starred and Marguerite de la Motte featured. Adapted by Jeanie McPherson and Douglas Zoty from "The Iron Chalice," by Octavus Roy Cohen. At the Broadway, New York, shown in conjunction with vaudeville week April 12. Running time, 70 minutes.

Alan Beckwith	Rod LaRocque
Beverly Vane	Marguerite de la Motte
"Squint" Scoggins	George Cooper
"Webb"	Walter Long
Andrew North	Gustav von Seyffertitz
Johnny Vale	Ray Hallor

An entertaining, perfectly cast, splendidly produced story on as gruesome a theme as any picture has yet used. Briefly, a down-and out man sells himself for a year's good fun, is insured for $100,000 in favor of another man, and at the end of the year promises to allow himself to be killed. The other man, to suit his own scheme, forces the man to marry a woman. Until the last minute the sceptre of death hangs ominously over the young hero's head.

Of course there is an "out," but the unrelenting tread of events to what looks like must be a cold-blooded murder thrills, chills and half-way panics the audience. For the scenario is airtight and foolproof. There is no deviation from the theme, little sentiment until the very last.

Rod LaRocque is the condemned man; Marguerite de la Motte the girl and Gustav von Seyffertitz the most cold-blooded villain the screen has yet revealed. LaRocque makes his first appearance in the down-and-out rig of a bum, while Miss de la Motte's entrance to the story comes when she is forced to marry him, the idea being that she is the sister of a boy who has double-crossed the villain, and the villain makes her marry a man she has never seen, in order to keep her within his power and thus keep an eye on her brother.

The cast couldn't be better. Von Seyffertitz especially is the incarnation of all the world's murderers rolled into one cool and crafty frame. George Cooper, in a semi-comedy part, also clicks throughout, while Walter Long is another villain, and it isn't on record that he ever fell down in such a part.

The production is almost a joy to behold, being so well directed and played. Nothing obtrusive to mar the interest, and the story itself is so gripping that lovers of such stuff will thrill to it. The only question which arises is that its gruesomeness might repel some people; but, on the other hand, almost anything of sufficient interest, whether gruesome or not, will be liked by audiences.

Okeh on these grounds for the first-runs, and the best of them, if LaRocque means anything. And ideal for the other houses. *Sisk.*

WILD OATS LANE

Producers' Distributing Corporation release produced by Marshall Neilan. Adapted by Benjamin Glazer from the play by George Broadhurst. Running time, 65 minutes.

Sweet Marie	Viola Dana
The One Shot Kid	Robert Agnew
Father Kelly	John MacSweeney

Central figure is a fatherly, fat, fine looking parish priest whose life is taken up with helping the poor unfortunates of the city's tenderloin. There is a love affair between a boy who is trying to go straight and a girl who has hit the bottom and is also trying to make the grade, but the priest still remains the principal figure, a right attractive one, too, from the standpoint of the family audiences to which this will appeal.

In the picture there is of necessity a great deal of crook stuff. To the everlasting credit of Neilan let it be said that his crook and police stuff is as real as any picture has yet revealed. The whole business gets a running start when the film opens with the young crook-hero in a third degree sweat box, taking questions that come from all sides out of the dark, while he, twisting and miserable, sits under the glare of a brilliant light. A plain clothes cop, Dillon, figures in many episodes and, although his name isn't programmed, he gives a nice grinning performance.

Some of the subtitles and action concern the raid and roundup of a prostie camp, but the so-called "moral lesson" drawn from the whole picture is so good it qualifies thoroughly for the daily changes and neighborhood houses.

Robert Agnew and Viola Dana are the two sweethearts, while John MacSweeney plays the priest. He has a 300-pound lead over anyone else in the film and shows some excellent acting of the Tom Wise-Maclyn Arbuckle brand. It was on the stage, incidentally, that Arbuckle played the priest's part, but whereas it flopped behind the foots, it makes okeh entertainment in front of the projection machines. *Sisk.*

RUSTLERS' RANCH

Blue Streak Western, released by Universal. From the story by W. C. Tuttle, directed by Clifford Smith and starring Art Accord. The Arena, New York, one day (April 8). Running time, about 45 minutes.

Art Accord is the kind-hearted and sympathetic westerner. He deals with the heroine, the kindly but about to be gypped old mother, the three and each dastardly in his own way villains and the hero's faithful dog and horsey.

This film allows the hero to foil the villains in their attempt to possess the girl and her mother's land. Known to none but the villains and the hero (and he only near the end) the land holds gold.

Accord, an expert at cowboy antics, is not a forceful actor. His gestures at times are so quiet and unassuming one could wish he be insulted or socked by a villain. Art is a well-built boy with a pleasing face.

Olive Hasbrouck, as the girl, is comely and played and fitted in this picture. A perfect type for any "western." And Edith Yorke, as usual, the mother. Duke R. Lee and George Chesbro, two "heavies" (very heavy), sneered audibly.

This Blue Streak is sure to get them, as do the rest of the shoot-em-ups. The boys, old and young, like them and those who relish rough cinema applaud gleefully as the rescue squad or hero approaches and appear disappointed when the end is reached. For that mob it is excellent if not perfect.

Pleasures of the Rich

Tiffany production based on Harold McGrath's "The Wrong Coat." Directed by Louis Gasnier, and starring Helen Chadwick. Running time, 55 mins.

Mary Wilson .... Helen Chadwick
Kate Wilson .... Mary Carr
Henry (Pushcart) Wilson ..... Marcin Asher
Frank Clayton .... Jack Mulhall
Mrs. Clayton .... Lillian Langdon
Maggie, the maid .... Dorothea Wolbert
Mona Vincent .... Hedda Hopper
Phyliss Worthing .... Julanne Johnston
Mrs. Worthing .... Katherine Scott

This one has a splendid cast, a few laughs, plenty of clothes, ditto atmosphere, but lacks the other necessities that pull a film play above the ordinary.

The tale starts fast at the breakfast table of Mr. and Mrs. Henry (Pushcart) Wilson. Henry is a wealthy grocer, who, as his middle monicker trys to portray, started with a pushcart and worked his way up to 40 trucks. The role is well played by Marcin Asher who has heretofore confined his efforts to program comedies. Helen Chadwick, starred, is the daughter of the Wilsons, being in love with Frank Clayton (Jack Mulhall), the son of the socially prominent Mrs. Clayton. Mamma objects to her son's choice, causing one of the several complications.

Hedda Hopper, as the wicked Mona Vincent, looked delicious to both the audience and Pushcart Wilson, the latter deciding to divorce his wife after 20 years of service, for the same Mona, only to find he had been played with. Though Miss Chadwick attempts suicide after 50 minutes of film, she is saved and love triumphs. Helen looked good, she being far ahead of other screen ladies in the art of forming legible words with her lips. When Helen talks subtitles are a burden.

A fashion show was neatly staged and richly gowned, but its feminine attire was equaled by Jack Mulhall's one-button and double-breasteds.

The cast is the picture. Nothing else matters. The story is uninteresting and therefore the players will be this film's mainstay in attracting attention on the outlying circuits.

DESPERATE GAME

Universal release of a Blue Streak Western (Lariat Productions). Starring Pete Morrison and directed by Joseph Franz. Story by George C. Jenks. At Ideal, New York (10c. grind), April 8. Running time, 51 minutes.

Weak and short. Pete Morrison, who looks like the cowboys made familiar by the "movies," is starred. Lightning, his "wonder horse," is featured. There was a time when audiences were unfamiliar with names of either horses or dogs, but since the vogue of Tom Mix's Tony and the canine Rin-Tin-Tin, animal titles are the rage.

Pete's horse, intelligent enough, is no exception. His coat is not fine nor shiny, which means a lot where animals are concerned.

The story is slim and unoriginal. It deals with the son of one ranch owner and the daughter of another, both just returned from school in the east. The sires want a marriage to settle a boundary dispute. The fathers are shortly satisfied, as are the boy and girl, for the match is made.

Morrison is a big boy and a good rider. His fighting is hard and realistic and his roping excellent. With a better tale and some background his talent would stand out. His type is that of Hoot Gibson, always popular in the rough and readys.

Dolores Gardner as the heroine is capable enough for this sort of release. In a better one she might be found wanting.

Just another one of those bing-bang things with plenty of fighting and shooting but woefully weak in the other departments. Costing a bit more than a cup of coffee, it may satisfy many cowboy aspirants and also its producers.

And no one is killed.

WATCH YOUR WIFE

Universal-Jewell. Story by Goesta Segercrantz. Directed by Svend Gade. Cameraman, A. L. Todd. At Columbus theatre, New York, April 9. Running time, 66 minutes.

Claudia Langham .... Virginia Valli
James Langham .... Pat O'Malley
Benjamin Harris .... Nat Carr
Gladys Moon .... Helen Lee Worthing
Alphonse de Marsac .... Albert Conti
Madame Buff .... Aggie Herring
Maid .... Nora Hayden

The romantic theme of "Watch Your Wife" is fashioned after a story that is as old as the hills. It's ancient stuff, wherein a husband and wife become divorced only to have them reunite after it looks as though both had found new affinities. But it's the way the separation, divorce and reconciliation are framed that makes for a film story. The comedy way out for this one would have made it worth twice as much to an exhibitor as it is in its present shape. An expert at comedy twists, turns and takes could have given the principals, Miss Valli and Mr. O'Malley, something more than just a feature vehicle.

There is much to commend in the directing, but the adherence to an out-and-out straight love motive held Mr. Gade within bounds. Allowing for a few stabs at comedy, lamentably thin and vaporish, there were plenty of chances for laughs, but somebody let the chance slip and the result is just a nice little picture pretty well enacted. At times the picture runs listlessly.

Miss Valli wears some good-looking clothes and occasionally rises to heights, while Mr. O'Malley is for the most part satisfying.

Helen Lee Worthing, of Ziegfeldian fame, is in this one, and still showing her figure and undies. *Mark.*

The Volga Boatman

Cecil B. De Mille Production, released through Producers' Distributing Corp. Story by Konrad Bercovici, adapted by Lenore J. Coffee. William Boyd, Elinor Fair, Victor Varconi, Julia Faye and Theodore Kosloff featured. Directed by Cecil B. DeMille. Opened for a run at the Times Square, New York, April 13. Running time, 108 minutes.

Feodor .... William Boyd
Princess Vera .... Elinor Fair
Prince Nikita .... Robert Edeson
Prince Dimitri .... Victor Varconi
Mariusha .... Julia Faye
Stephan .... Theodore Kosloff
Vasili .... Arthur Rankin

This picture from artistic and box office standpoint looks to be about as good as anything that Cecil B. De Mille has ever done. That is taking in a lot of territory, but in this particular instance De Mille has turned out a picture that has a lot of that quality known to the trade as "guts." It is not one of the wishy-washy type of society mellers with bedrooms and bathrooms that have been his wont at times. "The Volga Boatman" opened at the Times Square theatre in New York, legit house, scaled at $1.10 at the matinee and $2.20 at night.

Whatever fault might be found in the picture is probably in the cutting. There are a couple of spots where De Mille should have clipped and likewise a couple where he could have let his scenes run a trifle longer. Also some fault to be found with his leading lady, Elinor Fair, who seemed rather stiff and failed to rise to the heights of her role. And as that tells the worst that can be said of the picture, it is just as well to have it over with right at the start.

William Boyd walks away with all the honors in the title role, but at that he has strong competition from Victor Varconi as Prince Dimitri, the heavy.

De Mille does not appear to have been extravagant on this picture, but he has turned out a production that really looks like it has all the wallops necessary to put it over with a bang with the picture public. He has shot a couple of big scenes with a crumbling wall effect in one, where the palace tumbles down on the heads of the aristocrats of old Russia as a result of the gunfire from the Army of the Reds.

That is one wallop. Another came earlier when through suggestion alone De Mille shows the practical tearing of the clothes from the body of the Princess in the presence of the officers of the Russian nobility, who believe her to be a peasant woman and the wife of one of the Red leaders.

Then the big punch, when Prince Dimitri, her betrothed, walks in on the scene in an effort to torture the Boatman whom his men have captured only to discover that the woman whose very soul has been bared to delight a score of drunken nobles is in reality his own sweetheart. The latter is the "kick" scene.

The first part, which runs about an hour, is merely utilized to set the story. But there is an element of suspense that runs through it for the audience in their expectation of the outbreak which will free the hero from his serfdom. In about 50 minutes in the last half the picture builds upward to a climax that hits right at the heart in the finish.

There is one thing certain about "The Volga Boatman," and that is that the public goes away carrying the thematic melody with them. It is the "Song of the Volga Boatman," and it runs all through the musical presentation that Dr. Hugo Riesenfeld evolved for the production. He has done his work well and it is possibly the first time that an audience has issued from a picture theatre where a special has been shown carrying in its mind and on its lips the tune that has been forced on them in the theatre. They hum and whistle "The Song of the Volga Boatman."

Possibly they would have liked to have carried the air of that tune from "The Covered Wagon" with them. It was too elusive, but they know "The Volga Boatman" song and remember it.

It does a whole lot for the picture, too, for now when any one hears it after having seen the picture it will immediately conjure up that scene of those straining and striving serfs tugging at their ropes like so many canal boat mules, for that is what they were, yet singing their song of hope of a day of freedom.

Carrying through the picture is a comedy note supplied by Julia Faye as a camp follower in the Red Army and Theodore Kosloff as a mute blacksmith who tries to make love to her. Both supply touches that bring laughs here and there. The performance of Kosloff is particularly noteworthy. It ranks about with his Astec in the picture he played with Geraldine Farrar about five or six years ago.

At the finish of the picture where the Volga boatmen have turned the tables on the aristocrats, both men and women, and harnessed them to the boat to draw them to the seat of the government, is another effective wallop to that same impressive melody. In the final flash where the princess and peasant are together in their love and happiness, one feels that at least Billy Boyd has earned all that was coming to him. There isn't going to be any stopping that Boyd boy, he is just as certain to be a star of the first magnitude as it is certain that he carried away the honors of this picture. *Fred.*

Beverly of Graustark

Metro-Goldwyn release of the Cosmopolitan Production starring Marion Davies with Antonio Moreno featured. Adapted by Agnes Christine Johnston from the novel by George Barr McCutcheon. Directed by Sidney Franklin. At the Capitol, New York, April 18 week. Running time, 70 minutes.

Beverly Calhoun .... Marion Davies
Dantan .... Antonio Moreno
Prince Oscar .... Creighton Hale
General Marlanax .... Roy D'Arcy
Duke Travina .... Albert Gran
Carlotta .... Paulette Duval
Saranoff .... Max Barwyn
Mr. Calhoun .... Charles Clary

It has been noticeable in the recent Marion Davies releases that those in charge of her film destinies were giving her expensive and well known stories, the best of casts and scenarios prepared so that there was a situation every minute and a few opportunities for Miss Davies to either fall down or get kicked. Consequently, her most recent pictures have gotten money at the box office and have done more to gain her recognition as a legitimate star than all the advertising in the world.

And in "Beverly of Graustark" we have a well known story, a cast that is sterling and slap-stick situations every so often. On the other hand, Miss Davies falls down here because in her impersonation of a young prince, she cannot help looking like a girl—thus giving the picture a prince too effeminate for plausibility, while the scenario is incomplete and not sufficiently plain in spots.

But it is an entertaining picture which will be satisfactory to the general run of houses, even if not a knockout for the de luxe first runs. Enhancing its value considerably is a color sequence introduced at the end in which Miss Davies shows to real advantage.

The story concerns Beverly Calhoun, an American girl, who assumes the garments, etc., of her male cousin, heir to the throne of Graustark, who has been hurt but whose presence is imperative to forestall the plotting of a villainous general who would be king. Therefore Beverly passes as the prince until the royal personage recovers from his illness. Thus she gets herself a handsome bodyguard and falls in love with him, but when she slips into feminine clothes and finds that he is mad over her, the male garments get irksome—until she is found out. But then the real prince arrives, explains things and the film rides right into its happy ending—done on a massive scale in colors.

A good cast, with Antonio Moreno doing excellent work. Creighton Hale, while not so active throughout, is good when he gets a chance, and Roy D'Arcy villains in an obvious but effective 10-20-30 manner. The cutting has been done with a view to keeping the star in the foreground, it would appear, and it does seem that not a shot appears but what she's in the middle of it—but at that, stars are supposed to be omnipresent.

"Beverly of Graustark" is a good picture but could have been better.

Sisk.

A SOCIAL CELEBRITY

Famous Players picture. From story by Minte M. Katterjohn, adapted by Pierre Collings. Starring Adolphe Menjou, directed by Malcolm St. Clair. At the Rivoli, New York, week April 18. Running time, 62 minutes.

Max Haber	Adolphe Menjou
Kitty Laverne	Louise Brooks
April King	Elsie Lawson
TenEyck Stuyvesant	Roger Davis
Forrest Abbot	Hugh Huntley
Johann Haber	Chester Conklin
Gifford Jones	Freeman Wood
Mrs. Jackson-Greer	Josephine Drake
Mrs. Winifred King	Ida Waterman

A story that does not stand up and fails to fit the star with a supporting cast that does not do Menjou credit is why this is by far the weakest of the Menjou starring pictures Famous Players has turned out. "A Social Celebrity" will undoubtedly draw audiences into the theatre on the strength of the Menjou name, but the picture is far below standard. Menjou is accepted as the sophisticated star, and a wishy-washy milk and water story should not be given him. "A Social Celebrity" proves that if nothing more.

In Chester Conklin, erstwhile comic of the slapstick lots, F. P. has an actor that in his way is every whit as good as Emil Jannings. His interpretation of the role of the old Long Island barber here is much akin to Jannings in "The Last Laugh." All that Conklin now needs is a real chance. And in Louise Brooks it looks as though Famous has a find that might rank in the Colleen Moore class providing they handle her right.

As to the tale the film unwinds it matters not much what it is. Menjou is cast as the best barber in Huntington, L. I. He and his old dad are the only barbers there, from the picture. Pop Haber (Mr. Conklin) after opening up in the morning shaves himself with a safety razor, which goes for a wow laugh In the shop Kitty Laverne (Miss Brooks) acts as cashier. She and the barber's son are in love. She, however, decries the boy's lack of ambition and to stir this leaves Huntington and the barber shop flat in New York. It takes but a week for the boy to follow her. He can't locate her. She is working in a night club while he is clipping in a Broadway barbershop.

Comes a call for a barber in the home of one of the men about town. As Max looks the part the society boys decide to take him along as a count and foist him on their hostess that evening. They tog him out in dress clothes and the daughter of the hostess falls for him. But the next evening, in the same night club where Kitty is working, the barber is exposed for what he is, and his social lady friends leave him.

Nothing left but to return to Huntington, especially as Pop has come on the scene and informed the boy that business has been ruined by his departure. Kitty follows, like the brave little thing that she is, to be shown with him and a bouncing baby in the final shot.

In direction the picture has much to commend it, especially the scene with Menjou and Conklin as father and son sitting with their backs to the audience in the furnished room scene and the old boy consoling the youngster. Corking touch brought out here.

The cast has Josephine Drake in a character bit, Freeman Wood as the heavy, and Roger Davis in a comedy bit in which he looks like a cross between Harry Thaw and Jawn D. Jr.

Fred.

OLD LOVES AND NEW

First National picture, based on E. M. Hull's novel, "The Desert Healer." Features Lewis Stone; Barbara Bedford and Tully Marshall underlined. Adapted by Marion Fairfax and directed by Maurice Tourneur. At the Strand, New York, week of April 18. Running time, 80 minutes.

Gervas Carew	Lewis Stone
Marny	Barbara Bedford
Lord Clyde Geradine	Walter Pidgeon
Lady Elinor Carew	Katherine McDonald
Hosein	Tully Marshall
Kitty	Ann Rork
Denny O'Meara	Arthur Rankin
Dr. Chalmers	Albert Conti

Good program stuff, with Lewis Stone riding around bedecked in sheik's robes and eventually marrying the oppressed wife of a young drunkard, widowed by an elephant. The pilgrimage to the screen has left enough of the story on tap to hold up the interest, while Stone and Barbara Bedford have turned in performances that need no apologies.

A little lengthy in the time—80 minutes—Tourneur has made it hold with his direction. The tale is set in England among the lords and ladies, touches on the war, and finally wends its way to Algiers, where most of the dramatics occur. The English angle should make this film a cinch for the Canadian provinces, and they'll like it this side of the St. Lawrence and the lakes, too.

Stone, as Carew, is invalided home from the front to find his baby son dead and that his wife has left him for Lord Geradine, a youthful member of his own set, much given to being continuously in his cups and addicted to feminity. The hitch is that Geradine walks out on Mrs. Carew (Katherine McDonald) to wed Marny (Miss Bedford), whom he has met through her legless but commissioned brother (Arthur Rankin).

Carew folds up under the double blow, takes himself to the desert and becomes a patriarch to the Arabs. This is revealed after a title informs that the tale has leaped eight years. The Geradines are in that country for the crippled brother's health, and Marny's life is a hell until rescued from horse thieves by Carew. After that her titled but still stewed husband starts to let jealousy heighten his thirst with this climaxing in a hrose-whipping for Marny, during which Carew breaks in to retaliate.

The old adage that an elephant never forgets is the "out" for the couple, the pachyderm giving Geradine a tossing around that makes a chump out of a divorce court.

Stone continues to flash a dignified and vigorous front, and teams nicely with Miss Bedford. Tully Marshall is buried under one of those Arabian capes and in the script, while the reason for Miss McDonald playing a matronly role is simply a question of avoirdupois. This may be a "come-back" for Miss McDonald, she having married about a year and a half ago and announcing her retirement from the screen at that time. However, in certain "shots" she remains plenty to behold. Walter Pidgeon makes a smart villain, while Arthur Rankin pries loose what he can from a wheel-chair.

Tourneur has inserted what appears to be a genuinely blind child of above five years in the running, and it's strong for pathos. Also, the abrupt manner of revealing the brother as being legless is a "punch" that can't be ignored, which passage is ably aided by Miss Bedford.

A "class" picture of the upper social strata, with everyone deporting themselves accordingly, and assuredly major house program fare. The picture is better than the title.

Skig.

The Beautiful Cheat

Universal-Jewel with Laura LaPlant. One-half of double bill at Loew's New York for one day, April 16. Running time, 74 minutes.

Rather an exceptional picture for the Jewel label and more exceptional to be one-half of a double feature bill at the New York. More remarkable, the other feature is also Universal's and a good western ("The Border Sheriff" with Jack Hoxie). There's probably an inside explanation why the two U's were together when each could stand on its own. It may have been through "The Beautiful Cheat" running 74 minutes and "The Border Sheriff" with its 50 minutes balancing up on the total time. However, these two pictures probably comprised the best double program the New York has ever shown.

There are laughs, smiles, sentiment and good comedy in "The Beautiful Cheat." Also too much film. If the picture were cut to one hour it would be much better and this may easily be done. About the single fault is in the cutting. If U were more particular in picture making attention might be directed toward the force employed in some of the captions in an effort to capture a laugh. The point is too stronghly striven for, destroying its own effect. Yet one of the titles is about the best read in a long while.

It's a picture making story with three Jews and one Irishman the promoting operators. After a series of mishaps with backing, the climax is the president of the company receiving a wire reading.

"Studios burned down this morning. Insurance ran out yesterday. Am taking gas tonight. Abe Meyers."

Maritza Callahansky is the imported Russian actress, plain Mary Calahan, sent abroad by the picture men to return as a foreign star. The film adaptation of a story that ran in the "Saturday Evening Post," it lends itself easily to the screen and the director missed nothing in the making. It's really quite a comedy for Jewel and Universal could brag a bit about this one.

Miss LaPlant is splendid, all the way, and she has considerable work. It is balanced nicely in players with Alexander Carr playing the president. No one besides Miss LaPlant other than the players of the Baron character and Mary's father stands out.

Sime.

BLUE BLAZES

Universal release of a Blue Streak Western (Lariat Production). From the story in "Triple-X Magazine" by Frank C. Robertson. Starring Pete Morrison; directed by Joseph Franz. At the Arena (10c. grind), New York, one day, April 15. Running time, 41 minutes.

It's a funny thing about these Blue Streak "westerns." A guy from Broadway may see one and think it terrible. It is terrible—"artistically." But financially and as entertainment for the only type they aim to please they rate highly. And they undoubtedly make money.

They have been released since June, 1925, and since then about one almost every week. They cost little. A fairly well known cowboy actor, such as Pete Morrison or Art Accord, is starred and a "wonder horse" featured. Other than salaries and mechanical expenses the outlay is considerably low.

Interiors are few, the "great open spaces" being relied on for the scenic shots. And the interiors, when they happen, are seldom any more than the familiar inside of a ranch house or the cabin where the usual concluding fight is held.

The stories are all of the usual run, varying only in detail and then amounting to about the same in that. A tale that has run in one of the many western outdoor or adventure magazines can be purchased at a small price. It is not always necessary to buy a story when the producers have a staff of scenario writers. But with the magazine title trailing with the authorship, some ground, at least, is given the story.

Walk along 8th avenue or the outlying districts in New York or any other city and you will find frequent film places that play the so-called "double feature" days, having one of these Blue Streaks or a similar "small time" "western" as half of the program at least once, and many times three and four days a week.

The large amount of available "westerns" do not go over the demand, though. In the "go-in-for-a-dime-see-the-picture-and-blow" palaces they are liked, and immensely. No picture a kid enjoys like the "westerns." And the older boys are thrilled as in their youth.

It is no surprise that these picture plays make money, having the supply and demand angle at an almost perfect balance. And the producers, having laid out little money in the making, are probably off the "nut" on the first set of bookings.

Look at the large batch of Blue Streaks that Universal has for present and next season release. Then look at the larger batch now in the making and in preparation. Then look at the fact that Universal, while probably the largest in this line, is followed by a fairly large number of other companies in producing program "westerns." Then draw your own conclusions.

Pete Morrison is his usual big, smiling, hard-riding self in "Blue Blazes." "Lightning," Pete's horse, looked better and shinier in this picture than in the past. Les Bates, as the ever present villain, and James Welch, in his usual kindly old man character role, played excellently.

Barbara Starr, very sweet, did nicely as the girl who had come west to avenge her grandpa's death and recover 25 grand in a hidden cabin. Barbara, while familiar, cannot be recalled. She is a brunet. Times were when dark girls were used as vampires and only blondes as heroines in the "westerns." But time and the color of hair change.

THE TOUGH GUY

F. B. O. production, starring Fred Thompson and featuring "Silver King" (horse). Story by Frank M. Clifton; directed by David Kirkland. At Stanley, New York, one day, April 15. Running time, 62 mins.

Fred Saunders	Fred Thompson
June Hardy	Lola Todd
Mr. Carney	Robert McKim
Padre	William Courtwright
Bud Hardy	Billy Butts
Sam Jacks	Leo Willis
Silver	Himself

Here's your handsome, square-shooting, hard-riding, heroic and villain-routing cowpuncher — Fred Thompson, and with the proverbial bells on and the F. B. O.'s ace money maker for F. B. O.

They don't come more crowd-pleasing, with the possible exception of Tom Mix, than Thompson. And the other cinema calf-slingers don't get near the clean cut Fred where looks are concerned.

He is a girl's idea of a man—not a New York man, but a westerner—as verified in the heroine's exclamation by way of subtitle.

And Fred has plenty of opportunity to prove his worth in this film, especially in the first few moments, which are only too short. The pace set at the beginning is really great for this kind of release, and makes the later sob stuff, which would seem good in another picture, look somewhat weak.

Fred is foreman of the usual ranch, the crew of which is merely a tribe of murderers. To hold this gang in check Fred dons the make-up of a tough egg. But this toughness only covers his saintliness. Upon recovering money stolen from the local church, Fred shoots up the saloon and dance hall, pilfering hats, breaking lights and causing pants to fall through broken buttons. All this by his gun.

And then there is the girl, played by Lola Todd, a pretty miss, who is teaching school in the western town as a means of finding her lost little brother. Little bro. is cutely done by freckled Billy Butts. Billy is a clever kid, not much older than was Coogan when he started.

And the villain, played well by Robert McKim is after the girl's hand and would have won had not Fred found out the little brother first.

In this picture McKim is without his curled mustache. That is unusual. But McKim, with or without, is one of the screen's best trouble makers. His pantomime is of the first order, and his sneer still one of the darkest. An all-round villain, he.

"Silver King," Thompson's horse (not the mineral water), is a beautiful, white coated animal. And seemingly intelligent. But "Silver" is asked to do too much. He does many things usually allotted to humans. "Silver" has an "out" as the subtitles credit his acts to instinct.

The picture packs an unusual punch. Even its sob scenes run along at a fast pace, aided by several witty titles, Thompson's smile and "Silver King's" dramatics. With a competent Juliet, this horse could do a fair Romeo.

No kid and few men could resist "The Tough Guy."

HEADS UP

Harry Garson production released by F. B. O. Starring Maurice "Lefty" Flynn. At Tivoli, New York, one day (April 14). Running time, 50 minutes.

Breckenridge Gamble	"Lefty" Flynn
Angela	Kathleen Myers
Hallitosis Malofich	Kalla Pasha
Cortez	Jean Perry
Losada	Milton Gross
Biff	Harry McCoy
Commandante	Ray Ripley
Zeke	Raymond Turner
Spy	Robert Cautier

"Here comes the Americano now." Whereupon a group of Latin generals grab their swords and run.

Big Maurice "Lefty" Flynn is an adequate Americano. After subduing a large number of generals and revolutionists of one of the numerous phoney South American republics, he winds up by marrying the President's comely daughter.

"Lefty," as the wealthy American, Breckenridge Gamble, decides at his breakfast table that he is tired of the American servant problem and wishes to away. Applying as a messenger for an oil company he is sent with a vital letter to the President of Costa Casaba, or somewhere.

This Latin land is in a turmoil over taxes. The President has a sweet daughter, sought by a villainous general, Cortez, who also seeks the presidency. The President figures that the check, in form of "Lefty's" message, from the American company for the country's oil deposits will still the raging revolution and rout the wicked conspirators.

The check does save the country, but not until "Lefty" has kicked around a whole tribe of burlesque soldiers.

The film depends on its comedy and its pleasing star. It is an old story for pictures.

A corking lot of lowbrow laughs are packed, a good percentage of those being produced by the antics of Ray Ripley, who does a "nance" general. Ray's feminine antics had the boys upstairs in hysterics.

"Lefty" does some great leaping and fighting in "Heads Up." That he was once an all-round athlete is seen. Kathleen Meyers is not short of gorgeous and her medium height lends contrast to "Lefty's" tallness. Jean Perry and Milton (not Milt) Gross as revolutionist and President, respectively, played well.

THE BORDER SHERIFF

Universal, western, with Jack Hoxie. One-half double bill at Loew's New York, one day April 16. Added comment on this double bill is contained in the review of "The Beautiful Cheat," the other picture. Running time, 50 minutes.

Plenty of action in this western that speeds along through its 50 minutes of running time. No girl enters the film until after 1,500 feet. Comedy is begotten by a new stunt of tying up a crook by his heels is employed; also an "expose" of a possible way of smuggling dope over the border (in the horns of long horn steers), and rather a novel finish, where Hoxie as the sheriff handcuffs the heroine, to oblige her to go with him, against her will, she believing him to be a bad man.

The girl's father makes an enlightening explanation, but the sheriff does not remove the cuffs.

"Are you taking me to jail?" the girl inquires as the sheriff starts to leave, dragging her along.

"No, I'm going to take you to the minister," he replies, and the fadeout is the couple, still manacled, walking down a long road.

Very good western. Easily can stand up alone in any house liking that class of film. *Sime.*

MONTE CARLO

Metro-Goldwyn-Mayer production of Alice D. G. Miller's adaptation from Carey Wilson's story. Directed by Christy Cabanne. At the Stanley, New York, one day (April 14). Running time, 71 mins.

Tony	Lew Cody
Sally	Gertrude Olmstead
Prince Boris	Roy D'Arcy
Coorman	Karl Dane
Hope	ZaSu Pitts
Flossie	Trixie Friganza
Grand Duchess	Margaret Campbell
Greves	Harry Myers
Bancroft	Arthur Hoyt
Count Davigny	Cesare Gravina

How this one, with the strength of a brilliant cast alone, missed coming nearer Broadway than the New York theatre, which is on Broadway, but at which the picture played only one day, and the Stanley, on Seventh avenue, is hard to define.

It's improbable that the Metro people made this film as a whim, but that's apparent, if not true. When you have an attractive title as "Monte Carlo" and such names as Cody, Olmstead, Dane, D'Arcy, Pitts, Myers, Friganza, etc., you have something. Surely no such a layout is seen in Broadway's first run houses every week, and there are weaker or just as weak stories seen weekly in the same places.

In "Monte Carlo" are popular personalities brought on the screen for just a flash. For instance, Roy D'Arcy, recognized lately as highly competent, does a prince, and in this role is seen for no more than two minutes, if that long, and that at the very end of the film. But having a load of high-salaried players under contract, it is no more than right to give them enough work to keep up their fighting form.

This picture is not short of very good, relying on comedy and "situations" for effects. The bulk of the comedy is slapped on heavily by Trixie Friganza and ZaSu Pitts, both adept at slapstick. These two and Miss Olmstead, as three winners of a popularity contest conducted by a newspaper in a small American town, are awarded a trip to Monte Carlo. The girls are accompanied by the newspaper's star reporter, played by Arthur Hoyt in the usual good Hoyt manner.

At the French resort Lew Cody, as Tony Townsend, a young American thrown out of several hotels with his butler (done excellently by Harry Meyers) for failure to pay his board bill, is awaiting word and money from his wealthy American uncle. Uncle wires daily that if Tony returns to his job in the States he will get the money—or else. Tony drifts into the hotel where the three girls and the reporter are on the hunt for marriageable Counts, Dukes or even Princes.

After having his pants held by the hotel management, Tony grabs the wardrobe of the flighty Prince Boris, traveling incognito and not yet arrived. In the Prince's clothing Tony is treated royally, but not before he walks into Sally's room sans trousers.

The following action revolves around Trixie and ZaSu in their hunt for royal husbands. While Sally is delighted with Tony, believing him a Prince, the two comic ladies find their royal lads, one a Duke and the other a Count, and holding the titles despite they are waiter and doorman. Both ladies faint upon discovering their boy friends' occupations.

Several comedy situations evolved from the reporter's daily wires to his paper on the royalty hunt developments. And Harry Meyers as Tony's butler was great, but almost unrecognizable, appearing unusually tall. Miss Pitts, too, appeared taller than ever before, this being most likely due to type contrast, which was the only outstanding piece of directing.

There is no more girlishly sweet heroine than Miss Olmstead. She is beauty untouched. Mr. Cody was ever present with mustache and snappy uniforms. He lifts his eyebrows adequately.

A fashion show in colors is staged well.

FIGHTING EDGE

Warner Bros. production of the novel by William McLeod Raine. Directed by Henry Lehrman. At the Tivoli, New York, one day (April 17). Running time, 47 mins.

A cinema about the boys and their dealings with alien smugglers on the Mexican border.

Kenneth Harlan is Juan de Dios O'Rourke, of the United States border intelligence staff and on duty in Mexico. He is assigned to recover Joyce (W. A. Carroll), a brother staff member, held captive by smugglers.

The gang is headed by the wicked Gillette ("Red" Kirby). Miss Miller, Joyce's daughter, drifts into the crooks' den to find her father.

Some spine-tickling and reckless automobile riding is well done and holds most of the picture's thrills.

Just a rough one, but will please on the outlying circuits.

The meaning of the title is not disclosed, although fighting has a certain edge over love-making on Eighth avenue.

Shadows of the Law

Associated Exhibitors release produced by Arthur F. Beck. Adapted from story by Harry Chapman Ford and directed by Wallace Worsley. Clara Bow starred. Running time, about one hour.

Mary Matthews	Clara Bow
Dan Brophy	Ralph Lewis
Baron Lingard	Stuart Holmes
"Twist" Egan	William V. Mong

A crook story which has its beginnings on Welfare Island, where a girl known as Mary Matthews is just being released after serving a term for a crime of which a Baron Lingard accused her. The Baron, it seems, is a master-crook with his own gang of henchmen, a killer, mean and ruthless. Released, Mary goes to San Francisco to find that her father, Dan Brophy, is working with Lingard. A certain "Twist" Egan is also with Lingard. It is apparent the plot concerns itself with Mary's plan of revenge on the man who was responsible for her being needlessly committed to jail.

It's a well worked out story of the ordinary sort, excellently cast and directed. Miss Bow gives a good performance, but is backed by a cast of older men who come through like the troupers they are—especially that man Mong, who is one of the screen's real ace character actors.

"Shadows of the Law" fits well into the daily change program for which it was apparently intended.

Sisk.

QUEEN O' DIAMONDS

F. B. O. release, starring Evelyn Brent. Story by Fred Myton. Directed by Chester Withey. At the Tivoli, New York, one day (April 19). Running time, 55 mins.

Jeannette Durant	Evelyn Brent
Jerry Lynn	Evelyn Brent
David Hammon	Theodore Von Eltz
Le Roy Phillips	Wm. N. Bailey
Mr. Ramsey	Phillips Smalley
Mrs. Ramsey	Elsa Lorimer

Evelyn Brent is starred and has a dual role. She is the perfect crookess. One who could cop the gold out of your teeth while looking into your eyes. That's Evelyn.

Having never done much of anything other than crook roles, her sponsors realize her worth as that and keep her there. It appears that Evelyn will have to remain a picture crookess for a long time. She can do it—and profitably.

But Miss Brent also has her attainments as a "good" girl. In "Queen o' Diamonds" she is the innocently accused chorus girl and also a prominent dramatic actress with thieving aspirations.

And superb as both. But that she will remain a crook is here in proof. As the nice girl she is lovable, but as the crooked, sophisticated actress, great!

Miss Brent is Jerry Lynn, chorus girl. Then Jeannette Durant, tragedienne. Jerry is in love with David Hammon (Theodore Von Eltz), a young playwright with a piece he cannot interest the usual hard-hearted hannah managers in. They both reside in the same theatrical boarding house. Jeannette is the sweetheart of Le Roy Phillips (Wm. N. Bailey), mustached member of a ring of diamond thieves.

Jerry and Jeannette resemble each other. Excepting hair cuts, just alike. Attention to this is called by a newspaper story of the fact. The resemblance is where the gag lies.

Having double-crossed his fellow gangsters in the matter of a diamond haul, Phillips seeks to entrust Jeannette with the stolen jewels. Jeannette is kidnapped by the crossed crooks, and Jerry is tricked into impersonating her. While in Jeannette's rooms, Jerry meets Mr. Ramsey, London producer. Invited out to his Long Island home, she does not reveal her identity, seeing a chance to sell David's play.

Following a murder of one of the crooks, of which Jerry is suspected but which Phillips did, police, crooks and everyone else concerned congregate at the Ramsey home for the final blowoff. Phillips and the rest of his gang are walked to the cooler, as is Jerry's double; David sells his play and to top that, Jerry is engaged by Ramsey to star in it.

Miss Brent is the perfect crookess. It would take much to resist her stealing ways. She steals hearts.

SMILIN' AT TROUBLE

F. B. O. picture starring Maurice "Lefty" Flynn. Directed by Harry Garson. Author's name, if any, missed. At the Arena, New York, one day (April 19). Running time, about 40 mins.

Here's "Smilin' Lefty" again. This time it's "Whistlin' Lefty," too. "Lefty" is all over the place. And he has plenty of space to roam in this one.

He is Jerry Foster, young engineer assigned to the chief job with a couple of bad boys under him at a dam construction.

Much lively action about cheap cement the lowlives are slipping in the construction work with the eggs getting a nice rakeoff on the job. And Jerry fools 'em. But not until the dam of cheap cement caves in and drowns everyone but the principals.

"Lefty' is big, good looking, catchy smile, beautiful teeth and personality. But "Lefty' is not an actor. Being an actor and yet not actor has its virtues. Given something big, "Lefty" would flop. That's the virtue. He is the perfect type for this kind of "small time" cinema, and he's good right there.

For this kind of picture is liked and plenty where it is shown.

Theatre owners who cater to the class that like their picture plays moving fast and meaning little need not fear to book a "Lefty" Flynn model. Any one of his pictures will please the children.

Outside of a few phoney scenic shots held too long, "Smilin' at Trouble" is without apparent fault.

Two likely ladies, Helen Lynch and Kathleen Myers, are in it. Both are more than competent, Miss Meyers especially so. In the picture "Lefty' picks out Miss Lynch for his, but could have done as well, if not better, with Kathleen.

In writing of a picture such as this, the picture itself is not commented upon, as is the outstanding personality. And the kids will remember "Lefty" Flynn long after the plot is cold.

MAN RUSTLIN'

Produced by Jesse J. Goldberg. Released by the Independent Pictures Corp., via Film Booking Offices. Stars, Bob Custer. Story by William Branch. Directed by Del Andrews. Shown at the Columbia Theatre, New York City, one day, April 19, as one of double features. Running time, 43 minutes.
Mary Wilson................Florence Lee
Slim.................Skeeter Bill Robbins
Sheriff Jim Tucker.............Jules Cowl
Buck Hayden..................Bob Custer
Pop Geers....................Sam Allen
Smudge.......................Patt Beggs

As the title indicates: "western." Hoss ridin' buckaroo is Bob Custer. He's not the corn-fed type of gat-toting cowhand, but rigged to perfection as the kinda rough-riding bird that urges his superb mount to chain-lightning speed rounds up the dirty cow rustlers, licks 'em single-handed and captures the hull caboodle, whoopee and lickety split.

This picture is not unlike some other Goldbergs that have passed along, but has Bob Custer displaying the riding skill that has made him just as fast and important in "westerns" as some of the other heroes.

Bob may not be the handsomest of the screen cowboys, but he's just as quick on his feet, can pull some rough daredevil stuff and ride with any.

It was a lucky day for the westerns when the sweet-faced school marm took up the instruction of the three "r's" in the wild and wooly.

The young lady shows up in the school room at Desert City, Ariz.,

and, of course, there's the usual play by the sheriff, his side kicks and the bashful hero, Buck Hayden, for her smiles.

Usual pull at comedy byplay. And fighting, in which Buck out-wallops cow rustlers and turns them up by his lonely. But what makes the Broadway tenderfoot wonder is that Buck riding hoss' on into a villainous band of rustlers left his pistol in the holster and why the other shooters didn't pull when they were known to be quick on the trigger. Might have spoiled a few of the big scenes, hence the hand-to-hand smashing and socking.

Bob Custer handles himself well and in his thrilling moments gives all that could be desired. But the best acting was done by Sam Allen as old Pop Geers, the editor. He made a corking character out of Pop and his part was unquestionably a redeeming feature.

That the man who titled the film knew something about New York newspaper was evident as he referred to the New York "World' and called "William Randolph Hearst "Randle" instead of "Willie."

A "western" that is half and half.
Mark.

After Business Hours

Columbia production, starring Elaine Hammerstein. Story taken from Cosmopolitan story, with scenario by Douglas Z. Doty. Directed by Mal St. Clair. At the Columbus, New York City, as part of double feature, one day, April 19. Running time, 71 minutes.
John King.....................Lou Tellegen
June King............Elaine Hammerstein
Sylvia Vane................Phyllis Haver
Richard Downing............John Patrick
Mrs. Wm. Wentworth......Lillian Langdon
James Kendrick..............William Scott
Jerry Stanton...................Lee Moran

Not a thing new in the story as far as picture themes go, but fairly worked out through the direction of Mal St. Clair. St. Clair has put in some deft touches and set before the public a domestic story that would send home its moral to wives who would take any chance to cover up their gambling proclivities.

"After Business Hours" by reels made a despicable character out of June King, the wife who played poker, bet on the races and deceived her hubby because he just wouldn't trust her with money.

Everything looked blacker than Stygian darkness for Mrs. King. She had committed palpable theft and then followed it with forgery, until the audience began to quiver about the lips and figure it would have to be a corking film maker to get her out of the jams.

Some modern angles that left much for the imagination and incidentally made a corking ad for the radio.

Some fine scenes between Miss Hammerstein and Mr. Tellegen. Miss Hammerstein seems to have become more comely, handles herself before the screen with more confidence and ease; in fact, has improved immeasurably in her work. Mr. Tellegen seemed rather too matured for the husband at times, and that hair of his never seems to have gotten on to the modern ways of tonsorial dispatch. Tellegen showed real man-sized agility when he swung into his fight with Patrick. If it was a "double" it was magical camera work, and if it were Mr. Tellegen, he can still command a lead in present-day domestic revolutions.

There was undeniable consummate skill on the part of Mr. Patrick. As the rather imbecilic-like male modern he had the quivering lips, the bouncing eyelids and the nervous, fidgety mannerisms that betray the desires.

Miss Haver was splendid, and Miss Langdon did all she could to make an important role out of Mrs. Wentworth. Lee Moran got away soft with his work, and William Scott took care of his dramatic moments admirably.

The film establishes one thing clearly: Miss Hammerstein has not gone back in her screen work.
Mark.

THE MIDNIGHT SUN

Dimitri Buchowetski production, released by Universal. Featuring Laura La Plante and Pat O'Malley. From the novel by Lauridas Brunn. Directed by Dimitri Buchowetski. Opened for run at the Colony, New York, April 23. Running time, 111 minutes.
Olga Balashova...........Laura La Plante
Grand Duke Sergius..........Pat O'Malley
Alexei Oroloff ....Raymond Keane
Ivan Kusmin...............George Siegmann
Yessky ....Arthur Hoyt
Nickoll Oroloff ....Earl Metcalf
Duke's Adjutant..........Mikhael Vavitch
Second Aide ....Nickoll Soussanin
Opera Director ....Cesare Gravina
Barbara ....Nina Romano
Anisya ....Medea Radsina
Radical ....Albert Prisco

Second of the Universal productions that have reached the Colony in the guise of specials. "The Flaming Frontier" was the first. It lasted less than three weeks. "The Midnight Sun" is the second. While it is better than the other, no one will have to wear tinted glasses to get away from the glare of its success.

For the average neighborhood picture house "The Midnight Sun" will get by, but on Broadway or any other place where a week's run is the policy the picture can't stand up. It is just a meller for the low-priced admission houses.

Not even that Dimitri Buchowetski directed is going to save it. Buchowetski has done much better work than he displays here.

The story is of Russia in 1913, with the Romanoffs in power. The Grand Duke (Pat O'Malley) and Ivan Kusmin, banker (George Siegmann) fall in love with a young American girl in the Imperial Ballet. She in turn falls in love with a young officer just graduated from the cadet school.

It is to save this youngster's brother from exile that the girl goes to the Grand Duke's apartment. When he is about to send her home the young officer is the one summoned to accompany her. He becomes infuriated when seeing who the girl is and strikes the Grand Duke. He is arrested, court-martialed and ordered to be shot at sunrise.

The girl goes to the banker for his influence, but he uses the opportunity to lure the dancer on board his yacht to bring about her ruin. The girl's chum informs the Grand Duke. He orders out a destroyer, chases the yacht, saves the girl and then the two rush back to the execution yard of the "old fortress" just in the nick of time to save the young lover from death.

The handling of the latter portions of this melodramatic tale were such as to make the audience laugh.

The picture is split in two sections at the Colony. The first runs about 53 minutes. It is devoted to a lengthy planting of the story, entirely too much footage for the end achieved. The finishing half runs almost an hour, a succession of melodramatic episodes.

Laura La Plante as the American dancer seems to have hardened in looks, unless this was due to a poor selection in the matter of hats. With her hat off she was at her best. Pat O'Malley got away with the Grand Duke in good shape and Raymond Keane, new comer, as the young officer would seem to be something of a find, although somewhat stilted in his work at present. George Siegmann as the heavy delivered the best performance. Arthur Hoyt supplied what little comedy there was and did it very well. None of the balance of the cast played more than bits. *Fred.*

Mademoiselle Modiste

First National release, adapted from the operetta of the same title by Henry Blossom and Victor Herbert. Starring Corinne Griffith, with Norman Kerry and Willard Louis featured. Directed by Robert Z.

Leonard. At the Strand, New York, week of April 25. Running time, 63 minutes.

Fifi........................Corinne Griffith
Etienne.. ....Norman Kerry
Hiram Bent......................Willard Louis
Marianne................Dorothy Cumming
Mme. Claire.........................Rose Rione

With a couple of essential points of the original story of the operetta retained and enough new stuff to make it into a light comedy picture, "Mlle. Modiste" appears on the screen this week with Corinne Griffith as the star. The picture is presented by a trio that sounds like the Acker, Merrill & Condit of film business: Asher, Small & Rogers. On the strength of the Corinne Griffith name and that the picture is a dead open and shut bet for the exhibitor to tie up in a fashion show with one of his local stores, there should be a chance to get some money here.

Miss Griffith does fairly well in the title role, with Norman Kerry opposite—a likeable enough hero—but Willard Louis, in reality, runs away with the picture. He is just one of those hustling, go-getting types of American promoters who might do exactly the stuff he pulls when hitting Paris and getting an eyefull of trim calves and neat ankles.

The story is slim enough as it goes. Hiram Bent, a sort of a butter-and-eggish guy from this side of the Atlantic, strikes Paris with his ham sandwich along. She walks him into a modiste's shop, and when Fifi gets through with the wife, Hi has an ardent admiration for the saleslady's business ability. He proposes to buy out the modiste shop and install Fifi as manager, utilize American methods of promotion and publicity, and make his Paris trip pay for itself.

About that time the love interest is shoved in by horsepower, the hero's horse eating the phony apples off the heroine's hat.

The American promoter has obtained the promise of the girl that she will not divulge her identity to anyone until the shop with the name of "Mlle. Modiste" over the door is opened. The night before, he invites the principal buyers in and wines and dines them, with the idea of signing them up.

But the hero, who has trailed the heroine to the establishment, breaks into the picture. When he sees his girl apparently disrobing behind a screen and auctioning off her apparel, bit by bit, it is too much for him; he walks, after administering a bawling out. Then she consents to go to Deauville with Bent, to act as a walking model for the wares of the shop.

Further complications ensue, including an almost-duel. A couple of sequences look as though there is something quite risque, but this is washed over with the appearance of Hi's wife in the same room.

The picture as a picture is pretty weak, and the frightfully punny titles that Ralph Spence provided do not seem to help materially to bolster up the production. *Fred.*

THE RUNAWAY

.F. P.-L. picture directed by William de Mille. Clara Bow and Warner Baxter underlined. Adapted from a C. N. Buck magazine story, with Charles Boyle the photographer. At Rivoli, New York, week April 25. Running time, 69 minutes.

Cynthia Meade........................Clara Bow
Wade Murrell................Warner Baxter
Jack Harrison................William Powell
Lesher Skidmore............George Bancroft
Wade's Mother............Edythe Chapman

A yarn of Kentucky mountaineers, interrupted by the visit of a young moving picture actress, with William de Mille laying it on so heavy at times for dramatics that it made a Sabbath matinee audience giggle. The staying powers are invested in Clara Bow and Warner Baxter. The latter's performance is even throughout, with Miss Bow's flame brightening here and dwindling there. Despite the work of the pair it's not a good picture.

Pretty close to one of those things that might have been turned into a satirical tale of these southern hills. If such a temptation were on tap, de Mille leaned over backwards in dodging it. At least the action looks that, especially with Edythe Chapman, who plays the mountaineer mother.

There's a feud mixed up in the narrative, with the son striving to preserve the peace threatened by the invasion of the powdered and rouged screen actress. In toto, a weak peg upon which to hang a scenario with such paper hatrack folding up under the weight of 69 minutes.

Cynthia (Miss Bow) runs away from a Virginia town and her troupe "on location" when the accidental discharge of a revolver from across the street sends a bullet into Jack Harrison (William Powell). Harrison, at the time, is making well-mannered but questionable proposals to the girl. Cynthia, believing him dead, takes it on the run for the hills, to be found by Wade Murrell (Mr. Baxter).

Transported via horseback to the Murrell abode high up in the adjoining state, Lesher Skidmore (George Bancroft), blood enemy of the Murrell tribe, spreads the tidings that Wade has brought home a painted woman. The rest of the Murrell family tree call to demand either the departure of Cynthia or a new leader, but Wade's "Ma" goes to bat for the girl; she proves her bravery as one of the twain is about to shoot Wade, and the diamonds in the rough apologize.

Thence comes Harrison, recovered from his wound, but still believing Cynthia shot him. Bringing the breath of Broadway into the mountain country, he tempts Cynthia to return, but all is well when she resigns herself to a mountain existence with Wade by slipping into the mountain dialect to inform she'll linger.

Incidentally, Harrison kills Skidmore as the latter is about to shoot Wade. Which may give the impression that Mr. Baxter must have spent half the footage at the point of guns—and that's true.

The acceptance of Cynthia's tale by "Ma" Murrell and Harrison's verbal picturing of Broadway to the girl about "to go native," with her resultant reactions, are the outstanding passages where de Mille has broadcast his intent of the width of the film. Besides which the story doesn't convince. The only thing it does is to give Miss Bow another chance to romp as a silly kid, toned down by the seriousness of the backwoods people.

"The Runaway" belongs on a double feature program. If the names of Miss Bow and Mr. Baxter are considered strong enough to give it precedence on the outside, it's a mistaken conception. The picture will not entertain on the inside. *Skig.*

Other Women's Husbands

Warner Brothers' picture featuring Monte Blue and Marie Prevost. Directed by Erle C. Kenton. At Warner's, New York, week of April 24. Running time, 78 mins.

Dick Lambert......................Monte Blue
Katherine Lambert...........Marie Prevost
Marion Norton...................Phylis Haver
Philip Harding.............Huntley Gordon

Another light comedy for the Blue-Prevost team that reveals the same fault of others which have been assigned to this combination. Too much length. Something of a shame here, for the material is there and with more snap might have been a rollicking affair that would have clicked regularly through the footage. As is, it's a so-so marriage epic aimed for laughs, having its moments and also its weaknesses.

The best thing is a derby "gag" that may or may not be new. However, the way Kenton has handled it, it's surefire. Simple enough as worked out with Lambert (Mr. Blue) on his way to a "date," forgetting a diamond bracelet and returning to his house for it. Meanwhile, Harding (Mr. Gordon), his pal, has called on Mrs. Lambert. When the husband gets home he hangs up the hat without noticing the other derby. While upstairs Harding goes out and when Lambert again puts on the bowler it's too small and he starts to wonder who was calling. Both Lambert and Harding return to the former's home on excuses, each to get his hat. Mrs. Lambert gets the idea, seeing Harding trying to switch the derbies on a table, helps it along and when her husband insists he take his boy friend home, both go out with their own hats. Lambert doesn't know he has his own until he places it on his head, knows it at once to be his and starts to look at Harding. Inasmuch as Lambert has been playing around with Harding's girl it's a catch-as-catch-can contest—and that's the situation.

Light stuff and played nicely by the foursome. Miss Haver is the other member of the mixed quartet. But there's no "hoke" and neither the story or the situations, with that one exception, are strong enough to stand up minus the low comedy ingredient. That being the case, cutting for speed was the logical solution, but somebody evidently muffed it.

The tale carries on to a divorce court where Mrs. Lambert, after ribbed up by Harding, who acts as her attorney and would marry her, loses her inclination to free her husband while on the witness stand. Hence a make-up all around, a row with Marion being Lambert's "out" in that direction.

Blue can do this sort of thing, but that he must have help from outside the cast is equally as true of him as anyone else. Miss Prevost continues to impress as an in and outer in these concoctions. Miss Haver convinces in her role, while Mr. Gordon plays easily and not without appeal.

The picture has been nicely furnished in respect to interiors, these looking both solid and substantial. Also the titling breaks through upon occasion for snickers. That's why it's one of those regrettable releases—it means well and tries hard, but just misses a big laugh.

It's frothy and will amuse to a certain extent. Therefore, to add to the "buts," but they will not howl nor be tremendously interested. The picture carries enough "tone." There's a masquerade ball, in which the wife duplicates her rival's costume for undercover information from hubby, plenty of evening clothes around, automobiles and most of it takes place in a drawing room. The stock formula, perhaps, albeit neatly taken care of on the production end.

Cutting should greatly improve it. *Skig.*

The Exquisite Sinner

Metro-Goldwyn-Mayer release, directed by Josef von Sternberg. Adapted by von Sternberg from story by Alden Brooks. Titles by Joe Farnham and photography by Maximilian Fabian. At Loew's American Roof, in conjunction with vaudeville. Running time, about 70 minutes.

Dominique Prad...............Conrad Nagel
The Gypsy Maid...............Renee Adoree
Yvonne........................Paulette Duval
The Colonel...................Frank Currier
His Orderly..............George K. Arthur
The Gypsy Chief...............Mathew Betz
Dominique's Sisters { ....Helena D'Algy
{ ....Claire DuBrey

This is the picture Josef von Sternberg made for M-G-M after being highly touted for his "Salvation Hunters," as fine a box office frost as anyone film ever devised. "The Exquisite Sinner" is a corker in many respects and rates miles and miles ahead of some of the few weak sisters in the Metro list—films like "Time, the Comedian," etc., being referred to as the weak sisters.

This is a fanciful, wild and romantic sort of a story—the pictorial chronicle of a boy who would not be bound down by business but whose heart longed for the gypsy trails winding through Heaven-knows-where. And quite frankly, the story concerns itself with a boy and a gypsy girl. That's all there is to it, except that the boy comes from rich people and left a family chasing him. Between the efforts of the family and his fiancee to get him, and his romance down the Romany road, it makes a good yarn, especially as the boy is forced to feign insanity to get away from the doctors.

Conrad Nagel as the boy with a yearning to be free is corking, and Frank Currier is given a fine part, but once more it is Renee Adoree who runs away with the picture. As the wild, rough gypsy girl she steals every scene.

Sternberg's direction is good. He transgresses good taste in studio scenes at the beginning, one of which gives a posterior view of a woman whose middle is covered with a bath towel. There is a whale of a funny cemetery scene wherein a fellow delivers a long eulogy and loses his audience—to fall into the open grave. Not good taste, that scene, but funny.

"Exquisite Sinner" is an okeh first run on its own merits. But the chances are that the presence of no starring name is responsible for its first New York showing, being a Loew's first run. *Sisk.*

BROODING EYES

Banner Productions release, starring Lionel Barrymore. Adapted from the story, "The Man with the Brooding Eyes." At Stanley, New York, one day (April 21). Running time, about one hour.

Slim Jim Carey...........Lionel Barrymore
Philip Mott.........................Robert Ellis
Joan Ayre.......................Ruth Clifford
Pat Callaghan...............Montagu Love
Bell...................Lucien Littlefield
Slaney..................William V. Mong
Maria De Costa...............Alma Bennett
Agnes De Costa..................Dot Farley
Drummond.....................John Miljan

Lionel Barrymore does a lot of things with his eyes in this crook story founded on the activities of a band of London social outcasts specializing in blackmail and forgery while masquerading as a business firm. It's good screen drama, probably made for the daily changes and will do well in them.

Barrymore is Slim Jim Carey, the black sheep son of an illustrious family, heir to an earldom. Callaghan, his lieutenant in crime, believing him dead, assumes the leadership of the gang. He schemes to get possession of the estate, which is rightfully Carey's.

A girl, who proves to be Carey's daughter, is established partly by the gang's efforts to a place in society which is rightfully hers.

Carey is much alive. When the gang of crooks start annoying the heiress he obtains employment in her castle as a butler in order to protect her from his former companions.

Love interest is worked in with a romance between the girl and the barrister in whose office she was employed as a stenog before her elevation to royalty.

All the characters are well cast, the work of Barrymore, Ruth Clifford, William V. Mong and Lucien Littlefield being outstanding.

THE ROAD TO GLORY

William Fox production, starring May McAvoy. Directed by Howard Hawks. At the Stanley, New York, one day (April

24). Running time, about 60 minutes.

This picture will make perfect entertainment for any of the neighborhood houses specializing in daily change programs. It might even be worthy of showing before church organizations since half dozen or more morals and lessons are neatly sugar-coated.

May McAvoy is Judy Allen, daughter of a wealthy broker and member of the younger social set which delights in fast motor cars, the Charleston and all the other pleasures youth is heir to these days.

A series of misfortunes makes her lose faith in the Maker. Among these is the accidental death of her father, followed soon after by the loss of her eyesight. The latter came as the result of a joy-riding mishap some time before from which she had gleefully believed she had escaped unharmed.

Lewis Fenton is David, Judy's suitor. Spurned when learning she is doomed to blindness, he traces her to a lonely rustic retreat where she has taken refuge. There in the midst of his avowals of love despite her handicap, lightning strikes her bungalow, and the boy is seriously hurt. The shock, however, restores Judy's sight, while prayer and a surgeon restore David to health, happiness and a happy ending.

The final shot shows Judy vetoing a suggestion that they race a fast-stepping motor that has passed them on the road, whereas in the first hundred feet of the film she was all for it, thus cinching the secondary moral.

HER SECOND CHANCE

First National production. Anna Q. Nilsson starred. Directed by Lambert Hillyer. Scenario by Eve Unsell. Adapted from story by Mrs. Wilson Woodrow. At the New York theatre, April 22, one day. Running time, 75 minutes.

Constance Lee / Caroline Logan	Anna Q. Nilsson
Judge Jeffries	Huntley Gordon
Jim Devries	Mike Donlin
John Bell	Charles Murray
Maid	Dale Fuller
Nancy Wendell	Corliss Palmer

It was a lucky day for the makers of "Her Second Chance" when they cast Charles Murray as the private detective. The old-time stage craftiness and showmanship of this clever comic saves this film from doing a high nose dive. But this picture won't take any honors.

"Her Second Chance" drags in the backwoods of Florida, then switches to the heart of luxury in the big city and to the race track; again to the Florida woodlands.

In quick succession one sees Anna Q. Nilsson, who plays a dual role, so to speak, first as the ragged-attired Caroline Logan, who stops the law when it is about to evict her from her old home and fires a gun that wounds one of the men in the party, and then as Constance Lee, back from a two-years' stretch in prison, rich as Croesus and dressed fit to kill. It's film license to take a mountain girl and in a jiffy following two years behind the bars step into the gilded drawing room and wear clothes to the manner born.

The Florida girl is sentenced by the very young judge, who falls madly in love with her after the transformation. She has sworn to be revenged, and the corporation that gave her her riches, via one Mr. Beachy, by hook and crook, is determined that she fulfill that threat.

Through the film goes Murray and his comedy and his disguises; he pops in just when the film is running on three wheels.

Miss Nilsson does splendidly in the double role. She's athletic and was suited for the part, also looking comely in her handsome gowns. The remainder of the cast was adequate.

For the most part there is an apparent lavish expenditure.

Photographically much of the picture appeared to be in bad shape when seen at New York. Long stretches of footage were not only dim and dirty but spotted. It may have been rushed from the lab and again it may have been run too many times before properly washed.

The picture for the most part falls below expectations. *Mark.*

THE TAXI MYSTERY

Banner Productions, Inc., mystery film play from the story by Tom J. Hopkins. Directed by Fred Windermere. At Loew's New York Theatre, April 23. Running time, 57 minutes.

Nancy Cornell	Edith Roberts
Vera Norris	Edith Roberts
Harry Canby	Robert Agnew
Mrs. Jameson	Virginia Pearson
Willoughby Thomson	Phillips Smalley
Fred Norris	Bertram Grassby

Not much of a mystery. And not much of a picture. Just a melodrama that tries to be spooky and fails.

The evil designs of Fred and Vera Norris on Nancy Cornell, musical star, cause the supposed mystery. Vera is Nancy's understudy and looks like her (this being not peculiar for both roles are played by the same lady).

Two unprogrammed characters, as goofy detectives, several times accuse the wrong parties and show perfectly how not to be a sleuth. Theirs is the comedy end, little that it is. Edith Roberts, in the dual role, looked sweet enough in one, and hot-tempered enough to look wicked in the other. She is a capable actress. Baby faced Robert Agnew showed nothing out of his usual run in the young Harry role. He is always an outstanding juvenile. Distinguished looking Phillips Smalley fitted well as Willoughby Thomson as did Bertram Grassby as the villain.

But the mystery has not yet been explained. It is just that young Canby met Nancy in a taxi and for the most part of the film tried to find out if she was really the one he had met. That's the mystery.

With the picture unlikely for any kind of adults and misunderstandable for children, how it can make itself enjoyable and profitable over the outlying circuits is a bigger mystery.

BROWN OF HARVARD

Metro-Goldwyn-Mayer picture directed by Jack Conway. Based on the play of the same name by Rida Johnson Young. Features William Haines with Jack Pickford and Mary Brian underlined. Ira Morgan, photographer. At the Capitol, New York, week May 2. Running time, 80 mins.

Jim Doolittle	Jack Pickford
Mary Abbott	Mary Brian
Bob McAndrews	Francis X. Bushman, Jr.
Mrs. Brown	Mary Alden
Mr. Brown	David Torrence
Prof. Abbott	Edward Connelly
Hal Walters	Guinn Williams
Reggie Smythe	Ernest Gillen
Tom Brown	William Haines

More genuine college atmosphere here than any other film of the type has contained, and the younger element among the picture patrons should eat it up. It's entertainment all the way. William Haines, in the title role, plays it for full worth.

The Harvard undergraduate body and the Cambridge alumni could and probably will pick many flaws in the technicalities of the life as they know it at their alma mater, but to an outsider it smacks of being sufficiently genuine to waive all minor doubts. In fact, all college men will give the picture, its director and cast their due. The sincerity with which it has been made and the striving for detail are too obvious to be ignored. Plenty of credit all around for effort on this one.

Adapted from the play of the same name, it may be recalled that it was booed off the stage in Boston by Harvard students when it was done there a little more than 20 years ago. Previous to that, the piece was installed at the old Princess theatre, below 29th street on Broadway, with Henry Woodruff in the title role. It followed in the wake of "The College Widow," was ahead of "Strongheart," and enjoyed a successful run. At that time there was no reference to football in the script, the athletic kick centering around the annual crew races with Yale. Now it's a picture and in deference to the modern trend, a gridiron victory over the traditional New Haven rival is the big punch, although the crew race is still retained.

That spells action, and there's an abundance of it. A fist fight, the crew race and the football game take care of this angle. Outside of that Brown (Mr. Haines) is characterized as an extremely fresh freshman who doesn't "arrive" until the last quarter of the Yale game during his sophomore year. It's not one of those college hero things. On the contrary, Brown is just an average student with a pretty good idea of himself upon coming up from prep school, especially as concerns the girls. This leads to his going out for the Frosh crew when learning that Bob McAndrews (Mr. Bushman), his rival for the professor's daughter (Miss Brian) is out for a place in the shell.

Becoming second string stroke, Brown gets happily drunk in New London the night before the race, is called upon when McAndrews develops a pair of sore hands and strokes a loosing crew because he collapses before reaching the finish line. Generally snubbed for having broken training, he determines to quit school, but returns at the fall term on the suggestion of his dad to fight it out.

The following sequence is in the Harvard stadium with the boys in moleskins at practice. Not able to make a varsity backfield berth, Brown trails along as a scrub back until the Yale game, when he is sent in during the first half, but gets a bump on the ankle, and has to leave the field after his first play. More mutterings of "quitter," but Brown goes back in the final quarter with the score 3-0 for Yale, carries the ball almost the length of the field in a series of rushes and then McAndrews goes over for the winning touchdown.

Both the crew and football stuff have been well handled by Jack Conway. It's evident that he had an abundance of aid in these chapters. No doubt about the gridiron battle being the best the screen has yet held within a picture story, and the sweeping of the oars in the shell is authentic, too, even though Ira Morgan, camera man, made the mistake of grinding too slowly, so that the crews look to be pulling 100 to the minute. However, that's the only glaring slip.

Jack Pickford is in a purely secondary role, albeit the pathos of the story centers around him. As the undersized country boy, ignored by his classmates but rooming with Brown and worshipping the latter, he jumps from a sick bed and into a rainstorm to chase Brown and tell him that he has not been dropped from the squad, as his roommate has read in the college daily paper. This leads Doolittle (Mr. Pickford) to the infirmary, where he dies during the game, and to which Brown rushes immediately the final whistle has blown.

Brown weeps himself into Mary Abbott's arms, but the finish lightens to show him elected to an honory society and marching along arm-in-arm with McAndrews.

Haines is corking in the name part. He not only looks collegiate and like a halfback, but paces his performance to a nicety, in which glib subtitles are more than the usual help. Pickford convinces as the underdog, and young Bushman, Jr., makes a likeable "heavy," if he can be termed that. It's a fact that during the early stages of the footage the sympathy is all with Bushman, even during the fight he has with Haines over the girl because of the latter's presumptuousness in kissing her. And that's what should "sell" the picture. Brown is made neither a collegiate idol nor an athletic marvel. He's just second-string material, flops once because he's a foolish kid and cashes in after making up his mind to make good if the chance offers.

Miss Brian is strictly milk and water as the girl, but Mary Alden makes her mother role stand up, as does David Torrence as the father. Incidentally, Miss Alden's work while her son is supposed to be playing will get under the skin of many a mother.

For a college town "Brown of Harvard" is a cinch. The boys won't get much chance to kid it, for it's down to rock bottom on dramatics and Haines smacks too much of the genuine to be scoffed at. For youngsters from 10 to 15 it can't miss.

The football passages presumably were shot last fall at Cambridge, when Harvard eked out a stubborn moral victory by holding Yale to a no-score tie with the Blue a heavy pre-game favorite. Hence the celebration on the field was probably from the heart as far as Harvard was concerned. The "shots" of the stadium, campus and New London are "location." It is understood the university co-operated with this M.-G.-M. unit during the "shooting."

The game carries its flashes from the actual contest, and Conway presumably had his own cameramen grinding, while the yachts at New London are all there to add to the realism. Besides this, Conway has inserted a dance where the boys are in soft shirts and collars with tuxedos. They dance in the accepted collegiate manner. Verily, the picture is a treat as to the endeavor to be as true as possible.

A "sweet" picture, an outstanding performance by Haines and a neat piece of work by the director that the censors can pass with their eyes closed and which will "sell" itself upon the viewing. *Skig.*

THE GREATER GLORY

First National release, produced by June Mathis. Adapted by her from Edith

O'Shaughnessy's novel, "The Viennese Medley." Directed by Curt Rehfeld. Conway Tearle and Anna Q. Nilsson featured, with May Allison, Ian Keith, Jean Hersholt and Lucy Beaumont co-featured. To be released as a special in 11 reels. At the Strand, New York, week of May 2. Running time, 106 minutes.

Count Maxim Von Hartig...Conway Tearle
Fanny....................Anna Q. Nilsson
Corinne.......................May Allison
Pauli Birbach.....................Ian Keith
Tante Ilde................Lucy Beaumont
Gustav Schmidt..............Jean Hersholt
Dr. Herman Von Berg....Nigel de Brulier
Mizzi, his wife............Bridgetta Clark
Prof. Leopold Eberhardt....John Sainpolis
Kaethe, his wife............Marcia Manon
Otto Steiner..................Edward Earle
Liesel ,his wife.........Virginia Southern
Anna, Pauli's wife............Isabel Keith
Irma Von Berg, the stepmother.......
....................Kathleen Chambers
Leon Krum..................Hale Hamilton
Marie..........................Cora Macey
Countess von Hartig.......Carrie Daumery
Theodore von Hartig.........Thur Fairfax
The Scissors Grinder..........Boris Karloff
The Cross Bearer...........George Billings
Helga..........................Bess Flowers
Maid.....................Marcelle Corday

When this film was first announced it was to be a super-special for legitimate showings. Its title then was "The Viennese Medley." But a few weeks back orders were given to cut it from about 30 reels to few enough for regular houses. One cutter who had worked on it said he didn't see how it could be cut any more, but at the Strand this week it is shown in about 11 reels, a swiftly projected film with an epic theme. It misses both as a special and as a program release, and the salvation is a cast filled with "names" plus a production which cost somebody a prodigal sum.

Its claim to being an "epic" is the exposition of a theory that the World War caused many changes, and that when those Four Horsemen of the Apocalypse (War, Famine, Pestilence and Death) mounted their horses for a careening ride through the heavens their influence was so great that normal people did unheard-of things.

The medium of a single and well-bound-together family is used to exploit the theme. Thus, there is the old aunt, Ilde, and her brood of relatives. A musician, a professor, a doctor, a military man, etc., and her two nieces, Fanny and Corinne. The war wears them down to poverty, takes Corinne from the man she really loved and sends Fanny to be the mistress of a gross war profiteer. But in the end her aristocratic lover won out, and the sordid influence of War lost out when pitted against the ennobling influence of love.

Boiled down, that is the rudimentary plot of a very complicated scenario. which is still planting a story as the film nears its conclusion. The great fault with the scenario—and it is there that the fault lies—is that the entire family is manipulated throughout the story. Thus, unimportant people and unimportant things take up much footage in an attempt to drive home a point which the actions of the principal character, Fanny, drive home alone. Which means that many hammers are working to drive one nail and that the drivers are not skillful—so botchwork results.

The production is expensive. There are large sets utilized to set the Viennese atmosphere and thousands of extras are in the scenes marking mobilization in Vienna at the outbreak of the World War. It is all costume stuff, too. To properly show off the coming of the Four Horsemen there are tinted color scenes. With each stroke of a tragedy is a colored insert of the Horsemen riding their endless race. Another excellent thing is the advent of the D'Annunzio air fleet over Vienna, spreading pamphlets of amity and explanation instead of bombs.

Except for the work of May Allison as one of the young girls and Lucy Beaumont as the elderly aunt, there is little acting in the film to interest anyone. But it is interesting to see May Allison once more and observe the miracle which has kept her beauty of the earlier picture days as fresh as if it were the beauty of an hour ago. It's the first really big part Miss Allison has had after a period of some inactivity, and she fills the bill completely.

Miss Beaumont's role is strictly sympathetic, but she plays it with a nice distinction between what is sentimentality and banal saccharine bunk.

The director, Curt Rehfeld, is a newcomer to the ranks of the important megaphone wielders. Although his work here is adequate, it cannot be said that he has shown an inspired moment in the whole film.

"The Greater Glory," then, must be listed among the other costly but ineffective productions of the screen. Still its ambitious aims remain commendable even though the accomplishment reveals little deserving praise. The extremely long running time is also against it, and the chances are that if the sub-titles were displayed for a sufficient period the film would be five minutes longer. When reviewed, many sub-titles were flashed on and off so quickly that they could not be read.

Sisk.

DRIFTING THRU

Pathe Exchange release of a Charles Rogers Production starring Harry Carey. At the Tivoli, New York, one day. Running time, 45 minutes.

Harry Carey is the likable sort of hobo in this Western. He stumbles into all sorts of trouble and then stumbles out.

Starting out like a comedy, Carey is shown hoppin' freights, but dramatic incidents quickly follow when he breaks the bank in a gambling joint.

The owner of the place is killed by his faithless wife. Danny is blamed by the woman. Losing all his winnings in the scramble to escape the sheriff and his posse, he keeps on drifting by hopping from a horse back to a freight and then to a passenger train.

Back to where the crime was committed, he learns the woman who did the shooting and the foreman of the ranch are trying to swindle the girl from the city who has inherited the place. The girl happens to be the same one who had saved him from the sheriff's noose by hiding Dan in her stateroom when the passenger train was being searched.

The woman, following a runaway accident, confesses her crime on her deathbed, and Dan, having saved his benefactress from a swindle, wins her for a mate.

Usual "western," with the only inconsistency that Carey knocks half a dozen huskies cold with straight lefts while supposedly suffering from a bullet wound in the arm.

Skinner's Dress Suit

A Universal Jewel presented by Carl Laemmle, starring Reginald Denny and Laura LaPlante. From the story by Henry Irving Dodge. Directed by William Seiter. Shown at the Rivoli, New York, week May 2, 1926. Running time 75 minutes.

Skinner......................Reginald Denny
Honey.........................Laura LaPlante
Perkins..................Ben Hendricks, Jr.
McLaughlin..................E. J. Radcliffe
Tommy.........................Arthur Lake
Mrs. Colby....................Hedda Hopper
Jackson.......................Lionel Brahm
Miss Smith...................Betty Morrissey

Universal has remade "Skinner's Dress Suit" with Reginald Denny in the principal role and Laura La Plante co-starred with him on the film leader. The picture is just about as full of laughs as the original was and the mere fact that Universal was able to break into a Publix house on Broadway for a pre-release showing of the picture should be sufficient recommendation for the production.

It is a yarn of the suburban commuter who tries for a raise which is denied, but deceives his wife into the belief that he was successful in obtaining the advance, and through this she demands that he get a dress suit and step out with her. The husband and wife are a social success and although the hubby finally loses his job his social connections make it possible for him to win a contract that the firm thought they had lost and finally they offer him a junior partnership.

The story is told with an eye to laugh situation and William Seiter who directed made the most of the opportunities that the story offered. Denny as Skinner manages to handle the role nicely and when he and Laura LaPlante start giving Charleston instructions to their society friends there are any number of laughs and the pair show that they are equal to some nifty stepping.

Hedda Hopper in the supporting company manages to look very well. Lionel Brahm as the blustering Jackson who is a bit of a flirt also managed to score. Miss LaPlante looks better in this picture than she did in "The Midnight Sun," and her work shows that she is more at home in comedy than in heavy drama.

It's a pipe that this one is perfect for the warm weather programs in the bigger houses.

Fred.

Hell Bent fer Heaven

J. Stuart Blackton production presented by Warner Bros. From the stage play by Hatcher Hughes, adapted by Marion Constance Blackton. Featuring Patsy Ruth Miller and John Harron. At the Warner, New York, week May 1. Running time, 87 minutes.

Jude Lowrie ....Patsy Ruth Miller
Sid Hunt.........................John Harron
Andy Lowrie ....Gayne Whitman
Rufe ....Gardner James
Dave Hunt ....James Marcus
Matt Hunt ....Wilfred North
Meg Hunt ....Evelyn Selbie

"Hell Bent fer Heaven" was the Pulitzer prize play of several season's ago. As a picture it isn't going to win any prizes anywhere, simply because the theme of religious fanaticism has been somewhat subdued in the picture, which has been handled along the lines of the average old-fashioned screen meller with the usual floods that no longer have a novelty on the screen.

What the Warners should have done with this picture is to have announced a new star in Gardner James and sat back and heard the critics rave about a performance that would just about have been over their heads and by the same token given the film fans something to talk about, for they would have tried to dope out whether some one was trying to play a joke on them or if the little mountaineer who "got camp meetin' religion" was really the hero of the picture.

James certainly runs away with the picture and dominates every scene that he is in. Next to him is Evelyn Selbie in a character role of the mountaineer mother that she puts over in remarkable shape. Against these two the mere screen actors have no chance whatever.

It is a tale of the hills where feuds have raged in the past. The Hunts and the Lowries have been two contending factions, but Andy Lowrie and Sid Hunt have been pals and Sid is to marry Andy's sister Jude. But Sid went off to war, and the screen play opens on the day of his return.

Sid's return knocks out Rufe's expectations as far as Jude is concerned. He plans to set Andy against Sid and cause a renewal of the feud. The final line is "Well, Rufe taught us that there is no sense in havin' feuds."

Outside of the two players mentioned, James Marcus gave a corking performance as the elder Hunt, granddaddy of them all, while Wilfred North sufficed as the father of the hero. But both the featured players were last under the wire for histrionic honors in this picture.

J. Stuart Blackton's direction won't win any medals either if this picture is to be the entry in any contest of that kind.

Fred.

LOVES OF RICARDO

Los Angeles, May 1.

George Beban starred in own production of film and synchronized stage scene. Scenario, direction and dialog by Mr. Beban. Presented by Saul Magnus Paulais. At Metropolitan, Los Angeles, week of April 30. Running time, picture 82 minutes, play 23 minutes; total, 105 minutes. Seven reels, 6,800 feet. Two other reels enacted on the stage.

Ricardo Vitelli.................George Beban
Annetta..........................Lolita Lee
Steve Randall...........Monte Collins, Jr.
Marco Martinelli...........Albano Valerio
Flora Martinelli..................Mareokova
Tony Villano.................Signor Frondi

Also appearing on the stage, 27 members of the screen cast and George Beban's Italian String Orchestra.

"The Loves of Ricardo," the latest in George Beban's series of picture plays, is another one of those things in which Beban proves that he screens well as an Italian and then comes out on the stage at a critical moment to play his act with a peanut stand in support.

The star is a grocer and fruit merchant this time in a film with more action than there are Schmidts in Milwaukee. To enumerate some of the tried but true stuff used, there are fights, the Charleston, fake land deal, blackmail, bootleggers, U. S. Navy (applause), rum running, fire, auto going over cliff and thrilling rescue of lady in auto after it is over. The old hoke was brought all the way through with a new twist here and there and a touch of humor.

The story tells of Ricardo, played by Beban, who has adopted a beautiful girl, well photographed by Lolita Lee. He is in love with her and about to propose when she announces her engagement to a big poolroom man from Bowling Green. He allows the cue chalker to walk away with the girl and buys a piece of land that gets its irrigation when the tide comes in. While the water is high rum runners camp on the pasture, kidnap Ricardo and appoint him cook on their rum row yacht—by force. He floats the ship's parrot on a life preserver and it tips the dry fleet off. They rescue Ricardo; he returns to fight the heavy and win back his love, the only one, by the way, the title being misleading, unless the parrot and an old horse, Mussolini, are counted in.

The stage portion comes in during the wedding of Annetta, his ward, and Steve Randall, the heavy. The film fades into the same set on stage and the marriage celebration takes place, with Italian and jazz dances, some comedy and heavy emoting by Beban as the lover who is afraid to declare himself.

The production is unusual only in that the stage and screen are both represented. Beban draws applause with his dramatic moments. There are a few good laughs and some mediocre talent in the stage specialties. Beban dominates the entire opus with his fine Italian hand.

Billing and exploitation all on the Beban personal appearance angle and on the fact that stage and screen are synchronized in the attraction.

A large Italian draw can be obtained, since the picture is a fairly accurate portrayal of life in American colonies of that nationality.

SPEED MAD

Perfection Pictures presentation at the Arena, New York, one day (April 30). William Fairbanks, Edith Roberts, Lloyd Whitlock and Johnny Fox featured. Distributed by Columbia Pictures Corp. Running time, 50 minutes.

Little merit to this one, evidently perpetrated for the daily change grind houses. It has little or no plot and all of it is the old stereotyped stuff that flashed across the screens of neighborhood houses a thousand times.

Bill Sandford (William Fairbanks) is the speed-mad son of a wealthy indulgent father who, tired of paying his fines, sends the boy away with $5 and a $5,000 car. After ruining a milk delivery flivver, Bill volunteers to pay for the damage by delivering milk in his racer. While thus engaged he meets the girl, Edith Roberts, and the villain, Lloyd Whitlock, who threatens to foreclose the mortgage on her father's home unless she marries him.

To save her from a distasteful marriage he enters the amateur 300-mile auto race and is, of course, opposed for honors on the track by the would-be mortgage forecloser. The old familiar frame-up follows, but Bill's bull dog saves him from an abduction and a handily placed motorcycle and an aeroplane bring him to the track just in time to win the race and the girl for a flock of hurrahs.

The story is an open and shut affair to anyone who is even a mild movie fan.

The Wilderness Woman

Robert Kane production, released by First National. From story by Arthur Stringer. Directed by Howard Higgin. Featuring Aileen Pringle, Lowell Sherman and Chester Conklin. Shown at the Strand, New York, week May 9. Running time, 80 minutes.
Juneau MacLean............Aileen Pringle
Alan Burkett...............Lowell Sherman
Kadiak MacLean..........Chester Conklin
The "Colonel"..............Henry Vibart
His "Son"....................Robert Cain
The "Judge"...............Burr McIntosh
Squaw.......................Harriet Sterling

Considerable liberty was taken with the original story which Arthur Stringer wrote and which appeared in the "Sat. Eve. Post" under the title of "The Wilderness Woman," with the result that a comedy for the screen has been turned out. There are a lot of laughs in the screen version not present in the original. The picture proves to be a highly entertaining affair, but seems to lack in love interest. One of the principal faults is the total miscasting of Lowell Sherman in the heroic role.

The yarn is that of an Alaskan miner who makes a gold strike, gets a million from a New York syndicate from its representative, a tenderfoot, who journeys north to locate him and who comes to New York with his daughter. They are typical backwoods people and rely on the young tenderfoot to steer them right.

On the train east they run into a couple of sharpers, who pose as father and son. They propose to sell the old man the subway. The 'son' incidentally makes a play for the daughter, figuring to marry in on the old man's b. r. At the crucial moment the tenderfoot steps in and saves both father and daughter.

Aileen Pringle is the gold miner's daughter, and makes it look a million dollars, especially after she is dolled up. Chester Conklin as her father runs away with the picture. The "old boy," with his walrus mustache and glasses, trying to "make" the newsstand girl at the Biltmore, is a wow of a laugh scene. Sherman, however, does not ring true as the hero. It isn't his fault; he was miscast. He would have been better in the young con man's role.

Howard Higgin, who directed, made a fairly good job of it. There is a laugh scene early, with Miss Pringle removing Sherman's boots, and a couple of others later for the girl in her business with the young black bear in the hotel lobby, but the majority of laughs are garnered by Conklin. In his sequence with the three con men in a hotel room his handling of the "booze" is another punch. Tammany Young as a trick radio bartender in this scene is "oak."

"The Wilderness Woman" will get laughs, but it won't send the audience away talking or thinking about the picture.   *Fred.*

MONEY TALKS

Metro-Goldwyn-Mayer production, directed by Archie Mayo. Story by Rupert Hughes; adapted by Frederic and Fanny Hatton. At the Capitol, New York, week May 9. Running time, 66 minutes.
Phoebe Starling...........Claire Windsor
Sam Starling...............Owen Moore
Oscar Waters...............Bert Roach
Lucius Fenton...............Ned Sparks
J. Bradford Perkins......Phillips Smalley
Mrs. Chatterton...........Dot Farley
Mlle. Lucette..............Kathleen Key
Ah Foo.......................George Kuwa

Weak sister feature picture for Metro-Goldwyn. Far and away below its standard of more than a year. From the looks of the picture considerable change was wrought in the story by cutting and titling. The titles, by Joe Farnham, are about the only things that save the picture from utter condemnation.

For the small daily change houses

this one is about strong enough to be the better of two on a double feature bill, but as an attraction for a week's run in a de luxe house, impossible. Why it plays the Capitol is hard to understand, unless the fact is that M.-G.-M. is running short on product and want to hold back on their pictures of 1926-27 until after the summer is over. If they do this they are going to make a mistake, for the box office at the Capitol Sunday surely must have told a sad story as compared to other Sundays this season.

It is safe to predict that the Capitol the current week is going to have one of the weakest box office showings that it has had in months with this production. The only saving grace, as far as the picture is concerned, are the titles and the stage show that surrounds the film.

The story is one of a "go-getter" advertising man who has had a hard time battling to keep two leaps ahead of the sheriff. He finally gets a job to press agent a pleasure island that has been a flop, and he turns it into a health resort, getting a job at $50,000 a year, and thus wins his wife back.

The biggest part is devoted to the adventures of the prospective patients on their trip to the island. The skipper of the boat took the charter to cover his rum running activities. On the sea the boat is hijacked, and then there is a final rescue by the revenue men.

There was a chance here to get a lot of kick into the story, but they failed to come through with it.

Claire Windsor is a wishy-washy sort of a heroine, and Owen Moore is trying to do a female impersonation in the picture. His tussle in trying to don a pair of corsets is very antique both ways, but the funniest thing in the picture.

Someone with a good memory just lifted the furniture movers' idea from vaudeville, the one originally done by Bozo. That's in the picture in toto, which is a tip-off to every one to protect themselves in the clinches against having their material lifted without permission.   *Fred.*

The Little Irish Girl

Warner Brothers production made from C. D. Lancaster's story "The Grifters," and adapted by Daryl Francis Zanuck. Directed by Roy del Ruth with Dolores Costello and Johnny Harron featured. At Warner's, New York, May 8 week. Running time, 67 minutes.
Dorothy.....................Dolores Costello
Johnny.......................Johnny Harron
Jerry Crawford.............Matthew Betz
The Charleston Kid........Lee Moran
Grandma Weaver..........Gertrude Claire
Frisco Real Estate Man....Henry Barrows

A crook picture with the old twist of a reformed crook trimming the real villains, and the curse is taken off by the sweet motive which prompted the old crook's action. That's the plot of "A Little Irish Girl," chiefly a good film.

Dolores Costello is cast as the come-on gal for a flock of grifters, her particular racket being to pick out the suckers, drop a pocketbook with her card inside and then sit home answering the doorbell as they drop in, one by one. Once inside, her boy friends did a painless dry cleaning gag and the shorn lambs were shown the exits.

But she fell for one of the chumps. When her gang had to blow town, they went to a country hotel run by the young chump's grandmother. Planning to take the old lady over for a few grand, they framed with an impressive looking "real estate dealer" from Frisco to come in and play straight. But the old woman was once a quick thinker herself and in the end she trims the crooks and recognizing that the girl pines for an opportunity to go straight, she takes enough money from the smart guys to start the young fledglings on their own path

of righteousness—this touch preserving the high moral tone requisite to modern picture productions.

Not so much of a story but at that it is filled with enough situation to make it stand up and enough laughs to sprinkle them liberally throughout the footage. Miss Costello is all the trumps in the world in her part and if justice stays blindfolded then it is only a matter of time before this real actress displaces some of the phoney stars who are fading from view just as surely as the moon from the sky when daytime arrives.

The others are good, Johnny Harron showing up as a particularly capable juvenile. Direction is also good and the whole thing has been well produced. Okeh for the regular run of houses and backed by a good stage program, might slide by as the feature in a de luxe house.   *Sisk.*

LES MISERABLES
(EUROPEAN)

London, April 20.

The premiere of the Film de France super "Les Miserables," which has been secured by European (Universal), occurred at the Hippodrome. This Trade Show marks a distinct upward movement on the way these things are done here. Europe in the last few months has repeatedly won recognition outside the film world for its presentations, notably in the case of "The Midnight Sun," "The Flaming Frontier" and "The Cohens and the Kellys."

The premiere was attended by officials from the French, American, Italian and Swiss Embassies and Legations, while the French Ambassador, proprietor of "Le Matin," the producer of the picture and the leading people were guests at a banquet held at the Metropole hotel the same evening.

The "presentation" of the picture by Clayton Hutton, a member of U's European staff, was in itself noteworthy. The rise of the "tabs" disclosed Victor Hugo, who, in a brief soliloquy, spoke of the work he had done for humanity, while a small boy listened attentively. The weary poet slept and the boy tiptoed across the stage and stealthily opened a huge volume of "Les Miserables."

Immediately the leading character, Valjean, burst through the pages before the terrified kid, crossing the stage. This was followed by the other leading characters, Javert, Thenardier, Fantine, Cosette, Eponine. Each character crossed the stage and exited, to reappear in a tableau on a miniature stage erected behind the sleeping poet. The presentation was greeted with bursts of genuine applause as the players, the original French artists of the film, burst through the leaves of the huge book. The orchestra of the British National Opera Company in its entirety accompanied the picture under the baton of the composer of the music, Fernand Heruteur.

The film itself (it took four hours and a half to run in the Hippodrome) is a very artistic and sincere following of Hugo's novel. The production work and huge crowd scenes are alike brilliant and the acting is very far above the average. This feature, to be put out to the cinemas in two parts, will be followed by "Michael Strogoff" and Eugene Sue's "The Wandering Jew," both of which will, in all probability, be handled here by European (Universal).

Stop, Look and Listen

John Adams production, distributed by Pathe, from the musical comedy by Harry B. Smith. Larry Semon starred and credited with direction. One-half double bill at Tivoli, New York. One day (May 1). Running time, 59 minutes.

"Stop, Look and Listen" as a musical stage play was a success. As a picture it means nothing.

For its star it has Larry Semon. That should be considerable, but is not. Mr. Semon is a capable comedian. His facial expressions create immediate laughter. His acrobatics are of the best. But he has been seen in better pictures.

This comedy feature is nothing, other than one of the type of two-reelers Semon made and became identified with in former days.

The musical played about 10 years ago. Only the grown-ups remember it as a show. To the kids the title is only familiar through being connected with warning signs. Kids are the only ones who will enjoy it. For adults it will be found amusing at times, but too repetitious with stale gags and tricks. Semon's physical exertions are admirable.

Dorothy Dwan, about the best and sweetest leading lady Semon has ever had, is in it. Mary Carr, again a mother, played well, as usual.

As the shorter half of a program at the Tivoli on Eighth avenue, "Stop, Look and Listen" entertained only at intervals.

HURRICANE

Truart Production, directed by Fred Caldwell. With Alice Lake, Stuart Holmes and Jack Richardson featured. At Arena, New York, one day, May 6. Running time, 52 mins.

An exceptional picture exceptionally poor. The relation of the title to the picture is not seen.

In its embryonic state it may have had the possibility of turning into a fighting "thriller" for the younger generation. Whoever held the bag missed badly.

It's the story of the dissatisfied wife of the chief of American revenue service on the Canadian border. Not liking the woods, wife wishes away to the city and almost goes there with the man who later is exposed as a smuggler. She kills the smuggler and is forgiven by husband.

The acting at times appears amateurish and uninspired. Stuart Holmes, as always a villain, fails to do his best and Alice Lake, as the discontented wife, does her apparent worst. She is at a handicap in wearing but one costume, an unbecoming riding habit. Jack Richardson is unimpressive as either husband or border chief.

The trouble lies secondarily with Fred Caldwell's direction. But he may have been without material, financial and materially.

No acting, no development of story, no background of material, no heart or other interest—and no picture.

THE NIGHT WATCH

Truart picture, directed by Fred Caldwell. No author credited. Mary Carr featured. At the Stanley, New York, May 7. Running time, 39 minutes.

Why this was made is not known. Probably because it cost little.

It is a link, and a weak one, in the endless chain of dealing with the family feuds in Tennessee (or Kentucky). Same old story.

Running a little less than 39 minutes, it is one of the shortest seen around in a long time. That is its only virtue.

Mary Carr stands out in a mother role. Others in the cast are Charles Delaney, Muriel Reynolds, Raymond Rousenville, Ethel Schram, Charles W. Mack, Gloria Grey, Jack Richardson and Fred Caldwell.

SANDY

William Fox production from the story serial by Elenore Meherin. Adapted by Eva Unsell and directed by Harry Beaumont. Madge Bellamy starred. At Loew's New York May 9, one day. Running time, 64 minutes.
Sandy McNeil..................Madge Bellamy
Her Sister...................Joan Standing
Donald Keith.................Leslie Fenton
Ramon Worth..................Harrison Ford
Judith ....

A well-sexed flapper story which had such a nice sale as syndicated articles for those evening papers which feel that some of the inside pages should be well spiced for circulation's sake. According to several editors, Irish and Scandinavian, being interviewed to get all the angles, serial stories such as "Sandy," "Joanna" and others like "Unbound Passion," "The Frantic Virgin," etc., have put as much as 10,000 circulation on during their running period. Hence they must be read, and their following is great.

In "Sandy," things get pretty well involved and the gal with the "It" business goes through her paces with the men folk, but turns white in the end and saves the youth she loves from the gibbet, only to turn him over to another gal. The young flapper, being pretty tough, got a bullet around her heart, but kept on living.

"Sandy" is all right for the less toney first runs, and strictly on top of Money Mount for the regular places or where the story as a serial has been printed. In fact, "Sandy" has been played pretty thoroughly in the first runs. It showed in New York for the first time last week, very late.

Madge Bellamy acts mightly well in this, better than she's ever done before. Looks more like a human being and less like a China doll. Harrison Ford, as the heavy fellow, was also sufficient unto his role. The others played parts.

Harry Beaumont's direction, professional and neat, was so smooth that a good scenario was upheld and the full box office value of "Sandy" brought out. And that box office power is probably pretty considerable, all angles considered. *Sisk.*

WHISPERING SMITH

A P. D. C. release starring H. B. Warner. From the story by Frank H. Spearing, adapted by Eliott Clawson and Will M. Richie. Directed by George Melford. Shown at Loew's, New York, N. Y., double feature bill May 7, 1926. Running time 69 minutes.
"Whispering Smith".........H. B. Warner
Dicksie Dunning.............Lillian Rich
McCloud....................John Bowers
Marion Sinclair............Lilyan Tashman
Murray Sinclair............Will Walling
Bill ....Eugene Pallette
Lance Dunning..............Richard Neill
DuSang.....................James Mason
Seagrue....................Nelson McDowell
Bucks......................Robert Edeson

This is a combination western and railroad melodrama and as such stands above the average of the regular program picture that is turned out for consumption in the usual daily change of program houses. As a matter of fact this picture seems almost strong enough to stand up for a three day run in the combination vaudeville and picture houses. It has action and suspense and is capably enacted by a cast that stands up under inspection. H. B. Warner, who has the title role, manages to hold the audience every minute that he is on the screen and the supporting cast is most adequate.

One good idea about the story is the combination of both the western and the railroad angle. That takes it out of the class of either type. The story is laid in the western territory at a time when the outlaw element was prone to hold-up transcontinental trains and loot the passengers as well as the express cars. McCloud (John Bowers) has been appointed division super at a point where the usual stunt has been the derailing and wrecking of freight trains and the looting of the cars. The new super discovers that the head of his own track gang is the leader in this and fires him. Then a battle starts between the two. "Whispering Smith" (H. B. Warner), who is head of the railroad's secret service, is dispatched to the scene of action and he manages to clean up the gangsters.

Entwined with this action there are two love themes, and needless to say both heroes manage to win the girls that they are after.

George Melford has directed the picture with an eye to thrills and he manages to slip them to the audience. The suspense is maintained perfectly. Lillian Rich is a charming enough ingenue heroine while Lilyan Tashman takes care of the secondary love interest. Will Walling as the heavy gives one of his best screen performances to date. *Fred.*

FATE OF A FLIRT

Columbia production under the Waldorf brand. Story by Janet Crothers and direction by Frank R. Strayer. Dorothy Revier and Forrest Stanley featured. At Loew's New York, May 9, one day. Running time, 65 minutes.
Mary Burgess...............Dorothy Revier
Sir Gilbert................Forrest Stanley
Aunt Mary..................Clarissa Selwynne
Uncle John.................Thomas Ricketts

A well made and carefully handled independent production. The story itself is a light comedy with a wealth of funny stuff included between beginning and end, while its cast is unusually good.

The plot is the one about the all-American girl, who'd rather marry a bricklayer than a titled Englishman. So the boy who admired her, being a titled Englishman, had to bet his uncle that he could win her without revealing his identity. The stumbling block proved to be the girl's aunt and uncle. It was up to the young man to frame them for his side.

He did that by palming his valet off as a famous nobleman and the butler immediately coaxed the aunt to a roadhouse for the evening. Auntie looked forward to a real thrill to vary the monotony of her middle aged existence, while her husband, on the same night, attended the reunion of his class of '77. A bunch of gay old hounds they were, with their manicure patooties on their laps, eating bread and milk while the gals drank champagne.

On the same night auntie was out in the interests of True Love, and Uncle was just monkeying around, the girl and the boy (who had hired out as chauffeur to the household), happened to catch both the auntie and the uncle in their capers, so it was an easy matter to make them consent to a wedding.

Forrest Stanley makes a good leading man, good enough to be up in the major leagues, while Dorothy Revier is adequate as the girl in the case. Thomas Ricketts, as the old guy with adolescent ideas, got off most of the comedy, one of the gags employed showing him being pushed out of a taxi by a girl when he refused her advances. Old but funny.

"Fate of a Flirt" can be depended upon to give entertainment satisfaction. *Sisk.*

RACING ROMANCE

A. W. Ray Johnson production released through Rayart. Starring Reed Howes. Shown at Loew's, New York, N. Y., on double feature bill May 7, 1926. Running time 71 minutes.

This is one of the usual types of racing stories the only difference being that instead of the usual running horses trotters are used in this production. From a picture standpoint this one will stand up alone in the average two-bit or less admission houses, but where anything more is charged it will have to be played on a double feature bill as it was at the New York.

The story has all the regulation racing bits. The scene is in the bluegrass country. There is the old mansion and the stock farm that is about to fall into the hands of the heavy who wants to marry the young girl who is the owner and it looks as though he is going to win out, for he has a trainer for his trotters who is willing to do anything to assist his employer in achieving his desires. The heavy holds the mortgage and has liens against most of the live stock. It looks rosie for him until the hero—the boyhood sweetheart of the girl who went away—returns. He undertakes the training of the pride of the farm and develops the horse so that it can win and he drives it to victory, thus saving the farm and the horses and incidentally winning the girl for himself.

There is some fairly good comedy supplied by a trio of colored folk in the picture, but other than that it is just the usual melodrama hoke. *Fred.*

Aloma of the South Seas

Famous Players picture, staring Gilda Gray. Percy Marmont, Warner Baxter, Julanne Johnston and William Powell featured. From the play by John B. Hymer and LeRoy Clemmens, adapted by James A. Creelman. Directed by Maurice Tourneur. At the Rialto, New York, for six weeks' run, May 16. Running time, 87 minutes.

Aloma........................Gilda Gray
Bob Holden....................Percy Marmont
Nuitane........................Warner Baxter
Van Templeton.................William Powell
Red Malloy....................Harry Morey
Sylvia.......................Julanne Johnston
Andrew Taylor.................Joseph Smiley
Hongi.....................Frank Montgomery
Hina..........................Mme. Burani
Taula......................Ernestine Gaines
Sailor........................Aurelio Coccia

Gilda Gray made her debut as a screen star at the Rialto, New York, Saturday night in "Aloma of the South Seas." "Aloma" in its present shape is about 1,000 feet too long. It should be cut to snap up the action.

With that the picture looks as though it is a certain money maker, especially for the cities and towns where they have not had Gilda Gray in person. There is a certain curiosity on the part of the public to see Gilda Gray.

Miss Gray personally in this picture surprised even some of her most steadfast admirers. She has grown into a national figure from the time that she first made her advent in New York. First she came as a "shimmie" dancer, from that she developed into one of the foremost exponents of the Hawaiian and South Sea dancers, after which she stepped into the "Follies," followed this by a series of vaudeville appearances, and then blazed the trail in the picture houses with a record-breaking box office result for personal appearances. Atop of this she comes to the screen as a star in her very first production.

In adapting "Aloma" James Creelman, who wrote the script, and Maurice Tourneur lost much of the comedy in the play, but they did turn out a picture photographically beautiful. Some of the shots were works of art in their composition. In the matter of continuity the picture goes along smoothly enough, and were it not that certain of the scenes are held just a little too long it would click to greater advantage.

Gilda Gray does look great, and as the South Sea Island native girl gives promise of being able to do a lot more on the screen than she was given opportunity here. Surrounding is a strong cast, with Warner Baxter walking away with the honors of the supporting company. On the strength of his performance as Nuitane, Baxter should be in line for bigger and better things. Percy Marmont as Holden delivered a consistent and interesting performance. The heavy by William Powell was not made as much of on the screen as in the play.

A couple of old timers were Harry Morey and Joseph Smiley, both delivering in character roles. Frank Montgomery, playing Hongi, stood out at odd moments, while Julanne Johnston got by as Sylvia, a role that called for little.

The South Sea atmosphere has been cleverly carried through, and the addition of the native islanders for a background was well thought out, although several shots have too much footage.

"Aloma" on the strength of the Gilda Gray name will get the money.

The premier performance at the Rialto, given at midnight Saturday, found the house jammed with a most representative audience.

Fred.

THE RAINMAKER

Famous Players production adapted from Gerald Beaumont's story "Heaven-Bent" and made into a screen play by Hope Loring and Louis D. Lighton. Directed by Clarence Badger with Ernest Torrence, William Collier, Jr., and Georgia Hale featured. At the Rivoli, New York, May 16, week. Running time, 72 minutes.

Bobby Robertson......William Collier, Jr.
Nell Wendell..................Georgia Hale
Mike........................Ernest Torrence
Doyle.........................Brandon Hurst
Father Murphy...............Joseph Dowling
Chocolate......................Tom Wilson
Head Nurse...................Martha Mattox
Hospital Doctor.........Charles K. French
Dr. Wade.................Jack Richardson
Benson.................Melbourne MacDowell

Here's a picture that may need some exploitation to make the people know it's good. Which is against it to start with. How to overcome that should be told the exhibitor.

The plot concerns a jockey, Bobby Robertson, badly hurt in a race. At the hospital he fell in love with his nurse, Nell Wendell, a spirited girl with a dance hall past, but a determination to go straight. For looking after Bobby so carefully she was fired from the hospital and in desperation went back to Mike's dance hall in an oil boom town. Meantime, Bobby is incapacitated from riding, but because of a bad arm, was able to predict with uncanny precision the period when a rainstorm was approaching. So he sold his prayers around the track until the men who didn't own mud horses got sore and sent him away.

He went to the same western town which sheltered Nell. A drought set in. A mean oil promoter, scheming to grab land when people died from a resulting epidemic, kept the only doctor cornered until Nell cornered the lion in his den and had the doctor released.

But the drought was already on and hundreds were dying. A strict quarantine was set up. Nell took up nursing again and even Mike, the dance hall proprietor, and a square old guy, succumbed, leaving Nell and Bobby a stake to start on. The church which served as a temporary hospital caught fire and it was then that the jockey, also called The Rainmaker, got down on his knees and prayed—and it worked. Immediately the town was drenched.

The story sounds fishy, but so well done in film form it is entirely plausible. Young Collier, in a hard role, does so well he is immediately accepted as the kid who reformed through love. Miss Hale is letter perfect as the tough girl with the good heart, while Ernest Torrence carves one more deep notch for himself as Mike.

There's excitement in "The Rainmaker" and good direction. With the colored actor, Tom Wilson, handling most of the comedy, the laughs are of the rabbits' foot kind, but at that they're laughs and serve.

In all, it's a good film of the sort which pleases many and offends none.

Sisk.

WHY GIRLS GO BACK HOME

Warner Brothers production, directed by James Flood. Patsy Ruth Miller and Clive Brook featured. At Warner's, New York, week May 16. Running time about 60 minutes.

This picture may please the women—perhaps the girls more so than their elders. Therein lies its only strength. A girl eventually lands the man she fell for and who walked out on her. The girls like that. It seems the single thing in the film to play up or upon.

With a proviso—that it's no fair watching or judging a picture like this at Broadway and 51st street. They come a little bit too tough along Times square for this stuff. But the sticks, like Syracuse, where even the greased hairs believe they are destined and the flaps know they are, might take this right to their imagination.

It's all over a girl in the country who slobbered on the breast of a barnstorming hero of a sickly drama, meeting him in her father's hotel when the show went blewy.

So she followed him to New York on the same train, but he slipped out on the gal, afraid of consequences. She stuck on the main stem going into the chorus of a revue. And phoned her pasty he-vamp after he had become a Broadway hit as "the newest lover." But he coldly turned her phone call of congrats, too.

And then, what did she did? Nothing but! Right away, too. Through some publicity that broke just right, the girl from home became the dancing star of a dancing show, although she couldn't dance herself. (Latter just a detail).

And then, what did he did? Nothing but. Right away, too. He phoned her congrats as he had watched the premiere, without explaining how he was laying off on his own play the same evening. But she coldly turned his phone call.

Then she went back home. He went along on the same train, here evidently leaving his play flat without notice. And they made it up on the train—with the moral maybe if you love an actor, go into the chorus.

There will have to be something done about continuity, unless Mack Sennett changes his methods after 15 years. Mack, when the man touches a call button still shows that the buzzer inside is ringing.

Accepting that Kansas City is a part of the hinterland, will Mr. Will Hughes kindly send a review of this picture when it plays that town. Kansas City should be as nutty as Syracuse over the picture business.

Patsy Ruth Miller and Clive Brook or any of the others need not tell anyone they started a roar for themselves in this film. Miss Miller and Mr. Brook may enter a complaint on some of the close-ups, and as for acting, it's one of those keep-on-walking pictures.

Other specific demerits unhandy through Warner's theatre not believing in programs. And on a Monday night in this office a guy looking for a press sheet would be locally considered crazy enough to try picture acting or making himself.

Sime.

WET PAINT

Famous Players release, starring Raymond Griffith, with Helen Costello and Bryant Washburn underlined. Directed by Arthur Rosson; William Marshall, photographer. At the Strand, New York, week May 16. Running time, 78 mins.

He........................Raymond Griffith
She.........................Helen Costello
Her Brother..............Bryant Washburn
A Beautiful Woman......Natalie Kingston
A Husband....................Henry Kolker

A "gag" picture, using Shakespeare's "Much Ado About Nothing" as the "catch" line and flashing that in the opening sub-title. Proffering a hectic yarn that goes in 18 different directions it simply amounts to a series of "gags," with Griffith and Henry Kolker as a couple of happy stews.

Between the sub-titles and the action there's enough laughs to send this one across, but they won't come out talking the way they did on "A Regular Fellow" or "Hands Up." One reason for this is that the film is too long, 78 minutes, and the "stew" thing loses some of its strength after a while.

Griffith does a corking comedy drunk. Many of the 'gags' click, especially the one having Griffith driving a hook and ladder fire truck with no one at the rear steering wheel—thence becoming a terror of the road.

This leads into a real fire, where Griffith gets into the wrong house and a steam bath, previous to which a bandit holds up Griffith, also the husband and wife, whom he has become mixed up with through abducting the latter on the pretense he'll marry the first woman he sees.

Helen Costello and Bryant Washburn are restricted in support, the main burden falling upon Mr. Kolker, who capably meets the obligation.

Despite that it is an out and out silly farce, it's a full 60 minutes of laugh entertainment for any house. The extra 18 do not help, and there's enough of the "stew" bits running to permit scissoring. *Skig.*

BACHELOR BRIDES

P. D. C. release. C. Gardner Sullivan picture. Stars Rod La Rocque and features Elinor Faire. Adapted from the stage play of C. H. Malcolm, with W. K. Howard the director. At Broadway (vaude.-pictures), New York, week May 10. Running time, 74 minutes.

One of those comedy-mystery things from the "One Exciting Night" formula, with plenty of "hoke" and plenty of laughs. What connection there is between the title and the picture would take some deciphering. The same, to a lesser degree, might be said of Rod La Rocque in this vehicle. There's nothing much for La Rocque to do, the comedy butler tucking all the honors under his arm and winding up his performance by doing a neat laugh stew in the midst of the mysterious goin's on.

"Caught" at the Broadway where no programs are available there was too much cast record, hence the loss of this comedian's name. But he's a standout here to the extent he well nigh "makes" the film. La Rocque is cast as a silly Englishman, lays it on pretty thick, and only becomes normal during a couple of brief fistic encounters.

Elinor Faire is the wealthy American girl about to be married to the young Earl (La Rocque), and the panic starts when the family pearls, to be the girl's wedding gift, disappear off of a table.

An outside storm confines the action to interiors, and substantial in appearance.

W. K. Howard, the director, has painted in broad strokes. So much so that one of the three crooks who invades the house the night before the wedding is a laugh on his appearance, and the two Scotland Yard men have a distinct resemblance to Clark and McCullough in their unborn mule furs.

Slamming doors, shadows, secret passages, cut telephone wires and so forth are all in the routine, during which the butler is generally the "goat." The crossfire subtitle exchanges add to the merriment. It becomes very much a satire on the mystery plays and pictures.

This one is okay if lightweight. It won't mean anything to La Rocque personally, but the cast support is standard on all sides, with the butler's contribution rating first mention.

They laughed often and loud here, and the picture will repeat that elsewhere.

Skig.

THE SPEED LIMIT

Sam Sax presents Gotham production. Directed by Frank O'Connor and starring Raymond McKee. At the Stanley, New York, one day, May 10. Running time, 58 minutes.

Automobile racing picture of the familiar type but enjoyable as half an evening's entertainment in the one-day houses.

Concerning a young garage worker with a supposedly revolutionary process for making durable automobile tires and a girl. Also several naughties who plot to get the young man's secret process, aided by a good looking blonde. The young man drives in place of the champion auto racer, who is hurt in a spill, and wins, using the tires of his own make. But he is detained from reaching the track in time, as usual, by a villainous ruse.

Raymond McKee is the film's star. He has previously confined his efforts to two-reel comedies. Of a sudden the two-reel boys have taken a lurch at features. And without much success. But McKee shows possibilities, having a pleasing face. Better juvenile than comedian.

Ethel Shannon is the girl in the film. Miss Shannon cannot be recalled but is familiar. Probably familiar for quite a while. She looked older than her role in several close-ups. But a good actress and seems experienced. Rona Lee, large sized blonde, cops the beauty honors, though her role calls for a woman made attractive only by dress.

Bruce Gordon is admirable as the "dirty" worker. Others are E. W. Berman, George Chapman, James Conly and Charles Mack.

"The Speed Limit" would harm no late-run house. Being speedy, it will not only satisfy adults but also kids. Making no pretenses at anything else, it proves capable of supplying entertainment.

YELLOW FINGERS

Fox production made from the story by Gene Wright. Adapted by Eve Unsell and directed by Emmett Flynn with Ralph Ince and Olive Borden featured. On Loew's New York Roof, May 16, one day. Running time, 66 mins.
Captain Shane...................Ralph Ince
Niana..........................Olive Borden
DeVreis........................Armand Kaliz
Nona Deering...................Claire Adams
Rajah Jagore...................Nigel de Brulier

The theme of a native girl and a white man, with the girl's growing resentment toward a white woman who intends to marry the man, is the gist of this picture, set in the Malay Peninsula.

It also brings Ralph Ince to the fore once more as an actor, his sole recent activity in that direction having been an independently made version of Jack London's "The Sea Wolf" (recently shown around New York privately and has been taken over by P. D. C. for release).

Here Ince is a Captain Shane, trader and guardian of Niana, a native girl, to whom he is very dear, but whose relationship is unassailably pure. On a trip two of Shane's sailors rescue an American girl from a Chinese den in Bangkok. When telling her story, she is brought back with him. And she, a Miss Deering, eventually marries Shane, but not until Niana has been so distressed she entered into a vengeful alliance with Shane's enemies, only to repent at the last moment and turn the tables.

It's a well told melodrama, filled with action and fighting and also with enough of the South Sea undress business to get the mugs who like their brown ladies bare. Ince, as a hard boiled fellow with a good heart, does well, while the leading women, Olive Borden as the native and Claire Adams as the white girl are highly decorative. Miss Borden also throws in a few cooch dances which, if cooch dancing has any artistic or commercial value in the movies, rank high.

Satisfactory for the smaller houses and safe for the exhibitor whose main worry is to book entertainment and not names. *Sisk.*

MARRIED?

Owen Moore and Constance Bennett in the Herman F. Jans production of story by Marjorie Benton Cooke. Renown Picture. Directed by George Terwilliger. At the Arena, New York, one day, May 10. Running time, 55 minutes.

A real good program picture with plenty of pep, an interesting, if not

too original, story and some laugh getting gags by way of action and subtitle. Jack Thompson, Antrim Story, Julia Hurley, Gordon Standing, John Costelle, Evangeline Russell and others (names flashed on and off too fast) make up well balanced cast headed by sleek Owen, of the Moore boys, and Constance, blond and doll-faced daughter of Richard Bennett.

Something about the lumber holdings being blocked from producing if the land further down the rapids is leased to the villainous operators of the lumber company. Love story too.

A marriage via 'phone is a novel situation. One that could be played on with more ample material and made a legitimate farce. It will probably be seen later with some different colored fringe.

Clean-cut Moore is an appealing type and plays with sense in this picture. Miss Bennett does well merely by looking pretty, bored and smoking cigarets. The directing of George Terwilliger is excellent in spots and poor elsewhere.

At the Arena (two bit-grind) picture entertained highly.

SOMEBODY'S MOTHER

B. Berger presentation by arrangement with W. Ray Johnston. Produced by Gersten Pictures Corp. Written and directed by Oscar Apfel. Mary Carr starred. At the Stanley, New York, one day (May 15). Running time, 55 minutes.
"Matches Mary"..............Mary Carr
Pat.......................Mickey McBain
Peter......................Rex Lease
Peter's Wife.............Kathryn McGuire
Jim.....................Edward Martindel
Lawyer..................Robert J. Graves
John Foster.............Frank Whitson
Judge...................Albert Hart
Rex (dog)...............Himself

If there ever was a set-up for anyone, this picture is that for Mary Carr, its star. As the title infers, it is about a mother. There isn't a sweeter public mother in the world. And you can't help but love her and even weep with her, no matter how theatrical her movements and motives for action may be.

Rex Lease, as the boy, is fine looking and a good actor. Looks much like Cullen Landis, even to gestures and facial expression. A newcomer, he should be watched and he will go far. Kathryn McGuire, as his wife, also unfamiliar, looks sweet.

"Somebody's Mother" seems a sure thing to reach the good graces of the neighborhood sob sisters and mothers.

Three Weeks in Paris

Warner Brothers production made from the story by Gregory Rogers. Adapted to the screen by Daryl Francis Zanuck and directed by Roy del Ruth. Matt Moore and Dorothy Devore featured. Loew's New York Roof as half of a double feature bill. Running time, about 67 minutes.
Mary Brown...............Dorothy Devore
Oswald Bates..............Matt Moore
Gus Billikens............Willard Louis
Bruce Gordon.............John Patrick
Mary's Mother............Mary Cecil
Duc de la Porte..........Gayne Whitman

An improbable, tedious and generally uninteresting farce, impossible in more ways than one, filled with glaring anachronisms and so weak on its own feet that the hoak of the universe has been piled on for good measure.

In fewer words—a weak sister. *Sisk.*

NANA

Paris, May 3.
The trade show of "Nana," produced by Jean Renoir from the novel of Emile Zola, had the scenario written by Pierre Lestringuez, who has retained the local atmosphere

of the period of the story, 1868. The titling has been done by Mme. Leblond Zola.

Werner Krauss plays Count Muffat, supported by Jean Angelo as Count Vandeuvres. Catherine Hessling is a realistic Nana, the richly kept courtesan who rose from a chorus girl at the Varieties Theatre and caused many love tragedies.

"Nana" received a flattering reception.

SILENCE

Cecil B. DeMille production released by P. D. C. and directed by Rupert Julian. Adapted by Beulah Marie Dix from the stage play by Max Marcin. H. B. Warner, Vera Reynolds and Raymond Hatton featured. At the Times Square, May 20. Running time, 70 minutes.
Norma Drake }
Norma Powers }.........Vera Reynolds
Jim Warren................H. B. Warner
Harry Silvers...........Raymond Hatton
Phil Powers...........Rockcliffe Fellowes
Arthur Lawrence..........Jack Mulhall
Mollie Burke............Virginia Pearson

Here is the best movie melodrama in a long time.

This one has the great plot of the stage play, a handsome production, and H. B. Warner's real acting, so tense and expressive it makes an impression such as few bits of movie playing will ever make.

Perhaps the director, Rupert Julian, should be credited for a great part of the picture's success. At any rate, the picture itself is a real success and one of the finest in the entire lot which DeMille has released since with P. D. C. In that time DeMille has turned out some great audience stuff.

The story opens with Jim Warren waiting to be hanged. Beside him sits his attorney, nervously tapping his pencil on a desk; farther away are carpenters hammering at the scaffold; the pendulum of the clock swings relentlessly toward the hour, and Warren associates a swinging noose with the pendulum. To add to his mental brainstorm, a great bell begins tolling. And one of the fanciest pieces of work seen recently, the sum total of these various nerve-wracking noises is expressed through the medium of a multiple shot, all of them going at once in front of Jim Warren's drawn face.

Warren is going to swing because of another's guilt. Then comes the cutback which reveals him in early life as a crook but devoted to Norma Drake, whom he is to marry. But Mollie Bourke, the ward mistress, wants Jim for her own. When he gets into a jam, either he must marry Mollie or both he and Norma go up the river. So he marries Mollie and Phil Powers, who had worshipped Norma for years, married her to give a name to the baby.

The baby girl grows up out west where Powers becomes prosperous. The mother dies. Jim Warren disintegrates considerably, but in his wanderings he always manages to strike back at the little western town just to peer through the panes at his daughter.

One night a shifty partner tries to put the shake on Powers. Jim went to the house to warn him. While there the shifty one began abusing the woman who was loved by Jim but who married Powers. He called her an unspeakable name and a revolver shot rang out—fired by the woman's daughter.

Jim was going to swing for her crime, that's the whole story.

But it's so well handled that there is an ocean of sympathy all the way through for Jim Warren and the other characters are given sufficient play to turn in good performances.

"Silence" is one of the best pictures of the year.

It will thrill and interest almost any audience anywhere. In addition to that, it conforms to the best standards of modern movie making.

Exhibitors in booking this picture should realize that it was not shown at the Times Square, New York, at a $1.65 price by itself, but that the "Prince of Pilsen" accompanied it on the program. Only the completely bottled up condition of Broadway is to be blamed for making P. D. C. rent a theatre to show its product on the Big Street. *Sisk.*

Tramp, Tramp, Tramp

First National release of Harry Langdon's first feature length comedy. Produced by Harry Langdon Corp. and directed by Harry Edwards. Six authors credited with story. Titles by George Marion, Jr. At Strand, New York, May 23 week. Running time, 62 minutes.

Harry Logan....................Harry Langdon
Betty Burton....................Joan Crawford
Nick Kargas....................Tom Murray
John Burton....................Edwards Davis
Amos Logan....................Alec B. Francis
Taxi Driver....................Brooks Benedict

First big picture by a man who played in vaudeville several years **ago, and who wasn't even a headliner, although a well-rated standard act.** Into the movies he went, taking his vaudeville tricks, and within six months his two-reel comedies were much sought.

In "Tramp, Tramp, Tramp" he has done it. The film has a finish that will cause as much talk as Peggy Joyce's romances. That scene is where the hero and the girl are married a year or so later and look in through a window to call to their baby. And in the cradle is Langdon, dressed in baby clothes and goo-gooing away for dear life. The effect, of course, was gained by use of a large cradle and everything else in scale, so that his body might be properly dwarfed.

What precedes that part of the plot is the story of a shoe manufacturer who organized a cross-country walking race to advertise his product. Langdon was the sap entry. His progress across the land is a series of gags. In one place he gets arrested and stuck on the chain gang, and in another town he strikes a cyclone and, probably without realizing it, made himself the bravest man of the lot by heaving bricks at the black menace, although the swirling cone of wind was getting ready to leave of its own accord.

Langdon does some remarkable work in "Tramp, Tramp, Tramp." Aside from the expert handling of all the gags assigned him, he does several very long scenes in which facial expression is the only acting. Joan Crawford is borrowed from Metro to be a nice leading lady with little to do, while Tom Murray as a mighty hard-boiled walking champion is the only other member whose assignment amounts to more than a bit.

"Tramp, Tramp, Tramp," will be great for First National, ditto for the exhibitors. If Langdon can follow it with something as good or better, he is automatically installed as a pretty high muckety-muck among the Chief Screen Comedians.

"Tramp" has been released for some weeks; probably held back by the Strand. *Sisk.*

The Prince of Pilsen

Comic opera success produced by A. H. Sebastian, with Anita Stewart and George Sidney featured. Adapted from the Pixley and Luders original by Anthony Coldeway and directed by Paul Powell. Released through Producers' Distributing Corporation. Running time, about 60 minutes. At Times Square, New York, May 20, on run.

Hans Wagner....................George Sidney
Nellie, his daughter..........Anita Stewart
The Prince of Pilsen..........Allan Forrest
Princess Bertha of Thorwald.......... Myrtle Stedman
Bandit Chief....................Otis Harlan
Lady in Waiting....................Rose Tapley
Captain of the Guard.....W. von Brincken
Court Physician......Wm. Von Hardenburg

A funny, free and easy movie version of the famous operetta success. In it George Sidney is funny 99% and gets laugh upon laugh as the dumb little Dutchman who returned to his native town and was mistaken, in his lodge uniform, for the Prince of Pilsen.

The real prince was scheduled to marry the Princess of Thorwald on that day. So the Dutchman, Hans Wagner, being half stewed and willing to get real drunk, allowed himself to be hoisted in the royal coach and driven away.

Once in the palace, he still thought it was just a fancy lodge room and kidded his way everywhere. When told the princess was waiting, the old fellow figured it was nice to have the ladies' auxiliary in the same building.

Meantime his daughter has met **the real Prince of Pilsen and a nice romance ensues.**

With one more rendition of the operetta's stock gag, 'Vas you efer in Zincinatti," the picture fades out.

"Prince of Pilsen" has been handsomely produced, and three real performances are turned in by Mr. Sidney, Anita Stewart and Allan Forrest. Direction is okeh. Quite a flock of handsome sets and locations pass before the camera during this film's running time.

It qualifies for good houses and particularly likely to stand in favor where folks like their comedy alternated between the subtle stuff and the slapstick. *Sisk.*

VOLCANO

William Howard Production presented by Adolph Zukor and Jesse L. Lasky. From the play "Martinique," by Laurence Eyre, adapted by Bernard McConville. Featuring Bebe Daniels. Directed by William Howard. At the Rivoli, New York, week May 23. Running time, 48 minutes.

Zabette De Chauvalons......Bebe Daniels
Stephane Sequineau..........Ricardo Cortez
Quemba....................Wallace Beery
Maurice Sequineau..Arthur Edmund Carew
Cedriene....................Dale Fuller
Mme. De Chauvalons........Eualie Jensen
Andre De Chauvalons.......Brandon Hurst
Marie De Chauvalons.........Marjorie Gay
Pere Benedict....................Robert Perry
Auctioneer....................Snitz Edwards

Cut down to a screen running time of 48 minutes, "Volcano" makes a good picture.

It is just another instance of proving that there is a lot of unnecessary footage used on most of the feature productions that are being ground out. In this limited running time every bit of action necessary to the telling of the story of the former stage play that was entitled "Martinique" is there.

The average exhibitor, however, will say: "Well, if the feature runs only 48 minutes it is going to mean that I have got to dig up more than an hour of additional entertainment to fill in my show," and the chances are that this picture will because of this find its way into the double feature bills in the pop houses. That is going to be an error. Take it as it is and put shorts around it and it will stand up at the box office.

The volcano eruption effect is enough to send any audience out talking about the picture, and William Howard has turned out falling buildings and crumbling walls that stand up with anything De Mille ever did.

Bebe Daniels is at the head of a cast that includes Ricardo Cortez, Wallace Beery and Arthur Edmund Carew. Bebe shows more fire, verve and actual acting ability in **this picture than in anything that she has ever done within the recollection of this reporter. Everything that she does in this picture has a kick to it, and Miss Daniels proves herself considerable of an actress, one that is worthy of better stories than those that have been allotted her. Cortez at times seemed to be taking his work as a joke and laughed his way through a couple of scenes. Seemingly this young man is getting a little too sure of himself.**

Wallace Beery was his own reliable self in the performance he gave, and Carew was admirably fitted. But Dale Fuller really should come in for more than honorable mention, for she scored tremendously as a quadroon servant.

"Volcano" is good entertainment with a dramatic punch and a real thrill. *Fred.*

Chip of the Flying U

Universal-Jewel production starring Hoot Gibson. Adapted from novel by B. M. Bower and directed by Lynn Reynolds. Half of double bill at Loew's Circle, New York, May 24. Running time, 65 minutes.

Chip Bennett....................Hoot Gibson
J. G. Whitmore..........DeWitt Jennings
"Weary"....................Harry Todd
Della Whitmore.....Virginia Brown Faire
Walter Duncan..........Philo McCullough
Dr. Cecil Grantham..............Nora Cecil

As good a western comedy as Hoot Gibson ever turned out—and that's going some because this young fellow has himself a flock of admirers. In taking Bower's novel over for the screen, somebody was smart enough to gag it for a million laughs, and the result is an uproarious comedy, plus the natural appeal of Gibson. Meaning that without him it would still be a good picture—with him it's a better picture with a real drawing asset.

Chip Bennett is girl-shy. When the daughter of the ranch owner returns as a full-fledged doctor, he immediately takes a shine to her and is getting along great, although he has opposition in a "dude" from the next-door ranch.

Chip pulls a phoney accident and with the "doctor" nursing him for days, the romance progresses until his innocent deception is discovered and taken seriously. Even the girl goes back on him until he busts into a dance, tells the gang to go to thunder, grabs the girl and rides off to the parson.

For comedy purposes Harry Todd plays a sap cow-puncher for lots of laughs, aided by a freak trio of westerners who pull the slapstick effectively.

At the Circle, a neighborhood house catering to a mixed element, "Chip of the Flying U" was received with hilarity and enthusiasm.

There's no question about Gibson's popularity—even the rather awful "Flaming Frontier" won't be able to hurt it—and in so fine a vehicle as this it's a setup for the exhibitors and the producer, for while the film is well made, it wasn't produced on a million-dollar scale—rather a sensible thing at that because the use of genuine backgrounds trumps anything ever turned out by the best art department in Hollywood. *Sisk.*

THE BROWN DERBY

C. C. Burr Production, starring Johnnie Hines. Released by First National. Directed by Charles Hines. Special preview at the Playhouse, Rye, N. Y., May 21. Running time, 63 minutes.

Tommy Burke....................Johnnie Hines
Edith Worthing....................Diana King
Her Aunt....................Flora Finch
Her Australian Uncle.....Ralph Standing
The Bride....................Ruth Dwyer
Her Father....................Edmund Breese
The Groom....................Harold Forshay
The Heavy....................Bradley Barker

Johnnie Hines' latest comedy made for First National release has everything in it except the kitchen stove to get laughs. That is exactly what the picture does do. At the little Playhouse at Rye, N. Y., it was given a preview before an audience that jammed the theatre, an audience for the majority locals, although about a score of reviewers and members of the Hines company brought up from New York to see the picture tried out.

It is a corking exhibitor picture, for it does give the audience laughs and it runs only a little more than an hour.

There is an abundance of comedy in action and titles; a little romance, some sex stuff handled in a farcical manner, a couple of thrills in a motor car and motor boat race, and an abundance of gags.

It is handled well by the cast, but Hines predominates. In a spot or two the story hitches a little at present, but these can be fixed by the addition of a title.

Hines is a young plumber, about as good as plumbers come, although he is suffering from an inferiority complex. A rich uncle dies and leaves the young man his brown derby. This derby is known to have been a lucky omen to the old man, and as soon as the young plumber starts wearing it things begin to happen to him.

Through a series of circumstances he gets the photograph he has always admired from the case of the photographer's next door to his shop. **The address on the back of it is given to him by his assistant as that of a job. He walks in on the girl and is greeted as the long-expected uncle from Australia, whose name is A. Plummer.**

He is pressed into service as a best man for an elopement, the eloping pair being married by a crook whom they have surprised fleecing the real minister, and then the real minister marries the best man and the maid of honor, they permitting him to perform the ceremony in the belief that he is an insane man and trying to humor him.

The quartet all go to the same hotel, the couple really married taking separate rooms, while those not married are lodged together. The father of the girl who eloped appears on the scene, he having been placed in possession of the real fact by phone from the minister, and further complications ensue.

The action is fast all the way, punctuated with laughs that roll up.

Opposite Hines is Diana King, who scored nicely. (She is a sister of Lois Wilson, and this was her first lead). Ruth Dwyer filled well enough in what she had to do, while the balance of the cast was adequate. *Fred.*

SILKEN SHACKLES

Warner Brothers' production, starring Irene Rich. Story by Walter Morosco and Philip Klein. Directed by Walter Morosco. At Warner theatre, New York, May 23. Running time, 70 minutes.

Denise Lake....................Irene Rich
Howard Lake....................Huntly Gordon
Lord Fairchild....................Bert Marburgh
Tade Adrian....................Victor Varconi
His Mother....................Evelyn Selbie
His Father....................Kalla Pasha
Frederic Stanhope..........Robert Schable

A good little picture, filled with sophisticated twists and a deft finish which lifts it into that classy atmosphere where only the good pictures go. But it is burdened with a cheap title. The silken shackles referred to are those of marriage.

Denise Lake is a flirt. In Hungary she falls for a handsome violinist, who tells her that he is of the nobility and the war is responsible for his rather rundown condition. The girl almost falls, but her husband frames it with the violinist to make desperate love to her and then stand the gaff when the revelation comes that he was paid to do the heavy stuff. In the meantime, it is also discovered that the boy's parents are boorish peasants, so they are hauled in and instantly Denise is cured, thus running to the arms of her husband, but stopping on the way to drop a wink at another man.

The story runs smoothly, and as too many characters are not mixed up there is clarity throughout. Miss Rich, with a slicked down bob (new for her) and some very creme-de-la-creme fashion creations that looked like a cross between the early Vitagraph period and the later Milgrim influence, did good dramatic work all the way. Victor Varconi, the handsome young Hungarian whose "Volga Boatman" appearance made him many friends, played the violinist and proved quite satisfactory. Huntly Gordon was the prosaic husband.

For a first directorial job Walter Morosco has turned out a good film which should get itself a new title and then go out and please the folks. *Sisk.*

The Unknown Soldier

A Renaud Hoffman Production presented by Charles Rogers, released through P. D. C. Charles Emmett Mack, Marguerite de la Motte and Henry B. Walthall featured. Based on theme suggested by Dorothy Farnum, adapted by James J. Tynan. Shown at the Rivoli, New York, week May 30. Running time, 82 minutes.

Fred Williams.......Charles Emmett Mack
Mary Phillips.......Marguerite de la Motte
Mr. Phillips............Henry B. Walthall
His Sister.............Claire MacDowell
Mrs. Williams..............Ethel Wales
Corporal Fogarty............George Cooper
Peaceful Perkins.............Syd Corssley
"Mike" Ginsberg.............Jess Devorska
Rev. Dr. Mortimer...........Willis Marks

"The Unknown Soldier" as a title fitted perfectly for Memorial Day, especially as there was virtually a two-day holiday which the picture got the advantage of. However, taken as a straightaway picture entertainment, it is rather slow and draggy in spots, although it starts with considerable kick at the opening.

The bigger part of the "kick" to the picture is in the opening scenes, and there is a let-down from then on. There is punch here and there in the picture that is certain to get it over to the average picture house audiences, and the neighborhood houses and the smaller towns will like it the most.

A point about the story is the bringing back of the hero who has been in a hospital for over two years suffering from loss of memory from shell shock. It is a little sugary for Broadway but which will get to them with a wallop in the small towns.

The story deals with a factory mechanic among the first to enlist when war is declared against Germany by the U. S., and the daughter of the owner of the factory who goes overseas as an entertainer. They meet in France and are married, or believe that they are, although the one who performed the ceremony was a deserter who had stolen a chaplain's outfit to make his getaway.

The girl learns the truth the morning following the wedding, but the husband is on his way to the front and she cannot reach him. This scene is almost as effective as that of the little French girl's quest for her lover in "The Big Parade."

Finally mail reaches the boy informing him his wife is in a hospital with a baby at a certain point that is under fire. At the same time there is a call for volunteers to locate a lost company that has been cut off. The point is near the one where the wife is located and he offers to go, but misses the wife. That is the last of the war stuff.

The closing sequences show the burial of The Unknown Soldier in Arlington Cemetery, the scenes being the originals lifted for the feature, with the additional scenes cut in and perfectly matched. Finally the boy's mother locates him and brings him to the girl, who is still waiting with her nameless son for the father who didn't return.

The picture carries one along for a great heart throb at times, but there are other moments when cutting would help it along.

Charles Emmett Mack as the boy and Ethel Wales as his mother carry off the acting honors of the picture, with Henry B. Walthall a close second. A trio of characters played by George Cooper, Syd Corssley and Jesse Devorska fill i perfectly. Especially the latter in a scene where he is holding four aces in a dugout poker game and a shell gets him. Marguerite de la Motte seemed a little too matronly for her role. *Fred.*

RANSON'S FOLLY

First National release produced by Inspiration Pictures, Inc. Richard Barthelmess starred and Dorothy Mackaill featured. Adapted from the story by Richard Harding Davis and scenarized by Lillie Hayward. Directed by Sidney Olcott. At the Strand, New York, May 30 week. Running time, 76 minutes.

Lieutenant Ranson....Richard Barthelmess
Mary Cahill ....Dorothy Mackaill
Cahill, the post trader......Anders Randolf
Sergeant Clancy............Pat Hartigan
Lieut. Crosby........William Norton Bailey
Lieut. Curtis................Brooks Benedict
Col. Bolland.........Col. C. C. Smith, U.S.A.
Mrs. Bolland.................Pauline Neff
Mrs. Truesdale ....Billie Bennett
Post Adjutant...............Frank Coffyn
Judge Advocate......Capt. John S. Peters
Captain Carr................Taylor Duncan
Col. Patten ....Jack Fowler
Pop Henderson ....E. W. Borman
Abe Fisher ....Bud Pope
Drummer ....Forrest Seabury
Indian Pete ....Chief Eagle Wing
Chief Standing Bear........Chief Big Tree

Richard Barthelmess in an out and out western picture, the old "Ranson's Folly" story by Richard Harding Davis, filled with situation and plot enough for any man. By these tokens it is a good film.

Its cast is also good, although Dorothy Mackaill is about 500 times prettier and more winsome with her own hair than one of these 1492 wigs that some bright man must have suggested.

The central figure is the daring and reckless young lieutenant, Ranson, who first displayed his bravery when he disobeyed orders and took from a burning building two cans of nitro-glycerine which, if it had exploded, might have killed many people. He disobeyed orders to do this. Although court-martialed and disciplined he was called before his commanding officer and told that with the discipline went the fullest admiration for his bravery.

Shortly afterward the feats of a bandit, the Red Rider, became bruited about. Ranson bet his fellow officers he could hold up a stagecoach with a pair of scissors as his only weapon. He said he would and did. But simultaneously there was a killing by the Red Rider and the paymaster's wagon was looted. A churlish officer snitched on Ranson's bet and the blame was put on him. He was going through a court-martial and things looked bad. A death-bed confession from the real bandit saved him. So he kissed the girl, she felt his four-day old beard, remarked that it was rather rough, and then came the fade-out.

Barthelmess is properly daring in this film. It has been nicely produced, with a great many exterior sets. Long and expert cast. For several roles regular army officers were placed to assure no trespassing against the service regulations of the time, for this one is spotted about 1875 or so.

With the Barthelmess name "Ranson's Folly" is satisfactory. *Sisk.*

PARIS

Metro-Goldwyn-Mayer picture, written, directed and produced by Edmund Goulding. Features Charles Ray and Joan Crawford. John Arnold, photographer. At the Capitol, New York, week May 30. Running time, 67 minutes.

Jerry.........................Charles Ray
The Girl.....................Joan Crawford
The Cat....................Douglas Gilmore

Strictly a "movie" idea of Paris, its Apaches and what can happen to a wealthy American youth in that environment. The objective is light comedy, occasionally reached, but it's all a bit silly.

Jerry (Charles Ray), somewhat in his cups, roams around side streets until he stumbles into a cellar joint where the girl (Joan Crawford) and "her man" (Douglas Gilmore) are killing time by gazing soulfully into each other's eyes between impassioned embraces. This is repeated every so often for late comers.

You know that he's "her man" because the subtitles say so. Jerry gets one look at the girl, pays the Apache for a dance permit, steams the beauteous underworld devil up through his attentions to the girl and finishes by being tatooed with a knife.

The maternal instinct in the girl explains why she takes Jerry to her room, but she's not so much concerned with Jerry as shielding "her man," who will sojourn in solitude at the request of the gendarmes if they find out.

Inasmuch as "The Cat" has been hiding from uniforms ever since he could crawl under a crib it's an opportunity the law-enforcement boys fail to overlook. Jerry being disgustingly rich and correspondingly prominent, off goes "The Cat" to the Bastille to the strains of "My Man."

Jerry, harboring the desire to raise the girl above her lowly social scale, makes her a proposition of all for nothing. Recalling the Santa Claus legend, she moves right in. Considerable apartment and appropriate raiment.

But Jerry can't make the amour grade. Whereupon the girl returns to "her man" after he's done penance, writing a note to the effect that there ain't no Santa Claus and he'll get even when they meet.

Jerry hears of the prodigal's return, bounces in on a choking scene and goes to the mat with the Apache. After both soak up plenty of punishment the girl regains consciousness, feels her throat, realizes she's not so bad off as she might have been and, as Jerry is applying full attention to "The Cat's" ninth life, asks him to lay off, 'cause he's still "her man."

And there you are!

Goulding has laid the Apache thing on rather thick, dance and all. Nothing reasonable in the story, and very much of a celluloid fairy tale. None of the characters are genuine, whether you've been to Paris or not. Especially is this true of Gilmore as the handsome Apache with his boyish bob that has one curly lock drooping down to complete the circle just under his left eye. And it's probably not all Gilmore's fault, for, after all, he was under orders, too.

Ray is the smiling and nonchalant Yankee with a side-splitting remark on his lips for everyone. The titling substantiates this. At that Ray makes one or two minor pieces of business stand out as an inkling that he can deliver, no matter how poor the material.

Advance information on Miss Crawford among the "picture mob" had her strongly heralded as a "comer." Undoubtedly a "looker" (when profiled she can double for Norma Shearer in a closeup), Miss Crawford will nevertheless have to show more talent than in this instance to make that billing entirely unanimous. Good, yes, but perhaps suffering from the pre-boosting thing that always handicaps. And the Capitol audience apparently got no decided impression.

The picture has been well cameraed by Arnold, but Goulding's slums of Paris screen is melodramatic "hoke" that will draw snickers in some quarters, even away from Paris. *Skig.*

Looking for Trouble

Blue Streak Western, starring Jack Hoxie. Directed by R. N. Bradbury. From the story by Stephen Chalmers. At the Columbus, New York, one day (May 31) as half of double bill. Running time, 49 mins.

An unusually interesting cowboy film is this one of the series of Blue Streak Westerns (Universal). Jack Hoxie is starred and does his normal good job as a smiling, hard-riding cow lad. In it he is Don Quickshot. Why the last moniker is not apparent, for Don does little or no work with the irons.

Unlike its brethren, "Looking for Trouble" holds somewhat of a story. The scenarist exhibits some semblance of continuity, also unusual. Story includes the counterfeiting editor of the town's newspaper. The editor edits about the yellowest kind of a sheet. But Quickshot forces a personal apology and retraction from the editor after an untruthful and slanderous tale had been printed about the picture's heroine.

The usual couple of villains and Marceline Day as the girl. Miss Day is a sweet miss. Her graduation from "westerns," where not a few of the present-day female stars and near stars originated, seems certain.

Faults in the film can be found in the "night" shots and in one of Hoxie's fistfights. Hoxie hit his opponent on the point of the chin too easily and the receiver got to his feet much quicker than is natural for a man stiffly cuffed on the "button." It caused snickers. As for the "night" shots, they are too light to seem real. That is a common fault with "westerns." Either the green tint is too light or the Kleigs are badly played. But then, again, as much of the action in this type of film transpires in the late evening, it would probably be brutal on the eyes to try to distinguish the fast movement of cowboy and horse in a shot of heavy darkness.

SIBERIA

Fox production, based on Bartley Campbell's melodrama. Scenario by Eve Unsell and direction by Victor Schertzinger. Alma Rubens and Edmund Lowe starred. At Loew's Circle, May 24, as half of double bill. One day. Running time, 62 minutes.

Sonia Vronsky	Alma Rubens
Leonid Petroff	Edmund Lowe
Egor Kaplan	Lou Tellegen
Alexis Vetkin	Tom Santschi
Commandant	Paul Panzer
Beautiful Blonde	Lilyan Tashman
Beautiful Brunet	Helena d'Algy
Kyrill Vronsky	Vadim Uraneff
Andrei Vronsky	James Marcus
Governor	Daniel Makarenko
Ivan the Nameless	Harry Gripp
Feodor	Samuel Blum

This picture has a big production, a good cast and a great opportunity, but it didn't reach the grade, and accordingly is playing the double bills around New York and is aptly classified by that. Maybe it's okeh for the cheaper combination vaudeville houses and the daily change, but that's all. Costly and disappointing.

The story is the Bartley Campbell melodrama of the children of a rich Russian family who took up teaching of Leo Tolstoi and were automatically cast out. So they took themselves to a Russian village to teach the peasants. Quicker than you could say Michaelovitch Petranovosky they were sent into that land of natural refrigeration, Siberia.

That's where the monkey business starts. The girl, it seems, is beautiful and greatly to be desired, and the soldiers, it seems, are lustful men, always on the lookout for women. They treat their women folks terribly.

But the girl, of course, finds herself a protector, and from then on it's a scrap between a pretty high official and the protector, with virtue triumphing after outrunning a flock of zoo wolves over the snow.

Alma Rubens and Edmund Lowe, plus a mustache, have the big parts. The cast details the others, most of whom are reliable—and that goes for Victor Schertzinger, the director, but even with that much to the good, this one didn't shape up.

Sisk.

THE BOOB

Metro-Goldwyn-Mayer production. Adapted by Kenneth Clarke from the story by George Scarborough and Annette Westbay. Directed by William A. Wellman. Titled by Katherine Hilliker and H. H. Caldwell. Reviewed at Loew's New York May 26. One day. Running time, 64 minutes.

Amy	Gertrude Olmstead
Peter Good	George K. Arthur
Jane	Joan Crawford
Cactus Jim	Charles Murray
Harry Benson	Antonio D'Algy
Village Soda Clerk	Hank Mann
Fat Girl	Babe London

A terrible picture, the worst made by Metro since its merger with Goldwyn and Mayer. And so palpable are the efforts at comedy it was apparently remade and new stuff injected to give it even a semblance of a plot. As it is, the thing wavers between the carrying out of a comedy plot and establishment of a "boob" characterization.

In plot it concerns a boy who set out to prove to his girl that he wasn't a boob. With the audience he never quite established that point, but nevertheless and notwithstanding, the boy became a hunter of bootleggers and through some freak fell in on an important haul, made himself a hero and got the girl.

The alleged comedy consists of a handy-legged cowboy; a small colored boy; a village soda clerk doing the mug stuff while dining out in society, and for a big punch, an air hole blows the dresses of a fat girl over her head.

In places where M-G-M means good pictures, "The Boob" should never be shown. Far better for one like this to be shelved. *Sisk.*

ELLA CINDERS

First National release, presented by John McCormick, starring Colleen Moore, Lloyd Hughes featured. Adapted from the comic strip by William Counselman and Charles Plumb. Directed by Alfred E. Green. At the Strand, New York, week June 6. Running time, 67 minutes.

Ella Cinders	Colleen Moore
Waite Lifter	Lloyd Hughes
"Ma" Cinders	Vera Lewis
Lotta Pill	Doris Baker
Prissy Pill	Emily Gerdes
Film Studio Gateman	Mike Donlin
Mayor	Jed Prouty
Fire Chief	Jack Duffy
Photographer	Harry Allen
Editor	D'Arcy Corrigan
Director	Al Green

The comic strip, which has been appearing over the country relating the trials and tribulations of "Ella Cinders" has been adapted for the screen to serve as a vehicle for Colleen Moore. It gives a corking tie-up in almost every town of any size with at least one local daily. The result is there is a certain box-office value in the title which, coupled with the popularity of the star, is going to make the picture stand up fairly well at the majority of box offices. As a picture it must be labeled with the average of program productions.

The story is just one of those Cinderella tales in modern clothes, like a lot of our present-day musical comedies, only more so. Included in it is a touch of the life of "Red" Grange, as the hero is a football star-iceman. What more could anyone ask for than a stepchild for the heroine and a college football champ with lots of dough, who delivers ice for the fun of it, to work out a plot?

The ugly duckling wins the town's beauty contest for a movie star that was staged by a couple of sharpers. She gets her fare to the coast and then finds she has been hoaxed. She refuses to go back to her stepmother and drudgery, and sticks it out, finally breaking into a studio and making good under circumstances that pull lots of laughs.

In the finish the hero steals her away from in front of the camera and tells the director to get a new leading lady.

Colleen Moore more than makes good as the little family drudge, while Jed Prouty and Jack Duffy in comedy roles put a real wallop over. There is a brief minute of Harry Langdon in the picture, he playing one scene with the star for laughs, although not billed.

Al Green directed the picture and played the director in the cast. While Al may never become the screen's most wonderful leading man, he certainly did put this bit over.

On the matter of cost "Ella Cinders" looks as though it had been put on for a little nickel. *Fred.*

THE DEVIL HORSE

Hal Roach production, released through Pathe and starring "Rex," horse. Directed by Fred Jackman, with story by Roach. Photographed by Floyd Jackman and George Stevens, with titles by Malcolm Stuart Boylan. At special showing in Hotel Roosevelt June 1. Running time, about 65 minutes.

King of the Horses	Rex
Lady	A Silver Mare
The Killer	A Black and White
Dave Garson	Yakima Canutt
Marion Morrow	Gladys McConnell
Prowling Wolf, the Indian	Robert Kortman
Major Morrow	Roy Clements
Young Garson	Master Fred Jackman

This is the third of the horse pictures made by Hal Roach, the first being "King of the Wild Horses" and "Black Cyclone" the second. Now comes "The Devil Horse," best of the lot and an ideal novelty feature for an exhibitor whose audiences may be a bit fed up on blondined heroines and larded leading men.

The plot here is better than that of the other two. It is made to order and so constructed that it brings the heroic actions of the black horse directly into the sub-plot, which concerns some vicious Indians, a government fort and the daughter of the commander.

Chief Prowling Wolf, a very mean guy, is the Indian villain, and is set on getting the major's girl. To do this he stirs many tribes into warfare. Except for a wild and precarious ride made by "Rex" and Dave Garson, a frontier scout, they would have been successful. And so it ends that Garson wins the girl and "Rex" goes into an equine clinch with "Lady," a silver mare.

Previous to the beginning of the real story, it was "planted" that "Rex" hated Indians. As a colt he had been driven away from the boy who swiped milk that he might get strong and fill up those awkward legs which are the rightful, though erstwhile, heritage of any colt.

This boy turned out to be Garson many years later. Meantime the horse had galloped over the plains as a terror to any Indians, for he knew them by smell. Garson, too, hated the redskins because they had murdered his parents.

When "Rex" met Garson it made a great scene, because the Indians had bound him and left him where they knew the horse would soon appear. Looking on "Rex" as a fiend, the redskins naturally expected him to tear up Garson.

Somewhere back in the horse's memory (which the subtitles logically enough explain) was the recollection of a small boy feeding a tiny colt with a bottle and nipple. "Rex," instead of tearing Garson to pieces, made friends and before long was his pal. The situation of Garson trying to saddle the wild creature is included, and gives a corking excuse for some broncho-bustin' scenes the like of which the screen hasn't reproduced in many days.

"The Devil Horse," reel for reel, is as filled with thrilling situations and incidents as possible. Yakima Canutt, the world's champ cowboy and a riding fool, is the young hero. What he lacks in movie looks he makes up for in his rough riding, while the other actors of the cast are thoroughly satisfactory.

"Rex" gives a good composite performance, and insofar as the layman is concerned, he will not bother to figure out what labor may have been involved. He will take it for what it appears to be—a western story with a handsome horse as the leading character, and as such it qualifies in every way.

That it is better than "Black Cyclone" is the most succinct way to praise "The Devil Horse." And that is praise enough. *Sisk.*

SAY IT AGAIN

Famous Players picture, starring Richard Dix. Directed by Gregory La Cava. Story by Luther Reed and Ray Harris. Edward Cronjager, photographer. At the Rivoli, New York, week of June 6. Running time, around 75 minutes.

Bob Howard	Richard Dix
Princess Elena	Alyce Mills
Prince Otto V	Chester Conklin
Gunner Jones	"Gunboat" Smith
Baron Ertig	Bernard Randall
Count Tanza	Paul Porcasi
Marguerite	Ida Waterman
Prime Minister Stemmler	William Ricciardi

Richard Dix's name over the title should mean something in those localities where he is a favorite, but "Say It Again" is just a fair issue. Set in one of those hokus-pokus musical comedy countries, the yarn is a long time getting anywhere, with the hand-to-hand battle stuff the film's only action and placed next to closing. Nothing to rave about, but not a stage wait, either. It's one of those betwixt and between affairs.

The film's length is principally due to the sub-titling, which is hoked up in a fictitious language for giggles, with fade-in translations supposed to be the punch. There's a bushel of these. 'Way overboard into monotony.

"Gunboat" Smith is again teamed

with Dix and Chester Conklin is an added comedy starter. Both do well, although Conklin is not to the front as much as in a recent release of an opposition firm.

Mistaken identity is the key to the situation. Dix, blasting into a small kingdom, is adjudged the returning prince. Conklin is the true heir to the throne, but runs out when the reds start to heave bombs around. The princess had nursed Bob Howard (Mr. Dix) when he was wounded in the war, but has never seen his face because of bandages. Bob's pilgrimage is to find her.

That's the framework upon which is hung a deal of superfluous footage. But a good-sized Monday matinee was kept cheerful by events.

The fight comes when the mob learns that Bob is not the real prince, turns on the throne and makes the nation a republic, thereby doing away with any embarrassment concerning the princess marrying a commoner. During this sequence one member of the revolution gets the idea they should all kiss the princess, whence Dix and his pugilistic screen team mate swing into action.

Strictly summer entertainment to the last inch, and nothing for an audience either to ponder or wonder about. The girls giggle and apparently like Dix in the picture. The men chuckle at most of "Gunboat" Smith's and Conklin's activities, and the titles occasionally register.

The film eases by without being a standout.

Dix is nicely foiled by Alyce Mills as the princess, who, as far as known, is a new partner for him. Miss Mills looks good and clicks in the scenes where she has to. Dix, personally, is curtailed on histrionics, the action being practically a frolic for him in this respect.

However, Dix continues to look good, and the feminine gender will undoubtedly dote on him in uniform. The supporting players suffice and the sets make the grade. Nothing exceptionally lavish, but substantial.

La Cava could have chopped for heightened interest, but didn't; so "Say It Again" flows along at a normal gait. You can walk in on it, or leave it, without being disturbed. *Skig.*

ROLLING HOME

Universal production with Reginald Denny starred, in story by John Hunter Booth. Directed by William A. Seiter. At Colony, New York, June 6, for fortnight or more. Running time, 73 minutes.

Natt Alden....................Reginald Denny
Phillis....................Marian Nixon
Mr. Grubbell....................E. J. Ratcliffe
Dan Mason....................Ben Hendricks, Jr.
Mrs. Alden....................Margaret Seddon
Col. Lowe....................George Nicholls
General Wade....................Alfred Allen
Sheriff....................C. E. Thurston
Selectman....................George Marion
Selectman....................Alfred Knott
Pemberton....................Anton Vaverka
Office Boy....................Howard Enstedt
Aunt....................Adele Watson

The new Denny picture is based on a single idea and runs its length by virtue of a thousand situations, all surefire and admirably handled by Denny.

Here he is a smart and quick-thinking promoter, a fellow pursued by tough luck but whose letters home were written when he was riding high, so that when he omitted to tell the old folks of his lean days, they pictured him as none other than a genuinely wealthy power.

When writing he is coming down for a visit, they drag the band, bunting and fire engine out to meet him. The coincidence that he arrives in a Rolls-Royce, driven by a chauffeur-pal, only heightens the rich illusion.

The girl is the girl he left behind and came back to claim.

The gags are sure and Denny plays in the speedy and pleasingly flippant manner of an ad libbing comedian whose actions are never planned too far ahead. Supporting is Marian Nixon, uncommonly able and pretty, while numerous rural character parts are well handled.

Direction is good and no doubt responsible for much of the good playing.

An okeh first run this picture, especially where Denny means a draw. *Sisk.*

RANSON'S FOLLY

(2d REVIEW)

First National release, produced by Inspiration Pictures, Inc. Richard Barthelmess starred and Dorothy Mackaill featured. Adapted from the story by Richard Harding Davis and scenarized by Lillie Hayward. Directed by Sidney Olcott. At the Strand, New York, May 30 week. Running time, 76 minutes.

"Ranson's Folly" is not a good picture and must wholely depend upon the drawing power of Richard Barthelmess or Dorothy Mackaill or both. Where neither is a draw this picture cannot stand up.

It's silly to the point of aggravation, old fashioned in story and picturization, while its "western" tale is almost farcical all of the time and dreadfully farcical at the finale. Its direction is not any too brilliant, held down by the story's limitations, while the photography ofttimes is annoying through so many long shots.

This second review of a picture is brought about through a rule in the New York office of Variety that where two of its reviewers disagree with the printed review of a picture, a second review shall follow. In the notice on "Ranson's Folly" in last week's Variety it stated that it was a good picture in the opening paragraph and concluded in the final sentence of the criticism with the statement that with Barthelmess the picture is satisfactory.

Accordingly this second review is herewith for the information of exhibitors who may not be located in a "Barthelmess" territory.

For punches the picture holds only an ordinary prairie fire, and was badly cut at that point for its introduction, while the other is a stage coach holdup at a pretty late date for that kind of stuff in a class feature. Rest of the entire thing is applesauce.

Richard Harding Davis wrote his stories well in his day, which was long ago. This story read then much better than it films now. *Sime.*

BACKSTAIRS

Ufa picture without titles. Directed by Leopold Jessner. At Cameo, New York, for one performance, June 8. Running time, 51 minutes.

The Maid....................Henny Porter
The Lover....................Eugene Dieterle
The Postman....................Fritz Kortner

Imbued with the Continental touch of stark tragedy, this picture grinds out its story and lets it go at that, disregarding any attempt at a happy ending.

To those connected with celluloid the film will undoubtedly hold interest, but as regards the general public "Backstairs" seems destined to parallel the career of "The Last Laugh" as a box-office attraction over here. It is not for American consumption.

The story is a drab affair although realistic enough in its hopeless love of a semi-paralytic postman for a housemaid who in turn is entranced by a laborer. The pantomimic work of this trio is superb. Jessner's symbolizing, in lieu of subtitles, is also of high grade, although at one point the continuity becomes muddled. Three witnesses each received a different impression of the action.

An outline of the tale is that the maid sees her lover go away, doesn't hear from him for apparently weeks, and meanwhile the postman calls daily on his rounds while worshipping from afar. Finally the maid does get a letter and is overjoyed.

During a party in the house where she works the maid slips some of the refreshments to the postman in his cellar abode, there to discover that he has presumably forged the letter from her lover.

Evidently she becomes resigned to the postman's faithfulness. They are about to sit down to a modest banquet some time later when the lover returns. To the postman it is paradise lost. The lover is perturbed when explanations are forthcoming but can do nothing because of the mailman's physical condition. The maid leaves the two men in the room together and the next view is of the postman standing over his Nemesis with an axe in his hand.

The uproar caused by the murder leads to the maid losing her position on the spot, whence she calmly climbs to the roof and walks off to drop into the street. That's the finish.

The individual playing is brilliant. Kortner's bodily handicapped postman is genuine, and is comparable to Chaney's character work. Frau Porter's performance is also strictly high grade as is that of Dieterle, albeit he has the least to perform.

No mob stuff nor large sets. It's mostly interiors with the scenes of the apartment where the maid works causing wonderment because of their ugliness, even though accepted as a replica of the home of a middle class German family.

In restricted circles "Backstairs" will hold and may inspire discussion as an example of an untitled picture, but its tragic theme and treatment are not for normal consumption where toll is the objective.

Studio individuals will probably pay the picture its due in acknowledging the film has been well made and done, but it doesn't seem as if others outside of trade circles will be interested enough by the story to care.

It's seven years old and the understanding is that titles are to be inserted for general release. Jessner, who directed, is not a professional camera supervisor, while Carl Mayer, who wrote "The Last Laugh," is the scenario author and Paul Lein takes credit for the settings. *Skig.*

GOOD AND NAUGHTY

Famous Players production, starring Pola Negri. From the play "Naughty Cinderella," by Avery Hopwood, adapted by Pierre Collings. Directed by Malcolm St. Clair. At the Rivoli, New York, week June 13. Running time, 60 minutes.

Germaine Morris....................Pola Negri
Gerald Gray....................Tom Moore
Claire Fenton....................Miss duPont
Bunny West....................Ford Sterling
Thomas Fenton....................Stuart Holmes
Chouchou Rouselle....................Marie Mosquini
"Knockout" Murphy....Warner Richmond

New York and Florida take the place of Paris and Lido in the picture version of "Naughty Cinderella," with the story much revamped in certain particulars and Pola Negri in the role originated in this country by Irene Bordoni. As a picture, it does entertain for an hour, especially through the artistry of Ford Sterling who puts laughs into the action.

In a measure Pola gets a chance to act, to do something other than look beautiful. That is in the earlier portion of the picture when she is posing as a slovenly assistant in the interior decorator's shop. Pola does several things here that make her really worth while. There is a repression about her work that proves she is an artiste who when given the chance can score without clothes. On the whole, "Good and Naughty," which is the picture title of "Naughty Cinderella," is not exactly good or particularly naughty, but it looks like a good box office title.

Pola, as Germaine Morris, is a wealthy girl, crazy about interior decorating. She takes a post as assistant in a firm doing that work. She had heard that the more youthful of the two bosses would not engage a good looking girl because of the flirting propensities of his elder partner, so she appears sloppy and careless, gets the job and falls in love with the younger of the two men.

He is being pursued by the gadabout wife of a millionaire, and she wants him to go to Florida with her, so invents the excuse necessary by obtaining a commission for them to do over the winter home. On the eve of the departure the husband is shown getting the necessary preliminary papers toward securing a divorce, the name of the corespondent being left blank for the husband to fill in when he locates the "man."

Then comes the scheme on the part of the "assistant" to save the honor of the firm and likewise one-half of the partnership for herself from the designing blonde. When she appears all togged out for the fray, she is a lovely sight. In the end she straightens out the messed up affairs and wins the man she's after.

This story is all told with an eye for the laughs. It has been handled by Malcolm St. Clair to get the best comedy effect possible in the action, this being heightened by some snappy titles that are just as good on Broadway as they will be in the 4,000 "Troys" of this country that they are directed at.

Pola is great and looks the same. Miss duPont as a type is a splendid foil for the brunet beauty of the star with her blondness, but she is beginning to look gross. Tom Moore showed several flashes where he was really working while in other scenes he did not seem to get over as well as he might have.

Ford Sterling really took the picture away from everyone in a scene with him. Stuart Holmes just filled in. *Fred.*

The Social Highwayman

Warner Brothers production directed by William Beaudine and made from an original story by Daryl Francis Zanuck. John Patrick, Dorothy Devore and Montague

Love featured. Warner's, New York, June 13. Running time, about 70 minutes.
Jay Walker....................John Patrick
Elise Van Tyler............Dorothy Devore
Ducket Nelson..............Montague Love
Dr. R. R. Runyon...........Montague Love
Editor.....................James Gordon
Convict....................Frank Brownlee

Story an original by Daryl Francis Zanuck. While it isn't much of a story, it has bright moments and carries a fairish plot to a satisfactory conclusion.

Its subtitles are old gags and some very bad, while the absence of a star or a real feature "name" will undoubtedly be reflected at the box offices where this plays week stands.

Not that John Patrick and Dorothy Devore don't perform well enough, for they do, but one can't help but feel that without William Beaudine's direction, "The Social Highwayman" would have been pretty awful. As it stands, it passes muster, despite the hokum and subtitles and rests under the classification of a fair picture.

The plot concerns a cub reporter, Jay Walker, and the fight his paper is making against a city administration whose principal weakness is its inability to round up Ducket Nelson, a highway bandit. Walker, after making two or three bones, is given the assignment of running him in or getting off the paper. He trudges the roads for days in an effort to corral the desperado. The best he can do is to meet Dr. R. R. Runyon, medicine show expert, Ducket in disguise. Walker, seeking to impress the Dr., tells him that he is the bandit and the joke begins to grow. The Dr., to test the phoney Docket, orders him to do a holdup and show how easy it is. Out he goes, and a frightened young woman whom he meant to rob runs her car into the woods and meets both the fake bandit and the real one.

To fall in with the company, she relates how she once held up Monte Carlo single-handed. She is the niece of the publisher for whom Walker works, but that isn't discovered until later.

The picture's windup has Walker, the real bandit, and another convict fighting atop moving freight cars, while police watch from the side of the road. As the car pulls into a station the bandit is captured, Walker promoted, and the girl kissed.

Montague Love's performance as the bandit is the best thing. *Sisk.*

Wandering Footsteps

Banner production adapted from the novel, "A Wise Son," by Charles Sherman. Directed by Phil Rosen, with Estelle Taylor and Bryant Washburn featured. Made for independent market. At the Arena, New York, as half of a double bill, one day. Running time, 61 minutes.
Helen Maynard..............Estelle Taylor
Tim Payne..................Alec B. Francis
Billy......................Frankie Darro
Hal Whitney.............Bryant Washburn
A Neighbor..................Ethel Wales
The Matron..............Eugenie Besserer

A good story, not especially well adapted, but possessing enough sympathetic interest to hold. As a strictly commercial proposition it must be noted that its cast is hardly of the type to draw trade, for the "names" utilized (with the exception of Alec Francis) are those who **have slidden down from stardom, rather than those advancing to it.**

The story concerns young Hal Whitney, spendthrift and booze-fighter, who, on a spree, meets a gentlemanly old bum, Tim Payne, whom he legally adopts and then takes on a yachting trip. Once sober, he forgets all about the old fellow.

Meantime, his sweetheart is affronted by the presence of the old man, who looks pretty seedy. She leaves the trip with the boy friends befuddled over her actions. Because the newspapers have made so much of the story—the adoption of an old man by a young one—Hal looks the old fellow up and the conclusion is a reunion.

The real performance is given by Alec B. Francis as the bum, this dependable actor getting much footage and deserving it all. Bryant Washburn serves as the hero, while not so much can be said about Estelle Taylor, for a haughty bearing alienates the audience on her first appearance. The child actor, Frankie Darro, Ethel Wales and Eugenie Besserer have smaller parts and handle them well.

Daily change only. *Sisk.*

POWER OF THE WEAK

Jesse J. Goldburg production released by I. E. Chadwick for the independent market. Alice Calhoun starred. No director or author listed. At Loew's New York, June 11, as half of double bill. Running time, about 55 minutes.
Myra............................Alice Calhoun
Raymond..........................Carl Miller
The Father...........Spottiswoode Aitken

Weak picture except for its story. While commonplace and hackneyed, it embodies quite a bit of action and a good fight. Otherwise almost a total loss, inasmuch as Alice Calhoun's part, that of a woman boss in a lumber camp, is ridiculous at all times, the direction even making it more so.

The climax of the story has the woman worried that a certain load of lumber won't be out on time, the reason being that there is plotting within the ranks. A young man is given the blame. She lashes him with a bull-whip.

Then, according to a subtitle, his manhood surged and he was reborn. Immediately he went out after the villain, licked him to a standstill, made himself a big fellow in the eyes of the girl, and from that sequence went into one where the villains blew up a high bridge over which the lumber-train was passing.

This was badly done in miniature. At Loew's Roof the audience guyed it considerably, just as they did the finish, which had the hero and heroine mushing as logs swept by them in the current of the river.

Even with its action shooting galleries only will even want to consider this. *Sisk.*

TWO CAN PLAY

Embassy production released through Associated Exhibitors. Starring Clara Bow. Directed by Nat Ross. At the Stanley, New York, June 4, one day. Running time, 59 minutes.
John A. Hamis..............George Fawcett
Jas. Radley....................Allan Forrest
Dorothy Hamis....................Clara Bow
Robert MacFerth.......Wallace MacDonald

A little feature that has a story with a twist handled in such a manner that the audience is kept in suspense almost to the final fade-out. In that respect the picture is away from the ordinary program release, but it is one of those that had to be handled within a production figure and therefore it qualifies for the better class of daily change houses.

It is the story of a young girl who gets stuck on a society lounge lizard. Her uncle disapproving of the young man's mode of life, decides that he will get someone else to figure in her life and thus thwart the boy he looks upon as a fortune hunter.

The father selects a former aviator and then plans to set the three down on an isolated island where there is only an old sea captain and his wife, so that the girl will have an opportunity to judge between the two men. His plans go astray because the old captain is forced to come to the mainland to take his wife to the hospital, and the trio of young folk are left to their own devices. The result is the inevitable clash between the two men for the girl with the one that was looked upon as the bounder proving himself to be the best.

Clara Bow as the heroine handles herself admirably, while George Fawcett in the earlier scenes gives one of those usual masterly performances of his. The two men, Allan Forrest and Wallace MacDonald, scored, particularly the latter who registered right from the start.

Fred.

ENEMY OF MEN

Waldorf production from story by Douglas Bronston. Directed by Frank Strayer. At Arena, New York, one day (June 10) as half of double bill. Running time, 59 minutes.
Norma Bennett............Dorothy Revier
Dr. Phil......................Cullen Landis
Tony Caruso..............Ceasare Gravina
John Hurd....................Charles Clary
Roberti............................Leo White
Janet........................Barbara Luddy
Baby Janet..............Virginia Marshall
Miss Ordway..............Margaret Landis

Slow moving and ponderous cinema that borders often enough on the melodramatic to be boring. Seduction, murder and the beautiful working girl. The last named is not unusual in even better pictures than this.

The action seems uninspired with the exception of a few moments by Barbara Luddy, the wronged girl. These moments brought forth some likely talent. Cullen Landis, as a doctor-philanthropist, was badly cast. He is strictly a juvenile, and while his role called for a young man it looked poorly played by the theatrical young Landis.

Dorothy Revier is a fine looking girl.

Direction good. Bad projection spoiled several light moments that would have helped.

THE THRILL HUNTER

Waldorf production presented by Columbia Pictures Corp. Directed by Eugene De Rue and reviewed at the Stanley, New York, June 5, one day. Running time, 65 minutes.

A silly and impossible little picture but at that fairly amusing. The major portion of the plot is concerned with two fellows who drink "Peppo," wallop the tar out of half a city and then go into dreaming about the hunt for the prince of Grecovia.

The embassy is shown, a large country estate, quite a laugh in itself, because all the embassies in the U. S. are in Washington. They don't have throne rooms and a flock of cardinals hanging around to do wedding ceremonies and coronations on order. Here a young man is conscripted to be king of the country and right away they start to crown him. He battles his way out, rescues the girl, saves her father from a few bombs, and goes into a fade-out.

It is fairly amusing because of several chase scenes and other hokum comedy.

Haines gives a nice Harold Lloyd performance. Miss Bennett and Miss McGuire do those things assigned to them with no particular skill.

Filler for the small places. *Sisk.*

The Broadway Gallant

Richard Talmadge in an F. B. O. production. Story by Frank H. Clark. Directed by Mason Noel. At the Columbus, New York, one day (June 2), as half of double bill. Running time, 54 minutes.

This title was evidently slapped on for no reason. Anyway, "The Broadway Gallant" has nothing to do with the case.

The picture is a usual Richard Talmadge release in the usual double-quick action. Talmadge does some peach jumping, climbing, running and fighting, and holds the speedy tempo throughout. The kids flock to see his antics and relish in them as they did when Doug Fairbanks was leaping all over the screen.

First rate stuff for the youngsters and an okay hour of light entertainment for anyone.

Foreign Films

CRUISER POTEMKIN

Berlin, May 26.

The advances which the Russians have made between this film and the last of their products which has previously been released in foreign countries is nothing short of astounding. Where the "Postmaster," released in Berlin only a few months ago, was still technically unfinished and interesting only in spite of this, "Potemkin" is technically perfection.

One might even go so far as to say that the technical angle is here the most interesting.

The success of the film in Berlin is simply astounding. Profits from Germany can probably be conservatively estimated at not less than 1,000,000 marks. Whether the film will be a real success in America is another question. It is nothing more **or less than undiluted Soviet propaganda, and might even be forbidden by the censor on this ground. Should it be passed it seems doubtful that the average American film-goer will fall for it, because it is too evidently propaganda, and because it is too artistic.**

Its scenario concerns an actual historical incident which has been found by the Soviet government in the czaristic archives. In 1905 the armored cruiser "Potemkin" was lying off Odessa. The crew had been getting incdible rations and finally worm-ridden meat was brought on board. The sailors protested and refused to eat this.

The czaristic commander, true to the principles of his regime, decided at once to make an example. He portioned off 10 of the sailors, had them covered with a sail cloth and ordered the marines to shoot them.

At the crucial moment the leader of the sailors called to the soldiers: "Brothers, whom are you shooting?" After a moment of hesitancy the soldiers lowered their guns and mutiny broke out.

Within a few moments all the officers had either been shot or thrown overboard. In the struggle, however, the leader of the sailors was shot. His body was then brought by the sailors to Odessa and laid out in an open square. The news of the mutiny spread like wildfire through the city and the oppressed citizens, in the hope that the czaristic regime was about to fall, came to pay homage at the bier.

This rejoicing did not last long, as the city officials ordered the Cossack troupes to close in on the citizens. Coming from both sides of the big square and stairway leading up the hill they shot down mercilessly all in the way, cripples, old men, women and children.

This was only stopped by the cruiser opening fire on the city hall, where the authorities were ensconced.

The cruiser got news the entire Russian fleet was on its way to subdue them. They decided to go to meet it and die a heroic death in battle. The fleet, however, also sym-

pathized with them and let them pass through its lines without firing a single shot. The "Potemkin" then found refuge in a Roumanian harbor, where it was interned until the end of the Russo-Japanese war.

The direction of S. M. Eisenstein is original and powerful. There are moments in the film which even the most hardened conservative could not help being thrilled.

At the beginning the building up to the moment when the leader of the sailors cries, "Brothers," is positively nerve racking, and the mutiny comes almost as a relief. The shooting of the citizenry by the cossacks is harrowing in its individualized realism. Also the inexorable advance of the shooting Cossacks down the steps is interesting from a rhythmic angle.

The climax of the film is the sequence in which the "Potemkin" goes out to meet the fleet. One seems actually to be in the very bowels of the ship, seems to feel the very throb and pound of the engines, which increases from moment to moment.

Without sentimentality the sailors prepare themselves for the final struggle, the guns are loaded and all are waiting tensely for the first shot from the fleet. It is with a thrill of surprise that the sailors of the fleet answer the "Potemkin" and refuse to shoot on their comrades.

The photography by E. Tisse is fine throughout but occasionally is too "pretty" for the subject. Some night shots of the cruiser are too attractive and would much better fit into a picture of lighter type. *Trask.*

Die Fahrt Ins Abenteuer

Berlin, May 25.

Ossi Oswalda, featured, is a popular German film comedy star, still liked here. In the early days, under the direction of Lubitsch, she did pictures which were quite attractive. Now the hope of becoming an international star for her must be abandoned. Especially so if she goes on producing films like this "Trip Into Adventure." A feeble story, feebly directed by Max Mack. It really does not bear repeating, as it is merely a poor excuse to camouflage a travelog along the Mediterranean.

Although such well-known players as Willi Fritsch, Agnes Esterhazy and Warwick Ward are in the cast, nothing is made of them.

In short, this is a product suitable only to the daily change houses.

Special notice has been made of it here because it was given as the feature at the Ufa Palast am Zoo, Germany's leading first-run house. This proves better than anything else could that the Germans are no longer in any condition to supply their theatres adequately with class product, and it looks as if they must accept the American specials. *Trask.*

Footsteps of Aztecs

Berlin, May 24.

Interesting as an example of the educational films of which the Ufa is turning out from 20 to early. They evidently think this one of their best, as they gave a special performance of it at the Gloria Palast for a Mexican Commission traveling through Europe.

The picture was cranked by a German cameraman and taken under the direction of a German professor, Alfons Goldschmidt.

It really does not live up to its title, as only the first 500 feet are taken up with the Aztec culture. Here there are pictures of a few of the still existing Aztec monuments and several feeble attempts to reenact some of the characteristic ceremonies of the ancient Aztec life.

Then it skips off to a general view of modern Mexico from the business and scenic angle. Although difficult to make such a product seems to hang together; nevertheless, the mixture is a little too chaotic—some main line like a railway or river journey keeps the audience's interest more alive.

The film ends with the screening of a complete bullfight. This is camouflaged by titles which speak of the sport as revolting. That does not alter the fact that grucsome detail is spared, even to the maltreating of the defenseless old horses. This would have to be toned down in America.

Such educational films will unquestionably be difficult for the Ufa to dispose of in America, as they have neither the pictorial photographic beauty nor the sensational novelty that we demand. *Trask.*

PALM BEACH GIRL

Famous Players Picture, presented with Bebe Daniels starred. From the play, "Please Help Emily," by H. M. Harwood, adapted by Forrest Halsey. Directed by Erle Kenton. At the Rivoli, N. Y., week June 20. Running time, 73 minutes.

Emily Bennett	Bebe Daniels
Jack Trotter	Lawrence Gray
Aunt Jerry	Josephine Drake
Julia	Marguerite Clayton
Herbert Moxon	John Patrick
Tug Wilson	Armand Cortes
Sheriff	Roy Byron
Aunt Beatrice	Maude Turner Gordon

From a highbrow standpoint this may be one of the worst pictures Famous Players has turned out, but from an audience standpoint it is one of the best hoak comedies it has released in months. Full of laughs in action, in titling and situation, it has all the thrills any audience could ask for, and in addition the love theme, with the little ugly duckling of the family beating out her high-hat cousin for the heart of the hero. What could be more perfect?

Nothing as far as the Rivoli audience was concerned on Sunday, for they laughed and laughed and thoroughly enoyed seeing Bebe Daniels in a role that had her deathly afraid of the water, take a half dozen duckings in the old Atlantic at various times, and finally get so she actually seemed to enjoy it.

"The Palm Beach Girl" is just what the title implies. Bebe is the girl. She is a poor cousin from Iowa, invited to the winter resort by a wealthy aunt. The same aunt already has brought her sister and, the latter's daughter to the scene and remade them sartorially and socially. They resent the new arrival.

While on the train Bebe gets her face sooted up from a passing tug, and arrives on the scene looking so much like "colored folks" that she is compelled to ride in the station bus assigned to the servants, and a bell-hop who is a Charleston champ, according to his card, refuses a tip but tries to date her up.

Finally Bebe meets up with her relatives. After bathed and reattired in a flock of newly bought clothes that strip the Iowa from her, she starts to make a winning. Then the thrills begin. She manages to be perfectly seasick, always a gag laugh, and then gets mixed up with a bunch of bootleggers, who steal the boat of the hero.

Bebe returns after a night in the Everglades to his home, only to be jammed into a rather compromising position when the up-stage aunt and daughter drop into the boy's quarters. But she beats the barrier here and with the aid of a mechanic wins the motor boat race on which the hero has his "all" staked, and wins him beside.

The thrills portion is in the motor boat race. It is thrill mixed with comedy, and the suspense is perfectly maintained to the end of the race and the final fadeout.

Miss Daniels again proves herself in this picture and Josephine Drake in the little that she has to do just steps on the gas and makes the most of it. Lawrence Gray is a passable enough hero in this instance and Armand Cortes slips over a comedy character with effect.

Erle Kenton need not fear about his direction. If he can go on making them like this and gagging them as well he'll do. Geore Marion, Jr., did the titles and shows in spots that he has his dad's mania for collecting gags and putting them in scrapbooks as against the time he can use them. Some were bad, but the majority got laughs. *Fred.*

LOVEY MARY

King Baggott production, released by Metro-Goldwyn-Mayer. Adapted from the book by Alice Hegan Rice. Co-starring William Haines and Bessie Love. At the Capitol, New York, week of June 20. Running time, 63 minutes.

Lovey Mary	William Haines
Billy Wiggs	Bessie Love
Mrs. Wiggs	Mary Alden
Miss Hazy	Vivia Ogden
Miss Bell	Martha Mattox
Tommy	Jackie Combs
Baby Tommy	Freddie Cox
Europena	Gloria Holt
Asia	Mary Jane Irving
Australia	Annabella Magness
Kate	Eileen Percy
Stubbins	Russell Simpson
Miss Elchorn	Rosa Gore
Mrs. Chults	Sunshine Hart

"Lovey Mary," that quaint sequel to the equally quaint novel, "Mrs. Wiggs of the Cabbage Patch," one of the stage successes of more than 20 years ago, has finally reached the screen. What a picture is this! Full of human interest, jammed with homely humor that compels laughter, yet presented to the audience in such fashion as to make the majority wish there were more of it.

The title, "Lovey Mary," may not at this late date bring a record-breaking crowd to the box office, but those that do go will certainly leave with a feeling that they have seen something on the screen well worth their while sitting through.

And what a heroine Bessie Love proves to be in the title role! If anything she is better than Mabel Taliaferro in the original stage production which the Leiblers put on at the old Savoy. Bessie Love is Lovey Mary.

The supporting cast right along the line is superb. Vivia Ogden, who plays Miss Hazy on the screen, was in the original stage production in the same role. And then there is Mary Alden as the lovable Mrs. Wiggs, while in Jackie Combs as the two-year-old Tommy there seems to be a find in screen youngsters. He's great.

William Haines does not get before the camera until the picture is about half finished, but registers nicely. Russell Simpson plays the "answer to a matrimonially inclined maiden's prayer," and supplies the sinister interest to a marked degree.

This is one of those good clean pictures that make for a feeling of better understanding on everyone's part, and which do it in such a fashion that the lesson is tempered with wholesome comedy that sends away the tear to follow it with a laugh. It is a picture that should get a better box-office return than will probably be granted it on Broadway, at least. *Fred.*

PUPPETS

Al Rockett production released through First National. Drama, adapted from Frances Lightner's play (adapter not named on program billing). Milton Sills starred and Gertrude Olmstead featured. Directed by George Archbald. At Strand, New York, week June 20.

For anyone coming along and standing as well especially around New York as Milton Sills this "Puppets" thing is a pretty lightweight story to saddle upon him. Whether the women will like his Italian love making here can't be determined. They may if they can overlook the tiresomeness of the tale.

It's about 3,000 feet before any action arrives and that when a transport leaves the dock in New York. A series of bursting shell scenes, probably inserts, followed. And after that Sills as Nicki, the mannikin manipulator, is back in New York, deaf-stone deaf—but unable to read lip movements.

The picture just slops along. Probably runs around an hour that seems like a week. Toward the finish it's padded so heavily and badly that the only relief is when it ends.

Nothing can hold up "Puppets" but Sills, and it won't be his acting either that will do that—nor the acting of Gertrude Olmsted, although Miss Olmsted doesn't do so badly. At least she has the excuse of becoming wearied through Nicki lugging her around the place so much.

She had to be jogged again during the finishing fire, a blaze, and it should have been a laugh. While in the midst of this Nicki and his cousin were matching fingers in the good old way nearly every wop act in vaudeville has done it, only here it didn't get the laugh it should have had.

Francis McDonald is the serene and scheming villain who wanted Nicki's wife, whom Nicki had left immediately after marrying as they didn't give him much time to catch the transport that day. How Nicki had to go on a draft and Bruno (McDonald) didn't may be explained by the military laws of Italy. And Lucien Prival should take a look at himself playing Frank. He probably has drawn the hatred of every piano player in the world for looking the way he does, but he's not so far wrong at that—as a piano player.

That's all there is to the story, excepting that in the opening scenes, when Nicki is running his mannikin show, probably on the Tony Sarg scheme, he saw a face in the audience who looked up at him. It was Miss Olmsted as Angela, the drug store clerk around the corner. This started on the Bowery and ended at the same address.

Nicki got the drug store habit. He bought so much from Angela that the boss fired Angela for overselling. She also sold herself and got a job hanging around Nicki's loft-apartment.

Mr. Sill's will have to show a lot of b. o. strength to carry this over. If he can then he's strong enough as well to demand that he be properly fitted.

While the story here seems 80 per cent. at blame, the other 20 can be divided equally between the director and the adapter, which leaves the photography nothing, but it should get a demerit as well as the violet titling and the phlegmatic captions.

In short "Puppets" is all wrong.

Sime.

FOOTLOOSE WIDOWS

Warner Bros. release, featuring Louise Fazenda and Jacqueline Logan. Directed by Roy Del Ruth. At Warner's, New York, week June 19. Runnin time, 71 minutes.

Flo	Louise Fazenda
Marian	Jacqueline Logan
Jerry	Jason Bobards
Henry	Arthur Hoyt
The Senator	Neely Edwards
Mr. Dunn	Douglas Gerrard
Mrs. Drew	Jane Winton
Mr. Smith	John Miljan

This is a comedy built upon an idea that might have been borrowed from "The Gold Diggers," having as its two principals a couple of girls, models in a fashionable New York dress shop, who trim their boss out of a flock of clothes and slip to Florida to ensnare a millionaire husband for one of them.

The complications are from two J. A. Smiths stopping at the hotel the girls pick out, one a fortune hunter and the other a youngster who has made a fortune overnight in a new soft drink.

Of course, the girls pick the wrong J. A. S. He thinks one of the girls is a wealthy widow. He starts right after her. Meantime the real "J. A." falls in love with the "widow," and she in turn likes him.

The two principal roles are played by Louise Fazenda and Jacqueline Logan. The former walks away with the picture with her comedy, while the latter looks extremely well and impresses with her beauty. In the support Jason Bobards appears as a likable lead, while Douglas Gerrard and Neely Edwards furnish the greater part of the comedy. The former as a male modist with a monocle gets some corking laughs over.

The picture will not cause any record-breaking box-office results, but will entertain and make 'em laugh, which is about as much as they want at this time of the year.

A couple of early shots in the picture gives a flock of current Broadway shows free advertising in lights, as all of the Times Square district is shown.

Fred.

THE EARTH WOMAN

Mrs. Wallace Reid Production released by Associated Exhibitors. Story by Norton S. Parker, directed by Walter Lang. At Stanley, New York (25c. grind house), June 19. Running time, 70 minutes.

Martha Tilden	Mary Alden
Ezra Tilden	Russell Simpson
Sally Tilden	Priscilla Bonner
Steve Tilden	Carroll Nye
Joe Tilden	Joe Butterworth
Johnnie Mason	Johnnie Walker
Simon	John Carr
Mark McWade	William Scott

Rather sublimated old timer as to story and setting. Mrs. Reid has tried to lift it out of the ordinary with a title leader to the effect that the picture is dedicated to the women who helped in the pioneer work of building our country.

Even that leaves it just back in the hills of Tennessee, where moonshine is moonshine while men loaf and women work.

The redeeming feature is the splendid work Mary Alden does as the mother.

The story is of murder and attempted rape, lynching and finally a confession by three people each to save the other, though none killed the heavy.

Juvenile love interest is furnished by Priscilla Bonner and Johnnie Walker, neither with much to do. William Scott is the heavy and gets by. Carroll Nye looks as though he would be a bet in the future as a lead for juvenile roles at least. He is big and husky and looks good. John Carr as a half-wit registered nicely, and Russell Simpson in a character role as the father landed in good shape.

For the daily change grind houses where the audiences are not too particular, will pass.

Fred.

MY OLD DUTCH

Universal production based on Albert Chevalier's song and stage success. Directed by Laurence Trimble and produced with all-star cast. At Loew's New York, June 18, as half of a double bill. Running time, 80 minutes.

Sallie Brown	May McAvoy
Joe Brown	Pat O'Malley
David Brown	Cullen Landis
'Erb 'Iggins	Jean Hersholt
Mrs. Spudds	Patsy O'Bryne
Lady Diana	Jane Winton

This picture will mean more in England and its closely related colonies and strongholds than it will in the United States, for the story is one of the London coster mongers. While finely produced and marked by excellent acting it lacks punch where the local box offices are concerned.

Universal itself will hardly dispute that statement, for the U's foreign business is large and it is also known that at the present moment they have their own theatre under lease on Broadway, the Colony. Yet instead of putting "My Old Dutch" into the Colony, they have revived "Merry Go Around" and "Outside the Law" for showings there, while "My Old Dutch" is shunted into Loew's New York for a day's showing as half of a double feature bill.

The story concerns Joe and Sallie Brown, and Sallie is always referred to by Joe as his "Old Dutch." They are a young married pair, the husband a poor dweller in the cheap section of London. When their kid comes along their life is centered upon making a gentleman of him. To this end they assign a 50,000-pound legacy to the education of the son, who is taken from them at an early age and educated as a gentleman should be.

Afterward come reverses, the war, the old couple lose their home, and it is only the end that the boy comes to love the parents from whom he had been separated so long. And in the end, so the moral takes point, money isn't everything and that it is scant compensation for the lost love of parents.

May McAvoy beautifully handles the succeeding stages of age, which carry her from the freshness of girlhood into the decrepit and creaky period of old age, while Pat O'Malley, as her husband, is also corking. Jean Hersholt in a comedy character part runs away with his every scene.

The scenario of the film is a bit uneven, ditto the direction and cutting, the latter being particularly bad, as it closes many a scene before the scene has reached its effectiveness.

But "My Old Dutch" will suffice for the daily changes in good houses here; it will hardly hold up for a first run, but abroad should be judged on an entirely different basis, as the London atmosphere and angle is well handled.

And "My Old Dutch" is familiar to Britain as the immortal song hit of Chevalier.

Sisk.

THE LUCKY LADY

Raoul Walsh Production, presented by Famous Players. Lionel Barrymore, Gretta Nissen and William Collier, Jr., featured. At Loew's New York, New York, June 19. Running time, 62 minutes.

Grand Duke	Lionel Barrymore
Princess Antoinette	Gretta Nissen
Young American	William Collier, Jr.
Grand Minister	Marc McDermott

An old-fashioned story set in a mythical principality in southern Europe. For a program picture it will get by in almost any house of the class B variety. Not a film for a pre-lease or first-run house where the stay is longer than a day.

Well directed, and Lionel Barrymore as a Grand Duke who likes to play around with the girls and do a little drinking delivered an excellent performance. Gretta Nissen has a dual role, that of the Princess Antoinette in all her blonde beauty and then as Mlle. Toni, French girl, just playing around and looking her best in a brunet wig, and gave the better performance while in that character. Young Collier handled himself amazingly well and looked the goods. The boy is going to be one of the starring juveniles before long.

As the Princess, Gretta is in a convent, from which she plays hookey to see the performance of a traveling theatrical troupe. Here she meets the young American, who is immediately smitten by her. Back in the capital the Grand Minister hears the rumblings of Republicanism, and decides on a marriage between the Princess and one of the nobility, to stave off an uprising and at the same time secure his job. The Princess is sent for; her car breaks down on the road, and the American comes along, delivering her to her destination. Then the love interest begins in earnest.

Finally the Grand Minister suspects Mlle. Toni and the American of being accomplices of those advocating a republic, and sends them both across the border. The Grand Duke follows, and likewise the Grand Minister, when he discovers that in reality he has deported the Princess. But they arrive too late to prevent the marriage of the lovers.

Several very fine examples of photography, and on the whole a very fair program picture with a rather inane story.

Fred.

THE FIGHTING BOOB

Bob Custer starred in a Jesse Goldburg picture. Produced by Independent Pictures Corp. Jack Nelson director. At Arena, New York, one day (June 10), one half double bill. Running time, 43 minutes.

Handsome Bob Custer in a red-hot ranch tale. Most of the warm action transpires below the border.

The friendly feud of two rival ranch owners, causing one to send east for his nephew, who had been gassed in the war. Uncle doesn't know of his condition, thinking he may help in the fight.

"El Tigre" (Bob Custer), interrupts and poses as the nephew until the feud is settled and the several villains are neatly packed away.

Custer is a big boy and a hard rider. Joan Meredith has a sweet profile.

A fast moving "western" that is meaningless, but it will pack in the youngsters.

RUSTLIN' FOR CUPID

Fox production. Western drama by L. G. Ritz. Directed by Irving Cummings. Co-starring George O'Brien and Anita Stewart. Shown at Loew's Circle, New York, June 21, 1926. Running time, 64 minutes.

Bradford Blatchford	George O'Brien
Sibyl May Hamilton	Anita Stewart
Dave Martin	Frank McGlynn, Jr.
Tom Martin	Herbert Prior
Hank Blatchford	Russell Simpson
Mrs. Blatchford	Edith Yorke
Jim Mason	Sid Johnson

"Rustlin' for Cupid" is another of the celluloid ways a charming school marm falls in love with a young man whose dad is a rancher and who later proves to be a second Tom Mix in handling a cow pony.

There is splendid locale, an atmospheric play that is in favor of the picture, but the story at times is pretty thin.

That finale where the father, caught red-handed by the son, stealing calves, fesses up and makes the boy believe that it is in the blood, gives the romance a body bruise when such a sweet mother, the wife of the cattle thief, and a good son are the ones to suffer.

George O'Brien is every inch the hero—looks manly, fights and rides well and handles his melodramatic climaxes A1. And then there is the comely Miss Stewart, as attractive as ever, as the school marm.

The picture is corking in photographic values, and some scenes are very well directed.

As a "western" it will pass.

Mark.

BLACK PARADISE

Fox production, starring Madge Bellamy and Edmund Lowe. Directed by R. William Neil and made from an original story by L. G. Rigby. Scenario also by Rigby. At Loew's New York as half of double bill June 18. Running time, 65 minutes.

Sylvia Douglas	Madge Bellamy
Jack Callahan	Leslie Fenton
Lawrence Graham	Edmund Lowe
Ship Captain	Paul Panzer
Murdock	Ed Peil, Sr.

South Sea island story with the angle a crook had been engaged to marry a girl. He promised her to reform, but didn't. When the cops came he cut loose with her in a motor boat for the crook chief's schooner, outside Frisco's Golden Gate.

A detective came in pursuit and got aboard the boat, where he was set upon and put to work.

The boat's destination was the South Seas. There on an island the girl's fellow went for a native girl while she fell in love with the detective.

Murdock, the chief of the crooks, also tried to get the girl. His proposition was that if the detective was to be saved she must "pay the price."

That is laid on very thick, and the next scene shows her dressed up in next to nothing, ready to make the "great sacrifice," when the top blows off of a volcano and gives the technical department lots of opportunity for fancy miniature stuff. While the technical boys were taking care of this a boat rescues the girl and the detective, and they start the ride back to civilization.

A very sexy story, worse than "White Cargo" could ever be if filmed. The island scenes show hootchie-cootchie closeups that are suggestive to anybody while in addition the long soul-kiss stuff is worked overtime in many shots.

Madge Bellamy as the heroine goes around in few clothes, reaches the high point in the finale when she gets a chance to show all of her legs and 82 percent of everything else—the angle there being that such stuff sells pictures.

Maybe it does, but it will always remain a mystery why a state like New York, which has a censor board of people supposed to be able to interpret the law as it is written in black and white, allows such stuff to ride through uncut.

Picture is exciting and well made, the acting being good all through. It is a daily change subject and suitable for some places, but in houses where there is a good clientele or in places where Sunday films are wanted for that day, "Black Paradise" is unsuitable.

Otherwise, okeh. *Sisk.*

WITH THIS RING

B. P. Schulberg Production. Adapted from the novel by Fanny Heaslip Lea. Directed by Fred Windermere and released on a state's right basis. At the Stanley, New York, June 3, one day. Running time, 62 minutes.

The Villain....................Lou Tellegen
The Lawyer....................Niles Welch
The Girl....................Alyce Mills
The Hero....................Donald Keith

A pretty trite story, told with a so-so cast and in a so-so fashion.

The plot concerns a young fellow and his wife. They are first on the South Sea islands, where a shipwreck has placed them, but the woman later goes back to the States and awaits her man. A baby arrives but hasn't a name.

Enter the villain, brother of the hero.

He offers the gal a home but not his honored name. She slaps him in the face and the scullery maid bends a broom across his back and kicks him down stairs. At which juncture the man's lawyer enters and in a self-sacrificing mood offers her marriage. She takes him up. And they get married.

They make that very plain, for on the first night in, around bedtime, the lawyer says "Good Night" in a 96 point fullface voice. And the gal yells it back in five-point agate. So he says it again, this time in 72-point Cheltenham bold. And she again uses the swell-dulcet tones of agate, while the lawyer goes to dreaming (the producer didn't want the audience to get a wrong idea) of having a thousand kids around the house. A domestic fellow, if ever there was one.

Then the man comes back, sees his young son, pummels the devil out of his villainous brother, and an annulment is arranged so that she can marry the young fellow.

The cast doesn't mean 10 cents at the box office and the picture itself is strictly a filler for the daily changes. *Sisk.*

THE SPORTING LOVER

First National production. Produced by the Faultless Pictures Corp. Directed by Alan Hale. Distributed by First National. Shown at the New York theatre, New York, June 17, 1926.

Capt. Terrance Connaughton.Conway Tearle
Lady Gwendolyn Cavens..Barbara Bedford
Capt. Sir Philip Barton..........Ward Crane
Algernon Cravens..........Arthur Rankin
Paddy O'Dowd..........Charles E. McHugh
Michael O'Dowd..........John Fox, Jr.
Kate O'Dowd....................Bodil Rosing
Jockey....................George Ovey

As the title implies, deals with a sportive story, a race track romance, but with a dash of war flavor that has the hero and heroine meeting for some of the lovingest love scenes ever cameraed. When two "kissers" like Conway Tearle and Barbara Bedford get together a lot of the feminine screen devotees will die happy.

The champ kisser of the army wanted to call all bets off when he learned that his nurse was a rich girl. She will wed the villun if his horse defeats "Good Luck."

Just a story that has been told and retold since armistice day. But with Con Tearle and Barb Bedford kissing, the neighborhoods will fall. Otherwise just another picture. *Mark.*

EARLY TO WED

Frank Borzage production. Made by William Fox. Adapted from "Splurge," by Evelyn Campbell. Scenario by Kenneth B. Clarke. Shown at the Stanley theatre, New York, June 17, 1926. Running time, 75 minutes.

Tommy Carter....................Matt Moore
Daphne Carter....................Kathryn Perry
Mr. Hayden....................Albert Green
Mrs. Hayden..........Julia Swayne Gordon
Art Nevers....................Arthur Housman
Mike Dugan..........Rodney Hildebrand
Mrs. Dugan....................ZaSu Pitts
Mrs. Nevers....................Belva McKay
Bill Dugan....................Ross McCutcheon
Pelton Jones....................Harry Bailey

"Early to Wed" has no daring escapes, pursuits or gunplay. Yet its homey, wholesome story punch that cannot be denied.

Some corking comedy moments, but rising majestically above everything else is the present-day bluff and four-flushing that a young married couple play and fail to get away with.

Matt Moore, Kathryn Perry and ZaSu Pitts share the acting toplines, but Arthur Housman and Albert Green deserve as much praise. A lot of fun in the closing reels.

It may not mean a stampede on the box office, but anybody once in will get a load of entertainment.

This one is made to order for the neighborhoods. Typically American and will drive the truth home to the newlyweds, to the oldweds and to those contemplating matrimony.

It's worth seeing. *Mark.*

ROBES OF SIN

William D. Russell, Inc., production, distributed by Commonwealth. Adapted by George Hinely from a Louis Waldeck story. Directed by Russell Allen. At the Columbus, New York, one day (June 2), as half of double bill. Running time, 59 minutes.

Ruth Rogens....................Sylvia Breamer
John Rogens....................Jack Mower
Baby....................Lassie Lou Ahern
Cyler Bryson....................Bruce Gordon
Adelaide Thomas..........Gertrude Astor
Banjo Kid....................William Buckley
Mrs. Bryson....................Helene Sullivan

The old story of the discontented wife handled in familiar style. Must have been made some time ago, for skirts of the female players are down to the ankles, or maybe the producers are modest.

Detectives, bootlegger gang, the gang chief's kept woman and the unsatisfied wife. Miss Breamer plays the wife of a detective kept busy trailing booze and who has no time to devote to his spouse and baby. The wife falls in with bootleggers, ignorant of their occupation, only to learn at the clinch end that the gang is the one her cop-hubby has been searching for.

Miss Breamer has been idle for over a year. This picture was probably made before that. But it serves to bring back her face, which is of the screen's sweetest. Gertrude Astor is splendid as the mistress.

Of old stuff, "Robes of Sin" is a poor film, but the title should bring it along.

THE JUNGLE WOMAN

(STOLL-HURLEY PRODUCTION)

Sydney, May 25.

South....................Eric Bransby Williams
Mardyke....................Jameson Thomas
Eleanor South....................Lilian Douglas
Peter Mack....................W. G. Saunders
Hurana....................Grace Savieri

When Captain Frank Hurley made "Pearls and Savages" he turned out a splendid scenic feature. Going to London he interested Sir Oswald Stoll to such an extent that the Englishman agreed to help finance a company to produce a dramatic story in the tropics of New Guinea. In "Pearls and Savages" Hurley made some corking shots of tropical scenery and real native life. In "The Jungle Woman" he has relied mainly on the story, and in this respect he has failed badly.

The cast was engaged in London, with one exception, and the acting generally is very poor. Direction is about equal. Some of the scenes are good, with the native angle worked well. Beyond this the feature holds nothing of much interest.

The picture could have been better produced in Hollywood. Grace Savieri, an Australian girl, takes the acting honors.

The story has two chums seeking for gold in New Guinea attacked by natives. One escapes and tells the girl they both love that the other has been killed. With the help of Hurana, the other pal escapes and reaches the trading station in time to prevent the villain's marriage to the white girl. The native woman is bitten by a snake and dies.

Hurley has a lot to learn about the dramatic side of picture production before he can turn out a real winner.

The picture might have a chance in a daily change house, but that's all. *Garrick.*

VARIETY

UFA (German-made) picture, starring Emil Jannings and featuring Lya DePutti. Directed by E. A. Dupont, with story adapted by Dupont from the German novel, "The Oath of Stephen Huller," by Hollaender. Photographer, Carl Freund. Released over here by Famous Players under the F. P.-Metro agreement with UFA for interchange of pictures annually. Opened at Rialto, New York, June 27, for run, limited to six weeks. Running time, 92 minutes.

Boss....................Emil Jannings
His Wife....................Maly Delschaft
The Girl....................Lya DePutti
Artinelli....................Warwick Ward

"Variety" is a corking picture, made anywhere as it has been in Germany. It has variety, so much so many an American director may be only too eager to watch it the second time. And it will get away over here because there are several censor-approved box office kicks in it.

After that one who has not seen a German-made picture before for over seven years doesn't know where to start, this "Variety" film is such a paralyzer after that lapse and in comparison to seven years ago, in the progress by the Germans in picture-making.

No American producer could have made a better picture of "Variety" than this picture is, and that may be letting down the Americans easily. Certainly E. A. Dupont, besides his excellent adaptation, has put in novelties of settings, productions, direction and freakish photography that should make many an American blink in amazement, for this all to come and in one film from Germany.

And on top o' that, the cast—no better four principals ever have appeared in any one picture as far as this reporter can recall, whether native or foreign. The casting is perfect and the actors superb.

Seven years or more ago this same reporter sat through a series of German-made pictures, daily changes, for two weeks without missing a day at Weber's Music hall, then on Broadway near 28th street. The pictures were awful, nothing less. Subjects were morbid, productions cheap, characters haphazardly played, principals and casting generally terrible, and everything so all wrong that not one of those German-mades ever got distribution over here.

That impression then gained about German-mades remained so firmly intrenched that even when "The Last Laugh" was so loudly acclaimed by reviewers on Variety's staff, with the work of Emil Jannings particularly commended, that that could not alter the impression.

Meanwhile many American and some English pictures have been seen. The English have stood still, if not going backward. They did not seem to even pick up the fundamentals of better picture making from their sparse few that have reached these shores, while the Americans, as admitted, have swiftly advanced, but none have progressed as have the Germans if "Variety," the picture, may be taken as a model of their current output.

In "Variety" are spectacular pictures of carnivals, fetes and theatres that look real. They break in at just the proper times. Than there is a story with plenty of suspense, the suspense at one time being most intense; that is when there is a doubt whether the catcher in a casting act high above the heads of the audience at the Wintergarten, Berlin, will drop the flier in revenge. He does not, but the signs point the other way before the aerial act is concluded.

Yet with all of this goodness in everything and without a doubt that "Variety" has everthing to compose a comfortable draw, there is the reverse side; that amidst everything the matter of a sympathetic note was wholly neglected. There is nothing in this picture to endear it to an audience, nothing to weave a bond between the screen and the patrons, for it's a picture of double-crossing, twice, with the only possible object of sympathy, the wife of the triangle, seemingly too phlegmatic in the German way, meaning indifference to conditions, to grasp for sympathy from out front.

Mr. Jannings has been praised for his picture work, and never too highly, from what he does here. A pantomimist of rare calibre and a character player par excellence, he's the German acrobat, head of the act (or troupe) and the showman to the exact precision of the role. Mr. Jannings can play with his back to the audience and so easily that he does that here several times. A great actor.

Lya DePutti will take a lot of beating from the American vamps before they can safely say they have shaded her as the waif vamp in "Variety." She plays it, and how! The girl is a natural as a vamp, in looks and actions.

As a juvenile set in this frame Warwick Ward is exactly right. He makes up as the snappy foreign performer who realizes his position in the variety world of Europe and might have been an English acrobat with an Italian professional name. Mr. Ward probably has played romantic juvenile roles as well as villainous ones. He has a face to suit either.

Miss Delschaft as the boss' wife was taken for the type, a trifle heavy for acrobatics and forced to retire to become the piano player in her husband's dancing show on the carnival lot at Hamburg. What Miss Delschaft has to do she does well, like the others. There are any number of "types" among the extras. Most of these extras of now look like the German principals of those other days.

The story of the double-crossing is the tale of the film. The Boss, reduced from his high estate as head of the troupe to running a joint in a carnival, has thrust upon him a waif, seemingly from Java, left an orphan on the boat, "Berta Marie," when her mother died aboard ship. At Hamburg the mate takes her to the Boss' because she can dance.

As a "coocher" the waif gains admiration from the front when ballyhooing. When the Boss has to drive off a roughneck who climbed upon the stage to hug the girl, he decides it is about time to return to the trapeze, where he had been among the best catchers in his aerial line of casting work.

Meanwhile the waif (Miss DePutti) in the home-wagon of her benefactors and with the wife and a baby about, had been "making a play" for the Boss o' nights after the wife had retired. Repulsed often, she persisted, until following the climax of the roughneck, the Boss declared for her, saying they would silently leave that night, with the wife outside the dressing room, coming to call them to dinner, hearing his love confession.

Then another carnival with a double casting turn, the Boss and Berta, much devoted at this time and with the boss regaining his prestige as a bearer.

And following, the opening of the Wintergarten, Berlin, with Artinelli, aerialist, obliged to cancel through an accident to his partner in London a few days before. The Wintergarten management held open the spot for the Artinellis if he could secure another partner, with the boss and the girl located.

They appear in their triple casting act over the heads of the Wintengarten's audience, doing the regular casting (and good) besides an announced triple somersault.

At the opening night of the three-act Artinelli gave the girl a diamond ring for remembrance of their association, and the next morning enticed her into his room on the same floor with the Boss', after the Boss had left for his card playing rendezvous. That night Artinelli took the girl to a fete, returning around 4.30 a. m., creating something of a suspicion with the Boss, although soothed by the wilyness of the girl.

Again and at the card rendezvous an observer of the loving relations of Artinelli and the girl idly sketches a caricature of the Boss being deceived upon the marble top. Through forgetting his wallet the Boss returned to the restaurant, noticing the caricature upon the table which had been an object of mirth to the other professionals in the place.

Locating the young man who had drawn it, he received an admittance of that man having seen the love-making at the fete.

In knowledge of the probabilities the suspense starts, as the casting act goes on again the same evening, for the Boss visualizes the dropping of the seducing flier, and it is seen upon the screen. But the act goes on and through without mishap, with the Boss later asking Artinelli to tell the girl he won't be home until late.

When Artinelli enters his boarding house room early that morning, leaving the girl to go to her room farther down the hall, both apparently having been drinking, Artinelli finds inside his door the Boss, grim, silent, and resolute. The sombreness sobers up Artinelli. He appeals, but the Boss throws two knives on a table, saying he will count three.

Refusing all peace advances and after an unseen struggle on the floor, the Boss arises alone, to walk into his room where the girl is on the bed, washing his hands of the blood as the girl shrieks at the sight, and the Boss slowly walks back down the hall, down the stairs, with the girl screaming, falling and left behind, as he goes out of the front door to call a taxi to drive him to the nearest police station.

The picture opens and closes within a Warden's room, with the Warden at the opening telling the Boss his wife and child (now 10) have appealed for his pardon. The Warden asks the Boss to break his silence and tell his story, with the in between a switch-back and the finale a probable pardon.

The picture has been scored prettily for the "acrobatic" music, also in blend as the scenes proceed, with just the right tone and volume. It's an intricate score as well.

In the Wintergarten opening scene is a complete vaudeville bill, run off with abnormal speed through limited time appearance, but taking in everything, and neatly shifted in fade outs and ins.

This picture is doubly interesting to show people through the variety end. In Germany the picture was called "Variete," the German pronunciation and equivalent to the vaudeville of here. To preserve the original, "Variety" was decided upon for this country in preference to "Vaudeville."

Here is a paragraph that should have started the review and would have, were the American public sufficiently educated to acrobatics. This picture holds a remarkable trick photographic feat or an illusion, in the casting act. There is much freaking photography, such as the performers on the high platforms seeing nothing but a jumble of eyes beneath them, looking up; the Wintergarten's interior being whirled around as the trapezes swing back and forth, several of such and all unusually interesting in picture making as well as conception, but the trick is this casting act taking up the centre of the Wintergarten's amphitheatre, doing their casting, even the triple somersault and a blindfold leap, over the audience—without a net.

There is no casting act, no performer and no catcher who would permit it, that would work an act of this kind high in the air without a net stretched beneath. Just how this double scene was obtained cannot be explained nor are the substituted aerial acts known, being Germans.

In towns like Reading, Pa., noted for acrobats, this casting turn could be claimed to be doing the greatest acrobatic trick ever accomplished without a net, and the picture will bear that out.

Set in for six weeks at the Rialto, it's doubtful if "Variety" can hold up that long. It's a fine picture but not big enough for that length of time at this house, unless much heavier in box office strength than may be now credited to it. About three weeks should be enough, unless forced.

Miss DePutti is now over on this side and Mr. Jannings is due in the fall. A couple of foreigners like these will make the native boys and girls in pictures step. That will be worth their presence if nothing else, but Emil Jannings can set himself down for an American favorite in American-made pictures from the outset. *Sime.*

UP IN MABEL'S ROOM

Al Christie Production, starring Marie Prevost; starring Harrison Ford and Phyllis Haver. Directed by E. Mason Hopper. Adapted from the farce of similar title by F. McGrew Willis. Distributed through P. D. C. At Strand, New York, week June 27. Running time, about 62 minutes.

Mabel Ainsworth..............Marie Prevost
Garry Ainsworth, her ex-husband......
Harrison Ford
Sylvia Wells, a blonde.......Phyllis Haver
Jimmy Larchmont, a business man....
Harry Myers
Alicia, his wife.............Sylvia Breamer
Leonard Mason, a gay bachelor........
Paul Nicholson
Arthur Walters, a man about town....
Carl Gerard
Henrietta, his spinster sister..Maud Truax
Hawkins, Garry's valet......Wm. Orlamond

A picture for girls and women if for any one. They may find gags to laugh at here in the hoke farcical handling of women's lingerio and all the old stuff that goes with any bedroom farce. At the Strand Monday night the laughing was moderate in spots, with one healthy shriek as the man allowed a woman's combination to catch upon a chair.

This is a variation of the French door-slamming farce. Instead of jumping in and out of doors all of the time, some of the time is spent by the men hiding under beds or in chests. To a man it's very wearying, but the flaps and the mams seemed to enjoy it.

The women of the cast run far ahead of the men. Marie Prevost stars and easily leads the others, with the runner up Phyllis Haver. Other than those two none of the players in the picture need watch it, excepting Wm. Orlamond, as the butler. Whenever Mr. Orlamond got a real chance he stole the scene for a laugh away from everybody. This he did so handily in one scene with Harrison Ford that it could not be overlooked. But Ford was hard as nails all through any way.

Perhaps the Ford role was hard, and if so he added steel to it. That may be said also for the direction of E. Mason Hopper's. It continually looked as though while the film was in the making the director and principals met nightly to see what else could be done in the gagging way the next day. But this picture should not have cost so many days in its manufacture.

"Up in Mabel's Room" tells it all—all of the men were found in Mabel's room for one reason or another, with considerable of the reason therefore very silly—with nothing more silly than Ford's ridiculous direction-made shyness, if it were the director—and just as bad whoever's fault, even the original book's.

Nice large interior settings and one novelty production fit in a girl scene in a road house night club, whatever that is—in Hollywood.

Good enough for first runs during the summer. This was a proper time to break it. But the picture needs a strong push behind it to be sure of anything over normal grosses for this time of the season. ***Sime.***

LES MISERABLES

Washington, June 26.

Films de France (Societe des Cineromans) production. U. S. distribution by Universal. Directed by Henri Fescourt, assisted by Rene Barberis. Artistic direction, Louis Nalpas. Starring M. Gabriel Gabrio and Mme. Sandra Milowanoff. Pre-view showing under auspices of the National Press Club, Poli's, Washington, D. C., June 25.

Jean Valjean.............M. Bagriel Gabrio
M. Madeleine............M. Bagriel Gabrio
Champmathieu..........M. Gabriel Gabrio
Javert....................M. Jean Toulout
Mgr. Myriel...............M. Paul Jorge
Marius..........................M. Roset
Thenardier................M. G. Saillard
Gavroche...............M. Charles Badiolo
Fantine..........Mme. Sandra Milowanoff
Cosette..........Mme. Sandra Milowanoff
Gillenormand......................M. Maillard
Enjolras.................M. Paul Guide
Mlle. Baptistine..Mme. Clara Darcey-Roche
Cosetta (child)........Mlle. Andree Rolane
Epione..............Mlle. Nivette Saillard
La Thenardier..........Mme. Renee Carl

Universal has two phases upon which to sell "Les Miserables" in the United States: the fame of Victor Hugo and the almost equal fame of the title.

Judging from American standards to which the average picture-goer has been educated, "Les Miserables" is far from the great production touted.

The story, naturally, is extremely old fashioned, hence its greatest fault—the French producers have adhered what could be termed line-for-line to the Hugo script. Certain phases of the book are highlighted, but in general the film follows closely the original story.

The book is depressing, a reader actually "wallows" in misery, getting deeper and deeper in the depressing sufferings of the Hugo characters. A reader can lay down the book, but seeing the film is a different story. Here it ran close to three hours!

The old fashioned angle at times brought laughter, one instance in particular, and the big moment of the film, too. This was the famous reference to the girl's painted face and no (cut) hair. And the sufferings of an unwed mother failed to arouse any particular sympathy.

Both stories were presented at one sitting, but, according to James V. Bryson of Universal's London office, reported to have sold the film to his firm, it will be split and run as a serial over a period of two weeks, 10 reels each. This is new for over here and will give opportunities for publicity from another angle.

The Frenchman's direction does not line up. Lighting was bad. faces of characters back from the camera could not be seen; the battle scenes are like so much child play while the ordeal of the Paris sewers, which lives with every reader of the book, was an outright flop.

Photography, again in comparison, does not measure up, while for the cast its star is little Andree Rolane playing the child Cosette. M. Bagriel Gabrio does well with Jean Valjean as does Jean Toulout as Javert. For the balance of the cast, including Mme. Sandra Milowanoff, nothing can be said.

If Universal can dig up enough Hugo admirers who want their Hugo straight, this one may have enough pulling power to run up a profit. But it will have to be sold every minute of the way.

Meakin.

ROAD TO MANDALAY

Metro-Goldwyn-Mayer production, starring Lon Chaney. Story by Tod Browning and Herman J. Mankiewicz. Direction by Tod Browning. Titles by Joe Farnham. Running time, 66 minutes. At Capitol, New

York, week of June 27.

Joe	Lon Chaney
Joe's Daughter	Lois Moran
The Admiral	Owen Moore
Priest	Henry B. Walthall
English Charlie Wing	Kamiyama Sojin
Pansy	Rose Langdon
Servant	John George

They took a long running jump when they named the picture after Kipling's poem, because it has nothing to do with a "Burmah girl's awaitin'," or with "Come you back, you British soldier." It's a story of the underworld of Singapore, done more or less in the spirit of "Queen of the Opium Ring" of the ancient Theodore Kremer style, except that the screen has somewhat refined that bygone technique. However, the intent is no different.

There is a pretentious spiritual and moral theme that runs through the story, but it has all the aspects of being entirely phoney, while the underworld "kick" is the first consideration. It's a slumming party abroad screened with a sugar-coating to make it respectable to America, which includes censors and reformers.

Not a thing in the picture as presented at the Capitol that a censor could base a legitimate objection upon, but that's because of skill in handling rather than the motif. Outside of all these considerations, the film has a large-sized dramatic punch, which, after all, was the thing aimed at and achieved, and which will sell the picture to exhibitors and to the public.

Chaney has another of those characteristic roles. This time his deformity is a sightless, white eye. It is remarkable how this particular detail contributes a sort of mood and tempo to the whole production. The subject is built upon monstrosities — Oriental monstrosities — since the action takes place in Singapore and Mandalay (the town is the only connection with the Kipling verse).

Singapore Joe (Chaney) runs a dive in the slums of Singapore with all that a dive in the slums of Singapore carries with it. Here are mixed black, white, yellow and brown, male and female, and the delicate suggestion of the character of the place was scarcely necessary. The emphasis is on the female. His lieutenant is a renegade British naval officer (Owen Moore, in an ideal role) a wild rake of flaming past.

In Mandalay lives Singapore Joe's daughter, having no knowledge of her father, being brought up in a convent in all innocence. Joe sails his ship from time to time to Mandalay from Singapore, which is some undertaking, one being in Straits Settlements and the other in upper Burma.

On one of the trips the naval officer meets the daughter. Her purity so works upon him he reforms overnight, and forthwith we are moved to the interior of the Catholic cathedral—that's what it looks like—in Mandalay, where the reformed reprobate and the innocent maid are standing at the altar-rail waiting for the priest to marry them. It is plausibly established that the priest is Joe's brother.

Comes upon the scene at the crucial moment Joe himself. He is, of course, revolted at the thought of his dissolute lieutenant marying his daughter, essence of purity. A dramatic conflict between priest and dive-keeping brothers. The finish is that Joe abducts his former lieutenant and holds him prisoner in the Singapore dive. The dive manager is a snaky Chinese, called the "best knife man in the East," who has a grudge against Joe of long standing.

The daughter goes to Joe's Singapore dive—her journey is all in a handy title—and here is where the super-melodrama starts. She falls into the hands of the Chinese snake, who traps her in an upper room (there is eloquent comedy business by the regular customers downstairs to explain the possibilities), when Joe, the girl's father, happens along. He drives the Chinaman away.

Then a big scene between the girl and unknown father. Meanwhile the navy man is brought on the scene. Father and lover fight it out with knives, and the lover is about to be abolished violently when the girl stabs her father in the back.

Joe, although dying, remembers that his sinister Chinese enemy is waiting below. He manages to survive just long enough to bluff him off while the lover gets the girl out, then collapses from a balcony into his black, white, yellow and brown customers, in a sensational 20-foot fall. The girl and her lover escape, without Joe having revealed himself.

The cast is happily picked. Lois Moran puts over youth and innocence as no other screen actress who comes to mind. Chaney is splendid in a typical role, while Moore plays the boyish reprobate probably as convincingly as it could have been done.

The picture is Chaney, who unquestionably has a big following. At the Capitol Monday they had a good attendance at 2 o'clock and for the 4 o'clock show it was capacity downstairs. This, on a perfect June day, must have had some bearing on Chaney's draw. Besides Sunday night, perfect weather, biggest business in months.

The picture undoubtedly will go over big. It appeals to the modern taste for what is called "morbid," but which nowadays is spoken of as "sensational." The Grand Guignol, maybe, was ahead of the times.

At that, the picture isn't nearly as "strong" as the Knobloch piece of a few seasons back called "The Lullaby," or as "The Shanghai Gesture." But it is sensational enough to attract keen attention.

BORN TO THE WEST

Famous Players picture. From the story by Zane Gray, adapted by Lucien Hubbard. Directed by John Waters. Jack Holt, Margaret Morris, Raymond Hatton, Arlette Marchal and George Siegman featured. At Rivoli, New York, week June 27. Runnnig time, 62 minutes.

"Colorado" Dare Rudd	Jack Holt
Nell Worstall	Margaret Morris
Jim Fallno	Raymond Hatton
Belle of Paradise Bar	Arlette Marchal
Jesse Fillmore	George Siegman
Bate Fillmore	Bruce Gordon
Nell's Father	William A. Carroll
Dinkey Hooley	Tom Kennedy
Sheriff Haverill	Richard Neill
Mrs. Rudd	Edith Yorke
Sam Rudd	E. Allyn Warren
As children:—	
"Colorado" Dare Rudd	Billy Aber
Nell Worstall	Jean Johnson
Bate Fillmore	Joe Butterworth

One of the best westerns in a long, long while. It is one of the fastest action pictures that Broadway has seen in a year. Just bristles with excitement and seethes with suspense.

John Waters is a newcomer to the direction honors, this being his first assignment at the head of a company. If this picture is to be taken as a criterion of his work to follow, he certainly is a made man. Waters handled this picture with a deftness that bespeaks of long years of training as an assistant, and he has turned out a picture that will have the average audience on its head. It may not be a great box office winner, but it certainly is going to give every one that sees it a corking thrill.

The story is one of those typical of the Gray series. Laid in the west, it opens with a schoolday sequence that plants the natural rivalry between two boys over a girl. There is a fight between the two which ends in both being scarred, one on the forehead and the other on the back of his hand. When they meet again in after years the scars lead to the mutual recognition.

The girl also comes into the later sequence through having moved with her father into the new gold rush country, Nevada, where the father of one of the boys runs the dance hall and is boss of the town. His son is an all around bad egg, and when the hero shows on the scene real action starts. There are a couple of fight scenes that are corking, and the general gun battles in the dance dive are well worked out.

In the end a pitched battle between the miners of one strike which the town boss is trying to steal and the rough element of the boom town is one of the best staged film fights of its kind that has ever been seen. Here the miners win out and the rough element is chased out of town, with the hero rescuing the girl from the dance hall keeper's son and there is a happy ending.

Through the story there is a comedy element largely furnished by Raymond Hatton as the companion to the hero that registers in great shape. Jack Holt has the heroic role, with Margaret Morris playing opposite him, while Arlette Marchal does a dance hall girl in a corking manner.

The cast is a most adequate one, and for a fast moving western filled with thrills the exhibitor need look no further. Holt gives a great performance, and for the first time in a long while gets over his personality to the audience.

Fred.

THE STILL ALARM

Universal melodrama taken from the original of two—maybe three—decades ago—by Joseph Arthur. Helene Chadwick and William Russell featured. Running time, 65 minutes. At the Broadway, week June 28.

They haven't left much of the original. The story has been rewritten and brought up to date. The fireman and his bride have been married three years when the story opens in 1908. The situation set, years elapse in one short title. So we have the time of the action now in 1926.

A version of the famous old play was done by Selig in 1918 that kept reasonably within the limits of the old play, but this edition by Universal doesn't go much beyond admitting that the hero is a fireman, and it is at a fire that the crisis comes.

William Russell is no sprightly hero, so they turn him into the father. But it becomes necessary for the fireman to smear up a heavy at the fire for the sake of a woman. Wherefore, the new fireman hero must have a petticoat to rescue. The situation is covered by giving the hero a flapper daughter, saved from a fire the day his wife deserted him and adopted to sooth his grief.

She is a flapper, which calls for new amendments, since the modern flapper was unknown in the '90s. One change compelling another, they wander far from the story, so that it is unrecognizable.

Nevertheless, the basic appeal of the standard blood and thunder play of long ago remains to some extent, although the picture has been produced with an economy in places that injures its quality. The heavy, Richard Travers, is pretty bad, both in action and dressing. A suave millionaire who wears ill-fitting clothes has no place on the screen at this day and date.

The flapper daughter is better, and Helene Chadwick as the erring wife is a capital player, although why she should be playing middle-aged characters seems extraordinary. The piece is handled for an unfastidious clientele, and these points may pass, for there is sturdy melodrama in the action, and, of course, the flying fire engines and the fire-fighting episodes have an honest thrill. In particular there is one good bit where the fireman hero leads eight or ten trapped men from a burning building by means of a human chain linked along a dizzy ledge six stories above the street.

And then there is the good standby where the suave destroyer of woman's honor is properly beaten to a pulp by the honest hero. The picture has all these to make up for its hopelessly inartistic settings and numerous crudities in story and direction.

A picture to be bought and sold on a price basis for the less exacting. What it is doing in a Broadway house is something the arrangers of the Broadway theatre attractions will have to answer for, presently or in the hereafter.

EVE'S LEAVES

Cecil B. DeMille production, directed by Paul Sloane, featuring Leatrice Joy. Released by Producers' Distributing Corp. In the cast are Robert Edeson, Robert Long, Richard Carle, musical comedy old timer, and William Boyd, leading man. At Loew's New York, June 25. Running time, 64 minutes.

Familiar type of screen comedy-melodrama, the melodrama being in the action and the comedy in the titles for the most part. Discussion of the picture's merits involves the point whether fans like their heavy dramatics and their romance tempered with sophisticated kidding. The thing was never done before the advent of the movies. You got your melodrama straight and if there must be a humorous element it came from the "comedy relief."

The screen technique is to introduce the comedy relief and josh the heavy dramatics too. The result is confusing, and it would have to be a pretty nimble minded fan who would "get" the conflicting values. This is especially true of the present subject, because nobody seems to have been certain whether the mood was direct kidding or serious romance.

The direction of Paul Sloane, as to grouping, backgrounds and concentration of interest is first rate, but the uncertainty as to intent sets these technical excellencies at naught. Miss Joy is Miss Joy; that is to say, the actress is in a characteristic role, which calls for a coquettish hoyden. She rather overdoes it, as sometimes happens. Robert Edeson, one time matinee idol, has the inconsequential part of a gruff sea captain who seeks to keep his tomboy daughter in innocence of the world, while she instinctively yearns for feminine vanities. Hence the title, "Eve's Leaves." The ship, a magnificent square rigger, docks in a Chinese port, where the Chinese brigands kidnap the girl and her American lover.

The Oriental locale gives the picture good picturesque and romantic interest, and the farcical twist was bad judgment because it destroys these values. The only explanation that occurs is that as the production progressed, or after it was finished, the cynical studio mind rather revolted at the ten-twent-thirt grade of melodrama—such as the two lovers captured by the Chinese bandit and held prisoners while the bandit tortures the American boy to force compliance from the heroine—and gave it the comedy twist in the titles to make it smart, "classy" (abominable word) and modern.

Thus the naive melodramatic values the story originally had have been discounted. The action has good legitimate sex angles, and one comedy scene was splendidly managed—that where the heroine finds she loves the hero, who is tied hand and foot, and experiments with the hitherto unknown thrill of kissing. This was legitimate comedy, but the strained reach for horse laughs, particularly in the titles, was inexcusable, and spoiled what might otherwise have been an effective, direct and simple story.

MY LADY OF WHIMS

Dallas Fitzgerald Production. Starring Clara Bow Distributed by Arrow Pictures Corp. Adapted from the story "Protecting Prudence" by Edgar Franklin. At the New York theatre, June 25, one day. Running time, 64 minutes.

Prudence Severin...............Clara Bow
Wayne Leigh..........Camelia Geraghty
Rolf...................Francis McDonald
Bartley Greer.........Donald Keith
Detective........................Lee Moran

"My Lady Of Whims" is labeled a Dallas Fitzgerald production. Made last year, according to report, for the Arrow program, it stars Clara Bow.

It's a modern story with quite a comedy by-play in which Lee Moran works hard to garner laughs, the material lacking the real grounds for any uproarious fun-making. Even in the big climax scenes they drag away a fling at heroics to build up a laugh. This effort is only good for intermittent laughter.

The story as a whole has been done in a different way by other companies but this one gives Clara Bow considerable latitude to show her screen worth. Miss Bow is capable; she's cute and she's able to make her eyes help her out in many scenes.

Miss Bow has an ingratiating way; there are certain roles she can play to perfection although occasionally this young lady is miscast and then there's harm done to her reputation.

Part of this film is A1 and the other part doesn't "number" at all.

It entertains in spots and at other times burns up a lot of film footage.

It is not a film that anybody will lose any sleep raving about, but it does add credit to Clara Bow's reputation.

The cast in the main handles itself well with Miss Geraghty doing as much as she could with a minor role. Donald Keith works hard to please.

The photography was good. Just another feature.   *Mark.*

Hands Across Border

Independent production distributed by Film Booking Offices. Fred Thompson starred. Story by Frank M. Clifton and directed by David Kirkland. Titles by Malcolm Stuart Boylan. Running time, 60 minutes. At Stanley, New York, June 26, one day.

First rate melodrama of the Mexican border with loads of action, hard riding and story interest well developed. Nothing subtle about it, the picture's address being to the western and unsophisticated fan, and for this purpose the feature is first rate.

It has to do with border smuggling, counterfeiting, "bad men" from the American side, beautiful Spanish heroine, noble American society hero, commandeered in the U. S. Government service, U. S. Border troops, Mexican Rurales, all mixed up in an explosion of dramatica.

One of the features of the picture is the horse "Silver King," a splendid white charger, ingeniously worked into the story.

It is when the hero is in the hands of the counterfeiters he has been sent to catch that "Silver King," riderless, gallops to the spot and drops the plunger with his hoof.

For the rest there is an abundance of hard riding, beautiful settings,

---

a California horse show where the chain of events begins, a Mexican fiesta with dancing features, thrilling bit of horsemanship when the hero dashes through a big city railroad terminal to deposit the heroine on her train and such like incidents.

Several times Silver King is referred to as "she." But what matter these trifles. It's an uproarious melodrama, in which one may revel in unrestrained romance, and the verities of life do not have to enter. The picture makes no pretence to anything else and that is its large virtue.

This one plays romance wide open in the good old style and it gets over 100 percent.

Wehe wenn sie losgelassen

Berlin, June 17.
"Take Care When She Gets Started" is the best German film comedy yet produced. Its reception when shown at the Ufa Palast am Zoo was first-rate, and it looks as though it could hold out for a three weeks' run, an exception at this house. Henny Porten is the star. If the Germans can continue to improve in the making of comedies there seems to be no reason why they should not eventually be able to find a good American market.

The story is not brilliantly original, but is well handled from a technical point of view. The titles are bright throughout and at times get hearty laugh responses on their own. And there are gags of which Harold Lloyd need not be ashamed.

In brief: A wife believes her husband, a business man, does not appreciate her artistic leanings, and she turns to a young Turk named Ali Mocca for sympathy. He is a male gold digger, who seems to live by borrowing money from the husband. To cap the climax, she buys a Hungarian weaving loom, which falls apart, after succeeding in injuring everyone who tries to work it. The husband returns home one evening slightly lit and uses the loom as kindling wood in the fireplace. So the wife leaves home to earn her own living and show that she will not submit to a male tyranny. Ali Mocca, on whose understanding she counted, advises her to return to the financially-sound husband. She leaves him indignantly and tries various positions, among them that of film actress—but without success. She then changes clothes with a dowdy servant girl (a double role played also by the star) and takes a position in her own house. The husband realizes that it is the wife and just when he is about to disclose their to her she substitutes the real servant. So the end is a joke on the husband and a happy reunion.

Henny Porten, Germany's favorite screen star, is known to America through her performance as Ann Boleyn. She has developed into a fine actress and the difference that she makes between her characterization of the real maid and the wife playing the maid is film comedy of the subtlest sort. Unfortunately she is of that stature which is called junoesque. An inexorable 30 pounds stands between her and the American public.

Bruno Kastner gives a very pleasing and smooth performance as the husband, and Kurt Bois as the lounge lizard is superb.

FIG LEAVES

Howard Hawks Production by William Fox. Story by Mr. Hawks and scenario by Hope Loring and Louis D. Lighton. Running time, 68 minutes. Advance showing.

Adam Smith..................George O'Brien
Eve Smith.....................Olive Borden
Alice Atkins..................Phyllis Haver
Josef Andre...............Andre de Beranger
Andre's Assistant..........William Austin
Eddie McSwinggen..........Heinie Conklin

Picture of paramount feminine interest, and high general interest as well, both for subject matter and handling. The story is a novel comedy in treatment, although it might, under different management, have been a melodrama. From all sides it looks like a conspicuous winner because of its many avenues of approach to the fan public.

It deals in a fresh way with the husband and wife debate over clothes; has a startling fashion show done in exquisite color; there is a laughable prolog in the Garden of Eden which is a giggle from start to finish, and it winds up in one of those happy finales. Besides which there is the title, "Fig Leaves."

Story starts off jazzily with the introduction of Adam and Eve at the end of the honeymoon. They have an alarm clock. When a stream of sand fills a balance it drops a cocoanut on Adam's head. He eats grapefruit with a clamshell and the juice squirts in his eye. Over breakfast, the newsboy pitches in a stone newspaper. Adam reads the sporting page. Eve's attention is attracted to the bargain advertisements. This starts the subject of clothes. Eve "hasn't a thing to wear."

The title is "Ever since you ate the apple you've have the gimmies. First it was twin beds and now it's clothes."

They fight the familiar battle until the 8:40 local comes into sight. Sort of flatboat on land drawn by a dinosaur, with a ridge pole down the middle for the straphangers. Eve is an extreme brunet. She sees Adam fall into a semi-flirtation with a blonde commuter and returns to the cave thinking deeply. Enters the Serpent, and Serpent and Eve are deep in conference when the story switches to modern times.

Eve Smith and Adam Smith get along as luxuriously as a boss plumber and his wife would. The Garden of Eden scene is repeated in modern settings up to Adam's departure in wrath from the breakfast table. Then the Serpent enters, but this time disguised as a handsome blonde neighbor from across the hall, a hussy if ever there was one.

Eve is struck by an automobile belonging, as it happens, to the most expensive modist, Andre, in town. Out of this incident Eve gets employment as a model in Andre's shop, all unknown to Adam Smith. The stage is now set for the most elaborate (and most beautiful) fashion show the screen has shown this long time—if it has ever been equaled before is a question. Fox literature avers that Miss Borden's wardrobe cost $50,000, and after seeing the display in colors of the most exquisite toning, one wouldn't dare dispute the ciphers. The fashion salon, of course, gives opportunity for the display of a group of lingerie models which comes within an ace of having the sex kick of a night club show. However, the undraped girls never offend, probably because the whole scene and its background, as well as the models who take part, are of breath-taking beauty.

It so happens that during the salon Adams enters the shop, bent at last upon buying for Eve "the best cloak in town," and while the wife is posing in an evening dress' decollete back, front and otherwise, they come face to face. There is a

---

scene, of course, and Adam declares all bets off. Andre is hovering around during this episode. He has laid siege to Eve without success, and expects much from the departure of the husband. Instead, Eve reverts to the cavewoman, knocks the effeminate dressmaker spinning and flies back to Adam.

In the working out of this action they use the gag of the doctor's wife who was presented with an expensive fur coat. She hocked it, so the story runs, and had her husband redeem it. In the end she got a shabby garment, and the ritzy covering subsequently appeared on the doctor's nurse.

Only, in this case, they throw a new twist into it. It is the blonde from across the hall who suggests the scheme, having the husband find the pawn ticket in the hallway. The blonde neighbor substitutes another pawn ticket calling for a saxophone. When the husband brings home the horn instead of a mink cloak there is an explosion, just as the blonde is seen hurrying out to the pawnshop to gather in the treasure.

The picture is full of similar quick comedy surprises. It is expensively and beautifully mounted. It has subdued horse-play for those who like their laughs rough, and it has certain subtleties that the discriminating will appreciate.

Olive Borden makes a pretty heroine, and in the fashion show episode she is ravishing. Those big, dark, soulful eyes ought to carry her far in the picture field.

It is no trick at all to predict for this production a notable box-office record.

It's the Old Army Game

Famous Players picture by J. P. McEvoy; directed by Edward Sutherland. Starring W. C. Fields. At Strand, New York, week July 4. Running time, 70 minutes.

Elmer Prettywillie...........W. C. Fields
Mildred Marshall.............Louise Brooks
Tessie Overholt..............Blanche Ring
George Parker.............William Gaxton
Sarah Pancoast..................Mary Foy
Mickey.....................Mickey Bennett

A gag picture pure. Just why J. P. McEvoy was named as author is probably because he authored Ziegfeld's "Comic Supplement" (stage) that had more or less than three of W. C. Fields' former revue or vaudeville skits, "The Drug Store," "A Peaceful Morning" and "The Family Flivver" strung together with a bit of real estate romance, a fast moving land promoter who is believed to be a crook but turns out a benefactor, and a chance for Louise Brooks to strut her stuff.

Miss Brooks photographs like a million dollars and shows a screen personality that's "there." This girl is going to land right at the top in the picture racket and is a real bet at this time.

But for a summertime picture "The Old Army Game" is one of those that is pretty sure to send the audience away satisfied. It is replete with laughs, and that is ideal summer fare.

How great its pull at the box office will be is a question, but Fields is the type of screen comedian who can be built up and in time he will mean money.

Gag stuff comes natural to Bill Fields. From this picture he looks to have remembered pretty nearly every gag that he ever saw or heard of, and a great many are utilized. There are certain touches where Miss Brooks is given a chance with a gag scene, which shows the fine Italian hand of Eddie Sutherland, for the gags are a little more of the flapperish type.

The supporting cast doesn't matter much. There is Blanche Ring in a character role, and it's a pity that she was used in it, for B. R. is so well remembered that one hates to see her doing a flapperish old maid. As for Billy Gaxton, his face is great for the screen but his walk and the fact that his head is set rather too close to his shoulders do not make for the best screen appearance.

The story opens with a bedroom scene, with Fields as the village druggist, asleep. An automobile containing a woman is seen coming down the road. The auto and a train just escape a collision and the woman is disclosed ringing the druggist's night bell. He awakes and opens the store. All she wants is a 2c. stamp.

That immediately establishes the picture with the audience as a comedy.

Fields again tries to sleep. Household and tradesmen combine to make his morning nap a restless one. The false alarm brings the fire department swarming into the drug shop, and they all drink sodas when there isn't a fire. A couple come in for a "pint" and Fields has a good gag with an electric fan to ascertain whether or not they are revenue men.

With the real estate movement on he starts on a picnic with the family. They just about manage to wreck a Florida estate with their gags. At the finish Fields with a Ford in New York city is about as funny a gag as has been pulled in a long while.

The picture in reality is Mr. Fields and Miss Brooks; the former for laughs and the latter for sex interest, and that's about all. Between the two the audience is going to be satisfied. *Fred.*

PIECES OF CHINA

San Francisco, July 2.

Isaac O. Upham present "Adventures with picture camera in land of dragon. Travel de luxe, giving moving record of Mr. Upham's 10,000-mile journey covering one year in China." Photographed by Z. E. Shih; titles by Walter Anthony; cut and edited by De Leon Anthony. At Capitol (legit), San Francisco. Opening June 26 to $1 top. Running time, 95 minutes.

Most appealing thing about "Pieces of China" is the titles. They are clever, extremely witty and certain to keep any audience chuckling. Perhaps, the more erudite or curious will insist that they are not as informative as they might be, but **the deadly seriousness of the film itself, the almost schoolroomish exactitude of detail displayed by Mr. Upham in his "shooting" would make a less frivolous treatment in the matter of captions extremely tiring.**

The reaction one gets from "Pieces of China" is that Mr. Upham figuratively poked his camera into every nook and cranny of China. The consequence is that there is a mass of monotonous material, repetitions that are wearying. Besides, he shows only the surface of China. One is denied those little human interest episodes that would be a relief from the eternal geographical scenes.

The film starts with his departure from San Francisco and soon after hits his main subject with the arrival at Shanghai. Then comes Hong Kong. From this point on it hops and skips from one end of the Celestial empire to the other. Apparently, he succumbed to the dictates of vagrant whims. The locations are indicated by a black and white map.

The most interesting scenes were those of the interior of the Imperial summer palace in Peking and the views passing through the gorges of the Yangtzse River. Another incident showing minutely and with a touch of humor the catching of fish with cormorants was worth while.

Out of the eight reels a skillful cutter could assemble two reels of material that probably would make an excellent sub-feature on any regular program. As it stands, it probably never will click with the masses, although it doubtlessly will be of keen interest to non-theatrical exhibitors for school or college showings.

The photography at times is excellent and at others, atrocious, due probably to changing weather conditions.

Preceding the picture, Mr. Upham presented a prolog entitled "The Giant Sword," based on a Chinese legend and featuring in the cast Liu Yu-Ching, an Oriental giant brought to this country by the producer. This Chinese is over eight feet tall and makes his fellow Chinese actors appearing with him in the cast look like pigmies. Beyond that, he was scared to death. Liu Yu-Ching deserved considerable commendation for his histrionic ability. *Rivers.*

FREE LOVE

Produced and distributed by B. P. Schulberg. Cast headed by Clara Bow, Donald Keith and Raymond McKee. Story by Adele Buffington. At the Tivoli, New York, as part of double feature, July 3, one day. Running time, 52 minutes.

Marie Anthony	Clara Bow
James Crawford	Donald Keith
Tony	Raymond McKee
Jack Garner	Hallam Cooley
Otis Crawford	Charles Mailes
Judge Orr	Winter Hall

One of the main characters is a preacher, nothing but a straitlaced, mechanical, inanimate, automaton who seems shackled to convention to the extent of sacrificing one of the "leads" that should have been a "lead" in both action and deed.

One watches Donald Keith doing little as the young clergyman who is running the Settlement house where, according to a caption, exconvicts were going for religion and perhaps reclamation.

Hallam Cooley does some splendid work as the cool, crafty and unscrupulous master of crooks, and Raymond McKee as Tony just about hogs all the acting honors. This man's impersonation of the crippled crook, his smile and change of facial expression go a long way in helping this picture lift up its head.

Clara Bow is in a pretty difficult role, but has been cast so many times as the poor unfortunate who has done a prison stretch that it seems an easy trick for her to again enact Marie Anthony, who though innocent had been sent away just the same.

The picture drags every time the preacher is making sly glances at the girl.

The highlight is the raid on the "Nest," which saved the picture from doing a complete nose dive.

Story may have looked like the Woolworth tower on paper, but as picturized didn't have the punch. That "tame" parson blocked film traffic.

Some of the scenes, like the "third degree" for the girl and the court angle have been done so many times before the camera that they are older than Ann's grandmother. *Mark.*

SHIPWRECKED

Metropolitan Production released by P. D. C. From the play by Langdon McCormick, directed by Joseph Henaberry. Cast includes Seena Owen, Joseph Schildkraut, Matthew Betz, Clarence Burton, Laska Winter, Lionel Belmore, Irwin Connelly. At Loew's New York, double feature bill, July 2. Running time, 69 minutes.

They certainly do "things" to the play that Langdon McCormick produced as "Shipwrecked" on the screen. If McCormick could see the screen version he would never recognize it other possibly than the touch at the opening, where the girl tries to commit suicide.

As a box office attraction it is a pretty fair picture. The direction is rather good, photography fine, and the cast stands up very well, although Joseph Schildkraut does overact at times and is decidedly of the Lou Tellegen school before the camera. It is foolish to have him beat up real huskies in the picture. Seena Owen slipped over the wallop, while Laska Winter as a native girl looks good as a brown skin.

In changing the story they switched it from the New York to the San Francisco waterfront and instead of a steamer have a sailing vessel with the South Sea isles as the objective instead of Africa. The story used for the screen failed to compare with that of the play for real interest. The steamer sinking was far more effective than the sailing schooner.

Mr. Schildkraut is a galley assistant on the boat and the girl an escaped felon, she having shot a man who tried to "make" her and stowed away on the ship. When discovered the captain decides he'd like pleasant companionship on the trip, but before he can start anything there is a storm that virtually wrecks the boat, with the crew and officers putting off in a small boat, leaving the cook, his assistant and the girl on board.

The dismantled hulk finally drifts **to the shore of a south sea trading isle where the two decide to make a new start. The brutal captain appears later and tries to take the girl away, resulting in a fight between the former member of his crew and himself, which can have but one ending for picture purposes.**

The final scene discloses that the girl isn't wanted for a killing after all as the man she shot recovered.

Just so much blah as far as the story is concerned, but fairly well carried out. *Fred.*

NON-STOP FLIGHT

Emory Johnson production released by F. B. O. Story by Emilie Johnson. Directed by Emory Johnson. At the Tivoli, New York (15-25c grind), July 1-2. Running time, 60 minutes.

Lars Larson	Knute Erickson
Anna Larson	Marcella Daly
Marie Larson	Virginia Fry
Jack Nevers	C. Ogden
Jan Johnson	Frank L. Hemphill
Capt. Holm	David Dunbar
Olga Nelson	Peggy O'Neil
Eric Swanson	Bob Anderson
Pilots	Otis Stantz, Skiles Ralph Pope

Melodrama built around the non-stop flight that the U. S. N. fliers made from San Francisco to Hawaii. It is just a hoak meller that will, for the better part, carry in some of the smaller grind houses, but it isn't suited for a longer run, except where it comes in on a double feature bill, as it was at the Tivoli, where it ran two days.

It is a story of a sea captain who returns home to find his wife has left him. In reality she was kidnapped by a rival, but a forged note leads the husband to believe that she left of her own free will. Years later when embittered at the world he is piloting a tramp steamer engaged in the smuggling of Chinamen and opium into Mexico, the captain picks up a girl and an aged man from a desert island, where they have been living for over 20 years, after having been castaway when their sailing vessel was wrecked. The pair are an old sailor and the girl was born on the island. She is the daughter of the captain. He learns the truth just in time to save the girl from the hands of the leader of the Chinamen.

The non-stop flight is worked into the picture through the navy airmen coming down near the island so that the tramp steamer effects the rescue of them as well as the castaways. Just a dash of patriotic stuff to fill in with the meller stuff.

Lot of sea stuff and the news weekly stuff or the original hop-off, together with some fill-in shots, well matched up.

Of the cast Knute Erickson, as **the sea captain, gives a corking character performance, while Bob Anderson, as a comedy character, registered. The story amounts to nothing, and direction only fair.**

The picture looks like one of those things shot in a hurry to take advantage of the flying feat. *Fred.*

The Shamrock Handicap

John Ford production released by William Fox. From the story by Peter B. Kyne. Directed by John Ford. At the Stanley, New York (daily change, 25c. grind), July 1, one day. Running time, 69 minutes.

Sheila Gaffney	Janet Gaynor
Neil Ross	Leslie Fenton
Dennis O'Shea	J. Farrell MacDonald
Sir Miles Gaffney	Louis Payne
Molly O'Shea	Claire McDowell
Martin Finch	Willard Louis
Chesty Morgan	Andy Clark
Benny Ginsberg	Georgie Harris

A racing story as the title would indicate, but not of the usual type of race track tale screened. It is of jumpers, and the scene is Ireland and America.

That let the director, John Ford, in in all his glory. He loves anything Irish, and he made the most of the little human interest touches. **It is as much Ford's direction as anything else that puts this one over, for he did not have a particularly effective cast and his leads did not seem to get across at all.**

From a box office standpoint, the picture has little except for the daily change houses.

An old Irish nobleman has a great love for his home, his hounds, horses and tenants. In fact, he is so considerate of the latter he is facing actual poverty because he will not be hard on them in the matter of rents.

His financial condition finally causes him to dispose of part of his stable to a wealthy American, who also takes his young jockey to America with the horses. The jockey is injured in a race and crippled. While lying ill his former employer and daughter come over from Ireland, bringing with them two of their faithful retainers and their pride, a filly named "Dark Rosaleen." She is entered in the $25,000 Shamrock Handicap, which she wins, and the family fortune is recouped, so that they can all return to Ireland.

Janet Gaynor and Leslie Fenton are the leads, but the best work is by J. Farrell MacDonald, Claire McDowell, Willard Louis and little Georgie Harris. The latter gets a couple of good laughs over in front of the camera. One audience-scream registered was a title in Yiddish allotted him during the running of the great jumping race.

The steeplechase scenes are particularly full of thrills, furnished by the spills horses and jockeys take. *Fred.*

HANDSOME BRUTE

Perfection Production released by Columbia Pictures. Shown at Loew's New York, N. Y., on double feature bill July 2, one day. Running time, 61 minutes.

Melodrama based on the life of a policeman. Here it is a young copper who gums up the works when he gets on the force. After suspended, he rounds up a bunch of crooks and wins his way back.

Hokum for the smaller houses.

The story is rather poorly constructed and the direction leaves much. In general, though, the picture will do on double-feature bills in daily change houses.

At the New York the hard-boiled Roof, audience gave some of the serious portions of the picture the horse laugh Friday night.

The yarn has the young cop assigned to traffic duty, he leaving his post to get a supply of gas for a girl whose car won't run. Then he pinches the same girl that night when she is returning home from a masquerade in boy's clothes and climbing the porch to her father's home.

Of course, dad is the big jeweler of the town, and it is his business place the crooks have centered on.

This one could be titled into a comedy and be just as good. *Fred.*

Bigger Than Barnum's

Film Booking Office production, presented by Joseph P. Kennedy, featuring Ralph Lewis, Viola Dana, George O'Hara and Ralph Ince. Mr. Ince also directed, assisted by Doran Cox. Adapted by J. Grubb Alexander from the story by Arthur Guy Empey. At the Colony, New York, opening July 10. Running time, 60 minutes.

Peter Blandin.................Ralph Lewis
Robert Blandin...............George O'Hara
Juanita Calles.................Viola Dana
Carl Rabelle...................Ralph Ince
Princess Bonita.............Lucille Mendez
Jack Ranglin................Dan Nakarenko
"Bill" Hartnett.................George Holt
Ringmaster....................."Bill" Knight
Doctor.........................Rod Hathaway

A straightforward tale of the circus with romance, sentiment and a thrill, wholly clean but without a decided punch, for the story or the box office, other than to those who want to see a circus picture. For the latter this will be readily acceptable. However, it's strong enough in its romantic and heroic ends to stand up as a first run, for the intimacy of the circus backstage and under the big top as displayed means a continuous line of action.

Any recognized circus title was carefully cut out in the scenes from the wagons or the banners. Some of the interior tent scenes seemed studio, both as to interiors and rigging, while some drops appeared frequently. For the circus illusion portion the Barnes Circus and Barnes Zoo (coast) may have been especially employed.

Just now there are three circus pictures on the screen or about to be marketed. That is exclusive of "Variety," the German-made, just issued through Famous Players. If "Bigger Than Barnum's" follows in "Variety" anywhere, a hook-up could be made in publicity for this F. B. O. through a singular coincidence between the two pictures. In "Variety" the big aerial feat is accomplished without the aid of a net underneath and a net is not mentioned nor referred to, while in this "Barnum" picture, the story hinges upon the circus's proprietor demanding that his aerial wire act, 80 feet high, go through the act without the net, previously seen.

There are three in the Blandin wire turn, father, son and adopted girl, with the father the carrier. Upon the owner deciding there must be a danger draw to lift up the drooping business and selects the Blandin act to work without a net, the son, also a walker, refuses to accede, saying he will not endanger the girl's life. But the owner calls the son a quitter and appeals to the father's vanity, with the girl saying she will always go with her daddy.

Doing the act at the night show and without the net for the first time, the father falters, falls, and as he crashes downward to permanent disability, the girl catches the wire, regaining the strand and walking to the perch in safety.

The son, disgraced, called a "sawdust rat" for "quitting," becomes a wanderer but hanging around on the edge of his old companions. It leads to the second and final big scene, where the father is caught in a fire trap as the hotel burns, while the show is in winter quarters, and his daughter is there practicing.

Crippled, the father manages to drag himself to the roof and is on a ledge as the ladders are removed, firemen believing all are out. The son, watching the fire as a casual bystander, spies him. Climbing a telegraph ladder, he does the very thing he was accused of being yellow for refusing when it would risk the girl he loved. From the top of the telegraph pole he walks to the ledge on a wire, takes his father on his shoulders and returns to the pole.

Well cast in the principal (featured) roles, the players do nicely. Something of the story may have been lost through attention to circus

scenes but the adaptation has been smoothly done and the continuity holds the interest, also real suspense at a couple of junctures.

Viola Dana made a pleasant looking circus acrobat at times. At other times the photography is not so flattering to Miss Dana. She might ask for a couple of the negative shots to be taken out of the reel. One particularly is very poor.

Mr. O'Hara, playing the son, did very well in an agreeable juvenile role and looked his part. Ralph Lewis of course is standard.

Mr. Ince, who ably directed, though he did skip the startling as well as not falling for a box office punch through off-side stuff, left him with an even directorial score, but he gave his acting part a percentage boost by doing a big headed acrobat to a nicety and just escaping any villainy in it. Rather a good combination here for Ince, coming out better than would be expected.

This picture holds the film debut of Lucille Mendez, from musical comedy, and who married the same Ralph Ince last week. On the screen she is a performer, having but one bit of consequence, in the cook tent, where she slaps Ince's face for "feeling" although a monkey underneath the table was the culprit. Miss Mendez's brunet type cameraed rather well and one of the captions fitted her stage style of expression. Miss Mendez looks good enough to secure a picture place, plus intelligence in work.

Dan Nakarenko seemed by nature made to be a circus showman and boss of the lot.

"Bigger Than Barnum's" as here expounded as a title has no excuse, although it fits the picture for descriptive purposes.

F. B. O. appears to have the jump for this as a circus picture and should take full advantage of it. Steam should be put on the exploitation. It's questionable whether a circus picture should see the screen in the summertime when the tent shows are travelling. "Barnum" though, is good enough to show at any time. Technically it will interest show people and sentimentally all of the others, even the hard-boileds. *Sime.*

MEN OF STEEL

First National production. Milton Sills starred with Doris Kenyon featured. Directed by George Archainbaud. Story adapted by Sills from R. G. Kirk's short story "United States Flavor." At the Strand, New York, week July 11. Running time, 90 minutes.

Jan Bokak......................Milton Sills
Mary Berwick...............Doris Kenyon
Clare Pitt....................Mae Allison
Peter Masarick..........Victor McLaglen
Zachary Pitt..............Frank Currier
Captain Hooker Grimes....George Fawcett
Anton Berwick..................John Kolb
Frazer...........................Harry Lee
Wolfe..........................Henry West
Alex.........................Taylor Graves

A 10-reel picture, a big picture with some faults but so many thrilling virtues it should stand up beautifully as a de luxe program feature.

Its demerits may be set down as being in lengthiness and comedy, both deplorable. The story could be improved by tightening up, as it is strong, while the comedy consists of long distance spitting matches between two old fellows. The subtitles contain the words "spit," "out-spit," etc. This about ends the bad features, and both could be eliminated without hurting a handsomely produced film.

Locale is of the steel mills and concerns Jan Bokak, a young Bohemian, apparently, first seen working in the ore section of Minnesota. When the brother of his girl Mary is slain, he takes the blame to save someone else, but escapes capture and flees on one of the ore steamers. He is discovered by the ship's captain but a few minutes later he saves the captain's life, so the captain, though thinking him a mur-

derer, protects him instead of turning him over.

This captain, an old boyhood friend of the steel mill owner, Zachary Pitt, asks Pitt to give the man a job, but Jan, independent and filled with resentment toward any industrial baron, spurns the offer and tells them he'll get his own job. He does. His application to work and continuous studying after hours have advanced him to an important post on the hearth floor of the mill. Jan is also a leader of the men, preaching mild radicalism.

Pitt notices and admires him. When the "Red" agitators are successful in causing a great accident in the mills, Jan is hurt and taken to Pitt's home.

In convalescence, he meets Pitt's daughter, Claire, who admires his he-man vitality. Meantime, his old sweetheart Mary discovers that Pitt is really her father. After the death of her mother she comes to make known the facts. And as she enters the Pitt home she sees her Jan; now called John Brook, kissing Claire, for they are to be married. When Jan sees Mary, it is off for a while. When later accused of being a murderer, he runs to the mills to get the man who lied about him, and as a half-crazed crane operator attempts to pour molten steel upon them, the real murderer confesses. For a finale, Jan and his real sweetheart, Mary, now established as Pitt's daughter, are married, while Claire goes happily back to an old love.

Included among the thrills are the many industrial scenes; molten steel in its red, flaming color, also in the white heat state; the crash of a water tower into the molten steel with the subsequent spattering of the vicious liquid over many people (badly done in miniature but effective); and most impressive of all, the burial of a man who fell into a pot of molten metal.

Cast is excellent, with Doris Kenyon turning in a fine performance, displaying emotional stuff of high calibre. May Allison, as the other sister, never looked better in her hey-day of popularity, and from this film it would seem that Miss Allison's comeback is already a distinguished and decided success. Milton Sills as Jan is vigorous and adequate, although a bit prosaic once they take him from the rough clothes. Frank Currier and George Fawcett do well as the old fellows. Direction is fair, but that hardly matters, as the steel mill shots plus the story would carry this film through.

"Men of Steel" qualifies as a corker. *Sisk.*

THE TWO-GUN MAN

F. B. O. release, starring Fred Thomson and "Silver King." Story by Stuart Edward White. At Warner's, New York, week July 10. Running time, 71 minutes.

Dean Randall...............Fred Thomson
Dad Randall...................Joe Dowling
Ivor Johnson................Sheldon Lewis
Bowie Hill....................Frank Hagney
Texas Pete...................Ivar McFadden
Grace Stickley...........Olive Hasbrough
Dad Stickley...........William Courtwright
Billy Stickley...................Billy Butts
Sheriff Dalton...............Arthur Millet
Quong...........................Willie Fung

Fred Thomson has finally hit Broadway in a de luxe presentation house. His first picture is so far ahead of the majority of the rank and file westerns he has appeared in along the street in the daily change houses as far as story is concerned that he deserves the chance on the Main Street.

The box office return for the star won't be as big at this house as it should be, as the house is battling against the lack of a cooling system, although one is being installed, and Thomson's Broadway debut was made on one of the hottest days of the year.

But when this picture hits the towns that are Thomson's

element, boy, you are going to hear 'em rave. It will only be proof of what a real story can do for someone who is already a favorite with a reputation built up on mediocre stories.

Thomson and his horse, "Silver King," are a natural set-up for the towns that like western stuff, and most of them do outside of the big cities. That horse, with his name, is also a natural set-up for a publicity stunt, and with a date set for Thomson on Broadway far enough in advance it would have been a corking tie-up to have brought Thomson and the horse to New York with the Silver King water people in for a campaign, using the horse and the picture star as feeder to the regular advertising for the picture.

Another thing noticeable about this picture is the cast supporting the star. Sheldon Lewis is a corking heavy, and he more than makes good here, while Joe Dowling and Frank Hagney also lend excellent support.

It looks as though Olive Hasbrough is a comer. This girl appears to have a corking screen personality, and she certainly looks good in a role that doesn't give her anything too much to do. She will bear watching.

The story of "The Two-Gun Man" has all the action that any of the most rabid fans can demand. It starts with the return of the hero from France. He is in overseas uniform. On the way to the ranch of his father he sees his horse waiting for him, all saddled and ready to go. The horse is credited with knowing that his owner was returning that day. They might just as well have credited the animal with saddling and bridling himself. But as the youngster leaps to the animal's back from the touring car the action begins.

He is off across country, and from the heights of a cliff overlooking the desert he sees a water-hole tender shoot down the horse of a wagon train. From the distance of at least 1,000 yards Thomson with a revolver shoots the rifle out of his hands, and then as he reaches for it again clips the trigger off with another bullet. That's some shooting, kid, but the fans liked it. Of course, there is a girl in the wagon with her father, and the two have the three kiddies of a dead sister with them. At first the hero suspects the "family" belongs to the girl, but he is soon set aright.

Then the boy goes home, meets his dad, and finally becomes aware of the fact that dad has been trimmed by a bunch of rustlers, who not only have run off his cattle, but have obtained a mortgage on the ranch and are evicting the old man.

It causes the death of Randall, senior, and the boy swears to avenge him, but is stopped by the girl. Instead of committing murder he starts running off the cattle again. Finally, when the head of the rustlers offers $10,000 reward for the return of his cattle, the boy promises to deliver them, and does, atop of that running the real rustlers into the hands of the sheriff, leaving things right for a final fade-out for himself and the girl, who the rustler chief had locked in a room at his ranch.

Some great chase stuff and wild riding and some of the photographic composition is all that could be desired. The shots are all sharp and the photography itself particularly good throughout.

A couple of more stories like this for Thomson and the chances are that he'll become a regular Broadway fixture in westerns, for at present the only other western riding star that gets a chance at all on the Main Stem is Tom Mix, and before him there was not one but Bill Hart. *Fred.*

MANTRAP

Victor Fleming production for Famous Players. Featuring Ernest Torrence, Clara Bow and Percy Marmont. From the novel by Sinclair Lewis, adapted by Adelaide Heilbron. At the Rivoli, New York, week July 10. Running time, 68 minutes.

Joe Easter.................Ernest Torrence
Alverna.........................Clara Bow
Ralph Prescott.............Percy Marmont
E. Wesson Woodbury......Eugene Pallette
Curly Evans.................Tom Kennedy
Mrs. McGavvity.........Josephine Crowell
Mr. McGavvity.........William Orlamond
Lawrence Jackfish.........Charles Stevens
Mrs. Barker.................Miss Du Pont
Stenographer................Charlot Bird

Clara Bow! And how! What a "mantrap" she is!

And how this picture is going to make her! It should do as much for this corking little ingenue lead as "Flaming Youth" did for Colleen Moore.

Miss Bow just walks away with the picture from the moment she steps into camera range. Every minute that she is in it she steals it from such a couple of corking troupers as Ernest Torrence and Percy Marmont. Any time a girl can do that she is going some. In this particular role, that of a fast-working, slang-slinging manicurist from a swell barber shop in Minneapolis, who marries the big hick from "Mantrap," she is fitted just like a glove.

The picture itself is a wow for laughs, action and corking titles.

The story deals with a lawyer who is a divorce specialist, sick and tired of vamping females who come to his office with their troubles. To be rid of them he decides to go up into the Canadian wilds. His office neighbor takes him on the trip and in less than a week the two are at loggerheads.

The contrast to the lawyer characterization is shown in the owner of a trading store in the lonely country, who is woman-hungry and who goes to Minneapolis, wins himself the flip little manicure girl and takes her back to the wilds. There she is a trig little flapper, bobbed tresses, lipstick and powder puff and all the usual rolled stocking touches, practicing her flirting on the "untamed hes of the wide open," and boy, how she vamps with her lamps! And how they fall!

It is the storekeeper who comes across the campers just about the time when they are ready to kill each other. He decides he'll take the lawyer back with him to the trading post. He figures the law shark will be good company for the wife. When the lawyer gets a flash at her he just about shrivels. He keeps battling her wiles as long as he can. Finally she is too much for him, and he decides to go back and rejoin his camping companion, but the girl will have none of that. She's going too. When he refuses to take her she marches off down the trail herself and plants herself in his way as he comes along.

The two are finally lost when their Indian guide deserts them and are overtaken by the more or less irate husband, who sees the humor of the situation, although he has been played fast and loose with up to a certain point. Instead of shooting the man, he decides that he had better let his wife go to the big city for a vacation. This she does, stealing their boat and leaving both the men flat.

The final shot shows the lawyer back in civilization. A blond client is waiting for him in his private office, and it looks as though he is due to fall again. Back in the wilds the hick hubby is shown peeling his own potatoes while a neighboring trader and his wife are telling him he should be glad that he is rid of the flapper wife, he in turn defending her when she opens the door in all her flapper glory and applauds hubby.

While still in his arms receiving her return greeting she looks over his shoulder and spies a good-looking Royal Mounted Policeman and immediately starts giving him the eye. It is a wow of a finish.

Torrence is the hick hubby, while Marmont is the lawyer. These three carry all the principal action, with the balance of the cast doing fill-in bits. *Fred.*

SON OF THE SHEIK

Los Angeles, July 9.

John W. Considine production, directed by George Fitzmaurice, released through United Artists. Starring Rudolph Valentino and Vilma Banky. Pre-view engagement, with announcement picture will not be shown elsewhere within four months. At Million Dollar, Los Angeles. Running time, 70 minutes.

Ahmen, and The Sheik..Rudolph Valentino
Yasmin.........................Vilma Banky
Andre.......................George Fawcett
Ghabah.......................Montague Love
Ali...........................Bull Montana
Sheik's Wife..................Agnes Ayres

Los Angeles is given a four months' jump on the rest of the theatrical world in viewing Rudolph Valentino in his return to the role of a sheik.

In "The Son of a Sheik" Valentino not only is the dashing youth of the Arabian plains but he also plays his father, the Sheik. The double-exposure shots are not as clear as is possible in modern day photography. Naturally, the "son" is the predominating character, and in this role Valentino wins new laurels.

"The Son" is a sequal to "The Sheik," adapted by Francis Marion from the novel by E. M. Hull. It is best described as an interesting study in psychology, showing how a son of the Desert inherited the love, passions and hate of his father.

Valentino's love-making is of the passionate sort—the kind adored by flappers and even the more mature patron, but in this particular picture most of his work is devoted to a passionate hate.

Agnes Ayres, as a compliment to the star, reappears as the wife of the sheik. It is she who points out to the sire that he, alone, is to be blamed for any wildness or stubborness by the son.

Some exceptionally fine photography, especially the desert scenes, and the excellent acting of the supporting cast help to make "The Son of the Sheik" an outstanding success.

The story concerns the infatuation of the son for a dancing girl with a traveling aggregation of mountebanks. When surprised by her followers, including her father and a passionate admirer, and held for ransom, the son of the sheik is led to believe he has been tricked by the girl, which engenders hatred and a determination for revenge.

Valentino kidnaps the girl and takes her to his desert camp, where he submits her to humiliation and pain, refusing to heed her pleas of innocense.

At this juncture the father, angered by his son's disobedience in going into the desert, invades the son's tent, only to meet a stubborn resistence from the embittered youth.

But the sire finally convinces the boy he must let the girl go. She is sent away under escort. Her father and gang surprise them and the escort then learns the truth, that it was not the girl who betrayed the son but her villainous admirer with the traveling troupe.

The girl is returned to the dance hall whither Valentino once more follows her, this time in a repentant and humiliated mood.

There is a bitter fight, with plenty of knife play, the son of the sheik finally emerging unscathed, and with the girl again in his arms.

The new Valentino picture should go a long way to once more endear "the sheik" with picture fans.

SCRAPPIN' KID

Blue Streak Western starring Art Accord. Universal production. Story and scenario by E. Richard Schayer. Clifford S. Smith, director. At the Arena, New York, one day, July 12. Running time, 49 minutes.

Another Blue Streak Western. Short, snappy, and capable of exciting, as are its brothers.

Story of the hero, orphan girl, village gossipers, train robbers, reward offered for their capture, beaten up and captured by hero, collecting of reward by hero, paying off of mortgage with reward money by hero and clinch by orphan girl and hero.

Also forest fire, advances of robbers to orphan girl, kid brother, sheriff, banker's mean son, horse, dog and cow. Not to omit a dying mother.

A perfectly formal but enjoyable "western."

Art Accord is the hero. He is likeable and a hard rider. Velma Connor, typical "Western" heroine, is pretty and a neat actress. C. E. Anderson does the heavy.

Others in cast are Jess Delffbach, "Hack" Bell, Jimmy Boudwin and Edmund Cobb. Also "Buddie" and "Rex," Accord's well-trained horse and dog.

A forest fire, giving the cinema a speedy start, looks like the real thing and is good.

Shown as half of a double bill on 8th avenue, New York. As entertainment it had for its running mate an old tale of love in society and jungle atmosphere, beaten by a mile.

SHE

Lee-Bradford (English) production, featuring Betty Blythe. Adapted from novel of same title by Sir Rider Haggard with captions written by author. At Tivoli, New York, as half double bill. One day, July 7. Running time, 64 minutes.

Marcus Loew may take justification for his recent remarks to British producers and exhibitors on English-made pictures, on this English production, "She." Mr. Loew says if the English will send over good pictures they will find distribution. "She" is not one that will. As half of a double feature bill for one day at the Tivoli (Eighth avenue and 51st street), it may have cost the house $7.50 in rental, $7 too much.

A direct fault here and with everything else all wrong diverging from that is the one who decided "She" could be converted into a commercial film. With the book one of the best sellers of its day, that day was long ago, and in this day "She" in celluloid could never sell one copy of the H. Rider Haggard novel (with the H dropped as the Sir was conferred). The burning hit, as in the stage play, may have been depended upon for the kick. But it didn't mean enough in its draped nakedness.

Betty Blythe and Carlyle Blackwell are the two Americans in the cast, and leads, with Leander Cordova directing. Many may blame the director for the complete cipher made of "She" as a picture, but every demerit may be traced to the impossible story, except the terrible photography.

To make a serious pretense of a woman living 2,000 years is the first wallop given the film story and that wound it up right there. Afterward, although the director, actors and the rest went on in their serious vein, it was just a laugh for the roof audience at the Tivoli.

The scenes are merely a series of mythical, mystical strangenesses that never convince, never should have been tried in straight picture making, and only result in this picture being another slam against the British film industry.

Some while ago Miss Blythe went over to England to make pictures.

This may be the one she later started a salary suit over.

"She" (She-who-must-be-obeyed) was made entirely in the studio or on the north coast of Ireland, if Ireland has a north coast. The story plunges into a cannibal country where the flesh-eaters look like blackface comedians, acting even worse. A set fashion over there is that if a girl kisses a man and he returns the caress, unsolicited, they are married. Not a bad scheme for the girls, but dangerous over here, since the advent of automobiles, dark nights and lightless roads.

A column could be employed to detail the errors of this production, in everything, from settings, to acting, lighting and direction, besides mob scenes and range shots. But as a picture it is not entitled to over an inch in notice and only is receiving more through being English.

"She" may have been shown on this side before, possibly on states rights, in the shooting galleries for cheapness. It deserved no more nor that much. No record of it is in Variety's files nor is any previous local exhibition recalled. Also unlikely it will annoy any other New York audience. *Sime.*

THE NIGHT PATROL

F.B.O. release starring Richard Talmadge. Produced by A. Carlos. Story by F. H. Clark, and directed by Mason Noel. At the Ideal, New York, as half of double feature bill, one day, July 7. Running time, 60 minutes.

Dick Bradley	Richard Talmadge
His Mother	Mary Carr
The Girl	Rose Blossom
The Boy	Gardner James
The "Duke"	Victor Dillingham
His Girl	Grace Darmond

Richard Talmadge is now making his productions for release through Universal. In "The Night Patrol" he tries to be both a character actor and an acrobat. He is a better acrobat or stunt man.

The story has him as an Irish cop, in love with a girl. This girl's brother got in with crooks and the young cop himself arrested the boy as a murderer. Convinced the boy was guilty only on flimsy circumstantial evidence, the cop disguises himself as the Frisco Kid, crook, and by the aid of a cracked lip, putty nose and rough clothes, gets in with the crook gang which he believes guilty. He brings them to justice and at the last minute saves the girl's brother from electrocution.

The film isn't breezy except in spots, and a somewhat tragic theme pervades. Talmadge, though an excellent stunt man, isn't good enough actor to carry off the heavier moments, so the picture loses some of its effect.

Okeh for a day in the smaller houses, but not up to the usual Talmadge release. *Sisk.*

Hearts and Spangles

Presented by Sam Sax for Lumas Pictures Corp. A Gotham production. Story by Norman Houston and directed by Frank O'Connor. Wanda Hawley featured. Supervised by Renaud Hoffman.

Rex Barclay	George Chesbro
Bill Adams	Charles Force
Steve Carris	Robert Gordon
Peter Carris	Larry Steers
Grace Carris	Barbara Tennant
Dr. Carris	Eric Mayne
Harry Riley	J. P. Lockney
Bobby	Frankie Darro
Peg Palmer	Wanda Hawley

A poor story made into a poor picture with a fairish cast.

It is a circus yarn. A boy chucked out of college wants to go with the circus. He approaches the equestrian director, and that worthy tells him he can be a roustabout.

He falls in love with Peg Palmer, the bareback rider, and sticks with the show and the girl until the circus reaches his home town, where he tells his father of the expulsion, only to find that expulsion from school means expulsion from home. So he signs with the circus once more and soon becomes, so the subtitles run, "The King of Clowns" (although the picture only showed him doing stuff that a self-respecting clown wouldn't attempt).

The boy's romance with the bareback rider gets more and more serious, but the equestrian director, a mean sort of a guy, tries at every opportunity to hurt the girl.

Even in the ring, with her horse going around, he lashes her feet and, despite that equestrian directors aren't really that bad, it seems that this fellow attempts to act as though he was a small-town cutthroat in misplaced atmosphere.

His final mean act is to let the lions loose. One gets him and the other one almost ruins the young clown, but once the boys get after the lions, they run right into their cages and act like tired, toothless lions ought to act.

Wanda Hawley is the bareback rider, but about all Wanda did on the horse was to sit quietly while it walked slowly. Wanda's years are taking their toll. Robert Gordon was fair as the hero, and Frankie Darro turned in nice work as the kid.

Where circus details are concerned, this one is all wet; and, in addition, it's not very entertaining. At best, a daily change or half of a double bill for the galleries. *Sisk.*

Millionaire Policeman

Independent by Samuel L. Briskin, distributed through Banner. Production directed by Edward La Saint. Herbert Rawlinson featured, with Eva Novak playing opposite. Running time, 62 minutes. At the New York theatre, July 9, one half double bill, one day.

Starting with the title, the offering is full of crudities such as might suggest that it is the work of an inexperienced promoter. It has been made economically except for the cast, which represents a considerable sum, the people mostly being of note.

As a sample of the ineptitude that characterizes the whole feature it might be cited that emphasis is placed from the beginning on the fact that both the leading characters are typically Irish. But when they get to the "happy ending" before the altar, it is apparently a Protestant Episcopal minister instead of a priest who marries them.

The film has a scattered few of brisk action, but between the progress of the story lags lamentably. At the very beginning there is a sensational bit of riding. A girl friend of the hero is on horseback when her mount runs away over broken, mountainous country. The hero fails in courage to make the rescue, while a mounted policeman, by a daring exhibition of breakneck riding, does the trick.

Toward the finish the movement quickens, when there is a fire and the hero—who has now overcome his cowardice—makes a brave rescue which re-establishes him with his rich father and wins him the gal. Between times the story, if foggy, moves forward about as much by the titles as by actual happenings in action and besides is scarcely worth the telling. Picking the blonde and stoic Eva Novak for a peppy Irish heroine was not such good judgment either. Introducing a hero in an act of cowardice makes a poor start, and laying the scenes in humble surroundings doesn't give the story any added value.

A cop as a romantic hero is rather out of the conventional. There's nothing particularly gripping in the title "The Millionaire Policeman" that would make the populace rush to the gate, especially when there probably is usually an opposition around the corner advertising a picture called "Her Flaming Sin," with posters and billing to match the title. It is a fair presumption that the film was made for the lowest admission price houses. Even before that clientele it wouldn't get far. It's just one of those films that fans forget.

THE BIG SHOW

Made by Miller Bros. of "101 Ranch" from the story by L. Case Russell. George Terwilliger and distributed by Associated Exhibitors. John Lowell, principal cowboy with the show, and Evangeline Russell, also a member of the Wild West outfit, are featured. Running time, 65 minutes. At the New York July 9, one day, as one-half double bill.

Naive story of love and intrigue has been woven about the Miller Bros. "101 Ranch" Wild West show, with the wild west itself as a background and the regular people employed in the exhibition taking part. This includes John Lowell, Evangeline Russell, who works the elephants, and Joe Miller himself playing the part of Col. Jim, the circus proprietor, a minor part.

The players do not know much about pantomimic acting for the camera, and they don't look much like screen players, but this is an advantage rather than otherwise, adding as it does to the naive sincerity of the play.

"Naive" describes the production, but that only makes it more effective. All the neck-breaking feats of the Miller riders are worked somehow into the story. Almost the entire show is given, at one time or another, but always with the excuse that it ties up with the story.

For example, the "heavy" plots to rob the hero's trunk of "the papers" and naturally he picks the moment of the grand entry for the coup. Naturally, the excuse is sufficient for shots of the stirring "spec" of the show. At another point the heroine's baby sister is charged by a wild bull that escapes from a pen. Who should save the child but the hero? He does the trick by leaping from his horse to the neck of the bull and throwing the beast in full career.

For the climax they work in the elephant. The heavy has earned the big animal's hatred by feeding it a lighted cigar. Then when the villain is about to desert the woman he has pledged himself to wed, in a ceremony in the arena, the elephant breaks its chains and rushing into the crowded field, snatches the groom from the side of his bride and tears him to pieces. This bit of super-melodrama is capitally managed. The elephant reaches for the villain and seems to whip the man himself through the air and then trample him into the ground. A dummy is used, of course, but the substitutition is so well done the realistic effect is there.

There are many interesting views of circus life, such as a multitude of yoked oxen, aided by two elephants and gangs of men getting big circus wagons off a soft lot; the pictures of loading and unloading in the train yards and the dressing tent episodes all sustain interest, while the interpolated bits of the wild west show itself, with the wild riding cowboys, Indians and the like add a good deal to the feature.

Some amusing comedy is interspersed. One of the Indian chiefs with folded arms and impassive face is shown in majestic pose. The view broadens until it is shown that he is dictating a letter to his mission-educated daughter who takes it down on the typewriter. The letter instructs his bank in Oklahoma to credit him with oil royalties immediately to cover his checks drawn for a new runabout for his daughter. The clowns also are introduced into the action, Stump, the mule riding comic, playing the part of a sinister conspirator. This last twist has its own humor.

The romantic side of the film is somewhat injured by the fact that cowboy actors are notorious bad lovers on stage and screen, as well as in novels, the world over. Whatever the picture does, of course, will be velvet for Joe Miller and his enterprise, for it is worth while as an advertisement for the show. Aside from this it is a novel screen attraction from several angles, and well might stand on its own merits.

S-O-S-

Full title, "S-O-S Perils of the Sea." A Columbia picture, produced by Harry Cohn. Story by Tom Hopkins and directed by James P. Hogan. At the Arena, New York, for one day (July 7). Running time, 61 minutes.

Features Elaine Hammerstein. It is a heavy, ponderous, melodramatic piece, relying on two sinkings of ocean liners, one at the beginning of the picture and the other in climax for its kick. Joining the two disasters are some 45 minutes of story, not first rate.

A little girl-heiress is picked up at sea, after the boat on which she was crossing the ocean sunk (first sinking) by a sailing vessel, on which are two brothers, one good and other bad.

Growing up she learns to love the boy who is good, thereby creating the story's love interest. The villainous section is supplied by the bad brother. The bad 'un learns that she is heiress to the millions of a marine magnate, who had died, leaving orders with his right hand man to find the girl and give her the fortune.

Right hand man would get the dough if the girl isn't found—and he wants it.

The whole business ends in the final shipwreck with the bad brother confessing, as villains do.

Miss Hammerstein has become stouter. Her acting is still good, her change being only in appearance. She always did need a first-rate script to prove her acting ability. In this layout she is at a disadvantage. Robert Ellis is the male lead opposite.

The sinking of the first boat was superior to the second. The second vessel went down too fast. The bow tipped up too soon.

For comedy an old and devoted salt is continually bothered with flies. His line, "Where do flies go in the winter?" runs through the picture as a theme song. It fails to create laughs after the first dozen times.

THE SET UP

Universal blue streak western, featuring Art Acord. Story by L. V. Jefferson. Direction Clifford Smith. Running time, 58 minutes. At Arena, New York, July 1, one day.

A neat story of the brave sheriff who pursues the murderers of his sweetheart's father. What particularly distinguishes it is that it has an especially effective comedy turn in the use of a gang of boys who worship the hero, and in their efforts to imitate him help in running down the guilty desperadoes.

Some good surprises of a comedy nature through this story, so much so that this angle at times overshadows the romantic sub-plot.

For the rest the picture has hard riding, beautiful backgrounds and a trick horse. First-rate feature for a double bill, in which capacity it served at the Arena. Alta Allen is the heroine.

My Lady's Lips

Produced by B. P. Schulberg and released on a state's right basis. Directed by James Hogan. Alyce Mills, William Powell and Clara Bow featured. At the Ideal, New York, as half of a double feature bill, one day, July 7. Running time, 65 minutes.

Newspaper Owner..........Frank Keenan
His Daughter..........Clara Bow
Rita Blake..........Alyce Mills
Scott Seddon..........William Powell
Gault..........Mathew Betz
Smike..........Ford Sterling
Police Inspector..........John Sainpolis
Kit..........Gertrude Short

A hokum filled independent, produced with an excellent cast but rather tawdrily made. Crook story is interesting and exciting, so "My Lady's Lips" qualifies for daily changes and the cheaper combination houses.

The story is of a newspaper reporter who goes out to round up a gang of crooks, gets into their underground dwelling place, falls in love with a girl, eventually rounds up the gang, but lets this girl go free because she saved his life.

This girl, Rita Blake, was especially wanted by the police, so when the reporter couldn't produce her he went to jail for a year and she got free. The newspaper and the police, because he wouldn't produce the girl, figured that he had double-crossed them.

After released the reporter finds the girl is running a gambling house. In he walks and although he doesn't see her she sees him and orders the wheel fixed so he'll win. He does, and a great pile. A patron, sore because the hero usurped his place at the table, pulls a gun and fires. The girl jumps and gets the shot in the arm. As a fadeout she asks the man if he'll kiss the lips that once lied about him.

Alyce Mills is the girl and does good work. William Powell is badly miscast as the hero, he being the villain type. Clara Bow has nothing to do, ditto Gertrude Short, Frank Keenan and some of the others. But the cast as a whole performs well and puts the story over. Cutting would have helped the speed.

Schulberg probably made this one quite a while ago when independently producing. *Sisk.*

Her Honor the Governor

F. B. O. Production, presented by Joseph P. Kennedy. Story by Hy Daab and Weed Dickenson. Directed by Chet Withey. Pauline Frederick starred. At Warner's, New York, week July 17. Running time, 66 minutes.

Adele Fenway..........Pauline Frederick
Bob Fenway..........Carrol Nye
Marian Lee..........Greta Von Rue
Richard Palmer..........Tom Santschi
Jim Dornton..........Stanton Heck
Snipe Collins..........Boris Karloff

Melodrama of love and politics with a woman Governor placed in the spot where the old man usually was.

In some respects except for this change the story resembles a play at Weber's some years ago.

This is, however, good melodrama for the average picture audiences away from the big towns, with Pauline Frederick playing the mother role to perfection.

The question now remains whether or not Miss Frederick will retain her box office draw. With the middle aged and the more elderly role she undoubtedly still continues to have something of a hold, but a couple of flappers in the audience at Warner's expressed themselves adversely Saturday night.

Miss Frederick looks as good as ever on the screen, and that is going some, for she always was a mighty good-looking woman. When it comes to acting she has it so far over a lot of those the flappers go nuts over that one could never make comparisons.

The story opens with Miss Frederick as Adele Fenway making her inauguration speech on taking over the office of Governor of a state. The senior state senator, Jim Dornton (Stanley Heck) lets her know immediately he is going to be governor in fact and that she is merely a figurehead. But when she turns the tables on him and blocks the passage of one of his pet measures he turns on her. His first trick is to find the first wife of her late husband and let it be known that the state has a Governor who is an unwed mother, for the husband forgot to go through the formality of a divorce. All a part of the frame-up.

When the Governor's son seeks out the Senator to demand an apology a fight follows and later, when one of those involved in the scrap is found killed, the boy is accused of murder. While the mother-governor is fighting for her boy's life, she is impeached, but at the last minute the real murderer is discovered, likewise the records of the divorce of the first wife, and from then on all is smooth sailing.

It is a fairly good story and built as it is on woman's activity politically it has at this time a special value with "Ma" Ferguson breaking into print so often that they might almost hook this one up with "Ma."

The cast, while not particularly strong in names outside of Miss Frederick's, and Tom Santschi, has a couple of fairly good players in it. The juvenile lead is capably handled by Carrol Nye and Boris Karloff does a very good drug addict heavy. *Fred.*

THE PLASTIC AGE

B. P. Schulberg production for Preferred Pictures. Released through Commonwealth Film Corp. (Independent). Adapted from the Percy Marks best seller by Eve Unsell and Frederica Sagor. Directed by Wesley Ruggles. Allen Siegler and Gilbert Warrenton, photographers. Clara Bow featured. At Colony, New York, week July 21. Running time not taken, between 50 and 60 minutes.

Cynthia Day..........Clara Bow
Hugh Carver..........Donald Keith
Mrs. Carver..........Mary Alden
Henry Carver..........Henry B. Walthall
Carl Peters..........Gilbert Roland
Norrie Parks..........J. Gordon Edwards, Jr.
Merton Billings..........Felix Valle
Coach Henry..........Davji Butler

A nifty picture. It's made that way and plays that way. In it are yaps, saps, flips and flaps. What more could be said for what is strictly a boy and girl-made film?

For the flappers and their sundae buyers, "The Plastic Age" is perfect. Probably the book hit them as hard as this film is bound to. And the home run hitter will be Clara Bow as Cynthia Day, a tough little baby to hang around a college campus, but her excuse can be that she had no mother to guide her. At least in this film. And her reward can stand on her feet which she never allowed to slip, but seemingly not particular otherwise.

Ben Schulberg must have selected this picture as a sure-fire. It has been playing out of town for months. Schulberg has been with Famous Players (coast studios) for some time. Anytime would be the right time for this one. But perhaps Mr. Schulberg passed it over to the Commonwealth Film Corp., as a distributor, at its pleasure, with Samuel Zierler listed on the program as its president, if for no other identification or publicity purpose.

This story of college life abounds with girls, suggesting either a co-ed institution or else a seminary was planted in the next yard.

Donald Keith is the sap freshman of Prescott, who was the crack 440-yard flier in his home town high school, but he flopped at Prescott on the track after nearly making Cynthia and a few road houses. Without knowing it, Hugh Carver "busted" right into the class that holds Mickey Walker and Young Slattery. Though the picture fails to detail whether Carver ever won a foot race at Prescott after losing his first, he did win the big football match of the season for his college.

Mr. Keith does very well, as does Gilbert Roland, as a boyish semi-villain. All of the cast play well the young people, even "types," exceptionally so.

The picture takes its own jumping record, leaping three years over but one caption. The football game is excellent, and in the work out very much like Lloyd's "Freshman's" game, but without the ridiculousness, of course, that Lloyd stuck into his.

Somehow it appears easy to be a trainer in pictures. David Butler here is exemplary as the football coach, or maybe Wesley Ruggles so directed him he couldn't flop. Mr. Ruggles did very good directorial work in every way. His road house raid is a most logical bit of that kind of work, inclusive of the dancing preceding along with the fist fight between the two college rivals.

Laughs come out quite often, some very hearty, and others begotten by trivial snappy captions. Picture ends with a laugh, besides.

This film can't muff with the younger set. They'll sit glued to it. Clara Bow as a college cutie who knows all of the tricks, besides all of the boys, may set them a worse example than they ever believe a flapping kid could fall into. But for the boys it is proven here that the virtue of training brings its own reward to success, even though it is possible to get soused at a college ball.

How the adults will take to it is another thing. They will probably go solid against Clara and won't be so strong for Hughie. They may also wonder if Prescott College owned a faculty. For a go-as-you-please hall of learning Prescott is a prize pip.

But if Prescott did have a faculty it's odds on that Clara copped the pres and hid him under the bridge, too. *Sime.*

FAMILY UPSTAIRS

William Fox production. Story from play of same name by Harry Delf, and scenario by L. G. Rigby. J. G. Blystone, director. Reginald Lyons, photography. Release date, Aug. 29. At projection room screening. Footage, 5,917.

Louise Hellor..........Virginia Valli
Charles Grant..........Allan Simpson
Joe Hellor..........J. Farrell MacDonald
Emma Hellor..........Lillian Elliott
Willie Hellor..........Edward Pfel, Jr.
Mlle. Clarice..........Cecille Evans
Annabelle Hellor..........Jacqueline Wells

A sincere aim to produce a truly spiritual comedy of every-day life, done in clear and understandable terms and reflecting delicate and subtle human values. Moments of profound significance and moving pathos, all masked behind what on the surface is broad hokum comedy.

Picture is unique in treatment. It does put over a subtle theme of spiritual conflict in terms of direct action and it takes a commonplace story, tells it in every-day manner, and still crystallizes the soul stuff that lies behind the humdrum exteriors of its people.

The production should have wide appeal. For one thing, it has the surefire Cinderella pattern; its substance has to do with a family situation that in one phase or another is common to human experience, and it has both sentimental and comedy values of the strongest kind.

The picture has a wealth of "class," another term for literary excellence and it makes strong appeal to the low brow, as well.

That's a good deal to say of a screen pantomime, for the film medium does not ordinarily lend itself to such a delicacy of expression as is here revealed in its under currents.

Briefly what is disclosed is the budding of romance in the heart of a girl of fine instincts and high character, while her courtship is gradually wrecked by the efforts of her supremely vulgar mother to bring it to a climax. Here is the sensitive, sentimental girl at bitter odds with a coarse-grained and stupid mother.

This central theme is well focused and holds, surrounded with some of the best real-life character drawing the picture theatre has had in many a day. The whole family situation of wrangling husband and wife, the over sensitized older daughter, the lazy brother, the harrassed father and the precocious flapper-daughter, make a composite picture stunning in its fidelity to the apartment dwellers of the lower order in America.

The details are mean and sordid. Such things as the upheaval of a paperhanger's visit just as the girl's suitor is due to make his first visit, gives the point to the truth of the background, a background of petty squabbles, sloppy housekeeping and the dumbdora mother's shallow pretense to "refinement."

All these things come out easily and naturally as rather broad comedy—such for instance as the vulgar mother's misuse of pompous words—and a certain grade of fan will find them funny in an uproarious way. But in reality they are the materials out of which the girl's tragedy is being erected.

Not a little of the finest passages take real force from the daintily etched characterization of Virginia Valli, a capital actress who has never been so well fitted with a congenial role. Her artful restraint heightens its human appeal. J. Farrell MacDonald, as the father, a humble motorman who sympathizes with his the girl's dilemma but doesn't know what to do about it, draws a portrait that should go into the movie gallery of fame. The terrible mother is uncomfortably realistic and splendidly played by Lillian Elliott.

After these excellencies are pointed out, it may be well to observe that the production has few of those elements that seem to make for a smashing box office achievement. There is nothing sensational in it; the title is not calculated to inspire special interest, but as a creation in the sense of a high class, artistic bit of dramatizing life, it is notable.

THE CLINGING VINE

DeMille production from the play by Zelda Sears, adapted by Jack Jevne and Rex Taylor. Titled by John W. Kraft, directed by Paul Sloane. Supervised by C. Gardner Sullivan. Distributed by P. D. C. Star, Leatrice Joy. In projection room. Running time, 62 minutes.
Antoinette Allen...............Leatrice Joy
Jimmy Bancroft................Tom Moore
Grandma Bancroft.............Toby Claude
T. M. Bancroft...............Robert Edeson
B. H. Doolittle..............Dell Henderson
A. Tutweiler................Snitz Edwards

Rather pleasant entertainment that might have been a much better picture had there not been too much stress laid on the masculine side of the heroine early in the picture. An impression lingers as one views the picture that cannot be fought off, that a female impersonator is playing the girl. It persists in the mind as the picture unreels, despite one knows to the contrary.

Considerable liberty has been taken with the very charming little musical play which Zelda Sears originally concocted. The result is a rather light-waisted picture with one redeeming feature, in the way of laughs.

From the box office angle the picture will just be a program filler. It won't stand out nor pull any money, but if they are coming anyway it's able to entertain.

Leatrice Joy plays "A. B.," the secretary to T. M. Bancroft, president of a paint company. She is the actual head of the organization and domineers the situation. "T. M." is played by Robert Edeson. He slips over a character performance that few believed him capable of. It is a regular Theodore Roberts role, and he handles it perfectly. Laid up wit the gout, he has all his executives down to his country place at Stanford to discuss the purchase of a deposit of "emerald-ite," a mineral which heretofore they have had to import.

Jimmy Bancroft (Tom Moore), grandson of T. M., arrives. He had been hired by grandpa and fired by wire by A. B., so naturally is sore on her. It is grandma who steps in and saves the day. Grandma is played by none other than the musical comedy comedienne of Casino fame, Toby Claude. What a grandma she makes and how she handles the role. She's just a wow and gets laughs, too.

Grandma takes the frightfully masculine appearing A. B. and makes a frilly flapper with boyish-bob out of her and then sics her on Jimmy. He falls and so does A. B., for she is getting her first thrill. Before that her appearance suggested that she wore suspenders to hold up her skirt. It kept the boys away.

It is A. B. who slips over a deal for Jimmy's patent egg-beater and buys it for him, only to have a con-man, also a week-end guest, take the $25,000 right away from him. Then she evolves another scheme whereby the hero, despite himself, unloads a worthless farm on the con man, getting his $25,000 back and 100 per cent profit, which leaves the young couple in a position to marry.

Dell Henderson, former director, plays the con-man and handles the role right well. Snitz Edwards, in character, gets a few laughs, but none of the others than those mentioned mean anything. Miss Joy is charming enough at times, but one cannot, while looking at the picture, disassociate the idea that she is doing an "Eltinge."
Fred.

THE GOAT GETTER

Rayart released; produced by Harry J. Brown, with Billy Sullivan starred. Directed by Al Rogell and made from a story by Grover Jones. At the Arena Roof, New York, July 14. Running time, 63 minutes.
Billy Morris..................Billy Sullivan
Virginia Avery.............Kathleen Myers
Bradley.......................Eddie Diggins
Pie Eye.....................Charles Sinclair
Slug Geever....................Joe Moore

A fast-action, stunt-man picture, with Billy Sullivan starred. Sullivan puts more action to the foot than any of the other stunt fellows playing around in the independents. Where some of the others are getting to the stage where they've acquired a yen for character acting, Sullivan seems content to just keep moving and let the heavy dramatics

Flame of the Argentine

F. B. O. production from the story by Berke Jenkins and Krag Johnson. Adapted by Ewart Adamson. Directed by Eddie Dillon. At special (projection room) showing. Running time 62 minutes.
Ines Remires..................Evelyn Brent
Dan Prescott...........Orville B. Caldwell
Emil Tovar.................Frank Leigh
Marsini......................Dan Makarenko
Mme. Marsini..............Rosita Marstini
Nana......................Evelyn Selby
Donna Aguila...............Florence Turner

This is a hoke melodrama well enough pictured but so tritely titled as to make it ridiculous. Had this picture been properly edited and titled it would have stood up with any of the average program pictures slated for the better houses. But handled as it is it will go along in the majority of the daily change theatres without getting anywhere in particular.

Fairly well cast with but one exception, the male lead. He is Orville B. Caldwell, who doesn't seem to fit at all. Evelyn Brent as the heroine gives a fair performance, but the real honors must go to Florence Turner as the mother. She trouped all around the others with Evelyn Selby running second.

The story is laid in New Orleans and South America. The hero is a member of the Department of Justice while the heroine is a piano player in a New Orleans honk-a-tonk. The heavy, played by Frank Leigh, is the manager of a South American emerald mine for a wealthy widow whose baby daughter disappeared 20 years before. The child was drowned, but its nurse, fearing that she would be punished, concocted the story of a kidnapping. The heavy is aware of the true facts and in addition to stealing stones from the mine conceives the idea of providing an impostor for the long lost daughter so that when the widow finally passes on, he will be able to get the estate and the mines for himself. He picks on the honk-a-tonk piano player and takes her to South America with him to impersonate the daughter.

Under the influence of the kindly Spanish donna the character of the girl is regenerated and at the crucial moment she refuses to go through with part of the plot which had for its purpose the stealing of a very valuable emerald necklace. Then the heavy and his companions decide to throw discretion to the winds and attack the ranch house. The girl leads the defense and finally rides to bring aid, arriving with the troops in the nick of time to save the day.

Then it is disclosed that instead of being one of the plotters the hero is in reality a member of the U. S. Secret Service and the old donna also reveals the fact that she knew that the girl was not her daughter but as she always wanted one she adopts her.

Just hoke melodrama of the western type with a South American background, a couple of good fights and a little riding stuff.
Fred.

be handled by those in good standing with the Players' Club. As a result, Sullivan's pictures, notwithstanding their hokum plot and obvious but sure construction, pack a punch.

Sullivan plays a youngster who wants to get a crack at the boxing champ, but the champ, probably a midget cousin of Jack Dempsey, wasn't taking chances with unknowns. Sullivan followed him into a movie studio where the champ was to make a picture, and eventually he was picked to be the "set-up" in the film.

The fight turned into a real one and Sullivan won. The champ's manager tried to keep the story from getting into the papers, but, with some fancy horse and auto riding, Sullivan defeated the villains and got things ship-shape in time for the fadeout.

Fight scenes are great.

Good picture for the daily changes, etc., because it gives value. Made economically but with a capable cast and lives up to the entertainment standards set by Harry J. Brown in the previous stories in which he has produced Sullivan.
Sisk.

THE SEVENTH BANDIT

Charles Rogers presents Harry Carey. Pathe production. Scott R. Dunlap, director. Story by Arthur Preston Hankins, adapted by F. Richard Schayer. At Columbus, New York, July 14, one day, one-half double bill. Running time, 59 minutes.

This "western" is most unusual. It has some semblance of an interesting tale.

The story of a cowboy's revenge for the killing of a brother is familiar, but in its present state is well told, creating interest and some excitement.

Harry Carey is starred. He is popular with the "western" loving gentry. His role is that of an elder brother, reformed gunman, bashful with the girls, and is well played.

Harriett Hammond, nifty blonde, is the girl. James Morrison stands out as the younger brother. Trilby Clark, Walter James, John Dillion and Charles McHugh comprise the remainder of the cast.

As half of a twin bill, "The Seventh Bandit" was liked.

When Husbands Flirt

Waldorf production, produced by Harry Cohn. Paul Gangelin and Dorothy Arzner authors. Directed by William Wellman. At the Columbus, New York, one day (July 14), one-half double bill. Running time, 61 minutes.
Violet Gilbert...............Dorothy Revier
Henry Gilbert..............Forrest Stanley
Wilbur Belcher...........Thomas Ricketts
Mrs. Belcher..................Ethel Wales
Charlotte Germaine..........Maude Wayne
Joe McCormick..............Irwin Connelly

Light and enjoyable farce with plenty of hoke and some snappy subtitles. Comedy all the way and handled as comedy in a burlesque manner by all but one of the four principals.

Tale of the two married couples, newlyweds and old timers. "Situation" plot formed by blond gold digger who takes over the old guy and causes Mr. Newlywed to be suspected.

Dorothy Revier is Mrs. Newlywed. About the most beautiful of the younger set of brunets on the screen. Her features are fine and perfectly formed. A capable actress besides.

Good work is contributed by Thomas Ricketts as the elder husband. His excellent exasperation over the henpecking of his wife and the tentacles of the blond vamp, together with Malcolm S. Boylan's titles got the laughs.

Direction by William Wellman is good.

Attractive title should bring them

in and when in they will laugh. An 8th avenue audience laughed heartily.

MORGANSON'S FINISH

Tiffany Production. Suggested by Jack London's story of the same title. Fred Windermere, director. At the Stanley, New York. Running time, 70 minutes.
Barbara Wesley..............Anita Stewart
Dick Gilbert................Johnnie Walker
Dan Morganson..........Mahlon Hamilton
Ole Jensen....................Victor Potel

A story of gold mining in Alaska and a futile attempt to transfer Jack London's book zip to the screen. The four central characters do well and the story has possibilities of thrills at times, despite it is the old business of a villain trying to win the girl, but the picture is handled badly throughout.

Mr. London's tale of the young man, in love with an heiress and being hooked out of his job by the wealthy evil-doer, who desires the same heiress, created some interest years back. When the hero blows away to Alaska to find gold, accompanied by the villain (whose evil doing is not known) the story, the story's handling and the technical work flounder around until the end, when the works are prepared to take the count.

In Alaska the villain's attempts at putting the hero away by blowing up a mountain, throwing him over a cliff, etc., are in vain.

Johnnie Walker has the leading bit, with Mahlon Hamilton, in the title role, as the villain.

Walker is not for the lead in "Morganson's Finish." In this film he acts at his best but seems at loss.

Anita Stewart is about okay as the girl. Of the others, Victor Potel does, by far, the best. He plays a "dumb" Swede, and very well.

The ice and snow scenes are for the most part studio. Some of the shots are very bad. If genuine exteriors would have cost more they would have been worth it to the producers.

You Never Know Women

Famous Players' production of a story by Ernst Vajda. Adapted to the screen by Benjamin Glazer. Directed by William Wellman. Florence Vidor's first starring vehicle. At the Rivoli, New York, week July 24. Running time, 70 minutes.

Vera Janova..............Florence Vidor
Ivan Norodin..................Clive Brook
Eugene Foster..............Lowell Sherman
Toberchik.........................El Brendel
Dimitri..........................Roy Stewart
The Strong Man...............Joe Bonomo
Olga..........................Irma Kornelia
Manager.....................Sidney Bracey

This picture is sample of rejuvenated F. P. product, and it must mean that new life has been galvanized into the very scheme of their picture making. In addition to being one of the nicest program pictures in many weeks, it is flawlessly acted, brilliantly directed and filled with novel situations.

It marks the promotion of Florence Vidor to stardom, and if her future path is strewn with vehicles like this one there shouldn't be any hitch to really putting her over.

Ernst Vajda, the dramatist who left the Budapesthaus and came over here to try his luck at writing for the movies, has struck a real vein of sophisticated humor and story telling in this effort. While his first one didn't make much of a ripple, this one should. Much credit also goes to Benjamin Glazer, who did the adaptation, for that part of the work is smooth and in good continuity.

Plot concerns the love of an outsider for a girl with a Russian novelty troupe—acrobats, magicians, clowns, etc. The girl's partner and co-star is Norodin, whose great feat is escaping (after being manacled) from a box lowered into water.

Feeling the girl is not in love with him but wants a clear road to the outsider, he fakes death by failing to come up after one of his trick immersions. Actually he does come up, but after swimming under water gets out of sight of the spectators and appears a day or two later, as the outsider had turned villain and was trying to coerce an unwilling girl, who had just realized her love was really for her partner, supposedly dead.

The picture gets a fast start.

The first shot shows Miss Vidor, unidentified, walking by a building under construction. A girder is being hoisted, is in mid-air, and the cable begins to part. A rough workman jerks her to safety, and she faints. Meantime the outsider had witnessed the affair, and with his authority, dignity, etc., took the girl from the workman's arms into his own, commenting:

"I do this sort of thing so much better than you."

On that basis he forces the acquaintanceship, and because he is believed to have rescued her, his presence is tolerated, although the partner and the rest of the troupe resent him.

Many of the scenes—the majority—take place either in or backstage of a theatre. This troupe held about 20 performers. In their number was a clown, Toberchik (El Brendel), who did a tumbling-barrel act at the start; later had a trained goose go through many paces, and continuously clowned around in his ill-fitting clothes, so long familiar to vaudeville. Joe Bonomo, the strong man of Hollywood, is another of the troupe, his huge chest and massive form lending authority to his role, while Fortunello and Cirinillo, stage acrobats, are also in the line-up.

Miss Vidor played excellently all the way. Clive Brook gave a splendid performance. The same can be said of Brendel.

Wellman, at the megaphone, lifts himself into the ranks of the select directors by his handling of this story, for his direction is never obvious or old fashioned, his methods being neat and naive enough to express fully both the frothy and the serious parts of the story. Further in its favor, the scenario is so nicely contrived that suspense as to plot is always present.

A good picture in every sense. Admittedly done on the triangle theme, its novelty is so frefreshing the average spectator will believe, by the time "You Never Know Women" is over, that a triangle's interesting spots are not covered by three sides. *Sisk.*

THE WALTZ DREAM

Metro-Goldwyn-Mayer distributed film, made by UFA (Germany) with German cast and under German direction. At the Capitol, week July 25. Running time, 77 minutes.

Eberhard XIII..............Jacob Tiedtke
Princess Alix..............Mady Christians
Archduke Ferdinand.......Carl Beckersachs
Nicholas, Count Preyn.........Willy Fritsch
Rockhoff von Hoffrock...Julius Falkenstein
Lady Kockeritz...........Mathilde Sussin
Franzi...........................Xenia Desni
Steffi.........................Lydia Potechina

This German UFA bunch knows how to make pictures!

"The Waltz Dream" strikes the bull's-eye with a vengeance. Its players are unknown here; its director hasn't turned out anything that has previously met with success here, and the operetta itself hasn't had a vogue for a good many years, but this picture will make itself liked anywhere. That is, if the people appreciate a subtle, rollicking, naughty, romantic love story filled to the overflowing with the sweet and rhythmic measures of all the waltzes that ever came from Vienna.

The plot concerns Princess Alix, from Flausenburg, and a prudish little iceberg. Her papa, the king, is having a tough time getting her married off. They come hunting a husband in Vienna. The Archduke Ferdinand is the first target, but as the Archduke finds a kiss to Alix is the equivalent of marriage, he palms her off on his aid, Count Preyn. Count Preyn, a gay dog and good looking, takes her to a wine festival, and there the little princess gets stewed. Her prudishness vanishes, and she is just getting all primed for a large evening when the Chamberlain of her outfit takes her back. But Count Preyn has to marry her, and after going through several hundred court ceremonials, they come to the bridal chamber and the ceremonial of the tearing of the bridal veil.

Then the king tells him that the bride will summon him to the chamber when she's ready for him. But the princess, a shy little thing (sober), is too timid to call him in, although the empty side of the bed is on her mind.

So the count hops out, and to a beer garden, where he listens to a ladies' orchestra from Vienna play all the waltz tunes of his beloved city. To top things off, he starts a romance with the leader of the orchestra. Their romance develops until his status with her is ace high.

About this time the princess, desperate because she hasn't won the love of her husband (and she really loved him), calls for a Viennese woman to teach her the tricks—that's where the real fun begins. The husband's sweetheart is the woman called. She says the princess should wear her dresses shorter, quit the heavy under-dressing, etc., all shown in the film, where the princess in her heavy underwear stands beside the Viennese girl, who has a snappy layout of silk stuff. The Viennese girl then teaches the princess to play the "Blue Danube Waltz," which was the recurrent tune on the night in the wine garden.

Side by side the princess and the Viennese woman sat, and as the husband walked in, stirred to believe that the princess really recalled their one lovely night in Vienna, he took her in his arms, while the Viennese woman, on the other side of a screen, held the tears back and contented herself with the single statement, "That, after all, her romance was just a waltz dream."

The acting of Mady Christians as the prudish princess is splendid. Her "stew" is great comedy, while Willy Fritsch as her husband, also turns in nice work. Xenia Desni, beautiful blonde, is the Viennese woman, and she also contributes mightily.

The director, Ludwig Berger, gains some fine effects by use of multiple shots, visualizing the thoughts of the characters. The Vienna scenes were made on the ground, while the studio sets are heavy and plentiful.

"The Waltz Dream" is a first-class first run picture fit for the best of houses. When it strikes the daily changes, etc., its appeal should be just as great, for these actors get their story over with great clarity. Added to that is its tinge of naughtiness, which occurs in a spot or two, and is done with such a spirit that only a minister of circuit rider ancestry could find it objectionable. *Sisk.*

THE WISE GUY

Frank Lloyd production, released through First National. Story by Jules Furthman. Features James Kirkwood, Betty Compson, Mary Astor and Mary Carr, with George Marion, Sr., and George Cooper in cast. At Broadway theatre, New York, week July 26. Running time not taken, but under 60 minutes.

Picture butchered at its finish, probably through orders of the New York state censoring board, leaving the film unsatisfactory. Its entire continuity was banged into through the brusque cuts. There may have been others, but they were the most severe near the ending, reached abruptly and unlogically. In other states the full picture may be run.

Even with this handicap there's enough strength to the picture to hold it up, and for Frank Lloyd's direction much may be said commendably. Also the playing of all in the cast. But the subject-matter may be offensive, according to the audience.

In a big town of unbelievers this real purpose evidently of uncovering coin-getting reformers calling themselves evangelists will be appreciated, even cordially liked. But out in the sticks or in certain communities it's doubtful if the idea of converting a medicine show crooked fakir and his gang into an evangelistic crowd, allowing them to be seen going throughout the countryside converting cataleptics, will be accepted as proper for pictures, through the use of the cloth or the semblance to the church, suggested if not actually exhibited.

Not only that, but here it is permitted to be seen that the hula dancer of the medicine show and its faking leader or seller are living together, relations they continue after their conversion into the evangelistic group.

The little band of medicine show grafters secure their hunch for evangelism when noting that a small party of hymn singers near their stand stole their crowd away.

Not the least of the offensiveness, at least to some, will be the hypocritical attitude of the evangelistic leader, even toward his own people, and again later, when the only pure thing about the faking company, a girl, carried along after her father had died, develops crookedness of the past herself, with her father an ordinary second-story thief. While the phoney evangelist permitted to hold burial service is pretty raw for any set of people.

But one thing this does teach, and some of the show people in the same position might take a look (it will do them good), that even crooks when they accumulate money may also get religion. That's a peach if it's gotten right.

Notwithstanding the moral drawbacks, "The Wise Guy" is a good strong story and of sentiment of a kind. It's a pity that since some of it is shown in New York all of it could not be.

Still, after seeing "Variety" at the Rialto, and knowing of the double version of that made in Germany even before shown over here, maybe censoring isn't so much a question in pictures of a picture as it is of a payroll.

Discriminating exhibitors not playing to a miscellaneous or transient trade should view "The Wise Guy" before booking it. Exhibitors only can judge whether and how their audiences will accept this corking made film. *Sime.*

SILVER TREASURE

Fox production starring George O'Brien. Based on Joseph Conrad's famous novel "Nostromo." Directed by Rowland V. Lee and adapted to the screen by Robert N. Lee. At Stanley, New York, July 25, one day. Running time, 64 minutes.

Nostromo..................George O'Brien
Ramirez..........................Jack Rollins
Linda.........................Helena D'Algy
Giselle...............................Joan Rence
Mother Teresa................Evelyn Selbie
Solito, the bandit.............Lou Tellegen
Martin Decoud...............Otto Mattieson
Charles Gould................Stewart Rome
Mrs. Gould.....................Hedda Hopper

Based on Joseph Conrad's famous story of "Nostromo," a sea romance of daring and individual bravery, this film version is worthy of the original and has all the thrills of a real western feature, plus lots more romance than that type of film. The plot concerns Nostromo, a local hero on the Isle of Sylaco. Heralded far and wide as the good and brave man of the community, it seems his reputation is ever being put to a test—and always shows up on the right side.

Linda, daughter of the innkeeper, is supposed to be his betrothed, while in reality she loves one Ramirez, while Giselle, her cousin is the salvo of the establishment but deeply in love with Nostromo.

An Englishman, Gould, is the owner of a silver mine and fearing the attack of bandits, has Nostromo guide his silver train to the wharves.

A desperate battle with the bandits ensues, but by the trick of transferring the silver ingots to a hay wagon, the load goes safely through.

In the battle the mother of Linda received a bullet intended for Nostromo and on her death-bed, made him promise to marry Linda. He promised, although Giselle was his real choice. After this, Nostromo transferred the silver to a small sailing boat and planned to meet the vessel which would carry it to civilization outside the harbor, the supposition being that there they would be safe from the attack of bandits. In the night a bandit vessel ran down the sailing craft and wrecked it. Nostromo, now torn between his desire for Giselle and his forced wedding to Linda went crooked for the moment, and after he had rescued the silver itself, hid it on a rocky island.

Giselle repulsed him when she heard of his scheme that they would leave the island and be wealthy on the stolen money. Nostromo, conscience stricken to think he had entertained dishonest thoughts, confessed to the owner of the silver, who praised him for having the courage to make such a confession. A desperate struggle with the bandits won back the silver and with his own record purged, he returned to find that Linda's mother had released him from the marriage.

Action in every reel of this film, lots of it, while the backgrounds are elaborate and filled with thousands of supers. O'Brien in the lead does nice acting and fancy fighting, while the others, all of them thoroughly capable, round out an impressive cast. Joan Renee, a newcomer apparently, is the Giselle and gave an appealing performance, her wistful face recording nicely via the lens. Lee's direction is noteworthy in that the comedy touches are not forced. Indeed, the general attention to cast, direction and detail in "The Silver Treasure" should give the picture large commendation among exhibitors of every type, because it is a good, serviceable, "cloak and sword" romance, filmed as it should be filmed and played to the hilt by O'Brien.

Sisk.

SCANDAL STREET

W. E. Shallenberg production, from the story by Frank R. Adams. Arrow picture. Directed by Whitman Bennett. At the Columbus, New York, one day (July 24). Running time, 74 minutes.

Shiela Kane	Madge Kennedy
Neil Keeley	Niles Welch
Harrison Halliday	Niles Welch
Cora Foreman	Louise Carter
O'Malley	J. Moy Bennett
Julian Lewis	Colt Albertson

Some "inside stuff" on the film industry. Looked upon as that, it will probably find much favor. Unusually good and well made independent, holding a fairly interesting story and some competent acting by Niles Welch (at present in vaudeville).

Welch has a two-ply role. He is Neil Keeley, "the screen's greatest lover," and Keeley's "double." Madge Kennedy is featured and is at loss in that which the picture lacks—comedy. Without a laugh, the picture lapses into melodramatic moments that make one nervous. A giggle here and there would crack the suspense, but is not present.

Keeley and Shiela Kane, husband and wife, are co-stars in films produced by J. O'Malley. Both are popular. But Neil is an awful "stew," also quite a "chaser," causing his film work and wife to be neglected.

Harrison Halliday attempts getting a job as an extra. His likeness to Keeley strikes O'Malley and he is engaged. When Keeley lapses into a jag, as he frequently does, Harrison substitutes for long shots. Some studio work is shown with explanatory sub-titles.

Realism is inserted with the numbered slate and the director halting a scene to have the star powder her face.

Keeley is killed in an automobile accident. Halliday is persuaded by the producers to assume his name and place.

The story flops and flounders thereafter until the end.

Halliday falls in love with Miss Kane with blackmail stuff by a former sweetheart of Keeley's and a lawyer, who know of the replacement by Halliday.

Without a laugh Miss Kennedy is at a disadvantage. She is a comedienne and her eyes twinkle even in a crying scene. With a gag or two she would have made her role a toot-sweet. But as is she is just a brooding film star.

Louise Carter and Colt Albertson play excellently. Whitman Bennett's direction is good at times, very good at others, sometimes faulty.

MISMATES

First National release (Earl Hudson production) of Myron C. Fagan's stage play, co-starring Doris Kenyon and Warner Baxter. Charles Brabin directed. Charles Murray, May Allison and Philo McCullough prominent in cast. 70 Minutes at Loew's State, New York, week July 26.

A mother theme incongruously developed from a mismated marriage. It affords Doris Kenyon some excellent histrionic opportunities, of which this capable screen actress fully availed herself, but the entire proceedings become so inconsistent with the screening's progress that one wonders why it is all taken so seriously.

Phil McCullough is cast as a rich mother's darling. She refuses to acknowledge his wife of five years into the exclusive household.

The author and director would then have us believe that in order for the socially wealthy Winslows to gain possession of the adorable kiddie, they "frame" the wife into the penitentiary. Even up to that point much could be forgiven, but thereafter the mother, who has been summoned to manicure the warden's wife, effects her escape through the warden's household. Whether prison inmates are invited by public officials' wives to administer facial massages and manicures is besides the point.

But that escape!

Reaching the household where her baby boy is physically failing and crying for his "mumsy," one encounters an "exclusive social festival" that looks like a reel out of "Ben-Hur."

Why Mr. Brabin, the director, could not have made this a sane occasion in honor of the prodigal son and not try to out-Cecil DeMille with a Bacchanalian orgy, puzzles the intelligence.

What matters the acting after that story and direction? If there's an amusement demand for this sort of thing, "Buster Brown" should make a great sex scenario. *Abel.*

Men of the Night

Melodrama produced by Al Rogell and distributed by Henry Ginsburg under the Sterling Pictures Corporation trade-mark. Story by Florence Wagner. At Loew's State, New York, week July 19, as the film feature in conjunction with vaudeville. Running time, 71 minutes.

Dick Foster	Gareth Hughes
J. Rupert Dodds	Herbert Rawlinson
Trixie Moran	Wanda Hawley
Mrs. Abbott	Lucy Beaumont

One of the few independent films to be shown in Loew's State, New York (tied up between M-G-M and F. P. output). Although "Men of the Night" hasn't any star names to lend it a potent box office pull, it is a splendidly made picture and holds interest as a melodrama.

Al Rogell's direction is varied from the stereotyped stuff. Though nothing new was done, it was a different brand from the obvious, heavy direction usually given serious stories made by the state righters. Introducing a crook story, Rogell uses shadow silhouettes to express certain bits of action. His lighting and technical arrangement is so well worked out that the silhouettes register as well as if it had been done in the regular way.

The plot concerns an experienced crook and a young fellow over whom he held so much power that the boy was forced to be his accomplice. The crook operated an antique shop as a blind to other activities, and here a stenographer, sweetheart of the youngster, worked.

One night, after a job, the cops got on their trail. To throw them off the kid left their loot in the hands of an old woman sitting on park bench.

Struck by her kind face, he invited her to come and take care of their house, a scheme to which the older crook readily assented because he figured she would help divert suspicion from them.

The old woman duly became their "mother," with great interest in affairs, until the time arrives when she discovered they were crooks.

Realizing that the older fellow was too deep in to reform, she centered her interest on the youngster. One night, as he was to rob a safe, confronting him at the scene of the crime and by a twist of events, she was captured by the police, while the real robbers got away. Under the third degree she refused to reveal the identity of the crooks but the kid attempted to confess. At this time the old woman was found to be the sister of the wealthy woman who had been robbed, so the whole thing was squared.

Lucy Beaumont gives a good sympathetic performance as the old woman, while Herbert Rawlinson and Gareth Hughes do well as the contrasting crooks. Wanda Hawley, the sweetheart, isn't before the camera very much, but her few scenes fall rather flat.

"Men of the Night" is a good melodrama. While not first run material for big houses, it is suitable and satisfactory for vaudeville houses playing pictures. One and about the only drawback is that its featured names probably have little draught on their own account. *Sisk.*

THE WOLF HUNTERS

Ben Wilson production. Rayart picture. Adapted from the story by James Oliver Curwood. Directed by Stuart Paton. At Loew's New York, one day (July 23). Running time, 68 minutes.

Sergt. Steve Drew	Alan Roscoe
Minnetaki	Virginia Brown Faire
Helen Ainsworth	Mildred Harris
Ainsworth	Robert McKim
Roderick Drew	Carrol Nye
Le Grange	David Torrence
Cleave	Al Ferguson
Woomba	Joe De La Cruz

One of the numerous Canadian Mounted tales with plenty of "get your man" stuff but a good and intelligently entertaining picture.

Most of the enjoyment is provided by Virginia Brown Faire as a half-breed Indian girl. She runs away with the picture. Dark, young, large eyes, fine features and sassy action.

Alan Roscoe has the male lead, that of Sergt. Steve Drew, the "lone rider." He always rides alone and always "gets his man."

Villainous action by Bob McKim, that old standby and perfect cinema evil-doer. Mildred Harris has a comparatively small role, done poorly. She merely looks sorrowful in several closeups. She can play more advantageously.

The picture should make money in its rounds, for the Royal Northwest Mounted Policeman is always an attraction to the galleries.

PADLOCKED

Famous Players-Lasky production, directed by Allan Dwan. Story (serial) by Rex Beach, adapted for screen by Becky Gardiner. Continuity by Shelly Hamilton. Featuring Lois Moran, Noah Beery, Allan Simpson and Louise Dresser. At Rivoli, New York, week July 31. Running time not taken, around 60 minutes.

Edith Gilbert	Lois Moran
Henry Gilbert	Noah Beery
Mrs. Alcott	Louise Dresser
Belle Galloway	Helen Jerome Eddy
Norman Van Pelt	Allan Simpson
Mrs. Gilbert	Florence Turner
"Tubby" Clark	Richard Arlen
Monte Hermann	Charles Lane
"Sonny" Galloway	Douglas Fairbanks, Jr.
Blanche Galloway	Charlot Bird

"Padlocked," by Rex Beach, is said to have cost Famous Players for the film rights over $100,000. Whoever saw that value should make application for the X-ray diamond medal. Yet the picture as presented is quite apt to hit just above average business wherever playing, for it's of the sexy stuff, of the description that fits flappers who yearn. There's not enough in this film, however, to carry it along for a hold-over week unless some special stage attraction is sufficient to make the gross run high.

There's no fault here for the high-priced material to fall down on its estimated value except the Beach story itself. Beach wrote the story as a serial for "Cosmopolitan." Famous bought it early, after a couple of chapters had been published.

There's a large chance that Becky Gardiner, who adapted for the screen did more for actual results than the original Beach tale could have done. Little touches here and there, the nearest things to punches the story holds, look like an adapter's finish. While there may have been changes from the printed original, still the foundation must have been the author's. Allan Dwan in direction also jumped into every chance, but the story limited him as well.

While the acting might be said to have been the easiest of all. Lois Moran gives a corking performance as the girl. Two of the principals in unsympathetic roles were undeniably handicapped, Noah Beery and Charles Lane. Mr. Beery must have employed his own conception of a reforming country minister, while Mr. Lane merely walked through the part of a big city chaser who's after the sweet thing from the sticks.

Louise Dresser was in wrong in character as the procuress at the outset, but redeemed herself later, and always looked well. Miss Dresser's screen personality (and she had it likewise on the stage) dominates any scene she is in. Florence Turner played nicely as the minister's first wife, who passed out, and Douglas Fairbanks, Jr., made a neat flip youngster. Allan Simpson, as the opposite juvenile to Miss Moran, was in a loafing role.

If there's an outstanding performance here it's Helen Jerome Eddy as the catty, scheming neighbor who finally marries the widower. Miss Eddy made her role jump through hoops and the chances are that although the audience felt revulsion, she secured their admiration early. A character bit to attract was the drinking mother-in-law (unprogramed).

And now to Beach, his $100,000 story, picture producers and dramatists. Every American dramatist should see this film, to get a line on what a writing name appears to mean to picture people who can't dissect or analyze. Here's the tritest story that has been turned out on the screen in years by an author of Beach's repute. Generally looked upon as a virile writer, in "Padlocked," Beach wrote a mush story of the country girl going to the city to become a dancer in a cabaret and be saved in time. Fifteen years ago the two-reelers saved them much better and more quickly.

It's the type of story and picture that turned the screen sexward; it was the first sexy story the screen in this country ever exhibited as a continued tale. Beach made a couple of exceptions, neither original. He made the girl the daughter of a country minister and inserted a reformatory locale. A reformatory to send a girl to has been used before in pictures, a long time ago, and the name of the reformatory was mentioned; the Bedford in Weschester county. While a minister's daughter rushing to ruin is far from novel.

Otherwise "Padlocked" was skeletonized and written to rule, the most conventional of all picture subjects. If Beach did get $100,000 or more for this it may be said that any dramatist would have written a better story to order along the same formula for $7,500 or less. There's even a cabaret scene here. And the only bit that could call for attention as new is a kid party, very well done. While ringing in the second wife's family is all hoke and frequently used in comedy two-reelers. Yet this bit is the film's best comedy relief.

The dramatists, but recently got together and loudly set forth plaints for protection against their stage plays getting into pictures without their full consent and share. With the small actual percentage of stage plays reaching the screen, the dramatists could conclude it will be more profitable to write direct for films, if Beach can draw down that kind of money for this kind of slush. It's quite safe to hazard that not a recognized American dramatist would have voluntarily written anything like "Padlocked" at this late day.

As a picture, "Padlocked" is all right for the picture theatres. Many adults will yawn over it, but the growing younger set may see something different in it, but as a picturized story it's sloppy and worth about $15,000 net. Pictures like this should be thrown to the small, independent producers who need a sure-fire for state rights. *Sime.*

Devil's Island

Chadwick Pictures Corporation production. Released through regional exchanges. Story and scenario by Leah Baird. Directed by Frank O'Connor. Pauline Frederick starred with George Lewis and Marian Nixon featured. Titles by Mark Edmund Jones. At the Colony, New York, week Aug. 1. Running time, 65 minutes.

Jeannette Picot	Pauline Frederick
Jean Valyon	Richard Tucker
Guillot	William Dunn
Chico	Leo White
Andre LeFevier	John Miljan
Leon Valyon	George Lewis
The Commandant	Harry Northrup
Rose-Marie	Marian Nixon

In so far as the production is concerned this is an elaborate effort for an independent producer, but the story with its heavy drama is pretty old stuff and the burden of its sincere interpretation is almost entirely on Pauline Frederick and Marian Nixon, the latter as nice a little ingenue as the screen has had in a long time. George Lewis is featured, but his contribution is pretty colorless, either his fault or the fault of the director.

Story concerns a French surgeon sentenced to the penal colony on Devil's Island, off the coast of South America. After seven years he is released on parole to French Guiana, and at Cayénne, capital of that small territory, he finds his old sweetheart awaiting him. As a convict he must remain there all his life and the woman who marries a convict must do the same. The same penalty applies to any children born to them.

When their son arrives he has his father's aptitude for surgery. As he matures and after the father's death he becomes famous for his operations, which the titles tell us are so marvelous that they are unknown in Europe.

His mother plots for his escape, so that he can go to Paris and there receive the training which would develop a prodigy into a genius. But the boy falls in love with a dancer. Although he has a spat with her, the love sticks and the film winds up by a court of justice decreeing that the father should never have been sent to the Penal Colony in the first place and that France as a nation would attempt to rectify that by freeing his wife and son.

With their freedom they put in a request to free the girl, who is at the moment being roughly handled by the commandant of the land. The order for her release is broadcast by radio, and as the official is struggling with her they maneuver toward his radio set. Just as she is too weak to do anything else her release order comes through clear and strong, proving that justice did triumph and that static in the tropics isn't half as bad as in this temperate zone during the warm weather.

Miss Frederick's work as the mother takes her from a young woman to an old woman with gray hair, and she turns in many effective moments. Ditto Miss Nixon and Richard Tucker, the father. He isn't often seen around here, but in "Devil's Island" his work is marked by a sincerity which commends it. George Lewis seems to be an automaton, while Harry Northrup as the villainous Commandant worked strictly along the lines laid down by other villains.

"Devil's Island" isn't a wallop, neither is it a dud. It stands half way between the two classifications and in atonement for its too familiar situations allows Miss Frederick some excellent scenes. Moderate entertainment. *Sisk.*

The Savage

First National release, directed by Fred Newmeyer under the supervision of Earl Hudson. From original story by Ernest Pascal. Featuring Ben Lyon and May McAvoy. At the New York, July 30, one day, as half double bill. Running time, 63 minutes.

A two-reel knockabout comedy, spread out very thin to make a five-reel feature. Quality of its humor is childish and appeal is gauged to four-year-old intelligence instead of the 12-year level at which the average film fan is supposed to be—supposed to be, that is, by those who make a business of that kind of films.

Briefly the picture is monkey comedy, made for simians. On top of this plain intent they try to introduce a grossly conflicting subordinate theme of something like romance. The two elements are oil and water and they won't mix. The effect one gets is something like the spectacle of Romeo and Juliet doing a couple of neck falls.

It would be interesting to trace the making of such a picture from the germinating of the idea to its completion. For instance, whose bright idea was it to pick out for the characters of the monkey-hero and the girl opposite Ben Lyon and May McAvoy, two highly persuasive young romantic players? The intent obviously was to erect a romantic atmosphere and then degrade it with coarse horse play, a pretty idea indeed. It is pictures like this that inspire protests against "the low standards of the screen."

The story, such as it is, has to do with the jealousy of two scientists. One of them, in order to make a fool of the other, "plants" a civilized young man (Lyon) on a desert island, where he will be discovered in a state of nature by the other scientist and exploited in the civilized world as a "White savage living with the monkeys."

The second scientist falls into the trap, capturing the counterfeit "missing link" and bringing "it" home on his yacht. An affinity springs up between the "Whatisit" and the deluded scientist's beautiful daughter, the girl being the only person who can control the caged freak. The make-believe savage keeps up antics appropriate to his enforced character, until at a masquerade ball given by the duped scientists wife (where all the guests are dressed as monkeys) the scheming scientist attempts to expose the hoax and disgrace his victim.

It is then that the "savage" defeats the plot, beats up the schemer and carries off the girl he has learned to love. This leads to a revelation of the situation and the final lovers' clinch. This synopsis does not suggest all the "comedy" that pads out the footage, endless repetitions of knockabout and acrobatic buffoonery that hasn't a giggle in it.

Compared to this rubbish the slip-on-a-banana-peel school of fun is subtle high comedy.

The Love Thief

Universal production with Norman Kerry and Greta Nissen featured. Story and direction by John McDermott. At Loew's New York Roof, July 29, one day. Running time, about 70 minutes.

The Cook	Charles Puffy
The Princess Norrinne	Greta Nissen
Her Uncle	Marc McDermott
The Crown Prince of Mauralnia	Norman Kerry
The Chancellor of Mauralnia	Nigel Barrie

One of the Universal big numbers for its current program. Well produced, acted and directed, it frames up as pleasing entertainment of the lighter sort. Based on one of those mythical kingdom stories, this one has a serious plot which mixes nicely with that portion of the yarn which depends upon the purposeful light-headedness of the Crown Prince of Mauralnia, a young fellow who wears his uniforms and honors well, but who also is quite a devil with the women about court.

The Regent of Norvia comes to Mauralnia. He suggests it would be a nice thing for him to take over the actual government of the nation and let the Crown Prince, after his accession, be a mere figure-head.

Inasmuch as Norvia was much more powerful it seemed that the old king would consent, but the audacious Crown Prince gave the Regent a tough run-around.

Meantime he had met and fallen in love with a luscious blonde lady whom he met frolicking across the lawn. Not knowing she was the Princess Norinne he was to marry, he decried the condition of things which caused princes to wed princesses and forego the pleasure of real love.

As this gal was quite a looker he decided he could kick the old Crown Princeship overboard and get quite as much pleasure out of being a plain married man. He refused to marry the Princess Norrinne because he thought she was some one other than the girl whom he loved. Next he insulted the Regent from Norvia, and only by refusing to fight him a duel (which would have led to warfare) did he keep from killing that worthy. But the insult gave the Regent the upper hand, and the Crown Prince was drummed out of the army and sent into disgraceful exile, just as the court was preparing for his wedding.

The rest of the story?

Simply that the Princess loved him so much it didn't matter whether he wore his medals or not.

Norman Kerry is excellent in the leading male role. His easy manner explains why he is so high in the U list of stars, for he has what women like on the screen, a perfect carriage, figure and a fine face. Miss Nissen, the Scandinavian dancer, whose movie advent rather petered out into nothingness after she left Famous Players, is excellent in her part and screens like a million dollars. Perhaps the mistake made with her was in trying to make her a star overnight instead of letting her do supporting work for a while. Marc McDermott is the villain here and okeh, while Charles Puffy as the comedy relief and Nigel Barrie in the role of sympathetic adviser to the harum-scarum prince also scored.

Not a big first run, but "The Love Thief" should please most audiences, and in addition to that its tone is so good that it fits the Sunday houses. Its production details are rather elaborate and carefully carried out, so exhibitors need not fear receiving one of those mythical kingdom stories done on a dime scale. This one is well done. *Sisk.*

THE UNFAIR SEX

Associated Exhibitors' comedy-drama, with cast headed by Hope Hampton, Holbrook Blinn and Nita Naldi. Directed by Henri Diamant-Berger from the story by Eugene Walter, adapted by Arthur Hoerl. At the Stanley, New York, July 31, one day. Running time, 50 minutes.

Picture has many elements that should make for its value—splendid acting, close-knit story, production excellence, interesting title. But it does not, for some reason, register fully. The start is slow and dull, but presently the unfolding action speeds up and moves briskly to the finish.

The finale is novel, and it is the last incident that carries the picture's punch. Possibly the defect in the whole story is that the author had his attention fixed upon the surprise climax, and the progress of the action to that point had to be made to conform.

This scheme serves well enough in a short story, but in the case of this screen play, at least, it does not work out. The way it unfolds is something like this: A villain plots against a rich young woman by trying to alienate her young lover. His object is to steal her jewels.

He drugs and carries her to his apartment, evidently with the worst of intentions. When his schemes are all defeated by the timely arrival of the girl's heroic sweetheart, our deep-dyed villain takes his defeat in a spirit of jaunty sang froid for a surprise laugh.

In the writing this sounds well enough but as written and played the pattern is not satisfactory. Author and director know from the first that this villain is a comedy villain and in good time will be revealed in that guise. They have to shade his conduct during the action so that the revelation will not come as a hoax upon the spectator. But as this shading of purpose is gradually revealed, the effect is puzzling. The heavy's visible acts are melodrama, but there is something out of sight that makes him unreal and the spectator is puzzled.

Production and photography, beautiful. Some of the scenes are laid in a night club, where elaborate scenic effects are particularly impressive. Holbrook Blinn plays the comedy heavy as probably no other player could do it. If the part could be made effective, he is the one to play it. Miss Hampton has a rather colorless character in the rich society girl, dressing it handsomely and playing gracefully. Nita Naldi has a meatier role as the night club dancer, used to fascinate the society girl's fiance in the plot. The role overshadows that of Miss Hampton in interest, and, what is more important, earns more sympathy. Perhaps this detail adds to the confusion arising from the unusual situation previously mentioned.

THE SECRET SPRING

French production put on by Famous Players-Lasky. No billing matter in English. Directed by Leonce Perret. Story adapted from the novel by Pierre Benoit. Hugette Du Fluos of the Comedie Francais featured. At the New York one day, July, half double bill. Running time, 65 minutes. (Maker's name is not disclosed on main title.)

Picture of astonishing contrasts in merits and crudities. It has passages of appeal alternating with interludes of unbelievable roughness. There is a stag hunt on what looks like a manificent baronial estate, with striking shots of the leaping deer and the gayly caparisoned riders. There are some fine bits of pageantry in royal court scenes.

But where studio interior scenes are used they are of incredible shabbiness. The producer's idea of a royal boudoir would serve nicely as a stage setting for a Coney Island side show—all cheap tinsel and grotesque parody of regal splendor. Against these wretched backgrounds, whenever the story goes into natural scenery, effects are magnificent.

Even more surprising than the inexpert management of the settings is that the acting is altogether unconvincing. France has been noted through the ages for its gifted pantomimists, but there is no evidence in this picture of that tradition. The heroine (Mlle. Du Fluos) is a large, expressionless blonde who never for a moment suggests the Grand Duchess she plays. The leading man is a handsome youth, but an actor without force. None of the other players counts.

Add to these adverse elements that the story is shallow fiction of the juvenile kind, and the result is pretty discouraging.

What they started out to do was to film a romantic story of the Anthony Hope "Prisoner of Zenda" type, with a background of one of those mythical Balkan principalities where the atmosphere is ancient romance and the characters modern. This sort of thing demands the utmost plausibility in acting and background. Otherwise it turns back on itself in travesty. That's what happens here.

The narrative is not even clear. Characters become tangled, identities become confused, all because the continuity is badly handled and clearness and simplicity are sacrified to an intricate plot. There are too many subordinate characters, either developed too much or developed not sufficiently. It is possible that a whole cast of people, none familiar to American audiences, contributes to this sense of confusion, although a well-made, simple continuity would have avoided such a defect, especially if the types had been clearly differentiated.

In any event there is no excuse at this late day in the growth of the screen technique to make a picture so badly flawed in the basic and elemental principles of clearness of narrative and realism in settings.

If this is representative of the quality of French output, the future of native pictures in this market is indeed disheartening. Except for its beauty of natural scenery the film scarcely has a merit.

DON JUAN

Warner Brothers productions starring John Barrymore and featuring Mary Aster. Directed by Alan Cresland. Story written by Dean Meredyth, Byron Haskins and George Hollingshead. photographers. Titles by Walter B. Anthony nad Maude Fulton. At Warner's, New York, at $2 top, for indefinite run. Two performances daily. Running time around 30 minutes.

Don Juan	John Barrymore
Adriana Della Varnese	Mary Astor
Pedrillo	Williard Louis
Lucretia Borgia	Estelle Taylor
Caesar Borgia	WarnerOiand
Doanati	Montagu Love
Rena (Adriana's maid)	Helene Costello
Beatrice	Jane Winton
Maja (Lucretia's maid)	Myrna Loy
Leandro	John Roche
Trusia	June Marlowe
Don Juan (5 years old)	Yvonne Day
Don Juan (10 years old)	Phillipe de Lacy
Hunchback	John George
Murderess of Jose	Helen d'Algy
Duke Della Varnese	Josef Swickard
Duke Margoni	Lionel Braham
Imperia	Phyllis Haver
Marquis Rinaldo	Nigel de Bralier
Marquise Rinaldo	Hedda Hopper

John Barrymore's name on any picture gives that picture an edge for the box office. In "Don Juan" the added impetus is a walloping romantic story of pure box office strength through the character of the tale, this Don Juan being the symposium of all the great lovers of the world, in one, according to the legends of his ravishing career.

As a box office winner "Don Juan" is sure fire—it aims directly at the women for pulling power and that takes in everything. At $2 top it is quite apt to run at Warner's Broadway for six months and possibly a longer time. It's going to get repeats, plenty of them.

In design this film is perfect as a thriller. It sketches out the Juan life at a period when he's up against the Borgias, a devilish mixed two-act of their day. You never can decide which Borgia should hang first, Lucretia or Caesar, brother and sister, who are wicked enough to make one believe their relatives are bossing Hell.

While in the vivid contrast is the elegant Don Juan, a Barrymore role. It's straight juvenile stuff for him, and he plays it all of the way. The other contrasting figure is Adriana, the only girl Don Juan ever met who didn't fall for him on sight.

So Don Juan fell in love with Adriana, against his father's dying warning. Father, dying, is also shown at the opening. Barrymore playing the father and doing that equally well if not so recklessly. Don's father got the bump of his life upon returning home, unexpectedly and finding his wife had a lover. That's why Don, pere, told Don, junior, then a kiddie, never to trust women. In fact, as pere passed out the only thing he appeared to leave his son was a vendetta against the world with instructions to ruin it, starting with the women, any size or age.

Don was doing pretty well at his life's work when meeting Adriana. Adriana liked Don, too, but she had a dead line and held Don on the other side of it. It was so refreshing to Don to be repulsed that he took the chance of aggravating Lucretia to see Adriana, and then finally believed Adriana unfaithful when suspecting her of being the mistress of a dangerous looking Turk or Mex.

Lucretia Borgia in this picture may have her prototype many times over in Hollywood and perhaps New York. Lucretia didn't think there was a fellow living she couldn't make go over the jumps. Her single flop was Don. Because Don probably was working on the same side of the street and knew all of the tricks.

Anyway, Don got his Adriana and away, as Lucretia was just about to move downstairs to see Don beheaded—at her orders—that's the kind of a dame was Lucretia.

Several outstanders in this splendidly written, directed and produced feature. Not alone does Barrymore's superb playing become one of them, but his athletics, as well. Barrymore is doing stuff here that any of the "western" stars would like to do; things that Fairbanks couldn't have done better in his best outdoor day. A chase scene is a bear. It's of Don Juan carrying his Adriana away, followed by about a dozen swordsmen on horses, with Barrymore placing his charge in a tree, to return and knock off all of the riders, one by one or in twos. It beats killing them in lots on the ground.

Another scene, the long and short sword duel between Barrymore and Montagu Love, is about the best thing ever in this sort of battling. It ended with a twist when Barrymore, as Donati is disarmed, leaps to his shoulders over a flight of stairs, to continue the fight with his hands.

There is a scene in an English play, often done over here in the past, in an imitation or impersonation of David Garrick. Accepting any impersonation of Garrick at about 5 percent, and visualizing from that Garrick at 100, the quickest way of giving the personal impression left by Mr. Barrymore as Don Juan is that only a Garrick could have played it as well.

The complete surprise of the pre-opening at Warner's Thursday evening was the performance of Estelle Taylor as Lucretia Borgia. Miss Taylor may have done superior film playing, but no one in the theatre apparently was aware of it. She does it here, and undeniably. Her Lucretia is a fine piece of work. She makes it sardonic in treatment, conveying precisely the woman Lucretia is presumed to have been.

The other outstanding performance is that of Mary Astor's Adriana. Miss Astor, featured in the billing, has but comparatively little action, but fills the part so thoroughly that she is a dominating figure. Warner Oland is Caesar, the savage brother, and he looks the role, but his unsaintly sister stole everything away from him in the devilish line. Montagu Love, as the heavy and when opposite Barrymore never faltered; excellent always.

Plenty of sex throughout, but held down to pass any censoring. The picture is full of fire all of the way, and again, for that reason, notwithstanding the strong romantic tale, it must draw, and it will.

"Don Juan" having everything a box office picture should have may be said to be one of the best all around moving pictures of fiction the screen has seen. *Sime.*

THE SCARLET LETTER

Metro-Goldwyn-Mayer production of Nathaniel Hawthorne's story; adaptation, scenario and titles by Frances Marion, directed by Victor Seastrom. Starring Lillian Gish, with Lars Hansen, Karl Dane, Henry B. Walthall, Marceline Corday, Mary Hawes, William H. Tooker and Joyce Coad featured. At the Central, New York, for run opening Aug. 9. Running time, 98 minutes.

Hester Prynne	Lillian Gish
Rev. Dimmesdale	Lars Hansen
Roger Prynne	Henry B. Waltoall
Giles	Karl Dane
Governor	William H. Tooker
Mistress Hibbins	Marcelina Corday
Jailer	Fritz Herzog
Patience	Mary Hawes
Beadle	Jules Cowles
Pearl	Joyce Coad
Sea Captain	James A. Marcus

One error in the presentation of "The Scarlet Letter" is that it was brought into New York while the weather was still too warm. It is not a hot weather picture, and because of that the box office is apt to suffer heavily.

This latest M-G-M starring Lillian Gish is gripping, the story would make it that, but withal it is not a special when ranked with productions like "The Big Parade," "Ben-Hur," "Don Juan" and others of that ilk.

For the big picture houses, such as the Capitol, it is certain to be a money winner, and then in turn at the other regular houses, for the picture has appeal and woman appeal, but when it comes to figuring on it as being of road show dimensions, that's out.

Some 10 years ago William Fox made a production of this same story with the witch burning incidents of the days of the Puritans in New England. At that time it was Carl Harbaugh who directed, and the reviewer on Variety who witnessed the picture stated at the time it could have been made into a "big picture" had greater attention been given to the details. That is exactly what seems to have been done by the M-G-M organization.

They have paid attention to the smallest of details and the result is that they have a picture that will rank top with their program productions. Of course, the run can be forced at the Central for possibly four or six months, with the receipts just about getting the producers off the "nut" weekly, but it won't by a long shot ever arouse such box office interest as to have a line day after day after its second month.

Miss Gish makes of Hester Prynne, the little English Puritan maid, who, although married before coming to America, through the wishes of her father, to a man she did not love and expecting him to follow after, a really sympathetic character.

Hester and the Rev. Dimmesdale receive all the sympathy of the audience, but particularly through the toll that the little heroine is compelled to pay for loving. Lars Hansen, who plays the lead opposite the star, handles the role with a great deal of finesse. He is certain to be a popular favorite with the women after this picture. If ever deciding to screen "Hamlet" here is a boy that certainly looks ideal for the title role and from his performance here the chances are that he could play it to death.

Others standing out are Karl Dane as Giles, and Marceline Corday as Mistress Hibbins, both performances a good piece of character work, although Dane hasn't anything like his role in "The Big Parade" as far as importance is concerned. Henry B. Walthall plays the husband with a make-up suggestive of Shylock and mannerism much the same, though the reason for this is far from explained.

However, the direction of Victor Seastrom is pretty nearly perfect and the composition in some of the scenes bespeaks the highest art in picture photography.

"The Scarlet Letter" has a strong plea against intolerance, for it makes the laws of the Colonies seem highly ridiculous and laughable, as judged by our present day standards. Still there are fanatics enough in the land who will say that they should still be enforced.

The Central has been redecorated for this engagement. It was freely stated at the opening that the Shuberts were hoping that the M-G-M luck would still hold good and that it would lift the "curse" from the house. Possibly they will to a certain extent, but not in the manner in which most of those who previewed the picture predicted.

Making a comparison with "La Boheme," in which Miss Gish and John Gilbert are co-starred, "The Scarlet Letter" is a better picture, and with Miss Gish alone it should fare better at the box office than "Boheme." *Fred.*

Into Her Kingdom

First National release, produced by Asher, Small & Rogers, and starring Corinne Griffith. Adapted by Carey Wilson from a story by Ruth Comfort Mitchell. Directed by Svend Gade. At the Strand, New York, Aug. 8 week. Running time, 68 minutes.

Grand Duchess Tatiana...Corinne Griffith
Stepan, the peasant.........Einar Hanson
Ivan, the tutor........Claude Gillingwater
Senov, the carnival fakir...Chas. Crockett
Senov's wife................Evelyn Selbie
A farm hand.................Larry Fisher
Bolshevik Guard.............Tom Murray
Tatiana's maid..............Marcel Corday
Court Chamberlain......Michael Bleschkoff
American customer.........Alan Sears
Russian officers—M. Lodigenski, Maj. Gen. Ikanikoff, Maj. Gen. Bogomoletz, Lieut. George Blagoi, Lieut Gene Walski, Feodor Challapin, Jr., and George Davies.

This is one of the most costly (so it appears on the screen) regular releases yet put out by First National, and certainly the most ambitious financial effort put forth by Asher, Small & Rogers, who are producing the Corinne Griffith releases for First National.

Concerned with the legend of how a grand duchess, second daughter of the Russian Czar, escaped to America after being forcibly married to a member of the Soviet council, there is reason to believe that it is based on a newspaper story of some months back which related the claims of Russian royalists that a member of the Russ royal family was living incognito in the U. S.

Here the Grand Duchess Tatiana is the childhood ideal, the fairy tale princess of young Stepan Mamovitch, a peasant boy whose parents were sent to Siberia and who was himself thrown into a St. Petersburg prison. He was released during the revolution which shook Russia in 1918, and after his release became a commissar in the Soviet ranks.

The Grand Duchess, along with Czar Nicholas, the Czarina, the Czarevitch and others of the royal line, was condemned to death, but in the darkness of a cell her maid sacrificed herself for her mistress.

When Tatiana was brought (identity unknown) to the Commissar Stepan recognized her as his childhood love, then unattainable, but now, by the stroke of a Soviet-inspired pen, his wife to bully, master, browbeat and break. He told her he would do this, as the fiery spirit of the boy still harbored intense hatred of a royalist, for the exile to Siberia at royal hands was the death of his parents.

So they were married.

Later they escaped together to America, but the wife remembered her husband's threats. Once in a Jersey mill town, she became a shopkeeper while he worked in the mills. Finally, advised by a friendly tutor who had escaped with them, the husband went to the one-time Grand Duchess and with all humility told her he was wrong, that he truly loved her and that he would go to Europe to see the royalist factions and have her proclaimed Empress of all the Russias. He did this, brought the royalists to her humble home, but as she came down the stairs to greet them she bore a child in her arms and assured the distinguished visitors that her husband was mad—that his pet delusion was that she was the Grand Duchess Tatiana. The husband protested that he wanted to bring her into her kingdom. She, with typical movie reasoning, replied, as she looked at her child:

"Here is my kingdom."

It's a hunky story, but a good one filled with plenty of that rich girl, poor boy dope which audiences love. Unfortunate is the symbolistic insertion of a mystic figure, the Weaver of Fate, picking out varicolored cords, the red representing the girl and the brown the boy, and doing tricks with them. This was intended as symbolism. But symbolism, to retain its standing, should

always be nothing more than a subtle intimation of something else more tangible. Yet here it is all acted out, and is thus becomes sour. These inserts of the Weaver doing her stuff are in technicolor, quite out of tune with the splendid black and white of the film.

Miss Griffith's performance is excellent, as always, but the principal item of interest here is her leading man, Einar Hanson, apparently a Scandinavian actor. He is young, handsome, forceful, magnetic, and has a way which should hold him to a good position in pictures here. Hanson made a definite impression in this film. Svend Gade, the Swedish director, who made the unforgettable "Siege" for Universal last year, did this one, and turned out a smooth, excellent job.

In settings "Into Her Kingdom" stands out like a million dollars. The massive palace exteriors and interiors are all apparently studio made and they rank as fit to take their place in the grandest of specials. Moreover, they are always photographed well and add a great deal of illusion to the sore of a theme which people would like to believe but which wouldn't have been so good unless great structures of the type used had been made.

"Into Her Kingdom" is for the great picture-going mob. It should be handsomely received, for it is handsomely made.   *Bisk.*

OH BABY

Al Lichtman production presented by Carl Laemmle. Released by Universal. Written and directed by Harley Knoles, scenario by Arthur Hoerl. At the Colony, New York, week Aug. 7. Running time, 75 minutes.

"Billy" Fitzgerald.............Little Billy
Jim Stone...................David Butler
Dorothy Brennan...........Madge Kennedy
Arthur Graham...........Creighton Hale
Mary Bond..................Ethel Shannon
Aunt Phoebe................Flora Finch

When Harley Knoles sat down to write this screen story he must have had "Charley's Aunt" in his mind. At any rate, he has turned out a rather weak sister sort of an imitation of the old impersonation farce. For the average daily change house and some of the houses that run a split week, the picture will get over and draw laughs. Because of its comedy it's a fairly good warm weather attraction. It doesn't stand up with any of the average program pictures that manage to get de luxe presentations on Broadway, but it is fully as good if not better than "The Great Deception," current at the Rivoli.

The story is dependant entirely on Little Billy, who enacts the role of a midget prize fight manager. Billy has a contender for the heavyweight championship title, whom he is shaping up for a battle with another contender at Madison Square Garden. He also has a friend who wants him to impersonate his daughter for a few hours so that he can convince his wealthy old aunt that he has been leading a worthy life and thus get some of her money. Billy consents and a newspaper woman volunteers to pose as the wife for a few hours. They visit the aunt and there the complications arise when the old lady insists that they stay for the night and that a young lady guest put the little girl to sleep with her.

It is the night that the big fight is scheduled and the little manager finally makes his escape and gets to the ringside just in time to prevent his battler from being licked.

Later, when all concerned are having a celebration in a cabaret the aunt walks in on the picture and for a moment it looks as though the fat's in the fire, but Little Billy again saves the day.

A happy ending all around works out for a laugh.

Little Billy in particular looks as a great screen bet on the strength of his work in this picture, and ought to be find for a short subject comedy series.

The fact that all the sport writers are introduced and the radio public gets a chance to see Graham McNamee, the sport announcer, in action ought to add box office value to the picture. Capt. Irving O'Hay, who fought in about 11 wars, plays a bit with Billy in front of new Madison Square Garden and comes through with a good little laugh scene.   *Fred.*

SO THIS IS PARIS

Production and release by Warner Brothers. Ernst Lubitsch director, with Monte Blue and Patsy Ruth Miller featured. Farce comedy based upon French comedy "Revellion." No adapter programed. Not unlikely Mr. Lubitsch made or suggested lines of adaptation, also handling own continuity and building up story as he proceeded in the making. Preview at Cameo, New York (Film Arts Guild), Aug. 13. Now on run there at $1.65 top. Running time, about 80 mins.

Dr. Giraud....................Monte Blue
Mme. Giraud.........Patsy Ruth Miller
Georgette Lalle..........Lilyan Tashman
Mons. Lalle.............Andre Beranger
Maid........................Myrna Loy
Cop....................Sidney D'Albrook

A highly laughable farce comedy with the laughs heavy on situations, and humorous captions added to make an excellent total. The laughing of this Lubitsch directed picture seems big enough to make it a possible hold-over for several of the first runs.

Lubitsch has a snappy way of putting forward the laughs. He slams them over without unnecessary "planting" or using any of the rigamarole of the stereotyped.

Here, there is unusual photography also. At one time Lubitsch plays continuous scenes in what actually amounted to close-ups. He may have gotten a studio slant at the photography and taken advantage of it, or that may be a Lubitsch trade-mark. To bring the characters down front and keep them there, as in this film gives the picture a touch of individuality in direction that cannot be overlooked.

For straightaway directorial novelty Lubitsch handles a Parisian ball scene in a manner only equaled by the freaky shot or two of "Variety." In the massive crowded ball room, splendid in its own way, Lubitsch runs in a mass of mazy and hazy feet and heads, figures and legs; ofttimes clear, at other times misty. Double exposures and a dozen other tricks are there with one shot prominent, a stretch of bare legs as though an entire chorus lined up with nothing but legs showing in front, until the audience at the Cameo on the hottest night of the summer, involuntarily burst into applause.

A couple of laugh scenes were led by Monte Blue's "souse." Mr. Blue played it deliciously with just a bit of devilment. And otherwise Mr. Blue as a farceur is excellent.

It was close between Blue and Andre Beranger as the French dancer. Mr. Beranger looks like a pantomimist of rank. Some of his work here is so praiseworthy it must be seen to realize the grade. His postures, grimaces (no mugging) and bland fatheadedness force laughter, while all the time Mr. Beranger is always suggesting, without reaching an actuality, that in character disposition he is effeminate. That makes for an underlying continuous laugh whenever he presents himself.

Patsy Ruth Miller has range and much expression. Lilyan Tashman, as the frivolous dancer, looks the role and acts it well enough.

It's a question whether "So This Is Paris" is the best title that could have been selected since "Paris" has appeared in so many titles. But it may be as suitable as any other. The atmosphere and environment of Paris are faithfully held to.

Building up, this story is farce comedy and develops several angles in complications with two married couples living opposite each other drawn into a mass of lies and deceptions.

It permits of much gagging business, legitimately and logically fitted in. That is the strength of the picture. Hardly anything is foretold nor can it be guessed at, such as the ingenuous piece of business in the traffic cop scene.

Lubitsch will increase his long list of admirers through this "Paris." It shows the imported director's innate ability; that he is always the director and subject is secondary to him.

Frenchy in topic the tale lies wholly between the two families of two each. From a series of incidents the doctor discovers the dancing wife opposite is a former friend, while the dancer's husband (also her stage partner) contracts a fondness for the wife of the doctor, the latter having a "sheik" complex.

At the finale, without anyone having confessed to lying, doctor and wife are again in marital h rmony, while the dancer's wife is once again embroiled with another admirer, gained the night of the ball.

A corking comedy that should have been held back until the season. It has played some points over the map, but was first screened in New York as a preview last Friday night at the Cameo by the Film Arts Guild. Now running there and should do business in the small house. *Sime.*

GREAT DECEPTION

Robert Kane production released by First National. Featuring Aileen Pringle and Ben Lyon. Directed by Howard Higgin. At the Rivoli, New York, week Aug. 7. Running time, 61 minutes.

Cyril Mansfield	Ben Lyon
Lois	Aileen Pringle
Rizzio	Basil Rathbone
Handy	Sam Hardy
Mrs. Mansfield	Charlotte Walker
Lady Jane	Amelia Summerville
Gen. Von Frankenhauser	Hubert Wilke
Von Markow	Lucian Prival
Burton	Lucius Henderson
Maxwell	Mark Gonzales

Of all the straight out-and-out junky program pictures that have crashed into a Broadway de luxe presentation house this one is about the junkiest. At best, a mighty poor imitation of "Three Faces East," with the latter about 100 per cent a better picture. Rather than play this one, it would be a better bet to return "Three Faces East." Just what Robert Kane must have been thinking of when he tried to sneak this one over is a mystery. And how he got it on Broadway may or may not be a mystery. But the Rivoli's box office must suffer for this week as a consequence.

The story is one of those war tales laid in England and Germany. The kind of war film fiction rampant during 1917-18, and not half as well done as the majority of those seen in those hectic days.

A boy in a German school is English by birth. His dad is an Englishman and his mother German. The story opens with the last night of his student days when farewells are being said. One of his German companions tells him not to forget Germany when back in England.

Tho next shot shows the war started, and the boy is looked upon as a slacker at home, although he is secretly in the English spy system, while ostensibly in the pay of the Germans. He is flying back and forth between his own country and Germany, slipping the Germans misleading information while his own government gets the low down. His pal of school days is "caught with the goods" in England and "stood aginst the wall," having been betrayed by another German spy who wanted to strengthen his own position.

It is the latter who plays the heavy in the production and who tries to win the hand of an American girl in love with the hero. The heavy tries to compel her to do his bidding on the pain of having her lover exposed. Finally, he kidnaps the girl and takes her to Germany in a sub. At headquarters he faces the young Englishman, who has flown over to expose him. The Englishman is arrested and ordered shot within a few minutes, but escapes and rescues the girl, the two together with a loyal American mechanic get to their machine and fly back to safety after a battle in the clouds.

Miss Pringle is too mature a heroine to play opposite the slight Lyon. Lyon is far from appearing as heroic as he should in this role. The best work was done by Sam Hardy, who labored under a seeming terrific strain to inject a little comedy and succeeded fairly.

Balance of the cast meant nothing. *Fred.*

The Amateur Gentleman

Inspiration Pictures presentation releasing through First National and starring Richard Barthelmess. Adapted from story by Jeffery Farnol; Sidney Olcott directing. At the Strand, New York, week Aug. 15. Running time, 79 minutes.

Barnabas Barty	Richard Barthelmess
Lady Cleone Meredith	Dorothy Dunbar
Ronald Barrymaine	Gardner James
Sir Mortimer Carnaby	Nigel Barrie
Peterby	Brandon Hurst
Viscount Devenham	John Miljan
John Barty	Edwards Davis
Duchess of Camberhurst	Billie Bennett
Jasper Gaunt	Herbert Grimwood
Prince Regent	Gino Corrado
Captain Chumley	Sidney de Gray
Captain Slingsby	John Peters

A costume picture crammed with action and a not uninteresting story. Richard Barthelmess does a modified Beau Brummel, rides to win in an antiquated steeplechase race, rough and tumbles a bit and makes of it satisfactory fare for the bigger'n better houses.

Sidney Olcott directed and has woven nicely despite the impression a lessening of 1,000 feet might help. The finish resembles an opera finale when a three-cornered shooting affray concludes with all dropping, including the star. That he convalesces and weds the titled lady goes without saying.

The setting is England in the early nineteenth century with Barthelmess as Barnaby Barty, son of a former pugilistic champion turned inn keeper. A longing to prune and act as a gentleman swings into action upon the inheritance of a goodly sum (even for pictures) from an uncle. The youngster has to box his dad to win permission to make the London migration. During the trip he blackens the eye of Sir Mortimer Carnaby (Nigel Barrie) in favor of the Prince Regent, during a dispute over Lady Cleone Meredith (Miss Dunbar).

Acquisition of an ultra wardrobe, under guidance of a valet, and the buying of an unruly steed from Viscount Devenham (John Miljan) for the big steeplechase leads Barnabas into the center of the young bloods. This circle he conquers with the aid of Devenham and his middle name, Beverly.

Lady Meredith having a n'er-do-well half brother, to the hilt in debt, makes the complications with Sir Carnaby, the latter buying the brother's notes from a money lender. Young Barnabas beats his titled rival in the race and thwarts the latter's efforts to get the girl.

Mostly all studio stuff in sets, either interior or exterior, the frame work for the action nevertheless convinces. And the costuming digests easily. The steeplechase, with the gentleman riders in top hats and immaculately clothed, is away from the usual. Protographically the picture is standard and the titles please.

Barthelmess does Barnabas sincerely and well, ably supported by a good sized detachment of male cast members. There are only two women prominent, Dorothy Dunbar and Billie Bennett. Miss Dunbar has sufficient stateliness to fill her role of heroine, if somewhat limited as to footage allowed, while Miss Bennett is equal to being a light comedy foil.

Among the men the playing of Mr. Barrie and John Miljan stands out. With Miljan there is an interesting point. Having just "caught" this actor in a mediocre independent release, the difference in his two performances is astounding. In the minor film Miljan could be dismissed without a thought. His playing there apparently lacked everything outside of the mechanics. In this instance, among major company and subject to the demands of intelligent directing, his work ranks with the leaders of the film. Not that Miljan is new to pictures. Quite the contrary, and that but emphasizes the apparent difference either in morale or demands under these two conditions. All of which may or may not be true of free-lancing film players.

Barrie makes an acceptable "heavy," appropriately annoying during the late footage with no regrets when he passes out. Gardner James shows symptoms of restraint in playing the weak willed and well bottled half brother, nicely assisted in one scene by neat double camera work. Brandon Hurst clicks as the valet and Edwards Davis makes a compact job of the former fistic champ and father. In fact the support, as a whole, is excellent.

Nothing to be ashamed of by any-one in this release. The censors can't arbitrarily clip a foot and it gives Barthelmess all kinds of opportunities besides being sufficiently romantic. If not especially brilliant, then well made and an appropriate program feature. More of the same merit will never hurt its star. *Skig.*

The Duchess of Buffalo

Joseph M. Schenck production, with Constance Talmadge starred. Tullio Carminati featured. Released by First National. Adapted for screen by Hans Kraley from the Hungarian play, "Sybil." Directed by A. Sidney Franklin. At Capitol, New York, week Aug. 8. Running time, average for full feature.

Marian Duncan	Constance Talmadge
Lieut. Vladimir Orloff	Tullio Carminati
Grand Duke Gregory Alexandrovich	Edw. Martindel
Grand Duchess Olga Petrovna	Rose Dione
Hotel Manager	Chester Conklin
Commandant	Lawrence Grant
Maid	Martha Franklin
Adjutant	Jean De Briac

A picture with a title that is not explained. "The Duchess of Buffalo" is never referred nor alluded to during the running of the entire film other than the first title mention. That with other lapses might imply cutting before showing that knocked out several things, including a little continuity now and then.

Who's Tullio Carminati? He sounds new and what can he do to bring featuring But Tullio at least looked the part, and didn't overact in comparison or in contrast with Constance Talmadge.

The director, Sidney Franklin, and an actor, Chester Conklin, are responsible for the most and biggest laughs. Mr. Franklin got in a couple of roars. Once when Constance was bounced up and down on Edw. Martindel's knee. Mr. Martindel played the Grand Duke, taking everything for straight acting. The other bit was a kidlet sticking out its tongue as Constance started to kiss the child. That knee thing was good direction all through. Mr. Conklin as the excitable hotel keeper sent over plenty of laughs, most of them mild. At other times there was a semblance of tittering, for this is a tittering, flappering something.

Sometimes the locale appears to be in Russia. That's when it is snowing or there is sleighing. At other times it looks Viennese.

Not much reason in the plot to start the story and not much more to keep it going. Almost any old French farce of the banging door variety could have been used without the authors' names in full face

A lieutenant of the guards (no king in sight) wanted to marry an American dance girl in a show. The Grand Duke wanted to make the same girl also. Between the two the girl got a diamond breastpin and seems to have lost her job, while the Grand Duke got in a jam with his Grand Duchess. All the Lieut. received was an order to be shot whenever the sun came up for desertion.

However, as the Lieut, and his gal pulled the Duke out of his family trouble, the Duke revoked the shooting bit and ordered them to be married instead.

The picture started off as though it had been made because the titles were laugh punches, but even the titling commenced to fade as the tale started to wither. Still the title writer should have been featured, too.

Well produced picture for general assimilation by the usual picture house gathering.

Take a chance and guarantee 60 laughs—a laugh a minute. That always sounds good. If there are any squawks on the number, gross, tell them they are dumb and must have missed some. *Sime.*

SENOR DAREDEVIL

Charles R. Rogers presents Ken Maynard, "a brand new screen star," in this First National picture, directed by Al Rogell. Story and adaptation by Marion Jackson. Harry J. Brown, production manager. At the Colony, New York, Aug. 15; running time, 60 minutes.

Don Luis O'Flagherty	Ken Maynard
Sally Blake	Dorothy Devore
"Tiger" O'Flagherty	George Nichols
Juan Estrada	Josef Swickard
Jesse Wilks	J. P. McGowan
Ratburn	Sheldon Lewis
Pat Muldoon	Buck Black

A naive western melodrama with a wealth of whirlwind action against a background of remarkably beautiful western mountain scenery varied with wastes of cactus desert land. A super-hero, a miracle-horse, thrilling riding stunts, galloping desperadoes and the other ingredients make this a first rate picture in its class—which is to say high up among the run of program westerns, but scarcely in the special class.

As presented at the Colony the picture took on importance from its surrounding show and it will deliver entertainment wherever shown. Briefly it is a substantial commercial production with no special claim to high artistic grade. It has a number of capital screen highlights. One of them is a series of long shots showing a pack train of burros apparently a mile long climbing zig zag up a snow-capped mountain peak. Another punch comes in the wild rush of a prairie train of horse-drawn freighters in a rush through the swirling dust, racing against time to save a mining camp from plotters.

These last named shots take cumulative interest from the skillful way they are worked up by the underlying situation, and reach a climax in a stunning spectacular effect for the finale. The wagons under the lead of the hero have fought their way through three traps laid by outlaws. As they approach their goal, a mining camp hard pressed by famine, it becomes plain that nothing but speed can save the situation. At the last stage of the race against time, the train swings into the bed of a dried up lake, a hard, white, level floor across which they sweep with all the pictorial effectiveness of the chariot race in "Ben-Hur."

This is the smash and it is made to register for full worth as the climax of a scenic revel. Throughout the director has played up the fine scenery that serves as the locale.

Ken Maynard is the new cowboy hero and for riding he equals the best. In this picture he takes a number of falls from horseback going at full speed that are hair raisers, in one case leaping from his own galloping mount, tackling another rider and going over the second horse's head at grips with his antagonist. His riding is always an asset.

Maynard is a stalwart young man, likeable in appearance and rather flamboyant in his acting method, although this may be an unavoidable incident to this particular picture, in which he is called to play the super-hero. An educated white horse, billed as "Tarzan," contributes a good deal to the story.

This is the first of the independent westerns put out to take advantage of the vogue for that style of production. The hook-up with First National is understood to apply only to this picture, promoted by Brown, who is an independent of considerable activity. His releases have been put through Rayart up to this time. Maynard is being exploited as a newcomer, emphasizing the production rather than the star.

The story has only one defect. It gets into action rather late and the soft pedal is on the romantic interest. Dorothy Devore has a small, perfunctory part as a mining camp waif who runs a restaurant, and is the aid and comforter of the chief wagoner who freights supplies across the desert. The "planting" of the story is unnecessarily elaborate. Twenty-five minutes had elapsed before the exposition of the story was complete. However, once the situation is established, the action sweeps forward absorbingly.

Rush.

The Loves of Ricardo

George Beban production written and directed by Beban. Beban also starred. Presented by Saul Magnus Paulais with no distributor named. At the Rivoli, N. Y., and shown in conjunction with one 24-minute sequence played on stage by company seen in the film. Running time of film, exclusive of stage portion, 68 minutes.

Ricardo Vitelli	George Beban
Annetta	Amille Milaine
Steve Randall	Monte Collins, Jr.
Marco Martinelli	Albano Valerio
Flora Martinelli	Meeka Alrich
Tony Villano	Signor Frondi
Mike Fererra	Gullio Cortesi
Marie Fererra	Mrs. Gullio Cortesi
"Hap" MacGuire	Norman Ives
"Skeets" Riley	E. E. MacLeod, Jr.
Madge Anderson	Helen Huntoon

Exhibitors will understand that this picture is currently being played in first run houses in conjunction with a stage sequence which runs 24 minutes and in which Beban and a greater part of the film company appear. This review treats of the picture by itself, while another review under presentations department treats of the stage sequence, arriving at the general conclusion that with the stage stuff, the film qualifies as a first run attraction, but that in itself, it is suitable only for the intermediate houses.

Written by Beban, it is a hodge-podge of plot, which begins by having him as an Italian groceryman and the guardian of a beautiful girl, Annetta. He also has his horse, Mussolini, and with this pair he gets along beautifully until Steve Randall, a wise-cracking, smart guy, walks in and marries Annetta. Ricardo, the groceryman, turns the store over to them and goes to Florida, where he has bought land from a swindler, but didn't know until the tide came in that his land was under water. Because he talks back to some bootleggers landing stuff he is shanghaied to their boat and there he trains a parrot to say "Picka me up" and "I know where there's a lotta hootch." The parrot thus trained, he sets the bird adrift in his cage, supported by a round life preserver, which keeps the contraption above water. The parrot is picked up by a revenue boat, the bootleggers are driven away and Ricardo freed. He immediately goes back to his old home,

finds that Annetta is being mistreated and that Steve is blackmailing the wife of a wealthy Italian banker, friend to Ricardo. So Ricardo kicks Steve out of the house, goes to the city pound to buy back the horse which Steve has sold and sees Steve on the running board of a car—the woman he was trying to blackmail driving. The car has an accident; Steve is killed, the woman recovers and Annetta admits to Ricardo that she loves him. Happy ending.

It's a harum-scarum sort of a plot, written largely to exploit Beban's peculiar genius for portraying a certain type of Italian character.

The supporting cast is composed of unknown players of no especial distinction, and Beban's direction has leaned toward giving himself plenty of closeups, etc. But the story is so patently a device to create sympathy for one character and ill-will for his opponents that it must be judged on that basis. And it cannot be denied that Beban's part does get sympathy and that's all it goes after.

The film was made with an eye principally to the stage cut-in, but as a feature for the daily changes, stage stuff omitted, it suffices.

Sisk.

3 BAD MEN

John Ford production. Presented by William Fox. From the novel by Herman Whitaker, "Over the Border." Directed by John Ford. At special projection room showing Aug. 13. Running time, 75 mins.

Dan O'Malley	George O'Brien
Lee Carlton	Olive Borden
Layne Hunter	Lou Tellegen
Mike Costigan	J. Farrell MacDonald
Bull Stanley	Tom Santschi
Spade Allen	Frank Campeau
Joe Minsk	George Harris
Old Prospector	Jay Hunt

This feature falls just short of being a terrific knockout. But as an out-and-out western thriller it is a wow from beginning to end.

There are scenes in it as effective as the wagon train in "The Covered Wagon," and the thousands in the mad race across country when the government lands are opened to the public is bigger than anything of its kind that has been shown in a picture.

John Ford, who directed, has turned out a special in the fullest sense of the word—a picture that, while it cannot stand up in the $2 legit house attraction class, certainly will be a winner at the box office of the picture houses.

The picture is a walk-away for the three actors playing the title roles—Tom Santschi, J. Farrell MacDonald and Frank Campeau, with Santschi running away with the picture from the beginning. George O'Brien and Olive Borden supply the juvenile interest. There is a very compelling little romance.

The story is that of the opening of the Indian lands in the Dakotas. The three bad men impersonated are Mike Costigan, Bull Stanley and Spade Allen. They are wanted by the law authorities from Mexico to Canada, with a price on their heads in Canada and Mexico as well as in this country. They join the rush to the Dakotas. While they are cattle and horse thieves, they refuse to rob a little southern girl of her string of thoroughbreds after a rival gang had attacked the wagon in which she and her father are traveling and kill the old man.

It is then that the trio band together with the idea of protecting the girl. They do this to the utmost degree, finally laying down their lives in order that the girl and her young sweetheart shall have the opportunity to escape a pursuing gang led by Layne Hunter, a crooked sheriff, played by Lou Tellegen. Right here and now let it be said that Tellegen contributes a heavy of no mean proportions.

There must have been a whale of

money spent in making this picture. It shows it in the tremendous crowds used in scene after scene, and in the race scene there is almost as much thrilling stuff as in the "Ben-Hur" chariot race.

As for the cast, it has "names" in plenty to make it go over with the audiences. There is a lack of comedy in the picture, although MacDonald and Campeau supply what there is.

It is a real picture and one that they are going to go wild over in the localities where they are strong for westerns. This is a super-western and every bit as big as "The Iron Horse" was.

Fred.

THE SHOW OFF

Famous Players' screen version of George Kelly's play of same name. Scenario by Pierre Collins, with Malcolm St. Clair directing. At the Rivoli, N. Y., week of Aug. 22. Running time, 70 mins.

Aubrey Piper	Ford Sterling
Amy Fisher	Lois Wilson
Clara	Louise Brooks
Joe Fisher	Gregory Kelly
Pop Fisher	C. W. Goodrich
Mom Fisher	Claire McDowell
Railroad Executive	Joseph Smiley

"The Show Off" on the surface is a vigorous comedy, but it has a touch of deep and rather bitter cynicism. Its career as a film at the box office ought to be an interesting study because it will be something of a test of the screen public's capacity to support something of a novelty.

As adapted for the screen it has all the advantage of a cast of popular players. It has splendid handling of comedy values, and it is built on a theme that has in one form or another made for popular success. The essence of the story is that of a lowbrow blunderer who is a pest to everybody around him, but in the end makes good. The comedy is more or less superficial, while the satirical comment upon life is keen and rather biting.

It has serious drawbacks to popular appeal. For example, the environment of the whole tale is drab, commonplace, middle-class Philadelphia—scarcely an inviting background. The story is almost devoid of colorful romance and is absolutely guiltless of anything like sex interest. But it has comedy appeal.

The hero's absurd boastings are always good for laughs, and his exploit of driving a Ford car through Market and Broad streets, Philadelphia, is a revel of boisterous fun.

The picture is a novelty inasmuch as it departs from all the sure-fire formulas of the commercial picture. There is no pollyanna romance. Virtue gets no reward, and even after the vulgar lowbrow has saved the day he gives no more promise of being any less a pest than he was before. On the contrary, he has put everybody else under obligations, and, as the mother-in-law says at the finish, "Heaven help me from now on."

It's a curious story technique that chooses the least engaging of its character creations for the heroic role, as is here done. It may be true to life, but how will a convention-fed screen public take it? At a venture, they will accept the obvious laugh situations for their surface value and let it go at that, putting the production down as a fairly funny picture.

This Aubrey person, a $30-a-week clerk who talks like a captain of industry, has a good deal in common with "Babbitt," and if recollection serves, "Babbitt" as a picture broke no box office records. Incidentally, Ford Sterling's Aubrey is as skillful a bit of character portraiture as was Willard Louis' Babbitt. Lois Wilson, always a graceful player, has a pale part in the clinging vine, while Gregory Kelly, a most likable legit juvenile, is a passive puppet in the scheme of action. Louise Brooks looks the part of the modern flapper type, and Claire McDowell, as always, makes the mother role attractive and convincing. *Rush.*

BATTLING BUTLER

M-G-M feature presented by J. M. Schenck and starring Buster Keaton. Adapted from the musical comedy of the same name. Directed by Keaton and featuring Sally O'Neil. At the Capitol, New York, week of Aug. 22. Running time, 75 mins.

Alfred Butler	Buster Keaton
The Girl	Sally O'Neil
His Valet	Snitz Edwards
"Battling" Butler	F. McDonald
His Wife	Mary O'Brien
His Trainer	Tom Wilson
His Manager	Eddie Borden
The Girl's Father	Walter James
The Girl's Brother	Buddy Fine

Plenty scenarists had a hand in

this one with the picture a long time on the way. Result is that there isn't much resemblance to the show. But that's not of much account, the main object having been reached in turning out a laugh-getting comedy that should do business.

"Frozen Pan" Buster's face is as rigid as ever, besides which he gets an abundance of laughs out of pure gag stuff. It must be remembered that Keaton takes screen credit for having directed this one. And if so some of his stuff is excellent. At least one new wrinkle in a "goodbye" scene between he and the girl is bound to be copped by the other boys supervising camera action. It drew comment from the laity members present at the Capitol, which is fair enough.

The picture starts 'way ahead of the show in that Keaton opens up as a pampered son of wealth. A disgusted father sends him out to "rough it," and he goes plus a foreign car, valet and an elaborate camping outfit. Here he meets the girl (Sally O'Neil), whose backwoods dad and brother think little of Alfred (Buster Keaton) until the valet (Snitz Edwards) bridges the breach by explaining his young boss is "Battling" Butler, the lightweight boxer, about to fight the champ in his division.

Circumstances force the meek scion into marriage along with the other situation and he has to migrate to the genuine Butler's training quarters to make it look on the level. There he accidentally is of assistance to the fighter's wife, happenings make it look like "an affair," and Butler, become the champ, burns up.

Due to fight the "Alabama Murderer," the jealous champ frames with his trainer to teach the retiring Alfred a lesson by making him assume that ring engagement. The young bridegroom can't back out because his wife unexpectedly turns up at the camp and won't leave. Hence, the action takes Alfred into a training routine for his fistic battle with the "Murderer." And he believes it to be strictly on the level.

The night of the fight the scared youth is in a dressing room ready to go on when cheers announce the real Butler as the winner. It's okay with Alf, but the champ wanders into the room to put on the finishing touches by chastising Alfred a bit. The valet has locked Mrs. Alf into a store room, so she hasn't seen the fight in the arena, and believes her husband to have won. The bride w... to the dressing room door in t... to see her spouse taking an awful tossing around from one whom she thinks is a sparring partner.

Alfred gets one look at her in the door, knows he has to make good and the battle is on in earnest. Both are in trunks with gloves on and it's quite a private affair until a wild swing by Alf finally puts the champ on the floor. The finish has Alfred, still in his ring outfit, but with a top hat and cane, grabbed through habit during a hurried exit, strolling down a crowded street with his wife.

Not more than three or four actual scenes from the show included in the scenario, the boys having done plenty of rewriting as they saw fit. But the action carries along evenly and at a good pace to make it interesting. It's not a draggy picture and has its highlights. Keaton gets a salvo of laughs out of hoke induced by ring ropes and drew a howl out of a "situation."

Two camera men cranking has changed the lighting on various sequences, but it's not a serious difference in shading and probably won't be noticed. One slip seems to be a change of suits by Keaton during an upstairs climb.

Corking support from practically all members, the Misses O'Neil and O'Brien making their dual wives stand up and Edwards getting a full quota from his valet characterization. Behind this group comes Tom Wilson, very good as the trainer.

Keaton, of course, is practically in front of the camera all the way and is equal to the prominence. The ring stuff has been nicely staged with either a "situation" or a gag always on tap during the story. Few, if any, slow bits and in toto a picture on which Keaton and staff rate a bow. *Skig.*

The Lady of the Harem

Famous Players production made from the stage play, "Hassan," by James McElroy Flecker. Adapted to the screen by James Donohue. Directed by Raoul Walsh. Greta Nissen featured, with William Collier, Jr., and Ernest Torrence. At Loew's New York, Aug. 8, one day. Running time, 71 minutes.

Pervannah	Greta Nissen
Rafi	William Collier, Jr.
Yasmin	Louise Fazenda
The Caliph	So Jin

This picture was made by Raoul Walsh for Famous Players apparently when that firm was in the throes of a belief that pictures filled with semi-naked women would bring great box office returns. The failure of "The Wanderer" smashed that belief into bits, and now that "Lady of the Harem," a sumptuous and expensive production, has played but a single day at Loew's New York instead of a week at one of the F. P. theatres, it is proof enough that the undressed stuff proved a dud.

The stage play from which this was made, "Hassan," was a great triumph in England, and on that basis A. L. Erlanger last winter imported it for New York. The flop it did is memorable. In two weeks after its opening the scenery made abroad, the cast of over 150 and the advertising had gone for nothing. The play closed and only its picture rights remained. It may be that Famous figured on the pull this picture would have in England, where the play wes well known, but this hardly seems likely inasmuch as the adaptation to the screen has rearranged the incidents of the play to a great extent.

Not that this adaptation has hurt the play. As it now stands, the incidents which led to the climax run along to a nice enough conclusion, but there is no suspense. The plot is that the Caliph of Kornassah was a fellow who liked gold and women—plenty of both. So his soldiers stole Pervannah, a luscious blond, for him. Her lover, Rafi, got peeved, and with others oppressed by the Caliph's tyrannies, went on the warpath, organizing a crowd of expert dagger throwers. These terrorized the Caliph to such an extent that, disguised as a merchant, he went through the streets seeking those who were undermining his throne. But they got him first, and although believing him to be a traitor against their cause, yet not knowing he was the Caliph, they imprisoned him. Hassan, an ignorant candy-maker, was the means whereby he escaped.

Brought to court, Hassan was made a lord, but when he saw the Caliph preparing to torture Rafi before the eyes of his sweetheart, Pervannah, Hassan told the Caliph to his face that he was a skunk, and then forthwith became a leader of the people against the potentate. Result—the Caliph got a dagger or so in the back, Hassan took over the Caliph's duties, and Rafi and Pervannah were united.

Most of the roles are played well, but the directorial accent on sex, sex, sex seemed silly. Walsh kept parading the girls in front of the camera as if they were so many show girls, dressed sparsely to give the Winter Garden mob a thrill. Obviously he couldn't undress them too much because of the censorship restrictions, but even with what undressing the film now possesses it may not get by in the strictly censorial states. Moreover, it is not of the tone to be given a Sunday showing, for the Caliph's desire for the heroine is of a nature which will offend many.

Lavishly and well produced. Beautifully acted, especially by Miss Nissen and So Jin, the Jap who played the Caliph. Torrence is buried, while Louise Fazenda, playing a fancy strumpet who hid her friends under beds, was plainly "not the type." Miss Fazenda's long string of comedy parts in the past automatically disassociates her from the sort of a role she was given here.

For the daily changes, "Lady of the Harem," but not a first run of any importance. *Sisk.*

THE BOY FRIEND

Metro-Goldwyn-Mayer feature, adapted from John Alexander Kirkpatrick's novel, "The Charm Book," by Alice D. G. Miller. Directed by Monta Bell. In the cast: Marceline Day, John Herron, George K. Arthur, Gertrude Astor and Ward Crane. At the New York, Aug. 14, one day. Running time, 55 mins.

In addition to the common difficulties of concentrating the diffuse materials of a novel into the confinements of a screen drama, this story never should have been attempted in the film medium.

It depends not upon action and plot but upon the play of character and ideas. The result is that the story develops very largely in titles, and the screen views merely supplement the printed word, instead of the reverse, which, of course, should be the case. The action is all out of sight in the minds of the characters. As a result what was fully, probably interestingly, made clear in the novel is confused in the film play.

The essence of the story is that a small-town girl is happily headed for marriage to a small-town boy when she is thrown into the path of rich city people whose summer home is in the village. Her whole vision is changed. The life she lives, her family surroundings and her entire environment become distasteful as she contrasts them with the imagined thrill of living in the big city.

Around this theme a comedy story has been woven. Joe, the small-town sweetheart, becomes acquainted with an encyclopedia of worldly knowledge called "The Charm Book," peddled by a traveling book agent. He tries, by applying its absurd teachings, to make the small-town surroundings so attractive to the girl that she will give up her dream of a life in the city and marry him.

The working out of this idea brings about some rather boisterous comedy situations, and it is this comedy element that gives the film its chief value, such as it is. In the novel it is probable the reader's sympathy was drawn to the boy, but in the picture he comes forward as an unutterable fool. The same thing is true of the girl's mother, who acts as his accomplice in the benevolent conspiracy.

At no time does the human element register fully. The people who should win sympathy for their good intentions appear merely as ridiculous clowns because the picture medium does not permit of delicate shading of action and character. In short, the glaring faults are those common to the transpositions from novel to screen. Marceline Day is disclosed as an especially likeable actress. If anything could make the character attractive, her fresh youth and artless acting would do the trick. The players are all excellent with what they have to work on, but the whole production is short on definite human appeal, regardless of how rich the book may have been in that commodity.

It is probable that the small-town background, especially contrasted as it is here directly with the more elegant surroundings of the city people, reacts against the central characters. Here is a striking case of giving a drab setting to people to whom interest is invited, and a glowing and romantic atmosphere to the city people toward whom the spectator is supposed to be indifferent. It brings about a conflict of intent that must have an influence upon any audience, probably without their realizing it, but actual and disturbing, nevertheless.

PALS FIRST

Edwin Carewe production, First National release, of Lee Wilson Dodd's play, scenarized by F. P. Elliott and adapted by Olga Printzlau; titled by Ralph Spence. Harper Bros., book publishers, also given screen credit, unusual, although possible tie-up. Lloyd Hughes and Dolores Del Rio co-featured. Runs 60 minutes. At Broadway, New York, Aug. 9 week.

"Pals First" makes the fourth First National on Broadway this week (Aug. 9), with the Strand and Capitol holding other F. N. features. Whatever the merit of the other trio, this crook meller does not rate a full week's stand, being a fair crook meller, but nothing beyond that.

Lloyd Hughes and Dolores Del Rio, co-featured, click but half and half, with the Latin actress, an Edwin Carewe discovery (Mr. Carewe is also credited for this production), disappointing. Her Latin type for one thing does not jibe with the aristocratic southern atmosphere, in addition to which Miss Del Rio's personal accomplishments as a screen actress are negative. Her eyes, of Oriental type, are an odd combination with the Spanish features. Whatever registration is essayed is but mild.

The story is smooth and of no great melodramatic import. It carries with it a mild sort of suspense. A trio of crooks crashing the gate of the staid Louisiana mansion when the darky man-servant thinks he recognizes in one of the younger tramps the identity of Dick Castleman, reported drowned at sea. The young man (Lloyd Hughes) moves in with his two nondescript companions and after helping themselves they decided to see it through and offset the villainous cousin's machinations.

Meantime, the girl (Miss Del Rio), who had never lost faith in seeing her Dick alive, meets Dick and too believes him to be the right man, although the erstwhile sickly youth has improved through his peerage as a knight of the road.

The long and short of it is that the other two genuine tramps do a "turn to the right," and it develops that Castleman is the real heir to the southern plantation.

The implausibility comes with the obvious climax that the hero could naturally never live a deception. He attempts some sort of explanation at his original state in trying to land a "hand-out" at what was his own home, but it falls flat. One immediately thinks that if his clothes and boat passage were taken from him he could easily have wired for financial assistance and not taken to the road for such length of time.

Regardless, Ralph Spence's titles do much to hold it up, as does the comedian "count" of the hobo trio. These and other lighter touches relieve the background to some extent. Hughes is satisfactory in the leading male role.

One day program feature. *Abel.*

LOST AT SEA

Tiffany production, directed by Louis J. Gasnier. Adapted by Esther Shulkin from the novel "Mainspring," by Louis Joseph Vance. Reviewed at special showing. Footage, 6,400 feet; running time, 70 mins.
Richard Lane..............Huntley Gordon
Norman Travers............Lowell Sherman
Natalie Travers..............Jane Novak
Nita Howard............Natalie Kingston
Bobby Travers........Billy Kent Schaeffer
Olga........................Joan Standing

This picture has large possibilities in billing, having sex angles that might be exploited for returns. Here is a case where the subject-matter calls for a spicy title, while the title used doesn't suggest anything of the sort. There are cabaret incidents that would furnish a great pictorial lobby ballyhoo.

That is the film's value to the exhibitor. As a screen play it has its shortcomings. The long footage represents a good deal of wasted effort in the overelaboration of detail, some of it trivial and a great deal of it unnecessary. It takes the story an unreasonable time to make itself clear. At the start, for instance, the purpose is to make it plain that Travers is a selfish and domineering husband and father.

One significant episode would make that clear. Instead, about a reel is used to show that the parlor maid hates and fears the head of the house. The mother shows in pantomime that she is crushed by her husband's ill treatment. On top of that these four characters carry through a long dinner-table scene to reiterate several times that wife and son fear him, and for good reason.

The entire progress of the story is impeded and hampered with this same embarrassment of emphasis. Sometimes it leads to just the confusion it seeks to avoid. This happens in an incident where the wife, supposing her husband drowned, has married again. We know the husband is alive. But when the wife has to be enlightened by a telegram from the husband, the screen shows the radio operator receiving the message and the delivery by a messenger boy.

However, this radio message leads to a neat situation. The wedding guests have departed and bride and groom are about to retire. The portentous telegram lies among other messages of congratulation. The significance is whether they will see it tonight or remain in ignorance until the morning. This situation is skilfully kept wavering for a good bit of suspense.

There are several spectacular passages having to do with the blowing up of a steamship at sea with mob fights for the lifeboats. The cabaret episodes are well managed, and the best child actor in months is disclosed in Billy Kent Schaefer, used effectively for sentimental values. Besides, there is a trick dog, the boy's pet, which is a valuable asset.

The story moves with exasperating slowness up to near the end, where it takes a surprise twist. The returned Enoch Arden is found murdered in his own study. The new husband, entering in response to a telephone call from the wife, finds the body and is accused of the crime. Believing it was the wife's hand that committed the deed, he assumes the guilt. This looks like the beginning of a new mystery story on the tail end of a domestic triangle drama, but it is disposed of brusquely by the mechanical disclosure that it was an enraged paramour of the husband who killed him.

Out of all this confused pattern one misses anything like a motivating theme. The story is just a group of manufactured incidents without any direction.

The production itself is of the first order, another example of the frequent situation of flawless studio technique used on a story of glaring mechanical (in the literary sense) faults.

THE LAST ALARM

Production by Gerber Pict. Corp., presented by Wray Johnson, by arrangement with B. Berger. Story by James Frances Natteford. Directed by Oscar Apfel. Under the brand of Rayart Pictures. Cast includes Wanda Hawley, Maurice Costello, Theodore Von Eltz, Florence Turner, Rex Lease and Jimmy Aubrey. At the Stanley, daily change, New York, Aug. 6. Running time not taken. About an hour.

A melodrama with the familiar background of the gallant fire fighters and a climax in a three-alarm conflagration. The mechanics of the story creak audibly, but that commonly happens in screen melos and, as in this case, where the address is generally to the less discriminating fans, it doesn't matter much.

The "punch" situation is effective in a heavy-handed way. The appeal is obviously to juvenile thrill seekers. It will satisfy that section of the film public. Sophisticated fans would scoff.

One objection that might be entered against the "class" of the story is that it has a commonplace background. The whole situation is based on the (dramatically speaking) trivial situation of the theft by the "heavy" of receipts of a firemen's ball, a subject wide open for a jeer. The settings for this humble tale are quite as drab as its motivating situation. The parlor of the fireman's home, the ticket taker's office at the ball and a storage warehouse, where the heroine works and where the money is hidden after it is stolen, are the principal scenes of action. None of them is especially suggestive of romance of a heroic order, and these settings give the whole recital a dingy atmosphere.

The actual fire house has, of course, some dramatic value as a setting, but this is introduced only incidentally toward the end of the film. It is here that all the "punch" is concentrated, the rest of the long footage being used for self-conscious efforts to lead up to the fire. This "big scene" is effective, especially the shots taken apparently from the fire engine as the machine rushes pell mell through the streets of a crowded city.

The story is intricate. There are two firemen, buddies in the same station—Tom and Joe. Tom loves Joe's sister and Joe loves Tom's sister, making a compact foresome. Neither swain dares reveal his love, because neither has the means to support a wife.

Tom is treasurer of the firemen's ball. At the beginning of festivities he becomes involved with a rival suitor for the girl's hand, and they adjourn to the alley to fight it out. Tom, of course, vanquishes his enemy, but it's a whale of a battle, as it comes on the screen almost blow for blow. In revenge the defeated rival steals the receipts and secrets them in the secret drawer of a desk, borrowed from the storage warehouse where Joe's sweetheart (Tom's sister) is a stenographer.

Tom and Joe are suspended from the department, charged with mishandling benevolent fund money, and in the meantime the desk with the secret drawer is taken back to the warehouse. It so happens that the heavy goes to the storage place to recover the money just as the hero and heroine arrive there to search the desk. In his haste to reach the money in its hiding place the villain sets the place on fire as the other two searchers enter the vault.

So it comes about that all are imprisoned behind a steel door as the flames gain headway. All this has been brought about with infinite pains with some ingenuity and the abundant aid of coincidences. Theatrical device is never absent, and the whole business is always just make-believe.

The imprisoned characters call into the street for help; an alarm is turned in, and the familiar melodrama of the firemen to the rescue is turned on for a happy solution when the hiding place of the stolen money is revealed in a burning desk, and blazing timbers bury the heavy past all hope of salvage.

Maurice Costello plays the fireman father of the fireman hero, and Florence Turner has only a bit as the wife of the warehouse proprietor, who serves as comedy relief. The acting is almost as labored as the story, but sufficiently convincing for the type of play. *Rush.*

Return of the Lone Wolf

Columbia production of a crook drama from the novel by Louis Joseph Vance (C. B. C.). Adaptation by J. Grubb Alexander and directed by Ralph Ince, under the supervision of Harry Cohn. Running time, 61 minutes.
The Lone Wolf..................Bert Lytell
Marcia Mayfair....................Billie Dove
Mallison....................Freeman Wood
Morphew...........Gustav Von Sayffertitz
Liane Delorme............Gwendolyn Lee
Crane....................Alphonse Esthier

Well-managed polite crook story, done in the polite and casual style and with the high-toned society background of the "Raffles" series, of which this Louis Joseph Vance series is a later rival. A capital example of this type of fiction, admirably produced in all technical details and splendidly acted by all principals.

From the box-office angle the story has value from the large following built up by Vance for his romantic hero through enormous magazine circulation. The picture will attract and make good on all screens.

Several interesting angles are used in this chapter of the exploits of the society thief, such as the fact that the super-crook turns detective in order to recover from a rival gang of operators the fortune in jewels they stole from the woman the Lone Wolf loved and who turned him from his career of artistic crime into the paths of righteousness.

The atmosphere of de luxe society is skilfully established and well maintained, and it gives the rather unreal story a glamour of romantic setting which operates to its advantage. It is this aspect of the Raffles fiction formula that gives distinction to screen stories, lifting them above the level of mere crook tales and giving them a tone of romantic drama rather than crass melodrama. In this case the romance and the suspense have been extremely well sustained, so that the unreality of the material does not intrude.

All such tales are obvious make-believe, but here the fiction is so blandly naive that it almost escapes attention as the spectator's interest is held. The start is a fine example of compact exposition. Almost in the flash the foundation is laid and the story is well under way in terms of action promptly. From then to the finish progress of the story is steady and compact.

The film has a number of good surprises. When the Wolf is at bay in the crook's luxurious headquarters, he retreats behind a heavy curtain, through which he seems to poke a revolver barrel to hold off the crooks. When the hiding place is rushed, there is no Wolf in sight, the revolver being wedged into a piece of furniture so that it appears to be held by a hand. *Rush.*

HUNGRY ARMS

Independent production written and directed by Anthony Moran, starring Priscilla Moran. Special preview at the Bunny theatre, N. Y. (Washington Heights), Aug. 6. Running time, 58 minutes.
Priscilla O'Day............Priscilla Moran
Grandad O'Day,.........William V. Mong
The Mother ....Dorothy Devore
Rooming House Keeper.......Emily Fitzroy
Social Worker.............Cissy Fitzgerald
Colleen ....John Richard Becker
Dinty ....Buddy

Anthony Moran, former Oklahoma exhibitor, now producer and director of features starring his talented little daughter, Priscilla Moran, has come from the coast with his first production turned out independently. Last week the picture was given a preview in one of the neighborhood houses on Washington Heights, and the production seemed to strike a responsive chord with the audience and especially the women folk.

The story is replete with heart interest and fits the little star. It is one of those winsome affairs that creeps into the heart, brings a lump to the throat and follows with a little human touch that will bring a smile or a light laugh.

The picture isn't one that any one would want to slip into a Broadway house for a de luxe presentation. But it certainly classes with the average program picture that is shot into the neighborhood houses and the daily change bigger theatres on the Main Stem. At that, it might even stand up for a week at the Cameo or even the Colony if a special wallop of publicity was put behind. Some sort of a kid stunt with the "Daily News" and a tie-up with their Orphant Annie strip would get this picture a lot. Incidentally Priscilla Moran as "Orphant Annie" on the screen with a countrywide tie-up with the papers using the strip would be a mighty good bet right now. The Moran youngster seems to be particularly fitted for the role, more so than any one else that comes to mind at this time.

In this picture she is a little orphan who is living with her grandad, a huckster of green groceries. She discovers a foundling on a doorstep, brings it home with her and smuggles it into the rooming house where she and "granny dad" make their home. She insists on keeping the little babe, but after the two youngsters are asleep the grandad goes forth to apprise those on whose step the child was found that it is safe. On the way he is struck by an auto and taken to the hospital. In the meantime the mother of the child returns to the home of her mother, where she deserted it, and demands the infant be returned to her, being distracted at its loss, and a search is immediately instituted.

Priscilla with the baby is earning a living for both by selling papers, and finally enters the kiddie in the baby contest, where it wins the prize. But just at that moment the keeper of the rooming house in which she has been living and a social worker who have been searching for her and the baby appear on the scene and something of a chase ensues. In the end the little one is captured and the baby taken from her. The next day she slips into the orphanage where the baby is and kidnaps it just in time to prevent it from being adopted, taking it to the home where she originally found it. A reunion is effected between the distracted mother and her offspring, and as a result both Priscilla and her grandad are adopted, he to be the gardener and she to pick flowers for the baby.

There are flaws in the story to be sure and there are also some improbable moments, but what of it when the picture as a whole carries a corking heart kick. It undoubtedly shows that little Priscilla Moran is capable of some real things on the screen. *Fred.*

THE KICK-OFF

Excellent Pictures Co. release. Distributed regionally by Commonwealth Exchange. Story by H. H. Van Loan. Directed by Wesley Ruggles, and titled by Jack Conway (Variety). Loew's New York, Aug. 17, one day, as half of a double bill. Running time, 61 minutes.

This film, starring George Walsh, is a college yarn of the bad boys and the good boys. In other words, the hero comes to the school, a hick from the country, and is immediately rejected by the smart-alecky element but is taken up by those who believe in and trust his athletic prowess. The girl angle, too, is strongly played, for the villain who plots the ruin of the hero is after the same girl who likes the country boy the minute she sees him.

The crux, of course, is a big football game with the hero ordered into start, relieving the villain, who is disgruntled. The latter frames a wire to the hero and pronto, the lad leaps home expecting to find his mother dying. But his mother is actually at the game, waiting to see her boy rush down the field doing two touchdowns per quarter. Finding he has been tricked, the hero races back to the field, using an automobile and wearing that out; taking a buggy and driving that until the wheels come off, and making his last dash on the back of an old gray mare. He reaches the field, jumps into the game, and in the second quarter ties the score with a great touchdown. Then he's knocked out and taken to the showers, but a few minutes before the game is over he recovers and on a fake pass just romps down the field in the most approved Red Grange style.

George Walsh has the leading part. While a little stiff in some of the straight playing, does nicely in the football scenes, for here his athletic reputation takes care of itself. The leading feminine interest is Leila Hyams, and what a sweet-looking dish she is in the galloping tintypes! Looking like a million and coming through handsomely on what is probably her first screen appearance is her record.

There's a lot of punch in the titles for this one, which were turned out by Jack Conway (Variety's critic and slang expert). Here Mr. Conway has turned most of the titles into readable slang which got laughs at the New York. It's his first titling job and a good one.

"The Kickoff," as a picture, has sufficient action toward its conclusion to make it stand up, but it would seem more cutting would eliminate some stuff which slows up the approach to the climax. Otherwise okeh and nice for its field.

Sisk.

RACING BLOOD

Gotham production presented by Sam Sax and produced by Lumas. From a story by J. B. Smith. Directed by F. Richardson. Robert Agnew, Anne Cornwall and Charles Sellon featured. At Loew's New York Roof, Aug. 13. Running time, about 60 minutes.
Jimmy Fleming..............Robert Agnew
Doc Morton................Charles Sellon
Muriel Sterling.............Anne Cornwall
John Sterling...............John H. Elliott
Harris Fleming............Charles Geldert

An excellently produced film, insofar as external appearances go. With an unusual twist to its racing theme, it is thoroughly satisfactory as entertainment for the intermediate and smaller houses.

Renaud Hoffman did the supervision on this, according to the titles, but it looks like another of those supervisory jobs done with the eyes shut, for the newspaper section of the film is just as awful as are most newspaper sequences in best films. Specifically, one shot shows a sheet of copy paper with a story on it, the story having been written by a brand new cub reporter. He not only wrote the story but his own headlines as well, and then the story is shown, typed with no spacing between lines. Even a movie managing editor should get sore at that.

But the serious part of silly mistakes like that is not that they are just mistakes. When a picture containing such a "bull" gets into circulation and begins drawing reviews every newspaperman will call attention to and dwell on the error. And type wasted on explaining a fault will detract from the value of a good notice in the dailies, and "Racing Blood" is so good a yarn that it ought to get good notices.

The story concerns a boy and girl love affair during college days, but this affair is broken up when the boy receives a letter that his guardian has lost his entire estate betting on a horse race—and the winner is his sweetheart, for her father made the bet for her. So the boy cuts out as a cub reporter and at a circus auction sale has a horse handed him. This horse actually is Blue Boy, a famous racer, and lost by the girl's father in a train wreck. By coincidence the girl and her father come to the town where the boy is working to enter a handicap race, and he puts his gift horse, really the girl's, in the race as opposition to their own entry. At the last minute he finds out that the horse is the girl's. He won't ride. So she, anxious to have him win back his estate (and the betting has been fixed so he will) puts on a jockey suit and rides the steed, winning the race and the large purse.

That makes things up and up, so the pair do that well-known clinch fade-out. The picture, where acting is concerned, goes to Anne Cornwall, a fine representative of a fairly sensible flapper. Agnew does the sort of acting Agnew always does. Maybe some people like it. Charles Sellon, as a combination editor-auctioneer, gets laughs, while John Elliott and Clarence Geldert turn in excellent performances as the elderly men of the film.

The racing stuff is liberally supplemented by inserts from a library service, but audiences probably won't worry over that. "Racing Blood" should entertain the exhibitor's customers.

Sisk.

A DANGEROUS DUDE

Harry J. Brown production under the Rayart banner; directed by Mr. Brown. Presented by W. Ray Johnston. At the New York as half of double bill Aug. 6. Running time, 55 minutes.

A story of many strikingly good points. It is of the type that might be classified as an industrial melodrama, typically American and holding extraordinary interest in its spectacular moments.

The reason is not altogether plain for giving the story a background of newspaper life, for that phase of the story is altogether subordinate and does the production no particular good.

As a straight melodrama the story is great. All the real action takes place in and around a huge irrigation dam in course of construction, making a spectacular setting, with its impressive scenic setting in mountain country, the vast, half-finished concrete dam and huge pieces of machinery used on the job.

The heroine, Dorothy Dwan, is a daughter of the contractor, and although the romantic interest is light, the feminine element contributes to the situation. One thrill comes when the girl goes up in the concrete bucket raised 100 feet or more. The cable has been tampered with by plotters, and the girl is in peril at the top of the dizzy tower until the hero climbs up hand over hand on the scaffold work to the rescue. The camera work is especially good for this incident. Shots are taken from some great heights and the progress of the hero toward the rescue show him against the mountain landscape at angles that emphasize the giddy height.

At another place the hero is chased by his enemies and swings from the towering wall of the dam across yawning valleys and fearsome chasms like a super-acrobat sweeping through the air. All these stunt feats are neatly worked into the plot and make the picture. It would have been a better story if the newspaper angle had been left out. This part of the tale compli-cates a simple and direct narrative.

There are good comedy elements. The reporter-hero has a companion, an Irish taxi driver, with a fighting disposition. It is he who uncovers the plot and helps to defeat the plotters.

There are two rival newspaper publishers in the town. One of them, father of the hero, also is a contractor, who has the job of building the dam. The other editor attacks him in his newspaper, and schemes through his political influence to impede the work on the dam. The contractor-editor's son gets employment on the dam job, learns that concrete shipments are being held up and rotten materials are being delivered.

After fighting his way into knowledge of the situation, the hero at the last minute taps the telephone wires, arranges to block the delivery of bad materials and have supplies of good concrete rushed to the spot in a big fleet of trucks, just in time to defeat the schemers, avert a scandal from his father's name, and, of course, win the girl.

The progress of a fleet of powerful trucks through the mountains, rushing to the goal against time, makes a capital leading up to the climax and rounds the picture off to a hip-hurrah finale in a general fight.

THE MYSTERY CLUB

Universal production from the story by Arthur S. Roche. Directed by Herbert Blache. All-star cast. At the Broadway, New York, week Aug. 16. Running time, 65 minutes.
Dick Bernard.................Matt Moore
The Steward...............Charles Puffy
Nancy.....................Edith Roberts
Mrs. Vanderveer..........Mildred Harris
Thomas Burke..............Alfred Allen
Eli Sinsabaugh............Warner Oland
Club Members............{ Natt Carr
                        { Henry Herbert
                        { Jed Prouty

A mystery story with a weak denouement. That explains "The Mystery Club," and something else that isn't so good—Matt Moore minus his mustache has the leading part. Instead of the usual character sap stuff he plays a straight juvenile hero. Very unfortunate casting and not one in a dozen will recognize Moore.

A group of wealthy clubmen sign an agreement, with $25,000 posted, that each can commit a crime punishable by law and yet escape detection. They make this pact following an argument on the ease with which crooks get away with things.

Once the pact is sealed, mysterious things begin to happen. It is soon plain to them that some crooked gang on the outside has their number and is stealing their stuff.

First there is a jewel robbery, and it costs them $25,000 in dough to get the jewels back from a crook gang. Next a child is kidnapped, and it costs $25,000 to square that. Next one of their own membership is apparently stricken with paralysis and he, on what the others believe to be his death-bed, relieves them of $50,000.

The blowoff comes when their president is said to have been murdered, but that is phoney. Shortly afterward one of the crowd, Dick Bernard, captures the girl who pulled all the jobs. It turns out that she is a niece of one of the club members whose pet hobby was an institution to reform criminals and the various crimes she committed were done with the purpose of extracting money from the club members. This money was turned over to the institution, the hero kisses the girl and the old fellows admit they have been trumped.

It's fairly exciting at times, but the action is slow and this, taken with the fact that the element of sympathy is absent for anyone in the story, combines to make "The Mystery Club" a so-so film for the smaller houses.

The main fault, however, is that Matt Moore should try to play a juvenile hero. He has identified himself so thoroughly with another brand of playing that his return to the straight stuff is ill-advised.

Sisk.

Honesty—Best Policy

Fox comedy feature. Chester Bennett production. Story by Howard Hawks. In the cast, Johnnie Walker, Pauline Starke, Rockliffe Fellowes and Grace Darmond. At Loew's New York as half of double feature program, Aug. 20. Running time, 50 mins.

Here is a picture of strangely mixed purpose. Somebody in the cutting room must have realized that it might confuse the fans, and they wrote a title early in the picture explaining that it was a broad burlesque, so there couldn't well be any misunderstanding.

What it amounts to is a travesty on the crook melodrama, done in a vague way. The trouble is that the points are too subtle and then, realizing the mistake the other extreme is in horseplay. The idea is good enough, but the handling goes wrong.

The suspicion comes up that there was a conflict between the studio and the editor, and the original intent was changed when it came to the hands of the cutting room finisher. The story plan is this:

A comedy author brings his story to a magazine editor. The editor—a knock-about comedy character—agrees to buy the story if the author will read it to a jury of his stenographers and make them like it. The jury is brought in and the author goes into the story, a crook thriller. As the action of the tale progresses the effect of thrill, tension and suspense is indicated by the way the short-skirted girls tie their legs around the chairs, these bits being flashed back from the altogether serious dramatic scenes.

What happens in the minds of the spectators is that the crook action becomes so absorbing that serious interest is aroused in the make-believe thrill action of the crook and his girl pal. This more or less interest is from time to time jolted by the sudden return to the burlesque. The result is that the spectator time and again feels he is being hoaxed and made foolish by the picture. It's never safe to josh an audience. It's got to be extremely clever if done at all.

The dramatic scenes are exceedingly well done, both as to settings and acting. The action, too, is entirely plausible. If only they had overdone the flamboyant thrill stuff, that very excess of thrill might have served as the tip-off that would have guarded the spectator from taking it seriously even for the moment. But the crook incidents unfolded logically and interestingly, even to the introduction of a romantic finish to the crook story itself.

A travesty finale was brought in, having the author's wife crash the editorial jury room for a knockout conclusion in which the infuriated wife beats up the beauties of the jury box.

UNNAMED WOMAN

Embassy release distributing through Arrow Pictures. Story by Leah Baird, with H. O. Hoyt director. Cast includes Leah Baird, Katherine MacDonald, Wanda Hawley, John Miljan, Herbert Rawlinson, Mike Donlin, Grace Gordon and J. E. Beck. At the Arena, New York, as half of double bill, one day, Aug. 13. Running time, 62 mins.

Rather a feeble celluloid attempt to be risque. Poorly lighted and photographed, the moral at the finish doesn't hold much interest after an hour of hokum.

Written by Leah Baird, the script gives her every opportunity to stroll before the lens, for Miss Baird is in the cast. There's actually more prominence for the authoress than Katherine MacDonald, who, if the heat wasn't too much, seems to have been featured in the billing. Either way both are negligible as to performance.

Miss Baird plays an upper middle class money seeker, while Miss MacDonald is the innocent wife drawn into a compromising situation with Miss Baird's screen husband.

Incidentally, the shanghaied hubby, rushed to the altar while drunk, is as much in debt as his steerer. The moral is customarily at the conclusion when the hard-drinking and sensual man about town and his mercenary wife decide to turn over a new leaf. The motive for this is the spotless woman's feigning to take poison.

There is the usual impossible house party, swimming pool, costumes and all. Nothing in the picture impresses as above the ordinary, comedy touches included. Strictly a hoke film for the smallest of the small emporiums.

In cast names the lineup is not without quantity if they mean anything to the houses which this picture, of necessity, must find itself limited. Wanda Hawley does the accomplice of Miss Baird, railroading the supposed money man into marriage, and Herbert Rawlinson is the simon pure lawyer-husband of the socially embarrassed Miss MacDonald.

Constructed on the pattern of the "class" drawing room intrigues, this one misses a mile. The lighting is particularly atrocious for this day and date. Enough to make it a second rater without anything else.

Miss MacDonald, as previously noted since her return to the screen, is still somewhat overweight. On appearance she is at her best in hats and should adhere to them. Especially pour le sport. A couple of closeups showed her thus crowned to be the same good-looking girl she formerly was.
Skig.

Fighting Thorobred

Open market picture designated a "Billy Sullivan" production. Billy Sullivan started. Direction by Forket K. Sheldon. Leading woman, Marie Astaire. At the Stanley, New York (daily change). Running time, 50 mins.

Roughneck melodrama framed in haphazard manner, but acceptable feature for daily change type of house. Billy Sullivan is a mild edition of George Walsh and makes a likeable fighting hero.

The picture belongs to a certain type in its construction. It has two incidents—a horse race and a prize fight. To get these over a crude story structure has been erected entirely without finesse or skill, the point being to get the plot planting over with as soon as possible and spread unlimited footage on the two action episodes.

There is a three-round prize fight, shown practically blow for blow and a well managed horse race. The latter takes up what seemes to be an entire reel with close shots of the speeding horses, distant views of the grandstand and perspectives down the track at the quarter poles. This kind of material, of course, makes for a thrill and in this instance is very well managed.

The story takes a good deal of value from nicely handled comedy which somewhat compensates for its implausibility of detail, and it is this element and the emphasis on the high spots that give the production strength in its appeal to the neighborhood class of fans. The character of the rural sheriff is splendidly developed and there is a court room scene with a country judge doing a character bit that is worthy of notice. Titling is skilfully done. Most of the defects are in the rough construction of the story, a drawback that seems to be especially common in these independent enterprises.

First class technical ability appears to be plentiful in the independent studios. In this case the direction is excellent. So is the photographic quality, the management of scene composition and the designing of sets. But the technical staff were hampered with the story wished on them and apparently realized it.

Sullivan is a game boxer, product of the race track. Angered by the unsportsman-like conduct of the champion with whom he is matched, he is led into a brawl. In a rough and tumble the champion falls, fracturing his skull. Blood transfusion is necesssary and Sullivan submits to the blood letting, wrecking his chances in the ring.

He returns to the track to make a living selling programs. Here he meets the heroine, daughter of a southern gentleman in broken circumstances, but still owning the wonderful horse that is going to win the big stake race and re-establish his fortune. It is rather an unromantic detail that the heroine is running a refreshment stand at the track. Her father spends their last cent for moonshine liquor (which is out of character), and to make the next rack, they have to deadhead it on a freight. Smuggling a horse into an empty box car and getting it out again under the eyes of the train crew is a good deal of a gob to swallow.

All hands, including the horse, are arrested and are held under bail the day before the big race. It is here that Sullivan takes up the offer of the same champion to pay $250 to anyone who will stay three rounds with him in the ring. Billy makes the grade, pays off the fines with the $250 and then rides the horse to victory. Up to this time there has been no evidence of a love affair between the girl and the hero, but at the end of the race they fall into an embrace and all's well.
Rush.

The Gentle Cyclone

Fox production. From story by F. R. Buckley. Directed by W. S. Van Dyke, with Charles (Buck) Jones starred. At the Stanley, N. Y., Aug. 19. Running time, 65 minutes.

June....................Rose Blossom
Wales....................Buck Jones
Sheriff Bill....................Oliver Hardy
Thomas Marshall, Jr....................Reed Howes
Judge Williamson....................Jay Hunt

This story, which is more in the nature of a standard farce set in western atmosphere, is a corker in the Buck Jones series. With this one no exhibitor can squawk, because it has lots of laughs, some slapstick, plenty of hard fighting, and just as much fancy riding. Which should, by all the rules of movie-making, compose a thoroughly satisfactory action picture, and that's all these westerns claim to be.

In this instance there is a family feud on, with the heads of each family getting all the more peeved because two uncles, heads of the respective clans, are clamoring to adopt June, a girl with a big inheritance but an orphan. And with her adoption naturally goes the use of her lands to her guardian, so the feuding is continuous, furious and belligerent. In this mess comes one Wales, a redoubtable cowboy with a record of having whipped 40 men single handed; of having quelled riots by the simple process of whaling the tar out of the rioteers, and of having brought peace in his wake. Without going into detail, Wales stops all the argument by adopting the girl himself, falling in love with her, and then causing inter-marriages among the feuding factions, so that by the time the story nears its end everything is as near contentment as possible.

Through this well-contrived plot wanders a low comedy sheriff of the old Sennett variety, but everything he does is a roar, and the roars get bigger as the picture goes on. Played by Oliver Hardy, he is quite successful in providing the comedy relief, and the noisy approbation given this film in the Stanley is evidence of its appreciation.

Cast is okay, with Jones predominating and getting a close-up a minute, but holding his own in the riding business and playing his love scenes like a reluctant little boy. Rose Blossom is the heroine, while Reed Howes, the independent film stunt man, also gets a bit of footage in a few fights. Funny to notice is the effort to cover up his identity in the credits by calling him "Reed Hause."

But that doesn't make much difference, because he hasn't much to do, "The Gentle Cyclone" being largely given over to the funny feud and Jones.
Sisk.

BUCKING THE TRUTH

Blue Streak Western, released through Universal, starring Pete Morrison. Story by J. I. Kane, Milburn Morante directing. Cast includes Brinsley Shaw, Bruce Gordon, Charles Whitaker and Ione Reed. Half of double bill feature program at the Arena, N. Y., one day, Aug. 13. Running time, 52 mins.

They may turn two or three of these out daily on the U lot. This is one of 'em. As an example of factory production it's a fair exponent.

Just a western. No more, maybe less. If they had had cowboys in the old days you might say Aristotle prescribed the formula for this scenario and be close enough to claim a stand off on a bet. Hence, where intelligence isn't a burden and where they sit through these things from two to five times weekly, "Bucking the Truth" ought to have a chance.

Everybody rides and everybody draws a gun. What are mountains without a gun to an independent western? Pete Morrison is the innocent hero possed into galloping for his life and into a smuggler hideaway where he rescues the supposedly deceased sheriff in time to save the h--- responsible for his marathon in front of the gendarmes.

That's a magnanimous bit leading into his winning the feminine keeper of the town's eatery (Ione Reed).

Some sort of a wager running through the continuity, Morrison having ventured his opinion to an old timer (Brinsley Shaw) that the new west isn't as wild as the old west. (What a statement to make on the U lot.)

Morrison's horse "Lightning" also draws feature mention. A number of the western boys now have their pet steeds. This one appears a good looking animal, but his demonstrations of intelligence have been pieced together by the cutter.

None of the cast in this epic of the raw country is to the brim with histrionics. Morrison goes to the mat for fisticuffs a couple of times, Miss Reed alternately becomes frightened and passivle, and Brinsley Shaw is conservative enough to convince.

Showing at this house on a double feature bill, the picture needed the other half no matter if it were just the second title. At a 10c. top and during the dog days of summer —well, you can't have everything.
Skig.

Heartless Husbands

Produced by Sam Efrus and distributed on a regional basis by the Madoc Sales Co. A Sun picture. Directed by Bertram Bracken, with Gloria Grey starred. At the Stanley, New York, one day, Aug. 8.

Who this star, Gloria Grey, is, may be known to the producers of the film. It's easy to see that the public at large doesn't know her, because her face is unfamiliar and her acting of a poor quality. Therefore, the star stuff may be discounted, for she is a minor portion of a good story—badly cast.

The story concerns a heartless man who hated his wife to the extent that before her child was born he bruised her so that the child carried a birthmark. Then he denied paternity and divorced her.

The wife died, and the boy, a street waif, fell into the hands of Jim Carleton, safe cracker, who intended to bring the boy up in his trade until he came across a letter the mother had written begging that whoever took care of the boy should teach him integrity and honesty. This affected the old criminal, and after he was in Sing Sing doing a stretch, he had the boy sent to college and his true whereabouts concealed.

In college the boy became a football hero and fell in love with a sweet girl (played by Miss Grey). When he went home he found that a detective, Kelly, had it in for his foster-father because the old man, even though he had reformed, wouldn't squeal on a crook gang. Kelly revealed to the girl that the boy was living with an ex-convict, but that didn't matter, because it was shown at the same time that the man the girl supposed to be her father was in reality the heartless fellow who was the boy's real paternal parent.

Considerable punch of a melodramatic sort fits this story to the shooting galleries and their clientele, but the Hairbreadth Harry and Relentless Rudolph school of heroism and villainy is a bit too farfetched. And whoever played the young hero was altogether unfitted for the role. He was a man way past his college years, possessed of a heavy face and photographed none too well.

In more competent hands this story would have carried a wallop. As it stands now the wallop is considerably diluted, and therefore nullified.
Sisk.

SATAN TOWN

Pathe release produced by Charles R. Rogers with Harry Carey starred. From story by Jack Boyle, adapted by Marian Jackson. Directed by Edward Mortimer. At Loew's New York Roof Aug. 13 as half of double bill. Running time, 63 mins.

Bill Scott....................Harry Carey
Salvation Sue....................Kathleen Collins
John Jerome....................Charles Clary
Cherokee....................Richard Neill
Crippy....................Ben Hall

An excellent action-melodrama with the scene laid in the Alaskan territory after the height of the gold rush of '98. In a town labeled Satan Town and called the wickedest in the world, the hero, Bill Scott, comes to "get" a man who double-crossed him many years before. Not only does he get the man, but also finds an adopted child for whom he had almost stopped searching, consequently a happy ending all around and even happier than you think, for they even burn Satan Town down for a finish. And it makes a finish. The photographic work in this instance is corking, and a flock of frame buildings make a flock of flames.

Bill Scott first enters the picture after rescuing an orphan waif from being run over by a team. Taken with the kid's sad face, he gives a lawyer (crooked) $1,000 to send the kid to school as he hops a boat for Nome, but the lawyer double crosses him, and as the money keeps rolling for the youngster's care the lawyer is using it on his own daughter. The other girl in the meantime has grown up and has drifted into the Salvation Army. She's the sole good influence in Satan Town, and the protection Bill Scott offers her when he arrives goes great for a while and even greater when she discovers he is the man who once rescued her. Retribution is wreaked on the crooked lawyer, because his own daughter is inveigled into becoming one of the dance hall gals through falling in love with the procurer for the joint. When the crooked lawyer, who built and owns the concessions of Satan Town, finds out that his daughter is one of the painted ladies he has a fit, and Bill Scott, about to shoot him, figures he has been punished enough.

Plenty of swift action, lots of accurate shooting and the rest of the desperado-good man routine, but nicely handled and with Carey thoroughly at home throughout. Kathleen Collins, a pretty blonde, is fine as Salvation Sue, while Charles Clary and Richard Neill as a pair of skin-bound skunks, are also good. Direction is okay, and "Satan Town" as a picture qualifies as excellent and interesting entertainment.

Sisk.

West of Rainbow's End

Independent western by Rayart. George Blaisdell listed as producer, with W. Ray Johnston as sponsor. Direction by Bennett Cohen. Story adapted from novel of the same name by Victor Rousseau. Jack Perrin starred and "wonder horse," Starlight, featured. At Loew's New York as half of double feature program, Aug. 20. Running time, about 60 mins.

Good action western melo made on the tried-and-true formula. No effort to depart from the familiar plot or treatment, but the mechanical story is padded out with plenty of hard riding and an abundance of hand-to-hand battles with fists and guns.

It's a safe selection, because everything in it has been used scores of times and has never yet fallen down. The use of a freckle-faced kid for comedy helps, while Perrin is a likeable enough cowboy hero and a capital rider with acrobatic leanings.

The hero returns from France to find that in his absence a gang of land grabbers have taken possesion of his father's ranch. How they managed this is no part of the scenario, which concerns itself with the hero's exploits in recovering possession and winning the girl, who seems to have moved in as the ward of the land grabbers' leader, although her antecedents are clouded in the mists.

For a certain grade of film fans this arrangement is ideal. It works out that way here.

THE MODERN YOUTH

Sam Efrus presents this feature released by Sun Pictures Corp. Directed by Jack Nelson. Cast includes Gene Corrado, Olive Kirby, Rhea Mitchell, Alma Rayford, Joseph Girard, Charles Belcher, Lorimer Johnston, Milburn Morante, Ray Laidlaw, Charles Clary. At the Stanley theatre, New York, Aug. 13. Running time, 55 mins.

Showing how a man bearing an important secret service message must undergo a test to find out whether he is to be trusted with the important work at hand. It may all be in the license of film manufacture, but it is a little too much to swallow either as a whole or in part.

A former French army captain, tired of service and world war heroism, steps out of uniform to take a rest, see the world and especially America, following the war. Instead of taking life easy he becomes a secret agent of the U. S.

There's a plot that envelops the president of a republic and the action swings to Centralia, where a young woman, a prisoner in her uncle's house, is rescued by the captain in one of his sword siestas with the villains.

The film drags, but has several scenes fairly well staged. However, it's all rather ridiculous.

As shown at the Stanley the film was screened fast and showed rough usage.

Mark.

BEAU GESTE

Famous Players' picture and a Herbert Brenon production featuring Ronald Colman, by arrangement with Samuel Goldwyn. Adapted from P. C. Wren's novel of the same name with Brenon the director. Cameraman, J. Roy Hunt. At the Criterion, N. Y., for a run commencing Aug. 25. Running time, 129 mins.

Michael "Beau" Geste	Ronald Colman
Digby Geste	Neil Hamilton
John Geste	Ralph Forbes
Lady Brandon	Alice Joyce
Isobel	Mary Brian
Sergeant Lejaune	Noah Beery
Major de Beaujolais	Norman Trevor
Boldini	William Powell
Hank	Victor McLaglen
Buddy	Donald Stuart

A corking picture, but as a road show special not entirely surefire. The idea is that it will have to hold to just a few cities outside of New York to have a chance at $2. As a straight program leader it can't miss, although the running time of 129 minutes may keep it from equalling house records.

It's a "man's" picture, much more so than "The Big Parade." The story revolves around three brothers and their love for each other. And a great looking trio—Colman, Hamilton and Forbes. Beyond that the love interest is strictly secondary, practically nil. Which brings up the question as to how women are going to like it.

The picture is all story. In fact, only one cast member seems to get above the scenario. This is Noah Beery as the bestial sergeant-major. A part that only comes along every so often, and Beery gives it the same prominence in which Wren, the author, conceived it. It's undoubtedly one of the best portrayals Beery has ever turned in.

When all is said and done, Colman, in the title role, hasn't so very much to do. Hamilton equals him for footage and Forbes exceeds him. But that's a natural result of the script, as both Beau and Digby die before the finish. Colman's work invariably being even, he makes no deviation here but with the limited footage and action it serves to throw Hamilton and Forbes to the fore. Forbes, understood to be in his first picture, impresses all the way and will probably develop a future in celluloid. Hamilton also gives a sincere performance to leave his mark. But there can be no question that Beery is the outstanding figure of the picture.

The story smacks of rank melodrama, is just that in fact, but is so dressed up and served in film form that the hoke is dyed another color. "Beau Geste" is a well put together mystery story working backward to its solution. First you get the mysterious happenings and then the story which explains the solution after you've seen the finish. It's programed in those three parts —mystery, narrative and solution with the picture run off that way. A brief interlude of seconds marks the division between the mystery and story, while a full intermission precedes the solution. Under that routine the film took 97 minutes to reach the rest period and 32 to unfold the answer. Rather complicated and away from the conventional formula.

It starts out with Major de Beaujolais (Norman Trevor), heading a rescue battalion of the Foreign Legion, reaching the desert fort which has sent for him. The only response to his signals is a single shot from the fort. Closer examination reveals that the inmates of the fort are standing at their firing embrasures, but all are dead. Sending a bugler to scale the wall is a loss for the trumpeter fails to reappear. The major then conducts a personal examination, finding a deserted stronghold with the sergeant-major, senior man in the fort, lying dead, pierced through the chest by a French bayonet, and still no sign of his bugler. From the cold hands of a private, lying beside the sergeant, he takes a note admitting the theft of a famed diamond known as the Blue Water. His men, becoming nervous before this deserted tomb, the major opens the gates and asks for volunteers to make a further inspection. When again inside the walls he discovers that the bodies of the sergeant and the private, from which he took the note, have disappeared. His men, now approaching panic, he withdraws, intending to further investigate in the morning when suddenly the fort bursts into flames.

This passage of the troops becoming unnerved at the uncanny happenings is not as stressed in the film as in the book. However, this ends the mystery section, with Brenon questionably having tacked on dramatic sub-titles in an attempt to emphasize the unnatural series of incidents.

From here the tale goes back 15 years to an English estate where the Geste boys (Beau, Digby and John) are children companioned by Isobel. They are the wards of Lady Brandon (Alice Joyce), who is rearing them. A truant husband, unseen, is referred to as a spendthrift with the family's main possession being a magnificent diamond called the Blue Water. A wealthy Hindu bargains with Lady Brandon, and Beau overhears the conversation. At this point the story jumps ahead to show the children fully grown and played by the Messrs. Colman, Hamilton and Forbes, with Mary Brian as Isobel.

A cable from the erring husband says the Blue Water must be sold and the stone is brought to the table. The lights suddenly go out and come on again to reveal the diamond missing. Only the immediate family, plus Lieutenant de Beaujolais and a minister, are present. Lady Brandon orders the lights put out so that the guilty party can replace the jewel, but relighting shows the stone still missing.

The brothers laughingly admit in their rooms that each in turn has taken it. John awakes in the morning to find a note from Beau saying he has stolen the gem and has gone away with a postscript from Digby reading not to believe Beau, that he (Digby) has the diamond and has left. John packs, and also leaves to share in the blame, despite he and Isobel have been life-long sweethearts.

The next jump is to the barracks of the Foreign Legion's receiving post in France, where John, having joined, sees Beau and Digby already in uniform. Here the trio come across the despicable Lejaune, who breaks up the combination by despatching Beau and John to a desert fort and keeps Digby behind. Lejaune is after the diamond, having forced the information from Boldini, a private, caught in the act of snatching Beau's money belt after overhearing the brothers still chaffing each other about the Blue Water. Boldini has his hands pierced by bayonets for the attempt, a gruesome spectacle, but excellently played by William Powell.

Shortly following a couple of anti-Lejaune incidents comes the high point of the picture in an Arab attack upon the fort. Swarms of them, and attacking from all sides. Picturesque and an applause winner at the premiere. The attack comes just as a mutiny within the fort is about to break against Lejaune, but this is put off because of the Arabs. Picked off one by one, the soldiers are stood up in their embrasures after they've dropped by Lejaune to fool the attacking force. All drop, including Beau, which leaves John and the sergeant as the survivors. Lejaune is rifling Beau's person, the Arabs having withdrawn, when John pulls a bayonet. Lejaune is about to shoot him, but Beau grabs the killer's leg, the shot goes wild and John thrusts the bayonet through the hated officer's chest. Beau then dies in John's arms, leaving a letter for Lady Brandon. This terminates the story portion.

The solution part opens by again showing the arrival of the rescue battalion, with John firing the one shot at the column to give him time to escape in lieu of being tried for the murder of Lejaune. The bugler sent over the wall is Digby, who finds Beau dead, no trace of John, and is determined to carry out a childhood pact of giving Beau a Viking funeral. Digby hides while the Major makes his first inspection, and, as the latter is asking for volunteers outside the fort, carries Beau's body into the barracks room and prepares a bier. A Viking funeral demanding a dog at the feet of the deceased, Digby hauls the dead Lejaune into that position and sets fire to the cot, escaping over a back wall.

John and Digby meet in a depression of the sand dunes, and later run into two American members of the Legion sent back by the Major for reinforcements. The quartet becomes lost, one of their two camels dies, and Digby, knowing the four can never get through with one animal, leaves a note and plunges off into the desert to die.

The next migration is back to England, showing John on the Brandon estate to tell of Beau and Digby being dead and to deliver the former's letter. Beau's epistle informs Lady Brandon that, having overheard her conversation with the Hindu and knowing she had sold the Blue Water, he had stolen the imitation stone to save her embarrassment when her husband demanded that it be turned into cash. And that's the "beautiful gesture."

Brenon seemingly has followed the book very faithfully. So much so there are only two laughs during the entire film. One is when a close-up shows Lejaune being called names that can't be misinterpreted. And that's one fault with this release. There's no light and shade to it.

That many didn't like it at intermission but changed their minds about it at the finish, due to the story's composition arrangement, may be the tip-off on what is likely to keep it from being a "special." Nevertheless, the compound theme has been held together extraordinarily well, and it must have been a nightmare to the cutters. Brenon has taken one liberty in making the purchasing Hindu, for no apparent reason, wink at the family minister carrying the famed jewel during that early portion, and he may also be said to have left unexplained how the lights go out at the time Beau takes the stone. But they won't think of that till afterward, and if the picture draws that much afterthought it can't be a bad picture.

Scenically "Geste" is about the best example of desert shooting that has come along. J. Roy Hunt is flashed as the photographer, and has made an excellent job of it.

Alice Joyce is superb as Lady Brandon, with her dignity and poise, while Mary Brian means little or nothing as Isobel. William Powell as the stoolpigeon, Boldini, and Norman Trevor as the major are really the only outstanding figures other than the brothers and Lejaune.

Electric letters 11 feet in height proclaim "Beau Geste" as being at the Criterion, and it's liable to stay awhile. It's a well-done mystery-melodrama. The men will like it, but it's doubtful if the women will care for Beau dying with the sympathy in the character revealed by the climax after his death. Besides which there's that lack of change of pace and its length. Brenon has given too much time to planting the brother-love theme when the Geste boys are pictured as children. Any further cutting will likely be done through this sequence.

Either way, a great "break" for P. C. Wren, the author, as this is his first novel, and F. P. has also bought his second book. *Skig.*

ONE MINUTE TO PLAY

F. B. O. picture, starring Red Grange. Story by Byron Morgan. Sam Wood, director. Charles Clarke, cameraman. Reviewed in projection room. Running time, 78 mins.

Red Wade....................Red Grange
Sally Rogers..............Mary McAllister
John Wade..................Charles Ogle
Player 33..................George Wilson
Biff Wheeler...........Ben Hendricks, Jr.
Tex Rogers.................Lee Shumway
Toodles.................Lincoln Steadman
President Todd....................Jay Hunt
Mrs. Wade..............Edythe Chapman

This far-famed redhead may be a screen bet. His picture indicates that. At least Red Grange has a chance, for his performance here is far in advance of what might be expected, considering the conditions of his entrance into pictures. And his first release carries a wallop. It's in the finishing football game, of course, but it's a corker and should sell the picture.

Grange has a clean-cut appearance on the screen. A vein of awkwardness runs through his work, but the surprise is that it's so thin. If he's going to continue his studio career (and the understanding is that his next is to be an auto race tale), adroit direction and experience will help smooth the wrinkles.

However, three years of more publicity than any other football player has ever received has made Grange synonymous with the gridiron sport.

He belongs in moleskins, and as the release date will "break" as the sport pages begin to devote abundant space to the college squads in training, the film should have various tieups.

In eight reels the picture practically devotes all of its last spool to the game between Parmalee and Claxton. It's worth it. Grange, on the Parmalee squad, doesn't get into the fray until the last half, with the first two quarters ending in a noscore tie.

Sam Wood, directing, has pyramided this game action into undeniable tenseness. Technically it's the best football game yet screened, minus any clips from weeklies or collegiate film libraries. Also, it is spotted by corking camera work in "shooting" from different angles. One shot has Grange breaking through the line to plunge right into the camera while a "huddle" of the Parmalee team is taken looking up at the boys' faces. Good stuff and bound to cause comment.

Grange, under a cloud for supposedly having been drunk the night before the game, is sent in during the late moments with a 6-0 score against his team. His entrance marks the first forward pass of the game. After eating up much yardage it's all offset when Toddles, Grange's roommate (Lincoln Steadman), picks up a fumble and runs toward his own goal. The second march down the field culminates in a forward pass developing into a lateral to Grange (very much like the triple pass used against Pennsylvania last fall), whence he scampers over for a touchdown and kicks goal to make it a 7-6 victory.

The story starts with Grange about to enter Claxton as a freshman. His father (Charles Ogle) favors Parmalee, but the boy can't see that school because it has no gridiron record to speak of. Neither does the parent favor football, cutting the cards with his son to see if he plays or not, and, incidentally, pulling an ace from the bottom to cinch it.

On the train he meets the girl (Mary McAllister), bound for Parmalee. In an annual smoking car fracas between the returning students of both colleges he is laid out, and regains consciousness at Parmalee. Learning that the girl is also attending there, he passes up Claxton.

With a prep school reputation behind him, the college can't understand why he doesn't turn out for football, there being no freshman rule. When unable to stand the coventry any longer he breaks the agreement with his dad and plays. Toodles, ignorant of the situation, sends a press yarn home which features Red's exploits in the previous day's game. Father arrives the day before the Claxton battle. Having promised a good-sized endowment to Parmalee, Mr. Wade threatens to cancel the promise if his son plays.

Knowing that the money is vital to the college, Red sprinkles whiskey over himself, and let's the coach and his sweetheart see him. That makes it null and void as to his playing on the morrow, but the father, seeing his first football game, gets so steamed up that he goes to his son between halves, finds that the boy wasn't drunk, and tells him to go ahead.

Wood goes after comedy in the early portions and seems to have succeeded more in those spots where the effort is not so obvious. Theatrical license with undergraduate customs has been frequently tapped, but it will pass with the majority.

Football fans should go for this one. It will be noted that Player 33 gets cast mention. George Wilson may not mean anything in such a lineup, but they know him on the coast and all gridiron followers have heard of him. Considerable football player himself at the University of Washington, Wilson (since turned pro, as did Grange) is given plenty of footage here during the first half of the filmed game as a Claxton halfback. And he can move.

As sports go, Grange's gratis publicity will now begin to get less and less every fall, despite his pro-football team, which will play in New York. This season isn't too far away from the Grange waves of the past couple of falls, and "One Minute to Play" has that in its favor. Following this one, Grange must begin to click on his ability as an actor. That he shows promise of being able to do it is rather remarkable.

Grange will draw from the youngsters, and to that end the picture's "fair-play" atmosphere of amateurism has its influence. On the other hand, and pertaining to the same thing, it's regrettable that the father is shown cheating his son at cards. That one doesn't digest easily, especially in an adolescent and athletic theme.

Lincoln Stedman leads the support for performance value, while Miss McAllister makes an average heroine. Lee Shumway plays the coach believably, and Ogle is appropriately drastic as the father.

Grange and the game are the picture, however. It's an okay combination, although Wood seemingly has passed up a point by not showing Grange in semi-slow motion while carrying the ball. What a "winning play" could have been made out of that effect! *Skig.*

THE CAT'S PAJAMAS

Paramount comedy designated a William A. Wellman production. Screen story adapted by C. Hope Loring and Louis D. Lighton from the original by Ernest Vadja. In the cast Betty Bronson, Ricardo Cortez, Theodore Roberts and Arlette Marchal. At Loew's New York, one day, Aug. 29. Running time, 67 minutes.

A strangely mishandled Cinderella theme that doesn't jell. At times it is in the spirit of the Brothers Grimm and at others it smacks of Sinclair Lewis. Pretty fantasy on the one hand and on the other something like tart satire. It isn't fair to an audience to expect it to keep pace in sympathetic undersanding with two such conflicting elements.

It is entirely likely that the original made a charming story to read. Compared with the deadly literal screen the printed word is a vague suggestion. Working in the medium of the vaguer print the reader could make his own appropriate picture of the humble seamstress and the romantic young Caruso hero.

As a picture it is chaos. Sally can't be one moment the humble seamstress in her shabby flat with a broken old man, her father, to care for, and then at the behest of a studio director, become the poised woman of the world with a gift for high life intrigue. No more is it fair to cue a story as a fairy tale fantasy and then suddenly introduce a rather sarcastic episode poking fun at the artistic temperament.

The incident of the rupture of the romance of the stage dancer and the grand opera tenor in a mutual explosion of ill temper is a pretty keen lampoon on the artistic nature, done with rather a bitter touch. That furnishes the mood of the whole picture, and that feeling having been fixed one expects other elements in the story to conform.

Instead the spirit changes to graceful romance and the verities are shattered just as though a low comedian suddenly and without warning tried to play Hamlet or Romeo.

To make a bad matter worse little Miss Bronson has been made to overact the arch Cinderella outrageously and everybody has been keyed to the same excess. Pictorially the production has a wealth of beauty and many interesting elements have been worked in. There are attractive passages about the fashionable modiste's salon where the humble little heroine works. The touches of luxury that surround the dancer's home are rather magnificent, and the scenes in the opera house where the romance begins are extremely well done. The defects are mostly in the story itself, as usual. Technically the picture is a bit of high pictorial art. The trouble is that the shading of the comedy and the tone of the romantic interest clash.

The story has to do with a young and handsome grand opera tenor who is so much beset by worshipping women that he determines to marry swiftly to keep the petticoat horde at bay. He determines to marry the first woman providence points to. Providence appears in the form of the pet cat belonging to Sally. Sally brings the tabby to the opera and it escapes. Wandering about back stage it comes to the attention of the tenor, who, following the cat, comes upon the beautiful dancer of the company. On the spur of the moment he proposes marriage and is accepted.

They quarrel almost at the altar, and Sally, dressmaker's messenger bearing the bridal gown, is substituted as the bride. The rest of the picture has to do with the coquetry of Sally and her post-nuptial conquest of the temperamental tenor, a subject for travesty, rather than the saccharine idyllic treatment it here receives.

Miss Bronson is an exquisitely lovely little creature, but she should do her Cinderellas or Peter Pans straight and without any jarring notes of the comic commonplace. *Rush.*

THE WANING SEX

Metro-Goldwyn-Mayer production. Directed by Robert Z. Leonard. Norma Shearer and Conrad Nagel featured. Privately previewed.

A nice picture comedy, "The Waning Sex," made nice and nicer by Norma Shearer. This fresh-looking girl, who plays with charm, does a great deal for a picture that has its laugh punches. The film might not stand up so well without this girl, despite the excellent direction of Robert Z. Leonard.

Conrad Nagel, co-featured, gives a lukewarm performance in a wavering characterization. To plant a domineering point at the finish, Mr. Nagel wavered continuously. **Whether through direction or his conception of the role, it hurt the general value.**

Miss Shearer's freshness of youth is nowhere more evident than in a very fine swimming pool scene. And she was almost quaint in her manner of repeatedly baffling the vamp who was after her man.

Her man was a lawyer and she was an attorney also. The waning sex here could be either the male or the other. It looked like the woman would prevail. She said no consistently, until informing her sweetheart if he could beat her in two out of three contests they naturally fell into, she would marry him without condition.

The first was a swimming race, the next a court trial, the man winning the first and the woman the second. But when the woman was about to oppose him for re-election as district attorney, the worm finally turned, and that is the biggest laugh of the many.

When a director, Leonard or anyone else, can end a picture with a laugh and the biggest laugh in it, give him all the credit in the world.

As Jack Conway would say "The Waning Sex" is a push over. *Sime.*

Ermine and Rhinestones

Herman F Jans production released on a state rights basis by Renown. Story by Louise Winter. Directed by Burton King, with Niles Welch and Edna Murphy featured. At the Stanley, N. Y., Aug. 27. Running time, about 65 mins.

Pierce Ferring	Colt Anderson
Alys Ferring, his wife	Sally Crute
Billy Kershaw	Niles Welch
Minette Christie	Edna Murphy
Peggy Rice	Ruth Stonehouse

The moral of this one—and being a state righter it has to have a moral—is that a rhinestone finish on an ermine coat tends to make something genuine take on the tinge of cheapness. What all that has to do with this cheap and shoddily made picture is a little beyond anybody's guess. Nevertheless, that's the moral and it's not even a case of take it or leave it. Whoever pointed out that moral was so proud of it that it gets quite a few plugs before the last reel of this wearisome feature.

The story is about a flock of cheating couples, all of whom have their gay parties in fine homes on Long Island and behave with the manners of gorillas from the lower east side. "Such a bunch of bummers," as Looy dot dope would undoubtedly exclaim.

Billy Kershaw, who is a nice boy, is almost hooked by Peggy Rice, a gal who likes riches, etc., but who isn't particular how she throws herself around. Of course, in Billy she made a good catch, but began monkeying around and so lost him. Of course, she knew he was going back to a little girl he really loved, so she beat him to the girl's house and offered the sweet little heroine money to beat it. At that instant came a tapping at the door, and a mean, mean villain who had a grudge against the girl entered. Peggy, of course, secreted herself in another room, and the villain gagged the heroine and turned on the gas. When Peggy came from her hiding place the good gal was unconscious from the gas. Did Peggy help her? No, sirree, she didn't. Instead she smiled a dirty smile, made a dirty look and exited through a fire-escape window with one of those "and a good-night to you, my girl," the good-night business being italicized to impress upon the spectators the subtlety of her remark. Of course, Billy entered in time to save her, and after explaining that he was just engaged, not married, to Peggy, everything was all okay.

Poor story, poor direction, poor playing and of such a tone that it is unfitted for Sunday showings in the smaller places. An instance of the technical care is an interior upon which light pours from the top of the room. That the tops of rooms have ceilings and don't admit light is something most movie people recognized long ago—even if the legit stage (with the exception of Belasco) still believes in that little fairy tale.

"Ermine and Rhinestones" is a cheap meller, strictly tenth-rate stuff. *Sisk.*

Christine of the Big Tops

Banner production featuring Pauline Garon. Directed by Archie Mayo. At Stanley, New York, one day, Aug. 25.

One of those independents that will never fool anyone. It must have gotten into the Stanley, a 25-cent grind house, for one day on the strength of the Pauline Garon billing, or because the picture is a cheap renter. It's certainly cheap in the production end, and will only do for the hideaway theatres that takes 'em when they are cheap; the cheaper the better.

After the "Christine" title, indicative of a circus, not even a wagon show was employed for realism. A sectional canvass was rigged up, a few principals in circus togs and some extras shown and they let it go at that. For a picture with a circus title this is the biggest cheat of that kind ever made.

At one time an insert was employed of a regular circus, but that was but a flash and did more to expose the rest than anything else. A scrangy parade had "Barman's Big Show" as a play for Barnum's, and there was a semi-serious attempt at an unloading scene.

The single bit of direction that Archie Mayo may take credit for was the suggestion of a blow-down, that terrorizing circus life scene. This suggestion was rather well done. There's nothing in this picture that demerits Mr. Mayo. He was directing on a bankroll of probably 30 cents gross.

Miss Garon did well enough. This independent is one of those walk through films. No one can muff because no one has anything to do. They may have shot the entire picture in five days.

It's a conventional story, lightweight, of course, to get under the wire so inexpensively. A girl, the star of the unseen circus, feigns a sprain to inveigle the young physician traveling with the show. Afterward, when she really sprains her leg, no one believes it. In this scene an entirely unnecessary and unfaithful bit was put in when the owner of the circus, feeling for the sprain of the ankle, ran his hand up the leg of the costumed girl-patient. That was in direct contradiction of a title which read "We circus people protect our women." That is true. There are two great moral divisions of the show business, the circus and the stock (dramatic) company.

Mr. Mayo should have been ashamed of himself, even if ordered, to have libeled a fine class of people in the show business by this inexcusable bit that will never draw a dollar at the box office for this excuse of a feature picture.

"Christine" will probably get into the one-day-a-week stands, and let it stay there. *Sime.*

UNKNOWN DANGERS

Farce melodrama featuring Frank Merrill, athlete. Presented by Peter Kanello through Hercules Film Productions. Written and directed by Grover Jones. Cast: Gloria Grey, Eddie Boland, Marcain Asher, Emily Gerdes and Theodore Lorch. At the Stanley, N. Y., Aug. 26. Running time, 57 minutes.

The picture starts out to be a polite comedy, but the plan is lost when the action finally begins and proceedings turn into acrobatic knockabout. In this last respect it is effective as a laugh-provoker, but the preliminaries are extremely cumbersome.

This film might as well have gone into horseplay rightaway.

In the case of "Unknown Dangers" the story plan is to introduce the hero into a band of criminals, all of whom he supposes to be actors playing a hoax upon him. The means employed to establish this situation are most intricate. A firm of theatrical managers are angered that a dramatic reviewer has panned their show. They argue with the writer who persists that the play is based on absurd incidents that could not happen in real life.

While the debate is going on newspapers report the kidnapping of a judge's daughter by a notorious gang. One of the showmen determines to stage a reproduction of the gang's lair and lure the reviewer there. The actors in the company are made up to represent the gangsters and their girl victim, but the reviewer overhears the plot and permits himself to be led to the place as a lark. It then develops that the deserted house picked by the practical jokers is actually used as a hideaway by the real kidnappers, and it is this situation that the writer walks into.

Once the tale gets going it is amusing roughhouse, not particularly devised, but carried out with the utmost energy by the hero. It is just one hand-to-hand fight after another, with those swift entrances and tumbling exits that go into the Mack Sennett technique. By that time the underlying circumstances have been forgotten.

Some of the incidents are genuinely funny in a hokum way. A negro taxi driver, told to wait outside, but drawn into the proceedings, is funny. The efforts of the comic theatrical managers, who try to rescue the hero when they find they have sent him into a den of criminals, also have a good deal of effectiveness.

The five-reel comedy, then, turns out to be three reels of fair slapstick and two of wasted preliminaries. *Rush.*

THE STRONG MAN

Harry Langdon Corp. presents the comedian in his second full length feature. Directed by Frank Capra and released through through First National. At the Strand, N. Y., week of Sept. 5. Running time, 75 mins.

Paul Bergot	Harry Langdon
Mary Brown	Priscilla Bonner
"Gold Tooth"	Gertrude Astor
Parson Brown	William V. Mong
Roy McDevitt	Robert McKim
Zandow the Great	Arthur Thalasso

A whale of a comedy production that is bound to be a cleanup everywhere. It has a wealth of slapstick, a rough and tumble finish and in the earlier passages bits of pantimimic comedy that for legitmate and effective hour are notable in the whole range of screen comedy.

Langdon, until not long ago a maker of short subjects of the familiar gag school, has a comic method distinct from all the other film fun makers. The quality of pathos enters onto it more fully than the style of any other comedian with the possible exception of Chaplin. His gift of legitimate comedy here has a splendid vehicle.

There is one scene where the awkward hero is engaged in fighting off a bad cold while traveling in a crowded stage coach. He earns the enmity of his fellow passengers and his pantomimic display of helpless suffering mingled with indignation is an epic of laughable absurdity. In the same scene the business with a porous plaster was greeted with howls.

One of the remarkable things about the picture is the fact that its action and its comedy values are sustained for more than an hour. Besides this the finale rises to a climatic punch, although the finish as might be expected goes into roughhouse of the most violent kind. Something of the sort was imperative to provide mounting interest, and this the gag closing does.

At another point there is a rich episode of an adventure with a woman crook. The girl has "planted" a roll of money in Langdon's pocket to get rid of it when she is threatened with arrest. To recover the money she lures the boy to her apartment. He imagines she is making cave woman love to him, while she really is trying to salvage the loot and his coy retreat from her attack is the last word in comic misunderstanding. Gertrude Astor handles the crook role admirably here.

The story has a sentimental side that helps to give it light and shade. At the opening Paul Bergot (Langdon) is a young Belgian soldier at the front, delighting in correspondence with an American girl, named Mary Brown. The war scenes are turned to the travesty side when Paul can't hit his marks with a machine gun, but puts the enemy to flight with a bean shooter. Captured by a burly German, who, after the armistice, turns out to be a professional strong man; he is employed as the professional's assistant and they come to America. Paul takes up the search for his Mary Brown, a quest that leads to all sorts of ridiculous adventures. The strong man is engaged to perfrom in a rough border town where church people and bad men are engaged in a struggle for ascendancy.

The strong man is too drunk to go on with his act before an angry audience of a lawless mining camp, and the stumbling Paul is forced to substitute in the fear of being shot from a cannon to a trapeze above the crowd. Here starts a series of gags of never-failing ingenuity. The impressed acrobat swings up to the top of the proscenium arch and draws the stage curtain back on his return swing so that it covers the whole audience. Then he proceeds to stroll about as though on a prop stage sea, feeling for the heads of the boiling mob and "plopping" them with a seltzer bottle.

At the end of the battle the town's forces of evil have been defeated and the music hall dive demolished. These things lead to the happy finding of Mary Brown and the culmination of the war time romance.

A rich comedy that should take Langdon a step toward the class of stars, whose pictures figure for more than a week's engagement.

Rush.

HOLD THAT LION

Douglas MacLean Production released by Famous Players. From the story by Rosalie Mulhall adapted by Franklin Poland. Directed by William Beaudine. At the Rivoli, N. Y., week Sept. 4. Running time, 65 minutes.

Daniel Hastings..........Douglas MacLean
Dick Warren....................Walter Hiers
Marjorie Brand..........Constance Howard
Horace Smith-Smythe.......Cyril Chadwick
Andrew MacTavish............Wade Boteler
Professor Brand..........George C. Pearce

Douglas MacLean has turned out a very acceptable comedy for the better class houses in this one. It is a picture that is built for belly laughs, and gets them.

However, there are spots where the lighting is faulty, and the result is that the star looks tired and drawn. This is especially true in the early scenes in the office, where he and Walter Hiers as chums discuss the possibility of meeting the right girl.

Right atop of this discussion he sees a girl that he falls for and discovers that she is leaving on a trip with her father. He starts chasing her and continues to miss her at various points in Europe, finally catching up to her on the balcony of a hotel in South Africa. He has taken his chum with him on the trip and when the two are dressing to attend the big ball at the hotel, given on the eve of the annual lion hunt, he finds that his dress trousers are torn and his pal volunteers to take them to the tailor for him. While awaiting the pal's return he discovers the girl on the balcony, meets and talks with her without either being aware of his undressed condition. In his agitation he runs from his room, the spring lock behind him closes, and he is marooned in the hallway without pants. A couple of scenes that follow bring laugh wows. Finally he manages to steal a kilt from a Scotchman's room and goes to the dance to again meet the girl.

She and her father are going on the lion hunt, her dad wanting to secure a full grown specimen alive. All the lion hunters are talking of "the cat hunt," and the comedian does not get the significance of what they are talking of and therefore heartily accepts an invitation to join, topping that by making a bet with a lion hunter of $10,000 that he will bring in the first one alive. He wins out in the end through accident, the lion hunt being replete with laugh after laugh. The "shooting" here gives the impression the lion is constantly at the heels of the hero.

MacLean and Hiers carry the greater portion of the picture while Constance Howard makes an acceptable enough lead in a role that does not place any too great a strain on her.

Fred.

FINE MANNERS

Paramount picture starring Gloria Swanson. Story by James Creelman and Frank Vreeland. Directed by Richard Rosson. At Rivoli, N. Y., week of Aug. 28.

Orchid Murphy..............Gloria Swanson
Brian Alden....................Eugene O'Brien
Aunt Agatha......................Helen Dunbar
Buddy Murphy....................Walter Goss
Courtney Adams................John Miltern

Gloria Swanson in her last picture for Famous Players will do a great deal toward wiping out memories of her last two features.

Whoever is responsible for picking the story deserves credit, for it fits the star like a glove, is right in her wheelhouse, and allows her an opportunity for pathos and comedy that shows her at her best.

Swanson fans will rave over "Fine Manners." It is a Cinderella tale of a poor girl working in a burlesque show who is courted by Brian Alden (Eugene O'Brien). Orchid is interested, but her brother mistrusts Alden's attention and doesn't believe he has orange blossoms on his mind. Orchid protects Alden on one occasion by making him impersonate a waiter in a cafe when they are sitting when her brother enters. On another occasion he calls at the theatre in evening clothes and has to do his waiter stuff again on the way out when they discover the brother talking with the stage doorman.

Alden's high brow and socially ambitious aunt is informed of his love for the burlesque frail and tries to dissuade him. He insists he means to marry her. The aunt is implored by Alden to take the girl and make a lady of her while he is on a six months' trip to South America. Auntie accepts the assignment and Orchid moves from double Fifth avenue to Fifth. There she is taught the artificiality that passes for poise, etc. So much so that when Alden returns he hates her. She overdoes the blase thing for his benefit.

Her kid brother again appears on the scene, bent on killing Alden for not doing right by his sister Orchid. The girl is told to send for Alden and ask him if he intends marrying her or not. The brother meanwhile is hiding behind the curtains in her boudoir with a rod ready to shoot if the answer is no. It's a good dramatic situation, for it has previously been registered that Alden is about to call off the marriage and return to South America, so disgusted is he with his made-over fiance.

She and Alden meet in the bedroom and she manages to signal him to give her the right answer, saving his life and satisfying the brother, who leaves unseen. Then she breaks out as her real self, throws his clothes back at him, and steps out from behind a screen in her undies. Gloria has a cute figure, if anybody should ask you, but this is the first time she has permitted a close-up.

Walter Goss, as the younger brother, is a good type for the gorilla part, and Helen Dunbar, as the upstage auntie, is perfect.

This latest Swanson should be something of a clean-up for Paramount. The story has enough meat for popular consumption and will suit the Swanson fans, who are legion. Incidentally, the star has shed several pounds since her last picture appearance and has successfully regained the girlish figure she usually sports. Her eyes work overtime in this one, and her comedy training stands her in good stead when she enters the Fifth Ave. atmosphere to be transformed from a sword swallower into a pale society lily. One of her best.

Con.

DON JUAN'S 3 NIGHTS

Henry M. Hobart Production, released by First National. Directed by John Francis Dillon, titled by Gerald C. Duffy. Starring Lewis Stone. At Loew's New York, Sept. 4. Running time, 74 mins.

Johann Aradi........................Lewis Stone
Roberto ....Malcolm MacGregor
Ninette ....Shirley Mason
Baroness ....Gertrude Astor
Count De Courcy ....Kala Pasha

This is a wow of a boxoffice title for any town playing the Barrymore "Don Juan" picture. But as straight screen entertainment it does not stand up except in its clever titling. However, in the daily change houses the picture will get by in most cases on the strength of the cast.

Lewis Stone is the concert pianist who has left a trail of broken hearts all over Europe. Finally in Rome he falls in love with a little girl of 16 who is trying to look 20, but when he realizes that she is but a child he sets out to disillusion her, finally succeeding through the medium of throwing a drunken revel to which he invites any number of his former mistresses, and at the same time sending word to the youngster who is in love with the little girl that she can be found in a private dining room at the hotel.

Naturally the youngster shows up, rescues the girl and challenges the older man to a duel in which the youth is victorious and the pianist loses the use of one of his hands for life. But that doesn't deter him from continuing his philandering, and the final scenes show him starting out on a new romance.

Dillon, in directing, has tried to make it sexy and still keep it within the censorship bounds, succeeding very well in this respect. There are several minutes in the picture that have a real kick, the comedy scene between Stone and Kala Pasha being particularly effective.

Shirley Mason plays the young girl being kept in short skirts so that mother's age won't be revealed, and makes a charming looking little lady when she finally shows in evening frock. Gertrude Astor looks and acts a million dollars worth.

The big wallop is in the title, as against the Warner Bros. production, and the chances are that those producing the picture pulled the title just for that. There is no connection between this "Don Juan" and the original, and as for the added "Three Nights"—you can't find that in the picture at all.

Fred.

Honeymoon Express

Warner Bros.' feature, directed by James Flood from scenario by Mary O'Hara. Irene Rich and Willard Louis featured. Holmes Herbert, Helene Costello and Virginia Lee Corbin head supporting company. At Loew's New York Sept. 2. Running time, 64 mins.

Those who pick subjects for the screen appear to be much preoccupied lately over the American home and what's the matter with it. "The Honeymoon Express" is another discussion of the family situation, dealing with the effect of a philandering husband upon his faithful wife and upon his two daughters and a son.

The head of the family is a night club fan who regards himself as a sheik although he is 50. His wife is absorbed in her children and has served them to the exclusion of all other interests until she is a frump. A creature of habit, she disregards her husband's "affairs," but the effect upon the children is otherwise. One of the girls is disgusted with her father's open dissipations; the other girl takes advantage of the situation of family chaos to follow her own selfish and dangerous amusements. The boy becomes a night club butterfly in imitation of the sire.

From this start the story carries the family through its disruption when the mother leaves the home to a happy termination when she gathers the three children about her in the home she has built up herself, leaving the husband to go his own way. The picture starts out with a highly interesting basis for development, but the treatment does not quite come up to the theme. There is some keen insight, but the scenarist has compromised with "pretty sentiment" and the later chapters do not ring true.

The production is magnificent. The family is rich and lives on a scale of considerable luxury. The settings having to do with the home are as fine as anything that has been done in the studio—really fine, not in the ordinary way of film studio excess magnificence. Some of the pictorial compositions are notable for the rich effects of background, always in perfect taste and by the simplest means.

There are also good settings for the night clubs and for the "apartments intimes" where the philanderer spends his leisure with his favorite soul mates. As usual with pictures of this type, there is little dramatic action. Interest is centred in the narrative, and the conflict so necessary to silent drama is largely absent. For this reason the appeal of the picture is not especially broad. The comedy is subordinated, although there are many scenes amusing in a quiet way.

Altogether is a sweet sentimental picture with special interest for the women.

Rush.

A WOMAN'S HEART

Sterling Production. Adapted by Lucille de Nevers from the novel by Ruth D'Agostino. Directed by Phil Rosen. At Loew's New York, Sept. 3, as half of double bill. Running time, about 60 minutes.

Eve Waring..................Enid Bennett
The Other Woman....Mabel Julienne Scott
John Waring................Gayne Whitman
Ralph Deane....................Edward Earle
The Boy Friend..............Lewis Sergeant

This is the story of a woman who married a man she didn't love.

She regretted not having married Ralph Deane.

So she left her husband to go to Deane. Arriving, she found him with another woman and awoke to the fact that he wasn't so much.

Back to hubby, a sadder and a wiser woman.

It takes here 56 words, some of them superfluous, to tell that story. In the film it takes about 60 minutes, which shows what a padded out story it is. Its adaptation is the weakest point, for insofar as production, cast and direction goes, it is well and expertly handled.

Enid Bennett, as the wife, turns in a sobby performance, while Edward Earle, as the philanderer, does well. Ditto for the rest, but a sequence which introduces a flip kid sister and her dumb boy friend didn't belong in this story. In addition, both parts were poorly handled.

The print shown at the New York was apparently poorly cut, for one title was run twice, first in corrected form and afterward in what apparently was the original form.

A filler for the daily changes, inasmuch as cast, although competent, isn't of the drawing card type.

Sisk.

RISKY BUSINESS

De Mille production sponsored by John C. Flynn for Producers' Distributing Corp. Direction by Allan Hale. Scenario handled by Beula Marie Dix. Vera Reynolds featured in cast. At the New York Hippodrome Sept. 6. Running time, 73 mins.

Cecily..........................Vera Reynolds
Mrs. Strouds....................Ethel Clayton
Harold...............................Ward Crane
Ted........................Kenneth Thomson
Sarah.................................Sazu Pitts

Picture has those defects that frequently appear in stories adapted to the screen from novels. This one has dull explanations and is burdened with laborious building up of situations. It has a meaningless "box office" title and a featured player without any great following.

But the story is saved by one genuine and compelling situation, a scene of real human appeal. The comedy is quiet and effective at times and the playing throughout is of high quality. The defects are inherent in the story itself, but have been minimized by expert direction, which has given the picture good touches. There are two likeable kids and many fine settings.

Cecily is a spoiled society girl governed by an ambitious mother seeking to marry her to the millionaire Harold, although she loves

Dr. Ted, a young M. D., to whom she is secretly engaged. When the mother learns of the engagement, she schemes to have Dr. Ted's sister invite them to a week-end, hoping that Cecily will see the impossibility of finding happiness as the wife of a struggling country physician. She is aided in her plot by Harold, who has a luxurious country place near by.

The dowager's plan of disillusionment works out perfectly. Dr. Ted's sister is something of a drudge (Sazu Pitts plays this role flawlessly), harrassed by small means, household cares and two babies. The spoiled society girl is gradually brought to see that she could not stand such a drab life. One of the troubles with the story is that this phase of its development is laboriously built up. The weight of detail is oppressive, despite the comedy bits.

But it does furnish the background for the big scene. Cecily breaks her engagement to the doctor, fleeing for relief to Harold's merry house party. On a wild auto joy ride Harold runs down a child, and drives on heedlessly, despite Cecily's protestations. During a drinking bout at his country place Harold disgusts Cecily, and she runs away, wandering about the lonely countryside. Taking refuge in the first lighted house, the girl finds Dr. Ted performing a dangerous operation on the boy injured by Harold, and, being called into emergency service to help in saving the child's life, she realizes that she cannot waste herself on the vanities of society. Her romance with the doctor begins anew for a happy ending at the altar. *Rush.*

MISS NOBODY

First National release, directed by Lambert Hillyer; editorial direction by Wid Gunning. Adapted from the orignal story, "Shebo," by Tiffany Walls. In the cast are Anna Q. Nilssen, Louise Fazenda, Walter Pidgeon, Arthur Stone, Clyd Cooke and others. At Stanley, New York, one day.

Engaging comedy subject with no serious object. Not an especially plausible story, but the comedy spirit does not call for anything of the sort. The idea is fresh and amusing, and the comedy side neatly managed.

Briefly, the story plan is to have a well-bred girl turn hobo to escape an unwelcome environment and then picture her adventures with a gang of tramps led (as it turns out in the end) by a perfect gentleman in the person of a story writer posing as a hobo to collect local color. Several capital stunts are staged during the action, giving some dramatic kick to an otherwise comic story.

The runaway girl and the tramps are "riding the rods" of a freight train when a brakeman drops a coupling attached to a rope under the cars, where it will smear the interlopers. This incident is well worked for a thrill. Another episode has the tramps stealing a ride on a motor trailer when it breaks loose from its tow at the top of a mountain overlooking the ocean, with tricky shots of its precipitous descent backward along a winding road.

One of the tramps plays a polite lady killer in a particularly engaging manner for a first rate bit of low comedy. Walter Pidgeon is leading man, of the Thomas Meighan type, a young player of promise. Louise Fazenda has a first rate bit as a sentimental tough girl, and Miss Nilssen makes a captivating boy. The titling has been especially well done.

One of the outstanding merits of the picture is that it holds amused interest throughout by its naive comedy entirely unmixed with hokum. It has a touch of romance from the fact that although the girl thinks her disguise is perfect, the leader of the hobo band is aware of her deception, and as the story progresses it is made plain that he is falling in love with her.

A neat, quick finish when all the tramps are arrested as vagrants and the author reveals his identity to the friendly police turns off a thoroughly enjoyable comedy subject. *Rush.*

Through Thick and Thin

William Fairbanks vehicle produced by Camera Films Co. Distributed by Lumas Films Corp. Directed by B. Reaves Eason from a story by E. J. Meager. At the Stanley, N. Y., Sept. 1. Running time, about 55 min.

Don Dixon	William Fairbanks
Mr. Morris	George Periolat
The Dancer	Ina Anson
Miss Morris	Ethel Shannon
Blackie	Art Ortego
Mike Ryan	Ed Chandler
"Red" Grimley	Jack Curtis

A secret service story with the usual thrills. And better than usual because of a suspense which is maintained until the last scenes. Fairbanks, of course, does some rough-and-tumble scrapping up to his fighting par.

A secret service man is after a bunch of dope smugglers. Fairbanks goes to their Mexican hang-out, knocks out the bouncer, takes his job and then falls in love with a girl whose father he suspects of being "the man higher up." But the suspected man turns out to be a detective, merely using different and more subtle tactics to trap the smugglers. So, after rescuing the girl, who had been taken by the bad boys on a pretext, the plot is cleared up and there's a nice clinch.

Lots of action, plus a good cast. It is of interest to note that George Periolat, one of the real veterans of the picture-acting game, has a prominent part here. Fairbanks does excellently, while Ethel Shannon makes an attractive heroine.

But the part the mob will like is the fighting, and there's plenty of it. *Sisk.*

DIPLOMACY

Famous Players picture and a Marshall Neilan production directed by Neilan. Adapted from the stage play by Victor Sardou; features Blanche Sweet. At the Rivoli, New York, week of Sept. 11. Running time, 75 minutes.

Dora	Blanche Sweet
Julian Weymouth	Neil Hamilton
Countess Zicka	Arlette Marchal
Robert Lowry	Matt Moore
Baron Ballin	Gustav von Seyffertitz
Sir Henry Weymouth	Earle Williams
Count Orloff	Arthur E. Carewe
Marquise de Zares	Julia Swayne Gordon
Reggie Cowan	David Mir
Chinese Diplomat	Sojin

Just how closely Neilan has followed the play in screening this bit of writing can't be said. Speaking the contemporary jargon of the studios, "Diplomacy" chokes itself to death with "dramatic suspense." Almost everybody in the cast at one time or another becomes a "menace" and it's well-nigh a throwback to drawing room 10, 20 and 30. Just a program picture at best and a none too strong one at that.

Based upon an international treaty involving every country you ever heard of, the mysterious goins' on reach epidemic proportions. So much so a Sunday matinee audience at the Rivoli revealed intermittent tendencies toward disdainful snickers.

Neilan has jumbled up the characters when introducing them. It's a couple of reels before the witnesser has a chance to begin pigeon holing the players. Meanwhile there's something of a scenic on the screen, for Neilan was abroad and took some of these shots while there.

The interior of a Riviera cafe looks on the level and serves as a plug for Don Clark and his band. Also it appears that for the remuneration of sub-title mention, Carl Hyson and Peggy Harris evidently acquiesced to the suggestion of dancing before the camera. And they prance perhaps for 20 feet, Neil Hamilton informing Blanche Sweet that "That's Carl Hyson and Peggy Harris" for the payoff.

Everybody's gone diplomatic, according to this release. Miss Sweet, as Dora de Zares, isn't of the corps, but it appears as though she is to sustain the suspense. Her screen husband (Mr. Hamilton) has lost the precious document for which one Chinaman suffers a torture device, another of the high hat stratum gets shot and two more of the faction are found floating in the river, according to a title.

Earl Williams is monocled as the suave British representative, while Matt Moore is the subject of the "comedy instructor" in supplying comic relief. Moore, incidentally, turns out to be the in the nick of time American secret service man, and for a hurrah finale Neilan has printed matter which has Williams offering "Thanks to Uncle Sam" as his adieu.

After seeing it there doesn't seem to have been any necessity to have bothered with the authentic foreign scenes. They don't help here and anyway, it's doubtful if 10 percent of a first run audience believe "location" views at this day and date, due to the reading matter that has gone out for the daily press, magazines and appearing in the programs of "specials.",

The cast is lengthy but no one is of particular prominence. Miss Sweet looks good at varying intervals. Her work toward the climax, when Neilan really builds to arouse some degree of interest, is of par value although the impression remains that Arlette Marchal, as the unknown accomplice, steals the picture from her. Hamilton is curtailed and Williams does the calm, cool and collected conception of British diplomacy for all it is worth, maybe more, and no one yet has found out how much.

With so many coming and going, no one gets much of a chance to 'mge. before the lens, and in this instance the story suffers for it. On production the picture passes with the customary interiors.

Neilan hasn't done his best by this fearfully dramatic "Diplomacy." It's doubtful if the secret service of the world will appreciate the opening wording which dedicates the film to them. *Skig.*

SUBWAY SADIE

Alfred Santell Production released by First National Featuring Dorothy Mackaill, Jack Mulhall and Charles Murray. Story by Mildred Cram. Directed by Alfred Santell, under the production management of Al Rockett. Shown at the Strand, New York, week Sept. 12. Running time, 70 minutes.

Sadie Hermann	Dorothy Mackaill
Herb McCarthy	Jack Mulhall
Taxi Driver	Charles Murray
Ethel	Peggy Shaw
Fred Perry	Gaston Glass
Brown	Bernard Randall

A story of Fifth Avenue fashions and furs, the Bronx, subways, love and a smash-up. But atop of all this is the performance of Charles Murray as a taxicab driver who is assisted by a set of titles putting over the picture as a laugh hit.

Dorothy Mackaill, first of the featured players, looks great and handles herself wonderfully well as the heroine, while Jack Mulhall is the stereotyped hero of the films as far as his role here is concerned. He wouldn't even have registered that well if the title writer hadn't slipped a sequence of three or four titles that are repeated three or four times during the picture, making one remember that he is really in the cast.

From a box office angle the picture should get money if it is dressed up with an added attraction in the big houses. Right now those houses showing it might cop the spiral staircase scene, especially if they have a shallow stage and use it in conjunction with a fall fur fashion show, which would be sure fire.

Sadie Hermann is in the fur department at Sak's on 5th avenue, star saleswoman, of course, with an ambition to go to Paris. She lives in the Bronx with a room-mate, Ethel, who wants to be a good wife to some good guy. She kids Sadie's Paris complex by saying the chances are that she'll end up in the Bronx devoted to a better babies movement of her own.

The two travel to work via the sub each morn and there is a corking reproduction of the 149th street, Bronx, sub-station jam as the wage earners surge south to do their daily stunt.

Sadie and Ethel, jammed in the crush, are saved by Herb McCarthy, who dates Sadie up for the following Sunday and meets her in Central Park.

Then spring and romance, an engagement which is shattered by Sadie getting promoted to the post of Paris buyer of furs, a subway smash-up in which Herb is hurt and his telegram cause Sadie to miss her sailing only to find that Herb is the son of the owner of the subway, and if she marries him she can have a trip to Paris all her own.

Murray doesn't show in the picture until about the fourth reel, when he is the taxi driver called to take Sadie to the boat. But from the time he appears until the finish he just hogs every scene he is in.

There are laughs, and Murray makes them, although titles allotted to Sadie also pull giggles.

Al Santell handled the direction almost perfectly, although there was a little too much footage to a couple of the mush scenes in the park. A couple of novelties in the "Silver Slipper" scene that might be used effectively anywhere, and on the whole the action moves at a tempo that will hold the attention of almost any audience. *Fred.*

POKER FACES

Universal Jewel production, featuring Laura La Plante and Edward Everett Horton. Directed and also adapted by Harry A. Pollard. At Keith-Albee Hippodrome, New York, week Sept. 13. Running time, usual.

A very good comedy of the farce variety that can go in any first-run house. Unless "Poker Faces" was adapted from a popular selling novel, it hardly seems likely the title will mean any draw, but the picture may safely be played up in advance as a laugh-maker, for it is all of that.

The entire action takes place within 12 consecutive hours. That in itself for farce makes for speedy playing.

Here is a farce that reads as though from the French. It verges on the risque. Harry A. Pollard, the director, has skillfully jumped over all offensiveness without losing one whit of the suggestiveness. That's a trick. It is extremely clever directorial maneuvering Mr. Pollard has done in this picture, and often. It's so sexy that business should climb after opening, especially outside of the largest cities, through word-of-mouth advertising.

Captions frequently draw laughs as well. The titles are snappy and pithy. At one time a series in a row was of but one word each.

That happened during a family quarrel of the young couple, when Edward Everett Horton told his wife, Laura La Plante, she could not buy a new rug. The wife, remonstrating, said she would go back to work to obtain the things she wanted. Her husband forbade her ever to work again, with the consequence the wife slipped out immediately after he left, obtaining a position as secretary with the head of the firm her husband was working for.

Meanwhile the same boss informed the husband he was to pose for a week as the junior partner of the house, in order that he might entertain and secure a large contract from a visiting guest. After discovering his wife had fled, the husband received instructions to bring his wife with him to dinner that night, when they would meet the guest. The boss' idea was that as he had heard the wife was an attractive woman, she would be of decided aid. He had promised the husband $2,000 for the week's extra work if the contract should be secured.

To obey the instructions and in the absence of his wife, the husband procured a substitute wife from a theatrical agent's office, with the actress also owning a prize-fighting husband who told her she would have to return home by 11 that night.

Then the situation developed at the boss' home that evening of the guest arriving after he had seen a young man annoy everyone at the station. The young man was the junior partner, desperately in search of his wife, whom he believed had come to the station to take a train. When the junior partner walked in the guest recognized him as "the depot Romeo" (caption), with but a short time following the wife entering as the boss' secretary. Introductions amidst the embarrassment, with the wife believing at first her husband a bigamist, while the husband had to stand to see the guest make a play for his wife, the secretary.

This ran through an amazing maze of a farcical plot, finally winding up when the prize-fighter came around to learn something about his own wife, and finding the other husband with his wife in a locked bedroom, with the other husband in his underwear.

"Poker Faces" as the title comes from the husband gaining the rep for a dead pan.

The depot scenes are funnier than Harry Watson's phone skit when the phone skit was new.

Nicely cast, with Mr. Horton fitting the husband role in looks and action, while Miss La Plante probably has more opportunity for actual acting in this picture than falls to many a girl picture player in a dozen films. Miss La Plante is excellent, especially in the change of playing pace she often had to go through, while pantomimically the girl is a surprise.

The heavy or "menace" (Variety's New York reviewers are killed by that "menace" for the heavies that have come out from the coast), although here not strictly a menace, also did very well among a fine cast throughout.

A very good screen comedy for Universal or any other producer of pictures.

Perhaps it should be mentioned here as well as in the review of the Hip that those who may see this picture at the Hippodrome should not blame the photography. It is thought the projection is imperfect at the Hip. *Sime.*

HER MAN O' WAR

C. Gardner Sullivan production released by P. D. C. From the story, "Black Marriage," by Fred Jackson, adapted by Charles Logue, directed by Frank Urson, supervised by C. Gardner Sullivan. At Proctor's 58th St., N. Y., Sept. 13-15. Running time, 61 minutes.

Jim Sanderson	William Boyd
His Pal	Jimmie Adams
French-German Girl	Jetta Goudal
German General	Robert Edeson
Secret Service Head	Frank Reicher
Countess	Grace D'Armond
Peter	Junior Coghlan

One can't hand P. D. C. anything on this one. Being "just a war picture" and coming along at this time it doesn't click.

Up at Proctor's 58th Street, where the audience is one that usually revels in elemental melodrama, they handed this one the horse laugh. Even "the Yanks are coming," pulled in at the last minute to save the hero from execution as a spy at the hands of the Germans, failed to get 'em.

The story in brief is that of two volunteers from the American ranks who offer to pose as deserters, enter the German lines to find out about an underground passage to a castle so that the allied forces can tunnel their way to capture a big gun that has been holding up the advance. The men make the grade, are assigned to work on two farms, and the women fall in love with them. The farm that William Boyd is assigned to is that of a girl of mixed French and German parentage. She hates a deserter but still falls in love with this one. However, when the Countess, whose husband is commanding the sector, also falls for the American prisoner, she gets sore and tips off the General. The tipoff consists of delivering a shirt on which the directors of the tunnel under the castle's wine cellar are noted. There is an execution scheduled but at the last minute the little peasant girl relents uses a wireless phone and the Yanks arrive just in time.

Boyd handles the hero as well as can be expected, but Jetta Goudal, who is starred, does not convince as the heroine. Jimmie Adams, in a comedy role, registers nicely, while Frank Reicher and Robert Edeson have little better than bits. Grace D'Armond as the flirting Countess, is a million dollar blonde flash.

A poor picture that rates about one half of a bill on double feature day. *Fred.*

NO MAN'S GOLD

William Fox Western production, featuring Tom Mix and directed by Lewis Seiler. Story from the novel, "Dead Man's Gold," by J. Allan Dunn, adaptation by John Stone. In the cast: Frank Campeau, Eva Novak, Mickey Moore, Forrest Taylor, Harry Gripp. At the New York, Sept. 9, one day. Running time, 69 minutes.

A first-class cowboy melodrama, with all the merits that usually go into that class of picture, including scenic beauties and hard riding, and in addition a particularly interesting and tricky plot built up with much ingenuity.

The picture has a wealth of stunts which grow naturally out of the story instead of being dragged in, working up to a smashing climax when Mix, the dare devil cow puncher, takes a dizzy ride across a valley on the slender thread of a mine carrier in a suspended bucket that crashes through and demolishes the house where "bad men" are besieging the hero and heroine.

The locale of the action is in the high mountains, and the hero and his followers are beleaguered on a lofty peak, with the outlaws holding them at bay from a deep canyon. This situation provides a stunning pictorial background with camera shots of giddy altitudes and striking vistas. Also it makes possible the hero's feat of descending the sheer cliff by a rope, apparently lowered by Mix's horse, Tony, in an effective bit of tense melodrama.

The story gets under way promptly. At the very outset an outlaw shoots a miner from ambush in a plot to jump his rich gold claim. Dying the miner gives up the map, showing the location of his bonanza, but tears it into three parts, giving one part to the murderous outlaw, one part to a comedy character and the third, and vital, part to the hero. All three start for the mine, accompanied by the dead miner's orphaned son, Jimmy.

The outlaw's confederates scheme to follow at a distance and seize the mine when at length it has been found. The three have to keep together to that point, because none knows the other's section of the mapped route. They stop en route at a rodeo, which furnishes the excuse for some fine riding displays. It is here that Tom, the hero, meets and falls in love with the heroine before they go on their quest.

The girl learns of the plot to seize the mine after the trio have departed, and, following to warn Tom, she is captured by the skulking outlaws. Thus is furnished the romantic interest of the siege, when Tom and his little band are held at bay defending their narrow mountain pass.

The accumulated melodrama from here to the end when the hero wins out is a never-ending series of thrills. The use of dynamite to block the attack, the scaling of towering cliffs and finally the hero's wild ride through the air on an inclined cable, all make for smashing melodrama that keeps suspense a tip-toe to the final moment.

Mr. Mix plays in his familiar vein of casual comedy while his support is always convincing in situations that make up in "punch" what they lack in plausibility, which is all that one can say for stories of this type. *Rush.*

Mile a Minute Man

William Fairbanks' starring vehicle made independently by Camera Films, Inc. Distributor not named in titles, but probably Lumas, handling his last film. Story and adaptation by E. J. Meagher. Directed by Jack Nelson. At the Stanley, New York, Sept. 10, one day. Running time, about 56 minutes.

"Speedy" Rockett	William Fairbanks
Paula Greydon	Virginia Browne Faire
O. I. Rockett	George Periolat

A very cheap looking film, which looks, for all the exploitation it gives to Fairbanks' display of his muscles and figure, like it might have been written to order. It's a botch job where writing, production and acting are concerned, and even its thrill finish of a race is just applesauce by this time.

The reference is to the specific plot wherein the boy and the girl happen to be children of competitors in business, and of a feud thrown in to make it a bit more novel. That seems to be the sole difference known to the plot-makers.

It's the old Montague and Capulet stuff that Will Shakespeare wrote, but didn't collect royalties on.

Here the boy's father makes automobiles and the girl's mother does likewise. A race introduces the picture. Then the story goes to a home, where, the subtitles declare, "amateur theatricals are always enjoyed." In the subsequent scenes Fairbanks poses, in trunks only, to show that his chest is large, that his arm muscles are pretty good and that he's quite the masculine hero. Silly stuff and entirely irrelevant to the story.

Fairbanks has turned out some good action pictures. In this one he tries to be an actor—and he isn't. He's a good looking strong man capable of doing fancy fighting, racing and other stunt stuff. That he doesn't confine himself to the things he can do best is what ruins the film, for it is strictly N. G. *Sisk.*

THE HIGH HAND

Independent western distributed by Pathe. Story by Fred Beebe. Leon Maloney starred and also credited with direction. Josephine Hill playing opposite. At Loew's New York, Sept. 10, as half double bill. Running time, 65 minutes.

Leo Maloney goes along turning out westerns of fairly even quality. In this story he has a picture of better than average grade, due to a smooth plot plus abundant melodramatic action scaled against a capital undercurrent of genuine western humor.

It is this element that gives the picture its very unusual distinction. "The High Hand" is a reversal of the common situation. As a rule the acting is high class and the technical production is faultless, while the story is the weak factor.

Here it is the story that holds more excellence than either the acting, just adequate, or the production, which is negligible. The settings are all natural background or the simple interiors of ranch house or mining camp saloon.

The humor arises from the fact that the hero performs his super-human feats of valor and strength in a jaunty and mischievous spirit. Jack, the chivalrous cowboy, befriends a ranchman harassed and driven out of his home by land grabbers. Jack takes up the battle of the beaten rancher, when he finds that the conspirators against him are an unscrupulous lawyer and a dive keeper in Oakland.

Jack's reprisal against the two conspirators consists in robbing them and leaving a receipt for what he takes signed "The Collector." The money he sends to the sheriff for safe keeping, promising that at the proper time he will make an accounting for his unbusinesslike transactions. Meantime the conspirators, made desperate by the masked attack of "The Collector," hire Jack himself to run down and dispose of the mysterious "Collector," Jack taking the job and using it to further mystify and terrorize his crooked employers.

The climax is expertly built up, with the conspirators demanding a showdown from Jack, and Jack's agreement to produce "The Collector" in the dive at noon the following day. The situation is built up for cumulative value by alternate views of the crooks' preparations to entertain "The Collector" with violence and enthusiasm, and pictures of the clock as the hands approach noon.

Jack, of course, "gets the drop" on the outlaws, and leaves the dive keeper hanging on one of his own chandeliers and turns the other confessed thief over to the sheriff.

There is some romantic interest, although it is greatly subordinated to the melodrama. The playing is no better than fair but the picture, because of its well knit story, is almost actor-proof. *Rush.*

JACK OF HEARTS

Comedy drama made by American Cinema Association. Adapted from the stage play, "Jack in the Pulpit," by Gordon Morris. Adaptation by Frances Nordstrom. Directed by David Hartford, who sponsors the production. Cullen Landis and Gladys Hulette featured. At Loew's New York Sept. 10, as half of double feature bill. Running time, 56 minutes.

This independent is a warning against accepting a stage play at its face value and trying to transfer it to the screen in nearly unchanged form. As the story comes out it amounts to a set of titles, illustrated with pictures of people engaged in conversation.

The pantomime does not hold any drama. For long passages the action consists of two or more people engaged in conversation with more or less meaningless gestures and business. Then comes a title to explain what is going on. That process doesn't make a picture, and "Jack of Hearts" isn't a cinema story.

Confusion in character occurs early. An ingenue becomes confused with the leading woman until well into the story, because they both look somewhat alike. There are three or four subordinate men characters who are hard to distinguish and finally, even if the story were clearly and well told, it wouldn't be particularly interesting.

A young theological student desires to get first hand experience of life before he goes into the pulpit, and so goes to the big city against the desires of his aunt. In the city he is arrested and sent to jail when a crook plants a purse in his pocket to avoid arrest himself.

Released from jail, he takes job

after job, always defeated in his struggle for a living by the specter of the hounding police in the person of a detective. At length, discouraged, he returns home to find his aunt dead and crooks in control of her large fortune (a million dollars is mentioned casually in this connection). He takes the pastorate of the church, once held by his father, although how he accomplished this coup is left rather hazy. He is succeeding in his work as preacher and social uplifter, when, sure enough the detective appears and warns him he must leave town. This leads to the climax, the hero's last sermon in which he recites his sufferings until all hearts are wrung. The thief who planted the fatal purse confesses and the detective who is in the congregation, gives the spotless young man a recommendation to the church people. And so he marries the girl who had been waiting for him all this time, and they lived happily ever after.

Dull tale, dully told and acted without a spark of inspiration, making the venture a dead loss. *Rush.*

TIN GODS

Allan Dwan Production, starring Thomas Meighan, presented by Adolph Zukor and Jesse L. Lasky. Renee Adoree and Aileen Pringle featured. From the play by William Anthony McGuire, adapted by Paul Dickey and Howard Emmett Rogers, script by James Shelly Hamilton. Directed by Allan Dwan. At the Rialto, N. Y., for a run beginning Sept. 19. Running time, 79 mins.

Roger Drake	Thomas Meighan
Carita	Renee Adoree
Janet Stone	Aileen Pringle
Tony Santelli	William Powell
Dr. McCoy	Hale Hamilton
Dougherty	John Harrington
First Foreman	Joe King
Second Foreman	Robert E. O'Connor
Billy	Delbert Emory Whitten, Jr.

"Tin Gods" as motion picture entertainment may do well enough in the weekly change houses on the strength of the names in the cast, but as for standing up for a run even at regular picture house prices it won't do. Famous Players, placing the picture in the Rialto (opening with a special midnight presentation last Saturday) to follow "Variety," will be lucky if the picture holds up at the box office for three weeks to receipts that are half of what "Variety" got in its final week.

It is a fortunate thing that the Harry Langdon comedy, "Saturday Afternoon," produced by Mack Sennett, is included in the program. This three reeler saves the show.

There must be something all wrong with Thomas Meighan as to the selection of stories for him. For more than a year he has been slipping in this particular regard, and "Tin Gods" is just another of those things in which Meighan can just about get by. However, in this picture the star is overshadowed by one of the supporting players, Renee Adoree. As the little South American dancehall girl she just about walks away with what honors there are to be handed the cast.

Of the others the only one that does anything noteworthy is William Powell as the dandy that conducts the dancehall. He and Miss Adoree as a combination are a worthwhile consideration for future productions.

No question as to Dwan's ability as a director, but without material you can't expect him to work wonders. The story is slow in developing, and the principal theme, that of worshipping "Tin Gods" in so far as the seeking of personal aggrandizement is concerned, is lost sight of in the romance between the engineer and the dancehall girl. Up to the point that this romance comes into the story there is nothing, and then the romance goes along at a pace that has no kick in it for the audience. There is but one real punch to the picture; that is where the little dancer leaps from the span of the bridge which her lover has built when she believes he is going to return to his wife.

The story is that of an engineer who marries a wealthy girl. She dominates the household, and as a result he is overshadowed, while his wife goes in for politics. They have a child, a little youngster who is permitted to fall to death from the nursery while his mother is making a political speech over the radio. That is the straw that breaks the husband's back, and he accepts a commission to erect a bridge in South America. Once below the equator he doesn't do bridge building, but does manage to hoist a lot of booze into his system until finally he is taken ill. At this point the little dancer nurses him, and when he has recovered brings an expression of his love for her from him through a jealous play.

It is immediately after this that the wife is decisively beaten at the polls, and her political advisors attribute it to her being parted from her husband. She then decides to go after him and bring him back. When she arrives he tells her that she can at last give him real happiness, a speech which is overheard by the girl, who fails to hear him

say that it is his freedom that will achieve that happiness. With that comes the leap to death on the part of the heroine.

Meighan is worthy of better things. His role, while a sympathetic one, does not click, nor does the star for that matter. Aileen Pringle, in a most unsympathetic character, does the best she can, while Renee Adoree runs away with the picture.

"Tin Gods" will not help Tommie Meighan's prestige. *Fred.*

SPARROWS

Mary Pickford picture from an original by Winifred Dunn, adapted by C. Gardner Sullivan and directed by William Beaudine. Tom McNamara, Carl Harbaugh and Earle Browne in collaboration. Titling by George Marion, Jr. Released by United Artists. At the Strand, New York, week of Sept. 19. Running time, 83 minutes.

Mama Mollie Grimes	Mary Pickford
Richard Wayne	Gustav von Seyffertitz
Doris Wayne	Roy Stewart
Mrs. Grimes	Mary Louise Miller
Ambrose Grimes	Charlotte Mineau
Bailey	Spec O'Donnell
His Confederate	Lloyd Whitlock
Hog Buyer	A. L. Schaeffer
Splutters	Mark Hamilton
	Monty O'Grady

The Sparrows—Muriel MacCormac, Billy Jones, Cammilla Johnson, Mary McLane, Billy Butts, Jack Levine, Florence Rogan, Sylvia Bernard, Seessel Anne Johnson.

A view of this Pickford product explains why it was sent directly into program release instead of the usual course of a pre-release showing in a run theatre. The truth is the production is one of the few duds put out by Mary Pickford.

Of course, the star's name is more or less failure-proof. The picture will probably do something approximating the usual Strand total, and in all probability the name will draw generally for short or daily bookings, by virtue of the star's status as a national institution. But the picture itself is a dead loss.

Mary has always been a sort of lowly Cinderella, frequently in a drab background. But for the most part there has been some sunlight somewhere in the locale, even if only the radiance created by the Pickford character.

But in "Sparrows" there isn't a ray of brightness. For once a Pollyanna is submerged, smothered and muffled in sinister gloom. The surroundings are those of a terrifying nightmare—a baby farm deep in a miasmatic swamp infested by alligators and by the ogre Grimes who operates the place, a figure to spoil a night's sleep even for an adult.

The whole picture is played in the swamp locale. The photography is done in dim half lights and the whole business drips desolation. Miss Pickford's special style of sentimental comedy can make no headway against the penetrating gloom of the subject and locale. The dripping ooze of the swamp gets into the spectator's system and he leaves the theatre with the relief of escaping from a depressing incident. The fact is that the Cinderella stepmother technique has been overdone—laid on too thick—and spoiled the whole business. The detail that Grimes does away with his troublesome babies by "shoving them into the swamp," (which is ever present in shuddering reality) is rather a sickening bit of horror and is never allowed to get out of the foreground.

There are reels of agonies and the cumulative effect is oppressive. they even go into the minute particulars of the death by starvation of one of the babies on the farm, poeticised somewhat by a Biblical tableau after the manner of Little Eva's passing, but still not what one would voluntarily sit through on a fine autumn afternoon. There is little drama to relieve the tedium of agony, until near the end of the story, when justice is dealt to Grimes the Terrible, who sinks slowly to death in one of the swamp quicksand holes himself, a painful but entirely inadequate finish.

The baby farm is also a hog farm set in a stockade in the depths of a dismal swamp. Here are 10 abandoned waifs, among them "Mama Mollie," who tries her pitiful best to mother the oppressed brood. Grimes, who looks like Dr. Jekyll in one of his worst moments, misuses his charges cruelly, sinking them in the bogholes when they become troublesome. Led by cupidity, he agrees to hide the kidnapped baby of Richard Wayne, a wealthy citizen, and it is in defense of this baby that "Mama Mollie," followed by her nine small friends, escapes from the baby farm, braving the dangers of the terrible swamp.

The passage of their flight is the special nightmare. The band of urchins waded waist deep in sticky slime and mire; crawled across ugly tree branches with snapping alligators just out of reach and all but sank in the treacherous bog, before rescued by the police, engaged in running down the kidnappers. The finish has the youngsters all cared for in the Wayne mansion, for a happy ending.

The final portions of the picture, involving the chase of the kidnappers and the driving of Grimes to death in a bog hole, have a wealth of action, and throughout the story there are frequent episodes of typical Mary Pickford comedy, but everything is overshadowed by the horror and wretchedness, which supplies the controlling element and makes all else incidental. *Rush.*

THE CAMPUS FLIRT

Famous Players-Lasky picture starring Bebe Daniels. Clarence Badger production directed by Mr. Badger. From an "original" by Louise Long and Lloyd Corrigan. Ralph Spencer and Rube Goldberg titled, with H. K. Martin, photographer. At the Rivoli, New York, week Sept. 18. Running time, about 72 minutes.

Patricia Mansfield............Bebe Daniels
Denis Adams..................James Hall
Knute Knudson................El Brendel
Charlie Paddock..................Himself
Harriet Porter..............Joan Standing
Graham Stearns.............Gilbert Roland
Mae........................Irma Kornelia
Gwen.........................Jocelyn Lee

An amusing lightweight comedy for Bebe Daniels to romp in, and she frolics. Plenty of collegiate themes flickering on the soreens this fall, with this another one. But it's an okay example, having the twist of taking the feminine angle plus showing the girls in the midst of a track meet. Hence it's athletic, clean and funny. Fair enough for one release.

For attention the star is given a close run by El Brendel (formerly of Brendel and Burt in vaudeville). Brendel will undoubtedly do much more camera work if this first effort is a criterion. Here he plays a Swede waiter in a school dormitory extracting successive laughs throughout. His appearance is not unlike Langdon, but that doesn't mean he is mimicking. Not so, Brendel giving every evidence of taking care of himself.

Charlie Paddock, former Coast speed marvel, whom the dailies report as Miss Daniel's fiance, also breaks into pictures in this one. Paddock is sufficiently well known for his track exploits to draw out of curiosity. In fact, there is a parallel to be drawn between this boy and Grange, not that it means anything but it's an angle.

In the San Francisco picture box office story on page six or seven of this issue it will be noted that the Grange picture failed to mean anything out there. This is related because the Coast Defenders don't believe the redhead to be as great as heralded, due to a mediocre showing when his pro team played there last winter, and they don't think much of football played other than along the Pacific shore line anyway.

And Paddock is up against the same thing in the east. The repeated breaking of even time for the 100 and his wonderous stepping of many 220s out there is gazed upon skeptically in this section, simply because Paddock has never done anything to make those records convincing when running in this area. It's probably the East is East and West is West thing, both sections being jealous of their athletes—which isn't going to do the picture companies any good with their athletes in certain territory.

But that's away from "The Campus Flirt," and it's a good picture. Miss Daniels plays Patricia Mansfield, who has been educated abroad and pampered by a social designing mother but is sent to college to get along as best she can by a normal father. Wearing a high hat, undergraduate life is none too rosy for her until she starts to try to make the girls' track team.

A mouse is the cause of revealing her ability to hurdle and run, with Paddock's tutelage supplying the necessary form. He's done just that, strictly on the level. Miss Daniels actually runs as if she knew how, at least she makes it look good. Girls are generally awkward when they get above a walk, but not this gang. Badger has staged these track events well and made them interesting, Pat, of course, being delayed but getting to the field in time to win the relay and the meet for her college.

It must have been a strenuous picture for Miss Daniels. She takes quite a bit of pushing around besides getting into the water twice. Nice support is forthcoming from James Hall, opposite, but the love interest is secondary to the field work. Hall is in his inaugural film here, having been lifted by the film boys from musical comedy, where he was known as James Hamilton. Brendel, as previously mentioned, prominently stands out, and other contributing members suffice. Both production and photography pass as standard, with the titling additionally catching a few laughs.

Heartily approved here with a mild Sunday afternoon not keeping them from standing four deep downstairs at the second show. *Skig.*

FOR ALIMONY ONLY

William De Mille production. Presented by John C. Flinn. Distributed by P. D. C. Story and continuity by Lenore J. Coffee. Directed by William De Mille. Shown at the Hippodrome, N. Y., week Sept. 20, 1926. Running time, 72 minutes.

Mary Martin Williams.........Leatrice Joy
Peter Williams.................Clive Brook
Narcissa Williams.........Lilyan Tashman
Bertie Warin..............Casson Ferguson
Maid.........................Toby Claude

A story with a twist that is a little bit different from the average run. The picture itself ranks about with the average of the program releases, and it appears as though the audience at the Hippodrome liked it fairly well Monday night.

No particular big kick to the film, but it will serve to entertain.

Leatrice Joy is starred, with Clive Brook and Lilyan Tashman featured. After all, Lil is the surprise of the picture. Here she really appears natural in a role that calls for her to be the alimony-hunting wife who is detaining a pineapple on the side.

The story is that of a woman whose sole object in marrying is to land someone who can afford to make a handsome settlement either in a bulk sum or in installments in the form of alimony to be rid of her.

Peter Williams (Clive Brook) is her second victim. He gives up to be free. Later he meets with a little girl who is studying art, Mary Martin (Leatrice Joy), who wins him. Later, when thrown into jail for non-payment of alimony, it is she who hocks her rings to get him out and, atop of that, goes to work to keep him out.

Her duties as an assistant in an interior decorators finally take her to the apartment of the first Mrs. Williams, and she is there when her husband calls. She suspects all sorts of things, but in reality he is there to try to get the alimony reduced. Later his wife won't believe him and when he informs her that he has to dine with the former wife in order to get her to consider a reduction in the reparations she flies off the handle and makes a date with a fellow who proves to be none other than he who is living off of the first Mrs. Williams.

The two are at a roadhouse when first the magaimp's bankroll girl comes in, shortly to be followed by the husband and thirdly by the cops. Then the little wife No. 2 thinks fast and saves No. 1 and her boy friend from arrest by saying hat the entire party is there for the purpose of the marriage of Mrs. No. 1 to her boy friend. The cop, refusing to be conned, goes along to see that the hitching takes place. This frees Williams from further alimony payment.

There are a lot of laughs in the picture and the story runs along at a pace that holds the interest.

Leatrice Joy, with her boy's haircut, looks cute in it instead of masculine, as most girls do. Toby Claude in a maid's bit managed to register effectively in a couple of pieces of business. *Fred.*

FLYING HORSEMAN

Fox western featuring Buck Jones. Scenario by Gertrude Orr from original by Max Brand. Directed by Orville Dull. At Loew's New York, N. Y., on double bill, Sept. 17. Running time, 56 minutes.

This picture has all those attributes of speedy action, hard riding, fast moving plot and scenic smashes that go to make up the entertaining drama of the plains, and it has in an unusual degree one other quality. The outdoor shots have some of the most startlingly vivid bits of photography that have come upon the screen.

Photographic quality at this day and date goes without saying. It's pretty much all good. But when a series of views like this that arrest attention on the merit of the pictorial clarity and composition alone, it argues special merit. Most of the action takes place in the plains and in the mountains, at any rate in the open. Distant peaks and the details of the middle distances, with such things as dust clouds, stand out and the foregrounds with the real action are splendidly recorded.

The story is consistently interesting, has fair, quiet comedy, and a succession of stunts hold throughout.

Mark Winton (Buck Jones) is a care-free cowboy, unattached and rambling. He sees a lot of kids disporting in the swimming hole, and stops to watch. When the heavy, a land shark, seeks to whip the youngsters away, his ire is aroused and he takes up the fight for freedom of juvenile democracy. His antagonism toward the land shark (played by Walter C. Percival) leads him into many intrigues. He is suspected of horse stealing, and when the real outlaw is cornered and kills a deputy sheriff, the crime is fastened upon him.

The heavy, of course, is seeking to steal the ranch belonging to the heroine's father and is making dishonorable love to the girl. Also, the girl has a horse entered for the rodeo sweepstakes and expects to pay off the mortgage with the purse. All this is familiar, but it is good material when done as well as here.

When the heroine's horse is crippled by the heavy to keep it out of the race, Winton breaks jail and rides to victory and the defeat of the forces of evil. The sketch doesn't indicate the thrill of the race—a cross country event that has a world of kick. It becomes an obstacle race, with the outlaws posted along the way to bar the hero's way. They dynamite a bridge, forcing Jones and his beautiful white mount to cross on a slender tree trunk at a giddy height.

For comedy there is introduced the family of eight or 10 kids belonging to a widowed workman of the ranch. Mark finds them a gang of small bolsheviks, and drills them to discipline by turning them into Boy Scouts. The kids make a capital comic angle to the story. Gladys McConnell is the heroine, doing rather better with the role of a western heroine than usual. This is principally because she accepts a subordinate place in the story and merely tries to make the incidental part a graceful detail.

Altogether a high class program output. *Rush.*

ROSIE O'GRADY

Comedy-drama suggested by the old ballad of the same name by Maude Nugent. Scenario by Harry O. Hoyt. Picture directed by Frank R. Strayer under the supervision of Harry Cohn. Trade showing at Wurlitzer Hall, Sept. 17. Running time, 68 minutes.

Rosie O'Grady.................Shirley Mason
Victor MacQuade..............Cullen Landis
Uncle Ben Shapiro.........E. Alyn Warren
James Brady...............William Conklin
The "Kibbitzer"..............Lester Bernard
Friend of Uncle Ben..........Otto Lederer

Rosie, the heroine, is a foundling with a Jewish foster father and an Irish god-father. So far there is some shading of "Abie's Irish Rose," but the parallel goes no further. For the rest it's a Cinderella story of fair quality enlivened by some effective comedy and ending in a speedy elopement finish that holds interest.

Between them these two elements lift the picture to a little above average. There are times when it slows up for rather labored character bits that impede the action, but these passages probably will justify themselves for their humor. Such is the frequent interruption of a "kibbitzer" into the pinochle game.

The scenes, for contrast, shift from the pawnshop of Uncle Ben Shapiro to the mansion of Jim Brady, ex-policeman, who rises to wealth as a New York contractor. Both locales are well managed, especially the luxurious settings of the mansion. Here are first rate backgrounds, reaching that desired goal of magnificence that are in taste. Technical direction is always of a high order.

As much cannot be said for the acting. Of the cast the Jewish foster-father played by E. Alyn Warren is much the best. Cullen Landis does not properly picture the high-bred youth, and Shirley Mason is another of those over-saccharine Cinderellas.

On the doorstep of Ben Shapiro's pawnshop is left an abandoned girl baby with a note from its dying and widowed mother, begging the benign Ben to care for it. Jim Brady, cop on the beat, is present at the finding. Together they adopt the waif, naming her on the inspiration after the popular song being ground out by a street organ.

Victor MacQuade, scion of 5th avenue, becomes embroiled in a street fight while wandering among the tenements and Rosie is instrumental in his rescue. Becoming friends Victor invites Rosie on an auto ride, and unwittingly she is introduced into the MacQuade home where a "rags and riches" masquerade ball is in progress. The girl wins the prize for the funniest costume, departing in tears and furious at Victor, whose identity she has learned.

Policeman Brady meanwhile has achieved wealth, although he still keeps up his friendship for Uncle

Ben and Rosie (one wonders why he doesn't keep her better dressed). He enters the pawnshop to find the girl in tears and the situation leads to taking her to his mansion. Victor pursues her here to find her blossoming out in Paris frocks, and picking her up elopes with her in his roadster whether she wants to go or not. Uncle Jim gives chase, but is distanced. A rural traffic cop, who is also a justice of peace, arrests the elopers for speeding, and ends by marrying them in a neat comedy scene. *Rush.*

Lodge in the Wilderness

Tiffany production, suggested from the story of the same name by Sir Gilbert Parker. Directed by Henry McCarthy. Anita Stewart starred. At the Stanley, New York, Sept. 8, one day. Running time, about 60 minutes.

Virginia Coulson............Anita Stewart
Jim Wallace..................Edmund Burns
Dot ....Duane Thompson
John Hammond................Larry Steers

Just why a novelist with Sir Gilbert Parker's rep should be credited with this out-and-out outdoors story of romance, villainy, forest fires, prison and true love triumphant isn't clear and doesn't matter. It's a cinch Sir Gilbert would never have made a name for himself writing stuff of this sort, and it's just as cinchy that stuff of this sort makes good, interesting and actionful movies.

Here a girl owns a lumber camp. The manager, a suave looking fellow with smiles and sneers alternating over his face, tried to make love to the girl, but a handsome young engineer held aces and trumped the manager where the love business was concerned. But to make the plot curdle, the engineer was accused of murder and convicted, and it wasn't until a big forest fire came along (the hero having escaped prison in time to participate in the main heroics) that it was shown a half-wit had done the murder. Thus the hero was acquitted, he married the girl and defeated the villains.

Well made, this film, and furnished with a red hot forest fire for a thrill. This sequence runs quite a time and deserves its footage, as it is the clincher on what is otherwise a good feature of the outdoors. Anita Stewart starred does well and Edmund Burns makes an okeh leading man. *Sisk.*

KOSHER KITTY KELLY

Screen version of Leon De Costa's comedy with music. Released by F. B. O. as feature picture. Direction by James Horne. At the Colony Sept. 26. Running time, 62 minutes.

Kitty Kelly.........................Viola Dana
Officer Pat Sullivan...........Tom Forman
Mrs. Feinbaum....................Vera Gordon
Rosie Feinbaum.............Kathleen Myers
Moses Ginsburg........................Nat Carr
Morris Rosen................Stanley Taylor
Barney Kelly...................Carroll Nye
Mrs. Kelly....................Aggie Herring

A perfect treatment of the "Abie's Irish Rose" style of comedy, elaborately embroidered with hokum and rough-house humor. It is all very effective. In the direction and in the title writing the anything-for-the-laugh technique has been followed with absolute singleness of purpose. And the result is a picture the fans laugh their heads off at.

There could be no debate about the quality of the screen entertainment at the Colony Sunday afternoon. The audience laughed hard and often, and gave the film a convincing demonstration of applause at the final close-up. The testimonial was entirely convincing. The feature has the popular appeal in abundance, just as the Anne Nichols plays has, and inquiries and examinations into the whys and wherefores are waste of good typewriter ribbons. The "K. K. K." comedy on the stage, however, fared but fairly.

The fun does not depend upon the actors, for this screen version is no more than fairly well done, except in the characters of Mrs. Feinberg and Moses Ginsburg, played by Vera Gordon and Nat Carr. These two players sketch convincing Jewish characters with certainty. The other roles were merely so so. Probably almost any other set of experienced players could have done as well.

The subject-matter of social relations between the Irish and the Hebrews in the big cities appears to be innately funny to the generality, much in the way that almost any kind of dialect character appeals to the popular sense of humor. The comedy side has been handled effectively by the title editor. Its descriptive captions always have a funny turn. Mrs. Kelly warns her son Barney against his tough associates in a title, "I wouldn't trust that gang in a stone quarry," which is a good laugh and exactly what Mrs. Kelly probably would say.

Miss Gordon plays the Mrs. Feinberg type in a spirit of legitimate comedy, seldom edging into actual caricature, but making her scenes a riot when she does go in for horseplay. The love-making bits with Carr were uproarious. They did everything but neck falls in these passages, and they were greeted with gales of merriment.

The fun of the story lies in these two roles more than in the passages that involve the Irish and the Jewish factions in clashes, and the story probably could have been made as amusing if the racial conflict was a side issue.

The romance of the two mixed couples is really a side issue in "Kitty," wherein it differs somewhat from "Abie." That the characters of Mrs. Feinberg and Ginsburg are played as legitimately as they are saves the whole picture from being no better than a hoke burlesque. These two portraits are pretty faithful, subject only to the necessity of some comedy shading, and they lift the whole picture to some eminence. *Rush.*

YOU'D BE SURPRISED

A Paramount Production presented by Adolph Zukor and Jesse L. Lasky, starring Raymond Griffith. Story and screen play by Jules Furthman, directed by Arthur Rosson. Shown at the Rivoli, N. Y., week Sept. 25, 1926. Running time, 74 minutes.

The Coroner..............Raymond Griffith
Ruth Whitman..........Dorothy Sebastian
Deputy D. A...............Earle Williams
District Attorney.......Edward Martindale

Judging from the program at the Rivoli giving the cast of this picture, which is the same as appears in the press sheet issued by Paramount, and the cast matter that is on the leader to the picture itself there must have been considerable work done in the editing and titling to develop it into the hit it is proving from the laugh angle. The picture is "there," with the money's worth in laughs.

The story is a burlesque of a mystery melodrama. But instead of Edward Martindale playing the role of District Attorney, he is Mr. Black or Mr. Grey who is host to a party on a houseboat. Among his guests are the Browns, Greens and maybe the Reds. At any rate, it is a cast of colorful characters reading like the characters one would get in a program on the burlesque wheel.

The opening shots show a black cat wandering about among the feet of the guests on board. None is shown further than the knees until it is established that something dreadful is sure to develop. Then for the first full shot one has the host bearing an empty jewel case, stating that he has been robbed of a valuable diamond by someone abroad the boat. He says he wants the jewel returned and as he knows the thief, he will have the lights darkened while the empty case is in the middle of the floor. If the thief returns the jewel to the case nothing will be said. The lights are down, the action on the screen shows the players rushing hither and thither and when the lights again flash up the host lies on the floor over the jewel case with a knife stuck through his back.

At that moment a policeman arrives and asks for the host who had 'phoned that he has been robbed. The dead man is pointed out to him; he calls his sergeant who in turn summons the lieutenant who sends for the inspector, all in turn saying, "Don't touch a thing. This is a case for the coroner," which builds it up for the arrival of Griffith.

From that point on the laughs come fast, and Griffith finally manages to trap the real culprit after he has directed suspicion at everyone else in the cast.

Dorothy Sebastian plays opposite the comedian and scores triumphantly. She is a mighty clever little actress, and this picture should go a long way toward giving her a chance to do some real things. Earle Williams is the heavy and manages the role convincingly, but Tom McGuire, who is given screen credit but not programmed, plays the inspector of police in such fashion that if he walked down Broadway in that uniform he'd have half the New York department saluting him. There is a "harness bull" for your life.

The high credit for a picture must go to Arthur Rosson, who directed it. He has worked out a couple of bits of action that are distinct howls. Rosson's handling of the coroner's jury scene is perfect, and that bit of Griffith "crossing" the women in one room and the men in another is another howl.

The titles are also laugh winners and the picture, all in all, is one of the very best of the Griffith series to date. You can't go wrong on this one. *Fred.*

The Marriage Clause

Universal presentation of Lois Weber production from story ("Technic"), by Dana Burnet, adapted and directed by Miss Weber. Principals: Billie Dove, Francis X. Bushman, Grace Darmond and Warner Oland. Week Sept. 27 at Hippodrome, New York. Runs 74 minutes.

Spotty production, possessed of its fine moments, based on a naturally intriguing theme centering around the elevation and romance of a dramatic star, but offset almost fatally in spots with trivial elaboration and general piffle. The overlength running time of 74 minutes is not the only reason why a good deal could and should be cut to speed up the proceedings.

Francis X. Bushman is the famous stage director who discovers Billie Dove as a dramatic find for Warner Oland, the equally famous entrepreneur. Grace Darmond in a feminine "menace" role completes the dramatis personæ of the principals.

The title is derived from a restrictive clause against Miss Dove and Mr. Bushman marrying as they desire. After the prohibited three years are up and all obstacles removed, in order to round out a story, a new cycle of complications commences.

Each of the three opportunities for a kiss-and-make-up in real life could have been graciously accepted, but Miss Weber dragged it out, stalled the final "clinch" as must be the natural consequence of a screen romance, probably keeping in mind that hugely dramatic and intensely romantic near-deathbed scene for the ultimate climax.

Conceding the merits of that Romeo and Juliet affectation, there is much, much too much, interpolated in between that should come out for the sake of the distributor, the exhibitor and the patron.

Some day, just to be different and possibly overlooking the incidental qualification that it would also be more true to life, some director will show a first night audience as a cosmopolitan collection of bootleggers, wisenheimers, newspapermen and night club hostesses, the majority of whom do *not* wear dress clothes. Particularly will the director overlook that banality of introducing newspaper critics as bewhiskered professional characters, dressed in the height of formality and of the type that scurries back-stage like so many Johns to shake the prima donna's hands. It might occur to the same iconoclastic director that, if he desires such touch, the newspaper boys generally hie themselves to the nearest telegraph office to take possession of a typewriter for a "notice"; or if an afternoon sheet, a trip downtown to complete the review.

Miss Weber probably also knows enough about the show business to appreciate that on no occasion do flowers pass the footlights. Those kind of scenes seem an obsession with her.

Still the screen is the screen and the hinterland, for this is a type of picture that will hit the nickelodeons in no time, may not know the difference; or it may overlook much.

"The Marriage Clause" is interesting for the possibilities accepted by Miss Dove. With a hoydenish name that does not suggest the dramatic capabilities she evidences, Billie Dove bobs up as an important celluloid personage. Like her character, there's no telling what a good director could do with her.

Mr. Bushman throughout the 74 minutes of the screening left an indelible impression that he was great as "Messela" in 'Ben-Hur," a heavy role, and that he lacks somehow now in the male lead he has been cast for.

This is the second "outside" picture at the Hip under its new "grind" policy, Keith's having a P. D. C. film tie-up. It's nothing above a daily change program offering, despite the Hipp's week's booking. *Abel.*

THE BLOCK SIGNAL

Gotham Production presented by Sam Sax, released by Lumas Film Corp. From the story by F. Oakley Crawford adapted by Edward J. Meagher, directed by Frank O'Connor, supervised by Renaud Hoffman. Starring Ralph Lewis. Reviewed in projection room Sept. 24, 1926. Running time,

61 minutes.

"Jovial" Joe Ryan	Ralph Lewis
Grace Ryan	Jean Arthur
"Roundhouse" Rosen	Sidney Franklin
Jack Milford	Hugh Allen
Bert Steele	George Chesebro
"Unhandy" Andy	Leon Holmes
Jim Brennan	"Missouri" Royer

For a railroad thriller this one ranks with the better than average released in the independent market. It has the punch and the necessary kicks to make it worth while in the average run of houses. By that it must not be accepted that the picture ranks with the type that are usually shown in the de luxe presentation houses, but it will measure up with any of the regular run of program features.

The cast is a well balanced one and Ralph Lewis, who is starred, has something of a following in the popular-priced houses. Jean Arthur, Hugh Allen and Sidney Franklin, who are featured, go a long way to strengthen the cast.

The story is an out and out railroad romance with a series of thrills. There is a corking railroad wreck, another near wreck that adds suspense, and a couple of thrilling fights.

Lewis is the real hero of the story. He is an aged engineer who has been in the service for years and considered one of the crack men of the road. His eyesight is failing and because of this he is tricked into a wreck by a young engineer who is waiting for his chance to get a locomotive, and who also is the suitor for the old engineer's daughter. The old man is disgraced and placed as a flagman at a crossing.

While here he develops a block signal which automatically stops a train when the signal is set against it and finally he regains his former position with the road. The villain who succeeded him is dethroned and a young college man, who is in charge of bridge construction work, wins the daughter.

There is sufficient comedy element in the picture to make for a few hearty laughs. One thing about the production is the unusual lighting and production effects. They are most extraordinary for an independent type picture. *Fred.*

Doubling With Danger

A. Carlos presents Richard Talmadge in detective story. Scenario by Grover Jones. Directed by Scott Dunlap. F. B. O. release. Ena Gregory, feminine lead. At the Tivoli, New York (daily change), Sept. 23. Running time, 52 mins.

Better than average detective story with capital surprise finish. The production just misses making the best grade for this sort of thing, partly because of the absence of a leading woman and supporting cast that mean something. The technical side is of high quality; it has comedy values of good grade and several excellent character sketches.

The opening is brisk and gets straight to business. An inventor of an aeroplane silencer is telling his friend that a mysterious enemy is seeking to destroy him and gain his war machine secret. On the word he drops dead, shot by a mysterious gloved hand from the shadowy doorway. The friend takes possession of the papers describing the silencer, and the menace of the gloved hand is directed against him.

He retires to his country mansion and in the midst of a large house party puts himself under the protection of a detective. The sleuth is a comedy character with a trick of peeling and eating apples no matter where he is. The idea of giving a comedy twist to this role does not appear until later. From time to time the detective follows false leads in searching out the probable accomplice of the "Gloved Hand." At one time it is the rich man's private secretary (Talmadge), who, confronted by the sleuth with the evidence of a supposed former crime, explains that the crime was committed by a twin brother. The secretary receives a blackhand note from his supposed brother demanding money and the note is stolen by the butler, who (the audience is led to understand) is a real accomplice of the "Gloved Hand."

The secretary disappears, assumes the character of the brother and returns to take part in the theft of the aeroplane plans. This is accomplished and all the criminal band depart to a roadhouse, taking captive, with them, the rich man's daughter with whom the secretary is in love.

There follows lively fights and chases (sometimes with a comic twist) between the crook gang and the secretary, ending with his maneuvering of "Gloved Hand" into the cellar of the house where he remains until the arrival of the police. It then is disclosed that the twin brother was a myth and the secretary has been a partner of the comic detective who followed false scents to distract attention from the real search for the criminal.

The settings for the country house party are especially fine, both garden and swimming pool exteriors being lively with bathing girls and tennis players. The interiors are strikingly good for artistic composition. *Rush.*

ALMOST A LADY

John C. Flinn picture. Adapted by Anthony Coldewey from the Cosmopolitan magazine story, "Skin Deep," by F. R. Adams. Directed by E. Mason Hopper. Produced by Metropolitan Pictures Corp., and released by P. D. C. At Loew's New York Sept. 24 as half of double bill. Running time, 62 mins.

Marcia Blake	Marie Prevost
William Duke	Harrison Ford
Bob Blake	George K. Arthur
Mrs. Timothy Reilly—	Trixie Friganza
Mrs. Timothy Reilly	Trixie Friganza
Henri	John Miljan

Thanks to long service under the directorial wing of Mack Sennett, Marie Prevost is a leading woman with unquestioned comedy proficiency. She carries the stellar placement in this film handily.

As the title implies, Miss Prevost, as Marcia Blake, is a clothes model with a yen to be a lady. While she has many moments of enjoyable comedy with George K. Arthur, another graduate of the comedy byplay subjects, Trixie Friganza stands out like a beacon light as the rich woman who would knock society senseless. Barney Gilmore, as her husband, hasn't much to do but manage to keep his role from fading away altogether.

Harrison Ford is satisfactory as the young man who falls in love with Marcia while John Miljan scores as the owner of the modiste establishment.

There is romance in the film but the main try is for comedy, and thanks to the cast it registers. The backgrounds for the most part are fully adequate and the photography is very good. The Beach Club scenes in particular are photographically superb.

A picture that gives an hour of pleasing entertainment. *Mark.*

THE GOLDEN WEB

Gotham production. Story by E. Phillips Oppenheim. Adaptation and scenario by James Bell Smith. Directed by Walter Lang. Supervised by Renaud Hoffman. Distributed by Lumas Film Corp. Huntly Gordon, Lillian Rich, Lawford Davidson and Jay Hunt co-featured. At the Stanley, New York, Sept. 22. Running time, 62 mins.

Ruth Rowan	Lillian Rich
Roland Deane	Huntly Gordon
John Rowan	Jay Hunt
George Sisk	Lawford Davidson
Dave Sinclair	Boris Karloff

The team work of the cast will mean some profit for Sam Sax, the man behind the Gotham productions. The cast looks like ready money, and Lillian Rich is in one of her best screen roles.

The picture starts off in trip-hammer melodramatic fashion and then slows up when the locale shifts from a mining region to the big city. It is a modern story and well directed by Walter Lang.

There is considerable stretching of a court room scene and too much of Miss Rich on close-ups in this instance, but on the whole Lang has done some nice work.

That earthquake send-off at the start evokes dramatic intensity, and there is a novel and effective introduction of the two leads that build for romantic interest.

As an independent it stands up, entertains, and speaks much for the progress of Sax. *Mark.*

FORLORN RIVER

Paramount picture, featuring Jack Holt, Raymond Hatton, Arlette Marchal and Edmund Burns. Screen play by G. C. Hull. Directed by John Waters. At Loew's New York Sept. 22.

Nevada	Jack Holt
Arizona Pete	Raymond Hatton
Ina Blaine	Arlette Marchal
Ben Ide	Edmund Burns
Bill Hall	Tom Santschi
Hart Blaine	Joseph Girard
Les Setter	Christian J. Frank
Sheriff Stroble	Albert Hart
Magda Lee	Nola Luxford
Modoc Joe	Chief Yowlache
Deputy	Jack Moore

Once more Jack Holt does a lot of riding, with breathing space for a western romance of the usual Zane Grey mold. There is much "atmosphere" and, plus the cast, it's an okay western.

Burns makes a handsome leading man, but has to play second fiddle to Holt, as it's the latter who wins the girl. The "menace" was Tom Santschi, who made the role stand up.

Some unusual photographic shots, and the action should please the fans addicted to romance and gunplay. Special mention for Raymond Hatton as a hobo who becomes a cowboy.

Not the most expensive western Paramount has made, but it holds its own mainly due to the male principals. *Mark.*

PARADISE

First National production featuring Milton Sills and Betty Bronson. Produced under the management of Ray Rockett and directed by Irvin Willat. Story bby Cosmo Hamilton. At the Strand, New York, w ek of Oct. 3. Running time, 62 minutes.

Tony	Milton Sills
Chrissie	Betty Bronson
Quex	Noah Beery
Teddy	Lloyd Whitlock
Lady George	Kate Price
Lord Lumley	Charlie Murray
Pollock	Claude King
Perkins	Charles Brook
McCoustie	Ashley Cooper

A South Seas romance with abundant action here gives Milton Sills one of those he-man roles with which he usually scores. This time the story has a background of polite society, but the formula is the usual one of the super-hero in action against the white man bully of the tropics.

Action gets a peppy star with Sills as an aviator performing air stunts at an aviation meet to the admiration of the heroine. This passage brings on a stunt with a kick, in the pursuit of a fast automobile by a plane close to the ground along a country road. It ends when the plane crashes into a house.

Things drag for a time after this episode as the story moves to a society locale, but the action builds up again for a lively finish in a fight in the tropics, a treasure hunt and a neat comedy surprise twist for the climax, making a general score for a program feature.

A laugh finish instead of the sentimental clinch is the best thing in the picture. *Rush.*

IT MUST BE LOVE

Alfred E. Green Production, presented by John McCormick, starring Colleen Moore, with Jean Hersholt, Malcolm McGregor and Arthur Stone featured. From Brooke Hanlon's Satevepost story, "Delicatessen"; adapted by Julian Josephson. Released by First National. Shown at the Rivoli, New York, week of Oct. 2. Running time, 70 minutes.

Fernie Schmidt	Colleen Moore
"Pop" Schmidt	Jean Hersholt
"Mom" Schmidt	Bodil Rosing
Jack Dugan	Malcolm McGregor
Peter Halitovsky	Arthur Stone
Min	Dorothy Seastrom
Al	Cleve Moore
Lois	Mary O'Brien
Joe	Ray Heller

Colleen Moore, as the star of this feature, is proving herself a comedienne of rare qualities. The picture itself is a remarkable character study in human emotions, told in the terms of fast humor. It is the humor of the type that appeals to film audiences. At the Rivoli on Sunday the picture had the audience howling with laughter.

But "It Must Be Love" is going to do two things in addition to making film audiences laugh: it is going to land both Jean Hersholt and Arthur Stone in a class by themselves as character actors.

The combination of the name Colleen Moore and the title "It Must Be Love" should get business at the box-office. The picture itself will certainly entertain the customers.

"It Must Be Love" is the story of a Dutch delicatessen shop owner who still thinks in the terms of the old country, despite he has accumulated $80,000 running his shop on Market street. His wife and daughter assist in the store and live in the rear rooms.

Miss Moore is Fernie Schmidt, the daughter, with a hatred of the smell of the shop and a greater hatred of the husband-to-be that her dad has picked. This prospective bridegroom is the sausage maker who supplies old man Schmidt with his wares. He smells of the garlic with which he spices his weenies, topping this off with a taste for raw onions and scallions. His sartorial splendor is a celluloid collar and a ready-tied four-in-hand.

With the opening of the story it is Saturday ·night and Fernie is busy in the shop. Her manner of wrapping and packing back of the counter is the first laugh, this being topped almost immediately with another when she uses the smelling salts after selling a chunk of limburger.

Two girl companions want her to go to a dance, but, as pop's hand-picked prospect comes in, he forbids her to go, although mother finally squares it and sends him along with the girls.

At the door of the amusement park dance hall they lose the sausage maker and keep a date with three boys, previously staked out. But when Fernie gets home her dad turns her out of doors, because he believes that she is ashamed of him, her mother and the business.

Once away from home, she gets a job in a department store, where she runs across the boy of the dance hall, whom she really believed to be in the stock brokerage business. He said he was in stocks, and he is stock boy in the department stor. There are a couple of scenes hee that are surefire wows for laugh, and the finish of the love affair s at a Saturday afternoon picnic a which Fernie says yes to the stockroom boy.

The next day she's at home for Sunday dinner with the folks. Pop tells her that · he has bought a bungalow, and when she marries the sausage maker she can live with the old folks. At that point someone enters the shop. It is the stock boy who has bought the delicatessen from her dad with the $5,000 that he told her he'd saved. So she is right back to where she started, the only difference being that, with a husband of her own picking, she is going to be satisfied with the cheese and sausage smells.

Al Greene, who directed, kept the story coming along at a pace that held the interest at all times, and he slipped over a couple of laugh knockouts. One was the trick mirrors in the dance hall scene, used three different times, and each time the laugh tops the previous one. The other was the flop into the basement of the department store, followed by the note writing bit.

Jean Hersholt as the delicatessen shop keeper and Arthur Stone as the boob sausage maker give performances that will make the picture stand out as one of the best things that Colleen Moore has done since "Flaming Youth." That girl sure can troup, and the women in the audience love her to death. In this picture she handles herself perfectly and it is going to make a host of new friends for her. *Fred.*

THE DIXIE FLYER

Trem Carr Production, distributed by Rayart Pictures Corp. Story by H. H Van Loan. Directed by Charles Hunt. Eva Novak featured. At the Stanley, New York, Oct. 1, one day. Running time, 65 minutes.

"The Dixie Flyer" this time fools 'em. It is not one of the million or more racetrack romances, but is one of the million and more railroad stories.

After watching Eva Novak do some of the stunts which gave Pearl White her start in films, she should get all the play and prominence. She gives a stellar performance.

In the film the hero works on the railroad and mixes in with the type of men who use muscle. Through it all he wears a sombrero; perhaps not the regulation head shade, but what may best be known as a campaign hat. The hat didn't matter much, but just seemed out of proportion that was all to the work at hand.

The film is padded interminably; there are only a few real melodramatic climaxes that one would ex-

pect where there's deep villainy afoot. Miss Novak provides one of the big thrills in her scene on the car headed for the open bridge.

The picture will do in the neighborhoods. The bridge scene, preceded by the rescue of Miss Novak from the top of the car, save the picture from doing an outright flop.

Miss Novak is a hard worker; seems fearless, and while not a world-beater in her love scenes, she makes up for it in her stunts.

The photography in some sections excelled others. *Mark.*

THE GAY DECEIVER

John M. Stahl Production, with Lew Cody starred. Adapted from stage play, "Toto," by Maurice Hennequin and Felix Du Quesnel. Directed by John Stahl. Distributed by Metro-Goldwyn-Mayer Corporation. Supporting Cody are Marceline Day, Dorothy Phillips and Malcolm MacGregor. At the Stanley, New York, Sept. 29, one day. Running time, 83 minutes.

There have been any number of stage and screen themes where the central male character has been a gay old boy, a gay old roue, a gay old lover and in this Metro-Goldwyn it's "a gay deceiver," played by Lew Cody.

This picture lacks the punch; perhaps the best way to sum it all up is that it's lighter than film and that's too light for a box-office drag. Admitting Mr. Cody is popular, he's not popular enough to put this over as a blue ribbon proposition.

Mr. Cody plays the role of an actor who is in Paris doing his stuff, which runs to Shakespeare, but separated from his family. He has an affair on with a dame that's married, but the woman cares not beyond trying to keep her husband from knowing too much.

Mr. Cody makes quite a figure, to be sure, and handles himself nicely, but beyond looking nice in his stage clothes there's little for Lew to do that makes a big picture out of "The Gay Deceiver."

Photographically there is little fault to find with this one, but it seems stretched to almost the bursting point with little to commend it as a sterling standard b. o. attraction.

It seems even weaker than weak tea for Broadway, and it will perhaps grab its biggest favor in the neighborhoods.

The Cody role might have been slammed into a light comedy gag all the way and which might help it for American audiences, but the romance theme demands that it be handled a little more. straight although it swung into comedy channels at the close that helped the picture to lift up its head for a moment.

Where circulating libraries are getting a play on the "gay deception" stuff this film may get some attention but there is no use talking, it is a "weak sister."

What highlights are there which includes several nice scenes between the youthful lovers, played by Miss Day and Mr. MacGregor are so few and far between that the picture just wobbles along to the finish. *Mark.*

The Honeymoon Express

Warner Bros. production, starring Irene Rich, with Willard Louis and Virginia Lee Corbin featured. Directed by Jimmie Flood. At the Stanley, New York, Oct. 4, one day. Running time, 74 minutes.
Mrs. Lambert...................Irene Rich
Mr. Lambert...................Willard Louis
Becky Lambert.......Virginia Lee Corbin
Jean Lambert...............Helene Costello
Flint Lambert............Harold Goodwin
Jean's Sweetheart..........Jason Robard

It seems rather a shame that this picture did not get a real chance on Broadway in a de luxe run house. The picture would have made good on its own, and it certainly would have given Broadway a new star

possibility to talk about. That star possibility is Virginia Lee Corbin. Oh, boy! what a flapper ingenue she proves to be in this picture!

There is the possibility that the Warners fought shy of bringing this picture in on the Main Street, because Willard Louis, one of its featured players, died while the picture was in the making. As a matter of fact, the company went on shooting for three weeks after Louis' death to complete the picture.

That the production stands up is no mean thing to Jimmie Flood, who directed it. Originally Ernst Lubitsch was to have directed, but he was taken ill just as work was to start, and turned the direction over to Flood, who had been with him for a great many years. It was Flood's chance to make good, and he had to run into the hardest kind of luck, with his featured lead passing away.

The story is one of those rejuvenation tales. The story of a household where the mother has borne the burden of rearing three children while the dad was the playboy of the bright lights. One of the children, the daughter, Jean (Helene Costello) is of the serious type who attends to business and affects almost masculine attire. The other two children, the son (Harold Goodwin) and Becky (Virginia Lee Corbin) follow in father's footsteps and drink like dear old dad.

It finally comes to a showdown. Mother and the serious daughter step out of the home, leaving the trio of tipplers to shift for themselves. Mother betakes herself to a beauty parlor. While in a booth she overhears a flapper in the next one inform the attendant that she has hooked a prize chump in "Old Boy" Lambert, whereupon mother decides that it is time for her turning from the retiring position, and she takes the treatment from pedicure to a dye, bob and wave.

Meantime the son is off on a booze cruise, while Becky, the flapperish daughter, is chancing being sweet mommer to a young society kid who is playing the field.

But the chickens all come home to roost. First, there is father, who tries to "forgive" mother for walking out; then along comes sonny, who is ready to reform, and, finally, mother goes out and rescues Becky after she has run her young John over the side of a mountain in a speedy roadster when he refused to marry her after giving her the runaround for a couple of weeks.

When all the children are straightened out, mother gets them a new father. The latter touch is undoubtedly one of necessity because of Willard Louis' death, otherwise he would have been among the regenerated and also back in the fold.

But to get back to the outstanding performance of the picture, that contributed by little Virginia Lee Corbin. One must call her little, for it is hard to believe that here is the child actress of a few short years ago grown into a perfect blonde ingenue type who troupes like a million dollars and is a beauty that they are going to go crazy about on and off the screen. That girl handles herself like a woman who has learned all the tricks of the dramatic trade, and she certainly does display them here.

Of course, Irene Rich has the sympathetic role, and she makes the most of it in the characterization. An Irene Rich performance is always a satisfactory one, and this is no exception. Willard Louis' last screen appearance goes but to further emphasize how much he is going to be missed.

There are laughs aplenty in this picture and the action is always fast. With it all there is a love story that goes double, and above all that Virginia Corbin girl.

Fred.

The Speeding Venus

William C. Seastrom production. Directed by Robert Thornby. Distributed by Metropolitan Productions. Priscilla Dean starred. At the Dyckman, New York, Sept. 25, two days. Running time, 78 minutes.
Emily Carol...................Priscilla Dean
John Steele...................Robert Frazer
Chet Higgins...................Ray Ripley
Madge Rooney...................Dale Fuller
Speck Murphy...................Johnny Fox
Jed Morgan...................Charles Sellon

Around the idea of having the star drive a car overland from Detroit to Los Angeles, whereby she outwits the villain headed for the coast by passenger train, "The Speeding Venus" is framed. It's a meller that gets started slowly with two nephews of an auto manufacturer trying to invent a gearless car and also win the old man's secretary.

Like all romances where two men are after the same girl, one turns out to be a cad. He steals the other's plans, has another man run into the other's machine and tries to get to the Los Angeles auto show ahead so that he would be the white-haired boy in the eyes of the rich uncle who is on the coast awaiting the gearless car.

Priscilla Dean, as the heroine, not only favors John Steele, the other nephew, but has his car fixed and she and her girl friend, Madge Rooney (Dale Fuller) start on a whirl-wind drive to L. A.

An apparently absurd trick, but it is within screen premise, and, thanks to Miss Dean and Miss Fuller, a clever comedienne, it manages to hold interest.

Photography A 1, the "shots" in the open being exceptionally clear.
Mark.

KID BOOTS

Frank Tuttle production presented by Adolph Baker and Jesse L. Lasky, starring Eddie Cantor. From the play by William Anthony McGuire and Octto Harbach. Adapted by Luther Reed, script by Tom Gibson, titles by George Marion, Jr. B.P. Schulberg associate producer. At the Rialto, N.Y., for a four weeks' run, starting Oct. 9. Running time, 62 mins.

Kid Boots .... Eddie Cantor
Jane Martin .... Clara Bow
Polly Pendleton .... Billie Dove
Tom Starling .... Lawrence Gray
Carmen Mondora .... Natalie Kingston
Geroge Fitch .... Malcolm Waite
Polly's Father .... William J. Worthington
Carmen's Lawyer .... Harry Von Meter
Tom's Lawyer .... Fred Pendelton

Edd. Cantor has arrived on the screen. Jesse Lasky stated that Cantor was a "natural" for the screen before the rank and file in New York had seen the comedian's first screen effort, "Kid Boots." It looks that way.

The picture was shown at the Rialto for the first time Saturday night. There were three de luxe performances at which an admission of $5.50 top was charged. The result was that the police had to be called out to keep the crowds lined-up outside the theatre. Once inside the bunch got a chance to look at Eddie in person and on the screen.

Cantor is a "natural" in more ways than one, as far as the screen is concerned. In fact, he has such a sense of natural comedy that those working with him were often broken up and hard put to it as Eddie would improvise a piece of business that was not in the script. As far as pictures are concerned, Eddie need not worry as to his future. He is set if ever a comedian was, and with his first effort.

The box office need not fear Eddie Cantor, for he is going to pull money. He and his maiden effort on the screen are booked into the Rialto for four weeks, but if Publix can persuade Eddie to remain longer than that it is a cinch he will pull plenty of business.

Of course, certain liberties have been taken with "Kid Boots" for the screen. It does not follow the stage version, but is a corking comedy picture from all angles, and the supporting cast is all that could be desired. Billie Dove becomes more beautiful every day. And Clara Bow is just a world of merriment. Lawrence Gray looks and acts the part of the young millionaire sportsman, while Malcolm Waite, playing opposite Eddie, makes a splendid foil for the comedian.

Gags there are galore, but the greatest piece of business is where Eddie makes love to himself to kid along his girl who is watching from another table. That bit will go down in screen history as a classic.

The story opens with Eddie a tailor's assistant, who sells a misfit to a huge physical culture expert, who in turn comes back to clean out the shop. Then the chase which follows is another comedy wow, the chase leading right into the plot of the piece, which has to do with a chorus girl bride who has been getting a divorce from a young college husband, trying to get back into his home because she has learned that he has just fallen heir to $3,000,000. She has moved into his room at a hotel and is there awaiting him in undress costume. He has just saved Eddie from a beating at the hands of the physical culture guy so that when the wife's lawyer and a dick step in to make the evidence complete, Eddie is on the job and saves the day.

In order to balk the wife's scheme the young sportsman gets a job as a golf professional at a local resort and takes "Kid" Boots with him. The physical expert is on the job there as the swimming instructor and his girl (Miss Bow) falls for the Kid. The latter gets in Dutch with her when he tries to protect his friend from the wiles of the scheming wife. The girl thinks the Kid is falling for the vamp, he is willing to give her a little jealous play and that is where the self-loving bit comes in.

The real kick to the picture is the thrills provided in a cross mountain ride that the Kid and the girl take in order to get to the court house where the final decree of divorce is to be signed, and where the wife has presented affidavits to the effect that she has spent the night in her husband's room in the resort hotel. In reality, the Kid was in the room with her and his girl is burning up over it. That mountain ride on horseback with Cantor tied on his steed but finally bumped off over a precipice brings howls. The finish, a wedding ceremony preformed while the bride and groom run after a flivver in which the justice is facing them from the rear seat, gives the picture a final punch.

Cantor is a cinch for the box office on the strength if this one.

Fred.

THE QUARTERBACK

Famous Players-Lasky picture, starring Richard Dix, with Heather Ralston featured. Story by W.O. McGeehan and William Slavens McNutt, adapted by Ray Harris and directed by Fred Newmeyer; football game supervision by Fielding M. (Hurry Up") Yost. Runs 72 minutes. At Rivoli, New York, week Oct. 9.

Jack Stone .... Richard Dix
Louise Mason .... Heather Ralston
Elmer Stone .... Harry Beresford
"Lumpy" Geggins .... David Butler
Danny Walters .... Robert W. Craig
Nettie Webster .... Mona Palmer

Popular interest in collegiate athletics has had its inevitable reaction on the stage and screen with "The Poor Nut" (legit) and such notable screen productions as Lloyd's "Freshman," "Red" Grange's "One Minute to Play," and, from the opposite sex-point, Bebe Daniels' "The Campus Flirt."

In sequence, Lloyd did it farcically, Grange's stuff was a set-up because of the star's gridiron prowess, and Miss Daniels looked as much a co-ed as Sir Joseph Ginzberg.

Comes along Richard Dix with the football thing somewhat familiar on the screen and tops everything with a corking collegiate yarn that includes a modicum of realism. Although they still persist in making football heroes out of raw freshmen, it might be argued that the mythical hinterland colleges have not the plebe year restrictions as in the major institutions.

What recommends the Dix picture is the astuteness of the direction. At least the Hollywood undergraduates look youthfully collegiate and not like super-sophisticated clubmen. A delicate touch in softening up what might have been the "menace" of the proceedings was also wise. Despite the fact he is the opposing eleven's captain and the serious rival for her hand, college boys are boys the world over, and four years on any university campus does not breed schemers and "villains" (as in the Daniels film), a sense of wrong in the average case being but an exaggerated idea of rivalry for alma mater or amour.

These and other niceties make "The Quarterback" altogether wholesome in its footage without being in any wise maudlin or wishy-washy.

It is only natural for Jack Stone (Dix) to be reticent about disclosing his modus operandi on an early a. m. milk delivery route, since his girl friend and her associates seem to enjoy sorority and frat life so sumptuously. That's what makes the hero's frank fibbing so pardonable, the titles not sparing Dix when he is lying about this, that and the other thing, the girl, of course, learning everything on her own in time.

All football stories are built on the same formula, the hero making a grandstand finish for the winning touchdown despite any complication. Unlike Grange's feat in accomplishing it in one minute, Dix tops that with a last 20-second forward pass for the winning tally. The climax is derived from Dix's pseudo-professionalism, he having won a race at a county fair, defeating a noted professional 100-yard sprinter, with our hero avoiding the taints of C. C. Pyle-ism in refusing to accept the $200 prize, stating he competed for the sport alone.

Fielding H. ("Hurry Up") Yost has done well with the football formations, although there are some flagrantly open spots in the scrimmage scenes that look too "set" but possibly made necessary for ready perception.

The football scenes have given rise to several excellent photographic "shots," the camera seemingly being planted in an excavation to catch the thundering approach and the cleated hoofs of the gridiron gladiators as they are bucking the line. It is similar to the "Ben-Hur" shots of the chariot race.

Dix is immense in the title role. He is natural, manly and of serious enough mien, in keeping with the story, to lend character to the otherwise frivolous proceedings.

Opposite is the adorable Esther Ralston, who has stellar probabilities—not possibilities—that need no reminder from a reviewer to be readily recognized by the F. P. staff. Her wholesomeness, charm and sympathetic characteristics, particularly through smile and eyes, which Miss Ralston employs on occasion for deadly effect, recommend her flatteringly. She is not signaled out for featuring in the billing under the star's name for naught.

The trite summation that the rest of the cast is adequate is resorted to again because that's about all, each contributing evenly with David Butler, Harry Beresford and Robert W. Craig filling in intelligently.

An excellent film entertainment and should do heavy trade for the Rivoli this week. *Abel.*

THE BETTER 'OLE

Warner Bros. Production, starring Syd Chaplin. From the story by Bruce Bairnsfather and Arthur Eliot. Screen play by Darryl F. Zanuck and Charles "Chuck" Reisner, directed by the latter. Titled by Robert Hopkins. Opened at the Colony, New York, for run October 7. Running time, 97 mins.

Old Bill .... Syd Chaplin
Joan .... Doris Hill
Bert .... Harold Goodwin
Gaspard .... Theodore Lorch
Corporal Quint .... Ed. Kennedy
The Major .... Charles Gerrard
English General .... Tom McGuire
Alf .... Jack Ackroyd
The Blacksmith .... Tom Kennedy
General von Hinden .... K. Morgan
The Colonel .... Arthur Clayton

Another bull's-eye for Warner Brothers. In "The Better 'Ole" they have a picture built for laughs that will just about knock the average audience out of its seats. Likewise, chalk up another hit to the credit of Syd Chaplin.

Syd is unfortunate in having a great brother. For that reason his light has been kept under a bushel these many years. Syd would get a chance now and then, but it was mostly then, just because Charlie had the edge. But in the last year Syd, while with Warner's, has come along and into his own. And Charlie better watch his step. Syd has one thing which Charlie hasn't. That's versatility, which is acceptable to audiences. He can do one type in one picture and a distinctly different one in another. With Charlie it's different. The audiences want the funny shoes, the trick cane and the iron hat—and if Charlie doesn't give them what they want in a comedy, they don't want Charlie.

But coming back to "The Better 'Ole," it is an hour and a half of laughs, screeches and howls. Of course it's war stuff, but the same kind of war stuff that made "Behind the Front" a great box office film. Only this one is going to be greater.

It is jammed full of gags and hoak, some of it old and some of it dressed up by a twist, but all of it is funny.

Here is the spot where "Chuck" Reisner should come in for full credit. Reisner never did get much of a chance before this one to show what he really could do. But this picture, when the returns are all in, is going to put him where he should have been a long time ago—among the best of the feature comedy directors. Reisner was trained in the gag school of the stage, and he has plenty of stuff on the ball when it comes to hoaking a scene.

The picture is somewhat different than the play. It is the story of Old Bill, Bert and Alf, those three comic creations by Bairnsfather that came out of the war. Their troubles, tribulations and final triumphs are told here with a laugh and a gag. The picture opens with the boys in the trenches, takes them back to their rest billet, brings the Germans up and effects a capture of the town that they are in and finally has the Germans turned back again, a spy exposed and Old Bill made a sergeant.

In that paragraph the actual trend of the tale is told, but the action that makes it worth while is almost indescribable. Here are just a couple of the gags. Old Bill fills a rubber glove with milk from a cow in order to feed a litter of kittens. He ties the glove at the wrist and punctures the fingers with a pin, and while he is filling a second glove a suckling pig runs away with the first. Another gag is the prop horse with Bill in the head and Alf the hind-end. This is built and built until it is howl after howl, especially the scenes where the prop horse is placed with the real ones by a couple of drunken German soldiers after they have captured the town.

The war scenes are well handled and with this there is a little love story. This is never permitted to intrude on the comedy but the suspense has been built up in good style.

In addition to Chaplin there is a corking actor in Jack Ackroyd for the role of Alf. Tom McGuire is an imposing English general, while Harold Goodwin carries off the heroics in satisfactory manner. Charles Gerrard walks away with the heavy and Ed Kennedy more than makes good as Corporal Quint.

The only woman in the cast is Doris Hill, who acquits herself with honors.

Exhibs can't go wrong with "The Better 'Ole" if they let the audiences know in advance that it is the laugh of the year thus far. It has a Vitaphone accompaniment, and a good one, too, with a special score.

Fred.

THE TEMPTRESS

"The Temptress," with Greta Garbo and Antonio Moreno, adapted from novel by Blasco Ibanez. Directed by Fred Niblo. Cosmopolitan production; Metro-Goldwyn-Mayer release. At Capitol, New York, week Oct. 10. Running time, 95 minutes.

Elena .... Greta Garbo
Robledo .... Antonio Moreno
Manos Duros .... Roy D'Arcy
M. Fontenoy .... Marc MacDermott
Canterac .... Lionel Barrymore
Celinda .... Virginia Brown Faire
Torre Bianca .... Armand Kaliz
Josephiné .... Alys Murrell
Pirovani .... Robert Anderson
Timoteo .... Francis McDonald

Rojas	Hector V. Sarno
Sebastiana	Inez Gomez
Salvadore	Steve Clemento
Trinidad	Roy Coulson

Long heralded and immediately preceded by a brisk advertising campaign, the picture got away to a fine start, helped, besides other things, by a rainy Sunday afternoon and evening. The Capitol's ever widening circle of friends was out in force, and by 6 o'clock Sunday its Broadway block was almost impassable.

What the fans got was one of the most sumptuously produced pictures of the season. The screening is one unbroken succession of pictorial surprises in beauty. The settings are one long revel of loveliness. No better handling of background and composition has been seen this or any other season.

Flawlessness in this particular is unfortunately not matched by happy selection of story or of the star. Greta Garbo does not make the woman of sinister passion created by Ibanez. She is scarcely the screen type of aggressive vitality the character demands. Rather she might play the more anemic type, such as calls for dainty shading. This figure is drawn in bold strokes. It should dominate the story, whereas in its biggest moments it was secondary in its force of portraiture. That was the weak point of the acting. In other respects this cast is remarkably even and capable and of great box office value.

The story is typically Ibanez. It develops interestingly, holds attention and contains a wealth of dramatic "kick," but when it's all over one cannot put down the feeling that all its dramatic intensity is mere theatrical, and pretty phoney at that.

Its finale has an especially counterfeit ring. It is here that the Temptress is discovered as a woman of the Paris streets, sunk to the depths of drunkenness and degradation, blear-eyed and nodding over her cognac in a sidewalk cafe, when before her blurred eyes a dissipated tippler at another table takes on the likeness of the Christ, and she drops into his hand a ruby jewel, trophy of the only real love (which the audience knows was, in fact, more a guilty amour) of her life. **Maudlin sentimentality could not go much beyond this. Once more the movies spread it on too thick.**

However, these things are afterthoughts. While the picture is running the overpowering beauty of its settings, the picturesqueness of its people and the sheer play of its melodrama trick one into interest to the point of surrender to the situations.

Backgrounds have much bizarre charm, as, for instance, the hero's flight across an Argentine plain in a high wagon drawn by a score of horses and silhouetted against a stunning landscape that would nail attention even as a bit of still photography.

On the dramatic side there is a big incident when hero and a wild brigand fight a cruel duel with long whips, and another smashing effect in the collapse upon the hero of the waters of a flood when the big dam gives way.

It is these bits of melodrama that will carry the picture a long way. The sentimental and emotional aspects of the tale made no impression upon its first Broadway audience. Sunday evening they were disposed to be frivolous about it. One title, designed to be profound philosophy, to the effect that woman is the noblest work of God, got a distinct giggle. They applauded later in the wrong place, making it plain that something had failed to register in proper value.

The story starts at a masquerade ball in Paris, a remarkable bit of staging. Elena, unhappy wife (as later develops) of a Paris fop, and Robledo, Spanish engineer on leave from a vast irrigation work in the Argentine, meet and fall in love, Elena vowing she is free.

Elena's married state is disclosed. When it is further revealed that she was the mistress of a rich banker whom she ruined and drove to suicide Robledo breaks away, returning to South America. Thither Elena follows with her husband. One after another the white men in charge of the big work fall under her fatal fascination and go down to wreck, while Robledo alone holds aloof.

The actual guilt of the woman is left to the spectator. "Men have gone to ruin for you," charges the hero.

"Not for me; for my body," she defends herself. "Not for my happiness, but for their own."

And the author seems to leave the moral question on those terms.

In the end Robledo confesses himself defeated by the woman's fascination, and in a final contradiction she disappears (for his good, we are to suppose).

Years pass and Robledo is a famous engineer, returning to Paris with his fiancee. Here he runs across the wreck of the one-time vamp, but he can do nothing with the sodden creature, and the story perforce ends there, pessimistically and rather cynically.

And by the way, there is, curiously enough, no kick whatever in Ibanez' sex stuff. There never is. It takes an Elinor Glyn or a Mrs. Hull (she wrote "The Sheik) to get this material over. *Rush.*

Bardelys the Magnificent

Los Angeles, Oct 7.

King Vidor production, starring John Gilbert, presented by Metro-Goldwyn-Mayer. From the story vy Rafael Sabatin, adapted by Dorothy Farnum. Directed by King Vidor. At the Carthay Circle, Los Angeles, Sept. 30, for a run. Running time, 93 mins.

Bardelyn	John Gilbert
Roxalanne de Lavedas	Eleanor Boardman
Chatellernult	Roy D'Arcy
Viconte De' Lavedas	Lionel Belmore
Mmme. de Lavedas	Emily Fitzroy
Saint Eustache	George K. Arthur
King Louis XIII	Arthur Lubin
Ledjurow	Theodore von Eltz
Bodenard	Karl Dane
Cardinal Mcbelleu	Edward Connelly
Curloireuz	Fred Malatesta
Lafoare	John T. Murray

John Gilbert shows that he is romantically inclined, that he has that necessary ingredient called "It" by Mme. Glynn and that he is a carefree and all-around hurdler and acrobat, as well as masterful salesman of his talents in this latest King Vidor production. Gilbert scores a 100 per cent average in this work.

Vidor has turned out a most lavish and well-directed story. But he has not turned out a super picture or one that would warrant a $1.50 top. The picture has not those high spots or selling qualities that an audience is willing to give the top price for at two-a-day sessions and walk out satisfied.

It is a picture which will give satisfaction, if not more than that on a regular house program. Sold on the name that Gilbert has made for himself and giving the performance that the star does at the regular picture house admission price, it cannot miss. It was rather a bit too long in its early sequences here and dragged considerably. However, its cutting possibilities are not difficult and it may be easily held within 7,000 feet, still telling the story in a comprehensive way.

This picture originally was to have been made in techni-color. After deliberation at the studio it was decided that action was more essential and that this could be best shown in black and white. That is very true, as Vidor, an artist at the work of making pictures, brought out the beautiful points and situations in the picture just as easy and convincingly as well. He has put some new and novel touches to the romantic portion which other directors can well take cognizance of.

One is a scene between Gilbert and Eleanor Boardman on the lake. It is done in masterful fashion with the weeping willow branches sweeping over the boat, hiding one from the view of the other. Another is a trick shot where Bardelys is trying to escape his pursuers. He grabs hold of a canopy covering, turns it into a parachute and descends some 100 feet to the ground, landing feet up. It is a wow of a shot and possibly the most outstanding one.

However, with all these striking features, the subject is not handled in a serious manner. It seems as though the title writers were given a bit too much latitude. When the audience expected things to take a serious turn, a flip and fly title would shoot forth, leaving that unconvincing taste.

The titling is not of such consequence that it will hold back the establishment of the picture on its merits. It simply served as a sort of retard on its sincerity.

The story is that of Bardelys, a braggart in the court of Louis XIII, with respect to his conquest of women. The king and the entire court chide him on his romantic tendency and his willingness to smother with kisses any woman of the court. He is informed there is one woman who will not fall for him. A wager is made by Chalerault that he will fail with this girl, Roxalanne.

He starts off (after receiving instructions from the king not to do so) to win the girl. On the way he finds a man dying who proves to be Lesperon, a traitor to the throne. The latter gives him some letters and a locket. He is taken into custody by some of the king's troups, but finally pulling a Fairbanks works his way out and gets to the home of the girl with his pursuers on his heels.

Here again he does some more Barrymore and Fairbanks', scaling the walls of the castle to the chamber of the girl. She takes him in, binds his wounds, then turns him out after his pursuers have been unable to locate him. He falls en route to terra firma and is brought into the house with the girl's father feeling he is the one opposed to the king.

Finally, he has his romantic moments with the girl. They take the vow that they are man and wife until legally married. St. Eustache appears on the scene, showing letters sent to the rebel by his sweetheart. The girl exposes Bardelys as the traitor. He is arrested and condemned to be hanged with Chatellerault refusing to clear the identity. He is on the gallows with the girl meantime pleading with Chatellerault to save his neck and her promise to marry him if he does.

Chatellerault has sent word to the executioner to speed things up before the king arrives. Bardelys stalls the execution as the entourage of the king is seen in the distance, with the noose taken off the condemned man's neck while this goes on.

Bardelys manages to unloosen the ropes as he waits, does every one of the kicking-over tricks and climbing stunts that Fairbanks and Barrymore have done, knocking men off right and left with his athletic stunts until he arrives alongside of the king. The latter welcomes him, is told how he has been double-crossed and finally a duel is indulged in between the two enemies with Bardelys winning and getting the girl.

Miss Boardman, as Roxalanne, does her best to give a sincere interpretation, but does not seem to have that "It" which Gilbert has. This part was an ideal one for Renee Adoree, who would have given it the handling an audience expected.

John T. Murray, as "Lafosse," the court jester, put the big comedy moments into the affair. He has a neat and deft way of selling his stuff and looks like a sure-fire bet where comedy relief is required in a picture, whether serious or otherwise. Roy D'Arcy, as the 'menace,' was excellent. As the "junior" menace, George K. Arthur interpreted an idiotic character in superb fashion. Arthur Lubin, as the king, gave a clean and convincing performance. These and the others who also aquitted themselves well, were greatly aided in most of their scenes by the care-free Gilbert, who does not seem to want to hog the screen, and gives everyone a chance.

Despite all of the good points of the picture and the acting and directing in it, there is little likelihood it can get by at $1.50 top. For the regular film houses with the Gilbert following grosses should be more than satisfying, whether played for a week or day. *Ung.*

THE NERVOUS WRECK

Al Christie production, releasing through P. D. C. Adapted from play of same name. Directed by Scott Sidney, with Harrison Ford, Phyllis Haver, Chester Conklin, Mack Swain and Hobart Bosworth featured. At Strand, New York, week Oct. 10. Running time, 70 mins.

Henry Williams	Harrison Ford
Sally Morgan	Phyllis Haver
Mort	Chester Conklin
Jerome Underwood	Mack Swain
Jud Morgan	Hobart Bosworth
Bob Wells	Paul Nicholson
Harriet Underwood	Vera Stedman
Reggie DeVere	Charles Gorrard
Andy McNab	Clarence Burton

By stretching a point or two "The Nervous Wreck" could be classed as a good picture. But it doesn't look as if the lenient will offset the negative faction which is bound to emerge from a picture house shaking its respective heads over this one. That means it won't be so "hot" as a money draw despite the cast names.

The picture needs gags. It is woefully shy of 'em. Consequently the structure is inclined to bend too often. A 70-minute comedy is a tough proposition at any time. This one proves that theory, and the theorists have a corking chance **to compare notes between the "Wreck" and "Kid Boots" down the street at the Rialto.**

In this adaptation of the story which Owen Davis dramatized the legit version is followed pretty closely. "Boots," as a film, plays nothing like the musical comedy it was, but unfolds plentiful gags and easily takes the palm if a comparison between these two celluloid epics is made. Just a matter of treatment. Some bewailed that "Boots" left its original story flat when unreeled through a projection machine, yet the "Wreck" suffers for having been too faithful.

The best item in this Christie output is a gag at that. It's a wagon wheel attached to a Ford that keeps wavering as Harrison Ford and Phyllis Haver drive along narrow mountain roads. Otherwise it's pretty tedious watching Ford take pill after pill in the title role with Chester Conklin limited and Mack Swain on the receiving end of much debris.

There's too much of the two-reeler about it, and without the punch of a good twin-spool comedy. Scattered giggles was the best this film could extract from a matinee audience at the Strand.

Ford gets little sympathy as the medicine lunatic. Both Swain and Conklin outplay him when given an opportunity. Hobart Bosworth is negligible as the girl's father, and Miss Haver is the girl. Ford isn't a bad light comedian, either. He's done some corking work where the hero hasn't been laid on so heavy. The main fault appears to be with the story and the dearth of spasmodic punches to give it a push every so often.

In speaking of the first line houses the "Wreck" must needs be classed as a weakling. For the second string theatres it should be a bet, with the entertainment value increasing as the seating capacities grow smaller in the neighborhoods.

Too much fast and long length comedy competition these days for this release to gain definite recognition. *Skig.*

GIGOLO

William K. Howard production presented by the DeMille Pictures Corp. From the story by Edna Ferber, adapted by Garrett Fort; script by Marion Orth. Starring Rod La Rocque with Jobyna Ralston and Louise Dresser featured. Supervised by C. Gardner Sullivan. Released by P. D. C. At the Hippodrome, N. Y., week of Oct. 4. Running time, 80 minutes.
Gideon Gory..................Rod La Rocque
Mary Hubbel..................Jobyna Ralston
Julia Gory..................Louise Dresser
Dr. Gerald Blagden........Cyril Chadwick
Pa Hubbel..................George Nichols

It took two chances to get the slant on this picture that is herewith set forth. The first view of the picture was had at a pre-view given in a night club in New York, where it was presented without musical accompaniment and with very poor projection. The critic at the time thought the picture pretty bad but, willing to give it the benefit of the doubt, refused to review it until it was shown in a theatre. So he took a second look at the Hippodrome. All that happened was a verification of what he thought of the picture at the first showing.

It was slow and draggy, the story is mush, the direction bad and all that the picture really holds is the title and a corking performance contributed by the star.

The blame, if any, must be placed on the adaptor and the director. William K. Howard has proven himself a director capable of turning out great pictures in the past but what happened to him in this instance is hard to define. He was after a new technique, based on the symbolic idea, and the result killed the picture.

When first seen the picture ran 87 minutes. At the Hip it was cut to 80, and there is still room to eliminate about 20 minutes. Down to an hour it might have a better chance with an audience.

The story is pre-war, war, and post-war. The hero is a small town boy living where his father and grandfather were the operators of an iron mill. On his father's death his mother took him abroad and while in Paris married an English doctor who was after her dough. They return to the old home town and the boy renews a romance with a childhood sweetheart, but the doctor finds that his style is cramped here and he plays on his wife's vanity in order to get her to return to Paris. She causes her son to break off his love match and return abroad with them. All of this is told in endless footage.

Then comes the war. The boy goes into the French Flying Corps, the doctor grabs the mother's bankroll while the boy is away and gives her the air. The boy is almost fatally injured in a plane crash and it isn't until after the armistice that he is discharged from the hospital, and then he has a rebuilt face, necessitated by his injuries. He looks up his mother only to enter the apartment as she dies.

Broke and disabled he takes up the profession of a gigolo in a Parisian cafe. His manhood is submerged almost completely until finally his little sweetheart from back

home, with her mother and father enter the place, recognize him, and when he tries to infer she is mistaken she goads him into taking a crack at his stepfather who is there with another woman, and this brings the boy to his senses.

Once more back home he is working in the iron mill he once owned and again trying to win the girl.

Rod La Rocque gives the performance of his life from the time that he is first shown as wounded and in the hospital. Miss Ralston fails to convince and Louise Dresser cops the honors among the women.

It's a bad boy. *Fred.*

WINNING OF BARBARA WORTH

Los Angeles, Oct. 14.
Henry King production presented by Samuel Goldwyn, featuring Vilma Banky and Ronald Colman. Adapted from Harold Bell Wright's novel by Frances Marion. Titles by Rupert Hughes. Released by United Artists. World Premier at Forum, Los Angeles, Oct. 14, for indefinite engagement. Running time, 90 minutes.
Willard Holmes..............Ronald Colman
Barbara Worth..............Vilma Banky
Jefferson Worth..............Charles Lane
The Seer..................Paul McAllister
James Greenfield............E. J. Ratcliffe
Abe Lee..........................Gary Cooper
Tex........................Clyde Cook
Pat........................Erwin Connelly
Blanton........................Sam Blum

Samuel Goldwyn, since joining the United Artist group, has chosen himself nothing but boxoffice "naturals." "The Winning of Barbara Worth" in novel form sold around 2,800,000 copies. Goldwyn figured that if he spent around $1,000,000 on a story that had this reading circulation he was making a good investment.

Originally this story was to have been brought to the screen by Sol Lesser and Mike Rosenberg of Principal Pictures. They had had the release all set with U. A. Henry King came along and told Goldwyn he thought this epic of the reclamation of the desert lands was a highly dramatic incident for interpretation on the screen by him, and Goldwyn paid over $125,000 to Lesser and Rosenberg for the story.

Instead of going to Arizona and making his picture he went into the arid lands of Nevada, and instead of choking off and holding down the cost of production to a minimum, with the idea that the Harold Bell Wright name would carry it, he put every dollar necessary into the production. Then he started in on selling it 100 per cent, and to do that he made every possible tieup that would mean anything to the boxoffice. He got legislative and civic co-operation. He got ex-Gov. Thomas E. Campbell of Arizona, interested in reclamation work for 25 years, to see that the technical end of the production was right.

The treatment of the story is just a bit different from the novel which dealt with the reclamation problem. Frances Marion injected romance into the story, and plenty of it. Instead of making Jefferson Worth the hero, he had the story twisted around so that Willard Holmes the young engineer, would be the one to get the laurels. In building up the "Holmes" character, Miss Marion did an excellent piece of work, as it was almost essential in getting over the romantic portion of the story to force the love interest a bit. Then there was a possibility of carrying the story to extremes by making "Abe Lee," another romantic youth in the story, the villain, or vice versa.

The treatment at the start carried sufficient suspense to lead the audience to believe that Holmes was the interloper. However, as the story went along, it showed Holmes as the manly chap and lover, developing Lee into a sort of "brotherly" sort of chap instead of the fellow who would stand in the way. It was clever treatment and finely interpretated on the screen through the clever manipulation of the theme by King.

Taking a story of this sort and injecting besides the author's purport, entertainment is no child's task. King has performed a miraculous task. He has that entertaining spirit at tense moments, bringing out dramatic touch, which stood out at all times. The telling of the story, of course, was the big thing. Putting over the fine points of the yarn by showing a desert wind sand storm and then showing the progress of reclamation work and the destruction done by faulty construction was a mountainous job, well executed.

The principal actors were submerged by the important details of the story. But their labors are not to be discounted, even though Miss Banky through most of the picture just had to show her winsome and gorgeous self and personality by looking sweet and now and then indulging in love scenes with Ronald Colman. Her best acting was at the beginning, when she played a motherly role on the desert and had the sad task of burying her husband and making a cross for the grave out of the slats of the baby's cradle. That was a most significant dramatic touch and well worth while. Then, of course, to allow the finding of the baby to become plausible after a sand storm, the mother had to pass onto the beyond, permit the Worth expedition to find the child and later transform Miss Banky into the "rose of the desert."

Colman in his nonchalant manner interpreted the Holmes role most satisfactory and did a smart thing in playing in a straightaway manner instead of the egotistical, which another player might have done, and in this way could have lost the sympathy of the audience.

An outstanding performance was given by Gary Cooper as Abe Lee, played in a most sympathetic manner, and came near taking the stuff away from Colman. Cooper is a youth who will be heard of on the screen and possibly blossom out as an "ace" lead, of which there seems to be a scarcity on the coast right now.

Clyde Cook and Erwin Connelly, two vaudeville graduates, had the task of furnishing the comedy. Cook proved to be a marvel in getting over a sympathetic brand of comedy, with Connelly standing up as a "wow" of a foil. These two seem to have something in common, and if some producer wants to line up a couple of comics, here they are. They have the same possibilities of development that Charlie Murray and Arthur Stone have shown.

The story, briefly, is that of the Worth expedition going into the desert lands for reclamation purposes. They find they need money to carry on their work, and get in touch with James Greenfield, banker, who arrives on the scene with his foster son, Willard Holmes, an engineer.

Then the development process starts, a town springs up and endeavors are under way to bring the water from the gateway of the Colorado river to the arid lands. The new town of Kingston becomes prosperous.

Greenfield wants to double-cross his partners in the venture, fires all of the engineers who want to reinforce the gateway, and they, of course, flee to a high spot, which Worth decides to develop. Worth and his crew figure that Holmes is in league with Greenfield and Barbara repulses his advances.

Then Worth names his town Barbara and starts on his work of reclaiming that section. He runs short of cash and Greenfield does his "heavy" stuff and starts a riot among the help.

Worth makes a new connection which Holmes, unknown to him, has started, and the money is advanced to save the day. A 24-hour trip is made by horseback to get the money to the town. Lee and Holmes make it. They are ambushed by hirelings of Greenfield, and both wounded. Holmes gets back to save the day. Then Greenfield's town is menaced by the raging river. A flood wipes out the town, leaving Worth's new town the winner.

For massiveness of production, this film is incomparable in telling on the screen a new angle of the development of the west. Goldwyn paid heavy for the making of the flood stuff. He had to wipe out his towns in Nevada and then had to use miniatures to convey the destructive theme of the story. The epic had them cheering on the opening night

Sold from an entertainment and

educational basis, "Barbara Worth" should easily repay Goldwyn for his endeavors, as the Wright following will flock to see it and bring double their number with them. And though the story is not one which permits of intense dramatic acting and closeups for romantic players, the followers of Banky and Colman will not be disappointed in their endeavors. Most creditable performances are also given by Paul McAllister, E. J. Ratcliffe, Charles Lane and Sam Blum.

Selling this one in the regular way and tying it up with the proper organizations should bring this latest epic of the west to the fore of the big money-getting epics of the screen. *Ung.*

SORROWS OF SATAN

Famous Players-Lasky release of a D. W. Griffith production directed by Mr. Griffith and featuring Adolphe Menjou. From Marie Corelli's story, with John Russell and George Hull the adapters. Ricardo Cortez, Carol Dempster and Lya de Putti underlined. Harry Fishbeck credited for photography and lighting effects. Opened at the Cohan, New York, Oct. 12, for run at $2 top. Running time, 117 mins.

Prince Rimenez	Adolphe Menjou
Geoffrey Tempest	Ricardo Cortez
Mavis Clare	Carol Dempster
Princess Olga	Lya de Putti
Amiel	Ivan Lebedeff
Landlady	Marcia Harris
Lord Elton	Lawrence D'Orsay
Dancing Girl	Nellie Savage

D. W. again symbolizes good and evil with this "special," meanwhile out-deMilling deMille in sets and Bacchanalian revels, plus liberal suggestiveness. For all of that the picture is overshadowed in story and cast by its superb photography. Limited action comes very close to trying the patience more than once, and for that reason it's obvious that this latest Griffith epic is not a $2 film road show. As a program feature its career, of course, is assured. The names and production suffice for that.

The picture may linger for some time at the Cohan on the strength of its "dirt." There is the usually ruined young lady (Miss Dempster) after which comes the enticing of the poor lover (Mr. Cortez) to the upper social stratum by Satan (Mr. Menjou), masquerading as a fabulously wealthy prince, and later a broad display of passion by Lya de Putti when, as the Princess Olga, she figuratively strips her soul before the prince.

A great spot for this Hungarian girl. Between she and Griffith they've made it strong enough to be repulsive. In this slow moving script it's particularly dynamic and about parallels the way Menjou's entrance into the story has been constructed. But outside of New York the censors may and probably will scissor it.

And yet Harry Fishbeck's work at the camera dominates the film. Especially in the latter footage does this combination of photography and lighting become more prominent. Illumination of a mammoth staircase so that just the tops of the stairs are in relief and down which the figures come only picked out by a "pin" spot showing the bust of the characters must rate as a great piece of work.

At another point the cast members are shadowed and come well into the camera for a close-up before catching the light. It's an achievement in lens technique which makes some of the atrocious lighting in a few early scenes unexplainable. Three or four times the sequence switches to a white glare from subdued tones. So abrupt is this that it can't be missed, with the presumption retakes are responsible for the harsh notes in an otherwise photographic gem. Also a facial makeup which ends at the chin line on a bit player is a grievous error under this same white glare.

Dr. Riesenfeld has turned in a musical score paramount to this Paramount picture. It's a better orchestration than his effort on behalf of "Beau Geste," and that's a bit of all right, too. The instrumental accompaniment is half-way responsible for the wallop in Menjou's entrance. This comes when the young book critic is broke, denounces God during a raging storm with the door blowing open, a mammoth shadow approaching, and finally showing Menjou appearing within that shadow. A weird effect that made 'em all sit up.

The story is based on the legend of Lucifer being banished from heaven as a punishment, named Satan and told he must always attempt to undermine man's happiness. For every one resisting him he is to be rewarded with an hour at the gates of Paradise, but not until the world turns from him can he again enter the Realm of God. Satan's sorrow is that no one will or can resist him.

His connection with the struggling literary lovers is when he induces Geoffrey Tempest to desert his back room surroundings for wealth while reminding the boy that he can't promise happiness, despite an "uncle's legacy" of millions. Geoffrey, having induced Mavis into his room, deserts her on the day they are to wed and ultimately marries the Princess Olga, the latter eventually explaining her only reason for the alliance is her desire to be near Prince Rimenez, who is Satan in his earthly person.

It is during Geoffrey's sojourn among the wealthy that Griffith has wrung in the gorgeous party. It's what he had in "Intolerance," only modernly dressed. It shows a heavy production outlay and may mean something through depicting the physical reaction of the principal characters to the suggestiveness in the especially prepared pagan ballet. They can call it art but it's box office, too, no matter whose name is on the directorial end.

However, these incidents are divided into practically two hours of unreeling. Between times there isn't much to uphold matters. Menjou is his usually suave self with not too much to do, while Cortez doesn't impress as being susceptible to Griffith's method of direction. Miss Dempster leads the cast for plaudits, having long ago adapted herself to the Griffith school and getting the advantage of special "shots" under various emotions.

Miss de Putti needs only that one passage of self-revelation to impress but the tenor of her entire performance hints that something of the kind is on the way. Lawrence D'Orsay is also among those present but does nothing other than escort Miss de Putti.

Putting it all together there's not much reason why this couldn't have been boiled down to 80, or maybe 90, minutes and turned loose as a regular release. But it's Griffith and he's symbolizing the whims of mankind.

A program cast name (Dorothy Douglas) never does get on the screen. In lieu of that instance and that some of the "stills" in the souvenir pamphlets aren't viewed in the picture, it's easily imaginable how much cutting was done before this work was finally okayed.

Griffith has seemingly used a minimum of subtitles and if nothing else reveals himself to still be the master of the camera. Subtlety is the keynote of the director's attempt to suggest the causes for the different human weaknesses, although there's nothing timid about that one outburst from Miss de Putti. Fishbeck gets program credit for the lighting effects and camera work, and no matter who shares in on it there is no denying that this item is more than 50 per cent. of the picture.

There's too much time used in detailing the circumstances of the lovers in their cheap boarding house, this making for a lethargic first half hour from which the picture must recouperate. From there on the ultra drawing room stuff and Menjou's sex campaign will probably interest the average film audience, but not for $2 outside of New York. And there's nothing so positive about it being a money film at the Cohan.

It must get over on its sex appeal because of its limited action, as beautiful camera work has yet to put over any film that classes itself as a special and demands a high scale for the viewing. "The Thief of Bagdad" was an example of that. *Skig.*

Broken Hearts of Hollywood

Warner Bros. production, featuring Patsy Ruth Miller, Louise Dresser and Douglas Fairbanks, Jr. From the story by Raymond L. Schrock and Edward Clark. Script by Graham Baker. Directed by Lloyd Bacon. At Loew's New York, Oct. 6. Running time, 97 min.

Betty Ann Bolton	Patsy Ruth Miller
Virgina Perry	Louise Dresser
Hal Terwilliger	Douglas Fairbanks, Jr.
"Hop" Marshall	Jerry Miley
McLain	Stuart Holmes
Molly	Barbara Worth
Sheriff	Dick Sutherland
Director	Emile Chautard
District Attorney	Anders Randolph
Chief of Detectives	George Nichols
Defense Attorney	Sam de Grasse

Here is a picture that should be taken up by the parents and mothers' associations in every town that it plays. It is a picture produced with a purpose, the purpose being that youngsters must not expect to go to Hollywood and become screen stars over night. Another angle that the exhibitor can use is to go after the subscribers to the fan magazines and tell them that here is a picture that is going to give them a lot of inside stuff on conditions.

Besides that, the film is interesting. It is of the "Madame X" type, with the girl in the spot that was the son in the play.

It is the tale of a picture star who marries and leaves the screen. The lure of the Kleigs causes her to leave her husband and child and return to the studios. Here she takes to drink and soon finds herself on the outside. Her daughter is the winner of a local beauty contest back home, and she heads for Hollywood and pictures. On the same train there is a youngster who has won a popularity contest in his home town and is on his way to the coast for the same purpose.

The footage is here taken up with the attempts of the two kids to break in. The girl gets mixed up with a fast party in which there are a lot of outsiders, and the bungalow is raided. The boy, to get the money to pay her fine, takes a job as a stunt man and is injured. Then the girl, to get the money to help him get well, offers herself to the great lover of the screen, only to be taken by him into a living room where he introduces his wife and daughter. After that he slips her a check to help the boy out and gets her a job as his leading woman. Her own mother is selected to play opposite her in a mother role. When the youngster is a hit, one of the parasites of filmland steps in and takes her to his flat. The mother overhears the date, goes to the apartment to save the girl and has to shoot and kill the man to get the girl out. She takes the blame and goes on trial for her life. At the last minute the "kid" comes through and tells the real story and saves her mother's life. After this all is ready for the family reunited fadeout.

The picture gives a great whitewashing to the screen folk on the coast, and as such should be played up by exhibitors, as it will do a bit toward staving off some of the reform propaganda.

Patsy Ruth Miller and Douglas Fairbanks, Jr., contribute corking juvenile performances, but the real honors go to Louise Dresser, who walks away with the role of the mother. What she could do to the title role in a revival of "Madame X"! If anyone has that in mind he would better think of this actress. *Fred.*

The Prince of Tempters

Robert Kane production. Ben Lyon, Lois Moran and Lya De Putti featured. Scenario from E. Phillips Oppenheim's novel, "The Ex-Duke." Lothar Mendes, director. Released through First National. At Strand, New York, week Oct. 17. Running time around 70 minutes.

Monica	Lois Moran
Francis	Ben Lyon
Delores	Lya De Putti
Mario (later Baron Humberto Giordano)	Ian Keith
Mary	Mary Brian
Duchess of Chatsfield	Olive Tell
Apollo Beneventa	Sam Hardy
Duke of Chatsfield	Henry Vibart
Signora Wembley	Judith Vosselli
Lawyer	Frazier Coulter
Papal Secretary	J. Barney Sherry

Exhibitors can bank on the names in the cast of this Robert Kane picture drawing more than the picture will. They are far stronger than the film.

Besides Lois Moran, Ben Lyon and Lya De Putti, among the players and featured are Olive Tell, Ian Keith and Sam Hardy, good legit names and also worth playing up in the advance publicity. None of the legit trio does anything striking during the story. Mr. Keith, in pictures now for quite a while, has the opportunity, doing little with it, while Mr. Hardy takes care of a very sloppy comedy role that is not his fault but seemingly the idea of the new German director for over here, Lothar Mendes' comprehension of what Americans may think is funny. Miss Tell in a slight part makes it stand up on her looks. As a looker under the lights Miss Tell seems suited.

Held down by the story and direction are the featured players as well. Miss De Putti, the German vamp, with an elegant chance here, gets but little out of it, as her role is turned wishy-washy and she gains too much sympathy through it. Mr. Lyon as the male central figure is a major portion of the strongly romantic tale that holds too little action to ever attract attention on its own. Miss Moran, opposite, is splendidly nice for how she looks and carries herself rather than the actual work accomplished.

This may be Mendes' first directorial effort over here, or at least first for Kane. The picture drags and the very absence of any punch along the way makes it seem draggy when it may be moving rationally. Particularly early is there a labored attempt to plant the characters for the leap in years. It appears as though the film runs 2,000 feet before it starts going anywhere. Holding to scenes too long occurs frequently afterward. At least 10 minutes could be well and still cut out of this feature.

Two points only stand out in the direction, with the remainder if away from the usual American trend of direction, then of the usual German, mostly the cutting off of the head or bodies to show hands or feet or what the person is working at. In fact, the picture starts this way with a boy, a little trick here leading one to believe by the legs it is a girl.

One of the two novelties is the closeup of mouths only of two persons speaking rapidly to a girl between them in an endeavor to persuade her. The other is the little jaunty and saucy leap into the water performed by Miss Moran after Lyon brusquely kissed her while she was in a bathing suit on the brink of a pool.

There may be curiosity or interest in several of the scenes revealing the inside of a monastery, with some of the ceremonials performed by the monks exhibited. Also, the release from the order of a young monk, that he should go free into the outer world to secure a legacy and a title. That may be accurate Catholicity but doesn't sound it.

In direction otherwise, what might be called the straightaway, the picture runs very well, and in production there is no fault. How closely the book has been followed is not known. That is never necessary, however, in a picture film, as an adapted story stands or falls as a film, not to its resemblance to the book. And here the story does not stand well through it being mostly motionless.

The skeleton as outlined above about takes up the entire story, excepting the "frame" arranged by Mario with Dolores to "take" Francis, then the Duke of Chatsfield. Francis and Marion were novices in the monastery, with Mario rejecting his vows, Francis taking them and securing the voluntary release when it was learned he was the legitimate heir to the title and estates.

Dolores asserted she truly loved Francis and repented of the frame upon learning Francis loved Monica, his cousin. Dolores, after divulging the truth and hearing Francis declare he had no vestige of affection left for her, blew out by the poison route, a favorite exit for De Putti of late in filmdom. But as Dolores had fallen rapidly and worked faster upon Francis, it should not have been such a shock. She met him in the afternoon and had supper with him the same day. Both confessed their mutual affection, without Dolores even taking the time to change gowns.

Unlikely "Prince of Tempters" will advertise itself. Whole dependence should be placed upon the cast.

The comedy scheme referred to is of Hardy eating rapidly and gluttonously, with his mind always on food. It's an old burlesque favorite over here, as Mr. Mendes should have been advised. *Sime.*

FOOLS OF FASHION

Tiffany Productions production. Story from book by George Randolph Chester, "The Other Woman." Directed by James C. McKay. Mardleine Day, Mae Busch and Theodore von Eltz featured. At Loew's New York, one day, Sunday, Oct. 10. Running time, about 65 minutes.

Independent picture makers have their troubles, aside from the production that takes in financing as well as casting. Sunday at Loew's New York theatre, a one day "grind" stand, Tiffany had to be content to show its "Fools of Fashion" and without the house boards even carrying the label of the maker, the latter being deliberately left off.

Tiffany has an excellent picture in "Fools of Fashion" and especially for women. For what slim result a Sunday showing could have meant to Tiffany for trade purposes, at least its name might have been displayed outside on the boards and in the lobby. Picture people as a rule take Sunday away from the downtown district. As the New York exhibition by Tiffany was strictly for the trade as far as Tiffany was concerned, they probably derived little in trade publicity through the showing and nothing in billing exploitation.

However, the independents have persevered with the most substantial of them in business operation and production direction coming through. Tiffany is among these. One or two others have cheated their way upward, but that was excusable since they have survived.

The big producers who say they want competitors in production; that they must have them (and that is very true for the stability of the industry) are making no earnest effort to promote that rivalry when such an action as related here in the absence of the Tiffany label or forcing its picture into the New York on a Sunday for a Broadway display is considered.

For "Fools of Fashion" can stand up as a week's first run. It's a well made holding film with a couple of real kicks, and along the lines women will dote upon. Men will be divided over the picture. The first half runs a bit too mushily for the males, but in the latter half there's enough action and business to please every one.

In production itself the picture looks good. Almost entirely interiors, there is a solid atmosphere of luxury in the settings without anything garishly blatant. That's very sensible direction. However, it will strike the men why a real estate clerk could live as well as he apparently did and still be subject to annoyance by a bill collector for $125.

How closely the film tale follows the Chester novel is unknown. Regardless, the continuity is excellent with strong suspense toward the finale.

It's a story of a couple of young sappy husbands and their dress loving wives. To satisfy their fashion ambitions one of the wives coaches the other as to ways and means in which an a. k. roue figures. In fact, in a studio (artist) ballroom scene there were enough a. k.'s to start a stampede at Campbell's.

A favorite trick of the conniving wife was to find a pawn ticket on the street and have her husband redeem it, to learn that for the $10 or so it called for was a fur coat worth $1,000. The first time the other wife did it her husband upon calling at the pawnshop and seeing the fur cloak he could have had for the small amount turned around and sold it to the pawnbroker for $125 to pay the collector. Instead, he took home to the surprised women a measly piece of mangy black fur. Not a word left for the women to say.

That bit was really a gag, quite old as originally done, but here given such a new twist that there are laughs besides interest in it.

The other kick bit is a shower bath scene, with the wife inside curtains, revealing just sufficient to make the complete suggestion, and her husband in the bathroom handing her various articles as she calls for them. The scene is somewhat prolonged. Afterward the husband also is seen in the sho— but the wife does not enter the bathroom while he is there, although they later embrace in the parlor while in their lounging gowns.

The death of the designing wife is well worked, through having her drop from a ledge as her husband discovers her in a rendezvous.

Nothing particularly commendable in the playing. Whatever heavy credit there is belongs to James C. McKay as the director. He brought out everything.

The mushy early part is devoted to the newlyweds, their honeymoon and a year later. The year later will strike the men folks right at home, but the year before stuff must get the women.

While at the same time this picture is not a bad educational for single women, perhaps many a married one as well. It may also be something in the line of information for other sappy husbands.

Theodore von Eltz in the lead male role did a walk through; likewise Mae Busch, with what little acting of any moment there was performed by Marceline Day. Miss Day was frequently hurt in appearance by the shading of the photography, although in whole the camera work is first class.

A very good and worthwhile program feature film. *Sime.*

BLARNEY

Metro-Goldwyn-Mayer production from the story by Donn Byrne entitled "In Praise of John Carabine," adapted by Albert Lewin. Directed by Marcel de Sano. Starring Renee Adoree. At Loew's Circle, New York, one day, Oct. 9. Running time, 64 min.

Peggy Nolan	Renee Adoree
James Carabine	Ralph Graves
Marcalina	Paulette Duval
Blanco Johnson	Malcolm Waite
Peggy's Aunt	Margaret Seddon

A picture that might have been a "Little Old New York." Between the script writer and the director they muffed a corking chance to turn out a real box office bet. What this one lacked was the comedy relief "Little Old New York" had. Had the M.-G.-M. production department seen that was lacking in the script before starting shooting they could have saved the day.

It can be judged the kind of a picture it is when it did not get a first run showing at the Capitol or even the State in New York, both houses controlled by the M.-G.-M. organization.

It is really a shame that this good piece of property, as far as the story is concerned, was permitted to go to waste through faulty adaptation and mediocre direction. As a serial in the "Sat. Eve. Post" the story held the attention for the period that it ran. As a picture even cut to just a little more than an hour it is just so-so. At that there are a couple of corking bare-knuckle fights in it and they are the things that make the audience take notice.

It is a story of the early days of the prize ring in New York, telling of the last great bare-knuckl champion from Ireland, John Carabine, who came to this country and was first whipped by Blancho Johnson, later wresting the championship from him. What a chance for color and atmosphere in a story of that kind, but it was all muffed in transferring the yarn to the screen.

Carabine came to this country a stowaway, but his fare was paid by a little Irish lass on the same boat with him who happened to come from his home town and always harbored an affection for the fighting Irishman. Once here he gives her the go-bye and falls for a concert hall singer whom he marries. She in turn cheats with the champion and when the champ licks him in the first fight that they have, she runs off with him. Then the little Irish girl takes him back and with the aid of a relative from the old country manages to bring him back on his toes to an extent where he in a grudge fight that lasts for hours bests the champ.

Renee Adoree gives a corking performance as the little Irish lass, while Ralph Graves, as the boy, certainly covers himself with glory as far as individual performance is concerned. Malcolm Waite as the champion also stands out and the fight that the two put up certainly is a hummer. Paulette Duval as the vamp looked and acted to perfection.

It is a picture that will get by in the daily change houses, but that s all. *Fred.*

THE LILY

Fox picture and Victor Schertzinger production, latter directing. Adapted from play of same name. Features Belle Bennett. Cast includes Barry Norton, Richard Tucker, John St. Polis, Ian Keith, Reata Hoyt, John Roche, Gertrude Short and James Marcus. At Lowe's New York, Oct. 14, one day. Running time, 70 mins.

Schertzinger just missed making this an outstanding program release. A choppy sequence is keeping it from the first-grade houses, and yet those theatres are where this picture would have its best chance. The story must have attention to get over. It's deep and heavy. Belle Bennett gives it a brilliant interpretation, but in those emporiums where the audience is constantly shifting, such as Loew's New York, ""The Lily" is handicapped.

It is an old play adapted to the screen and suffering in the attempt to hold it down to program length. It depends on its story and the playing. There is meagre action. Miss Bennett as the unselfish and love-starved Odette is extremely human. The ability of this actress to make herself appear either 18 or 40 is remarkable. Here she plays a youngster of 17 or so. When the script jumps ahead she again is as genuinely the role. Miss Bennett is superb here.

The dramatic theme is not without comedy. Schertzinger extracts laughs from a selfish father (John St. Paul) and an elderly housekeeper, unmentioned, who gets a world of stuff out of characteristic gestures.

The father of the motherless Odette and Christiane forces the former to give up her first love because of sympathy for himself. Odette reconciles herself to a loveless life, but watches that a like experience does not happen to Christiane (Reata Hoyt).

The latter falls in love with a married artist (Ian Keith), who seduces her. Because of which their lone brother's engagement to a wealthy heiress is broken off. Furious at his younger daughter, the father is brought to task by Odette, who pours forth the thoughts she has been harboring for years. The father is something of a roue, being infatuated with a woman in Paris (action is in France) for whom he is slowly pawning all the household goods, including rare paintings, etc.

The artist's wife finally agrees to a divorce, that match being a family arrangement. It paves the way for Christiane's marriage and the union of Odette and the family lawyer, who has loved her for years. The finish has the father slipping a bronze statue under his coat, preparatory to another Paris trip, and the second laugh climax is allotted to the housekeeper.

To repeat, an excellently cast production that with better symmetry in the telling could have been a top notch release. It its present form seems destined for the secondary theatres where it must go up against that aisle action which detracts attention.

Perchance the ordinary celluloid audience will reject "The Lily" as entertainment. It must be said that one lobby remark from a patron was negative on this film. But the statement that "The Lily" is a good release still stands, and where they are inclined to take their film viewing a bit seriously this one will register. *Skig.*

WAR PAINT

Metro-Goldwyn-Mayer production, starring Tim McCoy. Pauline Starke featured. Adapted from Peter B. Kyne story of scenario, with continuity by Charles Maigne. Titles by Joe Farnham. Directed by W. S. Van Dyke. At Loew's, New York, one day, Oct. 16.

Metro-Goldwyn-Mayer's first own western in full length, and also the debut in western pictures of a new M-G-M star, Col. Tim McCoy, using for screen purposes Tim McCoy only, although the outside billing at the New York Saturday disagreed with the slide carrying the Colonel.

Assuming that in an initial film such as this is the star would be "protected" to quite an extent, no such evidence of "protection" is easily detected. McCoy works as though camera-broke, although, of course, much footage must have been used up in rehearsals. About the most important point he is lacking upon is expression, but there's not much call for that here.

As a rider Tim McCoy has a seat more closely to the military idea of the saddle than most of the other western jocks, though again that may be a matter of the saddle used itself. Some of the western boys may still be using the Mexican armchairs.

As chief of scouts at an army post in Wyoming in 1887, Col. McCoy did his full duty as an actor. In action he's very lithe and fast. Also, he fell in love with the girl within six minutes, commonly known as "on sight." Still, that may have been the Peter B. Kyne scheme of story telling.

"War Paint" is something a bit different in westerns. It takes in the Indians and the U. S. Cavalry. There is a skein in the tale that Mr. Kyne may have implanted to bring out that perhaps back in the days of the Indian extermination all of their uprisings were not wholly the fault of the red men. Nor does it appear in historical works that the red invited the white men to contaminate them. Perhaps the moving pictures some day will tell all of the truth about the American Indian and his decline.

A feature of the picture is the Indian sign language, guaranteed to be authetic. Col. McCoy speaks to the Indians in that language.

Plenty of riding and shooting action. Iron Eyes, a young chief, grew savage on his reservation when placed under arrest for "anarchy." Breaking his chains, he leads cohorts to the army post to avenge himself on White Eagle (McCoy), who defeats him in a knife battle within the first 600 feet of the film.

Meanwhile, the commandant of the post had become testy when informed by his chief scout he was all wrong in his judgment of the Arapahoes, the tribe remaining on their happy hunting grounds, a part of the reservation. The C. O. ordered out the cavalry to get the tribe if Iron Eyes were not delivered within 24 hours.

Iron Eyes in between led his red gorialls to the post, after the troop had left, and was besieging it when White Eagle did his stunts to break through. He brought back the troop as succor, but after he had brought the friendly Indians first.

So White Eagle was the champ go-getter of the post still and won the commandant's daughter, the gril he loved on sight but didn't know who she was until Pop introduced him.

Real Indian chiefs are programed as principals in their Indian roles.

A caption mentions the film was cameraed on a Wyoming reservation. In titles is a laugh here and there, also a comedy character "afraid of Injuns." Pauline Starke as the daughter doesn't have to do much heavy emoting. She is called upon to look flirty now and then, and does it more often then than now. But she's a brunet, anyway.

Mr. McCoy, from reports of his age (and he's no chick from those accounts), makes rather a good looking figure, whether afoot or astride. This picture at least gives him a running start for the western goal. It will require a couple of more before any real line can be gotten on him. From this one, however, the Colonel seems to be there also as a stunt-doer. How he will strike the women is something the women only will answer. But his chances for becoming a fad with the ladies look good.

As a western "War Paint" will be liked where westerns are okay. For this is okay. It has plenty of suspense, plus action and minus its weak romance.

Well made, but with some cheating on the extras. More cavalrymen and at least as many of the U. S. regulars as Indians would have better balanced that department. A better made western, though, and looking it, than those that usually come along the gross cost picture path. *Sime.*

MEN OF PURPOSE

Veterans Film Service presents. Data by Bruce Chester. Titles by Hoey Lawlor. At the Randolph, Chicago, beginning Oct. 2. Running time, 98 minutes.

Chicago, Oct. 15.

No help, in titles or otherwise, is asked for or by the veterans of the late war in this picture, shown and produced under the sponsorship of the American Legion. Despite that, a success, if possible, will aid the Legion.

The film holds no plot, no individual characters, no studio work nor interest, love or otherwise, to grip any of the finer senses, except, of course, patriotism. As that it stands strictly as propaganda.

It reviews the war in general, following the strife incident by incident, telling that now well-known story with no relief except in titles, and not getting mushy until near the end, when America and her soldiers are drawn into the drama. There the titles are relied on for some slight soft stuff.

It is produced by the Veterans Film Service, probably formed by the Legion solely for the production of this picture. It relies on data supplied by Bruce Chester, not known to have been previously identified in connection with the picture industry.

It is "A Monument to the Dead" and "Not a Story of Mankind, but of Men," according to opening titles. The film proper begins with the shooting of Archduke Ferdinand, whose assassination in Sarajevo, Serbia, June 28, 1914, is commonly believed to have given the Kaiser an excuse to start the war. It is explained that this scene is the only one in the film that is not genuine. It is a formal street shooting bit, with a crazy-looking assailant in the onwatching crowd shooting his irons at the Archduke and Duchess in a passing buggy.

The Prussian march on Belgium follows. From then on all scenes are of shelling and fighting on the battle front with variation only when another nation enters the struggle.

The authenticity of all the scenes is stressed. The faded, unclear condition of the film at times gives vent to that. If true, they are probably pieces of news reels and the work of staff photographers patched together. Some of the shots, especially those of the big guns in action, are thrilling. Numerous views taken by telephotography (explained by title to be taken by a camera with magnifying lense at long range, which camera is now used at prize-fights and ball games) give exciting pointers on the grimness of the hand-to-hand fighting. Bombarding, charging, fighting, shelling, falling men, falling airplanes, marching armies. With a proper musical score played by an orchestra in place of on the organ, the case when the film was reviewed, would have doubled the effect of these really staggering scenes.

There is much gruesomeness in the muddy and dirty conditions in which the pictures were taken. The wounded are frequently before the camera, as are the dead strewn on the battlefields.

The most famous characters of the war and the most famous events are shown in order with the war's progress. Shown are the Kaiser, Czar Nicholas, Marshal Joffre, Marshal Foch, King Albert, King George, Prince of Wales (then a boy), President of France, our own President Wilson, Theodore Roosevelt and others. Eddie Rickenbacker is once mentioned, but not pictured in scenes of an air battle.

The sinking of three vessels by German submarines is vivid. The shots were filmed on the deck of the enemy subs, probably having been official films of the German government.

The daring of the cameramen is stressed upon. From the picture it is seen that they risked death in numerous spots to get the action in picture. Film record of the famous battle in Argonne forest miraculously escaped destruction. The cameraman was killed and the camera shot through and partially destroyed.

Despite the frequency of gruesome scenes, none is prolonged to offensiveness. That is the film's main virtue.

The credit for procuring the data goes to Chester. If his job was difficult he deserves much credit. The picture estimates in millions at all times. It informes that the war took a toll of 9,000,000 lives and $180,000,000,000.

That "Men of Purpose" will commercially live is doubtful. Holding no story to promote sympathy, it is only an animated compilation of bits seen heretofore in newsreels, pictorial reviews and the numerous "books of pictures of the great war." As a reissue in 10 years from now it may be different.

Running time of almost 100 minutes is somewhat against it at the Randolph, a straight picture house in Chicago's loop. Doing nine shows a day there at 50 cents for all performances, it was making money in its second week. *Loop.*

THE OLD SOAK

Universal production adapted from play "The Old Soak," by Don Marquis. Adapted by Charles Kenyon. Directed by Edward Sloman. Featuring Jean Hersholt. At the Stanley, New York (25c. grind), one day, Oct. 11. Running time, 75 minutes.

Clement Hawley, Sr.	Jean Hersholt
Clemmy Hawley	George Lewis
Ina Heath	June Marlowe
Cousin Webster	William V. Mong
Sylvia	Mary Astor
Annie	Louise Fazenda
Mrs. Hawley	Lucy Beaumont
Lucy Hawley	Adda Gleason

Somewhere between the stage play and the screen version of Don Marquis' "Old Soak" all of the comedy that played so important a part in the play was lost. That leaves just a small-town meller that will please the average picture house audience in the daily change houses.

So long a time has passed since the play that it is doubtful if the average movie fan will remember the title as that of a play. However, in spots the picture will get some business.

The screen story stresses the love affair between young Clemmy and the chorus girl rather than the comedy element. Jean Hersholt, who plays the "Old Soak," gives a corking characterization, but to a great degree fails in the comedy end. Louise Fazenda as the servant girl isn't given a chance to get over with anything.

June Marlowe as the girl handles it very well. At times she is most pleasing and convincing. Mary Astor looks the million-dollar show-girl that she is cast for. The rather thankless role of the son was for George Lewis, who looks like a likely juvenile lead. He got all possible out of the character. William V. Mong as the hypocritical banker scored nicely, while the minor roles were well handled.

The picture itself does not look as though it cost very much to make. That is one of the angles that the Universal fell down on. One would think that with a piece of property as valuable as this it would have taken greater pains to put over a picture that would have clicked.

It is a cinch that there were enough comedy and laugh lines in the play to have made for better titling than the picture has. It could have been gagged over with titles to have made it stand up for a week's run on Broadway anyway. *Fred.*

WOMAN POWER

Fox release and Harry Beaumont production from a Harold MacGrath story. Cast includes Margaret Livingston, Ralph Graves, Lou Tellegen, Andre Randolph, David Butler, Ralph Sipperly, William Wallin and Kathryn Perry. At Loew's New York Oct. 1 as half of double feature bill. Running time, 60 minutes.

Not a bad picture for the smaller houses, although if paired with another feature the total result will have more value. Little excitement in the tale, but a mild comedy-drama that should kill an hour without causing talk one way or the other.

Adapted from a Harold MacGrath magazine story, the list of players includes two names familiar to legit Broadwayites. Kathryn Perry, of former "Follies" fame, is the girl, and Ralph Sipperly provides the comedy angle. Sipperly makes his role stand out as a crippled hanger-on of a pugilistic training camp, while Miss Perry looks okay and passes in a thin role.

Ralph Graves is the wealthy heir who becomes a weakling through his infatuation of a cabaret dancer (Margaret Livingston), and is cast out by his father after taking humiliating slaps in the face from the cafe performer's new flame (Lou Tellegen). The boy retires to the training camp to build himself up, and there commences an affair with the proprietor's niece (Miss Perry), who is adored by the rest of the pugs.

The comedy is split up among the fighters in a dining room, with the efforts of two of the boys to bring the girl and the reconstructing youth together when they realize she is smitten. The boy, of course, makes his moral comback, gets an okay from his dad on the girl and returns to the city to see the object of his former infatuation. This visit is to prove himself immune, and, upon meeting his former rival, he invokes the expected physical rebuttal, very much as Lionel Barrymore did in "The Yellow Streak" quite a few years ago.

Miss Livingston does well by the heartless vamp character and Graves makes the boy plausible. The athletes are "types," with the laughs depending on ill-fitting clothes, deportment, etc. Tellegen's work amounts to two bits.

Billing spread around the lobby had the names of David Butler and Miss Livingston prominent under the film title. Inasmuch as Butler is in a minor role it looked as if the names were selected at random. The actual screening was bare of any cast names made prominent.

The picture doesn't look expensively produced. The story makes no demands for heavy sets, but there is a cabaret scene and the usual exaggerated dressing room flash.

The drop-ins at the New York seemed satisfied, and the film should be able to keep up its head if kept in shallow water. *Skig.*

WINNING WALLOP

Sam Sax presents William Fairbanks in melodrama by L. V. Jefferson. Offered by Lumas Film Corp. (Gotham Productions). Directed by Charles Hutchinson. Bernard Ray, assistant director; James Brown, cameraman. Previewing, Oct. 8. Running time (hastened projection), 54 minutes.

Rex Burton	William Fairbanks
Marion Wayne	Shirley Palmer
Peter Wayne	Chas. K. French
Cyrus Barton	Melvin McDowell
Lawrence Duncan	Crauford Kent
Fight Manager	Jimmy Aubrey
"Pug" Brennan	Frank Hagney

Romantic melodrama of the prize ring with a background of society. Measures up as a valuable program release on the basis of neat playing, splendid technical quality as to production and photography and a wealth of fast action.

The film makes no pretense to be anything more than a fast melo. It hasn't a single moral precept, doesn't elucidate any theory and furthers no propaganda or cult. Just an entertaining bit of frank fiction about a college athlete who goes in for boxing, wins a ring battle and thereby overcomes the objections of a wealthy father to his suit for the heroine.

The action lags for a moment as the plot is "planted," but when it does get under way it moves swiftly and through varied episodes to a stirring climax. The finish, of course, is a prizefight staged in the Los Angeles Athletic Club, or at least views of an enormous crowd in that amphitheatre are spliced in convincingly with alternating shots close up as the battle goes on and at a distance.

The society scenes are extremely well managed, the polite atmosphere being especially well done in the settings. The photographic quality is particularly worthy of comment.

Shirley Palmer makes a thoroughly likeable young heroine. There is nothing about her of the untutored newcomer, in spite of her lack of previous featuring. She is a trim little pony type with dark bobbed hair and a charmingly ingenuous natural method. She may be a graduate of the bathing beauty coterie. She appears in one scene in scanty gym togs, and suggests that she would qualify in that field of art.

William Fairbanks, of course, is the super-hero of the familiar type, doing neatly the tasks that fall to the lot of such a character. The others of the cast are standard players of types, and all well known. The picture presents the unusual situation of an unknown feminine lead backed by veteran character players, instead of the reverse of that scheme.

Rex walks out on an austere father who objects to his concentration on the athletic field. He applies for a job as gym instructor in a society training camp for women run by Marion Wayne, his sweetheart, a wealthy girl with independent leanings. Some comedy here of fat girls reducing, etc.

The city boosters have framed a big prizefight for the publicity it would bring the town, and Marion's father is "in" for $100,000 if the fight goes a certain way. A business rival tries to make him lose the money, and, to guard against this, Rex is drawn in as challenger of the professional pug imported for the stunt. Plotters, seeing defeat, strike down the old man and try to fasten the crime upon Rex. He escapes. It is the night of the fight. To reach the ringside Rex leads the police on a perilous auto chase through the mountains, tricks them and strands them while he returns in their car, to go into the ring at the last minute and win. The way to this climax is strewn with fights, intrigue and romance in unflagging succession of action incidents, and these make it an entertaining picture. *Rush.*

THE HIGH FLIER

H. J. Brown production releasing through Rayart and directed by Brown. Stars Reed Howes, with Ethel Shannon and Cissy Fitzgerald also in cast. Story by Frank Clarke. At Loew's New York, Oct. 8, one day, as half of double bill. Running time, 62 mins.

A pretty fair comedy-drama independent, possessing aeroplane thrills as its main kick. Reed Howes jumps from a down and out doughboy to a bogus count, and finally rings in on the propeller invention, which means money, besides winning the daughter of 'plane manufacturer.

To get back the plans of the prop there is a hectic air chase, with Howes presumably making two exchanges of ships at high altitudes and finally dropping into a speeding car driven by the girl (Ethel Shannon).

What comedy there is is planted through Howes playing a count at the will of two of the girl's suitors, these boys being rich, harmless and full of ideas. It eventually turns out that Howes actually knows the real titled Frenchman, and both have collaborated on the much pursued invention plans. Brown has pieced the script together, allowing for plentiful action, with the aeroplane stuff rather veiled so as to make it a question whether a stunt man or he who cranked on the box is deserving of the credit.

No outstanding performance, although Howes does well by his dashing juvenile role and is evidently not without a sense of the comic. The women are not particularly prominent, such playing as does stand in relief coming from the male section.

The smaller auditoriums should be able to use this one without an added starter to strengthen, even though it be tried and true stuff. A few laughs and the thrills make it hold. They sat through it without effort at the New York. *Skig.*

THE YELLOW BACK

Blue Streak western (independent), featuring Fred Humes as the cowboy hero, supported by Lotus Thompson. Story, scenario and direction by Del Andrews. At the Stanley, New York, Oct. 9. Running time, 58 mins.

Satisfactory feature of the western type, neatly played by a small cast and with production costs small. Most of the action takes place in exteriors.

Story gets away from the familiar formula in only one particular, but this makes it something of a novelty. The cowboy hero does not throw a leg over a horse until the climax in the last reel, when he engages in a cross-country horse race upon which the fortunes of all concerned depend.

This race is the basis of the entire story being splendidly built up in daring riding, clever camera shots of horses going over barriers, speeding down dizzy inclines and rushing pell-mell across open spaces.

Andy (Humes) has an unreasoning terror of horses, heritage of some childhood fright and so finds it hard to keep a job as cow hand, the only trade he knews. He goes from ranch to ranch holding down his job briefly, but unable to conquer his terror of horseflesh. In all other situations he has plenty of courage. He saves Betty, the ranchman's daughter, from quicksand and gets a job from her father (Buck Connors), who is being forced off his land by a scheming neighbor who owns water rights necessary to the raising of cattle. Betty's father is gradually going broke and has not the money necessary to develop a well on his own land that will save the situation.

A purse of $500 is offered to the winner of the feature race at the local rodeo and Betty has entered her horse, Lady. Her father has bet his land against $5,000 with his plotting neighbor, when they pick Andy to ride the race.

The horse-shy Andy is in despair, as the race day approaches, but at the last minute he braces himself, and, spurred on by love of Betty, risks his life and conquers his fear, to ride the course to victory.

The picture is rather injured through the use of a Chinese cook for comedy purposes. Andy is made to confide in the cook, who appears to be his only pal. The comedy is scarcely worth while, and the association robs the hero of dignity. *Rush.*

ACE OF CADS

Famous Players production. Adolphe Menjou starred in this Michael Arlen story. Adapted by Forrest Halsey and directed by Luther Reed. At the Rivoli, New York, week Oct. 16. Running time, 70 minutes.

Chapel Maturin..............Adolphe Menjou
Eleanour..........................Alice Joyce
Sir Guy de Gramercy.........Norman Trevor
Basil de Gramercy..............Philip Strange
Joan.............................Suzanne Fleming

The suave and polished Adolphe Menjou in a romantic role made to order for his style of acting, a part with all kinds of romantic appeal and the attractive atmosphere of British society. An interesting little light drama, but very graceful in substance and background, without enough action for a kick.

The hero is a mate to Bertie in "Under Two Flags," and indeed this Arlen story has a good deal in common with that old epic of naive romance. A good, quiet story is well told in terms of quiet drama and acted with that tone of restraint.

Scenically, the production has much to recommend it. There are those rich but simple British interiors, splendidly realized; a good deal of spectacular flash in fashionable restaurant and gambling casino settings, and occasional glimpses of the Royal Guards, in which the hero is an officer. These last bits are probably cut-ins, but they are pat in their application to the action.

Lieut. Maturin is a gay youth among the London fashionables, quartered with his brother officer, the crafty Basil, son of Col. de Gramercy, commander of the exclusive regiment. Both are rivals for Eleanour, sharing their purses and their leisure.

Maturin swears off wine and gay ladies when he wins the hand of Eleanour, while Basil plots his undoing. It is Basil who arranges a bachelor dinner for Maturin and then tips off his fiancee, Eleanour, who bursts in just in time to catch her future husband apparently making love to a light lady of the evening—all details pre-arranged by Basil.

Horrified at the wreck of his happiness, Maturin drinks too much and becomes involved in a public brawl, an episode his Colonel takes advantage of to force him in disgrace from the regiment. There follows years of wanderings about Continental resorts while Maturin tries to forget.

Eleanour has married Basil, and now is a widow with a daughter, Joan, a headstrong girl, who resents the domination of Col. de Gramercy, her grandfather. Upon Maturin's return to London he is accidentally thrown into contact with Joan, with whom he plans a marriage to revenge himself upon the Colonel, in whose eyes he is a disgraced outcast.

The drama of the story comes in the clash between Maturin and the old Colonel, who tries to bully Maturin and then tries to buy him off. It is when Eleanour takes up the management of the affair that he is persuaded to abandon his project, giving up the girl and foregoing his vengeance only on the pleadings of his old sweetheart.

It is this episode that reunites the suitors of years before in a happy ending for a neat bit of sentimental romance. *Rush.*

RED HOT LEATHER

Universal production starring Jack Hoxie. Story by Albert Rogell. Directed by Albert Rogell. Distributed by Universal Pictures. Shown at the Stanley theatre, New York, Oct. 16, 1926. Running time, 59 minutes.

Jack Lane.................................Jack Hoxie
Ellen Rand..............................Ena Gregory
Daniel Lane.........................William Malon
Bob.....................................George French
Morten Kane.......................William Turner
Ross Kane..................................Tom Shirley

A most important member of this cast is a white horse called "Scout." He gives Jack Hoxie invaluable aid in this "western."

The story is of the old boy species that has always stood the test when a riding picture needed a plot—the mortgage on the farm, but here a ranch.

As the U camera experts were pretty busy in the past year at the more important rodeos, turning them to advantage in picture "westerns," this "Red Hot Leather" is given a rodeo background that proves the climax of the story.

Hoxie is a husky boy and some rider. He handles himself well, and once Universal slips him some regular celluloid continuity, this boy is going to show up all the more handsomely.

There are some corking photographic shots, the rodeo scenes in particular being unusually good. The riding is the big feature, with the rodeo section holding this one above mediocrity. Several comedy "bits" also help. *Mark.*

Shameful Behavior?

J. G. Bachmann presents the farce by Mrs. Belloc Lowndes, adapted by Douglas Bronson and directed by Albert Kelley for Preferred Pictures. Photography by Nicholas Musuraca. At pre-viewing Oct. 15. Running time, 58 minutes.

Daphne Carroll..................Edith Roberts
Curtis Lee.....................Harland Tucker
Jack Lee........................Richard Tucker
Mrs. Calhoun...................Martha Mattox
Joan Lee.........................Grace Carlyle
Sally Long.......................Louise Carver
The Butler...................Hayes Robertson

Strictly a light program picture for the daily change houses. The title is the only sensational thing about the production, which does not live up to its spicy suggestion. Best feature is the splendid technical production. In this respect the effort is on a level with the best. Settings, backgrounds, costuming and atmosphere are of high grade and the photography is faultless.

A trifling story, neither farce nor drama, holds the picture back. It has many dull moments and few lively ones. The central idea may have looked interesting in story form, but it doesn't work out in pantomimic action. It even doesn't get going until well along in the second reel and even after that it lags lamentably.

Daphne Carrol left home **an awkward kid. She returns from a French finishing school a very up-to-date young woman with modern ideas and dress. She has long been in love with Curtis Lee, serious-minded politician, who has old-fashioned views of what is becoming in the girls of society.** Daphne's picture accidentally is printed in connection with a story about an escaped lunatic named Sally Long, who is described as seeking her husband, armed with a big pair of scissors.

When Curtis absent-mindedly forgets a dinner engagement with Daphne the returning flapper decides to impersonate Sally and teach him a lesson. Carrying a huge pair of shears, she surges into Curtis' home, claiming him as her husband, which leads to something of a scandal among the reformers who are backing Curtis as a champion of high morals. These complications are worked up further when Curtis brings to the house a nurse to care for the supposed lunatic, the nurse being none other than the real Sally Long.

These involvements are none too convincingly brought about and the planting of so intricate a plot is laboriously managed. They aimed at **uproarious comedy, but it doesn't register, partly because everybody works too hard to pump up rough comedy to the destruction of any real humor. *Rush.***

THE LAST FRONTIER

Produced by Metropolitan Pictures Corp.; presented by John C. Flinn; featuring William Boyd, Marguerite De La Motte, J. Farrell MacDonald and Jack Hoxie. Adapted by Will M. Ritchey from the story

by Courtney Ryley Cooper. Directed by George B. Seitz. Released through P. D. C. at Loew's New York, Oct. 13, on day. Running time, 92 minutes.

Tom Kirby..................William Boyd
Beth..............Marguerite De La Motte
Wild Bill............J. Farrell Macdonald
Buffalo Bill.....................Jack Hoxie
Buddy........................Junior Coghlan
Lige..........................Mitchell Lewis
Cynthia Jaggers..........Gladys Brockwell
Pawnee Killer...............Frank Lackteen

"The Last Frontier" was originally destined to be an epic of the west of proportions to rival "The Covered Wagon." It was conceived in the mind of the late Thos. H. Ince as a picture that should be a splendid record of the last days of the west, but before Ince could carry out the production of the picture he died.

At that time, however, he had shot a great amount of footage of a buffalo drive in Canada in conjunction with the Dominion Government's process of thinning out the tremendous herd of buffalo on their great plains. Then the picture was taken over by Hunt Stromberg, who acquired a half interest, with the Metropolitan holding the other half. Stromberg finally sold his interest and the Met went ahead alone with the production. The result is an ordinary western that just about ranks as a program production.

A fairly good cast in the picture and some clever matching up so that the buffalo hunt shots could be fitted in with the studio production, for in the hunts scenes a number of persons were used as doubles.

The story opens shortly after the Civil War with an impoverished southerner starting for the great west, accompanied by his wife and daughter. Their wagon train is attacked and both of the parents are killed, and the girl, who was coming out to meet her fiance, Tom Kirby, blames him for the death of her folks in her grief.

This gives Lige, a hypocritical trader who is shipping and selling rifles to the Indians, a chance to take the girl to his home and later try to lure her away under the pretext that he is going to take her back east. In reality, he is running away from the town because his dealings with the natives have been discovered and he is in danger of being lynched. This leads [illegible] big scene, a buffalo stampe[illegible] soprano the Indians organized in o[illegible] but cover their attack on the town. In this stampede the double-crossing Lige and his mistress meet their death, while the young hero rescues the girl.

William Boyd gives a convincing enough performance as the hero, while the heavy of Mitchell Lewis is all that could be asked for. Jack Hoxie as Buffalo Bill makes the role of the great scout stand out, playing Col. Cody as a youngster.

Several touches of comedy, and Wild Bill and California Joe furnish them. Junior Coghlan, acting as the little father to to his baby brother after his folks have been killed off in the Indian attack, also contributes a worth-while touch to the picture.

As a western in the spots where westerns are popular it will get the money and please the audiences, but it does not rank in the class for which it was originally intended.

Fred.

THE MAGICIAN

Rex Ingram production released by Metro-Goldwyn-Mayer from the play by Somerset Maugham, featuring Alice Terry and Paul Wegener. Adapted and directed by Rex Ingram. At the Capitol, New York, week Oct. 24. Running time, 71 minutes.

Margaret Dauncy..............Alice Terry
Oliver Haddo...............Paul Wegener
Dr. Arthur Burdon.........Ivan Petrovich
Dr. Porhoet...............Firmin Gemier
Susie Boyd.................Gladys Hamer

Rex Ingram has turned out a very slow moving, draggy picture that has but a single thrill and that typical of the old days when the serials were the feature attractions of the average picture bills.

That story about Ingram returning to the United States to make his pictures and keep pace with the development of the screen technique in adapting and directing, certainly goes after seeing this work of his.

Ingram was one of the best script writers of a half a decade ago, just as prior to that he was one of the best cutters and he developed into one of the leading directors, but his last few pictures since he took up his residence abroad and is making productions there show that the boy is slipping.

Of course it might be that he is picking the wrong stories to start with, stories that have too much of a Continental angle to appeal generally.

At any rate the answer in regard to "The Magician" is that it won't do from a box office standpoint in this country. At the Capitol it undoubtedly will have a big week for it started off Sunday like a house afire, but it can't stand up sufficiently strong to warrant a second week and an Ingram picture should do that. When it hits the rest of the country it will droop at the b. o.

There is one thing that picture does do; it reveals a potential Jannings in Paul Wegener, who plays the title role. Wegener gives that characterization a startling fidelity and there are times when his work is on a par with some of the best things that Jannings has done.

Alice Terry, co-featured with Wegener, stalks through the picture as Trilby without showing a single flash of fire that would be worthy of comment. As for Ivan Petrovich, her leading man, his performance is convincing enough although in a number of shots he appeared to be suffering from an affliction of the left side. If that is true then it is to be regretted, for facially he does remind one of Conway Tearle as a type and he can troupe.

"The Magician" is more than anything else a personally conducted tour of certain parts of Europe. "Paris" with a shot of the city, "The Latin Quarter" with another shot, and the titles just as trite as the quotes indicate are a sample of what one gets. Then there is "Monte Carlo" presented in the same formula. Thanks for the buggy ride, Rex, it may save a trip abroad.

As for the story, it is that of a fanatic, a doctor of medicine who has gone daft on magic, and whose researches through the lore of the ancients had revealed to him a formula for the creation of human life by magic. The only hitch in the gag was in the fact that one had to kill to create.

The final touch necessary was the heart's blood of a maiden, one fair as to skin and hair and possessed of either grey or blue eyes. Miss Terry is just such, and the half-crazed magician prevents her marriage to the doctor hero of the story. Under his hypnotic force he compels her to marry him, although she is a wife in name only, the magician reserving her for his final experiment in the production of life.

At the last minute she is rescued by her unlucky suitor and her uncle, the crazed man, is cast into a fiery furnace of his own making, into which he tried to force the rescuer of the girl. The final scenes show the sorcerer's castle in flames.

Photographically the picture is pretty in spots, but it seems a long while to wait for a few minutes of real action before the fight over the furnace takes place.

Fred.

LONDON

British National Pictures, Ltd., subject releasing through Famous Players. From an "original" by Thomas Burke, with Herbert Wilcox, director. Features Dorothy Gish. No cast listed on program or screen. At the Rivoli, New York, week Oct. 23. Running time, 61 mins.

Another of British National's output featuring Dorothy Gish, but this time from the pen of Thomas Burke, he of Limehouse narration fame. Considering Burke's literary achievements in that direction this scenario is both porus and obvious. It would still be a weak story no matter who had written it.

Productionally it rates with the normal first run matter this country has become accustomed to expect. That is the action is nicely lighted, settings are to the point and the tone of the photography good. But neither Miss Gish nor her unnamed support can hold it up. That it runs but 61 minutes shows the good sense of Wilcox, directing, in not prolonging this simple Cinderella tale.

In toto, "London" can go into the major film auditoriums as a filler. It'll never break a record. Normal gross will be a pretty good week for it, and it's most liable to be responsible for receipt totals dipping a bit where it plays.

The action rises out of the slums of London, where Miss Gish is a pure ragamuffin sold in bondage to a scheming Chinaman from whom she flees, still chaste of course. That an artist has been nosing around and sees in her the likeness of his dead sweetheart leads to the mother of the deceased girl adopting the waif as the latter is discovered fainting from hunger by the wealthy lady's man-about-town nephew.

Having been taught how to handle a knife and fork, the former cotton-stockinged young lady is doing very well for herself in society, and especially with the nephew, until she who has claims on him steps in. Just what those claims are is not divulged, but it blights youth's young dream, and the disillusioned neophyte goes back to Limehouse. However, the artist pursues and persuades, and the climax shows them married.

It's an all-British cast outside of Miss Gish, and not a bad one. The men are not handsome brutes, but play capably and rather easily. The women, perhaps, lack looks, but it may be a boon to not have to gaze upon a series of rosebud mouths and baby faces. Whoever did the Chinese tong leader made that bit stand out, while the Mme. Fouchard of the story, who persecutes and sells the young damsel, has been coached in an arms akimbo manner that detracts.

Wilcox opens up with views of the already much pictured spots of London to show that the location is on the level. Later in the running he delves into a Henley regatta for a few interesting moments and has also included a few snaps of Paul Whiteman and his 28 men pretty well bunched on their stand in the Kit Kat Club. This scene, at least should prove to bandsmen who see it the handicap of which Whiteman complained at the Kit Cat.

Miss Gish has done this sort of thing before. Many times. It can hardly be termed an exacting role as far as she is concerned. At one point she turns in a particularly trim and neat Charleston and is standard in her conception of the underworld virgin. Little or no comedy in the picture, a point which would have helped had it been brought out, and Wilcox has been satisfied to depict the well-known Thames embankment against a back-drop.

A matinee Rivoli audience received it indifferently.

Skig.

LOVE'S BLINDNESS

Elinor Glyn production from original story by her. Pauline Starke and Antonio Moreno featured. Directed by John Francis Dillon. At Loew's New York one day, Oct. 23. Running time, 66 minutes. Released by Metro-Goldwyn.

Vanessa Levy...............Pauline Starke
Hubert Culverdale..........Antonio Moreno
Alice ....Lilyan Tashman
Benjamin Levy..............Sam De Grasse
Charles Langley............Douglas Gilmore
Marchioness ....Kate Price
Marquis ....Tom Ricketts
Col. Dangerfield, V. C.........Earl Metcalf
Oscar Isaacson.............George Waggner
Mme. De Jainon...................Rose Dione
Valet ....Ned Sparks

Elinor Glyn's latest story supervised by herself for Metro-Goldwyn-Mayer failed to get a Broadway de luxe week's run, and the first slant that the street had of it was at Loew's New York last week, where it was the bill for a single day.

Of course, M-G-M make the defense that so many of its productions are doing sufficient business to warrant holding over for a second week at the Capitol leaves it impossible to keep up with their release schedule and put all the pictures in the house that they would like to.

That would be all right if it were not that the organization could slip the pictures into Loew's State for a week's first run, and the possibility that the combination house would get a better result on business than following the Capitol with a picture. However, the fact remains that "Love's Blindness" went into the New York for a single day.

The picture is nicely cast and directed and the photography particularly good. The story isn't anything that one would rave about, rather one of those tales that the slaveys "back home" would just love to gush over, but which don't mean a thing in this country.

It is the tale of a money lender who married a daughter of the nobility and who promised his wife on her death-bed that their daughter should marry to the station from whence she came.

To that end he seeks out the young Earl of St. Austel, Hubert Culverdale (Antonio Moreno), who has backed an aeroplane company which cannot proceed without further funds. If it smashes, that will involve the young Earl's friends whom he got to invest, and suggests the marriage of his daughter.

The Earl, after considering overnight, consents. The two are married. The young bride (Pauline Starke) is much in love with the Earl and believes that he asked for her hand after seeing her at the opera, the marriage arrangement having been broached to her by her father the night after the opera. But the Earl does not see matters in that light, believing his bride to have been aware of the plot which her father engineered through the banks to refuse loans, which brought about his acceptance of the money lender's proposal.

'Tis a pretty tale, to read in the pantry, after you are through with the dishes and silver and the glasses are all back in place.

Miss Starke walks away with all the honors, and there are certain moments in the picture when she reminds one very much of Gloria Swanson. Given a chance she might be Gloria Swanson. All that she seems to need is the picture. Mr. Moreno is very conventional in his characterization of the Earl. Lilyan Tashman as a jealous Duchess, who had her eye on the

Earl and wanted to break up the pair after they were married, put a lot of real work in that character. Sam De Grasse as the girl's father was very convincing

But all in all it is just a program picture and not worthy of a general splurge nor more than a couple of days' booking at the most. It won't stand up for a week. *Fred.*

THE ICE FLOOD

A Universal-Jewel directed by George B. Seitz, starring Kenneth Harlan and Viola Dana. From the story by Johnstone McCulley, adapted by James O. Spearing. At the Hippodrme, New York, Oct. 18. Running time, 61 minutes.

Jack DeQuincy............Kenneth Harlan
Marie O'Neill................Viola Dana
Dum-Dum Pete............Frank Hengney
"Cougar Kid"...............Fred Kohler
James O'Neill..........De Witt Jennings
Cook ....Kitty Barlow
Thomas DeQuincy............James Gordon

Fair northwest lumber camp story that will do for the average daily change house, but it isn't strong enough to be played for a full week in a house of the type of the Hippodrome. If the Hip doesn't get better screen material it will lose out on the picture end and will have to take to showing second runs of better productions. As far as this picture goes it is a corking melodrama of the type that they eat up in the 10-15 houses, and as such will satisfy the average audiences.

Kenneth Harlan and Viola Dana are starred and both get the most out of it. Harlan as the son of the lumber king goes into the timber region to "clean-up" the camps in which his father is interested. He refuses to take his father's name and makes a bet that he can do it on his own. His dad does not know that the boy, who has just returned from Oxford, where he has finished his education, has been crowned light heavyweight collegiate fighter. The boy cleans up the bullies and stops the bootlegging that has made the camps fall off in work; at the same time winning the daughter of the superintendent.

To give the picture a kick there is an ice flood staged. This was to be the real thriller, but the manner in which the kick was cut into the story failed to give the desired suspense, for the shots with the heroine tied in a boat supposedly in the path of the onrushing ice were taken with little ice showing.

One corking fist battle between the camp bully and the hero, in which the men seem to batter themselves rather heavily, but when it is all over the hero hasn't even his hair mussed.

Don't go too strong on the picture because of the week's run at the Hip. It doesn't stand-up as of week run calibre, but was used at the Hip because the Hip can't get anything better.

George B. Seitz, who directed, handled the story in typical serial manner. *Fred.*

GREAT K. & A. TRAIN ROBBERY

William Fox release, starring Tom Mix. Adapted from book by Paul Leicester Ford's book. Lewis Seiler production. At Loew's New York one day, Oct. 21. Running time, around 56 minutes.

Probably the fastest picture in action ever filmed. This Tom Mix latest starts in action and never stops. It's through before you know it, leaving the impression the picture has not run over 30 minutes, whereas it goes 55.

Within the first thousand feet a witness will say, "That's a lot of action to start with," and wonder when it's going to slow down. It never does.

Action alone here would have placed this Mix in a Broadway first-run if one had been available. For intermingled with the melodramatics is plenty of comedy, much to real laughs.

There are thrills with the opening scenes, finding Mix sitting in a basket on a very long rope reaching up to the top of the Royal Gorge in Colorado, where the picture was mostly taken. Discovered by train robbers, Tom slides down the rope to land right in "Tony's" saddle.

From that moment the agile Mix starts to do things and never stops, winding up by swimming across a stream to capture a band of about 15 bandits, single handed. If you believe that you can believe some of the other things, but they happen, nevertheless, and through the way they are done, one can overlook plausibility.

Otherwise and in continuity this picture is perfect as a western. Mix doing new stunts and adding a love interest besides. In character he is a detective from Texas, sent for by the K. & A. Railroad to hunt down the train robbers. A secretary of the president of the road is in cahoots with the robbers, tipping them off on coin deliveries by express. Mix appears first in the picture as an apparent bandit himself, masked, and rescues the president's daughter, "the girl," who believes he is a highwayman.

Besides a western and a bandit story, this is almost a railroad tale in addition.

Tom Mix, always the great looking guy in a picture, has set a high mark for the "western boys" in this one. They will have to go a lot to approach it in action; and, in fact, Tom will have to do the same to keep up with his record here.

"The Great K. & A. Train Robbery" could safely be billed as the fastest-moving picture ever put on the screen. *Sime.*

DAME CHANCE

Releasing concern not flashed. Picture features Robert Frazer, Julanne Johnston and Mary Carr. Directed by Bertram Bracken. Cast includes David Hartford, Gertrude Astor, Lincoln Steadman, Jane Keckley, Joan Hathaway and J. T. Prince. At Loew's, New York, as half of double bill, one day, Oct. 15. Running time, 75 mins.

No reason in the world for this one to run an hour and a quarter. Sixty minuts would have been plenty. It's a slow moving actionless story of a financially pressed stock actress, who finally marries her masculine benefactor, after he has refused to take advantage of his position.

Incidentally, this film was Bertram Bracken's second directing effort on a double feature program. The other one was "Speeding Thru," and the better of the duo.

Julanne Johnston plays the depressed heroine, and Bracken has seriously handicapped his output by using up much footage of her depressed morale. The twist of the apartment donor being straight-laced is an interest-provoking angle, if unreasonable.

It is told that (J. T. Prince) has a wife in a sanatarium who had previously left him, and he is testing womanhood through Gail to regain his faith in the feminine. He falls in love with his experiment, and she with him, but the happy finish isn't reached until the wife dies.

Basically, the picture had a chance if concisely handled, but Bertram gummed it up by padding. Theatrically, it holds the usual exaggerated dressing room scenes with this such a recurrent fault among filmdom at large that it seems few directors have ever bothered to go backstage to take a look.

The cast is uniformly okay on performance, Miss Johnston apparently being under too many orders to gain predominance other than as regards footage. There seems little excuse to have featured Robert Frazer and Mary Carr. The latter might as well not have been in the picture for the brief moment she is viewed, while Prince overshadows Frazer. Gertrude Astor and Lincoln Steadman comprise the unessential secondary love interest.

Interior sets are substantial and help dress the film, but "Dame Chance" will never get out of the middle class auditoriums. Had it been handled properly it might have been outstanding among independent releases (and it is presumed this is an independent). It still could be given added value by substantial slicing. *Skig.*

HIS JAZZ BRIDE

Warner Bros. production, featuring Marie Prevost and Matt Moore. At the Columbus, New York (25c. grind), Oct. 14, one day. Running time, 65 minutes.

The Husband...................Matt Moore
The Wife......................Marie Prevost

This feature is of the type screen story that had its vogue about five years ago. The kind of a tale that Anita Stewart loved in the days that she was first under the Louis B. Mayer management. As a feature for the rank and file of grind houses it will do well enough on the double feature bills, but that is about all.

The story deals with the wives who, through their extravagance, drive husbands into debt and almost to ruin. In this case the story deals with two couples, one a government employe and the other a young lawyer. The latter is just marrying, with the government attache his pal and best man at the wedding.

It is his wife who puts the jazzy ideas into the young bride's head, and the result is that the two almost lose their lives on a pleasure steamer that is unseaworthy, but was passed by her husband because he needed the money slipped to him as a bribe to meet his debts, incurred by the wife. When the two husbands dash down the bay in a motor boat to save the day the young wife has a change of heart and starts housekeeping for the lawyer husband and casts off all her flighty friends.

The boat explosion and sinking are poorly done in miniature.

Marie Prevost has taken on dangerous weight. Matt Moore plays the sap husband with his usual finesse. *Fred.*

MIDNIGHT LOVERS

First National production co-featuring Lewis Stone and Anna Q. Nilsson in adaptation by Carey Wilson from play, "Collusion." John Francis Dillon directed; George Marion, Jr., did the titles, and Wilson also the continuity and editing. Ran 69 minutes at the Hippodrome, where it's in for the week of Oct. 25. Principal players with the co-features are Chester Conklin, John Roche and Gale Henry, first and last not given screen credit.

Sexy title is derived from the situation where the husband and wife, unwilling divorcees, are forced to spend the night in a common bedroom after it had all been arranged for the pair to separate.

The wife thereafter, to conform with English justice (London locale) is confronted with the problem on the morrow of making her solicitor believe she has complied with all the technicalities he has planned to ease her path towards a British divorce.

The husband takes it on his own to give both the barrister and the male interior decorator who has been playing a light heavy role (providing one can conjure up the vision of an interior decorator being that serious) with the usual happy ending eventuating.

It's a quasi-war tale. Lewis Stone is a flying ace. Anna Q. Nilsson is his bride of a fortnight. Thence his return to the front, where a meddling aunt is misled anent the husband's faithfulness. The wife, apprised of this, arbitrarily takes it upon herself to arrange the divorce. The usual screen misunderstandings that would ordinarily be explained away in a jiffy in real life accounts for the suspense.

Sort of lightweight in plot material, despite the adaptation from an alleged "play success," it is sustained by the directorial trimmings and the cast.

Chester Conklin has a few but effective comedy opportunities, and Gale Henry, she of the humorous physiognomy, who is equally unheralded and unsung by screen titling, holds up her end with a clown maid role. John Roche is the interior decorator, a good-looking boy and not altogether unsympathetic despite the "nance" part. Roche seems a new face on the screen, and while too finely chiseled a phsyog, he is well cast in semi-"heavy" roles.

For the rest, the opening military atmosphere starts the proceedings briskly. The flying squadron escorts the ace and his bride to the wedding nuptials and the miscarried flying honeymoon is a human sidelight.

A diverting picture, it runs a bit overlong and is by no means a week-stand offering at the Hip, where the house is starved for flicker material. Just a daily changer but withal a satisfying program feature, wherein the names of the featured pair must be made to count at the box office besides the picture's title. *Abel.*

MARRIAGE LICENSE

William Fox presents screen version of stage play, "The Pelican," by F. Tennyson Jesse (relative of Lord Tennyson, once poet laureate of England) and H. M. Harwood. Directed by Frank Borzage. Screen version by Bradley King. In cast are Alma Rubens, featured; Walter McGrail, Richard Walling, Walter Pidgeon, Charles Lane, Emily Fitzroy, Langhorne Burton, Arthur Rankin, Edgar Norton. At Fox's New Academy of Music, New York, week Oct. 17. Running time, 70 minutes.

A well-done play of sentiment with Alma Rubens in the emotional role of a mother torn between love of a man and love of her son. The part gives her an exceptional opportunity for emotional scenes and it is upon her acting that the force of the production rests.

She has every accessory of splendid backgrounds, direction and supporting cast, and the story has a certain grip that holds, although quiet drama without action in the more common terms of the screen. The settings are magnificent, with particular emphasis upon fine handling of light and shades in rich pictorial compositions. In this respect the whole picture is de luxe.

The purpose of placing the appeal on the high artistic quality of the film goes to the extent of giving it an "unnappy ending," which in this case rather heightens the sentimental role than otherwise. The substance of the story being quiet, restrained drama, the direction sees to it that the playing is in the so-called repressed style, a subdued treatment called for in this case and giving the play a certain charm.

The whole offering is appropriate to the new idea in the Fox establishment to provide high-class screen product of distinction and breaking away from the hokum variety of flicker melodrama. For high intelligence and artistic standard this picture takes its place with the best of the recent output from the Fox studios.

The heir to a British title brings home a commoner as his bride, to the resentment of his strong-minded and race-proud mother. The young wife is about to become a mother, but this does not deter the dowager in her determination to separate the couple. She is successful in having them divorced on trumped-up evidence and even carries out her purpose to have the young son disowned.

Years pass. The young boy has grown to young manhood in France, when the suffering woman meets and loves another. She is about to win deserved happiness in a new union when the boy's noble father comes upon the scene. In the struggle between the woman's love and her maternal unselfishness, she renounces her own happiness, to return again to the castle in order that the boy may have a noble name and a career.

The whole story is presented, in production and in acting, on a plane of dignity, without cheap theatrical device, leaving its appeal real and genuine. *Rush.*

SPEEDING THRU

W. T. Lackey picture releasing through Ellbee Pictures Corp., and directed by Bertram Bracken. Cast includes Judy King, Creighton Hale, Lionel Belmore, Robert McKim and E. L. duDuit. At Loew's New York as half double bill, one day, Oct. 15. Running time, 58 mins.

Auto race story sprinkled with a smattering of college atmosphere. At least the hero (Creighton Hale) is supposedly a student. It's a conventional tale and should find its level among the minor houses where it can pass as average fare.

The dirt track race is the obvious punch, the girl driving her father's car to victory after her sweetheart is slugged into a daze by hired cohorts of a rival manufacturer. The parent is opposed to racing his product, but the daughter realizes his financial straits and the triumph saves the family from going overboard.

Judy King plays the speed-mad daughter, while Lionel Belmore is the safe and sane father, with Robert McKim the rival production head seeking the all important foreign contract of 10,000 cars. All do acceptably minus lending anything approaching a particular luster to their work.

Bracken, directing, carries the film along at a fair pace and has seen fit to include a few news weekly shots in the race, one of an accident being vividly recalled because of its being an actual crash caught in slow motion and perhaps the best of its kind ever sniped by a camera.

Lightweight comedy attempts dot the sequence to mild effect, but it's mostly a matter of waiting for the race which signals itself in the title. Being on dirt, it is more spectacular than the board track events, and Bracken has laid it out to build up attention. *Skig.*

THE BLOCK SIGNAL

Gotham Production, releasing through Lumas Film Corp. Directed by Frank O'Connor and features Ralph Lewis. Cast includes George Chesebro, Sidney Franklin, Jean Arthur and Hugh Allen. At Loew's Circle, New York, as half double bill Oct. 18, one day. Running time, 66 mins.).

Railroad story harking back to the days when engineers had their own engines. Maybe they still do on the coast roads; that's where the yarn is laid, but on the big eastern lines the throttle boys now have to use any of about three moguls to make their runs. Anyway, the steel rail thing is generally interesting. Although "The Block Signal" is the usual cut and dried example it should be suitable for the minor screens.

O'Connor, directing, has thrown in a wreck, a fist fight while a train runs wild and various "shots" from other railroad films. He evidently thought enough of some of these lifted views to repeat 'em. They're unquestionably on tap twice and could advantageously be cut to once apiece, inasmuch as the film uses up six minutes over an hour, and that's unnecessary.

Flashes of a round house and the inside working of a cab while in action kept them looking, more so than the script.

This tells of a veteran pilot (Ralph Lewis) framed into a wreck by a scheming fireman (George Chesebro) who seeks promotion, and the former's daughter. Color blindness being an always present terror to an engineer, the younger man calls a signal wrong on his superior and then jumps from the cab. The resultant crash reduces the engineer to a flagman at a crossing where he continues his work on an automatic brake contrivance. The implausibility of one man wrecking two passenger trains for so slight a cause is not offset in the screen sequence.

Having to take out "Old Betsy," the engine, to haul the directors' special, the promoted fireman gets in a jam with his coal shoveler when the latter remonstrates with him for the way he is handling the beloved bus. Besides which the underling has fired for "Smiling Joe" and has suspicions about the new appointee. This leads to a hand-to-hand struggle all over the cab, with No. 8 coming the other way.

Joe sees "Betsy" thunder past, grabs his telegraph operating daughter, her fiance and his aged cronie, hops a hand car and all pump to beat the special to a certain switch. As Joe has attached one-half of his invention to his former engine it only remains for him to bolt the remaining portion to the ties, and then wait to see if it works. It does.

Lewis plays the grayed hair averagely leaving cast honors to Sidney Franklin, who does a Dutch yardman and has all the comedy. Jean Arthur is the girl and looks okay. Hugh Allen makes an indifferent fiance, this latter pair strictly comprising the love interest.

Some of the titling doesn't ring true and there's no production to the picture other than the train stuff. The film will have to slip by on the railroad angle. It has little else, but within its class should have a chance. *Skig.*

COLLEGE DAYS

Tiffany production. Story and scenario by A. P. Younger, who also adapted "Brown of Harvard" to screen. Directed by Richard Thorpe under Younger's supervision. Photographers James C. McKay and Edwin P. Willis. Marceline Day and Charles Delaney featured. In preview Oct. 18. Running time, 65 minutes. (Footage, 7,300).

Mary Ward....................Marceline Day
Jim Gordon....................Charles Delaney
Larry Powell....................James Harrison
Phyllis....................Duane Thompson
Kenneth Slade....................Brooks Benedict
Louise....................Kathleen Key
Bessie....................Edna Murphy
Mr. Gordon....................Robert Homans
Kent....................Craufurd Kent
Bryson....................Charles Wellesley
Carter....................Gibson Gowland
Prof. Maynard....................Lawford Davidson
Coach....................Pat Harmon
Dean....................William A. Carroll

A spirited bit of entertainment, having to do with young collegians and co-eds and ending up with a splendidly worked bit of hokum in a big college football game. The materials of the story are not new, but the virtue of the picture is the freshness given to familiar matter.

It is full of jaunty boy sheiks and short-skirted flapper shebas in their loves and intrigues, jazzed up with the slang of the campus and enlivened with suggestions of wild roadhouse parties, "necking" episodes and all the rest of the much discussed lives of the younger generation. The picture does not, however, fall into the error of trying to play these elements up in any cheap bid for sensational sex stuff.

There is some spicy flirtation stuff, but it is presented unostentatiously and as an incidental to the story itself, which concerns the little romance of Mary and Jimmy, co-ed and football star.

One of the agreeable things is the jaunty way the campus sheiking is handled in a mild comedy spirit but without buffoonery. The seriousness of the juvenile romance also is attractive. And behind these pleasant story elements there is a wealth of beauty in settings.

The football climax never fails. Here it is splendidly done. No gridiron battle has ever been done more convincingly than this elaborate staging of a game. It is said a score of Pacific coast pigskin stars were brought in for the scenes. The results justify the care taken, for even in a projection room the shots of the game have a first-rate dramatic kick.

Nothing is overdone in atmosphere. The picture catches much of the reality of the campus and it makes all these young people rather charming realities. There are comedy bits involving the raw country boy in his clumsy Romeo ambitions, but even here they never go into burlesque for an easy laugh. The young leads are altogether charming juveniles, Marceline Day giving her part much grace.

A hokum subject well done in the best of modern technic. *Rush.*

THE MIDNIGHT KISS

Fox picture and an Irving Cummings production, directed by Cummings. Adapted by A. A. Cohn from John Golden's stage play, "Pigs." Cast includes Janet Gaynor, Richard Walling, Tempe Pigott, Arthur Housman, Doris Lloyd, Gladys McConnell, Gene Cameron, George Irving and Herbert Prior. At Loew's Circle, New York, as half of double bill Oct. 18, one day. Running time, 56 mins.

How close this studio output adheres to the legitimate original can't be said. "Pigs," as a stage play, had a fairly prolonged sojourn in New York, and must have contained more than its film disciple. This unwinds as a lightweight comedy that has no connection with its name. The name can be construed as leading to a sex theme, but there's nothing resembling that angle in this rural episode.

It doesn't rate the first-string theatres, but can easily fulfill its obligation on a double-feature program and may stand by itself where the requirements aren't too drastic.

An 18-year-old girl and her flighty love affairs are secondary, the story revolving around a younger sister and her youthful boy friend. Hence it's really kid stuff, with the juveniles pulling the boy's father out of a money hole by selling 250 pigs at $10 the squeal.

This product has been fairly handled by Cummings, the director, although there doesn't appear to be much meat to it as a picture. However, it's noteworthy for being absolutely void of a villain or "menace." The bank note is the overshadowing cloud, and that only appears by title. The film has its slow spots, but holding down to 56 minutes doesn't make the burden so obvious.

The picture does this much. It should tip off the Fox staff that if they want to make a series of juvenile stories, along the lines of "Seventeen," etc., they've got a bet in Janet Gaynor and Richard Walling. This pair do nicely here.

Rigidly clean, the censors can't bother it, and, despite it's being almost exaggerated fair-weather stuff, they laughed at in in this house (Circle), and there's nothing mincing about the mob that drops in at this 59th street corner.

Gladys McConnell lends an abundance of appearance to the older sister role, and Doris Lloyd makes a mother bit noticeable. Tempe Pigott also turns in a couple of laughs on her own as the Grandma, allowing a goat to give her a bump for one of 'em.

An intermediate film that files itself as among the better of that class. No call for real expenditure on production, and it must have been a cheap one to get rid of, but the settings are appropriate. A title change would probably do this film a lot of good. *Skig.*

That Model From Paris

Tiffany Production, featuring Marceline Day, young find of that organization, supported by Bert Lytell. Director, Louis J. Gasnier. Author of story not given, but plot credited to Gouverneur Morris' tale, "The Right to Live." Others in the cast are Eileen Percy, Ward Crane, Miss Dupont, Crauford Kent, Arthur Hoyt and Otto Lederer. At the New York, Oct. 22 (half double bill). One day. Running time, 64 minutes.

Fairly interesting romantic comedy with a fashionable modiste's salon as its locale and the lovely Marceline Day as a model. The story is told in a light comedy vein and with an absence of dramatic splash. At one point it looked as though the ground was being laid for a fist fight between Bert Lytell and the heavy, but the opportunity was passed up in favor of a quiet finish.

This treatment gives opportunity for a capital emotional scene for Miss Day, who handled it very naively. The picture thus makes its appeal entirely upon the interesting romance and the excellent acting of the leading woman. Emphasis is put on a pictorial splash in a fashion show somewhat after the manner of "Fig Leaves," although this bit is not in the same class as the Fox revel in styles.

The settings and the artistic quality of the entire production are up to the high standard established by this producer in the past year or so, which is to say that these elements are remarkably well managed. Fine backgrounds are strikingly featured in the recent Tiffany output and with stories of dignity and intelligence, the technical excellence contributes much character to trade-mark.

The heroine obtains employment as a model with a fashionable modiste, thanks to the efforts of a gilded youth who has designs upon her. The girl arrives at the salon just as they learn a famous French model they expected to feature in a fashion display could not be present. The new model is pressed into service, instructed to cover her ignorance of French by pretending she knew no English except the word "No."

A son of the owner of the dress shop falls in love with the girl, but she holds him off by pretending not to understand his love making. It is here the gilded youth presses his claims upon the model, insisting that she come to dinner in his apartment. The girl is torn between her fear of this entanglement and her awakening love for the honest lover (Lytell).

In the end, the gilded youth's campaign of conquest is defeated by a suspicious mistress, while the sincere suitor is brought to understand that the girl is altogether worthy. Absence of strong dramatic material is the weakness of the picture and graceful playing its strength.

These materials make it a mildly interesting picture and not much more. *Rush.*

SO'S YOUR OLD MAN

Gregory La Cava Production presented by Famous Players-Lasky, starring W. C. Fields, with Alice Joyce and Charles Rogers featured. At the Rivoli, New York, week Oct. 30. Running time 67 minutes.

Samuel Bisbee................W. C. Fields
Princess Lescaboura...........Alice Joyce
Kenneth Murchison.........Charles Rogers
Alice Bisbee...............Kittins Reichert
Mrs. Bisbee.................Marcia Harris
Mrs. Murchison..................Julia Ralph
Jeff ....Frank Moneg̃umery
Al ....Jerry Sinclair

Boys, here is a combination that for laughs and gags would be hard to beat. W. C. Fields in "So's Your Old Man" is in the funniest picture he has made to date. He is one end of the combination; the other is Gregory La Cava (otherwise Mr. McAlpin), the same who directed a string of Richard Dix pictures that were such outstanding hits.

In "So's Your Old Man" no great outstanding comedy wallop, but it is a series of humorous situations and laugh compelling bits that follow along in an endless train from the beginning to the end.

The story looks as though it might have had the benefit of the fine Italian hand of one Tom Gerahty, leads up to a point where Fields can logically introduce his famous golf game. That piece of business proves funnier on the screen than on the stage, and that means a whole lot.

But don't believe the golf bit is the funniest kick in the picture. There are others and lots. Fields' souse bit with a trick pony will be a wow to any audience, and his pantomime in the stateroom of a Pullman, where he is relating to the Spanish princess the events leading up to his present state of dejection, is as clever a piece of film acting and direction as have been seen in a long while.

Fields is Sam Bisbee, a glazier in a small New Jersey town. He lives in a tumbled down sort of a house with his wife and daughter, the latter a pretty girl courted by the son of the wealthy Murchisons. The day the story opens young Murchison calls to inform the girl that his mother is going to visit her that afternoon.

Mother arrives and all goes well until Pa Bisbee comes in from the shop, which is back of the house, and where he has been celebrating with a couple of cronies.

He gums the works but tells the haughty Mrs. Murchison that in a couple of days he is going to be as much of the social elect as she is. He has invented an unbreakable glass for automobiles and has been asked to demonstrate it before a convention of automobile men in Washington. He goes there, having his flivver equipped with the glass, parks it in front of the hotel while he goes in to see the committee and then comes a piece of business. His car is moved while he is in the hotel. When he returns armed with bricks and a hammer to go through with the test he picks another flivver, smashes the glass, then selects another with the same fate and, to escape arrest, must beat it without getting his own car.

Returning home on the train he decides to end it all by the poison route, but his battle is smashed. A few minutes later, when the train gives a lurch, he is thrown into the stateroom of the Spanish princess. Noting a bottle of iodine on the table before her, he believes she is ready to take the same route and startes to dissuade her.

As he relates his story her sympathy is aroused and she registers a mental reservation to help the disappointed man out. She does not inform him who she is, but tells him he may call her "Marie."

On the train with him were a couple of the village's old women gossips. They spread the story of his ride with a woman in a stateroom. It is around the home town like wildfire before he is back five minutes. To get up courage to go home he seeks out his serious drinking pals and the trio stage a bat that lasts three days. Meantime the princess has announced her intention to visit the little town and the social elect arrange a reception but are flabbergasted when she asks for "Old Sam." The party starts for his home and runs across the old boy headed that way himself, he having purchased a pony to present to the wife as a peace offering.

From that point on the story tells of the acceptance by society of the Bisbees, for the princess remains at their home, and Sam is selected to tee off the first ball at the opening of the new Country Club. That heads into the golf game. Atop of that there arrives the chairman of the auto men's convention, who discovered the real car and tested the glass for himself, found it was as claimed and is ready to hand over a million-dollar contract.

Fields is great and one doesn't have to say more. Charles Rogers looks as though he is going to be a better and better bet as he develops, and Kittens Reichert is a girl that will bear watching. Alice Joyce is looking a little as though she were going in too strenuously for reduction and it is showing in her face, although she gives a corking performance.

But it is Fields and the funny bits well directed that will send this one over. Right now it might be claimed as a wow of a burlesque on the visit of Queen Marie and all the more appreciated because of this.

Fred.

TAKE IT FROM ME

Universal-Jewel presented by Carl Laemmle, starring Reginald Denny. Adapted from the musical comedy by Will B. Johnstone and W. R. Anderson. Directed by William Seiter. At the Hippodrome, New York, week Nov. 1. Running time, 65 minutes.

Tom Eggett................Reginald Denny
Grace Gordon..............Blanche Mehaffy
Dick....................Ben Hendricks, Jr.
Van..............................Lee Moran
Cyrus Crabb.............Lucien Littlefield
Miss Abbott......................Ethel Wales
Gwen Forsythe.................Jean Tolley
Mrs. Forsythe....................Vera Lewis
Taxi Driver....................Tom O'Brien

Best picture the Hip has had to date from the standpoint of real entertainment to the type of audience that that house is drawing. It has laughs and laughs are what vaudeville audiences want. Seemingly the Hip is getting more of a vaudeville crowd than it is a picture audience. Reason must be that the picture fans are wise the moment they look at the title and the release as to the value of a screen attraction. However, the Hip's box office this week with the Denny picture should show an improvement.

"Take It From Me" has been adapted to the screen in a manner to lend a couple of added thrills. It opens with a race track scene and from there goes into the department store where the biggest part of the action is laid and a fashion show is so very well worked out it is a real asset. It is at least different from the fashion show angle. Incidentally the exhibitors can work out a fashion show with it to advantage. They don't know enough about the picture business over at the Hip yet to take advantage of this kind of a lead, so they did not have one this week.

Denny plays the hero who has a department store left to him by an uncle to bo his, providing he can run it for three months and show a profit.

Playing opposite Denney is a little girl, Blanche Mehaffy, who, if given a chance, is going to make her mark in films. She is of the Marie Prevost type, but younger and prettier. She can troup, too, and in this picture registers like a million dollars.

Lee Moran and Ben Hendricks, Jr., play ex-vaudevillians who are the pals of the hero, while the fortune seeking fiancee of the hero is handled by Jean Tolley, who fails to impress, although the role is rather an ungrateful one.

William Seiter directed and turned out a picture that keeps moving, although some of his comedy stuff at the counters seems to have been dragged in by the heels.

But the picture is "there," and it will please any audience. *Fred.*

SYNCOPATING SUE

Asher, Small & Rogers present Corinne Griffith in the screen version by Adelaide Heilbron of Reginald Goode's stage play. Directed by Richard Wallace. Distributed by First National. Running time 73 minutes. At the Strand, New York, week Oct. 31.

Susan Adams..............Corinne Griffith
Eddie Murphy..................Tom Moore
Arthur Bennett...........Rockliffe Fellows
Joe Horn.........................Lee Moran
Marge Adams...............Joyce Compton
Landlady ....Sunshine Hart
Marjorie Rambeau......Marjorie Rambeau

A highly entertaining light comedy translated from stage to screen with a good deal of skill and played amusingly by a cast of favorite film players. Nothing particularly important happens, but these very natural and lifelike people maintain interest consistently through a longer-than-ordinary picture. The one flaw is a tendency to gag in titles, due probably to a desire to pull easy laughs.

The production is too good in all other respects to employ cheap tricks of that sort. Here again is observed the tendency of the enlightened school of producers to depart from the cruder methods of film drama. The story is in a cheerful comedy mood and it maintains just that quality throughout. At one point there was an obvious opening for one of those he-man fist fights, but the director declined the invitation and allowed his play to flow on smoothly to a laughing finish. This is the better way.

There are several touches of sophisticated high comedy, as in the incident of the hard-boiled girl piano player from tin pan alley bluffing about her visit to the theatre manager among her friends, although the visit was a failure. The attitude also of the hero toward his sweetheart is also authentic Broadway. Always the atmosphere is convincing and never theatrical, which is not as common in screen plays as it should be.

Susan plays a piano in a Broadway sheet music store, and of course, has stage aspirations and hates ivory banging for a living. Eddie is a trap drummer who comes to Broadway looking for a job. He rooms in the same boarding house as Sue. They become acquainted when they both start for home from the same spot, and the girl has her fellow lodger arrested as a flirt because she thinks he is following her.

From that unpromising beginning there springs a love affair. Susan's piano thumping so irritates a theatre manager who has his office above the music shop that he sends for her. He gives her a chance, more to further his own unworthy designs than because he thinks she will make an actress. As a Bernhardt Susan is a flop and she scorns to vamp the manager, who turns his attention to her sister. Meanwhile Eddie has made good on the quiet with the leading cabaret orchestra of the town and has a chance to sail with it to London.

Sue learns that her sister has gone to the manager's apartment and goes thither bent on a rescue. When Eddie learns where Sue is, he decides on the London trip, instead of crashing into the manager's home for a rough and tumble as the old screen technique would have had it. So when all is straightened out, Eddie is on the Berengaria just moving out of the dock, when Sue catches up to him to tell him she loves him and all is well.

This lays the foundation for a laughing finish with Eddie leaping into the water from the steamer deck and Sue taking a header from the dock to meet him, while a jazz hound from the orchestra throws Eddie his bass drum as a live preserver, making the final tableau a comic one for a change.

Corinne Griffith never has screened a lovelier picture. She here discloses a quiet knack for polite comedy that gives her a new and altogethr charming aspect. Tom Moore has a typical role, done in his best style. Marjorie Rambeau appears as herself for one brief bit in the music shop.

The picture is best fitted for the high class clientele. It may be looked upon probably as thin stuff by the fans who dote on blood, battle and slapstick. *Rush.*

A Gentleman of Quality

Wesley Ruggles production, presented by Sam Zirler, released by Commonwealth. Story by H. H. VanLoan, directed by Wesley Ruggles, titles by Herbert Cruikshank. Starring George Walsh. Loew's New York, New York. Double feature bill. One day, Oct. 29. Running time, 56 minutes.

Jack Banning ....George Walsh
Marion Macey...................Ruth Dwyer
Richard Courtney.............Brian Dunlevy
Dorenea ....Luri di Cardi
Spanish Joe..................Lucian Prival

A little independent production that serves its purpose well enough. It has got punch enough to make it worth while on any of the daily change bills, especially in the houses where there is a double feature policy. It has a name in George Walsh that stands up well enough in front of the house, and on the whole there is enough action.

Secret service affair that has to do with silk smugglers working in with Chinks. Walsh, as the hero, is a rookie member of the S. S. and runs down the band when all the experienced operatives have failed. Love story runs along with the action.

Wesley Ruggles, who directed, got the story moving in the early chapters and kept it moving right to the finish.

Ruth Dwyer plays opposite the star, doing well enough with what was assigned her, but Walsh is the picture. Lura di Cardi, cabaret dancer and also a member of the S. S., copped the honors between the two women. Brian Dunlevy, as the heavy, failed to get over, but Lucian Prival, an assistant heavy, bore a most marked resemblance to Von Stroheim in some of the director's early picture acting days.

Fred.

LADDIE

Joseph P. Kenndy presents Gene Stratton Porter's "Laddie." Produced and directed by James Leo Meehan. Story adapted by Jeanette Porter Meehan. Distributed by Film Booking Offices. At the Stanley theatre, New York, one day, Oct. 22. Running time, 78 minutes.

Paul Stanton ....David Torrence
Little Sister ....Gene Stratton
Leon Stanton ....John Fox, Jr.
Mother Stanton ....Eulalie Jensen
Candace ....Aggie Herring
Laddie Stanton ....John Bowers
Pamela Pryor....................Bess Flowers
Mahlon Pryor ....Arthur Clayton
Mrs. Pryor ....Fannie Midgeley
Shelley Stanton..............Eugenia Gilbert
Robert Paget ....Richard Von Early

Here's a picture that stands on both legs, thanks to the type of story, its homey, wholesome atmosphere and cleanliness. With the screen surfeited with other kinds of stories, "Laddie" stands out like a beacon light.

It's not an expensive production, although it has a long cast. There isn't a single city scene, aside from one "shot" or two supposed to represent inside residence. It is all confined to the country where two "farms" are used to carry the entire romance.

Barring several exceptions, the direction holds well, the basic idea of Mrs. Porter's story being adhered to without it becoming too preachy or dry.

James Leo Meehan has done himself proud with a story that many of the high-hat directors would have scorned to handle.

As Mrs. Porter wrote stories that dealt mainly with kids, this one has a child angle that cannot be denied. And with the children having a mighty big part in its general enactment it is a certainty that the picture will make its best score in the neighborhoods and add further to its lustre in the theatres outside the big cities.

There are two love stories, with the windup having a most intense dramatic moment when an enraged father starts gunning for the son whom he believed had disgraced the family.

Several scenes seem a little exaggerated and one out of aplomb is where Laddie is plowing with flowers in his hat and on the harness, and he is wearing a collar, tie etc.

Photographically splendid. Some of the big scenes are nicely connected, this adherence to continuity another feather for Meehan.

The cast balances nicely. John Bowers and Bess Flowers make a handsome, youthful couple. Very excellent work also done by Gene Stratton and John Fox, Jr. *Mark.*

APRIL FOOL

Produced by Sam Zilbalist from the play "An April Shower," by Edgar Allan Woolf and Alexander Carr. Directed by Nat Ross; titles by James Madison; featuring Alexander Carr. Released by Chadwick Pictures Corporation. At Loew's New York, one day, Oct. 28. Running time, 76 mins.
Alexander Carr..............Jacob Goodman
Duane Thompson...........Irma Goodman
Mary Alden...................Amelia Rosen
Raymond Keane..............Leon Steinfeld
Mr. Applebaum...............Snitz Edwards
Nat Carr...................Moisha Ginsburg
Joseph Applebaum.........Edward Phillips
The Children.............Pat Moore, Baby Peggy and Leon Holmes

Jewish comedy drama with laughs due to able titling by James Madison.

Alexander Carr should never have consented to tie up with the weak, sloppy story from which "April Fool" was adapted. As Jacob Goodman, presser in an east side shop who is fired for letting a pair of trousers burn while engaged in an argument over the relative merits of a book, Carr is given every opportunity to turn loose on pathos, but the picture is very dull at the beginning while the story lacks the concentrated continuity which would have made this a really big film.

James Madison, responsible for the titling, may be given full credit for saving the picture from certain failure. Madison's titles make up for the lack of "gags," suspense and interest in the story. The titles make the rivalry of Applebaum (Snitz Edwards) and Goodman for the hand of Amelia Rosen hilariously interesting instead of ludicrously stupid. "Marry me and I'll let you wish for anything you want," pleads Applebaum, while poor Jake Goodman is maligned in screamingly funny terms.

Every sub-title in the picture carries a laugh and these laughs will carry the picture. Nat Carr, as Moisha Ginsburg, a marriage and business broker, does it to perfection.

A scene in the early part of the picture that gets a laugh is where Moisha is trying to sell Jake a dreamy nag and a delapidated wagon for $90. Jake finally makes an offer, "For the wagon and the harness I'll give you $6 but if I must take the horse too I give only $4."

This picture will be a money-getter in some sections.

DANGEROUS VIRTUE

Lee-Bradford production, released by the Aywon Corporation. No producer or director named. Alfred J. Hitchcock credited with editing and titling. At Loew's New York. Double feature bill. Oct. 29, one day. Running time, 57 minutes.
Beatrice Audley...............Jane Novak
Leon de Brique............Warwick Ward
Sonia Roubetski..........Julanne Johnson
Marc de Rouqueville..........Hugh Miller
Laura Westonray........Gladys Jennings
Sir Neville Moreton........Miles Meander

One of the striking examples of why British-made films are not acceptable to American audiences. Just a piece of junk and far from worthy even a place on a double-feature bill at Loew's New York. Incidentally, the Stanley, a 25c. grind house further down the street, is giving better screen entertainment in the main than does the New York at 40c. Despite this, the New York is almost invariably crowded.

"Dangerous Virtue" is just a piece of film junk and nothing more. The answer is apparent that no producer or director is credited, and the note that American editing and titling were tried to whip it into shape, but even then there was nothing that could be done to save the picture.

The New York's audience laughed at it and practically hooted it from the screen in derision.

The story is a much-involved tale of a cold English maid engaged to a hot-blooded Frenchman. She repelled his affection even though they were engaged. To test him, she has a girl friend who is her opposite in type when the Frenchman returns from a trip home. When he arrives she informs him that she has decided to call off the engagement and at the opportune moment the friend walks in.

Immediately the fiance flops to the other side and in a short time he and the friend are engaged. Then comes the wedding. However, it seems that the "friend" had been compelled to act as a decoy for a gambling den in London and this she confesses to the man that she is to marry, in a letter that is to be handed to him prior to the ceremony by his former fiancee. She, however, fails in her mission and he does not get the letter until after the ceremony. Then he thinks it was a trick on the part of the girl who discarded him, and he turns on the bride as well. She commits suicide while still in her wedding finery and the cheated groom swears vengeance.

Two years later he returns to England, after having spent the interim in North Africa, to wreak his vengeance. He again lays suit to the hand of the English girl who once spurned him, and she reciprocates his seeming affection.

Finally he tells her that with two people so much in love with each other there is no necessity of marriage, and the girl after some thought practically consents to become his mistress. At the finish it is disclosed to the man she didn't intend to trick him but retained the letter to shield her friend. It was only delivered after she had swooned and the servants had taken the note from her hands while she was unconscious and delivered it to whom it was addressed. That patches things up for the happy ending.

The whole is atrociously cast and acted. Jane Novak never does get started, and the best performance of the entire cast is contributed by Julanne Johnson. Gladys Jennings has just a bit in two scenes. Warwick, as the hero, from his performance here would never find a spot before the camera in America

---

in a leading role, as "Variety" (film) indicates he might, and the heavy contributed by Hugh Miller was an out-and-out laugh. Miles Meander had an ungrateful role which he proceeded to butcher in most approved manner.

This is one to lay off of unless you want to show your audience how badly pictures can be made in England, or otherwise write a new set of titles and treat it as a comedy. *Fred.*

Justice of the Far North

C. B. C. presents the Norman Dawn production, "Justice of the Far North." Story and direction by Norman Dawn. An Arctic melodrama. At the Columbus, New York, Oct. 29, one day. Released by Columbia Pictures Corp. Running time, 57 minutes.
Umluk.....................Arthur Jasmine
Wamba ....Marcia Manon
Nootka....................Lasca Winter
Mike Burke..............Chuck Reisner
Izzy Hawkins............Max Davidson
Dr. Wells..................George Fisher
Lucy Parsons..........Katherine Dawn
Broken Nose McGee..........Steve Murphy

Outside the Columbus theatre the name of Max Davidson was the only principal played up in the billing. This was the house billing, as Davidson plays a secondary role to Arthur Jasmine's and others.

The best known of the picture is Chuck Reisner. In this thriller of the Far North Reisner plays the heavy.

One of the best actors in the picture was a dog, "Ilak."

It is an out-and-out love story of the frozen north, that part where it is really frozen, and the main character lives in an igloo.

A brilliant bit of screen work is done by Mr. Jasmine as the Eskimo hero, and exceptional work is also performed by Miss Manlon as Wamba and Miss Winter as Nootka. These characters are made to stand out all the way. Reisner makes a corking villain and knows his heavy oats.

An American romance is woven into the story that makes such a hero out of Umluk, whose Arctic sweetie is coaxed from her happy ice-padded drawing room by the man in heavy winter clothing. Only an illiterate, uncouth Esky woman could stand for a sheik with a makeup like Chuck Reisner's.

Davidson, featured in the billing, played Izzy Hawkins, rascally partner of Burke's in the fur business, Izzy and Mike cheating the Eskimos out of their fine hides.

Some fine photographic shots of the wild animals of the Arctic seas and several thrilling climaxes.

Corking buy for any neighborhood. Not a costly picture in the making but has scenes that give the story unusual locale and enough melodrama to steam it along to bully results.

And that dog, Ilak, bears watching. He will poke his nose right along with any of the others better known. *Mark.*

PLEASURE GARDEN

Released through Artlee Picture Corp. Adapted from the novel by Oliver Sandys. Featuring Virginia Valli, with Carmeletta Geraghty also billed. Alfred J. Hitchcock, director. At Loew's New York Oct. 26 as one-half double bill, one day. Running time, about 60 minutes.

A sappy chorus girl picture, probably intended for the sappy sticks where they still fall for this sort of a chorus girl story. Those are about the only places which could use "Pleasure Garden," other than the one-dayers, and Loew's New York, a one-dayer, doubled it up with "Dangerous Friends," even worse.

It's a tale of the smart chorister and another, the latter fresh from the country. The chorus girl from

---

the country proves the "smarter" in that way. About the film's best virtue is that it has been kept clean. The title, possibly attractive to the balcony low-brows, is merely of the name of the theatre where the chorus girls are engaged.

Thoroughly foolish story, illogical, implausible, which also takes in Carmeletta Geraghty's dancing.

Virginia Valli played a rather sympathy-getting "good" chorister, but that only in looks, with little else to look after. The male principals performed fairly.

Independents might better sidestep these 30c. stories. They don't make good pictures, and that goes double for most of the indies.

With the "Prince Ivan" character in this one, maybe the foreign market was in mind. In that case, and another version, the picture might tell a different sales price tale abroad. *Sime.*

Eucharistic Congress

Official motion picture record of the Eucharistic Congress of Chicago presented by His Eminence George Cardinal Mundelein. Prolog by S. L. Rothafel, musical score by Otto Singenberger and Erno Rapee. At the Jolson theatre, New York, for two weeks, November 8. Running time, 98 minutes.

The official motion picture record of the Eucharistic Congress of Chicago was presented for the first time publicly at the Jolson theatre, New York, Monday night. The picture is a religiously inspiring production, although a truthful record of the events leading to the four days of ceremonies held on Soldiers Field in Chicago and the final day celebrated at Mundelein, Ill.

It is to be presented as a road show in the principal cities of the country with the purpose to finance the sending of prints of the pictorial record to the world at large and the schools and churches of the Catholic faith the world over, so that all of the faith may witness what occurred at the first Eucharistic Congress ever to be held in America.

The picture in its effect is more than a record of the actual events, it is a revelation to all, no matter what faith or creed, that there is in this jazzy world of ours of today a tremendous belief and faith in God and His works.

Despite that, this picture is one that records the events at a Catholic conclave, it is one that all churches, no matter what their denomination, can point to as one of the most tremendous of all revivals in religious faith. It should be an inspiration to other denominations, this gathering of the Catholics from all over the world; something that should and must awaken in them a responsive chord to their own faith.

And how effectively was it all carried out. From the standpoint of the theatre one might say that here was staged the greatest of outdoor spectacles in scores of years. It drew a million people in one day alone in Chicago and that in itself should speak for master showmanship or an order that even those of the various fields of entertainment endeavor where huge amphitheatres are needed, might study to their advantage. A crowd of 1,000,000 crowded into one little town, and so well handled and policed that there isn't a single instance on the screen of ineffective handling.

As to the presentation itself:

There were a few moments prior to the picture taken up with speeches.

First, was an explanation by Msgr. Quille of Chicago (who acted as secretary to the Eucharistic Congress), as to the why and wherefore of the picture. He stated that he felt the film carried a message. Not a message for Catholics in particular, but a message to all mankind that religion was far from dead and that it is still the biggest thing in the life of the world today.

In addition to this, the monsignor distributed credits for the making of the picture, first mentioning that Martin Quigley of the "Exhibitor's Herald," Chicago, had made it possible to interest William Fox and Winfield R. Sheehan, president and vice-president, respectively, of the Fox Film Corporation in the project of making a picture that would be a historic record of the congress, and then topped that (to tremendous applause) with the fact that the picture, about to be shown, was a gift from the Fox Film Corporation.

This Msgr. Quille followed by relating that the first man he had met from the organization who was to have the direction of the filming of the congress was an A. P. A., a man named Hall (Ray Hall of Fox Varieties), whose assistance, according to the monsignor, was almost invaluable.

It was, Hall said, Msgr. Quille who wrote the titles and edited the film down to theatre length from the 30,000 feet shot.

He then credited S. L. Rothafel as a Jew for having staged the prolog and others of the same faith for their assistance in making the presentation possible, not mentioning names, but grouping them as musicians and newspaper men.

A humorous touch was added by the monsignor's mention that in the presentation he has had the most able assistance of "the two Hayses," meaning Cardinal Hayes of New York and Will H. Hays, president of the M. P. P. D. A., which led to a natural introduction of Will Hays and also of Secretary of Labor Davis, both of whom spoke.

The Secretary preceded Hays and made an address frequently punctuated by applause, his appearance being particularly appropriate, since it was he who carried and delivered the message of welcome to the Eucharistic Congress from President Coolidge.

Hays' speech was one that dwelt on religious tolerance so impressively it held the audience, although this usually excellent extemperaneous talker read his address. At its conclusion it was tumultously received and it certainly tied up the picture business for all time with the churches.

A gesture that exhibitors should not overlook, for it will in time react in their favor.

Then the picture itself:

It started in Rome and finished in Mundelein, Ill. Not a single thing that happened in the tour of the 12 princes of the church in their journeys to the congress was missed. Their receptions abroad, their welcome to America in New York, the tremendous crowds to receive them, the parades, the official welcomes by Mayor Walker and Governor Smith of New York, those of the state officials of Illinois and the Mayor of Chicago; their trip across country and finally the four days of the tremendous outpourings of the pilgrims at Soldiers' Field in Chicago culminating in a really tremendous spectacle at Mundelein, Ill.

The various Cardinals were greeted with applause on each of their appearances. The pictures of the crowds in Chicago and at Mundelein are really beyond description.

The picture of the Eucharistic Congress is being shown at the Jolson under a rental arrangement with the Shuberts, they being paid $3,250 weekly for the house. After two weeks the picture is to go to Boston, at the Boston O. H., and after that, in all likelihood, the third stand will be Chicago, with Baltimore, Philadelphia, Pittsburgh and other cities to follow.

In these cities it will be presented as a road show. For this purpose a special committee headed by Msgr. Quille has been set up in offices in the Longacre building, New York. Other members of the committee who are acting at the request of Will H. Hays are J. J. McCarthy, Pat Casey and Winfield R. Sheehan. Paul C. Mooney is managing director of the film on tour.

It was unusual to Msgr. Quille, acting as a showman, but he placed his position frankly before the audience, which on the opening night was in a considerable measure composed of gentlemen of the cloth of his faith, stating that he was trying to drive home the message of religion with the hope that the message would be accepted in the spirit in which it was presented.

After the road tour the film is to be generally distributed. In the event the exhibitor can not find a place for it on his regular program, or if the regular program will not permit of a break to admit it, it would be a good thing to take it on for special showings, through an arrangement with the churches and societies of his territory.

It is interesting and it is inspiring. No one will deny that.

Fred.

We're in the Navy Now

Edward Sutherland Production presented by Adolph Zukor and Jesse L. Lasky, starring Wallace Beery and Raymond Hatton. Chester Conklin and Tom Kennedy featured. An original story by Monty Brice. At the Rialto, New York, for a run, beginning Nov. 6. Running time, 60 mins.

Knockout Hansen .... Wallace Beery
Stinkey Smith .... Raymond Hatton
Capt. Stiffe .... Chester Conklin
Homicide Harrigan .... Tom Kennedy
Radio Officer .... Donald Keith
Madelyn Phillips .... Lorraine Eason
U. S. Admiral .... Joseph W. Girard
Admiral Puckerlip .... Max Asher

This looks to be the biggest laugh hit on the screen since "Tillie's Punctured Romance" came along years ago. It is a solid hour of laughs, one bigger than the other, and if they thought "Behind the Front" was funny then this one is going to be a laugh riot. Wallace Beery and Raymond Hatton are again the stars in a comedy of the world war, only this time the action takes place at sea on board a transport. With the two stars are Chester Conklin and Tom Kennedy, who help matters along in the fight for laughs.

It is all action and titles, both contributing a full share. George Marion, Jr., titled the picture.

At the opening of the picture Beery is a husky but dumb pug, managed by Raymond Hatton, the latter going 50-50 on everything except the beatings. At an athletic club K. O. Hansen meets Homicide Harrigan and the fight lasts to the extent of one punch, and Hansen is knocked clear of the ring and into one of the ringside seats. When he wakes up there the next morning his manager had faded from sight with the loser's end. A few days later, when the Navy is out recruiting with a parade, Hansen sees the manager, and a chase which follows takes both into the recruiting station, where they are whipped into line and before they can say a word they are singing the "Navy blues."

From that point on laugh follows laugh. They do everything that is possible to get them in Dutch, but both win decorations. They dump a boat load of visiting notables, including a foreign admiral, into the ocean, for which they are put to work peeling a couple of tons of potatoes. They see the captain locked in the ice box and can't help him until he is frozen stiff. They knock a spy cold and save the ship only to have the credit go to Homicide Harrigan, who is the chief petty officer of the boat they are on and who takes delight in making it tough for them. (It was he who was the tough sergeant in "Behind the Front.")

The picture belongs to Beery, Hatton and Kennedy, and the way they work together makes it seem too bad that the combination cannot be held together for additional pictures.

"We're in the Navy Now" is going to be a better box office bet than "Behind the Front," and that picture comes pretty near holding the box office record for the country of the 15th Birthday Group that Famous Players have turned out this year.

Lorraine Eason has the role of the heroine, and, with but little to do, manages to make herself more than noticeable.

Fred.

Everybody's Acting

Famous Players-Lasky comedy. An original story by Marshall Neilan, adapted by Benjamin Glazer and directed by Neilan. At the Rivoli week of Nov. 6. Running time, 65 mins.

Doris Poole .... Betty Bronson
Michael Poole .... Ford Sterling
Anastasia Potter .... Louise Dresser
Ted Potter .... Lawrence Gray
Thorpe .... Henry Walthall
Ernest Rice .... Raymond Hitchcock
Clayton Budd .... Stuart Holmes
Peter O'Brien .... Edward Martindel
Paul Singleton .... Philo McCullough
Bridewell Potter .... Jed Prouty
Barbara Potter .... Jocelyn Lee

An intensely artificial and "gaggy" picture, made entertaining by its splendid cast and by a certain vigor in its hokum comedy. The names in the cast insure its pull at the boxoffice, and its properity. But it is a pity the efforts of so brilliant an assembly of players could not have been applied to something more worthy.

The gist of the story is that four actors and an editor adopt an orphaned girl baby and bring her up in back-stage atmosphere, training her to all the accomplishments that will one day make her a successful actress. In due time she falls in love with the scion of a newrich family. The young man's managing mama makes inquisition into the girl's antecedents.

The syndicate of fathers call in the stage carpenter and the property room staff of the theatre to stage a fashionable menage in their apartment in order to impress Doris' future mama-in-law. The actors play the girl's father, his titled friends and the perfect butler, and out of this situation they work up elaborate effects. The girl refuses to take part in the hoax, confessing the deception to the boy's mother, who in anger ships the young man abroad.

The conspirators manage to slip the girl on the same ship confident the romance will grow in spite of mama, and then reconcile the mother to the situation for a happy ending.

As may easily be seen, this technique of a play-within-a-play lays itself open to all sorts of extravagances. For once Neilan falls directing, a victim of gross exaggeration. Everything is laid on thick. Too thick. The comedy growing out of the phoney home of luxury is terribly gaggy and most stagey at moments, although it has many low comedy laughs which save the situation. Hitchcock does a capital bit of work as the make-believe butler and has the big laugh of the play.

There are good bits mixed in with the hokum. Whenever a situation develops the five foster-fathers gather heads together for a conference and the relations of all five outside their common ward have rich possibilities. The sentimental side is managed with restraint, but it is the artificial plot devices that strain credulity. Betty Bronson does not lend herself well to artifice, for she is inclined to overact the cute child in any circumstances, and the surroundings here of artificiality and make-believe serve to emphasize the fact that she acts too hard anyway.

The picture is a medley of good and bad, but with the good predominating in sufficient weight to carry the picture through on its appeal to the average fan.

Rush.

FOREVER AFTER

First National release featuring Mary Astor and Lloyd Hughes. Adapted from Owen Davis' stage play and directed by F. Harmon Weight. At the Strand, New York, for six days, beginning Nov. 7. Running time, 64 minutes.

Theodore Wayne .... Lloyd Hughes
Jennie Clayton .... Mary Astor
Jack Randall .... Hallam Cooley
Clayton .... David Torrence
Mrs. Clayton .... Eulalie Jensen
Wayne .... Alec Francis
Mrs. Wayne .... Lila Leslie

War picture with a football game.

The gridiron footage looks like an added starter and is entirely incidental to the story, the season's epidemic of football films apparently being the excuse.

A pretty plain story with the audience 40 minutes ahead of the picture by calling the action and finish. Loew's New York has played many a release equal to this one, sometimes on double feature day. That's about where "Forever After" belongs.

There doesn't seem to be any pull to the title, yet the Strand was jammed Sunday night. But Sunday evening on "the street" is always a panic so proves nothing. This output is overly long in getting started, F. Harmon Weight using up considerable time in planting the idea that Jennie's mother isn't in favor of Ted Wayne as a son-in-law.

Jennie (Miss Astor) and Ted (Mr. Hughes) are very youthful at the opening, the former having her hair down her back and the latter the captain of his school's moleskin squad.

After about two reels you're pretty well convinced that Ted is non plus so far as Mrs. Clayton is concerned, and because he hasn't any money. The father thinks the boy is okay but has little to say in the matter. The pre-game theatre rally, the night before the contest, has the team on stage (not too authentic a bit) with the last half of the game fairly depicted until Ted runs the length of the field for victory. The celebration is offset when he gets a wire that his father has died.

A job in Boston takes him away but before going he stops to tell Jennie not to wait for him. The mother corners the boy and the result is that he tells the girl he doesn't care any more. And then the war. As a captain Ted wipes out a machine gun nest, is wounded and comes to with Jennie bending over the cot. After that it's a mere matter of being decorated and the clinch.

The war stuff holds plenty of action and easily outranks the football. Not much comedy, with both leads sticking neatly to their knitting plus Miss Astor's angelic appearance.

Nothing stands out during the hour of unreeling, with "Forever After" closely approximating that classification of "just a picture."

Alec B. Francis flashes forth for just a bit before he's killed off by Postal, with Eulalie Jensen making Mrs. Clayton very prim and proper, while wearing hats that only the wealthy would dare exhibit publicly. David Torrence is passive as the girl's dad and Hallam Cooley gets a superfluous amount of footage due to the director's prolonged introduction.

"Forever After" didn't get over as a show and bids fair to repeat as a picture.   *Skig.*

Return of Peter Grimm

Victor Schertzinger Production, presented by William Fox. From the play by David Belasco, adapted by Bradley King. Directed by Victor Schertzinger. Reviewed at projection room showing Nov. 4. Running time, 80 mins.

Peter Grimm.................Alec B. Francis
Frederick Grimm..................John Roche
Catherine.....................Janet Gaynor
James Hartman...........Richard Walling
Andrew MacPherson........John St. Polis
Rev. Bartholomey.........Lionel Belmore
Mrs. Bartholomey......Elizabeth Patterson
Marta ....Bodil Rosing
William ....Mickey McBan
Annamarie ....Florence Gilbert
The Clown ....Sammy Cohen

Victor Schirtzinger, who directed "The Return of Peter Grimm" for William Fox, has turned out a picture well worth seeing. It is a picture that is worthy to play any of the de luxe houses, and in the spots where it does play the big ones it will get money. The story is a heart throb affair and all of the kick that the play contained has been faithfully transferred to the screen. This is one of those pic-

tures that brings a sob to the throat and then gives you a laugh kick right after it.

In selecting the cast for the photoplay the choice was wise in regard to Alec B. Francis for the role that was originated by David Warfield. The supporting company is good, with Janet Gaynor as the little heroine, standing out as a "find." This little girl is sure to hang up a name for herself. Next in importance are Richard Walling and little Mickey McBan. The latter plays the little chap who goes on to join the departed Peter Grimm, and the manner in which the youngster troupes is something that some older players might watch.

In making the picture Schertzinger has worked out some really remarkable bits of photography in visions, and his handling of the "returned" Peter to walk through the household and right through the other characters of the story is little short of great. He remembered a trick or two from the T. Hayes Hunter dog and ghost picture made for Goldwyn some years ago. Schertzinger gets evtrything that there is to be had from the incident.

From a production standpoint there are a few spots that could have been handled a little better, particularly the lighting, for where it was sunlight outside it was night in the interiors. But in direction the action has been carried forward at all times without any killing of the footage. There are a few moments at the opening that might be speeded up, but after that there isn't a minute that is not utilized to advantage and the suspense toward the end is intense.

Fox has a box office bet in this picture. Also, it's a picture that measures up to the artistic standard that has been set for the product this year.   *Fred.*

Across the Pacific

Warner Bros. Production, directed by Roy Del Ruth, starring Monte Blue. Adapted from the play by Charles E. Blaney. At Loew's New York Nov. 4, one day.

Fast-moving "mellerdrammer" on the style of the "Injun-cowboy" pictures of 10 years ago, where the hero and the remnants of a glorious cowboy regiment are rescued at the last minute by a strong detachment of cavalry, the villainous Indians unmercifully slaughtered and the pure little blue-eyed white girl returned to the trusting arms of her wet-eyed dada by a blushing hero, etc.

In this case it is Uncle Sam's doughboys against rebel Philippinos who attempted to throw off the yoke of constitutional law and order shortly after the Spanish-American war.

Picture has been well made. It has lots of action, two good character actors, Ed Kennedy and So Jin, and it moves along fast excepting for a little while as Monte Blue agonizes over his fate over loving a sweet-looking, brown-skinned baby to learn the whereabouts of the rebel leader.

This gets him in wrong with Jane Winton, his white sweetheart, who thinks he cares for Myrna Loy, Marguerite, as he pretends to. But Monte was not that kind of a doughboy, although to judge from the way he kissed Myrna in one or two scenes one couldn't help wondering.

Ed Kennedy, as "Roughhouse" Ryan, runs away with the picture in a few comedy scenes, while in a death scene, propped up in Monte's arms in a heavy rain after having been shot several times, Ed makes the customers pull out the unused handkerchiefs. So Jin makes good as the lithe, despicable and ferocious Oriental villain. The high cheek bones and the glassy eyes are okay, but that wax mustache is

overdone, as it looks too fine and stiff to be true.

An opening love scene with Blue and Miss Winton out for a ride on the old-fashioned bicycle is so naive it is worthy of better surroundings. Picture ends up in a regularly planned war. Will make good if the movie public has forgotten the kind of pictures shown before the war or is ready to accept a novel interpretation of old stuff.

EXIT SMILING

Metro-Goldwyn-Mayer picture. Sam Taylor production. Co-featuring Beatrice Lillie and Jack Pickford. Story by Marc Connelly. Scenario by Sam Taylor and Tim Whelan. Directed by Sam Taylor. At Loew's New York, Nov. 6. Running time, 74 minutes.

Violet....................Beatrice Lillie
Jimmy Marsh..............Jack Pickford
Olga..........................Doris Lloyd
Orlando Wainwright......DeWitt Jennings
Macomber.................D'Arcy Corrigan
Cecil Lovelace..........Franklin Pangborn
Jack Hastings...........William Gillespie
Dave.......................Carl Richards
Jesse Watson..............Harry Myers
Canada Phillips............Tenen Holtz

In "Exit Smiling," Beatrice Lillie, the English comedienne of "Charlot's Revue" fame, makes her American bow as a film star possibility. That Miss Lillie, judged by her corking performance, will make the grade depends upon whether she cares to pursue celluloid ways.

This original story by Marc Connelly, legitimate playwright, whipped into screen shape by Sam Taylor and Tim Whelan, does well by the British girl.

Jack Pickford is given as much prominence as Miss Lillie in the picture credits, but he doesn't deserve it. His part is strictly secondary. Miss Lillie is in there all the time, working up ludicrous comedy bits and then showing versatility by switching to tense, dramatic work. She runs away with the picture as the galley slave of the traveling rep show which is making the crossroads and "sticks" in its own private car.

Sam Taylor rates a bow for his direction. He carries on nicely in depicting Miss Lillie as the big-hearted, sacrificial "drudge" who secretly loves the juvenile (Pickford) and gets him a job with the show, sees that he eats, protects him at every step and then fools the villain in order that the boy may return to his people undisgraced and watches the big thing in her life pass out.

Audiences won't like that ending. They will root for the boy to realize that the real love, an understanding one, is with the show slavey and not with the banker's daughter. Yet that evidently was not the Taylor idea.

Miss Lillie's work in this is said to have been sort of an experiment. "Exit Smiling" is well cast with De Witt Jennings capital as manager of the traveling stock company, and Doris Lloyd splendid as the leading lady. The remainder of the players also do nicely. Photographically the picture is also good.

The story is typically American, full of comedy and pathos.   *Mark.*

Private Izzy Murphy

Warner Bros. Production featuring George Jessel. Direction, Lloyd Bacon; story by R. Shrode and Edward Clark, scenario by Philip Lonergan. Robert Hopkins. In the cast: Patsy Ruth Miller, Vera Gordon and Nat Carr. At the New York Hippodrome, Nov. 8. Running time, 80 minutes.

A war picture with a New York Jewish boy as the hero and an Irish girl as heroine. That is to say, all the "Abie's Irish Rose" intent, dressed in pretty lavish sentiment and a wealth of hokum comedy including comic titles about "the Jewish organ," which means a cash reg-

ister. Elaborate business of the marriage broker for laughs.

Vera Gordon will be the tip off that the mother interest is played hard for the sentimental appeal. That's the kind of picture it is. All obvious trick and device employed with no subtlety and none of the simple, sincere artistry that hides the mechanicism behind a screen of unaffected naturalness. This is all theatrical makeshift. There isn't a trick of sentimentality or hoke comedy not rung in.

Much heavy acting by Miss Gordon, some of it genuine and some effective, but this angle dwelt upon with wearisome insistence.

The Jewish hero gets himself into the Irish 69th regiment with no intent to conceal his race, but by an error in the rush of volunteering. When his sweetheart's people learn that he is a Jew instead of an Irishman, there is a clash, and here the picture goes altogether wrong.

In "Abie" they handled this situation from the comedy angle. Here the story takes sides and deals with the episode with self-conscious delicacy that reveals the phoney inspiration for the whole line of bunk, including no end of flag waving. Whoever it was who framed the scenario to put in a defense of the Jewish war veteran's social status has committed a grave faux pas. Where the "Abie" technique was to deal with racial relations in a spirit of comedy, the picture has the whole 69th Regiment of Celts rush in to vindicate Izzy when his Irish sweetheart's father and friends would repudiate him. The whole treatment of the subject here is crude. It's all cheap, hip hurrah melodrama.

The picture in its story substance has plenty of false notes of the same kind. They deal seriously with the wrong things and the comedy motif is heavy handed hokum.

Izzy's name is really Goldberg, and he uses it for his delicatessen store in Hester stret. He has another establishment in an Irish locality, and his trading name here is Murphy. This is what leads to his getting on the regiment rolls as Murphy, when he volunteers to please his Irish sweetheart, who bids him farewell, promising to wait for him.

The girl's father, one O'Clahanan by name, has picked out a rising young Irish politician for her and does not get to know Izzy until he returns from overseas at the end of the war. When he learns he's a Jew there's an explosion.

Meanwhile there are many sentimental scenes having to do with the love of Izzy's mother, newly arrived from Russia, for her boy and her prayers for his safety.

The very orthodox parents of the Jewish boy, by the way, never show any objection to his marriage with the Irish girl, which again is not such true or tactful treatment of the story situation.

In the end Izzy's papa mentions complacently that it doesn't make any special difference what one's race or religion is because we're all children of God, and, strange as that may seem, the beautiful sentiment instantly removes all the elder O'Clanahan's objections to a Jewish son-in-law. Old O'Clanahan, in fact, becomes rather mushy with sentiment, and they have one of those "God bless you, my children" right then and there. From this you may perceive that it's a pretty bad picture.

It's too bad George Jessel makes his screen bow under such inauspicious circumstances. He makes a distinctly appealing screen figure, or would if he had a human part to play. Miss Gordon has one of those emotional parts, but it doesn't once ring true, although she brings to it all those natural gifts that have made her supreme in her type of character. Nat Carr has some rather funny bits as the marriage broker. Miss Miller is just a pale ingenue in a wooden role. Bernhardt couldn't have made it real.

Rush.

His New York Wife

J. G. Bachmann's story and screen play by Leon Abrams. Directed by Albert Kelley and titled by Robert Lord. Preferred Picture. In projection room, Nov. 4; released Nov. 15. Running time, 64 minutes (5,294 feet).

Lila Lake	Alice Day
Philip Thorne	Theodore Von Eltz
Alicia Duval	Ethel Clayton
Lila's Aunt	Edith Yorke
Julia Hewitt	Fontaine La Rue
Jimmy Duval	Charles Cruze

Production never rises above a childish story, full of astonishing crudities. The situation of a simple country girl from an even simpler rural village coming to the city and within a few days becoming a successful social secretary to a rich young matron.

These impossible details are just presented, and no effort is made to excuse them. Private detectives enter a fashionable apartment by force and there find a man and woman in what looks like a compromising situation. They arrest the man and lug him off to a police station, where a police sergeant takes charge of him and lets him go without any further formalities.

The picture starts out to be one of those mild stories about the village virgin who goes to the big city to seek her fortune, in this case lured by a fake theatrical agency promising to produce her plays.

It starts all over again as a society play when a rich woman seeks her lawyer's advice to save her son from marriage with an adventuress.

As a farce the story might have gotten over, but here the travesty comes in the middle of what had been a drama. After that the picture becomes a chase.

Alice Day could play the simple village maid very nicely, but here no acting could be convincing. The same may be said of Theodore Von Eltz as the leading man. Ethel Clayton is the society mother.

The title has very little to do with the proceedings. The New York wife is actually the least important character and with an explanatory title could have been left out altogether.

Rush.

UNKNOWN CAVALIER

Charles R. Rogers production, sponsored by First National. Ken Maynard starred. Story from a Kenneth Perkins short story. Scenario by Marion Jackson. Directed by Albert Rogel. Titles by Don Ryan. In the cast: Kathleen Collins, T. Roy Barnes and Otis Harlan. At Loew's New York (double feature day). Running time, 61 minutes.

A hard-riding western with a wealth of action, excellent pictorial quality and many merits. Story is on a well-known formula, but is compactly told in terms of fast action, and it has good comedy values.

Locale is the southwest desert country, and the sandy wastes figure in most of the backgrounds. One interesting setting is an abandoned mining camp in the middle of the bad lands, making a picturesque background.

The cattle district is infested with a bandit gang headed by a bad man called the Gila Monster, whose face has never been seen, even by his own followers. Maynard, the wandering cowboy, comes into the town just after the Monster has committed one of his outrages, it being clear to the spectator that the Monster is really a respected citizen working secretly in his outlawry.

Maynard is dispatched by the Vigilantes to capture the bandit, being given as guide across the desert none other than the outlaw himself, Suggs by name. Suggs overcomes the unsuspecting cowboy and leaves him to die of thirst in the bad lands, but he is released by his horse (Tarza), featured in the billing and takes up the chase anew.

Meanwhile Suggs has made it appear that Maynard was the outlaw, and upon his reappearance Maynard is seized by the Vigilantes, is put on one of those Bret Harte comedy trials and is about to be lynched when the heroine learns the true state of affairs and comes to the rescue. Maynard escapes and goes into the Gila Monster's den (the Monster's own men have never seen their chief's face), where he is received as the master bandit himself. In the end the hero rounds up the whole criminal gang and drives them into camp.

Throughout the story there is no end of spectacular horsemanship. In the bandit's camp Maynard gets possession of the bad men's mounts by his riding stunts, giving an exhibition of riding first two horses, then three and finally all four as he gallops away over a rise of ground, leaving the outlaws helpless afoot. In another place he rides a furious outlaw horse, breaking it to saddle. Throughout, the story develops to the accompaniment of pounding hoofs and reckless riding. This feature alone would carry the film for program purposes. It's simply a simple story, but well done.

Rush.

Dangerous Friends

Directed by Finis Fox. S. J. Bruskin production released through Aywon. T. Roy Barnes starred. Running time, about 55 minutes.

Terrible!

Trying for a comedy full length that carries nary a real laugh.

Its story of two married couples, each without children; one the nagging wife and the other the dominating husband, has had a thousand counterparts in pictures.

All of this stuff seems to have been written around the fundamental of the Harry Thornes' "Uptown Flat," a vaudeville standard farce for years, but years ago.

Its working out here is boresome. Everything is a couplet, one couple repeating—on the reverse, though—what the other does. It's one of the easiest pictures to walk out on that has been shown in a long while, even on a double bill, as this one was at Loew's New York.

If T. Roy Barnes thinks he is funny here, he should take another look.

For the shooting galleries and the one-nighters in the sticks.

The most important point in connection with this picture is that Burr McIntosh appears in it.

Sime.

UPSTAGE

Metro-Goldwyn production. Directed by Monta Bell. Adapted by Lorna Moon from original story by Walter De Leon. Norma Shearer starred. Oscar Shaw and Dorothy Phillips featured. Titles by Joe Farnham. Gaetano Gaudio, camera. At Capitol, New York, week Nov. 14. Running time, around 80 minutes.

Dolly Haven	Norma Shearer
Johnny Storm	Oscar Shaw
Sam Davis	Tenen Holtz
Dixie Mason	Gwen Lee
Miss Weaver	Dorothy Phillips
Mr. Weston	J. Frank Glendon
Wallace King	Ward Crane
Stage Manager	Charles Meakin

Monta Bell has done some exceptional directorial work on "Upstage." His big and little bits of direction, if anything, will make the layman like this picture of vaudevillians and backstage life.

With a vogue of stage plays seemingly, in the offing started by the smashing "Broadway," that may extend to the screen. If so, and the public can grasp all of Mr. Bell's subtleties, "Upstage" will be a box office draw. Otherwise it will have to hold itself up through Norma Shearer and the story as outlined.

But for the show business and for show people "Upstage" is ideal. Walter De Leon, who wrote the story, has been a vaudevillian. Perhaps Lorna Moon also, the adapter, and surely Joe Farnham knows his vaudy stuff as brought out by his humorous titles, no small part of this film.

But where did Monta Bell, a former newspaperman, find out so much about backstage and the vaudevillian? Mr. Bell tells he knows, not only in the booking agent's office scenes but in the Poughkeepsie "try-out" theatre. And he has given the vaudevillian a picture of himself that every vaudevillian, man or woman, will relish.

"Upstage" is great for vaudeville and for "Variety" (the paper). It's the story of a swell head. As it starts, one can almost recall the day when Billy Gould first brought Valeska Suratt into the old Rector's restaurant, after both had come east from Chicago. And Miss Shearer as made up and photographed in this picture does not look unlike Valeska did in those days, though Miss Shearer is the better looking although not quite as statuesque as Val always tried to make herself, on and off.

Leaving the home town to become a stenographer in New York, Dolly Haven (Miss Shearer) reads an advertisement of a theatrical agent in need of a stenog. Inquiring there, she finds the position filled, but accidentally runs into a conversation with Johnny Storm (Oscar Shaw), a song and dance man in need of a partner.

So Storm and Haven eventually try out at Poughkeepsie. After that they read a New Act notice in "Variety." It says the girl is there on the beaut thing; that "she is easy to look at and adds value to the act."

The country girl who fell into the show business took a decided brace on confidence after reading the notice. It went to her head. When Johnny couldn't handle her he let the girl slide to do a two-act with Wallace King (Ward Crane), a single.

Again Poughkeepsie and a tryout and again a "Variety" New Act notice flashed upon the screen (in the same style as this paper's New Act notices). The King and Haven notice read that Wallace King did not have enough alone to hold up a two-act with a girl who could do nothing. It suggested King go back to his single.

That broke up the second two-act, but Dolly still retained her "head." She interviewed Sam Davis (Tenen Holtz), informing the agent she "guessed" she would do a single herself. Sam guessed she might get a job in the chorus of a girl act. Dolly guessed herself out of his office, but went into the girl act's chorus after Johnny had declined her offer to "take him back."

This leads up to the pathetic punch and the moral of the story, about when an actor becomes a trouper. Weston and Weaver, knife throwers, early in the picture had mentioned they hoped to have their baby with them on Christmas. And Christmas they spent in Poughkeepsie.

Baby here was inveigled into one of the nicest bits a stage picture ever brought out, in a ventriloquist having his "dummy" carry on a conversation backstage with the babe. It was that dummy, however, left alone on the corridor, that led to baby falling over, onto the stage beneath, without mother or father aware of what had happened.

Bell here got into the heart of the show business without any blah stuff about "the show must go on." Their act was next. Weston and Weaver knew their spot and had to take it, but as they were on the stage and the husband about to decorate the board his wife stood against with knives, she saw her baby held in the arms of the stage manager in the wings.

Here it was that Dolly, with the girl act at the same house, got her chance. She motioned to the mother to take her babe and Dolly ran onto the stage, assuming her place before the knife thrower, who continued until Dolly, stricken with fear, crumped up and slid down upon the stage.

When opening her eyes to find Johnny Storm holding her, she asked Johnny if he had heard someone call her a "trouper." Johnny had. They decided to string together after that, with Johnny probably airing Dixie Mason (Gwen Lee), his present partner.

That trouper thing is the crux of the tale, started with a verse about "The Trouper" at the opening. Johnny had told Dolly she couldn't troupe and she couldn't even dance when first rehearsing. But Johnny saw she had "class" in her strut as she was walking out on him, and called her back to do that walk over again. It was a very natural bit.

There are many natural bits.

Photography throughout didn't always give Miss Shearer the best of it, and a few times decidedly the worst of it.

Speaking of "trouping," regardless of the proper definition, which isn't all heroism at least, Norma Shearer gave the best example in her knife throwing scene. From that scene alone you can set it down that Norma Shearer can act. It's one of the best bits she ever did; it's one of the best acting bits any American picture girl has ever done; it's splendid, and more so considering the double exposure involved.

This picture will be played because it is a fine picture, finely made, excepting the camera work, but to what extent it will draw over the average is problematical.

Yet the picture is holding over in San Francisco this week. Sunday at the Capitol, New York, it did over $13,000 on the day, nearly the Sunday record of the theatre. Even so, just what appeal this stage picture will have for the general public is in doubt. It will depend a good deal upon the house management and the advance. There is an excellent press sheet out for this film by M-G-M.

Though the public doesn't take too warmly to the picture, it will give recognition to Mr. Bell, to Mr. Farnham, Mr. DeLeon and Miss Shearer, besides which Mr. Shaw does very well as the s. and d. man, while the types around the agency and back stage are near-perfect. Mr. Holtz as the agent just missed, not enough to notice particularly, but just.

One of the truest stage stories ever pictured. *Sime.*

EAGLE OF THE SEA

Frank Lloyd Production presented by Famous Players-Lasky. From the novel "Captain Sazarac," by Charles Tenney Jackson, adapted by Julian Josephson. Featuring Florence Vidor and Ricardo Cortez. At the Rivoli, New York, week Nov. 13. Running time, 73 minutes.

Louise Lestron....Florence Vidor
Captain Sazarac....Ricardo Cortez
Colonel Lestron....Sam De Grasse
John Jarvis....Andre Beranger
Crackley....Mitchell Lewis
Beluche....Guy Oliver
Gen. Andrew Jackson....George Irving
Dominique....James Marcus
Don Robledo....Ervin Renaud
Bohon....Charles E. Anderson

Frank Lloyd has produced another sea tale for the screen. This time it is a tale of the pirates of the Caribbean of the early part of the 19th century, with the scenes in New Orleans and on a trio of sailing ships in the Gulf.

Florence Vidor and Ricardo Cortez are featured.

The picture is good enough entertainment in its way, but does not stand out as something extraordinary, which was expected coming from Lloyd. There are moments when the picture is as stirring as Fairbanks' "Black Pirate," but there are others when there is a lack of punch to give the audience a kick. It will get by, but won't break any box office records.

The feature opens with a series of street scenes in old New Orleans in 1815 when General Jackson is paying a visit to the city which he had saved from the hands of the British a few years before. At that time Captain Sazarac, a noted pirate, assisted in repulsing the English. For that the General secured a pardon for the sea rover and his crew.

But the pirate, it seems, would not stay put, even though some of his crew took on more honorable but less exciting employment. The captain again has a price on his head when the picture opens, despite which fact he is in New Orleans, drawn there by the lure of a pretty face belonging to Louise Lestrom, whom he rescues when her carriage horses run away.

Miss Vidor is Louise and Mr. Cortez the pirate captain whom she has captivated. A pretty romance follows, the two meeting at a ball given to General Jackson, who recognizes the pirate despite his mask, across the hall. He has him brought before him and gives him 24 hours to leave the town.

Louise is willing to finance an expedition to St. Helena for the purpose of rescuing Napoleon. Her uncle, who is in the intrigue, wants to set England and America at war again, so that Spain can come in and seize New Orleans. He makes his proposal to Capt. Sazarac to head the adventure, but he refuses to do anything which will injure America. The girl overhears the plans and the turndown which Capt. Sazarac gives her uncle and proclaims that she will broadcast there is such a plot. To prevent this her uncle and a Spanish diplomat contrive that she disappear on an outgoing merchant ship, giving forth the news that Capt. Sazarac had kidnapped her.

When the captain hears of this he seizes the ship intended for the Napoleonic venture and gives chase, rescuing the girl and starting to return with her, when his crew of cut-throats mutiny. He and his loyal followers are confined below decks. There is an attack by a Spanish frigate which has followed them with fortune first favoring one and finally the other, but the pirates victorious i the end. And the captain wins the girl.

The sea fights are well done. One of the best performances is contributed by Andre Beranger as a soused pirate with gallant inclinations.

Mitchell Lewis as the leader of the mutiny scored as did also James Marcus. Cortez was a pleasing enough gallant. *Fred.*

FAUST

Berlin, Nov. 3.

This film may be a disappointment—from the financial angle. From the artistic viewpoint there is some difference of opinion. Personally it is believed one of the best productions ever screened. But from the standpoint of taste and photographic brilliance it is doubtful whether there has ever been a production that surpassed it. It is not revolutionary as the same director's "Last Laugh" was but it has moments which will create a good deal of stir in the American studios. Here in Germany it won't equal the financial returns of "The Nibelungen."

The scenario by Hans Kayser is a combination of Goethe, the old Faust legend, and some modern variations. It has swift movement and gives much chance for the pictorial. Performances are on the whole very satisfactory, the Swede, Goesta Ekman, registering as both the old and young Faust. Camilla Horn was a good selection for Gretchen and gave naive charm to the part. In the dramatic moments at the end she did as well as it is necessary for a film actress to do.

Yvette Guilbert, the internationally known diseuse, was a happy choice as Martha and planted her comedy neatly.

Emil Jannings is a bit of a disappointment as Mephisto. He gives merely the conventionalized operatic conception of the role, where a more powerful, vital interpretation would have strengthened the story. Jannings' performance is unquestionably interesting but would be greatly improved if he could rid himself of the bad habit of mugging into which he has lately fallen. *Trask.*

THE SILENT LOVER

First National presents Milton Sills in screen version of Lajos Biro's play, "The Legionary." Scenario by Carey Wilson. George Archainbaud director. At the Strand, New York, week of Nov. 13. Running time, 67 mins.

Count Pierre Tornai....Milton Sills
Vera Sherman....Natalie Kingston
Cornelius Sherman....William Humphrey
Captain Herault....Arthur E. Carewe
Kobol....William V. Mong
Scadsza....Viola Dana
Contarini....Claude King
O'Reilly....Charlie Murray
Greenbaum....Arthur Stone
Haidee....Alma Bennett
Ben Achmed....Montague Love

Here's a "sheik picture," only upside down. The film distorts and makes ridiculous all those romantic elements that made Mrs. Hull's first desert picture a box office smash. The result is something like making a gag version of "Romeo and Juliet."

"The Silent Lover" has some low comedy that pulls laughs, but the whole pattern is hokum travesty and the results are not happy. Good pictorial values give the picture some interest, but a low comedy treatment of a romantic subject promises very little in popular appeal. Chances seem greatly against the picture registering on week runs where word of mouth advertising counts, putting it in the daily change grade. For this class of booking its impressive cast will bring trade.

The production is a jumbled medley of cross-purposes. A background of romance is built up with great pains out of the familiar materials of the French Foreign Legion, Arab sheiks, picturesque desert scenes and dashing horsemen. Having achieved a sentimental atmosphere, the story then proceeds to use it for burlesque comedy. The comic effects are obtained by the jazzy antics of a trio of Legion soldiers. It is enough to indicate the quality of the comedy to relate that Charlie Murray plays a Legion soldier named O'Reilly, exactly as it would be played on the Mutual wheel, and is supported by a fellow legionnaire named Greenbaum.

The effect of Irish and Hebe dialect pitchforked into the atmosphere of "Under Two Flags" is rather overpowering. Instead of laughing at it, the auditor is disposed to feel vaguely that the producer is laughing at fandom. There are times when the serious romance is given emphasis, but always a cynical twist pricks the sentimental bubble.

For instance, the romance of the soldier-hero and the heroine, tourist in the desert, is worked up with elaborate mechanism of heroic rescue, moonlight desert trysts, etc. Then when it comes time for the final embrace, it is the Algerian sheik who brings the lovers together because the sheik's favorite wife is sweet on the hero and the sheik wants to see him safely married and out of the way.

Contrasted to this cynical violence to sentiment, at another point in this wild narrative, the Legion officer and the same sheik meet man to man out in the desert to struggle to the death in one of those heroic battles with the lovely heroine as the stake. The trouble with the picture is that it has no definite design. The comedy and the romance seems to have been introduced by ungoverned whim and no sense of proportion. The effect as it comes to the spectator is exasperating. *Rush.*

JOSSELYN'S WIFE

Tiffany Productions society drama suggested by Kathleen Norris' story of same name. Scenario by Agnes Parsons, directed by Richard Thorpe. Harold Young, film editor. Pauline Frederick featured. Running time, 58 minutes (projection room speed); 5,800 feet. Set for release Nov. 15.

Lillian Josselyn....Pauline Frederick
Thomas Josselyn....Holmes Herbert
Pierre Marchand....Armand Kaliz
Ellen Marchand....Josephine Hill
Flo....Carmelita Geraghty
Mr. Arthur....Freeman Wood
Detective....Pat Harmon
Maid....Ivy Livingston
Butler....W. A. Carroll

This is the kind of drama the Laura Jean Libby fans used to love—which is to say it is false and artificial. Everything that happens is absurdly make-believe. The whole phoney dramatic situation arises from the fact that a loyal wife goes to the studio of her former lover. Her husband has asked her to have her portrait painted, and she knows the artist is going to make unwelcome love to her.

If she had refused to go, or had given some excuse, as any woman who had good sense would have done, there wouldn't have been any story.

Even so good an actress as Pauline Frederick can not make more than a dummy figure of the pure lady pursued by the amorous artist. The helpless lady victim of brute men is passe technique for stage or screen. The only emotion it excites is weariness and impatience at building up high-falutin' situations that have no basis, but the author's and director's poverty of resource.

Picture has some nice settings, but the playing is in no better style than the story, except for the always gracious acting of Miss Frederick. The men are just actors. Then never for a moment convey any illusion of real people.

It's a tiresome picture, appropriate only to the most unsophisticated clientele. *Rush.*

LADIES AT PLAY

First National production, directed by Al Green. Story by Sam Janney. Doris Kenyon, Louise Fazenda and Lloyd Hughes featured. Titles by George Marion, Jr. At Keith-Albee Hippodrome, New York, week Nov. 15. Running time, about 60 minutes.

A very nice comedy, with a good twist to the Sam Janney story and several laughs from the titles by George Marion, Jr. Al Green's direction keeps action on the jump and makes a fast moving picture.

In playing Doris Kenyon ran away from the others. Miss Kenyon has a roguish role, always looking fetching, and here the photography is more than worthy of passing notice.

In eccentric work Louise Fazenda was in the lead, closely held to, however, in the "drunk" scene by Ethel Wales. Virginia Lee Corbin did nicely as a sweetly slangy girl. She's improving rapidly and has looks. Captions were of distinct aid to her. Lloyd Hughes had no hardship in his simple juvenile role.

The story is another version of the marry-on-time or lose an inheritance. But here the heiress to six millions with three days to secure a husband was in love with no one. The best in sight as far she was concerned was the hotel's mail clerk.

The mail clerk gave her air when she broached marriage to him. It looked like a frame to the "collar ad kid," as Virginia called him. So Doris decided to "compromise" the clerk, but that failed, too, since there was too much compromising about.

As Doris had to have the approval of her two aunts to a husband, according to the terms of the will, and the old maidenly aunts thought two men in one room was safety first, it left Doris but another day to wind it up.

She decided to compromise the aunts, securing a couple of easy coin night club boys to do that little thing. They worked in on the aunts by claiming relationship, then took the old gals to dinner, filled 'em up with booze, removed them to their apartment, and Doris did the rest with a camera.

Quite unexpectedly a good comedy to be found at the Hippodrome, where it drew plenty of laughter. Despite plot and description, entirely clean.

Good for a first run anywhere but nothing extraordinary for a draw or self advertisement. *Sime.*

THE SMOKE EATERS

Trem Carr Production presented by W. Ray Johnston. Story by Arthur Hearl with C. J. Hunt director. At Loew's New York as half of double bill, one day, Nov. 12. Running time, 64 mins.

As a complimentary gesture toward firemen in general, and it's dedicated to the flame boys, this celluloid opus misses by many miles. Cheaply made, amateurishly titled, badly put together and minus pace, leaves little hope for "The Smoke Eaters" outside of the "shooting galleries." If trading upon the expected prestige M.-G.-M.'s "Fire Brigade" is perfect, the producer flopped just as badly.

The thrill sequences lack logic, much must be taken for granted and the big fire scene strongly suggests that Hunt was one of the directors who called out his camera men during the recent studio fires on the coast to take pot shots for future use.

It's possible this scenario was written around the opportunity to shoot the genuine fire stuff. Cullen Landis is the only cast member viewed in these scenes. He must have been hastily recruited for the occasion, as all he does is to run over a network of rubber hose covering the street.

It takes almost two reels before the script jumps 20 years, so that Landis and Wanda Hawley can enter the story. Previously a prolonged stretch depicts the sorrow of a fireman and his wife who have lost a child. When a passenger ship goes up in flames this same fireman rescues a man, woman and babe so that when no one claims the youngster he adopts the boy.

Technically, the film is extremely porous. Witnesses don't have to belong to the village fire brigade to note the errors. It's rank melodrama with nothing to relieve it. No comedy at all.

Even Baby Moncure, doing the lost tot of tender years, had a grouch during his scenes. The aquatic fire stuff is phoney and looks it, as does the close-up rescue work when the night club takes to flames.

It got on at the New York as one-half of those deadly double bills there, but to style it even "just a picture" gives "The Smoke Eaters" a break. *Skig.*

FLAMES

Associated Exhibitors, Inc., billed as "first time in New York." Designated as Lewis H. Moomaw Production, with Moomaw directing. Story by Alfred A. Cohn, who also supplied the scenario. Edited and titled by Frank Lawrence. In cast, Virginia Valli, Eugene O'Brien, Jean Hersholt, Bryant Washburn, Cissy Fitzgerald. Running time, 60 mins. At Broadway, New York, Nov. 15, week.

A first rate commercial production is this picture from the unfortunate Associated Exhibitors' list. It comes as a windfall to the Broadway, which generally is restricted in its choice of features from independent sources. In weight of cast names, in screen quality and in class the feature is far above the average of film material booked into Keith-Moss establishment.

The story is one of those romances of the open spaces, in this case the remote camp of a railroad construction engineer, to which the railroad magnate brings his daughter on a tour of inspection. The old formulas are used for situations, but they are well worked, and throughout the nature of the plot makes it possible to use remarkably fine scenic backgrounds of forest, river and mountain lake. Some of the scenic shots are notably beautiful.

Jean Hersholt does some very good comedy character work as a roughneck Swede boss of a construction gang. The dramatic high lights are one of those rough and tumble battles between hero and heavy and thrilling views of a raging forest fire, the fire being particularly well translated to the screen for vivid effect and realism.

The story itself doesn't especially matter. It is the familiar one of the rich girl trying to decide between a fashionable society man and the rough and ready railroad engineer.

A simple, naive tale, well and simply done. *Rush.*

West of Rainbow's End

George Blaisdell production. Directed by Bennett Cohen, presented by W. Ray Johnston, distributed by Rayart Productions. Starring Jack Perrin, with cast including "Starlight," the horse, and "Rex," the dog. Running time, 58 minutes.

A small town picture, but extremely doubtful if it will get across even before a none too exacting audience. The small boy pardner stuff has been worked to death in scores of westerns and the freckle-faced kid, Billy Lamar, is unnatural in this picture owing to the soldier's uniform which could easily have

been dispensed with. Milburn Murante, the faithful cowboy retainer, obviously created for "comedy relief," succeeds in looking ludicrous once, but never approaches anything like comedy. The titling is very poor. As an example of breezy western language is this classic: "He outsmarted us, gosh darn."

The ugly scar on the face of one of the villain's hirelings, Lew Stanley, looks exactly like a smear of raspberry jam in the closeups, while the chief vill'un, Palmer, played by Whitehorse, looks about as villainous as a Canal street pawnbroker on his day off. A youthful-looking sheriff, who tries to arrest the hero for stealing one of his own horses, appears to be the very image of a finale hopper dressed up for a masquerade ball.

The hero, Don Brandon, is shot at by the western villains several times from a distance of about six feet, but is not wounded once.

This western is devoid of anything strong in the way of love interest, hot fist fights or beautiful horses. There are no wonderful ranges literally covered with lowing herds of cattle, no strong, powerful men fighting for beautiful women. The vill'n is a man past middle age who shot and killed Old Man Brandon while Don was in France fighting. Whitehorse then appropriated the Brandon ranch, and when Don comes home finds his father dead and the ranch in strange hands.

Whitehorse, described as a land and cattle grabbing octopus, the ruthless, terrorized boss of the district, looks about as awe-inspiring as a cigar store clerk offering a substitute. Jack Perrin's face when he nonchalantly threatens the "villyun' with vengeance is as expressive as a porous plaster and he plays that way right through the picture. The only love interest consists of a couple of closeups of the heroine, Daisy Kent, looking softly after the departing hero. Of course, Don Brandon gets back the old homestead and wins the gal for his own, although how this is done is not made very clear. "Starlight" and "Rex" will do as animal stars.

SILENT POWER

Sam Sax production, with Ralph Lewis. Directed by Frank O'Connor. Supervised by Renaud Hoffman. Distributed by Lumax under Gotham label. At Loew's New York theatre, New York, one day, Nov. 13. Running time, 69 minutes.

An idea here, of a father in charge of a State prison "executioner's" switchboard who must swing the level that throws the juice into the chair where his son awaits death for murder. Of course the audience has a suspicion the boy awaiting the end is not the murderer, but the theme is such that nobody can sidestep its moral—that capital punishment should be done away with.

The story is held fairly well together, but had Sam Sax gone in for a liberal expenditure he might have made something bigger of it than told here.

However, Sax deserves credit for what he has accomplished, because the story will have its sentimental aspect taking effect in the neighborhoods.

That old gag about the sweetheart making a wild dash to the Governor on a last moment's appeal to save her lover has been done so many times it calls for something unusual to swing it away from the beaten path. Here it was the father, who had reconciled himself to the belief his boy was to be electrocuted but at a time when he was off duty during "killing time."

It runs that the man expected to throw the switch walks out and the father must fulfill the duty. He does it, and in one of the most dra-

matic bits of the film. The boy didn't die because the connecting wire had been cut.

Ethel Shannon, long playing leads in independents, does splendidly as the sweetheart of the condemned boy. Her strides in emotional work are much to her credit. She also photographs well and is effective in close-ups.

Ralph Lewis is the hero, in his characteristic way of grinning that becomes boresome. A thankless role is well handled by Vadim Uraneff. The acting of Charles Delany calls for special mention.

There are slight dashes of production investment, one in the night club scene where the girls are doing a number, but the story itself depends upon a rugged atmosphere of an outdoors. Photographically a boost for Sax.

It's a picture that should run the gamut of independent booking without any great fault-finding. *Mark.*

God Gave Me 20 Cents

Herbert Brenon production. Presented by Famous Players-Lasky. From the story by Dixie Willson, adapted by John Russell. Script by Elizabeth Meehan. Directed by Herbert Brenon. At the Paramount, New York, week beginning Nov. 20. Running time, 72 minutes.

Mary....................Lois Moran
Cassie Lang..............Lya de Putti
Steve Doren.............Jack Mulhall
Barney Tapman..........Wm. Collier, Jr.
Ma Tapman........Adrienne d'Ambricourt
Andre Dufor..............Leo Feodoroff
Mrs. Dufor..............Rosa Rosanova
Florist...................Claude Brooke

Here is a "Cosmopolitan" short story picked up for $2,500 for the screen, and the finished picture was selected as the opening attraction for the $10,000,000 Paramount theatre.

Of course, the business that the picture will do at the new Paramount must not be taken as a criterion as to how it will fare at the box offices the country over. Here the Paramount theatre is the attraction, and any picture could have rolled up a box-office record for itself. That is not saying that "God Gave Me 20 Cents" is a bad picture. Far from that, but it isn't a record-breaker, either.

In a measure, "God Gave Me 20 Cents," as a story, will measure up with "Broken Blossoms." As a picture it won't stand up as the latter did, but it will get business to a certain extent without knocking any audiences cold.

A lot of value is in the names connected with the screen production. First is Herbert Brenon, whose "Beau Geste" is just about burning the country up wherever it plays; also Lois Moran, Lya de Putti, Jack Mulhall and William Collier, Jr., a very effective box-office foursome of players.

The story is of the New Orleans waterfront. The action starts during the Mardi Gras, which gives opportunity for a lot of colorful shots and some very good comedy. There is sufficient underworld stuff to hold the interest and provide suspense and, atop of that, a pleasing little love tale.

The title is against the picture. It's a safe bet that many a 50c. admission house will have them walk up to the window with a duo of dimes to get in on the strength of that "20 Cents" bit in the title. That won't be true in the bigger houses in the bigger towns, but wait until it hits some of the smaller ones!

The way Lya de Putti handles herself in this picture tells that it makes all the difference in the world who is directing that girl. In this one she is almost as good as in "Variety." And she looks like a million dollars in some of the shots here.

As for little Lois Moran, that girl is a wonder. She troupes all over the place. Women are going to love her, suffer with her, and just about want to kill the sailor husband who they believe has walked out on her because of his former love.

Jack Mulhall is the sailor-husband, and Jack is looking better and doing better work than he has any time during the last five years. He gets the swing of this character and plays it. "Buster" Collier as a devil-may-care kid, delivers.

It is to the direction that the picture certainly owes a lot, and here Brenon again proves that he is a master craftsman. Brenon, who years ago was shooting big spectacles; Brenon, who just a few months ago topped a record of more than a year of consistent winners with that box-office smash, "Beau Geste," just goes out in this picture and proves that he has not been asleep to the tricky camera angle shooting the foreigners have been using to make them appear in the genius class. He goes right after them and does it himself. A couple of overhead shots in this make the picture worth seeing just from the technical viewpoint. Not only did Brenon figure the shooting, but he has stuck action all through it, and action that makes one believe one thing when another entirely is the case.

"God Gave Me 20 Cents" is a picture that is a little better than the average program feature Famous Players-Lasky has been sending out this year, and that is saying a lot.

Fred.

FLAMING FOREST

Cosmopolitan production releasing through M.-G.-M. and directed by Reginald Barker. From James Oliver Curwood's story, with Percy Hilburn, photographer. Renee Adorce and Antonio Moreno featured. At the Capitol, New York, week of Nov. 21. Running time, 70 mins.

Sergeant David Carrigan	Antonio Moreno
Jeanne-Marie	Renee Adoree
Roger Audemard	Gardner James
Alfred Wimbledon	William Austin
Mike	Tom O'Brien
Andre Audemard	Emile Chautard
Jules Lagarre	Oscar Beregi
Major Charles McVane	Clarence Geldert
Lupin	Frank Leigh
Donald McTavish	Charles S. Ogle
Francois	Roy Coulson
Bobbie	D'Arcy McCoy
Mrs. McTavish	Claire McDowell
Sloppy	Bert Roach
Ruth McTavish	Mary Jane Irving

Add another glorified western to the list, for this is it. Not such a much either, although it's been nicely handled, and some of it is in natural color, if that helps. At the Capitol they received it without emotion one way or the other.

An Indian attack on a fort and a forest fire, with the rescue brigade riding through double photography and the flames to save the home folks, consummate the film's punch. Meanwhile, Miss Adoree and Mr. Moreno uphold the love interest on a lightweight scenario thread which about serves the purpose and that's all.

Mr. Moreno is a sergeant in the Northwest Mounted, reason for the color. Barker evidently couldn't resist those red coats. Besides which the story has its historical side, for it supposedly depicts the entrance of Canada's famed police force into the northwest and the "heavy" happenings are evidently patterned after the Riel Rebellion, upon which subject they're not so anxious to talk up Canada way.

An extensive cast does adequately with their respective assignments, no one actually standing out, unless it is Gardner James as the crippled brother of Miss Adoree, who is finally incensed to do murder. Oscar Beregi is serious enough as Lagarre, the half-breed villain, and convinces.

Lagarre is steaming the Indians into a rebellious mood to establish himself as a monarch of the northwest when the Canadian Mounted arrive. This holds up his plans a bit, but not before he has persecuted the pioneers and evicted them from their homes.

It's at this point the Mounties appear, so the pioneers face about and replace the furniture. Jeanne-Marie's mother and dad have been killed at the instigation of Lagarre. When further goaded by a couple of the latter's hirelings, Roger, the brother, sneaks out and shoots his tormentors. This leads to complications, for Sergt. Carrigan (Mr. Moreno) is in love with the sister, and must arrest the boy.

The commander of the Mounties leads a detachment away from the post, whereupon the Indians light ye well-known beacon on the hilltop, and the battle is on. Carrigan eventually breaks through the Indian lines to bring back the departed force. The picture evidently gets its title from the Redmen firing the forest to prevent the return of the rescue column.

This bit is obviously propped up by dual camera work, but at times seems genuine and may fool some of the lays. That it's mostly exterior stuff goes without saying. Some of the backgrounds are picturesque, although the way they turn 'em out now you have to look eight times to make up your mind whether it's a backdrop. Guess not for this one.

The w. k. Northwest Mounted uniforms help the color bit, are the main substance of it, and no denying it dresses the release up a bit. It needs it, too, for the story isn't so strong. Miss Adoree and Mr. Moreno are passive as heroine and hero, their names promising more than their work accomplishes.

A thin vein of comedy runs throughout, besides which there are the wagon trains, fording of rivers and the climax battle. Barker has seen a few of the specials in the past few years and evidence of his patronage is noticeable here at various points.

Just average program footage at best, needing the "break" it will get from those who dote on their westerns.

Skig.

THE GREAT GATSBY

Paramount presentation of Herbert Herbert Brenon production, featuring Warner Baxter, Lois Wilson, Neil Hamilton and Georgia Hale in screen version of F. Scott Fitzgerald's novel, which Owen Davis dramatized last season. Screen play by Becky Gardner; adapted by Elizabeth Meehan. Footage, 7,296; 80 minutes. At Rivoli, New York, week Nov. 20.

Jay Gatesby	Warner Baxter
Daisy Buchanan	Lois Wilson
Nick Carraway	Neil Hamilton
Myrtle Wilson	Georgia Hale
George Wilson	William Powell
Tom Buchanan	Hale Hamilton
Charles Wolf	George Nash
Jordan Baker	Carmelita Geraghty
Lord Digby	Eric Blore
Bert	"Gunboat" Smith
Catherine	Claire Whitney

"The Great Gatsby" is serviceable film material, a good, interesting, gripping cinema exposition of the type certain to be readily acclaimed by the average fan, with the usual Long Island parties and the rest of those high-hat trimmings thrown in to clinch the argument.

Comes Warner Baxter, cast in a sympathetic role with a doubtful touch. Despite the vague uncertainty of Gatsby's illegal fortune from bootlegging (and Volstead violating in these post-prohibition days is not generally deemed a heinous crime despite the existence of a federal statute which declares it so), the title player has all the sympathies with him.

Then there is Hale Hamilton as the husband, a player who has been invariably cast on stage and screen as a manly and almost impossibly righteous husband or very dear, dear old friend of the family, and who is similarly cast here as the sire of the Buchanan household. He is the husband of Daisy (Lois Wilson), first betrothed to Gatsby.

The audience, in view of the general tenor of the triangular player's previous characterizations, finds itself somewhat befuddled. Along toward the last 20 minutes the wife calmly states she does not love her husband and that her affections are with Gatsby, from whom she was parted by the Great War. With that established, the audience's collective viewpoints are directed anew to the ultimate reunion of the wife of Buchanan and Gatsby, her first lover, particularly in view of Buchanan's apparent perfidy with a light lady.

The vacillating shades and touches make one wonder whether Brenon (or his scenarist) had not started out to alter the original Scott Fitzgerald story for screen purposes and was confronted with contractual obligations to the author, or other circumstances that prohibited such liberties. This is but a theory, since Fitzgerald is sufficiently established to command such special terms if he so elected.

The picture is no reflection on the original novel, an excellent volume, which, because of its literary form, permits a more faithful adherence to reality than the movies.

As a general entity the screen version of "The Great Gatsby" is good stuff. Fitzgerald will certainly have no quarrel with the filmization of his novel. All the niceties and un-niceties of fast Long Island life of the type Fitzgerald dotes on criticizing and exposing are capable of elaborate exposition. And where the exhibitor may look askance at the overlength of 80 minutes' running time and be tempted to apply the shears to the swimming pool orgies, etc., he is cautioned against this because for the average layman that footage will be most appealing.

The casting is excellent as far as the cast's personations of their roles are concerned. Baxter as Gatsby leaves nothing wanting. Neil Hamilton as Nick Carraway, cousin of the leading feminine character and a sort of disinterested onlooker, has an easy time of it.

Lois Wilson and Hale Hamilton are the uncertainties. Miss Wilson did her role too faithfully, it seems. After all, she is what parallels the "heroine" of a screen story, and she might have softened it up in general. With the trueness of her personation there is naught to be found, but for the paradoxical criticism it is too well done. Ditto for Hamilton. It may be a director's fault, of course. Georgia Hale as the free-and-easy wife did well.

The average screen reviewer, it should be mentioned here, is generally the type that is a stickler for any nicety in any flicker production. The artistic, to him or her (generally a her), represents the crux of cinema attainment, without any idea or eye to the box office end. From the artistic reviewer's viewpoint, therefore, "The Great Gatsby" would fetch something akin to a "rave." For a commercial commentator, the conflicting emotions from the audience reaction are something to be regarded.

"The Great Gatsby" has in its favor the general sophisticated tenor of the adaptation, intelligent handling of all the opportunities, and the novel's and play's additional prestige. Withal, it's a worthwhile program release.

Abel.

THE BLONDE SAINT

Marion Fairfax Production, presented by Samuel E. Rork, released by First National. From the novel by Stephen French Whitman, adapted by Marion Fairfax, featuring Lewis Stone and Doris Kenyon. Directed by Svend Gade. Shown at the Strand, N. Y., week Nov. 20, 1926. Running time, 69 minutes.

Sebastian Maure	Lewis Stone
Anne Bellamy	Doris Kenyon
Fannia	Ann Rork
Annibale	Gilbert Roland
Ilario	Secare Gravina
Vincent Pamfort	Malcolm Denny
Andreas	Albert Conti
Nino	Vadim Uraneff
Anne's Aunt	Lillian Langdon
Tito	Leo White

How this feature was ever picked by the Strand to stand off the possible opposition that might come through the opening of the new Paramount is a mystery. The picture is an ordinary program feature with no particular kick. The story moves along nicely enough, but one can see the outcome long before the first reel is ended. It only remains to see how they work out the paths the principals must travel before they get together for the fade-out. From a box office viewpoint there is nothing to the picture that is going to pull money in the de luxe houses. For the regular theatres where there is a change daily it will get by well enough.

Lewis Stone is the hero, an author with a past and the reputation of a roue, while to Doris Kenyon is assigned the role of the American girl who spurns him because of his rep, but who loves him nevertheless. She, however, makes up her mind that she will be a whole lot safer married to a very staid Englishman and so departs from Italy for England to be married.

The author takes the same steamer. When she refuses to break her engagement he grasps her in his arms and leaps from the steamer off the coast of Sicily.

From that time on the two are virtually marooned in a little fishing village where the "menace" takes the form of a plot to kill them both to secure the money of the man and the jewels of the maid.

A plague breaks out and the author devotes himself to the care of the suffering with the aid of the local priest. In the end the girl is won by his devotion to the unfortunates. When the English lover shows up to rescue her she decides she doesn't want to be rescued.

Ann Rork and Gilbert Roland handle a juvenile love affair very nicely, Miss Rork being particularly convincing in what she did. To Cesare Gravina must be handed the honors for a character interpretation that stands out.

The direction carries the story along at a fair clip. There are several moments of real suspense to the manner in which Sven Gade handled his Sicilian scenes.

Fred.

PALS IN PARADISE

P. D. C. release. From Peter B. Kyne story. George B. Seitz directing. Cast includes Rudolph Schildkraut, Marguerite De La Motte, John Bowers, Alan Brooks and May Robson. At the Hippodrome, New York, week Nov. 24. Running time, 68 minutes.

About rightly placed where it is. This picture slips by where a five or six-act vaude program is also present to share responsibility. For a straight de luxe house "Pals in Paradise" wouldn't look so good, but here it's okay.

It all centers around a gold rush town that sprouts in the desert when that certain young man discovers the vein after his Ford takes a slide off the road. A crook threesome is mixed up in it, as is the inevitable girl, with the old Schildkraut supplying the comedy as a storekeeper elected sheriff of the boom village.

The story of the boy and girl reaches complication proportion through the young woman's father having established the mine, but dying before striking wealth. Hence, when she comes out there's an argument, with the self-willed heiress almost marrying one of the crooks before Schildkraut, as the Jewish constable, hangs it on him at the finish.

Nothing slipshod about this one, and Seitz has held it together pretty well. That it's a western of the old school minus "names" keeps it from getting anywhere as a box-office proposition.

Bowers makes a clean-cut masculine figure of the young miner, although if any are around they'll probably only remember Schildkraut on the way out. May Robson is opposite as the nagging wife, and also gleans enough snickers to lighten the general dramatics.

Probably the comedy outstrips the story for interest. It's a cinch as to how the whole thing is going to turn out, it therefore being just a question of looking for the laughs on the way. Thanks to Schildkraut, they're there.

Where there's an added starter this one should get by. If it's standing alone it will depend upon the clientele of the house as to the grade of reception it will catch.

Skig.

Then Came the Woman

Sponsored by David Hartford Productions, Inc., under American Cinema Association. Titles by Frances Nordstrom. Features Frank Mayo, Cullen Landis. Mildred Ryan leading woman. Running time, about 57 minutes.

Story is built up around a forest fire, which furnishes the only action in the picture. Trouble is the action doesn't particularly lead up to the fire views, which are impressive in themselves, and nothing especially vital hangs upon the episode of the conflagration. To be sure, the heroine and hero are lost in the woods and threatened by the

flames, but the opportunity to give this situation a punch is not employed with much skill.

The rest of the action is sluggish and the feminine interest is not brought in until near the end. It looks like the story had been undertaken before the script was clearly determined upon. The story pattern is confused. In spite of defect good detail and excellent pictorial work make the production a better-than-fair program feature.

Bob is a wayward boy. He and his father clash, and Bob leaves home to seek his fortune. He reaches the lumber country, and there encounters Mr. Hobart, operator of large lumbering interests. The elder man takes an interest in the youngster, but they also clash, and fight it out man to man with bare fists. Hobart knocks Bob cold, and a firm friendship grows out of the combat.

Bob is making his way successfully under the tutelage of his guide and friend when Hobart sends east for the girl he loves, intending to celebrate her arrival with a wedding. Instead the girl falls in love with Bob. The young man here struggles between his love for the girl and his loyalty for Hobart. The young pair are picnicking in the forest when they are trapped by fire. It is Hobart who goes to their rescue, and out of the incident he comes to realize that "youth calls to youth," as the sentimental titles have it, and resigns in favor of his younger rival.

Some rather fair comedy is supplied by an Irish camp cook and her browbeaten husband. The scenic features are fine always. The director has avoided the fault of making his logging camp interior settings rough and crude, and has, rather, gone to the other extreme of making them rather too artistic to be convincing.

Altogether sums up as an average daily change program feature.

Rush.

COUNTRY BEYOND

William Fox production, of Canadian Northwest Mounted Police, featuring Olive Borden. Production by Irving Cummings. Titles by Katherine Hilliker and H. H. Caldwell. Story from the novel by James Oliver Curwood. At Fox's Academy, Nov. 22. Running time, 58 minutes.

Valencia	Olive Borden
Roger McKay	Ralph Graves
Mrs. Andrews	Gertrude Astor
Sergeant Cassidy	J. Farrell MacDonald
Martha Leseur	Evelyn Selbie
Joe Leseur	Fred Kohler
Henry Harland	Lawford Davidson
Father John	Alfred Fisher
Valencia's maid	Lottie Williams

A mechanical bit of magazine fiction made into a highly interesting picture by the very beauty of its scenic features and the lavish scale upon which the production has been made. Curwood grinds out enormous quantities of fiction of the kind magazine readers consume as fast as it is served. Probably this is as good a test as anything for material suitable for the screen.

This story is so treated in its unfolding in the magnificent scenery in Jasper National Park in Western Canada, and by the production magnificence that surrounds it when the action is transferred to back stage in a Broadway musical comedy, that the spectator is tricked into accepting it at much more than its intrinsic worth.

The settings on and about a lovely mountain lake, ringed by snow capped mountains and set off by fleecy drifting clouds, are beautiful beyond description. They would stand up as art shots for a scenic subject and they go a long way to strengthen a story that is pretty artificial, but effective enough as commercial romance. Capital acting also contributes to the quality of the production and expert direction does its part.

The picture is a good example of concentrated interest, for there isn't a foot of superfluous footage. The picture is the opposite of padding.

Besides these outstanding merits, it has a first rate twist in the character of Cassidy, constable of the Northwest police, played to the queen's taste by J. Farrell MacDonald, veteran character man of the Fox forces.

Instead of the familiar heroic figure of the Northwest Mounted constable, Cassidy is a rollicking old Irishman with a heart and a sense of humor. Olive Borden is a graceful heroine, inclined to overdo the lovely child of nature in the wilderness scenes, but coming into her own when the background of the Broadway musical comedy stage is more to her liking. Evelyn Selbie does a splended character bit and Fred Kohler is an impressive heavy, who looks the part and makes it real by his natural playing.

Valencia is the wild rose of the northwest forests left an orphan with the Hawkinses, rude backwoods people. Roger McKay meets her as he passes, hunted by the police for some prank. They fall in love, but Valencia's guardian wants to sell the girl to one of his friends.

At the nearby fashionable camp is Harland, producer of Broadway shows. He sees the girl dancing in a leafy clearing. He also falls in love with her, offering to make her fortune on the Broadway stage.

Harland furnishes to Cassidy, the Mounted constable, information of McKay's whereabouts and he has to take the fugitive into custody, much as he dislikes the task. Valencia's guardian is killed by his wife, driven to frenzy by his persecutions, and McKay, returning to find the body, supposes the girl has done the deed and takes the crime upon his own shoulders as he goes off to Vancouver.

Nothing is left for the girl but to take Harland's offer. Next she is seen as a reigning queen of the stage, in episodes backstage of unusual magnificence. To Broadway comes Cassidy seeking her out. There is a fight between the soldier and the theatrical manager and the rugged trooper of the Royal Mounted carries the stage beauty back to her native woods for a romantic reunion with her old lover, now cleared of the crime. They meet in their canoes out on the lake in a pretty idyllic series of views for the usual happy ending. Instead of the lover's clinch, the finale has Cassidy riding off into the landscape whistling his satisfaction at the happy ending of his plottings.

Rush.

THE GORILLA HUNT

Winkler Picture, presented by Jos. P. Kennedy, released by F. B. O. A film record of Ben Burbridge's expedition into Africa to capture gorillas alive. Reviewed at projection room showing. Running time, 52 minutes.

As a novelty this so-called feature will get by. It is rather a travelog, with a few thrilling touches at the end showing th giant gorillas in their native wilds.

However, it ranks with the majority of big game hunt pictures. As there has been but one of these on the market in several years there is no reason why this should not prove a box-office attraction and at the same time interesting. Considerable comedy element injected through native stuff and several young gorillas captured alive.

Ben Burbridge, with a number of friends, started at the mouth of the Congo, and for 1,000 miles traveled on a paddle wheeler up that stream. At Stanleyville they disembarked and started across country, with supplies carried by a small regiment of natives. Going through the country they met all sorts of hardships and dangers in their contacts with the natives, some of whom were cannibals, and the Batwa pygmies. The latter were the last of the tribes encountered right on the edge of the gorilla country.

One of the real thrills comes when a gigantic gorilla is seen directly charging the camera, only to fall dead just before reaching it because of a well-directed shot.

There is a lot of the native stuff very interesting, especially some of the dances staged for the visiting big-game hunters. A number of gag titles help this portion of the picture along.

The picture is big enough to play the small grind houses in the bigger towns for a week or so. It can be built up with a strong lobby display and snappy advertising, as such it would get over for better than average business at a house of the type of the Cameo in New York.

Fred.

MIDNIGHT MESSAGE

Designated a Goodwill Pictures, Inc., production. Story by H. H. Van Loan and direction by Paul Hurst. Cast headed by Mary Carr, with imposing support, including Wanda Hawley, Creighton Hale, Otis Harlan, Johnny Fox, Jr., and Stuart Holmes. Running time, 56 minutes.

A story of mixed merits and defects, done in the same sort of production. The big scene is the burglary in a rich man's home, followed by a spirited automobile chase.

But you never can be quite sure that the burglary isn't going to turn into a burlesque. At any time the possibility of the whole thing becoming a travesty is imminent, and the feeling rather takes away from the story interest.

Probably that was not exactly what the scenario writer had in mind. Apparently, he was trying for some such effect as Davis' "Gallagher," but it doesn't register. The picture has many fair laughs, though they scarcely pay for the effort. Something has missed. It isn't the actors, for they represent a high average of ability. Uncertain direction probably was the cause.

All kinds of pains are taken to build up the preparation for a burglary. And then when it comes off, it has no significance. The picture goes into details of the courtship of Wanda Hawley and Creighton Hale, and then it turns out to be a negligible side issue. They go to some trouble to establish the wealth of the family, and then make the rich man a comedy character, all to no purpose.

A surprise finish is used for a laugh. After a night of thrilling adventure, the rich man suddenly asks the boy, "What brought you to my house at such a time of night?" Johnny Fox, Jr., startled, recalls a telegram. It is delivered. The rich man (Otis Harlan) reads it with evidences of lively delight. He passes it all around and each character registers happy surprise. Then the dispatch itself is shown. It reads:

"It's a boy."

"HELEN."

You are to suppose that Helen is another daughter, although such a person had not been mentioned.

Rush.

THE BUCKAROO KID

Universal-Jewel starring Hoot Gibson. Made from Peter B. Kyne's "Oh Promise Me." Direction by Lynn Reynolds. Ethel Shannon leading woman. In the cast Burr McIntosh, Newton House, James Gordon and Harry Todd. At the Stanley, New York (daily change), Nov. 20. Running time, 70 mins.

A somewhat different western story, novel in the particular that all the emphasis is placed on the romance and the soft pedal is on the rough riding and typical cowboy stuff. The picture has a world of production class for one of its type. Instead of having for its setting dreary interiors, most of the action here takes place in scenes of some pretention, such as a modern hotel, the private office of a San Francisco banker and the luxurious home of the heroine, also in San Francisco. Other passages deal with ranch life, but there is some contrast and variety, giving special interest to the film story.

Altogether it is an intelligent story, simply and clearly told and with much fine background and dignified direction. The incidents are entirely plausible and the comedy is fresh and amusing without slapstick and rough-house, which in itself makes it novel for a western.

Gibson is a young ranch manager selected by his employer to reorganize a run down ranch belonging to a San Francisco banker. Gibson goes to Frisco to take the job. His first meeting with the crusty, but well meaning banker, results in a clash of tempers. Young rancher and crabbed banker are at grips when banker's daughter comes into the office and the young rancher falls for her.

When the rancher takes his daughter to lunch (here's where the fashionable settings come in) banker fires him and tells him to lay off daughter. Instead, rancher goes to the ranch and takes it over by force of arms, determined to make good for the sake of the girl's good opinion. Banker comes to the ranch personally to fire cowboy himself, but the tables are neatly turned upon him and he is forced to confirm young man in the job.

Girl likes cowboy, but leaves her answer to his marriage proposal open with a "perhaps." Two years elapse, cowboy has inherited a ranch of his own and has to leave banker's employ. He wants to borrow a large sum to develop his property. Banker willing to lend it on condition he give up daughter. If he persists in his suit, banker will break him. Cowboy promises that if banker interferes with his work he'll cut off the capitalist's ears, and here begins a good bit of broad fun.

Banker surrounds himself with bodyguard to the amusement of his daughter, who secretly sees to it that the cowboy gets his loan. Climax comes when cowboy and daughter at luncheon in the same hotel arrange the loan, while father is lunching with his bodyguard in another part of the restaurant. Cowboy and father come together in neat comedy scene and all is arranged.

Very entertaining program picture, probably the best of its kind Gibson has done.

Rush.

MONEY TO BURN

Sam Sax sponsors this Gotham production. Melodrama made from novel by Reginald W. Kauffman. Adaptation and scenario by James R. Smith. Walter Lang director. Distributed by Lumas. Ray June, photographer. Running time, 60 minutes. Seen in projection soon.

Dan Stone	Malcolm McGregor
Dolores Valdez	Dorothy Devore
Don Diego Valdez	Eric Mayne
Maria Gonzalez	Nina Romano
Manuel Ortego	George Chesebro
Senora Sanguinetti	Orfa Casanova
The Giant Negro	Jules Cowles
Bascom	John Prince
The Stranger	Arnold Melvin
Caramba, the monkey	"Josephine"

A melodramatic mystery play is here done in sumptuous style and with a good deal of fine production magnificence. The scope and splendor of the staging is an impressive feature of an interesting action thriller. Dorothy Devore and Malcolm McGregor are featured in a conspicuously well-selected cast.

The material classes as mere fiction of the "popular" grade, but so well is the production done that the film impresses as of a higher quality than its real substance would indicate. It is as though some publisher issued one of Harold Bell Wright's novels in a de luxe Russian leather edition. Pictorially the film is a revel of impressive beauty, while the story itself is sheer mechanical melodrama.

The locale is an aristocratic estate in Latin-America which lends itself splendidly, both to the unfolding of a romantic adventure tale and to the creation of fine scenic settings, both of which elements are employed for full value.

The story opens on shipboard. Dolores, South American heiress, on her way home from school in the States, falls in love with the young ship's doctor, Dan Stone. In defending her from a tipsy passenger Stone knocks the offender down and, thinking him dead, takes flight at Dolores' port.

The girl's guardian tries to force her into a marriage with Don Ortego, his partner in some mysterious business connected with the ancient church on the estates. The guardian moves about in a sinister atmosphere of intrigue. Dan wanders into his power and is received on the understanding that he must take charge of a mysterious patient, a man dying in a remote wing of the castle guarded by a huge Negro.

Dolores' suspicions are aroused by the warning she must not look into the chapel. A score of devices are used to heighten the air of grim mystery. The plot to marry the girl off proceeds to the altar, when a jealous mistress of the bridegroom breaks down all the plots by revealing to the American consul that the castle is the headquarters for a gang of counterfeiters who have been flooding the states with bad money. This leads to a grand battle as the American marines burst in upon the wedding scene to arrest the bridegroom, while the chief plotter and the hero engage in a running fight through the underground passages of the castle. The Negro guard of the mysterious invalid (who is the engraver used by the counterfeiters) supplies most of the comic relief.

The melodramatic material is abundant and the succession of action bits is constant, all of them effective in a purely theatrical way and holding attention closely. An ingenious bit of naive fiction made very effective through the manner of production. *Rush.*

OUT OF THE WEST

F. B. O. production. Starring Tom Tyler. Directed by Harry O'Connor. Distributed by Film Booking Offices. At the Stanley, New York. Running time, 57 minutes.

Bernice O'Connor..............Betty Welch
John O'Connor.............Alfred Henston
Jim Rollin.................Harry O'Connor
Tom Hanley..................Tom Tyler
Granny...................Gertrude Claire
Bide Goodrich............Ethan Laidlaw
Mascot...................Frankie Darro

This "western" has all the earmarks of a picturized version of a Frank Merriwell. It looks like the old Merriwell stuff with the home run hero at the bat. This may not sound like a "western," but it is a western crowd that plays; all cowhands with Tom Tyler, the big hero.

Not much to it, but some rough riding by Tyler and he's a rough rider all over the lot. There are several good laughs, one not intended, but spontaneous just the same. This unexpected laughter came when little Frankie Darro discovers the hero a captive in a cave on the day of the big game he is to pitch. Little Frankie conceives the idea of attracting the guard outside. As the guard steps into the open he is socked on the bean from above by a rock or boulder flung downward by Frankie. Tyler is a hard worker. He takes his screen assignment pretty seriously, but he is not afraid to mess his physiognomy up in the rough stuff. Frankie Darro is a child of the movies; he knows his onions right now, and he's only a whisper, so to speak.

Gertrude Claire made a pleasing and effective character of the old grandmother.

Economically speaking the picture is right; otherwise it will suffer in comparison with "westerns" now surfeiting the market. *Mark.*

Prisoners of the Storm

Universal-Jewel starring House Peters. Lynn Reynolds production, directed by Mr. Reynolds. Adapted from the James Oliver Curwood story, "The Quest of Joan." Cast includes Harry Todd, Walter McGrail, Peggy Montgomery, Clark Comstock and Fred de Silva. Running time, 66 minutes.

Taken from the Curwood story, "Prisoners of the Storm" is naturally of the northwest and snow stuff. It's average double feature day material minus any particular kick, despite a snow avalanche that hems in the principal parties. This house viewed it quietly and without visible or audible response.

It doesn't rate the 66 minutes consumed and probably an entire reel could have come out and no harm would have been done. Pretty slow in spots. Those who are tired will sleep for there's nothing to keep 'em awake.

Two prospectors have hit a vein and intend to follow each other to the trading post a day apart. The elder man is anxious to see his daughter, so is the first to leave and is murdered en route. A northwest Mountie has tipped off the girl (Miss Montgomery), that her Dad (Harry Todd), is coming in loaded with money, and the post doctor (Fred de Silva) overhears the information.

The father failing to show up starts the Mountie (Walter McGrail) on a search when he attacks Bucky Malone (House Peters), who is following his partner in from his diggings.

The officer is convinced Malone has murdered his partner and in the scuffle hurts his leg. Malone drags him to a cabin and when the sergeant falls ill goes for the post physician. The girl accompanies him and all are snowed in.

Then the avalanche, the struggle to get out with the doctor finally confessing the crime. Malone and the girl reach for each other at the finish inasmuch as the man has fallen in love with a photograph her father possessed.

Obvious scenario minus a twist or outstanding punch. Peters does well enough as the handcuffed hero, with Miss Montgomery a passable heroine. McGrail seemed to get more out of his role of the Mountie than anyone else, with Harry Todd taking care of the comedy early in the running before bumped off. De Silva was rather a white-haired villain, the dirty deed being done by sub-title.

Minor screen material bound to play that class of theatre. *Skig.*

The Student of Prague

Berlin, Nov. 10.

Gruesome thriller which might have emanated from the imagination of Poe.

A student in the Prague university is badly in debt and wants money to win the rich heiress with whom he is in love.

The devil, disguised as an old merchant, gives him the necessary fortune but, in exchange, takes his reflection in the mirror away from him. This reflection then takes on an evil existence of its own. It fights a duel in his stead and kills an opponent whom the student has given his word to spare. The heiress throws him over and everybody shuns him. Driven to desperation he is followed through the night by his reflection. At last the reflection returns to the mirror from which it was taken and signifies, by pointing at its heart, that the student shall shoot it there. He fires, the mirror breaks to pieces, and he realizes, from gazing into one of the fragments, that he now can see himself again in the glass. But in shooting his reflection he has at the same time wounded himself mortally.

Not a bad story for the Caligari type of treatment. Werner Krauss was the best possible choice for the Devil, and Conrad Veidt might be supposed an adequate one for the student. But the director, Heinrich Galeen, hasn't been able to get much out of his actors and only the last half reel chase of the student by his reflection is really thrilling. While Conrad Veidt again proves himself to be without sufficient depth and variety to carry a star role. *Trask.*

WHAT PRICE GLORY

William Fox Production from the stage play by Laurence Stallings and Maxwell Anderson. Directed by Raoul Walsh. Featuring Victor McLaglen, Edmund Lowe and Dolores Del Rio. Titled by Malcolm Stuart Boylan. At the Harris Theatre, New York, for run beginning Nov. 23. Running time, 116 minutes.

Captain Flagg............Victor McLaglen
Sergeant Quirt.............Edmund Lowe
Charmaine...............Dolores Del Rio
"Cognac Pete"..........William V. Mong
Hilda of China............Phyllis Haver
Carmen of the Phillippines....Elena Juardo
Lieut. Moore..................Leslie Fenton
Private Lewisohn............Barry Norton
Private Lipinsky..........Sammy Cohen
Private Kiper...........Ted McNamara
French Mayor.............August Tollaire

To settle the question right off the bat let it be said that the event of "The Big Parade" a year ago has not taken the edge off of "What Price Glory." As a matter of fact "The Big Parade" has made an audience for "What Price Glory."

More than that, the latter film has nothing to fear at the box office of the effect of the first one. From the looks of things it is safe to predict that the Fox picture is going to be just as great a hit in the legitimate houses as the Metro-Goldwyn-Mayer one is. Yet while they are both by the same author and both are war pictures, still they are totally unlike each other. You can mark "What Price Glory" down in your little red book as one of those pictures that is "in" and look back at that book a couple of years from now with the satisfaction that you picked a winner.

The chances are that "What Price Glory" will be just as big at the box office as "The Big Parade" was, providing it is as deftly handled as a road show. One thing the Fox people do not want to do and that is to rush in all over the country with road shows right off the bat. The thing to do with this one is to lay back, pick the spots and play about six of the big cities this season. Philadelphia, Boston, Chicago added to New York and Los Angeles already opened, and possibly San Francisco should be all that are hit this season, and then late next August strike out with about 12 companies in the week stands and get the money.

"What Price Glory" is a picture that they are going to talk about. They are going to gag that "bird" thing around. They who see the picture are going to start tipping off on the cuss words used, words that can only be gotten by lip reading, but the bunch that goes to see the picture will watch for that rough stuff. And that word of mouth advertising that is going to result is the thing that is going to get about the country like wildfire and go a long way to make the picture.

The more one thinks of this picture the more angles there are to judge it a surefire money maker from. It's a picture that has everything except an out and out love story of the calibre of the one that there was in "The Big Parade." But where it lacks in that it certainly does make up in sex stuff and comedy. And comedy that is comedy. Comedy that will appeal to the variest lowbrow and still click with those who have no hair at all.

There is a wallop right in the beginning in the two short sequences showing both Flagg and Quirt as sergeants of the Marines in China and the Phillippines. Right here the conflict between the two men whose trade is soldiering, over women is set down and in the sexiest manner possible, yet with a light touch of comedy that hits the audience right between the eyes.

Then the picture goes right into France. The world war period begins with the arrival of the marines the first of our soldiers to get "over there." They are in a little French village back of the lines, and it is here and in the trenches that all the following action takes place.

Flagg, captain now in his own beloved U. S. Marine Corps, takes his company into the village and comedy begins from that moment. His striker Private Kiper (the fellow with the ever-ready "bird") and Private Lipinski that the bowl arolling. The action alternates, a laugh, a bit of sex stuff and a thrill and heart-throb from then on.

The picture keeps moving along at a pace that has one on edge always and wondering. The wonderment does not start until Flagg's old rival with women, Quirt, appears. He is still a sergeant, but the best in the Corps, the only thing is that he is "too wise," and that's why he can't rate a commission. But from that point the audience begins to wonder. The question is which of the men, or maybe both, has made the grade with the charming Charmaine. Of course they never find out but they do a lot of guessing.

Both men are on the make and both are trying hard. They are free with their hands and kisses. Charmaine does not appear to repulse either in this respect until the final shots of the picture, when she does express her preferment for the sergeant, although he marches right off to the front again though suffering from a wound.

A title just before the ending tells the story better than words here set forth could. It is to the effect that they go to the front once and come back, they go twice and come back—but the third time, never. They are uttered by Charmaine as she watches the two men that have battled each other for her favors march off arm in arm to fight together the common enemy.

So much for the story, itself.

Now for the picture "What Price Glory."

In the first place if this is a sample of what Winnie Sheehan can do on the Fox lot in the way of making pictures for that organization he should never be permitted to get away from the lot. The result will be that William Fox will not only run up profits of a figure that he has never had before but he will get his pictures in houses where he never expected that they would be unless he could drive up with a machine gun and force them to book.

Then as to the cast. It is one of the most perfect things about the picture. Victor McLaglan stands out bigger than he ever has in any picture, and this production is going to "make" him. He is the hard-boiled Capt. Flagg, and the women are going to love him. His role gets far greater sympathy from them than that of Sergeant Quirt, which Edmund Lowe plays, and Lowe in this picture is doing his greatest bit of screen acting. No one thought Lowe could get away with Sergeant Quirt when he was cast for it. Lowe has fooled them, he IS Quirt, hair cut and all.

And as for the Charmaine of Dolores Del Rio, that girl doesn't have to go any farther; she is made if ever an actress was. Of course it may have been due to a great extent to the direction, but she registers like a house afire. It is no wonder that she had the whole army after her! She's worth it, in the picture.

But with it all one cannot overlook Leslie Fenton, who in a brief scene in a dugout dressing station certainly gives the impression of a shell fire crazed man if there ever was one enacted before the camera. With the comedy in the hands of Ted McNamara (the "bird" artist) and Sammy Cohen as the Little Heb private, there is nothing more to be asked for.

In the early sequences Phyllis Haver slips over a dame on the "make" that will send the boys walking right up to the screen and lay their dough on the line, and Elena Jurado, the Phillippino lady who is also a member of that profession, isn't hard to look at either. William V. Mong as the father of the girl gives a corking characterization to the grasping inn keeper who wouldn't hesitate to make a few francs even at the cost of his daughter's shame, while August Tollaire as the French village mayor was good for a couple of laughs, one when the boys "took" him in the crap game and the other when the "striker" went down to "dust him off" for the wedding.

To Raoul Walsh a great deal of credit will have to go. He has turned out a picture that places him right in the front rank of directors. His handling of the war stuff is little short of marvelous. In the shooting of those scenes the camera staff, which comprised J. B. McGill, John Marta and John Smith, must come in for a full share of praise.

Having seen the picture twice, once with and one without the musical accompaniment, one must say that Erno Rapee did compose a masterful score for the production. True, there are times when the music seems rather too forceful, but in the main it does lift the production tremendously.

No one can go wrong playing "What Price Glory," no matter what kind of a theatre it is. Any of the legit house managers, especially those that played "The Big Parade," who don't go after this one, are fast asleep.

It's a natural, anywhere, east or west, north or south, and the laughs are going to stop any foreign criticism such as the "Big Parade" received.

In other words it's a "bird" and that goes both ways. *Fred.*

THE CANADIAN

Famous Players-Lasky production starring Tom Meighan. Adapted from W. Somerset Maugham's play, "The Land of Promises." Directed by William Beaudine. At the Paramount, New York, week Nov. 27. Running time, 78 mins.

Frank Taylor	Tom Meighan
Nora	Mona Palma
Ed Marsh	Wyndham Standing
Gertie	Dale Fuller
Pop Tyson	Charles Winninger

Small cast celluloid of the Maugham play that rates above the other stories Tom Meighan has had handed him of late. It's a quiet bit of screen telling depending on the story, cast and direction to send it across.

There are no battles, snow avalanches, cyclones or Indian stuff. It's just a study of the Canadian wheat fields with a farm hand finally winning the love of a cultured girl come over from the "old country."

It's not timed when Canada was in its infancy. Modern threshing machines are in action, etc. In fact, the picture was so timely it is understood Meighan walked out on it to see the Dempsey-Tunney scrap. According to this sidelight yarn, the star left the troupe flat in Calgary and hied himself to Philadelphia with the picture unfinished. This necessitated the company staying on "location" for another week or 10 days carefully shooting "stills" for reproduction sets in the east, where the film was finished. The switch is not noticeable, although skylines seen through the windows of Meighan's supposed Alberta cabin are obviously the result of a scene painter's artistry.

It might be said that the picture takes too long in unwinding itself, especially in lieu of the limited action. There are places that could and will be cut as 78 minutes is a lot of time in the big program houses unless it all has some bearing on the matter. A little of "The Canadian's" footage isn't entirely necessary, but at that there isn't much waste.

Beaudine has extracted full worth from each player in his meagre cast, particularly Dale Fuller. Miss Fuller plays the extremely plain wife of Ed Marsh, an Englishman come to Canada to farm and refill his pockets. It is his sister, Nora, whom Frank finally takes to wife because she and Mrs. Marsh can't get along under the same roof.

The electric condition between Gertie and Nora finally blisters the house when the two women have words before the farm hands. Gertie demands an apology from her well-bred sister-in-law. She gets it, and before the "hands," but Nora can't stand the gaff and throws herself at Frank with the proposition that she'll be no more than housekeeper for him, despite the ring.

Frank's cabin is worse than her brother's home, so Nora is between and betwixt and becomes worse off when Frank forces his way into her room, after having slept in the combined dining room-parlor for weeks. That's the finish for Nora, only a sprained ankle keeping her from making the next train. Frank brings her back; he's a much subdued husband, takes to the barn for sleeping quarters and they begin to get along more amiably.

Frank believes Nora wants to go back to her cultured England, and when he harvests intends to bank roll her return passage. Meanwhile, Nora's aunt dies and leaves her $2,500. That's the sailing o. k. with Nora reluctantly leaving for home and country. Pop Tyson (Mr. Edinger) has the situation purposely misses the train he's driving Nora to catch and the married couple are finally brought together, despite themselves, having been silently in love with each other anyway since the fourth reel, maybe the third.

Miss Fuller's performance is a capital effort. Perhaps the best of the cast. It's a forceful character as she plays it, and Beaudine has given her a few comedy chances, as well. Winninger is the laugh relief and fulfils that niche capably. Miss Palma, as Nora, plays her with reserve, making a rather colorless girl win some sympathy. Meighan, of course, is the hardy son of toil, looks it and sends it from the screen to the audience.

Beaudine has made a neat job of this stage adaption. It should prove a boon to the Meighan fans who have been waiting some time to see their star in a story that had some sense or merit to it. *Skig.*

Belle of Broadway

Columbia Picture produced by Harry Cohn. From the story by J. Grubb Alexander and Jean Peary, adapted by J. Grubb Alexander. Directed by Harry O. Hoyt. Featuring Betty Compson and Herbert Rawlinson. At the Stanley, N. Y., Nov. 24, one day. Running time, 62 minutes.

Marie Duval	Betty Compson
Paul Merlin	Herbert Rawlinson
Mme. Adele	Edith Yorke
Count De Parma	Armand Kaliz

Unusually fair picture for the independent market. Good enough to stand alone in the daily change houses in these days of double feature bill, and that is saying a whole lot.

Theme is one of the stage and rejuvenation, in itself interesting. In addition are a couple of names for the smaller houses, Betty Compson and Herbert Rawlinson. Here they are playing leads instead of being supporting players, which is a change of late for them.

Story laid in Paris in 1896 where Madame Adele makes her debut in "Du Barry." Married to a musician in the pit of the theatre in which she is playing he departs for parts unknown, taking with him the boy born of their marriage.

Story jumps to the present. Mme. Adele, worn, aged and without funds, except enough to eke out a more or less precarious existence, visits the theatrical agents. Can't land a job. One tells her that if she could look as she did 30 years ago he would put on a revival of "Du Barry."

On returning to her theatrical boarding house, a young girl studying dramatic art, in a moment of jest, dons the old actress' costume. The resemblance is so marked the idea is born of substituting the young girl for the former star.

It works out and the town is again crazy about the one whom they suppose to be Adele. Her old admirers flock about her and one in particular tries to make the grade. He insists that she come to his apartment for supper. When she does he unmasks the masquerade and then tries to compel the girl to accept his attentions. She is rescued at the last minute by a young admirer whom she met before the masquerade was started.

As good old coincidence is dragged in he proves to be the son of the old star.

Miss Compson plays the dual role. Edith Yorke is the former star, doing very well with it. Miss Compson should watch her step in profile shots. Rawlinson as the hero does well enough. Armand Kaliz, former musical comedy tenor, serves as the menace.

Picture is well directed and some stock shots are cut into it with perfect continuity. *Fred.*

Wild Horse Stampede

Blue Streak Western, released by Universal. Story by W. C. Tuttle. Direction of Al Rogell. Starring Jack Hoxie. At Tivoli, New York, one day (Nov. 24).

Nothing sensational in this except the tough, red-shirted finale hoppers who clutter up the great wide-open spaces have seldom been known to have their eyebrows picked a la Broadway chorus girl. Cow-hands wouldn't go in for these extravagances even if there were any beauty parlors on the Cross L ranch.

A dog called "Bunk" may now walk around with his tail in the air for getting a heavy laugh in one scene where he plays dead. Then, when he figures the villains have forgotten him, warily opens one eye while remaining perfectly still, to slip off. "Bunk" doesn't look so magnificent in the long shots, but the close-ups of his face are interesting. Clever.

Jack Hoxie as Jack Parker succeeds in corralling 1,000 wild horses within 10 days with the aid of his horse, "Scout." With the money they represent he figures he "won't be 'shamed to arsk Jess Hayden to be mine." But Champion William A. Steele also wants little Jess. While Jack is busy corralling the ponies the former makes love to the lass, much against the father's wishes.

Enter the mysterious woman whom Jack allows to use his cabin. Follow complications, which end up in a horse stampede in which the bold, bad man is trampled to death. The mysterious woman turns out to be a very close relative of Champion; in fact, his wife.

Picture moves along at a canter. Stampede camera shots are okay, but produce nothing in the way of an innovation.

Prowlers of the Night

Blue Streak western released by Universal. Story and direction by Ernst Laemmle. Starring Fred Humes. At the Stanley, New York, one day, Nov. 26.

Freddie Humes looks more like a cowboy than most of the permanent hair wave college kid specimens. Although he isn't great on the emotional stuff Humes acts naturally, smiles a shy, awkward little smile, and moves with diffidence in the presence of the one and only. More like a cowboy than a polished club man in a riding outfit.

As Sheriff Norton, Fred is on the trail of a gang of bank robbers which he finally locates. The girl, Barbara Kent, is the daughter of the leader of the gang and is given a chance to waste a couple of hundred feet of perfectly good film by weeping copiously on Norton's shoulder for no apparent reason.

The picture boasts one solitary laugh. Humes wanders into the village store to buy a gift for the girl and is asked if he wants something "for the wife or something nice?"

A couple of good camera shots of horses flying over a rocky embankment and lots of pretty mountain scenery. One scene of a snowcapped mountain with its head breaking in the blue skies looks more like a beautiful painting than a bit of nature's handiwork.

Story is hackneyed, plot contains no surprises and the action hardly a thrill.

Hair Trigger Baxter

J. J. Goldberg film releasing through F. B. O. Starring Bob Custer. Directed by Jack Nelson. Cast includes, besides Custer, Lew Meehan, Eugenia Gilbert, Ernie Adams, Murdock MacQuarrie and Hugh Saxon. At the Stanley, New York, one day (Nov. 24). Running time, 54 minutes.

Story of a rancher's son who cleans out a tribe of rustlers to save his parent. Previously he rescued the girl from dance hall persecution, and all is well in 54 minutes.

Good-looking boy, this Custer, besides which he handles himself so as not to overplay. Maybe the director should cut in for credit on this point. Otherwise "Hair Trigger Baxter" is a typical western, with nothing to make it a standout among the species. The supporting cast contribute little more than their figures to carry out the yarn, Custer practically sustaining the burden alone.

Picture patrons have been watching films of this order for years. And it's the old story again. Custer looks as if he could play superior fare. His appearance should be pleasing to men as well as women, and he shows possibilities of being able to troup. But these kind of stories won't help him. *Skig.*

A REGULAR SCOUT

Fred Thomson production released by F. B. O. From the story by Buckleigh F. Oxford, adapted and directed by David Kirkland. Seen in projection room. Running time, 58 minutes.
Fred Blake.................Fred Thomson
Olive Monroe.............Olive Hasbrouck
Luke Baxter............William Courtright
Steve Baxter.............T. Roy Barnes
Mrs. Monroe...........Margaret Seddon
Buddy Monroe.........Buck Black
Ed. Powell................Robert McKim
Scar Stevens.............Harry Woods
Silver.....................Silver King

A corking Fred Thomson action western that has a corking tie-up made to order. It is a Boy Scout picture that will make every kid in every town want to join the Scouts, and in addition the picture will prove real estertainment for the Thomson fans. It is a rare combination certain to please the grown-ups as well as the youngsters.

After all, the name of Fred Thomson is sufficient gauarantee at the box office in enough spots in this country for the exhibitor to just stick up the notice that "another Fred Thomson picture" is the attraction.

Another touch cannot be overlooked. Imagine, if you can, any other producer who had Mary Carr in the cast overlooking the fact

just because she was in the first reel, and did not run through the picture. In the majority of cases they would have had her name right after that of the star, but here it wasn't on the cast sheet.

The feature starts with Fred Thomson as the rodeo champion of his territory. While the boy is out adding to his laurels as a rider of bucking horses along comes a hard character who first begs a meal from the boy's mother and then strangles her so that he can loot her purse.

Thomson starts after the murderer and finally lands him in the slums of Los Angeles. There is a struggle and the murderer is slain. The hero flees, but not until he has learned from the effects of the dead man, that he had planned to return to his mother who had been seeking him all over the country. He then decides to pose as the slain man to wreak further vengeance on his relatives. But, instead, he falls in love with his supposed sister, rescues a younger brother, who is a Boy Scout, from what appeared to be sure death, is accused of the murder of the scar-hand dead man, only to be saved at the last minute.

There are a lot of kicks in the action and the Boy Scouts play no small part. When the heroine of the story is kidnapped the kids go off on the trail. It is there with a thrill and at the same time carries a laugh.

Of course Silver King, Thomson's horse, plays an important part in the story, and the way that horse is handled in a couple of shots certainly puts him in the star class. *Fred.*

FLASHING FANGS

F. B. O. picture, starring dog, "Ranger." Adapted for screen from story, "Always Faithful," by Ewart Adamson. Directed by Henry McCarthy. Running time, 54 minutes.

Film dog stars are still leaping into place before the picture camera. Some show superior canine intelligence to others, but all in the end are just in time to pounce upon the cruel villain who has the fair-haired heroine in his grasp. Ranger is no exception. Nicely trained animal and does very well in his main climax of outfighting the bad man of this film, who has chained the girl to the corner of his shack.

This is perhaps about the only film now in existence that shows how easy a band of men can raid a hoosegow and take a man out for a little necktie party. Of course the hanging is nipped in the bud, but it is well staged as far as it went.

Cast just cast.

Cheap in the making; story not strong and ancient in construction with rental chances hinging solely upon the dog. *Mark.*

THE FALSE ALARM

Columbia picture releasing through Commonwealth and produced by Harry Cohen. Frank O'Connor directing from story by Leah Baird. Cast includes Ralph Lewis, Dorothy Pevier, John Harron, Mary Carr, George O'Hara, Priscilla Bouner, Lillian Leighton. Running time, 59 minutes.

Another ode to the fire departments and probably on the "hunch" started by Louis Mayer's "Fire Brigade." There have been plenty of these around this district lately but this much can be said for "The False Alarm"—it's about the best of the independent attempts to date.

For one thing the story has some body to it, an item which the others have lacked. In this instance the family juvenile follows his father's footsteps into a fire house and on his first alarm fal's prey to an inherited fear of fire. Leaving his trapped father to be rescued by others, Joe Casey (John Harron)

becomes ostracized and forbidden his home. He goes to the steel mills to overcome the weakness. That he makes good is obvious, so he finally comes back to marry the family's adopted daughter (Dorothy Revier) and to once more rate a uniform.

Meanwhile there is the counter story of Joe's brother (George O'Hara) mixed up with crooks and responsible for Bessie Flannigan's (Priscilla Bouner) predicament. Trapped in an apartment fire, Joe would rescue Bessie and the brother fights him to allow the girl to perish as a means of dodging his responsibility.

A comedy attempt during the running, but it doesn't get anywhere. However, the cast do well by this screen yarn. Mary Carr and Lillian Leighton convince in mother roles while Ralph Lewis is the stern father and fire chief. Miss Revier has no dramatic call but Harron extracts plentifully from the substance in the part of the boy who must come back.

Some of the fire stuff is colored. Not entirely necessary but not too detrimental either. O'Connor has carried it along with a fair degree of speed and the result is that this edition should be able to play the secondaries to satisfaction. No panic, mind, but okay. Other than the de luxe palaces, the emporiums should like it. *Skig.*

OH, WHAT A NIGHT

Sterling production released by Sterling Pictures, Inc. Directed by Lloyd Ingraham. Featured players, Raymond McKee, Edna Murphy, Ned Sparks and Charles K. French. Running time, 57 mins.

Quite a smattering of "Seven Keys to Baldpate," "Seven Days" and whatnot in this one. But a youngster runs away with the picture.

It concerns a young playwright who goes to the apartment of a stage director, where he may write a new third act of his play that has gone into rehearsal. The writer soon finds himself in all kinds of trouble, starting when the fat manager of the hotel apartment is robbed of his watch and chain and puts the playwright under suspicion. This is followed by a robbery at the apartment house when a second-story worker gets hold of a string of pearls that have been dropped into the pocket of the playwright's coat as he is mistaken for the jeweler's messenger.

Of course there is a girl and she is Edna Murphy. Watching the work of this blonde convinces that she is improving.

The main male roles are handled by Raymond McKee, as the playwright, and Ned Sparks, as the burglar. Comedy scenes are nicely worked up and effectively.

From start to finish there is a rough-house, mistaken identities, chases galore, with the kidnaping of the baby that was supposed to have swallowed the pearls and its subsequent recapture on the roof of the apartment house, all intended for laughs.

What success the picture obtains is due to the principals and that little kid. The latter is almost uncanny in the unusual work performed. *Mark.*

THE DEVIL'S TOLL

Big Horn Ranch Presentation, distributed by Metro-Goldwyn-Mayer, directed by Clifford Smith. Starring Francis McDonald.

Compared to some of the westerns turned out recently this one is a classic. Tom Santschi, as the heavy, is much more convincing than he ever was as the lead in other pictures of this kind, while in Kathleen Key, beauty-famished fans can take a look at one of the prettiest girls ever lassoed into appearing in split skirts.

Kathleen can roll her eyes too and shows up well in camera shots from every angle. She appears with long, black curls, in a floor-sweeping dress fitting tight at the hips and higher, in the style of 20 years ago.

Francis McDonald, as Frank Darwin, has flown to an impregnable shack in the hills to forget the scorn of some woman, name unmentioned.

McDonald puts over a much more creditable performance than the usual run of western heroes but, owing to lack of a powerful appearance, is quite unconvincing in the strength display scenes. Picture shows good direction.

OLD IRONSIDES

James Cruze's Paramount production presented by Adolph Zukor and Jesse L. Lasky. From the story by Laurence Stallinsg, suggested and adapted by Harry and Walter Woods. Score by Hugo Riesenfeld. At the Rivoli, New York, for run, opening Dec. 6, 1926. Running time, 117 minutes.

The Girl.......................Esther Ralston
The Boy.......................Charles Farrell
The Boatswain................Wallace Beery
The Gunner..................George Bancroft
The Cook....................George Godfrey
Commodore Preble......Charles Hill Mailes
Stephen Decatur..........Johnny Walker

No matter what the production of "Old Ironsides" cost, the executives of the Famous Players-Lasky organization were able to go home Monday night after the opening at the Rivoli and sleep wel' for no matter what investment the picture represents they are sure to get it all back and a whole lot more.

The opening performance was attended with a lot of pomp and ceremony, gold lace and naval officials, including the Secretary of the Navy and a flock of society folk. It's doubtful if the Rivoli ever had so many Rolls-Royces standing in front of its door at one time.

But these, together with the regular run of picture fans who managed to buy their way into the house and a flock of picture people were brought to their feet at the close of the first part of the picture when the screen opened up to twice its regular size and revealed a picture of the Frigate "Constitution" sailing directly at the audience. That was the biggest "kick" delivered to any audience in a motion picture theatre in years. What an impression it made on the high ranking naval officers who were present. They got a kick out of it, too, and a kick that they'll remember for a long while.

"Old Ironsides" is a cinch for a year on Broadway at $2 top, and what a road show it will make. They are going to eat it alive, for their is no grown up or kid who doesn't recall:

Ay, tear her tattered ensign down!
Long has it waved on high,
And many an eye has danced to see
That banner in the sky.

and recalling it conjured up visions of Tripoli and pirates, sea fights and deeds of daring which put the United States navy on the map and freed the seas that all merchantmen might travel unmolested.

With these mental pictures in mind they will want to see this picture, and seeing it they won't be cheated, for the picture will have all that they'll expect and a lot more, too

And how Jimmie Cruze has made this picture. He has put the comedy relief in such spots as it was needed most and it is comedy of a type that will have the average audience howling with glee. And as for the battle scenes, the fight before Tripoli will be to naval pictures what the battle scenes of "What Price Glory" are to the visualizations of the late war.

"Old Ironsides" as a picture has everything that one could ask for. There is a love story that stands out tremendously, there is a comedy element ever present in the personages of Wallace B..ry, George Bancroft and George Godfrey (the latter the colored heavyweight pugilist who is a whale of a screen comic as paired up with Beery and Bancroft), there is the patriotic element which just goes to prove that George M. Cohan was right when it comes to waving the flag for an audience in this country, and above all the stirring spectacle as embodied .. the battle scenes.

In some quarters it is said that "Old Ironsides" cost something li.. $2,400,000 to produce. If that is true it was worth it, for it is a picture that will keep on sending the dough home from the four corners of the earth for years to come. It can't grow stale and right now with the hook-up of the "Save 'Old Ironsides'" campaign it is sure to be a natural.

Laurence Stalling, who did the tale for the picture, has taken a couple of liberties with history to plant a love story, but he has done this so skillfully that no one is going to object. He starts his story at the session of Congress in Philadelphia, with Thomas Jefferson delivering his famous "Millions for defense but not a cent for tribute" address—then leaps to New England to show his hero leaving the farm to enlist in the navy to do service on the "Constitution." From that point the story of the love affairs of the hero and heroine take precedence over the Tripolian situation, except for a brief minute just before the closing of the first part.

The hero is shanghaied onto the barque "Esther" together with a gunner's mate of the "Constitution." On the "Esther" is the daughter of the owner of the craft, journeying to Italy to meet her father. The farm boy is whipped into a seaman at the end of a rope but becomes so proficient that he is taught the handling of the wheel.

The girl falls in love with him despite his lowly position. All goes well until the ship is becalmed in the Mediterranean and attacked by pirates from the Barbary Coast. They are taken to Tripoli and sold into slavery.

The captain of the "Esther" makes a plea that he be permitted to secure ransom for the woman and himself, but the girl is so pretty that she is selected as a gift to the Sultan while the crew are put to work in the quarries. Berry, Bancroft, Godfrey and the hero are shackled together, but make their escape during the night and in an open boat put out to sea, picked up a few days later by the "Constitution."

Meanwhile the "Philadelphia" is shown chasing a pirate craft into the harbor of Tripoli, where she runs aground and is captured. The daring feat of Stephen Decatur in entering the harbor with a few men and blowing up the captured ship is one of the real patriotic kicks.

Then finally the "Constitution" comes sailing into the scene and with blazing guns bests the great forts, sinks the Tripolian frigate and captures the fort.

There are no words that can be set on paper that will convey the thrills to be found in this sea battle or the hand-to-hand encounters on the decks of the ships, slippery with the blood of those fallen in the fray, the toppling great masts of the ship as they are chopped to splinters by the constant cannonading, the slithering sails that are rent and torn by shot and shell, the furious give and take of it all, and at the same time there is present that ever-saving comedy touch that sends the picture along at a pace that makes the audience believe it has not seen enough of it.

For the finish the victorious crew of the 'Constitution" is shown as the "Esther" is leaving port, again manned by her own crew who have been released by the pirates, with the lovers reunited on the deck, and the boatswain of the out-going ship can not refrain from shooting a last wise crack of the day to his former companion, the gunner, who is remaining with the man-o-war.

Charles Farrell, who plays the hero, is a find if there ever was one. He has been around pictures for a time but has never done anything as outstanding as his work in this picture. He got his chance here, and from now on is made. Esther Ralston, as the heroine, is truly magnificent. She holds her own every minute.

Charles Hill Mailes is the stern, old Commodore Preble, while Johnny Walker as Stephen Decatur clicks in a manner that he has not since the days of "Over the Hill."

But the biggest kick of the picture, after all, is the new Magnascope, an arrangement which permits of the throwing of a picture twice the size of the one usually projected on the screen. This is the real punch. The manner in which it is first introduced is most impressive. The picture runs along for an hour until just before the closing of the first part the screen opens up to the full width and heighth of the stage and the "Constitution" comes sailing at the audience, only to turn her broadside just as she comes in front of the camera.

In the second part the story is again resumed on the regular screen until the battle scenes arrive, and then again is the full-stage screen used. What a thrill and what a kick! *Fred.*

FAUST

Ufa-Metro-Goldwyn-Mayer picture featuring Emil Jannings. Adapted from the Goethe version. F. W. Murnau, director; Carl Hoffmann, photographer. Titles by Katherine Hilliker and H. H. Caldwell. At Capitol, New York, week Dec. 5. Running time, 76 minutes.

Cherub ....Warner Fuetterer
The Evil Spirit...............Emil Jannings
Faust.........................Gosta Ekman
Marguerite...................Camilla Horn
Her Mother.................Frieda Richard
Her Brother Valentine....Wilhelm Dieterle
Her Aunt Martha..........Yvette Guilbert
The Duke.......................Eric Barclay
The Duchess..................Hanna Ralph

A Berlin review some time ago of this picture in Variety expressed doubt as to its financial success. From the initial box office reports coming in on "Faust" the conclusion to be drawn is that the German verdict is not to be scoffed at, but there is this angle to the situation: if the public does become b. o. shy at "Faust" it will be mostly because of the title. Anyone who sees it is bound to talk about it. The picture can't miss from that tangent. And as for the possibility of the title keeping them away, the opening Sunday at the Capitol disproves that theory, at least for New York.

With a high wind and blizzard this house was practically filled when the four o'clock matinee performance began. Four hours later, with the wind still hitting it up, but the snow having stopped, a double line turned the 51st street corner to extend another 100 feet. So that shows either the title doesn't hurt or those who saw it in the afternoon talked much and fast about it.

"Faust" is not a performer's picture. With or without Emil Jannings it would be pictorially as good. Murnau, directing, and Hoffmann at the camera, have made the cast secondary. It's really a cameraman's picture. The boys who crank will probably take a good look. It's likely there's so much expert camera work flashed that the American photographers will see this one twice.

Murnau has done with this one what Griffith tried or wanted to do in "Sorrows of Satan." Running along similar lines Murnau's symbolizing is far in advance of what "Sorrows" held. And a couple of effects and the photography in general is about all the latest Griffith release has to offer.

This Ufa product is a studio made film if there ever has been one. Exteriors and interiors flaunt the studio trademark, yet all of the sets and the manner in which they have been lighted and pictured offsets any resemblance to the commonplace. There's nothing ordinary about "Faust," even if most of the credit goes to those behind the camera instead of those in front of the lens.

How much trick photography and how many fantastic sets go to make up this release is guess work. One report is that Murnau had an electrically driven camera placed on a swinging and circular piece of scaffolding atop a regular elevator plunger to "shoot" the passage of Mephisto (Jannings) and Faust (Ekman) through the air on a flying cloak. The appearance of Mephisto's head and shoulders above a village, his blowing of the black plague over the town, the burning of words upon a paper scroll, dazzling light flashes that blind the action momentarily, etc., are all there. Beautiful work throughout that is unfamiliar to this country's audiences but which they'll get plenty of as soon as the home technical staffs have a chance to take a look at this epic from across the Rhine.

Berlin states that the story is based on the Goethe version plus the scenarist, Hans Kayser, having interpolated a few modern touches. Opera regulars will probably be the only ones to note the deviations and it doesn't make much difference anyway. However, there is a comedy passage between Jannings and Yvette Guilbert that, while strictly elementary, got results at the Capitol. Possibly because of the weight of the main theme.

Murnau has taken the story of Heaven and Hell at cross purposes over the soul of Faust and symbolized it with a production that must have cost all kinds of money. The legendary tale loses nothing as this German director tells it in celluloid and it's certain that no stage performance could ever relate it as it is told here. An odd rhythm is given the film through the cast generally entrancing and exciting in spasmodic rushes. It's all fantastic with the weird happenings usually signalized by vapors pouring up from beneath the action.

Jannings' performance infers that he was entirely subservient to his director, and all other cast contributions are in a similar vein. The result is that no one predominates, although the work of Jannings, Gosta Ekman and Camilla Horn, as Marguerite, is bound to receive favorable comment.

If "Faust" isn't a "Last Laugh" then it's the next thing to it and only because it lacks the personal note the "Laugh" possessed. It's certainly as artistic in design, even more so. The applause with which a matinee audience greeted the climax was far beyond the usual for this house and the manner in which they were talking about it indicates it will hold over.

To offset the title doubt it could be mentioned that Yvette Guilbert, famed French diseuse, is making her first film appearance in America in "Faust." Besides which Jannings' name means something.

It's a corking picture that holds tension from start to finish. If they will come in to see it the picture will sell itself in the first 500 feet. One of the best that Germany has sent over and worth an hour and a quarter of anybody's time. *Skig.*

MICHAEL STROGOFF

Universal Film de France Triumph, presented by Carl Laemmle in conjunction with Jean Sapene. Adapted from Jules Verne's melodrama. Directed by V. Tourjansaky. At the Cohan, New York, for a run, starting Dec. 5. Running time, 105 minutes.

Michael Strogoff...............Ivan Moskine
Nadia Fedor.............Nathalie Kovanko
Ivan Ogareff.....................Chakalouny
Marfa Strogoff..............Mme. Brindeau
Zangara.....................Mme. De Yzarduy
The Grand Khan...........................Defas
Gen. Kissoff..........Prince N. Kougoucheff
Alexander II........................K. Gaidaroff

Some one with Universal made a colossal mistake. The blunder is trying to put the picture over as a $2 attraction. The trick that should have been pulled with this one was to have kept it off Broadway and to have gone to the exhibitors all over the country that play the Universal product and told them that this was a $2 picture, but that it would be given to them instead of road showed. And the exhibitor would have been tickled to death, for in the small towns "Strogoff" will make money. But on Broadway, or State street, or Tremont street, or Market street it will never get past the post at $2. At the Cohan on Sunday afternoon the audience laughed at the picture.

The fault lies not with the picture nor with the story, but with the manner in which the story was made into a picture. "Michael Strogoff" was a standard melodrama in the one-night stands in this country until about 10 or 15 years ago. It was one of the annual events in the small towns. Those who never saw it at least heard of it, and the chances are will want to see it in film form, but they won't give up $2 for it.

The manner in which the French adaptor and director literally took page after page of the Jules Verne story and slapped it on the screen makes the picture utterly impossible to the better class of audiences. In the first place, the cast is over-made up and hasn't the slightest idea of what this picture thing is all about. Then they went out and shot a series of chases, evidently still believing that the good old days are still here. The chances are that had the picture been made by an American company, including Universal, it would have been 100 per cent better in screen entertainment. They must have labored plenty in the U. offices trying to whip this one into shape.

Some shots in the picture are good and certain scenes worked out in a stencil color process are fairly effective, but on the whole the picture is what is termed in the trade "a Joe McGee."

Of course, the big scene is the blinding of Michael Strogoff by the decree of the Khan of the Tartars. This was exceptionally well worked up in color and was the one smash of the picture. In fact, the second half is the only portion in which anything worth while occurs.

In the cast there are but two people who amount to anything, and both are women. The remarkable performance of the film is in the hands of Mme. Brindeau, playing the mother of Strogoff. She is the real trouper and overshadows all others with the exception of Mme. De Yzarduy, as the gypsy sweetheart of the traitor, Ogareff. Universal says it is going to bring Ivan Moskine, featured in the title role, to this country. It doesn't make any difference yes or no. The leading woman, Nathalie Kovanko, just about gets by, and that's all.

In the picture houses for a three or four-day run "Strogoff" should be okay, but outside of that it's just one of those pictures that can be passed up. It's worse than "Sans Gene" that Gloria Swanson made in Europe and hasn't anything like the Swanson name to carry it along.

Fred.

THE POTEMKIN

Amkino Production presented by Leon S. Zamkovoy. Directed by S. M. Eisenstein. At the Biltmore, New York, for a run beginning Dec. 5. Running time, 68 mins. No cast given.

Something radical must have happened to this film prior to permission for its showing in New York being granted. Otherwise those who saw the film in its original form must have been overenthusiastic or off their nut from a showmanship standpoint. As this screen version of the mutiny aboard a Russian cruiser now stands it may interest a few Russians in this country, but it is utterly devoid of entertainment and box office value.

The authorities need not fear that the showing of this picture will cause any unrest among the lower classes in this country, for not enough of them will see it to make any difference. Those that are out-and-out reds, and those that are inclined to socialism will undoubtedly find great things about the picture, but hardly anyone else will.

There were stories months ago of a tremendously powerful motion picture that had been sent into this country by the Russian Soviet and that it was being kept under cover until such time as it could be shown. Those few who were permitted to see the picture privately raved about it. It was the picture of the "Potemkin" revolt. Word went along the street about the picture, and when announced that it finally was to be shown publicly there were a lot of people in the trade who wanted to see it. They were there Sunday night, and they walked out of the theatre very much disappointed.

In the first place, the showing was to have started at 8:30, but it was nine when things got under way. There was an overture that lasted minutes upon minutes, and then a scenic was shown, and after that there was an intermission. After intermission came an intermezzo, and then a presentation, which consisted of a reproduction of the deck of a battleship and a double sextet of male singers indulging in some Russian songs. Well enough for the Russians that were present, but the balance of the audience was bored to death by the proceedings up to this point. However, they had come to see the picture, "Potemkin," and they stuck.

The picture opens with a title to the effect that this is a reproduction of the uprising of the crew of the cruiser, Prince Potemkin, in Odessa harbor in 1905, the reproduction made possible through the official records from the Russian Navy archives of the original mutiny. The initial shots on board the cruiser show the men complaining over the food being served, the inspection of that food and its being passed by the ship's doctor. Then the men refuse to go to mess when the food is served, and the commander calls them to quarters and asks those that are satisfied with the food to take one step forward out of the ranks. All the officers and six members of the crew step out. In the ranks there is a movement started by one of the crew for all hands to muster at the front turret and the crew breaks ranks without orders from the officers. This enrages the commander to such an extent that he calls for the marines and orders a group of the men shot to death. The marines refuse to fire when ordered to do so, whereupon the seamen of the ship acclaim them as brothers, arm themselves and attack their officers, throwing them overboard.

In command of the ship, they take the body of their slain leader to Odessa and place it under a tent on one of the docks so that the city may be informed of their story. The city hears, heeds and offers support to the revolting crew, whereupon the Cossacks set upon the citizens and a massacre occurs —the Odessa massacre, which aroused the world.

The next day the Czar's fleet is seen approaching to capture the mutineers, but when the fleet arrives its gunners refuse to fire on the Potemkin, which steams out to sea. The ship is later interned by the Roumanian Government and the men informed that if they return to their own country they will be given fair trial, but according to a title presented here, the government broke its word, shot the ringleaders immediately on their return and sentenced the balance of the crew to exile in Siberia.

That is the story of "The Cruiser Potemkin" as depicted by film.

To Russians this may all mean something. As a pictorial historical record for the archives of the Soviet Government it may also mean something, but to the average American, unless he be an out-and-out red, it doesn't mean a damn. And that's that.

Fred.

Love 'Em and Leave 'Em

Famous Players-Lasky film. Directed by Frank Tuttle, featuring Evelyn Brent, Lawrence Gray and Louise Brooks. Based on the play by John Van Altsyno Weaver and George Abbott. Adapted by Townsend Martin. At the Paramount, New York, week Dec. 4. Running time, 62 mins.

Mame Walsh....................Evelyn Brent
Janie Walsh....................Louise Brooks
Bill Billingsley..............Lawrence Gray
Lem Woodruff..................Osgood Perkins
Miss Streeter..................Marcia Harris
Mrs. Whinfer......................Vera Sisson
Mr. McGonigle..............Arthur Donaldson
Miss Gimple......................Elsie Cavanna

This is a very human document, interesting and amusing, and for the greater part will prove satisfactory to audiences. It isn't a knockout, but rates as a consistent picturization of the story of a love affair between a window dresser and a wrapper in a department store. The picture is capably directed with an eye to its comedy values as well as the love story, and the general atmosphere is such that it will hold the average audience anywhere. The title alone should be enough for the box office.

The cast has three featured members—Evelyn Brent, Lawrence Gray and Louise Brooks. It would have been just as well to have reversed the order of the names, for Louise Brooks, playing an entirely unsympathetic role of the flapper sister of the saleslady runs away with the picture. The story is rather lightwaisted. Two sisters live in a typical boarding house frequented by the department store sales help, and the older sister is in love with a young hat clerk, who, through her efforts, becomes an assistant window dresser. The younger girl is a flighty dame, strictly "on the make" as far as the boys are concerned, and any male is fish for her net. The elder girl has promised mother that she will always take care of the youngster, so she proves to be self-sacrificing and lets the flapper practically walk all over her.

When vacation time comes around she starts off to the country. She and the window dresser are, to all intents and purposes, engaged and only awaiting the time when he shall get his raise before they are married. But while Mame's away Jane makes hay, to the extent that the older sister's unexpected return finds the two of them in the hallway exchanging good-night kisses.

Jane has been harking to the "wire" that a track tout living in the boarding house has been slipping her, with the result she is "in" the Welfare Fund for $80, and it's the night that she is supposed to kick in. She manages to put the blame on the older sister, and then tells the latter the truth, with the result that she goes after the tout, who has been holding out to get the kid's money back. Of course, the window-dressing "sweetie" comes in just in time, when the girl and the tout are mixing it, and saves the day.

Evelyn Brent has the only sympathetic role in the story. She is the self-sacrificing sister at all times, while the flip wise-cracker is Louise Brooks, and the hero of Lawrence Gray is just a self-centered chump who knows he's good and that's all there is to it.

It's Frank Tuttle's direction as much as anything that puts the picture over. There was a chance to cut in all sorts of stuff, and the chances are that the majority would have done. But Tuttle resisted in favor of wild dance stuff at the Welfare Fund Ball and likewise a chase after a Rolls-Royce in which the owner of the department store is taking the younger sister home after the ball, and a few other little things like that. The result is that the picture is just a simple, straight-forward tale that clicks, even if it won't enthuse anyone.

Fred.

FRENZIED FLAMES

W. T. Lackey film, directed by Stuart Paton. Distributed by Ellbee Pictures Corp. At Loew's New York as half of double feature program, Dec. 3. Running time, 72 mins.

It's the age of fire laddie pictures. They are coming along in droves. "Frenzied Flames" burns up a lot of celluloid making a hero out of a dead fire chief's son who was a coward at heart but tried to live it down.

It is a fireman's life, both at home and in service. When the son of Mother Grogan (Mary Carr) went into the department he was well liked by his fire laddy buddies save one boy and it was Joey who just about caused Danny Grogan to pass out of the picture.

Later Danny drives the chief's car over an embankment to save a kid, and isn't even nicked. When Danny's girl is being attacked by the "menace" while the place is afire, Danny rescues her and also gives the bad boy a larruping. Heroics are very much on the mock and make-believe.

That drawn-out fire and rescue is too much for even the most imaginative brain.

The cast is just fair, with Miss Carr about the best in her usual mother role. Cullen Landis continues to hold poses and assume dramatics that are unnatural.

Just a picture at best.

Mark.

TIN HATS

Metro-Goldwyn-Mayer picture. Edward Sedgwick production, with story and direction by Sedgwick. Titles by Ralph Spence. Ben Reynolds, photographer. At the Capitol, New York, week Nov. 26. Running time, 70 minutes.

Jeck Benson....................Conrad Nagel
Elsa Von Bergen..............Claire Windsor
"Lefty" Mooney..............George Cooper
"Dutch" Krausmeyer...........Bert Roach
Top Sergeant.....................Tom O'Brien

Not to be compared with the current war "specials" but not out of its class if matched with "Behind the Front." It doesn't run off as funny as the latter named picture but comes close enough. Preceding films in a similar vein may hurt its drawing power, but this release will entertain, once they're past the box office. A matinee audience at the Capitol found plenty to laugh at.

As in other films of the type the story doesn't amount to a thing. What little love interest there has been dragged in and the rest is simply a matter of comedy episodes. Conrad Nagel and Claire Windsor are, of course, the "names," with Nagel of a doughboy trio and Miss Windsor a German girl whom Nagel finally wins. But the heart thing is merely an excuse for "situations."

Nary a battle scene. Closest approach is the announcement of the Armistice just as the boys are about to go over the top.

George Cooper plays the hard boiled "Lefty" Mooney and Bert Roach does the plump "Dutch" Krausmeyer. Combined with Nagel this threesome go through experiences ably abetted by Ralph Spence's titles. These wordings are at least 25 percent. of the picture despite that at times they become platitudinous.

Story opens with the three boys bound for France aboard an army transport. With the armistice just as they're about to see action, "Dutch" has to figure how to grab some medals to take back to his girl friend. A photography shop seems overboard on length for the results secured, after which the boys return to their camp site to find their outfit has moved to parts unknown. Hopping bicycles they unknowingly pedal into Germany where they are mistakenly greeted in a village as dictators.

Here Benson (Mr. Nagel) resumes his pursuit of the proud and evidently wealthy Elsa (Miss Windsor) and the boys are given the key to the town.

Takes a mystery turn when Benson inveigles his pals to a castle where Elsa has gone, doors shut behind them and pictures on the wall suddenly develop human eyes. Nobody knows what it's all about, the final explanation being that Elsa's servants are trying to frighten the triumvirate away.

Finish is on a transport again, showing Benson with his Elsa, "Lefty" married to a Fraulein whom he couldn't lose, and "Dutch" possessed of a raft of stolen medals.

More unfunny than funny on paper, but Cooper and Roach make it stand up plus the titles. The picture doesn't look money and probably rates as a moderate cost production. The Castle sets carry a phoney atmosphere, and the use of a back drop in one exterior is too obvious. Also the camera work is prone to reveal faulty passages every so often.

Lightweight in toto but should entertain if its predecessors haven't killed it off. No smash, just all right. *Skig.*

FOR WIVES ONLY

Metropolitan production, distributed through P. D. C. From play, "The Critical Year," adapted by Anthony Coldeway. Starring Marie Prevost and featuring Victor Varconi. Directed by Victor Heerman. At the Hippodrome, New York, week November 29. Running time, 64 minutes.

Laura Rittenhaus	Marie Prevost
Dr. Rittenhaus	Victor Varconi
Dr. Carl Tanzer	Charles Gerrard
Dr. Fritz Schwerman	Arthur Hoyt
Prof. Von Waldstein	Claude Gillingwater
Housekeeper	Josephine Crowell
Countess Von Nessa	Dorothy Cummings
Butler	William Courtright

Marie Prevost must have thought that she was going to get another chance in this picture, as she had in "The Marriage Circle," that she made a couple of years ago while she was under contract to the Warner Bros. In that picture she had Ernst Lubitsch as a director, and in the cast were Florence Vidor, Monte Blue and Adolphe Menjou. What a picture it was.

This might have been as good, but it did not have the subtle direction of Lubitsch, although Victor Heerman tried hard with what he had in hand. The result is just a program production of very ordinary caliber.

It is possible that Miss Prevost, now a star, wanted to have everything her own way. Because o' that there is no woman in the cast other than a character woman with a chance. Dorothy Cummings has a role supposed to offset that of the star, but she is on for only a brief moment, early.

The story is supposedly a burlesque of lodge affiliations. The scene is Vienna, where Dr. Rittenhaus is the most popular physician in the city. Not because he is a good doctor, but because all of his women patients are in love with him. A friend, a professor, with an ambition to become the head of a hospital, sees in the handsome young doctor a means to an end and persuades him to accompany a good looking countess to the country to select a site for the institution, knowing that if the young doctor will accompany the countess she will present the hospital with the site.

But the idea of her husband leaving to remain away over night does not meet with the approval of the doctor's wife. She concocts a scheme to arouse his jealousy. The doctor decides he will leave his wife under the guardianship of his three male friends and associates, as well as lodge brethren. She kids them all with the result each believes she is in love with them. In the end they are all trying to elope with her when the husband returns in time to save the day.

The story had posibilities, but they were not brought out. *Fred.*

STEPPING ALONG

First National release of a C. C. Burr picture starring Johnny Hines and featuring Mary Brian. Directed by Charles Hines and adapted from Matt A. Taylor's story, "The Knickerbocker Kid." Cast includes Dan Mason, William Gaxton, Ruth Dyer, Lee Beggs and Edmund Breese. At Loew's New York (daily change) Dec. 4. Running time, 82 minutes.

Charley or Johnny Hines, it doesn't make much difference, allowed this one to run almost an hour and a half. That probably explains why it never made First National's Broadway house, the Strand. There's not a comedian on the screen who can remain funny for 82 minutes or surround himself with a story that holds up for that length of time. There have been so many examples of prolonged comedy films that the supposition to be drawn from a projection room screening and a watch must have been obvious. But no one bothered about it.

House managers who play this "serial" will likely return the print in ribbons. They can cut it blindfolded. A comparison shows "Stepping Along" is just one minute short of "Barbara Worth," as the latter is currently running at the Strand. There's 1,000 feet that can easily come out of this Hines output. If further boiled down, to consume around an hour, the picture will be additionally enhanced.

Comedy situations are extended until they lose their kick. Some of the incidents haven't any kick, but they're in there just the same, and so it goes. Hines hoofs his head off in this tale. Not running, dancing. And he's not a bad buck and wing guy. Anyway, he's showing everything from time steps to a Charleston.

Maybe Charlie and the camera man became so engrossed watching John hoof that nobody hollered "cut." It's all here and by the time it's over you're at least convinced Johnny can hop the buck.

The story is of a news stand boy who eventually digs up enough votes to become an assemblyman. A favorite of an East Side district, with the political boss to help, Johnny Rooney (Hines) finally makes the grade. Meanwhile, comes a political outing where a troup of midgets substitute for babies and comedy and would be funny if not on the screen long enough to grow beards.

Another dragged-out item takes place back stage with the curtain going up to reveal the hero before the lights and having to dance because two threatening stage hands await his exit in either wing. Funny? Sure, but not for almost a reel.

There's also a chase. This comes when the young political aspirant trails the villain who has his birth certificate 'cause he must prove he's a legal citizen. Done via a fire department car, someone got the idea audiences are too dumb to absorb the inference of an F. D. and a brass bell—so they've tinted the car red. Useless and unsightly.

It's simply a matter of having butchered a script that might have made rollicking film house fare. Hines is a flip film comic who can handle himself, but they're liable to become fed up with him if they sit through this one. Edmund Breese foils nicely during the chase footage, while Mary Brian here gives a neater performance than in other pictures of more importance. But it doesn't much matter what anyone does. They're all buried under endless reels. Billy Gaxton plays the light-heavy acceptably, while there's not anything particularly lavish about the production. East Side street scenes are studio made; stage stuff is on the level and the amusement park thing has been done on location. The rest of it rates as minor interiors.

Somebody fumbled this one away by playing with it too long. It could have been made into a fast moving laugh provoker. Too late now, with scissors the only help left. *Skig.*

SIN CARGO

Tiffany Production, featuring Shirley Mason and Robert Fraser. From story by L. R. Brown, adapted by J. F. Natteford. Directed by Louis Gasnier. Reviewed in projection room Dec. 3. Running time, 64 mins.

Eve Gibson	Shirley Mason
Capt. Matt Russell	Robert Fraser
Harry Gibson	Earl Metcalfe
Jim Darrell	Lawford Davidson
Mary Wickham	Gertrude Astor
Capt. Barry	Pat Harmon
Customs Official	William R. Walling
Cooper	Billy Cinders
Butler	James Mack
Charley Wu	K. Nambu

The type of picture that the average neighborhood house audience takes to its heart and loves. It isn't for a de luxe presentation theatre, but it has a flock of "kicks" and thrills despite the story being "just one of those things."

There is smuggling, the attack on the girl, near murder, a strip poker game, a wild party on a yacht and finally the heroine and the hero are happily married. In addition to this action there are sufficient "names" in the cast to make the picture stand up, and then there is the title, "Sin Cargo." That ought to look inviting on almost all neighborhood marquees.

The action is laid in San Francisco. During the first reel and a half all the "menace" and enough of the plot are planted to inform what the answer is going to be. Harry Gibson and his sister live together. Harry owns a ship in the Far East trade engaged in a smuggling project, the owner being in partnership with a chinaman. His sister, however, is unaware of the facts. The brother engages a captain for his boat and the sister falls in love with him. The captain is also ignorant of the true purpose of his voyage. Brother has entered into the smuggling scheme because he has been "hooked" in the stock market, and is counting on the success of the plan to meet a check that he has out for $20,000, this being held by his "best friend," who is likewise a suitor for the sister's hand. But this "best friend" gets sister alone on his yacht and instead of "walking home" she has to "swim home." Later, when the captain returns, he is accused of smuggling by customs officers and loses his license. He then becomes a common sailor and is dropped by the girl at the same time. Following events disclose the situation, and after her brother and the villain have both lost their lives the girl and captain are in the final clinch.

Shirley Mason is the only woman in the cast that has anything to do and although Gertrude Astor is named, she shows only for a brief moment. Of the men Robert Fraser as the captain gives a fair enough performance, while Earl Metcalfe as the cad brother registers strongly enough. The heavy of Lawford Davidson is all that could be asked.

For an independently made picture this one shows a lot of class as to sets and is above the average in this market. *Fred.*

THE HIDDEN WAY

Associated Exhibitors' picture labeled a Joseph de Grasse production. Mary Carr and Tom Santschi principal players. Story by Ida May Park. Directed by Joseph de Grasse. Released via Pathe. At the Tivoli, New York, "double feature day," Dec. 1. Running time, 57 minutes.

Mother	Mary Carr
Mary	Gloria Grey
Bill	Tom Santschi
Harry (Kid)	Arthur Rankin
Mulligan	Ned Sparks
Sid Atkin	Wilbur Mack
The Woman	June Thomas
The Child	Billie Jeane Phelps

Stage and screen stories having crooks and yeggs doing some good in life other than to crack heads and safes are no longer a novelty, nor are they ascribed as unusual entertainment. "The Hidden Way" belongs to that category but in many scenes proves a corking eye-absorber. In others it drips into commonplace channels. Despite its wobbling toward the finish this picture in the main will hold attention. It has a celluloid tension that is in its favor.

Two "jail birds" are just out of the big stir when they meet a knight errant of the road called Mulligan. As the three hold a roadside session, there is a runaway, a girl being drawn by a horse pell mell toward an approaching train. Bill, one of the trio, essays to save the girl and the crash is averted. It's a thrilling photographic "catch," de Grasse making this standup right at the start.

The girl is Mary. She takes the three wayfarers to her home where her sweet-mannered and smiling mother feeds them and gives them shelter. Mary falls in love with Harry, the youngest of the lot. The girl's mother wins Harry over first and then Bill, but Mulligan is just a thieving derelict.

Mulligan and Bill attempt a fake pass in "salting" a natural spring; an accident makes the water prove the real thing and subsequent developments make for the finale through Mulligan robbing the others after they have formed the Nu-Life company and are marketing the water.

There is a bit of "menace" to the film in Sid Aitken, betrayer of the woman later loved by Bill, and who causes the latter's reformation through her angelic child.

The atmosphere is of the country where open spaces are pastures. Mary Carr plays the mother and ..akes her a lovable character. The girl is Gloria Grey, who gets what there is out of the part. Tom Santschi has never appeared to better advantage than as Bill, while young Rankin does not overact as the younger crook. Ned Sparks is good as Mulligan. Sparks is among the best as a character comic.

Little Billie Phelps as the child is a natural for the screen and Miss Thomas was effective as far as she went.

"The Hidden Way" seems to be one of Associated's best bets in general screen entertainment for the neighborhood. *Mark.*

Shadow on the Wall

Gotham Productions sponsored by Sam Saxe and released through Lumas. Eileen Percy and Creighton Hale featured. Also in cast Sally Rand, Edward V. Mong, Dale Fuller, Jack Curtis and Hardee Kirkland. At the Columbus as half of double bill, Dec. 2. Running time, 59 mins.

A mediocre story in a mediocre production, destined for just the purpose it here serves—half a double bill in a two-bit scale daily change house serving an eighth avenue neighborhood.

A low ruffian, thief and thug holds captive the young hero whom he terrorizes into committing robberies. The youth is compelled under threat of beatings to masquerade as a long lost child of a millionaire, for purposes of profit to the burly criminal. The only trouble with the idea is that they use Creighton Hale as the timid imposter, and he makes a pretty husky Oliver Twist to engage the sympathies of grown-up picture fans. The whole story falls down on this point, and it isn't much of a yarn at that.

Situations are forced and there is little suspense or sustained interest. Beginning in the squalid home of the thug, the action moves to surroundings of wealth, when the heavy forces his victims to present himself as the long-ago kidnapped son on the sole evidence of a package of baby clothes. The father subjects the pretender to a strange test. The missing child's twin brother lived to young manhood, but at the time of the story is dead. However, a room is kept where the dead twin's shadow has been marked on the wall, and all who claim to be the kidnapped child are put to the test of matching the shadow. As it happens, the pretender matches the shadow perfectly and is accepted on this basis as a member of the household.

The boy falls in love with the supposed daughter of the rich man, and then abandons his masquerade in shame, returning to the thug's home to thrash him on general principles. He accomplishes his purpose and when he has the bully at his mercy the beaten man confesses that our hero is in reality the kidnapped son of the millionaire. That ought to end the story, but it doesn't. The hero now is faced with the apparent fact that the girl he loves is his sister. More footage is used to make it plain that she is merely the rich man's adopted daughter.

Nearly all these developments come late, for almost anybody can anticipate them and the kick is lost when they appear. It's all old routine and mechanical drama and not especially well devised or arranged.

The picture's only virtue is its acting, the bedraggled woman played by Dale Fuller being noteworthy.
Rush.

THE RIDING RASCAL

Universal featuring Art Acord, directed by C. S. Smith. Olive Hasbrouck leading woman. Others in the cast: Dudley Henderson, C. E. Thompson, W. A. Steele and Les Sailor. Half double feature bill at the Tivoli, New York, Dec. 4. Running time, 56 minutes.

A nicely designed western, using familiar material and devices, but handling them with skill for story and scenic effect. The big scene is a battle between the hero and a band of cattle rustlers, when he holds them at bay in a rocky mountain pass as a sheriff's posse rides breakneck to his assistance.

This bit of film drama is staged in a bleak upland setting of boulders and dizzy cliffs, some stunning long shots of the fight being interspersed with views of the galloping rescuers over rough trails.

Acord is a first rate cowboy hero for the purposes of these melodramas. He does not attempt much character shading, but plays in a direct and simple way that fits such stories. Olive Hasbrouck makes a good leading woman with her charming appearance and a graceful simplicity of method. A capital bit of comedy character work is contributed by Les Sailor as the ancient prospector-hermit who befriends the hero when he is hard pressed by the "bad men" and helps to capture them.

Acord is a mysterious squatter in the cattle country infested by rustlers. Suspicion of the ranchers is directed toward him because he is a stranger to the country, and he has to fight the male population to preserve his self-respect. The real cattle thieves go on with their schemes and manage to throw the blame upon Acord—who is in reality a Texas Ranger.

The Ranger goes through the usual hair-breadth escapes, is captured and escapes several times while the climax is worked up. The action is nicely laid out and sustains interest to the finish.

A commercial film expertly made and sure in its appeal to that large section of fandom that can't get too much of cowboy picture romance and adventure.
Rush.

STRANDED IN PARIS

Paramount production, starring Bebe Daniels, with James Hall, Ford Sterling and Iris Stuart featured. From the play, "Jenny's Escapade," by Hans Bachwitz and Fritz Jacobsetter, adapted by Herman J. Mankiewicz and John McDermott; script by Ethel Doherty and Louise Long. Directed by Arthur Rosson. At the Paramount, New York, week Dec. 11. Running time, 67 minutes.

Julie McFadden	Bebe Daniels
Robert Van Wye	James Hall
Count Pasada	Ford Sterling
Theresa Halstead	Iris Stuart
Countess Pasada	Mabel Julienne Scott
Herr Roberson	Tom Ricketts
Mrs. Van Wye	Helen Dunbar
Mrs. Halstead	Ida Darling
Pettipan	George Grandee
Schwab	Andre Lanyo

Concentration is the theme of this Bebe Daniels starring production which has a flock of laughs in it and at times becomes a bit risque in a farcial manner. Just how it will work out at the box office is going to be something of a question, for the picture is just a little shy on kick. A number of its laughs are through the George Marion, Jr., titles.

It is a story of a department store sales girl who gets a free trip to Paris as the guest of a foreign perfume company that worked the idea out as a publicity stunt. Miss Daniels is the girl and she gets the lucky envelope which contained the order for the steamship passage when the airplane showers the ground with the samples of the powder they were trying to plug.

On the boat she meets a wealthy young man and starts to concentrate on him with the idea of compelling a proposal. In this she is successful. Later in Paris she discovers the establishment she is supposed to reside at has been gutted, at the same time a couple of Apaches steal her pocketbook and her suitcase so she is very much up against it.

At this point she sees a display card in the window of a fashionable modiste shop to the effect that an English speaking girl is wanted. She walks in and takes the job, and is sent to Deauville to deliver a consignment of clothes, but has the wrong tickets handed her at the railroad station and is compelled to assume the identity of the Countess Pasada and is headed in an entirely different direction from where she was supposed to go, finally winding up at a famous spa where her clothes create a sensation.

But as she is registered as the Countess Pasada trouble looms. With the appearance of the Count, who registers and is ushered to her suite of rooms, he remaining there over night. Further complications come with the arrival of the real Countess, who knows that her husband is in the habit of playing about a bit and is always prepared to take care of her end of things with the aid of a shooting iron.

To make it more difficult the young man to whom she is engaged appears on the scene and believes the worst possible of the situation as he sees it.

Finally the tangled affairs are straightened out and all ends happily.

Miss Daniels gives a corking performance and works hard for her laughs. She has a couple of bits with a wire-haired terrier that are screams. James Hall, playing the lead opposite the star, looks to be considerable of a juvenile leading man bet. Ford Sterling just ambles through the picture, getting a punch bit here and there.
Fred.

CORPORAL KATE

P. D. C. release. Vera Reynolds featured. At Keith-Albee Hippodrome, New York, week Dec. 13. Running time about 70 mins.

"What's all the shootin' for?"

Certainly no one will ever be able to tell after seeing "Corporal Kate." P. D. C. appears to spend enough money on its pictures but doesn't get its money's worth for the screen. This will probably land in the daily change houses. It might be a help in the neighborhoods for the double bills.

It's a war picture with comedy asides or attempted comedy. Sometimes it's almost ghastly. Such as when Becky Ginsburg was dying, she wanted Jack Clarke to kiss her, just once, and the caption read: "I know Jake doesn't love me."

"Jake" didn't but he kissed her anyway as she died neatly and without getting any dust on her uniform, in sight of the audience.

Whoever the director was, he had an odd sense of humor. Placed two girls in a pig sty and permitted the pigs to run around them. After which one of the girls sprayed perfume from an atomizer all over the place. It isn't every picture audience which enjoys a pig-sty as much as the director apparently did.

Story of France in war time with a couple of American girls in khaki traveling together as entertainers for the soldiers, named Kate Reilly and Becky Ginsburg. During the picture they sing and dance. Of course, the singing could not be heard but it could not have been as bad as their dancing.

Over there they meet a soldier and both love him. These girls weren't confidants. Becky didn't know Kate loved the soldier and Kate didn't know Becky did until Beck started to die on the lot. But captions had killed off Becky long before so it really made no difference.

Some of the war stuff looked like inserts. A little of it seemed on the studio level, although why the Germans kept throwing bombs into one spot for a couple of days or a week must be a picture secret. No battle action by the American troops. After the cannonading grew tiresome someone rode up to where the loving soldier was hugging the girl and told him the troop was moving up. Perhaps it moved.

Plenty of dirt spilled and a couple of shacks ruined, but war, according to this loving soldier, isn't as tough or wasn't in France as one might believe from reading about it. He had a lovely time himself.

The story started out to prove how long a girl could withstand a request for a kiss. They turned that into a laugh to let the war go on.

About the best and only touch in the picture was when an aviator alighted but for a few moments to greet his sweetheart, a Red Cross nurse, affectionately fondling her and after saying they would be married the following week, he flew away, with his fiancee watching and waving. There was a real touch in that, so much away from the remainder for reality or sentiment that someone around must have thought of it.

"Corporal Kate" may be a title to draw the veterans. But they won't be elated over it and may blame the theatre instead of the producer. About the only sincere playing was the soldier-lover as the juvenile—he did very well and in the proper tempo to the right spirit.

Not a big time picture.
Sime.

MANON LESCAUT

Ufa (German) production. Lya de Putti starred. Directed by Arthur Robison. Photographer, Theodor Sparkuhl. At Cameo, New York, for two weeks ending Dec. 12. Running time not taken.

Manon Lescaut	Lya de Putti
Des Grieux	Vladimir Gaidarow
Marshal des Grieux	Eduard Rotheuser
Marquis de Bli	Fritz Greiner
Son of de Bli	Hubert Meyerinck
Manon's Aunts	Friday Richard and Emilie Kurtz
Susanne	Lydia Potechina
Tiberge	Theodor Loos
Lescaut	Siegfried Arno
Claire	Trude Hesterberg
Micheline	Marlene Dietrich

Despite its second hold-over week by the Film Arts Guild (renting Cameo) at 75c. top in the 600-seat house, "Manon Lescaut" is far from anything approaching a big or holdover picture for the large first-runs. It's U F A-made (German) and has Lya de Putti starred.

That Miss de Putti is starred will be the picture's best draw, although this French romantic story, adapted from the novel of considerable fame of the same title, should pull the readers of the book to a lesser degree since the novel is aged, so much so the royalty on it probably has run off.

U F A must have made "Lescaut" a long while back. That is mostly based upon de Putti in it. She looks very different from the de Putti of "Variety," "Prince of Tempters" and others, with "Satan" not forgotten. In this picture de Putti is quite slim, of more charm in naivete appearance, but of less pantomimic ability than in those more recently coming to America with her or made over here. There must have been a long lapse between "Lescaut" and the others.

In "Lescaut" de Putti displays but little acting ability. Her biggest scene for emotion, when repulsed by her lover, went flat, for de Putti refused to emote. She blandly looked, turned and walked. A little more spirit was evident in her escape from the prison wagon. Otherwise she was just a nice, sweet, handsome country girl, but even then bringing out a natural strain of vampishness when in the inn, where she captured a couple of men, to prevent herself being sent to a convent by her two old maiden aunts.

Any one regularly watching films may give more attention to de Putti in "Lescaut" than the picture itself. She's an odd girl on the screen, this de Putti of Berlin. There seems to be the devil in her always, but the devil always doesn't come out. Not much doubt she was held down in "Sorrows of Satan," but she was allowed to go in "Variety," and de Putti will have to go a long while before equaling that performance.

Unless she again is fortunate enough to secure the combination of a director like Dupont and an actor like Jannings in one picture.

"Lescaut" is the exotic romance of a couple of love-embraced younglings. More than the ordinary tribulations of the free lover clan. But Manon seems to have plied her innocence into no little commercialism. While she beguiled Griex, her fervent lover, easily and often, when the time for real happiness arrived she died in Griex's arms. He didn't bury her in the sand in the picture as he did in the book (from memory).

It's not as sad an ending as it may sound. Every one seemed to have had a lot of fun while it lasted. While the two lovers were often troubled, through finances and people, this Griex boy (Vladmir Gaidarow) put in enough loving when he got started to last over many a depressed period. And the kid could kiss! And how! And where!

These little touches of box office sex help the film as it runs along, but the film runs too long.

The picture should be cut according to the American idea. Nice interior settings, average photography, quite dimly at times; too many long shots and nothing very big, while the comedy is also heavy in the German way.

Good cast and nice direction. Nothing exceptional in either or the picture as a whole.

Playing up de Putti and the title strongly should send this in for a week anywhere. That "Manon Lescaut" is one of the standard works of romance might be made the stronger publicity.

And remembering that this is a costume play of a French period.

After seeing "Lescaut" it may be said that more than one American director apparently recalled the book well enough to borrow a scene or two for other pictures from it, and without credit. *Sime.*

Girl From Coney Island

Alfred Santell production for First National release. Four leading characters co-featured. Directed by Alfred Santell under the production management of Al Rockett. Adapted from Gerald Beaumont's story. Alternative title of "Just Another Blonde" billed. At Strand, New York, week Dec. 12. Running time, 54 minutes.

Jeanne Cavanaugh........Dorothy Mackaill
Jimmy O'Connor..............Jack Mulhall
Diana O'Sullivan............Louise Brooks
Kid Scotty.............William Collier, Jr.

Quiet bit of modern comedy romance presented in a highly entertaining picture, done in a fresh and engaging spirit. The picture has in it a good deal of the charm of the story, "Checkers," that enjoyed its vogue both in book form and on the stage some years ago. It deals with the sophisticated courtship of a young sower of wild oats who quits his occupation of gambler when he falls in love with a wise and understanding girl, employed as a hostess in the Luna Park (Coney Island) dance hall.

It is part of the appeal of the picture that there is no apology for these two unconventional occupations, both young people being presented for what they actually are. And under the surface of sophistication they turn out to be rather serious minded, even sentimental, although you have to discover their softer side for yourself. That's the merit of the treatment. All its points are made by inference and indirection, but the subtle suggestion is eloquent.

For the greater part of the action the audience is deliberately misled to suppose that it is the blonde who is the sweetheart of the hero, only to have the tables turned at the end, when it is revealed that the woman-hating boy has been led to the altar in a sentimental conspiracy of his pal and the pal's girl. The story device, particularly in its deft working out, is worthy of the resource of an O. Henry.

Jeanne, blonde, and Blackie, brunet, are pals, one as the dance-hall hostess, the other as a Luna Park ticket seller. Jimmy is managing a dice game in a gambling house, while his pal, Scotty, is the overseer of the game. The two pairs are inseparable.

It is Scotty who first awakens to love, as disclosed in his confessions to Jimmy, who is a hard-boiled woman-hater, and advises against getting "tangled up with a dame." The blonde's photograph on Scotty's bureau reveals the situation to the partner. Scotty confesses he isn't making much headway with his courtship, begging the wiser Jimmy to meet the girl and do his "Romeo broadcasting."

Jimmy meets Blondie and falls for her hard himself. But his loyalty to his pal makes him proof against temptation. Scotty plays around at a distance, preserving a mysterious complaisance toward the situation of his girl falling for his pal. All four go to the airplane races, and Jimmy and Blondie go up. Their plane loses its landing gears. Faced with peril, Jimmy forgets his fealty to Scotty and confesses his love, receiving the girl's confession of love in return.

They are smashed up a bit in landing. When he leaves the hospital Jimmy is for beating it from the scene of what he thinks is his guilty disloyalty until Scotty reveals that it was really Blackie he loved and he just threw Blonde at Jimmy so all hands could marry and make a foursome of it.

The wild airplane ride has a movie stunt kick, but that is the least of the picture, which takes its interest from the likeable young people it reveals. The four players, who comprise all the cast that matters, have particularly happy roles. Louise Brooks is notably agreeable with her quiet, demure handling of a bobbed and understanding young sophisticate. The titles are neatly done. As a sample, Blondie notices the discreet distance Jimmy keeps

in dancing. "Afraid I'll scratch your fenders?" she says. "Nope," wisecracks Jimmy, "but I've just had the body washed and polished, and I'm careful."

A cheerful, intelligent bit of entertainment that is bound to attract. *Rush.*

THE FIRE BRIGADE

Metro-Goldwyn-Mayer picture, featuring Charles Ray and May McAvoy. From the story by Kate Corbaley. Adapted by Robert Lee. Directed by William Nigh. For run at the Central, New York, beginning Dec. 20. Running time, 94 minutes.

Helen Corwin..................May McAvoy
Terry O'Neil..................Charles Ray
James Corwin............Holmes Herbert
Joe O'Neil....................Tom O'Brien
Mrs. O'Neil............Eugenie Besserer
Jim O'Neil..........Warner P. Richmond
Capt. O'Neil..............Bert Woodruff
Bridget....................Vivia Ogden
Fire Chief Wallace......DeWitt Jennings
"Pegleg" Murphy.............Dan Mason
Thomas Wainwright........Erwin Connelly

You can't get away from the old kick there is in a horse-drawn steamer with three white horses abreast flying to a fire, especially as in this case, where the horses in their mad charge manage to breast and finally beat out one of the big motor-driven fire trucks. That is the big kick to "The Fire Brigade," which Metro-Goldwyn-Mayer presented in New York for the first time at the Central Monday night.

"The Fire Brigade" is not a $2 picture, but it is a darn good special, and it is by far the best of the fire pictures on the screen to date. There is enough color stuff to take it out of the F. B. O. class, which organization up to this time has seemingly had the edge on the fire, police and post office departments as the backgrounds for stories.

Atop of that, it is about as good a sob puller as "Over the Hill" was, and that is saying a lot. Story itself doesn't mean very much, but the manner in which William Nigh came through on the direction means all that there is to the picture. The background of plot outside of the fire department stuff is just about as good as the modern story was in "The Ten Commandment" and about on the same lines —that of a crooked contractor and a phony philanthropist who gives a little with one hand and gyps in chunks with the other.

But for the small-town boys it'll get the pennies, especially as there is an arrangement whereby M-G-M turns over 25 per cent of the net to the fire departments of the country, which in New York is to be utilized for the establishment of a college for the training of fire-fighters. That tie-up makes it perfect for the big ballyhoo, and a strong ballyhoo means money in the box office.

Speaking of ballyhoo, the marquee of the Central theatre collapsed Monday afternoon between five and six, sagging down to the sidewalk in front of the theatre. The accident, it is believed, was due to the fact that there were too many men working atop of the structure. M-G-M executives stated that not a bit of weight more than the marquee had previously carried was placed on it.

The Norden Sign Co. and the Strauss Co. were both on the job trying to clear away the wreckage, but were unable to pull loose that remaining portion of the marquee that clung to the building. At about 7.30 the fire department was called on, and for over two hours they hacked and hauled, finally getting the debris free to be carted away.

Two pieces of apparatus standing in front of the theatre, with the searchlights playing on the building and police lines formed to handle the crowd, had the effect of clogging Broadway traffic for hours. Chief Kenlon personally took charge of the operations and directed the men.

And a lot of wise New Yorkers on their way to the theatre remarked: "Isn't it wonderful how far these picture people will go in order to get advertising?" That remark was heard four times in half a block while trying to get into the theatre, the management having used the side doors of the Central as the entrance because of the blockade on the front.

The first reel is mighty slow and draggy, but after that it starts to build steadily until hitting a wallop of a climax. A wise piece of showmanship was displayed in presenting the picture without an intermission, for the picture isn't big enough to stand a wait.

The story opens with a comedy sequence showing "Grandpop" O'Neil, retired fire captain, conducting a rookie school in which he has his grandson Terry (Charles Ray). Terry is the youngest of three boys, all in "the department." Their father was a fireman and lost his life at a blaze. His two older boys, Joe (Tom O'Brien) and Jim (Warner P. Richmond), have followed in father's foosteps. Before the end of the picture they follow him all the way, both losing their lives fighting the flames. Jim passes out in a chemical blaze (a corking bit of staging), but it doesn't daunt Terry, who wins his right to a uniform and badge at a rookie field day.

The fire in which Jim lost his life leads to an investigation on the part of the fire chief, who discovers the building was one of those erected by a certain contractor who seems to have the "inside" when it comes to bidding on city jobs. The chief makes a protest to the building board when the contractor is awarded the contract to build the city orphanage, and for that the chief is ordered removed. Politics is the reason, for the boss of the town, who poses as a philanthropist, is the silent partner of the contractor.

It is with the boss' daughter Helen (May McAvoy) that Terry falls in love. She reciprocates until her dad finds out and turns the boy from the door. When the chief is ordered removed and has but a month more on the job he assigns the boy to make an investigation of the orphanage, with the result the boy turns up the proof that the father of the girl he is in love with is in reality a murderer of firemen through his building of flimsy structures.

The girl also learns it by overhearing her lover's denunciation of the father, and leaves home.

Right atop of that, a gigantic fire sweeps the town. Among the buildings in flames is the orphanage. With the fourth alarm sounded the old horse-drawn steamer of the rookie school is called into action. Young Terry goes with it, coming through with glory, making rescues and finally fighting his own way out of the flames to rescue a little tot, taking a jump from the roof with her.

In production the picture must have cost a pretty penny, even though the co-operation of the fire department of either Culver City or Los Angeles was obtained. The color shots of a garden party given by the boss' daughter to aid the building fund of the orphanage were about as beautiful a series of Technicolor shots as have been shown in some time, and Miss McAvoy certainly looked amazingly well in this sequence. Later the color shots of the big blaze gave the picture an added kick.

Mr. Ray and Miss McAvoy carry off the leads most satisfactorily, with the latter having a shade. The real honors go to DeWitt Jennings as the fire chief and to Eugenie Besserer as the widow who loses the two sons. She is the element that brings the sob, and the manner in which she does her role is a work of art. Bert Woodruff as the retired fire captain contributed a few good laughs, while Tom O'Brien and W. P. Richmond as the elder brothers did their best work in the fire-fighting scenes. Vivia Ogden in a comedy role had little to do.

In the regular picture houses this is sure to click, for it is an out-and-out hokum thriller of the type mass audiences eat up. *Fred.*

SUMMER BACHELORS

Fox release of Alan Dwan production, directed by Mr. Dwan. Adapted from Warner Fabian's novel. Featuring Madge Bellamy. Photographed by Joe Ruttenberg. At the Capitol, New York, week Dec. 18. Running time, 58 minutes.

Derry Thomas............Madge Bellamy
Tony Landor..................Allan Forrest
Walter Blakely...................Matt Moore
Beverly Greenway...........Hale Hamilton
Willowdean French..............Leila Hyams
Preston Smith...........Charles Winninger
Martin Cole...............Clifford Holland
Mrs. Preston Smith...............Olive Tell
Bachelor No. 1...............Walter Catlett

A Fox feature picture in the Capitol (Metro-Goldwyn-Mayer house), and easily meeting the assignment.

As the title suggests, it's a light fabric from the jazz age, containing much cocktail shaking and the sex angle. Fast moving and with laughs sprinkled in every reel, it makes an entertaining hour that will never bring on brain fever.

It skips from apartment parties to cabaret and summer resort pastimes, revealing Madge Bellamy as Derry Thomas, a youngster convinced that marriage is not for her, but eventually surrendering to Tony Landor (Allan Forrest), who weds her while she is under hypnotic influence.

Willowdean (Leila Hyams) is Derry's girl friend. Both are familiar with the habits of the boys whose wives run away from the city's heat. Not that the girls have any off-color affiliations, although the implication is that Willowdean has had an unofficial affair. The letter is much taken up with a timid scientist (Matt Moore) whom she grows to love enough to give up when his mother-in-law shows her his crippled wife. But Derry is satisfied with her framed marriage after about to take a tour with one of the lonesome husbands.

It's one of those yarns that's right in the pocket of the flaps and cakies—big autos, fast boats, parties, risque situations, good-looking boys and girls well clothed. Titles are briskly worded, much thumbing of address books, and the comedy is supplied by others in the corps of summer bachelors, mainly Charles Winninger and Walter Catlett. Everyone frolics around Derry and Willowdean.

Jammed into 58 minutes, there's something doing all the time. Improbable, undoubtedly, but it's tart, and if not particularly smart, gains the niche at which it has been aimed.

Miss Bellamy plays easily and looks well in the central role, closely followed by Miss Hyams. The latter has been flirting with pictures on and off for some time. Other than an exceptional appearance, Miss Hyams here gives the best performance she has turned in to date and should become a familiar screen figure.

Allan Forrest is the suave hero. Matt Moore does well by the retiring scientist who falls under the spell of Willowdean, while the Messrs. Hamilton, Winninger and Catlett do the antics of the wifeless males left to their own devices. Olive Tell is glimpsed but briefly as a returning but broad-minded spouse.

Settings are solid, having that "money" front, and the photography does the action justice. One passage of the picture brought a gasp and giggles when Miss Bellamy takes a midnight swim, evidently unclothed, to be joined by Forrest, who sports a bathing suit. The giggles cropped out when Forrest showed up and the gasp was in order upon his swimming around to the same side of the float as Miss Bellamy. If Dwan meant it that way it's a bit daring and may be censored, but it's more logical that Miss Bellamy is in a flesh-colored one-piece suit. Dwan passed up bringing out this point. A caption could square it for the censors.

Drew hearty laughter at the Capitol and rates de luxe showing in the better houses. A lively picture that will hold 'em all. *Skig.*

THE POPULAR SIN

Famous Players-Lasky production made in the Eastern studio. Florence Vidor starred, with featuring for Clive Brook, Greta Nissen and Philip Strange. Director, Malcolm St. Clair, from an original story by Monta Bell, adapted by James A. Creelman. William Le Baron associate producer. At the Paramount, New York, Dec. 19. Running time, 68 minutes.

Yvonne Montfort............Florence Vidor
Jean Corot.......................Clive Brook
La Belle Toulaise.............Greta Nissen
George Montfort............Philip Strange
Alphonse Martin ....Andre Beranger
Lulu ....Iris Gray

A smart, compact bit of high comedy on the screen, produced and played in a spirit of engaging elegance. Distinctly a class product, although its appeal as a picture would go to every grade of fans and is bound to be popular with the women on the score of its sumptuous display of clothes, among other things. The picture has intelligently handled sex angles and in its acting is as nealy flawless as any screen feature that comes to mind.

What the story amounts to is a discussion conducted in a vein of jaunty sophistication of the divorce evil, the restless changing of mates among the rich. Only here the debate is conducted in terms of polished politeness and aplomb.

Yvonne is the serious minded but resigned wife of a "chasing" Parisian rounder. She knows of her husband's "affairs" and is pained by them, but does not raise the issue. George buys railroad accommodations for himself and his newest flame over a week-end. When the tickets are found in his coat by Yvonne, he pretends he planned a trip to celebrate their wedding anniversary. George then makes up a business engagement to keep him in Paris and Yvonne goes to the train alone.

During a week or so at a French resort she meets and is captivated by a novelist, Jean Corot. They confess their love and agree to part honorably. Only George steps in at the critical moment, and they are caught in what looks like a compromising situation. Divorce and a new matriconial deal are the remedy.

Jean and Yvonne take up their life, but Yvonne finds much ground for jealousy in the feminine adulation that surrounds her new husband. After many painful experiences, most of them altogether imagined on the part of the wife, she witnesses what looks like a love scene between her husband and La Belle Toulaise, an actress for whom he has written a successful play.

Once more they resort to the divorce lawyer and Jean marries La Belle, who turns out to have many lovers in her train, including by chance the abandoned George. Jean finds a strange door key in the mesh bag of wife No. 3, and looking into this situation confronts his light-minded spouse and his old friend George living en famille.

Here is a scene rich in suppressed merriment. While the two men are engaged in a brisk and sprightly discussion of the matter, La Belle, piqued at being ignored, threatens suicide by leaping to the street. The lover is agitated; the husband calm and judicial as the actress stands poised for the leap. She stands poised until the husband lets the lover go to the rescue and then she faints.

All agree that divorce is the only way, and as Jean leaves George presents him with the key to the home occupied long since when George and Yvonne were Mr. and Mrs. Jean makes his melancholy way there only to find Yvonne dreaming over his (Jean's) portrait, for a happy and romantic finale, pointing the moral that love after all endures.

Florence Vidor, most charmingly feminine, has an ideal role and finds herself happy in playing it. Her costumes alone are worth the price of admission to any woman from Judy O'Grady to the Colonel's lady. Clive Brook and Philip Strange reap new honors by the smooth, casual playing of two very worldly parts. Throughout the settings are a revel in good taste and unobtrusive splendor.

Perhaps this isn't a picture that will stir up a great deal of talk, but its merits will make headway for it inevitably. *Rush.*

The White Black Sheep

Sidney Olcott Production, presented by Inspiration Pictures, Inc. Released by First National, starring Richard Barthelmess. Patsy Ruth Miller featured. Story by Violet E. Powell. Adapted by Jerome N. Wilson and Agnes Pat McKenna. At Strand, New York, week Dec. 18. Running time. 74 minutes.

Robert Kincairn......Richard Barthelmess
Zelie.....................Patsy Ruth Miller
Enid Gower.............Constance Howard
Yasuf.......................Erville Alderson
Col. Kincairn...........William T. Hooker
El Rahib..........................Gino Corrado
Kadir...............................Albert Prisco
Dimos...............................Sam Appel
Col. Nicholson........Col. G. L. McDonnell
Stanley Fielding.............Templar Saxe

There are more than a couple of raps coming to this picture. The first might be one of those "What the well-dressed picture actor should not wear," and the answer would be for Richard Barthelmess to lay off of the dress clothes he wore in this picture. It made him look like a fellow without any neck and a hunch on his back.

Then Sidney Olcott has turned out a picture that doesn't get anywhere outside of a couple of suspense scenes toward the end of it. The third rap will to a great extent exonerate Olcott, and that is the story is one of those things the screen has had time and again, and a great many times a whole lot better. Total all three of these and the chances are that you'll find the answer—"A cluck."

Patsy Ruth Miller runs away with the picture as far as the story is concerned.

Robert Kincairn, a young Englishman of good family, whose father is a colonel in the army, is living beyond his means and doing a bit of gambling that compels him to assume debts to cover his losses. His father believes the worst of him when he practically assumes the theft of a wallet containing £400. In reality he refuses to be searched, so that he will cover up the girl he is engaged to.

Turned out by the father, he enlists in the army under an assumed name and is stationed in northern Africa as part of the British garrison in the Arab country. The Arabs plan an uprising, and the boy who, after a fight in a cafe, has been carried off to safety by a Greek girl in love with him, is listed as a deserter. He obtains information as to their plans, escapes from a prison and arrives in time to save the garrison.

Of course, the commanding officer has changed from the time that the boy has disappeared, and when he returns, he finds that his dad is in command. A reconciliation follows and the boy is permitted to marry the Greek girl who saved his life. Not much of a story there, is there? And what there is of it already has been done, hasn't it?

In addition to Miss Miller there are three performances contributed by Erville Alderson as a deaf and dumb beggar, Gino Corrado and Albert Prisco as the leaders of the revolting natives that stand out. None of the others means very much.

The picture is just one of those program features, no better nor worse than the average. *Fred.*

The Adorable Deceiver

F. B. O. film featuring Alberta Vaughan. Story by Harry Hoyt; adaptation by Frank Clifton and Doris Anderson. Philip Rose, director. In the cast are Cora Williams, Harlan Tucker, Daniel Makarenko, Jane Thomas, Frank Leigh. At the Tivoli, New

York, as half double feature bill, Dec. 4. Running time, 60 minutes.

When they picked Alberta Vaughan to play a hoyden heroine, with all the coquettish mannerisms of a Betty Bronson, they hung a heavy handicap on the piece. Miss Vaughan is by disposition and by established reputation a low comedienne, a lady clown given to the custard pie school of humor.

Called upon to do a character that called for whimsical femininity she missed the point. The choice of this actress probably was made with the roughhouse finish in mind. In these passages she did very well, but to make the material fit the player, they had to switch from a romantic comedy to a slapstick farce, which was not what they apparently started out to make.

The story starts out with Miss Vaughan a sort of comic Zenda princess, forced to flee during a revolution. This was gagged up somewhat but had a good stunt during an escape by a fast auto chase. She and her father, the king, emigrate to America where they go broke after pawning all their possessions.

The princess grasps herself a job as a lady princess and in an attempt to sell a car to the hero she gets jailed for speeding, but makes the friendship of the rich youth and is received into the home of his mother, a social climber, who takes the joke of her son that the girl is really a princess, and undertakes to exploit her for social prestige.

Meanwhile a crook and his woman accomplice have foisted themselves on the dowager as members of European royalty. In the working out of the story it is the real princess who exposes the fraud, prevents the theft of jewels and sidetracks a social scandal, winning the love of the rich young man as a result.

This simple narrative is at times entertainingly unfolded to the accompaniment of amusing gags. For instance, the princess when she becomes involved in a losing argument takes off one of her high-heeled slippers and wades into her opponent. The finish is a complicated chase of the woman crook by the princess, culminating in a knockdown and drag out and hair pulling fracas between the two women, which is not especially funny as it is done and far from graceful.

Miss Vaughan doesn't always seem sure whether she is a polite comedienne or a slapstick lady clown. Indeed, nobody seemed to be quite sure what effect they wanted to convey and in consequence the picture is neither one thing or the other.
Rush.

While London Sleeps

Warner Brothers' crook melodrama of the old school. No star featured and no billing on display to give production details. De Witt Jennings, Helene Costello and Otto Matiesen promin-n. in the cast, and the dog Rin Tin Tin is featured. At the Broadway, announced as "First showing in New York," week Dec. 13. Running time, 72 minutes.

Mystery about this one. On the face it must have been made several years ago at least, and then shelved as a weak sister. The clothes of the only woman in the cast are of a fashion not less than three years passe; the photography is not even passable, and most of the action is timed like slow-motion film, so that the butler walking to the door to answer a ring seems to float through the air.

The direction is by one H. P. Betherton, a name that doesn't recall anything. Technique pretty terrible. Long stretches of action that amount almost to close-ups of still life.

At one point there is what should be a thrill-inspiring shock when a savage ape-man from the Indian jungle climbs into the bedroom of the sleeping beauty to abduct here. The thrill is canceled when any-

body can see that the ape-man is being hoisted through the trees to the bedroom window by a cable hooked to the back of his coat.

Most of the picture equally crude. Acting also terrible. They have a leading man named Walter Merrill doing the polite juvenile in a style that recalls Harry Langdon forcibly. The picture ought to have been left to rest on the shelves for the sake of the good name of Warner Brothers.

It is seldom that a picture comes to light these days where the technical details are not plausibly handled, and no case comes to mind of a product by a going producer that has not at least clear, flickerless photography.

There is one bit in "While London Sleeps" where the camera shifted along a line of sitting characters. So inexpert was the management of photographic method that the different figures passed by a series of starts and jerks that almost blur the faces.

The picture is presented in all seriousness as a thrilling melodrama, exploiting the dog "Rin Tin Tin," the only convincing actor in the outfit, and gets more closeups in an hour than Gloria Swanson ever enjoyed. The melodrama is laid on so thick it gets into unintended comedy. *Rush.*

When the Wife's Away

Columbia production, directed by Frank R. Strayer. Story by Douglas Bronston. At Loew's New York as half of double feature program, Dec. 3. Running time, 67 mins.

Mr. Winthrop..............Geo. K. Arthur
Mrs. Winthrop..........Dorothy Revier
Uncle Hiram............Thomas Ricketts
Aunt Minerva................Ina Rorke
Chicago Dan..............Ned Sparks
Joe Carter..............Harry Depp
Detectives ....
Lincoln Plummer and Bobby Drumm

Several sure-fire laughs in this output, although the story padded out. The fun centers in the female impersonations by two of the principals, Harry Depp and George K. Arthur. Mr. Arthur makes about the niftiest and most bedimpled "girl" in pictures.

This is an independent that will hold up its face anywhere through its farcical theme. A young married couple rent an imposing house to put over a phoney front on a rich relative. The same house has been "leased" by a pair of crooks, one dressed as a woman. The police are on the trail of the latter, also a duo of correspondent school hick sleuths. In a series of twists and turns the climax finally narrows now to the big roundup where a general wig uncovering takes place.

Ned Sparks, former expert stage farceur, is making rapid strides in pictures. A skilled pantomimist, he knows how to work up a screen bit. Miss Revier is attractive as the wife of the young man who must pose as a butler one minute and make a quick change to woman attire the next. The latter is expertly handled by Mr. French, who, the captions state, has been "loaned" by Metro-Goldwyn-Mayer for this picture.

In the main the picture is typically farce, and independent exhibs will please with it. *Mark.*

THE TIMID TERROR

Romantic comedy. F. B. O. release (Jan. 9). Directed by Del Andrews from the story, "Hi Taxi!" by Walter A. Sinclair; adapted by Gerald C. Duffy. Running time, 56 minutes. (Footage 4,872.)

Talbot Trent..............George O'Hara
Mrs. Trent..............Edith Yorke
Dorothy Marvin..............Doris Hill
Howard Gramm..............Rex Lease
Amos Milliken..............George Nichols
Mrs. Milliken..............Dot Farley

Entertaining comedy of youth with a background of a business

office. Of distinct appeal to the younger generation of both sexes. It deals in a light and cheerful way with their lives.

Story fictionizes and dramatizes the aspirations of the young strugglers in city business places; has broad and effective comedy, and is neatly acted by the three leading characters, Talbot, Dorothy and Howard.

Types of the two young men are sharply drawn. Talbot is the earnest but timid young bond salesman, constantly getting into hot water, while Howard is the cock-sure, egotistical pusher who plays rather cruel practical jokes on Talbot. Both boys are rivals for the attention of Dorothy, the boss' secretary, and both contend for the new job of manager for the Cleveland branch. Howard is the typical under-dog.

Howard has a smart runabout, while Talbot does his traveling on the hoof or by the commuters' 7.42. He realizes that he must have a car if he's going to win the girl, but the best he can do is a worn-out taxicab, presented by a friend. The taxi only gets him into more hot water with his girl, until at the finish it works out his salvation.

The foundation of the story is laid with rather tiresome elaboration, but when the action does get going it speeds to a swift, satisfactory climax. Both young men make splendid types in the hands of George O'Hara and Rex Lease, while Doris Hill is a pretty, graceful figure of the young American business girl.

Production is at all times adequate, although simple settings are all that are called for, and no great outlay is represented. *Rush.*

GOING CROOKED

Fox release of a George Melford production featuring Bessie Love. Based on the play by Winchell Smith, William Collier and Aaron Hoffman. Directed by Melford, with Charles Clark, photographer. Reviewed in projection room Dec. 9. Running time, 60 minutes.

Marie Farley..............Bessie Love
John Banning..............Oscar Shaw
Mordaunt..............G. Von Seyffertitz
Doyle..............Edwin Kennedy
Car Driver..............Leslie Fenton
Mother..............Lydia Knott

Crook story that takes a couple of reels to warm up. It's migration from stage to screen hasn't helped any for it unwinds as a stagey melodrama reminiscent of the old mystery serials.

A nice production is behind the story, but the habits of an antique dealer, the head of a jewel thieving gang, are a bit too thick to be swallowed without coughing a couple of times.

To relieve the suspense there is the familiar comedy and ridiculous detective. It's practically a dressed up 10-20-30, with Bessie Love neatly handling a sappy role and Oscar Shaw hitting as the prosecuting attorney, to offset the rehashed methods used in presenting the film.

The love theme has opposition in the circumstantial evidence conviction that is sending a healthy and honest youth to the chair. An armored truck guard has been shot by Mordaunt, head of the gang, but the blame is tagged on to the youth who was driving the machine. The rescue or reprieve doesn't take place until the boy is actually in the chair. It is accomplished by telephone.

Meanwhile, through Marie (Miss Love), John (Mr. Shaw), is able to secure a confession from Mordaunt, and Marie is exonerated of former theft charges because of her aid in the matter. She was forced into the gang against her will anyway.

Melford has made it pretty theatrical so that it seldom convinces. Lydia Knott is the mother of the convicted son and stands out. Leslie Fenton hints at being a bet for more important work. Miss Love looks good and gets a chance to romp in evening dress when the

action briefly swings to a summer resort. Von Seyffertitz plays the conventional scowling, scheming heavy.

Doesn't rate de luxe house showing but okay for the daily change and otherwise, although these audiences, too, will be reminded of the old serials. *Skig.*

Tell It to the Marines

George Hill Production presented by Metro-Goldwyn-Meyer starring Lon Chaney. Eleanor Boardman, William Haines and Carmel Myers featured. Story and script by Richard Schayer; titled by Joe Farnham. At the Embassy, New York, for run, Dec. 23. Running time, 97 minutes.

Sergeant O'Hara	Lon Chaney
Private "Skeet" Burns	William Haines
Norma Dale	Eleanor Boardman
Corporal Madden	Eddie Gribbon
Zaya	Carmel Myers
Chinese Bandit Leader	Warner Oland
Native	Mitchell Lewis
General Wilcox	Frank Currier
Harry	Maurice Kains

"Tell It to the Marines" is a sure-fire box office if there ever was one. It isn't $2 box office stuff, but it is just what the doctor ordered when it comes to the picture houses. It's a special and that goes 100 per cent.

That it has Lon Chaney as the star isn't going to drive anyone away from the money window, for he certainly has a great box office following, especially among the men. It's a funny thing, that Chaney following among the boys, the boys who don't care for the pretty face actors. They figure that a guy with a pan like Chaney's getting by on the screen gives them about an even break on life after all. Many may say that it is out and out propaganda for the U. S. M. C. (back in the old days they used to say the initials stood for Useless Sons Made Comfortable), but the chances are that any fellow seeing what the hero of this yarn had to go through before he made the grade would lay off the Marine Corps if he is looking for a soft snap. There sure is a lot of flag waving and red fire to the picture and this, coupled with that stirring Marine anthem that begins with "From the Halls of Montezuma" would certainly steam up anyone who had the slightest iota of national pride.

Atop of that, despite the "Marine" title, it isn't a war picture but a corking comedy that abounds with laughs and gags.

Dick Schayer, who wrote it, turned out a good yarn, and Joe Farnham, who stuck the titles in, did his work well, but it was George Hill's direction that turned out a whale of a picture at what looks to have been about a little nickel of cost. The Marine Corps and the navy certainly stood off the cost sheet on this one. Some day this boy Hill is going to get a real chance, and they had better watch him strut his stuff when that time arrives, for he is a real picture producer.

The story starts with a young tout from Kansas City trying to take a free ride at the expense of Uncle Sam to the Marine Base in San Diego, Cal., in order to get to the track at Tia Juana, Mexico. He invades the wash room just before the train gets in and gets gabby with an old gent in civvies who is none other than a Marine Corps general. To him he confides how he is beating the government out of his carfare.

When the train pulls in the general is the first to alight. He steps over to a hardboiled leatherneck sergeant who is sporting six hash marks on his sleeve, which denotes 24 years in the Corps, and tips him as to the young man and his intentions. When the tout tries to make off he is confronted by the sergeant who takes him in tow, but he makes his escape in traffic and hops the train to the track. But he comes back, as they all come back—and—broke. When turning up at the barracks at the base broke and hungry he walks in on the same roughneck sergeant who is politeness itself until after the tout takes the oath and then his troubles begin.

Finally, he tried to duck drill by reporting sick and the treatment that he gets makes him only too willing to get back in line again, for they slip him the castor oil cure. But he has met the nurse at the base hospital and as he has dubbed himself "America's Sweetheart," he starts after her. He falls short at first. One of those fresh punks that nothing in the world can feaze; insult means nothing and rebuff rolls right off his back, so he walks right in on her again, this time having hired a drive-it-yourself fliv.

While he is pestering the girl the sergeant, who is also in love with her, walks up, places her in the car and steps in himself with the punk acting as driver. Down in the town they two step out and the sergeant goes one way while the girl continues another with the punk with the fliv following her and compelling her to get into the car in order to avoid a scene in the street. Result, he tries to get fresh, and she gets out and walks to the trolley line. He, having ditched the car, follows and is without a cent, so the girl has to pay his fare back to the base.

Coming in after hours, he is sent to the brig. When a detachment is ordered for sea duty the girl relents and goes to the sergeant and pleads for the boy, and the sergeant takes him along. A reconciliation between he and the girl first coming to pass.

Then it is a case of marine life on shipboard, in the Philippines, a tustle with the bandits in China, the rescue of the girl and then back to God's country again with the girl and the recruit, now a full-fledged marine with all of his conceit knocked out of him and a real boy anyone would be proud of. He and the girl are married and want the sergeant to come in on their farm proposition with them, but he preferes to stick to the service.

Chaney is starred as the sergeant, and has the sympathy of the picture, but William Haines, as the tout, really takes it away from him because his role is built up as strong as the hero. Eleanor Boardman, as the heroine, has little to do, but does that very well.

Eddie Gribbon, as a marine corporal, gets over a flock of laughs in his first handling of the "boots," as rookies are called, and finally ends up as the buddy of the hero.

The picture is full of action, laughs and holds a lot of love interest. In addition, the photography is great. Some shots worthy of an artist's brush.

William Axt did the score. In the main, it is stirring, with but one criticism; in the accompaniment to the castor oil sequence.

The chances are that "Tell It to the Marines" will undoubtedly get from five to six months at the little Embassy and get money, too. When it reaches the picture houses it will be a clean up. *Fred.*

TWINKLETOES

First National production, presented by John McCormick, with Colleen Moore starred. Adapted from Thomas Burke's novel of the same title. Directed by Charles Brabin. At the Strand, New York, week Dec. 25. Running time, 80 minutes.

Twinkletoes	Colleen Moore
Chuck Lightfoot	Kenneth Harlan
Dad Minasi	Tully Marshall
Cissie	Gladys Brockwell
Hank	Lucian Littlefield
Roseleaf	Warner Oland
Bill Carsides	John Phillip Kolb
Lilac	Julanne Johnston
Inspector Territon	William McDonald

Here's a chance to see Colleen Moore wearing a blonde wig and delivering a performance in a serious manner.

Seemingly that is an error for a natural screen comedienne, but in this case Miss Moore shatters precedent and more than makes good as the little slum child of London's Limehouse district in the screen version of the Thomas Burke novel, entitled "Twinkletoes."

The original story was considerably emasculated for the screen. All remaining is a rather sordid tale on to which has been tacked a pastoral finish to permit the lovers to clinch. It is understood that the censors would not have permitted the story in its original form, but as a matter of fact that is all that there was to the tale, that ending that had sudden death, rape, imprisonment and the turning down of the woman squealer by the fellow whose attentions she craved.

As a picture it will serve well enough to entertain, but it certainly isn't anything to write home about, except for the performance that Miss Moore delivers in the aforesaid blonde wig. But Miss Moore: Remember what happened to Mary Pickford when she stepped out of her natural characterizations and tried for the serious and then for the costume roles. Better stick to flappers of the sort that made you a star.

Burke's story is that of a widower sign painter who brings up his daughter in the Limehouse district. She is beloved by all, a witty chit with a natural bent for dancing.

Dad, to further this inherited gift, does a little smuggling on the side in order that he may buy instruction for her. The girl is unaware of her father's association with the thieving gentry. She gets into a neighborhood theatre as the feature of their local show, and is a hit. On the same night the wife of Chuck Lightfoot, local pugilistic champ, who has fallen in love with the girl, squeals on her father, with the result that the old man is pinched. When the youngster hears it she permits herself to be plied with wine, and when drunk the ballet master of the theatre takes her to his rooms to wrong her, but she fights him off and makes her escape. (In the original story it was the opium pipe instead of wine, and instead of escaping she remained in his rooms, not caring because of the shame of her father's guilt.)

One of the best performances of the year is that which Gladys Brockwell contributes as the gin-bibbling slattern wife of the prizefighter. It is a veritable gem of a characterization that carries the ultimate conviction. Tully Marshall is self-sufficient as the father, as is also Kenneth Harlan as the lover, both their performances being topped by the character interpretation that Lucian Littlefield delivers as Hank, who drinks "steady." Warner Oland's Roseleaf was also worthy of notice and complimentary comment.

Charles Brabin, who directed, did well enough with the direction of the story, his best bits being the fight stuff at the opening of the picture and the stage stuff with the shots of the cockney audience in front of the house. *Fred.*

VALENCIA

Metro-Goldwyn-Mayer picture starring Mae Murray and featuring Lloyd Hughes. A Dimitri Buchowetzki production. Buchowetzki the director and responsible for the story in conjunction with Alice D. G. Miller. Percy Hilburn the photographer. At the Capitol, New York, week of Dec. 25. Running time, 55 mins.

Valencia	Mae Murray
Felipe	Lloyd Hughes
Don Fernando	Roy D'Arcy
Don Alvardo	Max Barwyn
Captain	Michael Vavitch
Cafe Owner	Michael Visaroff

A week ago the Capitol had a Fox film leading its program, the story around concerning that innovation being that the house believed the next three or four M-G pictures to come in would be holdovers. And being the week before Christmas it looked like an appropriate spot to save the expected fortnight run pictures. But that Fox film was better entertainment than "Valencia," and the only thing that will hold this program leader over will be the rampant holiday spirit that now exists until after the first of the new year.

"Valencia" classes itself as a nice production placed on celluloid by high-grade camera work but lacking a story. Hilburn, as the camera, has played up the personal appearance of Mae Murray for full worth and she turns in a better performance than this screen yarn merits. Buchowetzki, directing, undoubtedly knows what he's doing and how he wants it done, but has presumed that Continental morality will be accepted by American film house audiences. That's a difficult order from the start and especially here where the girl is supposed to win sympathy. Yankee patrons like their heroines pure. The big cities may not be so fussy, but the general attitude is that the first feminine character must abound in virtue no matter what happens to the remaining characters. In this story Valencia (Miss Murray) is a cafe singer of unknown (to the audience) who fascinates a sailor (Mr. Hughes). He escorts her home and spends the night. After that what matter that the new governor (Mr. D'Arcy) is pursuing the girl. The action intimates that the incident of the sailor is of no importance to Valencia, that she doesn't love him, and when Felipe, the Spanish gob, proposes marriage she laughs. And there passes any chance that Miss Murray may have to get under the skin of the witnessers. From that point the picture must depend upon its light comedy concentrated in the governor and his conception of himself as a gift to all womankind.

Later events show Felipe as deserting his ship because of his love, Valencia's ultimate amorous surrender after he has supposedly departed, finding the boy in her room with the governor following and Felipe revealing himself when the official becomes a little too energetic. The girl then makes the conventional bargain with the governor for the imprisoned boy's release, he is placed on a boat for foreign shores, the gov can't stand Valencia's constant crying, and she flees to the dock in time to sail in the arms of her amour.

Not much of a story and, as previously stated, will seemingly be incapable of catching sympathy or holding interest. That Buchowetzki has completely told it or cut it to 55 minutes is in the film's favor. It's one of the shortest program leaders the Capitol has had in some time and rates as something of an innovation on this angle.

It's a Spanish theme, principally located in Barcelona. Settings are eye filling, and despite the lack of genuine action the pace is fast. Miss Murray looks good all the way and plays the careless Valencia to make the role convincing. Lloyd Hughes is a good foil, and Roy D'Arcy is again the suave masculine "chaser" of many mannerisms. The latter drew snickers every so often but the comedy highlight is where he becomes annoyed at Valencia's unending sobs at the time of their rendezvous and finally dismisses her.

A Christmas matinee gathering remained unmoved by the picture, and they are free with applause here when the feature is to their liking. *Skig.*

HOME SWEET HOME

Independent by John Gorman Pictures. John Gorman wrote scenario and directed. Roger Heman is set down as assistant director. Featured are Mahlon Hamilton and Vola Vale. In the supporting company are Hugh Allan, leading man; Lila Leslie, Archie Burke and Mildred Gregory. At the New York, New York, Dec. 24, half of double bill. Running time, 53 minutes.

This is a silly picture, mostly inexpertly moulded in its story plan, although produced with a good deal of technical excellence as to its acting and backgrounds. The trouble is that it deals in an altogether serious way—absurdly serious in places—with a subject that calls for light comedy treatment.

It is enough to indicate the sloppy sentimental vein to record that one of the chief dramatic incidents has to do with a sweet young girl who gets herself into something like delirium tremens by eating bon bons loaded with liquor. The moral here is that the loose ways of the idle rich are destructive of all virtue. Of course, as it comes on the screen it is a comedy riot instead of dramatically intense, as was intended.

In a greater or less measure the whole picture goes to pieces for the same reason. The episodes that are designed to point the serious moral kick back upon themselves for a giggle. For instance, the story is designed to show that contentment comes only to the simple home, while the homes of the idle rich are full of moral iniquity.

The simple home pictured has all the atmosphere of a cheap flat furnished on the installment plan, and the people who live in it are stuffy and tiresome. On the other hand, the home of wealth and evil is a dream of decorative beauty, and the people who appear in it are lively and apparently gay, even if they are more or less lit on gin and oranges.

The virtuous young man from the small town, who upbraids the heroine for what he considers her rowdy ways, is a good deal of a young fool. The young prig from the small town in the end takes the fashionable flapper from her Long Island home and puts her back in an installment flat, and Mr. Gorman apparently meant it to be a happy ending. But one had an uncomfortable feeling that the young wife was going to have a dull time of it after the Long Island parties.

By the way the small-town boy was played by Hugh Allan a young man who could do something with a decent part. He almost made this impossible role attractive. His acting and that of Vola Vale were the only worthwhile details of the film, which otherwise was awful.

Rush.

HER BIG NIGHT

Universal-Jewel, starring Laura La Plante. Directed by Melville W. Brown. Story by Peggy Gaddis. Scenario by Melville W. Brown. Cast includes Einar Hanson, Zasu Pitts, Tully Marshall, Lee Moran, Mack Swain, John Roche, William Austin, Nat Carr and Cissy Fitzgerald. At Loew's New York, one day, Dec. 23. Running time, 74 minutes.

If this Universal-Jewel never starts any box office sizzling, it will start credit in the new starring bonnet of Laura LaPlante. Adapted from Miss Gaddis' story, "Doubling for Lora," telling of the trials of a department store girl who, to cop some quick money, agrees to double as an actress whom she resembles. In so doing she gets in bad with her sweetie.

Miss La Plante is in the dual role and A1. Miss LaPlante is fast acquiring the ropes of a gilt-edged film comedienne. She has looks and personality to carry her along to success with it.

The picture is good in spots; drawn out at intervals and skids along and then is yanked out of its ordinary run by some corking scenes in which Miss La Plante is the dominating figure.

Tully Marshall, as a reporter, is one of the old school, hardboiled and never accepts anything until it is positive.

The picture, thanks to deft directing, works out nicely, and the old wise dog of a newspaper man is nicely outwitted, naturally relished by the fans everywhere.

Lee Moran as the personal representative of the actress, and he has some tall jumping around to help carry out the "double" gag.

Cissy Fitzgerald does nicely, and the juvenile Mr. Hanson, as the sweetheart of Miss La Plante, is clean cut, withal a satisfactory lad all the way.

This picture will give satisfaction in the outside exhibiting territory. At the New York the audience appeared to like it immensely. And that New York crowd of regulars sees about all the independents, as well as the regular output of the other feller's.

Photography unusually good, and this is a big asset to any picture.

Mark.

DESERT VALLEY

William Fox production starring Buck Jones, with Virginia Brown Faire and Malcolm Waite featured. From the novel by Jackson Gregory, script by Randall Faye. Directed by Scott Dunlap. Reviewed in projection room Dec. 23, 1926. Running time, 57 minutes.

Montgomery Wilson Fitzsmith	Buck Jones
Mildred Dean	Virginia Brown Faire
Jefferson Hoades, Jr.	Malcolm Waite
Timothy Deann	J. W. Johnson
Sheriff	Charles Brinley
Deputy	Eugene Pallette

One of the usual type of Buck Jones western which, if anything, has a little more story behind it than the average of these pictures. For the spots where they take the westerns as a regular fare this one will provide them with sufficient thrills and excitement to appease their appetite. In the daily change houses it should fit as well as any other western when it comes down to the question of box office value.

Buck Jones is a roaming cowboy who wanders into Desert Valley and there finds that the ranchers are losing their cattle by thirst because Jefferson Hoades (Malcolm Waite) has cornered the water supply and is holding up the cattle men for an exorbitant rate.

Jones sees cattle dying from thirst and opens up the pipe line and permits the animals to slake their thirst. Later he hits the ranch house of the Deans, it having been this rancher whose cattle he saved. Seeing a couple of pies on the window sill cooling he helps himself. Caught by the cook he retreats into the house and runs into a girl in a bathroom. He tries to escape but is caught and jailed.

He escapes from the little hoosegow and makes his way into the desert again, only to run across the same girl and on this occasion she is in the hands of the water profiteer, who is trying to make love to her. He saves the girl from the situation and learns that her father is accused of breaking the pipe line and up on trial for it. He returns to the town, tells the true story and is turned out for the crime. But he is recognized as having broken jail, and a chase ensues. In the end he bests the heavy water-hoarder and has the ranchers drive him from the country. That leaves the way clear for the usual happy ending.

Buck does well enough as the hard riding, hard fighting buckaroo, while Virginia Brown Faire is all that could be asked as the heroine. The "heavy" of Malcolm Waite is really worth while, and the prediction is made here that he is going to be heard from in the future in bigger pictures.

Scott Dunlap, who directed, stuck some rather ill-advised stunt stuff in the scenes of the escape, with Buck climbing over house tops and in full view of anyone who wanted to take a pot shot at him.

The chase stuff, however, furnished the necessary suspense element.

Fred.

HER FATHER SAID NO

F. B. O. Production from the story of H. C. Witwer. Continuity and titles by Al Boasberg, directed by Jack McKeown. Reviewed at projection room, Dec. 22. Running time, 77 minutes.

Charlotte Hamilton	Mary Brian
Danny Martin	Danny O'Shea
Al Conklin	Al Cooke
Kit Goodwin	Kit Guard
John Hamilton	John Step-ling
Matt Doe	Frankie Darro
Herbert Penrod	Gene Stone
Betty Francis	Betty Caldwell

One of those romances of the roped arena tales that H. C. Witwer chooses and writes. It is no better and no worse from a story standpoint than most of his stuff. As a picture it contains sufficient element of entertainment to make most of the audience like it.

Nothing that will pull them in, but it will satisfy. The picture could stand about 10 minutes of pruning.

One element for the box office is the name of Mary Brian, a Famous Players-Lasky star, in the lead.

The story is of a pugilist and the daughter of a wealthy man, adverse to prize fighting and prize fighters. The girl meets the contender for the welterweight championship while he is doing his road work, her car having run out of gas and stalled. She thinks that he is part of a college football squad, also doing road work. Later, when discovering he is a fighter, she is so deeply in love she cannot give the boy up. But her dad says "No," and that leaves the proposed match up in the air.

After the contender is robbed of a decision over the champ he undertakes the management of a health farm and the girl's father and the young man dad favors decides to take the "cure." The girl goes with them. The men sign a contract to remain in the sanitarium for 60 days until the cure is completed. While going through the stunts the youngsters marry and run off, with father giving his blessing from the dormitory window.

Lot of corking comedy episodes in the rest cure sequences, especially with the former trainer and manager of the pugilist putting the old boy and the favored suitor through their paces. Both are on a diet. When it comes to the boxing portion of the training they refuse to put on the gloves until told the winner will get a lamb chop to eat. The titles are good, although Boasberg has dug pretty far into the bag for them at times.

In direction Jack McKeown moved the picture along in good shape and the spots where he hooked his radio stuff into the fight was well done.

Miss Brian takes the honors, while Danny O'Shea as the hero registers pleasingly. Little Frankie Darro as an orphan that becomes the training camp mascot certainly does lend himself for the sob stuff element. Betty Caldwell in a minor role proved to be meaningless.

Fred.

ATTA BOY!

A. MacArthur presents Monty Banks in the full length comedy, directed by Edward H. Griffith and distributed via Pathe Exchange. In the cast Mary Carr, Virginia Bradford, Virginia Pearson. Titled by Harold Christy. At the New York, New York, Dec. 24, half of double feature bill. Running time, 65 minutes.

This independent production exploits Monty Banks, comedian of the custard pie school in a rather important way. Cast and production represent considerable outlay. The result is distinctly promising. The comedy shows vast ingenuity and resource in keeping the gagging in motion over the five or more reels.

For so sustained an effort the average of interest and laughs is high. There is some evidence of padding in the elaboration of incidents such as the hotel detective's chase of the innocent young man suspected of being a bootlegger, but the development of the situation and the building up of incidental stunts is very well managed.

They have borrowed some of the Charlie Chaplin technique of giving the sentimental twist to the knockabout comedy. Here it is rather crudely done, but at that it is effective because the mechanics of the sympathetic relief are basically right, even for horseplay.

There is a first rate stunt episode involving camera tricks. The dumbbell comic is making his escape from pursuers, when he drops a ladder from a fire escape, the bottom resting in a parked automobile. While the patsy is at the ladder top about to descend, somebody starts the machine, and he is whisked up and down mountain roads, to the edge of dizzy precipices and through trees, swaying in the air at the top of the ladder.

This situation is worked for all it's worth and builds up a lot of shocks, thrills and surprise laughs. The whole picture is rather remarkable for its speed and variety of comic action. These things are perhaps mechanical, but they also are ingenious and generally amusing. Of course, it's all slapstick, and it misses the quality of the big feature length comedies because the clown does not develop character, but is merely the dummy for mechanical gags. But for plain gagging the picture is there.

Rush.

THE CARNIVAL GIRL

Louis Lewyn presents Marion Mack in "The Carnival Girl." Directed by Cullen Tate. Story by Raymond Cannon. Cast includes Gladys Brockwell, Frankie Darro, George Siegmann and Allan Forrest. Released via Associated Exhibitors. At the Tivoli, New York, on double feature day, Dec. 9. Running time, 55 minutes.

At the Tivoli the house apparently didn't think so much of the box office prowess of the star as Gladys Brockwell was played up in outside billing. Marion Mack is a decided brunet who isn't one bit afraid of work.

The picture didn't impress much in the first part. It was tame and amateurish. Miss Mack as a tight wire walker wore an outlandish outfit for such a stunt but worked it in nicely later when going to a party given by the officers of the fleet. And the distance her wire was from the stage was a laugh; it was barely off the floor.

At first it looked as though the shooting was of foreign background until things got swinging into rum-running theme, with the romance a long way around to the big climax.

Miss Mack does well with what she has to do, but the story could have easily been told in two reels. Frankie Darro was a commanding figure. This youth is a corking film actor.

A blazing dory or schooner was overdone but will make the thrills in neighborhoods.

In summarization there are some splendid scenes, nicely staged and effective, but the picture is padded to its disadvantage; the opening is very slow and just about crimps any action that follows.

The best work was done by George Siegmann. As a "menace" he is there.

This picture will run best on double feature days, as it did at the Tivoli.

Mark.

Redheads Preferred

Tiffany Gem Production presented by M. H. Hoffman. From story by Douglas Bronston, directed by Allan Dale. Edited by Harold Young. Reviewed in projection room Dec. 15. Running time, 53 minutes.

Henry Carter	Raymond Hitchcock
Angela Morgan	Marjorie Daw
John Morgan	Theo. Von Eltz
Mrs. Henry Carter	Cissy Fitzgerald
Mrs. Bill Williams	Vivien Oakland
Bill Williams	Charles A. Post
Office Boy	Leon Holmes
Miss Crisp	Geraldine Leslie

Anita Loos, authoress, says that "Gentlemen Prefer Blondes." Douglas Bronston, author, says, "Redheads Preferred." The chances are someone will come along with "Brunettes Common" or "Blackheads Barred."

But in this picture the redhead, after all, is just the "bunk." She's a brunet, but wears a wig to fool her husband, who, when soused, has a redhead complex.

Picture is a rather good little farce, more or less of the bedroomy type, built for laughs and a little touch of high life added with an artists' ball. Three couples, all married and all involved in one another's affairs, to provide good screen fun.

Playing up the title and taking a chance with a contest as to what is really preferred locally by the men should get some discussion and pull money for the exhibitor.

The story starts with a little twist, unusual. A bride and groom on their honeymoon in their suite in a hotel. First experience of the kind for either and both extremely bashful. Notice on walls of room that lights are turned out at midnight. Husband looks at watch and sees that it is five minutes to midnight. Just then a fuse blows and the lights go out. When on again the two are disclosed in negligee, to their consternation.

After a couple of years of married life in which they take each other very much for granted, the husband is taking out an out-of-town buyer for a night at the artists' ball. The out-of-town buyer knows a lady who's married. Her husband is a traveling man. She consents to get another girl for the young husband. He wants a redhead, but when he walks in to the apartment the traveling man's wife recognizes him as a friend of her husband's. She cannot have her girl friend along on the party for the girl friend is none other than the wife of the young husband. However, she is fixed up with a red wig and a mask and the quartet are off.

The night brings complications for the day following. They are very laughable with the three husbands and wives very much mixed up, all trying to square the other.

Direction is fairly well handled with some of the ballroom sets rather flashy.

Raymond Hitchcock is one of the featured players, with Marjorie Daw. Hitchcock, in his farcical role, registered very well, especially in his costume from "The Galloper," which he wore for the ball scene. Miss Daw was effective as the injured young wife. Cissy Fitzgerald, as the dominant wife of the out-of-towner, with but little to do did that little very well.

"Redheads Preferred" as a regular feature will get by with the average audience because it will make them laugh. *Fred.*

DANCING DAYS

J. G. Bachmann presents "Dancing Days," with Helene Chadwick, Lillian Rich, Forrest Stanley, Robert Agnew, Gloria Gordon, Sylvia Ashton, Thomas Ricketts. Story by J. J. Bell. Directed by Albert J. Kelly. Distributed by Preferred Pictures Corp. At Tivoli, New York, Dec. 11. Running time, 57 minutes.

This one teaches an animated lesson to the married ginks who go in heavy for the modern dances, and hotfoot it so much that they forget all about the dear ones at home. This one also takes a slam at the saxophone, which becomes a pest as far as the bird was concerned who neglected his wife to do his stuff to the crooning, moaning sax, played by the girl who had vamped him by her dancing.

"Dancing Days" is happily and nicely presented. There is quite a strain of comedy with the twin beds and single bed "bit" surefire laughs.

Helene Chadwick as the Charlestoner dresses the part throughout, making herself a most attractive blonde. As the "opposite" woman, Lillian Rich, fine-appearing, splendid actress, handled the neglected wife to perfection.

The men were Forrest Stanley and Robert Agnew, the former as the husband who went wrong with his dancing feet and the latter as the night club baby who could go to sleep on a dime, dancing the latest hot stuff.

Photographically picture near faultless. Some unusual shots, with the collision of the two autos at the finish excellently staged.

As an independent this picture holds up in story and cast.

Picture caused no end of laughter, the tag coming when the twin beds went out of the home and the "single" went back following the reconciliation of husband and wife. *Mark.*

LAZY LIGHTNING

Universal western, starring Art Acord. Story and scenario by Harrison Jacobs. Directed by William Wyler. At the Stanley theatre, New York, one day, Dec. 16. Running time, 55 minutes.

Dickie Rogers	Bobbie Gordon
Lila Rogers	Fay Wray
Uncle Henry Rogers	Arthur Morrison
Dr. Hull	William Welch
Sheriff Boyd	Vin Moore
Rance Lighton	Art Acord

In "Lazy Lightning" there is the man who would stoop to anything to turn up some money to squash his gambling debts. Yet the real "menace" was a contagious disease —diphtheria—which held the center of the film in the big moments and provided the real reason for a wild ride through a raging rainstorm by the hero, who, in making the dash, got a bullet in his shoulder for his trouble.

One thought the doctor would never get there in time when the little boy in the picture became very ill. He did, and then he said it was diphtheria and that only serum could save his life. Some one had to go for the serum. Uncle Hank, who knew that by the boy's death he would inherit one-half of the Rogers ranch in San Jacinto valley, offered to go. He did. But he planned that it would never reach home in time. But he reckoned without the hero, in the person of Art Acord.

Art rode like the devil possessed to bring back the serum. There is a fight and the ride. The drop into the river by the horse and rider, and then the auto plunge which snuffed out the unk's life, were finely photographed.

There's a girl, to be sure, but she is second fiddle to the crippled boy, who moves a very lazy cowhand to heroic deeds. It is pretty hard to make any audience familiar with Acord's rough riding and lariat manipulations swallow that character of the lazy man—a bimbo lazier than the famous Bacon "Lightnin'" character.

There are some efforts to whip comedy into the film. Much of it falls with a thud. Just about one legitimate laugh or two in the whole caboodle of farcical by-play.

There is a twitch or two at the heartstrings, due to the bully acting of the boy playing Dickie. All that stuff cutting back to the film interpretation of the stories told the boy by the lazy man were rather thin attempts to work up comedy. May be all right for the kids, but Art Acord's horse can do more for them than any of that mythical piffle.

The lazy man won the girl, saved the boy and was instrumental in the "menace" getting it two ways from the middle. The picture in the main is a "weak sister," despite its sentimental tug through the care of a big man for a crippled boy. *Mark.*

Butterflies in the Rain

Universal Jewel, featuring Laura La Plante and James Kirkwood. Edward Sloman, director. Story by Andrew Soutar, adaptation by Charles Kenyon. Also in the cast, Edward Davis, Robert Ober, Dorothy Cummings and Rose Burdick. Running time, 70 minutes. At New York Hippodrome week Dec. 20.

Reporting the current feature at the Hippodrome as another of those things is getting to be routine. This is no exception.

It starts out to picture the atmosphere of English society of the upper class, specifically the landed gentry, and then handles the subject as it might be handled from the viewpoint of a South Amboy, N. J., socialist.

The daughter of the aristocratic house of Carteret living on an estate near London (played by Laura La Plante) has all the characteristics of a badly brought up small-town flapper. Her two brothers are the Mutual burlesque wheel type of Englishmen caricature. The Carterets despise their neighbor, a rich young commoner. So they jump their horses over his walls, ride on his lawns and then, after they have insulted him, invite him to dinner so they can humiliate him.

On the other hand a real lord is introduced. The author treats him with worshipful reverence, a particularly fine bit of screen snobbery. After being properly snubbed, the rich young commoner, of course, falls in love with the Cartaret girl.

They have been married a month, the story goes on, when the husband has occasion to go into his wife's room. This broad-minded and modern bride shrinks, cowering behind the bed coverings when her husband enters. At this point it was more than the audience could stand. They exploded in giggles.

Anyhow, that's the literary subtlety of the whole picture. The film is rich in absurdities as crude as this. The rest of the story has to do with the misfortunes of the coy bride, who goes for a tour in Spain with a gang of blackmailers posing as society people. They involve her in a scandal and threaten to ruin her and her husband unless they are bought off.

Here the real lord comes to the rescue (in the acting he's wooden, but the author conceived him as the only heroic character in the cast). He exposes the blackmailers. But meantime the rich commoner has gone broke by one of those convenient turns in the stock market. So the haughty wife and the now impoverished commoner are reconciled to start life all over again, happy in each other—but broke.

This significant happy ending where everybody is broke but affectionate is the sure mark of the picture made for the more unsophisticated fans. Some day a scenario genius will have a couple of lovers at the end both contented and solvent.

Meanwhile pictures like "Butterflies in the Rain" will continue to regale the daily change neighborhood houses to the profit of the producers. But why do they pick this kind for the Hippodrome? And for a week! *Rush.*

A ONE MAN GAME

One of Universal's Blue Streak Westerns, featuring Fred Humes. Directed by Ernst Laemmle, story by William Lester. In the cast, Harry Todd, Norbert Myles, Clara Selden, Fay Wray and Lotos Thompson. Half of double bill at the New York, New York, one day, Dec. 18. Running time, 70 minutes.

Familiar type of western picture with a simple, obvious story to carry along the wild riding and fine scenic background. Has some rather silly comedy incidents that don't help, but it is saved for the purpose of all westerns—the entertainment of juvenile fans of all ages—by its lively action.

Bob (Humes) is a prosperous ranchman, director of the local bank. He is far away at the round-up when his partner summons him to come to a director's meeting to defeat the granting of a fraudulent loan to the heavy. To make the trip in time he has to commandeer an automobile on the road occupied by two wealthy women relatives of his partner.

They snub him as a roughneck rowdy, but he makes the meeting in time, and by defeating the plan of the villain earns his enmity. Bob buys polite clothes and lays off the cowboy chaps and boots, masquerading as the Duke of Black Butte as a hoax upon his partner's fashionable relatives. The cowboy's idea of a duke supplies a sort of comedy that may be funny to wild west fans, but in a Broadway house is dull.

The villain and his crew of bad men abduct Bob and hold him prisoner while they go off to rob the bank, having misdirected the sheriff to a remote mountain pass. Of course, all Bob has to do is to knock down his two or three husky guards after the manner of screen heroes and ride off at a breakneck gallop to engage with the bank robbers. The sheriff's posse also is warned in time and dashes back.

All this is familiar and obvious stuff, but it seems to register unceasingly. Here the action is energetically sustained, the principal object. *Rush.*

OBEY THE LAW

Crook society play with comedy angles. Bert Lytell featured. In the cast, Edna Murphy, Hedda Hopper. Adapted from Max Marcin's story and directed by Al Raboch for Columbia. At the New York, New York, one-half double bill, one day, Dec. 18. Running time, 52 minutes.

This subject is not up to the high standard recently set by Columbia for its product and it falls down in the usual way—the story values. As to its technical makeup, the picture has been well done in all those particulars of first-rate backgrounds, lighting, grouping and titling.

Probably the fatal defect is that the hero's action is absurd. He is a smooth "Raffles." When his old pal's daughter is about to marry a rich young man he steals a valuable jewel in order that the old man may have a suitable present to give her at her bethothal. There is nothing the matter with this idea as the basis of a light comedy story. The trouble comes when the thief is caught and goes to jail, refusing to defend himself.

The building up of the story has been in a comedy vein, so that when it is shifted to the seriously dramatic side, one gets the idea that the whole business is trivial. The motivation is all wrong. The hero, of course, should have been forced by some compelling circumstance to commit a crime—something more impressive than a whimsical desire to please a flapper and her father.

Details are mismanaged all through the film. At the opening a sister of the rich young man who later is to marry the hero is introduced in a way that leads one to suppose she will play an important part in the story. After the brief introduction the character disappears entirely.

The action starts out with the crook's daughter, and it is not until the recital is well along that Lytell, the crook, turns out to be the principal character to whom attention is directed. Sympathies are concentrated upon the crook and his pal, but the important things happen to the young lovers who are entirely secondary.

The girl doesn't know her father is a crook just out of jail, and never does learn it. Why it was necessary to show the old man in his prison surroundings isn't plain. It gives the story a sordid, uncalled for twist. When the rich young lover learns that his father-in-law to-be is a jailbird he just waves the detail aside complacently—another case of crude motivation. Certainly the audience was entitled to know why a man of social position didn't mind taking a jailbird into the family. As far as the screen evidence went, this socially impeccable young man had rather a taste for papas-in-law fresh from the hoosegow.

These things are a matter of treatment rather than of the substance of the material. If the story had been consistently comedy they would have passed unnoticed, but when it took the dramatic turn it became full of implausibilities. So that it sums up as just a naive "movie." *Rush.*

"Romance of a Million"

Preferred Pictures Production presented by J. G. Bachmann. Directed by Tom Terris, from the story by Elizabeth Dejeun. Featuring Glenn Hunter with cast, including Gaston Glass, Alyce Mills and Jane Jennings.

Aside from the fact the title has no connection with the story, "Romance of a Million" is fair entertainment with no special box office value. With fine treatment from the camera Alyce Mills makes a presentable heroine. Gaston Glass carries the burdens of a polished villain with ease, but ends up in a ludicrous scene in the last reel disguised as a woman. He looks too funny and kills some of the effect previously created.

In a reformatory at the age of 14 for some connection with embezzlement, Glenn Hunter is finally discovered by a millionaire uncle.

Glass is the other nephew who thought himself the sole heir to the Dunbarton fortune. The uncle provides that $500,000 be held in trust for each of his nephews, the inheritance to pass from one to the other should either disgrace the name.

Gaston tries to get Glenn in wrong by planting stolen articles in his room, stealing money from his aunt's safe and making false insinuations. Climax comes when a valuable necklace is stolen from a woman guest who refuses the cash value, but insists on having the necklace because of sentimental value. Gaston disguises himself as a mysterious Russian woman and offers to return the necklace for $100,000. He is foiled at the last minute and unmasked by Glenn's gal, none other than the vivacious Alyce.

Glenn looks just the harmless, inoffensive sort of an unsuspecting youth who would stand for the raw deal handed him by the handsome, well-groomed cousin. Almost anyone else in the role, it seems, would have broken the sneering cousin's map just for the fun of it, if for not other reason. An ineffective detective, Bobby Watson, worked in for comedy purposes shoots wide of the mark.

1927

BERTHA

(THE SEWING MACHINE GIRL)

Fox picture and an Irving Cummings' production, featuring Madge Bellamy. Directed by Cummings. Photographed by Abe Fried. Adapted from Theodore Kremer's story of the same name. Cast includes, besides Miss Bellamy, Anita Garvin, Sally Phipps, Ethel Wales, J. F. Macdonald, Paul Nicholson, Arthur Housman and Allan Simpson. At the Hippodrome, New York, week of Jan. 3. Running time, 65 minutes.

Bertha, 1927 model, is probably somewhat different than the demure miss around whom Al Woods wove a stage production once upon a time. In fact, there's no doubt about it.

Find a woman who'll admit she saw the original version for verification. Ask Al himself, or his wife, or his brother, Marty.

Yea, verily, the new Bertha is quite a dame. She poses in lingerie that the first Bertha would have crammed the cover of the box upon, struts like no mannequin ever really strutted, except to a "hot" band, rides in fast motor boats and on a yacht and yet has this in common with her namesake—she's just as chaste (or chased). Possibly the pursuit is a little faster, internal combustion motors and cabarets being what they are today, but the villain is there and still pursuing.

Both girls unquestionably have "it," whether the covering is muslin or silk, and Madge Bellamy has a plentiful amount. The Fox gang are well aware of the fact, if you aren't, so they tagged Madge—she's "it" and Bertha, streamlined, convertible, '27 model, f. o. b. Fox.

Give this girl clothes to wear, be she well covered or otherwise, and the boys'll be interested. The womenfolk may not become overly impressed, but they're not going to get the boy friend out of the theatre without some kind of an argument. And that's the way Miss Bellamy screens.

From "Summer Bachelors" to "Bertha." A stretch of years between what each of those titles signifies to the public, but pretty much the same role in either instance for this featured player.

The scenarists have presumably used the original yarn as a mat on which to do nip-ups, head spins and hoke falls with the theme. It starts in a "sweat shop," of course (something to square the title), but it's not long before Bertha lands in a silk establishment, where she eventually models and catches the eye of the wealthy and dastardly manager. Falling in love with the assistant shipping clerk, she's about to walk out on him in favor of taking up designing in Paris. This at the instigation of the aforementioned manager, who, business not being so good, or great, declares himself in for visits across the pond when, suddenly, his bootlegging of stock comes to light.

Inveigled to the manager's country estate, the jam starts for Bertha through a motor boat dash to the yacht and then away for South America. It's to the credit of someone that they garnered a motor boat that looks as though it could dash and a yacht that impresses as if it could make Sandy Hook without foundering if anybody on board happened to sneeze.

Bertha, poor gal, is unaware of her boss' intent until the yacht starts to move. But don't forget the shipping clerk. Has this boy been on the trail? He has. Plus six cops and a Cadillac.

And do they reach the palatial private steamer in time? They do. And does the heavy take the sock? Positively.

But who do you suppose the clerk turns out to be? None other than the president of the firm Bertha has been working for. Young, good looking and rich. Perfect.

Well, that's this generation's Bertha, and the Fox crew has paid something to make her what she is today.

No puffed sleeves and no bustle, says you. Plenty of limb and a lingerie parade, says I. Would you know the old girl, doggone 'er? You would not.

Had they titled it from the original phrasing and emphasized the gestures, while playing it in modern dress and atmosphere, the picture might have become a yell as a satirical poke at the old timers. As it now runs off no one can believe it, no matter how broad-minded they may be, while the title that reveals the clerk as the wealthy owner will draw an outright laugh anywhere.

Nope. All this Bertha is blessed with is that Miss Bellamy has "it"—and that lingerie display. *Skig.*

HOTEL IMPERIAL

F. P.-L. picture, starring Pola Negri. Story by Lajos Biro, adapted by Jules Furthman. Directed by Mauritz Stiller under the supervision of Erich Pommer. James Hall and George Siegmann featured. At the Paramount, New York, week Jan. 1. Running time, 67 minutes.

Anna Sedlak	Pola Negri
Paul Almasy	James Hall
Gen. Juschkiewtsch	George Siegmann
Elias Butterman	Max Davidson
Tabakowitsch	Michael Vavitch
Anton Klinak	Otto Fries
Baron Frederikson	Nicholas Soussanin
Maj. Gen. Sultanov	Golden Wadams

Just another war picture.

Great things were expected of the combination of Mauritz Stiller-Erich Pommer-Pola Negri, but the result is just a program picture.

In the spots where Negri draws the picture will do well enough, in Central Europe they undoubtedly will go wild over it, but in the major portions of America it won't bust any records. At the big new Paramount it is apt to do things because it was placed in that house New Year's week and opened with a special midnight performance New Year's Eve, but the tale is told in the fact that the picture was originally intended for a run of eight weeks or so at the Rialto and then was switched into the Paramount for a single week on Broadway.

In direction and camera work the picture stands out, but the story isn't one that is going to give anyone a great thrill. Stiller and Pommer have done their work well, and they have made Pola look like a gorgeous beauty in some shots, and effectively handled her in others, such as her scenes with the Russian general, but to what avail is good direction and supervision, plus acting when the story isn't there?

It has to do with the advance of the Russian armies into Galicia after their defeat of the Austrians. The Hotel Imperial is located in one of the border towns of Austria-Hungary. Here a fleeing Austrian huzzar seeks rest and is caught behind the lines of the nemy when they move into the town.

Pola Negri, as the hotel slavey, shelters him and suggests that he act as the waiter to cover himself. The Russian general makes the hotel his headquarters and falls for the girl. The waiter, in turn, loves her also and she reciprocates his feeling. He later slays a Russian spy who has just come through the lines with valuable information before he can turn it over to the commander of the Russians and then makes his escape, rejoining his own forces.

They attack the Russians, defeat them and reoccupy the town and the young officer and the hotel slavey are reunited, she being congratulated by the commander-in-chief of the Austrians for having helped in the defeat of the Russian, and the officer is given a couple of days' leave to marry her.

A corking leading man is James Hall, and he appears to have the stuff that will make him worth while. He has an "air" that denotes that he is capable of real things in picture work. George Siegmann, as the Russian general, puts all that there should be into the heavy. Undoubtedly in the prints of this picture that will be shown abroad Siegmann will be shown stripping Pola to the skin when he starts to remove the dresses and jewels which he has presented her with when discovering she has tricked him and is in love with what he assumes is nothing more than a waiter.

But, on the whole, the picture isn't one that is going to come, though, at the end of 1927 as one of the top 20 of the year, even though two master craftsmen of the industry imported from abroad had their hands in the making of it.

Fred.

A LITTLE JOURNEY

Metro-Goldwyn-Mayer production based on Rachel Crothers' play of the same name. Directed by Robert Z. Leonard. At the Capitol, New York, week Jan. 1. Running time, 67 minutes.

Julie Rutherford	Claire Windsor
George Manning	William Haines
Alexander Smith	Harry Carey
Aunt Louise	Claire McDowell
Alfred Bemis	Lawford Davidson

Romantic comedy is here done in the quiet, simple style that is the newest fashion in the screen. "A Little Journey" is a gem of a production in its development of a graceful, charming little love story in a technique at once dignified, charming and impressive.

Time was when a movie was either "dramatic," in which case it was violent, or "comedy," in which case it was all custard pie or gagging. A love story was either played out in action of heroic proportions or in the spirit of the comic strip, and there was nothing approximating high comedy. Pictures of the "Little Journey" kind are a new and encouraging departure.

There is almost no action (action in the old sense of "movie roughhouse") from beginning to end, and there isn't a gag in the picture. But there are several passages which reach something like tenseness, and the means are of the simplest. For one, the incident where George, the young lover, breaks the news to Alec, the rich traveler, that it is he whom Julie loves, is managed in pantomime with telling effect. There isn't even a gesture to express the emotional conflict involved, but the changing moods that flit across the faces of the two men convey a world of drama.

The picture is made up almost entirely of everyday commonplaces—beginning and progress of an everyday love affair between two entirely everyday young people on a railway train. But so real are the people, so real and faithful to life are their actions and so commonplace are the surroundings that they engage and hold one's attention as feverish, invented fiction never could.

It is a picture that is made effective without the usual aids of screen story. In place of the usual beauty of background there is here only the bare surroundings of a railroad sleeping car aisle. But somehow the commonplace environment heightens the effect; perhaps because it comes as a novelty to a fan surfeited with scenic extravagance in the pictures.

The playing of the cast of three—for the compact little story is wholly in the hands of this trio of actors—is as fine in its unaffected naturalness as the genuine little story in its delightful artlessness. Claire Windsor achieves the difficult miracle of underacting an ingenue role instead of overplaying all over the set. Harry Carey fits into the acting scheme most appropriately, conveying his meanings with an economy of gesture and facial expression that is remarkable. William Haines had more scope as the rather sophomoric young lover, but he never was guilty of overemphasis and was always true to the vital-spirited young suitor.

The story has to do with Julie, traveling across the continent to marry the middle-aged Alec, and her encounter with George, young gogetter on his way to a new job in Chicago. What starts on George's part in a mild flirtation develops between Albany and Englewood as a life-and-death love affair.

The young pair strike a romantic spark, when Alec clims unexpectedly aboard the train, having come east to surprise his bride-to-be.

In the old screen technique the values could have been expressed only by a fist fight between the two men from the locomotive cab to the observation platform, preferably as the train was crossing a dizzy trestle over the Grand Canyon.

Here the whole thing is adequately expressed in half a dozen quiet scenes; the dramatic conflict is conveyed in spiritual terms, and the sentimental value is amazingly eloquent. Of course, the older man resigns for a happy ending for the lovers. In nothing is the high and intelligent quality of the picture shown than in the titling—terse, direct and simple to the last degree.

It goes without saying that the picture is not a box-office epic. By the very nature of the production that would not be expected. But it will please the best class of picturegoers and it will add appreciably to the prestige of Metro-Goldwyn-Mayer. *Rush.*

LADY IN ERMINE

First National release, starring Corinne Griffith. Produced by Asher, Small & Rogers. Adapted from the operetta of the same name. Screen play by Benjamin Glazer. James Flood, director. At Strand, New York, week Jan. 1. Running time, 65 mins.

Mariana	Corinne Griffith
Adrian	Einar Hansen
Archduke Stephen	Ward Crane
General Dostal	Francis X. Bushman
Mariana's Maid	Jane Keckley

This Corinne Griffith picture will be accepted.

Having been adapted from an operetta, it's full of musical comedy uniforms, with Francis X. Bushman leaving the heroics to become a heavy. It goes back as far as 1810 and is based upon an Austrian invasion of Italy. The Shuberts produced it as an operetta about four years ago. Whether the stage version carried the same sex angle as this celluloid adaptation is a question. It's probable that the scenario has been switched to magnify the spice. Anyway, it's there, and forceful enough to keep the patrons in a state of anticipation, even if nothing actually happens.

Miss Griffith is permitted to appear as a bride, in some sort of an Empire gown, supposedly nude, except for an ermine cloak, and in uniform. That's enough for one film and for this girl who invariably "sells" her appearance for all it's worth although a hideous headdress doesn't help. Plus the various types of uniforms floating around in front of castle exteriors and interiors the film is picturesque enough but not to the point where the costume thing becomes an impediment.

It opens with a military wedding taking place on the eve of battle. Mariana (Miss Griffith) becomes the wife of Adrian (Einar Hansen), the latter immediately departing for the front. The Italian detachment takes the wrong direction, however, and the Austrians come in the other way, the officers making the castle their headquarters. General Dostal (Mr. Bushman) commands the invaders and must needs keep an eye on the Crown Prince (Ward Crane), both for military and personal reasons, as each has an eye for the feminine. One look at their hostess and the personal duel is on between the men, while the jeopardy tangent is supplied when the bridegroom rushes back to his homestead in disguise upon the news of the invasion from the rear.

The spice is weaved in through a family heirloom, a picture called "The Lady in Ermine." It is of Mariana's great grandmother, who paid the price to save her husband from death during a war with France. When Dostal eventually dooms Adrian to death he repeats the demand to Mariana, and she is supposed to come to him clothed only in ermine.

But Dostal falls asleep and dreams that Mariana keeps the bargain, giving Miss Griffith a chance to wear the white wrap while remaining as pure as it looks and saving her husband at the same time. Which may or may not satisfy everybody.

Fair screen fare that will stand up in the big league houses. Bushman and Crane wear their uniforms well and please as light heavies. Other cast members remain secondary, except for an old-man role which the player (unnamed) makes a standout.

Plenty of attendance at the Strand Sunday afternoon, with little doubt that the Griffith name was greatly responsible.

Averagely directed. Miss Griffith and that dash of ginger figure to make it financially sound. *Skig.*

CHEERFUL FRAUD

Universal Pictures starring Reginald Denny. Directed by William A. Seiter; K.R.G. Brown, author. A.L. Todd, photographer. Gertrude Astor and Gertrude Olmstead underlined. At Paramount, New York, week Dec. 23. Running time, 77 mins.

Sir Michael Fairlie	Reginald Denny
Ann Kent	Gertrude Olmstead
Mr. Bytheway	Otis Harlan
Mrs. Bytheway	Emily Fitzroy
Steve	Charles Gerrard
Rose	Gertrude Astor

A light comedy yarn for Universal's principal star that slipped by at the Paramount without causing much comment one way or the other. It's not a "gag" picture, but relies on the situations in the story for its merriment, and these come through a mistaken identity theme.

Reginald Denny plays a titled Englishman who takes a position as a private secretary in a newly rich family so as to be near a young miss whom he has seen and traced to the estate. It evolves that she is secretary to the socially ambitious wife with circumstances bringing about an invitation to Sir Michael Fairlie, already in the house as the master's underling.

A crook, having hidden in Sir Michael's apartment, gets the invitation and accepts, the complications starting out from that point, augmented by the hen-pecked husband having to stand off a visit from a lady who is in waiting for coin in lieu of mash notes, which she holds. The latter recognizes the crook posing as Sir Michael. When he attempts to grab the family jewels, it leads to a chase in which Denny and the thief (Charles Gerrard) battle it out in a speeding automobile.

Denny and Otis Harlan carry the main laugh responsibilities, the star having the advantage of situations, while Harlan adds the personal equation to his total. Gertrude Astor registers as the invading woman, and Gertrude Olmstead makes a nice-looking heroine. Emily Fitzroy is the newly-rich wife, getting in a laugh bit every so often.

It's practically all interior work, and U has turned out some neat-looking sets as background. Seiter, directing, might have chopped a little. The tale isn't strong enough to rate the hour and 17 minutes it consumes. The wild auto ride while the boys are battling in the back seat doesn't convince or impress as a thrill. Just incidental, and the picture would be as good without it.

Denny's performance is up to scratch all the way. He has pretty well established that he can take care of any story in the light comedy vein that comes his way, but he is suffering the same as his contemporary screen thespians — from lack of material.

"The Cheerful Fraud" isn't a bad picture. Nothing great about it, either, but it will do. And that goes for the major houses which consummates a big percentage rise for a U release.

While Famous Players - Lasky slipped this U in for holiday week at the Paramount, they tried to keep it secret, it seemed. In the theatre's advertising the title of the picture was run without the least display, not even full face to the type, and in position it was placed beneath the name of the stage production.

Just one of those things, you can suppose. *Skig.*

THE THIRD DEGREE

Warner Bros. production, starring Dolores Costello. From the play by Charles Klein, adapted by Graham Baker. Directed by Michael Curtiz. Louise Dresser featured. In projection room Dec. 31. Running time, 75 minutes.

Annie Daly	Dolores Costello
Alicia Daly	Louise Dresser
Underwood	Rockliffe Fellowes
Howard Jeffries, Jr.	Jason Robards
Mrs. Chubb	Kate Price
"Daredevil Daly"	Tom Santchi
Mr. Chubb	Harry Todd
Baby Annie	Mary Louise Miller
Detective Chief	Michael Vavuch
Howard Jeffries, Sr.	David Torrence
Detective	Fred Kelsey

A story of circus and carnival life with a society element as a later background. The whole is handled in a manner to make an impressive screen story, especially as it has Dolores Costello as the star and heroine, as a high-diver and wire-walker who wins the millionaire's son when all the trials and tribulations are over. For the box office, the picture should be a money-getter in the average neighborhood house or small-town theatre.

With Miss Costello starred, Louise Dresser is featured, playing the mother of the young circus girl. The twist to the story is more or less along the "Madam X" lines, with the mother finally confessing to save her daughter's husband from being convicted of murder.

Miss Dresser as a circus performer is the wife of "Daredevil Daly," diver, tight-rope walker and knife-thrower. She deserts him to elope with the ringmaster of the small circus they are touring with.

On the night of the elopement Daly is riding a motorcycle in a slatted bowl with his little baby hanging from his neck. He sees the wife and her lover in an earnest conversation and has a premonition of what is taking place. An accident occurs and he and the baby are hurled over the top of the bowl, the child falling safely, but he sustaining a fracture of the skull. He, however, is physically strong enough to prevent the wife from making off with the child when she leaves, and after that drops dead. The Chubbs, owners of the little circus, take the girl and rear her. Fifteen years later they are running a side-show at Coney Island, at which the girl, grown to young womanhood, is the star attraction. She walks a tight-wire high above the audience and then does a 100-foot dive into a small tank. She is courted and married by the young son of a millionaire, but when he takes her to his home his father turns them both out. The millionaire has married a second time, and his wife is none other than Annie's mother.

The father of the boy decides to break up the marriage of his son and engages a private detective. He is the former ringmaster with whom the young bride's mother eloped. The detective lays a plan for the young bride and the husband believes the worst. He goes to the detective's home. There is a rough-and-tumble fight, with the result that the boy is knocked cold.

Atop of this his wife's mother enters and shoots the detective dead when he threatens to expose her past to her husband. The boy, when he comes to, is arrested for the crime. At first his wife tries to take the blame by confessing that she committed the crime, but later her mother confesses.

Miss Costello and Miss Dresser give rather good performances, although Miss Dresser overacted at times. Jason Robards as the lead opposite the star was disappointing.

In the matter of direction, Curtiz has tried for the same effects that made "Variety" a sensation in this country, but in this case he rather overshot the mark. It must have been one of those instances where someone on the lot told him that his trick camera stuff and direction of the freak shots were great and that he ought to put more in the picture. He took the advice, with the result that there is too much of a good thing.

But it is a picture that the public in the main will like. *Fred.*

ONE HOUR OF LOVE

Light dramatic story by Tiffany. Story by Leete Renick Brown. Scenario by Sarah Y. Mason. Directed by Robert Florey. Film editor, James C. McKay. Milton Moore and Mack Stengler, photographers. For release Jan. 15. Running time, 70 minutes (6,500 feet).

"Jerry" McKay	Jacqueline Logan
Patrick Quarry	Robert Frazer
J. W. McKay	Montagu Love
Joe Monahan	Taylor Holmes
Neely	Duane Thompson
Gwen	Mildred Harris
Vi	Hazel Keener
Louis Carruthers	William Austin

This picture has everything—except story. The story is an immature romance scaled to something less than school-girl intelligence. What the producer started out to do probably was to make a light romantic comedy based on the situation of the modern young female playing the pursuer in courtship. It is conceivable that such a picture might be made amusing.

The trouble here—and this is a point upon which a good many film directors have slipped up—that values become distorted in the screening of the script, which may have looked right in print but doesn't translate into pantomime smoothly.

Jerry McKay is a frivolous young thing, the spoiled daughter of a rich father, very modern in her independence. A sort of lounge lizard young man of her set proposes and is jestingly accepted upon condition that he stand the test of riding with Jerry at her customary speed without losing his nerve. He makes good by a trick, and they are engaged.

Jerry goes with her father to look over a dam building improvement he is promoting, and there this very self-sufficient young flapper and the engineer in charge of the work, a square-jawed young man, have a clash of wills.

Jerry swears she will make him propose and makes a bet with her girl pals she will hang his scalp to her belt. To this end Jerry devotes herself to the conquest. At the climax Jerry and the engineer are driven into his house on the work during a violent storm, and it is there that he makes love to her in the hearing of Jerry's three girl pals, concealed in the next room.

When the trio are discovered the engineer in fury orders them out, while he keeps the girl—to all appearances—in his rooms all night, with every indication that he intends to teach her a lesson. You are permitted to imagine what happened when Jerry returns home next morning, much bedraggled in appearance, to face her father and her friends. But all is smoothed over by the girl's simple statement that she remained in the house alone, while the engineer spent the night elsewhere.

The result is that nothing happens, nothing has happened, and the spectator was deliberately misled. Nothing does happen, except in the titles. The picture action is poorly laid out for effect. The girl carries on a cheap bit of conquest. This is expressed in the visible action. That she is really falling in love with her intended victim comes out more in the titles than in what happens.

In the same way the audience is led to suppose that the couple part for good. But in the very next view, without explanation, they are back making up in the engineer's home, and they do make it up without any reasonable action to show how or why.

The acting is very well done, although the girls—all four of them—are inclined to overdo the sweet young thing.

There are comedy values that ought to score with the easily amused, and the backgrounds are adequate. A picture that will find its audience among the neighborhood type of fans. *Rush.*

JIM THE CONQUEROR

Producers' Distribution Corp. western, featuring William Boyd in story by Peter B. Kyne. Directed by George B. Seitz. In supporting cast: Elinor Fair, Tom Santschi, Tully Marshall, Marcelle Corday. At New York Hippodrome, week Dec. 27. Running time, 62 minutes.

A western action picture, "Jim the Conqueror," best thing P. D. C. has done in months in respect to cast, production and story value. In a market overflowing with material of the same sort and of generally good quality, this feature probably will not attract special attention but should please along with the general run of features in its division.

The picture has a good deal of class for a western, partly from its capital cast and from a well-made story which has been enriched with excellent screen treatment. *Rush.*

Blonde or Brunette

Famous Players-Lasky picture starring Adolphe Menjou and featuring Greta Nissen and Arlette Marchal. Directed by Robert Rosson. Adapted from the play "An Angel Passes," French comedy. At the Paramount, New York, week Jan. 8. Running time, 62 mins.

Henri Martel	Adolphe Menjou
Fanny	Greta Nissen
Blanche	Arlette Marchal
Grandmother	Mary Carr
Mother-in-law	Evelyn Sherman
Father-in-law	Emile Chautard

The dignified, but with a twinkle, Menjou between the Misses Nissen and Marchal, both of whom he marries in the story. He finishes by going back to Miss Nissen, the original sweet thing who turns modern after the ceremony, but becomes herself again following a divorce.

Strictly a featherweight plot which the boys have tried to build up with subtitles and the cast names. Just an average program picture they've been slipping into the Paramount while the curious are still swarming through the doors.

Basically this one is a French bedroom farce, but on the screen it's not quite fast enough to equal farce tempo. Located in France, the settings are all interiors to the extent it's doubtful if the picture gets a breath of fresh air for more than a couple of hundred feet. A pure example of a studio-made film and well produced.

From an audience standpoint Miss Nissen in various stages of undress and under as many flitting emotions, runs away with the picture. Quite a portion, this girl, and here she's the entree, main course and demitasse. The farce bedroom situations develop in her grandmother's home, where the old lady plays innocent to try and get she and Menjou together again, although knowing they're divorced and that Miss Marchal is the present official bride.

Circumstances force Menjou in and out of his former wife's room while the threesome is making frantic efforts to hide the truth from grandma.

That's about all there is to it despite an opening passage showing Menjou well fed up with a fast set which won't let him alone. Miss Marchal is angling for him until he meets the non-drinking and smoking miss whom she turns into a jazz nut, as she's still angling.

If the pace doesn't reach a farce rating the resultant situations are swift enough to make the opening seem slow. However, it's only a 62-minute picture, so there's nothing actually draggy about it. Just fluffy stuff that will have to sail by on Menjou's name and Miss Nissen's appearance.

It was received quietly at the Paramount. Snickers, yes, but nothing uproarious in the reactions nor applause to stamp approval at the finish. *Skig.*

Flesh and the Devil

Clarence Brown production, presented by Metro-Goldwyn-Mayer. Starring John Gilbert with Gretta Garbo and Lars Hanson featured. From the Hermann Sudermann novel, "The Undying Past," adapted by Benjamin F. Glazer. At the Capitol, New York, week of Jan. 8. Running time, 91 mins.

Leo von Sellenthin	John Gilbert
Felicitas von Kletzingk	Gretta Garbo
Ulrich von Kletzingk	Lars Hanson
Hertha Prochvitz	Barbara Kent
Uncle Kutowski	William Orlamond
Pastor Breckenburg	George Fawcett
Leo's Mother	Eugenie Besserer
Count von Rhaden	Marc MacDermott
Minna	Marcelle Corday

Here is a picture that is the "pay-off" when it comes to filming love scenes. There are three in this picture that will make anyone fidget in their seats and their hair to rise on end—an' that ain't all. It's a picture with a great kick, a great cast and great direction.

Clarence Brown ranks with the best of the imported directors when it comes to handling sophisticated stuff. Brown is the first of our own directors to show something that carries the conviction that he knows what it is all about when he decides to adopt the German technique in the making of pictures.

This film is a battle between John Gilbert, starred, and Gretta Garbo, featured, for honors and if they don't star this girl after this picture Metro-Goldwyn doesn't know what it is missing. Miss Garbo properly handled and given the right material, will be as great a money asset as Theda Bara was to Fox in years past. This girl has everything. Gilbert has to keep moving to overshadow her, even though she has a most unsympathetic role.

There is one other girl in this picture that is going to bear watching in the future, Barbara Kent. She came through this one with flying colors. Lars Hanson also did a neat piece of work here.

But as to the picture itself—it is certain to be a box office smash, no matter where they play it. It looks as though it should be big enough to smash the record at the Capitol this week and possibly hold over next week for another record. After they get a load of this love making the audiences are going out and talk about it, and send others in.

The story is laid in a small German or Austrian town. Two boys and a girl have grown up together. The boys have, as kids, sworn eternal friendship through a blood bond. They are both at military school when the picture opens and about to start on their annual holiday. Back home there is a ball and Leo (Gilbert), the more sophisticated of the two, sees a girl that he admired at the station. He dances with her, but fails to learn her name. Next they are disclosed in her boudoir back in the city. Her husband walks in on the picture and the youngster then knows for the first time that she is married. The husband strikes the boy, and it calls for a duel. The general impression is given out by the two principals that the cause is over a card table row. The husband is killed. He was a powerful man and the military authorities take notice of it and "advise" foreign service for five years for the youngster. Before going he asks his bloodbound friend to seek out the widow and console her.

After three years away Leo is pardoned by the Emperor and returns with one thought, that of seeking out his former love and marrying her. But on his arrival he discovers that she has wed the friend. Then a series of incidents occur that almost brings on a duel between the friends. The woman is the cause. She wants the one for his wealth and the other for a lover, and is willing to do anything to gain her point. In fact, after agreeing to elope she tries to change things so that she will still remain under her husband's roof and hold the other man as a sweetheart.

Leo rebels at this and while a tremendous scene is at its height, the husband enters. He believes the tale his wife unfolds and challenges his friend. The two meet the next morning on the same spot that they swore eternal friendship and just as they are about to fire their pistols the husband sees the truth. In the meantime, the little girl of their childhood days, also in love with Leo, has been pleading with the wife to tell the truth and to prevent death. The wife finally harkens, and in crossing the ice to the scene of the duel falls into the lake and is drowned. Then the happy ending when the spring comes and the blossoms bloom.

A corking story, exceptionally acted and cleverly directed. A lot of glory to be distributed among all concerned. *Fred.*

Bred in Old Kentucky

F. B. O. picture presented by Joseph P Kennedy. Directed by Eddie Dillon, from the story by Louis Weadock and C. D. Lancaster. Featuring Viola Dana, with cast including Jerry Wiley, Jed Prouty and Josephine Crowell. At the Stanley, New York; one day, Jan. 8.

Light racktrack film, with the usual doped horse, dirty work and the hero's naïve innocence. Makes fair picture as independent.

Jerry Wiley is a good male lead, but his part as the wealthy young race horse owner who doesn't know anything about the thieving trainer whose crooked plot ruined Viola is not drawn in forcibly enough.

Iron-hatted, check-suited Jed Prouty makes an interesting, amusing but somewhat impossible bookie. His exact position in the picture is indefinable. He is not villainous enough to be the heavy and not straight enough to be considered by the pure little girl who spends her waking hours in the stables dressed in overalls.

One scene gets laughs. Miss Dana is ejected from her room by an irascible landlady whom she owes $40 The bookie sees Viola the same day and proposes that she hand out tips and bring him custor[illegible] percent commission. Viola refuses, but when lunch time comes round the third she has missed out on, the spirit begins to weaken. And when the landlady rushes up to her and demands an introduction to an "honest" bookmaker, Viola hails Jed.

The latter turns over half the landlady's money to Viola, who uses $40 of it to pay her rent. The landlady takes the $40 and hands it to Jed to be bet on the same horse. And Jed hands $20 of it to Viola. The whole scene transpires in a restaurant around three tables.

The horses are not the kind people would bet all their money on. At the start Viola banks the family fortune on a specimen which looks as if it wouldn't raise a leg to save its life.

THE PERFECT SAP

First National picture adapted from the stage play, "Not Herbert." Directed by Howard Higgin. Ben Lyon and Pauline Starke featured. At the Strand, New York, week of Jan. 8. Running time, 60 mins.

Herbert Alden	Ben Lyon
Polly Stoddard	Pauline Starke
Ruth Webster	Virginia Lee Corbin
Tracy Sutton	Lloyd Whitlock
Roberta Alden	Diana Kane
Stephen Alden	Byron Douglas
Mrs. Stephen Alden	Christine Compton
Fletcher	Charles Craig
Nick Fanshaw	Sam Hardy
George Barrow	Tammany Young
Cissie Alden	Helen Rowland

Neat bit of nonsense with a dramatic climax for screen purposes built up beyond the play possibilities. Picture takes a wealth of comedy interest from a variety of amusing characters, the progress being designed for laughing purposes with the punch drama reserved for the finale.

Some of the incidents of the story are better on the screen than on the stage, and the piece that was a so-so success behind the footlights makes first rate picture entertainment. It will be graded somewhere in the same class as "Seven Keys to Baldpate," a little milder in comedy, but somewhat in the same level of well made screen product. Good for a week anywhere, with the better grade of clientele preferred.

The character of Herbert, wealthy young dabbler in the science of crime detection, has in it something of the Bunker Bean, and Ben Lyon plays it with an engaging simplicity. Tammany Young has a good low comedy role as a roughneck crook, while Virginia Lee Corbin does a vamp nicely. Charles Craig has a comedy old man role made to order for him. The others play satisfactorily but do not matter especially.

The production is elaborate and supremely well done—so much so that the settings merge into the story without ever intruding upon one's attention. Herbert has fitted up a trick apartment for himself to aid in his study of the detective profession and such devices as periscopes, sinking rooms and trap doors are introduced for good comic effect.

The robbery at the masked ball is a good bit of staging, and the events leading up to it, chase and capture of the crook, are well managed. Titling is expertly done. The wording is brief and covers the situations without any straining for laughs. In that way it is in keeping with the tone of the picture, allowing the complications to generate their laughs naturally, a treatment, by the way, that is happily becoming more and more fixed as recognized technique. *Rush.*

NOBODY'S WIDOW

Donald Crisp production made by DeMille Pictures Corp., released by P. D. C. From the play by Avery Hopwood, adapted by Clara Baranger and Douglas Doty. Leatrice Joy starred, Charles Ray, Phyliss Haver and David Butler featured. Shown at the Hippodrome, New York, week Jan. 10, 1926. Running time, 67 minutes.

Roxanna Smith	Leatrice Joy
Hon. John Clayton	Charles Ray
Betty Jackson	Phyliss Haver
Ned Stevens	David Butler
Roxanna's Maid	Dot Farley
Mlle. Renee	Fritzi Ridgeway
Valet	Charles West

This one is so far and away ahead of the usual program features that P. D. C. has been turning out that it is almost an occasion for cheers. The picture is a farce comedy idea that has been well worked out in the picturization and with a couple of rough moments looks to be about as right a bet for the box office as the Hip has had as yet from the allied releasing company. For the general run of houses the features will stand up and it has a cast that should mean something at the box office.

Leatrice Joy is starred with Charles Ray, one of the trio of featured members of the cast playing opposite her. Miss Joy handles herself perfectly through this picture, does a little display of her physical charms that should interest the boys in front. The same might also be said of Phyliss Haver. She sure offers to be "a girl friend" to the boys. Charles Ray is Ray in dress clothes and that is all, while David Butler means nothing to either the story or the B. O.

As Roxanna Smith, Miss Joy marries the Hon. John Clayton (Mr. Ray) in England. After the marriage he confesses that in reality he is a duke, but, of course, that doesn't make his American bride exactly angry. A few moments later, when she steps into his apartment at the inn where the wedding took place and finds him in the arms of a French girl, all bets are off and the wife decides to become a widow, returning to America.

The scene shifts to California, where the widow's best friend, Betty Jackson (Miss Haver) welcomes her home again.

From then on she is royally entertained and all the men are intrigued by the handsome young lady wearing widow's weeds, until the husband shows.

She, however, compels him to keep her secret and woo her all over again. He is given a week for his courting. Meantime his wife leads him a merry chase, finally on the seventh day when he proposes again she rejects him. He says that he'll keep his promise to her to remain dead at least as far as she is concerned, but not to other women and that brings a change of heart on her part. But the complications are not over as yet.

The widow's best friends has decided that a duke wouldn't be so bad for herself and is on the make. As she is a grass widow and knows her male sex, she gets him into her rooms for a private dinner and the two are there when the widow and the grass widow's new fiance come in the door.

Then the trouble starts all over again, only to be finally straightened out when the duke's wife decides to elope with the grass widow's fiance just "to teach 'em both a lesson" with the result that the husband discovering the plan follows post haste to mountain inn arriving in time to save the night.

There are a number of laughs in the picture, but they occur at distant intervals, which makes the picture slow moving in spots.

Fred.

HOME-STRUCK

Ralph Ince Production presented by Joseph Kennedy, released by F. B. O. Story by Peter Milne, adapted by Ewart Adamson. Directed by Ralph Ince, starring Viola Dana. Reviewed at projection room Dec. 29. Running time, 62 minutes.

Barbara Page..................Viola Dana
Lyn Holmes..................Alan Brooks
Dick Cobb..................Tom Gallery
Warren Townsend..................Nigel Barrie
President Wallace..................George Irving
Nick Cohen..................Charles Howard

Story of the theatre and banking circles that shows that the boys in the banking business are a whole lot wilder than those that are of the stage. Incidentally, it shows that the stage girls are straightlaced as compared to some of the so-called society flappers. As a whole it is one of the nearest approaches to real life that has come along on the screen as depicting theatrical life. Incidentally it is a fair little melodrama that will get by almost anywhere.

Unusually strong cast for an F. B. O. release. The star is Viola Dana. She is still petite enough to get away with a dancer's role. Viola does dance, and there is one flash of a dancer's legs in it that shows that Vi must have done some real hoofing in her day.

In addition there are three strong roles for the men, and they are admirably cast. Alan Brooks has the sympathetic role of the press agent in love with the girl, who makes the sacrifice for her that she may be happy with the man she loves, who is a young bank employee, played by Tom Gallery, while Nigel Barrie plays the heavy and gets all that there is out of the part. Charles Howard in the role of a theatrical manager looks like Freddie Goldsmith, the lawyer, and smokes a cigar like Al Woods.

The tale has Viola Dana working on the end in the chorus and putting over a little comedy stuff (incidentally very much along the line that the Mendoza girl did in "Jessie James" prior to her marriage to Ralph Ince, who directed this picture). She is about to be put under contract by the management as a principal when she decides to marry instead. Having been "born in a theatre, cradled in a Pullman berth and lived in hotels all her life, she is keen for the chance to get a little home of her own, so she turns down the P. A. when he proposes and takes the bank clerk, refusing the management's contract. The young bank employee believes that life is nothing but a series of parties, and to hold up his end dips into the bank's funds at the suggestion of one of his fellow employees, who is keen to make the wife.

That employee tips off the bank president, and then when they try to make the pinch the husband has disappeared. The double-crosser then offers to square the account if the bank president will drop the case. With this arranged he tries to collect from the wife, but at that moment the former press agent-sweetheart walks in and clears the scene.

The girl returns to the stage, eventually becomes a star, and then hubby returns for the final clinch.

Lot of action and the wild party stuff fairly well staged under Ince's direction, who knows his party and stage stuff very well indeed. If this is Alan Brooks' first picture he looks like he is sure to be a bet, for he's natural before the camera.

Fred.

One Increasing Purpose

William Fox production from the story by A. S. M. Hutchinson, adapted by Bradley King. Directed by Harry Beaumont. Edmund Lowe and Lila Lee featured. In projection room Dec. 30. Running time, 98 minutes.

Sim Paris..................Edmund Lowe
Elizabeth Glade..................Lila Lee
Charles Paris..................Holmes Herbert
Linda Travers Paris..................May Allison
Dr. Byrne..................Lawford Davidson
Mrs. Andiron..................Emily Fitzroy
Mr. Glade..................George Irving
Andrew Paris..................Huntley Gordon
Old Gand..................Josef Swickard
Alice Paris..................Jane Novak
Jule..................Nicholas Soussanin

Another of those stories of English life by the author of "If Winter Comes." It is a very much jumbled-up affair regarding life in England after the war and in its present shape, much too long for American consumption. At least 15 minutes could be cut. Scenes showing Edmund Lowe walking around London taking in the sights might well be dropped as far as this side of the Atlantic is concerned, although they should be kept in for prints going to British possessions.

The picture has a corking cast, and it could be well advertised as an all-star production by the American exhibitors. The chances are, however, that it will not be a particularly strong box office card, except for those who may have read the book.

Sim Paris, played by Lowe, has gone through the war unscathed. He has been a major, and while his comrades-in-arms have been knocked off right and left, not a single scratch has fallen to his lot until he becomes convinced his life has been spared for some greater purpose.

When returning to England he discovers that one of his elder brothers is so wrapped up in making money that he is losing the love of his wife; another brother, who has been taking care of an invalided relative for years in expectation of a remembrance in the will, is also about to lose his wife, she having fallen in love with a doctor who has been in attendance. The male nurse has discovered the secret and tries to blackmail the woman, finally succeeding in making her state that she was present with him when the invalid died and that before passing away he directed that the nurse should receive $5,000.

The returned officer walks in on this state of affairs. While he pays slight attention at first, after a visit to the home of the widow of a former comrade in the army and noting the happiness that prevailed in the home, he believes that his mission is to straighten out the affairs of the others and he proceeds to do so.

One would think that Lowe would have taken a lesson to heart from the success that he achieved in "What Price Glory" and stopped walking through pictures as though he felt sorry for himself, but he hasn't. Here again he is up to his old matinee idol tricks and registering wholly negative in the role assigned him. Lila Lee was pleasing enough opposite him, but May Allison in what she had to do was easily in the forefront. Jane Novak also contributed a very effective performance. Josef Swickard and Nicholas Soussanin, in character roles, scored.

The fault with the picture lies principally with the adaptor, who evidently tried to follow the book too closely. He should have cut away from some of the detail and tried to get a picture story that was not so involved out of it.

Fred.

EXCLUSIVE RIGHTS

J. C. Bachman presents this independent. Based on the story, "Invisible Government," by Jerome N. Wilson, screen version by Eve Unsell. Directed by Frank O'Connor. Photographed by Andre Barlatier. A Preferred Picture. Running time, 62 mins. (projection room time).

Stanley Wharton..................Gayne Whitman
Catherine Courtwright..................Lillian Rich
Mac Morton..................Gloria Gordon
Mack Miller..................Raymond McKee
Flash Fleming..................Gaston Glass
Night Club Hostess..................Grace Cunard
Bickel..................Sheldon Lewis
Boss Morris..................Charles Mailes
Sadie Towner..................Shirley Palmer
Bat Hoover..................James Bradbury, Jr.
Garth..................Fletcher Norton
Specialty Dancer..................Jimmy Savo

A picture with promise of special interest from several angles. One is the atmosphere of night clubs, where much of the action takes place, and the other a high powered melodramatic climax in which the hero, unjustly condemned for a murder he did not commit, is carried directly to the electric chair, apparently doomed. Whether the brutality of the death chair passage will revolt or attract is a question.

It is skillfully done in this instance to give a maximum of dramatic kick. The night club scenes are well managed with good pictorial shots of the semi-nude girls, the hard-boiled hostess, and the specialty people, notably an eccentric dance by Jimmy Savo, used for the purpose alone without being concerned directly in the story.

For some reason the producer does not exploit these night club bits in his billing matter, thereby missing a good bet. Instead, the billing emphasizes the death house angle and its political phase, which doesn't mean a thing. This story stands up on its own merits, both as a production in the best modern manner and for its innate grip of interest.

Death house and night club are both hung on the story thread of a corrupt political boss and his scheme to break an honest governor who refuses to further his manipulations. One of the governor's lieutenants is framed on a murder charge in order to force the state executive to pardon the boss' political henchman, convicted of murder and threatening to squeal. The cabaret is the boss' hangout and it is there that the murder takes place while the girls are working in the floor show.

The acting is extraordinarily convincing for a melodrama, and settings are always in the best of taste. In some of the earlier passages there is some crudity in planting the situation, and a little of over-elaboration, but when the action gets down to its pace it is a capital example of sustained suspense, with a fine building up of tension and a swift, surprise finale.

Rush.

Sunshine of Paradise Alley

Chadwick Pictures presentation from the play by Duncan Thompson. Directed by Jack Nelson under the personal supervision of Jesse J. Goldburg. Starring Barbara Bedford, with cast including Max Davidson, Bobby Nelson, Frank Weed, Kenneth McDonald, J. Park Jones, Lui Lorraine, Gayne Whitman and Nigel Barrie. At Loew's Circle, one day, Jan. 10.

Unpromising Jewish East Side life start, switching quickly into the easily recognized, aged-in-the-wood thriller with a couple of new trimmings. While the story holds nothing new, the picture is packed with old reliable gags and a few thrills.

Kenneth McDonald furnishes part of the excitement when he batters down a door with his bare fist, blood oozing over the panels through the force of the impact of the naked flesh against the wood. The grim look on his face, the powerful, effortless thuds on the door, the fateful "die-or-get-there" look on his face, register big.

Gayne Whitman registers well as the polished, wealthy banker who plans to destroy Paradise Alley in favor of factory buildings. Barbara Bedford, of course, is Sunshine O'Day, everybody's sweetheart. She looks much better with hair frizzled and put up and rolled stockings a la rough house.

Nigel Barrie is the heavy, a gentleman who "prefers bonds" and dear little Sunshine. For coveting the latter in his apartment he gets a present of several jaw-breaking socks from the boy friend McDonald.

Max Davidson as Solomon Levy furnishes the right touch of humor, and J. Park Jones, the assistant villain, carries on nobly as a sneak-thief and fly-by-night hoofer.

Bobby Nelson is too ragged as "Bum," but puts over the sob stuff according to demand. Of course everything ends happily. Barbara doesn't really love the wealthy young banker, after all. Just friends! Kenneth is the lucky dog in the final finals. Paradise Alley is to be torn down in spite of all of Sunshine's pleas, but instead of building factories the owner promises to put up new dwellings with two kinds of water and bathrooms.

Striving for Fortune

Samuel Zierler presents independent picture released by Commonwealth, featuring George Walsh. No director's name given. In the cast Beryl Roberts, Joe Burke, Tefft Johnson, Louise Carter and Dexter McReynolds. At Loew's New York (double feature day), Jan. 7. Running time, 62 mins.

A capital screen idea is here spoiled by bad treatment of a romantic plot. The kick of the picture is the building and launching of an ocean liner (the actual yards of the New York Shipbuilding Company being used and the liner is real).

The dramatic action takes place in the environment of the shipyard and so has an intensely interesting background for certain melodramatic episodes, such as the rescue of the heroine when she tries to work the big electric crane as a lark; the actual casting of big ship parts with white hot steel, riveting gangs at work and the growth of the ship in its timbered network of ways as hero and heavy fight their battles.

So far as the story sticks to the building of the ship, the humble workman, Tom Sheridan, opposing the hull boss, who seeks to delay the job through treachery, the tale is thoroughly absorbing, but when the love story is dragged in the interest lags, principally because the love thing is not vitally tied up with the center of interest, which is the completion of the ship on time.

There are a number of punch scenes. The villain gets possession of the big crane, raises a five-ton casting high in the air and is ready to drop it upon the almost-finished ship when the hero rushes to the controls, and in a hand-to-hand fight saves the day. There are a number of these melodramatic passages neatly worked into the shipyard scenes that in themselves would make a worth-while industrial picture.

The launching is a splendid bit of spectacle and has its dramatic action as well, with the hero saving the ship from destruction when the villain opens the seacocks to sink her as she takes the water. Two women love the hero, the ship builder's daughter, and the daughter of a fellow workman, but the producer seems to have realized that this romantic element was out of the focus, for it is almost ignored at times and again emphasized.

If this love element had been properly evaluated in the whole composition, the picture would have been a high-class program feature. Instead, it is just a crude melodrama done in highly interesting settings. *Rush.*

The Masked Woman

First National release of June Mathis production presented by Richard A. Rowland; written for screen by Miss Mathis from play by Charles Mere, and directed by her husband, Balboni. Gerald C. Duffy did the titles. Anna Q. Nilsson, Holbrook Blinn and Charles Murray co-featured in cast, which has Einar Hansen and Ruth Roland also among principals. Ran 60 minutes at the Broadway, New York, in conjunction with vaudeville show, week Jan. 10

"The Masked Woman" is conventional triangle stuff with sophisticated Nice, Riviera and Paris locale. It impresses more because of its sumptuous trimmings rather than the basic theme of a sophisticated Turkish nobleman coveting another but unwilling addition to his harem. The fundamental dramatic suspense is derived from a virtuous wife's fight to protect her honor with the usual silly complications through the husband being conveniently called away on long-distance consultations so as to give the Turk his innings. It is only because of the lavishness of the production that the picture is held up sufficiently to qualify as a one-day program feature, despite the flattering week's stand at this house which doesn't mean much either way.

Most noteworthy in the film is the possibilities of Holbrook Blinn as another Menjou in the same type of a sophisticated light "menace." Blinn did excellently here and with Charlie Murray foiling well as his butler, the male two-thirds of the featured trio ran away with things. Miss Nilsson did little beyond acting sweet 'n pretty.

There is much that lacks conviction in the entire proceedings. One possibly does not bother to analyze it at first glance and it all progresses smoothly up until the fade-out when the wife decides to accept the dead nobleman's heritage of millions with the caption, "think of all the poor war-orphans of France we can make happy," or words to that effect. They tittered at that one.

Her original intention was to reject the wily Turkish Casanova's enforced inheritance, realizing how he had trickily branded her from his grave, but a jealous lady of the evening pops up conveniently to rant against the unfairness of this saintly wife getting the financial "breaks" although "she wouldn't even let him touch her last night." That's great as a convincer in the eyes of her doubting husband and so another heroine's honor has been saved.

Einar Hansen is not particularly effective opposite Miss Nilsson as the medico-husband but then, the opportunities are limited. Histrionically, Blinn and Murray monopolize the most attention.

One senses a constant titular apology via the captions that "although she doubted the Turk's message, the possibility of the truth attracted her to his apartment" (at an indiscreet hour). Similarly the orphanage atmosphere is dragged in to build for the inheritance finale.

The sartorial and scenic trimmings are okay if familiar. There's the usual Monte Carlo gambling scenes; Folies Bergere or similar night club scene; the flock of "dames" running around the Turk's domicile so that he is literally "knee deep in frails," plus the salaaming Oriental menials, etc. Good hinterland hoke and bound to go with the customers at pop scale. *Abel.*

THE MUSIC MASTER

William Fox presents the Allan Dwan production of the William Klein play produced by David Belasco and made famous with David Warfield. Scenario by Philip Klein, son of the author. Lois Moran and Neil Hamilton featured, with Alec. B. Francis starred in the Warfield roll. Running time, 80 mins. At the Strand, New York, Jan. 15.

Anton Von Barwig	Alec B. Francis
Helene Stanton	Lois Moran
Beverly Cruger	Neil Hamilton
Andrew Cruger	Norman Trevor
Richard Stanton	Charles Lane
Joles	William T. Tilden
Jenny	Helen Chandler
Miss Husted	Marcia Harris
Mrs. Andrew Cruger	Kethleen Kerrigan
August Poons	Howard Cull
Pinac	Armand Cortes
Fico	Leo Feodoroff
Mrs. Mangenborn	Carrie Scott
Pawnbroker	Dore Davidson

Allan Dwan's picture is a beautifully done sentimental story, set in exquisite taste, acted with admirable restraint and containing honest heart throb, altogether worthy of the fine tradition of the piece. But it is old fashioned, out of line with the screen mood of this year of grace and there is the situation that weighs for and against.

The older generation will love "The Music Master," but the chances are against it inspiring the younger fans educated to a taste for more highly seasoned screen fare.

Viewed apart from the aura that surrounds an institution of the theatre more or less hallowed by the passage of years, this chronicle of a broken-hearted old musician does make quiet entertainment, judged by modern standards.

The producer has bravely refused to compromise with the new order of things, touching the original with a hand almost of reverence. The comedy that was a distinct part of the charm in the Warfield play has paled in the picturization. Notably the spaghetti eating incident is altogether missing. When it was produced that passage attracted more attention than the star's emotional acting, together with its surrounding atmosphere of humble Bohemia in the New York boarding house.

The only comedy element remaining is the romance between Poons and Jenny and here even this is dealt with in a rather sentimental way. Emphasis has been thrown to the sentimental character of von Barwig and in spite of the flawless playing of Alec B. Francis in the title role the sentimental side does at length become oppressive. The trouble is that the whole pattern of the narrative belongs to a by-gone period, together with straight fronts and balloon sleeves.

The role of the heart hungry music master by Mr. Francis stands out for grace and finished etching in portraiture, but it isn't the music master of Warfield's. This is a sort of etherealized music master and the thing that contributes principally to the change is the absence of von Barwig's flavoring of dialect, the distortions of speech that made him so sympathetically human.

The picture is done with amazingly few titles, best evidence that the director's hand was sure and the dramatic values were right. Of course the lines "If you don't want her," etc., came upon the screen. Another title was the line at the meeting of von Barwig and the man who had despoiled his home—"The world has revolved a few times since we met," says the music master. But on the screen it's a pale speech, while in the play it was momentous as drama.

The picture play has a gorgeous wedding scene, perhaps to compensate somewhat for deficiencies elsewhere in emotional punch, quite the loveliest nuptial ceremony of the season.

The wedding scene is like the rest of the screen version in that it completely satisfies the sight, but it doesn't deliver the essence of the thing that made the play the sensation of the decade.

In the cast besides Mr. Francis, Lois Moran stands out like a lighthouse as the music master's lost daughter. For youthful charm this young actress is comparable to anyone. *Rush.*

THE POTTERS

Famous Players-)Lasky picture starring W. C. Fields, featuring Ivy Harris and Mary Alden. Adapted from J. P. McEvoy's stage play of the same name. Directed by Fred Newmeyer, with P. C. Vogel photographing. At the Paramount, New York, week Jan. 15. Running time, 71 minutes.

Pa Potter	W. C. Fields
Ma Potter	Mary Alden
Mamie	Ivy Harris
Bill	Jack Egan
Red Miller	"Skeets" Gallagher
Rankin	Joseph Smiley
Eagle	Bradley Barker

W. C. Fields' pictures have been reported in and outers ever since he took to the screen. Whether that's so or not it looks as though "The Potters," which he has turned out, is the best light comedy the new Paramount has housed to date and a picture that will overcome any of Fields' early film shortcomings when the country at large gets a flash at it. The bigger the house and scale the better they will like this picture.

"The Potters" is all Fields. It's doubtful if his ability as a pantomimist has ever shown to better advantage on a screen. They ate it up at the Paramount during a Sunday matinee, laughed all the way and thoroughly enjoyed it. That condition will repeat itself in other houses. It's fast, clean and wholesome. And if the story is along well known lines, even unto the house anticipating what's coming, it but adds to the credit of Fields and Newmeyer, who directed, that it continues to entertain.

As a Broadway show this script carved out a neat run for itself under the guidance of Richard Herndon who produced it in 1923. The play was a study of a middle class drudge. The picture retains the middle class background but it's been hoked away from the drudge idea to show Pa Potter (Mr. Fields) as an office worker with a high finance complex who throws the family savings account into an oil speculation. The oil thing tips off the story and its finish immediately. Yet Fields holds the picture together despite its obvious characteristics. The four $1,000 shares of stock are worthless, of course, with the one share that the gyps throw in as a gift turning out to be the bonanza.

Simple? Certainly. But a delight as Fields plays it.

The counter story is of the daughter of the family (Ivy Harris) in love with a $30 a week clerk (Skeets Gallagher) who rubs Pa Potter the wrong way every time he walks by the house.

Fields is best foiled by Mary Alden, who plays the conservative Ma Potter, well aware of her husband's misdirected financial ideas. The scenes between these two are standouts with Gallagher and Fields also making the situations count every time they get together.

An instance of two former vaudeville performers fencing in the good of the cause, with the early schooling showing its value. This may or may not be Gallagher's first effort before the camera. Anyway, this boy carries a corking appearance to the screen and should be able to find plenty to do around the studios.

Ivy Harris, if the memory isn't too far off, is a product of the Paramount school. Okay too, although not given much to do. The same generalization apparently covers Jack Egan as the heir to the Potter troubles. Joseph Smiley and Bradley Barker are cast as the oil manipulators.

Fields always has been known for his accomplishments as a pantomimist. It's what brought him to the front as a comedy juggler until he finally got away from juggling altogether. If there is any doubt as to his ability as a screen subject this performance should smother it. Little bits crop up all through the picture that ordinarily wouldn't mean a thing but which Fields' turns into laughs. The film opens with a guffaw and his chasing of a taxi which holds his grip for blocks, finally catching it to ride but a few feet and then having to pay the fare is a new gag wrinkle which got what it deserved. A shot of pathos during the late footage serves as a neat change of pace. Also a word for the titles, which aid the momentum.

An all-around good film, on which the technical staff as well as the cast can take a bend. There may not be enough slapstick in it to thoroughly amuse the "shooting galleries" but it's human and everyone can understand it.

Which may explain Fields' brilliant performance. He's human here, and funny. So much so it may prove a lesson in pantomiming to many of his contemporary screen comics. *Sid.*

SPANGLES

(Nellie Revell)

Universal release of Arthur T. Beck production. Screen adaptation by Leah Baird of story by Nellie Revell. Hobart Bosworth and Pat O'Malley featured. Nellie Revell starred as author in billing. Directed by Fank O'Connor. Captions by Walter Anthony. At Loew's, New York, one day, Jan. 12. (Previously played the Keith-Albee split week vaudeville theatres in New York and Brooklyn, perhaps elsewhere). Running time, around 60 minutes.

"Spangles," by Nellie Revell, is now in book form. Readers of it will form their own opinion of the adaptation of the Revell story by Leah Baird for this picture. In former days Miss Baird starred in feature pictures, some produced by her husband, Arthur T. Beck, who also produced "Spangles." It's an open question always for stage or screen whether there should be so close communion between writer and producer; also if such team work is not apt to become set, routined or from habit. However, this is a very fair view of a circus and can fit in for the mediums, even the shorter run neighborhoods, because of the possibilities in the advance publicity on Nellie Revell, a nationally known figure in and out of the show business.

Miss Revell was brought up on the circus lot, so she knows her sawdust. Her "Spangles" between covers fully substantiates that.

Here "Spangles" is a romantic mellerdrammer told in somewhat of a stolid style, relieved with but the slightest of comedy, and only the circus itself through its animals providing a sole thrill here or a bit of mild excitement there. If there should have been more of either, maybe the Bairds can blame it upon the directer, Frank O'Connor, although Mr. O'Connor may be said from the outsider's view to have done very well with what he had to do it with.

The circus employed looks like Al Barnes', since the picture was made on U's coast lot. Barnes has a zoo out there as well as a circus that travels within the coast zone. The herd of elephants looked too large for Barnes' show on road travel, while there was a harnessed rhinoceros, recalling the Wallace-Hagenback Animal. The opening pageant held a glitter and numbers, with the performers somewhat at long distance when performing, while the Hippodrome track appeared to be in front of a poorly painted drop.

And the star of the troupe, "the world-famed bareback rider," Spangles (Marion Nixon), did no bareback riding either by herself or through a double. This seemed to sound the economy of the thing as well as at other times when holes appeared that could have been made enlivening.

An animal trainer (Gladys Brockwell) was screen named Mlle. Dazie, the same as in the book, and named by Miss Revell after her friend, Mlle. Dazie Fellowes. The book 'Spangles" is dedicated to May Wirth, who is the greatest bareback rider in the world without any doubt.

Hobart Bosworth gives a likable characterization as the boss of Bowman's Circus. Pat O'Malley as the hero and juvenile who falls in love with Spangles while escaping from the police, has a walk-through part, except when he drives in the chariot race, with a bit of business neatly lifted from "Ben-Hur." As a lifted bit it should have been much better done and to a real thrill instead of its present befuddled finish.

But O'Malley as Dick wasn't guilty of the murder and Spangles didn't marry the circus owner, but Dick.

The real kick, however, in the picture and story that can be set down as Miss Revell's own is that of the elephant Sultana killing the circus' boss. The boss previously had beaten the elephant. One of the captions said an elephant never forgets a kindness or forgives an injury. That is circus lore.

No outstanding captions by Walter Anthony. It's a wonder Universal did not have Miss Revell write the captions. She should be an uncommon caption titler for any picture with her writing talent and witty streak.

Miss Nixon also walked through, but she did look the role; in fact, the characters, even to the freaks, looked like it, although the cook tent held screen liberty, and some more of that was displayed in labeling it "Circus Hotel."

"Spangles" will hold an audience's interest without exciting, exhilarating or thrilling them. As a picture and Nellie Revell's first theme for the screen it speaks very well for her future career in the films if she may be induced to continue. Miss Revell's experience in everything pertaining to the show business, besides her newspaper work, must have equipped her as an ideal scenarist of ideas. And she expresses herself very well in the story way. *Sime.*

STAGE MADNESS

Fox release of a Victor Schertzinger production. Story by Polan Banks, scenario by Randall H. Faye. Virginia Valli, Lou Tellegen and Richard Walling featured. Cameraman Glenon McWilliams. For release Jan. 9. Reviewed in projection room. Running time, 60 mins.

Madame Lamphier..........Virginia Valli
Andrew Marlowe........Tullio Carminati
Dora Anderson..........Virginia Bradford
Pierre Doumier..............Lou Tellegen
Jimmy Mason.............Richard Walling
H. H. Bragg.................Tyler Brooke
French Maid................Lillian Knight
Maid...........................Bodil Rosing

A picture that lends itself especially to sensational billing, which gives it value for all grades of houses. Subject deals with backstage, has the theatre of Paris and Broadway as its background and purports to be the life record of a stage star, all elements of box office pull. Story has several out-standing scenes and situations and the production is elaborate and showy; particularly a series of shots at a ballet performance in which the heroine has her big dramatic moment.

These are the strong points of the feature. Its weakness is a scattered and rambling story which moves by fits and starts rather than in an ordered progress to its climax. The single narrative has the materials for at least three screen plays and this makes for an embarrassment of treatment.

The audience is called upon several times to accept shifts of interest. There is almost a complete story in the marriage of the stage star, her restless urge to return to the stage and her break with her husband when she obeys the summons of the footlights. There is a certain unity in the passage where the famous dancer finds herself suddenly superceded in popularity by a young and talented girl protege, and there is distinctly an entire dramatic unit in the final complications where the star kills her lover and throws the blame upon her younger rival who presently turns out to be her long lost daughter.

But the success of the production will be insured by the high-light incidents. These have plenty of punch. The scene of the great dancer's downfall is splendidly built up with all the spectacular incidentals of a stage ballet pageant. There are fair comedy incidentals of a mild kind, such as the fluttering enthusiasms of the French player folk and later the scheming of an American press agent who insists upon insuring the French artist's legs for $100,000, to her vast disgust.

Miss Valli wears some striking costumes in the later footage and the scenes of the ballet rehearsals have the girly atmosphere of a semi-undressed revue. *Rush.*

Wings of the Storm

Fox film, featuring William Russell, Reed Howes and Virginia Faire. A J. C. Blystone production. Story by Lawrence W. Pedrose; scenario by L. C. Rigby and Dorothy Yost. At Loew's New York, Jan. 5. Running time, 62 mins.

First-class program picture of the action type taking special interest from its scenic beauty. The story is set in the Rocky Mountain locale and has to do with the adventures of a forest ranger, his dog and a rich young woman who goes into her own lumber camp to detect the dishonesty of her superintendent.

A neat turn in the unfolding of the story is that it seems to be told from the viewpoint of the ranger's dog, the police dog Thunder.

The use of a forest ranger in place of the familiar cowboy is agreeable, but the story formula is about the same, made up of the scheming heavy, brave, noble and hard-riding hero and heroine in distress. Moving side by side with the story of the humans is the story of the dog, which was born a weakling pup, had to overcome a streak of cowardice, fought for a mate and won his honorable degree by saving the heroine.

For the melodramatic punch, the hero and heroine are trapped halfway down a mountainside, while above them the villain threatens death by rolling logs in an avalanche upon them. This novel bit is well worked and makes a high spot in the hero's race against time to snatch the heroine from the path of the avalanche.

The mountain scenery is magnificent and the dog gives a remarkable performance. It is made to quit in a fight with another hound, turn tail and slink off, and then, when the story demands, return to the fight and carry it off to victory. In another place the dog, carrying a call for help from heroine to hero, plunges into a roaring mountain torrent, is tumbled about among the rcoks, and climbs gradually to the opposite bank in a fine bit of dramatic action.

A great picture for the fans, especially so for the younger division. *Rush.*

WIDE OPEN

Scharlin-Taylor picture starring Dick Grace. Directed by J. W. Grey. Cast includes Grace Darmond and Lionel Belmore. At Loew's New York as half double bill, one day, Jan. 14. Running time, 52 mins.

Dick Grace must be a stunt man elevated to stardom for this picture. Couple of aeroplane shots appear to have Grace out on the wings without a double, hence that conclusion. Grace isn't much of an actor nor is this much of a picture.

A nine o'clock audience at the New York guffawed at it in no uncertain terms, and even applauded to have it stopped. But if that's the worst the best should also be mentioned—the mid-air stunt stuff stopped the laughing and the demonstration.

It's a melodramatic and conventional story badly put together. That's what the house was ridiculing. Grace plays a former service air pilot who becomes attached to a rival 'plane plant of his Dad's. The girl (Grace Darmond) is also an equation as is that the two fathers were former business partners.

No particular production frames the story and nary a soul in the cast stands out. Purely for the smallest of the small and even within those confines only rates showing on a double bill. *Sid.*

Tom and His Pals

F. B. O. production directed by Robert de Lacy from the story by Frederick Arthur Mindlin. Featuring Tom Tyler. At the Stanley, New York, one day, Jan. 15. Cast includes Frankie Darro, Helen Lynch, Dicky Brandon, Barney Furey, Frank Clew, Doris Hill, LeRoy Mason and Wesley Hopper.

Slight variation from the "tried and true" type of western. Frankie Darro, child star, exceptionally good. This impression is gathered because of the contrast furnished by Dickey Brandon, the other child actor in the picture.

A ranch is selected by a movie company on location as a suitable site for some "shooting." The director and his "yes" man good for laughs. On arrival at the station the company is greeted by a gang of fierce Indians who turn out to be innocent ranch cowboys. More laughs.

At evening meal the director registers humorous disgust because he can only get a smell of the food before he is asked to pass something to one cow hand or another. When finally free to attack his plate the chink lifts it.

Tom Tyler, though sincerely in love with Doris, can't help admiring the blonde leading lady and almost loses the "girl." A fight in a speeding train with the villain is poorly staged, as the wild swinging blows are easily seen going wide of the mark.

MAN-BAIT

P. D. C. release of John C. Flinn presentation of Donald Crisp's production. Story from play by Norman Houston. Scenario by Douglas Z. Doty. Principals include Marie Prevost, Douglas Fairbanks, Jr., Louis Natbeaux, Kenneth Thomson, Sally Rand, Eddie Gribbon, Betty Francisco. Ran 70 minutes at Keith's Hippodrome, New York, week Jan. 17.

How this flicker goulash got into a week-stand house is explainable only by the Keith-Albee hook-up with P. D. C. On its merits it's one of those film abortions one might encounter at the Stanley or at Loew's New York as half of a doubleheader.

The many shortcomings provide opportunity for dissection, but it's hardly worth it.

The story, or Doty's adaptation, was muchly awry basically, which is some alibi for Crisp. The title-writer further fuddled it by seemingly obeying somebody's instructions to jack it up with jazzy titles. The result is sad. The quips and puns are elementary, more like out of "College Humor."

To top it, it's one of those dese, dose and dem dumbells who is being "polished" for a society match. Besides the society stuff being ludicrously impossible, the conventional clinch with the rich bachelor himself falling for the comely moron, adds further to its banality.

Yet Crisp permitted the introduction of that dance-hall bouncer and his frail at the heroine's coming-out party, so what else matters? The gal was supposed to have coached up enough to make a decent stab at the debut formalities, and she seemed to be managing quite well but for the creep-joint beefer's nickel-a-dance penchant.

A free-for-all is the wind-up of the social event. The title tries to cover this up with the explanation the heroine, after some energetic persuasion, won her way, since the rough but hearty mokes are her pals.

The casting is not happy. Marie Prevost has taken on weight. She doesn't fit the role.

Douglas Fairbanks, Jr., is all right, and that goes for the rest with the exception of Louis Natbeaux, impossible as the "chaser."

A happy thought is Kenneth Thomson, who reminds of Wallace Reid and may be somebody's "find" along similar lines, providing Mr. Thomson can be developed on the s. a. stuff. He lacks animation, although his conservative bachelor role held him in check. *Abel.*

FANGS OF JUSTICE

Sam Bischiff production, directed by Noel Mason Smith; story by Adele de Vore. Featuring dog "Silverstreak," with Johnnie Walker and June Marlowe. At Loew's Circle, one day, Jan. 10.

Should do well in the double bill semi-weekly change houses. Brilliant work on the part of the animal star appears to all. Able direction and closely-knit, nicely worked out story resulted in an even picture which gathers momentum as it goes along.

Johnnie Walker is the take-it-easy son of a wealthy builder, and June Marlowe is the girl whom Johnnie realizes he loves when it is almost too late.

June isn't extraordinarily interesting and hasn't a very interesting role.

"Silverstreak" is a fine-looking dog. Majestic, powerful, intelligent in the closeups, he puts up three exciting battles and had them shouting advice from the gallery more than once. It is "Silverstreak" who hides the will of the suddenly stricken master in a clothes box and later climbs a ladder in a vain endeavor to save the child.

THE STUPID PRINCE

W. Ray Johnstone presentation, produced by Morris Shlak, featuring Bobby Ray, at the Stanley, New York, one day, Jan. 14.

Revolves round princely double, hired to get three fireworks salesmen into the home of millionaire so that they may present their wares. Trio forget about selling firecracker and start lifting sparklers, once in on the party.

Mostly made up of the old reliable stock gags.

THE KID BROTHER

Harold Lloyd production released by Famous Players-Lasky, starring Harold Lloyd with Jobyna Ralston featured. Authors and director not credited on program. Opened for a run at Rialto, New York, Jan. 22. Running time, 83 minutes.

Harold Hickory..............Harold Lloyd
Mary Powers..............Jobyna Ralston
John Hickory..............Walter James
Leo Hickory..............Leo Willis
Olin Hickory..............Olin Francis
Sandoni..............Constantine Romanoff
"Flash" Farrell..............Eddie Boland
Sam Hooper..............Frank Lanning
Hank Hooper..............Ralph Yearsley

Harold Lloyd has "clicked" again with "The Kid Brother," about as gaggy a gag picture as he has ever done. It is just a series of gags, one following the other, some funny and others funnier.

From the box office angle the picture should be sure-fire, although somewhat longer than his last previous offering, this one running more than an hour and twenty minutes, while the former ran less than an hour. That will necessitate an earlier opening to get in the number of shows to get all the money.

Lloyd is somewhat different in this picture than he has been heretofore. In this case he is the younger son of a family of three boys who live with their father, a widower. Had the mother lived it is easy to see that Harold, the baby, would have been mother's boy. As it is he does the housework. Cooks the meals, washes the dishes and the clothes. His opening scene shows him performing the latter task with the aid of a butter churn. An ingenious mechanical arrangement for the wringing out and hanging of the clothes with the aid of a kite which carries the clothes aloft as they come from the wringer.

The story is laid in the feud country where old man Hickory is the sheriff and the town is Hickoryville, so it is easy to see that he is the leading citizen. He and the two big boys haul logs while Harold tends the home. There is a project on to build a dam for the town and a local subscription has been started and the money placed in the care of the sheriff.

While he is at the town committee meeting along comes a wagon show. When they stop at the sheriff's home to try to get a license it is Harold who signs it. He is all dressed up in father's vest with the badge of office and gun and everything.

That night when dad finds out that a medicine show has made a pitch and that the boy has given them a license, he orders the youngster to go down and close up the show. There are a couple of gags here that get over for howls, especially that of causing the amateur sheriff to disappear and his final hanging up against the back of the stage securely handcuffed. But as a result of this gag the banner flash of the trade is set afire and the wagon destroyed. That leaves the spieler, the strong man and the little girl who continued running the show after her father's death flat on the lot.

Harold takes pity on her, brings her home, walking in on the two older brothers sitting in their night shirts. This sequence has laugh following laugh with the two older boys trying to remain unseen by the girl.

The spieler and the strong man turn off the sheriff's strong box and he is accused of having made away with the funds himself—especially after his two sons are unable to locate the crooks. Then Harold comes across them by accident. After a series of thrills and laughs he manages to deliver the strong man who has already made away with the spieler so as to get all of the money for himself to the angry mob which is just about to hang his dad as a thief.

Jobyna Ralston plays opposite Lloyd as the little medicine show girl and handles herself perfectly. Walter James as the comedian's father got a chance to show what he could do after having tried for a long time and acquitted himself with honors. *Fred.*

Tenactles of the North

Rayart production, W. Ray Johnston presents, from the story by James Oliver Curwood. Directed by Louis Chaudet. Carries finale tag line, "A Ben Wilson production." Co-featured players, Gaston Glass and Alice Calhoun. At the New York theatre, New York, one day, Jan. 21. Running time, 55 minutes.

The "North" indicated here is supposed to be the Arctic. "Supposed" and nothing more. It may have been the intention to make this Curwood "outdoors" a big production, but it pulled a smashing dud, face down.

Little to commend it despite the apparent camera effort to make the far, far northland, but the icy, frigid scenes won't.

The New York audience didn't think much of it. Some of them sighed when the end came.

One wonders if Mr. Curwood could recognize in this production any of the realistic scenes his book describes. *Mark.*

PARADISE FOR TWO

Famous Players-Lasky release, directed by Gregory La Cava under supervision of William LeBaron, F. P.-L. associate producer in charge at the Long Island studios. Richard Dix starred with Betty Bronson featured; Andre Beranger sub-feature. Program confuses authorship credit in this manner: "Story by Howard Emmett Rogers; adaptations by Ray Harris and Tom J. Crizer; screen play by J. Clarkson Miller." Usual release running time. At Paramount, New York, week Jan. 23.

Steve Porter..............Richard Dix
Uncle Howard..............Edmund Breese
Sally Lane..............Betty Bronson
Maurice..............Andre Beranger

A pleasant little comedy of no especial merit other than in the titles written by Robert Benchley. It's not big enough as a story for Richard Dix, who has been coming along so fast Famous should take care of him in the story line, now that he has been sewn up. Exhibitors might better play up Dix and Benchley rather than to dilate upon the picture otherwise.

This may be Benchley's first titling. If so, he's set. He's on "Life" and is widely known.

The story doesn't permit of much, not even for Dix, and that is where Benchley came in. Outside of very commonplace farcical situations, that will draw laughs from the women, there isn't much to giggle at here, other than the captions. No stooping here in wordings to hokum, vulgarity or slapstick for a laugh. When a good laugh could be word-fitted to a scene, Benchley stuck it over a mile or more. A few are peaches in their nicely guaged fitness.

Nor is Dix or anyone else called up to do anything of importance. It may be said the interiors are almost elegant in their furnishings, but that is all, other than the picture looks to be a comparatively inexpensive one for a F. P.-L. regular program release.

In story the thing is 1,000 years old, measured in the French farce mileage. It's of a bachelor who must wed within two days to receive the fortune left by his father, held by his uncle in trust. As unk is to be the referee, the son and a theatrical agenting friend framed to have a young girl aspiring to the stage play the pro tem wife. After that the ancient complications.

Edmund Breese was the Foxy Grandpa uncle, Andre Beranger the agent who seemed to have the French pantomime idea of screen acting, and the extras if doing piece work wouldn't have been paid for over one hour.

Rather a vapid film for a comer like Dix, a boy who should be sent forward with every picture. Stories like this ought to be worth $25 for three and then turned over to a comic maker for one-reelers.

This Dix film, however, is a first-runner because the laughs are there, the silly farcical thing and from the captions.

And another good title wasted. *Sime.*

THE NIGHT OF LOVE

United Artists release of Samuel Goldwyn picture directed by George Fitzmaurice. Features Ronald Colman and Vilma Banky. Story by Leonore Coffee, with G. S. Barnes and T. E. Brannigan, cameramen. At Strand, New York, week Jan. 22. Running time, 83 mins.

Montero..............Ronald Colman
Princess Marie..............Vilma Banky
Duke de la Garda..............Montague Love
Dame Beatris..............Natalie Kingston
Gypsy Bride..............Laska Winter
Gypsy Dancer..............Sally Rand
Jester..............John George

Costume picture highly flavored with romance. It's length, 83 minutes to unwind, has a depreciating effect for the action is not always interesting. In a few particularly slow spots balcony patrons were audibly snickering. Film is highly theatric, smacks very much of the studio and doesn't get off the screen to convince at any point. Yet, no one will deny the production effort and picturesqueness.

A tough one to rate as "yes" or "no," although the Colman-Banky names may tilt the scales for a decisive answer. Colman's performance is bound on all sides by the mechanics of pantomiming before the camera. He plays a Gypsy Robin Hood and screens as being too well aware of the fact to merge into the role. Miss Banky looks sufficiently gorgeous to demand interest for herself, but cannot make this heavily weighted love story stand up for top rating.

Yet with "The Flesh and the Devil" at the Capitol with its Gilbert-Garbo team drawing into its third successive week, it may be the team rather than the picture that will draw regardless. On this basis where Colman-Banky have established themselves this should likewise operate for the b.o.

In script the scenario is a cross between the traditional vendetta attributed to Latin races and an out-and-out sequence made popular by Mrs. E. M. Hull in "The Sheik." "The Shiek."

Montero (Mr. Colman) has his Gypsy bride snatched from him on the bridal night by the dastardly duke (Montague Love). When the titled villain weds, the Gypsy leader reverses the former situation but on a more gentlemanly basis. Where the duke threatened Montero's bride so that she kills herself, the latter turns his fair-haired captive over to the care of tribeswomen after she has needlessly jumped from a castle window. As is expected each falls in love with the other. The duke, being the husband, stands in the way and rather than return to him Princess Marie chooses the church. The duke disguises himself as his wife's confessor, she discovers the ruse, a forged note for help draws Montero to the castle and he is to be burned at the stake. The Princess saves him, the duke is killed in the ensuing riot, and that's that.

The authoress, Lenore Coffee, is also credited with the scenario. This may explain the superfluous footage through her disinclination to cut. Fitzmaurice evidently allowed the version to stand. Some of the sets are massive and there are plenty of people running around. Photography is good and passes as a highlight.

The picture starts out tempestuously enough with the reason for the strife between Montero and the duke, but when the love theme creeps in, there it is and it's a long while before the continuity gets back to the personal hostilities.

Minus around 1,000 feet should do this latest Goldwyn release a world of good. Those who liked the Colman-Banky combination in "Barbara Worth" will probably be attracted by the billing of these two again.

Monday the Strand was confident "The Night of Love" would do sufficient business to warrant holding over for a second week. A big Saturday and Sunday, the latter a miserable day as to weather, was the basis of that optimism. But this picture doesn't register as of holdover specifications. A fairy tale story dressed with colorful settings and in its present state not vital enough to class as more than passive entertainment.

THE LAST TRAIL

Lew Seiler production starring Tom Mix, presented by William Fox. From the Zane Grey story adapted by John Stone. At the Hippodrome, New York, week Jan. 24. Running time, 53 minutes.

Tom Dane..............Tom Mix
Nita Carrol..............Carmelita Geraghty
Kurt Morley..............William Davidson
Ben Ligget..............Frank S. Hagney
Sheriff Joe Pascal..............Lee Shumway
Deputy Pete..............Robert Brower
Tom Dane Pascal..............Jerry, the Giant
Jasper Carrol..............Oliver Eckhardt

In "The Last Trail" Tom Mix has turned out one of the fastest action pictures that he has had in a long while. It starts with a zip and bang and never leaves the pace for a minute, right up to the finish. Both Tom and Tony get a lot of action in this one and there are more thrills in it in a minute than there usually is in a whole five reels of the average western.

In this one there is a free-for-all stage coach race that comes near rivaling the famous chariot race in "Ben-Hur." It is replete with thrills and spills. From a box office angle this one is sure to be better than the average Mix and that is saying a lot, for his average is always high.

Also, in this picture there is something of an added attraction in the fact that Mix has Jerry, the Giant, a cute youngster working with him almost throughout the picture. Carmelita Geraghty, who played a small role in Mix's last picture, "The Canyon of Light," is his leading woman and she more than makes good. That girl is going to go to bigger things on the screen before she is through.

The picturization of the Zane Grey story opens with an Indian fight. Mix saves the life of the wife of Joe Pascal and Joe, in return, promises to name his first born in his honor. Ten years later Mix, as Tom Dane, is still riding the west, when he gets a note from his old friend to come and see the youngster that bears his name. Pascal in the meantime is the sheriff at Carson City and the stage line, which is carrying the gold, has been repeatedly robbed until the sheriff decides to drive the stage through to the railroad with a guard. Soon after leaving Carson he is attacked by the bandits, and they are chasing the stage across the country when Tom rides into the picture to help give battle. The robbers are driven off, but the sheriff is mortally wounded. As he is dying, he places his son in care of the man that the youngster is named after.

The contractor of the stage line is afraid that he is going to lose out because of his inability to protect his freight. A representative of the U. S. Express arrives and suggests a free-for-all stage coach race to decide who shall get the contract, the leader of the bandits, who, under cover, is one of the big shippers in town, lines up his hold-up men as the contestants.

But the old contractor has a daughter that Tom Dane has fallen for and he decides to help the old man out in the race. It is one of those last-minute starts, and Mix and a half dozen others start the race, driving four-in-hand lumbering stage coaches with the others all banded against him. He finally comes through to victory, even though he has but a team and the two front wheels of his coach left at the finish, arriving just in time to jump on Tony's back and start off on another race to catch the leader of the bandits, who is trying to escape with the girl and the loot taken from the stage coach office. That makes for the hurrah finish for the final fade-out.

Interspersed in all this melodrama is sufficient comedy to slip the audience a couple of hearty laughs, especially the work done by Robert Brower and a blood-hound with a pair of trick ears that are worked on wires from the looks of things. William Davidson slips over a good performance as the heavy without overacting.

An extra good Mix western.

Fred.

The Canyon of Light

Benjamin Stoloff production, starring Tom Mix. Presented by William Fox. Story by Kenneth Perkins, adapted by John Stone. Featuring Dorothy Dwan, Barry Norton, Ralph Sipperly and William Walling. Reviewed in projection room Jan. 21. Running time, 62 minutes.

Tom Mills....................Tom Mix
Concha Deane...............Dorothy Dwan
Ed Bardin....................Carl Miller
Jerry Chanks..............Ralph Sipperly
Ricardo Deane...............Barry Norton
Cyrus Deane.........William Walling, Sr.
Joe Novado........................Duke Lee
Ellen Bardin..........Carmelita Geraghty

A combination war and western that leans principally toward the latter, although the war stuff is very well done. The opening of the story has Mix as a leader of the cowboys when the call comes for "the sons of the Rough Riders, who made history in '98." They all ride off to enlist, but just before the train pulls out Mix, as Tom Mills, rescues a girl who is on hand to see her brother off.

Before that, it is planted he is leaving his ranch in the care of his sister and her husband. Then come the war flashes, with Mills and his buddies acting as motorcycle dispatch riders in France. When one of the trio is sniped and passes west, he hands Mills his picture to take home to his father and sister. When the remaining two get back things start to move. From that point it is a typical Mix western, with hard riding, shooting and hand-to-hand fighting. From a box-office angle it is a fairly good Mix, with a little different twist added by the war stuff.

Mills comes back to the ranch to find it practically gone to rack and ruin; his sister's husband has deserted her and is heading a band of highwaymen who have been holding up stage coaches, banks and generally terrorizing the neighborhood. His sister is on her deathbed, and she begs to have her husband brought back to her before she passes out.

Mills rides out to find him, and arrives just in time to take him from a lynching party.

He gives his brother-in-law his coat and tells him to hurry home and see his wife, but instead the bandit leader rides off to the haunts of the gang. Mills then delivers himself to the sheriff to pay for the escape of the bandit leader. The sister has died, and he cares for naught else. It is given out that he is to be hung. The bandit leader is tipped off to what has happened, and, having found the pictures of the dead soldier in the pocket of the coat Mills gave him, decides to impersonate him.

But instead of hanging Mills the sheriff has used this as a ruse, for he turns Mills loose with instructions to "get his man," which he does in the end. But not until he defies the gang at a barbecue that is being given in honor of the phony "Tom Mills." They turn the tables on him, rob the house and make off with the sister of Mills' dead buddy. Mills goes after them and cleans up the gang single-handed, rescues the girl and then rides back to glory.

It is a little overdone at times, but on the whole it will be satisfying to the Mix fans and to those who are rabid western picture bugs.

Fred.

FINGER PRINTS

Warner Bros. burlesque crook mystery play, adapted from the story of Arthur Somers Roche. Directed by Lloyd Bacon. Screen story by Raymond L. Shrock. In the cast Louise Fazenda, Warner Richmond, Helene Costello, John T. Murray. Running time, 65 minutes. At the Broadway, New York, Jan. 24.

Seven to five Arthur Somers Roche would never recognize this hoked up, jazzed up, gaggy arrangement as his story. Whoever did the screen version apparently tore loose with a sole desire to pull laughs from juvenile audiences in the neighborhood houses.

The method is a cross between the custard pie comedy technique and the methods they use in building up melodramatic serials. That is to say, no device is too crude or violent to serve its purpose. There is not a legitimate laugh in all seven reels, and the best of the picture is in the gag titles.

The story starts out seriously and ends up in a surprise dramatic twist, but between it is delirious. In between they have made it like Byrne Brothers' "Eight Bells," with trick comedy, grotesque comedy bits and absurd character gags. The custard pie and the wooden mallet were the only comedy devices passed up.

At the opening a legitimate situation is built up, in which a daring crook has made his getaway with a pile and hidden it, just before his arrest and dispatch to jail. His accomplices now want to find the treasure and split it up among themselves. They capture the kid sister of the master crook and take her to a lonely house in the country, where they attempt to force from her the secret of the cache. So far it has developed as a crook play with some promise.

At this point it turns back on itself and goes into futuristic comedy. Panels open in walls, people are snatched into openings and disappear in the grip of a mysterious power. All this to the accompaniment of gage titles and clowning by the entire cast, including the comic servant girl played by Louise Fazenda.

Development of the story is suspended for the time being while trick staircases slide people from top to bottom, a hand appears from the wall and shoots down one of the crooks so that a burlesque coroner may arrive with a prop coffin which is made the subject of more trick humor.

At the finish it turns out that the travesty deputy sheriff and the low comedy servant girl are both operatives from the secret service, who capture the whole gang and then fall into each other's arms.

A picture frankly made and offered to the simplest grade of movie fans. It will please them. *Rush.*

NEW YORK

Famous Players-Lasky production, directed by Luther Reed. Adapted by Forrest Halsey from story by Barbara Chambers and Becky Gardiner. Featuring Ricardo Cortez, Lois Wilson, Estelle Taylor, William Powell and Norman Trevor. At Paramount, New York, week Jan. 30. Running time, around 70 minutes.

Michael Angelo Cassidy......Ricardo Cortez
Marjorie Church ....Lois Wilson
Angie Miller..................Estelle Taylor
Trent Regan................William Powell
Randolph Church...........Norman Trevor
Buck ....Richard "Skeets" Gallagher
Helena Matthews..........Margaret Quimby
Izzy Blumenstein ....Lester Scharff
Jimmie Wharton.............Charles Byers

"New York" was a happy thought on this for a feature picture. It's about all it has, but the title may be enough away from its namesake.

As "Broadway" is the best title selected in 10 years for a comedy or comedy-drama, which that stage smash has, so "New York" will operate wherever it is worked up. But this one can't be gone too strongly on for New York as is. It isn't. More of a little east side west side stuff and taking your choice, 3d or 10th avenue.

Not much in the loose melodramatic story. Its principal trouble is too much story and too little New York.

A polite leader of a gang is the hero. He's also a song writer and also tried for murder, convicted, but with screen license released without the audience seeing how that occurred. It may be believed, however, that a witness of the death told the truth, but that must have been as circumstantial as the evidence which convicted the song writer, etc. Still, at that time the picture had run long enough. In fact, if it runs 10 minutes less any time it will be a better picture.

The names may do something. Ricardo Cortez is in the principal role, carrying several expressions, apparently trying to send himself into different moods as his song writing advanced him in life. He was partially successful and looked better when dressed up.

Lois Wilson had a walk through role until the murder trial. Then she cried a bit, but otherwise quite nice in an office bit when dodging a kiss. Playing the role of a millionaire's daughter becomes Miss Wilson.

For good screen performances it can go 50-50 between William Powell and Estelle Taylor. Miss Taylor was the fiendish girl of the east or west side in love with its leader, but sidestepped by him, linked to Trent Regan (Mr. Powell). The only ginger in the picture is where Angie Miller (Miss Taylor) framed for her sweetie, Trent, to bump off Mike Cassidy (Mr. Cortez). That brought about her death. Mr. Powell looked more speakeasy than either avenue, but played well. This wasn't supposed to be a tough gang, but just a neighborhood bunch that stuck.

Norman Trevor may have played for one day, but his name goes up. Skeets Gallagher had a soft job as a piano-playing partner of the song writer. Leon Scharff as Izzy Blumenstein, a Yid politician, must have started to make up as Abie Kabibble and quit in the middle.

Yes, there's a cabaret scene.

One of those just-get-bys, but the farther from New York the easier.

Sime.

LUNATIC AT LARGE

First National release of a Fred Newmeyer production, supervised by Earl Hudson and starring Leon Errol. From the story by J. Storer Clouston. At the Hippodrome, New York, week Jan. 31. Running time, 59 minutes.

Sam Smith.........................Leon Errol
Beatrix....................Dorothy Mackaill
Bill and Henry...........Kenneth McKenna
Mandel Essington............Jack Raymond
Dr. Wilkins......................Warren Cook
Maxwell..........................Tom Blanke
Lunt............................Charles Slattery

They are giving this Leon Errol feature film credit at the Hip for pulling the biggest Monday matinee and night business that the house has had in weeks, and the Hip management can't understand how the Strand let this picture get away. It has a great comedy wallop and is filled with laughs and thrills. Of course, the Hip boys did a wise trick. They held off on the picture until the new Leon Errol show came into town and then started the picture the Monday after the opening of the revue.

The picture is one of the last made at the Biograph studios for First National under the supervision of Earl Hudson. It was reported that there was trouble over the picture, and this may have scared off the Strand. However, it's a film that can go in anywhere and make good on its own. The fact that Ralph Spence titled the production is one of its particularly strong points.

The opening scene has a quartet of terrible looking hoboes riding in what appears to be an automobile of the vintage of 1900, and carrying on an airy conversation regarding the situation in the financial marts and politics. It is finally disclosed that the boys are in an old wagon, being pushed from the rear by Errol. Errol is the galley slave to the tourists, but finally makes his escape, only to be eased into a lunatic asylum through exchanging places with a supposed millionaire, whose handsome limousine is parked against the road.

In the madhouse he learns of the plight of a fellow inmate whose twin is really mad, but who, through a crafty move, has managed to switch places with the sane brother, who is about to be married. Errol undertakes to make his escape and break up the wedding and save the day for the sane brother. He manages to do this by the time the final iris is ready.

Incorporated in the picture are all of the famous Errol falls, his former vaudeville smashing of the statuary and the armor bit, all of which proved to be howlingly funny to the Hipp audience.

Errol has the picture to himself and just about does as he pleases, although Newmeyer's direction puts over a laugh punch in several spots. The story is carried along at a fast clip.

Dorothy Mackaill is featured with Errol the star of the picture. She hasn't a great deal to do, but is okay and looks mighty pretty. Kenneth McKenna gets a great chance in the dual role of the twin brothers, and there is a piece of trick photography of the double-exposure order that is as good as anything that has been seen. There are a number of minor roles, Harry Lee managing to put over a good "nut" in one of the early scenes. Charles Slattery will be a laugh to any of the old mob from Doyle's, up near 125th street, where he was the Tommy Lyman of his day in Harlem.

"The Lunatic at Large" is a good laugh bet that has a comedy wallop.

Fred.

UPSTREAM

Fox release of a John Ford production, featuring Nancy Nash, Raymond Hitchcock, Earle Foxe, Sammy Cohen, Ted McNamara and Francis Ford. From "The Snake's Wife," by Wallace Smith. Adapted by Randall H. Faye. Reviewed in projection room Jan. 27. Running time, 61 minutes.

Gertie King.......................Nancy Nash
Eric Bashingham..................Earle Foxe
Jack La Velle................Grant Withers
Miss Breckenbridge...Lydia Yeamans Titus
Star Boarder............Raymond Hitchcock
Campbell Mandare.........Emile Chautard
Callahan and Callahan..................
Sammy Cohen, Ted McNamara
Sister Team.....Ludy King, Lillian Worth
Soubret...........................Jane Winton
Gus Hoffman.....................Harry Bailey
Juggler...........................Francis Ford
Deerfoot..........................Ely Reynolds

Looking at this picture reminds of those good old days when Helen Green wrote the "Actor's Boarding House" stories. Whoever penned "The Snake's Wife" must have had a look at the Green stories, for this was so like one that it might have been a lift. But it is a good story and it makes a good picture, one that's strong enough for any of the Broadway houses. No outstanding star in the lineup, but the cast as a whole makes up for that. Any number of laughs, and for the wise Broadway mob it will be a set-up.

It's a tale of a vaudeville actor's boarding house, where the knife-thrower is in love with the girl that works in his act. But she is in love with an out-and-out ham who is going in for Shakespearean roles, coached by a broken-down legit player of the past. There are the sister team, the juggler, the comedian, the pair of hoofers (played by Sammy Cohen and Ted McNamara, the duo that scored so heavily in "What Price Glory") and other local color necessary to the boarding house.

Earle Foxe plays the wealthy young Bashington, suffering from extreme ego and who finally makes the grade as Hamlet when he goes to England. He comes back and walks in on the wedding of the knife juggler and his partner, and takes it for granted that it is a prearranged reception for him. Finally he is kicked out, and even that doesn't shatter his ego, for he picks himself up in time to get the right pose for the cameramen who are grinding away on him.

Raymond Hitchcock as the star boarder manages to register most effectively, and Harry Bailey, former manager of the Alhambra and of touring companies, has turned actor to play the role of the manager to the star in this picture. Not bad at all, Harry.

Another old-time touch was to see a former director, Emile Chautard, playing the broken-down legit actor, while Lydia Yeamans Titus as the boarding house keeper fitted perfectly.

Just wait till Mrs. Sparrow, down in Baltimore, gets a load of this one.

Fred.

Slums of Berlin

Produced by National Film A-G Corporation of Berlin (Germany). Distributed by Imported Pictures Corp. over here. Directed by Herhard Lamprecht. Adapted from story by Prof. Heinrich Zille. In third week at Cameo, New York. Running time, around 60 minutes.

Robert Kramer............Bernard Goetzke
His Father.......................Paul Bildt
His Financee ....Margaret Kupfer
Emma ....Aud Egede Nissen
Steve ....Arthur Bergen
Regine ....Mady Christians
Her Brother.......Christians Bummerstedt
Rottman, the Photographer..............
The Washwoman..............Frigga Braut
Her Husband......................Georg John

"Slums of Berlin" as a title must have been slipped on for the box office.

Should have been "Bums of Berlin."

Or "Bums of Anywhere."

"It's also a bum picture.

Crime, vagrants, crooks, poverty, squalor and what not of any city's lower life in this picture, with immature adaptation, almost total absence of continuity as though whole chunks had been cut out, uninteresting story for what could be gleaned of that, simple direction and ordinary acting with mostly obscure photography.

What more could be included in a bum picture?

Few exhibitors over here will play this depressing feature film. Only then its excuse can be that it is for a German neighborhood or city. The Germans or native born German-Americans must be holding it to the three-week run in the small Cameo. No Americans will care for this picture; they don't want to see the besodden on the sheet; they may be seen daily on the street.

Germans from their Fatherland may wish to recognize the types from the home town. No doubt there are types in this—tinny types that don't mean a thing.

It's also a type of picture that reverts back to the German-made underworld picture of 10 years ago. Were it not for the attempted bits in direction copy from Dupont and Bernard Goetzke's obvious tries to ape Emil Jannings in expressive pantomime, together with use of eyes to further that, this picture could have been suspected of having been a revival.

You can't even kid the picture. It's a weary, dreary waste of film and time.

What there seems to be of a story is of an escaped or released convict, vainly trying for work, finally attempting to jump into the river when saved by a woman of the streets. The latter becomes attached to him, while he seems to be immeshed with a couple of other women, one of whom is married.

In his efforts to obtain work and his desperation at not finding it, the viewer is conveyed into the slums to meet the bums.

Whatever the original story held in sentiment has been killed out through the adaptation or the cutting until there is left but a whirligig of celluloid going along as though relating the vagaries of ragpickers.

Film Arts Guild presents this picture (as it has others at the Cameo). That seems to be another name for B. S. Moss.

A picture like this will do more to set back the advancing opinion of Germany's picture progressiveness than any of its purient or lacivious films could possibly do.

It's like a detailed illustrated intimate view of the poorhouse.

And the case-hardened comment must be made that since this is a picture from Germany and in these days, it must be accepted as a reflection in part at least of the taste for films in Germany—the land of the Kaiser's kulture. Perhaps the Kaiser made the adaptation—he's been loafing around in recent years.

Sime.

Johnny Get Your Hair Cut

Jackie Coogan starred in production by Metro-Goldwyn-Mayer under the supervision of Coogan, Sr., and a large staff of assistants, including titles by Ralph Spence and a couple of aids. Archie Mayo concerned as director. Running time, 75 minutes. At Loew's, New York, one day, Jan. 29.

Awkward and inept picture exploiting Jackie Coogan. Finds its level promptly in a daily change house, to which it belongs. If this picture had been built around anyone but the youngster who was hero of a national vogue a few seasons back it would have been lost.

The picture runs 75 minutes, and its only gripping scene is a horse race, which takes up probably three minutes in unwinding. This climax is very well done mechanically, but after 70 minutes or so of planting the interest and building up the underlying situation it would take more than a horse race to compensate.

It is as though the maker of the scenario had given the entire play over to dramatic preparation for the climax and had disregarded any idea of holding interest in the story itself. The character and situation necessary for the race could have been established in a brief reel or so, so that about six reels of this entire footage is a dead loss. There is nothing like tension, no progress in story interest and, except for Jackie, no building of character that really counts.

The result on the spectator is that he is bored stiff before they get to the meat of the affair and the picture is sunk half-way through. It is made up of trivial bits about a boarding house where jockeys live during the Tanforan meeting; the schemes of a crooked horse trainer to make one of the jockeys throw a race and Jackie's success in getting a mount that he rides to victory, saving the day but not much else. As a matter of fact, there wasn't anything vital at stake in the race at that, except a natural desire to see the highest paid child actor in the world make good, even if that was a foregone conclusion.

The devices to sustain interest are ancient and hackneyed. The crooked trainer who wanted a horse pulled is almost as old a trick of the theatre as the mortgage on the farm. The only incident that warranted details was the cutting of Jackie's hair, and this was done rather brusquely.

The story staggers along draggily. At one point Jackie has to go to a wealthy racing man and plead to have his horse entered. This incident, the outcome of which could easily be forecast, was stretched interminably. After the racing man had agreed, he changed his mind, and it had all to be done over again, for no reason except, perhaps, that they had decided upon a 75-minute picture.

As it stands the picture could be cut two reels and bettered. And as it stands it makes dull entertainment, even for Jackie's most ardent fans.

Rush.

A Captain's Courage

Designated Ben Wilson production on Rayart's list. Story from the original by James Oliver Curwood. Scenario by G. Pyper. Directed by Louis Chaudet. Running time, 70 minutes. At the Stanley, New York, Jan. 29. In the cast: Eddie Earl, Jack Henderson, Richard Holt, Al Ferguson, Lafe McKee and Dorothy Dwan.

Especially badly done picture in almost all respects. The story as it comes upon the screen is trash, the acting is entirely worthy of the material and the production is astonishingly cheap and shabby. The story fault probably lies in the transcription from the written word. Curwood is too experienced a maker of popular fiction to do anything as bad as this looks in its celluloid version.

The story is laid in 1853 and the locale is the shores of Lake Michigan. Pictures of historical reference have to be done in a large way to be impressive, as in the case of "The Covered Wagon" and others in its train. This period and locale has nothing of picturesque costuming to recommend it in a pictorial way, which makes it worse.

The hero is a nice-looking movie actor, that's all. The heavy wears the falsest false beard, copied in faithful detail from the Smith Brothers, whom he resembles closely. His acting is a bad as his make-up, which doesn't seem possible until you've seen both. The direction is terrible. Hero and heavy have one of those he-man fights for life that inspired even the simple-minded Stanley audience to unseemly laughter. When you make a 25-cent scale audience of fans laugh at the wrong place, all is lost. This fight, by the way, is one of the longest on record.

The two silly actors stand up in fierce attitudes and pose. Then one makes elaborate preparations to strike a terrific blow. The other shows that his entire attention is taken up with receiving the stroke so as to register it with emphasis. From the time the blow stars until it knocks the opponent 40 feet, the receiver of the swing would have had time to swim away. This goes on for the better part of a reel.

The heroine is of the 1853 model, a foolish, gesticulating actress even in so personable a pantomimist as Dorothy Dwan. There is no semblance of building up a story. Things just happen, and then the titles explain what has taken place. At the finish two groups of men meet off stage somewhere in a hand-to-hand conflict for possession of an island in Lake Michigan, and the winning faction gets into the picture after all the fighting is over. That's the kind of picture it is. Everything of interest takes place in the titles, and the action sort of illustrates the text. Even the photography isn't always good. Some of the action takes place on a sailing vessel becalmed in a bay. The spectator is made to understand this when he is shown a model in the tank. Everything that happens on the ship is set in a studio set of the cabin or forecastle, or on a section of the deck, apparently (certainly this is the way it looks) built on shore overlooking the water.

Rush.

STOLEN PLEASURES

Leah Baird story directed by Phil Rosen. Features Helene Chadwick and Dorothy Revier. Gayne Whitman and Harlan Tucker also in cast. At Moss' Broadway week Jan. 31. Running time, 61 mins.

One of those independents for which no one apparently will take production or releasing credit. Nothing in the exterior billing or lead slides to indicate where the picture comes from. It's a story that Leah Baird must have tossed off in a hurry and that Phil Rosen could have directed from memory. Situations and business are stock stuff.

It may be the last independent film Helene Chadwick will be gleaned in for a time, this former fairly well-known girl having again signed with a major company. Here she gives a standard performance while not being called upon to stress the histrionics. The same for Dorothy Revier. Both play wives of faulty husbands, complications leading to a roadhouse mixup. The roadhouse had to be burned down to get Miss Chadwick home in her underclothing. And it's not for comedy unless you construe it that way.

The story starts out to reveal the devastation which jealousy can cause, gets fumbled around and winds up in a light vein. It's a small cast picture, only being five members kept tabs upon by the continuity. Titles are hit and miss but a couple of interiors look good.

The women overshadow the men on appearance and work and should prove sufficient to carry this one into the minor daily change or double feature emporiums.

The attendance at the Broadway didn't particularly care for it but got a few laughs during the late footage. The same will probably take place wherever shown.

Picture at Moss' Broadway for full week, evidencing how helpless Keith-Albee appear to be on the picture end.

Sid.

THE AUCTIONEER

Fox release of an Alfred E. Green production. Adapted from stage play of same name. Scenario by L. G. Rigby and John Stone. At Fox Audubon theatre, New York, Jan. 24. Running time, 60 mins.

Simon Levi......................George Sidney
Esther Levi..........................Doris Lloyd
Moe...............................Sammy Cohen
Ruth...............................Marian Nixon
Dick Eagan...................Gareth Hughes
Paul Groode.......................Ward Crane

"The Auctioneer" has enough in its favor to make it a worthwhile major house booking. It is a wholesome picture, has comedy and pathos.

Photographically it is splendid. As a production is runs along economic lines until it hits the house party given by Simon Levi, when he takes possession of an elaborate home.

In the first caption the audience is informed the story starts in 1908 and then the action shifts to 18 years later. This brings it up to 1926 and gives the production a latitude that modernizes it completely.

George Sidney, in the role of the auctioneer, makes a lovable character of Levi. The romantic theme of the youthful lovers is a secondary consideration, but Miss Nixon and Mr. Hughes make this undercurrent felt. The "menace" in the story is capably handled by Ward Crane.

Sidney stands out all the way and the continuity gets a gouge here and there to permit him a few extra comedy bits.

The theme is deftly handled and so worked out that it will not offend anyone.

The picture gains strength as it goes along and will hold. *Mark.*

THE TRUTHFUL SEX

Columbia Pictures production directed by Richard Thomas from the story by Albert Shelby Levino. Featuring Huntley Gordon and Mae Busch, with cast including Ian Keith, John Roche, Rosemary Theby, Leo White and Richard Travers. At the Stanley, New York, one day, Jan. 27.

Tale of a domestic tragedy where the wife lets hubby have "her" own way. A silly squabble over forgetfulness starts off the fireworks and leads to the usual complications.

The story is weak for a screen flicker, or has suffered from improper adaptation. The gagging is clever and, with the humorous subtitles, the only worthwhile feature of the picture. Mae Busch and Huntley Gordon handle their roles with ease.

The baby boy, Junior, is introduced very nicely with "Three hundred and sixty-five quarrels later." Junior, as is usual with late arrivals, picks the middle of the night as the appropriate moment to bawl. Father says he should be fed and Ma answers, "The doctor said he's to be fed only every three hours." "Well, explain that to him, will you?" roars the wrathy male parent.

"Half of the baby is mine, anyway," wails the frau, "and he's not to be overfed." Hysterical laughter from the female customers as the comeback is flashed, "Well, then, feed my half and go to bed."

Picture drags at the beginning and fails to lead up to a satisfactory climax. Introduction of Ian Keith as a safecracker is hardly warranted but he does well with the ineffective part handed him.

The Overland Stage

First National release. Picture with Chas. B. Rogers, Ken Maynard and Kathleen Collins. Story by Marion Jackson. Directed by Alfred Rogell. At Loew's New York, Jan. 26. Running time, about 60 mins.

A "western" going back to the old days when the Bad Lands were wild with wild Indians.

There is much that is not explained or interpreted by the film. But it has the western atmosphere, the old overland calvacade, the stage coach, all the trimmings and Indians, some real. No denying its atmosphere, but the story misses fire.

Ken Maynard is a corking rider and his horse is also splendidly trained. The main strength of the picture is Maynard.

Nothing here to throw a rave about.

The picture is noticeably padded and there are a lot of mock heroics.

Okay for the neighborhoods where they like outdoor stories. *Mark.*

WHEN A MAN LOVES

Warner Brothers production, based on "Manon Lescaut," starring John Barrymore. Adapted by Bess Meredyth, directed by Alan Crosland. Presented in conjunction with a Vitaphone program and Vitaphone accompaniment for a run at the Selwyn theatre, New York, Feb. 3. Running time, 110 minutes.

Chevalier Fabian	John Barrymore
Manon Lescaut	Dolores Costello
Andre Lescaut	Warner Oland
Comte de Mortfontaine	Sam De Grasse
Louis XV	Stuart Holmes

Warners are seemingly attempting the impossible by presenting two "specials" on Broadway at the same time and both starring John Barrymore. The pictures are alike inasmuch as they are both "costume" screen plays. Possibly they can get away with it, but if they do it won't be that their latest presentation, a screen version of "Manon Lescaut," holds as much interest as did their first, "Don Juan."

In "When a Man Loves" they again have a "three star combination," the same as they had in "Don Juan." Barrymore is the first of the trio, Dolores Costello second and the third, the director, Alan Crosland. But they have lacking that admirable actress, Estelle Taylor, who contributed so much to the first picture. Likewise there is lacking in the latest production anything in the nature of comedy to relieve the long drawn-out sequences that become tiresome.

"When a Man Loves" is principally worth sitting through for the last reel or so, action taking place on a ship that is bringing the hero and heroine to the French penal colony in Louisiana. Before that there is a scene in which Barrymore gets an opportunity to display his swordsmanship in a fight on a flight of stairs in which he bests about a score of the gallants of the Court of Louis XV. In watching this scene progress one could not fail to think back to the days of "A Gentleman of France" and recall the manner in which the late Kyrle Bellew handled himself in that famous stair duel scene. Such a comparison is not favorable to Mr. Barrymore or the manner in which the scene is handled.

As it stands at present this film is entirely too long. There are long stretches where the story drags almost to a point where one would prefer taking a nap, but there are other moments that amply repay for sitting through the picture.

These are the shots when Dolores Costello is before the camera. That girl is beautiful, she can act and does. Of course the picture is almost wholly Barrymore and every opportunity is given him to get all the footage possible.

Warner Oland plays the role of a dissolute brother of Manon who is willing to barter away his own sister's virtue to a wealthy roue of the court and does so. But the girl has fallen in love with the poor but more youthful Fabian, so when the time comes that he manages to win himself a bankroll she is quite willing to discard her more elderly protector for her first love, for love and wealth are more to be desired than mere wealth alone.

Oland handles himself decidedly well and the scheming De Mortfontaine of Sam De Grasse is a delightfully conceived and executed piece of character acting. Stuart Holmes makes Louis XV decidedly picturesque but not any more so than the dashing Richelieu contributed by Bertram Grasby.

From a production standpoint there are few things left to be desired, but a moving dock hardly gives the impression of a ship moving out to sea.

Those that have seen "Don Juan" will want to see "When a Man Loves," but it is safe to predict that they will not be impressed as much by the latter as by the former. *Fred.*

IT

Famous Players-Lasky release; story by Elinor Glyn; directed by Clarence Badger; Clara Bow starred and Antonio Moreno featured; at the Paramount, New York, week of Feb. 5. Running time, 64 mins.

Betty Lou	Clara Bow
Cyrus Waltham	Antonio Moreno
Monty	William Austin
Adela Van Norman	Jacqueline Gadsdon
Mrs. Van Norman	Julia Swayne Gordon
Molly	Priscilla Bonner
First Welfare Worker	Eleanor Lawson
Second Welfare Worker	Rose Tapley

Elinor Glyn's "It" came to the Paramount last week, and it is the best picture that the big, new Broadway house has had to date. Therefore, it would not be surprising if the house managed to turn in receipts for the current week that should come close to $80,000.

"It" is that kind of a picture. Not a "Flesh and the Devil," but one of those pretty little Cinderella stories where the poor shop girl marries the wealthy owner of the big department store in which she works. It's done with a dash of Glyn suggestion playing on that too fulsome word of motion picturedom, "It."

Incidentally, in "It" Madame Glyn makes her debut as a picture actress. A chance to see Elinor without a tiger skin; but it seems that they all get that way sooner or later, especially later, for the older they are the crazier they are to do just that sort of thing. At that, Elinor makes a pretty good sort of a grande dame "extra" in a restaurant scene. To make sure that no one will miss her, she has "added attraction" billing on the film program and is introduced by her own name when she makes her entrance.

But you can't get away from this Bow girl. She certainly has that certain "it" for which the picture is named, and she just runs away with the film. She can troupe in front of a camera, and the manner in which she puts it all over the supporting cast in this production is a joy to behold.

Antonio Moreno, principal supporting player, looks just about old enough to fall for the Bow type of flapper, in fact, just a little too old and too ready to fall. But the chances are that Madame Glyn did the greater part of the casting, as far as males were concerned. If that is the case, give her credit for having picked the best "silly ass dude" type that has been seen on the screen in a long while, William Austin. He's immense and furnishes the greater part of the laughs.

"It" starts in a department store, where the father has just turned the business over to the son. His Percy pal comes in to congratulate him and makes a tour of inspection with him. He is all het up over the Glyn story of "It" in a magazine and starts looking for "it" among the shop girls, ending up with being sure that he has found one in Betty Lou (Clara Bow). He picks her up on the street when the store closes, and as she holds a secret admiration for the new "boss," sees in him a means to an end and lets him date her up for dinner. That night in the Ritz she "makes" the boss, at the same time making a bet with him that the next time he sees her he won't recognize her. She wins her bet, for when she is called into his office to receive a call-down for having insulted a customer she has to almost fall over him to make him see who she is.

From that time on there are propositions and complications, but in the end the little girl hooks him after a thrilling struggle in the water, having eased her way into a yachting party that the boss is giving.

Judging from what the screen shows, "It" is nothing more than the determination on the part of any young flapper to hook a certain man and going to any length to land him.

But the combination of the title, played as it is and with the name of Elinor Glyn, it's going to make the picture a mighty good box office bet.

George Marion, Jr., is to be given credit for having titled the picture, the wordings drawing gales of laughter at the Paramount. However, Clara Bow really does it all, and how. *Fred.*

McFADDEN'S FLATS

Asher, Small & Rogers present Charlie Murray and Chester Conklin in the screen version of the old musical extravaganza exploited by Gus Hill. Picture directed by Richard Wallace from adaptation by Rex Taylor. Distributed by First National. Running time, 78 minutes. At Strand, New York, week Feb. 6.

Dan McFadden	Charlie Murray
Jock McTavish	Chester Conklin
Mary Ellen McFadden	Edna Murphy
Sandy McTavish	Larry Kent
Mrs. McFadden	Eggie Herring
Patrick Halloran	DeWitt Jennings
Edith Halloran	Dorothy Dwan
Mrs. Halloran	Cissy Fitzgerald
Russell Halloran	Freeman Wood
Bridget Maloney	Dot Farley
Hat Salesman	Leo White
Interior Decorator	Harvey Clark

Much shrewd showmanship displayed in this screen translation of Gus Hill's stage roughhouse of slapstick. Moments in the film story when it approaches high levels of sentiment and herein is displayed a genius of the studio. On the screen "McFadden's Flats" is an intelligent bit of comedy with touches of deft humor, material transmuted from the crudest and least promising materials in the original.

The creators of the picture have realized a vital element of comedy, in the fact that the banana peel technique straight is perhaps the lowest form of buffoonery, and it is admissible into civilized entertainment only when it is employed to heighten and intensify pathos or at least something of sentimental import. Somebody concerned in the manufacture of "McFadden's Flats" has used nice judgment in this particular, because it is the thing that raises it above a trick bit of low clowning. The trouble is that they didn't go quite far enough.

The picture gives one the impression of a conflict in its producing personnel. It looks as though somebody had argued to soft pedal the hoke, the gagging and spread the slapstick thin, while somebody else in the directorate argued "give 'em the old knockabout good and strong." The compromise is generally good, but it does sometimes spill over.

The picture has been titled with conspicuous skill. It is there that most of the gagging takes place, some of it hokum, but most of it effective in getting laughs. The reception at the Strand Sunday night augured well for the production. They laughed loud and long at its gags, and they absorbed its semi-serious passages with silent attention—best proof that the material was genuine.

The picture is probably a business builder for week engagements, on its comedy merit. *Rush.*

THE GENERAL

United Artists' release, starring Buster Keaton. Story and direction by Buster Keaton and Clyde Bruckman. At the Capitol, N. Y., week of Feb. 5. Running time, 77 minutes.

Johnnie Grey	Buster Keaton
Capt. Anderson	Glenn Cavender
Gen. Thatcher	Jim Farley
Southern General	Frederick Vroom

Annabelle Lee..............Marian Mack
Her Father..................Charles Smith
Her Brother.................Frank Barnes
Union Officers..........................
Joe Keaton, Mike Donlin, Tom Nawn

Buster Keaton's first comedy for United Artists is entitled "The General," and is the attraction for the current week at the Capitol. That house, after four weeks of record business with "Flesh and the Devil," looks as though it were virtually going to starve to death this week. There was far from a heavy play for the picture the first three days of its run, and there is a reason. "The General" is far from funny. Its principal comedy scene is built on that elementary bit, the chase, and you can't continue a flight for almost an hour and expect results. Especially is this so when the action is placed entirely in the hands of the star. It was his story, he directed, and he acted. The results is a flop.

The story is a burlesque of a Civil War meller. It opens with what looks like a real idea, but never gets away from it for a minute. Consequently it is overdone.

Keaton has the role of a youthful engineer on the Watern and Atlantic R. R., running through Georgia, when war is declared. He tries to enlist, but is turned down, as it is figured that he would be of greater value to the cause as an engineer. His girl, however, won't believe this, and tells him not to see her again until he is in a uniform.

A year later he is still running his train, while both the brother and father of his sweetheart have been wounded. The girl is on a visit to her dad when 10 Union daredevils steal the train in the middle of Confederate territory and start off with it, intending to burn all bridges behind them, so that the line of communication and supplies for the enemy shall be cut. The girl is on the train, and Buster, sore because his beloved engine has been stolen, gives chase in another locomotive. The chase takes him right into the Union lines, where he overhears the plans of the staff and, also becomes aware of the fact that his girl has been made prisoner.

He helps her to escape, and the next morning the two steal the engine back again and start to return to the Confederate lines, this time with the tables of the chase turned, the Unionists chasing the locomotive with the escaping pair. Back in the Confederate lines the young engineer tips off the commander of what he has done and what the plans of the Union forces are, so that they are enabled to block them and win a battle. Just for that Buster is enlisted in the army as a lieutenant, and dons his uniform, with the girl looking on.

There are some corking gags in the picture, but as they are all a part of the chase they are overshadowed. There isn't a single bit in the picture that brings a real howl. There is a succession of mild titters, and that's about all.

No one besides the star has a chance to do anything, and Marian Mack looks as if she might register if given a chance.

"The General" is a weak entry for the de luxe houses. It is better geared for the daily change theatres, as that is about its speed.

Fred.

Getting Gertie's Garter

P. D. C. release presented by John C. Flinn starring Marie Prevost. Charles Ray featured. Adapted by F. Willis McGrew from stage farce of Avery Hopwood and Wilson Collison; E. Mason Hopper directed. Others in cast include Sally Rand, Harry Myers, Fritzi Ridgeway, Lila Leslie, William Orlamond, Dell Henderson, Franklin Pangborn. Ran 70 minutes at the Hippodrome, New York.

Title and the basic theme augured well for a good flicker had the technical qualifications been up to par. As it happened, "Getting Gertie's Garter" in film form gets nowhere It's a long time getting started, drags, runs over-long and by the time things commence to happen it makes little difference anyway.

The casting isn't the happiest, Charles Ray being catapulted into a farce role with which his natural hesitant style does not jibe. As a result, in one moment he is hey-hey'ing his staid aunt into a jazz dance (following the collapse of a hot cup of tea) and in the next breath Ray is his usual hapless self, floundering about in the typical Ray manner of shyness.

The recovery of the incriminating jeweled garter with the lawyer's photograph encased is familiar in theme and it: screen presentation does nothing to offset the obviousness of it all.

Just another P. D. C. of play at the Hip.

Abel.

HELD BY THE LAW

Universal production, directed by Edward Laemmle. Scenario by Bayard Veiller. Ralph Lewis, Margurite De LaMotte and Johnnie Walker featured. At Moss' Broadway, New York, week Feb. 8. Running time, about 60 minutes.

A very good mystery-detective-crime story, without sufficient drawing power for the b. o. in any one thing to mark it as exceptional for a U. of this type. Well made, directed and played picture, just missing in that one essential, a box office punch.

Yet, wherever the meller or tense suspense dramatic or mystery story is liked, this one will do the trick, either for a week or a day.

In story writing, continuity and tension, Bayard Veiller, whose forte has been this kind of stuff for stage or screen, has done his best. There are little twists to the big story that hold continuously, a real twist toward the finale, scenes of the death house at Sing Sing, even to the chair, but withal, there it is, as nicely directed picture of this description as one could ask for, but one that must draw strictly on its merits as a made story. If that gets it much, it will be in a neighborhood where they talk over their film mellers with every meal. Nothing startlingly original in theme; it's more the way handled.

Not a laugh to stand off the dramatics, other than in one caption, thrice repeated.

It's a tale of an elderly man condemned through jury conviction of the murder of his friend, whereas a nephew of the dead man did it, all conveyed to the audience, making it somewhat more interesting in the working out. How they uncover the real murderer is clever writing, and the closeness of the wrongly condemned to the chair is harrowingly carried forward, but without undue dragginess.

Margurite De LaMotte makes an impression with her sad sob stuff as the daughter, and there is a two-sided love affair.

"Held by the Law" will get circulation because it's a good picture. But if there could have been sent into it just one wallop, Universal would have had a peach release.

Sime.

THE FIRST NIGHT

Tiffany Production, directed by Richard Thorpe, featuring Bert Lytell and Dorothy Devore. From the story by Frederica Sagor, adapted by Esther Shulkin. Reviewed in projection room Feb. 4. Running time, 53 mins.

Dr. Richard Bard..............Bert Lytell
Doris Frazer.................Dorothy Devore
Hotel Detective..............Harry Myers
Mimi }
Jack White }..................Frederic KoVert
Mr. Cleveland...............Walter Hiers
Mrs. Cleveland...............Lila Leslie
The Drunk....................James Mack
Miss Leeds....................Hazel Keener
Mrs. Miller...................Joan Standing

This is one of those bedroom farces that has as its principal "kick" the female impersonating of Frederic KoVert, although both Bert Lytell and Dorothy Devore are billed over him. For the regular run of houses it's strong enough to pull laughs, and there is a spot here and there where this one is good enough to fill in for a week.

For the screen this film is built just about the way that A. H. Woods builds his bedroom stuff, only they don't go as far, for it is on the screen. There isn't a thing in it that is censorable, and it would have been mighty easy to make the titles a little too raw. Instead, they have built for laughs both in action and titles.

It is the tale of a patient who gets stuck on a good looking doctor who specializes in women's cases. She throws over her former fiance for the doc, with the result that the boy who is cast off decides to manufacture a "past" for the physician. In the army he had been in one of the regimental musical comedies playing a "girl" role, so he decides to impersonate a French wife of the doctor's.

He manages to get away with it for almost five out of the six reels, but in the end he is hoisted by his own petard. Both the doctor and the house detective, whom he has fooled, taking a couple of socks as he is revealed without his wig.

The title is derived from the fact that the doctor and the girl elope and for their honeymoon seek out the hotel where the former sweetheart of the girl is stopping. The female impersonator has already convinced the house detective that he is really the deserted wife of the doctor and has enlisted aid on the promise that they will become sweethearts when "she" is revenged on the faithless husband.

With the arrival of the newlyweds things begin to happen. There are chases through the halls, mix-ups in rooms, etc., and a final straightening out of the whole affair when the impersonator's wig comes off disclosing his real identity.

Bert Lytell handles the role of the doctor nicely enough, but Dorothy Devore does not show up so well. As a matter of fact, KoVert makes a better looking gal than Miss Devore. Harry Myers, as the house detective, furnished a flock of laughs as also did a little negro lad, not programmed, who played a page boy in the hotel scenes. Walter Hiers was stuck into the picture for a few laughs, and his scenes are the only ones that are overdone. The hall-chase stuff, which he and Lytell indulge in run too long.

The picture will get laughs, and after all that's what counts.

Fred.

THE WAR HORSE

Lambert Hillyer Production, presented by William Fox. Starring Buck Jones. Story by Buck Jones and Lambert Hillyer, script by the latter. Reviewed in projection room Feb. 3. Running time, 53 mins.

Buck Thomas....................Buck Jones
Audrey Evans...................Lola Todd
Captain Collins...............Lloyd Whitlock
Lieutenant Caldwell..........Stanley Taylor
Yvonne..........................Yola D'Avril
General Evans.................James Gorden

It looks as if all the western stars on the Fox lot were bitten by the war bug, while the boys were making "What Price Glory." It is only a few weeks ago that a Tom Mix picture was shown with a war angle to it and now comes Buck Jones with another yarn that has a war complex with France as the locale. So don't look for too much western stuff in this picture even though it has Jones as the star. Right here the advice is for Buck to stick to Stetsons and chaps.

The story is very human, has a lot of action and thrills and there isn't anyone that will find fault with the cowboy who follows his own horse to France when that animal is taken by the Army for service. That is the opening of the story. A ranch where they are furnishing animals for the artillery and a shipment being passed on by an officer who finds that he is a couple of horses short so that he takes over Buck's "Silver Buck." The horse wrangler follows, enlists and comes up with his horse again in France.

From then on it is a story of the war with a dash of love interest, for Buck falls in love with a beautiful ambulance driver and when he turns out to be a hero and saves the battery from an ambuscade, she naturally melts in his arms.

There are a lot of thrills, a couple of corking fights and some touches of comedy. How they ever managed to manufacture the mud in this one in California is a mystery, but there's enough to splatter everyone.

Lola Todd plays the lead opposite the star and looks like a good bet. She has looks and pep and some of that "It" that they are talking about these days. The rest of the cast just about fills in.

Fred.

REMEMBER

Columbia Pictures presents "Remember," featuring Dorothy Phillips. Produced by Harry Cohn. Directed by David Selman. Story by Dorothy Howell. At Loew's New York, one day, Feb. 4, one half of double bill. Running time, 55 mins.

Ruth Pomeroy.............Dorothy Phillips
Jimmy Cardigan............Earle Metcalfe
Constance Pomeroy.............Lola Todd
Slim Dugan..............Lincoln Stedman
Billy.....................Eddie Featherstone

"Remember" has no relation whatsoever to the popular song of that title. Apparent saving here on salaries, which may enable the Columbia-Cohn combination to realize a profit on the film. Many interiors. Outside the war scenes is one of those economical productions that need not be ashamed of being part of a double feature day program.

It was at its biggest climax perhaps when the blinded hero fell downstairs and then regained his sight to gaze upon the real Connie who was not as he had believed upon his return from war the Pomeroy girl that he had loved and had married. Yet the audience got the biggest kick out of the war scenes. Some of them looked real.

It's a sob story, the sacrificial efforts of Ruth Pomeroy to cover up her sister's chucking over of Jimmy Cardigan when he was over there.

The main work is centered in the leads, with Miss Phillips acting the more matured role of the older sister with credit. Metcalfe was acceptable yet seemed to be showing age. Little for any of the rest to do.

Somewhat padded but with the war scenes saving it from falling from exhibitive grace altogether.

Mark.

THE SPEED COP

W. Ray Johnston presents Rayart picture, starring Billy Sullivan. Directed by Duke Worne. Story by Grover Jones. At Loew's New York, one half double bill, one day, Feb. 4. Running time, 64 mins.

At best a travesty on justice, with the story too commonplace to give it much thought other than giving Billy Sullivan credit for his herculean efforts to make the picture stand up on both feet. Sullivan not only photos well but he fights in the manner the educated birds of today with the many fight cards staged weekly. In a Tux he is a Beau Brummel.

A rich girl speeds faster than a comet and with a stand-in with the judge has the arresting motor cop invited to her home in a supposed scene of ridiculing him.

While a pity to waste so much film yet it boosts Sullivan's screen standing.

Mark.

THE RED MILL

Cosmopolitan production releasing through Metro-Goldwyn-Mayer. Adapted from the musical comedy of the same name and stars Marion Davies. Directed by William Goodrich (Fatty Arbuckle). H. Sartov, the photographer. At the Capitol, New York, week of Feb. 12. Running time, 72 mins.

Tina........................Marion Davies
Dennis........................Owen Moore
Gretchen........................Louise Fazenda
Willem........................George Siegman
Captain Edam........................Karl Dane
Burgomaster........................J. Russell Powell
Timothy........................Snitz Edwards
Governor........................William Orlamond
Innkeeper........................Fred Gambold

An idiotic screen morsel substantiating the contention that the average intellect of a picture audience parallels an 11 or 13-year-old youngster. And the kids are about the only ones who are going to giggle at this portage from stage to studio. It starts mark timing with the title and 72 minutes later is in the same spot.

The Capitol is evidently suffering a reaction from "Flesh and the Devil." That one lingered four weeks and was doing well enough to have remained another. Then came "The General" and now "The Red Mill." Mothers who accompanied their children to this house Saturday afternoon were asking the tots "shall we go" after only seeing half of the feature's footage, but the offsprings wanted to stick. The adults were up to the neck with boredom, and the morale won't be any different no matter where this one plays.

As a show "The Red Mill" was a success. Marion Davies is starred in the celluloid version, but it's not fair to altogether blame her for this kindergarten effort. Personally she does as well as she can, but her surrounding contributors, technically and otherwise, have left her dangling in the air. It was directed by Fatty Arbuckle under the program name of William Goodrich.

The story doesn't amount to a whoop. If it's being sexless is an attribute, then it's also senseless, the gags become as monotonous as puns, and the titles (Dutch girl's mixed phrasing) are trying on the nerves. In fact, outside of production it's pretty awful.

Tina (Miss Davies) is a kitchen slavey who sees the debonair Dennis and becomes all agog. It takes much too long for the chase and the capture. Low comedy falls on an ice pond are supposed to cause hysterics among the patrons, a pet mouse breaks up a wedding, and Miss Davies spends about 500 feet trying to set up a trick ironing board.

Miss Davies being innocent of responsibility for having been a party to this conspiracy allows the director an out in pleading guilty, and he should and will. The story isn't there for the simple reason there is none. A musical score and dance numbers filled in the vacancies in the original libretto, but there's nothing to break its dullness as a scenario.

Louise Fazenda and Snitz Edwards attempt to "mug" their way to laughs, Owen Moore plays a girl-crazy youth, George Siegman is the harsh inn keeper, and the captions try to make these characters plausible and funny. Sartov, at the camera, has done justice by his assignment, but it's a waste of time to bother about the remaining component parts.

Sid.

THE THIRD DEGREE

Warner Bros. production starring Dolores Costello in filmization of Charles Klein's melodrama, directed by Michael Curtiz. Louise Dresser, Rockliffe Fellowes and Jason Robards co-featured. Photography by Hal Mohr. Runs 80 mins. At the Paramount, New York, week of Feb. 12.

Annie Daly........................Dolores Costello
Alicia Daly........................Louise Dresser
Underwood ....Rockliffe Fellowes
Howard Jeffries, Jr........................Jason Robards
Mrs. Chubb........................Kate Price
"Daredevil Daly" ....Tom Santchi
Mr. Chubb ....Harry Todd
Annie (as a baby)......Mary Louise Miller
Clinton ....Michael Vavitch
Howard Jeffries, Sr........David Torrence

For all its reminiscence of "Variety," the Ufa importation, "The Third Degree" is alibied because of its original Charles Klein source. A popular melodrama a number of years ago, it does not quite impress according to present day detective standards, since the "third degree" is stressed in the title. It's draggy and overlong, the 80 minutes being 15-20 overtime and capable of amputation with ease.

The "Variety" parallelism is not confined to the circus theme start, but even more so as regards the trick photography which distinguished the Ufa product. Whoever Hal Mohr, cameraman of "The Third Degree," may be, he does as well if not better than the foreign lens expert.

The circus start plants the alleged lowly antecedents of the heroine and her mother (Miss Dresser). The mother's remarriage into society creates a social barrier for the daughter (Miss Costello), who in maturity, is unbeknown to her mother.

Follows thereafter the usual complications of the prospective son "confessing" to a murder committed by his mother under "third degree" inquisition, the discovery of the relationship, etc., for the conventional clinch.

There is worth-while material in the running time which, with judicious editing will shape up as a tight one-hour feature. The camera stuff should not be axed, but much of the introductory detail can go.

Dolores Costello is now quite a flicker "name," and to those not well acquainted with her the delicious Dolores will take care of her own laurels. The gal is a "looker" and knows her groceries on histrionic registration before a lens.

The supporting cast is okay, but not distinguished in any wise. The cameraman next to the star deserves the most individual credit.

"The Third Degree" as a title, with the star's assistance, is all right, but it is not a week stand feature. A Warner booking into the ace Paramount house is the tip-off on the rental, this being explained by the strong stage attraction—Paul Whiteman.

Abel.

TAXI TAXI!

Universal light comedy-drama, starring Edward Everett Horton, with Marion Nixon featured. Directed by Melville W. Brown from story by Raymond Cannon. In the cast also are Burr McIntosh and Edward V. Mong in character parts. Running time, 58 minutes. New York Hippodrome, week Fez. 14.

Light character comedy in which nothing of moment happens except a mild flirtation that leads to a travesty wedding b't at the finish is no sort of material to support a weak vaudeville entertainment in the huge Hippodrome within a biscuit toss of Broadway.

It hasn't anything to appeal to the naive mob that patronizes that establishment. A bad picture that had some semblance of a kick would be better material.

The picture isn't a bad example of the new mode of fluffy story. It has a wealth of mild laughs, but no rich comedy values. Worst of all, it hasn't any people whose names mean anything in the front.

Technical production is first rate, both in the settings and in the action such as it is. Best shots are those of a gay cabaret, and anybody who depends upon cabaret stuff to carry a picture over at this late day is up against it. The rest of the picture aims at quiet character humor of a sort of Bunker Bean character who gets himself mixed up with a gang of crooks when he buys their Lizzie taxicab in order to get his girl home dry during a rainstorm.

The mild escapade leads the couple to a rural church, where under the girl's promptings they present themselves to be married by the country pastor. While the ceremony is in progress the police come up in pursuit of the crooks' taxi and interfere with the wedding. Also the girl's guardian crashes into the situation. Here comes in the comic situation which has been a long time in arriving.

The boy and girl run round and round the church, with the guardian in pursuit, and each time they pass the vestry window the minister shoots at them a line of the marriage service, such as "Do you take this woman" on one trip, and so on to the finale, "I pronounce you man and wife," just as the pursuing guardian catches up, too late.

Rush.

THE MAGIC GARDEN

F. B. O. production with Raymond Keane, Margaret Morris and William V. Mong co-featured. Adapted by J. Leo Meehan from story by Gene Stratton-Porter. Directed by J. Leo Meehan. At private projection rooms, New York, Feb. 9. Running time, 73 mins.

Amaryllis Minton (child).......Joyce Coad
Mmaryllis Minton (adult)..Margaret Morris
John Guido (child)..........Phillipe Delacy
John Guido (adult) ....Raymond Keane
Paul Minton ....Charles V. Mong
Maestro ....Cesare Gravina
Countess di Varesi...........Paulette Duval
Peter Minton (child)......Walter Wilkinson
Peter Minton (adult).......Earle McCarthy
Mrs. Minton ....Hedda Hopper

Allan Siegler, in charge of camera work, has done an exceptional job. His photographic results are really cinematic art. Irrespective of the story that ran quietly along to a quiet finale with the child-day sweethearts reunited, the picture elicits one's wholesome admiration for its camera triumph.

The story is not unusual, and it did not shape into the colorful, entertaining story that "Laddie," which F. B. O. also released and which was another Gene Stratton-Porter story. Both are kid stories in the main, and there is the usual sentimentality, yet this one seems to drag interminably.

The picture displays money expenditure and the adaptation no doubt strives to run true to the author's form, yet the theme forced the main characters to move to and fro for long stretches like automatons.

William Mong makes John Forrester of natural interest and effect. Joyce Coad just about walks away with the picture up to the time she had to give way to the adult transformation with Margaret Morris stepping in. She's a clever kid.

The picture will unquestionably find its biggest reception from the kids. For the adults not so engrossing.

Mark.

METROPOLIS

Berlin, Feb. 5.

The long-awaited film for which Ufa has been beating the gong for the last year. It is said to have cost 7,000,000 marks (about $1,680,000), and the picture looks it.

Nothing of the sort has ever been filmed before; its effect is positively overwhelming. From a photographic and directorial standpoint it is something entirely original. Brigitte Helm, in the leading feminine role, is a find. If she has really never acted before, Fritz Lang, directing, cetrainly did an extraordinary piece of work with her.

Also Heinrich George, Fritz Rasp and Gustav Froehlich deliver exceptional performances.

The weakness is the scenario by Thea von Harbou. It gives effective chances for scenes, but it actually gets nowhere. The scene is laid in the future, 100 years from now, in the mighty city of Metropolis, a magnified New York. It is ruled by a millionaire, who lives in the upper city and whose son falls in love with a girl of the workers, who lives below in the city of the toilers. This girl is preaching good will to the workers in the catacombs below the city.

An inventor has discovered a way to make artificial human beings, and at the request of the millonaire gives this creation of his the form of the girl. She preaches destruction to the workers, and they destroy the machinery which regulates everything in the city. Only through the aid of the boy and the real girl can the children of the workers be saved from inundation in the lower city. The workers turn against the evil marionette and burn her on a scaffold. The boy and the girl are united, and peace is closed between the millionaire and the workers.

Too bad that so much really artistic work was wasted on this manufactured story. However, if put across with strong publicity, it may be possible to get out the money invested in it.

Love's Greatest Mistake

Edward Sutherland production, presented by Famous Players-Lasky from $50,000 Liberty Magazine serial. Evelyn Brent featured. Story by Frederic Arnold Kummer; adapted by Becky Gardiner. At the Paramount, New York, week Feb. 19. Running time, 72 mins.

Jane........................Evelyn Brent
Don Kendall........................William Powell
Harvey Gibbs........................James Hall
Honey McNeil........................Josephine Dunn
William Ogden........................Frank Morgan
Sara Foote........................Iris Gray
Lovey Gibbs........................Betty Byrne

A surprisingly interesting picture, considering the slight fanfare that accompanied its initial showing in New York. One reason for it not being more impressive at first glance is the fact that there isn't a star name anywhere in the cast. That lack is entirely overcome by the picture itself.

It is a comedy drama of a phase of life today in New York. As a matter of fact, it might well have been suggested by the Dorothy King mystery and several others of like ilk that followed a short time afterward. The picture may not draw the first day, but business will build, for it will get word-of-mouth advertising.

Incidentally, it is Josephine Dunn who runs away with the film, despite that Evelyn Brent is featured. Miss Dunn looks like a potential Garbo. This one shows that the girl has pretty much everything needed to carry her through, and if she is supplied with the right type of roles, there is no reason why she shouldn't land in the big money.

The story opens with Honey McNeil (Miss Dunn) on her way to

New York from Bangor, Me., to visit her married sister. On the train she meets William Ogden, a banker, who becomes smitten with her beauty. She tells him that the married sister has always been the quiet one of the family, and therefore she is afraid her visit is going to be a dull one. Then the sister is flashed. She is married to a traveling man, off on the road, and sister is entertaining a cake-eater type of lover. He seems to be the sheik of that particular set, for the modiste in the picture also has him for a lover, and his boast is that for five years he has been able to live without working. William Powell has this fat role and makes the most of it. The twist, however, gives the audience a flock of laughs. In fact, the picture abounds in just those twists and the consequent laughs.

The little Maine girl goes about with her banker, while the sheik and the modiste try to frame so that they will be in on the "shake" when the right time comes. There is also in the background a young architect (James Hall), in love with the girl, but seemingly without enough speed to get her.

Finally, when the banker is about to go abroad, he offers Honey a string of pearls, but she turns them down. He puts them in a hiding place in his apartment in her presence, with the information that whenever she changes her mind and wants them they'll be there awaiting her. When Christmas arrives and the banker is abroad, the young architect takes her to his home to meet his mother, and on her return to her sister's apartment Honey discovers that there is someone in there that has been making a search. She is attacked and ordered to give up the banker's letters, but refuses. The architect returns to the apartment in time to save her life, and she is removed to a hospital, where the story of the attack gets into the newspapers.

The banker, on landing, dashes to the hospital, and his first question is regarding his letters. The girl turns them over to him, being considerably disillusioned by his instinct of self-preservation. Later the sheik tries to pin a blackmailing scheme on the banker, but is unsuccessful, and for revenge plants the story with one of the tabloid scandal sheets. The young architect, seeing the story, believes the worst, but still wants the girl to marry him. But she, sensing that he thinks that she has been under the protection of the banker, refuses him again.

The finish is another gag that will wow wise audiences. It has the two youngsters entering a hotel room when a person suggesting the house dick from all angles arrives, but he turns out to be the justice of the peace that they have sent for to marry them.

Surefire and will get dough after they know what it's about.

Fred.

DON'T TELL THE WIFE

Warner Bros. production starring Irene Rich. Huntley Gordon and Lilyan Tashman featured. Scenario by Rex Taylor. Directed by Paul Stein. Shown at the Hippodrome, N. Y., week Feb. 21, 1927. Running time, 63 minutes.

Mrs. Carter........................Irene Rich
John Carter......................Huntley Gordon
Suzanne..........................Lilyan Tashman
Henry...........................William Demarest
Magistrate............................Otis Harlan

An entertaining if not a particularly strong picture. It is a production that could have been helped materially with snappy titling. The situations of the story lend themselves naturally to that, but it was a bet that was overlooked. Originally it must have been the intention to make the story one entirely Parisian in flavor, but at the last minute three of the principal characters were changed to Americans.

Irene Rich is the star and she gives her usual finished performance in the role of the wife who is struggling to win her husband back from a Parisian vamp. But though administering the same sort of medicine to her husband as he is slipping her in his affair with the other woman, she almost loses him for good.

The yarn is that of a trio of Americans from Peoria, Ill., who are abroad. The Carters are in the big money and Henry, also from Peoria, is just a hanger-on. Henry is dashing about with Suzanne, a Parisian beaut, and takes her to a party at the Carters. Suzanne looks over John Carter and decides that he would be just about right for her, bankroll and all. She makes her play and hooks him and the next night they go stepping while Mrs. Carter remains at home. She, however, knows what's up and sends for Henry and urges him to make love to her just as John Carter is coming in the door and John gets an eye full.

A week or so later John makes an excuse that he has to go on a business trip and Mrs. Carter, again wise that something is on tap, switches his suit case for her own, first having forged a note from Henry in loving terms and placed it where hubby can't fail to find it. On the train he opens the bag and comes across the note, and although his sweetie is in the next compartment he feigns illness, has the train stopped, and dashes back to Paris in an ambulance with sweetie on the front seat with the driver.

He gets home before the wife returns and when she comes in with Henry the big scene is staged. John decides to let Mrs. Carter have her freedom but insists that Henry shall marry her, he offering to give Henry $1,000,000 to support the wife. The kindly-hearted old magistrate, a friend of the Carters and fully aware that they are both stalling, proceeds to trick them into the belief that he has obtained a separation and proposes that a double wedding be held immediately so that a double honeymoon can begin. After performing a ceremony he leaves the two couples to themselves, thinking that after an hour or so he'll return and tell them that it was all illegal and they are not divorced, but he fails to account for the whims of women. Both of them want to get as far away from the other as possible, the result being that they both make off to the country to the chateau of the Carters. The old magistrate follows and finally rights things, and in the end Suzanne and Henry are spliced.

Otis Harlan plays the old magistrate and puts it over. Lilyan Tashman makes the most of the vamp role and looks great in her silk trick pajamas. Huntley Gordon slipped over a finished performance as Carter, and the comedy Henry of William Demarest was all that could be asked for.

A few laughs are there and a couple of bedroom touches will get the small town gang. *Fred.*

DON MIKE

F. B. O. production, presented by Joseph P. Kennedy. Starring Fred Thomson, with cast including Silver King, Ruth Clifford, Noah Young, Albert Frisco, William Courtwright, Tom Bates, Norma Marie and Carmen Le Roux. Story by Frank M. Clifton; directed by Lloyd Ingraham. Reviewed in projection rooms Feb. 16.

Leading role in a story of this sort forced Fred Thomson to do a Fairbanks. Thomson is a bit awkward in spots, but shows up well under fine treatment from the camera with soft focus close-ups. The story holds, even if not new, placing Thomson as a Mexican grandee torn from his high estate by a wandering American jailbird whom he had befriended.

Noah Young, the leering, uncouth, straggler bossing an outfit which almost perished in the desert from thirst until rescued by Don Mike, is not only an effective heavy, but registers for laughs. The titles are very bad.

Thomson does some fine stuff in a knife throwing exhibition, stopping Don Luis, the mayor, from panicing a servant girl.

The climax is effectively worked in with the outcast Don Mike, dressed in a monk's garb, attending the wedding of the girl as the officiating priest. He cleans up the room by swinging two long ropes in circles, sharp daggers attached to the ends. Thomson then polishes off the heavy in a solo at the latter's own request. The American Army, under an extremely foolish-looking General Fremont, is thrown in for good measure.

Silver Horse, the star's dumb sidekick, adds interest to the production.

Okay outside of the major stands.

THE MONKEY TALKS

Raoul Walsh production presented by William Fox. Story by Rene Fauchous, adapted by L.O. Rigby. Olive Borden and Jacques Lerner featured. Directed by Raoul Walsh . Reviewed in production room, Feb. 17. Running time, 62 minutes.

Olivette..............................Olive Borden
Jocko Lerner.......................Jacques Lerner
Sam Wick..........................Don Alvarado
Bergerin............................Malcolm Waite
Lorenzo.....................Raymond Hitchcock
Firmin..............................Ted McNamara
Malsie................................Jane Winton
Mata...............................August Tollaire

Raoul Walsh has turned out a true box-office bet in "The Monkey Talks." It's a picture that is a decided novelty, has a wealth of suspense, a tremendous love interest, and sufficient comedy to make it carry anywhere. The picture ought to get a de luxe presentation at one of the Broadway houses for it is strong enough for that.

"The Monkey Talks" was first presented as a play in New York by the Selwyns in conjunction with William Fox. It had been a sensation abroad but in New York did not quite click. However, the picture is sure to have more popular appeal.

It is the story of the trials and tribulations of a trio operating a small wagon circus in France. They are about two leaps ahead of the sheriff when the handy man of all work with the show runs across his former captain in the flying corps. The latter is down and out and despondent because of having been jilted by a woman lion tamer. He is persuaded to join the show. The sheriff finally catches up, seizes the show and the quartet are thrown on their own resources.

It is the little man of all work who is finally utilized to gain fame and fortune for them all. He can imitate a chimpanzee perfectly, and so the four get to Paris where they are a sensation with their talking monkey. They are sworn to keep the secret so all four live together. At the theatre they are playing there is Olivette, a wire walker, who falls in love with the former flier, now acting as trainer of the chimp. But little Jocko Lerner, the human monk, also loves her. The quartet is on the high road to wealth when the lion act appears at the same house and the lady tamer tries to win back her former admirer. When he scorns her she plans revenge by kidnapping Jocko and the replacing him with another chimpanzee. A thrill and a happy ending follow.

Raoul Walsh has turned this out full of atmosphere and replete with suspense. Olive Borden, as the youthful wire walker, is a joyous bit of beauty and the performance of Jacques Lerner is a marvel. He is "Consul the Great" all over again, a perfect chimp. Don Alvarado, opposite Miss Borden, shows great promise and should go a long way in pictures. Raymond Hitchcock is his old self and pulls many a laugh.

A real bet and worth playing up.

Fred.

HILLS OF KENTUCKY

Warner Bros. production, starring Rin-Tin-Tin. Adapted from the Dorothy Yost story, "The Untamed Heart." Adapted by Edward Clark. Directed by Howard Bretherton. Jason Robards featured. Reviewed in projection room Feb. 18. Running time, 70 mins.

The Grey Ghost.....................Rin-Tin-Tin
Steve Harley......................Jason Robards
Janet..............................Dorothy Dwan
Ben Harley.........................Tom Santschi
Little Davey...............Billy Kent Shaeffer
Puppy..........................Rin-Tin-Tin, Jr.
Nanctte...................................Herself

One of the best action pictures, with Rin-Tin-Tin as the star, that has been turned out in this series. In a great many respects it ranks with the very picture that Strongheart was starred in, and was by far the best that that dog actor ever turned out. This picture is surefire with any audience, and with dog lovers it can't miss.

In addition to the canine star, there are Jason Robards, featured, and Tom Santschi as the heavy, with Dorothy Dwan playing the ingenue. Billy Kent Shaeffer as a little crippled boy lends a touch of heart interest that is going to make it a great picture for the kids.

It's a story of the hills of Kentucy, as the title indicates. Prior to the opening of the yarn the farmers have been compelled to turn their dogs loose because they did not have food enough for themselves. The dogs form in packs and range and forage after the fashion of wolves. A little puppy is turned loose by a little boy because his father commands it. When the story itself starts this pup has grown to be the leader of the pack and is known as the Grey Ghost.

In a part of the hills are two Harley brothers, one inclined to be a bully and the other a rather diffident youngster. There comes into the picture at this time a young school teacher with her crippled child brother. Both of the Harley men fall in love with her. The bully wants to master her physically and the younger wants to marry. Naturally she falls for the latter. The crippled boy in the meantime falls in with the Grey Ghost, who is lying in a thicket after having been injured. The boy helps the dog and the animal permits it because of his early memories, although he is decidedly man-shy. The two become friends and the dogs saves the boy from the pack when they attack him. This is a scene with thrills.

Incidentally there is a moment when there are three suspense sequences being carried on at once: The two brothers fighting over the girl in the woods, the dog swimming down the stream toward the falls for the youngster's crutch, and the little fellow himself trying to fight off the dog pack. This carries a wallop, is well worked out and, to the majority of the audiences, the "fake" on the dog stuff, when the Grey Ghost, perched on a ledge, fights off the pack, won't be noticed, as it is done so well.

The dog in the final scenes manages to aid his mate to escape from the farmers that are hunting the pack, saves the life of the heroine after he has drowned the heavy in the stream, and for the finish he and the mate are part of the household when the hero and shero are married and have a two-year-old youngster of their own.

It's a "best of the show" bet, and if you know dog shows you know what that means.

Fred.

WANDERING GIRLS

Columbia picture. Directed by Ralph Ince. Story by Dorothy Howell. Produced by Harry Cohn. Distributed by Commonwealth Film Corp. At Moss' Broadway, New York, week of Feb. 21. Running time, 51 mins.
Peggy Marston............Dorothy Revier
Peggy's mother............Eugenia Besser
Mrs. Arnold............Frances Raymond
Jerry Arnold............Robert Agnew
James Marston............William Welch
Maurice Dumond............Armand Kaliz
Maxine............Mildred Harris

A modern story that is fast growing old: the daughter of straightlaced parents taking her fling at wild parties. Starts out with a title that jars from the start, for the simple reason you anticipate seeing a raft of flappers running the gamut of high life and the like in a big city. It deals with the ups and downs of one girl while another has not only wandered from home fires but has become a sneak thief.

By way of treading close to stage and professional names there is Maurice and Maxine as a fashionable dancing team taking society's money for exhibitions and their jewels at the same time. Maurice played by Armand Kaliz, long in vaudeville. He is the "menace," with Mildred Harris as his guntoting moll, who later kills him when he has thrown her over.

Mildred Harris does some excellent work, while Miss Revier has the looks, carries herself well all the way and is the standout. This girl is improving right along.

Allowing for cinema premise, the story runs through to the usual reconciliation of the runaway girl with her parents and the straightening out of a messy jam in which she has gotten through starting out to earn her own way in the world.

In toto, the Misses Revier and Harris hold it up.

Mark.

FAITHFUL WIVES

Platinum Pictures production and also handles the distribution. Story adapted from "The Faithful Sex." Directed by Norbert Myles. Running time, 63 mins.
Tom Burke............Wallace MacDonald
The Mother............Edythe Chapman
Tom's Sister............Doris May
Tom's Wife............Myrda Dagmarna
The Child............Phillipe de Lacy
The Widow............Dell Boone
Buck Randall............William Lowry
Charles Austin............Niles Welch
Governor Turner............William Conklin
The Lawyer............Bill Brown

To all appearances this independent was turned out in Hollywood in 1920. It has a modern story, yet the attire of the women is of the long-dressed kind that makes the picture look ancient. At the Stanley was an audible snicker in different sections by the women who had to laugh when the old-fashioned dresses appeared.

The story is not new, of an innocent man sentenced to die either by the electric chair or the gallows, and saved at the eleventh hour.

The Stanley looked over the "names" and played one up outside, Niles Welch. But even Welch can do little with this one as a box-office proposition. It has little kick to it other than a fight on a train. Strange to relate the hero was tossed off and into a hospital cot, showing up in time, however, to save the state necktie party.

Much stress laid on the mother of the boy about to die, who is continually rolling her eyes about and literally spilling captions that almost wrote themselves.

This film will do well to get a chance on a "double feature" day.

Mark.

FLYING HIGH

Sam Sax production, featuring William Fairbanks, Alice Calhoun leading woman. Directed by Charles Hutchison and marketed in open market. Carries name of Lumas on production end. Others in the cast: John Wells, Leroy Mason, Cecile Callahan and Jos. Gerard. At Loew's New York as half doube-feature bill Feb. 18.

A "stunt" melodrama with a wealth of highly flavored action. "Flying High" suggests a different kind of story. On first guess you'd look for a comedy, while the picture itself is a thriller of air transport banditry, in itself an attractive subject for thrill fans.

The film makes good abundantly on that basis. It's stunt features have plenty kick and then some, but the melodramatic thread upon which they are based is futile and juvenile. With a well-constructed narrative background the film would have stood up. Now it has only the air stuff to recommend it.

These are spectacular. In one incident the hero (a commercial flyer) takes his sweetheart for an aerial joy ride. From the clouds they witness the attack of an airplane bandit upon the air mail. The hero goes to the assistance of the hard-pressed express messenger and beats the bandits off with his revolver.

From that the story goes into a cumbersome plot, having to do with a society woman who is a spy for the air thieves; her husband, who runs an aerial express company to mask his operations as the bandits' master mind. This angle opens up the possibility of ringing in the fancy dress ball stuff that has been so much overdone and which is entirely out of order in this story.

All the society side of the story does is to distract attention from the melodrama of the air. A neat dramatic trick was the planting of a smoke bomb in the automobile of the flying highwaymen by the hero's comedy relief partner, so that their hiding place among the mountains could be spied out by the hero scouting high up.

This led to a capital thrill incident, with the hero making a parachute descent into the bandit's hiding place from his own plane. The climax is a bit too elaborate. So much that was really spectacular and thrilling had gone before that when the capture of the bandits came along it was rather trivial. The reason for this was that several subordinate air stunts earlier had a stronger kick than the culminating episode of the hero's rescue of his sweetheart from the bandit's plane, and instead of this being the top of the crescendo it was a distinct let down.

Crude as some of the episodes are the picture even now could be much improved by the elimination of heavy footage and concentration on the aerial episodes, with a consequent centering of interest on this phase. As it stands now "Flying High" is a good proposition for the neighborhoods, where a good percentage of the fans are juvenile either in years or taste.

Rush.

BURNING GOLD

W. T. Lackey sponsors this independent bearing the trademark of Elbee Producing Co., and handled through Commonwealth. Director, Jack Noble. Story by Stuart Payton. In the cast Herbert Rawlinson, Mildred Harris and Shirley Palmer. At Loew's New York as half double feature bill, Feb. 18. Running time, 65 mins.

Typical independent in manner, method and personnel. As half a double bill it is about getting its deserts. One of those long drawn out and "plotty" subjects, in this case dealing with crooked oil lease operators.

The action takes place in the oil fields, a locale that ought to be handled with utmost caution. An oil field is a pretty drab setting for movie romance as it is here employed. Along the same line a director who dresses his heroine—if even but for the moment—in dingy overalls and boots takes chances on audience reactions.

The big moment is the burning of oil storage tanks. Apparently the effects in this passage were clips from news reels, with the story action cut in to match. The fire stuff makes an impressive background, but the story action is rather forced and foolish. Besides the presence of the girl at the burning well doesn't mean anything.

A clumsy melodramatic story has been woven, shaped with no dramatic instinct and worked out with no appreciation of dramatic values. The best of the effort is the fire stuff as a detached spectacle and the quality of the photography, exceptional in giving some tone of picturesqueness even to such unromantic settings.

Rawlinson : among the most artificial of screen leading men and does not shine in a machine-made story. Mildred Harris is cast for a dead loss role as a hard-boiled gold digger, throwing the meat of the whole picture to an unknown ingenue, Shirley Palmer, who has not —in this instance at least—a sympathetic personality.

For the daily change houses, and then only as a makeshift when standard names and product are not available.

Rush.

HUSBAND HUNTERS

Tiffany Production presented by M. H. Hoffman. Story by Douglas Bronston, adapted by Esther Shulkin, directed by John G. Adolphi. Reviewed in projection room, Feb. 18. Running time, 61 mins.
Marie Devere............Mae Busch
Bob Garrett............Charles Delaney
Letty Crane............Jean Arthur
Sylvester Jones............Walter Hiers
Helen Gray............Duane Thompson
Cynthia Kane............Mildred Harris
Bartley Mortimer............Robert Cain
Jimmy Wallace............Jimmy Harrison
Rex Holden............Nigel Barrie
Mr. Casey............James Mack
Mr. Cohen............Marcin Asher
Archibald Springer............Alfred Fisher

Jack Adolphi, who directed, has turned out a corking box office picture for Tiffany. It is one of the films that just about bristles with s. a. but only right up to the mark and not over it. This film is going to make the boys step up to the window, lay down the coin and catch a thrill. Yet it's not so raw as to offend the girls, and there you have it.

A lot of names in the cast, none of them means much when it comes to performance before the camera. However, they all do their bit. Mae Busch, as a wise-cracking chorus dame who carries a copy of Bradstreet's with her on all parties, slips over the best individual effort, with little Duane Thompson, in a similar role, running second.

As for the story, there isn't anything that's new. Tried and proven true material that the fans eat up. A little of the usual formula of stage meller is depicted on the screen with something of the "Golddiggers" touch.

Of course there is the sweet young thing (Jean Arthur) who comes to the big town to get a job in the chorus, but who doesn't fit because her clothes don't make sufficient flash when she gets into a manager's office. The particular office she goes to has an angel who is a devil with the girls. This is the heavy (Robert Cain). The latter likes his ladies in groups and favors playing two or three at a time. In this particular case he has been attending Cynthia Kane, small town choir singer, whom he has promised to make a prima donna and marry, when he gets his divorce. Then Letty Crane, as the mushy ingenue character is named, steps in and he makes a play for her. Result Cyn gets wise, takes him out in his motor car after the show dressed in the wraps of the girl that he is expecting, and the two go over a bank and

are killed. That leaves the road clear for our hero.

Mildred Harris does the wronged choir singer, and is a bit plump. The hero is Charles Delaney, who looks not unlike Teddy, Jr. Walter Hiers manages to get a couple of laughs over, while Nigel Barrie sticks his profile and moustache into the picture for a few scenes. Why he doesn't click to greater advantage is a question.

Some good spots in the big scenes. The stage stuff for the revue is corking and a cabaret show has all the ideas that Joe Smith put on at Healy's Golden Glades when they had the ice there. It looks great as done here.

This one is good box office for the regular run of houses outside the de luxe theatres.

Fred.

STARK LOVE

Famous Players-Lasky picture, written and directed by Walter Woods. At the Cameo, N. Y., Feb. 27. Running time, 70 mins.

Rob Warwick	Forrest James
Barbara Allen	Helen Munday
Jason Warwick	Silas Miracle
Quill Allen	Reb Grogan

Here is an unusual picture. It's different in so many ways that you can't really get to where the wallop of the production is. One thing about it is if there are any highbrows in the neighborhood they are going to rave over it. And the low brows will get enough raw melodrama to please them.

The picture is a slice of life cut from the raw—life in the Carolina mountains where for more than two centuries the families of the pioneers have been living and bringing children into the world. The women working and the men loafing, and dying, all unconscious of the progress of the outside world.

There are no actors in the picture except the mountaineers themselves, although the ingenue belies that claim for the production. She looks as though she at least has been to one of the towns or cities near home. She may have originally come from the mountains, but she suggests too much of the outside world in the way that she handles herself. She has a certain amount of "it" and uses it, but find the woman who has never turned it on if she had it.

The idea originated with Karl Brown, cameraman, who was in the mountains some time ago making a picture. He prevailed on Jesse Lasky to finance the project and then went south to get the picture. The result is a freak, but not a freak that is to be classed with "Nanook of the North" or any of the like because this has a story that is real gripping meller.

It tells of the love of a mountaineer boy, the oldest of his family, for the daughter of their nearest neighbor, she likewise the oldest of her family. Their fathers and mothers are friends. The boy has obtained a book and is teaching himself to read, his success in this particular leads him to crave further education, and finally he desides to accompany the itinerant preacher out of the hills to the settlements, sell his horse and go to school. When he reveals his ambition to the girl she tells him to go, for if she had the opportunity she would give up all that she possessed to do the same. The boy goes forth, sells the horse, makes arrangements at a school and then enters the name of the girl for the course of study. He then walks back to the hills to give her the tidings for the arrangement he has made and the sacrifice that he is making for her.

When he gets back he discovers that his mother has died and that his father had on that very day made arrangements with the parents of the girl that she was to become "his new woman," tend his house, rear his children that remained and bear him others, and that he would marry her the "next time the preacher came." The boy sees red when he realizes that he is to sleep on the floor in the very room where the girl he loves will be in the arms of his father. The cabins that they live in have but a single room. The boy and the father come to blows when the youngster protests, and the result is that the youth is beaten down and cast into the rapidly flowing creek in front of the house. The old man then bars the door and is about to take the girl when she raises an axe and holds him off until she gets out of the door.

Seeing the boy in the creek, unconscious, and being carried off by the stream, she wades in to save him and both are carried off down stream. Later they are shown wandering down into the valley where the settlements are.

It's a story that holds, and the action is cleverly maintained with just sufficient of the native comedy in it to give an occasional laugh.

Its money getting qualities, however, will depend entirely on the amount of effort that is put behind it by the exhibitor in exploitation and publicity. The picture will have to be plugged before ti opens. After that it'll take care of itself.

Fred.

BLIND ALLEYS

Famous Players-Lasky picture, starring Thomas Meighan. Evelyn Brent and Gretta Nissen featured. Story by Owen Davis, screen play by Emmet Crozier, directed by Frank Tuttle. At the Paramount, New York, week Feb. 26. Running time, 68 mins.

Capt. Dan Kirby	Thomas Meighan
Sally Ray	Evelyn Brent
Maria D'Alvarez Kirby	Gretta Nissen
Julia Lachados	Hugh Miller
Dr. Webster	Tom Chalmers
Gang Leader	Tammany Young

Thomas Meighan is not going to set the world afire with this especially written script by Owen Davis. Incidentally it does not speak any too well for the author, even considering that Meighan at this day is more or less hard to fit. "Blind Alleys" might have better been called "Coincidences," for that's all it is. Just one coincidence after another all through the picture, and there are certain portions of the sequence designed for sustained suspense, at which the Paramount audience laughed.

Withal it is a picture that will prove entertaining enough in the ordinary run of houses, and will do some business because Meighan has not as yet disappointed all of his following through bad stories. Gretta Nissen, opposite the star, gives as good a performance as could be expected from her role, while Evelyn Brent, as the heavy, an unthankful role at its best, runs away with the honors.

The story has Meighan as the captain of a passenger steamer between New York and South America. In a South American city he meets and marries a Latin-American society girl and brings her back to New York. The first night they are on Broadway he leaves the hotel to get some flowers and fruits and is struck by an automobile owned by a doctor who is in the car and who also has a private hospital to which he takes the man. Meighan, when he becomes fairly conscious the next day makes his escape from the hospital and tries to find his way back to his hotel. He collapses on the street and is taken into a boarding house. From then on it is a case of husband trying to find wife and wife trying to find husband, with each one missing the other by just a second. That's where the laughs come in. As a matter of fact this might make a good comedy properly titled.

Meighan's name will have to carry it.

Fred.

Affair of the Follies

First National picture starring Billie Dove. Features Lewis Stone and Lloyd Hughes. Adapted from a Dixie Willson story, June Mathis doing the scenario. Millard Webb the director. At the Strand, New York, week of Feb. 26.

Hammersly	Lewis Stone
Tamara	Billie Dove
Jerry	Lloyd Hughes
Sam the Waiter	Arthur Stone
The Inventor	Arthur Hoyt
Lew Kline	Bertram Marburgh

Just what destination this role of celluloid has picked out for itself is not quite clear. It doesn't matter much, for no one is going to lose sleep over it even in a theatre. The "Follies" in the title explains that it's another back stage picture, not so far back and not good enough to be up.

Webb, directing, has used plenty of time taking close-ups of Miss Dove. Though this girl is a soothing and sightly screen lotion, candy is candy and the palate will object. No particular story, or if the original script read as a possibility, June Mathis has gummed up her fielding average in getting this one over to first for the put out.

Hammersly, a wealthy bachelor, dotes on Tamara of the 'Follies," but she will have none of him because of Jerry, the struggling clerk. Jerry wants to do the right thing, a justice of the peace is an accomplice and so Tammy and Jerry are one until the latter loses his job. Tam, having quit the stage to wear a ring, hikes it back to the ballet and Jerry bids her silent bon voyage. No Jerry, no happiness and Tammy finally goes to supper with Hammersly at his home where Jerry follows. However, Ham is strictly above board, explains to the young husband that he still holds the exclusive rights so that's that and "An Affairs of the Follies."

Giggles here and there with Arthur Hoyt extracting nicely from a bit role. Miss Dove looks well and may equal the responsibility of having her name above a picture's title if given a story. Hughes continues to be a good looking juvenile just wandering around in this one while Stone is his usual standard self in portraying the man about town who always "plays cricket" in or outdoors.

Al Rockett gets credit for producing this picture and backgrounds are standard throughout. There is the usual stage stuff, Tammy being one-half of an adagio team, and one or two interiors look solid. Not a too expensive effort, probably below average.

All of which may go to prove how essential a dastardly "menace" is, particularly if there's nothing to tell without him. Nary a blow is struck at any time. In fact, the picture's most violent emotion is expressed in a few trickling tears from Miss Dove. You can't get the suave Stone to explode and there's no one for Hughes to take a sock at.

Nicely cameraed and all that sort of thing, but just touring and in doubt where it will stop overnight.

WHITE GOLD

Produced by De Mille Pictures Corp. and releasing through P. D. C. Jetta Goudal starred, with Kenneth Thomson and George Bancroft co-featured in support. Adapted from the play by J. Palmer Parsons. Directed by C. Gardner Sullivan. Shown at Wurlitzer Hall, Feb. 24. Running time, 58 mins.

Dolores Carson	Jetta Goudal
Alec Carson	Kenneth Thomson
Carson	George Nichols
San Randall	George Bancroft
Bucky O'Neil	Robert Perry
Homer	Clyde Cook

"White Gold" has only one feminine character, played by Jetta Goudal, but she carries the role creditably and the story holds up all the way.

While Miss Goudal is starred and does a nice piece of work, George Bancroft is there like a lighthouse in a storm. As the cool, unscrupulous stranger who rides by the Carson sheep ranch and tosses a coin to see whether he will stay, Mr. Bancroft is the "menace" to the manner born. Bancroft's scene where he has a gun poked into his ribs is a corker as well as the one where the man is aroused to the attack on the girl while her husband sleeps in the bunkhouse. Here are shown three simultaneous "shots" of Bancroft in different moods, and it sure is finely cameraed.

The locale is a sheep ranch in Arizona. Into this drab environment goes the Mexican dancing girl who was woeed by young Carson on a trip to the city; there the husband's father resents her presence and schemes to put her in bad with the boy, and does. The ending leaves a dark brown taste in the mouth.

There's a caption "judgment" with succeeding "shots" to show that the girl shot and killed her attacker, yet she goes out alone into the sands of Arizona when her hubby's dad claims he shot the man because he found him in the son's bedroom with the latter's wife. The boy then sticks to his father. That's all, but it is well told.

Photography is adequate and the picture sustains interest from start to finish.

Clyde Cook is in the film for comedy relief. Some of it is effcetive.

When Dolores is seen taking the revolver from the folds of her outer wrap as she walks alone from the ranch and tosses it into a mudhole, one is then left to draw his own imagination as the picture stops then and there without one realizing the end comes so quickly without things being set right in the husband's eyes and causing her great love to be reconciled along the lines that one naturally expects where justice should be done.

The ending will cause comment. Perhaps favorable, perhaps not. Either way the effort is commendable.

Mark.

Alaskan Adventures

San Francisco, Feb. 25.

Here's a sleeper. Whoever goes in for travel stuff, for adventure, the picture different, can peg this one for a natural. It is better than Kleinschmidt, Snow's African Hunt or Rainey's Big Game all rolled into one—because it is human and there is a reason to the story, outside of collecting at the box-office.

Pathe slipped into a great bet when it had "Alaskan Adventures" tossed into its lap.

Captain Jack Robertson is, or was, a sourdough. He put in 16 years mushing around Alaska, always with a yen to make a movie of his country. Then he "came out" to the states. He tied up in the camera section of a local department store and met Art Young, world's champion archer. The two of them framed to go back to make a movie of the real Alaska with the added kick—they'd take no firearms of any sort—just Art Young's bow and arrow. So far, so good, but the money for the expedition? J. M. Allen of Oakland supplied that.

The film starts at the southern shores of Alaska and follows to the Yukon, to Bering Sea, into Siberia, into the maw of ugly old Katmai, the volcano, and back to civilization.

Young goes salmon fishing with his bow and arrow, knocks off wild mountain sheep, deer, bull moose and Kodiak bear, but there is no killing for the lust of killing.

The kill is for food, when they want to build a boat, when they need clothes. There isn't a scene in the 6,100 odd feet that will offend any woman no matter how humane she may be about the killing of wild animals.

There is a mutt dog who attaches himself to the pair and who furnishes more laughs, heart interest and drama than two-thirds of the high priced movie stars. They call the mutt "Wrong Start."

There is also the breaking up of the ice in the Yukon River; 2,000 miles of ice six feet thick that crashes its way to the ocean within 60 hours, and there are more thrills in this than the river sequence of "Way Down East."

There are scenes that for sheer natural beauty will make the heart of you leap out of your chest, if you've got a heart. You'll see a herd of thousands of reindeer—the males separating to "go over" the glacier pass while the females choose the easier roundabout course, the mother bear and her three cubs fishing for salmon. There are shots of "the midnight sun"—taken every 20 seconds from nine at night to three in the morning that are believed the first camera record of this phenomena.

Into the rotten country of the volcano Katmai, Robertson and Younk trek on the tip that "there's plenty of game and fish"; instead they found poison gas and a 60-mile gale blowing powdered pumice into their eyes and lungs.

On the back stretch they caught the icebergs off Siberia. There is one scene where a 'berg comes up from the bottom of the ocean, sticking its ugly head through floes. It looms up as big as the back payments of France's war debt. Here's one spot where a good organist can lift the spectator out of his chair.

They say Robertson and Young spent two years in shooting 20,000 odd feet of film. If this is true they're going to be well paid for all their misery when blase New York gets a peep at their record, for Broadway is a sap for adventure —especially those who have never been west of Seventh avenue.

Whit.

THE SONORA KID

F. B. O. production presented by Joseph P. Kennedy starring Tom Tyler. From the story "Knight of the Range" by William Wallace Cooke. Directed by Bob DeLacy. Reviewed in projection room Feb. 24, 1927. Running time 57 minutes.

Tom McReady..............Tom Tyler
Phyllis Butterworth....Peggy Montgomery
Aunt Marie...............Billie Bennett
Chuck Saunders...........Mark ·Hamilton
Arthur Butterworth.......Jack Richardson
Tough Ryder..............Ethan Laidlaw
Doc Knight...............Barney Furey
James Poindexter.........Bruce Gordon
Sheriff..................Vic Allen

This is a slap dash western with a comedy element of a souse medicine man and his colored boy in armor as a ballyhoo to break up the action stuff. There is a love story in which Tom Tyler, the hero, naturally bests the crooks and wins the hand of the ranch owner's daughter in the most approved film western style. The picture is one that will be generally liked in the smaller towns where they go to that western stuff.

Incidentally this Tom Tyler looks like a comer for the small towns as a western hero and it is possible that F. B. O. is building up a corking new bet in the boy. He manages to ride well and looks like a go-getter. In this particular picture Peggy Montgomery playing opposite him does very nicely in the ingenue heroine role and looks very well indeed.

The story isn't particularly strong and for the greater part the picture is shot in exteriors. Phyllis is romantically inclined and dreams of the days when knights were bold. To a certain extent her father's ranch foreman fills the requirements, but pop has other ideas and brings a chance acquaintance from the city home with h'm with an idea that he'll make a suitable husband for the daughter. Of course he turns out to be a crook in masquerade. The hero bests him and his outlaw companion and co-worker after they have kidnapped the girl with an idea of compelling her to marry the city crook. And then father relents and lets the young couple marry. *Fred.*

GIRL IN THE RAIN

A Carloma production, starring David Butler. Claribel Campbell in the cast as feature. At Loew's New York on double feature bill Feb. 25. Running time, 48 mins.

This is a Joe McGee, if there ever was one. How the picture ever got on even a double feature

bill on a Loew daily change house will be a mystery. From the looks of things the chances are that Claribel Campbell or someone interested in her must have bankrolled the picture; otherwise there is no excuse for her being in the production. The cast, in addition to David Butler, contained Hale Hamilton; but why two fairly good actors should be saddled with so palpably an amateur is going to be one of life's mysteries.

Butler plays a double role in the picture, with the double exposures so raw that they got a laugh from the audience.

The thing to do with this one is to pass it up. *Fred.*

LET IT RAIN

Douglas MacLean production. Presented by Famous Players-Lasky. Story by Wade Boteler, George J. Crone and Earle Snell. Directed by Eddie Cline. At the Paramount, New York, week March 5. Running time, 67 minutes.
"Let-It-Rain" Riley......Douglas MacLean
The Girl.................Shirley Mason
Kelly....................Wade Boteler
Major of Marines.........Frank Campeau
Butch....................Jimmy Bradbury
Bugs.....................Lincoln Steadman
Marine Captain...........Lee Shumway
Three Crooks.............{ James Mason
                        { Edwin Sturgis
                        { Ernest Hilliard

Douglas MacLean has turned out another laugh winner in this picture, which, if anything, is better than his last screen effort and can run a race any old day with "Tell It to the Marines." Naturally the comparison has to be made, because this picture also is a marine story. But it is different from the "Tell It" picture. Here the action is laid almost entirely on board ship except for a couple of brief hotel sequences and one exhilarating comedy wallop which takes place in the mail car of a train. This brings roars of laughs and slips the great kick into the picture. It looks as though MacLean has scored a box-office bet in this one that is going to be as great as that steeplechase picture that he did some time ago.

He has the role of the leader of the marines on board the particular ship he is assigned to. He is a sergeant and has as his buddy Jimmy Bradbury. The two are constantly framing pranks and gags to be played on the gobs. The latter in their section are led by Wade Boteler, a tough gob as ever paraded a hash mark. He and Doug are constantly crossfiring each other with rather rough although playful gags. Both are in line to be promoted if they will ever stop gagging long enough to study for their commissions.

Then the girl steps into the picture in the person of Shirley Mason, whom both try to cop. She slips them her card, with her address as a fashionable hotel, and both believe that she must be extremely wealthy. When they finally call they find her the telephone girl.

It is good, wholesome fun with a dash of melodrama, and, wonder of wonders, MacLean plays a love scene in this picture, for once in his life, as though he really enjoyed it. He's usually shy about that love stuff. *Fred.*

THE TAXI DANCER

Metro-Goldwyn-Mayer picture featuring Joan Crawford and Owen Moore. Adapted from a story by R. T. Shannon, with Harry Millarde directing. At the Capitol, New York, week of March 5. Running time, 64 mins.
Joslyn Poe...............Joan Crawford
Lee Rogers...............Owen Moore
Doctor Kendall...........William Orlamond
Henry Brierhalter........Marc MacDermott
Kitty Lane...............Gertrude Astor
Stephen Bates............Rockliffe Fellowes
James Kelvin.............Douglas Gilmore
Aunt Mary................Claire McDowell
Charlie Cook.............Bert Roach

Just another southern girl come north to be pursued by men, but not unentertainingly. If anyone peeks too hard they'll find plenty of hoke scattered in this unwinding, although after the opening flash of the depreciating plantation home it'll be more or less expected.

But for all of that the cast is liable to see this one through to average receipts. It impresses as a small town picture where the reformers get themselves on the censoring board to see the dirt that's to be censored. Not that this film is overboard on dirt. But it holds its share of spice, sex and general atmosphere upon which the moral sleuths dote to snipe.

Joslyn Poe (Miss Crawford) comes up from Virginia to be a dancer in New York. Aiming for ballroom exhibition work she finally lands in a dancehall, where her boarding house friend, Lee Rogers

(Owen Moore), former card sharp, keeps an eye on her. Her girl friend is the means to a class club party where the youngster is introduced to the dancing king of the day, and both fall. A flat party results in an attack on Joslyn, the dancer makes a bluff he wants to fight in her defense, calls it off when alone with his opponent. but the latter won't quit. A wild swing of a miniature statue saves the dancer, but kills the other man, and the cops drive in.

Miss Crawford could be termed as an in and outer on this picture. Every so often comes a flash of power that may indicate this girl has something, while at other times she's too coy and clinging. That may be direction, too, albeit Millarde has handled both script and players well. There isn't much waste footage at any point.

Moore is only glimpsed at sparse intervals, yet makes something of his role of a card sharp. Joslyn is about the only character in the lineup that's on the level. Others are roues, questionable women, card sharps, etc. Douglas Gilmore is suitably despicable as the weak-willed dancer and Rockliffe Fellowes makes his presence felt if only for a minute or two. Gertrude Astor and Wm. Orlamond are the comedy sidelights in addition to Ralph Spence's titles. And these aren't bad. Some can't miss where a sense of humor abounds. It's mostly all flip chatter and should register.

"The Taxi Dancer" is one of those pictures that will do well in one town and flop in another. The flaps and their undergraduate or counter monarchs will remain interested while older men won't find it hard to gaze on Miss Crawford and her array of nightgowns. The world-wide police force authorized by a ring will be the most likely faction to object, and if not that to register disapproval by staying away.

Fairly well met at the Capitol with the title laughs smoothing over some of the slow spots. *Sid.*

THREE HOURS

First National picture, starring Corinne Griffith. Adapted from story "Purple and Fine Linen," with James Flood directing. At Strand, New York, week March 5. Running time, 59 mins.
Madeline Durkin.........Corinne Griffith
James Finlay............John Bowers
Jonathan Durkin.........Hobart Bosworth
Gilbert Wainwright......Paul Ellis
The Governess...........Ann Schaefer
Baby Durkin.............Mary Louise Miller

Corinne Griffith's last for Asher, Small & Rogers and First National hints at being one of those pictures that will roll off the laps of men but which the women may like. The male population at the Strand Sunday afternoon wasn't overly interested, but the symbolized death of a child had a few of the girls blowing their noses.

"Three Hours" is a cut-back story revolving around the havoc caused by a jealous husband. The resulting anguish is strictly mental. So, while that may be natural enough, it puts a premium upon action. And that's an ingredient this release lacks and is possibly the explanation why the masculine seat-holders will remain indifferent.

Madeline Durkin, divorced wife of the wealthy Jonathan Durkin, many years her senior, lifts the wallet of James Finlay (Mr. Bowers), rich globe-trotter, to secure clothes. Years of waiting for permission to see her daughter have finally brought a summons from the father on the child's birthday.

Meanwhile Finlay has followed the woman who has "cleaned" him and is about to turn her over to the police when she starts to tell her story. Thence the return to former days and the depicting of an unhappy marriage. Having refused a lover because of a sense of duty to her marriage vows, Madeline is humiliated at a party by her husband when he sees his wife and the suspect conversing in the garden. Little money and no friends bring about the last stand of larceny, Madeline telling all this to Finlay over a dinner table.

Only half convinced, he escorts her to her former home, where the husband sends the mother of his child up to the daughter's room. The youngster lies in her bier. The clinchless finish has Finley much concerned plus the supposition that he stands by and eventually marries the former Mrs. Durkin.

Miss Griffith looks as good as ever and gives an even performance, although histrionic honors must go to Hobart Bosworth as the husband incapable of bridling his jealousy. It's a small-cast picture weak in male principals outside of Bosworth. No other women are concerned beyond Miss Griffith, thus centering the interest on but two characters. The lover (Paul Ellis) simply flits in and out and is too much of the parlor type here to gain sympathy for either himself or the wife who loves but rejects him. Bowers is dormant throughout. Outside of the attention Bosworth draws, the only appeal from the screen is in the bond between the mother and her child, a beautiful youngster in the person of Mary Louise Miller.

Almost entirely studio-made, the interiors are of substantial appearance, while Miss Griffith's personal sightliness speaks for itself. That about sums up the "dressing" phase.

Neither great nor bad, and on its feminine appeal apparently a better matinee picture than as after-dinner entertainment. Which brings about the conclusion its sphere is in the neighborhoods, where the Griffith name should mean something and where mothers predominate.

A woman's picture.   *Sid.*

RUBBER TIRES

A. H. Sebastian presents for Alan Hale-DeMille Pictures Corp.; production released through P. D. C. Harrison Ford and Bessie Love in cast. Story by Frank Woods, adapted by Zelda Sears and Tay Garnett. Ran 62 minutes at the Hippodrome, New York, week March 7.
Mary Ellen Stack..............Bessie Love
Pat Stack..................Erwin Connelly
Charley Stack.............Junior Coghlan
Mrs. Stack.....................May Robson
Bill James..................Harrison Ford
Adolph Messer................John Patrick
Mexican....................Clarence Burton

They have everything in this one, and still it lacks punch. It's a combination of auto racing, wild west "bad man" stuff and simple bucolic romance, with no distinguishing common bond to sustain it.

Title is derived from the motor theme, the crux of which revolves about an ancient vehicular relic that is worth $10,000 to the motor car manufacturers as part of an advertising campaign. It so happens that the heroine's family selects the antique from the junk heap and in that wise is susceptible to a small fortune.

The poor Stack family had decided to sell their New York belongings and drive across the continent to take up residence on the coast. From the proceeds of the furniture sale, they acquired the ancient auto. After a number of trials and tribulations, including the actual physical parting with that car, the Stacks recover it, although they had traded it for a better vehicle, but for the unusual antique value of their original bus.

Harrison Ford, as the persistent swain who happens along always at the right moment to get the hapless Stacks out of a ditch or an accident, is opposite Bessie Love, the "brains" of her family. May Robson and Erwin Connelly as the parents and Junior Coghlan, the mischevious youngster, complete the family personnel.

This is one of those quickies that can't be taken too seriously. Mayhaps an auditor will exact a chuckle

here and there, but it will never stand analysis.

For one thing, one never saw such consistently moderate good weather. It was sunshine all the way and the director wisely overlooked those persistent storms considering the open work of that barouche. Then, too, while the hero was not at first particularly welcome, he had eased himself sufficiently into the good graces after being of practical aid in three or four emergencies, to have made it logical that his own car should be permitted to follow close behind the Stacks' vehicle. But no! that would have spoiled the heroism when he happened along at the right moments.

Like most all past P. D. C.'s, at the Hippodrome, this wouldn't be worth more than a day's rental—usually a flicker like this is encountered as part of the double-header at Loew's New York—excepting for that company's tie-up with K-A.   *Abel.*

LADYBIRD

Chadwick production with Betty Compson featured. At Academy of Music, New York, week March 7, as half double bill. Running time, around 60 minutes.

A tricky memory without paper or pencil for help and this written 17 hours afterward is responsible for absences of many names and technical information on "Ladybird" as well as Fox's "Love Makes 'Em Wild," both wrongly on a double bill at the Academy Monday night. Neither should have been linked up with another, as either is well able alone to provide amusement in its own class. "Love" is a comedy—this a mystery story with detective leanings.

For anything up to three days where mystery with well sustained suspense is useful, "Ladybird" is there. It's a well made and directed independent, all excepting its Mardi Gras scene. In New Orleans the showmen say that never has the stage or screen caught the Spirit of Mardi Gras as it is. This bears them out. Chadwick's Mardi Gras scene is as far from the real as Hollywood is from New Orleans.

In "Ladybird" the story carries and that's enough. Its players need but to follow it. There are so few stories that may be said of in pictures. Miss Compson, is in an attractive role here and looks attractively in it. She goes into a maze of adventures, to locate the chief of a crooked band she accidentally runs into while subbing for a dancer in a New Orleans cabaret.

Her quest came about through the girl's determination to leave her guardian and earn her own living, the guardian objecting to her heavy purchases.

The story opens youthfully and sexy, but gets right down to cases. When set in New Orleans, it goes the gamut of mystery, with the girl in detective role. Implausibilities don't mean a thing here because they are interesting. At times the tension is quite high.

Chadwick should be able to sell this one, if he can find something besides the Compson name to hang the publicity upon. Its title "Ladybird" won't help, unless from a well known story, and the titles are so flat they can't aid either. Still there is comedy sprinkled here and there, enough for relief.

An excellent mystery picture.   *Sime.*

Loves Makes 'Em Wild

William Fox release. Comedy, adapted from a magazine story. At Fox's Academy, New York, as one-half double bill, week March 7. Running time, around 60 minutes.

A Fox full-length comedy that is

worth a week's run in any man's film house where they would rather have entertainment than names or naked knees.

Plenty of laughs in a light story nicely carried forward, although a bit padded in sections. It's well made, holding that class finish Fox has been putting to his pictures of late, and, in fact, the comedy here will hold up so well it may be excused that Fox slapped no "box office name" into the cast.

But, at that, John Harron and Sally Shipps, in the juvenile leads, are interesting enough or will be to the youthfuls to make them relish the principals as well as the fun of the film.

It's about a meek young man in fear of losing his job and awaiting the time until he will be independent through saving sufficient to have a weekly income. Meanwhile he is noting in a diary the **browbeaters who take advantage of him. They include the assistant boss, janitor and the elevator man.**

When a quack doctor tells the mild-mannered boy he will die in two weeks, the boy declines a cure and steps out with a companion to spend the $4,000 he has saved, within two weeks at the Ritz.

An urge is within him through a stenog in the place. Her Howarth eyes get him, but they can't hold him. Later, though, when the stenog hears he's at the Ritz and steps in on his party the boy goes wild, cleans up his enemies and returns to a graduated job at much money.

There are several gags worked as bits, thereby fitting into the story. One is Jimmy Barry's best, that of the pantomimic flirtation; but there are several others that the picture itself owns, and very good. Titles are so so, with a great chance lost in them.

The low comedian (name not caught) has a big bit in trying to get $100 bills girls at a banquet shunted into their stockings or breasts. He tries for the bills by getting the girls to dance and shaking them up until the bills drop out on the floor. It's entirely new as far as known and a dandy. He's also copped the "bird" bit from "Glory" (Fox), and it's a howl.

Well balanced company, and the caster should have credit there.

Good performance all of the way, with no one pushing any one else out of focus. More of this balanced stuff in cast and work would make many another picture better, as it has this one.

There's only one way to bill "Love Makes 'Em Wild," and that is to say:

"Come in and laugh."   *Sime.*

MIDNIGHT WATCH

A Rayart Picture, presented by W. Ray Johnston. Story by Trem Carr. Directed by Charles Hunt. Shown at Loew's New York, N. Y., on double feature bill. Running time, 56 minutes.
Bob Breemer..................Roy Stewart
Chief Callahan..............David Torrence
Rose Denton..............Mary McAllister

A society crook melodrama with the college boy detective as the hero. The story is just so-so and the acting about the same. The production, however, is good and there is sufficient suspense to make the picture stand up in the daily change houses, especially where double feature bills are the vogue. At Loew's New York last Friday it was the strongest link of the bill with the names of the three members of the cast above played up in the billing.

Roy Stewart has the role of the college boy copper, who is in love with the social secretary of a wealthy family who is accused of the robbery of a pearl necklace. Through this theft he manages to run down the leader of the underworld, who moves in the same so-

cial set as the employers of his sweetheart.

But he does not accomplish this until he has been "broke" and returned to harness by his chief who didn't like his over assurance that he was on the right track. He is put in uniform and on on "the midnight watch" from which the picture gets its title.

Stewart manages well enough as the hero, while Mary McAllister is sweet as the "shero" of the cast. David Torrence does well enough as the chief of police, although he has little to do.

The audience is "in" all the while **on who the real crook and king of the underworld is so that does away with a lot of the mystery that could have been sustained had it not been disclosed early in the picture which one of the characters was the ringleader.**   *Fred.*

THE LOVE OF SUNYA

United Artists release produced by the Swanson Producing Corp. starring Gloria Swanson. From the screen story by Earle Browne based on the Charles Guernon and Max Marcin play, "The Eyes of Youth." Directed by Albert Parker. At the Roxy, New York, week beginning March 12. Running time 72 minutes. Cast, Gloria Swanson, John Boles, Raymond Hackett, Robert Schable, Flobelle Fairbanks, Anders Randolf, Pauline Garon, Ian Keith, Andres De Segurola, John Miltern, Hugh Miller, Ivan Lebedeff and Forrest Huff.

For her first release under the direction of United Artists, Gloria Swanson chose to make a new screen version of "The Eyes of Youth." It originally served as a film starring role for Clara Kimball Young about eight years ago. That was at the time that C. K. Y. was supposed to be about washed up in the picture business, but the role of that picture brought her back with a bang.

As much cannot be said for Miss Swanson, for this picture proves to be an extremely draggy affair, even though the star personally achieves a triumph in her characterization. The part gives her every opportunity to make good and she does so with a vengeance. But the picture is not what could be honestly termed a box office knockout. It is doubtful what it will do in its second week at the big new Roxy where world's records were shattered during the first two days of business.

There has been little change in the story of the heroine of "The Eyes of Youth," who through the medium of a reincarnated Hindoo priest and the crystal that he bears enables her to see what the future holds in store for her in the event that she chooses either of two men with whom to spend her life. The girl is really in love with a young man but holds ambitions to become a great singer and the opportunity is offered her. At the same time her family is in financial difficulties and her father seeks to marry her off to a man of wealth. The question is which of the three men will she choose.

The crystal first reveals her career as a singer being exploited by the impresario and living the life of a demi-mondaine with he reaping the profit while she pays as a woman is supposed to, with unhappiness and being compelled to see the man she really loves shot down before her eyes when the bullet is intended for him who has been exploiting her.

The second sequence shows what she would endure as the wife of the wealthy man who would tire of her after five years for a flapper who would lead him to frame her so that a divorce could be obtained. Here she is shamed and without friends, wandering the streets an outcast. The dope portion of this that was in the original has been omitted.

Then having seen the end of both of these paths the girl turns to her young lover in defiance of her father's wishes.

Nothing about the picture which makes it unusual except the direction and the corking performance by the star. The supporting cast is adequate with De Segurola standing out in the role of the impresario.

Albert Parker got some corking shots with his direction, but the picture should have been edited with more of an eye to speed of action. The slow tempo makes it appear as though the picture was two hours in length, while in reality it is about an hour and 15 minutes in showing. *Fred.*

METROPOLIS

UFA production, German-made, released through Famous Players-Lasky. No player starred or featured in American presentation. Without press sheet as yet available, technical information not at hand. Opened at Rialto (Publix), New York, March 5, indefinitely. Running time, 107 minutes.

John Masterman....Alfred Abel
Eric, his son....Gustav Froelich
Rotwang, the inventor..Rudolf Klein-Rogge
Joseph....Theodor Loos
No. 7....Heinrich George
Mary....Brigitte Helm

"Metropolis" has mass appeal over here, but without class appeal of any character. It's a weird story, visionary all of the time, without any degree of unusual imagination and ofttimes monotonous. Withal, a puzzling film that might deceive the most expert picture showman, either way. Yet it holds something that holds the picture audience and will draw to a picture house.

That may be its weirdness or its production or photography or subject matter of 100 years hence or so, or its attempted massiveness of scenes—or that it reels off like a Henry Ford dream—mechanical—human labor of the future.

Without a press sheet exactly what is striven for must be doped out. It appears to be that the mechanical can never wholly substitute for the human labor, nor must Capital entirely exhaust its working people or that the human physical elements may never be mechanically transposed.

These things will fling an ordinary picture audience at their limitations into a turmoil of thought, meanwhile held to some suspense by the supposed vastness of it all; big machinery halls, the huge crowds of labor people; mythical ultra-modern city of 100 years hence with its underground living abode for the laborers, or the perpetual lock step with its dirge that runs throughout the film.

After all of this for the serious side and before the picture has been running very long one is inclined to laugh at its plain absurdities, its open face scheme of story and the merciless persecution of poor Mary. Mary is probably the most chased girl of the screen. They chased her everywhere every minute, up alleys, into rooms, over roofs and what not. If Mary saw a chance to escape the open door closed just before she reached it. The only thing muffed was a blackface comedian to get the laughs in this stupendous scene of a "Haunted House."

And Eric, the son of his father, who went down into the subterreanean town for the first time in his 20 years to see the village and Mary. Caught by the skirt as he was wrangling with some vamps in burlesque wheel costumes, Eric fell for the dame. That was Mary, also about 20 and the first time she ever had seen inside of a two-story home. Mary had large blue eyes. Someone had told her to stare and plenty. Mary did.

Down in the village to which the workmen went in elevators holding 1,000 people or more, from appearances, Mary was a sort of Aimee McPherson evangelist without the scandal. Mary preached peace, before and after she landed Eric (a much better German name than John for a young chaser).

But Eric wasn't Mary's only chaser. The other was Rotwang, an inventor. After he had perfected Metropolis as a one-man town belonging to John Masterman, Rotwang, who looks like David Belasco did 15 years ago, started to pull the final surprise upon his Masterman. He had fashioned a human figure of metal. All required was to get his lights working properly, to send or pour any human he pleased into the figure—and he selected Mary, but before capturing Mary, Rot had to chase her about 18 miles of hallways.

He put everything of Mary's into the figure, excepting Mary's peace loving soul, but a caption said a soul couldn't be placed into steel, probably having in mind a few theatrical managers. So when the No. 2 Mary came forth, she was a hell-raiser, preached socialism to the workmen and started the machinery going the wrong way.

It led to a flood, to the workmen going upstairs, to the real Mary saving the children, to Eric getting his Mary and to the Masterman taking a tumble to himself.

In all of this is trick photography and trick production. Probably there never has been a picture made with so much seemingly trick production stuff. Nothing appears to be on the level in this film. In the trick photography is one bit of swirling electric lights that can't be figured out by any method.

In the production end seems to be several massive sets that either were magnified from miniatures or drawn as sketches and vitalized. The impossible unison of the movements of humans suggests this. In any event the effect is big for the 17 percenters. But the photography of "Metropolis" does not compare with that of "Variety," which it slightly suggests, although the production end here lies over the other like a tent, whether it's faked or no.

A letter recently received by Variety (this paper) and written by the Aktiegesellschaft fur Spiegeltechnik of Berlin advised that in the UFA picture "Metropolis," shortly to be shown in New York, appeared 13 scenes of the firm's system called the Schufftan Process.

No one in New York who could be reached had heard of the Schufftan System. It may be like the "Valley of the Lepers" in "Ben-Hur." But "Metropolis" appears to have some sort of a process introduced to make the immensity of the effect or to aid it, in much the same way pictures have found how to multiply crowds as must have been done here also. At times the crowds look enormous.

But "Metropolis" will make the commoners talk if no more than to say, "You must see that crazy picture."

From understanding the German version was a pretty clumsy affair. Over here and especially recut by Channing Pollock, there is quite good continuity, as far as that could be gotten, while Mr. Pollock's captions have a dignity in language and phrasing that lends greatly to the impressiveness. Without impressiveness this picture would have to fall down because of its blooeyness.

Brigitee Helm as Mary did nicely in acting when assuming the No. 2 dual role. That forced her to the other extreme of expression. Alfred Abel as the boss of the works did well the cold, stern driver of men and money. Gustav Froelich, the son, had a heavy part he played lightly for value and must have been selected for his juvenile appearance. Theodor Loos was Joseph or No. 7, probably Joseph, and with plenty of beard. He made it resemble Russian more than German, also beating off a mob of several thousand, as did Eric at one time. How those Germans, single handed, can handle mad mobs in pictures is pretty close to a mirthful miracle.

For UFA to say this picture cost almost $2,000,000, if not meaning marks, sounds like the bologna, unless the actors got it or the processes were unusually expensive. It is more easily believable that the picture was comparatively cheap for the eyeful results obtained.

Some sex stuff here and there and a cooch dancer! Yes, sir, a coocher. In the revigorated mechanical figure, and a pretty good coocher, too, but not so thick around the hips as German coochers generally are. But then you must remember that this young lady was made to order.

Houses that played "Variety" won't miss with "Metropolis." It's the same UFA and its weirdness will at least stand up. But don't invite the readers of "The American Mercury" to see it. *Sime.*

THE SHOW

Tod Browning production, released by Metro-Goldwyn-Mayer. Starring John Gilbert, with Renee Adoree and Lionel Barrymore featured. Story by Charles Tenney Jackson. At Capitol, New York, week March 12. Running time, 70 minutes.

Cock Robin....John Gilbert
Salome....Renee Adoree
The Greek....Lionel Barrymore
The Soldier....Edward Connelly
Lena....Gertrude Short
The Ferrett....Andy McLennan

Something of a question as to how the role that John Gilbert is playing in this picture will react regarding the player in the future productions. It seems to have been something of a mistake to cast Gilbert as a highly egotistical panderer such as he here portrays. It undoubtedly will hurt his general popularity with the women, for while he is a great lover there is nothing romantic in the character, it being a sordid role of the type which tends to degrade. One thing it does do, and that is to give Gilbert an opportunity to troupe. He does do that to perfection. From a box-office angle the picture is certain to do business, for with the names of John Gilbert, Renee Adoree and Lionel Barrymore up in the lights for a single production, how could it be otherwise?

Something about the story suggests touches of "The Merry-Go-Round" and "Lilliom." Just a blending of the two, with the result that there is a new yarn.

The scenes are laid in Hungary, where the hero is the barker making the openings for an illusion show and doing the lecture on the inside. He is a hellion with the ladies, and cops 'em right and left. The "blow-off" for the chumps is a tabloid version of "Salome," which gives an excuse for a cooch dancer. In this spot Tod Browning grabbed off a double for Renee Adoree who could throw a mean wiggle. And boy, what a "grind" she staged!

A shepherd from the hills brings down part of his flock to dispose of them and likewise his daughter for a little trip to the city. Daughter sees the barker and falls like a ton. He lets her buy him his supper. She also pays for their joint photographs, and in all is right on the way to be a general chump for the boy.

But things happen fast that night. The Greek (Mr. Barrymore) and one of his gangsters know that the shepherd has a roll, and they bump him off, expecting to get the money, but he was wise and left it with his daughter. When hearing of the murder she rushes to the one person that she knows—the magimp—with her troubles, and he is willing to take care of her after he sees the roll that she is packing.

At that point the coocher, who has been in love with him right along, but who had to discard him because the Greek, with whom she had been carrying on an affair, interfered, breaks into the barker's apartment and chases the country girl out of the room, she being turned out by him after he administers a beating. When the police are after him for the money that he grabbed from the girl, the dancer shields him in her apartment. He remains there for some little time until the Greek gets wise to what is going on. He steals one of the poisonous reptiles from the pit show and puts it into the barker's hiding place, only to be bitten himself a little later.

In the finish the Salome dancer is back on the show and the boy is once more making the openings, the two of them having "found" themselves when the dancer's brother is hung and her father dies. The closing flash shows the two working and a couple of dames standing in front of the show looking on, one of them remarking: "They say that she hid him in her apartment for months and she lived there all alone with him," to which her companion, also a wise-looking little flapper, retorts: "Well, who wouldn't?"

Gilbert and Miss Adoree certainly play their roles right up to the hilt, and Barrymore as the heavy furnished a flock of menace where it was most needed. Edward Connelly as the blind father of the dancer also contributed a studied characterization. Gertrude Short as the "butter and egg girl" from the country likewise slipped over a good performance.

Tod Browning handled the direction very skillfully, for it would have been all too easy to slop over in a lot of spots in this story, and that would have gotten the picture in dutch with the censors.

Joe Farnham, who titled, did not go out of his way to contribute anything brilliant in this respect for this picture. He has done far better work in the past. *Fred.*

SENSATION SEEKERS

Universal production. Billie Dove and Huntley Gordon featured. Adapted from Ernest Pascal's story, "Egypt." Lois Weber director. Cast also includes Raymond Bloomer. At New York Hippodrome week March 14. Running time, 65 mins.

This Universal picture runs along in a far-fetched groove until near the close, when the punch comes in a water scene where a yacht collides with another boat and sinks. It goes down Billie Dove as the girl and Huntley Gordon as the rich suitor more than earn their money.

Photographically the picture measures up, and in some of the main climaxes Lois Weber has done a splendid job of directing.

While an apparent small-town environment is used the way that some of the fast-living men and women jazz things up in search of a night thrill may start something.

A preacher—he's a good fellow at that; doesn't pull off any of the kind of stuff that Elmer Gantry, Sinclair's preacher-man, does in his latest book that is causing no end of present-day gossip—is one of the main principals in this U picture.

The story up to the destruction of the yacht was preachy and more preachy, but, boy, oh, boy! what a camera kick that capsizing of the yacht with the girl and the drunk sweety gives!

That closing water stuff just about saves the picture.

Mr. Bloomer appears as the parson, and he never appeared to better advantage if he didn't have too many "doubles" working for him. In a number of pictures where strenuous athletic work is required Mr. Bloomer is known to have been "doubled"; there's a reason, of course, when a man is making a picture and wants it finished without his leading man carted away to a hospital for physical repairs.

Miss Dove is an eyeful from a camera angle and she knows how to wear clothes.

That raid was about the poorest seen in films since Volstead got his name in constitutional print.

Any of the neighborhoods will get a kick out of that final scene with Miss Dove and Mr. Gordon in the sinking boat. That's real picture stuff. *Mark.*

THE BELOVED ROGUE

John Barrymore in "The Beloved Rogue," United Artists' picture, directed by Alan Crosland. Screen play by Paul Bern. Photography by Joe August. Titles by Walter Anthony. At the Mark Strand, New York, March 12. Running time, 129 minutes (139 minutes with prolog).

Francois Villon............John Barrymore
Louis XI.....................Conrad Veidt
Charlotte de Vauxcelles.....Marceline Day
Duke of Burgundy............Lawson Butt
Thilbault d'Aussigny.........Henry Victor
Jehan.....................Slim Summerville
Nicholas.......................Mack Swain
Beppo......................Angelo Rossitto
Astrologer..................Nigel de Brulier
Villon's Mother.............Lucy Beaumont
Olivier........................Otto Matiesen
The Abbess...................Jane Winton
Margot..........................Rose Dione
Duke of Orleans..........Bertram Grassby
Tristan l'Hermite..........Dick Sutherland

For the elaborateness of purpose, for the time consumed and for the recklessness with which huge bodies of extras were assembled, the new picture delivers an astonishingly low average of entertainment. It will draw because the name of Barrymore will take care of that, but the feature will scarcely go in for more than a week for slightly more than the run of grosses.

Seen at an early afternoon performance on the day it started for the Strand, the reviewer could not see it as a builder, but it looked rather like one of those pictures that starts at its best under heavy exploitation and then will run its course only pretty well.

The extreme length of a romantic costume subject, for one thing, is against it. Besides, as a purely romantic offering it has its defects. Much of the glamor is missing in the hero, who is for most of the time rather a disheveled sort of person—a picturesque enough rogue at all times, but not always the height of splendid romance. Briefly, this Don Juan doesn't always glow in triumph, but often plays the underdog.

The story isn't in the Barrymore "groove," but more in that of William Fairbanks'. There are scenes scattered through the long footage, that Fairbanks would revel in. He could make them live, shining with vitality. The best Barrymore could do with them was to give them a sort of gay grace, which was not the point at all, since the production is on an enormous scale and called for kick and voltage.

The story, of course, is a variant of the old Francois Villon who has served in "If I Were King," "Don Caesar de Bazan" and innumerable other romances. He is the jaunty scalawag, the only real and intense thing about him being his deep patriotism.

Louis XI condemned him to death for some harem scarem deviltry, and then pardons and receives him into prime favor when he saves the royal ward, Charlotte, from forced marriage with a henchman of the plotting Burgundy. Later Burgundy abducts the girl to his own castle stronghold, there to force upon her a marriage that will further his schemes for seizing the throne.

Villon goes back to his ragamuffin companions, his scheme being to demand the Paris beggars' rights to free entertainment at a royal wedding, in the hope that once within Burgundy's gate he can effect a rescue. From this point the melodramatic romantic action is swift and pictorially striking, but the part screamed for Fairbanks. Villon climbs the tower where Charlotte is held prisoner, is shot by archers, captured, tortured under the sneering eyes of Burgundy, and then exposed naked and broken before the jeering populace. It is here that he notes and appeals to his beggar companions for succor, and in response their steps out King Louis himself, disguised as a vagabond, but backed with an army of beggars who reveal themselves as royal soldiery.

The humiliation of Burgundy and the return of Villon as the King's favorite follow, with the marriage of the hero to his long-worshipped Charlotte.

Pictorially the picture is strong. The romantic backgrounds have been skillfully designed, and the massing and grouping of large numbers of people have been managed with boldness that is particularly striking. *Rush.*

The Gallant Fool

Rayart production, presented by W. Ray Johnston. Story by George W. Pyper, directed by Duke Worne. Starring Billy Sullivan with cast including Hazel Deane, Rath Boye, Frank Naker, Jimmy Aubrey and Frederick Shumann-Heink. At Loew's Circle, one day, March 15, as half double bill.

Story weak and ancient. Direction below standard, evidently due to lack of material. Picture too obviously constructed with a view to low figures on the expense sheets.

Billy Sullivan makes the perfect young American. He'd probably be pointed out with pride, even on Broadway. The princess in distress, Hazel Deane, is not so good, and Frederick Shumann-Heink might be a crown prince and might not.

The mob scenes are sure to raise laughs if this film is ever shown in higher grade houses. The alleged "mobs" are composed of about two dozen extras.

Frank Baker is overdrawn as the villainous prime minister, while the royal army is not shown to contain more than a couple of dozen soldiers at any one time.

Jimmie Aubrey, as valet-chauffeur to the American, gets faint legitimate laughs, while a group of queerly dressed brigands also register for same.

The double love motif sags throughout and the change in places transforming the American into a crown prince is not effected in a manner to create suspense.

THE SNARL OF HATE

Sam Bishoff presentation, directed by Noel Mason Smith, featuring "Silverstreak." Story by Edward Curtiss and Noel Smith. Cast including Johnnie Walker, Mildred June, Jack Richardson and Wheeler Oakman. At Loew's Circle, March 15, one day, half double bill.

Penny-thrillers tame in comparison to this one. Under careful direction usually boring desert scenes have been cut to right length and presented in fashion that holds.

Johnnie Walker is two people in this picture. The odd man is his bearded brother, killed early by a human vulture who preys on luckless prospectors. The whole of the first half of this picture is quite mixed, except for the animal star fight scenes.

Scene switches to the city, where the smooth-shaven twin tracks down the murderers through the discovery of a mating glove by Silverstreak in the home of "the gal's" guardian.

Walker stages a night club scrap with Wheeler Oakman, assistant villain, realistically. He has the knack of seeming to hit hard down pat, getting tense silence instead of laughs.

Mildred June displayed to good effect.

"Snarl of Hate" is more than a title. The dog registers a snarl in comparison to which hate is a mild passion.

The Fighting Failure

Nat Levine presents "The Fighting Failure," with Peggy Montgomery featured. Story by Mary Eunice McCarthy. Directed by E. G. Boyle. Cast also includes Lucy Beaumont, Sidney Franklin, Ernest Hilliard and Richard Travers. At the Stanley, New York, one day, March 11, Running time, 64 mins.

Only thing missing from this one is the kitchen sink; the meller dish as served heaped to overflowing with all the old Jack Dalton stuff, plus some of that that has surfeited the screen from all angles.

The "failure" is a pugilist who is set for a big bout, but his ma slips him K. O. drops handed her by a supposed pal of the pug and she to keep him from the ring puts the "silencers" in his soup. He then ducks west to the open spaces, where any passing stranger of the J. B. ranch can drop in and get a cowboy's job. Of course, the bad boys that plotted against him in the ring move out there and one can guess the rest.

By way of trying for comedy, an over-fed Jewish man steps off of a Bronx express, so to speak, and becomes a romantic cowboy.

There's so much villainy that one couldn't dent it with machine gun fire.

It is funny about some of those parlor-made westerns; the eastern audiences are given the impression that everything goes on the western ranches these days.

This one will be lucky to get bookings where double features are a necessity. *Mark.*

THE WRECK

Columbia Pictures Production. Featuring Shirley Mason and Malcolm McGregor. Written by Dorothy Howell. Directed by William Craft. Distributed by Columbia. At Loew's New York on double feature bill March 11. Running time, 59 minutes.

Just an ordinary program picture unravelling a combination underworld and mistaken identity story with a train wreck incorporated.

The underworld theme is very Chautauqua and the other element or counter story too sacchariny for any but the yokels of the hinterlands, if there still is such a crop in captivity.

Shirley Mason does what she can as the unfortunate young wife of a yegg being railroaded to the pen for something her husband has done.

While en route the train is wrecked, and through a toss in the lap of a strange handbag she is identified as the wife of Robert Brooks and rushed to his mother's home.

The real wife, killed in the wreck, had gold-digging tendencies, according to Robert. When confronted with Ann he carries on the ruse so as not to disillusion his mother. Ann's husband, believed dead, turns up to plague the couple with his presence, but later meets death in an auto accident.

Not overburdened by action, save in two spots, both wrecks. Just an ordinary potboiler. *Edba.*

CHARLES XII

(SWEDISH)

Los Angeles, March 22.

Although Eric Von Stroheim has been talking for years about producing a picture that will require two sittings for the complete unreeling, it remained for the Swedes to present the first production in divided projection.

"Charles XII" is in 24 reels, covering the entire life of one of Sweden's most popular monarchs from the time of his ascension to the throne at 15 until his death. It is said to be the most expensive picture produced in Sweden to date, representing $350,000. Started by the Historic Film Company of Stockholm, organized especially to make this one picture, a wealthy Swede, Herman Rasch, had to come to the rescue when the production cost far exceeded first estimates.

The picture was intended primarily as educational. It adheres closely to historic fact, particularly in regard to the odd half-crazy character of the king. Hjalmar Bergman, who made the adaptation, wove in a little love story between a Swedish sergeant and the daughter of a major's widow but it is essentially a chronicle of military and political events rather than a plotted narrative.

The presentation in America is being made by W. J. Adams, who has handled a number of Swedish travelogues in this country. Thus far it has exhibited in Boston and Brooklyn, the intention being first to tap the communities where there is a Scandinavian element.

The direction of John W. Brunius is intelligent and workmanlike. Photography is straightaway, in general good, although not up to American standards in lighting. Acting is of a high order. Gustav Ekman, as the king, gave reality to a man who is one of the most bizarre figures in history. Mona Martenson, who played the sergeant's sweetheart, is to be brought to this country by Metro-Goldwyn-Mayer, it is said. None of the characters has any particular prominence. Great stretches of footage occur between the appearances on the screen of the king himself.

At Philharmonic Auditorium were unreeled 12 reels one night and 12 another. Subtitles entirely in Swedish.

The picture is totally impractical in length, theme and character for straight commercial exhibition, as it is simply a patriotic proposition. The number of characters and battles is almost confusing, although with English subtitles this confusion would be greatly minimized.

Charles XII is a national hero of Sweden. He was a sort of Lincoln among monarchs, plain, severe, asking no one to do anything he would not do himself. He lived without style or ostentation in daily contact with his people and at the head of his army, suffering their privations and exposing himself to their dangers. He was killed in battle.

Coming to the throne when a mere boy, his cousin, the King of Poland, in league with the Czar of Russia and the King of Denmark, attempted to take advantage of his youth, but the lad quickly halted his enemies, administering a series of smashing defeats. The schemers and charmers of the courts were powerless before Charles XII's directness and bluntness. He was a woman-hater all of his life. From this arose legends that Charles XII was really a woman.

Such a character is novel, different and interesting.

EVENING CLOTHES

F. P.-L. picture starring Adolphe Menjou. From the play, "The Man in Dress Clothes," by Andre Picard and Yves Mirande. Directed by Luther Reed from the continuity by John McDermott. Running time, 59 minutes. At the Paramount, New York, week March 19.

Lucien	Adolphe Menjou
Germaine	Virginia Valli
Lazarre	Noah Beery
Fox Trot	Louise Brooks
Henri	Lido Manetti
Germaine's father	Andre Cheron

Adolphe Menjou in another typically engaging high comedy, all fluff and class and made amusing by its jaunty grace. Presumably the story is of French origin and the producers would be wise to make their selections for this star from Paris. Menjou has a big draw among the women, to whom his sophisticated types are fascinating. The French do these things best.

Here Menjou is happily fitted with an appropriately suave piece calculated to enhance his feminine following. The whole production has a delightful suavity with a background of elegance, both star and production shrewdly designed to attract the women fans. "Evening Clothes" will draw through the star and will entertain on the screen, besides adding to the prestige of Menjou.

The production in its artistic nicety keeps pace with the spirit of elegance in the story of French high life. It is pretty much done in interiors which approach perfection of style and quiet taste. The story is told with a bland sort of restraint. In spots where the director might have splurged in the familiar style of overdone movies he has used judgment.

One notable instance—the first of the sort that has come to notice—the action moves into a Paris night club. To any director working along stereotyped lines, this episode would have been the inescapable cue for a floor show involving half-naked dancers. Nothing of the sort appears in "Evening Clothes." The story holds itself to its characters and to its action, and ornamentation for the sake of mere display is rigidly put aside. The play has good sex values, always handled with utmost delicacy.

That is the spirit of the whole picture. The hero lives in a luxurious apartment, but so skillfully are the sets designed that the backgrounds merely create incidental atmosphere in accord with the characters, and then do not intrude. This is a triumph of designing genius. It expresses the newest technique in the studio. Probably it does the product no good with the vast generality of fans, who want their comedy rough and their splendors of high life on a more lavish and obvious scale, but such pictures as this one will gain friends among the more intelligent of the screen public.

The story itself is light and entirely without surface drama. Germaine makes a marriage of convenience with Lucien, rich but rather crude country nobleman. His manners offend her and she revolts against what she terms his boorishness. Her aloofness startles Lucien on their nuptial night—a scene managed with conspicuous smoothness—and he takes measures next morning to change the situation.

Turning three-quarters of his fortune over to the bride-in-name-only, he goes to Paris, there to acquire social polish. His tutelage takes him among the women of the night clubs, where his adventures are varied and spicy, but he remains true to Germaine. When he goes broke, one of the ladies of the evening he has entertained returns to pay back her fee, explaining "there was no sale." The girl (neatly played by the trim Louise Brooks) explains to the wife, who has come to ask her husband for a divorce, the moral or "sporting" status of a girl who welches on a rich marriage. This gives the near-bride a new angle on the affair, and she comes to Lucien's rescue with money, agreeing he is a thoroughbred. *Rush.*

WHITE FLANNELS

Warner Bros. comedy dramatic feature, featuring Louise Dresser as a character old woman. Story by Lucian Cary; scenario by Graham Baker. Picture directed by Lloyd Bacon, Ted Stevens, assistant. Cameraman Ed Du Par. Running time, 67 minutes. At Warner's, New York, March 19, in connection with a new Vitaphone program.

Mrs. Jacob Politz	Louise Dresser
Frank Politz	Jason Robards
Anne	Virginia Browne Faire
Ed	Warner Richmond
Jacob Politz	George Nichols
Paul	Brooks Benedict
Berenice Nolden	Rose Blossom
Paul's sister	Rosemary Cooper

Louise Dresser, up to now one of the best of the grande dames on the screen, is here disclosed as a character actress of fine abilities. In a dull and colorless part, as the mother in a coal mine town and against the drab background of a miner's cottage, she stands out from the story by sheer power and delicacy of delineation. She gives to the difficult role deft shadings and a certain insight that almost makes an impossible picture absorbing.

When you have made this acknowledgement to Miss Dresser you have about covered all that is worth while in the film, which otherwise in story and direction is graded for the daily changes and not so forte at that. It has no dramatic punch, no color, except the grime of coal and its monotonous locale and no effective situations. Part of the action is set in the university to which the young miner-son goes to better himself, but this staging is cheap and false and never once convinces.

With the single exception of the mother role the characters are dull and uninteresting people, as they come on the screen, and they are made no better by the handling they receive at the hands of the supporting cast. The characters are all fiction and they are played by just actors directed in a theatrical way for the most part to get their effects in the old-fashioned melodramatic style.

That Miss Dresser could draw a convincing and compelling picture of a humble, dogged Polak mother who schemed and plotted for the betterment of her son in a curious combination of blunt determination and keenly subtle intrigue. The bit where she sees a boarding house waitress about to marry the boy and defeat her ambitions for him, and the episodes where she starts a counter-plot was delicate drama of the best kind, superbly played by the veteran ballad singer and pantomimist.

That the scene of the college dinner was grossly overdone in maudlin sentimentality, was no fault of Miss Dresser. She played with restraint while the scene was hooped up for hokum sympathy of the crudest. The waitress (played by the way of Rose Blossom, a dark-eyed girl who has dramatic possibilities, not realized here) gets the boy, after all and the old woman's dreams for the future of her son are shattered when he is dropped from college. The author seemed to think this was a happy ending, and it may have been when the story was in print. But in its screen translation it didn't work out that way, to the satisfaction of at least one viewer. But that was only one glaring flaw in a picture that never once was convincing in its general aspect. *Rush.*

THE DEMI-BRIDE

Metro-Goldwyn-Mayer production made from the story by F. Hugh Herbert and Florence Ryerson. Norma Shearer starred and Lew Cody featured. Directed by Robert Z. Leonard. At the Capitol, New York, week March 20. Running time, 76 minutes.

Criquette	Norma Shearer
Philippe Levaux	Lew Cody
Monsieur Girard	Lionel Belmore
Gaston	Tenon Holtz
Madame Girard	Carmel Myers
Lola	Dorothy Sebastian
School Teacher	Nora Cecil

Despite the box-office draft of the star, Norma Shearer, "The Demi-Bride" is a tedious picture, and, all told, just fair. Its story is one of those oft-told things about the girl who had to work like the devil to get herself a husband and then it turns out that the poor fellow, once hooked, falls in love with his wife.

Here the atmosphere is French and the girl is Criquette, daughter of a man whose second wife is somewhat of a stepper and whose stepping partner is a well-known rapscallion named Philippe Levaux. Inasmuch as the girl Criquette has set her cap for Levaux and as she catches her step-mother holding hands (yes, it's a clean French atmosphere that this picture portrays) she has enough on the pair to make them readily amenable to any of her whims. And her main whim is to marry Levaux.

So when her father gets hep to her stepmother's carrying on, Criquette saves both Philippe and her stepmother from exposure, tricking the scene to make it appear that she is calling on Philippe and that he is anxious to make arrangements for a marriage.

Once the marriage has been pulled, the picture does perk up a bit, for upon arriving at Philippe's apartment after the marriage the bride and groom discover one of the other girl friends lying on Philippe's bed in a thoroughly pickled condition. This gal had gotten stewed for the singular purpose of wising up the young bride to the kind of a man she had married, but by this time the husband was so thoroughly in love with his unwanted matrimonial acquisition that there seemed no chance of his straying from the path that marks wedded happiness. And this fact provided a happy ending.

The film itself is entirely studio made, the exteriors being far, far in the minority, while the interiors are not particularly elaborate. These facts, plus the small cast (Shearer, Cody and Myers are the only ones with anything to do) stamp "The Demi-Bride" as an unambitious production which must have depended strongly on the story itself. But as the story itself doesn't hold up, the picture is a disappointment, although there is a remote possibility that where the line "Demi-Bride" can be used to recall memories of "Demi-Virgin," something may be done. But to put this one over, a smart selling campaign is required of any theatre.

What Every Girl Should Know

Warner Brothers picture, directed by Charles (Chuch) Reissner. Patsy Ruth Miller featured. At Broadway, New York, week March 21. Runs about 60 minutes.

"What Every Girl Should Know" as a title here must be not to let the soup burn.

After watching this maudlin story for an hour or more, that's the nearest relation it carried to hold up the supposed box office title.

It's about a boy, support of his sister and little brother, who got sent away for driving a booze truck of cases he presumed contained glassware. That left his relatives for the municipal home, where they were finally rescued by a wealthy window with a grown up son.

The rest had its complications, including a tennis match, but hurried through without an explanation of what happened to the conspirators who nearly separated the lovers. It was quite sad.

Almost as sad as Patsy Ruth Miller trying to play a 17-year-old girl.

No credit here for anyone, taking in the director. Chuck Reisner, and also the tennis match, about as poorly handled in method and execution as any athletic game could be.

Strictly a title picture, and a deceptive one in that. Nothing here but the title may be depended upon, other than Miss Miller's fans, and they will be disappointed in seeing her play this role, unless the age is taken out of the caption. Neither do the captions help by themselves.

Sime.

EASY PICKINGS

First National release starring Anna Q. Nilsson, with Kenneth Harlan and Billy Bevan featured. George Archainbaud directed; Frank Griffin produced; from story by William A. Burton and Paul A. Cruger. Runs 61 minutes. Hippodrome, New York, week March 21.

Mary Ryan	Anna Q. Nilsson
Peter Van Horne	Kenneth Harlan
Stewart	Philo McCullough
The Detective	Billy Bevan
Tony	Jerry Miley
Dr. Naylor	Charles Sellon
Remus	Zack Williams
Mandy	Gertrude Howard

This one will sell itself to the pop priced exhibitor on the strength of that naive fade-out when the mystery melodrama viewed on the screen ends with the conventional clinch and irises into a picture auditorium where the audience within the film story is shown getting up to leave. Among them are Anna Q. Nilsson, Kenneth Harlan and Philo McCullough, heroine, hero and villain, respectively, of the photoplay, who are viewing themselves. Other members of the audience are endowed with titles commenting on the musculine appeal of the hero, and one fan questions Miss Nilsson what her middle initial stands for.

Without that it's mediocre stuff which the producers probably figured would not do. There is no getting away from the fact that the familiar hoke of the secret chambers in the mysterious house, the black-hooded figures, the spooky lights-off and lights-on, along with the artificial frenzy built up by the sure-fire darky maid and butler, are popularly appealing. There is enough of the spook stuff to grip attention, although one views it with tongue-in-cheek and snorts at the needless extension of it all.

For a time it becomes rather confusing, this being explained by two of the sympathetic characters alternating as the unknown masked quantity. Of course, some details, on analysis, are never cleared up.

It's one of those stories about a will, the crooked lawyer, the unwilling female dupe who is coerced into personating the rightful heir, the hero's attachment for the pseudo-villainess—and the inevitable banal explanation that she is not a crookess after all; she was trapped in the house looking for documents which will prove her father was the man whose invention was stolen by the dead man. No use trying to unravel the involved plot.

It holds audience interest, which is sufficient unto the purpose thereof, although the ultimate audience reaction with the exit march would be one of tolerant tittering were it not relieved by the novel conclusion of a story within a story.

It's above the usual P. D. C. par that has been holding forth at the Hipp, and that's something else again.

"Easy Pickings," not particularly a good title, moves along briskly and has some good people in it. Billy Bevan meriting his featuring through a semi-nut detective role. Bevan is a slapstick comedy graduate.

Abel.

Winners of Wilderness

Metro-Goldwyn-Mayer picture, starring Tim McCoy. In the co-feature lines appear Joan Crawford and Roy D'Arcy. Directed by W. S. Van Dyke. At Loew's Circle theatre, New York, March 19. Running time, 76 minutes.

Allegorically and pictorially "Winners of the Wilderness" stacks up and makes a pretty story from a historical viewpoint. Otherwise its efforts to make a red-blooded American style romance stand up look pretty thin at times.

It is one of those very brave and expensive attempts to make a screen epic or opus out of the days before George Washington and his army began to fight. And it succeeds in showing the last days of the proud old soldier leader, General Braddock, who marched toward Quebec but was cut down on the way by the French and Indians.

There are some beautiful scenes of men and women dolled up in the wigs and old fashioned raiment of 1768 but all these scenes do not a big picture make, although they burn up a lot of footage and money.

It's a tough break for Tim McCoy, the dashing wild west Colonel of "War Paint," who, despite his immaculate British army outfit and wig, does some of the stunt stuff which helped him stand out in "War Paint," his first, and also for M.-G.-M. The army regulations, strict adherence to court etiquette and all that sort of fol de rol that perforce goes with characters of such a period seemed to handicap McCoy as the intrepid soldier who dared risk anything to have a little petting scene with the daughter of his enemy.

McCoy has the figure, the presence, in fact his military bearing makes him every inch the part, but for one to imagine in this jazzedy age that soldiers of the McCoy stripe in Washington's early days pulled the kind of heroics and daredevil stunts he did is a little too much. The film makers apparently strived hard to bring out real facts, real incidents and make them as natural as possible, but they gummed 'em all by putting McCoy through a roof-to-roof hurdling scene or doing a pole vault to the back of a horse ready to carry him and his girl fast from armed pursuers.

The picture starts slowly and then gets even slower, with the younger generation in the audience ready to walk. At the Circle there were audible twitters and an occasional guffaw from some of the boys and girls who appeared to dislike the powdery wigged lovers bowing right and left, and so on.

There are some bully scenes with the Indian portion about the most realistic. Since the screen has been getting the kind of war pictures like "The Big Parade" and "What Price Glory?" such pictures like "Winners of the Wilderness" seem a little too ancient for a general smash, despite stunt stuff.

Credit for Joan Crawford as the French girl on looks, dressing and love scenes. And Roy D'Arcy managed to dish up plenty of "menace" rascality and cruelty to hold up some romantic tension from a meller standpoint.

On a general summing up "Winners of the Wilderness" may prove an animated reference for the American boys and girls who dote on American history. It's impinging in that respect.

"Westerns" seem McCoy's forte; he's pleasing in appearance and graceful for all that but his style appears to be best suited for the wild and woolly.

Mark.

THE ROUGH RIDERS

Famous Players-Lasky release of a Victor Fleming Production. Original story and research by Hermann Hagedorn. Screen play by John Fish Goodrich. Opened as a road show at the Cohan theatre, N. Y., March 15. Running time, 137 mins. In two parts.

Col. Theodore Roosevelt	Frank Hopper
Stewart Van Brunt	Charles Farrell
Bert Henley	Charles Emmett Mack
Mary	Mary Astor
Hell's Bells	Noah Beery
Happy Joe	George Bancroft
Stanton	Fred Bohler
Col. Leonard Wood	Col. Fred Lindsay

It is said that this picture cost F. P.-L. $1,410,000 to make. That's a lot of money and the picture doesn't show it. There was considerable trouble with the film before it was finally ready to be shown, and when it finally did arrive on Broadway it proved to be more or less of a disappointment. It doesn't measure up as a road show and it will only get money on the strength of the popular appeal in the memory of the late Col. Roosevelt.

It will be the lure of the Roosevelt name that will draw the public in. It will be a case of playing this one as a road show along the lines of come in, get the money and get out. It won' stand up for runs at all.

The picture is entertaining enough along motion picture lines of the average program production. In the picture houses as a special it will get over after the brief road show dates are played.

One can judge the big kick in the picture with the opening scenes in which the character of Roosevelt appears. The audience is awaiting him, and when he finally shows up they go after a hand for him, but after that the actor part comes to the fore and with it a realization on the part of the public that it isn't their idol after all, but just an actor portraying him.

Interwoven in the historical facts is a love story that concerns two of the enlisted men of the Rough Riders who go to Cuba with the regiment, and one of whom remains there forever. They are both in love with the same girl. Likewise there is a comedy element furnished by Noah Beery as a western sheriff and George Bancroft as a horse thief. The latter, to escape the sheriff, joins up, while the latter also does the same thing to be sure of his man when the fracas is over. The two go through the entire story with lots of laughs.

The young love interest is carried on by Charles Farrell, Mary Astor and the late Charles Emmett Mack, recently killed in an automobile accident a few weeks ago on the Coast.

Col. Fred Lindsay had the role of Col. Leonard Wood, in command of the Rough Riders when Roosevelt was Lieut. Colonel.

The action takes place in the mobilization camp in Texas and in Cuba, with the historic charge up San Juan Hill as the big punch. There are numerous comedy scenes, and the one in particular that kicks is the shooting up of the picnic during a band concert when the Rough Riders, who are the invited guests, mistake the firing of a gun as part of the band selection as a signal to begin shooting.

The war stuff in the light of the films of the World's War is rather tame, but there is all that old glitter and pomp of the commander on horseback, the waving of the sword and hand-to-hand fighting stuff that gets over.

The tie-ups will have to be with the camps of Spanish War Vets and things of that sort to get money on the road.

Fred.

SLIDE, KELLY, SLIDE

Dear Chick:

Strap on your sliding pads, hook into the Embassy and grab yourself a grand stand seat for "Slide, Kelly, Slide." You'll see William Haines playin' the freshest busher that ever busted into the big league, and you'll see him cured finally through his love for Mickey Martin (Junior Coghlan), a rod ridin' homeless kid that Kelly picks up at the training camp and practically adopts.

The story is a pip, the direction of Edward Sedgwick is big time, and the titles by Joe Farnham would pull a laugh from a blue law inventor. Mike Donlin, who used to pull them into the right field seats at the Polo Grounds, plays a coach in the deaf and dumb opus and also was the technical adviser. You can shoot the roll that Turkey Mike steered them past the usual boots that these baseball pictures develop. This one is 99 per cent. and would have been 100 if the Yanks wore grey uniforms when playin' the White Sox in Chi. That wasn't Mike's fault.

But this guy Kelly will kill you. He's signed with the Yanks, comin' up from a class XX bush and reports in Florida where the club is trainin'. He has wired Macklin (Warner Richmond), the manager, not to worry if the club don't look so good, as he is on his way. Macklin has to look up the rookie list to even peg him.

On the way to the camp Kelly is the life of the party and tells the club car how good he is. In the day coach he meets a couple of regular big leaguers and hands them out trick cigars. A swell lookin' dish vamps him and he pays for her lunch. She frisks him but he's not hep until leaving the train.

The gang stand for Kelly because he's a whale of a pitcher but his head gets so fat it scratches up the walls.

There's an old cruller-legged catcher with the Yanks, who tries to steer Kelly right but the rookie is such a riot in the big league he think's he wrote the book. The catcher's daughter is in love with Kelly and she tries to cure him. He's hopeless.

The club gets so sore on him they can't win and the pay off comes when Kelly gets plastered on the eve of an important series with the White Sox. Mac indefinitely suspends him. The old catcher tries to reason with Kelly after finding him in his daughter's room, where she has hidden him to save him from being caught drunk, but Kelly bawls him out and tells him he's been saving his job. When the old apple grabber hears this he decides to resign. Mac won't hear of it and induces him to stay. They are all off Kelly, even Mickey, now the club's mascot.

The club comes through, wins the pennant and goes into the World's Series with St. Louis. The deciding game comes along and the Yanks have run out of pitchers. Mickey and the gang beg Mac to let Kelly pitch but he can't see it. Finally they persuade him and Mickey, overjoyed, starts to tell Kelly. On the way to Kelly's flat the kid, who is on a bike, is run into by a taxi and rushed to the hospital.

All wait anxiously outside the operating room. Mickey, after comin' out of the ether, wants to know if Kelly is goin' to pitch, Mac sends in word yes.

Kelly pitches the last game but hasn't his regular stuff. He's up to his neck when Mickey arrives in a wheel chair. That was the cue for St. Louis. Kelly shuts them out and socks a homer in the last inning, hitting the dirt as he comes into the place for the first time. Formerly he came in standing up. He didn't have to slide. He blew a ball game that way.

Haynes will have the frails rootin' for him all the way in this one. Sally

O'Neil will also turn a lot of caddies back to baseball, and Karl Dane, as "Swede" Hansen, could crash the player's gate in any park.

Baseball in a picture isn't supposed to have an appeal for women that will make it good matinee stuff out of New York, but this one may fool them. This Haines kid has a following like a World's Series ticket line and any woman who lamps this boy will tout her neighbors into going.

At the Embassy the matinees have been holding up but that don't mean anything in New York on account of its cosmopolitan population. The lay offs would fill the house indefinitely.

Everybody concerned with "Slide, Kelly, Slide," has hit .400. Get a load of it. Your pal, *Con.*

The Yankee Clipper

Los Angeles, March 24.

Rupert Julian production for C. B. de Mille Corp., starring William Boyd. Presented by Producers Distributing Corp. Story by Denison Clift, adapted by Garrett Fort and Garnett Weston, with Rupert Julian directing. At the Forum, Los Angeles, for indefinite engagement, beginning March 23. Running time, 96 minutes.

Hal Winslow..................William Boyd
Jocelyn Huntington............Elinor Fair
Mickey......................Junior Coghlan
Richard.........................John Miljan
Portugese Joe................Walter Long
Mr. Winslow................Burr McIntosh
Queen Victoria....................Julia Faye
Zachery Taylor..............Harry Holden

Rupert Julian has taken every license a director can to make this one a melodramatic spectacle that might bring the red blood to the fore of those who are interested in American history of the Clipper days of the early 19th century. However, he has not made a super-spectacle or a $1.50 two-a-day picture. What he has turned out is a piece of commercial merchandise for the program houses, which, if sold from the exploitation possibilities that a picture based on Yankee progressiveness offers, will bear fruit and profit to exhibitor and producer.

Though William Boyd is starred and Elinor Fair has second place, none other but six-year-old Junior Coghlan cops the bacon. Rupert should be given credit for taking the comedy portion of the picture and turning it over to this youngster, who acquitted himself in remarkable fashion and who no doubt in a short time will be grabbed off by some producer and starred in juvenile pictures. This kid need not be afraid of having to follow in the footsteps of Jackie Coogan or Wesley Barry. From what he has done here and in "Slide, Kelly, Slide," Junior should be able to give either of these youngsters cards and spades.

He plays a dock waif who smuggles aboard the Yankee ship in a potato sack; is added to the ship's family and chews a wad of tobacco throughout the opus as though he were born with a cud in his mouth. The kid also knows dramatic value and timing, and has a way of getting sympathy by a turn of the head and a twitch of the eye.

Boyd is the Yankee skipper in a sort of a sympathetic, hard-boiled fashion, and gets away best on the romantic and heroic end and not on the rough stuff which one would expect from a skipper of a ship with a mutinous crew.

Miss Fair as the fem lead is great to look at, but seemed to have her eye more on the camera than on her fellow players with whom she was playing scenes. Seems as though she should not be cast opposite her own husband where romance is concerned, with the screen end of it seeming to be just necessary and not realistic.

John Miljan as a cowardly English lover of the heroine gave a convincing and not overacted performance. Walter Long, doing the so-called rat ship "menace," was big in his characterization, but his work did not seem to ring as true as it might have. Julia Faye was flashed in the early moments and as a most attractive queen. Other players, including Burr McIntosh, were flashed on and off, but had no roles which might bring forth special mention.

Garrett Fort and Garnett Weston turned out a commercial adaptation of this Denison Clift play, but got pretty well away from the original idea in trying to get the box-office into it.

If this picture is intended for the $1.50 top houses, it has missed, as its production cost hardly went over $325,000, with the picture hardly having any big moments in it which would merit its competing with the $1,000,000 and over productions now being road showed.

The biggest and most thrilling of the many melodramatic portions is a typhoon encountered by the "Yankee Clipper" after it rounded Cape Horn on its way back from China. One sees plenty of water splash, lightning, etc., but it seems obvious that most of the stuff is of the miniature and studio variety, with the audience hardly taking it seriously outside of the momentary impression it will make.

Story is that of England building a fast clipper ship to get the Chinese tea trade. America at the same time turns out the "Yankee Clipper" for the same purpose. Both ships reach China at the same time.

Jocelyn, who is out seeing Foochow with her finance, is attacked by Chinese beggars, with Hal Winslow coming to her rescue. He falls in love and finds the villain has an affair with a Chinese girl. Chinese merchant invites her father, played by Louis Payne, to tea with the skipper of the American ship. He tells them that the first ship to reach Boston Harbor with cargo will get the tea trade for the world.

Both ships are ready to sail when the girl with her fiance come to bid the American skipper good-bye. American shanghais the girl and throws her lover in the hold, and racing for America starts. The American ship leads till it hits typhoon, when it is badly damaged, while the English ship goes through okay.

After the typhoon a mutiny takes place on "Yankee Clipper" through shortage of water. Boy captain and his loyal crew overcome mutineers, after which it is found that the English sweetheart had cached some of the water.

Ship is gotten into shape, pursues the English boat and sights it within five miles of Boston Harbor. Wind there is slack, so American skipper tells crew to get out blankets, hold them to wind for breeze to keep boat moving while the English boat is crawling. Of course, American ship beats English boat into harbor by a nose, and America has commercial supremacy of sea, with hero winning heroine.

First 50 minutes, or half of picture, very long and draggy. Looks as though it were cut very close, but some oriental atmospheric scenes good to look at and quite impressive, but might be cut to 10 per cent of its present footage, or even be eliminated, and the story would be more concise and holding. Kick is in last portion of picture. Though ending is obvious, action holds interest.

Heavily exploited and with local tie-ups from the shipping and patriotic angle, this one, which has plenty of the flag, should not miss in the picture houses. *Ung.*

LONG PANTS

Harry Langdon's third feature length comedy for First National. Story by Arthur Ripley. Direction by Frank Capra. At the Mark Strand, New York, week March 26. Running time, 70 minutes.

The Boy.....................Harry Langdon
His Mother...............Gladys Brockwell
His Father.........................Al Roscoe
The Vamp.....................Alma Bennett
Langdon as small boy.......Frankie Darro
Priscilla..................Priscilla Bonner

A bit of a let down for Langdon. It hasn't the popular laughing quality of his other full-length productions, principally because the sympathetic element is over-developed at the expense of the gags and the stunts that made "The Strong Man" a riot.

By anybody else the picture would be hailed as a great production. Langdon's name and work will make it a substantial box office property. The pull of the name was evidenced at the Strand Saturday and Sunday, when queues were continuous. The point is that the picture is amusing and satisfying, but it is not up to this up and coming comedian's best.

The opening is exceedingly quiet. It is here that the picture seeks to build up a sympathetic background for the Boy, giving a semi-serious twist calculated to heighten its subsequent clowning.

Langdon does the boyhood scenes in his inimitable style, but the humor is a bit fine for the generality of fans.

Later on, when they get into rougher material, there are several highly effective comic passages. One of the best was the incident where Langdon, who has unwittingly helped a woman criminal to escape jail in a packing case, sees what he thinks is a policeman sitting on the box. He takes up a position across the street and tries by half a dozen absurd ruses to draw away the cop.

The picture builds up in speed of action when the lady crook the hero innocently rescued from jail gets into a fist fight with a woman cabaret dancer whom she blames for her arrest. Harry all this time registers merely his typical nervous, futile protest, and for the moment the story gets out of his hands.

A swift finish is used. The whole situation, elaborately built up, is unceremoniously dropped, and Harry is seen returning from the nest of crooks he has stumbled into to his quiet home and his simple sweetheart. This brusque transition is rather confusing.

Besides the incident with the cop there is an elaborate comedy situation about half way. Langdon has become enamored of a woman criminal without, of course, knowing her character. While he wants to go to her in the city, his parents force him into a marriage with a village girl. In his absurdly naive way he decides the only way he can escape is to take the village bride out into lovers' lane and shoot her.

Much laughable material is used here in Harry's painstaking but futile preparations for his scheme, and his decision not to carry it through when he loses his pistol, gets caught in a bear trap and jams his hat down over his eyes as he takes aim. Some pretty obvious devices are employed here, such as his slipping trousers and efforts to control his suspenders.

The opening shows Johnny, a kid in knickerbockers, reveling in super-heated romances from the public library. When he gets his first long pants he starts out to do a Don Juan, with such complications as may be imagined. *Rush.*

WOLF'S CLOTHING

Warner Bros.' production, starring Monte Blue, with Patsy Ruth Miller, Douglas Gerrard and John Miljan featured. Story by Arthur Somers Roche. Adapted by Darryl Francis Zanuck. Directed by Roy Del Ruth. At the Roxy, New York, week March 26. Running time, 70 minutes.

Barry Blaine........................Monte Blue
Minnie Humphrey.......Patsy Ruth Miller
Johnson Craigie...................John Miljan
Herbert Candish..........Douglas Gerrard
Vanelli..........................Lewis Harvey
Vanelli's Pal.................Ethan Laidlaw
Hotel Manager...................J. C. Fowler
Hotel Doctor...............Walter Rodgers
Hotel Detective...............Arthur Millet
Crook "Doctor"..........John Webb Dillon
Millionaire.........................Lee Moran

This is one of the best Monte Blue starring features that has been turned out in a long while. For the average theatre it may be a riot. However, the picture does not measure up to what is expected of the film fare at the Roxy. Yet a Sunday afternoon audience at the big house laughed uproariously at the mystery farce, which has it weakest point in that it finishes up as one of those dream things, through the action having been manufactured in the disordered brain of a subway guard who has been run down by an automobile and taken to a hospital. One thing about it, though, is that the action is fast and never lags. Had the titling been snappier it would have been a hundred per cent picture.

In support of Blue, Patsy Ruth Miller looks great and handles herself cleverly. The comedy characterization of Douglas Gerrard as a society detective of the "silly" Englishman type, does much to lift the laugh element in the film. The balance of the cast, with the exception of John Miljan, who plays a supposedly crazed youth of wealth escaped from a sanitarium and does it very well indeed, is sufficient to the needs.

In the regular picture houses anything up to a four-day run will find this one standing up. *Fred.*

Fashions for Women

Famous Players-Lasky production, made on West Coast. Esther Ralston starred, for first time. Adapted from the play, "The Girl of the House" by Armont and Marchand into scenario by Percy Heath. Directed by Dorothy Arzner, F. P.'s first woman director. Raymond Hatton featured on film titles, but on theatre program Einar Hanson also featured. At Paramount, New York, 70 minutes running time. Week of March 26.

Celeste de Givray } ....Esther Ralston
Lolo Dulay }
Sam DuPont..............Raymond Hatton
Raoul de Bercy................Einar Hanson
Duke of Arles............Edward Martindel
M. Alard..................Agostino Borgato
M. Pattibone.................Edward Faust
Mimi..........................Yvonne Howell
Restaurant Manager........Charles Darvas

Corking good picture, flooded with ladies' figures, more fancy clothes than have been flashed on the screen recently, a swell little plot, good acting, good direction, photography that makes Esther Ralston look like all the world's beautiful women rolled into one blonde, and heart interest which, if a bit hackneyed, also okeh. The point is that as program pictures go, "Fashions for Women" goes much further.

Dorothy Arzner, scenarist and assistant director for quite a time on the coast, has handled her first megaphone for F. P.-L. with genuine skill and with a keen eye to closeups of Miss Ralston. Maybe on an initial starring venture that is okeh. However, Miss Ralston has an unaffected appearance on the screen and where some of the veteran grande dames who are still doing duty as ingenues get a trifle tiresome, Ralston wears well.

Plot is about a celebrated Parisian woman, Celeste de Givray, not only the best dressed woman of Paris but the best loose 'un. Her press agent, Sam DuPont, who operated swiftly and well, framed a big stunt to draw attention to her face-lifted beauty.

The stunt was to take the gal out of town until the final night of the fashion fete, then to spring her on the mob and with her new face (plastic stuff got a good laugh through a novel introduction) knock all her competitors into the ashcan.

To go through with the preliminaries of the fashion show it was necessary to get a substitute, so a cigarette girl whose name used to be Lulu Dooley in New York but Lolo Dulay in Paree, was hired. As her aviator, a Vicomte Raoul de Bercy was engaged, the angle being that the Vicomte had just gone broke on the Bourse and as a nobleman, plus his rep as an ace, he would fit well into the story when it broke on the front pages. Now the rub was that the cigarette girl passed as the real Celeste de Givray and the Vicomte, whom she used to admire when he came into the restaurant where she worked, refused to have much to do with her because of her rep.

Things were further complicated by the press agent, DuPont, an unconscionable liar. When it was all framed for the real Celeste to blow in, things went wrong because Celeste changer her mind and married a Duke of Arles, one of her boy friends. Being a duchess, she refused to go back into the fashion show business. This left the little cigarette girl up a tree because the Vicomte failed to believe she was really on the level until he saw the papers which announced the deception.

Lovely gowns are in every foot. Ermine negligees; bath in milk, numerous underpanties, chemises and other intimate items, all of which look like a million dollars on the svelte little Ralston figure, just round enough. Settings are typical examples of studio magnificence, the film being well handled in that respect, and the injection of much action, even in the fashion episodes, keeps the film from slowing down.

Miss Ralston rates her stardom and doing a dual role here, handles both with ease. Raymond Hatton does his comedy part beautifully, neither too rough nor too polite—and at the same time leaving off so many of the gags which have been associated with him in comedy. Einar Hanson as the adored man hasn't a great deal to do, but he does well, while Ed Faust and Agostino Borgato do comically as two French dressmakers—maybe they're kidding Poiret or Patou—it hardly matters.

A good picture and a cinch for exploitation. For the usual spring fashion shows which many of the de luxe houses give in conjunction with the department stores in their cities, this is a setup and was probably made with that idea in mind. At the Paramount no tieup was utilized, but this should and probably will be tied up right and left with the new styles.

THE NIGHT BRIDE

P. D. C. release. Story adapted by Zelda Sears. Supervised by F. McK. Willis. E. Mason Hopper, director Marie Prevost starred. Harrison Ford featured. In the company, Robert Edeson, Frank Pangborn and others. At the New York Hippodrome week March 28. Running time, 60 mins.

A picture of mixed aims and purposes that does get over some hoke comedy but misses utterly what seems to have been its first design—the screening of a witty comedy verging upon farce. They have managed to get the polite atmosphere in the surroundings and backgrounds, but the story lands uncertainly somewhere between a custard pie revel and a rough knockabout farce.

Of wit it has none and depends principally upon such devices as the hero pretending illness to escape an embarrassing situation, being forced to take a dose of castor oil. That incident marks the picture for its class and grade, meaning net, just another program comedy.

The entertainment falls in that no man's land between the out-and-out roughness comic and the polished style represented by the recent French adaptations used for the exploitation of Adolphe Menjou. Either of these two types has large possibilities. But there is small excuse for the in-between which alienates the unsophisticated fan who wants his custard pie and the discriminating customer who enjoys a witty, clever picture.

In the instance of "The Night Bride" a fine technical treatment has given the story splendid backgrounds in polite society, but the story pattern is more of the "Charley's Aunt" order. One of the high lights was the spectacle of a cissified man secretary floundering about the house all mixed up with a bride's intimate trousseau. From this episode and the castor oil chapter you can figure out the rest.

Marie Prevost overplays sadly in one of those cutie, tomboy, flapper roles, and Harrison Ford was never destined to shine as a suave unctuous comedian. That stopped the picture, no matter how exquisitely they dressed up the star or how perfectly they designed the settings to reflect the atmosphere of wealth in mansion and country club. Harrison trying to make a sleep-walking incident funny was not stimulating. The Hippodrome audience laughed intermittently at the rougher knockout, while the long flirtation passages were received with languor. *Rush.*

BREAKING CHAINS

Cambridge, Mass., March 26.
Produced by the Moscow Art Film Studio and presented in Boston under the auspices of the International Workers' Aid.

This Russian film shows all the crudities of ill-equipped studios and poor workmanship. Bereft of any semblance of plot unity, the picture is noteworthy for the few good scenes and the excellent facial pantomime of the actors.

Katja, a young girl of the working class, loses her father in the revolution of 1917. She is called for by her grandmother from the country and taken to a little village where the workers are just forcing the factory owner to sign his plant over to them. This owner's son was the man who killed Katja's father. The owner and son flee to Paris, and there spend all their money. After a time the son returns to his home, now a community center for the workers, and tries to get his jewels hidden in a room now occupied by Katja.

The girl has, meanwhile, fallen in love with the engineer of the plant. She is temporarily won over by the polished aristocrat, but when his evil schemes come to light she falls back on her old fiancee. The villain is shot, the father is never heard of, the girl never discovers that the villain was the murderer of her father, and into this confused tangle of loosely hanging threads are injected Lenin's death and loads of incoherent pictures.

The actors in the film are unnamed, but they have the usual Continental quality of conveying their thoughts without aid of titles. Although the lighting of the scenes was poor—evidently no Kleig lights—the faces stood out well enough to attract attention.

As was to be expected, the audience went wild over every mention of the Soviet, showing that for them the quality of the film counted for nought. Symphony Hall, Boston, where the picture was shown, was filled to capacity (2,500) at $1.10 top.

The picture has nothing to recommend it to the public at large and will only be of limited propaganda value. Cannot be compared to "Potemkin" or any of the German productions. *Gross.*

Thru Darkest Africa

Sub-titled "In Search of White Rhinoceros." Wild animal picture. Presented by Captain Harry Eustace, who, with wife and natives only humans appearing on screen. At Cameo, New York, week March 21. Running time, around 45 minutes.

This is a mild animal hunt picture, mostly grazing scenes, with a plentitude of titles in an attempt to cover up its weaknesses. At the Cameo, doubled up with the Chaplin reissue, "Shoulder Arms," and Chaplin picture featured over this, the gross at the Cameo, though both pictures be held over, will be no indicator of the drawing strength of "Thru Darkest Africa."

A sort of story-suspense is obtained in the animal film through the captions pointing toward a white rhino, which is the quest. It is finally seen and described as the white rhino with white-blue sides, leaving the auditor to guess what he pleases.

The most interesting point the film touches upon is the graveyard in Africa of all tusked animals, something no one ever has claimed to discover excepting a solitary Englishman. The picture places the graveyard in a bed of quicksand. That could say that there has been an animal radio working for years in the jungles of the Dark Continent.

It is difficult for anyone to detect in a wild animal picture, and especially of the hunt or exploring variety, what may be an insert or an assembly. Through experience of viewing many animal pictures, one comes to observe that somehow whenever the opportunity presents itself one or more of the hunters manages somehow to get before the camera, together with the animal or animals. When not seen and animals alone only showing, the reason is open to conjecture. It could be the danger or impossibility in a few instances.

Mildness of the picture counts against it. Action only is suggested in the titles, with expectancy highly worked up through them to see two rhinos battle. Another caption, when the rhinos were in sight, opposite each other, stated that rhinos might glare at each other for hours before starting to fight. That is what they seemed to be doing on the screen. Finally one ran off, "badly gored" the caption added, which was news to those in front. An ostrich appeared to have a ball playing aim with one leg and seemed to have hurt Capt. Harry Eustace, the explorer, who filmed the pictures, or his wife, or a cameraman. Mrs. Eustace appeared anon, also about a dozen native blacks.

At one time the caption foretold of onrushing elephants, but they weren't seen onrushing, although with another caption three dead elephants were on the ground.

If the captions and expectancy of blunted anticipation can support a draw for "Thru Darkest Africa," it has a chance. That is doubtful. There have been too many animal pictures for a mild one to arouse more than cursory interest at this time. That the Eustaces missed a capacity water hole is almost unbelievable. The first Rainey had a water hole, and it since has been the stock in trade of all animal pictures.

This is not belittling the Eustaces or that their visit to Africa was not as dangerous and fearless as is that of any of these high-nerved hardy adventurers, but it must be said that commercially "Thru Darkest Africa" is far from sensational in the animal film line. If inserts have been employed to tighten up the picture, that was permissible but failed to add to its value. *Sime.*

Quarantined Rivals

Feature length farce made from the original by George Randolph Chester. Producer Gotham Productions; distributed by Lumas Film Corp. Designated Sam Sax production. Director, Archie Mayo. Featured players are Robert Agnew, Kathleen Collins and John Miljan. In projection room, March 24. Running time, 70 minutes.

Independents do not often try a polite screen farce. Knockabout comedy or melodrama cost no more and are infinitely safer. This experiment is better than a fair program picture, just missing substantial commercial value. Its principal defect in the form presented for a trade showing is that it is too long. An hour and a quarter is a terrific stretch of time to sustain polite farce on the screen.

The earlier footage is tiresome, but when the complications have been wound up toward the finish the day is saved. It does seem that shrewd editing of the first four reels would cure the flaw. The idea appears to be to exploit the name of George Randolph Chester, who as a magazine writer had a big following.

Very little of the spirit of Chester is left in the screen version of his story, which runs into the complications growing out of a young couple in love being marooned in a quarantined home with a severe mama of the girl, a roughneck plumber, a barber and his newly married manicure-bride.

Possibilities here suggested for exits and entrances, unexpected clashes and inricate maneuvers are plentiful. To make it more uproarious the climax comes after the mixed household have retired for the night, and such comic episodes invite the guffaws of the fans as the young lover, escaping from the venegeful plumber and barber, takes refuge in mama's bed.

Kick comes at the finish when the hero, who was last seen exiled in pajamas to a balcony where he invited pneumonia, is discovered sharing half the twin beds in his sweetheart's bedroom, the discovery being made by the girl's hard boiled mama. The explanation, of course, is that they had summoned a minister at 3 a. m. who stood in the garden and married them as they leaned over the balcony. So censors of Ohio and points west again are thwarted.

The picture is a conspicuously good one in its physical makeup. A good deal of truly elegant atmosphere has been put into the settings, which faithfully produce in effect a home of wealth and refinement. The acting also is satisfactory, particularly by the heroine, Kathleen Collins, a graceful young woman who has beauty and character besides. She plays with considerable judgment and is one of the ingenues who understand that coquetry is not school girl kittenishness.

On the comedy end it was John Miljan as the plumber who stood out. Indeed, these two have the picture to themselves, Miss Collins on the polite side and Miljan for the comedy. The leading man, Robert Agnew, runs to mugging, playing a polite part much as Monte Banks would handle a two-reel roughhouse. Certainly, that wasn't what George Randolph Chester meant. *Rush.*

BRONCHO TWISTER

Fox western melodrama with story by Adele Rogers St. John and designated a Orville Dull Production. Tom Mix starred with Dolores Costello opposite. Comedy role by Jack Pennick. Dorothy Lloyd, ingenue. Running time, 60 minutes. At Fox's Academy, New York, March 21.

A typical melo of the plains with this riding star at his best. Scene is picturesquely set in the plains and hills of Arizona, where some tricky scenic work has been done by an expert cameraman who repeats the fox trick of getting remarkable sky and cloud effects into the action backgrounds.

This picture will get to the Mix admirers, for it is one revel of riding and fighting action, culminating in a whale of a screen situation.

The hero is in a Spanish mission ranch house tower used for the storage of dynamite by the rancher. Thither he has brought the heroine to save her from an unwelcome marriage dictated by her evil stepfather. A third member of the beleaguered party is a comedy buddy of the hero and his pal during service with the Marines during the war

The trio are surrounded by shooting enemies and protect themselves by dropping cans of dynamite upon them from the tower balcony. This situation is worked up with variations as the climax of the single-handed hero prevailing, of course, against a score or so of enemies and making his getaway by a trick and his good right arm.

This episode is the culmination of abundant action in the earlier footage. Two neighboring ranchers, the Mortons and the Bradys, are at feud when Tom comes home from the World War. His father has been wounded in an ambush and Tom goes out after the murderous clan. His meeting with the beautiful heroine, stepdaughter of the enemy feud leader, complicates his task, but his difficulties are made into the materials for a first-class western thriller, with Tony playing an important part, Miss Costello making a highly satisfactory Spanish heroine and Jack Pennick, an unknown, contributing first-rate comedy values as the ex-Marine who wanted to be a cow puncher but had no talent for sitting in the saddle. A shrewd touch given to this character was his sudden switch from a low comedy tumbler to the heroic role of the girl's rescuer in the hero's momentary absence.

A good action picture, done in the best Tom Mix manner, and warranted to bring out in full force the Mix fans. *Rush.*

CHARLES XII

PART 2

Second 12 reels of "The Life of Charles XII" is a tedious succession of military maneuvers; not very clear or definite. The Swedes are at war with the Russians, then the Poles, Turks and, finally, Hungarians. Here the weakness of the whole 24-reel production is most apparent. To adhere strictly to historical facts in chronological order they have sacrificed interest at the shrine of veracity. The historical films produced some years ago by Yale University had the same fault.

Battle scenes at times very poorly done, notably in the clashes of cavalry. The mounties milled around and flourished vicious - looking broadswords, but no one was even wounded. An extra engaged in a hand-to-hand fight with three of the "enemy" was plainly laughing.

In another case a Swedish general cornered in battle is fighting off several soldiers. An extra is right behind him with a fixed bayonet, but does nothing except mark time and look bewildered as if he got into the camera's eye accidentally. At no time were there enough extras used to give the illusion that there was really an army engaged.

During the various military movements a young soldier is repeatedly wounded, but always revives with such remarkable promptness it grew funny. The angle on the boy is that he's the director's son.

The second 12 reels, it is understood, were made a year after the first 12. Immeasurably duller and looks cheaper.

Whole production impossible for the United States; strictly for the Swedish public schools.

(A Review of the first part in 12 reels of this picture appeared in Variety last week).

Somewhere in Sonora

First National release produced by Chas. H. Rogers. Directed by Albert Rogell. Adapted from "Saturday Evening Post" story by Will Levington Comfort. Starring Ken Maynard, with Kathleen Collins featured. At Loew's New York Circle, one-half double bill March 21.

With great picture possibilities in the Comfort novel, this film has been brought down almost to the level of the usual westerner.

Would be bad judgment to rely on this one alone for results, but may do as extra entertainment with strong vaude program.

There is a time and a place for trick horses, but they are not plausible in stories of this sort. The motif of revenge has always been strong for interest, but the "do or die" spirit is expressed only in titles not in action here. Ken Maynard is a little stilted in spots, but shows up well in the fight scenes.

Starts off with fine exhibition of trick horsemanship at a rodeo. The pride of the ranch is accused of wrecking the rival coach, and to spare his employer public shame leaves for Sonora, incidentally to seek the latter's son.

The girl fights shy of the conquering hero for the first three reels, but succumbs when he is wounded in a fight with Monte Black's bandits. Frank Leigh registers capably as the suave but dangerous leader of the Brotherhood of Death.

The rescue scenes are interesting only from the action. A free-for-all rough and tumble staged in a saloon constitutes one of the most realistic scenes of this sort ever shown on the screen.

If the picture was intended to hit the first runs it has shot wide of the mark. It is almost totally an action picture, none of the people in the cast being given any opportunities to display trouping ability. Why First National went to the trouble and expense of buying the screen rights to this story is a mystery, unless there was an original intention to follow the Comfort novel which was later lost sight of.

The Brotherhood of Death was obviously created by Comfort as an additional pulse-quickener. In the film it is merely a title for a group of bandits.

A few laughs furnished by two of the lead's cronies and another in which the former makes the girl take driving lessons with her arms round his neck.

BURNT FINGERS

J. C. Barstyn production released by Pathe. In the cast Eileen Percy, Ivan Doline, Henry Mowbray, Edna Murphy, Jane Jennings, J. Roy Bennett, George O'Hara and Wilfred Lucas. At Fox's Academy, New York, March 24. Running time, 64 minutes.

Picture of mystery hokum neatly laid out with the main purpose the preservation and building up of suspense. Some of the methods are old fashioned, but the picture does achieve its purpose of piquing interest. The technical production is excellent, with convincing backgrounds executed in the best style of the studio.

Grades as a good program picture with special appeal to the less sophisticated clientele to whom the night club life of London should have appeal and to whom mystery melodrama has a big thrill. Reviewed at the new Fox house it was half a double feature, with the main billing for Buster Keaton in "The General." That about sets the weight and grade of the Pathe release.

Alone it couldn't support an important three-day engagement but it is a capital secondary screen offering. Complications are built up effectively around the murder of a night club dancing idol. It is established that the heroine was in his apartment on the night of the killing seeking to recover from him letters which compromised a woman friend of hers.

She is accused, is cast off by her fiance and berated by her family, but befriended by a high government official who moves quietly through the action, his interest being undisclosed until the denouement, when it is revealed that the murdered man was a foreign spy and he was slain by treacherous accomplices. The night club scenes are rather well done for the desired effect of rather obvious melodrama and spectacle. Indeed, all the hoke is skillfully put over. Atmosphere of high life and elegance has the usual value that goes with these elements, a murder in high life being worth two brutal killings and an elaborate fight in the slums.

Ought to be a better attraction in the hinterland than in New York. It has details and atmosphere that the small town will revel in. *Rush.*

THE BROKEN GATE

Designated a Tiffany Gem. Suggested by Emerson Hough's novel of same name. Directed by James C. McKay; continuity by John Francis Natteford. Film editor, Harold Young. In projection room March 25. Running time, 59 minutes.

Aurora Lane................Dorothy Phillips
Don Lane.................William Collier, Jr.
Ruth Hale....................Jean Arthur
Judge Lucius Henderson...Phillips Smalley
Miss Julia...............Florence Turner
Ephraim Adamson........Gibson Gowland
Johnny Adamson.........Charles A. Post
Mrs. Ephraim Adamson. ....
                Caroline "Spike" Rankin
Invalid.......................Vera Lewis
Sheriff Dan Cummins......Jack McDonald
Constable Joe Tarbush....Charles Thurston
Gossip......................Adele Watson

A tiresome picture about the small town lives of small and mean people. In its earlier passages drags lamentably and even after it gets into melodramatic speed—with a couple of murders and an almost lynching party—it does not grip. The reason probably is that the whole business is too theatrical and too false to engage sympathy.

Weighs in for the daily changes with preference for yoking up with a stronger attraction for a double feature bill.

The cast makes the picture look important and certainly the excellence of the acting brought out all the value there was in the script. Even with this advantage the story never gets anywhere. A drab village as a background argues against engaging atmosphere; it is hard to be interested in cheap, mean characters whom the story persists in treating seriously, and finally the whole thing is done in a heavy-handed way that belongs to a by-gone period in the studio.

Dorothy Phillips plays a mother role in a perfect drizzle of tears. That is against the picture as the role is here played, because endless close-ups of tearful mamas never get anywhere on the screen. Dull rural types are ready made for comedy, but here they are dealt with seriously.

One of the high light scenes has to do with a half-witted boy and his brutal father arousing the village to drive the persecuted mother out of town because she was regarded as an immoral character. This, of course, was mere acting.

Not a moment of the highly-colored action that was anything else. One could no more swallow a village milliner being mobbed because she was seen to kiss a young man (her son, although the villagers didn't know it) than one could observe the poor widow, her equally poor son and a humble friend depart in one of those $6,000 automobiles when all the troubles had been cleared away.

They just put the automobile in and didn't bother to explain who had financed it. That's the kind of a picture it is. They want a certain effect—a confession of murder from a subordinate character—to save the hero from hanging. All they have to do is to drag in the subordinate character, who can be most easily spared, and have him confess.

It will have to be a pretty dumb fan clientele that will take the picture seriously. It is one of those productions that needs a set of travesty titles to save it. *Rush.*

CALIFORNIA IN '49

Arrow presents Neva Gerber in "California in '49." Ben Wilson production. Story by Karl Coolidge. Co-directed by Ben Wilson and Jacques Jaccard. At Loew's New York as half of double bill, one day, March 25. Running time, 63 mins.
John Augustus Sutter.......Charles Braley
Arabella Ryan................Ruth Royce
Judge Coleman...............C. Coffey
Cal Coleman.................Ed. Cobb
Robert Marsdon.........Wilbur McVeagh
Sierra Sutter...............Neva Gerber

On the credit sheet it read that this picture was shot by four photographers. The way this picture jumped and galloped it was a certainty the four were pretty busy cranking.

The period was back in 1846 and there is no telling when it was made. It showed plenty of wear. As a picture it is for the most part out of focus, out of continuity, and is incoherent.

One sits and wonders how can pictures get that way. The men, sturdy pioneers of the great west in the days when all pioneers were sturdy and Indians were Indians, are shown in coonskin caps and buckskin outfits; fighting the real cold weather and rigors of a country full of snow and privations, yet one sees them in comparatively mild weather a few minutes later, with the trees taking on the first indications of an early spring.

Neva Gerber does a lot of riding, but her handling of a horse isn't sufficient to lift the head of the one she rides.

The credit lines were right: Four cameras shot the picture and they shot it to pieces. *Mark.*

CASEY AT THE BAT

Famous Players-Lasky picture starring Wallace Beery; featuring Ford Sterling, Zasu Pitts and Sterling Holloway. Hector Turnbull production directed by Monty Brice. Story by Turnbull, with Sam Hellman and Grant Clarke credited with titling. At the Paramount, New York, week April 2. Running time, 59 mins.

Casey	Wallace Beery
O'Dowd	Ford Sterling
Camille	Zasu Pitts
Putnam	Sterling Holloway
Spec	Spec O'Donnell
Trixie (Florodora Girl)	Iris Stuart
McGraw	Sydney Jarvis

Not a smash and a picture that looks like limited box office. Wallace Beery, personally, has his comedy moments. Many of them, but the situations aren't always there, wherefore crop up passages that well nigh reveal the gag men wrecking their brains for bits and scene punches.

Beery is Beery, and the multitude like him. He can stay in comedies for so long as he likes, and he likes, according to his new F. P. contract. As Casey he's the town junkman and playing on the village nine until a big league scout (Ford Sterling) looks him over. With one hand surrounding a pitcher of beer and the other grasping a bat, Casey socks one of the scout's shoots out of the lot—which means open sesame to the East River bridge leading into Manhattan.

Laid in the '90s the costuming of both men and women draws its share of snickers while it gives a chance to revive memories of the old semi-circular wooden double decker at the Polo Grounds. That era also allows Casey to go off his nut on Broadway and take the Florodora Sextet on a party. The famous sextet is shown in action although the Paramount organist never paid any attention to it and passed up "Tell Me, Pretty Maiden," entirely.

The plot punch hangs on the scout and Casey's self appointed manager (Sterling Holloway) trying to frame the star of the Giant's out of the World Series. Nothing sinister in the methods of keeping Casey away from the ball park on the all important day and all aimed for comedy, yet smacking of the stigma which will ever follow this country's national sport since '22. The kid mascot finally gets Casey to the grounds, after he has been made to believe he's sick. With his back to the pitcher while addressing the crowd, he has two strikes called on him. The finish is a terrific swing for an inglorious strikeout with the bases full in the ninth inning, thereby holding up the theme of the famous sport poem of the same name.

The happy twist is that Casey can't understand how he struck out, traces the twosome and it is finally brought out that the balls were switched so that the opposing pitcher was using some kind of horsehide that had a jumping bean in it. A title explains that the game is to be played over the following day.

No mob or real baseball stuff. Just comedy hoke with Beery, an illiterate ball player, explaining the simplicity with which he's framed. Love interest is tried for through Zasu Pitts being the village girl who comes to the city to see Casey clean up. Holloway, also being in love with her, has misread one of her letters to the athlete. It's a long time before the principals patch up the difference.

The titles help in spots and Beery always. But the yarn is not basically there. In the central Atlantic south, where they're baseball and golf crazy, "Casey" will probably suffice as a picture. For those sections of the country which take their diamond pastime more as a matter of course it's something else again. Too much stretching of the imagination to make it reasonable. That it all supposedly takes place before 1900 allows for many liberties, although according to the snatches of the game witnessed it could just as well have been anywhere previous to 1908.

Sterling supplies his standard aid and Holloway is adequate. The latter is a screen recruit from "Garrick Gaieties" and as far as known is in his first major production. Previously he was playing in two reelers, also comedy.

Sydney Jarvis' impersonation of McGraw, as manager of the Giants, means nothing other than the association of the McGraw name with the game. Miss Pitts is rather colorless as the somewhat snappy heroine, not through her own faults but rather because she has nothing to do.

"Casey" isn't going to burn up any turnstiles or weary many ticket takers. It won't do Beery any harm, and if that is true it's only plausible that this one may not do him any good. Following "Behind the Front" and "Navy Now," Beery, perhaps, can afford an indifferent release at this time. And that's about what "Casey" is.

Looks like an inexpensive picture minus a sporting thrill or mass grandstand or game attack to send it across. *Sid.*

SEE YOU IN JAIL

First National picture, produced by Ray Rocket and directed by Joseph Henabery. Story is from the original novelette by William H. Clifford. Jack Mulhall starred with Alice Day, and Mack Swain featured. Running time, 60 minutes. At Strand, New York, week April 2.

Jerry Marsden	Jack Mulhall
Ruth Whitney	Alice Day
Glottenheimer	Mack Swain
Marsden Senior	George Fawcett
Roger Whitney	Crauford Kent
Jailer	John Kolb
Inventor	William Orlamond
Valet	Leo White
Attorney	Carl Stockdale
Judge McCurd	Burr McIntosh
Rollins	Charles Clary

Another light comedy, this time with a pervading spirit of youth and good humor that hold interest fairly. Calculated for satisfactory service in the twice-a-week establishments. In general it goes into that large bulk of product that pleases while stopping short of real distinction.

Most of the polite comedy stories fall into this class, leaving the exceptional rating to those pictures of outstandin~ dramatic force, on one hand, and the comedies with a touch of the custard pie technique, on the other. "See You in Jail" is a capital bit of production and direction. Director and cast got out all there was in the story while the technical designer gave it the perfection of settings and scenic accessories.

The picture is full of mild chuckles, but there isn't a really hearty guffaw in the whole 6,000 feet. This is the fault of the story, of course, for young Mulhall plays the part of the rich young man hoboing it temporarily neatly and with judgment. Mack Swain, recruit to drawing-room comedy from the roughhouse school, is here wasted. The moustached giant who used to tower as a menace behind the wee comic of the Keystone two-reelers doesn't get anywhere with a business man role. Alice Day stands out in a "cute" role which she handles trimly and without over-emphasis. George Fawcett and Burr McIntosh have bits typical of their style, making the cast really impressive for names. Crauford Kent is lost in a colorless part.

Mulhall is the ne'er-do-well son of a millionaire milk distributor. The old man puts him on his own after an escapade. He goes broke in a distant city. A millionaire has been arrested for speeding and his lawyer picks up Mulhall from a park bench to substitute for him on a jail sentence. The millionaire has a pretty sister and, of course, the young people fall in love. Mulhall goes to jail in de luxe fashion with a lot of other rich men there for the same offense. He is forced to enter a business deal to sustain his masquerade as the millionaire and when the financier refuses to have anything to do with the project, his sister backs the hero. It turns out to be a bonanza, and Mulhall's angry father is appeased by the success of the boy he had despaired of.

There's very little action in this, most of the laughs coming from the titles instead of situation, a state of affairs that seems to be common to stories of the kind. However, it's all cheerful, handled in good taste and gives an agreeable screen hour. *Rush.*

The 4th Commandment

Universal production, from story by Emilie Johnson. Directed by Emory Johnson, who adapted the story for the screen. Belle Bennett featured, with Mary Carr given second line billing. Photography by Arthur Todd; titles by Carroll Owen. At Colony, New York, week April 2 with new Vitaphone unit as stage attraction. Running time not taken; about usual, one hour.

Gordon Graham	Henry Victor
Marjorie Miller	June Marlowe
Virginia	Belle Bennett
Edmund Graham	Leigh Willard
Mrs. Graham	Mary Carr
Ray Miller	Brady Cline
Mrs. Miller	Catherine Wallace
Frederick Stoneman	Frank Elliott
Mrs. Smith (Sonny's wife)	Kathleen Myers
Sonny	Robert Agnew
Sonny (little boy)	Wendell Phillips Franklin

In "The Fourth Commandment," if little else, there is the performance by Belle Bennett. With such slim findings for local exploitation in this Universal picture, exhibs had better go heavy on Bennett.

Otherwise this is a story of daughters-in-law and mothers-in-law. Perhaps good enough in the neighborhoods where the neighbors hear first hand gossip through second-hand sources. Flaps won't like the story because they will know it can never surround them, although there is a fly flapper here as one of the in-laws.

It's mushily weepy for those to whom it gets to, hard form similar experience. It's of the mothers-in-law given air by their boys' wives, the daughters making it a choice of "put her out or I'll leave this house" and the sap sons-husbands made to look like simps.

A repetitious tale, as the first daughter-in-law gets the same dose as a mother she slipped to her mother-in-law years before. And on top of everything else after she had done the deed long ago to have it kick back on her in after years when she had married another man, and he committed suicide, she went back to the first home, to be welcomed by her former mother-in-law and still loved by her ex-husband—instead of getting the boot at least from the man. That's rewarding double-crossing virtue.

The finale is almost as tiresome as most of the rest of it, with the opening scenes painfully padded. There is some slight action and the scenes are well built up to with Emory Johnson's direction as well as continuity most and praiseworthy.

Mary Carr is the first mother, a cinch role for Miss Carr, who is the standard mother player of the sheet. Kathleen Meyers is the second daughter-in-law and makes it very flapperish in the beginning. Rather well too.

But it's Belle Bennett who is about all that there is to the Commandment that says be nice to your parents. What Commandment is that about "Thou Shalt Not Commit Adultery?" What a b. o. bulger that could have been for Carl and U. With that Commandment the Colony at 50-75 cents would have had capacity at 4 o'clock Sunday afternoon, something it did not have.

U may have had a good idea in this mother picture. But it didn't work out. If you have not had a mother abused by your wife or never had to bawl out your wife for your family, this "Fourth Commandment" will not interest, unless careful note is taken of Belle Bennett's fine performance. *Sime.*

WHISPERING SAGE

Fox Western starring Buck Jones. Designated as a Scott R. Dunlap production. Story by H. S. Drago. In supporting company: Natalie Joyce, Emile Chautard, Carl Miller and Joseph Girard. Running time, 60 minutes. At the Academy, New York, April 4, splitting the bill with the Douglas MacLean comedy, "Let It Rain," Famous Players.

Western melodrama of the familiar kind, high in photographic quality, rich in action and with one point of novelty. The story plants a colony of Basque immigrants in the Nevada desert. It is in the picturesque settings of their transplanted bit of Spain that much of the heavy story has its locale.

For contrast to the American cowboy atmosphere the old world settings are especially effective, besides putting a romantic element into a Western, a value that for some reason seems to be utterly lacking in that type of screen story. It is in this detail that gives the picture its special touch of distinction.

Jones does the cowboy hero in his always acceptable style of quiet playing. In Natalie Joyce, leading woman, who seems to be a newcomer, the cast has a strong set. She is thoroughly in the picture for the Spanish type and plays with a good deal of restrained force and reserve. With this role as a sample she looks like a possibility for more ambitious parts calling for the flashing, dark-eyed brunet type.

Except for the pictorial novelty of the Spanish motif, the formula is familiar. A scheming American ranchman desires to seize the land held by his neighbors, and employs a gang of gunmen to drive them out. The victims here are the Basques, fiery-tempered people, who resist. Spaniards are aroused to mad fury and gather in a concerted attack upon the rancher. As it happens the schemer has just departed to burn the old world settlers out of their homes.

Jones is the usual roving cowboy who meets the beautiful Spanish girl and espouses her side of the feud. When the gunmen arrive at the Basque village the cowboy here is there alone with the girl, a few women and children, their sole defense against the desperadoes, while the men of the settlement are seeking to carry the war into the enemy's country. There is a long sequence of gun fighting between the besiegers and the lone defender, ending with the return of the Spaniards and the saving of the situation by the timely arrival of the U. S. marshal.

All materials that are common to most western melodramas, but here neatly done for maximum effect. Picture has good cumulative values, building up to the finale with excellent suspense. First-class program feature with special value to those houses where the Western is entrenched. *Rush.*

HEY HEY COWBOY

Universal Western, starring Hoot Gibson. Story continuity and direction by Lynn Reynolds. Photography by Harry Neuman. At Loew's New York as half double bill, one day, April 5. Running time, 65 mins.

Billy	Hoot Gibson
Doolin	Slim Summerville
Emily	Kathleen Key
Billings	Clark Comstock
Decker	Nick Cogley
Evans	Wheeler Oakman

Last production made by the late Lynn Reynolds. He is also responsible for the story and scenario.

Brisk, breezy little Western, with plenty of action and a lot of neat touches good for laughs.

Plot conventional, but because of Reynolds' workmanlike treatment and the excellence of Harry Neuman's photography it stands out above the average picture with a riding-shooting star.

Hoot Gibson recently pulled a walk-out on Universal, protesting against the stories assigned to him. So long as the productions maintain the level of this one Gibson need not fret himself on the score of losing his small town following.

Gibson has Kathleen Key as leading woman here. Miss Key is decorative and strong on personality. She gets across an impression of brains, lacking in so many of the young women facing cameras. Slim Summerville, the tall, angular comic familiar to Universal's short subjects, provided giggles in a role of legitimate scope. He is better working quasi-genteel than straight slapstick. Wheeler Oakman realized the gentleman rancher who did the dirty work.

Two ranchers have a feud secretly fostered and inflamed by **their dude neighbor with designs on their property. The dude is playing up to the pretty daughter of one of the cattlemen. Each of the cattlemen has sent to a detective bureau in the city for an investigator to get the goods on the other. Gibson plays one of the dicks, with Summerville his rival.**

Familiar stuff, but done well.

LIFE OF AN ACTRESS

Chadwick Pictures release. Jesse J. Goldburg production, directed by Jack Nelson, from play by Langdon McCormack. Photography by Ernest Miller. Running time 68 minutes. At Loew's, New York, one-half double bill one day, April 5.

John Dowen	Bert Sproute
Mother Dowen	Lydia Knott
Nora Dowen	Barbara Bedford
Bill Hawkes	John Patrick
Hiram Judd	Sheldon Lewis
Jacob Krause	James Marcus
Mooch Kelly	John Hyams
Bobby Judd	Bobby Nelson

This title may have value in the sticks and, with several fairly known names, there may be a sale angle. But it's a dull picture by any standard. It's draggy, poorly directed and holds bad photography.

Caught kissing an actor, Nora Dowen is browbeaten into an unwelcome marriage with Hiram Judd, rich farmer. An insight into the kind of egg Hiram is shows him paying off the minister who performed the marriage in small change. Hiram then turns to his young bride and tells her to hurry home, as she will have to get up early and cook breakfast for the harvest hands.

Despite the fact that Hiram is supposed to be a miser marrying for a housekeeper, the home to which he brings his bride is swell. **Looks like they utilized a set standing in the studio when making the picture. It's the tip-off on the whole production end. The set wasn't even dressed to carry a suggestion of what it was supposed to represent. The farmer sits at a ritzy flat-top desk in an upholstered high-backed chair and drinks wine from a decanter.**

After two hours of married life Nora runs away and joins a traveling wagon show. She has a baby later, but sends it home for her mother to keep until she makes good on the stage. The baby falls into the hands of Judd, who brings the child up to hate its mother. Hiram teaches the child hatred systematically. Each day the little boy is required to recite in front of his mother's picture that she is a bad woman. However, the kid secretly loves the picture of his mamma.

Some years later the subtitle announces Nora as the star of a fifth-rate New York company. The "fifth-rate" description is the title writer's. Later, the manager of the company receives a letter addressed "Princess Theatre, New York."

In the end the rich farmer is bumped off by a train, allowing the actress to wed the actor who kissed her in the first reel.

Barbara Bedford, ordinarily an attractive leading lady, looked very little like herself, and John Patrick, identified with fly youth parts, just as figurehead as the actor. Sheldon Lewis gave a ragged performance as the farmer.

Detail extremely careless from start to finish.

Had 'em yawning at Loew's, New York, on a double feature bill.

THE PRICE OF HONOR

Columbia release (Harry Cohn-produced) released on states' right market by Commonwealth Film Corp. handling New York and New Jersey rights. Directed by E. H. Griffith from scenario by Dorothy Howell. Ran 60 minutes at Moss' Broadway, New York, week April 4.

Principals: Dorothy Revier, Malcolm McGregor, William V. Mong, Erville Addison and Gustave Von Seyffertitz.

Here's a five-reeler that says nothing but says it rather interestingly, a directorial foresight to overcome the negative qualities of the script. It is ofttimes difficult for the average film artificer to unreel a flicker yarn interestingly. By the same token the task is at least twice as hard when handicapped by an inferior story, which may or may not be to the director's (E. H. Griffith) credit.

The sustaining of the interest is obtained by judicious switching of locale and some clever cutting and editing to maintain a fast clip.

After the hour's footage had had its screening—and long before that, for that matter—it was obvious that at best the only excuse for it all might be a coupled film prayer against circumstantial evidentiary convictions and capital punishment; the latter particularly if obtained through the first cause.

What the production has in its favor is some effective acting by the cast, prominent among whom are Dorothy Revier and Malcolm McGregor opposite each other.

It's a "buy" for a daily change exhibitor and the capital punishment and circumstantial guilt catch-phrases may be ballyhooed for benefit of box office.

Abel.

FRISCO SALLY LEVY

Metro-Goldwyn-Mayer production, directed by William Beaudine. From the story by Alfred A. Cohen and Lew Lipton. Featuring Sally O'Neil. Titles by Joe Farnham. At Capitol, New York, week April 9. Running time, little over 60 minutes.

Colleen Lapidowitz	Sally O'Neil
Isador Xavier Lapidowitz	Turner Savage
Stuart Gold	Roy D'Arcy
Michael Abraham Lapidowitz	Leon Holmes
Patrick Sweeney	Charles Delaney
Isaac Lapidowitz	Tenen Holtz
Bridget Lapidowitz	Kate Price
Rebecca Patricia Lapidowitz	Helen Levine

Those who have been proclaiming against a superabundance of films dealing with Jewish-Irish domestic life will proclaim less loudly after a look at "Frisco Sally Levy." There can be no divided opinions on this production. It constitutes a highly pleasing evening's entertainment, averaging a dozen laughs to the minute. This is not a great picture, and it does not set out to teach any moral lessons. The objective of the makers was a comedy, and as such it ranks with the best of its kind.

It is a long while since so many hearty, legitimate laughs have been heard at the Capitol. The situation provided for the characters to work in presents comedy possibilities to the audience immediately. A meek little man named Isaac Lapidowitz (Tenen Holtz) married an Irish girl called Bridget. Two boys and two girls resulted from the union. As Joe Farnham has it in the titles, "They met in front of a cigar store and became united."

Michael Abraham (Leon Holmes) and Isador Xavier Lapidowitz (Turner Savage) are the two boys. As a team of juvenile comedians these two youngsters are unsurpassed. Holmes is short and stout and dogged; Savage is long and lean, freckled-faced and timid. They have been very ably drawn out by William Beaudine to show comedy effects equal to and greater than some of the finest adult comedians.

With the aid of Farnham's irresistibly funny subtitles, Holmes is really the laugh hit of the picture during the first 15 minutes, continuing to make the crowd break into shrieks at close intervals even unto the final curtain.

There is a conspicuous absence of hoke and prop gagging. Almost every one of the laughs is on straight comedy. A St. Patrick's Day parade is shown in fine, clear colors. Isaac and Bridget, breaking through to the front of the crowd, yell, "Hullo, Pat!" to one of their acquaintances in the parade. And immediately every one of the carefully tailored, frock-coated, top-hatted gentlemen turn about with military precision and raise their hats in unison. Then there are laughs with closeups of an ambulance and a German band leading the Irish patriots.

After having been misplaced or misdirected in innumerable productions, Tenen Holtz has at last been given a role from which he will probably derive no little benefit. The Jewish tailor and clothes repair man is a colorless character if taken without laughable eccentricities. He is obnoxious if overdrawn and too Jewish for comfort. The border line between the two extremities is indefinite and unfixed, but Holtz puts it over in this picture.

There is a slight slowing up as the "drammer" is planted, but interest does not slacken too much. Roy D'Arcy enters as a rather purposeless and indefinite villain. His sole wrong, until near the end, when the foul man desires to press the fair lady to his breast, consists of gazing evilly at the gal, Sally O'Neil. The latter leaves home because daddy despises the suave stranger and becomes a night club dancer.

Miss O'Neil is okay as the girl, but does not show up strongly enough, mainly because the love interest was handled as of secondary importance to the comedy. A little episode where Gold (Mr. D'Arcy) is being entertained at home by Colleen and Bridget panics the ladies.

It seems that Isador Xavier and Michael Abraham had no special liking for the polished visitor, bestowing their unsolicited favor on the poor but respectable motorcycle cop as a boy friend for Colleen. On the other hand, although the young men were in night gowns and on the point of retiring, they cherished certain longings for a luscious strawberry shortcake reposing on the kitchen table, waiting to be served to the guest. One at a time they crept through to the kitchen, where they carved the heart out of the cake and replaced the top. Later on the insatiable Michael Abraham made another trip and polished off the strawberries. These he replaced with stuffed fruit of a similar nature which he tore from a hat belonging to Colleen. It knocked them into hysterics in the boxes, the orchestra and in the gallery.

On account of not having to battle any powerfully despicable characters, Charles Delaney, male lead, is presented in a weak light as a motorcycle cop. Kate Price (Bridget) handles her Irish assignment admirably.

Approximately 40 per cent. of the laughs are in the Farnham titles. William Beaudine has done nobly, especially with the fadeaway scenes. In denoting change of time and action in certain cases a scene just fades out, giving way to the next before the title is flashed.

"Frisco Sally Levy" doesn't mean anything as a title and there is no particular box-office draw in any of the names. But they'll come fast after the first showing—for a laugh.

AFRAID TO LOVE

Famous Players-Lasky Production starring Florence Vidor. Directed by Edward H. Griffith. Adapted by Doris Anderson from "The Marriage of Kitty," by (Mme.) Fred de Gresac. Titles by Alfred Hustwick. Running time, 58 mins. At Paramount, New York, week April 9.

Katherine Silverton	Florence Vidor
Sir Reginald Belsize	Clive Brook
John Travers	Norman Trevor
Helen De Seminiano	Jocelyn Lee
Rafael	Arthur Lubin

The sort of polite society comedy with which Florence Vidor has been identified since coming under the Paramount banner. The title means nothing so far as having any application to the plot is concerned. Lightweight picture, but with good production and swank style sufficient to send it over.

Basically the story hinges on a freak will, that ancient device of playwriting for excusing and explaining any sort of a farce predicament. Sir Reginald Belsize has been left a wad of dough, but with a distinct proviso that he is not to marry Madame DeSeminio, Peruvian widow. Sir Reggie's dead uncle seemed to know that the madame was not on the up and up and specified particularly against her.

A makeshift marriage to get the coin is arranged. Kitty Silverton, a nice girl but broke, consents to become Lady Belsize temporarily until the money can be cinched and a divorce arranged. She falls in love with Sir Reggie and he with her, the Peruvian dame is outwitted, and that's it.

Clive Brook, who has been Miss Vidor's leading man in several pictures, again does the polished but bewildered Englishman. He and Miss Vidor team nicely. Norman Trevor and Arthur Lubin have bits. Jocelyn Lee as the Peruvian dame fits the worldly part ideally.

MATINEE LADIES

Warner Bros. production starring May McAvoy, with Malcolm McGregor featured. Directed by Byron Haskins. Adapted by Graham Baker from story by Albert S. Howson. Photography by Frank Kesson. Running time, 65 mins. In projection room, April 8.

Sally Smith....................May McAvoy
Bob Ward...............Malcolm McGregor
Mrs. Aldrich..................Hedda Hopper
Mrs. Smith.................Margaret Seddon
Tom Mannion...............Richard Tucker
Maizie Blossom................Jean Lefferty
Madame Leonine..............Cissy Fitzgerald
Man About Town.........William Demarest

Straight program stuff, with May McAvoy to pull 'em in. Okay, is offered without a lot of blah of great or big.

The plot is nobody's business so far as origin is concerned. It has the principal idea of "Cradle Snatchers," that of college students playing gigolo to discontented wives. It also has the menace luring the heroine to his palatial houseboat with the hero fishing the gal out of the sea after a storm has wrecked the boat. That situation is as venerable as any in the movies.

This is the first production made by Byron Haskins, former camera man, in his new capacity as director. It has some of the over-done touches that might be expected from a lens expert suddenly given a megaphone. In general, however, considering the time-worn material, Haskins did well enough with his initial assignment.

Smart titles could have added much. Those that it contains are extremely uninspired, with one or two bordering on the ridiculous, such as when Miss McAvoy is made to say in response to an invitation: "I'll go if you promise it isn't one of those wild parties."

"Matinee Ladies" are supposed to be married thrill-hunters who take a little necking with their afternoon tea. Bob Ward (Malcolm McGregor) has been forced by necessity to become a professional dancing partner at these four o'clock petting siestas. He loves the cigaret girl (Miss McAvoy). Their romance is threatened on one hand by the rich Mrs. Aldrich (Hedda Hopper), who has aspirations against Bob's manly idealism, and on the other hand by a "millionaire bootlegger" (Richard Tucker), who wants the gal.

Miss McAvoy and Mr. McGregor make a good team of lovers and are very apt to register at box office. Tucker was his usual and competent self, with Mrs. Hopper fitting her role nicely. William Demarest (formerly of Demarest and Collette, vaudeville), did a butter and egger and impressed as a possibility in screen comedy characters.

The Notorious Lady

First National release of a King Baggot production. Presented by Sam E. Rork. Features Lewis Stone, with Baggot the director. Adapted from Sir Patrick Hastings' novel, "The River." Cameraman, Tony Gaudio. At the Strand, New York, week April 9. Running time, 63 minutes.

Patrick Marlowe...................Lewis Stone
Mary Marlowe............Barbara Bedford
Kameela..........................Ann Rork
Anthony Walford............Earl Metcalfe
Manuela Silvera.........Francis McDonald
Marcia Rivers...............Grace Carlyle
Dr. Digby Grant............E. J. Ratcliffe
Williams.......................Guniss Davis

No better or worse, above or beneath the general run of program pictures. At best "just a picture" of the type to which Lewis Stone seems chained. Stone rates better fare than this, for the simple reason he can handle it, especially in lieu of his being featured. But the average fan won't get a headache from trying to decipher the story, while the highbrow element will scoff because it's sympolic of nothing in particular. The titles have a tendency to eliminate any chance of that, and the main title is not entirely a true tip-off.

The shooting galleries, double program and thrice weekly change houses need have no fear of this one. It will suffice, too, for the major theatres, but will need surrounding program strength if there are to be any fireworks at the box office.

In toto, a story of a wife who blasts her reputation on the witness stand by a lie to save her husband from a death penalty. That he believes her confession swings the action to Africa and a diamond hunt.

Freed on the "unwritten law," Patrick Marlowe (Mr. Stone) hies himself to the hot climate, from where emit reports of his death. Mrs. Marlowe (Barbara Bedford) takes the journey to solve the mystery of her husband's demise, and eventually becomes engaged to a fellow-traveler, Walford, played by Earl Metcalfe. The despondent wife is also the object of a pursuit by the wealthy Silvera (Francis McDonald), the story's "menace," and, as Walford is seeking adventure, a diamond hunt expedition involves not only him but Silvera and Marlowe, the latter under an assumed name.

Silvera is at the bottom of a camp uprising against Walford and Marlowe, the latter men finally escaping to their antiquated and small vessel through the aid of a native girl (Ann Rork). Arrival at the home port brings forth revelations; Walford releases Mrs. Marlowe from her engagement to him, and the subdued Patrick is only too willing to take her back upon realization that she lied to save him.

Nothing outstanding in a production way, although there are plenty of natives running around during the jewel hunt. The fight against Silvera and his hirelings is a ripple, and Baggot has carried the natural suspense along to the escape. One corking shot is of a spear just missing Stone's head in the water. Maybe a rubber-headed stick, but a fairly long "shot" and unfaked.

No heavy emotional displays by any cast members, Stone playing the strong-willed husband capably and Miss Bedford's appearance making her male conquests believable. McDonald is a fair enough heavy and Metcalfe slips by as the honorable and generous lover. Minor roles are in the hands of Ann Rork, showing up nicely and very seriously as a native, and Guniss Davis, who registers in the last half.

Baggot has inserted a comedy touch through a persistent deck walker on board ship. If that sounds unimportant, the Strand audience gave each flash of this character a solid laugh, and it helped.

As a whole, Baggot seems to have directed conservatively on histrionics, possibly holding the players down to too great an extent to give this conventional screen yarn any particular sparkle.

Will slip by without causing any disturbance one way or the other.
Sid.

Rose of the Tenements

F. B. O. production, starring Shirley Mason, presented by Joseph P. Kennedy. From the story "The Stumbling Herd," by John Morosco. Directed by Phil Rosen. Cast includes Johnny Harron, Lolita Lee, Evelyn Selbie, Scott McKee, James Gordon, Mathilde Comort, Kalla Pasha, Sydney Franklin. At the Stanley, New York, one day, March 10.

A drab, colorless presentation offering little in either entertainment or box office value. New York's pictorially hackneyed East Side is used as the locale without variations.

Two adopted children, boy and girl, are shown going through emotional stages, not at all uncommon in real life, which are not dramatized to an extent where the mob can be made to forget the obviously ordinary scheme of affairs.

Shirley Mason is the girl who must hide her great love under the pretense of being Johnny's sister. Situations under these circumstances offer great opportunities obviously slighted by the directorial megaphone. The mob scenes, the fights and the clinches, leave much to be desired, although Harron shows unmistakable signs of promise.

Sydney Franklin, whose name isn't even flashed on the screen, steals the laugh hit of the picture with a screamingly funny interpretation of a sissified Yiddish overgrown schoolboy.

For the finish the boy forgets his anti-war friends, realizes dormant amorous longings for his adopted sister, and joins the army. An unsatisfactory denouement that leaves them cold because the actuating circumstances are not played up or portrayed with sufficient strength.

LIEBE

Berlin, April 2.

This picture played four weeks at the Capitol in Berlin where the average successful run is two weeks. There can be no doubt that it got over strongly in Berlin, but that was due entirely to the personal popularity of Elisabeth Bergner. This actress is Germany's best-liked woman star.

The present attempt, "Love," is a lot of weak tea said to be dished up from a story by Balzac. It is just nothing at all about a flirtatious married lady who falls for a general after dangling him at her apron strings for some time. He, however, believes she is merely playing with him, and when he does realize the truth it is too late. She has entered a convent and there the general finally finds her just as she is dying—for no particular reason.

The director, Paul Czinner, practically never gets her fantastic charm and pathetic appeal across, for the reason that he builds the film around her as the star. She is continually trying to register something in the close-ups when she jitneys if the Keith-Orpheum-When she does get the right director and scenario there'll be no stopping her.

THE SEA TIGER

First National picture, Carey Wilson directed. Adapted from novel, "The Runaway Enchantress," but adapter not mentioned. Milton Sills starred, with Mary Astor opposite. In support, Alice White, Marie Fitzroy, Larry Kent, Kate Price. Running time, 58 minutes. At New York Hippodrome, April 11 week.

When a First National picture appears at the Hippodrome a few blocks away from the Mark Strand, which holds the first National franchise, the situation speaks for itself. It is obvious that the Strand waived the privilege, and especially with the Hip's limit of $1,000 for any picture.

"The Sea Tiger" is a bizarre story made up of clumsy melodrama and inept trick effects. One of the "big" scenes has the seafaring hero push out to sea alone in a frail sailing craft during a raging storm to rescue his brother. The trickery of the effects are apparent to the most simple minded. One episode is a violent fight between two girls, both rivals for the same suitor, a passage that would be offensive to a clientele educated to improved screen standards.

For another thing, the subject matter would not appeal to women fans, alone enough to set it back at the b. o. Why they called it "The Sea Tiger" is something else again. The hero is leader of the fishing fleet, but, far from being a tiger, is is a mild enough sort of person, given more to the humorous and genial mood than to anything wild. The idea of two girls engaged in a violent struggle for the affections of a swain is rather inverted romance, even for the wide open and catch-as-catch can technic of the screen. One of the girls is a modest and womanly character, the other a scheming, gold-digging vamp. The latter seems to have it all her own way until the end, when the gentle, suffering lady goes goofy and throws her bodily off the lot in the champ free for all ladies knock-down-and-drag-out of the decade.

The picture has a certain picturesqueness in setting and characters, the locale being the Canary Islands. The water shots are extremely pretty and the technical production is well managed for pictorial effect in composition and backgrounds. One of the high spots is a fight at the Easter carnival among the fisher folk, when the hero goes into one of those heroic struggles with a prize-fighter bully. The bully was about the size of Bill Edwards when Bill was in trim. When Milton Sills bested him in a rough and tumble it didn't seem right.

That's the kind of picture it is. They propose to show action, and why be annoyed with restrictions of plausibility?

Weighs in for the daily change, where it should prosper. *Rush.*

ARIZONA BOUND

Famous Players-Lasky western, starring Gary Cooper. Directed by John Waters from R. A. Gates story, adapted by Marion Jackson. Titles by Alfred Hustwick. Photography by C. Edgar Schoenbaum. In the cast, Betty Jewel, Jack Daugherty, El Brendel, Charles Crockett and Christian Frank. Running time, 59 mins. At 5th Ave., New York, April 11, first half.

Famous Players' answer to Metro-Goldwyn's Col. Tim McCoy is this Gary Cooper boy who, like McCoy, has been made into a full-fledged star overnight and without previous camera experience. Paramount now has three western stars, Fred Thomson, Cooper and Warner Baxter, the latter replacing Jack Holt in the Zane Grey series.

"Arizona Bound" is no great shakes, but it has been well made. John Waters, who handled the megaphone, has done a tight job. The picture moves with zip undiminished to the final triumph of the hero.

A rambling cowboy happens into a western town the day a big gold shipment is leaving by stage. Two factions are planning to rob the coach. Buck O'Hara (Jack Dougherty), who drives the stage and has public confidence behind him, heads one scheme to cop the dough. A stranger (Christian Frank) plans to hi-jack the shipment. The cowboy is embroiled and implicated as one of the bandits. He narrowly escapes lynching, and in the end retrieves the gold, establishes his innocence and wins the girl.

Comedy relief is supplied by El Brendel doing his goofy Swede characterization. Betty Jewel furnishes the love interest.

Cooper is a tall youth, with a boyish smile and enough swagger to give him character. "Arizona Bound" will give him a respectable introduction to his future public, but as a picture it's just program.

EASY PICKINGS

First National release produced by John McCormick. Story by William A. Burton and Paul Kruger, directed by George Archainbaud. Starring Anna Q. Nilsson. Cast includes Phil McCullough, Jim Miley, Jack Williams, Kenneth Harlan and Charles Sellin. At Fox's Academy, New York, part of double feature program, April 11, three days. Running time about one hour.

Good old mystery picture with the disappearing body, quivering negro servants, comic opera detective, crooked lawyer and the usual resulting effects are not treated in any unusual manner. As an attempt to give a city audience an absorbing problem to worry about the picture flops. It incorporates part of "The Gorilla" disappearing technic in addition to every hackneyed and time-worn device known to the average picture house or legit theatregoer.

In smaller towns where these mystery combinations are not so well known there may be a chance. The story tellers and continuity writers are mostly to blame. Even with an ancient theme there is always an opportunity through the creation of new twists and the insertion of new angles.

If "Easy Pickings" was intended as a filler in the split week houses it has been cut to the right pattern.

Title would indicate a crook underworld story. This is merely a case of a dying millionaire who wants to cut his niece out of his will at the last minute because of her failure to appear at his bedside. The lawyer finds a strange woman in men's clothes prowling about near the safe and forces her to take the place of the missing niece who has been killed in an accident. He then poisons the old man before he can change the will, the arrangement being that the girl will turn her half of the estate over to the lawyer on the pain of being sent to prison.

Indefinitely mixed up in this is a strange chauffeur, dark vaults and underground passages, and impromptu love glances exchanged between the niece and the nephew.

Miss Nilsson is in an unsympathetic role. Her rather striking appearance is not shown to good effect. The central figure, always in and out of the picture, is shrouded in black and fails to raise either curiosity or interest because it is not definitely established whether it is working for good or bad cause.

The colored couple are okey, working well with old material. The comic subtitles have been flashed on many sreens before.

The picture is probably figured to make money for the producer, with all of the shots confined to two interior settings and an inexpensive cast with the exception of the star, with the balance of the shooting on a lawn. Good particularly where Miss Nilsson has followers.

IRISH DESTINY

Photoplay based upon historic incidents of the Irish Rebellion of 1926. Written and produced by Dr. I. J. Eppel. Presented at Daly's, New York, March 30, under Dr. Eppel's auspices. Made and produced in Dublin, Ireland. Running time, 95 mins.

This may be "The Big Parade" and "What Price Glory" of the Irish cinema, but it is doubtful whether its appeal will interest others than those from the ould sod who have followed press reports of the Irish uprising in '26, which established the Irish Republic.

Dr. Eppel, who scenarized and produced the film with a cast of actors recruited from the various theatre movements of Ireland, has adhered strictly to history of the Irish combat, weaving only the required love interest into proceedings. But withal he has succeeded only in grinding out a picture with class instead of public appeal.

Political intrigue and the machinations of the "Black and Tan" are vividly pictured. However, despite efforts of the author-producer, and granting that such efforts were made, the political propaganda of the Celt creeps into the picture frequently and undoubtedly mars its box office value from a popular appeal slant. It will have its effect in bestirring loyalty of the Irish lad over here, but little else. Letters from home have probably depicted that which is shown in this film in a more homely, but understandable way.

From a melodramatic angle the battle scenes are well reproduced and a coherent love story sustained of a boy who upon his wedding eve enlists with the Republican army and does himself proud.

The film's local future lies in auspices, tie-ups with Irish societies, etc. As a general release it cannot get far because of its limited appeal. *Edba.*

Mme. Wants No Children

Feature length comedy of manners. Released by Fox. Story from the novel of Clement Vautel. Maria Corda, French actress, starred. Directed by Alexander Corda. Titles for Fox release by Katherine Hillaker and H. H. Caldwell. At the Academy of Music, New York, March 31. Four days as half double bill. Running time, 60 minutes.

This subject apparently comes into the Fox list by purchase or distribution arrangement, being manifestly made abroad—in France for choice, since the action takes place entirely in Paris. It is by long odds the best French product that has come to attention so far, although its commercial value for America is doubtful.

Here it is presented as half of double-feature bill in conjunction with "New York" (F. P.-L.). It is one of those quiet comedies such as the last two of the Menjou releases. It is in the same vein of humor and done with a fine regard for atmosphere and background that characterize the best of the American pictures. For the average American fan, however, the story idea is pretty finely spun. The thing that acts against it is the absence of any box-office name.

Just a light, fluffy story about a gay French bachelor and a Paris flapper. She wants to jazz around at night clubs, accompanied by a frivolous flapper mother and a sister while he seeks the comforts of home. The six reels deal with the conflicts arising out of such a situation on the honeymoon, the departure of the young husband for the apartment of his former mistress, and the sudden realization of the wife that she has a rival. All of this leading, of course, to a final close-up in a maternity ward.

This is exceedingly light material to spread out over an hour of flickers. All that has been done in delicate humor, neatly etched characterization and comedy complication has been done, but the picture does drag, principally because the family situation is not especially appealing to an American audience either in substance or treatment.

Maria Corda, star, does not play the light scenes with any finesse, suggesting that her forte probably is in emotional roles. This contributed to the failure of the film to register fully. The production is a splendid one. The settings for a story of Parisian high life are models of grace and elegance and, with skillfully picked character types, create convincing atmosphere.

The American speaking stage has not had successful translation of a French comedy in years, although innumerable importations have been made. The French excel in this type of police semi-farce, but if they fail to attract on the speaking stage, what chance has a celluloid version before the less sophisticated screen clientele? *Rush.*

The Man From Hardpan

Pathe Pictures starring Leo Maloney. Story by I. Beebe. Shown at the New York theatre, New York, as part of double bill Saturday, March 18. Running time, 68 mins.

Robert Alan..................Leo Maloney
Elizabeth Warner.........Eugenia Gilbert
Sarah Lackey....................Rosa Gore
Henry Hardy.........Murdock MacQuarrie
Jack Burton....................Ben Corbett
Sheriff ....Albert Hart

While this one is one of the best that Leo Maloney has yet done for the screen it skidded off just at a time when its story was threading slowly and surely into real continuity, carrying a punch that had all the earmarks of putting over a bully good story under the Maloney label. Then it struck soft sand or whatever it was that shot the picture back into the usual run of Maloneys.

A Maloney means a western, but as westerns have become so thick it behooves the Maloney makers to attach themselves to stories with a reason for the romance and the villainy.

That idea of having the hard-panned mother palm her no-good son off as the half-owner of the ranch paved the way for a dramatic tension that ran high and thrilling for a time, but got too stagey and impossible.

In casting Miss Gore as the mother, this independent found a woman who went in for the part in a most commendable way as far as acting was concerned, as she gets a lot out of this thankless role. She became a little too dramatic toward the close, but in the main was the proper cool, calculating and deliberate woman.

The athletic, hard-riding Maloney, of course, dominates the picture. On his strong-arm prowess in out-riding and outfighting and even out-drawing or outgunning the bad boys in his pictures has built up quite a following in the neighborhoods.

A pleasing asset to this Maloney is the work of a dog that does some unusual stunts and shows remarkable canine sagacity. That dog, horse and Maloney are a surefire combination when it is a long time between the Mix and Thompson pictures. *Mark.*

PLAY SAFE

Feature length comedy starring Monty Banks for Pathe release. Cast includes Virginia Lee Corbin, Charles Gerrard, Charles Mailes, Rosa Gore and others. Direction Joseph Hennaberry. Story credited to star. Photography by Blake Wagner. Running time 58 mins. At Loew's Circle, New York, one-half double bill, one day, April 4.

Monty Banks' expansion from two-reelers to full length comedies is of recent date. In "Play Safe" he seems to be trying to emulate the type of picture and comedy done by Harold Lloyd in his early successes for Pathe. There is a "chase" sequence reminiscent of "Girl Shy" and some stuff on top of a runaway freight train cut from the same cloth as the "dizzy" scenes in "Safety Last." Also Banks goes in for an under dog characterization, the poor boy who triumphs over enemies and adversity more by dumb luck than anything else.

However, beyond this outward similiarity resemblance of Banks to Lloyd ceases. "Play Safe" is simply a two-reeler done in five. Banks is constantly tripping over himself, constantly pursued by a pack of wolfish thugs, and constantly ducking missiles which bounce back and hit his opponent. He peels a banana, throws away the fruit and eats the skin. And that about tabs the quality and date of the gags.

The story is credited to Banks. He is one of the common people. The rich young heiress who owns the mill in which he works is hounded by a crooked guardian (Charles Mailes), who connives a matrimonial alliance of the girl with his son (Charles Gerrard).

Picture contains laughs, but not enough to justify its claims to being a straightaway comedy. The plot is a mere flimsy skeleton on which the gagmen worked. No heart interest because there is no reality or illusion to the characters. Virginia Lee Corbin, who has frequently shown to advantage in flaming youth roles was blankly negative in this one.

Production inexpensive and direction of Joseph Hennaberry on a dead level. Strictly program and with Banks as yet hardly even a "name."

RED CLAY

Blue Streak Western, distributed by Universal. Directed by Ernst Laemmle; from the story by Sarah Saddoris. Featuring William Desmond, with cast including Ynez Seabury, Marceline Day, Albert J. Smith, Byron Douglas, Billy Sullivan, Lola Todd, Noble Johnson. Titles by Ruth Todd. At Loew's New York, one day, April 8, one-half of double feature program.

William Desmond, as one of the best screen Indian chiefs. In pictures of this class. "Red Clay" is an interesting story well told. It runs to the realistic, showing the probable results of an attempt by an Indian to mix with a white girl.

Here it is a case of a congressman preaching that the Indian is equal and even superior to the white man in many respects. Desmond is drafted and while overseas saves the life of a man who later turns out to be the son of the congressman. The man does not know who his rescuer is. Returning home, he registers objection to having his sister go out with an Indian. In spite the latter is a soldier, a scholar and a star football player.

Desmond is fatally shot in the end and dies in the arms of the man he rescued after making himself known. The death scene is not explained properly and not staged well. Marceline Day lacks appeal and the supporting cast is weak.

Good enough to hold up the three-day stands that like this stuff.

THE KING OF KINGS

Cecil B. DeMille's super-production in 14 reels, with scenario, original, also continuity, by Jeanie Macpherson, featured on billing. DeMille's name above title and not less than one-half its size. No players featured. Frank Upson, assistant director (to DeMille); second assistants, Wm. J. Cowen and Roy Burns; art director, Mitchell Leison; chief photographer, Perevell Marley, with Fred Westerberg and J. A. Badaracco, assisting; associate editor, Clifford Howard; technical engineers, Paul G. Sprunck and Norman Osunn; film editors, Anne Bauchens and Harold McLernon; research, Elizabeth McGaffey. P. D. C., distributors. At Gaiety, New York, opening April 19 for run. Time of film, 2 hours and 35 minutes, exclusive of one intermission. Scale, $2.20 top.

Jesus, The Christ............H. B. Warner
Mary, the Mother........Dorothy Cumming
The Twelve Disciples—
Peter....................Ernest Torrence
Judas.................Joseph Schildkraut
James.........................James Neill
John......................Joseph Striker
Matthew.....................Robert Edeson
Thomas...................Sidney D'Albrook
Andrew.....................David Imboden
Philip....................Charles Belcher
Bartholomew..............Clayton Packard
Simon...................Robert Ellsworth
James, the Less...........Charles Requa
Thaddeus...................John T. Prince
Mary Magdalene.........Jacqueline Logan
Caiaphas, High Priest of Israel........
Rudolph Schildkraut
The Pharisee...................Sam De Grasse
The Scribe................Casson Ferguson
Pontius Pilate, Governor of Judaea.....
Victor Varconi
Proculla, wife of Pilate.....Majel Coleman
The Roman Centurion......Montagu Love
Simon of Cyrene,...........William Boyd
Mark...................................M. Moore
Malchus, Captain of the High Priest's Guard.................Theodore Kosloff
Barabbas...................George Siegmann
Martha............................Julia Faye
Mary of Bethany.........Josephine Norman
Lazarus.................Kenneth Thomson
Satan............................Alan Brooks
The Woman Taken in Adultery. Viola Louie
The Blind Girl.........Muriel MacCormac
Dysmas, the Repentant Thief.........
Clarence Burton
Gestas, the Unrepentant Thief.........
James Mason
The Mother of Gestas.........May Robson
Maid Servant of Caiaphas......Dot Farley
The Galilean Carpenter.......Hectar Sarno
The Imbecile Boy............Leon Holmes
Captain of the Roman Guard..Jack Padgen
Soldiers of Rome.........Robert St. Angelo, Redman Finley, James Dime, Richard Alexander, Budd Fine, William de Boar, Robert McKee, Tom London, Edward Schaeffer, Peter Norris, Dick Richards
An Executioner...............James Farley
Guests of Mary Magdalene—
Eber, a Pharisee............Otto Lederer
A Young Roman........Bryant Washburn
A Roman Noble...........Lionel Belmore
A Rich Judaean............Monte Collins
A Gallant of Galilee.......Lucia Flamma
A Prince of Persia...................Sojin
A Wealthy Merchant......Andre Cherron
A Babylonian Noble....William Costello
Slave to Mary Magdalene.....Sally Rand
Charioteer................Noble Johnson

OTHER PLAYERS

ACTRESSES

Emily Barrye	Jane Keckley
Elaine Bennett	Lydia Knott
Lucy Brown	Nora Kildare
Edna Mae Cooper	Alice Knowland
Kathleen Chambers	Kadja
Josephine Crowell	Isabelle Keith
Frances Dale	Celia Lapan
Millie Davenport	Alla Moskova
Anna De Linsky	Gertrude Norman
Lillian Elliott	Patricia Palmer
Angelka Elter	Gertrude Quality
Dale Fuller	Hedwig Reicher
Evelyn Francisco	Rae Randall
Margaret Francisco	Reeka Roberts
Winifred Greenwood	Evelyn Selbie
Julia Swayne Gordon	Semone Sergis
Inez Gomez	Peggy Schaefer
Natalie Galitzen	Anne Teeman
Edna Gordon	Barbara Tennant
Eulalie Jensen	Mabel Van Buren

ACTORS

Jere Austin	Bertram Marburgh
W. Azenberg	George Marion
Joe Bonomo	Louis Natheaux
Ed Brady	Richard Neill
Fred Becker	Robert Ober
Baldy Belmont	Louis Payne
Charles Clary	Al Priscoe
Fred Cavens	Herbert Pryor
Colin Chase	Edward Pjel
George Calliga	A. Palasty
Malcolm Denny	Warren Rodgers
Victor De Linsky	Hector Sarno
Dave Dunbar	Josef Swickard
Denis D'Auburn	Bernard Siegle
Kurt Furberg	Carl Stockdale
Sidney Franklin	William Strauss
Jack Fife	Walter Shumway
Bert Hadley	Phil Sleeman
Fred Huntley	Charles Sellon
Brandon Hurst	Mark Strong
Edwin Hearn	Tom Shirley
Stanton Heck	Charles Stevens
Otto Kottka	Paul Wiegle
Edward Lackey	Will Walling
Theodore Lorch	Charles West
Max Montor	Fred Walker
Earl Metcalf	Wilbert Wadleigh
James Marcus	Stanhope Wheatcroft

"King of Kings"

Tremendous is "The King of Kings"—tremendous in its lesson, in the daring of its picturization for a commercial theatre and tremendous in its biggest scene, the Crucifixion of Christ.

That scene alone, minus the crucifixion and of the storm only, with the ravages of God upon the Romans for the crucifixion of Jesus, as illustrated here by an electrical storm of high intensity, concluding with an upheaval of the earth, or earthquake, engulfing the peoples amongst the falling rock and earth as The Christ remained pinioned to the cross, with a dove circling around His head, can carry the whole.

There yet remains, though, so much that could and should be said about this Cecil B. DeMille stupendous outworking in celluloid of an inspired thought. It is still a jumble to one who little knows the Bible and perhaps but little more familiar of his own faith. As outstanders in this mass of Biblical reproduction of the Miracles, Parables or legends, whatever they may be called, and with no dispute of any claim, are the illustrated pictures of the only religion known to the civilized world, God and Christ. Yet here and throughout, which may be the religion of God or Christ, is another religion this picture always points to, the Truth. It's the teaching of Jesus on the film and so must have been His word in the Bible.

"The King of Kings" looks predestined to provoke many and strong arguments, according to the faith, and likely of all faiths. If achieving that end, and it may have been an aim, although the picture has been scrupulously produced to prevent adverse religious criticism, this DeMille celluloid monument will be a super-production for years to come. It should be, for the effort, the nerve, the investment and the results are entitled to that and more.

And to the one who knows so little of religion, his own or any other, this "King of Kings" strikes as almost providentially presented at a moment when the North American side of the universe appears concededly to have about gone crazy in its ideas and opinions of movements and notions or morals. Were the clergy, including in that ministers, priests and rabbis, to **urge their people and their children to see this picture, the Church might find increased congregations and be happily free from antagonizing the theatre, for "The King of Kings" should make more churchgoers. It most certainly will further respect for religion.**

As to Biblical accuracy, naught may be said, excepting that some screen license must have been taken by Jeanie Macpherson's splendidly sketched scenario and continuity, as far as continuity could be surmised. At least the story runs logically, building up finely to its impressive, gripping finale.

The auditor is carried away at times; "the picture" is forgotten. Many Scriptural incidents have been repeated, but with the only comparative scenes those Biblical ones of "The Ten Commandments" or "Ben-Hur." As a Biblical reproduction it must be said that "Kings" far surpasses either or both. This may be due to the presence of the impersonation of The Christ in this picture as impersonated by H. B. Warner. In "Ben-Hur" He was indicated only by a hand, and in "The Commandments" not at all.

Whether "The Kings" is of the life of Christ or episodic of Christ as related seems of no moment. **Those scenes reproduced, of Jesus called the carpenter and healing the multitudes, always the poor, oppressed by the Roman High Priest, starting with the redemption of Mary Magdalen and ending with the Ascension following the Crucifixion, are realistically supernatural, of sublime holding power and convincing. Those are great points for a great director.**

Mr. DeMille has singularly denoted the accepted version that Jesus was not killed by the Jews. That may amaze the masses, though it does arrive somewhat belated, as far as the Jews are concerned.

Technicolor is employed in two sections of the 14 reels, at its commencement and near the finish.

As to the impersonations there is almost as much which might be said. Mr. Warner is the accepted likeness of Jesus. He grows theatrical or moving picturish at odd times, probably unavoidable. The same inability to escape when under make-up creeps up and out here and again with all, but never lingering nor interfering with the reality of the impression.

In scenes such as The Last Supper, the seduction of Judas by the Romans to betray The Christ, the healing Miracles, the driving out of the evil spirits from Mary or the **carrying of the Cross by Jesus (one of the most excellent in execution after the Crucifixion of the picture) there is a naturalness that is entrancing, remembering these scenes are visualized reproductions.**

In appearance, the impersonators are beyond comment, since if there is a model, it must have been on hearsay in the first place. In settings, however, and often, the moving picture as etched out resembles the finest of oil paintings by the greatest of masters. They are superb.

And the acting is no less. Calling this as it must be called a performance, the Schildkrauts (father and son), after Mr. Warner, come first to attention, the father as Caiphas, the High Priest of Israel, and the younger as Judas, the traitor. And again no less Ernest Torrence as Peter, Robert Edeson as Matthew, and perhaps others likewise of the Twelve Disciples, whose desertion of Jesus is brought out pathetically, almost, while His reappearance amidst them after the resurrection is an inner thrill.

Jacqueline Logan is Mary Magdalen. It is Miss Logan who has the sheet almost entirely to herself in the first few hundred feet before **the depth is within reach. Her ride to locate the Carpenter and wean Judas away from His influence is beautifully staged, led up to and consummated by her conversion. Mary appears but infrequently thereafter. Another excellent performance among the women was Mary of Bethany, as played by Josephine Newman. The little blind girl did unusually well in action when blind and upon her recovery. She is Muriel MacCormac. Mark (if the young boy) and played by M. Moore, while taking the role very well, was too often in evidence at all times and in all places.**

If there is a discord it is the Pontius Pilate as the governor of Judea of Victor Varconi. He appeared too youthful for the power allotted and smoothly shaven, although it may be historically or biblically correct.

There are other performances and players in this huge cast that call for comment. But the picture itself too often drives the mind into channels far removed from the acting or the people on the screen. To thoroughly see or know "The King of Kings," over one viewing is required. It's an exposition of sacredness, religion, truth and faith that should be seen as often as possible; the more so, the better man, woman, boy or girl.

It seems impossible that the same screen holding this De Mille film's fountainhead could also send forth another and different picture that might be officially censored, but that's pictures and it's so. Yet those others will come and go, but "The King of Kings" will live forever, on the screen and in memory.

No one can afford to pass "Kings" by unless it is the scale. If it ultimately reaches the picture houses, then all will see it. And all should see it; the sooner the better for all.

Commercially, with Mr. De Mille making this super at a cost of $2,300,000, the picture should make money. "Ben-Hur," at its unbelievable production cost of $8,000,000 and with Marcus Loew expecting that "Hur" will eventually break even, is the basis for that. Also there is a circulation today for a super film, including, of course, the foreign market, as well as the opposite ends of all native picture exhibition, of a mighty sum. It might almost be predicted that "The King of Kings" will not only erect itself as the greatest picture ever produced, but it will reach the largest gross ever earned by a motion picture.

Cecil B. De Mille deserves both.

Sime.

MR. WU

William Nigh production for Metro-Goldwyn-Mayer starring Lon Chaney. Directed by Mr. Nigh. Adapted from the novel of Louise J. Miln by H. M. Vernon and Harold Owen. Continuity by Lorna Moon. Titles by Lotta Wood. 7,400 feet. Running time 80 minutes. At Forum, Los Angeles, April 13, for run.

Mr. Wu.........................Lon Chaney
Mrs. Gregory..................Louise Dresser
Nang Ping......................Renee Adoree
Mr. Gregory..................Holmes Herbert
Basil Gregory....................Ralph Forbes
Hilda Gregory..........Gertrude Olmstead
Ah Wong...................Mrs. Wong Wing
Mr. Muir..........................Claude King
Loo Song......................Anna May Wong
Little Wu..........................Sonny Loy

From an artistic standpoint "Mr. Wu" cannot miss. But from a commercial standpoint it looks as though this Lon Chaney starring vehicle, even though the star is calculated to get them in, will not be a big box office attraction. It is too gruesome and draggy an epic to make the folks out front want to say, "Here is another Chaney natural, don't miss it."

William Nigh is not to be blamed because his product is not commercial. No doubt the studio officials wanted the story to follow along the lines of the original novel and play, which called for the heroine being done away with, as well as the father. The last 2,500 feet of this film are as highly dramatic as any audience would want to witness. The story held the Forum audience in suspense with the continuity of Lorna Moon being perfect and consistently carried out.

However, the first half is a draggy, cumbersome series of sequences for the purpose of establishing and carrying along a plot, but proving most uninteresting. The story throughout is carried along in a heavy dramatic way. It might have been pepped up had a good gag man been called in to inject some comedy moments. There were plenty of opportunities to inject a laugh without interrupting the tale, but it was a miss, as not even an actor with comedy possibilities is in the cast.

Chaney started by playing the grandfather of Mr. Wu in the initial scenes. Then Wu grew up and became a mandarin with Chaney changing appearance and char-

acterization in accord. It was a walk-away for him.

Louise Dresser did not seem to have any chance at all. It was just a case where they missed out with her only scenes in which she could demonstrate her acting ability coming when Wu had sent for her and her daughter and tricked them into separate rooms. With Wu telling her that she must sacrifice one or the other for the crime the son had been accused of, Miss Dresser gave a heart touching mother performance by even wanting to sacrifice herself. Wu was to order the execution of the son and she stuck the dagger into his heart as he reached for the bell. It was as fine a piece of acting as could be accomplished. Renee Adoree as the daughter of the great Chinaman gave the performance she is noted for, and proved that she still has that sensuous appeal which always clicks.

Ralph Forbes seemed to be a bit out of place as the juvenile. He played it as though uneasy. His love making was not convincing, nor were any of his scenes played in that romantic way a white youth should employ in a romance with a yellow girl.

Gertrude Olmstead as the daughter had no chance at all. She just walked into scenes and out. It was really unfair to cast her for a part of this type. Anna May Wong as the companion of Nang Ping, played it in a loyal and sympathetic way. Claude King might have had a chance for comedy and stabbed at it several times, but was negative.

The story is that of the son of a great Chinese who is married according to tradition, loses his wife after childbirth and becomes wrapped up in the welfare of his daughter. He is all set to marry her off according to custom when a young Englishman makes love to and seduces her. The father hears of it from a servant. The latter is killed by the father to keep the affair quiet. The father orders the daughter to entertain the English folks, and the youth appears. The young couple have a final farewell with the girl fainting as the boy starts to leave. He is captured and put in a torture chamber.

The father takes the girl to her room and when she learns he knows, the girl confesses all.

As the Chinese custom is that a girl who disgraces herself must be killed, the father tells her coldly, and she goes to her doom at his hands. Then he sends for the family of the boy, mother and sister. The girl is taken into a chamber where there is a bandit ready to do to her what her brother did to the girl. The mother is fully informed and shown her children, and their possible fate. She tries to sacrifice herself.

Then the gong and dagger scene.

This picture is shown here for $1.65 top. It is not a special or two-a-day product. It can only draw on the reputation of Chaney. Chaney fans will not rave over it, especially in the hinterland. The production is artistic and beautiful from every angle, though it did not reach $250,000 in cost.

In the key cities it will no doubt get over to good business for a week's run, but in the smaller communities it might be safe to hold the bookings for this down to a minimum of play dates for a star picture which will not get anyone unduly excited. *Ung.*

KNOCKOUT REILLY

Paramount production. Richard Dix starred; Mary Brian and Jack Renault featured. Directed by Malcolm St. Clair. Titles by John W. (Jack) Conway. Adapted from "The Hunch," a story by Albert Payson Terhune, with scenario by Pierre Collins and Kenneth Raisbeck. At Paramount theatre, New York, week April 16. Running time about 60 minutes.

Dundee Reilly..................Richard Dix
Mary Malone..................Mary Brian
"Killer" Agerra..................Jack Renault
Pat Malone..................Harry Gribbon
"Spider" Cross..................Osgood Perkins
Mrs. Reilly..................Lucia Backus Segar
Kewpie Dugan..................Larry McGrath
Buck Lennard..................Myrtland La Varre

Richard Dix revels in a picture like "Knockout Reilly," and puts it over so far there's plenty to spare. His admirers will go for this one strong, and although it's of the prize fight variety, Dix makes it stand up so well with its continuous action that he will get them all, old and young, boys and girls.

As a fight picture, it's a pip. Any fan will admit that much. No better fight at Madison Square Garden can be recalled than the one put up by Dix and Jack Renault, with Dix going right through with it. No doubling. It's too tough to have been rehearsed and when Dix says he had two ribs fractured in that battle, you'll believe it after seeing the picture.

An exhibitor might claim that this pictured fight is better than any championship scrap, and the screen will bear him out.

Quite a neat story for a film of this kind. Also snappy captions, the latter written by Jack Conway of Variety. "Knockout Reilly" is Jack's first as a title writer on the big time. He has done very well. Some of the captions fit the situation so acutely and humorously that the laughs come spontaneously. There is a spontaneity about Jack's writing anyway, and he has carried it into captions, also brevity, another virtue.

It might have been suspected that a virgin title writer would have gone in for a wise crack at every chance or to have padded, but Jack did neither. He slipped in a laugh when needed or where the situation called for it. When it was straight, he made the caption straight, thereby disclosing that he's not alone a loose word writer or a caption writer of slang, but can put on the ritz when required. It looks like Jack is set for titling, although that means Variety must take it on the chin through losing him.

Men all over will like the fight scene, an excellent reproduction, with Joe Humphrey as the announcer and Patsy Haley as the referee. Good performances right down the line, not overlooking Jack Renault's. This must be Renault's debut also on the sheet. He's acting here as well as fighting. This will probably set Renault for pictures, as he's athletic, looks well—and can act! It's no child play part Renault has. He must look fierce, show emotion and almost assault a girl. He does them all and well. His glare in a close up is a nightmare in its reality. And how that boy can slam, but Dix socked him right back and won the championship of the world.

Coincidences were neatly worked in from the start. They never faltered even to the girl inventing an excuse that enraged Knockout Reilly to the degree that he finished off "Killer" Agerra, after Reilly was all but out with the bell saving him at the count of nine.

Several characters known in the sporting world are seen around the ringside. Cast is uniformly in balance and in keeping with the atmosphere of the picture. Mary Brian does nicely and looks well.

"Knockout Reilly" is an okay Paramount, a perfect fit for Dix. *Sime.*

ANKLES PREFERRED

Fox picture featuring Madge Bellamy. Adapted from story by James Hamilton and directed by J. G. Blystone. Glen MacWilliams, photographer. At Roxy, New York, week April 16. Running time, 58 minutes.

Norah..................Madge Bellamy
Barney..................Lawrence Gray
Ted..................Barry Norton
Hornsbee..................Allan Forrest
Flo..................Marjorie Beebe
Virginia..................Joyce Compton
Jim..................Arthur Houseman
McGuire..................J. F. MacDonald
Goldberg..................William Strauss

They pick 'em for this girl. True, they may generally be pretty much alike, but the results are there.

"Ankles Preferred" is a picture that tells its story in the title. Hence, Miss Bellamy is again to the front with a substantial display. Besides that there is the usual gown establishment. This allows for some more modeling by this Fox featured player. But a program leader for any theatre, be it of the bigger'n better type or where there's only one aisle and the screen is high. Miss Bellamy has "it" for the boys, and the women will like the costumes worn. That seems to be the regular formula which the Fox bunch slips their Madge.

In this instance "Ankles" is a flip comedy sustaining three love affairs. The girls all slave for a living and live together while the boys are well this side of financial independence.

Nothing to ponder over, with gags running all the way from taxicab stuff to walking home, and trite sayings put into the mouths of the characters by some neat titling. Not an actual howl during the unreeling, but no denying the number of laughs various bits provoked, or the stamp of approval a big Saturday matinee audience placed on it.

Lacking much as to story, this piece of studio merchandise could easily have become a bust. Deft handling, production and playing send it across.

Miss Bellamy starts behind a department store counter, has an ambition to get ahead by brain power and finally winds up convinced that the boys don't want their girl friends to do anything but look pretty. To learn this lesson she prematurely gums up the plan of McGuire and Goldberg, proprietors of a modiste shop, by announcing at a party that the firm has promised her a trip abroad if she persuades the "money man" to lend the Irish-Jewish partners some more money. Her announcement comes when Hornsbee promises her "anything," after which he walks out, but with Nora (Miss Bellamy). The resultant auto journey is interrupted when Nora jumps from the car because of Hornsbee's presumptions. This leads to a battle between Barney, the young advertising suitor, and Hornsbee.

Barney, having procured the job for Nora but objecting when the modeling gets a bit too exposive, is out of favor for remonstrating over the employers providing her with an apartment and clothes. Nora's two girl friends are also in a turmoil, so the last 500 feet is given over to straightening out the difficulties—each for a laugh.

The younger element among picture goers should dote on the exaggerated depictions of their own troubles, while the sex tangent to the theme has yet to miss with the adults.

Miss Bellamy, as usual, looks good and plays adequately. Lawrence Gray foils nicely, this pair evidently getting so they don't have to strain for team work. Marjorie Beebe and Joyce Compton send home their impression, with Arthur Houseman allotted the closing laugh. J. F. MacDonald and Wm. Strauss make their modified Potash and Perlmutter characterization stand up.

Blystone has given the vehicle pace to the extent it's on and off the screen under an hour. Little superfluous footage involved plus a couple of subtle touches that the wise mob will recognize.

A box office title and a box office picture. *Sid.*

THE BRUTE

Warner Bros. release. Directed by Irving Cummings from novel by Douglas Newton. Scenarized by Harvey Gates. Stars Monte Blue, with Leila Hyams featured. Photography by Abe Freed. Running time, 70 mins. In projection room, April 15

"Easy Going" Sondes..................Monte Blue
Jennifer Duan..................Leila Hyams
Oklahoma Red..................Clyde Cook
The Eel..................Carroll Nye
Felton..................Paul Nicholson

With an Oklahoma oil boom town as the background for most of the action, this western stacks up as different from the regular formula. There are some clever touches in the oil town "atmosphere." Ignorant Indians suddenly grown fabulously rich by the discovery of oil on their lands created some funny and unusual "nouveau riche" stunts. Because of the locale and fighting, this rates as a dandy action picture.

One millionaire brave arrives in town driving an old-fashioned glass-cased hearse. In the hearse where the coffin usually rests is his squaw and offspring. The automobile of another Indian strikes the brave's fancy, and he makes a trade of hearse, squaw and kids, and all in reutrn for the flivver. Other Indians strut about wearing oyster-size diamonds and in general acting like people crazy from sudden wealth.

Monte Blue, who began in pictures as a cowboy, rising eventually to polite continental farce, is back in the stirrups as a son of the ranges. He is the foreman of a ranch in Texas. Opposing the evil influence of Felton, keeper of a gambling and girl house. The latter frames him. Horsewhipped and driven from the state in disgrace, the cowboy appears some years later driving a mule team in the oil country of Oklahoma. Meanwhile the gambler has followed the oil boom and has opened a big joint in the oil town.

A gusher has been brought in near Felton's saloon. The shooting geyser of oil is spraying the saloon, threatened with ruin by saturation. Felton offers $3,000 to the man or crew of men who can cap the gusher. Not knowing who made the offer, the cowboy accepts and succeeds in bringing the gusher under control. This feat gives him immediate celebrity in the oil town. He discovers that Oklahoma Red (Clyde Cook), his pal from Texas, is one of the richest men in town, and has declared the cowboy is on one-half of everything.

The love interest is handled by Leila Hyams, formerly of vaudeville and legit, recently signed by Warner Brothers for leads. She has become an inmate of Felton's establishment because her brother, a weakling, is in debt and fear of Felton. The cowboy loves the girl, but does not know of the circumstances of her case, and misunderstands. Miss Hyams looks very good for pictures. "The Brute is her first featured assignment. She photographs well and has a personality different from the common run of Hollywood ingenues.

Clyde Cook, identified with two-reel comedies, was hardly recognizable as himself in his new type of characterization. He looked and acted the part of the goofey ranch hand. In giving him a chance in features the casting director's confidence was vindicated. He is the latest of a long list of slapstick comics to go "straight."

Paul Nicholson, coming to the fore among heavies of the films, registered as Felton. Still another comparatively newcomer is Carroll Nye as the weakling brother.

The final fight between the gambler and the cowboy is a darb. After breaking down several doors to get at him, the cowboy attacks the gambler with a long mule whip which snaps the gambler's revolver out of his hand. They fall over rails and have a bang-up fight, with the gambler finally dragged out of his saloon by one foot and made to eat mud. The kids in particular will love that fight.

Orchids and Ermine

First National picture starring Colleen Moore and featuring Jack Mulhall. Alfred Santell director, with story by Carey Wilson. Strand, New York, week of April 16. Running time, 69 mins.
Pink Watson...................Colleen Moore
Richard Tabor..................Jack Mulhall
Hank ....Sam Hardy
Ermintrude ....Gwen Lee

Fairly similar to "Ankles Preferred" (Fox) playing across the avenue at the Roxy. So alike in one instance that both pictures have passages taking place in the rain and on top of buses where the main character twosomes are struggling to become acquainted without an introduction. However, both pictures are liable to achieve their objectives, laughs, this one mainly on the strength of Ralph Spence's titles. One of these is a yell.

And yet Miss Moore turns in a nice performance. Always the clean-cut girl, "Orchids and Ermine" is as proportionately spic and span. Playing a hotel phone operator, Miss Moore is accosted by the usual run of lobby males, but it's all in the nature of gags without a hint of "blue." Complications arise through Richard Tabor arriving at the hotel and changing places with his valet to avoid the women chasing his money. Hanks, the underling, eventually hooks up with the wise flower stand girl, and, of course, Miss Moore grabs the genuine scion. An anti-climax is the trouble encountered in establishing Tabor's true identity.

Carey Wilson hasn't turned in much of a story. As a result it's up to Santell's direction to keep it going, and Spence has relieved him of half the responsibility with a set of titles that are as concise a piece of work as any light comedy has carried around here in some time.

Well constructed settings set the action off and Miss Moore gets a chance to appease the feminine eye when she invades a modiste shop to don the ermine and orchids she has been craving.

The picture has a tendency to slow down every once in a while, but a title comes along and lifts it up.

Miss Moore is about due for a "wow" picture. This one is not it, but neither will any house that plays it have to blush. It's clean and light entertainment, again hoking up the pedestrianism of girls who take auto rides and the struggles of the working girl to marry for love and grab money at the same time.

Jack Mulhall looks good opposite Miss Moore. Sam Hardy appears to be above his role as the valet. Gwen Lee extracts abundantly from her assignment of the wise-cracking flower girl, while the bit players come and go. However, the conception of the effeminate manager of the modiste shop stands in relief.

An old subject refreshingly treated but basically too well worn to make it a smash. If it weren't for the titles the picture would be ordinary. At that Spence's contribution is the only item that really justifies the 69 minutes of running time. *Sid.*

LOVERS

Metro-Goldwyn-Mayer picture, designated John M. Stahl Production. Ramon Novarro starred, with Alice Terry in support. Adapted from the stage play, "The World and His Wife." Running time, 56 minutes. At Capitol, New York, week April 15.
Ernesto........................Ramon Novarro
Teodora.........................Alice Terry
Don Julian....................Edward Martindel
Don Severo...................Edward Connelly
Pepito......................George K. Arthur

Dona Mercedes............Lillian Leighton
Milton.......................Holmes Herbert
Alvarez.........................John Miljan
Senor Glados...................Roy D'Arcy

A screen play of stunning pictorial beauty, photographic excellence and fine acting, but lacking in the prime essential—sustained dramatic interest. On the speaking stage it may have had a grip but in screen form it is weak in action, meager in development, and tepid in character interest.

It takes an enormous footage of titles to make the exposition clear. Much of the film merely shows people talking to each other in pairs, trios or in groups with titles to explain what they said. There is no real drama in this.

Only spirited scene in the six or so reels is a duel with swords between hero and heavy. The director seems to have realized that he had to spread out his little conflict pretty thin to make it last for the scene is drawn out, even if the denouement is pretty easy to forecast.

The point of the story is the evil that may be worked by vicious social gossips. In a play such a point might be adequately developed but the screen version does not achieve any absorbing interest in the telling. The picture more depends upon the strong attraction of its principal players and upon the unquestionable beauty of its production; also its "sweet" title. In technical treatment of backgrounds, settings and composition of the groupings the production is a marvel of artistry.

Ernesto lives with his guardian, Don Julian, middle-aged diplomat lately married to the young Teodora. The society gossips of Madrid (locale modern Spain), wag their tongues over the possibilities of a young wife and a young and handsome ward in the same household, reports of which wicked tattletale first puts the thought of anything wrong in the minds of all three, who have until now gone on happily in mutual faith.

Ernesto resents an overheard sneer in a club and gets himself into a duel; Don Julian takes on the challenge and is killed in the encounter. Ernesto then kills his foeman. Time passes (also film footage) and in the end are Ernesto and Teodora sailing on the same ship for Argentina, apparently with a marriage in the future. In the stage version it may have been dramatic material to trace the working of the poisonous slander to its evil end, but the film does not preserve that unity, being diverted from the real issue by the necessity of getting some direct and positive action into the telling. *Rush.*

Children of Divorce

Paramount production starring Clara Bow and Esther Ralston. Adopted from Owen Johnson's novel of the same name and directed by Frank Lloyd. Gary Cooper, Einar Hanson and Norman Trevor featured. At the Rialto, New York, for a run on a "grind" policy, week April 16. Running time, 72 mins.

The Cast.
Kitty Flanders ....Clara Bow
Jean Waddington ....Esther Ralston
Ted Larrabee ....Gary Cooper
Prince Ludovico de Sfax....Einar Hanson
Duke de Gondreville......Norman Trevor
Katherine Flanders ....Hedda Hopper
Tom Larrabee ....Edward Martindel
Princess de Sfax .....Julia Swayne Gordon
The Secretary ....Tom Ricketts

"Children of Divorce" doesn't appear to have enough power behind it to warrant the assumption that it should have a house to itself. Despite that the Johnson novel is being advertised as in its second printing, plus the follow up on "It" for the Clara Bow name, "Children" will probably have its trouble rolling up sizeable grosses at the Rialto for six weeks.

Readers of the book say the picture is not a genuine copy of the original script. Whether or not, this society drama shapes up as interesting program fare, that's about stretching its reels as far as

they'll go. It's a society drama of the type of which the American picture patron has had more than a smattering. Cocktail parties, unhappy marriages and a dramatic ending.

A slight twist given is that the principal youngsters are supposed to have reared themselves because of their parents' inclination for the courts.

Rich settings, lots of clothes and all players adopting drawing room mannerisms. A parlor picture with everybody putting it on a bit, including Lloyd who directed. Action has its natural moments but the role held by Miss Bow doesn't always ring true as screened. That may be due to over-direction or over-playing, besides which it has to go up against the contrast in Miss Ralston delineation, that of a wealthy and reserved girl, taken conservatively. It's possible that Lloyd has shaded too heavily between these feminine roles. Anyway, Miss Ralston wins all the sympathy (as it should be, according to the story), while Miss Bow takes the slap as the selfish and mercenary youngster.

There's no "menace" other than Kitty's temperament.

Miss Ralston rings true on her "class" impersonation and there is little doubt that both starred girls take the picture away from the men. Gary Cooper will likely find himself more at home in westerns and Hanson doesn't get much of a chance albeit he registers mildly. Norman Trevor, Hedda Hopper, and the remaining members are pretty much secondary all of the while.

Good program material because, at least, it has been technically well treated. The Misses Bow and Ralston will hold it up long enough together with its curiosity tide to warrant a week's sojourn in the larger houses. *Sid.*

NAUGHTY NANETTE

F. B. O. picture featuring Viola Dana. Directed by J. Leo Meehan from a story by C. H. Smith. Allen Seigler, cameraman. Reviewed in projection room. Running time, 50 mins.
Nanette Pearson.................Viola Dana
Lola Leeds ....Patricia Palmer
Bob Dennison..................Ed Brownell
Lucy Dennison.................Helen Foster
Bill Simmons....................Joe Young
Grandpa Dennison...........Sidney DeGray

Viola Dana trying to do a mild "Kiki" in a flyweight vehicle that may appease the flicker fanatics in the lesser emporiums. Strictly middle class stuff. Not much sense to it at any time.

The yarn carries a picture studio angle which might have been enhanced to strengthen the anemic script. However, Miss Dana trots around in short dresses and a figurative chip on her shoulder to ultimately reconcile a wandering and starving granddaughter to a wealthy grandfather. Meanwhile she cops the heir apparent for herself.

Supposedly a comedy output and will perhaps register in the villages. In other harbors there's liable to be an embargo on laughs. Miss Dana is in the title role as a fresh extra girl loved by an assistant director (Joe Young), who in turn is pursued by the script girl (Patricia Palmer). As the story works out, the character of the secondary supervisor wins all the sympathy, so Nanette finally winds up on the arm of the scion (Ed Brownell), a figure which evokes no interest whatsoever. In reality the attention centers itself on the sickly feminine wayfarer (Helen Foster) whom Nanette adopts, and the young director. Perhaps due to story construction, but this five-reeler hints that there may be possibilities in hooking up Young and Miss Foster as a juvenile team for yarns to be told via moving images.

Miss Dana is awarded a large share of lens time, but is handicapped by the odds. As to personal value, "Naughty Nanette" won't mean a thing to her, and she doesn't mean much to "Nanette." That's simply because it's one of those inane roles.

Meehan's direction is obvious throughout. Prolonged grimaces by Miss Palmer impress that she's vexed while Miss Foster appears to be almost expressionless. Yet this girl seemed to have something with which to cut loose if called upon.

Mediocre production, but the camera work meets the needs. Not altogether a humpty-dumpty and maybe can amuse when the Fords stand wheel to wheel on Main Street Saturday nights. *Sid.*

CAMILLE

First National release of Joseph M. Schenck presentation. Norma Talmadge starred. Gilbert Rowland featured and Fred Niblo director. Photographed by Oliver Marsh. At the Globe, New York, for a run beginning April 21. Running time, 96 mins. $2.20 top.

Camille ....Norma Talmadge
Armand ....Gilbert Rowland
Olympe ....Lilyan Tashman
M. Duval ....Maurice Costello
The Baron ....Harvey Clark
The Duke....................Alec B. Francis

A high-rate program release. It's doubtful if even First National believes that "Camille" can stand up as a $2 showing for any length of time.

Norma Talmadge never looked better in her life and the picture is an excellent technical example of photography and production. But to be a $2 attraction a picture must be vital. There's nothing vital about this latest version of the Dumas story.

Heavy interiors, gowns, etc., give the film an abundance of class, and the romance of the theme may get under the skins of the minority. Romantic tales are evidently riding the crest, taking "Flesh and the Devil" and "A Night of Love" as examples. "Camille" has a chance to follow up if released fast enough to be included on the incoming or maybe outgoing tide. Otherwise, Fred Niblo and Miss Talmadge have dedicated a pretty love story to the screen that lacks the punch to make it a standout.

As running at the Globe, in two halves, dramatic intensity only twice arises to make an audience forget it is watching a picture. This is when Armand returns to his suburban cottage to find Camille has left him, and when he next meets her in a gambling parlor escorted by her first financial amour, the Baron.

For some reason Niblo omitted the traditional sympathy that goes with Camille's death or a pull on the heart strings where she gives up Armand at the instigation of his father. For a demi-mondaine supposedly in the throes of the first and only real love of her life, Miss Talmadge gives in much too easily as Niblo has screened it.

In these times when hotsy-totsy film fare is splashed across the screen in unmistakable gestures, Camille's quick and well-nigh emotionless acceptance of the pater's demands is very apt to leave an audience cold. And that also goes for the aftermath of her asking the older man to kiss her as a daughter. No thrill there, either. The picture has a tendency to miss where it should grip.

And through it all Miss Talmadge looks beautiful. Never better, besides giving a sterling performance. This probably will be of decisive aid to the picture. It needs it.

Opposite Miss Talmadge is Gilbert Rowland. Fandom in general is liable to tab these two as a "cute" screen couple. That being so, it'll be enough. If they like this pair together "Camille" is going to do business in the regular program houses. For $2 it hasn't the stamina to stand up as full and satisfying entertainment.

Other than Miss Talmadge and Mr. Rowland no one shines except Harvey Clark. The latter does adequately, too, especially in his scene with Rowland when both men are at white heat over a gambling table, with Camille as the undertow that is dragging on their nerves. Beyond that nobody will ever know that Lilyan Tashman is in the picture and the couple of hundred of feet which include Alec Francis will never mean anything to him. The same for Maurice Costello.

Eye-filling sets and Miss Talmadge. That seems to have been the formula followed. Both are sufficient for program needs.

Niblo's direction includes a couple of new camera tricks. During the sequence of Armand's anguish over Camille's desertion the boy's mental agony is brought out by a series of dissolves bringing his face closer and closer to the lens until he completely fills the screen, the finish of this string going back to a three-quarter shot of the figure to pick up the action. The dissolve chain has a tendency to kill off the dramatic interest, but it is a new angle and worthy if not overly prolonged.

Another is the symbolism of night life by feminine limbs "shot" from between steps ina long stairway so that the effect is of women walking over the camera as they ascend. A new twist to the train covering the camera bit, and effective.

The picture is split into two parts, running 50 and 46 minutes respectively. How close this version adheres to the original story is probletmatical, although Chandler Sprague's continuity keeps this conception together nicely.

As a starter Camille is driven from her home into the arms of a wealthy admirer by parental cruelty. When meeting Armand she has tramped many a mile on the primrose path. Her adoption of the rose for the lily, as signified by Niblo, takes quite a while in the telling, although not so her surrender to Armand. This makes for inconsistency, but by stretching a point may be included under dramatic license.

The two throbs in the unreeling belong to Rowland. That doesn't mean that he steals the picture, for otherwise he would be smothered by Miss Talmadge. Camille's death is insignificant and will likely leave a house unmoved. Yet Miss Talmadge never loosens her hold on massed attention so long as she is on the screen.

Narration is through Armand reading the diary of his deceased love after she appears to him in a vision. So they know Camille is dead before the picture has gone 500 feet. Even if the story is so familiar as to be traditional, this is going to hurt.

You may not believe the story, but you'll believe Miss Talmadge's performance. *Sid.*

ROOKIES

Feature length comedy from Metro-Goldwyn-Mayer, featuring Karl Dane and George K. Arthur. Story by Byron Morgan; directed by Sam Wood. Titles by Joe Farnham. Running time 75 minutes. At the Capitol, New York, week April 23.

Sergeant Diggs....................Karl Dane
Greg Lee....................George K. Arthur
Betty Wayne....................Marceline Day
Zella Fay....................Louise Lorraine
The Judge....................Frank Currier
Colonel....................E. H. Calvert
Seageant O'Brien....................Tom O'Brien
Corporal O'Sullivan........Charles Sullivan
Sleepy....................Lincoln Steadman
Smarty....................Gene Stone

Here's a cleanup all over, and a money picture everywhere. "Rookies" has everything. It maintains sustained laughter for more than an hour by its wealth of legitimate low comedy; it has a neat little romance and a whale of a thrill for the finish.

All these things go into the count for a popular smash, but the special quality that gives the production its kick is the swift succession of surprise laughs. It starts out as a rollicking chuckle, progresses into broad fun and ends with a great tag kick with a terrified sergeant of the regulars descending from a runaway observation balloon in a parachute and fighting off an inquisitive hawk.

They have packed in an astonishing quantity of punch laughs, starting promptly and carrying on with remarkable resourcefulness to the end. There is one bit where Karl Dane as the roughneck drill sergeant is bawling out the clumsy recruit in the Citizen's Training Camp (George K. Arthur) that is particularly rich in comic pantomime. Dane looks as though he might eat a timid recruit alive, while Arthur, heretofore a player of bits in society pictures, is a shrinking little fellow. His expression of shocked protest at the sergeant's lurid address is as funny as anything Mack Sennett ever did in his travesty.

But "Rookies" never descends to burlesque. It's most uproarious moments are legitimate, as when the rookie draws away the soldiers crowding about the belle of the camp by sounding a fire call on a stolen bugle. Logical situation always backs up the comedy. In another place the vengeful soldiers are waiting for the rookie to come from a call on the local belle so they may wreck him. In the dark the rookie engineers another uniformed victim into their hands while he goes casually on his way to bunk.

The whole thing is done in an artless, unaffected way that gives it added flavor. Nobody tries to be funny, playing in that artless earnestness that is the essence of farce. Even the extra people have been drilled by an inspired director into the same serious and intense style of playing. There is an inspection scene where the dull witted sergeant tries to polish up a squad of misfit citizen-rookies that is another low comedy scream.

There are five reels of this unbridled frolic and then for a change of pace they stage a thrill finish that would serve to top off a big melodrama for its sheer sensation. The heroine and her aged uncle, present to watch closing maneuvers of the citizens' training camp, have gone aloft in an observation balloon, accompanied by the sergeant as escort.

The balloon breaks away from its moorings and floats away, presumably bearing all hands to destruction. The little recruit, watching from the ground, gets permission to go aloft in an aeroplane carrying parachutes. How they managed to get it on the screen is a marvel, but every detail is recorded with convincing detail, as the plane circles and jockeys above the balloon the rescuer drops from the plane to the netting of the big bag, clambers perilously down to the basket and accomplishes his mission. There is a gasp in every foot of this episode, made especially realistic by the fact that the aerial shots are projected with the distant ground as a background with all the effect of dizzy heights.

Hero and heroine descend in the same parachute for a comedy love clinch as they streak through the air, the girl trying to make her skirts behave. Joe Farnham contributes to the effectiveness of the picture with some crisp title writing. *Rush.*

SPECIAL DELIVERY

Paramount picture, starring Eddie Cantor. Directed by Wm. Goodrich. Story original by Cantor. Titled by George Marion, Jr., with Harry Hallenberger, cameraman. At Paramount, New York, week April 23. Running time, 65 mins.

Eddie.................... Eddie Cantor
Madge....................Jobyna Ralston
Harold Jones....................Wm. Powell
Harrigan....................Donald Keith
Flannigan....................Jack Dougherty

Eddie Cantor's second for Paramount is a gag picture with a thread of a story to give its hoke some semblance of coherence. Too much Cantor and a continuous series of practically unconnected comedy scenes makes the picture strain for laughs.

They've gone back into the files for a lot of stuff. Even unto a midget playing a baby and Cantor tying toy balloons to a market basket for an ascent which he stops by a shotgun, the punch being the drop of the basket on his head. The top laugh sequence comes through a fire engine chase to a steamship dock that has Cantor at the rear steering gear of one of those elongated hook and ladder trucks. Also not new, but about the high spot for "Special Delivery."

Love interest in this one, with Cantor opposite Jobyna Ralston. It doesn't look as though the popular stage comic can make an armour theme stand up. What pathos he has is not nearly so affective when playing the lover. It should be a happier solution for all concerned if Cantor is isolated from the direct love thing, but is given a hand in its ultimate and proverbial conclusion. In this case, and with that funny "pan" of his, it would be of more value to have him lose the girl, closing out to a laugh in which a "tear" might be imbedded. There's nothing romantic about Cantor in celluloid and no use dodging the issue. It will help him to say away from it.

Cantor is supposedly the son of a family long in the postal service. He's out to start at the bottom with the early possibility of capturing the swindler who has veen using the mails and whom the department is after. Following to or three reels of gags in tracing Cantor on his mail route, a series of coincidences picks up the trail of the phoney promoter (Wm. Powell), whence follows the chase to catch the South American boat. Jones, the swindler, has pursuaded Madge, lunch counter girl, to sail with and marry him on board—she having accepted the proposition because Jones looks prosperous and on Cantor's earlier self-sacrificing advice. Enough to kill off the interest of any film audience in the girl. The climax, of course, is the capture of Jones, the saving of the girl and Cantor accepted by his father as a hero.

The manner in which the film unreels hints that the cutter must have had the hardest job because of having to splice it together. Various scenes reveal Cantor's own conception of clowning mannerisms, although a comedy fist fight with the heavy rates its due.

No other cast member means anything, and production background is negligible. Paul Kelly is listed among the playing group, but doesn't appear.

Cantor's name over the title may draw 'em in, but the picture won't satisfy the mob. His next will have to be just that much stronger to stand off "Delivery" and to re-establish the start "Kid Boots" gave him. If not dynamic that one was, nevertheless, okay for a first effort.

However, other established laugh provokers have had their troubles in getting set before the camera. Cantor is also evidently in the throes of such a struggle. All comics, screen or stage, have one thing in common—the emphatic need of material. That material is missing here.

A highlight of "Delivery" at the Paramount Saturday afternoon was the way the organist on duty played it. No comedy effects, but a straight accompaniment so well executed that the house was listening, as well as watching. And it helped a picture that needed help. *Sid.*

THE HEART THIEF

P. D. C. release, featuring Lya dePuti and Joseph Schildkraut. At Keith-Albee Hippodrome, week April 25. Running time, around 60 minutes.

If the scheme here were for P. D. C. to sell a feature picture upon the names of Lya de Putti and Joseph Schildkraut, that concern should have secured its exhibs contracts in advance. There's nothing else to the picture, excepting the ever-poor projection at the Hip.

Seems too bad to have wasted the featured players here, when there are other independents with possibly good stories who would have done much better for and with them. Mr. Schildkraut and Miss de Putti have perfect walk-through roles, and that's about all they do, other than their unconsciously funny "Romeo and Juliet" bit that didn't mean a thing and the two sword battles by Schildkraut for action. Though what looked like a wop jazz orchestra furnished the R. & J. serenade.

It's about a young man hired to break up a betrothal of an elderly lord and a young girl. He's to make the girl and disgrace her. Paid for it besides. Sounds like a New York nite club crowd. But it's set in a foreign country. The young man discovers the girl he is to besmirch is his first and only love, so he earns his money easily. Even that or anything else is applesauce.

If this can hang around the one-dayers nobody should complain except the audiences.

Great stuff, that, slipping anything costing under $1,000 for rental into the K-A Hip for a week stand, and that week can be written either way. *Sime.*

HIGH HAT

First National release, with Mary Brian, Ben Lyon and Sam Hardy featured. J. A. Creelman, director and co-author of story and scenario with Melville Baker. Cameraman, William Schurr. Running time, 65 mins. At Loew's Circle, New York, one day, April 23.

High Hat........................Sam Hardy
Millie..........................Mary Brian
Director........................Lucien Prival
Assistant Director.........Osgood Perkins
Props...........................Jack Acroyd
Jerry McCoy.....................Ben Lyon
Stars...........................{Iris Gray / Ione Hones}

The boys and girls who avidly consume the monthly editions of the fan magazines will probably love this "studio" picture, with its supposedly inside stuff on picture making.

Authors have kidded their subject and poked some fun at the picture mob. They have caricatured Erich Von Stroheim so broadly that it's as clear as plate glass. Lucien Prival looks enough like Von Stroheim to be a relative. He wears a high, short Austrian haircut and a monocle.

There is a novelty to the picture that recommends it. The story and direction slop over at times, but in general its burlesque note holds it up.

Sam Hardy plays High Hat, an extra of little importance in the studio, but a big guy in a lunch room when the picture mob talks shop. He tells Pola Negri marriage would interfere with his career, and he shows John Barrymore how to kiss the girl. These thoughts are expressed in subtitles. Toward the end of the picture an "opening night" at a picture house gets in some shots of well-known stars. Hardy has shown a wide versatility before the camera and makes the conceited extra register like the authentic article.

Ben Lyon again does a boob. First National started out to make a heavy lover of this lad, but evidently discovered he was a little too boyish to carry conviction as an exemplar of passion. This time his boob character is lazy, always sleeping and falling down when given responsibility.

The only actual plot complication has to do with a string of supposedly valuable pearls used in the making of a picture. A press agent's yarn of their value results in their being stolen. The little seamstress (Mary Brian) to whom they were entrusted quits her job, leaving a note that she will work her fingers to the bone the rest of her life to pay back the value. About 75 years ago Guy de Maupassant the French author, used that idea for "A String of Pearls" with the irony that the jewels were fakes in the first place.

A darb of a gag at the finish closes the picture with a laugh. High Hat has been beaten up and is "out" on the floor. Fearing he may be dead, an assistant director places a mirror to see if breath will vaporize the mirror. The presence of a mirror immediately revives the ego and the body of the extra.

Women Want Diamonds

Edmund Goulding production for Metro-Goldwyn-Mayer, featuring Pauline Starke, Owen Moore, Lionel Barrymore and Douglas Fairbanks, Jr. Story and direction by Goulding. Photography by Ray Binger. Running time, 55 minutes. At Loew's American, April 21-24.

Picture based on a pretty delicate subject for the film trade, and the consequent cautious handling weakens it too much for any particular recognition as an unusual venture. But even in its lukewarm condition several of the states may define censorable qualities in it.

When playing program houses, as here, the film will have no trouble in getting along. The larger stands, however, may need extra exploitation to get full value out of it.

Plainly told, the story is of a girl, past unknown, first amid luxurious surroundings and later identified as the mistress of a rich bachelor posing as her uncle. The bachelor also is paying an elderly lady to act as the girl's mother.

Evidently the bachelor protests but mildly when she starts a romance with a young ultra-society youth just, as she says, for laughs. The kid takes things seriously, though, and causes a blowoff by threatening to the "uncle" that he will elope with the girl if immediate consent to marriage is not forthcoming. When the bachelor tips him off to the girl's real status the kid breaks down and wouldn't touch the girl with a ten-foot pole.

This gives the girl an idea as to how she actually rates, and sows the first seeds of discontent with her lot. Later, taking a liking to her chauffeur, who lives with his sister's family, she is drawn to him by witnessing the death in a maternity hospital of the sister while the husband is also lying near death from automobile injuries and the three kids are home wailing for their parents.

While the husband is recuperating in a hospital she acts as mother to the three children, with a mutual affection growing warm between the girl and chauffeur. But she is unwilling to let the chauffeur in on how much she thinks of him, considering herself unworthy. He in turn is somewhat backward, as he considers her beyond his class.

The girl decides that she can't stand the gaudy life any longer and starts to leave the bachelor's apartment. He interprets her departure as preliminary to elopement with the chauffeur, and threatens to expose her if she doesn't remain with him. Protesting hysterically, she suddenly tells the chauffeur herself and flees from the apartment.

It is several months later before the chauffeur again finds the girl. Meanwhile he has become a cab driver and thinks that the girl is still mistress to the bachelor. Happening to see the bachelor in a hotel, he finds that the former maid in the apartment has replaced the girl, who is now a hospital nurse. He hurries there, and the fadeout clinch follows.

There are evidences of more than average expenditure in the picture, in players and production. Interior sets are massive and brilliant. The casting, with Pauline Starke as the wayward beauty, Lionel Barrymore the bachelor, Owen Moore the chauffeur, Douglas Fairbanks, Jr., the society kid, and several well known faces among the support, seems somewhat better than the story merits.

Miss Starke, niftily gowned and handling her part easily, fails to draw sufficient sympathy, probably because it calls for too much affected posing. The fault is not with her. Barrymore is perfect as the bachelor, and Moore rates very good as the chauffeur. The society kid, played by Fairbanks, Jr., is a comparatively minor role which still registers effectively. Fairbanks looks better here than in any previous picture.

Photography given many opportunities for beauty in the attractive sets. Direction apparently was affected by surroundings, with the characters becoming noticeably stiff in the more decorative spots. In the simpler scenes it was at its best.

ALTARS OF DESIRE

Metro-Goldwyn-Mayer production, directed by Christy Cabanne. From the story by Martha Thompson Davless. Starring Mae Murray with Conway Tearle featured. Cast includes Robert Edeson, Maude George and Andre Beranger. At Loew's Lincoln Square, April 18. Running time, about one hour.

Although the title denotes nothing of the purport of the picture, it was probably retained, very properly, as a draw. "Altars of Desire" is not as strong a production as it should be on account of the garbled story material, but it is still a good bet for the three-day stands and even full weeks in certain locations.

Christy Cabanne's direction is unimpeachable when considered that he really had nothing much to work with except Mae Murray. She still looks as good as the best of them under the soft lens. Some of the shots where Mae is shown under the blind dusk or early dawn in various stages of undress are sure fire.

Conway Tearle is spared as many full-face closeups as possible, the back of his neck, shoulders and side views being concentrated upon. Andre Beranger proves himself as a strong type "comedian," partly heavy, with his interpretation of feeling on discovering that an aged spinster has flattened his top hat.

Miss Murray is the unsophisticated girl whose father insists she go to Paris to acquire polish. She returns with a lot of new clothes, new ideas and a funny French count for whom she snubs here former sweetie. The boy is loyal, though, in spite of everything and stands by until the end when it is shown that the Count has a wife through a former marriage.

The Gay Old Bird

Warner Bros.' production. Directed by Herman Raymaker, from a story by Virginia Dale. Adapted by Edward Clark. Running time, 66 mins. At Loew's New York, April 21, one day.

Angus Brown.....................John T. Murray
Mrs. Angus Brown................Jane Winton
Arthur Jones....................William Demarest
Uncle...........................John Steppling
Maid............................Louise Fazenda

As flat as a pancake.

Plot so old and so familiar it's more of a legend than a story.

Newlyweds quarrel. In the wife's absence another woman and baby are pressed into service to win the promised financial favors of a wealthy uncle who shows up suddenly.

Story credited to Virginia Dale, but hardly qualifies even as a rewrite. It is not know whether this is the Virginia Dale identified with the Chicago "Journal" as picture editor. If so, it points a moral or something for producers.

At the New York the unreeling did not produce one laugh, although there were a few snickers. The net result was a large cipher.

Jane Winton, who does vampires and chilly-hearted dames as a rule, played the wishy-washy bride. Her bungling hubby and his "fixing" friend were John T. Murray and William Demarest. Both recruits to the films from vaudeville.

Featured is Louise Fazenda, doing a goofey housemaid characterization such as made her well known years ago in the two-reelers. Clumsy housemaids seem to have gone out of style as themes for popular humor. Louise was plenty clumsy, wore mid-Victorian underwear, registered dumb and no laughs.

To make it worse, it runs over an hour.

NAPOLEON

Paris, April 16.

French-made super production by Abel Gance, dealing with the earlier life of Napoleon Bonaparte, particularly episodes of the French revolution, made by the Societe-Generale de Films (French corporation) and since bought for world distribution by Gaumont-Loew-Metro-Goldwyn.

Released at the Opera as a special gala in favor of local charitable organizations assisting war victims.

The scenario deals with historical facts in the life of the future emperor up to the war in Italy, before he even became First Consul. The picture does not include the period when the hero was known to history as Napoleon I.

The Opera showing was a triumph and there is every sign of "Napoleon" being a universal success. The triple screen, whereby (in certain portions of the picture for war scenes) the screen is increased to thrice the ordinary size caused a sensation for the lay public. The extended vision is obtained by projecting three reels from separate lanterns on three screens, the pictures synchronizing.

Details of the execution were given out for press use, wherein we are told the French government provided 5,000 troops, as supers, for the episode depicting the siege of Toulon, and the rallying of the famous army in Italy. Rock salt estimated at over a ton was used to imitate hail and half a ton of boric acid as snow. Though no deaths were to be deplored during the making of the picture, in which thousands manoeuvered with fire arms, many accidents occured, 220 claims having since been filed with the insurance companies.

The rain during the siege of Toulon is somewhat exaggerated, but the scenes during the Revolution are particularly impressing.

Albert Dieudonne in the title role is excellent. A special score by Arthur Honegger, of the new school of music grade, accompanies.

It is a splendid achievement but still needs careful pruning. *Kendrew.*

The Heart of Salome

Fox release, featuring Alma Rubens. Directed by Victor Schertzinger. Story by Allen Raymond. Scenario by Randall H. Faye. Cameraman, Glen MacWilliams. Running time, 63 mins. In projection room April 21.

Helene...........................Alma Rubens
Monte Carroll....................Walter Pidgeon
Count Boris......................Holmes Herbert
Redfern..........................Robert Agnew
Chauffeur........................Tom Dugan
Henri Bezanne....................Barry Norton
Mme. Bezanne.....................Virginia Madison

Rather heavy love "drammer," not too convincing in plot. Packs a moderate entertainment punch.

Her love "insulted and despised" because the hero discovers she is a thief's accomplice, the heroine (Alma Rubens) does a long brood with her love souring into hate and murderous desire for revenge.

This phase is very moving picturish. It is impossible to adequately sketch the mental processes that would create a psyscose of this nature. Particularly not with 200 feet of film and most of it long shots. And without conviction in this vital point that the real guts of the picture is lost.

It's particularly hard to swallow, with the thought in mind that at any moment the heroine's Salome-like desire for her lover's head and life will be lifted and she will snap out of her passing madness to again be a "good woman."

Holmes Herbert, with his hair combed so as to give him "bangs," does the "master criminal," to whom the heroine is attached by bonds of fear. The hero is kidnapped by henchman of the arch-felon and taken to a castle, a misty, weird place much like the castle of the crazy guy in Rex Ingram's picture, "The Magician." The hero is manacled to a bench in an enclosed court, through which runs a stream of turgid, vermin-infested water. He is parched for a drink, but cannot touch the poisoned water.

Master criminal and the heroine still in her mood of hatred call upon the hero and taunt him. She tells him she hates him for what he called her. That was a subtitle, which read: "You are lower than a woman of the streets. She at least is honest in her trade."

The settings in several instances were too obviously "faked." A harvest moon playing upon a pond of water in the early sequences was a flop so far as illusion was concerned. And that castle was just "painted on the scenery." Victor Schertzinger's direction is so-so, though perhaps he deserves credit for keeping the picture from becoming ridiculous.

BITTER APPLES

Warner Bros.' melodrama, starring Monte Blue, with Myrna Loy in support. Story by Harold Macgrath. Directed by Harry Hoyt, who also made the scenario. Running time, 55 minutes. Released April 23. Reviewed in projection room.

John Wyncote	Monte Blue
Belinda White	Myrna Loy
Stefani Blanco	Paul Ellis
Cyrus Thornden	Chas. Hill Mailes
Joseph Blanco	Sydney de Grey
Mrs. Channing	Ruby Blaine
Wyncote's Secretary	Patricia Grey

A straight - from - the - shoulder melodrama. Concerns itself not at all with plausible probabilities, so long as it gets the action punch over. It does that plenty.

Story is a medley of he-man fights, sex intrigue, pirate ships, revenue cutters and caveman love-making, stirred with a pitchfork and served hot to fans who take their screen romance in the raw and care not for the verities.

For this type of clientele the picture will deliver gobs of thrills, but sophisticated audiences may object to having the hero and heroine rescued from pirates sailing on tropical seas by a U. S. revenue cutter. A lot of the picture is as hard as this to swallow, but it is rich in rough stuff by way of compensation.

Monte Blue fights a whole crew of sailors from one end of a three-masted ship to the other as one incident. And the rest of the action is typical of Harold Macgrath, best seller in the red-hot fiction field. The picture is excellently made as to its technical side, with a good deal of elegance in its settings and some convincing storm effects when the ocean liner is wrecked.

They work a variation on the tropical island idea here. Instead of the hero and heroine being cast away when all are lost on board, they are knocked senseless when the ship hits a reef, waking up to find the storm abated and themselves alone on the ship caught on the rocks.

The girl had married the hero for spite, intending to make his life terrible, but, as you know is going to happen, she falls in love with him instead. And after he saves her from the messy pirates—it should be mentioned that the pirates come along and take them off the wrecked ship—there's nothing to it. She goes for her gallant hero for the works.

This Myrna Loy is an exotic looking girl, a real looker for such parts as Nazimova would revel in, but hardly for an unbridled melo.

The picture is a good example of the machine-made story done on an accepted formula. It should lend itself well to florid lobby display and hectic billing on the romantic side, with special appeal to naive screen fandom. *Rush.*

The Western Whirlwind

Blue Streak Western released by Universal. Directed by Al Rogell from the story by Rogell. Starring Jack Hoxie, with Margaret Quimby in female lead. At the Columbus, New York, April 21, one day, one-half of a double-feature program.

The only outstanding characteristic of this gem is poor camera work and bad makeup on Hoxie in the closeups. Otherwise picture is constructed along the lines of the usual western.

Jack is the returned soldier who finds his father has been murdered by the "gang" during his absence overseas. He becomes sheriff, but his mother makes him promise not to do his duty as often as possible so as to keep out of danger.

No one can sympathize with this attitude, as Jack looks bullish enough to clean up the gang, especially with a sheriff's badge on his chest. He is branded a coward, and only when the little white-haired mother's house is cleaned by bandits does she release Jack from his promise.

The audience at the Columbus razzed the picture in spots. In one scene the "menace" calls the new sheriff "yella." The sheriff leaps forward with battle in his eye, and the mob sits back awaiting a good scrap. Instead a vision of the little mother rises in front of Jack's eyes, and he walks on, crushed, to the accompaniment of silent haw-haws on the screen and loud squawks in the theatre.

CHANG

Wild animal picture produced by Merian C. Cooper and Ernest B. Schoedsack, also the producers of "Grass." "Chang" released through Paramount. Titles by Achmed Abdulla. At Rivoli, New York, week April 29. Running time, about 70 minutes. House scale, top, nights, 99c.

On the front page of the Rivoli (Publix) program is "A Request," signed "The Management," in which patrons are asked not to explain the meaning of "Chang," the title of the best wild animal picture ever made.

"Chang" may be Siamese for elephant. And the elephant here places this splendidly cameraed and made film into the $2 road show class.

What it is doing at 99c top in the Rivoli can't be figured any more than for the reason of such a request to keep silent on the biggest exploitation point of the picture.

Nowhere as far as known can a herd of 90 or 100 or more elephants be seen and especially in a jungle. The nearest approach to that might be the trained herd with the Ringling-Barnum Circus, around 40 in all, and then seen but in groups of five performing in a ring or in the menagerie peacefully awaiting peanuts.

Which might people prefer to know about, that chop suey title or 100 wild elephants in action?

Even before going into details on "Chang," mention must be made of the camera work, primarily, the photography, fine, under the conditions it must have been taken in and around, and the apparent danger the camera men seemingly and continuously exposed themselves to. No news camera man has anything on the boys who took this picture, whoever they are, probably Merian C. Cooper and Ernest B. Schoedsack, producers of the picture, placed with Paramount for release.

Every kind of wild animal is here. Most of them come head on to the camera, many at close range. With the elephants a camera or two must have been buried. They come right out of the sheet. It cannot be positively stated, of course, that these elephants are wild. In Siam every rancher may have his own elephant barn, but they look wild enough. But 100 altogether as a sight is worth $2, as much as any other picture that may be shown with a remarkable sight or scene that never before has been seen and may never be again, in another picture or elsewhere.

Perhaps some one decided, however, that the picture is not long enough for road showing. At least it is for a special run. And it's made long enough through its story and the cutting, for there are two or three anti-climaxes, where one believes the picture may stop, to have it go forward, even with the elephant scene, the best of all in up-building.

First, there is shown a baby elephant captured, and that seemed very tame, after tigers and leopards have been bowled over. Then the mother of the baby comes along, to wreck the hut her child was chained to. And then the herd, a vast number of the big tuskers that could not be counted at any time. It was an elephant roundup in fact, the natives chasing the mammoths ahead of them, through carrying branches of trees before them to make the human moving body resemble walking trees.

The elephants are sent along over land and water until packed into a corral that did not, however, contain all of them, but enough to again defy a count.

As a moving picture, however, and a wild animal film, the elephant portion is but its biggest incident. Towering above all else as an animal picture is a melodramatic story of native life in the jungle. Its continuity is perfect and the tale logical in all angles excepting here or there when the natives are doing chase stuff or escaping.

The picture carries a native cast, men and women, with two principals. No white appears in it. Animals also become unconscious actors and take their roles as they appear to frighten or drive away the little native family attempting to erect and maintain a home in the jungle, at some distance from the nearest village.

Father and mother with two young children and domestic, also wild, pets. There is a constant vigil against the jungle breeds. Leopards come in to steal their meals, tigers are seen in the jungle depths and traps and snares are made and laid. This latter will be particularly interesting to children. In fact, as a natural history lesson there could be none better than "Chang."

It all leads up to the big herd, with several bits of comedy for laughter gained through the antics mostly of a pet white chimpanzee, also a tame monkey. No names are programed other than the producers and Achmed Abdullah as the title writer. Some of the titles are a bit too flip for a writer of that name. Early in the picture, however, are some excellent straightforward captions, probably by the accredited author of them.

The first animal picture was Rainey's, that of the water hole, something other animal pictures closely followed. This "Chang" is the first animal picture having a scenario and with just an immense jungle for the background. Besides "Chang" carries more of a thrill than the other pictures of its sort, in total, for there seems danger frequently and the ferociousness of a tiger or leopard here and there is most realistic. As in the scene where the native is high up in a tree and a tiger attempting to climb it. Or when the leopard fastened onto the swinging dummy. That's when an orchestra seat is worth any price.

"Chang" is a remarkable moving picture. *Sime.*

CABARET

Paramount production, with Gilda Gray starred. Tom Moore and Chester Conklin featured. Directed by Robert G. Vignola. Adapted from story by Owen Davis, with scenario by Becky Gardiner. Titles by Jack Conway (Variety). At Paramount, New York, week April 30. Running time, about 60 minutes.

Gloria Trask	Gilda Gray
Tom Westcott	Tom Moore
Jerry Trask	Chester Conklin
Blanche Howard	Mona Palma
Andy Trask	Jack Egan
Jack Costigan	William Harrigan
Sam Roberts	Charles Byer
Mrs. Trask	Anna Lavsa

"Cabaret" runs flat for the most. It has not the snap or ginger a story called "Cabaret" should have. In fact, about all that "Cabaret" now holds is Gilda Gray and her name, and for this film her name must mean more than anything else. That should mean enough if properly boomed, for her stage career has been connected with cabaret entertainment.

Not a stand out of any character in this picture. Of course, Miss Gray's celebrated, usual and expected Annapolis dance is there, with its heaves and its hips, but shimmy dancing grew so common they were doing in on the cafe floors with nothing on. Even the cabaret scenes, while elaborate, are tepid, with a few dancing girls and Miss Gray, who heads the bill at this celluloid night club.

As better illustrating what this melodrama under a fly name means in story, there's barely a chance, and then only seldom, for Jack Conway (Variety) to let loose a laugh in the captions. It's that kind of a tale. All Conway could do was to aptly fit the situations with sets of words. Very good wording and excellent titling in that respect, but anyone knowing Jack and hearing the name of the picture would imagine it would be a fine gagging chance for him on captions. A couple or so of good laughs in the titles, but that's all. The story is so strongly dramatic all of the way there's no room left for comedy, either on the sheet or in the titles.

Chester Conklin is another sufferer from the same cause. The best he could do was a little mugging now and then as a taxi driver. Even Conklin, almost always sure fire, can't pick up over a couple of giggles.

The story itself is mild all of the while until very close to the finale, when murder complications help to heighten the tension. It has the outline of "Broadway," but misses its subject-matter. Freuently along the road to there the vapid tale was tiresome. It's one of those open-face mysteries that looks even more so until a twist comes about 1,500 feet from the kiss.

None of the players do any work beyond the ordinary. In that it's a self-player. Tom Moore is a detective, Mona Palms the bad woman, William Harrigan the cafe proprietor, squawking about bad business but carrying at least $500 in cash in the safe, and Charles Byer the dirty villun. Miss Gray's role is another walk through. It got to be a question how everyone looked more than what they did or would do. Whether different direction would have spiced it up, who can tell? The picture is finished.

The story starts in the cabaret, with the detective calling on the cabaret star, back stage, taking her home, for the first time, as she said, proposing to her on the way. By the time they reached home the couple were so friendly that the girl's father, the taxi driver, had to shake them up to break their hold. That settled all plausibility.

Although the girl didn't mind kissing the fellow all over the lot, stage and cabs, she said he didn't know her well enough to marry her, but changed her mind after the dick had saved her kid brother from a murder charge. The guy knocked off was the villun, but he was doing his part well enough to have stuck it out with the others.

Smart moving picture detective work did the rest.

This is Miss Gray's final picture for Paramount. Her next will be for Sam Goldwyn, through United Artists, and Sam had better get right to work on a story. *Sime.*

VENUS OF VENICE

First National picture, starring Constance Talmadge and featuring Antonio Moreno. Wallace Smith story directed by Marshall Neilan. At the Capitol, New York, week April 30. Running time, 70 minutes.

Carlotta..................Constance Talmadge
Kenneth..................Antonio Moreno
Jean..................Julianne Johnston
Journalist..................Edward Martindel
Marco..................Michael Vavitch
Ludvico..................Arthur Thalasso
Giuseppe..................Andre Lenoy
Bride..................Carmelita Geraghty

Nonsensical, dumb and dull.

Constance Talmadge looks good, and that lets the picture out. The story isn't there, and Marshall Neilan has done nothing with it. Loge inhabitants at the Capitol Saturday night were distinctly bored.

Venice means water, so Miss Talmadge has ample opportunity to display her aquatic ability. After 70 minutes the only thing the house is convinced of is that Connie possesses a mean crawl. Every 500 feet Neilan has her diving, and as they're all straight dives the plunging becomes monotonous.

No reason at all for running over an hour. It could be cut 20 minutes and still lack the requisites of de luxe house fare.

Productionally the picture is pretty. The canals and a masque mall are not hard to gaze at. But the story: Carlotta is the aid of a crook ambling about as a blind peddler. Running from the gendarmes, she drops into the gondola of Kenneth, who immediately succumbs and instigates a reform campaign. The social affair behind masks is a great opportunity for a grab at a pearl necklace, Marco lifts it and Carlotta steals it from him to mark her turn to the right. A swimming finale in which Kenneth is pursuing Carlotta closes.

Neilan has padded plenty to get the required footage. It may have looked good in script, but that opinion is completely reversed on the screen. It must have been obvious in the projection room as well.

One cast member stands out on performance. The Misses Talmadge, Johnston and Geraghty have appearance and are called upon for little more. The same holds true of the men, with Michael Vavitch, as the sham blind beggar, the only individual to convince.

This half of the Talmadge sisters needs special material at all times. A good yarn with Constance has its points, but a bad story makes it rather hopeless. Aimed at being a light comedy, there are few snickers, with George Marion, Jr., apparently realizing the futility of helping it by titles.

Not first-run house material and in need of concentrated strength on the surrounding program to make any kind of a showing. *Sid.*

MOTHER

F. B. O. Production starring Belle Bennett. Suggested from novel by Kathleen Norris. Directed by Joseph Leo Meehan. Cast includes Mabel Scott, Crawford Kent, William Bakewell, Joyce Coad, Sam Allen and Charlotte Stedis. At the Hippodrome, N. Y., May 2. Running time, about 60 mins.

This is nothing more than an ordinary picture relying solely on the title and the star for drawing power. Evidently intended as a neighborhood card, the production should fulfill its destiny.

As far as Belle Bennett is concerned, this new film will not increase her stock of laurels.

"Mother" is a hackneyed proposition all around. Giving credit to Kathleen Norris for the idea is as funny as charging a bootlegger with concocting the yarn.

Audience reaction to the film was nil. It didn't make 'em cry, laugh or think. It is an old story that will stand repeating in certain sections. The billing carries Belle Bennett, "who appeared in Stella Dallas."

It seems that Mother in this case is quite the patient, long-suffering creature every one knows her to be. The characterization is not dramatized to make it mean anything in the way of entertainment. And as far as could be judged from those who attended no one seemed particularly interested in a regular household routine that is common property. The story consists of a series of connected incidents with no central pivot.

Mom is blessed with a wise-cracking kid who becomes disgusting at times through sheer brightness and a little girl. Also a vague husband whose duty it is to register extreme failure during the first half of the picture.

With an inherited $10,000 friend wife sets hubby up as an architect on his own after he is discharged by employers. Hubby prospers and, although a well-meaning parent and household bulwark, lets himself be chased by another woman.

The idea through it all is that mother refuses to take offense at anything, forgives the guilty, cheers the suffering, helps the poor and so on. Just about enough cloying sweetness to ruin any one's appetite.

In spite of the mishandling, Miss Bennett manages to look well and play well, even if not up to her former standard.

THE CLIMBERS

Warner Bros. production starring Irene Rich in Tom Gibson's adaptation of Clyde Fitch's play of that name. Directed by Paul Stein. At the Colony, New York, week of April 30. Running time, 80 mins.

Duchess of Aragon..................Irene Rich
Pancho Mendoza..................Clyde Cook
Duke Cordova..................Forrest Stanley
Laska..................Flobelle Fairbanks
Countess Veya..................Myrna Loy
Martinez..................Anders Randolph
Juana..................Dot Farley
Queen..................Rosemary Cooper
Duke of Aragon..................Nigel Barrie
Ensign Carlos..................Joseph Striker
Miguel..................Hector V. Sarno
King Ferdinand VII..................Max Barwin
Clotilda..................Martha Franklin

"The Climbers' 'was a Clyde Fitch stage success in which Amelia Bingham came to fame many years ago. From hearsay, the play was a modern comedy-drama of contemporary American life. As far as the film version is concerned, it's an entirely different affair. It's a far cry from modern comedy-drama to a play with characters out of the pages of history dating back to the Spanish Inquisition.

Furthermore, the title is a misnomer, excepting for the opening shots at the Spanish court, where one of the nobility during the reign of Ferdinand is characterized as seeking high political and social favors at court.

The action following the banishment of the Duchess of Aragon is shifted to Porto Rico, where the erstwhile lady is depicted as a cruel taskmistress in the administration of her extensive landholds.

The dramatic interest revolves about the long lost daughter and the romance is contributed by Forrest Stanley as El Blanco, a notorious bandit, alias the Duke Cordova, who was also banished by royal mandate.

It's pretty long drawn out stuff, running 80 minutes and sags intermittently for this and other reasons. An attempt at plenty of action is not unsuccessful, the shifting situations presenting a kaleidoscopic scenario. However, there is plenty of room for judicious chopping.

Miss Rich gives an intelligent performance and Stanley as the sympathetic brigand is a dashing vis-a-vis. Clyde Cook doesn't get started somehow, although there are opportunities for comedy relief.

With Vitaphone coupling at the Colony, "The Climbers" will do for a week's stay, but is otherwise a good daily change program feature. *Abel.*

THE DENVER DUDE

Universal-Jewel, starring Hoot Gibson. Story by Earle Snell. Directed by Reaves Eason. At the Columbus theatre, New York, on double feature bill, April 29. Running time, 62 mins.

Rodeo Randall..................Hoot Gibson
Rodeo's father..................Charles Newton
Colonel Lamar..................Howard Truesdale
Slim Jones..................Slim Summerville
Henry Bird..................Rolfe Sedan
Patricia Lamar..................Blanche Mehaffey
Bob Flint..................Robert McKim
Boston fop..................Glenn Tryon
The fop's mother..................Mathilda Brundage
Sandy McTavish..................Henry Todd

The Hoot Gibson U's may not be improving in point of story, but by the great horn spoon the supporting cast is perking up in talent. This Gibson western is all west and a yard wide in one respect, namely, a lot of wild, reckless daredevil work astride a horse's back by Hoot.

By way of starting it off with wild and woolly animation, there are shots of cowboys at rodeo play, a pastime that looks zippy and exciting before the camera.

There is plenty of villainy in this Gibson with Bob McKim taking gilt-edge care of the role all the way. And right here a pin can be stuck as to the film valuation of a nice looking gal in these westerns. Miss Mehaffey not only looked athletic when in her riding togs, but she was always a pleasing bit of femininity throughout. That was a help to the story. The moment Gibson doffed his western raiment and bedecked himself a la dude; it came close to being an effeminate delineation in so far as the type was concerned, but the real effeminate role was handled by Glenn Tryon.

It's not an unusual picture; interesting in spots, has some bully photography and the shots of all of Gibson's horse accomplishments are a feature. The picture will more than hold up on double feature days, but may not hit it so vibrantly when billed alone.

Tryon is the boy that has been doing a lot of two reelers under Pathe release for some time. It was reported in the east that he was being groomed to step into Harry Langdon's shoes on the Mack Sennett lot. Anyway, here he is supporting Gibson; all that his role called for he did and did well. In an opposite comedy role was Slim Summerville as the stewed, elongated cowpuncher and still another, Henry Todd, as a Scot bagpiper.

The cast worked hard, but the story isn't there to make it a stand out. *Mark.*

Pleasure Before Business

Independent feature comedy offered by Sam Zierler of Commonwealth. Produced under direction of Harry Cohn (Columbia). In cast: Max Davidson, lead; Virginia Browne Faire, ingenue; Pat O'Malley and Rosa Rssanova, character old woman. Running time 59 minutes. At Broadway, New York, week May 2.

Another screen exploitation of the "Abie's Irish Rose" idea, although here worked out with a comedy melodramatic climax that made the crowd at the Broadway sit up. Much of the humor is in the form of titles such as a thrifty Jew who has suddenly turned prodigal with inherited money, begging the family "not to be Scotch," when they object to his extravagances. Gagging of titles is skilfully done for the registering of hoke points, effective with small time fans, for which the film probably was designed.

The story has some good action. Jewish cigar maker suffers a breakdown and is warned by the doctor to rest. His wife tells him he has inherited a fortune from his uncle Max, to get him to quit business. Meanwhile they give him the money saved for the daughter's dowry. The cigar maker embarks upon an orgy of spending. He buys clothes by the truckload, such things as checked plus fours to go with a dinner coat. He buys a yachting suit and then a yacht to go with it.

In a last splurge of spending he bets $5,000 on a 40-to-1 shot and learns just before the race starts that the story of the fortune was a hoax. All hands rush to the race track to try to salvage the $5,000 wagered, only to find that the money can't be recovered. Just then the race starts, and of course, the long shot wins for a happy finale in a driving finish of a horse race and the marriage of the dotless daughter to the doctor, capping a romance that has served as a sub-motif of the whole story.

Davidson is a fine type for the spendthrift old man playing effectively without trying too hard. Miss Rosanova fits into the picture. There is a laughable comedy character in the daughter's former lover, laughable, that is, to audiences who still find these rehashed "Abie" things entertaining. That's

where the picture grades—good for laughs with that kind of audience. "Abie" pictures are sure getters in the right spots, but no novelty.
Rush.

THE SCORCHER

Rayart picture starring Reed Howes. Story by Robert Symonds. Directed by Harry C. Brown. Cast includes Hank Mann, Harry Allen, Ernest Hilliard, George Chapman and Thelma Parr. At Loew's New York, New York, Saturday, March 18, half of double bill. Running time, 52 mins.

Looked like the Glidden tour on motorcycles the way the footage burned up here to establish supremacy among a number of bike riders in an up-hill, down-grade contest, with Reed Howes, of course, riding the winning bike.

Pretty hard to hold romance and story together when motorcycles are whizzing so fast that it was almost impossible to keep track of them until a cut-in where announcements were made how the riders were progressing.

Every attempt to make something big out of a motor race fails to lift this film's head above salvage, and if it hits the double feature days it will just about obtain its compensation.

One of those impossible stories with a weak attempt to inject comedy through the athletic hero named Mike O'Malley framing up a repair biz with an "arab" named Goldberg, with a palpable try at Milt Gross dialect thrown in.

Looked like a lot of film waste to make Howes as the lead important in the eyes of his lady love who, as might be expected, is the daughter of the president of the very rich company which can do right by our boy, Mike, if he sees fit, and which he does later, as all films of this stripe reveal when it comes time for "iris" or the "fade out."

There are a few brief interesting minutes otherwise the picture submerges Howes, story and everything else. The camera got a workout, and full credit must go to the way its operator caught those scenes in the open where the motorcycles are doing their stuff.

Seemed the easiest thing in the world for the president's daughter to be hanging around the dirty, smeary, grimy workshop where the young hero was in overalls.

If Howes worked throughout this picture then he must have been mighty glad that the motorcycle work was over, for it sure appeared like hard work and lots of it.

Nothing to commend here beyond the photography. *Mark.*

SPUDS

John Adams presents Larry Semon in a full-length comedy. Story and direction by Larry Semon. Photography by H. F. Koenekamp. Released by Pathe. Running time, 59 mins. Half double bill one day, April 12, at Loew's New York.

Captain	Edward Hearne
Sergeant	Kewpie Morgan
General	Robert J. Graves
Bertha	Hazel Howell
Spy	Hugh Fay
Madelon	Dorothy Dwan
Spuds	Larry Semon

A Hollywood press agent termed Larry Semon "the man with the million-gag mind." If a few of the million were original Semon might get by in the feature-length division. As it is, his few efforts in the big league section have been merely expanded two-reelers. In the shorts Semon for some time was the most outstanding survivor of the custard-pie traditions. His failure to click as a five-reel comedian is attested by his now being with Paramount as a non-acting gag man and "chase" director.

"Spuds" is hokum all the way. Some laughs and a few bright moments, but mostly an over-effort and straining for humor where there is none, that palls on an audience.

"Spuds" is a hard-luck buck private in the war. He is first seen buried in an avalanche of potato peelings after a protracted period of kitchen police. The top sergeant is forever picking on "Spuds," with the latter performing miracles of bravery and daring in a dumb way, without credit or recognition. An armored pay car is stolen while under the charge of the captain, who, it seems, knew Spuds in private life. The captain is placed under arrest. Spuds by accident chances upon the stolen pay car and recovers it from the Germans.

The parts are all bits with the exception of Semon's and Kewpie Morgan as the big and tough sergeant. Dorothy Dwan (Mrs. Semon) has a minor in-and-out role of a French waitress.

"Spuds" has no human interest, and the gags, although well dovetailed at times, never mean much.

Cyclone of the Range

F. B. O. release, starring Tom Tyler. Directed by Bob De Lacy from original story by Olive Drake. Photographed by Nick Musuraca. Running time, 55 mins. In projection room April 20.

Tom Mackay	Tom Tyler
Mollie Butler	Elsie Tarron
Seth Butler	Harry O'Connor
Jake Darkin	Dick Howard
Frankie Butler	Frankie Darro
The Black Rider	Harry Woods

A pleasing mixture of those western ingredients which patrons of the adventure stands enjoy and expect. Contains speed, constant action, unpretentious love theme and a rippling of comedy throughout. Consequently it can't fail to click in the places where they crave lots of pepper in their film fares, even at the expense of reasonability.

Nothing new in the plot, but its pace keeps it from being tiresome. Story deals with Tom Mackay, roving cowpuncher, out to avenge the murder of his elder brother at the hands of the Black Rider. Securing a job on a ranch, he immediately falls for the owner's daughter, thus getting in bad with the outfit's foreman, who is having a one-sided courtship with the girl himself.

Don Alvarado, owner of an adjoining ranch and secretly the Black Rider, also is hot after the femme. Earlier fighting in this looks somewhat puny, but the climax fight is heavy whaling and should get enthusiasm. Photography makes little attempt at beauty, being simply a clear portrayal of action and very good as that.

Tyler, clean-cut western type, gives a normal healthy characterization in this picture, while Elsie Tarron, the ranch owner's daughter, is mostly a subsidiary to the action and has no real opportunity to register. One of the cast, Harry Woods as the Black Rider, indulges in a little acting and doesn't hurt things at all.

Frankie Darro, kid actor, is much in evidence as sole comedy material, and as directed shows himself naturally adapted to juvenile humor. Not far behind Tyler in interest attraction. Other support is suitable. An action picture with a punch.

HILLS OF PERIL

Fox production directed by Lambert Hillyer, starring Buck Jones, with Georgia Hale. Scenario by Jack Jungmeyer. At Fox's Academy of Music May 2-4 as half of double-feature bill. Running time about 55 minutes.

Corey Ford, who burlesques anything and everybody for the lighter magazines, once wrote his idea of the average western story. It was almost identical with the plot of this, even to the name of the hero. Which is sufficient indication that "Hills of Peril" gets along quite well in the average western classification. It's even better, considering that Buck Jones improves any story he carries.

His feminine opposite, Georgia Hale, didn't s. a. at all in this picture. Photography didn't give her half a break, except in one instance where they fuzzed her up. Picture weak on this angle.

Story concerns Buck Laramie, roving cowpuncher who enters a bad Virginia town and immediately gets into a fight for the cause of law and order. Ellen Wade is for wiping out the liquor mysteriously coming into town, and warms up to Buck when he displays his virtue.

The mayor of the burg and his gang secretly are making the bad liquor afloat—in Ellen's mine, unknown to her. In a melee the local sheriff is killed and the better element want to give Buck the star.

He refuses, and they turn against him. Doing a solo, he captures the liquor makers, cleans up the town, and then explains that he refused the star before because he couldn't have worked so well with it.

They offer it again. He takes it—and the girl.

Fist and gun fights throughout. Fast chases on horseback. Mr. Jones smiling and mauling.

Crowd will like it.

MILLIONAIRES

Warner Brothers' release featuring George Sidney, Vera Gordon and Louise Fazenda. Suggested by E. Phillips Oppenheim's "The Inevitable Millionaires." Directed by Herman Raymaker. Running time, 58 minutes. At the Arena one day, April 28, as half of double bill.

Meyer Rubens	George Sidney
Esther Rubens	Vera Gordon
Reba Rubens	Helene Costello
Sara Lavin	Louise Fazenda
Maurice Lavin	Nat Carr

A picture without a trace of youthful love theme. To replace it are a humorous characterization by George Sidney and a slight evidence of elderly matrimonial affection after the first 45 minutes' worth of film. No go; a picture, like a horse, doesn't stand up so well without any neck. They might have rung in an Irish policeman to fall in love with Sidney's daughter. Lack of love theme hurts muchly.

"Millionaires" must have support for any but the smaller houses.

The plot is easy; an old reliable. Meyer Rubens, tailor on the east side, is heckled by his wife because her sister has married into money and makes frequent visits to Meyer's shop to put on the dog.

In an effort to get quick money for the sake of the frau, the tailor purchases some apparently worthless oil stock from his sister-in-law's hubby. But the well comes in, and the Rubens family are in the millions.

The rest is mostly comedy around the former tailor's attempts to hobnob with the ultra. He's a flop, naturally, and his wife becomes so disgusted she is persuaded by her sister's husband to seek a separation. The gent wants control of the dough, and is willing to get rid of both his wife and his tailor brother-in-law for the sake of it.

Ever willing to help his wife, Meyer permits himself to be framed with a dame in a hotel room. Then he sadly goes back to his old tailor shop where he belongs. And his wife follows.

The story takes little footage. Gags are played extensively, so much so that they resemble a patchwork of skits. And all pretty familiar. One is the blundering millionaire at a social dinner, eating and acting all wet; another is a golf game, wherein Meyer plows up the course; the third major event is a horseback ride, Meyer again having comic difficulties.

With no love to carry things along, George Sidney bears the burden of responsibility throughout. His comedy is neat stuff. As is, however, the picture is too much for him to carry alone with satisfying results, and Sidney misses a chance to score as he has done in later pictures. (This one is several months old.)

Vera Gordon has a somewhat unsympathetic part as the nagging wife, but otherwise does her typical Jewish mother. Louise Fazenda is in a minor part with no real chance for comedy. Nat Carr, as the sharp-witted brother-in-law, has a couple of effective spots. The major portion of his appearances, however, is dummy stuff. Other characters are negligible—even Helene Costello.

Direction and photography, while good, can't help much, and the picture misses by several yards.

WOLVES OF THE AIR

Sterling production, with Johnny Walker and Lois Boyd featured. Story by J. Francis O'Fearna. Direction by Francis Foard. Running time, about 55 minutes. At the Arena, New York, as half of double bill, April 28.

Dirty work in the airplane game with a title to draw the ones who like it, enough action and comedy to satisfy that crowd. Therefore this is okeh in the action class.

Johnny Walker, the youngster, went to France for the big debate and returns to find his father's airplane factory in the hands of an unscrupulous character, has little besides action, and he couldn't miss on that if he tried. Lois Boyd, gingham gal, who loves him but doesn't get him till the end, smiles real sweetly and clicks on that alone.

Couple of other names in the film —Mildred Harris as Walker's fiancee, secretly a hophead and out for the boy's money, has little to do besides ditch Walker when he goes broke. Maurice Costello also has surprisingly little to do as Walker's father, dying quite early in the picture. Their names look well on the billing, though.

The comedy team are Billy Betcher and Bud Jamison, with plenty to carry, and doing it well. They help along considerably. Gayne Whitman villains around in a cultured and entirely suitable manner.

The kid builds a plane to enter a race against one put out by the man now in control of the factory for the government's air mail contract. Villain spoils things something terrible, but Walker's plane is all right at the start of the race. With Walker at a hospital with a wounded buddy, the gingham heroine drives the plane herself.

Most of the mid-air tricks are faked, but there's some excitement in 'em. The picture also was helped along in early war scenes by newsreel inserts.

Considered, though, as a typical speed affair, with comedy intermissions, this one should go along quite well.

MEN OF DARING

Universal release directed by Albert Rogell. Story by Marion Jackson. Cast includes Jack Hoxie, Ena Gregory. Running time, 65 mins. On double feature bill at Loew's New York, one day, April 29.

Well above average western dealing with the gold rush to the Black Hills of the Dakotas around 1875. An announcement states the picture was made near Deadwood, S. D., and the scenery indicates as much.

Among the emigrants is a small group of religious fanatics who seek not gold but the doing of evangelical deeds. They are en route to join a larger wagon train proceeding cautiously through the danger zone of the Badlands infested with hostile Indians and rendered more hazardous by Black Roger, a bandit. This latter particularly may or may not be historical. The Indians are mentioned by name as Blackfeet, Sioux and Cheyennes.

Three former army scouts led by Jack Taylor (Jack Hoxie) join the pious trekers. The head of the religious cult, who wears a puritan-like cape and hat and carries a staff in the form of a cross, is killed. He passed on the shepherdship of his flock to the scout, who isn't much on expounding the scripture to his flock, but gives them some high-class protection from Indians and bandits. A romance between the scout and a girl with the religious colony (Ena Gregory) develops.

Direction good and all essential production details well handled. Plenty of action and lots of fighting.

DOWN THE STRETCH

Universal release. Directed by King Baggot from the story by Gerald Beaumont. Co-featuring Marion Nixon and George Agnew. Cast includes Jack Daugherty, Otis Harlan, Ward Crane, Virginia True Boardman, Lincoln Plummer and Ena Gregory. At Loew's New York, one day, April 6.

Containing an unusually strong cast, with the exception of the featured players, this picture could have been turned into a much better small town box office bet than it is with more attention to story and direction.

Continuous, undiluted suffering grows obnoxious. George Agnew is a jockey who has to make weight in order to ride the favorite in the big race. He fasts for days and days to get down to 110.

No sympathy for the boy, because the trainer is a villainous character who is responsible for the death of one jockey who was overstarved. The feeling is that Agnew is not starving for a worthy cause. No subtitles could overcome that.

In small parts, Jack Daugherty and Ena Gregory as the square young race horse owner and his girl make a charming pair and seem worthy of better things. Marion Nixon displays no exceptional talent, and, in addition, has the uncompromising position of urging a young man on the point of death to continue starving.

Otis Harlan, blackface comedian, figures for laughs, with Lincoln Plummer, the best trouper in the outfit, as an unconcerned but vicious, overbearing figure when it comes to starving jockeys to make weight.

7th HEAVEN

Fox production. Adapted from Austin Strong's stage play by Benjamin Glazer. Directed by Frank Borzage. Edited and titled by Katherine Hilliker and H. H. Caldwell. Settings by Harry Oliver. Lou Borzage, assistant director and Ernest Palmer, camera man. World premiere at Carthay Circle, Los Angeles, May 6. Running time, 115 minutes.

Diane....................Janet Gaynor
Chico....................Charles Farrell
Col. Brissac....................Ben Bard
Gobin....................David Butler
Madame Gobin............Marie Mosquini
Boul....................Albert Gran
Nana................Gladys Brockwell
Pere Chevillion............Emile Chautard
Sewer Rat....................George Stone
Aunt Valentine Vulmir......Jessie Haslett
Uncle Geores Vulmir.......Brandon Hurst
Arlette....................Lillian West

Abundance of war pictures that have hit the clear and been placed in the road show or $2 class. With anything now coming along with a tinge of war in it, there is a bit of skepticism as to its success. However, no fear in any direction as to the success of "Seventh Heaven." It is a great big romantic, gripping and red-blooded story told in a straight to the shoulder way and when the last foot of some 11,000 or so feet is unwound, if there is a dry eyelash on either man, woman or child, they just have no red blood.

This Frank Borzage production is an out-and-out hit and one on the $2 order. It is going to click as big if not bigger than any of its predecessors. Though "The Big Parade" got a big start on it, there is no reason why this one will not turn in the shekels just as fast and as consistent as the M-G-M product.

Borzage is entitled to the blue ribbon for this one. He has made a great picture which is going to do the William Fox bankroll lots of good: secondly, he brought to the fore a little girl who has been playing parts in pictures for two years and made a real star out of her over night. They have been saying that ever since Irving Cummings selected Janet Gaynor for a role in "Johnstown Flood," that she had it on the "ball." But it took Borzage to take this young woman and let her smack the ball full on the nose by elevating herself into the Lillian Gish grade. She has become a little comedienne over as pretty a scene when Charles Farrell on being called to war, as could be made.

Borzage can also take credit for bringing Farrell over the hurdles. Farrell, of course, had the youthful lead in "Old Ironsides." They said he was excellent. But his work in that opus did not come one-two-forty with his performance in this picture.

David Butler comes into his own as Gobin. Butler has always been considered a good character lead, but now he can step out as an excellent one. George Stone, until recently a vaudevillian, has his first shot at a part in the cinema. He played the rat in the devoted and cringing fashion it should be, and gave a realistic performance that could easily have been distorted. Stone got one chance at comedy and went over on all six. This youth is another of those comedy finds that Fox has like Sammy Cohen and Ted McNamara.

Ben Bard was a most unconvincing menace. As a rule there is something sympathetic or appealing in the make-up of a heavy. That was lacking in Bard's performance.

Emile Chautard was a sweet, sympathetic and loyal character as the priest. He played it as those French priests enact the part in real life, and had the sympathy of the audience throughout. Albert Gran as "Papa Boul," taxi driver, made one believe they were in actual contact with a "one lunger" bandit of the Paris highways. Gladys Brockwell as the drunken and cruel sister did well in her short appearance on the sheet. Marie Mosquini, Jessie Haslett, Brandon Hurst and Lillian West were among those flashed on for a bit and away, upholding their acting dignity in what they had to do.

A new trick shot that Ernest Palmer introduced was showing the couple walking up seven flights of stairs. It was by synchronizing two cameras, one overlapping the other as the shots were taken, giving every movement of the couple as they climbed.

There were not more than 2,500 feet of actual warfare in the film. Balance of the story is romance. A big punch is the march of the taxi cabs and trucks and pleasure cars with troops 30 miles from Paris to the Marne to stem the advance of the Germans. This scene was a great kick but might have been better had the cabs been more compactly placed in the advance to the front, and had not they been so evenly spaced in the miniature. This, however, would not be so noticeable to the lay person as it is to one who sees the technical stunts performed.

The first 2,000 feet seem a little slow, but from that spot on one cannot take his eyes off the silver sheet. The story just holds and grips from then on to the finish. Folks will wait for it always, due to the intensiveness of the anti-climax footage.

This one cost Fox around $1,300,000 and took over six months to make. But the investment was well made as it will be bound to run six months in some of the bigger key cities and bring home the bacon aplenty. *Ung.*

SENORITA

Paramount picture starring Bebe Daniels Features James Hall and William Powell. Story by John McDermott, with Clarence Badger director. Titles by Robert Hopkins. At the Paramount, New York, week May 7. Running time, 71 mins.

Senorita....................Bebe Daniels
Roger Oliveros................James Hall
Ramon Oliveros............William Powell
Don Hernandez............Josef Swickard

A feminine "Mark of Zorro" and a corking light comedy with plenty of action. Able cast support, with a more or less hectic South American ranchers' feud as the background. Miss Daniels swings from chandeliers, duels eight or nine men at a time, hops off balconies and is generally all over the place disguised as a boy. Good material for this girl, and she can handle it.

Miss Daniels hasn't been around in some time, although her last couple of pictures have sent her well along the road to revived box office interest. This one will add to its rejuvenation.

"Senorita" is swift, amusing and clean. These 70-minute light comedies aren't so easy to turn out, but this one runs 71 and checks in as an exception. If a familiar story, Clarence Badger has cut it to the bone and paced it so fast that there's always something on tap. Whether they know what's coming or not, they'll wait to see it just the same. The clinch climax is the picture's weakest point. It can't follow the preceding action. A comedy finale would have made this release pretty close to 100 per cent.

Miss Daniels romps, and how. The number of times "doubles" have been called in for the stunts doesn't matter. The footage is too busy clicking off its even time for every hundred yards to make this a defect. And the star is particularly well foiled by William Powell as the light comedy "heavy," who would steal her grandfather's cattle and sell them without his cousin's knowledge.

Being the granddaughter of a proud South American grandfather, Miss Daniels is smuggled into the world as a son. The grandparent sends in a call for his supposed boy when matters get too hot between the Hernandez and the Oliveros. Being more boy than girl, Francisco changes clothes upon arrival so as not to disappoint her relative. The scrap between the two ranching factions and the ultimate love affair between the rival young leaders takes up the rest of the time, a duel of swords between Roger and the girl winding up when she is injured and her tightly wound bandana loosens.

Nice program material aimed for laughs and getting them. No howls, but steady giggles and bound to keep a house smiling. Miss Daniels plays it for full worth under Badger's supervision, and has evidently reached that point where the film-going mob is looking ahead for her pictures, wondering when she dosen't show every so often.

The musical comedy James Hall is not the standout here that he has been when previously opposite Miss Daniels. In this instance he simply suffers from being buried under the performance of Powell, who has turned in a corking piece of work. Other cast members, unprogrammed, also handily contribute as to comedy values.

Sturdy sets give the action adequate background, while nice photography and titling, despite a couple of well-worn gags, add to the total.

Neither Paramount nor Miss Daniels can go wrong on "Senorita." In those localities where the latter is weak this picture figures to start filling in that handicap. *Sid.*

CONVOY

Robert Kane production in association with Victor H. and Edward R. Hakperin. Dorothy Mackaill and Lowell Sherman featured, with Lawrence Gray, William Collier, Jr., and Ian Keith, sub-featured by Strand program. Picture directed by Joseph C. Boyle. Scenario by Willis Goldbeck from adaptation from story of "The Song of the Dragon." At Strand, New York, week May 7. Running time around 75 minutes.

Ernest Drake............Lowell Sherman
Sylvia Dodge............Dorothy Mackaill
John Dodge ....William Collier, Jr.
Eugene Wyeth............Lawrence Gray
Smith ....Ian Keith
Mrs. Wyeth ....Gail Kane
Mr. Dodge................Vincent Serrano
Smith's Assistant............Donald Reed
Eddie ....Eddie Gribbon
Jack ....Jack Ackroyd
Ione ....Ione Holmes

"Convoy" is a series of sea warfare scenes surrounded by a structure of a very light melodramatic secret service story. Neither the sea sights nor the tale carry weight, leaving the picture barren of sensationalism and weary in plot.

A slide stated the U. S. Navy cooperated in the making. Just what the Navy did should be specified for the sake of the Navy. As a recruiting propaganda picture, this one won't. What sparse comedy is in it is made to come from the gobs or recruiting.

What the Navy must have done is to provide some sea war films, about the best of which is the genuine sinking of a warship (not American). Other scenes of this sort appear to be mostly the w. k. applesauce.

In story the single point is that a girl of social standing was induced to do some secret service work to uncover the deliverer of the enemy of transport departures from this side. The man she had to land was in love with her. Upon instructions from superiors to "remain with him for 24 hours without leaving him for a minute," the girl did so, with intimations that she "gave more than her life for her country."

Nice stuff for pictures and for the Navy, whether the Department's staff, gobs or the intelligence department. A little more of the intelligence department of the Navy upon the scenario of this film and it might have turned out a better picture.

And if not enough, they killed the girl's brother over there but brought back her boyish sweetheart, who discovered the girl standing beside the flag-draped coffin of the brother, in full view of the audience.

Dorothy Mackaill is the girl. She always appeared as desperately striving for expressions she could not register. Startled or abashed, whatever it was, Miss Mackail's gave only the impression of a big but unsuccessful effort. And that's all she had to do except to be arrested for street strolling in front of the Navy Yard while seeking information about her brother from the gobs, instead of Washington. Miss Mackaill's best bit was when she bade her brother good-bye. Still that was a little over-fervent.

Lowell Sherman plays the spy, one of those 'igh 'at guys of the villain-still-pursued-her type that Charles Withers loves to reproduce in his "Opry House" travesty. Several names are feature in roles wholly unimportant. Any sort of an actor could have done them. Otherwise production cost looks low enough for a First National program release.

A large chunk of continuity appears missing just before the spy was captured and immediately after the girl is presumed to have spent the 24 hours "without missing a minute with him." This may have been censored.

Some of the sea pictures could have been taken from the news reels or taken from boats in any bay.

Very weak picture for its purpose and publicity.

Billed as "The Big Parade of the Navy," "The Big Parade" has justifiable action. *Sime.*

Understanding Heart

Romantic drama made by Cosmopolitan, released by Metro-Goldwyn-Mayer, screen version of the Peter B. Kyne novel. Directed by Jack Conway; titled by Joe Farnham. Running time, 67 minutes. At the Capitol, New York, week May 7.

Monica Dale..................Joan Crawford
Bob Mason................Rockliffe Followes
Tony Garland...Francis X. Bushman, Jr.
Kelcey Mason.................Carmel Myers
Sheriff Bentley..............Richard Carle
Uncle Charley................Harvey Clark
Bardwell.........................Jerry Miley

For some reason pictures that have for their dramatic punch episodes of a forest fire do not get anywhere. This is no more satisfactory than others on the subject. The story doesn't "build" to a cumulative climax, doesn't particularly engage sympathies and generally is dull.

No particular fault seems accountable for the meagre result. It's just one of those stories that lags. The forest fire is effectively enough screened and the scenic details of snow-capped Rockies are strikingly fine. The acting is always satisfactory in an artless and unobtrusive way, with Francis X. Bushman, Jr., standing out as a jaunty young forest ranger and Joan Crawford playing a rather picturesque role with her usual grace, looking more like Pauline Frederick than ever.

Ordinarily, Kyne is strong on the he-man, red-blooded romance, but this one falls down on vigor. A fan public that has been surfeited with World War trench and artillery battles, lies back yawning when they try to pump up action out of getting a force of rangers off to combat with advancing flames in the woods.

The heroine and two suitors are marooned by the fire on a remote mountain peak with no escape except down an impassable cliff. At the last minute an airplane, sent by the government, maneuvers overhead and drops parachutes so they can float to safety. They are one parachute short, but a rainstorm arrives in time. It leaves the thrill seeker blah.

Screen translation must have been considerably revised. The meaning of the title is vague and its application foggy. Two comedy characters, a western sheriff, soused throughout the picture, and his pal, get more footage than the straight characters, some of it funny, but funnier in the titles than in the action. Their antics weaken and cheapen the drama rather than sharpen it by contrast.

All the "big" scenes seem to come as an after thought and accidentally rather than being built up in strength and emphasis.

Action is rather perfunctory. For instance, there is a scene in which the two rivals have one parachute between them. Which will be saved? But before this situation has had time to sink in one suitor socks the other in the jaw and proceeds to fasten him in the device. He is still at the task when the rain begins to fall. Things just happen.

Just a program picture. *Rush.*

THE LOVE THRILL

Universal-Jewel, starring Laura La Plante, Story by Millard Webb and Joe Mitchell, with Webb directing. Gilbert Warrenton, cameraman, and titled by Albert DeMond. At Roxy, New York, week May 7. Running time, 52 minutes.

Joyce Bragdon...........Laura La Plante
Jack Sturdevant.................Tom Moore
J. A. Creelman...........Bryant Washburn
Paula...........................Jocelyn Lee

Probably "Love Thrill" had to do a nip-up to get into this theatre, and would never have "crashed" if it hadn't been that the Roxy has had "Alaskan Adventures" penciled in for some time. At that this U-Jewel is as good as some of the stuff that has been lately bouncing along the Alley. But that doesn't mean it rates de luxe house leadership. Strictly a lightweight and somewhat inane.

Story rambles without getting anywhere. It has no personal "menace." Bryant Washburn threatens to do the dirty over a dinner table for two in his apartment, but this turns out to be a phoney, so the only suspense is whether Joyce is going to sell an insurance policy to save her father and the old homestead.

Assuming the widowship of a supposedly dead author to get to the latter's wealthy friend is the formula. Miss La Plante and Mr. Moore simply walk through the script. It all takes place indoors, and the four-wall handicap about signifies the amount of action.

Put it to music and the summation would be: Not for just a week, not for just three days, not for just two, but one day. *Sid.*

THE MISSING LINK

Warner Brothers picture, starring Syd Chaplin. Story by Chuck Reisner and Darryl Zanuck. Directed by Reisner. Dev Jennings cameraman. At Colony, New York, with Vitaphone accompaniment, for run on grind policy starting May 6 at benefit performance. Running time, 71 mins.

Arthur Wells.....................Syd Chaplin
Beatrice Braden..................Ruth Hiatt
Col. Braden......................Tom McGuire
Lord Dryden..................Crauford Kent

A jungle comedy that never actually gets into the heavy foliage, but has Syd Chaplin the scared explorer having to overcome lions, a comedy monk and a huge man-played gorilla, from which the film gets its title. It's a laugh program leader.

The picture is in at this house for a run on a grind. How long it will stick is problematical. Four weeks looks to be top.

It's all Chaplin, with no other cast member cutting any particular figure. Gags, and more gags through the real exploring scientist hiding his identity in the person of his valet (Chaplin) because of a timidity toward women and the host's daughter. Chaplin, of course, eventually captures the desired gorilla and the girl.

Most of the comedy surrounds Chaplin and his difficulties with Akka, a great monk, without which the film would be lost. As the household pet this animal attaches itself to the fear-stricken valet, and a chase around the house, with the monk pursuing, is the standout laugh sequence. The film has been well cut through this passage, and they'll howl at the antics of the animal.

Not much to the story. Chuck Reisner evidently had a tough time getting it under way. Chaplin starts out as a starving poet who bungles himself on board ship after a series of mishaps and is saved from the crew by Lord Dryden when the latter gets the idea to change places. Starting in London, the locale switches to Africa.

Five or six lions are turned loose on Chaplin, the majority of this action taking place within the African homestead. This is provocative of some excellent fake camera work, as also a couple of phoney sets of the ship's landing.

Plenty of laughs, and Chaplin works his head off. They liked it at this opening benefit performance and the grind audiences will also approve. The picture has its slow moments, but that standout strip between the comedian and the large-sized monkey will carry it.

Erno Rapee has capably scored the feature for its Vitaphone accompaniment, using the jungle motif, which all Broadway film houses have evidently adopted, and which is currently and heavily stressed through "Chang." *Sid.*

HIS FIRST FLAME

Mack Sennett production, Pathe release. Harry Langdon starred. Directed by Harry Edwards from story by Arthur Ripley and Frank Capra. At Strand, New York, week April 30. Running time, about 55 minutes.

Harry Howells..............Harry Langdon
Ethel Morgan.............Natalie Kingston
Mary Morgan.....................Ruth Hiatt
Amos McCarthy...............Vernon Dent
Hector Benedict............Bud Jamieson
Mrs. Benedict....................Dot Farley

A gag picture, running through a story of no consequence, but with laughs enough from the Harry Langdon gags to make this picture stand up as that kind of a comedy. It's the last full length Langdon made for Mack Sennett, and its release (Pathe) at the Strand, New York, shortly, follow Langdon's latest First National ("Long Pants").

It's about a blundering boy home from college with a bachelor uncle, foreman of a fire company and deadly on all women, trying to thwart his nephew's ambition to marry.

As a rule—and it seems inviolable in pictures—all dead pan comics must follow the gag line. That means padding to lead up to the laugh punch. It's so here, but Langdon, when he laugh-punches, does so with a kick, and you laugh, no matter who you are or what you think.

Still there's quite a lot of padding as in the fire rescue scene. Here the comedy punch is the weakest.

For immobility Langdon holds to about the most stern mug of all and all of the time. He barely broke into a slight smile once during the running. A funny guy who seems to be steadily forging forward, one of those slow but sure sort that eventually lands in the Chaplin-Lloyd circulation class.

Quite a nice production even to exteriors, with support correspondingly. A couple of misses with reminiscent vaudeville names, Natalie Kingston and Ruth Hiatt, prettily show before the camera as sisters. They care nicely for their comparative little, and the same for the others. It's a Langdon picture.

Wherever Langdon has made himself this can follow right in, either before or after "Long Pants." *Sime.*

THE CLAW

Universal production directed by Sidney Olcott. Norman Kerry and Claire Windsor co-starred. Running time, 59 minutes. At Hippodrome, New York, week May 9.

Marquis of Stair................Tom Guise
Major Kinsella.....Arthur Edmund Carewe
Deidre Saurin..............Claire Windsor
Maurice Stair..............Norman Kerry
Judy.........................Helene Sullivan
Nonnie..........................Pauline Neff
Scotty.....................Nelson MacDowell
Zambula..................Dick Sutherland

This picture looks as if it was planned to be great shakes, but failed. It seems almost impossible that Sidney Olcott, big timer, should be so careless about detail. Picture is dotted with sloppily handled scenes.

It's a peculiar dish of stew. British frontier stuff in Africa, javelin-throwing savages, rich weakling who has come from England to make a man of himself. Material wasn't so bad and should have made a better picture. Olcott has failed to get suspense, and there isn't a laugh, despite the presence of Nelson MacDowell to supply comic relief.

Three principal characters are not clearly defined. Arthur Edmund Carewe is a sympathetic villain, and Norman Kerry an unsympathetci hero. Claire Widsor's contribution is her usual attractive appearance and little else. Not a gown or any feminine interest.

Scenes, supposed to be in the jungle, are "studio" all over.

Briefly, the plot concerns the coming to Africa of the rich weakling and later the girl he loves, who is infatuated with the charming menace.

Not for fastidious audiences.

Outlaws of Red River

Fox western starring Tom Mix. Scenario by Harold Shumate from a story by the late Gerald Beaumont. Direction by Lew Seiler. Titles by Malcolm Stuart Boylan. Photographed by Dan Clerk. Running time, 62 mins. In projection room, April 14.

Tom Morley.........................Tom Mix
Mary Torrence..................Marjorie Daw
Ben Tanner...............Francis McDonald
Sam Hardwick..............Arthur Clayton
Dick Williams.......................Duke Lee
Mr. Torrence.................Lee Shumway
Mrs. Torrence..............Ellen Woonston
Capt. Dunning.............William Conklin
Mary (as a child)........Virginia Marshall
Tom (as a child)..............Jimmy Downs

The pictures of Tom Mix do not vary greatly in plot or entertainment average. In this one Tom is seen as the boy who grows up cherishing a vendetta for the men who murdered the people with whom he came west as a lad. The daughter of the chief bandit when Tom finally discovers the gang proves to be his boyhood sweetheart who was kidnapped by the outlaws.

This is practically identical all the way with plots that have previously served Mix, not to mention other western stars. In this instance, thanks to a well though-out scenario by Harold Shumate and brisk direction by Lew Seiler, the hackneyed plot skeleton is not noticed.

"Outlaws" opens with Mix chasing a group of bandits. Pretending to be shot and falling from his horse he lures the bandits from their ambush and plugs the chief, escaping before the others can cover. From then on there's an abundance of action, escapes, shootings, high-handed villainy and some good free-for-all fighting between the outlaws and the Texas Rangers, of which Mix is a member in the picture.

Marjorie Daw did not show to

good advantage. Miss Daw, once a prominent film ingenue, has not been in the fore for some time. In a couple of shots she was her old girlish self but mostly the camera revealed her a little wan.

Francis McDonald, handsome enough to be a leading man, got a lot of nastiness into the menace role. It was while fighting with McDonald during the making of this picture that Mix was accidentally burned by gun powder from which it is understood he is still laid up.

A rip-snorting wild west melodrama, the Mix fans will go strong for "Outlaws of Red River."

The Mysterious Rider

Paramount production supervised by B. F. Fineman. John Waters director. Adaptation by Wyndham Gittens. Titles by Alfred Hustwick. Cameraman, Edgar Schoenbaum. Running time, 65 mins. One half double feature bill at Columbus, New York, one day, April 20.

Bent Wade........................Jack Holt
Harkness........................Charles Sellon
Lem........................Tom Kennedy
Mark King........................David Torrence
Miss King........................Betty Jewel
Rancher........................Guy Oliver

Up to standard as a western, with the masked rider angle subordinate to the issue of the struggle of settlers to keep their homes and ranches against the forces of the law.

The ranchers have arranged with Harkness, a lawyer, to buy an old Spanish grant held by him on their property. They raise $20,000 but in the meanwhile Harkness accepts an offer from the millionaire for a hundred grand.

Bent Wade (Holt) is framed. Acting for the ranchers he has received from Harkness a receipt for the $20,000 but the receipt has been written in disappearing ink. That's a little like the old Craig Kennedy "Exploits of Elaine" stuff. There may or may not be such a thing as disappearing ink and the public may or may not be disposed to place any credence in it. But that's the plot, anyhow.

The big punch of the picture is when the settlers are evicted from their property. The millionaire has brought in gangsters from the city and has had them sworn in as deputies. The gangsters wear city clothes but ride horses in true western style. They have cleared the land and the settlers are almost out of the valley when one settler, maddened by the injustice, turns back and is shot cold by the city gunmen. That determines the settlers to fight. They put up a barricade and a pitched battle ensues.

In the end Holt forces the truth from the lawyer and the millionaire relinquishes his claims. Holt and the millionaire's daughter clinch.

Direction good.

A Princess on Broadway

J. C. Barnstyn Production released by Pathe. Directed by Dalls M. Fitzgerald from the story by Ethel Donahar. Starring Pauline Garon with cast including Johnnie Walker, Dorothy Dwan, Ethel Clayton, Ernest Wood, Harold Miller and Neely Edwards. At Loew's New York, one day, April 8, one-half of double feature program.

Pauline Garon draws some attention with appearance in the chorus girl part, but loses out as a Russian princess. Other members of the cast play aimlessly under apparently lax direction. A try for comedy is unproductive.

The picture has been cheaply produced and shows it. Photography poor and story ancient, of the chorus girl who becomes a princess to gain publicity to carry her through the lead in a new play.

Miss Garon receives some rough treatment from the camera under certain angles, giving her face an elongated appearance. The same happens to Miss Dwan.

Neely Edwards shows possibilities if provided with material.

The Bachelor's Baby

Columbia production. Adapted from "The Girl Who Smiles" from an original story by Garret Elsden Fort. Directed by Frank Strayer. Cast headed by Helene Chadwick, Harry Meyers, Midget Gustav, Edith Yorke and Pat Harmon. At Loew's New York Theatre, one day, April 1, as part of double bill. Running time, 62 minutes.

In this Columbia independent an old formulae has been employed. Deceit practised by a young couple in love to fool the old folks plus a series of farcical stuff made by trick photography.

A young man and his sweetie to put on a front they are married and have a baby reaches a climax where they palm off a midget as their offspring. Of course the lilliputian is married and there is the devil to pay when the expose makes things merry for all hands.

There's a comedy chase that finally lands the clouds, with the trick cinema stuff good for laughter for those who like that sort of screen dish.

Not very well connected, overdone and overdrawn, but successful in a measure of causing some light enjoyment.

As summarized at best, it will stack up best where another feature is also offered the patrons at the same admission.

The story may have read well, but didn't come out that way on the strip. *Mark.*

ALL ABOARD

C. C. Burr presents Johnny Hines in a First National production. Directed by Charles Hines from a story by Matt Taylor. Cast includes Edna Murphy, Henry Barrows, Babe London, Frank Hagney and Sojin. Running time 66 mins. At Hippodrome, New York, week April 18.

Neither First National nor Johnny Hines will gather any prestige with this picture. It looks cheap and it's not funny.

Opens with Hines reading a book, "How to Remember Not to Forget." Beside him his breakfast toast is burning. He is pictured as an abnormally forgetful young man but as the emulsion unwinds this idea is lost track of in the avalanche of hokum.

Although a shoe clerk Hines has studied foreign travel. Without previous experience or qualification is able to become guide of a "conducted tour" to Egypt. He endears himself to the travel bureau magnate by discovering—on a map—a shorter route to the Pyramids.

A sheik abducts the girl and Hines' business is to rescue her. It's all very dull, very mechanical and very badly directed.

Trading on Hines reputation may not leave him any.

RICH BUT HONEST

William Fox comedy-drama of the footlights. Story by Arthur Somers Roche; scenario by Randall H. Faye. Directed by Albert Ray, assisted by Horace Hough. Set for release May 22. Running time, 56 minutes (5,480 feet). In perfection room.

Florence Candless..............Nancy Nash
Bob Hendricks..............Clifford Holland
Dick Carter..............Charles Morton
Diamond Jim O'Grady..............
J. Farrell MacDonald
Barney Zoom..............Tyler Brooke
Heinie..............Ted McNamara
Maybelle..............Marjorie Beebe
Archie..............Ernie Shields
Mrs. O'Grady..............Doris Lloyd

Amusing light story with sexy angles, heavy emphasis on silk stockings and shapely legs, and for a surprise twist at the finish rather sophisticated angle on stage door Johns vs. humble chivalry. Picture has good entertainment quality for all grades of audiences and takes special interest from its wise backstage material done in the "inside stuff" intimate style popularized by the stage play, "Broadway."

Characters are modern. Heroine, Florence, is a young "Charleston" fan who frequents dance halls and takes part in dance contests, but below the surface appearance of worldliness a bit of a Puritan. Her pal, Maybelle, is the "Patsy" type. Both work behind the counter in a department store. Florence's beau is an auto mechanic.

Her figure and dancing talent bring Florence to the attention of a theatrical manager and she joins the chorus. A bright bit is the scene where Florence falls down on the steps at rehearsal and by chance the manager "discovers" that the humble Maybelle is a natural comedian and dancing clown. The resplendent Florence is relegated to the living pictures, where she needs only dumb beauty, while Maybelle, the Patsy, gets in the show as a featured principal.

This reverses the conventional formula and makes a shrewd bit of wise action. Another touch that does violence to hoke romance is the development that the rich John who falls for Flo turns out to be a suitor of honorable intent, while it is the poor mechanic who was playing all the time for an informal honeymoon at the seashore.

The Charleston contests and the rehearsals of the "Follies" gives opportunity for much footage showing the girls in all their unadorned shapeliness and rounded knees and curving legs get more closeups than usually go to the movie queen's profile.

The picture has capital comedy values besides the cynical slants mentioned. The John takes the heroine out in his roadster and they park in a country lane for the usual business in that familiar screen situation. But here it has a novel outcome. To carry out the stall that the car had broken down, the John phones for the wrecking car from a distant garage. When the wrecker arrives at the spot, who should be in charge but Florence's mechanic sweetheart, Bob.

Bob, suspicious, takes the John's car in tow and brings it in in the wildest and most thrilling tow the world ever saw. The tow car hits it up to 60, snapping the roadster about behind on sharp turns like the tail of a kite, the John and the girl holding on for their lives.

Brisk modern comedy with plenty of sex kick, variety of incident that never flags and first-class, novel comedy angles. Production on the order of same company's "Ankles Preferred," but better in many respects. *Rush.*

Mountains of Manhattan

Gotham Feature, distributed by Lumas. Featuring Dorothy De Vore, Charles Delaney and Kate Price. Directed by James P. Hogan from the story by Herbert Clark. At Loew's Circle, one day (May 9), as half of double-feature bill. Running time, 63 minutes.

Gotham just missed making "Mountains" into a good program picture desirable for the better independent trade. As is, it can't be classed above fair.

The film story was there: the former boxing champ of the army discards the gloves for his mother's sake and takes up engineering, putting in his days laboring on uprising Manhattan skyscrapers. But the kid brother gets sick and the prospective engineer takes on one more fight to send the youngster to Denver. Also, there is a fist fight with an agitator on the girders of a building skeleton. With several fights under his belt, our hero has become superintendent of construction and son-in-law of the constructor.

Cast was there: Charles Delaney, comparatively new, puts up a nice front in the male lead and registers very favorably. Dorothy De Vore photographs as a logical desire for marriage; and Kate Price does her customary Irish mother in considerable unwasted footage.

Photography was there: good shots in the skyscraper sequence and a rating average throughout.

But the direction wasn't there, out to lunch or someplace in several spots where it was in demand. Too much strain for dramatic and comic effects, made more noticeable by the quality of the normal scenes.

Which is why the picture is not better than fair.

DON DESPERADO

Pathe western directed by Leo D. Maloney. Story by Ford I. Beebe. Cameraman, Ben White. Running time, 62 mins. In projection room, April 20.

Leo McHale........................Leo Maloney
Doris Jessup........................Eugenia Gilbert
Nathan Jessup........................Frederick Dana
Joe Jessup........................Morgan Davis
Franchy........................Bud Osborne
Aaron Blaisdell........................Charles Bartlett

Nothing unusual about this Western except that it was taken on location with snow on the ground. It stacks up as better made all the way than Maloney's previous productions.

There's a moral to the plot. Men who advocate lynching change their ideas when the person nominated for the hemp happens to be one of their own family.

Nathan Jessup is a hot tempered mine superintendent, leader of an agitation to lynch "Frenchy," brought in by the deputy sheriff (Maloney) as a highwayman and murderer. By a subterfuge Frenchy frames a stranger as the real bandit. The stranger is Jessup's son.

A love affair between the deputy and Jessup's daughter has been broken up because of the deputy protecting "Frenchy" from the mob led by Jessup. With the new complication involving his son, Jessup admits his ideas were wrong and appeals to the young deputy, who makes everything come out okay.

Ford I. Beebe, who has authored many scripts for Maloney, is responsible for "Desperado." Eugenia Gilbert is an attractive feminine lead and again opposite Maloney. Frederick Dana, an unknown, gave a very competent performance as Jessup. Maloney did some good trouping. He has been characterized by more acting and less "action" than many of his contemporaries in cowboy opera.

RED SIGNALS

Sterling Pictures production, directed by John P. McGowan. Adapted by William Armstrong from novel by William Wallace Cook. Earle Williams starred, Eva Novak and Wallace McDonald featured, with cast including Thomas Moran, J. P. McGowan, Robert McKenzie, Billie Franey, Frank Rice. At Loew's Circle, March 28, one-half double bill.

Fair program filler for double bill houses.

Railroad picture, no different from any of the innumerable others. Usual train wreckers, actual wrecks, scheming foreman and weakling district boss, honest old engineer, charming daughter and newly appointed superintendent.

Although Earle Williams is featured, Wallace McDonald shoulders the major burden of the story as the super's hobo brother who turns out to be a detective.

McDonald is skilfully planted early in the story. The two tattered tramp companions with him, Frank

Rice and Billie Francy, drive away all suspicion that the boy is anything but tramp. Incidentally these two boys are comedians of no mean ability.

J. P. McGowan, the director, gave himself the role of heavy No. 1. He does well with it, looking ferocious in spots. Eva Novak will take some swallowing as the sweet young thing, even from soft lens.

Code of the Range

Rayart picture, presented by W. Ray Johnston through arrangement with Morris Schlank. Directed by Schlank and Ben Cohn from a story by Cleve Meyer. Photographed by W. Hyers. At Loew's New York one day (May 6) as half of double feature bill.

The mild Jack Perrin, his horse, and dog, carrying on in a considerably unreasonable western that still manages to entertain. Its entertainment values will support it in the regular western haunts, and, as here, it looks okeh on a double-feature bill.

One or two spots grate on the average customer; particularly the murder of the villain by Rex, the dog, in a brutal affair. Another is the cowing of the assistant villain by Starlight, the horse. This assistant villain has a gun on him, but apparently prefers to be mauled by hoofs rather than be cruel to a dumb animal.

Other mythical spots are entertaining enough to be consumed with ease.

Perrin is a cowpuncher out for revenge on the gent who seduced his sister into a dance hall by advertising for a school teacher and then finished her off before he blew town.

Casting good. Nelson MacDowell, an old two-gun character with a weakness for animal crackers, turns in an exceptional account of himself. Pauline Curley, with little to do besides look frightened during fights, does that effectively. Lew Meehan is the chief bad man, with fair support in Chic Olsen.

Perrin, while working mildly, carries the burden handily. A juvenile, name uncaught, registering well in a minor role.

This line-up could have stood a better story.

DESTINY OF RUSSIA

Written, directed and produced by K. S. Rymowcyz, of Warsaw, Poland. Released by the United Import Film Corp. of New York. At the Commodore, New York, May 6. Running time about an hour.

Only possible market for this film lies in neighborhoods populated with Ukrainians, Russians, Poles and Slavs. Picture very badly done, the titles are written in ungrammatical English and the camera work sloppy. At the Commodore this film drew some business because of the nationality drag in the East Side neighborhood.

Picture is told mostly in the titles. Every flash of a scene on the screen is followed by reams of explanations in bad English. The story for the most part is historical, of the do. nfall of the Czar, the rise and fall of the various governments succeeding and the final establishment of the red rule.

The producer throws the Bolsheviki into the light of an overbearing group of men crazed with sudden power and wreaking vengeance on all those who were not totally in accord with their aims. Production is made up of clips from various news reels showing Lenin, Trotzky and the former Russian royal family at public functions. In these scenes the faces and figures are seen only from a distance. The actors playing the political personages for the balance of the picture make very poor im-

personators and know nothing of screen work. Make-up is like huge black smears on their faces, and all carry themselves with a hunted, unnatural appearance.

"Love" interest centres round a professor and his daughter. Two students, one an evil Bolshie and the other a peaceful scholar, both set out to get the girl. The "gal" in this picture is clumsy, unspeakably ugly, walks like Big Bertha on roller skates and in every one of the five shots shown breaks into tears for no special reason.

The names of all the people in the cast are mercifully omitted. But for those interested in making a study of how not to act and how not to make a picture, this film offers a lesson with a million laughs.

Rymowcyz is now in America and probably has seen enough of real pictures to know just how impossible his is.

UNEASY PAYMENTS

F. B. O. release, starring Alberta Vaughan. Directed by David Kirkland. Story by Walter Sinclair. Photographed by Charles E. Boyle. At Columbus one day (May 4) as half of a double feature bill. Running time, 55 minutes.

Strained farcical treatment of a fairly humorous story fizzles this into a melancholy flop. The picture will have a tough time getting by anywhere alone.

It's a tale of a young gal who wins a Charleston contest in Farmdale, Mo., and comes to Broadway for recognition. Getting a job as a chorine in a cabaret, she takes the advice of one of the owners, buying a truckload of furnishings and finery on the installment plan so that she can put up a front.

But the other owner of the cabaret, repulsed in his efforts to do wrong by the girl, withdraws his okay on all her accounts. The installment boys clean out her apartment and track her to the cabaret. There they take everything off her but a breastband and a pair of panties.

With the show in full progress, the girl slips onto the floor in her negligee, does her Charleston, and cops the hit of the show.

Then for no particular reason the youthful and heroic part owner of the cabaret says: "What a fool I've been," and takes her into his arms for a necking fadeout.

Picture's best bet and one hope for getting by is the semi-nude comedy in the cabaret. Alberta Vaughan wears as little here as she can, and the effect was visible among the boys at the Columbus.

Jack Luden, juvenile, carried on as though he had never faced a camera before, and most of the support was similar. Gino Carrado, light-heavy, exception. Miss Vaughan, considering the story, did well enough.

Photography ranges from average to bad.

Situations are handled too ridiculously even to rate as farce.

The One-Man Trail

Presented by Westwood Productions through the Hollywood Producers Finance Ass'n. Featuring Monte Montague and Eva Gregory. At the Arena one day (May 9) as half of double-feature bill. Running time, about 50 minutes.

Something peculiar about this one.

On a hunch that most of the photography in it looked prehistoric, "Variety's" records were resorted to. In 1921 Fox released a picture of the same title featuring Buck Jones. The story also was identical—of the cowboy out to find the guy who abducted his sister.

That reviewer thought it was terrible.

In the present release the subtitles are antique affairs. In a close shot the hero will be riding a white horse and in two seconds will be galloping along on a black one (in a long shot). In a few shots the hero is recognizable as some other fellow. All action lacks sequence.

If the Westwood boys didn't use all of the 1921 film, in which Buck Jones couldn't be recognized, they wasted money.

Because the 1927 version is also terrible.

Pirates of the Sky

Pathe, released from Productions, Inc. Directed by Charles Andrews; photography by Leon Shamroy. Adapted by Elaine Wilmont. In projection room May 4. Running time, 50 minutes.
Bob Manning..............Charles Hutchison
Doris Reed................Wanda Hawley
Bruce Mitchell............Craufurd Kent
Jeff Oldring..............Jimmie Aubrey
Stone.....................Ben Walker

Charles Hutchison, stunt man, not as active as usual in an average adventure picture. Too many preliminary "stills" handicap the few major action scenes. Customers will accept "Pirates," but won't talk about it.

Hutchison is a wealthy amateur criminologist who is called upon by the U. S. secret service department from time to time when a case becomes too difficult for them. Air mail robberies have baffled them.

Hutchison's two main bits are a mid-air change of planes, and a drop from a plane to a haystack.

He has comparatively good support in Wanda Hawley and Craufurd Kent as the refined gang leader. Jimmie Aubrey, playing Hutchison's service man, lends considerable to the picture in his comedy as a Sherlock Holmes student addicted to disguises.

Picture hurt by the lack of early action, but still rates as average.

HEART OF A COWARD

Duke Worne production presented by W. Ray Johnston. Released through Rayart Pictures. Directed by Duke Worne. Starring Billy Sullivan. Cast includes Edyth York, Jack Richardson and Myles McCarthy. At the Arena, New York, one day, May 4. Running time, 48 minutes.

Lack of good story material and plot construction, inferior direction and poor cast limit this picture to a small sphere of houses. Continuous production of hackneyed themes of this sort in this crude manner will eventually break up the market now being sold.

Billy Sullivan looks fairly presentable in the lead, but shows no ability as an actor in the present instance. Supporting cast not good.

Story is of a country boy, a coward because of his literary ambitions, which keep him immersed in a world of make believe. This would be a fine theme if carried through to its logical conclusion, but the directorial megaphone steps in with a girl, the usual necessary "menace" and the wealthy publisher, turning the story into the dime novel class.

Fist fights are unconvincing and amateurishly staged. An automobile wreck does not score for the desired effect. The gal is lustreless and insipid and the denouement entirely divorced from the story that the script originally started out to tell.

Only novelty is that the arm of the law gets a break. When the girl runs out to get help the cop is standing on the corner.

The Devil's Masterpiece

Presented by Stanford F. Arnold. Handled by Goodwill Pictures. Story by Mason Harbringer. Directed by John P. McCarthy. Photography by Lyman Broening. Running time, 59 mins. Double feature bill at Loew's New York, one day, April 29.

A short bank roll, an unknown cast and a star (Virginia Brown Faire) of little name or note do not produce pictures that mean much. This one is a state rights proposition designed for a limited market and for that market good enough to suffice and even satisfy. There have been a lot of worse "quickies" than "The Devil's Masterpiece."

A melodramatic plot with a background of Royal mounted cops and dope smugglers manages to sustain interest fairly well. The leading man (Gordon Brinkley) on the trail of the man who murdered his father is unable to explain to the girl he meets and loves that he is a mountie working in civilian clothes to trap the dope gang. She misunderstands and believes him one of the gang.

While "The Devil's Masterpiece" is fourth rate as a picture in the climes where they play fourth-rate pictures, this one will possibly seem pretty good.

The Kentucky Handicap

W. Ray Johnston presentation, directed by Harry J. Brown and released by Rayart. Story by Henry Roberts Symonds. Starring Reed Howes with cast including Alice Calhoun, Josef Swickard, Robert McKim, Lydia Knott, Will Malone and James Barabury, Jr. At the Arena, New York, one day, May 5.

A new race story telling of the old southern estate falling into ruin and finally passing into the hands of receivers until even the boy's only race horse is mortgaged and almost prevented from running at the last minute.

Further innovations consist of doping the horse and the male lead being ruled off the racing books for trying to lose his race and kill his own horse. For a pathetic touch there is the blind old mother who thinks all is well.

No action, no story, no trouping. Direction could be worse.

Alice Calhoun seems to have possibilities, but wears bad clothes and gets rough camera treatment, making her look unattractive.

SALVATION JANE

F. B. O. production, starring Viola Dana. Directed by Phil Rosen. At the Stanley theatre, New York, one day, May 5. Running time, 62 mins.

For some unaccountable reason this picture seemed in bad shape in its projection presentation at the Stanley theatre. Latter part, in particular, was murky and apparently much used or sadly in need of retakes. Either way the impression was unfavorable to the film. And, furthermore, it gave the star much the worst of it.

Where closeups of Miss Dana were shown it made the star appear old, with her makeup somewhat bleary, which no film lady likes at any time and especially when her film is being shown to New York fans.

The story at best is a threadbare theme; the old gag about the girl who became a thief so that her grandpa could have the things to sustain life.

Cast shows no exceptional screen speed or class beyond carrying the characters along at a rate that does not build up the climaxes effectively.

What chance the picture might have had was killed by the condition of the print. *Mark.*

ANNIE LAURIE

Metro-Goldwyn-Mayer production directed by John S. Robertson from the story by Josephine Lovett. Titled by Marion Ainslee and Ruth Cummings. Oliver Marsh, photographer. Starring Lillian Gish with Norman Kerry featured. At the Embassy, New York, May 11. Indefinite. $1.65 top. Running time, about 80 minutes.

Annie Laurie....................Lillian Gish
Ian Macdonald..............Norman Kerry
Donald......................Creighton Hale
Alastair......................Joseph Striker
The Macdonald chieftain..Hobart Bosworth
Enid...........................Patricia Avery
Sandy........................Russell Simpson
The Campbell chieftain.....Brandon Hurst
Sir Robert Laurie..........David Torrence
Cameron of Lochiel..........Frank Currier

Every Scotchman in America will want to see this picture. It will no doubt surprise thousands to learn that innumerable Macdonalds, now considered human beings equal in many respects to other people, were once regarded as the outcasts of Scotland, the barbarians of the hills.

"Annie Laurie" is a strong picture. Its story is well planned, closely knit and while the title may indicate a strictly historical legend which would detract from universal popularity, such is not so. There are many ways of filming blood feuds. This one has been made interesting, through a broad directorial touch. The film should draw almost anywhere.

"Wild men have a way with woman." That is the underlying love motif running through the battles, the rampages of the Macdonalds and Campbells, the theft of sleek Campbell women from sleek Campbell men by the bold, powerful Macdonalds.

The narrative starts with a rush. The mutilated body of a dead Macdonald is sent to the chieftain with a note to the effect the same treatment will be handed out to all Macdonalds found on Campbell grounds. That night the Macdonalds raid the Campbell grounds and Alastair captures the daughter of the Campbell chief. When a truce is called Enid refuses to return to the fold, preferring to remain with her kilted hubby. And no one could blame Enid after taking a flash at Alastair.

The King of England finally attempts to end clan warfare through peace treaties. The Campbell chief is appointed arbitrator. He abuses his power to dictate to the Macdonalds, knowing that the latter will not accede and that they will, therefore, be wiped out by command of the king.

During the peace advances the "Cub of the Wolf," Ian Macdonald, makes a play for Annie Laurie, daughter of the governor. Annie and the governor are neutrals, but both seem to have a natural preference for the more civilized Campbells, rather than the uncouth, but honest, Macdonalds. Donald (Creighton Hale) here essays the sissified dandy, the son of the Campbell chief, as a foil for Norman Kerry's tremendous strength and skill at sports. Climax is reached when the Macdonalds are tricked into housing the Campbell troups, and the bridge to the beacon light, by which the Macdonald clan may be summoned, is destroyed. The Macdonalds are hemmed in and no help seems forthcoming.

Lillian Gish, fleeing up a mountain like a frightened bird to light the beacon, pursued by gun shots from a guard, drew a storm of applause. The closeups were fine and succeeded in conveying the hazardous situation almost to the throbbing heart beats.

Then, of course, came revenge. When the Macdonalds stormed through the gates and Ian leaped upon the debonair Donald from above, almost tearing him apart.

Hobart Bosworth is the strongest character as the Macdonald chieftain. His simple smile as Donald entered the room, the outstretched hand of welcome, and then the sudden shot from the Campbell gun, constituted one of many tense moments. The slow, weighty fall of the chief leaves so strong an impression it might almost be heard.

Russell Simpson does well with a small but significant part. He has the catch line of the story, "Wild men hae a way with wimen." For the fadeout Sandy is brought up life size on the screen, saying his choice mouthful at the happily married couple.

Seemingly scheduled for a fair run at the Embassy, it is not probable that "Annie Laurie" will get $1.50 in many spots out of town. But when it finally hits the picture houses there is little doubt of its success.

THE RESURRECTION

United Artists release of Inspiration Pictures production of Count Leo Tolstoy's novel of the same name. Scenario by Edwin Carewe and Finis Fox, assisted by Count Ilya Tolstoy, son of the Russian novelist. Cameraman, Robert Kurrle. Rod La Roque and Dolores Del Rio featured. Running time, 95 minutes. At the Strand, New York, week May 16.

Prince Dmitri.................Rod La Rocque
Katusha Maslova...........Dolores Del Rio
Major Schoenboch.......March MacDermott
Aunt Sophya...................Lucy Beaumont
Aunt Marya.........................Vera Lewis
Princess Olga............Clarissa Selwynne
Princess Sonia..................Eva Southern
Old Philosopher.........Count Ilya Tolstoy

A de luxe screen production, finely wrought in its interpretation, but having pessimistic and depressing material. Inspiration gets a mark for its courage in holding to the unhappy ending of the original. This may increase the artistic merit, but it is doubtful if it will benefit the box office.

The length is another thing that reacts against it. Running time of more than an hour and a half for the feature had them hopping at the Strand, although the rest of the program had been cut to the bone. It seems to be impossible to give the picture a varied supporting program and hold within the time limit.

The stars' names seemed to be a potent draw. Sunday in the early evening the line stretched from the box office around the 47th street corner, an unusual occurrence at this season, with outdoors inviting.

The drama is sombre and utterly unrelieved by lighter passages. For screen purposes a splendid adaptation has been made, dealing with the spiritual values of the work rather than satisfied with its surface drama. For this credit goes to Finis Fox, American novelist, who has done outstanding work. The acting is always impressive, particularly on the part of the two featured players. Edwin Carewe has not compromised with the screen's demand for obvious.

The picture never becomes theatrical in scene or expression. The whole atmosphere is of dignity and impressiveness. Scenically the director spread himself somewhat. The bits showing the mile-long line of Siberian exiles on the march across the snow-buried waste places is a whale of a pictorial bit. This whole passage is striking for its bleak backgrounds. The prison scenes, while they impress as authentic, are monotonous despite their realism (or maybe because of that very element, a comment that goes for the whole picture).

There is the usual expanse of close-ups found in pictures of this kind which deal in spiritual values rather than in drama in terms of action. One neat device is employed. In a sort of prolog a Moscow cobbler is chatting with a philosophical visitor (played by Tolstoy). "The sole of this shoe," says the philosopher, "is much like the soul of man. Each peg that gives it form is like the succession of experiences that forms man's character."

Thereafter with each episode in the lives of the principal characters there is a fadeback to the cobbler driving another peg into a shoe—a recurring thread that emphasizes the spiritual development of the history as distinguished from a mere recital of melodramatic incidents.

It is this quality throughout that distinguishes the picture as an artistic effort, but it is doubtful if it will pull at the box office in a way commensurate with the production effort. Both subject matter and treatment are against big money taking.

Rush.

THE TELEPHONE GIRL

Paramount production directed by Herbert Brenon. Madge Bellamy, Holbrook Blinn, Warner Baxter, May Allison, Hale Hamilton and Lawrence Gray featured. Adapted from the William C. DeMille play, "The Woman." At Paramount, New York, week May 14. Running time, slightly over one hour.

Kitty O'Brien..................Madge Bellamy
Jim Blake.......................Holbrook Blinn
Matthew Standish...........Warner Baxter
Grace Robinson..................May Allison
Tom Blake....................Lawrence Gray
Mark Robinson.................Hale Hamilton
Van Dyke..................Hamilton Revelle
A Detective..................William E. Shay
Mrs. Standish....................Karen Hansen

Direction and acting go to make "The Telephone Girl" a most interesting drama on the sheet, and a good looking production in toto. As a Paramount regular release it should stand up anywhere.

There's acting in this film. Also the extremely skillful direction by Herbert Brenon. No one seems more adroit at suspense and tension than Brenon, whether it be only in a baby size picture for his directing hand like this or the bigger ones.

And Holbrook Blinn is such a sterling actor, on the stage or screen, that he likely kept all of the other principals on their toes when in scenes with him. Blinn doesn't tear up scenery or pose all over the lot before the camera—he just acts and how he can. Madge Bellamy, first in the featured billing, is a wistful, pleasant picture as the smart little hotel switch board operator.

May Allison had the really difficult role, an erring wife with the error having occurred before she married the governor of some state. It finally came out though in a hot political battle, where her husband's opponent for re-election was his wife's companion on that erring trip, evidenced by a road house register bearing the man's right name, "Matthew Standish and wife." There may be that much honesty in the coast road houses and it indicates perhaps a righteous indifference for a loving hideaway, but around New York they don't even register—much the safer.

That road house stuff starts the picture away to a sex complex and then develops into an untangling of the political intrigue. The phone girl downstairs got the angle of the framing about to happen through hearing it go over the phone. She also picked up an incriminating number and refused to reveal it, although bombarded with money offers and threats.

It was in the scenes with the foolish wife that Miss Bellamy did her nicest and most wistful playing. She suggested much more there than the captions said. While Miss Allison, in her role that carried much shading, got nearly all of the shades, turning in a brilliant performance.

Frequently Brenon gave in a flash an expectancy of consequences, without at any moment disclosing a hint as to outcome. This held to the suspense without a waver and does much for the favor this picture will find.

Camera work and titling in harmony with the whole.

Besides the list of playing names, it wouldn't be a bad scheme for exhibitors in publicity to bear down on the moral of this story; that sin never dies.

Sime.

IS ZAT SO?

Fox picture featuring George O'Brien and Edmond Lowe. Adapted from the stage play of the same name and directed by Alfred E. Green. At the Roxy, New York, week May 14. Running time, 66 mins.

Ed Chick Cowan.............George O'Brien
Hap Hurley.....................Edmund Lowe
Marie Mestretti...............Kathryn Perry
Robert Parker...............Cyril Chadwick
Sue Parker.........................Doris Lloyd
Florence Hanley.................Dione Ellis
Major Fitz Stanley......Richard Maitland
G. Clinton Blackburn,
Douglas Fairbanks, Jr.
Little Jimmy Parker.....Philippe De Lacy
Gas House Duffy...........Jack Herrick

Nice program stuff that can **shoulder the responsibility. They liked it and laughed at it here. "Is Zat So?" is a commendable program leader that lightly entertains and should both draw on the title and entertain 'em.**

Nobody means anything in the film outside of George O'Brien and Edmund Lowe as the dumb prize fighter and manager respectively. The former's interpretation runs more true to form than his co-worker, but both get over.

Three fights in the footage. One shows O'Brien taking it on the chin in the ring, another when he gets it while performing in the Fifth avenue parlor and the third is an insert over the heads of the girls who are listening in while he wins the championship.

Young Fairbanks plays the wealthy young rounder who adopts the fighter and his manager as his trainers, and plays it pretty well. Alfred E. Green has forced emphasis on Fairbank's drunk at the opening of the picture and although a bit young for the role, if comparing to the way the play was cast, he nevertheless gets it on the screen satisfactorily.

In regard to the play, the film starts ahead of the original script in making O'Brien a street car motorman who socks a truck driver, which gives Lowe the idea he can make a fighter out of the trolley pilot. Thence onward, the picture closely follows the legit version with only a few sidelights.

Kathryn Perry and Dione Ellis, blonde and brunet, foil each other on appearance, but have little to do, Cyril Chadwick is the semi-heavy as the overbearing husband of Fairbank's sister to whom the latter finally administers a thrashing.

O'Brien makes the fight stuff convince and handles himself well with or without the gloves. Lowe is opposite and competent, but will suffer in the eyes of those who have seen him in "Glory." Sue Parker is cast as the society sister and for some reason Green has allowed her to insert a bit of "mugging" that is all out of character and in direct opposition to the supposed setting. More hoke, almost bordering on the vulgar, is a scene wherein O'Brien and Lowe raid the mansion's icebox and parade around the luxurious surroundings munching bones thick with meat.

No cheating on interiors for this one. Lots of good looking sets and all solid. It will get by, easily.

Sid.

IRISH HEARTS

Warner Brothers production, directed by Byron Haskin. From the story by Bess Meredith and Graham Baker. Starring May McAvoy, with Jason Robards in support. Cast includes Walter Perry and Warner Richmond. Moss Broadway, New York, week May 16.

The only Irish in the picture is in the title. It starts out as a meller-drammer of the most lurid type,

and finishes up with a last-minute reel of hilarious slapstick. There is nothing to draw except the title, and this should be effective only for the first day or two when nationality trade will quit because the picture hits neither specifically nor generally.

The trouble commences when the little Irish girl loses her Killarney clover, the emblem of luck. She allows herself to become a neighborhood goat, suffers greatly from back talk, etc., and manages to love her boyhood sweetheart, despite the latter has deceived her frequently.

A reformed prize fighter brings her back to her former self with a gift of a clover pin identical to the one she lost. This serves an excuse for May to upset a wedding feast, pelt her former sweetie with decayed fruit and vegetables and exact satisfaction in full measure from all concerned.

Highly improbable in spots and uninteresting in others. In one scene, at a ball held at the Hibernian Club, the comedy "heavy" forsakes the gal for another. And May is shown sitting alone, with her back against the wall, all evening. This little scene would be pathetic were it not that May was the most attractive girl in the hall.

Had the picture started out with elaborate comedy touches there might have been an excuse for the ending. In the present instance the comedy broke in cold and registered for heavy laughs in the last few minutes. Handicap too great to overcome.

One Chance in a Million

Sam Sax production, distributed by Lumas Pictures. Featuring William Fairbanks, supported by Veora Daniels. Directed by Mason Noel Smith. Photographed by James Brown, Jr. At Loew's Circle one day (May 16) as half of double-feature bill. Running time, 55 minutes.

An action picture handled well enough to carry one day alone, although more suited to double-feature bill as at Loew's Circle.

William Fairbanks is a secret service dick out to coral a gang of jewel thieves, with plenty suspicion falling on him because no one knows about his legal affiliations until pretty late in the footage. Another element of mystery is carried until the last by the secret identity of the gang-leader, who doesn't turn out to be a butler, but someone almost as bad.

The big noise, though, is the action; and the picture has enough to satisfy. Molling fistfights rate first, with skidding automobile chases a close second. Photography here is better than usual.

Fairbanks is both energetic and brutal. Miss Daniels, his support, looks pretty and expresses nicely. Speed is this one's merit.

MARRIAGE

Fox release, produced by R. William Neill. From story by H. G. Wells; scenario by Gertrude Orr. Photographed by R. J. Berquist. At the Columbus, one day (May 11), as half of double feature bill. Running time, 56 minutes.

Marjori Pope................Virginia Valli
R. A. G. Trafford...........Allan Durant
Daphne Pope............Gladys McConnell
Sir Roderick Dover......Lawford Davidson

H. G. Wells isn't very brilliant on celluloid. Or possibly his interpreters were at fault.

"Marriage" in print had evident picture possibilities. "Marriage," the picture, herewith blooms as one of "two splendid features" grinding for 20c in a one-day stand.

Which indicates that the name of one of the world's most famous living authors was wasted. If a John Doe had written the story it wouldn't be waste; but Mr. Wells, who must have been paid highly for the picture rights, should have been handled with more care.

A bad break in selecting only one name for the cast. If the picture had developed stronger this would be overlooked, but names would be of considerable assistance as it is.

If the name of the author and the possibilities of the printed story were disregarded, "Marriage" would stack up as a fair program picture. But the lithographs give Wells such heavy billing it is impossible to considered the film as other than a disappointment.

Unwinding somewhat tediously, the picture shows, in situations, where a successful marriage is simply a mutual sacrifice. (The hoi polloi have had the same thought—only they call it a 50-50 proposition.)

The man pays too much attention to his work, sacrificing its money rewards for ideals. The wife induces him to sell a formula instead of giving it to the world, as he had planned, and then neglects him to some extent as she takes up the social activities money has brought her.

A misconstrued love triangle sets in and the hubby leaves for Africa. Wife follows but is repulsed. As she sets out through the jungle a lion attacks her and hubby comes to the rescue. He gets badly mauled and is nursed through several delirious African days by his wife.

Which leads to the closing subtitle about mutual sacrifice.

The forte in lineup is Virginia Valli—the only name. Allan Durant, the husband, looks in character but doesn't impress. Support is fairly efficient.

Only action punch is in the lion battle and that looks too phoney towards the finish.

The major weakness is direction, giving plenty of slack to a scenario that should have been held tightly throughout. Photography average.

A rather unfortunate affair.

Outlaws of Red River

Fox western starring Tom Mix; designated a Lewis Seiler production. Directed by Malcolm Stuart Boylan from story by G. Ramont. At Fox's Academy, New York, May 11. Running time, 49 minutes.

First class program picture of its kind with Tom Mix in a likable action role. Story follows the familiar formula of the Texas Ranger in pursuit of the bandit gang, but here the picture has a finale of novel angles. Romantic interest only fair, even for a cowboy film, but production takes merit from its splendid pictorial locale apparently in the southwest, with desert waste spaces fringed by abrupt sand peaks.

These elements of the landscape give a broken, rugged sky line skillfully utilized for hair-raising feats of horsemanship and remarkable falls by the hero. The photographic quality of the entire picture is noticeable for its excellence. The precipitous sand hills give the whole picture distinctive scenic character.

The steep slopes rise abruptly from the very edge of the desert and the sides of the ridges look impassable. But Tom and Tony make nothing of the giddy grades. Tony zooms up along the narrow ridges, silhouetted against the sky for striking effects. In one case Tom does a fall from horseback, rolling down what looks like an almost perpendicular sand precipice for 50 feet or so. This is when he is being led out into the desert, a captive; for expected death.

Tony continues up the ridge and then turns and joint Tom in a slipping, tumbling descent. The hills again enter into the climax when Tom and the posse have the bandit band beleaguered in their mountain fastness. First they attach a time fuse and dynamite to a wagon wheel which is sent driving down the hillside against the bad men's stockade to make a breach. Then Tom mounts to the driver's seat of a stage coach without horses and—by means of lines tied to the wagon tongue—guides it in a thrilling mad ride smack into the bandits' fortress, where the gun play finishes the story.

Romantic angle has to do with a kidnapping of a baby girl by outlaws. Years later the child's playmate (Mix) is a ranger, beut upon pursuing the kidnappers. He is directed by the governor of the State to clean up the Red River gang. Gaining entrance to their lair by a ruse, he finds that the kidnapped girl—now a grown woman—is among the outlaws, having been brought up by their kindly leader as his daughter.

With the clearing up of the thief hunting job, Tom, of course, wins the girl through the death of her pretended father at the hands of mutinous bandits.

Story elements stereotyped, but pictures made to stand out by its incidental details. *Rush.*

SPIDER WEBS

Artlee Pictures Corp. presents Niles Welch and Alice Lake, with J. Barney Sherry, Edna Richmond and Maurice Costello in "Spider Webs," adapted from the story, "The Fast Pace," by H. G. Logalton. Adaptation by Charles Horan. Directed by Wilfred Noy. Part of double feature bill at the Arena, New York, one day, May 16. Running time, 46 mins.

Flora Benham..................Alice Lake
Bert Grantland...............Niles Welch
Chester Sanfrew..........J. Barney Sherry
Joe Dickson.................Martin Faust
Nick Sinclair.................Bert Harvey
Jeffrey Stanton...........Maurice Costello
Mrs. Stanton..............Edna Richmond

The name right off the flash indicated deep-dyed villainy. Sure enough it soon plunged head over heels into the old game of blackmail wherein an innocent girl is used to obtain the letters of the married woman who fears exposure and wants them back. And a lamp of the cast also indicated that it might be good, but that was only a thought, as the cast became almost hopelessly lost in a plot that any high school boy could have devised for a screen story.

Real flashes of heavy expenditure and again many interiors that showed where economy is sometimes a blessing without disguise for the independent makers.

Some excellent shots of Broadway, Park avenue and the Penn station and for a moment with these especial spots in line of camera focus also deceived the audience that the story would do itself proud.

Before the fadeout for the final embrace everybody in the picture was getting messed around; cops were dragging Miss Lake away to the cooler, and upstairs Welch and the villain's agent, Faust, were engaged in a roughhouse encounter that had them fighting for ages.

The cast and the meller that flows and flows through its celluloid veins may give the picture a chance on a double-feature day. *Mark.*

The Broncho Twister

William Fox production, directed by Orville Dull. Story by Adela Rogers St. Johns. Potographed by Daniel B. Clark. Starring Tom Mix. At Stanley, New York, one day (May 11). Running time, 61 mins.

Tom Morton.........................Tom Mix
"Jinx" Johnson................Jack Pennick
Paulita Alvarez..............Helene Costello
Jasper Brady...................Paul Nicholson
Dan Bell.........................Malcom Waite
Tony, the horse..................(Himself)

A picture moving with such swiftness it pays the price in reasonability. It's a question, though, whether the enormous Tom Mix patronage worries about impossibilities. Either way, Mix is good entertainment in this film and should draw as usual.

He's an ex-marine, returning to his father's ranch and taking up a feud started in his absence.

A partial tally had Mix destroying 20 of his antagonists during the 61 minutes of film, a portion with straight pistol work and the remainder with cans of gunpowder. This does not include those knocked unconscious by Mix's fists nor those whose deaths were not certain. Nor what he might have done as a marine.

Sweet feminine appeal in Helene Costello, who has considerable more film devoted to her than most of the western sisterhood receive. Also good character support from Jack Pennick, playing a fighting sap ex-marine who follows Mix to the ranch.

Mix is more energetic than he has been in some time. In other ways he's his normal western self.

There shouldn't be complaints on this one, despite impossible story.

WHEN A DOG LOVES

F. B. O. production. Directed by J. P. McGowan from the story by John Morosco. Starring Ranger, dog, with cast including Harold Goodwin, Helen Foster, Frank McGlynn, Jr., and Henry McBann. At the Stanley, New York, May 13, one day.

Another that baffles comprehension. For no particular reason the heavy insists on attacking a harmless mongrel without an evil thought in the world. It is true that, according to the subtitles, the dog should be harboring a gnawing, unquenchable hatred for the "menace," but Ranger refused to register.

In almost every case where the dog is supposed to lunge at the man with extreme ferocity, it is the man and not the dog who does it. Frank McGlynn, Jr., is actually seen forcing the hound's jaws wide open.

The "action" was intended to center round the loss of the dog and a valuable necklace. A little boy finds the dog and brings him home.

A reward is offered for the dog and the "menace" tries to steal it and the necklace so as to collect a double reward.

Harold Goodwin, "wealthy clubman," finds his necklace being worn by Helen Foster. After knocked on the head a few times, thrown down stairs and chased about miscellaneously he decides to marry the gal and let her keep the choker.

An extremely poor production owing to bad direction, an impossible animal "star," and poor supporting cast. Story, to start with, is cold.

The Heart of the Yukon

H. C. Weaver Productions, Pathe released. Written and directed by W. S. Van Dyke. Photographed by Abo Scholtz and Dave H. Smith. In projection room May 11. Running time, 58 minutes.

Jim Winston.................John Bowers
Anita Wayne...............Anne Cornwall
Jack Waite...................Edward Hearn
"Old Skin Full"...........Frank Campeau
"Cash" Gynon............Russell Simpson
Yukon Madge...........Nell Barry Taylor

One of those pictures immediately associated with five acts of vaude. It rates among the nicer average of this classification.

The film was made near Tacoma, Wash., with all outdoor scenes shot in snow. Action occurs during the Alaskan gold rush days, when he-men, saloons and women were the rage.

Into the coarseness of it all steps little Anita, homely as the devil and from New England. She's looking for her father, whom she has never seen, so that she may divide the fortune mama left her. Actually her old man is the town's foremost booze hound, but the saloon owner convinces her that he's the father.

Hanging around the saloon

wisens the girl up on beauty culture, and she turns pretty. The fake father then gives himself away by kissing too hotly for a blood relative, and the hero comes to the rescue for a finale kiss. And the real old man is also cured of his likker habit.

Anne Cornwall puts over the transformation from homeliness to beauty with reasonable makeup assistance. The part fits her like a glove. John Bowers, looking mild as usual, was passable in a burly role. Support was very good, Frank Campeau shining in a drunk you could almost whiff.

The picture's action rests in several fistfights, with the supposed big spot, a race between two dog teams, missing by yards in expected punch. This race was preliminarily played up all through the early portion of the picture, and its actual weakness hurts.

Direction best in handling of details. Photography uniformly good. Entertaining program film.

The Mother

This Russian film has had one of the few really big successes in Berlin, even to such an extent that film houses opposite and alongside of each other played it the same evening.

Although not the money-maker in North Germany that "Potemkin" was, it will probably about even up as the censorship will find no ground to forbid it in South Germany. In America its appeal may be stronger than that of "Potemkin," as it tells a regular story.

Maxim Gorki's short story, from which it is taken, concerns a mother whose son conceals strikers' weapons in the house. The police come and arrest the son on suspicion and the mother, believing that she will save the son by doing so, discloses the hiding place of the revolvers. As a result, the son is committed to jail and the mother inveighs against the injustice of the court. A demonstrating party of workers marches out to the prison, and at the same time the convicts start a revolt from within. The officials get wind of the affair, however, and the prisoners begin before they get any help from outside. Most of them are shot down, only the son escaping by leaping onto floating ice on the river. Cavalry have been also warned of the march of the workers and charge down upon them, shooting the son and riding down the mother who holds the red flag aloft.

The direction of the 23-year-old Pudowkin is undoubtedly workmanlike and concise, but in nowise epoch-making. Moreover, he uses the very bad and outmoded trick of continually comparing the action of humans with natural phenomena. The players are generally competent, especially the bits which are peculiarly interesting on account of their characteristically Russian qualities.

JUNGLE BELLES

Bray Cartoon, programed especially compiled for Paramount theatre, New York, where it is for week May 14.

Set in the woods, the sketch artist is seen, moving, before his easel. His views take up considerable of the time and the cameraman must have thought very well of the artist, as he is given several close-ups. Usual cat stuff and chasing, with some animals worked in.

The personal entrance may be new to this sort of work. But for a short the time might better be devoted to attempts for laughs. If the artist wants a test, give it to him, Paramount. *Sime.*

ROUGH HOUSE ROSIE

Paramount picture starring Clara Bow and featuring Reed Howes, Arthur Housman. Directed by Frank Strayer from story by Nunnally Johnson. Titled by George Marion, Jr. At Paramount, New York, week of May 21. Running time, 63 mins.

Rosie O'Reilly	Clara Bow
Joe Hennessey	Reed Howes
Kid Farrell	Arthur Housman
Ruth	Doris Hill
Arthur Russell	Douglas Gilmore
Lew McKay	John Miljan
W. S. Davids	Henry Kolker

Clara Bow's return to flippancy and much more at home than in sedate drawing rooms. She's also back to fluffy bob, which will help convince those who missed "It" as to whether this girl carries out the modern version of that pronoun.

And "Rough House Rosie" isn't a bad picture. Nothing great about it, either, but the program houses will screen it successfully.

On the other hand, here's the prize fight angle again. "Knockout Reilly," "Is Zat So?" and now this one. They'll all be across the street from each other in many a town, with it even money and take your choice. "Reilly" tops the trio on the fight thing, "Zat So?" has an edge on laughs, and "Rosie" names Miss Bow and George Marion's titles as its chief defenders.

Rosie quits a candy factory to become a cabaret performer. The feminine urge to be a "lady" gives any tuxedo an approach to her acquaintanceship. The first one she falls for turns out to be a crook.

Meanwhile Joe (Reed Howes) is training for a championship bout, and Rosie finally hooks on to a social youngster who is an open sesame to the Bohemian set.

Joe is taking it on the chin, consecutively until Rosie attends a parlor party, where the husbands and wives are mixed up, when she decides she'd better go downtown and watch Joe struggle for the title. Joe is in tough shape by the time Rosie reaches the ring, but with the knowledge that his light o' life is in the arena, he stages a comeback, and while Rosie is turning on the personality for the champ Joe slips one to the button and it's all over with the other fellow.

Miss Bow capers around the screen and will likely please her own particular audience. At that, it seems as though all cast members run second to Marion's titles, the best job this writer has had on Broadway in some time. Arthur Housman is a standout as the cynical manager of Joe, while Reed Howes may surprise the general clientele as the latter character. Every so often Howes flashes a bit of neat trouping, far superior to anything he showed when handsome only before the independent cameras.

That may be to the credit of Frank Strayer, who directed. The latter has carried the theme along for certain action and it doesn't drag. Considering the well-known trail which the script follows, this isn't a bad feature of the production.

Light and merry at many points. They'll know the story by the end of the first 1,000 feet and may become restless during a cabaret passage, but after sitting through it the average cinema audience is apt to approve. *Sid.*

FIGHTING LOVE

Jetta Goudal featured in DeMille production. Directed by Nils Olaf Chrisander. Distributed by P. D. C. Story from Rosita Forbes' novel, adapted by Beula Marie Dix. Running time, 67 minutes. At Roxy, New York, week May 22.

Donna Vittoria	Jetta Goudal
Gabriel Amari	Victor Varconi
Filipo Navarro	Henry B. Walthall
Dario Niccolini	Louis Nathcaux
Princess Torini	Josephine Crowell

A picture of conspicuous beauty in production, but one in which the romantic story elements somehow do not grip. It has good spectacle features and the usually fascinating atmosphere of African desert, with a background of soldiers, fighting and intrigue.

The weakness on a guess arises from the fact that it was written in novel form with a man hero and the woman a subordinate interest. Adapted to present uses, the feminine character is moved into the center, and somehow values are disturbed. In any event, the story takes more interest from its splendid settings than it does in its substance.

The production is magnificent. Some of the shots of Italian interiors are arresting pits of picture composition. The stage tricks are capital; such, for example, as the deft use of symbolism in the passages where the old soldier's young wife is constantly brought face to face with the young officer whom she tries her best not to fall in love with. Always they look at each other across a flame. Several times it is candle light; another time it is a camp fire.

But these are mere story-telling devices. The trouble is that the story itslf doesn't grip. Col. Navarro, the old soldier, is the only heroic character. The young lovers are merely passive and lose sympathetic appeal, while all the romantic interest of the story is directed toward them. They triumph in a "happy" ending, while the old soldier who has engaged sympathy dies in the end to insure their future.

Story is weak on action drama. Much of it develops in quiet pantomime, with the action in the titles rather than the visible form, always a weakness. In this case it arises, of course, from the difficulty of adapting a written story to the screen.

The playing is always skillful, particularly the old soldier as done by Henry B. Walthall. Victor Varconi is a fine-looking leading man, playing with restraint, while Miss Goudal brings her exotic beauty to a role that rewards her best efforts scantily.

Several scenes of wild Arabs fighting in desert towns, well enough done, but they do not stand out as striking mass effects, principally because the underlying situation is not there. For instance, Col. Navarro and his command are besieged in a desert town and are starving because the Governor wants the old soldier killed in order to win his wife. Nothing of the siege or fighting is shown. The titles convey this part of the story, and the incident gets into view only when the Italian command (the locale is Tripoli) surrenders.

Later on the Colonel and the treacherous Governor meet. There is a fight to the death, this being the only dramatic kick. At the opening is an elaborate exposition of a self-willed old noblewoman, who thereafter fades entirely out of the story.

All these things tend to diffuse and dissipate interest in what should have been a clear-cut, concise narrative. *Rush.*

BEWARE OF WIDOWS

Universal production starring Laura La Plante. Directed by Wesley Ruggles from story by Owen Davis. Cast includes Paulette Duval, Catherine Carver, Heinie Conklin, Walter Hiers, Tully Marshall and Bryant Washburn. At the Hippodrome, N. Y., week of May 23. Running time, about 60 mins.

A likable comedy of good entertainment value, this picture constituted the best part of the program offered at the Hipp this week. While there is nothing new in the story material and slapstick is frequently called upon to help out solid laughs are heard strongly and continuously.

Laura La Plante is there on looks, makeup and comedy. Looks a little peevish in the scenes where tears form the major part of the scenic setting, but gets a few laughs to make up for loss in appearance. Tully Marshall, Walter Hiers and Hienie Conklin furnish most of the comedy in the latter part of the picture.

Story is of a good-looking doc perpetually surrounded by some of the prettiest widows in creation. Not satisfied with this state of affairs, it seems that the doc had taken a girl friend unto himself some time previously. The g. f. is jealous of the lovely widows, and for good reason.

When the doc and his g. f. go up to the mountains to be married a designing widow (Catherine Carver) lures him into her bedroom at the very moment the g. f. is waiting at the minister's.

The result a squabble, and when the girl repents she finds the boy friend about to marry another.

Catherine Carver is poorly dressed and looks unattractive. Paulette Duval, another widow, shows up well in several scenes and seems scraggy in others.

Direction not too good.

Princess from Hoboken

Tiffany production with Edmund Burns starred on New York theatre's billing. Blanche Mehaffey and Lou Tellegen featured. Scenario by Sonya Levien, directed by Allan Dale. At Loew's New York as half double bill May 17. Running time, around 60 mins.

Terence O'Brien	Edmund Burns
Sheila O'Toole	Blanche Mehaffey
Mrs. O'Brien	Ethel Clayton
Prince Balakrieff	Lou Tellegen
Princess Karpoff	Babe London
Mr. O'Brien	Will R. Walling
Pa O'Toole	Charles McHugh
Ma O'Toole	Aggie Herring
Whiskers	Charles Crockett
McCoy	Robert Homans
Cohen	Harry Bailey
Tony	Sidney D'Albrook
Immigration Officer	Broderick O'Farrell
Pavel	Boris Karloff

"Princess From Hoboken" starts off and quite well as a comedy, with the possibilities plenty, but it slides into the dangerous dramatic undertow toward the finish, dying out through that. It might have been a good comedy picture as a comedy; as a hybrid, it's an uninteresting mixture.

The comedy prospects probably deceived whoever selected the story, which looks to be an original, although with the only novelty in its theme the treatment of an impersonation. That the Tiffany picture was on a double bill at Loew's New York need not prejudice it; it's a good one-dayer by itself for downtown daily changes and is apt to stand up in the neighborhoods for three days. Women may favor it more than the men.

A well-made film, with a finish in production and photography, the latter in the closeups and larger figured views being especially noteworthy. Too bad that this independent producer did not switch the scenario entirely to comedy. From the manner in which it is run, either the story writer or the director became entangled with the problem of extracting the girl from her masquerade, going into dramatics to obtain that and thereby spoiling the comedy tale up until that time.

Easily starting in the telling of the opening of a Russian restaurant with a Russian Princess as the star dancer and attraction, excellent planting is smoothly made for the impersonation of the Princess by the daughter of the restaurant's chef. This is resolved upon as a desperate expedient, when the real Princess, delayed in arrival until after the crowd is in the new cabaret, for the premiere, arrives and is seen to be a big, beefy-looking Swede more than Russian, not the beautiful, dashing bankrupt

Princess advertised. There's a real good laugh in this.

When Blanche Mehaffey, as Sheila O'Toole, becomes the Princess Sonia Alexandrerovna Karpoff, there is more humor in her attempted simulation of "Me speek no Engleesh," and the courting of her by Edmund Burns as Terence O'Brien. The deception is finally revealed through a series of dramatic incidents closing the tale, involving her discovery by Prince Alton, a scheming Russian, eventually uncovered by the police as a swindler, some missing jewels, plots, suspicions, and so on.

Mr. Burns looks very good on the screen and gave a nice performance, with Miss Mehaffey a close second at times, although often wavering in her work. Charles McHugh made up and played the chef unusually well, with Lou Tellegen as the Prince handling his easy role with ease. Charles Crockett, called Whiskers on the program, looked a Russian 100 percent, and then some.

Just why picture people seem to believe there is more value in dramatics and mellerdrammer than in comedy cannot be fathomed. This same thing often occurs in picture making, killing off what may have been a good comedy by inverting into a bad drama. A good comedy is worth its weight in gold celluloid, while dramas are worth 30c. a dozen.

It would be wise money spent when a story suggests comedy to have it switched into all comedy at all hazards.   *Sime.*

DRIVEN FROM HOME

Chadwick production, presented by Jesse J. Goldburg. Directed by James Young from a play by Hal Reid. Cast includes Sojin, Anna May Wong, Melbourne MacDowell, Margaret Seddon and Ray Hallor. Virginia Lee Corbin starred. At Stanley, New York, one day, May 19. Running time, 65 minutes.

An old-time melodrama, with lots of plot, has been made into a fairly good programmer.

It's a blood-curdler, in which a wealthy parent with a yen to be the father-in-law of a bum count disowns his daughter for refusing the count, and sends her, suitcase in hand, from his palatial home.

Lurking in the background all through the picture, and ready to nab the dame for his villainous purposes, is a Chinese chop suey magnate. This angle could have been left out, as there is little or no suspense created thereby, the whole white slave thought being soft pedaled and sloughed over.

Virginia Lee Corbin, starred, is the gal who prefers 'em poor but honest. There are sympathetic characters, easy to understand plot, and a bit of comedy, which, though badly handled, will probably please in the spots for which this one is destined.

All in all, not so good, but a long ways from being bad.

HORSE SHOES

Monty Banks production, distributed by Pathe. Featuring Monty Banks. Directed by Clyde Bruckman from story by Banks and Charles Horan. Jean Arthur leading woman. Running time, 56 minutes. At Fox's Academy, New York, May 19-22, as half double feature.

Monty Banks here does fairly well in a full-length comedy. It has its moments of merriment. The best is an uproarious passage where the comic hero is forced by circumstances to share a Pullman berth with a young woman not his wife. Some of the gags are close to the line, but shrewdly pass muster.

The acrobatic feats of Banks trying to get undressed in an upper berth mostly taken up with hand luggage is capital knockout, and at the Academy evoked boisterous

laughter. This style of fun finds Banks at his best. He essays quiet humor at times in this picture, but it gets him little.

The story doesn't burden the screen, except that it calls for a few tiresome sequences. These story-planting bits are perfunctory and brief, and the footage delivers a high average of laughable knockabout which is directly to the purpose.

Story winds up nicely to a climax in a courtroom scene about as unrestrained as "Irish Justice," good for laughs and puts a brisk finish. A sustained comedy of feature length probably is the most difficult thing to make in the whole range of screen production. This one gets close to the mark, but not quite, partly because of story short-comings and partly because of Bank's style, the knockabout becoming tiresome from many repetitions.

The idea is the two-reel technique applied to a six-reel subject.

Rush.

Silver Comes Through

F. B. O. western starring Fred Thomson and Silver. Directed by Frank Cliften. Photography by Mack Stengler. Cast includes Edna Murphy, Harry Woods, William Courtright, and Mathilde Brundage. Reviewed in projection room May 18. Running time, 58 mins.

F. B. O. has come through with the usual type of Fred Thomson western and where that star and his cream-colored horse have the balcony whistling, this latest flicker will probably please. Anywhere else it's liable to be one long yawn.

Plot is the old one about the gambling ranch owner who bets everything he has, including his land and cattle, on the outcome of a horse race. Just before the race his prize entry has an accident and the hero's despised but sturdy equine cops the dough in spite of the efforts of the menace to foul the race.

Direction is fairly reasonable except at two points. The picture opens with Thomson deliberately going after a mountain lion without his gun. The meat-hungry cat jumps him, but Thomson overcomes the lion with the might of his bare arms. That's too big to go down the average throat. At another point Thomson mounted on Silver jumps from the open door of a moving freight car landing on a steep incline by the roadbed and never so much as a strain to either man or horse.

The usual modest bankroll for a Fred Thomson picture calls for plenty of exteriors in this one. Photography is competent.

SPEED CRAZED

Duke Worne production, distributed by Rayart and presented by W. Ray Johnston. Featuring Billy Sullivan. Story by Suzanne Avery. Photographed by King Grey. At the Columbus one day (May 20) as half of double bill. Running time, 50 minutes.

All details indicate that "Speed Crazed" was turned out in a hurry and that a minimum of thought was devoted to it. Nevertheless, it's good as juvenile stuff and acceptable material for double bills.

Billy Sullivan, of the clean-cut heroic type, perpetuated by writers for the "American Boy," cavorts around as the fellow who drives the racing car of his sweetheart's old man to victory. Naturally there are countless obstacles to overcome, which lead to fist fights auto chases and such.

The race stuff, a combo of newsreels and special closeups, is okeh. One clip of a car somersaulting several times would have been a darb if they hadn't close-upped the hero crawling from under it and continuing the race.

Casting is sufficient, as there's little acting to be done. Photography average.

Fair entertainment, not to be considered seriously.

IS THAT NICE

F. B. O. release. Directed by Del Andrews from story by Walter Sinclair. Photographed by James Cronjager. At Stanley one day (May 21). Running time, 50 mins.
Ralph Tanner..................George O'Hara
Doris Leslie....................Doris Hill
John Gorman................Stanton Heck

Farcical handling of a cub reporter tale to mediocre results. Some funny incidents and quite a few unfunny ones. Total spells one day.

In criminating papers in the crooked politician's safe, and it is up to the cub reporter to get them. He gets them, of course, with the aid of a girl who turns out to be a daughter of the local judge.

All incidents are bled for laughs. The cub stumbles around on skyscraper windows, makes wild automobile chases and dons various disguises. Title writer probed to the hilt for gags, finding some and hitting wild for plenty.

With the director also out to have his laugh at any price, things pan out a trifle too ridiculously to catch on as farce.

The photographer alone of the technical boys kept his eyes open for comedy, turning out some good skyscraper and chase stuff. Closeups weren't as good, expressing a distinct dislike for makeup at times.

George O'Hara is funny when they work him mildly. In the far-fetched farce he has a tough time. Doris Hill is sweet in the face and displays ability as a light actress. Support almost entirely at the mercy of the story, but still convinced that it is competent.

Those scattered laughs are the only forte.

The Wrong Mr. Wright

Universal production. From the stage play by George Broadhurst. Featuring Jean Hersholt with cast including Enid Bennett, Dorothy Devore, Walter Hiers, Edgar Kennedy. Directed by Scott Sydney. At the Tivoli, New York, one day, May 19.

Weak production built up around a player not yet sufficiently strong to assume comedy leads.

Jean Hersholt is given a "character" role, a "part" from which he is expected to draw first honors. As a stage play, the story may have had popular appeal through dialog and comedy interpretations not suited to the screen.

The awkward son of a teddy bear manufacturer, Hersholt is wrongly suspected by a detective of absconding with some $10,000. Enid Bennett must vamp him into a confession. She's vamped instead.

Situations complicated, but not comical. No laughs in the titles and the director attempted to carry off the burden of the laughs with Hersholt's change in attire, old-man make-up and a couple of comic fights.

Miss Bennett looks interesting in the love-making scenes, and puts a little feeling into these shots as well. Supporting cast not so good, Walter Hiers trailing without much to do, and miss Devore similarly placed.

THE PRAIRIE KING

Universal picture, starring Hoot Gibson. At Loew's New York as half double bill, May 17. Running time, around 60 mins.

"The Prairie King" doesn't mean a thing to anyone except a bug on westerns, and even a bug would have to be pretty buggy to like this one. That there is a vast mar-

ket for westerns is displayed by the utter contempt the scenario writer or director of "The King," if either, had for any intelligence that even a western picture audience might hold. That Gibson is a western draw in certain sections may well be believed through that very thing.

Action slight, comedy absent and badly striven for with but faint result, and story stupid.

Probably nothing more silly in story ever put on screen than here, when Gibson leaves his elderly pal to defend a mine against three bandits while he goes to a "Fiesta" to look after nothing.

Very tiresome, with Hoot's elderly pal the best actor in it, which doesn't mean much either. But it's the best glaring western ever seen. How those tough guys do glare at each other.   *Sime.*

Japanese-American Film

Los Angeles, May 25.

Independently produced by Kato Ediguchi productions. Directed by E. L. Zeer; featuring Harry Abbe and Tuki Mayeda. Previewed at the Westlake, Los Angeles, May 24.

This picture is probably the first of its kind to be made in this country. No title as yet, but the subtitles are in Jap hieroglyphics.

Continuity is at no time clear, with evidence of a good deal of cutting and in bunches.

Picture is stopped three or four times during the performance to allow the screen actors to go on with the story on the stage. The only thing novel about this is that it's done by Japs, with the exception of the two players in the film who are white, boy and a girl.

Japanese musical instruments are used for accompaniment, with a little singing on the side.

Stage part is the best of the whole thing. Whipped into shape it might be worth something.

All of the players on the stage appear in the picture. A quartet of Jap kiddies, as cute as they make 'em, put on some native dance routines that are entertaining and mirth provoking. Tuki Mayeda, featured child actress, solos with some more of this, including a toe number.

From the limited translation made from the stage by Harry Abbe, other featured Jap player, and from the observable continuity (what there was of it), the story in the film has to do with a Jap father, taking his son with him, leaves his nativity, wife and daughter, to come to America to make his fortune.

Years later find the father and son prosperous farmers, adjoining an acreage worked by a school chum of the Jap boy and his sister.

An impending love affair between the Jap lad and the white gal is evident, though nothing comes of it, due to noticeable cutting. (Probably in view of the picture being shown in white territory.)

The mother and daughter, accompanied by a half wit friend of the family, whose relationship is never comprehensibly explained, are brought over from Japan. The devoted half wit is told to go, leaves, strikes oil somewhere and later returns full with dough.

The narrative ends abruptly, with more cutting the cause and ends on the stage.

Abbe, as the half wit, and the little Tuki gal, as the child daughter, are the best bets on stage and screen; particularly Abbe, a good comedian and pathos handler. The little girl is the best versed in American lingo and has stage personality.

Whole at present running 73 minutes is in a crude shape. Photography and settings okay in spots but show lack of material (and money) with which to work. Tinting for some of the scenes, especially garden, would aid to a great extent. Also the insertion of American titles with gags. Direction can't be judged properly, due to the chopped continuity.

With entire revamping and expert cutting, this production should provide suitable program material for picture houses; particularly where Japanese settlements are in number.

A MILLION BID

Warner Bros. production, starring Dolores Costello. Directed by Michael Curtiz from a story by George Cameron. Adapted by Robert Dillon. Cameraman, Hal Mohr. Running time, 63 mins. At Paramount, New York, week May 28.

Dorothy Gordon............Dolores Costello
Geoffrey Marsh...............Warner Oland
Dr. Robert Brent.........Malcolm McGregor
Mrs. Gordon....................Betty Blythe
George Lamont..........William Demarest
Lord Bobby Vane..........Douglas Gerrard
The Gordon Maid.............Grace Gordon

A tiresome, never-ending laughless picture based on the ancient plot of the society mother who sells her daughter to a middle-aged millionaire.

Dolores Costello weeps and wails and goes out of her mind, but does little else of moment. Malcolm McGregor, the lead, is miscast. In appearance McGregor is hardly old enough to be riding the rumble seat of a hospital ambulance, yet the picture represents him as an eminent surgeon of immense reputation in the medical profession because of his success in delicate brain operations.

There is a story in the trade to the effect that this is not the picture made by Warner Brothers originally under the title "A Million Bid." The original production having turned out well, this makeshift was substituted, it is said, to take care of the title and the year book, while the good picture is reported to have gotten a new title.

The bewhiskered trick of intercepting letters and thereby separating the lovers is the cause of all the grief in "A Million Bid." And the grief is more with the people who paid to get in than with the actors.

Better pass it up.

CRADLE SNATCHERS

Fox production of stage play of same name. Howard Hawks, director, with scenario by Sarah Mason. Titles by M. S. Boylan. Lead film title features Louise Fazenda and J. Farrell Macdonald. At the Roxy, New York, week May 28. Running time, 59 minutes.

Susan Martin..............Louise Fazenda
George Martin.............J. F. Macdonald
Ethel Drake....................Ethel Wales
Howard Drake.........Franklyn Pangborn
Kitty Ladd..............Dorothy Phillips
Roy Ladd...................Wm. Davidson
Joe Valley..................Joseph Striker
Henry Winton.................Nick Stuart
Oscar...........................Arthur Lake
Ann Hall.........................Dione Ellis
Ike Ginsberg.................Sammy Cohen
Osteopath.......................Tyler Brook

They howled at this one in spots at the Roxy Sunday afternoon. Every so often the picture becomes almost as funny as the original stage version. Usual studio liberties have been taken with the script, and the picture keeps building up for three-quarters of its footage, to peter out as it concludes.

Nothing wrong with the climax other than the screen version of this comedy lacks the dialog which topped off the final curtain of the show. In lieu of the laugh situations which have preceded, it's not surprising that the picture can't establish a finish on the strength of a subtitle that was Mary Boland's line, "and for God's sake learn some Spanish." That's a little too strong for the screen, so the wording has been toned down.

Probably the most remarkable angle of transplanting this "smash" comedy to celluloid lies in the manner in which the three college youths have been duplicated. As a screen threesome they overshadow the women who play the neglected wives seeking revenge by hiring the youths as escorts. Each of the male youngsters does exceptionally well and Hawks has directed them splendidly through the "punch" sequence of the house party that winds up when the husbands walk in, and then carries on for a further twist as the three flappers come in on the husbands.

The kids are corking, with Arthur Lake, as the very blonde Swede, and Joe Valley, as the Spaniard from Brooklyn, particularly standing out because of the concentrated comedy in the roles. Nick Stuart plays the third boy legitimately and quite as capably as the others, but lacks the standout material with which to work.

Compared to the stage cast the women here suffer more than the others. However, the picture unwinds an impressive example of team work by the players. So much so that there doesn't appear to be any reason for featuring anybody other than to possibly give the film a name for billing purposes. The main title is bound to attract, and as evidence of this there were many people present at the Roxy who had dropped in because of having seen the show, and audibly compared the film with the legit version as it went along. And favorably.

Louise Fazenda is to advantage in the Mary Boland part, although not threatening to overcome the impression the latter has left as Susan Martin. The same is true of Ethel Wales and Dorothy Phillips, in that anyone who views this Hollywood effort is bound to recall the manner in which Edna May Oliver and Margaret Dale played these assignments.

As a whole the scenario adheres to the path blazed by the play. The opening is different, for the film starts in college and immediately establishes the three boys. Some ad libbing also permits Sammy Cohen to hop into the sequence for a female comedy impersonation depending mostly on "situation," followed by a girl coming in to complicate the embarrassment on the strength of out and out hoke.

A number of the titles are direct from the show, others being corresponding appropriate. A first-class production helps, although a distinct change in lighting, or photography, is an unusual flaw at this day and date. This happens as the husbands catch their wives and the kids late in the footage.

With or without the play in mind "Cradle Snatchers" makes a corking program leader that guarantees laughs. It will amuse and entertain in any class of house and before any type of audience. The story and situations are too surefire to miss.

Sid.

THE CLOSED GATE

Sterling distributing a Joe Rock production, directed by Phil Rosen. Adapted from Manfred Lee's same titled story. Jane Novak and John Harron featured. At Hippodrome, New York, week May 30. Running time, around 65 minutes.

Quite a production in looks for this independent producer and with holding qualities through much hoked sentimentality. It just misses being a very good program release, to become just a fair picture of the mush sort that should stand up in the neighborhoods. That it gets a week at the Keith-Albee Hippodrome is because that house has a rental money limit on its pictures. Still, this film will bring out many a handkerchief.

Early in the picture the story seems forced and the manner the auto accident was handled entirely stops interest thereafter for several hundred feet. The sobs are thrown in heavily through the death of a roll chair invalid mother, but again not so heavily when the son, cast out by his father and going to the big war, lost his memory through shell shock.

It's through the draggy finale when the hardened widower softens toward his only son whom he had believed lost in France that there's any real feeling. That's done quite well, although Johnny Harron appeared to be on piece work the way he deliberated whether he should recognize his dead mother's picture.

No one other than the father gave more than an ordinary performance. Father looked and acted his role. Jane Novak should put in a damage claim against the photographer, although the cameraing in the usual run is very nice.

Miss Novak is the nurse who brought the memoryless soldier back, married him and then removed the boy to a sanitarium near his old home, without once during the entire running permitting a caption to say amnesia. His cousin was on the board of directors for the sanitarium. On a tour of inspection the boy thought he knew his cousin, his face looked that way, but the cousin denied it to the wife. But there was a maid named Bridget, etc.

At the start with the son sweetly attentive to his invalid mother, the father spent his leisure bawling out the boy. One evening at dinner the young man didn't like pop's chat and walked out, going to a roadhouse. Coming back one of the girls insisted she would drive her roadster alone. But the boy wouldn't listen to that, so he hopped on the running board, helping her to steer in that position, doing about 50, and the car ran over a cliff. That was the botched portion.

When mother saw the newspaper account of the accident, stating that the girl had died and her son was in the hospital, she succumbed. That turned the father one hundred and eight percent against his boy, and sent the kid to war.

It isn't all mother stuff, however. There are a few war shots, of the narrow gauge kind but good enough, and the picture cost something to make. Far beyond the class of the usual kind of releases from this calibre of inde.

Sime.

TERROR OF BAR X

F. B. O. release, produced by Bob Custer Productions. Directed by Percy Pembroke, from published story by Gage M. Johnson. Photographed by Ernest Miller, with titles by Ruth Todd. At the Stanley, New York, one day (May 25). Running time, 63 mins.

Bob Willis............................Bob Custer
Doris Hunter.......................Ruby Blaine
Henry Hunter...................William Ryno
Percival Petree....................Jack Castle
Jim Ashland.......................Duke R. Lee
Hoke Channing..................Walter Maly

Plot is quite venerable and there is an absence of mechanical distinction, yet "The Terror" is a unique western program that should receive more general favor than the great majority of its cowboy brethren.

Its uniqueness is achieved simply by giving the love theme prominence equal to that of the plot action. The favorable results through this formula do much to overcome numerous technical weaknesses.

Right after the characters are introduced Custer takes Miss Blaine into his arms for a gentle but overpowering kiss. A few minutes later they're at it again; in fact, every time they meet there is a period of osculatory or necking activity. The total effect is not half as blubbery as it might seem. Miss Blaine is one of those girls who exudes a desire for sturdy masculine protection.

Antiquity is the story's outstanding point. The hero loves the rancher's daughter, but likewise does the local gambling-hall proprietor. The g. h. p. holds a note on pa's ranch, and threatens to foreclose. Custer gets the dough and pays off, but is implicated in a stage coach robbery.

Direction is strong on love theme, but shows ragged in some action spots. The old-fashioned stage coach robbery doesn't click so wel. with a subtitle speaking contemporarily of Will Rogers.

Casting very good. Custer, as lead shares considerable of his importance with Ruby Blaine, and the combination is all to the good. Miss Blaine is excellent as a lover but a trifle weak in looking miserable. She's far above the usual western ingenue. Support is in quality with the featured.

Photography average.

This combination of action and heavy love theme screens with exceptional western results.

BABE COMES HOME

Newark, May 30.

First National production starring Babe Ruth in Gerald Beaumont's story, "Said With Soap"; scenarist or titler not mentioned; Wid Gunning, director. Ran 55 minutes at Branford, Newark, N. J., May 30. In at the Branford for entire week as flicker backbone of Baseball Week program.

Babe Dugan,
"Babe" (George Herman) Ruth
Vernie....................Anna Q. Nilsson
Laundry Girl..............Louise Fazenda
Georgia...................Ethel Shannon
Laundry Driver............Arthur Stone
Peewee, Third Baseman........Lou Archer
Angel Team Manager........Tom McGuire
Mascot....................Mickey Bennett

This First National feature has played around the country for a number of weeks although not reaching nearer to Greater New York than Newark where it was reviewed at the Branford. As a film star, Babe (George Herman) Ruth, delivers almost as handily as on the diamond, which is saying much both ways for the King of Swat.

The title is appropriately fitting, a consistent pun on the circuit clouter's favorite exploit on the diamond.

The story has been judiciously neutralized for universal appeal to include the domestic touch for benefit of the femmes, although unlike the background of "Knockout Reilly," the great American pastime is popular with both sexes and not limited to one particular field. However, Wid Gunning played safe and the object of the title is stressed to mean everything in relation to the hearth and the fireside.

A romantic background revolves about the proverbial rose-covered cottage, the scene of a pre-nuptial split between Babe Ruth and Anna Q. Nilsson on the very eve of their wedding. Miss Nilsson objects to the slugging star of the Angels' tobacco chewing proclivities, and the quartet of hand-decorated cuspidors with which Babe's teammates have presented them, are ruled out. One situation leads to another in a well directed domestic squabble scene, and the couple part.

The crisis on the battleground, the usual ninth inning, but this time it's just a league pennant race, instead of a World's Series, comes with Miss Nilsson breaking through the stands to hand her amour a healthy plug of tobacco.

This situation is conservatively built up, with as much of the Frank Merriwell heroics eliminated as could be consistently accomplished without nullifying the effect. It is but another of the many other fine little touches in a simple baseball romance.

"Babe Comes Home" has a natural box-office appeal in its star who rates high as a space grabber. Think of baseball is to conjure up Ruth. That's why Ruth is worth plenty at the gate. No need to catalog this batsman. Coupled with a story structure like this and Ruth will win new followers for baseball, if such a thing is possible. The picture has been wisely directed in that Ruth's prestige on the diamond is not over-stressed but more taken for granted, and the romantic phase is more to the fore.

Miss Nilsson personates a laundress who complains of all ballplayers generally and Babe Dugan (Ruth) particularly as an exceptionally dirty and untidy group of a .letes. She pens Babe a short but harsh note. He comes back twice as rough and that's the beginning of things.

Louise Fazenda has the comedy relief. Ethel Shannon shows favorably.

Tom McGuire as the manager was probably cast because of his resemblance to John J. McGraw.

Abel.

PRIMITIVE LOVE

Billed as "A true story of life and love among the Esquimos." Taken by Capt. Frank E. Kleinschmidt, explorer, who spent a year with the Arctic people, accompanied by his wife. Running time, 60 minutes. At the Cameo, New York, week May 28.

Ok-Ba-Ok.................Modern Caveman
Sicca Bruna......................His Wife
Wenga.................Flapper Daughter
Amutuk...............Sensible Daughter
Patunuk.................Suitor of Wenga
Itak......................Rival for Wenga
Annok ....Grandmother

Interesting travel or educational, with several fairly thrilling episodes of eskimo hunts, but the whole film does not carry out the title in a romantic sense. It is an unstudied picturization of native life. In that lies both its strength and weakness for public exhibition.

Scenically it is absorbing with its limitless wastes of frozen sea and land, its muffled figures and their quaint habits and weapons. Behind all this there is the drama of their existence against the odds of arctic hardships, with starvation and death from cold just a step ahead. But the spectator has to build much of the atmosphere for himself, and the subject does not qualify as a feature to support a program anywhere.

Elements of romance and drama are not well staged for effect. These need the aid of art and subterfuge. Here it is the titles that tell most of the drama, while the action by native actors—the real thing, of course—are rather drab.

The hunting scenes and capital shots at an Arctic blizzard are the best, with the courtship episodes blah. One hunt bit has the natives far at sea and among the ice floes harpooning a big polar bear swimming from ice field to ice field. Another has the killing of a polar bear in hand-to-hand fighting with spears and arrows. There are real thrills here. A hunt from an ice cake in which an enormous walrus is the quarry, being stalked among the ice and dispatched by harpoons, has a kick, too.

A semblance of story in the courtship of the hero's daughter by two rival tribesmen, but it is merely a slim thread upon which to hang the scenes and text showing the strange lives of these far-north peoples. It never reaches any intrinsic interest. In this respect the picture is greatly inferior to "Nanook of the North," a similar subject made under the auspices of the Hudson Bay Company in 1922.

"Nanook" took particular interest at the time from the circumstance that polar regions were much in the public eye because of explorations then figuring in the news, and that gave it popular value. No such aid is at hand for "Primitive Love," which is merely a good short magazine subject stretched out to dull feature length.

The bill is filled out with an "Aesop Fable," revival of Charley Chaplin in "The Cure," which has been the rounds lately, and an unusually good issue of the Pathe News reel.

Rush.

ROAD TO BROADWAY

Released by the Motion Picture Guild, Inc.; presented by Louis T. Rogers. Howard Mitchell, director. Names of photographer and author missed while getting a drink of water. At the Arena, New York, one day (May 25) as half double-feature bill. Running time, 60 minutes.

Mary Santley.................Edith Roberts
John Worthington.............Gaston Glass
E. Norbert Richter...........Ervin Renard

As the footage mounts up the trade value slides down. What looked like a nice program in the first few minutes of play goes off its nut and breaks its back with several tons of plot. Very few doormen in full uniform will take tickets for "Broadway."

A dame comes to New York in search of film fame. To do it she bucks the wishes of her old man back in Louisville who wants her to settle down and marry his friend's son. A film publicity man uses her for a gag, wherein she does a phoney loss of memory and wakes up in a hospital unidentified and mysterious. She's wearing a funny ring and her pocketbook is full of French money.

The hero enters and claims he knows her; he doesn't. Several Frenchmen enter and claim her. One of them gets her and threatens to murder her because she's a Russian traitoress.

Hero enters again. Being from Louisville, he proceeds to duel the Frenchman with swords. Police enter and break it up.

New York reporters—all three of them—get the story, and it's a great publicity break for the film company. (You see, the cops and the French villains are all phoneys, hired by the film company in this gag to exploit their forthcoming picture. The reporters don't get wise, leaving the scene immediately at the command of the director.) Hero turns out to be the gent from Louisville, whom the girl had never seen and, therefore, didn't want to marry.

Miss Roberts looks pretty, but must act pretty silly. Gaston Glass is similarly handicapped. Direction, annoying. What a plot. Otherwise the picture has no evident possibilities.

CHEATERS

Tiffany Production directed by Oscar Apfel from story by Harry Kerr. In cast: Pat O'Malley, Helen Ferguson, George Hackathorne, Alphonse Ethier, Max Davidson, Claire McDowell, Heinie Conklin. Running time, 62 mins. On double feature bill at Columbus, New York, one day, May 25.

Crook picture with hackneyed plot and lacking the directorial finesse that might have excused the story. Pat O'Malley heads the cast, which includes some fairly well-known movie "names." In spots and with the cast line-up "Cheaters" will be seen by audiences without a feeling of having been cheated, but it's not for the critical houses.

George Hackathorne is playing Half-Wit Paul, shell-shock victim with kleptomaniac tendencies. In the unfolding he is the befriended ward of Allen and Mary, two former crooks now employed respectively as clerk and cashier of a hotel. The master crook, Kingston, from whom the pair had hoped themselves free, returns to demand their assistance in the theft of a society woman's jewels held in the hotel safe. After a series of conventional complications the master crook is popped off when escaping after being placed under arrest.

Alphonse Ethier, whose specialty of kind-hearted detecting is familiar to followers of the independent screen, again performs as a shrewd but amiable plain clothesman who acts as judge and jury on his own cases.

For a fade-out the lovers try to clinch with humorous results because of the handcuffs that bind them together.

PAYING THE PRICE

Columbia production directed by David Selmar. Cameraman, George Meehan. Cast includes John Miljan, George Hackathorne, Eddie Phillips, George Fawcett, Marjorie Bonner, Priscilla Bonner. Running time, 62 mins. On double feature bill at Loew's New York, one day, May 27.

Columbia has turned out a highly moral and fairly dramatic yarn dealing with the consequences that followed the taking of a shot of hootch by a pious church-goer not used to drinking.

Because the picture is so very moral and because it oozes over with sweet sentiments and Godly people it may be figured as good for the lesser communities, but a pain in the neck for the big towns.

Dorothy Howell's well-thought-out scenario that leaps the picture right into the action at the start and keeps it moving fairly consistently is an important factor to the picure.

David Selmar has performed a brisk business-like job holding the action to the groove and managing to round off the absurdities that might otherwise have crept in due to the wishy-washy story which has a very boyish minister of the gospel as its hero and the two Bonner sisters looking very dumb as the wrong gals.

It is never made clear whether one or both of the girls were ruined by the sheiky villains after the drugged lemonade affair. The father kills the scoundrel and is on the jury when an innocent boy is being tried for the murder. The jury decides to bring in a verdict of not guilty and to forget the story told them by the father. The minister and the eldest girl marry for the finis.

Because of its production standards this one rates as okay.

THE BUSHMAN

Denver, May 25.

Independent animal picture produced by Denver African Expedition and locally presented by H. E. Ellison. East of Denver distribution to be handled by Players of Boston; west of Denver by H. E. Ellison. Reviewed at Broadway theatre, Denver, May 25. Actual screen time about 97 minutes. As shown with one machine, about 110 minutes. Directed by Dr. C. Ernest Cadle. Photographed by Paul Hoefler. Cut and titled by Fred Myton of Paramount.

Just another animal picture, this time without the real thrill shots which "Chang" and others of this style have led the public to expect.

As screened, the picture holds only four titles after the introductory card, but Fred Myton loaned to H. E. Ellison by Jesse Lasky is on the ground now and planning his titles on the basis of audience reaction. The cutting of the first two reels shows the master hand of this boy who has been specializing on the Zane Grey Westerns for Paramount. For a travel picture and composed mostly of "atmosphere" shots of the first towns encountered on the African coast these first two reels have an amazing tempo.

After these first two reels the picture degenerates mostly into repetition of long shots of herds of strange animals. The picture's title is based on the small people of the African interior and many shots of this tribe, their dances and hunting habits are shown. Some of the photography is good and some not so good, the general average being far below the recently shown "Gorilla Hunt," for instance.

A scene which caused much comment was of the approach of the Bushmen on a portable phonograph; while similar to a scene in "The Gorilla Hunt," this one is much more prolonged and more carefully handled. The reaction to an Al Jolson record using the word "Pickaninny," which the lecturer explained is the only word carried over to our idiom by the Africans, is especially creative of interest.

As shown, the picture's main value is in the lecturer whose talk is synchronized in the manner formerly used by the late Lyman Howe. The Players, of Boston, a concert bureau handling explorers, has booked the man and picture for the east, the western manager planning to use him also either with clubs or local sponsors in preference to regular theatre dates; although several of these are also planned.

CALIFORNIA OR BUST

F. B. O. production, directed by Phil Rosen from the story by Byron Morgan. Featuring George O'Hara with cast including Helen Foster, John Steppling, Johnny Fox and Irving Bacon. At the Arena, New York, one day, May 26.

Five reels out of a two-reeler. Story is too threadbare to carry the length and action is there for slow. A fairly good film, aside from those defects. A few laughs at the opening where three rubes and a rog gaze steadily at a checker board until lunch hour. The committee then adjourns only to return and resume inactivities an hour later.

O'Hara and Miss Foster are a presentable team for the spots this film is intended. Supporting cast rather good, considering type of production.

Story is of a country mechanic who has built a fast automobile from stray parts. He proves its value to the wealthy automobile manufacturers after the expert engineer has pronounced it n. g. and is invited to superintend production. Will hold them.

When Seconds Count

Rayart release of a picture starring Billy Sullivan. Directed by Oscar Apfel, with Mildred June as "the girl." At Loew's, New York, as half double bill one day. Running time, 53 mins.

One of those things that has all it can do to stay with the double feature runs. No more than a time destroyer for the intermediates.

Sullivan has plastered so much make-up on his face that he looks ghastly while supposed to be a youthful and erring scion of wealth. Dragging a hard-boiled cabaret dancer to his father as a prospective daughter-in-law instigates the family blowoff. Sully takes it on the run for a small town where Dad is building a dam. A crooked supervisor of construction, complications and a phone operator. No production, but the usual action. Haphazard release that isn't going anywhere in particular and will just stop here and there before calling it a season. Cast members will probably regard it as satisfactory if their names aren't mentioned. *Sid.*

AVENGING FANGS

Pathe release, produced by Chesterfield Pictures Corp., and directed by Ernest Van Pelt. Featuring Sandow, the dog, supported by Kenneth McDonald, Helen Lynch, Jack Richardson and Max Asher. Story by George Pyper. Photographed by Jimmy Brown. Reviewed in projection room. Running time, about 50 mins.

Too many unintentional laughs in this picture hold it to the minor spot on a double-feature bill.

Sandow, the dog, was too playful to agree with the subtitles, feeling pretty happy over things when the printed inserts would have him grim and merciless.

The story is a cipher. Sandow and his master's pal hit for the west in search of the people who bumped off the master back east. They get the villains all right, and for a surprise ending practically everyone but the bad men turn out to be members of the secret service, or indirectly connected with it.

Direction is weak and casting is identical. Photography is average. Sandow won't be proud of this, if he's interested at all.

HARD FISTS

Blue Streak western, starring Art Acord. Written and directed by Paul M. Bryan. Running time, 56 mins. One double-feature bill at Tivoli, New York, one day, May 26.

Done on a shoestring with plot No. 654, this Art Acord picture will be valuable where a strict western diet is the rule and low rental the best seller.

Yes, there's a Ky. col. in it.

AFTERMATH

Los Angeles, June 2.
Produced by National Film A-G Corporation of Berlin (Germany). Directed by Erich Waschneck from an original story. Edited and titled for the American screen by Alfred Hustwick. Presented by Walter W. Kofeldt, Inc., at the Forum, Los Angeles, May 24, for run. Running time, around 90 minutes.

Louise von Wilkuehnen	Jenny Hasselquist
Her Son	Hubert von Meyerinck
Henry Raschoff, Governor	Fritz Alberti
Zeremski	Hans Adalbert Schlettow
Nadja	Olga Tschechowa
Marlene	Camilla Spira
Duban	Hugo Werner Kahle
Waldo	Oskar Homolka
Steward	Albert Steinrueck
Innkeeper	Wilhelm Diegelmann
Horsedealer	Siegfried Arno
Butler	Max Maximilian

Time—1919.
Place—Rupolsia (Eastern Europe).

The same people making this one also made "Slums of Berlin," which met with disaster when brought over here about four months ago. "Aftermath" is a fair program filler with its province in the east, in the cities where the foreign element may support it.

American treatment in continuity and plot evolvement is evident throughout "Aftermath." There is little in the story aside from a few twists here and there to distinguish it from a number of other foreign laid plots made in this country.

Photography is good without being above ordinary; and the same goes for direction. The first half of the picture is by far the better and gives promise of an interesting conclusion.

However, with the unfolding of the second part it can be seen nothing of the sort is going to occur.

From the exploitation touting handed out for this film before the opening, one was led to believe that a disclosure, at least in part, of what the Great War left in its wake of blood and disaster was going to take place. The title is misleading. There is no aftermath of the war to speak of. If there was any originality most of it must have been cut before it reached this country. What happens at a time designated as 1919 could have happened before the war or any other time.

The story revolves around a German noblewoman left a widow during the war, but still amply provided for. An only son is still in the service, keeping his identity concealed when entering his home town near the borderline between Russia and Germany, upon a furlough to visit his mother and sweetheart, the latter a barmaid. Town is invaded by an outlaw band from the other side, with the leader of the band, accompanied by his lady love, taking possession of the nobleman's home and declaring martial law.

He falls in love with his hostess, makes advances to her and is tolerated because of the mother's fear for the safety of her son, who smuggled himself into her house with the aid of his sweetheart under the cloak of a servant.

The cast, according to the program, is made up of various European nationalities. Of these three are outstanding. Olga Tschechowa does well as Nadja, the outlaw captain's sweetheart. The girl, in looks and manner, bears a resemblance to Pola Negri and is a possibility for the American screen. Hans Adalbert Schlettow convinces as Zeremski, the outlaw captain. Fritz Alberti registers solidly as the Governor. The rest of the principals do nothing to write home about.

Shown here at $1.65 top, the picture will not pick up any money. Alongside "The Last Laugh" and "Variety" it doesn't stand a chance. No value for the small town exhibitor. Running time needs plenty of cutting.

TILLIE THE TOILER

Metro - Goldwyn - Mayer production, directed by Hobart Henley. Starring Marion Davies. An original story founded upon the comic strip cartoon of same title by Russ Westover. Titles by Ralph Spence. At Capitol, New York, week June 4. Running time, around 60 minutes.

Tillie Jones	Marion Davies
Mac	Matt Moore
Pennington Fish	Harry Crocker
Mr. Simpkins	George Fawcett
Mr. Whipple	George K. Arthur
Sadie	Estelle Clark
Bill	Bert Roach
Bubbles	Gertrude Short
Mr. Smythe	Arthur Hoyt
Ma Jones	Claire McDowell

Mildly amusing program release and getting into the mild class only through a few of the captions written by Ralph Spence. In cities where the Hearst papers can splash publicity upon this, as they do on all Cosmopolitan pictures, this film should reach the normal gross, also in towns where the youngsters have gone wild over "Tillie the Toiler" in cartoon strip form, if any have gone wild. Otherwise "Tillie" is just a picture.

In the cast George Fawcett draws a laugh or so as the boss, and Bert Roach does well as the self-exploiter, while Gertrude Short, the kidlet, not only does nicely but is made to do more so by a couple of the Spence captions.

Marion Davies and Matt Moore, the leads, aren't overburdened by work or effort. Miss Davies is Tillie, and the funniest thing she did was when winking. Picture started off with large possibilities through that wink, but changed its pace and plodded along thereafter, with probably Spence called in as a life saver.

Tillie here secures a job as typist in the office where her sweetie, Mac, is the bookkeeper. She flirts while at lunch with Pennington Fish, who had a mother and a car of his own. Tillie got in the car and got Fish, having heard he was wealthy. She wanted a rich husband to repay her mother with less work and a better home. But Tillie loved Mac, eventually turning down the Fish, with Mac getting an elevation in the office.

In between not much doing. Little action, no sex stuff and the romance a little dizzy often. Not even a big cabaret scene.

"Tillie the Toiler" should have been a very good light picture for Miss Davies. It isn't and the fault appears to have been with the story or scenario builder. Every one else did what they were called upon to do, from Hobart Henley, the director, to the kid actress. But there wasn't much to do. That's where Spence came in.

One of Spence's gags was: "The kind of a man who got married in the back yard so the chickens could get the rice." *Sime.*

The Heart of Salome

William Fox production directed by Victor Schertzinger, from the story by Allen Raymond. Scenario by Randall H. Faye. Featuring Alma Rubens, with cast including Walter Pidgeon, Holmes Herbert, Robert Agnew, Erin Labissoniere, Walter Dugan, Barry Norton and Virginia Madison. At the Roxy, New York, June 4. Running time, about 55 minutes.

Not a picture that can be run by the ace houses depending entirely on the film for the rent money. With vaudeville or as 50 percent of a program the film will do, providing the balance of the bill is strong enough to carry it.

Slow-moving and devoid of any outstanding story twist or personality for audience appeal, "Heart of Salome" also offers a representative lesson on miscasting or lack of a good cast. The material on hand was obviously scanty and the director's only chance was in getting a modern vamp with a Valentino type of screen lover for human interest.

It is a difficult matter to draw sympathy for a Parisian girl, the

assistant of a blackmailing thief. The girl's job is to get the victims drunk on wine and her beauty and slip out with the plans or whatever it is before they start necking. The idea conveyed that the girl did not love the villain. But her only virtue was that she loved the young American engineer. This is not enough of an excuse and anyway she didn't show her love strongly enough to win support among the audience.

Alma Rubens looks like a type French girl in the picture, but not like the kind men are interested in. The first essential, s. a., is sadly lacking in her makeup. Cast as a whole is poor. Schertzinger accomplished about as good a job as possible considering the material he was given to work with.

TIPTOES

British National Corporation's production, made in England and released over here by Paramount. Directed by Herbert Wilcox (English). Starring Dorothy Gish with Will Rogers and Nelson Keys (English) featured. At Proctor's Fifth Avenue, June 6-9. Running time trifle over 60 minutes.

If the names of Will Rogers and Dorothy Gish on a picture over here, even English made, can draw any money, "Tiptoes" will; if not, then not, for the picture is nearly a perfect blank. What makes it a perfect blank as a picture and story is the inane direction, with the total absence of sympathy, the latter to be as well blamed upon the direction.

Here is a story of an American vaude three-act, two men and a girl going to Liverpool to "try out," doing an open face flop to an extent they are closed in by the front cloths, and then having the girl assume the masquerade of an American heiress to inveigle an English lord, with the story hoping you believe she is a "good gurl."

Whether she is or no, not one will care after seeing the London hotel suite occupied by the Americans at $50 a day, without a cent in the world between them, only "a good gurl." It's merely making a con trio of them.

This picture is not only a libel on Americans, but on American vaudeville and its artists. The attempted interpolation of comedy or the remorse of the girl will never excuse it. And the Americans can forever throw "Tiptoes" back into the faces of any foreigners who may say that American pictures furnish illusions, whether of Americans or conditions.

In its working out the picture is simple, altogether too simple, not only in direction and incidents, but in the work of Messrs. Rogers and Nelson Keys, the latter the English single turn (variety) and musical comedy comedian who has been on this side. That, however, doesn't mean a cent for the value of his name in the U. S. Both of the men are made to be awkward, almost cockney, song and dance vaudevillians, without either permitted to do any screen comedy.

According to this picture the people want to see Bill Rogers when he's talking, not acting, for the Fifth Avenue held far from capacity Monday night with the picture, his name and Miss Gish's largely billed outside.

Scenario adapted from the Guy Bolton play of same name, produced in New York some time ago. Made by British National, an English producing concern promoted by J. D. Williams, American, who is reported no longer connected with it.

Paramount has the American distribution. Early reports were that the picture would not be released, perhaps because of the libels or just because it's nearly a picture, but if Keith-Albee want to buy it, why not? Anyone else except for the one-dayers should not take a chance unless certain that the Rogers-Gish combo will do the b. o. trick. The shooting galleries or the sticks where the sight of Will Rogers might mean something, away from a Vitaphone, can handle it if cheap enough for the gamble, but whomsoever sees Will Rogers here and have not seen or heard him previously will be disappointed in our Bill.

Miss Gish looks nice at times and the other times may be blamed upon the English. *Sime.*

THE TENDER HOUR

First National picture starring Billie Dove and featuring Ben Lyon. Alec B. Francis and Montague Love underlined. Story by Carey Wilson with George Fitzmaurice directing. At the Strand, New York, week June 4. Running time, 75 mins.

Marcia Kane....................Billie Dove
Wally Mackenzie....................Ben Lyon
Grand Duke Sergeivitch....Montague Love
Gorki....................Constance Romanoff
Vicomte Chinilly..........Alec B. Francis
Tana....................Laska Winter
Rough-House Higgins......T. Roy Barnes
Pussy-Finger....................Buddy Post
The Wrestler............George Kotsonaros

F. N. is presumably grooming Billie Dove to succeed to the niche formerly held by Corinne Griffith previous to the latter going over to United Artists. If that's the case, First National undoubtedly has a chance to do it, but Miss Dove is going to need stories. Better than this one.

This girl has an abundance of beauty with which to gain a male following while the clothes she has been wearing in her recent pictures are bound to draw feminine attention and attendance. That being so, the best thing the story pickers can do is get some tales for Miss Dove.

"The Tender Hour" is practically a 400-foot picture. That is, the punch action and title laughs are all in the last half of the last reel. Ahead of that is much heavy unwinding on lavish sets, impressive costumes by Miss Dove, an Egyptian stage ballet and not much story.

As far as the plot is concerned, it's very familiar. Marcia Kane believes her juvenile lover dead, so marries the Russian duke under persuasion of her father, who has an eye on the latter's oil holdings. But Wally isn't dead, and turns up just after the ceremony. Following this most of the footage is used to get Marcia out of the predicament, meanwhile depicting too much anguish by the lovers.

Comedy is introduced through Wally, on a stew, falling in with a hard-boiled threesome from the States, impersonated by T. Roy Barnes, Buddy Post and George Kotsonaros. Pretty much rough and tumble from then on with the wallop 'way at the finish in the laugh-getting titles.

Lots of production to this one and good performances by Miss Dove and Montague Love, the latter as the heavy "heavy." Ben Lyon looks okay as the lover, but doesn't convince physically when up against in the hand-to-hand calisthenics. The comedy trio are invaluable as a bolstering influence, but Alec B. Francis has little to do.

Fitzmaurice has "traveled" his camera in the opening passages almost as far as the combined mileage of Lindbergh and Chamberlin. The lens never seems to stop moving and the effect becomes monotonous. However, the sets give the audience plenty to look at while the Egyptian Ballet appears, an added tidbit not necessary in view of the lengthy footage and the expense it involved.

Nothing to classify this one as a "smash" and saved by its late comedy. Should draw moderately and too lightweight to mean anything to Miss Dove other than from a physical standpoint. *Sid.*

SLAVES OF BEAUTY

Fox production. Directed by J. J. Blystone from the story by Nina Wilcox Putnam. Featuring Olive Tell and Earle Foxe, with cast including Hebert Holmes and Margaret Livingstone. At the Hippodrome week June 6. Running time about 65 minutes.

Fair program picture built up from interesting story. Angle of mother and daughter fighting for the same man, even though the daughter is only doing so to prove a point, is not played for full value.

The love story of the middle-aged woman was allowed to overshadow interest in the younger couple too much, reducing the latter to the status of nonentities.

Story is of an old-fashioned husband who invents a beauty clay through which the wife becomes wealthy from a beauty parlor. The husband sticks to old clothes, wifie stays young, and finally starts chasing the handsome manager in her employ.

Papa wakes up, establishes a rival beauty parlor and takes away all of mama's business, following divorce proceedings. Mama repents after being shown the kind of blackguard the manager really is. Sounds very good, but doesn't look half so good in the picture.

The Whirlwind of Youth

Paramount presentation starring Lois Moran; directed by Rowland V. Lee. adapted by Julien Josephson from A. Hamilton Gibbs' novel, "Soundings." Runs 60 minutes at Paramount, New York, week June 4.

Nancy Hawthorne.............Lois Moran
Heloise....................Vera Veronina
Bob Whittaker...............Donald Keith
Cornelia Evans................Alyce Mills
Lloyd Evans....................Larry Kent
Curley....................Gareth Hughes
Jim Hawthorne..............Charles Lane

"Soundings," the Hamilton Gibbs novel source of this Paramount flicker, metamorphosed into the racy title of "The Whirlwind of Youth," suggests from this trite adaptation that the book was probably a rather interesting study of flaming youth on the half shell.

As presented it has its moments, but sums up as pretty familiar stuff about the 18-year-old heroine laboring under suppressed amorous desires and unrequited love. The object of her affection is the original "it" kid, played by Donald Keith, whose S. A. seems deadly for any and all femmes.

The manner of registering Keith's lady-killing qualities is to show him wrestling and kissing the gamut from English flappers to torrid senoritas, with a native French gal in between. If nothing else, the Keith technique on the screen should click with the adolescents, particularly frails, which may mean he will set a pace for himself on the screen in that role. And considering everything else, Keith does pretty well.

Vera Veronina, who is featured, is just fair as the hot Spanish mamma. Alyce Mills is tepid in an inconsequential role. Larry Kent—isn't or wasn't he a Paramount Junior star?—acts conventionally manly through 60 minutes of the running time, but suggests greater possibilities if given the opportunity. Gareth Hughes, whose screen veteranism exceeds the Junior Star idea, is absolutely wasted in a minor role not commensurate with his prestige. He makes a few brief appearances in the opening shots.

Individually Miss Moran, who is solely starred above the title, sustains the picture. She is an optical treat and can do her stuff before the lens, in and out of close-ups.

It winds up with the kissing papa falling for Miss Moran in a behind-the-front romance, he as a British army officer, she as a nurse.

The picture has two box office assets, youth and romance plus, which should carry it. Coupled with the Whiteman orchestra as the big musical noise at the Paramount this week, both should do business. *Abel.*

FOREST HAVOC

Ellbee picture, presented by W. T. Lackey. Directed by Stuart Paton. Photographed by Al Prince and Wm. H. Tuers. At the Tivoli, New York, as one half double bill, one day (June 4). Running time, 65 minutes.

Ronald MacDonald..........Forrest Stanley
Lenore Renwick........Peggy Montgomery
John Garue....................Ernest Hilliard
Sandy McRae....................Harry Todd
Sarah Bolton..................Martha Mattox
George Renwick...........Sidney De Grey

The 65 minutes running time indicates that this picture is relied upon to carry itself in most places. Although presented here with four shorts and another feature and booked in for only one day, the reaction to it noted among a certain element in the audience is fair reason for okehing it as a solo feature in one classification of houses. This embraces those theatres whose patronage has been built up on a diet of thrills and old-fashioned melodrama. For theatres whose customers expect a modern type of picture the verdict is nix.

Technically the picture hits high and low. The presence of two themes, adventure and love, running side by side and each having its big moments is the one sign of intelligent directing. That the big moments are spoiled by crude handling is unfortunate.

Titles are weak. They can't handle emotion without slobbering over the magnificence of it all, and they fail to account for lack of continuity in the film. Taking the picture strictly on its word, it seems that the hero met the heroine, married her that night, and became the proud father of a bouncing boy either the next day or a few hours later. Lapses of time must be guessed at by the audience.

Story is of a crooked lumber camp boss, who is stealing logs from the owner. He is also engaged to the old man's daughter. A young assistant gets the girl's attention; and after the youngster rescues her in a forest fire she marries him and has that baby.

In the rescue the youth was hurt, and he later goes blind. The monotony of living with a blind man gets the girl after a while, and she is almost persuaded to blow with her previous love.

The hubby hears of it and pulls a blind fight with the villain. In the battle he regains his sight and recovers the love of his wife. The lumber graft is also exposed.

The cast is emotionally weak, but good enough on straight stuff. Forrest Stanley and Peggy Montgomery have the looks and fair talent. Support sufficinet.

Despite its weaknesses there is a limited market for this as a single feature. The customers it draws will overlook the technical sadness.

SAVAGE PASSIONS

Made by Nat Levine in association with Alpine Productions, Inc. Alice Calhoun featured. Directed by Fred S. Allen from original story by Mary Eunice McCarthy. In the cast: Lucy Beaumont, Eddie Phillips and others. Running time, 56 minutes. Half double feature bill ("Pleasure Before Business," another independent). At Loew's New York, New York, one day, June 2.

An arresting box office title is here displayed. Instead of a South Seas romance as might be expected, the title reference is to the unbridled hates and fighting instincts of the Tennessee mountain feudists, their fierce prides, sullen resentments and bitter rivalries with the law.

Out of this material the producers have made rather an interesting picture, interesting in its types. The principal factor against it is that the subject matter has little broad interest. The romantic side is made rather secondary, center of attention being directed toward the young lawyer who tries to bring to the settlement of a back country dispute the arbitrement of the legal machine instead of the traditional resort to rifle bullet.

It scarcely needs saying that for screen purposes there is more drama in one gun fight than in 10 arrests for murder by legal process. Hence the whole picture is the contrary of drama. Settlement of a mountain feud by resort to the courts may have a fine ethical precept, but for picture purposes it is like two husky lovers deciding who shall have the girl by matching pennies.

In the end, of course, the feud has to be settled by a man-to-man fight in which hero and heavy battle, but this came only at the tail end of rather a tame five reels. Mountain scenery makes a fine setting for the action and the players are notably authentic in appearance and manner.

Picture probably was made at a minimum cost, the settings being either the inexpensive out of doors or the simple cabins of the mountaineers. Serves for its present purpose as a program filler, the arresting title being an asset. *Rush.*

HEAVEN ON EARTH

Metro-Goldwyn-Mayer production, directed by Phil Rosen. From the story by Harvey Gates. Featuring Conrad Nagel and Renee Adoree, with cast including Gwen Lee, Jessica Gordon, Marcia Mave and Pat Hartigan. At Loew's American, June 2-5. Running time, about one hour.

A good box-office title and irresistible story appeal stupidly directed and miscast.

It is on stories of this kind that some of the greatest picture successes have been based. An autocratic, all-powerful aunt, accustomed to directing the destinies of the largest silk mills in Southern France and incidentally ruling the social, political and financial destinies of the townfolk, has raised an apparently emotionless nephew under the same restraining policy. The idea was to prepare for the inevitable break when the young man's passions would assert themselves.

As far as Phil Rosen was concerned, it was sufficient that a tremendously powerful character such as the aunt should exist only in the subtitles. The woman in the role was quite pleasant, if at times a little firm, but far from the ruthless tyrant described.

Conrad Nagel is the nephew. He looks the clean-cut young American business man, and putting on a pair of velvet breeches and a tam doesn't change the impression. The break is quite passionless, and the disappearance from home handled too easily to cause eye tension.

Renee Adoree is the gypsy caravan girl whom the wealthy young man meets and loves. They travel together along the country roads, living in a freedom often dreamt of but never achieved. The love scenes here offered some fine opportunities, but the director kept his young man scrupulously as emotionless as before the break from home.

Metro can even now take this story and with slight changes by another director the results will probably be so far different from this production as to be presentable for sale as another production.

Picture is too lustreless for the first-runs, hardly reaching usual M-G-M production standards. It has not played the Capitol on Broadway, but got one day at Loew's New York.

BLAZING DAYS

Blue Streak western, directed by William Wyler from story by Florence Ryerson. Featuring Fred Humes, Eva Gregory in support. At Columbus one day (June 2) on double-feature bill. Running time, 55 minutes.

This is a pic-ture," a wes-tern pic-ture. Not a good pic-ture; not a bad pic-ture. It's a wes-tern picture.

It is a-bout cow-boys and love. Of course, you are not old e-nough to real-ly know what love is, but it is a-bout kis-sing.

You will like this pic-ture. It has a stage-coach rob-ber-y—what a big word! It means naught-y steal-ing.

The la-dy is out-west with her bro-ther. He has a sick-ness in his che-st and he wants to get well like you would if you had a sick-ness in your che-st.

The cow-boy out west loves the la-dy. But some-one robs the stage-coach, and every-one thinks the sick bro-ther did it. Be-cause he gets a lot of mo-ney and won't tell where he got it. He real-ly won it in craps (those shak-ing things) or cards, but he's a-shamed to tell. So sis-ter and the cow-boy think he rob-bed the stage-coach, and the cow-boy thinks the sis-ter hel-ped, be-cause she is try-ing to pro-tect her bro-ther.

But things look ba-ad! Cow-boy thinks the sis-ter is al-so a thief, so he does-n't love her any mo-re.

Gue-ss what? Cow-boy finds the ba-ad vil-lin man who lo-ves the girl, too, real-ly rob-bed the stage-coach. He makes the ba-ad man tell every-bo-dy, and so every-thing is all right.

Kind of sil-ly. But gu-ess what. Lots and lots of grown-up peo-ple think and act just a-bout like you chil-dren do, and the pic-ture is made for them.

Fun-ny kind of peo-ple. Go to see these pic-tures o-ver and o-ver, and don't se-em to ti-re.

But re-mem-ber, if e-ver you see **one of the-se gro-wn-up peo-ple co-ming out of a the-a-tre where th-ese pic-tures are be-ing shown, run and run and run as fast as your lit-tle legs can car-ry you.**

Be-cause—w-ell——

SHE'S MY BABY

Joe Rock production released through Sterling. Directed by Fred Windemere. Featuring Earle Williams, Bobby Agnew and Mildred Harris. At Loew's New York as one half double bill one day, May 31. Running time around 65 minutes.

At Loew's New York this day were two independent features, this one Sterling (Rock), and the other Lumas (Sax), with either capable of standing up by itself for longer than a day.

It was just a break for the double bill and, of course, the independents had to suffer.

Loew's New York uses nine features weekly, having two double feature days. It's certain that among the nine last week were two poorer pictures than "She's My Baby" (Sterling) and "Sinews of Steel" (Lumas).

Had "She's My Baby" better captions and a better title, it would have been in the first rate program release rank. The picture is too good for the indefinite farcical title of "She's My Baby" with its flippancy relation only understood by a few fly people in large cities. The **story is so well done that laughing captions would have accentuated its worth. Instead the captions sounded ordinary, machine-made, denoting that little money and less attention had been given.**

Repeatedly "She's My Baby" steadily missed becoming a big comedy film. As it was, though, there are many laughs in it, a lively taut story and a neatly made feature besides.

The story started with a newly wedded couple, honeymooningly loving, but immediately jumping to 20 years after, when everything's a scowl between them. Their daughter has grown up; there is a phoney prince around making a play for mother and a cabaret soubret is after the old man, with the daughter taking late night rides to road houses. Ranged alongside for the soubret is a tough husband she wants to lose, a young lover crazy about her, besides the married man who is also a lawyer.

This lightly and swiftly works out to a reunion of the squabbling parents, and the wedding of their daughter to the demoted lover of the soubret, first taking in a fight with the soubret's tough husband who refused to be divorced.

Of the many cabaret scenes in pictures, one came out here almost startling in its novelty idea, if especially built. Otherwise it may be a coast nite club, but the same idea, a jail interior for a cabaret, was spoken of for New York without ever fully put into execution. Tables are in cells and the big room is set like the corridor of a prison. Without the garishness of the usual cabaret setting, this one is a peach.

The late Earle Williams as the father did well. Younger people of the picture all right with nicely balanced cast for an independent, making it apparent that some money was spent on the acting end as well.

This picture is okay for split weeks and anything less. *Sime.*

SIMPLE SIS

Warner Bros. production directed by Herman Raymaker from the story by Melville Crosman. Featuring Louise Fazenda and Clyde Cook with cast including William Demarest, Myrna Loy, Billy Kent Shaeffer and Cathleen Calhoun. Previewed in projection room June 3. Running time, 60 minutes.

A colorless production of negligible entertainment or box office value.

Louise Fazenda seems unsuited for straight comedy purposes, and Clyde Cook without his trick mustache is worse.

"Simple Sis" is billed as a comedy, but there isn't a real laugh in it. The director didn't stretch his imagination and it looks as if no gag men were employed to inject spicy bits, which sometimes have the effect of changing the entire appeal in otherwise poor productions.

The story, without an original idea, is unsuited for the lead players. Miss Fazenda is not called upon to be funny, but to play straight love stuff. Cook is neither comical nor pathetic as an earnest lover.

Action starts in a laundry where the ugly duckling falls in love with a timid truck driver. Billy Kent Shaeffer, as Buddy, shows up very well and has all the earmarks of developing into a good juvenile actor if properly handled.

The Unknown Cavalier

First National western starring Ken Maynard. Directed by Al Rogell. Story by Kenneth Perkins, adapted by Marion Jackson. Cast includes David Torrance, Otis Harlan, T. Roy Barnes, James Mason, with Kathleen Collins featured. Running time, 62 mins. On double feature bill at Columbus, New York, one day, June 4.

Fast-moving outdoor drama with shooting and riding and fighting enough to satisfy the cowboy fans.

First National has done a good production job barring some crudities. The idea of a gang of bandits not knowing who their leader is and that leader masking himself with one arm which he keeps in front of his face whenever doing his stuff is a little hard to accept, as is also T. Roy Barnes trying to do comedy and succeeding only in being silly.

The plot is out of the familiar western catalog. Intent upon a lynching a posse of vigilantes is determined to hang the hero, who has been framed by the real bandit. The important business of this western is to get in a lot of action. The characters, like the plot, moves at a gallop.

Ken Maynard is a zip-roaring saddle acter with enough of looks and personality to carry him through the love passages, brief and innocuous. Kathleen Collins, featured, makes an appealing candidate for the clinch and can wear riding breeches.

Put it down as an okay western.

Say It With Diamonds

Chadwick production, starring Betty Compson. Directed by Jack Nelson. Cameraman, Ernest Miller. In cast: Earle Williams, Jocelyn Lee, Armand Kaliz, Betty Baker. Running time, 58 mins. At Loew's New York one day, June 2.

"Married" comedy of the type generally classified as "smart," with the husband and wife really in love despite bickerings and frivolous fights. Chadwick can offer it as parring its average—meaning it's a pretty fair independent release.

Trouble starts when there is a mix-up over a wedding anniversary present. Husband has bought a diamond-studded comb. Wife has seen the comb, unknown to the husband. She gets a diamond lavaliere instead. Inquiring about the comb, the husband explains truthfully he sold it to a friend. Subsequently the comb makes its way to the sweetie of the husband's friend.

Picture runs fairly smoothly, though getting pretty slapsticky at one or two points. It is probably the last picture in which the late Earle Williams appeared. Miss Compson looks good and wears some clothes which will give picture dame appeal.

Okay for family audiences despite sex theme.

SINEWS OF STEEL

Sam Sax production, released through Lumas (Gotham). Features Alberta Vaughn. Directed by Frank O'Connor. Titles by Delos Sutherland. At Loew's New York, one-half double bill, one day, May 31. Running time, around 60 minutes.

Rather a good one-dayer for an independent. What is remarked in the review of "She's My Baby" for this double-day feature bill at Loew's New York goes for this one as well, the other half of it.

Rather a self-confessor of a title, or just another mill or plant. The plot foundation of these things should be hidden instead of billed. "Steel" in any title for an independent is another of those 30c. stories, but here, however, it's something beyond the stereotyped, made so mostly by the Frank O'Connor direction and the Gaston Glass acting, with nice comedy nicely done by whomsoever played the nance.

The women don't count particularly here, that taking in Alberta Vaughn, with the other girl not doing any more but looking much better. Glass carries the picture along by his breeziness and fast work, whether in business or fighting. One marathon fight he indulged in was skillfully handled by the director. You don't see them fighting all over Hollywood and back again, but in snatches.

It's the tale of the boy beating pop in business, in the steel mill way. All idiotic and rough on the steel men, but made likable through ingenuity mostly, and some thought given to the output.

This is the best Sax made picture

seen in some time. There may have been better, but it does look as though the smaller and cheating Indes of the past had concluded there isn't enough gross in circulation left for their pictures of the former type. They are going to gamble, maybe, to get more profitable trade.

It's about time. If this is a sample of that attempt, as "She's My Baby" may have been produced through similar thought by Sterling, there's a chance for them to dig in with product of this class.

Where an independent can make a picture look well and give it some substance at the production cost of what Sax or Rock will spend, or the other grade of independent, like Tiffany, F. B. O. or Columbia, they are doing something that will make the old-line companies look up before long.

For these and the other pictures at their production cost, sold on that valuation and beating any of those $200,000 or $300,000 regular program releases so far below in rental that they become inviting to exhibitors who find they can slip one in often enough to get away with it to a profit in rental, even before the box office is considered, must sooner or later, if the pace can be held to, make an impression on the trade. Even unto that other and first-grade film-maker who will wonder what is the matter with his own organization when these little fellows on a shoe-string bankroll, comparatively, can turn out pictures that at least will make a showing. Maybe it's the small bankroll that forces this, but whatever it is, there it is.

This is a whole story in the picture business today, but it may be confined to this, as it is confined in its interest. But this much should be said, that the present independent picture makers are doing better and at a lesser cost than some of the biggest producers did in their start under the same circumstances. With many of the independents it's a question of proper financing. Good, sensible picture makers, those who can produce at a minimum of cost, those who are doing their best and hardest without wasting money should be financed. They eventually will land —either as a picture producer on their own or as a picture producer for a larger concern.

The big picture makers cannot afford to overlook that comparatively, in production cost and production, they are being beaten up, down and around by these little fellows, who have not a thousand stars under term contracts, who don't remake and who don't let their best feature go beyond $40,000.

And more than that, if the $30,000 or $40,000 picture is but one-fifth or one-sixth or one-eighth of the cost of those modern first-run productions, then these pictures at least look one-half as good as the high cost ones. Since production and overhead are now engaging the greatest attention of the greatest picture makers, any of them may make more money by taking off their high hat.

But there is another if: that the independent must depend upon an independence among exhibitors. If the exhibs are to be swallowed up by the chains, where will be the outlet for the inde picture?

It must be a headache for the independent producer who sits up to figure it out.   *Sime.*

THE OUTLAW DOG

F. B. O. release, featuring Ranger, the dog, in a story by Ewart Adamson. Directed by J. P. McGowan. Photographed by Joe Walker. At the Tivoli, New York, as one-half double bill, one day (June 4). Running time, about 50 minutes.

Essentially for juveniles of all ages. Ranger, the dog, is presented as being able to read and understand such commands as "Go flag the limited and bring assistance. It's up to you, Ranger!"

Ranger discovers that he is falsely accused of attacking his master and hits out for the open spaces via blind baggage. The dog pauses though to read a sign offering $1,000 reward for his capture.

He drops off at a hick station to help the young station agent in a battle with two bums to save a payroll. Later, when the bums attempt to get another payroll by dynamiting a bridge so that the passenger train will plunge into a river, Ranger steps in to flag the train, saving also the payroll and a few hundred lives.

It must be said for the dog that it does the things naturally enough. Should get some money from the kids.

GOOD AS GOLD

Fox western starring Buck Jones. Directed by Scott Dunlap. Murray Leinster's story adapted by Jack Jungmeyer. Cameraman, Reginald Lyons. Running time, 52 mins. In projection room, June 2.
Buck Brady }
Sonny Holman } .... Buck Jones
Janet Laurier .... Frances Lee
John Gray .... Charles K. French
Thomas Tilford .... Carl Miller
Timothea .... Adele Watson

Good average Buck Jones feature. Following the simple familiar plot is a task for the eye only.

A boy grows up vowing vengeance against the man who murdered his father and stole his gold mine.

Only in the movies could two thieves be hero and villian. The hero does his grand larceny with a romantic swagger and has a presumely virtuous motive.

Frances Lee is the leading lady. At one point she runs around in lingerie. That is sex-plus for these westerns which are usually neuter gender. And a little sex in the cowboy dramas would be a welcome relief from the constant rotation of all western stars between about half a dozen standard plot situations.

A MILLION BID
(2D REVIEW)

A second review of this Warner Brothers picture, "A Million Bid," becomes necessary through a statement in the first review, in Variety of June 1, last, to the effect:

"Better pass this up," at the end of an unfavorable notice.

That comment should not have been made by Variety's reviewer on this or any other picture with Dolores Costello in it. Despite the quality of the picture itself, Miss Costello has quickly ranged a following. Odds are that despite "A Million Bid" is not much other than an ordinary program release, Miss Costello's fans may overlook that through her presence, for she has never looked as well in appearance as in this film.

When "A Million Bid" played the Paramount, New York, during the week the first review appeared, the house did a gross of $66,000, as against $63,000 the previous week. The Paramount also had in its increased week the first Lindbergh pictures that must partially account for some of the gross, but still must be credited Miss Costello as well, for the picture by itself is not a drawing card nor could it secure, alone, through its story any favorable verbal comment or publicity.

Variety's attention was attracted toward its first review of "A Million Bid" by John Hamrick, of Seattle, a theatre operator of that and other northwestern cities. Mr. Hamrick's wire is reproduced on another page of this picture department. Upon receipt of the message two other Variety reviewers requested the Warners to run the film off in the projection room.

If the last line comment quoted above had not been on the first notice, that notice could have stood, although it did not give enough detail as to the picture or its making. The first reviewer appears to have formed his opinion mainly upon the story permitting a young man, and much too young for the honor, to be proclaimed an eminent surgeon, performing an extremely difficult operation, much beyond his years or possible experience.

The story is aggravatingly illogical throughout; never convinces in any one iota, and never grips. The last is the most important. Early in the unreeling the illusion is socked by implausibility, and that continues steadily, even to and including the finale.

Direction frequently suggests olden methods, with the most likeable points the production end, very good; some successful tries at a little difference in camera work and the looks of Miss Costello along with the acting of Warner Oland. To be also charged against is the lamentable and vain efforts by Douglas Gerrard and a box of candy to get a laugh. A collision at sea was but fairly done, one of those self-exposers, but the interior bits of the wrecked yacht together with an onrushing water or flood scene were much better. Malcolm McGregor is the youthful surgeon and lover. As the latter had to be a juvenile, the miscasting was inevitable, but it did provide a large wallop. No captions that count.

It's a two-fold familiar tale, with the first section a mother's aspirations for her daughter, to wed a millionaire the girl near detested, losing her sweetheart through the mother's machinations, and the other half the surgeon's position when believing himself the lawful husband and father, to be obliged to decide whether he should perform an operation upon the legal husband, returned some years after the wreck with loss of memory. It had been presumed that he had been drowned at that time, the wedding night. His unloving wife, who repulsed his advances, was being overcome just as the collision between the two boats occurred.

A murky atmosphere to the finale is that the legal husband, regaining his reason and recognizing his wife, and now a mother, as the innocent but illegally wedded wife of the surgeon who had brought back his reason, decides to permit the young couple to believe the operation had not been successful, thereby remaining in his former status of an unknown and going out of the picture and their lives.

This left the wife and her child without a name, also precluding the possibility of an application for a divorce since that would divulge that her first husband had not died, etc. The remainder of the story is just as convincing.

Mr. Hamrick stated in his wire he considered "A Million Bid" a super special and that he has advertised it for a run of several weeks at the Blue Mouse, having seen, with Mrs. Hamrick, the picture in New York. If Miss Costello is strong enough in Seattle to hold this picture in for over a week, Mr. Hamrick and that young woman are very fortunate.

Other exhibitors if booking "A Million Bid" should do so only for their customary minimum limit, and then depend wholly upon the Costello girl, going as strongly as they please on her, for she is a very sweet looking young woman throughout this film. But where Miss Costello is not established or unknown, this is not the picture to take a chance with.   *Sime.*

ENCHANTED ISLAND

Tiffany production and release. From original by John Thomas Neville. Directed by William G. Crosby. Henry B. Walthall featured. Photographers, Jos. A. Durbray and Stephen S. Norton. At Loew's, New York, one-half double bill, one day, June 7. Running time about 65 minutes.
Alice Sanborn .... Charlotte Stevens
Tim Sanborn .... Henry B. Walthall
Bob Hamilton .... Pierre Gendron
Red Blake .... Pat Hartigan
U. A. Washington .... Floyd Shackleford

A No. 2 "Chang." And a first run for the best from Tiffany.

Tiffany bills "The Enchanted Island" as an unusual picture. It is. It's almost an animal picture, prettily disguised with romance and melodrama.

Taking into consideration that the producers of "Chang" had to go to Africa and remain there a long while, this Zoo-supported Tiffany film is all the more unusual.

It's more like a fairy tale and a delight for children, while adults will much appreciate the beauty of the setting and the story, at the some time becoming much puzzled as to how this picture was made. The Tiffany press sheet mentions the locale of the picture, as a deserted volcanic island off the California coast, with the Zoo animals transferred there. That's very frank on the Tiffany press department's part and commendable, as the instinct here would have been to be "smart"; but since this picture may create talk as to manner executed, it might be advisable for exhibitors not to use the exploitation of production secrets for advance publicity. It should be of more value to the box office to keep 'em guessing.

Illusions from inserts are plentifully and skilfully handled—very skilfully. So much so that frequently it calls for an expert to detect the maneuvering of the situation and photography, the latter being exceptional also, technically as well. One sees a girl (Charlotte Stevens) playing with a leopard (actually) and chasing other animals who should be wild out of her father's little cabin. The animals embrace almost all species, including lion and elephant. And again, when the volcanic eruption occurs, one could almost make affidavit that the lava is flowing over the island.

It's the nearest to "Chang" in the wild animal line that has been seen; but it's not "Chang," and far from it. But that does not prevent "The Enchanted Island" from being a romantic novelty film. Its poorest point is the title. Too bad a better one could not have been thought up for it. The "Enchanted" suggests the fairy trend of the story, but this film needed a more virile name to give it a kick before starting.

A sort of a Robinson Crusoe tale, it opens on a picturesque island with wildly dashing waves against the shore. There are a father and daughter marooned for nine years through a "circus ship" disaster, with the girl now grown up. Off the steamer path, hope has been abandoned of rescue. The only humans on the island, their home has become the barn for all of the animals. The daughter is on familiar terms with each, whether in her home or meeting them in her wanderings.

A terrific and interesting storm at sea, probably an insert, with three castaways washed up on the shores. One the huge, uncouth mate, Blake; another a youth, the son of the shipwrecked boat's owner, and the boat's colored male cook. About the single piece of wreckage recovered amounting to anything appeared to be a case of liquor, over which the brutal mate assumed sole proprietorship. Sighting the three men, the father, after talking it over with his daughter, clips her hair and dresses her as a boy for her protection.

Later, when the mate discovers the girl's hair in an overturned urn, he becomes suspicious, with the outcome he kills the father upon his refusal to turn his daughter over to him. But the daughter and the young boy meanwhile had grown chummy, with the boy unaware of the other's sex until she kissed him when injured by the mate.

Thereafter follows the eruption, the attempt of the mate to kill the boy and his rescue by the colored cook, who dragged the mate and himself over a cliff into the volcanic stream. Boy and girl escape upon a raft, to be sighted by the first ship that so coincidentally happened along after nine years, with no date given when the raft was built.

The young couple wandering through the woods are sweetly romantic and climatical, since this is supposed to be an island in the tropics. There is the only bit of blue when the boy suggests they go swimming and the girl acceding in her male dress until unbuttoning her shirt, when she remembers—and calls it off. Later a girl in the perspective through a pretty shot is seen bathing au natural, with the mate watching her. That started the first fight when the boy discovered he was taking a peek. Another of the discrepancies, but immaterial.

Exhibs taking this picture from Tiffany and showing it before playing "Chang" will get full value. The way to publicize is to say there is no other picture like it. While "The Unchanted Island" is not as big as this notice sounds, there being no other way to soft pedal on it, the film is a little dandy and well worth playing anywhere.

And one-half of a double bill at Loew's New York, with the maker's label not displayed anywhere excepting upon the picture's first slide. That's what the indes are up against.

In acting Pat Hartigan steals the picture. He's a rough mate and plays it 'way up. Miss Stevens exhibits plenty of nerve, with Walthall having a walk through role before bumped. Pierre Gendron as the juvenile missed a mile, but he seems new. Floyd Shackleford, whether colored or blackface, got a few unneeded laughs, for here's a picture calling for no comedy. No extras employed. *Sime.*

THE UNKNOWN

M-G-M picture, starring Lon Chaney. Story and direction by Tod Browning. Norman Kerry and Joan Crawford featured.. M. Gerstad, photographer. At Capitol, week June 11. Running time, 55 minutes.

Alonzo........................Lon Chaney
Malabar........................Norman Kerry
Manon........................Joan Crawford
Zanzi........................Nick de Ruiz
Cojo........................John George

Probably one of the shortest Lon Chaney pictures of recent days in falling five minutes shy of an hour on the screen. With "Mr. Wu" the Capitol had to speed up projection, as Chaney's actual gestures in that one were so slow, but on this release the booth boys are evidently unwinding normally.

Smart, holding this one under an hour. The story will hint it could go in somewhere for a run, but it doesn't work out that way. Browning's brain-child will also read as ghastly, but again there's another "but."

A good Chaney film that might have been great.

Chaney and his characterizations invite stories that have power behind them. Every time Browning thinks of Chaney he probably looks around for a typewriter and says "let's get gruesome." In this instance he has again outlined strongly for the character actor. Possibly as brilliantly as in "The Unholy Three," although what momentum he has gained on paper has been lost in discretion.

The tale concerns an armless fakir in a gypsy circus who loves the proprietor's daughter. The girl has come to detest all men for their constant pawing, hence the welcome companionship of Alonzo (Mr. Chaney). None of the circus troupe knows that the latter is physically normal, except his helper. Alonzo fakes by strapping his arms to his sides.

As retribution for a beating, Alonzo strangles the girl's father, with the police seeking the murderer, who has left fingerprints of two thumbs on one hand. Believed to be armless, Alonzo escapes the investigation; but to make certain he will win Nanon (Joan Crawford) and that she will never know who killed her father, Alonzo blackmails a doctor into amputating both his arms. After weeks in a hospital he returns to find her enfolded by Malabar, the strong man (Norman Kerry).

Taking that story and doing it uncommercially Browning could probably have made it one of the top pictures of the year, with the irony of Alonzo's armless return the logical finish. Directing down and to the box office (and why not?), there is an anti-climax—the death of Alonzo and the arm-in-arm finish of Nanon and Malabar.

Smoothing over the horror of the amputation has been successfully accomplished through the familiarity of seeing Chaney armless during most of the preceding footage, and nothing nearer an operating room is viewed than a hospital cot upon which Alonzo is supposedly recovering. But this saps the story of some of its strength, as does the following anti-climax, although it's well staged.

This item concerns Malabar and Nanon doing a vaudeville act, in which the former holds two horses as they pull in opposite directions on treadmills. It is explained that if the treadmills were suddenly to stop Malabar's arms would be torn from his body. Figure the rest out for yourself; for, as expected, Alonzo throws the brake, a stagehand stops one horse in time, and Malabar is able to hold the other rearing animal while Nanon frantically tries to quiet it until Alonzo dashes to her rescue, and is himself killed by the plunging hoofs.

Browning has chopped to the bone in the cutting room. It's logical to suppose that there was ample footage "shot" on this yarn. And that's smart, too, because it crams the picture with action and interest, something Chaney's preceding vehicle didn't always hold. Sweet photography and production all the way, while Miss Crawford never looked better in her life than before Gerstad's lens. Both she and Kerry turn in neat support, as do the others in this small-cast feature.

Chaney does various things with his feet during the picture, such as eating, smoking, etc. Some are obviously not Chaney's legs, and in one or two instances the large dimension of features before a close lens makes some of this work seem out of physical proportion. At that the effect, on the whole, is good and well done.

Another Chaney-Browning program release that will reinforce the value of this combination.

"The Unknown" is a paradox, in that it is not as great a picture as it might have been, but will undoubtedly have its compensation in the gross rentals. *Sid.*

RUNNING WILD

Paramount production. Directed by Gregory La Cava. W. C. Fields starred and Mary Brian featured. Story by Mr. La Cava. Adapted by Roy Briant. At Paramount, New York, week June 11. Running time, around 60 minutes.

Elmer Finch........................W. C. Fields
Elizabeth........................Mary Brian
Jerry Harvey........................Claud Buchanan
Mrs. Finch........................Marie Shotwell
Junior........................Barney Raskle
Mr. Harvey........................Frederick Burton
Mr. Johnson........................J. Moy Bennett
Amos Barker........................Frank Evans
Arvo, the hypnotist........................Ed Roseman
Truck Driver........................Tom Madden
Rex........................Himself

"Running Wild" is in as a laugh film. It will amuse all audiences for a week or less.

And it will send W. C. (Bill) Fields quite some forward in starring picture circles, besides giving him most likely a wider circulation than any or all of his previous picture productions have done. Bill Fields is a consummate pantomimic comic, along legit lines, who can handle the comedy, high or low. He classes with Charlie Chaplin in this, and, like Chaplin, Fields got his training in vaudeville, as a dumb juggling turn. Chaplin was a knockabout, also in the dumb-act class. As European pantomiming actors are more common than over here, and especially over here in vaudeville nowadays, that Fields emerges as he does on the sheet redounds all the more to his prestige and credit.

As with most good film comedies, when they are good they are all good. "Running Wild" is marked for good story and direction by Gregory La Cava, with good gags and playing, the gags not being segregated for their own laughs, but blending in with the story. There's as much difference between just gags and story gags as there is between factory and pantomime acting. With all helped to more and ofttimes louder laughs by captions, although the titles are not uniform in standing up.

It seems a happy thought that brought about the story in the way it has been done, making an original really out of an old plot plan—that of the worm turneth. An entirely new gag as far as known is Fields, late for work and walking rapidly to it, dodging the cracks on the sidewalk. His superstitions include ladders and horseshoes. Later, when picking up a horseshoe for the good luck he so badly needed and throwing it over his shoulder to cinch the omen, the piece of iron crashed through a jeweler's window.

That started a chase, right onto the stage of a vaudeville theatre where a hypnotist was soliciting subjects. He had one and impressed Fields for the other. Before either knew what it was about both were under his influence. The "Professor" told the other he was Lord Fauntleroy and Fields that he was a raging lion, strapping boxing gloves on each. The lion accepted the suggestion so thoroughly that he whipped everyone on the stage and escaped before he could be stopped.

Still under the influence and making his pet slogan, "I'm a lion," he whipped and roared himself through a business day, then went home to straighten out the family that had been browbeating its only provider. Even the dog at home took a chunk out of Bill at pleasure, and his stepson, always crying for "Ma," had been an especial aversion. Fields, a widower with a daughter, had married a widow with a son. The joined family was on a strictly 90-10 basis. Fields was the 10 percenter through his timidity, one of those envelope turnovers on Saturday nights and a home-made dummy for the remainder of the week.

Continuity near perfect, with a performance not so far second to Fields by Barney Raskle as the fat ma-calling pest. Ed Roseman did the hypnotist nicely, he reappearing to take Fields out of the trance after the latter had fully established himself at home and in business while hypnotically the lion.

Mary Brian, featured, and the daughter, looks nice, but doesn't do much for a featured player, even a girl. Producers in Hollywood seemingly like to feature Miss Brian but in roles that call for little exercise, and the girl also looks capable of doing more than modeling.

A story like this is a fortune for any film comedian in itself, but it needs a comic of the Bill Fields high calibre to make "Running Wild" the sure fire that it is. *Sime.*

LOST AT THE FRONT

First National production, produced by Frank Griffin. Directed by Del Lord from the story by Mr. Griffin. Titles by Ralph Spence, co-starring Charlie Murray and George Sidney. At the Strand week June 11. Running time about 60 minutes.

Michael Muldoon............Charlie Murray
August Krause ....George Sidney
Olga Petrovitch............Natalie Kingston
Von Herfiz............John Kolb
Adolph Meyerburg............Max Asher
The Inventor............Brooks Benedict
Captain Kashluff............Ed Brady
Captain Levinsky ....Harry Lipman
Russian Girls.....Nita Martin, N. Romane

Only two other burlesques on the war are in the same rank with this picture for box office values. It is strictly a burlesque, perhaps a little more indelicate than the others. But for every lack of delicacy there is a whole regiment of laughs.

The titles are responsible for approximately half of the comedy. It's a tossup between Charlie Murray and George Sidney for the balance of the honors, which are plenty.

There really shouldn't be so many laughs in a picture because after the female brigade gets through screaming at the "impersonation" scene they haven't much breath left to carry on with.

Sidney and Murray in long dresses, with colored handkerchiefs à la Moscow over their heads, "borrowed" from two Russian girls, are a joyous eyeful to start with. When they begin to vamp two drunken Russian officers with all the wiles and artifices of village belles nothing can hold them.

"Be hard to get," whispered Muldoon to August. The figures of the boys are far from girlish and August looks stouter than ever bouncing on the knee of a dyspeptic looking officer. Muldoon again utters well ground fears that the "boys will try to get fresh."

Muldoon's trousers finally appear through the skirts and the two soldiers are laid out with vodka for the exit from this scene.

Preceding the love battle the brave boys tack themselves on to a brigade of women prisoners heading for medical quarters, where they are to be fumigated. August cringes in a corner afraid to open his eyes and Muldoon buries a worried face on his shoulder.

They finally put on the sheets without removing their clothes, and are pushed toward the showers. A gigantic woman soldier picks up August and insists on undressing him, or rather "her." The scrap takes place behind closed doors, with August finally emerging sans shirt and sans head covering, clutching his trousers grimly.

Story is rather slim. August enlists with a determination to end the war through a discarded radio set which he has been convinced can cause explosions at will by a turn of a knob. Muldoon, an Irish policeman and a pal of the bartender's, knows of the machine and goes to war to find August and tell him that America is in and to stop using the machine to destroy the allies.

Titles pull the story along here and in some of the war scenes with remarks like: "The Germans had to disguise themselves as sandwiches to make the Russians come out and fight."

Olga Petrovitch, a sculptress, is woven in rather carelessly. Getting Muldoon into the Russian army is the best she does, but appearance is okay and reproduced well in front of a camera.

Murray and Sidney work well as a team, although the wide differences in appearance are not realized upon to the fullest extent.

SECRET STUDIO

William Fox production, starring Olive Borden. Story by Hazel Livingston; scenario by James K. McGuinness. Victor Schertzinger, director. Running time, 60 minutes. At Roxy's, week June 11.

Rosemary Merton..............Olive Borden
Sloan Whitney..............Clifford Holland
Elsie Merton..............Noreen Phillips
Larry Kane..............Ben Bard
Mae Merton..............Kate Bruce
Pa Merton..............Joseph Cawthorne
Nina Clark..............Margaret Livingston
Mr. Kyler..............Walter McGrail
Mrs. Kyler..............Lila Leslie
The Plumber..............Ned Sparks

A highly flavored, sexy story, written in the spirit of "True Story" and "Confessions" magazine, but screened with fine taste. The result is a bit of artificial fiction, but done with such impressive skill that it almost tricks the mind into believing it worth while.

It probably will touch a popular taste which revels in high life, spicy and dressed up romance and racy atmosphere. The technical production is magnificent; the story is just another of those superficial tales lacking in any distinctive quality Very likely as a satisfactory box film.

In all things except the story conception the picture is splendid. It is acted convincingly by the star and her supporting company. In all probability it was written to order for Miss Borden's exquisite figure, which furnishes the principal kick of the footage when it is on display in scanty draperies. The high pressure episodes in an ultra Bohemian studio are a good deal forced. Nothing in real life could be quite so exotic as this.

Clifford Holland is a handsome and vigorous lover without working too hard at it, while Ben Bard is successful in suggesting the sinister snarer of virtue. A capital bit of comedy is supplied in the relations of Ned Sparks, a rural plumber courting the heroine's sister in the little home town and engaged in a bitter feud with the girls' father whom he defeated in an election for sergeant at arms of the local lodge.

The backgrounds of the Bohemian studio and later settings for an artists' ball are finely worked out to suggest extreme but ominous luxury. The display of half-clad girls

is pretty ultra but always cleverly managed, for instance, there is one shot of what looks like a girl wearing nothing but a short fur jacket, an effect that would do for a snappy post card view. But when the girl moves she turns out to be a fully dressed guest at the party who has been sitting on a plaster model of a pair of legs. Deft treatment of a number of delicate scenes gives the kick but takes out the sting in like manner.

Another dramatic high light concerns the painting of the heroine in the nude, a bit conveyed with a maximum of sensation but also free of offense. If the creator of the story had had the resourcefulness of the director who gave it form the result would have been something more than a fair program picture as it is.

The narrative has to do with the familiar material of the small town girl who comes to the metropolis to make her fortune and falls in with a designing portrait painter who tries to make a conquest of her while she is serving him as a model. He almost accomplishes his design and is only saved by the intervention of the usual rich art patron who takes her out of all this to marry her. Familiar materials, but here visualized with skill that makes the spectator sometimes forget its triviality.   *Rush.*

VANITY

P. D. C. release featuring Leatrice Joy, supported by Charles Ray. Produced by C. Gardner Sullivan, directed by Donald Crisp. Running time, 60 minutes. At New York Hippodrome week June 13.

Second rate program picture made up of a multitude of trivialities, postures and phoney drama. Everything is overdone from the labored elegance of the star and the self-conscious elegance of the society atmosphere to the sentiment. It's a picture where one is able to identify the aristocratic heroine by picking out the lady who registers high disdain for the butler. That about covers the general tone of the product.

A rather effective melodramatic passage is that in which the pampered society girl is lured to the cabin of a tramp steamship on the eve of her wedding and there held captive under pretty terrifying circumstances by the brutal skipper. He is killed in a fight with a bestial negro cook who makes gestures toward attacking the girl, until she gains possession of the skipper's revolver and kills him.

Materials are here for a punch, but the scene's effectiveness is diluted by the false train of happenings that lead up to this high point of melodrama and by the artificial make believe.

It is hard to get interested in a heroine who is introduced lounging in her boudoir in a negligee that never could have any existence outside the "Follies." There is a comic opera exaggeration about every detail of the building up of backgrounds. The purpose, of course, is to convey the sense of great elegance; the effect that actually gets across is unintentional travesty. The whole picture is utterly lacking in plausibility. Even when the action in the scene mentioned reaches its height, one is never lost in suspense because the people never have been real.

There is an elaborate wedding scene where the shots have been so badly arranged that one gets only a confused idea of which are bride and groom and which the wedding guests. Even the photography is bad in this passage.

Apparently the story grew from the attempted assault scene. Some of the planting of character and incident is inexpressibly crude and

labored. For instance, the heroine runs a recreation hut during the war. This is necessary to plant an acquaintance with the rough sailor who later takes advantage of the passing acquaintance to get the girl to his ship on pretext of having her christen it. But the recreation hut episodes are used for dull comedy and stretch out interminably.

Just a mediocre screen idea.   *Rush.*

Is Your Daughter Safe?

Los Angeles, June 11.

Presented by S. S. Millard. Directed by Lou King and Leon Lee from story by Max Abramson. Produced at Chadwick Studios, Hollywood, Calif. Indefinitely at California theatre, Los Angeles. Women only admitted from 10 A. M. to 6 P. M.; men only from 6 P. M. to 10 P. M.

CAST

The Girl..............Vivian Winston
The Boy..............Jerome Young
The Beast..............Henry Roquemore
The Madame..............Georgia O'Dell
The White Slaver.............."Slim" Mahoney
The Deceiver..............William Dennis
The Victim..............Bernice Breacher
The Doctor..............Palmer Morrison
The Governor..............Winfield Jones
The Rounder..............Joe Bonner
The Gambler..............Hugh Saxton
The Maid..............Hazel Jones
Ladies of Leisure—Vera White, Hortense Petra, Virginia Hobbs, Alta Faulkner, Dorothy Jay, June D'Eon, Mildred Northmore, Ann Porter, Mildred McClune, Geraldine Johnson
and
Hon. Mayor William Hale Thompson of Chicago
and
Members of the Chicago Vice Commission.

Possibly the strongest and most daring of so-called hygiene and sex warning pictures ever made. Did any of the legitimate producers turn out this quickie as was done in four days, they possibly would be heading for the South Sea Isles if Will H. Hays ever got on their trail.

Millard who made this one, or at least had it made, did so because he had cleaned up a bankroll on a lot of cutouts from other films that were made as far back as 15 years ago and sold under the name of "Is Your Daughter Safe?"

This one opens with a shot of a physician discussing the vice legislation with the Governor of the State. The physician tells the Governor how bad conditions are with a flash to a shot of William Hale Thompson and his vice commission of Chicago discussing the problem. Then one sees a shot of the old time line around Chicago in full operation, after which a number of feet of this same district with the lid on are seen. Then they get into the story of the safety of the daughter.

In the play "Sex" which May West produced one got an earful; in the screen version of "Is Your Daughter Safe?" they get an eyeful. The film exposes and shows the new racket which has taken place of the old time line. It introduces the gold digger, street walker, apartment house and the call house. It shows how the gold digger and the street walker buy their wares and how the apartment house and call houses are operated. Of course, it is always necessary to tell parents that their daughters are never safe when it comes to the automobile. The picture starts with the auto racket, the stalled car and the girl starting to walk home, after she had accepted a ride from a strange man who pulls a new one by walking with her. On the way home he assaults her and disappears.

Comes a sequence showing the workings of the procurer or the cadet. This is done through a girl having vainly tried to obtain employment. She becomes tired and stops to rest on a park bench. The girl is delivered to the woman operating an assignation house with the procurer or cadet getting his 30 pieces of silver.

The full workings of this joint are shown. While the inmates are carrying on, a scene is shown where one of the girls tries to cache a little luck money, but is caught by the madam who reprimands the girl in a subtitle saying, "Don't hold out on me again."

Another scene is of the girl as she approaches a live one on a park bench and gives him the routine. The pickup on the park bench turns out to be a sweetheart of childhood days. The chap takes a flash at the swell front which the girl presents and proves that he is not a mug by the title "I knew you would make good."

This reporter has seen many of the Lilies of the Field stage and screen. But this one is the prize pip. If the censors let it get by in communities where they want to see hot stuff, it is a cinch this will be a wow.

The methods of selling this one are by starting off with a lecture showing slides of various phases of social diseases. The lecturer tells the customers that he is selling a book on sex for 50 cents which solves all of the social problems as well as warns against the pitfalls that come in the way of all young. He offers to answer pertinent questions after the spiel. For an outside ballyhoo here they have been using a live girl sitting in a glass case in the lobby who seems to be contented with the scarlet life. It is a flash for the boobs.

If communities will stand for it, no exhibitor can go wrong on the ballyhoo or picture and the lecture. However, the lecture is the strongest this reporter has heard in connection with so-called white slave pictures. It makes a great impression on the audience, male or female, and proves to be the means of the promoter cleaning up with his men only and women only performances.

While the producer of this picture admitted that his original picture of a group of cutouts did not stand him over $150 gross, this one looks to be a splurge and must have cost every bit of $3,000.

THE SUNSET DERBY

First National production, directed by Al Rogell, Mary Astor, Willie Collier, Jr., and Ralph Lewis featured. Titles by Mort Blumenstock. Photographer, Ash Fisher. At Moss' Broadway, New York, week June 13. Running time, under 60 minutes.

As a title "The Sunset Derby" foretells what to expect, and here no one expecting will be disappointed. Only instead of the horse getting the bad breaks, it's the jockey. And notwithstanding the same title might lead anyone to believe the picture was made by a sharpshooting outfit, it's a First National. And just about able to stand up on the one dayers where there have not been too many $15 "Kentucky Derby" pictures around of late.

That's about the main fault here —the waste of money on a film horse race. You see two running races in this one, and much of and about the track. Its story doesn't mean a thing, although in a house where there's a gallery it may pull a yell when "The Queen" wins. She had to win because the picture didn't have another 100 feet to go either. That left the finish quick and kissy.

It's a story that should have been turned down. Al Rogell, the director, considering what he was handed, did overly well. Its best bit is a piece of comedy, of "The Queen" stolen by a peddler and hitched to his cart, upon hearing the bugle at the track and seeing the horses running past, ran away to join in the race, spilling the garden truck in the process—and winning. The next best are the captions. This title writer, billed as Mort Blumenstock, has a nice snap to his stuff.

Another little bit that will be appreciated by those following the races is that of the injured jock, having been badly thrown, losing his nerve on the second try. Photography very good in the main.

Willie Collier, Jr., as the jockey, does nicely, with Ralph Lewis taking what there is to grab in the playing end. Mary Astor as the daughter had a heavy thoughtful role. "The Queen" was something of an actress, too. A couple of elderly roles were well done and the track scenes with races looked realistic enough. *Sime.*

DUTY'S REWARD

Ellbee production, with Eva Novak, George Fawcett, Alan Roscoe, Lou Archer and Vincent Brounet as principals. Directed by Bertram Bracken. Distributed by Ellbee Pictures Corp., New York. At the Stanley, New York, June 10. Running time, 60 mins.

There isn't a solitary thing new about this independent. The melodramatic kick is centered on the big building which is built of very bad cement, a condition understood by those in on the villainy side of the film. Of course, it collapses, the hero saves the heroine and all ends well.

There's a stretch of comedy by-play through the efforts of a newspaper man to run down the deep-dyed villain who stalks through the picture. The dashing young hero, however, is a motorcycle cop.

There isn't much to the picture save the building collapse. This is effectively staged.

Lucky if it strikes the double feature programs. At the Stanley the only player given special house billing was Miss Novak. The men run ahead of her on work. *Mark.*

THE WESTERN ROVER

Universal Blue Streak western. Directed by Albert Rogell from story by George Hively. Starring Art Acord, with Ena Gregory, Charles Avery and A. J. Smith in support. Photographed by Edwin Linden. At Loew's New York one day (June 10) on double-feature bill. Running time, about 60 minutes.

A western suitable for opening and closing on the same day, and that a weekday. Even better as the minor member of a double-feature bill.

Acord plays the son of a Chicago packer who sets out to make good. The opening has him as the star rider in a one-ring circus that has just gone broke, and he and the clown of the outfit hook up with a near-by ranch as cowpunchers. The ranch happens to belong to Acord's father, so he proceeds to expose the foreman's trick of delaying contract shipments so that the Chicago packer will go broke. In getting the shipments of cattle through on time Acord also wins the gal from the foreman.

Direction and photography okay for this type of picture.

Cast looks about the same as it did last week, although Ena Gregory is a trifle thinner.

Code of the Cow Country

Pathe film starring Buddy Roosevelt. Directed by Oscar Apfel from Betty Burbridge's scenario. Cameraman, Ray Ries. Running time, 46 mins. Reviewed in projection room, June 8.

Jim West....................Buddy Roosevelt
Red Irwin..........................Hank Bell
Helen Calhoun...................Elsa Benham
John Calhoun...........Melbourne McDowell
Ted Calhoun....................Sherry Tansey
Bill Jackson...................R. Richard Neil
Dutch Moore.....................Walter Maly
Tallas..............................Frank Ellis
Dolores..............................Ruth Royce

A bright and smart little western, inexpensive as to production. Well above the entertainment average of the open space opuses turned out by the independents.

This one has something in common with the real west. A gambling-dancehall is movieish but otherwise plot and characters seem plausible and probable.

Buddy Roosevelt is an unknown so far as metropolitan audiences are concerned, but probably is a likely contender for small town and kid popularity. He looks and performs okay before the camera.

Sherry Tansey, playing a spineless brother of the heroine, looks like a perfect type for roles requiring weak character and might be recommended for such parts to the bigger companies. The cast also includes that competent actor, R. Richard Neil, doing his usual "menace," and Melbourne McDowell, familiar old timer. Elsa Benham makes an appealing girl lead.

In analysis the plot is familiar stuff but has been done neatly. Plenty of action, some laughs, love interest and a general total that gives the picture a degree of class in its division.

It is produced by Lester F. Scott, Jr.

Tracked by the Police

Warner Bros. production. Directed by Ray Enright. Starring Rin-Tin-Tin, with Jason Robards, Virginia Browne Faire and Tom Santschi featured. Cameraman, Ed Du Par. At Loew's New York one day (June 8), as single feature. Running time, about 58 mins.

In the dog picture market this one rates among the more desirable, although the juvenile title will prove a hindrance in drawing trade for metropolitan stands. A limited customerage was noted at the New York, where the picture held forth for one day on its own merits.

The story has Rin-Tin-Tin and his master (Jason Robards), who were in the big fight together, back in the U. S. A. working on an irrigation dam. The dog's duty is to keep an eye out for meddlesome characters while the master is busy supervising construction work. A rival company is hard at it trying to ruin the dam, but, thanks to Rin, everything turns out all right.

As a little extra love interest, the dog falls for a classy canine named Nanette and takes up sizable footage in necking scenes. The human romance is carried by Robards and Virginia Browne Faire with average success.

Rin himself does little scrapping. There's one good battle between the lead and the heavy. The thrill burden is toted by scenes wherein the dam is partially destroyed and the rushing water almost eliminates both the dam and the heroine.

Direction and photography are an asset. Titles get weak at times, explainable in the fact that it's hard to tell just why a dog is gifted with human intelligence.

ON TIME

Tiffany release of Truart picture, starring Richard Talmadge. Directed by Henry Lehrman, with story credited to William Marshall. Edited and titled by Ralph Spence. Cast includes Stuart Holmes, Billie Dove, George Seigman, Charles Clary and Tom Wilson. Running time, 62 mins. At Arena, New York, on double-feature bill, June 8.

This is 'way past being merely bad.

Broadway has a legend that when "The Tavern" was placed into rehearsal the humorous possibilities of its serious situations were noted by George M. Cohan who rewrote it into a travesty. Something of the sort seems to have been attempted by Henry Lehrman, director of this puzzle. Seemingly realizing how bad it was going to be, Lehrman attempted to kid the whole business. The result is terrible.

There are crazy Chinamen, a wild-eyed, bushy-haired guy with an operating room where the bathroom should be, a fantastic dwarf, a symbolic devil given to leering and trap-door exits, and a miscellaneous assortment of Desperate Desmonds in silk hats. Through this nightmare of idiots and maniacs Richard Talmadge follows his customary course of acrobatics, while Billie Dove, Stuart Holmes and Charles Clary presumably got half a week's salary pro rata.

Ralph Spence, called in to do something with the titles, also botched his job. Granting he had no material to work with, there is still no excuse for using the same pun twice in one picture.

Where they buy film by the foot this one will not be any worse than some other monstrosities of the state right market.

THE JAZZ GIRL

Louis T. Rogers release, featuring Gaston Glass and Edith Roberts. Directed by Howard Mitchell. At Loew's New York, one half double bill one day, June 7. Running time, around 55 minutes.

Another good title blown.

"The Jazz Girl" should have been above a corking lively story suitable to the billing. Instead it's a stupid tale of a girl tired of modern society turning amateur detective to catch rum runners, and meeting a reporter sent out for a story on the same thing, which each believing the other to be in the liquor traffic. The boss runner himself stands between the two.

Story forced, with the impression left whoever responsible made it up as they went along.

It also brings out sharply that to be good screen actors there must be material. Here at least the actors were unable to rise above it, and that's likely true for all screen stories. Not only Gaston Glass as the reporter and Edith Roberts as the girl were pitiful at times, but the direction most often was even more so.

"The Jazz Girl" will do for the double bills and the smallest, but the chances are that Louis Rogers, its producer, could have made more selling that title than he will out of this mis-product. *Sime.*

TOPSY AND EVA

Los Angeles, June 17.

United Artists production, starring the Duncan Sisters, based on the stage play by Catherine Chisholm Cushing. Del Lord, director; production consultant, Myron Selznick; continuity, Scott Darling; title by Dudley Early. About 7,000 feet. Running time, 80 mins. At Grauman's Egyptian, Los Angeles, June 16, on run at $2 top.

Topsy........................Rosetta Duncan
Eva...........................Vivian Duncan
Simon Legree...............Gibson Gowland
Uncle Tom...................Noble Johnson
Marietta......................Marjorie Daw
Aunt Ophelia.............Myrtle Ferguson
George Shelby....................Nils Aster
St. Clare........................Henry Victor

"Topsy and Eva" is going to get a lot of money as long as it is shown on the same bill with the Duncan Sisters, its stars, making personal appearances. That money, however, will come from the de luxe and first run houses. The production is not an expensive one for a special, standing around $300,000.

In houses where the Duncan girls do not appear it is going to be a different story. The picture is not going to draw heavy grosses and it is not going to please all around, especially with the trade that has reached the stage of adolescence. It will do, however, and nicely for the kiddie matinees.

Rather a hard time was had in getting this picture finished for a screen showing. The Duncan girls had engineered a deal whereby the picture would be made by First National. Blanche Merrill was called in to write the screen story from the Catherine Chisholm Cushing play. Something happened, and United Artists took it over. Then Lois Weber came along and did something to the story, as she was to direct it. Exit Miss Weber, and Del Lord was signed to direct.

From what this reporter saw on the screen he did not know whether Del Lord, too, had something to do with the story end. Anyway, it was just as well that no one was given screen credit for the adaptation as possibly no one would have craved it. Scott Darling was credited with the continuity; there again no one can see how that matter was handled and how closely the script was followed.

"Topsy and Eva" on the screen is nothing but a lot of burlesque gags and situations on the "Uncle Tom" story with a bit of drama and pathos here and there. What drama is in the picture that has any effect on a patron might be credited to D. W. Griffith, who was called in about 10 days before the picture got its initial showing to straighten things out. He no doubt did his best, but is probably not bragging about it.

Titles are very good in most instances, with a few a bit off color and probably after their Coast premiere will be discarded by orders of censors. These comedy titles are funny, but just a bit too broad for screen safety.

The story opens with miniature shots being shown on the screen of the stork racing a doctor to the home of the St. Clares and winning out in delivering Eva ahead of him. Two months later a black stork raises havoc by going through rain and lightning and after being driven away from the homes of colored folks, drops Topsy into a barrel. Then the incidents which lead to the slave market where Uncle Tom and Topsy are sold to the St. Clare family.

In the situation surrounding the sale Topsy has great opportunities for comedy. She gets them over, though in many instances the efforts are a bit crude and grotesque. However, an audience will laugh and that is all that is wanted.

One gag which seems a bit nauseus is where Topsy after biting some of Simon Legree's chewing tobacco gets on the auction block and becomes sick. During her comedy antics she turns away from the crowd and gets rid of the cud. More to this and it is nothing pleasant to witness on the screen.

After the sale, everything goes well at the St. Clare home until Legree comes to foreclose on Christmas eve. He takes Uncle Tom and Topsy away. Brutal to them, Topsy gives him a whaling at every chance. Meantime, Marietta, the niece of Legree, finds he is not on the level, and is locked in a room by him.

Slaves are brought to the Legree home. Immediately after their arrival Young Shelby appears, having been commissioned to turn over the St. Clare jewels to Legree for Topsy, so that the life of Eva might be saved.

Topsy meantime raises cain with Legree and makes a getaway. Shelby and Legree start to mix it with result that it is a great battle, with Topsy slugging the slaves, trying to help Legree.

Marietta hands Topsy note to St. Clare, which says the latter is to administer the estate of her dead father. Shelby is unable at first to help the girl to her freedom, as he is knocked cold by Legree and his men. Topsy makes one of those comedy getaways, grabs a saddle from his horse, throws it on a fence, riding down hill, chute-the-chute fashion, on it for long distance and then starts the tramp through a cemetery, etc., to the St. Clare home, with Legree and his bloodhounds on the trail.

They catch up with her after a time, and she gets rid of Simon by throwing him from a cliff during a battle in the snow. Then Shelby makes the house with his sweetheart, Marietta, and Topsy coming in on the scene shortly afterward. Eva is, of course, on her death bed, but when Topsy comes on the scene, comes to life.

After lots of clowning at the expense of the others, Topsy gets alongside of Eva on the bed and every one then knows the story of "Topsy and Eva" as the Duncan girls tell it, which in no way should have any effect on the next "Uncle Tom" picture, which Universal will release.

Rosetta Duncan, as "Topsy," took the whole cake with her comedy. She was all over the screen most of the time, and it was really too bad the story was not a bit more consistent, as she would have done far better. Vivian, as Eva, looked nice, but her role called for little acting.

Possibly someone will get an idea for a series of short subject pictures on the doings of "Topsy and Eva." If they do the girls will, with proper material, have a cinch of a time in cleaning up through their screen efforts.

Gibson Gowland did Simon Legree in as brutal a fashion as one would want to see this famous villain. Nils Aster, as George Shelby, looked good, but had little opportunity to show just how good he would measure up on the screen. Noble Johnson, as Uncle Tom, had little chance to shine, either. He played in the meek fashion of the play and had no big moments to get over. Marjorie Daw, as Marietta, was just on and off. Henry Victor, as St. Clare, gave a convincing performance. Myrtle Ferguson did likewise as Ophelia.

The picture down to around 6,800 feet or so could stand little trimming, due to the nature of the episodic tie-ups. It will have to be played in its present way as cutting would not be beneficial.

With the Duncan girls remaining with the picture for nine months doing their stage work, it is a cinch that the Joe Schenck organization and the girls will not lose anything. Then when it goes on regular program, its best chances seem to be the kiddies, for it will be able to repeat for several years at special kiddies show. *Ung.*

ALIAS THE DEACON

Universal-Jewel production, directed by Edward Sloman. Jean Hersholt featured. Titles by Walter Anthony. Screen adaptation from stage play of like name by John B. Hymer and Leroy Clements. At Roxy, New York, week June 18. Running time, around 70 minutes.

The Deacon	Jean Hersholt
Nancy	June Marlowe
John Adams	Ralph Graves
Mrs. Clark	Myrtle Stedman
Cunningham	Lincoln Plummer
"Slim" Sullivan	Ned Sparks
"Bull" Moran	Tom Kennedy
Willie Clark	Maurice Murphy
George	George West

Universal has made "Alias the Deacon" stand up as a week-stand program release, but that's about all. It's not exceptional in any one item. Instead it's irritating at times in its slowness, and if the time caught in the dark, around 70 minutes, is correct a considerable cut should be made.

What appears to be the punch of the picture, a prize fight, tumbles over through direction. Old style direction here of breaking into the fight with attempted comedy that never lands, also asides while the fight is progressing just knocks it, although the fight itself or what is seen of it is not done badly at all. But after the Dix fight in "Reilly," a screen fistic battle has got to go some and fast to follow it.

Taking the screen story as it runs and without regard to the stage hit it was adapted from, that stage play not having been seen, "The Deacon" is lacking in tenseness. It starts in a box car with a girl disguised as a boy one of the rail riders. That's not so refreshing. Thereafter, though, the boy she met in the box car marries her at the finish, there is no reason disclosed why the girl is wandering around as a roughneck, where she came from or who or what the boy is or was. Although for convenience when he fights a pug, Bull Moran, a slide tells he was an amateur boxer at college. Perhaps a story of these two young people by themselves and why they left their home towns to become hobos would be more interesting than this story of the "Deacon."

The Deacon character is a sanctimonious card cheating grifter, rolling into town to fleece natives and being run out of each county by the sheriff. To make such a crook a soft-hearted meandering philanthropist as is done here is like asking some one to swallow carbolic to find out if it burns. And the gage of bringing back the wop murderer for the Deacon to nab in a barber shop after the Deacon had stolen $1,200 playing cards from a sports promoter, with no good reason to do it, is another sop to the lowbrows. How the women will take to this combination of bums and crooks is problematical.

A scene of an auto racing to catch a train is pretty old film stuff, although it's the nearest to suspense or a thrill in the film. Some one had the good sense to stop the car beside the train at a crossing instead of a narrow escape.

Jean Hersholt played the Deacon rather well. He studied the role in appearance and gave it a complacency of expression that sent him, personally, very well over. He was helped a trifle by captions. Walter Anthony wrote the captions, but muffed many a chance to send over a homer. It's a peach picture for a fly title writer. Photography does better, especially in the only part when a few tricks look very good.

June Marlowe did nicely in a small way as the runaway girl. Myrtle Stedman as the operator of the country hotel had but little to do, making it easy for that actress. Ned Sparks, the standard hotel clerk of the stage in years gone by, is the heavy here, the manager of the prize fighter. As a matter of personal choice that pug, Bull Moran, as played by Tom Kennedy, did as good work as any one in the film, and Mr. Sparks' performance is somewhat nifty also. Sparks can mug and knows how not to overdo it.

Maurice Murphy as the landlady's young son is a lively little kid, pushing himself forward. He should be in the running for stronger boy roles. Ralph Graves as the juvenile had a conventional part, barring the fight exhibition or as much of it as he did. Probably chosen to size up alongside the pug. *Sime.*

FRAMED

First National film drama release featuring Milton Sills. Designated a Charles J. Brabin Production and produced by Ray Rockett. Adapted from "Dawn of My Tomorrow," by George W. Sutton, Jr. Adaptation and continuity by Mary O'Hara. Running time, 59 minutes. At the Strand, New York, week June 18.

Raoul Hilaire	Milton Sills
Diane Laurens	Natalie Kingston
Alphonse Laurens	E. J. Radcliffe
Arthur Remson	Charles Gerrard
Moola	Edward Peil
Lola's Husband	John Miljan

A particularly wooden drama, molded into shape for a male star. Appeal is to the naive of the fan public. Every contrast is in extremes, lest any subtlety might be "above their heads." Story is jumpy, suggesting that the continuity maker concentrated on the action elements and argued that audiences would be impatient over details of knitting episodes smoothly and logically.

It takes three minutes of a court-martial, including titles, to convict the hero of something or other. Then Bang! like that, he is an overseer of blacks deep in a South American diamond mine. Almost in a breath he is introduced to the heroine, aristocratic French girl, who happens—why worry about why—to be sojourning about a back country Brazilian diamond mine.

Even more brusquely than this the girl goes into the mines just in time to be trapped by what the title calls a "mud rush," a remarkably gooey screen effect, albeit it furnishes the only punch in the six reels. Hence it calls for some comment. The diamond searchers are working in mine galleries apparently cut through stiff clay earth. Soft river earth or mud breaks through the walls and oozes along the galleries. Of course, hero and heroine are imprisoned in a gallery end and rescued only at the last minute from a messy death by the hero's efforts. The creeping up of the river of mud, however, had a kick, even if one anticipated almost everything that happened.

Then the romance is standing up and the hero is sent to a penal settlement in the swampy and malarial interior for a diamond theft he didn't commit, but which was fixed upon him by a rival for the girl. Our hero is discovered almost immediately in the prison camp. Thither comes the man who framed him, at length caught in his own crimes. Plotter is dying of a fever and begging for the only quinine in the place, possessed by the hero.

Hero laughs scornfully and refuses succor, but appears the vision of the departed girl begging him to show mercy to their enemy—discipline for the hero's soul, of course. So he plays samaritan and in return the expiring heavy makes confession of the framing. Almost instantly the hero is back on the Riviera in Panama hat and white flannels, and it takes less time than this telling for the final embrace.

All juvenile, mechanical make-believe, without a semblance of illusion to carry a grown up along with interest. Picture's only value is Sills' name. His leading woman, Natalie Kingston, is as artificial as the story. Production and photographic quality excellent. *Rush.*

RITZY

Paramount production starring Betty Bronson in an Elinor Glyn story. James Hall featured. Directed by Richard Rosson, Charles Lang, photographer, with George Marion, Jr., titling. At Paramount, New York, week June 18. Running time, 63 mins.

Ritzy Brown	Betty Bronson
Harrington Smith	James Hall
Algy	William Austin
Mary	Joan Standing
Nathan Brown	George Nichols

When Elinor Glyn desires to become silly by pen, the strain is evidently not great. This is one of those times, the result being a weak, light comedy that's neither here, there or anywhere. It will have to draw on the Glyn authorship, as it has little else.

The diminutive Betty Bronson hasn't done much since "Peter Pan," and it stands to reason she isn't going any place in stories of this order. Noted for her risque tendencies as an authoress, Miss Glyn has presumably taken the oath for once, swept clean all corners, but in doing so has forgotten to replace the furniture. Hence, "Ritzy" is an empty room, around which Miss Bronson and James Hall wander. Incidentally, granting that the latter has built up a flapper following, his name may be of some aid. Whatever pull this boy has the picture needs. Rialto going for Miss Bronson.

Chas. Rosson's direction and Geo. Marion, Jr.'s, titles are limited by the script. The director could do nothing but follow the conventional trail. His highlight is a windshield cleaner, removing the moisture from the glass to show the leads, at the finish, nicely snuggled in the front seat of an auto, a hand down from the window cleaning bit first used in a Mary Pickford film. Marion is only able to slip through a laugh at well spaced intervals.

In the story Ritzy Brown is a small town girl nursing dreams of marrying a title. Plus a wealthy father, the fulfillment is not impossible. It's when Harrington Smith (Mr. Hall), the Duke of Westborough traveling incognito, makes a business visit to the Brown home. For no discernible screen reason Smith sees gold under the youngster's snobbishness and cares enough to induce a friend to play the duke and turn the girl away from her social ideas.

The rest is concerned with that stock situation, William Austin playing his customary English fop and Joan Standing paralleling him as the ugly duckling cousin whom Austin eventually snares.

Meanwhile, Ritzy is spanked by Smith on board ship, a fake wedding ceremony is arranged in London for her and Algy (Mr. Austin) and the girl goes out on a tear when Smith tells her it was all a joke. The "tear" consists of going to the apartment of an Oriental, whom she imagines is a base villain having evil designs on her. All the man wants to do is to get rid of the silly youngster. The best situation in the picture and inadequately worked up.

Production, of course, is standard, although the photography reveals various changes in lighting.

"Ritzy" has its points as a title. The independents would probably have run riot with it. However, the authoress has only used it for a lead and failed to follow up.

No particular fire to Miss Bronson, while Hall saunters through familiar routine. Austin actually does more work than anyone else, and on valuation can claim first rating. The usual applies to Miss Standing in going through the picture minus makeup to let the freckles show and emphasize the homely cousin who must always play second fiddle. If for nothing else this girl deserves credit for that.

"Ritzy" is not strong enough to be classed as other than an anemic "filler" by major houses. *Sid.*

Black Diamond Express

Warner Bros. dramatic picture, directed by Howard Bretherton. Monte Blue starred, supported by Edna Murphy. Story by Mark Canfield. Myrtle Stedman, Clare MacDowell, Carroll Nye in cast. Running time, 64 minutes. At the Broadway, New York, week June 20.

Best thing of the kind Warners have put out in some time. Story is light but takes on importance from the manner of telling. Good part for Monte Blue as a rough diamond railroad engineer drawn into a love affair with a society girl.

Slow at the start but builds up in dramatic interest with splendid sequence of the hero piloting a runaway Pullman down a long winding mountain slope to foil a band of desperadoes who have held up his train and killed the railroad official riding in his private car.

This episode is splendidly backed up with neat shots of wild mountain scenery, vistas of dizzily winding railroad track skirting breath-taking precipices. Ingenious handling of familiar plot gives full value to situation background of the melodrama. Each incident takes force from suspense in the situation.

Blue comes nearer to his old form in this production than in any of the action pictures he has been concerned with lately, and his passing into maturity is forgotten. Edna Murphy makes one of those gushing blonde heroines of which the screen has a surfeit. She is overshadowed here by Myrtle Steadman, who gives a world of grace and poise to an inconsequential role of a matron, and illustrates how such a part should be played.

The story was probably written around the railroad incident, explaining its early slowness, but the quickening interest for the action passages is ample compensation. The interiors are handled in the best of the modern technique, making convincing setting without distractive attention from the story essence and the direction is always expert.

Latter half of action is skillfully knit and delivers a maximum of suspense, the necessary element in stories of this kind. Picture will please partisans of Blue and deliver abundantly before the grade of audience classified in the trade as "action" or "westerns" fans. *Rush.*

TIME TO LOVE

Paramount prodution starring Raymond Griffith. Directed by Frank Tuttle. Cast includes Vera Veronina, William Powell and Josef Swickard. At Hippodrome, New York, week June 20. Running time, 51 mins.

Supposedly good little scenarios that turn out to be bad little pictures and are threatened with the shelf have a habit of being leniently punished by being sent below 42d street to the Moss and Proctor houses or east of Broadway to the K-A or out of town for Mr. Proctor or other K-A's. That goes for the major producer-distributors. Papa Par was evidently displeased with this one, for it's hiding over on 6th avenue this week sans any title of credit for direction, story, etc.

There's nothing but the main wording which heralds Ray Griffith as starring in a Frank Tuttle production released by Paramount. There's a reason. It's a good one. The picture is spotty. Too weak on laughs to stand the strain of a full week of de luxe presentation. It's where it belongs here, and otherwise looks as if three days anywhere will be plenty.

Only three persons actually concerned in the story, therefore a small cast production. Griffith opens as a despondent lover, casts himself from a bridge and into the lap of Vera Veronina, who is riding in a gondola. Love as he lights (to cop "Old Gold's" new slogan) and the action goes after farce when Griffith discovers the young woman is under a forced engagement to his best friend, William Powell. Inasmuch as the latter expects Griffith to fight all his duels the situations crop up to climax in Griffith stealing the girl during the wedding ceremony, an auto chase and final seclusion for the pair in a basket which turns out to be attached to a target balloon.

Every so often some funny stuff crops out, but the inconsistency of the comedy is what hurts. No titles to help nor outstanding "treatment." All things considered, Griffith does pretty well from a personal angle. Whatever merit the picture has can be mainly credited to him. Miss Veronina doesn't overly impress, and although everyone agrees Powell did all right in "Beau Geste" his conception of a well-dressed Frenchman in this instance is a winged collar and a crooked right arm at all times.

Nice interiors set the action off, photography is okay and a pip of a sport Renault for transportation. But that practically all the technical staff have seen fit to hide tells the studio opinion.

Can easily stand up for one day and probably okay for three, but has got to have something to help under the latter period, and the b. o. price has got to be right. A remake in part might have saved it.

It couldn't get on Broadway and the Hip never pays over $1,000 for playing a picture seven days. *Sid.*

MOON OF ISRAEL

F. B. O. distribution of a Sacha (German) production featuring Marie Corda. Adapted from Sir H. R. Haggard's novel; directed by Michael Curtiz. At Roxy, New York, week June 25. Running time, 65 mins.

Merapi, Moon of Israel	Marie Corda
Prince Seti	Adelqui Miller
Userti	Arlette Marchal
Ana	Ferdinand Onna
Amenmeses	Oscar Beregi
Moses	Henry Mar
Pharaoh Menapta	A. Weisse
Pampasa	Reinbold Haussermann
Laban	Georges Haryton
Khi	Emil Hayse

This is the picture Paramount bought to keep out of the way of Cecile DeMille's "Ten Commandments" back in '23. The main confliction between the two pictures was and is in the punch sequence of the sea opening and closing to save the pursued Israelites. Paramount held on to this German production since that time, finally selling it to F. B. O., the present distributor. Allowing that the purchase price was right, F. B. O. should turn a very fair profit.

"Moon of Israel" is a spectacular specimen depicting the miracle of the sea more clearly, if less dramatically, than the DeMille's.

The sets, mob stuff and "effects" are all on a huge scale. So much so that for the 65 minutes it runs it is always worth watching.

The reason for this one being on the shelf for such a length of time evidently lies in the treatment of the love theme, a tepid affair compared to modern screen amours. Marie Corda must shoulder some of the blame for this because the well known grotesque German make-up for a camera that kills off any chance of catching the American acceptance of feminine beauty. Perhaps Curtiz can also be singled out for the stiff and formal manner of the lovers, Miss Corda and Adelqui Miller. Hence, the love story is secondary to the production's mass attributes.

The locale is Egypt, with the Jews in slavery under Pharaoh Menapta. Persecution is depicted, the duel of Gods brings destruction, plagues, "signs," etc., all for big mechanical effects that impress despite that other films have held the same things. The story winds itself around Prince Seti, heir to the Egyptian throne, who ultimately renounces his title by favoring Merapi's people.

Performances by the men are sterling to the point of over-shadowing Miss Corda. Curtiz has handled his big ensembles excellently, photography is good, and the continuity is all right, despite the two reels which have been deleted.

In the matter of the sea thing the effect here is so similar to that which DeMille used in the "Commandments" as to cause astonishment among those who can graphically recall the scene as revealed in the latter picture. The canyon through the water is even more clear here, but the bit of water rolling back and then rushing to submerge the pursuing Egyptians is an exact duplicate. If memory serves, the DeMille method called for four different shots, with the walls of the opened sea made possible through a gelatine composition. The replica is so obvious as to immediately impress that someone "copped" from someone, and if Sid Kent hustled "Moon" out of the way it's logical to presume Curtiz had his first.

"Commandments" and "Ben-Hurs" notwithstanding, "Moon of Israel" looks good enough to go into any first run house for a week and make money for both ends. Its basic spectacular features are sufficient to overcome the weakness in story and the performance by the men hold that angle together. If the love interest is tame, there are too many production "fireworks" to make a material difference.

The picture rates exploitation and will fulfill the promises of the billing. The Annies and Jimmies aren't used to seeing this sort of thing before having heard all about it, unless they give up heavy dough at the b. o., so "Moon" promises to be a novelty in that respect.

That Paramount didn't want to handle it doesn't necessarily count. The idea is that F. B. O. has it, it's a big picture that calls for handling and will draw a response if the people are made to know it's in town.

Running comment at the Roxy was favorable during the screening, and from lay persons who had seen all the Biblical "specials." The Roxy gross at the end of the week should be indicative, as the stage show is currently not powerful enough to smother, as usual, the screen end of the program. *Sid.*

RUBBER HEELS

Paramount production and release. Ed Wynn starred, with Chester Conklin and Thelma Todd featured. Directed by Victor Heerman. Writers' and adapters', if any, names not caught. At Keiths Hippodrome week of June 27. Running time, 60 minutes.

A tur-ru-bul picture, boys, to sic onto a beginner like Ed Wynn as his first flicker. Paramount may have paid Eddie for going through the motions, but the exhibs if they give the money back to Par will be nuttier than the nuts at the Paramount studios who ever let this hunk of junk go to a finish.

Wynn will be frazzled through this picture, and may deserve it for ever believing he could be a dead pan film comic, but Paramount should be rapped first for releasing, and twice for making it. That takes in Victor Heerman, who probably thought he was directing, the side line staffs, if they were alive, and all the others, from the Quince who owned the gem chest to his lady friend, with Chester Conklin and his collection of dummies.

In New York they tell, those folks coming from the coast, how in the evening when all is quiet, no more conferences and the studios are stilled, they gather in the projection room to look at the "rushes." It sounds bu-tu-ful, but if the Paramount bunch looked at any of the rushes of the "Heels," they must have had goggles or something else on. And here the plural "Heels" goes double.

Had "Rubber Heels" opened last week in New York it could have accounted for Paramount dropping to 95 on the 'Change. At least it would have been a more logical reason than anyone in Times Square thought of for the drop.

If this picture were cut to one reel, including the Niagara Falls scene (which is quite a piece of film work, but not enough to stand off the rest), "Rubber Heels" without identifying Wynn in the picture, might find a ready market at the one-reel price. As it is the Wynn picture must be worse than the first Keystoner was.

Prior repo's said Paramount would not exhibit this film. The reports were smarter than Paramount, although here it is at Keith's Hippodrome, probably after having been turned down as a part of double feature day at Loew's New York—for one day. The Hip has it for the full week! That's cruel on the Hip, but the booking is the single laugh.

If Wynn had had a chance at the pictur racket, this would have killed it. But he hasn't. Ed makes good on the stage as a funnyman and should be tickled over that, after seeing himself on the screen. Although not many will see his film try.

Still he was entitled to intelligent aid if nothing else, and he got nothing. Most of the time Wynn doesn't appear to know what he is doing, with seemingly no one of intelligence around to inform him. There's protection for a considerable investment.

Whoever wrote it, if ever written, is doing a hideaway. Maybe the 42 writers Metro let out. As an out, if Paramount says anyone framed it with this picture, that excuse would be as good as any. Wynn might have told them what a comical cuss he was once on the stage as an amateur detective of many disguises. They must have believed him, for he's doing the same stuff here, trying to recover a disappearing chest of kingly jewels. The chest looked like a couple of tons, but they handled it like a feather.

Those picture fellers know a lot of tricks about everything but stories. At one point they jumped continuity as though the cutter fell asleep before an audience could.

Eddie should have told them about the hats. Maybe the hats would have been better. They carried Ed in and out of vaudeville some years ago, then into production and then into—way into—Paramount, if the tales about the jack paid Eddie as salary for his first are as nearly true as they sound foolish.

This one must have cost Paramount plenty. Location was Niagara Falls in the winter, but how they ever let it get beyond the first 1,000 feet is a bigger mystery than why it is worth while making dumbbell pictures for only dumbbells.

This is the leader of all of the pains-in-the-neck. *Sime.*

Old San Francisco

Warner Brothers production starring Dolores Costello. Directed by Alan Crosland, from D. F. Zanuck's story. A. Coldeway scenarist, and Hal Mohr, cameraman. Vitaphone synchronized score by Hugo Riesenfeld. At Warner's, New York, for a twice daily run commencing June 21. Running time, 88 mins. Top $2.
Dolores Vasquez..........Dolores Costello
Chris Buckwell............Warner Oland
Terrence O'Shaughnessy...Chas. E. Mack
Don Hernandez Vasquez..Joseph Swickard
Don Luis.....................John Miljan
Michael Brandon........Anders Randolph
Lu Fong............................Sojin
Dwarf ....Angelo Rossitto
Chinese girl..............Anna May Wong

A good enough program picture but even in conjunction with Vitaphone, problematical successor to the 19 weeks "When a Man Loves" finished here just ahead of it. In other words, "Old San Francisco" looks like about eight weeks and will have to develop fast to get that through tackling the heat.

Two men carry the picture, Warner Oland and Joseph Swickard. Former plays the "heavy" with Swickard as the grandfather of the girl. Opposite Miss Costello is the late Charles E. Mack. Swickard has played so many Spanish grandees he probably stands up for the national anthem of that country, while Oland has been doing the dirty to heroines and heroes since the Pearl White days. Both are very well in this picture and overshadow the star for the reason she has been handled with care other than to look delectable.

As the title suggests, the wallop is down at the finish in the 'Frisco "fire" of 1906. This has been well cameraed in miniatures and double photography, the latter on the Bitzer style. The collapse of buildings is graphically pictured and the flames are in color. A "shot" of the present day city intermingles with the final clinch of the principals. This is added to by the Vitaphone attachment for the earthquake portion.

Story revolves around the old Spanish rancho of the Vasquez descendants deeded to the family by the King of Spain when the first explorers arrived in that Pacific area. A nine minute prolog plants the ancestry and the family pride with the '49 gold rush starting the financial misfortunes. This is the prolog. When the scenario picks up Miss Costello and the Vasquez estate are down to their last monies and Chris Buckwell (Mr. Oland), boss of the Tenderloin, is after the property. Brandon, negotiating for Buckwell, takes his nephew, Terrence, with him and the first glance at Dolores signs up Terry to the Vasquez cause.

Buckwell, of course, frames to get the girl and the ranch, and is in reality a Chinaman, and when Dolores makes that discovery the vengeance of his countrymen, whom he has persecuted, is exploded. Kidnapping the girl to a secret hiding place takes place just ahead of the earthquake whence Buckwell and his followers are killed with Terrence rescuing Dolores.

Parts of the story and Crosland's direction are distinctly theatrical in too many spots to make this picture a standout special. Oland is at home again in sliding back secret panels, finding his way through hidden passages, etc., while the director has laid on the proud spirit of the Vasquez to overflowing. Neither do those Irish brogue titles allotted to Terrence help, although these cease after the latter becomes acclimated. However, Swickard extracts much from the role of the Spanish grandfather and makes it convincing in the face of the overemphasis.

Miss Costello makes a lovely appearance, struggles with the villain, is put on display for a group of Chinamen and takes up the sword when her grandfather suddenly succumbs during the general turmoil. Her scenes with Mack are well played and directed but the main histrionic power comes from Oland and Swickard due to material and the proverbial "sweetness" concentrated on the heroine in stories of this type. Miss Costello is the only girl of prominence in the film, Anna May Wong being the sole contestant in this respect and doing what amounts to no more than a few bits.

Productionally the picture is solid and impressive. Shots of the old Barbary Coast hold interest and the 'quake stuff will make them look. Continuity has been nicely timed so that the suspense keeps building and the 88 minutes consumed is not too far out of proportion albeit there is room for scissoring.

Plus a creditable Vitaphone score

"Old San Francisco" looks like standard stuff with or without the mechanical accompaniment.

Despite its serial tinge, as a regular film house program leader this one looks capable of taking care of itself. *Sid.*

THE FIRST AUTO

Warner Brothers production and release, featuring Barney Oldfield, speed motor driver. Story by Darryl Francis Zanuck, scnario by Anthony Coldeway, directed by Roy Del Ruth, titles by Jack Jarmuth. Assistant dicetor, Ross Lederman; cameraman, David Abel. Running time, 75 minutes. At the Colony, New York, June 27, on grind run.
Barney Oldfield...........Barney Oldfield
Rose Robbins ....Patsy Ruth Miller
Hark Armstrong.........Russell Simpson
Jim Robbins...............Frank Campeau
Dave Doolittle..........William Demarest
Steve Bentley.................Paul Kruger
Elmer Hays.................E. H. Calvert
Banker Stebbins........Douglas Gerrard
Bob Armstrong...........Charles E. Mack

If you can associate an early century Ford model with a dramatic idea you'll enjoy "The First Auto." The feat was a little too much for the premiere audience, who took the screen story very quietly. This in spite of the festive nature of the premiere, attended by Barney Oldfield in person, a benefit performance and the presence of a number of vaudeville and musical comedy stars who took part in the Vitaphone bill that preceded the picture.

The combination of so fundamentally funny a subject as early automobiles, the costumes and social absurdities of the period of 1895 and the trick costumes that go with the period, and a dramatic theme of the conflict of the old and the young generation are hard to reconcile. Certainly they don't blend in this production.

It is funny in the wrong places. When intense in its melodrama it is almost a travesty.

You couldn't blame any audience for being confused. Ancient Fords are one of those things that are arbitrarily funny. For screen uses it is a convention that it must explode or collapse; its uses for anything but low comedy is unthinkable. Here the grotesque first attempts at auto making (and they have assembled a marvelous collection) are used for comedy relief, but in the background the horseless carriage is the basis of the domestic motif. That's where the hopeless incongruity comes in. It can't be done.

It is conceivable that the introduction of the automobile and the consequent effect upon the institution of Old Dobbin had its dramatic side at the time, but it isn't dramatic any more. It's just funny. The story deals with a father who is a lover of horse flesh, owner of fast steppers and proprietor of a livery stable. His son goes in for the new fangled devil wagons, and father and son are separated. The old man goes broke in the livery stable business. Brooding over his loneliness and failure he goes a bit off in mind.

When son comes back to the old town to drive in an automobile race, the father is tricked into doctoring his car so it will explode on the track, not knowing the driver is his own son. The car does explode, but the boy survives and the near-tragedy brings the old man back to a sense that progress is inevitable.

For the finish this hater of gas buggies steps into view out of a Rolls Royce, to be an interested spectator at an aviation meet, where he learns that the fliers can go up to 200 miles an hour. The closing gag finds him looking for his son, only to learn that he has gone to a horse show.

There are several first rate comery relief passages, genuine in their fun and cleverly devised. But the srious drama spoils the whole affair because this material has no business in the story. Technical production first rate. Something of the atmosphere of the early century is caught in a fine view of a public square, with crowds moving about and a steady stream of 1905 cars passing.

The picture has been well managed in several particulars. It has some very amusing satire on the social habits of the post-Victorian period; its types are picked and played with much skill. But the mortgage-on-the-farm style of melodrama puts the damper on the whole affair.

A comedy set of titles might save these passages and help the whole picture, for joshing is the only treatment possible. *Rush.*

WEDDING BELLS

Paramount production and release. Raymond Griffith starred. Directed by Erle Kenton. Story and adaptation by Grover Jones, Keene Thompson and Lloyd Corrigan. Titles by George Marion, Jr. At Paramount, New York, week June 25. Running time, around 60 minutes.
Algernon Schuyler Van Twidder
.............................Raymond Griffith
Miss Bruce...................Ann Sheridan
Tom Milbank..............Hallam Cooley
Miss Markham.............Iris Stuart
Milo. Mimi de Lyle........Vivien Oakland
Mr. Markham.............Tom S. Guise
Judson (valet)...............Louis Stern
Detective.................Edgar L. Kennedy
District attorney............John Steppling

Neat, clean, steady amusement in this Raymond Griffith "Wedding Bill$." It's a mild laugh all of the way, with a thrill at the finish, besides some rattling flip captions by George Marion, Jr. It probably will stand out on the Paramount program as an enjoyable picture of the wholesome kind.

The thrill is an adaptation of Harold Lloyd galloping around a skyscraper. Here Griffith does it and there's some audience ahs.

Story and continuity in perfect unison and near-perfect as well, each, for their celluloid purpose. The tale has but a couple of drawbacks, neither really noticeable, but there. One is two men conniving to trim a woman who is trying to trim one of them, and the other the blackjacking woman so continuously present in a house where she doesn't belong.

In running, this picture outfarces any French farce. It does more things with a diamond necklace than any Frenchman ever thought of, and to top it off, a pigeon flies away with the bauble around its neck. That's what started the chase with the pigeon alighting upon the top of a very tall building, Griffith going after it, finally sliding down to the ground on a band of ticker tape.

Quite some production at the start. Griffith as a perpetual best man is shown presiding as such in three different weddings on the same day, he making them on schedule and falling asleep standing up at the third.

For another wedding the following day comes a balk. The prospective groom for whom he is to be best man informs Griffith it looks as though a crimp has been put into the works through a Russian dancing dame he has been toying with threatening to blow the party via his letters unless a $20,000 necklace he had kiddingly promised her comes to life.

Griffith proposes a scheme of securing a necklace on approval, slip it to the dame, then cop it from her and let her be vamped as well as vamping. That sounds so good to the groom he tells Griffith to do it himself.

The necklace is procured on approval by Griffith, with the time limit five in the afternoon, that day, for its return. Then the farcical complications, with the necklace doing a record hideaway among the people concerned and a safe, until the Russian finally casts it into a fancy pigeon coop that is a special prop for the wedding. As Griffith releases the two birds to take the necklace, he having seen the woman cast it in the cage, the birds fly out of the window, and one has the necklace around its neck.

Griffith plays smoothly and likably. He's a debonair fixer, with an added laugh as he stages a bunch of AK's for a football formation he did at Harvard, calling off to them numeral signals, which are in reality the combination of the safe in the next room. He also falls for Ann Sheridan, who joins him in the chase for the necklace, also meeting her for the first time in the jeweler's in the morning and buying her wedding ring before 5 p. m.

Vivien Oakland is the vamp, doing fairly. For a Russian dancer she seemed a bit chilly and even the captions couldn't warm her up. Tom S. Guise did nicely as the father-in-law, and Miss Sheridan looked well, giving some expression at odd moments. But the play is all Griffith, with Erle Kenton, who directed, entitled to plenty of credit for turning out this well-written and put on picture.

The gags of the early part are neatly blended in, with the latter portion holding the out and out gags, and the latter get the best laughs. *Sime.*

CAPT. SALVATION

Cosmopolitan dramatic feature adapted from the novel of the same name by Frederick William Wallace. Screen version by Jack Cunningham. Directed by John S. Robertson. Distributed by Metro-Goldwyn-Mayer. Titles by John Colton. Running time, 87 minutes. At the Capitol, New York, week June 26.

Anson Campbell	Lars Hanson
Mary Phillips	Marceline Day
Bess Morgan	Pauline Starke
Captain	Ernest Torrence
Zeke Crosby	George Fawcett
Peter Campbell	Sam De Grasse
Nathan Phillips	Jay Hunt
Mrs. Buxom	Eugenie Besserer
Mrs. Bellows	Eugenie Forde
Mrs. Snifty	Flora Finch
Old Sea Salt	James Marcus

A truly notable picture, set apart for a number of reasons. Most important is its departure from screen custom in respect to its dignified treatment of a theme commonly touched upon in a spirit of cynicism. This is the first picture that has come to this writer's attention in which formal religion is vindicated as a high dramatic motif.

Beginning with the popularity of "Rain," the picture producers took the cue that a light treatment of religion was a popular asset, and there have been more cheap, shoddy film slurs upon certain aspects of the church than are at all called for.

Here a genuine spiritual theme is dealt with in a thoroughly sincere, dignified way. The material is woven into a story that has true drama, fine grip, a thrill in incident and situation and, most important, heart interest and intellectual appeal. Whether it will exert an exceptional pull from the generality of screengoers in New York is a question. This is unimportant in the broad view.

What it will do is to create good will throughout the country among those people who have been frankly hostile to "movies" because of a tendency, real or imagined, to deal frivolously with certain conventions of society. In a way "Captain Salvation" ought to do for the screen something of the same service that the stage production of "Ben Hur" did for the drama in making friends for the theatre among non theatregoers.

Coming upon the heels of the controversy over Will Hays' prohibition of plays for screen production, the appearance of this splendid photoplay is particularly timely as frank propaganda in the interests of winning favor and consideration for the screen from that element which has scoffed at pictures as beneath intelligent consideration or as an institution that was, in effect if not in intent, opposed to the older social conventions.

As a technical production, in details of settings, composition of backgrounds, delicacy of photographic effect, the film is flawless. By some trick of method the picture achieves the goal of conveying atmosphere. It makes no difference what the background is, always it is real and actual.

An unimportant bit, for example, where the heroine is hastening to the wharf to meet her lover, returning from the sea. She goes through a village street. The screen has pictured countless village streets, just village streets. But this one is that particular village street—a street in Maple Bay in 1840. Again they have an "old fashioned fish fry" in a jolly old sailor's shack and that's what it is. It isn't a movie set at all. Ordinarily a shack in a picture would do for a boy scout's camp or the old mill where the dirty work is done in the third act. But not so here. This is a sailor's shack where this particular fish fry was held.

These two trivial scenes are cited to make the point. The effect of reality is immeasurably finer for the highlights. Always the sense of actuality is there and the beauty of it is that there is no evidence of meticulous care. It is just unaffected naturalness that is the essence of art.

One thing contributing greatly to this "feeling" is the happy casting. Lars Hanson is a new hero to the screen. He comes with no great trumpeting, but the trumpeting will begin with this picture. He is a find. A pantomimist of bold but subtle method, he does some remarkable acting here. He has the knack of graphic expression in brief, crisp action; he can indicate subtle values without facial distortions and possessing something like eloquence in repose. Hanson is one of the few screen actors who gives the spectator's imagination a chance. That makes him a great screen personage.

Pauline Starke here has a part that will advance her. There is something about her performance. Her always vivid feminine quality has an extraordinary opportunity in the role of the Jezebel of the waterfront. Marceline Day in the quaint costume of 1840 makes a charming picture. David Torrence plays a brutal, sardonic captain of a convict ship, a sinister, evil creature, played with a grotesque touch of grim humor that is tremendously interesting. George Fawcett as a queer old salt rounds out an all-American group of gifted actors, happily associated in this extraordinarily fortunate combination of play and players.

The story deals with Anson Campbell, a youth in a narrow little New England sea town. He has returned from the theological seminary, his education completed, but with the call of the sea in his heart and uncertainty over the realness of the call to gospel ministry. The action has to do with the stirring battle of the boy's soul to find its call. The bigoted village turns against him when he befriends a fallen woman cast among them. He goes to sea to escape his disappointment, shipping innocently enough on a convict ship on which also the waterfront Jezebel takes passage. Still the girl's friend, he defends her from the captain, to escape whom she kills herself.

It is in the hold of the convict ship, when the girl dies surrounded by the dregs of humanity that Anson finds his call to sail the seven seas as an evangelist.

The merit of the production is that these spiritual values are expressed deftly in valid drama.

Rush.

WAY OF ALL FLESH

Paramount picture starring Emil Jannings. Belle Bennett, Phyllis Haver and Donald Keith featured. Directed by Victor Fleming from P. P. Sheehan's story. Adaptation and screen play by Lajos Biro and Jules Furthman respectively. Julian Johnson credited with titles and Victor Milner, cameraman. At the Rialto, New York, on grind, commencing June 25. Running time, 90 mins.

August Schilling	Emil Jannings
Mrs. Schilling	Belle Bennett
Mayme	Phyllis Haver
August, Jr.	Donald Keith
The Tough	Fred Kohler

The last time Emil Jannings was at this house "Variety" was his picture. It remained quite a while, much longer than this current picture will linger, but it's not true comparison to parallel the two pictures. "The Way of All Flesh" has neither the fire nor composition of "Variety" yet, as a sample of what Jannings is going to do on this side, it suffices to the extent that it will probably draw them back to see his next film. Fair enough.

No specific punch to this initial made-in-the-U. S. A. Jannings release. It really amounts to a study by the star of a middle class character who succumbs, just once, to the feminine and must forever after live in hiding while his family believes him dead and enjoys prosperity through one of the sons' violin concerts. Starting in 1910, the story weaves its way up to the present year, giving opportunity to display three characterizations in as many makeups.

First as the bewhiskered gruff and trusted cashier of a Milwaukee bank, second as under the influence of a demi-mondaine, thereby shorn of his facial growth, and finally as a broken example of indiscretion cleaning up park playgrounds and peddling chestnuts.

This all takes an hour and a half to tell which, incidentally, is more than necessary and above what house managers are going to allow when it is in the regular program houses. There is much that will and can come out. However, it's only just to say that as unwinding at the Rialto the leaning toward tediousness is not serious enough to handicap the interest Jannings evolves and sustains.

Fleming has followed the German method as the average American screen audience has come to recognize it. Possibly because he believes it the best for the results in a story of this type or, perhaps, due to Jannings' choice in the matter. Milner, the photographer, cooperated nicely for double exposures, dissolves, etc., while Fleming has suggested things here and there by bits that demonstrate thought on the subject, albeit there is nothing revolutionary to be seen. A well made picture lacking brilliance will sum it up technically.

In substance the story revolves around the incident of Schilling (Mr. Jannings) being entrusted with valuable bonds to be sold in Chicago. On the train he meets Mayme (Phyllis Haver), obviously attired for the character, who ultimately leads him to a drunken sleep in a hotel where she rifles him of his consignment. Awakening and realization take Schilling back to the cafe of the previous night, where a fuss with Mayme leads to her lover, recipient of the bonds, crashing a chair over the frantic cashier's head.

Schilling is dragged to the railroad tracks, where he regains consciousness as the chair wielder is relieving him of his valuables. The struggle ends as Schilling accidently pushes his assailant in front of an on-rushing train. As the latter has taken all identification marks on Schilling, the finding of the disfigured body is presumed to be Schilling with newspaper accounts crediting him with a valiant battle gainst bandits.

The finish is Schilling, as a beggar, outside his own home on Christmas eve peering through the windows and finally disappearing up the street in a blizzard. A stock situation held up by Jannings.

Picture is not without comedy, although this is concentrated in the early footage and making its appearance in directorial attempts for naturalness. After Schilling discovers he has been robbed it's all drama, heavy-footed and actually heavily lensed on Jannings' feet, very much as in "The Last Laugh."

Belle Bennett, in another mother role, is dormant through frugal opportunities. She hasn't had so little to do before a camera in some time. Miss Haver does well as the seductress, while Donald Keith makes the violin playing son a sincere contribution.

Most of the production is studio made, although there are theatre and amusement park sequences, the last named inviting various camera angles, one or two of which stand out.

As regards Jannings, he does here what anyone will expect of him if familiar with his work. His characterization is a fine piece of acting and holds a wealth of detail. This, his first domestic made picture, is assuredly creditable. Not great, but program material that will appease those who scoff at pictures for their impossible situations and sugary sweetness. For the rank and file it's a little more serious than the average diet and figures to keep them looking no matter how lightly they dismiss it after it's over.

Sid.

BROADWAY NIGHTS

Robert Kane production, released by First National. Lois Wilson starred, Sam Hardy featured. Directed by Joseph C. Boyle. Adapted by Forrest Halsey from story by Norman Houston. At Strand, New York, week June 25. Running time, around 55 minutes.

Fannie Fanchette	Lois Wilson
Johnny Fay	Sam Hardy
Baron	Louis John Bartels
Bronson	Philip Strange
Dancer	Barbara Stanwick
Night Club Producer	"Bunny" Weldon

An old-fashioned story filmed under a modern title and both wasted. About the only one to get any value out of this will be Arrow Collars, and if the Arrow Collar people did not pay for the production, they should have. As a picture it is less than so-so. It could be said that it's a "Robert Kane Picture," to describe it, according to the others Kane has been turning out, all seemingly amounting to the same in the end.

According to this picture "Broadway Nights" is one in a nite club and another at the opening of a musical show. That's a swift way to disappoint an audience expecting any picture to at least make a semblance of living up to its name.

Besides are several views of Times Square or the Broadway lane lighted up. That's where Arrow Collars come in. In all of the electrical signs, often displayed, "Arrow Collars" is the only one distinctly and always visible. In the olden vaudeville days almost any national advertiser would pay for a drop to have its name on it. Some paid cash, too. And this is a picture, supposed to exhibit throughout the world.

This story runs to two young people meeting at an amateur night in a theatre when one, the girl, got the hook by request. They then doubled up for a vaudeville act, later to do the same thing matrimonially; then go into a cabaret, to get fired, after which the husband, a piano player, went back to shooting craps, his favorite diversion, with apparently the world's record as a loser. One caption mentioned "After 20 Passes," and that sounded like a liberal estimate anytime for Johnny Fay to go broke.

The dice finally weaned his wife away. She went into a musical comedy, to get a hit (unseen) over night and a sumptuous apartment. But she still loved her husband, better than the producer, who loved her, and as Johnny was lonesome, too, now that he had turned composer and stopped gambling, it worked out all right, with Lois Wilson as the star of the new show, in the principal number that would have sent any girl leading it back to the chorus in stock burlesque.

Just about a one-dayer for the neighborhoods, where the women like sadness, a baby and weeps.

Very well balanced cast, with Louis John Bartels and Philip Strange sub-featured. It may be Bartels' first picture. He played with good judgment, but that is also true of Mr. Strange, although perhaps the credit goes to Joseph C. Boyle, the director. There's not much else to credit Boyle or anyone else with as there's not much for any of them to do in this sort of a tale that was a popular kind of a moving picture 10 or more years ago.

Though no titler mentioned, Jack Conway (Variety) must have written the captions. There's no one who can write in the Conway style, and these were unmistakably Conway's. Some were nifty, considering the disadvantages of story. In that it was another "Cabaret" for Conway.

Sime.

Land Beyond the Law

First National picture starring Ken Maynard. Directed by H. J. Brown with Dorothy Dwan as "the girl." At Loew's New York as half of double bill, one day, June 24. Running time, 69 mins.

A wild riding western that's got enough of that riding to see it through as a solo program leader.

Why it was on a double bill at the New York is one of those things. It can stand by itself in the average picture house, and three days is not stretching a point. It holds more action and better riding than many of this film stripe flashed in the Broadway de luxe houses of late. Most of it is by Maynard, who does some great work.

One of the titles gives credit to the 500,000-acre Miller and Lux ranch in northern California for the cattle scenes. These are excellent with a stampede graphically pictured for the climax. Meanwhile, Maynard is the deputy sent to clear infested Oklahoma of its rustlers. Inasmuch as there are so many cow thieves that hijacking is going on, Maynard swears in one gang as assistant deputies, and comedy and retribution follow.

Maynard is possibly not the world's greatest actor, but on a horse he can keep a cameraman pretty busy. In this instance he runs the usual gamut of vaulting mounts, etc., but reaches his high point when disconnecting the running gear of a wagon from a pair of galloping horses and riding the animals astride during a chase.

There's a lot of stuff that's implausible, for that matter, but the action is so fast that who cares? Laughs here and there, not much story, with lots of horse flesh. Maynard's animal, Tarzan, is to the fore plus human understanding—no almost about it.

A majority of the "trouping" comes from those billed under Maynard. Dorothy Dwan passes as the heroine, but the men, of course, predominate. Exteriors are pleasant and there is a tense situation in a dance hall. It's all about the struggle of a touring band of cattlemen to get their herds into open country.

Padded in spots, the 69 minutes could be handily cut. It would amplify the natural action of this film anyway. Granted that any picture playing the New York catches sympathy through not having made a Broadway house (similar to a chorus girl always having an edge on a principal when stepping out of the line to do a bit) the fact of "Land Beyond the Law" being on a double bill is a puzzle after viewing it. It's better than the billing. Not strong on acting, names or story, but "pie" for all western fans with enough horsemanship to focus the enemy eye on the sheet. *Sid.*

BACKSTAGE

Tiffany production and release. Original by Sarah Y. Mason, directed by Phil Stone. Photography, Jos. A. Dubray and Earl Walker. Features Barbara Bedford and Willie Collier, Jr. At Loew's New York as one-half double bill, one day, June 21. Running time, around 65 minutes.

Owen Mackay..........William Collier, Jr.
Julia Joyce..............Barbara Bedford
Myrtle McGinnis..........Alberta Vaughn
Fanny.......................Eileen Percy
Jane......................Shirley O'Hara
Frank Carroll.............Gayne Whitman
Flo.........................Jocelyn Lee
Mike Donovan.............Guinn Williams
Charlie..................Jimmy Harrison
Harry....................Brooks Benedict
Mr. Durkin................Lincoln Plumer
Landlady....................Marcia Harris
Referee......................Louis Carver
Eddie.........................John Batten

A good picture of chorus girls, but "Backstage" lacks a decided kick. It should be interesting and particularly in those sections where there is a large fan trade of the youngsters. This picture can play anywhere. It has been kept scrupulously clean and sets forth the good, hard working chorus girls who must make their way by themselves.

Tiffany can sell "Backstage" with confidence, and it will satisfy, but will do only average business. Although average business nowadays on the feature alone is something very worth while.

The best direction bit put in by Phil Stone is a chorus girl number in a production, where the girls are opposing football teams. It's done very well. You see a flying twisted bunch of girls' legs, and with 11 girls to each side this a gingery sightly sight.

Sarah Y. Mason wrote the story. Perhaps Mr. Stone put in a couple of touches, such as the prospective "angel" and the producer of the show together. That's smart show stuff. But the authoress worked out her story along the lines of all chorus girls are not without ambition. Here they are set forth as in rehearsal, without the manager able to make a salary advance until landing a money man. Meanwhile, the girls go hungry and are driven from their boarding house.

Considerable light comedy with Alberta Vaughn given the best of that. Eileen Percy, also as another of the chorus girls, has a chance for laughs through borrowing anything she sees, slipping it down her waist and claiming it must have been lost. Rings or pins if worn by men are her chief annexing delight.

A neat situation is brought about, though not a new scheme, by having Barbara Bedford, after turned out of home, tell Gayne Whitman, as the "angel," that she lives at the Hotel Drake. He obliges her to go through with it, and accompanies her there, she taking him to his very own suite, claiming it as her own. Dropping his own key on the carpet, he picks it up as though lost by the girl and unlocks the door. She enters to find a note left by the backer's companion from another show, saying she had gone away for three weeks.

Miss Bedford remains in the apartment with her chorus girl friends and their Johns calling. They start to raise roughhouse, but are stopped when the man's companion suddenly returns. This leads to the finale.

Another good comedy scene is a taxicab bit. On the rainy night the girls were turned out, they saw a taxi parked on the curb with the driver asleep just inside the garage. No place to go and wet, they take possession of the car, pull down the blinds and sleep until the morning when the driver awakes, discovering them. Miss Vaughn kids him, also a cop, and attaches the hick driver as her steady. Inside the cab the girls had partially disrobed.

Another disrobing scene is in the apartment, but since this is a chorus girl picture disrobing means little, although it looks good.

Usual implication by the backer that the girl he wants to make, Miss Bedford, will be elevated from the chorus, but the good girl note runs throughout, the love interest, never strong, centered upon Miss Bedford and Willie Collier, Jr.

Mr. Whitman does an excellent performance in the role of the wise sucker. Guinn Williams as the producer, also played well and with restraint. He didn't wear a derby at an angle nor did he have a half smoked cigar stuck to one side of his mouth. Chorus girl end also nicely subdued, but peppery.

Principal girls gave an even performance in a well balanced cast that in Alberta Vaughn and Eileen Percy holds names of as much if not more importance for billing than Miss Bedford or Mr. Collier. The four names may be featured. You can't tell at Loew's New York where everything not on the screen is buried, because the picture is an indepenednt. It was also on a double feature day, with the other half a Fred Thomson (F. B. O.). That's enough to tell a lot. *Sime.*

CALIFORNIA

Metro-Goldwyn-Mayer production starring Tim McCoy with Dorothy Sebastian featured. Directed by W. S. Van Dyke from Frank Davis' adaptation of a Peter B. Kyne story. Cameraman, Clyde De Vina. In cast, Marc McDermott, Lillian Leighton, Frank Currier. Running time, 56 mins. At Loew's American, New York, June 23-26.

The association of W. S. Van Dyke, director; Tim McCoy, star, and Dorothy Sebastian, leading lady, continues in this fairly good "action" production. The Tim McCoy pictures were projected to fill a need in the M-G-M program, and they should pass the test pretty well, or have to date.

Peter B. Kyne authored this story, which deals with California in the days of its Mexican provinceship. While the sub-titles studiously avoid mention of Mexico, alluding to it as a "foreign power" when at all, the villainy is attempted by Mexicans and thwarted by the always-efficient American hero, so that the picture hardly qualifies as one that will make any hit south of the Rio. On the other hand, there is still no reason why it should be offensive.

In the course of military maneuvers of no great excitement or conviction, McCoy has a tempestuous love affair with a haughty senorita who feels duty-bound to hate him because he is an American, but loves him because he is such a dashing fellow. Miss Sebastian, whose brunet beauty is very Spanish, is an entirely plausible reason for a romantic brody on the part of the American. Incidentally, Miss Sebastian gets a lot more pep and animation into her performance than she has heretofore. She seems to be graduating from the class of the beautiful and dumb.

The production standards are sufficient, although the military clashes, notably the cavalry stuff late in the picture are strictly sham battle.

NO MAN'S LAND

Hal Roach film released by Pathe. Directed by Fred Jackman from the story by F. Richard Jones. Starring Rex, the horse. Features Barbara Kent and James Finlayson. At Loew's N. Y., June 17, as half double feature program.

Excellent western production suffering from padding. Too long, but otherwise okay.

It's one of the very few western pictures with real laughs. A closeup on a checker game which is to settle the fate of the crippled miner and his daughter sets a high standard of comedy. The lighter attempts, far from detracting, add to the dramatic punch in the film.

Finlayson shows up strongly as a character at which many actors in westerns have aimed but have never achieved. The easy, almost supercilious attitude masking polished strength has been so often portrayed with ridiculous results that Finlayson should prove a treat.

The story is simple but carries tremendous appeal. Had the producers wanted to make a higher grade production they could easily have done so.

The outlaws, one beyond redemption, find a gold mine belonging to another. Instead of shooting the owner they have an accident happen to him which breaks his legs.

The miner's daughter (Barbara Kent) is then at the mercy of the two outlaws. The girl is prepared to fall in love with someone and she takes a liking to the younger of the two men. This mainly causes the split between the two cronies who had not liked each other too much previously.

Rex and a white mare are nicely woven into the story. Two donkeys and the miner furnish the comedy.

Miss Kent looks and acts well. A couple of the almost nude scenes will not stand much chance with the censors out of town.

MODERN DAUGHTERS

W. R. Johnston presents this Trem Carr Production featuring Edna Murphy and Bryant Washburn. J. S. Wodehouse did the story with C. J. Hunt directing. At Loew's New York as half of double bill, one day, June 24. Running time, 60 mins.

If all modern daughters were as hair-brained as this particular one, there'd be a lot of spanking—and that'd be that. Unfortunately, an indulgent father figures there's only one specified use for a hair brush. Add to that a suave villain who owns the outlying village "dive," plus the editor of the town paper, who fears not the politicians, sees something worth reclaiming under the blonde bob—shake well, stir three times and start on your vacation.

This is one of those hippity-hop things that those who delight in rolling hoops and playing pom-pom-cuckedy-coo will watch while munching lollypops to exit and wonder if dubiously they'll ever be like that. For adult consumption it is strictly among the flyweights. Where anything goes for one day "Modern Daughters" should rate as a filler, although added program value is desirable.

There is the usual beach swimming and bathing suit dancing party arrived at through much hysterical driving, whence the editor's innocent car is forced over an embankment. But such a slight tumble doesn't upset this journalist (Bryant Washburn). It's such a trivial matter that he even joins the kids' party. This and that, and more of that, finally winding up with the hero and heroine (Edna Murphy) being framed into the roadhouse the night of the long expected raid.

Inasmuch as the menace takes a pot shot at the editor, misses and kills the father, there comes the w. k. search for the Governor, who must grant the stay of execution, as, of course, the ed. is on his way to see the noose, reported currently playing on the Coast.

Looks very much like a "quickie" of no story potency. Miss Murphy has a screen appearance that rates a chance in something better, while Washburn can prove he's done better things.

On double bills, probably yes, but only alone where there is not more than one daily paper in the town. *Sid.*

What Happened to Father

Warner Bros. production of Mary Roberts Rinehart's story. Directed by John G. Adolfi. Cameraman Willard Van Enger. Running time, 50 mins. In projection room, June 17.

Father............................Warner Oland
Betty.......................Flobelle Fairbanks
Detective Dibbin.........William Demarest
Mother..............................Vera Lewis
Victor Smith........................John Miljan
Tommy Dawson....................Hugh Allan
Violet........................Cathleen Calhoun
Gloria............................Jean Lafferty

Moderately amusing light comedy in the "worm that turned" division. So high-salaried a writer as Mary Roberts Rinehart uses plot formulas quite as old and hackneyed as any minor scenarist it seems.

After years of being domineered by a strong-willed wife, the affable but absent-minded husband has a series of dumb adventures culminating in an assertion of his manly rights in the household.

In this instance, father is an Egyptologist given to long abstractions over ponderous volumes. On the q. t., however, he has a secret ambition. He is the author under a nom-de-plume of librettos for musical comedies. While attending the rehearsals of his show, he is lured to one of those wild parties so frequent back stage, according to the movies. There he meets the "angel" behind his producers. The angel is the self-same Mr. Smith engaged to marry the Egyptologist's daughter on the following day. The plot merely asks the audience to believe that a father who is professedly fond of his daughter has never seen the man she is marrying.

Warner Oland, character actor of a wide range, was seemingly on strange ground in this role, but carried it through acceptably. He is featured. Sub-featured is Flobelle Fairbanks, a niece, according to report, of the great Doug, and William Demarest, once of the two-a-day. Miss Fairbanks is one of several young leading women Warners are grooming. She makes an appealing figure for the camera. Demarest is doing very well for so new a recruit to the studios. The cast also includes Vera Lewis, ever the aggressive, and John Miljan, ever the menace.

Production good, and there are some laughs contained in the subtitles whose authorship is uncredited. In summary, "What Happened" falls into the in-between category.

Silver Comes Through

F. B. O. production and release. Fred Thomson starred. Directed by Lloyd Ingraham. No writer mentioned. At Loew's New York, one-half double feature bill, one day, June 21. Running time, about 55 minutes.

Fred	Fred Thomson
Lucindy	Edna Murphy
Zeke, ranch owner	William Courtright
Stanton	Harry Woods
Mrs. Bryce-Collins	Mathilde Brundage
Silver King	Himself

Fred Thomson, the "western" star, is rated highly intelligent, besides being a crack western rider and player. But in "Silver Comes Through," an ordinary Kentucky Derby sort of story told in another way, he permitted two incidents that reach the limit to absurdity. And the picture is so flat otherwise that it will sell only where Thomson can sell anything.

The big noise is a four-mile steeplechase, well done and made fast with good camera shots of oncoming racers over a rough, treacherous course. That's okay by itself and should hold up the picture notwithstanding, if only dumbbells watch it. But right in the center of the race when Silver King, with Thomson riding, goes to a fall, Thomson hangs around, feeling the horse to see if injured, and then argues with the villain, who also had taken a fall at the same spot. Accusing the villain of tripping his horse, Thomson starts a fist fight, finally knocking his man into a creek. He then remounts and goes on to win the race. The only thing Thomson overlooked was to have had his dinner, too.

The other logical fluke was when Thomson caught up with a freight where Silver King had been placed, following the villain's theft of the horse. Knocking out the two attendants in the box car, Thomson mounted the horse and drove him out of the car while the train was moving. You saw them sliding down a hill, but Thomson reached the race track just in time to get in under the flag for the start.

No locale mentioned, but as the ranch owner with his niece and the horse, besides the horse race, were there, if it weren't intended for Kentucky it should have been.

The seeming contempt of some of these westerners for their audience is beyond comprehension. Here is a story that must have been written in the making, dependent upon the steeplechase, and those two bits enough to ask whether the western picture makers or their audiences are crazy.

Playing all right. Nothing difficult other than the riding.

Thomson is going over to Paramount. Maybe he's there already. He'd better get an author. *Sime.*

Tongues of Scandal

Sterling production, produced and directed by Roy Clements from a story by Adele de Vore. Cameraman, Leon Shamroy. William Desmond and Mae Busch co-starred. Running time, 54 mins. On double feature bill at Arena, one day, June 22.

A peach of a drama for the independent market. It represents first-class production standards all the way, is well cast, neatly directed for the most part, and carries a story less hackneyed than ordinarily. It is plenty strong enough to stand on its own, although in the congested big cities it may get shoved in, as at the Arena, as a double-header.

Mae Busch and William Desmond are two pretty well-known camera celebs whose names in connection with "Tongues" ought to possess some box office drag.

The action concerns the aristocratic Rhodes family. A younger son (Ray Hallor) while traveling in Europe has had an affair with a girl. His mother cables the American consul to prevent the marriage. As a result the girl who is with child commits suicide and the Rhodes family comes near to a bad scandal.

The older son of the family is Governor of Kentucky and engaged to marry a girl from a far-off state. She is the sister of the girl suicide, and by accidentally discovering some documents on her wedding night she believes the governor is responsible for her sister's tragedy.

The bride's purpose becomes one of ruining her husband instead of loving and helping him. The governor is up for re-election and she is the opposition's best ammunition. By continually causing the tongues of scandal to wag through her daring conduct she is turning the public against her husband. In the end, of course, she learns the truth, and the pair are reunited.

In some of the delicate sequences the director almost let his subject slip away from him, but despite this the job as a whole is very good. The lighting, acting and sets are in keeping with high-grade production standards. Miss Busch carries sex appeal, and if the picture is laughless it will not be minded where a two-reeler is slipped in on the bill for balance.

Heroes of the Night

Gotham Production produced by Sam Sax. Directed by Frank O'Connor. Supervised by Renaud Hoffman. Story by James J. Tynan. Cameraman, Ray June. Co-features Cullen Landis and Marion Nixon. Distributed by Lomax Corp. At Columbus theatre, New York, one day, June 25. Running time, 65 mins.

Tom Riley	Rex Lease
Joe Riley	Cullen Landis
Mary	Marion Nixon
Jack Nichols	Wheeler Oakman
Bull Corrigan	Robt. Honans
Mrs. Riley	Sarah Padden
Reporter	Lois Ingraham

It hasn't been many years ago when Sam Sax could have made two mellers out of the stuff that has been crammed into this one. There is enough action to satisfy the independent exhib who craves lots of fighting and what-not in his film fare these days. There are some sections of this one that old A 1 tension; has a real punch, but the over-zealousness to give too much just about removes the big effects desired.

Story of two Irish boys, one a fire laddie and the other a cop, who fall for the same girl, yet throughout are fighting villains and fires in the way audiences demand, so that their heroes face death many times in effecting rescues and making arrests.

There is some of the old-time plot wherewithal that is worked overtime, you know the kind about the newspaper woman who uncovers an election plot and the subsequent overthrow of a gang determined to cop the spoils at any cost and one of the dashing heroes of the "night" rushing in and fighting his head off to place justice where it belongs.

Some corking photography. Enough fine shots to keep a camera shooter like June working for moons to come. And a lot to the direction that spreads a feather or two in the cap of the megaphone handlers.

An old, old story, but given enough screen latitude to satisfy the boys and girls who revel in fist fights and rise from their seats when the fire engines are on their way to a big "studio" fire. It's all in the works and the audience knows the finale by heart, but it's melodrama served redhot and at a dime or two bits, not so bad. *Mark.*

THE FLYING MAIL

A. Carlos production and Pathe release. Stars Al Wilson in a story by F. H. Clarke, crediting Mason Noel as director. Cast includes Carmellita Geraghty, Harry von Meter, Eddie Gribbon, Kathleen Myers and Frank Tomick. At Stanley, New York, one day, June 18 Running time, 45 mins.

An air mail story thinly spread over a series of stunts with Al Wilson as the principal chance taker. An explanatory pledge-slide states no double or trick photography is employed. The actual unwinding on the plane to plane stuff, leap from motorcycle to suspended ladder from an under carriage and a hand-to-hand fight on a wing of one of the air machines bears out the guarantee. For a one-day stop-over, or to split honors with another film, "The Flying Mail" should satisfy, minus sensationalism.

Wilson is cast as a mail flier framed by crooks to believe he is married after emerging from the fog of a drug, delayed so that the bandit-aviator gets his plane with the money. Then the chase to square himself with his employer and the latter's daughter. Another robbery is rung in and Eddie Gribbon as an amateur detective for comedy.

The padding awkward and unrelieved by interesting cast support, inasmuch as the players have nothing with which to work. Gribbon is capable of better things than this, but does as best he can. Neither of the women, the Misses Geraghty and Myers, could have lost weight, while this was in the making. Harry von Meter is the villain.

Not much attempt at love interest, the concentration being on the thrills and comedy. The finish of the struggle on the wing has a nice twist in both men clinging to each other and making a descent to earth by parachute. Not too clearly cameraed. However, at least one man attached to a parachute leaves the plane in the midst of the struggle.

Wilson is evidently more at home stunting than acting, but is adequate for this occasion. One fair-sized interior is flashed, but otherwise production is mostly concerned with aeroplane rentals. *Sid.*

The Little Adventuress

P. D. C. production, directed by William DeMille. Vera Reynolds featured. Adapted from the A. A. Milne stage play, "The Dover Road." At Tivoli, on 8th avenue, New York, one half double feature, one day, June 20. Running time, 60 minutes.

To say that "The Little Adventuress" might please the motherly neighborhood women is saying all this picture is entitled to. It's broad farce, utterly silly in the making. While the broadly farcical matter at times will bring a few laughs from the kind of women mentioned, they are just as apt to fetch snorts from the men. One day should be plenty anywhere, and like the Tivoli, to double it up may be the safer way.

The little adventuress is a little fool and the other woman no smarter. With that as the basis and remembering the title, the director attempted to slip in too much. He tried to mix devilment and innocence, sex and prudery, callousness and gentility, until all of the characters are playing in a false key and the net answer is the hokum bunk.

If "The Dover Road," a play from which this thing was adapted for screening purposes, ever meant anything as a run on Broadway, then (without wasting the time to look up the record) it must have been through the kindness of Joe Leblang, the helpful one-half cut ticket man. It's 30c. top at the Tivoli. If many of these went in there, even for the far west siders, cut rates would shortly follow also.

It's just the silliness of the story. Everything else okay. Too bad the director and the cast should have been wasted. For these films do cost money.

Besides Vera Reynolds, featured, were Phyllis Haver, Robert Ober, Theodor Kosloff and others. It made little difference who was who on the screen. Whether Miss Haver was the wife, which she was, or Miss Reynolds the little adventuress which she wasn't, or what roles the men played or else.

After the yawning period started in early, who was who became the least, while "The End" was the most important of a stupid picture. *Sime.*

His Rise to Fame

Commonwealth production, starring George Walsh. Directed by Bernard McKeever from a story by Victoria Moore. In the cast: Martha Petelle, Ivan Linou, Bradley Parker, Mildred Reardon, Peggy Shaw and William Nally. Running time, 56 mins. On double-feature bill at Tivoli, New York, one day, June 15.

Not a bad little picture, despite all it lacks (plenty) in production, lighting and directorial detail. The story is straightforward, with considerable action. The same story produced right with a bank roll might come close to being an epic among the prize-fight operas. It has a kinship with the cauliflower profession and its invariable affinity with honkey-tonk cabarets that gives the picture a vitality better productions have not possessed.

George Walsh, starred, is a roustabout whose boss in firing him in the first 100 feet of film calls him a dissipated gambling bum, or words to that effect.

Besides reading the racing charts, George maintains a vest pocket directory of phone numbers, and is, all in all, a very human and affable guy for a movie hero. In a cabaret he falls for a girl entertainer, but, getting into a fight, takes it on the jaw from a pug and retires in humiliation. To make good with the dame and also in shame that his elderly mother should go out looking for work, due to his shiftlessness, George buckles down and is presently discovered by the proprietor of a gymnasium to be a potential fighter.

The crooked promoter (Bradley

Parker), with a yen for the cafe entertainer (Peggy Shaw), frames to foul George in his first fight, so that he will make a poor showing and the girl will think him a coward.

From then to the denouement it's familiar stuff.

The Broadway Drifter

Excellent Production presented by Sam Zierler. Directed by Bernard McVetty, from the story by William B. Laub. Starring George Walsh, Dorothy Hall featured. Cast includes Arthur Donaldson, Gladys Valerie, Bigelow Cooper, Nellie Savage and Paul Doucet. At the Stanley, New York, one day, June 8.

A poorly directed picture, tiresome and chockful of tedious detail. At its best the story is hackneyed. Not worthwhile beyond the short stand grinds.

George Walsh is still a good bet for some independent producer running shy of leading men or male stars. But "The Broadway Drifter" shows exactly how George should not be handled.

Dorothy Hall is okeh as the female lead without a chance in a production of this sort. Everything that could be done to detract from interest in the two young people was done. At the most inopportune moments, just as the scenes are beginning to get warm, the uncle is shot in, for no good reason, to crab the love scenes by raising his hands in blessing.

The climax hinges on the exposure of Walsh as the son of a rival airplane manufacturer. As the assistant to the girl's uncle he was in a position to steal certain "plans." He could easily have proven that he had not been near the paternal mansion for six months, but the director apparently insisted that the uncle refuse to accept an explanation.

Cheap sets, action taking place in three or four interiors.

FAST AND FURIOUS

Universal production and release. Starring Reginald Denny. Directed by Melville W. Brown from story by Denny. Adaptation by Raymond Cannon. Running time, 64 minutes. At Paramount, New York, week July 2.

Tom Brown	Reginald Denny
Ethel	Barbara Worth
Miller	Claude Gillingwater
Dupont	Armand Kaliz
Joe	Lee Moran
Hodge	Charles K. French
Coachman	Wilson Benge
Doctor	Robert E. Homan
Shorty	Kingsley Benedict
Englishman	Edgar Norton

As far as known this is Denny's first effort to provide his own story. It's a good story along familiar Denny lines, well thought out, based on sound farcical principles and good for quite a few laughs. That "Fast and Furious" falls somewhat shy of the satisfaction-giving qualities of earlier scenarios not authored by the star is not necessarily his fault. Nor is there any vital flaw in the direction of Melville Brown. The fault can probably be blamed on luck.

No reason why the Denny fans and the regular Denny stands shouldn't go for this one. It's a funny picture qualified merely by the statement that it's not as funny as Denny is generally expected to be.

Denny built his story around a speed maniac who gets bested on the road by a speed crank. After leaving the hospital his former affection for automobiles has become a pronounced aversion. His nerves jump at the sight of every gas buggy he passes and the honk of a horn drives him mad. Accordingly he charters a hansom cab and sets out to find the daughter of the cranky guy. He is, of course, mistaken for a great racing driver and obliged to drive the crank's entry in the sweepstakes to make good with the pretty daughter.

Barbara Worth, one of the Wampas' selections, is the heroine. She registered nicely and exhibited a Greta Garbo bob. Claude Gillingwater as the cranky father had the only other role of length.

The Flag Lieutenant

British-made picture distributed by Paramount. Adapted from story by Majors W. P. Drury and L. Trevor. Cast includes Henry Edwards, Fred Raynham, Fenlas Lewellyn, Hayford Hobbs, Humberstone Wright, Forrest Harvey, Lionel D'Aragon, Lilian Oldand and Dorothy Seacomb. At the Capitol, Montreal, week June 26. Running time, 101 mins.

One of those pictures indorsed by the British Admiralty and showing at the Capitol, Montreal, during Canada's Confederation Week (Dominion's Diamond Anniversary), and therefore well seasoned with propaganda for king and empire. It's a naval film that, minus the reams of padded celluloid which carries it over an hour and a half on running time, could go into the States and stand up in the daily change houses.

Substitute his majesty's marines and sailors for our well-known screen formula of "the Yanks are coming," and you have the story of the isolated fort attacked by a horseless Mediterranean tribe. It brings the British navy to the rescue plus the sidelight story of the characters which, once it gets under way, holds interest.

This tells of a marine major and a young naval leutenant who are pals, with the major never having had a chance to stand out during 23 years of service. The youngster has flitted in and out of numerous scraps to win decorations, despite a frivolous attitude. Dispatched on a destroyer to save the fort, the major is in charge of the landing party, but an ammunition shortage makes it a tough situation in face of the new arrivals.

The major determines to break through the enemy lines to get word to the anchored destroyer, the fort's wireless being destroyed, but is wounded in the head as he climbs over a wall and loses all memory of the incident.

Meanwhile the young lieut carries on, gets word to the ship, returns and remains quiet when the major is given credit for the heroism. Complications ensue through no one being able to find the lieutenant during the battle. He is ostracized upon returning to the fleet and is headed for a court-martial. The major's fiancee finally happens upon the solution, tells the admiral. But nothing is announced outside of official vindication of the lieutenant's name, the major retaining his decoration and promotion and the lieut winning the admiral's daughter. There is no villain.

Shots of a naval regatta, the fleet cheering the king, etc., are all included, besides seaplanes finally saving the fort. Over and above the propaganda angle, if sufficiently cut, this one should stand up for a day, maybe three, on the theory that the American public might like to take a look at someone else's defense system for a change.

The battle stuff has been camaraed well enough, but the direction on the actual story is unquestionably bad, mostly for the reason that the director apparently couldn't find a means to end his scenes and received no help from the cutter. At least 30 minutes can come out of this picture with no harm done. Most of the padding is within the opening four reels. Neither is it the naval stuff, the waste being in the try for comedy.

Henry Edwards plays the title role, registering better in the serious sequences than when doing comedy. There are indications that he can handle a laugh assignment, but not here where there is no material with which to work. More giggles supposedly come from an ordinary seaman and a marine private who team throughout the film. Lillian Oldand is the admira's daughter, opposite Edwards, and is away from the American conception of a screen heroine. Nothing doll-like about Miss Oldand, who nevertheless has charm, dignity and a sweet appearance on the screen. The only other woman, Miss Seacomb, is a trifle heavy, but turns in some nice work. She is blonde, while Miss Oldand is dark. The men are uniformly okay, if a bit stiff, while there isn't much of a production effort outside of the battle items.

Ostensibly booked at this house for Canada's week of concentrated patriotism, "The Flag Lieutenant" will please, should draw business and figures to repeat the score in any of the provinces with or without governmental emphasis.

To those who have heard time and again of the mediocracy of British films this particular effort may be something of a surprise. It has a number of faults, but not so many that astute cutting would have saved it for favorable comparison with some of the better independent releases to which the U. S. exhib is accustomed.

Neither the name of the company or director could be caught in the opening title, due to plush curtains which masked the screen.   *Sid.*

DEARIE

Warner Bros., production featuring Irene Rich. Directed by Archie Mayo. Adapted by Anthony Coldeway from story by Carolyn Wells. At Roxy, New York, week July 2. Running time 65 minutes.

Sylvia Darling	Irene Rich
Stephen Darling	William Collier, Jr.
Ethel Jordan	Edna Murphy
Samuel Manley	Anders Randolf
Luigi	Richard Tucker
Paul	Arthur Rankin
Max	David Mir
Englishman	Douglas Gerrard
Maid	Violet Palmer

One of those typically formula prepared mother-love stories that the Warner Brothers must provide for Irene Rich. It is no different from any of the other ones where mother must sacrifice herself for son; latter not appreciative and then reaches his senses when something almost tragic happens. Not an expensive production, but a most satisfactory one for the program houses, as the exhibitor will never be hi-jacked for the rentals with the summer season the great time to show it in first run houses. Will not break house records, but should always keep the exhibitor out of the red.

Miss Rich has opportunity here to show her emotional and devotional sides. The background for this is perfect with her performance practically the same as it is in all pictures of this type. William Collier, Jr., as the spoiled and weakling son, gets away with his role nicely even down to the point of retribution.

Edna Murphy is the girl but has little opportunity. She is a looker and might do things if given the chance. Anders Randolf as a millionaire publisher who always wants to do things accomplishes his mission in a parental way without at any time having an ulterior motive.

Richard Tucker showed up well as the cabaret keeper, who respects his star and sees that everything comes out right in the end. Arthur Rankin and David Mir, school companions to the boy, and who edge him on, give excellent interpretations.

Archie Mayo directed and got several good touches in that they had exceptional comedy value. One is where the boy acts his story to the publisher. Another in cabaret where "Dearie" does one of those Tex Guinan's and asks for the "Give the girls a hand," etc. Toward the finish the story drags a bit with what seem several anti-climaxes. About three minutes can easily be cut from these ending scenes without affecting the story value any.

Photography very good, with settings adequate.   *Ung. .*

Naughty But Nice

First National release produced by John McCormick; directed by Millard Webb. Based on story by Lewis Alen Brown entitled "The Bigamists." Scenario by Carey Wilson. Starring Colleen Moore. At Strand, New York, week July 3. Running time about one hour.

Berenice Summers	Colleen Moore
Paul Carroll	Donald Reed
Judge J. R. Altwood	Claude Gillingwater
Alice Altwood	Kathryn McGuire
Paul Ames	Hallam Cooley
Mrs. Altwood	Edythe Chapman
Miss Perkins	Clarissa Selwynne
Uncle Seth Summers	Burr McIntosh

All Colleen Moore was given in the story was a series of more or less hackneyed situations from which she was asked to derive humor. She has put every ounce of facial dexterity and genius for mimicry into the picture with the result that in addition to selling herself as one of filmdom's greatest comediennes, she almost succeeds in lending an illusion of cleverness and comedy to the story. The illusion is strong enough to satisfy the mob out front and the picture can be counted on for good returns, given a fair break with the weather over the summer.

Brown's original story may possibly have been different. In its present state the tale is of the freaky country girl whose uncle has suddenly grown wealthy through oil. She is sent to a finishing school in the east with the usual awkwardness attributed to country maidens. Suffers the usual sneers, etc., until the roommate puts her wise to beauty parlors and bobbed hair minus spectacles.

Romance flirts with Berenice from the moment she falls off the train attired in a masculine raccoon coat which a catalog had assured her was extremely "collegiate." While powdering her nose Paul Carroll, the village cutup, flies past in a cream-colored limousine, splashing mud all over the Berenician countenance. After that it's love at first sight with the girl, while Paul turns up the aristocratic nose and deposits her at the servants' entrance of the school she was to attend.

After Berenice is all polished up to look beautiful for the school dance she cuts the boy dead but later repents.

Serious complications finally set in owing to the girl's lying propensities. Judge Altwood's daughter, Alice, is vaguely identified as the roommate. To avoid a reprimand from the school teacher for being in a hotel lobby unchaperoned Berenice tells of a visit to the fictitious "Gardners."

Miss Perkins accompanies the girls to the room. They enter to find a young man before a mirror putting on a shirt. The only flaw in this scene is that he hasn't his trousers on. Hide and seek for a few seconds, the inevitable discovery and ensuing embarassment. The young man, Hallam Coolley, gets behind a trunk.

Meantime the judge and his wife have been advised their daughter is visiting the Gardners. They enter the room as the two girls are leaving. On the spur of the moment Berenice says she is Mrs. Gardner, married the same day.

Coolley is in the diplomatic service and is ordered to Judge Altwood's house for duty. There the well meaning Mrs. Altwood insists on putting Berenice into the same bedroom with her alleged husband for the night.

The high spot for laughs is where Coolley is behind the trunk trying to get his trousers on and almost does a half dozen times, but for interruptions. He finally gets them on backwards.

A strong cast in support of Miss Moore. Can't miss with this one.

THE CIRCUS ACE

Fox production and release. Tom Mix starred. At Hippodrome, New York, week July 4. Running time, 57 minutes.

Tom Mix in a good story is a double pleasure.

"The Circus Ace" as a story probably ranks any regular program release a western star has had in years. It's consistent with proper continuity, and while the basic ingredients are of the formula, they are secreted here as far as the picture going public is concerned.

For the western fans, this picture is there a mile; for the Mix fans, it's perfect and at the Keith-Albee Woolworth stand for a week, all of the fans besides those who grow stubbed-nosed looking at westerns will take to the film.

It's a nice evenly balanced picture, and that it has a new leading woman or at least one who sounds new, Natalie Joyce, a girl who can do something else besides wearing make-up, may be lending an added charm. Miss Joyce is an athlete or gymnast. Despite any doubling or camera faking, the girl handles herself like an aerialist. This is made evident when she goes into the cradle to take off on the trapeze. Even though that cradle were on the ground a girl couldn't do it the way she does without experience. And Miss Joyce can smile without her mouth looking like a purple chasm.

Background is a small town tent outfit, one ring, one lion and one elephant. Also a boxing kangaroo that lands some of the several laughs in the running. Mix does stunts in and about the circus, acrobatics, climbing, jumping, riding, shooting, lassoing—in fact he works in almost all of his tricks.

At one time it seemed as though Tom was about to set a new world's record by lassoing an elephant, but instead he roped the girl on the animal.

The picture starts at a fast pace with a balloon ascension with Miss Joyce as the parachute jumper. Imagine a balloon ascension with a two-car show! Nellie Revell will die over that one.

Mix is a careless cowboy, always whittling wood. His whittling grows into a steady laugh as the picture progresses, also giving a pretty little fadeout, as, after the customary marriage, the "little chip of the old block" is seen to have picked up his pop's best habit. Tom hauls the girl off the parachute, crabbing her act and she bawls him for it.

But Tom likes the gal and wants another lamp. So he watches the circus parade the following morning. Seeing some toy balloons escaping he stops the calamity by shooting them while in the air. The shots frighten the elephant his lady friend is gracing, and the big beast starts off on a swift gallop, with Tom racing after to lasso the jane.

Then comes the villain, the political boss of Sage, Ariz. If there is a tank in Arizona by the name of Sage, its political leader had better take air or else. The boss wants the gal, holds a mortgage on the show but is willing to forego payment if, etc. And then Tom with "Tony," and the kid whittler.

An excellent Mix picture, so much so it may be said that "The Circus Ace" is the best picture the Hippodrome thus far has played, although to give the Hip due consideration, it had to play the P. D. C.'s.

The Roxy could have used this Mix film. It would have been a good change for the Roxy picture end and a great chance to send Mix away over, on Broadway, for "The Circus Ace" is more interesting as a program release than 70 percent of the stuff the Broadway houses have been using in recent months. *Sime.*

STREETS OF SORROW

Drama of German origin, designated Sofar Flm production. From novel by Hugo Bettauer. Directed by G. W. Pabst. At Cameo, New York, week July 2. Running time, 95 minutes.

Greta Rumfort....................Greta Garbo
Maria Lechner....................Asta Nielsen
Lieut. Davy, U. S. A.............Einar Hanson
The Butcher of Mercholr Street........ Werner Kraus
Councillor Rumfort...............Jaro Furth
Rosa Rumfort.....................Loni Nest
Maria's Father...................Max Kohlhase
Maria's Mother...................Silvia Torf
Mr. Rosenow......................Karl Ettlinger
His Wife.........................Ilka Grunting
His Daughter, Regina................. Countess Agnes Esterhazy
Dr. Leid, a lawyer......Alexander Mursky
Lia Leid, his wife...............Tamara
Don Alfonze Canez........Robert Garrison
Egon Stirner, his secretary..Henry Stuart
Col. Irving, U. S. A.........Mario Cusmich
Frau Greifer.....................Valesca Gert
Fraulein Henriette........Countess Tolstoi
Frau Merkel..............Edna Merkstein
Else.....................Hertha von Walther
The Waiter..........6.....Grigori Chmara
Trebitsch........................ Raskatoff
An American Soldier........Kraft Raschig

The picture's only commercial value is the presence at the head of the cast of Greta Garbo, featured in the Cameo billing. It's a lobby asset rather than a screen recommendation, for the role is a poor one of a rather furtive and bedraggled heroine which does not gain much sympathy.

The picture has minor virtues and major defects. The principal drawback is that it's fearfully long and dull, besides being hard to follow in its complications. The central idea is good. It deals with the middle class enmity in Europe toward the post-war social upstarts, rich war profiteers and dealers in the necessities of life who oppress the poor and become wealthy on hard-wrung profits. Probably the novel dealt more adequately with these materials.

The screen story gets them tangled up with shoddy melodrama in what one takes to be the red-light district of Vienna. Probably the unabridged picture would have a sex kick in some of the scenes in the equivalent of a house of assignation, but these passages have been deleted for American exposition. What is left is a long-drawn-out and generally prosey picture that bores.

The pure girl who is lured into the house of ill-fame doesn't deliver much of a sensation here. Neither does the murder mystery. One solves the mystery immediately and there isn't any suspense.

Some of the character types—the pompous butcher and the two fat, sleek profiteers among others — are excellent in portraiture, and the settings are generally interesting because they are different from the level of sameness in American productions. But the women are impossible. Nothing stimulating about a semi-slum high life. A pretty dingy lot are these Vienna daughters of joy. Several elaborate bits are introduced apparently with the intent to exploit the gay night life of Vienna. It doesn't register gaiety, but rather drab squalor.

The story constantly jumps about in confusing manner — something like a Dickens novel. This is the result of poor continuity construction. They have tried to screen the whole book instead of using skillful selection and making a clear-cut, unified story out of the matter chosen. Pictures made from novels often have this grave defect, a particularly annoying one in this case.

Photography far from high grade. Often the quality is thin and sometimes blurred, the best effects being in the handling of heavy light and shade masses. Worst of all, the whole affair has an atmosphere of artificiality and the consequent absence of illusion. *Rush.*

RIDING TO FAME

Ellbee picture, presented by W. T. Lackey. Director not billed. Photographed by K. C. MacLean and Leonard Cline. Cast includes Gladys McConnell, Arthur Rankin, Bert Tansey, Rosemary Theby, George Fawcett, Henry Sedley, Dora Baker. At Loew's New York, one day, July 1, on double-feature bill. Running time, 60 minutes.

Outside Loew's New York, George Fawcett was getting exclusive billing on this picture. Inside, Mr. Fawcett unhappily died almost immediately after the picture opened, but not before the picture had his "name" in its lineup.

This hiring of a "name" for just a few feet of film and giving him extensive billing is a common trick among the quickie factories. In case that doesn't peg the type of film this is, it might be mentioned that in the three separate horse races the same grandstand shots are used. A chubby gent in the foreground became quite well known before the picture had ended.

Still, this stuff has a market. Several people leaving the house were heard to remark that it was "nice." And if they think so there must be plenty more like 'em.

Technically, the picture is rancid. Director neglected to carry his love theme and the fadeout of the juvenile team with a baby between them looked almost immoral. There had been no reason given previously for that.

Numerous "cheater" insertions for the horse races were too obvious and tended to hurt some genuine shots. Acting muffed almost all around.

The title isn't in the story. It's about a crippled dame left one horse and no dough by her old man. She wants to be operated on so she can walk. Three former employes of her dad manage to win a race for her, and get some coin. Then she marries the jockey.

Photography not annoying.

If you book it, Finnegan, it's in again, out again.

AINT LOVE FUNNY?

F. B. O. production and release with Alberta Vaughn featured. Story by Lila Gedley and Kay Klemore. Directed by Del Andrews. At Arena, 8th avenue, New York, one-half double bill one day, July 1. Running time, 53 minutes.

"Aint Love Funny?" may be a self-answerer as a usual thing, but here the answer is "No." This F. B. O. near-comedy on a double bill at the Arena could be a one-dayer anywhere else. Not over that with the far side neighborhoods preferred, or in such houses as don't care how long they run if they are cheap enough.

Nothing particularly the matter with the picture, except that it failed to turn out as designed. A nice performance by Alberta Vaughn is its single recommendation. There are some types that will strike some neighborhoods as humorous in their looks and make up; there are a couple of laughs also for the same neighborhoods, but there's mighty little comedy in the picture or in Neal O'Hara's titles. If Mr. O'Hara is new at titling, that's an excuse; if not, he'd better snap 'em up and plenty.

It's about a girl who wants to go to war, but her father and fiance interpose an objection just about as she is going on the transport. Back home, pop tells her she can do anything if only remaining at home. With her fiance not going across, she returns his ring a couple of times, and then invites doughboys waiting for their boat to come up to the house. They do in squads and companies. It drives father to his club.

Over there, through a couple of location scenes, the same soldiers receive a form letter from her, all saying that upon their return she will marry them. Each receiving the letter, cherishes it and when returning, flock up to her house in a mob for her promise. To evade them, the girl confesses her love for Elmer Murphy, a former plumber, thought to have been killed. Elmer arrived the same day, probably by airplane. To escape him after an ordinary chase the girl marries her fiance in a justice's court.

Babe London is the other girl and needs to be fitted with a role or clothes. She's all heft. The men play all right for what's needed.

It didn't just turn out, that's all. And two people had to write it. For the regulars it's a yawner. *Sime.*

FIRE AND STEEL

W. T. Lackey presents "Fire and Steel" with Mary McAlister, Burr McIntosh, Philo McCullough, Cissy Fitzgerald and Jack Perrin in the cast. Directed by Bertram Bracken. Distributed by Ellbee, at Stanley, New York, July 1, one day. Running time, 62 minutes.

Hot times around a steel plant any old day in the year it is running on all furnaces. That "hot" applies to the heat necessary to turn out finished steel. Now and then a picture concern comes along and figures a steel story just about fills a long felt want, very often filled in the past.

In this one the plot was almost

lost in the running once the furnace scenes were being shown and for much of the way the players seemed to be running around in circles.

Story pretty thin, hackneyed in theme. It made one wonder how old this picture could be. Credit must be given the director and the camera man for some very fine shots inside the plant.

Several players tried hard to make mountains out of molehills. Even the lustre of such "names" from the dramatic annals as Burr McIntosh and Cissy Fitzgerald failed to lift the picture very high. They handled several scenes nicely but there was too apparent a "padding." *Mark.*

NO CONTROL

P. D. C. release featuring Phyliss Haver and Harrison Ford. Directed by Scott Sidney. In cast, Jack Duffy, Tom Wilson. Running time, 60 minutes. On double bill, Tivoli, New York, one day, June 30.

Limited time, thought and bankroll seemingly in this expanded two-reeler. Silly plot of the farce type and indifferent score on laughs taking the reaction of the Tivoli audience as the gauge.

Phyliss Haver and Harrison Ford are featured. Miss Haver's value here is her increasing box office power. Ford also may have a following, particularly where this picture is apt to be played as he's been in nothing else but for quite a spell. The weight of that drawing power should be the answer for the exhibitor who asks himself: "Shall I book it?"

In the hodge-podge of hokum is the toothless Jack Duffy, of two-reel fame, and Tom Wilson with his familiar blackface character.

There is a horse with lots of speed but an unreliable disposition. He is afraid of lions. Radio ear phones are attached to the equine ears and the roaring of a lion is broadcast for the special benefit of the nag. The $10,000 purse is won by the horse who thinks a lion is at his heels.

Frank Condon, a scribe of some note, is credited with the story.

Shamrock and the Rose

Chadwick production. Adaptation of Owen Davis play. Directed by Jack Nelson. Cast includes Mack Swain, Olive Hasbrouck. Edmund Burns, Maurice Costello, Wm. Straus, Dot Farley. At Loew's New York one day, July 1, on double-feature bill. Running time, about 55 minutes.

Owen Davis may have written something like this, and again maybe not. The files carry no record of such a play. And the story is a puzzle in familiarity.

If any of the smaller stands have had much luck with the Jewish-Irish pictures they can use this one. It's like the rest, except not so good. Photography terrible. Yet a day in the one-days all right.

Two families, one Jewish and other Irish. Irish son loves the Jewish daughter, but the parents don't like the idea. Family feud on for some time. After the youngsters have secretly married, reconciliation.

Yes, there have been other pictures something like this.

Acting isn't bad. Mack Swain does a slapstick Irishman with good results, and William Straus, the racial antithesis, gets his comedy, also. Others do enough for the money. Costello has a minor part, although given exclusive billing outside the house..

Photography is the worst of the picture; direction fairly close second.

Modern Commandments

Paramount production and release. Starring Esther Ralston with Neil Hamilton featured. Based on a story by Jack Lait. Screen play by Doris Anderson and Paul Gangelon. Continuity by Ethel Doherty. Titles by George Marion, Jr. Direction, Dorothy Arzner. At the Paramount, New York, week July 9. Running time, 69 minutes.

Kitten O'Day	Esther Ralston
Tod Gilbert	Neil Hamilton
Aunt Ruby	Maude Truax
Ueno	Romaine Fielding
Speeding Shapiro	El Brendel
Belle	Rose Burdick
Sharon Lee	Jocelyn Lee
Disbrow	Arthur Hoyt
Benny	Roscoe Karns

Here is a type story that might warrant keeping Esther Ralston in the ranks of the Paramount stars. Though Miss Ralston in the past has always required something which had fashion parades, etc., to show off her ability to wear clothes, this one has substance enough to give her a chance to demonstrate she is a bit of a comedienne outside of being cataloged as a clothes-horse.

The picture so far as actual production outlay is concerned does not appear to cost anywhere near the figure of some of her preceding productions and ranks much higher from the box office angle. By no means a super production, but one that can take its place among the regular program releases and hold its own with the buyers of picture house entertainment, especially the women.

Though the Ralston pictures in the past have been defined as "women" pictures, this one being based on a smart cracking story of Broadway will also interest the male of the species. It is based on a magazine story of Jack Lait's and has received a free and comprehensive interpretation for the screen by Doris Anderson and Paul Gangelon. The continuity by Ethel Doherty seems to be faultless and handled by a fem does not miss any of the high-lights which the author possibly would have liked brought out on the screen.

George Marion, Jr., turned out a lot of snappy crackers as captions which no doubt may be utilized by the gag conversationalists of the speaking stage to good results.

Dorothy Arzner, who directed this one, handled another Ralston before it. From the manner in which she did the megaphoning here she might be teamed with Miss Ralston and given latitude in the selection of story for this star. If this is done, Miss Ralston should prove to be a great draw for Paramount, which she is not today, though coming along nicely.

The story deals with the trials and tribulations of a young composer who has written a song for the star of a musical show on the main stem. Of course, he cannot get to the star or her producer. Poverty stricken, he goes to a boarding house where Kitten O'Day is maid of all work, helping her aunt. He spills everything to the girl. She knows how to reach the producer. She visits the office, but finds she cannot get to the main guy. Then she learns that he is about to leave in his car.

She hoaxes the chauffeur to let her sit and wait. The producer comes out with the star, from whom he is trying to make a getaway. They discover Kitten in the car. The star squawks and Kitten socks her.

That makes a hit with the producer, who asks Kitten to go along. Then she broaches the song stuff to him. He in turn tells her that he wants to have some one on hand who can keep the star off his trail.

A deal is made; he clothes Kitten, gives her a car, etc. But the young composer disappears from the boarding house before the good news arrives.

The girl goes back and tells the producer she cannot find the hero. He then informs her it is necessary to have him sign a contract, otherwise the song cannot be used.

The show goes into rehearsal with Kitten in the chorus. Being a rookie the girls decide to initiate her. First they show her the "Ten Modern Commandments" on the wall, which are "Get Your Man," printed on 10 different lines in graduated type.

Something new occurs then in initiation. Instead of the old Keystone dough and custard pie tossing at the victim, a cold cream battle takes its place and all are smeared up, including the star, who enters on the scene. The heroine gives her a dose and runs her out of the dressing room.

Then she is in right with the other girls, who have no yen for the upstage dame. Rehearsal goes on with the boy still trying to get his song introduced. He is hanging out at the stage door when a messenger comes out looking for a piano tuner. Our hero volunteers, and when found faking says he has no tools. It is discovered that the piano player had let a cigar butt drop inside the instrument. It clogged the keyboard. Incidentally, it is discovered that the piano has been obtained gratis as the name of this upright is shown in a close-up.

Being on the stage, the young man decides he is going to have his inning and get to the star. He sits on top of a ladder when the tune of his song is wafted from the piano. He looks at his composer's copy and then falls against the switchboard, blowing out a main fuse he grabs in his descent. He gropes around in the dark with a flash and finds our heroine, who, of course, wants to get him to the home of the producer so the number can go on. He is pushed into the car of the girl friend with the star wanting to go along. En route she tells him the car belongs to the girl, insinuating, of course, that she is the favorite of the producer. The boy becomes enraged, meets the producer and socks him on the beezer. That upsets the latter, who boils, and when the girl comes to square, says the song is out. The star being on hand, hears it.

The girl then locks the boss in the bathroom with his valet and goes to the theatre. She gets after the star and tells her she will knock her cold if she does not use the song. Meantime a detective finds the composer, takes him to the producer's home, and when the latter is released one of those farce chases lasts to the theatre. There the number is ready to go on, when the boss calls for the halt. The heroine pleads, and finding success far off, pulls the switch and blows the main. She rushes out with a flashlight, has the tune struck up, and proceeds to lead the number. The chorus backs her up with the result, naturally, being that the composition is the hit of the show, the star is shown up and all are happy.

Plentiful use of gags and comedy sequences that make this one an amusing and laughing comedy dramatic picture. Neil Hamilton as the composer does not seem to have the chance he requires to show the ladies what a nice and manly looking lead he can make. He appears to have one of those rushing-in-and-out parts which do not give him the romantic possibilities he requires to get the okay of the fans. Jocelyn Lee is ideal as the trouble-making and turbulent star. She is good to look at and has that necessary "it" to classify as a fem menace. Arthur Hoyt in the role of the timid star shy producer gives a most commendable characterization. El Brendel is flashed on and off, given no opportunity, nor are others of the cast.

For the regular program houses this should be most satisfactory, and on a vodvil program can share the billing above the average variety program and prove good drawing card. *Ung.*

SINGED

William Fox production and release. Directed by John Griffith Wray. From the story by Adela Rogers St. John. Featuring Blanche Sweet. At the Roxy, New York, week July 9. Running time, about 60 minutes.

Dolly Wall	Blanche Sweet
Ben Grimes	Claude King
Royce Wingate	Warner Baxter
Wes Adams	Clark Comstock
Wong	James Wang
Mrs. Cardigan	Ida Darling
Jim	Alfred Allen
Amy Cardigan	Mary McAllister
Howard Halliday	Edward Davis
Ernie Whitehead	Edgar Norton

The entire force of the story is lost in the picturization. Continuity was not properly prepared or the director failed to capitalize his opportunities. As produced the story is hackneyed. Capably handled the people in the cast might still have done something with it.

Dolly Wall, shoddy hostess in a mining town saloon, stakes a tin-horn gambler to an interest in an oil well. It proves to be a gusher. This prolog is entirely too long drawn out and without interest. Characters introduced through this opening are barren of human interest.

Royce Wingate is not characterized as a "bad" man with a streak of something worth while in his make-up. He is shown as a blank individual, neither good nor evil, doing nothing that matters much either way.

Blanche Sweet has been given a role from which it would be difficult to extract honors. The hard-boiled hostess, uneasy in the big city, about to lose her man, could incite a certain sympathy if sufficiently hoked. Miss Sweet looks vapid and purposeless. Enough to enlist support for the man in his desire for a cleaner girl like Amy Cardigan.

The sensational rise to great financial power following a good opening break in another part of the country, is an ace, always to be played up for good returns. Carelessly glossed over in this picture and meaningless.

Climax is where Wingate shoots Dolly as she threatens to throw acid in his face unless he calls off his engagement to the society girl. A complete change of heart when he discovers the bottle containing water instead of poison.

Mary McAllister, appearing for a few shots only, does well in a part which might have been enhanced for better effects.

Warner Baxter is somewhat misplaced in the role of a grifter. He also fails to hold as the "financial power."

Not a film to be depended upon by picture houses without added attractions of proven drawing powers. Will do in the neighborhoods on the split week basis.

Camera quite unkind throughout to Miss Sweet.

SHATTERED

Exceptional photoplays committee of the national board of review presents, through Fifth Avenue Playhouse projection methods, a German-made tragedy, featuring Werner Kraus; at the Fifth Avenue Playhouse, week of July 4, 1927. Cast, Werner Kraus, Mme. Strassman, Ed Posca, Pearl Otto. Running time, 43 mins.

The tiny Fifth Avenue Playhouse at 66 Fifth avenue, near 12th street, is an indigenously and intensively New York city institution. The Little Theatre movement in the movies has not yet gained general ground. New York now has several, of which Mike Mindlin's converted little art theatre, seating 264, is the pioneer success.

Recently it has made a policy of playing German films of the sort not regarded as desirable for general release on this side, but of sufficient cumulative pulling power, to have developed a steady clientele at this out-of-the-way bijou playhouse. That is, it is out of the way for all but the Greenwich Village contingent, and on the occasion of this reporter's visit, it seemed that they, rather than the society mob, supposedly its chief patrons, were in the majority.

It is a cozy little joint, with an art foyer studded with original modern paintings, and where cigarets, orangeade and coffee are served gratis. It is a one-floor house in a big office building, airy and neat and prettily decorated. The orchestra is a piano and violin, and between programs renders "concerts," rather good. The pictures are a complete set, with newsreel, feature comedy, a special educational and the foreign drama. The prices are 75 cents, and up to $1 on Saturdays, Sundays and holidays.

"Shattered" is a grim, ultra-natural story of the typical German latter-day style, continental in every respect, including its cheapness of production. It has four principals, all the settings are practical, indoor and out, and the action stark, brutal and usually true.

The ingenue is unbeautiful and unmade-up. The father is the principal character. He is a trackwalker. The division superintendent comes to his home, seduces his slavey daughter. The mother hears the unsavory business, steps in on it, goes stumbling forth in the snow to pray at a crucifix, and there is frozen to death. The old man finds her and carries in her stiff body, the finest bit of acting in the film, and a lesson in reality on celluloid.

The villain refuses to marry the girl, who tells the distracted old giant, whereupon he goes in and strangles the visitor, after he carts the dead body of his wife across snow floes in a sled to the churchyard, as poignant a hundred feet of film as ever was photographed. He then goes mad, flags an express train and almost wrecks it, and numbly gives himself up. That's all. The fate and future of the daughter are not revealed.

Almost Ibsenesque is this simple tale by Carl Mayer. It has a place in the theatre, though perhaps not in many theatres. Kraus is next to Jannings as the exponent of that style and technique, and has been seen and approved in America many times. As a character man who deals in truths before the lens, he has no superior in the known spheres of acting.

"Crime and Punishment" and a UFA, "The Way to Strength and Beauty," are announced to follow. The first named, if not too terrifying, might find its way uptown, as the story is a semi-classic from the modern Russian.

The big boys of the films should watch the Fifth avenue exhibits—any one of them may click off a fortune. *Lait.*

Callahans and Murphys

Metro-Goldwyn-Mayer production and release. Comedy, made from the novel of the same name by Kathleen Norris. Directed by George Hill. Marie Dressler and Polly Moran featured. Running time 66 minutes. At the Capitol, New York, week July 9.

Mrs. Callahan	Marie Dressler
Mrs. Murphy	Polly Moran
Ellen Callahan	Sally O'Neil
Dan Murphy	Lawrence Gray
Grandpa Callahan	Frank Currier
Monica Murphy	Gertrude Olmsted
Jim Callahan	Eddie Gribbon
Timmy Callahan	Turner Savage
Terrence Callahan	Jackie Coombs
Mary Callahan	Dawn O'Day
Michael Callahan	Monty O'Grady
Mr. Murphy	Tom Lewis

A medley of hoke and slapstick raised to the level of brilliant character comedy by legitimate acting by Marie Dressler and Polly Moran, veterans of farce; by deft handling of genuine humor and by skilful title writing. Perhaps the least of the credit is due the titling, for at times it does descend to gagging.

But the playing of the two featured women is never out of key. They have here done a fine bit of portrait drawing, and it is the utter fidelity of their work that gives the whole picture its value. The comic situation is ingenious always, but it is the shrewd acting of this pair that lends to the roughhouse slapstick its point. Without them it would at times get into the roughhouse class, but they never let the affair get out of their hands to descend to pure hokum.

One passage is where Mrs. Murphy and Mrs. Callahan meet at a St. Patrick's day picnic. They had quarreled and then become reconciled over the beer glasses. The possibilities of the situation for low comedy can easily be imagined. These two wring the opportunity dry for honest laughs, but they never overstep that vague line that separates legitimate comedy from vulgar horseplay. It's all robust fun and one continuous riot of laughter, but the business is never once offensive. Of hoke there is plenty, but it's the best kind of wholesome hoke and tremendously effective.

The picture in its style of appeal is another "McFadden's Flats," with the two Irish matrons in place of the Charley Murray and Chester Conklin roles. That makes it additionally appealing and extra funny. For there is true sentiment in this picture. Indeed a sure fire laughing comedy seldom is really funny without its touch of pathos.

Besides the two women, Eddie Gribbon contributed a sincere bit of playing in the rough and ready role of Jim Callahan, putting a world of tenderness into the blundering big brother character.

A boy and girl romance is in the story but merely a detail. The actual body and substance of the production are the character relations of the two women. They fight and make up and fight and make up, in an unbroken series and the final scene finds them ready to clinch over whether the new baby is a Callahan or a Murphy, when the supposedly abandoned daughter of the Callahans turns out to be the secret wife of the Murphy boy. Up to then it had looked as though it was a romance gone wrong.

"The Callahans and the Murphys" is a money picture because it is a continuous laugh, but it is more than that. It is a fine faithful transcript from life, and therein it is a bit of art, a credit to its producers, its director and its excellent cast. *Rush.*

Prince of Headwaiters

Samuel E. Rork production. First National release, starring Lewis Stone. Directed by John Francis Dillon. Adapted by Jane Murfin from the story by Viola Brothers Shore and Garrett Fort, published in "Liberty." Running time, 85 minutes. At Strand, New York, week July 9.

Pierre	Lewis Stone
Faith Cable	Priscilla Bonner
John Cable	E. J. Ratcliffe
Mae Morin	Lilyan Tashman
Barry Frost	John Patrick
Elliott Cable	Robert Agnew
Beth	Ann Rork
College Boys	Cleve Moore, Dick Folkens Lincoln Stedman
Susanne	Cecille Evans
Judy	Marion McDonald
Elsie	Nita Cavalerie

A first class program picture, strong on sentimental appeal but a little weak in dramatic action. Excellent modern bits and takes interest from the elegance of its fashionable atmosphere and high life background. Theme almost a parallel of that which motivated "The Music Master"—the yearning of a humble father for the child he cannot well acknowledge, in this case a boy instead of a girl.

The picture has good comedy values growing out of a party of rich college boys who come to New York for a lark and tie up with a bevy of peppy flappers as companions. **Good light comedy episodes in the tea dansants and fashionable restaurants with flip comments on modern youth, gin and the like. One title bearing on the tea dansant goes, "If you know the holds, the steps don't matter," typical of the tone of this lively passage.**

Acting is unusually satisfying. Stone's role fits him well, fine medium for his suavity. This intelligent screen player has come to represent in pictures something of what Kyrle Bellew did in romantic plays of a generation ago, the acme of the social graces. Ann Rork handles a rather pale role with natural ease, and Lilyan Tashman is convincing as a blonde gold digger. The college boys play plausibly also. The director wisely has decided that the Rah! Rah! type of collegian is passe and gets some likeable effects out of the jaunty quartet.

Stone is the headwaiter at the Ritz. As a youth he had married a rich American art student in Paris, but they had been separated by the girl's rich and snobbish American family. He never knew he had a son until the boy is revealed to him accidentally years later when he becomes involved with a notorious blackmailer. It is then the headwaiter goes to the boy's rescue. *Rush.*

DANCE MAGIC

Robert Kane production, released by First National. Directed by Victor Hugo Halperin. Featuring Ben Lyon, Pauline Starke, Louis John Bartels. Adapted by Clarence Buddington Kelland from story, perhaps of similar title. Running time, about 55 minutes.

Hopeless!

If this picture gets into the double-dayers, that'll be lucky. Or at the utmost, the neighborhood one-dayers where they wish pictures had had a Hollywood before the old man made them move into the country.

Here's a bad picture, a really slovenly written story, and the entire fault is in that story. If Robert Kane, the picture's producer, selected the story himself, there is no out for him, but if it were wished on him he has the squawk of 1927.

It seems unnatural that amongst a First National experienced crowd of picture makers, such a mess as this could have been turned out and how. It's quite likely that if all of the inside stuff about this film were made known, it would be quite interesting.

At one time when Pauline Starke walked into the theatrical man's office in New York, direct from Ridley Bridge and with her gripsack in one hand, the scene looked exactly like a Universal of 10 years ago, when U was slipping 'em out fast for the yaps. Even a U of 10 years ago would look foolish now, and this is even worse than that. Sid could make a better picture than "Dance Magic" any Sunday night up at the house with his amateur camera and lights, besides saving 5,500 feet of film and an entire organization.

That's what "Dance Magic" suggests—amateurishness, all of the way through. Toward the finale when the melodramatics get to work, chunks appear to have been cut out, either by the censors or a sloppy cutter. Nothing here for the official censors to object to, unless they don't care for amateur pictures running up to $85,000 or more.

The story is as old as picture making; it's the girl from the country who wanted to be a Broadway star, and was, for one night, when she went home and confessed her sins, publicly in church. Her sin was dancing. She swore nothing else sinful had occurred during her New York stay, nor in the apartment of the theatrical producer.

For blah stuff this is a pip.

Of course everything kept step with that story, from direction to acting to cameraing.

With notes coming due and payrolls to meet it must hit a lot of people as an inexplicable mystery where money comes from that flows so easily into pictures such as "Dance Magic." *Sime.*

RICH MEN'S SONS

Columbia picture, adapted from the story "The Lightning Express." Distributed by Commonwealth. Harry Cohn, producer (director). Ralph Graves, who plays the feature part, listed as director. Shirley Mason co-featured. George Fawcett also in featured names. Story credited to Dorothy Howell. Running time, 85 minutes. At the Broadway, New York, week July 11.

Columbia picture made with an eye to economy but a considerable show obtained. Dramatic action is spread pretty thin over nearly an hour and a half of story, with only one real punch in an auto race between hero and a fast express train.

Fair comedy helps make up for lack of speed but the net result is just a so-so program picture. Acting pretty artificial Ralph Graves is always the self-conscious actor and Shirley Mason not much better. Both labor and struggle to make points. Very theatrical pair. Mr. Fawcett is the finished character old man—the only real personage in the cast of too painstaking players.

The two leads take rods and rods of film for close-ups that add nothing to the effectiveness of a story that is stereotyped. Several distinctly objectionable incidents. The hero is a lazy son of a rich man, who avoids his father's demand that he go to work in the railroad business, by threatening to expose the old man's escapade with a blonde. Even comedy treatment doesn't excuse this.

The circumstance is planted for comedy purposes. In the end when the son gains a favor at his father's hands on threat of exposure, it is revealed that the photograph which was the means of the exposure has been changed to the portrait of the boy's honest sweetheart. But the story device, neverthless, leaves a bad taste.

Settings are plain, but skillfully contrived to give the effect of good taste and the surrounding atmosphere is that of richness and refinement desirable in productions addressed to the neighborhood clientele. Photography fair.

That seems to characterize the whole production—it is merely a so-so job. *Rush.*

Not for Publication

F. B. O. production and release. Directed by Ralph Ince from Robert Wells Ritchie's story, "The Temple of the Giants." Scenario by Ewart Adamson. Cameraman, Allen Seigler. Running time, 60 minutes. In projection room, July 6.

Big Bill Wellman	Ralph Ince
Commissioner Brownell	Roy Laidlaw
Phillip Hale	Rex Lease
Beryl Wellman	Jola Mendez
Eli Barker	Eugene Strong
Editor Pike	Thomas Brower

"Not for Publication" is not for release until October 19, so the trade showing in a projection room was plenty far in advance.

Ralph Ince, who doubles in brass in most of his productions as both actor and director, and pretty good at both, has a part well suited to his type, that of a political czar. The story is laid in an environment of political conspiracy and journalistic enterprise. The hero's paper is out to expose Big Bill Wellman. In the process of exposing the young reporter finds that Big Bill isn't such a bad egg after all and his younger sister is quite delightful.

It all makes for a picture of undoubted interest.

Introduced in this feature is Jola Mendez, young Central American cutie. She is a sister to Lucille Mendez, whom New York remembers as the peppy chorus girl. Lucille married Ince and so sister Jola gets her chance in the celluloid operas. She has an interesting personality, lots of animation and for a first effort is okay in "Not for Publication."

Featured with Ince is Rex Lease, breezy chap of likable personality. He is the bright reporter. Eugene Strong was a bit too sardonic, especially when exiting laughingly.

"Not for Publication" is a good all-round picture of the dramatic category.

THE BETTER WAY

Columbia picture, directed by and featuring Ralph Ince, with Dorothy Revier co-featured. Supporting cast includes Eugene Strong, Hazel Howell and Armand Kaliz. Story by Harry O. Hoyt. Photographed by J. O. Taylor. At the Arena, New York, one day (July 7) on double bill. Running time, 65 minutes.

This picture has been released outside of New York for several months. In Chicago it was at the Englewood neighborhood house, playing for four days with five acts of cut-rate vaudeville. That booking was quite a break for the film.

What it is best fitted for is one-day projection—if with another picture to help along, so much the better.

The footage contains a small portion of genuine acting, concerned primarily with the telling of a story that has a plot twist. There's a plain little dame (Dorothy Revier), stenographer for a broker who plays heavy on the market and women. Ralph Ince, the bookkeeper, loves her as she is. But the little gal overhears a tip, stakes her savings, and wins. Which calls for a trip to the beauty parlor and the transformation of a moth to a butterfly.

With the steno beautified, the broker notices her for the first time. He gives her a couple of more tips, and when she's dirty with dough tries to get his reward in necking and such.

But she won't play, so the broker gets sore and gives her a phony tip. She tells the bookkeeper to invest all she's got, but in order to reform her and reverses the instructions, so she'll go broke again and be her plain little self. Naturally she cleans up, with the bookkeeper stepping in just in time to rescue her from advances of the broker and get her for his life partner.

There are some "cheater" shots of the Stock Exchange much dimmed by time. The rest of the photography is of the sort that records action without any attempt for the unusual. Direction is aimed at the third wrinkle in foreheads of patrons unhampered by too much intelligence. Subtitles carry the same idea, carrying it almost too far. It took three sets of titles to put over the idea plainly that the mean broker was giving the girl a fake tip so that she'd lose her dough. The first explanation was sufficient for anyone over eleven.

Plainly made for the unsophisticated neighborhoods, where it should get along for a day.

BEAUTY SHOPPERS

Tiffany production and release. Directed by Louis Gasnier from story by Travers Lane. Cameraman, James Dubray. Running time, 62 mins. At Loew's New York, one-half double bill, one day, July 5.
Dick Merwin...................Thomas Haines
Mabel Hines......................Mae Busch
Sam Billings.................James Marcus
Peggy Raymond..................Doris Hill
Maddox........................Ward Crane
Mme. Helene....................Leo White
Mald..........................Dale Fuller
Art Patron................Cissy Fitzgerald

"Beauty Shoppers" comes in somewhere between the two-reelers F. B. O. used to produce with Alberta Vaughn and the lingerie operas Fox has been turning out with Madge Bellamy and Olive Borden. It's that kind of a picture, and that kind have been enjoying a strong echo at the b. o.

Louis Gasnier directed competently, neatly, even smartly, up to the final reel, when his early days in the peep show business got the best of his 1927 judgment in one sequence where the stylish and classy Mae Busch is seen in dressing gown chasing down the street after a garbage wagon, which she overtakes, climbs aboard and starts hunting for some liver pills belonging to her rich old hubby, who, she has suddenly discovered, is a gold mine only as long as he lives. That should forthwith be ordered cut from all prints. It's a sour note in the whole proceedings.

Doris Hill is the young heroine with the swell and much displayed gams. Like her prototypes in the films, she registers more sex appeal than mental vigor, which is, commercially, an advantage. Also new is Thomas Haines, the boy she cares for. The balance of the cast are standard players.

Ward Crane villains as an art gallery proprietor who is after our Nell. Nell has drawn some pictures, but through a fluke the pictures of an artist of real merit have been mixed with her pictures. She is accordingly accused of theft, with the art guy trying to make the most of her fears of going to the lock-up.

The secondary plot revolves about Nell's worldly room-mate, who ropes in a "Scotch" millionaire in order to escape the humdrum of manicuring nails.

"Beauty Shoppers" has color and a sufficient quantity of class. It is very much out of the ordinary run of independent program releases.

THUMBS DOWN

Banner Production released by Sterling Pictures. Directed by Phil Rosen. From the story by Gladys E. Johnson. Cast includes Creighton Hale, Lois Boyd, Helen Worthing, Scott Seaton, Vera Lewis and Windham Standing. At Loew's New York, one day, July 8, one-half of double feature program. Running time, about 55 mins.

A powerful romance for two-year-olds.

Outstanding part of this independent time-killer is the inclusion of an elderly "society" dame with a fish-like face. While a total loss in this production this facial characteristic might be well employed for comedy purposes.

Gladys E. Johnson is reported the author of the original script. It seems that a wealthy young man loved a stenog. His mother objected to stenogs mainly because they had not attended finishing schools.

Hundreds of feet of good film are devoted to showing how a ma-in-law can make things uncomfortable. This should prove an inspiring film for couples about to commit matrimony.

The "punch" is in the gal's secret. It finally leaks out that her old man is in jail for another's offense. The ma-in-law, it seems, is not so upset about this as she was because the girl was trying to get the old boy out.

The young man had in the meantime turned against the wife. As suddenly he changed his mind. The "menace" consists of the ma-in-law's cross-examination of the stenog to learn something of her family connections.

HERO ON HORSEBACK

Universal production and release. Starring Hoot Gibson. Peter B. Kyne story. Cameraman, Harry Neuman. Directed by Del Andrews. Running time, 64 mins. On

double bill at Loew's New York, one day, July 5. In cast, Ethelyne Claire, Edwards Davis, Edward Hearne and Dan Mason.

Hoot Gibson squawked some time ago about the stories Universal was giving him. To square matters U promised him some real yarns from the presumably clever pen of Peter B. Kyne. This is one of the "promised" gems. If anything, it's worse than the scripts the cowboy got previously.

Written for a magazine with the carrying power of a smart literary style, "Hero On Horseback" might rate despite its basic plot absurdities. Reduced to celluloid, it lacks that essential to all good stories, whether written or screened—the illusion that the action is really happening and that the characters are real.

Hoot is a cowboy with a gambling mania. He has gambled away his ranch cow by cow. When finally broke, an old boy whom he has staked returns with the news that he had discovered gold and sold out for $100,000, one-half of which is Hoot's. Hoot buys out the local bank, becomes its president and establishes a faro department where cowboys gamble with money they have borrowed from the bank on I. O. U.'s.

Del Andrews' direction is okay and the picture is made well enough.

Where the Trail Begins

Sam Bischoff production. Directed by Noel Mason Smith. Starring the dog "Silverstreak," with Johnny Walker featured. At Loew's Circle, New York, one day, July 11—one-half double bill. Running time, about 55 minutes.

Animal star used in a series of stock pictures with little or no variation in plot or business. Films are practically all alike but should prove interesting nevertheless to dog lovers and juveniles.

"Silverstreak" is a great dog actor. He puts over a new trick or two in almost every new release, providing the only change of diet. Johnny Walker must be getting plenty to agree to look as foolish as he does in this one. Walks into a part where all he has to do is get beaten up by some individual with a mustache. After the massacre Johnny wants to know the man's name.

Long shots of mountains covered with snow. A mate and three pups appear with "Silverstreak" to good results.

Okey for a change and strong enough on its own where the dog has a following.

ON ZE BOULEVARD

Metro-Goldwyn-Mayer production and release. Directed by Harry Millarde. Story by Hugh Herbert and Florence Ryerson. Cameraman, Andre Barlatier. Running time, 47 mins. At American Roof, New York, July 7-10.
Gaston.......................Lew Cody
Musette....................Renee Adoree
Count Guissac...............Roy D'Arcy
Gaby...................Dorothy Sebastian

Despite it is loaded with laughs "On Ze Boulevard" did not get a regular Broadway first run release by M-G-M. Probably shortness of running time (about 47 minutes) responsible. At least it denotes heavy deletions.

It is a funny story of a French waiter who wins a lot of dough in a gambling pool. He promptly goes off his nut on a spending spree.

His sweetheart remains hard-headed and practical and continually kids him. A couple of high hat percentage artists spot the overdressed ex-waiter for a sap and try the badger game but are out-slicked by the astute sweetheart.

All of the four principals do great

work, with Lew Cody and Dorothy Sebastian particularly showing unsuspected talent.

Director Harry Millarde did a first class job keeping the plot within reason at all times and avoiding the too obvious hokum. Hugh Herbert and Florence Ryerson should be singled out for commendation on the well-knit and sprightly yarn. And may be the unknown cutter got away in for his share of the result.

Catch as Catch Can

Sam Sax production, directed by Charles Hutchison. From the story by L. V. Jefferson. Starring William Fairbanks, with cast including Jack Richardson, Rose Blossom, Larry Shannon, William Shumway, George Chapman. At Loew's Circle, New York, one day, July 11—one-half double bill. Running time, about 55 minutes.

Slow-moving film, with nothing to recommend it for anything outside of the grind houses.

Story is slim and devoid of interest. The manager of the baseball team is accused of throwing a game. The gal's kid brother did it, but the stronger man feels capable of standing the strain.

Strictly States Rights and then!

THE BLOOD SHIP

Produced and distributed by Columbia. Story by Norman Springer. Scenario by Fred Myton. Directed by George B. Seitz. Running time, 62 minutes. At the Roxy, New York, week July 18.

Newman	Hobart Bosworth
Mary	Jacqueline Logan
John Shreve	Richard Arlan
Capt. Swope	Walter James
First Mate	Fred Kohler
The Knitting Swede	James Bradbury, Sr.
Nils	Arthur Rankin
Cockney	Syd Crossley
Second Mate	Frank Hemphill
Rev. Deaken	Chappell Dossett
Negro	Blue Washington

Harry Cohn, production head of Columbia, need never take his hat off to anyone when it comes to the production of action sea pictures whose entire tempo is action, fight and more fight. In "The Blood Ship" he has turned out as thrilling and blood-curdling a tale of shanghaiing for the high seas as anyone could conceive.

Being an Independent producer, Cohn naturally had to conserve as far as cost was concerned. He went far ahead of his general production allowances for program pictures, probably tripling it. But he turned out a product which is on a par if not excelling that of concerns who spent four times as much for their product and just got one of those so-so pictures of the sea.

There is nothing at all about this picture which resembles the quickie or cheater. George B. Seitz was the director, and the leads were handled by Hobart Bosworth, Jacqueline Logan, Richard Arlan, Walter James and Fred Kohler, each of whom is known as "big league" picture players and who have and are still appearing in productions made by the first-line producers. There was no stinting in general production, as a five-masted schooner was used for the sea scenes and a supporting cast was chosen which showed exceptional merit in handling their individual chores.

Bosworth, of course, copped the top honors, with Miss Logan as the only woman in a role which required emotional ability as well as a faculty to troupe.

The story is that of a captain of a ship known as the hell hole because he shanghais his crew, beats the tar out of them, kills one now and then, makes port, gives them a chance to desert so he will not have to pay off and starts all over again at the same racket. In the end he meets his master, and later a series of blood-curdling incidents and sequences come to his waterloo. He is thrown to the sharks as a companion of his first mate.

Walter James as the captain gives a realistic performance of the bully who never fears as long as he has his coherts around him and his revolver handy. Bosworth, playing the role of a sailor who shipped to get the man that double-crossed him, stole his wife and kiddie and then railroaded him to prison for a murder he did not commit, is vindicative until he gets his man. He has several big and gripping scenes with James. Particularly one, where he is handcuffed and hung by the wrists to get a beating with a leather-spiked strap, and another, after being freed by the girl when he comes face to face with his enemy, takes the strap away from him and beats him to death, after which he tosses his body to the sharks.

A negro, who is programmed as Blue Washington, runs right into the top-notch acting class in this vehicle. He seems to have a great sense of comedy knowledge and provides considerable relief, which is accented by clever captions. After being cowed by the first mate and a stool in the crew, he finally gets the first mate, beats him in one of those regular battles, works him to the rail, tosses him overboard and gloatingly turns to the rest of the cowed crew to say, "I got my man."

This he did because the mate would not let him minister to the wants of a dying sailor who had been kicked to his death by the captain and mate.

Arthur Rankin as that "pasy" voyager gave a most commendable performance. Fred Kohler, noted for his work as a heavy, did his stuff as the mate. Richard Arlen, who was borrowed from Paramount for the juvenile lead, had no easy task on the romantic end. He had plenty of fighting to do and showed that he is a good two-fisted lead as well as able to hold his own on the love-and-sympathy stuff.

James Bradbury as the Knitting Swede, who ran a dive where sailors were drafted for the payless voyage, is a character type one relishes on the screen. Chappell Dossett as the Rev. Deaken, the fighting parson of the Seamen's Mission, shanghaied because he wanted to clean up the Knitting Swede's joint, played in an even tempo and gave it a sincere touch.

"The Blood Ship" is one production that will satisfy the patrons of the de luxe, neighborhood or general run houses. It is away from the regular formula type of program picture, and will probably gross as much as many of the big producers' touted outputs. *Ung.*

ROLLED STOCKINGS

Paramount production, featuring five "junior stars," James Hall, Louise Brooks, Richard Arlen, Nancy Phillips and El Brendel. Directed by Richard Rosson. Story by Frederica Sagor; screen play by Percy Heath. Editing and titling by Julian Johnson. Running time, 65 minutes. At the Paramount, New York, week July 17.

Jim Treadway	James Hall
Carol Fleming	Louise Brooks
Ralph Treadway	Richard Arlen
The Vamp	Nancy Phillips
Rudolph	El Brendel
Mr. Treadway	David Torrence
Coach	Chance Ward

An exceptional picture of college life is here presented. As a commercial picture it has good points in the casting of a quintet of up and coming players who already have attracted attention and in the exposition of a gay and cheerful story of youth that must have its appeal to the younger generation.

As a literary product it is yet more notable. For once the motif of college athletics has been handled as a background rather than the center of interest. The screen story is a vast improvement upon the labored idea of a college sporting event upon which hangs the outcome of a romantic situation such as the long run of the football hero that lifted disgrace from the halfback.

Here there is a thoroughly interesting situation of the younger and older brothers, both students, in love with the same girl. The romantic narrative works out naturally and interestingly as the main theme, while the boat race, which is the action high light, is merely a situation bearing on a human drama rather than the drama itself.

The campus atmosphere is splendidly done in a vein of high comedy rather than the familiar rah-rah travesty. These young people are real in settings recognizable in life. College pictures usually have the tone and mood of a Mack Sennett riot.

"Rolled Stockings" isn't a particularly happy title. It suggests bare-kneed flapper co-eds, which doesn't apply here, for, above all things, these young people are likably real, and presented in a distinctly sympathetic treatment. The casting of the young stars is fortunate. Miss Brooks, who has done several excellent things, here finds a role for her demure charm with its tricky suggestion of mild sophistication. Hall is the dashing, cock-sure older brother, a part that could easily be ruined by too smooth and unctuous playing, but here deftly balanced. Hall is almost too formally good-looking to make a perfect screen type, but is saved by character in face and bearing.

Arlen is an exceptional juvenile, having a certain rugged masculinity that goes further on the screen than mere good looks. Here the part calls for just his make-up. He plays the blundering, headstrong, but warm-hearted kid to a nicety. The production is well balanced. The college background has about as much elegance as it can stand, but the director has escaped the fault of overdoing, finding a highly agreeable middle ground.

It may be that the absence of campus hoke will react against the picture in some quarters. It has none of the usual gagging and horse play that the mob expects in its college pictures. In the same vein the titling is balanced to accord with the sincerity of the handling. It makes its appeal much higher than any college film that comes to mind. This is true both of its story substance and its style of staging. Evidences of such a tendency toward higher tastes are to be found in the modern screen mode. A dignified picture of college life wouldn't have seemed feasible a few years ago.

The story is a tactful handling of the older and younger brother theme. Jim, the older, is a junior, disposed to "ride" his younger freshman brother. They are rivals for Carol. Jim seems to be the favored suitor, until Carol finds that he has had many flirtations and transfers her favor to Ralph. Ralph seems now to be the victor. But Jim wins back his lost ground by honest reform.

Ralph has gained the coveted seat of stroke on the crew, and the night before the big race seeks out Carol to clinch their engagement. He finds her sealing her engagement to Jim with a kiss, and in furious resentment at what he regards as a stab in the back from fate breaks training and goes off to a disreputable roadhouse. Discovery there will mean expulsion and heartbreak for the boys' father, himself an old stroke in the same college.

Jim speeds to the roadhouse. Here their wills clash. Ralph refuses to leave. The coach, who means discovery, is on his way. Jim tries force, but the trained oarsman is more than a match for him. While Jim can stand up and keep coming, Ralph will have to go or keep knocking him down. His will wins the day. Ralph departs just in time to escape the coach and their father, while Jim takes the blame and faces expulsion.

A quick shift to the rowing race, nicely staged for its dramatic effect, and then a brief and rather obvious twist to a happy ending. *Rush.*

The Great Mail Robbery

FBO production and release. Directed by George B. Seitz. Story by J. Hawks and Peter Milne. Cast includes: Theodore Von Eltz, Frank Nelson, Jean Morgan, Lee Shumway, De Witt Jennings, Cora Williams, Nelson McDowell, Charles Hill Mailes and Yvonne Howell. At the Hippodrome, New York, week of July 19. Running time about one hour.

Fast-moving, clean cut film, well handled both before and behind the camera. Photography clear even in the night scenes.

Story woven round the mail robberies of last year. Opening is of a water-drenched arm rummaging in a sleeping car, the fingers finally emerging with gold certificates clutched in their grip despite revolver shots.

Locale then switches to a marine base where Captain Macready, Theodore Von Eltz, is told to proceed into the mountains with a detachment of fighters. He is advised to take along the sergeant for sleuthing purposes. Said Sergeant, Frank Nelson, doesn't prove to be much of a sleuth but is great on comedy, adding just the proper touch of humor to the details.

There is a mysterious Major Howard, Lee Shumway, said to have been thrown out of the marines. Proving himself a first class gun man he is welcomed into the outlaw fold. A hackneyed situation but handled from a slightly different angle and with fresh faces in front of the camera can be accepted as novel.

The train robbery is realistically handled with every modern weapon in present day banditry, including machine guns, employed.

Here the law proves stronger than the gunman by bringing unconquerable reinforcements in the form of airplanes. Tear-bombs are thrown down on the outlaws, cornered in a hole in the mountains.

The girl, Jean Morgan, photographs well and shows up to better effect generally than the averaage leading women in these roles.

The Gingham Girl

F. B. O. Production and release. Adapted from Daniel Kussell's musical comedy by David Kirkland and Rex Taylor. Continuity by Ewart Adamson. Directed by David Kirkland. Lois Wilson and George K. Arthur co-starred. Running time, 65 minutes. At the Capitol, New York, week July 16.

Mary Thompson	Lois Wilson
Johnny Cousins	George K. Arthur
Pat O'Day	Charles B. Crockett
Letty O'Day	Hazel Keener
Sonia Mason	Myrta Bonillas
Harrison Bartlett	Jerry Miley
Mazie Le Lewer	Betty Francisco
Mildred Ripley	Derlys Perdue
Haden	Jed Proty
Mrs. Trask	Maude Fulton

David Kirkland missed in making "The Gingham Girl" an almost flawless comedy for the screen. This picture could have been one of the best bets that the summer season has had, if bungling in unraveling for the screen of this stage tale had not been made. There are various ways of figuring, with it really hard to tell which way the mistakes have been made.

Either Kirkland and Taylor in writing the story thought they might skip material sequence in telling the yarn and leave it to the audience to take happenings for granted even though periods had been skipped; or Ewart Adamson in providing the continuity figured that with the original premise having been established that future sequences would not have to be developed in telling the tale; then again it might be conjured that what seemed to be most material to the telling of the tale had been eliminated in the cutting to hold down footage.

Whichever way this was done someone erred, and badly, as this picture might have given F. B. O. a good foothold in the de luxe class A houses. The production is more expensive than F. B. O. is accustomed to turn out and has a cast which was an exceptional one for their class of productions.

Starting off it gives promise of telling a sweet romance of a youth and girl in a small town who are in love, with both eventually going to the big city. The boy is the village cut-up and tries to do the rounds in the big town and show up the smart folks of the community through his wise angles on affairs. The girl having been making cookies in the home town has more business-like intentions. She bakes her cookies, goes around and gives away free samples and is finally staked by a chap who had been in the home town from the city and wanted to back her.

Meantime the young fellow messes himself up and proves to be a chump. Then for no reason at all, without previous explanation or planting or the fact by celluloid interpretation the girl is head of the big cookie concern, the boy strolls in doing odd work, runs into her and, of course, the partner is forced out through the boy's making it known he represents the biggest concern in the business and is going to buy the guy who had been spurned by the heroine.

Mr. Kirkland never stuck to story at all in the adaptation. He gagged it up and let his gags milk themselves out in carrying the sequences too long. He had Maud Fulton do a characterization of Mme. Elinor Glyn, foreign to the play and grossly exaggerated to the extent that the discoverer of "It" may take it as a personal affront. However, Miss Fulton gave a fine performance and helped Arthur get a lot of good comedy results when they were in together.

Arthur seems to run away with the picture. He had a natural setup and given a chance to hoke it was a pipe for this little screen comic. There was nothing that he did not get away with in the low comedy line. Miss Wilson as the country lass simply had to smile. She had but one chance to shine in the classy raiment and this opportunity permitted her to outshine the rest of the clothes horses surrounding her.

Betty Francisco in the gold digger role proved to be a wonder. The part fitted her to the 'steenth portion of an inch. Jed Prouty showed up well as the wise drummer giving the hick boy the steer on how to do the big town up brown. Jerry Miley, the heavy, seemed entirely out of place. He just did not seem to understand what acting was all about. Derlys Perdue had a bit that gave her chance to show that she knows how to be jealous. Hazel Keener amounted to little as a small town vamp. Probably not the girl's fault, as there were too many alleged camp characters in the picture.

Whoever titled the picture must have been reading up during the past few years as well as being able to show that he was an ardent admirer of burlesque comics who crack the smart sayings.

"The Gingham Girl" has plenty of situations which are mirth provokers and no doubt will get by where an audience is not so concerned about straight story telling, or unfolding of a constructive plot.

In these regions folks will say it is a durn sweet little picture, but in the regions where people are able to and will pick out flaws they will possibly say, "How did some one muff such easy points!" *Ung.*

THE POOR NUT

First National Production, presented by Jess Smith. Directed by Richard Wallace from the play by J. C. and Elliott Nugent. Screen adaptation by Paul Schofield. Starring Jack Mulhall, with Charlie Murray featured. At the Strand, New York, week of July 16. Running time over 60 minutes.

John Miller	Jack Mulhall
"Doc"	Charlie Murray
Margie	Jean Arthur
Julia	Jane Winton
"Magpie" Welch	Glenn Tryon
Wallie Pierce	Cornelius Keefe
"Hub" Smith	Maurice Ryan
Professor Demming	Henry Vibart
Coach Jackson	Bruce Gordon
Colonel Small	William Courtwright

With everybody in Hollywood bragging about the tremendous overflow of charming young women all battering upon the directorial doors leading to an appearance in pictures, it seems strange that from all of these should have been selected two flat specimens such as Jean Arthur and Jane Winton. Neither of the girls has screen presence. Even under the kindliest treatment from the camera they are far from attractive and in one or two side shots almost impossible. But the picture has laughs, human interest, appealing story, and should be a strong draw.

This is not a profitable film for Jack Mulhall, although he makes good in a comedy role which was not cut any too well to his order. Charlie Murray ,as the college athletic trainer, steals the picture for laughs.

Aside from poor judgment in selecting feminine players Richard Wallace has done a fairly good job. He has put as many laughs as it is possible to get into a picture, relying on mugging and other business from the principals for these effects, rather than on prop gags.

The psycho-analytical scene should have been the high spot for laughs, with Miss Winton trying to cure Jack of his inferiority complex. Missed out here to comparatively little comedy with Murray getting the big laughs just by shaking his head lugubriously or winking an eye.

Mulhall succeeded in holding one scene. As the bashful botany student about to be welcomed into the class frat he suddenly overturns a plate of hot soup over his trousers.

Story is of a dreamy book-worm, wrapped up in the study of plants, who writes lovingly to a co-ed at another university whose picture he saw in a paper. He tells the girl he is the best athlete at college.

The day of reckoning finally arrives when the two colleges are to meet on the field of war, and Julia arrives to meet her "big college man" for the first time. She finds a bespeckled, dilapidated "John" Miller who is not even on speaking terms with a running suit.

But Miller had decided to train, and the coach had noticed a natural swiftness which bore all the signs and indications of championship form. Then the last-minute race with the usual results.

THE SATIN WOMAN

Sam Sax production. Mrs. Wallace Reid starred. Written and directed by Walter Lang. Released by Lumas. Seven thousand feet. In projection room July 13.

Mrs. Jean Taylor	Mrs. Wallace Reid
George Taylor	Rockliffe Fellows
Jean Taylor	Alice White
Maurice	John Miljan
Maria	Laska Winters
Mons. Francis	Chas. Buddy Post
Claire	Ruth Stonehouse
Mae	Gladys Brockwell
Countess	Ethel Wales

Looks as though Mrs. Wallace Reid slipped Sam Sax a "jo-jo." Unless there are some picture fans really anxious to again glance at the Wallace Reid name on introductory titles or they want to see the widow of the late film star when she makes personal appearances with the picture, it seems unlikely that the production will get over the barrier as did some of her previous starring efforts for this concern.

If an exhibitor figures in handling this one from a heavy exploitation angle and wants to carry it for daily or split-week runs, he might get trade with it, but it is hardly possible that the silent drama followers will do any bell ringing in its behalf.

Sax let Mrs. Reid go the limit on this one, too, on expense. Fashion show and summer resort as well as high-class cafe scenes, with Mrs. Reid wearing plenty of gowns that in real life would have a rich man gasping for breath if he had to stand the gaff.

Sax also surrounded the star with a corking good cast for an independent production. Names of some mean something at the box office, but only in one or two exceptions do they get a chance, and then it appeared as though they were checked so that the star could demonstrate how dramatic and emotional she could be. Mrs. Reid seems to take the "eskimo pie" when it comes to "close-ups." She has more in this film than many a big money-drawing star gets in a half-million-dollar production. All meant nothing, as when it comes to acting this lady just gets out on the limb and stays there.

She is the wife of a rich sportsman and prefers teas, society and fashion shows to her husband and daughter. Husband walks out after falling for another woman who helped him while away idle hours, leaving a note telling her not to allow the child to lead a lonesome existence.

She has the awakening when her hair turns white within a year. She takes the kid to Florida, which, according to sub-titles, is a summer resort. There the kid meets a sheik ballroom dancer.

A countess appears to tip the mother the sheik is one of those boys whom women support.

Meantime the former husband and his new wife split and he asks for forgiveness. The mother, not wanting the girl to make a bad pick, tells the kid they should blow back to the father.

The kid, as strong minded as her mother was in her younger days, puts the damper on the old gal and tells her to mind her own business, as she had been a flop herself.

Finally the mother makes a play for the sheik and is caught in a compromising position with him by her former husband and his dancing partner.

The dancing partner, of course, being jealous, starts pumping lead and shoots the mother, who was sacrificing herself for her daughter, instead of the male target. The sheik makes a getaway to join the countess, who is his wife and who was working a blackmail game with him.

Mother recovers and family is reunited.

Walter Lang, who wrote story, continuity and directed, seems to have tried to handle a bigger load than any one man's shoulders could carry, even though the story was one of those formula mother-love things.

Rockliffe Fellows as the neglected and spurned husband did a good piece of work, though taking the role a bit too seriously and not coming to the emotional stage in the final chapters, when it might have been expected.

Alice White has one of those walk-in-and-out parts, getting little chance. Miljan was good as the insipid, scheming dancer, with Ethel Wales fine as the confederate. As the jealous dancing partner Laska Winters did not seem to know what it was all about.

Ruth Stonehouse and Gladys Brockwell, in character roles, were able to show little, as it probably was figured that would not be so good for the star. Charles Buddy Post flashed on and off, doing nothing.

Had Sax spent this money on his regular ones instead of on this special, seems as though he would have gotten something that would make the box office talk up loud instead of softly, as it may on this one. *Ung.*

Crime and Punishment

Adapted version of "Raskalnikov" by Dostoievsky, a novel; made by the Moscow Art Theatre, and with their staff of players; presented at the Fifth Avenue Playhouse, running time 93 mins.

Here is a thoroughly Russian story, thoroughly Russianly filmed. That isn't a categorical "knock"; there is much the American movies can learn from the near-East Europeans. But there is more than much that they do which it would be better than well for the American producers to forget.

Dostoievsky is of the pessimist school so popular of recent years in Russia. He starts with the premise that this mundane span of mortal tenancy on earth is a pre-doomed period of sorrow, tragedy and disillusionment. He proves it—as far, at least, as the vagaries of his characters herein go their destined distances.

We thus are thrown into an atmosphere of abject poverty—but poverty of the kind not known today in the U. S., and scarcely or reluctantly recalled by those of us who knew it when. This is miserable, unclean, inexpressible, lousy, degrading poverty.

A high-minded student, irreligious, writes brochures on the inequalities of society. He takes his own stuff seriously. He goes to pawn his watch. He returns and butchers (with an ax) the female loan-shark; her aged sister enters accidentally, and he has to dispatch her.

He makes a miraculous escape, and thereafter is driven by ghostly visitations of conscience, horror, fear and holy promptings to become a maniacal screen nuisance.

The "drama" is registered mostly in comings and goings, exits and entrances. The head, face, midriff and feet are employed to lend significance to the grim effects of avenging inner-realizations on the sentitive, sensitized youth.

A counterplot sends him a street-walker whom he worships in a more sacrosanct than sexual sentiment. She equips him with a rosary and a regret. After that he becomes, filmly speaking, a pain. The action practically ceases and he registers nothing but his inner feelings. These, mostly, are elusive and vague.

It turns out to be a 6,000-foot reeler that could be better told in 2,000 feet, if it must be told at all.

Dostoievsky has gathered a limited following of the eccentric rather than the esoteric. The "billing" brags that this presentation is a most faithful interpretation of his tale. Unfortunately—it is.

While this is the sort of raw, red-blooded, reeking stuff that keeps the cozy, hospitable and chummy Fifth Avenue Playhouse "unique and extraordinary," the particular exhibit herein reported will add no outside revenue to Mike Mindlin's coffers.

Already "Crime and Punishment," a semi-classic greeted by the cognoscenti, has been revealed to several mid-metropolitan communities. They turned thumbs down on it. They knew their onions.

This is not an American vegetable and cannot be promoted into one. It has its "points," but it will click in this land of milk and money. Bricklayers, drawing $10.50 per diem; critics getting almost as much, etc., will never, never believe it. *Lait.*

On the U. P. Trail

Sunset production presented by Arthur J. Xydias. Directed by Frank S. Mattison. Cullen Landis and Roy Stewart featured. Cast includes Sheldon Lewis, Kathryn McGuire, Earle Metcalfe, Milburn Moranti, Hazel Howell, Fred de Sylvax and Felix Whitefeather. At the Arena, New York, one day, July 14.

Given an opportunity in this insignificant independent, Kathryn McGuire displays exceptional talent in the leading fem role. With dark, curly hair, she photographs well and registers chockful of charm and vivacity. Although draped in long, springy dresses of another decade, Miss McGuire's bearing indicates that she can wear clothes.

Aside from this girl the cast is dull and strictly small time. Cullen Landis is not the "type" as a hardy pioneer wagon train protector. Roy

Stewart as "Buffalo Bill" is a howl. Bill Cody has been made into a shrewd heckler and business man for the purpose of this film. He is seen hunting buffalo and delivering mail only rarely with the balance of his time taken up with rescuing Indians instead of pursuing them.

As a whole the picture measures up to the standards of the smaller independent production with the name of Buffalo Bill on the billboards to be figured. The story is garbled and thoroughly hashed where it should have been a little more simple if intended for the country trade.

The story of Buffalo Bill and the Union Pacific Trail was never like this. According to the film version the railway wanted to pass through a certain territory on which Bill had built a whole town, anticipating this move. Accordingly, Bill should have grown tremendously wealthy which would have released him from riding round the country with a wild west show until he died.

Several shooting and fist fights in the latter part of the picture should prove interesting. A stampede of buffalo is cold with the animals too scattered, seemingly ambling homeward instead of rushing madly.

The World at Her Feet

Paramount society comedy from the French. Story by Georges Berr and N. Verneuil. Directed by Luther Reed under production supervision of B. P. Schulberg. Florence Vidor starred; leading man, Arnold Kent. Richard Tucker, Margaret Quimby and David Torrence in cast. Running time, 70 mins. At Loew's State, New York, July 18.

These French triangle stories never seem to bull's-eye at the box office, though this one is a first-rate sophisticated comedy with excellent wise humor and a lot of sparkle. It has much elegance of atmosphere and a brisk play of wit.

The answer seems to be that the fans run to either low comedy in domestic stories or high intense drama, and the graduations between the extremes don't register. There have been a score of suave comedies of this sort on the Broadway screen, but not one of them sticks in memory as a commercial success. The same thing is in a measure true of the speaking stage. Not for seasons has there been an outstanding success from Paris, at least a comedy tone with French finesse.

This picture in an artistic way is an ideal vehicle for the grace and feminine charm of Florence Vidor, and it has been staged with great suavity and effectiveness. It has a certain dramatic kick also in a neatly turned situation, where the wife, confronted with the loss of her husband to a philandering blonde, tricks the blonde's husband into a compromising position to save her husband from complicity in a divorce scandal.

It's all very smooth and casual, without theatrical parade, and perhaps the screen public wants its dramatic punch delivered with more force than grace, as in this instance. The French are a discriminating, fastidious people, sipping their pastimes like old wine. This American people gulp their screen and stage sensations like straight redeye.

The fun of the story is the situation of a reversal of the neglected wife, victim of a husband absorbed in business. Here it is the woman who ignores her husband while she devotes her energies to carving out a career for herself. The humor is distinctly subtle, and here is developed with great adroitness, set off by a scenic production of distinguished elegance. Some of the interiors are pictorial gems, and the whole spirit is that of breeding and refinement. The kick is all in the climax, and the patient and painstaking "planting" and building up of situation and denouement at times is rather wearisome to a public accustomed to rough and ready drama and Keystone comedies.

The point is that the studios here have turned out a polished bit of high comedy and served it to a public appetite that doesn't especially relish such daintily seasoned fare. An artistic achievement foredoomed to commercial neglect. *Rush.*

THE GREY DEVIL

Rayart production starring Jack Perrin. Directed and adapted by Bennett Cohn. Running time, about 50 mins. On double bill at Arena, New York, one day, July 19.

This picture is a moving picture with the stress on the "moving." No valuable footage is wasted on any Lubitsch sublety or Von Stroheim innuendo.

Nine actors are given screen credit, yet so fast is the picture that the patron hardly gets a good look at any except Jack Perrin, featured.

The characters are mere moving symbols who gallop by the camera lens. They divide easily and naturally into two major divisions, evildoers and right livers.

Perrin is the main protagonist of the latter. Cliff Lyons is in the corner for the evil doers. Throughout the picture right liver is on the giving or receiving end of some mighty wallops.

Horses are stolen, men are drugged, others are murdered, nobody stops a minute in one mad round of villainy and fisticuffs that is probably going to be relished with loud acclaim in some parts.

At the Arena "The Grey Devil" was teamed on a double bill with Metro - Goldwyn - Mayer's "Frisco Sally Levy," a long yawn. M-G-M's cost sheet would probably show at least $75,000. "The Grey Devil" is a "quickie," hardly figuring much above $12,000. Audiences may smile indulgently at its brusque ways but they won't get a chance to yawn.

RANGE COURAGE

Universal Blue Streak Western starring Fred Humes. Directed by Ernst Laemmle from a published story by Gene Markey. Photographed by Al Jones. At Loew's New York one day (July 15) on double-feature bill. Running time, 57 minutes.

Adhering faithfully to the accepted idea as to what a western should be, this film automatically denotes its own market.

Story is of a youth who spends five years abroad and then comes back west to be known as a dude.

Direction handles material capably enough, considering the story's average worth. Photography is of the better cowboy classification.

Acting is better identified as action.

TARTUFFE
(The Hypocrite)

Ufa production and release (direct, over here). Adapted from Moliere's play by Carl Mayer. Directed by F. W. Murnau. Photography by Carl Freund. Starring Emil Jannings. Werner Kraus and Lily Dagover featured. At the Strand, New York, week July 23. Running time about one hour.

The Old Gentleman..........Herman Picha
His Housekeeper............Rosa Valetti
His Grandson...............Andre Mattoni
Mr. Orgon..................Werner Kraus
Elmira, His Wife...........Lily Dagover
Dorine.....................Lucie Hoeflich
Tartuffe...................Emil Jannings

The name of Jannings, rapidly becoming a box office asset over here, should bring them in. But everyone going out will carry a report detrimental to Jannings, the picture and the theatre.

One of the queerest sensations is seeing an alleged "boob" audience high-hatting a film. That is what happened at the Strand Saturday afternoon. The feeling seemed to be unanimous, "An impossible picture."

Jannings does not even appear on the screen until half of the picture has been run. As usual, the German actor does his stuff and, in this particular instance, gets the laughs in the few opportunities there are

The situations are beyond the realm of understanding of the present generation. No doubt, as a play, there was a piquant touch of pointed French wit in the story of a wealthy simpleton who believed a philandering rogue masquerading as a pious gentleman to be a saint and therefore urged his pretty-wife to believe also. But French humor, seen through German eyes, and finally placed before an American public, is bound to suffer in the process.

The film does bring forth a cast of exceptional merit with the exception of Werner Kraus, who was really kept so busy running around that it seemed impossible for him to do himself justice. Rose Valetti, as the scheming housekeeper who was slowly poisoning her master, is worthy of good spotting in any picture where such roles are to be depicted.

For the start there is a somewhat lengthy prolog leading up to the point where the nephew, wishing to save his wealthy uncle from death, disguises himself as the owner of a traveling cinema and so gains entrance and permission to show a picture entitled "Tartuffe."

The curtain parts and Orgon is shown returning home to his lovely wife after a long trip. His brow is furrowed and he is no longer his carefree self. Hardly touching his wife as he runs to his room, Elmira soon joins him and after a few minutes behind closed doors appears with a sigh of unmistakable significance.

Organ prostrates himself before the saintly guest "Tartuffe." Elmira knows the latter to be a hypocrite and in all probability a thief and tries to frame him in her room with hubby behind the curtain. The latter is just foolish enough to look through the curtains and "Tartuffe" catches sight of him in a mirror. Back to the saintly stuff and accepting the confession of the young wife that she loves him, Tartuffe resists the petting impulse and exits, saying he will pray for her.

Organ is convinced and writes a testament leaving his estate to Tartuffe. Elmira conspires another frame that night. The priestly person enters her room and soon puts away enough wine to unsober him. He tears his clothes off, parts the curtains leading to a bed and draws the bed clothes aside invitingly. He then plumps himself into the bed and stretches his arms forth. Meantime the camera has recorded aggravatingly soft closeups of various parts of Elmira's anatomy.

Organ has been brought to the scene meantime and as Tartuffe confesses to Elmira in drunken glee that he is no priest she pulls

the doors open and Organ enters—cured.

This picture will prove the delight of the censors. By the time they are finished cutting the suggestive scenes there may be 35 minutes of film left.

A degenerate priest trying to "make" his benefactor's beautiful wife should go especially well in Catholic districts.

What little humor there may have been in the original play is entirely lost, leaving only an impression of sordid buffoonery. The laughs, both of them, are in Organ's following Tartuffe like a galley slave, feeding him and brushing flies from his priestly mug.

The picture has been well handled from a production standpoint and Murnau's fine directorial touch is very much in evidence.

Seems a total loss as far as the box office is concerned despite that Jannings may draw the first day or two.

DEMPSEY-SHARKEY
(FIGHT PICTURE)

Presented by Tex Rickard; filmed by Goodart Pictures, Inc., at the ringside, Yankee Stadium, July 21, night. About 18 minutes.

The motion picture of the Jack Dempsey-Jack Sharkey fight July 21 and exhibited the following afternoon is to be rated among the most interesting screenings of the summer. There was such a welter of discussion after the battle that not only the 80,000 who witnessed the event were interested in seeing the pictures but many others who read the opinions of the opposed experts or heard the details over the radio.

The claim of foul hitting by Dempsey was expected to clear up the dispute over that point but even the slow motion view of the seventh round, which lasted only 45 seconds, does not either prove or disprove the claims. One looking at the picture and believing there were two foul blows might think the pictures show them. Those who argue against the foul see nothing wrong at all.

The reason lies in the fact that the picture cameras happened to be spotted where Dempsey's back was showing at the precise time. The motions of his right and left hands to Sharkey's stomach may be seen in direction only, not the actual landing of the socks. A still taken from a broadside angle which appeared in the "Evening World" the day after the fight gives a much better idea of the low blows delivered by the ex-champ, but that picture referred to an earlier round. When the blows to the stomach or groin and the left hook to the chin sent Sharkey down groveling, the men were much closer together.

The slow motion section clearly showed the pain on Sharkey's face just before he took it on the button. He had dropped his hands and turned partly around to protest to the referee, Jack O'Sullivan. Like a flash came the left hook that felled him. Then came the warning from the referee to the fallen man to get up or he would start counting. Then the count after, it is said, Bill Duffy in Dempsey's corner yelled to the referee to do so. When Sharkey was carried to his corner by Dempsey and a second from Sharkey's camp, the beaten man's ankles were virtually flapping on the canvas. It looked as though he had been given a long count.

Portions of the picture show some low blows which O'Sullivan claimed struck Sharkey's legs. The slow motion pictures did not reveal the referee's warning to Dempsey to keep 'em up. There was a slow motion bit at the end of the fifth round when Sharkey tapped Dempsey in the face after the bell rang. As a matter of fact Dempsey had landed one just before that, at the time the bell clanged or slightly afterward. The blows did not hurt the ex-champ and the referee in parting the men is seen to smile. Under the rules Sharkey could have been disqualified.

As to the fighting up to the time of the sudden ending it looked pretty even most of the way, with Sharkey getting in the cleaner blows and Dempsey forcing the milling. The first round shows Dempsey taking it plenty, but his woozy condition at the bell is out. At the ringside it looked as though Dempsey led after the second round because of his boring in and continuous body punching. The pictures show it was a slugging match from start to finish, with both men letting 'em go. Dempsey is proven to be a real fighter of the mauler type, able to take it and taking it but coming back for more. He backed up or side-stepped only a few times, as did Sharkey.

The pictures are not as exciting as the ringside saw it but they are clear and well photographed. Had the men been at a different angle they might have cleared up the fouling dispute. There is no waste of footage, such as showing the men in training. Instead of that old stuff the picture gets right down to the battle.

There was some cutting because the entire film was run off in 18 minutes whereas that period was consumed by the first six rounds alone. The other views and titles would have made it last longer, unless the projection machine was speeded. It didn't seem so. The boxing commission viewed the pictures before they were released, probably to get a line on the alleged foul blows. Persons at that showing said stills would have to be printed before any decision could be arrived at. The titles are partial to Dempsey all the way.

The International Newsreel inserted three rounds of the fight in the weekly news release. Those views were copped, it is said, by means of a telescopic camera spotted in the stands. *Ibee.*

MAN POWER

Paramount production starring Richard Dix in Byron Morgan's story, adapted by Ray Harris and Sam Mintz; continuity by Louise Long; titled by George Marion, Jr.; Clarence Badger directing. About an hour at the Paramount, New York.

Tom Roberts	Richard Dix
Alice Stoddard	Mary Brian
Randall Lewis	Philip Strange
Judson Stoddard	Charles Hill Mailes
Ptomaine	Oscar Smith
James Martin	George Irving
Albert Rollins	Charles Clary
Rev. Guthrie	Charles N. Schaeffer

Not an overly strong Richard Dix feature but satisfying with a male Cinderella idea for the theme. As a hobo, Dix drifts into the scene on a box car, and winds up winning the boss' daughter.

The picture proceeds pacifically until the punch when the manly heroism is the dominant keynote. Dix chauffeurs a tractor with its cargo of dynamite, to blast an avenue for the watery avalanche which threatens to sweep devastation in its path through Peaceful Valley. The timely arrival of the T. N. T. is necessary for the deviation of the aquatic torrents. Coupled with this situation is the flop tractor manufactured by the heroine's father. Something is the matter with it and the old gent faces financial ruin in view of his heavy investment in a dud product.

The giant caterpillar plods its weight through the muck and mire where the hubs of ordinary trucks are marooned, and proves itself doubly, including its pilot.

Considerable suspense is injected into this situation. Down below in Peaceful Valley's citadel, the kiddies are in the midst of an Xmas celebration. A modern Paul Revere mounted on a flivver is racing from household to household to warn the inhabitants that the dam is going and that they should take to the hills.

Mary Brian is a fetching vis-a-vis. She is an eyeful as ever before and extending herself a little more, although most of everything revolves about Dix and the tractor. Oscar Smith as Ptomaine, Dix's colored wartime buddy, supplies satisfactory comedy relief. The rest of the cast is sufficient unto the purpose, but not distinguished.

It's a good action story and with the Dix name should register at the gate. The vigorous title is an asset. *Abel.*

PAID TO LOVE

William Fox romantic comedy. Story by Henry Carr, scenario by William N. Conselman. Directed by Howard Hawks. Running time 80 minutes; at Roxy's, New York, week July 23.

Crown Prince Michael	George O'Brien
Gaby	Virginia Valli
Peter L. Roberts	J. Farrell Macdonald
King Haakon	Thomas Jefferson
Prince Eric	William Powell
Maid	Merta Sterling
Servant	Hank Mann

Rather a saccharine romance, done in the vein of Anthony Hope's "Prisoner of Zenda," only much more so. The director seems to have realized that the sentiment was getting rather maudlin, for he gave the picture a satirical touch. Ironical humor and mythical kingdom in the Balkans refuse to blend. If you're going to do "Zenda" romance, you positively have to do it with a straight face. Otherwise the customers get confused. That's what happens here. But sex stuff is to the fore and with much production beauty, the film is good program material.

Virginia Valli plays the super-heroine role flawlessly. George O'Brien is almost believable as the picturesque crown prince, and the scenic settings of the story are exquisite beyond telling. The regal atmosphere is conveyed remarkably well. Interiors are spacious and beautifully designed and some of the shots of de luxe seashore scenes —the action takes place on the Mediterranean coast—are stunning.

Picture's appeal is to the more naive of the fans who will love it for its voluptuous romance. To the wise crowd the device of having a comedy American millionaire slap the Balkin king on the back is pretty rough hokum. They go even further than that. There is a comic scene in which a valet, absorbed in stolen peeks at the royal lovers, unconsciously turns and throws his arms around the monarch, registering frightened embarrassment when he realizes his faux pas. Hokum could go no further.

The dramatic punch is a rather tricky bit. The heavy sits unobserved in the bedroom of the heroine, while she disrobes and then makes dishonorable love to her, revealing that she has been brought to the palace, hired to "amuse the household." The story turns on this incident, for the girl supposes that she is present on a diplomatic mission. At least the story would have us believe so.

The whole device is hard to swallow.* Virginia Valli is one of those girls who makes her living in a Paris dive, doing an Apache dance in the floor show and associating with the underworld. Still she is a pure girl. In the picture. In the end, of course, they make her a duchess so she can marry the handsome crown prince, and that's another headache.

These crudities are unfortunate, for the picture on its technical side is a splendidly done bit of work. Some of the shots are startling in their pictorial beauty, such, for instance, as a view of rain-swept countryside at dusk with a gnarled cyprus tree as the only landmark. The interiors are the last word in dignified elegance and the acting matches the settings in its quiet suavity. *Rush.*

TWELVE MILES OUT

Metro-Goldwyn-Mayer production and release. Directed by Jack Conway. Titles by Joe Farnham. Adapted from the play by William Anthony McGuire. Starring John Gilbert. Ernest Torrence and Joan Crawford featured. At the Capitol, New York, week July 26. Running time 85 minutes.

Jerry Fay	John Gilbert
Red McCue	Ernest Torrence
Jane	Joan Crawford
Maizie	Eileen Percy
Trini	Paulette Duval
Chiquita	Dorothy Sebastian
Hulda	Gwen Lee
John Burton	Edward Earle
Luke	Bert Roach
Irish	Tom O'Brien

A tale of modern piracy on the high seas. It has its humble beginnings with mere low-lived, uninteresting gun smugglers as the piece de resistance. But as the story is masterfully unwound, and a group of characters, as real and as strong as it is possible for humans to be, are introduced, the theme veers toward hi-jacking, war among bootleggers for the possession of each other's cargoes, nothing more than piracy under another name.

It is a great story as related on the screen, its three principal characters taken by a powerful cast. The picture is a surprise. It promises nothing but delivers a lot. At the best it is expected to be moderately amusing. Instead it turns them inside out laughing, sends a hundred thrills and chills running up and down a thousand respective spines and finally leaves them happy and philosophical with but one query that is an answer in itself, "Is this not life?"

Red McCue and Jerry Fay were friends—in a way. They played each other a lot of tricks that were more or less off color, for instance where Jerry, seeing his boat seized by revenue officers, exchanged with Red for $2,000 and his boat and Red then being arrested for possessing a gun-runner. And Jerry, being the wise-cracking kid, always poking fun at poor old Red for being ugly and stupid. Besides, Jerry was pretty and always stole Red's women.

But Red forgave him. After he got out of the clutches of the Spanish officials, according to Joe Farnham's titles, he turned over a new leaf and took up diamond smuggling in Holland. And when Jerry happened in on the same place what should Red do but corner his pal in a room and give him the bitter taste of a stout leather whip just to show there was no ill-feeling.

Then Jerry got back at him in New York by stealing 500 cases of scotch from his pal, both now in the bootlegging business.

While innocently engaged in loading liquor there is an incident where Jerry is chased by a rum guard. He makes for shore, puts the stick up sign on a man and a woman in their own home and makes himself comfortable until the revenue cutter passes. Then the formally-attired gent wanting to be smart tells the woman to remember Jerry's face for court identification. So Jerry takes them both along.

Here, up against plain sea water, the gent does the cowardly business and Jerry incidentally discovers the pair are not married, only engaged. After that it's a case of trying to make the dame just as he had done a hundred times before. But Jane is not that kind of a girl and finally it sinks through to Jerry. And by the time it hits Jerry the girl has fallen just as hard.

Spying hi-jackers rushing down Jerry orders guns on deck. He then notices white caps on men on board the pursuing boat and orders all the guns thrown overboard, figuring he is being caught by revenue officers. But the figuring is wrong and he is hi-jacked by none other than his old pal, Red McCue.

But Jerry no longer cares about the booze, it's the girl he wants to keep safe. The blubbering "John" here almost spills the beans and registers for one of the biggest laughs by rushing up to Red and, believing him to be a revenuer, protesting, "Officer, you can't take me away like this. I left my fiancee in the Hold." To which he gets a reply, "That's all right, borrow one from one of the men."

Then Red discovers the girl in the room downstairs. "Lay off, Red," Jerry warns him, "she's different. She's not the kind we've been stringing with." But he can't put that sort of an idea through Red's head. McCue is one of those boys to whom all women are alike.

So Jerry tries to kid him out of it. He accuses Red of being drunk and inveigles him into a drinking bout. And finally the man to man fight on the slippery deck of the skidding sloop, punching each other through the rigging, tearing nails into each other's flesh, Jerry hammering away at a chin built like the rock of Gibraltar, and the girl steering straight for a revenue cutter on his orders, with a jail term awaiting him at the end of the scrap.

At the point of exhaustion Jerry picks up a gun and Red finds another. Jerry is shot in both arms but not before he has put three bullets into Red. Side by side they sink to the floor, friends again. And Red, about to pass out, insists that Jerry show him how to pop a bottle by slapping it at the bottom.

The revenue officers board and ask whose ship it is. "Mine," says Jerry. "He's a cock-eyed liar," roars McCue, "it's mine," thereupon turning over cold.

Joan Crawford is a riot, registering like a classic for form, appearance, looks and ability. Two more pictures like this for Miss Crawford and she's set. In this film she knocks them for looks. And she wears only one gown. She has them raving, with the women commenting on her appearance more than the men. Only in one scene, with tears running down her cheek, is the effect somewhat spoiled.

A few titles too many at the opening, but since every one carries a big laugh overcome the slight defect of too much talk without "action."

John Gilbert at his best will bring them in bigger numbers after the first day.

Can't miss.

Rejuvenation of Aunt Mary

P. D. C. production and release. Film version of the famous old comedy with May Robson, the original stage star, supported by Phyllis Haver, Harrison Ford, Arthur Hoyt, Franklin Panghorn, Robert Edeson. At the Hippodrome week of July 25. Running time 52 minutes.

Of all the Keystone flickers, the sort optimists thought gone and limboed, here bobs one that must have done a stowaway for 10 years in somebody's overmatter vault. Statistically this may prove to be a modern product, but visually it is pure pre-war. Its photography is watery-weak; its indoor shots are pale gray, and its action and "plot" are bunkum, hokum and soakem, even to pie-throwing.

The story is preposterous. Fancy a prim old virgin lady who meets a sweetie of her childhood, suddenly goes night-clubbing and gets soused. In a raid she is pinched and comes up before him, through a "coincidence" her naughty but good-looking nephew gets freed after he has run into the judge and been pinched for speeding, and on the last second gets to race his car.

A dirty dog rival ditches him, overturns the speedster, hurts the mechanic. The axle is bent. No other mechanic will sit with him. Auntie tears into overalls—Auntie! Fully 60, and now sober!—and he goes. But that isn't all. His own baby-doll, auntie's trained nurse, fearing for her safety, leaps into a huge ambulance, pushes the driver aside, and gives chase. The cars go at a rate not less than 10,000 miles an hour, and that is no kidding (with a bent axle!).

The "hero" wins after hitting a hot dog stand; auntie catches a gooey pie and throws it backward, gumming up the dirty dog, and the ambulance still pursues—a tremendous closed truck, driven by an inexperienced girl, jerking and winding between a dozen flying racing cars. Of course, the leading man wins. And the ambulance is second!

Only 10 per cent. of the absurdity of this whole crying crime against what was once a reasonably amusing light comedy. It is an insult to the venerable years of an artist like Miss Robson, who knew it in its days of decent dignity, to be hornswoggled or shanghaied into being made the ridiculous butt of such worthless trash.

If it were uproariously amusing that might compensate somewhat—a player is a player and comedy has been the instrument of much talent, much art, even much genius. But this brand of brazen claptrap, which cries out the vulnerable vulgarities with which the screen is constantly charged, at no time attains the legitimate standing of those old-time katzenjammers of Fatty Arbuckle, Ford Sterling, Chester Conklin—not to say Mabel Normand and Ben Turpin.

Miss Robson plays her role tragically well. More's the pity. A trouper of seasoned parts, her noble work makes the entire spectacle the more insolently ironical. And poor old Bob Edeson, himself a player who has been through and over, he slinks through his debasing bit like a one-time gentleman caught picking up cigaret butts in daylight.

Miss Haver looks sweet and acts ditto. Harrison Ford is just what he always is, a "straight man" who never gets a hair rumpled and who does everything with one expression. As a comedian, Franklin Panghorn is hard put to keep himself and the audience from shedding tears. That is only partly his fault. No supposed-to-be-funny man ever had such wooden-headed material handed him. Arthur Hoyt, as a sour and dour disappointed sap, is screamingly unentertaining at all times.

The distorted story is so soppy with shrieking and reeking consistencies, even for film-farce, that they could not be detailed here in two columns. At no time is there a flash, even an approach to that conviction which a farce requires as well as a tragedy. The titles, blunt duds, are the only speaking things that could take it seriously; and when they aim to be rollicking they are most serious.

The photography is the poorest that this reporter has observed in the last several years, or else a poor print was unreeled here. It was at no time sharp, not even in the outdoor takes, except the interpolated newsreel footage of the race. The lighting was underdone throughout on interiors.

Some of the sets were fine. But they didn't belong here. The nephew, who has to "touch" auntie constantly, lives in a mansion, fitted up like Henry Ford's rather than Harrison Ford's. He fakes being a doctor, and the place is turned "within an hour" into a sanitarium where his young drunk cronies "act" as patients. This gets some crude laugh effects in spots, but misses throughout because it is incredibly silly and we are asked to conceive that any human being above the age of two could swallow any part of it.

This is, in all, a third-rate dime-house program release. It is the best argument for block booking ever projected and should be shown to the Interstate Commerce Commission as an argument to prove that this system is imperative—from the producer's standpoint.

Lait.

MATA-HARI

Los Angeles, July 18.

Produced by National Film A-G Corporation of Berlin (Germany). Starring Magda Sonja. Directed by Friederich Feher. Presented by Walter Kofeldt at the Broadway Palace, Los Angeles, week July 18. Running time, around 105 minutes.

This picture is much too sombre in tone to get very far. Evidently the National Film A-G Corporation of Berlin is determined to keep on making European war stories. In the first place, an hour and forty-five minutes of melancholia is too much.

An Oriental dancer, Mata-Hari, is believed to have been executed in Paris in 1916 for treason. Newspapers and magazines carried accounts of this woman, who was supposed to have been a famous spy, dealing with her escapades and intrigues in European court circles. Her identity was never fully established.

The plot on the screen concerns itself with political situations and a love affair between Mata-Hari and a Russian peasant. Leading up to the climactic finish where the heroine faces the firing squad, nothing daunted, is the story of the dancer-spy who is the inamorata of a Russian grand duke until she meets the peasant, Grigori, while escaping from the duke's palace during a wild orgy. The duke learning of her lover causes his arrest. The woman is given the opportunity to save her sweetheart's life by securing certain plans of an Austrian fortress. She obtains them by bartering with Russian military papers, only to find that she has been duped. She agrees to accept the death sentence willingly, so that her peasant lover may be spared.

The scene of the execution, with the rattle of the drums for a fade-out is striking, but too long and weary a procession. Direction in general is just fair, with not enough high spots. A leaning toward the risque is evident in intention but is not carried out to the extreme. The scene of the wild party at the palace has the heroine clad only in a wrap. The garment is allowed to slip off just as the lights go out. No trick shots or outstanding bits of photography. Magda Sunja in the title role is intelligent in her expressiveness and displays a good deal of acting ability of the Pola Negri type. Her sensitiveness is keen, with moods and emotion registering pleasantly. Of the others in the cast Fritz Kortner's "heavy" was convincing, with Alexander Murski true to character as the duke. Matteus Wiemann, as the peasant, was commendable in his character only as far as the love scenes.

An Oriental title for a European story is misleading. Where the foreign element from Germany and Russia might take a chance with a familiar title, the odds are for them passing this by. The running time will have to be chopped by yards. The cutting is none too good. No bet for the small town exhibitor.

DEATH VALLEY

First Division Production, directed by Paul Powell. From the story by Raymond Wells. Cast includes Carroll Nye, Rada Rae, Sam Allen, Raymond Wells, Grace Lord and "Rex," dog. Previewed in projection room July 22.

An epic of the west characterized mainly by a sordidness through frequent repetition of colorless scenes and idiotic expression.

The crux hinges on a dirty look, figuratively and literally. Raymond Wells does it. Raymond wears the long black mustachios of meller-drammer and lunges forward with hunched shoulders in the manner most approved of in barnstorming circles. With a few hisses the atmospheric surroundings would be complete.

There is a certain desire on the part of any audience to know why Raymond looked at that nice young boy in that way just because he happened to strike gold on his first day on the claim. Others might figure that the look should have been the tip-off. If Raymond had any designs on the young man's gold it would have been wiser not to have registered such covetousness in public.

The hero flops badly from his first introduction. When Raymond hands out that dirty look everybody figures the fun is due to start. The young man smiles up confidingly instead of pushing the gruesome nose between the heavy's ears.

If the producers would care to pay a comedy writer enough for a set of laugh titles for the picture it could easily be turned into the outstanding comedy western of the season. There is a serio-comic scene where the unknown woman is threatened with a fate worse than death unless she steals the boy's gold for Raymond.

This is worked through a painful ruse. The woman is to be found wandering in the desert by the boy. To lend a touch of reality to the proceedings Raymond places the woman against the wall and punches her face three times. This is probably the first time a picture has been shown of a man deliberately punching a woman in the face and three times, too.

Contact between the heavy and the male lead is entirely avoided. The latter doesn't even raise a hand either in praise or censure.

Story stupidly handled. Scenes are practically all exteriors with two shacks for the interiors.

The cast is so far below the standard of the average western cast as to be beyond classification.

There's a dog in it too.

White Pants Willie

First National production presented by C. C. Burr, starring Johnny Hines and directed by Charles Hines. Story by Elmer Davis. Cameraman, James Diamond. In cast: Leila Hyams, George Kuwa, Walter Long, Henry Barrows, Margaret Seddon. Running time, 50 mins. At Loew's American, New York, July 14-17.

The Johnny Hines pictures have been pretty seedy the past season, with even the yesmen admitting everything was not all it should be. "White Pants Willie" appears to be the official beginning of a bigger and better life for Messrs. Burr, Hines, et al.

Some dough spent for the story, which ran in "Liberty." It's the old idea of the hero being mistaken for somebody famous, this time a crack polo player. Despite its basic familiarity, it's a good yarn that might have served Reginald Denny's genteel hoke methods. It has been made up into a fairly good, though not big league, comedy. The Hines organization showed admirable restraint, but couldn't quite conquer several temptations to hurl a little custard.

Hines is a lowly garage mechanic of an inventive turn. His ideas of grandeur find expression through the wearing of a pair of white flannels purchased from Sears-Roebuck. His boss, the garage prop., bullies and finally fires him. With the assistance of a disgruntled Chinese laundry worker who poses as his chauffeur, Johnny rides up to a swell country hotel in a borrowed limousine. Tipping lavishly and wearing his white pants, he sneaks in as the real thing and gets passed as a polo player. From then on the complications follow conventionally with dumb luck making him a hero and winning a millionaire's backing for his invention.

Leila Hyams is the millionaire's daughter not called upon to do anything of importance, but looking great. Miss Hyams is understood to be under contract to Warner Brothers and loaned for this film. George Kuwa, playing the comical Chinaman, rates mention for his legitimate farcial work.

Despite **hat boxes that walk** through lobbies and hot water bags hidden under skirts, "White Pants Willie" is a distinct step out and away from the spilt-soup-and-ripped-seam type of low slapstick that has kept Johnny Hines from making capital of the advantage gained when a First National release was obtained for his pictures some time ago.

THE MOJAVE KID

F. B. O. production, directed by Robert North Bradbury. Story and continuity by Oliver Drake. Cameraman E. T. McManigal. Running time, 50 mins. In projection room, July 20.

Bob	Bob Steele
Thelma	Lillian Gilmore
Silent	Buck Connors
Big Olaf	Bob Fleming
Bill Dugan	Jay Marley
Panamint Pete	Theodore Henderson
Zeke Hatch	Nat Mills

F. B. O. introduces with this one a new saddle king, Bob Steele, who will be seen in a series of action yarns of the great open areas. Steele is a young-appearing chap though possibly it's his slight stature that gives the impression of being on the lean side of 20. Most of the cinema cowboys are big guys with enormous lungs and bulging biceps. So Steele on a basis of size alone is unique. And if F. B. O. continues to surround him with stories as good as "The Mojave Kid" it seems certain that whether boy or man, he'll click with the fans.

F. B. O. necessarily operates on a policy of moderate priced western productions. No dough is wasted, but at the same time they generally manage to get plenty to show for the outlay. In "The Mojave Kid" it is unlikely that more than a couple of inexpensive studio sets were built. The free and plentiful scenery of mother nature was resorted to.

The Mojave kid is the son of a prospector who had disappeared 12 years before. He follows three bandits whom he believes have knowledge of the fate of his father. Discovering themselves followed the bandits fire at the kid and leave him for dead. The Mojave kid is uninjured through a ruse of wrapping his blanke around a log.

In the "valley of the lawless" is a colony of hard hombres who are keeping the long-missing prospector prisoner in the hope of one day forcing from him his secret of a hidden gold mine. The leader of the tough mugs is a man of his word. An inter gang feud develops. It is the means of the kid, his father and the heroine escaping to make the final clinch.

Photography excellent and the close-ups always clear, unusual in western pictures. Direction is businesslike and competent, with the celluloid assembled intelligently. The cast acquit themselves well in parts suited to their types.

First rate western all the way.

The Fighting Hombre

F. B. O. release. Jesse Goldburg production starring Bob Custer. Story by Estrella Ward. Jack Nelson director, with Ernest Miller at camera. In the cast Mary O'Day, Carlo Schipa, Zita Ma-Kar, David Dunbar, Bert Sproute and Walter Mailey. Running time, 54 mins. At Stanley, New York, one day, July 22.

Plots of cowboy pictures are pretty well standardized and an experienced judge can generally etch out the whole from the ground work of the first reel. But here is something a little different. Instead of the hero being wrongfully accused of murder in "The Fighting Hombre" it's the heroine who gets pinched on a homicide charge, with the hero working to establish her innocence.

F. B. O. has an acceptable western picture in this one. It moves swiftly as an outdoor melodrama should and it moves with dovetailed continuity. Two details bespoke carelessness. The menace was alternately referred to in sub-titles as Hopkins and Goldstud, with quotes around the latter on one occasion. There was no reason for this and it would tend to confuse.

Late in the picture, with the heroine going into a neck with the hero her dress was sweated badly under the arms.

Mary O'Day, playing the heroine, is in some respects ideal for westerners. She is more or less baby dollish, yet rides and shows enough vitality to plausibly have been raised in the cow country. She imparts enough sexiness to be interesting and can wear riding breeches.

Carlo Schipa, playing a sympathetic Mexican character, stood out as a type and a trouper. He is an unknown who ought to find a niche for himself in the films. Also new, and a good type, was Zita Ma-Kar, playing a Mexican gal wronged by the villain.

The camera work was faulty here and there, when Ernest Miller seemed to be shooting directly toward the sun with an open shutter. Brisk and peppy in the main and maintaining a good production standard (for westerns), "The Fighting Hombre" rates better than okay.

HANDS OFF

Blue Streak Western released by Universal. Directed by Ernest Laemmle from the story by J. Allen Dunn. Starring Fred Humes, Marian Nixon featured. Cast includes Nelson McDowell and Bruce Gordon. At Loew's New York, one day, July 22, one-half of a double feature program. Running time around an hour.

Ernest Laemmle has progressed further with his Blue Streak Westerns than many directors who have been doing the same work for twice as long. He has evidently learned to produce type pictures of a quality which will please wherever westerns are liked.

With the opening scene the director avoided the pitfalls that others easily fall into. An old prospector is dying. Without the usual tearstorms he dies, placidly, naturally, as most people leave this earth. And before his senses leave him he makes the stranger, Fred Humes, promise to act as guardian for the girl and the claim.

Humes is accompanied by two ancient, bushy-browed prospectors who furnish much more than the usual quota of comedy. McDowell and Gordon are a fine pair of type funsters whose abilities should be commercialized to a greater extent.

There are laughs in this picture that few westerns of the cheaper grade have ever achieved or even come near reaching. This Mutt and Jeff team is a riot in the smaller towns and with proper material would doubtless hit any set of customers.

This western is also original inasmuch as the schemer does not own the sheriff, body and soul. For once in a thousand times here is a small town official more like what he is than what some people think he should be.

By-play between the boy and the girl is minus most of the awkwardness usually attributed to such scenes in westerns. A couple of snappy fist fights and some fine riding about completes the action.

POOR GIRLS

Columbia production directed by William James Craft. From the story by Sophie Bogen. Cast including Dorothy Revier, Ruth Stonehouse, Edmund Burns, Lloyd Whitlock and Marjorie Bonner. At Loew's New York, one day, July 22, one-half of a double feature program.

Not a chance. The first half of the title is a fit adjective for the cast, story and direction.

Because she discovers her mother a rich but honest night club hostess Dorothy Revier leaves home and makes for a departmental store without asking the old lady why and wherefore. No audience can root for the gal when they know mother has done her darndest to make enough money to meet the gas bills and her daughter's drug store accounts.

And if the gal does leave home for a try at a job, what of it? There are doubtless hardships attached to such an undertaking, but the move was entirely unnecessary and could have been straightened out in a five-minute conversation.

Miss Revier has a tough assignment and handles it gracelessly.

Edmund Burns and Lloyd Whitlock are both stilted and unnatural.

Two-Gun of Tumbleweed

Pathe production directed by Leo Maloney from the story by Ford I. Beebe. Starring Leo Maloney. At Loew's New York, one day, July 8; one-half of double feature program. Running time, about 55 minutes.

While not original, the cold-blooded "mysterious" heavy angle gives this western a slightly different touch. Joseph Rickson troupes very capably, in comparison with the balance of the cast, as the dangerous outlaw with just a spark of decency in his makeup.

Instead of playing Rickson for the foil all the way through Maloney brought the Bar C foreman into the pictures plus a total loss in a sheriff. This detracted from the interest in a possible scrap between two worthwhile characters.

Leo Maloney directed himself in this effort. He screens, too, stout for pop appeal and lacks other essentials in a western star.

Most of this film seems to be made up of chin arguments instead of action. Maloney proves himself a very good debater. Being the director, Maloney was in a position to allow himself to win all the arguments.

For the climax is a gently staged shooting. It does not rouse a particle of suspense.

Where they like westerns with action they won't care for this one. The love interest, as in most westerns, is nicely skimmed over.

Rickson photographs well as a possibility for better things.

Mile a Minute Man

Lumas release, presented by Camera Pictures, starring William Fairbanks, with Virginia Brown Faire in support. Directed by Jack Nelson from a story by E. J. Meagher. Cameraman, Art Reeves. At Columbus one day (June 28) on double feature program. Running time, 45 minutes.

A passable racing picture, considered from the miniature expenditure angle.

Plot is standard, except in a final twist. This ending has the leading light deliberately lose the race because his gal is riding against him and she's promised to marry him only if her car wins. Such an ending is somewhat disquieting and will disappoint many a panting heart.

As for acting, Miss Faire is coyly cute while big husky Mister Fairbanks (he busted a set of handcuffs by just pulling his arms apart and showing his teeth) is called upon for muscle rather than mentality.

Until the time of the race the picture is a patchwork of incidents, some having nothing to do with anything in particular.

Still, suitable for its field, although not for posterity.

Perils of the Jungle

Produced and distributed by Artclass Pictures Corporation (Weiss Bros.). A serial in ten chapters of two reels each. Running time of chapters, about 12 minutes. Directed by Jack Nelson under supervision of George M. Merrick from the story by Harry P. Crist. Photographed by W. C. Thompson and Bert Longnecker. Viewed in projection room July 21.

Phyllis Marley............Eugenia Gilbert
Rod Bedford.................Frank Merrill
Kimpo......................Bobby Nelson
"Brute" Hanley.........Albert J. Smith
Stephens ....Walter Maly

In the days when you paid your nickel and at the end of the first show had to turn in your ticket stub so they could keep you from sitting through it all again, serials like this were quite the stuff.

But kids are still kids, and if they won't flock to the neighborhood house to see this one something's all wrong. It's a phantom of the past—a blood and thunder thriller whose each chapter ends with death just around the corner for some member of the cast.

And for a serial "Perils" is well done. The story, of course, is as illogical as catsup on grape nuts; but who can be consistent when there is a ton of wild action to be packed in each chapter?

The fact that the picture was made in California speaks well for some of this "wild" stuff. The lions, for instance, cut up like they were on the level, and several other brands of animal life do likewise. The elephants, as a rule, fail to get into the savage spirit of it all, but put in a few impressive moments.

Set into the wild animal atmosphere is a story of an adventurer in Africa who joins with a girl seeking her long lost sister and the sister's son. Also, there is an item of gold and diamond treasures, the location of which is denoted on a map. Half of the map is held by the adventurer; the other by his girl friend. Two white villains of the cast and the native bad men provide the difficulties.

The sister is eventually found. She is enthroned by the blacks as a witch goddess, while her little son is identified as the mystery boy who was discovered by the searchers quite early in the story.

Frank Merrill, the male lead, is manly looking. Eugenia Gilbert, the girl, has little acting to do; but she's pretty and photographs well.

Bobby Nelson, as the little mystery kid, handles a major part very professionally, and undoubtedly will cop favorite honors among the juvenile customers.

Direction is best in the animal stuff, some of it being done expertly. A weakness is evidenced in handling emotions, but as these are secondary to situations it doesn't show so plainly. Photography good.

This serial should be a draw in the neighborhoods.

MME. POMPADOUR

Paramount release of British National Pictures, Ltd., production starring Dorothy Gish ("courtesy of Inspiration Pictures, Inc.") and featuring Antonio Moreno. A Herbert Wilcox production, supervised by E. A. Dupont. Scenario by Frances Marion, based on Rudolph Schanzer and Ernst Welisch's work. About 60 minutes at the Paramount, New York, week July 30.

Madame Pompadour..........Dorothy Gish
Rene Laval................Antonio Moreno
King Louis XV................Henry Bosc
Comte Maurepas........Jeff McLaughlin
Duc de Courcelette.............Nelson Keys
Gogo.......................Cyril McLaglin
Madame Poisson..........Marcel Beauplau
Belotte.........................Marie Ault
Premier....................Tom Reynolds

Once in a while England sends over a good one. This is a good one. Of course, the exotic Pompadour theme is almost sure-fire box-office with half-way decent treatment. The Wilcox production is above British par—judging from other importations—and it shapes up rather complimentary, even for an American producer.

Nothing condescending or tolerant about this championing of the Hollywood megaphone wielders, but all this is generally acknowledged for the general run of foreign pictures, not excepting the German, which only occasionally can click with a "Variety" or "Metropolis." And the same E. A. Dupont who turned out "Variety" made this "Pompadour." So figure it out.

Dorothy Gish gives a dignified and softened performance. Her amour for the radical artist who later becomes her bodyguard (Tony Moreno) until Louis XV gets hep to the cheating is great stuff for the femmes. It is a better woman's picture, in truth, than men's. The frails will go for it, and the way they buzz at the romantic ruses is enough of a tip-off.

Costume stuff a great flash, and some lavish interludes are introduced for the last reel and a half. A couple of fine directorial touches in contrasts, moods and shades dress it up.

Henry Bosc as the jealous Louis and Jeff McLaughlin as the menace did exceptionally well, on a par with the featured pair.

A money picture.

Abel.

PAINTING THE TOWN

Universal release, produced by William James Craft (Jewel). Story and scenario by Harry Hoyt. Titles by Harry Demond. Photographed by Allen C. Jones. At the Roxy, New York, week July 30. Running time, 62 minutes.

Hector Whitmore..............Glenn Tryon
Patsy De Veau..........Patsy Ruth Miller
Raymond Tyson............Charles Gerard
Fire Commissioner..........George Fawcett
Secretary ....Sidney Bracey
Wilson.........................Max Ascher

Once the cash customers lamp this picture they'll start passing out the favorable remarks. With a comparatively unknown youngster carrying star honors, though, it may prove a little tough getting patronage started. Exploitation is needed to put it over right.

Glenn Tryon is the newcomer. If you know your two-reel comedies he's not so new, and his clowning in this feature length is apt to surprise. That pan of his, while not so homely, is nevertheless a natural laugh. With plenty of prop situations to mirror it along, he finishes with a good foundation on which to build a standing rep.

William James Craft produced and directed. His story called for a frivolous brand of comedy, but he took advantage of the w. k. license and borrowed his wow punches from the farce department. A series of legit laughs in the middle of the footage tends to show up the farce work, including the highly hoke ending, but the damage is slight.

The tale has Tryon as Hector Whitmore, young hick inventor with all patents pending, coming to the big city with an automobile he has invented for the use of the fire department. This car goes 150 miles an hour and stops within two lengths.

Young Hector also has a half-way invitation from a "Follies" star whom he met while tending his gas station back home. He looks her up at the theatre. A party follows the show. Hector turns out to be the big noise with his exploding cigars, clown antics and other trick incidentals.

The "Follies" girl has a boy friend trying to sell cars to the Fire Commissioner. When this guy lamps Hector's car he realizes he's lost unless dirty work is done.

Upon Hector's big chance to demonstrate the nasty gent has glixed the brakes so that the car looks like a flop. Never daunted, Hector waits for his next chance, and, with the help of the show girl, gets the Fire Commissioner into the trick car, making him sign a contract while tearing up and down Broadway.

This Hector role is meat for Tryon. It calls for a wise guy pranker who thinks he's the berries, but is, underneath it all, just a simp with a nice heart. Tryon works something like William Haines, although much more farcically.

Feature honors are shared by Patsy Ruth Miller, whose name is more known to the box office. She is the "Follies" dame with satisfying results, but overshadowed throughout by her partner. George Fawcett as the Commissioner has a good character role, while Charles Gerard handles the menace work.

Craft's direction brought out several healthy laugh situations. One gag, having a magician at a theatre party smash a watch to bits in a trick, thinking it was the hick's and later discovering it was his own, brought a roar at the Roxy. This bit, not new, was handled expertly. Several other bits also drew heavily.

Titles work hard for results and hit fairly, with the exception of a few foolish cracks.

Although there's some box office risk in taking on the first effort of an unknown comedian, this picture has "names" in the cast and will establish its worth inside a theatre.

LONESOME LADIES

First National comedy drama featuring Lewis Stone and Anna Q. Nilsson. Directed by Joseph Henabery. Story by Lenore J. Coffee. Running time, 60 minutes. At the Strand, New York, week July 30.

John Fosdick	Lewis Stone
Polly Fosdick	Anne Q. Nilsson
Mrs. St. Clair	Jane Winton
Helen Wayne	Doris Lloyd
Motley Hunter	Edward Martindel
Bee	Fritzie Ridgway
Dorothy	De Sacia Mooers
Mr. Burton	Capt. E. H. Calvert
Mrs. Burton	Grace Carlisle
Butler	Fred Warren

Another light society comedy made with fine atmosphere and acted with intelligence and taste, but lacking in compelling interest. It's just a well made picture from tepid, humdrum materials. There isn't a character on view who engages the sympathy or even the interest of the spectator and there is scarcely an incident that grips.

The picture has comedy of a sort, but it's terribly polite and subtle comedy. Of drama there is scarcely a vestige. The picture goes to the extreme in the new mode of quiet story exposition. At one point there is a situation that could have been made the means of something like action. A husband, separated from his wife by scheming women, finds his mate dining alone with a bachelor of unsavory reputation in the bachelors' apartment.

Husband, who has every reason to believe that his honor is involved, stands in the middle of the room and frowns hard at the man who apparently has broken his home. So the bachelor sheepishly slips out by the back door and the husband takes his wife home, where they resume their former domestic life of newspaper reading and yawning.

That incident is typical of the entire production. It achieves triumphs of boredom and does it with remarkable elegance. The action is always on the brink of something stimulating, but never delivers. One long episode is devoted to the business of a peppy widow making amorous advances to the deserted husband. Widow wears one of those revealing negligees and undulates all over the sumptuous drawing room, while the husband tries to make her attend strictly to the business of giving instruction to her architect. But nothing happens. It may be as well that the screen is outgrowing some of its melodramatic excesses, but the new craze for the other extreme is as bad or worse.

The materials here are commonplace and well worn. Husband neglects his wife for business. She declares herself and goes to live her own life with a group of hard-boiled divorcees living on alimony. One of the alimony ladies has her eye on the husband and devotes herself to keeping them apart while apparently acting as the go-between seeking their reconciliation. It is she who brings about the intimate-dinner situation the husband steps into, an episode that brings husband and wife together.

The story is not calculated to attract women, since it deals with the sex in a cynical vein. The wife's a fool and her women friends are either dishonest or dumb, while the widow angling for the lone man of the scenario in a serio-comic way will draw no cheers from the feminine fans.

The players handle their unsympathetic roles with what grace is possible in the circumstances, which, to be sure, are little enough, and the settings are created with striking skill and artistry. If that makes a movie, you can have this one. *Rush.*

Judgment of the Hills

F. B. O. release, produced by Leo Meehan. From story in "Cosmopolitan" by Larry Evans. At Hippodrome, N. Y., week Aug. 1. Running time, about 60 minutes.

Margaret Dix	Virginia Valli
Tad Dennison	Frankie Darro
Brant Dennison	Orville Caldwell

That title should never have been tacked on this release. The picture's too good for it and the title's apt to hold the picture down.

Although well made, "Judgment" looks like only a medium money-maker as an inde output. The story it tells was in its highest favor several years ago, since slipping to apparent oblivion with one freak exception, "Stark Love."

"Judgment" is the story of an illiterate brute living among the Kentucky hills with his kid brother. The big bro gets lit every so often with the town's loafers, and demonstrates his amazing strength for their particular delight.

The town's school teacher sees the pair and persuades the elder to let his kid brother attend school. Thus she cultivates their acquaintance but makes plain her disgust with Brant's drunken tactics.

The war comes along and Brant is called, but despite his strength and bully tactics he proves fearful of having his body marred by bullets. He runs away. His younger brother, persuaded by the school teacher that it is for the best, exposes Brant's hiding place, and the drunk is jerked into the army.

When the armistice is signed and the men start milling back, the town decides that Brant should have become a changed man. A big celebration is made ready for him.

But he steps off the train dead drunk and staggers to the saloon with his old pals, neglecting the celebration in his honor.

In the saloon he starts his old stuff. One of his tricks is to break a brick with his first. As usual, he steps outside the saloon and calls for the kid to fetch him a brick. The kid, with tears in his eyes, does so, but in a rage he hurls the brick at his brother and derides his drunken show-off displays.

That turns the table. Big bro sees what a sap he is and pleadingly indicates that he'll be okay from then on. He also eyes the school teacher in a manner that indicates there's be love later on; but it isn't in the picture.

Direction and photography combine admirably to put this picture across technically. Settings, characters and scenery provide a natural rustic atmosphere, conveyed effectively.

Virginia Valli is the school teacher. She looks a trifle too sweet for the rest of the outfit, but manages to do her bit besides providing a "name" for the picture.

Frankie Darro, juvenile, known mostly for his work in "quickie" westerns with Tom Tyler, here is head and shoulders above any of his previous stuff. Orville Caldwell, male lead, also comparatively unknown, just fits his role, which may account for his previous nonentity. He is highly convincing here.

The absence of heavy love theme is not noticed so much until the picture ends. It is a slight disappointment.

Even if it doesn't get much big booking this film will be a treat for the smaller houses.

The Way to Strength and Beauty

UFA presents a seven-reel patchwork of newsreels and educational propaganda; at the Fifth Avenue Playhouse, July 30.

The title sounds as though this were something written by Mary G. Baker Eddy. But it turns out to have not been written at all. It is a German feature and played in stock in one Berlin theatre for two years. It seems to have been collected from many sources, and is plotless.

The nudity in this propaganda for nature-living, exercise and outdoors far outstrips anything ever permitted before on the American screen. It must have been a looloo in Germany, for what still survives here and is seen at the snug little Fifth Avenue playhouse is plenty naked.

Women entirely undraped flicker and flit through, usually with their backs turned and always on the way to enter the waves or go into some classical al fresco dancing. In other portions girls bare of any suggestion of covering from the waist-line up also "act"—that is, they are maids in the Roman baths, etc., and are out-and-out movie whereas the all-nude ones make the pretense of being rather "natural" than naked.

To the point of monotony, the titles reel off arguments, pleas and propaganda for us to get back to mother earth and the simplicity of early savagery.

To this end newsreel bits from all countries, revealing all manner of athletics, sports, exercise, are screened. Here and there a diagram of anatomy is utilized. Men, women, babies are shown, the men as nude as the women.

Germany, especially since the war, has been beset with fresh-air and nature-culture cults. They have magazines of their own and in portions of the empire whole cliques live entirely clotheless, subsist off raw vegetable foods, and serve the gods of grace and strength.

To those who can take such plans sincerely, there must be a good deal of kick in the display. To those who see the pornographic appeal of women's figures displayed, these exhibits offer the big shot of all times to be so entertained in a movie-house chair.

It makes one blink to behold, in this land of the free, such frank exposure. The dumb-looking German women who disport before the lens, healthy and strapping Gretchens with not much of what we regard as "It" in our film tastes, are fine specimens of potential motherhood if nothing more. They are not pert or saucy. Their hair is not bobbed. They are not Sennett cuties. But they are very sturdy heifers, and as exhibits of what air, water, grass and calisthenics can accomplish, they are convincing testimony.

Glorifying the human body has, of course, wide potentialities, and they are utilized to illustrate many forms of many centuries and many countries. Here and there the hand of a slick director is seen to contrive methods for revealing nudity and yet alibi plausibly with naive titles crying aloud for us to prolong our lives, improve our minds, heighten our pep, purify our souls in God's fresh and free sunshine instead of in stuffy, synthetic city surroundings and the hypocrisy of garments.

This healthy, primal plea, which should find a home anywhere, will still encounter lots of smoke if it attempts to tour around America. The nakedness would shock the hinterlands into a panic of protest. If it can get by, it can get money. It will never be seriously followed here by mature folks who see any good in it, but should draw adolescent boys and superannuated men whose eyes pop at the sight of feminine curves.

Of course, at the esoteric Mindlin playhouse, it's a laugh. The patrons there are wised up, and the house titles kid everything. But there is no other theatre on this continent with that spirit, so what this film did here cannot serve as a guide-light to general projection. Here it did business. *Lait.*

ROARING FIRES

Elbee production directed by A. B. Barringer. From the story by A. B. Barringer. Cast including Alice Lake, Roy Stewart, Lionel Belmore, Bert Berkeley, Robert Walker, Culvert Curtis. At Loew's New York, one day, July 29; one-half of double program.

By eliminating a few more scenes with titles substituted in their stead this would have been a novelty as the first short story ever filmed.

The roaring fires are strictly a figment of the director's frenzied imagination. Between hot scenes of an insipid looking female talking or arguing a couple of shots of burning tenements are thrown in for effect. Closeups of Trusty Dobbins hot-footing it to the rescue are far from exciting.

The directorial touch is clumsy. There is a story of the old fireman, with the last three horses, dreaming of by-gone glory. A fair situation sadly neglected.

Story is of a wealthy girl reforming the slums with speeches. The old man refuses to make the fire traps safe.

A heroic fireman is thrown in without regard for anyone's feelings. He's a flop as far as the audience goes, but makes good with the gal. Extremely limited in scope.

GRINNING GUNS

Universal western, starring Jack Hoxie. Directed by Al Rogell from script by Grover Jones. Photographed by Wm. Nobles. Cast includes Ena Gregory, Bob Milasch, and George B. French. At the Stanley, New York, one day (July 28). Running time, 55 minutes.

This stable sachet is recommended because quite a portion of the cowboy addicts at the Stanley seemed to think it was good. If they like it in New York their brothers of similar bean will like it in Muskogee, Okla.

Mr. Hoxie this time is a rambling gent traveling about the west with a tough pal. The pal thinks Hoxie is a bandit, and has hooked up with him to pull a few jobs. It later turns out that Hoxie is looking for the author of a certain book.

He finds the author, a fiery little guy who is running a newspaper in an ungodly town, and saves him from the wild bad men who are persecuting him for trying to bring order into the hamlet.

Hoxie and his gun then take over the paper. Every tough guy in town is made to subscribe at the point of a gun. Hoxie prints each week the name of a ruffian who must leave town or take the consequences.

With things finally cleaned up and the menacing saloon owner dealt with, accordingly, Hoxie takes the editor's daughter into his arms.

This, according to a date line in the paper, occurs in 1919. Guns are toted about by one and all. The saloon is one of those things identified with the gold rush days. Everyone rides around on horses, and there isn't a single Ford in the footage.

The one man guilty of some actual performing is Bob Milasch, carrying on as the rowdy pal of Hoxie. He draws several legitimate laughs on his own score and does considerable for the picture. Others as usual.

Photography is up to standard. Direction showed a weakness for farce at times, and averaged as not so hot.

But the addicts won't care.

RAMBLING RANGER

Universal Western. Jack Hoxie starred. Del Henderson directed. Running 46 mins. On double bill, one day, Columbus, New York, July 28.

A western picture without speed is like an airship without a motor, it's not going to get very far. Starting with a title that has no significance, "The Rambling Ranger" unfolds a commonplace western plot.

It may be held as a doubtful principle for westerns to hinge their appeal on the adopting by the hero of an infant foundling. Jack Hoxie or any bridle specialist will be liked better when riding, shooting, strong-arming or cliff-leaping than when registering dumb bafflement over a baby.

There's a menace here, but a little too milk-and-watery for orthodox villainy. About the limits of his daring is to make faces behind Hoxie's back and to steam up the Mothers' League of a small western village to take Hoxie's adopted baby away from him. Small boys in Crookston, Minn., or Strawberry Point, Ia., are going to have a difficult time refreshing up any venom against a wrist-slapping villain or any enthusiasm for a do-nothing hero.

The production is rock bottom minimum. All exteriors barring a couple of shacks, a country store and a sheriff's office.

Even the scenery is dull.

YOURS TO COMMAND

F. B. O. production and release, starring George O'Hara. Story by Basil Dickey and Harry Haven. Directed by David Kirkland. Cameraman James Cronjager. In cast, Dot Farley, Shirley Palmer, Jack Luden, Vin Moore, William Burress, William Humphrey. Running time 53 minutes. At Stanley, New York, one day, July 30.

A sad yarn of the "Bringing Up Father" genus. Besides sporting a hero with the name of O'Hara, "Yours to Command" details the exploits of a newly-rich Irish family who come to New York and are framed by some society highbinders. It all makes for a fairly breezy little feature that will satisfy outside the big first runs.

George O'Hara is a good looking chap with an easy, natural manner before the camera. F. B. O. gave him stellar honors following his appearances in a couple of its series of two-reelers which evidently sold him to the provinces. He hardly qualifies as yet as a big city "name."

O'Hara is driving through Oklahoma in a ritzy car. Lost in a forest of oil derricks a girl school teacher shows him the way out but mistakes him for the chauffeur, not the owner of the car.

Later they meet in New York. He carries out the masquerade as chauffeur to guard her and her family against the jewel thieves who have insinuated themselves into the family's good graces by flattery.

Picture holds a sizeable quota of laughs, runs along swiftly and always keeps the hokum within decent bounds.

LIGHTNING LARIATS

F. B. O. production and release. Starring Tom Tyler. Directed by Robert De Lacey from a script by George Worthing Yates. Jr. Cast includes Dorothy Dunbar, Ruby Blaine, Frankie Darro. At the Columbus, New York, one day (July 29) on double-feature bill. Running time, about 55 minutes.

This western has the advantage of a venturesome departure in western scripts. Balancing this is the disadvantage of little action. Which makes its chances just the same as those of the average western.

The story concerns an Arizona ranch owner whose property is covered with notes held by a friendly old neighbor. This neighbor has a pretty daughter with a nasty temper who is confident that she'll eventually marry the young rancher.

When it's time to foreclose on Tyler's ranch, the old neighbor fills his stomach with likker and gets up enough temporary courage to refuse his daughter's demands and sends her back home with a spanking. Suitable casting and an unusually refined brand of western directing.

Spirit Lake Massacre

Sunset Production. Directed by Robert North Bradbury. Cameraman James S. Brown, Jr. In cast, Bryant Washburn, Anne Schaeffer, Jay Morley, Shirley Palmer, Thomas Lingham, Chief Yowlache. Running time, 50 mins. On double feature bill at Arena, New York, one day, July 29.

The Indian, once the partner of the film cowboy, has largely disappeared. Indian pictures in the never-ending output of westerners are sufficiently infrequent to afford refreshing relief from the monotony of masked riders and sheriff's posses. So "Spirit Lake Massacre" can be recommended for the exhibitor whose patronage is largest when his feature is full of horses and fighting.

Anthony J. Xydias is slated as the producer of the didoes here under discussion. No great banking resources were required for the financial end. It's a "quickie," but, in justice, a much better production than that slang term generally implies. The photography is clear and good, saying a lot for a "quickie."

It details the dream of power came to Sitting Bull, who sets out to do a lot of tomahawking. Usual love story between the young scout and the prairie flower, this time a minister's daughter. The young scout is Bryant Washburn, who looks about as western as Times Square. He wears a waxed mustache and a general air of dramatic stock. Being the only name in the picture, he's featured.

A real Indian, Chief Yowlache, plays Sitting Bull and proved a better actor than any of his white brothers. Picture is replete with fighting and has publicity angles for the small town.

BARBED WIRE

Paramount production and release. Starring Pola Negri; featuring Clive Brook and Einar Hanson. Adapted from Sir Hall Caine's novel, "The Woman of Knockaloe," with adaptation by Jules Furthman. Directed by Rowland V. Lee. At the Paramount, New York, week of Aug. 6. Running time, 67 mins.

Mona	Pola Negri
Oskar	Clive Brook
The Brother	Einar Hanson
The Father	Claude Gillingwater
The Commandant	Charles Lane
The Neighbor	Gustav von Seyffertitz
Hans	Clyde Cook
The Sergeant	Ben Hendricks, Jr.

London caused Sir Hall Caine, author of the original novel from which this picture is adapted, quite some annoyance when this film was first shown there. So much so that the well-known writer answered the cries of "pro-German" in the British press to defend his story and the makers of the picture. Viewing of this release will convince that the author was fully justified in his defense. It's an interesting and unfamiliar portion of the late war which must have made good reading in book form and undoubtedly has more body to it than 80 per cent of our screen program leaders. It's of a French girl who falls in love with a German prisoner of war. German-Americans especially will eat it up.

A well-made production from start to finish with one flaw. The star, Pola Negri, does not convince in appearance or performance as the French peasant woman ultimately driven from her home by neighbors because of befriending one of the enemy.

The general rule is that should the star of a picture lack the requisites to meet his or her responsibilities in a production, then that particular production is doomed. "Barbed Wire" is an exception. Miss Negri's performance may handicap the film as a whole, but the story plus the work of Clive Brook, Claude Gillingwater, Clyde Cook (comedy) and the assembling of its component parts more than offset her deficiency.

Some believe that Miss Negri invariably is camera conscious, others that except under the guidance of certain directors she is lost. In any case this particular episode reveals her first and always the actress to the extent that any house will be so aware of that fact that the star will never "get off the screen." She must be vindictive, yielding; she must have strength, she must have fire and here she has neither. Just the actress being mightily helped by a competent supporting cast who, in turn, are abetted by capable direction and support from the technical staff.

The picture unquestionably held the attention of a capacity audience for the full 67 minutes it was on the screen Monday night. The story is responsible for that plus the performances of the men. Miss Negri is practically the only woman allowed personal footage.

The high point is when Mona (Miss Negri) goes home after justifying Oskar at a court martial for attacking a French sergeant. Her neighbors turn against her, but the German prisoners (war) behind the wired fence tip their hats as she walks past them.

Worth taking a look at for those who have never liked Negri because of the theme it carries which, in reality, is propaganda for the pacifists. No offense whatsoever to any nationality, seeking neither to place the blame of the war on one people or another.

Granted that it's war stuff. But with a new twist and well done.

Sid.

THE STOLEN BRIDE

First National production directed by Alexander Korda. From the story by Carey Wilson. Starring Billie Dove, with Lloyd Hughes featured. At the Strand, New York, week Aug. 6. Running time over one hour.

Sari, Countess Thurzo..........Billie Dove
Franz Pless..................Lloyd Hughes
Ilona ....Lilyan Tashman
Baron von Heimberg.........Armand Kaliz
Count Thurzo........ ....Frank Beal
Lieut. Kiss......................Cleve Moore
Archduke ....Winston Miller
Sergeant ....Bert Sprotte
Dancer ....Yola d'Avril

Painstakingly woven with close attention to geographical detail this is but another variation of the princess-and-peasant theme. The director wastes too much time getting the opening planted, detracts from the atmospheric appeal by too much explanation in titles, and fails to handle the mush scenes with convincing delicacy when he finally does get down to work.

There are evidently opportunities in the script which should have resulted in a better picture than has been turned out. While not novel, a story of this kind is of the reliable stock-in-trade. In addition there are two charming players in Billie Dove and Lloyd Hughes with whom to carry out the "action." Both are handled stiltedly and lose much of the appeal and sight attraction they have radiated in other productions.

From the opening scene directorial weakness is noticed in the play of two children, the youthful Sari and the cobbler's boy. The little girl gives him a set of soldier toys, asking him why he does not remain in Hungary instead of going to America. The boy picks up a toy soldier holding a horse for an officer as the answer. A fine scene pointless on account of the manner presented.

The reconciliation between Sari and the boy 20 years later in Central Park is a waste of footage. Instead of building the cobbler's son, Korda has just allowed years to pass over him. When he is reintroduced the customers don't know if he's a drugstore cowboy or president of a bank. The girl has a title but no personality. Both the leading players had parts worthy of powerful delineation with neither properly directed.

Events leading up to the action of the picture place the male lead in a foolish light. Forgetting to become an American citizen, Franz is drafted into the Hungarian army for three years. Any man who lives in a country 20 years without becoming naturalized doesn't deserve and won't get sympathy over trouble arising from this stupid oversight.

Being shanghaied into the militia, Franz incurs the enmity of Heimberg and is appointed personal valet to the Baron. The latter has been picked as Sari's husband by Count Thurzo. Thurzo is another characterization possessed of contradictory qualities. He is shown well inclined toward his daughter, yet brutal in forcing her to marry the Baron, announcing the engagement at a public military dinner without telling the girl beforehand.

Franz gets himself slapped around the royal joint for a couple of reels, unable to hit back without inviting death. He finally unlooses but it isn't much of a scrap although the baron tears down a curtain with the weight of his fall. If there had to be a fight it might have been a good one.

The gal insists unto the bitter end that she will yet defeat the will of her father, but seems helpless, and aside from becoming hysterical does nothing. Miss Dove should not be allowed to become hysterical—it spoils her looks. She looked forbiddingly unattractive in a few scenes. Maybe a kind word to the camera man would help some.

Franz also does nothing much except hide in a bedroom for a night. He is then allowed to escape by the baron to preserve silence about the night in the bedroom with the Countess. This was not as hot as the description.

The happy ending is arrived at through Ilona who wanted her "Heimie" untouched. She substitutes, allowing Sari to escape in her clothes. The baron is saved from utter mediocrity by his action in accepting Ilona, saying, "We did have a lot of fun together, didn't we?"

Military scenes are correctly represented with numerous beautifully constructed interiors. An expensive production. Has moderate box-office value through being a flash picture with a good cast.

ADAM AND EVIL

Metro-Goldwyn Mayer production and release, featuring Lew Cody and Aileen Pringle. Original by F. H. Herbert and Florence Ryerson, with R. Z. Leonard director. Andre Barlatier, photographer. Titles by Ralph Spence. At the Capitol, New York, week Aug. 6. Running time, 73 mins.

Adam Trevalyan } ....Lew Cody
Allan Trevalyan }
Evelyn Trevalyan...........Aileen Pringle
Gwen De Vere....................Gwen Lee
Dora Dell......................Gertrude Short
Eleanor Leighton............Hedda Hopper
Mortimer Enkins...............Roy D'Arcy

One of those marital farces most generally approved by the French, but in this case very apt to be enjoyed by that great American public, rural and otherwise. Lots of ginger all the way, and while they didn't laugh so loud at the Capitol, a Monday matinee drop-in crowd giggled plenty.

This entire studio unit stands responsible for a well-constructed piece of work. It's an instance where Ralph Spence's titles fail to dominate. The latter has supplied artificial respiration to so many "bad boys" that to see his name on the lead title is to immediately think "lemon." However, there's nothing pale or sour about "Adam and Evil." It'll tickle more people than Tunney and Dempsey would like to play to.

The story is a twin brother series of complications with the wife (Miss Pringle) in between and Lew Cody playing both brothers. This is productive of some sweet double photography even unto the two Codys exchanging money by hand. The yarn is set in a fair-sized town with most of the action and fireworks on tap at the local hotel. Sets substantial throughout. A feminine male pursuer (Gwen Lee) jams things up nicely, the laugh climax sequence being Adam sending his brother Al up to make love to the ever ready Gwen in a hotel suite, meeting the wife there but following instructions as he's never met his sister-in-law.

Cody gives this effort a good-sized shipment of spice while Leonard has supervised with intelligence and for pace, achieving both. A bit more broad in its humor than the type Lubitsch turns out so well but well able to hold its head up in its class. Miss Pringle does nicely as the comically persecuted wife and Miss Lee informs that she's present both early and late. No one will ever know that Roy D'Arcy is in the picture due to meagre opportunity. Hedda Hopper looks good and plays well.

Leonard and Spence have combined to use W. C. Fields "Elmer" bit. If without permission it's a crime, for this piece of business, identified with Fields, is a classic of its type. Co-operation between director and titler is a necessity for the action would be meaningless minus wording and vice versa. It's a sure laugh, although footage demands that less time be given it than Fields utilizes to build it up.

Anyway, here's a picture that will probably be more welcome in the higher priced houses than in the "galleries." The faster they think the better they'll like it. Leonard has given it that momentum and Cody is an apt follower of pace here.

Sid.

DR. MABUSE

Decla-Bioscop melodrama directed by Fritz Lang, presented at Fifth Ave. Playhouse, Aug. 6; running time, 63 mins.

Dr. Mabuse..............Rudolf Klein-Rogge
Countess Stolst...........Gertrude Welcker
Cara..................Auge Neggede Nissen
Brother..............................Alfred Abel
De-Witt....................Bernhard Goetzke
Hull................................Paul Richter

When Abraham Lincoln was a young man he wore no whiskers. When he was elected President, he grew a bush. Later, maybe as a war economy measure, he again shaved 'em off. He thought better of it once more, and at the time of his tragic demise, had a luxurious hirsute equipment. During the second non-beard period, a sculptor named Volk chiseled in bronze an immortal head of the martyr.

What has all this to do with "Dr. Mabuse?"

This much: the leading man, Bernhard Groetzke (not the title role performer) is the uncanniest replica of the Volk Lincoln-head imaginable. And that is a tip-off to an American audience on the grade of "It" exemplified by German leading men. Our Abe was a great Emancipator, but no one would pick him as a great romancipator. Nobody but Fritz Lang, who is regarded as some pumpkin in Germany, and who directed "Metropolis," "Siegfried" and other hunsuccessful features. Probably the worst features he ever directed were Groetzke's.

Abe Lincoln De-Witt Groetzke is the Chief of Police of Vienna, and he has to cope with "the Great Unknown" (not "the Great Onion"), who is the wickedest, weirdest, woesomest and wearisomest mastermind in all film history—which lets out a lot of American actors and directors.

He has the "Evil Eye"—not evil eyes, just one; he "concentrates" through a monocle. And he "mesmerizes" his victims.

Back a couple of decades or so, when this generation of reviewers were kids, the lurid paper thrillers were called "Libraries." The word "dime-novel" was not then an artistic oprobrium. A dime was a lot of dough. The "Libraries" cost a nickel. And they were passed from one hand to another. And among them was one called "The Mesmeric Eye." It gave the growing youngsters who today control the destiny of the nation and say they don't choose to run again shivers up their unformed spines. Well, here it is, "Made in Germany," and called "Dr. Mabuse." (The M is in for no reason!)

His racket is "controlling" rich weaklings, male and the hippier sex as they differ over there; he gambles for high stakes at incredible games in unbelieveable "clubs" after absurd coincidences and via grotesque and abominable plots, hooks the chumps of both species, and is there with every crime from rape to disguises. He is nailed in the end through the love of the unshaved Lincoln for the "Countess" whose brother the dirty beast has victimized, and he meets a horrible end in a sewer, which is a fitting "location" for this film to wind up in.

This delirium was shot somewhere about 1920, judging by the fashions of dress. Sending it over here now is probably a violation of the Armistice for which we fought, bled and pay income taxes. It proves that the German spirit was not broken—only twisted. It also proves, if one has the gift of analysis, why Germany thought it could conquer the world: if it thought this was a movie, it could think anything.

It may also prove that the "block booking system" obtains in German films projected on this side. It should prove something. If not—why it is here?

The titles are ungrammatical, misspelled and constructed in the reduntant and florid English indicative of an authority on our language who studied it in Heidelberg. And Sammy Mindlin's patrons are of the few movie collections who know their spelling, punctuation and grammar.

The theme (as the title would have it) is "psychio-analyses." That is German-American for mental hypnosis shot through a monocle. And it is the "power" of "the Great Unknown," who would be caught by the sheriff of Duchess county or the assistant warden of Matteawan before he got around the corner in Wappinger Falls. He is as "unknown" as the Woolworth Building and as subtle as Peggy Hopkins disguising herself as a gold digger.

The German ladies look and act like scrubwomen out of work. They emote hysterically, they love torridly, they hate like vitriol, and they smell like limburger. In the battle of sex-allure between the crook-nosed crook, Mabuse, and the Volk-Lincoln Groetzke, they leave nothing undone except the shoulder-straps of their then-snappy gowns (this to lend sex appeal).

The scenic detail, while not lavish, is skillful. The lighting is perfect. As a lighter, Fritz is no sap. His characters light a nasty cigaret. Indeed, he has "technique." But in that he isn't alone. A Chaplin of the same vintage (Mabel Normand leading lady) followed and proved that Fritz was "playing the book" as it then obtained.

Yes—this is a good picture (of Abraham Lincoln when he had no chin-piece).

Lait.

NEVADA

Paramount release and production. Starring Gary Cooper. From a Zane Gray Western story. Featuring William Powell and Thelma Todd. Titles by Jack Conway. At Loew's Lincoln Square, New York city, Aug. 8-10. Running time, 60 mins.

May be the day will come when the exhibs will throw their hands up on all westerns and cry quits. And again may be not. Meanwhile the cry and hue is still raised, and to supply the demand Paramount must ride along with the rest and turn out "westerns." The dose or deluge of the stories of the wild and woolly has been going on ever since the first film was made, and it must be worse than a Chinese puzzle these days to figure out some angle that hasn't been shot literally, figuratively and every other way for the screen.

But still they come. Paramount has Gary Cooper now riding the plains, tall, two-fisted, gun toting and lightning fast on draw, who has done his darndest to step into the shoes of Jack Holt. Cooper does well but the stories seem to be getting thinner.

In this one much of the old stuff is rehashed and the old, old chase of rustlers is done over for those who perchance didn't see Bill Hart or Broncho Billy do it in the earlier days.

There isn't much to the story that couldn't have been told in two reels. One of the very fine things in favor of this Par western is the camera work. Some of the finest shots ever produced by the m. p. crank turners is on view in "Nevada." The photographic work for the most part is about the best turned out by Par in a long time.

Riding along with Cooper, who makes quite a masculine figure in the togs of the cowboys, is little

Ernie Adams, who works very hard to make his role stand out.

The titles are credited to Jack Conway, formerly of Variety. This capital slangist doesn't get much of a chance to slam in any wisecracks although a number of the captions are palpably of the Conway brand and laugh getters. Yet the style and type of story confined Conway to straight titles that were necessary for the good of the romance. Jack did a splendid job of the captioning.

There is something graciously refreshing about the youth and charm of Thelma Todd; she registers effectively and attractively and makes a very prepossessing heroine, but in some of the close-ups her lips looked as though they were shedding goose oil.

Now and then the story hangs with bulldog tenacity onto its continuity and then sweeps into some corking shots of the great western slopes, then into some of those ungodly chases over hills and through chasms after the bad men of the picture that nobody seems to care for other than to bring the picture to a close somewhere.

It is a western, nothing more, and as such serves its little niche. Gary Cooper is improving in his work and serving his masters well in everything but his love making. There comparisons creep in and as a consequence Cooper suffers thereby. *Mark.*

THE LAST OUTLAW

Paramount production, starring Gary Cooper; Jack Luden and Betty Jewel featured. Arthur Rosson director; author, Richard Allen Gates; adaptor, J. Walter Ruben. Scenario by Ruben and John Stone. Footage, 6,032. Half of double-header at the Tivoli, New York, one day, Aug. 6.
Buddy Hale....................Gary Cooper
Ward Lane.....................Jack Luden
Janet Lane....................Betty Jewel
Bert Wagner.................Herbert Prior
Butch............................Jim Corey
Chick.............................Billy Butts

Gary Cooper is Paramount's new western star whom they are trying to put over. Cooper first came to attention in "The Winning of Barbara Worth" and was finally starred in "Arizona Bound."

Co-featured in this western are Jack Luden, Par picture school alumnus, and Betty Jewel, opposite Cooper in "Arizona Bound."

Par can stand a western star and has a personality bet in Cooper, but they're not doing right by him if "The Last Outlaw" is a sample of the best story material they can offer. The blood-and-thunder title is very Biograph-y in its import and the plot is just as Broncho Billy with its cattle rustling, double-dealing sheriffs and other central ingredients.

Cooper does some good work, rides fast and flashy on his horse, "Flash," and impresses with his gun totin' generally. Screen mechanics are against him. He labors against story shortcomings and creaking directorial machinations.

Betty Jewel, opposite, is almost dragged in for her entrance. Miss Jewel is a satisfactory vis-a-vis, and Jack Luden (of the Luden cough drop family, being groomed for Paramount stardom) clicks in a brief secondary opportunity.

Topping everything is the lovable Billy Butts, a Jackiecooganish youngster, who, now that Jackie has reached the "awkward age" between childhood and boyhood, impresses as a likely possibility along similar lines. Young Billy Butts as Chick is rather improbable as a wanderlust cowboy's pal, but the youngster registers regardless.

"The Last Outlaw" was caught as half of a twin-feature bill at the Tivoli, an 8th avenue neighborhood triple-jitney parlor, and that's about

its metropolitan speed. In the hinterland it should hold up as a daily changer on regular programs. *Abel.*

A Royal American

Rayart release. Harry J. Brown (or Burton) production, directed by the producer. Reed Howes starred. At Loew's New York one-half double bill one day, Aug. 5. Running time, 58 minutes.

A very lively picture all of the way, with a well balanced cast and a first class athlete in Reed Howes in the lead. As an action picture away from the western (this is mostly on board ship), "A Royal American" qualifies for any of the houses wanting this type of picture. It would go in many of the other houses also and might be welcomed as a novelty in them, although without drawing power on title or names.

Action starts within the first 500 feet through a couple of corking fist fights between sailors on shore leave and Howes. This same Howes is not a bad actor either. He's a powerfully built and quite good looking fellow. Women will go for him.

It was thought the early action would be difficult to follow, but when the brutal captain and crew of "The Hawk" shanghaied Howes, more and swift action raced along on the boat, bound for South America with a cargo of contraband guns and ammunition.

Several chases on and around the decks, some of them foolish, but all holding a bit of a thrill, while Howes clambering up the ropes to the peak of the five-masted schooner was well done and taken.

It developed that Howes was of the coast patrol. He signaled a coast guard boat that wound up the picture when arresting the tough captain of "The Hawk."

Only women in the picture were the excellent, but unknown, player who did the elderly Mother Meg of the sailors' saloon in the early portion, and the rather nice girl, personally and as an actress, who did the niece, also shanghaied, but not doped by the boat's crew.

It's the most evenly played picture for an independent of its class seen in months. Even the minor roles were well cast.

This Reed Howes if properly handled should go forward. As a stunt athlete who can do things, look well and act, he seems to be there. For the thrill houses, a pipe. *Sime.*

Drums of the Desert

Paramount production and release. Zane Grey western novel, with Warner Baxter and Ford Sterling in cast. At Loew's Circle, New York, one day, Aug. 8, as half of double feature bill.

Zane Grey has a faculty of weaving primitive wild west cowboy-and-Injun stuff into a 20th century setting. He again accomplishes it admirably in "Drums of the Desert."

It is an intelligently conceived western and as Paramount has produced it, a tight flicker feature. The valuable oil grants are the basis of this Grey plot, with the outlaw whites seeking to mulct the Indian reservation of its dower rights.

Warner Baxter is the only square-shooting white who would protect the redskins' interests.

A field battle between both factions could have been built up a bit more, up to the point where the troopers intervene and turn the tables.

Baxter stands out in the principal male role and Ford Sterling gets something with his comedy relief, although it's an assignment away from the usual dapper and foppish Sterling characterizations.

Plenty of action throughout, mostly outdoors, and is an inexpensive Paramount production in toto. There couldn't be a particularly high exhibition value placed on this one and regardless, for the exhibitor, it's a good western buy. It has the Grey story as the Paramount feature. *Abel.*

Woman Who Did Not Care

Gotham production, presented by Sam Sax. Released by Lumas. Starring Lilyan Tashman. Philip Rosen directed from story by Rida Johnson Young; supervision of Carroll Sax. Released on states' rights basis. Half of double feature at Loew's Circle, New York, one day, Aug. 8.

For a state's rights release (Lumas) "The Woman Who Did Not Care" more than hits the mark. It is a society comedy-drama flash, with Lilyan Tashman in a difficult, unsympathetic part, and carrying her assignment. The obvious twist that the apparently insouciant woman, gold digger made so by economic determinism, can really be made to care if the right boy friend comes along, takes the curse off of it all, for the getaway.

From the drab boarding house start, where Iris (Miss Tashman) is subjected to countless cruelties by the rough male boarders, the action quickly shifts to a life of ease and means. Staking everything on a slim heritage, she sets about cutting a social swatch as a means to an easy existence.

From one boy friend she drifts to his father. The old boy has the scene all set for the nuptials when the breezy mariner-son (original b. f.'s brother, in other words) makes his presence felt, and the girl is willingly shanghaied on a yacht.

It's a bit silly, this concentration of her digging proclivities on the one family, but it's rather well done. After playing son against father, another son comes along and makes her "care."

Philip Rosen has handled the direction well. It's a conservative production, and yet it makes a flash. There are little touches such as close-ups of Iris' sartorial transition from drabness to luxury, that are pips. One shows off Miss Tashman's nude form within the glass-encased, vapory needle shower.

Arthur Rankin as the weaker of the sons, and Edward Martindel as the old boy, sustain the important male roles along with Phillip McCullough.

Running an hour at Loew's Circle as half of a double-header, "The Woman Who Did Not Care" could have satisfied on its own. It's a strong independent program feature. *Abel.*

THE SILENT HERO

Rayart release, presented by W. Ray Johnson. Directed by Duke Worne, from story by H. H. Van Loan. Starring "Napoleon Bonaparte," a dog. Robert Frazer, Edna Murphy, Ernest Hilliard, Joseph Girard, Harry Allen in support. Photographed by Ernest Smith. In projection room, Aug. 8. Running time, 55 minutes.

New dog star, launched with production support that instantly rates him above several, though not all, canine contemporaries. Where dogs bark for the box office this picture may be taken on with assurance that it will be liked.

The new dog star looks okay. He can act nasty when asked, and fights without that playful spirit noted in others.

In this film his master leaves for the north and gold, first presenting the pup to his wealthy sweetheart. Later the villainous menace has the dog railroaded out of town and then leaves to jump the hero's gold claim, only to be frustrated by the dog, who has met up with his master.

The picture has two healthy looking fights, both including the dog.

All scenes are directed and photographed very well and played by a competent cast.

Titles hurt a little by being too bookish.

A well made dog film.

MARRIED ALIVE

Fox production and release. Emmett Flynn producer. Adapted by Gertrude Orr from a story by Ralph Straus. Matt Moore featured with Margaret Livingston, Claire Adams, Lou Tellegen, Emily Fitzroy and Eric Mayne in support. Photographed by Ernest Palmer. At Loew's New York, one day (Aug. 4). Running time, 53 minutes.

A hopeless combination of tragedy and comedy.

Probably the story from which the adaptation was made rambled along in Michael Arlen's manner. The picture, however, takes its tragedy seriously and its comedy lightly. It tells of a college professor, who approves of polygamy among the lower forms of animal life, going to the seashore for a rest and there meeting with a man who reveals he is married to several different women. Prof. sets out to tell the various wives of their husband's dastardliness. One is an actress and she doesn't mind. Another is a preacher's daughter, and she is heartbroken in touching style. Another is a lady of royalty and she falls in love with the prof., who returns it. Another is an old battle axe, who married the scoundrel first and therefore is his only legal wife. The Prof. finds this out and then is free to marry the lady of royalty. A tough job trying to tell this story. Continuity is at times completely lost. The way the characters jump about indicates it was butchered heavily in the cutting room. And the idea of trying to make a comedy out of it is all wet.

The censors will display no love for this picture. Nor will the customers.

A good cast, replete with names, wasted.

The Master of Nuremburg

This is the first film that Ludwig Berger has directed since his successful "Waltz Dream." It shows the careful preparation and minute labor which has gone into its making. Unquestionably it is one of the best pictures produced in Germany within late years. The cast all suit their roles, continuity is good, and when one says that Berger's direction is up to his former efforts that is sufficient praise.

The scenario is taken from the libretto of Wagner's opera, "Die Meistersinger von Nuernberg" and skillfully adapted.

Rudolph Rittner proves that an actor of the old school can today be as effective as ever. He has real charm and power. Maria Solveig plays her first important film role and proves herself worthy of the opportunity. Finely etched character roles are given by Julius Falkenstein, Veit Harlan, and Max Guelstorf.

The only objection to the film is the scenery which, although competent, is not in any way exceptional. All scenes were undoubtedly taken in a studio.

The film ought to get a good break for its first run in New York at one of the big houses, as it can be hooked up with Wagner's popular music. Outside of the big cities it is a more doubtful proposition but may be put across if well handled.

Primancrliebe

Never heard of the director, Robert Land, although it is understood that he has made a couple of small films before this one. Surprise was all the greater, therefore, to find this one of the most finished products of the season. Land understands how to handle actors before the camera. Here is undoubtedly the biggest directorial talent which has made its appearance in the German film industry for the past two years. Judged from all angles, his work in this instance can be compared with that being done anywhere in the picture industry today. He is not a comer, he is already there.

"Primanerliebe" (Students' Love") concerns the love of a young high school boy, Rolf, for Ellen, the daughter of the headmaster of his school. One of his comrades, a nervous, hysterical type, is driven to suicide by the uncomprehending severity of his teachers. Rolf also gets himself in badly with the school authorities by writing a radical essay against war and by protesting publicly against the way his dead schoolmate was treated. He is expelled. The boy is in deadly fear of his uncle, who believes in only the strictest sort of discipline. Rolf steals a revolver with the intention of committing suicide, and goes to say goodbye to the girl. He comes just in time to save the girl from an assault by an opera singer, whom he shoots in the arm. At the court trial the whole matter comes out and the guardian and the girl's father come to the realization of their mistaken policy.

Not a single bad performance in the film. Wolfgang Zilzer and Grete Mosheim are engaging and moving as the young lovers. Fritz Kortner, as the guardian, plays with a restrained finish which places him in a class with Jannings and Krauss. And then the wealth of characterization in the minor roles played by Jaro Fuerth, Paul Otto, Adolphe Engers, Hans Albers, and Martin Herzberg.

The theme as handled is undoubtedly to Continental to appeal to a general American audience. For the artistic theatres it is a sure-fire bet, however, and no American director should fail to see it.

The Patent Leather Kid

First National release of Alfred Santell production from story by Rupert Hughes. Directed by Alfred Santell, production management of Al Rockett (billing). Titles by Gerald C. Duffy. Adaptation by Adla Rogers St. Johns. Scenario by Winifred Dunn. Photographed by Arthur Edison with associate photographers. Ralph Hammeras and Alvin Knechtel. Art directors, Stephen Goosson and Jack Okey. Film editor, Hugh Bennett. Richard Barthelmess starred. At Globe (legit), New York, opening Aug. 15 for run at $2 top. "Running time around 110 minutes.

Patent Leather Kid...Richard Barthelmess
The Golden Dancer............Molly O'Day
Puffy ....Arthur Stone
Capt. Breen ....Lawford Davidson
Jake Stuke..................Matthew Betz
The Tank Crew................Fred O'Beck
Cliff Salm, Henry Murdock, Charlie Sullivan, John Kolb and Al Alborn
Mobile Molasses ....Raymond Turner
Sergeant ....Hank Mann
German Officer...............Lucien Prival
French Doctor............Nigel de Brulier

A run picture for those run houses that the film trade now has, but not a road show film. That means "The Patent Leather Kid," with Richard Barthelmess, will be a hold over when going into the regular picture houses.

For Barthelmess, perfect, even if Barthelmess is made to play what at times is a repulsive role, that of a slacker during wartime, and admittedly so. When in France he must display such outward fear that one of the several extremely well-worded captions, often with a giggle to them, and more than a giggle often, asked him not to brag of his fear.

Barthelmess is such a big portion of this long film, in action and work, that he must come before the picture itself. Others of the cast almost rate up to him, that little Molly O'Day, who always holds to her role of the east or west side New York girl who fell for a prize fighter, and Matthew Betz as the fighter's manager, giving a near-matchless performance.

There are agonizing periods in the second of the two parts the picture was run off in at the Globe Monday night. In one spot the agony is made pretty strong and prolonged. It seemed for a moment as though a surgical operation without the employment of ether was about to be displayed on the screen. If ever there, it had been taken out, and just as well. That bit went quite far enough as it was. Here it was that Miss O'Day gave a realistic explosive exhibition of emotion under great stress that in itself was quite well performed, but with flaws before and after the outburst, not her fault, but in holding the mush scenes too long. That girl looks and plays well.

One defect against the wholesale acceptance is that the picture as it runs is too stagey. Too much of it seems staged. And the romance is given an awful wallop through its inception. It is set in the suggestive manner of a cabaret cooch dancer (Miss O'Day) going to a prize fight with her 5th avenue boy friend, there to razz the Patent Leather Kid, and later to join him at the entrance of the arena, blow her 5th avenuer, and slip away with the pug in his roadster, he taking her home and at the doorstep telling her from thence onward she is his girl.

All of the whitewashing captions, romantic mushing and crushing and the girl's persuasive powers toward making a soldier of the fighter never square the love end.

No striking comedy, but some mild laugh matter here and there. Biggest laugh is when Miss O'Day knocks out the manager with a pitcher, and the Kid immediately knocks her cold for doing it.

When recovering consciousness the girl caresses her assailant, with a caption of the kid saying:

"You have a pretty nose, but keep it out of my business."

Probably the reddest red-fire finish any picture ever has had. The Patent Leather one, in battle and perfoming a valiant act for which he was decorated, after all of his professed cowardice, is under the care of his sweetie. He had gone across as an entertainer and became a nurse.

The boy is paralyzed, hands and feet. American soldiers march past. He had just attempted to move his hands at the doctor's request, but had been unable to do so. He wants to salute the flag. The girl salues for him, she standing at attention. He grips himself and says he will salute, moving his hands, then his feet, then standing semi-erect, then erect, and then saluting, for the band meanwhile, along with the house orchestra, has been playing "The Star-Spangled Banner." As the boy stands to salute, the entire house is standing with him to the final curtain.

If Mr. Rockett will stick in a dissolve there of Miss O'Day and have it come out Aimee McPherson, it will be a great plug for Aimee's faith followers and may help business.

In the second part are war scenes, with tanks predominating. It's war and with a thrill. But the war is over. This is straight war stuff and not uncommon in pictures, excepting that one long line of tanks may be new. Some bayonet work is exhibited, and that is new also to the screen. It was not carried far.

In story the picture runs from the Patent Leather Kid, whom everyone seemed aggrieved against because of his egotism and looks, winning one fight and losing another, to be drafted into the army in 1917, after he had been knocked out by a set-up, who socked the Kid while he turned his head in the ring to listen to the music of the soldier band then passing.

The asides and the cabaret stuff are in the first section, with a Y hut in action and as a hospital in the second half. Lawrence Davidson is the 5th avenuer, later a captain of the A. E. F., into whose company the Kid and his crony trainer, Puffy (Arthur Stone), were assigned. Another in the fight bunch is Molasses (Raymond Turner), who looked the negro, although possibly in blackface. If the latter, his make up exceptional. Betz passed out of the picture at the end of the first part, when bidding his protege good-bye, and Stone got killed in action.

Amplifiers were employed, probably from discs, for the ringside noises of the fights. No doubling for Barthelmess in the ring scraps, he doing them very well, with each going less than two rounds. While the boxing was not unusually punchy, it was brisk and well covered up.

No prolog to the picture, it starting off the show at the premiere near 9. With an intermission, the film stopped at 11:13. Effects back stage arranged by Joe Plunkett, are of great assistance in conveying the war illusions. Another aid is the pleasing musical accompaniment. The score is unnamed.

The Globe's exterior lobby or entrance has stills of Barthelmess plastered so thickly that the star, though accustomed to seeing himself in repose and motion, must have faintly blushed at least if ever getting a flash of this grouped collection. There are over 200 pictures of Barthelmess only in the Globe's lobby. And if he ever wants a perfect double for himself Barthelmess should call in Charlie Morrison, the hustling vaudeville agent.

But Barthelmess is giving a fine performance as the Patent Leather Kid. He shows moods easily, has plenty of expression and sends himself away across.

Captions held up better earlier than later, but average very high.

First National has a picture here it can go strong on, if letting the road show thing slide. Though a different kind of war picture, the war end itself is not so different.

At the $2 top at the Globe it's problematical how long the picture will run. The Barthelmess drag must enter into that. Against it is the prize fighting, that may discourage some feminine trade. But it should ride at least eight weeks to good grosses at the Globe, and then ease off for perhaps four weeks beyond that. But in the 99c. toppers or run houses, or even above, the run should be from four to six weeks.

And for the top de luxes, if the femmes go with it, a certainty.

Cost plenty. *Sime.*

WINGS

Paramount picture and a Lucien Hubbard production. Directed by Wm. Wellman from John M. Saunders' story. Harry Perry credited with photography. Titles by Julian Johnson. Opened at the Criterion, N. Y., for a twice daily run Aug. 12. Running time, 139 mins., split by an intermission, 65 and 74 minutes in respective halves. $2 top.

Clara Preston.......................Clara Bow
John Powell................Charles Rogers
David Armstrong.............Richard Arlen
Cadet White....................Gary Cooper
Sylvia Lewis...............Jobyna Ralston
August Schmidt.................El Brendel
Celeste.......................Arlette Marchal
Air Commander.............Richard Tucker
Sergeant....................Gunboat Smith
Mr. Armstrong.............Henry Walthall
Mrs. Armstrong......Julia Swayne Gordon
Mr. Powell...................George Irving
Mrs. Powell..................Hedda Hopper
French Peasant............Nigel de Brulier

Paramount has got itself a $2 picture. In fact, the most legitimate of the specie it has had since "The Covered Wagon." The air stuff in this one is going to keep it at the Criterion a long time and they're going to turn out for it when it takes to the road. "Wings" is there.

This super is not just a $2 entry for Manhattan. It's a road show—on the strength of that air stuff, a combination of beautiful flying and great camera work. There are thrills and a couple of gasps in it. When the action settles on terra firma there is nothing present that other war supers haven't had, some to a greater degree. But nothing has possessed the graphic descriptive powers of aerial flying and combat that have been poured into this effort. All of which will carry the 12,600 feet of film currently being unloaded for the populace twice daily. Try and get in—for awhile, anyway.

And the picture is being staged. Midway in the first part the switch is made to Paramount's Magnascope, which spreads the screen and projection across the entire stage. This is retained until the finish of the first half. The same thing occurs in the second part, so that much more than half the footage is magnified. More effective than in either "Ironsides" or "Chang," because of the terrific action. Add to that back-stage effects simulating the whine and drone of the motors, in two tones to denote the American and enemy planes, with the music abruptly halting every so often to allow full dramatic intensity, and the result will get under anybody's skin.

This high altitude war game has been given plenty of technical attention from actual "shooting" to presentation. The total on this phase speaks for itself and the rewards will be heavy.

Some of the Magnascope battle scenes in the air are in color. Not natural but with sky and clouds deftly tinted plus spouts of flame shooting from planes that dive, spiral and even zoom as they supposedly plunge to earth in a final collapse. Automatic cameras (reported to be mostly Devrys) have registered the personal equasion of what goes on inside a cockpit of a falling plane. Some of these shots of aviators dying with their planes going out of control are realistic enough to make a house "freeze." Who these boys are isn't known. They're not the main characters in the story, just individuals of a combat group pictured as both American and German, all fighting.

Rolls, dives, slips, loops. They're all there. Spectacular enough without the added constructive potion of make believe that signifies the urge for self-preservation. Manoeuvers that the average person has never seen performed in the air, space eaten up so fast that there's no calculating the rate it's consumed at, besides the jockeying of the planes to get on each other's "tail" before pouring out their stream of lead. So much to see that it actually can't be minutely consumed at one viewing.

Trench warfare and tank action, too. All on a big scale and well done, but secondary to the airplanes.

The story? An average tale. And yet it was human enough Friday night to make 90 per cent. of the women in the house cry. The director, Wellman, can take credit for that, as the tale is laid out for but one situation: that of the American flyer, John, unknowingly shooting down his pal, David, after the latter has escaped from behind the enemy lines in a German plane. John discovers what he has done when David's machine crashes.

What seems to have even more power is Wellman's depiction of David's (Richard Arlen) departure from his family for training camp. The director is ably abetted in this by the cast membership of Arlen, Henry Walthall and Julia Swayne Gordon. Both Walthall and Miss Gordon are again histrionically prominent during the anti-climax footage when John (Charles Rogers) comes home to deliver his dead friend's decoration and mascot to the bereaved parents.

Arlen, incidentally, has gone through the picture minus make-up. At least the cameras register him that way. Consequently he looks the high bred, high strung youngster who would dote on aviation and backs it up with a splendid performance that never hints of the actor. Rogers' effort is also first rate, the important point here being that these two boys team well together.

There not being so much of Clara Bow in the picture, or a straining for her to turn on that "it" personality, she gives an all around corking performance. The way the film unwinds it's a sure thing this girl has been cut out of a lot of time on the screen. El Brendel's comedy is spasmodic and mostly early in the first half, while Gary Cooper is on and off within half a reel. Jobyna Ralston only crops up occasionally but is significant in the love theme, as both boys love her. An accidental incident makes John believe he is favored when it is David whom she cares for, and David knows. Clara (Miss Bow) having worshipped John from afar throughout the picture finally gets him, and that winds up the unreeling. Other players listed are relegated to what amount to bits.

The most planes counted in the air at once are 18. But there are the pursuit and bombing machines captive balloons, smashes and crashes of all types, with some of the shots of these "crack-ups" remarkable. Fake stuff and double photography, too, although no miniatures in regard to the air action are discernible if used. The bombing of targets, in this case a French village, is familiar through the newsreels, but John is shown coming down in his machine to spray infantry, wreck a general's automobile by killing its occupants with his dual guns besides destroying a couple of captive balloons.

Probably the standout of the crashes rests between the destruction of a giant bomber and the shooting down of a plane that isn't more than 20 feet in the air as it takes off. How they got the latter shot will likely keep those interested guessing for some time.

No preliminary stalling, the story being down to cases and working up interest at the end of 10 minutes. Training camp stuff is quickly dispensed with and the two boys are overseas and on their initial dawn patrol, where the first and best air fight of the picture takes place, before the screening is much more than half an hour old. Musically the score is not as stirring as that for some of the other war supers.

When "Wings" was pre-viewed in San Antonio last spring it was in 14 reels, and that aviation-mad town went off its collective head about it. It is understood that the criterion showing has been curtailed to 12,600 feet, and may soon lose some more of its yardage.

To be a genuine road show a picture must be vital and of universal appeal. The industry, to date, has known just six of these, namely: "Birth of a Nation," "'Way Down East," "The Ten Commandments," "The Covered Wagon," "The Big Parade," and "Ben-Hur." Irrespective of the wave of interest in aviation that is currently sweeping the world, add "Wings" to the list. Because its flying is vital. *Sid.*

AFTER MIDNIGHT

Metro-Goldwyn-Mayer release. Written and directed by Monta Bell. Titles by Joe Farnam. Photographed by Percy Hilford. At the Capitol, New York, week Aug. 13. Running time, about 65 minutes.

Mary....................Norma Shearer
Joe Miller....................Lawrence Gray
Maxie....................Gwen Lee
Red Smith....................Eddie Sturgis
Gus Van Gundy....................Phillip Sleeman

Norma Shearer's name on this makes it substantial box-office stuff. Picture is of the type that neither benefits nor is hurt by word-of-mouth comment, leaving a dully passive impression on its viewers.

In it Miss Shearer has opportunity to do her usual transformation from moth to butterfly. What her heavy following wants and expects. But this is set in a story that develops from light comedy into tragedy with a not-so-hot degree of finish.

The practical and economical heroine rooms in New York with her spendthrift sister (Gwen Lee), working as a cigaret girl in a night club while her sister kicks in a chorine lineup. The wild sis is out for parties and b. & e. men; the other is saving and scrimping so that she can settle down with an ex-bandit she has reformed.

Comes the day when the little gal has saved a thousand bucks and her sweetie has enough dough to set himself up in the taxi business. Miss Shearer invests her grand in a Liberty bond. Then her sister comes home from a party and displays a bond for the identical amount, explaining it was one of the favors at the party.

Promptly struck with the irony of life, especially after seeing her sweetie in a drunken party which he had been forced into, Miss Shearer blows her bond for clothes and sets out to cut up. She becomes so soused her sister starts to drive her home from a party in a borrowed car. With the drunken girl beside her fooling with the steering wheel, she swerves over an embankment and is killed.

This leaves Norma and her boy friend to soliloquize in the fadeout that they were failures for not trusting each other, while the supposedly greedy and wild sister wasn't so bad after all. (Usually said in obituaries.)

Audience won't appreciate that so much, although they will find numerous little incidents of merit in the story. The various types, for instance, are handled very well.

The story has a strange angle. With scenes and clothes indicating a present-day story, there is the combating idea of prominent Liberty bonds, the scarred face of the minor menace and the presence of a man on crutches at one of the wild parties. These things indicate a time not so long after the war, but no mention of date is made.

Miss Shearer plays well, hurt now and then by unflattering photography. Miss Lee, the wild sister, is highly convincing. The ex-crook is handled by Lawrence Gray suitably.

The star will draw with little help from the story.

The Fighting Eagle

De Mille (PDC) Pictures Corp. production. Produced by C. Gardner Sullivan. Released by Pathe. Adapted from Conan Doyle's story, "Brigadier Gerard." Rod La Rocque starred, with Phyllis Haver and Sam de Grasse featured. Directed by Donald Crisp. At Strand, New York, week Aug. 13. Running time, around 60 minutes.

Etienne Gerard....................Rod La Rocque
Countess de Launay....................Phyllis Haver
Talleyrand....................Sam de Grasse
Napoleon Bonaparte....................Max Barwyn
Josephine....................Julia Faye
Col. Neville....................Clarence Burton
Major Oliver....................Alphonse Ethier

An ordinary program release for P. D. C. (De Mille), but above the average of the P. D. C.'s of last season. It's strictly for Rod La Rocque, and he must draw the business rather than the picture itself, unless there are sufficient readers of the Conan Doyle work over here enough interested to make the traffic brisk. Held for a week at the Strand, it will not shove the gross there above the average unless there is real theatre weather this week.

Principals all do well and greatly push along the impression, although the unnamed title writer, with a nicety of expression in his captions and just the proper tinge of comedy, should be highly credited.

You will meet some well-known people in this film, starting with Napoleon, as played by Max Barwyn. At times Barwyn did resemble Nap and at others a Hebe comedian. Talleyrand and his intrigues, Josephine and a countess or so, with plenty of soldiers, also.

That sets the picture in the period class, but the working out of the story takes this away from the costume thing, since it's a tale of an upstart soldier reaching the rank of colonel and bragging about everything on his way up, having commenced as an inn keeper. His self-importance as done by La Rocque is so well put on the screen and in the captions that one must laugh even while resenting the boy's nerve.

It is easily believed that the Doyle book read much better than this picture has been filmed. That is not La Rocque's fault, though, and his performance is of high grade, it being a natural for him. Sam de Grasse as Talleyrand suggested all of the treacherous ingenuity that has come down in the history of that double crosser.

Phyllis Haver has a nice part, that of the Countess de Launay, standing high in the Emperor's favor and in the ranks of the secret service. Miss Haver sent over the impression she was a smart dame, despite her good looks, although the beautiful and brains combo doesn't seem to hit many actually on the stage or screen.

It was the Countess who yanked the youth out of the hill country inn to save her from the scheming Talleyrand, as she was returning from Spain with important papers.

Important papers run throughout the telling. There are many extravagant scenes, some very nearly low comedy, impossible to accept otherwise. Considering it all, Donald Crisp put much intelligence into his direction, and it has counted.

For the impersonations it may be said that there is a real illusion in each.

But after it's all over there's nothing to remember. *Sime.*

SERVICE FOR LADIES

Paramount picture starring Adolphe Menjou. From an Ernest Vajda story, and directed by Harry D'Arrast. Titles by George Marion, Jr., with Harold Rosson cameraman. At the Paramount, New York, week Aug. 13. Running time, 65 mins.

Albert Leroux....................Adolphe Menjou
Elizabeth Foster....................Kathryn Carver
Robert Foster....................Charles Lane
King Boris....................Lawrence Grant

Clean-cut and well constructed, Adolphe Menjou release that has nothing serious about it and scampers along to solid entertainment. Up to scratch as neat program matter and has every chance of being approved in all corners.

In the de luxe houses it will be something of an inside angle for the audiences as to how the class restaurants wish off certain kinds of food they want to get rid of by "recommending" it via captain and waiter. Menjou plays the major domo of a smart hotel's restaurant who becomes smitten with a feminine guest of the hostelry and follows her to the Continent. His struggle to hide his vocation plus the final decision to escort her to a table, in his official capacity, upon the return to Paris, leads up to the climax of the management promoting him to a full managership after the girl has confessed she doesn't care what sort of position he holds.

D'Arrast has given it speed while Menjou is to the front plus his usual smooth performance. Action is both in and outdoors with a flash at winter sports. The picture has been well dressed, holding an ice carnival as its main exterior.

Opposite Menjou is Kathryn Carver, who foils adequately. Other cast membership is noticeable in the person of Lawrence Grant, who obtains a good deal from a small role of a king traveling incognito. Marion's titles are breezy and Rosson's camera work is standard all the way, including a novel introduction of the carnival sequence.

Obviously pleased a capacity audience Sunday afternoon and bids fair to duplicate all around.

Sid.

HIS DOG

Pathe production and release. Directed by Karl Brown. From story by Albert Payson Terhune. Adapted by Olga Printzlau. Featuring Joseph Schildkraut, with cast including Julia Faye, Robert Edeson and Sally Rand. At Hippodrome, New York, week Aug. 15. Running time, about one hour.

Too long drawn out for direct appeal to dog lovers and not sufficiently hoked to play on public sentiment.

Opportunities for turning on the water works are plentiful but ignored, according to the plan of laying on an artistic coating.

Story is of a truck gardener who goes to town once a month to collect his pay, settle his bills and get soused. On his way home one evening, kicking a can along the road, Olsen stumbles over a wounded collie. He brings the dog home, sets his leg, and they become friends.

In time they become such great pals that the man has to choose between liquor and remaining a bum, or the dog. He sticks to the dog.

Too many subtitles and the dramatics start in late, when the picture is almost over. The artistic touch is missing at the finish where it would be most appropriate. With a drunken mob in a speeding car about to kill a little girl, the dog leaps across the road carrying the child out of danger.

Olsen's girl, who had always been afraid of dogs and had tried to make him get rid of this one, breaks down and the man lets loose a few more observations on canine bravery.

The leading lady trails the cast for showing in this picture. The collie is great on looks, a good actor and, narrowed down to two reels, could have made the film an outstander.

A full week at the Hip tells nothing. It's a fill-in.

EAGER LIPS

I. E. Chadwick production released by First Division Pictures. Starring Pauline Garon, Betty Blythe and Gardner James featured. Running time, 52 mins. On double bill at Loew's Circle, New York, one day, Aug. 15.

Backgrounded by what is represented to be Coney Island. It partakes only superficially of any of the flavor of midways and will in no way conflict or dull the edge of the flock of carnival pictures announced for future release by other companies.

"Eager Lips" is simply the old time plot of the libertine who masquerades as a marrying man in order to cop the dame. He happens to own some ballyhoo joints and the dame happens to be a dancer with a competing outfit.

It would have been just the same if she had been on the notions counter at Macy's and he a sinister merchant of butter and eggs.

Not a bad picture, though. Directed nicely if a bit draggey and photographed clearly. Pauline Garon, Betty Blythe, and, to a lesser degree, Gardner James, qualify as names familiar to movie fans and, by deduction, possessing drawing power. Short of the de luxe houses the picture can be used for up to three days.

Promising to keep a protecting eye on the orphaned daughter of a dying actress the tough bimbo (Betty Blythe) has a hard time steering the kid, who is heady and stubborn. The oily guy from the next show wants to grab the kid because she is a business-getter on the ballyhoo end. He promises marriage and the kid goes over, leaving her friends and the boy who loves her flat.

The denouement follows when the worldly-wise dame does a little private vamping and shows up the oily guy in his true colors.

Quite some sex is injected in the vamping sequence when Betty Blythe uncorks some of the elixir of T. N. T. that was her specialty of yore.

Also the director has her and Miss Garon run around quite a bit in some ducky chemises. It all helps to make the footage interesting.

The Valley of Hell

M-G-M western starring Francis McDonald. Directed by Clifford Smith from story by Isadore Bernstein. Cameraman, George Stevens. In the cast: Edna Murphy, Anita Garvin, William Steele. Running time, 54 mins. At Loew's Circle on double bill, one day, Aug. 15.

Undiluted western melodrama, lightning paced and sure to have the kids whistling and stamping and adults interested despite a superior snicker every now and then when the hero's exploits seem just a bit too miraculous.

There's a sweep to the yarn that brushes aside needless plot detail and rushes forward in a mounting crescendo of sheer action. Nobody pauses to do any meditating in this busy opera. It's bang-bang from the main title to the clinch.

Francis McDonald is a new type of western hero. More of a cowboy and less of a polo player than Jack Holt, he resembles the latter in being a strong, silent guy, hair-triggering and bluffing his way through crowds of hostile gun-toters. He can burst through the swinging doors of a desert dance hall and strike a revolver from his antagonist's hand in a truly William S. Hart manner.

The plot has the usual no-good gambler with the weakling brother, his pure and pretty sister from New Hampshire and the mysterious rider, possessed of superhuman brawn and machine-like alertness. The mysterious rider is a pal of the Indians who taught him his stuff.

Good production values and a pip of a western all the way.

The Silent Avenger

Lumas release of Gotham Production with Sam Sax producer. James P. Hogan director. Story by Frank Foster Davis, who also supervised. Starring "Thunder," dog. At Loew's New York, one half double bill, one day, Aug. 9. Running time, 55 minutes.

Probably a usual dog story, but without as much action as expected either in a dog or western film. But enough in this, plus a few laughs to please the younger set who go for these dog tales.

"Thunder" as a police dog has a corking trick in winking at the proper moments. Otherwise he's a police dog with the instincts of those animals, with this one looking like a Belgian.

An excellently staged battle between the dog and a tame or trained bear. Also "Thunder" makes a great show of attacking through seizing the person attacked by the arm or wrist.

While a police dog can easily crush any bone in the human frame, it can also, if friendly inclined, seize a person by the arm and push him over without even scratching the skin. The traits of police dogs are the fascination to those knowing them. It may be the size of the animals and their instincts which attract and hold others.

In "The Silent Avenger" "Thunder" goes along with his pal, the son of a railroad president, seeking the right of way over a Tennessee farm. A struggle is on between two roads for it. The son, reforming of his wild oats days, goes to secure the privilege, to re-establish himself with his father.

He secures the rights, marries the farmer's daughter and thwarts a couple of villains, while the dog rescues everyone worth it around the premises.

Action doesn't really start until after about 45 minutes of the 55. In the remaining 10 is packed much, including fights and the rescue of the girl from the approaching express, she having kindly lain down on the rails.

The story didn't need a writer, merely a memory, but that probably goes for all of them. *Sime.*

Tumbling River

Fox production directed by Lew Seller. Adapted from the J. E. Grinstead novel, "The Scourge of the Little C," by Jack Jungmeyer. Starring Tom Mix. Dorothy Dwan and Wallace MacDonald featured. Cast including William Conklin, Stella Essex, Elmo Billings, Edward Peil, Sr., Buster Gardner, Harry Gripp. Previewed in projection room Aug. 11. Running time, about 50 minutes.

Not quite as much action as in the average Tom Mix western. Two juveniles, Elmo Billings and Stella Essex, are employed with apparently disastrous effects. Probably intended to make a play for juvenile audiences, but miss out through bad awkwardness. Totally unnecessary.

Any original material there may have been in the book has been passed up, production being cut according to type. Three tramp cowboys are played up for weak comedy.

The girl is a habitual hero collector, bringing home various specimens whom she endows with fictional strength of character. Her father treats them all contemptuously.

"Tony" and another horse named "Buster" troupe better than any one else in the picture with the exception of the star.

Down the Grade

Lumas release of Gotham Production by Sam Sax. Directed by Charles Hutchinson. Starring William Fairbanks. Cast includes Alice Calhoun and James Aubre. At Loew's New York, one day, Aug 12, one-half of a double feature program.

Okay where it's intended for state rights.

No one will try to lure William Fairbanks away from Gotham on his showing in this picture.

Considerable action in automobile, motorcycle and airplane chasing with the climax in a runaway train being cut loose on board.

Deals in a surprisingly original manner with the sleuth hired to protect a railway company payroll who is tipping off the gang. The audience is further surprised and thrilled to discover that the sleuth is in reality the leader of the hold-up mob.

Fairbanks plays the good-for-nothing son who thinks more of booze parties and women than honest endeavor. He turns over a new leaf and some one else's motorcycle simultaneously and goes into the mountains to clean up the gang.

Alice Calhoun as the girl lacks conviction.

LES MISERABLES

Film version of the Victor Hugo classic, originally done in 32 reels by the Cineromans Cie in France, and now edited down to 11 reels for American presentation by Universal. Musical setting for this engagement by Hugo Riesenfeld. Directed by Louis Manpas. At the Central theatre, New York, Aug. 22, for a run. Running time 140 minutes, including intermission.

Jean Valjean	
M. Madeleine } ....M. Gabriel Gabrio	
Champmathieu }	
Javert ....M. Jean Toulout	
Mgr. Myriel.............M. Paul Jorge	
Marius.........................M. Rozet	
Thenardier.............M. G. Saillard	
Gavroche.............M. Charles Badilole	
Fantine }	
Cosette } ....Mme. Sandra Milowanoff	
Gillenormand.............M. Maillard	
Enjolras.............M. Paul Guide	
Mlle. Baptistine.Mme. Clara Darcey-Roche	
Cosette (Child).......Mlle. Andree Rolane	
Eponine.............Mlle. Nivette Saillard	
La Thenardier...........Mme. Renee Carl	

This version in its boiled down form has all the breathless haste and fierce economy of a "synopsis of chapters already published" in a magazine serial. Not for a single moment does it live and breathe with any touch of human interest. Instead it is a long and tiresome parade of stiff and stilted melodrama.

The result of a determination to present a large design on a small canvas could scarcely be otherwise. This is merely a machine shaped skeleton of the lurid passages in the great novel—the scaffold upon which Hugo wrought his epic. It has no suggestion anywhere of a transcript of life.

In its literary quality as here presented it has no merit. As a film its technical quality is astonishingly poor. Photographic texture is distinctly bad; settings give little or no illusion and the acting is unequivocally bad—in short the whole enterprise falls short of even mediocrity.

There are moments of shocking crudity in acting and staging. One has the feeling that a great literary work has been degraded to cheap melodrama in some of the episodes. Javert registers grave though by tucking his hand in his breast suggesting the travesty of the "ham" actor in a comedy quartet. Thenardier expresses crafty cunning for all the world as Eddie Cantor might in a comedy scene. These crudities probably are nothing more than the inept treatment of a tremendously dignified and solemn subject. A mediocre actor playing King Lear would be twice as absurd as if he were dealing with an inconsequential role.

It is possible that in its original 32 reels the production might have had some sweep. If anybody should be able to translate "Les Miserables" to the screen, surely it would be the French, inspired by their intense national pride in the Hugo tradition. But if the larger pattern had dignity, spirit or compelling grip, it has been lost in this transcription. It must have been a staggering physical task to cut the film from 32 to 11 reels, and to preserve any fidelity to the written story in its human quality seems to have been impossible.

Character exposition is lost in the mad dash to cover the vast ground of material presented in one of the longest books in any language. Motives are obscure. For instance when Javert in the end is confronted with the conflict of either compromising with his conscience, or sending Valjean, who had just saved his life, back to prison, the screen device is brutal. Javert is shown staring down into the Seine. A title explains brusquely what is on his mind; and, presto! Javert is a splash in the river.

The business of getting over the passage takes up probably 75 feet of film. And thus is dismissed an episode that has the material in it for a three-act drama. That's the trouble with "Les Miserables." There is a super-film in every chapter and any effort to crystallize the whole book within the limits of a picture is absurd. William Farnum once figured in a version, but, if memory serves, that adaptation departed somewhat radically from the book in sequences and merely dramatized a few characters and passages instead of attempting the impossible of a full recital.

The 11-reel arrangement is planned for a twice-a-day showing. Another arrangement has been done in eight reels for regular release. This version entirely eliminates the character of Fantine which takes up neatly half the longer edition, and concentrates on the more spectacular passages of the Revolution which involve some big crowd effects in the views of fighting behind the Paris barricades. These bits are well done compared to the earlier chapters, which have for the most part backgrounds of squalor and misery.

As it stands the picture has very little appeal as art and none whatever as entertainment. "Les Miserables" never had much of a kick as light summer reading in book form, and about three weeks ought to use up the patronage of high school students who go or are sent because everybody ought to know what "Les Miserables" is about.

Rush.

UNDERWORLD

Paramount picture directed by Josef Von Sternberg from story by Ben Hecht. Adapted by Charles Furthman and scenarized by R. N. Lee. Running time 75 minutes. At the Paramount, N. Y., week of Aug. 20.

"Bull" Weed..............George Bancroft
"Rolls Royce"..............Clive Brook
"Feathers"..............Evelyn Brent
"Slippy" Lewis..............Larry Semon
"Buck" Mulligan..............Fred Kohler
Mulligan's Girl..............Helen Lynch
Paloma..............Jerry Mandy
"High Collar" Sam..............Karl Morse

Par. intended "Underworld" as a special for a run at the Rialto or Rivoli. What it might have done in that class can't be said but the Ben Hecht story under Von Sternberg's treatment shapes up as a whale of a film yarn. It has everything from romance to thrills and the underworld stuff is the big wow generally.

The title itself is half the battle. Whatever morbid or other interest actuates human curiosity in anything pertaining to the underworld, it certainly works well with this picture. The opening day the crowds seemed abnormally large even considering the weather and the Saturday half holiday.

"Underworld," without mentioning Chicago as the scene of the ensuing machine gun warfare between the crooks and cops, evidently is a page out of Ben Hecht's underworld acquaintance with the Cicero and South Side gun mob. The "hanging by the neck" death sentence is another tip-off that New York, at least, is whitewashed, and it makes one wonder how the Illinois and other midwestern censors will feel about some of the niceties of highway robbery, footpadding, double-crossing, martial warfare with the authorities, and other fine points in underworld misbehavior. As far as New York is concerned, it's a pip picture.

There's a wallop right through and yet the film retains romance, clicks not a little on comedy (through the medium of Larry Semon) and even whitewashes itself with a "moral" that banditry cannot successfully defy the law and that the wages of sin is death.

Hecht could have made "Underworld" a true biography of Cicero with its "alky" gun mob, with a little switching of the motivation, but instead of bootlegging, our hero is a jewelry store sampler. If his "moll" fancies a bauble he politely excuses himself and fetches it forthwith.

George Bancroft as "Bull" Weed, a sympathetic crook, explains why Paramount re-signed him by his performance in "Underworld." Bancroft will be heard from importantly from now on if again given half the opportunities that are in this picture. Clive Brook, cast as the regenerated drunkard, and Evelyn Brent, as Bancroft's girl, complete the outstanding trio. Larry Semon, doing a foppish shady character, impresses with his mannerisms as a dandy and dude. Semon does more legitimate work than ever before in his character, in just these few scenes.

The triangle situation of "Bull's" protegee, the reclaimed drunk, who falls for and is loved by "Bull's" girl, is the basis of "Underworld." Around this is woven a fast moving, spirited tale, replete with action and situation.

Fred Kohler as "Buck" Mulligan, a rival gang leader, bumped off by "Bull" following his attempt to steal "Feathers" (Weed's frail), does excellently as the "menace."

The punch is a wow. "Bull" Weed has made his escape from his death cell. He suspects Feathers and "Rolls Royce" of duplicity. Royce wants to be true to his pal despite the girl's inclination to "start all over again clean, etc." Back in their hideaway, an avenue of escape through a secret chamber is closed to the fugitive murderer. "Rolls Royce" alone has the keys. The latter makes his way through the pitched battle between the machine-gunning officers of the law and the trapped convict, and thus proves his loyalty. With escape in his grasp, "Bull" recognizes the greater claim "Rolls Royce" has on "Feathers" and eases them out through the secret passage, and surrenders himself to accept his penalty.

"Underworld" runs 75 minutes and while it might stand a little chopping it grips right through. Between Bancroft, Brook, Brent and Semon it should do great gate.

Abel.

MOCKERY

Metro-Goldwyn-Mayer picture starring Lon Chaney. Written and directed by Benjamin Christensen. Titles by Joe Farnham. At the Capitol, N. Y., week of Aug. 20. Running time, 66 mins.

Sergei..............Lon Chaney
Dimitri..............Ricardo Cortez
Tatiana..............Barbara Bedford
Gaidaroff..............Mack Swain
Mrs. Gaidaroff..............Emily Fitzroy
Ivan..............Charles Puffy
Butler..............Kai Schmidt

It would be difficult to select the factor contributing most forcefully to the ineffectiveness of the production. It's a hodge-podge mixture of **half-formed ideas and emotions, morbid but not introspective enough to register as art; slightly pathetic but striking no sympathetic chord or line of thought with which the customers would be in accord.**

Lon Chaney is put through a routine of pug-ugly mugging, but even this flops, as somehow he hardly achieves the ferocious power of facial characterization he has often managed to convey in other productions.

The theme is dull, trite and uninspiring on account of the limitations in handling. Revolutionary stories have proven of vast appeal only when picturized on an elaborate scale.

Background and preparations fail to carry. But for the costumes the revolution might have been in South America; there is nothing except the titles to tell that Russia is the locale.

Christensen tried to show that a walkout of three or four servants, a solitary uprising of discontented villagers and two or three shooting scenes contained the essence of the untold number of bloody battles, murders of women and children and haphazard attacks on women of every class, which followed the overthrow of the czarist regime.

This is a difficult subject, however **—a Russian peasant of such intellectual limitations as to be bordering on imbecility. Given an individual of this sort, the director insisted on making him behave quite rationally instead of taking advantage of the situation thus created for the purpose of making impossible situations** possible.

Tatiana, the countess, was on dangerous territory, disguised as a peasant woman. She had to get to a military stronghold. Seeing a peasant gnawing a bone, she promised him food and a job if he would accompany her. At the border she told Sergei (Chaney) to say they were married. Later they entered a hut where they were to spend the night, and Sergei was flogged by Bolsheviki for refusing to reveal the identity of his alleged wife.

For his services Sergei was later given a job as a servant in the house of Gaidaroff. Sergei became jealous of Dimitri, the captain. He felt that the countess had betrayed or forsaken him. The cook told him how to get the countess in the end. There was to be an uprising. The idea couldn't sink through to Sergei.

Finally the feebly staged revolution. Following some slight hesitation Sergei threw off the bonds of mental serfdom with a mighty effort and constituted himself equal to anyone on the top floor. With the promotion he elected himself a fit candidate for an unpremeditated attack on the countess.

The beauty and beast effect is entirely lost in these scenes. The contrast is not strong enough, since Chaney does not look as repulsive nor Miss Bedford as beautiful as it is intended to convey. Mostly a chase through a couple of well-furnished rooms, and then the soldiers arrive.

When several of the villagers were held to be shot, the countess is asked about Sergei, and she advises that he be allowed to remain unharmed because he had remained faithful. But Sergei almost loses his life in the following scenes in a successful effort to save the countess from another attack from the male kitchen help.

The picture may be figured to draw on the strength of Chaney's box-office value the first half of the week. It lowers the star's batting average considerably.

Hard Boiled Haggerty

First National picture starring Milton Sills. Adapted from "Belated Evidence," by Elliott W. Springs. Scenario by Carey Wilson, with Charles Brabin directing. At the Strand, N. Y., week of Aug. 20. Running time, 73 mins.

Lieutenant Haggerty..............Milton Sills
Germaine..............Molly O'Day
Klaxon..............Arthur Stone
Major Cotton..............Mitchell Lewis
Brigadier General..............George Fawcett
Cafe Dancer..............Yola d'Avril

A well seasoned aviation lieutenant who gets a pair of twin daughters mixed up and is almost court martialed because of the mistake. That's "Haggerty," and nt has a good chance to survive at the various box offices despite the anchors Brabin has tied to it every time a love port heaves in sight.

Brabin, not the speediest director in the world, has sprinkled this one with enough closeups to take care of two normal pictures. Don't tell a director where to place his closeups. They say. Well, if the ethics of the studios permit, somebody should take the subject up with Charles in a general way. No kiddin', there are enough heads of Molly O'Day in this one to make **those Barthelmess "stills" in the Globe's lobby blush.**

And it's a fair picture for Sills. Rough and ready characterization holding situations where strong men stifle their man-to-man emotions, but not so much that the camera can't catch it. Sills gets a D. S. C., yet the ring around his neck where the makeup ends offsets the embarrassment. Nothing doll-faced about Sills. Probably why the men like him. Here he's an aviator in the midst of the war, shot down and in turn shooting down his opposing "stick" wielder. Air stuff, and for those who haven't viewed "Wings" okay.

Haggerty has a habit of popping off German planes, watching them fall and then flying on to Paris to dodge M. P.s. Dodging himself into Germaine's (Miss O'Day) apartment the love interest is on, only to become complicated when the Irish boy's major tips him off that the girl isn't all she should be. Sock, and into the conference which will lead to a court-martial unless one of the men speaks. The major finally gives in and the girl admits everything. Haggerty disillusioned.

It all comes out in the Armistice when the major learns that his well-meaning tip concerned the twin sister of Germaine. Bringing both girls before Haggerty squares everybody concerned so that it looks as if Germaine will see the Atlantic.

Arthur Stone supplies comedy as Haggerty's mechanic with a true weakness for going a. w. o. l on the assignment. ..ves for Miss O'Day on her Globe performance, but nothing to cause hysterics here. However, nice and may 'be too much of her because of Brabin.

Sills convinces. He seldom does anything else. At least this boy is always trying. The scene where he renounces his uniform before the board of inquiry carries a kick and marks the high spot of the director's effort. Strictly an all male affair with the inclusion of Miss O'Day suddenly turning town scamp to save her lover, too theatrical and taking the edge off of an interesting sequence.

"Haggerty" has some laughs and one good touch of drama. How many program pictures have more? It should do business for the boys and their theatres. Especially as these same boys can undo a few things Brabin has done with an ordinary pair of scissors.

Sid.

For the Love of Mike

First National release of Frank Capra production. At the Hippodrome, New York, week of Aug. 22.

Mary..............Claudette Colbert
Mike..............Ben Lyon
Abraham Katz..............George Sidney
Herman Schultz..............Ford Sterling
Patrick O'Malley..............Hugh Cameron
"Coxey" Pendleton..............Richard (Skeete) Gallagher
Henry Sharp..............Rudolph Cameron
Evelyn Joyce..............Mabel Swor

Lack of expert directorial continuity and allied creative skill counts against "Mike" which, as a basic idea, had possibilities. The George Sidney-Hugh Cameron Jewish-Irish alliance goes one better with Ford Sterling ringing in the Dutch.

Title is derived from Michael Otto Abraham O'Malley, a doorstep foundling reared by his three dialect "dads." The old boys go the limit for the love of their Mike (Ben Lyon), and the yarn winds up in Yale with Michael, etc., captain and stroke of the varsity crew. With no author or scenarist credited, it may be one of those made-on-the-lot productions.

The usual gambling complications are again resurrected and our hero is faced with throwing the race to Harvard as a settlement for $1,500 in I. O. U.'s. Mr. Capra does not bother to explain how gamblers are permitted to drift in and out of the New Haven oarsmen's quarters, or how the Yale coach would permit letters of disturbing import to reach the crew.

The Hipp singled out Sidney, Sterling and Lyon for triple featuring, although Hugh Cameron, as the Irish third of the trio of "fathers," does some effective work. Claudette Colbert (memorable for her work in "The Barker") makes her screen debut here but is given limited opportunities. She registers in what she does. Mabel Swor, another legit (musical comedy) alumnus, makes an impression as the blonde campus vamp who "steers" for a Park Avenue "joint." Skeets Gallagher is unusually effective as the coxswain who suspects Ben Lyon's obligation to the gambler.

Rudolph Cameron as Henry Sharp, the roulette operator, has a Lowellshermanesque personality and augers well for future flickers in sleek light-heavy roles. Intelligently handled Cameron will develop into a convincing personality. The picture has a couple of news shots interwoven. The first is the 20 years ago melting pot scene and an airplane shot of the regatta may or may not be a cut from the news reels.

The Hipp's urgent need of film accounts for the week stand at this K-A house; otherwise it rates a three-day booking. Not particularly distinctive in any sense, "Mike" has three good names to play up, and the Jewish-Dutch-Irish idea, with the collegiate evolution, recommends it for general box office appeal in any neighborhood. *Abel.*

Love Makes Us Blind

Booked and billed in "support" of a Ufa, this reporter still thinks the far-north scenic, "Alaskan Adventures," is the topliner at the Fifth Avenue Playhouse.

The foreign baby is a manifestation of heavy-footed and thick-spectacled Germans in a festive mood. The result is epitomized in that classic vaudeville nifty, "Look —he wants to play!"

Even the redoubtable Emil Jannings clowns it; Conrad Veidt sports a Keystone mustache, and the rather sexy Lillian Dagover (the spirit of it is tipped off in Mindlin's satirical program, wherein he calls her "Lil") wigs up and makes a monkey of her stolid young husband; George Alexander, not of the Ufa stock outfit, plays a minor but excellent share.

It isn't much of a picture, any way you take it. But Art Young, champion bow-and-arrow shooter, and a companion and a comical dog, making a tour of Alaska and into Russian Sibera across the Bering Sea, is a thriller—a full-size feature, with all the cut-outs restored. Roxy showed a miniature release of this, all boiled down to the "important" chunks. There is more to films than importance. Anybody who loves the outdoors, and city people are far from immune, will feel the pulses pounding faster over this one.

Through it all for comedy (and much funnier than "Love Makes Us Blin?") runs a dog of questionable ancestry, aptly named "Wrongstart."

Restored to its original size and shape, and shown here that way, "An Alaskan Adventure" is a candidate for program use anywhere and everywhere. It runs full-length, about 50 or a few more minutes. And it hasn't a dull or stale foot in it.

Business Sunday night was over capacity, with the Villagers and long-distance Fifth Avenue Playhouse fans standing out. This is a rather remarkable tribute to the current program and the house

---

policy, for there isn't another thing of any kind open within eyeshot of this extraordinary bijou theatre on a Sunday; yet the private cars were lined up for a block on both sides and around all corners.

Mindlin seems to have perfected the movie mousetrap that Elbert Hubbard wrote about. *Lait.*

THE COWARD

F. B. O. production directed by Alfred Raboch from a story by Arthur Stringer. Cameraman, Jules Cronjager. Running time, 62 mins. In projection room, Aug. 17.
Clinton Philbrook...........Warner Baxter
Alicia Van Orden............Sharon Lynn
Leigh Morlock..............Freeman Wood
Pierre Bechard..............Raoul Paoli
Darius Philbrook...........Byron Douglas
Marie.....................Charlotte Stevens

A predicted bell-ringer for almost any house.

"The Coward" stood out in a projection room where reviewing conditions are all against a picture. By inference it should be correspondingly stronger when projected in a theatre.

A simple enough yarn telling the familiar tale of the weakling son of great wealth who is stung into a realization of his own softness by the bullying of a self-made and disagreeable millionaire. He goes to the northwest, plunges into the woods with a burly French Canuck, and emerges with the strength and heart of a lion.

While Arthur Stringer's story has given an intelligent and believable plot foundation it is the direction of Raboch that figures as the picture's main strength. Raboch is a new director only recently given a megaphone, according to report, after serving his apprenticeship as an assistant. On a basis of his work on this production and on another, not yet released, it is understood he has been assigned to direct a forthcoming film for United Artists.

One sequence here was a little demanding of credulity. That is where the made-over hero carrying a man on his back scales the perpendicular side of a cliff by sheer muscular hold of a rope. However fabulous such an exploit may seem, it will probably not constitute any great obstacle to the enjoyment of the average patron.

There are several crackerjack fights and Raboch has managed to make it seem like real stuff.

In the cast are two new camera faces. Sharon Lynn, the femme lead, is a classy gal with a knockout wardrobe. The women will be interested in some of her rather extreme styles. Raoul Paoli, playing the hefty French woodsman, is a candidate for the title of "a find."

A dandy picture with a hackneyed title.

SNOWBOUND

Tiffany production directed by Phil Stone. From the story by Douglas Bronston. Cast includes Betty Blythe, Lillian Rich, Robert Agnew, Harold Goodwin, Pat Harmon and Dorothea Wolbert. At Loew's New York, Aug. 19, as one-half of double feature program. Running time, 65 mins.

A lightweight farce with an appealing cast and a couple of comedy scenes figured to fit the patronage of the bi-weekly changes.

Much unnecessary detail adds to an already bewildering series of circumstances. By pursuing a less cumbersome and clearer course the director had an opportunity of injecting elements of greater merit in humorous situations. The predicaments of the hero become so involved at times as to put the audience into a predicament—to walk out or not to walk becomes the question.

A will is again held responsible for resulting in trouble. The boy must be married in order to receive a legacy of some three million odd dollars. Finally the time comes,

---

as it has a habit of doing. But the beneficiary of the will is not married. He is in no hurry, but his chief creditor wants to be paid and gets his secretary to act as the wife. The girl's boy friend is a motorcycle cop—the same one whom the hero had overturned in a rush trip. These are only a few of the complications which are finally settled through the simple expedient of having the girl pass out, temporarily, in a faint.

Story should have had a better chance with expert treatment. "Snowbound" seems to be slightly exaggerated as the title.

HULA

Paramount production and release. Clara Bow starred, with Clive Brook featured. Directed by Victor Fleming. Titles by George Marion, Jr. Adapted by Doris Anderson from novel by Armine Von Tempski, with scenario by Ethel Doherty. At Paramount, New York, week Aug. 27. Running time, around 60 minutes.
"Hula" Calhoun.................Clara Bow
Anthony Haldane..............Clive Brook
Mrs. Bane.................Arlette Marschal
Harry Dehan................Arnold Kent
Margaret Haldane............Maude Truax
"Old Bill" Calhoun............Albert Gran
Uncle Edwin..............Agostino Borgato

One paragraph could tell the entire tale of this "Hula" picture. It has Clara Bow and is bent over to meet the picture house reflex. That makes it okay for the usual film theatre attendance.

Probably Clara in her gayest mood, as she does a slight cooch at one moment, the only excuse for the title, although the locale is Hawaii. But, then, again, at another time Miss Bow's mouth has such an overdose of carmine that it seemed as though the horse she wouldn't get off had kicked her there. Or a cold sore or just a bad spot that she and everyone else around overlooked, unless the director, Victor Fleming, was running this thing through on a time limit. At other times Clara's sometimes pouting lips resembled a raspberry ice. And Clara is no stranger to make up.

And after you like this film in its flighty way you'll get a laugh out of the idea of a man jumping into a narrow stream to save a dog. That catches up with the egg and chicken gag: who swam first, man or dog? Clive Brook did the swim. He and the dog were saved from the rapids by Miss Bow hanging onto a limb of a tree with one hand and giving Clive her other.

That brought them to the bank soaking wet, up and down. But it didn't prevent Clara and Clive from sitting on the river's edge to make love. Being all wet means nothing to picture lovers.

A few other things you may tingle at, but this sap and flap picture will get to 'em just the same, those in the orchestra, mezzanine and balcony, for Clara must be Clara. She's it doubly now, especially to the femmes.

Probably Ethel Doherty, who did the scenario, being a girl, knew how to send this the straightest way across inside of a film pallais. And being a girl, Ethel sent it in for the gals, catching the boys on the side, for the first shot of Clara is in swimming, showing her from the bust up, and that's no bust of a shot, either.

When they wanted to show what Clara owned on the inside, they only let them see by suggestion, such as when Clara wanted Clive to look where she had hurt herself, starting to lift up her skirt. Clive wasn't nearly as excited over that as the audience, for he turned his head away. But the cutter or the cameraman killed what might have been quite a sight, although Clara showed it, anyway, before and after in one way or another. Clara didn't get to be it on impulse.

"Hula" is a pretty fair b. o. title, even if Gilda has used it almost all up in action, and no chorus girl nowadays isn't without a couple of wiggles in her routine or hips.

But just as Clara told the dinner party watching a couple of natives going through the straw practice that she would show it to 'em proper, and started to get hot on the left to right stuff, Clive picked her up and carried Clara away. That cheated the house of another extra 35c. worth, for Clara looks to be a cut-rate wiggler.

Mr. Brook didn't have to do much besides the swim, standing for Clara's kisses and seeing that his hair kept parted. That couple do a lot of kissing in this film, but somehow Clive seemed to maneuver

Clara sideways. That left it to guess he was long distancing it from that carmine. Fair enough, too, for why should an actor take a chance? But Clara is some kisser when she starts. If Clive hadn't taken more care of her make-up than she did of his'n, the smears would have been terrible streaky.

In Hawaii Clara seemed the pampered daughter of the care-free family of Calhouns. She lived alone, away from the homestead with a native philosopher for cook. He told her some day she would meet a man and love him. When Clive arrived from England, Clara took one look and picked him.

Before the Englishman knew it he was loved. And then Clara tried her naivete. She's naive in spots, and at other times pretty fresh, but it all gets over.

Toward the finish the picture went to a jam. Clara had made Clive confess he loved her, although Clive has previously informed the near-hula prancer that his wife was in England. There they were. It couldn't go much longer that way, and the wife wouldn't divorce him. So they brought the wife over on the next boat and pulled the jam out of the hole on the home grounds. Lovely!

Everybody's all right, even to Clara's horse, and the gal can ride.

Geo. Marion's titles, though, are not up to their usual mark.

Paramount has the right idea with the Bow girl. While she's running in high, send her in front often. It will take three bad ones to start to kill her off, and, like Chaney, et al., until then she may be safely played by any house as often as Par will let her go to the screen. *Sime.*

Smile, Brother, Smile

First National comedy drama feature, starring Jack Mulhall and Dorothy Mackaill. Adapted by Rex Taylor and Al Boasberg's story and directed by John Francis Dillon. Produces by Charles R. Rogers. Running time, 65 minutes. At the Strand, New York, week Aug. 27.

Jack Lowery....................Jack Mulhall
Mildren Marvin...........Dorothy Mackaill
Harvey Renrod...........Philo McCollough
Fred Bower....................E. J. Ratcliffe
Mr. Potter...................Harry Dunkinson
Mr. Saunders..................Ernest Hilliard
Mr. Markel.......................Charles Clary
Mr. Kline..............................Jack Dillon
Daisy.................................Yola d'Avril
The Collector.......................Hank Mann
Three High-powered Salesmen
T. Roy Barnes, Jed Prouty, Sam Bloom

Entertaining light program subject, very modern and done in a neat comedy spirit. Toward the end the director sacrifices all dramatic interest in his quest for laughs and at times the fun runs to pretty rough gagging in the Mack Sennett vein. It got the laughs, but at great cost to the human interest that had been painstakingly built up.

Jack Mulhall does splendidly as a rather dull shipping clerk whose future appeared to be limited by the shipping room until his girl practically forced him to go out after something worth while by way of a job.

Jack takes to the road as a salesman, only to run against a plot by a rival concern which threatened to wreck his career as a commercial traveler. It was then the girl again came to his rescue, framing a sales device that won out for both.

Here is a story that ought to interest the younger generation who read "Success" magazine. The characters of the shipping clerk and the phone girl are nicely created and capitally acted by these two engaging young screen players. Dramatic material is extremely light, but the everyday incidents are interestingly presented in a story that takes its very punch from commonplaceness. It is a cross section of present-day life.

Perhaps the gagging was found necessary to compensate for the lightweight dramatic element. Jack's adventures as a salesman are jazzed to the point of broad farce in action and titles, the comedy being rather forced. As, for instance, when the small town hotel pages "Mr. Cohen" in the lobby and the entire gathering of loungers starts for the phone.

Jack is selling beauty preparations. When a double crossing rival defeats his sales it is his girl who conceives the idea of a public demonstration of transforming a human fright into a ravishing by means of the treatments, the girl herself being the subject. This scene is jazzed up to the point of burlesque, but it is full of broad laughs, and is so introduced that there is a surprise kick at the finish. Miss Mackaill does extremely well with a rather trifling role.

It's a picture that will please the fans, but probably will not prove an especially strong pull aside from the strength of the featured players, who are coming to mean more and more in the lobby. *Rush.*

The Desired Woman

Warner Brothers production and release. Featuring Irene Rich. Adapted from a Mark Canfield story and directed by Michael Curtiz. At Hippodrome, New York, week Aug. 29. Running time, about 60 minutes.

Lady Diana.........................Irene Rich
Capt. Maxwell....................Wm. Russell
Larry Trent................Wm. Collier, Jr.
Lieut. Kellogg....................John Miljan
Sir Sydney Vincent........Richard Tucker

An Irene Rich picture that takes some weird detours to make all ends meet. Not strong enough to stand alone for a week anywhere, but okay for a day, and probably three, because of the cast names which should have some degree of fetching power.

No matter where it plays, the story is going to be familiar. It's about another military garrison in the desert with a woman the cause of a lieutenant's court-martial. Even the thesis that the wife of the brutal post commander is too old or the youthful officer, and the philosophy that youth forgets easily upon which the picture ends, is hardly new to the screen.

Meanwhile there is little to hold this one up unless it be the performance of John Miljan as an fiicer who loses his mind and whom Trent (Buster Collier) is forced to kill in self-defense.

Miss Rich has turned in too many standard performances to need defining in this epic of the sands. In fact, it's a pretty heavy burden to place on her shoulders, despite its lack of weight. And the b. o. responsibility will be hers because she's featured. Collier plays the boy who would run away with his superior's wife, doesn't "suffer" any too well before the camera, but otherwise is convincing enough. Miljan takes cast honors because of the fireworks in his role and of which he takes full advantage.

Curtiz, directing, doesn't seem to have done much with his subject exept follow routine lines. In getting Diana (Miss Rich) from the desert, and as the wife of the stony hearted Maxwell, to London where she is suddenly announred as Lady Vincent, the action calls for a great break from the patron's imagination. Either the blame belongs to Chrtiz or to whoever cut the film. But as the story is inclined to be jumpy throughout, it's possible this closing flaw will be a matter of indifference.

Photography is uniformly good, while including a few good looking desert scenes. Not much action even in the skirmish between the post defenders and Arabs.

Won't help Miss Rich's personal drawing power, and will have to be "sold" to the public sight unseen. Little or nothing in this release to make them come out talking favorably. *Sid.*

THE BUSH LEAGUER

Warner Bros. production starring Monte Blue. Directed by Howard Bretherton from a story by Charles Saxton; scenarized by Harvey Gates. Leila Hyams, Clyde Cook, William Demarest and Richard Tucker featured. Running time, about 55 mins. At 5th Avenue, New York, Aug. 29-31.

Warners contribute this one to the cycle of baseball pictures. It is just fair, lacking the authentic baseball atmosphere of "Kelly."

Monte Blue is doing a sap and not, incidentally, adding anything to his feminine following thereby, his sap being without sympathy.

Monte is a pitcher and a whiz, but his real interest is in gasoline pumps. While negotiating with some big business men for the marketing of his invention he forgets that he is supposed to be pitching his club to a victory in the game that clinches or loses the pennant. He arrives for a ninth inning, single handed snatching defeat from the visiting club.

Leila Hyams heroines as the heiress that owns the ball club. In a whole series of gross exaggerations it is as easy to believe in her attachment for the boob pitcher as in any of the other far-fetched details of a meaningless yarn.

Clyde Cook was good as a kibbitzing veteran. Cook, once a slapstick comedian of two-reelers, is not quite "definite" as a serious character man but shows growth in his new department.

The plot includes the usual effort to frame a game with the noble hero and his rough but honest pal scorning the proferred banknotes.

No highlights or suspense in a strictly routine programer.

Firemen, Save My Child

Paramount production and release. Wallace Beery and Raymond Hatton starred. Josephine Dunn and Tom Kennedy featured. Directed by Edward Sutherland. Story and scenario by Monty Brice and Tom Geraghty. Caught outside New York. Running time, about 60 minutes.

Elmer.........................Wallace Beery
Sam.........................Raymond Hatton
Dora Dumston..............Josephine Dunn
Captain Kennedy..............Tom Kennedy
Walter...........................Walter Goss
Chief Dumston................Joseph Girard

"Firemen, Save My Child" as a title bespeaks the low comedy it is. Not travesty or burlesque, just the hoke that makes laughs. Thusly it becomes a first rate laughing regular program release of its class.

That is mainly because Wallace Beery and Raymond Hatton are again teamed up, but not altogether those boys. They play what has been written for them. That's where Monty Brice and Tom Geraghty, the preparers of the script, come in. Those writers have given this male duo some comical work, and aimed right at the picture audiences which will like it.

The fundamental idea of the film is funny in itself; that of the daughter of the chief of the fire department under the impression she can call any of her father's companies to her assistance if she wants to go home, have her car pulled out of a ditch, or so forth. And the company she picks on most is that one where Beery and Hatton were impressed into service while going through a chase. Beery wanted to catch Hatton, because the latter trimmed Beery in a con game. They had been school mates and this also comes out in the final reel, as it is shown in the opening portion, a school room set.

A couple of the best hoked bits are the old Ed Hayes piano moving stuff, worked here on the upward way to the seventh story of an apartment house, and the gag of an Italian fruit merchant seeing his stand wrecked everytime the hook and ladder swung around his corner to go to the girl's home. The final time as the wop catches sight of the truck coming down the street, he kicks over the stand to beat them to it.

Of the two leads, Hatton appears to just edge out Beery in the results. It's a matter of roles. As the con man Hatton must perforce be flip while Beery is the boob, Hatton horning in for the credit whenever Beery turns a trick.

A hoke comedy that will slip in just right for the weekly houses if spotted proper; between a couple of pictures without hoke in either. Perhaps heavily worked up and on the strength of the "Navy" film, this could be pushed into a holdover, but these two names will have to be very strong in the locality to make "Firemen" go that far. A corking week, however, should be the reward of good exploitation for the picture is there for that. *Sime.*

NELSON

Toronto, Aug. 26.

British biographical picture starring Cedric Hardwick. Produced by British Educational Pictures, Ltd., with co-operation of Admiralty. Director, author or photographer not named. Cedric Hardwick, as Admiral Lord Nelson, and Gertrude McCoy, as Lady Hamilton, only billed. At Tivoli, Toronto, for run. Running time, 68 minutes.

Hollywood has nothing to fear from this one largely because of woefully weak trick photography on which the picture obviously depends. French, Spanish and British navies sail into action without a ship moving. Roar of cannons doesn't even rock the boats.

Other than that, a picture that should please throughout the British Empire. A God-send to Australia and England, where a certain percentage of English pictures must be shown.

Cedric Hardwick, from the legit stage, does the part of the weakened and blinded Lord Nelson with commendable restraint. Gertrude McCoy satisfactory in a retiring sort of way as Nelson's paramour, Lady Hamilton.

Opens with Nelson, a boy at school, tempted by pals to rob an orchard. He does the trick, then refuses the fruit. The story proper has him aboard a sailing man o' war on the lookout for Napoleon's fleet. Photography aboard ship excellent.

Two main battles; at the Nile and Trafalgar. Picture makes most of the famous message: "England expects this day that every man will do his duty."

Photography and direction good in hand-to-hand struggle as enemy sailors board the "Victory," then driven back only to surrender their own ship.

Death scene of Nelson one of best ever done in England.

Few love scenes with Lady Hamilton and the break with his own wife by Nelson, rather hurried over but with historical accuracy, even to the illegitimate daughter. Canadian censors let this go.

Picture should get a full week in the larger British houses throughout the world.

Now in third Toronto week, fifth at Montreal. *Sino.*

Rose of the Bower

Comedy drama of underworld bearing the brand of American Cinema Corp. and designated "A Hartford Production." Edna Murphy starred. Running time, 65 minutes. At Loew's New York, one day, Aug. 26. Half double bill.

Another one of the "Sidewalks of New York" craze. Just fair in all departments, story juvenile and frankly designed for the neighborhoods. Useful as here employed as half a double feature bill.

Satisfactory melo in many particulars. Has plenty of action and progress of story is fast. Gets promptly into underworld atmosphere and engages interest at outset. Action lags for brief period and then picks up, well sustained from middle to end. Edna Murphy does not do particularly well with a hoyden role, over playing the "cute" side of the character.

Comedy contrasts are neatly done by Irish character man and Hebe juvenile. A lost baby formula is basis of the tale. Crook rushes into thieves' den offering to sell satchel full of loot so he can make quick getaway. Satchel turns out to contain baby birl. Child adopted by crook, who brings her up. Through no fault of her own, she is involved in a murder case and on trial is about to be found guilty, when she turns out to be the long-lost daughter of the district attorney.

A flash-back goes to the beginning, where the district attorney and his wife are about to part in a family quarrel. He demands that she leave their baby with him. To take her child the mother hides the little one in a portmanteau. In a railway station a hard pressed crook, to escape pursuit, substitutes his hand bag filled with loot for the mother's bag holding the baby. A railroad wreck, in which the mother is killed, disposes of the search, while the baby really is delivered to the underworld.

In the story there are fairly good passages in society settings when the heroine goes to the home of a school mate for vacation. Nothing but familiar hoke, but it is handled in workmanlike manner for useful program material. *Rush.*

The Secluded Roadhouse

Presented by Fred J. Balshofer, of Balshofer Productions. Featuring William Barrymore, supported by Carol Wines, Winifred Landis, Carl Silvera, and Bud Osborne. Directed by Robert J. Horner from a story by Iris Kenyon. Photographed by Lauron Draper. At the Arena, one day (Aug. 26), as half double bill. Running time, 45 minutes.

Destined to live and die in the shooting galleries.

It tells of a young cabaret dancer named Gilda Gay and of her love torn between an upstanding young highway policeman and the sneering owner of the joint. Don't ask why, but she decides to marry sneer-face and goes auto riding with him. The cop finds out.

"I don't think his intentions are right," says the cop. Whereupon he rushes to headquarters, secures about 15 other bike riders, and pursues the girl. He pursues her to the cabaret, to a shipping dock, and then pursues her in a boat.

That's all that can be fathomed. Bad photography, too.

The cast is unknown and knows nothing about acting. William Barrymore is featured apparently for no reason other than that his name has a familiar sound. He is not related.

As the picture unwound its weary way Friday afternoon the manager of the Arena grabbed a young fellow by the shoulder and yanked him to his feet. He shook him and he jerked him and he slapped him slap after slap in the face. The youth, trembling in fright, broke away and ran down 8th avenue. The manager brushed his hands casually.

"Not in this theatre," he muttered. "A woman has a right to see a show without having anybody feeling her legs."

Too bad.

Maybe that kid would have liked the picture.

But the manager shouldn't have blamed the boy so harshly for going after a little excitement.

Ahd he only felt one leg, the lady said.

HIDDEN ACES

Independent underworld melodrama bearing the stamp of Louis T. Rogers Production, released by Pathe. Charles Hutchison starred, with Alice Calhoun feminine lead. Directed by Howard Mitchell from story by J. F. Wallefore. In the cast: Paul Wiegel, Barbara Tennent. Running time, 70 mins. At the New York, New York, Aug 27 as half double bill.

Neatly managed crook story, better in its construction and technical treatment than the acting, which reverses the usual order. The novel point here is the by-play of heavy crook melodrama contrasted with unexpected comedy.

Every time the straight action reaches a tense climax it takes a swift twist to the comedy side, the surprises giving the whole affair a certain attractive flavor. A lot of good character is developed smoothly and unobtrusively.

Opens with the docking of an Atlantic liner, where a Russian princess disembarks, watched through the customs by the master crook, intent upon stealing her jewels. The pursuit continues through night clubs, where the crook learns that another thief, in the person of a girl outlaw, has got herself engaged in the princess' service.

Thereafter the story is the contest between the woman and the man crook to get the gems from the sap major domo of the princess. They scheme against each other with often amusing complications, when the police get into the chase. At the finish there is a whooping auto pursuit with stunt features, all ending when it is disclosed that the girl is a secret agent of Scotland Yard and the man crook is really an American Secret Service operative, while the sap major domo and the princess are in fact desperate smugglers.

The story progresses swiftly, with wealth of incident and good suspense. A jaunty bit of love interest comes in the neat suggestion of a love affair between man and woman crook, used in a romantic finish. Titling is well done to emphasize the rather subtle humor of the whole business.

Picture probably would do better with the wise fans than among the less knowing, who usually resent the introduction of irony in their melodrama. Certainly worthy of a better grading than half double bill as here booked. *Rush.*

GARDEN OF ALLAH

Metro-Goldwyn-Mayer release and production. Adapted from Robert Hichens' play of the same name. Directed by Rex Ingram, with Alice Terry and Ivan Petrovich featured. Photography credited to Lee Garmes, Monroe Bennett and Marcel Lucien.. Willie Goldbeck, scenarist. At the Embassy, New York, for a twice daily run commencing Sept. 2. $1.65 top. Running time, 96 mins.

Domini Enfilden	Alice Terry
Boris Androvsky	Ivan Petrovich
Count Anteoni	Marcel Vibert
Lord Rens	H. H. Wright
Suzanne	Mme. Paquerette
Father Roubier	Armand Dutertre
Sand Diviner	Ben Sadour
Ayesha	Rehba Ben Salah
Batouch	Gerald Fielding
Hadj	Claude Fielding

Metro-Goldwyn-Mayer has been afraid of this picture. Possibly still is. The way it unwinds at the Embassy it registers as straight program fare that doesn't threaten to upset booking schedules by demanding holdover showing. If it gets over to that extent in the big film houses indications are that M-G-M will be satisfied.

Ingram sent over two versions of his latest work. Inasmuch as the film was due at this house last June it's easily realized that the studio execs thought some changes should be made. So the director asked them to hold off until he had again cut the footage and requested that they gaze upon his second version.

The understanding is that the print at the Embassy is the outcome of Ingram's follow-up scissoring. There is still another conception, maybe two, as cut and spliced on the Coast. Those who have seen all from the cutting room claim the California effort is the best through holding suspense by retarding the revelation of Boris as a Monk and the switchback sequence that reveals his revolt against his religious vows. As currently playing there is no suspense, and it's a straightforward story into which Ingram has not transfused a great degree of directorial acumen. Still, the Ingram-cut film at the Embassy is the only one scored, so that settles that.

The story has body and share of fame behind it to lift it above the usual screen tale. Religious angle of the Monk leaving the monastery to hide his identity, wed and repent, after telling his wife of his transgression so that he returns to the monastery, may cause talk which will help attendance.

In any case, Ingram has uncovered a screen bet in Petrovich, who, it is reported, was sponsored for the part by Miss Terry. Petrovich's appearance indicates that he will be favorably received by women and men. Too, his work throughout is capable.

Miss Terry does little emoting and will refresh the memories of those who have viewed her in other releases. Marcel Vibert lends outstanding support to the main pair, with other cast members contributing as expected.

What faults "The Garden of Allah" has may either be attributed to the making or the cutting. No question that in certain passages the story becomes dull as it pauses. Running 96 minutes, there is much that the program houses will delete and which should be of advantage to the picture. Opening night it ran without intermission.

At odd moments some of the photography is beautiful as regards desert scenes. Yet the sandstorm, the kick of the play, doesn't impress here as much more than a flurry against the big stuff that has been hitting the screens of late.

A main idea again is that possibly Ingram has been staying away from this country too long. Antique directorial technique is especially noticeable through the manner in which he has introduced what comedy bits the story affords. Consequently, Ingram is "telegraphing" each supposed laugh, with no laugh resulting.

In toto this foreign-made product is something of a ponderous film that looks suitable for the program houses on the strength of its title and the names in the personnel. The tab readers won't like it, but they'll probably come into view it, while the more intelligent clientele is figured to receive it mildly. *Sid.*

THE JOY GIRL

Fox production and release, starring Olive Borden. Directed by Allan Dwan. From the Saturday Evening Post story by May Edginton. At the Roxy, New York, week Sept. 3. Running time over one hour.

Jewel Courage	Olive Borden
John Jeffrey Fleet	Neil Hamilton
Mrs. Heath	Marie Dressler
Mrs. Courage	Mary Alden
Herbert Courage	William Norris
Flora	Helen Chandler
Vicary	Jerry Miley
Hugh Sandman	Frank Walsh
Valet	Clarence Elmer
Isolde	Peggy Kelly
Chauffeur	Jimmy Grainger, Jr.

Considering the imposing triumvirate responsible for construction, story and leading role the result is not over satisfying.

Neil Hamilton and Olive Borden form a cute, likeable team of youthful lovers. Given an outdoor background, with just the right mixture of grass, trees and soft lens closeups, the impulsive movements of the pair, the girl especially, are catchy and unexaggerated.

Lighting and photography bad in several spots. Most of the scenes are at a distance. This gives the principles slim opportunities to register anything that resembles acute emotion.

Marie Dressler is subjected to long distance shooting and dark lights in almost every scene. She has to put her work over through motions of body, arms and legs. With an assignment offering every chance for surefire low comedy Miss Dressler doesn't do any mugging.

As Mrs. Heath, wealthy widow of a millionaire oil man, she is being played by Vicary, a chauffeur, for the bankroll. The love scenes are intended for laughs, but miss through lack of face work. Miley is given the camera breaks, but doesn't register, except as a colorless character. Miley has the spicy role of the chauffeur in his master's clothes and car, out on the make, but doesn't seem to grasp any of the abundant opportunities.

Action is allowed to weaken too often from a production viewpoint. The girl is described fully and repeatedly as a fortune hunter. Because she is out for money for her mother's sake doesn't let her out with the average movie fan who places true love above everything.

The millionaire flops for the girl, but being disguised as his own chauffeur she will not marry him, though she cares.

Jewel finally marries the real chauffeur, thinking him wealthy. The marriage is later discovered null through a previous marriage with the wealthy Mrs. Heath.

Color photography used in several Palm Beach scenes very effective. Gets everything, including neckties and the sunshine.

Will do in the smaller of the first runs, though box office returns are not expected to be above average.

SWIM, GIRL, SWIM

Paramount production and release. Starring Bebe Daniels and featuring Gertrude Ederle. Clarence Badger directing. Story by Lloyd Corrigan. Cameraman, J. Roy Hunt, with George Marion, Jr., titles. At Paramount, New York, week of Sept. 3. Running time, 69 minutes.

Alice Smith	Bebe Daniels
Jerry Marvin	James Hall
Gertrude Ederle	Herself
Helen Tracey	Josephine Dunn
Mr. Spangle	William Austin

Another of Bebe Daniels' light

comedy sport pictures, with a couple of high spots to offset the midway footage that stays well within any speed limit. The story makes the star an undergraduate again, and will be a worthy box-office successor to the preceding pictures of this type to which she has been assigned.

One gag in particular drew a whoop out of a Sunday matinee audience that goes down as the biggest yell heard in a picture theatre since MacLaglen discovered who was giving him the razz in "Glory." It may not hit with such spontaneity in other places. It happens during a co-ed's class rush, the objective of which is to get a greased ball across a swimming pool and into a barrel on the other side. Alice (Miss Daniels) is the sap on her side; the ball accidentally pops into her lap during a scrimmage, and she's off for the pool while the others still struggle. Reaching the water and unable to swim, she starts to puff up her water wings for the crossing as the mob comes up behind her. And the house rocked.

Not much of a plot holding the film together, but the situations consistently win giggles. The windup is a girls' intercollegiate race, with Alice getting a late start, but crawling out front in the last 50 yards. As prescribed by formula for such a tale, there is a wild auto dash to get the heroine to the starting line, in this instance the means being an ambulance, with motorcycle cops believing they are clearing the way for an emergency case. The central portion of the picture is turned over to a channel swim, which Alice accidentally wins to become the heroine of the campus. Gertrude Ederle slips into the action when Alice has got to make good for her school, and goes to Trudy for instruction.

It's reported that Badger turned this release out fast enough to make it one of the quickest jobs Paramount has had in months. With Ederle drawing $7,000 a week, it is understood the swim champ was held only a fortnight. Trudy isn't necessary to the story, although rating as an interesting sidelight. So, if that's worth $14,000, okay.

Miss Daniels has been doing very well in the athletic series she has been turning out. These have brought her back after undeveloped love stories threatened to bury her. "Swim, Girl, Swim," won't impede the return trip so far as the public is concerned.

Miss Daniels goes almost halfway through the yarn as a shell-rim bespectacled young lady with tight drawn hair, cotton stockings, etc., before getting a chance to turn on her full appearance value.

A couple of rough sequences calling for acrobatic falls indicate a double has been used, but there's plenty of shots showing the star ploughing through the water. A high dive from the top of the ambulance as it stops upon a bridge drew exclamations from the house. Giving the picture a total of two demands upon the vocal chords of an audience. Nothing remarkable about the dive—just well spotted and pretty.

Miss Daniels handles herself capably all the way, with James Hall again opposite, this time as the head of the student-body and, of course, the other half of the love theme. However, William Austin and his well-known English fop characterization run the star a close second for cast honors. As a professor Austin gets a lot of assistance from the George Marion captions. Miss Daniels, Hall and Austin are the only members that count, with Trudy as the added starter to intrigue the curious.

Incidentally, Miss Ederle is only in the water for about 20 feet of film, although always in a bathing suit.

Enough gags to hold it up in the big program houses with a cheap production nut and good photography. *Sid.*

THE STREET

Karl Grune's German-made picture, featuring Eugene Klapfer and Egede Nissen; at the Fifth Avenue Playhouse, Sept. 4, week; running time, 67 mins.

This long-waited overseas opus makes its American premiere at Mike Mindlin's atmospheric and esoteric Fifth Avenue playhouse, where the special titles usually kid the special features. In this instance even Mike takes this effusion seriously and unreels several hoch-hut blurbs to the effect that this is a symbolical conception and that it is hot material.

This scrivener could discern nothing symbolical, nor did he sizzle. Which puzzled this scrivener, for on this individual occasion he was quite sober—for a Sunday evening.

What he did catch was an American projection of a German melodrama of French life. It seemed to have all the dimensions and physical aspects of a fleshly plot-story, and only in a spot here and there, when in his discontent the principal figure saw shadows, cut-ins of busy street scenes and the like, was there other than a consecutive, concerted and co-ordinated running story.

And not bad, at that.

If those Germans wouldn't always pick their actors so homely and middle-aged, they might work up some foreign rights. In this instance Eugene Klapfer, seldom off the screen. He is in his late forties, a bit baldish, paunchy and dressed like a tank-town evangelist. He carries an umbrella—from the moment he leaves his house and through all the vicissitudes of the action, and back again to his tragic return, he never lets go that flopping, clumsy umbrella. Maybe that's the symbol. Symbol of what? There is no bad weather in the picture anywhere. Maybe it's there to show that into each life some rain must fall.

He is first as a bored husband with a wearied wife of his own age. She cooks his soup. He dreams of streets—life outside the humdrum monotony of his own. Suddenly he bursts forth, revolts, runs into the street. The wife puts the soup in the oven. He is on his way.

He acts like a semi-lunatic, walks like one, falls like one for the crudely obvious decoy of a pair of unsubtle crooks. They fleece him at cards, she lures him to the house—as she also does another and even sillier old boob—and when the second yokel is badgered, resists and is murdered, the first is left to be enmeshed in the toils. Through the unwitting blab of the decoy's baby, he gets out, returns home, staggering with liquor, grief, disillusionment and the weight of the umbrella.

His faithful, worried wife has fallen asleep. She wakes up, rubs her eyes—goes to the oven to get the soup—and he probably never runs away again. But, maybe he does. For he leaves the umbrella right near the door. However, it now stands on its head. Maybe that means it'll be all upside-down now, anyway if the umbrella is the symbol.

Maybe it isn't the symbol at all. Maybe it's the sex-appeal. The film hasn't any other. Surely not Eugene. And more surely not Egede Nissen, the vamping lead, who at her most irresistible looks like a lunchroom waitress, dresses like a chambermaid on a night off, and acts like a rep-troupe second-business character woman.

With Edna Purviance at her best in a Chaplin revival, "The Immigrant," following, and of about the same production vintage, one gets a contrast that eloquently demonstrates how broad is the Atlantic between German and American casting.

"The Street," with all its faults, could be remade, today in Hollywood, and could be sent back to show all the Germans, including Karl Grune, how to turn out a movie—symbolical—or at least bimbolical.

As a novelty, as "something different," this should please the filmworms who seek the unconventional. The Germaniacs who make the Fifth Avenue hideaway a habit, like it. Business was turnaway Sunday eve.

For American general consumption—just fair-to-midlin.' *Lait.*

LIFE OF RILEY

First National release, produced by William Beaudine. Featuring George Sidney and Charlie Murray. Produced by E. M. Ascher. Running time 70 minutes. At the Mark Strand, New York, week of Sept. 3.

Meyer, Police Chief	George Sidney
Riley, Fire Chief	Charlie Murray
Montague	Sam Hardy
Penelope Jones, Widow	Myrtle Stedman
Molly O'Rourke	June Marlowe
Steve Meyer	Stephen Carr
John King	Edward Davis
Aaron Brown	Bert Woodruff

A first rate low comedy idea is here worked out into a good laughing picture, serviceable for program purposes, but missing by a wide margin any better classification because it has been written down to the supposed level of the usual film fans.

If they have missed any of the familiar gags it was an oversight. They're all there, beginning with the "fly-paper-in-the-dark" and ending with the burlesque bit of the comic lovemaker who caresses a man, supposing him to be his sweetheart. It ought to be a clean up where the clientele never tires of westerns.

But it doesn't get into the class with such comedies as "McFadden" or "Callahans and Murphys." They had a background of human interest and reality for their vigorous humor. This is just a knockabout farce, of the "Mutt and Jeff" grade. Some of the comic devices are pretty rough, but always get laughs and that apparently was the frank design of the producer.

The picture has a story as the basis of its clowning, dealing with Meyer, chief of police, and Riley, store keeper and head of the village fire department. They are rivals for the hand of the Widow Jones, and in all things friendly enemies.

Riley has invented a fire extinguisher, but when it is to be demonstrated for development, an enemy fills the chamber with benzine instead of the right chemical and as a result Riley's store burns down.

Riley and Meyer go into the building to rescue the widow. In the smoke Riley actually rescues Meyer for the hilarious climax. Then the extinguisher gets a fair test and Riley makes a mint, wedding the widow.

In the telling the producer has adopted the burlesque wheel system of getting laughs. Some of the scenes are carried out in the spirit of burlesque "bits." All pretense of legitimate comedy is abandoned and anything goes for laughs. The gagging is strong arm stuff at times, but all done in a frank, naive way, so that the picture really comes along as a two-reel custard pie comedy stretched out to six reels. *Rush.*

Clancy's Kosher Wedding

FBO production and release. Comedy of feature length, starring George Sidney. Directed by A. E. Gilstrom. Story by Al Boasberg, adapted by J. G. Hawks. Running time, 60 minutes. At the New York Hippodrome, week Sept. 4.

Nobody ever alleged that "Abie's Irish Rose" was subtle, but neither the daddy of all the Irish-Hebe stories nor any of the masterpieces that it inspired ever went as far as this smear in simian fun.

Picture starts out with a sort of tacit understanding that a fat man slipping on a banana peel is refined wit, and from that basis goes on into what it conceives to be vigorous low comedy.

The fun consists of neck falls for the most part, varied by swift kicks delivered upon intimate surfaces of fat character women's persons and then more neck falls.

When that style of merriment palls—and how it palls—the title-writer is called in to supply uproarious gems of humor, to wit: "The sun can't shine in Ireland when it's raining in Jerusalem"; or "He'll (juvenile in fireman's uniform) put an end to Delancey street fire sales." Another bon mot is "There are three races here, Irish, Jewish and innocent by-standers." It's a parade of all the stale Mike-andable gags in "Judge's" files.

Nobody ever worked harder or at more expense of good taste to be funny. Scenario men, actors and directors just shut their teeth and gagged regardless, picking a bit here and an idea there until the appointed five reels were accomplished.

A politician's picnic is introduced as in "The Callahans and the Murphys," only more so. The fight is precipitated by a comic Jewish character who sings for the crowd "Ireland Must Be Heaven," the general melee beginning promptly on the line of the lyrics "Ireland must be heaven for my mother came from there." That ought to start something with both sides of the Mike-andable entente.

If the comedy is bad, the sentiment is worse. Of course, the daughter of the Jewish Capulets and the son of the Irish Montagues are in love with each other, the girl being forbidden to meet her sweetheart, first because he is an "Irisher" and second because her parents apparently favor the suit of a Jewish prize fighter. The literary ethics of this episode are delightful.

The prize fighter robs the Cohens deliberately and then presents them with their own money on condition that they persuade the girl to go to the picnic with him. They agree to this pretty arrangement. That should please the Jewish fans.

Much of the comedy arises from the fact that Cohen and Clancy run adjoining stores on Delancey street, both second-hand clothing stores. Clancy in the second-hand clothing trade on Delancey is a quaint conceit. They are apparently always at war, but in reality sympathetic friends.

For the finish young Clancy and the prizefighter are matched for a ring battle for a purse as a means of settling their feud over the girl. Cohen backs the pug, betting his store against Clancy's shop. The battle is shown in detail. As a graphic prize fight the spectacle is a bust.

Young Clancy wins, of course, although the girl tried to double-cross him and the picture turns to maudlin sentiment, with Cohen broke and forced to start all over again, until Clancy turns up, inviting him to enter a partnership.

When the picture aims to be funny it is terrible, and when it gets sentimental it is nauseating.

And this reporter is neither Jew nor Irish. *Rush.*

THE GUARDSMAN

Film Arts Guild (Symon Gould, director) presents Viennese film production of Franz Molnar's "The Guardsman," produced by Pan Films, A. G., of Vienna; directed by Robert Wiene. Edited and titled by Dimitri Stephon and Symon Gould. American premiere at 55th St. Cinema, week Sept. 3. Running time 55 minutes.

Wife..........................Maria Corda
Husband ....Fritz Abel
Critic ....Biela Friedell
"Mamma" ....Alma Hasta

As with so many of these art-y importations, their premier exhibition governs future distribution, which accounts for no releasing source being credited. Films of this nature solicit a suitable exhibition auditorium for proper audience reaction before closing the business details.

Symon Gould, who is the leading spirit in the Film Arts Guild, which has the program presentations in charge at the 55th St. Cinema, seemingly imported the picture on his own, editing, adapting and titling it for the American market in collaboration with Dimitri Stephon.

The 55th St. Cinema has elected to herald the picture as a filmization of "the Guild success," referring to the Theatre Guild, although as a screen offering it does not compare with the Guild's stage production.

Nor are Maria Corda and Fritz Abel (also billed as Alfred Abel) as the leading players comparable to Miss Lynn Fontaine and Alfred Lunt, the Guild play personators of the same roles.

Something basically artificial about most foreign characterizations that disqualifies them for American acceptance, excepting only when the character studies are necessarily grotesque. Then they ring true and impress unusually.

In this Austrian filmization of the eminent Hungarian's play—and Molnar is certainly more native to Vienna than America—the local talent does not compare with the Guild players' treatment.

Maria Corda as the capricious actress-wife is at times very biography-y in her cinema histrionics, and Fritz (or Alfred) Abel, as the doubting husband, leers and "emotes" needlessly, although for the main impressive and working hard. Alma Hasta as "Mamma" (Nannette, the housemaid) and Biela Friedell, as the critic, fared well in the only two other important parts.

"The Guardsman" has the advantage of the Guild rep, the Molnar "name" and the present vogue for foreign film productions, but does not hold up even alongside of some of the lesser UFA's.   *Abel.*

THE WINNING OAR

Excellent (brand) picture, presented by Samuel Zierler. Starring George Walsh, with leading lady unbilled. Directed by Bernard McEveety; photographed by Marcele Pigard. At the Rivoli, New York, two days (Sept. 1-2). Running time, 65 minutes.

Already marked for states rights. Starting weakly as a college story, this mess jumps several years and and turns into a mystery melodrama with several whopping necking scenes thrown in.

George Walsh, a young college student, has secured his gal's promise that she'll marry him if he wins the boat race. He wins, but she marries instead a gent who looks like Ben Turpin, because this guy'll foreclose some notes on her old man if she doesn't.

Hubby is a booze sponge and a lady massager. Poor wife is heartbroken. Walsh has gone into the law business and is already district attorney.

The girl's husband gets shot and everybody thinks she did it. The trial is held, with Walsh forsaking his D. A. job to defend the girl, and the jury deliberates for 40 hours because one little fellow won't admit the dame is guilty. Finally the little runt breaks down and admits he killed the wicked husband.

So the jury turns in a not guilty verdict and Walsh and the flame are free to marry.

About those necking scenes. They're raw enough to make a plumber's helper sit on a hot stove. Party scenes brought in to show how foul the poor girl's husband is. Hey! Hey!

Direction, photography, story and cast are n. g. Newsreel clips furnish most of the collegiate boat race.

God's Great Wilderness

David Hartford production, released by American Cinema Ass'n. From original story by Spottswood Aiken. Scenario by Frances Nordstrom. Cameraman, Walter Griffin. In cast: Russell Simpson, Lillian Rich, John Steppling, Mary Carr, Joseph Bennett, Edward Coxen and Wilbur Higby. Running time, 56 mins. At Arena, New York, one day, Sept. 5.

Spottswood Aiken, veteran character actor of the screen, turns his hand to story weaving. In "God's Great Wilderness," as far as known his maiden scenario effort, he gives Director David Hartford a yarn that has all the sentimental voltage and Adam's apple agitation of one of the late Gene Stratton-Porter's epics of life among the backwoods fundamentalists.

The thing is simple. It deals with the meanness of a man who ran the general and only store in his native village. He overworked his wife, beat his son, cheated his customers, and was just naturally disagreeable. He sows mean deeds and reaps a harvest of bitterness. His wife dies, his store is burned, his son runs away, and he is left high, dry, poor and lonely.

In contrast, returning good for evil, the family of the rival grocer shower him with little kindnesses in his downfall, and the old codger takes to reading the Bible. His heart is softened and he is a new man—humble, reasonable and proud of his grandchild, who meantime appeared on the scene.

All this is part and parcel of the kind of literature the tall grass settlements read avidly, with tears streaming down their beards. The novels of Gene Stratton-Porter and Harold Bell Wright sell by the millions, and when adapted for the films have proved good box office. "God's Great Wilderness" is that sort of a story.

Direction good and production standards okay up to the point where it was deemed necessary to fake a mountain torrent which sweeps two horsemen off a bridge. This was a bad job to boot.

Cast is competent, with familiar names and faces. Lillian Rich gets top billing, but Russell Simpson as the crabby old skinflint does the big work. Simpson has had a vogue of late as a domestic tyrant and Adam Sowerguy. He gives a convincing, forceful interpretation.

LADIES, BEWARE

F. B. O. production and release. Starring George O'Hara. Directed by Charles Giblyn. From story by J. G. Hawks. Cameraman, Jules Cronjager. In cast: Alan Brooks, Kathleen Myers, Nola Luxford, Jimmy Aubrey, Mario Carrillo. At Stanley, New York, one day, Sept. 1. Running time, 54 mins.

About par the average of the George O'Hara pictures for F.B.O. Should deliver reasonable satisfaction when booked in the right house on the right day or days (up to three, if plural, being safe gauge).

Showmen will not be particularly concerned that what might have been a darb of a crook comedy was turned out minus the big sock. Neither, probably, will the majority of fans examine into the matter very closely, so the "if" is only interesting as a passing commentary on the picture trade.

A slick jewel thief goes to a country estate and introduces himself as a detective, warning the wealthy family that one of their house guests due to arrive the next day is a smooth crook with designs on the wall safe.

The guest arrives and a fertile situation is created. But for no purpose. Where finesse and other refinements of script and direction were needed a fast production schedule and the venerable old slapstick successfully kept the picture in the "just another" class. Natural, not gag, comedy possibilities were ignored without effort, or probable thought of development.

Alan Brooks played the guest and conveyed an interesting personality that, more than anything else, suggested the lost opportunities of the plot germ. Brooks is of the legit, having done a little work in previous F.B.O. pictures. He's no Adonis, but an actor who knows his tricks and is able to get into the lens the force he sends across the footlights. He dwarfed the rest of the mob.

Kathleen Myers, fetching blonde, can pout and get away with it. Jimmy Aubrey, another of the custard pie comics to go into training for the features, displayed commendable restraint.

Production standard as regards lighting, sets and photography is first class.

Splitting the Breeze

F. B. O. production and release, starring Tom Tyler. From story by Frank Clark, directed by Robert De Lacey. Running time, 50 minutes. On double feature bill at Arena, New York, one day, Sept. 5.

Plenty of riding and gun-play in a fast-moving western that will appease the customers of the one, two and three-day grinds.

It's the familiar situation of the hero wrongfully accused of everything in the statutes. Uncovering of the real culprit, breaking up of his gang and ultimate denouement when the girl, somewhat ashamed that she should have doubted our boy, Thomas, falls into his arms, is visible without the aid of binoculars before the picture has gotten around its first curve.

F. B. O. has teamed a kid with Tom Tyler. The kid, about 12, rides like a whirlwind and is the only one maintaining faith in the hero when things look darkest. Incidentally, the idea of putting a kid into the midst of a fiesta of western rough house is ingeniously calculated to mean plenty of juvenile trade at the box office.

And "Splitting the Breeze" is a box office picture for houses using this type of cowboy drama.

The Lost Limited

Rayart production, directed by J. P. McGowan from story by Walter Griffin. In cast: Reed Howe, Ruth Dwyer, Dot Farley, George French, Henry Barrows, Billy Franey. Running time, 50 mins. At Stanley, New York, one day, Sept. 3.

This railroad story will be usable for the one-dayers, but it may be just as well to date it for double feature night. It's pretty weak in every respect. Story is sieve-like in its careless disregard of intelligible continuity. Direction is spotty, with only the photography getting by as first rate.

The climax is centered on a collision of two trains. For this some library stuff, evidently of a stunt pulled some years ago at the South Dakota state fair or at the old Brighton Beach race track was used. A flukey imitation would have been better.

Whole picture is eloquent of a short bankroll. The heroine, Ruth Dwyer, appears throughout in overalls, making the picture a minus so far as the women fans are concerned.

It does not rate extended notice. But cheap merchanise for the house after approximately 5,000 feet of celluloid and not caring beyond that.

CAT AND CANARY

Universal production and release. Directed by Paul Leni (maiden American production) from stage melodramatic success by John Willard. Ran 75 minutes as the premiere film feature of the Colony, New York, under U's direction.

Annabelle West	Laura La Plante
Paul Jones	Creighton Hale
Charles Wilder	Forrest Stanley
Roger Crosby	Tully Marshall
Cecily	Gertrude Astor
Harry	Arthur Edmund Carewe
Susan	Flora Finch
"Mammy" Pleasan..t	Martha Mattox
The Doctor	Lucien Littlefield
Hendricks	George Siegmann
Milkman	Joe Murphy
Taxi Driver	Billie Engle

"The Cat and the Canary," by John Willard, was one of the early mystery meller successes on Broadway. It is of the same pattern so prolifically copied by the other mystery thrillers.

What distinguishes Universal's film version of the C-C play is Paul Leni's intelligent handling of a weird theme, introducing some of his novel settings and ideas with which he became identified. It is the German director's first American production.

The play is one of those haunted house and eccentric recluse's will combinations. Mysterious panels and difficult codicils of the will complicate matters, including the necessary murder, theft of jewels, suspecting of everybody, including Carl Laemmle, of committing the murder, and the inevitable audience-guessing as to "who did it?" Leni cleverly shifts the character's moods and shades with plausible pliability, so that by the time the denouement is eagerly awaited everybody on the screen, including the heroine and the cameraman, are possibly "it."

The story and the Leni direction could carry almost any cast, although the combination of players above seem unusually well suited to the proceedings. Mayhaps Flora Finch put it on a bit too thick and Arthur Edmund Carewe overplayed somewhat, but they were satisfying. Laura La Plante looked pretty and acted calmly for the main. The honors went to Creighton Hale and Tully Marshall, and Martha Mattox in an uncertain characterization was successful in making her aloof personality complicate matters, as was Leni's purpose.

The film runs a bit overlong and is susceptible of amputation. Otherwise it's a more than an average satisfying week-stand feature for the Colony or any of the first-run houses. Great for the neighborhoods.

Abel.

SHANGHAIED

F. B. O. production directed by Ralph Ince. Starring Ince with Patsy Ruth Miller featured. From story by Edward J. Montague. Cast, Gertrude Astor, Alan Brooks and Tom Santschi. At Hippodrome, New York, Sept. 12. Running time about 60 minutes.

Title bespeaks action and lurid melodrama. With featured players beyond what is considered the prime of life for picture people the only chance is either in powerful, dramatic characterizations or with a speedily moving yarn providing for fist fights, struggles and what is known as "action."

Aside from the title there is no trace of any of these elements. Neither of the leading players are known as strong character actors and from their work in this picture it is highly improbable they will derive any further rating as such. With action wearisome, untouched by hokum and libraried all the way through the production misses.

Miss Miller is introduced as the "spawn of the waterfront." The location is Frisco and spawn from a waterfront such as that is a tough handicap for the girl to overcome. In addition she's a cafe dancer, manhandled as she makes her way through the crowded tables.

Skipper Haley is rolled for the works by the proprietor of the cafe and in revenge he shanghaies the girl. Here the customers have to swallow a hard one. Once on board ship the girl suddenly turns evangelistic and threatens to swat everyone who tries to get fresh. She even acquires a liking for the sea and does the hornpipe on board a greasy deck attired in kitchen overalls.

So the days roll by slowly and the minutes seem like hours for the mob out front. For the fiftieth time Skipper Haley's grim jaws tighten as he registers determination. Striding up to the gal, he grasps her puny arm in his big mitt and hollers at her, "The sea's too good for you. Get back to the gutter where you belong." And he sends her.

A year later in a chink joint the gal is again picking pennies off the floor, poor but virtuous, saving it all to repay the skipper for the money he had been robbed of. Haley finds her there and what could have been explained in the first reel, without spending all that money on making the picture, was finally ironed out.

Santschi is in it, too. Once he says, "That'll take us four days out of our course, cap'n."

COLLEGE

Joseph M. Schenck production; United Artists release. Buster Keaton starred. Directed by James W. Horne. Story by Carl Harbaugh and Bryan Foy. Running time, 65 minutes. At Mark Strand, New York, week Sept. 10.

The Girl	Ann Cornwall
Her Friend	Flora Bramley
A Rival	Harold Goodwin
His Friends	Buddy Mason, Grant Withers
The Dean	Snitz Edwards
Crew Coach	Carl Harbaugh
Baseball Coach	Sam Crawford
A Mother	Florence Turner
A Son	Buster Keaton

Strong-arm comedy here is only partly effective. Buster Keaton's odd twists of indirect humor never get a chance to function, so determined have the scenario writer and director been to get on a series of gags that would be fool-proof. Instead of leaving the laughs to come from this genuinely funny comedian's pantomime, they seek to make assurance doubly sure by turning out a slapstick picture on the theory that the mob always falls for stencil humor.

A sample is in the boat race scene, where Keaton, the dumbbell coxswain, has lost his rudder. He rescues the tiller and straps it around his waist, then seats himself a-straddle the stern of the shell and steers his crew to victory by executing shimmy movements that direct the boat's course. The tone of the picture is like that, and it is more often dull than funny.

When Keaton gets a chance for his own characteristic oddments of humor he is a joy. This comic gets capital effects from a character background and a situation in which there is some element of pathos. In some of the passages of the new film these things are provided.

The underlying situation is that he is an earnest young boob making his way through college and intent upon doing well in his studies. But his sweetheart wants him to shine on the athletic field. Here his knack of unconscious burlesque has something to work upon and they have not loaded him down with cheap gags. His performances in field games are very funny. But the synthetic gags are not.

The picture will do business because the Keaton name assures that, but many pictures of this grade will find him marking time rather than advancing. Not so many distinctive screen humorists of the first grade that we can afford to have Keaton go into the slapstick, jazz gag business. There are plenty of comics to supply the banana-peel customers, while the Chaplin - Lloyd - Keaton - Langdon group is limited.

They'll laugh at "College," but it will go down as just another program comedy resting for its pull on the excellent things Keaton has done before, rather than building on its own merits.

Technical production well handled. They have brought in a crowd of real young college athletes to fill in the background. The boat race is a splendid bit of staging outside of its travesty features, and the shots at field games are interesting on their own. College atmosphere is neatly suggested and pictorially the film is expertly made. As much cannot be said for the titling, hoked up to the last degree.

Rush.

SOFT CUSHIONS

Paramount production and release. Directed by Eddie Cline. From story by George Randolph Chester. Starring Douglas Maclean. At the Paramount, New York, week Sept. 10. Running time, over 60 minutes.

Young Thief	Douglas Maclean
Girl	Sue Carol
Slave Dealer	Richard Carle
Fat Thief	Russell Powell
Lean Thief	Frank Leigh
Police Judge	Wade Boteler
The Notary	Nigel de Brulier
The Wazir	Albert Prisco
Chief Conspirator	Boris Karloff
The Sultan	Albert Gran
The Police	Fred Kelsey

Just a fair Paramount program picture, with Douglas Maclean and the title perhaps to be counted on for a draw.

In some far-off Eurasian land there lived a handsome, lovable, nimble-witted rogue whose nom de promenade was Aslan the Fox. Aslan was many, many centuries ahead of his times. Had he lived to see modern vaudeville he would never have been obliged to eke out a precarious existence by divorcing the simple sucker from his jack. For Aslan was the Houdini of his day. No bonds could hold him and no walls were thick enough to harbor his presence for more than a limited length of time.

One day there arrived in town a prehistoric yokel, attired in broadcloth and velveteen, with knee-length britches. He stooped to pluck an errant straw from his sock and so gained the attention of Aslan and his two partners in crime.

As a hero Aslan could be understood. But the corpulent knave and the lean thief were just a couple of dishonest crooks. And more than once they attempted to do wrong by little Aslan only to be foiled and baffled. After the yokel was robbed Aslan was deeply intrigued by a pretty face gazing at him tantalizingly from a window in the house of a slave dealer.

The girl was Sue. A dismal name for a girl who looks like that. Virginity is written all over her round little map in milk-white letters. Aslan went in and decided to buy her. A thousand something or others was the price, so the fox left a deposite of 40 and promised to return later with the balance.

Sue dreamt of soft cushions. She claimed the stars had shown her she would be the Sultan's favorite some day. On that day Aslan promised to pull the beard of the Sultan. For saying so and committing the error of stealing a door-knocker Aslan was arrested and brought before the Kadi.

The latter knew nothing of golf, but became possessed of a strict sense of justice—the minute he saw Sue. He judged thusly: "I will confiscate the money because it was stolen and I will keep the girl because she was bought with stolen money."

Tremendous possibilities in this story, but neglected. Titling is an attempt at modern slang mixed with biblical phraseology and registers less than 30 percent for comedy. Interiors lavish and beautiful. Gagging seems mostly to flop.

Maclean does not seem to be comfortably cast. There is need for the Chaplin type of comedy here. Maclean is a little awkward in an atmosphere of flowing robes and turbans.

Sue Carol is a highly attractive leading lady. Scantily attired, she scores best in one of the final scenes where she black bottoms for the white-bearded Sultan.

Maclean's support, Russell Powell and Frank Leigh, as the two other thieves, is not sufficiently strong. These boys contribute very little of their share of laughs.

Cruise of the Hellion

Duke Worne production, presented by Rayart Pictures. Story and continuity by George W. Pyper. Cameraman, Walter Griffin. Running time, 61 mins. In projection room, New York, Sept. 12.

John Harlan	Charles K. French
Jack Harlan	Donald Keith
Diana Drake	Edna Murphy
Captain Drake	Sheldon Lewis

A touchdown for Rayart. As fine an independent as ordinarily encountered in a year's unreeling. That is should satisfy practically anywhere seems certain and, by the same token, that it should make money for producer, distributor and exhibitor seems in the bag.

It's a sea story with all the reliable stock in trade about hairy-chested brutes and black mutiny on a three-master.

Tom Santschi is the brute, a whole waterfront of big muscles and bad disposition all in himself. With a realism that makes for awe, he beats Donald Keith, not once but many times, until it would seem the younger and smaller actor was black and blue. This fight stuff is great. When the kid finally k. o.'s the big bruiser it creates a scene packed with gallery and kid appeal.

The captain of the ship is quite a tough hombre himself when nursing an alcoholic edge. The kid has to fight him as well as the bullying first mate. In the struggle for a pistol the first mate plugs the captain from ambush, and the kid thinks he did it.

Ship is carrying gold. The kid, the girl and Peg-Leg, the sympathetic old salt, throw it overboard. But their ruse is discovered and the kid is forced to don a diving suit and go over after the chest. The first mate frames for his henchman, who also goes down in a diving suit to bump off the kid, once the gold is found on the ocean's bed. Lots of good melodrama in this sequence.

Francis Ford, usually a director, returns temporarily to the grease-paint to give a well-pointed interpretation of the one-legged old jack tar. Edna Murphy is her usual vivacious blonde self.

One Woman to Another

Paramount production and release. Directed by Frank Tuttle. Based on the stage play by Frances Nordstrom. Screen adaptation by James L. Campbell. Titles by George Marion, Jr. Starring Florence Vidor. Paramount, New York, week Sept. 17. Running time, over 60 minutes.

Rita Farrell	Florence Vidor
John Bruce	Theodore von Eltz
Mrs. Gray	Marie Shotwell
Olive Gresham	Hedda Hopper
Rev. Robert Farrell	Roy Stewart
The Niece	Joyce Marie Coad
The Nephew	J. Boudwin

With the exception of a few scenes where the two juveniles score laughs with their childish pranks, the picture depends on Geo. Marion's titling, rather than on complex bedroom situations, for comedy. On this account mainly, but also owing to the matronly bearing of the star, the production on the whole is weak and unsuited for the full week major stands unless supported by an impressive stage show.

Neither the star nor the title can be counted upon as a strong draw. In addition, construction is poor. The obvious reason for the ineffectiveness of the picture is that the play has been thrown on the screen via sub-titles. Picture mostly consists of a series of shots of people talking cleverly in spots, but only talking. A switch in locale is not a physical change but merely another title.

Action is telegraphed ahead, elaborated on and described in sub-titles. In the case where John Bruce, the eligible bachelor, is spied by an envious ma and her unwed daughter, a regular discussion arises between the two women. It is carefully and laboriously explained, in the dialog, that the girl intends to make a play for John despite that he is engaged to Rita. So that, when she really does it, it is of little interest.

Miss Vidor is unconvincing as the sweetheart. Von Eltz, despite the mustache, looks younger than the girl and thereby handicaps the star considerably. The picture is intended for light comedy but the result is less than featherweight.

Somewhere Olive Gresham is described as a friend of Rita's. Her raison d'etre in the story is to address Rita at intervals thusly, "As one woman to another I tell you—," and so on. It is Olive who warns Rita to come home if she expects to retain Bruce.

Von Eltz registers nicely in the closeups but is not intended for this kind of stuff where there is but little opportunity for the rest of him. The boy is built both for speed and action, and there's neither in this picture.

Story is of a girl trying to swipe someone else's man and unable to do so, gets herself "compromised" in the hope that he will be conventional enough to marry her on that account. Not an original idea and given the usual treatment.

THE DROP KICK

First National picture, produced by Ray Rockett. Directed by Millard Webb. Adapted by Winifred Dunn from Katherine Brush's "Glitter," serially in "College Humor." No photographer or title writer billed. At the Strand, New York, week Sept. 17. Running time, about 65 minutes.

Jack Hamill	Richard Barthelmess
Cecily Graves	Barbara Kent
Eunice Hathaway	Dorothy Revier
Brad Hathaway	Eugene Strong
Molly Alberta	Alberta Vaughan
Bones	James Bradbury, Jr.
Ed Pemberton	Brooks Benedict
Mrs. Hamill	Hedda Hopper

This picture has several weaknesses but should be a moderate money-maker with the Barthelmess name.

For exploitation purposes it contains the 10 college boys selected in recent nation-wide film tests, and

its tie-up with "College Humor," which furnished the story and assisted in the collegiate film tests. Considering all this, it seems strange that the comic monthly gets no mention in the billing.

As customary, the picture bears little resemblance to the story. One instance is appropriated, a football game is tacked on, and the adapter has thus given birth to a practically new idea.

In it Richard Barthelmess is a heavy necker and football hero with magnificent talent at drop-kicking. His mother is mildly priming him for marriage to a sweet little daughter of an old friend, but Richard prefers skirts with a broad outlook on life.

At college the wife of the football coach is out to make the youngster. She puts her husband in debt by buying truckloads of clothes and forces him to steal from the athletic funds in order to meet bills. Driven frantic by the certainty of disgrace when his thefts have been discovered, the coach kills himself after writing a note to Barthelmess.

The new widow finds the note and alters it so Barthelmess thinks the coach killed himself to let Barthelmess marry his wife. And the kid, thinking himself honor-bound and being connected scandalously with the widow in false campus rumors, consents to marry her, although he hates her.

The young collegiate's mother hears about it and scents a frame-up. She calls on the widow and gives her a juicy amount of dough to lay off the youngster. Barthelmess doesn't know of this and goes through most of a football game in rotten condition because of his worries. He gets jerked out and razzed mercilessly by the crowd, then gets fighting mad and goes in to win the game in the last minute of play with a 40-yard drop kick. Afterwards he learns he is free from the widow and takes the sweet little girl in his arms for the finish.

The college and fraternity scenes are authentic enough, although collegiates all over the country are going to wonder what kind of students razz one of their own players when he's not playing good football. Shots of university social life are quite on the level, especially the views of various ways to neck.

Casting ranges from good to poor. Those 10 college film test winners won't be recognized by anyone but their mothers, as they rarely face the camera and can't be singled from other extras. Barthelmess remains young-looking enough for college and handles his part well. The sweet little girl, Barbara Kent, is a little too heavy for heroine work and doesn't draw the sympathy she should.

Dorothy Revier is the thankless widow and puts it over with surprising grim voluptuousness. At one time she gets Barthelmess on a bed with her. Eugene Strong, her husband and the unfortunate football coach, rings in with a batch of good acting. Albert Vaughan is used for a few necking shots.

Photography was off in spots, possibly due to a bad print. Most of it was of the better class. The football game is a weakness in production, failing to impress as much as most of its predecessors in college pictures. This may be attributed to the idea of having a drop kick winning the game instead of a long and hazardous run down the field.

Titles started weakly to be funny and then changed to serious and better stuff.

The Strand crowd Saturday afternoon were food for contemplation of the possibility that women will be kept away because of the title. It may be well to make a special play for feminine trade.

MAGIC FLAME

Samuel Goldwyn production, United Artists release. Ronald Colman and Vilma Banky starred. Henry King, director. Story adapted by June Mathis from stage play "King Harlequin," by Rudolph Lothar. Running time, 100 minutes. At the Rialto, New York, Sept. 18, on run. 99c top.

Clown	Ronald Colman
Prince	Ronald Colman
Aerial Artist	Vilma Banky
Ringmaster	Augustino Borgato
Chancellor	Gustave von Seyffertitz
Aide	Harvey Clarke
Wife	Shirley Palmer
Husband	Cosmo Kerle Bellew
Utility Man	George Davis
Manager	Andre Cheron
Visitor	Vadim Uraneff

Romantic novelty splendidly produced and capitally acted by these two highly satisfactory screen players, again in partnership in a graceful story that fits them trimly. All the elements that go to make a class boxoffice picture are here in combination—names, adequate production and interesting story. Colman and Banky together should be a draw on their own.

The novelty gets into the situation this way: The story has its basis in the familiar "Prisoner of Zenda" formula—the trick of a modern story of modern characters in romantic medieval settings—but in this case the whole business is projected on a background of a traveling circus.

By the turn of events the clown of the sawdust ring has to impersonate a corrupt king. The pattern has subtle irony, of course, but the thing is trickily worked out in terms of rather delicate comedy, so that the satire does not appear on the surface to mock the romance, which has free play.

If your ideas are tuned to syrupy romance you will find it here; and if you relish a suggestion of tartness in flavoring—both lemon and sugar in the tea, so to speak—you'll find that, too, in "The Magic Flame."

But you have to look for it, because at first glance it's all sugary and sweet, perfect for the flaps who just love the handsome Colman and the ravishing Vilma.

On the straight romantic side the picture takes great appeal from a particularly fine artistic production. There are shots that have the real feeling of the old world in their pictorial composition. There is a bit where a group of peasants are watching a circus parachute jumper in the skies that has something of the quality of the masterpiece, "The Angelus," in its handling. Picturesque bits of an European circus with its houses on wheels and finally there are fascinating bits of camera trickery showing the stately Miss Banky doing a trapeze act high up under the circus canvas.

The difficulties usual to filming a dual personality role are skilfully handled, principally by the director attempting little acting involving the two characters played by the same person. Here as in the whole picture there is evidence of smooth and intelligent direction.

The story does not give much suggestion of the excellent quality of the picture. The clown and girl aerial star in the circus are in love, when Baretti's Circus plays a Mediterranean town. A corrupt prince casts his eye upon the girl and schemes to possess her. He lures her to his room in the hotel, where he masquerades as a count. Hard pressed, she makes her escape by dropping from his window and gaining the ground through the branches of a tree.

The clown follows to her rescue, and in hand-to-hand combat kills the royal philanderer to whom he bears a remarkable resemblance. Terrified, the poor clown sees himself destroyed by his deed, but the way to escape opens before him when the hotel servants accept him as the count without question.

The sudden death of the king of the distant principality brings the

clown to the throne, although he is intent only upon escaping the situation that keeps him away from the circus and his sweetheart. The girl, believing her lover slain by the vicious prince, journeys to the castle to avenge her dead love. She becomes involved in royal intrigue and nearly accomplishes her mistaken mission when recognition brings a happy finale.

The picture has neat and rather charming bits of quiet comedy, some of its dramatic passages are thoroughly absorbing, and in spite of its 100 minutes in length the picture sustains interest, leaving a good impression. *Rush.*

THE CLOWN

Columbia production. Sold for States right release to Commonwealth. Directed by W. James Craft from story by Dorothy Howell. Featuring Johnny Walker and Dorothy Revier. With a cast including William Mong, John Miljan and Barbara Tennant. At Loew's New York one day, Sept. 15. Running time, about 60 minutes.

This picture was made under the supervision of Harry Cohn, of Columbia. One of the best for the market aimed at and considering what the production cost for a picture of this kind averages.

Though given hackneyed and time-worn story material, the film holds with its ancient melodrama. Very little time wasted in the opening. Without a subtitle the director conveys the impression that a murder is to be committed. Craft was also clever enough not to indicate who was to pass out. It was in the storm.

Dorothy Revier, handled nicely by the camera, makes a very suitable leading woman. Only a couple of faulty camera angles, which the undiscerning eye of the small town movie fan in most cases passes up, offer a slight but distinct contrast to Miss Revier's otherwise attractive appearance.

Until Johnny Walker gets into the picture this production differs from the average States right through closely knit detail, minus gaps and telling of the story through the characterizations and action rather than voluminous subtitles. And after Walker's entry the conversational titles are kept down as far as possible.

Opens with Mong, half owner of a circus, nuts about his handsome young wife and baby. Exits to pacify the lions and on return finds the careless villain necking with the traitorous spouse. Murderous anger gleams in Mong's eyes as he advances with a club. A storm rages and when a beam is unloosed the wife gets it in the neck and drops dead. Mong is accused of the murder by the heavy and is sent away for life.

John Miljan, the heavy, like other heavies in States righters, sports a mustache. But he doesn't annoy the customers by continuously flaunting or caressing it, as is the wont of most other thespians.

Time passes, the baby grows up and the circus plays the prison where the old man has been given free board. The latter escapes and after sundry misadventures visits vengeance on the heavy by having an unfriendly lion chew him up.

Walker spends his time carrying pails of water to the elephants and has a good scrap with one of the trainers for his bit. Mong does well with the role of the old clown—considering. At any rate, he doesn't lay it on too thick.

2 GIRLS WANTED

Fox production directed by Alfred E. Green. Based on the stage play by Gladys Ungar. Scenario by Seton I. Miller. Starring Janet Gaynor. In projection room Sept. 15. Running time, 82 minutes.

Marianna Miller	Janet Gaynor
Dexter Wright	Glenn Tryon

Jack Terry	Ben Bard
Sarah Miller	Marie Mosquini
Philip Hancock	Joseph Cawthorn
Miss Timoney	Doris Lloyd
Edna Delafield	Alyce Mills
William Moody	William Tooker
Mrs. Delafield	Pauline Neff
Johnny	William Blatcher
Michael	C. L. Sherwood

Janet Gaynor's first starring production is below standard of the average programme. If this is a reward for her fine work in "7th Heaven," Miss Gaynor should decide against further rewards. The stage play has been unceremoniously mauled in the screen adaptation. Due to be plugged on the strength of the star's work in "7th Heaven" plus the advertising value of the title, it can only detract from Miss Gaynor's recently acquired popularity.

Direction and, evidently, adaptation are jointly responsible for a story starting nowhere, bent toward no place in particular and arriving 82 minutes late. Laughs are few and weak and almost altogether doubtful with ace house audiences.

Waste of footage is too obvious to escape comment. Picture starts off with Marianna looking for a job. Shown walking along the street, told the job is taken, and photographed walking all the way home, where the sister awaits. Plenty of time is devoted to explanations that the girls are hungry.

Marianna is kept grinning idiotically throughout. They frame a meal with a bottle of milk, an egg and a doughnut. The lady who runs the house nearly catches them. They drop the egg outside and spill the milk in putting out a small fire. And not a gag in these lengthy scenes to relieve the monotony.

But for the crude direction and lack of comedy business the picture would have a chance on merit in addition to the sales possibilities in the star and the title of the well-known play.

Love scenes with Glenn Tryon are awkwardly done. The girl finally lands a job as secretary, through Wright's recommendation, with Wright's competitor. She ends up by unintentionally locking her employer in his safe.

Hancock wants to buy out Moody for 200 grand less than his property is worth, and the girl tries to block the deal by warning Wright. The latter has been opposed to the proposition all along, and finally Hancock's nephew quietly puts him out with a Mickey Finn. Then the conventional last-minute rescue and the finish.

Sarah, the other sister, is in the picture to be spoken to at rare intervals. At these times she listens intelligently, then stolidly continues her labors.

Titling lengthy and profuse, signifying weakness since the story is meant to be told via action.

BULLDOG PLUCK

Bob Custer production released by F. B. O. Directed by Jack Nelson from the story by W. B. Foster. Starring Bob Custer. Supervised by Jesse J. Goldburg. Cast includes Hugh Saxon, Bobby Nelson, Veora Havlin, Victor Melzetti and Richard Neill. At the Arena, New York, one day, Sept. 19.

Hard to discover just what phase of the proceedings the title was based on, but aside from that there is a little more interest than in the usual western story and enough action to take care of the red-blooded fans.

The male lead is not a fugitive from justice, nor a detective in disguise, but the leading citizen of the community, the owner of the gambling saloon and the only hotel, and a model of young manhood as exemplified by the west.

Rumpus starts when Custer does a Jimmie Walker and decides that both saloons should close at midnight, owing to sundry shootings and robberies. As a blue law enforcer Custer still holds water because he does a lot of hard riding, shooting and scrapping on the side. In addition he shows an inborn love for children through his action in buying the girl's little brother a cowboy suit.

No trace of the ordinary romance. On meeting the gal the first time he orders her off a lot to save the party from a flood following a rainstorm. The next time he tells the gal not to buy stolen horses from the heavy. the third time he lets her win money at his bank. And the pair get to loathe each other with every passing scene until near the finish when the girl discovers that the man she thought friendly was the outlaw of the district, while Custer was the wealthiest and most influential citizen.

Action moves along evenly at a good pace.

LOVE OF PAQUITA

Hi-Mark Productions film, starring Marilyn Mills. Cast includes Floyd Ames, Walter Emerson, Wilbur Mack, Robert Fleming and Adar Bruno. At the Columbus, New York, as part of double features Sept. 10. Running time, 60 mins.

According to the lobby display, two horses share honors with the star. Miss Mills may not be a beauty winner, but she is one of the most attractive riders of all screen women who can do their stuff astride a horse's back.

"The Love of Paquita" is melodramatic throughout, with a near-hanging one of its climaxes. The work of all principals seems secondary to that of two horses. Both animals are fine screen workers.

The entire locale is Spanish, the picture carrying out its atmosphere effectively all the way. Story drags in spots and some scenes are given too much camera range.

But the horses will keep this picture alive in the neighborhoods.

Picture hardly has the weight to run alone, but appears suited for double feature days. *Mark.*

STRANDED

Joe Rock production; Sterling release. Story by Anita Loos, directed by Phil Rosen. Cameraman Herbert Kirkpatrick. William Collier, Jr., and Shirley Mason costarred. Others: John Miljan, Dale Henry, Florence Turner and Shannon Day. Running time one hour. On double feature bill at Loew's New York, one day, Sept. 16.

Anita Loos devoted to her typewriter in the manufacture of "Stranded" a minimum of attention and effort. Her purpose seems to have been to provide in the simplest terms a skeleton plot upon which to hang a sermon from the Will Hays office on the dangers of trying to get into the movies on a small bankroll.

The heroine comes to Hollywood from the inevitable Iowa. She is long on self-esteem; short on brains and dough. In this picture she finds out that it's pretty tough sledding when a nice little girl wants to remain a nice little girl and live in Hollywood.

Lurking in the background is the menacing figure of a boulevardier specializing in virgins. Only when she has been ejected from her rooming house, only when her mother back in Iowa needs $500 for an operation, does our Nell decide to sell out. The timely arrival from Fernwood, Iowa, of the boyhood sweetheart saves Nell at the very brink of a De Mille boudoir set.

Seems likely that dates will be available for this picture because of its propaganda usefulness. It is also a fairly interesting picture through its studio stuff. Some of the direction is terribly careless and the plot is asthmatic.

But the production itself has enough merit to stand up for short bookings.

PAINTED PONIES

Universal production and release. Directed by Reaves Eason from the story by John Hamlin. Starring Hoot Gibson. At Loew's Circle, New York, one day, Sept. 19.

Whoever John Hamlin may be, he makes no startling contribution to western literature in this tale of the west which bears a striking similarity to all other western stories.

Hoot Gibson is the champ from the Northwest who seems likely to win all the prizes in the Toptown rodeo, and the local Toptown champ is determined that this shall not be so, even if he has to shoot someone.

The gal, Ethlyne Clair, appears in a few scenes to encourage Hoot in the rodeo, which is well staged and has lots of plain and fancy riding on both horses and steers. The rodeo scenes carry the bulk of picture.

Hoot Gibson is okay, production well made, as far as type westerns go, and the picture may be counted on for the usual returns in the spots where they like 'em that way.

RIDING FOR LIFE

W. Ray Johnson presents by arrangement with M. R. Schlank. Distributed by Anchor Films. Starring Bob Reeves, supported by Bob Fleming, Hal Waters and Alyne Goodwyn. Story by Joe Kane; photography by Ray Cline. At the Arena one day (Sept. 9) as half of double bill. Running time, about 50 mins.

Bob Reeves, a moon-faced cowboy, rides fast and fights hard in an average sample of western moronia. It will be liked in its one-day hangout.

Reeves is a young rancher accused of robbing $30,000 from the express office with his kid brother. A northern outlaw really did it, but this can't be proven at first because the outlaw knows about a shady spot in the kid brother's past and threatens to snitch if exposed. By dint of hard fighting and fast riding the brothers capture the outlaw and are proven innocent.

The s. a. is handled by Alyne Woodward, who looks fair as a rancher's daughter and snuggles comfortably in Reeves' arms. Her difficulty in love is brought out by having the $30,000 in the express office deposited there by her old man, which makes it bad for Reeves when thought guilty.

Photography and title lettering good. Other technical departments fair.

Tunney-Dempsey Fight

Ten-round heavyweight championship of the world battle between Gene Tunney, title holder, and Jack Dempsey, former world's champion, at Soldier's Field (Stadium), Chicago, night Sept. 22, Gene Tunney given decision at end of 10th round. Pictures taken from elevated stand inside enclosure by Goodart Pictures Corporation, claiming exclusive picture rights to event. Running time of fight film, 30 minutes. Running time of fight film with trailer, showing training quarters of both fighters, about 42 minutes. At Castle theatre in Loop, Chicago, on run to grind to 75c top. First showing at noon Sept. 23.

Five of the ten rounds of the Tunney-Dempsey battle Sept. 22 in Chicago, as seen in the ring and on the screen, are worth mention only. The other five are immaterial and do not count to any real effect in the general result other than to create disputes as to which of the remaining rounds either of the fighters was entitled to.

Goodart Corp., the picture taker, has some excellently moving pictures of the battle. It was a clear, fairly warm evening. Two sets of films were taken, one the usual action pictures and the other the slow motion.

The pictures, added to the ringside impressions, reveal that Dempsey did not hold his fighting head at the crucial moment for him; that Tunney does not seem to possess a knockout punch, at least for Jack Dempsey, and that to settle the title of championship of the world for any class in a 10-round bout is the heighth of absurdity, though perhaps not financially.

Slow motion of the spectacular 7th round brings out Dempsey's temporary loss of his quick thinkery. Around the ringside Dempsey's fast one-two had been seen and it was thought that those two or three blows sent Tunney to the mat. Additionally Dempsey sent in a few more short jabs to Tunney's map while he was topping over.

As Tunney slid to the floor, about 12 feet to the right from Dempsey's corner, Dempsey walked direct to the ropes and about 10 feet to the left of his own corner. The referee, acting under an Illinois State boxing rule, did not count while he walked over to Dempsey, telling him to go to a neutral corner or the other side of the ring. The pictures will disclose that Dempsey still appeared confused, turning and walking the short distance to his own corner, whereupon the referee again instructed him to go to the other side, when Dempsey walked over there as the referee started to count.

Meanwhile Tunney, on the mat and in a squatting position, may be seen watching. As the referee started the count, Tunney intently kept his eyes upon him, looking all of the while as though he could have arisen at any moment. At nine on the film this count fades out and Tunney actually rising to his feet is not seen. Other small portions of the pictures seemed to be edited, for no reason or importance.

As Dempsey came toward him, Tunney, upon his feet, commenced to back away, doing a fast one step backward and circling the ring, with Dempsey following. At one instant Dempsey motioned with his hands for Tunney to come in. An observer will believe at this point of the bout and picture that Dempsey was uncertain of his legs, or of Tunney's left hand. William A. Brady said to another fighting expert before the bout and in New York:

"Tunney has the best left hand of any fighter who ever lived." His companion did not disagree on that statement.

In either event Dempsey could not maneuver Tunney into a corner or against the ropes, they mingling, however, a couple of times during Tunney's backward glide. Each time Tunney fully protected himself, making an equal exchange of blows with his challenger.

In the 4th round Tunney had his opportunity to annihilate Dempsey.

It was in this round as well as the 9th and 10th that Tunney evidenced a weakness in his punch. In the 4th Tunney landed a terrific right to Dempsey's jaw as he had the latter in the northeast corner of the ring. Dempsey faltered. Tunney, with his man against the ropes, piled plenty of blows upon his chin and head but Dempsey weathered it, and nicely stood up during the next round.

Tunney's claim of Dempsey often using the barred rabbit punch, plainly seen by the onlookers, is even more thoroughly noticeable upon the screen.

In the 8th round slow motion is again employed as Tunney scored his knockdown on Dempsey. At the ringside this knockdown seemed to be a clip on the chin as Dempsey slipped, but the slow motion brings out that Tunney caught Dempsey on the jaw and Dempsey went down to come up again before the referee had passed two, Tunney meantime walking away.

Up until the 9th round the fight could have been called a draw, figuring that Dempsey's knockdown so cleanly counted for a lot in his favor. But Tunney, in the 9th and 10th, particularly in the 10th round, punished Dempsey severely in blows if not physically. A cut in the eye that started bleeding would lead one to believe Dempsey was injured more than he had been. The 9th and 10th rounds with each having registered a knockdown placed Tunney far away on points with the decision going to him without audible protest in the arena.

That the opinion of fight experts that only a knockout should decide a championship bout, and especially for the world's heavyweight crown, is most plausible. If Dempsey's legs did not go back on him, and he had not stated or admitted that they did, Dempsey might have repeated his 7th round performance at any moment he could again crack Tunney in the same manner. That Dempsey appeared to have expended his reserve energy in that 7th round spurt or that he was outpointed later might not have counted against his repetition. While Tunney, in three rounds with the opportunities and in the 4th when he was fresh, failing to knock out Dempsey either showed the champion was fighting with extraordinary caution or that a knockout following the 10th round by him was unlikely.

In the majority those around the ring at the conclusion of the bout thought that if the battle had continued Tunney would have won by a knockout, claiming Dempsey was all in. But Dempsey had been in an all-in condition much more in the 4th round.

The win by Tunney and the pictures will dissipate all talk of a frame of course. But had Dempsey won, that the fight had been in the bag would have been all too prevalent. The pre-publicity on the fight had been foolishly directed, all seemingly with the objective of creating a suspicion of fixing, and this held down the betting until, with the odds in Chicago going to evens on the eve of the battle, sent there through sentiment and Dempsey's admirers, merely brought forth further distrust.

No marked demonstration for either fighter as they entered the ring, Tunney five minutes behind Dempsey. That lack was another reproach for the attending publicity. Nor was there fervent bubbling during the ten rounds excepting at those few points when the audience was brought to its feet. Enthusiasm was about 50-50 around the ringside for the battlers.

The 30-minute fight reel is preceded by a trailer of the fighters in their training quarters, running about 12 minutes. Regular picture houses of Chicago side-stepped the picture rights, through the Dempsey-Sharkey fight film having had no extreme drawing power in the city. A picture exhibitor in the Loop having three store shows, each seating about 350 people, got the exclusive for the Tunney-Dempsey film, starting it on a grind in each place at 75c. (usual admission 25c.), and did business from the outset on Friday (23rd.).

That seventh round may have been the drawing card. An audience when the picture was seen inclined just a bit toward Dempsey, again probably swayed by sentiment or newspaper reports.

If the Tunney-Dempsey fight film is circulated beyond the confines of Illinois, it may be played with a surety as regards the box office, now or in the future. As a fight picture it is a good one by itself, and that seventh round argument will probably remain open for decades. *Sime.*

SUNRISE

Fox picture directed by F. W. Murnau. Scenario by Carl Mayer. Has Movietone symphonic accompaniment, sight-and-sound device controlled by Fox. Katherine Hilliker and H. H. Caldwell did editing and titling; cameramen, Charles Rosher and Karl Strauss. Running time, 90 mins. At the Times Square, New York, Sept. 23, on a twice-daily run at $2.

The Man	George O'Brien
The Wife	Janet Gaynor
The Maid	Bodil Rosing
The Woman from the City	Margaret Livingston
The Photographer	J. Farrell Macdonald
The Barber	Ralph Sipperly
The Manicure Girl	Jane Winton
The Obtrusive Gentleman	Arthur Housman
The Obliging Gentleman	Eddie Boland

"Sunrise" is a distinguished contribution to the screen, made in this country, but produced after the best manner of the German school. In its artistry, dramatic power and graphic suggestion it goes a long way toward realizing the promise of this foreign director in his former works, notably "Faust."

The screening of "Sunrise" was rather an epic undertaking. What Murnau has tried to do is to crystallize in dramatic symbolism those conflicts, adjustments, compromises and complexities of man-and-woman mating experiences that ultimately grow into an endearing union. The dramatic action of this humble hero and workaday heroine is spaced between one drawing and another, but in that scant interval there is packed an emotional lifetime.

Many elements enter into the success of this ambitious effort. Murnau reveals a remarkable resourcefulness of effects; the playing of George O'Brien and Janet Gaynor and their associates is generally convincing and the story unfolds in settings inexpressibly lovely and appropriate.

Nor should be neglected credit as a detail contributing vastly to a satisfying whole, the accompaniment of the Movietone. Here is a sound obbligato that contributes subtly to the effect of sight drama instead of detracting from the essential pantomime by its distracting blare. Here the incidental music blends smoothly, suggesting the mood of the scene, but without intruding into the conscientiousness. In many scenes (honking autos, when dreaming lovers block a street, is a case in point) sound effects are introduced. This has been managed with skill. One accepts the sound as part of a real situation. It never suggests its own mechanics, and herein is the whole difference.

Perhaps one reason is that the sounds have been handled judiciously. They do not attempt too much. One passage has to do with a young couple honeymooning in a sort of sublimated Luna Park. The sound effects here have full swing. On the other hand, one of the dramatic high lights was a terrific storm far out on a lake. There was almost no attempt to get sound effects here, probably because sound would have seemed foolish by its inadequacy.

The musical accompaniment was reproduced with flawless delicacy and under absolute control, merging into the entertainment and apparently disappearing as a separate element.

Murnau has a knack or a gift or a genius for broad effects. He can convey subtle meanings by trick photography or by treatment of backgrounds. As instance, for example:

The Man, involved in a scarlet affair with The Woman from the City, while his young wife is heart broken, wanders about his farm, revolving in his mind the City Woman's poisonous suggestion that he murder the wife. It is evening. As he strides about the neglected fields, the camera eye roves before him, taking in what must have met his own. Ghostly whisps of white mist swirl about in the desolate, miasmic march. Unkept growths show wraithlike from the ooze. The whole dark prospect is a reflection of the man's distemper of soul.

This gloomy passage over, the young couple, reunited, are in a sort of dream city, spending a dream honeymoon. Where should they wander but into something of a super-Coney Island. Here the background is a confused medley of merry-go-round, toboggan slide, chute-the-chutes woven into grinning clown-faces, laughing boys and girls, booming bass drums and blaring trombones—all helter-skelter in a potpourri of double and triple exposure. This is mere trick photography, but it register as part of a fine pattern of expression.

Always there is meaning in the background, such meaning as a painter skillfully weaves into his canvases. The young couple come into a big city, she in flight, he in tender and conscience-stricken pursuit. Instead of bluntly labeling it "City," Murnau selects one graphic detail or background to express the idea. The set is a section of an enormous girder of a bridge with a corner of a building and bustling traffic moving back and forth. A panorama of Times Square couldn't have fixed it more definitely.

The picture is full of this technique of crystallizing signficant trifles to suggest much. The Woman from the City is characterized in a twinkling by summoning an old peasant woman haughtily to brush off her dainty high-heeled pumps while she holds her skirts above her knees.

At the very outset of the picture the attention of the audience is transfixed with a capital bit of trick photography. A title says it's vacation time, and the screen melts into a Gargantuan railroad terminal in a glass dome, through the sides of which may be seen the rivers of holiday seekers moving from town to country, while a nightmare of trains weaves back and forth. Smack through this bedlam of motion an ocean liner cuts her way through a half-scene ocean; a white sailed yacht ploughs among the rushing railway trains and a union-suited bathing girls dives from a springboard into the pandemonium. Giddy, hilarious vacation is pictured on the spot.

All these things lay upon a story as simple as it is human. The Woman from the City snares the young farmer. Under her hypnotism he listens to a plan to drown the young wife; sell the farm and go off to the city. Still under the spell, he takes the girl out upon the lake, but at the act he revolts and pulls desperately back to the shore. The frightened wife takes to flight, leaping upon a trolley car, regardless of where it is going. Horrified husband catches up, and while he pleads for forgiveness they roll into the city.

Wife is gradually quieted and they go upon a holiday, a sort of second honeymoon. All is well, with them when they start back to the farm, sailing the lake in the moonlight. A storm comes up and their boat is wrecked. The Man reaches shore safely and organizes a hunt for his missing wife. The Woman from the City supposes the wife had been murdered according to the plan she had suggested, and, meeting the Man, is about to be strangled when the timely rescue of the wife saves her.

A grim touch is given to the story. The City Woman had fixed it for the Man to float ashore after drowning his wife on a bundle of reeds, and it is this that saves the wife from drowning. *Rush.*

THE STUDENT PRINCE

M-G-M picture featuring Ramon Novarro and Norma Shearer. Adapted from the operetta of that name and directed by Ernst Lubitsch. John Mescall the photographer; Hans Kraly, continuity; titles, Marian Ainslee and Ruth Cummings. At the Astor, N. Y., for a twice daily run starting Sept. 21. Running time, 105 mins.

Prince Karl Heinrich	Ramon Novarro
Kathi	Norma Shearer
Dr. Juttner	Jean Hersholt
King Karl VII	Gustav Von Seyffertitz
Heir Apparent	Philip De Lacy
Lutz	Edgar Norton
Kellermann	Bobby Mack
Court Marshal	Edward Connelly
Old Ruder	Otis Harlan
Student	J. S. Peters

Lubitsch took his tongue out of his cheek when he directed this special. He had to, and in doing so he also took any kick right out of the picture, if any were there in the script for him. "The Student Prince" was and is a nice little love story, should figure as a fair enough program undertaking, but where they're going to pay $2 for it is a problem. Not at the Astor, where the picture will be doing very well if it's still in the house after the Christmas holidays. It will never be road showed and runs off as if it would be much more comfortable in the Embassy. The title of "The Trail of '98" alone makes it seem probable that the gold rush film will be in here, and soon.

It looks as though the director had been miscast. Not meaning that Lubitsch hasn't done well by Heidelberg. Quite to the contrary considering the paper material with which he had to work. It's not farce and it's not drama. Just a pretty love story of peaches and cream that may have put perfume in the director's cigars as he supervised. In toto, everything is okay except the story—and Novarro's makeup. The yarn isn't there for $2, that's all. It's doubtful if the boys and girls are going to get excited about it in the program houses. They'll like it, perhaps, but they won't rave for the simple reason there's nothing in the unwinding to stir 'em. And a picture has got to slip under the skin to get over and stay there cross country.

This may be an instance where a song synchronized attachment would have helped plenty. The male chorus put over the operetta and the massed singing could have been an aid to the film. But there are no voices, and the Heidelberg student body isn't overly impressive as screened. A program describes the school's old dueling customs, yet there's no such affair in a picture that cries for action.

"The Student Prince" theme is no doubt familiar. If not it concerns an heir to a throne who is forced to give up his love for a tavern maid because of duty to his country. And on the point of the Prince marrying the Princess his dead uncle had selected, the film ends.

Lubitsch has cameraed the love scenes between Prince Karl (Mr. Novarro) and Kathi (Miss Shearer) with restraint, and to that extent these bits will please the fastidious, although the tab readers may not think they're so hot. And neither has Lubitsch directed over anybody's head. It's all obvious and understandable. Fairly close to methodical.

The claim is that it took a year to make this feature, yet this doesn't show. Productionally there are some rich interiors counterbalanced by a sprinkling of back drops on exteriors. Mescall's camera work is average, with soft focus closeups of Miss Shearer not especially flattering. Still, she looks fair despite the dress of a generation ago, which puts the picture practically in the "costume" class.

But nothing can stand off Novarro's facial makeup. This is ghastly under certain lighting conditions and at no time allows him to completely spin the illusion of the character he is playing. Due to that makeup Novarro is always the actor here despite a performance that is creditable. Miss Shearer's personal efforts are a highlight and Jean Hersholt stands a good chance of outlasting both in the memory of fans on this release because of a sympathetic role plus a corking performance. Others in the cast are incidental.

Music from the show predominates in the score and a short prolog with a male chorus of 22 precedes the screening. There is no intermission.

"The Student Prince" isn't strong enough to stay at the Astor for any extended length of time on its merits. If it gets over with the program house public it will be due largely to the women, for men won't care for its emphasized sentimentality. And that appears to be its field, the major first runs, with the Shearer, Novarro and Lubitsch names to help.

As Loew's has a long lease on the Astor, M-G-M can force it if it cares to. But even under that consideration the picture doesn't impress as having the necessary vitality to make it a Broadway standout.

Sid.

WOMAN ON TRIAL

Paramount production and release. Directed by Mauritz Stiller. Pola Negri starred. Screen play made by Elsie Von Koczain from the drama, "Confession," by Ernest Vajda. Running time, 63 minutes. At the Paramount, New York, week Sept. 26.

Julie....................Pola Negri
Pierre Bouton....................Einar Hansen
Gaston Napier....................Arnold Kent
John Morland....................Andre Sartz
Paul....................Baby Brock
Henrietta....................Valentina Zimina
Brideaux....................Sidney Bracy
Morland's Lawyer....................Bertram Marburg
Julie's Lawyer....................Gayne Whitman

One is rather startled as "The Woman on Trial" progresses to find the flaming, sophisticated Pola Negri carrying on in the role of a persecuted mother, given to tender broodings over her child. How the fans will adjust themselves to this violent innovation is a question. The quality of the play in which this usually vivid actress is concerned here doesn't help a pretty difficult situation.

It is thoroughly theatrical and strangely alien in tone and locale. It is a super-sentimental affair, moving sluggishly and coming to life only for a few minutes toward the end, when the vitality is rather the flamboyant emotional acting of the star, than anything stirring in the play itself.

The picture takes a form made effective several times lately on the stage. Opening in a courtroom, where a woman is on trial for murder, the body of the story is a fade-out representing her testimony. What is gained by telling the story at second hand does not appear. As a direct recital it would be mild enough.

It all starts in a Paris art studio, where many bad plays and worse pictures have had their beginnings. Julie is madly in love with Pierre, who is in terrible health and can't sell his pictures. One knows instinctively beforehand that Pierre is going to be ordered to the country to rest, while Julie is going to sacrifice herself to meet the sanitarium budget.

A lot of other things can be forecast with similar correctness by any reader of fiction. Julie marries a millionaire, who treats her scandalous. Six or seven years later this is still the situation, while Pierre is getting weaker and weaker, although he doesn't communicate with Julie—doesn't even suspect it is she who buys his pictures. Julie by now has a son. Little Paul is five or six.

Word comes to Julie that Pierre is dying and would love to see her. She goes, and is followed by her jealous husband, husband and wife facing each other across the bed of the apparently expiring Pierre. A divorce follows—heaven knows why—and Julie gets the child. The scheming husband plots to rob her of little Paul, and to that end compels one of Julie's old artist friends who owes him large sums of money to compromise Julie, proving her a woman of evil character. It is upon these grounds that the father proposed to regain the child by court writ.

The scheme succeeds, except that when the child has been taken away, after a fairly spicy scene in the artist's studio, Julie shoots the traitor. That she didn't bump off the husband as her impulse would be was the ground for complaint for dramatic force and sporting justice. The artist-traitor was pretty small game after all.

At the end the jury brings in a verdict of innocent, the courtroom cheers and there is an artistic final shot, showing Julie and little Paul playing on a pretty beach, while Pierre, entirely himself again, approaches in the golden sunset.

Such is the gushy history that is laboriously and ponderously unfolded in settings that are artistically fine, especially in their foreign atmosphere, and played out painstakingly by capable actors, who must have known at the time that this sort of sentimental slush was futile.

Rush.

LOVES OF CARMEN

Fox production and release. Featuring Dolores Del Rio and Victor McLaglen. Directed by Raoul Walsh, with scenario based on story by Prosper Marimee. Cameramen, Lucien Andriot and John Marta. Titles by Katherine Hilliker and H. H. Caldwell. At Roxy, New York, week Sept. 24. Running time, 85 mins.

Carmen....................Dolores Del Rio
Don Jose....................Don Alvarado
Escamillo....................Victor McLaglen
Micaela....................Nancy Nash

Plenty of hell, sex and box office in this latest film biography of a well known Spanish damsel. The male population is going to eat it up, the censors in a couple of the states are going to find something to do, and meanwhile it's going to make dough besides increasing the prestige for Winnie Sheehan's idea of a pulsating maiden.

The '27 fall model of "Carmen" as Raoul Walsh and Dolores Del Rio have turned her out carries more dynamite than all the preceding film characterizations of this cigar factory vamp. And that explosive power is going to clear a path to the b. o. They go out talking about this one. And the next time Miss Del Rio shows in another picture they're going to come back.

Figure out all the versions of "Carmen" you've seen, stage or otherwise and toss 'em off, for this is "it." A long way from the "Carmen" the Metropolitan vocalists give voice to every winter (wouldn't some of those coloratura sopranos like to have Dolores' figure), but if there's any question as to the authenticity of this interpretation, who cares? Here's a screening that will be understood in any language.

Everybody knows the story, so that's out. The basic tale is recognizable if double exposed behind the flashing bare legs of Dolores. And these particular limbs are all over and through the picture. But the situations aren't such to horrify anybody or need heavy slicing. Yet every suggestion is subtly presented.

Production and camera work are splendid, with Walsh giving pace to the finished work. Besides Miss Del Rio's high voltage work is that of Victor McLaglen and Don Alvarado. McLaglen is the hard-hearted toreador whom Carmen pursues and finally snares, while Alvarado plays the love-sick officer at whose hands Carmen finally dies. Both men lend impressive support, with McLaglen so reminiscent at times that you can still see his "Glory" uniform draped on him. That's something this boy will probably never live down.

And with all the emphasis on the sex thing, still a light vein runs through prominently enough to make it almost seem as if cast and director were well nigh winking at the original script. Which makes it appear all in good fun and may soften up the rigid blue pencilers when they come to view it.

Smart showmanship slipping this into the Roxy instead of trying to make a special out of it. It's not a $2 picture but could go into any of the Broadway grind-run houses (Rivoli and Rialto) and make good. As a program picture it's a pip with Walsh's handling of the subject and Miss Del Rio's performance dominating.

Every foot of "Carmen" is there.

Sid.

Rose of Golden West

First National release and production. Directed by George Fitzmaurice. Mary Astor and Gilbert Roland featured. Screen play by Bess Meredith. Adapted from the story by Minna Carolina Smith and Eugenia Woodward. Running time 65 minutes. At the Strand, New York, week Sept. 25.

Rosita....................Mary Astor
Juan....................Gilbert Roland
Gomez....................Gustav von Seyffertitz
General Romero....................Montagu Love
Senora Concha....................Flora Finch
Thomas Larkin....................Harvey Clark
Mother Superior....................Roel Muriel
Russian Prince....................Andre Cheron
Secretary....................Romaine Fielding
Orderly....................Thur Fairfax
Commodore Sloat....................William Conklin
Senorita Gonzales....................Christina Montt

A charming romantic story, delightfully acted by the beautiful Mary Astor and a satisfying company. Sumptuous production, with flashes of inexpressibly' beautiful landscapes and picturesque costumes, mark this historical love story of Spanish mission California of 1846. Measures up as a high-grade program picture that will please, particularly, the women.

Makes no pretense to high dramatic climax or sensational punch, but does deliver a pretty bit of light entertainment through its spirit of grace and youth. The box office angle probably will be that it will please established clientele, but won't pull beyond that.

Pictorially, the film is notable. The camera has caught some scenic shots as background for the action that nail attention for their beauty. Vistas through wind-warped firs at moonlit waters, with a convent gleaming white against the forest; rocky mountain passes backed by distant valleys and peaks, and picturesque, massive interiors, give to the whole picture an atmosphere of loveliness that heightens the flavor of its sentimental romance.

For the most part the action is tepid, but there are lively passages. A runaway coach bearing the heroine as it goes careening along rough mountain roads, with the hero dashing to the rescue, has a moment of thrill.

Throughout the photography is extraordinarily fine. Some of the closeups, particularly those of Miss Astor, have the quality of fine portraiture. One in particular, showing the convent girl in the candlelight of an ancient altar, is an interesting bit.

Picture is full of interesting character studies. Montagu Love, who has had more misfit roles than any other actor on the screen, is here well fitted as a jovial Spanish overlord, careless of habit and bored to death with politics. He handles it splendidly. Gilbert Roland does some spectacular horseback riding, but has few acting opportunities that count, while Miss Astor is the embodiment of youthful charm. Gustav von Seyffertitz has a characteristically sinister role.

Some elaborate spectacular scenes are fairly well managed, and, for once, a Spanish picture doesn't go in heavily for guitar strumming and Spanish folk dancing.

The film has grace, intelligence and charm, but no stimulating kick. It leaves a pleasant but mild impression, and is quickly forgotten. On the sex side, it wouldn't get an indignant reaction from a volunteer film censor.

Rush.

THREE MILES UP

Universal production and release. Starring Al Wilson, stunt flyer. Directed by Bruce Mitchell. Story by Carl Krusada. Cameraman, William S. Adams. Running time, 56 mins. On double bill at Loew's New York, one day, Sept. 16.

A turk in production standards but possibly possessing a box office angle in certain types of town or neighborhood because of its dare-devil hero and his air stuff.

A returned war ace is forced back into his criminal ways by the "master mind." He goes up with a haul of diamonds while pursued by the cops.

Wishing to get away from his evil life and associates the ace fakes an accident in mid-air and jumps. Parachute fails to work. He lands, unconscious in the yard of the heroine, whose father, a colonel, is a staunch admirer of the aviator. Nursed back to health, his scars are gone when the bandages are removed.

The denouement is conventional melodrama with a "novelty" angle in the big comedy bore turning out to be a dick. This character, supposed member of the gang, has hay fever all through the picture and is pursued by a God-awful spinster. He being a federal cop is the tip off on the quality of the story, continuity and treatment.

The punch is where Wilson makes a change from one plane to another by lassooing the passing plane and swinging free. Air stunts are effective in this respect, and the only feature of the picture.

GENTLEMAN OF PARIS

Paramount production and release. Starring Adolphe Menjou in polite comedy from the story, "Bellamy, the Magnificent," by Roy Horniman, adapted by Benjamin Glazer. Directed by Harry D'Abbadie D'Arrast. Running time, 65 minutes. At the Paramount, New York, week Oct. 1.

Marquis de Marignan	Adolphe Menjou
Jacqueline	Shirley O'Hara
Yvonne Defour	Arlette Marchal
Henriette	Ivy Harris
Joseph Talineau	Nicholas Soussanin
General Baron de Latour	Lawrence Grant
Henri Doufour	William B. Davidson
Cloakroom Girl	Lorraine Eddy

Another saucy recital by Menjou, the bland, done in the best spirit of French comedy. That's about the best that may be said of the picture, which is a lightweight in appeal, particularly lacking in feminine interest. The story provides another of those pastel shaded backgrounds for the debonair star, a cream puff of a production, but a graceful and sightly cream puff for those who have a taste for such confections.

Play has a lot of neat, tricky bits in the light comedy vein. Such is the episode of the indignant husband who bursts upon the Marquis and his lady friend in the private room of a night club. The Marquis blushingly admits he has a woman companion behind the curtain, but it's not the intruder's wife. The trick is that he had hidden with the wife a girl attache of the place when she came to warn him of the husband's approach. It is the girl who shows her blonde tresses through the curtain to prove the hidden woman is not the brunette wife.

It is of such bits of wicked suggestion that the picture is made up. The risky atmosphere is set at the beginning, when the Marquis' valet, seeking him in a hurry, phones all his supposed haunts. Valet picks up the phone and one glimpses, at the other end of the line, a lovely lady awakened and reaching for her bedside phone. In one case it is the lady's husband who reaches the phone, to the confusion of the valet when he is answered by a masculine voice. These passages are neat in their delicate suggestion.

The story grows to a climax when the valet discovers evidence that the Marquis is concerned in an intrigue with the valet's own wife, and determines upon revenge. To humiliate his master, he "plants" a playing card up his sleeve and then brings about the accusation that he cheated at play. Thereby the nobleman is disgraced, but by pretending suicide he arouses the really loyal valet to hysterical confession.

The production is a splendid bit of technical work. The smart atmosphere that goes with the haute monde surroundings are splendidly carried out in action and settings, the French tone of the interiors being particularly convincing.

Graceful society comedy daintily done, but, of course, terribly thin fare for meat-eating picture fans.

Rush.

A MAN'S PAST

Universal production and release. Directed by George Melford. Taken from the play, "The Diploma." At the Colony, New York, starting Oct. 1. Running time, about 70 minutes.

Paul La Roche	Conrad Veidt
Yvonne Fontaine	Barbara Bedford
Dr. Fontaine	Ian Keith
Lieut. Destin	Arthur Edmund Carewe
Prison Doctor	Charles Puffy
Sylvia Cabot	Corliss Palmer
Dr. Renaud	Edward Reinach

Conrad Veidt is the gent John Barrymore brought back from Europe and announced as quite an actor. Veidt was already known slightly for his work as the murderous somnambulist in "The Cabinet of Dr. Caligari," German film.

Apparently Universal is out to make some of the dough Emil Jannings is bringing in for Paramount. Veidt is primarily an actor, measuring not in the least to the standard accepted for heroic types in American films. Like Jannings and Lon Chaney, this newcomer to Hollywood is practically devoid of sex appeal; and in his first American picture he registers less forcefully than his two confreres.

This picture, while intelligently produced, will be found lacking in holding power. This is attributable to several long periods wherein the story might just as well have been told in a series of "stills," so passive is the action.

It is of a doctor sentenced to 10 years in a French prison on the Isle of St. Moir because he has deemed it merciful to kill patients afflicted with incurable painful diseases. In a prison brawl, the official doctor is killed and the officer in charge seriously wounded. A young lieutenant, newly added to the military staff of the prison, promises the imprisoned doctor that if he can save the life of the official he will be rewarded with immediate freedom.

Veidt saves the officer's life, but the latter is ungrateful and refuses to carry out the promise made by his subordinate. Veidt escapes to the mainland. A brother surgeon, slowly going blind, persuades him to disguise himself and perform operations which he can no longer accomplish of his poor eyesight; Veidt consents, and thus prevents his friend from being discharged from the hospital, where he is employed.

Hospital officials in Algiers want the weak-eyed surgeon on their staff, and, when the fellow at last goes blind, Veidt assumes his friend's name and accepts, taking the sightless fellow and his sister with him.

In Algiers, Veidt is believed to be the brother of his friend's sister. He finds the deception painful, as he is violently in love with the girl. Later the young lieutenant from the St. Moir prison is transferred to Veidt's station in Algiers, and recognizes the former convict.

Fearful of being exposed, Veidt tells his blind partner of the lieutenant. The blind youth inveigles the lieutenant into a chess game and shoots him as they play. With the lieutenant at the point of death, the secret of Veidt's identity is almost secure. But his physician's nature gets the better of him and Veidt nurses the officer back to health. The lieutenant later rewards him with his freedom and the renewal of his license to practice medicine.

The picture starts tensely with scenes of the prison squalor and the almost immediate brawl. As the footage unreels the physical side of the story is submerged in exposition of the mental attitudes of the characters. Diminishing of movement is injurious to any moving picture.

Because of the foreignness of story and atmosphere it seems certain that "A Man's Past" will draw strongest on the other side. The popular American audience will patronize it moderately.

Veidt's work, without comparing it to that of contemporaries, may be called good acting. The s. a. is blotto.

Ian Keith puts over his rather dreary part as the surgeon who goes blind. His features are strong and highly expressive. Barbara Bedford is not called upon for much acting ,but does her share capably. Corliss Palmer, the prize beauty, is a minor in the cast. She attracts attention when pressing a man's hand to her breast and asking him to feel her heart. This portion may not be in to delight Kansas.

Direction shines in handling groups, detail and significant expressions; it slips in letting the picture drag. Photography good.

THREE'S A CROWD

First National production and release. Starring Harry Langdon. Directed by Langdon from Arthur Ripley's story. At the Strand, New York, week of October 1. Running time, 56 minutes.

The Girl	Gladys McConnell
The Man	Cornelius Keefe
The Odd Fellow	Harry Langdon

Harry Langdon had previously threatened to direct his own pictures and in this one he's done it. "Three's a Crowd" is no sensation but neither is it a cluck. So it shapes as fair program material with the comedian leaning toward he serious and stressing pathos more than is his habit.

At the Strand juvenile patronage seemed particularly delighted Sunday while the more elderly secured their share of laughs.

Those who don't like Langdon aren't going to be won over by this release. It's too quiet and lacks the necessary explosive mirth to overcome that handicap. Those who do favor the comic, however, will be satisfied. There are spots in the picture where Langdon is brilliant, but on the other hand slow passages also creep in. It's not a high geared vehicle and Langdon has held down the hoke, which may explain.

In script it tells of Langdon as a trunk hustler who lives alone and finds a prospective mother in a snow bank. Shelter and a comedy search for medical aid brings the baby into the world with Langdon happy as he has craved someone to look after.

As the girl has left her young husband it's only a question of time when he is going to show up. This happens, the family reunites and Langdon is back where he started. The gag finish is Langdon going back to the fortune teller who told him everything was going to be all right.

Langdon's work outside the door while waiting for the baby to arrive is the highlight of his personal performance. As previously known he has little trouble in winning sympathy and his pantomiming to such an end has a definite effect, the criticism being that there is too much of this in lieu of needed laughs to give the film added power.

A moderate production forms the setting as the action takes place in a tenement district. Photography is average. In this respect the director-comedian reveals a penchant for lingering over fadeouts at the end of scenes, pausing almost a full minute over some of these with himself as the central figure.

"Three's a Crowd" is not of the spontaneous type but it's clean and jogs along at a fair gait with enough laugh incidents to hold interest. Supporting cast members handle little more than bits.

Sid.

THE BUGLE CALL

Metro-Goldwyn-Mayer feature starring Jackie Coogan. Directed by Edward Sedgwick from story by C. Gardner Sullivan. Supporting company headed by Claire Windsor and Herbert Rawlinson, with Tom O'Brien and Harry Todd. Running time, 60 minutes. At Loew's Lincoln Square, New York, Sept. 19-21.

Picture is a childish affair that might have been made into a two-reel filler, but as a full-length feature with any box-office potentiality it doesn't measure up. What can be said of the chances of a screen offering that makes Claire Windsor look like a frump and the vigorous Herbert Rawlinson like a simp?

The result is a good deal of a bust. One of the troubles is that no woman, even Miss Windsor, can wear the simpering curls of the '70's, together with the costume eccentricities of that period, and still do anything but a comedy role. Here she has a sympathetic part opposite Jackie Coogan, and the result of tender and sentimental business and the silly get-up creates something akin to travesty. The scene is laid in a frontier army post in 1870 something.

Rawlinson, tricked out in mutton chop whiskers and a civil war uniform with the flat-topped cap that hasn't been picturesque since 1892, may have engaged in heroic business in the script, but his part on the screen set up a distinct impulse to giggle. This was the discordant background against which young Jackie was called upon to be cunning, mischievous and amusing. If the surrounding atmosphere had been perfect it would have been a full job for this boy of awkward age. As it was, the day was lost early and never regained.

The sentimental passages, having to do with the boy's grief for his dead mother and his resentment at the introduction of a stepmother, were just tiresome.

The role handed Miss Windsor was a gem. All she had to do was to carry a trick comedy costume, win the sympathy of the spectator from the boy hero and be graceful in an insipid character. Sarah Bernhardt couldn't have done it.

Who was it, one wonders, on the M-G-M lot who thought up the bright idea of making a beautiful stepmother heroine playing opposite a boy star?

That's only one item in a smear of tangled fiction elements. The heroics of the soldiers fighting the Indians on the western plains took on a reverse twist, with difficulty in distinguishing between straight dramatic action and comedy relief. There was one lively episode in which the juvenile star was shown saving the garrison from an Indian attack, all of it done in the dime novel style, and one never could be sure whether the intent was comic or straight.

The always convincing emotional acting of Jackie could make no headway against the surrounding absurdities, and the picture skidded badly, comedy as well as drama.

Might get past as material for Saturday afternoon in the neighborhoods where the screen addresses itself to the school children, but as adult entertainment it's a dead loss.

Rush.

MUMSIE

Film version of Knoblock's stage play, produced by Herbert Wilcox. Trade shown at the London Hippodrome, Sept. 2, for world's trade.

Mumsie	Pauline Frederick
Sud Murphy	Nelson Keys
Nobby Clarke	Frank Stanmore
Colonel Armytage	Herbert Marshall
Noel Symonds	Donald McCardle
Edgar Symonds	Rolf Leslie
Carl Kessler	Arthur Barry

London, Sept. 17.

This is Wilcox's first independent production since he finished "Pompadour" and his British National contract. It marks a great advance on his previous work, though "Pompadour" was a pretty good film. But in "Mumsie" he has told a story coherently, and the story is good sob stuff. A number of female hard-boiled eggs wiped away channels in their face powder as they came out, and on its tear appeal it ought to be good.

Pauline Frederick has a role which suits her age, and plays with becoming restraint. She is better directed than for many a picture, and this film should put her back into favor quite a bit.

Pre-war scenes in the French village are excellent, and the air-raid stuff is more natural than this sort of thing is usually. Good thumbnail sketches of village characters brighten up the general action and lighting and photography are keeping.

While this touches the over-worked war, it is not a war film, nor is it a bad imitation of Hollywood. It might have been made snappier on the Coast, but not so sincere nor so genuinely sobby.

Not a world-beater, but good enough to stand on its own feet in any type house, and promising for Wilcox's future.

LADIES AT EASE

First Division release, presented by I. E. Chadwick. Directed by Jerome Storm. Featuring Pauline Garon, supported by Gertrude Short, Gardner James, Raymond Glenn, Lillian Hackett. At the Hippodrome, New York, week Oct. 3. Running time, 55 minutes.

A comedy pictured in primary humor and aimed at the patrons of neighborhood and small town houses. Although the Hip has it for a week, it is a one-day picture.

Stripped of its naive mispelling of famous institutions—Ziggy for Ziegfeld and "Foolies" for "Follies"—the story is of two girls modeling underwear in a luxurious shop, who steal the boy friends of two "Follies" girls. The showgirls have the models fired. The models lock the showgirls in their apartment. Then they swipe the girls' costumes and do their act in the "Follies."

So bad is the impromptu routine of the models, the audience acclaims them geniuses, and Ziegfeld immediately offers them a stupendous contract. But an "angel" also wants the girls to star in a show he contemplates, so Zieggy agrees to let the "angel" finance the show.

To cap it the former models go back to the old shop all dressed up and laugh at the erstwhile showgirls, who have taken to modeling for a living.

Pauline Garon and Gertrude Short are the models. Miss Short is fairly funny in two instances and Miss Garon in none. The direction by Jerome Storm makes every last one of the characters seem like juvenile actors, each waiting for someone to tell him or her what to do next.

All that drew laughs in the Hip were the subtitles.

There is an actual parallel to part of this plot—the case of the Cherry Sisters.

That there are many people who like their comedy easy to understand is what will give this picture its play in small houses. Nix for the better crowds.

THE RACING FOOL

Rayart picture, presented by W. Ray Johnston and produced by Harry J. Brown. Starring Reed Howes. At Victory two days (Sept. 15-16) on double feature bill. Running time, 50 minutes.

Suitable for week-day trade in small houses. Plot is quite familiar but capable direction and a handsome, somewhat talented star do much to offset that angle.

Reed Howes, the star, has been batting around for the independents quite a while. Recently he was in "Rough House Rosie," Paramount picture starring Clara Bow, and gave a good account of himself.

This picture is built around automobile race shots. It's about the son of an auto manufacturer who succumbs to the daughter of a rival manufacturer. Howes is to race for his old man. When the other fellow's daughter, not knowing his identity, asks him to race for her father, he has to refuse.

The menace agrees to race for the girl's old man on a half-hearted promise that he'll get the gal in marriage. He intends to throw the the race, having a grudge on, and Howes hears of it. At his dad's request he calls off driving the dad's car and wins the race for the girl's father.

Racing shots are above average and brought off after a series of highly keyed and interesting situations.

Prior to that is more excitement when the hero rescues the girl off a runaway horse and tumbles with her down a steep hill.

Good action picture in comparison with most inde products turned out along this line.

In its own particular class will be liked.

THE HAUNTED RANGE

Davis Distributing Co. release, starring Ken Maynard. Directed by Paul Hurst and photographed by Frank Cotner. Cast includes Alma Rayford, Fred Burns, Bob Williamson and the Six Hollywood Beauties. At the Arena, New York, Sept. 22, on double featured bill. Running time, 55 mins.

Ken Maynard is under contract to First National. This picture is some months old, being made by an inde previous to Maynard's F. N. hookup.

Technically the film is a laugh from start to finish, but it has the usual amount of action and the people who see it in the houses it will play aren't bothered by technicalities.

As Westerns go, this one is quite novel. Featured equally with Maynard on the boards outside the Arena were the Six Hollywood Beauties in bathing suits. The producer inserted the girls by showing them in swimming while some cowboys peeped through the bushes. The girls are on the screen about one minute, long enough to feature them in billing. The girls aren't beautiful, but aren't bothered with Chaney's worry of being stepped on, and a good lithographer took care of them on the display paper.

Story concerns Maynard's clearing of a murder mystery. His father died suspected of killing a neighboring rancher, and since his death a ghost has been riding the range. Maynard inherits the ranch if he can clear the mystery. He does, capturing the ghost rider and identifying him as an employee of the murdered rancher and the killer himself. Love interest is worked with the daughter of the murdered rancher. She won't speak to him until he has proven his father's innocence.

Action points are a horse race between Maynard and the son of the murdered rancher, and a rescue of the heroine by Maynard from a guy out for forcible necking.

Alias the Lone Wolf

Columbia production and release. Directed by Edward H. Griffin from the Louis Joseph Vance story. Bert Lytell and Lois Wilson featured. In support Ned Sparks, Paulette Duval, William V. Mong. At New York Hippodrome. Runs about 65 minutes.

If "The Lone Wolf" has a following that can stand "Alias the Lone Wolf," then this picture may have a chance to do business. Otherwise it's simple and insipid, loosely directed and more loosely played, with the "detective situations" at times quite irritating.

Bert Lytell must have had the loaf of his picture life while making this one. He just lolls through, in and out of impossible escapades and tricks, finally letting out the secret that he is really not a crook but a Secret Service man all of this time.

It's crook vs. crook, in fact a band of the latter against the solitary Lone Wolf, until the U. S. S. S. gets into it. And it was simply delicious to hear the girl who tried to smuggle jewels into the country call the Lone Wolf a crook. Maybe that's why Mr. Lytell commenced to loaf.

If there is no great following for

"The Lone Wolf" around, but there may be for a western, then the western lovers may go for this one.
Sime.

BORDER BLACKBIRDS

Pathe western starring Leo Maloney. Directed by Leo D. Maloney from a story by Ford I. Beebe. Cameraman, Edward Kull. Cast: Eugenia Gilbert, Nelson McDowell, Morgan Davis, Tom London, Dan Coleman, Allen Watt. Running time, 56 mins. At Loew's New York, Sept. 23, on double feature bill.

Westerns made under Pathe label with Leo Maloney starred constitute somewhat of a closed corporation as to star, leading lady, director and author. They seem to be always the same. The joint efforts have been represented by westerns of averagely good entertainment and production quality. The pictures have not been up with the best but neither have they been down with the humpty-dumpties. "Border Blackbirds" is typical.

It's the stock situation of the outlaw who attempts to set his crimes laid on the hero. The outlaw in this case is in league with a bank president and a mine superintendent in that generous custom of western films.

Ultimate denouement is achieved with sufficient plausibility and virtue and innocence are honored in due course.

The Flight Commander

London, Sept. 30.

Film version of story by John Travers. Presented by Gaumont-British. Directed by Maurice Elvey. At the London Hippodrome, Sept. 29, preview. Running time, 100 minutes.

Flight Commander.Sir Alan Cobham, K.B.E.
Mary..........................Estelle Brody
John Massey.................John Stuart
James Mortimer........Humberston Wright

Eleven months ago Sir Alan Cobham was in the headlines everywhere after his world flight. Someone evidently supposed that made him a box office bet. The result is almost everything in the film is sacrificed to bringing in Cobham, and the story, thin to begin with, suffers.

Estelle Brody is miscast. She is a good comedienne but in the heavy and rather unsympathetic role here is wasted. Gaumonts appear to be running the artists named, together with Bromley Davenport and Alf Goddard, on stock. Result in this picture is not successful. Good work is done in a minor role of a French sailor by William Pardue, a ringer for Douglas Fairbanks.

Cobham puts in a world air route, and, Massey goes to the East in charge of depot. Mary, daughter of local missionary, is about to marry Mortimer, big concessionary, when John arrives. The two fall in love but give Mortimer a square deal, John deciding to go away.

Inspired by Bolshie wireless operator, natives break out against whites on wedding day. John is lost trying to send a radio message and Mary's love for him comes out. Mortimer goes out and brings him in, sends radio to Cobham, and is killed. Cobham arrives, bombs village, and troops come in airplanes to clear it up.

Plenty of material for a thriller but story interest lost by concentrating on Cobham. Attempt to introduce angles for America and France by putting matelots and doughboys in the story. One of the latter is effectively played by Cyril McLaglen, brother of Victor.

Chinese village sets are about the best exteriors yet built here. But film does not live up to them. Elvey has obviously labored under the handicap of airway propaganda, which seems to be film's aim, and fighting stuff in riots very unconvincing. Photography patchy.

On Cobham's name, good for the half-weekly change houses, but not likely to stand up elsewhere.

A Sister to Assist 'Er

London, Sept. 28.

Adapted from the late Fred Emney's vaudeville sketch and other sketches by John Le Breton. Directed by George Dewhurst. Preview, Sept. 27, Palace, London. Running time, 72 minutes. Controlled by Gaumont-British Co.

This cockney humor, so acceptable here, where it made Fred Emney's fame and fortune, is an English vaude classic. As a film it suffers from the attempt to put humor of dialog into action. All the leering inflections of voice which made it so funny to English people on the stage disappear when the lines become screen captions.

But nothing in which Mary Brough appears could be unfunny, and for smaller houses in industrial areas it will be a scream here. For any other country, even where they speak English, it will be as comprehensible as Chinese drama to an Aztec, it is so saturatedly cockney.

Making such extremely "local" films as this is no way to get British pictures into a world market.

THE JAZZ SINGER

Warner Brothers production and release. With Vitaphone synchronization. Starring Al Jolson. Featuring May McAvoy and Warner Oland. Adapted from the play of the same title. Alan Crosland director. Hal Mohr, cameraman. Captions by Jack Jarmuth. A. A. Cohn credited with scenario. Opened at Warner's, New York, twice daily, run, starting Oct. 6. Running time, 88 mins.

Jakie Rabinowitz (later Jack Robin) .... Al Jolson
Mary Dale .... May McAvoy
Cantor Rabinowitz .... Warner Oland
Sara Rabinowitz .... Eugenie Besserer
Moisha Yudelson .... Otto Lederer
Cantor Josef Rosenblatt .... By Himself
Jakie (13 years old) .... Bobbie Gordon
Harry Lee .... Richard Tucker
Levi .... Nat Carr
Buster Billings .... William Demarest
Dillings .... Anders Randolf
Doctor .... Will Walling

Undoubtedly the best thing Vitaphone has ever put on the screen. The combination of the religious heart interest story and Jolson's singing "Kol Nidre" in a synagog while his father is dying and two "Mammy" lyrics as his mother stands in the wings of the theatre, and later as she sits in the first row, carries abundant power and appeal. Besides which the finish of the "Mammy" melody (the one that goes "The sun shines east, the sun shines west" is also the end of the picture with Jolson supposedly on a stage and a closeup on the screen as his voice pours through the amplifiers.

To a first night Broadway mob that finale was a whale and resulted in a tumultuous ovation. Jolson, personally, has never been more warmly greeted than at this premiere. He was there, in person, also.

But "The Jazz Singer" minus Vitaphone is something else again. There's really no love interest in the script, except between mother and son. It's doubtful if the general public will take to the Jewish boy's problem of becoming a cantor or a stage luminary as told on celluloid. On the other hand, with Vitaphone it can't miss. It is understood that W. B. has prepared two versions of the film, with and without Vitaphone, for the exhibition angle.

Jolson, when singing, is Jolson. There are six instances of this, each running from two to three minutes. When he's without that instrumental spur Jolson is camera conscious. Yet for his first picture the Shubert ace does exceptionally well. Plus his camera makeup this holder of a $17,500 check for one week in a picture house isn't quite the Al his vast audience knows. But as soon as he gets under cork the lens picks up that spark of individual personality solely identified with him. That much goes with or without Vitaphone.

The picture is all Jolson, although Alan Crosland, directing, has creditably dodged the hazard of over-emphasizing the star as well as refraining from laying it on too thick in the scenes between the mother and boy. The film dovetails splendidly, which speaks well for those component parts of the technical staff. Cast support stands out in the persons of Eugenie Besserer, as the mother; Otto Lederer, as a friend of the family, and Warner Oland as the father. Oland recently left this theatre as a Chinese dastard in "Old San Francisco" and comes back as a Jewish cantor, so if his performance isn't what it might be, it's excusable on the territory he covers.

May McAvoy is pretty well smothered on footage with no love theme to help, but being instrumental in getting Jakie, nee Jack Robin, his chance in a Broadway show. She is also a performer in the story.

Heavy heart interest in the film and some comedy, plus adept titling, which helps both these ingredients. The pathos makes the picture a contender for Jewish neighborhoods, minus the voice feature. With Jolson's audible rendering of "Kol Nidre" this bit will likely make a tremendous impression in such houses. Or any audience for that matter as, after all, anybody's religion demands respect and consideration and when as seriously presented as here, the genuineness of the effort will make everybody listen. Besides which the story has the father dying as his son sings for him with the boy's voice coming through a window as the parent passes on.

By script it tells of young Jakie running away from home to eventually become a vaudevillian. Bobbie Gordon plays this early sequence with Jolson's entrance in Coffee Dan's cellar restaurant in 'Frisco, where he gets up and does two songs, "Dirty Hands, Dirty Face" and "Toot, Toot, Tootsie, Goodbye."

In the sticks a wire comes for him to join a Broadway show. He returns home to see his mother, where he sits down at a piano to run over one of his songs, "Blue Skies," for her. At this point is some laugh patter as Jolson affectionately kids his mother. As he goes into another chorus, his father entrances, to order him out of the house for the second time. The scene switch is then to the dress rehearsal on the day of the show's opening with Yudelson and his mother pleading with him in the dressing room to come to the synagog that night and sing on the eve of Yum Kippur because of his father's illness.

Worried about his father, torn between his first big chance and a natural impulse to throw up everything and go to the synagog, Jolson comes out in "one" to do "Mother O'Mine, I Still Love You" as she stands in the wings and listens. Convinced that her boy belongs to the theatre, she returns home where Jolson follows, dons the Cantor's talis and leads the choir.

Crosland has done no stalling in these passages, the scenes moving fast with just the boy's decision to the inferred mental struggle shown through his appearing in the home. Following "Kol Nidre," the final scene has Jolson in "one" during a performance, his mother in the first row as he sings "Mammy" to her, and the finish of the song closes the picture.

George Jessel originally did the show and was supposed to have done this picture. Jessel is still out in the play and doing big business. When the show first opened on Broadway last year talk was that the story was based on Jolson, so now with Jolson actually doing it the psychology is perfect.

Louis Silvers gets credit for having arranged the Vita-synchronization with the projection booth switching machines for Jolson's songs, the change over generally coming on a title. An odd factor is that the orchestral accompaniment to the story is scratchy, but when Jolson sings it's about the best recording Vitaphone has turned out to date.

Jolson in "The Jazz Singer" is surefire for Broadway. With his songs that holds good for any town or street. Exclude Vitaphone and there crops up the problem that it amounts to a Jewish mother-son-religious story with Jolson not yet enough the screen actor to carry it. It's running for a consecutive 88 minutes at the Warner and will have totaled a lot of screen hours by the time it reaches the end of its stay.

As presented with Vitaphone, it's a credit to everybody concerned.

Sid.

The Road to Romance

Metro-Goldwyn-Mayer production and release. Directed by John S. Robertson. Titles by Joe Farnham. At Capitol, New York, week Oct. 8. Running time, 60 minutes.

Jose Armando .... Ramon Novarro
Serafina .... Marceline Day
Popolo .... Marc McDermott
Don Balthasar .... Roy D'Arcy
Castro .... Cesare Gravina
Drunkard .... Bobby Mack
Don Carlos .... Otto Mathieson
Smoky Beard .... Jules Cowles

A story of pirates, plenty of water on the side, and Ramon Novarro.

One must like Novarro a lot to like the picture, but those who do, will.

Otherwise it's too grossly exaggerated, travels too much along the w. k. buccaneer lines, and has too many holes in the tale for it to strike beyond an average week, even in a Novarro town.

A captain of the Spanish dragoons was sent incognito to an isolated island to rescue a young lady the undisclosed chief of the pirate wanted to marry. He intended to marry her, that tough bird, and didn't mind telling her ill brother that the day he died his sister would be hisn.

The brother died before his time, as it were, through one of the pirates stabbing the wrong fellow.

But he didn't marry the girl. The captain from Spain thwarted him there. It's 3/1 Capt. married her himself.

Pretty nice girl, Marceline Day, but mostly she hugging walls here. It was a terrible country and company she landed in, although you could tell she was asking for water without a caption.

Novarro did a neat bit as a nance aside in a court scene to fool the judge, the crafty Don Balthasar, who was played by Roy D'Arcy as Frank Keenan used to play his western gambler. But D'Arcy did a good job.

Joe Farnham's captions were severely straight and rather good, excepting that one that said:

"You're under arrest as a pirate on the high seas."

Every single in vaudeville could be pinched for the same reason.

Sime.

We're All Gamblers

Paramount production and release starring Thomas Meighan. Directed by James Cruze from the story by Hope Loring. Based on the play "Lucky Sam McCarver" by Sydney Howard. Titles by Jack Conway. At the Paramount, New York, week October 8. Running time about one hour.

Lucky Sam McCarver .... Thomas Meighan
Carlotta Asche .... Marietta Millner
Georgie McCarver .... Cullen Landis
Monty Garside .... Philo McCullough
Mrs. McCarver .... Gertrude Claire
Gunboat .... Gunboat Smith
Spec .... Spec O'Donnell

Small time stuff. Doesn't seem to be any sense at all in so openly knifing a name like Meighan and this picture is nothing but another nail.

In the tank towns, where Meighan still draws, it may be all right, but the box office power should be figured only on the name value of the star. Not a thing in the picture.

Slovenly direction. Surprising in a degree in a veteran megaphone wielder like James Cruze. The script wouldn't get an okay from anyone but an incompetent supervisor. It's dreary, draggy and monotonous. Situations are carelessly handled, none built up for interest and practically all flat.

"Gamblers" has been playing all over the country. It comes into New York at the tail end of its first run trip.

The leading lady, Marietta Millner, is of the average type and of average ability. It seems to be a gag, all these loud, continuous squawks about the everlasting search for talent. Pictures like these leave nothing but a suspicion that someone is playing favorites.

The title, like the story, some of the cast and the picture, doesn't mean a thing. It has no bearing on the production. There are better stories in the records of emergency ambulance calls. That's what this one is built up around.

Starting off with the New York of many years ago is shown the tattered, forlorn figure of a little boy on a stormy winter night, seeking shelter in a cold packing case. The kind-hearted copper on the beat finds him and gets him shelter and a home with Mrs. McCarver. The opening is handled coldly.

Sam grows up to be a prize fighter and he won't sign a contract unless the little, gray-haired Maggie McCarver is there with his lucky sweater. He gets run over by Carlotta's car before getting a chance to pose in the ring for any kind of a fight and then comes long scenes of Lucky lying on a cot in the hospital.

For no great reason the locale switches to night clubs. Lucky runs one and it is a howling success right from the start. The titles say so but no explanation about how it's done.

Cullen Landis puts a little feeling into it on occasion but he hasn't much of a chance with the poor material.

AMERICAN BEAUTY

First National production and release. Starring Billie Dove. Featuring Lloyd Hughes. Directed by Richard Wallace from a Carey Wilson story. At the Strand, New York, week Oct. 8. Running time, 64 mins.

Millicent Howard .... Billie Dove
Jerry Booth .... Lloyd Hughes
Claverhouse .... Walter McGrail
Mrs. Gillespie .... Margaret Livingston
Gillespie .... Lucien Prival
Waiter .... Al St. John
Madame O'Riley .... Edythe Chapman
Claire O'Riley .... Alice White

Screen material that isn't going to get Billie Dove anywhere. A beautiful girl in a couple of nice frocks walking through some good-looking sets reveals all. Not enough body to the story to make it other than just another picture.

One more poor girl after luxuries, but choosing South America and the moderate salaried boy friend after getting in a jam over a "borrowed" dress from a repair establishment. A proposal from New York's richest bachelor, rush to the train to take off with the mining engineer and the loss of a shawl that displays the star in her undies as the suddenly united lovers scramble on to the outgoing observation platform.

He of wealth isn't even a villain, has honorable intentions, but is passed up when Millie (Miss Dove) is spotted with the beauteous gown by its right owner at a society gathering.

The best thing in the film seems to be the view of the Grand Central Station, New York, from the inside.

Numerous soft focus shots of Miss Dove, and she looks good, as usual. Hughes, opposite, simply kills time and doesn't even have to get into a tux. Other players do about as much, with Walter McGrail as the moneyed rival for the hand of the feminine hotel restaurant checker. Al St. John has a couple of bits as a waiter.

The title is derived from the name of an evening dress, but "American Beauty" wanders aimlessly and practically without the ingredients any film must have to hold interest. The Dove fans may approve the flash of their favorite in negligee, but it'll take a wild imagination to enthuse over anything else in the footage.

Nothing there despite a production that's worthy of a better script.

This one won't do for the best runs.

Sid.

THE GAY RETREAT

Fox production and release. Featuring Ted McNamara and Sammy Cohen. Story by William Conselman and Edward Marshall. Adapted by Murray Roth and Edward P. Moran (Roth solely title-credited). Titled by Malcolm Stuart Boyland. Directed by Ben Stoloff. At Roxy, New York, week Oct. 8. Running time, 60 minutes.

Sam Nosenblum..............Sammy Cohen
Ted McHiggins..............Ted McNamara
Bob Wright....................Gene Cameron
Betty Burnett...............Betty Francisco
Joan Moret.........................Judy King
Charles Wright.............Holmes Herbert
Edward Fulton.............Charles Gorman
Jerry.........................Jerry the Giant
Dog ....Pal

Ted McNamara and Sammy Cohen's impression as a comedy team in "What Price Glory" prompted their featuring, possible future, in Fox comedies. "The Gay Retreat," Stoloff production, is their maiden effort, and flatteringly introduces the duo.

The feature is but a glorified slapstickers in five reels, but as screen entertainment, regardless of the ingredients, it clicks.

"The Gay Retreat," as the title suggests, is another of those impossible war comedies. Sam Nosenblum and Ted McHiggins are the chauffeur and butler in the Wright huosehold. Young Bob Wright is refused enlistment because of somnambulistic tendencies. Through the usual hoke situations they find themselves in Flanders fields, catapulted into enemy strongholds and emerging accidental heroes.

The "situations" are variations on some tried-and-true slapstick formulae, although Director Stoloff has evolved plenty of new hokum with the author's able assistance.

After Ted and Sammy capture a Hun battalion and cop a few medals, much to the annoyance of an officious top-sergeant, the fade-out finds Sammy and his zoftig Froggy returned to America with a Junior. The kid (Sammy Cohen) is featured for some comedy horseplay, showing the comedian in miniature (camera effect) toying with the bottled product from contented cows, and featuring a shnozzle that's a replica of his pop's.

Plenty of action. Gene Cameron, Betty Francisco and Judy King, heavy mama, are adequate.

Picture is no world-beater and is not going to do more than favorably introduce McNamara and Cohen. Fox by systematic production will have to follow up the idea of putting the team across. The Fox outlets insure a cinch profit for "The Gay Retreat," which is a frugally produced feature, utilizing sets and props of a calibre and number not much beyond the character of the average Fox-Sunshine comedy. That's an idea of the production conservatism, not obvious, but economic, because nothing more was necessary. Most of it is outdoors, with a couple of interiors.

Given half a chance on script and direction McNamara and Cohen can be made an important Jewish-Irish combo of a character akin to Sidney and Murray, but not as A. K. Both are youngsters, natural in their mannerisms, with a great sense of comedy interpretation, regardless of the impossibility of the situations. They carry the elemental emotions to a degree beyond the average. When they act scared or startled or aggrieved,, their pantomime requires no titles for interpretation. That's a natural asset few comedians command.
Abel.

In Moment of Temptation

F. B. O. production and release. Directed by Philip Carle. Kit Guard featured. From story by Laura Jean Libbey. At Loew's New York theatre one-half double bill one day, Oct. 4. Running time, about 60 minutes.

Polly........................Charlotte Stevens
Ed...............................Grant Withers
Martin Breen..............Cornelius Keefe
Alice Gage..................Marie Walcamp
Blunty...............................Kit Guard
Timothy Gage................Tom Ricketts
Leetch.......................John McKinnon

This aged old story of a girl's rise to home and husband from a lowly position is different in several ways from the customary of the mush turned out by Laura Jean Libbey, the original "Confession" writer. Although the late Miss Libbey never realized that.

This story will have appeal exactly to the masses of those workers who can appreciate her position of cash or wrapping girl in a large department store. There is too little intelligence in the story to appeal to anyone else, except those who may be dumber. There should be an audience for this. With its soft sentimentality, if given another and more likeable scenario, it could have mildly attracted with all classes.

What is said in the film review of "Lightnin'" in this issue could almost be duplicated for this one as far as story is concerned. It might be slipped in that the title, "In a Moment of Temptation," doesn't mean a thing.

Laura Jean Libbey had a huge following for the sugar-coated stories of the Horatio Alger sort of girls she wrote of. In her day she was the antithesis in literature of Ouida, with the latter as popular in her style.

The brief happening here that wallops the sympathy for the girl is that after having been abused through being charged with a crime of which she was innocent she decided to go wrong. Acted as the inside agent for a crook, gaining entrance to a mansion through a window of which she was to allow the thief to enter. But a cop chased the thief away on the outside, and the girl, inside, was uncovered by a lonely old man, an invalid in a wheel chair.

The old man took a liking to the girl and believed her story. He even encouraged the young man who was to have married his niece to marry the cash girl instead. He also stated an intention of adopting her. And then permitted his niece to leave him and his home.

After that it was all applesauce, as much as it had been applesauce previously.

This situation of being in the old man's home, with the young man wooing her, is all there is to the story. The rest is the planting, including the snatching of a purse off the counter in a lively department store with the robber (the girl's sweetie) getting safely away. More applesauce.

Charlotte Stevens as the girl did her best when soulfully gazing, which was almost always. Marie Walcamp as the niece has the outstanding role, and plays it to that position as the female menace. Kit Guard is featured on some of the billing, but is in the secondary role as a genteel crook tired of the game. Grant Withers is the juvenile, doing well enough in a walk-through part. Grant Withers is the crook-sweetie, another walker.

This picture will find its place, for at least it is clean as they go nowadays. It is, for that reason mostly, given a better working out, it could have counted upon a pretty good circulation. Now it's the neighborhoods mostly where there's shop or factory hands, and probably the small towns where they don't care or wherever they don't care.
Sime.

LIGHTNING

Tiffany production and release. Directed by James C. McKay. Adapted from a Zane Grey story by John Francis Natteford. Film editor, L. O. Ludwig. Art director, George E. Sawley. George Stevens, cameraman. At Loew's New York theatre, one-half double bill one day, Oct. 4. Running time, around 60 minutes.

Mary Warren..................Jobyna Ralston
Dot Deane..............Margaret Livingston
Lee Stewart.....................Robert Frazer
Cuth Stewart..................Guinn Williams
Simon Legree....................Pat Harmon

A picture should have a little logic, and with a little of that, "Lightning" might have been a worthy release by Tiffany. As it is, it's a western "horse" picture and a first rate western, quite well produced. But it's either badly directed or was poorly adapted or was terribly written by Zane Grey in the first place. If from a Zane Grey book, it now looks impossible of having been faithfully adapted. Zane Grey is a powerful writer of the open, but this is far from a powerful picture.

It's just as well to stick in a general pan here, for both of the pictures on this day's split, the other being an FBO, suffered from the same thing—carelessness in story.

If the story in pictures is the thing after all, and producers wasted years before they decided it was, then why not give the same attention to the story before starting to make, as in the rushes afterward? Independents of the Tiffany-FBO rank have a very good economical reason for almost anything they do in picture making. Neither is getting the price for its hardily sold product that it should and probably will in time, but that is not sufficient excuse to permit a story to go to bat that has holes in it a mile wide, while some bits of direction are so negligent that a retake should have been taken.

In some of this mis-direction the actors were also at fault. Four people can't live on a desert through the night in a blinding sand and windstorm, walking or riding and not one of them have even a fleck of sand, dirt or mark on their faces the next morning. Not in the U. S. deserts. Nor can a picture make a girl steal $400 from a chump, having her look like a coin digging hustler and then expect sympathy to follow.

Nor use impossible coincidences and expect plausibility or belief. It's like impossible magical tricks—they expose themselves because they are impossible.

Here two girls to keep a show engagement in Salt Lake flew from St. Louis, the plane coming down on the desert when the pilot had to land. Here in the desert waste the two girls met the two cowboys they had frisked in a Chicago joint. With the attempted comedy here of the hands trying to boss the girls a flop in itself, as much so as their unreasonable lovemaking the next morning, without a full explanation having been made, except it stopped further production cost. The two cowboys got there through chasing a wild horse leader, "Lightning," which could be a brother of Hal Roach's "Rex." Much the same horse stuff is in this, with "Lightning" linked up with a white mare, etc. So those two cowboys chased that wild horse, possibly from Hollywood to the desert, which may be in Arizona, if that's the route from St. L. to S. L.

As a western, okay. But it could have been more with the horse attachment. Everything should be watched.

When some indes can make their $50,000 feature films look 50 per cent as well at least as the $200,000 programmers from the ritzy producers, it's worth watching, no matter what the picture may cost.

Nothing about the title. "Lightnin'" was made and sent through so long ago that "Lightning" here means nothing but "Lightning" outside of the trade.

Some splendid backgrounds, an excellent cabaret scene, with a little bit of the "Uncle Tom" travesty worth while. Production all right right along, including the small time sand storm.

Neither Miss Ralston nor Miss Livingston could be "sweet" because the storm prevented; it made them raw and uncouth, especially Miss Livingston, who copped. Mr. Williams, as the gun toting cowboy, did too much mugging and was never funny, while his side partner, Mr. Frazer, was the reverse, too reserved. Pat Harmon got program mention for a four-second bit. His name must be worth a lot—somewhere.
Sime.

NAUGHTY

First Division Picture. Produced by I. E. Chadwick. Principal players, Pauline Garon, Johnny Harron and Walter Hiers. Directed by Hampton Del Ruth. At Loew's Circle theatre, New York, Sept. 26, half of double feature, one day. Running time, 53 mins.

"Naughty" is a jellyfish affair, that could have been told in two reels and with little or no moral and withal a feeble attempt to make a feature out of a very thin bit of scenario fabric.

A girl is told by a fortune-teller that she will go on a vacation, meet a doctor, fall in love with him and so on. She does.

They are married by a burglar in a minister's garb. They go home and the husband is called away by the very same burglar and a fat boy friend spends the night there, as hubby is out in a driving rain in his car. He and the wifey are shown together in several scenes, each in sleeping attire, pajamas to be explicit and a lead up to where the wife taps on the wall for the fat boy to come to her room. He does and even edges close to her bed at her request, only to be told there's a man under the bed. Hubby returns. Friend is holding wifey who has fainted.

The mistaken situation gag with the captured burglar helping straighten things.

It has nothing to commend it anywhere beyond a very fine rain nicely photographed. The naughty idea is slowly worked up to and even then it doesn't cause any undue excitement. The cheap magazines tell a whole lot more and don't mince so much in the telling.

One can scarcely believe his eyes in the change in Pauline Garon, who plays the wife. Not long ago this little blondy miss was acquiring avoirdupois that was slowing up her impressions of former days. But she has grown almost as thin as her days before pictures. And she is really more like the Garon of yore.

Johnny Harron as the hubby tries his best, aided by a man-sized upper lip adornment. Walter Hiers was the fat boy. The usual Hiers maneuvers, grimaces and gestures.

This picture just about does a nose dive through its palpably weak story.
Mark.

The Lady from Paris

American premiere of a foreign feature produced by Gloria Films, directed by Menfred Noa, Vilma Banky starred; at the Edith Byron Totten theatre (capacity 250), Sept. 25, 1927. Released by Nathan Hirsh of Agwon Co. Running time, 72 mins.

Yvonne Barron...............Vilma Banky
Valescu ....Ernest Reicher
Prince ....Gibson Thane
Bobby Miller.............George Alexander
Sadie ....Valerie Ward

The little Edith Totten theatre on 48th street, west of Broadway, after a series of theatrical vicissitudes in attempting to fit a house of 250 capacity into the frantic competition of Broadway, opens with a film policy somewhat a la 55th Street Cinema and the Fifth Avenue Playhouse. The policy is foreign films, first runs desired; the prices, 50 cents top weekday afternoons, 75 cents evenings and all day Saturday and Sunday.

There is no "presentation" of any sort. The fifth Avenue has a three-piece orchestra and individual titles, smoking lobbies, free cigarets and orange drinks. No lobby or anteroom at the Toten house. Just straight projection with an organ, very good instrument and very well handled by a girl billed as Eopy. In so tiny an inclosure the vibrant and reverberant organ is emphasized, and pleasantly so.

"In "The Lady from Paris" (not to be confused with Chaplin's "A Woman of Paris") Miss Totten has not made an entirely happy pick. From the wardrobe revealed it is likely that this European opus first saw the light of projection about six or seven years ago. Photography is of the poorer foreign grade, the direction is awkward and raw, and the cast, even including the skittish Vilma, is inartistic. In appearance the cast is far easier on the eye than most of the troupes on the other side. In acting, no improvement.

The story is a wild hysteria of coincidences, doubles, master-mind crooks, disappearances, disguises, fiendish and diabolical double-crosses and a gallant prince.

The girl is a mysterious party, in cahoots with the super-thief, yet the savior of the prince, whom she grabs off for herself. It is dubious whether it was on the strength of this endeavor that Miss Banky got the call to Hollywood, the Mecca and Golconda of the movies. Anyway, Manfred Noa, director, seems to be still cupping his hand to his ear in anticipation of his. If he waits on what his 7-reeler exposes he'd beter get a stout prop for his elbow.

Whether the screen, the projection or only the film was poor material, the result as it danced about before the eyes of the beholders was reminiscent of the early Keystones in optical reaction. The blacks were grey, the whites were muddy. The shooting in the first place was none too slick. Nor was the scenic background conducive of many interludes where Nature's lighting would have helped. Almost entirely indoor, and shoddy indoor at that, sets. The economy exercised is painfully obvious, though this flicker cost far more than most of the recently imported old-timers from over there.

Business Sunday at the peak of the evening was heart-breaking. There were scarcely 10 people in. That means little, however, as the house had just opened with its new attraction, and it is so small that it cannot profitably go into extensive display advertising. Miss Totten may put this over as Mike Mindlin, with much better facilities and far smarter treatment but nowhere near as strong a location, has surely done. *Lait.*

WILD BEAUTY

Universal-Jewel production and release, starring Rex, horse. Principal players, June Marlowe and Hugh Allen. Story by Sylvia Seid. Directed by Henry MacRae. At Loew's Circle, New York, Monday, Sept. 26, as part of double feature. Running time, 60 minutes.

Same Rex of Pathe (Roach) days, yet in this U horse special is another animal that shows remarkable horse training and at times takes all the thunder away from Rex. This other equine actor or actress, as the picture gives it, is named Valerie, and shows bully training.

It is along the lines of other wild horse films, with a love story attached that holds interest. Both look well and ride well. June Marlowe in particular registers effectively. She is graceful in movement and apparently rides as though she had trained well.

There are some very pretty shots and, though footage must be allowed for the wild horses to show their stuff, there are some exciting moments for the lovers of melodrama. The stampede of horses, with the heroine on foot before the onrushing animals, was not only splendidly staged, but camaraed effectively.

Rex makes himself as wild as anyone would have a horse of that calibre behave. The fight scenes between the horses may be phoney balony, but they pack a lot of realism just the same.

There is villainy afoot, but none of it reaches the knock-em-down-and-carry-em-out phases.

A horse race is well done. It's a cross-country affair, and sustained interestingly and a help to the film.

The plot's a little thin, but, as vaporish as it may be, the work of those two horses, Rex and Valerie, bear watching.

Unquestionably a nice frame for the neighborhoods and where they know more about horses than they do about autos, this one will prove all the more popular. The kiddies will like this one. *Mark.*

THE RED RAIDERS

First National production, starring Ken Maynard. Directed by Albert Rogell from Marion Jackson's story. At the Hippodrome, New York, week Sept. 26. Running time, about 65 mins.

Typical screen yarn of the settling of the west when some Indians were bad. Certain army officers did nothing to impede the Red Man's destructive tendencies, and these factions always seemed to get together. Looks like a three-day prospect for those spots where they never tire of the plains and horses. Otherwise one day is plenty.

No direct or drastic villainy here and less of a love theme than that. Therefore it's mostly Maynard's riding on "Tarzan" and the to-be-expected Indian attack on the stockade, which arrives on time. Okay, too, after it gets started, but too long getting there. Meanwhile there is comedy from the troopers, some of which clicks.

The thin love thread makes the girl a negligible personality. Nary a member of the cast is really called upon to "troupe." High spots are Maynard's riding of a bronc, supposedly "Tarzan," but an instance of where a horse can have a double as well, and the previously mentioned Indian offensive against the settlers with Maynard bringing the troops back at the gallop to save the burning situation.

Everything takes place outdoors, with the cameraman taking advantage of the exterior opportunities. Chase and battle stuff has been well photographed, plus some of the falls from horseback worth a gasp or two.

Punch is in the second half of the film, and if it had a story behind it "Red Raiders" would be worth while.

Maynard had one at this house not so long ago worthy of Broadway showing. But the Main Stem is off westerns. This one isn't that good, although Maynard's horsemanship will get over if they'll put something else besides that asset in the making. *Sid.*

THE FAKE

Film version of Frederick Lonsdale's play. Produced by Neo-Art, England. Adapted by George A. Cooper and directed by Georg Jacoby. Running time, 96 mins. At the New Gallery, London, Sept. 9.

Geoffrey Sands..............Henry Edwards
Ernest Stanton, M. P....Norman McKinnell
Mavis Stanton..................Elga Brink
Hon. Gerrard Pillick.........Miles Mander

When the censor has passed this it will certainly get a West End pre-release. Yet if it had been made in the States there would have been a howl here at making a Member of Parliament—and a Peer—a "fake" who sacrifices his daughter to a degenerate, said booze and dope fiend being a member of the English aristocracy. We can do this, but you mustn't unless you want to get slammed for Anglophobia.

Direction and female lead are both German. This was in consideration of an advance against distribution in Germany, but it is understood the German firm making the arrangement cannot come through with the money after all.

Outstanding points are Mander's acting. He hogs the film all through with a great performance as the brutal husband who sinks lower and lower till he dies of an overdose given by wife's tame friend. Henry Edwards, as the latter, is too restrained, making the character priggish. Elga Brink gets by, but she is not another German find. Not a good looker, and no pep, besides being a bit too big physically.

Photography and direction outstanding. Cabaret scenes some of the best ever done.

Appeal abroad on title mainly—till they see it, and then on direction. Mander's acting the real high spot, but none of the cast known in America. Most female fans prefer dissolute husbands to be regenerated by love or else replaced by a he-man. In this case the injured wife is left flat. But it will book big here.

Hollywood doesn't make them better than this.

THE GHOST TRAIN

Adapted from Arnold Ridley's play. Produced by C. M. Woolf. Directed by G. Bolvary. Running time, 84 mins. London Hippodrome, Sept. 13.

Teddie Deakin.................Guy Newall
Saul Hodgkin..................Louis Ralph
Charles Murdock.............John Manners
Peggy Murdock...............Anna Jennings
Richard Winthrop...........Ernest Verebes
Elsie Winthrop............Agnes Kerolenko
Miss Bourne........................Ilse Bois

Getting films into the Continent by using a mixed cast and a foreign director is becoming a fashion. This one has an Austrian director, two Germans and a Hungarian in the cast. One of them, Ilse Bois, is the hit of the film as a female temperance reformer who gets lit up by emptying the hero's flask believing it to be medicine. A great comedienne.

There is a lot of good trick stuff—traveling dissolves from close-up to mid to long-shot, and some effective overlapped close-ups. Camera work on the whole reminiscent of "Variety" in effects, but clearer and sharper.

Direction and acting very good. Railroad stuff excellent and in spots novel, but some "ghost" shots of trains very fakey.

Will clean up here. Women bookers at pre-view were on their toes for it. Ought to be good for America if well exploited. Plenty of angles, and the picture will stand up to boosting.

In an already over-long series of war films this stands out as ambitious in scope and historical fact. It places on record for the first time a battle front hitherto unused filmographically and an episode of the war which, though soon forgotten in the greater issues, did much to mould the future course of the world struggle.

Big moments are when the smoke of guns blows away and men lie still, in shattered heaps on sinking decks and around the twisted chaos of turrets. It is patriotic to the 'nth degree, and will probably gross nearly as much over here as "Ben-Hur." But its value in other markets is problematical.

As an essay in the soulless mechanics of naval warfare and as a contribution to English history it is outstanding. As a contribution to motion picture history it offers little.

HER DISCRETION

Biltmore Production directed by Herbert F. Jans. Based on the novel by Hamilton Thompson. Featuring May Allison and Mahlon Hamilton. At the Columbus, New York, one day, Sept. 8.

Resembles a series of slides more than a motion picture. The story is unraveled with monotonous detail through a procession of still scenes aided and abetted by equally dull titles.

It is obvious that the directorial wand was decidedly uninspired in addition to being curbed through limited cost. While the story is not above average merit, independent producers have been turning out better pictures with lesser material.

The country maiden, wife of the captain of the U. S. Coast Guard, is meant to be a simple, unassuming miss. But not slovenly. May Allison, in ground length skirts, looks far older than she really is. Faulty make-up and bad camera studies influence her appearance unfavorably.

The strong, silent, powerful hero-husband (believe it or not) is endowed with the name of Trueman Tisdale. As such his sole endeavors along the line of husbandly protection are limited to a furrowing of the manly brows and a steely look in the grayish eyes. Even when his talkative ma tells him the young wife has been spotted in the arms of a gent named Nate, his noble nature forbids him from registering anything more potent than a puzzled, uncomprehending look.

This picture has the unique but doubtful distinction of telling the climax in titles. The wife's flight to Boston from the tiny seaport is explained in a note to Trueman. The villain's attempt to attack her is roughly told in a letter to her girl friend. The husband's trip to Boston and his return with wifie is limited to the captions. There is not even mention of a scrap with the betrayer.

For the clincher Nate is again shown following the girl through fields of new mown daisies. As he attempts to seize her, Trueman just reaching the top of the cliff, Martha turns on him fiercely, saying. "I am true to my man. If it would add one day to his life I would kill you." And with that devastating remark she daintily gathered up her skirts in her dimpled fingers and resumed her light, mincing trot across the field.

Nate remained stunned for fully a second as a result of the crushing attack and then, screwing his mustache (he had a mustache) more tightly to his sneering lips, resumed his chase.

Neither the man nor woman wanted to shoot Nate more than once. While they were arguing about who should do it Nate climbed onto a cheap young tree, placed near the brink of the cliff, and crashed to the rocks below as the weak sapling yielded.

To assure the customers there would be no excuse for an arrest someone sent two fishermen to the spot just as Nate fell.

THE KID SISTER

Columbia picture directed by Ralph Graves from story by Dorothy Howell. Photographed by J. O. Taylor. At the Stanley, New York, Sept. 21. Running time, 63 mins.

Helen Hall........Marguerite de La Motte
Mary Hall.......................Ann Christy
Thomas Weber..........Malcolm MacGregor
Ted Hunter.................Brooks Bennedict

A film that will entertain middle class picture audiences but cannot stand up in the better houses. Marguerite de La Motte and Malcolm MacGregor, the leads, are sufficiently known to exert a draw.

There is unusual flash because of the theatrical angle. Miss La Motte, the elder sister, is a "Follies" girl who steadfastly walks home from auto rides. Her kid sister comes to New York on a visit, and with intent to cut up. She meets a bozo on the make, and gets into a roadhouse brawl when the guy starts his pawing.

The elder sister is having an honest affair with one of the stagehands who, unknown to her, is a millionaire paying the stage manager to let him work. Later she finds out he's rich and throws him down. But when her sister gets into the jam and needs $5,000 bail she agrees to let the millionaire walk in if he'll pay the ball.

The rich youngster accepts the bargain and balls the sister out. Then he takes the other sister to his house, leads her upstairs, takes her into a bedroom, and introduces her to his mother.

There is backstage stuff, cabaret scenes, and shots inside the theatre. The story is slow in unwinding but has its sex interest to hold.

Miss La Motte and MacGregor are capable in the minor acting required.

Ann Christy, the younger sister, has a pep personality well suited for this role.

Fair direction and competent photography.

THE GIRL FROM RIO

Gotham production released by Lumas. Directed by Tom Terris. Story by Norman Kellogg. Presented by Sam Sax. Carmel Myers starred. Walter Pidgeon, Mildred Harris, Richard Tucker, Edouard Raquello. Running time, 61 mins. At Loew's New York, Sept. 23, on double feature bill.

The directorial methods of Tom Terris include a pronounced penchant for semi-long shots and fadeouts. Both procedures keep "The Girl from Rio" in the magic lantern class. At times beautiful effects are achieved. There are moments that look class and should impress customers. But never is there enough drama to blow up a ripple in a tea cup.

Carmel Myers is featured as a Brazilian coquette who falls for a young English coffee buyer. The coquette lives in great opulence under the patronage of the richest man in Rio de Janeiro. He threatens to be nasty when she gives him air, but ends by sending she and her boy friend off to England with his blessing. Nothing is ever very clear except that the richest man in Rio must have been a terrible boob.

The picture contains an opening stanza in technicolor and much soft focus photography. Neither will compensate patrons for the almost total lack of action or suspense. The acting is competent.

OUT ALL NIGHT

Universal release starring Reginald Denny. Directed by William Seiter from an original story by Gladys Lehman. Running time, 65 mins. At Colony, New York, week Sept. 24.
John Graham................Reginald Denny
Molly O'Day................Marian Nixon
Dr. Allen................Ben Hendricks, Jr.
Uncle Billy................Dan Mason
Rose Lunde................Dorothy Earle
Chief Officer................Lionel Braham
Purser................Robert Seiter
M. S. Kerrigan................Wheeler Oakman

They'll laugh at and like "Out All Night." They may also notice that Seiter, directing, has been extremely careless in certain details and has permitted extraneous matter to mar the smooth running of the farce.

There was, for instance, the scene where Dan Mason, bearded and aged about 60, fell on the floor weeping because his niece would not sign a theatrical contract which held a clause forfeiting a $100,000 bonus if she married during its life.

There are other badly handled details and inexcusable discrepancies not heretofore identified with the well-oiled Denny farces directed by Seiter.

The picture emerges, however, as a good laugh getter along conventional Denny lines and can be recommended as a probable moneymaker.

Sailor's Sweetheart

Warners' production and release. Comedy starring Louise Fazenda and Clyde Cook. Story by George Godfrey; scenario by Harvey Gates; directed by Lloyd Bacon. Running time, 52 minutes (5,685 feet). Released Sept. 24.
Cynthia Botts................Louise Fazenda
Sandy McTavish................Clyde Cook
Claudette Ralston................Myrna Loy
Detective................William Demarest
Mark Krisel................John Miljan
Lena Svenson................Dorothea Wolbert

Knockabout comedy is amusingly maintained for a bit less than formal feature length, subject always to the fact that it is extremely difficult to hold up knockabout beyond the usual two-reel extent. They succeed here rather better than usual, thanks to fast chase action, knockabout stunt stuff and farcical complications, all strung on a light thread of story and helped by the familiar character types of Cook and Miss Fazenda.

Production goes to ambitious lengths. One sequence takes place on a big ocean liner about to sail. It is here that the farce story is briskly planted, going promptly into the old Keystone technique, time-tried and accident-proof.

Miss Fazenda plays the comic old maid—plays it with all the low comedy trimmings, but manages to get into it something of a sympathetic equality. Cook is always the clown, his comedy coming entirely from his own grotesque acrobatics.

Picture is one long chase. Pretty nearly all long comedies are. But it is split into fragmentary chases. One time it is a prying old man spying upon Louise, who by an accident has a man in her bedroom. Another time it is Cook's efforts to escape a bulldog. Of course, the old maid gets drunk unintentionally. No old maid farce would be complete without this formal incident. But here for once they don't overdo it and it has materials for genuine comedy.

Cynthia, spinster school teacher, is lured into a marriage by a designing sheik, but discovers his true character as they are about to sail. She falls overboard and is rescued by one of the sailors. The pair of them are picked up by a bootlegger gang, and after many adventures with coast guards find themselves free, but handcuffed to each other.

They gain Cynthia's home, stealing into the spinster's bedroom. The sheik husband pursues, and, catching up, is exposed as a bigamist, leaving Cynthia and her sailor lover to make a match of it.

Program picture standing up for ordinary uses on the strength of its low comedy hoke.   *Rush.*

GALLOPING THUNDER

F.B.O. western starring Bob Custer. Directed by Jack Nelson. Richard Neil, Frederick Lee in cast. Running time, 54 mins. At Tivoli, New York, Sept. 21.

Typical western and will please western fans. A well, if cheaply, made picture, with action aplenty.

It's the familiar yarn of the wolf in sheep's clothing, the friend of the family secretly plotting to steal the gold shipment. He does steal it and his henchmen are guarding the express car containing the bullion. The car on the downgrade while the villain is inside wrestling with the heroine and the hero is on top of the car.

Lots of horses, some humor, and an appealing blonde heroine.

BORDER CAVALIER

Universal production and release, starring Fred Humes, western. Story by Basil Dickey. Directed by William Wyler. In cast: Joyce Compton, lead; Ethel Pierce and cowboy group. Running time, 55 minutes. Half double feature bill at New York, New York, one day, Oct. 7.

Spirited filming of the oldest of old stuff. Whole formula is here: land shark, cow country divekeeper, hard-riding hero, honest rancher and beautiful daughter, not to speak of the dance hall girl.

These materials are spread out over a workmanlike production, attempting nothing elaborate, but making a simple tale interesting enough by its direct telling, with plenty of hard riding, abundance of hand-to-hand fisticuffs and a flavoring of honest comedy, supplied by the cowboy band.

Plot and counterplot are fast enough to give the effect of a chase, and any western that has the chase technique can't miss with those addicted to this type.   *Rush.*

THE RING

London, Oct. 4.
Original story by Alfred J. Hitchcock. Produced by British International Pictures. Directed by A. J. Hitchcock. Running time; 100 minutes. Preview, Capitol theatre, London, Sept. 30.
"One Round" Jack Sander....Carl Brisson
The Girl................Lilian Hall-Davis
Bob Corby................Ian Hunter
George................Gordon Harker
The Showman................Harry Terry
The Promoter................Forrester Harvey

Hailed as the greatest British film yet produced, this picture merits unusual attention for many reasons. It is the first offer from Elstree since those studios were taken over and reorganized by British International Productions. It is, at last, the performance of the long-deferred "promise" of Hitchcock, and it is an intelligent contribution to the effort of this country to produce real motion pictures.

This is not to say it is a superfilm. Outside its newspaper-made boom in the home market, which will create a huge demand for it in the boxoffice—and rightly so—it is hardly more than a good program picture, looked at from first-class American standards.

For the story is trite and not too convincing, and the cast does not contain a name known to the American "fan." That is not an insuperable difficulty, for Jannings and Negri were unknown when "Passion" was first put on Broadway. But the climax of the story, when the young wife leaves her husband, aspirant for heavyweight honors, apparently to go to the man who holds the title, and then calmly returns to hubby when he has become champ, is likely to tax the credulity and offend the moral traditions of screen heroines in the eyes of the American moviegoer.

Circus booth, training quarters and ringside sequences are remarkably well handled, one shot in the latter being a striking lesson to the German school of the way in which symbolism can be allied to reality. Hero gets the K. O., falling on his back. The familiar German screenful of whirling spots is cut in. But they sort themselves out, become less and less defined as mere spots and finally come into focus as the arc lights on the roof of the hall.

A noticeable point of direction is the use of trick endings and openings to sequences in place of fades or cuts. In some cases this is achieved by throwing the scene out of focus and picking up the next sequence out also; in others by traveling the camera right up to a wall or a character's back till the screen is blotted out, then traveling it away till the next scene comes clear in.

Carl Brisson, known here and on the Continent as a musical comedy star, is overshadowed by the acting of the heavy, Ian Hunter, who, thinned down a bit physically, could be put over as a world star with little difficulty. He is a first-rate film actor with an engaging he-man personality and a strong flapper appeal.

Gordon Harker, on the screen for the first time, nearly steals this one as a hard-boiled cynical trainer. His sense of screen comedy is acute and restrained at the same time, and he makes his points with lips and eyes in a notable fashion. He is a comedy Tully Marshall.

Hitchcock gets more out of Lilian Hall-Davis than any Continental director has yet done, and at times makes her reminiscent of Lya de Putti. But the story gives her a rather unsympathetic and incredulous role and her sudden revulsion in favor of friend husband is not too convincing.

Photography by John Cox is first-rate, trick and effect stuff well-nigh perfect.

Bob Corby visits a circus, sees a girl at a boxing booth paybox, and falls in love. He is persuaded to go in and K. O.'s the hero, "One Round" Jack in four rounds. Bob and his manager disclose their identity, and Jack gets a job as sparring partner. He aspires to championship honors. Meantime his wife, former paybox girl, flirts with Bob.

Jack gets into the last eliminating contest, becomes chesty and objects to wife's goings on. She walks out on him, and at the fight for the championship turns up to jeer. Her sympathies revert to husband when she sees him getting a lacing. She goes to his corner and eggs him into winning, and he knocks Bob out.

Sheer hokum, and hoked heavily by the director in parts. The circus atmosphere and the excellence of the ring scenes, some of the best ever done yet, will get it over.

"The Ring" has been received with loud cheers by the press here. While most of the expressions err on the side of generosity it is perhaps good they should. The film is a distinct effort to make good here as a producing center, and so ought to be welcomed to the full.

There is a big angle in this film, exploited the right way, for America: its complete difference from Hollywood product. It rather gains than loses in drama and suspense by the absence of glittering artificiality. Hitchcock may be classed as a leading exponent of the "naturalistic" school, for his methods make the action seem to be happening in fact rather than to have been staged.

This "entertainment plus difference" appears to be an asset for the American market.

JESSE JAMES

Paramount production and release. Fred Thomson featured. Directed by Lloyd Ingraham. Story by Frank M. Clinton. Biographer and technical advisor, Jesse E. James. At the Rialto, New York, starting Oct. 15, on run. Running time, 75 minutes.

Jesse James....................Fred Thomson
Zerelda Mimms....................Nora Lane
Frederick Mimms............Montagu Love
Mrs. Zerelda Samuels..........Mary Carr
Frank James....................James Pierce
Bob Ford........................Harry Woods
Parson Bill............William Courtwright

Exhibitors away from the western classification of house and with a possible draw from the nice people in any town, had better look at "Jesse James" before playing it. It's not for the nice people; they will resent this picture and its idea if not scheme of cleansing Jesse James. It's strictly a film for the roughnecks and the gallery. The larger the town or city with its larger motley crew of gangsters, stick-ups, dips and crooks in general, the larger will be its draw from amongst that lot.

That a bad man can be a good man only when he's a dead man may be Paramount's excuse to turn out "Jesse James" as the reason to charge more for Fred Thomson as a western actor than FBO did when Fred Thomson made westerns without disguise. "Jesse James" is a camouflaged western, but nevertheless a western, of superior production for that type of picture. That it has been sent into Publix Rialto, New York, for a special 99c. run doesn't alter the fact.

Paramount looks to have taken a long chance on censure and censor in the attempt to idealize this gunman, robber and murderer, Jesse James. He was probably the first gangster in America following the civil war, having aptly graduated from a band of cutthroats. Here the film tries to square Jesse James, having little to do or say or show with his brother, Frank James, as notorious. The James brothers were known 30 to 40 years ago, with but little difference between the two in their evilness, although Jesse was looked upon as the leader of his brother and of their band of robbers and murderers.

The James brothers terrorized their state (Missouri) for years, yet Paramount in "Jesse James" would present that life taker in a heroic frame. Not only that, but here they have a northern girl of gentle breeding falling in love with him, refusing to expose him as a southern spy while she was in the home of her scheming southern uncle, then occupied by northern officers. And afterward, when he went into banditry, brazenly and boldly, and without the slight justification this picture attempts to forward, she continued to love him, and according to the picture married him, or was with him at his violent death.

In this picture Jesse is seen brought in dead, on a stretcher, with Parson Bill, in the room, remarking on a caption, "Jesse was wrong and he had to go this way." The previous view on the screen was Jesse avowing his love for the northern girl, who remained south after the war, ostensibly from the picture, to be near Jesse. He said, at that avowal he was not in a position to mention his love. Therefore, it must have been a long jump from that scene until his death. Which may have been a part cut out. It also gives the poorest and most abrupt finish to a long picture the screen has had for years.

It is mentioned and programmed that Jesse E. James, presumably a close relative of either of the James boys, had been the biographer or advisor for the picture. Therefore it may be assumed he was prejudiced.

Thomson as Jesse James seems always poised for a pose toward the heroic, volunteering during the war when of Quarntrell's Guerrillas (Confederate and most terrible of all guerrillas), as a spy, and to hardly carry the southern flag to the top of a crest shelled by the union forces. This portion was a sloppy bit of direction, although direction otherwise generally good and ofttimes excellent.

Even Quantrell's Guerrillas are made to shine as "gentlemen" when in swimming au naturel and informed a couple of "young ladies" were also in the water on the opposite side of the stream. These "Southern gentlemen" then scrambled for the shore and clambered into their clothes, while the two girls, clad Quakerish and mumbling about one showing an ankle beneath a bathing suit, meanwhile carrying parasols as they bathed, also ran out of the water toward their home.

Which is or may be not historically correct in this besodden picture. You tell.

Jesse James or his band may be seen here holding up trains, stage coaches or robbing banks. Always outright thievery, and no effort to coat it with the Robin Hood charitable system.

The love story may have been intended for the principal squarer, but whatever merit that tale may have will also be resented by nice people of the North, for the Northern girl is dragged ahead, with and behind Jesse James throughout. Not only did she protect him as a spy but as an outlaw.

Dick Turpin or Capt. Kidd, though either or both a legend, at least had some romanticism for a background.

This is Thomson's first for Paramount. He was slipped over to Par by F. B. O. on some kind of a deal. Thomson may have reserved the right to select his own subjects and may have picked Jesse James, but Paramount will have to stand for it. He plays Jesse in his customary manful way, but he will be unable to get away from the impression held by all elders in this country of Jesse James, the bandit. Thomson is not picturesque, although he tries for that in appearance, including short side burns and dress, while the uniform of the Quantrell's Guerrillas, probably that at least accurate, is something akin to a Robin Hood make-up in the feathered cap, anyway.

Montagu Love is the heavy heavy here, and first heavy, since Jesse James is also a menace, though juvenile. Love is Frederick Slade in character, who always is seeking to frame Jesse, of whom he is in constant dread. Love gives an excellent performance, always in character and always in looks. Frank James is played by James Pierce, a negligible role, while Harry Woods as Bob Ford did well enough in everything but make-up; he was a bit too dandified for Missouri in 1866. William Courtwright is Parson Bill, making it a worthwhile characterization and with some prominence.

Nora Lane is the Northern girl (Zerelda Mimms) and appears to have implicitly followed directions. That is probably a virtue in Hollywood by itself. Mary Carr is her usual mother.

An air of bravado is given to the picture by the acrobatic Thomson, who is also an actor. That bravado is not warranted if he took from outlawry from force of circumstance, but, if, as seems true, that Jesse James was a bandit in his heart, with his companions and in his life, then that bravado but bears that out.

For "western" houses and audiences, a pushover; for nice houses, caution; for the gallery anywhere, some appeal, and for the picture industry—not so good.

"Daniel Boone" probably never got its production half way back. "Underworld" will make a barrel of money. And "Underworld" is an underworld picture; it sets forth a condition that exists. That's the excuse for underworld pictures, even those made by the Germans.

But it's a matter of judgment whether advisable to rewrite a murderer into a hero.

For this is an uncalled for, useless and dangerous story of "Jesse James" on the screen. *Sime.*

East Side, West Side

Fox production and release. Directed by Allan Dwan. Based on the novel by Felix Riesenberg, adapted by Alan Dwan. Starring George O'Brien, Virginia Valli featured. At the Roxy, New York, week Oct. 15. Running time, over 60 minutes.

John Breen....................George O'Brien
Becka..........................Virginia Valli
Pug Malone............J. Farrell Macdonald
Channon Lipvitch..............Dore Davidson
Mrs. Lipvitch................Sonia Nodalsky
Josephine........................June Collyer
Gerrit Rantoul..................John Miltern
Gilbert Van Horn............Holmes Herbert
Judge Kelly.....................Frank Dodge
Grogan..........................Dan Wolheim
One of Grogan's Gang..........John Dooley
Policeman......................John Kearney
Fight Second..................Edward Garvey
"Flash"......................Frank Allsworth
Engineer.....................Gordon MacRae
Engineer.......................Harold Levett

Not strong enough to stand up alone in the first runs for a full week.

Picture has been directed with an apparent indifference or worse. The story is jumpy, incoherent and at no time interesting. This is the impression given by the screen treatment.

Miss Valli hardly gives the impression, on the screen, that she could torment anyone sufficiently to cause — well, what happened. Miss Collyer, in the first few side shots, looks too mature for comfort. After turned down by Miss Collyer, the second woman in the case, George O'Brien goes out on a drunk, leaving everyone to guess whether he was hurt or happy. If it were left to the judgment of the customers the majority vote might be that he was happy.

Far too many subtitles. Too much conversation to explain circumstances and situations which would be received more readily if handled in the subtle manner they should have been.

A good-sized laugh where O'Brien has punched his ring opponent into insensibility when the latter is suddenly transported to another world, attired in a green velveteen coat and Robin Hood hat surrounded by a group of dancing nymphs. Then he is carried out of the ring.

Title sounds good and a picture built up on the lines suggested by the title might have clicked. The story opens on the riverfront, with John Breen (Mr. O'Brien), his mother and stepfather living on a brick barge. The barge is wrecked, the parents drown and the boy gets to the city he has dreamed of living in. He is also determined to find his own father, who allowed his family to send the boy's mother away because she didn't fit into the circle.

Breen becomes a pretty good prizefighter after being virtually adopted by Van Horn, who is in reality the father. But Breen becomes tired of punching mugs around the ring and is given a chance by Van Horn to become a builder. Following are shots of Breen going down 'way under the earth to dig up dirt. It isn't very interesting after the prizefighting racket. And a little more s. a. in **the picture and less dirt would have been better.**

In the attempt to use all of the story material the result is a series of unconnected incidents rather than a closely knit whole. Lacks conviction and doesn't seem likely to attract patronage.

TELL IT TO SWEENEY

Paramount production and release. Directed by Gregory La Cava, featuring Chester Conklin and George Bancroft. Story by Percy Heath and Monte Brice. Adapted by Percy Heath and Kerry Clark. Running time, 62 minutes. At Paramount, New York, week Oct. 15.

Luke Beamish..................Chester Conklin
Cannonball Casey..........George Bancroft
Jack Sweeney.....................Jack Luden
Doris Beamish......................Doris Hill
Supt. Dugan...................Franklin Bond
Old Man Sweeney.......William H. Tooker

The locale of a railroad furnishes the inspiration for a succession of gags, stunts and more gags as the peg upon which to hang the laughable comedy of Chester Conklin. It's a shrewdly managed piece of work. It has wealth of action of a more or less dramatic nature, but nothing is allowed to interfere with the laugh-provoking genius of the imbecilic Conklin.

As a serious-minded, sentimental and altogether dumbbell railroad engineer Conklin is as funny as he ever has been, his funniments being heightened by the hair-breath escapes through which he passes, all the time in a sort of waking daze.

A capital foil for the weazened Conklin is the burly George Bancroft, a rival engineer on the line and suitor for Conklin's daughter. These two divide their attention between fighting and helping each other through a five-reel series of marvelous misadventures, all growing up into a climactic maze of nonsense when they are driving an engine on a vital race against time, and still carrying on their feud.

The trick of this elaborate comedy situation is that it has all the obvious paraphernalia of a railroad melodrama, while the characters go through their thrilling experiences in the manner of Keystone comedians. Effect is rich burlesque.

Whole story is told in that spirit. There is a romantic sub-plot that contributes rather than rivals the comic element. Conklin's daughter is in love with the railroad superintendent's son, while the towering **Bancroft seeks the girl's favor. Bancroft is the road's champion wrestler, and the super's son is lured into challenging him to a contest at the picnic. Looks like a play for romantic interest when the two get together, but instead a surprise twist brings the shrimp-like Conklin into the match against the bulky Bancroft for a laughing explosion.**

This low comedy scene is well worked up. Conklin has bet his roll on his daughter's sweetheart, and when he is absent chooses to go into the ring to save his bet. When he is getting the worst of the battle he steps aside to confer with the bookmaker on a proposition of getting a bet down on his antagonist. It is of such stuff that the picture is made

In the end Conklin wins the wrestling match because, when it grows into a cross-country chase, Bancroft rolls down a hill and knocks himself unconscious just as Conklin falls on top of him.

And so the picture resolves itself into a Keystone of feature length, packed full of laughs and holding interest to the end. The railroad train stunt stuff is amusing from its speed and the unflagging ingenuity of absurd twists.

A fast laughfest that will reach all classes of fans. *Rush.*

SPRING FEVER

M-G-M production directed by Edward Sedgwick. William Haines starred; Joan Crawford and George K. Arthur featured. Vincent Lawrence's play adapted for screen by Albert Lewin and Frank Davies; titles by Ralph Spence. Running time, 60 minutes. At Capitol, New York, week Oct. 15.
Jack Kelly ....William Haines
Allie Monte...................Joan Crawford
Eustace Tewksbury......George K. Arthur
Mr. Waters.................George Fawcett
Martha Lomsdon.............Eileen Percy
Johnson.......................Edward Earle
Pop Kelly...................Bert Woodruff
Oscar...........................Lee Moran

Elevated to stardom, William Haines is seen in a type of harmlessly egotistic character akin to his "Slide, Kelly, Slide," the baseball picture. Haines is labeled Kelly in this exposition of the guid auld Scotch game of golluf.

Golf theme is put on a bit too thick. Despite the pleasant qualities of the plot and production, there's too much stance and niblick to "Spring Fever" for it to bogey with the general run of film fans.

Haines is a likable personality and should travel far. This picture, however, will not help him much.

As Jack Kelly, our hero is introduced as a golf bug and a wiz on the course. His boss is another addict but n. s. g. at it. Kelly shows him a few things about putting, driving, etc. The long and short of it finds Kelly somewhat of a favorite in the packing business where he was a lowly shipping clerk.

The Old Man gets Kelly a guest card at an exclusive golf club and in the brief two weeks of the shipping clerk's vacation he woos and wins Joan Crawford and generally slays the femmes with his golfing prowess. It more than fulfills his bragadoccio at the game.

The atmosphere has gone to Kelly's head. Impressed with the convenience of the idle rich he poses as one of them. After eloping with Miss Crawford who was somewhat enamoured with the golf pro of the club, Kelly confesses on their wedding night that he is not what he seems. The punch is derived from a crucial championship game for a $10,000 purse, with the heroine turning up to cheer Haines to victory.

There isn't much punch to "Spring Fever," and the premise of misleading a rich girl into a marriage under false pretenses, despite the ensuing confession, is not well-founded for popular appeal.

The players do well all around and Ralph Spence's titles contribute effectively on the comedy end, but the director, Sedgwick, could not cope with a weak theme. "Spring Fever" is from Vincent Lawrence's play of that name, a very light comedy. *Abel.*

PUBLICITY MADNESS

Fox production and release. Directed by Albert Ray. From story by Anita Loos.

Running time, 60 mins. At Hippodrome, New York, week Oct. 10.
Violet Henley.................Lois Moran
Pete Clark...................Edmund Lowe
Uncle Elmer.................E. J. Ratcliffe
Oscar Hawks.............Arthur Housman
Henry Banning.............Byron Munson

Wildly absurd story with a hero of the breezy Reginald Denny type that cops everything on sheer bold nerve. Direction none too deft and holes aplenty in the script, but sum total satisfactory and ought to deliver outside the de luxes.

Probably because of his characterization of the roi-snorting topsergeant in "What Price Glory" and the illiterate prizefight manager in "Is Zat So," Fox has given Edmund Lowe the assignment of the heavy zaphyr salesman.

Lowe started with Fox as a kid glove Adonis, and has worked into the human sort of thing. He turns in a good, properly ozoned performance in this instance.

Picture timely. Thinking that a flight from the Pacific coast to Hawaii is impossible, the hero, high-prssure bunk artist and press agent, puts up $100,000 of his firm's money. With the headlines of Lindbergh making the Atlantic, he realizes that the Hawaii hop is possible and someone is apt to make good on the $100,000 prize. So he enters the race himself, and in an utterly ridiculous manner gets to Hawaii, thereby saving his firm against having to make good on his publicity stunt.

Lois Moran is seen in a new guise, less the weeping innocent and more the pert chic with sex appeal. Maybe Fox is training her for more romantic parts. Sheehan hid wonders with Madge Bellamy by transferring the focus from her large baby eyes to her gams.

E. J. Ratcliffe, Hollywood's busiest millionaire business executive "type," is here seen in Pecksniffian side whiskers, and Arthur Housman has a bit.

The plot holds lots of laughs, thereby condoning the atrocious licenses it takes with plausibility and probability.

SLIGHTLY USED

Warner Bros. production and release. Comedy, featuring May McAvoy and Conrad Nagel. Story by Melville Grosman, scenario by Graham Baker. Director, Archie L. Mayo. Cameraman, Hal Mohr. Running time, 60 minutes. Released Sept. 3. Seen in projection room.
Cynthia Martin...................May McAvoy
Major John Smith............Conrad Nagel
Donald Woodward............Robert Agnew
Helen Martin ....Audrey Ferris
Mr. Martin.................Anders Randolf
Aunt Lydia ....Eugenie Besserer
Gerald ....Arthur Rankin
Horace ....David Mir
Grace Martin...................Sally Eilers

A particularly inept comedy, addressed apparently to the high school girl grade of intelligence. One of those gushing, juvenile pictures that explain why film reviewers die young or live on to surly old age. Film inspires especially violent impatience because it uses clever players to act out such desperate drivel, and the camera work and technical production are fine beyond the ordinary.

Here is a picture that in its literary substance is the utterest rubbish, and it is played out in settings of superlative artistic beauty and in terms of splendid photographic values. There are graceful modern interiors that could supply fitting backgrounds for a Pinero society play, while this childish story makes them look foolish.

It isn't conceivable that the picture would be interesting to anybody above the level of the gum-chewing dumbdora stenographer type. It deals with a terribly cute flapper who pretends she has married a distant aviator in order that her two younger sisters may escape the ban of their father against suitors. In the whole realm of screen characters there is no type that inspires quite the same homicidal impulses as the

sweet young thing who is determined to be cute. Whoever it was that brought May McAvoy into this role has done no service to that charming young player. It must have been the same source of creative art that put Conrad Nagel, stolid and substantial juvenile, into a role that called for a graceful low comedian, if a low comedian can be conceived as graceful.

The rest of the people do not matter so much, consisting of a stereotyped father, a prop comedy old woman and a flock of fluttering young things, male and female.

Cynthia is the oldest of three sisters. Papa has decreed that the two younger girls may not become engaged until Cynthia is wed. Cynthia returns home announcing she is married, and on the spur of the moment says her husband is a Major John Smith, picking the name out of a newspaper reporting the Major's air hop to South America. In order to back up her story Cynthia writes a wifely letter to the absent aviator, whom, of course, she has never seen, and by mischance it gets into the mail and is duly delivered.

Meanwhile Cynthia falls in love with a young bond salesman, who makes casual love to her in order to sell papa a line of bonds. Cynthia appears to make all the love making, although she has taken on the wedded status, a situation that has a false ring about it.

The girl causes a death notice to be printed in the newspapers in order to rid herself of the fictitious husband. The device succeeds perfectly in the movie manner to which anything is possible. Only Major Smith turns up later and complicates things. He poses as Major Adams, the best friend of the "late Major Smith," and there ensues a series of episodes designed to be exquisitely comic. The counterfeit Major describes with hard-working comedy business the tragic death in the jungle of the "late husband" and otherwise makes himself a nuisance while the heroine squirms uncomfortably as the results of her hoax pile up upon her.

In the end the Major crashes into Cynthia's bedroom to declare himself the real Smith and urge his position as acknowledged husband. There are possibilities in this passage, but they are not fully developed, and by that time the picture has lost its hold on interest. *Rush.*

THE FIGHTING THREE

Blue Streak Western released by Universal. Directed by Albert Rogell from the story by William Lester. Starring Jack Hoxie, horse and dog. Cast includes H. Rocquemore, Buck Conner, Olive Hasbrouck, Marin Sais, Fannie Warner, William Dwyer, William Malan, William Norton Bailey. At the Arena, N. Y., one day, Sept. 23.

Jack Hoxie and Olive Hasbrouck should be kept in continual action. As soon as they stop to mug the entire effect is spoiled and the picture slows up while the pair exchange more or less meaningless subtitles.

Besides Hoxie registers effectively on horseback on the long shots while the girl similarly, on the stage, looks better from a distance.

The dog and the horse are unconvincing as a pair of scrappers. While okey for atmosphere and appearance, the animal stars are not good troupers and any attempt made to use them as such, as in this picture, is ridiculous.

This is western story routine No. 1, and maybe some of the customers have forgotten all about it. The gal is a chorus girl. On the day of her return to the home town her remorse-stricken dad kicks the bucket leaving her a large estate. The cowboy friend has married her meantime.

An evil nephew, William Norton Bailey, convinces the gal that the man she married murdered her aged pop and she shoots but fails to kill Hoxie.

Then the arrival of the sheriff, but pop was only half killed.

The fans at the Arena went heavy for the fight stuff and it gets exciting in spots. Production not considered of any special value outside of state's rights.

Two Arabian Knights

United Artists' release, produced by Caddo Co. Lewis Milestone directed from a Donald McGibney story, adapted by James T. O'Donohue and Wallace Smith. Titles by George Marion, Jr. William Boyd and Louis Wolheim co-featured; Mary Astor sub-featured. At Paramount, New York, week of Oct. 22.

Private	William Boyd
Anis Bin Adham	Mary Astor
Sergeant Peter McGaffney	Louis Wolheim
Emir of Jaffa	Michael Vavitch
Shevket	Ian Keith
American Consul	DeWitt Jennings
Ship Captain	Michael Visaroff
Purser	Boris Karloff

Paramount acquired a good comedy flicker in booking this United Artists' release which has William Boyd and Louis Wolheim in a farce of the Great War. This is the Boyd of pictures and not Bill Boyd of "What Price Glory," the play.

There is little pretext at a continuity that can stand analysis. It is primed exclusively for laughing purposes from the opening shots where McGaffney (Wolheim) and Phelps (Boyd), who hate each other heartily, disregard the shot and shell and general holocaust on No Man's Land and lace into each other. They look up to view Germans with drawn bayonets trapping them.

In the prison camp Wolheim, because of his higher rank, is again put in command of the American doughboys, much to Phelps' disgust. In short order Phelps proves of service to the sergeant and a fast friendship develops between the good-looking private and the tough searg who has among his personal effects a handbill calling for his arrest and imprisonment in the States on a confidence game charge.

The "Arabian knights" thing develops when the twain make their escape in garb pilfered from Arabian allied prisoners. They find themselves shipped to Constantinople and from there to Arabia, where Boyd rescues the Oriental-veiled heroine (Miss Astor).

Their many adventures include some effective rescue and escape stuff of acceptable cinema thrill character. Boyd and Wolheim work well together.

Some of the comedy business in "Two Arabian Knights" is questionable and certain to be curtailed by the more conservative state censor bodies. One bit has to do with Boyd identifying the heroine's male bodyguard as a eunuch. Wolheim in another bit, where the pair have been without food for a couple of days, decides to milk a goat for their breakfast. He is shown swishing his hand and remarking "wrong kind of goat." There is still another.

Plenty of laughs, however, and in this era of comedy demands, the feature should click at the gate generally. Mary Astor is fetching, although she has little to do.

Abel.

THE FAIR CO-ED

Metro-Goldwyn-Mayer picture starring Marion Davies. Directed by Sam Wood. Adapted from the George Ade play of the same name. Running time, 57 mins. At the Capitol, New York, week of Oct. 22.

Cynthia	Marion Davies
Davy	John Mack Brown
Betty	Jane Winton
Amy	Thelma Hill
Monitor	Lillianne Leighton
Herbert	Gene Stone

Snappy, jazzy comedy of college life from the modern feminine angle, done in a breezy way with much shrewdly invented and briskly staged comedy incident. Picture has special appeal from its spirit of youthful nonsense and provides the best light role Marion Davies has had in some time.

Some of the hilarious college pranks have been gagged up vigorously, but the gagging has been done with a delicate hand, and there is a certain realism about the campus atmosphere which is nicely built up. The Ade original furnished a substantial foundation upon which to work. Probably the Hoosier humorist is the American writer best qualified to handle the subject and his hand is apparent here in what is easily the best American college comedy available.

So much for the basic material. The production has taken many liberties with the text, but it has kept to the spirit if not the letter of the play. Indeed in some respects the film is better than the stage version. Some of the campus crowd scenes are capital and an especially persuasive bit is a sentimental scene in which the young heroine, after she has flippantly flouted the convention of loyalty to alma mater is made to feel the urge of young enthusiasm toward an ideal. The treatment of this passage is a gem of direction, a touching little episode projected swiftly and naturally into a melieu of bustling comedy.

The blonde and tomboy Marion fits trimly into a part cut to her measure. As the flirtatious basketball star of Bingham college she had a conspicuous opportunity to spread eagle on the gym floor in "shorts" and the trimmest of trim jersies, all duck soup for a one time "Follies" girl. There is a bevy of flapper basketball beauties who are a relief from the bathing beach variety of pulchritude. The picture stages a girls' basketball match that has all the spectacle and dramatic kick of one of those "a minute to play" football stories.

It's easier to watch and vastly more absorbing as done here, for the girls stage a real game with all the old tricks worked to a fare-the-well for the climax of the winning goal. The fact that the opponents are sightly femmes goes to intensify the grip.

The picture has good sentiment, nice romantic interest, and best of all effective comedy. It is upon this last element that the film will rest safely. The students come back after vacation to Bingham where the faculty has forbidden student motorists. They arrive in every possible kind of trick conveyance, from a burlesque Roman chariot drawn by a pair of Missouri mules, to a bicycle squad. This absurd parade is elaborated for a wow. There is some good girls' dormitory stuff, dealing with coed feminine types, rivalries, jealousies and hazing.

Excellent titling stands up independently as a laugh getter. The lackadaisical heroine is wearily watching the girls' basketball practice when the team captain (heroine's dearest enemy) asks her, "Why don't you try for the team?"

"I do not chose to run in 1928," is the comeback.

There is a running fire of this sort of gagging, up to the minute and thoroughly pat to the situation. Production is excellent, especially the campus mass meetings. The picture has some hokum, but it is masked behind a general feeling of sincerity in the whole work.

Rush.

HIGH SCHOOL HERO

Fox production and release. Story by William Conselman and David Butler. Directed by David Butler. Running time, 62 mins. At the Roxy, New York, week of Oct. 22.

Pete Greer	Nick Stuart
Eleanor Barrett	Sally Phipps
Mr. Merrill	William N. Bailey
Bill Merrill	John Darrow
Mr. Greer	Wade Boteler
Mr. Golden	Brandon Hurst
Allen Drew	David Rollins
Coach	Charles Paddock

Breezy, speedy laugh-laden comedy of 18-year-olds. While several well-known players are in the cast, essentially its the work of unknowns. That may detract to a degree from picture's box office value, but the film can stand and deliver on its own intrinsic merits.

William Conselman and David Butler wrote the yarn. Seton Miller made the scenario. Butler did the directing. The indication is that all ages will be amused and the flaps and jellybeans, an important percentage of picture attendance, will probably be flattered at a picture dealing with their own kind. For "High School Hero" is exclusively adolescent in theme and story.

The big laughs are derived from one of those amateur plays known to every high school auditorium in the country. The action has been extremely well worked out. Humor is based on spontaneous situation, not arbitrarily grafted "gags." The mishaps are natural, the sort of mishaps that can and do mar the dramatic efforts of high school Thespians. The play is being done by the Latin class in a Roman setting. All the friends and parents are in the audience. The genial prof., played by Brandon Hurst, and well, has fits in the wings as one faux pas after another wrecks his Caesarian tragedy. This is rich audience material.

Nick Stuart and John Darrow, newcomers, are promising juveniles. Their camera deportment is natural and easy and they photograph great. Both lads should go forward and upward. Another young novice, David Rollins, also seems to have possibilities. Young Sally Phipps impersonates the cause of the trouble between the boys. She has been seen previously in other Fox pictires and is cute.

The picture will produce laughs and satisfaction.

THE CRYSTAL CUP

First National release. Produced by Henry Hobart. Directed by John Francis Dillon from Gertrude Atherton's story, adapted by Gerald Duffy. Running time, 62 mins. At Strand, New York, week of Oct. 22.

Gita Carteret	Dorothy Mackaill
Geoffrey Pleyden	Jack Mulhall
Eustance Bylant	Rockliffe Fellows
Polly Pleyden	Jane Winton
Mrs. Carteret	Edythe Chapman
Mrs. Pleyden	Clarissa Selwynne

First National has bacon in this package. Production, story and cast join in a siren song of the box office. Essentially it's a victory for the script, although the production of Henry Hobart and the direction of John Francis Dillon deserve plaudits. The point is that other First National pictures of recent release have cost as much and been as well directed as this one, but have not clicked particularly well because the stories were dull or trivial. In this case the story is novel and interesting.

The theme is sex antagonism. Learning in her childhood to hate all men, the heroine grows into a beautiful and disdainful young woman. Finding herself the object of obvious attentions, she gives up wearing attractive frocks and effects a very mannish get-up. This makes for rich "natural" comedy. Dorothy Mackaill has the part which just oozes with gravy, and does the job wonderfully well. The fans will like her in her masculine tuxedo and will enjoy seeing her light a match with her thumb a la Bill Hart.

To escape talk the man-hater finally makes a deal for a platonic marriage with a novelist, played by the efficient Rockliffe Fellows. They are to be man and wife in name only, but it is made clear that the novelist is playing fox and has no intention of observing the rules of cinema cricket. In the end the heroine finds her true love in a young surgeon, and resumes wearing silk stockings and other feminine trappings.

It's a pleaser.

Back to God's Country

Universal production, distributed by Universal. Directed by Irvin Willat. James Oliver Curwood story adapted by Charles Logue. Renee Adoree starred. Running time, 68 mins. At the Colony, New York, week of Oct. 22.

Renee Debois	Renee Adoree
Bob Stanton	Robert Frazer
Captain Blake	Walter Long
Jean Debois	Mitchell Lewis
"Frenchie" Leblanc	Adolph Milar
Jacques Corbeau	James Mason
Clerk	Walter Ackerman

Story of the frozen north having box office strength from name of author and star. Curwood is something of a cult among magazine readers of the "Cosmopolitan" class and his work commands an enormous popular interest. Rene Adoree, of course, has the huge prestige of the "Parade." These two elements are more than sufficient to insure the draw of any picture.

The feature makes good on the screen. It has several good stunt bits, a clean cut romantic story and much pictorial beauty in its snow scenes, some of which may be manufactured, but all of which are thoroughly convincing. Wealth of action carries good suspense and the climax is a dramatic chase that is surefire, having the heroine fleeing with the wounded hero in a dog sled with the heavy in keen pursuit behind another team of dogs. Comedy is rough and tumble with nothing to recommend it to discriminating fans, but vigorous enough for the general following of this type of film.

There is a point of novelty in the introduction of a deep sea sailor into the story of the north woods. The action takes place in a trading post apparently on the seaboard where a trading schooner, with its dissolute captain and raggamuffin crew, calls twice a year or so. The captain's roving eye falls upon the daughter of a backwoods trapper, at the post to sell his winter's catch of pelts. The trapper kills a crook in self defense and the captain tries to force the girl to marry him on threat of turning the woodsman over to the authorities for murder.

It is here that an American engineer comes to the rescue, because he has fallen in love with the girl. Thus the story becomes a contest between engineer and sailor. It all gets down to a dog sled race through a blizzard, a device well worked in its scenic features and storm effects, building up to a capital climax, when a fierce dog, which the girl has treated kindly and which the heavy has beaten, turns the scales in favor of the fugitives. Battle between dog and man is fought out with a good deal of realism, ending when the dog drives the snow-blinded villain over a cliff. This **drop into a frozen river from a height, the sight of the villain crashing through the ice and his short struggle, furnishes a capital finale kick.**

Rush.

ONE ROUND HOGAN

Warner Bros. production and release. Directed by Howard Bretherton from a story by George Godfrey. Monte Blue starred. Running time, 60 mins. At Hippodrome, New York, week of Oct. 24.

One Round Hogan	Monte Blue
Tim Hogan	Jim Jeffries
Helen Davies	Leila Hyanna
Joe Morgan	Frank Hagney
Fight Promoter	Robert Perry

Nothing new in a fight picture, though it may be new for Monte Blue, one guy in the films that has the build to look like a heavyweight. This picture as a production and as an audience picture is about par with the Warner Bros.' output starring Blue. Where the latter is a fav the picture will be liked. Elsewhere the betting is even.

The plot deals with the son of a prize fighter who is himself a pug. The elder Hogan is impersonated by none other than the famous Jim Jeffries. Gunboat Smith entered the

movies, bringing a pan rich in dramatic topography. Jeffries has none of the scars o' his trade, so has to do more acting. His acting is okay, too. He acts rings around Dempsey.

Through a combination of circumstances in the plot Hogan, the son, thinks he has killed his best friend in a knockout. The friend has been killed by the brutal manhandling of his manager. Young Hog develops a complex. He is afraid to hit anyone and is called a coward. The parent is broken hearted.

In the fight to clear his name young Hogan is being pummeled. He has no heart because his girl is sore at him. She listens in at the radio, hears, weakens, comes to the arena and the tables are turned on the villain, who gets knocked for a row of what have you.

It's very conventional, and within that definition reasonably entertaining plus the fight stuff to put it over. Jot it down as moderate.

The Irresistible Lover

Universal production supervised by Carl Laemmle, Jr. Directed by William Beaudine from the story by Evelyn Campbell. Featuring Norman Kerry and Lois Moran. At the Colony, N. Y., Oct. 21.

J. Harrison Grey	Norman Kerry
Betty Kennedy	Lois Moran
Dolly V. Carleton	Gertrude Astor
The Lawyer	Lee Moran
Hortense Brown	Myrtle Stedman
Mr. Brown	Phillips Smalley
Jack Kennedy	Arthur Lake
Mr. Kennedy	Walter James
Smith	George Pearce

Light farce handled in the lofty, modern manner, with plenty of laughs in the titles and trouping to take care of some of the weak situations. Can be relied upon to hold up the picture end for the full week.

Kerry is correctly handled but Miss Moran walks off with everything. Steals the picture with looks, action and ability. The kid gets the dames as well as the male admirers.

Titles carry most of the comedy, though the gag writer is not even billed. The boy sends them across, hot, fast and right over the plate for the laughs that interpret themselves into cash at the box office.

Story deals with a wealthy young bachelor with a penchant for ladies' boudoirs. He finally tires of being chased by husbands and sued by chorus girls and falls for a sweet, simple miss whom he bumps into in a traffic jam. The gal doesn't give him a tumble until he is almost killed saving her purse with the tag-day money.

Lee Moran is the legal fixer for most of Grey's law suits by broken-hearted ladies. When Grey starts in on the Betty the lawyer figures it's another frame and breaks up what promised to be smooth work. Straightened out for the usual clinch finish.

RACING ROMEO

F. B. O. release produced by Sam Wood, featuring Red Grange. Story by Byron Morgan. At the Hippodrome, New York, one week, starting Oct. 16. Running time 64 minutes.

Red Walden	Red Grange
Walt Brown	Walter Hiers
Hattie Wayne	Trixie Friganza
Sally	Jobyna Ralston
Rube Oldham	Ben Hendricks, Jr.
Lorraine Blair	Marjorie Zier

With the fame of Red Grange, the football player, somewhat dimmed, it is well that the youngster was provided considerable acting support and a fast-moving script in his second picture for F. B. O. This picture should draw nice money on short stands.

About a year has passed since Red made his film debut with "One Minute to Play." Since that time he has been relegated to the background by such as Lindbergh, Ruth Elder and Grover Whalen. Consequently it matters little that in his second picture he is a racing auto pilot, driving a battered machine labeled "77" (his famous gridiron numerals).

Red, a garage keeper in a hick village, always enters the annual local race and always loses. Finally he decides to give up the race attempts and marry the village belle. On his wedding day he is driving to the ceremony with the girl's aunt, only to be inviegled into a play for the road by a guy who wants to pass him. The resulting wrecking activities so endanger the aunt's life she induces her niece to call the wedding off. So Red goes back to racing, winning the next race from the champion dirt track driver of the world, who is on the village track making a motion picture. With such honors, Red wins the girl back.

The picture has its best fast stuff in the race scenes, with the speeding cars shot from all angles spewing clouds of dust into the air. Several wrecks are shown, one looking as though it hit the camera shooting it.

Among the talent, Trixie Friganza took more honor than the script alloted her as the huffy aunt and helped the picture quite a bit. Walter Hiers showed well as Red's mechanic, although his opportunities were few. Jobyna Ralston is all right in a part requiring little.

Grange would have looked much better in a football picture, but he manages to act more convincingly than you'd expect a football player would.

Production concentrated on the racing interest, which will benefit the picture in the stands it plays.

CHAINED

Ufa production and release. Directed by Carl T. Dreyer. From story by Herman Bang. Adapted for screen by Thea Von Harbou and Carl T. Dreyer. At 55th St. Cinema.

Michael	Walter Slezak
The Master	Benjamin Christensen
Princess Zamikow	Nora Gregor
Adelksjold	Alexander Murski
Madame Adelksjold	Grete Mosheim
Herzog Von Monthieu	Didier Aslan
Switt	Robert Garrison

Here the German producers have chosen to tell a story of a great devotion, according to their own admission. Accordingly almost every foot of film contains at least one evidence of devotion in connection with something or other. The servant is devoted to the master, the master to the boy, the boy and the princess emote devotion mutually, and even the hard-looking critic seems to have the complex.

There is enough story material for three poor pictures and not enough for one good. Three individual themes, each in need of separate treatment to be effective, have been hastily thrown into one mass of incomprehensible detail and subtitles.

Situations are neglected, possibilities over-looked, direction botched and generally mismanaged. It's another one of those foreign pictures and may be taken as a typical reason why German producers cannot sell here to any extent as long as they work in this manner.

The story starts with a gathering of people in the home of a famous painter. Laborious conversation, transmitted via subtitles, results in an explanation that the young man used as a model had helped in making the artist famous. Instead of a flash back, if the producers had started out at the beginning, telling the story of the poor art student whose sketches are worthless, adopted by the famous painter and finally ending up by murdering his benefactor for love of a woman, it would have at least been a connected story.

As it is the master dies of dispepsia or some other unromantic disease while the young man, it is vaguely implied, is guilty of neglecting the old boy through shorter and less frequent visits.

Entire production is impossible. Six of the 12 members of the audience in the house laughed during the most dramatic situations. It's a continuous laugh, crude, alien and not worth the celluloid printed on.

The princess, Nora Gregor, walks with a waddling movement reminiscent of the old Mississippi steamers. The lead, Walter Slezak, screens well in spots and could be used in local productions.

Switt, the art critic, is a good buy for comedy on condition that he be allowed to think he's playing heavy roles. He looks and acts like some of the Variety critics. Everything is lousy; nothing is on the level. Everybody should get at least two dirty looks a minute. He eyes everything with suspicion. A perpetual sneer is firmly engraved on his upper lip. He never combs his hair and walks as if he owns Germany.

Herzog Von Monthieu has a little play of his own. He seems to be deeply intrigued with Madame Adelskjold. The madame is not only married but her husband is alive. This does not deter Monthieu. Why this matter is brought into the picture is not fully explained. It is supposed to hinge on the fact that Monthieu was one of those present in the opening scene.

Everyone unfortunate enough to be present in any opening scene in a foreign production must evidently undergo a searching scrutiny and have a personal story brought in with the main plot.

If the foreign producers expect anyone here to believe they are being conspired against by the local distributors in an endeavor to keep foreign product out they would do well to keep pictures like "Chained" at home. They weaken their case considerably with the introduction of such "masterpieces."

Junk of this kind has no place here even in art theatres, that seem to stand for anything if it's cheap enough. Less thought about low rentals and more devoted to the b. o. might give these arty affairs a break, unless they have a subscription list under cover.

THE FRONTIERSMAN

Metro-Goldwyn-Mayer production and release. Directed by Reginald Barker. Tim McCoy featured, supported by Claire Windsor. Scenario by L. G. Rigby; titles by Tom Mirana. Running time, 53 mins. At Loew's American, New York, on last half bill.

Aim here was akin to that in "The Covered Wagon"; that is, the filming of a romantic-action incident taking interest from its patriotic appeal. For some reason the punch doesn't eventuate, possibly because the material is ineffective, the costuming is awkward rather than picturesque, and certainly the comedy is pretty fierce.

Indian warfare furnishes the suspense and locale in the Andrew Jackson period. Tim McCoy plays John Dale, trusted lieutenant of Jackson and scout for the militiamen.

Instead of confining itself to the rugged frontiersmen and Indians, the picture brings in scenes in the metropolis, where the military uniforms of the time and the feminine dress have something of a costume effect at variance with the pioneering atmosphere of the rest. The costumes are not graceful to our modern eyes, and the supposedly courtly manners of the epoch seem to us rather silly.

Thus, when the hero slaps an offender's face as a challenge to a duel, there is a giggle instead of a thrill. That's a sample. The action delivers mixed sensations, some of them comic when the intention is serious. Anyway, the medley costume magnificence and frontier simplicity are confusing.

The gallant captain is delegated by Jackson to escort his niece to a remote frontier fort, where she is to meet her father. Hero has just been disappointed in love and is indisposed to flirtation with a blonde. The heroine (Miss Windsor) teases him on the subject of his amours, and this is supposed to furnish a light comedy passage. Miss Windsor was a poor choice for the hoyden.

When they approach the fort they find the entire garrison massacred by the Indians, and thence the race back home. They make the settlements safely, and the rest of the picture is a pumped-up patriotic appeal, the militia being shown in all manner of shots riding gallantly to deal summary vengeance on the redskins. Some of the battle shots are fairly effective pictorially.

Fair enough program picture for the juvenile fans. Otherwise just a release. *Rush.*

THE SWELLED HEAD

Columbia release, directed by Ralph Graves. Adapted from "Sidewalks of New York." Cameraman, Conrad Wells. Running time, 55 mins. At Loew's New York one day, Oct. 21, on double feature program.

Lefty Malone	Ralph Graves
Bill O'Rourke	Johnnie Walker
Molly O'Rourke	Eugenie Gilbert
Kitty	Mildred Harris
Mother Malone	Mary Carr

Columbia has a conventional but interesting prize fight film in this story of a truck driver with a sock. He fans a couple of set-up and gets an enlarged cranium pronto, taking a lacing and a let-down in conceit when he comes up against his first real opposition.

The prize fighter is played by Ralph Graves, whose varied cinema career has included romantic leads for D. W. Griffith and slapstick two-reelers for Mack Sennett. In this case he is also director. The megaphone work is never bad and occasionally clever. The opening sequence is a bit reminiscent of those Sennett shorts, but apart from that Graves remembers that the director of a feature has responsibilities.

Eugenie Gilbert is the wholesome colleen who gets neglected during the truck driver's brief opulence as a pug. There is the usual home-and-mother sentimentalism, with that busy parent, Mary Carr, getting cured of an undefined paralysis when listening over the radio to a first-class mauler knock the stuffing out of her overconfident offspring. This miracle is accomplished without a solitary bead or a word about the good book.

Looking very spiffy and improving as an actress, Mildred Harris impersonated a lady of the night clubs. The truck driver might have been a champ if he had passed up the lady's flat.

Some laughs, a trace of drama and a good prize fight make this a good box-office property. A one-day at the New York, but stronger than that for the smaller metropolises.

CANCELLED DEBT

Banner Production, released by Sterling Pictures. Directed by Phil Rosen. Star, Rex Lease. Cast includes Charlotte Stevens, Florence Turner, James Gordon, Ethel Grey Terry. At Loew's New York on double feature day. Running time, 58 minutes.

Some film makers seem to be doing the old stories over and over again. In the hazy future, say 1950, the plot of "The Cancelled Debt" will still be bobbing along on the screens.

The formulae is dosed up good here, with a young girl whose dad is political boss falling in love with a motorcycle cop, going from the early sunrise eating hour to the night club with the usual clash with the underworld, and Mr. Cop emerging victor.

A plain story plainly told; nothing new in any way, although the camera for the most part does A1 work.

A funny incident occurred at the New York, where this old-fashioned meller was being shown.

An outside display card had Robert Gordon featured. Robert Gordon is known to the Broadway film fans and Rex Lease isn't. Subsequently the only acclaim Rex got was on the regulation lobby cards gotten out by Banner. Such is fame! There is a James Gordon in the picture, playing one of the principal roles in support of Lease as the cop.

Several tense minutes and a laugh when the girl jumps into the free-for-all fight in the warehouse office when her sweetboy cop is getting mauled about the place.

A lot of license in many spots. Perhaps picture will get better attention on double-feature days, as alone it would wabble along like a dog on three legs. *Mark.*

FINNEGAN'S BALL

San Francisco, Oct. 10.

First Division release, presented by Pallas Photoplay. Produced by Graf Bros. studio, San Mateo, Calif. Directed by James Hogan; supervised by Max Graf. About 6,250 feet, running time, 1 hour. Premiere, Rivoli, San Francisco, starting Oct. 8.

Molly Finnegan..........Blanche Mehaffey
Maggie Finnegan............Aggie Herring
Danny Finnegan, Sr.........Chas. McHugh
Danny Finnegan, Jr.........Mimi Finnegan
Patrick Flannigan..............Mack Swain
Flannigan, Jr.................Cullen Landis
Judge McCarthy..............Kewpie Mogan
Lawyer O'Connell...............West Clark

The first full length comedy feature produced by the Graf Bros. at their studio just outside of San Francisco, is an adaptation of the old stage farce played a quarter of a century ago by Murray and Mack.

The producers selected a well-balanced cast and side-stepped anything which might be repugnant to the Irish race. In its finished form, "Finnegan's Ball" is a picture that will get a lot of laughs from the average picture fan. There will be little place for it in the de luxe houses.

The action starts back in Ireland, where Finnegan and his family are awaiting funds from Flannigan, who has become a successful contractor in New York. Love affair between the Finnegan girl and the Flannigan boy.

Flannigan makes good his promise to send for his old crony, whom he likes so well he cannot be happy unless he is quarreling with him, but an employee embezzles the money.

Determined to get to America at any cost, Finnegan and his family with a pet hen embark steerage. Flannigan has met several ships and seems again doomed to disappointment when he discovers his friend with the steerage immigrants. A fight naturally follows and this little feud of the two friends is carried right through the picture. Everybody gets involved in these fights, excepting Molly and Jimmy, the youngsters.

Flannigan gives Finnegan a job carrying the hod on one of his jobs, but is constantly in hot water and constantly being fired. One day comes the lawyer from Ireland with the news that Finnegan is heir to a mansion and a huge fortune. Finnegan moves into the new home and puts on the ritz. With his wife, they ararnged an elaborate ball, so they can invite everybody but Flannigan. Molly sees to it that her sweetheart and his dad attend, though they affect a disguise.

The elder Flannigan is unmasked and a fresh free-for-all is just started when the lawyer returns to tell Finnegan the estate belongs to another by the same name.

Flannigan then takes his old friend into partnership.

Charles McHugh gives an excellent performance as the fiery, fighting Finnegan and Aggie Herring is great as his wife, also pugnaciously inclined. Blanche Mehaffey is a pretty colleen and Cullen Landis satisfies as the sweetheart. Mack Swain is a pompous and over-lording contractor.

Editing and cutting faults are numerous and some of the titling is not up to standard. But it has plenty of good comedy, of the hokum kind, and that is what will get it over with a large class of picturegoers who go in for that type of entertainment.

BECKY

M-G-M-Cosmopolitan production and release. Directed by John P. McCarthy. Sally O'Neil and Owen Moore featured. Scenario by Marion Blackton. Cameraman, John Arnold. In cast: Gertrude Olmstead, Harry Currier, Mack Swain, Claude King. Running time, 58 mins.

This is the M-G-M picture which played the Chicago theatre, Chicago, largest of the Balaban & Katz houses, but did not play the Capitol, New York, M-G-M's own movie parlor. It is like "On Ze Boulevard" and some other M-G-M's that never crash the Capitol, a picture of limited de luxe strength but possessing boxoffice elements for the smaller capacities and prices.

"Becky" is rather a hodge-podge in plot. There are two heroes. The heroine is a pert young cash girl in a department store whose ability to attract the opposite sex is equalled only by her own determination that "they shall not pass" the bounds of propriety. She is, as played by the sprightly Sally O'Neil, kin-sister to the naughty-nice heroines of First National, Paramount and Fox: Colleen Moore, Clara Bow and Madge Bellamy.

Perhaps of all the flappers in the movies Sally O'Neil is the one who comes closest to look like the real article. She is the perfect prototype of the gum-chewing young freshie who knows how to slow up sheiks and get them thinking about furniture and time payments. "Becky" is therefore, in spite of a loose scenario and rather stilted direction, fundamental boxoffice.

Galloping Thunder

F. B. O. western release, produced by Jesse Goldburg. Starring Bob Custer. Story by W. Bert Foster. Directed by Scott Pembroke. Running time about 65 mins.

Kincaid Currier...................Bob Custer
Judith Lamb.....................Anne Sheridan
Oliver Lamb......................J. P. Lockney
Dallas Savage..............Richard R. Neil
Lash McGraw...............Fernando Galvez

Regulation western stuff produced by Jesse Goldburg for F. B. O. release. Lots of movement and a fair enough production based on a cowboy yarn of familiar ingredients.

Hero loves the daughter of his boss, but she taunts him by pretending to like a visiting rancher who is a bad boy. The hero leaves on the assumption his affections are not reciprocated.

In a neighboring county the hero goes to work for the railroad. He is the means of recovering a missing express car containing a bullion shipment. The eventual reconciliation of the hero and the gal follows his rescue of her from the hazards of a runaway train.

Anne Sheridan, appealing blonde, makes a spiffy heroine and the ever-sinister Richard Neil creates sufficient menace.

Not much suspense to this opry, but an aceptable filler for the houses that change their programs at frequent intervals.

Mask of Lopez

Harry J. Brown presentation for Monogram-Biltmore release. Directed by Al Rogell. Fred Thomson starred. In cast, Dorothy Ferguson, Dot Farley, Dick Sutherland. Running time, 53 minutes. On double feature bill, one day, at Arena, New York.

Seemingly old and probably a western re-issue, this picture is all action and ought to be okay for the daily changes. It has Fred Thomson for star and that name is presumed to mean quite a bit in certain quarters.

The plot deals with a tyrant who wears a mask and has a set ritual in executing his prisoners. A glass of wine and three cakes are placed on a table. Firing squad is all set. Signal to pop is the breaking of the third cake. Climax is when the hero and the real Lopez have changed positions.

The hero is wearing the mask and the bandit is set for a dose of his own medicine with his gang not knowing they are about to execute their own leader through never having seen his face. The timely arrival of the reliable cow hands extricates the hero from his subsequent difficulties.

For short runs and small rentals.

FOR LADIES ONLY

Columbia production, distributed in eastern territory by Commonwealth. From the story, "Down With Women," by George F. Worts. Directed by Henry Lehrman and Percy Pembroke. John Bowers and Jacqueline Logan featured. Others in cast: Edna Marion, Ben Hall, William H. Strauss, Templar Saxe, Kathleen Chambers, Harry Rocquemore. Running time, 70 minutes. At the New York, New York, half double feature bill, one day.

"For Ladies Only" is a light comedy dealing with a flock of girls in a business office who force the handsome young manager to re-employ them after he had fired the whole force. It is pretty juvenile in its humor, and addresses itself to the flapper taste. Comedy is obvious and strained and drama lacking.

Picture makes a perfect running mate for a routine western, with which it was yoked in this performance. Fans who enjoy the familiar type of cowboy picture will also like the comedy. That characterizes "For Ladies Only" completely.

Roughened up and with a chase finish, the story would have been a lively two-reeler; spun out laboriously into feature length, it is badly padded.

Bevy of pretty stenographer girls flutter through the action, giving the picture some life, but the femmes never do anything except flutter. One scene with something of a kick had the girls lined up at the office windows looking at a passing parade, with camera shots rich in rolled stockings and silken knees. Useful for lobby flash, the bit being played up in lobby display at the New York. John Bowers is one of those leading men who fares poorly in this comedy type. A player like Jack Mulhall might have done something with the part, but it is lost here.

Jacqueline Logan is much too "legitimate" in style for a comedy role that calls for farce treatment. Both leads out of their element doesn't help in getting the picture over. There are moments when the stenog girls are much more interesting than the leading character.

Picture is only fair in technical treatment, lacking the fine photographic effect that usually marks the Columbia product. Settings are good, with no occasion to strive for elaborate effects except in a hotel lobby sequence and the girls' apartment. Both backgrounds first rate.

Picture is one of the betweeners in the excellent line this independent has been putting out. *Rush.*

BULLDOG PLUCK

F B O western starring Bob Custer. Directed by Jack Nelson from story by Bert Foster. Cameraman Ernest Miller. In cast, Hugh Saxon, Richard Neill, Veora Daniel and Victor Mezetti. Running time, 52 mins.

Speedy bronco opera made well and acted acceptably. It contains the somewhat tongue-in-cheek situation of a professional gambler, also the town's reformer, to smashing mirrors, bottles and lights in a rival joint that "violates law and order" by staying open after 12.

That angle would give fastidious patrons quite a few chuckles, but it is obvious this picture will not be booked for fastidious audiences, so that's a hazard that need worry no one.

Lots of whipping out of six-shooters and other western pastimes as the good sinner battles the bad sinner for the championship of Boulder Gulch or whatever the name of the town is. Bob Custer stars and makes a good job of it.

Made for the box offices that front on Main street.

Return of Boston Blackie

A First Division release presented by Chadwick Pictures Corporation. Directed by Harry Hoyt, Featuring Corliss Palmer, Raymond Glenn and Strongheart, the dog. Supervised by Arthur Beck. Continuity by Leah Baird from story in "Cosmopolitan" magazine by Jack Boyle. At the Stanley, New York, one day (Oct. 22). Running time, 70 mins.

With a script continually calling for impossible situations, this picture couldn't be good even if it were made well. It is a one-day program and should be at its best in the double-feature houses.

The story is of a crook just out of jail vowing to go straight, but later deciding to pull his last job for the sake of a girl. This dame's father has been fooling with a night club hostess, even so far as to give her the family heirloom jewel piece. The daughter recovers it by theft and wants to get it back into the safe so the mother will never know about the old man's playing around.

Assisting in the labors for justice is Strongheart, the dog actor. He is utilized to rescue and make escapes when progress is roughened by a villain's various efforts.

The casting is not good and is shown to poor effect in a weak brand of photography. Raymond Glenn, as the crook, accomplishes best results with his part. Corliss Palmer, the girl, is too large to draw sympathy, and for some or no reason wears a white outfit that makes her look larger.

A lengthy string of incongruities must be blamed on the directing.

The low type of audience will, as usual, derive some entertainment from this. They seem to go for anything.

FORBIDDEN WOMAN

William C De Mille production. Distributed by Pathe. First major release under new regime. Directed by Paul L. Stein. From an original story by Elmer Harris. Adaptation and continuity by Clara Beranger. Jetta Goudal starred, Victor Varconi and Joseph Schildkraut featured. Running time, 70 mins At the Paramount, New York, week of Oct. 29.

Zita..........................Jetta Goudal
Sheik..........................Ivan Lebedoff
Sultan..............................L. Snegoff
Zita's Maid...................Josephine Norman
Col. Gautier.......................Victor Varconi
Jean La Coste...............Joseph Schildkraut

Exotic drama, with the emotional stuff laid on thick. Has more the quality of Elinor Glyn than Elmer Harris, and may pull with the women. Men will call it sloppy sentiment. Very artificial and theatrical, but has a certain screen effectiveness. The production is uncommonly beautiful and the acting graceful in spite of the stilted story.

Good judgment to swing Jetta Goudal and Joseph Schildkraut into a romantic combination, a team that matches Colman-Banky, and since the enterprise addresses itself deliberately to the femmes the selection is perfect. On this basis the picture has the marks of a money-maker.

But a little of this heavy Oriental romance goes a long way with men. This one overdoes everything from atmosphere to coincidence. The locale is the foreign legion in Algiers. That background has taken the limelight away from the Royal Northwest Mounted. "The Sheik" started it and "Beau Geste" carried the vogue another step forward. It's beginning to lose its novelty.

Some of the sentimental passages would be absurd in other hands than Schildkraut and Miss Goudal. The heroine is outstanding in her clinging gowns and picturesque headdresses, while Schildkraut, of course, is even handsomer than necessary. Any couple carrying around that much combined pulchritude couldn't possibly be ridiculous, and their parts here pass muster, but by a narrow margin.

The Arabians are hard pressed by the French, bent on conquest. The aged sheik calls upon his granddaughter (Miss Goudal), daughter of a native mother and French father, to go into the enemy's camp and obtain military information. In pursuit of this plan she marries the French colonel. He goes secretly to Paris on a military mission. When the wife-spy follows by ship, she meets and falls in love with a famous violinist, Leon, who turns out in due time to be the colonel's brother.

The outraged husband ultimately compels his brother to enlist under him in Africa as a penalty for what he supposes is his treachery. It doesn't sound reasonable, but that's the scenario.

The production itself is a splendid bit of work on its technical side. Every aid of artistic settings, voluptuous photographic effects and fine pictorial arrangement is given to the picture, and almost gives it dignity in spite of the story's overdone sentimentality.

Will make a good box-office showing, but as the opening fanfare in Pathe's campaign it falls somewhat short of the De Mille prestige.

Rush.

THE MAIN EVENT

De Mille Pictures Corp. production, released through Pathe, co-featuring Vera Reynolds and Rudolph Schildkraut, directed by William K. Howard. Continuity by Rochus Gliese from story "That Makes Us Even," by Paul Allison. Runs 60 mins. At the Roxy, New York, week of Oct. 29.

Glory Frayne.............Vera Reynolds
Regan, Sr............Rudolph Schildkraut
Margie ....Julia Faye
Johnnie Regan............Charles Delaney
Red Lucas.............Robert Armstrong
Slug—Nutty Fighter..........Ernie Adams

This fight picture is just a so-so feature flicker. It will do as a daily change for the neighbs but would never have made a full week at the Roxy except for the all-Pathe week in the Broadway picture houses, with presumably the added inducement of an attractive rental.

Not only can't "The Main Event" stand analysis, but they view it with polite skepticism. The elements are so flimsy and the ingredients so thin it is really to William K. Howard's credit that he turned out the relatively good job that he did.

The backbone of the plot has to do with a night club danseuse in love with Red Lucas, pugilist. Lucas is to meet Johnnie Regan (Charles Delaney), the sympathetic leather pusher. Johnnie is smitten with the dancer's charms in the Royale Night Club, and effects a contract only to find Glory (Vera Reynolds) miffed when apprised he is the Johnnie Regan who meets her beau in the near future. Red Lucas is a trifling Lothario and has Margie (Julia Faye) in reserve.

Margie and our heroine are roommates and pals and the incongruity of Glory muffing all the significance of Margie's playing around with Red, not to mention that a night club dame should know her onions better than a bucolic recruit, makes it incongruous. There was a time when scenarists wished that situation on the trusting and trustful maiden from the sticks.

Glory is led into framing the hero by keeping him up late, which too is the razzberry, particularly with such faithful father-managers as Rudolph Schildkraut is supposed to be.

The punch, of course, as in these formula pug pictures, is the big bout, hence the title. With Regan punch-drunk at the hands of Kid Morpheus on the very eve of the main event, he still manages to pull the kayo.

There is one variation on the fight plot in that the girl in the ringside seat is not featured as the beacon of light and hope to spur her hero to victory. Instead, the heroine is temporarily under fire, because of her double-crossing penchant, and the pug's sight of her goads the groggy Regan to best her designs as well as his opponent. For the finish it is explained that Glory is through with Red and that she grew to love Johnnie Regan, etc., for the usual clinch.

Miss Reynolds is not particularly sympathetic as the female lead. Delaney is effective as the male lead and Schildkraut does excellent work as the old sport who manages his fighting son. It's a character departure for Schildkraut, trim and neat in a Tad role and not be-whiskered and Semitic as have been the majority of his screen performances.

Abel.

Angel of Broadway

Pathe DeMille release. Presented by William Sistrom. Direction of Lois Weber. Story by Lenore J. Coffee. Leatrice Joy starred, with Victor Varconi featured. Running time, 64 mins. At Colony, New York, week of Oct. 29.

Babe............................Leatrice Joy
Jerry..........................Victor Varconi
Big Bertha........................May Robson
Goldie.............................Alice Lake
Gertie ....Elise Bartlett

For New York this title is a dud, but in the hinterland it may well be esteemed box office. Pathe has, in fact, a very good commercial property for the territory west of Hoboken. It's weepy with religion and socky with night club stuff. It's the sort of story Harold Bell Wright might author and the sort of production, with a heavier cost sheet, F. B. Q. might produce.

Lois Weber, one of the two women directors in the business, has done exceptionally well. Aiming at the tear ducts of the great sentimental American public, she will probably be rewarded with quite a gush. The theme of her story is blasphemy.

It is a pageant of good and evil. The scene is alternately laid in a Salvation Army mission and a high hat night club. The heroine (Leatrice Joy) is an employe of the latter ;the hero (Victor Varconi) a devotee of the former. The night club gal gets a load of the Salvation Army soul-saving technique and burlesques it in the night club. The blasphemy troubles her, however.

Canon Chase and other reformers contending that the Hollywood film makers offend the moral sentiments of the religious might look at this one. A more obvious effort to please the religious element could hardly be conceived.

The picture introduces Elsie Bartlett (Mrs. Joseph Schildkraut). She symbolizes the woman who has sinned and the sad end she comes to. Her acting, for a neycomer to the screen, was conspicuously good. Miss Joy handed in a well rounded performance. Victor Varconi seemed too handsome for a truck driver and too debonair for a saint in the slums. May Robson did a sort of Texas Guinan in the night club and used Tex's line, "Give the l'il girl a big hand."

The script is credited to Lenore Coffee, a Hollywood scenarist who writes directly at the box office.

This one is brimming with the stuff the hoi polloi likes. Good direction, production and acting have helped, but a large chunk of the credit rightfully belongs to the writer.

DRESS PARADE

DeMillo picture distributed by Pathe. Directed by Donald Crisp. Story by Major Robert Glassburn, Major Alexander Chilton and Herbert David Walter. William Boyd starred. Running time 66 minutes. At the Strand, New York, Oct. 29.

Viv Donovan .... William Boyd
Janet Wallace .... Bessie Love
Stuart Haldane .... Hugh Allan
Major Steinhold .... Louis Natheaux
Mealy Snodgrass .... Maurice Ryan
Cadet Dawson .... Walter Tennyson
Commandant .... Clarence Geldert

A romantic story of West Point here is done in a sentimental way, with heavy emphasis on the patriotic angle. Played by William Boyd, the subject and star compel interest. The whole film has been shot in actual settings at West Point and some of its production devices are notable.

For example it is related that the quarters occupied by the screen hero and which is used as a background for numerous passages, is the one occupied by General Pershing during his cadet days. An imposing array of views of the cadets in review and about their classes and meetings have a kick, and some of the sentimental passages would be tremendous if they were presented rather more casually.

One gets the impression that the producer is trying to stuff the patriotic and sentimental appeal down one's throat. In one scene the young cadet hero goes into the chapel to fight out a moral difficulty involving a point of honor. There his eye wanders over the hallowed battle flags; bits of the academy's cherished traditions of the young soldier code cross his mind. Of course, he makes the right and honorable decision, but it wasn't necessary for the title writer to slop all over to make even a dumb audience understand the sentimental values of the issue. Trouble is the screen doesn't give the spectator any credit for human intelligence or average imagination.

However, the physical production is magnificent and some of the dramatic tricks are splendid. For example there is a smashing trick. The hero supposes he has been disgraced and dismissed from the Academy. He is in his quarters (Pershing's old room) and sunset review is in progress. One gets glimpses of the marching squadrons through the window, sees the grieving cadet confined to his room stiffen to salute at the sunset gun, with a view of the parade ground over his shoulder through the window. The effect is a stunner. Things like this carry their own meaning and title lines, no matter how eloquent, gild the lily.

There were possibilities in the basic story, which concerns the gradual moulding of a soldier and a gentleman out of a roughneck, by his association with the West Point institution. It is dramatic subject worthy of fine treatment. Here it is done in a heavy handed way. Boyd's Donovan is often just an objectionable smart aleck, which is fatal. The love affair between the boy and girl is pretty juvenile romance. To tell the truth Boyd doesn't look either the roughneck or the finished cadet. He's pretty mature in appearance for one thing. So is Bessie Love who plays the girl gracefully enough. Hugh Allan makes a splendid young soldier, the character drawing the sympathy that was meant to go to the hero. The subordinate characters are all excellent, especially the soldierly Commandant played convincingly by Clarence Gelbert.

The film will carry, however, on the name of Boyd and it will entertain as a pictorial. But the story and the innate drama are not there.

Rush.

TEA FOR THREE

M-G-M production and release. Directed by Robert Z. Leonard. Adapted by Roi Cooper Megrue from a play by Carl Sloboda. Cameraman, Andre Barlatier. Running time, 62 mins. At Capitol, New York, week of Oct. 29.

Carter.............................Lew Cody
Doris..........................Aileen Pringle
Philip...........................Owen Moore
Harrington..................Phillips Smalley
Annette....................Dorothy Sebastian
Butler......................Edward Thomas

As a play "Tea for Three" was smart, gay and successful. As a moving picture it is dull and possessed of little box-office value beyond its title. It represents the poorest work of Robert Z. Leonard, a director who has turned out some dandy sophisticated comedies for M-G-M. The old tricks and the familiar formula failed this time.

The acting is uniformly poor. Repeatedly Lew Cody and Owen Moore look at the camera, and a butler character fails to be the source of the laughs evidently anticipated.

Lacking the brilliant dialog of the stage success and the drawing-room presentation given it at the Maxine Elliott some seasons ago, the story becomes unforgivably stupid.

It concerns a married couple. The husband is a peculiar dolt with two principal faults: First, he breaks luncheon engagements with his wife in order to make more money; second, he is quite crazily jealous.

There is a bachelor friend, very breezy but quite honest as regards his attachment to the wife. The reality of the characters never exists. The whole procedure is pointless and wearisome. Played on a bill with an expensive stage show at the Capitol, and should be gauged with that circumstance in mind.

THE WISE WIFE

William C. DeMille production distributed by Pathe; directed by E. Mason Hopper. Phyllis Haver starred. Arthur Somers Roche story adapted by Zelda Sears and Tay Garnett. Running time 56 minutes; at the Cameo, New York, Oct. 29.

Helen Blaisdell.................Phyllis Haver
John Blaisdell.....................Tom Moore
Helen's Father...................Fred Walton
Jenny Lou.................Jacqueline Logan
Carter Fairfax.................Joseph Striker
Jason, the butler.............Robert Bolder

Light social comedy of no great moment mostly because the people concerned are not interesting people. Story has to do with the long-married and sedate husband suddenly falling for a shallow flapper and deciding to play with the notion of young love again without taking any long chances. Girl is just a flirt. The action has to do with the campaign of the loving wife to meet the situation.

There are perhaps possibilities in the subject matter of an older and wiser woman turning the tables upon a young rival for her husband, but this story does not develop anything but hackneyed comedy ideas, such as making the flapper darn husband's stockings; fixing it so that his snoring in an adjacent room keeps her awake and having the sentimental husband confronted with the young beauty when her face is plastered up with beauty clay.

Everything in the story is easily anticipated. Nothing happens by way of surprise and the wife does nothing especially clever to win her point. Indeed, anybody in the audience would be inclined to sympathize with her husband if he walked out on the wife and grabbed off the girl in the end, and that was not the impression the author or the director intended. Probably they picked too good looking a girl for the flap role in Jacqueline Logan. Jacqueline wading bare legged in a trout stream would turn any settled husband's head. Phyllis Haver suggested only the capable wife where the intent was to make her the sophisticated and fascinating woman.

The picture is an obvious affair designed for the fan multitude at its lowest mental terms. The titling has such gems as this:

"If you were my husband I'd give you rough on rats."

"If I were your husband I'd take rough on rats."

That's about the tone of the whole production, although in its settings it is excellent both in the outdoor locations and in the interiors. Like most of the mediocre pictures of the kind, the surroundings and atmosphere are beautiful, convincing and appropriate, but the subject matter is dull.

Just a commercial program release. *Rush.*

A HARP IN HOCK

Pathe release. Renaud Hoffman production. Rudolph Schildkraut starred. Story by Evelyn Campbell. Cameraman, Dewey Wrigley. Running time, 62 mins. At Broadway, New York, week of Oct. 31.

Isaac Abrams.........Rudolph Schildkraut
Timmy Shannon...........Junior Coughlan
Mary Banks....................May Robson
Nora............................Bessie Love
Dr. Mueller.................Joseph Striker
Mrs. Shannon..................Elise Bartlett

Excellent performances by Rudolph Schildkraut and Junior Coughlan accounts for 60 percent of this picture's average of merit. A title which suggests terrible things proves to be quite a human and interesting little story of the attachment between a lonely and ostracized old Jewish pawnbroker and a little Irish boy, who comes under his guardianship through a combination of circumstances.

The neighbors believe old Abrams a hard-driver because of his profession. Instead of being a Shylock the old man is warm-hearted and kindly.

There is a thread of romance, but essentially the picture is between the old man and the kid. The menace is in the form of district antagonism toward the old man on account of his trade and nationality. The kid is whisked off to an orphanage and the old man's heart is broken. Everything comes out okay, of course, though it would have been more satisfying as well as truer to life if the neighborhood gossip had remained stubbornly bitter against the pawnbroker until the end instead of weakly and unconvincingly shaking hands.

The production is good, the direction intelligent and the acting excellent. Schildkraut comes very near being the best character actor now before the camera. He gets a world of conviction into his work.

As a boxoffice proposition "A Harp in Hock" is okay with limitations. It's clean and pleasing.

Girl in the Pullman

Pathe-DeMille comedy, directed by Earl C. Kenton. Marie Prevost starred; Harrison Ford leads the support. Running time, 57 minutes. At the New York Hippodrome, Oct. 31.

A hard working, tensely directed farce, with its comedy arising from its laboriously contrived complications. Addressed to a simple grade of fans, it will make a satisfactory program release. It lacks any pretense to high quality and devotes itself to rough and tumble hoke situations and titles.

Basis of play is situation of divorced physician, about to marry again, becoming involved in hilarious situations when he and the new wife on their honeymoon find themselves in the next compartment on a Pullman train to the ex-wife who still loves her husband and intends to win him back.

The possibilities are readily seen for opening and closing doors; for bride and wife coming upon hero in all sorts of remarkable situations; intrusions of other passengers because they are awkward or because they are goofy, etc., etc., etcetera ad infinitum. It's all done so laboriously and with such determination to be funny that the thing rather defeats itself. But it has some genuine moments of low comedy, as, for instance, the nutty remarks via titles of an eccentric fellow passenger who cuts the Pullman car away from the train so that it runs wild down the mountain side and who thinks he's teasing the others by keeping their peril a secret.

Marie Prevost is called upon to do some of the hardeset-working cutie-cutie flirtation stuff that ever gave an audience a sense of intense weariness, while the usually smooth and easy Harrison Ford as the doctor is out of his element in such business as dropping an electric apparatus over a patient's head and then going away and forgetting him. Why they picked Ford for the part instead of Ben Turpin was a miscue.

The fact is that polite farce is effective on the screen only once in a score of times. If the new combination is going to shoot for fans who dote on westerns, which is a tactful way of referring to the low-brows, they would be wise to play their farce straight along Keystone lines. These dressed-up hokum polite comedies are usually blah.

That's the trouble with "The Girl in the Pullman." It has the custard pie technique but tries to disguise it as polite farce. The title, with its suggestion of spicy doings, is the best thing about the picture.

The physical production is on a high level. Settings and the atmosphere are in the best modern style. There's nothing the matter with the Pathe-DeMille technical staff. So far, the weakness appears to lie in the department that picks the stories and dictates their making into film. *Rush.*

THE LOVE WAGER

Pierpont Milliken "Platinum" production. Story and direction by Clifford Slater Wheeler. Cameraman, Earle Walker. In the cast: Lucy Beaumont, Arthur Rankin, Sheldon Lewis, Jane Grey, Gaston Glass, W. W. Watson, Dorothea Raynor and Lenore Bushman. Running time, 54 minutes.

This one is eligible as a flop in all major departments of production: script, direction and cast. Conceivably, it may have cost something. At least, a little more than the average quickie. But it all spells turk.

The story is absurdity itself. It opens with a scene of Arthur Rankin driving off in an automobile. His mother, the frantic-faced Lucy Beaumont, waits up for him. Along about 3 a. m. she comes out and falls asleep, sitting on the stone stoop of the porch, where she remains until 8 a. m.

Then, getting a wrap from the house, she goes off, presumably, to report her boy's absence to the nearest police station.

Poor lady, she never gets there! The boy, returning home in the automobile, kills his mother.

We next see him in the penitentiary with a 20-year sentence—plenty for accidental manslaughter.

A couple of close-ups of Sheldon Lewis, the kid's cellmate, and then the body of the boy hanging from the bars, he having suicided with his belt for a noose.

In his pocket is a note for the cellmate to introduce himself to a wealthy girl friend, not figuring in the story until then.

There's a pearl necklace involved and a bet made by a rich clubman (Gaston Glass) that he can earn his living for six months.

The plot is silly and hard to follow, jumping about ridiculously in an amateurish effort to gather up the various threads.

Taking everything for stiffness and newness is W. W. Watson playing a millionaire. If there's an angel in this woodpile, intelligent suspicion would indict him. Lenore Bushman as the femme lead was equally stiff and without the timed co-ordination of movement necessary to loom natural before the camera. Experienced members of the cast fared little better. Lewis was posey and Glass suffered from an embarrassment of profile close-ups.

Just so many feet of foolish film.

SILVER VALLEY

Tom Mix production for Fox. Directed by Ben Stoloff. Story by Harry Sinclair Drago. Cameraman, Dan Clark. Running time, 50 minutes.

Tom Tracey.............................Tom Mix
Sheila Blaine......................Dorothy Dwan
Black Jack Lundy.........Philo McCullough
Silent Kid...........................Jocky Hoefli
Hayfever Hawkins...........Tom Kennedy
Slim Snizer..............................Lon Poff
Mike McCool................Harry Dunkinson
Wash Taylor.....................Clarke Comstock

"Silver Valley" is both a good western and a good Tom Mix western. It has a plurality of action, an assortment of laughs and the sure touch that a well-seasoned organization gets into a picture.

Tom, fired for wrecking his boss' ranch with a bum invention, becomes the sheriff of a town with a high mortality rate among sheriffs. He shows up the master mind of the gang and wins the gal, the appealing Dorothy Dwan.

For a different touch the rendezvous of the gang is the crater of a defunct volcano. The volcano comes to life and spurts lava all over the villain.

Photography excellent. Dan Clark, Mix's regular cameraman, is ace high for fast-action stuff, always keeping the galloping smooth and the horse in the middle of the focus.

Should be a characteristic Mix bull's-eye for the box offices that front on Main Street.

SALLY OF OUR ALLEY

Columbia production and release directed by Walter Lang from a story by Edward Clark. In the cast: Shirley Mason, featured; Richard Arlen, Alec B. Francis, Paul Panzer and Kathlyn Williams. Running time, 56 mins. At Loew's New York one day, Oct. 22.

It seems there was a little lass in a tough but warm-hearted neighborhood. She had for "daddies" three argumentative tradesmen—a Wop, a Yiddisher and a Scot. And a lad of the district, a fine, upstanding machinist, loved her. Then came the sudden revelation of a wealthy aunt.

The transplanted alley rose in the hot house of snobbish wealth, the bad manners of her old friends when attending her party in the swell new diggings, and all the usual hokum.

A formula picture all the way and not a good one.

THE BOY RIDER

F. B. O. production and release. Featuring Buzz Barton, boy hero. Directed by Frank Rice. Story by Frank Terence Daugherty. Others in cast, Lorraine Eason, William Ryno, Frank H. Clark, Lewis King. Running time, 58 minutes. At the Stanley, New York, one day.

Here's a first rate idea neatly carried out. "Buzz" Barton might be a boy of 14 from his appearance, although he's, of course, older than that. In this picture he is the hero of a good action western, playing a boy wanderer in the wide and open cow country. He has adventures with bad men, cattle rustlers, saves the beautiful hero and pals around with a picturesque old-timer of the plains.

The layout is pretty much as it would be in one of those Frank Meredith on the ranch stories done into a screen play. For Saturday afternoon or a holiday in the neighborhoods it ought to draw the juvenile population to the last youngster.

At that it's as entertaining a film for grownups as the average western, for it has intelligent comedy, good characterization of the old timer and a plot lively and plausible, even if it doesn't get away from the familiar pattern.

Boy hero, separated from his folks, falls into the hands of a gang of cattle thieves who take him on intending to use him in their business. Kid gets wise to character of his associates and turns the tables by hog-tieing the leader with a lariat. The bad men are about to take their revenge when the Old Timer comes to the rescue. Old Timer and youngster become friends and team up.

Presently they find the heroine in distress and undertake to rescue her from the same band of cattle rustlers holding her for ransom. This takes them on many desperate rides and wild pursuits and into many hand-to-hand fights. "Buzz" rides a beautiful little piebald pony that will win the hearts of all the boys on first sight.

Kid and Old Timer make the world safe for pretty western heroines and then travel on their way.

Old Timer is woman-shy and much of the comedy arises from his discomfort when heroine teases him.

Picture was taken almost entirely in the open spaces and the scenic features are fine. Plenty of action and plot complications, all handled neatly. Story is told in a simple, direct style that makes it rather charming in a naive way. At least it gets away from the super-hero cowboy and for that much novelty, it is to be commended. *Rush.*

LUCKY SPURS

Chesterfield (State rights) production. Bill Patton starred. Directed by V. V. Clegg. Running time, 52 mins. At Arena, New York, on double-feature bill, one day, Oct. 19.

Despite some atrocious photography this is a likely small-town picture preaching a moral against booze, and hymning the praises of the sweet, clean, manly life. They go for that in the Harold Bell Wright belt.

The picture, additionally, tells its story in a forthright manner. Here and there careless cutting and bad continuity hurt, but in the main it's a well-told yarn.

Nobody in the cast even looks familiar, yet the acting is fair enough. The production was bankrolled on a shoestring, but doesn't look half as cheap as the majority of quickies.

Put it down as a better-than-average film.

AFLAME IN THE SKIES

F. B. O. production and release. Directed by J. P. McGowan from a story by Mary Roberts Rinehart. Cameraman, Joe Walker. Running time, about one hour. In projection room, Oct. 26.

Inez Carillo.....................Sharon Lynn
Terry Owen......................Jack Luden
Major Savage.........William Humphreys
Joseph Murdock.............Robert McKim
Saunders......................William Scott
Grandfather Carillo...Charles A. Stevenson

Dandy action picture and a satisfaction-giver for practically any house. Based on a tale by Mary Roberts Rinehart, it succeeds in being a western without the usual drawbacks of that type of picture.

Two aviators, one of them young and handsome, have pitched a camp in the New Mexican desert for the purpose of experimenting with a luminous smoke screen. Twenty miles away the hacienda of a rich old landowner is the scene of a plot to slow poison the old man to death while the villain grabs off the daughter.

The aviators, of course, enter the equation and are the means of ultimately busting up the plot. Some novelty is injected through the hero making love and calling for help by skywriting.

The hero is Jack Luden, who looks like William Boyd. Sharon Lynn, an appealing brunette, kept busy by F. B. O. in a great many of its releases, is the gal in the trim riding breeches. The menace is played by the late Robert McKim in what was probably his last role. William Scott, once a leading man, plays a bit.

An entertaining picture and promising box-office feature.

JAKE THE PLUMBER

F. B. O. production and release. Directed by Edward Luddy from original story by himself. Jess De Vorska featured. Running time, 53 mins. In projection room, Oct. 19.

Jake the Plumber........Jess De Vorska
Sarah Levine.................Sharon Lynn
Mrs. Levine................Rosa Rosanova
Mrs. Schwartz..............Ann Brodie
Fogarty.......................Bud Jamison
Mrs. Lewis................Carol Halloway
Mr. Lewis..............William T. Tooker
Sadie Rosen............Dolores Brinkman

F. B. O. introduces herewith a new comedian—Jess De Vorska. He has done some work in two-reelers, but never attracted particular notice. His principle qualification as a funny man seems to be an extremely homely face. The present cycle in screen comedies appears to be that the homelier the pan the greater the assumption of humor in the owner. Neither he nor the picture seemed funny in a projection room, yet the suspicion was born in reviewing both that there is a box-office appeal tucked way in this dumb opera.

It's a yarn about two Jewish families. The story is trivial and the gags generally without point. At all times the impression of looking at a two-reeler and not a feature is given. Yet the hokum and the silly sentiment may be swell to many moviegoers of the hinterland.

The Romantic Rogue

Rayart production, directed by Harry J. Brown. Starring Reed Howes, supported by Ena Gregory, James Bradbury, Syd Crossley and Cuyler Supplee. At Stanley, New York, one day. Running time, 50 minutes.

A featherweight comedy, non-sensical and with a title good enough to draw business one or two days.

Reed Howes acts the last of a line of patent medicine manufacturers, all previous to him belittling the qualities of their rejuvenating fluid by dying of heart failure.

Howes is an athletic type, good to look at and especially appealing to feminine viewers. He employs a dumb pan for comedy. The film also has an elderly comedy team—James Bradbury and Syd Crossley—with good humor. Ena Gregory, the heroine, looks unfamiliar and not so coy as in her cowgirl suit.

Harry J. Brown, the director, went for fast moving farce situations without regard for reality. The result is somewhat silly but suitable fare for lesser minds.

LITTLE BIG HORN

Independent production released by the Oxford Exchange. Directed by Harry L. Frasier. Roy Stewart featured. Story by Carrie E. Rawles. Shown at the Tivoli New York, on a double feature bill. Running time, 56 mins.

Gen. George A. Custer.........John Beck
Lem Hawks.....................Roy Stewart
Betty Rossman................Helen Lynch
Capt. Page...................Edmund Cobb

The entire film hinges on that fatal day, June 25, 1876, when that intrepid Indian fighter, General Custer, and a small army band were massacred by the redskins at Little Big Horn bend. There is a feeble attempt to run a romance along with the incidents leading up to the death of Gen. Custer, but it doesn't run true to form. Even Roy Stewart, the rough rider of many a film, failed to carry it to any dramatic heights.

The picture for the most part is a drab story. Aside from showing as much in detail as possible how the Indians got togteher for the clash that killed Custer it has no moral or lesson; mainly historical, a stark tragedy of the plains, showing bodies strewn all over 40 acres or so of land.

On double feature bill it may do.
Mark.

THE FIGHTING SAP

Distributed by F. B. O. Copyrighted in 1924 by Monogram Pictures Corp. Starring Fred Thomson with his horse, Silver King. Directed by Albert Rogell from a story by Marion Jackson. At the Columbus, New York, one day (Oct. 26) on a double-feature bill. Running time, about 55 minutes.

One of the ancient order of adventure pictures, made at minimum expenditure for only the most naive of audiences. The 1924 copyright mark may mean it is being now exploited to capitalize on Fred Thomson's later hook-up with Paramount.

In a dizzy order of sequences Thomson acts the sappy, geologically inclined son of a rich miner. He proves his worth at last by besting, with only the aid of his horse, a gang of desperadoes who have appropriated one of the old man's gold mines.

One bit has Thomson tied to a post with a can of explosives at his feet. Silver King, the horse, pushes the can to a spot where it will do no harm and then comes back to untie his master.

"Perils of Pauline" reincarnated.

Dog of the Regiment

Warner Bros. production, directed by Ross Lederman. Featuring Rin-Tin-Tin, with Tom Gallery, Dorothy Gulliver and John Peters in support. Scenario by Charles R. Condon from story by Albert S. Howson. Cameraman, Ed Du Par. In projection room Oct. 26. Running time, 45 minutes.

This dog picture is better than average, and should draw well among the younger element.

The story is said to be based on Rin-Tin-Tin's life. A young American attorney, in Germany to assist in the closing of a deceased client's estate, falls in love with the young mistress. Forced to return to America by the start of the world war, the attorney joins the U. S. aviation forces.

Flying over German lines, he is dropped and later taken prisoner. He finds his sweetheart, now a Red Cross nurse, with her dog also doing first aid. After several thrilling episodes in which Rin-Tin-Tin acts as chief rescuer, the couple are once more united. Rinty barks happily as his two loved ones embrace.

It is impossible to present naturalism in a picture featuring a dog of pretended human intelligence, but a good attempt has been made here. Rinty is supported by several skillful players in this film, and the director and photographer did well.

The Flying "U" Ranch

F. B. O. production, directed by Bob De Lacy, starring Tom Tyler, supported by Frankie Darro, Nora Lane, Barney Furey, Bert Hadley, Ruth Lansing, Olin Francis and Dudley Hendricks. Photographed by Joe Walker. At the Stanley, New York, one day (Oct. 22). Running time, 50 minutes.

Average horsey aroma for the cowboy addicts.

Somebody has been robbing the old man's cattle. Tom Tyler, cattle detective, comes to the ranch as "The Stranger" disguised as a Spaniard. Incidental to unraveling the mystery thefts, Tyler falls in love with the belle of the ranch, a visitor from the city. His rival for the belle is a neighboring rancher whom Tyler later identifies as the cattle thief. He vanquishes the villain by drowning him during a fight in deep water. Unfortunately, the actual drowning isn't shown. There are the regular little assistant plots to make things exciting, such as the stolen paper, the dance hall conflict between villain and hero, etc.

Tyler's pictures seem to be selling well in their certain market, so there is no use suggesting that his director deviate from aged cowboy stories. The customers seem not to notice they've seen each picture anywhere from several times to several hundred.

Photographed clearly and directed simply. Very simply.

BIRDS OF PREY

Columbia production and release. Featuring Priscilla Dean. William James Craft directed, from a story by George Bronson Howard. In the cast—Gustav von Seyffertitz, Ben Hendricks, Jr., Sidney Brackey, William Tooker, Hugh Allan. Running time, 53 mins.

An attempt has been made here to produce a crook picture along the lines of "The Unholy Three," box office winner of a season or so ago. There is the same central situation of a band of crooks, one a midget who impersonates a child. The whole thing misses because of inexpert script treatment. It ends weakly by having an earthquake kill off all the gang except the heroine while they are in the act of robbing a bank.

What an earthquake! Apparently it affected only the bank, but it did a good job there. No two brick were left together, and when rescuers filched the hero and the gal out of the wreckage they had plenty of plumbing wrapped around their necks.

Having a master mind criminal in the plot, Columbia cast Gustav von Seyffertitz for the part. He's been the master mind before and no doubt will be it again. His was the best individual performance in the face of a dumb plot and drab direction.

Being a second rate production all the way, "Birds of Prey" will be just a can off film, even where tastes are simple and dispositions lenient.

BREED OF COURAGE

F. B. O. production directed by Howard Mitchell. From the story by John Stuart Twist. Featuring Ranger, dog. Cast includes Jeanne Morgan and Sam Nelson.

Ranger is not a good actor, inclusive of all the progress he has made since last seen. In the fight scene he is one of the tamest in the business. Several shots are especially crude. The heavy practically drags the dog toward him instead of the animal attacking. In several cases the menace falls to the floor, pulling the dog down on top in semblance of a fight.

Jeanne Morgan photographs very nicely, looks attractive and indicates possibilities. She is given a difficult assignment but carries it through gracefully. Direction is bad all the way through. Sam Nelson, male lead, rates in the class with the picture.

The story encompasses a mountain feud. The McQuinns had shot another family off their own grounds and the surviving girl comes back from teaching school to assert her rights.

The young man from the district attorney's office, Nelson, does all the last minute rescues and other business with Ranger given a chance to eat a dynamite fuse to prevent an explosion.

Ranger is given another dog as a mate to work with.

Few possibilities aside from states' rights.

UNCLE TOM'S CABIN

Universal production and release, adapted from Harriet Beecher Stowe's story of the same name. Directed by Harry Pollard with Charles Stumar and Jacob Kull cameramen. Story supervision, E. J. Montagne; continuity by Harvey Thew and A. P. Younger. Musical score by Dr. Hugo Riesenfeld. At the Central, New York, for twice daily run commencing Nov. 4. Running time, 141 mins., split by an intermission; $2.20 top.

Uncle Tom..................James B. Lowe
Cassie..........................Eulalie Jensen
Eliza.....................Margarita Fischer
Eva St. Clare...................Virginia Grey
Topsy................................Mona Ray
Miss Ophelia.................Aileen Manning
George Harris...................Arthur Carew
Simon Legree................George Siegmann
Little Harris....................Lassie Ahern
Mr. Shelby........................Jack Mower
Mrs. Shelby....................Vivian Oakland
St. Clare...........................John Roche
Lawyer Marks............Lucien Littlefield
Mrs. St. Clare................Gertrude Astor
Haley..............................Adolph Milar
Harris (slave owner)...........Skipper Zeliff
Phineas Fletcher.........Nelson McDowell

"Uncle Tom's Cabin" is probably the best big picture Universal has ever turned out. And yet it's not a $2 road show. It may be $2 for exploitation purposes, but cannot expect to get beyond that.

"Uncle Tom" is a good picture but not great. Its main fault at present is length. Its complex is the necessity of telling three stories in one and to hold these themes both together and up.

As run off principal attention centers on Eliza and George Harris, who although colored, carry what love interest there is to appeal to a general public. Drama is signified in the relations of Legree and Cassie while the sympathy goes to Uncle Tom. Topsy and Eva are an incident in a story already filled to the brim but a sidelight which will make the women sniffle. Musical accompaniment is not noteworthy although a mixed chorus chants a spiritual at odd moments offstage.

Eliza and her husband, George, run throughout the performance. The story opens with their wedding and closes as they are reunited after a long separation and a series of privations. Uncle Tom and Legree are dead.

In 141 minutes of unreeling something must stand out and certain scenes do. Eliza's famed flight across the ice has been well cameraed and didn't need the applause which started from the back of the house. Mona Ray's interpretation of the impish Topsy screens as an understanding reading of the part, and if Eva's death was overly drawn out it was no fault of hers. George Siegmann and Eulalie Jensen, especially the latter, give the top performances.

Lincoln's Emancipation closes the first half and Sherman's march to the sea is instrumental in winding up the story. How much theatrical license has been taken to get that Georgia expedition into the picture is immaterial inasmuch as "Uncle Tom's Cabin" would have a tough time in the South anyway, and the flashing of Sherman's men simply clinches and likely queers its chances below the Line.

Harry Pollard has given the picture a serious and good presentation. From a directorial standpoint the most damaging misdemeanor is the erratic pace. Perhaps inevitable in a film that postpones intermission for 80 minutes with the finish still 61 minutes away after it resumes. Reported to be in 13 reels, "Uncle Tom" can still lose at least 1,000 feet. The technical staff has done nice work in production, sets, lighting, etc., so in this wise it may be said that the scenes as made can stand. It's the sequences that need curtailing, particularly the aftermath of Eva's death, which is symbolically signified.

The players have been uniformly well chosen. James B. Lowe gives a human performance in the title role; Margarita Fischer will not meet the general conception of Eliza on appearance; Edmund Carew is adequate as the runaway slave; someone has tried to make Lassie Ahern too cute as Eliza and George's child, and Virginia Grey is sufficiently angelic as Eva. However, the cast kick is in Cassie, Legree, Topsy and Uncle Tom, and in that order.

Those river boats peculiar to the South, the stern wheelers, are made colorful (a tipoff on what U. can do with "Show Boat" if going after it properly) with a certain amount of the plantation stuff also keeping eyes on the screen.

Famed and as well known as it is, there still remains the question of how familiar with "Tom" is the present generation under 30. They have seen it satirized enough and heard of it, but how many know the story or the glamour of its past? How interested they are in it or whether they'll believe it an educational matter to see it, is Universal's problem. It's going to take a lot of plugging and there's many a state that may shy at the three cornered flogging of Uncle Tom.

U. is supposed to have spent over $1,000,000 on this program super. After viewing it that figure is plausible enough, especially considering a tooth which ultimately sent Pollard to a hospital resulting in a six months' production delay.

But "Uncle Tom" only occasionally grips and never brings a lump to the throat. If they can't be stirred it's not $2, and it's an axiom among a few that if a picture doesn't indicate coast to coast throbbing qualifications there's no use trying to force it. Road showing a picture means something more than just going into a theatre on sharing terms and hanging out 2.15 and 8.15 signs.

Not forgetting to give someone credit for putting over an opening that had no sun arcs present to jam up Broadway and at least made this premiere one of the most pleasant of the season to date. *Sid.*

THE GAUCHO

United Artists release. Starring Douglas Fairbanks. Produced and copyrighted by the Elton Corporation. From a story by Elton Thomas. Directed by F. Richard Jones. Photographed by Tony Gaudio. Running time, 102 mins. World premiere at Grauman's Casino, Hollywood, Nov. 4.

Mountain Girl.....................Lupe Velez
Girl of the Shrine,
Ceraine Greear, Eve Southern
Ruiz...............Gustav von Seyffertitz
His First Lieutenant......Michael Vavitch
Gaucho's First Lieutenant..Charles Stevens
The Padre..................Nigel de Brulier
Black Doom Man.......Albert MacQuarrie
The Gaucho.............Douglas Fairbanks

Doug Fairbanks is at it again. He still knows how to do those acrobatics, and just the Fairbanks of old serving up his regular routine of tricks in new dishes.

The story of "The Gaucho" is credited on the screen to Elton Thomas, but that person is none other than Doug. In doing so, however, he does not hog the picture, but permits a little Mexican girl, new to films, in on the racket, and this baby is over. She scored 100 per cent. plus and is established as a feminine Fairbanks.

This youngster, who got her first shot at screen work on the Roach lot, is Lupe Velez, and is not more than 16 or 17, a beauty and has that freshness that goes with youth. When it comes to acting she does not have to step aside for anyone. They put on a rave about Dolores del Rio for more than two years out here. Now it's going to go for Lupe. This kid has a great sense of comedy value to go with her athletic prowess. She got her start with Fairbanks, and it won't be long now. Doug deserves the credit for letting the youngster get the break.

Carded as a $1.50 attraction, it is a toss-up whether the picture can road show or run on the two-a-day plan in general. With a strong supporting stage show it is a cinch. Otherwise it can come along as a special and clean up with the gang who like Doug. They get thrills they will carry away and think about for a long time after seeing the picture. Though the first 30 minutes or so seem a little slow, the picture then settles down. Looks as though better than $500,000 has been expended, and the picture shows it. There are several new novelties, with the general theme based on a miracle.

To please the little mountain girl, the Gaucho has a house moved from its base by 100 horses to the town he has come to take because there is an abundance of gold there. A novelty and worth while. Then there are scenes of troops in large numbers going through a mountain pass which is a gorgeous sight. The big punch is a stampede of cattle to save the day for the Gaucho. A tremendous herd sweeps the town, driving everything and everybody before it, with the Gaucho and his mob coming in and taking possession on the dust. A pip of a scene.

The picture opens in technicolor with a little girl falling from a ledge into a canyon and lying prostrate. It looks like death. But there comes a halo from a rock, showing there is life in her body. The natives come forth, watch the miracle and join in prayer with the girl. Word spreads about the miracle, people come from all around, the girl prays for the healing of a few and soon they call the town Miracle City. Then begins the action in black and white. The town grows up, a shrine is built and gold pours in. Ruiz, the Usurper, hears about it and sends his aide (Michael Vavitch) to take it. Then the Gaucho is flashed. He and his outfit are in the mountains. A reward of 10,000 pesos is on his head. He starts for a town, tells his men he will go alone and that they should ride in the long way over the pass. Doug starts his hop-skip-and-jump stuff. Rushes the natives and, of course, holds sway. The little girl, played by Lupez, seems to be the only one unafraid. She just makes for him, beats up another dame who tries to cut in and sticks fast to the Gaucho. He decides to head for the Miracle City. The kid wants to go along. She is eating her supper. So he has his men tie ropes to the base of the building and 100 horses pull the house while he and the girl are inside. On the outskirts he learns that the men of the Usurper are in possession. So the Gaucho decides to take the army single-handed, telling the men to follow in when their flag is hoisted. Of course he is recognized, and chase after chase follow. Finally he corners the head of the army and forces him to go on the balcony and announce that the Gaucho has been taken prisoner, orders the latter's flag hoisted and then tells his men to stack their arms. With the trick over, the Gaucho's gang comes into town unopposed.

Deciding to have peace all around, the Gaucho puts on a big feast and then orders that prisoners put in jail by the Usurper's men be brought forth. They are turned loose, with the exception of a leper. Doug sentences him to do away with himself, saying if he were in the same plight that is what he would do. The leper, however, sticks around. Doug goes to the room of a beautiful girl he saw when coming into town. She holds him off and finally the mountain girl comes in. She runs at the other girl. Doug tosses her around and is cut by a dagger, but gets rid of the girl. Reclining against a window sill the leper grabs his hand. A struggle follows, with the leper telling him to do what he said he would under the circumstances. Doug goes to put the gun to head, but is followed by the girl, who tells him of the miracle shrine. All he need do is pray. Both pray. He puts his hand into the spring and, of course, is healed. Meanwhile, Ruiz hears of the Gaucho being in possession and sets forth for the town to take him. Gaucho's lieutenant double-crosses him and has the followers withdraw to another town. The mountain girl tells that Doug is in the shrine with the other girl, becomes remorseful, but too late, and he is captured with the padre and the miracle miss. They are to be hanged, but the heroine does a Paul Revere to his followers. Doug has figured a way out of the bastile and meets his troops on the outskirts of the town. He devises the way to take the town by a cattle stampede and, of course, saves the girl and priest who are about to be executed.

Outside of the performance of Fairbanks and the girl, the other players are just in the cast, although Eve Southern stands out as the miracle girl. Picture well titled and photographed and will get over with all of Doug's fans. In some spots they may be a little skeptical about the leper sequence, but it is so deftly handled that there should be no aversion to it.

With a Fairbanks picture not having been on the market in more than a year, it looks as though this one will get an okay all around.

Ung.

MY BEST GIRL

Mary Pickford production. United Artists release. Story by Kathleen Norris. Directed by Sam Taylor. Scenario by Hope Loring. Cameraman, Charles Rosher. Running time, 64 mins. At Rialto, New York, for run, commencing Nov. 5.

Maggie Johnson................Mary Pickford
Joe Grant.........................Charles Rogers
Ma Johnson......................Sunshine Hart
Pa Johnson.................Lucien Littlefield
Liz Johnson.............Carmelita Geraghty
Mr. Merrill....................Hobart Bosworth
Mrs. Merrill.......................Evelyn Hall
Millicent Rogers...............Avonne Taylor
Judge................................Mack Swain

Plenty of hoke in this latest Mary Pickford. It's the old tear-behind-the-smile, clean, wholesome, family type of fun. No crocodiles in this one. May be less art, but more box office.

"My Best Girl" is for anything up to a week, but will hardly be held for longer periods except where U. A. has its own house or a partnership.

"Girl" is a typical Mary Pickford formula. Mary is the brains and character of an incompetent, shiftless but well-meaning family. The father is a mail carrier, a creature of habit and pressure. The mother, like certain women characters in Dickens, has a penchant for funerals—anybody's and all funerals. The other sister is a hotsy-totsy, and keeps company with a shady gent.

Mary is a stock girl in the five-and-ten. She falls in love with a new clerk, not knowing he is the son of the owner. The boy is betrothed to a society miss, but the father insists he makes some sort of a showing in the store before the engagement is announced.

That's the plot. It has been well cushioned in the conventional corners with gags from the combined mentalities of Allen McNeil, Tim Whelan, Hope Loring, Clarence Hennecke and Sam Taylor, the exgagman, who megaphoned the job. Kathleen Norris authored this yarn to Miss Pickford's measure.

The cast is good. Charles Rogers overcomes his good looks with a display of naturalistic humanness. In this instance he is more the old type of screen hero. Miss Pickford is her usual sweet and likable self, seeming very much flesh and blood despite being the only white sheep in a tribe of black ones.

The entire production is high class.

QUALITY STREET

Metro-Goldwyn-Mayer production, directed by Sidney Franklin. Marion Davies starred. Adaptation from the J. M. Barrie play. Scenario by Albert Lewis and Hans Kraly. Titled by Marion Ainslee and Ruth Cummings. Hans Sartov, photographer. At the Embassy, New York, for a run, starting Nov. 2.

Phoebe Throssel............Marion Davies
Dr. Valentine Brown........Conrad Nagel
Susan Throssel........Helen Jerome Eddy
Mary Willoughby..............Flora Finch
Nancy Willoughby.........Margaret Seddon
Henrietta Turnbull........Marcelle Corday
Patty..........................Kate Price

A costume play of quaint charm, beautifully produced, "Quality Street" provides a graceful, sentimental role for Marion Davies. It recalls the same actress' agreeable performance in "Little Old New York.

What makes the new picture notable is that the producer has managed to screen a worthy transcription of the Barrie comedy, which does not lend itself naturally to picture treatment. Something of the elusive quality of Barrie's sentimental humor is here somehow caught and conveyed. And that alone marks the effort as worth while, because Barrie is a difficult subject to catch and fix in screen terms.

Contributing toward this achievement is some of the best and sincerest acting Miss Davies has ever done in a part that ideally fits her type of blonde beauty and that supplies a temperamentally happy medium for this actress's comedy talent.

The production is a marvel of pictorial beauty, the men with their brave boots and jaunty cockaded hats, the women with the sweeping but discreet frocks of the empire and the period rooms that to this day are the despair of interior decorators. All have been created in a delightfully real background for the romantic story of the little English girl who waited for her lover to return from the wars, faithful to a hope rather than a pledge.

The group of character types that made for "Quality Street" as much of its charm as did the sorrows and joys of its romantic hero and heroine have been exquisitely recreated. Helen Jerome Eddy as the timid but loving sister of the hapless heroine gets a world of fragrant and charming sentiment into the building of the fluttering Susan, while the trio of village gossips, played by Flora Finch, Margaret Seddon and Marcelle Corday, are a delight.

To the title writers also is due a tribute. Some of the lines have as much atmosphere in them as the scenes they illuminate, all written in the quaint stiltedness that marked the language of the day. For it was the "prunes and prisms" era, and the little comedy pokes fun at the social customs as well as the speech of the epoch in a dainty, almost tender, way that only Barrie could command.

Probably picture tradition would have justified the building up of action passages, such, perhaps, as the hero's adventures in the wars, but instead this picture holds to the Barrie play in all its color and shading. And, what is more important, makes it interesting in its high comedy and sentimental appeal.

Beauty of the settings alone are an enormous asset. There is one passage devoted to the homecoming of the hero in a stage coach that is built up into a bright episode. The dashing horses, swaying coach and the misted landscape, the bustle as it changes horses in a tavern stop, has all the charm and beauty of a fine old print vitalized into motion.

The possibilities of a box-office smash are probably remote. The picture is not designed to that end by its very nature, but it will contribute enormously to the prestige of the star and of the producer.

Rush.

SHANGHAI BOUND

Paramount production and release. Directed by Luther Reed from the story by E. S. O'Reilly. Screen play by John Goodrich and Roy Harris. Starring Richard Dix, Mary Brian featured. At the Paramount, New York, week of Nov. 5. Running time, over 60 mins.

Jim Bucklin.................Richard Dix
Sheila..........................Mary Brian
Payson ....Charles Byer
Louden...................George Irving
Shanghai Rose................Jocelyn Lee
Smith........................Tom Macguire
Yen...........................Frank Chew
Local Agent...................Tom Gubbins
Algy..........................Arthur Hoyt
Scarface.....................Jetsu Komai

May not break house records, but the kind of a picture that builds patronage. Compactly constructed, from studio and story angles, efficiently directed, the players properly cast, an interesting story, speedy all the way through and, topping everything, Dix's name with an assured following.

The megaphone wielder is probably responsible for the light, entertaining manner in which the story is prsented.

Even in the most melodramatic moments there is a hilarious touch, but managed so that it does not detract from the strength of the situation, rather enforcing them.

Dix has to be a rough, domineering sea captain without descending to real or affected brutality which, in pictures, is usually the sign of a warm understanding heart.

The story is planted in one of the smaller Chinese ports upon which a bandit chieftain has laid hold. His plan is to unite the Chinese against all white invaders. Bucklin is almost caught while with a friendly Chinese. Tied up in a white apron Bucklin looks like a waiter, and when the party of supercilious Americans command him to bring food he kids them along until the angry mob outside had wrecked the tourist car, killed the chauffeur and taken their belongings.

On the down river run to Shanghai, Bucklin has the underwater fight with the Chinese. Photography is remarkably clear in these scenes. The party on board Bucklin's ship is rescued by a yacht, but Bucklin is left alone in the waters, despite Sheila's protest.

The usual fadeout with a pretty background in Shanghai.

THE DEVIL DANCER

Los Angeles, Nov. 4.

Samuel Goldwyn production. United Artists release. Starring Gilda Gray, with Clive Brook. Story by Harry Hervey. Fred Niblo production, with adaptation by Alice D. G. Miller. Titles by E. Justus Mayer. Cameramen, George Barnes and Thomas Brannigan. World premiere in conjunction with Gild Gray stage act, Million Dollar, Los Angeles, Nov. 3. Running time, 73 minutes. U. A. release.

Takla.........................Gilda Gray
Stephen.......................Clive Brook
Sada......................Ada May Wong
Ivan........................Serge Temof
Hassim..................Michael Vavitch
Sa lik Lama.........................Sojin
Ta a...........................Ura Mita
Arnold Guthrie..............Albert Conti
Isabel...............Clarissa Selwynne
Ka im.........................Kala Pasha
Grand Lama................James Leong
Lathrop..............William H. Tooker
Aubrey...................Claire Du Brey
Julia..........................Nora Cecil

Gilda Gray has the best picture of her career. She is handled remarkably in a photographic way; does plenty of dancing and acquits herself capably from the acting end.

This picture is much better than her "Aloma of the South Seas" and "Cabaret." With Miss Gray appearing in person and properly exploited, it should play to big results from the box office in the key cities and the one-week stops. It is also a good bet for the European and Latin-American markets, but for the small towns, where they do not know the shimmy queen, it is another matter.

Sam Goldwyn will have to figure on the personal appearance to get the better part of his $500,000 nut in the American field. He probably will get production cost and considerable profit as a whole on the investment, but it will not reach stupendous proportions.

The production was a complicated affair for him. It started off with Al Raboch directing. Then Lynn Shores, who was his assistant, came along and got the megaphone, with Raboch reverting to the assistant position. This state of affairs did not last over six weeks, when Fred Niblo came on the Goldwyn pay roll to do a picture. He was drafted for this one and finished it. On the screen he is given sole credit, with the other directors ignored. Just what they did and he did is not obvious, but evidently Niblo pulled the production out of the "woods."

The story is that of a missionary and his wife, traveling in the Black Lama country of the Himalayas. The man is killed; the wife gives birth to a child and dies. The infant, of course, is Gilda, and she is brought up in the faith of the Lamas. She sees no whites and believes in the native creed.

When at maturity the tribe's dancer, played by Anna May Wong, commits an indiscretion with one of the men, both are buried alive. The ritual performed calls for one of the females of the tribe to dance the curse of the devil off. That job falls to Gilda.

Clive Brook, English adventurer, comes into the walled town with his man Friday, played by Kala Pasha. They make up as members of the tribe. Brook sees the white girl and, of course, finally, in the Doug Fairbanks fashion, gets her to flee, and takes her into the white settlement. He introduces her to his people and announces he is in love.

His sister, played by Clarissa Selwynne, does not like the bringing up of the girl, and frames with a trainer and owner of nautche dancers to get her away. He kidnaps her and tries to make her one of his own. She repulses him, but, loving the dance, always performs wherever they go.

The story as it goes along developed into plenty of melodrama and holds suspense. Possibly the screen story does not coincide with the original yarn of Hervey's, who is an authority on the tropical wild tribes. It suffices from the entertainment standpoint. There are plenty of mob scenes, with a carload or two of blacks used in the big ones for atmosphere.

The supporting cast is exceptionally good, with the Gray dances as hot as ever. Plenty of them, and if the Gilda fans of the "shimmy" days still have a desire to see her shake it up, what she does in the picture is worth the price of admission.

Brook gives a sincere performance and struts his stuff right in the tight fight spots.

Kala Pasha comes on early, but what they see of him is great. He is a comic that comics on the screen, with every expression of the pan being sure-fire for the laugh. Michael Vavitch as the Nautche thief gives a typical cruel whip lashing character. The others of the cast flash on and off.

Direction meant a great deal, and if the majority of the stuff was shot with the megaphone in the hands of Niblo he should get the certificate of merit. He had a great camera crew who knew angles and how to show Gilda emoting and dramatizing. The titles by Edwin Justus Mayer were of the necessary storytelling kind, with little chance for anything extraordinary.

Ung.

BODY AND SOUL

Metro-Goldwyn-Mayer production and release. Directed by Reginald Barker. Adapted from the story by Katherine Newlin Burt. Titles by Farnham. Running time, 70 minutes. At the Capitol, New York, week Nov. 5.

Hilda ....Aileen Pringle
Ruffo ....Norman Kerry
Dr. Leyden................Lionel Barrymore
The Postman................T. Roy Barnes

An out-of-the-ordinary picture. This drama of a disgraced doctor, humble maid servant and young hero in the surroundings of the Alpine peaks doesn't classify itself with any of the familiar screen forms. Its oddity and the fine background of the mountain snows, together with Lionel Barrymore's acting, are the chief recommendations, for the story is without humor. It has much gloom in its telling and comes to a rather oppressing and pessimistic ending.

For moving delineation of character and graphic playing of strong dramatic passages Barrymore is remarkably impressive, even for a player of his prestige and accomplishment. His creation of a broken man striving to catch somehow a fleeting bit of romance and happiness, his slow realization that the game is against him and his gradual collapse under brooding and drink make a compelling chapter on the screen. But serious subjects of this sort, however well made and however sincere in aim, are faced with the routine tastes of the fan public and there is no way to gauge their result. This one will be either a bust or a clean-up, with Barrymore's acting possibly the factor to turn the scales to the right side.

Some idea of the quality of the story may be gained from such passages as that where the once famous surgeon, in drunken madness and also because his mind was a little turned from introspective brooding, takes seriously the jesting suggestion that he burn a brand upon his young wife to satisfy his jealous suspicions, and proceeds to carry out the plan. He drags the girl through a blinding snowstorm to a smithy and there heats his office seal in the forge, pressing it upon her shoulder.

The girl is taken off by her young lover. When the handsome boy is crushed in a fall from a mountain snow field it is the half demented and altogether drunken husband who is summoned to save his life. Here is staged a passage of pretty heavy drama, with the surgeon locking himself in the room with his dying rival, there to make up his mind whether to restore him to life or let him die. He compromises with his wife to let the boy live on her promise to return to him, and carries out his part of the compact, only he himself is caught in an avalanche—and a remarkably realistic avalanche it is—on his way back to the tavern, presumably leaving the girl and her maimed lover to make the best of their lives together. Scarcely what you'd call a happy ending.

The production is as out of the ordinary as the story. The settings carry out the picturesque foreign atmosphere which seems to pervade the whole production. The snow scenes are particularly splendid, both in quiet pictorial effect and in the storm scenes that make an appropriate background for much of the heavily dramatic action. There are few dull scenes and the story is carried to its climax with relentless economy of detail.

A fine production, finely conceived and admirably carried out, but not a great popular success from the nature of the work itself.

Rush.

PAJAMAS

Fox production and release, featuring Olive Borden. Story by William Conselman with J. G. Blystone directing. At the Roxy, New York, week Nov. 5. Running time, 57 mins.

Angela Wade....................Olive Borden
Daniel Wade.....................John J. Clark

John Weston..............Lawrence Gray
Egbert Forrest................Jerry Miley

One of Fox's snap releases throwing one-third of its s. a. trio to the front in the person of Olive Borden.

Get the Misses Borden, Bellamy and Del Rio on a screen, all at the same time, and something is liable to burn. And the title to this one, "Pajamas."

Fox is reaching into the hat and pulling one of these out well nigh every week. The intelligensia may not think so much of the billing, but Jim and Jake are going to drop in to find out what it's all about. In this case they won't be overly thrilled, but they won't be disappointed either.

It's a flip and flimsy story harking back to the daughter of wealth who again is her charming and selfish self, always according to all screen ethics. A small cast picture that will get by on the work of Miss Borden, Lawrence Gray and the exterior sets. Not a bad scenic artist at that for the last half locale is the Canadian Rockies, and they don't throw up those mountains over night. So if the film looks good, give some credit to the cameraman.

John Weston is down from Canada to close a business deal with Angela's father. Induced to jump into one of those Hollywood swimming pools with all his clothes on, when it comes time to sign the papers the sheets are worthless. It's a hurried trip back to Canada by 'plane, and Angela sneaks into the pilot's cockpit. A midair mishap maroons the pair after a parachute descent, and there they fall in love after continuous quarreling.

The action has laughs if it doesn't cover much mentality, and there's always that background to look at if not interested in the story. However, nobody's line of vision is going to get very far away from Miss Borden.

This is the Fox unit which originally stopped off at Banff, became dissatisfied with something or other and jumped to Lake Louise. There they located and were out on location as early as six in the morning, coming back to talk it over with Rod and Vilma, who were honeymooning at the time.

A lead title gives credit to Lake Louise for the scenery, but maybe what happened behind the hotel desk at Banff caused the Canadian Pacific by-line to be dropped.

"Pajamas" will do as program fare.   *Sid.*

THE COLLEGE WIDOW

Warner Brothers production. Directed by Archie L. Mayo from the play of the same name by George Ade. At the Strand, New York, week of Nov. 6. Running time, 67 mins.

Jane Witherspoon........Dolores Costello
Billie Bolton............William Collier, Jr.
Hiram Bolton............Anders Randolf
Prof. Witherspoon......Charles Hill Mailes
Prof. Jellicoe...............Douglas Gerrard
Jack Larrabee................Robert Ryan
Jimmie Hopper............Sumner Getchel
Don White...............Big Boy Williams

Following "The Fair Co-Ed" (M-G-M), this film is further proof that George Ade's college stuff is easily adapted to picturization. "College Widow" is a fast, snappy comedy that can be brought into the full week houses without fear of box-office trouble.

The previous and current horde of college pictures have worn the novelty off campus capers, but this one seems strong enough to withstand the handicap.

Story shows how the college president's daughter employs her sex appeal in recruiting a football team for the school. At a board meeting the trustees complained they were losing students and money by specializing in education, and threatened to kick the college

head out if the football team didn't beat its big rival the following year. The daughter, doing her stuff in the summer resorts, manages to collect a crew of candidates, each thinking he is the big motif in the gal's life. Playing the boys along through the season, the girl keeps them from getting wise until just before the big game.

When the light hits them, the players declare a walkout at first, but later decide they like the girl well enough to win the game for her old man's sake.

The love theme centers on the girl and a millionaire's son who has been kicked out of 12 colleges. He is one of the s. a'd football experts, falling for the girl so hard he uses an assumed name and works his way through school because his father thinks he is enrolled in the rival college.

Casting has been handled well, almost all of the players being naturals for their parts. Miss Costello's charm is the big idea, and she has it in abundance. Collier, as the millionaire's son, acts a likeable wise guy without strain. The football huskies probably are actual. One of the more prominent is Big Boy Williams, who used to raise dust at Oklahoma University.

The big game is well handled. It's a combination of closeups blending with long shots of regular games (for shots including stadium crowds) and done very well.

Good comedy direction by Mayo.

THE HARVESTER

FBO release of Leo Meehan production. Adapted from Gene Stratton Porter's novel of the same name with Orville Caldwell and Natalie Kingston featured. At Hippodrome, New York, week Nov. 7. Running time, 66 mins.

A sleeping potion de luxe. It's a bet that no picture this season has been as slow as the molasses movement this film clings to the first 20 minutes. For over a reel it's practically a nature study. Anyway, the Hip doesn't know the difference, as it's used to the bad boys.

Why F. B. O. ever went to work on this script is one of those things for Sweeney. It may have been okay in book form, and if remembered rightly the novel had a big sale, but it in no way shapes as screen material as finally produced. The title will have to draw, as the cast features two strangers, Oliver Caldwell and Natalie Kingston. And there's a dog in the running for those inevitable cute scenes with the dejected hero.

Gathering herbs for a living, the harvester dreams of a girl who finally appears, but is racked by outstanding debts. In fact, she has a debt for every situation. So after they wed, in name only, it all comes out when she reveals she has promised herself to a doctor who served her dying mother gratis. But the doc is regular, spurns the girl's gesture of appreciation and she finally learns to love her husband.

This is all heavy going with 50 minutes having passed before there is a threat of a story twist that will catch interest. To further impede the snail's pace, the husband brings the body of the girl's mother to their home for a second burial. So the audience sits through a funeral procession and a scene at the grave. Little or no production concerned.

Camera work average and a fair performance from those involved. It's a picture the booth boys can speed up past 95 without a guilty conscience. It took the Hip 66 minutes to get rid of it.

Daily change and double feature subject and none too strong in either instance.

Four youngsters no older than 12 nor less than 9 sitting, unaccompanied in the Hip balcony smoking cigarets. But that's got nothing to do with F. B. O. It comes under

the head of theatre management. And just comment. For the Hip needs biz, and how.   *Sid.*

SURRENDER

Universal production and release. Directed by Edward Sloman. Story by Alexander Brody. Mary Philbin starred. Ivan Mosjukine featured. Running time, 60 mins. At Proctor's 5th Ave., three days, starting Nov. 3.

A picture of East European Jews, interesting as conveying a glimpse of customs and peoples strange to America. The action takes place in a Jewish village situated in a war zone for which Russian and Austrian troops are contending. It is a modernization of "Lea Lyon," a famous old play.

The girl (Mary Philbin) is the daughter of the rabbi (Nigel de Brulier). She meets and likes a Gentile peasant only to learn later that he is a Cossack prince. Unless she comes to his rooms by a certain hour he says his soldiers will set fire to all the homes in the village. She goes (to save her people), but the Cossack (Ivan Mosjukine) proves unexpectedly gentle. He looks at the stars and in subtitles deplores the fact that the same stars that look down on lovers look down on armies of killers. He ends up by saying: "Oh, God, what beasts men are." That's the cue for grand renunciation.

There is more trouble; the girl is stoned by her people in return for her sacrifice, the rabbi dies, there are wars and years and in fadeout the reunion of the Cossack, now a comrade of the commune, and the languishing belle. It's not very real, but because of the foreign background the picture may be interesting to the majority of audiences.

Catalog it as fair to middling.

THE LAST WALTZ

Ufa production. Paramount release. Directed by Arthur Robinson from Oscar Strauss' operetta, scenarized by Alice D. G. Miller. Running time, 62 mins. At Paramount, New York, week of Nov. 12.

The Queen..................Sophie Pagay
The Crown Prince.....Hans von Schlettow
His Aide.....................Willy Fritsch
The Princess................Liane Haid
The Countess................Suzy Vernon
Her Maid......................Elsie Vanya
A Minister of State............Fritz Rasp
A Lady in Waiting..............Ida Wust

Credentials from Ufa and Paramount will not make this a good picture. The best that can be said for it is that it manages to be reasonably interesting, but not distinguished, smart, box office or unusual.

It contains some of the worst makeup that ever made a pretty actress look like something else. The French film companies are supposed to be pre-eminent in the undisciplined use of mascaro, but with this picture Germany officially enters a bid for consideration.

Exhibs who may have found Ufa's "Dream Waltz" of b. o. strength should not believe "The Last Waltz," a sequel in standard or value. The picture may be played, but on a conservative basis.

The plot is derived from an operetta. The inevitable crown prince is somewhat of a cad. His conceptions of honor are warped. He needs to be primed to do the magnanimous thing. He fights with his friend and aide, Count What's name, and sentences him to be shot at sunrise. The ladies get together and the future crown princess delivers a timely lecture which saves everything including the count.

It is not likely this film will create a mandate from the American people for the prompt importation of any of the players. The acting is good, however. And the direction is passable. Willy Fritsch plays the count. His work in Ufa's "Dream Waltz" made many mark him for Hollywood. He does not show to similar advantage this time. If Hans Adalbert von Schetlow, playing the crown prince, should come to America he will have to check part of that moniker at Ellis Island.

Photography good, and a few laughs.

SORRELL AND SON

United Artists production and release. Presented by Joseph M. Schenck. Directed by Herbert Brenon from the novel by Warwick Deeping. Featuring H. B. Warner. At the Rivoli, New York, Nov. 12, for a "grind" run. Running time, over 60 mins.

Stephen Sorrell..............H. B. Warner
Dora Sorrell.............Anna Q. Nilsson
Flo Palfrey..................Carmel Myers
John Palfrey.................Lionel Belmore
Thomas Roland............Norman Trevor
Buck....................Louis Wolheim
Dr. Orange................Paul McAllister
Fanny Garland...............Alice Joyce
Kit Sorrell...................Nils Asther
Molly Roland.................Mary Nolan

Little doubt that this picture will make money, a lot of it. It's a big draw in every better class theatre in the country; not only on account of the well known novel, but because an age-old and ever beautiful story has been superbly mounted, ably directed and well played.

Whether this picture will appeal in the 10 and 20 cent houses is problematical. It would not be fair to attempt to analyze the production technically. It becomes cheap melodrama toward the finish. It is composed of the usual elements—sobs, tears, gray hairs and a tragic finish for the British officer who remained a gentleman through the trials that thousands of British officers were forced to undergo in post-war England. But the appeal to the finer sensibilities is irresistible; there's a thoughtful tear in every situation. It may be ever so lightly overdrawn but no sob story ever told in pictures has had a universal appeal unless given that additional shading.

The only reason "Sorrell and Son" is not a $2 picture is because there is no longer any such thing. There aren't two 'alleged $2 pictures in New York that could get out on the road and break even, discounting any idea of a profit.

It may be a cinch to pull the mother love thing for box office angles, but the love of a father and a son may be intensified many times, although a precarious proposition in constant danger of suffering in screen treatment. While the movie mob is always willing to accept and ready to understand the heartaches of a mother, they don't fall so hard when it's the old man who is suffering. Perhaps for this reason it is noticeable in the early scenes that Brenon manages his contact between father and son in a manner that defies criticism.

Captain Sorrell, awarded the Military Cross, comes home to find his wife packing up to go away with a new husband. No hysterics and no pleas. The affair is handled naturally. She wants to go because Sorrell has no money. He doesn't want that kind of a woman for a wife, so it's even.

In scrupulously formal attire, top hat, frock coat, cane and gloves, the Captain looks for a job as sales manager. He can't get it. He becomes a hotel porter. That is no exaggeration. It is only too true, even if they don't like the idea in England.

Flo Palfrey (Carmel Myers) was Sorrell's first boss. She scrutinized the Captain carefully. He is obviously a gentleman and she a bad girl. The idea of being able to order a British officer around, making him clean spittoons and wash the floors, appeals. The manner in which Miss Myers handles this scene is great, and for that reason it is doubtful if it will pass uncensored.

Flo finally gets her hubby drunk and the Captain in her room wiping a mirror late at night. She is in a disturbing state of undress but Sorrell walks out on her and it costs him his job.

Through it all the father and son theme is never once relegated to the background. They're pals. Kit grows up a famous surgeon and then mother puts in a claim for her son's affections. She shows him night life in London, even framing a dame on him. But the boy can't see her as anything but a drunken old woman trying to be young again, and he leaves.

One of the big scenes is where the boy, now married, lies awake crying, listening to the moans of his father dying in the next room.

Mickey McBan and Betsy Ann Hisle, playing Kit and Molly as children, work like veterans, with a pleasing absence of awkwardness. Nils Asther, as Kit the man, does not seem to register very strongly. Mary Nolan photographs nicely and stands out in her minor role.

Alice Joyce, as the housekeeper of a class inn, is placed in one scene that has little chance out of town. That is where Louis Wolheim, as the head porter, is caught in the girl's room, attired in a dressing gown, with the girl screaming for help.

The closing scene, where Kit has to give his father an extra strong dose of morphine which he knows will kill, can be passed over safely. It is doubtful if that ending will rouse much comment. It seems a logical finish. A dying man asks to be put out of his misery a few hours or a few days sooner and his son, unable to withstand the agony his father is in, has to comply with the request.

It does not seem possible that this picture will miss. Title, story and names are bound to carry it. Besides, it's a good picture.

Breakfast at Sunrise

Inspiration production. First National release. Directed by Mal St. Clair. Constance Talmadge starred. Story by Fred Cresac. Running time, 62 mins. At Strand, New York, week of Nov. 12.
Madeleine............Constance Talmadge
Loulou........................Alice White
Marquis..................Bryant Washburn
Georgianna................Paulette Duval
Queen.......................Marie Dressler
Champignol...................Albert Gran
General....................Burr McIntosh
Prince........................David Mir
Lussan.....................Don Alvarado
Madeleine's Maid........Nellie Bly Baker

First National has a pleaser here. It's of the sophisticated genus. Light but diverting, and trifling but smart. Very apt to be consistent at the box office.

It is by Fred de Gresac and directed by Malcolm St. Clair, one of the few directors commanding respect out Hollywood way when they consider a drawing room dido.

A young woman, pretty and rich, wants to pique her lover. So she marries a young man, handsome and poor, who also wishes to pique his faithless mistress.

That the two eventually fall in love is inevitable. In the minor complications before the ultimate clinch there is much gay, sly, humor.

Don Alvarado plays the lead to establish himself as a comer. He was formerly with Fox. Bryant Washburn, who has been using Ed. Pinaud's on his mustache these many years, comes out of the independent studios to enact the puzzled marquis for Inspiration.

Production, cast and direction of high order throughout, and Miss Talmadge looks very good.

THE SILVER LINING
(BRITISH MADE)

London, Nov. 4.

Original story by Bai David. British International production. Made at the Elstree Studios. Directed by Thomas Bentley. Distributed by Wardour Films Go. Running time, 90 mins.
Mrs. Hurst...................Marie Ault
Thomas Hurst..............Pat Aherne
John Hurst.................John Hamilton
Letty Dean......................Eve Gray
Mrs. Dean..............Mrs. Fred Emney
Mrs. Akers............Sydney Fairbrother
Gypsy......................Moore Marriot

This is the third successive picture from the Elstree Studios, and the third time isn't lucky. Better than "Poppies in Flanders" in direction and story, it is spoiled by so blatantly stupid a blunder in the theme, coming in the last thousand feet, one gasps at the thought even a moron could have switched a story (it appears to have been done in the editing and not in the making) into such dumb bathos.

For five and a half reels the picture promises fairly well, in spite of John Hamilton being miscast and acting as if he knew it. A succession of the swift and clean dissolves the plant atmosphere of English village life almost perfectly. No studio stuff, but shots stolen some place which has not been discovered by trippers and still clings to coal-oil lamps and thatched roofs. Life in a store is almost up to "'Way Down East" stuff of this sort; gossips, male and female, finely chosen and directed. Marie Ault's old mother was far above the work of Mary Carr in these parts, and looked real. But Pat Aherne registered much more au studio than au naturel, and as the other son John Hamilton was null and void.

Eve Gray seems to be regarded by British International as a find, but only maybe so. A moderate

trouper, she is not photogenic enough to be adopted by the fans.

There is Widow Hurst, with two sons, one a steady worker, the other lazy. Mother keeps a village store, and son John consumes the stock and has it charged. Thomas is going to marry the village belle, which also gives John a grievance. So, when the Lady of the Manor lends the bride a string of pearls to wear at the wedding John frames the theft with a gypsy poacher, and puts a charge of buckshot into his brother's arm at the same time. The thief, says John to the police, is wounded in the arm, and at the altar Thomas cannot conceal his injury and is denounced and arrested. To spare his old mother, he won't go back on his brother, and goes to jail. When his time is up, brother John gets scared, falls weeping on mother's shoulder, and says: "I have done him wrong; I cannot face my brother"; goes out and has a shine with gypsy over the pearls—all this time seemingly hidden in a hole under a tree—gets shot up, makes a dying confession, and joins the hands of good brother, girl and mother. Then dies.

But the film is dead before that. Fair to middling village drama to the point of telling mother what a bad boy he was. From then on slop, slush and an entertainment blackout.

Photography by William Shenton and G. Pocknall brilliant. Direction better than casting.

British International will have to do better than this if it is to measure up outside the home market.

Frat.

PITFALLS OF PASSION

Produced and released by S. S. Millard for state rights market. Story and direction by Leonard Livingstone. Cameraman Ted Tetzlaff. Running time with trailer on "Mysteries of Sex" about 80 minutes. Reviewed in projection room, New York, November 11.

Variety's reviewer was shown the unexpurgated master print of this newest of "sex hygiene" pictures. That unexpurgated version is raw meat for the foreign market. Whole scenes suggest the proverbial entertainment of stag smokers. The body of the action is backgrounded by a fashionable house of prostitution with a tuxedo clientele. Without rigid cutting of these chemise scenes the master print (film uncut) is impossible for most of the United States.

With "Pitfalls" as cut for over here, goes a trailer, scientific and gruesome, with visual evidence of the festering ravages of social diseases. Medical charts explain the development of the two different germs. It can be truthfully advertised that this part of the show is educational. Also with each print a "doctor" is included to give his message of uplift and sell his little pamphlets in the lobby.

The story itself is not particularly apropos for its professed purpose of pointing a lesson. The only thing it points out is that some young men are by nature easy converts to "easy living."

There is Jimmy, fresh from the farm. He has eloped with, but not married, his country sweetie. After Jimmy's passion and money have gone he listens to the sinister suggestion of Louie, poolroom bum.

This results in the young girl being bartered to Madame Francine, proprietress of a high hat establishment. Louis takes most of the dough with the near-husband getting a cut.

Jimmy is not again seen until, trying to escape from dicks, he runs into the hospital ward where May is being treated for the diseases she was acquired in her crimson life. He has been plugged by the cops after having—in a subtitle—murdered the woman he was living with.

May rises in her cot to gloat that

he has gotten his for his perfidy and weakness.

To avoid trouble with censors Millard will have to eliminate many scenes and implications in "Pitfalls." He will also be wise to call in at least three mats pictured in his press sheet.

Some new subtitles with a view to tying up the theme with its "educational" alibi are needed. As viewed the life of a prostitute is primarily a soft if a slightly sneering-at-human-nature one. The heroine is seduced with too much ease to allow any strong conviction that she was particularly remorseful. When taking to the toboggan she arrives at a cash register house and as the madame rings up $2 the girl's reaction seems entirely economic.

The production represents some money. Photography clear and good. Cast is unknown, with Prudence Sutton, Hollywood extra, having the lead and starred on the main title. She cannot act but neither can Leonard Livingstone cop any particular laurels at the directorial job.

"Pitfalls of Passion" is, however, a better job all around than the average "sex hygiene" picture.

(Picture reviewed by Variety before release for judgment in case advertising copy mentioning film submitted. It will be accepted provided no attempt is made to advertise that the unexpurgated version will be sold in the United States.)

SHE'S A SHEIK

Paramount production and release. Directed by Clarence Badger from the story by John McDermott. Screen version by Lloyd Corrigan. Starring Bebe Daniels. Richard Arlen and William Powell featured. At Paramount, New York, week Nov. 19. Running time, about 70 minutes.

Zaida.......................... Bebe Daniels
Captain Colton.................. Richard Arlen
Kada............................ William Powell
Wanda Fowler.................... Josephine Dunn
Jerry........................... James Bradbury, Jr.
Joe............................. Billy Franey
Sheik Yusiff Ben Hamod.......... Paul McAllister
The Major....................... Al Fremont

Bebe Daniels now blossoms forth in the feminine version of the cycle of light, frothy, amusing costume comedies which have taken hold in recent months.

Titles sell the picture at the beginning and keep it sold, bolstering up weak comedy situations and smoothing over uneasy spots in the story. Megaphone wielder has done well, the studio desert backgrounds are as the movie patrons would want to be and considering, also, the star and the snappy title, production rates moderate money.

The mixture of American slang, clothed and glorified in Quaker or Bible English, results in a brand of humor highly pleasing to picture house trade.

Placing the girl in the position usually taken by the male, as the physical aggressor in love manoeuvers, is not exactly unique in the annals of film production. Giving the girl color as a lady sheik, however, furnishes as suitable idea for putting the story over along novel lines.

Powell scores two ways, as a comedian and as the menace. The ludicrous tint applied to Kada (Powell), the fierce Arabian desert bandit whose flowing garments are ripped to pieces by a girl in a fencing bout and who allows himself to suffer other indignities, serves to heighten the general farcial effect aimed at.

The opening scene reveals two pious figures engaged in earnest debate regarding the physical charms of the girl Zaida. In answer to a query as to why he is shaking the moths from his beard one reverend gentleman replies that he is out to buy permission to wed the girl, whom he classifies as "a hot number."

Zaida, of Spanish parentage, would marry only into the Christian faith, declining to choose from the swarthy brethren among whom she had always lived. When she finds her man he is on the verge of falling for a blonde of no mean physical attraction. Zaida then boldly has the Captain captured and brought to her desert camp. After a few days in a cage formerly occupied by Zaida's pet leopard, the gallant French Captain succumbs to the lures of his forceful captor.

Kada's vanity fills in for another laugh when the Captain tears a chunk of his carefully barbered beard and then dumps him on the cold, inhospitable sands of the desert. Kada's private barber weeps bitterly as he informs his master that hair Nos. 40 to 85 inclusive are missing.

For the climax a lifelike battle is staged between the Arabians and the outnumbered French troops.

Richard Arlen does not register as the submissive Captain. Not built for the spotting. *Mori.*

IN OLD KENTUCKY

M-G-M production and release. Directed by John M. Stahl. Suggested by Charles Dazey's old melodrama. Cameraman, Max Fabian. Running time, 57 mins. At Capitol, New York, week Nov. 19.

"Major" Brierly.................. James Murray
Nancy Holden..................... Helene Costello
"Skippy" Lowry................... Wesley Barry
Mr. Brierly...................... Edward Martindale
Mrs. Brierly..................... Dorothy Cummings
High Pockets..................... Stephen Fetchit
Dan Lowry........................ Harvey Clark
Lily May......................... Carolynne Snowden
Uncle Bible...................... Nick Cogley

A poor picture. Inconceivably asinine in story and with kindergarden tecnnique. Nobody should be misled by it playing the Capitol for a week. Ruth Elder on same bill and counts for any draw.

James Murray, Helene Costello and Wesley Barry are the "names" of the picture. Throughout Murray walks a zigzag. He is drunk because he went to war and found out that where there's a battle there are corpses.

Miss Costello, badly gowned, has nothing more than a bit. Barry also has a bit, unessential to plot or action. He at least will be interesting to the fans as this is apparently his first cinema appearance since he "grew up" and became a married man.

Charles Dazey's old melodrama "suggested" this picture. It has "suggested" 500 others, none good. The M-G-M studios appear to be excessively receptive to suggestions. Maybe somebody ought to develop a "no" habit out there. Pictures like this should be easy to dodge.

The old family nag here goes through the world war, is wounded in battle and left for dead, sewed up, shipped back to America and by a curious coincidence next appears at an auction sale in Kentucky. The old massa buys back the nag for $180, giving a phoney check to cover the amount. The nag lives to win the Kentucky Derby and to pay the grocery bill that has accumulated during the war. It made a pauper out of old Brierly, who two years before had owned a string of expensive race horses.

This picture will be a horse on a lot of exhibs.

Husbands or Lovers

Rimax production, released by Emblem Film Exchange. Directed by Paul Czinner. Based on the Russian work entitled "Nju." Co-starring Emil Jannings and Conrad Veidt. Elizabeth Bergner featured. At the Cameo, N. Y., Nov. 20. Running time, 60 minutes.

The Husband...................... Emil Jannings
The Wife......................... Elizabeth Bergner
The Lover........................ Conrad Veidt
The Child........................ Nils Edward
The Maid......................... Migo Bard

A winner for art film houses and good enough for regular program theatres in spots. Construction is polished, the story powerful and told in a forceful, connected manner. There is a conspicuous absence of sub-titles, and these are more in the nature of comment. The story is told in pictures.

Without Jannings the film would lose just the additional value that rates it higher than the average foreign-made production. And that not at all on account of what pulling power Jannings has here, but solely on his individual merit in this particular production.

Jannings lands the few laughs there are and delivers the touch that lends conviction to strong, dramatic situations.

Elizabeth Bergner and Conrad Veidt are implausible. Veidt does not make the grade either as the lover or the heavy. Miss Bergner looks slovenly, frowsy hair blowing from her ears into her face in a most ungainly manner, and has cultivated an extremely unlovely walk. Her mannerisms are unattractive, and if the picture hits the regular runs the reaction may be that the husband should have let a woman like that walk when she wanted to.

Veidt does not register for the kind of man who would be supposed to win the affections of a happily married woman from her husband and child.

It's a little too hot in spots for regular fan fare. Some of the bedroom scenes stand little chance in small towns, and the structure is primarily based on a theme that may meet with opposition from censors.

Story is of a woman who takes an inexplicable liking to a passing stranger. She meets him at a ball and he writes a poem to her on confetti paper. Because hubby is getting a little stout the wife decides to blow him and her child. If it's question of passion, it seemed that the husband was far more attractive than the pale, anemic poet Nju (that was her name) picked on.

Jannings' prophetic warning to the wife of the risk she runs in an endeavor to keep her home is reflected in a large bedroom mirror. It shows the wife, deserted by her lover, sinking to the depths, standing on a street corner swinging a purse, being picked up by a drunk, taken to a room and given money. Every action is mirrored in detail. Finally comes the scene in the room of a disorderly house. The man leaving her puts money on the table.

Despite the graphic description of danger, Nju left her home for the man she wanted.

As hubby predicted, the lover forsakes her after a few days, and the gal, in desperation, jumps off a cliff on a rainy night. When he learns of her death the poetic genius repents, but bears up remarkably well under the strain.

THE GORILLA

First National production. Directed by Alfred Santell from the play by Ralph Spence. Photographed by Arthur Edison. At the Mark Strand, New York, Nov. 19. Running time, 72 minutes.

Garrity.......................... Charlie Murray
Mulligan......................... Fred Kelsey
Alice Townsend................... Alice Day
Uriah Townsend................... Tully Marshall
Cyrus Townsend................... Claude Gillingwater
Stevens.......................... Walter Pidgeon
Marsden.......................... Gaston Glass
The Reporter..................... Brooks Benedict
The Cook......................... Aggie Herring
The Butler....................... Syd Crossley

"The Gorilla" is a box office tonic for more reasons than one. It is an entertaining picture, the title boasts a reputation gained from the stage play, and the story makes good exploitation material.

The play had its punch in the flow of wisecracks from the two detectives. In the picture this humor has been transposed to pantomime, and effectively, by Charles Murray and Fred Kelsey. Murray, of course, has the richer part, and the picture unquestionaly belongs to him.

Except in a few serious instances, the story is done in broad comedy. It concerns the mysterious murder of a wealthy recluse, who lives with his daughter and house staff in a mansion on the Hudson. Every one in the cast is made to appear suspiciously leering or embarrassed at intervals in order that all may be connected with the crime.

To make things more intricate, it is made plain that a gorilla has been committing a series of murders in the city, and one is in the house at the time. Solution of the mystery takes care of the main puzzling factors. Presence of the typical mystery play incongruities must be executed as combining "to make it harder."

Murray has a meaty part as the detective, adding one more to his string of reliable comedy performances. His partner, Fred Kelsey, is primarily the straight man, and a capable one. He is familiar through numerous detective roles. Extra humor is rung in on the story with a butler, played by Syd Crossley, an Englishman with a permanently incredulous air.

Other character parts are handled by Tully Marshall, Claude Gillingwater and Aggie Herring, all three established as capable actors. Brooks Benedict acts a supercilious reporter from the "Herald Tribune" for a probable laugh from that paper's staff. The love interest triangle consists of Alice Day, Gaston Glass, and Walter Pidgeon, satisfactory, but no more. This because they are allotted little individual footage.

Technically the picture is distinctive in photography, being handled with an expert treatment of lighting values and perspective. Sets are highly atmospheric.

Effective direction by Santell makes a good job.

COLLEGE HERO

Columbia Production and release. Directed by Walter Lang. Story by Harry Symonds. Cameraman Joe Walker. Running time one hour. At Keith's Hippodrome, New York, week of Nov. 21.

Rodney St. Clair................. Ben Turpin
Jimmy Halloran................... Rex Lease
"Happy" Cantfield................ Robert Agnew
Mary............................. Pauline Garon
Coach............................ Charles Paddock
Goggles.......................... Churchill Ross

After a strenuous autumn of cinema football the movie fans who attend the films with any kind of regularity ought to be nearly fed up on collegiate pictures. Columbia has turned out a fair enough production, but what is there new that any scenarist could write or any director insert into the basic situation of good old Podunk winning the big football game in the last two minutes of play?

Incidentally, the title and, to an extent, the characters of this one resemble Fox's "High School Hero" released a few weeks ago. It has the situation of two boys moon struck over one girl. That was in "High School Hero." Columbia treats this angle more seriously.

Ben Turpin, the gallant Rodney St. Clair of umpty-teen Mack Sennett two-reelers, emerges from a semi-retirement to perform with his old popular slapstick technique the role of the dormitory valet. He got some laughs and will be welcomed by the fans.

Charles Paddock, the running man, seems to go from one Hollywood studio to another impersonating head coaches. He will probably be one of the few to regret the passing of football pictures.

Rex Lease kind of lifted himself into first place in the two-some with the ubiquitous Bobby Agnew. During the craze for flaming youth pictures Bobby was busy doing wayward sons. He seems not to have been in demand for the gridiron operas due probably to his slight stature. Rex Lease is comparatively new.

Pauline Garon, the Canadian cutie, was denied her usual quota of close-ups and the picture was that much shy of sex appeal.

The direction of Walter Lang was workmanlike and managed for the most part to hold the improbable yarn in bounds.

Pencil it in as a moderate pleaser.

13TH JUROR

Universal production directed by Edward Laemmle from Charles A. Logue's adaptation of the stage play by Henry Irving Dodge. Running time, 60 minutes. At the Colony, New York, Nov. 20.

Henry Desmond.................... Francis X. Bushman
Helen Marsden.................... Anna Q. Nilsson
Richard Marsden.................. Walter Pidgeon
The Politician................... George Siegmann
The Housekeeper.................. Martha Mattox
Sergeant Duff.................... Fred Kelsey

A well-sustained bit of film drama, giving an especially striking role to Francis X. Bushman, who makes a better middle-aged character then ever he did a young hero. Something of the once rather overpowering beauty of this former idol has softened and mellowed.

For the not inconsiderable portion of the fan public who take their drama straight and unsmiling, "The 13th Juror" ought to prove first-rate entertainment. To the sophisticated the play takes itself rather seriously and absurdities creep in, but the story is direct and absorbing in its naive way, working up to a melodramatic climax that for theatric effect is not without its kick.

Story is set in atmosphere of fashion, having to do with the situation of a gifted and unscrupulous criminal lawyer, who, after a successful career in getting real criminals free of the law by his legal trickeries, finds himself at last caught in the toils, charged with a murder, and able to clear himself only by dragging in the name of the woman he loves.

Of course it's old stuff, but here presented with intensity and obvious aiming for effect that carries it through. A Sunday afternoon crowd at the Roxy might giggle at it, but the sentimental customers of a Washington Heights neighborhood will love its emotional splurge. Atmosphere of wealth and luxury is well carried out. Anna Q. Nilsson makes an appealing heroine, being here cast as a sort of walking part and having no occasion to act with delicate meaning. Bushman plays the forceful, masculine type still and is effective in a stagey part.

Story is built up to its climax through a maze of complications and with increasing values, is generally plausible and the production in a pictorial sense is thoroughly workmanlike. *Rush.*

GOOD TIME CHARLEY

Warner Bros. production and release. Featuring Helene Costello. Directed by Michael Curtiz. At the Roxy, N. Y., Nov. 19. Running time, about 60 mins.

Rosita Keene............Helene Costello
Good Time Charlie..........Warner Oland
Bill Collins..................Clyde Cook
John Hartwell............Montague Love
John Hartwell, Jr.............Hugh Allen
Elaine Keene..........Julianne Johnston

There is nothing quite as futile in pictures as a sob story without sobs. That's why this one doesn't register. Where there should be pathos there is only vague, sentimental appeal. The story is there but Curtiz has failed to tell it on the screen. This boy might do well as a writer, he allows emotions of the cast to be described via subtitles.

This is a concrete example of what can happen to a sob story if handled "with restraint." Not a chance in the major houses.

The beginning of the story plants Good Time Charlie as a small time stock actor with an overdeveloped ego. He figures himself the greatest actor of the times. The director did not concentrate on this figure, allowing the story to run out of his hands. The daughter, instead of the old actor, becomes the center of interest as the picture proceeds and interest in both therefore lags.

After 15 years of stock Charlie, Rosita and Bill Collins are playing in an East Side cabaret. The menace, Hartwell, who was responsible for the death of Charlie's wife, had in the meantime reached the heights as a producer on Broadway. Rosita gets her chance but the old man is left in the saw dust joint.

The girl marries Hartwell's son. The latter is cut by his pop who also has the girl blacklisted because she left his show flat. Bill had saved a grand with which he intended having Charlie's eyesight repaired, but when Charlie gets the lowdown on what happened to Rosita he hands her the money to go to London and start over.

It misses in picturization. The grip on audience attention is not there.

NEMESIS
(GERMAN-MADE)

Produced by Ufa. Directed by Dr. Asagaroff and W. Starewitsch. Featuring Warwick Ward, Camille Horn and Gustav Frolich. At Capitol, Haymarket, England, Nov. 7, on run. Running time, 108 minutes.

According to Funk & Wagnall, "Nemesis" means "retributive justice." If that is so, the fellows who made this film ought to be forced to see it twice a day for 10 years. They would get off light at that!

It would be difficult to conceive anything more childish masquerading as a new idea in cinematography. The kindergarten school fable of the industrious ant and the lazy grasshopper, familiarized in Lafontaine's Fables, has been taken literally and made with models on the "one turn one picture" process. As a trifling novelty this might pass, but some moron has given birth to the idea of making a human analogy and cutting it in and out of the "bug" stuff. The result is incredibly dull and wearisome, giving one to wonder where the much-vaunted merits of German production have strayed!

One little girl loves being gay, while the other little girl does her sums and her chores scrupulously —the little prig! Big boy is going to marry the industrious girl, but gets vamped by the "grasshopper," and they go off to Paris for a gay time.

Boy forges father's name to a bill because he is broke, and the good little girl sells a house uncle has left her to meet the bill. Gay girl goes off with another, boy goes after her and gets all beaten up, returns home and marries good girl. Bad girl comes home, in full snowstorm, falls fainting with hunger and repentance beside the old home door, is taken in and fussed over by mother.

Find your own moral.

All the sets are studio-built, and the streets, especially in the "back home and broke and it's snowing" stuff, look it. Some of the pseudo-exteriors are shot against a plain grey backing!

Warwick Ward does best as a sort of half-villain, and the boy of Gustav Frolich is not too bad. Camilla Horn is wasted in a part that does not suit her, and the girl who plays the industrious wench looks as if she had gone to the cupboard to steal jam in the dark and drunk the vinegar instead.

Best is the insect stuff. The models act far better than the humans. Real time and trouble were taken with this part. But, from the result as a whole, it was hardly worth it.

The best that can be said of this is that if picture theatres were infant schools it might be a wow. Even the Capitol's press agent announces "'Nemesis' will not be retained." *Frat.*

THE FURTHER ADVENTURES OF THE FLAG LIEUTENANT
(British Made)

Original story by Lieut.-Col. Drury. Adapted by George Cooper. Produced by Neo-Art Productions, Ltd. Released through W. P. Film Co. Directed by Will P. Kellino. At Marble Arch Pavilion, preview, Nov. 4. Running time, 100 mins.

Richard Lascelles, D. S. O., the Flag Lieutenant..............Henry Edwards
Col. William Thesiger......Fred Raynham
Admiral Sir Berkeley Wynne
Fewlass Llewellyn
Sybil Wynne..............Lilian Oldland
Pauline Alexander.............Isabel Jeans
The Sinister Influence........Lyn Harding

As a photoplay, this is a joke. It may not be a bad joke for the distributors, credited with having booked it to the Provincial Cinematograph Circuit for $40,000, which is around an average of $380 a house. And they claim they have booked the film in the United Kingdom to $250,000. Maybe. If they have, it only shows what you can get away with. Whether the exhibitors will also get away with it on release is a different problem.

It looks like it cost around $100,000 to make, and with the same amount of money it should have been possible to have made a film. But not with this story.

There's a lot of footage of flags and ships and seas which mean nothing, then there's a lot of semi-acting all over warship decks, in wardrooms and in hotel lounges, which means little more. None of the cast seems quite to know what it is all about, a point on which they share a fellow feeling with this reviewer.

There's some kind of story about a sort of Russian agitator who is a "sinister influence" on the Chinese. There's a vamp who steals the secret orders from the warship (by having a Chink washerman open the safe in the admiral's cabin and slip the papers into her parasol while the ship is fully manned).

There's a couple of comic sailors —no, one's a marine—played by the Brothers Egbert, vaudeville old-timers; there's a hero who dashes around and a shero who looks as if she were lost in the mazes of a crossword puzzle set by grandma. And he saves her from the villain, gets the papers back, the vamp commits suicide (best thing she does), and the admiral blesses them, my children.

Direction is old-fashioned and uninspired, though the crowds are well handled. Sets very elaborate, and shipboard stuff the real thing. Photography good; acting as well as the direction will let it be.

This is the second production by the company, which made "The Fake." They will have to do a whole lot better with their next to hold up their reputation and bookings.

Though they may get out on this film financially, it will help neither them nor British pictures when it gets into the theatres. For, while the public may want hokum mainly, it does want it with thrills or a strain of intelligence. And this film has neither. *Frat.*

SAILOR IZZIE MURPHY

Warner Bros. production and release. Directed by Harry Lehrman from story by Edmund T. Lowe, Jr. Starring George Jessel. Cast includes Warner Oland, Clara Horton, Otto Lederer, Audrey Ferris and John Miljan. At Moss' Broadway, New York, week Nov. 14. Running time, over 60 minutes.

Does not rate among the unusual program productions of the season. Comedy situations are strong but cast does not play them for full worth. George Jessel, as the star, shows less than average ability of a featured screen comedian. This is only his second film try.

Compared to some of the productions released by Warner Bros. this year this one towers far above on quality.

Clara Horton, the girl playing opposite Jessel, screens as a pretty new flapper type. With proper exploitation she should prove a profitable investment. The girl carries the draggy spots in the picture on appearance.

Story is of an escaped bunch of lunatics, the leader with a perfume complex. Dressed in sailor costumes they gain control of a yacht with the purpose of prosecuting the wealthy owner because he crushes innocent little flowers to manufacture perfume.

Izzy Goldberg, chasing the perfume manufacturer with a summons containing a claim for $10,000 as compensation for physical injuries when thrown out of the latter's establishment, boards the yacht as a sailor named Murphy. He is expected to shoot down the owner of the yacht.

Warner Oland does well as the perfume manufacturer. Otto Lederer adds a little comedy as Izzy's business partner.

GOLD CHEVRONS

Collection of official war pictures, taken by the U. S. Signal Corps. Here billed as "New York Troops in the World War" and bearing the mark of Sales Picture Corp., distributor. Views deal mostly with the Rainbow Division of New York in their operations at Chateau Thierry and with other New York troops in the Argonne, including the "Lost Battalion." Running time, 65 minutes. At Cameo, New York, Nov. 12.

Group of official war pictures here has apparently been assembled as an Armistice Day after-thought. No notation is made of government auspices or benevolent purpose in the presentation. To all appearances the showing is a commercial enterprise. In connection with the film, Private Clayton K. Slack, one of the 53 soldiers to whom was awarded the Congressional war medal, makes a personal appearance, reciting humorous personal experiences of the war for about 10 minutes.

Some of the lobby material makes it seem that the film, or parts of it, have been used before. One stand had a previous title covered up with script reading Gold Chevrons." The "Lost Battalion" views have been exhibited before, under the late Col. Whittlesbey's sponsorship, if memory serves.

The pictures in themselves make a thrilling document. Some show the hottest kind of trench action; advances of troops under fire; in one instance what purports to be an actual picture record of an engagement between a German and an American combat plane in the air. Several views show troops advancing under machine-gun and shrapnel fire, and the spectator can readily see men drop wounded. One bit shows a squadron of cavalry rushing across open fields and caught as an enemy shell explodes among them.

Graphic bits show the handling of wounded Americans at field dressing stations, enemy prisoners being brought in, some acting as stretcher bearers for American casualties; artillery laying down barrages, and such details.

There is a biting realism about some of the intimate views, but shots at large engagements need a good deal of imagination. The actuality isn't nearly as dramatic to watch in panorama as the effects staged for dramatic purposes.

But the sidelights of the picture here are thoroughly fascinating. Such things as a wounded American brought into a dressing station and sitting up to puff a cigarette; Americans dealing with German captives for souvenirs and the like are strikingly human.

A heightened effect is given to the American advance by the interpolation of film records from the German war office showing the action from the German side. One shows the Americans coming on against German machine-gun fire, the camera being apparently stationed just behind a German gun. A title asserts that these inserted bits are from the official German record.

An interesting war exhibit, but of doubtful commercial value, except as a feature for special occasions. *Rush.*

WOMEN'S WARES

Tiffany production and release. Directed by Arthur Gregory. (No other technical credit on print reviewed). At Hippodrome, New York, week Nov. 14. Running time, about 70 minutes.

Dolly Morton..................Evelyn Brent
Bob Crane......................Bert Lytell
Maisey Duncan..............Gertrude Short
Jimmy Hays....................Larry Kent
Cissie Fitzgerald, Richard Tucker, and Myrtle Stedman.

For short dates, moderate coiner. For full weeks, fragile.

A tale of a girl who becomes sore at men when her boy friend tries to make her. She starts on a career of getting things from the men and thumbing her nose when they ask for payment in a necking way.

She gyps a guy out of an apartment by threatening to tell his wife and sets herself up in style. When a nice fellow comes along he takes her for what she seems to be starts to paw. This breaks her heart and makes her see.

For some undisplayed reason she goes back to her first love and leaves the nice fellow thinking ill of her. The audience does not follow in sympathy with this move, because of handling and uneven casting.

Evelyn Brent is photographed disadvantageously at times. She contributes satisfactory acting, not up to her previous work. Bert Lytell is the disappointed nice fellow with little to do. The juvenile is Larry Kent, who looks like 10 different actors in as many different scenes. Peculiar camera work makes him all the shades between brunet and blond.

Playing Miss Brent's girl friend, Gertrude Short may draw laughs from naive customers. She is a comedienne with one of the most acute cases of over-acting seen in many months. Directors should hold her in check, as she pulled the same boner in a recent picture with Pauline Garon.

Direction apparently handicapped by script, but still not satisfactory.

The Rose of Kildare

Gotham production. Released by Lumas. From story by Gerald Beaumont. Directed by Dallas Fitzgerald. Cameraman, Milton Moore. Running time, 58 mins. At Stanley, New York, one day, Nov. 11.

Barry Nunan..................Pat O'Malley
Rose.......................Helene Chadwick
Bob....................Henry B. Walthall
A Gambler.......................Lee Moran
His Pal.......................Edward Brody
Young Nunan..................Carroll Nye
Elsie..........................Ena Gregory

Fairly well done and interesting picture based on one of the yarns of the late and prolific Gerald Beaumont. It will be okay as a programer, but contains nothing for splurging on publicity.

The action starts in Ireland, proceeds to South Africa and concludes in the U. S. An interlude of 25 years is spanned. The years whiten the hair and deaden the eyes of Pat O'Malley, but Helene Chadwick is her same girlish self as an Irish colleen and as night club proprietress in America.

A romance between the son of one and the daughter of the other finally brings the long-separated Irish lovers together. The boy who loved in Ireland, now a district attorney in America, calls off a raid on his lady's gambling establishment.

Direction and production are better than the scenario, which is not well knit, due, perhaps, to the lack of unity in time and action.

THE SWIFT SHADOW

FBO production, directed by Jerome Storm from script by Ethel Hill. Starring Ranger, dog. In cast Al Smith, Sam Nelson, Wm. Bertram and Lorraine Eason. In projection room Nov. 16. Running time, 50 minutes.

Good emotional stuff for the dog market, directed efficiently and photographed well.

It shows the conflicting urges of a dog trained to obey his first cruel master, but befriended by a second. The first is a criminal, who uses the dog as an aid in his crimes. He kills the father of the dog's second master. Later, when the two men meet, Ranger is ordered to attack his friend, but winds up by going after the former master.

A story of this sort does not require implausible exposition of a dog's intelligence, relying rather on natural canine instincts. This is in the picture's favor.

Lorraine Eason, providing the love interest, rates high in the feminine lead. She is exceptionally pretty and has a primary knowledge of acting sufficient for films of this kind. Possibilities of advancement are evident.

"Swift Shadow" is okay.

AT THE GREY HOUSE

UFA (German) presents the American premiere of a "Romance of the Moors," by Thea von Harbau, directed by Arthur von Gerlach, featuring Lil Dagover; at the 55th Street Cinema, Nov. 12.

Old Grieshaus...........Arthur Krausneck
Viscount Heinrich............Paul Hartman
Viscount Detlef............Rudolph Forster
Owe Heiden.................Rudolph Rittner
Barbara.........................Lil Dagover
Greine.......................Gertrude Welker
Matte.........................Gertrude Arnold
Enzio.................Hans Peter Peterhaus
Christof.....................Jahn Christen

This reviewer's first visit to the 55th Street Cinema. Probably assigned there because regularly covering the Fifth Avenue playhouse. No reason at all for any such assumption. No more than having an expert viewpoint on a night club band because one has reviewed a symphony orchestra. Fifty-fifth Street's entry is so punk an imitation of Fifth Avenue's that detailed comparison would be distressing. Attempt at similar policy, but with none of the finesse, sense of humor, sophistication and nifty skill shown at Mike Mindlin's wigwam.

Comes now "At the Grey House." It's a UFA. The initials may mean UnFunnyAbsolutely. If this isn't the worst moving picture in the world, it will do till the worst comes along. Soppy, sloppy, as natural as a wooden duck, and as intelligent. This is a wild shot at being Ibsenesque. Without the consent of Ibsen.

The action is slow. Old men abound, with lots of Heinie horsemanship of no consequence. Then the startlingly original idea of having master's son fall for servant's daughter. Program calls her "lovely Lil Dagover." She may be lovely in spirit. Spirit doesn't close-up very good. Not for lovely Lil, anyway. But she looks like a servant's daughter. But not one that the master's son would lose his inheritance over.

She plays with tame animals, looks coy and is so surprised when the bad actor who plays the lover lets her in on his pash. His wicked brother takes advantage of the situation to get the Grey House and the bankroll that were to have been the bad actor's heritage when the whiskered old gent drops of heart disease very awkardly—very awkwardly for the love-struck son and very awkwardly for film technique.

It runs on forever. In time justice is done. Nobody cares.

The slides or titles, in the inane attempt to do a Mindlin before the theatre "proudly offers" the above described film, asks "permit us to introduce the Screen Master of Ceremonies." Permit granted. Permit revoked after optically "listening" to the screen master. Meaningless, not bright, never interesting and usually not lucid as to what he is flopping about because not lucid as to what he is driving at.

"Thank you for coming" ends the program. They should. *Lait.*

SECOND TO NONE

Toronto, Nov. 10.

Regal Films (Canada) release. Produced in England by Brittania Films, Ltd., with co-operation of the British admiralty. Direction, titling and photography not credited. Continuity rewritten from short stories by "Bartimeus." At Pantages, Toronto. Running time, 74 minutes.

Bill Hyde..Micky Brantford, Moore Marriott
His Mother......................Grace Vicat
Commander Brian Douglas. ...Ian Fleming
His Mother..................Daisy Campbell
Ina..........Aggie Brantford, Benita Hume
Old Lemon.....................Tom Coventry
Mr. Levine.....................A. B. Imeson
Tubby............................Johnny Butt
Curley............................Alf Goodard

Here is one of the best British films released on this side, although built along routine lines. It is a story of love and life in the British navy in peace and war.

Opens with a couple of kids in love. Girl's mother dies. She runs down to the docks to sympathize with herself, and an old skipper asks what is the trouble. He stops the tears by telling her her mother is in heaven, just beyond the horizon—where his ship is soon sailing.

Girl jumps aboard as a stowaway, but is found next day just before fire sweeps the vessel and blows it up. She is the only survivor, picked up by a British man o' war. The commander takes her to his mother's home.

Skip eight years to find the girl grown up and her kid lover, now an ordinary seaman in the navy, sharing her favors with her ward, the commander of the boat. A German spy, also trying to get the girl, is in the offing as the heavy. The commander wins the girl and there is a big celebration aboard to mark the engagement. Bill, the seaman, deserts.

When war is declared the spy looks him up, but Bill gives him a beating, returns to his ship, serves with distinction and is killed in a subsequent naval battle.

Photography is excellent, particularly that of the blowing up of the small steamer at sea and the naval battle that closes the film. Part of this is cut from news reels, but the trick camera stuff, heretofore a big weakness in English films, has been convincingly done.

The work of the two children, Micky and Aggie Brantford, brother and sister, is excellent. Ian Fleming, experienced on the English legit stage, is convincing as a naval commander while in uniform, but rather wooden in his few love scenes.

Camera was unkind to Benita Hume as the grown-up Ina. Her best scene was in bidding good-bye to Moore Marriott as the childhood sweetheart after she had married the captain. Marriott is inclined to be overdramatic in spots. Daisy Campbell and A. B. Imeson are good in bits.

Some good shots of the British seamen in training at Portsmouth serving as entertainment and propaganda. Most of the shots, including all interiors, were made aboard H. M. S. "Tiger," renamed "Determination" for this picture. Much of the comedy was a revamp of the punishments shown in the F.' P. "Navy Now."

Direction rather obvious and hurried in spots, but this picture is a godsend to those countries compelled to exhibit a certain percentage of British films. Here in Canada it can stand a week in the ace houses.

Sinclair.

BY WHOSE HAND

Columbia production and release. Directed by Walter Lang from the story by Marion Orth, under supervision of Harry Cohn. Starring Ricardo Cortez with cast including Eugenia Gilbert. At Loew's New York, Nov. 18, one-half of double feature program. Running time about 60 mins.

An acceptable small time production that can be used in the smaller houses. Considering the cost, the picture has been well made and capably directed. Cortez photographs nicely though the girl is minus attraction.

It's a crook drama spotted in an atmosphere of evening clothes. A mysterious operative known as X-9 is called upon by the chief of detectives to bring in "The Shadow." The face of the operative is kept from the audience, only the back of his head being shown during the phone conversation.

Three men, accompanying a fat, rich old lady, are each suspected of stealing her jewels. Even the gal is implicated. It's jewel thief plot No. 319, Series B.

IN THE FIRST DEGREE

Sterling Pictures production, directed by Phil Rosen from a story by Reginald Wright Kaufman. Cast includes Bryant Washburn, Alice Calhoun and Gayne Whitman. At the Columbus, New York, one day, (Nov. 17) on a double feature bill. Running time, 55 minutes.

Here is a combination of two reliable plots; the tale of the girl who is almost forced to marry the villain to help her father out of financial difficulties, and the bromide of the hero who is saved in the nick of time from the electric chair, to which he has been sentenced for a murder he did not do.

The combination as told and directed is for short program dates. Right triumphs completely and villainy is repaid with death, which is as it should be for houses where melodrama is regarded highly and accepted unhedgingly.

Bryant Washburn is the villain, Alice Calhoun the heroine, and Gayne Whitman the hero. All three are capable actors whose popularity has waned. Of the three, Washburn is best fitted to present standards of picture actors.

Fair meller for the minimum price mob.

The Spotlight

Paramount production and release. Starring Esther Ralston with Neil Hamilton featured. Directed by Frank Tuttle. Adapted by Hope Loring from the Rita Weiman book, "Footlights." Titles by Herman J. Mankiewicz. At Paramount, New York, week Nov. 26. Running time, about 60 minutes.

Lizzie Stokes................Esther Ralston
Norman Brooke................Neil Hamilton
Daniel Hoffman..........Nicholas Soussanin
Maggie Courtney............Arlette Marchal
Ebbetts....................Arthur Housmann

A lightweight Paramount regular program release, but good enough to hold up in the first runs as such. It's one of those pictures that had better be shifted into the house with the strongest stage attraction. Drawing power by itself will be meagre unless sent into a downtown or community theatre that draws the flaps and yaps.

To the sophisticates this picture will be a pain, as probably the Rita Weiman book it was adapted from must have been, if this adaptation is at all faithful. The story is of a theatrical manager who makes a stray girl in his office a blazing Russian stage star within three months. The best thing in the film is that of the camera work in showing the lapse of time simultaneously with backgrounded pictures of the girl laboring in her rush to cultivate a Russian accent, the language and manners, beside wearing a brunet and dandy wig.

The outstanding figure is the shrewd and cold blooded theatrical producer. But two other principals, Esther Ralston as the converted Lizzie Stokes into Olga Rotosky and Neil Hamilton as the lover. For some reason Hamilton doesn't fit the role. He looks too youthful against the be-wigged and wise stage star, despite the character calls for a novice at playing.

Direction means but little. Sparse action, sparse anything, even to the principals which might have left this one of Paramount's cheapest for the regular product. At times for the theatre scenes a few extras are employed.

Illusion is seldom perfect, and the story is straightaway, leading up to a cold flopping finale.

Beneath her black wig Lizzie Stokes is a blonde, and Hamilton told her he didn't like blondes. And the manager told her Norman Brooke was in love with the Russian star, not Lizzie Stokes. After a while Rotosky confesses to Brooke she is Lizzie Stokes and pulls off her wig in proof. So he loves Lizzie Stokes instead. 99c. for that!

Comedy nil except for some bright flashes here and there in the Herman Mankiewicz titles, and also some good straight captions.

Nicholas Soussanin as the theatrical man is very convincing. Perhaps that is why in part that the others are not. Direction is about as insipid as the story. Still that story has its appeal to those dreamers of front page stories and roto sections.

This one will barely breeze through in the majority of the houses it plays. Show people may give Miss Ralston credit for her attempted impersonation of Nazimova, but it's in the dress and wig only. *Sime.*

THE 13th HOUR

M-G-M production and release, featuring Lionel Barrymore and Jacquelin Gadsdon. Based on stage play by Douglas Furber and C. M. Franklin, with latter directing. Titles by Maximilian Fabian. At Capitol, New York, week of Nov. 26. Running time, 53 minutes.

Professor Leroy..........Lionel Barrymore
Mary Lyle...............Jacquelin Gadsdon
Matt Gray.................Charles Delaney
Detective Shaw.................Fred Kelsey
Polly.........................Polly Moran
The Dog.........................."Napoleon"

Why don't the boys give Pearl White a break and bring her back? She's gotten out of more traps, dungeons, cages and torture cells than Houdini. And she did it years ago; so these modern mysteries and dilemmas wouldn't feaze her. They are not liable to feaze anyone else, either, if this one is an example of the Coast studios' new mystery complex.

Plain, unadulterated melodrama, while you wait—and you don't have to wait long. That's its best point, it doesn't last long—on and off in 53 minutes.

Those who pay balcony prices for their film fare may like this from sewer-to-parlor-to-cops routine, while the 25-35-centers will possibly squeal with delight as hairy arms creep out of clothes closets and from behind secret panels, etc. It figures as good cheap admission fare, but what it'll do in the handsome chalets is something else again.

In this case the professor (it's always a professor, and the Roxy has one this week, too) has a mania for killing people to get their jewels. Matt Gray's idea is that he and his dog can decipher these one a. m. killings for which Professor Leroy (Mr. Barrymore) offers substantial coinage.

Is the killer-thief the "prof" himself? No one else.

And Mary (Miss Gadsdon) is his secretary. A few film feet hint at the designs Leroy has on Mary. Matt and the comedy-relief detectives invade the house, and thence the room-to-room stalking, as Leroy gazes into an instrument which makes Marconi seem feeble-minded and shows him who is in "room six" and what's going on.

The dog brings about the ultimate capture after a chase across the roof and a plunge therefrom. Meanwhile, Polly Moran has been given a couple of inane titles to utter after chastising two or three of the Leroy gang, as is the habit of all good newspaper women in pictures.

Barrymore probably snickers to himself over these roles. He certainly must chafe when recalling "The Claw" and "The Jest." Barrymore trying to outwit American youth for screen entertainment! What chance has a villain got in a picture You can see defeat in his eyes as he gloats over his first victory. He knows it won't last, so he quickly adopts a grim expression and a stoop to conform to the standard conception of an Id and cagey rascal who takes any means to gain his end.

But the hero! And the heroine, Jacquelin Gadsdon! New? A good-looking girl who will have to get out of the clutches of the master minds before she gets into those of a fan public. She shows nothing here but promise. However, if it's her first time out from the M-G camp as a featured player, it's not a bad effort and she's likely to get on if the stories are right. Charles Delaney, as the boy, plays fairly enough, takes it on the chin early in the running, but also gets it on the lips before everything is over.

One youngster was muffling shrieks of delight during the picture and a balcony laugh sounded raw enough to be a "plant." But that can easily be the tip-off on this reel opus. Its forte is in the balcony and the cheap admissions.

What it's doing in the Capitol, you figure out. Maybe it's to start Miss Gadsdon. *Sid.*

Wreck of the Hesperus

Produced by De Mille Pictures Corp., released by Pathe. Suggested by Henry Wadsworth Longfellow's poem. Screen adaptation by Harry Carr and John Farrow. Directed by Elmer Clifton. At the Strand, N. Y., week of Nov. 27. Running time, over 60 mins.

Captain David Slocum.....Sam de Grasse
Gale Slocum............Virginia Bradford
John Hazzard................Francis Ford
John Hazzard, Jr............Frank Marion
Singapore Jack....................Alan Hale
Deborah Slocum................Ethel Wales
The Bride..............Josephine Norman
Zeke..........................Milton Holmes
Cabin Boy.....................James Aldine
First Mate......................Budd Fine

It was a bad suggestion and the result is a headache.

They walked out on it at the Strand Sunday evening and they'll probably walk elsewhere. Painfully long drawn out, the cast is inconsequent, and the story is told in a dull, tedious, lifeless monotone.

There isn't a tense situation throughout the picture—while the story needs powerful characterization to get over. The central figure, Captain Slocum, is played by Sam de Grasse, who does it more like a butler than a sea captain.

Marion, juvenile lead, is badly spotted. He is buffeted around, unable to display any quality which would gain interest from an audience.

That is mainly the trouble throughout. None of the characters are rendered interesting enough to get attention. They're practically all colorless. The girl, Virginia Bradford, is attractive against the proper settings. Side shots weaken her.

The storm scene, for the finish, is well done, but there have been so many.

Longfellow may mean something to the youngsters, but the picture won't. *Mori.*

VERY CONFIDENTIAL

Fox release of a James Tinling production featuring Madge Bellamy. Story by J. K. McGuinness. In cast: Pat Cunning, Joe Cawthorn, Mary Duncan, Marjorie Beebe. At Hippodrome, New York, week Nov. 28. Running time, 59 mins.

If this picture had any kind of a chance to make the first run grade it wouldn't have played any place in New York but the Roxy. Whenever the Fox boys allow Miss Bellamy to get away from the "cathedral" there's something wrong, and the Fox office knew enough to keep "Very Confidential" off Broadway. Over at the Hip it doesn't matter.

This one doesn't hold. It rambles along displaying some fair sport stuff. It has arms and legs but no body. Miss Bellamy hops herself into a nice looking V-bottom boat to steer a weird course over a lake and then pilots a low slung car to win a feminine hill climbing contest. Inasmuch as she's a sales girl posing as a famed sportswoman, those are the comedy complications, and the titles are unusually bad.

No screen credit for producer, director or author. Only the Fox label and the cast. It's just as well. The further they can keep it away from the following Miss Bellamy is acquiring the better off for all concerned.

Joe Cawthorn, of former Julia, Donald and Joe fame, plays the wealthy father of the society boy whom "Madge" is chasing. Okay, too, although beyond Cawthorn and Miss Bellamy the players shed little light on the subject.

However, the girl enrolled as "Madge's" sidekick scored every so often for comedy. In fact, there were a surprising number of laughs from the Hip attendance. On that order the picture should be a fair three-day bet and figures good one day entertainment without needing a second feature to bolster. *Sid.*

Peaks of Destiny

(GERMAN MADE)

Ufa (German production, released in U. S. by Paramount. Leni Riefenstahl starred, with Louis Trenker and Ernest Peterson featured. Story or adaptation by Dr. Arbild Franck. In the absence of mention of the director's name that may be assumed also to be Dr. Franck. At Moss' Cameo (400 seats), New York, week Nov. 27. Running time around 65 minutes (question whether six or seven reels; time not taken).

Others in cast: Frida Richard, Friedich Schneider, Hannes Schneider, Edmund Meisel.

"Peake of Destiny" seems more scenic than anything else. It's in reality a picturization of the Swiss Alps. While there is a story running through, it's nearly all outdoors, with but little if any cost in that for staging scenes, while the interiors are nothing at all. Outside of the cast's salaries this production, including location, if any, probably did not cost $5,000.

Best places for it over here are the one-dayers and the houses where westerns are preferred. There's considerable action, but it's mostly all on skis. There are ski races and jumps, with all of this stuff dragged out.

Again there is suspense painfully tried for in the German way, with one mountain climber attached to the other by a rope, holding his companion whom he had forced over a high cliff by the same rope from late afternoon until next morning. You can imagine how that long distance suspense was mangled. It involved the girl struggling through the snow for assistance.

They made the girl a vamp, also in the German way, and in unvamping her at the finish the impression was left she didn't know whom she loved and didn't care.

Entire film is dragged out. Easily 1,500 feet could go out of this version. There's not enough stability to the vague, wabbly story to stand for the dragginess.

The story might have stood up for a two-reeler. It's of a flirty dancer who lost her fellow but found him again in the mountains with his mother. He preferred the mountains, a caption said, as they made him forget, so he probably had something on the mountains.

Most interesting character and best player of the picture is Ernest Peterson, a good and likable juvenile. He is a personable boy with a pleasant smile, and played well all of the time. Louis Trenker, the co-featured lead, was too heavy, in the German way also. He hitched on the Jannings glare, too. Perhaps when Jannings gets a few weeks off he will return to Berlin and give them a new mode over there.

Leni Riefenstahl as the dancing flirt seemed a victim of the cameraman. At times she suggested a looker and at other times a cook. Her acting, however, is better than her dancing. Frida Richard played a Mary Carr mother very nicely. No one else of importance.

Ufa shouldn't send over pictures like this as a sample and should take off the billing, as here: "Producer of 'Metropolis,' 'Variety' and 'Passion.'" Those who have seen those pictures won't believe this billing. Or they may inquire why didn't Ufa make another such. *Sime.*

THE WIZARD

Fox production and release, featuring Edmund Lowe. Adapted from the play "Balaoo," by Gaston Leroux. Directed by Richard Rosson. Titles credited to M. S. Boyland and photography to Frank Good. At the Roxy, New York, week Nov. 26. Running time, 61 mins.

Stanley Gordon..............Edmund Lowe
Anne Webster.................Leila Hyams
Paul Cariolos........Gustav Von Seyffertitz
Judge Webster..............Norman Trevor
Ape......................George Kotsonaros

More horror. Laid on thick. But the great American public brought it on themselves. They "went" for the serials back in the early days of screendom, and it looks as if the cycle has come around again. The new dish is evidently gorillas sprinkled with apes. Shake well, add the mental power of a tabloid reader and be horrified.

Silly and a waste of time. But so is "The Wizard."

Another ingenious professor who playfully grafts the face of a fiend on the skull of a huge ape and trains it to fetch, carry and kill while the prof. chuckles in his secret den. The last line of the cast will tip off the plot, and Kotsonaros gives the best performance in the picture. He waddles, glowers, fights and gets shot. Odds on that Leila Hyams was ..iore scared in Sherry's than she is supposed to be. Everybody is scared—except the audience.

This picture hasn't got enough sense to it to even create an illusion of horror. All it can do is keep some imaginative youngsters awake for a couple of nights. And that won't compensate for low grosses.

And Fox or the theatre has acquired a tinting complex. It shows in this epic. A yellow robe over the ape as a disguise. It's unquestionably yellow. Candles on a birthday cake. See them glow, even in long shots. The girl fires a gun. Watch the flash. Why? Somebody ought to remember it's mostly black and white on a screen and these tintings are much like an actor hopping in and out of character. A hundred percent, or nothing. They're even tinting some of the subjects in the newsreel. It's doing the product no good, either. Partial tinting can't get over. It detracts more than it adds and causes the attention to waver.

But ."The Wizard." That's Von Seyffertitz! He's out ·to revenge the sentencing of Paul Duval to the chair. What Paul did you'll never find out. However, it crops up in a title that he was the wizard's son. It explains Coriolos' feud on the Webster family, Miss Hyams and Norman Trevor. ·Mysterious notes inform the victims that they're "next." One disappears from the midst of a dinner party.

It's all very annoying until the cub reporter (Mr. Lowe) gets on the trail. He's got to get a big story or lose his job. He doesn't 'phone in about painting an elephant, but he does go to the mat with the ape which suddenly overcomes the effects of the operation and · goes pure ape with its ancestors.

And there's hell to pay.

Coriolos, a dirty dog at best, uses the whip once too often and dies at the hands of the "thing" he has conceived. Anne shoots the beast, Stanley phones his beat on the town's blood curdling mystery and obtains himself a bride.

Write and 'play down to your audience. They did. Rentals should be very good in Russia and Roxy will have a grouch all week? *Sid.*

OUT OF THE PAST

Peerless production. Directed by Dallas M. Fitzgerald from script by John S. Lopez. Featuring Mildred Harris and Robert Frazer. At Loew's New York (Nov. 4) on double feature bill. Running time, about 60 mins.

There isn't a chance for any but minor bookings. Crude and frank is this film's melodrama, the technical side of picture making is as plain as the water mark on a kid's neck.

When the ladies open their mouths the lips are exposed white beyond an outer rim of rouge. Miss Harris 'glides around with head held high because when she lowers it the camera raises havoc. Robert Frazer, an actor, exposes others in the cast whenever he's in the same frame with them.

In several spots, where things get too pathetic, comedy utterly foreign to the story is brought in to form a protecting cover. The titles boast such heart throbs as "Thus Was Wrought a Miracle" and "Fate's Grim Jest."

A girl loves a soldier who is reported killed. At the persuasion of her mother she marries a broker, whom she doesn't love. The broker goes broke because of dissipation, and blows for the tropics after

leaving evidence he has committed suicide. The supposed dead soldier comes back and is about to marry his former sweetheart. The broker comes back, too, but after seeing things through a French, or possibly Italian, window, sets off down the dusty road with head hung low.

Throughout it all the fiddlers in Loew's New York drew their bows slowly across the strings, producing beautiful little notes that tugged earnestly at the heartstrings.

But sometimes even that doesn't help.

TIRED BUSINESS MAN

Tiffany production and release. Directed by Allan Dale. Starring Raymond Hitch-·cock. Scenario by John Francis Natteford. Cast includes Blanche Mehaffey, Mack Swain, Charles Delaney, Margaret Quimby, Gibson Gowland, Dot Farley and Lincoln Plumer. At the Columbus, N. Y., Nov. 6. Running time, 50 mins.

About the only thing missing is the good old custard pie. The picture has Raymond Hitchcock doing all the stunts of the low screen buffoon of long ago.

Hitchcock works very hard, painfully so at times, to keep the picture's head above water. but the film falls short of his anticipated fun-making results.

It's a commonplace story, Hitchy doing the alderman who, when his wife's away, plays flirtatiously with a stenographer. At tea she soils her dress so that the host obliges with a dress of his wife's until the other dries. Hitchy's pants catch fire and he rushes upstairs in his home for a change, and before he gets the substitute wife returns, and the fireworks start.

At the Columbus the picture disappointed. It will have to find solace in double-feature fare. *Mark.*

Galloping Fury

Universal-Jewel production. Directed by Reaves Eason from Peter B. Kyne story. Starring Hoot Gibson, supported by Sally Rand and Otis Harlan. Photographed by Harry Neuman; titles by Tom Reed. At Loew's New York (Nov. 4) on double-feature bill.

Peter B. Kyne's story made good material for this western, and an unusual and interesting picture (for a western) was the result.

It deals with a ranch whereon a peculiar mud is discovered by the hands. The boys find that by placing it on their faces they can remove all sorts of blemishes. Two city gents get wise and seek to swindle the old owner out of his possible rise in the beauty clay market. But after numerous adventures the city guys are balked, and the ranch foreman (Hoot. Gibson) embraces the niece (Sally Rand) of one of these city guys. The other city gent is, of course, Hoot's villainous rival.

Gibson, Harlan and Miss Rand are easily satisfactory as the featured trio. Direction and·photography okay.

HAZARDOUS VALLEY

Ellbee release. Directed by Alfred Neitz from script by A. B. Barringer. Cast includes Virginia Brown Faire, Vincent Brownell, David Torrence, Sheldon Lewis and Burr McIntosh. At the Stanley, N. Y., one day, Nov. 2. Running time, 62 mins.

Story of a youth who goes to his father's lumber camp and personally sees to it that the all-important shipment of logs is delivered on time. The difficulties overcome are fostered by his father's rival, who later sees the light when his own daughter is in the arms of the courageous youth.

Cheaply produced and acted with various degrees of ability. Best is David Torrence as the crooked rival. **Vincent Brownell is a handsome if a bit untalented juvenile lead. Miss Faire is sweetly satisfactory.**

Picture can do three days with neighborhood vaudeville or one day alone. Doesn't rate anything better.

BOY OF THE STREETS

Rayart production directed by Charles J. Hunt. From story by Charles T. Vincent. Featuring Johnny Walker. Cast includes Mickey Bennett, Henry Sedly, Betty Francisco, Edward Gordon and Charles O'Malley. At the Stanley, N. Y., Nov. 5. Running time, 55 mins.

Mickey Bennett, the kid player, makes the picture. The boy has a knack for facial expression unusual in juvenile players. Screens well and is a good actor.

Good direction responsible for fine results with ordinary material in story. There is, however, an obvious cheapness in production that keeps the picture in the daily change class.

Miss Francisco is at no time plausible in the role of the little girl about-to-be-taken-advantage-of.

Walker is the big brother doing his last safe-cracking job in order to get enough money to send the kid to the country. On account of his dog, the little boy is hurt and taken to the girl's home. By a coincidence this·is the spot picked to be looted of valuable papers which would place the district politics in other hands. The big brother is caught in the act but the girl saves him on account of the kid.

A lot of action crammed into the last half with the reformed yegg rescuing the gal's pap from jail and getting her brother out of the hands of a blackmailer.

The Tigress

Columbia Production. Hollywood release. Directed by George B. Seitz. Scenario by Harold Shumate. Cameraman, Joe Walker. Jack Holt starred. Others include Dorothy Revier, Frank Leigh, Phillipe De Lacy. Running time, 54 minutes. At Broadway, New York, week Nov. 28.

Inexpert continuity, thick-fingered direction and some of the worst technical treatment seen in some time have made a very weak picture out of a plot situation of intrinsic entertainment value.

Many will wonder after seeing this one why Jack Holt was so squeamish about playing gentlemen cowboys for Paramount. He certainly gains no distinction in "The Tigress." Nor does anyone else.

Action is in Spain. A band of gypsies poach on the deers in a neighboring estate. The menace murders the chief gyp in cold blood and says the Englishman, the Earl of Reddington, who owns the estate, did it.

The chief's daughter, crack knife-thrower, sets out to revenge her father. She is thrown from her horse and put to bed unconscious in the Earl's place. The Earl allows her to mistake him for a valet.

Not even as good as it may sound.

HOUR OF RECKONING

Presented by George Davis, produced by John E. Ince. Directed by John E. Ince from the story by Frederic Chapin. Cast includes John E. Ince, Herbert Rawlinson, Grace Darmond, J. J. Darby and Harry von Meter. At Loew's New York, Nov. 18, one-half of a double feature bill. Running time about 60 minutes.

A cheaply made film, dealing with no particular subject that might be relied on for unusual exploitation. Rawlinson, in the lead, holds up in his department.

Story is of the manager of a safe manufacturing concern who gets those certain papers that the owner of the company is hiding. The gal's father, an inventor, is unable to prove his claim for money without them.

Owner's son is locked in a safe,

toward the close of the narrative, and can be saved only by the manager. Because the latter's sister is married to the boy the hero saves him. The iron-hearted papa then breaks down and makes everybody happy.

LOVE

Metro-Goldwyn-Mayer production and release, starring John Gilbert and Greta Garbo. Adapted from Tolstoi's story, "Anna Karenina," and directed by Edmund Goulding. Wm. Daniels, photographer; titles by Marion Ainslee and Ruth Cummings. Musical score credited to Ernst Luz. At the Embassy, New York, for a twice daily run, starting Nov. 29. Running time, 84 mins.

Anna Karenina....................Greta Garbo
Vronsky..........................John Gilbert
Grand Duke.....................George Fawcett
Grand Duchess...................Emily Fitzroy
Karenin.........................Brandon Hurst
Serezha.......................Philippe De Lacy

It's an idiom that your American public stands for what it likes and a lot that it doesn't. That may not prove anything, but they were on their feet two deep behind the last row in this 596-seater Saturday afternoon and lobby announcing S. R. O. until Monday night. Tie that! The Embassy hasn't even approached it in some time. The house has finally got itself a picture that's going to do some business.

"Love," plus Gilbert, plus Garbo, is a clarion call to shoppers. Shoppers mean women, and women mean matinees. Big ones. Try and keep the femmes away from this one. They've all apparently got a Gilbert-Garbo complex tucked away somewhere. The men, too. They like Garbo, but the girls are going to pay off this production cost, and some more besides. And how often do the exhibs get a "matinee" picture?

"Love" isn't $2. That is to say, it couldn't stand up as a road show. Its setting is about perfect in this house of intimate atmosphere, with no clamor of the mob coming and going. It doesn't start until 3 p. m., no intermission, and they're out by 4:30. Plenty of time for three shows daily on the week-ends. The feature should stay here at least 12 weeks, figuring that "Flesh and the Devil" would have been good for 20 and without thinking twice about it.

What is there to tell about the Tolstoi story? Its locale is Russia in the time of the Czar. Anna (Miss Garbo) has a husband and a young son, Vronsky (Mr. Gilbert), a military heritage and a desire for Anna. For screen purposes it's enough that both are of the aristocracy, which permits Miss Garbo long, stately gowns and Gilbert a series of uniforms that would make a buck private out of the student prince. There are rich interiors, appropriate exteriors and an excellent officers' steeplechase to get the action figuratively off of a couch for a while. Besides which Miss Garbo and Mr. Gilbert supposedly care for each other in the script.

Under Goulding's guidance anyone may rest assured this couple are quite apt to get that idea across, although if the censors think they're going to have a picnic through being the only ones permitted to see things, it's going to be an uneventful private showing. Goulding has throttled passion 'most all the way. The dailies would probably call that "repression" by the director; Variety merely states that he has laid off. Anyway, Goulding hasn't let the title run away with his sense of discretion. Possibly has leaned over backwards to the extent of keeping this picture from becoming a "rave."

The girls get a great kick out of the heavy love stuff. They come out of these pictures with their male escorts and an "I-wonder-if-he's-learned-anything" expression. They claim the screen's the closest they can get to it. But pity the modern lover. He's so tired from holding up a raccoon coat he can't compete, so no wonder there's an aching heart for every clinch in Hollywood.

On the other hand, Goulding has used good judgment. If conservative, it's something not many similar pictures have had, is not going to interfere with rentals and can't cause a protesting chirp from other than the extreme fanatics who think that if a boy tips his hat he should do right by the girl.

Peculiar combination this Gilbert-Garbo hookup. Both sprang up suddenly and fast, Miss Garbo from nowhere. The latter isn't now as big as she should or will be, always remembering it's the stories that count. Neither has she been in enough pictures of late. But if handled, and she will allow herself to be handled, she's the biggest skirt prospect now in pictures.

With "Love" to urge on the demand for this couple, M-G-M can isolate both players so as to only appear together. With the start they've got Miss Garbo and Mr. Gilbert are in a fair way to become the biggest box office mixed team this country has yet known. It's comparable to the following certain stock company dual leads have enjoyed, simply magnified by the field.

Both are strong away from each other and have proved it. But combine that double strength with a reasonable story and what, or who, can stop it? Also what producer wouldn't take this couple and be satisfied to turn out just two pictures a year? As a team they can do that. Apart they can't.

When all is said and done, "Love" is a cinch because it has Gilbert and Garbo. Without them it would be a nice program leader. *Sid.*

WILD GEESE

Tiffany-Stahl production released through Tiffany of Martha Ostenso's "Pictorial Review" prize novel. Phil Stone directed from A. P. Younger's adaptation. Belle Bennett featured. Runs 69 minutes. At Roxy, New York, week Dec. 3.

Amelia Gare....................Belle Bennett
Caleb Gare...................Russell Simpson
Judith Gare....................Eve Southern
Sven Sandbo....................Donald Keith
Mark Jordan....................Jason Robards
Lind Archer....................Anita Stewart
Martin Gare.....................Wesley Barry
Ellen Gare.........................Raida Rae
Charlie Gare....................Austen Jewel
Mrs. Klovatz....................Evelyn Selbie
Mr. Klovatz...................D'Arcy Corrigan
Bart Nugent.....................Bert Starkey
Skull...........................Jack Gardner
Parson............................James Mack
Marshal...........................Bert Sporte
Mrs. Sandbo.....................Bodil Rosing

Martha Ostenso's novel, "Wild Geese," won for the authoress $13,500 in cash prizes in the "Pictorial Review" competition in addition to accruing royalties from the nine translations of her yesteryear's best seller. As a novel, it was a poignantly graphic insight on a Minnesota household's existence under the tyranny of a domineering head of the family.

Transmuted to the screen, Phil Stone's celluloid painting is almost as gripping as the authoress' word-painting, and yet "Wild Geese," the film, does not compare with "Wild Geese," the novel.

The answer is simple. The basic backbone of all stage or screen performance is action, be it dramatic, comedy, hokum, but it must be action. Thus, "Wild Geese" is a little more exciting than one of Mencken's "Prejudices" scenarized.

Reduced to its fundamentals, Caleb Gare's browbeating of his family and the ultimate death of the despot as a means to the liberation of the Gare tribe's natural reactions is pretty familiar stuff. It was Miss Ostenso's treatment that distinguished her novel, and while the Stone direction, the Belle Bennett and Russell Simpson screen characterizations, and the supporting cast's vivid interpretations are equally as distinguished, the composite produces nothing but a desire for something to happen. Everything is draggy, retarded and fairly soon obvious.

Tiffany-Stahl's ambassadorial entry into the Roxy is by no means a handicapping try. Very likely "Wild Geese" will do business here for the Roxy is just the type house a picture of this nature will please.

The sophisticated downtown film fan that contributes to the Roxy's staggering grosses will rather fancy the deft treatment of each character. He will appreciate to more or less conscious degree that Director Stone was wise in restraining Simpson's portrayal of the tyrannical father, making him a domineering but not fiendishly impossible sire. Miss Bennett's intelligent interpretation of the cowed wife is equally creditable, reserved and less sobby than usual. And so on down the line. An exception might be Eve Southern, whose blond tresses were poor wig outfitting.

Thus, "Wild Geese" is conversely questionable for mass appeal in ratio to its artistry. Somewhat subtle and generally sluggish, the mob of hinterland fans might not cotton to it as much as it deserves. It is the type of film the fanciful stylist reviewers will enthuse about but overlook the box office possibilities.

"Wild Geese" has much in its favor to offset this through a generally economic production cost, so taking it by and large, Tiffany-Stahl emerge creditably. *Abel.*

Valley of the Giants

Charles J. Brabin production, released by First National. From the story by Peter B. Kyne. Directed by Charles Brabin. Starring Milton Sills; featuring Doris Kenyon. At the Strand, New York, week Dec. 4. Running time, over 65 minutes.

Bryce Cardigan....................Milton Sills
Shirley Pennington...............Doris Kenyon
Buck Ogilvy.......................Arthur Stone
John Cardigan..................George Fawcett
Rondeau............................Paul Hurst
Pennington......................Charles Sellon
Felice.............................Yola d'Avril
Big Boy............................Phil Brady

A fast-moving meller, with a light sprinkling of comedy and a somewhat unimaginative title. Good program picture and the story strong enough to make it stand up full week in support of vaude or other stage show. For the split week and lesser stands it's a ready made coin getter.

Based on Kyne's popular novel this tale interestingly unwinds round the battle of an ancient pioneer lumber king and a newer eastern lumber merchant with a domineering complex.

Pennington (Charles Sellon) as Cardigan's enemy is miscast. He looks more like the country general store proprietor than a lumber man.

Miss Kenyon, opposite Sills, is badly treated by the camera after the first introduction and that is inexcusable. She looks attractive in the first few shots, but is painfully lustreless after that.

Pennington, according to the story, owning the local railway line, plans to cut off railroad service for the Cardigan lumber mills with the intention of gaining control of the latter's possessions. Cardigan's outstanding notes have been taken up by his competitor. The old lumber man finally negotiates a loan of half a million from a friend and there is then the difficulty of getting a franchise from the city council, which is controlled by Pennington.

Arthur Stone (Buck Ogilvy) as the smart city gent, is framed to pose as a Chicago millionaire and creates a carload of laughs in the scene where he gets the city council stewed enough to agree to a franchise. The obstinate councilman and Buck's helper, both unbilled on the program, are at least equally responsible with Stone for the skilful comedy touches in this part.

It fits Sills. *Mori.*

MAN, WOMAN & SIN

Metro-Goldwyn-Mayer production and release. Written, directed and produced by Monta Bell. Starring John Gilbert. Jeanne Eagles featured. Cast includes Gladys Brockwell, Marc McDermott, Philip Anderson, Hayden Stevenson, Charles K. French and Aileen Manning. At the Capitol, New York, week Dec. 3. Running time, over 65 minutes.

Box office possibilities not above average with the exception of localities, where Gilbert is strong enough to draw on name, aided and abetted by the alluring title.

Production has been handled smoothly—too smoothly. Considering the weakness of the story, inept characterization, miscasting and lacking a suitable climax, Monta Bell did exceptionally well as a director. As a screen scribbler and producer, not so good.

From no conceivable angle, is the story one which could meet with popular approval. In smaller cities and towns, especially, it is unlikely to draw favorable comment, though moderate business can be figured on account of the star and the title.

The try for comedy, though raising an occasional laugh, is not in line with the general tone of the picture which seems inclined to morbidness. These kind of pictures react unfavorably in more ways than one.

There is an impression, from the opening scene, that tragedy stalks the path of the ragged little boy who makes himself a target for workers on coal trains so that he can collect the stray bits of fuel to bring home to his mother. Despite the impression, the grip on interest is not affected because the characters are not built up interestingly enough. The story isn't there.

The first reel or so is devoted to showing that poorly dressed kids don't stand much of a chance with families of more substantial means. For no special reason the poor little boy walks into a haunted house, in front of which an awed group is gathered in heated argument, and comes out alive.

That is evidently intended to plant a germ for futuristic deduction, but it doesn't. The boy grows up. A long-winded process, as most people know, usually most uninteresting and stereotyped. Hundreds of feet of film showing boy saving pennies and, later on, dollars, in a large earthen jar. Even the mother love racket doesn't hold attention.

Dreary scenes of mother and son talking, later arguing. Boy shown in the press room of a newspaper folding newspapers. Becomes a reporter after saving one of the city room's regulars from severe handling in a "cabaret" purposely miscalled with the scene showing the place to be nothing but a cheap joint.

Boy falls for the society editor, not knowing she is friendly with the newspaper owner. Fairly nice girl, the society editor (Jeanne Eagels), but that camera may have been cruel in some scenes. Miss Eagels looks haggard in spots, contradicting the description in the subtitles. Under the soft lens the legit recruit handles herself pleasingly. She has the only role in the picture with any color to it.

Finally, a scene in the society editor's apartment. The reporter had come to ask if it were true that the publisher of the paper on which he worked had a claim on the girl. The old boy opens the door of the apartment with a key and wants to know what the young man is doing in his apartment, picking up a bronze statue for an attack. During the struggle the older gent is killed. Nobody cares. Everyone might have been just as happy if all three had dropped in that scene.

Court room scenes; old stuff. To save her reputation, the girl perjures herself. The tottering mama gets her to submit new testimony after the conviction of the boy and the death verdict. The self-defense plea, with the girl's testimony, frees the boy. *Mori.*

GET YOUR MAN

Paramount production and release starring Clara Bow. Adapted from Louis Verneuil's play with Dorothy Arzner directing. Charles Rogers featured. Titles by George Marion, Jr., with Albert Gilks cameraman; at Paramount, New York, week of Dec. 3; running time, 60 mins.

Nancy Worthington	Clara Bow
Robert de Bellecontre	Charles Rogers
Duc de Bellecontre	Josef Swickard
Marquis de Villeneuve	Harvey Clarke
Simone Villeneuve	Josephine Dunn
Mrs. Worthington	Frances Raymond

Typical Bow picture that will appease this girl's following. No rave but okay.

Miss Bow has adopted the hair-off-one-ear coiffeur which makes her look a la Negri profile. It's not becoming and if Miss Bow cares to look it up she'll find that Paramount wouldn't renew with Pola for $10,000 weekly mainly because her type is mostly welcome some 3,600 miles from here. However, in this instance Miss Bow does her usual flip flap and it's enough for program purposes.

Another case of titles helping plenty, although the story carries the principals into a wax museum where the boy and girl become locked in and have to spend the night. Well handled, this passage is the real excitement of the footage and will tickle the populace.

To clinch it, Clara frolics around in undies as she tries to compromise the bo" she's after in his home. But if these are stock situations Miss Arzner has handled them sufficiently well to make it breezy, and easy on brain power.

Charles Rogers, opposite Miss Bow, shows signs of becoming too actory from haircut to shoes. With the story set in France there's nothing Latin about Rogers in the first place, he'll never be a male vamp to the public at large in the second, and the third guess is that the more he studies the ways and means committees on a campus the more natural he'll be with a better chance of getting over. It'll take more than his performance in "Wings" to make this boy.

Miss Bow turns loose some nice trouping in various spo'- and is urged along by the performance of Harvey Clarke as an elderly connoisseur of women who falls for the fresh American youngster. As he's the father of the girl to whom Robert is bethrothed, it's through him that Nancy frustrates the engagement. Josef Swickard also lends valuable assistance.

Simply a lightweight farce with the Bow name on it. She has had better leads and will have better films. *Sid.*

CHEATING CHEATERS

Universal production and release, directed by Edward Laemmle, starring Betty Compson. From play of same name by Max Marcin. Running time, 60 mins. At the Colony, New York, week of Dec. 4.

Nan Carey	Betty Compson
Tom Palmer	Kenneth Harlan
Lazarre	Lucien Littlefield
Steve	Eddie Gribbon
Tony	Cesare Gravina
Mrs. Brockton	Sylvia Ashton
Mr. Brockton	Erwin Connelly
Mrs. Palmer	Maude Turner Gordon
Mr. Palmer	E. J. Ratcliffe

Crook society play came practically ready-made to the film producer. A faithful, and therefore adequate, transcription has been accomplished. Danger in picturization was that the screen version might miss the delicate balance between smooth comedy and flamboyant farce. Peril has been successfully avoided.

The situation of two gangs of crooks, each unaware of the other's character, operating against each other in fashionable surroundings to which they are alien, could readily be misjudged. Gagged up too much the effect would be lost, while the underplaying of the comedy might waste some effective material. Laemmle has managed his subject matter with good judgment.

The fact that the heroine is in reality a detective is neatly concealed until the last minute as in the play. All in all, the production is an excellent job. It has good laughs, first-class suspense, interesting pictorial qualities and sustains interest. A valuable program subject.

Has a brisk opening with heroine leaving the jail, where she has been planted to make an opening for entrance to the crook gang's confidence. Goes into amusing revelations of society crook circles and then promptly moves into the society atmosphere, with such bits as butler who can't resist picking supposed aristocratic guests' pockets, or reaching for his "cannon" when he thinks danger threatens.

Love interest between heroine and youth, unwilling member of the rival crook gang, develops incidentally without halting crook complications. The finish is brought on promptly and in good action passages, to the surprise finish, where the girl detective herds in both gangs and accomplishes her task. First-rate acting helps ensemble effect, together with technical production in the best modern manner.

Kenneth Harlan makes a rather mild part attractive by his unassuming style, while Eddie Gribbon as the tough gun-toting yegg has the outstanding comedy role of the cast. Sylvia Ashton, too, has her moments as the woman crook playing society dowager.

A touch of novelty enters into the opening, when the main title becomes a sort of animated affair, instead of the usual stilted acknowledgment of credits. At the start the screen shows a darkened room. Presently a burglar enters from a window and his electric flash plays about the place. Gradually the bright disk of the torch comes nearer and nearer until it takes up most of the screen, when the title appears in its circle. Nothing else is disclosed except the Universal name and the state license notice. The picture is on its way immediately with an appropriate introduction. *Rush.*

The City Gone Wild

Paramount production and release. Directed by James Cruze. Thomas Meighan starred. In the cast Louise Brooks, Charles Mailes, Wyndham Standing, Mona Gray. Running time, 58 mins. At Hippodrome, New York, week of Dec. 5.

James Cruze shot this one in a hurry as a windup to his contract with Paramount. It is the same picture the press departments of West Coast Theatres, Inc., handled so roughly a few weeks ago. In San Francisco the name of Meighan was blocked out of the 24-sheets and in Los Angeles the picture was wrapped in a "take-a-chance" week.

"City Gone Wild" is as good as the average Meighan picture and much better than "We're All Gamblers," which Cruze also directed. The plot is fairly novel and for Meighan quite revolutionary.

Tom is the smart lawyer to a bunch of crooks. He is continually getting his gangster-clients free on some technicality. The district attorney is, however, a personal friend of his, although his enemy professionally. The two men love the same girl and the girl's father is that often mentioned but seldom seen "man higher up" in crime.

The gang stuff is a la "Underworld"—machine guns and plenty tough. The two main yeggs each have a moll carrying their gat in the pocketbook. Very authentic in these little details is the picture.

Not a picture to be played up, but its action should carry it through.

AFTERMATH

Presented by Collwyn Pictures, Inc., distributor not mentioned. Advance notices attributed work to Ufa, while main title bears name of "National A-G-Films." Directed by Erich Waschneck. Cast all foreign. Running time, 78 mins. At the Cameo, New York, week Dec. 4.

Nadja	Olga Tschechowa
Zeremski	Hans von Schlettow
Louise von Wilkuhnen	Jenny Hasselquist
Henry Raschoff	Fritz Alberti
William Wilkuhnen	Hubert von Meyerink
Marlene	Camilla Spira
Corporal Walde	Oscar Homolka
Adjutant Duban	Hugo Werner-Kahle
Kitchen Maid	Frieda Braut

Picture has all the earmarks of German manufacture both in its merits and defects. The latter predominate. A story of anarchy following the war in Europe ought to have possibilities, but they are not developed here, for the production is a wretched sample of second rate output.

The acting is mostly bad and the photography crude, particularly in close ups. There is only one minor character who has any idea of playing before the camera. He is Fritz Alberti, a high-bred looking figure. Direction is heavy to the point of absurdity. Inconsequential scenes are padded out endlessly and climaxes, long postponed, amount to little when they do eventuate.

The whole business has the appearance of inexperienced producers and players. Titling is barbarous in its crudity.

The only items worth while are occasional fine glimpses of old world settings and the acting of a few minor players as ruffian types. There are several mob scenes that are impressive by reason of action and settings, but the principal story episodes are impossible.

Action takes place in an unidentified principality called Despotia, or some such name. After the war the territory is in dispute and has no government. Guerrilla bands roam the land under bandit chiefs and oppress the old nobility and gentry. Such an outlaw band is captained by Zeremski, whose uniform is partly Cossack and disposition altogether so. He and his ruffians billet themselves upon the estates of Louise von Wilkuhnen, robbing the place and the chief, after a drunken revel pictured in elaborate and often offensive detail, is in the way of committing the ultimate outrage upon the widow herself, when he is laid low by her son. Whereupon all the good people of the story escape on horseback to the nearby border and are safe, while the despoilers rage vainly.

It's all clumsy fiction. Hans Adalbert von Schlettow, as Zeremski, tries to play the jaunty young braggart, but the close-ups reveal him as a middle-aged man. He is attended in his crimes by Nadja, whom the script may have set down as his infamous paramour, but who in the playing by Olga Tschechowa was just a large, plump blonde girl, trying to be devil may care and making tough going of it. Everybody overacts. These Continental pictures when they're good are very, very good, but when they're bad——
Rush.

PRINCE OF LOVERS

(BRITISH MADE)

Gaumont production. Directed by C. S. Calvert. Scenario by Alicia Ramsey. Based on the biography of Lord Byron. At the 55th St. Cinema, New York, week Nov. 28. Running time, about 60 minutes.

Lord Byron	Howard Gaye
Isabella Milbanke	Marjorie Hume
Lady Caroline Lamb	Mary Clare
Augusta Leigh	Marjorie Day
Cam Hobhouse	David Hawthorne
Sir Walter Scott	W. D. C. Knox
Lady Jersey	Viva Birkett
Tom Moore	Eugene Leahy
The Prince Regent	Beliendom Powell
Madame de Stael	Mrs. Saba Raleigh
Southey	James Bonatus
Ada Augusta Byron	Eileen Onions

With the basis for a likeable production in the story of the eventful career of one of Britain's immortals, the picture has been deprived of entertainment value through miscasting and unbusinesslike direction.

The expense of a director is wasted, since the story is told almost entirely in the titles. There is no action of any kind. With a topic which would best flourish, as far as box-office value is concerned, if handled in a light, breezy, sophisticated style, an air of morbidness, inexcusable in film entertainment of any kind, pervades.

The story carries more than enough material for mugging, trouping and climaxes. None of the possibilities were properly developed. In the hands of capable producers the same picture could be remade even now, with little doubt that it could register not only as a good program picture, but as a special. All it needs is specialized treatment.

Lord Byron as a character, if popular legend is adhered to, would gain interest and attention. Howard Gaye dies with the role. As a great lover Byron is certainly a back number, according to the way he has been framed here. It is inconceivable that the stilted, awkward, somewhat stupid person of this film would gain much headway with the dames; not in A. D. 1927, and doubtful if at any other period, even his own.

With the story underdeveloped, colorless and weak, the central character is undermined, and with him so presented the picture flops.

There is no excuse for sloppiness in costume pictures. That the ladies in the picture wear the loose apparel of their times does not warrant their looking unkempt and ungraceful. Costume productions have often been chosen because of the interest value to be derived from showing former modes and the picturization of old styles added to the value of the films made here. In this one the costumes detract.

There are laughs when the "beauties" are introduced. No sense in having a sub-title tell of a pretty lady and then a flash of her on the screen showing a dame who wouldn't stand a chance with the chorus of a third-rate burlesque show.

"As beautiful as a statue and as cold," is the sub-title introduction to Isabella Milbanke. Maybe there are hidden beauties of the spirit, but that should have been explained. Certainly the physical aspect of the lady in question is far from prepossessing.

Besides, who wants statues? The story seems to indicate that this baby wasn't so hot. She, or her old man, had a lot of money, and Byron knew it. Since there is no ardent love affair preceding the marriage, there is nothing to prevent the patron of the art theatre from assuming that Byron married her for the bank roll.

Byron is set forth as a drunkard. There are likeable stews. This one is obnoxious. Movie fans and others will stand for almost anything from characters they can like and admire, but there is little of either feeling for the Byron of this picture.

It seems a shame to waste a perfectly good title. The story, minus the badly advised introduction of Byron's mother and step-sister, tells of a great poet who was also supposed to be a great lover. Byron is shown reading lover letters from admiring females to prove this.

The poet gets into the bad graces of the aristocracy, among whom were formerly all his friends, and he leaves England. Later he joins the Greeks and dies from a cold or something—quite unromantically. No Grecian battles with the Turks are shown. That would have been worth while, but it would have cost money.

There are enough American-made film flops. *Mori.*

Isle of Forgotten Women

Columbia production and release. Directed by George B. Seitz. Scenario by Norman Springer. Conway Tearle starred. Others in cast: Dorothy Sebastian, Alice Calhoun, Gibson Gowland, William Welch. At Loew's New York, one day, Nov. 23. Running time, 58 mins.

The excuse and interest of this picture is Dorothy Sebastian in a state of semi-nudity. Dorothy was borrowed by Columbia from M-G-M to enact a walnut-skinned pippin of a south Pacific isle. Between yawning at Conway Tearle in a series of fevers, hallucinations and injustices, the customers will probably keep awake for the appearances of Miss Sebastian. It is, however, an ordinary and dull effort.

Tearle looks poorly in this one, probably his first screen appearance since he tried to boost his salary to $3,500 a week.

The story is familiar and venerable. A bank cashier is wrongfully accused of embezzlement and forced to flee the country. He goes to the tropics and is tempted by a voluptuous hip-wiggler. He resists her wiles and keeps his ideals. Alice, his faithful sweetie from back home, arrives to take him back just after the shredded wheat flame gets killed protecting him from a gin-crazed white man.

Girl From Gay Paree

Tiffany-Stahl production and release. Directed by Phil Stone from story by Violet Clark. Cast: Lowell Sherman, Barbara Bedford, Malcolm McGregor, Margaret Livingstone, Walter Hiers, Betty Blythe, Templar Saxe, Leo White. At Stanley, New York, one day, Nov. 24. Running time, about 65 minutes.

Misses being a good buy for full week stands on account of slovenly handling by director. The story, while not extraordinarily new, is still interesting, and every member of the cast is a fairly strong player, registering for results in the respective roles. It does not seem that Phil Stone was especially restricted in money. Settings are all appropriate, and if cheap give no impression of that.

The title, though hackneyed and seemingly unattractive, may serve very well in the towns where the novelty of Paree in any form is still fresh and acceptable.

In semi-nude costuming Miss Bedford photographs well in several shots. Not so good in the close-ups. If the camera effects had been watched more closely the production as a whole would have resulted more favorably.

Story is of a small-town girl with a yen to make the chorus in the "Follies." Broke and friendless, she is chased into a job in a cafe by a cop. For $1,000 she is to impersonate the wickedest woman in the world, who was scheduled to appear at the cabaret but canceled her contract at the last moment.

A feature writer on one of the daily newspapers flops for the gal and publicizes her to the extent of several columns. The wickedest woman in the world, hearing of the impersonation, leaves Paris for New York with dull and uninteresting complications following in place of a bright finish.

McGregor is too weak for spotting as the lead, both on appearance and ability.

Okey for the split weeks and daily changes. *Mori.*

BLACK JACK

Orville Dull production released by Fox. Directed by Orville Dull from story by Johnston McCulley. Starring Buck Jones. Cast includes Barbara Bennett. At Loew's New York, one day, Nov. 25, one-half of a double feature program. Running time, about 60 minutes.

Wherever westerns are liked this one will please. It's fast and handled in light comedy vein.

Introducing Black Jack as the dangerous gambler who is demoralizing the male population of the town, there follows a scene in which Jack is shown losing 17 cents. After the reform element had broken up the game the jedge and his henchmen gather in a barn, take off their coats and go to it for real jack.

The gal is the holder of one of three pieces of a lead coin which, if joined together, would reveal the hiding place of the gold. Black Jack holds another piece and a ranch hand has the third piece. Villainy stalks into the lives of these simple folks via the unscrupulous ranch owner. *Mori.*

The Light in the Window

Trem Carr production released by Rayart. Directed by P. Scott Pembroke from story by Arthur Hoerl. Featuring Henry B. Walthall and Patricia Avery. Cast: Henry Sedley, Tom Grady and Cornelius Keefe. At Loew's New York, one day, Nov. 25, one-half of double bill. Running time, over 60 minutes.

Dull, trite, miscast—impossible. Unintelligent direction and produced cheaply at cost of interest and saleabality.

Hundreds of feet of closeups of Patricia Avery and Walthall. Wasted. Neither player registers on the screen here except as lifeless. With thousands of girls dying for a chance on the screen they had to put a player like Miss Avery in the leading fem role. And then they tried to make a heroine out of her, besides. Miss Avery may do in comedy and that without the slightest change of expression.

This one would get the booby prize in a competition for the best independent productions of the year. Where this kind of a picture can be sold is a mystery.

It is explained that the old shoemaker loves his daughter so much he won't let her go out, even with a girl chum. That kills the old man as a noble character. The girl finally gets out, meets a pair of young men she knows nothing about and marries one of them.

Hubby is arrested for stealing a car he had paid for. Doesn't sound right. The girl, alone and homeless, finally lands in a cabaret as a cigaret girl. Husband turns up to claim her and is thrown out by a couple of bouncers.

And the rest doesn't matter either. *Mori.*

The Adventurous Soul

Select production released by Hi-Mark. Directed by Gene Carroll from story by John J. Moreno. Starring Mildred Harris. Cast includes James Fulton, Arthur Rankin, Chas. K. French and Tom Santchi. Supervised by Harriet Virginia. At Loew's New York, Nov. 29, one day, one-half of double bill. Running time, about 60 mins.

Faulty direction and supervision. With the exception of the juvenile lead, Fulton, who looks as if he'd like to fall asleep and pass out completely, the cast is good, considering it's only a daily change picture or less.

Story treatment is haphazard and partly responsible for the poor results. Attention is split several ways. A shipping clerk with a yen for the open seas, wayward son wasting the opportunities offered by a wealthy shipowning dad, and a girl given no definite status.

Evidently first intended to work up the shipping clerk as the central figure but the director divided between the shipowner, the son and daughter instead.

For an adventurous soul the clerk is not given any glamorous tinge which would so impress an audience. Though hackneyed the story offered several opportunities for a good production. All muffed.

In desperation the old man frames to have his son shanghaied and given the rough treatment on one of his ships. The lad, through some peculiar coincidence, listens in on the plot from behind the usual curtain and leaves home. The shipping clerk, calling on the girl, is taken instead and makes good at the branch office as assistant manager under the name of his employer's son.

Miss Harris is interesting in spots but kept too much in the background while the sub-titles have it out on the screen.

No love interest—no action—no box office. *Mori.*

Temptations of Shop Girl

I. E. Chadwick production released by First Division. Directed by Tom Terriss. Starring Betty Compson, with cast including Pauline Garon, Armand Kaliz, Raymond Glenn, James Gludder, John F. Dillon, Cora Williams and William Humphries. At Loew's New York, one day, Nov. 29, one-half of double bill. Running time, about 60 minutes.

Even worse than the title sounds. Only smart stuff pulled by the author was when he had his name kept off the billing.

As a high pressure blonde Betty Compson is decidedly nit. Pauline Garon, with a couple of exceptions, looks too hard for one of such obvious youth. The flighty, young sister role doesn't suit or she doesn't make it look right.

This picture may have been dumbed up purposely. It couldn't be any more uninteresting if it has. No highlights worth a second thought. It is hardly worth a play even in the split weeks. If shown in any spot where people are accustomed to any kind of fairly good programers they'll walk.

Story revolves mainly around the kid sister, a gal with a penchant for stealing expensive dresses on the advice of a small time yegg for whom she has fallen. The "chief" is located in far too luxurious surroundings to be bothering with the theft of an occasional gown.

Miss Compson does the big sister stuff and takes the blame for the missing dresses, later framing her sister's betrayer.

Unconvincing. *Mori.*

THE CROSS BREED

Produced and released by Bischoff Pictures. Story by Wells Ritchie. Cameraman, Ray June. Directed by Mason Noel Smith. Johnnie Walker starred, with "Silverstreak" (dog) featured. In cast: Gloria Heller, Chas. K. French, Frank Glendon, Henry Hebert, Joseph Mack, Olin Francis. On double bill, one day, Nov. 30, at Tivoli, New York.

A sinking of the stomach when another police dog was flashed on the screen at the Tivoli was the first reaction of a professional movie-goer. After Rin-Tin-Tin, Peter the Great, Peter the Second, Dynamite, Thunder, Ranger and the other canine "stars," a new mutt is just an additional strain.

It may be significant that after such a sorry first impression this picture gets a good notice. In spite of the dog this is an exceptionally pleasing melodrama and a picture that should deliver satisfaction outside the exclusive precincts of the deluxe.

Nothing particularly new but neatly handled. The dog remains a dog, not a mind-reading, miracle-performing, semi-human, cued quadruped. Toward the end the pup does seem to get a little clairvoyant but not absurdly so, as in some other woof-woof operas. And at no time does "Silverstreak" indulge in those prolonged dog soliloquies.

In the story dog and man are both cowards and both achieve bravery only when goaded to fury by the affronts of a bully. The boy has inherited a big lumber camp which powerful interests are after. Attempts to intimidate him, drive him off his own property or make him sell are tried with the final villainy the blowing up of a bridge to prevent the delivery of a train-load of lumber.

Cast and direction good. Production while not expensive is first class.

A blonde leading lady, Gloria Heller, is a cute biscuit that some big producer should grab. She photographs like big money and registers intelligence as well as (sex) appeal.

"The Cross Breed" is okay.

WOMAN'S LAW

Peerless production. Directed by Dallas M. Fitzgerald. Featuring Pat O'Malley and Lillian Rich, supported by Ernest Wood, John Cossar, Harold Miller, Audrey Ferris, Edward Cecil and Sam Allen. Story by H. Tipton Steck. At Stanley, New York, one day, Nov. 30. Running time, about 65 minutes.

H. Tipton Steck must have been bursting with things to tell. His story makes a long and complex picture that is rather tedious and not up to more than one day in a house.

The girl (Lillian Rich) doesn't really love any man, but she almost marries the villain in order to keep her father out of prison. An attorney helps the girl shake off the villain and is going to marry her, but the villain kills him. Then some one kills the villain and every one thinks the girl did it.

A Northwestern mounted cop is commissioned to get the girl, and marries her, thinking she is some one else. When he finds out who she is he cringes, but a letter arrives at that moment telling how the villain was killed by some one else. (And as complicated as it reads.)

Location ranges from California to Canada, and the heroine wears everything from a bathing suit to a lumberjack outfit.

Pat O'Malley is the mounted cop and looks all right in his uni. Ernest Wood is a sneering villain with a mob of razzberry scowls, making it overly plain that he is undesirable. Lillian Rich makes fair headway with an incongruous part.

Direction isn't good.

Land of Hope and Glory

(BRITISH-MADE)

London, Nov. 12.

Produced by Napoleon Film Company. Original story by Valentine Williams. Directed by Harley Knoles. Preview, Plaza, London, Nov. 11. Running time, 110 mins.

Despite Sir Edward Elgar's musical setting for the preview, the film's title, and the advance press it had, this is the sort of stuff to put "out" in "quota." The first few hundred feet look like its being a good patriotic picture, and then it switches into the story.

The story! For the love of meller! Foreign spies stealing them papers—in this case aeroplane plans. Foiled, aha, and by the police. Son who has invented 'plane gets back to that old homestead (complete with aged mother and blacksmith father) in time for mother's 60th birthday, having made fortune with 'plane.

Harley Knoles has done more than most directors could have done with a bromide script. Some of the opening and closing shots are nearly inspired. Cast, which includes Enid Stamp-Taylor, Lynn Harding, Ellaline Terriss and Robin Irvine, does its best.

May be a first feature for second rate houses. But already the fans are writing to the newspapers asking producers to let up on the flag-waving stuff and make some straight movies.

HELEN OF TROY

First National release and production featuring Maria Corda, Lewis Stone and Ricardo Cortez. Based on the John Erskine novel, adapted by Carey Wilson, with Alexander Korda directing. Photographers, Lee Garmes and Sid Hickox. At the Globe, N. Y., for three weeks commencing Dec. 9. Running time, 87 mins.

Helen	Maria Corda
Menelaus	Lewis Stone
Paris	Ricardo Cortez
Eteoneus	George Fawcett
Adraste	Alice White
Telemachus	Gordon Elliott
Ulysses	Tom O'Brien
Achilles	Bert Sprotte
Ajax	Mario Carillo

A corking program release that figures to particularly delight what is currently smart in picturegoers. De luxe house loge clientele should enjoy it thoroughly and others will signify hearty acceptance, but pot and pan Annie may have her doubts because there are no custard pies bombarding the walls of Troy.

At that there's nothing subtle about this original satire as screened. Situations, bits and titles are broad, and those situations, with the titles, make the picture. First National has given it a splendid production, including some trick camera work that commands admiration. As far as being a $2 picture is concerned, there is no problem, as F. N. has no intention of road showing "Helen." The producing concern has three weeks to go on its lease of the Globe, so this release is simply filling in for exploitation purposes on a twice daily basis over that period. It's likely to do all right under these restrictions, too.

The picture is nothing like the book. Robert E. Sherwood adapted "Road to Rome" on the Erskine plan and Carey Wilson, making the "Helen" film adaptation, evidently had vivid memories of the play. More so than the novel. So "Helen" on the screen is more like Sherwood than Erskine, although the latter will collect, and rightly, inasmuch as he's the instigator of the whole thing. Erskine was on the stage at the opening, before the picture, offering what was probably the best verbal introduction any New York film has ever had. It was funny and it was short. It also served to introduce Maria Corda in person.

Those who saw this girl in "Moon of Israel" are going to be surprised. The difference between the German and American idea of makeup. Miss Corda looks good here and in certain spots the camera makes her look great. For "Helen" she's "the type," and plays it nicely if a little blank at times. In future pictures this will have to be overcome. On performance no one touches Lewis Stone, even if he is still reaching for his coat lapel despite wearing armor. Few will know that Cortez is in the picture.

"Helen" is all comedy, including the score, and the big houses can do no better than to use the Edouarde orchestration. Satirizing ancient myth in general and Helen's affairs particularly, the titles are topical, while the music is mainly based on pop dance tunes. Wheeling the giant wooden horse inside the gates of Troy is accomplished to the strains of "Horses, Horses, Horses," etc. The film kids the husband-wife complex throughout, the king, following the conquest of Troy, making a beeline for Helen's dressmaker to destroy the shop. Meanwhile he has been trying to go fishing since 9 o'clock. When it looks as if Helen is about to take another vacation with her second prince, the king is convinced he's going to get in his trip, and that finishes the picture.

No battles and no slow spots. The action is lively all the way, with Miss Corda in various stages of flight clothing. The "Helen of Troy" contest First National has tied in on

with the New York "Graphic" doesn't register as the best thing in the world for this actress. The "Graphic" is too well known for its physical culture pictures of women, and for all you can tell from the "stills" the paper has been using, Miss Corda might be a bathing girl.

However, "Helen" rates as a program plum. It's well made, lively and funny. The smart set will dote on it, and it's broad enough not to be over the heads of the John Held, Jr., models here or abroad. *Sid.*

London After Midnight

Metro-Goldwyn-Mayer release produced by Tod Browning. Directed by Tod Browning from the story by Tod Browning. Scenario by Waldemar Young. Starring Lon Chaney. At the Capitol, N. Y., Dec. 11. Running time over 65 minutes.

Burke	Lon Chaney
Lucille Balfour	Marceline Day
Sir James Hamlin	Henry B. Walthall
Butler	Percy Williams
Arthur Hibbs	Conrad Nagel
Miss Smithson	Polly Moran
Bat Girl	Edna Tichenor
The Stranger	Claude King

Will add nothing to Chaney's prestige as a trouper, nor increase the star's box office value. With Chaney's name in lights, however, this picture, any picture with Chaney, means a strong box office draw.

Young, Browning and Chaney have made a good combination in the past but the story on which this production is based is not of the quality that results in broken house records.

Marceline Day shines dimly in a role relegated to the background with the love interest while the murder mystery gets the play over everything. Miss Day gets across definitely and would do better with an appropriate part. Conrad Nagel is futile and unimpressive as the juvenile. Polly Moran gets only slight returns on her comedy, mainly because this element in the picture is suppressed. No closeups of Miss Moran and as a mugger this girl has proven a topnotcher. Walthall delivers finished and expert business.

Lack of interest in Burke (Chaney) may be attributed to the circumstances in which this character is placed in the story, having no interest in common, either with the audience or the other characters in the production. If Burke had been linked with the girl there might have been a touch of sentiment.

Burke is pictured as a detached character, mechanical and wooden. As such the only audience appeal is that of curiosity and that is not strong enough.

The story is based on a theory that under a hypnotic influence a criminal will repeat a crime, under given circumstances, regardless of the length of time that has elapsed since he committed it.

Opening with the death of Balfour, beside whose body is found a note confessing suicide, Hamlin, the executor of the estate, argues with Scotland Yard Inspector Burke that it couldn't have been suicide. The scene is planted in the same surroundings five years later.

Burke hypnotizes Hibbs, Balfour's nephew, in an attempt to discover if he had killed his uncle but draws a negative. He then works on Hamlin, after having created an atmosphere of mysterious, unearthly characters in Balfour's former residence.

A double for Balfour is placed in the library of the Balfour home and Hamlin, under Burke's hypnotic influence, imagines himself five years back. He has an argument with Balfour in which the latter refuses to allow him to marry Lucille, pulls

a pistol, and orders Balfour to write a letter in which he admits suicide before shooting him.

The usual suspicions, planted while the situations are worked out, succeed in leaving an impression of mystery regarding the outcome. *Mori.*

Now We're in the Air

Paramount feature length comedy, with Beery and Hatton. Directed by Frank Strayer. Story by Monte Brice and Keene Thompson. Adaptation by Tom J. Geraghty. Louise Brooks second feature. Running time, 70 minutes. At the Rialto, New York, indefinitely.

Wally	Wallace Beery
Ray	Raymond Hatton
Grisette Chelaine	Louise Brooks
Lord Abercrombie McTavish	Russell Simpson
Monsieur Chelaine	Emile Chautard
Professor Saenger	Malcolm Waite
Top Sergeant	Duke Martin

Another hilarious incident in the hectic lives of Wallace Beery and Raymond Hatton, this time even more sprightly and unrefined than the predecessors. Gags aplenty, slapstick, inflated bladder—anything to coax the honest haw haw. It does that with vast ingenuity and an utter disregard of the finer aspects of wit and humor.

There is plenty of assault and battery upon the prominent personal rear elevations of the principals; comedy falls in astonishing variety; some of them elevated to the sphere of something like art by the ponderous resources of the modern picture studio.

Then there is the highly indelicate incident of a near-sighted soldier trying with poor success to milk a prop cow in which the comedians are hiding. This is fun that poises perilously balanced between vulgarity and robust amusement. A spinster aunt would say it was indictable, but the broad-minded matinee audience (where do all the young men come from in the afternoon?) seemed to be pretty unanimous that it was a comedy riot. It's for the fans to say.

Despite its horseplay, the picture has a world of honest fun in it. George Marion has planted a lot of rich titles through the footage. All credit to this wit, who has been much more restrained in his captions than the actors and director in their business. Indeed, it is the clever sparkle of the written word that helps to take the curse off the extreme clowning of the picture. It sort of paves the way for a self-respecting laugh at screen material that a lot of people would be rather ashamed to confess they thought funny.

The technical production against which this slapstick is scaled for effect is absolutely amazing. An astonishing amount of elaborate detail has been provided for these two clowns to work with. Squadrons of aeroplanes are employed, in the air and on the ground. And enormous masses of people are brought into play just to give point to some of their crude funniments.

You may deplore the methods, but in spite of yourself you must agree to the kick and the hilarity of the performance. It is unquestionably funny. The fan mob will find it so and will probably pile up a lot of money for it, but one does wish that this talented pair could do something a little more restrained, even if it did cost them something in the esteem of the simple but honest majority.

Beery and Hatton are a couple of American simps who are intriguing to get the wealth of their Scotch grandfather, an old aviation fan who is trying to get into the World War as a flyer. They wear Scotch kilts to please him, and that costume, as they employ it, doesn't add to the refinement of the humor. They are eternally losing some essential garment. Anyhow, they become entangled with the aviation forces, get carried over into the enemy lines by mistake in a runaway circus balloon, are returned in an enemy plane and almost get shot as spies.

Much of the action takes place in the air, and with the thrill of flying on a foundation of custard pie comedy, the effect is confusing but extremely funny.

Louise Brooks has an altogether pale and negative part, but this snappy young brunette justifies herself by just being present in any visible capacity.

There you are. It's a de luxe custard pie two-reeler spread out into a feature, but the fans will regard it as a treat and act accordingly.

Rush.

FRENCH DRESSING

Robert Kane production. Directed by Allan Dwan. Under First National distribution. H. B. Warner, Clive Brook, Lois Wilson and Lilyan Tashman co-featured. From original story by Adelaide Heilbron. Running time, 60 minutes. At the Strand, New York, Dec. 10.

Very smooth comedy of high life, of genteel atmosphere, great pictorial beauty, with appeal to all classes of fans. Strong cast and fetching title insure draw, and the picture itself will satisfy. Belongs to the type becoming more and more popular, polite romantic action taking its interest from deft handling of character and incident rather than dramatic force.

The inside facts of the production are that it was just 14 days in actual studio work, sets and all other details being ready to hand when the shooting began. And still there is no sign of roughness or haste. The picture couldn't be smoother in its suave ease if it had been stretched over two months instead of two weeks.

If a picture like this, calling for the most delicate adjustment of action and background, balance of character and incident, can be carried through so promptly, a rough-and-ready dramatic ought to take even less time. The film is said to be one of the most economical in negative-cost Kane has ever released. For its kind it is one of the neatest pieces of work Kane or anybody else has sponsored.

In the first place there is a wealth of fine material in the story, light in texture as it is. The plan of telling a story completely with four characters and putting the four roles in the hands of players of superlative skill in their types works out extremely well here, and capable, experienced players to work with must have done a vast deal to simplify the problems of the director. The results speak for themselves.

It is always difficult to gauge how much of a given effect is attributable to actors' performance and how much to the materials they work with. In this case it is particularly hard to weigh relative values because the literary substances are excellent and the performance of the cast is impeccable in its artless flow. And many other things contribute. The picture is a revel in elegance of modern costume, of persuasive scenic settings and those other elements that go to make up a composite atmosphere.

The picture has fine sentiment, and for once it never becomes maudlin or mushy. Plot deals with a wife who in pique runs off to Paris for an easy divorce, although she really loves her husband, but is irritated by certain trivialities. A highly fascinating Frenchman rushes her, in the absence of her husband, until the two men meet. Here is a delightfully jaunty scene. Frenchman and American measure each other. Each observes the other wears the red ribbon of the Legion of Honor, and they depart to conference. It takes two close-ups and one brief title to convey a world of unexpressed drama, where the ordinary "movie" technique would have had two artificial actors generating high-power scenes all over the place. That's one of the distinctions of the picture—it gets much of subtle suggestion by indirection.

You don't know for the moment what the conference of husband and lover really brought forth. But later it works out into a neat surprise trick. The angry wife appears to surrender to the French lover, but in the end the situation is deftly twisted for an unexpected outcome, graceful and with a smart little sentimental turn of high comedy.

Rush.

LADIES MUST DRESS

Fox production and release. Featuring Virginia Valli. Lawrence Gray and Earle Foxe underlined. Scenario by Reginald Morris; M. S. Boylan, titles; Glenn MacWilliams, cameraman. Directed by Victor Heerman. At the Roxy, New York, week Dec. 10. Running time, 56 mins.

Eve	Virginia Valli
Joe	Lawrence Gray
Art	Hallam Cooley
Mazie	Nancy Carroll
George Ward, Jr.	Earle Foxe

Routine comedy enlivened by snap titling and getting away fast. It's so lively off the mark that although only running 56 minutes it slows up perceptibly before the finish. A program leader that will entertain on the inside even if there's nothing much else to draw other than the title.

It's a shopgirl-stenographer friendship with Miss Valli as the old-fashioned and much too heavily clothed typist, foiled by Nancy Carroll as Mazie, the baby-faced miss who rolls 'em and wears 'em to snare despite a husband behind the opposite counter. The Don Juan son of the store owner complicates the yarn which has Eve going to his apartment to extract Mazie, thereby convincing Joe (Lawrence Gray) that a good cigar is a smoke, because Mazie is out of sight under the bed.

The majority of laughs are early and in the mouth of Mazie as she argues with hubby and comments on Eve's undergarments as she forces the latter to undergo a transformation in apparel. Credit this to M. S. Boylan and his titles, Miss Carroll also registering the inferences punched over by word.

Really a picture where the secondary characters stand out because of scene sequence and titling. Miss Valli is practically a figurehead, Miss Carroll, Gray and Cooley topping her on performance.

Simple theme and simply made, Heerman emphasizing speed and the cutting room voting the idea unanimous. No heavy production and nothing tremendous in salaries.

But it makes 'em laugh, and that's enough.

Sid.

HONEYMOON HATE

Paramount production and release. Directed by Luther Reed. Based on the Saturday Evening Post story by Alice M. Williamson. Scenario by Ethel Doherty. Titles by George Marion, Jr., and J. Herman Manckewiecz. Starring Florence Vidor. At the Paramount, N. Y., Dec. 12. Running time, over 65 minutes.

Gail Grant	Florence Vidor
Prince Dantarini	Tullio Carminati
H. Banning-Greene	William Austin
Mrs. Fremont Gage 1	Corliss Palmer
Mrs. Fremont Gage 2	Shirley Dorman
Miss Molesey	Effie Ellsler
Bueno	Genaro Spagnoli

Skillfully blended for the screen by expert scenario work, embellished by Marion's and Manckewiecz's laughter-provoking titles, the two outstanding male characters vividly enacted by William Austin, comedian, and Carminati, lead, make this enchanting magazine story equally entertaining as a picture, if not more so.

The Prince has lost a little of the statuesque, unbending fomality in the picturization, together with an ironic subtlety, which it would have been difficult and perhaps unsatisfactory to reproduce, while his charm has been retained and enhanced.

Carminati registers powerfully on the screen. He evidences possibilities, but would be well advised to change his name to one which could be more easily remembered if press agented.

Florence Vidor as Gail Grant shows little of the capricious arrogance accredited to the Pittsburgh steel magnate's daughter and less of her grace and beauty, according to the story.

The early part of the picture is somewhat dampened by the ineffectiveness of the star. Austin as the floundering Englishman mouthing Marion's ludicrous puns in flowery book English brings on the laughs while strengthening the action at the same time.

Story deals with the haughty heiress, accustomed to buying everything in sight. A clerk in an antique shop in Venice refuses to sell her a rare piece of tapestry when she loudly brags of cutting it into a gown. The clerk turns out to be the owner of the palace, obliged to sell antiques since the ravages of the war.

The Prince hires out as the girl's guide, with the preliminary intention of taming her. Later he changes or loses his mind, and they marry.

An argument about the honeymoon trip to Paris the wedding night leads to complications, and Herbert Banning-Greene unwittingly, though cleverly, serves as the means through which the girl gains her object.

Mori.

HOME MADE

First National comedy, presented by C. C. Burr, starring Johnny Hines. Directed by Charles Hines. From the story by C. B. Carrington. Running time 70 minutes. At the New York Hippodrome, December 12.

Lead	Johnny Hines
Leading Woman	Marjorie Daw
Mother	Margaret Seddon
Grand Dame	Maude T. Gordon
Old Man	Edmund Breeze

There's this much to be said for the Hippodrome's pictures. They don't arouse much expectation. The big playhouse has been a sort of dumping ground for movie trash for months and months and months, and now when you go there you pretty well know in advance what you're up against. Maybe that's why the balcony is empty at two bits. The neighborhoods at the same price have better stuff.

This Johnny Hines subject is about low water mark for production, story interest and everything else that goes to make a screen entertainment. It has a dull, slow start, gets duller as it progresses and ends staggering. What sort of a business position has a big playhouse almost in Times Square worked itself into when this sort of material is all it seems eligible to play there?

Story starts in a poor farmhouse, where boy helps his mother to make fruit preserves to sell to passing motorists. Cruel stepfather drives him away from home. It takes 12 minutes to plant this.

Boy has adventures on Pullman when he beats his way, meeting fashionable girl. Then he gets to the big town and takes job as waiter in exclusive hotel, intending to try to do something with mother's preserves. You know instinctively that he is going to pour soup down a society man's back. Yep, he does. You can foretell most of the other comedy devices in advance.

Fate brings him to the same fashionable girl's home as a waiter when she gives a party. He frames with girl to do comedy and then introduced as a guest. The comedy is pretty. Anyhow, the party is radioed and Johnny gets a chance to put in a plug for mother's brand of jam. This makes Heinz 57 rush up with huge contracts and somehow he marries the girl, taking her away from the rich suitor.

Ho-hum! (Business of stifling a bored yawn.)

Rush.

SHIELD OF HONOR

Universal action melodrama presented by Carl Laemmle. Directed by Emory Johnson from the story by Emilie Johnson. Neil Hamilton featured. Running time, 67 minutes. At the Colony, New York, Dec. 10.

Jack MacDowell	Neil Hamilton
Gwen O'Day	Dorothy Gulliver
Dan MacDowell	Ralph Lewis
Robert Chandler	Nigel Barrie
Mrs. MacDowell	Claire MacDowell
Howard O'Day	Fred Esmelton
Rose	Thelma Todd
Red	David Kirby

A vigorous action drama of sure fire material, the high points made up of an airplane chase by the hero, a police aviator, who rounds up a gang of diamond thieves in a thrilling action fought in the clouds and on the ground. The mechanics of the air stuff are convincing and the climax has a fine thrill.

Story is labored in parts, as usually happens in these he-man pictures. Planting of situation is labored, as usual, but the thing builds up to an effective crescendo, its excuse being that it was worth waiting for and worth all the preparation.

In its politer passages technical work has been well done. Backgrounds are appropriate to the fashionable world. Cast is entirely satisfactory, with Neil Hamilton as the young aviator, a thoroughly attractive figure, and one the women fans will love. Comedy is light, but what there is of it is neatly contrived, while sentiment is laid on pretty thick, which is probably as it should be for the clientele it is addressed to.

The type of picture done in this straightforward style couldn't miss. Society deb is chosen to christen first airplane in Los Angeles police department and meets the handsome young aviator. Presently they are in love, and the police are called in to trace a big diamond robbery. Deb's father, being the Tiffany of the city, is innocently concerned in the crime, his own secretary being the master mind of the criminals.

Culmination of many-sided plot at length brings the heroine into her father's office the night the gang is preparing its final coup, and she is locked in the vault, while the diamond thieves make their getaway, the leader taking to the air in his own plane, leaving a subordinate to dynamite the jewelry store. Another angle is that the jewels are turned over to a girl confederate who is to take the Santa Fe Limited and wait for a signal to drop them on the track to be picked up by the waiting airman.

This brings us to the air pursuit and battle. It all takes place at night, which gives it still more effect, for in the air battle both sides bombard the other with flares. There are nose dives, tail spins and hairbreadth landings, not to speak of a hand-to-hand fight when hero and heavy finally face each other on the ground.

Then back to the jewelry store, which now has been blown up and is on fire as the rescuer arrives. The fire stuff is also well worked, with the other subordinate angles of the story brought in for a gradual culmination and finale. Another division of the story deals with the hero's father, a faithful veteran of the police who is retired against his will upon reaching the age limit. This is played for good strong sentimental values. If memory serves it was Universal who made a similar film dealing with firemen. Anyhow, the idea is nicely developed here. Throughout the picture the service of the police is lauded in titles, and this angle probably has its side in figuring the potentialities of the production. It doesn't need any aid of the sort, but a special exploitation feature will be that much more to the good.

Feature has good vigorous appeal, no pretention to class, and for its purpose is an expert bit of work. Ought to prove valuable program subject for Universal, with returns well above the average. *Rush.*

THE ARCADIANS

(BRITISH MADE)

London, Nov. 24.

Presented by A. C. & R. C., Bromhead. Produced by the Gaumont-British Co. Directed by Victor Savile. From the musical comedy by Mark Ambient & Alex M. Thompson. Scenario by Ben Blue. Preview at the London Hippodrome, Nov. 21. Running time, 84 minutes.

Smith, alias "Simplicitas"........Ben Blue
Mrs. Smith..........Jeanne de Casalis
Eileen Smith..........Vesta Sylva
Jack Meadows..........John Longden
Sir George Paddock.....Huberston Wright
Peter Doody..........Gibb McLaughlin
Sombra..........Doris Bransgrove
Chrysea..........Nancy Rigg

Twenty-odd years ago "The Arcadians" was a successful musical comedy. The late Alfred Lester helped to make it, and it made him. A committee helped to make the screen version. They are not likely to go down to fame for it. And whoever wrote the captions should never be allowed to handle a typewriter or a pen again—at least for the purpose of title-writing.

Included in the cast, for no apparent reason but to make the film cost money, are Tracey and Haye, Balliol and Merton, Teddy Brown and Band, Lola and Luis, Ivor Vintor, Donovan Sisters and Tiller Girls. Most of these vaudeville topliners are seen only for a flash, and Vintor plays a page in about three flashes and a close-up! A good new title for the film might be "The Vaudevillians' Holiday."

The story has been brought up to date, with airplanes, cuts from a news reel of the Derby, and jazz bands. In fact, the director has gotten everything into it but motion picture.

Exteriors in the Arcadian scenes look rather like Coney Island grottoes, and the robes of the girls, what there is of them (robes, not girls) tone so much with the sets the players often get near to vanishing altogether from the screen.

There are some good opening shots, especially gag dramatic shadows on the glass door of an office, and for a while the film moves fairly fast. But when Smith gets to Arcady, from then on the rest of the picture doesn't matter. Where it is not a news reel it's a nuisance. And when it is considered in the light of what America did with "The Merry Widow," and what Germany did with "The Waltz Dream," it's a tragedy.

The cast has done its best, which is saying a lot. And the director has done his best, which is not saying so much. But the title-writer ought to write wisecracks for a delicatessen-store wrappers.

Smith owns the Green Mill Club, and Mrs. Smith owns him. He is refused a drink extension on "Borstal Boatrace Night" (sample of the humor of the captions), and when the police enter the club in search of a crook, Smith thinks they are after him for exceeding the time limit. He bolts.

Escaping in an airplane, he drops out when he finds the crook (whom he thinks is the chief of police) is the pilot, and lands in Arcady. Here he teaches the Arcadians the Charleston and the "Dark Base" (another sample of the wit), and with two of the corypheès is sent back to earth by the High Priest (ringer for Theodore Roberts' Moses) to convert the world to truth.

He reopens the club with an Arcadian atmosphere, and finds his wife flirting with a jockey who has framed to lose a big race so Sir George Paddock can beat Jack Meadows to it for the girl. With the aid of the two Arcadians he puts the jockey away, rides the horse himself and wins. His wife recognizes him, and is persuaded by the Arcadians to take him back.

In the club scenes quite effective use is made of swinging the Sun-arcs and tinting the shot differently, a method first used here by Harley Knoles when he made "Carnival." Camera-traveling is indulged in a lot, sometimes usefully, and at others with no apparent reason except the director thought it was a good idea.

Cut to six reels, it should go quite well here in the provinces, but hardly the lowest-browed audience will fall for the existing titles. One priceless piece of "humor" is a newspaper insert of racing news, telling that "Gluepot will stick; Cabbage is a bit green, but may get ahead; Watertap is sure to run; Oscar has been scratched, which made Oscar 'wild.'"

If producers here think that is "what the public wants," then heaven help the public—and the producers. *Frat.*

NO PLACE TO GO

First National release. Produced by Henry Hobart. Directed by Mervyn Leroy from the story "Isles of Romance," by Richard Connell. Featuring Lloyd Hughes and Mary Astor. Cast includes Hallam Cooley, Virginia Lee Corbin, Myrtle Stedman and Jed Prouty. At Loew's New York Dec. 9, half of double-feature program. Running time over 60 mins.

Likeable picture losing its standing as grade A product through direction. With surefire comedy titles it would have been a smash. For the smaller houses and split weeks it should stand up nicely.

The opening scene creates a laugh. A white girl is shown rushing madly through a dense African jungle. She comes to a clearance and, trying to make her escape, finds herself confronted by a giant negro with a spear. On all sides similar terrifying savages begin to close in. The girl falls to the floor in a faint, comes back to life in a few seconds and starts in on the Charleston, accompanied by the colored gents. The scene broadens, revealing the floor show of a night club.

The story then deals with a young girl possessed of a yen for a cave man. She is fond of the boy friend, but intimates that she must be taken by force by the man who wants her.

The girl's mother takes a party on a yacht trip to the South Seas, and the girl prevails on the boy friend to leave the ship one night and row for one of the islands to live life as she thought it should be.

Unromantic rain dampens happiness, and the boy's preference for food and golf where the girl wants smoething else adds nothing to her pleasure. They are almost captured by cannibals when the girl thinks of the night club scene and begins to Charleston. The colored boys like it and join in, giving the pair a chance to escape.

Mother arrives with a rescue crew to take them off the island, and insists that they be married. After the marriage the girl pulls the old gag of painting a dividing line across the floor. Gets scared dreaming of the cannibal scene, and rushes to hubby's bedroom at night, allowing for the happy ending. *Mori.*

WOLF FANGS

William Fox drama built about the trained police dog, Thunder. Directed by Lew Seiler. Story by Seton I. Miller and Elizabeth Pickett. Scenario by Seton L. Miller. Running time (projection room), 52 mins. Released Nov. 27.

Thunder..........Himself
Ellen..........Caryl Lincoln
Neal Barrett..........Charles Morton
Pete..........Frank Rice
Bill Garside..........James Gordon
White Fawn..........Herself
Zimbo..........Himself
Oswald..........Himself

A picture of well-sustained action and intelligent interest, backed by scenic shots of great beauty. The high spot is a thrill battle between the dog hero, "Thunder," a magnificent animal, and a savage-looking canine brute, his rival for leadership of the dog outlaw pack, which preys upon the flocks.

The story is shaped along somewhat the lines of Jack London's "Call of the Wild," with the human interest and the dog actors neatly interwoven so that the absorbing story of the sheep herder's pup turned wilderness renegade, and the interesting romance of the herder's daughter and a forest ranger move forward hand in hand to a gripping climax, splendidly built up.

None of the dog pictures has been better managed. Here a whole group of the animals is used for the pack that ranges the peaks of towering mountain country, making sallies upon the grazing flocks of sheep and outwitting the herders through the strength and cunning of Thunder, their leader. Ingenious escapades of the dog are filmed with convincing detail.

One scene has the renegade pack running wild among the terrified sheep, and another has the epic battle between "Thunder" and "Loto," his rival for leadership, to all intents a desperate battle of fang and claw to the death. This episode is a whale for kick and takes increased force from the dramatic situation that brings it about.

"Thunder" was once a pup cuddled by Ellen, the herder's pretty daughter, until the cruel sheep tender's brutality sent him an outlaw into the woods. When he is grown he takes command of the wolfdog pack, but always with a loyal memory of the girl.

A year later Ellen, back in the pasture land, is driven out of her home by the cruelty of the same herder, her stepfather, and in her flight to the cabin of Neal, the forest ranger, is pursued by the hungry pack and held captive on a rocky cliff, just out of reach of the snapping jaws.

It is here that "Thunder" finds his once loving mistress. He challenges the snarling pack in her defense, and this brings on the battle between "Thunder" and "Loto," his rival for command of the forest, a gripping dog fight and a breathless screen situation.

The picture is full of big screen drama. There is a capital episode when Ellen hides the wounded dog in the garret of the cabin, while her stepfather searches to find and destroy "the sheep killer." The dripping of blood from the ceiling (as in "The Girl of the Golden West") leads to discovery in a neatly made scene. Another high light is the sequence in which the dog speeds through the forest to the girl's aid when she is threatened by her brutal master, a passage strongly built up with alternate shots of the man slashing at the girl with a whip and the canine hero racing through the moonlight toward the rescue. The climax to this passage comes in a battle between man and dog all over the place, with a thrill to the running celluloid foot.

The picture was taken in Mt Baker National Park in Oregon, high pine country with magnificent scenic shots, particularly with the dogs posed on craggy heights and with the towering, snow-capped Mt. Baker rising ten thousand feet in the background.

An exceptional program picture of this popular type. *Rush.*

SPEEDY SMITH

Rayart production. State rights release. Story by Grover Jones. Directed by Duke Worne. Billy Sullivan starred. Hazel Deane featured. Running time, 48 mins. At Columbus, New York, on double feature bill, one day, Dec. 7.

Billy Sullivan, serial star and cinema athlete, goes through five reels of conventional movie stuff which enables him to get in some boxing with a pug about twice his size. He disposes of the pug in short order and beautiful style.

It's all about $500, which sum is required to bring to the small town an eminent eye specialist to save the sight of the heroine's mother. A visiting carnival offers the half-grand to the gent who will step up and sock the champ-yun of eurup for a goal.

Production, direction and acting strictly third class, but for the third class houses the picture's okay.

THE SLAVER

Crescent picture. Milton Schlank production. Story by James Oliver Curwood. Directed by Harry Revier. Cameraman, Del Clauson. Pat O'Malley starred, with Carmelita Geraghty featured. Cast includes John Miljan, J. P. McGowan. Running time, 54 minutes. At Stanley, New York, one day, Dec. 7.

An in-betweener. Not bad, despite being something of a "quickie." Holds enough interest to get by.

Director has allowed some absurdities and conspicuous incongruities to creep in, but an abundance of fist fighting and hairy-chested sea-going deviltry will probably hold the interest where the customers are not too fastidious.

Dynamite angle through a negro tribal chief on the coast of Africa making a deal with a dissolute white sea captain to buy a white girl. Supposed to be "squared" by a negro cabin boy sacrificing his life, saving the girl from the black nabob.

James Oliver Curwood's name in connection with this picture can be played up, although the poorest story that author ever wrote.

BACKSTAIRS

(GERMAN MADE)

American premiere of UFA German-made production. At 55th St. Cinema, New York, running 50 minutes. Leopold Jessner directed; Carl Mayer authored; Paul Leni's settings.

Possibly the stolid German mind can appreciate the drama or suspense of a triangle situation concerning a scullery maid, village postmaster and heavy lover of unidentified occupation, but whoever thought it would please American film fans evidences reason why he should not operate a picture house.

Intended as a character study, probably with "The Last Laugh" in mind, it is unexciting, uninteresting and uninspiring.

Were it deftly handled or in some wise distinguished as a screen character study a la Jennings' "Laugh, Laugh," there might be some saving grace for it all, but as it is, it just isn't.

Paul Leni, now a Universal director, whose settings in past UFA successes were outstanding, again registered with the limited opportunities for his grotesque scenic ideas, but otherwise, directionally, creatively and histrionically, "Backstairs" is a grand bore that makes the 50 minutes' running time seem twice as long. *Abel.*

One Glorious Scrap

Universal-Blue Streak western. Fred Humes featured. Directed by Edgar Lewis. Francis Ford, Shorty Hamilton, Betty Day in cast. Running time, 50 mins. At Arena, New York, on double feature bill, Nov. 25.

This is pretty poor, even as westerns go. It is one of the cheap releases handled by Universal for the non-fastidious settlements.

There are two sets of characters, the goods and the bads. The bads are out to gouge the goods by controlling the water supply and forcing the ranchers to sell for little or nothing. The goods hire a rainmaker, a sort of travelling charlatan, who could impose on no one above the comparative mental average of a Hollywood cow puncher. The rainmaker is not only a fake but secretly in league with the town banker, a misanthrophic old bunny who wants to bankrupt everybody. His son, a fresh guy with fancy clothes, tries to force the girl to marry him. Mr. Humes knocks him for a row and marries the gal himself.

Those who buy film by the foot will not mind this one.

RANCH RIDERS

Universal production (Ranch Riders Series) directed by Wm. Wyler. Starring Ted Wells, supported by Garry O'Dell, Lillian Gilmore and Wilbur Mack. Story by William Lester; photographed by Milton Bridenbecker. At Arena, New York, one day, Nov. 30. Running time, 50 minutes.

A simply dramatized western story, not overburdened with mentality taxation and providing a standard number of thrills. It will be liked in its haunts.

Wells rides into a girl's life and saves her gold mine from a tough gang. Location of the mine was secret until the girl's weak-willed nephew snitched. A fast finish is provided when Wells pursues the gang and knocks them off one by one, all knocking off done on horseback.

Suitably directed.

SKYHIGH SAUNDERS

Universal production and release. Directed and written by Bruce Mitchell. Starring Al Wilson, supported by Bud Osborne, Elsie Tarron and Frank Rice. Photographed by Wm. S. Adams. At the Tivoli, New York, one day (Dec. 7) on double feature bill. Running time, 55 minutes.

Aimed 'way too low to satisfy the metropolitan cowboy fans. Only for double feature houses, with good support, and remote stands.

Plainly the trouble is terrible comedy. With most of this cut out, the picture would improve considerably. Al Wilson, the star, plays a dual role. There are twin brothers, one of whom is supposed to have died in France, but actually is chief assistant to a gangleader who smuggles in the States with airplanes.

The other brother is a member of the U. S. Air Patrol, and comes west to break up the smuggling. In air combat the government bro kills his outlaw bro, then assumes his identity to wipe out the gang. He also marries the girl after telling her he isn't his brother.

The supposed humor is worked by Frank Rice as a mechanic, and a blackface gent. Whoo-ee, what hooey! Three mugs in the Tivoli balcony ripped loose a section of brass rail in their agony.

The airplane stuff is okay and held attention. Otherwise, blotto.

IN OLD KENTUCKY
(2d Review)

A somewhat too harsh notice was printed in Variety a few weeks ago on "In Old Kentucky," Metro-Goldwyn-Mayer. At best it's just a fair picture following 100 other race track stories of southerners, their horses, women and boys.

The Variety reviewer who gave this picture a panning had his justification. There are a couple of idiotic sequences. One is too utterly ridiculous to believe it was in for any other reason than that M-G thought anything could be put over on its public. That was of a race horse sent to France in the war, shell-shocked over there and sewn up wounds still showing, winning the Kentucky Derby a couple of years afterward.

Another was to bring the only son of the family back from the war, in uniform, and to stagger off the train to greet his folks drunk. The director here wouldn't even waive this offensive bit to wait for the boy to get stewed in his civies.

Much mush stuff, but the M-G finish to the film, and a colored comedian hold up the picture. He's just a lazy, no good roustabout, wheedling money out of the colored help, but he's no mean pantomimist. The Charles T. Dazey meller has been twisted about to place some of the locale in France, but in any way the subject has been handled, it doesn't matter. Yet for those who can still stand for these Kentucky Culnel, Suh, and the filmsy, fleeting horse race, "In Old Kentucky" may be set down as a superior in that class, and that's all.

To say it is utterly impossible and would be a horse on the exhibitors playing it, as the fresh comment did say in Variety's previous notice, was going a bit too far.

Two other Variety reviewers, watching this picture in M-G's projection room, through courtesy of its press department, and at the request of an exhibitor out of town, who deterred from playing it on the first notice, agree on the above.
Sime.

PASSION ISLAND
(BRITISH MADE)

Pathe of England production, directed by Manning Haynes. Story by W. W. Jacobs, with Pyrcy Stony cameraman. Randle Ayrton among cast. Reviewed in projection room, New York. Running time, 86 mins.

Poor little movie, don't you cry,
You'll play the Keith houses bye and bye.

("Tip Toes" did)

Had this one been turned loose in '17 it would still have been five years behind. It runs just short of an hour and a half, too. Even the operator in the projection room booth was ready to call it quits at the end of the second reel.

If England can cry over block booking, America is entitled to a few tears if it ever is shown such screen product as "Passion Island." The picture couldn't be saved by cutting 3,000 feet, and "quickies" are program features in comparison.

The picture strangles itself with footage in unfolding a story that could have been made into suitable material for the daily change houses. As it stands it's doubtful it even the shooting galleries would be interested, and maybe the K-A houses will pass it up. You can't tell. Whoever sent it over must have done so with charges prepaid and a prayer.

"Passion Island" is Corsica, Napoleon's first yard, the story pushing off on a last half vendetta that sees the girl's brother, a priest, murdered by her lover's scheming friend, Beppo.

Twenty years later the lover returns to Corsica with his daughter, the mother having died, is recognized by Beppo and the blackmail starts until the daughter is Beppo's objective.

Following a confession by Beppo that he knifed his victim's brother-in-law, the father kills and then shoves his persecutor over a cliff.

It's an hour and a half out of anybody's life to be regretted.

The picture may have cost $15,000 to make. Interiors are skimpy and there's probably not a salary in the cast. Camera work is monotonous. There isn't as much as a fade anywhere. The best bit is Beppo trying to recall a voice when he hears the wronged man speak after 20 years; pictured by various faces appearing within Bep's ear.

A likely looking boy and girl are among the players but remain helpless within such environment. But no one in the cast has a chance, as Haynes, directing, has made it so tedious that any audience will get sick of looking at it.

The damn thing is endless. *Sid.*

SERENADE

Paramount comedy-drama starring Adolphe Menjou. Directed by H. D'Abbadie d'Arrast. Story and screen play by Ernest Vadja. At Paramount, New York, week Dec. 17. Running time, 55 minutes.
Franz Rossi...............Adolphe Menjou
Gretchen...................Kathryn Carver
Josef Bruckner...........Lawrence Grant
The Dancer...............Lina Basquette
Gretchen's Mother........Martha Franklin

Another of those debonair comedy-dramas with which Menjou is almost inseparably associated. This one has the usual grace, delicacy of treatment and pictorial beauty, but it is even lighter in substance and structure than the others. At that it sustains interest and builds up to a first-rate crescendo of suspense, only in the last minute to develop a serio-comic surprise.

It is astonishing that these delicate film plays can sustain attention as well as they do. This one is meaty with small trifles that amuse, as though a brilliant after-dinner speaker paused in his address to illustrate with a pointed anecdote.

The story has to do with a gifted composer who tries to keep his wife at home and out of his career at the theatre. He is really a devoted husband, but he will have little affairs on the side.

Menjou is happy in these delicately shaded characters; he is so humanly and gracefully amusing while maintaining a sort of naive earnestness, oblivious to his own absurdities. It is largely due to his own character drawing that such light material stands up.

Of course, in the end the homey wife intrudes upon her husband's activities in the theatre, and promptly discovers his little affair with the stage dancer. Here the comedy takes an unexpected turn. The missus merely disappears, turning up at a later performance with a resplendent male escort and sitting in the most conspicuous box. She lets it be known that she is staying at the Hotel Schoenbrun (locale is Germany).

Thither hurries the now repentant husband, suspicious of unutterable things. The wife's maid takes his card, returns to report that "madame is preparing for bed," showing him the door. Husband notes a silk hat and man's opera cape hanging in the foyer. He waits in the hotel corridor. Three waiters enter the apartment bearing supper service for two. The maid leaves for home, depositing at the door two pairs of shoes, which tell a tale of their own.

By this time husband is in a frenzy. He crashes in to find his wife calmly waiting before the spread table—alone. The hat and cloak are his own and so are the shoes. Embrace as the porter gathers in the shoe. Wifie was just showing him what could be done, a shill escort having been engaged.

Plot is made to order for the delight of the women which circumstance probably will register at the boxoffice in addition to the star's own pull with the petticoat clientele. Lawrence Grant does a delightful old man character bit as the musician and philosopher. Kathryn Carver, blonde and unemotional, was appropriately uninteresting as the homey wife. Lina Basquette as the high-voltage vamp dancer furnished the eloquent contrast.

Settings and atmosphere have that unobtrusive beauty that is the ultimate in studio art. *Rush.*

GIRL FROM CHICAGO

Warner Bros. production directed by Roy Enright. Myrna Loy and Conrad Nagel featured. Scenario by Graham Baker. At the Roxy, N. Y., week of Dec. 17. Running time, 61 mins.
Handsome Joe..............Conrad Nagel
Mary Carlton...............Myrna Loy
Steve Drummond..........William Russell
Bob Carlton ....Carroll Nye
Dopey ....Paul Panzer
Colonel Carlton............Erville Alderson

Underworld melodrama with some of the crudest theatrical devices imaginable, but with a highly effective climax that saves the day. This is what they'll talk about, forgetting the absurdities, a consideration that will make for the boxoffice on week dates.

The kick is in a machine gun battle between a police squadron and a gang of gunmen. The play was simply built up to this finale. Trouble is it wasn't planted artfully. Aristocratic southern girl learns that her wandering brother is awaiting execution for a murder he did not commit. She visits him in prison and learns the killing happened in a night club where a gun crowd hold forth. They did the killing and planted a gun on the boy.

Sister goes out to associate with the gang in the hope of discovering the real killer, apparently either Handsome Joe or Steve. Joe and Steve promptly become rivals for the "new skirt." It is early revealed that Joe is really a police sergeant who has wormed his way into the crooks' confidence in an effort to trap the real murderer.

Story progresses to point where Joe's real identity is discovered, and he is in the girl's apartment. The whole gang, led by the jealous Steve, go there to take vengeance. Joe is trapped, but before the killers get him cornered he has telephoned word to police headquarters.

As the gunmen open fire you see the police bandit squad on their motorcycles swing from headquarters on a race to the rescue, and while the battle progresses in the apartment, alternate shots of the flying squadron tearing through the city streets at night are flashed. Meanwhile the indoor fight is indicated mostly by darts of flame as pistol shots stab the dark. Joe and the girl retreat from room to room holding the killers at bay, until just as the detective's ammunition gives out the cops open up with machine guns. This is a running fight that starts blocks away and ends only over the expiring master crook, who confesses he did the killing for which the brother is about to pay the penalty.

This action is convincing and grips. The implausible part is the subordinate plot. The girl entering an association with the criminals also is careless enough to bring with her photographs of herself and her brother and leaves them around the apartment. That's a tough one to swallow. The reasonableness of a gently reared girl going among gangsters is enough of a tax, but that can be accepted as possible if improbable. Of course, the purpose of such clumsy devices was to make short cuts to the big scene.

Myrna Loy has a certain wistfulness, resembling Marie Doro in type. The role does not particularly suit her, but she carries it off well enough. Conrad Nagel is in one of the best theatrical parts that has come his way recently, a role with good comedy shading and several big moments. He does nicely with it. William Russell is great in the master crook's part and excellent types are well placed.

Production is first rate, with cabaret introduced in just the right way; that is, incidentally to heighten the main action rather than as a display for its own sake. Good character drawing by Russell and convincing bits by subordinate characters. *Rush.*

MAN CRAZY

First National release of a C. R. Rogers production, directed by John F. Dillon. Featuring Dorothy Mackaill and Jack Mulhall. Adapted from Grace Mason's magazine story, "Clarissa and the Post Road." At the Strand, New York, week of Dec. 17. Running time, 58 mins.

Clarissa Janeway	Dorothy Mackaill
Jeffery Pell	Jack Mulhall
Grandmother Janeway	Edythe Chapman
James Janeway	Phillips Smalley
Van Bremer	Walter McGrail

A conventional picturized story better adapted to the split week houses than for a full week's stand before 3,000 seats. "Man Crazy" will find the going easiest when playing the intermediates because at best it's just a picture. The Mackaill-Mulhall combine represents whatever strength it has.

Rather a shame, too, for there's a chance for this couple if given sufficient script material. Miss Mackaill is not unattractive to male patronage, while Mulhall doesn't keep women out of a theatre. But stories such as this one aren't going to get them anywhere as a team. Individually the picture means more to Miss Mackaill than her co-worker.

Clarissa is simply one more wealthy deb fed up on social high jinks. So much so she erects an attractive lunchroom on the post road which transcends her grandmother's estate. There she meets Jeffery Pell, who operates an express truck carrying valuable shipments.

Unaware she is heiress to plenty, Jeff proposes and is accepted. But not until Clarissa has scared off bootleggers who have held him up and has spurned her betrothed social equal at a dinner party. Jeff, of course, eventually announces himself as the grandson of the Pell, who granny recalls as her first beau.

Meanwhile, F. N. has presumably adopted the same method for Dorothy that Fox has applied to Madge Bellamy. You see more of Miss Mackaill in each picture. Did F. N. take up that option? Anyway, Miss Mackaill frolics around in one of those sunken tubs, is in negligee at various times and always seems to have an expanse of limb displayed by one means or another. That this girl can stand the expose will be testified to by the public if they'll ever give her some stories.

Mulhall does well by his conception of the gentleman truck driver, Walter McGrail is a land mark as the rejected suitor and Dillon has forced Edythe Chapman to far overplay the exasperated grandmother. The latter also totes the most wig-like wig that's been in a Broadway picture in some time.

F. N. releases generally possess nice interiors, and more are here included. The eccentrically bodied express truck should also catch the interest of auto fans. As a whole it's rather a pity to waste the production on this routine story. But the "Saturday Evening Post" published it!

Mostly straight titling and a couple of snickers in the action. The best thing Dillon has done is to keep it moving to clean it up under an hour. No screen credit for any member of the technical staff as shown at the Strand.

Won't get over in the big houses unless it gets plenty of help and will have to dig for its moderate returns outside the first run. *Sid.*

NIGHT LIFE

Tiffany-Stahl production and release. Directed by George Archainbaud. Alice Day and Johnny Harron featured. From story by Albert Shelby LeVino and continuity by Gertrude Orr. Chester Lyons, camera. At Keith's Hippodrome, New York, week Dec. 10. Running time, about 55 minutes.

Anna, waif	Alice Day
Max	Johnny Harron
Nick, his coadjutor	Eddie Gribbon
Manager	Walter Hiers
War Profiteer	Lionel Braham
His Wife	Kitty Barlow
His Daughter	Dawn O'Day
His Daughter	Mary Jane Irving
His Daughter	Audrey Sewell
Amorous Swain	Earl Metcalf
Amorous Maid	Patricia Avery
Chief of Detectives	Archduke Leopold
Merry-Go-Round Manager	Snitz Edwards
Beer Garden Waitress	Violet Palmer
Landlady	Lydia Yeamans Titus

Can you imagine the Keith's Hippodrome? At last it has a good picture. Even the house staff enjoys the novelty.

It's "Night Life," by Tiffany, and an excellent program release; excellent in every department, especially with the direction of George Archainbaud. While the Gertrude Orr continuity is no slouch.

Tiffany-Stahl has a picture here that stands up under the title, although that title as a matter of fact more strictly is for the box office than the story. And as box office it's good anywhere.

In story it's interesting, with a good tale well told nicely spread out over the sheet. It dips into pre-war at Vienna without any war stuff used, comes back to Vienna and remains there until the finish.

The picture starts with a magician and an audience plant in a beer garden cabaret. The war call comes and they go. Upon their return they are hungry and broke. But the profiteers come along in their gas wagons. Which suggests to the plant that since the palming magician is a bear with his mitts, that they go into the pickpocket racket rather than to die standing up and starving.

The dip trade seemed pretty good in Vienna around those days, showing that many had money, even if the soldiers didn't. But there were other starvers and one a girl. She tried to work the same side of the street and the magician caught her as his watch started to go south in her hands.

Without permitting the novice to know she had gone up against an expert, the young palmer took her home, fell in love with the girl and thereby incurred the enmity for her of his partner, the plant and locater. As locater the plant located desirable stuff to lift for the lifter.

That led into complications, concluding when the plant took a 90-day slap he had tried to hang onto the girl instead, with all vowing that marriage and the right stage road thereafter would be better.

Glorified crooks are not so healthy in pictures, but here the moral rubs off the rest.

Acting is not the least of this picture, after giving Mr. Archainbaud the credit he should have for carrying this story as he has done. The outstander is the plant, Nick, a bulky Syengali, who dominated his youthful protege. Nick is played by Eddie Gribbon and finely. This Gribbon in a straight role such as this surely does furnish evidence of knowledge of character and how to do it. His is a perfect performance of an unsympathetic role.

Alice Day has an appeal in her screen make up that gets over despite it. She pantomimes rather well. Johnny Harron is the youthful magician, playing Johnny Harron nicely.

The laugh and about the only one is quite neat. When the crime partners get to the row point, Harron, sore, socks Gribbon twice, right on the button each time, and Gribbon never moves. Then Gribbon with a counter knocks Harron across the room for the count of 100.

Picture worth while, and above the Hip standard as well as stand. Although in there for the week before Christmas, the chances are that "Night Life" through its title and production will do some business for that house this week.

And also taking them as they have come in weekly releases along Broadway during the season thus far, "Night Life" could have taken its place for a week on the Big Alley.

On the program is billed Archduke Leopold as "Chief of Detectives." He's probably in the picture. Maybe as a test or publicity. *Sime.*

THE LOVELORN

Cosmopolitan production released by Metro-Goldwyn-Mayer. Directed by John P. McCarthy based on the "Advice to Lovelorn" column by Beatrice Fairfax. Screen adaptation by Bradley King. At the Capitol, N. Y., Dec. 17. Running time, over 60 mins.

Georgie Hastings	Sally O'Neil
Ann Hastings	Molly O'Day
Bill Warren	Larry Kent
Charlie	James Murray
Jimmy	Charles Delaney
Joe Sprotte	George Cooper
Ernest Brooks	Allan Forrest
Beatrice Fairfax	Dorothy Cummings

An unsatisfactory picture for the big towns. It's small time in theme, direction and production. A gamble if intended for full week stands, with the odds unfavorable.

The boy who wrote the titles is not given any program billing. He should have been featured above the ghastly, unattractive feminine person who presumes to be the star and he certainly deserves more credit than the directorial brain responsible for the creation of a film that mirrors his incompetence in every scene.

The titles are a real asset to the picture, carrying laughs as well as building the story. Every member of the cast, with the exception of Molly O'Day, photographs badly and impresses mildly as far as audience interest is concerned.

The finish is unconvincing and a conclusive damper on an unentertaining offering.

The story, or possibly the screen treatment, resulted in a flimsy basis for a picture. It concerns a girl who wrote letters to the editor of a "Lonely Hearts" column. That stamps her as a nitwit with every big town audience in the country.

Ann Hastings is the girl who worships at the fountain of wisdom as represented by a Miss Fairfax. Her problem is with a younger sister, Georgie, whose flair for picking up strange men who own flashy limousines is viewed with alarm by the maternal Ann.

Then there's some connection with a boy named Bill whom Georgie scorns. He turns to Ann for sympathy and winds up by proposing marriage. Ann decides, finally, that Bill is still in love with Georgie and intends to give him up in favor of the younger sister. Both sisters are handed a letter from Bill in which he says he has decided to give them both up in favor of marrying money.

The gals don't take it hard and encourage the advances of two young men they previously repulsed.

Shots of Miss Fairfax writing letters to the lovelorn are thrown in at intervals.

At best it's only for the frequent changers. *Mori.*

THE LONE EAGLE

Universal production and release. Directed by Emory Johnson. Featuring Barbara Kent and Raymond Keane. From story by Lieut. Ralph Blanchard. At Colony, New York, week Dec. 17. Running time, 60 minutes.

Lieut. Wm. Holmes	Raymond Keane
Mimi	Barbara Kent
Capt. Richardson	Nigel Barrie
Sven	Jack Pennick
Red McGibbons	Donald Stuart

An abundance of technical faults and plenty of cheating, but okay for the U-supplied houses, the daily changes and maybe the split-week theatres. The air stuff will carry this ordinary story, lacking prominent love interest. The same case as "Wings," only on a much smaller scale.

The air "dog fights" reveal foot after foot of double photography with one sequence of two planes falling in flames repeated three times. But maybe the patrons won't notice it, nor the California hills under the final duel between the German ace and the untried American youth. Some of the bombing of a village is in miniature, but the Kelly Field lieut.'s determination to down the vanquisher of his pal got applause here, so that offsets it.

Attached to a squadron of the British Royal Flying Corps, young Holmes is under suspicion of cowardice after his first fight because he has ducked the battle. That his gun jammed is something that's hard for his flying mates to believe, especially as McGibbons, clown of the unit, "takes it" to let him get away. The duel with the German leader comes about through a challenge from the enemy aviator to meet the man who downed his brother.

Holmes wants to vindicate himself, draws the number and goes up to be shot down by the black cross flyer. Saving himself by parachute, after climbing into the fuselage with the "umbrella" loosely strapped on, Holmes again goes up, this time in a plane that has no guns, to join the free-for-all which has developed. He clips the German's wing off with his undercarriage, and the following shots are armistice stuff, succeeded by the homecoming with Mimi as his wife.

Other than the altitude action, Nigel Barrie and Donald Stuart hold the story together by their performances, Barrie as the flight commander and Stuart as the carefree McGibbons who knows he is going to get it and doesn't care. The latter is the actual highlight personality of the picture. Neither Miss Kent or Raymond Keane give much to their roles in establishing the love angle. Johnson has permitted the girl too much breast-heaving when under emotion, and Keane is only on top when undergoing his first touch of fear. Miss Keane is also the better fit as a young Frenchwoman.

The air stuff may fool the majority of witnessers At least there's enough of it to keep them interested. Youngsters present at the Colony Sunday were on the edge of their chairs as one indication. However, Johnson has rounded up the film's most convincing moments within the barracks of the flyers, which Stuart completely dominates.

The picture has pace, better and more air stuff than "Hard-Boiled Haggerty," despite the phoney filming, but won't feaze "Wings." The Colony orchestra used a melody which ran throughout the "Big Parade" for "Eagle's" accompaniment.

Sid.

THE SOMME

(BRITISH MADE)

Toronto, Dec. 9.

Regal Films of Canada, Ltd., release, of Britannia Films Production. Made with co-operation of British government and Canadian war museum. Running time, 74 minutes. Titling and publicity done in Canada.

Here is a full length feature film running 74 minutes with never a woman seen. Not even in the background.

It tells the story of the British efforts on the Somme before and after. As a historical picture, partly rebuilt from actual scenes via news shots, it attempts to tell no acted romance. There is no plot.

In British countries this will be a smash. Partly from patriotic purposes, partly because there are enough Somme veterans in nearly every city to make it worth while and partly because of the compulsory law.

For Canadian exhibition Tom Daley sliced it up and inserted Canadian events all through. Result has flag wavers in continual applause.

Outstanding shots come on the charge of Scotch Highlanders against stiff odds at night, heavy bombardment from behind the lines (actual shot) and the first use of tanks.

Some low comedy worked in on the ration party and the tank angle, but mostly the picture sticks to facts, undressed. It is sufficiently accurate to record those instances in which British troops were beaten back by smart machine gun work or hung on the wire in front of enemy dugouts.

The few instances in which trick camera work has been done is a big improvement over earlier pictures of this type. Maps to illustrate the progress of the battle don't mean much and an epilog showing the cities from which troops came is superfluous.

Picture obviously not intended for American exhibition. *Sinclair.*

Winds of the Tampas

Superlative production released by Hi-Mark Sales. Directed by Arthur Varney from the story by Elinor Ewing. Cast includes Ralph Clovinger, Edwards Davis, Claire McDowell and Ann Drew. At the Stanley, N. Y., Dec. 15. Running time, over 60 minutes.

It's a type production, monotonous, unrelieved by any touch of interest. A fairly good story given poor directorial treatment and, from the result, made with both eyes on the expense account.

The girl playing opposite Clovinger, unbilled on the screen, should get attention. She overcomes bad makeup, faulty camera studies and inept direction with poise and screen presence.

According to the tale, presented with an Argentinian background, an aged rancher is the object of a gift of hate from a foster brother whom he had tried to wrong years before by making a play for a woman they both wanted. The annual poison gift is beginning to get on the rancher's nerves.

The youthful son, Don Juan, just back from his studies abroad, is told to enter the service of the foster brother and prevent the shipment of the gift for the year.

Juan finds his foster uncle possessed of two daughters, one of whom he wants while the elder wants him. A brilliant fellow, Juan, with a remarkable lack of tact. After being told to lay off the younger gal by the irate male parent there are several scenes showing him making ardent, but awkward, love in the hallways of the house in broad daylight. In the same clever manner he is caught prowling around the building by his foster uncle.

The aged rancher should have been described a lunatic. Knowing the danger to his son he writes him a letter urging the speedy destruction of the annual gift. Through this letter the boy is trapped and flogged. The law of the Pampas, according to this version, provides that a spy be flogged and then sent out on horseback, hands tied behind his back, to face the desert winds alone.

With the gradually diminishing number of shooting galleries and states right exchanges it may soon be a difficult matter to sell pictures of this kind, but it seems they intend to keep on making them until the dime house is extinct.

Mori.

LUCK OF THE NAVY

(BRITISH MADE)

London, Nov. 25.

Graham-Wilcox production. Story by Mrs. Clifford Mills. Directed by Fred Paul. Featuring Evelyn Laye and Henry Victor. Pre-view, London Hippodrome, Nov. 22. Running time, 110 minutes.

It is hard to believe this film runs 110 minutes. It seemed years. Not alone in time, either. Technique, story, continuity, appeared to belong to a dim and distant era. One thing, the critics of the film bill can't blame this one on the government measure to help the British film industry. Because it won't.

Someone must have taken all the sheets out of a hack writer's card index, thrown them in the air, and made a film from the situations on those coming down face up. And how!

First there are feet and feet and feet of warships and waves, then the admiral's sailor son (of course, an officer) comes home. Then he goes away again, while the villain, who loves the heroine, discovers his own mother is a spy, and becomes one, stealing plans from a naval drawing office where he works in his spare time.

Hero does gallant deeds abroad—in a caption—heroine hegisters l-o-o-o-ve for him.

Again he comes home. He l-o-o-oves her, too. No one but he has the new navy code. The spies want it. Trapped, he writes it on the back of her photograph and gives it to her. She thinks she is getting the frozen mitt, but no! She, too, is trapped by the spies.

Fights, gunplay in which no one ever gets hit. Rescue by totally unarmed crowd of sailors. Villain perishes in aeroplane while trying to escape.

Back in the dim and ancient past of, say, 1918, Universal and Fox made this type (I do not say "this sort") of movie for the long grass, and did it well. Why anyone, especially with an era of revival in British films, should make this one now, I can't even guess. All the futile stupidities which obsessed part of the public mind during the late war have been brought in—spy-mania, old men spouting lip-patriotism and molesting boys who have not given their bodies to be mangled for "glory." Girls in war uniforms making their idle, silly play out of tragedy (and wearing war period clothes while the cast as a whole wears contemporary dresses of the present mode).

The whole film is a jumble of crude and commercial flag-waving, old-time stock melodrama, screaming to the gallery for applause, and moronic lack of even the lowest standard of audience intelligence.

If this were representative of the new British film producing industry, then there would be little left to do but shed the tears and raise the headstone.

But luckily it is not. It is merely a monument to a type of ineptitude which must disappear if this country is to take any serious place in the ranks of the world's film producers. *Frat.*

BRASS KNUCKLES

Warner Bros.' production, featuring Monte Blue and Betty Bronson. Directed by Lloyd Bacon from story by Harvey Gates. Photographed by Norbert Brodin. Cast includes William Russell, Georgie Stone, Paul Panzer and Jack Curtis. Reviewed in projection room Dec. 9. Running time, 68 mins.

One of the underworld cycle of pictures brought into vogue by the success of the film bearing that name. This picture is lacking in qualities desirable for de luxe stands but will go as intermediate program stuff.

A prisoner (Monte Blue) frustrates an attempted jail break. He is paroled, and visits the daughter of a man sentenced to die. The girl is in an orphan asylum and later escapes to live with Blue, who thinks she is just a kid. Later, one of the prisoners, who has vowed vengeance on Blue, is let out of the pen. As the girl has never seen her father and doesn't know where he is, the prisoner impersonates her dad and later tries to make her.

Blue comes to the rescue, staging a corking fist fight with the villain. Then, realizing the girl's womanly charm, he takes her in his arms.

Betty Bronson is the type for a girl supposedly looking younger than she is. Her perfomance averages moderately favorable. Monte Blue, surrounded by a cast of shorts, looks like a giant, and conveys the idea of good-natured brutality well. William Russell as the heavy is good. Support capable.

Should be suitable for the split-week houses.

THE ROMANTIC AGE

Columbia production and release. Directed by Scott Florey. Featuring Alberta Vaughn, Eugene O'Brien and Stanley Taylor. Photographed by Norbert Brodin. At the Tivoli, New York, one day (Dec. 7) on double feature bill. Running time, about 55 minutes.

An anæmic climax and miscasting drag this picture down to the weak sisters. If relied upon for more than one day it will show its frailty.

Eugene O'Brien plays listlessly as a middle-age fiance. Stanley Taylor, acting the younger brother of O'Brien (and his rival), gets along fairly until he attempts emotion. Alberta Vaughn is capable, but glixed with several instances of silly direction.

Characters are inconsistent. Miss Vaughn deliberately tries to make the younger brother, when she is engaged to the older, but turns on the kid when he gives in. Little sympathy for her. Stanley Jones, juvenile, starts as a likeable kid and is then made to appear suddenly vicious.

After disruption of their romance by the youngster, O'Brien and Vaughn are reunited in a fire scene. O'Brien goes into a blazing building to get some papers, but can't get out. Several minutes later Miss Vaughn goes into the building the same way O'Brien did. Then they await death in each other's arms, neglecting to leave the building through the door they came in by. Firemen cut a hole in the roof to save them. All this is done in heavy dramatics. Laughed at in the Tivoli.

First half of the film, directed in a light breezy way, looked okay. The last half killed that impression.

Hook and Ladder No. 9

F. B. O. production, directed by F. Harmon Weight from story by John Moroso. Cast: Cornelius Keefe, Edward Hearn, Lucy Beaumont, Dione Ellis, Thomas L. Bower and Johnny Gough. Photographed by Lyman Broening. At the Stanley, New York, one day (Dec. 2). Running time, 62 minutes.

Being straightforward handkerchief melodrama, this picture will be most appreciated by unsophisticated customers. Best for the neighborhoods and small towns. In the blase places it would encounter tough sledding.

A tale of two firemen, one of whom marries the girl they both love. The other carries on morosely for a few years. Then comes the big fire scene; the disappointed lover rescues his former pal's wife and kid.

His death is problematical. Advance trailers say he passed away after the rescue and the press sheet scenario says likewise; but the film refutes this theory by having the fellow say he'll be all right in a minute, and he's breathing at the fadeout.

Weight aimed rather low in his directing, in several instances making his situations markedly unreasonable to afford grandstand plays for the characters. Fire scenes are okay, mostly actual shots.

Edward Hearn as the disgruntled lover has a pathetically humorous part and handles it well. Cornelius Keefe, the successful rival, has looks, flashing smile and a fair knowledge of acting. Dione Ellis, the girl, is a sweet type. Good support.

Immortals of Scotland

(BRITISH MADE)

Toronto, Dec. 8.

Regals Films Canada release. Biographical and historical picture made in Scotland. Running time, 80 minutes.

Here is a long and rather dreary life story of Bobbie Burns and Sir Walter Scott. Weak on plot, strong on scenic beauty and worth a maximum of three reels. Split up with song and dance as it was by Lloyd Collins at the Regent and plugged on the patriotic angle of demanding British picture it might get a break in England and Australia, but for Canada the answer is no, and for the United States a couple of them.

High spots in the lives of the two men of letters are accurately shown in native surroundings. Shots in and around Ayrshire where Bobbie Burns was born and bred are pictorially excellent but as a program picture it doesn't mean a thing. With women's organizations and patriotic groups writing the papers to insist upon the showing of more British pictures this one comes as a black eye.

Sinclair.

RIDERS OF THE WEST

Rayart production, featuring Ben Wilson. Cast includes Fangs (dog), Neva Gerber, Ed LaNiece and Bud Osborne. Director's name kept off paper. At the Arena, New York, one day (Dec. 14) on a double-feature bill. Running time, 50 minutes.

Too crudely handled for appeal to any but juvenile western fans.

Apparently Ben Wilson was to have had starring honors, but a dog in the cast was later given that spot in billing to sell it as a canine picture.

Fangs, the dog, is a good natured pup entirely averse to fighting and acting. He is not sufficiently trained to be offered as a star.

The story has Ben Wilson serving a sentence for a murder he didn't do, and later taking a job as sheriff in a tough town to save a girl's gold mine and incidentally discover the real murderer. An unusual amount of time is devoted to lengthy explanatory subtitles, some of them useless.

Ben Wilson impresses faintly in this, as does Neva Gerber opposite him. Direction is pretty anemic.

German Pics

Berlin, Dec. 12.

"Am Rande der Welt" ("At the Edge of the World"). The director, Karl Grune, has turned out several films which had a moderate success in London and Paris. The present film is one of those pacifistic pictures in which all the characters remain abstractions, you never for a moment get interested in them. Brigitte Helm of "Metropolis" has a few personal moments, but these are entirely her own. Grune is suing the Ufa, charging his film was cut in such a way as to ruin it. But as there is not a single scene that has the spark, I can't see how it could have made much difference.

"Berlin"—An attempt by the Berlin branch of the Fox Film to put the German metropolis into a five-reeler without using any story. A few moments are good, but as a whole it is very one-sided, being without humor, merely concentrating on movement. Some of the photography is adequate, but most of it not above the level of a news weekly.

"Orient Express." — The interesting idea of a station master in a small town to whom chance brings a lady of society from the big city. In the end she leaves him, but has made him contented with his humble lot. One of the best German films of the season, discreetly directed and played by Lil Dagover and Heinrich George.

Jack London via Moscow

"Suehne" ("Atonement"). — This Russian film made by the official Soviet film company is taken from a short story by Jack London. In the gold district of Alaska a workman, who finds a rich claim for his employers, shoots two of them because they are not going to give him any share of it. The third and his wife guard the man through a long winter, in order to bring him to justice. Toward spring the three are not able to stand the strain any longer and at the request of the murderer the other two hang him.

Undoubtedly the most brutal film that I have ever witnessed. Its sheer cruelty is unbelievable. It is unthinkable that it could be given in America. Technically considered, the photography is bad, and, although the acting has extraordinarily powerful moments, it is as a whole amateurish.

"Die Hose" ("The Underwear")— Taken from a well-known comedy by Sternheim, it again proved that it is foolish to make pictures of plays which depend on dialogue. Moreover, Hans Behrendt's direction is indefinite and muddled. Werner Krauss and Rudolf Forster stylised their roles while little Jenny Jugo is just conventional. But, worst of all, the film is never funny.

"Das K. und K. Ballettmaedel" ("The Royal Ballet Girl")—Old-fashioned story laid in Vienna before the war. Only interesting on account of the performance of Dina Gralla in the title role. Each year this young actress is winning a stronger position in the German film world and should soon class up as one of the real stars.

"Ramper"—The stage play by Max Mohr could have produced an even more interesting film, as the idea is excellent. An explorer is lost for 30 years in the Arctic regions and becomes almost an animal, losing the use of his tongue and his memory of human things. He is finally captured and exhibited in circuses as a man-beast. There the head of an insane asylum finds him and brings him back to his normal self. After an unhappy affair with the doctor's wife he returns again to the north. The leading role is splendidly played by Paul Wegener, but the direction by Reichmann was jumpy and lacking in strength.

"Casanova"—Although produced in Paris this film was partly financed by German capital, its scenario is by a German, Norbert Falk, and several of the leading roles are taken by German players. Here the reception was good and, though forced at the Gloria Palast, there is no doubt it will do satisfactory business in Germany. The story is on the style of Barrymore's "Don Juan" film with Iwan Mosjoukin in the title role.

The film covers a lot of ground, bringing Casanova from Venice to Russia under Catherine the Great and back again. There is also no main love interest as Casanova flits from affair to affair. But the picture undoubtedly has sex appeal and should get over in America. Mosjoukin is no Barrymore but he is manly and graceful. The little German, Jenny Jugo, is fresh and charming and the Italian Rina de Liguore is a real picture find.

"Die Tolle Lola" (Crazy Lola). Continually roasted by the press, Richard Eichberg's films go right on appearing at the big Ufa theatres. It must be that the German public likes them, but judged by the standards of American comedy they are of the crudest. The present effort is one of the worst he has turned out. Lillian Harvey, its star, is now trying to break her contract with this producer.

"Napoleon"—Really a French product, it may be of interest to learn the German reception. Candidly, it was a flop. It is the opinion of this reviewer that this chilly affair can never have any success outside of France and there only on account of the subject matter. Here it is reported that the director, Abel Gance, has gotten American capital to help him make a continuation. American pictures are meeting their usual success and failure. "What Price Glory" had a most satisfactory Berlin run and has cleaned up wherever shown. "Sunrise" has been well treated by the press and looks as though it would do splendid business. "Chang" was looked forward to as being a big sensation and rounded off 12 weeks at the Nollendorf. The last few weeks of the run were undoubtedly forced, but there was no question of the reality of the success. Reports from the provinces, however, say that many theatre owners have been running it as part of a double header.

December 28, 1927

CHICAGO

DeMille Pictures Corp., production released by Pathe and featuring Phyllis Haver. Adapted by L. J. Coffee from the stage play of that name, with Frank Urson directing. Cameraman, Peverell Marley. At the Gaiety, N. Y., for a twice daily run commencing Dec. 23. Running time, 98 mins.

Roxie Hart......................Phyllis Haver
Amos Hart.......................Victor Varconi
Casley..........................Eugene Pallette
Katie...........................Virginia Bradford
Reporter........................T. Roy Barnes
District Attorney...............Warner Richmond
Flynn...........................Robert Edeson

"Chicago" shouldn't go under $2 examination. It's not a top price picture and no one pretends that it is. It is aimed for the regular picture houses where, with 1,000 or 1,500 feet deleted, it will be at home and is quite apt to play host to a consistent stream of guests.

Pathe has got another year to go on the lease of the Gaiety, if it so wills, and is retaining the house for exploitation purposes. Heads of the firm figure this double-edged treatise on Chicago court procedure to play a profitbale six or eight weeks, after which another film will be brought in.

As a translation from the stage the picture is a good twin. It at least adheres closely to its predecessor, except for what may be termed a prolog and epilog. On reels the story both starts ahead of and finishes after the play. The epilog is the strongest drama in the script from a screen viewpoint. This has Amos, the husband, throwing Roxie out of the house after he has stood by her despite that she killed her lover and has gone publicity mad during the subsequent trial. Amos is also the buoy, marking the main difference between the studio and stage vision. Before footlights Amos was very much of a sap. In the picture he is transformed into a dynamic husband, who steals to pay counsel fees, finally tells the wife to take air with the finishing inference that he will wed the young house maid who has admired from afar since reel one.

"Chicago" will neither thrill or grip the higher admission donaters. However, the trial sequence discloses a couple of shots of three gum-chewing and typical department store misses, who hang on every word and gesture. It's likely this is the clientele that will be the most interested in Roxie. She's not an easy character to play, and Miss Haver can't win much sympathy for her on a screen because the role doesn't call for it, and this actress isn't the heart-pulling type.

Yet, Roxie is liable to do much for Miss Haver in a trade way. She has always been able to interpret these care-free maidens, but has been at a disadvantage when cast as a sweet young heroine. What she promised in "What Price Glory" she has accomplished here. Miss Haver makes of Roxie a mincing, pouting, snarling dame who is all dame; nothing more and nothing less. A good piece of work.

Victor Varconi stands out as the husband who mentally battles to save his self respect by ordering his notorious wife out of his home. Robert Edeson turns in a sterling performance as Roxie's scheming lawyer from whom Amos steals the money to pay trial costs. Other cast members do little more than bits, including T. Roy Barnes, as the reporter.

"Chicago" has comedy and action. Not enough to warrant a 98-minute showing, exclusive of an intermission, but sufficient for program display. Production is high grade throughout, as is the camera work. Titles hold a few laughs and the undercover duel between Roxie and her lawyer during the trial is a laugh high light. The courtroom, of course, is the main comedy sequence showing the reaction of the jury to Flynn's saintly description of his client, and that client's knees.

Substantial cutting room attention should give "Chicago" enough pace to carry it through the program houses without boxoffice or censor worries. *Sid.*

THE GAY DEFENDER

Paramount production and release. Starring Richard Dix and featuring Thelma Todd. Story by Grover Jones with Gregory La Cava directing. Cameraman, E. Cronjager; titles by Henry J. Mankiewicz. At the Paramount, New York, week Dec. 24. Running time, 65 mins.

Joaquin Murrietta	Richard Dix
Ruth Ainsworth	Thelma Todd
Jake Hamby	Fred Kohler
Ferdinand Murrietta	Robert Brower
Comm. Ainsworth	Fred Esmelton

Southern California is being saved again for the Spaniards; this time by Richard Dix. It's the Murrietta ranch plus the dead United States commissioner's daughter, Ruth (Thelma Todd). Dix has side burns and a mustache, but it's still a tough job for him to look Spanish. He ought to remain this side of the border.

Other than that, neither Mexico nor Spain will have anything to squawk about, because the villain is an American, "Gay Defender" is just a western and not a good one. Production is okay, but it's wrapped up in the well worn bundle of the wealthy heir taking to horse to save the peasants.

A side issue is the hero under suspicion for killing the commissioner after the latter has hurrahed his refusal to frame with Jake Hamby to bear down on the surrounding property for the gold therein.

The only thing the script left out is the attack on the girl by the heavy.

Beyond that, Dix is on his way to be hung when he escapes to go on a vegeance campaign aboard a white horse.

None of the cast do well by it. If it weren't for the Dix name it probably would never have reached a Broadway house. And this stereotyped product isn't going to help Dix. It'll make 'em wary of his next one. He's a screen athlete, but rather ludicrous under this makeup.

Besides that, flicker fans will probably now have to undergo a fad for George Bancroft laughter from all heavies. Dentists should welcome the era. Fred Kohler laughs "Hamby" through this reel opera. Miss Todd wears crinoline and bonnets and seems satisfied.

No punch to the yarn, easily recognized after the first 10 minutes. Those who await a twist will be disappointed. It won't mean anything in the big first runs or split weeks.

Dix had better go get himself something with which to follow up. He'll need it. *Sid.*

A HERO FOR A NIGHT

William James Craft production, released by Universal. Starring Glenn Tryon. Directed by William James Craft from the story by Harry O. Hoyt. At the Colony, New York, week Dec. 24. Running time, about 60 minutes.

Hiram Hastings	Glenn Tryon
Mary Sloan	Patsy Ruth Miller
Fred Knox	Lloyd Whitlock
Samuel Sloan	Burr McIntosh
Bill Donavan	Bill Allash
Nurse Mack	Ruth Dwyer
"Bobbie"	Himself

Robert, or Bobbie as he is known, is the chief laughter-getter in an otherwise laughterless picture. Bob is a monk with a routine. He wears glasses to look at bathing girls.

Glenn Tryon is in danger of being killed off as quickly as he was ballyhooed into stardom by Universal. Comedies need smart gag men and plenty of them. Story and situations here are weak. Titles are clever, but only occasionally, mostly too familiar from frequent usage.

Story is of a taxi driver with a flying bug. Never in the air but took correspondence lessons and built a queer-shaped machine from two flivvers and a gramophone.

The boy falls for a ritzy looker whom he brings to the hotel from the station in his cab. She turns out to be the daughter of Sloan, the shaving soap manufacturer.

Sloan is recuperating from illness at the resort and Hiram tries to sell him the idea of sponsoring a trans-Atlantic flight. Turned down.

On the night of a dinner given to flyers, Hastings breaks in unexpectedly and when a call is made for backers, the monkey jabs a fork into Sloan's seat and the old boy jumps up.

Hiram pulls a couple of crazy antics, gets himself chased out of the hotel and the flight is all off until the gal discovers her old man is in danger of losing all of his money unless he reaches New York in the morning.

They get into Hiram's plane and land in Russia. Sloan's stock goes up on account of the publicity and the conspiring knaves are ruined.

Moderate money picture in smaller houses. *Mori.*

SILK LEGS

William Fox comedy production and release. Directed by Arthur Rosson, starring Madge Bellamy. Story by Frederica Sagor, adaptation by Frances Agnew. Titles by Delos Sutherland. Under supervision of William Councilman. At Roxy, New York, week Dec. 24. Running time, 56 minutes.

Ruth Stevens	Madge Bellamy
Phil Barker	James Hall
Ezra Fulton	Joseph Cawthorn
Mary McGuire	Maude Fulton
Mrs. Fulton	Margaret Seddon

Arresting title and sexy lobby display matter that goes with it make picture a pull. Production is a good flash for the program patrons. Nothing in it to draw censor fire.

Plenty of lingerie display, but all smartly done and handled neatly as legitimate story material. Plot has to do with the rivalries of a girl drummer selling one brand of silk hosiery and a young man on the road for another brand.

Very modern in substance and literary treatment. Certain slick style of comedy not without effectiveness and light vein agreeably carried out in titling. One of the early captions says we've progressed from the stone age, through the gold age and this is the age of silk legs, when a satin complexion and silk legs are the heritage of every woman, rich or poor. That sets the motif of the screen action.

Modest girl drummer finds herself in a losing battle with a fresh man rival for a competing brand of stockings. He deals with women buyers and his system is to "feed 'em, flatter 'em, fondle 'em and forget 'em." Desperate, she determines to use her own sex appeal upon the men of the firms.

The first battle comes when the boy arranges a lingerie exhibition in his hotel sample room, to which he has invited the head of a dealer firm, supposed to be a bit of a chaser. The ruse is a reprisal against the girl drummer who has vamped the tired business man.

The undress flash is in this lingerie display, an exhibition that has a neat touch of spice, but is so shrewdly shaded with bland comedy that it gets over safely. The point of the story is that the girl drummer invades the lingerie show with her own brand of stockings on the sly and puts the deal over for her own house.

Suspense is carried on from here by a rather clever device. You suspect that the old man who buys the order is really chasing the girl and that idea is nursed along to the last moment when it develops by a surprise twist that the girl reminds him of his own departed daughter and he was bringing her to his home to let his wife meet her.

The hero, who, of course, has fallen in love with the girl drummer, follows and battles his way in for another well developed bit of comedy finale.

Works out as a smart sophisticated sexy comedy, the atmosphere of elegance being emphasized by a beautiful production in backgrounds and costuming and a splendid cast of five, making it a clear, compact story with character and suspense values capitally balanced.

Maude Fulton has a first class character comedy bit as a flashy old maid buyer, handling the role with the same fine intelligence and restraint that have always marked her work on stage and screen. James Hall, as the lead, is bringing a good deal of good judgment to one of those show off characterizations that calls for nice shading.

Madge Bellamy has the gambs to make the part stand out, a pair of props that are an artistic little production in themselves. She is the wide-eyed appealing type, also that tones the candor of some of the business, while her comedy registers satisfactorily.

Modern light subject that will attract the flapper element and their boy friends, too, by its flash and its sex angles. *Rush.*

THE LOVE MART

First National release starring George Fitzmaurice production starring Billie Dove in Benjamin Glazer's adaptation of "The Code of Victor Jallot." Edward Childs Carpenter's original. Gilbert Roland and Noah Berry featured. Week Dec. 24 at Strand, New York. Running time 75 minutes.

Antoinette Frobelle	Billie Dove
Victor Jallot	Gilbert Roland
Captain Remy	Noah Berry
Jean Delicado	Armand Kaliz
Louis Frobelle	Emile Chautard
Fleming	Boris Karloff
Poupet	Raymond Turner

A good title, a winsome star, constantly handicapped by poor stories and direction, and one good situation comprise the box office appeal of "The Love Mart" as a titular reference to a slave market scene wherein the star as the pseudo-octoroon slave is auctioned off to the highest bidder, who proves to be the hero.

Running 75 minutes, with Miss Dove not brought into the action until after 15 minutes have been devoted to Gilbert Roland's advent into the old New Orleans scene of 100 years ago, it is altogether too slow and unsatisfactory a film feature.

Everything is mild and pacific in its transition with the big dramatic punch in the scene wherein the coveting dandies who once wooed the Belle of New Orleans now bid for her physical possession on the auction block. This circumstance is brought about by the return of Capt. Remy whom Antoinette Frobelle's father had given up for dead and who, as the new master of the Remy holdings, had brought up Antoinette as his own daughter, the offspring of a prosperous and respected merchant.

With Remy's return, not only does he strip Frobelle, his former overseer, of his belongings, but contrives to make Antoinette believe she is the unaccounted octoroon slave, and submits her to the ignominy of a public auction.

The motivation for the big scene is altogether too lethargic and the audience is inclined to impatience by the time the punch arrives.

Slowly but surely Miss Dove, who has the makings of an ace among feminine stars, is being killed off by the same brand of inadequate stories and undistinguished direction. Her last three or four have all been in the same negative vein. Although prolific in her output, evidencing a heavy production schedule, the mass turnover is not conducive to her personal prestige at a time when there is ripe opportunity for a smash production.

Roland as a male lead is too striking a "type" to click in the end. That full mane of hirsute adornment lays itself open too much to discussion, may or may not prove to be an asset on the matter of fan argument. Noah Berry as the heavy turned in a neat piece of work and Armand Kaliz, from vaudeville, is coming along in sleek "menace" roles.

The picture can stand chopping to speed it up. As a box office proposition, the star and the title (which latter is open to considerable exploitation possibilities) will do much to impress as a draw despite the other shortcomings of the flicker. And of course the F. N. enfranchisements and the moderate production investment insure a profit from the start, regardless of merit. *Abel.*

Legionaires in Paris

FBO production. Directed by A. E. Gillstrom. Story by Louis Sarekey. Titles by Jack Conway. Co-starring Al Cooke and Kit Guard, with cast including Louise Lorraine, Virginia Sale and John Anson. At Keith's Hippodrome, New York, week Dec. 26. Running time over 60 minutes.

Hardly measures up to any of the big war laugh specials released during the past year but an entertaining program picture for double feature houses or with strong stage shows.

Titles carry most of the laughs in this house. Of course the customers never got the idea of Pratt Falls, N. Y., the town where part of the action takes place. The titles were by Jack Conway.

With expert gag men on this job it could have been a laugh riot instead of a mere programer. Worth the open play dates, however, and will probably get them.

Al Cooke and Kit Guard deliver nicely as a team on straight as well as slapstick comedy. The title should appeal to the American Legion members of which there is a considerable draw to count upon.

Story starts in Paris with a couple of stewed doughboys falling for a fake murder and giving up a bankroll to the brother of the stricken man. Chased by a gigantic Gendarme, who is a laugh on account of his enormous size, the boys finally land in Pratt Falls, N. Y., as a couple of waiters in a one-arm eatery.

An election of the Legion is held to pick two delegates to attend the convention in Paris, and the two fugitives are chosen. They still figure they're wanted in Paris for murder but are forced to go to represent Pratt Falls.

A French general whose life the pair had saved during the war sent a detachment of police to greet them on their arrival. The legionaires figure they are being pursued on the old murder charge and the rest of the picture is devoted to chase episodes.

The girls are both ungainly, photographing badly and detracting from the value of the picture. *Mori.*

QUINNEY'S

(British Made)

London, Dec. 13.

Gaumont-British production. Adapted by John Longden from Horace Annesley Vachell's novel. Directed by Maurice Elvey. Photographed by Percy Strong and Basil Emmott. Censor certificate. "Universal." Preview, London Hippodrome, Nov. 6. Running time, 104 minutes.

Joseph Quinney	John Longden
Susan Quinney	Alma Taylor
Sam Tomlin	Wallace Bosco
Posy	Frances Cuyler
Jim Miggott	Cyril MaLaglen
Mabel Dredge	Ursula Jeans
Lord Melchester	Henry Vibart

A film which presents a problem outside itself, one touching the fundamentals of picture production on this side. As far as it goes, a good film. But the doubt in the mind of the reviewer is whether it goes far enough.

With the theme and the wide familiarity the public has of the novel and the stage play, it is not difficult to see, viewing this film, the result which might have been attained by spending more money and using wider vision.

It does not look starved—just underfed, lacking that smooth polish which is so great an asset in many big corporation-made American movies.

So, while this is a good picture, it is not a good enough picture. It gets out of the "local" class but misses getting into the international. That is why it presents a problem, for it is impossible to tell whether the producers are aiming solely at the home and colonial markets. If so, they have succeeded fully. If they intend this as a shot at the wider market, they need to open their purse strings and enlarge their ideas of universal entertainment manufacture.

Direction is very good and at some moments nearly inspired. It just misses these spots by going on to show what it has already rather skillfully suggested. For example, the coming of Susan's child is conveyed by nuances of expression, and, having got the point over rather brilliantly, the director proceeds to travel a shot from Susan's face to the ground at her feet and show—for heaven's sake! a pair of baby socks.

Again, when the child is born, Quinney, waiting in a room below, sees a passing show of the nurse going up the staircase—surely a sufficiently obvious method of planting the birth. But, no, the director cuts to a shot of the nurse entering a door at the head of the stairs! These make one feel as if certain shots have been started by the director and finished by the stage carpenter.

Joe Quinney loves things—old furniture and china—more than he loves people. After he marries Susan it takes more than her objection to "fakes" to make him see there are real things in life. Then he sets up to build a reputation as a dealer who only handles genuine antiques, but pumps against a gang of crooked dealers, one of whom is his old partner, Tomlin.

He succeeds, but has some fake stuff planted on him by one of his own workmen, with whom his daughter Posy has fallen in love. He gives back the six thousand for which he had sold the fakes, but his patron turns it over again to him for an Etruscan vase which Joe had been saving to give his son, if ever he had one.

Joe believes his workman has an affair with the stenog, and gives him the six thousand bucks to clear out. He goes, and Joe finds Posy is really in love with the boy, and sends her after him.

End is different from the novel, in which the workman stays in his shady character and goes off with the stenog and the dough.

For the first four reels the film stands up pretty well as a clean, sweet story. Thereafter the cleanness and sweetness remain, but the story loses out. It drags because the interest wavers.

Longden, playing Quinney, doesn't grip the part. He appears conscious he is a young man playing a middle-aged role. The much-boomed Frances Cuyler doesn't convince. But Alma Taylor makes a rather astonishing comeback, screening young and reasonably pretty in the early part and trouping well in her "later on" sequences.

Shortening, to snap it up a bit, and changing captions in most cases where they have not been lifted from the novel or the play will make it a film of quiet charm. But exhibits, mainly shy on stuff without sex and gore, may be afraid of it. They needn't. *Frat.*

Wages of Conscience

John Ince production, presented by Superlative Pictures and Hollywood Producers Finance Corporation. Cast includes John Ince, Herbert Rawlinson, Grace Darmond, Harry LaGarde, Jasimime and Margaret Campbell. Script by Mrs. James Hall; photographed by Bert Baldridge. At Stanley, New York, one day, Dec. 24. Running time, 58 minutes.

Most of the boys quit turning out pictures like this quite a few years ago. Audiences accustomed to modern stuff will squawk at "Wages"—if they aren't kept away by the title. When played, it's for one day.

Leading parts are handled by once-prominent names—John Ince, Grace Darmond and Herbert Rawlinson. Most of others are noticeably amateurish, hinting that casting may have been handled through the Ince-connected school of picture acting. Mrs. James Hall, who wrote the story and did the continuity, gets mammoth billing for some reason unfathomable by an observer.

The heroine is introduced as just a "Pawn in the Game of Life." She is forced to marry the wrong guy, while her real boy friend is framed into a life sentence for murder by her hubby.

So she has a baby which looks like her, and then she dies, only to play the daughter role 20 years later.

Hubby is wracked by his conscience and goes nuts. Framed guy escapes after 20 years and falls dead when trying to kill his framer.

Mrs. Hall, who wrote it, lets the framer live because he would welcome death in preference to the "Wages of Conscience."

When the picture ended, five gents were asleep in the Stanley balcony.

Ince directed this very crudely, and his work was made to appear more unfavorable by the photography and hackneyed subtitles. His acting is better, as the framer. Miss Darmond and Rawlinson don't appear forte, not all their fault.

Just a pawn of some kind.

POLICING THE PLAINS

(Canadian Made)

Produced and released by Policing the Plains Film Co., Ltd. From book of the same title by R. G. McBeth. Direction, adaptation and titles by Arthur David Kean. At the Royal Alexandra, Toronto, Dec. 22. Running time, nearly 120 minutes.

Britannia	Margaret Lougheed
Officer	Col. T. A. Wroughton
Commanding Police	Alfred Crump
Officer of Police	Donald Hayes
Sergeant Major	Jas. G. Harrison
Corporal	Jack Downing
Interpreter	Joe Flieger
Indian Scout	Norman Randall
Statesman	Senior Heaton
Canadian Girl	Dorothy Fowler
The Aunt	Roberta Scully
The Cousin	Gertrude Smythe

This first feature length all-Canadian picture will cause no panic in Hollywood. Made over a period of three years and at a cost of $125,000, the owners find themselves without a releasing agency, as none of the regulars are willing to take them on. They have therefore decided to road show the picture themselves.

The film purports to be a history of the Royal Northwest Mounted.

As such it is a historically accurate and interesting effort but as a program release it cannot be taken seriously.

It is a Canadian "Covered Wagon" produced without substantial resources. Yet it is a beginning. Given an even break in distribution it should pay for itself.

There are four main faults. Too long, too many titles, no experienced actors and dark photography. Kean, who has had wide experience making pictures for the Canadian government, has done a good job in direction. Particularly the Indian mob scenes. But cutting room work was certainly attempted by an inexperienced hand.

The main idea is to show how the Mounties kept peace and maintained order on the plains. It starts with a cabinet council in Ottawa, where the force was first suggested, shows the recruiting depot in Toronto, the departure for the west, treking through the plains and establishment of posts.

Encounters with whisky runners and horse thieves, a Buffalo hunt (actually filmed at Wainright National Park) and the turning back to the United States of Sitting Bull and his 3,000 Sioux are high lights equal to the best in American westerns.

Kean has attempted to show there was no lawless gun regime and no violent outbreaks with the red men, but rather a peaceful invasion in which the police played as much the role of interpreter and banker as strong arm man. By this he loses most of the dramatic climaxes that dot Hollywood westerns. The buffalo hunt, is the real high light.

There has been no attempt whatever to introduce comedy relief and the heart interest is very weak. Two or three of the cast men show promise. The camera was unkind to Dorothy Fowler in the only feminine part of consequence.

An epilog, showing the present activity of the mounties in preying on smugglers of narcotics, brings the film up to date but detracts from the story.

With half the titles cut and with at least 2,000 feet dropped this pioneer would be a better picture. As it stands it will have to drag them in on curiosity. There have been thousands better than this. Thousands worse, too. *Sinclair.*

SAN FRAN NIGHTS

Gotham production, released by Lumas. Directed by R. William Neill from "Fruits of Divorce" by Leon DeCosta. Cameraman James Diamond. Titles by Maude Fulton. Running time, 60 minutes. In projection room, New York, December 21.

John Vickery	Percy Marmont
Flo	Mae Busch
Red	Tom O'Brien
Flash	George Stone
Ruth	Alma Tell

A neat number for Gotham and a better than average independent picture.

Story of some novelty has been directed with intelligence by R. William Neill and acted by an excellent cast, including three names, Percy Marmont, Mae Busch and Tom O'Brien.

Action concerns divorce more than San Francisco. Placing the story against a Barbary Coast background was not necessary though it may have been so in the original script. While there is nothing typically San Franciscan about the story for box office purposes the new title is a great improvement upon "Fruits of Divorce," original label.

Marmont is a lawyer with his nose in his books and gets air from his wife. He drifts via the booze to a dance hall in the wide open sector of the San Francisco that used to be.

There he is befriended by Flo, dance hall girl, whom he had saved from the copa. Subsequently he becomes the lawyer for the underworld and earns the enmity of vice interests.

A gangster named "Flash" tries to steam up Flo's guy to bump off the lawyer.

George Stone, who played "Flash" is a darb of a crook type. For a congenitally nasty gunman Stone has a perfect mug. Pale, disagreeable and with ice water in his veins, the character of "Flash" is high drama.

The work of the other players uniformly good. Production standards first rate and no noticeable skimpiness.

CASEY JONES

Trem Carr production released by Rayart. Directed by Chas. L. Hunt from the story by Arthur Hoerl. Based on the song by T. Lawrence Seibert and Eddie Newton. Cast includes Ralph Lewis, Kate Price, Al St. John, Jason Robards, Anne Sheridan and Brooks Benedict. At Wurlitzer Hall, Dec. 20. Running time, about 60 mins.

A good idea gone wrong. An invitation audience at Wurlitzer Hall failed to become enthusiastic. Looks like one of the usual states right supers.

Ralph Lewis doesn't make the grade. Perhaps he wasn't permitted to. The sob situations are there, but are not put over. The death of Casey's little girl brings tears only to the eyes of the cast.

The story unfolds sluggishly. The heroic Casey, Jr., baggage master, has a message to deliver to his chief in the evening. As he nears the Ayres mansion, riding a bicycle, a man is seen trying to force a girl to take a drink. She turns it down. Casey, Jr., to the rescue and the romance is pushed into the arena. Jason Robards and Anne Sheridan, juvenile leads, do their bit to relegate the picture to a low standard.

It's a railroad story with a couple of train wreckers. The menace falls into his own trap and Casey Jones, engineer, remains triumphant. *Mori.*

CARRY ON!

(British Made)

London, Dec. 14.

Britannia Films, Ltd., production. Distributed by the Gaumont-British Co. Original story by Dinah Shurey and "Taffrail." Directed by Dinah Shurey. Photographed by Randall Terraneau and D. Dickson. Censor certificate. "Universal." Preview, Marcle Arch Pavilion, London, Nov. 2. Running time, 90 minutes.

Mick Trevorn, the boy	Micky Brantford
Mick Trevorn, the Man	Moore Marriott
Oliver Trevorn	Wyndham Guise
Mrs. Trevorn	Leal Douglas
Molly, the Girl	Aggie Brantford
Molly, the Woman	Cynthia Murtagh
Admiral Halliday	Frank X. Atherley
Bob Halliday, the Boy	Lewis Shaw
Bob Halliday, the Man	Pat Aherne
John Peters	C. M. Hallard
Sylvia	Trilby Clark

Another "Second to None" but a bit more hoked. Not likely to mean a thing outside British territory, but pretty good for the mob in its own limits.

Story has been used often but has everything the dumbell wants. In fitting the card-index theme to a naval occasion the scenarist has furnished a script which would have been topical in 1918, but now makes the film appear like a die-hard's attempt to sing a hymn of hate six months after everybody's kissed and made it all up.

The British navy lent two ships to the lady who directed the film—a destroyer (the ship, not the lady) and a battle cruiser. They play the leads both in parts and in sets. Scenes round the guns during a fight are more convincing than is usual in these naval films, and some naval maneuver stuff is very nicely photographed.

Story mechanism is a variation on the dream solution, the main action taking place in retrospect while the old admiral and the fisherman (Oliver Trevorn) tell the boy, who is about to enter the navy, the tale of the family traditions.

Nothing to get sobs and sniffles from the working-class woman fan is left out, and though the film is weak in story, poor in acting and patchy in direction, it will pull them in and send them out satisfied here. Where audiences are picture wise it will only get by as a second feature. In foreign markets it wouldn't get by at all.

As a contribution to movie making it's out of focus. As a local box-office hit it is on the spot.

Frat.

WAS HE GUILTY?

Aywon release (state rights), written and supervised by Carlton King. Director, Frank Grandon. Cameraman, Carl Widen. William Boyd starred. At the Columbus, New York, on double bill Dec. 22. Running time, 49 mins.

Jed Bascombe..................Carlton King
Homer Moore..............Joseph W. Girard
Marion Moore ....Vivian Rich
Jack Bascombe ....William Boyd

It will come as a surprise to many to know that William Boyd has been in pictures so long. Judging by styles, treatment and photography this one was made around 1919. The leading lady is Vivian Rich, who has not been seen on the screen for many moons.

Yet with all the lapsing of time it isn't, even now, a bad picture measured by the standards of the state right field. Those exhibs who buy emulsions by the foot will likely get more this time than they expect.

The title means nothing, and, in fact, will hurt by its banality.

Boyd's present prominence gives the picture a "star."

The story told is of a returned soldier who falls into the morphine habit. His father, the town marshal, having been told by a doctor that only by rigid confinement can the boy break the drug's grip, deliberately frames his son as a thief so that the boy is sent away to the pen, where he fights and wins.

Upon his return to society, cured, he takes up his career as an engineer and the step-father of his sweetheart is exposed as the secret head of the drug ring.

Some unintentional humor in the titles, but in general the picture, despite its age, is not as incongruous as films generally seem eight years later.

GUN GOSPEL

Charles Rogers production released by First National. Directed by Harry J. Brown from story by W. D. Hoffman. Screen adaptation by Marian Jackson. Starring Ken Maynard. Cast includes Virginia Brown Faire, J. P. McGowan, Noah Young, Romaine Fielding, Bob Young. At Loew's New York, one day, Dec. 23, one-half of double bill. Running time, about 60 mins.

Fast moving western loaded with action, trick riding and gun play. Story treated interestingly; cast screens and plays well.

A trio of mountaineers are blamed for raids on the ranchers. Rustlers headed by one of the ranchers whose plans are to scare the other

settlers into selling their properties at a low price.

Oldest of the mountaineers is shot and killed in a chase headed by the menace, posing as a protector of the village. Before passing out the old mountaineer makes his young companion promise never to use a gun.

Rope work is called into action and serves to create suspense and interest. Situations follow in logical conclusion to the point where the boy is forced to use firearms to protect a household in which a dying rancher and his daughter are in danger.

The guise of a minister, adopted by Ken Maynard for strategical purposes in the story, is used to good effect.

Mori.

RAGTIME

First Division release. Based on the story by James Ormont. Directed by Scott Pembroke. Cast includes Marguerite de la Motte, John Bowers and Robert Ellis. At Loew's New York, Dec. 23, on double feature program. Running time, about 60 mins.

Impossible outside of states right market. Cheaply made with poor cast. Story weak.

Deals with the theft of a song hit from the composer's piano. The gal is making a name for herself in the musical world via the classics when her picture appears on the covers of a ragtime number and she is barred from her circle.

She first blames the piano-pounder but later learns the hoofer stole the photograph from the boy she gave it to.

Drags and is monotonous.

Mori.

IF I WERE SINGLE

Warner Bros. production and release. Directed by Roy del Ruth from story by Robert Lord. Featuring May McAvoy and Conrad Nagel, with cast including Myrna Loy and Andre Beranger. Previewed in projection room, Dec. 23. Running time, 60 minutes.

Moderate money picture for smaller houses and split weeks, but by no means suitable for large downtown theatres.

Conrad Nagel photographs badly here. He leaves a poor impression, delivering with an expressionless countenance.

Direction is faulty and results in a rambling, loosely connected picturization.

Primarily the story is not interesting enough to carry the production. An insignificant incident served as the excuse for a series of situations which fall flat because none is built up to gain attention. Comedy dull and shows need of gag men.

A happily married young man, according to the story, flirts with an unknown young woman, leaving her with a lighter given him by his wife. The unknown turns out to be the wife's school friend.

Hundreds of feet of film devoted to showing verbal arguments. Hubby leaves home in the early hours of the morning to keep a date with the girl. Wife follows with a music teacher and both couples finally land in the same auto. The car is held up, and, following that, the music master and the girl drive off suddenly, leaving the couple to walk back home in a rainstorm.

Could have had a chance if intended as a farce and handled properly.

Mori.

GUN HAND GARRISON

Rayart western, featuring Tex Maynard. Directed by Edward R. Gordon from a story by Arthur Hoerl. Cameraman Er-

nest Depew. In cast, Edward Helm, Ruby Blaine, Charles O'Malley, Jack Anthony, Art Witting. Running time, 50 minutes. At Stanley, New York, one day, Dec. 21.

Fair to middling westerner. Some of the directorial detail is ragged and careless, but plot holds lots of action and that's what they want in cowboy drama.

The usual formula about crooks after the property of innocent people and blaming their own murders on others. Poetic justice dished out is ample to bring all the culprits to the reward of wrong doing in the movies.

Tex Maynard (brother of Ken Maynard) is featured with "Rayart's Rough Riders." Tex is an upstanding, nice-looking, go-getting prairie Galahad with the customary versatility in getting out of tough corners, eluding sheriffs and such.

Practically all exteriors with some shacks mean bankroll tap moderate. Result is okay. Photography good and interest-provoking qualities reasonable.

RANGER OF NORTH

FBO production, directed by Jerome Storm. Starring Ranger, dog. Story by Ewart Adamson; photographed by Charles P. Boyle. At Arena, New York, one day Dec. 24, on double-feature bill. Running time, 43 minutes.

Weak stuff. Just for kids.

"Ranger," dog, saves his pal from death several times and helps him secure hidden treasure for girl and her grandfather. This, despite three villains.

Jerome Storm made this into overripe melodrama. Photography good and support fair.

Much below the average "Ranger" picture.

THE SLINGSHOT KID

F.B.O. production and release featuring Buzz Barton. Story by John Twist and Jean Dupont, directed by Louis King. On double bill at Tivoli, New York, Dec. 24. Running time, 50 mins.

"Red"........................Buzz Barton
Hank........................Frank Rice
Clem Windross................Buck Connors
Santa Fe....................Jay Morley
Betty.......................Jeanne Morgan
Foreman.....................Arnold Gray

Buzz Barton is the 12-year-old kid cowboy offered as an ace bid for juvenile trade by F.B.O. Buzz is a bet and there's showmanship in the decision to build around him. With Jackie Coogan pulling in his chin at a military school and Wesley Barry grown up, the screen is without another boy star. Buzz may be it.

"The Slingshot Kid" is a breezy, speedy, well produced and directed western detailing the experiences of Buzz and his adult side-kick, the walrus-mustached Frank Rice. They outthink, outgeneral, outride and outshoot a gang of ruffians and cattle rustlers led by a youth named Santa Fe Sullivan, played with a week's growth of beard and a lot of venom by Jay Morley.

However, improbable their luck and ingenuity, Buzz and Hank provide what the western clientele desire—action and plenty of it.

1928

THE CIRCUS

Charlie Chaplin production, written and directed by Mr. Chaplin, who is also its star. United Artists release. Assistant director, Harry Crocker; photography, Rollie H. Totheroh. Cameramen, Jack Wilson and Mark Marlatt. At Strand, New York, opening Jan. 6 for limited run. Running time, around 70 minutes.

Circus Prop.-Ring Master.....Allan Garcia
Step-Daughter.............Merna Kennedy
Rex, Tight-Rope Walker....Harry Crocker
Head Property Man........Stanley Sanford
Assistant Property Man........John Rand
Magician.....................George Davis
Old Clown.................Henry Bergman
Pickpocket....................Steve Murphy
A Tramp....................Charlie Chaplin
Spectators, Clowns, Circus Performers, Policemen, Tent Men, etc.
Locale: Somewhere in the "Sticks."

For the picture patrons, all of them, and for broad, laughable fun—Chaplin's best.

It's Charlie Chaplin's best fun maker for other reasons; because it is the best straightaway story he has employed for broad film making, and because here his fun stuff is nearly all entirely creative or original in the major point.

In clinging to a tale of logical sequence, without the expected interpolations or detached incidents, Chaplin's "Circus" for speed, gags and laughs has not been equalled on the sheet. But it's very broad, for Chaplin makes no attempt at subtlety in this one, with the probable reward that those who see it will see it again—at least.

One might say that much cutting was done to bring this picture to 70 minutes, but in that cutting they bunched the hits. It's zippo with the laughs often running on top of each other.

The outstanding example of this is toward the finale when Chaplin substitutes for the wire walker of the circus. Using a pulley wire at first for the impossible tricks in the air, Chaplin does some straight walking, but falls off, and clinging to the wire, climbs underhand to the bicycle for the ride for life thing to the performers' entrance, the same as the regular wire walker. But Chaplin misses the catch by the attendants in the entrance and keeps on at lightning speed, full tilt into a drug store across the street from the circus lot. Dazed and out on his feet, Chaplin walks to the curb and bows. For show people this bowing bit will be a terrific laugh. Lays may not pick it up as readily, but this entire sequence was a scream.

Again and throughout, Chaplin as a wandering tramp falling into the circus is blundering about, with each blunder more laughs. Through blundering he becomes the star clown and drawing card of the wagon show. Show people will again enjoy the circus' owner telling the other clowns to put on "The William Tell bit" and "The Barber Shop business" as a rehearsal, to test out the new clown aspirant, and each time Chaplin giving the bit another and funnier ending. Or the bit through which his blundering with the assistance of a pile of plates and a kicking mule made the tramp the new boss clown.

Whether intentional or not by Chaplin, there is a fine bit of sarcasm in his ideas on circus clowning. In a somewhat learned article recently on the great clowns of all time, and not over seven mentioned, Charlie Chaplin was included. His "Circus" vindicates that writer.

Being the superior pantomimist he always has been, this particular upbuilding of new clown business before your eyes is almost a revelation, or it will be to John Ringling and Jerry Mugivan, besides their 150 clowns.

Heretofore, and whether in the arty or the broad manner, Chaplin has been prone to adapt for his gags. That absence here is noted. It could be said that the pulley wire safety hooked into his back was adapted, but merely in the basic and never applied previously in this way. It's the single point of adaptation in the picture, other than a simple bit that Mr. Chaplin should order out, and that is the only place for critical comment.

A sick horse must have a pill. Chaplin is ordered by the boss hostler to blow a pill out of a tube down the animal's throat, with the hostlers holding its mouth open. As Chaplin starts to blow into the tube the pill rushes toward him and goes down his throat. Chaplin says the horse blew first. Very funny. Later the boss hostler comes around, wanting the pill back. He gives Chaplin a kick in the rear when Chaplin drops the pill from his mouth. This kicking bit is poor in every way and the oldest comedy trick of the small-time travesty magicians.

Pathos to a limited degree is stuck in through Chaplin attempting to protect the bareback riding daughter of the circus owner, the father brutally abusing the girl (Merna Kennedy, the only girl programed). The tramp falls in love with her, but when the handsome new wire walker arrives the tramp is cold. That is why Chaplin took to practicing wire walking—to rival his rival.

As a matter of fact, Chaplin did practice wire walking, and only for this picture, doing it about three feet from the ground, as shown in the picture. Despite the pulley and another trick employed to keep in on the wire, Chaplin is an expert wire walker. It may strike some of the thoughtful as worth thought that a man in his 40's and a comedian, of position and wealth, should go to the extremely difficult task of learning to walk a tight wire for a five-minute scene in one picture. But to let Chaplin as a comedian or a pantomimist stand aside for a minute, for the Chaplin who could, as a showman, visualize that bit as big enough to be worth the unusual effort, and then to find that his judgment was so accurate, his wire-walking scene is the biggest laugh-make of this picture.

The finale is real Chaplinesque. Taking the wire walker to the girl and joining them the tramp declines an invitation to go into their wagon, but returns to the empty lot as the wagon circus starts for its next stand. Seated on the plate left within the ring he watches the circus depart, then trudges in the other direction, again the tramp, permitting his back and wiggly legs only to be seen for the curtain.

There's a lot of other stuff—ever so much; for "The Circus" as a comic film is a corker.

THE ENEMY

Metro-Goldwyn-Mayer production and release. Directed by Fred Niblo. Lillian Gish starred. Adapted from Channing Pollock's play of the same title by Willis Goldbeck. Continuity by Agnes Christine Johnston. Oliver Marsh, photographer; titles by John Colton. At Astor theatre, New York, Dec. 27, on twice-a-day run at $2 top. Running time, 96 minutes, exclusive of six-minute intermission.

Pauli Arndt.....................Lillian Gish
Carl Behrend.................Ralph Forbes
Bruce Gordon...............Ralph Emerson
Professor Arndt.............Frank Currier
August Behrend...........George Fawcett
Mitzi Winkelmann..........Fritzi Ridgeway
Fritz Winkelmann..........John S. Peters
Jan..............................Karl Dane
Baruska.........................Polly Moran
Kurt......................Billy Kent Shaefer

It is hard to see how this screen version of the much-discussed war play by Channing Pollock can exert a strong pull from the screen public. The physical production—such matters as imposing scenic and spectacular effects, effective acting and tricky dramatic niceties—is worthy of Fred Niblo, which covers that aspect of the matter.

But the subject-matter is not timely, and in the transition from stage to screen the adapters have committed mayhem and a little arson upon the material they worked with. It doesn't seem reasonable that Niblo did some of the things of his own free will. He's too well balanced a showman.

The picture has a happy ending in the return of Carl, the husband, but that was to be expected in a picture version and is good judgment. New ideas that do violence to the original are such episodes as Pauli, in the extremity of seeing her baby starving for lack of the money to buy it food, going into a Vienna bagnio in a scene that is a good deal more literal than it need be.

Lillian Gish doesn't register powerfully in this sort of stuff. You have to be pretty naive to accept Lillian as a creature of sin without an involuntary twitch at the corner of the mouth.

It is all out of the spirit of the stage play, which made its argument with some measure of restraint, while the picture tries to drive home its message of the cruelty of war, but still would make the whole business a whooping melo-ning when the picture was reviewed he was the only character whose first appearance brought spontaneous applause from a moderately filled house. It was patent that most of the people present had seen "The Big Parade" and the applause for Dane was a kick-back.

"The Enemy" has some fine military shots, made especially effective from the fact that soldiery is always shown on glittering parade, for a cutting contrast to the squalor and wretchedness of the war. These passages are handled with a sort of admirable legerdemain.

There are also tricky bits of dramatic effect. Hero and heroine are sedately walking from their wedding altar to the stately strains of the organ postlude when a military band passes in the street, war having been declared. The camera tells the whole story in a study of the bridegroom's feet, torn between the stirring march of the brass band and the subdued measures of the organ.

Graphic bit at the opening, too. A brilliantly colored figure of Mars, done like a stained glass window, is thrown on the screen, and across it there goes the tramp, tramp of marching soldier-feet in ragged puttees and an occasional trim officer's boot. This camera trick is repeated many times, and toward the last loses its punch.

As a special it doesn't measure up, although it should be a mild drama. As long as the tempo holds to homely sentiment it registers.

That is to say, that the story of the romance beween Pauli and Carl is interesting up to the husband's departure for war. Here the visible world is bright with sentiment and cheerful things, sharpened by the background of looming conflict and wretchedness. After that the horrors get too close and the thing becomes rather morbid if not maudlin.

The death of Pauli's baby would have been ample to create the necessary contrasts. All the other sordid and unnecessary detail leaves a bad taste.

Karl Dane has an inconsequential role in "The Enemy." On the eve-

ning when the picture was reviewed he was the only character whose first appearance brought spontaneous applause from a moderately filled house. It was patent that most of the people present had seen "The Big Parade" and the applause for Dane was a kick-back.

"The Enemy" has some fine military shots, made especially effective from the fact that soldiery is always shown on glittering parade, for a cutting contrast to the squalor and wretchedness of the war. These passages are handled with a sort of admirable legerdemain.

There are also tricky bits of dramatic effect. Hero and heroine are sedately walking from their wedding altar to the stately strains of the organ postlude when a military band passes in the street, war having been declared. The camera tells the whole story in a study of the bridegroom's feet, torn between the stirring march of the brass band and the subdued measures of the organ.

Graphic bit at the opening, too. A brilliantly colored figure of Mars, done like a stained glass window, is thrown on the screen, and across it there goes the tramp, tramp of marching soldier-feet in ragged puttees and an occasional trim officer's boot. This camera trick is repeated many times, and toward the last loses its punch.

As a special it doesn't measure up, although it should be a mild
furore as a general release.

This presentation has a prolog lasting about five minutes. The super-sentimental appeal is rather clumsy, just as it is in the picture.

Rush.

THE DOVE

United Artists' production and release. Starring Norma Talmadge. Features Noah Beery and Gilbert Roland. Adapted from Willard Mack's play of same name. Directed by Roland West. Oliver Marsh photographer. Titles by Wallace Smith. At Rialto, New York, for a grind run, commencing Dec. 31. Running time, 90 mins.

Dolores...................Norma Talmadge
Don Jose Sandoval.............Noah Beery
Johnny Powell..............Gilbert Roland
Billy..............................Eddie Borden
Gomez.......................Michael Vavitch

"The Dove" ain't what she used to be. That goes in the face of the production, cast and glass work United Artists gave it in the screen version of this melodrama. Not only that, but Dolores, alias the Dove, is no longer the toast of a Mexican dancehall. She's not even in Mexico. To get away from the foreign government squawks the locale is now Costa Roja, "somewhere on the Mediterranean coast."

However, Dolores (Norma Talmadge) is still the toast of "the best damn caballero" and speaks by broken-English titles. That's the main trouble with the picture, she does little else.

Noah Beery, as the egotistical and pursuing "heavy," steals the honors. Okay for Beery, but not the box office. Few villainous assignments and the men playing them have been able to hold up first line product. Yet, Beery's replica of Holbrook Blinn's work in the stage role is not to be confused with his performance in "Beau Geste." That being the case, the efforts of Miss Talmadge and Gilbert Roland are less by perspective. Houses with a stage presentation, news weekly, overture and shorts will chop from the 90 minutes the feature is allowed here.

The story keeps very close to the play, a synopsis of which includes Don Jose as the country's bad man, who is after Dolores and applies the pressure when Johnny Powell (Mr. Roland) gets himself in a jam over a shooting affray. Dolores promises she will give all to save her sweetheart.

A double escape and capture ends in Powell up against a wall in front of a firing squad with Jose in command. But just before triggers are pressed, Dolores scoffs at her nemesis, ridicules him for his "best damn caballero" claim, piques his ego and to uphold his boast before his people he sets the couple free.

"The Dove" doesn't threaten to get under the skin and hasn't the dramatic intensity of the play. It's spasmodically slow. Roland doesn't look like a gambling dice player and must have realized it, according to the results.

Miss Talmadge continues fair of face and form but doesn't seem to have been trying, possibly the outcome of having no high voltaged moments. Under suppressed emotion Miss Talmadge is not as impressive as when turning on the works. In this instance, anyway.

Marsh's camera work is a predominate feature throughout. Although how anybody is going to mistake the exteriors as being laid in any other spot than Mexico is something for the boys to figure out when the "squaring" commences. Mountainous sets, closely resembling some of the backgrounds in "The Gaucho," are well cameraed and reveal excellent care in glass technique. Too much traveling by the camera is an eye strain.

Summed up, the picture is Beery, camera work and production. Add to that the Talmadge drawing power and it figures to stand up as a program leader. But "The Dove" isn't a reason for scrapping stage presentation. *Sid.*

A TEXAS STEER

First National release of a Sam Rork production. Directed by Richard Wallace. Will Rogers starred. Louise Fazenda, Douglas Fairbanks, Jr., Lilyan Tashman, Mark Swain, Ann Rork, Sam Hardy and Lucien Littlefield featured (on Strand's theatre program). Adapted from the stage comedy by the late Charles H. Hoyt. Titles by Mr. Rogers. At Strand, New York, week Dec. 31. Running time, about 70 minutes.

Will Rogers	Maverick Brander
Louise Fazenda	Mrs. Ma Brander
Sam Hardy	Brassy Gall
Ann Rork	Bossy Brander
Douglas Fairbanks, Jr.	Fairleigh Bright
Lilyan Tashman	Dixie
George Marion, Sr.	Fishback
Bud Jaimison	Othello
Arthur Hoyt	Knott Innitt
Mack Swain	Bragg
William Orlamond	Blow
Lucien Littlefield	Yell

An average film comedy of the straight kind with a farcical touch, plus Will Rogers, starred, and plus Will Rogers' titles. It will easily stand up for the First National's first runs for a week, but is scarcely a hold-over in that class.

Sam Rork, the producer, or F. N. should carry a billing line that this is not a cowboy picture, to remove the possible impression on its name from those off westerns and also those unknowing of the Hoyt stage comedies. And if they do not care to do so now that the press sheet is out, the local exhib should.

All of the laughs are not in the Rogers' captions. Some come from bits of business, and those probably are foreign to the original script. The two best are the "one-horse town" gag (business) and the other when Rogers as the congressman from Texas goes before the House without having on his pants.

Starting as a comedy, in the Hoyt farcical style with the Hoyt story seeming quite well followed in sequence, the picture ends as a comedy meller, including a kidnaping, escape and chase.

Looks as though Bill, after he got that Press Club night in Washington, a peach plug not duplicated for influence in years, sorta sewed up Washington on privileges. He did more on its streets than might have been done in Los Angeles, and for a period it seemed as though "A Texas Steer" had gotten the exclusive rights to the steps of the Capitol.

Congress is shown in session with the scene deftly handled for the illusion of Rogers before the House.

At the start the Rogers captions wholly hold the story and the laughs, most of them giggles here, Bill building up on his laughs with one caption starting as big a snort as did the one-horse town business.

It opens on a Texas ranch where Rogers as Brander is with his cowboys. An election is being held in his town, Red Dog, engineered by his wife for his election as congressman. He's elected without having discovered he was even running.

Pursuing the wife's social ambitions, the Brander family move to Washington, with the ensuing matters surrounding country boobs in new hi' 'at quarters. A special shot here of the Willard hotel, Washington (name not mentioned). Thereafter it becomes a matter of lobbyist with a dame trying to frame the Texan legislator from voting in favor of the Eagle Rock (Texas) dam.

The whoopee scheme is carried right through the picture, with Richard Wallace, the director, doing quite well considering that idea is there, although the picture as a whole does drag. It's always working up to a gagging point.

Mr. Rogers makes up well, dresses the rural role and holds attention without that quaintness that might be deemed attachable to the Brander role. His rep gets the attention and his captions do the rest, besides his name that is a large part of the week's guarantee for this film.

Not much for the youngsters of the picture. They look all right.

Louise Fazenda has the semi-comedy part and her dressing for it will be a laugh all alone for the women. Lilyan Tashman played the vamping blonde, but there was no hard work in that. Sam Hardy did the villain, another walk through role.

Three musketeers from Red Dog do a great deal of the whoopee stuff, doing a little too much of it. A nance social secretary was rung in for laughs and if you think Bill won't reach for a laugh, listen to this in a title, when one of the roughnecks was asked to go up stairs in the hotel by the social sec whom he thought was a girl; caption:

"I'll buy a bottle of beer, but I won't go upstairs."

George Marion, Sr., did a neat character bit in blackface as Fishback, who wanted to be minister to Dahomey, but couldn't locate Dahomey.

Lot of stuff here for local publicist to work on, although probably all suggested by the smart First National press department.

Mr. Rork has a very nice and sweet looking daughter in Ann Rork. She was a picture as Bossy Brander, looking out of the hotel window.

To convey a story of this caliber to the screen and make it stand up is no slight performance. It was a good pick for Rogers, they fitting one another, and it's also a good example of what intelligence in picture making can do.

2 FLAMING YOUTHS

Paramount production and release. Co-featuring W. C. Fields and Chester Conklin, with Mary Brian and Jack Luden sub-featured, in a John Waters production from original story by Percy Heath. Scenarized by Heath and Donald Davis; titles by Jack Conway and Herman J. Manckewiecz. Runs 55 minutes. At Paramount, New York, week Dec. 31.

Gabby Gilfoil	W. C. Fields
Sheriff Ben Holden	Chester Conklin
Mary Gilfoil	Mary Brian
Tony Holden	Jack Luden
Simeon Trott	George Irving
Madge Malarkey	Cissy Fitz Gerald
Slippery Sawtelle	Jimmie Quinn

"Two Flaming Youths," with a comedy team in Fields and Conklin that can be developed into another Beery and Hatton as its stars, is a most satisfying laugh feature. Judiciously running a bit short rather than padding it to the conventional 60 minutes, it is a bright comedy from fade-in to fade-out.

The Percy Heath yarn has substance with the stars' courtship of the ex-burlesque queen who presides over the village hostelry; for the youngsters the sub-romance concerning the winsome Mary Brian and Jack Luden makes a secondary romantic strain.

Fields as the financially embarrassed carnival showman, with his troupe of hungry freaks clamoring for food and compensation, invades the county of which Conklin is sheriff. Conklin is giving Madge Malarkey (Cissy Fitz Gerald) the heavy rush, with matrimony in view, but Fields' suave and worldly manner clicks with the hotel owneress. Fields' intentions are ulterior, counting on the certainties of the three squares as an incentive.

Such complications as the sheriff mistaking the showman for a wanted criminal on whom there is a $1,500 reward; the complications arising from two rival county sheriffs claiming the reward, with each wrestling for the physical possession of the real Slippery Sawtelle, and kindred hokum makes for a great 55-minute laugh.

Fields as the barker is quick to capitalize every opportunity for ticket sales. When Conklin is catapulted into a dug-out wherein the boxing kangaroo is established, Fields vends stubs for the set-to in the pit between the pugilistic animal and his unwilling opponent.

In that setting Fields' native talents for juggling are consistently introduced. His capabilities with the cigar boxes, balls, shell game, etc., are neatly dovetailed into the action under the intelligent direction of John Waters.

The finale has the town "plute" marrying Madge, leaving the rivals for that fickle mama's heart, hand and hotel good friends, but not before the sheriff beats Simeon, the wealthy codger, at a little shell gaming, and splits the take with the carnival man.

Jack Conway and Herman J. Manckewiecz are credited for the titles, and, without intention to deprecate the latter's abilities, the gags and the laughs are all in the *Con.* style. That is obvious, particularly in the nifties built around the burleycue mama and the outdoor gimmick. The laugh titles are more than passably satisfactory, for in a feature of this nature the quips establish the key to the situation even before the action indicates it.

"Two Flaming Youths" will satisfy any exhibitor and his patronage. *Abel.*

WEST POINT

Metro-Goldwyn-Mayer production and release. Starring William Haines and featuring Joan Crawford. Directed by Edward Sedgwick. Story credited to R. L. Schrock. Titles by Joe Farnham. Ira Morgan, cameraman. At the Capitol, New York, week Dec. 31. Running time, 90 mins.

Bruce Wayne	William Haines
Betty Channing	Joan Crawford
Bob Sperry	Neil Neely
"Tex" McNeil	William Bakewell
Bob Chase	Ralph Emerson
Captain Munson	Leon Kellar
Coach Towers	Major Raymond G. Moses, U. S. A.

A good M-G-M program picture with comedy, action and color. Despite it's another tale of the cadet corps and includes more football, the film both entertains and holds to the last frame.

William Haines does his now familiar characterization of the fresh youngster which has dominated his releases. Having done this in "Brown of Harvard," still the best college picture of the bunch, Haines seems particularly at home in undergraduate themes.

In fact, there is much in common between "West Point" and the Harvard yarn. If memory serves the final score of these two screen football games were the same, Haines being sent in with the score 3 to 0 against his team. Against Yale he carried the ball the length of the field in short dashes to let the "heavy" go over for the touchdown, but here he scores himself on the Navy.

The interpolated gridiron shots are of the '26 Army-Navy game in Chicago. Most of the stuff looks to have been reprinted from Fox News negative, and care has been taken to see that Haines' jersey is numbered 10, the numerals Harry Wilson, halfback, carried. Hence, actual game shots reveal No. 10 doing some neat running off tackle. It's Wilson, but the script dovetail makes it Haines. It consummates a nice bit of careful direction and cutting. In one instance the formation the Navy used when it turned loose its initial long pass against Army in the first quarter of the Chicago struggle is duplicated by the camera teams so that the cut into the newsreel shot completes the pass which the Navy's back is seen to toss in closeup. That's pretty close attention to detail, but worth it.

As in "Brown of Harvard" and "Slide, Kelly, Slide," Haines has his physically weaker and hero worshipping pal in a hospital during the big game. It seems a formula the producers are afraid to vary and while good, still it can't go on forever. And "West Point" is also favored by a corking performance in this standard role, this time from William Bakewell, who gives Haines a run for honors. Joan Crawford has little to do other than look good, which she does from habit. Others, although secondary, are okay.

Where Bruce Wayne comes from the picture never tells. Subsequent action reveals he's a flip youth who thinks pretty well of himself and has money. The fastest and funniest passages concern his entrance to the Point, where the upper classmen immediately start to rag and chase him to formations. A scrimmage between the plebe and varsity squads, with Haines running wild, abruptly terminates his plebe year whence he is shown in summer camp as he becomes a yearling.

Meanwhile, Wayne is constantly pursuing Betty, daughter of a hotel proprietor, who can't reconcile herself to the ego the boy displays.

Sport page publicity goes to Wayne's head so that he is benched gives out a newspaper interview charging favoritism, is bawled by the coach and retaliates by crying "to hell with the corps."

A student committee meets to "silence" Wayne, but he is saved by his roommate, Tex, who pleads for him after being struck by his hero. Wayne tenders his resignation to the superintendent, but as the team is entraining for the Navy game he repents, asks for another chance, and although none of the squad will speak to him, makes the trip. An injury in the last quarter sends him into the game, which he finishes with a bad arm and where he apologizes to the team after the final gun.

Even this part of the Plot Series FB92 was in the reverse for Marion Davies in "The Fair Co-Ed," but basketball there.

All shots of the Point are interesting with mess hall scenes, including comedy by title—taken from cadet custom of questions and answers by plebes. Commencement scenes of the graduating class doing officers front and center are assuredly picturesque as are any shots which include the corps as a whole or in part. Theatrical license has been taken with the demeanor of Wayne, and if a bit far fetched no one is going to squawk.

Edward Sedgwick has drawn the relationship between Wayne and McNeil with a fine sense of understanding and has carried the action along smoothly and well. The football sequences have been excellently handled with Ira Morgan, cameraman, borrowing the shot of a "huddle," which first popped up in Grange's "One Minute to Play"—that of the lens peering up into the faces of the players as they gather for signals. One or two closeups of individual players have a backdrop duplicating an end of the Chicago stadium for realism. Okay, too.

Joe Farnham's titles are crisp if including a couple of old gags.

"West Point" will do in any house. It's in Haines' backyard—he plays it, and so does Bakewell. *Sid.*

BABY MINE

Robert Z. Leonard production, released by Metro-Goldwyn-Mayer. Directed by Robert

Z. Leonard. Based on the stage play by Margaret Mayo. Screen adaptation by Sylvia Thalberg. Titles by Ralph Spence. Co-starring Karl Dane and George K. Arthur. Featuring Charlotte Greenwood. At the Capitol, New York, week Jan. 7. Running time, over 60 mins.

Oswald....Karl Dane
Jimmy....George K. Arthur
Emma....Charlotte Greenwood
Helen....Louise Lorraine

Enjoyable picture. More laughs in the sub-titles than it is possible to count and still keep track of the story, and a couple of sure-fire muggers in Dane and Arthur. Smart gagging and a story that holds attention despite its necessary slightness are the rest. Charlotte Greenwood does not register as a comedienne, while Louise Lorraine is also weak in straight support.

Dane cops most of the laughs. The boys are roommates at a college of chiropractors. Oswald (Dane) is pictured as a heavy-handed youth inadvertently crushing statues and paper weights by mere touch. Jimmy is set to wed the one and only when she tells him of an older sister who must commit matrimony first before she can be free. The older sister turns out to be a gawky, long-legged creature. Jimmy frames her on Oswald.

The scene where Oswald and Emma become playful and throw sashweights at each other in gleeful abandon may be classed as slapstick, but delivery is novel. Dane's mugging puts every piece of business across.

While dazed from a blow on the head Oswald is married to Emma. He runs away on waking the next morning. Jimmy later discovers him and get him back for Emma by telling him that he is the father of a child. Oswald comes back by airplane before the schemers have a chance to get a baby.

In the rush all three bring home a baby, and Oswald is told he is the father of triplets. The third baby is a midget. While in his swaddling clothes the midget acquires a flask of liquor, which he empties into the milk bottle and consumes with great relish. He finally strips, and is last seen smoking a long, black cigar while a horrified old maid runs out of the room in terror.

There are 14 laughs in the first 20 sub-titles and almost as many in the picture during that same period. Good title and with proper exploitation picture should get money.

Mori.

CHINESE PARROT

Universal-Jewel production and U release. Directed by Paul Leni. Hobart Bosworth, Marian Nixon, Edmund Burns, Albert Conti and Anna May Wong featured. Adapted by J. Grubb Anderson from the similar titled story by Earl Derr Biggers; story also appeared in "Satevepost." Titles by Walter Anthony. At Colony, New York, week Dec. 31. Running time, around 65 minutes.

Sally Phillimore....Marian Nixon
Sally Phillimore (older)....Florence Turner
Philip Madden....Hobart Bosworth
Jerry Delaney....Hobart Bosworth
Robert Eden....Edmund Burns
Martin Thorne....Capt. Albert Conti
Charlie Chan....K. Sojin
Alexander Eden....Fred Esmelton
Maydorf....Ed Kennedy
Louie Wong....George Kuwa
Prospector....Slim Summerville
Prospector....Dan Mason
Nautch Dancer....Anna May Wong
Gambling Den Habitue....Etta Lee
Jordan....Jack Trent

A very good Universal program of the thrilling mystery stuff, made by Paul Leni, who also directed U's "Cat and Canary." This picture will do more than nicely for the U trade and elsewhere for the strictly fan patronage, but as a story or a thriller or a mystery, it's terrible applesauce.

This epic, opus or vehicle strings out over some pearls with a grouch on or in them. Whoever monkeys with them goes dead or dead broke. Large pearls, too, every one, large even in a film. Worth a lot of dough, and one gal sold her soul for 'em, thereby losing a steady lover. That loving boy was so steady he hung around, but in the offin', for 20 years to get the pearls and the girl who turned him down.

Meanwhile the girl had had a daughter, her original hub had bumped himself off, and there she was with only a daughter, a discarded lover and a thousand pearls or so, waiting in Frisco for a chink sleuth to drag the junk over from the straw skirt country.

The mystery of the story is whammed in with the mysteries of photography ..t times. At times it's good photography, creepy, freaky and ofttimes hazy. It jumps to Chinatown, and there's the mob waiting to grab the shiners, but the Chink detect gets past the crowd, while the deserted lover tells the women folks to bring the stuff to his place in the desert the next night.

His place in the desert is a bearcat for style. There they wear tuxes day and night. Also the Chink sleuth as a Lon Chaney cook-waiter, and if he weren't doing a Chaney it was because Chaney can't stoop that low. Another two inches lower and the Chink would have been doing Bugs Baer's lizard gag on Lon.

Much sneaking along the hallways in that swell joint in the sand. Also shooting and the parrot. The parrot could understand Chinese and translate it into English. And with a better memory than an act stealer. But that's about all the relativity between the title and the story.

Really the most mystery was how a Chinese coolie could so easily walk off a ship and off the wharf on United States territory.

So then they gave the pearls to an Indian, calling them beads, and told him to give them to his squaw, without asking if he had a squaw.

Love stuff, but not strong.

E. Sojin played the Chink, and from the name he is. He did good enough, considering he had the meat role. Florence Turner was the weepy mother, al ays with the glyc. Marian Nixon, the daughter, with Hobart Bosworth in a dual role that had to be neatly handled without double exposure toward the finish. Bosworth is always the good actor.

Anna May Wong looked oke as a cooch dancer in the prolog, but she passed out on the knife route, slipped her by a treacherous looking brute. That meant one day's work and featuring.

Edmund Burns is the juvenile, always looking ready to go, but appearing in trouble over getting set. The picture is now listed at 7,300 feet, so maybe a lot of footage had to be chopped.

Still, withal of general appeal to a low or high percentage of appreciation, according to your pressure or mind. But again okay, with Leni's directorial work quite outstanding when you think of what he must have had to sidestep in this to prevent duplication on the "Cat and" thing.

GATEWAY OF MOON

Fox production and release. Featuring Dolores Del Rio. Based on play by Clifford Bax; John G. Wray directing. Chester Lyons, cameraman. At the Roxy, New York, week Jan. 7. Running time, 48 minutes.

Toni....Dolores Del Rio
Arthur Wyatt....Walter Pidgeon
George Gillespie....Anders Randolf
Henry Hooker....Ted McNamara
Gottman....Adolf Millar
Mortlake....Leslie Fenton

Probably the worst picture Fox has sent into the Roxy. The same company had "'Very Confidential' over to Sixth Avenue and the Hippodrome; "Gateway of the Moon" should have taken the same trail. It's only asset is Dolores Del Rio's name, and that isn't yet strong enough to be acknowledged a surefire draw everywhere. The film's title certainly means nothing.

"Gateway of the Moon" is constructed around a legend of Trader Horn's country. Jungles 'n' everything, with Miss Del Rio in a costume equally as appropriate on an Hawaiian beach. Her mother is supposed to have been an Indian, but her father was white and is dead. Cared for by an uncle "whose only redeeming trait" is a love for his ward, said uncle turns out to be a dirty dog, conniving to get the railroad construction crew drunk and sneak coin.

Meanwhile the chief engineer from headquarters arrives and, because the cards have told her to expect a lover, Toni (Miss Del Rio) starts to chase Wyatt all over the lot. He will have none of her, but she saves him after he has been shot by her uncle's accomplice, and maybe he takes her back to town with him.

There's one passage where the male youngster, who hasn't become acclimatized and knows of Gillespie's goin's-on, is sent out and deliberately left to die in the jungle. This brings on a sequence of alligators, and, inasmuch as the house staff continues to tint its features wherever they deem it showmanly, they are yellow alligators. The tinting idea helps a shack fire scene, but it's still a questionable habit. All this to music from "Rose-Marie" as played by the organist.

Miss Del Rio does nothing in the picture. She might as well have saved the effort for a good story. The same goes for the others, although Anders Randolf and Adolf Millar are as villainous as possible. Walter Pidgeon, featured on the program but not in screen title, gets a break if everybody just says it's a bad picture and lets it go at that. Wray, directing, has done nothing with an anemic story.

The film is only running 48 minutes at the Roxy. It can't be slashed much shorter than that, even for the daily change houses, where it belongs. It's not for any city's Broadway for seven days. A bad boy.

Sid.

Gentlemen Prefer Blondes

Paramount production and release. Directed by Malcolm St. Clair. Adapted from story and play by Anita Loos. Cameraman, Harold Rosson. At Rivoli, New York, for grind run starting Jan. 14. Running time, 75 mins.

Lorelei Lee....Ruth Taylor
Dorothy Shaw....Alice White
Gus Eisman....Ford Sterling
Henry Spoffard....Holmes Herbert
Sir Francis Beekman....Mack Swain
Lady Beekman....Emily Fitzroy
Mrs. Spoffard....Trixie Friganza
Judge....Chester Conklin

On the screen "Gentlemen Prefer Blondes" lacks the sophistication of the play and the demand upon the imagination created by the Anita Loos diary. Miss Loos has "adapted down" and "sapped up" to the film public, Malcolm St. Clair directing likewise, undoubtedly from the basic knowledge that it had to be done. It's good de luxe program fare, but no more or no less. No howls, but steady laughs, with the titles, surprisingly, only fair.

Ruth Taylor's Lorelei, as directed, is merely a copy of June Walker's stage performance. So close, it tabs Miss Loos as the direct coach of this former extra girl who is making a personal tour with the picture. Miss Taylor looks good, a corking pick for the baby-stare type, and impresses as a neat possibility as regards future releases with direction making or breaking her within her next two pictures.

And as close as Miss Taylor's performance follows that of Miss Walker, Alice White's is just that far away from the cynical sophistication of Edna Hibbard as Dorothy, the girl friend. Miss White looks like a high school flapper all the way. Mixed in with heavy money men, the ease with which these two kids make the boys come across doesn't readily digest. At various points in the unreeling Miss Taylor also resembles a youngster in her very early 'teens.

Opposite the two girls are Ford Sterling as the button monarch who is educating Lorelei, Holmes Herbert as the wealthy bachelor whom the blonde snares into marriage, and Mack Swain as the old Britisher who unknowingly bankrolls Lorelei into buying his wife's diamond tiara. It's a heavy contrast in characters, maybe too much so.

If all that's against the picture, then the assets include this s. a. the Misses Taylor and White spread across the screen, the comedy in the theme, the production background and the support of Sterling and Swain.

The picture dips in and out of the original script, starting in the Arkansas hills where Lorelei's father is a gold miner. Her male conquests with her hair still down lead to the stenog job, the boss of which she ultimately shoots and kills when finding him with another girl. A comedy jury acquits, and the judge (Chester Conklin) stakes her to the California fare for a try in pictures.

On the train she meets Eisman (Sterling) and after becoming a film extra it's Eisman again, New York, and then the European jaunt which sequence is given the most footage.

The scenario only uses the incidents of the diamond tiara, cutting out the manipulation between the girls and the French lawyers, and Lorelei steering Eisman into ptomaine poisoning to get him out of the way so she can grab Spoffard. Figure for yourself how much has been ignored.

The inclination of Spoffard, an announced moralist, to pour over risque magazines and visit questionable places under the guise of duty, is retained and can go as a slap at the national reform element.

Viewing of "Blondes" will indicate the extent to which Paramount has gone to set Miss Taylor off on the right foot. It's the dominant note of the release. The story, naturally, revolves around her, but the technicians have gone further than that to make her stand out. Various touches in the running reveal how carefully this girl has been handled, and has she been dressed? And how! For the women and eyefilling for the boys.

Miss Taylor isn't so flappery during these passages but spasmodic flashes of rolled stockings fail to help the illusion of the ultra in gold diggers she's trying to represent, while some of Miss White's skirts hang above the knee. If any one believes something like 16 can make the world go broke, then the studio has turned this out to the life.

But "Blondes" is a suitable program entry. There's nothing to stand off just how far Lorelei is supposed to have gone with the man she shoots and her benefactor. Neither is there anything to condemn her. Witnesses are simply left to draw their own conclusions. If there's any objection to that, the film's materialism will hardly teach this younger generation anything it doesn't know.

It's a sweet picture for Ruth Taylor and as produced probably consummates one of the greatest "breaks" any girl has ever gotten in pictures. If she gets as much attention in her next release, and can follow up on the ability shown here, the girl is an odds-on choice to land somewhere. *Sid.*

THE FOUR FLUSHER

Universal production and release; directed by Wesley Ruggles. Adapted from the play by Caesar Dunn. Co-starring George Lewis and Marian Nixon. At the Colony, New York, week of Jan. 14. Running time, about 60 minutes.

Andy Whittaker..............George Lewis
June Allen..............Marion Nixon
Robert Riggs..............Eddie Phillips
Jerry..............Churchill Ross
Tom..............Jimmy Aye
Ira Whittaker..............Burr McIntosh
Cashier..............Patricia Caron

Clean comedy, carrying plenty of laughs. It's a "type" story, but the director puts it across with a speed that makes it interesting. Leading players both photograph well and are attractive enough to sell the picture as a good programmer. Patricia Caron, given only a few shots as a cashier in a shoe store, registers as a movie face.

The four-flusher is a shoe clerk who goes out on his own, after being given $10,000 credit by the bank. An unknown uncle has visited the bankers and left the money in trust for Andy, with the request that the latter should not be told. Andy offends unc by stepping on his straw lid a few times, and the latter tries to stop his nephew's credit. But the boy has already invested the money in stock and fixtures for a shoe store, and the banker cannot call his loan for three months.

Interwoven love interest, of course, and Andy's arch-supporter, an invention, triumphs at the last minute. The creditors are paid off and the menace gets his justice.

While the story sounds trite and insipid, the picture grips and holds attention. *Mori.*

WIFE SAVERS

Paramount production and release. Starring Wallace Beery and Raymond Hatton. ZaSu Pitts and Ford Sterling featured. Adapted from the musical comedy, "Louis the 14th." Ralph Cedar directing. A. Gilks, cameraman. Titles by George Marion, Jr. At the Paramount, New York, week Jan. 14. Running time, 57 mins.

Louis Hozenozzle..............Wallace Beery
Rodney Ramsbottom..............Raymond Hatton
Germaine..............ZaSu Pitts
Colette..............Sally Blane
General Lavoris..............Tom Kennedy
Tavern Keeper..............Ford Sterling

A capacity Sunday mob got its b. o. worth out of this one. It should give the Beery-Hatton team a neat push on sale and entertainment value. Give Cedar, the director, a little credit, too. As far as known this is the first time he has handled these male comedians.

Just what relation there is between "Wife Savers" and "Louis the 14th" is obscure. Both have the Alps as their location; otherwise never the twain shall meet is the rule. Laughs and a lot of 'em. Spotty, perhaps, but when they crop up there's no mistaking 'em. And as it's all boiled down to less than an hour the quiet interludes are never over-long. Besides which, the picture finishes on a howl—a comedy film's favorite ace.

As a whole it's Beery's screen. Little doubt about that, with Hatton getting what laughs he has by ill-fitting clothes while doing semi-straight for the big fellow. Beery gives a corking performance as the awkward Alpine guide whom the heavy would like to bump off so he can wed the girl (Sally Blane). Meanwhile Beery has to marry Colette to save her for the second lieutenant (Hatton), who has returned to America. The action starts during the war with Beery in a service bakery. That permits of slapstick with the dough.

A high light is that most of the laughs are the outcome of situations. A few gags, but not many. The scream portions are reached when Beery takes a party up a mountain where every time any one sneezes it starts an avalanche. This leaves the ungainly guide in some precarious positions, helped along by Marion's titles. A hoke three-cornered duel takes place in Colette's house the night of the marriage and Hatton's return, and the yell finish sends Beery to the barn to sleep, where he lays down on a nest of eggs in a nightgown to wake up as they hatch and exclaim: "My God, I'm a mother!"

Snow and mountain stuff is all studio, but made to look good, with the comedy dominant enough to cover all prop technicalities. ZaSu Pitts has a bit where the sequence kids the Gilbert-Adoree motor truck separation in the "Parade," and Miss Blane is also confined to a limited action area. The latter, however, shows enou' to impress if for nothing else than that she's not of the doll face type. Ford Sterling lends valuable support in working with Tom Kennedy, the "menace."

The picture's war opening may cause a wave of disappointment to sweep an audience, but that won't last long. The laughs at the Paramount were too strong to leave any doubt concerning the entertainment qualities in this one. *Sid.*

THE DIVINE WOMAN

Metro-Goldwyn-Mayer production and release. Gladys Unger's stage play, "Starlight." Directed by Victor Seastrom. Greta Garbo starred. At Capitol, New York, week Jan. 14.

Marianne..............Greta Garbo
Lucien..............Lars Hanson
Legrande..............Lowell Sherman
Mme. Pigonier..............Polly Moran
Mme. Rouck..............Dorothy Cumming
Jean Leary..............John Mack Brown
Gigi..............Cesare Gravina
Director..............Jean de Briac

No denying Greta Garbo. Her beauty is of a simple sort; nothing exotic or hectic—just a super-pretty blonde. And Seastrom knows just how to handle her. If she had better stories than "The Divine Woman," which is not bad, but nowhere near great, she would have such a flying start that it would be hard to overtake her in the movie market.

In this instance she is a peasant girl from Brittany, and here and there the incidents suggest anecdotes of the life of Sarah Bernhardt, though this thread is not consistently followed. She comes to Paris to find fame as an actress. The man who brings her there is her mother's lover, played by Lowell Sherman in his best manner. She falls in love with Lucien, a private soldier, and gets him into all sorts of grief, including arrest as a deserter and prosecution for stealing a dress she admires.

The romance is a rough-and-tumble, cute and juvenile. Greta flirts charmingly, and Lars Hanson, whose features do not indicate Scandinavian origin, takes his love-making quite seriously, which gives a fine effect to her work. In the later reels she, too, shifts to a less frivolous view of life, and after she has attained her triumphs as an artiste she abandons all that she strove for to devote herself to her Lucien.

The villain is not a "heavy" in this instance, nor is he asked to be. The worst that can be said of him is that he has "a way with women" and could scrub his morals a bit. But he doesn't harm the heroine.

There is considerable comedy besides the hefty emotionalism at the critical turns of the action. The photography is perfect and the scenic ambitions seem directed at realism rather than magnificence.

Garbo's name, of course, assures any picture an advance demand. But in this one she and the director have created more substance than that, and "The Divine Woman" should rank high among the program releases of the year. If John Gilbert were in it, this might play as a special. *Lait.*

COME TO MY HOUSE

Fox production and release. Directed by Alfred E. Green from the story by Arthur Somers Roche. Scenario by Marion Orth. Starring Olive Borden and Antonio Moreno. At Roxy, New York, week Jan. 14. Running time, 55 mins.

Joan Century..............Olive Borden
Floyd Bennings..............Antonio Moreno
Fraylor..............Ben Bard
Murtagh Pell..............Cornelius Keefe
Renee Parsons..............Doris Lloyd
Jimmy Parsons..............Richard Maitland

The trouble with this picture is that its entire effect is ruined by closeups of Miss Borden's toothy smiles. In its screen treatment the story is improbable and uninteresting. The picture is draggy and the major situations lack suspense, a directorial fault. The murder scenes are not shown, being merely referred to in the subtitles.

This is Miss Borden's last picture for Fox. It seems ma'e that way

The woman-hating bachelor, according to this yarn, asks a girl he meets for the first time to come to his house late at night after a party is over. The girl, Joan, had finally agreed to marry her persistent suitor, Pell, though she didn't care particularly. Following the announcement of her engagement the girl goes to the home of her new acquaintance.

She is spotted by a blackman artist and warned that unless she is prepared to pay in cash he will spread the story. Joan rushes to the city to get in touch with Bennings. He promises to take care of the blackmailer.

Subtitles tell of the murder. On trial for his life, Bennings refuses to state the reason for his crime. Joan confesses at the last moment, risking her reputation to set him free.

Court scene cold. *Mori.*

THE SILVER SLAVE

Warner Bros. production and release. Directed by Howard Bretherton. Starring Irene Rich. Adapted for screen by Peter Milne from story by Howard Smith. At the Roxy, New York, week Dec. 31. (Reviewed in projection room.) Running time, 65 minutes.

Bernice Randall..............Irene Rich
Janet Randall..............Audrey Ferris
Tom Richards..............Holmes Herbert
Philip Caldwell..............John Miljan
Larry Martin..............Carol Nye

A society picture, attractively produced and based on the familiar dramatic situation of a mother compromising herself with a rounder to show her daughter what a cad he really is. It is entertaining as a whole for any type of audience and should bring average money to full and split week houses.

The usual s. a. failing of pictures whose stars play matronly roles is overcome in this instance by Audrey Ferris as the daughter, who can act moderately and looks hot in a bathing suit or low-neck gown.

Irene Rich is a natural as a mother, conveying the maturity of her part and at the same time appearing appealingly pretty. Similarly attractive is Holmes Herbert as her suitor, also a seasoned actor. Carol Nye, the daughter's righteous boy friend, is all right in an easy role, and John Miljan as the man of the world is able to be somewhat likeable, though villainous.

The theme concerns the destructive qualities money sometimes influences over love. A widow marries one gent when she loves another, because one has dough. He dies, but she won't marry the other because her late husband's will cuts her off if she does, and she wants to raise her daughter right.

Later she alters her viewpoint and encourages her daughter to marry a poor but honest boy. The daughter, spoiled, says nix and goes after a rich and naughty guy. By compromising herself with the vag in the presence of her daughter, the mother shows him up as a heel. And the mother's original lover sees all and takes her in his arms.

The story is planted in classy interiors and summer resort scenes. Bretherton did a pleasing job all around.

WOLF'S TRAIL

Universal production and release. Directed by Francis Ford. Star, trained dog, Dynamite. Story by Basil Dickey. Half double feature day at Columbus, New York, one day, Dec. 29. Running time, 50 minutes.

Made by Universal years ago. Apparently U is using where exhibs demand a real low case buy when figuring on a double feature day. It is that kind o' a picture.

Story of the outdoors, with a Texas Ranger palming himself off as a two-fisted gun-toter of "one-gun" fame. He goes right into a den of moonshiners. "Dynamite," the police dog, is there, too.

Not much to hold this one up other than the dog.

Old age is just about lambasting this one to a frazzle. It won't be long before U won't be able to give it away. *Mark.*

PRETTY CLOTHES

Sherling production and release. From story by Peggy Gaddis. Directed by Phil Rosen. Co-featured are Jobyna Ralston, Johnny Walker and Gertrude Astor. Cast also includes Lloyd Whitlock, Charles Cleary, Jack Mower, Lydia Knott. One-half double feature, one day, Dec. 26, at Loew's Circle, New York. Running time, 60 minutes.

An independent that has a light story, but does well in a way with its cast, although Jobyna Ralston has little to do. Bulk of the screen work falls on Gertrude Astor and Johnnie Walker. Miss Astor just about walks away with the film.

Photography is immense. Some corking shots. Story is clean, wholesome and will stand up in the neighborhoods.

There appeared to be a tendency to pad out some of the old home scenes where the mother, ill, awaits the return of her little daughter, who has fallen for a rich boy only to have her love affair burst until the end.

It's the old gag of the poor working gal who longs for pretty clothes and gets them, only here she retained her baby innocence by insisting that she got them as a loan.

Picture will show to best advantage on double feature days. *Mark.*

TWO "FORTUNE HUNTER" REVIEWS

Below are paralleled reviews on Warners' "Fortune Hunter." One was caught last week in Warners' projection room and the other at Keith's Hippodrome. The projection room running was 80 minutes; at the Hip 68 minutes.

In the projection room the picture was run off to the Vitaphone musical accompaniment, with Hip having but its house organ.

As it is the first time a Warner picture has been caught the same week with and without the Vitaphone attachment, and additionally through the projection room and theatre showing by two different reviewers, the reviews are paralleled.

There is no talk or singing in the Vitaphone scored picture, Vita giving the accompaniment only.

FORTUNE HUNTER

Warner Brothers' production and release. Starring Syd Chaplin. Adapted from Winchell Smith's play by the same name and directed by C. F. Reisner. Amongst cast: Erville Alderson, Helene Costello, Paul Kruger, Thomas Jefferson and Clara Horton. At the Hippodrome, New York, week Jan. 9. Running time, 68 mins.

Playing Broadway's reformatory for pictures over which studio supervision has had little or no control. The tough part is that the good independents occasionally slipping in at this house have to suffer before they even start from the stigma left by their big brothers. "The Fortune Hunter" is a staunch supporter of the Hip's current film entertainment record. That it is playing there is the story of its possibilities and limitations.

A bad picture for the Chaplin-Reisner combine. That John Barrymore once played this comedy on the stage isn't going to help the film. That was too long ago. A 68-minute unreeling left the idea that the picture is strictly a subject for the twice and thrice weekly changes. If it stays a week anywhere the stage or screen support will have to be heavy.

Neither the director or the star seems to have bothered to break in or try out any new gags. Plenty of gags, though, and most of 'em of the vintage we'd like to have our Scotch. Chaplin uses a soda fountain faucet to squirt it around promiscuously, sweeps enough dust out of a store to have the village fire fighters come running and does a comedy love scene with a dummy, the illusion of the wax figure being alive obtained by Chaplin's use of one of his arms—a throwback to Buster Keaton choking himself when Ma and Pa Keaton were in the act. Beyond that, there's some boarding house stuff with a fresh kid and a bean shooter. This sequence eventually gets into the dining room for footage which a pair of scissors would help.

Chaplin starts out as a cafe's strong man with jurisdiction over the dance floor. Flashing a former jailmate in a tuxedo leads to the information that the pal has married small town money, the latter offering to bankroll the comedian's entrance into the same village and for a similar purpose—the financial split to take place after a marriage.

A fraudulent front sets Chaplin with the church element, he's pursued by the banker's daughter (Helene Costello), but falls for the old druggist and the granddaughter, who are about to be dispossessed. How he puts the drug store over takes up the rest of the running, until he weds his boss' ward.

Picture has no outstanding production to assist in holding it up and there's very little to it outside of Chaplin. And when Syd Chaplin is not too funny in a Chaplin picture the result is likely to be quite unfunny. In this instance it's a case of too much Chaplin in too much punchless action. Something like a quarter of a house at the Hip snickered fairly consistently, but at no time threatened to howl. Just one of those passably amusing items that should do all right on the Syd Chaplin name where the b. o. tariff isn't too high. Nary a supporting cast member stands out.

In a situation such as this, Chaplin and Reisner probably lighted Murads. *Sid.*

FORTUNE HUNTER

Warner Bros. production starring Syd Chaplin, directed by Charles F. Reisner. Full musical score by Vitaphone. Helene Costello featured. Scenario by Bryan Foy and Robert Dillon, from the play of same name by Winchell Smith. Sandy Roth, assistant director. Ed Du Par, cameraman. Projection room. Running time, 80 minutes (6,639 feet).

Nat Duncan	Syd Chaplin
Josie Lockwood	Helene Costello
Betty Graham	Clara Horton
Handsome Harry West	Duke Martin
Sam Graham	Thomas Jefferson
Blinky Lockwood	Erville Alderson
Roland	Paul Kruger
Betty Carpenter	Nora Cecil
Dry Goods Store Owner	Louise Carver
Sheriff	Bob Perry
Waitress	Babe London

Winchell Smith's whimsically sentimental play of 1910 or thereabouts has been made into an uproarious gag comedy for the screen, one that will cash in with the average of fandom because of its sometimes heavy handed humor. In short, it's another of those play transcriptions that makes terrible art but first rate business.

Chaplin, in the role once glorified by John Barrymore on the stage, has his moments. Indeed this is one of the best things he has done. Compared to "Charley's Aunt," it is subtle and delicate, of course, but even that leaves something to be desired.

Syd has his moments of legitimate farce, and it's upon one of these and upon the full length Vitaphone orchestral accompaniment that the picture will win its way to a pretty certain box office success. The passage in question is entirely a studio invention and has no basis in the play.

Nat's engagement to the village belle has been announced without his consent and he is scheming to break it without jilting her. To this end he sits upon a sofa with a wax clothes model at his side and so manipulates his own hands that it looks like a violent necking party. All the people at the bazaar see the performance through door hangings and assume the worst.

A fine bit of gag trickery, vigorous enough to upset a screen audience and sure to provoke comment. The rest of the story is similarly dressed out in broad humor, most of it hoked up to a fare ye well.

The soda clerk who cracks a bad egg into a lady customer's glass is a fair sample of the humor, worked up as it is with elaborate business of agony and discomfort of everybody thereabouts.

Much of the fun is of this style, although Chaplin's pantomime in the drug store window, selling a cure-all to the rube population is at times genuinely funny, and the comedy fire in the drug store (it's really floating dust that looks like smoke), and the travesty local fire company's efforts to quench the "blaze" has a certain touch of Sennett effectiveness.

The picture discloses Chaplin, in short, as a comedian with possibilities in a legitimate way. He has scenes that disclose some of the family knack of vivid pantomime, and here he does without any grotesque accessories of make up or dressing. It's a one-part piece, of course, and everybody works up to the star, but Chaplin does put over adequately a straight comedy role as distinguished from his former broad farce effects.

A glaring bit of miscasting puts the rather insipid Clara Horton in a sympathetic role, while the vivid Helene Costello is Josie Lockwood, who represents in this particular bit of fiction the role of Cinderella's step-sister, a part in which she is quite thrown away. The rural types are excellent, furnishing an endless variety of incidental comedy while the simple settings serve as an appropriate background without achieving anything important in a production way, as, of course, was inevitable.

The opening has a neat twist. Nat is a bouncer in a dance hall (instead of the poor but well bred young city dweller, as in the play) The place is a resort of the tough mob and the dance floor is a roped arena like a prize ring. Couples getting up to dance have to climb through the ropes and this is made the occasion of some really funny titles and shots at a lot of girls' legs. It makes an arresting start for the film, even if it does rather punish Smith's original play. *Rush.*

ON YOUR TOES

Universal production and release. Starring Reginald Denny. Story by Earl Snell with Fred Newmeyer directing. Ross Fisher, cameraman. At Colony, New York, week January 7. Running time, 60 mins.

Kane Halliday	Reginald Denny
Mary Sullivan	Barbara Worth
Jack Sullivan	Hayden Stevenson
Mello	Frank Hagney
Grandmother	Mary Carr
Mammy	Gertrude Howard

Reg Denny in the ring again and really a throwback to the "Leather Pushers." Therefore, more of a picture to the liking of male patronage. The women have certified that prize fight titles or padded arena lithos will keep them away, besides which the love interest here isn't too strong. Hence, the men should like it, and get a few laughs, but the picture won't get both sexes on a vote.

The "Leather Pushers" rehash is brought in through Kane Halliday (Denny) actually being the son of Kid Roberts, the central figure in Witwer's ring series. And Jack Sullivan (Hayden Stevenson) is again cast as the hero's manager although, here, he doesn't personally tell the story to the camera as formerly or as in the "Collegians." A technical blunder is that Sullivan looks no older in guiding the son than when he was splitting percentages with the boy's dad.

Comedy in the yarn is brought about through Kane, Jr., having a doting grandmother who wants him to be an aesthetic dancer. A failure in his New York studio, young Kane, unaware of his father's ring prestige, finally dons the gloves after flattening Sullivan's heavyweight prospect in a taxicab row. The main laughs center around the training camp, prior to the big fight, when grandmama arrives and Kane turns the quarters into a studio to line up his hard boiled retinue for an improvised routine of ballet work. That the battle and victory over the champ is only won after the grey haired parent arrives at the arena to stop the struggle, and decides to stay to see her boy win, follows in natural order. The girl in the case (Miss Worth) is the manager's daughter. Another comedy touch is that whenever Kane gets mad his ears wiggle, a family trait. This runs throughout the film and never failed to draw a giggle.

The picture couldn't have cost U. much as the company has made so many of these ring stories. Close-ups of Kane and Mello going to it during the championship bout show a vacant balcony as background, but otherwise the ring stuff looks natural and Denny makes it realistic. Not as good as some of his previous lens affrays, however. Cast support is okay all around with Denny's performance a good one.

Laughs, action and pointed for the men. If not aimed, that's the mark it will have to hit to get anywhere. "On Your Toes" looks like a tough matinee proposition but should appease night clientele. *Sid.*

THE WARNING

Columbia production and release. Directed by George B. Seitz. Jack Holt starred. Cast includes Dorothy Revier, Pat Harmon, Frank Lachteen and Norman Trevor. Photographed by Ray June from adaption of story by Lillian Ducey. At Broadway, New York, week Jan. 2. Running time, 78 minutes

A money-maker for Columbia.

The houses buying their stuff from the independents will be surprised when they get a flash of the production. Seitz did a job of directing that lacks nothing in putting the story over forcefully and he was aided not a little by Ray June at the camera, who can shoot with the best of the boys working without the aid of magic.

The one bad boy is that the hero turns out to be secret service operator No. 24. Probably that will scare away some of the de luxe houses, but it will make things all the better in other quarters.

Jack Holt has a role here that fits him and he swaggers through it with enough romanticism to catch the admiration of any flap. As a mysterious ship owner, past unknown, he is in company with a gang of Hong Kong opium smuglers.

London Charlie, one of the boys has a secret service dame captive. Holt fights the mob off and lets her escape, later making it appear he took her to his room for a make and she blew out on him.

The gal gets her partner and the Chinese police primed for a raid on the gang's cavern headquarters, only to be betrayed by her partner, secretly a member of the smugglers and delivers her back to them.

Again Holt pulls a fighting rescue this time with a machine gun and hand grenades. In the hospital, recovering from his wounds, he takes the gal (s. s. 63) in his arms when he is revealed as s. s. No. 24.

This plot reads very honkytonk, but is skillfully handled by Seitz. Especially impressive in production is the sequence in the smuggler's cavern, a mammoth place with a towering series of stone steps. Shots of the mob rushing Holt and the girl, at the top with the machine gun, impart quite a kick for any audience.

Holt has good support in Pat Harmon as London Charlie, with whom he stages a corking fist fight early in the footage. Dorothy Revier as the femme interest shows lack of expressive ability, looking permanently incredulous, but has looks. Others are okay.

Seitz and June deserve plenty of credit for this film.

Let 'Er Go Gallagher

Pathe release of a De Mille production. Starring Junior Coghlan. Directed by Elmer Clifton. From the story by Richard Harding Davis. Cast including Harrison Ford and Elinor Faire. At the Hippodrome, N. Y., week of Jan. 16. Running time, about 60 mins.

A Pathe release finally built along lines intended to harmonize with box-office results. Not an exceptional production, it rates well as a program picture for use on the tail-end of strong vaudeville or in the split-week film stands. Junior Coghlan, juvenile player, is not sufficiently appealing to carry the picture as a star, though he merits more than average consideration.

It's a newspaper yarn with the most interesting character, the swell-headed cub reporter, handled in an unsympathetic vein and so causing a partial loss of interest.

This same cub is shown as a stew, asleep on the job several times while a murder story is breaking. It is difficult to drum up attention after that.

Action revolves round a thug known as Four-Fingered Dan. The kid, Junior, a tattered newsboy, witnesses an actual shooting and hands the reporter a front-page yarn. After being discharged for failing to keep on the story, incidentally losing his gal, the cub figures his only chance to regain prestige is to capture the yegg himself for the purpose of a first person story.

The newsboy trails the thief into the woods, is almost killed when discovered, and saved through the appearance of the reporter and a sleuth from headquarters. *Mori.*

A Chinese Bungalow

(BRITISH MADE)

Toronto, Jan. 6.

Oscar Stahl English production, released by Regal Films. From stage play by same name. Direction, titling or photography not credited. At Tivoli (F. P.), Toronto. Running time, 56 minutes.

Yuan Sing	Matheson Lang
Richard Marquess	Shayle Gardner
Harold Marquess	George Thirwell
Abdul, servant	Clifford McLagan
Chinese servant	George Butler
Chinese servant	Louis Miller
Ayah	Evelyn Gardiner
Charlotte	Genevieve Townsend
Sadie	Juliette Compton

One of the best general program celluloid melodramas to come from England. If released in the U. S. should prove competition to the common garden variety of home product.

The title means nothing except to link it up with the stage play. Something snappier would be a help.

Seldom, if ever, before has the entire cast of a stage success been chosen for the film version of the same piece, but that is what happens here and the legit actors make a good job of it.

Matheson Lang, whose hobby seems to be Chinese parts, is not quite hep to the tricks of picture makeup, but his performance leaves nothing short.

An English girl in the chorus of a revue playing near Singapore is abducted by servants of Yuan Sing (Lang), a wealthy and educated Mandarin. She grows to love him and becomes his wife. Her sister (Miss Townsend) joins her in the elaborate "bungalow."

Harold Marquess, just out from England, breezes in from a nearby rubber plantation, falls for Mrs. Sing and gets in some hot lip work while Charlotte protests and the Chinese servants peek around corners.

Sing returns and coldly lets them all know he is wise. The boy lover suddenly dies from fever. His brother comes to find what it's all about. He falls for Charlotte. Sing meantime has fallen for her himself and gives her the chance to marry him or see her sister killed.

Marquess smashes in to start shooting, but the Mandarin calms him, serves wine and tells him one of the glasses contains poison. It is for him to choose. He picks the good glass and when nothing happens to himself tells Sing he is bluffing and leaves with the two girls. Fadeout on the Chinaman dying from a painful poison.

The work of the five principals shows England to be rapidly getting over the awkward stage in film production. Miss Townsend, looker, was particularly effective as the distraught wallflower who suddenly finds herself much in demand. George Thirwell as the juvenile was a trifle frightened. Titles, in Chinese type, were good.

This one will certainly be in demand in Canada. *Sinclair.*

THE NEST

Excellent production, featuring Pauline Frederick and Holmes Herbert. Directed by William Nigh, from story by Paul Giraldy. Cast includes Jean Acker, Ruth Dwyer, Rolland Flander, Reginald Sheffield. Photographed by Jack Brown and Harry Spradling. At Tivoli, New York, one day (Dec. 28) on double-feature bill. Running time, 78 minutes.

Inferior photography is a drawback for this picture. Otherwise it seems good enough for the neighborhood split-week vaude houses not too particular about their pictures. These houses might take a chance on it as is, but its natural destination is the daily change.

Pauline Frederick and Holmes Herbert with plenty of picture experience behind them, and William Nigh, who directed, furnish the film's value. They had a workable story by Paul Giraldy, and did nicely with it considering the probable budget and the rather faint talent among the support.

Those two cameramen, though—

Story is humanely handled, concerning a widow's tribulations with a wild son and daughter, who between them appear set on raising the particular dickens. The kid gets mixed up with a dame who frames him for the works and he gets as low as forgery before she's through with him.

Daughter marries before she's old enough to know, and starts having trouble with her husband.

Back of these two problems is the widow's fight to retain her attractiveness despite overwhelming worries and her pride in refusing to marry the executor of her estate, who loves the widow and wants to help her show the kids where to get off.

Miss Frederick plays understandingly and has good support in Holmes Herbert, who looks like a matured John Barrymore. None of the juvenile parts is more than fair, with Reginald Sheffield as the wayward son getting best results.

Jean Acker as the vamp looked flat.

THE AIR PATROL

One of the Universal "thrill" series. Story by the star, Al Wilson. Directed by Bruce Mitchell. Cameraman, W. S. Adams. In the cast, Elsa Benham, Taylor Duncan, Jack Mower, Monte Montague. At Columbus, New York, one day, Jan. 4, on double feature bill. Running time, 48 mins.

Aviation pictures threaten to become as numerous as the dogs'. Simple, sure method of getting "action" into 5,000 odd feet of film. To date the stunt flyers have offered some unenticing flickers, due principally to the slim bankroll.

"The Air Patrol," while a long way from being either expensive or clever, is an improvement of a sort over some that have been seen.

Al Wilson authored his own script on accepted patterns. He does some plane-to-plane hopping and other stunts appearing more foolhardy than real. There is a sorry effort to inject comedy relief in the person of one Monte Montague and there are a dozen minor male characters, all wearing mustaches. Elsa Benham wears curls and looks a bit silly.

Fourth-rate stuff for customers with elementary tastes.

THE RAWHIDE KID

Universal production and release. Starring Hoot Gibson. Directed by Del Andrews from story by Peter B. Kyne. Cast includes Georgia Hale, Frank Hagney, Wm H. Strauss, Harry Todd. Photographed by Harry Neumann. At Tivoli, New York, one day (Dec. 28) on double-feature bill. Usual feature running time.

Somewhat below the average Hoot Gibson footage, but the western fans probably won't notice that. There's some healthy socking, as always, and a finale of fast horseback stuff.

Hoot appoints himself defender of a Hebe peddler and his daughter, who came west to corner a virgin market. Within a short time the peddler has half the town and the villain the other half.

Each stakes his share on the outcome of a horse race, in which Hoot bests the villain for the peddler and gets the gal for himself.

Hebe character is a novelty in westerns and well acted by William H. Strauss. Georgia Hale looks fair, and Hoot is Hoot.

Story weak because of incongruity—even considering it's a western. Directing good in spots and fair in others.

STAGE KISSES

Columbia production and release. Directed by Albert Kelly. Kenneth Harlan and Helen Chadwick co-featured. Cast includes John Patrick, Phillips Smalley, Ethel Wales, Frances Raymond. At Loew's Circle, New York, one day, Jan. 7. Running time, 66 mins.

Rehash of a story that has been done time and again in the pictures. Nothing unusual in it, could be told in two reels. Double feature placement.

A rich boy falls in love with a girl who must earn her living on the stage. She tries to live like other well regulated domestics, but a compromising scene where another man is found in her boudoir sends the hubby off his nut with the belief that like stage kisses his marriage is phoney boloney.

But the love stuff is the real thing for the gal. She schemes to show both her husband and his rich old daddy how she had been a victim of circumstantial evidence. She enacts a similar scene on her son's father and it works.

Not much of a kick, although set up by wife with the old man well staged. It may have looked stronger on paper than it did on the screen.

Helen Chadwick as the wife gets much from her part. Kenneth Harlan is big-lettered. Phillips Smalley, as the father, makes him look foolish as an actor. Number of very good shots, interiors and exteriors, yet noticeable wastes of celluloid. *Mark.*

TARAS BULBA

[POLISH MADE]

Produced in Poland. Directed by J. M. Ermolieff. Based on the novel by N. V. Gogol. Cast includes J. N. Douvan-Forzow, Joseph Rounitch, Helen Makowska and Oscar Marion. At the Fifth Avenue Playhouse, New York, Dec. 28. Running time, over 60 mins.

Taras Bulba might have been a ferocious Cossack leader in his day, but in pictures he looks like a comic opera version of an escapd convict with the hives. Hardly a figure to fire the imagination of American youth or capture the adoration of the flappers.

Taras, according to this version, struts through life with a stomach as big as a 100-gallon barrel of vodka. His facial decorations consist of two long sausage-shaped mustaches. From the center of his shaven dome droops a solitary lock of hair, also formed like a frankfurter, and looking as heroic. The Tarasian countenance, when not buried in a huge mug of booze, is almost always in repose when photographed. At times the great actor deigns to affect anger or joy but only at rare intervals.

Through the war scenes drifts a tender love motif between a mud-complexioned mama and one of Bulba's sons. There is a gold mine in these cheaply made, grotesque European productions. Someone will yet grab a picture like "Bulba" and turn it loose as a farce after recutting and burlesquing with subtitles.

The story is meaningless as far as American audiences are concerned. It seems that once upon a time the Russians were cruelly oppressed by the Polyaks and other factions, which were later harnessed under the sovereignty of a czar. Taras Bulba led a group of Cossacks who protected one of the Russian boundaries.

His two sons went with him after leaving school. One of the boys flopped for the daughter of the Polish Governor and forsook his father's troops to join the Polyaks. This boy was later caught on the field of war by his old man and shot. The other son was captured by the Polyaks and hanged. Then they got the old boy and burned him alive. Anyone who would stop to look for a pipe while being chased by a regiment of angry soldiers, especially Polyak soldiers, deserved to be burned.

They'll pass this up without losing any sleep. And, if anyone should ask, Polyak is the way it's pronounced. *Mori.*

BROADWAY MADNESS

Samuel Zeiler presents an "Excellent" (brand) (state rights) picture. Directed by Burton King. Story, scenario and titles by Harry Chandlee. Cameraman, Art Reeves. Marguerite de la Motte featured. Cast includes Louis Payne, Donald Keith, Tom Ricketts, Orral Humphries, George Cowl. At Loew's New York on double bill, one day, Dec. 29. Running time, 53 minutes.

A better than average state righter. Usual hokum about the Broadway wise dame regenerated by the moral influences of a small town and one of those clean-minded juveniles.

Production has enough class to get picture by without the stigma of being a "quickie."

Cabaret scenes will appeal to the yap communities as being quite hotsy-totsy. Towns having cabarets will find it funny. Especially droll is the enthusiastic applause given the table-singing cutie.

The gold-digger takes a detour out of Times Square for the purpose of collecting a legacy of a quarter millio. Nobody has ever seen the real heiress, who died in the gold-digger's arms.

The masquerade calls for a two-year residence in a one-street village, as the money is in trust for that time.

There is villainy from a New York racketeer, who wears a wall-paper shirt, and the small-town skinflint who is getting the use of the money, which really belongs to the clean-minded juvenile.

Well-known players and fair direction make "Broadway Madness" an okay program.

WHEN DANGER CALLS

Sam Sax production, released by Lumas. Directed by Charles Hutchinson from story by Ben Allah. Cameraman William Reis. William Fairbanks and Eileen Sedgwick featured. Cast includes Hank Mann, Ethan Laidlaw, Don McDonald, Sally Long. At Stanley, New York, one day, Jan. 7. Running time, 54 mins.

Meritorious subject well handled around conventional fire department heroics. It concerns the efforts of a young fire inspector to condemn fire traps over the opposition of politicians. Good effort in its class.

Marsden, a chiseler, unloads a group of tenements on the heroine. He knows they will be condemned as the result of a recent tragedy in another tenement. The heroine is running a mission for 'boes and doesn't understand the attitude of the fire inspector toward her property, which yields her the money to carry on her work.

Eileen Sedgwick, away from the screen for some time recovering from injuries received doing stunts in western and railroad yarns, plays the heroine. Fairbanks, capable athletic star of the minor leagues, impersonates civic virtue acceptably. Hank Mann, one time comic of walrus mustache and large pants, works straight as a slightly dumb handy Andy, who is the inspector's man Friday. He gets some laughs without pies.

Fire stuff is good, some of its probably library clips, but effective.

Siren of the Tropics
(FRENCH MADE)

Paris, Jan. 8.

Maurice Dekobra did the scenario on this French picture produced for Centrale Cinematographique by Nalpas 'and H. Etievant, mostly in the suburbs of Paris. The apparent object is to feature Josephine Baker, colored vaudeville performer still playing in a local revue, who reveals herself a fair screen actress, while there are some thrilling scenes, with good camera work, picture cannot be listed as a successful release.

Plot: Berval is sent to the West Indies by capitalist, Severo, to get him out of the way from Denise, to whom the young fellow is secretly engaged. Severo, although married, wants the girl himself, and he instructs his confederate, Alvarez, to prevent Berval returning. On his arrival in the tropics Berval saves a colored damsel, Papitou (Miss Baker) from Alvarez's forced embrace, and the girl henceforth becomes his willing slave. She is able to help Berval when he falls down a precipice, due to the treachery of Severo's assistants. Meanwhile, Mme. Severo and Denise have arrived in the village to take .the victim home. They are followed to France by Papitou, who boards another steamer by a subterfuge leading up to brisk comedy, but she has lost trace of her beau. The beautiful negress becomes a children's nurse in Paris, is found by an impresario and becomes a popular star. She eventually finds Berval and is innocently instrumental in his marriage with Denise being canceled. In the end Papitou explains how she was hoodwinked by Severo, brings about a reconciliation of the lovers, and quits broken hearted, returning to her native clime.

The film is being released this week by Aubert. *Kendrew.*

FIGURES DON'T LIE

Paramount production and release. Directed by Edward Sutherland from the story by B. F. Zeidman. Screen adaptation by Grover Jones. Titles by Herman Mancklewicz. Starring Esther Ralston. Cast includes Richard Arlen, Ford Sterling, Eulalie Jensen and Natalie Kingston. At Loew's American, New York, four days starting Dec. 29. Running time, over 60 minutes.

Program picture good enough for full weeks in minor houses. No originality in the gagging but nice delivery by Ford Sterling and Miss Ralston, with old material, gets laughs. Many worse than this have been shown in Broadway houses during the past few weeks. It was probably figured that the names here would not be strong enough to draw in the straight picture houses.

Story is about the assertive, self-sure young man who laughs himself into a sales managing job on conceit and wise cracks to keep it by showing he can sell insurance.

Comedy inserted through arguments with the gal, whom he tried to make on the street and later discovers in the office of the man he sold his idea to.

Sterling, as the absent-minded employer with strings on his fingers as reminders of appointments, was a continuous laugh to the customers here in the picture's limited way.

Greater care might have been shown in closeups of the fem star. Looks okey, and especially so in bathing suit. But camera caught her face at some queer angles with the results unsatisfactory in those cases.

Richard Arlen in it too, but no chance to shine. *Mori.*

YOUR WIFE AND MINE

Samuel Zeller production "Excellent" (states right) picture, featuring Phyllis Haver. Directed by Frank O'Connor. Cast includes Stuart Holmes, Wallace MacDonald, Barbara Tennant. At Columbus, New York, on double bill, one day, Dec. 28. Running time, 50 minutes.

Usual sort of product resulting from a decision in Hollywood to make a farce comedy dealing with a scramble of husbands and wives. Laughs are non-existent for any one of any sort of sophistication, but conceivably may be present for the naive settlers of the distant provinces.

The moral of these leaping lithographs appears to be that hubby should not fib to wifey. It leads to fist fights and police stations and the eating of "humble pie" by the hubby. This picture shows a hotel dick placing under arrest and dragging through a crowded lobby a whole floor full of assorted spouses.

Picture qualifies as regulation state rights stuff, fair as to production and directorial quality and with several well-known players in it.

Cautious exhibs will look at it first.

SECRETS OF A SOUL
(GERMAN MADE)

Ufa production. Directed by G. W. Pabst. Featuring Werner Kraus and Ruth Weyher. Scenario by Colin Ross. Cameraman, Guido Seeber. At the 55th Street Cinema, N. Y., Jan. 12. Running time, 63 minutes.

Neither the stage or the screen has ever been very successful in getting across dramatic entertainment when the theme rotates about the self-torture of a quasi-demented neurotic. This German film comes about as near to holding the spectator's interest in the subject as anything yet attempted. But it falls considerably below popular standards of diversion.

It is labeled "a graphic explanation of the theory of psychoanalysis" and is all of that. From the standpoint of a trade paper it may be dismissed simply by saying it is not a commercial subject and will not receive commercial exhibition save by Mike Mindlin. It is, however, an interesting film well done and valuable as a possible indicator of the form pictures might conceivably take in the dim distant future.

It's safe to say that only in Germany would the theme be used, and only there could it be used with such intelligence. Without any of the conventional ingredients of dramatic action, a clinical study of a mind temporarily twisted is dissected and made absorbing.

Photography is excellent, unusual and arresting throughout. Ditto for direction. Werner Kraus looks like another Jannings here. Espe-

cially powerful is a scene where he gets shaved while suffering with a horrible phobia-fear of a razor. Menjou did a similar bit, out for comedy, in a recent picture.

CONFETTI
(BRITISH MADE)

London, Jan. 4.

First National British Production. Story by Douglas Furber. Directed by Graham Cutts. Art direction, N. G. Arnold. Photography, Roy Overbaugh. Censors' Certificate, U. Running time, 72 minutes. Previewed at Hippodome, London.

Count Andrea della Zorro..Jack Buchanan
Dolores ....Annette Benson
Carlo ....Robin Irvine
Roxane ....Audree Sayre
Grand Duchess Maxixe..Sydney Fairbrotner

This, the first British film to be made as a quota contribution by First National, succeeds on one score and fails on three.

Technically it is almost without blemish; continuity, sets, lights, dressing all there. Cast pretty good, too. But the total effect is as if some one had spent a lot of time putting a diamond polish on a piece of bottle glass. For the story is card-index stuff and all the cars in the Nice carnivals have been seen so many times.

Besides which, the picture never comes to life. There's no punch in the direction; the artists under-act or overact, according to their immediate moods. The film gives the impression of the director having little interest in it outside some of the mob scenes.

Count Zorro (not related to the Fairbanks family of Zorros) is 40 and still looks youthful. Dolores is 30 and looks even more so. He loves her and she loves him, and he is about to propose on the first night of the carnival when Grand Duchess aunt arrives with Roxane, a baby flapper, whom she designs for Andrea. He falls for her till he finds she is in the kindergarten class in ideas and tastes.

Then he swings back to Dolores, and the baby girl hooks up with little boy Carlos, aunt having meantime explained to Andrea her idea was revenge for having been disappointed in a youthful love affair of her own. Ends with confetti cutter, who has run through the picture as a kind of Greek chorus, turning out to be the love of the Duchess' ill-spent youth.

Not so much of a story, but possibilities aplenty for character building and clashes, which are missing. Sydney Fairbrother mugs too much as the Duchess and makes what should be an ironic figure almost grotesque. Audree Sayre has been canvassed as a find, but does not show it in this film. She is self-conscious and naive and occasionally appears as if she is a bit camera shy. Fair looker and may have possibilities when more forcibly directed. Annette Benson looks good and troups well, but the two men, Buchanan and Irvine, have little to do. Both can act, but they don't have to in this.

Just a program picture with a higher polish than this class usually gets. Little dramatic value and not a kick. *Frat.*

A CHANGE OF HEART
(FRENCH MADE)

Paris, Jan. 15.

The novel of Maurice Dekobra, now in the limelight, serves as the scenario for this French picture released by Paramount. The writer has a circle of readers and his name should attract at present.

The title is fairly well known as a "best seller" of the moment, and the screen version of Marco de Gastyne closely follows the book. The action is laid in New York (with views of the city), and Venice, the picture being creditably produced by Natan.

Mrs. Turner, wealthy widow, is courted by many suitors. By the terms of her late husband's will she loses the fortune should she marry and then divorce, the money going to a daughter by a former marriage. Dextrier, handsome aristocrat, on his uppers in New York, is enlisted by a corporation, headed by a rejected prince, to win Mrs. Turner's hand, and easily marries the widow. The couple spend their honeymoon in Italy. For some unexplainable reason Dextrier becomes tied up in an intrigue with his wife's step-daughter, now a drug fiend. This leads to a separation, the man returning alone to France.

Annette Benson impersonates the rich widow, but does not seem at home in the part: Choura Milena makes good as the step-daughter; Philippe Heriat is the villain, showing himself a true actor, while Olaf Fjord holds the part of the young husband with distinction.

It is doubtful for the Anglo-Saxon market because of the poor story. Productionally, it might surprise.

Kendrew.

THE LAST COMMAND

Paramount production and release. Emil Jannings starred. Directed by Josef von Sternberg. Supervised by Joseph Bachman. Adapted by John F. Goodrich from original by Lajos Biro. Titles by Herman J. Mankiewicz. Opened on run at Rialto, New York, January 21; 99c. top. Running time, 90 minutes. Present length, 8,154 feet.

General Dolgorucki..........Emil Jannings
Natascha.....................Evelyn Brent
Leo..........................William Powell
Adjutant................Nicholas Soussanin
Serge, valet.................Michael Visaroff

Jannings must be fitted. He's an actor. Maybe that is why Jannings is always the actor. He gets the **stories. And "The Last Command"** is no exception, either side. It's exceptional for a regular program release, even for Paramount, and a model for every newspaper writer anywhere to advocate that their readers see it, if giving no other reason than it should be seen to elevate the common impression of the popular price screen.

Perhaps the flaps and their saps will not rave over this picture. There may be too many whiskers in it for the girls and not enough mush for the simps, but a picture such as this breaks in neatly and nicely as against the background of the screen's vapory array of mostly nothing at all in substance.

A few more similar program pictures and it's possible, but barely, that the babes might be partially educated away from doll maps and funny mustaches. Yet there are enough American followers of this imported star, though here but a comparatively short time, to compose his own audiences and enough of others to appreciate what a really fine photoplay is "The Last Command."

Jannings is an elegant and eloquent actor. That covers it all on that end. But it must be surmised that he is no less a director, the latter in no disparagement of Josef Von Sternberg's work here, but more because every time a Jannings picture comes out, all of the actors in it are acting.

Evelyn Brent you will like immediately, and William Powell, giving a corking performance in a double sided role.

Story made quite interesting through its base and that base is a studio in Hollywood. To bring it out more sharply and push in the mellers, a cut back goes to Russia in the early days of the war and the revolution. There Jannings is the commander-in-chief of the Czar's armies in the field. This picture's working title was "The General."

Imperialistic in Russia and the cousin of the Czar, whom he defied when instructed to have a play offensive for that guy early one morning, the general, overthrown and overwhelmed by the revolutionists, drifts to Hollywood, to become a $7.50 a day extra waiting in a rooming house for a call.

It comes when a Russian picture director requiring a movie army recognizes a photo of the general as the same who whipped him in Russia in 1914, when the director then was a starving actor-revolutionist.

They make him a general again, at $7.50 daily, with many studio scenes, to lead a movie army of Russians. This he does, shaken and halting until the director calls for "music" and the Russian Anthem is played, mostly on the piano. Now the general is himself once more, again employs his whip to strike down the foolhardy and goes to his death on the picture platform while leading his suping forces.

You believe it all because Jannings is doing it, although the death finale forbids any applause at the finish.

Plenty of direction and as much photography. There doesn't appear to be a miss or skip either. When considered that a picture of this magnitude was 90 percent made on the Paramount lot in Hollywood, one may marvel over what there is yet to arrive in picture making, saying that if nothing else and remembering the army before the Russian headquarters in the field.

Herman Mankiewicz's titles are no small part of the interest, always perfectly placed and phrased. They hold a couple of laughs, although the subjects matter limits that.

A most substantial high grade picture with the Paramount's press sheet for "The Last Command" describing it accurately with its screamer front page head saying: "Another Great American-Made Jannings Hit."

SIMBA

(WILD ANIMAL FILM)

Martin Johnson African Expedition Corp., Daniel E. Pomeroy, pres., producer. Billed as "A Natural History Picture." Cameraed by Mr. and Mrs. Martin Johnson, with native cameramen as assistants, in Africa. Titles and prolog by Terry Ramsaye. At Earl Carroll theatre, New York, first public exhibition for twice daily run Jan. 23 at $1.65 top. Running time, around 105 minutes.

There are four standout scenes in "Simba" (meaning "Lion"), the Johnsons' animal picture. Two are new to the screen and two may have to go out to preserve what there is of feminine patronage for this character of film.

An elephant herd in the wild, and seemingly wild without trainers or of the ranch type, and a herd of lions. The lion herd is probably the largest ever viewed on the screen. A caption so announces and claims 14.

The questionable scenes for the good of the picture are those of two lions tearing a zebra apart, with this view held overly long in any event, and the other of colored natives on a lion hunt who spear the animals to death, with two instances of the latter. To men this spear hunting is interesting, but not to women. It is doubtful, however, if the picture can afford to lose the spearing views. There isn't enough to the picture as a whole in its remainder to stand the loss of very much, although the vultures could be omitted without harm. All animal pictures have had that stuff, also the water-hole bits, though the Johnsons picked up a couple of new species to Americans at large at one of the water holes.

Crocodiles in abundance, rhinos in numbers and also wild boars in lots are more extensively pictured, and more, in fact, in groups than heretofore seen. The boar bit is well done on the lens end, and there is much dangerous camera work in this film with as much more pictured. Mrs. Osa Johnson is given the shots that seemingly first kill an elephant, then a boar, although no shots were aimed apparently at one of the lions, even when he was about to catch a native when dashing in among the spear carriers, the spears being their only defense.

Something new in wild animal hunting is the flashlight pictures taken of lions drawn to a trap by a zebra as bait. These become stills, showing the beasts bewildered by the flash.

The picture in its running length has plenty of pastoral scenery, also some grazing and much travelog, the latter prettily effective at times.

Billed as "A Natural History Picture" and on a probable hook-up with an historical society, the opening night's audience drew many of what must have been students viewing the scenes from that angle. From that angle this is quite a picture; from the box office slant at $1.65 it's not a heavyweight for the price as animal pictures go, and without submitting comparisons.

A descriptive caption told of the Johnsons remaining in their African location for four years, during which these views were taken. Variety has printed that the Johnsons went to Africa on their last trip in behalf of an institute or society, with the Johnsons reserving the commercial exhibition rights to the film, the title remaining vested in the sponsoring society.

The Johnsons, like the others, must be given all of the credit in the world for their nerve, not only in taking some desperate chances (which may be seen at times), but also for remaining in that jungle for four years.

The opening program was not inspiring. It started with moving scenes of the Johnsons at home and on hunting trips. Mostly travelog again in the latter, but containing the usual African native dance shots. Then a song of "Safari" to a lilting but quite familiar melody and sung by Frank Munn on a Brunswick disc, from which source Mr. Johnson's introducery talk emanated, and again a very brief talk by him ended the picture.

In between the incidental music also was from canned discs, not so fancy for $1.65.

A good advance sale was reported for this picture before it opened, extraordinary in itself, and asserting that the tie-up, whatever it is, is the picture's strongest draw. That was made evident Monday night, when the name of Daniel E. Pomeroy was applauded as it appeared on a slide. Mr. Pomeroy is the president of the Johnsons' business corporation.

Terry Ramsaye did some nice captions here, making them breezy and light often, and calling attention to the danger to the camera operator just as often.

A nice setting was given to the stage in a couple of animal cast figures, one on either side of the stage, and both said to have been borrowed from the Museum of Natural History.

BEAU SABREUR

Paramount production and release. Gary Cooper, Evelyn Brent, Noah Beery and Wm. Powell featured. Adapted from Percival Wren's story. Directed by John Waters. Cameraman, C. E. Schoenbaum with titles by Julian Johnson. At the Paramount, New York, week Jan. 21. Running time, 67 mins.

Major Henri de Beaujolais——Gary Cooper
May Vanbrugh...............Evelyn Brent
Sheikh El Hamel..............Noah Beery
Becque......................William Powell
Suleiman the Strong..........Mitchell Lewis
General de Beaujolais.......Frank Reicher

An ordinary Paramount program leader which has its best chance to get b. o. results through the story being called a "sequel" to 'Beau Geste." Billing is tagged that way, but there doesn't seem to be any further connection. Both take place on an Algerian desert. That's the closest relationship between the two films.

No mystery in this one. Just a straightaway story that's none too strong. Young Beaujolais (Gary Cooper) must get the French treaty to El Hamel (Noah Beery) to stand off native uprising and save the territory for France. Evelyn Brent is mixed up in it as an American authoress seeking atmosphere, and William Powell is the insurgent Foreign Legion member who leaves the service to steam up the disciples of Allah. A complication is that El Hamel holds up the treaty so he can secure the authoress, but finally relents on this phase for the best subtitle in the picture

Cooper makes a passable hero, Miss Brent leaves the imprint of having been miscast and Beery is under heavy wraps histrionically and physically, so that he doesn't help much on performance. His name, however, will probably mean something on the "Geste" hookup.

Battle stuff won't cause any excitement and it doesn't look like a heavy production outside of the extras on horseback. It's nice enough on camera work, plus a glass shot that gives the effect of a mirage of a city in the desert.

This tale is far under the horsepower of which "Geste" could boast, and all in all is amongst the weakest features the Paramount has shown lately. It's hardly likely to receive favorable word-of-mouth exploitation.

Sid.

SHARP SHOOTERS

Fox production and release from story by Randall H. Faye. Titles by Malcolm Stuart Boylan. Featuring George O'Brien and Lois Moran. Directed by J. G. Blystone. At the Roxy, N. Y., week of Jan. 21. Running time over 60 mins.

George.....................George O'Brien
Lorette..........................Lois Moran
Tom ....Noah Young
Jerry ....Tom Dugan
"Hi Jack" Murdock.....William Demarest
Flossy ....Gwen Lee
Grandpere ....Josef Swickard

This version of gob life on land packs a hefty wallop. Story is familiar, but the gagging in business and titles is smart and fast. Laughs are numerous. As a whole, one of the best programers turned out by Fox this season.

It is difficult to dissociate Lois Moran from her cute roles. Though she is unconvincing as the cheap cooch dancer in the Morocco cafe, she retains her personality appeal and that counts more with the fans than realistic characterization. O'Brien plays straight, while Young and Dugan, a couple of comedians, get full value from the spotting they have been given.

Story deals with the popular impression of the sailor with a girl in every town, the sharp shooter who avoids permanent entanglements. In a Mediterranean port a French dancer falls for George and believes his advances are real, despite that he tries to make her understand he is through when his ship leaves port.

Back in New York, George brings his local girl a pair of garters. A scene follows where George bends down, with nothing shown of George. The girl's face indicates that George is putting on the garters. First she grimaces, finally becomes angry, and winds up by playfully socking George.

Lorette follows George to New York, where his two mates figure the girl is on the level, and show George the fallacy of attempting to evade the laws of fate by punching him into submission. The ceremony takes place at sea.

The unwilling husband snubs his wife at the beginning. When he later decides to stick she has left home to go back to a river cafe where she had first worked. George leads a detachment of the navy to the joint. The mob fight scenes are well staged.

A couple of hot scenes stand little chance with out-of-town censors.

Mori.

A RENO DIVORCE

Warner. Bros. production. Written and directed by Ralph Graves. Screen adaptation by Robert Lord. Starring May McAvoy with cast including Ralph Graves, Hedda Hopper, Robert Ober and Anders Randolf. At Academy of Music, N. Y. Running time, about 60 minutes.

Story has no connection with the title which seems to indicate a spicy theme entirely lacking in the picture. What little opportunity the production has to be interesting is stilled by Ralph Graves, who scores a triple bust—as director, author and actor.

Every conventional piece of business known is used. Footage could be cut 50 percent. With an exceptionally strong bill at this house during the week, the picture was played only to fill in. That is about all the spotting it is worth, either to fill in or in the split weeks.

May McAvoy, with an unproductive role, manages nicely. Hedda Hopper registers for a blank.

Story begins with a youthful vice-president of a steel plant who seems inclined to favor art over steel. His father orders him out because he refuses to settle down to work.

Tramping through the streets, the painter is hit by an auto conveying the gal. Sympathy overcomes reticence and she takes him to her home to recover.

A couple of the girl's friends had been divorced. The male divorcee makes a vain play for the gal. She is willing to accept him as a friend, and when rejecting him with a kiss is spotted by the artist.

Minor complications follow with a scene where the drunken chauffeur enters the girl's room and tried to attack her in revenge for being discharged. The artist is accused and ordered to leave. The chauffeur is immediately after discovered in the girl's room.

The divorced wife (Miss Hopper) decides to wed again and picks the artist as the gent to be so honored. He doesn't seem flattered but accepts a steamship ticket to Europe as part payment for a picture he had painted of the woman. On the boat he finds himself occupying the same suite with her and is getting ready to leave when found by the poor, little rich girl.

They didn't stick through the picture here. *Mori.*

ARIZONA WILDCAT

Fox production and release, starring Tom Mix. Directed by R. W. Neill. Story by Adele Rogers St. John. In the cast, Dorothy Sebastian, Mickey Moore, Ben Bard and Cissy Fitzgerald. At Fox's Academy of Music, New York, first half week of Jan. 23. Running time, 56 mins.

A western to be sure, but somehow one that nobody needs to apologize for. The story is full of capital angles. It has an amusing comedy start with the hero as a kid (Mickey Moore), organizing an amateur rodeo which leads up to some interesting horse tricks by youngsters, ending in a runaway team with rescue by the boy hero on horseback.

A twist to the western motif is the idea of hooking it up with a high society atmosphere. This is contrived by having the cowboy hero go in for breeding and training polo ponies, which he supplies to the society polo fans. Heroine is the childhood sweetheart, now grown up and moving in the haute monde of the Pacific coast. Her brother is a polo player, and buys his mounts from Tom.

Thus, when one of brother's teammates is knocked out on the ever of an important polo match, he sends for Tom to take his place. Here we turn to the polite atmosphere for the dramatic finale, which is a polo game before a society crowd, building up to an excellent effect with fast play and good shots at the flying horses.

The heavy is the polo leader on the opposing team, a blackguard, who, of course, is only after the heroine's money. When his side is defeated and the government secret service is closing in on him for mail frauds, he abducts the girl, and it is here that Tom dashes off the polo field for the usual pursuit.

The climax is worked up with stunt riding effect rivalling the stuff that made Fairbanks famous. The kidnapper takes the girl to one of those Spanish mission palaces familiar to followers of the California made movies, and riding his mount up outside staircases, the hero gallops into the room where the villain is struggling with the girl. The stunt of riding back and forth about the house is elaborated while Tom puts the heavy's retainers to fight, finally throwing the girl across his saddle and dashing off down the steep steps and away.

It's all veritable movie hokum, exaggerated and flamboyant, but it does give a certain dime novel dramatic kick, in the way that is familiar to Mix fans. The point is that it gets away from the stereotyped westerns, goes into a fresh locale and takes interest from its society atmosphere of luxury instead of the everlasting dreary ranch house and corral.

Nicely played, with good comedy values in a hard-boiled and serious minded cowboy who falls hard for heroine's short skirted French maid. Will please the Mix fans. Picture has ingenuity and a certain elegance that raises it above the typical western to a punch melodramatic subject. *Rush.*

THE DESERT PIRATE

F. B. O. release, featuring Tom Tyler. Directed by James Dugan. At the Stanley, New York, on double-feature program, Jan. 21. Running time, 62 minutes.

Part of this picture threatened to get away from the stereotyped westerns, but it is swept into the old mill stream and founders.

Tyler puts a lot into his film characterization of the former gun-toting sheriff who eschews all the gats, yet walks into the den of killers and licks them single-handed with his fists. The picture is better than some of the other Tylers.

With the kid and dog connection it can't miss in the neighborhoods with the youngsters. Nothing unusual, but it gives unmistakable evidence that any semblance of a real story will go a long way towards giving Tyler a better break.

Some excellent photography and some very well directed sub-climaxes. A good sob scene between the hero and the kid should help. *Mark.*

Thanks for Buggy Ride

Universal production and release. Starring Laura La Plante, with Glenn Tryon featured. Directed by William A. Seiter. Titles by Tom Reed. Editorial supervision of Joseph Franklin Poland. Runs 60 minutes. At Colony, New York, week of Jan. 21.

Jenny....................Laura La Plante
Joe....................Glenn Tryon
Mr. McBride....................Richard Tucker
Joe's Pal....................Lee Moran
Dancing Master....................Jack Raymond
Harold McBride....................David Rollins
Landlady....................Kate Price
Trixie Friganza....................Trixie Friganza

All about a would-be songwriter, dancing instructress and both their efforts to sell McBride, the hard-boiled and flirtatious music publisher, a song for $10,000 in order to buy that bungalow, etc. With all the basic elements of any film—the usual boy-girl-menace-success formula—this is tricked up with a touch of the theatrical, although all of that is atmospherically unfaithful. Light stuff, but satisfactory for the young people as a one-dayer.

Miss La Plante as the dancing teacher and Glenn Tryon, song plugging from a truck, meet accidentally. Follows Tryon's efforts to sell his boss, McBride, a song manuscript. This is complicated by the gay old boy having been rebuffed by Miss La Plante. McBride does not know of our heroine's relationship to our hero, and so when the songwriter makes a date to demonstrate his stuff, with Miss La Plante assisting on the vocalization, it doesn't work out so well.

Thereafter Miss La Plante does a cork impersonation in order to crash an exclusive gathering of vaudeville's who's who, allegedly met for a demonstration of the publisher McBride's new song effusions. What a tin pan alley pipe dream that is! Anyway, Trixie Friganza, playing herself, is smitten with the hero's song, and the rest writes itself.

Title is derived from song hit of that name, which is theme of the picture.

Outside of Universal's own Colony, "Thanks for the Buggy Ride" is not a week-stand picture. *Abel.*

Ginzberg the Great

Warner Bros. production and release. Directed by Byron Haskins from story by Arthur Caldewey. Starring George Jessel with cast including Audrey Ferris, Theodore Lorch, Gertrude Astor, Douglas Gerrard, Jack Santonio. At Moss' Broadway, New York, week of Jan. 23. Running time, 60 minutes.

Byron Haskins, director, or whoever translated this continuity into action, denatured comedy scenes, spoiled continuous action and killed what little love interest it was intended to convey. All the makings for a good picture in this instance and the result is a filler for the double feature programs or the daily changes.

George Jessel, its star, is unfortunate in being its star.

Audrey Ferris is a convincing type but is kept out of the picture with the exception of a few scenes which couldn't have been kept out under any circumstances. Under proper guidance Miss Audrey would have a chance to develop. Despite cruel camera shots she maintains an attractive appearance.

Story is of a small town boy in a tailor shop with a yen to shine on Broadway as a magician. He finally gets to Broadway and does a nose dive, starting as a cleaner in a dime museum and winding up by rounding up a gang of criminals.

He returns to his home town, unaware of success, admitting failure, but is again kicked out of the tailor shop. The head of a vaude circuit whose stolen jewels were found through Ginzberg's ingenuity comes after him with a set of metropolitan newspapers, in which Ginsey is given full page spreads, and offers him a contract. *Mori.*

BACK TO LIBERTY

Commonwealth production and release. Directed by Bernard McEveety, from story by Arthur Hoerl. Starring George Walsh, with cast including Dorothy Hall, Edmund Breese, Gene Del Val and De Sachia Moones. At Loew's New York, Jan. 20, on double-feature program. Running time, over 60 minutes.

Far better than the average state right production. The picturization of this closely woven story is done with little waste of footage. Action is continuous, with no stops for lengthy closeups.

George Walsh works with a stolid front, but lacks expression in those spots where a little emotion would be suitable. Edmund Breese cops trouping honors as the ringleader of a gang of jewel thieves with a standing in society under another name. Dorothy Hall does well as the girl.

The leader's only daughter has been brought up in schools without learning of her father's activities in the underworld. Walsh, as one of the yegg's associates, meets the daughter and visits her home several times before being introduced to her father. The latter wants to keep his daughter away from the boy and dissolves partnership with him and another member of the gang (Gene Del Val).

The boy refuses to accept the money, and declares intentions of going straight for the gal, but the other member of the combination quarrels with the chief over the loot and later returns to kill him. Suspicion is worked into a case around the boy as the murderer. But the accused refuses to reveal the identity of the chief on account of the girl. The girl plays around with the real murderer and gets a confession, with a dictaphone and a set of sleuths planted in an adjoining room.

Good crook picture, with screen treatment efficient in retaining interest while dealing with mechanics of the plot. *Mori.*

FRECKLES

FBO production and release. Directed by Leo Meehan from story by Gene Stratton-Porter. Titles by Jeanette Meehan, continuity by Dorothy Yost. Previewed in projection room Jan. 18. Running time, 60 minutes.

Freckles....................John Fox, Jr.
Swamp Angel....................Gene Stratton
McLean....................Hobart Bosworth
Bird Woman....................Eulalie Jensen
Wessner....................Billy Scott
Duncan....................Lafe McKee

In smaller towns they may like it because it's a clean picture about the outdoors. Production must have been made with a definite market in view. It is slow-moving, uninteresting and lacking in acting talent, but similar nature pictures have clicked with the fresh air fans before, and this one probably will too.

The two juvenile players, John Fox, Jr., and Gene Stratton, have little if any makeup on. Both faces register clearly on the screen, but are incapable of creating anything but an expression of blankness. Miss Stratton, it is claimed, is only 15. She is a granddaughter of Gene Stratton-Porter.

Action is laid in the timber lands run by McLean. The story centers round a one-armed boy, refused recognition everywhere on account of his deformity. Freckles undertakes to guard the Limberlost from timber thieves. Despite his physical disability the boy guarantees to deliver the forest without the loss of a single tree.

First attempt of timber thieves is foiled when the boy is warned by the Bird Woman, a naturalist, exploring the woods with the Swamp Angel. The second time the boy is captured and tied to a tree while the gang goes on with the operation of cutting. The Swamp Angel appears on the scene and though the boy is not released she notices the rope at his feet and runs for help after making the leader of the gang, Wessner, believe that she suspects nothing.

The boy is hurt with the fall of a tree and refuses to get well, figuring his love for the girl hopeless. She makes him understand, toward the close, that his standing with her is aces up if he would only get well.

The fight scene with Freckles and Wessner is effective, while there is an undercurrent of sympathy for the single-armed boy running all through the picture.

Hobert Bosworth delivers strongly in a minor role. Eulalie Jensen also does well on appearance in a matronly role. *Mori.*

FRIEND FROM INDIA

C. B. DeMille production; Pathe release. Starring Elinor Fair. Directed by Franklin Pangborn from story by H. A. de Souchet. Cast includes Franklin Pangborn, Ethel Wales, Louis Natheaux, Edgar Norton, Ben Hendricks, Jr., Thomas Ricketts, Jeannette Loff, Tommy Dugan. At Proctor's 5th Ave., N. Y., Jan. 16-18. Running time, 60 minutes.

The comedy idea in this picture is much like that in the screen "Charlie's Aunt." Here also a female impersonator vamps an elderly gent while the broken mirror scene is duplicated in detail.

Aside from that the picture is dull, consisting mainly of the usual chasing episodes. It is light film fare with a poor title. Rates as a filler only.

Story is of a penniless nephew threatened with disinheritance by a wealthy aunt unless he brings home the Hindoo prince he has been talking about.

While attending a Chinese lottery the joint is raided and the nephew with another, who has been following a fortune teller to learn the location of a girl, are pursued by police.

The nephew brings the stranger home after a hectic night, and the latter is forced to impersonate the Hindoo prince. Two other fakirs arrive during the party. It is finally broken up by a pair of headquarters sleuths.

Pangborn hogs the picture, keeping Miss Fair in the background all the way. *Mori.*

CALL OF THE HEART

Universal production and release starring the dog, Dynamite. Story by Basil Dickey. Directed by Francis Ford. Principal players Joan Alden and Edmund Cobb. On double feature program, Arena, N. Y., Jan. 19. Running time, 60 mins.

Dynamite is a pretty busy dog in this crazy quilt western. In fact, he seems to show to better advantage than in several others. Dynamite is a pretty good canine actor and does just the sort of things the boys and girls like. And he is always on time.

One sequence has the males fighting all over the lot with some long tugs on the imagination, but from the number of people employed this one probably cost a little more than some of the other Dynamites.

The dog and a youngster who does some yeoman work to hold up the story tension, carry away the honors. *Mark.*

STAGE KISSES

Columbia production and release. Directed by Albert Kelly under supervision of Harry Cohn. Helene Chadwick feminine lead. At Stanley, New York, one day, Jan. 18. (Release in Nov.) Running time, 65 minutes.

In reality the picture is a starring film for Helene Chadwick as the cabaret dancer who marries a rich man and then regrets it. All the "fat" falls to her, while the male lead has a sort of waiting role.

It's primarily a picture for women and a good program subject for the purpose; nice production on the technical side, but story weak in action. Long passages are built up for the kick and when the climaxes do come they seem diffused.

The whole punch of the film comes when the heavy, a former suitor who is peeved at the dancer's marriage, frames to be found in her room by her husband, the girl being entirely innocent. She is cast off as an unfaithful wife.

Early sequences in cabaret are fairly lively and throughout the technical production is on the high plane established by the Columbia people. Kenneth Harlan as a weak hero in a polite comedy drama is rather fatal. The story has no low comedy laughs which also reacts against it.

Just a fair program release. *Rush.*

BARE KNEES

Gotham production, released by Lumas. Directed by Erle C. Kenton from story by Adele Buffington. Cameraman James Diamond. Scenario and supervision by Harold Shumate. Players include Virginia Lee Corbin, Jane Winton, Forrest Stanley, Johnnie Walker, Donald Keith, Maude Fulton. In projection room, Jan. 19. Running time, 53 mins.

Despite many improbabilities and absurdities, "Bare Knees" is a first rate Gotham release, with breeze and sex.

It tells the fable of two sisters, one staid, conservative, married and industriously respectable, the other snippy, snappy, jazzey and unconventional. The picture argues the hot baby is the better of the two.

Gotham has assembled six players, possessing considerable individual and collective box office magnetism. Plus an okay production and directorial job, the picture should be welcomed by the indies.

Virginia Lee Corbin does well as flaming youth, but needs to be steered away from certain stock mannerisms of conveying flippancy. She has been kept pretty busy doing flaps since graduating from pinafores.

Jane Winton is attractive except when emotionalizing in close-ups. Nature gave her a beautiful but comparatively phlegmatic face.

Maude Fulton, who has written scenarios and titles for the flickers, was a surprise as a goof house maid. While overdone, her characterization showed possibilities.

"Bare Knees" will make for audience entertainment.

THE CHEER LEADER

Sam Sax production, released by Lumas. Directed by Alvin J. Neitz; from the story by Lee Armauth. Supervised by Sam Bischoff. Starring Ralph Graves, with cast including Gertrude Olmstead, Ralph Emerson, Shirley Paulner, Harold Goodwin, Donald Stuart and Duke Martin. At Loew's Circle, New York, one day, Dec. 30. Running time over 60 minutes.

Well made independent production, with likable cast. One of the usual college stories. Okey for split weeks.

Direction weak. Ralph Graves is sandwiched in between two other male characters. None of the boys is given any coloring.

The menace is introduced at the beginning as the college hero. The two schoolboy friends are shown as a couple of chumps. There is a doubt as to which of the three is meant to be the outstander until 20 minutes after the picture is started.

The football captain plants seeds of jealousy and hatred by telling one of the boys the other had fixed with the coach to get on the team. Both had been working for the same position. In a fit of heroics the lead tells the coach he can't play and his place is given to his roommate.

Usual complications with the last-minute rushes and getting the girl back. *Mori.*

WHEELS OF DESTINY

Rayart Pictures. Directed by Duke Worne. Story by Joseph Anthony. Cameraman, Walter Griffin. Forrest Stanley and Georgie Hale featured. Cast includes Ernest Hilliard, Miss Dupont, Jack Herrick. On double bill at Loew's, New York, one day, Dec. 29. Running time, 56 minutes.

Title will hurt this one. Besides being banal, the label has no point and no relativity. The picture's a pretty fair number in toto, however, excepting the unattractive billing.

Story wanders all the way from a research laboratory to the midway of an amusement park. The metamorphosis of a scientist into a carnival spieler is accomplished by a convenient attack of amnesia.

Forrest Stanley is the guy who got banged on the head. Georgia Hale (once leading lady to Chaplin) is the unspoiled darling of the 10c side show. Miss Dupont plays a less-than-human society snob, and Ernest Hilliard is the disagreeable boy friend.

As with most of the Duke Worne productions, excessive speed in the writing and making hurts. There are loose ends to the script, ragged details, and illogical makeshift devices. A scene calling for a series of dissovles was clumsily faked.

An average Rayart picture.

The Hour of Reckoning

John Ince production. Capitol release. Directed by John Ince. Co-featured, Herbert Rawlinson and Grace Darmond. Cast also includes Virginia Castleman, John J. Daly, John E. Ince, James B. Lowe, Edward Middleton, Harry Von Meter. Story by Frederic Chapin. Half of double feature day at Columbus, New York, one day, Dec. 29. Running time, 68 minutes.

Enough deep-dyed villainy in this one to supply a half-dozen pictures.

Picture made in 1925 when the Charleston was in vogue, but aside from that the villainy is much along the old, old lines. Picture shows wear and tear and yet gave evidence of having some splendid photography. With John Ince directing some of the climaxes are capitally staged and the picture as rattle trappy as it is has some dramatic scenes that are nicely sustained by the principals.

The work of both Miss Darmond and Rawlinson stands out. In this picture one who knows that James B. Lowe is the negro of present day "Uncle Tom's Cabin" fame finds him working hard to make a role of a butler, dippy on the subject of hypnotism, stick a few comedy points in a stodgy dramatic. As an independent it may suffer comparison with some of the present day stories of jazz and dissipation, but at that it will in a measure give some satisfaction on a double feature bill if the other half can hold any weight at all. *Mark.*

Daredevil's Reward

Fox production starring Tom Mix. Directed by Gene Ford from story by John Stone; photographed by Dan Clark. Cast includes Natalie Joyce, Lawford Davidson, Billy Bletcher, Harry Cording and William Welch. Reviewed in projection room Jan. 13. Running time, 55 minutes.

Many a manager's "out" is Tom Mix. "All I have to do is put Mix's name out front and they come back like prodigal sons," he says. "There's affection and trust in their eyes again when they lay down their dough. They take for granted that Mix will never go up against less than 20 guys. There's a man for 'em."

And here's another picture for the boys. It suffices that Mix outwits his not-less-than-20 men, rides his horse like a sedan, and turns out the lights by shooting across the room at a button. His necking is a little squeaky, but that's so with all rugged men.

As usual, the plot is trimmed with novelties. Tom is a Texas Ranger, and gets a line on the thieves by appearing in various disguises, including two comedy portions as a medicine man and a waiter. The whole thing is done in that half satirical manner that makes Mix a favorite among some of our best minds. Natalie Joyce is a determined but appealing heroine.

Mix starts where the other westerns leave off. His pictures have some of the fastest footage to be found: his rescues are hotter, his shootings more numerous, his pursuers more multitudinous. Which is why he rates aces with "the boys."

A Bowery Cinderella

Samuel Zierler release of an Excellent production. Pat O'Malley and Gladys Hulette co-featured. Story by Melvin Houston. In the cast: Kate Bruce, Pat Hartigan, Leo White, Rosemary Theby, Ernest Hilliard. At Loew's New York Jan. 13 on double-feature bill. Running time, 57 mins.

Samuel Zierler has been presenting a conspicuous number of better-than-average state rights productions of late. They are labeled rather banally "Excellent" pictures. Almost any other trade-mark would be an improvement on that. Also banal is the title of this l. t release, but behind the 1912 tag there's a neat film for the indie r ·et.

While photography leave something to be desired, the picture has been produced with flashiness and competence. The plot deals with backstage life and the w. k. studio debauch which involves an innocent chorine in a divorce scandal. Her sweetheart, a newspaper reporter, breaks in on the scene with a detective and finds the girl in a compromising situation. The scenarist brings about a cheerful denouement.

Pat O'Malley has little to do, but does it well. Miss Hulette, a pleasing personality, stands out, as does Ernest Hilliard, who looks like a hundred other film heavies but manages to be good, nevertheless.

An oke effort.

DARING DEEDS

W. Ray Johnston presents this Duke Worne production, starring Billy Sullivan. Story by Suzanne Avery. Cast includes Molly Malone and Earl Metcalfe. Distributed by Rayart. At the Columbus, N. Y., on double feature program, Jan. 14. Running time, 57 minutes.

Recent aviation wave probably prompted this one with Billy Sullivan as the hero. A wishy-washy meller at best.

Production looks like a Scotchman's donation and Sullivan's heroics are far overdrawn. Supporting cast do litttle to aid. "Daring Deeds" will best sidestep headaches on double feature programs. *Mark.*

BLOOD WILL TELL

Fox western, starring Buck Jones. Directed by Ray Flynn. Kathryn Perry featured. At Loew's New York Jan. 13 as half of double-feature bill. Running time, 54 mins.

Buck Jones' last picture for Fox is a conventional western without much action or values. It is unsuccessful in creating anything remotely akin to suspense. Therefore it must depend upon its star for any usefulness it will have to the average exhibitor.

The customary routine about the cheating foreman and the stranger who hires out as a cow hand, later revealing himself as the real owner of the ranch.

The picture is helped materially by the presence of the attractive Kathryn Perry. Jones has his horse and his 12-year-old buddy who knows he's not a crook. Eleven out of every dozen westerns this season have the cowboy with a kid saddle partner. The ranch scenes differ somewhat from the regulation cowboy locales, though seemingly having been taken in California amid trees and vegetation.

"Blood Will Tell" is just one of the machine-made in-betweeners.

ON THE STROKE OF 12

W. Ray Johnston presents this Rhem Carr production. Adapted by Arthur Hoerl from the play by Joseph LeBrandt. Directed by Charles J. Hunt. Cast includes David Torrence, Jane Marlowe, Lloyd Whitlock, Danny O'Shea, Charles West. Distributed by Rayart. At the Columbus, N. Y., on double feature program, Jan. 14. Running time, 67 minutes.

Irrespective of other things in this Rhem Carr film, the photography stands out. Seldom does any cameraman smear himself with so many good shots. The photography becomes more noticeable as the story rides and should prove a selling argument.

The story goes along nicely in dramatic tension and continuity up to the moment where the girl looks from an upper stairway and sees her sweetheart bending over the lifeless form of his father, from whom he has become estranged. At this juncture the picture skids to become utterly improbable, silly and preposterous.

From an airplane to the deck of a ship, then the topmost rigging, the water and whatnot. A nose dive into tawdry melodrama.

The cast does well, David Torrence being immense as the rich old daddy. Danny O'Shea continues a capable lead, while Lloyd Whitlock makes villainy plenty villainous. June Marlowe goes through creditably.

Camera work is the high mark and the crank shooter should be given ful credit. *Mark.*

FANGS OF THE WILD

F.B.O. production and release featuring Ranger (dog). Directed by Jerome Storm from a story by Dorothy Yost and Dwight Cummins, adapted by Ethel Hall. Cameraman, Robert DeGrasse. In the cast: Dorothy Kitchen, Sam Nelson, Sid Crossley and Tom Lingham. Reviewed in projection room, Jan. 12. Running time, 45 minutes.

Well-dovetailed scenario plus business-like direction and good camera work makes this a standout for a dog picture. Only in one sequence, towards the end, does Ranger get beyond the bounds of plausibility as to canine intelligence.

The plot concerns a treacherous, superstitious, bullying mountaineer who is after Nell. Nell's property has coal in it and the handsome young engineer from the city comes to buy the land. Deviltry is concocted by the Cumberland meanie and the cause of right triumphs only after desperate struggles and the timely and remarkable assistance of the faithful dog.

Millionaire Orphan

Fred J. Balshofer production. William Barrymore, star. Written and directed by Bob Horner. First distributed by Balshofer Productions, Hollywood, now handled by Biltmore Exchange, New York. At Arena, N. Y., double feature, one day, Jan. 4. Running time, 55 mins.

William Hampton.........Jack Richardson
Norman Davies.................Hal Ferner
Fay Moreland...............Pauline Curley
Jack Randall..............Wm. Barrymore
Henry Moreland ....Rex McIlivaine

För an independent that had a title that read like ready money this one never got anywhere, with the hero fist-fighting from one to a half-dozen men from the start to finish. It will do well to stand up on double feature days. The name may sound as hefty as the title, but Bill is called upon to do too much. So much so that in the Arena's 8th Ave. neighborhood the boys and girls laughed at the most hippodrome villainy ever staged.

The story seemed thrown together on the lot. *Mark.*

DRUMS OF LOVE

United Artists production and release. Directed by D. W. Griffith. Story credited to G. J. Lloyd. Karl Struss, photographer. Assistant cameramen, Harry Jackson and Billy Bitzer. Score by C. W. Cadman, Sol Cohen and Wells Hivley. At Liberty, New York, for twice daily run starting Jan. 24, at $2 top. Running time, exclusive of intermission, 115 mins.

Princess Emanuella..........Mary Philbin
Duke Cathos De Alvia...Lionel Barrymore
Count Leonardo De Alvia....Don Alvarado
Bopi.........................Tully Marshall
Duke of Granada..............C. H. Mailes

D. W. has turned himself out a program picture in that cycle which enfolds "Flesh and the Devil," "A Night of Love" and "Love." For program and b. o. purposes it rates with any of these if not as dynamic.

Highly romantic with a tragic ending, "Drums of Love" is technically as great as anything that has come out of Hollywood within the past 12 months. And that includes "Sunrise," as well as "Flesh and the Devil." Whether this is the best program feature Griffith has ever made is an open question, for they still talk of his "Avenging Conscience," which this director turned out some 13 years ago. But there is no doubt that this tops anything he has done outside of that one.

Doubts have been expressed as to whether the beauty values here can overcome the tragic double killing at the finish. But if the love story, the appearance of Mary Philbin and Don Alvarado and the performance of Lionel Barrymore can't make this release box office as well as artistic, then there'll never be anything but clinch finishes until they push a button to watch and hear entertainment in the parlor.

"Drums of Love" is a loge section film. The art centers will dote on it. That's sure. It's basic appeal is to the playgoer who thoroughly enjoys the Theatre Guild. Yet, the accentuated love theme is easily potent enough to get off the screen and reach the last rows up and downstairs.

Women are bound to like it and the men won't get tired of gazing at Miss Philbin the way Griffith presents her.

The shock of having the husband knife his wife to uphold the family honor she and his brother have smirched, and then turn to his brother and do the same to him, kissing both before each thrust, centers on the girl. By the time Cathos (Barrymore) reaches Leonardo (Alvarado) with the blade, the worst of the cold shower is over. It's not as abrupt as the finish of "Love," but there's no need of regret for having included it.

The script is based upon the story of Paolo and Francesca. This screens as a triangle of two brothers, one handsome, the other deformed, with the girl forced to marry the ruling big hearted brute to save her people. The locale is South America in the 19th century.

Into this Griffith has woven superb camera work, a delicacy of interpretation and a performance by Barrymore that is this actor's outstanding camera achievement to date. The placing of a blonde wig on Miss Philbin is a revelation. At various times she resembles Alice Terry, Mary Pickford and Marilyn Miller, and looks better than all three. A wig and a good cameraman. Add to this that Miss Philbin can act and she totals a pretty fair piece of work for one picture. Better than "Merry Go Round."

Griffith, as famous for his form clinging negligees as De Mille for his bath tubs, is part of the answer. The rest is lens technique, lighting and the knowledge of how to handle people. Witness the work of Alvarado.

Beautiful shots are constantly cropping up without over shadowing the story or resorting to double and triple fades and trick stuff.

Bitzer is listed as an assistant cameraman.

The scene where Emanuella enters Cathos' chamber the night of their marriage is a classic from all angles, and various other sequences are as eye filling if not so trying on the nerves.

Appearing to be 90 per cent studio-made, Griffith is reported to have turned "Drums of Love" out without waste both as to cost or time, unusual for him. The story lacks that necessary vitalness to make it $2, even for a swing around the key cities, but it should carve its own path within the program houses as to financial returns, for which it was made. It would be perfectly set within such a house as the Embassy in New York.

To those liking a story with some sense to it transformed into a well made picture, this is all wool and yards wide. Technically, it's a triumph. Hence, there remains the question of that finish. But Greta passes on in both "Flesh and the Devil" and "Love" and there is nothing cheery about Jannings' closing footage in "The Way of All Flesh" or "The Last Command." It will make them talk and, perhaps, argue. And if anyone hears 'em arguing they're going to drop in to find out what all the shootin's for.

It won't be easy to cut this picture from 115 minutes, but when they drop it down to around 90 most of the clipping will probably take place in what is now the first half. A few battle scenes, reminiscent in tactics of the "Nation," help the early footage along, and the accompanying score is excellent.

"Drums of Love" will get the support of those who have been yelling for "better pictures" and may feel censorship in certain sections.

It's a sweet comeback for Griffith and a corking picture. *Sid.*

13 WASHINGTON SQ.

Universal production and release, directed by Melville W. Brown. Starring Alice Joyce and Jean Hersholt. From the play of the same name by Leroy Scott. Titles by Walter Anthony. At the Roxy, New York, week of Jan. 28. Running time, 70 minutes.

"Deacon" Pyecroft...........Jean Hersholt
Mrs. De Peyster..................Alice Joyce
Jack De Peyster..............George Lewis
Mary Morgan.................Helen Foster
Mathilde ....Zasu Pitts
Olivetta..................Helen Jerome Eddy
Mrs. Allistair.........Julia Swayne Gordon
Mayfair.....................Jack MacDonald
Sparks..........................Jerry Gamble

Entertaining picture, with its appeal to the intelligent among the screen public and likely to be voted mild by the gum-chewing clientele. Away from the Universal style, U ordinarily making program pictures for the masses. Will please as a program release, without setting any high marks as an independent draw. Stars and title not figured as a pull.

But will please regular house following, on the score of its clean-cut romantic story, its atmosphere of elegance and comedy that is robust while not rowdy. Beautifully produced and acted with crisp competence. Mystery element is turned to comedy purpose and the thrills are not worked up. Has a world of mild laughs, but they never get beyond the polite classification.

All of which adds up to an average picture for better class patronage. The kind of film the screen critics demand in their crusades for better pictures, but the kind of product the mob doesn't crowd in to see. Would be poor opposition for a name star with a hot title.

Zasu Pitts, in the comedy role of a lady's maid who always gets her long words mixed up, has the prize character and plays it. Here is a character comedienne who has seldom been supplied with parts that would advance her. In this picture she gives a finely balanced performance in a part that could have been clowned to death. Alice Joyce, as an aristocratic mother, has a charming and graceful figure, but aristocratic mamas do not make popular pictures. Jean Hersholt plays the sympathetic crook part that came near making the piece when it was on the stage. It isn't a screen part, calling for too little significant acting and too much illumination in titles. Most of the interesting things the crook does are conveyed by title.

Romantic story is just a side angle of interest. Sympathetic interest is bound up in the mother and the crook, and what grip the story has in its celluloid form is confined to these two. For the rest, there is little action in the cinema meaning of the word, and an impatient flapper fan might call it dull.

These defects are inherent in the story material, for it has been produced in faultless taste. The settings showing an aristocratic home in Washington Square are remarkably well done. A room in Washington Square is just that, instead of a de luxe furniture display set out in Grand Central Palace. Acting is scaled on the same moderate and reasonable plane.

It's satisfying playing of this sort of material, but the substance of the story never once gets hold of the sympathies. *Rush.*

BUCK PRIVATES

Universal production and release with Lya de Putti featured. Directed by A. Melville Brown. At the Colony, New York, week of Jan. 28. Running time, 60 mins.

Anne............................Lya de Putti
John Smith............Malcolm MacGregor
Hulda................................Zasu Pitts
Major Hartman..............James Marcus
Sergt. Butts..................Eddie Gribbon
Capt. Marshall..........Capt. Ted Duncan
Cupid Dodds...................Bud Jamison
Mose Bloom..........................Les Bates

Nicely balanced comedy feature with agreeable romantic interest and some beautiful scenic shots. Story is set in Europe just after the armistice and deals with the comedy side of the A. E. F. Not a suggestion of war stuff in it, except the uniforms.

American troops in Germany have been given permission to pass through Luxemburg on their way out of the Rhine country. They descend upon a picturesque village and the hero (Malcolm MacGregor) is billeted with a giant pacifist and a beautiful daughter, whom he is forbidden to address or look at. Villagers set up the rule that soldiers may not fraternize with native maids and any girl caught being friendly toward a uniform shall have her head cropped.

The hero, a private, has as a rival for the lovely Lya, his top sergeant in the laughable person of Eddie Gribbon, who is a better clown than ever he was a baseball player, which is a compliment. Hero wins the girl, but sergeant butts in and is caught kissing her against her will in the moonlit garden. He is up for court-martial and can only escape by marrying the girl.

Lya's maid (Zasu Pitts), playing the part with her usual gift for awkward grace, is substituted, and the misinformed hero kidnaps her at the very altar, leading to a hip hurrah motorcycle chase for the finish.

Picture is a neat blending of romantic story and vigorous comedy. For the most part the comedy is intelligent and free of the ordinary grade of film gagging, but at the finish it goes a little Sennett. To tell the truth, this finish gives a peppy period to an otherwise quiet picture and makes it something of a rowdy, but effective entertainment.

Production is in the best manner of Director Brown. Foreign atmosphere is capitally built up in the settings and the characters. This scenic element gives the picture a good deal of engaging beauty in its backgrounds. One love scene between hero and village girl is a charming episode, particularly in pictorial surroundings.

Acting is remarkably uniform in its excellence. Zasu Pitts once again steals a good deal more of interest than she was entitled to in the script. This actress has a veritable genius for doing the impossible with drab roles. Gribbon is a low comedy treat and MacGregor makes an engaging young leading man. The role of the Dutch heroine is out of Lya de Putti's line. Character bits are made to stand out. Nothing more realistically military has been seen than the captain of the company, and men villagers such as the barber who plants the shearing idea. Title writing is crisp and bright, as when the hard boiled sergeant says on his way to his own wedding, "I feel as nervous as a pullet about to lay her first egg."

Good, honest comedy with qualities that will appeal to the best grade of fans, and enough robust fun to please the flaps' saps. *Rush.*

THE HAUNTED SHIP

Tiffany production and release. Directed by Forrest Shelton. Adapted from Jack London's "White and Yellow.". In cast: Dorothy Sebastian, Montague Love, Tom Santchi, Ray Hallory and Alice Lake. At Keith's Hippodrome, New York, week Jan. 23. Running time, 48 mins.

One of those rough and ready yarns calling heavily on the imagination to make it credible. As a picture it appears capable of holding up on single day stands.. Strictly a meller and making up in a mutiny for the absence of a storm at sea.

Montague Love is the heavy-fisted master of the schooner who fifteen days before has cast his wife and young son adrift on a raft, believing the boy isn't his and that his first mate (Santchi) is responsible.

For that, fifteen years the first mate has been shackled in the ship's hold where Gant (Montague Love) administers floggings to make his victim confess. A switch to South Sea locale shows the boy, full grown, (Ray Hallor) as a nondescript beach comber who is shanghaied aboard Gant's craft along with "Queenie" (Dorothy Sebastian), shipwrecked member of a theatrical troupe.

Gant is after the girl and the boy seeks his unknown father for vengeance. The relationship crops out and aided by the crew the boy overthrows Gant, releases the first mate and everybody deserts the ship Gant has fired.

All but Gant and the first mate who are trapped in the hold as the ship sinks. The boy and girl cling to a crate and are washed ashore on some undetermined coast where the picture ends.

Miss Sebastian gets a certain s. a. into her characterization while Love plays his usual burly brute effectively. Santchi never comes out from behind his beard and only goes into fistic action during the memory cutback. Hallor is neither good nor bad as the boy.

It's elemental love and hate drawn in broad strokes and should appease the cheaper admission clientele. Footage in a low dive will interest from the flesh angle. Story's pace is carried along at a fair clip and photography okay. *Sid.*

THE THRILL SEEKERS

Superlative Pictures production. Cast includes Lee Moran, Jimmy Fulton, Ruth Clifford and Robert McKim. Distributed by Hi-Mark Productions. At Stanley, New York, on double feature program Jan. 29. Running time, 57 mins.

Too much phoney melodrama knocks this one cuckoo. Old type of deep-dyed villainy starts early and wallows in such a quagmire of palpable dramatic impossibilities that it was too much of an overdose even on double feature day. The story is the kind that has been cameraed to a whisper, but may survive the double feature demand and bring back the original investment to its independent makers.

Hero and his side kick butler take a lot of punishment physically, yet they come right back for more, and the principals pummel each other all over the screen.

Picture smears itself with a deluge of heroics that became such mockery as to make the audience giggle.

Story never has a chance, but cast does its best. Some consolation. *Mark.*

A RACE FOR LIFE

Warner Bros. production and release, starring Rin-Tin-Tin. From a story by Charles R. Condon, directed by Ross Lederman. Cameraman, Edward Du Par. In projection room Jan. 27. Running time, 48 mins.
Virginia Calhoun...Virginia Browne Faire
Robert Hammond.............Carroll Nye
Danny O'Shea.............Bobby Gordon
Bruce Morgan............James Mason
Tramp...................Pat Hartigan

Bearing in mind there is a definite following for these canine dramas, "A Race for Life" may be recommended for the very apparent skill it demonstrates in the art of constructing a theatrical scaffolding around a quadruped leading man.

As Rin-Tin-Tin is the professional father of all the cinema pups and has been a star and a moneymaker for a longer time than any other woof-woof hero, it is not surprising that there is a certain factory-like efficiency in the turning out of these pictures. There is certainly nothing in this one that could be called even a new variation of old stuff. Yet it possesses a confident manner, as if director, scenarist and dog trainer were sure of their goal and driving straight for it.

Enjoyment of a picture such as this requires a naive and sentimental disposition plus a regard for dogs. Where and when dog pictures are exhibited in big cities it is invariably as one-half of a double-feature bill.

In the smaller communities, however, the dog opera can and does stand alone, unaided and unapologetic. For these stands "A Race for Life will probably be okay. There is enough heart tug of a sort to have the kids whistling at Saturday matinees.

Bobby Gordon plays Rin-Tin-Tin's boy friend and is the only player with much to do. Gordon may be the lad he is represented to be, but the many-sided versatility of his boyishness suggests advanced years and considerable trouping.

WEB OF FATE

Dallas M. Fitzgerald production released by Peerless. Story and direction by Fitzgerald. Lillian Rich featured. Cast includes Eugene Strong, Henry Sedley, Edward Coxen, Frances Raymond. At Loew's, New York, on double bill. Jan. 27. Running time, 49 mins.

A fair state righter, without much support from "names" of any sort. Lillian Rich, featured, is the only one with any probable box office registry.

It is a drama of high jinks amongst the swells and depends upon the w.k. device of two gals who look alike, the innocent one being blamed for the murders and one thing or another of the loose bimbo. The usual misunderstandings are okayed in the end, when newspapermen discover the hard-boiled jane, thereby saving our Nell from the hoosegow.

Lillian Rich, turned blonde, uses a sneer to identify the n.g. gal.

When playing the heroine she seems very sweet. It isn't a bad nical detail are above "quickie" job of duo-characterization.

Production, continuity and tech-standards.

MANEGE
(GERMAN MADE)

Berlin, Jan. 25.
By far the best picture which Defina, partially financed by First National, has yet turned out. It may be the best German film of the year. Following in the footsteps of "Variety," it unquestionably stands on its own feet.

The two partners of a tight-rope-walking act have quarreled over a woman and for years have not spoken to each other, although continuing their act. In the circus in which they are playing, a frail little girl is performing a leap-the-gap sensation, certain to end in making her a physical wreck. But she is so under influence of her brutal stepfather that she goes through with it nightly.

The younger of the acrobats, Ralph, tries to threaten the stepfather into discontinuing the act, but without success. Then he tries to force the manager of the circus to stop it by inciting a strike among the other performers. This also fails. Gaston, his brother, feeling that he really has been at fault in their estrangement, goes to the stepfather and during a quarrel knocks him down. The police come to get him that night at the close of his turn, which he goes through with the knowledge that they are waiting for him.

Solution is happy.

Direction by Max Reichmann is competent and often full of intensity. He will bear watching. Mary Johnson as the little girl has a helpless naivete, very moving, and Kurt Gerron has a Jannings-like brutality. Raymond van Riel and Ernst van Duren are more than adequate as the brothers. *Trask.*

THE WHITE SHEIK
(BRITISH MADE)

London, Jan. 20.
Produced by British International. Released by Wardour Films. Directed by Harley Knoles. Adapted from Rosita Forbes' novel, "King's Mate." Photography, Rene Guissart and J. J. Cox. Previewed at the London Hippodrome, Jan. 17. "A" censor certificate. Running time, 95 minutes.
The White Sheik........Jameson Thomas
Martengo................Warwick Ward
Rosemary Tregarthen....Lilian Hall-Davis
Menhebbe...............Clifford McLaglan
Zarifa..................Julie Suedo
Pat.....................Forrester Harvey
Jock...................Gibb McLaughlin

Mrs. Rosita Forbes is an explorer. And a novelist. They claim she was an active assistant on this film in choice of location and in direction. So maybe Harley Knoles isn't to blame.

Anyway, it is the first film British International made — before "The Ring" and those shown since—and it has been the last of this set of productions to be previewed. There is a fine cast, some good photography, lots of Moorish mud huts, streets and sandhills. Natives juggling muskets. A couple of comic soldiers, two good troupers who just have to come in and be funny and go out.

Story? What there is goes something like this: A girl wanders into the foothills, gets lost, is captured by Riffs, who have a mysterious white leader. (Yes, he is the title part.) Villain, who pursued her before she was lost, is one of the white men gone Riff, and as the White Sheik won't let her go back to poppa in Fez, in case she tells of the secret passage to the Riff stronghold, villain promises to help her escape.

She goes to his hut, is attacked, rescued by the White Sheik, who marries her — platonically — for her own safety. Villain fights a duel with hero, is wounded, frames to murder him, girl saves him, and discovers she loves him. And it's as blah as it sounds.

Nothing, apart from the story, specially calls for criticism. Likewise nothing calling for recommendation. Just dull and pointless. *Frat.*

LOVE OF JEANNE NEY

(GERMAN MADE)

Berlin, Jan. 25.

A disappointment after the splendid work done by the same director, G. W. Pabst, in "Secrets of a Soul." Taken from a novel by Ilya Ehrenberg, said to be good, it never got to be a picture scenario. It is not anywhere near concentrated enough.

It begins interestingly enough in the Crimea, where a young French girl falls in love with a bolshevik agent. But when the two meet again in Paris the atmosphere is disturbed by the introduction of a burlesque detective, the girl's uncle.

This character is murdered, and the youth is suspected of the crime. The girl discovers the real murderer, an international swindler.

Only good performances are by Uno Henning as the male lead and Brigitte Helm in a minor role. Edith Jehanne, French actress, did not pan out at all in the female lead.

Trask.

SADIE THOMPSON

United Artists production and release. Starring Gloria Swanson. Adapted from original story by W. Somerset Maugham and directed by Raoul Walsh. Cameramen: Oliver Marsh, George Barnes and Robert Kurrle. Titles by C. Gardner Sullivan. At Rivoli, New York, for run on grind starting Feb. 4. Running time, 94 mins. 99c. top.

Alfred Hamilton.........Lionel Barrymore
Mrs. Hamilton............Blanche Friderici
Dr. McPhail..................Charles Lane
Mrs. McPhail............Florence Midgley
Joe Horn.....................James Marcus
Sergt. Tim O'Hara..........Raoul Walsh
Sadie Thompson...........Gloria Swanson

After viewing "Sadie," silent but in motion, a lot of the boys are going to say, "Well, what was all the shootin' for." Was Sadie going to reach the screen or not? She was. She wasn't. Rumor this. Rumor that. And here she is. With so much "poison" extracted that she's fangless. Nobody's going to get excited about the old girl. She'll be a good program picture, that'll be that and they'll forget her. The women will probably go stronger for this one than the males.

Little doubt that the script has been handled with kid gloves. Barrymore is neither Davidson nor a reverend. He's Hamilton and a reformer. Program credits make no reference to "Rain" the play, the picture having been adapted from the "original story" by Maugham. However, the presentation is conveying the idea of "Rain" by a stereoptican downpour effect prior to and through the opening titles.

The scene in which Hamilton enters Sadie's room during the night is not more than barely hinted at, finishing with Barrymore standing at the door. For a few previous feet is shown his mental struggle to overcome Sadie's physical attraction for him, but nothing more than a faltering hand reaching out to stroke her hair is flashed. The pause before the door takes Barrymore out of the picture, as he supposedly kills himself on the beach before morning, explained by the following action and title.

Sadie's costume, her struggle to articulate above and over a wad of gum and her familiarity with the Marines is sufficient to establish her character at the beginning. But there's likely to be a wide difference of opinion on Miss Swanson's interpretation of the role. And at least that difference will be better than indifference—for the picture.

A long sequence in which Sadie berates Hamilton for having her deported, following him from room to room as she rages, is excellently played by the star, although at other times, particularly during the first two reels, her hard-boiled walk, gestures and facial expression seem out of proportion. She's let her hair grow, too.

Barrymore's performance is okay and Raoul Walsh, assuminig the double duties of actor and director, does well by both. He plays O'Hara with whom Sadie eventually sails away. Charles Lane makes a minor bit count, and Blanche Friderici rises to her occasion late in the running. Production and photography are all that they should be, with no special reason for the full 94 minutes the film is using at the Rivoli.

"Sadie Thompson" isn't great, but it's big program material with the Swanson name and "Rain" rep to help.

They've let Sadie down and gently.

Sid.

HER WILD OAT

First National release. Produced by John McCormick. Starring Colleen Moore. Directed by Marshall Neilan. Adapted from Howard Irving Young's story. At Paramount, New York, week Feb. 4. Running time, 65 minutes.

Mary Brown..................Colleen Moore
Philip Latour.....................Larry Kent
Tommy Warren.............Hallam Cooley
Daisy ....Gwen Lee
Dowager ....Martha Mattox
Duke Latour..................Charles Giblin
Miss Whitley.............Julanne Johnston

Nice, bright comedy; nice and bright especially in its substantial little star, bright in its captions and as bright at times in its business, while the production when needing to be nice, is nice. And a staple Colleen Moore program release for First National.

It may be Miss Moore's first time in the Paramount on Broadway. If that house has its own clientele, aside from the Strand where she is so well known, the Paramounters won't forget her after "Wild Oat."

Film starts novelly and swiftly with Miss Moore, as an orphan, operating a lunch wagon. She's saving her earnings, to take a vacation, and finally does that when she gets a fellow who the girl believes is looking for a job. But he's not. Soused one evening, that young fellow got his clothes taken away by panhandlers and when appearing at the girl's all-night rumbler for a cup of coffee he looked a panhandler himself.

Afterward with his face washed but still wearing the jumper suit he had borrowed, he told the girl he had a job as chauffeur and was driving down to the beach, where his boss lived at a $30 a day hotel.

When the lunchroom young woman decided to go to that hotel and did, it seemed as if the picture would blow up, with the French farcial ingredients immediately mixed in. But it didn't, for that's where the business or gags started, commenced by a publicity agent who thought he would star the girl as a duchess and picked "Potage de Granville" off of the menu card for her name, making it the Duchess de Granville. Then the real Duke of that name on the scene, and her young man his son, besides mixing her into the centre of it as the Duke's latest wife.

Very well done, this part, and sent the picture through flying from laughs only.

Marshall Neilan's handling okay all of the time, with some nice bits also from his end. Extra good photography with much of the screening in the open.

But as the pensive lunchwagon girl, Miss Moore displays that intelligence of knowing her work that makes stars of the Moore grade endurable in pictures. There are not so many.

And it won't do any harm to all of the parties interested that the Colleen Moore picture is at the Paramount this week.

Cohens-Kellys in Paris

Universal comedy production and release. Directed by William Beaudine, featuring George Sidney and J. Farrel MacDonald. ~~At Colony, New York,~~ week Feb. 3. Running time, 70 minutes.

Mr. Cohen.........................George Sidney
Mr. Kelly...............J. Farrel MacDonald
Mrs. Cohen.........................Vera Gordon
Mrs. Kelly.............................Kate Price
Patrick Kelly...............Charles Delaney
Sayde Cohen ....Sue Carol
Paulette ....Gertrude Astor

Another chapter in the Jewish-Celtic screen embroglio inspired by "Abie's Irish Rose," and the best thing of its kind to grow out of that much overdone vogue. There is a good deal of genuine comedy in the new "Paris" version of Universal's "Cohens and Kellys." It is heavily overlaid, of course, with heavy-handed gagging, but basically there is a deal of legitimate fun in the scrappy Kelly and his partner Cohen.

The subject is so innately amusing that even the laborious and determined efforts of the director and players to make it funnier doesn't quite defeat its intrinsic humor. In all probability the broad effects will enhance the fun for the fan mob, but to the fastidious it does seem to be stretching it when Kelly and Cohen go to a cabaret and become involved in a riot when they think the Apache dance is on the level and interfere with the assault on the woman dancer.

Picture is full of this sort of thing. Perhaps it is necessary to put a certain amount of banana peel comedy into a picture of this kind to make certain that all the 12-year-olds of all ages will be amused, but it does inspire impatience in the adult spectator.

However, there are passages of robust comedy that are laughable on their merit, the titles throughout are skillfully fashioned, the action is fast and well sustained and the production is first class in a technical sense.

Titles were supplied by Al Desmond and the introductory crack is a fair sample. It goes, "Irish and Jewish partners have quarreled ever since David played with a harp and called it a lyre." That is submitted as perhaps the neatest thing that has been pulled on the "Abie" situation.

This time Cohen's daughter Sadye and Kelly's son Patrick are in Paris, the girl for voice training, the son to study art. They marry secretly. Summoned home by the old folks' cablegram, they pretend they are only engaged, and both sets of parents start immediately in wrath for Paris.

Usual and inevitable seasick scenes on shipboard. It must be admitted that Cohen's mal de mere is funny and the stunts are ingenious.

In Paris the marriage is revealed for more violent demonstrations of enmity by Kelly and Cohen. They decide to make the best of it.

At this point Sadye demands a divorce because Pat has had a blonde model in his studio. Thereupon Cohen and Kelly seek out the blonde model in a night club to square things.

This episode departs widely from the story for the sake of acrobatic comedy when the model's French gigolo misinterprets the intentions of the two elderly Americans who seek the girl in her dressing room. There is more of the same sort of thing when Kelly and Cohen meet the girl in her apartment, and, of course, it all ends in an uproarious chase.

Vera Gordon contributes her Jewish mother type, flawless in comedy or drama, while Kate Price plays the Irish mama in excellent comedy vein without overdoing. Sue Carol is a pretty youngster, acceptable in a mild way, while Charles Delaney gets something definite out of the boy role.

MacDonald plays the Irish father up to the hilt for low comedy. He has tricks of manner, such as a curiously oblique lifting of the eyebrow when he is angry, that are first-rate comedy contrivances.

Sidney plays the Jewish family man with rich unction. Even in his most extreme comedy moments Sidney is Cohen in real life. He is never a conventionalized comedy type—and no comedy character in the whole range can be more hoked up than the middle-aged Hebe—but always a human being rather than a stencil. Sidney here has to do a lot of hoke comedy, but it is always the material that is mechanical, never the method of the player.

Picture will be a clean up, for the title will attract the fans who enjoyed earlier chapters of the same theme, and the picture itself will make its way on low comedy laughs.

Rush.

LOVE ME

(AND THE WORLD IS MINE)

Universal production and release. Starring Mary Philbin and Norman Kerry. Adapted from the story, "Affairs of Hannerl." Directed by E. A. Dupont, with Jackson Rose, photographer. At the Roxy, New York, week of Feb. 3. Running time, 67 minutes.

Hannerl.............................Mary Philbin
Von Vigilati.....................Norman Kerry
Mitzel. ....Betty Compson
Van Denbosch...................H. B. Walthall
House Manager............George Siegmann
Billie...................................Albert Conti

"Love Me" won't hold up for a week in the big houses and may have its troubles getting the production cost back.

E. A. Dupont' first directorial effor in this country, and he must have taken a couple of looks at "Merry Go Round" before starting. With Miss Philbin and Kerry having been in that picture, the similarity between the two is emphasized. But there's no comparison on merit. "Merry Go Round" was quite a film.

Dupont used up a lot of footage to tell a commonplace screen story. Locale is gay Vienna, with the war creeping in and the lovers marrying as the boy starts for the front. Meanwhile the simple maiden (Miss Philbin) has been cast from her aunt's home because the Austrian officer kissed her while billeted there. She has turned to an old friend, Mitzel (Miss Compson), of the opera ballet, whose boy friends must have money.

Interwoven is Van Denbosch (Walthall), middle-aged bachelor, who adopts Hannerl and wants to marry her. Dramatic climax is that Hannerl casts aside the bridal veil to dash to the station as Von Vigilati (Kerry) goes to war. An impromptu three days' leave allows him to hop off the thrain so as not to make a fool out of Hannerl's wedding gown.

Picture is slow and Dupont hasn't been able to draw the love tragedy of boy and girl, both needing money and not caring delicately or strongly enough to make anyone concerned over whether they get together or not. Neither could the director resist newsreel shots to herald the war declaration, one passage holding five scenes within the celluloid frame. In fact, the story doesn't do other than just amble along, lacking the punch to accelerate a pace that never threatens to violate the law.

To see Miss Philbin under Griffith and then Dupont is to watch not only two performances but two distinct girls unrecognizable except by name. Miss Philbin proved her ability in "Merry Go Round," and such stories as this are probably the reason she has been blanketed these many months and a few years. In "Love Me," a bad title anyway, she is just a fair-looking miss with no mass or sex appeal, and this consequently throws Miss Compson into added prominence, although she, too, has been better than in this film. Kerry's performance is spotty, but Walthall is good throughout, with Siegmann meeting requirements in what little he has to do.

Production is rife with back drops and some of those interior opera views of which U has many in its library. Photography is very plain, with Miss Compson's makeup bordering on the German idea. *Sid.*

SOUTH SEA LOVE

FBO production and release. Directed by Ralph Ince. Patsy Ruth Miller starred. At the Hippodrome, New York, week of Feb. 6. Running time, 70 mins.

Dull picture obviously designed to cut in on the South Sea thing, rain and "Sadie Thompson." This one is a flash in the pan and a dud. About up to the Hippodrome grade.

Fairly capable cast struggles to no purpose with a discursive and rambling story which begins back stage on Broadway and then brusquely switches to the South Seas where hero goes in search of a fortune in pearls. By theatrical devices that would make a hack writer for the dumbbell magazines blush, hero, heroine and heavy are all brought together in the jungle settlement, just as the rainy season starts. The trio are housed up until they go coo-coo and the heavy gets a sock in the jaw from the hero, which naturally makes him confess that it was his plotting that brought about all the misunderstanding between the two loving hearts.

So they send the heavy comfortably back to civilization, while the hero and the heroine, who had been a musical comedy star during working hours back on Broadway, settle down to sweet domesticity in the fever laden islands. Fans of an intellectual condition that would swallow this trash deserve to get it.

Production has some lovely tropical shots, even if the characters do paddle with the river tide both coming into the settlement and going out of it. Must have been one of those belt line rivers. There's another fascinating bit. The heroine, driven quite frantic by imprisonment in a lonely shack during the months of rain, is so wrought up that when she has a quarrel with her lover she tries suicide by throwing herself in the same river. Instead of sinking she floats gracefully off with her head well out of the water until the natives go up to the camp, call the hero and he swims out to tow her ashore none the worse for her experience.

Story has no pattern or shape, merely rambling and doubling back on itself. All in all you get a confused impression of the heroine's character, as though you were watching Theda Bara playing Little Eva. Faults are of course in the script and the direction. Miss Miller looks good, even when being paddled up the tropic river dressed for a dansant including gloves. That's the kind of a picture it is. A beautiful river, but can't keep your mind on the dramatic interest for concentrating on the gloves. Hasn't a single spark of comedy of any kind.

Hippodrome spreads upon lobby display suggest hot love story, with girl in shredded wheat skirt spooning among the palms with stalwart hero. If that idea persuades them to buy, they'll be plenty peeved.

Rush.

Phantom of the Range

FBO western featuring Tom Tyler. Directed by James Dugan from story by Oliver Drake. Cameraman, Nick Musuraca. In the cast: Charles McHugh, James Pierce, Marjorie Zier, Frankie Darro, Duane Thompson. Reviewed in projection room Feb. 1. Running time, 46 mins.

Attached to a story of some novelty—in the beginning—is a title that cannot remotely be associated with the plot. While the title of a western is probably the least important part thereof, "Phantom of the Range," for a story about a stranded actor, seems unduly careless.

The picture is launched interestingly with a barnstorming troupe of one-nighters giving their show in a western tank town. The leading man (Tom Tyler) is an ex-cowboy and a bum actor. The troupe goes blooey when the manager skips with the dough and the cowboy has to go back to being a "hand." Disgusted at finding the ranch is a milk cow ranch, he is walking out when the gal taunts him with being a snob and a ham actor. He sticks to prove he isn't.

Thereafter the ex-actor becomes the champion and protector of the family against the real estate agent who is indifferent to the principles of Rotary.

Regulation western stuff and okay in that classification for the regular western stands. *Land.*

The Law and the Man

W. Ray Johnston's Tremm Carr production, released through First Division. Adapted by Arthur Hoerl from story by Octavus Ray Cohen. Directed by Scott Pembroke. Hap Depew, cameran. Gladys Brockwell and Tom Santchi featured. At Loew's New York one day, Jan. 31, one-half double bill. Running time, 60 minutes.

Dan Creedon....................Tom Santschi
Margaret Grayson........Gladys Brockwell
Ernest Vane....................Robert Ellis
Quintus Newton..............Tom Ricketts
Miss Blair.................Florence Turner
Jimmy..........................Jimmy Cain
Stanley Hudson..........Henry Roquemore

"An unusual story" states the First Division press sheet on this picture, and it is, in its class. A feature film that can make the split weeks nicely and hold up for them. It's a well-made independent and splendidly carried along in its continuity through the adaptation by Arthur Hoerl of the Roy Cohen tale, "False Fires."

Direction by Scott Pembroke is skillful. Ready to go mad-melodramatic at any time, Mr. Pembroke has held it down and admirably, even in the courtroom scene. That makes for the better effect with the more intelligent picturegoer.

It takes the threadworn political story and turns it right around. It is like seeing the customary tale on the other side, played backward as it were. Here the political boss of a small town, 60,000, to win the good opinion of the girl he loves, reforms himself. He throws out the crew of grafting officeholders put in by him, asks the girl, who is a lawyer, to accept the nomination for district attorney, and agrees with her that she can go the limit in her prosecuting office.

During this the girl thinks she is in love with another, an architect and a bad boy. She is engaged to marry the architect. That is a shock to the politician when discovering it, but, despite that, he determines to win the girl, and does.

While doing it he protects the architect, who becomes a forger, and for a climax, when the district attorney is impeached, the political boss voluntarily takes the stand to assume under oath the crime he thought the girl he loved had committed to save her fiance.

You don't catch a story like that on the screen every day. It's much better in the unreeling than in this description. It's also much better visually expressed by Tom Santchi and Gladys Brockwell as the leads. Mr. Santchi could not have played it better if he had lived the role, and that's enough to say for his work. He poured a lot of feeling into it and made that leap off the screen. Acknowledging the director's imagination, and there's plenty of that here, Miss Brockwell also gives a grade A performance. She's not the outlandish woman lawyer with spectacles, but a balanced girl who believes in her official duty. It must have been direction with Miss Brockwell. There's no girl of the screen capable of handling this kind of a characterization without direction.

For a play without the s. a. spilled all over. one must admire the love motif as here advanced. Hardly a prettier scene could be wished for than the political boss when about to propose to the girl, being set aside by her as she walks away, to kiss her fiance at the end of the ballroom. It was a wallop to the boss, and he showed it in suppressed emotion, not by chewing up scenery.

In comedy relief is Tom Ricketts as a country editor, always lighting a cigar. Somewhat overdrawn in all ways. Another smirch is the political boss' overconfidence in his stenographer, to the extent of revealing his heart.

That double bill day at the New York again means nothing here. Perhaps the producer believes his courtroom scene is the kick, but the punch is the story. That' different, and that it is different should be played up.

Production in keeping and well produced.

THE RUSH HOUR

Pathe production and release. Supervised by F. McGrew Willis. Directed by E. Mason Hopper from story by Frederick and Fannie Hatton, "The Azure Shore." Screen adaptation by Zelda Sears. Starring Marie Prevost. Cast includes Harrison Ford, Seena Owen, Ward Crane, Dave Butler. At Keith's Hippodrome, New York, week Jan. 30. Running time, 60 mins.

Screening this picture about the most effective means of clearing house. Draws honors for dullness and monotony unrelieved by the n. It.s the type of picture made five or more years ago, and only third rate at that time.

Story is of a girl who wants to go to Paris. She lives in Jersey, must get up early in the morning, and is part of the usual morning hour rush. She doesn't like rushes. Also, she both likes and dislikes her sweetie.

The girl finally decides to go to Paris. She hides on board a steamer and is discovered. Ordered to work her passage she becomes seasick and experiences similar exciting adventures on board ship.

Finally, picked up by a team of con workers who figure to use the girl as a bait for the wealthy mark, the girl gets to the Riviera.

The female half of the crook team becomes jealous of her and tells all.

Meanwhile the mark has proven himself such a great guy that by the time they bring the hero over from Jersey the sympathy of the audience is with the boy who gave up 100 g's so that the girl could get a commission.

Ending unsatisfactory.

Miss Prevost okey on appearance.

OUTCAST SOULS

Joe Rock (Hollywood) production for Sterling release. Directed by Louis Chaudet. Priscilla Bonner featured. At Loew's New York, one-half double bill, one day, Jan. 24. Running time, around 60 minutes.

Useless waste of celluloid. Not only the picture drags terribly all of the time but most of everything illogical and what's not is not explained. The finish reels off as though entirely cut out to make the proper running time.

The episode some while ago of a husband and wife having been arrested in Cleveland for necking in their machine and the traffic cop sued for damages appears to have suggested this film.

At the start the young couple meet in the afternoon, going out in his roadster the same evening. They are taken to the station house for the same reason. Telling the cop they were married, they informed the desk lieutenant they wanted to be. So he phoned a justice of the peace at 2 a. m. and they were married, going to the girl's home to advise her mother and then going to a hotel, all within 18 hours.

Later the father of the husband meets the mother of the daugher, while the latter is acting as a decoy on a sight seeing bus. The father pays $14 to sit with the mother on each bus until it's her time off. Then he procures a marriage license, with neither knowing the other and not knowing their children are married.

After that you can go to sleep or go nuts.

THE BANDIT'S SON

FBO western featuring Bob Steele. Directed by Wallace Fox from story by Frank H. Clark. Cameraman Nick Misurcara. In the cast: Ann Sheridan Tom Lingham, Stanley Taylor, Bobby Mack, Finch Smiles, Hal Davis. At Arena, New York, one day, Jan. 21. Running time, 53 minutes.

A slight variation of the western plot formulas. The variation, though unimportant, is welcome. Perhaps the single outstanding fault of all westerns is this overpowering attachment to one or two plots.

FBO lays down a good idea in "The Bandit's Son," but doesn't do much with it. The situation of a man living honestly and decently in a community for 20 years, but unable to gain any standing because of old stories about his having been a bandit in his youth, is capable of dramatic development. The scenario, however, handles the intriguing idea of a reformed bandit with all the trite conventionalized machine routine of the movie factories.

It is just a little absurd in the particular of the young scoundrel (Stanley Taylor) who is a cold-blooded murderer, a bully, gambler, and son of the sheriff. When escaping after the truth comes out he pauses to grab the heroine and gallop off. The hero is not two minutes behind him.

The movies will no doubt continue to represent men fleeing from the law as having the inclination or foolhardiness to add kidnapping to their other crimes.

Production, cast and direction okay.

HEROES IN BLUE

Rayart release, presented by W. Ray Johnson and directed by Duke Worne for producing unit bearing his name. Story by Leota Morgan. Cast includes John Bowers, Sally Rand and Gareth Hughes. At Stanley, New York, Jan. 14 (one day). Running time, 57 mins.

An economically produced flicker that will satisfy the neighborhooders and go well in the hinterland through tie-ups with the local police and fire forces. As title implies, "Heroes in Blue" glorifies the pavement pounders and the smoke-eaters.

Around the Dugans and the Kellys is built this meller. Sally Rand of the "Smoky" Dugan clan is opposite John Bowers, a young cop whose sire is a veteran flat-foot. The Dugan's stepson is a pyromaniac responsible for the series of incendiary fires and simultaneous robberies. A young member of the Kelly tribe, on the detective squad, is killed by the Dugan bad boy, as is Kelly pere. The double murder by the heroine's stepbrother is avenged by her own father, "Smoky" Dugan, who dies with the hoodlum in the punch conflagration of the footage.

The ingredients are trite, but satisfactorily handled. The mother stuff, the constant battling by the checker-addicted senior Kelly and Dugan, Mamma Kelly's fortitude in worrying about her husband and two sons, and the romance between the fire-eater's daughter and the cop's son make for an okay neighborhood flicker that will do for a single day's booking.

Story and title seemingly were devised with an eye to the small town exhibitors and exploitation hook-ups.

One naive title between the leading pair has Bowers telling Miss Rand that they'll go to the movie tonight and see John Bowers and Sally Rand. *Abel.*

THE FEARLESS RIDER

Universal "western" production and release. Directed by Edgar Lewis. Fred Humes featured. At Loew's New York, one-half double bill one day, Jan. 24. Running time, around 55 minutes.

Usual western type, with Fred Humes knocking out seven or eight men in a small room, before his own four men arrived to capture them all.

More story than customary. This would be a strong recommendation for "The Fearless Rider" if the tale did not run so mechanically, although the youngsters won't detect that, of course.

Not much riding and very little shooting. Just a bad man, the doctor and druggist of the village, trying to steal a gold mine from the old miner who had a good-looking daughter, who Humes first saw as the picture opened, although both had been living on opposite sides of the range for years.

Humes given little to do, but that one scrap. A fair western of the second class.

THE BATTLES OF CORONEL AND FALKLAND ISLANDS

(British Made)

British Instructional Corporation production. Presented by A. C. Bundy. Released for America through Artlee Pictures Corporation. Directed by Walter Sanders with J. V. C. Arton, assistant director. Picture's supervisor, H. Bruce Wolfe. At Cameo, New York, week Feb. 12. Running time, around 80 minutes.

Billing

Actual reproduction of these vivid and historical naval engagements, created with co-operation of British admiralty and Navy league.

37 Battleships—37,000 Men

Including the following battleship actors:
H. M. S. Barham for H. M. S. Invincible
H. M. S. Malaya for H. M. S. Inflexible.
H. M. S. Cardiff for H. M. S. Good Hope.
H. M. S. Concord for H. M. S. Monmouth.
H. M. S. Conquest for H. M. S. Glasgow.
H. M. S. Coventry for S. M. S. Sharnhorst.
H. M. S. Seres for S. M. S. Gneisenau.

None of the ships that were in either engagement still existed at the time of the making of this film, with the exception of one. All were sung by enemy action and the remaining one was broken up at the conclusion of the war.

This pictured reproduction of a couple of naval engagements between England and Germany early in the war amounts over here to a couple of hot scenes stretched out to 9,000 feet or so. In between for the padded footage are some useless scenes and considerably of that inane. As, for instance, at one time using perhaps 50 feet to show an anchor being weighed.

High interest in the picture will be with the English and the Germans. Over here those who went to war on land or sea may want to see it and that leaves for its draw an 85 per cent male audience. Its title should attract boys curious to see even a picture battle of the cruisers.

Much may depend upon the press work and there should be plenty handy with the subject, the memories it can recall and the people engaged. Although the picture's own billing is incredibly extravagant and should be toned down to facts. It says 37 warships and 37,000 men. As a matter of fact both engagements on the water involved 12 battle boats and there are not enough extras by some 36,000 to live up to the billing.

There are two actual engagements that will break even for those concerned. In the first engagement at Coronel, the Germans defeated the English, sinking two English boats with the odds five Germans to two English ships. At Falkland Islands, where each had five warships, the English wiped out the entire German fleet, without a ship's casualty of its own.

A bit of propaganda may have been of record or inserted at Falkland Islands, to bring out the humaneness of the English in attempting to give the Germans a chance to surrender, also the English sailor boys saving the Germans who went overboard from their boats. Again at Coronel a bit is interjected that places the Germans in a favorable light, and again when the German admiral, in accepting a bouquet at the celebration of his victory, tersely remarked, "These will be handy when it comes my turn."

In between the battle scene are wide spaces, filled in by what not, including the First Sea Lord's office in London and the Sea Lord himself, Lord Fisher, and well played by the unnamed actor. If there are impersonations here of the originals of the ships' highest officers, including the rear admirals and admirals, Americans cannot detect it. Besides, the names of the players are not programed.

In acting Admiral Sudcree (English) gave the best performance.

In warfare the engagements were about limited as could be expected to flashes from the big guns aboard the boats, with the usual cut offs. Sinking of boats may be seen in the dim distance, suggesting camera trickery in that of course. Smoke-stacks toppling over and supposedly into the ocean with nothing but the stacks seen would be a simple studio operation in California.

Suspense is altogether maintained for what it's worth through the captions, with the titling in a straightforward way, carrying this picture along. The story, if there is one, is that of the Sudcree fleet returning to the scene of the Coronel disaster with Fisher's instructions to Sudcree to wipe out the German fleet that gave Admiral Braddock and England about their first defeat of the war on water. The reproductions are claimed authentic, through the co-operation of the British admiralty.

It must be noted that for both countries their admirals chose to go down with their ships. That's the real and only thrill.

Near ludicrous is that portion of the picture showing the haste in which Admiral Sudcree equipped the "Invincible," then in drydock. It's so minute in details, even to supplies going aboard, that Sudcree had his boat start off the ways at exactly 6 p. m., the exact minute and the day he told Lord Fisher the boat would be ready to leave.

Nothing new in the film, except the reproduction. Battle scenes afloat and on land have been too numerous in individual productions and in the news weeklies to leave anything other than the reproduction here as a novelty. And one must be patient to watch 9,000 feet of flowing film to see 1,500 feet of action.

As a production otherwise, okay, with direction excellent. Direction here is the best thing in the entire picture. There's a mass to handle all of the time and it is well done, as far as the director did it, in every way.

But the picture calls for a small house, with the Art Theatre type preferred or those of around 1,000 capacity. The picture can only depend upon the men.

Cameo is about a 400-seater. Picture was booked in for two weeks and likely will be held over as expected. Business Sunday afternoon capacity at 3 with about 200 waiting in the lobby. Around 6 another lobby line of 100 was outside.

FOUR SONS

William Fox production and release. Directed by John Ford. Starring Margaret Mann, 10 years modest studio struggler and now star overnight. Story from original by Miss I. A. R. Wylie. Adapted by Philip Klein. Production editors, Katharine Hilliker and H. H. Caldwell. Musical setting and incidental sound effects by Movietone. Opened Feb. 13 at the Gaiety, New York, in on $2 scale, indefinitely. Running time, 100 minutes. Special musical score by S. L. Rothafel, assisted by Erno Rapee.

Mother Bernle.............Margaret Mann
Her Four Sons—
Joseph.......................James Hall
Franz.........Francis X. Bushman, Jr.
Johann..................Charles Morton
Andreas..................George Meeker
Annabelle......................June Collyer
James Henry.............Wendell Franklin
Major Von Stomm..............Earle Foxe
The Postman.................Albert Gran
The Burgomeister..........August Tollaire
The Schoolmaster............Frank Reicher
The Iceman..................Jack Pennick
The Innkeeper...............Hughie Mack
Johann's Girl....................Ruth Mix
Captain.......Archduke Leopold of Austria
Staff Surgeon...Ferdinand Schumann-Heink

A profoundly moving picture of family life in Germany during the war, giving a sympathetic insight into the effect upon the humble people of rural Bavaria of the great struggle. As an artistic creation the production is magnificent in the amazing effectiveness of its fine realism and in its utter simplicity. As a boxoffice attraction at the high scale its fate is in the balance.

In its favor are some of the finest and most touching passages of high sentiment ever shown on the screen, and the dramatic elevation of Mrs. Mann to picture eminence, which bids to exceed in public interest the sudden stardom of Mary Carr. The abundant excellence of the creation itself and the fascinating circumstances of Mrs. Mann's triumph are enormously valuable assets, and will probably suffice to give the Fox people another "Over the Hill."

Any obstacle that might have been anticipated from the risk of selling a sympathetic treatment of the German side of the war has been minimized by developing an American side to the story and by its happy ending, with the mother happily joined with her surviving son, by now a prosperous merchant in New York. The same thing works out in the tone of the story. While some of the sombre war-time episodes—the news of the death of three sons coming upon the grieving mother at home — are compensated by the lighter, sentimental sequences at the end, the picture leaving a cheerful effect.

The film is an achievement in artless realism. There isn't a moment when it does not live, and the whole production is utterly guiltless of theatrical device. Simple people, kindly and happy, are suddenly engulfed in the conflict, and tragedy comes upon the gentle villagers, among whom stalk the hated military martinets. It is the arrogant military class that plays the villain. The people are the pitiful puppets.

The story itself does not bear telling, so simple and unadorned is the commonplace history of a widow and her four sons. Joseph goes to America before the war, marries and has his own little delicatessen shop, and a baby is born. Then the war comes. The other three brothers go to the front and one by one are killed. There is no "war stuff," the war tragedy is enacted in the homely cottage of the lone mother. Joseph goes overseas in the A. E. F., leaving his wife to handle the shop. The story leaves him while the mother back in Bavaria is slowly broken as the war machine takes her three remaining boys—Franz, the handsome; Johannes, the strong, and, finally, Andreas, the beautiful.

Armistice Day finds her destitute of life and joy, while Joseph returns from France to America to find that his business had grown to a rich chain of stores.

His first move is to send for mother. From sombre tragedy the picture here takes on a tender and livelier quality. Mother has to go to school to learn her letters for American immigration purposes. Upon the Ellis Island examination she goes to pieces and is detained. But quite innocently she wanders out of the detention pen, reaches the city and meanders around under the care of kindly cops, who at length bring her safe to haven in Joseph's very modern apartment, where the frantic Joseph, returning from his search, finds her cuddling the baby before the fire.

Mrs. Mann's playing of the big role is a miracle of unaffected naturalness. Her Frau Bernle lives from the moment the film starts to its finish. She looks the part and she plays it with utter absence of effort or consciousness as a stately and white crowned old mother might go about her household tasks. And if this isn't art so much the worse for the trained and inspired acting profession.

Something of the same effortless simplicity has been communicated to the whole cast. The picture is rich in fascinating characters, such as the pompous but kindly old German letter carrier (Albert Gran) whose agonizing task it is to deliver the casualty notices to Frau Bernle; the Burgomeister of the village (August Tollaire), and the Innkeeper (Hughie Mack), besides a host of others.

The picture will be the making of James Hall, hitherto just a young leading man. As Joseph he creates a splendid portrait with a wide range of clean cut playing. Earle Fox makes a graphic study of the cold-blooded military officer type.

One of the high lights is his suicide at the explicit invitation of his rebellious regiment upon Armistice day, dressing himself in all his decorations for it.

In a pictorial sense the production is a revel in beauty and significant detail, with camera shots that are arresting. Such are the views of departing soldiers seen marching through the gay village streets from the vantage point of the church belfry; the panorama of the farming countryside swathed in morning mists; the church steeple with the tolling bells reflected in the still mill pond and a myriad of such color shots. Happy character bits likewise go to the building up of eloquent atmosphere and bit by bit the illusion of reality in place and people is created and never lost through nearly two hours.

Movietone is again employed with excellent discretion. It supplies an appropriate score and interpolates a few sound effects. When the young villagers are bringing in the hay, snatches of their song are brought out; again in the only battlefield sequence a faint voice is heard through the mists crying "mutterchen," and for one passage (where the stricken mother dreams her brood are again gathered about the supper board) a male chorus sings faintly as though at a great distance, or as though a choir were singing in a far off organ loft in church. The treatment follows closely upon that employed in "Sunrise," avoiding emphasis that might clash with the illusion.

There can be no question of the work's merit. There is only one bare chance for it to fall short of enormous popularity, the possibility that the screen public will shy off from a serious war picture at this time, when the subject has been pretty well exploited. That's quite remote, very remote, for a picture of this class and strength. *Rush.*

SPORTING GOODS

Paramount production and release. Starring Richard Dix. Directed by Malcolm St. Clair from story by Tom Crizer and Ray Harris. Titles by George Marion, Jr. At Paramount, New York, week of Feb. 12. Running time, over 60 minutes.

Richard Shelby	Richard Dix
Mr. Jordon	Ford Sterling
Alice Elliott	Gertrude Olmstead
Henry Thorpe	Philip Strange
Mrs. Elliott	Myrtle Stedman
Regan	Wade Boteler
Timothy Stanfield	Claude King
Mrs. Stanfield	Maude Turner Gordon

Light comedy harboring several strong situations which, combined with George Marion, Jr.'s titling, create sure and plentiful laughter.

Dix is ably supported by Gertrude Olmstead in the leading fem role. Cast delivers enjoyable business all the way through, Sterling and Dix dividing comedy honors in one of the two hit comedy situations.

Dix is a sporting goods salesman, also the inventor of a new type of golf suit guaranteed to give players more freedom for arms and shoulders.

On the strength of the car and his obvious acquaintance with Stanfield, a financier, Dix, the girl and her mother, go for a ride into town when their car breaks down on the road.

Sterling, as Jordon, head of a department store and a golf bug, is induced to go out on the golf course and watch the easy style of Dix's garment. Jordon is convinced. It begins to rain and the suit begins to grow longer, the coat finally reaching below his knees and the trousers stretching to the floor.

In another scene, where the menace lays plans to embarrass Dix in a poker game, the latter is called to the phone three times. Each time two of the players leave the table and the other slips a deuce into Dix's cards in exchange for another card. Every time Dix returns to the table to pick up his hand he notices the deuces growing. Mugs humorously when he finally spots the four deuces and wins four grand.

Production handled neatly and carried along at a good rate of speed. Dix's reception by the manager of the hotel and a regiment of redcaps create more laughs.

Not exceptionally strong but high class program fare which should get money. *Mori.*

ROSE-MARIE

Metro-Goldwyn-Mayer production and release. Featuring Joan Crawford, House Peters and James Murray. Adapted from operetta of same name and directed by Lucien Hubbard. John Arnold, cameraman. At Capitol, New York, week February 11. Running time, 70 minutes.

Joan Crawford	George Cooper
James Murray	Polly Moran
House Peters	Lionel Belmore
Creighton Hale	Harry Gribbon

The way the cast reads at the head of this notice is also the manner in which the Capitol program is listing the "principal players." It's a bad idea for an ordinary program feature that will serve as a fair open week filler, preferably during the hot weather when the mountain scenery won't be hard on the eyes and thoughts of vacation days.

How the uninitiated are going to pick out who's who in this one is a problem. Maybe they're all hiding, including Edmund Goulding, whose name doesn't crop up anywhere. This is the picture M-G-M scrapped after sinking $50,000 in it, gave it out as a press story, started to remake with Goulding and felt a bit sorry about it all. Lucien Hubbard gets screen credit for directing. How much of it actually is his is guess work.

But that cast idea. No character parts on program or in a lead title. Identifying the players as they appear with their names italicized down in one corner of a title is still a pretty fair system.

Especially value when trying to put over a new personality. In this instance it seems to be James Murray. Few at the Capitol this week will be able to pick him out, except by deduction. As the studios seem afraid to leave anything to the imagination of their followers, why give that same public credit for being able to decipher an incomplete cast listing system.

Murray looks like a bet for featured roles. Judging on this performance it's doubtful if stardom will ever enfold him. He's not the type. No one will ever associate Murray with the collar ad boys, but he's a masculine appearing youth whom the men will probably accept more readily than women. Formerly a member of the Capitol's uniformed staff (doorman) this is Murray's first picture there, and he's due at this house again next week in "The Crowd."

"Rose-Marie" isn't as bad as the advance reports rated it. It's just a picture with whatever following Joan Crawford has picked up to help. It's up in high altitudes, with the famed red coated force liberally sharing the story. The heavy dramatic incidents and the slow-motion miniature ice break climax figure to hold enough interest to make it passable with the average audience even if familiar. Eliminating 750 feet would help plenty.

Continuity jumps around and just what becomes of the heroine's husband isn't quite clear. But "the end" has her going downstream with Murray who has been under suspicion for murder since reel two. A questionable inclusion is the inferred intention of attack by Murray on Miss Crawford, the rough and ready boy seeing the light when the girl starts to pray for protection. Titles, uncredited, are rather awful and too many in number. Photography is okay.

Miss Crawford doesn't do badly, Murray is pretty fair and House Peters makes the sergeant reasonably convincing. "Pigeon" Polly Moran also rings in on a dance hall scene, and presumably George Cooper serves as an adequate menace.

Capacity Saturday matinee audience accepted the picture without comment either way, and gave it a light smattering of appalause as it closed. Sufficiently trimmed down, "Rose-Marie" should fill in on one of those "dog day" weeks for a break even or slightly better gross with title a possible aid. *Sid.*

THAT'S MY BABY

Universal production and release starring Reginald Denny. Directed by Fred Newmeyer from original story by Denny; Albert De Mond titled. At the Roxy, New York, week of Feb. 11. Running time, 55 mins.

Jimmy Norton	Reginald Denny
Molly Moran	Barbara Kent
Sylvia Van Tassel	Lillian Rich
Pat	Tom O'Brien
Lucien	Armand Kaliz
Pudge	Jane La Verne
Mrs. Van Tassel	Mathilde Brundage
Perkins	Wilson Benge
Second Butler	Charles Coleman
Valet	Art Currier

Reginald Denny's magnanimousness in permitting the four or five-year-old Jane La Verne to steal the picture from him goes double, considering that the star also authored the story which gives the kiddie actress the opportunities she has.

Little Miss La Verne is a female Jackie Coogan and will be heard from soon and often if handled right. Universal has a better bet in the kidlet than Baby Peggy was. Considering the child actress' performance, the existent shortcomings of the story and direction don't really matter. After all, if the purpose was to give the youngster an opportunity, some concession to faithfulness must be made.

In a somewhat fantastic manner Denny meets little orphaned Pudge. Becoming an unwilling "father" on the eve of his marriage to a social climber and a feminine fortune hunter, whose affection is obviously influenced by the hero's financial rating, the youngster is instrumental in halting the nuptials and uniting the sympathetic nurse (Barbara Kent) with Denny, these being the "parents" the orphan selects for herself.

When there is danger of the action falling down, rescue and accident scenes, among other things, are interpolated and so, for 55 minutes, the audience overlooks much of the realistic standards and is entranced by Jane La Verne's performance. Albert De Mond's breezy titles also help.

The kiddie overshadows Denny, and the rest of the support is accordingly slighted, although Tom O'Brien as the breezy traffic cop makes most of his opportunities.

"That's My Daddy" is not a costly production nor a great one, but will make money, please generally and above all impress because of little Jane La Verne. *Abel.*

CONEY ISLAND

F. B. O. production and release. Directed by Ralph Ince from story (probably original) by J. J. O'Neill. Lois Wilson and Lucila Mendez starred. Titles by Jack Conway. At Keith's Hippodrome, New York, week Feb. 13. Running time, about 63 minutes.

Joan Wellman	Lois Wilson
Joy Carroll	Lucila Mendez
Tammany Burke	Eugene Strong
Bob Wainwright	Rudolph Cameron
Hughey Cooper	William Irving

"Coney Island" can play any picture house, and that takes in the biggest, for a week. It's a corking action-romantic meller with Coney Island as its title and background.

Just one of those happy things that F. B. O. happened to hit. Though that does not remove any of the glory for J. J. O'Neill, who wrote this worthwhile story, or the excellent direction of Ralph Ince.

Without knowing what F. B. O. spent for this "Coney Island," if it cost $300,000 it would not be a whit better—and Joe Kennedy didn't go for that amount—not for F. B. O. this season.

The Coney Island scenes get Ahs from the audience. Especially when the audience is carried up and down the roller coaster. While the big coaster is called "The Giant Dipper" on its front and the admission is 10c., it and its dips look like the One Mile Streak at Luna Park, where the gate is 25c. Of course, this could have been taken at one of the beach resorts on the Pacific.

Applause breaks out several times in front. The loudest is when Lucila Mendez K. O.'s the heavy by kicking him on the chin, and another when the cops arrive to balk the gangsters. The way the gangsters started to wreck the joint on the platform of the coaster is perfect and speaks as well for Mr. O'Neill's outdoor detail throughout. Or perhaps it was Mr. Ince.

Scoring at the Hip was most apt. Music embodied many pop numbers, all alluding to the situation at hand. Two or three fights and a general melee toward the finish with the gangsters, but the best battle occurred in the dressing room of the cabaret show between Miss Mendez and another girl. Miss Mendez runs away with the entire film. The co-star, Lois Wilson, has a placid role, one of those sweet parts as a ticket taker at the coaster with the ride's owner in love with her.

Miss Mendez is a flip dancer and utters many of Jack Conway's fast captions, with none of those too high or two fast for the audience. Several get their laughs and the others neatly fit into the atmosphere. In a story of this character the caption writer, if he can do it, and Conway can, should be allowed to go as far as he likes. When will the producers learn that one of the best word things liked mostly by the American public is slang, even if they don't always understand it. It's something by itself to talk about. All book and periodical publishers have discovered that much.

Tale is consistent and handled that way. The ride's prop. must have a clear July 4 to get over. Otherwise the political boss of the Island will cop his coaster. Intertwined is the millionaire who likes the cabaret girl but falls for the cashier and goes to work as an engineer on the ride under an assumed name.

The finish is the picture's only weakness. Probably no one could think of anything else. At least it helps to keep a clean picture clean. It's too quick and illogical, but a minor defect in an otherwise bear in its class.

Besides which this film permits of a clown, carnival or circus ballyhoo in front of the house or on the street. The Hip has a mechanical clown in front making a good ballyhooed flash.

"Coney Island" is by far the best picture the Hip has had. That says very little for a house that has held the worst, but this F. B. O. will do business this week for the Hip because it more than makes good under one of the gingerest of names. And a name that should draw by itself.

THE WHIP WOMAN

Produced by Robert Kane. Released by First National. Story by Forrest Halsey and Leland Hayward. Directed by Joseph C. Boyle. Presented at the Greenwich Village theatre, New York, for a two weeks' engagement, starting Feb. 11. Running time, 53 minutes.

Sari	Estelle Taylor
Michael	Antonio Moreno
The Baron	Lowell Sherman
Countess	Hedda Hopper
Mill Haldane	Julanne Johnston

Pronounced and continuous razzing greeted the unreeling of this crude film on the opening. Subtitles so trite that the spectators anticipated them; director ineptness so conspicuous that it seemed funny; acting that reflected the general quality of the production, all combined to spell turkey in caps. Why talk about quickies and state righters when Robert Kane, a moneyed producer, releasing through an important organization like First National, can go so far wrong

The story takes place in Hungary, where Sari, a peasant girl, has a large horse whip as a Hungarian equivalent to roller skates. She gives the boys a dose of the lash whenever they get fresh. She drives a plow by day, and at night has a rather indefinite status in a local wine shop. Her hatred of men is intense, and nobody has ever caught her when she didn't have her whip with her.

She beats up a young aristocrat, but later saves him from fulfilling a suicide urge. At this point she knocks him on the head. The hero and heroine throughout the picture wallop one another plenty.

Dragging the aristocrat to her home which, a subtitle tells us, has never been entered by a man, she undresses him and puts him to bed. The next subtitle reads:

"An Awakening Such as Sari and Michael Had Never Imagined."

This shows them the next morning, the girl in the high Hungarian bed, the man on the floor mattress, with a resulting Pullman car effect.

The ripening of love is a matter of but a few feet of film. The conventional complications from the direction of the aristocratic family are in due time circumvented, and the picture closes with an assurance that they were married. *Land.*

OPENING NIGHT

Produced by Hollywood Pictures, released by Columbia. Directed by Edward H. Griffith. Producer appears on title sheet as Harry Cohn. Lobby data is scanty. Stars Claire Windsor and John Bowers. Story by Albert Payson Terhune. At the Academy, New York, Feb. 13 Running time, 56 minutes.

Several of Jannings' pictures with an unhappy ending appear to have inspired the idea among producers that the time is ripe for that sort of screen material. Here it doesn't work out satisfactorily. The tale is artificial; always one is conscious that the people and events are being manipulated by the dramatist, director and actors entirely to gain effects and without regard to what people would logically do in real life.

Events are not well knit. For instance, a man, believed to have been lost at sea, returns to find his wife being won by a rival. Because he has played the coward during the sinking of a liner, he voluntarily fades out of the picture, leaving fortune and loved ones behind, and taking a job as washer in a garage. You can't help but think he could have disclosed himself and nobody would ever have known of the disgrace, and so the whole business seems foolish, rather than heart rending as the picture would have it.

Sentiment is spread on pretty thick. By a coincidence the hero in his capacity of automobile washer is called upon to wash his own Rolls Royce, when the car comes back after having taken the wife and her new husband on their honeymoon. He climbs into the ritzy tonneau and picking up the trick speaking apparatus, as was his wont when he was prosperous, he murmurs to the absent chauffeur, "Home," and thereupon drops dead. The pathos is laid on so thick, here as in other places, that it defeats itself and one is disposed to meet it with levity.

The picture has not been happily cast. The lobby billing features Claire Windsor and John Bowers, although the principal character (role is typical of the sort Jannings plays) is done by an actor who never gets into the step or spirit of his character, partly because he is rather an obvious stagey actor and partly because it is an extraordinarily difficult role, of a middle-aged man who has both to draw sympathy, and still establish that audience attitude that will accept his ultimate defeat at the hands of fate. Jannings might do it, but not just a mechanical actor.

The Windsor and Bowers roles are very incidental. The happy outcome is theirs, but nobody cares. The story is loosely woven, does not rise to a climax and is extremely slow in development. The technical production has been nicely handled. Several passages have a first rate trick of expressing dramatic values in symbolism, such as the husband throwing a loving note to his wife on the steamer dock. It is wrapped in a gold coin. The coin reaches the hands of the husband's rival, while the loving message floats into the water. Again the same trick is employed when a child makes the husband a gift of a handkerchief, with which he later wipes his face when he has been struck by missiles from a mob which reviles him as a coward.

Just a good idea gone wrong.

Rush.

MARIA STUART

(GERMAN MADE)

Berlin, Jan. 26.

Resounding flop. Anton Kuh wrote the scenario and Friedrich Feher directed it under the supervision of Leopold Jessner of the State Playhouse, Berlin. Jessner has been much criticized for spending his precious time on this work, as he has not staged a single production at his own theatre this season.

This is particularly justified, as he does not seem to have any idea of film direction.

Madga Sonya, tooted lately as a coming star, is superficial as Maria. Even such a fine performer as Fritz Korner made nothing of his role.

Trask.

THE CROWD

Metro-Goldwyn-Mayer production and release. King Vidor starred as its director. Eleanor Boardman and James Murray, co-featured. Story by John V. A. Weaver and Mr. Vidor. Titles by Joe Farnham. At Capitol, New York, week Feb. 18. Running time, 98 minutes.

Mary	Eleanor Boardman
John	James Murray
Bert	Bert Roach
Jim	Daniel G. Tomlinson
Dick	Del Henderson
Mother	Lucy Beaumont
Junior	Freddie Burke Frederick
Daughter	Alice Mildred Puter

A drab actionless story of ungodly length and apparently telling nothing. Yet quite possibly written for the greater mass of the usual class attending picture theatres, and if so, should be liked by them, especially in the neighborhoods.

The longness of the picture suggests it was designed for a Metro special, but on what, only its authors, John V. A. Weaver and King Vidor, must know. Superficially it reels off as an analytical camera insight into the life, worries and struggles of two young, ordinary people, who marry and become parents.

Their lives may be the same more or less of hundreds of office clerks or others of that salary earning power. The husband is a plodder and dreamer, achieving nothing, however, but two children and an $8 raise of salary in five years. For this he seems in constant reprimand from his wife and her family. Casting aside his permanent desk job through mental strain over the death by a truck of his little daughter, the young husband tries other jobs in vain, until his wife, disgusted, finally slaps him in the face and walks out.

That is the sole bit of action. But she walks back and the film proceeds to its wearying finish, a finish at the Capitol's first showing Sunday that was very vague. Another print must have been in use, as others who saw the next unreeling mentioned a different finale. If they are trying out two finishes, the one that will leave the film the shorter should be selected.

As it is, 2,000 feet could come out of this picture, and the more the better. To those who can't fall into the atmosphere of this tedious subject it is endless and useless. Whole sequences could be taken out. One particularly is the birth scene, the entire hospital views.

If the objective here was to mark the rush of the crowd, the breaking away or through the common or to swing along with the tide as the easiest or customary way, the lesson isn't there. Nothing stands out in story excepting that a girl who should not expect more than she received wouldn't stand for her husband's lot. If an excerpt from Life, that alone kills the excerpt. If, meant to express that even a drudge may have an underlying strain of commercial value, such as the husband's ad slogan, that was smothered also.

King Vidor, the director, has interjected a little of everything, including freaky photography and hokum, the latter taking in a bit of comedy, but it fades into the monotonous and deadly detail of it all.

James Murray is the young husband and catches the spirit at times, more in looks than anything else. Murray is a type who must be fitted, as here. Both he and Eleanor Boardman had the opportunity for a big scene when seeing their child trampled over by a moving truck while walking toward their home. Both parents muffed the chance by a mile. For the record, little Freddie Burke Frederick as their 5-year-old son gave more expression as he walked alongside his father, looking up into his face, than the entire cast did in the other 8,950 feet, except Miss Boardman.

Miss Boardman played well in the sweetly style, as wife and housekeeper, until bringing out some spirit in that face slapping. While Vidor had Murray contemplating suicide by jumping beneath a railroad train because he couldn't get a job that stuck, after working in one previously for several years. And then everybody deliriously happy when the young husband gets a job as an advertising sandwich man.

Joe Farnham's captions in regulation fashion for this kind of a film and breaking through for a laugh when the subject matter permitted.

This picture may create a diversity of opinion among the different sets who see it. Those of the shelves should go for the picture in the larger houses, while the downstairsers in the main may be bored. It's a picture worth watching for effect on the picture public in general, of an unmoving story with no offside stuff except one sleeping car episode on the couple's wedding night, another unnecessary sequence but which may have been suggested while the rushes were run off.

If this is an original and the program mentions no adaptation, then it follows through the undue length that the story did not work out filmlike as its conceivers hoped for.

A Girl in Every Port

Fox production and release. Starring Victor McLaglen. Written and directed by Howard Hawks. Titles by Malcolm Stuart Boylan. Cameraman, William O'Connell. At Roxy, New York, week Feb. 18. Running time, 64 mins.

Spike Madden	Victor McLaglen
Chiquiti in Buenos Aires	Maria Casajuana
Salami	Robert Armstrong
Girls in Panama— Natalie Joyce, Dorothy Mathews and Elena Jurado	
Marie in France	Louise Brooks
Girl from Bombay	Sally Rand
Gang Leader	Francis MacDonald
Lena in Holland	Phalba Morgan
Lena's Husband	Felix Valle
Other Girl in Holland	Gretel Yoltz
Girl in South Sea Islands	Natalie Kingston
Girl from Liverpool	Caryl Lincoln

The boys will find this picture to their liking, but what the dames may think is something else again.

The plot deals with a Damon and Pythias friendship between two rough and tumble seamen. This pal stuff between two guys has never made any great hit with the ladies, and when the eulogy of male friendship includes several back-handed slaps at the feminine gender the reaction may be a matter of legitimate conjecture.

"A Girl in Every port" is packed with sex, but has not romance; it has a dozen ingenues and no heroine. Of all the beautiful bimboes encountered by the sailors in their world travels not one is on the up-and-up, and the one (Louise Brooks) who inspires McLaglen to day dream over settling down in a cottage for two is the biggest gold-digger of all.

The picture is a series of hoke adventures with dames and gendarmes. It holds a lot of laughs and still maintains a human note on the comrade angle. McLaglen is great as the heavy-hitting bozo. His buddy is played by Robert Armstrong, legit actor, newly recruited to the screen and looking like a good bet.

Confusion in the program makes it difficult to identify the girls individually. They are a zaftic bunch of hot-looking mamas.

Miss Brooks has the longest session in front of the camera. This gal is solid with the jellybean trade. She is often and favorably mentioned whenever the boys go into executive session on the opposite sex. With all the merited praise of her face and figure little has been said to date about Miss Brooks' acting. It's one of those things you don't mention.

Malcolm Stuart Boylan's titles seemed involved and obscure in thought on several occasions. Howard Hawks made a good job of directing with the exception of an overdone bit of melodramatic acting by McLaglen upon the discovery by him of what he supposes to be the perfidy of his buddy.

The picture is entertaining and ought to click. The possibility of an unfavorable feminine reaction because of the cynical attitude towards sex matters should not prevent the picture obtaining moderate box office rating. It's okay for de luxe first runs anywhere. *Land.*

PAUL AND VIRGINIA

(FRENCH MADE)

Paris, Feb. 13.

This screen version of the famous work of Bernardin de Saint Pierre was produced by Robert Peguy some time ago, and is now being released, after an unexplained delay, by Societe Mauricienne du Bon Film. As the action (well known) is laid in the Mauritius Island, picture is almost entirely exteriors. The fame of the story may attract, but the picture is not likely to become famous.

Virginia was a maiden of high birth in the island of Maurice when it was a French possession, who played in the woods with Paul, son of a servant. They grew up together, and their deep affection continued. When Virginia sailed for France to visit a relative, Paul waited patiently for her return, but she was shipwrecked. The youth, unable to subdue his grief, also died, and the two mothers wept over the two young lovers united in death.

Jean Bradin is excellent in the part of Paul, with Simone Jacquemin pretty as Virginia. *Kendrew.*

Shepherd of the Hills

First National production and release. Featuring Molly O'Day. Adapted from Harold Bell Wright's novel of same name. Directed by Al Rogell, with Alec B. Francis, John Boles and Matthew Betz underlined. At Strand, New York, week Feb. 18. Running time, 76 minutes.

The Shepherd..............Alec B. Francis
"Sammy" Lane..............Molly O'Day
Young Matt..............John Boles
Wash Gibbs..............Matthew Betz
Old Matt..............Romaine Fielding
"By Thunder"..............Otis Harlan
Ollie..............Joseph Bennett
Little Pete..............Maurice Murphy

"Shepherd" registers as a mild western which will need all the publicity it can get on the hookup with the Harold Bell Wright novel of the same title. The story, taken from any angle, is familiar to both picture fan and the prolific fiction reader. In this instance it's not cattle, but sheep, with the familiar "sky pilot" toned up and repressed a bit. The answer to his prayers for rain saves the settlers. Not "smash" box-office, but likely to figure moderately through whatever strength the title possesses and the performances of Francis, Boles and Betz. Scenic qualities also an asset.

It's the story of the hills and a drought which threatens to ruin the ranchers. The stranger among their midst, the Shepherd (Mr. Francis) becomes their oracle and secretly knows that a youngster with a peculiar mental twist is his grandson, the son of his boy whom he advised to desert the country girl for a career. The daughter of Old Matt (Fielding). The latter befriends the aged city minister, come to the hills for peace.

Secondary motive is the love interest between young Matt (Boles) and "Sammy" (Miss O'Day), who is engaged to a native with big-town ideas (Bennett), for comedy. Betz plays the heavy who would see the settlers desert their land so he can grab it.

High spots are the ultimate roundhouse swings young Matt and Gibbs exchange and the destruction of a supply train the former is bringing in by a landslide which Gibbs' followers instigate. As the settlers turn against the Shepherd, the clouds roll up and it starts to pour, making everybody happy.

As the fight has convinced "Sammy" that Matt's her boy, it's all satisfactory at the finish. A dramatic passage is donated to Little Pete, almost dying, during which the dead mother's father discovers the Shepherd is the youngster's other grandfather and is about to brain him when stopped by a shadow symbol of the cross.

Picture doesn't move any too fast, but the underlined players help to make it stand up, and its scenic background is worthy. Photographically, the best inclusion is a cutback to Little Pete's father and mother, camaraed through a checkered screen which immediately identifies it. Looks good and doesn't hide the action.

Miss O'Day has little to do and is probably being featured on what may have resulted from "The Patent Leather Kid." No reason other than that for her being emphasized here. Report of F. N. forcing her to reduce is quite plausible after this viewing. She's something more than pudgy in this film. *Sid.*

LOVE AND LEARN

Paramount comedy production and release. Starring Esther Ralston. Directed by Frank Tuttle. Leon Chandler, leading man. Production supervision, B. P. Fineman. From story by Louise Lang, adaptation by Florence Fyerson. At Paramount, New York, week Feb. 18. Running time, 57 minutes.

Fairly amusing farce with a good deal of bedroom stuff neatly framed and played in an artless manner that robs it of offense. Won't pull much business but should please regular clientele. Picture is played without any explicit billing about the house or even in the program, as part of a blind show under the rather attractive title of "Take a Chance Week" at the Paramount. Shrewd bit of showmanship, possibly being used as a device to help a picture that is without a strong "name" draw for lobby display, although the title would be an asset in a box office estimate.

Amusement value lies in the ingenious complications devised in a hotel, where heroine seeks to save political candidate from being framed by a woman tool of his party opponents, only to find herself innocently occupying the other double bed while the candidate, equally guiltless, slumbers in the same room.

Miss Ralston contributes a good deal of blonde beauty and some grace to the eternal flapper role, but cannot be said to raise a moderately diverting picture beyond just that. There isn't much an actress can do with the hoyden flapper type these days when there are so many roles of the sort, except to play it without too much simpering, and this Miss Ralston achieves.

Picture generously gagged up with comedy bits and laughable surprises. It gains in speed as it goes along and climaxes in a brisk solution of both the romance and the tangle for a good average of laughs from both titles and action sequences. The bedroom scenes are skilfully managed, so that there is a maximum of sex kick and filmy lingerie without offense, largely due to the absence of any smirking emphasis upon the subject in the Avery Hopwood manner.

Rather, the whole business is managed with an altogether charming youthful candor and naivete. A girl in lacy step-ins and a young man in dressing-gown can be cheerfully innocent in the same hotel room, if the intent is to make them so. The situation becomes risque only by aforethought and design. Here it is quite without guile or double entendre, which makes all the difference between black and white—or white and pale lavender, if you like.

Settings are cheerful and bright and serve admirably for background. And picture is smoothly enough handled to keep it on a high comedy plane under circumstances where very little might have made it pretty rowdy. *Rush.*

Streets of Shanghai

Tiffany-Stahl production and release. Featuring Pauline Starke. Directed by Louis J. Gasnier from J. F. Natteford's story. Cast: Kenneth Harlan, Margaret Livingston, Eddie Gribbon, Jason Roberds, Sojin and Anna May Wong. At Hippodrome, New York, week of Feb. 20.

A yarn of the Marines with enough familiar names and faces floating through it; production and action to let it stand up in the intermediate houses, no matter how they split the week.

Pauline Starke is the foreign miss at the mission, upon whom the Chinese "heavy" has designs. Kenneth Harlan is the soldier boy who has his love affair gummed up by Miss Livingston as a hit and run girl who compromises him in the barracks.

The kick footage is the attack on the mission by the heavy's followers, with much gun play, convulsive deaths and Eddie Gribbon saving the situation.

T-S is following the Fox idea of tinting any and everything that hints at light and lends itself to color. It's neither good nor necessary.

Cast principals play this one okay and Gasnier keeps it moving. Titles carry a chuckle or two and a couple of pretty solid laughs crop out during the running. A Monday night Hip audience laughed and later applauded the rescue.

The Yanks are coming and all that sort of thing, but the boys and girls who stand for the 50c. tap at this house gave sound evidence of approval. *Sid.*

BUTTONS

Metro-Goldwyn-Mayer production and release. Produced, directed and written by George C. Hill. Screen adaptation by Hayden Talbot. Titles by Ralph Spence. Starring Jackie Coogan. Cast including Gertrude Olmstead, Lars Hanson, Roy D'Arcy, Paul Hurst, Jack McDonald. At Loew's American, New York, Feb. 20-22. Running time, over 60 mins.

Because of several deviating twists to the story which lower concentrated interest in the whole this picture misses as a full week's attraction in major houses.

George Hill has shown highly profitable capabilities in the slapstick line, but apparently the effort of compiling the story and assuming charge of production in addition to directing interfered with his knack of wringing laughter from cold audiences.

Although one of the characters, the slow-witted physical culture trainer on the trans-Atlantic liner, is framed to cause laughs, the rewards are meagre, unsubstantial in volume and far from frequent.

For small town audiences, and especially where the juvenile element is considerable, the picture rates as a moderate draw.

The story is weak, as it has been built around a character, the youthful star, whom it would be difficult to equip satisfactorily with material.

Jackie Coogan is not handled sympathetically. He acts with restraint, and while that sort of thing should appeal to the high hat critics, these are not the people producers seek to please. Coogan as a sobbing, tattered London waif, though previously done, might have succeeded in winning sympathy. The natural manner in which the boy is introduced and routined throughout is admirable, but it is at no time boxoffice.

Love interest is stifled early. The captain, played up as the heroic figure, finally discovers that his fiancee is not a good girl. The girl fails to please as a type because of her acceptance of the attentions of a man like Henri (D'Arcy). The latter, foppish, unattractive lounge lizard, rouses a feeling of contempt which is transferred to the girl because she is willing to play his game, though only temporarily.

"Buttons" (Coogan) serves as a page on board a British ship on which the action is laid. The sinking of the ship shows the boy returning, after all the others had left, to die with his captain. The pair are saved for the closing of the story. *Mori.*

THE SIREN

Columbia production and release. Featuring Tom Owen and Dorothy Revier. Byron C. Haskin directed from story by Harry Shumate. Cast includes Jed Prouty and Norman Trevor. At Loew's New York. Running time, 65 mins.

Interesting meller for the honky tonks. Harry Cohn may be given entire credit for turning out a production of this quality against the cost limitations.

Continuity is kept moving with one or two exceptions. Trevor has the cinch part of the picture, as the card sharp who almost succeeded in framing the girl for his murder, though still living, but muffs an easy bet.

Owen and Miss Revier make an interesting team. Miss Revier, especially, looks good. When seen several months ago her appearance spoiled any chance for effectiveness. Expert makeup and good camera treatment has resulted in a distinct change.

Film catches interest from the opening. A girl on a lonely road, caught in a storm, one of the tires of her car punctured, is shown climbing through the window of a log cabin. She removes her clothes (flashes of bare shoulders and knees), gets into a gown and falls asleep. The owner of the cabin, arriving with the opening of the duck shooting season, finds her there.

Meet in the city at a reception given by the girl in her mansion. Menace is introduced as a well groomed card manipulator, stuck on the gal. The latter won't stand for his cheating the boy friend and orders him out of her house.

Later the heavy returns. A fight starts during which the curtains catch fire. The girl shoots the trouble-maker. The house burns down and Cole (Trevor) is generally accepted as dead. He has, however, been saved by his partner. He forces the latter to accuse the girl of murder, figuring on his changed appearance, facial burns, to make him safe from recognition. Court scenes are not handled convincingly.

Story leads directly to the chair, a noose being placed round the girl's neck, with a last minute confession by the sharper's partner. *Mori.*

JAWS OF STEEL

Warner Bros. production and release. Starring Rin-Tin-Tin. Directed by Ray Enright from story by Chas. R. Ceman. Cast includes Jason Robards, Helen Ferguson, Mary Louise Miller, Jack Curtis and Buck O'Connor. At the Tivoli, New York. Running time, about 60 mins.

The dog star is still a knockout. That's all there is to this picture, but it's enough to carry it over successfully in the split weeks and daily changes.

From 15 to 20 minutes could easily have been cut. Picture moves along monotonously except when the dog is in action. Every movement of the animal is interesting. Even at play, and not doing tricks, he is a spellbinder. Some of his actions are almost human and as a trouper he ranks far above the regular run of two-legged actors appearing in films.

Robards and Miss Ferguson photograph badly. Mary Louise Miller, chubby baby player, steals scenes where the dog is not shown.

Story revolves around a pup who is lost by a family moving to a small town to work a gold claim. The dog grows up to be a killer but always remembers his childhood playmate and returns to amuse the little girl though knowing he may be captured. Saves the little girl's life by his presence and reveals the murderer of an old prospector who had found gold, thereby clearing himself with all folks. *Mori.*

Wickedness Preferred

Metro-Goldwyn-Mayer production and release. Directed by Hobart Henley from story by Florence Ryerson and Colin Clement. Titles by Robert Hopkins. Co-starring Lew Cody and Aileen Pringle. At Loew's American Roof, New York, Feb. 16-19. Running time, over 60 mins.

Anthony Dare....................Lew Cody
Kitty Dare....................Aileen Pringle
Baby Burton....................Mary McAllister
Homer Burton....................Bert Roach
Leslie....................George K. Arthur

No amount of editing, cutting or skillful directing could have saved this from the shooting galleries. Titles, by Robert Hopkins, harbor a multitude of laughs, but not of a kind to score with other than Class A house trade, where the picture is out of place.

Most of the film is told via titles, more like a foreign production in this respect than the output of a highly organized American studio.

Shorn of titles and inopportune by-play, the story is of the man and the girl on the island who try to live with the sky as a roof and the great outdoors as a home. This time it's done by two married folks, a flighty, half-grown, girl-wife, and a novelist with an efficiency expert for a wife.

As usual, physical discomforts soon prove that civilized conveniences with the former mates are preferable.

Miss McAllister photographs as a desirable blonde, despite having the role of an empty-headed girl with a flare for romantic novels. Lew Cody is used mainly for buffeting purposes, rarely producing any legitimate comedy.

Silly, unsuitable and uninteresting story material. Fault of the pickers. Just money and time wasted. *Mori.*

BRASS KNUCKLES

Warner Bros. production and release. Directed by Lloyd Bacon from the story by Harvey Gates. Starring Monte Blue. Betty Bronson and William Russell featured. At Moss's Broadway week Feb. 13. Running time over 60 mins.

Slow-moving, badly directed picture based on a type story without any new twists.

Action opens in a prison. Convicts stage a break, but are stopped by two of their own gang (Blue and another), who figure that recapture is inevitable.

Released from prison, the two ex-convicts adopt a little girl, daughter of a fellow-jailbird.

Russell plays the heavy. Incensed against the man who stopped the jail-break, he revenges himself on being released from prison by framing a charge of immorality on the grounds that the girl is "living" with them.

The charge is disproved, but the heavy has meantime secured documents proving himself the girl's father or guardian.

Usual fist fight and clinch for the finish.

Title acquired as the menace used brass knuckles.

Time-killer only. *Mori.*

FASHION MADNESS

Hollywood production, released by Columbia. Starring Claire Windsor. Directed by Louis Gasnier from original story by Victoria Moore. Continuity by Olga Printzlau. Cameraman, J. O. Taylor. In cast Reed Howes and Laska Winter. At Loew's New York, one day, Feb. 13, as half double bill. Running time, 60 minutes.

Lavish sets and clothes; society stuff and melodramatic hokum, but "Fashion Madness" as a program picture is considerably better than some higher priced films the bigger colleagues have turned out in the past six months.

Society and the north woods are oddly, but interestingly, combined. Everything is evening clothes, clubs and milady's domicile before the spoiled daughter of the Wall street big boy is spirited away by her husky man-about-town friend. Medium for the abduction is the friend's yacht and the site where the story unfolds is in his mountain cabin.

Claire Windsor, as the girl, does some of the strangest work of her picture career. All of it shows her off to advantage, from the ball room gowns to the trim riding habit up in the hills. Reed Howes makes an ideal leading man for her, and is also given the opportunity to use all of his neck ties.

Some of the most effective work is accomplished by Laska Winter as the little Indian rival of the society damsel.

The climax, although more far-fetched than the rest of the story, should provide a punch in off-Broadway houses.

BOWERY CINDERELLA

Excellent production, released by Commonwealth. Directed by Burton King. From story by Melvin Houston. Cast includes Pat O'Malley, Gladys Hulette and Rosemary Theby. At the Arena, New York. Running time, about 50 mins.

Not likely it will ever be seen outside of the state right market. Cheaply construted, badly played and crude direction. It spells "quickie" in every scene.

Plot No. 658, in which the wealthy villain has designs on the poor gal. He puts her and her sick mother into a comfortable apartment. Just as he is about to exact a kiss from heavily rouged lips, who should appear at the doorway but the boy friend, broad husky and ready to go.

This fight scene is more funny than dramatic. Once home, the boy discovers that he has sold a play, an advance payment being conclusive proof. A flash of the vine-clad cottage finishes. *Mori.*

Trial of Daniel Westhof

(GERMAN MADE)

Ufa production and release. Directed by Fritz Wendhausen. Cast including Imre Raday, Erna Morena, Karin Evans and Eliza La Porta. At 55th St. Playhouse, New York, Feb. 17. Running time about 60 minutes.

This picture is but another argument in opposition to claims of suitability made for foreign productions. While it easily fills the requirements of art theatres and is bound to meet with approbation from that class of patrons, it is impossible as a general release.

Fritz Wendhausen has done well. There is little fault to find with the direction, judging only from the foreign production methods applied. The film is chockfull of good ideas, technical and otherwise, many of which could be used to enhance the value of American pictures. But the whole has been assembled in a manner decidedly and distinctly alien to the tastes and desires of the American public.

The script has suffered either in the writing or in the adaptation because the characters depicted are not faithful to themselves. There is, for instance, Lessing, first shown as a highly educated, hard-headed, unemotional lawyer of the foremost rank. It does not seem possible that a man of that calibre, steeled to scenes of violence and crime, accusations and rebuttals, a lawyer who has doubtless conducted brutal cross-examinations and in no awe of the court room, would break down and confess a murder which some one else had already pleaded guilty to. It would take more than a mere charge, flung by a half-grown girl in a state of frenzy and over anxiety to protect her lover, to cause a character of that kind to break down suddenly and sink to the floor, clutching his throat and shrieking his guilt.

Characters cannot be painstakingly built up through five or six reels and then torn down at a moment's notice. It is simple enough to understand the emotional reaction of the stupid, half-witted hero who, believing he had murdered a man, rushed to the nearest police station and gave himself up.

Audience sympathy is ruthlessly and continuously bothered throughout the picture. The hero would get no consideration from audiences of the regular type. According to the story the boy wanted to stop the marriage of a millionaire to a creature with whom he had had amorous relations. No one could be deluded into believing that such a marriage could be stopped by the boy refusing to let the money-lender out of his room on the wedding day. A proceeding of that nature might delay the marriage.

The hero, from the opening until the closing reel, is played as a sap without any kind of appeal, to atone for his obvious lack of sense.

There are interesting directorial items spotted through the picture. Some of these have been used in "The Last Laugh" and "Variety," while others seem new. A small part played by the lawyer for the defense approaches genius in its admirable handling.

As a whole picture hasn't a chance outside of the art picture houses. *Mori.*

GOLDEN YUKON

Sam Pisor production. Aywon release. Neil Shipman starred and credited as author and co-director with Bert Van Tingle. Cast includes Alfred Allen, Lillian Leighton, Hugh Thmopson, Ah Wing, C. K. Van Auker. At Tivoli, New York, one day, Feb. 16. Running time, 53 mins.

Not a bad states right number, although probably made some time ago or possibly a reissue. Plot brings back your old friend, white slavery. Innocent and trusting girl is taken to Alaska by an unscrupulous gent, who commits bigamy and tries to commit murder.

Crazy miner with tales of a bonanza kicked around by the rabble, only to be proven right in the end.

Acting, production and photography, fair. *Land.*

JOLLY VINEYARD

(GERMAN MADE)

Berlin, Feb. 4.

Comedy by Karl Zuckmayer, one of the most successful of late years But the film will not meet the same kind fate; for America it is without chances.

Concerns life in the Rhine district during vintage time, and is just as coarse as life there probably really is.

Seductions are handled in a jocular vein. At the end about eight couples decide to get married—afterwards!

Its figures are the rich vineyard owner, his daughter, his housekeeper, the sailor who loves the daughter and is loved by her in return, a swindler who gets the daughter into a compromising position and asks for her hand, and two comic German wine salesmen from Berlin.

In the cast only Camilla Horn as the daughter and Friedrich Lobe as the traveling salesman stood out. *Trask.*

SOFT LIVING

William Fox production and release. Produced by James Tinlin. From story by Grace Mack. Starring Madge Bellamy. At Roxy, New York, week February 25. Running time 60 minutes.

Nancy Woods....................Madge Bellamy
Stockney Webb....................John Mack Brown
Lorna Estabrook....................Mary Duncan
Billie Wilson....................Joyce Compton
Philip Estabrook....................Thomas Jefferson
Rodney S. Bowen....................Henry Kolker
Mrs. Rodney S. Bowen....................Olive Tell
Office Boy....................Maine Geary
Hired Man....................Tom Dugan
Swede....................David Wengren

Good title, minus names and a story based on a mere thread of an idea which nears extinction in the process of the narration, represents the unattractive total upon which this production may be judged.

Continuity is dull and draggy. Not a punch in the picture. Story unconvincing.

It's another version of the brutal treatment given the newlywed wife with the object of teaching her to appreciate the true worth of her papa. In this case it's lightly disguised under the heading of divorce and alimony.

According to the story the secretary to a divorce lawyer has a vague, half formed ambition to marry a money man with the object of retiring on alimony, following a divorce. She is given further encouragement by Lorna Estabrook, an old and experienced divorcee, who has milked several wealthy husbands.

The girl secretary, Nancy Woods, finds that Stockney Webb, the man she agrees to marry after a three-day courtship, is in love with her and it doesn't seem fair. But, through an open door Webb overhears Lorna advising Nancy on the wedding day how to carry out divorce and alimony proceedings.

Webb stays away from the bride during the honeymoon. Later, Lorna comes on the scene with the intent of getting Webb for her own while giving the impression that she is compromising the boy to help Nancy secure a divorce.

Laughs light and sparing. One title tells the story. The secretary, looking at an alimony check, says: "I get $35 a week for making good and she gets $1,000 for failing."

Madge Bellamy interesting in several brief interpretations. Best is where the girl does sample court routines, teaching prospective alimony-seekers how to vamp judge and jury. John Mack Brown is suitable male lead. Support capable. *Mori.*

LATEST FROM PARIS

Metro-Goldwyn-Mayer production and release. Starring Norma Shearer and featuring George Sidney. Directed by Sam Wood from A. P. Younger's original. Titles by Joe Farnham, with William Daniels, photographer. At Capitol, New York, week Feb. 25. Running time, 73 minutes.

Ann Dolan....................Norma Shearer
Sol Blogg....................George Sidney
Joe Adams....................Ralph Forbes
Abe Littauer....................Tenen Holtz
Bud Dolan....................William Bakewell
Louise Martin....................Margaret Landis
Bert Blevins....................Bert Roach

Light comedy of no particular importance but with the Norma Shearer name and enough laughs to see it through for program purposes. Productionally the picture doesn't fulfill what the title promises. Miss Shearer, however, looks good all the way, gets a chance to be kittenish here and there, and does well with the assignment as a whole. Looks like a good matinee film.

Main trouble with the feature is that the love story doesn't convince. Miss Shearer as Ann Dolan, the star of a clothing firm's sales department, falls for Adams (Forbes), a rival salesman, who apparently hasn't much but nerve and allows himself to be forced into an engagement with Louise Martin (Miss Landis).

How a girl with Ann's supposed mentality can become weepy over

Adams, as Forbes plays him, is something the scenario asks you to believe. Rather an imposition on the script's part, although if girls prefer blondes, too, they may take to Forbes. But it's doubtful if he'll ever get the men or a majority of the women.

Against the Potash and Perlmutter background most of the story takes place in a small town which other than cast salaries and an overlong studio snow sequence makes the "nut" on this one appear most reasonable. The snow thing has the lovers walking into the open minus wraps or hats and so enthralled with each other that they saunter along unmindful of the weather for close to 1,000 feet. The start of this bit is a solid laugh, and follow-up snickers are strung out.

The prolongation tempers the first impression. As a 73-minute picture it would have more punch if cut eight or 10 minutes. Lobby stills displayed scenes which never cropped out on the screen, so the boys and their scissors have likely been at it already.

The star flaunts various costumes, mostly of the sport type, which should catch the feminine eye, and seem particularly adept in a short bit where she solos a rehearsal with herself on bawling somebody out.

It's all carefree and gay, with George Sidney doing capably with the heart interest when it looks as if Ann is going to lose her man. Farnham's titles do their part and the camera work is standard.

"Latest from Paris" registers as a bright little picture for Miss Shearer from a personal angle. It will neither make nor break box offices. *Sid.*

THE LEOPARD LADY

Pathe release of a De Mille production. Directed by Rupert Julian. Adapted from play, and features Jacqueline Logan, Alan Hale and Robert Armstrong. J. J. Mescall, cameraman. At Colony, New York, week Feb. 25. Running time, 67 minutes.

Paula	Jacqueline Logan
Caesar	Alan Hale
Chris	Robert Armstrong
Berlitz	J. Bradbury, Sr.
Hector	Dick Alexander

Maybe Keith-Albee has an argument as to why it won't pay any more for pictures than it will for a No. 3 act. "Leopard Lady" could be a reason. This picture might also clarify, to some extent, when K-A hasn't helped Pathe or Pathe K-A.

Film features like this don't make it tough for the opposition. Here's a mystery thriller that's a perfect fit for the third-grade houses or where it can linger only one day. The saps may shiver and a couple may squeal, but nearly everybody is going to get a laugh out of a ridiculous sub-title that pops up in the midst of a dramatic scene. How any pre-view projection room could fail to detect it is a marvel. Studio must have just labeled the film "cut and send," without bothering to take another look.

Johnny Mescall, now screen credited as J. Joseph Mescall, has tricked up the photography to snare early attention, and Rupert Julian, directing, has undone that good work by stringing out, endlessly, a deal between the secret service head and Miss Logan, which takes place in the latter's dressing room.

Berlitz, the silent cop with a white mouse Julian evidently thought was a scream, will give Paula 20,000 kronen if she'll clean up a circus that either leaves robbery or murder in its wake. The money wil lallow the girl to quit and join an officer in the U. S. merchant marine.

The tent show's part owners' trained ape has been bumping everybody off. For what reason nobody'll ever know. Paula's cats eventually turn on her, but Caesar saves. For that she's about to let him get away, when Chris comes in a little the worse for wear after a tussel with the ape. That takes all the sentiment out of Paula as far as Caesar is concerned, and as the boys fisticuff about a bit she socks the Russian strong boy from behind.

And here it is that Chris is made to say, "Now I know you love me."

Well, sir, you should have heard that third of a house laugh.

Finale has Paula cornered by the ape, which she eventually induces to shoot itself with an automatic pistol. "Ape commits suicide"—great for the tabs and those composite photos.

Picture might have been all right if it hadn't been butchered.

Very dramatic most all the way, Miss Logan, like the rest, is prone to overplay. And that's direction. Each of the principal players has turned in good performances in other pictures, but not here. Miss Logan was once in a film called "Java Head." Neither before nor since has she looked as good as her opening shot in that one. She still has appearance, but Julian has made her go 'way overboard in a flirtation sequence and has timed the story spasmodically.

A much hoked dramatic release that occasionally shows flashes of what it might have been, good for the big independent neighborhood houses. Now, if they play it, they'll be taking a chance. *Sid.*

SAILORS' WIVES

First National production and release, directed by Joseph Henaberry from story by Warner Fabian. Featuring Mary Astor and Lloyd Hughes. At the Hippodrome, N. Y., week of Feb. 27. Running time, about 60 mins.

A weak sister. May be used as a filler in the split weeks, or with strong stage show support. Misses as a first-run house feature. Pictures loses out because of story which may have been fine reading, but does not translate into action or even interest on the screen.

Tells of a girl who, knowing she is to lose her eyesight, runs from the man she loves and has promised to marry. When he finds her later she tries to impress him as a flirt who did not mean what she said when she first met him.

Girl finally shoots herself when she becomes blind, and bullet lands at an angle which relieves pressure doctors had been afraid to attempt to alleviate via an operation. She regains her sight.

Miss Astor looks and carries herself well, but film without climaxes, vital love interest or action. Production rates among the seconds. *Mori.*

Battles of Falkland Island

(BRITISH MADE)

(Canadian Review)

Toronto, Feb. 25.

Produced by H. Bruce Woolfe for W. and F. Film Service, Ltd., with co-operation of British Royal Navy and technical committee from (late) Imperial German Navy. Released in Canada by Regal Films Ltd. Directed by Walter Summers. Scenario by Harry Engholm and Capt. Frank C. Bowem, R. N. Cast not directly named. Filmed in the Mediterranean. Previewed at Tivoli, Toronto. Running time (fast), 75 mins.

From the standpoint of the British Empire, particularly Canada, where British films are seldom seen, this history of two naval battles is sure fire and a money maker. It is a triumph of direction in the mass and strictly impartial as to the merits of the crews in these South Pacific and South Atlantic fights.

Belling credits "35 ships and 10,000 men," which is an exaggera- Billing credits "35 ships and and in a few spots too much time is wasted on details, but despite this the picture does not lag and holds suspense throughout its 8,000 feet.

Aside from actual battle scenes, which are excellent even unto trick photography, hitherto a serious drawback of British productions, the story is in the behavior of its characters. How the German Admiral Von Spee refused to drink "Eternal damnation to the British Navy," but preferred as a toast "The health of a very gallant foe." How this same admiral refused to leave his battered ship when a boat drew up alongside him and how Cradock, the British commander, fights rather than run away when badly outnumbered in ships and guns.

The story is simple. Cradock has a small fleet near Coronel in the south Atlantic. He hears the enemy is in the vicinity and tries to prevent them getting into the open sea, where they could attack Allied commercial ships.

His only battle cruiser develops engine trouble and is left far astern. Coming up with a much larger German outfit than he expected, he is advised to run away, but stays to fight and is sent to the bottom. The Glasgow, a light cruiser, escapes, and the missing battle cruiser never gets into the engagement.

England gets the wind up, and Lord Fisher, first lord of the admiralty, orders a large squadron southward under Admiral Sturdee. He is told the fleet, led by the Invincible, cannot leave for five days after he has told them to go, but insists they weigh anchor by six p. m. Dec. 6. Feverish work in the dockyards gets the boats ready, and they push off on a record run to the Falklands.

Meantime, at a big banquet in Valparaiso, where he is acclaimed a national hero, Von Spee announces his intention to capture the Falklands and make them useless as a British coaling station. When his ships reach the harbor Sturdee's fleet is coaling and unable to sail.

The Germans go about but Sturdee chases them into the night and sinks all but one without loss of a ship.

The characters of Lord Fisher and Admiral Sturdee are the best interpretive bits put on the English screen. Photography is good, particularly on inside shots, and no "we won the war" stuff mars the close-ups of gunners, stokers and bridge officers. Where individual acts of heroism were done by Germans this is faithfully shown, such as where Sturdee orders cease fire against "Gneisnau," which is crippled except for one gun and rapidly sinking. The lone gun keeps barking, and the ship goes down stern first with a sailor waving the German naval flag far up on the prow.

Practically no comedy relief but some human interest stuff when the Glasgow, survivor of the first fight, finds itself out of coal in pursuit of a German cruiser. Furniture is smashed and thrown into the fire, and eventually the chaplain's treasured organ goes in, too.

This is "The Big Parade" of the sea. Sure of real money in the British Empire and Germany and should also draw in the U. S. *Sinclair.*

COMRADES

James Ormont production, releasing through First Division. Directed by Cliff Wheeler. Cast includes Helene Costello, Gareth Hughes, Donald Keith and Joseph Swickard. At Loew's New York on double feature program one day, Feb. 24. Running time, 60 mins.

Fair enough and moderately priced independent that will suffice where they're used to dropping in regardless of titles. Yarn is familiar, but has sufficient pace to hold it to its limited purpose, and the Helene Costello name may help.

Delves into the war after starting in a military prep school where the two pals (Hughes and Keith) are introduced, one a physical coward. When the draft is called the younger and braver of the two takes his friend's place under promise that the latter will step in the following year when he reaches 21 and his name will be called. Sister of the weakling overhears the promise, so that gets the silent hero back his ring. France and the usual heroism and cowardice, with the local papers crediting the wrong boys in each case because of the name switch. Homecoming of the youths carries on the situation until a mentally deranged father, who has lost his sons in the war, pulls a gun on the supposed coward, whence the lad who couldn't force himself out of a trench steps in front of his companion to receive the bullet. A dying confession puts everything right, including the knowledge that he has overcome his fear.

Cast work is better than the production. War stuff is ordinary with the military academy barrack scenes not true, except of the "boy scout" schools. Picture will have its troubles standing up alone for three days. It is fair one-day material, but will be more at home with a companion to share the burden. *Sid.*

Little Mickey Grogan

FBO production and release. Directed by Leo Meehan. Frankie Darro (kid) starred. Jobyna Ralston and Crawford Kent featured. From story by Arthur Guy Empey. At Loew's New York, on double feature program.

Fair enough picture for the single dayers. Or in the small towns where it may be held according to the rental.

F. B. O. may be desperately trying to put across a kid actor, Frankie Darro as Mickey Grogan. For the information of F. B. O. and its staff, if it means anything, the reviewer who watched the picture at the New York on a double bill, without previously knowing the title of either, was surprised upon emerging from the house to find the title was "Little Mickey Grogan."

The attempt to make a kidlet a star may be very good if it can get over, but not in a story of this nature. The boy is incidental, notwithstanding what may be tried. It's like the dog films; they don't convince.

Taking the reviewer's unbiased opinion as he watched the film, thinking the kids in it were incidental for comedy and that the story hinged upon Jobyna Ralston, it may prove to the producers that if they are to star or feature kids there must be kid pictures.

It's impossible to carry conviction with impossible tales for children Kids can not be made too mature.

This Frankie Darro is a nice kid actor, following direction. But his face will never be a screen panic, and there is no outpouring sympathetic feeling toward him. Sending the boy onto the city's dumps to salvage what he can and letting him meet the girl there, or in fact putting these children into the centre of misery does not help them as film favorites.

Here the story is so so, machine made. An architect is losing his sight, but regardless of that never attempts to help himself by wearing glasses. That's a fatal oversight that must have started with the script and was never caught. And another was the burly lover of the girl. Calling him a prizefighter could not square that.

Still the kid angle as incidental helps a little and makes it a one-dayer.

Shooting Stars

(BRITISH MADE)

Two entirely opposite opinions on one English-made subject, "Shooting Stars," by members of Variety's London office staff. Both are printed herewith for future decision.

Oddly enough the favorable comment on this British-made is by an American (*Jolo*), while the adverse opinion is by an Englishman (*Frat*).

Neither ventures to say what chance this picture might have in the U. S. The American at least should have so stated. All reviews of foreign-mades when reviewed outside the U. S. or Canada for Variety should carry this opinion, which may be qualified to any extent.

London, Feb. 2.

Original story by Anthony Asquith. Scenario by John Orton. Produced by British Instructional Films, Ltd. Directed by A. V. Bramble. Distributed by New Era Films, Ltd. Lighting by Karl Fischer. Camera-men, Stanley Rodwell & H. Harris. Pre-viewed at the Plaza, Feb. 1. Running time, 72 minutes.

Mae Feather ....Annette Benson
Julian Gordon ....Brian Ahearne
Andy Wilks ....Donald Calthrop

There is no other film critic in this country faced with the difficult position before me. Film production is starting here as a serious industry; the public pockets and the banks' coffers are at last open; there is sound finance, as well as finance which is nothing but sound and will end in fury.

And I have written for and supported the establishment of film-making in this country to a far greater extent than has any other qualified writer. I am assailed now because I do not slobber praise over every British film I see. I am accused of "attacking" British productions because I do not join in the chorus chanted over pictures which the film-going public later reacts against from the very fact of their having been oversold.

I know, before anything yet appears, the trade press and the newspaper critics will claim "Shooting Stars" as a masterpiece—and once again a few tyros will hail each other as superior to Griffith and mightier than Lubitsch or De Mille.

That does not prevent me from saying this is a rather stupid and childish attempt to make a motion picture. When in a three-verse piece of doggerel over the signature of Anthony Asquith, I read a claim that the climax "out-Wells Wells," I was fearful. And after I had sat through an hour and a quarter of silliness I knew I had cause to be fearful!

It has been claimed loudly that this picture would strike an entirely new note on the screen; that it would revolutionize film production. If that were all the film might just be passed up as meriting no attention. But it will be sold to the public as the work of a genius, and once again British films will get a black eye when this one gets to the screen. If the "friends" of British films would realize the enormous harm they are doing by their slavish praise they would temper it with a little sane comment.

Some of this film is devoted to a sneer at the type of film fare the general public makes its entertainment. The rest is imitative of the Ufa "absence-of-lights" complex, traveling the camera till the looker-on becomes dizzy, and an even more ordinary story than the one jeered at by implication in the film itself.

Mae Feather is a film star, married to her leading man. She loves a slapstick comedian working in the same studio. Mae gives the comic the key of her apartment, supposing husband will be away on location.

Husband is cleaning a gun in readiness for a day's shooting, not expecting to work, and Mae slips a cartridge into her bag in mistake for her lipstick.

Andy, the comedian, gets to Mae's apartment just as the news has come through on the radio he has been badly hurt. It was a "double" who was hurt, however, and Mae's relief at seeing Andy, together with the comedian's possession of the key, raise hubby's ire and he announces divorce intentions. A contract to go to America has just been signed by May. It has a penalty clause for scandals. As the next day a shooting sequence is to be taken in which villain fires at hero (hubby), she loads gun with the stolen cartridge.

Only one barrel is fired and husband escapes. Then gun is borrowed for a comedy scene with Andy in another picture, and he gets killed by the cartridge intended for friend husband.

Time elapses (a typical stroke of genius is a blank screen for a few seconds) and husband has become a famous director. Mae is now a crowd worker, and even her husband does not recognize her as she goes to him after a day's shooting is finished and asks "Don't you want me any more?" He shakes his head and goes on reading his script, while she makes a long, long exit right down the floor, stands silhouetted against the door and then closes it behind her. Finish. And about time!

Acting and photography are both good. The rest is inexcusable.

Frat

London, Feb. 10.

This picture was reviewed by a member of Variety's London staff, a man of vast newspaper experience, and especially in films, together with a technical knowledge of picture making possessed by few of the film critics. There is no question of the honesty of his criticism, but this confrere in the same office takes issue with him on his opinion in the present instance.

The writer made a canvas of the picture colony, the "wise" folks of show business in the West End and elsewhere, and has not received one opinion coinciding with this (his own), with the exception of a prominent official in the Famous-Lasky office.

Visitors to the Plaza were heard to remark—droves of them—that it was "terrible." The picture did excellent business at the Plaza during the week and was retained a second week, but the writer is willing to concede this was due to the fact that the story emanated from the brain of Anthony Asquith, son of Margot Asquith and Lord Oxford and Asquith, former prime minister of England, and hence the picture for the first week was a draw of no mean proportions from "the best people." Perhaps for the same reason it has been booked for 65 of the provincial cinematograph theatres, more or less under the direction of Lord Ashfield.

It is understood the picture was peddled about in film circles in America with no takers, which may, or may not, be another argument in favor of the original film review aforementioned.

The viewpoint of the writer is that the picture is too modern for the average moving picture patron, who is confronted with the difficulty of carrying in his mind a story within a story and even then part of another story within the inside story.

From the outset he is intrigued by the opening of the picture which begins with a closeup of the conventional clinch and closes with the shutting of a door. If one stops to consider for a moment, it is the exact reverse of ordinary picture routine. It appeals in no small measure to the imagination.

The only chance for anything of this sort here would be if it were made by a continental producer (shall we say German?) and then the English audiences would not be expected to understand it and would remark on its artistry. But, made by a native producer, it apparently hasn't the proverbial Chinaman's chance.

The experiment of playing the picture in the P. C. T. houses will be worth watching.

Jolo.

While it is true that almost every English critic goes into ecstasies over continental art productions, box office experience has shown that the public does not necessarily take the same angle. Examples are "The Street," directed by Karl Grune, newspaper success 100 per cent, and a box office failure in about the same ratio. Also chief critics' angles are Lubitsch's "Variety," where the symbolic and technical devices, which in almost every case passed over the heads of the audiences.

"Caligari," "The Golem" and "Destiny" are three other outstanding continental pictures which did not repeat their newspaper success at the box office.

This state of affairs has become so recognized to the majority of provincial film salesmen that they figure when a picture is hailed as a big artistic success by the London critics, there will be very considerable difficulty in booking it.

Frat.

Burning Up Broadway

Sterling production. Directed by Philip Rosen from story by Norman Houston. Supervised by Joe Rock. Starring Helene Costello. Cast includes Robert Frazer, Ernest Hilliard, Sam Hardy, Max Asher and Jack Rich. At Loew's New York. One-half of a double feature program. Running time, about 50 mins.

A speedy, entertaining production making up in action what it lacks in polish. Fine offering for the small theatres.

Very little of Broadway in the picture. Story deals with rum runners whose chief operates a speak-easy. The young man from the west, on his first trip to New York, is taken into the place by a friend just to get a glimpse of life in the raw. The boy falls for one of the chorines and, on returning a second time to press his attention, is slugged by the proprietor, who has fallen for the girl himself.

From planted wires the audience is given the idea that the boy's friend is the leader of a gang of hi-jackers who are planning to stage a holdup on the bootleggers. The girl's actions, her half-hearted attempt to appease the heavy while not encouraging his attentions too strongly are clothed in mystery.

For the finish the girl is revealed as in the employ of the revenue department working with the supposed leader of the hi-jackers, also a Government man.

Mori.

WOMAN WISE

William Fox production and release. Directed by Albert Ray. Featuring William Russell and June Collyer, supported by Walter Pidgeon and Theodore Kosloff. Titles by Malcolm Stuart Boylan. At the Academy, New York, Feb. 27-29. Running time, 60 minutes.

A novel film comedy that has many things to recommend it. Delivers neat and compact entertainment without going to extremes of slapstick and still holds genuine laughter. It isn't often that polite film story telling has this balance of intelligent fun, getting surprises and laughs from situations that are away from the Sennett technique.

The whole business is expertly shaped. Picturesque backgrounds in oriental atmosphere of U. S. Consul's office in Persia. Soldier of fortune from nearby camp of American oil prospectors gets involved with native woman and consul in saving him from native dignitary, recognizes in him an old buddy. Natives want to shoot prospector for flirting with their women, but hard-boiled guy won't compromise. So consul knocks him cold until he can smooth things out, then he makes him at home.

The entertainment lies more in the incidental comedy tricks than in the story itself. There is one rich bit, where a prospector's dog, scream of a woolly-up, has a flirtation of his own, which apparently turns into a fight, for the pup is seen departing from the rendezvous in a sadly wrecked condition. The departure is done in slow motion and is a scream.

Another dog scream bit is later.

The film has a world of action to support its hour of running time. The native bandits at the order of the Pasha besiege the consulate, where there is a fine, full gun battle, with victims falling from high walls into the lawn lake; desperate riding of picturesquely costumed orientals and finally the summoning of the American gang from the oil camp for one of those to-the-rescue sequences. Behind all there is excellent scenic locale, fine photography and good character playing.

This Walter Pidgeon is coming to the fore as a leading man. He plays naturally and makes a clean-cut human figure without a hint of the familiar actor type, good looking enough without being too handsome to distract attention from his character. June Collyer has a pale part, playing it gracefully, which was about possible.

William Russell makes a mistake every time he plays a role that is not pure comedy. He has a great role here in the he-man who boasts of his knowledge of women, but gets double-crossed every time he hooks up with a dame. And he does it well. It is a good deal more convincing than the heroic stuff that ends up with a clinch. It isn't always easy to take Russell seriously as a straight hero. Here a comedy role fits him perfectly.

Kosloff is sunk in an impossible heavy part, impossible in itself, but used only as a foil and feeder for the straights.

First-rate light comedy-drama that will please any grade of clientele on the three-day or straight week booking plan.

Rush.

MOTHER MACHREE

Fox production and release, synchronized with Movietone. Based upon the song of the same name. Directed by John Ford from Rida J. Young's story. Belle Bennett, Victor McLaglen and Neil Hamilton featured. Titled and edited by Katharine Hilliker and H. H. Caldwell. Chester Lyons, cameraman. At Globe, New York, for twice daily run starting March 5. Running time, 75 minutes. $1.65 top.

Ellen McHugh (Mother Machree)	Belle Bennett
Brian McHugh	Philippe DeLacy
Brian McHugh (in later years)	Neil Hamilton
Terrence O'Dowd	Victor McLaglen
Harpist of Wexford	Ted McNamara
Rachel Van Studdiford	Eulalie Jensen
Edith Cutting	Constance Howard
Mrs. Cutting	Ethel Clayton

The first half hour of "Mother Machree" is as bad as the last half hour is good. That, in itself, is enough to establish its status as a $2 picture. However, it's not a $2 picture in value or price. This latest Fox entry is at the Globe for $1.65 top. If it stays any length of time it'll take some forcing, but there's not much question on its capabilities as program material.

And it may serve to put the quietus on the Irish societies which have been up in arms against Hollywood of late.

Preceded by a full 38 minutes of Movietone, in a mixed news and talent unfolding, it's not a bad evening at the Globe, starting at 8.40 and out by 10.45. A brief intermission divides the two halves, with Movietone bringing back some shots it has previously used, such as the B. & O. railroad demonstration of progress and Gertrude Lawrence. Another Charlot Revue luminary also makes her appearance, Beatrice Lillie. Both good, with Miss Lawrence still the highlight of any performer yet recorded by this device. Miss Lillie, before a film audience, is a study for her enthusiasts.

In the main feature and in the title role Belle Bennett is a fixture. That is to say, this former stock actress has become identified with these characterizations. Although not surrounded with the power of "Stella Dallas," her latest effort will cost her nothing in prestige. She is ably foiled by Neil Hamilton, who plays her grown son, and Victor McLaglen, as the Irish carnival strong man who follows her to America, becomes a New York cop and then joins the 69th to keep an eye on young Brian for her.

Rida Johnson Young has evolved an effective mother story which John Ford, directing, gets under way in too slow a manner. It opens in 1899 in an Irish village on a night when Ellen McHugh's husband is killed during a storm. Convinced that in America lies the best future for her boy, Ellen makes the crossing to meet discouragement until Terrence arrives and induces her to join a side show of freaks disguised as the "half woman."

Placing of the boy, Brian, in a fashionable school comes about through the principal taking a fancy to the youngster. Ultimate discovery of the mother's occupation leads the principal to offer Ellen the proposition of either letting her adopt the boy or dropping him as a student.

The youngster's innocent desire to be with his companions decides Ellen, whence she becomes employed as a scrubwoman in a 5th avenue residence. Her ability to handle a baby leads to the position of housekeeper.

Story jumps years to show the girl Ellen has practically raised, in love with Brian, now a lawyer but believing his mother dead. Revelations are made all around the night war is declared. Brian and Terrence depart, come back, and the picture quickly draws to a close.

It's for the mob, and they'll like it. Ford has an uncanny knack in handling babies. In "Four Sons" his mite in a bathtub is a standout sequence, and here Miss Bennett's handling of the babe nobody can make stop crying will hop off the screen to effect both sexes. There's a tear in Brian discovering who his mother really is, but no basic and sustained pull on the heart as in previous big mother films.

The flash of war stuff looks like over matter from "Glory," and is just an incident without even a closeup of the principals involved. Production is always to the point, without any attempt to cheat, and Lyons' photography loses none of it.

As to cast, it's all Miss Bennett, Hamilton and McLaglen, the former naturally taking precedence and especially in the late passages under a gray wig. Also a word for the late Ted McNamara, who covered his assignment adequately and draws many a giggle when it is both necessary and welcome, a matter of editing as well as playing.

And not the least of "Mother Machree" is the score. The song, of course, is the basis, and there's an interlude where Hamilton sits down at a piano to play and sing it to perfect synchronization. Doubtful if the actor actually vocalized, but just as good as if he did, and if he did, give the boy a great big hand.

Movietone reproduction in this house sounded faulty, dominated by tonal vibration. Not even that, however, can offset the merit of the assembling of selections. It was inevitable that the score would delve into Victor Herbert's "Eileen." It does—and how! The scene wherein Brian and Edith become engaged is musically as effective as anything of the kind any picture score has ever had. Switching from the lovers to the ballroom, the melody is retained but a waltz rhythm is interwoven by cellos as the camera pans from the dancers to the principals in another room.

The basic undertone of drums to catch the pulse of the first war hysteria is also excellent, while the weird shriek of bagpipes and drums also figures to cause a tingle. S. L. Rothafel and Erno Rapee are credited with the orchestration.

Houses with or without Movietone don't have to worry about "Mother Machree." It's substantial program material. It has enough of all the ingredients except, perhaps, excitement to carry it. *Sid.*

THE SHOWDOWN

Paramount production and release. Directed by Victor Schertzinger, starring George Bancroft. From Houston Branch's novel, "Wildcat," adapted by Hope Loring. Continuity by Ethel Doherty. At the Paramount, New York, week March 3. Running time, 77 minutes.

Cardan	George Bancroft
Sibyl Shelton	Evelyn Brent
Wilson Shelton	Neil Hamilton
Winter	Fred Kohler
Goldie	Helen Lynch
Hugh Pickerell	Arnold Kent
Kilgore Shelton	Leslie Fenton
Willie	George Kuwa

A picture of considerable dramatic vitality, cynical in some of its phases and a wide departure from the screen formula of romantic story. Anything that follows lines away from the stereotyped takes a chance on results, and for that reason "The Showdown" is a gamble. Logically, women ought to shy away from its rather brutal romantic import, and they probably won't like the subject. Which puts it in the class of good pictures that don't make money in proportion to high literary and production quality.

Here is the romantic situation that raises the question mark: Cardan (played to the hilt by George Bancroft) is a globe-trotting roughneck oil prospector. He breaks pioneer trails to strange places in search of oil, always pursued by one Winter, field scout for a big oil corporation. The two are bitter but admiring enemies, living out a sort of Capt. Flagg-Sergeant Quirt relation. Their life and death rivalry in oil and women is the essence of the story.

Cardan is first in a new tropical oil field and drilling when Winter arrives intent upon taking away his well if it comes in. Cardan's dance hall sweetheart from nearby settlement makes a visit and Winter tries to cop her, but fails. A second woman comes into the district, an aristocrat following her husband into the desperate wilderness. Cardan ignores her at first, while Winter stands by shrewdly waiting for the tropics to break the woman so he can step in and grab her.

The crooked oil scout's purpose is a challenge to Cardan, his ancient enemy, and Cardan devotes himself to the defeat of his rival. As it lies, two brutal men set themselves out to the conquest of a woman, not because they love her, but because each desires to defeat the other and satisfy a long-standing grudge.

Upon this theme the picture evolves much keen and tricky drama, craftily working up to the climax clash of the two men. The play of other characters upon the central situation is cleverly managed for fascinating minor incident. Such is the passage where the dance hall girl and harassed aristocrat meet; where a foppish dude essays to try his hand at the conquest of the proud wife and is unceremoniously disposed of by the impatient main contenders.

The kick comes when Winter tries brutally to take the woman by force and he and Cardan go into a rough and tumble. Cardan wins the fight, and the exhausted woman, broken by hardship and terror, recognizes that she is the winning man's property and admits herself ready to accept the situation in those terms.

Husband returns at this juncture. Cardan could eliminate him if he wanted to, but doesn't. Instead he agrees to play cards with the husband for the oil well—and presumably the woman also. They play and Cardan relinquishes oil and woman by throwing down winning cards in order that the woman may escape back to civilization.

On the surface, of course, it is an act of nobility, but the inference is plain, that, once won, Cardan didn't want the woman at all. It was the defeat of his hated antagonist that inspired him from the first. Which from a romantic angle is considerably zero minus from the feminine point.

The picture is played with exquisite irony. Except for the very graphic fist fight done in true flicker elaboration, the tension is always present but under the surface. The two principal men characters are always ostensibly in polite relation, but each with a knife up his sleeve, figuratively speaking, and this play of acting one thing and indicating another is carried out with utmost finesse. It's a subtle treatment and it does carry with it the penalty of slow surface action. But the picture is rich in suspense in spite of its seeming slow progress.

Bancroft makes Cardan a memorable screen creation. This reviewer does not recall any characterization of quite the same flavor and tang. Cardan's a tough egg without any of the graces or the noble virtues that go with screen heroes, but a first-class fighting hater, richly true and human.

The action of the whole cast is admirable, especially admirable in its simplicity. Even Evelyn Brent's heroine in distress isn't overdone while the brazen dance hall girl of Helen Lynch is a nice balance between no-better-than-she-ought-to-be and pity-the-poor-girl, which alone is a triumph for the silent drama.

Picture has good comedy values for contrast, low comedy bits being supplied by a Chinese servant, who roots for Cardan when he bets on the cards or engages in fights. *Rush.*

FINDERS KEEPERS

Universal comedy, directed by Wesley Ruggles. Adapted from Mary Roberts Rinehart's story. Laura La Plante starred. Titles by Tom Reed. At Colony, New York, week of March 4. Running time, 56 minutes.

Barbara Archibald	Laura La Plante
Carter	John Harron
Colonel Archibald	Edmund Breese
Percy	Arthur Rankin
Bozo	Bill Gorman
Ken	Eddie Phillips
Chaplain	Joe Mack

One of Mrs. Rinehardt's always amusing stories has here been turned into a hoke comedy film of feature length, plentifully gagged-up and clowned for the mass fan trade into a fair program picture. It should do business and please the element for which it was cut and measured.

It has rather tedious passages, all leading up to the point where the heroine crashes into a wartime training camp to be married to one of the citizen-soldiers by the regimental chaplain. To this end she disguises herself in a regulation uniform borrowed from the hero's pal and arrives just in time to be thrown into a hasty line-up of the regiment for review.

As the reviewing officer goes down the files examining each soldier's equipment, the girl's trousers break loose and begin to drop. This sequence is played upon and built up for much slapstick and it tells the story of the picture. It's all laboriously forged fund, not particularly well done, but obvious enough so that nobody can fail to perceive that it's funny, and behave accordingly. At the Colony Sunday evening they laughed uproariously, putting the stamp of approval upon the picture, which ends all argument. Nevertheless, it would have been just as amusing if Miss La Plante had not worked the coquettish young thing so hard. It isn't within reason that a regular army colonel's daughter would regard army routine with wide-eyed ignorance, nor snub a lieutenant on the principle that the commission made him objectionable. It's a cinch Mrs. Rinehart committed no such error. At least, she probably got around it somehow.

There are several good soldier types, principally the top sergeant of the hero's company and a tough recruit with a trick of shooting buckshot from between his teeth, a device that has been used before. Camp scenes are impressive, with hordes of extras or some military unit employed, but otherwise the picture does not represent large money. Edmund Breese plays the Colonel-father in the sappy style such a part deserved.

Just a commercial picture, well aimed for the clientele of below-medium grade of screen taste. *Rush.*

THE SMART SET

M-G-M production. Story by Byron Morgan. Directed by Jack Conway. Cameraman, Oliver Marsh. Titles by Robert Hopkins. At Capitol, New York, week March 3. Running time, 63 minutes.

Tommy	William Haines
Nelson	Jack Holt
Polly	Alice Day
Durant	Hobart Bosworth
Sammy	Coy Watson, Jr.
Cynthia	Constance Howard
Mr. Van Buren	Paul Nicholson
Mrs. Van Buren	Julia Swayne Gordon

The Haines formula is now well known. Take one good-looking young man, give him the nerve of eight salesmen, the "line" of a dozen sophomores, the athletic prowess of Red Grange, Lou Gehrig, Bobby Jones or Tommy Hitchcock, throw in a pretty girl, add complications, some wistfulness, snappy sub-titles, and stir well for laughs.

"The Smart Set" is the application of the Haines formula to polo. The young man is a regular rinktum-scoot heavy necker, inveterate kid-der, full of pranks, conceit and horse laughs. He is a member of the international polo team about to engage the British team for the championship.

Because of his grandstand complex the youngster tries to play a one-man game, and is finally dispensed with. That he eventually saves the day for Old Glory in the final chukker of the last game with 18 seconds to play goes without saying. That he changes horses in midfield and at a gallop, that he drives in the winning goal with a broken mallet is a matter for technical comment among poloists.

"The Smart Set" is a speedy, laughy, immensely entertaining improbability. It will be a box-office tonic anywhere, and should be another "Slide, Kelly, Slide."

The story is by Byron Morgan, and skillfully worked out. Robert Hopkins, credited as the title writer, is new to Hollywood, having been signed in the east about three months ago by Harry R pf, this being his first assignment. He has done an excellent job, overlooking a couple of bromides, a rewrite on "no matter how thin you slice it, it's still boloney," and maybe an unnecessary title here and there.

Haines is good, as usual, in his freshie characterization. This young man has a natural, easy, camera personality, never goes too far, and makes it all seem plausible. Alice Day, sister of Marceline, is a standout in the picture. After a long novitiate with Mack Sennett, Alice got her chance only recently with a major company.

She photographs intelligence as well as sweetness and charm. She should find a vogue for a long time to come.

Jack Conway's direction is efficient, classy and workmanlike. It's a very good program picture all the way. *Land.*

IF I WERE SINGLE

Warner Brothers production and release starring May McAvoy and Conrad Nagel. From Robert Lord's story, with Roy Del Ruth directing. Titles credited to Joseph Jackson, with Barney McGill cameraman. At Roxy, New York, week March 3. Running time, 61 mins.

May Howard.................May McAvoy
Ted Howard.................Conrad Nagel
Joan Whitley.................Myrna Loy
Claude Debrie.................Andre Beranger

One more of those thin-skinned comedies the studios turn out by the gross, some more gross than others. Much along "Adam and Evil" lines and sprinkled with a fair share of laughs. Small cast picture that keeps itself active and figures to be of just average b. o. value.

Story gets a young married couple all excited when the husband starts to flirt, the third party turning out to be a friend of the wife. The latter's effeminate music teacher also gets into the mixup. When hubby and the other girl take the closed car for a jaunt, wife and her music guide are under a blanket in the rear of the car.

Cast foursome does nicely with it and titles and situations give it gentle shoves whenever it threatens to become backward. Producers probably figure picture needs whatever strength the McAvoy and Nagel names can give it, and rightly. Couple in support are also good, especially Beranger as the nance musician who dotes on the wife. Myrna Loy does well enough, but should keep out of full length shots. Nothing unusual on the production and with photography just straigh camera work.

Light program material that will appreciate any support a house can construct around it. *Sid.*

Chicago After Midnight

FBO production and release. Story by Charles K. Harris. Ralph Ince director-star. Cast includes Jola Mendez, Helen Jerome Eddy, Christian Frank, Frank Mills, Charles Sullivan, Carl Azell, James Morris. At the Hippodrome, New York, week of March 5. Running time, 60 minutes.

More inside stuff on the mad-bad life of the cabarets. The high finances and incidental shootings of the bootleggers and their triple-crossing contemporaries, the high-jackers, stool pigeons, sly cops, show girls. A seven-layer cake of melodrama.

Nothing new in or about "Chicago After Midnight." It's plain, unadorned gun play. Up to and maybe including some of the lesser deluxes it's an acceptable thriller.

Fastidious customers will find its thrills a little dull. It is not the first, and probably will not be the last, movie based on the general thesis of "Broadway." But the hootch-gangster angle has not been well developed in this instance. The plot has as many holes as a New York side street.

Ralph Ince, a capable actor and director, officiates in both capacities as usual. He has a very unsympathetic role. Whatever the girls in the tank towns may think of him for love interest, from the masculine viewpoint he seems a much more plausible romantic lead than the wishy-washy youth who promised to do right by Jola Mendez. This was just one of several points where the story and script was damp.

Miss Mendez, Ince's sister-in-law, is developing. Her sister, Lucilla, is also a new acquaintance of the fans. Too early to gauge reaction, but if properly steered the girls should be okay. Difficult to catch other names off the long roster of players. Whoever played Bill Boyd's pal was good, as was the stool pigeon waiter. Helen Jerome Eddy, an infrequent player these days, had a mere bit.

Chicago atmosphere included most of the Balaban and Katz houses, the Frolics, Colisemo, Rainbo Gardens and Randolph Street. The two cabarets in which the action transpires resemble almost anything else. By the time "Broadway" is finally transmuted into celluloid it's basic theme will be as old and standard as the one about several cowboys chasing several other cowboys up a hill. *Land.*

FEEL MY PULSE

Paramount production and release. Starring Bebe Daniels and featuring Richard Arlen and William Powell. Directed by Gregory LaCava from H. E. Rogers' story. Titled by George Marion, Jr.; J. Roy Hunt, cameraman. At the Paramount, New York, week Feb. 25. Running time, 66 minutes.

Barbara Manning.................Bebe Daniels
Uncle Wilberforce....Melbourne McDowell
Uncle Edgar.................George Irving
Sanitarium Caretaker......Charles Sellon
Patient.................Heinie Conklin
Her Nemesis.................William Powell
Her Problem.................Richard Arlen

Of no particular purpose but mixing Bebe Daniels up with a bunch of rum runners in an exteriorly sedate sanitarium. Not as strong as some of this star's previous comedies and more given to snickers and light chuckles than successive laughs. Yet, a 9.30 mid-week, well-filled house guffawed enough to check it as okay, if mild, for the general flicker mob.

Star doesn't look as good as in other pictures. Maybe because of staying too long in one dress. Romps around and gets in a gun shooting rough house at the finish but hasn't the situations to let her build up to a punch. Device of making Miss Daniels a much sterilized heiress of an anti-germ uncle, and the girl's wide range but most proper vocabulary, is right in George Marion's lap. Titles help the pace and in odd instances solidly register.

Arlen plays the undercover newspaper member of the bootleggers whom the innocent Barbara orders to drive her to the sanitarium, which has been willed her. The caretaker had turned it over to the rum boys, headed by William Powell. Ultimate attack by hijackers and Powell's intentions toward Barbara burst forth at the same time, whence Arlen goes to work saving the girl and unks arrive with the revenue men. The pot shooting and fight is mostly comedy, with the breaking of a chloroform bottle in the midst of the rumpus, responsible for a slow motion insert that gets the desired reaction from witnesses.

Won't cause hysterics, but enough action and comedy to get it by after the moerate name display on the cast has induced them to drop in. *Sid.*

GUNS AT LOOS

(BRITISH MADE)

Stoll production released by New Era Films. Original story by Sinclair Hill. Scenario by R. Fogwell and L. H. Gordon. Photography, D. P. Cooper. Directed by Sinclair Hill. Preview at the Plaza, Feb. 9. Censors' Certificate "U.". Running time, 84 minutes.

John Grimlaw.................Henry Victor
Clive.................Donald McArdle
Diana.................Madeline Carrol

Still another war picture. That's about its only fault. Story is nothing much, but it is full of thrills, even if most of them have been copied from "The Two Orphans" and "Ben-Hur." Camera work is highly effective, direction reasonably good and acting all right. Bits are effectively done by Bobby Howes and Hermione Baddeley.

Preview audience was largely sold by the use of the magnascope, switched in on sequences of saving a battery of guns, with upward pit shots making horses and wheels rush out of the screen. Shots of gun limbers turning over while retiring at the gallop also were well done.

Madeline Carroll is by way of being a find, and with more forceful direction ought to get somewhere. In this film she is allowed to droop too much, probably in an attempt to look soulful. But she has looks and obvious ability.

Until the last half reel Henry Victor is convincing. But when he comes home supposedly blind, he loses grip and never gets it back. Bad cutting is probably the cause, for the film as a whole needs editing, and the final sequences, showing Victor making a speech to strikers on their defection from duty, is tedious and lets the film down at the close.

Donald McArdle as the other aspirant for the love of the heroine, is not well cast, and shows to nothing like the advantage he did in "Mumsie."

John Grimlaw is an ironmaster, and uses brutal methods to speed up the output of shells. He is in love with Diana. So is Clive. Both propose on the eve of their departure for France, but the lady is not sure. Under fire Grimlaw loses his nerve and is taunted and bullied by Clive into regaining it for the sake of the girl. Later, when forced to retire from shortage of shells, Grimlaw saves his battery and is blinded by a shell. He gets home to find a strike at his factory, appeals to the strikers to go back to work, and Diana decides she loves him.

Character building is not this director's forte, most of the story on this angle coming from captions; otherwise it is very sketchily washed in. Artillery action and munition factory shots very well handled, but models too obvious in front-line shots, probably due to overlighting or none too careful photography.

As a whole, a good patriotic picture and box office for this country and the colonies. For the foreign markets it means nothing. *Frat.*

The House Without Love

(FRENCH MADE)

Paris, Feb. 11.

This picture is adapted from a story by Andre Theuriet, produced by E. Champetier for George Petit, and is listed as a good French issue, without any pretensions of super-importance.

Action is laid in France in the small store of Hyacinte and Germain, bachelor brothers, who sell anglers' supplies and do a bit of fishing on their own. But the arrival of Laurence, a lass, with her mother, cousin of the brothers, upsets the tranquillity of the household. Germain falls in love with Laurence, and in order to secure a comfortable home for her mother the girl accepts his offer of marriage. The other brother, disagreeing with the union, introduces a handsome swain into the family, hoping the young wife will be led astray. Germain sees her chatting with the young man and imagines Laurence is unfaithful. He announces that henceforth they will live together as strangers, and thus the home becomes "The House Without Love." After much suffering the wife is proved innocent, and the repenting husband opens his arms once more.

Acting is suitable for this sentimental yarn, with Henri Baudin and Jean Coquelin playing the two brothers. Arlette Genny is charming as the mistrusted Laurence, Madeleine Guitty, as funny as ever, is in a minor role. It is a romantic portrait of village life in France, and can be classed as a fair French film for home consumption. *Kendrew.*

STRAIGHT SHOOTIN'

Universal production and release. Directed by William Wyler from the story by William Lester. Starring Ted Wells. At the Columbus, N. Y., on double feature program. Running time, about 40 minutes.

One of the usual westerns. Here the bad men try to get the gold mine of the old prospector by starving him to death. The latter's partner betrays the whereabouts of the mine.

Enough riding, shooting and fist fights to meet the needs of the market it was created for. *Mori.*

ADVENTURES IN PYGMY LAND

Produced under auspices of Smithsonian Institution and the Dutch Government. Shown for first time in regular picture house at 55th Street Playhouse week Feb. 25. Running time, 75 minutes.

Camera travels through explored and unexplored areas of Dutch New Guinea during the expedition of Dr. Matthew W. Stirling are interestingly grouped in this historical travelog, titled "Adventures in Pygmy Land." Beautiful scenic effects are achieved and a close photographic study of the undersized inhabitants in the mountainous regions of this island is accomplished. The action, however, could be speeded up considerably were some of the footage dealing with repetitous river scenes eliminated.

The picture as a whole compares by no means in interest or box office value to the multiplicity of its kind which have preceded it on national screen.

Under the supervision of Dr. Stirling, an ethnologist at the U. S. National Museum, the picture was made by the Smithsonian Institution with the material co-operation of the Dutch Government.

Many of the so-described pygmies have the physical proportions, at least photographically, of the civilized explorers. Comparisons of this kind have a tendency to minimize the importance of the discovery by the average lay audience. Many of the shots, although enthusiastically titled, will constantly remind sophisticated fans of scenes and activities of natives which they have witnessed in other productions of the travelogue variety.

A continuous drag in the running is almost irritating to those prefering action.

DRESSED TO KILL

William Fox production and release. Directed by Irving Cummings. Story by Howard Estabrook. Edmund Lowe and Mary Astor featured. Titles by Malcolm Stuart Boylan. At Roxy, New York, week of March 10. Running time, 60 minutes.

Mile-Away Barry	Edmund Lowe
Jean	Mary Astor
Nick	Ben Bard
Professor	R. O. Pennell
Ritzy Hogan	Robert Perry
Joe Brown	Joe Brown
Silky Levine	Tom Dugan
Biff Simpson	John Kelley
Detective Gilroy	Robert E. O'Connor
Singing Walter	Ed Brady

Romantic underworld picture using the "Raffles" formula of gallant and polite but daring crook (played by Edmund Lowe) thrown into a romantic adventure with beautiful heroine (Mary Astor). Combination couldn't miss with the generality of fans. It's a sure-fire Fox programmer; good anywhere and a certain draw if well exploited. And, if properly handled, probably a hold-over.

This version has several angles to vary the stereotyped crook story. Heroine instead of turning out to be a detective is a girl seeking to recover bonds for the theft of which her lover, bank official, is in prison. Another difference is that the polished crook works with a gang of tough gorillas, and in the end has to sacrifice his life to their hate to save the girl. Both points heighten and sharpen the sentimental appeal.

Much of the action takes place in a night club used as a rendezvous by the "mob" and this phase of the story is basis for some excellent underworld melodrama, such as discovery of a stool pigeon and "taking him for a ride"; cool verbal fencing with police officials who crash in with threats of arrests. The grim atmosphere of desperate criminals is nicely established, even to a certain ominous humor that runs through the sequences. Such is the passage where the gunmen bump off the stool pigeon, and then appear in elaborate mourning garb at his impressive funeral, with the baffled detectives watching them.

Whole story is told against background of elegance. Master crook lives in a mansion and the night club is a luxurious affair, all of which gives picture a certain tone. Much of the action is rather unconvincing, plausibility being deliberately sacrificed to dramatic effect. You just have to accept the fact that heroine goes willingly to remain over night in the master crook's apartment, and gets away with it by coyly locking her bedroom door and leaving him to sleep on the living room couch, which, it is made plain, was far from his intent.

Such discrepancies are rather lost sight of in the pure melodrama of such things as the carrying out of an elaborate plot to hold up and rob a fashionable furrier's shop, carried out in a jaunty spirit of sang froid, until the scheme goes wrong. The crook's crimes are always graceful and unhurried, symphonies of social grace which lend them a disarming attractiveness.

Even at the end when the hero gives himself up to the machine gun fire of the gangsters to save the girl (with whom he has fallen in love, of course) he does it in the same debonair fashion, and drops dead before a propaganda billboard reading "You Can't Win," an impeccable figure in faultless evening dress, hence the title "Dressed to Kill." It's that "You Can't Win" of this police vs. crooks that gives the film a high moral percentage.

In its elements the whole business is an impossible bit of fiction, but so shrewdly has it been filmed, so cleverly the story woven into character, humor and thrilling incident, that it tricks one into eagerly accepting it.

For ethical reasons the hero has to be killed at the end, and this does leave rather a sombre finish, but that is relieved by a well contrived comedy tag sequence, showing the rounding up of the tough gangsters by the police and the humiliation of one of the characters, a pompous gunman who looks like a society leader and talks like a thug, character played with nice sense of comedy by Ben Bard. Indeed the type bits are all well played.

Of the two principals, the best that may be said is that they never obviously over played, in itself no small achievement for a story of this sort. Mr. Lowe indelibly stamps himself here, while Miss Astor can bless the caster who placed her in this one.

Strong credits go other than to this unusual cast; to Irving Cummings as director, splendid, and to Howard Estabrook's smooth scenario and continuity that's made really remarkable here in what it tells and how it tells it to come out in a picture, and Malcolm Stuart Boylan's captions. Mr. Boylan's captions are an example of good judgment in a crook film meller. He employed just enough of the underworld jargon to get laughs, and plenty of the speeches he places in the mouths of the slimy characters get other laughs.

In this film are some actual underworld characters, known from coast to coast amongst their kind. Among them is Joe Brown, who has operated enough joints in New York in other days to make him composed in this, to him, familiar picture and he is. It's surprising how some of the otherwise "extras" brought in for types become actors here because they are playing themselves. Even Lowe's sleek crook is modeled after a recognizable Broadwayite.

There will be many who will see this picture more than once. It's of general appeal, but particularly so to men and the young people.

Rush.

Heart of a Follies Girl

Sam E. Rork production, released by First National. Directed by John Francis Dillion, from story by Adele Rogers St. John. Billie Dove starred, with Larry Kent and Lowell Sherman featured. At Strand, New York, week March 10. Running time, around 65 minutes. (Program states Richard A. Rowland (Pres. F. N.) presents, but slide mentions Rork as producer).

Teddy O'Day	Billie Dove
Derek Calhoun	Larry Kent
Roger Winthrop	Lowell Sherman
Caroline Winthrop	Clarissa Selwynne
Florine	Mildred Harris

Around 180 captions in this picture; not a laugh in the lot. That may tell it all. There isn't much left excepting captions to tell of. Other than its three names and title, it hasn't a thing. Those may be enough for three days in the neighborhoods. Nothing beyond that. And whatever one may like in this picture will be ruined by its sloppy, vague and silly finish.

That finish looks as though the whistle had blown at 6,000 feet, or that the bankroll had, or that someone got tired. Saying "enough." The only wonder is that they got to the 6,000th foot, even with those titles.

"The Heart of a Follies Girl" may have been an inspiration as a title. If the writer, Adele Rogers St. John, knows aything about the inside of those dames, she doesn't tell it here, and John Francis Dillion, who directed, is certainly minus. While, according to Billie Dove, a "Follies" girl is a chump in her heart and a dumbbell in her head. That never before fitted one of Ziegfy's wisest.

How could two title writers, as here employed, compose 180 captions on a semi-comedy and make them as deadly dull? They couldn't advance Mildred Harris as a flip "Follies" damsel. But the captions at that but typify the entire picture. It recalls features of 10 years ago. The only two real laughs are undisclosed and must be detected, not much trouble.

The biggest is in the finale. From the story a middle age downtown John is smitten on a number leader in "The Follies." On her birthday, not feeling so good or perhaps having forgotten to dye his hair, he sends his secretary to present his regrets, some flowers and take the gal out for eats. The boy does it all. He starts at midnight, going to a nite club (for something to eat!). According to an ever-present clock, at 2 o'clock, they are in love, on the level, without either having touched booze.

In his loving way the young man believes posing is best, so he trails along as a friend of his boss instead, meanwhile stopping long enough in the swift courtship to forge his employer's name for a check to buy the dame an engagement ring. Though doubting whether the "Follies" girl loves him, he asks her, proposes and then gives her the ring. Any of Ziegfy's wisest, if receiving a ring at the moment of a proposal would know it was either a phoney or in general use.

When the girl tells the John she's engaged, and to his friend, he brings in the sec, everything is uncovered and the boss sends the kid for a stretch for the forgery.

There he is, the poor boy, in prison, and the girl married him just before he was convicted. A "Follies" girl! But the John came in one evening to her dressing room. It was New Year's eve. Her husband would be paroled. But the husband in jail after there for some time, discovered three bars in a window and probably chewed them away. The same night he came home, still New Year's eve, but later.

He wasn't paroled; escaped.

"You get right back in that jail," said the other half. "Is that nice, busting out of jail?"

She wouldn't tell him of the probable parole, maybe thinking he would believe she had been cheating with the boss. More like it. But the young man didn't like to go back to jail. "You don't know what a terrible place it is," he said to his wife, unaware of some of the dressing rooms or jams a "Follies" girl gets into in her day.

This all comes out in those stiff-necked captions that tell most of the story, anyway. But the wife pleads with him to go back to jail. She pashes him up until he promises, and her big argument is this:

"What will our children think of you? Don't you want your children to be proud of their father?"

Oh, boy! In 1928.

So he went back to jail.

Whether he got his parole or children no one will ever know.

Still, as only a forger rather than a jail-breaker, all kids should be proud of him.

Everything seems to go wrong in the picture. It's one of those hand-kissing affairs. Is that coming back, too? Only in this one, when Larry Kent kisses his beloved, she wants to denote ecstasy, and she looks as though Larry had bitten her hand instead. Or face. Miss Dove is full of grief all through. She registers everything but naturalness.

And Mr. Kent, also in the good old way, and not so old, rushes up to a door, opens it in an awful hurry, and then stands in the doorway. If no rush, why the hurry? But otherwise Mr. Kent does well, especially in make-up after his escape.

Lowell Sherman—okay. Role right in his lap, and a loaf.

And the cameraman or director got a new scheme here. It's a close-up in three jumps, frequently repeated. It looked as though the studio had run out of movable platforms or the photographer was wearied. First a long-distance shot, then a short distance, and then, look! now! close up!

Outside the names and title this one should be sold with the promise of refund if dissatisfied, and then engage another cashier for the refunds.

Czar Ivan, the Terrible

(Or "Wings of a Serf")
(RUSSIAN MADE)

Sovine of Moscow production; released by Amkino. Directed by Juri Tavitch. Period programmed as second half of the sixteenth century. Billing refers to no data or adaptation and makes no claims of authenticity, historical or otherwise. May have been contained on opening slides, not seen. At Cameo, New York, seating 400, on 42nd street, near Broadway. Theatre's complete capacity at scale and policy $11,000 (record) weekly. Running time, about 60 minutes.

Czar Ivan	L.M. Leonidoff
Kurliator	M. Arkanoff
Lupatoff	V. Makaroff
Fima	S. Garrel
Nikita	I. Klukvin
Malluta	M. Katchaloff
Fedka Basmanov	N. Prozorovsky
Drotzkoy	N. Vitovtoy
Tzarina	Safnat Askaradva

As a heathenish pictorial exposition of a barbarous, tortuous and unreasonably cruel Czar of the Russians, "Czar Ivan" as a film is solely suited for the neighborhoods over here where there may be a Russian colony or in a city containing a large number of Russian immigrants, such as New York. The only other picture exhibition places this film will be endured are the Art theatres. It's perfect for them. Although if a picture theatre has proven its clientele likes the somber or gruesome, 1,000 per cent. more than the worst of the Lon Chaneys in that respect, then "Ivan" can take its try there.

Plenty of whiskers, of course, and they fit in. Not many women and no girls to attract. Men in profusion, all kinds and most of them nightmares. But one or two stand out for looks, notably Klukvin as Nikita and (chancing it) Makaroff as Lupatov. Both of these have strong faces, with Lupatov light on the brush and Nikita using a mustache only. Yet some s. a. is worked in when the Czarina makes a bold play for Nikita, before and while she was keeping him from losing his head through expert amputation at the behest of her disorderly husband, Ivan. At one time Nikita almost fights to save his Czarina from a charge of assault.

Ivan picked up a grouch against Nikita because the youth thought he could fly, and did. Through the air, fastened in between a pair of wings that never wavered or flickered as Nikita flew before the grand stand, the Czar and his retinue, besides some English merchants the display had been arranged for. Ivan said Nikita must be in league with Satan. It's about the only thing in the picture Ivan said or did that he could not be blamed for.

And, of course, Ivan couldn't foresee that centuries afterward there would be a Soviet Government or that he would be used so hardly and brazenly for a propaganda picture by it.

That was a point calling for some information on authenticity, since Nikita 300 years ago was trying to do a Lindbergh without having then heard of Lindy. Another bit was a spinning wheel that Nikita made work after the wheel stopped, following its inventor going blind. That is what set Nikita in right with the Czarina, but it cost them both their lives before the finish.

As the Czar became finally wise that the Czarina was a double-crosser, he killed her himself, by choking his wife, the only good deed of the picture and the single time the Czar in person committed murder or torture—if you except the moment he threw a bowl of scalding soup into the face of his Clown. But as the Jester up to that minute had done nothing to make either the audience or the Czar believe he was funny, that may have been justified in 1650.

When Ivan bumped off Mrs. Ivan he sent for a priest and told the prelate to pray for her, thus bringing out that Ivan wasn't really sore for catching his wife going wrong; he seemed only a little peeved.

While the Czarina was no slouch either as a vamp. When flashing Nitika and deciding she would grab him, the queenly one said to a hanging-on admirer: "Upstart! I'm through with you!" And he was through, so much so he duly took a ride by the Czarina's knife in his back, possibly known as the quick way over there. While a ranking Prince whom the Czar took a dislike to went through a trap into the sewer, the same route Nitika finished up on, making the finale of the picture somewhat disappointing.

What should have happened could have been Nitika tearing off the Czar's whiskers and beneath you could see Nitika, by double exposure. Maybe they don't know about double exposure yet in Russia, or perhaps that would not have been historically correct. But it might have given the picture its only giggle.

Still, there may be laughs and applause for this "Ivan" film when before Russian immigrants. They will relish any of the royal family given the worst of it, particularly Ivan getting the works from Mrs. Ivan.

In the torture chamber is a variety of ways and means to make them squeal. You see some in operation. They look guaranteed to make the victims come across.

Rather a well-made and produced picture. It goes shy on extras often. Crowds or guards aren't as heavy in numbers as the scenes call for, but they were nicely manipulated by the director. Acting is evenly balanced, with Sainat Askardva as the Czarina no mean pantomimist, and also the Czar, Leonidoff. The Czar had a habit of screwing up one eye and glaring with the other. Whenever he did it, that meant Campbell's in the morning.

Photography does not run evenly. At times the contrast is so marked as to suggest inserts from other Russian, perhaps Ivan, pictures. But the continuity is held to quite well without time lapses denoted.

In Russia, and likely on the Continent, this picture should have been welcomed by those of the republics as a picture and as a recital of what their forebears had to endure if not go through. That makes it no less a good picture over here for those who may want or who can sit through it. Its seamy side of a day forgotten calls for no bringing that back to the picture houses of America, which prefer that their people return home to sleep peacefully after seeing a picture show.

And whiskers are almost extinct over here.

THE SECRET HOUR

Paramount production and release. Directed and produced by Rowland V. Lee from story by Sidney Howard. Screen adaptation by Rowland V. Lee. Starring Pola Negri. Jean Hersholt featured. Harry Fishbeck, photographer. At Paramount, New York, week March 10. Running time, over 60 mins.

Annie.......................Pola Negri
Luigi.......................Jean Hersholt
Jack.......................Kenneth Thomson

Very dull, bordering on stupidity in spots. Picture stands little chance despite Pola Negri, Jean Hersholt and the Paramount label. A poor picture all the way through, based on a story which is the limit for dispassionate and lengthy title explanations, it spells bad business for any downtown house showing it and will be a chaser for the neighborhoods.

For the arty houses this production is a cinch. It holds only a lukewarm love interest, is completely without action of any description, harbors characters as colorless and insipid as possible.

According to this tale it seems that Luigi, wealthy orange planter, decided to go to San Francisco and get himself a wife. In a restaurant he spotted a good-hearted waitress. Being timid he could not approach her so he went back to the farm and sent her love letters with a picture of his hired man.

The girl accepts a marriage proposal by mail and on arriving at the orange farm finds her suitor an old, grey-haired man instead of the youth whose photo she had been sent. She falls in love for the hired man, just as she had fallen for his picture, and the twain commit matrimony during the "secret hour."

When Luigi recovers from his accident the girl tells him she has married Jack. The old man forgives them but the audience never will, or the old man either.

Over 60 minutes to tell a tworeeler.

This is the film version of the stage play, "They Knew What They Wanted," with the censorable material eliminated. *Mori.*

THE COUNT OF TEN

Universal production and release. Directed by James Flood. From story by Gerald Beaumont. Screen adaptation by Harry Hoyt. Starring Charles Ray, with James Gleason and Jobyna Ralston featured. At Colony, New York, week March 10. Running time, over 60 mins.

Billy Williams.......................James Gleason
Johnny McKinney.......................Charles Ray
Betty.......................Jobyna Ralston
Mother.......................Edythe Chapman
Brother.......................Arthur Lake
Boland.......................Chas. Sellon

Clean-cut, entertaining comedy of the type which can be played any place, any time, but especially suited for neighborhood family trade. Plenty of laughs and Charles Ray gets most of them with nothing in the lines and a difficult part to handle.

Though James Gleason, making his screen debut in this picture, is given practically all of the comedy lines and the fattest role in the picture, he does not rate over average as a comedian, though good support for Ray, however.

To judge from the laughs which greeted every endeavor at comedy business Ray is still the original and best-liked of the loveable, country yokel type, whether in city clothes, tailor shop or as a boob fighter, as in this instance.

The star carried this picture from the opening scene to the close, and delivers as good comedy what is nothing but a cheap, trashy type story remodeled by Harry Hoyt for screen purposes.

One of the unforgettable scenes is where Ray is courting the girl. Too bashful to get very far the young lady decides to help and maneuvers herself into his arms while Ray remains with his mouth open and eyes staring. Created a storm of laughter and applause.

Ray photographs well and interestingly. The story, though outworn and commonplace, has been tailored around him with an expertness which speaks well for the screen adapter, Hoyt. Pictures of this kind are not only wanted but badly needed in the neighborhoods, and this production should meet with as hearty a welcome generally as it got here. Not advisable for downtown first runs, however, though it ranks better than average seen on Broadway in recent weeks.

Miss Ralston registers nicely in the opening shots but later falls down on her assignment on account of bad photography. Some of the scenes, especially where the girl has to pull sob stuff, should be eliminated if the leading woman is to retain the sympathy of the audience. In the sob scenes Miss Ralston's face assumes expressions which disfigure her.

Story is of the prize fighter who allows his wife and her family to spend all of his money. Finally faced by the problem of securing five grand in a hurry he fights the champ with a broken hand. Later learns the money is to be used to pay his brother-in-law's gambling debts but that wife did not know of the plot. *Mori.*

LAST MOMENT

Experimental production made in Hollywood under independent auspices. Zakoro Film Corporation (name of promoting group) sponsors. Produced by Samuel Freedman and Edward M. Spitz. Directed by Dr. Paul Fejos, from his own story. The doctor is described as "a bacteriologist by profession and not previously identified with motion pictures." In on sharing terms on run at Greenwich Village theatre, March 11. Rest of performance is supplied by interpretative dancer, Tamiris; pianolog by Clara Evelyn, American debut of English singer and revival of "'Op-o'-Me-Thumb,'' playlet (once done by Maude Adams) with Lillian Foster starred. Running time of picture, 54 minutes.

He.......................Otto Matiesen
(As a child).......................Julius Molnar, Jr.
Innkeeper.......................Lucille La Verne
A woman.......................Anielka Elter
Another woman.......................Vivian Winston
His first wife.......................Isabelle Lamore
His second wife.......................Georgia Hale

An interesting, freaky and slightly morbid arty picture, creating talk among (and be hailed as epochal by) the art theatre groups, but in now way a picture with general commercial possibilities. Production is said to have been made in eight days at a cost of $13,000. If that is true, it shows no indication of having been pinched for money, the technical production and the settings measuring up to good studio standards. Acting also is dignified and adequate by all trade standards.

A program note makes a great ballyhoo of the fact that the film is the creation of one person, Dr. Fejos, who was "left entirely unhampered by supervision in carrying out his ideas." Program continues, "The film thus represents that rare thing in motion picture production—the creative effort of one man working along experimental lines."

The film does introduce a novel technique. Instead of following the screen formula of dramatizing a theme in orderly sequences, leading up to a climax and concentrating dramatic attention upon one personal or story element, it goes on the basis that a human life—any human life—has a large content of drama. That being the case, a brief prolog crystallizes a whole life time by the device of picturing the operation of a man's mind as he is drowning.

From that point the film picks up the same life at babyhood and carries it through to death, briefly touching upon its salient incidents, all leading to the culminating circumstances that brought the subqect to the still millpond on suicide bent. Having thus pictured the successive steps that made him a suicide, the prolog, which had epitomized the life in a series of fantastic flashes, is repeated exactly as at the beginning. The flashing summary of a lifetime first shown is mere meaningless phantasma, but when it is repeated, it does take on some significance, and the whole business, although merely a theatrical device, has a kick, even if the subject matter and mode of telling is morbid.

The grip of the story lies in the development of the unrelated incidents that make up the man's life. Dr. Fejos, one suspects, is a student of the Freudian idea, and he uses it as a scientist would. That is, he looks for the common experience and tries to present them uncolored by conventions of fiction.

The picture has plenty of romance, but it is utterly uncolored by poetry—always somebody else's romance under clinical inspection rather than romance emotionalized for the benefit of the audience. Always the story is a cold, unmoved recital of the more important things that happened to make up a human existence, as an impersonal historian might record the life story of Hamlet, seeking to point out the exact influences and experiences that culminated in his final madness.

Lighting and photography at times are at fault. The picture has not that clarity of vision that the commercial productions have but this may be due to an effort to get art effects in misty composition, and the mere suggestion of detail. Acting is remarkably well balanced for an effort of this kind.

It's a picture for the Greenwich Village faddists to chew over. But it is strictly limited to that sort of appeal and interesting because of perhaps pointing the way for something in the way of screening realistic narrative. This much it does —it demonstrates that stern realism can be made absorbing on the screen. *Rush.*

THE NIGHT FLYER

Cecil B. De Mille production. Pathe release. Directed by Walter Lang under the supervision of James Cruze. Starring William Boyd. With cast including Jobyna Ralston and Philo McCullough. At Keith's Hippodrome, New York, week March 12. Running time over 60 minutes.

Out of place in any first-run house and not good enough for the first and second-class neighborhoods.

More than ever before William Boyd is here revealed as a type that could easily be popularized and turned into box office under proper directorial guidance and with fairly good story material.

Planted in a bizarre costume period with the locale of the most uninteresting kind and story lacking the essentials of either drama or comedy, Boyd still emerges a handsome, cheerful mugger, distinctly impressive.

Support is weak. Jobyna Ralston looks badly in the closeups. She has been framed to look as unattractive as possible in shapeless clothes of some ancient period, her hair braided and tied in a knot in the back of her neck with the weirdest effect imaginable resulting.

The queer appearance of the girl and a somewhat similar effect produced because of the clothes with which the star is surrounded spoi love interest. Picture then depends on two action scenes, neither strong enough.

It's the story of the old engine destined to the scrap heap. The crack engineer overturns the fast mail train on its trial run, and the fireman, Boyd, brings the mail in on the old 99, to the cheers of the multitude and the handshakes of the president of the road, who figures to get the government mail contract on the strength of the trial run.

This feat squares the conquering hero all 'round, and especially with the gal, whom he almost lost by stupidly getting soused the night of her birthday party.

Betwixt and between are a couple of near-battles with the glowering, heavy-set villain, in which the hero comes out second best, sequences which put a dent in the star's standing as a hero. *Mori.*

DAWN

(English-Made)

London, March 2.

Original story by Reginald Berkeley. Produced by British Dominions Films. Directed by Herbert Wilcox. Scenario by W. & F. Film Co. Private view, London, March 1. Running time, 90 minutes.

There is a fortune in this film if it could be released in a number of big theatres all over the country simultaneously. Then the public, worked up by the controversy, would pack the houses day and night to see it . . . for as long as the morbid interest held out.

But it has not the merit, as a motion picture, to get it over by the ordinary release channels. Once the flash of its immediate publicity dies away, the film will die with it.

It is a pity Sir Austen Chamberlain did not see it instead of writing the letter which started all the fuss. He would hardly have found anything to justify the idea it was likely to cause international complications or arouse bitter feelings.

It has practically the same appeal as detailed newspaper accounts of an execution; an appeal to morbidity and inverted sadism which it is surely not the function of the picture theatre to gratify.

Herbert Wilcox has been exceedingly clever in focussing the attention of the world on himself through the banning of the film here. Equally clever, if it is admitted anything is justified that draws the mob, was his selection of the Cavell incident as an excuse for giving what almost amounts to a public execution . . . a form of horrific sensation which every civilized country has long since abandoned.

One feels it would not have been impossible for T. P. O'Connor to have refused to pass the picture on this ground, and that it is a pity the authorities were manoeuvered into making it a political issue. The German objection has aroused the very feeling it sought to prevent: a storm of anti-German sentiment based on emotion but not on evidence or fact.

How far it is within the province of the reviewer to approach these matters may be open to argument. But questions of morals are not confined to affairs of sex. A general conclusion can hardly be avoided that politically before its release and emotionally after its release (if that ever takes place) it is morally harmful.

Apart from which, viewed as a motion picture, it is not entertainment. It has not the excuse of glorifying Nurse Cavell. She appears rather in the light of a courageous fanatic doing something which, in the circumstances, was opposed to the law, knowing the risks and paying the penalty unflinchingly.

Far from creating the impression the German authorities committed an atrocity, it makes it seem they merely committed a blunder in not being sufficiently opportunist to realize they would have gained more by clemency than by what appeared to them—and to Nurse Cavell—to be the justice of war.

As a story it is unrelieved gloom, and marches slow as a funeral car. An escaped Belgian soldier arriving home is in danger of death if he is recaptured. Nurse Cavell hides him in her hospital, and then evolves the plan of assisting escaped war prisoners to get back to their own land and army. Her organized system of aid is discovered, after notices have been issued warning that it is a capital offense; she is tried and, despite the strenuous appeals of the American Ambassador, executed.

One of the firing party is shown to refuse to fire. He is shot out of hand by the officer in charge of the firing squad. Nurse Cavell faints when this happens and the actual scene of her shooting is avoided by cutting off at a point at which the officer unstraps his revolver holster and walks out of the picture toward where she lies in a swoon. The picure ends on a close-up of the graves of the nurse and the soldier who refused to raise his rifle against her.

Technically the picture is adequate, but nothing more. Some of the street shots, taken in Brussels outside the hospital, are obviously taken recently while traffic is held up and without atmosphere of wartime occupation by an invader. Attempts to get this by marching a squad of a dozen German soldiers through the set-up rather heighten the lack than relieve it.

Except Sybil Thorndike, as Nurse Cavell, cast is unnamed, but includes Marie Ault, Mary Brough and Micky Brantford. Acting competent but not inspired. Many of the extras played as German soldiers would have made fine Cockney Tommies.

Frat.

PRIMANERLIEBE

(GERMAN MADE)

Produced by Robert Land and released through Ufa. Cast foreign, including Fritz Kortner, Greta Mosheim and Wolfgang Zilzer. At Fifth Avenue Playhouse, week March 12. Running time, about 65 minutes.

Ufa's New York representative has told of his company having certain pictures slated for release in America only in cultural centers. "Primanerliebe" evidently is one of these foreign efforts intended for consumption of American sophists.

An average audience, even in the tank town, would consider the theme extremely primary, but this picture, if reviewed by an audience previously accredited with an appreciation for things subtle, could find food for thought.

This, with the exception of the titles, which the greatest accredited sophist cannot kid himself into believing subtle, and the editing of the picture. A better job with the shears could have been done by the average script girl in any of Hollywood's quickie plants.

Leading titles tell of Germany's adult stars being weaned away to the land of big money and blare of self-ballyhoo. As the result Germany, if the titles are worthy of even monetary consideration, is now being forced to pick on the younger element—thus the reason for this picture and so many others from that country being forced to base their stories on themes dealing with adolescence.

At any rate the kids do their best. Regular school activities with boys holding secret frat meetings in opposition to war among nations; and authority of their "profs" and elders.

The stand that they should be able to apply themselves to their books when the spirit moves them; that they should be licensed to meet their girl friends in clandestine meetings by garden walls—all is substantiated when the cutter's shears spell finis on that part showing the old uncle and teacher and all the other members of the faculty despairing over wisdom in expelling the young man, when that young man follows his boy friend on the suicidal path.

Film editing, more than anything else, has made "Primanerliebe" deny the theme which the titles said it started out to teach. American sophists may be willing to argue it out among themselves, but good old American audiences won't waste the time.

Le Chauffeur de Mlle.

(FRENCH MADE)

Paris, Feb. 27.

One of the best French comedy pictures of the present season, creditably performed by Dolly Davis, French star.

Picture produced by Henri Chomette, for Argus Film Co., and released through Armor Film Corp.

Dolly is herself in the picture "Chauffeur de Mademoiselle" (title needs no translation).

Dolly, dressmakers' model, marries the young artist, but as they cannot live on love and water, the modest home soon emits S. O. S. Dolly has a wealthy aunt who dislikes men in general, and the niece neglects to announce her marriage.

Aunt takes Dolly to her gorgeous country mansion, leaving the husband in Paris. The artist soon gets tired of waiting and visits his wife.

Still afraid to confess, she has her husband admitted to the servants' hall as chauffeur.

But a jealous maid informs the aunt that Dolly has an amorous affair with the chauffeur, visiting him at night, and this leads to a revelation when the old maid watches them together.

Meanwhile the aunt has fallen in love herself with an elderly nobleman and is willing to frogive her niece.

Simple scenario, nicely told, with suitable settings in Paris and along the Mediterranean. Several amusing situations, and nicely acted.

Alice Tissot (aunt), Ollivier and Albert Prejean are worthy partners for the charming Dolly Davis.

Kendrew.

HAM AND EGGS (at the Front)

Warner Bros. production and release. Directed by Roy del Ruth from the story by Darryl Francis Zanuck. Cast includes Tom Wilson, Carl Dane, Heine Conklin and Myrna Loy. At Loew's Circle, New York, one day, Feb. 24. Running time, about 60 mins.

This colored version of war life, handled in a comical vein, though barren of novelty and coming in the wake of a flood of various war pictures, should get a good play in the neighborhoods and in the split-weeks. It has been well handled in production. Despite that most of the gags have been previously used, the laughs are there and in sufficient quantity.

Action starts in the training camp in the South, in the U. S. A., with four colored boys playing poker. For the climax of this scene three of the players each flash four aces and a joker, while the fourth brings forth a royal flush. It registered with the customers here.

The two buddies, Conklin and Wilson, are selected to bear the featured roles. At the front, story takes a twist with the introduction of a team of serio-comical enemy spies. Myrna Loy, also in blackface, plays the femme spy and is ordered to ingratiate herself with the two buddies to relieve them of a message which they had unwittingly intercepted and of which they did not know the importance.

Usual complications. Action slows up too often. Picture would gain greatly in value if continuity had provided for continuous business.

Mere idea of a colored regiment at the front should be sufficient to draw business with proper exploitation. Picture can support good stage shows in better type houses.

Mori.

FAITHLESS LOVER

State righter, produced and distributed by Krelbar Pictures Corp. (Sherman S. Krelberg, identified with numerous open market concerns for years). From the novel by Baroness D'Arville, adaptation by Jack Murray; directed by Lawrence Windom. Eugene O'Brien starred, Gladys Hulette and Raymond Hackett featured. Reviewed in projection room. Running time, 57 mins.

Austin Kent ....Eugene O'Brien
Mary Callender............Gladys Hulette..
Harry Ayres ....Raymond Hackett
Mrs. Seeton ....Jane Jennings
Bert Rogers................James S. Barrett
Charles Dunbar.........George de Carlton

Slowly paced romantic drama taking its kick from climax sequences when dam breaks and dramatic rescues are brought about during a wild flood. Story is loosely woven and requires enormous footage of titles. It is in the printed word that the story is told up to the finale. Flood action shots only moderately well done with newsreel clips, models of the dam and views of what convinces as the collapse of a real dam dovetailed.

Neither strikingly bad nor strikingly good product, but a picture that will serve its purpose before screen audiences of indifferent standards such as the state right independents generally serve. Krelberg proposes to do eight features of this kind in addition to a like number of westerns. This is his second of the dramatic group. At a price the film should serve, for it has possibilities in billing. Novel by Baroness D'Arville sounds intriguing; wedding and society scenes furnish excuse for fashion display ballyhoo, although the truth is the women are not particularly smart in appearance. Eugene O'Brien may still be a draw among the fem fans.

Story itself is blah. Earlier passages consist mostly of couple of people standing in conversation, or even one character, usually O'Brien in closeup, and then a deluge of titles explaining what he is saying to her or she to him. At one time hero disappears and is supposed to have been killed, instead of which he has suddenly lost his memory. He reappears and the mystery of his absence is covered up in a title which explains that he was driving alone when suddenly everything went blank. Crude adaptation work.

Gladys Hulette is an unconvincing actress, principally because she is made to do absurd things. O'Brien plays smoothly in another dumbbell part. That of an able engineer who falls in love with a society girl who loves a handsome young bonehead. The engineer gives the young boy a $10,000 job in order that he may marry the girl, although anybody could have told him that the pup wouldn't make the girl happy. In the end, of course, the juvenile wrecks the dam, accuses the girl of having an affair with their benefactor and is providentially killed in the flood. It doesn't take much intelligence to tell in advance all that's going to happen. Trouble is that the novel doesn't stand up in treatment on screen.

Rush.

ALMOST HUMAN

Pathe production and release. Story by Clare Beranger based on Richard Harding Davis' "The Bar Sinister." Directed by Frank Urson. Lucien Andriot, cameraman. John Krafft, titles. Cast: Vera Reynolds, Kenneth Thomson, Majel Coleman. At the Arena, N. Y., March 6. Running time, about 60 mins.

"Almost Human" is made almost a picture by John Krafft's titles. Were it not for these connecting links, occasionally as bromidic as the sequences in the story, the picture would be just a conglomeration of dogs, with a "human" now and then bobbing up over the horizon.

Why Vera Reynolds and Kenneth Thomson, as well as Urson, should have been mixed up in such a story will probably remain a secret. However, their names, coupled with that of Davis, the author, and lobby ballyhoo, may pull from the outside. On the inside there will be one big disappointment. Tempo is way under rating for the kids, and the story, ill described as trite, has anything but the Richard Harding Davis trend which it claims.

TENDERLOIN

(Partially through this picture being virtually the first try at character-talking from the screen, and owing to the hard-boiled first-night audience seeing it too cold-bloodedly, two reviews are printed by different Variety reporters. One is of the opening night and the other on the reception the third night by a wholly lay audience.)

First Night

Warner Brothers production and release. On the Vitaphone. Program mentions "Produced and reproduced by Western Electric system and apparatus." Directed by Michael Cortiz from story by Melville Crosman. Scenario of E. T. Lowe, Jr. Dolores Costello starred, with Conrad Nagel featured. Cameraman, Hal Mohr. At Warner's on run March 14. Running time, around 85 minutes. $2.20 top.

Rose Shannon	Dolores Costello
Chuck	Conrad Nagel
Professor	Mitchell Lewis
The Sparrow	Georgie Stone
Lefty	Dan Wolheim
The Mug	Pat Hartigan
Detective Simpson	Fred Kelsey
Cowles	G. Raymond Nye
Aunt Molly	Dorothy Vernon
Bobbie	Evelyn Pierce

Stripped of its mechanicals "Tenderloin" is a very ordinary film crook meller. That of itself could react against its experimental debut as the first actual talking picture, wherein the characters speak their film roles. This speech is indulged in four or five times, in groups and once by but two people. Of the picture's 85 minutes, perhaps 12 to 15 minutes in total are of the talking dialog.

The Warner Brothers, on the Vitaphone as the speech medium in this picture as an experiment, undoubtedly understood it might look and sound primitive in spots during the spoken dialog. To what degree a talker can or will go or the many angles this production suggests can not be predicted at this time by any one. Critics of the dailies in the main may comment upon the picture as it is, not the possibilities it presages nor the probabilities it may hold.

Holding in mind the quality of "Tenderloin" and that that quality will prevent it becoming a draw of any moment anywhere and especially at Warner's at $2, unless the novelty of screen talking is strong enough to overcome the picture itself, the talking picture appears to be a matter of the voice and the calibre of the dialog to be employed, together with the situation involving both. Here in the first talking scene, a third degree sort of expose at police headquarters, several men aggressively browbeat the girl (Dolores Costello). Her slight voice is pitted against the harshness of the males', the dialog is consistent and a rather good impression in general is received.

Later as the situation wavers in strength, again a group of voices and here the girl's voice is lacking, in volume as well as force. And again in a bedroom scene, the girl and the heavy alone with the man threatening, the woman appealing and resisting, her voice and the dialog could not hold pace with the situation. The audience laughed.

And still again, similarly, with the situation once more rather than the voices, until the screen with the talk resembled a bit from Charles Withers travestied "Opry House" skit of vaudeville. And the audience here laughed outright, to a disturbing limit.

Singing "Sweet Adeline" for the finale cinched that laugh. The picture could have and did logically end three minutes previously.

A wise first night audience may be blamed for that, although another review that is going alongside of this one, may denote more clearly the public's reception on the third night. That smart collection of picture first nighters caught the crudities of "Tenderloin," talking or otherwise. That they laughed as they did but merely evidenced that they came into the theatre prejudiced against the innovation. Some left still prepudiced, and reasonably so, since all are entitled to their opinions.

Neither this picture nor the next or another after that, perfect or not in the speaking way, will foretell the future of the talkers. That decision will have to come from all of the picture goers and that means after the theatres of this country shall have become generally wired. At present there are but a comparative few. However, between Movietone (Fox) as a news reel feature-novelty and the success Vitaphone (Warners) have so far met with in a middling way with its subjects, going to heights with its first full length song film, "The Jazz Singer" with Jolson, together with these talking character pictures that both Vitaphone and Movietone intend to produce, it looks as though all or at least a large majority of theatres, including the vaudfilm houses, will have to go wire, sooner or later.

Vocally the talking picture will appeal mostly from the trained voices of the stage. Notably here with Mitchell Lewis the best voice of "Tenderloin," and Conrad Nagel, both stage trained. Miss Costello is not an elocutionist, nor does she evince more vocal instruction than may have been given her for this film. That she falters at times when speaking cannot be unexpected, from Miss Costello or any other of the picture players who find themselves unable to speak in action through not having control of their voice. In fact, Miss Costello's main fault in talking is the very lack of sympathy between her emotional expression and speech that is the basic principle of the Vitaphone's projection.

Yet, for the other end, Georgie Stone, playing Sparrow, a small fellow with but a few lines toward the finish of the picture, revealed that he has comedy in his light tone. The chances are Mr. Stone has never spoken before on the stage or screen. If that be true, and assuming that his comedy voice may cast him importantly in the talkers, it could be argued that anyone with an appealing voice on the screen, with any sort of personal appearance, may go skyward as a talking character, if the talking pictures become popular.

This is not unlike the unknowns made by radio, through their voices. Unseen they became universally popular to radio's invisible audiences.

Another angle is whether the voice on the screen does not suggest something missing, with that missing element the physical self. This is undeniably felt. The voice, though issuing from the picture player, seems a thing apart, albeit synchronizing. It may mean that show patrons want their pantomime as is rather than an addition that tries to bring the picture too closely to a stage play, leaving the two as the talking image against the talking person. That in its way should lend itself to the promotion of the stage play. This may be found and profited from possibly by stock companies, if "Tenderloin" plays in a city holding a stock. Quite easily the stock might invite the locals to see its stage players after witnessing the film talkers. The edge will be with the stage. This brings up whether a picture shall be a picture only, as people have grown accustomed to and like, or a mixture.

Now the talking picture as here exhibited is a mixture, and a bad one. Captions run along to the Vitaphone score. As talk starts the music stops, then picks up again, with no one aware when it will be a caption or conversation on the screen. That the novelty question must enter is also in view, but how much is the problem.

"Tenderloin" through its deficiencies as a underworld film and as a talking picture may be dismissed on its own account. Possibilities of the talker are more interesting.

As a picture "Tenderloin" tells of a nice girl, a cabaret dancer, mixing up with a crook. Comes a bank robbery, the girl accused of implication, the crook's realization she is a "good girl after all," his determination to go straight and the girl's belief in and love for him. About the only thing worth while in a semi-familiar story is some freak photography.

Chances are that its director, Michael Cortiz, was but one of many. Perhaps a dozen or more of the Warner people were watching and suggesting during this experiment. It may be believed that a picture director realizes but little more of what may be required, so far, for a talking picture than the actors in it. And, for that matter, who does know in this day? Perhaps the Western Electric's engineers would be the best directors of the talkers.

Miss Costello, when passive or pantomiming and feeling at home, did her usual, as handsome as ever. But with the burden of dialog, consciousness of action while talking, the results, as mentioned, not so forte. Mr. Lewis as the heavy, always at home, and Mr. Nagel, too. This may have been why no scene including Miss Costello talking was shown in Vita's 15-minute trailer on this picture that was at Warner's for two or three weeks with "The Jazz Singer." Only the men appeared in talk in the trailer. Still the caption writers should stand some blame for this, at times, inane dialog.

Adequate settings, with a couple singularly pretty in their rural and romantic simplicity, but the lovers did not talk. Maybe the flappers will prefer to hear the love passages spoken on the screen rather than the dramatic stuff. That is worth trying, also.

As a new departure in the show business, "Tenderloin" is blazing the way, but as to what way, who can tell?

Third Night

A good small town picture, to judge from the impression on a third night audience, if the inane anti-anti-climaxes are removed. The picture should logically end where the girl is trailing the wagon on which the boy friend is being taken for a trip to the cooler.

Following the cold reception this production got, both as a straight film and as a talker, from the opening night attendance, two of the talking scenes in the middle of the picture were removed, leaving only two speaking sequences.

The third degree scene, halfway through the picture, is powerful. The talking and singing sequence at the end of the picture is also interesting but comes too late because of poor construction of the film.

With the Vitaphone dialog sequences the picture will draw patronage as a novelty though not exceptionally so. As an instance of the possibilities in talking pictures the two sequences appeal strongly.

The direction of a picture suggests that Curtiz was not given a free hand and, if so, it lets him out on responsibility.

Georgie Stone (the Sparrow), formerly a song and dance man in vaudeville, makes a great showing with a small but effective role in the picture. In the closing talking sequence, Stone, who had been getting laughs on appearance throughout, registered doubly on the comical tone of his voice.

Conrad Nagel, Stone and Pat Hartigan, singing "Sweet Adeline" for the finish, will surprise picture fans, Nagel especially so.

Picture is gripping in spots, but continuity is jumpy and direction faulty in others. *Mori.*

CONSTANT NYMPH

(ENGLISH MADE)

London, Feb. 28.

Screen adaptation of the play by Margaret Kennedy and Basil Dean. Continuity by Alma Reville. Produced by the Gainsborough Pictures Co., Ltd. Directed by Adrian Brunel under the supervision of Basil Dean. United Kingdom distribution, W. & F. Films. World rights controlled by the Gainsborough Pictures Co. Preview and premiere at the Marble Arch Pavilion, opening Feb. 20. Censors' certificate "A." Running time, 110 minutes.

Sanger	George Heinrich
Linda	Mary Clare
Tessa	Mabel Poulton
Paulina	Dorothy Boyd
Toni	Benita Hume
Lewis Dodd	Ivor Novello
Ike	Peter Evan Thomas

With the material there was nothing wrong. As a novel, and hardly less as a play, "The Constant Nymph" held many fundamental elements of dramatic clash which, in the hands of a sympathetic adapter and director, should have made a great film.

Yet the result, dragging on through some 10 reels, is rather as if a provincial newspaper reporter had taken the story and reduced it to newspaper headlines, and still another and equally provincial reporter had written a screen story from those headlines. For the struggles between temperament, the blossoming of an over-strong adolescent love, the awful and inevitable sadness of attempts by people to dominate those they assume they love—all this is left out, and nothing remains but the dry bones of story, clothed in respectability and "refinement." Linda is made to appear as Sanger's wife, which is not the case in the novel.

The essence of the Sanger household atmosphere is conveyed, in the novel and on the stage, by two episodes. One is the illicit holiday which Toni takes with Ike before marrying him; the other is the intrigue between Linda and a traveling ballet master—an intrigue revealed to the rest of the family by the sudden death of Sanger.

Both these episodes are left out of the film, and even the curtain is made "respectable" by removing the venue of Tessa's death from a Brussels house to a dowdy sitting room in what appears to be a rooming house.

Perhaps too much was expected from Basil Dean's first picture. But however much was anticipated, very little has been realized save the fact it takes something wider, faster and more broadly understanding than stage technique to obtain satisfactory effects on the vivid canvas of the screen. As portrait painters both the director and Basil Dean have failed with a theme calling fundamentally for such treatment. They have consequently failed to register the character clashes on which the story depends so much, and instead of a tragedy which sweeps all the chords of emotions and weaknesses, they have played a commonplace melody and filled it with discords.

The saving grace (but a common factor of that kind in so many films) is the Tyrolean scenes in the first part of the picture. These, taken around Achensee, not far from Innsbruck, hold all the appealing quaintness of the Tyrolean atmosphere and costume, set against a magnificent background of emotionless mountains, aloofly unconscious of the petty human turmoil at their feet. But not for long is this held. The film swings back to London, to small ideas, little silly people, formless actions, motiveless doings.

Besides which, it holds almost every scene far too long. The action is at once slow and inchoate, the direction lacking fire, the acting (save in the case of Mabel Poulton and Frances Doble as the misunderstanding and misunderstood wife) spineless. Ivor Novello looks well, and when he is not called on to be dramatic gets over satisfactorily. But in the tenser moments he is melodramatic and needs a director who either can or will restrain his over-emphatic movements, especially the elevator work with his eyebrows.

As told by the picture, the story goes that Lewis returning to the Sanger chalet, and with him comes a ballet master to get an opera from Sanger. Linda, Sanger's third matrimonial effort, starts an intrigue with the dancing man, interrupted by Sanger's sudden death. Then Lewis writes to an uncle of the family in England, who comes to look after some of the children. One departs with the vituperant Linda, who takes the ballet master with her also. Ike marries another, and two are sent to school in England, Lewis meantime falling in love with and marrying the kind uncle's daughter.

Lewis' wife has ambitions for her husband, but they are of the Greenwich Village type, and Lewis is a real artist at heart, and, being so, regards nothing of importance save his own feelings.

Tessa and Paulina, the two sent to school, break away and come to Lewis' house. His wife especially takes a dislike to Tessa, and accuses her of being Lewis' mistress. So, Lewis being sick of his menage, and Tessa wanting also to get away, they bolt to Brussels on the night of Lewis' successful debut as a composer-conductor.

In the apartment house, straining to open a window while Lewis offhandedly writes a letter to Tessa's uncle, the girl falls dead from a heart seizure, and the final fadeout is on Lewis burying his head on her cold breast.

A lot had been promised for the trio of girls who should have stood out in this story: Mabel Poulton, Dorothy Boyd and Benita Hume, and one hoped here were some coming young "finds" for British films. But, with the exception of Mabel Poulton, who makes the most of the Tessa part despite inadequate direction, the others are almost passengers. So once again we are faced with the forlorn fact of a British film being oversold with little to justify the advance ravings. *Frat.*

GARDEN OF EDEN

Walter Morosco presents United Artists production, U. A. distribution. John W. Considine associated in production. Lewis Milestone director. Corinne Griffith starred. Story based on play by Rudolph Bernauer and Rudolph Osterreicher and American stage play by Avery Hopwood. Scenario by Hans Kraly. George Marion, titles. At Paramount, New York, week of March 17. Running time, 75 minutes.

Toni Le Brun.............Corinne Griffith
Rosa ....Louise Dresser
Henry von Giessing........Lowell Sherman
Madame Bauer...................Maude George
Richard Spanyi................Charles Ray
Col. Dupont............Edward Martindel
Musical Director..........Freeman Wood
Railroad Conductor............Hank Mann

This picture has everything, star, cast, romance, title, comedy and intrinsic interest quality. A feature for anybody's house on any booking basis.

Universal appeal of the Cinderella theme is the foundation upon which a fine production has been built and carried out with all the resources of the modern studio. Stands out among the best for beauty of setting and fine pictorial effect. Principal locale is Monte Carlo and the background is a fashionable hotel with atmosphere of luxury.

Beauty of star, beauty of production and human appeal set this one in as a winner from the getaway, with special pull from the women fans.

Story grips from the first. Toni, humble young singer in Vienna, is lured to a questionable resort in Budapest, supposing place is an opera house. Turns out to be shady night club that sells innocent country girls to rich philanderers. Girl refuses to go on stage in seminakedness and is tricked into appearing as a "Puritan" in costume which is transparent when lighted from backstage. She is maneuvered into a private dining room with a scheming roue and rescued by the wardrobe woman of the establishment, who befriends the girl when she is discharged.

Older woman persuades girl to go with her on a vacation, and to the girl's amazement, takes her to the most expensive hotel in Monte Carlo. Woman confesses that for 50 weeks of the year she is a humble seamstress, but enjoys a pension that gives her two weeks of the luxury she knew before the war when she was a Baroness and her husband was alive.

At the hotel the Baroness meets old friends, among them a colonel who pays ardent court to the girl. His rich young nephew becomes his rival and the two struggle for the maid's hand. Youth wins. At the very altar the heroine's humble birth is revealed, although the Baroness has now adopted her legally and she brings a real title to the marriage.

Sneering relatives learn that all the bride's jewels, even her wedding dress, are the gift of the bridegroom. It is made falsely to appear that he would back out of the ceremony. Whereupon the girl strips to the "underwear which I provided for myself," running through the assembled guests clad in a scanty step-in. Here is a first rate high comedy sequence delightfully climaxed when bridegroom and Baroness capture the girl, who takes refuge under the bed covers and the ceremony is performed on the spot. Spicy little kick in this passage, but the whole thing is carried out in a charming vein of graceful comedy, innocent of suggestiveness.

Louise Dresser as the fairy godmother adds another stately role to her growing gallery of engaging portraits; while Charles Ray brings his old boyish awkwardness to a part that was made to order for him. Corinne Griffith in all her ingenue beauty is caught in some stunning camera studies and throughout plays a delightful comedy role with vast charm.

The picture is meaty with amusing comedy passages. There is the scene where she and the young man signal each other across the hotel court by snapping the electric light on and off. Presently everybody in the rooms facing on the court is signalling. Later on girl and her protectress disagree about turning off the bedroom night light. One snaps it on and the other turns it out, and presently the whole hotel is back at the wig-wagging. Titles are skilfully designed to emphasize the innate humor of the situation but never descend to gagging on their own, admirable restraint for George Marion, Jr., who can gag with the best of 'em when the situation calls for that treatment.

Picture that will score at once with the class clientele and with the westerns' following. "Garden of Eden," by the way, comes from the facts that the hotel where the romance runs its course is called the Hotel Eden, enough connection to get a good box office title by.

But while a certain feature for the regular houses it just misses that punch which might have classed it as a special, or surely for a U. A. 99 cent house run. Perhaps that is because it really ranks as a comedy.

Rush.

The World War as Seen Through German Spectacles
(GERMAN MADE)

London, March 3.

Ufa production. Distributed in the United Kingdom by Wardour Films. English version edited by Boyd Cable. Censors' certificate; U. Running time, 60 minutes; an episode. Released in 10 5-reel parts. Preview at the Capitol, London, March 1.

The pre-view of this Ufa film was declared to have been postponed on account of feeling over "Dawn." But postponement was only for two days.

Part shown covers the opening of the war to the end of 1914. It is partially an official record and for the rest studio reproduction. Several shots are used two and three times. Naturally, the reconstruction of the invasion scenes in Belgium and by the Russian army in Eastern Prussia are made with a German appeal.

Interesting as a document from the German point of view as popularly expressed, and for America as denoting the early stages of the struggle before America was implicated.

Cannot be regarded as movie theatre entertainment, and its appeal is limited to education by comparative methods, when (and if) they exist.

Boyd Cable (Lieut. Col. Ewart) spoke from the stage after the preview and suggested the average man's idea of fair play was a good reason for showing the film in picture theatres. So much feeling akin to the mob state of mind during the war has already been stirred by ill-advised concentration on the making of war films here and by the distorted limelight thrown on the Nurse Cavell film episode, there is little doubt Boyd Cable is out in his estimate.

On the whole, except the difference in uniforms and in some cases in scenery, there is little or nothing in this film which has not been seen in most other war pictures. And in any case the picture-going public is already showing its satiation with this theme by staying away from the more recent releases unless they have a strong story value apart from gunfire and shell bursts. *Frat.*

THE NOOSE

First National production and release. Richard Barthelmess starred. Alice Joyce, Lina Basquette, Thelma Todd, Montague Love and Robert T. Haines featured. Scenario adapted from the stage play by Willard Mack and H. H. Van Loan. At Strand, New York, week March 17. Running time, around 75 minutes.

Nickie Elkins........Richard Barthelmess
Buck Gordon..................Montagu Love
Jim Conley............Robert E. O'Connor
Tommy..............................Jay Eaton
Dot..........................Lina Basquette
Phyllis.........................Thelma Todd
Seth McNillan..........................Ed Brady
Dave...........................Fred Warren
Bill Chase.................William Davidson
Mrs. Bancroft.....................Alice Joyce
The Warden..............William Walling
The Governor............Robert T. Haines
Craig.........................Ernest Hilliard
Priest.........................Emile Chautard
Judge.......................Romaine Fielding
Cabaret Girls......Yola d'Avril, Corliss Palmer, Kay English, Cecil Brunner, Janice Peters, Ruth Lord, May Atwood

"The Noose," with Richard Barthelmess, gives First National a drawing program feature that will stand well up to follow Barthelmess' great hit in "The Patent Leather Kid." It's an extremely well directed and played drama, with meller tendencies, a touch of the underworld with a real cabaret scene one of the standouts, but underneath the rest a virile story of suspensive qualities that are all taken advantage of. It's in.

This picture is said to have been taken under the natural light, or at least the cabaret scene was. Natural light is indicated throughout. If the first of that kind, its defects can be remedied if natural light is thought beneficial. While the trade may detect a different lighting scheme, it's doubtful if the lays will. At times the photography is misty and not always uniform in light, a greyish tint often appearing. That followed into the cabaret scenes for the side rooms employed there, but on the floor the lighting was evenly bright. At the Burbank studios when this scene was taken it was said that the heat from the big arcs was terrific on the people beneath them.

Toward the finish of "The Noose" extraordinary suspense is maintained and it's two-sided. First is whether Nickie Elkins will be hanged, and he is walking toward the gallows for some time, while the other is whether the Governor's wife will confess to her husband that Nickie is her son. Neither happens. What did happen was that Mrs. Governor 'phoned the warden over her husband's private wire ordering the execution stopped, and the Governor, when advised, calling the boy before him, to intimate that a pardon would be forthcoming.

Nickie had shot and killed his father, Buck Gordon, within five minutes after Buck had told the lad who his parents were. His mother was the Governor's wife, said Buck, and if he were sent away for killing another gangster, Nickie would have to appeal to his mother to save him. Upon Nickie's refusal, Buck said he would shake down the Governor's wife himself then for freedom and coin. Nickie said he wouldn't and, to prove it, shot his father, who had brought him up from babyhood without Nickie aware of his father or mother.

Other than the cabaret scene, no action of moment. A bit of shooting, but the play's action very

Barthelmess' Nickie a natural for him, although Barthelmess is more likable in action. That's where he shines. Nevertheless, Barthelmess has a distinctive individuality on the screen, and it's very valuable, for few own it. He always suggests impulsiveness, and that's suspense in itself, continually.

Lina Basquette does Dot, the cabaret girl, nicely. In the prison and Governor's room scenes, Miss Basquette was admirable. She's in love with Nickie, who was about to be regenerated by a "nice lady from uptown" just as he bumped off his suddenly discovered dad. Thelma Todd as the nice lady only had to see that her very blonde hair was marcelled.

Alice Joyce had a difficult emotional role as the Governor's wife. She looked the part, excepting when opposite Barthelmess, when she appeared too young, but Miss Joyce will probably not be miffed over that. She had to express extreme heart anguish and yet refrain from confessing to her husband even for a commutation or pardon that the condemned boy was her own son. That made it quite a serious moment of acting for her and also an unreal character, but she got by well enough under the conditions.

Jay Eaton as Tommy, the stager of the floor show, minced it up a little for a laugh; the girls behind him displayed good coaching and legs. William Walling as the warden had but one chance, but made that bit look very good. Montagu Love did the heavy Buck. That was soft for him, doing his best in looking the role. Robert T. Haines was another who perfectly looked the Governor, giving the part all of the dignity it called for.

John Francis Dillon's direction keeps this story moving fast all of the while.

Barthelmess' backward leap into the front rank of the male b. o. cards will be helped along by this one.

ODETTE

(FRENCH MADE)

Paris, Feb. 28.

This is taken from the popular work of Victorien Sardou and realized under praiseworthy conditions by Luitz Morat, who has not done anything better since his "Petit Ange."

"Odette" is an excellent French picture, for small time, with good photographic work, with a suitable cast comprising Francesc Bertini in the title role, surrounded by Warwick Ward (English) and Mlle. Simonne Vaudry.

Count Clermont suspects his wife of infidelity and drives her from home. He even raises a monument over a pretended grave to lead their child to believe her mother is dead.

Many years later Odette attempts to recover her daughter, but the girl refuses to recognize her mother, convinced by other relatives the visitor is an imposter and only a friend of her deceased parent.

Unable to regain her child and husband the poor woman prefers to seek death.

Somewhat antiquated in these days, "Odette" was a melodrama with a tremendous run in the mid-XIX century and constituted an attraction in the Sardou repertoire.

Story pleases less today, although making an impression on local movie fans. Released under favorable conditions by De Merly.

Kendrew.

Legion of the Condemned

Paramount production and release featuring Gary Cooper and Fay Wray. Directed by W. A. Wellman from J. M. Saunders' story. Harry Gerard, photographer. Titled by George Marion, Jr. At Rialto, New York, on run starting March 17. Running time, 74 minutes. Top 99c.

Christine Charteris.........Fay Wray
Gale Price.........Gary Cooper
Byron Dashwood.........Barry Norton
Charles Holabird.........Lane Chandler
Gonzalo Vasquez.........Francis MacDonald
Robert Montagnai.........Voya George
Richard DeWitt.........Freeman Wood
Commandant.........E. H. Calvert

Over matter from "Wings" and yet very apt to do plenty of business on the '28 coast to coast interest in aviation. Okay for program material, although not to be compared with Paramount's similar and preceding super, despite turned out by the same combination of Wellman and Saunders, director and author respectively.

A lot of stuff in this one that didn't get into "Wings," notably the solo raid on a German troop train by the plane Gary Cooper is supposed to be in. It's really the boy who flew for "Wings," and likely to be vividly recalled by numerous audience members because of the black streamer on the helmet which Buddy Rogers affected and which somebody forgot to tack on Cooper. Stills of this aerial machine gunning of the train appeared outside the Criterion for a while, but never reached the screen inside. It's understood the Paramount road show department requested that other sequences cut from "Wings" also be deleted here, and this has been complied with to a certain degree. At least at the Rialto.

A flash of the St. Mihiel sector, which "Wings" heavily plugged in the newspapers, is in the original "Legion" print, but is out at the Rialto. It's better out all over, for those who have seen "Wings" can't fail to spot it.

On the other hand, this "sequel" has much to recommend it from a program viewpoint. Its main asset is action supplemented by a good "type" cast, some members of which don't even get program or title mention. The main weakness is an 11-minute cutback to pick up the love story after an interesting two-reel start without it.

To establish the spirit and desire to die in the personnel of this particular pursuit squadron, the picture pushes off by showing a Spaniard shooting a South American husband as he flees with the wife; another youth laughed out of suicide by a girl after going broke at Monte Carlo; a kid kills his girl companion in a drunken auto smash in England, and another boy is generally bored with everything in New York and Harlem. This is all short, fast and to the point, with the next flash the French air base, all four boys in uniform and drawing high card for the sure death assignments. In the midst of the first drawing enters Gale Price (Mr. Cooper), who loses to the British youngster (Barry Norton), and the latter hops off to drop a spy in enemy territory.

A great face, this boy Norton. Dangerously close to being too pretty, but perfect here in uniform and answering Wellman's best bit of direction when he stands up to be shot after being caught with his passenger. As a matter of fact it's the standout bit in the picture, and early. Thence a return to the base, and Gale, who assumes the next such mission by physical force.

And into the flash back of Gale, as a reporter, and the reason for his being of the Legion. Assigned to cover an embassy ball, he takes Christine (Miss Wray). Not knowing she's in the French secret service, the bottom drops out of the evening's love declarations when Gale finds her in a private room on the knees of a German baron and apparently drunk. So that's Gale's excuse for wanting to die in a hurry. Compared to the opening quartet of causes, it makes just a foolish kid of the big, hulking he-man reporter who should have stuck with his typewriter.

But when Gale looks up to see who he's to drop behind the German lines it's Christine. Quick explanations and the amour is on again; but duty calls and they take off. Supposed to call bock for her in 10 days, Christine is trapped and placed at the same spot to act as a decoy to snare her returning pilot. Her warning gets through too late to stop Gale, but his companions are rampant on retribution, and the pursuit squadron becomes a bombing detachment. Just as the firing squad is about to open up on Christine the boys start bombing, the execution is postponed and Gale and Christine are rescued. Follows Gale's unanimously agreed discharge from the group who have lost interest in their blood pressure.

The poison has been subtracted from the enemy executions by depicting the German officers showing every courtesy to the prisoners and regretting that it has to be done. Whoever plays the German officer in charge of the firing squads does it in the Von Stroheim manner and competently enough to receive program or title billing. Likewise for "Toto," the mechanic, who uncorks as snappy a salute as any of the military pictures have had and makes his entire performance stand up.

These two plus the male foursome at the opening are strong enough to overshadow the principal duo, Cooper and Miss Wray. The latter, however, looks good, but Cooper is up against a pretty fair assortment of trouping from the male contingent. Gerard's photography, if he was also in on "Wings," is good, and Marion's titles carry a snicker or two for diversion. Plenty of wiggles by a colored miss in a supposed Harlem cabaret are also cut from this version.

"Legion," as a picture, is all right, but no rave. It should particularly thrive in those centers where "Wings" has paved the way. As an indication, the Rialto was one of the few Broadway houses to have a b. o. line as early as 2:30 on a cold and wet Sunday. As for hurting "Wings"—not a chance. *Sid.*

HUNTINGTOWER

(ENGLISH MADE)

London, Feb. 22.

Produced by Welsh-Pearson Productions, Ltd. Directed by George Pearson. Screen play by Charles E. Whittaker, from the novel of John Bucham. Paramount release. Photoplay by Roy Overbaugh. Censors' Certificate "U." Pre-release at the Plaza, February 19. Running time, 72 minutes.

Dickson McCunn.........Sir Harry Lauder
Princess Saskia.........Vera Veronina
John Heritage.........Pat Aherne
Mrs. McCunn.........Lilian Christine
Speidel.........Moore Marriott
Prince Paul.........John Manners

The Plaza is running "Huntingtower" in a two-feature program, "Serenade," with Menjou, being the other. Atmosphere is provided by a Scottish prolog in a Highland glen set, with a couple of pipers, two Highland fling dancers, and a male vocalist, who closes on a Lauder chorus, "Roaming in the Gloaming."

The film runs seven reels, and gets many laughs, but they are not all played for. For it is not possible to take either the story or the method of its unfolding seriously. Russian Bolsheviks, complete with fur hats, running about a Scottish castle, landing at their sweet will from the sea; rescues by half a dozen small boys and about three men, armed with nothing more lethal than golf clubs; a Princess immured in a tower by desperadoes who want her jewels and her life—all these ingredients might have made an admirable burlesque. But the Plaza audience, apparently expected to take the film as a drama, laughed in many places where the director's obvious intention was to be dramatic.

The story is thin, and never decides to concentrate on any particular character, with the consequence it swings in an unco-ordinated fashion from Lauder to the female lead, and from her to a funny but rather incredible gang of Glasgow street urchins. This uncertainty of purpose appears to come not so much from story treatment as from direction.

Lauder is—just Lauder. His quaint little figure, his rhythmic strut, his mixtures of comedy and pathos expressions are all there. Like the rest of the cast, however, he has moments when he does not appear to take the business seriously, and to feel the whole story is so unreal it verges on funniness.

"Huntingtower" is a curious film, and not easy to review. Settings, exteriors, locations, cast, photography are all first-class, yet the picture lacks both conviction and appeal.

On Lauder's name alone it will be a box office attraction, but it will not establish the Scottish comedian as a screen artist. Nor will it enhance the reputation of George Pearson, who of late has not fulfilled the promise of his earlier Betty Balfour pictures, and, in actual fact, has done nothing worthy of note since "Love, Life and Laughter."

It was anticipated Pearson would make other quota films for Famous, and whatever the other reasons may be why he is not doing so, one of them may be "Huntingtower."

Frat.

BRINGING UP FATHER

Cosmopolitan production, released by M-G-M. Based on newspaper cartoon strip by George McManus. Directed by Jack Conway. Titles by Ralph Spence. Cameraman, William Daniels. At Capitol, New York, week March 17. Running time, 62 minutes.

Jiggs.........J. Farrell MacDonald
Dinty Moore.........Jules Cowles
Maggie.........Polly Moran
Annie Moore.........Marie Dressler
Ellen.........Gertrude Olmsted
Dennis.........Grant Withers
The Count.........Andres de Segurola
Mrs. Smith.........Rose Dione
Oswald.........David Mir
Fiedelbaum.........Tenen Holtz
The Dog.........Toto

A few months after its costly run-in with the Irish societies over "Callahans and Murphys," M-G-M takes a long shot in releasing another Irish roughneck comedy. They hope it will get by, and it may because of some very obvious efforts to placate any resentment. The picture is slapstick for comedy purposes. It can certainly be argued that there was no conscious thought of ridicule; indeed, quite the reverse. Nevertheless, it does not flatter the Irish. It represents an Irish wife and mother as a vile-tempered nagger, who makes the life of her husband a hades of petty subterfuge and scheming to have a little innocent fun now and then.

Polly Moran's impersonation of Maggie is shot through with vulgarity. Her manners, dress and attitude are shanty. Her telephonic conversations with her sister-in-law leave no doubt as to the adjectives and expletives employed.

Ralph Spence is responsible for the subtitle in which Maggie says to the young duke:

"I'll kick the pants off that butler for calling you 'mister.'"

Twice during the picture one Irishwoman actually does kick another. The spectacle can hardly be expected to please the sentimental Irish who weep over "Macushla."

The picture is funny in spots and plain dull in others. It is dullest when an attempt is made to paint a contrasting picture to Maggie in her sister-in-law, married to Dinty Moore.

The plot is extremely sketchy. Where or how Jiggs got all his money is never explained and who or what the young duke is never seems very clear. Gertrude Olmstead as Jiggs' daughter is pretty and a needed relief. The cast is a good one and makes the characters seem as plausible as the hokum permits.

Spence's titles drew laughs on three or four occasions, but were old and mothy for the most part.

The Hearst tie-ups and attendant publicity will probably be valuable, although there is an increasing tendency to discount the value of the Hearst plugging, because of overdoing it in the past. Nevertheless, McManus' cartoon strip has a following that may want to see the picture and who, very likely, will think it quite a cinema.

Still, in the final analysis, it is just a so-so picture. *Land.*

MODERN DU BARRY

(GERMAN MADE)

Ufa production released through Universal. Featuring Maria Corda. Directed by Alexander Korda. At Colony, New York, week March 17. Running time, 75 minutes.

Toinette.........Maria Corda
King of Andalia.........Jean Bradin
Cornelius Corbett.........Friedrich Kayssler
Count Martel.........Alfred Gerasch
General Padillo.........J. V. Szoreghi
Juliette.........Hilde Radnay
Aunt Fifi.........Julie Serda

Even Germany has a couple of good reasons for a quota. This is one under the "make 'em play our pictures—good or bad" plan. And it's bad.

Change the title to "From Scullery Maid to Queen" and that tells all. Except that Maria Corda has a good cry over every male sign post on the route. By disposition she's prone to give in every so often, but for American consumption, maybe not. There's nothing to hang Toinette's loose morals on, except that she bounds from a salesman, to a count, to an extremely wealthy protector and then a king —with the salesman getting the best break. He doesn't have to stick through and watch Toinette sob over the titles and habits of man. Between men she manages to become a mannequin, a stage star and almost breaks up her king's kingdom.

That's covering a lot of territory in an hour and a quarter. As you may guess, it's pretty well disjointed. Besides which, Maria is back to her "Moon of Israel" make-up; eyelashes that you'd need a niblick to play out of; black hair, and a hard-boiled looking bob.

Korda directed, too, recalling the brave days of old. Between them the Yankee impression is going to be negligible. Those who saw "Helen" and remember won't believe it's the same combination.

Productionally the picture holds some genuine Paris street stuff, but Korda reverts to the tree and fields as a symbol of love and to alabaster statues for dejection. Miss Corda is either up against one or the other, according to the mood. When she isn't weeping. But maybe nobody was in the mood. It's quite possible. Anything is possible.

Here's a picture that proves nothing, except that Germany also has its quickies. And that Miss Corda can out-tear Jane Cowl. What grief! All the glycerin in Germany. Poor little gal. Money, clothes, home and jewels. And still crying. She wants her king and Corbett, the bold, bad billionaire won't let her have the kink. Because he owns all the oil wells in Andalia, the army hasn't been paid off and the king's got to come to him for coin. Why didn't he think of America? Corbett'll even marry Toinette. But the former housemaid spurns the offer. Her Majesty or nothing. But when the power behind the throne learns that "she really cares" he calls off the small time revolution he has inaugurated and puts the king back to work. Just for Toinette. And she finally stops crying.

Only thing the picture reveals is that Jean Bradin, playing the king, might be a bet for pictures over here. The C and K OrdAs rate a couple of rousing blushes. *Sid.*

NAMELESS MEN

Tiffany - Stahl production featuring Antonio Moreno and Claire Windsor. Directed by Christie Cabanne from the story by E. Morton Hough. Cast includes Eddie Gribbon. At Keith's Hippodrome, New York, week March 19. Running time over 60 minutes.

A good neighborhood picture with an excellent cast, fine direction and story rendered interesting through treatment.

The names in the cast, though not high power, should result in additional attendance. Moreno and Miss Windsor still photograph well and maintain suitable appearance as leads in a story with love interest.

Gribbon, with limited business, creates laughs frequently with mugging that can't miss getting results. Steals the picture.

The continuity writer missed out on a story which might have resulted in a great picture instead of a mere programmer. It is told in the titles toward the end, "You were a great pal, Blackie, but a bum crook," the secret service man saying this.

Throughout the picture the pair were not played as pals. Had the interest there been stronger the production would certainly have made a Broadway house.

Story revolves round a sleuth who goes to prison for six months to gain the confidence of a youth who had participated in a robbery and who had hidden the money where no one could find it.

Blackie (Gribbon) tries to shanghai the girl and grab the swag for himself toward the end of the last reel but is killed in a shooting match where the sleuth is almost bumped off too.

Blackie's attempt to imitate the smooth, easy manners of the sleuth, especially his envy of the latter's spoon trick, runs through the picture and results in a steady vein of comedy.

Love interest might have been handled more skillfully. *Mori.*

THE FARMER'S WIFE

(BRITISH MADE)

London, March 4.

British International Pictures production. Directed by Alfred Hitchcock. Distributed by Wardour Films. Adapted from Eden Phillpott's play. Photography by Jack Cox. Censors' certificate U. Running time, 100 minutes. Preview at Astoria, London, March 2.

The Farmer	Jameson Thomas
Araminta	Lilian Hall-Davis
Churdles Ash	Gordon Harker
Thirza Tapper	Maud Gill
Dunnybrig	Gibb McLaughlin

Eden Phillpott's stage play of Devonshire manners depended mainly on its comic dialog, which in turn depended largely on the spoken philosophy of Churdles Ash, old farm-hand. To make the play into a movie, interest has been switched to the various attempts of the farmer to get a new wife. Out of what appeared such thin material many folk held off when the rights were on offer, but Alfred Hitchcock has made a fine photoplay.

As a cross-section of English rural life with sufficient broadness of interest to make it universal in appeal, it is one of the first pictures made here which looks like a real high-grade photoplay.

The subject prevents it from being in the super class, despite technical excellence in acting, settings and photography as well as direction. Some of the Devonshire exterior sequences are a revelation in beauty without retarding story. In fact, there is not 100 feet of padding throughout, though the tale would not suffer if the first half reel were cut out. It shows the death of the farmer's first wife and strikes a discordant note on which to open a comedy. The situation could just as well have been planted by a caption, with the action jumping straight into the situation of the farmer wanting to make a second matrimonial venture.

Unlike Hitchcock's two previous pictures, "The Ring" and "Easy Virtue," this film is free from imitation German symbolism and other attempts to placate the highbrows. The director has treated a broad subject in a broad, forthright fashion. He evidently has found his real medium in a subject not calling for subtlety.

To the smallest "bit" of an ostler, the types are chosen with unerring accuracy. Families attending an afternoon tea party at the house of the village postmistress are a delight, particularly the kids. Most of these players have not been on the screen before, once again proving Griffith was right.

Farmer Sweetland, middle age, loses his daughter when she marries, and decides to take another wife. With the aid of his housekeeper he makes a list of the women around who will jump at the chance. From one to the other he goes, full of his own magnificent condescension. He is turned down first by a fox-hunting widow, next by a dried-up spinster, then by a near-young fleshy dame with a tendency to hysteria, and finally by the mistress of the village inn. He finally gets an angle on his own swelled headedness, and finds a wife at home in his housekeeper.

As a story on paper it does sound thin, but the situations are well played up, with much comedy support from the cynical old help and a half-wit village gaffer. Three effective shots of a foxhound pack in full cry are also worked in without disturbing the continuity.

Jameson Thomas is over-young for side whiskers, and should be playing younger character leads. But he gives a first-class performance, with Lilian Hall-Davis in the best work she has yet done. Maud Gill plays the role she had in the **stage version and with as much success.**

"The Farmer's Wife" is a film which will do more to put British movies over than all the war and flag-wagging pictures in a bunch. It is different, and even if it is not a great picture, it is entertainment that does not need an audience born here to understand. *Frat.*

TRAGEDY OF YOUTH

Tiffany-Stahl production and release, directed by George Archainbaud. From the story by Albert Shelby LeVino, continuity by Olga Printzlau. Titles by Frederick and Fanny Hatton. Film editor, Bob Kern. Photographer, Faxon Dean. In projection room, New York, March 16; running time, 64 minutes.

Frank Gordon	Warner Baxter
Paula	Patsy Ruth Miller
Dick	Buster Collier
Mother	Claire McDowell
Father	Harvey Clark
Diana	Margaret Quimby
Porter	Steppin Fetchit
Landlady	Billie Bennett

A domestic problem play handled skillfully in the sentimental style of romantic fiction that has enormous vogue among the women. Something on the Mrs. Southworth technique, with a touch of "Snappy Stories" to give it a modern smart fillip. This sort of material bound to be duck soup for neighborhoods, especially, and for the femme fans of that grade.

Picture produced in the best manner and neatly acted. Settings reflect atmosphere of elegance appropriate to the subject of modern married life among the wealthy. Whole affair is strictly modern in settings and literary treatment.

Some of the episodes are shown in a good deal of elaborate detail, the purpose being to play up the sentimental angle. Effect is sometimes that of slow tempo, particularly in the earlier sequences. However, picture picks up in dramatic speed as it approaches it denouement, and on the whole the effect is satisfactory.

Theme is another play upon modern headlong youth, subject being dealt with in sympathetic way. Boy and girl fall in love because they enjoy dancing with each other. Girl's father and mother advise against marriage on the ground of their extreme youth, but they won't listen. They have been married a year, when husband neglects wife and gives all his attention to his hobbies, one of which is bowling. Youngsters are growing apart.

Wife meets handsome neighbor during one of her lonesome evenings, and the two suddenly realize they are in love with each other. Girl has savage quarrel with selfish husband, but he pretends an attempt at suicide and in fright she consents to reconciliation, sending the other man "out of her life," as the title has it.

Lover sails away. His ship is wrecked and news is brought that he has been lost at sea. Young husband, who has resumed his courtship manners toward wife while there was competition in sight, now ignores her again. She leaves him in a new quarrel, just as news arrived that lover was not drowned at all but returned on a rescue ship.

Finale shows wife in romantic married scenes with second husband, while gay husband is stepping out with a blonde charmer, announcing as they go upon night club dance floor, "All right for you. Gorgeous, I'm in circulation again."

Comedy side lights are plentifully besprinkled throughout story, the titling being especially good for its bland humor. Good picture for certain specific clienteles, especially for the less worldly type of woman fan. Men will find it dull and the "wise" bunch will scoff. *Rush.*

THE GOLDEN CLOWN

(HEART, OF A CLOWN)

(Swedish Made)

Joe Fleisler, Esq.,
Cell 888,
55th Street Playhouse,

Dear Joe:—Ever since a couple of cloak and suiters transformed this 55th street garage into a temple dedicated to the cinematic art and the accumulation of American shekels, it has been my painful duty to sit in solitary confinement, week after week, and pass judgment on sundry atrocious offerings which European producers claimed were motion pictures. The reason I say solitary confinement, Joe, is because I was usually the only umpchay in the house.

Friday night, Joe, last Friday night, walking down from Seventh avenue I saw a little cluster of people outside the theatre. I thought maybe you were giving away an Ampico with every subscription and I took the count when I saw the boys planking down six bits each, cash money, merely for tickets.

"Art has triumphed at last," I breathed disappointedly. I was disappointed because experience had taught me that art as exemplified by the arty picture houses consisted of a six-weeks-old newsreel, a couple of scenics and a foreign feature flicker that couldn't get a showing anywhere else.

So when the gagged western, consisting of a single shot of a muddy-faced hombre mugging a dame, flashed on the screen I figured the booze the night before and I had crashed the wrong joint.

But I stuck. And when "The Golden Clown" flashed on the screen I knew I spotted right. Everything on the program okay except this. What the cloak and suiters refused to understand, Joe, was that the customers in the neighborhood couldn't stomach straight picture stuff of this kind and you and Mike Mindlin had to come up from Fifth avenue to show them how.

The only difference between your show and the kind of show that resulted in the defeat of the noble aspirations of the c. and s.'s is the comedy. You have to give the folks a couple of laughs. You have the laughs but you put a crimp into the works by showing the "Clown" straight and with an introduction about America not going for sob stuff.

According to your screen scribbler the 55th Street Playhouse could not see the loss of this "dramatic masterpiece" to America and salvaged it for the benefit of posterity and the box office. Minus this introduction, which handed me a hefty haw, the customers might have hollered at some of the stuff in the picture and that would have done you and the box office more good eventually. If the leading man's loud-checked, velvet-collared coat, reaching down somewhere near his toes, the bulgy pants and the Harry Langdon pancake lid shouldn't be played for comedy, what have you?

Nobody in the house got the tragedy anyhow. Just because the happily married gal done wrong by kissing the hair-dresser, fashion creator, or whatever it is, and the famous clown went on a drunk is not a sufficiently powerful situation to call for a sob contest from the customers. 'Course that's not your fault, Joe, but trying to sell that kind of stuff on a Republican ticket won't work out after a while even if it gets returns for the present. Somebody will start gagging these foreign made pictures and clean up.

As a whole it looks like a good show for the neighborhood. And from the crowd in the house Friday night your bunch shows that it takes more than putting the "art" shingle on the door to get business.

And say, Joe, nobody seems to remember that line you pulled when you first started plugging the art picture racket, "Walk up and save the evening." It's as good as new. *Mori.*

ALEX THE GREAT

F. B. O. production and release. Story by H. C. Witwer. Directed by Dudley Murphy. Cameraman Nigel Neeler. In projection room, New York, March 14. Running time, 60 minutes.

Alex............Richard "Skeets" Gallagher
Ed............................Albert Conti
Muriel.....................Patricia Avery
Alice..........................Ruth Dwyer
Brown......................Charles Byer
Smith....................J. Barney Sherry

This is the story of a Vermont rube who sold 50 automobile trucks to a department store proprietor by recognizing a picture of the prop's pet cow, Betsy Ross, hanging on the wall.

It's just as bad as it sounds.

Richard "Skeets" Gallagher, who has performed an odd chore or two now and again for the bigger film companies, gets probably his first major opportunity in "Alex the Great." He is always winking at some one, alternately indicating flirtatiousness, insolence or chumminess. He is about as convincing as near-beer on the screen, and that goes for the rest of the cast as well.

Dudley Murphy, the director, has made a generally botched job out of a typical H. C. Witwer fresh guy yarn. The detail particularly is clumsy, unnatural and annoying.

"Alex the Great" is the sketch but not the fulfillment of a comedy. Where the customers please easily it may be liked, but it seems probable that its draggy telling of an incredible story will bore most people to extinction or the exits.

Land.

JALMA LA DOUBLE

(FRENCH MADE)

Paris, Feb. 26.

Another creditable French picture for week runs, of a dramatic comedy category, made by Cineromans Films de France, with Roger Goupillieres producer. It should meet with success.

"Jalma la Double," adapted by M. Bouquet, tells of two French travelers in Turkey releasing a pretty princess from the cruel Sultan who schemes to imprison her, his niece, so she will not prevent him from be coming the ruler of the district which he has unjustly proclaimed himself to be.

Picture shows Turkey suffering under the reign of Abdul-Hamid and his clan. Lucien Dalsace, de Bagratide, Chakatouny, and Mlle. Groza Wesco are the protagonists.

Kendrew.

Service of Transportation

(INDUSTRIAL)

At the request of the Stanley Advertising Company Variety reviewed this industrial film in the Engineering Society Auditorium, where it was shown March 16 to 600 members and guests of the New York Railroad Club. It is probably the first instance of a theatrical trade paper considering an industrial film critically.

Stanley Advertising features its affiliation with "800 theatres and a 5,000,000 weekly circulation." "In the Service of Transportation" is strictly propaganda for the American Car and Foundry Company and too long and too local for any but non-theatrical distribution.

Distribution and circulation is generally the crux of screen advertising, the point big business wants enlightenment upon, and the stumbling block for the average industrial film producer lacking regular outlet for his product. The background of the Stanley theatres gives the Stanley Advertising an edge, but in this particular instance it seems improbable that many, if any, of the affiliated 800 movie parlors can or will play a four-reel plug.

The picture is fairly good throughout but starts badly with a series of faked bird's-eye views of various plants about the country. These might have been sneaked in, but spotted at the opening they stood out like a sore thumb. As all of the actual shots were made in Pennsylvania this side of Pittsburgh, and as the fakes were quite some railroad fare further inland it looked skimpy.

Frank Zucker's photography is clear and commendable. There were too many factory interiors shot from overhead moving cranes, however, with this angle, effective once or twice, becoming stereotyped. Applause greeted one scene when a moulten red boiler cylinder was hoisted from a burning oil vat. Colored stock was used here for effect.

Stanley shoots without script, as do most industrials. This places a heavy burden upon the cutting and editing and results in a certain lumpiness that continuity would eliminate. Even without story or continuity, merely collecting and splicing 4,000 feet of miscellaneous celluloid, Stanley has succeeded in registering the magnitude of American Car and Foundry operations. Members of the New York Railroad Club were familiar with its general character, but to an outsider it's all news and eyeopening. The audience applauded posed camera studies of Clemuel Woodin, founder of the company, and his son, William Woodin, its present president

Heretofore industrial film makers have not enjoyed much repute. Anybody who knew where to hire a camera and could crash the gate of a business office to put on a sales talk was an industrial producer. They operated on a shoestring and with the same ability or reliability possessed by the glib racketeers who offer to make saps movie stars for $50 and up.

The number of business men who have been stung is legion. Yet, it is possible to predict that in spite of this motion pictures for advertising purposes is a field of great possibilities. Stanley reduces its standard print to 16m. size and sends it free of charge into the homes of amateur projectionists through dealers and a mailing list.

There are three well-known industrial producers in New York—Stanley, Castle and Bray, and one in Chicago—Rothacker.

Land.

PANAME

(FRANCO-GERMAN MADE)

Paris, March 1.

Screen version of a novel by Francis Carco, of the Paris underworld, known in local slang as "Paname." After a run in Berlin, it is shown under the title of "Paname n'est pas Paris" for French exhibition.

A good work, interesting in many respects, with views of the French capital, after a prolog in New York.

Many cities of Europe are seen, at a glance, during the run of this film, produced by N. Malikoff for the Alliance Cinematographique Europeenne. Leads are held by Jaque Catelain, Charles Vanel, Ruth Weyher, Lia Eibenschutz, Olga Limbourg, Mic, J. F. Martial and Malikoff.

Kendrew.

WILFUL YOUTH

Peerless production released through Capitol. Directed by Dallas Fitzgerald from story based on novel, "Whispering Pines." Edna Murphy and Kenneth Harlan featured. In cast: Jack Richardson, James Aubrey, Barbara Luddy, James Florey. At Loew's New York, one-half double bill, one day, March 13. Running time, 65 minutes.

"Wilful Youth" is a couple of paces ahead of the average quickie meller. Dallas Fitzgerald uses the familiar double-crossing brother sequence, the wronged girl falling off the cliff and the right girl refusing to abide by the dictates of the money-mad mother, with judgment.

For program stuff in ordinary houses, or possibly for the weak end in a double-feature bill in better second runs, this will be found to possess a sufficiently satisfying continuity executed by an even more satisfying cast.

Kenneth Harlan uses his mitts too often for the sunnyness of his role. This gets a laugh now and then, especially when he takes a healthy sock at the lumber foreman for a move made quite obviously in jest. A later tilt with his brother is an up-and-down affair, during which the audience can almost picture the director-referee on the lee side of the camera.

The tempo is generally good for a production of this calibre. Tightening up some of the drawing-room scenes and eliminating many explanatory titles would increase the speed and build up the intensity of that kind of a climax, which shows the brother a crook, murderer and open-handed advocate for suicide.

HIS HOUSE IN ORDER

(ENGLISH MADE)

Adapted from Sir Arthur Wing Pinero's play. Scenario by P. Mannock. Produced by Ideal Films. Directed by Randle Ayrton. Photography by H. M. Wheddon. Censor's Certificate "A." Preview at the Palace theatre, Friday, Feb. 24. Running time, 72 minutes.

Annabel Jesson .... Sheila Courtenay
Filmer Jesson .... David Hawthorne
Major Maurewarde .... Eric Maturin
Hilary Jesson .... Ian Hunter
Nina Graham .... Tallulah Bankhead

A very contradictory film. Technically, it is full of defects. Lighting, make-up, sets and direction are all old-fashioned. The continuity is so full of signals that nothing comes as a surprise, in fact, one waits with irritation for things to happen and have done with it, so obviously have they been telegraphed earlier.

Nevertheless, the film carries its story through with more entertainment and rather more conviction than most of the much more expensively draped and modernly directed pictures seen here. It tells a probable story, and the cast looks like it might be human beings to whom such things are happening.

But the theme is lacking in conviction save as a leaf from the past, and the tendency to stilted direction, as of the stage of a generation ago, emphasizes the feeling.

It is the first appearance of Tallulah Bankhead in motion pictures, and while one may hope it will not be the last, it is also to be hoped her next shows her to better advantage. Not as an actress, but personally. Her make-up was wrong, she was not well lit, and some of the angles used from which to photograph her ought to be avoided. Like most of the other artistes in this film she got into the spirit of the character quite well, but the poverty of technical aids shows.

David Hawthorne succeeded in making Filmer Jesson as provincial and pompous as he ought to be, but Eric Maturin as the near-villain was very stagey.

Seen only in the early part Sheila Courtenay, as the falsely pedestalled wife, made a good job of her part but the easiest and most natural player was Ian Hunter as the brother who spills the story of the first wife's cheating. He has had more screen experience than the rest in the film, and it shows in his work. He had no opportunity of repeating his run away, as in "The Ring," but he took most of the honors all the same.

Just a fair program film, its merit being an absence of pseudo-intellectuality and imitation symbolism.

Frat.

A TRICK OF HEARTS

Universal production and release. Hoot Gibson, star. Reaves Eason, director. Story by Arthur Statter, suggested by Harry Irving Dodge's "The Horse Trader." In cast: Georgia Hale, Joe Rickson, Rosa Gore, Nora Cecil. At Tivoli, one day, March 10. Running time about 65 minutes.

A western with an old angle, but not used enough to make it as stereotyped as many of the more abused bromidic sequences. It provides Hoot Gibson with something better than his usual.

Hold-ups, but the house is let in that they are phoney. A real bad man who helps Gibson work up the climax and rescue the girl.

Gibson fans will eat this up because of the laughs provided with hard riding. Instead of pulling the he-man stuff from the start Gibson masquerades as a woman to thwart the town of its ambition to emulate a Tex Ferguson administration.

Foolishness winds up in a lot of merriment as well as a punch for audiences of this kind.

MALDONE

(FRENCH MADE)

Paris, March 7.

The Societe des Films, Charles Dullin, presented the last realization of Jean Gremillon to the press and trade last week at the new Salle Pleyel. Despite its unnecessary length, "Maldone" pleased the guests, but much pruning will be required to make this picture a commercial proposition, particularly for exportation.

There are some wonderful photographic views of canal life in France, and it must have cost a pile of money to produce. The story, by Alex Arnoux is rather slight, but it affords opportunity for Charles Dullin to renew his screen success.

Plot: Maldone runs away from home when young and becomes a teamster, towing barges. When his brother is killed by being thrown from a horse Maldone becomes the heir to the ancestral property and a faithful old man servant sets out to find him. Maldone is found in a small town where he is smitten by a pretty gypsy lass, but he is persuaded to quit his former free-and-easy environment to inherit the family manor.

The happy-go-lucky youth marries a rich neighbor's daughter, has a child, and life becomes boresome. He loves his wife but still thinks of the gypsy and his former freedom. This preys on his mind; he has fits of spleen and gets impatient with his affectionate, passive wife. To throw off this increasing irritable despondency Maldone travels with his wife (an occasion for the usual cabaret scenes, with jazz accompaniment), and chance will have it that he runs into the arms of his former gypsy charmer, become a prominent actress.

He returns to his country home, now in a hypochondriacle state, which continues until he can support the quite domestic existence no longer. He dons his old clothes and sets off on horseback for his former haunts, the picture depicting his certain transmutation to a lunatic. The technique of this picture is worthy of all praise, some of the exteriors being splendid aquatic views of the Gatinais district. Dublin impersonates the unfortunate Maldone with skill. His gradual metamorphose to the crazy condition is good acting. Genica Atanasiou, as the gypsy Zito, Marcelle Dullin, Andre Bacque, Roger Karl and Isabelle Kloukowski are likewise well remarked in the cast.

Kendrew.

BRANDED SOMBRERO

Fox production and release. Starring Buck Jones. Directed by Lambert Hillyer from story by Cherry Wilson. R. Lyons, cameraman. In cast: Leila Hyams and horse "Eagle." At Loew's New York, one-half double bill, one day, March 13. Running time, 55 minutes.

Too much time taken to explain what the "Branded Sombrero" is all about gets this Buck Jones special off to a slow start. Lost time is made up in the last-half with the speed of a battler out for the edge in the final round.

Fans, no matter how rabid they may be about movement, will find it tough going to follow Buck Jones once he decides to pay the debt the old man, on his death-bed, reveals he incurred through rustling.

Love for the village queen leads him into jail, overtaking a fast freight on his horse "Eagle," capturing the bad man who is out to "break" her in order to snap on the marital band, and a score of other things.

When she understands that his wayward brother parl...d his share of the estate on gaming tables and followed the old gent's track steps in order to pile up the chips, everything glimmers on the silver sheet.

Yep, Buck Jones' people will leave the house satisfied that they have put away a good meal.

Les Transatlantiques

(FRENCH MADE)

Paris, March 2.

Adapted from a well known book of Abel Hermant by Pierre Colombier, "Les Transatlantiques" is one of the best productions of Henri Diamant Berger, dealing with the pleasant adventures of an American family in France. The film closely follows the novel, with Aime Simon Girard, Marcel Vallee, Jim Gerard, Jean Dehelly, Daniele Parola and Pepa Bonafe as principles.

This cast is excellent, but the picture is not a big drawing card, notwithstanding much material suitable for universal movies.

Kendrew.

SPOILERS OF WEST

Metro-Goldwyn-Mayer western. Directed by William S. Van Dyke. Tim McCoy starred. Marjory Daw heads supporting cast in which William Fairbanks is featured. At Loew's American, New York, March 12-14. Running time, 52 minutes.

Hard-riding western taking special merit from its historic interest, the action taking place on the western frontier during the Indian fighting that followed the Civil War.

Spectacular Indian-fighting stuff is done splendidly, scenic backgrounds are fine and melodrama is dealt with in terms of Fenimore Cooper instead of the Old Scout dime novel style.

Picture has the material to hand thrills to the youngsters, but still has enough intelligent control to be accepted as interesting fiction by grown-ups. In the neighborhoods it should be of a quality to please both the matinee and the night customers.

For a wonder it is a western with fair romantic story interest. McCoy is an army lieutenant assigned to clear out the trappers from Indian lands in 30 days, by which time the Indians threaten to go on the war-path against the squatters and all whites. McCoy undertakes job, supported only by a handful of Indian police (a historic detail that isn't often played up in movies or fiction).

Settlers are all driven off with some riding action and clashes, and then the lieutenant runs against a settlement around a trading post operated by the beautiful heroine, a determined gal who won't move and is ready to back up her decision with a rifle.

Before the campaign has gone on long, of course, the brave soldier is in love with the girl, but determined to go through with his duty. There is a good scene where she covers him with a rifle, declaring she will shoot if he approaches up to a certain mark. Lieutenant walks steadily toward her, and she weakens. Then a hidden sniper picks the soldier off, and while he lies wounded in the girl's cabin the 30-day armistice expires and the redskins go off on the warpath.

They are massed in the hills, holding at bay a troop of cavalry sent to the relief, when lieutenant recovers sufficiently to realize the situation. He goes off on a desperate ride to get to the Indians and mediate the strife before there has been bloodshed. By this time the girl knows she is in love with the brave officer, so she rides after him and all is well when the warriors are reassured by their trusted soldier-friend, and agree to make peace.

Gathering of Indians in a mountain-flanked plain; maneuvers of the cavalry to gain a high position to defend, hero galloping to the rescue through hills and canyons and water courses, all make a pictorial rave.

One of the few "westerns" that command and deserve serious attention. And a miniature "Birth of a Nation" for the small-boy trade.

Rush.

THE LAW OF FEAR

FBO production and release. Adapted by Ethel Hill from story by William Francis Dugan. Directed by Jerome Storm. Supervisor, Robert North Bradbury. Cameraman, Robert De Grasse. In New York projection room, Feb. 29. Running time, 47 mins.

The Dog	Ranger
Marion	Jane Reid
The Sheriff	Sam Nelson
Steve Benton	Al Smith
The Hunchback	

A dog picture with most of the stigma that goes with woof-woof operas removed. The mutt remains, happily, subordinate to the melodrama.

Picture brims with action. It is liberally seeded with fisticuffs, moving horses and other sure-fire ingredients of cinema thrillers. Photography is excellent and the scenery hand-picked from the best the west has to offer.

The mysterious bandit this time is a sort of Dr. Jekyl and Mr. Hyde, peaceful if a bit snotty, rancher by day, a toothsome, distorted fiend by night. A pleasant relief from the usual development of this classic western plot. Al Smith plays the two-timing lad and goes exceptionally well. Smith is an unknown, although the thought occurs that he may be the owner or trainer of "Ranger."

After all, even villains are human beings and a dog is still a dog.

"The Law of Fear" is a good melodrama.

Land.

THE CLEAN-UP MAN

Universal western featuring Ted Wells. Story by George Morgan. Directed by Ray Taylor. Cameraman, Milton Bridenbecker. At Tivoli, New York, one day, Feb. 29, on double feature bill. Running time, 48 mins.

Again the mystery rider, the unknown gang leader in reality a supposedly respectable citizen. Again the unjust accusation of the hero, although in this case they do not try to lynch the hero.

This is a Universal western and neither worse nor better than most of its kind. Where these pictures have given satisfaction in the past "The Clean-Up Man" will suffice equally well.

If Ted Wells has a following the individual exhibitor must be the judge. He looks new to this reviewer. And quite a handsome lad for a cowboy star. Most of the saddle Thespians are more rugged than comely. He gets considerable less footage than Peggy O'Day as the heroine. She turns out to be a private dick in the end. Even the kids will have that figured out before the picture's into its first chase.

Reasonably fair sample of a conventional one-day westerner.

Land.

Canyon of Adventure

Charles R. Rogers western, distributed by First National. Albert Rogell, director. Ken Maynard, star; Virginia Brown Faire, lead. Story by Marion Jackson, produced under supervision of Harry J. Brown. Half of double bill at Loew's New York, New York, one day, March 16. Running time, 65 minutes.

Typical hard riding western but here with a certain additional interest from picturesque locale of Southern California in '49. Plots and counter-plots of Spanish landholders around Americano hero. **Plenty** of fighting action, abundance **of** picturesque costuming and some **beautiful** scenic shots.

All obvious melodrama directed to **the** simplest fan tastes and for that **purpose** extremely well done. Ken **Maynard** and his white horse, "Tar**zan,"** are a great team for this sort **of** thing and here handle the as**signment** very well. Picture has **good** comedy in its rough and ready **western** outlaw types. They work **up** a whale of a fighting climax **when** hero is besieged in hacienda **of** Spanish heavy.

"Tarzan" takes a signal to the **outlaw** band which has befriended **the** hero and they ride to the rescue **while** hero holds the horde of natives **at** bay in sword combat.

All routine material, but sure-fire **and** presented for full value. **Picture** is first rate subject for the daily **change** houses and a strong number **for** double feature programs, as **here.**

Rush.

BROKEN MASK

Morris R. Schlank presents Crescent Picture, distributed by Anchor. James B. Hogan, director. Cullen Landis and Barbara Bedford featured. Story by Francis Fenton. Also in cast: William V. Mong, Wheeler Oakman, James Marcin, Pat Harmon and Phillipe DeLacy. At the New York, New York, one day, March 16, half double bill. Running time, 60 minutes.

One of those independents. Little to recommend it, even for the modest daily changers except perhaps price. Relegated to the week-end of double bills, as on this program.

Fatal defect is use of a comedy idea as the basis of a dramatic subject. Story has to do with an Argentine man dancer working in a New Orleans night club whose face has been so marred by scars that he cannot get ahead in his profession.

A sweetheart from the Argentine has become a dancing star in the theatre. When they meet, she per**suades the hero to have his map done over by a plastic surgeon, and thus made handsome, become her partner. All this is accomplished in due time and the dancing pair become the greatest in their line.**

They fall in love, of course, but meanwhile the same plastic surgeon has fallen in love with the girl.

On their marriage eve, he gives the hero some treatment that brings back all his old scars, making him so ugly the Doc thinks heroine will refuse to marry him. Instead of which hero cuts the doc all to pieces with one of those Argentine cattle whips and heroine declares she loves him for his sterling heart and not his patched up pan.

Story is dull in the telling besides absurd in material. Long passages are devoted to sentimental business between dancing heroine and her ancient papa, refugee from a South American revolution. Girl is supposed to be a whirlwind of a dancer, but doesn't put it over.

Few cabaret scenes are sightly enough and the settings are always adequate but the only action is the doctor-hero fight, which doesn't support the whole hour of flicker.

Rush.

WOMAN WISE

Fox production and release. Directed by Albert Ray. Scenario by Randall H. Faye. In cast: June Collyer, William Russell, Walter Pidgeon, Theodore Kosloff, Duke Kahamamoku. At Loew's Circle, one day, March 2. Running time, about 50 minutes.

Slap bang direction and shooting from a story too small to fit, even on the Hollywood cuff, contribute largely in making "Woman Wise" the kind that will register blah even in oiliest tank towns.

"It's a Fox Production" should be taken off on account of the really worthwhile material coming out of the Fox lot. The most wholesome reaction is that of having witnessed a newsreel of attacking Persians spliced into a Mack Sennett comedy, with a fraction of a reel of the popular "Poverty Row" drama.

By the time the thing is over, the fan can only remember that a fairy-like pasha is after the scalp of an American because of a girl. The consul has to be socked on the jaw before he is wise that the girl loves him and not his friend.

Apparently, the last couple of feet inspired the title.

SKINNER'S BIG IDEA

FBO production and release. Story by Henry Irving Dodge adapted by Matt Taylor. Directed by Lynn Shores. Cameraman Phil Tannura. Titles by Randolph Bartlett. In projection room, March 7. Running time, one hour.

Skinner	Bryant Washburn
Hemingway	William Orland
Carlton	James Bradbury, Sr.
Gibbs	Robert Dudley
Perkins	Ole Ness
McLaughlin	Charles Wellesley
Dorothy	Martha Sleeper
Jack	Hugh Trevor
Mrs. Skinner	Ethel Grey Terry

About 1923 Bryant Washburn starred in "Skinner's Dress Suit," one of those typical fantasies of getting ahead in business. Story has been since used again for Reginald Denny.

Now comes the sequel. Skinner, established success, is taken into the firm of McLaughlin & Perkins, placed in complete charge during the absence of the senior partners and told that his first job is to fire Hemingway, Carlton and Gibbs, **three old bunnies who have gotten mouldy by 20 years of faithful but uninspired service for the firm.**

Skinner hates to air the genial old men, especially because they are so honestly delighted at his own promotion. His heart is about broken when the old boys give him a surprise party at his home.

The big idea that came to Skinner was to rejuvenate the vets. This he does by psychology, planting a bright young actress in the office as a secretary, and then kidding, brow-beating and annoying the old timers out of their drowsiness, making them think, act, use initiative and snap out of it.

The story, the idea, the sentimentality of the whole thing is just what the average American loves. It's a business romance, the romance of a business such as nobody probably ever knew, an office in which making money is too easy to be important, but it's pie for the home towners.

Additionally there is a little heart-tug now and then, some laughs, pure, unruffled love between the actress and the big boss' son. It shapes up, in toto, as a neat number for FBO and the average non-deluxe exhib.

Land.

OPEN RANGE

Paramount production and release. Directed by Clifford B. Smith from the story by Zane Grey. Screen treatment by John Stone and J. Walter Ruben. Cast including Betty Bronson, Lane Chandler and Fred Kohler. At Loew's New York, one day, March 2. Running time, 60 mins.

Excellent western pleasing in every aspect. While consisting of the usual ingredients the treatment of this production sends it over as a change of diet from the usual type of western.

Most commendable feature is its continuous and exciting action. Satisfactory lack of lengthy overdrawn sequences and even the love scenes, usually crude beyond description in westerns, are well done, due mainly to Miss Bronson's appearance and experience.

Principals, Miss Bronson, Lane Chandler and Fred Kohler, register as strong performers. Kohler, as the heavy, is unusually convincing, though Chandler is somewhat light in the lead male role.

Story is of the wandering cowboy who is suspected of rustling cattle and persecuted by the real rustlers. For the gal and the good of the community the boy hunts down the gang. Everything points to a quick and happy finish when it develops that the leader of the rustlers is a half-breed, mostly Indian. The Indian leader offers the menace protection and at the last minute an old-fashioned Indian-cowboy battle takes place.

To save the settlers, the "hero" stampedes the stolen cattle through the main street of the town, which is packed with redskins. He then saves the girl and her family from a fire and concludes an otherwise uneventful afternoon with the gal against his manly chest. Anyone could have written it, since it's been written before. *Mori.*

FLYING LUCK

Pathe production and release. Produced by Monty Banks. Directed by Herman Raymaker from story by Charles Horan and Monty Banks. Screen adaptation and continuity by Charles Horan and Matt Raylor. Monty Banks starred with cast including Jean Arthur, J. W. Johnstone, Kewpie Morgan, Eddy Chandler and Silver Harr.

Feature length comedy of this kind impossible except in daily changes or in spots where anything will go. This one merely a two-reeler padded with extra falls and ineffective mugging as filler for the additional running time.

Monty Banks is far too light to carry full length feature comedies, rating more in the two-reeler category if anything. Sergeant Duff (Kewpie Morgan), obviously intended as a foil, is an excellent type of overgrown boob heavy. He steals most of the scenes for laughs when played against Banks.

The story is simple and laboriously handled in the screening. It is similar to several other air stories seen in pictures recently, concerning the amateur airplane bug who takes correspondence school lessons in flying, but winds up by winning a contest, race, air polo game, war, mail delivery, speed test or whatever seems easier to shoot at the time on location.

In this case the dub wins the air polo match for the army through a trick played on him by the other workers on the flying field.

Laughs scarce, business uninteresting and response light.
Mori.

PHANTOM RANGER

Universal production and release starring Al Wilson. Story and direction by Bruce Mitchell. In cast Lillian Gillmore, Mary Cornwallis, Larry Steers. At Arena, New York, one day, March 16. Running time, 45 minutes.

Although every effort has seemingly been made to make "The Phantom Ranger" an action picture,

with speeding cars, planes and horses, as well as motorcycles, the average audience will arise feeling worse than if it had sat through two hours of the poorest foreign stuff.

The main trouble is the total lack of continuity. Coupled with a cast that never gets away from direction, the acting as a whole could have been done better by amateurs.

Al Wilson, the stunt flyer, does a lot of stock movements. Part of the time only does he use a real plane.

Too many nonsensical antics that fall flat even of comedy's bounds make this a hocus-pocus of stuff, not worth the negative it is printed on.

THE MASKED ANGEL

I. E. Chadwick production. Starring Betty Compson. Directed by Frank O'Connor from the story "Remorse" by Evelyn Campbell. Screen adaptation by Maxine Alton. Photography by Ted Tetzlaff; titles by Leon Lee. In projection room, New York, March 15. Running time 55 minutes.

Betty Carlisle.................Betty Compson
Jimmy Pruett.................Erick Arnold
Luther Spence...............Wheeler Oakman
Lola Dugan....................Jocelyn Lee
Cactus Kate..................Grace Cunard
Wilbur Ridell.................Lincoln Plumer
Detective Bives.............Robert Homans
The Nurse.....................Jane Keckley

Badly directed; enough so to kill possibilities except where the picture can be used as a filler. Story trite and dull, minus picture angles of any kind.

The star owes her fine appearance here mainly to the brilliant work of the photographer. Photography would place this picture on a par with anything turned out by the major studios if backed up by suitable story and continuity.

Action only in the subtitles, poorly written and constitute another unwelcome feature of the production.

Story is of the cabaret girl who did wrong but refuses to go back to her old lover. She accidentally meets a blinded soldier in a hospital and friendship soon blossoms into love.

Later, happily married in the cottage bought with a soldier's pension, the menace turns up to tell the soldier of his wife's record. The girl first intends to shoot her lover but the light of understanding shining in her tear-dimmed eyes, she tells all in the hope that her soldier-husband will understand. He does. *Mori.*

SATAN AND WOMAN

Samuel Zierler presents an "Excellent" production. Distributed by Commonwealth. Directed by Burton King from story by Mary Magruder. Cameraman, Art Reeves, Claire Windsor starred. Principals include Cornelius Keefe, Tom Holding, Edith Yorke, Vera Lewis and Madge Johnston. At Loew's New York, one day, March 9. Running time, 64 minutes.

Every now and then the professional movie-goer runs into a states right proposition that stands out like a royal flush. "Satan and the Woman" is such a picture. It has neatness, class, intelligence, good cast, well directed and a good story well told. It's deserving of playing much better theatres than it probably will play under the states right handicap.

Claire Windsor is starred. She looked like a million bucks and flashed some natty dressing that materially assists the picture in maintaining an air of distinction. Her name probably will count in the majority of stands.

The title is a misnomer. Satan has nothing to do with it, even by remote symbolism. It's a yarn about a small town where a gloomy old dame is boss of the works. She lives in a mansion on a hill and owns most of the town; her house

overlooks. Her granddaughter lives in the town, unacknowledged and a social outcast, because of the haziness surrounding her parentage.

Tale not wholly original but related in visual terms with effectiveness and nicely sustained quality.

Picture free from skimpiness. Sets look the part and like money. A masquerade dance is not too gaudy and yet sufficiently close to flashiness to add "production" to the final result.

Some of the circuits might find this number worth considering.
Land.

THE TRAIL OF '98

Metro-Goldwyn-Mayer production and release, based on Robert W. Service's novel of same name. Features Dolores Del Rio, Ralph Forbes and Karl Dane. Directed by Clarence Brown. John Seitz, photographer; Joe Farnham, titling. At Astor, New York, for twice daily $2 run starting March 20. Running time, 127 minutes, exclusive of intermission.

Berna.......................Dolores Del Rio
Larry........................Ralph Forbes
Jack Locasto................Harry Carey
Lars Peterson...............Karl Dane
Salvation Jim................Tully Marshall
Samuel Foote.................George Cooper
Old Swede....................Russell Simpson
Mrs. Bulkey..................Emily Fitzroy
Mr. Bulkey...................Tenen Holtz
Grandfather..................Cesare Gravina
Mrs. Peterson................Polly Moran

"Trail of '98" is going to be road-showed at $2 next fall and will get money at that figure. It's more spectacle than story. For that reason whether it will line up with the preceding Big Six road shows is a question. The most advantageous point in its favor in this respect is that J. J. McCarthy is handling its special career. Of this there can be no doubt. No prolog, a McCarthy habit. Bang! Right into the picture. For program purposes the picture is there a mile.

"Trail" probably holds more spectacular sequences than any of the real $2 pictures since "10 Commandments." Yet, its story never brings a lump to the throat although, at various times, it grips. Dramatic intensity in the love theme is lacking until about the start of the final two reels. A touch of genuine pathos has sometimes been found to be worth a big effect and that pathos, which makes the feminine eye damp and the male swallow once or twice, is what "Trail" lacks.

"Big Parade" was a natural after the first half of the picture, not because of its corking war scenes but because of the interest involved in the characters and the unusual human script background against which they were etched in celluloid; "'Way Down East" had its soul-stirring ice flow to the falls, which the screen has yet to top for both pure drama and action at one and the same time; "Commandments" had its color and the opening of the sea, although it is generally admitted that the modern story of the second half put this one across at the legit scale; "Covered Wagon" possessed the foundation of a people opening up a territory, epic and understandable wherever the civilized brain functions; "Ben-Hur" unfolded its chariot race, famed story and superlative production, while who can deny that "Birth of a Nation" had all of these, and more?

Then, on a basis of comparison with these six leading films of the industry, and this latest M-G-M super rates their measure, is it incongruous to say that "Trail's" closest parallel is "Wings," a picture currently threatening to force its way into this select group? In actual story the air film is weak, but holds two passages which make the women cry and seep under the masculine skin, while the aeroplane warfare commands intense attention. "Trail" doesn't reach this emotional peak albeit its spectacle high spots are inspiring, aided by Fantom Screen. That novelty screen twice mysteriously moves down stage to fill the entire proscenium opening and then retires, upstage, to continue the story on a normal 16-foot "picture." Hence, this latest of the big ones may be said to have its story shortcomings, is shy of that quality which makes an attendance consistently forget it's a picture, but the spectacular scenes will see it through.

No question that Brown, directing, and Seitz, photographer, have accomplished great pieces of work in filming a snow slide and raging rapids. And the maximum presentation value for these scenes, 20 minutes apart, is reached through the gradually magnified and moving screen. The white avalanche appears to be slow-motion miniature technique, but is handled so realistically that it seems as if the snow were hurtling into the laps of those in the orchestra. But none of the main characters are in danger so, as far as the story is concerned, it remains an "effect"—although a pip.

The rapids are something else again. With Berna (Miss Del Rio) in a boat which gets out of control, Larry (Ralph Forbes) jumps from his craft to steer his sweetheart to safety. Nothing miniature about this mad water and if there's any fake about it in the long shots, other than the dummies, then it's amongst the best that have been evolved.

On the camera end, particularly important in this picture, Seitz has turned out foot after foot of double photography and what hints at being glass "mountain" backgrounds. Excellent work which only falters to become especially obvious as the fleet of stampeders approach Dawson City by boat and in centering on the vessel the boy and girl are in. In a maze of so much trick stuff it's remarkable that Seitz has turned out such a smooth job.

The story doesn't really tighten up until Larry returns laden with gold to find Berna become a dance hall girl and the victim of Locasto (Harry Carey), claim jumper and general menace. Bitter at the boy for having left her, Berna hurls the gold into his face crying, "Everything's too late." This leads to a hand-to-hand battle between Larry and Locasto that flashes the best finish any two-man screen struggle has ever had. The lover throws a kerosene lamp which strikes Locasto and explodes, covering him in flames so that he becomes a living torch. Plunging blindly out of the room, enveloped in flames, Locasto falls from the balcony on to the main floor of the dance hall, sets fire to the building and Dawson City burns.

This is all packed into the last two reels, is standout action, new, and actually is the first chance the audience has had to submerge itself in the love interest. Extreme finish has Berna and Larry reunited and working a hydraulic mining company in conjunction with Salvation Jim (Tully Marshall) and Lars Peterson (Karl Dane), Larry's partners.

First half of the picture, 66 minutes, centers more on Salvation Jim, Peterson and Samuel Foote (George Cooper) than the love duo with the struggle to reach Alaska always dominant. Brown's introduction of the news of the gold strike spreading across the country is a sweet piece of showmanship in traveling the camera across a map, focusing on various states and then sharply irising in and out through this map to pick up the principal players as they start for the west coast and Alaska. Chilkoot Pass is worthy of getting the big screen and would be particularly valuable in the second half, during which this new effect is not used, if continuity would permit. The boy and girl's first sight of Alaska is also impressively handled by the camera.

During this opening half, Brown has allowed the stampede to the north to smother Berna and Larry. When the lovers are occasionally spliced in the tempo of the running slows up, the result of prolonged scenes between the two and, in turn, perhaps the outcome of somebody's guilty conscience in having neglected this phase. General theme, the rush for gold, is carried along evenly enough, but reaches that stage where everything is prone to become incidents. A bit where a youngster whistles to his dog he has sold Peterson, who is on a boat, and the animal dives from the top deck to swim back, is a highlight among these.

The second part, 61 minutes, also has its standout incidents, notably Foote's death by freezing as he finds gold and after having made a deal with Locasto to fix it so Larry won't come back to Berna. Another is that of a brother shooting his brother when one returns with gold and refuses to split after pledges of sharing half and half. Cooper is exceptionally good in his bit and earlier runs up a score for himself in foiling for comedy with Dane.

"Trail" has laughs. Divided between Dane, Marshall and Cooper, the former runs away with these honors by means of an excellent performance and a role of sufficient elasticity to permit him to go into a rage and wreck the claim registry office. Breaking up of the ice in the Yukon is also well done.

First cast mention can go to Dane and Carey, the latter the least hoked heavy around in some time. Miss Del Rio's name won't do this film any harm nor will her personal contribution. Held down most of the way, nevertheless when called upon she responds to make them remember her. This looks like Forbes' best effort New York has seen, and Tully Marshall, as always, is standard.

A well put together score, stressing a march, is credited to David Mendoza and William Axt and with 36 pieces in the pit it gets what it deserves. Orchestra is carrying two drummers, something even the Broadway musicals don't bother about any more. Another aid is Joe Farnham's titles.

Fantom Screen, a device on rollers, is an improvement upon Paramount's Magnascope because the picture can double its size in moving down front and then reduce to normal as its retreats up stage. All at will. Working in conjunction with a special projector holding a wide angle lens, this illusion's main achievement lies in the reduction following the enlargement, no matter if the public will only remember the big flash. Shrinking to normal size is done to take up the story and keep the characters from appearing out of proportion. To help and mask the transition the screen comes forward and goes back on titles.

Paramount's use of its Magnascope has been limited in that once the big screen is used it has to be retained, or the abrupt switch to normal is ridiculous. Comparable to the difference between standard and 16m film projection. Anyway, it's a surety that no future M-G-M picture holding any spectacular features will ever come in without it for $2; other companies will undoubtedly use it, if they can, and after the directors glimpse the possibilities they'll "shoot" their big stuff with Fantom Screen in mind. A tremendous effect.

Over $1,000,000 tied up in "Trail," but this will come back, and plenty more with it. Its spectacular features assure this because, plus the new screen, there's going to be talk and they'll go in to find out. Absence of an emphasized love theme may make an extra effort for feminine trade necessary, but there'll be little hesitancy on the part of men in okaying it.

"Trail" is shy of a strong love story, until its final 20 minutes, and a tear. Other than that it has everything—and J. J. McCarthy to handle it. *Sid.*

MARIA MARTEN

(or "The Murder in the Red Barn")
(BRITISH MADE)

London, March 15.

Gaumont-British picture. Produced by Ideal Films, Ltd. Directed by Walter West. Censors' Certificate "A". Running time, 75 mins. Preview at the Palace theatre, March 8.

William Corder..............Warwick Ward
Maria Marten..................Trilby Clark

Hardly necessary to detail the rest of the cast, for this film does not matter that much. Supposed to be based on the "bath of blood," stage meller recently played at the Elephant theatre downtown, it leaves out all the elements of drama which made the crude stage version a thriller.

Suspense is almost entirely lacking, no speed or punch, and the direction is so respectable that the atmosphere is lost, save for costumes and wigs.

Stage version told how Corder persuaded Maria to disguise herself and leave home secretly to meet him at the Red Barn, where he slew and buried her. Film shows him explaining to her parents she had better slip away as a boy and meet him at the barn to go to London to be married. It does not seem to have occurred to the director the rest of the story contains no mystery or anything else after that.

Acting, lighting and sets passable, but theme and direction without grip and interest. It will book here on its title. *Frat.*

TWO LOVERS

United Artists release, produced by Samuel Goldwyn. Directed by Fred Niblo. Starring Ronald Colman and Vilma Banky. Based on the novel "Leatherface" by Baroness Orczy. Screen adaptation by Alice D. G. Miller. At Embassy, New York, March 23, on run. Twice daily, $1.65 top. Running time 100 minutes.

Mark Van Rycke..........Ronald Colman
Donna Lenora de Vargas....Vilma Banky
The Duke of Azar..............Noah Beery
Prince of Orange..........Nigel de Brulier
Gretel.................Virginia Bradford
Inez..................Helen Jerome Eddy
Madame Van Rycke......Eugenie Besserer
Ramon de Linea...............Paul Lukas
Meinherr Van Rycke,
Bailiff of Ghent..........Fred Esmelton
Jean.......................Harry Allen
Marda.....................Marcella Daly
Dendermonde Innkeeper.....Scott Mattraw
Innkeeper's Wife....Lydia Yeamans Titus

The Colman-Banky combination in the lights plus the title leaves little to guess work as to the box office probabilities, regardless of story and construction. While the production does not rate in the special run class it seems likely to have a profitable run at the Embassy of two or three months, considering the small house capacity and the drawing power of the starring team.

In the picture houses, as a program release, its draw is assured. The screen yarn has been cut and patterned to one of the formulas always successful with the picturegoers. In addition are a couple of hot sequences which, in themselves, should draw attention locally and where they are allowed to remain in out of town.

One scene shows one of the minor menaces chasing a barmaid up into a room. There he prepares to attack her, savagely tearing her dress around the shoulders and waist. It stops here with the appearance of Leatherface, masked avenger of the downtrodden Flems, who kills the attacker Ramon, following a gripping fight with knives.

Other scenes guaranteed to rouse both feminine and masculine interest to a high pitch take place following the marriage of the Spanish governor's niece and the Flemish bailiff's son.

Though married the girl does not love her husband and the boy sets out to win her confidence before assuming his rights as a husband. Bedroom scenes are enticing, especially since the leading players register high power sex appeal in photography. Miss Banky gets the men and Colman is surefire with the women, though each scores strongly with both sexes.

The only possible excuse for the use of the Baroness Orczy novel for story material, instead of telling a staff writer to grind it out in a week or two, may be that the producers feared a plagiarism suit from the author of "Robin Hood." The same theme has been used in innumerable pictures, credited to various authors. It has been the basis for the many Fairbanks pictures, "The Mark of Zorro" among others.

All the producers got for their money is the period costume setting. Nothing in the picture warrants the title, which, though weak, will draw attention.

Noah Beery is kept down to a stereotyped role and has evidently been watched by the wary director to prevent him stealing the picture, as in other instances in the past. But even as the usual heavy, Beery lends an air of distinction and character.

Action is in the Netherlands in 1572 when, according to the story, the Spaniards had dethroned the reigning prince and were exercising tyrannical power over the Flemish nation.

Appears a strange figure, magically out of the air in the most unexpected spots, clothed in leather jacket and mask. For this reason he was called "Leatherface." His duties were to save the Prince of Orange every time he was threatened with capture by the Spanish soldiers and protect the peaceful unarmed Flems from the military marauders.

The Duke of Azar was looking for an excuse to destroy the city of Ghent but hadn't specific proof to gain the King of Spain's consent. He married his niece into the leading Flemish family for the purpose of discovering treachery, getting the convent girl to agree by telling her she would end all strife and bloodshed if discovering the plans of the rebels.

Though loving Ramon, a Spanish captain, Donna Lenora agrees to the plan. Mark Van Rycke (Colman) wins her love but on finding him to be the despised Leatherface, tells her uncle. When learning of the Spanish plan to burn Ghent, her sympathy reverts to her husband's people. She does a Paul Revere on a stormy night, warns the Flemish patriots and is instrumental in their regaining possession. *Mori.*

OLD BILL

(FRENCH MADE)

French made picture, released on this side by Red Seal Films. Producer, Edwin Niles Fadman. Story from Anatole France. Maurice de Feraudy, French dramatic actor, starred. At 55th Street theatre ("art theatre"), New York, week of March 19. Used as program filler, supporting feature, "An Alaskan Adventure," novelty subject. Running time, 22 minutes.

"Old Bill," or "Cranquebille" as it is called in French, is crude in its technical making; its photography is bad by American standards and its scenic production is extremely faulty. But these are minor defects as the fatal thing about it is that it is entirely unsuited to American audiences in subject, tone, atmosphere and everything else. It runs but 22 minutes, which might suggest anything.

What Anatole France wrote as a graphic sketch of a humble Paris peddler may have been a fine piece of writing, but it isn't a picture at all. The whole is alien to the theatre and especially to the screen. Its atmosphere is gloomy and sordid, action is petty and annoyingly trivial and it has no pictorial value.

"Old Bill" is a peddler of vegetables, hawking on the Paris streets. He delays over one sale and the gendarme orders him to move on. Policeman thinks peddler is impertinent and arrests him for talking back. Bill goes to jail for 10 days.

In that time his customers forget him and his business drops. In desperation he is about to jump into the Seine when a street gamin whom he once befriended in a boyish fight comes to his rescue, gives him a meal and Old Bill goes about his business, telling the youngster he has saved his life.

Picture hasn't a spark of comedy, nothing but a dreary recital of a dreary chapter in a dreary life, pictured in tone of utter realism that makes it even duller. Glowingly graphic perhaps on the written page can't alter the screen impression. *Rush.*

THE BIG CITY

Metro-Goldwyn-Mayer production and release. Lon Chaney starred. Betty Compson, Marceline Day and James Murray featured. Directed by Tod Browning. From an original by Mr. Browning, with scenario adaptation by Waldemar Young. Titles by Joe Farnham. At Capitol, New York, week March 24. Running time about 65 minutes.

Chuck Collins	Lon Chaney
Sunshine	Marceline Day
Curly	James Murray
Helen	Betty Compson
Red	Mathew Betz
The Arab	John George
Tennessee	Virginia Pearson
Grogan	Walter Percival
O'Hara	Lew Short
Blinkie	Eddie Sturgis

Not much better than a lightweight underworld picture for a Metro-Goldwyn-Mayer program release, but with the possible novelty of showing Lon Chaney playing a human being in modern dress. That means Chaney is doing straight work with his own face in plain view. On that score "The Big City" should at least bring the week's average to any house without undue stage assistance.

In fact, the players and playing are superior to the story. Latter is of the cheating-cheaters sort, with some tricks of crooks fairly interesting. For the picture itself the best that may be said of it is that it ends with a laugh. That happens with a picture about twice yearly. Here Joe Farnham, in charge of captions, stuck in a corker at the finish. When the chief crook reforms and tells his girl he's going to marry her, she's overwhelmed. Rushing toward him for a pleasurable hug, he repulses her, saying: "Listen! I ain't going to buy you nothing. I'm just going to marry you." It's one of those wise titles the entire house gets.

The film tale is of one outlaw gang using its wits against the other, starting in the hold-up of a cabaret, with one gangster leader using guns while the other uses his head. The head user wins out. Picture runs neatly in its several channels, but there's not much to it, through the commonplace foundation. And no punishment for the wicked.

Chaney as Chuck Collins, one of the crook leaders, is a consummate actor, in this as well as in character or otherwise. And at least in "The Big City" Chaney accepted a story he knew he'd fit.

A most surprising performance is given by Betty Compson as Chuck's girl, a much better piece of playing than Miss Compson was thought susceptible of performing. She makes this role very effective and it's second only to Chaney's.

Another excellent bit of work is contributed by Marceline Day, a boob among sharks. She's blandly innocent in looks and actions and a great contrast to the fly skirt of Miss Compson's.

James Murray is again at the Capitol this week, probably his third or fourth consecutive appearance there, and each time in a role that suits him. That says the M.-G.-M. casters know their people. Murray does better in this than the others, although he must have grown tired in rehearsal of Chaney knocking him out.

Mathew Betz plays the other gangster chief with a furious scowl and makes it stand up.

Around Times Square most attention may go to Virginia Pearson's impersonation of Texas Guinan, as hostess of the nite club where little girls get big hands or the collar. At times Miss Pearson really suggested Tex, but only at times. The scenario writer for some reason didn't permit the impersonator to be as smart as Tex would have been, in a raid, hold-up or anything else, for Tex is always

prepared for either or more in her nite clubs.

Walter Percival and Lew Short ably did the headquarters detectives who were always on the heels of the gangsters, but several rods away. Mr. Percival carries nicely the burden of that work, although wearing a mustache.

Farnham's captions didn't bid for laughs as a rule, but were aptly worded and suited, up to the laugh-finishing one.

To insure attention to "The Big City," the heavy publicity should be placed upon Chaney as himself, without disguise, just to see the difference. It's quite a difference, too, but the same Chaney, and finely supported.

THE LOST SHADOW
(German Made)

Dear Little Exhibitor Boys and Girls:—Tonight Granny is going to tell you a bedtime story about a bad, bad man called Dapertutto; a great, strong, kind-hearted boy whose scenario parents had the bad taste to name him Sebaldus, and a charming feminine creature answering to the fascinating appelation of Babby.

All those little boys and girls who solved the mystery about Grandfather and whether he slept with his beard under the quilt will derive an equal amount of joy from the narration of this tale. That is, if anyone can be interested in a hero called Sebaldus.

This Sebaldus, or Baldy as he was called by his intimate friends, lived a great many years ago. I, personally, doubt the heroic propensities of the middle-aged, bulky, unromantic looking specimen such as Baldy was, but Karl Meyers, who wrote the story for Ufa, says he was a hero, and who can tell?

Whatever his physical limitations, Baldy had a heart of gold and a set of fingers which drew the most entrancing melodies from a violin. So Baldy was in great demand among the aristocracy of his community.

Then there sprung up an intimacy between Babby and Baldy which rapidly blossomed into love—the real article, dear little boys and girls. No crack about it, because when Baldy saw his beloved through a window he always became excited, paced the floor of his dingy bedroom excitedly, tore up sheets of music which might have been symphonic masterpieces, thumped himself on the head violently and generally behaved more like a nut than a hero. But the people in the Fifth Avenue Playhouse, where this story was spread on the screen last Wednesday night, thought Baldy was doing a song and dance. They laughed. How aggravating!

Babby loved Baldy but she wanted him to tip his mitt so she made him insanely jealous by talking to a male cousin, grinning wickedly, whispering in his ear, wiping her nose with his handkerchief and otherwise carrying on terribly unladylike. But since Babby looks like Louise Fazenda in comedy makeup, it is to be feared that the tragedy is not poignant.

On this peaceful scene came Daperutto, the shadow man. Tutty had lost his best shadow and couldn't put on his show. Quickly grasping the situation between Baldy and Babby he called the former into the garden and spoke:

"Would'st win the hand of yon fair maiden e'en so that she will follow you like your very shadow?" or words of that kind.

Baldy thought Tutty was the nuts, but he said, "Uh-huh."

"Then list!" commanded Tutty. And Baldy listed.

As a result, Baldy signed away his shadow to Tutty. In return Tutty whisked a magic violin out of the air which he gave Baldy with the information that if he played on it

Babby would follow him to the ends of the screen.

That night Baldy and Babby walked into the garden. Suddenly, coming into the moonlight, Babby saw her shadow, but none from Baldy. Turning on him fiercely, she cried: "Unfortunate man, where is your shadow?" Before Baldy could ask her if a man had to have a shadow to get married, the girl did a faint. And all the guests pitter-pattered out of the house to revive Babby, the gypped.

For a while it looked sorta tough for Baldy. When the neighbors discovered he didn't have a shadow they figured him and his violin a creation of the devil and went for him with whisk-brooms and other instruments of period warfare calculated to put physical dents into the musical genius. On top of that Babby went into a convent.

It all worked out however. Baldy went near the convent, played his magic violin and the gal went with him, but on the condition that they find Dapertutto, give him back his evil instrument and regain Baldy's shadow.

Of course, this is all a play. Baldy is none other than the famous Paul Wegener, who played in "The Golem," and still looks it. As a film attraction this story and the manner in which it was played proved amusing and caused continuous gales of merriment, ofttimes suppressed by more serious-minded patrons of the Fifth Avenue Playhouse who murmured something about the sanctity of art and so on.

Granny will now quit you, little children, but promises to try to find out what causes continental producers to believe they can create motion pictures of a pleasing nature. *Mori.*

RED HAIR

Paramount production and release starring Clara Bow. Featuring Lane Chandler. Directed by Clarence Badger and adapted from an Ellnor Glyn story. Titled by George Marion, Jr., with Alfred Gilks, photographer. At Paramount, New York, week of March 24. Running time, 73 mins.

"Bubbles" McCoy	Clara Bow
Robert Lennon	Lane Chandler
Judge Rufus Lennon	Lawrence Grant
Thomas L. Burke	Claude King
Dr. Eustace Gill	William Austin
Minnis Luther	Jacqueline Gadsdon

Independent out of town exhibs testify that Clara Bow hops into their houses and is a high rated name draw despite the second run and 90 days later clauses. "Red Hair" isn't going to change that status on this round-eyed personality girl. Bow plus Glyn equals underwear, and that goes in this release, and plenty.

Flaps and the wide-panted males will like it because it won't make them think and Miss Bow hasn't looked as well in many a picture. A natural color start, featuring the star in a white bathing suit with her red hair against a blue sky, is symbolic of something or other—but what's more important will probably make many a guy struggle to remember that the wife and kids come first.

Story doesn't mean a thing other than it makes Clara a gold digging manicurist who presumably reforms afer an aquatic rescue by Robert (Lane Chandler).

Comedy complication is that Bubbles (Miss Bow) has been consistenly "taking" three middle aged desk holders who turn out to be the guardians of the wealthy Robert. The quintet play bean bag with the situation until at the formal engagement party Bubbles gets steamed up over an ermine coat she has rented and starts throwing her sartorial gifts back at the doners.

This includes dress, stockings, undies, etc., until she's subject to drafts except for an enfolding parlor drape. Gagging the lady in ermine lets Bubbles fly into the

garden with nothing but the costly wrap about her, whence the guy from whom she rented the coat calls to snatch it back as a cop has informed it's stolen and he must return it. It sends Bubbles into a garden pool for protection with Robert and a blanket finally the means of a second rescue.

Picture could loose a full 1,000 feet and have more punch. But Miss Bow's appearance here, better than she has looked in many a day, will square a lot of things. Chandler, featured, gives a straightaway performance upon which the star capitalizes, while Lawrence Grant, Claude King and William Austin do well as the three guardians constantly on the make for Bubbles.

Production is in proportion, with Gilks' camera work giving it a break. Marion's titles step out every so often for attention.

If Haines has to be fresh and Bow undressed, figure out for yourself what'll happen if they ever do a picture together. Both are signed, sealed and delivered as to formula before their pictures open. Yet, they keep on dropping in to see 'em.

And Clara is still top 90 days later. That goes for "Red Hair," too. *Sid.*

VICTORY
(BRITISH MADE)

London, March 16.

Gaumont-British production. Presented by C. M. Woolf. Directed by M. A. Wetherell. Distributed by W. & F. Films, Ltd. Story by Boyd Cable. Photography by Joe Rosenthal and F. Young. Censors' Certificate "U". Running time, 100 minutes. Preview at the London Hippodrome, March 5.

Seth Lee	Moore Marriott
Major King	Walter Butler
General von Doorn	Griffith Humphreys
Kapitan Wein	Douglas Herald
Marie Dulac	Julie Suedo

After Wetherell made "The Somme," he was regarded as one of the white hopes of British production. For this film under review, he joins the a. k. class. It is long since anything quite so poor, as is most of this motion picture, has been offered to a war-ridden public.

Boyd Cable has taken all the crude elements of the most violently sensational wartime legends and thrown them into a semblance of a story. So thin, even then, is the structure on which Wetherell has built a scenario that the picture is at least one third padding. And padding with no motivation except to bridge bad continuity.

The whole film is a farrago of the war fever period idea of Germans and their behavior, and can serve no purpose in peace time. Coming from an author who made a speech pointing to the need of a fair statement of the other side of the case, when a German war film was shown only four days earlier, the paradox is deplorable.

Starting with the German advance in '18, refugees are seen leaving their homes and the elements of a story begin with a girl leaving her ruined chateau at the urgent request of a stranded British airman, who gets back to headquarters and is then deputed to drop a disguised Canadian officer over the enemy lines. His machine is brought down and with the spy he shelters in a cottage where lives a French agent of the secret service. Strangely enough, the cottage is close to the chateau, the girl has returned and the German headquarters are at her home. A lot of impossible stuff with secret messages sent by pigeons, the girl, at the demand of the Canadian officer, sacrifices her honor to the German staff captain in order to get some essential information, and when the German retreat begins the spy system is discovered and the Canadian is shot. The girl and aid officer are saved at the last moment by the news coming through of the Armistice.

Splendid shots of tanks in action

relieve an otherwise weak film. Nothing is left out; comic paper German soldiers, musical comedy cockney soldiers, humor concerned with decayed fish and wounds in the pants.

Except Moore Marriott, a minor Lon Chaney in the matter of disguises, cast is ill fitted. Direction gives the impression the director felt the whole thing to be incredible, except the war stuff.

It is to be hoped "Victory" will close the long list of war films.

Frat.

WOMAN AGAINST THE WORLD

Tiffany-Stahl production and release. Directed by George Archainbaud. Harrison Ford and Gertrude Olmstead featured. From story by Albert Shelby Levino. Continuity by Gertrude Orr. Chester Lyons, cameraman. Edited by Desmond O'Brien. One-half double feature bill. Loew's New York, one day, March 20. Running time about 60 minutes.

Schuyler Van Loan..........Harrison Ford
Carol Hill..................Georgia Hale
Bob Yates...................Lee Moran
Bernice Crane...............Gertrude Olmstead
Mortimer Crane..............William Tooker
Mrs. Crane..................Ida Darling
Reporter....................Walter Hiers
City Editor.................Harvey Clark
Maysie Bell.................Sally Rand
Housekeeper.................Rosemary Theby
Warden......................Charles Clary
Detective...................Jim Farley
Chauffeur...................Wade Boteler

Fairly suspensive mellerdrama that can act as a substitute in those houses unable to pay rental for the more notable features along this life-saved-from-hanging way. Can stand up for itself in the neighborhood dayers, although half the bill at Loew's New York when caught.

It starts as a newspaper story, but jumps right into a murder mystery when a chorus girl is found dead. Through the girl reporter and the leads discovered by the police, a wealthy young man on his wedding night is torn away from his bride in the hotel suite, charged with the murder. He admits having called on the chorus girl that morning, a call that delayed his wedding two hours. He called at her request to pay off, which he did, giving the chorine $10,000 in cash. A flashback reveals it and denotes he committed no other crime at that time.

Upon learning the facts the girl-bride walks out and divorces him before his conviction. Then commences the long suspensive grind of the man awaiting execution with the clock moving around as per usual, gradually reaching midnight of March 31, when the kid must swing.

But there are developments after 11 the same evening; the stoppage of the fast flyer, a confession obtained from the chorus girl's former chauffeur, a prisoner on the train, who killed the chorus girl, and also that day, her maid, with the girl reporter persuading the warden over the phone to postpone the hanging just as the clock was at 11:59¾, etc.

It unfolds much better than the skeleton might lead one to believe. Though Gertrude Olmstead is co-featured on the main billing with Harrison Ford, Georgia Hale as the reporter runs away with the picture. She had fallen in love with Schuyler Van Loan when first interviewing him.

Miss Olmstead as the disappointed bride has a triple-ply squawk in this picture. If Miss Olmstead were not well known, it might be her film finish. Her close-ups are terrible. At times she looks around 60 and her facial features are really distorted by the photography.

Lee Moran as the boy reporter competing with Miss Hale also runs ahead of Ford in the playing. Ford's role is unsympathetic, even though about to be hung. If the audience is not sore at him for giving up to the gold digger, it will be for having mixed with her in the first place. Harvey Clark plays sanely a city editor, and the city

room of the daily on the screen is not made to look like wild hotsy totsies.

A nice bit of direction is the forced confession with a blackjack threat from one of the detectives. Quite a bunch of anguish spread throughout, but the suspense is holding, sometimes a bit gripping, and a very good picture of its class.

Peculiarly, perhaps, there is a hanging suspense sequence not altogether unlike this of "A Woman Against the World" in the current First National's release, "The Noose."

SQUARE CROOKS

Fox production and release. Directed by Lewis Seiler under the supervision of Philip Klein. Adapted from play of same name. Cast includes John Mack Brown, Dorothy Dwan and Robert Armstrong. At the Broadway, New York, week of March 26. Running time, over 60 minutes.

Moderately interesting program production if spotted in grade B houses or split weeks and in neighborhoods.

Value of the picture rests almost entirely on one continuous piece of business, juggling of the missing pearls and hair-breadth escapes. Without action of any kind and only a slight love interest, the summing up leaves nothing but the foregoing conclusion as to box-office possibilities.

Only chance with a story of this kind was to build a central character. But here five different people and a juvenile player divide interest, with the baby drawing first honors.

As a play "Square Crooks" drew moderately on its comedy, which has not been transferred to the screen. Story is of two crooks trying to go straight, with a bull throwing them out of jobs as soon as they get set by telling their employers of their past.

Soon after they are discharged from their last position a necklace is stolen in the home of their employer, and the enemy sleuth insists on pinning the crime on the two boys. Vindication, a reward and jobs result for a happy finish.

Mori.

LITTLE BUCKEROO

F. B. O. production and release starring Buzz Barton. Directed by Louis King from original by Frank Howard Clark. Roy Eslick, cameraman. In cast is Peggy Shaw. At the Tivoli, one day, February 25. Running time, 50 minutes.

A little more galloping, shooting, roping and marrying than the average western. But "Little Buckaroo" is a great deal better than the average because of directorial insistence to stick to continuity and because of the live wire kid star who plays into the hand of every newsboy and Boy Scout in the land.

Youngsters in the Tivoli went wild over it and the average adult mentality in the audience also got a partial share of amusement.

From the time the girl's prospector father is shot on the desert to the time Young Buzz and his old side kick swear vengeance over the bones, there are a couple of stage coach holdups which introduce the girl and pave the way for concluding action.

One of the strangest marriages ever screened occurs in this picture when an unknown cowboy to save her from ruffians books her for the altar, practically "sight unseen." Discovery of the villain by the youthful Buzz makes the marriage a successful one since it bares frameup after frameup and shows the old sheriff as the most susceptible of the village's louts.

All in all, gloriously hoked, but there 100 percent in the right western box office.

WIFE'S RELATIONS

Columbia production and release. Starring Shirley Mason. Directed by Maurice Marshall. In cast: Gaston Glass, Ben Turpin, Armand Kaliz, Arthur Rankin, Flora Finch, Lionel Bellmore, Maurice Ryan, James Harrison. At Loew's New York, half of double feature, one day, March 23. Running time, 55 minutes.

Dusting off the old gags, ceilings that give way to the flow from broken plumbing, comics that flop down chimneys and fling meat cleavers, all of the stuff popular in two-reelers of yesteryear, are worked into this feature length in Columbia's "The Wife's Relations."

More reminiscent than ever is the resurrection of Ben Turpin in chef's garb; the same old Ben, holding true to old form in hogging the best number of the loudest laughs.

Without Ben the picture, even though it boasts one of those tried-and-true wealthy - daughter - poor-inventor plots, in which a big house is borrowed to make a splurge with papa, would just be a dragged-out two-reeler.

Flora Finch gets the hand with Ben. These two comics make the principals take a back seat because they, together with a couple of good titles, will sell it in many a second and third-run house.

WE AMERICANS

Universal production and release. Adapted from play of same name and directed by Edward Sloman. Features George Sidney and Patsy Ruth Miller. J. J. Rose, photographer. At Colony, New York, twice daily run, starting March 28. Running time, 97 minutes.

Mr. Levine..................George Sidney
Beth Levine.................Patsy Ruth Miller
Phil Levine.................George Lewis
Pete Albertini..............Eddie Phillips
Mrs. Levine.................Beryl Mercer
Hugh Bradleigh..............John Boles
Mr. Schmidt.................Albert Gran
Mr. Albertini...............Michael Visaroff
Mrs. Bradleigh..............Kathlyn Williams
Mr. Bradleigh...............Edward Martindel
Helen Bradleigh.............Josephine Dunn

Universal has sent this feature into the Colony for exploitation purposes. No idea of roadshowing, but Broadway angle again figured to have added weight on other main streets or to keep Colony open at a profit. Regardless of what it does at the Colony on the twice daily schedule, "We Americans" lines up as excellent program material.

Nothing fancy about this release, either in script of directing. Straightaway story of America's mixed populace told so that a tear creeps in every so often, revolving about three families—Jewish, German and Italian. Secondary theme is the problem with the children, and thence branching off into the love story between Beth Levine (Patsy Ruth Miller) and Hugh Bradleigh (John Boles), the "Able" idea with, in this case, a society background.

Corking performances by George Sidney and Beryl Mercer, with Sidney the standout.

One of the best attributes is that after all the storm and strife, taking in the war, the film ends on a laugh title. Neat headwork, productive of a finishing punch which will help the word of mouth. This is the best titled U film that's been around in months—and no program or screen credit for the title writer!

Nary a film fan is going to be able to misunderstand this one. Strictly elemental in script, Sloman has told it plainly and, plus Sidney and Miss Mercer, that's its charm. Localed on New York's east side, no lavish sets are called for. U gets a break, but all sets are appropriate. For the Colony showing the picture is allowed to run over an hour and a half. This won't be necessary in other houses, and adroit scissoring will help. About 75 or 80 minutes ought to be able to expose everything.

Story principally deals with old man Levine, pants presser all his life, and his daughter and son, who are the average modern youngsters. Beth is an apprentice on interior decorating, while Phil (George Lewis), is splitting his time between the Polo Grounds and Madison Square Garden. Levine orders Beth out of the house because of irregular hours; the war takes the boy, and the Levines are alone.

Unable to either read or write, a night school prof induces them and their neighbors, the Schmidts and Albertinis, to take up the mental struggle, on the theory that maybe it's the parents and not the children who are wrong. A flash at the trenches lasts just long enough to show Phil giving his life to save Hugh, and Mrs. Levine receives the government's regrets as she's in the middle of Lincoln's Gettysburg Address.

The affair between Beth and Hugh reaches its conclusion after the war, when the social and wealthy Mrs. Bradleigh learns that it was Beth's brother who saved her son. With the two families congregated in the Levine flat, in walks the old man who, when informed of the proposed match, says, "What can I lose?" And that's the finale.

Action is well sprinkled with comedy, titles adding their share, with a high spot a pinochle game, during which Mrs. Levine continuously stops behind her husband's chair to kibitz a bit. Pathos concentrates on the death of the son, but is also made significant and effective when Beth leaves home and the Schmidts realize America has declared war on the Fatherland. Albert Gran pries much from this passage, while Miss Mercer rises to each of her scenes. Patsy Ruth Miller has adopted an unbecoming coiffure to play the Jewish daughter, but it's in keeping, and no one is going to find fault with her performance. John Boles, ut of musical comedy, is a likable juvenile, and other cast members make it worth while. Sidney is excellent all the way.

The one discrepancy, either in casting of playing, points to the school teacher, while a technical error is that the titles delay too long in identifying some of the characters. This misstep, of course, can easily be rectified.

How closely the picture follows the play doesn't matter. "We Americans" figures as a good b. o. title and justifies the admission tap and rep of any program house.

Sid.

Children of No Import'nce

(GERMAN MADE)

Produced by National Pictures. Directed by Gerhard Lamprecht. From the story by Q. Heilbron Korbitz. Cast includes Ralph Ludwig, Margot Misch, Fee Wachsmith and Bernhard Goetzke. At 55th St. Playhouse (Art house, 400 capacity), New York, week March 31. Running time, 60 minutes.

Preceded by Nan Britton (New Acts), who bragged to a capacity audience of her love for her illegitimate offspring, evidently for the purpose of increasing sales of her book, "The President's Daughter," this nauseatingly crude shriek of protest against society unwound with all the irritating slowness and uninteresting, lengthy detail that characterizes a foreign-made production.

Lamprecht, dignified with the title of director of the conglomeration of illogical sequences, and those connected with the production seem to have been imbued with the false impression that there is entertaining drama in pure, unalloyed poverty. As a result, the picture is nothing but a newsreel which might have been shot in the slums of any metropolis.

Without the titles, no 'story. Nothing explains that the children were born out of wedlock. The entire picture could have been made on the streets of New York at a cost of $5,000 by any cameraman given the titles to put meaning into the scenes. The plight of the unfortunates has not been dramatized. That might have made the picture as great as it is now, in an equal degree, stupid.

The story is of three children placed under the care of a married couple. They are not taken care of properly for food and clothes, and a little girl dies of starvation. The real mother appears to shed tears for about a hundred feet of film.

The little boy is adopted by a wealthy woman, but his father shows up and insists on putting him to work on a barge. The boy runs away, is returned, jumps in the river, and winds up in the arms of the kindly woman who adopted him.

What it proves or where the audience interest lies does not seem evident. Made under the supervision of experienced film producers, a story of this kind has a chance, but the returns would be limited and would not warrant the production cost.

Accompanied by the stage ballyhoo regarding the necessity of giving illegitimate children legal status, the picture is limited to arty picture houses.

Mori.

DOOMSDAY

Paramount release and production starring Florence Vidor, with Gary Cooper featured. Directed by Rowland V. Lee. From Warwick Deeping's novel. Adapted by Doris Anderson; scenarized by Donald W. Lee. Running time, 65 mins. At Paramount, New York, week of March 31.

Mary Viner.................Florence Vidor
Arnold Furze....................Gary Cooper
Percival Fream...........Lawrence Grant
Capt. Hesketh Viner..Charles A. Stevenson

A homely, actionless drama is "Doomsday," adapted from Warwick Deeping's novel whose "Sorrell and Son" presumably accounts for his tungsten billing on the Paramount marquee.

More of a character study than a reflection of contemporary life, the keynote of all of Deeping's writings, it hasn't the dramatic appeal of "Sorrell" nor the skillful cinematic transmutation with which the Herbert Brenon production was endowed. As a result, "Doomsday" is pretty sorry stuff even for the average programs, much less a full week at a key city stand, discounting, of course, a booking with a strong stage presentation.

"Doomsday" is not a Biblical prophecy, but applies to Capt. Arnold Furze's Doomsday Farm which Mary Viner spurns as her home and hearth in favor of the aged Fream's sumptuous manse. The old man's darling idea, in true screen style, pans out a flop and the obvious and inevitable reunion with the vigorous and manly Gary Cooper anticipates the author.

Unfortunately for raconteurs of Deeping's calibre, the screen formula of physically picking your leading characters for the ultimate clinch, regardless of the author's efforts to weave the romance in another direction, nullifies any literary machinations of the story creator. Hence, the high pressure Woolworth sales experts and the gum-chewing, gum-shoeing, hotsy-totsy strutters know sure as shucks that in spite of the luxurious props, Miss Vidor will give Cooper and his humble hut the ultimate break.

Florence Vidor looked suprisingly well. At one time she seemed headed for the Alice Joyce type of roles, but in this picture she handles her conservative ingenue in good style. Supporting cast acquit themselves well, although Grant is a vacillating character as the aged suitor. A directorial attempt to make him appear a bit unsympathetic, to offset the favorable circumstances, is obvious and misses fire.

Picture will not satisfy the fans and will not add anything to Miss Vidor or Cooper, although it will probably spell a profit through the assured Paramount-enfranchised outlets.

Abel.

STAND AND DELIVER

Pathe release of a De Mille production starring Rod La Rocque and featuring Lupe Velez and Warner Oland. Directed by Donald Crisp from Sada Cowan's story. At Strand, New York, week March 31. Running time, 57 mins.

Roger Norman.............Rod La Rocque
Jania..........................Lupe Velez
Ghika.......................Warner Oland

Pathe's going to have its troubles getting the dough back that's in this one. Not that there's a stupendous amount involved, but the film looks $100,000, the story isn't there, and it'll take whatever draw La Rocque has to make it break even.

Picture is not without novelty in that it turns to Greece for its locale. It's a happy thought that it unwinds in less than an hour. La Rocque plays the post-war overly bored Englishman who reads of the rampages of a Grecian bandit and sets sail for adventure. Next peek at Roger (La Rocque) has him an officer in the Greek army, where he accidentally kills his superior in protecting Jania (Miss Velez).

This sends him into the mountains with the girl, where both are captured by the brigand, Ghika (Warner Oland). Getting a message through to his former compatriots, the soldiers arrive just after Roger has returned to battle Ghika over Jania and the outlaw is toned down. A government declaration that immunity will be granted any law-breaker turning over another of the same stripe extracts the sting of what may be waiting Roger for having socked his commanding officer. Whether the latter is killed or not is left to choice.

Comedy spots the telling with Roger, a woman-hater, but afflicted with the hero worship of Jania, whom he has rescued from a bandit raid. They marry, of course, and finish has both back in London. La Rocque gets out of the customary scenario jams by quick action, although Crisp has directed much better than in this effort. In the matter of Lupe Velez, it appears as if this miss is becalmed. Rolling up an inaugural rep for herself opposite Fairbanks, the youngster shows nothing here other than a heaving chest habit. Picture won't serve to advance Miss Velez. Only other cast promontory is Warner Oland, who does well enough with the heavy.

Tame release, having only the La Rocque name and its production to recommend it as de luxe program fare. A picture that the K.-A.-O. houses will welcome from necessity, but doubtful if others, beyond the splits and galleries, will bother about except as a filler or because of a rental break.

Sid.

FLYING ROMEOS

First National production and release. Directed by Mavyn LeRoy from the story by John McDermott. Featuring George Sidney and Charlie Murray. With cast including James Bradbury, Jr., Duke Martin, Fritzi Ridgeway and Lester Bernard. At Keith's Hippodrome, N. Y., April 2. Running time 60 mins.

Weak story construction, no original gagging and without support in the titles, the picture falls short, but may serve as a filler in the split weeks.

Audience appeal is limited despite the mugging of the featured players. A strong team but not strong enough to make up for lack of comedy business and uninteresting continuity.

Story concerns two barbers, Cohen and Cohan, in love with the manicurist. Both are supposed to be shortsighted, but the average audience may forget to consider that and then the dame is out of luck. She never impresses as capable of attracting attention.

Casting a girl who photographs unattractively in the lead fem role destroys interest. Any one of several hundred girls who have appeared in small bits in films during the year would have done better and none could have appeared to worse effect.

To get the gal, who loves aviators, the boys go in for flying. They do some fancy air stunts by accidentally running wild in a 'plane and are then forced to pilot in a coming race.

Gags include the usual ferocious instructor whom the barbers have wronged and in one sequence laughing gas is used to promote laughs.

Mori.

UNDER TONTO RIM

Paramount production and release. Directed by Herman C. Raymaker, featuring Richard Arlen and Mary Brian. J. Walter Ruben made screen story from original of Zane Grey. At American, New York March 26-28 (split week). Running time 50 minutes.

Picture with all the merits of a good melodramatic western and something besides. Plenty of hard riding, cowboy super-hero, bad men and gambler in cahoots to jump mine claims and lovely heroine victims of desperados' plots. These things are inseparable from such subjects and are here in abundant quantity.

But what raises the film to the best grade of program release is a certain authenticity, that for want of a better designation one might call "Covered Wagon" quality. "Under Tonto Rim" represents to the cheap western what "The Last of the Mohicans" does to "Dead-Eye Dick" or the difference between a slipshod potboiler and a work of art.

If more westerns had been made like this Paramount, the cowboy stars wouldn't be going away to escape the curse of the designation "western."

"Tonto Rim" establishes at the outset a fine atmosphere of historical interest. It opens with a gold rush to the new strike up in the cow country ("strike was made right under Tonto Rim"). Atmosphere is convincing and the photography of these early scenes of the pioneer trek to the new country is surpassingly lovely.

Then into vivid sequences of a rough mining camp where the former cowboys have all turned placer miners; dance hall dive has been set up in the raw mining camp. Good character types contribute good touches of comedy. Gambler bully schemes to jump new claims with assistance of gang of two-gun desperadoes and to that end intimidates young land recorder into doctoring the government registration books.

They jump hero's claim and kill his father, the old man with his last breath gasping that the murderer was a gambler who shuffled cards with one hand. Hero goes on trail with nothing but that clue.

Mine jumpers' war grows to crisis until miners organize vigilantes who are slowly being forced out of the country until under leadership of hero they line up for a pitched battle with the desperadoes. This scene is staged on a table land plain with hard pressed bad men taking refuge in a rocky knoll and vigilantes besieging them like Indians, riding around the rocky refuge in circle.

This climax is built up through a long dramatic chase which has splendid culminating values. Whole picture is remarkably well paced for increasing tension. Comedy incidentals are extremely well managed.

An incident is where the desperadoes are pursuing the miners and have to dash through a camp of the vigilantes, left in care of the women. One old crone hides behind a tent and as each desperado gallops past she steps out, sloughs him with an enormous club and then steps back under shelter to cut a fresh notch in the bludgeon. It was a series of roars at the American. Other excellent comedy was provided by a pair of ancient prospectors.

Richard Arlen is a new film cowboy, young, good looking and a smooth-player of heroic roles. Mary Brian looks charming and is less futile than usual for cowboy romance heroines.

If it weren't that "westerns" aren't any more for de luxe houses, this one would rate a week at any.

Rush.

You Can't Beat the Law

Trem Carr production, released by First Division. Charles Hunt, director. Story by H. H. Van Loan, adapted by Arthur Hoerl. In cast: Lila Lee, Cornelius Keefe, Warner Richmond, Betty Francisco. At Loew's New York one day, March 27, one-half of double bill. Running time, 55 mins.

A rookie cop who can tell his captain that black is white just naturally doesn't swing a stick on the force, and, it is feared, will be just as out of luck on the screen in "You Can't Beat the Law."

Cornelius Keefe, the good-looking bit player, swings into a lead with Lida Lee. As the sister of a crook and the sweetheart of a cop, she finds things rather hard going toward the end. When the cop tips off he is going to yank in her brother, she lets it out that she will be the tip-off. Okay with the cop, since he takes the case out of his superior's hands and evades the crook firing squad when his girl goes in for some more fancy double-crossing.

From start to end this production, based on a trade-mark made famous by police throughout the country, is the direct antithesis of what any non-moron newspaper reader assumes to exist in blue circles.

It's one of those indie mellers which popularize "Poverty Row."

FANGS OF DESTINY

Universal production and release. Starring "Dynamite" (dog). Directed by Stuart Paton. Story by George Morgan. In cast: Edmund Cobb, Betty Caldwell. Featured at Columbus one day, March 28. Running time, about 60 mins.

As a gun-carrier, messenger boy and ace sprinter of some part of Hollywood's plains, "Dynamite," which Universal is trying to popularize as another "wonder dog," does his stuff in this "western thriller," titled "Fangs of Destiny."

The "destiny" part of the title just makes it more difficult. "Dynamite" steals every sequence, even to the point of depriving rustlers of their well-known shootin' irons.

These babies, unlike the garden variety of film cattle stealers, are out to break a neighboring rancher because thar's oil in them thar feed lands.

The picture may hum—but in unknown box offices.

Fourfooted Ranger

Universal western production and release. Featuring "Dynamite," dog, and Marjorie Bonner. At Loew's New York, one day, March 30, as half double bill. Running time about 60 minutes.

Ordinary western, of cattle thieves with the foreman of the adjoining ranch their leader. Under those circumstances why they had to wait until this picture opened to start to steal the cattle is one of those film complications.

Edmund Cobb is the hero or Texas Ranger and his police dog, "Dynamite," is the fourfooted ranger of the title. "Dynamite" looks like a police dog in repose and that's remarkable enough here, for he looks like a German toy mountain lion when he's running. Otherwise it's a dog that will bring many a laugh to owners of police dogs if they see this one, although "Dynamite," like the other dog picture actors, may be one of any 200 in Hollywood. These dog collections of celluloid merely go to bring out how the children must like the pictures.

Cobb, although he may have been the director instead, is out to get the beef and hoof hustlers. About the most work he does is when held up and in a room at the ranch, he phones the sheriff to bring on the posse. The sheriff does and that ends the story. But just before Cobb and the menace, the foreman, put up about as poor an indoor fight as two men could do while on any payroll. So even if Cobb is the director instead, this picture can't help him.

The funniest thing in sight was one of the actors slide-named as Pat Rooney made up to look like an old tin-type of General Grant. His acting wasn't any better. Francis Ford was the villun and a good bad man. Miss Bonner as the girl played, rode or fought back over hundreds of feet.

Where dogs are in on the grinds, this will probably get a look-in. If it does, it will be a money maker for U., for it's nearly all outdoors and could have been made in any two back yards.

MARRY THE GIRL

Hollywood production; Sterling release. Produced by Joe Rock and directed by Philip Rosen. Barbara Bedford featured. No other credits caught, with no need for anyone to regret that. At Loew's New York one half double feature bill, one day, March 30. Running time, around 56 minutes.

One of those indies that if the notice isn't written within 30 minutes after the film ends, it's hard work to recall what it was about. Which says that giving it half the double day bill at the New York gave the Rock-Rosen product an edge. This may be an old boy through having Rosen as the director. Whatever it is it isn't there.

A story that can carry an impersonating mother and child through 5,000 feet and fold up without letting the audience know if she really was a widow, divorcee, or a mother or who the kid actually belonged to, sorta indicates lapses of memory or concentration at whatever quickie plant this was turned out overnight in.

That's the story; the impersonation to get an old man's money. The day the o. m. had a heart attack and had just finished drawing up a new will, they told him about the deception and everything else, but still he wouldn't die, and looked fit to play golf again as the whistle blew.

Barbara Bedford is the impersonator in a walk through part. The child, Freddie Burt Frederick, is made too smart for his years; overly knowing until his up glances and general info about things he should not know are a pain in the neck. When this boy is just a kid as he always should be, he's quite likeable. That's probably when there aren't too many on the sidelines shouting at him.

Picture may make the grinds or at the art theatres; anywhere they don't want to and won't pay rental.

TEMPORARY SHERIFF

Ben Wilson Star Westerns series. Rayart production. Dick Hatton, star. Cofeatured, Bill Patton and Martin Turner. Directed by Hatton. Half double feature bill, Arena, New York, one day, March 28. Running time, 50 mins.

No bouquets due this one. Condition and plot about spoiled any chances it had, even on a double feature day close to Broadway. An old-fashioned meller now dead on the screen.

Fist fights among men, always on the draw, overdone so much the kids tittered. When kids titter, the feature is blooey.

Condition of the film indicated that it might have been made so far back that even the exchange lost the date of its birth. *Mark.*

WALLFLOWERS

F. B. O. production and release. Directed by Leo Meehan from book by Remple Temple Bailey. In cast: Hugh Trevor, Mabel Julienne Scott, Jean Arthur, Lola Todd, Charles Stevenson, Mrs. Temple Pigott, Crauford Kent, Reginald Simpson. One half double bill one day, March 29, at Loew's New York. Running time, about 60 minutes.

So tiresome a picture it is with difficulty concentration can be given it while unreeling. Only persons mentioned in the main billing are Leo Meehan, who directed, and Temple Bailey, writer of the adapted story. F. B. O.'s press sheet gives no programming, using the names of the below-average players as a lot in a short story mentioning them by name. Lucky to hold its spot at the New York as one of the two features there on a double day bill. Even a double bill with it needs something a little more than ordinary for the other half.

If the Temple Bailey novel held any interest generally it must have been through telling the tale much more convincingly than does this picture. Here it's saddening and boring mush mostly, with the only outstander the step-mother of the juvenile, a scheming woman, played by Mabel Julienne Scott, and she at least stuck some spirit into her role. The rest ambled along as though the director had told them to work it out themselves.

Several times the film gets way into low on acting and is always that on action. A phoney will, the juv repulsing his stepmother, now widow, to marry the girl, one of the wallflowers, a bunch of ivory figures that are made mystic and the final outcome, each as exhilarating as this cold type recital.

The title was grabbed because at a ball one evening, two of the girls did sit out alone against the wall for about 40 seconds. Had the picture given an insight into the lonesomeness, desolation and despair of the always-fellowless girl, it might have meant something.

If these are of the F. B. O. stock company, then among the women other than Miss Scott, F. B. O. can stand a few good-looking girls. Men were much better but that doesn't say much either.

HEART OF B'WAY

Duke Worne production, released through Rayart. Directed by Duke Worne from story by Arthur Hoerl. Starring Pauline Garon. In cast, Robert Agnew and Wheeler Oakman. At Loew's Circle one day, March 26, as half double bill. Running time, 65 minutes.

When "Heart of Broadway" strikes the farmingdales there'll be another epidemic among the agriculturists to keep the gal at the kitchen sink. It's bromides of this kind, showing the White Way as the mouse-trap for out-of-towners, that keep so many stenogs in the embryonic state until the "yeggs" here give them a hand across the street.

For an outsider who clips off a bit of applause from the neighbors but wins the discard from her tight-lipped aunt, the girl, played by Pauline Garon, sees more of Broadway in a couple of weeks than a dozen "Follies" girls in a couple of lifetimes.

Duke Worne follows the path of least resistance and a gunman falls in love with the country dame before she has a chance to emerge on a night club floor. The proprietor decides he wants the moll, so the gunman bumps him off.

There is a session, a clear parody on Fox's "Dressed to Kill."

The kid she loves falls for his liquor again, and pops up just in time to be nicked by the cops for the job. The girl saves him with skill not even found in a country girl devotee of underworld novels. The gunman, true to dear old Broadway "tradition," gets half of a detective's gun in the plexis, interfering with plans to knock off the jane. He calls for a fag and the bull lights it!

No wonder the folks 'way out in Texas raise the hand when little daughter mentions chances for a career in Manhattan.

SPEEDY

Paramount release of Harold Lloyd Corp. production, starring Lloyd. Directed by Ted Wilde with Walter Lundin cameraman. Titles by Albert DeMond. At Rivoli, New York, for grind run starting April 7. Running time, 87 minutes.

Harold "Speedy" Swift.......Harold Lloyd
Jane Dillon....................Ann Christy
Pop Dillon....................Bert Woodruff
Steven Carter...............Brooks Benedict

If Harold Lloyd has topped the Paramount list of stars on sales value for the past two seasons, and he has, "Speedy" is going to make it plenty tough for the rest of the boys and girls to catch up to him. This is a pip comedy on which anybody can write a catch line for reprinting and be right. Picture is great three ways: for the theatre, Paramount and Lloyd.

Only possible fault is its length, and with 10 minutes out the film will practically be fool proof. Action brings back Coney Island in all its mid-summer glory, and although the amusement resort has taken a lot of camera punishment, Lloyd has got enough gags running to make it stand off whatever repetitious liabilities are there. At the same time, this is where a pair of scissors can be applied; notably the ride home in the truck, where Lloyd and the girl (Ann Christy) frame up a prop parlor with furniture, and a dog chasing a rubber and air-filled frankfurter.

It's a gag picture but what gags. A general melee between a gang of roughnecks and the old tradesmen on the street which the horse car serves, and which the elderly cronies use as a club house every night, is the best comedy battle in seasons. For instance, the old Chinese laundryman heats up his iron and plasters it on all and sundry of the opposing faction as they bend over while scrapping and the champ quoit pitcher knocks the hard-boiled boys off by tossing horseshoes to their chins. It's all because the railroad wants the franchise which old man Dillon holds for his horsecar. He'll only sell at his price and the car must run once every 24 hours for Dillon to retain his rights. Meanwhile, Jane, the daughter, is Lloyd's objective.

A lot of wild driving in the film, once with Lloyd wheeling a taxi and again when he hooks up a team of horses to the horsecar, after it's been stolen, and rushes across town to make the once daily trip. Most of this is genuine New York stuff, shot all over the town, but some of it's Los Angeles, too. Anyway, the mad taxi gallop is a standout sequence, and there's plenty of laughs as Lloyd rushes Babe Ruth to the Yank stadium, the Babe turning loose some pretty fair mugging at the horrors of Lloyd's driving.

Story starts with Lloyd behind a cafeteria counter serving sodas. He's a baseball nut and flashes the score to the kitchen crew by a showcase in which he arranges doughnuts and crullers to correspond with the innings. Not being able to hold the job, Lloyd drifts to the taxi thing, and then the horsecar finish.

Only three principals who mean anything. Other than Lloyd there is Miss Christy, opposite, and Bert Woodruff playing the old dad. Woodruff is particularly good, and Miss Christy suffices in her scenes with the star.

No question that the outstanding feature of the film is the brainwork behind it. In other words, the gags. Lloyd has a rep of having the best of the comedy constructors around him on the Coast, and "Speedy" will about prove it.

Among everything else there's a bit where Lloyd, in a new suit, looks down to see it completely spotted. Rubbing fails to erase anything but when he looks up he's under a woman's spotted parasol. Another has Lloyd dreaming of marriage, so the fade is to a crib and twins—each wearing shell rimmed glasses. Camera work is excellent, titles often make their point and the action seldom slows up.

"Speedy" is a corking program

laugh provoker. The spots where it'll fall down, you'll be able to count on 10 fingers. *Sid.*

STREET ANGEL

Fox production and release. Directed by Frank Borsage. Featuring Janet Gaynor and Charles Farrell. Adapted by Philip Klein and Henry Roberts Symonda from the play by Monckton Hoffe. Continuity by Marion Orth. To Movietone accompaniment at Globe, New York, opening on run April 9. Musical score by Roxy, assisted by Erno Rapee (conductor at Roxy theatre). Program credits Western Electric for recording and reproducing sound on Movietone. $2 top. Running time, 85 minutes.

Angela....................Janet Gaynor
Gino....................Charles Farrell
Lisetta....................Natalie Kingston
Mascello....................Henry Armetta
Polce Serg....................Guido Trento
Policeman....................Alberto Rabagliali

Another of those superior program pictures William Fox and Winnie Sheehan are accumulating so rapidly, with each making the heart of the exhibitor playing the Fox stuff beat a little faster every time. That this special exploitation at the Globe at $2 may not do more than break Fox even, if that, for the Broadway run, is fine promotion for Fox and those same exhibitors, for it spreads the fame of Fox and the film. To say that Fox's "Street Angel" is sure box office for any picture theatre for a week or longer sums it up for the commercial end.

In "Street Angel" is revealed the rapidly progressing studio ideas. Long and continued shots are in the picture of streets and alleys, that at first glance appear impossible of studio manufacture but doubtlessly were.

"Street Angel" may become noted for this, also for its photography. At times the closeups of Janet Gaynor are nothing short of startling cameos on the sheet. In one she and Charles Farrell both seem to have hit upon the third dimension for their bust views. Yet there is an overdose of the wall-shadows.

Technically there is much to admire throughout. Practically the picture is merely the illustration of a narrative, and held so closely to the narrative any illusion is submerged, tension is missing and the suspense, if any tried for, does not make itself manifest, leaving it all of the time a picture.

In story the ordinary picture gazer can anticipate the developments, with one serious error committed in this non-holding tale, toward its end. It's when the artist painter believes what a street walker told him about the girl he lost on the eve of their marriage. What the girl told him was the truth, that his girl had been in prison for a year for attempted robbery while soliciting, but that as an artist and seeing her purity through her eyes before and after her imprisonment should have been sufficient to have not accepted the first breath he heard against her. It reacts against the logic of a class picture.

And that the painter saw the soul of Janet Gaynor through her eyes may not have been alone his secret, for someone on the Fox lot must have seen the same thing a long time ago, since Miss Gaynor is now under a Fox contract. Many a picture will be made in Hollywood that calls for the soul and eyes of a Gaynor. They will have to be provided and they also need something else that Miss Gaynor owns—a sense of acting that permits her to get over her portion. Miss Gaynor is in the title role of "Street Angel" and plays it all of the while, though none of the characters draws real sympathy.

Charles Farrell is the painter, made up as a strangly Italian youth in looks, since he seems to be a vagrant artist, doing odd painting around the country side. With the scene set in Italy and Naples for the opening, Miss Gaynor was rescued from the police after receiving a year's sentence and escaping, by the touring circus. Through that circumstance she met the painter who was showing in opposition to the little wagon outfit.

Miss Gaynor had been arrested for soliciting when attempting to gain 20 lire in that way to fill a prescription for her dying mother. But the men she made advances to, even rough as they were, thought she was just funny. Each walked away from her annoyance. Desperate, she made an effort to snatch change on a lunch counter and was caught.

In the beginning the picture is light with some slight mirthful minutes, while the love making of the leading pair is sentimentally likeable, even though that it is only the unreeling of a story is continuously impressed. Toward the finish the pad starts to come out. It's draggy there in spots and for the picture houses the film can easily stand cutting.

Mr. Farrell in his proper person might look like a favorable juvenile. Here, without ever having his hair combed and mostly heaven gazing upon his beloved, the attention perforce and willingly goes to the girl instead.

Young people will take to the young couple and their romance, marveling at the will power of both. They compose a good team for Fox.

Secondary roles well cast and played. Natalie Kingston as the street walker does very well, while there is real comedy in a quiet manner begotten by Henry Armetta as the circus manager. A sample of Italian love making apart by itself is given in one of the traveling circus wagons when the strong man denotes his passion for the fortune teller by pulling her about by her hair.

A very good picture for Fox and Janet Gaynor.

THE VORTEX

(BRITISH-MADE)

London, April 2.

Produced by Gainsborough Pictures, Ltd. Directed by Adrian Brunel. Adapted from Noel Coward's play by Elliott Stannard. Titles by Roland Pertwee. Photography by James Wilson. Distributed by the W. & F. Film Co. Preview and run, Marble Arch Pavilion, March 26. Censor's certificate "A." Running time, 75 mins.

Nicky Lancaster....................Ivor Novello
Florence, his Mother......Wilette Kershaw
David, his Father........Sir Simeon Stuart
Bunty Mainwaring............Frances Doble
Tom Veryan....................Alan Hollis

Except for the Novello and Coward fans over here, this is a not-so-good program picture; not too good for the general audience here and little hope any other place. Coward's play was cynical and, at its moment, sophisticated. But it has been emasculated for the screen, fitted with a happy ending, and looks cheaply made.

Sets are not effective and the photography is patchy, in some places very good and in some the reverse. There is some slovenliness in lighting, too, and in one case shadows from the set are clearly seen on the street backing.

Nicky Lancaster is a composer who falls in love with a girl scribe who comes to interview him. His mother is keeping her youth by running around with a boy friend, Tom Veryan. Latter has had a love affair with Bunty (the girl scribe), and at the Lancaster's country house Nicky finds his girl and his mother's boy friend embracing. He creates a scene and so does mamma, the latter ordering the girl out of the house. Nicky upbraids his mother, tells her he has one consolation left—"coke." Whereat she throws his dope sachet through the window, asks the girl not to go, and promises to drop her boy friend and grow old gracefully.

Story doesn't grip and it's not possible to believe the characters or their actions. A mechanical production lacking the saving grace of mechanical precision.

Wilette Kershaw lacks almost everything needed for the screen and fails to register any emotion. Frances Doble screens well and with better direction might have possibilities. She has youth and looks in her favor. Ivor Novello is as usual, a good looker and an easy mover, but nothing more. Rest of the cast does not matter.

Obviously booked before it was made, as the release is for April 23, the chief thing coming out of this picture is the risk exhibitors run when they book sight unseen.

Frat.

SKYSCRAPER

DeMille Studio production; distributed by Pathe; directed by Howard Higgin. Ralph Block, associate producer. William Boyd starred. Adapted by Elliott Clawson and Tay Garnett from story by Dudley Musphy. Titles by John Krafft. At Paramount, New York, week April 7. Running time 70 minutes.

Blondy, a steel riveter......William Boyd
Slim, his buddy....................Alan Hale
Sally, a chorus girl..............Sue Carol
Jane ....Alberta Vaughn

A program picture of the very top grade, made so by its excellent sentimental vein, touched and colored with delightful comedy and all tinged with a certain whimsical quality faintly suggestive of O. Henry. The title may not get it much at the boxoffice but word of mouth will make it a money picture. Women will like it, for the story's romantic element is shrewdly paced. Beautifully acted and ably directed. Altogether a release that will do more for Pathe prestige than the whole five subjects splashed on Broadway in one week as a ballyhoo some months ago.

Story of a husky, young steel worker (Boyd) driving rivets on a New York skyscraper, playing pranks among the dizzy girders of the sky line, and a jobless girl who by accident gets into the chorus. The settings are the steel skeleton of a towering unfinished building. Quivering vistas of the traffic in the streets far below supply a tension and suspense far more dramatic than any theatrical situation.

Here's where the screen has it on the stage. Boyd wants something from his coat pocket. He seizes a rope and swings across a frightful chasm to a distant ledge of steel. You hold your breath and grip your chair. An admiring young apprentice (Wesley Barry plays the role) imitates him in the stunt. He delightedly makes the trip back and forth. No trumped up "situation" on the stage ever inspired the suspense the audience feels as the poor kid misses his footing and drops into eternity.

The introduction of Boyd and his little girl friend is a neat bit. Theatre adjoins the building job and chorus girls have come up on the roof in their rehearsal togs to practice. Iron workers kid the half-dressed choristers and Boyd swings out across the fearful gulf on a derrick line to be lowered to the theatre roof to beg a cake from the girl's lunch basket.

That leads to a trip to Coney Island where they fall in love. Then girl goes "on the road" with the understanding they're engaged. Boyd is crushed by a falling girder when he sacrifices himself to save his pal, and, like a prideful young male, determines to break it off rather than be the girl's crippled mate.

The girl comes back but Boyd, concealing his crutches, pretends he's ditched her (a sequence here is admirably played for sentimental effect without once slopping over). It is the pal who steps in to save the situation. He bawls Bill out as a "quitter" who's wedded to his crutches, seeking to make him mad enough to overcome his injuries. He even makes a play for Bill's girl and scoffs at him as a dead one. Bill gradually forces himself painfully to make his cripple muscles function. In the end, when the pal puts a crowning insult upon him in the presence of his girl, Bill goes into action in a first fight up among the girders and comes out winner.

Through this dramatic action there are woven unceasing comedy bits. The pal (great part for Alan Hale) has a gold tooth that is forever coming loose and getting lost; Bill is continually turning practical jokes upon the stupider companion, such as slipping trick dice into the crap game. And they are always in a fight of some kind. They are about to clinch with each other when the foreman bawls them out. Instead they knock the foreman cold and lean him against a wall, plant a gin bottle in his pocket and he goes off in the patrol wagon. The picture has a wealth of incidents of this kind and a low comedy laugh is always on the heels of a sentimental bit.

Story is splendidly built to its climax which is high power. The comedy is just as cunningly managed and the composite is a beautiful bit of screen fiction. Titles by John Krafft are brightly written, fit in pat and are never self-conscious.

Rush.

MOULIN ROUGE

(BRITISH MADE)

London, April 1.

British International Pictures production. Directed by E. A. Dupont. Story by E. A. Dupont. Distributed in U. K. by Wardour Films. Censor's Certificate "A." Running time, 144 minutes. Presentation and run at Tivoli, London, opening March 22.

Parysia....................Olga Tschekowa
Margaret (her daughter)..........Eve Grey
Andre....................Jean Bradin

Dupont took almost a year to make this picture and is credited with having spent about $500,000 on it. Certainly the film is very gorgeously mounted and the Parisian stage sequences are terrific. But the story is thin and tiresome, sympathy is lost in two of the chief characters early on, and not regained, and the shots of the Casino de Paris, front and back stage, are endless repetition.

But shortened to about 110 minutes from its present 144, "Moulin Rouge" will be a big hit on the Continent on its title and the suggestion running all through. As a highly colored tourists' guide to Paris and on the real stage stuff done so well at the Casino de Paris it should have real American box office value. Properly boomed, the film would stand up in any house in the States.

The first 1,500 feet are a prolonged tour of Paris by night, with atmosphere of the type the tourist expects before he has been to the gay city. Paris' commercialized "thrills" for foreigners are used to create atmosphere, and the much-abused censor again reveals his innocence and lack of sophistication by leaving in some shots which appear suitable only for South America. This is not being squeamish, either.

Far too much footage is expended in repeating sequences of illuminated Paris streets at night and on the Moulin Rouge stage show to the detriment of story development. As a result the film lacks audience grip. At least three reels could come out.

Parysia is the rage of Paris. She has a daughter, secretly engaged to Andre, and the boy's aristocratic father objects to the alliance because of Margaret's mother being a revue actress.

The girl is naive and simple, and the boy falls heavily for the mother, who goes to the father and gets his consent to the marriage. Andre intends to commit suicide by disconnecting the brakes of his racing car, as he cannot face the prospect of loving the mother and marrying the daughter. He is going to the country to fetch his father in for the wedding and frames the "accident" to happen on the way. Calling on the girl and her mother before he goes, he is taken ill, and Margaret takes the car to fetch papa.

When Andre recovers he tells Parysia of her daughter's danger and goes off in a high-powered car to overtake her. Side by side the cars race till he is able to pull her from the seat, but crashes in so doing. The girl's life is despaired of, but she is saved by an operation. Andre wakes up to his folly, recognizes the age of Parysia, marries Margaret and departs for Nice and honeymoon.

The outstanding feature is the photography, superb. Direction is extremely fine in all the stage and cabaret sequences, but when handling individual characters Dupont seems to have little grip. The scenes in which the mother goes to plead with the old man gave a fine opportunity for dramatic situations, but all that happens is that Parysia weeps a little when the old man refuses and goes out. He sees her handkerchief on the floor, picks it up, looks at it and then writes her a note changing his mind. The rest of this sequence is taken up by the arrival and departure of Parysia's automobile.

Acting fair. Olga Tschekowa undresses almost as much and as well as Mae Murray used to do, and fairly exudes sex appeal from a French angle. She can put emotion onto the screen, but is mainly seen in undress as a stage star.

Jean Bradin carries side whiskers and looks continental without being sympathetic. His acting is mechanical and hard; he needs a better make-up and more intimate direction.

Eve Grey, British and the only native angle in this film, looks like making good. She needs pep to put her over, having the native failing still of looking too respectable. Her role loses audience sympathy from an unnecessary and out-of-the-part episode in which she gets "lit." The fans will not like this, because they can't feel sorry for her after it.

Frat.

THE CHASER

Harry Langdon production and First National release. Directed by Mr. Langdon, who is starred. No author cr adapter named. A. H. Grebler, title writer. At Keith-Albee's Cameo (seating 400) on 42d street, New York, week April 7. Running time, 58 minutes.

Wife....................Gladys McConnell
Husband....................Harry Langdon
Her Mother................Helen Hayward
His Buddy...............William Jaimison
The Judge................Charles Thurston

Poor judgment is in evidence in comedy, "Chaser" (First National) at the Cameo, or its Broadway first run. Since the Strand has the F. N. franchise for New York that's a tip off as to the merit of the picture all by itself. No de luxe downtowner will probably play the picture if they first see a couple of alleged comedy fun bits in it.

Mr. Langdon is starred and slide-announces he directed the picture, so the fault is all his own, although as he likely is responsible for the gags, his blame can go double. For Langdon has some odd ideas about bathroom comedy and both of them are in the first 30 minutes of the picture. Whatever is worth while is in the latter section.

While one might suspect that Langdon's greatest needs are a director and author, still it might be a personal mental balance that would permit him to select newer and better subjects, the latter taking in ideas and gags. Or else be content as a dead pan comic who apparently can get more put of his face than he can out of his head.

Any screen comedian who thinks the castor oil and choking chicken bits are funny to even 15 percenters in the deaf and dumb racket had better write idiotic after their names. Yet for children the castor oil bit may be a laugh and in the neighborhoods perhaps the whole thing will be thought funny enough, but Mr. Langdon must figure someone else besides the kids and the women after wash Mondays.

For the first 30 minutes of "The Chaser," it's drear. But the last half is better with the best laugh here and of the film gotten by William Jaimison. Langdon probably had to let the Jaimison laughs go to get the picture anywhere. The most Langdon could show was a runaway auto going over bumpy ground and then down hill, most of it done before.

It's about a young married man with a nagging wife and a worse mother-in-law. Langdon is made up too young for the husband. A little more dependence upon himself and less on gagging for long worked up points would give more weight to any of his pictures. The husband is called a chaser by his m-in-l because he doesn't get home until 8:30 evenings.

Now and then a laugh in the titles, but only now and then. Gladys McConnell does fairly as the girl and Helen Hayward the usual type mother-in-law, with Jaimison grabbing the picture for any worth grabbing there.

PARISIENNES
(BRITISH-MADE)

London, April 2.

Isepa Production (Sweden). Directed by Gustave Molander. Distributed in the U. K. by Gaumont Co. Story by Paul Merzbach. Censor's Certificate "A." Running time, 100 mins. Preview at the London Hippodrome, March 27.

Armand de Marny........Miles Mander
Nita Duval.............Margit Manstad
Jeanne Duval.............Ruth Weyher
Dr. Leon Monnier..........Louis Lerch

A very Continental comedy, a much better title being "Wives for Exchange." Continuity and direction is old-fashioned, characters being introduced in closeups with name and role captions at the beginning of the picture. Story is inclined to be told in the back-and-forth method, and would improve with editing. Many of the captions are too stilted.

Armand writes plays and has a fresh love affair with every one. His latest is Nita Duval, but when the proprietor of the theatre wants to put in another leading woman, or close down the theatre, Nita walks out on the playwright and marries a doctor.

Returning from the honeymoon they meet Armand who rushes Nita into a resumption of their affair, while the doctor proceeds to fall in love with his wife's cousin. Armand is accidentally shot by Nita during a visit to his apartment, and Jeanne (her cousin) takes the blame so Nita's husband shall not know where his wife was. Convalescent, Armand realizes the position, tells the doctor his wife was the "lady with the pistol" and reveals she is at the moment in his apartment. After wanting to shoot Armand, the husband sees that he doesn't love his wife but wants the cousin, and turns his spouse over to the playwright, who puts her in his next production, marrying her meantime.

Not so bad for the first run houses here, but a little too sex spicy for the family theatre. Unlikely to get a chance in America, not through any fault of story, but from direction and setting. Dressing of the sets looks as if all furniture and props in store had been brought on and pushed in.

Acting is good. Miles Mander, who made his first real hit in "The Fake," and, except in appearance, is a near Menjou. Margit Manstad troups well and looks full of "it," but they should never photograph her with her chin down. Ruth Weyher, who was in "Doktor Caligari," has more talent than this film shows.

Better for the Continent than here, and better for here than America.

Frat.

LADIES NIGHT

First National release of an Asher, Small and Roegers production. Featuring Dorothy Mackaill and Jack Mulhall. Directed by Edward Cline. At Strand, New York, week April 7. Running time, 71 minutes.

Helen Slocum..............Dorothy Mackaill
"Speed" Dawson..............Jack Mulhall
Pa Slocum..................James Finlayson
Ma Slocum...................Sylvia Ashton
Mr. Spivens.................Harvey Clark
Edwin Leroy...................Reed Howes
Sweeney.....................Guinn Williams

Breezy, thin-skinned comedy better than many of the Mackaill-Mulhall series. Immeasurably helped by a support cast that makes itself a decisive factor. Not mincing matters over delving into pure hoke when it has to, "Ladies Night" satisfied at this house and bids fair to do that nationally without breaking records.

James Finlayson, playing Helen's (Miss Mackail) father, plus a Chester Conklin makeup, and Guinn Williams as Sweeney, Speed Dawson's (Mulhall) pal, are the particular luminaries on value contributed. Sylvia Ashton, doing old man Slocum's overweight wife, and who eventually takes the action into a turkish bath, also makes her comedy bits stand up. A cast oddity is that a "quickie" hero becomes a heavy in faster company. Reed Howes taking the slap toward the finish after making a play for the girl.

Cline, directing, hasn't done much stalling, the result being continuous and sufficient movement to keep them looking at the screen. Speed and Sweeney are ironworkers, with the former giving up his Don Juan ideas after meeting Helen, who sells her parent's lunch boxes at a street counter. Bought out by a firm, the Slocum's move uptown and ma starts going social by undertaking a diet.

It ends in a four-cornered row, whereupon Helen and her mother walk out and into a turkish bath, while Speed and the old man accidentally meet at a stag where a cooch dancer is performing. That the all-male affair is next door to the bath building sends Speed and Pop Slocum through a window and among the women when the cops stage a raid. Ma gets locked out on the roof, swathed in towels, and is pinched as the missing cooch dancer. Meanwhile the parent and his would-be son-in-law are having their troubles dodging the well-steamed femmes and Helen. They get home in time to stop Leroy (Howes) getting fresh with Helen, the latter having left the boys to their fate. Climax is a laugh developed between Speed and Sweeney, with Helen also present.

Gags, and some of 'em okay, spot the picture, with titles clicking every so often. No need for big sets, and these are absent, but the picture can stand the lack of a scenic splurge. Mulhall nicely shades his conception of the fast-working boy whom Helen finally slows down, and Miss Mackaill is no strain on the eyes in another conventional role.

Mulhall and Miss Mackaill have been badly in need of a program comedy of merit. This seems to be it. Anyway, "Ladies Night" should boost their entertainment stock, and about two more of the stripe figures to stamp them with definite drawing power, even at this late date.

Sid.

THEIR HOUR

Tiffany-Stahl production and release. Story and continuity by Albert Shelby Levino. Directed by Al Robach. Cameraman, Faxon Dean. In projection room, New York, April 6. Running time, 60 minutes.

Cora......................Dorothy Sebastian
Jerry ....John Harron
Peggy........................June Marlowe
Cora's Father..............Holmes Herbert
Cora's Fiance...................John Roche
Mr. Shaw....................Huntly Gordon
Peggy's Father...............John Steppling
Peggy's Mother............Myrtle Stedman

This Elinor Glynish title concerns the escapade of a pampered daughter of wealth and a shipping clerk. Dorothy Sebastian, borrowed from M-G-M, plays the silver spoon baby and John Harron is the $40 a week kid that week-ends with the swells and goes off his nut. The story of the rich girl who has everything in the world stealing the sweetheart of her poor working girl cousin is interesting and away from the beaten track of cinema plots.

June Marlowe is the poor cousin, demure and reserved in her prettiness, where her cousin is bold and vivacious. "Their Hour" has lots of sex appeal, that generally meaning box office appeal as well.

The rich cousin has a private aeroplane, no less, and takes the twine and sealing wax lad out for a ride, conveniently stranding near a rural inn 300 miles away. In the inn, with separate but nearby rooms, the brazen lass vamps the impressionable but upright guy and they have "Their Hour."

The arrival of the rich dame's fiance brings to the boy realization that he has been making an idiot of himself. He beats it, hotfoot, for his original sweetie, who forgives all. Nice sentimental little yarn tinged with eroticism of the thin ice school. Production and direction good and picture should deliver.

THE ISLE OF LOVE
(FRENCH MADE)

Paris, April 2.

Featuring the late Claude France, who died some weeks ago under tragic circumstances, "L'Ile d'Amour" (adapted from "Bicchi," by Saint Sorny) has received a favorable reception, released by Franco Film Co. As a drawing card, the name of Mme. Mistinguett, with her dancing partner, Earl Leslie (American), is also invoked, the couple being introduced into a scene representing the gala given by an American millionaire for the inauguration of a hospital he has endowed. Action is placed in Corsica today. Bicchi is a solid, handsome young native of the island, not particularly fond of work, but full of adventure and courage. He becomes the guide of a young American widow, niece of the millionaire mentioned. At first Xenia treats Bacchi as her servant during their mountain climbing, but one day the young man saves a child's life at the risk of his own. Henceforth Xenia takes an unusual interest in the brave lad, who is now violently in love with her, running the risk of a vendetta for her sake.

Bicchi is accused of a murder committed while he is visiting Xenia at night. Not to compromise the woman, he refuses to prove the alibi. However, Xenia informs the magistrate of her lover's whereabouts at the time of the crime, and he is released, later being shot by the victim's father who still believes Bicchi guilty. Xenia nurses him back to health and together they travel, the rustic mountaineer now having become an elegant gentleman, finally returning to the Corsican home which is the Island of Love.

Pierre Batcheff is a fitting partner for Claude France in this picture, and they form a splendid couple. Indeed Batcheff is a bit too elegant for this role. The other parts are well taken.

Jean Durand is producer and he has turned out an excellent picture, of its kind, though not destined for feature runs.

Kendrew.

Beware of Married Men

Warner Bros. production and release. Featuring Irene Rich. Directed by A. L. Mayo. Cast includes Clyde Cook, Audrey Ferris, Myrna Loy and Rush Hughes. At the Hippodrome, New York, week April 9. Running time, about 55 mins.

Side street farce that has only the Irene Rich name to redeem it. Is best adapted to the double feature and multiple change programs. It can't and won't stand up for more than three days, top, and will have its troubles doing that.

Marital theme delves into farce when the principal characters get mixed up in the married man's apartment, doors slamming, everybody in and out of rooms, etc., but all minus pace. Action got a couple of laughs out of a Monday night audience at the Hipp, but not enough for a 50-minute comedy.

Miss Rich plays secretary to a divorce lawyer with whom she's in love. Side issues are a headstrong kid sister, the playful husband who would like to give this youngster some time, the wife stalking the husband and her hoke detective. One sequence takes Miss Rich into the husband's suburban home disguised as an old maid and claiming to be a member of the Welfare League. This is to frighten the chaser into leaving her sister alone. He sees through the disguise, feins a heart attack and the following footage tells that Miss Rich has fallen asleep in a stiff backed chair, slept through the night and is therefor compromised. No later threats develop from this situation.

Silly stuff made additionally unimportant by the manner in which it has been handled. Production is good enough, but bad lighting, particularly atrocious in closeups, offsets whatever interior values may be in the picture. Clyde Cook and Audrey Ferris do fairly with their respective roles of the comedy detective and sister. Myrna Loy is among the cast and also Rush Hughes, who has been away from pictures for some time. Hughes had a corking start on the old Goldwyn lot, but gave up his idea of eventually becoming a director to come east. Here he does just a minor bit, but still looks good enough to go after the juvenile thing, seriously. *Sid.*

FOREIGN DEVILS

Metro-Goldwyn-Mayer production and release. Directed by W. S. Van Dyke from story by Peter B. Kyne. Starring Tim McCoy, with Claire Windsor featured. Cast includes Cyril Chadwick, Frank Currier and Sojin. At Loew's New York, as half of double bill, April 6. Running time, 60 minutes.

Western idea planted in China, with the Boxer uprising and a couple of wars thrown in for action. Not a chance in any smart neighborhood house, but in the smaller stands it can't miss making them applaud when the troops come marching down the dusty road to save the handful of Americans about to be massacred for the good of China.

Story makes the picture interesting, and this survives despite what has been done to kill it in production. A fine love theme, slight, but witty and intriguing, has been mechanically handled and robbed of most of its charm.

Claire Windsor, in addition to photographing well, puts across a strong, convincing role as the English girl. It's exactly the conception prevalent in the hinterlands as to the looks and bearing of mid-Victorian women. McCoy registers the soldier type nicely but is weak in love scenes. Supporting cast okay and mob stuff well handled.

Opens with the situation of the brave captain who unwittingly suggested that the young lady should not go out exploring Chinese temples the following day because of the outbreaks against the whites. The boy is promptly sat upon and has to ride to the outskirts of the town the next day to save the gal and her monocled escort.

Finishes with the arrival of the allied armies, the British navy, the U. S. marines, etc. *Mori.*

Why Sailors Go Wrong

Fox production and release. Directed by Henry Lehrman. At Roxy, New York, week April 7. Running time, 60 minutes.

Doris Martin....................Sally Phipps
Sammy Cohen..................Sammy Cohen
Mac ....Ted McNamara

Title a possible handicap. Under it is a clean, fast, light comedy with about 60 laughs a minute. Maybe the average won't be so high elsewhere, but it registered that heavily with the Roxy audience Saturday night.

Cohen and McNamara get all the laughs and put the picture over on the gagging with which they have been supplied. Nick Stuart and Sally Phipps, the latter especially, register unfavorably. Stuart, however, hasn't much opportunity to put anything across. According to the script, he is kept locked up in the cabin of a yacht while most of the action is taking place. Keeps him out of the picture. Miss Phipps photographs uninterestingly. Cold and expressionless.

Story is light, used merely as a convenience in support of the comedy team and stretched to suit the moods of the gag writers.

An engaged couple are offered a yacht cruise by the girl's boy friend who had lost the race for her heart. The girl arrives, with her father, and is taken on board ship, the menace leaving instructions behind that if Wright (Stuart) should arrive to keep him from reaching the boat. Wright makes the boat by swimming, is caught and locked in a cabin.

Storm follows, and it throws Cohen, McNamara, the girl and her father on a desert island where, according to the titles, the natives subdivide tourists instead of lots. Spot is great for the comedians, aided and abetted by a couple of lions, a monkey that gets the biggest laugh and wild natives.

The monkey is first shown in the early morning awakened by the snores of the sleeping sailors, Cohen and McNamara. After figuring it out the monk comes down from his branch and tries to shut off the snores by sticking its hands, feet and tail into the mouths of the snorers, finally sitting on their faces.

The usual rescue, but a riotously funny closing scene where the two boys have an alligator strapped to the earth and are feeding him castor oil to make him cough up the five grand in bills which he swallowed.

Gagging smart most of the way and surefire all the way. Titles weak at times, but contribute one or two strong laughs.

Should do well in first runs. Bettel title, would be better. *Mori.*

Beyond London's Lights

FBO production and release. Directed by Tom Terriss. Story by J. J. Bell, adapted by Jean Dupont. Bob DeGrasse, cameraman. In cast: Gordon Elliot, Adrienne Dore, Lee Shumway, Florence Wicks, Templar. Saxe, Blanche Craig, Herbert Evans, Jacqueline Gadsven. At Loew's New York, April 3, one day, one-half double bill. Running time, 55 minutes.

"Beyond London's Lights" is a light but nicely put together melodrama. In houses where pictures of this kind are shown it should register.

Contrary to the average meller, there is a well sustained rather than jerky suspense. It is unusual in that the story is unfolded more by the physical actions of the characters, excluding the brandishing of guns and the profuse use of blackjacks which might be indicated to some by the title. In the latter respect consistent use of pipes by male members of the cast, a mug of beer and a touch of fog are used to keep the story within the limitations of Piccadilly.

A river scene with a pretty girl emerging from a bath to meet a chauffeur who insults her. Watching the mechanic being bowled over by the single blow of an aristocrat, opens the picture. Thereafter is developed the meat of the story in well arranged sequences in which the girl hits it for London when she finds that her rescuer is engaged to a haughty heiress. All parties come together in a modiste's shop where the girl is a model, the artist who gave her a lift an admirer, and the engaged couple prospects.

The way in which the chauffeur, detailed by the girl's father to "fetch her home," plays the heavy role is decidedly amateurish. He succeeds in getting well potted when deciding to use force. This, with a few feet in the early reel, is the only rough part in the production.

DESPERATE CHANCE

Morris Schlank production distributed by Anchor Film and featuring Robert Reeves. Directed by J. P. McGowan, Story by Charles Saxon. Lead played by Ione Reed. Cast includes Lon de la Mothe, Charles Whittacker, Gypsy Clarke and Harry Furley. Half of double bill at the Arena, New York, April 6. Running time, 50 mins.

A western quickie of the cheapest sort. Daily change, 15-cent gate and double bill as represented in this house, about the ultimate in film modesty and that fixes "A Desperate Chance" in all departments. Best thing about it is that it has fine scenic background, California scenery being absolutely free to independent producers.

Other things that are fairly inexpensive are hard riding and western cowboy heroes, and the settings of a mining camp main street, porch of a wild and woolly hotel and a shabby office. Scenarios about bad men land-grabbers can't be very expensive, either. And that's all right. With these economical elements, no reason why an independent couldn't make an interesting western story. But there is no excuse for a big husky like Reeves putting up a fist fight with an under-sized heavy that is a travesty. The enormous Reeves just makes an open handed gesture at the menace and the menace fades into a coma. Nothing in filmland is funnier than these fights, unless it is Ben Turpin's moments of passion.

For the shooting galleries this kind of thing seems to be just as good as intelligently produced pictures. At the performance witnessed, the audience passed up a well made romantic society play, "A Reno Divorce," but fell for the western junk hard. When Reeves hamed it all over the lot they applauded with obviously sincere enthusiasm. McGowan directs a lot of quickies of this class, and has been doing so for a number of years. In all probability he has learned that it is just this crudity that makes the films salable for shooting gallery fandom.

This one was a mild riot here; in a deluxe house it would have been a burlesque of stuffed shirt acting and mock heroics. Making these cheap westerns for the tenement clientele must be a trade in itself and no general film standards apply. Anyhow, a late afternoon crowd gave "A Desperate Chance" the *Rush.*

THE PINTO KID

FBO production and release starring Buzz Barton. Directed by Louis King. Roy Eslick, cameraman. Story by John Twist and Jean Dupont. In the cast: Frank Rice, Gloria Lee, Walter Shumway, Hugh Trevor. At the Stanley, N. Y., one day, April 9. Running time, 55 mins.

Horatio Alger's kid of the plains scores again. This time it's in "The Pinto Kid," tailored to fit young Buzz Barton's measurements.

With his familiar side-kick, the Gump-like Frank Rice, Buzz proceeds to rescue a girl and her horse from quicksands as the introduction to his latest exhibition of riding and rope slinging. This leads into an unusually good story for this type of production and well pieced together by John Twist and the rapidly rising Jean Dupont.

A bit of comedy that will squeeze laughs is provided at intervals by the grandfathers of the sheep and horse ranchers. A fistic encounter and later a gun duel behind rocks, each believing the other has kidnapped their niece and nephew, will break out grins in many an adult.

The abductions, promoted by a would-be land buyer, are hardly convincing, but they give little Buzz an opportunity to gallop on his pony, change clothes with the heroine and push the villain into a pool. Perhaps the biggest guffaw will be when Buzz finally hooks the bad man to a rock and proceeds to paddle him as he dangles.

THE DEVIL'S SKIPPER

Tiffany-Stahl production and release. Starring Belle Bennett. Founded on Jack London's story, "Demetrios Contos." Adapted by John Francis Natteford. Directed by John G. Adolfi. Cameraman, Ernest Miller. In projection room, April 6. Running time, 58 mins.

The Devil Skipper.............Belle Bennett
Mate..............................Montagu Love
John...............................Cullen Landis
Skipper's Daughter.........Mary McAlister
Her Father.......................Gino Corrado
Seaman.......................G. Raymond Nye
First Mate.......................Pat Hartigan
Second Mate..................Adolph Millar
Arabian Trader..............Phillpi Sleeman
Planter's Father..............Frank Leigh

Fairly interesting picture because of the twist given to the usual "sea wolf" stuff in having the wicked captain of the sinister ship turn out to be a woman.

History tells of a woman pirate, so the improbable situation has that much corroboration.

The story, written by Jack London, has a theme kinship with "The Shanghai Gesture." In both stories an innocent girl is delivered into the brutal hands of the scum of the seven seas. Escaping the ultimate implications of such a fate, both women, hardened and bitter, rise to positions of power and years later attempt to wreak their vengeance upon the man.

Belle Bennett as the girl who grows up to be the skipper of a slave ship sneers and scowls. Her continued grouch seems a little thick, particularly as, to meet censorship requirements, she is never subject to anything more than the threat of a gang attack. For 20 years she is able to boss the hell ship through the devotion and constancy of Montagu Love, her first officer.

Love, here, always competent whether striving for that tug at the heart or for hisses, is the epitome and embodiment of pure, disinterested, platonic friendship.

Miss Bennett's forte of maternal roles is rather left-handed under the circumstances. A last minute injection of the mother stuff, through the inevitable discovery that the girl she is about to give to her crew is her own daughter, not very convincing.

Tiffany-Stahl has perhaps been inspired by the success of Columbia's "B[illegible] Ship" and Rayart's "Cruise of the Hellion" indie pictures dealing with rough, tough and nasty sailors, but since the late Jack London wrote this before "Shanghai," there's no suggestion in that direction.

"The Devil's Skipper" is a good picture in toto, despite the basic theme's unprettiness. It has been directed and acted well, holds action and drama, and will probably be rated an okay programer wherever showing. *Land.*

THE STRONGER WILL

Excellent production released by Commonwealth. Directed by Bernard McEveety from story by Harry Chandlee. Stars Percy Marmont. Cast includes Rita Carewe, Merle Ferris, W. B. Butler, E. L. Bissoniere and Howard Truesdell. At Loew's New York, as half of double bill, April 6. Running time, 60 minutes.

No story, poor screen adaptation, cheap production. Badly directed, miscast and improperly acted. No excuse for selection of a story of this type, even by a minor independent producer, unless it was to be had free of charge. Better screen material in the daily true stories run in the local tab newspapers.

Wall street finance king, never shown either financing or kinging, is engaged to marry the gal at the time of the opening scene. He has to leave for Mexico on business, and while gone the girl figures it out and announces her engagement to another. The power comes back and shows the miss that unless she marries him he can put her father into bankruptcy. They marry but live in separate bedrooms for the first few screen minutes. Husband then proves that the man she had intended to marry while he was away had been interested only in the money end. All ends happily in a nursery, with the heavy suddenly become the hero. Most subtitles.

Mori.

THE PIONEER SCOUT

Paramount western production and release. Starring Fred Thompson. Story by Fred M. Clifton. Co-directed by Lloyd Ingraham and Alfred Werker. On double feature bill at Tivoli, New York, one day, April 5. Running time, 56 mins.

Fred Thomson, with Paramount, has returned to a type of production identical with the standard of westerns made for him by FBO. "The Pioneer Scout" may have cost more, but that seems doubtful. It's strictly outdoor stuff, with a cave scene about the only set of importance.

The story is typically western, each development being visible miles away. Old wagon train days, gang of thieves who dress as Indians, the menace with a hook for a hand, horses beating up the dust and men beating up each other.

Romantic element is negligible. It's all action, but little drama and except for Fred Thomson, or western fans, hardly interesting.

Its value to exhibs will be in accordance with these facts as applying to their audiences. *Land.*

MAD HOUR

Robert Kane's production. First National release. Directed by Jos. C. Boyle, under the supervision of Allan Dwan. Based upon the Elinor Glyn book, "The Man and the Moment." Continuity by Tom J. Geraghty. Featuring Alice White, Lowell Sherman, Sally O'Neil and Larry Kent. At Strand, New York, week April 14. Running time, about 75 minutes.

Cuddles	Sally O'Neil
Aimee	Alice White
Jack Hemmingway, Jr.	Donald Reed
Elmer Grub	Larry Kent
Joe Mack	Lowell Sherman
Hemmingway, Sr.	Norman Trevor
Red	Eddie Clayton
Inspector	James Farley
Modiste	Rose Dione
Lawyer	Tully Marshall
Maid	Margaret Livingston
Chauffeur	Jack Eagan
Jail Matron	Kate Price
Police Matron	Mary Foy
Bride	Iona Holmes

Funny kind of a picture "Mad Hour." Funny because it's apt to please the flap specie or, again in the countryside and neighborhoods, where they believe what they read, and this through the picture's opening scenes. These latter are held up through their "moral lesson," the bunco for getting them in there, as they are a bit raw and loud, with a bedroom scene rawer and louder.

Otherwise the picture is full of more holes than the Swiss national product. And the title is or the box office, with the Elinor Glyn name tacked on. The late Laura Jean Libbey used to write this kind of mush with the reverse. Elinor seems to slap it on, and the scenarist probably landed some more slaps. And if you don't hear those on the sides lines at Burbank hollering, "Make it hotter!" then you have no imag.

Right off the reel it goes warm and keeps on heating up, until the juv and the gal, while stewed, get married, to wake up the next morning in a hotel room's double bed. From the way they accepted that situation one might be almost convinced it was a daily or morning occurrence with both. That's why there is no sympathy in this picture, even when the poor gal had to go to jail as the other also had to in "Street Angel," both for a year, and perhaps the same jail set, and both gude gurls.

Then the irate Hemmingway, the elder, came in, disowned the son and the hotel bill came due just in time for a crook to get the girl-wife to deliver some stolen jewels. The police got her and she got a year. Here's where Elinor needed a dramatist.

While in jail her baby was born, her husband annulled the marriage, and the day her sentence expired she reached the Hemmingway home as her former husband was marrying the girl he had been engaged to before the stew party came off.

Sad, yes, indeedy.

But the finish was sadder—and costlier. The mother without a husband and with baby taken away, borrowed the bridal auto, raced it down the roads, thought of everything that had happened in the past, with only the screen watching the speedometer. What could happen? It did. Over the cliff to finis.

That stewing up in the early part is the morality tale, of how young girls drink booze in roadsters when college boys have enough money to buy it. The moral seems to be a terrible slam at prohibition, for why should college boys buy booze when they have rich fathers? Don't the old man ever buy? Which composes another moral: the older you get, the smarter—maybe.

But here the booze, the stews, the party and the marriage in the middle of the night may intrigue the sticks, and also perhaps others. It's the only possible savior for this picture, made well enough and directed quite nicely, but not any too well played by anyone excepting Donald Reed. He has the sap college role and worked it neatly both ways.

Other than Sally O'Neil, who did better every so often with a low average, the other featured players, Alice White and Larry Kent, were lost in the shuffle, with Kent out early. While Lowell Sherman had another walk through, he is probably earning more money more easily than any actor in Hollywood. If he ever gets a role with work in it besides wearing a high hat, he should holler.

Strictly a two-people picture, with many characters named, to make it harder, and 75 minutes for the film is much too long. First National appears to be getting to the 75-minute line on all regular features. Unless it's a request from the exhibs, they should save the footage.

"Mad Hour" is worth taking a chance on if the advance publicity dares go into the subject of how young people go wrong, or why. For that's the only guts in this pale story. And as that occurs in the first part and the picture can't be run backwards, it must be borne down on to make the film stand up.

L'EQUIPAGE

(FRENCH MADE)

Paris, April 7.

After a flattering trade show this patriotic picture has been put into the Imperial Cinema here under favorable conditions by the Alliance Europene. The story of "The Crew," adapted from the novel of G. Kessel, deals with the war, mainly with the aviation section.

Performances with airplanes are a thrilling attraction, and in "L'Equipage," distributed by the Lutece Film Co., there are many air thrills.

There is also a good plot, slight as it may be, with strong dramatic effect. A young lieutenant, newcomer, is drafted to an aviation camp for the first time. Without apparent reason he is at once disliked by his future companions, and everything possible is done to make him feel uncomfortable. A fellow officer takes pity on him, and the couple become friends when they share the same flying machine, one as pilot, the other as observer. Then the two men fall in love with the same woman, married to the lieutenant.

Soon the latter learns his friend is carrying on with his wife. Duty calls them and they leave together for a combat in the sky. The airplane returns with the lieutenant wounded and his companion dead. The wife, while weeping silently for the deceased hero, nurses her husband back to life, and for the first time the young lieutenant finds true happiness.

It can be said frankly "L'Equipage" is a good French film. The photographic work is excellent, the aviation stunts interesting and the acting first class. The roles are held by Jean Dax, Geo. Charlia, Camille Bert, Pierre de Guingaud and Mme. Claire de Lorez. *Kendrew.*

LOVE HUNGRY

William Fox production and release. Romantic comedy, directed by Victor Herrman. Lois Moran featured. Story by Randall Faye. Titles by Frances Agnew. At Roxy, New York, week April 14. Running time, 56 minutes.

Joan Robinson	Lois Moran
Tom Harvey	Lawrence Gray
Mamie Potts	Marjorie Beebe
Ma Robinson	Edythe Chapman
Pa Robinson	James Neill
Lonnie Van Hook	John Patrick

This whimsical romance of youth and commonplaces in the setting of middle-class society in a big city makes cheerful entertainment. Light story, simple and unpretentious in its appeal, it takes on substance from its atmosphere of youth and optimism.

There isn't a moment of real drama, but these loveable young people engage one's sympathies and their rather trivial adventures hold the spectator's willing attention. A picture that is slow in its development, trifling in its import, but still holding through the human appeal. Daintily made little romance in the background of a New York rooming house.

Tom is a young and not very successful writer making his home with Ma Robinson, who has lived a life of drudgery as the loyal helpmate of her small clerk husband. Joan, their daughter, is a humble chorus girl trouper, seeking, as she says, to grab herself a rich husband so she can do something for wornout pa and ma. Joan comes home from a discouraging adventure on the road, accompanied by her pal of the chorus. Goldie, the rough-and-tumble gold digger by her own confession. Tom and Goldie get on each other's nerves, but he falls hard for Joan. He is working on a story about being happy and married at $40 per. On this issue Tom, Goldie and Joan clash.

Tom introduces Joan to his millionaire friend, Lonnie, giving her a chance to grab a ban' roll. Lonnie falls, but in the end it turns out that it was Tom she loved all the time. Ma supplies the clincher argument on the "happy-at-$40-per" idea when she tells the youngsters she wouldn't change pa for any millionaire.

Good comedy bits in constant succession. Girls are invited to the Ritz by the millionaire and, by a misunderstanding, have to pay the $16 check. They blackjack Tom to make the loss good, after having to walk home in tight shoes. Goldie awkwardly tries to promote the millionaire for Joan and nearly spoils the plot.

Marjorie Beebe as Goldie runs away with the picture. This girl has a comedy knack that is priceless, doing low comedy bits with a certain naive grace altogether captivating. She is funny without ever being vulgar. Lawrence Gray makes a splendid young lead, natural in his clean-cut style, while Lois Moran, with her fragile beauty, is the perfect ingenue lead.

This combination of manly leading man, amusing comedienne and romantic ingenue suggests the possibilities of such a trio for exploitation in a romantic comedy way, after the manner of the straight romantic couples. With stories like "Love Hungry" such a trio would become standard.

Feminine appeal is strong in this picture, based, of course, upon its sure-fire Cinderella motif. Release will please generally, with special pull for class clientele. *Rush.*

SEALED LIPS

(SWEDISH MADE)

Swedish-made feature based on a story by Guy de Maupausant. Directed by Gustaf Molander. Mona Martensson and Louis Lorch featured. At 5th Avenue Playhouse, New York, week of April 14. Running time, 66 minutes.

Program for the lower 5th avenue movie parlor mentioned this Swedish number as "introducing the new school of Russian cinema technique." That may be put down as a petite piece of baloney. "Technique" is a fine-sounding word but it doesn't mean much for "Sealed Lips."

It's not bad barring some subtitles which form a ridiculous combination with some of the scenes. Also laugh-provoking is the sequence where the fabulously naive girl blindfolds her lover and on the pretty suggestion of playing a game leads him into a church where a priest is waiting to marry them, with the young man knowing nothing about it and already possessing a wife.

Script is based upon a yarn by de Maupasant. It traces several years in the life of a girl leaving a convent, brushing shoulders with lust and tragedy, her return, disillusioned, with the intention of taking holy orders, and her ultimate reconciliation with her lover.

Mona Martensson alternately photographs well and badly, either due to make-up or camera angles. Louis Lorch is an averagely good looking, romantic lead, but a little negative otherwise. The old man role is exceptionally well played.

Possibly the Russian technique talk refers to the failure to cut some scenes soon enough and the contrary habit of cutting other scenes abruptly.

"Sealed Lips" is fair "art" theatre material but of little utility for straight trade purposes. *Land.*

A Night of Mystery

Paramount production and release. Starring Adolphe Menjou and featuring Evelyn Brent and William Collier, Jr. Directed by Lothar Mendes, with Harry Fischbeck, photographer. H. J. Manckiewicz titling. At Paramount, New York, week April 14. Running time, 60 minutess.

Captain Ferreol	Adolphe Menjou
Therese D'Egremont	Nora Lane
Jerome D'Egremont	William Collier, Jr.
Marcasse	Raoul Paoli
Gilberte Boismartel	Evelyn Brent
Marquis Boismartel	Claude King

Indifferent Menjou film which needs all the surrounding program help it can get. With the star's name a draw, the picture's entertainment qualities are short of what that exterior billing implies.

A straightaway murder plot without a change of pace. Little action and no comedy. Short on love interest, too, due to Menjou's supposed fiancee (Nora Lane) being but a continuity figure. Evelyn Brent does nothing, although featured. If the star is strong enough to stand off one of these, okay, but there'll be cries for help if another one of this stripe is turned loose.

No mystery for the audience as to who is the murderer. The problem is for Menjou, as a French officer, to extricate his sweetheart's brother (Collier), who is innocently on trial. Complication is the killer's threat that if Menjou talks he'll tell of the affair between Menjou and the wife of the judge who is sitting on the case. As America's tab readers don't like their heroes smirched by a married woman, there'll not be much sympathy over here for Menjou in this role. Nor for anyone else in the picture, with the possible exception of the bride to be, and she's made to appear colorless.

Action never gets outside the studio, and Mendes, directing, presumably figured there was no room for anybody with a sense of humor to work on it after getting the script. Manckiewicz, titling, also apparently under strict orders to cease clowning. Not even any sympathy for the accused brother, as he previously has sneaked his sister's necklace to borrow on it.

Nobody stands out in the cast. Menjou again is strictly the gentleman, plus stiff hipped bows and a great pair of officers boots. Plot lets Mankie turn loose an hurrah title on "woman's honor."

Picture is based on Victorien Sardou's play, "Ferreol," with the screen play by Ernst Vajda. That's probably what's the matter with it. It's French in origin, French on the screen and best adapted for French consumption. Film has the asset that it will be better for Menjou abroad than here. Despite the standard production background, "Night of Mystery" is mediocre material for the States, will see many a "red" week and may have been a cause in the discussion between the star and Paramount executives. When Menjou needs Whiteman it looks bad for Menjou. *Sid.*

CRIMSON CITY

Warner Bros. production and release. Directed by Archie Mayo. Story by Anthony Coldewey. In cast: Myrna Loy, Leila Hyams, John Miljan, Anders Rudolf, Richard Tucker, Anna May Wong, Sojin and Mathew Betz. At Broadway, New York (Vaude-picts) week April 16. Running time 59 minutes.

Second string production grade of this producer which explains it first run presence at the Keith-Albee establishment just off Times Square, a house that has to dig for its new material. Becomes available for the Broadway because it doesn't rate class house for exploitation and still is too good a lobby flash to waste on the Hippodrome.

Picture's best asset is the locale of the native quarter of Shanghai which lends itself to lurid lobby billing playing up Oriental mysticism, yellow peril characters and the thrill that goes with the mysterious Orient. Title also carries some boxoffice weight and cast of familiar screen names has value with fans.

Story on the screen is strained melodrama with leering Chinese menace and all the tricks of Oriental melodrama from the days of "Queen of the Opium King" up to date. Sophisticated movie goers will be prone to jeer at its labored melo, while the simple minded will fall for the tried and true hokum.

Technical production is of the best quality with settings, groupings and stage management capably managed and the photography exceptionally good. In short a workmanlike product turned out for the daily change clientele and making good in that classification.

Story is another model No. 7945, Series B, on the "East Is West" theme of Oriental maid about to be sold into salvery as property of a wicked, cruel, and what is worse, A. K. mandarin, and falling in love with the brave white outcast down on his luck and a fugitive from the white man's law.

For the Broadway, with its record of dull and dumb screen entertainment, it is a good feature, but for a house that caters to a wise fan public, blooey.

Material is handled in directorial sense far better than the subject matter merits and the acting is rather more than adequate. *Rush.*

WOMAN WISE

(3D REVIEW)

Through confliction and delayed record filing two reviews of this Fox picture recently appeared in Variety, written by different staff members in different issues, and expressing diverse opinions, pro and con.

As seen cold in a projection room by two other Variety reviewers, the picture seemed unworthy of the effusive puff and undeserving of the severe slam. It is not a good picture, but as a neighborhood and small town proposition on short engagements, it can slip by without occasioning any comment one way or the other.

No request was made of Variety for another review. Attention to the conflicting notices was drawn by exhibitors, with the Fox press department courteously arranging for the projection room showing.

Both prior reviews mentioned Mack Sennett, whose two-reel technique was discerned in "Woman Wise" by one of the previous reviewers and reported missing by the other.

The picture deals with the woman-hating American consul in a Persian town and his woman-loving buddy. A pretty girl arrives from the United States to act as the consul's stenog. The local potentate, robed in satin, plans deviltry.

Plot development and direction are rather seedy and the panning review is correct in the statement that this film is well below the production standards of the recent Fox output, but the suggestion that the trade slogan, "It's a Fox Production," should be deleted, was unnecessarily captious.

The picture is conspicuously miscast in William Russell playing a role for which a younger man was needed. Walter Pidgeon, the romantic lead, will probably have femme appeal, and the boys will like June Collyer, one of the Wampas chicks, in pictures about a year and coming fast but hardly a "name" as yet.

Theodore Kosloff, the one time dancer, plays the dressed up potentate. Kosloff has been in eclipse for the last several seasons, and his return herein may interest fans. He does the meager role very well, especially in make-up for it.

A Sealyham terrier with ears that wiggle will likely be considered rare fun by the kids and non-fastids, and there is also some slapstick to make the push-overs giggle. The picture has much of a western-brigandage sort and lots of action, and that adds neighborhood value. *Land.*

STOP THAT MAN

Universal production and release. Arthur Lake and Barbara Kent co-featured. Directed by Nat Ross. Cast includes Eddie Gribbon, Warner Richmond, Joseph Girard, Walter McGrail, George Seigmann. At Hippodrome, New York, week April 16. Running time, 59 mins.

Highly improbable farce here represents an entertainment average that will suffice in the stands under the full week grading. Much of the picture is undisguised slapstick but reasonably successful in its determined snatching for laughs, so, in toto, a moderate pleaser.

Arthur Lake, who a couple of years ago did a schoolboy series for Universal, is co-featured with Barbara Kent, practically an unknown outside of having the Wampas' endorsement.

Through the kiddishness of Lake and the negative impression of Miss Kent, "Stop That Man" may be said to be without love interest. It stands or falls with its hokum.

Lake plays the kid brother of two hefty Irish cops. While posing in the uniform of one of the brothers the kid gets them into a scrap through helping a crook break and enter a residence. Later, by sheer dumb luck, he captures the crook, trusses him up, hitches up a couple of horses and goes gallôping to the police station in an old rickety horse trolley.

At the Hippodrome laughter was fairly frequent, with the audience showing a disposition to accept the film simply for what it pretends to be, a farce designed for giggling purposes. *Land.*

DEAD MAN'S CURVE

FBO production and release. Directed by Richard Rosson. Phillip Tannura, cameraman. In cast: Sally Blaine, Douglas Fairbanks, Jr., Kit Guard. At Columbus, one day, at Loew's Circle. Running time, 60 minutes.

No second-run house, including quite a few of the first-runs, can go wrong on "Dead Man's Curve." In the language of those houses, this is a picture; full of the old stuff, to be sure, but directed in such a way as to work up a high-powered suspense.

Young Fairbanks plays a Lindbergh, so far as facial expression goes. Even though his pan fails consistently to register, his racing car tilts along at a pace that will get 'em all going.

The gags of doping the winning car the night before are better oiled in this one. The suave one's bribe to get to the car provides the young hero with the necessary entrance fee. The manipulations for the auto manufacturer's daughter only result in the daughter financing the lad's new motor.

The race is one of the longest that has ever been unreeled on any screen. The audience doesn't weary however, because the plot has already sold itself.

A WOMAN'S WAY

Columbia production and release. Directed by Edmund Mortimer. Ray June, cameraman. In cast: Warner Baxter, Margaret Livingstone, Armand Kaliz. One day, at Loew's Circle. Running time, 60 minutes.

Heavy in spots, light throughout with a story based along very conventional lines, "A Woman's Way" gains something from Margaret Livingstone, Armand Kaliz, some good roof-top and Parisian cellar shots.

Those who do not analyze the story will take to the picture. Kaliz' Parisian crook is rendered with a suavity, so often overdone. Miss Livingstone plays a cabaret singer, while Warner Baxter handles a modest part with moderate ability.

Everything winds up bloodily but happily.

The Adorable Cheat

Chesterfield production supervised by Lon Young. Directed by Burton King from story by Arthur Hoerl. Lila Lee starred. Cameraman, M. A. Anderson. In projection room, New York, April 13. Running time, 57 mins.

Marion Dorsey	Lila Lee
George Mason	Cornelius Keefe
Cyrus Dorsey	Burr McIntosh
Will Dorsey	Reginald Sheffield
Howard Carver	Gladden James
"Dad" Mason	Harry Allen
Mrs. Mason	Alice Knowland
Roberta Arnold	Virginia Lee

Chesterfield formerly released through Pathe but presently is a states righter.

"Adorable Cheat," the first picture made under the new arrangement whereby Lon Young, last with Gotham as publicity director, becomes production supervisor, was made in Hollywood in about 10 days, and despite that, or because of it, is a fast-moving, interest-holding picture.

For the states right market this is a spiffy number all the way. Intelligent and restrained, doing wonders with a small bankroll and hiding its miracle-working so that except for a handful in the trade, nobody will suspect the size of the cost sheet. The sum expended on this picture is reported to be around $10,000. While Chesterfield may not like this figure publicized, if true, it stands as an eloquent testimonial to those concerned and if they can continue to turn out pictures of this quality at that figure, or a little better, they will be the marvel of the business.

The first point in favor of "The Adorable Cheat" is the story, well-knit and plausible. It is credited to Arthur Hoerl who functions exclusively for the indies and should have plenty of assignments.

Lila Lee is starred and while the "Cuddles" kid has passed from public focus of late she looks extremely attractive here and will be liked. Cornelius Keefe, new leading man, who appears on the ascendant in Hollywood, makes a good impression. Gladden James, some years ago one of the busiest of the screen's "no-good guys," and seen but little for some time, does a cad with his accustomed finesse in nastiness.

It's a yarn about a shipping clerk that fell in love with the president's daughter without knowing who she was. Complications at a week-end party in the fashionable home of the manufacturer.

Neat stuff. *Land.*

ABIE'S IRISH ROSE

Paramount production and release. From Anne Nichols' stage play. Directed by Victor Fleming. Titles by Julian Johnson and Herman Mankiewicz. Harold Rosson, cameraman. At the 44th Street, New York, April 19. Running time, 129 minutes. Opened for run as a special at $2.20 top.
Solomon Levy...............Jean Hersholt
Abie Levy..................Charles Rogers
Rosemary Murphy...........Nancy Carroll
Patrick Murphy......J. Farrell MacDonald
Isaac Cohen................Bernard Gorcey
Mrs. Isaac Cohen..............Ida Kramer
Father Whalen.................Nick Cogley
Rabbi Jacob Samuels.......Camillus Pretal
Sarah.....................Rosa Rosanova

Discussion of "Abie's Irish Rose" film status as a commercial proposition is futile. With its prestige as a national institution, built up by its amazing box-office record, the picture will, of course, attract and prosper in the picture houses.

Miss Nichol's play has been translated literally from the stage, and the picture adds nothing, while it does detract a good deal. The picture is not as good a picture as the play was a stage performance, something inherent in the situation surrounding its creation.

Stage drama often is heightened when it is transferred to the screen, but this production demonstrates that the studio has already developed a comedy technique that is immeasurably superior to that of the stage. The truth is that the humor of the film "Abie" remains exactly the same as the humor of the stage "Abie"; that is, the fun is all in the titles (as it was in the dialog) rather than in the intrinsic substance of the story.

Two hours and 10 minutes of title gags is scarcely going to be hailed by film fans educated to the standards of the picture house where the greatest of the laugh-makers never risks more than an even hour and has to pack that limited time with clever fun that is basically laughable in pantomime and doesn't have to be interpreted in printed words. "Abie" proves conclusively that, certainly in comedy, the screen has nothing to learn from the stage.

What the film theatre gets from "Abie" is the commercial advantage of the best publicized title in the world. The play material itself is a handicap. Hollywood could turn out a score of funnier comedies on the same subject. What is more, Hollywood has done just that little thing. Several of the films inspired by "Abie" have been much funnier in substance than the film translation of the original. Which doesn't prove anything except that the screen has grown away from the theatre into a technique that is its own, and that "Abie" on the screen is nearly all straight drama excepting the comedy captions.

All the screen could do for "Abie" was to make its background more elegant and to magnify its settings. Some fine production has gone into the war sequences and a few of the sentimental passages have been shrewdly intensified. The picture takes a good deal of interest from dramatic tricks — devices, by the way, which belong to the screen entirely. For example, nothing could be more effective than the bit early in the picture which covered a lapse of time in a graphic way.

The point is that "Abie" is growing up in the great melting pot of New York's east side. He is among the school children in the schoolyard. They are assembled in lines reciting the school pledge to the flag; a bell rings, and they march in many files to their classrooms. While the kids go tramp, tramp across the yard, the scene dissolves slowly and the marching children become the American soldiers marching down 5th avenue in 1917. Here in 30 seconds was conveyed a high-powered emotional kick. The picture has a number of such details. They are all strictly picture devices, and they are effective on the screen, while the material taken over from the stage play has to express itself entirely in titles, and loses force.

The picture doesn't grow in ascending values to a climax, a treatment essential to a gripping picture. It takes over two hours to lead up to what in substance is a rather feeble gag, when the antagonistic fathers, Jewish and Irish, at length come around on Christmas eve to see the offspring of their cast-off children. Levy demands to see his "granddaughter," while Murphy is anxious to hold his "grandson." The sex of the child leads to new and violent argument until friendly priest and friendly rabbi disclose the presence of twins, a situation any auditor could have forseen. Even the climactic gag is tipped in advance.

The laborious sentimental play upon bigotry, continued reference to the brotherhood of Jew, Celt and the rest of mankind—including the Mohammedan — is wearisome and seems for the most part to have been pushed in.

Under the Constitution, and specifically in the subway rush hours, these things go without saying. There is something also not so very tactful about the elaborate technical exactitude of the Jewish and Roman Catholic customs, even to the point of assuring the audience in a program note that a real rabbi and a real priest acted as expert advisors in these details. If these things are right they will speak for themselves to such auditors as are concerned in their correctness.

Of the acting many nice things will be said. The outstanding performance is that of Jean Hersholt as Solomon Levy, an eloquent and sincere performance of a role that in its elements might not have been very genuine under less skillful treatment. Nancy Carroll and Charles Rogers make a charming pair of young people, especially charming in their artless grace and youthful good looks. J. Farrell MacDonald is just a comic Irishman, while Bernard Gorcey as Solomon's attorney friend is a strong asset in his low-comedy role.

Settings are excellent, with fine intelligence in expressing appropriate mood and restraint from overdoing both the magnificence of the high-toned backgrounds and the poverty of the east side. War shots are fine, especially some of the hospital locations. The sentimental passages have been fairly well developed, but the dependence upon the comedy motif has nullified this angle. It is possible that this was a mistake. It is strange that the sentimental side of "Abie" has attracted so little attention. Hollywood's faith in the power of the grand old gag is probably the reason.

Rush.

(Rush, Al Greason, is of the Protestant faith.—Ed.)

MADRE

(ITALIAN-MADE?)
(With Eleanora Duse)

No screen credit given producer, distributor or cast with exception of subtitles hailing it as the first and only film in which the late Eleanora Duse appears. At the 55th Street Playhouse week of April 21. Running time, approximately 40 minutes.

As a decided novelty in film technique, because of antiquated lighting which blurs the greater footage and over-acting of an unknown foreign cast, "Madre" is hardly worthy of enrollment in filmdom's archives as a testimonial to one of the most famous tragediennes the world has ever known. While it stars the late Eleanora Duse in what is described as her first and only play on the screen, yet it shows this tragedienne in anything but her real self as known on the legit stage of yesterday.

Apologies that Duse abhorred make-up are profusely subtitled for her being seen through practically the entire production with a black

hood over her head. It shadows her face, with only occasional white flashes, from recognition. In the last few feet a moment for study of her face is provided. At no time, however, are there the close-ups which would have made this foreign picture, with all of its crudeness in craftsmanship, a historical gem.

The outstanding feature in the life of a mother who watches an illegitimate child grow up in the ways of the world is the way that Duse uses her hands. They are especially effective at the death scene, despite distractions provided by absurdly over-acted neighbors and that of the son, who would hardly be a credit to a phoney movie school.

"Madre" with its star will be an attraction for the thousands who have witnessed her perform and for the millions who have known her through the public print; at the same time it will be a great disappointment.

THE PATSY

M-G-M production and release starring Marion Davies. Directed by King Vidor. Adapted from Barry Conners' stage play. Cameraman, John Seitz. At the Capitol, N. Y., week of April 21. Running time, 64 minutes.
Patricia Harrington........Marion Davies
Tony Anderson...........Orville Caldwell
Ma Harrington.............Marie Dressler
Pa Harrington.............Del Henderson
Bill.....................Lawrence Gray
Grace Harrington..........Jane Winton

Barry Conners' stage play has been converted with liberal licenses into a dandy laugh picture for de luxe program requirements. In it Marion Davies does some really great comedy work. "The Patsy" would be a good opportunity for the soft-pedaling of the customary Hearst hokum publicity to see if the picture and the star cannot stand up and get by without the bolstering.

Many of the laughs come from the subtitles, with about half taken verbatim or with slight changes from the play. Ralph Spence gets sole credit for the title job, but should split credit with Conners. The picture follows loosely the general story of "The Patsy," that of a younger sister who is imposed upon by an older sister and her mother, who favors the butterfly daughter. Pop takes sides with The Patsy, being somewhat of a Patsy himself.

Efforts of the younger girl to attract the attention of the man who is courting her sister forms the basis of the comedy and plot. Toward the end, with a generous employment of screen liberty, Miss Davies does a series of imitations of Pola Negri, Mae Murray and Lillian Gish. The imitations are great and reveal Miss Davies as a skillful mimic. Audience broke into applause on the Gish interpretation. Corking fan stuff, especially in the smaller communities where screen gossip is a matter for table conversation. Gloria Swanson once did some imitations of other stars in a picture she made for Paramount.

"The Patsy" is an excellent laugh picture.
Land.

The End of St. Petersburg
(RUSSIAN MADE)

Berlin, April 9.

Out with the adjectives of praise for this Russian government made picture. How those Moscovite boys are keeping pace! Now they are right up at the top from the directorial and photographic angle. I've never seen a better photographed picture anywhere. And think of what their films looked like three years ago!

This director, Pudowkin, has here created a film which deserves to be classed with "Potemkin," and perhaps this is the better of the pair.

How those people do act—not a moment of exaggeration or grimace! They live it.

The story is simple. It concerns

a peasant boy who comes to the city to get work. A strike starts and he takes a position as strikebreaker. Without realizing what he is doing, he betrays a relative, a strike leader. When understanding, he beats up the owner of the factory.

The world war breaks out, and he and the strike leader are mobilized. During the Russian revolution the boy proves himself a hero for the cause and is tended by the worker's wife.

Story is of no interest to the general American public, but every American picture actor and director, if securing the chance, should look at this film. *Trask.*

THREE SINNERS

Paramount production and release. Directed by Rowland V. Lee. Pola Negri starred. From play "The Second Life," by Bernauer and Osterreicher. Adaptation by Doris Anderson. Screen play by Jean de Limur. Julian Johnson, titles. At Paramount, New York, week April 22. Running time, 68 minutes.
Baroness Gerda Wallentin......Pola Negri
James Harris...............Warner Baxter
Count Dietrich Wallentin......Paul Lukas
Count Hellemuth Wallentin,
                          Anders Randolph
Raoul Stanislaw..........Tullio Carminato
Valet to Dietrich..........Anton Vaverka
Cuntess Lilli....................Ivy Harris
Prince von Scherson,
                    William von Hardenberg
Baroness Hilda Brings....Olga Baclanova

One of those supposedly worldly-wise plays of polite European society and Continental locale of great elegance. Pretty thin material for an hour's film running. Magnificent physical production, but another story which offers Pola Negri a pale role for her vivid type of acting. It's a programmer of moderate worth, dependent upon the star's name.

Very artificial people, and plot is based on the hard-to-take supposition that a man meets the wife he has wronged perhaps five years after and, failing to recognize her, falls in love with her all over again. This isn't a particularly thrilling situation. The principal appeal of the picture for women is that it furnishes Negri with opportunity to wear some stunning clothes and appear in a white wig, which makes her more beautiful than any disguise she has lately assumed. It is another merit that the drama moves in surroundings and atmosphere of high life, always an asset in the picture theatre.

The production has to make its way on these grounds, for its story is without punch, develops in leisurely style and is loosely woven. It was probably picked because it seemed appropriate to put Miss Negri back in the atmosphere of Continental polite society, in which she first came before the American public, surroundings to which this exotic actress properly belongs.

As the picture comes upon the screen it is the settings, the pictorial accessories that are of interest, while the story material itself is tiresome. Pola Negri, dressed in a dream creation of an evening gown, wearing a white wig and presiding over the gaming tables of a Paris casino, is a spectacle to create talk among the fans, the women fans particularly. But they will reject as absurd most of the pumped-up dramatic situations.

The play is old fashioned in its artificial motivation and there isn't a spark of humor in the whole business. Under the circumstances it is to be expected that the acting will be stilted and false as the play.

Rush.

Dans L'Ombre du Harem
("In the Shadow of the Harem")
(FRENCH MADE)

Paris, April 13.

Excellent French-made picture, which has met with a flattering reception. Produced by Leon Mathot and Andre Liabel, it forms another of the Oriental series of late. Initial release of the new Paris International Films Co. through the Franco Film Corp.

Scenario is taken from a drama by Lucien Besnard. Montfort, an engineer residing with his wife and infant son in one of the North African protectorates, carries on a flirtation with Djebellen'nour, favorite of the ruler of the country, Emir Abd-en-Nacer, whom he chanced to meet in the palace. The clandestine rendezvous take place in the home of Lella, sister of the princess.

A rival denounces them, and all the women folk are thrown into prison. As for Montfort, the emir swears to get even with the European. A few days later Montfort's child is kidnaped, and the mother is informed by an anonymous letter that the emir has had her son removed to his harem.

The child will not be harmed and will be returned to the mother if she consents to visit the palace for one night. The governor and the woman both entreat the emir to forego this terrible vengeance of "an eye for an eye," but as Montfort first offended, the Oriental insists on the price of the wife's sacrifice to save her child.

However, the emir respects the woman, insisting, nevertheless, on letting the husband believe she had become his mistress. Later the situation is explained, with Montfort obtaining his wife's pardon.

Leon Mathot impersonated the ruler in fine style. Louise Lagrange was the wife, and her sincerity contributed much to the realistic impression. Several interesting scenes with good photographic work. of sacred customs of the Arab chiefs.
Kendrew.

BURNING DAYLIGHT

First National production and release. Directed by Wid Gunning from the story by Jack London. Starring Milton Sills, with Doris Kenyon featured. At Strand, New York, week April 21. Running time, over 60 mins.
Burning Daylight............Milton Sills
Virginia....................Doris Kenyon
Dutch Oven Danny............Arthur Stone
French Louie................Guinn Williams
Jack Kearney................Jack McDonald
Martha Fairbee..............Jane Winton
Morton....................Lawford Davidson
Johnson.....................Frank Hagney
The Stranger................Harry Northrup
Percival Blake..............Stuart Holmes
Edwin Dossett...............Edmund Breese
John Letton.................Howard Truesdale

Not the kind of a picture to please attendance at the first runs. Primarily of the blood and thunder variety, it belongs in the neighborhoods, the second and third runs and so on down the list. With Sills considered a fairly reliable draw it should do reasonably well in its place.

Action in Alaska, with a couple of well done fist fights, is strong and gripping, but strong man stuff applied too broadly in spots. Continuity is jumpy and sub-titles carry too much of the burden of telling the story.

Comedy light, resting on the absurdities of miners suddenly wealthy, in society. Construction of many of the situations rough and mechanical especially the punch scene near the finish, when Burning Daylight makes the San Francisco brokers return the millions they stole. Here the girl who has sponsored his entrance into society and introduced him to the financier who later fleeced him on the stock market, crashes into the room with some remark about the "sucker," the latter appearing from behind the door.

Sills has a good role but not as effective as it might have been with proper screen adaptation. It should have been the story of the square-shooting gambler, jumping from Alaskan gold fields to the stock exchange merely because the stakes were higher. Instead it deviated into many channels, detracting from the interest and weakening the story.

Doris Kenyon makes a suitable lead opposite Sills but the characterization of a dance hall girl who will

---

only sing to entertain men cannot be conveyed realistically. *Mori.*

THE PLAY GIRL

Fox production and release. Starring Madge Bellamy and featuring Johnny Mack Brown and Walter McGrail. Directed by Arthur Rosson. Titled by N. Z. McLeod, with R. J. Bergquist photographer. At Roxy, New York, week of April 21. Running time, 50 minutes.
Madge Norton..............Madge Bellamy
Bradley Lane.........Johnny Mack Brown
David Courtney...........Walter McGrail
Greek Florist............Lionel Belmore
Millie....................Anita Garvin

Underweight comedy picture that classes among those entries which are just able to poke their nose past the post to stay in the money. Nothing to get excited about, with the film's best point the kidding of the girl by the semi-heavy when she resents his advances after coming to the latter's apartment for an isolated dinner. It's almost as weak as a former Bellamy film which Fox let the Keith-Albee Hippodrome have over on Sixth avenue.

N. Z. McLeod's titles hold a couple of laughs and are sprinkled with smiles to give this release a 50 per cent. entertainment rating. The star has looked and worked better in other pictures, here depending upon an undressing comedy sequence to get her across. Clara, Corinne, Dot M. and Madge have become the screen's principal mannequins for lingerie; all have a habit of looking pretty good when so presented, and as the studios have found this formula holds its b. o. advantages, the angle may again be okay in the case of "The Play Girl."

It's another instance of the girl hurling her gifts in the face of the doner until she's forced to grab male clothing for coverage, only to discover the rescuing garment is a swallow-tail coat. Previously Walter McGrail has cynically applauded Madge's indignant demonstrations at his advances, also asking her if she does "Camille." Action gets down to a chase basis at one time.

Story starts out with Madge as a salesgirl in a hotel florist shop, where she meets young Lane in Courtney's rooms upon delivery of some posies and with Lane unaware of her presence and skipping about in athletic shirt and trunks. Losing her job leads to Millie (Miss Garvin) suggesting that Madge become a good-time Annie, and the latter starts out to learn the way of her mercenary girl friend. Following the predicament with Courtney, Madge decides she doesn't want to play around and okays Lane's ideas on marriage.

Brown is reputed a former Coast gridiron luminary who looks all right but needs interference by directors before he'll threaten to break loose behind the juvenile lines. McGrail does well as the hero's lawyer with a femme complex, while Anita Garvin fills the role of the philandering girl friend full of advice. For Miss Bellamy it's an ordinary piece of work from all angles.

Arthur Rosson directed and Bergquist cameraed, the latter making some good-looking interiors screen that way. Rosson refrained from padding a weak script, so that the picture is on and off 10 minutes under the hour.

Just a comedy, and a light one that will need stage show oxygen in the better houses and is best suited to split weeks. *Sid.*

THE MATINEE IDOL

Columbia production and release. Starring Bessie Love. Directed by F. R. Capra. Cast includes Johnny Walker, Ernest Hilliard, Lionel Belmore and David Mr. At K-A Hippodrome, New York, April 23. Running time, 66 minutes.

Solid laugh and hoke picture with a misfit title just shy of rating a demonstration in any of the program houses. As it stands the film is surefire for those abodes using split-week policies and doesn't need a

---

second feature to bolster. A few more thousands spread between production and cast would have made this one worthy the de luxe sites across the country.

Main appeal lies in the broad histrionics of a tent troupe doing a Civil War drama. The company is so rotten a revue producer engages them for his Broadway show for laughs. They're a New York comedy riot and the ingenue's heart is broken. Meanwhile, and through circumstances, the blackface star of the musical (Johnny Walker) has played a northern soldier super under the canvas and, due to the cork, is able to hide his identity from the daughter of the traveling show's proprietor when they reach New York.

Opening night in the big town is when the girl realizes how she and the players have been duped, flight into a downpour brings the male star in pursuit, and when the rain washes away his makeup she sees it's the boy who has been working in her company as a soldier.

The story finishes in the "sticks" again, with the "name" comedian once more applying for a job in the girl's company.

It's a picture a good organist can have a circus with. The chest heaving and gesturing drama lays itself open to all kinds of kidding sobs. Besides which there's the pianist in the pit doing "effects."

The first time it was flashed they laughed from their toes in this house. The second time, supposedly when the "actors" are seriously working in the Broadway house, they laughed some more if not quite so loud. Titles are a decided help, and Miss Love's youngster who has the entire responsibility of the troupe on her shoulders, and who is just as bad as any of 'em, is as good a piece of work as she's been seen in in some time.

Walker doesn't particularly impress as the Broadway star, and the remainder of the cast just suffices. Capra, directing, passed up chances to emphasize the pathos when the girl and father realize their performance is being laughed at, although he's allowed the miss to walk down to the footlights and do a Dick Bennett in bawling out the premiere house—which they take as more comedy. A traveling camera to a closeup in at least one spot might have brought a lump to many a throat, but the film is too concerned with laughs. All of which it gets, and that's fair enough.

For a company that has a rep for building its pictures around titles, "The Matinee Idol" as a name is a cluck for this Columbia release. It has no direct bearing on the story and may make prospective patrons skeptical. However, once they're in there'll be no doubt that they'll like it.

Any house that wants to take this picture for laughs only, first routining it from the pit orchestra or organ for kidding, with music and effects, can't help but send it over, and should make a good laughing feature of it. *Sid.*

SHOOTIN' IRONS

Paramount production and release. Directed by Richard Rosson. Adaptation by J. W. Ruben and Sam Mintz from novel "Arizona Bound," by Richard Arlen. Harry Gerrard, cameraman. In the cast: Jack Luden, Sally Blane, Fred Kohler, Richard Coryle. At Tivoli, New York, one day, April 11, as half double bill. Running time, 55 mins.

"Shootin' Irons" is one of those westerns where they worked and worked on the story with the hope of achieving a novel finis. This Paramount seems to have accomplished by averting a double hanging in proving that the stage coach was held up by the hero only that he could save his sweetheart's father from arrest; and that, after all, the police were after the wrong man.

Although the yarn is one of the most unconvincing that Paramount

---

has turned out in a long time, yet the usual riding and gun-toting will carry it through with western audiences. The romance arouses only a minimum of interest and sympathy, because Sally Blane's pan simply refuses to respond to the director's coaxing for emotion. Studio tears fall when occasion demands, but the mouth remains a slightly curved line.

Jack Luden entertains, but the story curbs his ability in that it inspires him with a gusto and strength which enables him to carry on through nearly half of the footage with a bullet in his shoulder. Despite the wound, which at first lays him low, he is able to ride, shoot and even engage in a fistic encounter with the heavy Fred Kohler. As Kohler is really heavy, it makes the battle, in view of the other odds, worse claptrap than might be expected in some quickies.

For Kohler, it must be said that "Shootin' Irons" gives him a chance to show what he could do in a real story.

THE RAIDER EMDEN

(GERMAN MADE)

Emelka production released by Columbia. Produced under the auspices of the German Admiralty. Titles by Joe Weil. At the Cameo, N. Y., week of April 28. Running time, 60 mins.

Another foreign made, prefaced with some patriotic remarks regarding the advisability of forgetting wartime hatreds. This epic makes its bow as a picturization of the heroic and humane elements within the "enemy" ranks.

Film shows how the destroyer Emden, in the opening months of the war, attacked and captured defenseless merchant ships of other nations, though leaving the passengers and crews unharmed.

Among other "exciting" incidents in the life of the Emden are shown scenes of the ship leaving port heaving anchor, sailing smoothly through calm seas, signalling, morning drill, meal time, and so on. Not one real battle scene.

Cold even for the sure-seaters Best art house picture on the program was "The Vision," of the Music Master Series, done in technicolor. *Mori.*

Turn Back the Hours

Lumas release produced by Gotham. Directed by Howard Bretherton. Adapted by Jack Jungmeyer from the old play of the same name by E. E. Rose. In the cast Myrna Loy, Walter Pidgeon and Sam Hardy, featured, Josef Swickart and Sheldon Lewis. At Loew's New York, April 27, as half of double bill. Running time, 53 mins.

Fast picture with one fatal defect. In the producer's anxiety to speed up action he has robbed his hero of sympathy at the outset and never explains away the taint in his character.

Probably the play took care of this detail, but it is a flaw in the screen production that robs the whole thing of value. Opens with hero being read out of the C. S. Navy on charges of cowardice. The circumstances of the officer's disgrace are never set forth, and the impression is that his conduct was beyond defense. That stops a screen hero, and the fact that he finally makes good later doesn't raise the curse altogether. A hero who isn't justified is a dead loss to the fans. This detail could have been straightened out in the script or in the studio.

But when they deliberately show the man as a coward in the early action, on top of the dismissal from the sea service, they've wrecked the picture, and no amount of subsequent heroism squares it, particularly because they never explained his first yellow streak.

Thus a good, fast action story with picturesque angles is spoiled. Broken by his disgrace the officer sails for distant lands as a stowaway. He is nearly lost at sea, but is rescued by Tiza, Spanish girl living with her father on a South Sea isle. This role is played by Myrna Loy, who is miscast.

The island is ruled by an outlaw band, the leader of which desires the girl. Rest of the story has to do with hero's fight to defeat the brigand's vicious designs upon the girl. Climax is nicely built up, which has hero and heavy in a hand-to-hand combat on the roof of a tropical mansion, just as an American man o' war arrives on summons of the girl's father, and the Marines come to the rescue at the last minute.

Grades as weak end of double bills although it has material that deserved something better. *Rush.*

ROSES OF PICARDY

(BRITISH MADE)

Montreal, April 29.

Canadian Educational Films, Limited, release, starring Lillian Hall Davis and John Stuart. Based on R. H. Mottram's novel "The Spanish Farm." Directed by Maurice Elvey. All-British cast. At Princess, Montreal, eight days, from April 29. Running time, two hours.

Touted as "greatest English production" and "the one you have been waiting to see," it is hard to see how they get that way. It is about 60 minutes too long and the padding is thick.

Plot is of Flemish girl with two lovers, one French, the other English. She is apparently about equally fond of both. When one is away, the other comes in. The whole story—if there is a story—centers around these two but in such haphazard form that the audience doesn't know what it's all about for the most part.

In between are scenes in billets and of fighting, without any particular interest, having been done dozens of times and with nothing new in this presentation. Supposed to be all kinds of symbolic meanings in these, but unless you were told, you wouldn't notice them.

The heroine is not inspiring and the two heroes have no special kick. Scene opens with shot of French village after the war with hero watching a rubberneck car from which the information is megaphoned that nothing happened here. Ironic, then, but judging by the following picture, it is only too true.

Based upon a book that made a reputation in Great Britain, the picture cannot follow the subtle shades of character drawing and description contained in the original.

As an example of breaking of continuity, there is a point toward the end of the picture where the hero and heroine are about to meet. The whole of the action is held up for a long five minutes while page after page of a long letter are reproduced in script on the screen. It is difficult to read and boring as well and by the time it is through, the audience has forgotten what went before.

The picture ends with the English and French lovers being brought together by the heroine and forced to shake hands. It is hard to know exactly why ,since, beyond the odd kiss immensely lengthened out, the Englishman has been strictly pure.

"Roses of Picardy" might go in a British country if accompanied by much patriotic tub-thumping. Elsewhere it would likely be taken off after the first night.

QUESTION OF TODAY

(VITAPHONE PLAYLET)

(8 Mins.)

Chicago, April 27.

Here you have an affair upon Warner Brothers' Vitaphone involving a chief of police, a sailor, a society dowager and an ultra-modern society debutante. The theme of the story is very moral. A sailor has been arrested for accosting the society girl on the street. He had just returned from a six months' whaling trip.

As the story goes, the sailor was headed for a dance hall when he saw the girl. She had him arrested. The society dowager calls on the chief of police to tell him he must put a stop to the moronic advances made to girls on the street.

The chief calls her bluff. He summons the sailor, a husky, brutish chap He summons the girl, a sexy, shallow little thing with a dress that the sailor likens to a "wet bathing suit." He lectures the girl and the dowager, and tells them that if they prosecute the sailor he'll prosecute them for playing bridge for money and violating the Volstead act.

It is just one of those things treating on the subject of present-day feminine attire and its effect upon the passions and imagination of we bestial men.

Altogether a very ridiculous piece of story. It hands a laugh and a few naughty giggles to the girls of the audience who wear "wet bathing suits." It gives the men an "I-told-you-so" puff.

Rather melodramatic and overacted, but gets over. *Loop.*

VEIL OF HAPPINESS

(FRENCH MADE)

French production, based on novel by Georges Clemenceau. Released through states rights. Cast: All Oriental players practically unknown here. At Fifth Ave. Playhouse week April 28. Running time, about 65 minutes.

A production having for its finale the signature of France's ex-Premier, dealing with a Chinese fantasy of which Clemenceau is also credited with the authorship, made its American bow at the Fifth Avenue Playhouse. Titled "The Veil of Happiness," the theme, one of the purest fantasy, attempts to illustrate the blissful existence humans would lead were they materially blind to the misgivings of their fellow men.

A few sets, one a most artificial cherry orchard, add to the monotony of overfootage made more so by slow moving Orientals who comprise the entire cast.

Cut down to a two-reel film drama with a lot of cumbersome titles eliminated, this story might really come somewhere near bringing to the screen the philosophical objective of the author.

As the picture now runs it is totally minus any particular interest and devoid of suspense, exclusive of two flashes. One of the latter is when an ex-convict, seeking alms from the blind aristocrat, recalls pictorially the murder for which he was punished. The other is when the lord, his sight restored by the potency of a witch doctor, gouges out his own eyes after he discovers things about him the opposite of what he imagined during his long blindness.

Properly edited into a short subject "The Veil of Happiness" would get over in high-brow houses.

Van Dal and Delac, French independents, produced the picture in France.

THE SWILIN' RACKET

(Amateur and believed assembled) Produced by Varick Frissell, member of the Royal Geographic Society. At 55th Street Playhouse, New York, week April 21. No release arrangements. Running time, about 45 minutes.

"The Swilin' Racket" deals with the capture of seals in the ice fields off the coast of Labrador.

Photographed by Varick Frissell, a youthful New Yorker turned explorer, this educational is unusually interesting since, unlike many of its kind, it holds its various shots together with the thread of a story dealing with the competition among sealing vessels and the hazards to which their crews are exposed.

Steamers cracking their way through the ice fields until points are reached where seamen tugging on a long line have to assist the propeller; men spearing and shooting seals and jumping from block to block of ice, where the field has been broken up; a vast panorama of the ice country—all of these sequences lend interest to a film which would be well-nigh perfect were a few of repetitious scenes aboard ship eliminated.

Love Makes Us Blind

(GERMAN MADE)

Ufa production. Conrad Veidt, Lil Dagover and Emil Jannings featured. At 55th Street Playhouse, week of April 28. Running time, around 60 mins.

Heretofore, says an inserted subtitle preceding the first scenes, German pictures have been serious, but now America may see the mental giants of Ufa in lighter mood turning out a comedy drama. And, another subtitle continues, it is noticeable that in their humor the Germans aim higher than Mack Sennett.

This may be a comedy but it's not particularly funny, so, however high minded and artistic it's not as successful as Mr. Sennett's efforts, which are generally funny.

Actually an expanded anecdote about a man who cheated on his wife and how she won him back by donning a wig and fooling him. Not to novel. "Love Makes Us Blind" is interesting chiefly as showing the interior of the Ufa studios in Berlin with Emil Jannings out of character. That's worked in through a group of society people making an amateur movie for charity.

Conrad Veidt, generally a heavy, attempts to do a goof and succeeds beyond his expectations. Lil Dagover, the sensuous Ufa lady, does a Clara Bow by running about in her unmentionables. The Germans may be ahead of us in camera angles, but they've a lot to learn about lingerie.

All in all the film is a dull and inferior sample of the Ufa brand. *Land.*

WAGON SHOW

First National production and release starring Ken Maynard. Screen play by Ford I. Beebe. Directed by Harry Brown. At Loew's Circle, N. Y., one day, April 28. Running time, 60 mins.

First rate western with a circus background that will please the kids from seven to 70 in the neighborhoods, and even the better class houses. Neat love story which is subordinated to the circus stuff puts this flicker over.

A couple of those "hey rube" rumpuses on the lot heighten the action effectively when story shows signs of lagging. High spot is reached when Maynard leads a galloping circus parade onto the lot in time to prevent a riot on the part of outraged citizens who thought the honest wagon show owner was slipping them a phoney performance.

Plot revolves about the Greater Beldan Shows playing the tanks in Montana. In addition to bad weather Col. Beldan has the sharp methods of the Sayres Mammoth Shows to contend with. Maynard, acting as guide for Beldan, steps into the breach when star of the circus runs out on him and ties up with opposition. Maynard puts on a fine exhibition of plain and fancy riding and the Beldan show is on the verge of getting out of the red when the Sayres outfit steals half the wagons the day of an important engagement. Maynard brings them back and the final clinch finds the circus man's daughter in his arms. Maurice Costello, as the square shooting circus man, delivers a realistic performance.

Okay all the way.

The Little Yellow House

FBO production and release. Based on novel by Beatrice Burton. Adapted by Dorothy Yost. Continuity by Charles Kerr. Directed by Leo Meehan. Cameraman Al Siegler. In projection room, April 18. Running time, 62 minutes.

Rob Hollis	Orville Caldwell
Emmy Milburn	Martha Sleeper
Mrs. Milburn	Lucy Beaumont
Mr. Milburn	Wm. Orlamond
Perry Milburn	Edward Peil, Jr.
Wells Harbison	Freeman Wood
Grandmother Pentland	Edythe Chapman

A story of the type familiarized by Harold Bell Wright and the late Gene Stratton-Porter, "The Little Yellow House" is family stuff with a strong moral lesson on the evils of drink.

The troubles of this particular family originate with the boozing habits of the father. He is one of those amiable weaklings who is sure to be drunk when most needed or when most inconvenient. Besides keeping his family in poverty he continually humiliates them by staggering in at card parties and whatnot.

The grandmother is wealthy and wants to help the family, but the drunk's devoted wife won't leave the little yellow house to which she came as a bride. Finally, faced with the danger of losing her daughter, the mother consents to leave the yellow shack and go to live in the mansion of the grandmother.

Charley, the chronic stew, is warned that the first time he shows up drunk, out he goes.

In due time Charley appears carrying a load. The grandmother, furious, orders him from the house. He goes out reeling and steps in front of an automobile for a quick curtain.

The wife turns on the mother, accusing her of having killed Charley by sending him out when pie-eyed, and the family moves back to the yellow shack, but daughter takes an apartment in the wicked city and announces her purpose of living her own life.

It's applesauce after that, with the daughter finding the rich man a villain and going back to her humble lover, who has meanwhile stepped from a Chevrolet to a Buick, and now wears a white shirt instead of his former khaki open at the neck.

The cast is a good one, although it seems remarkable to have Lucy Beaumont, who specializes in mother roles, represented as the daughter of Edythe Chapman, whose age must be about the same. Martha Sleeper daughter of an old-time executive of Keith's, has the lead and does very nicely.

The picture may be rated as a moderately successful effort of in-between box-office weight. *Land.*

The Woman Tempted

(BRITISH MADE)

Wardour production released by Aywon. From novel by Countess Cathcart. Directed by Maurice Elvey. Screen play by Sidney Morgan. In cast Juliette Compton, Warwick Ward, Malcolm Tod, Nina Vanna, Mrs. Haydn-Coffin and Joan Morgan. At the Cameo, N. Y., week of April 21. Running time, 60 mins.

This siren story freely adapted from one of the literary contributions of the lady who brought about the discovery of "moral turpitude" holds little but a trite story, poor photography and plenty of mugging. It's of mediocre value for the two-bit grind houses.

Picture sets out to prove that charity covers a multitude of sins, the flaming Mamie using it as a cloak while strictly on the make.

Louise Harding (Juliette Compton) deprived of romance by a marriage of convenience, sets out to strut her stuff when she is left widowed and wealthy. Taking up charity work she ruins the life of one man and is about to grab herself another when the fiancee of the first man bumps her off and retires to a convent.

Miss Compton gives a good performance as a vamp, but Elvey's direction lacks imagination, simplicity and restraint. Warwick Ward is given little opportunity to show to advantage here.

PUT 'EM UP

Universal production and release, starring Fred Humes. Story by George H. Plympton.. Directed by Edgar Lewis. On double features program at Tivoli, N. Y., April 18. Running time, 50 mins.

Tom Evans	Fred Humes
Benny	Benny Corbett
Pewee	Pewee Holmes
Helen Turner	Gloria Grey
Mullins	Harry Semels
Jake Lannister	Tom London
Pop Turner	Charles Colby
Tradin' Sam	Buckley Starkly

Deep-dyed villainy stalks, rides and runs through this one, with Fred Humes as the western hero. The dirty work in the small town starts early and the captions fairly sizzle in their bloodthirsty dye. An old-fashioned western.

The villain and his trusties try their cussedness on a trader, a Hebe who sticks with the hero and saves his life, and his business, too. One shot after another has the plot getting thicker and thicker until the gal is kidnapped and forced to stand for a marriage that is frustrated at the last minute.

Picture is made pleasant to some extent by the work of Humes and Miss Grey. Latter isn't a bad looker and she and Humes give a touch of youthfulness throughout. Captions were atrocious but made so by the way the villainy starts to get hot from the opening. *Mark.*

Valley of Hunted Men

Pathe release, produced by Action Pictures. Directed by Richard Thorpe. Buffalo Bill, Jr., starred. Story by Harrison Strong. Titles by Frank Ingraham. In the cast: Kathleen Collins, Alma Rayford, Oscar Apfel, Frank Griffith. At Loew's New York April 27 as half of double bill. Running time, 54 minutes.

Excellent action story for the daily changes, with Mexican border locale for fine picturesque effect and some stunning photography to give it punch. Scenic backgrounds in which horseback pursuit is set and fighting between border patrol and outlaws is dandy detail.

Picture has good comedy value arising from the whimsical behavior of the cowboy hero who goes into the lair of border smugglers in a campaign to lure them into pursuit from the Mexican to the United States side of the line. Outlaws, by the way, are all renegade Americans or Europeans, tactful arrangement to avoid objections of the Latin-American republic.

Story nicely made and does not follow the worn-out formulas. Bad men are running arms into Mexico and rum into the U. S., and there is not the usual land-grabbing heavy seeking to steal heroine's ranch. Heroine is niece of the master mind of the smugglers.

Tom Mallory (Buffalo Bill, Jr.), cowboy, goes into border service. He's impatient with tactics of his unit, which has been chasing the smugglers three years. He agrees to round them up in three days. Framing to set off a smoke signal for aid, he goes into the the camp of the outlaws, just across the line, and sets himself to so provoke them by his impertinence that they will attack them. One of the gang has a daughter, who falls in love with the hero, and when he repulses "r (because he loves another girl in .e camp) she pretends he has affronted her. This works into the cowboy's hands, for they set out to get him. He leaps to the saddle and sets off through the plains, with the bandits in pursuit.

Tom lights smoke signals and then leads the pursuers into the hands of his waiting comrades, first having provided for the escape of the second girl, with whom he has fallen in love. Tom's series of insults designed to sting the bandits is an excellent movie trick. It provides the comedy and also brings on a series of fights.

Picture is action from start to finish, logical and well sustained. First-class products for the western fans. Rates better than double feature material and worthy single feature for the daily changes. *Rush.*

MY HOME TOWN

Rayart Picture presented by W. Ray Johnston, also styled a Trem Carr Production. Directed by Charles J. Hunt. Cast includes Gladys Brockwell, Gaston Glass, Henry Sedley, Violet LaPlante. Shown at Stanley theatre, N. Y., double feature, April 28. Running time 63 mins.

Story takes country boy, throws him into ill repute in his home town under circumstantial evidence and has him hit the big city and become enamored of a gal with wicked ways. The smart city gal finally throws him back into his mother's arms because she really and truly loves him. There is nothing new, novel or strange in that sort of picture stuff.

"My Home Town" carries its country boy and city gal theme along to what is supposed to be one of the smash climaxes where the woman to send the boy away from her stages a phoney love scene with another man and finally socks her rural sweetie smack on the side of the jaw.

Not a lot to commend in this one.

Much of the photography towards the latter half of the film didn't seem so good and there were apparent shots that made the figures seem somewhat distorted and the closeups in particular looked poor.

All told a picture that may slide by best where doubled with another film and at the Stanley with a Harold Lloyd it gave passable satisfaction. *Mark.*

THE SPORTING AGE

Columbia production and release. Starring Belle Bennett. Directed by Earle Kenton. Ray June, cameraman. In the cast: Holmes Herbert, Carrol Nye, Josephine Borio. At Loew's New York, one day, April 21. Running time about 60 minutes.

Snatches of a train wreck, racing track and paddock and plane plunging into the sea would make "The Sporting Age" one of Columbia's best action films were it not for slow intermediate action in garden scenes and studies. Clipping the latter to the extent of even a half reel would bring the production into Class A as a program attraction.

The train wreck, which renders the race track man temporarily blind and prolongs an affair between his wife and his secretary, could well be given more footage.

A unique shot is secured by the camera being focused downward while a plane is swirling toward the sea.

Failure to secure any marked climax is the chief weakness of the story. The audience is let in on the fact that the husband has recovered his sight too early for any particular suspense up to the point where the wife and boy friend become cognizant that their actions have been watched.

The secretary also helps to minimize consistent interest during long lawn scenes by a marked inclination toward too virtuous an interpretation of his role, rendering the romance wishy-washy.

SO THIS IS LOVE

Columbia production and release. Starring Shirley Mason. Frank Capra, director. Ray June, cameraman. In cast: William Collier, Jr., and Johnnie Walker. At Loew's New York one day, April 17, one-half double bill. Running time, 60 minutes.

Willie Collier, Jr., is hardly a match for the stockily-built Johnnie Walker in the ring contest for the championship of Greenwich Village, but, nevertheless, he acquits himself quite convincingly in Columbia's "So This Is Love." The picture will probably make its way in other places where Columbia has succeeded.

Following several socks on the chin which Collier, as the dressmaker, sustains from the fist of Walker as the big glove boy of the Village, the youth persists in his attempts for the hand of the delicatessen storekeeper. He becomes a pug and winds up in a contest for the title.

Some of the funniest work is accomplished by Shirley Mason when she feeds the champ on everything she has in the store before he meets her boy friend. After the latter is bumped all about the ring Shirley suddenly recalls the pickles which she has fed the champ. The closing shot witnesses the boy friend in her arms after he has pummeled the champ's plexis into submission.

From the angle of second and third-run box office—not a bad picture.

AIR MAIL PILOT

Produced by Superlative Pictures and distributed by Hi-Mark (Nat Nathanson). Earl Metcalfe starred. Blanche Mehaffey leading woman. DeWitt Jennings featured. Half of double bill at New York, one day, April 13. Running time, 57 minutes.

Good example of this style of commercial quickie; a picture expertly made to appeal to the very naive fan element and for this purpose first rate. Melodramatic action is swift even if it is illogical and sometimes crude. Plausibility of story is sacrificed deliberately to the prime purpose of staging a fast action drama

The punch of the film is the hero's pursuit of mail robbers fleeing in an airplane, culminating when the hero climbs from his own plane to that of the fugitives while the heroine drives the airship up in the clouds. There follows a desperate hand-to-hand fight between the hero and the robbers all over the plane's wings. After that the hero jumps and parachutes to earth safely, while the robbers turn and drive head on into the girl's plane, with the girl also jumping and landing safely.

The effects are fairly well managed and probably the picture packs a kick for the juvenile mind of any age; but the thrills are piled on so thick the whole business skids rather close to travesty. Acting is on a par with the type of picture, rather stilted and altogether hokum. An occasional touch of comedy is rather better done, as, for instance, the finale, where two lovers, brought together in safety, fall into an embrace, but are dragged across a field in that pose by the wind-blown parachute to which the girl is still attached.

A good deal of ingenuity has gone into the staging of the air battle thrill. Much of it holds the illusion of really being in the air. Dovetailing of real air shots and trick photography has been neatly done, and to the uninitiated the sequence has all semblance of reality. Not so good were the shots of hero and heroine off on a dash through a raging rainstorm.

Ground shots have been taken at a real air port and bits of arriving and departing mail planes are briskly interesting. An error occurs in having the hero and scheming heavy (also aviator in the mail service) so much alike that the spectator is often not quite sure whether the uniformed airman is hero or villain.

Despite its crudity picture is a serviceable product. If these quickies would hold to plan of making straight outdoor action pictures instead of trying for the subtle program play subject, exhibitors playing double bills would have more satisfactory material to pick from. This one would be a valuable item in the neighborhoods, and for the minor daily changers would support the body of a bill by itself. Subject lends itself admirably to good lobby billing. *Rush.*

The Man Who Laughs

Universal production and release, directed by Paul Leni, with Conrad Veidt and Mary Philbin co-featured. Based on Victor Hugo's novel. Adapted by J. Grubb Alexander. Cameraman, Gilbert Warrenton. At Central, N. Y., for $2 run, starting April 27.

Running time, 124 mins.
Gwynplaine....................Conrad Veidt
Dea...........................Mary Philbin
Duchess Josiana............Olga Baclanova
Queen Anne..............Josephine Crowell
Dr. Hardquannone........George Siegmann
Barkilphedro.................Brandon Hurst
King James.................Sam De Grasse
Lord Dirry-Moir.............Stuart Holmes
Ursus.........................Cesare Gravina
Wapentake....................Nick De Ruiz
Lord High Sheriff............Edgar Norton
The Spy......................Torben Meyer
Gwynplaine..............Julius Molnar, Jr.

"The Man Who Laughs" is the third picture based on the writings of Victor Hugo to be handled by Universal as a special. The first was "Hunchback of Notre Dame," a money-maker and prestige-builder. Last fall U had "Les Miserables," French-made and, to date, a good grosser, if spotty, demonstrating that the name Victor Hugo possesses a definite pulling power.

On the premise that Hugo's reputation as a classic is a beneficient factor it may be predicted that "The Man Who Laughs" possesses additional strength above and beyond its intrinsic entertainment qualities.

"Man Who Laughs" may be okay at $2 for a few of the bigger cities and for extended non-reserved seat runs in the others. For program purposes it should be a standout, although possibly handicapped by the reaction against costume pictures. Five or six years ago it might have been a smash. Today it's a pretty good specimen of a familiar type of movie plus an unusual angle in the stenciled grin and also plus the name of Victor Hugo. The production bankroll must have been sizeable but U should get a good gross back.

The picture in its full length is draggy, notably in the second half. When reduced for general release purposes this slack material can be taken in, but the weakness will remain as regards the absence of an adequate climax. After all the intricacies of plot, sub-plot, treachery, cruelty, agony and general grief the ending seems banality itself, especially with the last minute inclusion of one of those scenes where Rin-Tin-Tin gets his man. This scene is unnecessary and somewhat too harrowing as it close-ups the dog's fangs sinking into the man's throat. The dog, until this point, has been entirely casual, allowing Mary Philbin to have a playmate.

Miss Philbin incidentally is zero in this picture. Any pretty girl would have done as well. The part is sheer posing all the way, negative and uninteresting because Dea is a blind girl and never knows what's going on. After Miss Philbin's fine work in "Drums of Love" this sort of a role seems a waste of time and talent.

The plot, sketched briefly, concerns a grin carved upon the small son of Lord Chancharlie by order of King James of England in 1690. The boy, abandoned, is brought up by a traveling montebank and in time becomes Gwynplaine, "The Man Who Laughs," a famous clown. He again comes in contact with royalty when King James' successor, Queen Anne, becomes peeved at Duchess Josiana, whose wealth is founded upon the estate of Lord Chancharlie. Disliking the Duchess, and learning of the existence of his son, the Queen, to humiliate the Duchess, orders the "man who laughs" raised to his rightful position as peer of England and to marry the Duchess.

The toothy clown with his perpetual grin makes an interesting, if gruesome, character. Men are more apt to be intrigued by the situation than women. The grin makes it difficult for Conrad Veidt to do much acting. Glycerine tears do not quite succeed in conveying soul torture nor in creating romantic illusion.

"Man Who Laughs" will appeal to the Lon Chaney mob and to those who like quasi-morbid plot themes. To others it will seem fairly interesting, a trifle unpleasant, and intermittently tedious. There have been so many of these 17th century movies there is no longer novelty in the background, and the continuous villainies of the kings, courtiers and others gets monotonous. The picture is, however, happily different in that absolutely no attack is made on the heroine.

Production, direction and photography are excellent. Indeed, the megaphone work of Paul Leni puts the picture over even where the script leaves loose ends in its not always successful efforts to negotiate the tremendous mass of Hugo's story material. The scenes of Southwark Fair, near London, are interesting, if historically authentic, as revealing how ancient the carnival racket is.

The types are well chosen. Sam DeGrasse in a short sequence and a great make-up was a vivid King James. This medieval mind with its religious bent seemed immensely interesting. Brandon Hurst, with his best sneers, made real the character of the king's jester, "whose smiles were false and whose jests were cruel." Stuart Holmes was rather nondescript as Lord Dirry-Moir. Unessential to plot or story it was not quite clear whether he was supposed to be a monumental imbecile or a cunning court politician. At first sight he seemed to be of the comic relief, but subsequently it seemed otherwise.

Josephine Crowell made a splendid Queen Anne, crusty, jaundiced and catty. Ceasare Gravina did his customary beaming boy. Olga Baclanova, in a role of color and vitality, quite outshone Miss Philbin, costarred with Veidt. Miss Baclanova has an interesting blonde personality.

Land.

GLORIOUS BETSY

Warner Bros. production and release with Vitaphone, directed by Alan Crosland. From the play by Rida Johnson Young, with screen adaptation by Anthony Coldeway. Photographed by Hal Mohr. Starring Dolores Costello, with Conrad Nagel featured. At Warner's, New York, for $2 run starting April 26.

Betsy Patterson............Dolores Costello
Jerome Bonaparte............Conrad Nagel
Preston.........................John Miljan
Colonel Patterson.........Marc McDermott
Princess Fredericka..........Betty Blythe
Napoleon..................Pasquale Amato
Captain St. Pierre.........Michael Vavitch
Captain De Fresne......Andre de Segurola
Ship Captain..................Paul Panzer
Aunt Mary..............Clarissa Selwynne

Despite its obvious play for the favor of picture fans through a superabundance of love sequences and heart interest, the picture misses on these counts through lack of directorial ability along those lines and the weakness of the male lead, Conrad Nagel, as a convincing hero with either sex. Nagel cannot do a Douglas Fairbanks satisfactorily.

Love scenes are crudely done and, excepting second and third-class audiences, can't get by. Studio work on this production equals anything turned out by the major producing companies, with photography and settings of the highest order.

While not in the $2 class and hardly expected to stay more than four or five weeks at the Warner, if that long, the picture still merits attention in the first runs on account of the Vitaphone angle, which should draw on its novelty. Without the talking sequences production should do nicely in the neighborhoods for a full week. This is on account of the high standard of studio production rather than construction of the story, direction or acting.

Miss Costello, limited to two or three talking sequences, is again at a disadvantage with her lines sounding unnatural. Singing of "Le Marseilles" by one of Jerome Bonaparte's captains is effective on account of strong delivery. The plantation scene in which negroes are grouped for a southern melody is also appropriate and further demonstrates the value of vocal effects in pictures. Speaking lines, even when delivered well, do not impress favorably because none added anything of special interest, like useless lines in a stage play and wouldn't be missed if eliminated.

Story of this sort called for a centering of forces on the male lead with a powerful player in that part. Attempt to throw burden of heroism on the girl doesn't quite grip. The girl is forced to give up her husband on the Emperor's orders, and her action cannot be construed as bravery.

Action revolves round an unknown French tutor, who is engaged to give lessons to one of Baltimore's richest and fairest. The humble teacher's expertness with a sword and abundant supplies of cash rouse comment. He wins the girl's love and gets her promise to marry him before revealing his identity as Napoleon's brother.

With the announcement of Jerome's betrothal to the girl comes the news that Napoleon is Emperor of France. The latter expects Jerome to make a political marriage and nullifies the American nuptials. According to history the story ended there, but the screen adaptation brings Jerome back to Betsy and his baby son.

Mori.

Across to Singapore

Metro-Goldwyn-Mayer production and release. Directed by William Nigh. Based on the story by Ben Ames Williams, "All the Brothers Were Valiant." Ramon Novarro starred. Joe Farnum's titles. At the Capitol, N. Y., week of April 28. Running time, 78 mins.

Joel Shore...................Ramon Novarro
Priscilla Crowinshield....Joan Crawford
Capt. Mark Shore......Ernest Torrence
Jeremiah Shore............Frank Currier
Noah Shore................Dan Wolheim
Mathew Shore..............Duke Martin
Joshua Crowinshield....Edward Connelly
Finch..........................James Mason

Six or seven reels of highly dramatic violence, most of it theatrically effective, but it doesn't make a top-grade picture, principally because it depends upon artifice, and the genuine human interest and emotional grip are lacking. A skillful studio product, but never a human document, which makes the difference between a great work and a merely salable commercial product.

On its technical side the film is a marvel of artistic excellence. Its settings are the finest kind of pictorial compositions, both ashore and on the majestic square-rigged ship; period costumes (of the '50s) are picturesque, and sequences in Singapore dives, sinister, shadowy waterfront glimpses in strange ports are arresting bits. There is a thrilling passage of the ship rounding Cape Horn in a "snortin' nor'wester" that is a marvel for kick, indeed the first really convincing sea storm this reviewer has ever seen filmed.

Picture is one succession of fights, mutinies, bloodshed, hate, love, passion and wickedness. But these high emotions never once achieve the conviction of reality because the material is always the creation of make-believe. It's all a story, brilliantly visualized by all the arts of the studio, but you never lose the sense of motives and movements dictated by a stage manager. Not one incident or character really lives.

Interest centers in Mark and Joel Shore, oldest and youngest of four seafaring brothers. Mark falls desperately in love with Priscilla Crowinshield, daughter of a neighbor, and playmate of the boyish Joel, and without the girl's expressed consent their engagement is announced in the village church on the eve of Mark's sailing for the Orient. This also is Joel's first trip at sea.

Priscilla is cold at the farewell and Mark broods about it as the ship plows through the sea, drinking all the time. In Singapore he goes on a speee and through a plot is left behind. An evil mate throws Joel into irons and brings him home, charging he 'deserted Mark and left him to die. Joel, blaming Priscilla, seizes the ship and takes her back to Singapore, firm in the belief that Mark is alive and can be saved. They find him crazed with drink and brooding, and he turns upon them. The crew mutinies and Mark, seeing the boy about to be killed, comes to reason, leads the fight against the conspirators, and, although he is victorious, dies from his wounds, leaving the young people to each other and happiness.

The hurry and rush of melodramatic action leaves small time for the building up of romantic sentiment, and this is a weakness in the story. Picture is an almost unbroken succession of fights, man against man, man against mob, and mob against mob, and the ceaseless riot of violence after a time palls. Outstanding performance is that of Ernest Torrence as the elder brother, ship master and fighting giant, an actor with distinctive qualities that make him proof against artificial roles.

Novarro doesn't convince as a rough-and-ready fighting hero and the romantic angle of his character is rather pale. Joan Crawford has a passive part to which she brings much appealing beauty. Some of her earlier comedy sequences are prettily done.

Another of those program pictures that really addresses itself to the naive fan, but gets by in important houses because its elaborate and expensive production makes it look better than it is in substance.

Rush.

PARTNERS IN CRIME

Paramount comedy feature, directed by Frank Strayer, starring the clown duet of Wallace Beery and Raymond Hatton. Story and scenario by Grover Jones and Gilbert Pratt. William Marshall, cameraman; titles by George Marion, Jr. At the Paramount, New York, week of April 28. Running time, 65 minutes.

Mike Doolan..................Wallace Beery
"Scoop" McGee...........Raymond Hatton
"Knife" Reagan..........Raymond Hatton
Marie Burke.......................Mary Brian
Smith ....William Powell
Richard Deming.................Jack Luden
Barton ....Arthur Housman
Kanelli ....Albert Roccardi
Chief of Police...........Joseph W. Girard
B. R. Cornwall................George Irving
Dodo..........................Bruce Gordon
Jake........................Jack Richardson

Picture that has moments of inspired farce by this always amusing pair. Not so rough and ready in its gagging as some of its predecessors, but as laughable as the best. Story is a timely satire on the vogue for underworld subjects, and the cream of the fun is that Beery and Hatton are a couple of knockabout low comedians planted in the midst of a deadly serious crook melodrama.

The fundamental situation is funny and the studio has gone the limit in framing farcical twists to what is on the surface a thrilling melodrama. The epic gag of the whole business is a climax in which, while rival gangs of gunmen are engaged in one of those pitched battles in a luxurious mansion, the two boobs by accident set off a whole packing-case of police tear-bombs, and crooks, cops and innocent bystanders go off in a paroxysm of sobbing and a rain of tears.

Beery is a boob detective and Hatton a caricature of the star reporter of the screen. The bandit gang is robbing a store when Beery ambles along and, by his own awkwardness, is laid low by the clothes dummies. Hatton's reporter is working on the robbery, unaware that he is the counterpart of the most desperate criminal of the lot. He and Beery are rivals for the same girl, and Beery gets a job as waiter in the night club where she sells cigarettes. He mistakes the gunman for Hatton and knocks him cold, thereby winning the friendship and admiration of a rival master criminal, who hires him as a bodyguard.

That leads him into the lair of the gang just in time to get into the thick of the gangs' battle, into which also the reporter is led in his search for news. They are horrified witnesses of all kinds of bloodshed growing out of a dispute over $10,000 of stolen money, which first gets into Beery's hands and then into Hatton's, sudden death being the penalty to anybody holding the loot.

This situation is carried along with remarkable building up of comedy trick and dramatic incident. Melodrama is built up skilfully and then turned to a laugh, and the give-and-take thrill and laugh are a dizzy continuation. The sequences are packed with low comedy roars and the tear bomb finish is a panic.

A light romantic thread runs through picture without interfering with its real purpose, the idea being that the girl for whom the two comedians are fighting is really in love with the polite juvenile, but at the finish even the romantic subplot is drawn into the comedy situation of the two reunited lovers going into the hot clinch bathed in the synthetic tears, and the comedy effect is rather devastating.

Picture is made with all the theatrical trimmings of an elegant crook melodrama, with the sinister master crooks behaving with that exquisite poise that is the mark of the modern screen underworld drama, and the polished settings that go with the story type. All of which points and heightens the absurdity of the Hatton and Beery clowning. Even if the subtle satire of kidding the polite crook film is a bit fine for the generality of fans, there is enough of obvious horseplay to touch their funny-bones. Good, wholesome laugh session, bound to prosper on its own and due to the reputation of the comedy partners.

Rush.

THE BLUE DANUBE

Pathe release of a Ralph Block production for DeMille. Leatrice Joy starred, with Joseph Schildkraut and Nils Asther featured. Directed by Paul Sloane from John Farrow's story. At Strand, New York, week April 28. Running time, 67 minutes.

Marguerite	Leatrice Joy
Ludwig	Joseph Schildkraut
Erich	Nils Asther
Helen Boursch	Seena Owen
Herr Boursch	Albert Gran
Baron	Frank Reicher

Ordinary screen tale given some reason to stand above the daily change houses by the performances and names of Joseph Schildkraut and Leatrice Joy. Story, so close to the "Student Prince" type that the organist plays that score unconsciously, goes for Sweeney, as the audience is at least one reel ahead of the action all the way. Light business will mark its distribution path.

Productionally "Blue Danube" is a commendable effort, mixing up a few glass shots for the stretch toward exterior magnificence. Interiors are substantial, and the camera work on Miss Joy and Schildkraut is smooth.

Tale is simple enough, with Miss Joy as a tavern maid who falls for the military young baron (Asther). War is declared on the eve before their wedding days, and the wordless separation is brought about by the deformed and crippled violin maker (Schildkraut), secretly in love with Marguerite. A scheming uncle of the young baron forges a letter to a brewer in trying to arrange a match with the latter's daughter, the cripple intercepts Erich's real message to Marguerite, and it's not until after the latter marries the hunchback for spite that the lovers get together again. Erich returns the night of the wedding, the cripple gives up in despair, kills himself and all's well.

Not enough action or suspense to make this a standout release. The younger Schildkraut demonstrates his versatility as being able to play either juvenile or heavy and sustains his record as uniformly good on either end of a story. Nils Asther cameras too pretty as the dashing officer, while Miss Joy stands well the rigors of long closeups. Sloane, directing, has put one or two good bits in the running, but Albert Gran, to the front lately, has little to do in the cast.

Good-looking picture, but that's about all. Cast names may mean something to it, but short of hinting at being a sure draw.

Sid.

THAT CERTAIN THING

Columbia production and release, starring Viola Dana, with Ralph Graves featured. Story by Elmer Harris. Directed by Frank R. Capra. Titles by Al Boasberg. On double feature program at Tivoli, N. Y., April 18. Running time, 69 mins.

Maggie Kelly	Aggie Herring
Molly Kelly	Viola Dana
A. B. Charles, Sr.	Burr McIntosh
A. B. Charles, Jr.	Ralph Graves

Those who don't think the independents are trying to make good pictures had better take a look at "That Certain Thing." Here is an indie that gives A-1 entertainment. Especially in the neighborhoods.

The story holds up, even if a little old in general theme. But it is welded into a strong, laugh-comedy romance materially aided by Boasberg's titles. It's all about a poor girl who acquires a millionaire.

Directing is splendid and the work of the small cast immense. Both Miss Dana and Ralph Graves are exceptionally good.

Photographically and otherwise "That Certain Thing" will help Columbia. It's wholesome, full of fun, and has that touch of neighborhood kin that will make it acceptable anywhere.

Mark.

THE LITTLE SNOB

Warner Bros. production and release, starring May McAvoy. Directed by John Adolphi. Cast includes Robert Fraser, Alec Francis, John Miljan, Virginia Lee Corbin and Frances Lee. At Tivoli, N. Y., on double-feature program, April 12. Running time, 52 minutes.

Old gag about a poor gal being smitten by the upper crust bug to the extent of being ashamed of the old home bunch. The Warners have done this one well. It carries a strong little preachment on snobbery effectively worked out by May McAvoy working alongside of the Misses Corbin and Lee.

Coney Island starts off the action, where the snob is shown with her lover, a barker for concessions. The girl's dad is Col. Banks, who runs the Kentucky Derby, another Island concession, with wooden horses. The kunnel sends the daughter away to a "finishing" school, and the snobbery begins. The bursting of the ritzy fireworks comes when the poor girl's school pals declare her dad is dishonest, crooked and so on. There is, of course, a happy finale for the old crowd.

Light, airy film padded here and there. However, it has a moral. Some corking photography and splendid direction where the school parties are on. Work of Miss McAvoy stands out, as it's the kind of a role she dotes upon.

Mark.

Phantom of the Range

FBO production and release. Starring Tom Tyler. Directed by James Dugan from original by Frank Howard Clark. Cast includes Duan Thompson, Charles McHugh, Margaret Zier and Frankie Dorro. At Stanley, New York, one day, April 20. Running time, about 60 minutes.

Plenty of action in this better than average western that will more than please the kids in the neighborhood houses. The grown-up, too, will like it as the story is told with a directness that reflects credit on Director James Dugan. Only fault seems excess footage given to scenes in which Tom Tyler kayoes at least three men in order to save the poor ranchman from being swindled.

Plot has to do with Tyler as an actor, stranded in a tank town and forced back to his original occupation as a cowpuncher. Here the girl takes him in hand and proceeds to bring him to earth.

Leading lady of the stranded troupe, meanwhile, has allied herself with a real estate swindler bent on grabbing the farmer's land. She frames the actor-cowpuncher and he loses his jos, as well as the girl, granddaughter of the farmer. He returns in time to knock the realtor and three of his men cold in one of those parlor rough and tumbles, prevents the land grab and wins the girl.

Top Sergeant Mulligan

Morris R. Schlank production featuring Wesley Barry and Lila Lee. Story by Francis Fenton. Directed by James P. Hogan. At Loew's Circle, New York, as half double bill, one day, April 23. Running time 55 minutes.

Just another comedy on the war with Donald Keith playing the title role and Gareth Hughes in a minor part. Only good gag in the film has Barry as a recruit peppering his superior officers and Sergeant Mulligan continuously with buckshot propelled by his teeth and tongue.

Barry tagged with the gag monicker of Mickey Neilan is himself enlisted for service while out helping the recruiting officers with his vaude partner, Lila Lee. At the training camp he encounters topkick Mulligan who proceeds to make life miserable for the rookie.

On top of that the sergeant, Y. M. C. A. worker and the captain make a play for his girl.

In France Mulligan and Neilan are sent spy hunting and are captured with a labor unit after putting on cork. Taken to Berlin they get their man and bring him back after the war is over and get the bird from their buddies.

Meantime the girl the rookie has left behind with an entertainment outfit gets hitched to the "Y" worker.

Film doesn't measure up to comedies of the same type that have previously been seen and will help little to re-establish the freckled faced Barry as a draw.

Horseman of the Plains

Fox production and release starring Tom Mix. Directed by Benjamin Stoloff from story by Harry Sinclair Drago. Cameraman Dan Clarke. Cast includes Sally Blaine, Charles Conklin and Charles Byers. At Academy, New York, April 26-28. Running time 45 mins.

A western modernized in everything except plot. The plot is No. 666 about the family ranch that will be foreclosed unless the family nag wins the big race. But despite this hackneyed old yarn, the picture is entertaining.

Explanation of paradox: good direction.

Benjamin Stoloff has megaphoned life and breeze into the mortgage classic. The picture moves with zip and is distinctly better than the Tom Mix average for the last dozen or two.

Stoloff even has Tom acting like a romantic juvenile, going into clinches with the heroine. That in itself is sort of revolutionary. Heretofore Mix's screen romances have been Bostonian in their neuter gender purity. The final fadeout generally showed Thomas patting the girl on the arm with a look of sheer brotherliness.

A novelty too is the race, a combination affair started on foot, including laps in a chariot, hay wagon, speed car and ending with stage coaches.

Only 45 minutes in the running and something popping every second. Great for western fans.

Land.

PHANTOM FLYER

Universal production and release. Written and directed by Bruce Mitchell. Stars Al Wilson. Cast includes Lillian Gilmore, Don Fullen, Mary Cornwallis, Larry Steers, Buck Connors, Bill Jones, Myrtis Crinley. At the Columbus, N. Y., one day. Running time, 60 minutes.

It seems that a gang of rustlers were making off with the Crandall stock, and an aviator arrived, literally out of a clear sky, to save the gal and prevent the old man from losing the homestead. The flyer, Al Wilson, photographs nicely but looks a little clumsy in action because of his stocky build. Story has been built around the star's air stunts, which are okay but lack suspense. Girl looks good.

A little different from the usual small-town western on account of the air stuff. Should do all right in the same spots.

Mori.

THE APE

Collwyn production released through states rights. Directed by B. C. Rule. Claimed to be based on actual police record. In cast: Ruth Stonehouse, Gladys Walton, Basil Wilson, Bradley Barker. At Stanley, one day, April 16. Running time, 60 minutes.

Shot in the old Triangle Arts studio in Riverdale, "The Ape" is a little inferior in technique to the product which came out of Yonkers a decade ago. The story, a jumbled mess of cart before the horse detail, is brought to the screen with a school boy's appreciation for technicalities. Messed up with this is a cartload of the most explanatory titles. These take up half of the footage.

All kinds of hands that are played upon by a baby spot and figures that shadow themselves on window sills attempt to provide the mystery. The action confines itself to four sets with a fleeting shot of the Hudson. Foolish fights in the dark which, fortunately, will not cause an eye strain because of not the semblance of suspense, take up one-fourth of the running time. The thing is blah all the way.

It will go punk in every house except with the sure seaters delving into filmdom for exhibits from its bloomer days.

GYPSY OF THE NORTH

Rayart release, produced by Trem Carr. Directed by Scott Pembroke from story by Arthur Hoerl. Featuring Georgia Hale, with cast including Huntley Gordon and Jack Daugherty. At Loew's N. Y. Circle April 30, one-half of double feature program. Running time, 60 minutes.

It so happens that it was not Steve Farrell, the ruthless gambler, who shot and killed the tenderfoot for his stake, but the suave, oily owner of the mining town's only saloon. This revelation socks the heroine right in the pit of the stomach, to judge from the pained look in her eyes. The gal had left a starring role in a Broadway production to hunt down Steve, who, she thought, had killed her beloved brother.

This stirring drama of the frozen north is guaranteed to rouse the maximum yawning powers of any grown-up audience in towns over 10,000 population. Leading woman rather dull, though Huntley Gordon still photographs well and fills his role capably.

Title of the picture is derived from the name of the gal's Broadway show. When she hits the northern trail she calls herself the gypsy.

A couple of strong fight scenes, always in place in stirring dramas of the north, are missing.

Mori.

THUNDER RIDERS

Universal production and release. Directed by William Wyler from story by Basil Dickey and K. Krusada. Featuring Ted Wells, with cast including Peewee Holmes, Dick L'Estrange, Bill Dyer, Julia Griffith, Charlotte Stevens, William A. Steel and Leo White. At Loew's N. Y. Circle April 30. One-half of double feature program. Running time, over 45 minutes.

Another western of the usual quality intended for the usual spots. Attempt at comedy seems unsatisfactory though it may get over before an appreciative audience.

Story of the eastern heiress arriving on the ranch to take over her father's estate. Guardian and gang of cowboys stage phoney western atmosphere, but the gal is wise and acts up to it.

Finally, during the masquerade, the hero is locked up while the girl's eastern boy friend runs off with her to force a quick marriage. Much to everybody's surprise it appears that the blue-blooded Bostonian is an ex-convict.

Lots of wasted footage but a few well-staged fist fights.   *Mori.*

The Wild West Show

Universal production and release. Starring Hoot Gibson. Story by Del Andrew. In cast: Dorothy Sullivan, Allan Forest, Monte Montague. At Loew's New York one day, April 17, one-half of double feature. Running time, 55 minutes.

Hoot Gibson again dons woman's clothes. This time in "The Wild West Show" as the swift Bulgarian bareback rider.

A windstorm buckles the carnival tent just at a time when Hoot's rescue of the impoverished circus owner's daughter is opportune.

Circus receipts have been promoted by Cowboy Gibson's rally among the neighbors for the little aerial girl, played by Dot Sullivan. A heavy in the show confiscates the money and plants Hoot with the empty money sacks. Justice asserts itself in finding the ready cash in the pockets of the guy who would cop not only the daughter but also the entire show.

One of the keen cutters of this picture is the cock-eyed knife-throwing sequence in which a visually impaired dame chucks butcher knives around Hoot's ears and arms.

Taken from the first reel, the picture is one which Hoot may count on with all of his followers.

Cruise of the Speejacks

Paramount release. Written, directed and produced under the supervision of A. Y. Gowen. At the 5th Ave. Playhouse, N. Y. Running time, 75 mins.

Picture is nothing but a long scenic covering a 40,000-mile honeymoon cruise around the world made by A. Y. Gowen, an American millionaire, in a 90-foot boat called Speejacks.

Film evidently made many years ago and finally taken off the shelves for a try in this "art" house. Painfully uninteresting despite the subtitles attempting to throw adventure into the usual travelog shots.

In addition, picture has not been properly cut and edited.

At best could only serve as a two-reeler. Route is through the Panama Canal across the Pacific, through Asia and Europe and back to America.

Might have been interesting but the shots taken were what the amateur producers thought interesting and unusual, resulting in the filming of everything that has been seen before, and since.   *Mori.*

WON IN THE CLOUDS

Universal production and release. Starring Al Wilson. Directed by Mitchell Bruce from story by Otis Turner. William S. Adams, cameraman. In the cast: Helen Foster, George French, Myrtis Crinley, Joe Bennett. At the Tivoli one day, April 14; one-half of double bill. Running time, 45 minutes.

"Won in the Clouds" is a little better than the average in this class called by Universal "Thrill Series." This one, with Universal City and a part of Burbank converted into an African jungle, is a direct reminder of "The Perils of Pauline" kind.

Al Wilson's stuff is the same as in his predecessors. One wallop from his fist is all that is necessary to lay out an opponent. The same kind of a battle in mid-air on the wing of his plane that he staged in "The Phantom Rider" is to be seen in "Won in the Clouds."

Considerable footage is devoted to titles. They tell about a diamond mine owned by Al's father and about the treacherous foreman who would run away with Al's girl and crab the works in general.

Constant use of horses in chasing planes back and forth from the mine to the savages' hangout.

Diversion when Al rests up at either place to exercise his mitt.

GERMAN PICTURES

(ALL GERMAN MADE)

Berlin, April 15.

THE WORLD WAR (Part II)

The Ufa picture treats of 1915-16, in other words from the beginning of the trench warfare in France to the turn of the tide against Germany. A further part will show Germany's defeat and the founding of the republic.

It is undoubtedly an improvement on Part I, as most of it is studio or directed shots and the actual war scenes are cleverly fitted in. Also the animated maps are technically better done and make the battles tactically easily understandable.

But the picture has still as little interest for other countries as did the first. With all its attempt to be objective it is still naturally out of the question that the German side should not be taken.

Even here in Germany the picture has not gone over as expected, for the simple reason it is a compromise, not anti-militaristic enough for the pacifists and not patriotic enough for the fire eaters.

SPIONE ("SPIES")

Fritz Lang's "Metropolis" being admitted a financial failure, he has gone back to the style of his early success, "Dr. Mabuse." He has gone back so thoroughly one might almost believe that his wife, Thea von Harbou, had made a direct copy of the former scenario by Norbert Jaques.

Here again is a mysterious criminal, the head of a fantastically large band of crooks. At the end he is again captured after a monumental struggle with the police.

The trick in these affairs is to make the audience believe in all the monstrosities—if they once doubt, it turns from suspense to comedy.

Lang's direction was in nowise extraordinary. Klein-Rogge, as the leading crook, was flat and thin. Willi Fritsch, Gerda Maurus and Lien Deyers were pleasing, but they could not make up for the boring surroundings.

DONNA JUANA

Elisabeth Bergner, Germany's most successful stage star, is still trying to express herself in pictures and has not yet succeeded.

This comedy taken from an old Spanish play is but partially acceptable.

Miss Berger plays a young girl who, in order to win her lover, disguises herself as a boy in tights. For those who know her on the stage there are moments where her charm crashes through, but for the general public these must be very few and far between.

When will Miss Berger decide to let Paul Czinner select a really first rate director?

QUEEN LOUISE

Terra picture, great stuff for the German public and will show a nice profit on the Reich alone.

This queen who made the shoes famous is the favorite German historical figure with this the first attempt to put her into pictures.

Her life was not particularly dramatic but how they love to see her running around a la Lillian Gish in her empire style robes.

The film is tastefully enough directed and Mady Christians in looks does all honor to her Queen Quality.

DER ALTE FRITZ
("The Old Fritz")

A sincere attempt to present Frederick the Great as he really was in his latter days. Nothing of the crotchety sardonic old man is left out. And Otto Gebuehr plays him with real subtlety and power.

The director, Gerhardt Lamprecht, deserves a credit mark for taste and ability.

As little interesting for Americans as a Washington or Lincoln picture for Germans.

SCHULDIG ("GUILTY")

Good competent program material.

A man released from life imprisonment, to which he has been unjustly sentenced, finds his wife has become the mistress of a dance and opium dive keeper. In order not to interfere with his wife's supposed happiness, he takes a position in the same restaurant and is not recognized, owing to the change wrought in jail.

The dive owner is getting tired of the wife and considering going after the daughter, also working there. He has succeeded in making a dope fiend of the wife and is only stopped from seducing the girl by the husband who kills him.

This time the husband is guilty but aquitted.

Johannes Mayer proves that he has learned a lot from America. Suzi Vernon, Willi Fritsch and Hans von Schlettow are all up to their roles.

FRAU SORGE ("DAME CARE")

An excellent picturization of the famous Sudermann novel by the German First National.

Director Robert Land follows up the good work he did in "Primanerliebe" and shows himself an international comer. Wilhelm Dieterle and Grete Mosheim are excellent in their roles, and Fritz Kortner, as the father, gives a masterly performance. There isn't any better picture acting being done anywhere in the world today.

Mary Carr, from America, starred here in the title role. She is always good and here delivers her usual fine performance. But Miss Carr is not a particularly good type for this role. Several low salaried German performers could have done as well with it. And her name won't get it beyond the American "art" theatres anyhow.

ALRAUNE

Titilation for the gooseflesh. All the horrors of "Metropolis" and quite a lot more concentrated into one short fillum.

Hans Heinz Ewers, scenario writer, makes Edgar Allan Poe look like an amateur.

A coldblooded doctor brings to life a child, the daughter of a hanged criminal and a prostitute, in a fashion which cannot be printed, even if screened.

When the girl grows up, he falls for her, but she learns what he had done to her and gives him the very coldest of shoulders. He expires in the gutter, the dirty dog.

Heinrich Galeen squeezes all the horror juice out of it, and Brigitte Helm, the vamp, is at least 200 per cent. When will some American director take a look at this extraordinarily fascinating girl. She has an individuality of her own.
    Trask.

THE BIG NOISE

Robert Kane production, released by First National. Alan Dwan direction. Chester Conklin featured. No other credits given on program or screen this week at Strand, New York. All slides, if any, but title and Dwan as director removed, picture going direct from the second Dwan slide into the action. Other names in cast susceptible of featuring are Alice White, Sam Hardy and David Torrance.

John Sloval................Chester Conklin
Sophie Sloval....................Alice White
Ma Sloval......................Bodil Rosing
Philip Hurd......................Sam Hardy
Bill Hedges........................Jack Egan
William Howard..............Ned Sparks
Managing Editor.............David Torrance

A corking comedy on the screen and would have been a great film laugh maker all of the way had not the comedy end turned flat toward the finish. Previously, however, there had been enough laughs, some howls, and continuously, to stamp this as a crackerjack program comedy that any exhib can go the limit on in saying it holds plenty of fun.

Despite it has Chester Conklin, there's no outward hoke. That and the gags are smoothly slipped in and all go with the story. It is the story that forces the paleness after about two-thirds of the run, as the logical tale must be logically carried to a finale.

There isn't a newspaperman anywhere who won't enjoy this picture. Whether it's a slap or burlesque on a tabloid daily's methods, or a sort of satirical dreamland idea of bringing a boob into the limelight, to let him sink back into the darkness of the tenement, it's fine either way. There is much sublety to it all of the while. Mr. Conklin's playing is no small part of this.

A Coney Island scene, not lengthy, is made funnier than any of the other comedy bits from the freak rackets of the merrygorounds, while there is a scene that will be a howl for the arty groups where Conklin, in a hospital bed but not sick, is prevented from speaking to his wife nor can she speak to him.

And the daily tab that used Conklin's subway worker as a mark for its mayorality candidate is a constant laugh for the posings and flashlights. Captions break in every so often and as strong points. When the daily, after Conklin had fallen off the subway platform and nearly run over by a train but not hurt, going to a hospital because he was sleepy, went to Conklin's home to get the big story complete, the reporters found the wife had but a grown up daughter.

So they sent for the kids in the tenement and had a group picture taken, the kids bawling "We want our Daddy," with the mother in the centre. When Conklin saw the picture in the paper, he rubbed his head, saying to a nurse, "How long have I been here?"

Bodil Rosing does the mother nicely and Alice White is a flippant kid (daughter) who does one of the best bits of comedy business seen on the screen in a long time, when she is kicking the door while being kissed. Other roles are far below in importance but all well cast.

Production excellent for a comedy and looks expensive. Extras are used in profusion.

For a good laugh, see "The Big Noise."

At the Strand all billing slides on the picture were taken off, if there. Only two credit slides, name of picture and another solely devoted to Allan Dwan as director. Nor did the program furnish any more information, excepting the cast.

Through no credits having been displayed on the screen when "The Big Noise" recently played the Strand on Broadway, credits were omitted in Variety's review.

Ben Hecht wrote the story as an original comedy satire. Tom Geraghty adapted it for the screen, as produced by Robert T. Kane for First National, with Allan Dwan the director.

THE ORCHID DANCER

(FRENCH MADE)

Paris, April 29.

This is the picture Ricardo Cortez came to France for, giving rise to a grouch in some of the trade press on account of an alleged exorbitant salary paid a foreign performer. Since "La Danseuse Orchidee" has been produced by Leonce Perret this pecuniary criticism has been dropped. It's probably the finest work Perret has done, and much of the success is due to the acting of Cortez.

Adapted from a novel by J. J. Renaud, the romantic scenario has a cast of Cortez, Xenia Desni, the Russian operetta actress; Louise Legrange, French picture comedienne in the title role, and Gaston Jacquet, local star.

The plot is of Luicha, supposed to be earning her living as a governess in Paris, who returns to her native village in the Pyranees for a vacation. Yoanes (Cortez), her childhood friend, resumes his former affection which flares into a passionate love. He asks her to become his wife, but the girl only promises her answer another day. Following morning Yoanes learns that Luicha has left the village, and he follows her to Paris. There he discovers his sweetheart is the celebrated dancer surnamed The Orchid, the mistress of a wealthy wine merchant.

Yoanes meets Luicha and rushes away in despair. Intending to emigrate, just as the boat is sailing he goes ashore, thus becomes stranded, having left his baggage and money on board. Yoanes wanders to Paris and gets a job as a dancer in a fashionable resort until sacked. His next situation is as a super in a picture studio of Franco Film Co., where he is introduced by Marise (Xenia Desni), the leading lady, whose acquaintance he made at the dancing resort. He becomes known as a cinema actor under the name of Jean Barliave, and happy with Marise, to whom he owes so much for his rapid progress, until chance leads Luicha to the studio, where the couple meet again.

The Orchid dancer has quit her champagne dealer, has an engagement at the local Eldorado, and Yoanes there visits her.

During the performance a fire breaks out in the theatre, Yoanes (present in the audience) saving the dancer. However, he is badly burned, and is nursed by Marise during Luicha's absence, who is obliged to leave for London to fulfill an engagement. During his illness Yoanes continually calls for Luicha. Marise reads some letters, realizes he will never care for her other than as a friend, so she disappears when the Orchid Dancer returns.

The story, on the lines of a best seller, is a little too drawn out, but there are thrills. The fire in the theatre is realistically depicted.

An excellent French picture.

Kendrew.

HONOR BOUND

Fox production and release. Directed by Alfred E. Green. From the story by Jack Bethen. Features George O'Brien and Estelle Taylor. At Roxy, New York, week April 29. Running time, over 60 minutes.

John Ogletree.............George O'Brien
Evelyn Mortimer............Estelle Taylor
Selma Ritchie.....................Leila Hyams
Mr. Mortimer.....................Tom Santchi
Dr. Ritchie......................Frank Cooley
Blood Keller..................Sam DeGrasse
Gid Ames..............................Al Hart
Skip Collier.......................Harry Gripp

A slow-moving, uninteresting story without color that allows of little for anyone or anything. Can't rate a better classification than filler, unless, of course, the names of George O'Brien and Estelle Taylor are poignant enough to stand off the dullness.

Miss Taylor is excellent in the picture, carrying the burden of the real playing, and doing that well, as she always does when actually acting. Her single action portion was a whipping scene at the finish. She flung the whip or rope with precision. Leila Hyams made a sweet-looking nurse and giving a considerable quantity of expression to her continuous compassion for the mistreated hero.

Mr. O'Brien as that self-same mistreated one isn't so nifty here, in appearance or work; he's held down by the story. But O'Brien or someone else never should have permitted him to come through a bad fire scene with an exceptionally clean face and a cleaner shirt. It's not the sort of a picture for this extremely well-built and attractive young man. O'Brien looks 150 per cent all man, and it's an error to have him hide that.

Tom Santchi gave a nice performance as the mine owner and Harry Gripp as a prison trusty and stool made up to look it exactly.

The story also limited direction, with Alfred E. Green doing well enough there when opportunity presented, such as the lashing scenes. A miniature fire not so good. Photography at times fetching, in the close-ups especially of the busts, but at other times nothing to mention.

Opens with a scene in O'Brien's bedroom after midnight. Enters the woman who wants to flee with the young man because she can't stand her husband's brutality. Hubby enters next, punches the hero to the floor and is killed in the scuffle with his wife.

The boy takes the prison slap in preference to implicating the woman, who later marries wealthy operator of a coal mine run with prison help. She imports O'Brien from another prison to be her chauffeur. Suspicions of the second husband are aroused, and he has O'Brien sent into the mines to dig coal.

A convict nut finally sets fire to the jail. O'Brien's innocence is established and he and the nurse mix.

FLIGHT COMMANDER

(BRITISH MADE)

Montreal, May 6.

British production directed by Maurice Elvey. Cast includes Sir Alan Cobham, Estelle Brody and John Stuart. Running time 75 minutes. At the Capitol, Montreal, week May 5.

Advertised as "not a war picture," it is not a flying picture either except for a few feet of planes at the start and finish. Otherwise it is a meller of the most pronounced type with the name of Sir Alan Cobham to weight it. A few closeups only of the latter, and, while his name carries in British countries, he would not be much of a drawing card elsewhere.

Plot shows daughter of missionary in Chinese territory just married to elderly merchant immediately after arrival of merchant's assistant who is brought by Sir Alan in person to the station. Assistant and she fall in love at first sight and she divulges her share of it to her husband when the natives, having arisen against the Europeans owing to the machinations of the usual communist, capture her lover.

Hubby swallows this unpleasant morsel in strong silent man fashion which used to be popular a score of years ago, goes out to search for him, walks right through armed natives, shoots up their leader and the communist, and wirelesses for relief. He is shot several times in the process, sometimes at a distance of inches, but gets his message through before he topples over dead.

Planes arrive, save the station and presumably all ends happily for the lovers.

John Stuart as the lover was billed in "Roses of Picardy" as the "darling of the Empire." He is a joke on this side. When he walks up and down with chin sunk on manly bosom registering grief and renunciation, all he gets from the audience is a laugh. He is fighting desperately all through the picture and it must be at least four times he is shown with three or four coolies clinging to his limbs, with a fifth taking a flying leap at his neck. Even coolies, armed with rifles, aren't so dumb that they wouldn't shoot in preference to taking socks on the jaw for the amusement of movie fans. He wears lovely white pants with a perfect crease throughout these encounters, and the pants look nearly as smart in the final closeups as they were when he was best man at the wedding before the scrap began. These are minor points but they tell like the devil in ruining any illusion of real action.

Estelle Brody as the heroine is no rave. There isn't much subtlety in her acting and if the captions didn't tell what she was doing you would hardly guess it. She tells her husband she will make him a good wife, despite her love for the other man, and then does little else during the fighting but moan "John! John!" which of course is not her husband's first name. When John at last turns up, she clings round his neck while hubby is pulling the hero stuff and incidentally committing suicide to save her and the rest of the party.

A quantity of comic relief with an American, English and French sailor trio and a maid. They all love each other and the girl about equally, but naturally she picks the Britisher in the finish.

No kick on that in a British picture, but all this material is little more than padding. The fighting is another flop. Every now and again coolies and Europeans rush across the garden firing at each other at point blank range and without cover. Result: garden full of dead coolies while Europeans are unhurt.

After the third encore of this, house starts to laugh. Practically no suspense anywhere in the picture.

Doubtless there are good British made pictures, but this isn't one of them.

UNDER BLACK EAGLE

Metro-Goldwyn-Mayer production and release. Directed by W. S. Van Dyke. Dog actor "Flash" featured in billing. Ralph Forbes and Marceline Day head cast. Titles by Madeleine Ruth. Original story by Norma Houston; screen play by Bradley King. Running time 50 minutes. At Loew's American, New York, April 30-May 2.

Many elements against picture. Story is sympathetic treatment of German side of the war; hero is a pacifist in substance, even if he does rise to heroism at the last, and most of the dramatic interest of the story has been thrown to the dog "Flash." It is doubtful if the majority of the fans will react favorably to any or all of these angles.

Even if the details mentioned do not raise direct opposition in the minds of an American audience, they do complicate a simple and straightforward dramatic story. A hero beset with conflicting emotions such as love of girl and horror of war is lacking in aggressive appeal. Of course, a hero who conquers dread and fear is much more the hero than the man who is naturally brave and does not have to fight down his own terror before he can accomplish heroic deeds, but that intricate situation is not easy to express in black and white celluloid. This hero is altogether too much a composite to be accepted wholly as a hero. There is always a doubt of his character.

The dog "Flash" is the more ad-

mirable character and a remarkably good actor too. The sequences involving this pup are fine, so fine indeed that they shadow the roles of the humans. Some splendid shots of the animal in comedy bits, such as his bored indifference at the love making of the romantic leads and his quizzical inspection of hero's painting of the heroine, with head cocked to one side and an expression for all the world like critical uncertainty. The dog does all a dog can do to carry the picture and interest in his exploits measures the value of the release. Great for dog lovers; for the generality of fans, not so hot.

Technical production is fine and war sequences of which there are a great deal are excellent. Big mass effects of marching soldiers have been well managed and some of the scenic shots are of the best. Scenario has great resource in contriving situations, but the subject matter of the romance itself reacts against highest interest.

Salable subject for the neighborhoods and fine for the younger element which will take the swift action for full value and remain unconscious of the details that distract. For a sophisticated clientele picture will be just a film. *Rush.*

EASY COME, EASY GO

Paramount production and release, starring Richard Dix and featuring Nancy Carroll. Adapted from Owen Davis' play of the same name, with scenario by Florence Ryerson. George Marion, Jr., titled, and Edward Cronjager, cameraman. Directed by Frank Tuttle. At Paramount, New York, week May 5. Running time, about 65 minutes.

Robert Parker................Richard Dix
Barbara Quayle..............Nancy Carroll
Jim Bailey....................Charles Sellon
Mr. Quayle....................Frank Currier
Winthrop.......................Arnold Kent

Fair program comedy that won't burn up records, but holds sufficient entertainment to warrant average trade within those emporiums which it will play. Picture has its high and low spots, the trouble being too much distance between those points.

Studio has taken its liberties with the original play script, but warrants the license through some excellent pieces of business. Marion's titles are in keeping with the general pace, spasmodic, with Richard Dix cast as a radio announcer fired by his father or profanity and never overcoming the habit. Circumstances make him the innocent accomplice of an elderly bank crook, which sponsors a lot of laughs in a smoking room scene on a train.

Action gets into a sanitarium, where the president of the bank, which the old man has robbed, and his daughter have gone for a few days, and the crook is also forced to go for protection. Then starts Dix's attempt to return the missing pay roll with the comedy culprit spreading the information that the young man suffers from a delusion of telling people they've been robbed. It terminates as the detectives catch the old man and Dix gets the girl.

Dix does well by the role and can't be blamed if the feature is overlong. Miss Carroll, hitting Broadway for the first time in "Abie's Irish Rose," continues to appear a corking screen bet if somewhat at a loss at times in th's picture. Charles Sellon as the light-fingered Bailey is the comedy fulcrum, and Frank Currier, cast as the girl's father, is also prominent on performance.

Picture lacks nothing productionally and has enough spontaneous laughs to see it through the big houses. But careful scissoring should make it a better and faster comedy than it is running here.

Sid.

ADVENTURE MAD
(GERMAN MADE)

Ufa production released by Paramount. Directed by Lothar Mendes. No featured players. Story by Robert Liebman. Cameraman, Fritz Wagner. Cast includes Nils Asther, Eric Barclay, Nina Vanning, Lillian Hall-Davis, Paul Graetz. At Loew's New York, one day, May 4, on double bill. Running time, 65 mins.

Introduced to Broadway via the double-header route, this Ufa picture is a peculiar blending of Hollywood and Berlin technique. It is better than the average German films playing the "art" houses, but in no wise comparable to the Ufa's that have been handled by the big companies heretofore. Paramount's name and trade-mark appear on the main title, but inconspicuously, the German label being prominent.

Story is ridiculous. The situation is of a tremendously wealthy and tremendously bored English nobleman residing in his Italian villa and surrounded by clocks, a mania. The nob's chief clockmaker is a villain who has read a book on the uses of cuckoo clocks in crime. With the Englishman half crazy from the tediousness of his existence, the clockmaker plans to hypnotize him and get the combination of the vault in which is kept vast treasure trove. The fantastic conspiracy takes all hands to Cairo and thereby gives the film its chief interest to Americans because of the unusual background.

Lothar Mendes, now with Paramount, directed this one, and did as well as could be expected in view of the unbelievable yarn. Cast contains several faces that may be fairly familiar to American fans, particularly the disciples of the "art" idea. Nils Asther is now with United Artists.

Picture not without some interest. The plot, at least, is not hackneyed and the foreign settings and touches help. Photography is pretty good. Paramount should be able to peddle it to the smaller houses for short engagements. *Land.*

THE ESCAPE

Fox production and release. Featuring Virginia Valli, Nancy Drexel and George Meeker. Adapted by Paul Schofield from Paul Armstrong's play. Directed by Richard Rosson. Cameraman, Kenneth Hawks. At Roxy, New York, week May 5. Running time, 58 minutes.

Jerry Magee................William Russell
May Joyce....................Virginia Valli
Jennie Joyce..................Nancy Drexel
Dr. Don Elliott.............George Meeker
Trigger Caswell.........William Demarest
Jim Joyce....................James Gordon

Another picture reminiscent of "Broadway," and pretty dull from the standpoint of habitual moviegoers. In the provinces, neighborhoods and minor rialtos they may easily find it an absorbing cinema. The scenes down cellar beneath the night club where a drunken chemist manufactures pre-war rye and blows cubweb dust on the bottle while the hard-boiled customer upstairs waits is apt to pack a great thrill for the burgs.

Some years ago Lambert Hillyer made a picture with similar scenes showing a bootlegger mixing up a tub of hootch with a dirty broom. Because of this and other things in the picture calculated to make the prohibitionists chirp, the picture breezed by the censor boards with several risque scenes untouched. Not that there's any risque stuff in "The Escape," but simply as an illustration that these touches are great for the tight belts.

The story starts out interestingly. A young doctor riding the rumble seat of a Bellevue ambulance meets a girl in the slums and a friendship is formed. The doctor meanwhile has been hitting the booze. He is kicked out of the hospital when caught by one of the staff surgeons. Discouraged and disgraced the young doc goes to the dogs and is mixing the booze for a gunman's night club when the girl of the slums, now a cafe hostess, discovers him.

That's about all except that the girl has a younger sister, something of a nitwit, who is running around with Trigger Caswell, a tough customer. A gun fight in the night club on New Years' Eve kills off all the bad boys and the young doc, now sobered up, the hostess and the kid sister blow the joint just as the cops break in. Fade out on the sun, title reading "Escape," and pointing the moral and the story's title; escape from environment.

Production and direction are fair, photography okay, acting ditto. George Meeker, featured, is a blonde young leading man being groomed by Fox. He's a distinctive type and not a bad trouper. Nancy Drexel, also given billing, is one of the new crop of pretty babes. William Demarest, ex-vaudevillian, who has graced the Warner pictures chiefly, appears in this Fox opus with a mustache.

"The Escape" will probably be an in-betweener. *Land.*

WOMEN WHO DARE

Sam Zieler Excellent production for state's righters. Featuring Helene Chadwick. Directed by Burton King. Story by Langdon McCormick. Adapted by Adrian Johnson. Cameraman, Art Reeves. Cast includes Charles Delaney, Jack Richardson, Grace Elliott, Frank Beale, Henry Barrows. At Loew's New York one day, May 4, on double feature bill. Running time, 62 mins.

"Excellent" pictures, three years on the market, have during the past season been turning out some crackerjack features, with the trade growing conscious of a new independent with some pretentions to class. "Women Who Dare" is not one of the best this comparatively unknown company has turned out. Particularly in the last reel is it below standard. Nevertheless it is pretty good, told nicely, and deserving of exhibitor consideration. Its presence on a double bill in a New York daily change grind should speak only for New York.

The story is of a rich girl doing charity work in the slums. Her father is an extensive owner of tenement properties but blind to conditions in them. He is one of the sheltered Brahmins who leaves everything to his renting agent. The hero is a self-centered young millionaire. The girl ultimately brings the boys around to her way of thinking.

The end suddenly brings in Chinatown cellar dives with sliding panels, a queen of the underworld, a king who is polygamous, and the w. k. fight for maidenly virtue. That's the baloney in an otherwise tasty stew.

Production okay all the way. Direction and acting ditto. *Land.*

Turn Back the Hours

Sam Sax-Gotham production released through Lumas. Directed by Howard Bretherton from story credited to stage play by Edward E. Rose. Norbert Brodin, cameraman. In cast: Walter Pidgeon, Myrna Loy, Sam Hardy, Josef Swickard, Sheldon Lewis, George E. Stone. At the Stanley, one day, May 5. Running time, 60 minutes.

A gaucho atmosphere of an independent order pervades "Turn Back the Hours." At the same time the hopeless effort to make the theme "original" results in Shakespear's Juliet reversing positions with Romeo and after climbing the trelis, exclaiming: "I'll do it. I always wanted to shave someone."

Thereupon Myrna Loy, as the beautifully gowned senorita in a gorgeously appointed homestead on a midocean island of bad men, plasters the bristles which Walter Pidgeon acquired before the aggressive heroine had pulled him in the waters. Pidgeon's acquaintance with the deep came after the navy had shorn him of his ensign's buttons because of cowardice.

Of course, the coward winds up as the hero, but not until after a Mussolini of the island, who parades around like Fairbanks did in "The Gaucho" on a set closely resembling one of the street scenes in the U. A. picture, has many opportunities before the camera.

In storming the home a lot of shots are fired aimlessly. So many attempts to inject comedy are made that the picture, with the exceptions of the opening and closing footage, appeals more as a burlesque on a meller.

A naval destroyer arriving at the last minute gets the best audience reaction. The commander who discharged Pidgeon salutes him as a comrade and the girl, at last positive that he is a hero, embraces him to the fade-out.

You Can't Beat the Law

Trem Carr production, released by Rayart. Directed by Scott Pembroke. Story by H. H. Van Loan. In cast: Lila Lee, Cornelius Keefe, Betty Francisco, Warner Richmond. At Arena, New York, one day, May 8. Running time, 60 minutes.

Good underworld story in which the copper is glorified and the crooks who laugh at signs bearing the flicker's title come to no good end. Heart interest is supplied by having the cop in love with the innocent sister of the gun mob's leader. One weakness in film is that the uniformed policeman does considerable sleuthing.

Plot revolves about Cornelius Keefe as a cop who had been run down by a gang of crooks making a getaway in a speeding car following a jewelry store stick-up. Discharged from the hospital, he gets permission to tail the mob that has been pulling a series of jewelry store jobs, believing it to be the same that nearly knocked him off.

In a cabaret he meets one of the ladies of the mob who unwittingly tips him off to the gang's hangout. Before going to make the pinch, J. Keefe calls on his sweetheart (Lila Lee), and shows here a photo of Warner Richmond as the leader of the gang he is tracking down.

Lila recognizes the rogues gallery picture as that of her brother, and pleads with the cop to go easy on him. Torn beetween love and duty, he decides on duty. Lila goes to warn her brother that he is in danger. They'll like this one in daily change houses, if they like action and gunplay.

BLONDE BY CHOICE

Gotham production released by Lumas. Starring Claire Windsor. Directed by Hampton Del Ruth from a story by Josephine Quirk. Clarence Hennecke screen credited for "comedy construction." Titles by Paul Perez. Cameraman, Ray June. Don Diggins assistant director. Cast includes Allan Simpson, Walter Hiers, Bes Flowers, Louise Carver, Leigh Willard. At the Arena, New York, one day, May 2, on double feature bill. Running time, 53 mins.

A trifle silly and not helped by the artificially added "comedy construction" of Clarence Hennecke. Walter Hiers was shoved into the middle of this picture and apparently told: "Get funny." One of the comedy gags on board a yacht has Hiers absent-mindedly pulling off a woman's skirt to use as the black cloth for a camera. Which tells everything.

Picture will get by in the remote neighborhoods. It is far below the average of previous Gotham pictures in which Claire Windsor has been starred. She needs comedy dramas.

The story of "Blondes" refers to a young woman with a progressive beauty salon in a dead hick town and of the young millionaire that comes into her life. There is no substance to the story and the effort to convert it into farce is rather disastrous. *Land.*

ARIZONA CYCLONE

Universal production and release, featuring Fred Humes. Story by William Lester. Directed by Edgar Lewis. At the Circle, New York, May 7, as half of double bill. Running time, 50 mins.

Not a redeeming feature to this flicker. It looks as if those responsible started out to make a western comedy, changed their minds, attempted melodrama and finally succeeded in producing something for the daily grinds that is just so many reels. Story is weak, direction ditto. Subtitles and comedy worse than that.

Humes plays a double role—Larry Martin, foreman of the dear old Triple X ranch, and his cousin Tom, the stick-up man known as the Arizona Cyclone. The Cyclone, Larry's double, plans to grab off 18 grand in cash that Larry's employer has in the ranch house. Larry is lured to town and Tom goes back to the ranch to lift the dough. When the ranchman discovers that Tom is not Larry, just as his daughter, Kathleen (Margaret Gray) had previously learned, the battle is on. Larry, however, escapes his captors, the Cyclone's confederates, and returns to the ranch in time to save the money and win the girl.

Just one of those things that mean nothing, even as the minor portion of a double bill.

Phantom of the Turf

Duke Worne Superior production, distributed through Rayart. Directed by Duke Worne from story by Leata Morgan. In cast: Helene Costello, Rex Lease, Forrest Stanley. At Loew's New York, one day, May 2, as half double bill. Running time, about 60 minutes.

A rich old man of mystery dies, apparently a suicide. His good young friend is made administrator with instructions to dig up an unknown daughter and son and make them his beneficiaries. It is obvious right off the bat the administrator is a crafty young man and that the lawyer who gives him the legal dope knows more than he reveals.

Anyhow, this is how Duke Worne launches into a story which smells a little of the stable but concentrates on mystery, double-crossing among gentlemen crooks, love, and finally—the horse race.

Not a bad program picture; in fact, one of the best Worne has turned out. Should register as big in houses that have shown Worne product.

RAMONA

United Artists' release of an Inspiration and Edwin Carewe joint production. Dolores Del Rio starred. Adapted by Finis Fox from Helen Hunt Jackson's 50-year-old novel. Cameraman, Robert Kundle. At the Rivoli, New York, May 12 for a grind run. Running time, 78 minutes.

Ramona....................Dolores Del Rio
Alessandro....................Warner Baxter
Felipe....................Roland Drew
Senora Moreno....................Vera Lewis
Juan Canito....................Michael Visaroff
Father Salvierderra..........John J. Prince
Marda....................Mathilda Comont
Sheep Herder....................Carlos Amor
Bandit Leader....................Jess Cavin

"Ramona," the novel, is in its 92d printing. "Ramona," the ballad, is one of the spring's outstanding song hits. Those two tie-ups are valuable for "Ramona," the picture. As a screen story, as drama, spectacle or entertainment the film is weak. But with the background, the popularity of the novel, the probable drawing power of Miss Del Rio, the class production and the publicity impetus of the song, it will doubtlessly be a winner both for U. A. and the exhibs.

The picture has important sales points, strong exploitation angles and has been given a special campaign by Inspiration which probably realized the picture had to be built up to get across.

Trouble with the story is that there is almost none in a pictorial sense. It takes a full half hour to establish the characters, and about the only action is when Ramona defies her guardian, the stern Senora Moreno, to elope with Alessandro, the Indian sheep shearer. Thereafter Ramona is seen for a brief sequence happy with her lover and their babe. This quickly passes and a series of drab tragedies ensue. The Indian villagers are massacred by outlaws, the baby dies because the white doctor will not treat an Indian, Alessandro is accused of horse stealing and is murdered in cold blood, and Ramona goes wandering in the swamp, her mind a blank. Finale has the girl restored to her white foster-brother, regaining her memory and everybody smiling but without arousing at any moment anything gripping or tense.

Carewe has sneaked in a little heat in the scene where Ramona and the Indian spend their bridal night, and Miss Del Rio was eloquent in this sequence. She overacts markedly throughout with the closeups as numerous as the deaths in the picture.

At the start the continuous episodes to illustrate her girlishness are a bit tedious. Too obvious that director, scenarist, cameraman, sales department, and everybody else were more anxious to build up Dolores than the story.

Warner Baxter, trying to look and act like an Indian, does well enough and certainly makes a better brave than Dix and some of the other Hollywood male leads who have attempted bronze skinned interpretations. Baxter has a symmetrical build and shows up well in a couple of costumes from thighs to the waist. Alessandro was probably the only Indian of his time with a vaccination mark.

Roland Drew, a new young lead, is the white foster brother. He is mustached, marceled and soft-eyed, more apt to appeal to women than men. However, he acquits himself capably.

Picture is packed with great scenery, some monastery stuff being included to capture the spirit of the novel. Camera work, credited to Robert Kundle, is excellent and a substantial percentage of the merit in the picture. One or two giggles, but essentially it's a somber, straightaway narrative, draggy in the telling although interesting in the color derived from the background.

Importance of the song in helping the picture is pronounced. It is scored almost entirely by this melody. At the Rivoli a phonograph device broadcasts the tune to passersby. It is the first case of a picture having a song of familiar title break in advance.

The song is just getting into its full stride as the film goes after its quota. That's not an accidental break, but a smart showmanly stunt worked out by Inspiration.

"Ramona" will make money.

Land.

KENTUCKY COURAGE

Alfred Santell production for First National. Screen version of the John Fox, Jr., novel, "The Little Shepherd of Kingdom Come," Richard Barthelmess starred. Titles by D. Wuelle Bentham and Rufus McCosh credited with titles. At Strand, New York, week May 12. Running time, 72 minutes.

Chad Buford..........Richard Barthelmess
Melissa Turner................Molly O'Day
Old Joel Turner...........Nelson McDowell
Maw Turner................Martha Mattox
Tom Turner....................Victor Potel
Dolph Turner..............Mark Hamilton
Caleb Hazel..................Wm. Bertram
Old Tad Dillon................Walter Lewis
Daws Dillon................Gardner James
Tad Dillon....................Ralph Yearsley
Nathan Cherry......Gustav von Seyffertitz
Jack, the dog.................................Buck
Major Buford..........Claude Gillingwater
General Dean.............David Torrence
Mrs. Dean.....................Eulalie Jensen
Margaret Dean..............Doris Dawson
General Grant...............Walter Rogers

Not a happy screening of the novel that was a best seller. The picture never once gets under the skin of its characters. Whole sentimental feeling of the work is missed, and it becomes just a fair commercial product.

Principal fault probably is in the production. Settings are terrible for one thing. Some of them are crude beyond telling. Even woodland backgrounds have a phoney look. The "feel" of the whole thing is artificial and manufactured, and as the story unfolds that air of artificiality communicates itself to the characters.

The story doesn't build. It is jerky and uneven. Situations are not made to grow to a high point, and endless footage is lavished on trivialities.

John Fox may have made his characters glow with nobility on the printed page, but as they come upon the screen the people and the locale generally are mean and sordid. Certainly they're shabby and a drab atmosphere is fearfully depressing through the eye of a camera.

The two women of the picture are uninteresting. Melissa, the mountain girl (Molly O'Day), hasn't a spark of charm as played, and Margaret, in the hands of Doris Dawson, is just an Elsie book blank in crinolines. The Barthelmess part is flat and tastless. In its sentimental phases it is underplayed, and when the frail Dick wipes up the field with a husky mountain bully, one sits back and stubbornly declines to lend one's self to so crude a make believe. There are limits to a fan's surrender to autointoxication.

Whatever the technical defects may be or whatever the shortcomings in acting or creation, the picture just doesn't engage interest. It will get just what the Barthelmess name will pull and very little else.

Rush.

HANGMAN'S HOUSE

Fox production and release. Directed by John Ford. Victor McLaglen featured. From novel by Donn Byrne. Editor, Margaret V. Clancy. Titles by Malcolm Stuart Boylan. Cameraman, George Schneiderman. At Roxy, New York, week May 12. Running time, 57 mins.

Citizen Hogan...............Victor McLaglen
Connaught O'Brien............June Collyer
Dermott McDermott............Larry Kent
John Darcy.......................Earle Foxe
James O'Brien, Lord Chief Justice.... Hobart Bosworth
Anne McDermott............Belle Stoddard
Neddy Joe.......................Joseph Burke
Colonel of Legionaires..........Eric Mayne

A comedy-drama natural for the screen with many angles of appeal. Not the least is that the story deals in a dignified dramatic way with the Irish gentry which in itself is something of a novelty for the screen, where anything Celtic is a comedy convention. This reviewer doesn't remember any other picture subject dealing with Irish society in a serious drama.

Here the locale and characters are treated in a fine literary way and the scenic backgrounds (picture apparently taken in Ireland) are remarkable for their pictorial beauty, so much so that the photographic quality of the whole production is one of its outstanding merits. Besides there is a thoroughly interesting story, with fine, unaffected character drawing, a strong tug of suspense, and although the action has an abundance of dramatic force, it is never merely theatrical.

Contributing as much as anything else to the admirable effect is the very capable acting of a well chosen cast.

For once here is an Irish picture play that should please the Irish. It has throughout its whole telling a feeling of entire sincerity. It doesn't on the one hand travesty the Celt, and it doesn't go out of its way to pat him on the back, two attitudes that have done a good deal to justify Irishmen's bitter objections to stage and screen representations of himself and his people.

The picture has its comedy bits, but they are always done in an artless and kindly way. Humor always sympathetic and genuine, giving evidence that the original novel was written by a Celt with all the loving warmth of the Irish for the homeland and the home people.

And this material has been transcribed to the screen with something approaching reverence. An element that enters is the titling of Malcolm Stuart Boylan, as trim a bit of literary workmanship as has come to attention lately. The explanatory notes are always in tune, crisp, unforced and innocent of gagging or striving for effect, either of comedy or drama, and this result is the ultimate of the titling art, an art that supplements without intrusion.

The same happy feeling is achieved in the photography. George Schneideman has caught some of the most striking touches of composition seen on the screen since those swamp land shots in "Sunrise," which they often resemble. There are bits of mist-draped landscape that actually inspire real emotion; vistas of moorlands in dim morning lights, glimpses of an old gate and driveway to a castle that give the feeling of fine old prints. From start to finish the pictorial side of the production is a revelation of camera possibilities.

The film has good theatrical values. There is a splendidly built up sequence of a steeplechase with dandy trick shots of horses going over the obstacles and mounts and riders taking astonishing falls. There are passages of first rate dramatic tension built up toward the climax, where the heavy burns down the castle just as the hero who has been trailing him to avenge a wronged sister comes to grips with him. One episode takes the story among the Foreign Legion where the hero, an exile from Erin with a price on his head, is serving until he is summoned home to do vengeance for his dead sister.

All these things, valuable screen material intrinsically, are logically blended into a capital story, building into a strong crescendo.

Victor McLaglen has a distinctive, out of the ordinary role, and he plays it to the last ounce.

Larry Kent and June Collyer are the romantic pair, playing daintily. Miss Collyer was a happy choice for the heroine, for her high bred type of beauty harmonizes perfectly with the role.

Altogether a screen output that calls for unrestrained applause.

Rush.

THE 50-50 GIRL

Paramount production and release. Directed by Clarence Badger. Bebe Daniels starred. Adapted by Ethel Doherty from story by John McDermott. Not programmed, but on slides. Titles by George

Marion, Jr. Photographer, Roy Hunt. At Paramount, New York, week May 12. Running time, around 65 minutes.
Kathleen O'Hara............Bebe Daniels
Jim Donahue..................James Hall
Engineer..................William Austin
Buck, the Gorilla Man..George Kotsonaros
Oscar.......... ....Johnnie Morris

Aside from some of the kids at matinees and the few k. m's. who will see this film comedy, there are about two actual laughs for anyone else in the entire running. One of those is from the titles. Otherwise it's a perfect blank, though it has Bebe Daniels and her rather nice ways of playing. But the picture will need plenty of stage show support and should be given it.

A boresome thing to the limit, containing but two angles and each of those of the extreme silly sort for this day of the show business. One is the exchange of places by man and woman, one of those "50 Years From Now" skits that was thought to have been barred from the stage or screen by common.consent 10 years ago. The other is mystery thrills in a cave, such as the children might cry out about when going through the "Coal Mine" at Luna Park. This bit seemed taken in one of those summer park concessions.

The cave stuff is terrible, in conception, direction, execution and any other thing you may want to think about. While the kitchen cooking stuff by James Hall is probably as nauseating as he must have thought of the thing cooked up for him to do.

Miss Daniels' performance overshadowed that of Hall's, but allowing Hall the discounts for his undeserved handicap of the character. Second was Johnnie Morris in a fop role, and the rest didn't mean a thing. Even George Marion's captions away below his average, but he has the story excuse also.

One would hardly think it needs money to make moving pictures after seeing "The 50-50 Girl" with the name of Paramount on it.

CIRCUS ROOKIE

Metro-Goldwyn-Mayer production and release. Starring Karl Dane, George K. Arthur, and featuring Louise Lorraine. Directed by Edward Sedgewick from own story, in collaboration with L. Lipton. Photographed by M. B. Gerstad with Robert Hopkins titling. At the Capitol, New York, week May 12. Running time, 60 minutes.
Oscar Thrush..................Karl Dane
Francis Byrd............George K. Arthur
Belle......................Louise Lorraine
Bimbo........................Fred Humes

Standard comedy of no particular brilliance, turned out on the seemingly mass production basis that has sponsored so many others of the ilk. Karl Dane puts on a new suit, is spattered by Arthur's Ford as it passes through a puddle, and that starts the feud that travels all over the circus lot. They'll laugh a few times and forget it.

Not over-long on sprightly gags, with the ever-present situation being the undersized member of the team in constant danger of being annihilated by the big husk. Meanwhile Arthur is trying to make some headway with the trapeze artiste, daughter of the owner of the show. The little guy finally gets up on the swinging cross-bar for trick photography and a final fall into the net.

The supposed thrill is when the big ape (Fred Humes) gets loose on a train, attacks the girl and frightens the engineer and fireman from the cab. Impending wreck has a twist in the circus train liable to overtake a freight ahead of it.

Robert Hopkins, M-G's veteran title writer, whose name seldom flashes on a credit caption, has done much to help the picture; but at best it's not more than a filler for the big houses. Its sudden placing at this theatre was probably due to the management's fear of the revival scheduled, "The White Sister," against the Paul Ash opening down the street at the Paramount. The Capitol's strong stage show will help this film this week, and it can stand like treatment cross country.

If there's any cast choice it goes to Dane as the dumb employe to whom the ugly tempered ape takes a fancy. Humes makes the animal unusually realistic and Arthur spends most of his time displaying a frightened and innocent pan.

Louise Lorraine, as the girl, is a mild 50 per cent. of the equally mild love interest, but holds enough to hint she may eventually show something.

Picture takes an even course, neither reaching the heights nor plumbing the depths. One of those pictures that men forget and short of creating anxiety as to when the next Dane-Arthur release will be along. Half houses will mark its path.

Sid.

STEAMBOAT BILL, JR.

United Artists production, directed by Charles F. Reisner. Cameramen, Dev Jennings and Bert Haines. Story by Carl Harbaugh. Buster Keaton with Ernest Torrence co-starred. At Rialto, New York, May 12, indef. Running time, 65 mins.
Steamboat Bill............Ernest Torrence
First Mate....................Tom Lewis
Mr. King....................Tom McGuire
Mary King..................Marion Byron
Steamboat Bill, Jr..........Buster Keaton

This is the last comedy Buster Keaton made under his United Artists contract. It was held back for several months, getting itself concerned in several wild rumors, all of which were a million miles from facts. Whatever may have been the real reason why United Artists took its time about releasing this one, it had nothing to do with quality, for it's a pip of a comedy. Lovers of comedy and picture house regulars will like this latest Keaton film. It's one of his best.

Carl Harbaugh wrote the story and supplied the comedy construction, while "Chuck" Reisner's direction extracts the last drop of juice from the situations and gags.

The story concerns the efforts of an old hard-boiled river captain (Earnest Torrence), to survive on the river in the face of opposition from a brand new modern rival boat, put in commission by his rival (Tom McQuire). The old-timer hasn't seen his son since he was an infant. The son arrives (Buster Keaton), and things begin to happen, fast and furiously.

The son falls in love with the daughter of the rival owner. Matters reach a climax when the old tub of Steamboat Bill is condemned. In a rage, he confronts his rival and accuses him of jobbing him. A battle ensues. Torrence is jailed for contempt, after he has torn up the condemnation notice.

Keaton appears to try and rescue the father. He is carrying a huge loaf of bread. Inside he has concealed enough tools to free Ireland. His efforts to get his father to accept the bread are one of the funniest scenes in the picture.

A wind storm which takes the roofs off houses and raises cain in general, is also used as a frame work for several very funny gags for Keaton. The old vaudeville stunt of a falling set with the victim emerging unharmed because it held a center door fancy which framed his body, is twisted into a corking screen gag through the added thrill of apparently seeing a whole side of a house fall, and Keaton remain standing upright, oblivious of danger because an open window fell around him.

During the wind storm Keaton is riding a hospital cot. He also has some funny stuff when he is blown into the ruins of the town's theatre. He finally grabs a tree for protection. It is uprooted and gives him a ride to the river. He lands back on his dad's tub in time to save the girl and his father. The latter is in the jug and about to be drowned when Keaton, by using pulleys to replace the engineer, starts the old stern wheeler and cuts the jail in half, releasing the old man.

After this Keaton saves everybody, including his father's rival and a minister, the latter just in time to unite him to the heroine.

An excellent cast gave Keaton and Torrence big league support. The late Tom Lewis as the first mate, Mr. McGuire as the rival owner and Marion Byron as the girl, contributed heavily.

The picture looks like a heavy production outlay and warrants it, for the effects obtained are thrilling. The windstorm is a gem and the river stuff interesting and colorful.

Keaton does some back breaking acrobatics in his awkward attempts to master seamanship, some of the falls looking dangerous. The gags maintain an even tempo of laughs, and are all new to picture house audiences, although several are reminiscent to a vaudevillian.

Con.

THE LIGHT OF ASIA

(INDIA-MADE)

Produced by the Mimansu Rai Group in collaboration with the Emelka Production Co. of Munich, Germany. Directed by O. F. Osten. Cameramen, Willy Kiermeister and Joseph Wiersching. Screened for the first time in America by the Film Arts Guild. At Carnegie Hall, New York, May 11. Running time, 90 minutes.
King Suddohodhanna..........Sarada Ukil
Queen Maya, consort...........Rani Bala
Gotama, son...................Himansu Rai
Gopa, his wife..................Seeta Devi
Devadatta....................Profulla Kuma
Asita, the Seer...............Dyanananda

"The Light of Asia" is a story of India and has a theme that carries six of the principals through the entire production, the locale, people, habits and customs all being typical of that tropical country. It apparently has been a long time reaching the American screen. Several years ago it was on the London silver sheets. In New York it was screened at Carnegie Hall for a few limited extra scale performances.

To the average American movie devotee "The Light of Asia" will hold interest through its native cast, its colorful surroundings and its picturesqueness, yet cannot approach anything exceptional or sensational through its snaillike story pace. That story does its best at times to approach real romance of the heart-throbbing love type but submerges itself in propaganda that is palpably of a religious aspect and which naturally takes the kick out of any try for melodrama.

On the whole "The Light of Asia" as summed up depicts in a lavish and pictorial way that despite the belief that India is rock ribbed in idol worship, filled with degenerates and thrives on the lowest form of illiteracy, that there is a real light, an enlightenment and a real atmosphere that is good propaganda for the country.

It does give a vivid picture of how even royalty can toss off its silks and satins to spread spiritual morale that has wide reaching results.

"The Light of Asia" is a sort of a paradox. It's a spectacle and pageant and again it isn't. During one of the big scenes where the royal offspring of two Indian families are joined in wedlock there is a wedding procession and ceremonial reminiscent of recent articles in the United States press when Nancy Miller, an American girl, was married to an Indian Maharajah.

That Nancy Miller wedding is so fresh in the minds of Americans that perhaps that alone may create additional curiosity on this side to see "The Light of Asia."

One sees elephants and camels in their every day work and processional duties, the former in particular being interesting as they stroll along the narrow streets of India with packed-in humanity on either side.

Some disjointed phases and some tall imagining to be done at different points. The caption or title, all the titles in English for the American presentation, reads that the King's son, who has left his attractive dusky bride, his luxurious home and everything that regal splendor can do for him day and night, to become a wanderer, a nomadic beggar, having seen "the light" that impels him to carry spiritual encouragement to the sidewalks, has been for 40 days and 40 nights under a native tree before deliverance comes. Yet during that long siege the young man looks just as fresh and clean as the first day he started on his aimless wanderings.

Everything is in keeping with the story; it is undeniably all in all a native India proposition and that in itself is something of a change from the Hollywood studio built scenes of the deserts and Far East.

Any effort to put this one on a $2 plane with road shows or American mades of that class is going to leave this foreign one a hopeless last, through its lack of a direct melodramatic smash or action that holds the necessary kick.

Some bully good photography, much of the coloring type that makes it a little bit more than usual, and again it has some terrible shots.

This film may get something on its foreign embellishment but very doubtful if it could go into any American city and stand up at advanced prices.

For those who read, delve and follow cults; who are enthralled by anything that savors of the tropical mysticism and who are fed up on westerns, deep-dyed melodramatic subjects and delight in something typically historical, allegorically and otherwise, will get an eyeful in this made in India picture.

At Carnegie Hall the audience was appreciative and expressions as the folks filed out indicated that it held interest, yet none was a rave.

Out in the northwest where Nancy Miller is best known this one should prove a magnetic draw. Even in the crossroads where they only see the elephants and camels in the news reels or occasional circus "The Light of Asia" should prove a curiosity.

Mark.

CARMEN

(FRENCH MADE)

Albatross production, released by the Eastern Film Company. Featuring Raquel Meller. Based on novel by Prosper Merimee. Directed by Jacques Feyder. In cast, Louis Lerch, Guerrero de Xandoval, Gaston Modot. At Greenwich Village, New York on run, starting May 5. Running time, about 75 minutes.

Arty, in one way or another, ever since it was built about a decade ago, the Greenwich Village has now gone art movie under management of Harold Meltzer and James Riley, who also run the Greenwich Village Inn. They have the house under a five-year lease.

This French flicker of the famous story of Carmen, the gypsy, that has been used and abused on many a movie lot in recent years, is a real achievement for several reasons, not the least of which is that it was shot in Ronda, Spain, the actual locale of Merimee's yarn. Another is Raquel Meller as Carmen and Louis Lerch as Don Jose. The story in this version of "Carmen" closely follows the novel, instead of the operatic version used for previously screened "Carmens." This "Carmen" is okay for any cut house and ditto for the grinds.

The story of the gypsy cigaret girl who vamps the soldier and leads him to murder the banditry for love of her needs no retelling for every moviegoer over the age of ten would recognize the plot as the basis on which most vamp stories for the screen are founded.

The picture was shot with the Spanish hill country as a background, with no studio sets and no trick photography. Story is simply and directly told in a strange and little known land. The latter, its winding streets, hot fields and sand-duned hills, have been used to excellent advantage by Director Feyder.

Louis Lerch, young French actor, comes close to running away with the picture at times. As Carmen's lover he is called upon to kill all who would steal her from him and in the duelling scenes, is superb.

Meller, the Spanish diseuse, looking a little heavier than when on this side a few years ago, gives a realistic performance. Her Carmen is no flapper, but a full grown woman who takes her loves where she finds them and flings them aside whenever the gypsy in her craves freedom.

The high spot is the bull fight. This one looks like the most authentic affair of its kind ever shot and holds a kick for most anyone. All the prelims leading up to the kill are shown. Then the picador steps out to confront the maddened and practically exhausted bull. With half a dozen or more spears buried in his hide, the bull prepares for his last charge. He lunges at his newest tormenter and as he does so the picador buries his sword up to **the hilt between the bull's eyes. Most of this is proof that bull fighting is no child's play. All is shown, only the actual kill being cut.**

In addition to the duels and bull fights, the picture has a battle in the mountains as the soldiers attack the gypsy stronghold. Here the soldiers are doing plain and fancy pratt slides down sand dunes while in pursuit of the bandits. One of the soldiers stops suddenly in his descent and catching his arm in an exposed root takes a pot shot at the enemy. It's a fine touch for a hearty laugh.

At the Greenwich Village grinding the flicker last week brought about $3,000 with 50c. tops and two-bit matinees. Some of the carriage trade that found its way down to the latest sure seater sniffed at the prices, so that this week the scale has been titled to six bits.

Looks like the Greenwich Village will provide plenty opposition for the Fifth Ave. playhouse, especially if the new operators can grab a good flicker to follow "Carmen." Also they're giving away free cigarets, as well as tea and coffee over at Sheridan Square.

AFTER THE STORM

Columbia production and release. Hobart Bosworth starred in screen billing. Directed by George B. Seitz under supervision of Harry Cohn. No other members of cast featured in billing. Players include Charles C. Delaney, Maude George, Eugenia Gilbert and George Kuwa. Author not credited on screen. At Keith's Hippodrome, New York, week May 7. Running time 65 mins.

Moderately entertaining sea meller as good as anything shown at the Hippodrome in recent times, which says or means little. Here for a full week this independently produced picture can make the grade in the smaller houses if properly handled. Suspense is lacking and love interest weak on account of insufficient strength of the players to whom these roles have been entrusted, but had these deficiencies been overcome the picture would have merited attention in the first runs.

Hobart Bosworth is a strong personality and a fair name draw in the spots this film is intended for. He screens well here.

Comedy attempts with a Chinese **cook aboard ship poor and results negligible though one piece of business, throwing the cook's plaster gods into the ocean, registers for a laugh.**

Action is powerful and gripping and, though not abundant, is enough to carry the picture. First fight scene is well handled and rescue sequences in a storm, the boy and girl out on the ocean in a small boat, convincing and impressive.

Story not so good. Involves a father and son, captain and first mate of their ship, the former harboring an insane hatred against all womankind because he believed the first had betrayed him to the revenue officers when he was a smuggler in order to get the reward. The second, a loose woman of Singapore, had married and later deserted him when he was finally caught and thrown into prison for five years.

The flashbacks are more interesting than the spot story and better results might have been obtained, had the continuity been written in the present tense, starting at the beginning and working up to the clincher instead of going back and holding up progress.

Charles Delaney and Eugenia Gilbert, as the youthful pair, not very interesting. Need more polish. Maude George delivers a correct impersonation of a bum out for sailor money.

They'll like it where action takes precedence over, and the audience is not oversensitive to the finer shades of dramatic interpretation.

Mori.

THE FLYIN' COWBOY

Universal production and release. Starring Hoot Gibson. Story by Arthur Statter. Directed by Reaves Eason. At Loew's Circle, New York, one day, May 12. Running time 60 minutes.

First rate western with a dude ranch for some neat clowning, a gem robbery and a one man wild west show. Hoot Gibson has been getting better stories of late. His horse is almost as familiar as Tom Mix's Tony and when he rides out after the bad 'uns on the neighborhood screens, Hoot is greeted with cheers by the kids.

Olive Hasbrouck plays opposite and gives a fine performance as the blase easterner who is thrill-proof. Both the writer and the director also deserve credit for the way Olive goes over. A novel twist is given the heart stuff by having the femme who is really nuts over Gibson pretend indifference while he is putting on a one man rodeo more for her benefit than the rest of the dude ranch's guests.

A good finish is provided by having Gibson slide down a mountainside and concealing himself in the fork of a tree. There he ropes the two Chicago bandits who are headed for the border with a lot of ice belonging to the girl.

Tag this one for the "western" houses.

TEMPEST

United Artists production and release. An original story by C. Gardner Sullivan. Directed by Sam Taylor. Supervised by John W. Considine, Jr. John Barrymore starred, with Camilla Horn and Louis Wolheim featured. At Embassy (seating 569), New York, May 17, on run. $2 top. "Running time, 105 minutes.

Sergeant Ivan Markov......John Barrymore
Princess Tamara.............Camilla Horn
Sergeant Bulba.............Louis Wolheim
The Peddler..................Boris De Fas
The General................George Fawcett
The Captain.................Ullrich Haupt
The Guard.................Michael Visaroff

A high type of an intelligently written, directed and produced picture of the popular description that fits perfectly into the Embassy, on Broadway, at $2 top. In the regular picture houses it's a holdover. If it's not, that will be the exhibitor's fault, for United Artists has thoroughly performed its portion here.

Additionally to what may be called the model modern picture making this film represents, it has John Barrymore, a strong romantic draw. U. A. now has another heavy b. o. card in Camilla Horn, the German girl, debuting over here in this American made.

It's a toss-up for the top credit, if that may be named. It can't well be; for C. Gardner Sullivan in his original plot turned out a striking tale of quite some suspense and marked continuity. It's carried forward splendidly. To what effect may be understood when this hour and three-quarter special ran through without an intermission the opening night and without losing a person to its very end.

With the locale laid in Russia, the setting is always adequate, even to the snowy finale, when the young couple flee the country across the Austrian border.

Mr. Barrymore and Miss Horn as opposites do a very forceful couple of young people, widely contrasted with the girl a Russian princess while Barrymore becomes a frowned upon peasant commissioned army officer, promoted from the ranks.

Miss Horn looks to be of a wide range, at least in expression. She's a handsome blonde on the screen (and off) and chameleon-like in her expressions. Unless the director of the camera caused the varied facial expressions this imported girl exhibited, Camilla Horn immediately becomes a distinctive film actress over here.

Barrymore set forth all of his talents, taking in make up. When in solitary confinement, left alone for days, he grew a beard. At the finale of that dungeon scene Barrymore could have played the Savior in "The King of Kings," for that's how he looked. Not as much action as usual for a Barrymore romancer. No acrobatics, no fighting or duelling, and but one kill, toward the finish.

One of the delights of the picture, however, are the scornful, verbal battles between Barrymore and Miss Horn. There are several of these, each one a peach for interest.

Nothing even suggesting a particle of miscasting. Louis Wolheim as another peasant sergeant has his moments, and mostly subdued, with a certain commendable restraint placed through the picture upon everyone.

George Fawcett was excellent as the Russian general commanding. He had to undergo one scene similar to that Emil Jannings went through as a Russian general in "The Last Command"—that of being degraded and humiliated by the victroious Russian revolutionists. Much of this sequence, minus the sentences and executions, was not unlike that in "Command."

Ulrich Haup did a fop army captain rather well, though he did, as a Russian officer in uniform, wear a monocle.

Boris DeFas' Russian peasant agitator posing as a pedler singularly suggested Trosky. This was held to after the Bolshevists were in power, with the Pedler sending the aristocrats to the firing squads.

Many scenes and some of pictorial notice with several mobs handled exceptionally. Photography always superior, while the picture swept along so evenly on its story crest that it looked more like an unfoldment than a tale.

One attractive bit was when Barrymore in confinement and close to insanity, seeing visions and images in his weakened mind, finally hears Wolheim calling to him. Barrymore thinks it's but another vision. He looks blankly at the other man, carefully feels his chin, mouth, nose, eyes and then falls weeping into Wolheim's arms Superb.

The story starts with a Russian cavalry regiment in quarters. Barrymore is studying for the elevation; uselessly his comrades tell him, as no peasant has been commissioned for 10 years.

Almost at the outset the big kick of the picture occurs. The men have gone in swimming with their uniform trousers on. Down the stream three girls are also bathing. A detached cavalryman steals their hanging clothes for a joke. Wolheim intercepts him, takes the clothes with a smirk and starts to return them. He is stopped by Barrymore who says he will be the gallant.

As Barrymore returns the outfits, he is thought by one of the girls, Miss Horn as the Princess, to have **taken them. Lightly clothed she steps up to and withers him. When he expostulates that he did not take the dresses but merely was returning them, she snatches his whip and beats him fiercely across his naked chest. When she is exhausted and through, the soldier takes her in his arms, kissing her. The girl is furious, but does not report him.**

Again he meets the girl when her father, the general, through his affection for Barrymore, procures the commission, and again when the Princess says to the Lieutenant, as she is dancing with him through her father's intrigue: "It needs more than a title and a uniform to make an officer and a gentleman."

Maddened, Barrymore leaves her and stocks up with booze. Blind drunk he mistakenly falls into her bedroom and proceeds to fall asleep on her couch. When returning later, the girl, alone, with her maid having gone, discovers Barrymore asleep. She rings a bell, calling her father and the captain, the latter her fiance. As the bell rings, Barrymore tells her it ends his army career, but that it doesn't his love for her.

Barrymore is sentenced to five years and stripped before his company. There is no more pathetic scene to picturize than the stripping of a service officer of any country and this is just a little more pathetic than the others.

Then war in 1914, the rush to the front, the poverty of Russia, the Revolution and the release of Barrymore, up to the detention of the Princess, the execution of her father and fiance by the order of the Pedler, now the Red commissioner in charge of the district, and also the Pedler's charge against Barrymore for treason, because he had seen Barrymore holding the aristocratic general as the latter was dying.

So Barrymore killed the Pedler, not a bad idea at that moment.

And they fled to Austria, one of three finales reported having been made for this expensively produced picture.

It was a picturesque finale for a very, very fine picture, a huge mark for United Artists and all concerned, and a decided asset to the American picture industry.

Before the picture opened Miss Horn, in the audience, was brought forth and introduced by Major

Bowes. Miss Horn nicely recited a press agent's thoughts on sudden emergencies, and the audience reacted quickly to Miss Horn's most pleasing personality.

Dr. Hugo Riesenfeld provided a light and pleasing musical score.

Sime.

Something Always Happens

Paramount production and release. Starring Esther Ralston and featuring Neil Hamilton. Directed by Frank Tuttle from his own story, with Florence Ryerson adapting. J. Roy Hunt, cameraman. H. J. Mankiewicz titles. Running time, 49 mins. At Paramount, New York, week May 19.
Diana.............................Esther Ralston
Roderick.........................Neil Hamilton
Chang-Tzo ....Sojin
Perkins..........................Charles Sellon
George...........................Roscoe Karns
Earl of Rochester................Lawrence Grant
Clark............................Mischa Auer

Short mystery-comedy that should serve its purpose as summer fare on the program route. No particular kick to the story, but they squealed and laughed here over the haunted house idea.

It's all because the American girl finds the Earl of Rochester's abode too dull, and she's engaged to wed the son. The family owns a particular jewel for which Chang-Tzo is in jail. When the Chink breaks loose, young Roderick takes the stone to a vault.

On the way a stop is made at an isolated house; Roderick disappears inside, doesn't come back, and Diana follows. Thence the mysterious moving chairs, figures, etc.

This is the first "scare" sequence, after which the comedy link comes as the girl discovers Roderick has framed with friends to give her a thrill, and she in turn starts to mystify them.

The third and serious twist is when Chang-Tzo gets into the house and the chase and fake fights suddenly become on the level.

It moves fast, run off here under 50 minutes, with enough action, thrills and giggles to hold it up. Mankiewicz's titles no panic, but Tuttle has made it a compact example of competent direction and cutting, and Hunt has nicely taken care of the camera end.

Miss Ralston does well with her light role, while Hamilton retains his usual good appearance and takes easily to the knockabout script. Charles Sellon is a cast asset, and Sojin plays the heavy who becomes a factor late in the footage.

Production unit hasn't made the mistake of trying to drag this one out to an hour or more, and that's its principal strength. Brief and fast enough to carry its point.

Sid.

DON'T MARRY

Fox production and release. Produced by James Tinling. Screen billing features Lois Moran and Neil Hamilton. Story by Phil Klein and Sidney Vanfield. Screen adaptation by Randall Faye. At the Roxy, New York, week of May 19. Running time, over 60 minutes.
Priscilla Bowen......................Lois Moran
Louise Bowen........................Lois Moran
Henry Willoughby....................Neil Hamilton
Gen. Willoughby.....................Henry Kolker
Aunt Bowie.........................Claire McDowell
Hortense...........................Lydia Dickson

Excellent comedy, well acted, expertly directed and produced, and nicely photographed with a degree of quality in the laughs certain to register strongest with audiences in the first-run houses.

Story and continuity are clever. Action interesting at all times and fast pace keeps going without a lapse. Ranks among the best programmers on the Fox lineup.

Story concerns a modern flapper encumbered with an old-fashioned aunt whose clothes date back a decade and who controls the girl's inheritance. The kid is alive, likes to wear natty bathing suits, and auntie thinks it's a cardinal sin to expose anything above the ankle.

Girl meets a fresh young lawyer whose ideas on women's behavior coincide with her aunt's. The young man is the son of the girl's elderly friend, also a lawyer. The pair frame a scheme whereby the girl plays twins, being a modest cousin, Priscilla, on the side. She gets attention in the modest role and then gets the boy sick of everything prim, gawkish and old fashioned.

Incidents worked around the double play of character lead to a series of funny situations. While changing costumes the girl's clothes are locked in her car. She has to get into her bedroom in a nightgown and, in trying to elude her aunt, is obliged to hide in the boy friend's room. More gags, and the girl is finally discovered in a compromising situation.

Lois Moran delivers some fine bits and secures able support from Hamilton. Henry Kolker and Claire McDowell also score.

Mori.

BILLY KERNELL'S CREDIT

Los Angeles, June 5.

In *Variety's* favorable review of "Don't Marry," with Lois Moran, all credits were mentioned excepting Billy Kernell, who did the titles for the film.

HOT HEELS

Universal production and release. Glen Tryon starred and Patsy Ruth Miller featured. Directed by William James Craft. Tod Sloan, former jockey, in cast and probably featured by press sheet. At Keith's Hippodrome, New York, week May 21. Running time, around 55 minutes.

A kind of a comedy picture that is good for the three-day neighborhoods and, of course, lesser time, because it has the fun stuff the community folks think they like. It could have been a first runner if better judgment has been employed first by the writer and again by the story department and again by anyone who passed on the story besides the caster.

It starts off with the Charlie Withers' bucolic opry house scheme of the old time Jack Dalton meller, that will get its laughs. After that the film goes into a plot, quite simple in text, and winds up as a race track picture, this time the Havana Steeplechase.

Captions ordinarily should have had much to do with this story. These didn't, but one title did; it was the laugh hit of the film and read: "Listen! I hear footsteps approaching on horseback."

Now you know what kind of hoke is in it.

Or again when the orchestra drummer tore a strip of linen as a girl in riding breeches mounted her horse. How much longer before that will be declared out among gag stealers?

The theatrical troup of the terrible meller (comedy) which stranded before an audience looking as though it had been packed into a projection room, was saved by the drummer-orchestra leader who also ran the country hotel. That hotel was full of gags, such as sliding steps. Here though sending ice water and valises to their different rooms by pulley wires was a funny enough idea to have been carried much farther. Which may go to express the common impression that a gag stealer when hitting upon an original can't detect it himself.

One of the best bits of a long while was the Apache dance between Glen Tryon and Patsy Ruth Miller. Had the story turned right there to have that couple repeat their accidental good and comedy dance to Broadway prominence, "Hot Heels," the name of a horse, could still have carried that title and would have gotten into the first runs. It might have gotten any-

---

where without the horse race and minus its bad casting.

So the horse that was stranded with the troupe which also had him in an imaginary race of their meller, finally won the Steeplechase in Cuba, freed the troupe over there which had stranded again, and foiled the silly vallain.

Mr. Tryon looks quite good, first time seen on the screen. He plays lightly even as a juv and looks well, and appears to have a range in his work. It was an error to cast Miss Miller opposite him here, as much so as it was to have an audience believe that Tod Sloan at his present age could ride in a race. But it's a great plug for Tod.

Not much else there excepting the horse, which looked much better than the race. More especially so with the latter this week as the news reels are showing the original Kentucky Derby of last Saturday.

Just another chance muffed. Probably doesn't matter much, stories are so plentiful.

DAUGHTER OF ISRAEL
(FRENCH MADE)

Billed as product of Bell Pictures, Inc., distributed in the U. S. by Nathan Hirsh, New York state righter. Directed by Edward Jose. Betty Blythe starred. Titles for American edition by Merritt Crawford. Story taken from French novel, "Jacob's Well." At Cameo, New York, week May 19. Running time, 88 minutes.
Agar.............................Betty Blythe
Igor............................Wallstein
Leon............................Mathot
Paul Elzear.....................Malcolm Tod
Rabbi Beriah Moses..............Ernest Maupin
Guitele.........................Annette Benson
Reine Avril.....................Henriette Delanoy
Cochbas.........................Andra Nox

A particularly clumy bit of "continental" producing. Scenario, direction, acting and everything else except some of the real foreign settings unbelievably crude. It is enough to indicate the grade of the subject to report that Betty Blythe, who must weigh 150, plays a young hoyden.

In one sequence she does a barelegged dance which edges toward travesty, and in another appears at a masquerade in black lace tights.

All the players use the artificial foreign make-up that grates upon the American fan, and the photography even exaggerates the theatrical appearance of the characters. The backgrounds are even more make-believe, and there isn't a moment in the whole hour and a half that creates anything approaching illusion. The acting is terribly serious, almost to the point of involuntary burlesque. Whole thing is hopelessly old fashioned, belonging to the "Stand back, Jack Dalton!" school of melodrama.

No idea of well-knit action. Story rambles interminably. Apparently they began at the start of the novel and worked painstakingly through to the last page. The screen result is emphasis upon trivial details and dismissal of important climaxes with scant attention. Thus what may have been an absorbing novel becomes anaesthetic as a movie.

Story has to do with the granddaughter of a rabbi in Constantinople who is taken up as a protege by a music hall star and gets an engagement in Alexandria as a dancer, working in a cafe which turns out to be a dive. She is rescued by a benevolent old man who is developing a Zionist colony at Jacob's Well in Palestine. The old man falls in love with her and they are married, although she loves a younger man in Constantinople.

Some of the foreign backgrounds, such as the Constantinople plaza overlooking the sea, the harbor shipping and scenes in tropical Palestine are interesting, but the production as a screen offering is a complete bust. Subject isn't even material for retitling for burlesque purposes. Crawford, in giving an American set of titles, has used discretion by handling the captions

---

briefly and covering the ground as tersely as possible. *Rush.*

THE YELLOW LILY

First National production and release, starring Billie Dove. Clive Brook featured. Directed by Alexander Korda. Author not credited on screen or program billing. At the Strand, New York, week of May 19. Running time, over 65 mins.
Judith Peredy.....................Billie Dove
Archduke Alexander................Clive Brook
Kinkeline.........................Gustav von Seyffertitz
Archduke Peter....................Marc McDermott
Eugene Peredy.....................Nicholas Soussanin
The Archduchess...................Eugenie Besserer
Mlle. Julie.......................Jane Winton
The Mayor.........................Charles Puffy

Sweet box-office attraction, provided it will be permitted to run uncut elsewhere.

A young archduke, looking like a Roxy usher, with a leather pouch on his back, who has had his own sweet way with the ladies, finally meets the girl who wouldn't trade except for a wedding ring. The duke chases the girl all over the town of Tarnavar, Hungary, and finally corners her in her own bedroom in the middle of the night. That's enough to send shivers up and down miscellaneous feminine spines anywhere.

With the little girl cornered and in nothing except a chemise, the duke suffers a shock. "I hate you," she subtitles, but there's a strange look in her eyes. She really loves the duke. And just as it seems everything should be cleared up, the girl's brother, the doctor, bursts into the room. The archduke is shot and the girl and brother go to jail. You can't fool a brother, it seems.

For the finish the picture takes a familiar turn, the duke defying regal authority and promising to marry and protect the gal forever.

Seems to be particularly good program picture for the full-week stands. Titles, not credited, are badly written, and photography poor in spots. In latter case Miss Dove's face gets harsh treatment. Clive Brook makes an excellent lead, and balance of cast deliver fine performance. *Mori.*

THE CHORUS KID

Gotham production released by Lumas. Virginia Brown Faire featured. Story by Howard Rockey. Adaptation and supervision by Harold Shumate. Directed by Howard Bretherton. Cameraman, Charles Van Enger. Titles by Casey Robinson. Production manager, Carroll Saxe. At Loew's New York, one day, May 9. Running time, 60 mins.
Virginia Brown Faire, Sheldon Lewis, Hedda Hopper, John Batten, Bryant Washburn, Thelma Hill, Tom O'Brien.

Exceptionally meritorious independent film. Used alone at Loew's New York, where indies are generally dumped in on double feature days. The production looks first class in every respect and is okay for de luxe houses.

There is a new and interesting twist given to the ancient hokum about the good little chorus girl. It would have been a darb of a story for First National to use for Billie Dove instead of their inanity of "Heart of a Follies Girl." Virginia Brown Faire, less well known, makes an agreeable and plausible chorine and the picture is far better than the First National's effort in the same direction.

Gotham has assembled a "name" cast even to having Sheldon Lewis in a bit so small he can scarcely be recognized.

Story has chorus girl coming into a small nest egg through an oil investment. Having been born in a dressing room and brought up in a trunk the girl figures she has missed her girlhood. She hikes off to a swell finishing school, misrepresenting her age as 17 and trying to recapture her departed kid days.

She gets thick with one of the school chums and goes home with her to spend the holidays. The chum's pop is a natty widower with dough (Bryant Washburn). A fashionable widow (Hedda Hopper) is out to cop the rich daddy. Of course the chorus kid gets the orange blossoms.

Tom O'Brien contributes some smiles. Miss Hopper looks marvelous and Washburn fits the part like a glove. Thelma Hill, of two reelers, is a cutie.

Gotham can plug this one. *Land.*

OLD AGE HANDICAP

Trinity Pictures Corp. production, releasing through First Division. Directed by Frank S. Mattison from magazine story by Tod Underwood. Adapted by Cecil B. Hill. Photographed by Jules Cronjager. Titles by Putnam Hoover. Starring Alberta Vaughn. Cast: Gareth Hughes, Vivian Rich, Olaf Hytton, Mavis Villers, Bud Shaw. At the Stanley, N. Y., one day, May 18. Running time, 62 minutes.

Even with Gareth Hughes' dead pan this is a nice picture. It's the kind which will get the okay of every parent-teacher association in the country. Put together in interesting style, above that attained by the average indie, this Trinity picture should satisfy the bigger percentage of fans.

At no time, however, does the film get so moralistic as to be obnoxious. There's a splash of sex throughout, which hits a climax in a roadhouse to which the bad boy of the town has lured the sis. A lot of bright material before he succeeds in feeding her her first drink, and then the dancer of the joint (Alberta Vaughn) stalls aff the rest until the big brother arrives. A wise but good gal in love with the brother, she makes the big sacrifice of her own to save the young girl. Miss Vaughn even rides the family's old nag to victory in a race framed by a banker. It winds up logically, happily and morally.

THE CHORUS KID

Gotham production released by Lumas. Directed by Howard Bretherton. Screen play by Adele Buffington, adapted from Howard Rockey's story. Virginia Brown Faire and Bryant Washburn featured. In cast: Hedda Hopper, Tom O'Brien, Thelma Hill, John Batten and Sheldon Lewis. At Loew's Circle, New York, one day, May 20, on double bill. Running time, 60 minutes.

Lightweight flicker built around a highly improbable story. If neighborhood patrons are willing to overlook such items as a May-December marriage and a chorus girl, born in a trunk, raised on the stage and still ashamed of her birthright, this one will slide by on a double bill. Otherwise it's thumbs down.

Plot revolves about Beatrice Brown (Virginia Faire), chorus dame in a Broadway revue, who, when she gets her hands on a chunk of dough, decides to go to boarding school and thereby recapture a youthful experience she has missed. At the fashionable finishing school she is befriended by the daughter of the president of the oil company responsible for her sudden wealth. Latter frowns on show folk, but falls in love with his daughter's chum, who has concealed her past from her new-found friends.

Mrs. Garrett (Hedda Hopper), a widow, is the menace on the make for the wealthy oil man. She throws a wrench into the romance between the middle-aged man and the girl. Resultant misunderstanding is patched up after girl is ordered out of the house where she is a vacation visitor. Following the girl's denunciation of bigotry, smugness and bias of wealthy folks in general and her pursuer in particular, there is the usual clinch with the suitor's daughter on the sidelines applauding his choice of a wife. A few wisecracking titles about the only thing worthy of commendation.

THE DESERT BRIDE

Columbia production and release. Directed by Walter Lang. Betty Compson starred, with Allan Forrest, Edward Martindel and Otto Matiesen featured. Photography, Ray June. Adapted by Elmer Narris from the Ewart Adamson story, "The Adventuress." Continuity by Anthony Coldewey. At the New York, one day, May 11, as half double bill. Running time, around 60 minutes.

Diane Duval	Betty Compson
Captain Maurice de Florimont	Allan Forrest
Colonel Sorelle	Edward Martindel
Kassim Ben Ali	Otto Matiesen
Private Terry	Roscoe Karns
Beggar	Frank Austin

Not very impressive, this Columbia's "Desert Bride," with a small time sand storm as the only kick.

Best in the picture in every way is Betty Compson, who looks nice and does well.

Billed as adapted from "The Adventuress," the film scenario would indicate that the adventuress portion of the novel had been toned or tamed down. Nothing vampy here, nor any gold digging, with the girl made the niece of an English army officer in Egypt or India.

Allan Forrest barely made it as the love-making captain, chief of the Intelligence Department. It's a sort of mild secret service story with an Arab chieftain or Pasha waiting and scheming to get ammunition the captain had seized.

Much meller and Arab extras, with the soldiers busting in gates just in time.

Looks like the price of the story was the inducement for Columbia.

One dayers and double bills.

OVER THERE

Based on official U. S. and allied government motion pictures of the World War, put together by Super Film Attractions. Release undecided; probably state rights. Private showing before press and representatives of D. A. R. in Hays office projection room May 16. Running time, about 60 minutes.

Six-and-one-half reels of official war film from government archives are pieced together under the title of "Over There." The selections, according to Sidney Lust, Washington exhibitor and president of Super Film Attractions, required research work extending over the past three years and the co-operation of two government officials.

At the close of the preview in the Hays office, Mrs. Newton Chapman, national chairman of the Daughters of the American Revolution, endorsed the film in behalf of her organization. She described it as being as unbiased as could be expected in its treatment of the credits and conditions. She also said that it afforded a great relief in comparison with other war pictures because "it is not saturated with sex appeal and deals with the cold realities of the war."

"Over There" possesses unlimited exploitation possibilities. The D. A. R. okay is only one of many that capable handling will bring this film. As to its entertainment qualities, "Over There" is in a very crude technical state. It is practically devoid of sequence and is full of repetitious shots. There is such a lack of continuity, which even well-placed and significant titles might ensure, that the action as now edited reacts strongly of a disjointed conglomeration of newsreels.

Historically, excepting the assurance that the feature represents excerpts from government records, "Over There" is practically nil. This is due to a careful avoidance on the part of the titles to enumerate dates or places where various bombardments and charges have taken place.

From the angle of pure showmanship and with the material at his command, Lust can improve his venture a thousand per cent. After the titles, a re-editing that will get the action more in line and work up a suspense, which the feature now lacks to the point of being monotonous, will provide the essentials which may make this a clean-up at every box-office.

Cutting out several thousand feet of marching scenes and artillery work, played to death by the newsreels and by Hollywood as well, and substituting more close-ups and material not to be found in the common garden variety, will make this feature worthy of the exploitation which it can get, even in its present raw state.

SUNSET LEGION

Paramount production and release, starring Fred Thomson. Directed by Lloyd Ingram and Alfred L. Werker from original story by Frank Clifton. Cast: William Courtright, Edna Murphy, Harry Woods. Titles by Garrett Graham. At Loew's New York May 19, one day. Running time, 70 minutes.

Fred Thomson has cranked out one that will click with the mobs. Picture features Thomson and his horse as quick change artists. From the dumbell cowboy and the sleepy white horse, Thomson and Silver King don black satin and scare the town's bad citizenry.

Dual roles of horse and rider help the suspense in the early footage. From the meek cowboy who breezes into the town just after another wagon load of gold has been lifted by the bartender's gang, Thomson suddenly turns into the shooting, wild-riding demon. He cops the evidence which shows the beer pourer up before the legal bar, but keeps it under cover until love-interest is aroused between the black outfit and the daughter of the mine owner. Girl is Edna Murphy.

Holding off the township at a country fandango while Thomson dances with the gal is one of the standout sequences. The climax at the mine brings out Thomson as the leader of the rangers. Lots of familiar gags, but used to excellent advantage.

The Lion and the Mouse

Los Angeles, May 22.

Warner Brothers production (Talker) release. Directed by Lloyd Bacon. Cameraman, Norbert Brodin. May McAvoy and Lionel Barrymore featured. Vitaphone talking production, based on the play by Charles Klein. Scenario by Robert Lord. Edited by Harold J. McCord. Titles by Jimmie Starr. At Warner's theatre, Hollywood, beginning May 21. Running time, 65 minutes.

Shirley Rossmore	May McAvoy
John (Ready Money) Ryder	Lionel Barrymore
Judge Rossmore	Alec Francis
Jefferson Ryder	William Collier, Jr.
Dr. Hays	Emmett Corrigan
Smith (Jeff's valet)	Jack Ackroyd

Paraphrasing the title of the picture, it is not a lion, nor yet is it a mouse. The truth rides somewhere between the sizes of the two. Great production it is not, because basically it lacks the interwoven essentials of such a structure. What success it registers is due to its novelty, the appeal and the interest that reside in the human voice from the screen, even though that voice sometimes be indifferently reproduced.

Added appeal in emotional scenes undoubtedly comes with the voice. It is this factor which strengthens the closing scenes of the picture and which will serve to lift this subject over the hurdles and help it to make a lot of money.

This picture was advertised as "the first talking motion picture," thereby carrying the impression it was to be a 100 per cent dialog subject, even if accompanying sound effects were absent.

In the interest of historical accuracy let it be set down "the first talking motion picture" is yet to come. A casual mental record of the sequences, 13 in all, showed the first to be a dialog between Lionel Barrymore and Alec Francis. Then, for seven consecutive sequences, the titles were working full blast, with not a single word vocal. The concluding five sequences were dialoged. And the interest chirked up appreciably as a result, in spite of unevenness in volume and clarity.

The reviewer purposely took a seat near the rear of the balcony in order that whatever there might be of the vocal order could be compared with the spoken drama of the legitimate. The newcomer does not stand the test with credit, not in its present state of development.

Angles of contrast between the old and the new are many. In the new, when looking on a close-up suddenly flashed out of a long shot, one naturally, coming into the same room with the players, as it were, expects the voice to be raised, even as he looks for a lessening in volume when from a close-up the players are removed to a distance. But the voice holds unchanged in volume, whether the speaker be near or far.

Again, when in close-up the actor speaks, synchronization to the patron seated 200 feet from the screen seriously is impaired. At that distance from the stage the auditor in a legitimate drama cannot note the movement of the players' lips and so detects no difference between lip movement and sound. In the screen's colse-up, however, the disparity between movement and sound sticks out, especially if the enunciation be indistinct or low or both. And in some instances in this picture that was the case.

Especially was this true where May McAvoy first came within the range of the microphone. Her voice hardly carried to the back of the house, giving the impression it was insufficiently robust. Yet, in a later sequence it came clear and strong, showing earlier lack of cohesion between the monitor and the director. Upon the former, it may be explained, ordinarily rests the responsibility of regulating volume as it may be indicated to him by the loud speaker in his sound-proof room adjacent to the recording stage.

Where in an ordinary silent picture the onlooker is annoyed by an absence of agreement between the movements of the lips and the words put into the speaker's mouth by the title writer after the picture is photographed the unpleasant impression is intensified immeasurably where a silent sequence follows one vocal.

In a majority of cases where the voice was recorded the words came from a single close-up. Rarely from a two-shot, and not more than once or twice were there three persons within the range of the camera when any talking was heard.

One major error in "The Lion and the Mouse" seems in making the first sequence vocal. That action materially damaged the illusion, as the person following the story, after having been told it was a "talking" picture, continually was wondering when the voice would be recovered—or if it was not going to be after all. And after a half dozen silent sequences file by the impatient customer is about ready to give up the guessing match.

Even with over 50 per cent of the picture silent, the settings practically all are interiors. Scenic and outdoor photographic embellishments are lacking, and the absence is felt.

There are six in the cast as furnished. Actually there were but four, as two of the six had little to do. All were perfect ladies and gentlemen, except John Ready Money Ryder, who so far fractured the conventions as to declare and reiterate his son was a liar and to denounce Shirley Rossmore as a thief. But now a blow was struck. The absence of that physical action may be felt in industrial and other sections where raw meat is demanded.

The clearest voice, consistent in quality, was that of the oldest player, Alec Francis. He had not so much to say as some of the others. Young Collier's voice sounded differently in different sequences, in one place as if someone else were speaking the lines he apparently uttered. The volume seemed too great or the tone too heavy or too basslike for the frame from which it came. In the quarrel between son and father, for example, it seemed the voice of the father was accompanying the movement of the lips of the son.

Barrymore's voice accomplished many of the things the player sought to make it do. Not always, however—patently due to mechanical inequalities—was it distinct even when sufficient in volume. Again, it came clear when low.

This half picture, half photographed stage play, is worth seeing. It is eloquent of what the future holds for the screen—and that sentiment rather than one of critical annlysis will animate the average picturegoer.

STREET OF SIN

Paramount production and release. Starring Emil Jannings and featuring Fay Wray. Directed by Mauritz Stiller. Story by Joseph Von Sternberg and Benjamin Glazer, latter supervising. Chandler Sprague, scenarist, with V. Milner and Harry Fischbeck, photographers. Titles by Julian Johnson. At the Rialto, New York, for grind run starting May 26. Running time, 62 mins.

Basher Bill..................Emil Jannings
Elizabeth..........................Fay Wray
Annie.......................Olga Baklanova
Mr. Smith................Ernest W. Johnson
Iron Mike................George Kotsonaros
Cronies of Basher Bill....{John Gough / Johnnie Morris}

A pause in the Jannings series. About the best thing that can be said of it is that it won't seriously interfere with others to come. It lacks smash box office potentialities and is far short of being a holdover feature. Yet the Jannings name should turn in satisfactory weeks for the theatres and its full circulation won't hold many regrets by Paramount other than that the star might have been given better material. But Jannings probably has a say in his subject matter, so he can shoulder his share of the responsibility for "Street of Sin."

Picture has production, photography, Jannings' vulgarities as a Limehouse bully and Olga Baklanova, playing his woman, to see it through. These count enough to class the film as first line fare.

Why Fay Wray is featured in this Jannings feature is one of those studio mysteries, although she's on the '28-'29 as a starred and featured player. If anybody deserves magnified mention it's this Olga Baklanova, who does a Jack Conway prostie well enough to equal or eclipse the work of Jannings and edge in on Mae West's "Diamond Lil" sans the "ice."

Miss Wray has been given a Salvation Army bonnet, folds her hands, looks good in the slum surroundings and waits for Basher Bill (Jannings) to break into her room. Meanwhile, Annie (Miss Baklanova) has turned over her night's earnings to the Basher, been thrown out for holding out and taken back and burned up by her man suddenly taking the veil because of his yen for Elizabeth (Miss Wray).

It's all curtains when Annie, frantic with jealousy, tips off to the cops who did the amusement part stick-up and the bobbies ride into Harmony Row for a gun play raid. The Basher takes a bullet from one of his gang's guns and expires after he has saved the babies in the Salvation Army center, the spot his former co-workers have picked for defense.

A number of tots are used, mostly all crying. There are one or two smiles in the way Jannings handles them. But nothing to equal the three-part yell of surprise, contempt and mirth which greets Jannings' morning ablutions when he gargles, spits the water into cupped hands and then returns it to his face for an economical cleansing. There are a few other touches, not quite so rough, but on the same pattern. That first one is going to disgust a lot of people, probably please the art mob and amuse others, but it doesn't seem entirely necessary. All it needed was "sound" to make it doubly sure to register and turn a few more stomachs.

Camera work of Milner and Fischbeck has aptly caught the intended filth of the locale with Stiller's direction particularly to the fore if he handled Miss Baklanova. Picture looks to have been abruptly chopped in a couple of places which, although it explains the brief running time of 62 minutes, is just as well.

Jannings gives a standard performance without highlights and has a couple of spots where he appears a bit foolish. Notably where Elizabeth prays him out of the idea which has brought him into her room, her linen or cotton nightgown being a help, and when "Iron Mike" hits him on one side of the jaw so that he turns for the second punch because of the girl's teachings. Remainder of cast is replete with types.

Josef von Sternberg and Benjamin Glazer are credited with the story, probably also suggested by Jannings. *Sid.*

Laugh, Clown, Laugh

Metro-Goldwyn-Mayer production and release. Directed by Herbert Brenon. Lon Chaney starred. Adapted from David Belasco-Tom Cushing stage play by Elizabeth Meehan. Cameraman, James Yonghowe. Titles by Joe Farnham. At the Capitol, New York, week May 26. Running time, 65 minutes.

Tito..........................Lon Chaney
Simon......................Bernard Siegel
Simonette...................Loretta Young
Giacinta...............Cissy Fitz-Gerald
Luigi..........................Nils Asther
Diane...........................Gwen Lee

Another romantic play with a semi-tragic finale, the fortunes of which are always anybody's guess. In this case, Lon Chaney as the star should be almost an insurance of a draw.

Star's name value is the film's best asset. Production is excellent in Herbert Brenon's best style. Element of uncertainty comes entirely in the character of the story, built upon aging man's hopeless love for young girl and his death to open the way for her mating with a young lover. Any way you look at it the fan's simple reaction is unfavorable to the bumping off of a character that had aroused sympathy. That's what happens here.

Chaney does some splendid acting as the clown who makes the world laugh while his heart is breaking with a vain love. Sentiment sometimes gets a bit sloppy, but this actor always has the situation in hand and carries through some passages that call for dainty treatment and nice judgment.

Rest of the cast is up to its assignment, although Loretta Young is rather a pale personality for the principal feminine role. Story develops with irritating slowness. It has a good screen climax in the episode where the clown brings about his own destruction while making a sensational "death-defying slide on the wire" in the theatre in order to free the girl he loves from the sacrifice of marrying him. This scene is similar to the finale of "Excess Baggage" story.

There is no true screen action in the whole picture, as commonly happens with stories brought from stage or book. Progress of action therefore has to be expressed in facial pantomime and the consequence is an over-abundance of closeups and plenty of titles. Comedy is almost absent, coming in such sequences as the clown's visit to a specialist for treatment of his melancholy, only to be told that he ought to go see Flit, the clown, to be cheered up and replying that he is Flit himself—the subject of a hoary old gag.

Background of the circus and stage is here exceedingly well pictured, but that locale is no longer a novelty as it was probably when the Belasco play was on the boards. Certainly it's not a screen novelty at this time.

In the absence of dramatic action here, back stage atmosphere doesn't mean much. The picture never once establishes tension or suspense, is entirely without vigorous comedy and its romantic appeal is practically nil. Al that's left for audience effect is Chaney's acting, and a scenic production that has a good deal of beauty, small ground for film fan response at best.

Result is a program picture that will have to do business on the prestige of its star but won't add to it. *Rush.*

LADY BE GOOD

First National production and release. Directed by Richard Wallace from the stage musical of same title. Dorothy Mackaill and Jack Mulhall featured. Credit slides removed from screen by Strand, New York, where it is playing this week, May 26. Running time, 69 minutes.

Jack..........................Jack Mulhall
Mary.....................Dorothy Mackaill
Murray........................John Miljan
Madison......................Nita Martan
Texas West.......................Dot Farley
Trelawney West..............James Finlayson
Landlady....................Aggie Herring
Dancer..........................Jay Eaton
Dancer......................Eddie Clayton
Assistant ....Yola d'Avril

A picture of small time vaudeville in the main, it looks to have been played and directed in the small time way. Which means that the farther away from Broadway it goes the better chance it has with the rurals. As a first runner in the de luxes it needs plenty of stage or other film support, and more than it has currently on the stage at the Strand.

If anything were needed to show up this picture back stage story it's the small time stage unit vaudeville at the Strand this week. Coming before or after the picture, it's a toss up as to which may be preferred.

Jack Mulhall plays a small time magician with plenty of live props. His girl assistant is Dorothy Mackaill. They are always together, in theatre and the boarding house when both are starving, with the director making it evident they are not doubled up. Toward the finish when there hasn't been a laugh for 2,000 feet, the director made three principals throw paste and powder over each other, Mr. Mulhall, Miss Mackaill and Nita Martan. If that's considered funny or filthy in Hollywood, it will be no place else.

Neither of the two mixed teams looks small timey. The other is John Mijan and Miss Martan, as adagio dancers. Mijan looks as much like one of those dancers as Roscoe Arbuckle. It would have been better if a piano player had been cast for the role. Miss Martan was okay as his opposite, although a bit heavy.

Mr. Mulhall and Miss Mackaill seemed too healthy to be starving, missing 13 meals at a time. At one point, when Miss Mackaill pulled out the waist of her dress to prove how thin she had gotten, Mulhall tried to do the same with his coat, but foolishly had on one of his regular garments.

Mijan is the villain, trying to make the magician's assistant, who is Miss Mackaill. The magician said a real trouper, in a title, wouldn't bust up another artist's act. Name of title writer not mentioned. If adagio dancers are real troupers it must have happened very recently.

There's the boarding house keeper who wants her room rent, the expected suggestion of the girl that the magician kill his prop animal pets for meals, which he refuses to do, and everything else that might be looked for from some one writing about something of which he appears to know nothing, and also played as well as directed that way.

Still these back stage plays seem to hold interest in the sticks and "Lady Be Good" had a w. k. stage name. So did "Abie's Irish Rose."

Picture runs 69 minutes and can be cut to anything above 55.

No action is the worst mark against the film. After that it's the scarcity of comedy in a story of this character, with but a laugh or two in the ordinary captions.

You can walk in or out on this picture at any time.

HIS TIGER LADY

Paramount production and release, starring Adolphe Menjou. Evelyn Brent featured. Directed by Hobart Henley. Adapted by Ernest Vadja from Alfred Savoir's play, "Super of the Gaiety." Cameraman, Harry Fischbeck. Titles by H. J. Manckiewicz. At the Paramount, N. Y., week of May 26. Running time, 57 minutes.

Henri.......................Adolphe Menjou
The Duchess..................Evelyn Brent
Mme. Duval.......................Rose Dione
Stage Manager...............Emil Chautard
Duke.........................Mario Carillo
Count....................Leonard de Vesa
Marquis....................Jules Rancourt

A typical Menjou cream puff. Unreal, unconvincing, unimportant, but moderately amusing because of a novel slant on the usual masquerade idea.

Menjou, an extra in a Parisian revue, falls in love with a beautiful and haughty duchess. To win her he borrows from the theatre wardrobe the costume of a rajah. Having awakened her interest and bluffed his way up to the point where she confesses her love, the extra reveals the deception and leaves. The next day the duchess shows up at the theatre as one of the chorus, and the final clinch indicates that they will take the vows.

Picture represents Evelyn Brent as a posey, indolent dame who fancies tigers because they have claws and scratchy habits. The idea of the slumbering histrionics is evidently to convey an impression of a volcano in repose. Put down the tiger part as baloney. It would have been a better picture minus the Elinor Glyn sash hitters.

Miss Brent looks great, however, and wears a couple of nifty gowns. Menjou's performance is smooth and pleasing. There's nobody else in the cast to speak of or about.

Film is okay for the spots where Menjou is a fav. It will be quickly forgotten. Menjou has been getting some palookas lately, and it may be a pertinent point whether a strictly so-so picture is good enough at his present stage of popularity. A very moderate moderate. *Land.*

THE NEWS PARADE

Fox production and release, featuring Sally Phipps, Nick Stuart and Earle Foxe. Directed by David Butler with J. A. Valentine and C. Wagner cameramen. Titled by M. S. Boylan. At Roxy, New York, week May 26. Running time, 67 mins.

Nick Naylor....................Nick Stuart
Sally Wellington..............Sally Phipps
Ivan Vodkoff......................Earle Foxe
Newsreel Editor............Truman Talley
A. K. Wellington..........Brandon Hurst
Prince Oscar.......................Cyril Ring
Snappy Walpole.......Franklin Underwood

First of the newsreel romance pictures to come in and leaving the field wide open for the others on the way. Fox has taken the subject and simply glorified a fresh free lance cameraman for comedy, hoking it up so that it runs off like one of the old serials. It misses the newsreel boys just as the many newspaper and college pictures have falsified press and campus. Its chief contribution is that Fox has modestly refrained from plugging its own news service and Boylan has titled so as to boost the newsreel in general.

Rather a shame the studio has botched a corking idea as there's a lot of material which could be pieced together about the hit and run camera boys to make good program material. Newsreel men will scoff at this opus. It's too broad to convince the public of anything other than being a mild slant on a profession of which it knows little.

That the pictured angle is miles away from the genuine article is the story department's fault. The yarn doesn't show any of the real cameramen, except as a background, although the Fox News offices on Tenth avenue are flashed as is Truman Talley, actual head of the Fox News service, who is introduced by name in a title which describes him as "the hard boiled, straight shooting chief of the newsreel staff."

Nick Stuart plays the forward kid who goes camera with a home made "box," so ridiculous and cumbersome as to even overtax the imagination of the much duped fans. It's particularly out of proportion when the other boys line up on Curtis Feld with their Akeleys and Debries.

Nick, of course, gets the closeup of the parachute jumper which brings him a tryout assignment from Talley. It's a window cleaning stunt shot allowing for the familiar dizzy footage as the principal struggles to get his stuff from a board hung out of a 20 or 30 story window.

Love interest creeps in when Nick is told to get A. K. Wellington, financier, with a horror of being photographed. This takes the action to Lake Placid, Palm Beach and Havana, Nick constantly running into the millionaire's daughter as he tries to "shoot" the old man. Finish is in Havana where Wellington and his offspring are abducted and Nick performs a rescue to save both of them and get his footage as well.

Simply a series of gags strung together haphazardly.

Laughs at the Roxy ran up a suficient total to designate it as satisfactory for the split week and lesser houses, but it has neither the story, cast nor merit to send it into the de luxes without some doubt. Boylan's titles are spotty although he has slipped a couple through for the mob when the old man Wellington says, "Just call me A. K., girls," and then in describing a group of falling ice skaters as "The Pratt family of Great Falls." Jack Conway's original title squib slightly changed.

Picture holds neither good farce nor drama. Just low comedy situations which are continuously shy of 100 percent and tend to weary. Stuart is shown grinding his camera aboard a fire truck rushing around New York, the two sport Genes (Sarazen and Tunney) are briefly seen during the Palm Beach passage, and an aquatic put-put chase needed a couple of fast motorboats to help the abduction suspense in Havana.

Sally Phipps gives her light heroine a nice appearance and Stuart is in his element. Earle Foxe is as legit as he can be as the broadly drawn menace, with Brandon Hurst actually top for comedy in playing A. K. Wellington.

Would have been better if Fox had undertaken to screen this subject on the level and gone into more detail as to the enterprise and energy involved in turning out 104 newsreels a year. "News Parade" can't class as anything but an ordinary feature with a serial tinge. **Patrons will still be in the dark on newsreels after this viewing, which doesn't make it impossible for Fox to do the subject again—but do it.**

And anyway, the Fox News bunch deserve a better dedication. *Sid.*

DECAMERON NIGHTS

(GERMAN-MADE)

Ufa production of Herbert Wilcox (Englishman) picture, featuring Werner Krauss and Lionel Barrymore. Photographed by Theodor Sparkbul. Setting by Erich Czerwonsky. At Greenwich Village theatre, New York, on run. Running time, 60 minutes.

The Soldan....................Werner Krauss
Saladin, son...............Lionel Barrymore
King of Algrave............Albert Steinruke
Perdita..............................Ivy Duke
Torella....................Bernhard Goetzke
Teodora, wife.......................Xeni Desni
Count Ricardo..................Randel Ayrton
Violante, wife....................Hanna Ralph
Imliff.........................Samson Thomas
Abbot..........................Hans Sternberg
Musical Arrangement by Andre Pola

Even Lionel Barrymore, Werner Krauss and a title pointing toward a salacious story will do little for this English-directed Ufa film, made in Germany three or four years ago, either from an artistic or a box office angle.

Taking one of the tales from the "Decameron of Bocaccio," legend of the Crusades, Herbert Wilcox (English) has turned out a commonplace, unconvincing story with a shoddy and obviously manufactured background.

It concerns itself with a scheme of the Saracen soldan, played by Werner Krauss (German) and a Christian king to unite their resources and conquer the world by the expedient of marrying the soldan's son to the king's daughter.

The prince (Lionel Barrymore—American), and the princess, neither aware of the other's identity, meet and fall in love at sight. The prince carries the maiden home to his father, who kills his son for defiance of the paternal mandate.

The princess falls dead on the prostrate form of her lover as her father comes in to identify her and clear up matters.

The plot is as old, of course, as the "Decameron of Bocaccio," if not older. As unwound in this picture, it is crude and tiresome; not helped any by the presence of a professional English beauty (Ivy Duke) as the princess. Miss Duke is a statuesque blonde, somewhat inflexible in motion and not quite young enough for a picture princess.

The picture is vague in detail, badly lit and carelessly cut. The sets look faked.

Krauss and Barrymore are as good as their roles will permit, but that isn't enough.

Anyone lured by the title to expect something racy is doomed to disappointment. Even the dirt—not that there's much—is dull.

CROOKS CAN'T WIN

FBO production and release. From the story by J. J. O'Neill. Director not credited on billing, screen or program. Features Ralph Lewis with cast including Thelma Hill, Sam Nelson, Joe E. Brown, Eugene Strong, Charles Hall and James Eagle. At the Hippodrome, N. Y., May 28. Running time, over 60 mins

Opens slow, but gathers momentum upon the introduction of the crook element halfway. Finishes powerfully with a miniature war between police and gangsters, in which a machine gun is used. Well made picture, of its kind, and should do moderately well in its intended spots. Casting is okay except for the featured player, Ralph Lewis. Thelma Hill photographs well and delivers in restrained, but effective manner.

Joe Brown, from musical comedy and on a police assignment, packs an infectious grin. He should do well under intelligent direction. Held down here through lack of comedy business.

Story is about a family of cops, the retired policeman still proud of having served in the force and anxious to see his adopted son succeed in his chosen field. The youngster nabs a bank robber the first day out, but is later dismissed for leaving his post and refusing to explain that his younger brother had sent him a note asking for help. The boy gets a job as a truck driver and then frames with the newspaper men to get the police commissioner to stage a raid the night the silk thieves plan another of their holdups. *Mori.*

YOUTH ASTRAY

(GERMAN MADE)

Produced by Matador Films, Berlin. Released here through Artlee Pictures Corp. Directed by Peter Ostermayr from story by Dr. Hohn Brandt and Alfred Halm. German cast, featuring Nina Vanna, Mart Johnson and Andre Mattoni. At Cameo, New York, week May 29. Running time, 70 minutes.

High-class audiences in the first and better second runs throughout the country will welcome "Youth Astray" as a well-mounted, cleverly directed and acted presentation of a theme long hacked on the screen, stage and in the novel.

Its very realism and naturalness of this German treatment of two classes of parents and two types of offspring just over the boundary of adolesency are refreshing and excellently sustained entertainment, compared to the tawdry, artificial hodge podge interpretation of the average Hollywood director on this subject.

Despite the straight strokes of semi-undress on the part of the wealthy sensual widow and the clear-cut advances of warm youth creating a regretful aftermath for the innocent daughter of parents made indifferent through social aspirations, the production has a verve appealing at all times to sophisticates. Yet it socks home the ending which sums up the teaching of parents to their collegiate sons and daughters.

For a foreign picture, "Youth Astray" is superbly edited. Well worded and pointed titles are used and are few in number. Theme moves in perfect continuity at a pace that cuts its 70 minutes' running time in half. Double and triple exposures advantageously substitute three-fourths of the incidents usually deemed necessary of a wordy explanation by foreigners.

THE CHORUS KID

(THIRD REVUE)

Goth production realesed by Lumas. Story by Howard Rockey. Adapted by Harold Shumate. Directed by Howard Bretherton. Casey Robinson titled, and C. Van Enger cameraman. Production manager, Carroll Saxe. Cast: Virginia Brown Faire, Sheldon Lewis, Thelma Hill, Hedda Hopper, John Batten, Bryant Washburn and Tom O'Brien. At the Stanley, New York, one day, May 24. Running time, 67 minutes.

Variety, having last week printed two conflicting reviews on this picture through error, saw this picture again for the third time, and continues to believe it's pretty fair material for a solo attraction in the daily change houses. Preceding criticisms had different aspects with the reviewer who caught it on a double bill evidently influenced and inclined to underrate it from that reason.

Its story does call for a rubber imagination, but cast and production give it sufficient initiative so that it holds its own. Stanley theatre though Thelma Hill the only name worth marquee lighting, when in reality none of the femme lineup stands out like Hedda Hopper. It's doubtful if Miss Hopper ever looked better in a picture, and, playing a scheming widow, the script made Washburn a chump in passing her up for the chorus youngster. But the author couldn't figure Miss Hopper's eye appeal when writing.

Gotham has slipped this one a couple of impressive and rich interiors. They help plenty, besides which, being a backstage story, there's quite a flash of feminine underpinning early in the running which will hold the boys in their seats.

Neither the Misses Hill or Faire classify as finishing school undergraduates. They even have trouble making the grade as something just as good. It's not so much the trouping as the appearance. The studios always have had worry in genuinely picturing college youngsters, and are invariably farther from the mark when called upon to characterize the co-eds and girls of the exclusive schools. About time a director or supervisor spent a day at Vassar, Smith or National Park so that they'd know what all the shootin' was about.

Miss Faire does well enough by the chorister who cashes in on some oil stock and invades a seminary because of a childhood spent off the fairway. Yet, cast honors are enfolded by Miss Hopper and Mr. Washburn, who plays the father of Miss Faire's roommate (Miss Hill). Sheldon Lewis is only flashed as a stage manager, with Tom O'Brien struggling to give a light comedy role some weight.

No need of the picture running over an hour, and clipping will help. Nice production cast work, and names that figure to mean something in the lesser houses make it worth attention. *Sid.*

DAWN

(BRITISH MADE)

Presented by Arch Selwyn at the Times Square, New York, on run, twice daily, at $1.65 top. Produced in England by Herbert Wilcox for the British and Dominion Film Company. Directed by Herbert Wilcox from the story by Capt. Reginald Berkeley. Screen adaptation by Reginald Berkeley. Featuring Sybil Thorndike. Running time, 80 mins.

Nurse Cavell	Sybil Thorndike
Madame Ada Bodart	Madame Bodart
Phillipe Bodart	Gordon Craig
Madame Rappard	Marie Ault
Her son, Jacques	Micky Brantford
Madame Pitou	Mary Brough
Jean, her husband	Richard Worth
Widow Deveaux	Colin Bell
Her Daughter	Dacia Deane
Col. Schultz	Cecil Barry
German A. P. M	Haddon Mason
British Airman	Maurice Braddell
Lutheran Priest	Edward O'Neill
Pres. Court-martial	Griffith Humphrey

In a 10-minute introduction, preceding the feature picture, Helen Ware (legit) hails this production as the most pretentious anti-war propaganda to date. "It was a labor of love," said Miss Ware, "made by warm hearts to benefit suffering human beings."

It may have been a labor of love, so, and once again, Love's labor lost.

The picture can make a little money only if expertly and extensively publicized and then only in certain localities in large cities. At the Times Square it is due for a short run at moderate grosses only on account of the publicity created through the European discussion which was echoed here, also, recently. Its draw is the foreign population, English or others.

There is nothing objectionable in the film to any nation or any creed. Neither is there anything of merit or interest in it. As an educational, perhaps, it can be used, but educationals are not commercial ones here.

The story, the situations, the locale, the characters—all are bleak, colorless creations lacking the essentials of popular American appeal. The leading character, Nurse Cavell, despite her obviously fine intentions, strikes no sympathetic vein. She is here a stiff, starched officious person. Titles are not enough, in themselves, to create likeable characters on the screen.

It is fairly well known over here in picture circles that the producer of "Dawn," in England, finding himself stuck with a picture, determined to start a little "Cavell" discussion in the hope that the publicity would put the film over. The publicity ran away from him and resulted in holding up the showing of the film over there. From that international publicity resulted.

The importers of this picture in America must have known that the picture depends on ballyhoo. The usual spot for a picture of this type is in the sure-seaters and it will probably end up there.

As far as New York is aware the picture is being shown in its original state, without any cuts. It was Selwyn's original intention to produce the sequence on the stage of the theatre with a legit speaking-playing company. This would have been more effective than the screen version, which is quite uninteresting, as it merely suggests the execution.

It is understood that Selwyn got the picture under a percentage arrangement, with little cash involved.

Briefly, the story is of English Nurse Cavell in Belgium, whose love for suffering humanity caused her to break the military laws. She hid escaped English prisoners, helped them get well, and later shipped them out of the danger zone. One of the men was finally caught and told about the Cavell operations. The German action in executing a woman who had been supplying the enemy with men seems justified. The treatment by Germans of enemy prisoners, as shown here, pictures the Germans as kind-hearted. But the clincher is in the execution scene. One of the soldiers in the firing squad refuses to raise his gun and the officer in command lets him get away with it.

Without the publicity attending this picture couldn't last a week anywhere at 75 cents top. It has been exploited to get a play in New York from the British element and possibly from the Germans.

A 15-minute newsreel preceding "Dawn," billed as "Memories of Conflict," "Official War Scenes," has some of the most thrilling war shots ever shown in a theatre. Had it been possible to embody material of this kind in a feature production it would have been strong enough to stand up at $2 on Broadway at a profit. It's unreleased war scenes, either official or deleted from news reels. The scenes are gruesome but gripping. They compose an undeniable preachment against war, as many are almost close-ups, probably by telephoto (long-distance) lens.

The sinking of two ships, one a cruiser with 2,000 men aboard and the other a merchant vessel, is an unforgettable spectacle. Final shots of the cruiser sinking, bottom up, shows hundreds of men clinging vainly for some support. Only 76 of the 2,000 were saved. The picture shows hundreds of men drowning.

These war shots, edited and cut by Al H. Young, easily form the best part of the program at this theatre.

Added

In the out of town version of this picture the most powerful sequence, which has been eliminated by the state censors for the New York showing, is to be retained. That is the execution scene. As one of the soldiers refuses to raise his gun and fire at Nurse Cavell the officer in command of the firing squad shoots him. The nurse drops to the ground in a faint. The officer then raises his revolver to shoot her himself.

Another scene cut in New York is where a German civilian official goes to make a final plea to the military governor who had ordered the nurse's execution. The military governor is shown at the theatre, implying indifference to the fate of the woman he had ordered killed.

Mori.

End of St. Petersburg

(RUSSIAN-MADE)

Sovkino Production directed by W. J. Pudowkin. U. S. exhibition rights with Arthur Hammerstein. Scenario by Natan Zarchi, with D. W. Bartlett production editor. Cameraman, A. Golownia. Score by Herbert Stothart. At Hammerstein's, New York, for twice daily run starting May 27 at $1.50 top. Running time, 93 mins.

A Peasant	Alexis Davor
His Father	Peter Petrovich
His Wife	Olga Korloff
His Mother	Anna Baranowska
A Worker	Paul Petroff
His Wife	Katrina Kaja
Factory Manager	Natan Golow
Capitalist	W. Obelensky
Kerensky	Serge Alexandrowski

Russian Revolution picture and nothing to grow hysterical about. Story stresses the overthrow of Kerensky as the big moment in Russia's independence, doing away with the Czar by a title. Well directed and replete with "types" but below the camera standard of the big German and program American pictures. Carries no love story and general appeal over here limited. Every sure-seat (art) house in the country should welcome it, and under that classification it fits.

If the Soviet Government turned over the city of St. Petersburg to Pudowkin for the making of this picture, as stated in the advance press stuff, there's no doubt the director passed up plenty. At least he's done nothing with the metropolis and its population other than to symbolize the reign of Nicholas II by oft repeated flashes of frowning statues and by a traveling camera inside the famed Winter Palace which leads up to the finish.

The capital-labor equation is presented in the form of a munitions factory. A principal fault of the story is that it continuously promises a gripping climax of a country in revolt which never fully arrives. Allowing that the pictured street skirmishes are facsimiles of the manner in which Russia actually gained its freedom, there's not enough spectacle concerned to interest a Yankee public which still believes the Czar was the main hurdle. The Kerensky aftermath is probably vital and true to Russia, its students and sympathizers, but the average American isn't that well informed and the bare and weak dramatic statement of that fact as made here doesn't sufficiently convince of the Kerensky middle class menace.

Picture's appeal is in its presumed authenticity and peasant characters—dirty, dull-witted, and dumbly suffering, who are slow to find themselves. It opens on a farm where a peasant, excellently played by Alexis Davor, must stay in a field and plow as his wife dies in childbirth. Trudging to the city with his mother to seek work through relatives, the boy stumbles into a nest of revolutionists. He is advised to go back to the farm as there is going to be trouble. When "the worker" and thinker (Paul Petroff), his relative, calls off the men as war increases the demands upon the munition factory, the slow-thinking but big and bulking widower becomes a strike breaker, innocently involving his kinsman when he tells his co-workers that he knows who started all the trouble. Grabbed from the mob by factory officials to repeat what he knows to the military, on promise that his relative will go free, the peasant makes his way into the office of Lebedewer (W. Obelensky), the factory head and capitalist figure, where he attacks the factory manager. Then, evidently smartened up by somebody, chants, "I want the highest," and goes for the throat of Lebedewer. Four or five soldiers subdue him after which he is beaten and thrown into prison until released to go into the trenches.

War stuff conforms to the foreign ideas of realism, stressing death in various gruesome postures. It runs the usual gamut and winds up as the soldiers return to St. Petersburg to support Kerensky.

A title states that the Czar has passed. Kerensky is shown addressing the troops whence "the worker" appears, also speaks to the soldiers, and the peasant steps from the ranks to substantiate his kinsman.

Pudowkin has handled his cast and continuity extremely well. An explanatory title tells that there is only one actor in the personnel. If the picture appears to jump and skip it's more the fault of the photography because of practically no dissolves and lack of irising. It's simply a matter of abrupt cutting from scene to scene. Various camera angles stand out with the registering of Russia's vast expanse and the drudgery of the factory adequately impressed.

The director has evidently concerned himself with adhering to fact and symbolizing everything else. This means that the power of dramatic license has been lost in important passages which might sell the film to the public. If admirable it also serves to temper those sequences calling for spectacle. Titles attempt to take the curse off the propaganda by stressing the term "Democracy," yet this film is apt to sponsor many an idea in mining and industrial centers. It's influence within a large city will be negligible.

"The End of St. Petersburg" is too sincere an effort to be taken lightly. It infers integrity to fact throughout and that minority which takes its screen educationally will give it attention. However, its photography keeps it from being a rave.

For public approval the picture unwinds too much like a well illustrated text book. There is no love theme and it holds but two laughs, both of which concern an unimportant pickpocket. It is, perhaps, Russia's "Birth of a Nation"—for Russia.

Only those program houses which definitely know their town and patronage can afford to say "yes" on this film sight unseen.

For the Hammerstein showing the picture is mightily helped by Herbert Stothart's score, among the best ever written for a Broadway screening, splendidly interpreted by an exceptionally full orchestra. The presentation is without prolog or an intermission.

It belongs in the "art" theatres where it should be of holdover qualifications.

Sid.

FAZIL

Fox production and release featuring Charles Farrell and Greta Nissen. Directed by Howard Hawks. Story by Pierre Frondaie. Adapted by Phillip Klein. Scenario by Seton I. Miller. Cameraman, L. Wm. O'Connell. Film editor, Ralph Dixon. At Gaiety, New York, June 4, for twice daily run at $2. Running time, 75 mins.

Prince Fazil	Charles Farrell
Fabienne	Greta Nissen
Helene Debreuze	Mae Busch
Ahmed	Vadim Uraneff
Jacques Debreuze	Tyler Brooke
Rice	Eddie Sturgis
Aicha	Josephine Borio
John Clavering	John Boles
Gondolier	John T. Murray
Iman Idris	Erville Alderson
Zouroya	Dale Fuller
Ali	Hank Mann

Large and liberal doses of good solid box office sex and sheik stuff predict a dollar studded future for this Fox production. Outwardly it's a woman's picture, but there's no reason why any mugg should complain with the array of femininity in the harem scenes. Not to mention Greta Nissen, a high-tension emotional vibrator, who with this picture emerges as one of the screen's nifty neckers.

It's been a long time since Miss Nissen has had a major assignment, although it must be all of four years since she first came to the camera. She looks great, wears clothes well, is a pretty fair actress and oozes with that w. k. stuff. "Fazil" ought to advance her markedly.

Charles Farrell, separated from Janet Gaynor in a totally dissimiliar role to his types in "Seventh Heaven" and "Street Angel," goes after the flap vote with a virile desert polygamist characterization in a business-like performance. Always bearing in mind that essentially and basicly the story and the characterization are baloney.

"Fazil" is primarily a woman's picture because it is devoted 100 per cent to the grand pash with little action or humor. The love palpitations are unceasing from start to finish.

The Arab prince meets the chic Parisienne with ignition setting in immediately. It's one long honeymoon thereafter intensified by the sex antagonism that develops when the Arab seeks to impose his absolute will upon his wife and dominate her every thought. Fighting for her personal liberty as a woman and an European yet loving the Arab with his Oriental ideas, the Parisienne suffers and loves in surroundings that should exercise a strong imaginative power over feminine audiences.

Picture holds a sad ending but it's not apt to be a serious impediment. Story could hardly end otherwise than in the death of one or both of the lovers. It's both. The death scene has been dramatized to the nth degree.

Some minor parts, scarcely more than bits, are assigned to Mae Busch, Tyler Brooke and John Boles. The latter, a clean-cut leading man, is the boy that is left in the lurch when Fazil first casts his flaming orbs on the gal.

Production is excellent. Especially unnecessary, however, and rather gruesome was the scene early in the unreeling when Fazil orders the decapitation of a runaway servant. Just as the handy man is about to cleave off the head the Mohammedan time for prayer arrives. The executioner puts down his gigantic sword, goes through his devotional formula, picks up the sword when finished, and quietly lops off the hapless retainer's head.

Photography is credited to L. William O'Connell, who has done a first rate job all the way. Howard Hawks' direction is good. Perhaps a major share of the flowers belongs to the men who handled the script. Sheik thing was done to death a few years ago and it is notable that this story manages to add a few new wrinkles to a seemingly exhausted theme. The harem scene referred to brings in a flock of Hollywood's shapeliest. Fazil, having left his wife in Paris, returns to his sandy province to forget with the harem as the anti-toxin.

"Fazil" is utterly unreal, mushy and trite. But it looks to be commercially strong because it possesses what the women have indicated they like. Its $2 career will be limited but for the general release it should be a big dough picture. *Land.*

THE DRAG NET

Paramount production and release. George Bancroft starred; Evelyn Brent and William Powell featured. Directed by Josef von Sternberg. Original by Oliver H. P. Garrett; adapted by Jules and Charles Furthman. At Paramount, New York, week June 2. Running time, about 70 minutes.

Two-Gun Nolan	George Bancroft
The Magpie	Evelyn Brent
Dapper Frank Trent	William Powell
"Gabby" Steve	Fred Kohler
Sniper Dawson	Francis MacDonald
"Shakespeare"	Leslie Fenton

Before "The Drag Net" opened Saturday at the Paramount, out-of-town reports on its accumulating week's gross seemed to say that here was a surprise draw—and it should be that, at the Paramount as well as any other regular picture house. As an underworld with unusual rapidity and plenty of action it must compare most favorably with, if not above, that other "Underworld," also directed by Josef von Sternberg.

"The Drag Net" for its swiftness and some tenseness may reflect more credit upon its cutter than the remainder of the technical staff, for that is the way it looks. It's cut in and out with incredible swiftness at times, all in action and no action or sequence prolonged. For that the picture is a model, helped, of course, with its scenes and photography as well as by its director. The latter has slipped in many a curious little shot, just enough and fitting, while his mob handling for the involved scene of rounding up the crooks is A1. If this von Sternberg is the boy Chaplin picked and who flopped with that Salvation film on his first try, he has fully redeemed himself, and seems to have plenty in his bean.

Oliver H. P. Garrett, who wrote the corking story, is one of Menkiewiczs recruits, from the New York 'World,' and this is probably Garrett's first. He has an interesting tale of the downbelows, cops vs. crooks, the latter in a gang with William Powell their sardonic and cynical leader. Twist is where the gang gets the best of it, through framing George Bancroft as the captain of detectives, into believing he had killed one of his own men, Donovan.

That lead Bancroft to resign after he had started a furious drive to clean up Gangville, giving the boss crooks 24 hours to leave town. Among the crooks is a girl friend of Powell's. Bancroft falls for her and she for him, the girl walking on the crook leader after seeing how the chief detective operates with his two-gun stuff. And as a lead shooter Bancroft appears to have it on the "western" boys; he did everything with the guns excepting shooting around a corner. Probably overlooked that.

It's the liveliness of this well-made picture, the promiscious murders and the general hell bent of the whole thing that holds. It opens with action, a murder trial with one of the gang accused. A stool, about to testify against him, is shot dead on the witness stand from the window of an adjoining house by one of the gang.

Later that same shooter was killed by the boss crook for talking too much. All he said was that Bancroft had been framed over Donovan's murder. It was at a little celebration party in a nite club. So the head gangster eased out the talker to a side room and left him there, lifeless, as the party proceeded.

The girl brought Bancroft back and the gang was wiped out when she told him he had been framed. That took the drink craze away from him, but the young woman never did say whether she had been Powell's girl, immaterial, anyway, down below as between a cop and a crook.

Bancroft is a strong personage in the setting as the bull dog detective. He's playing it all of the time. Evelyn Brent is the girl, always doing well in playing but not always looking so well. In a few scenes, though, she looks peachy with those close fitting hats. Powell is the debonair crook, suggesting everything the role expects of him. Other characters on both sides do their bits, with Francis MacDonald predominating as The Sniper.

Production in high for film of this story character. Slight but sufficient comedy.

THE LIVING IMAGE
OR
THE LADY OF PETROGRAD
(FRENCH MADE)

French producer unknown and unprogrammed or billed. Distributor in United States, Phoenix. Directed by Marcel L. Herbier. No story source mentioned on program or screen. Probably original; not good enough for adaptation otherwise. Emmy Lynn, Jaque Catelain and Roger Karl featured. At Cameo (sure seater), New York, week June 2. Running time, around 55 minutes.

Countess Svirska	Emmy Lynn
Mme. de Cassel	Claire Prelia
Capt. Ditmitriff	Jaque Catelain
Henri de Cassel	Jaque Catelain
Gen. Count Sivirska	Roger Karl
Charanon	Gaston Jacquet
Louis	Bondire

A primitive story along primitive picture ideas for over here is "The Living Image," French made. It's questionable if this picture will do business even in the sure-seaters. Sunday afternoon at the Cameo at 2, with a Chaplin two-reel revival, "The Count," added to regular film bill, not 30 people in that 499-seater.

For America "The Living Image" as a title was a stupid selection. And the alternative sub-title, "The Lady of Petrograd," is little better, though at least the secondary name signifies something. For Russia possibly the story appeals, or the characters, or the Russian revolutionary opening. Locale is intended for Russia, and at the opening, St. Petersburg, but moves to France.

Opens with the commencement of the czar's overthrow, with a few stray mobs in view trying to batter down palace doors that had plate glass in them. The Bolsheviks maybe didn't know enough in those days to break the glass instead. Gen. Count Svirska and his women folks are at home and worried. Capt. Ditmitriff has warned the general the rebels are about to bust out. Before the general takes any steps, however, to protect his family or himself, he shoots down the captain cold bloodedly.

The captain had a mutual love affair on with Mrs. Svirska. The latter knew her sweetie had been bumped off by hubby, but she stuck to the A. K. after the Svirskas had fled the border in safety, to the Riviera. That's about all of the revolution, and inexpensive.

Down in the sunshine of lower France the countess sees Henri de Cassel, "the living image" of her captain. She falls for him, as she had for the other, with both going strong for her. So the A. K., by this time looking about 50 years older than his wife, tries to kill Henri. He fails, and raves. Mrs. Svirska tells Henri's mother to keep him away from her, as the Svirkas are going to Eze, wherever that is. It was like the old gag of "Don't you dare come to my room 508!"

Henri goes to Eze, and they let loose two dogs on him. But the general killed one of the dogs 15 feet below Henri on a wall as the A. K. shot at Henri. So you know what kind of a pistol expert he was. Then Henri shot the general, who should have died, anyway, of apoplexy in the first 500 feet.

And that was the end of that.

But Henri's mother, Claire Prelia, is the most magnificent patrician-looking woman of the world's screen. Hollywood could use her for any dowager role.

Jaque Catelain in his dual role played it with his mouth open. Perhaps the makeup stuck when his lips were closed. Otherwise he's not the brand of American-favored juv. Good looking enough excepting for his mouth, but without force.

Emmy Lynn may be liked on the Continent, and she can make up her mind she's set for there. Nice enough in the plump style, with possibly the photography giving her much the worst of it at times. Also at times the film is heavily tinted, too much so and too much of it.

Roger Karl seems an excellent character actor. As the A. K. General he did a good job of a thankless role. Another character and bald-headed, probably taken by Gaston Jacquet, as the general's personal aide, was attractive in the oddity of the entire makeup for it.

At the Cameo when there is a terrible picture terribly cheap, they ring in a Chaplin two-reeler, as they are doing this week. If the feature at those times gets credit for any business, it should go to the Chaplin instead.

Yet, while things like "The Living Image" can't get over anywhere else, there still may be a market for them in the Russian communities or neighborhoods. Like "Ivan the Terrible," more terrible than its title. Yet its American distributors cleaned up $40,000 over here showing it to the Russians and their families.

It would seem from the Russian revolutionary pictures that Russia will never tire of the subject on the screen. This is about the 10th foreign-made of recent months with the revolution, or some of it, in them. Perhaps this is put out just now because of "The End of St. Petersburg," at Hammerstein's. If so, the title should be altered to "The Beginning of the End of St. Petersburg"

Lay off.

The Strange Case of Capt. Ramper
(GERMAN-MADE)

Defu Production, released in North America by First National. Directed by Max Reichmann. Story by Curt J. Braun. Paul Wegener featured. At Roxy, New York, week June 2. Running time, 79 mins.

Captain Ramper	Paul Wegener
Tony	Mary Johnson
Jim Chocolat	Kurt Gerron
Freddy	George D. Gurtler
Professor Barbazin	Hermann Vallentin
The Strange Doctor	Hugo Doblin
Chocolat's Father	Dillo Lombardi
The Captain	Raimondo van Riel
The Thick One	Harry Grunwald
The Thin One	Max Schreck
The Old One	Plotz Larell
The Giant	George Schmieter
The Ship's Boy	Karl Balihaus

First National is releasing and Roxy is showing this German flicker. That gives it distinction over and above the general run of imported pictures that hit the sure-seaters and not the deluxes. It is somewhat better than the contemporary German pictures seen on this side during the last season or two but possesses characteristic faults of most German, or foreign, films as appraised from the American viewpoint.

It is draggy running about 80 minutes at the Roxy Saturday and with the stage show apparently shaved down to accommodate the extended screen period. Love interest negligible. No youth in the picture and not so much as a single mild giggle throughout the 80-minute stretch.

Nor is there any essential dramatic conflict. No clashing of wills or muscles to speak of. Few of the ingredients considered essential to popular entertainment are present.

The story is of a man lost in the Arctic wastes for 15 years. He becomes a big, hulking, ape-like creature with mind a blank. Discovered and captured by the crew of a whaling ship he is brought back to civilization where a famous brain specialist ultimately restores his thinking powers. The man, however, has lost his taste for civilization and his thoughts are of the "quiet and purity of the North."

At this point the Germans trot out their set formula of symbolic dissolves. The squalor, vice, intemperance, viciousness, poverty and misery of a big city are handled in a cycle of impressions to prove that civilization is corrupt and rotten and life among the polar bears much to be preferred.

The picture has in its favor a certain timeliness from the aviation angle. Captain Ramper is represented as starting for the North Pole in an aeroplane prior to the war. Wrecked in the barren country he is given up as lost. The presentation at the Roxy included a short spoken prolog mentioning the recent disaster of General Nobile and his dirigible. One of the characters thereupon recalls the strange case of Captain Ramper and the house goes dark for the picture.

Direction generally good, photography ditto. Doubtful whether the plot will interest the average American, although there is plenty of market for the grotesque and bizarre in fiction. Much must be accepted without question in following the story development.

Acting is good, types interesting and production adequate. The net result fair to middling screen fare badly in need of a lot of cutting.

However, the record of recent foreign pictures, the absence of the things that sell easiest in these parts, and the sombre theme indicate that "The Strange Case of Captain Ramper" will be just another non-combustible. *Land.*

Clothes Make the Woman

Tiffany-Stahl production and release. Written and directed by Tom Terriss. Cast: Eve Southern, Walter Pidgeon, Charles Byer, George Stone, Duncan Renaldo. At Hippodrome, New York, week June 4. Running time, 65 mins.

Another demonstration of how the Czar got slapped, which gives the late Nicholas II just three Times Square vetos this week—Cameo, Hammerstein's and Hip. This particular conception of the Russian revolution carries a "Last Command" pattern in that the action switches from a Hollywood studio to the Communists' backyard and then to a California "lot" again. It won't do for other than the daily changes.

Central idea has the principal

duo re-enacting their harrowing experience in Russia before the camera, within identical sets which terrify the former princess. It's all pretty choppy, jumbled and not well cast. Besides which a few inane titles are included. So it's too much of a burden to make this release other than suitable material for the minor houses and in neighborhoods which aren't too particular.

Walter Pidgeon plays the film extra suddenly become a star in one picture. Production heads and supervisors, perplexed by obtaining a follow-up yarn, listen to the boy who starts to relate a true story. **This carries the action into the rather hokey Russian uprising culminating in a misfit idea of how the czar and his family were assassinated. Being the story of himself in Russia, the newly crowned screen light goes on to relate how he saved the princess, how she escaped at the border and how he has never seen her since. It's a great tale to the studio heads and they start production with a finish to the script.**

Leave it to the hero to find the lost princess (Miss Southern) in the mob of extras. He, of course, picks her out to play opposite him to simply duplicate their former experiences. All's well, plus love interest, until the cellar scene, which marks the end of the Romanoffs.

Hero, gun in hand, intends to miss the princess when ordered to fire, but a cartridge has been mistakingly loaded in place of a blank, and he actually shoots her. He finishes the picture with a double and goes back to his sweetheart as she convalesces.

What "Clothes Make the Woman" as a title has to do with all this only Tiffany-Stahl can explain.

Cheap picture to make as one series of sets double and flashes of the family killing are simply repeated later when the film company is supposed to be "shooting." None of the players give it anything beyond a stereotyped reading, while the director, Tom Terriss, shows little ingenuity and no finesse in establishing his points. Action is stilted with the titles of no aid.

Basic idea could have been molded into a nice piece of work, but the studio developed too many thumbs. Film may offset some of its weak points by Main Street interest in the studio stuff. Not much of it, but enough to keep them looking and it reveals the mechanics of one traveling camera effect.

Ordinary at best without hope or promise of accomplishing anything above a Class C showing. *Sid.*

DEVIL'S TRADEMARK

FBO production and release. Directed by J. Leo Meehan from story by Calvin Johnson. Continuity by Dorothy Yost. Al Seigler, cameraman. In cast: Belle Bennett, William V. Mong, Marion Douglas, William Bakewell, William Desmond. At Stanley, New York, one day, May 25. Running time, 70 minutes.

One of those freakish story angles characteristic of many indie pictures makes "The Devil's Trademark" less impressive and lighter than the average program meller.

It deals with a pair of married crooks who go straight with the arrival of their first child. The husband, however, obstinately persists for a score of years in looking for the criminal taint in his offspring, it being the agreement that if such manifests itself his wife will okay his return to the burglar's kit.

The story is brought to the screen in a shoddy way, with the son left hanging literally in mid-air when the picture ends. The sacrifices of the wife in paying back stolen goods are robbed of any dramatic value by her consistent assent to the husband's frequent reference to the children and his eagerness for them to enter crooks' row, so that he can quit the straight and narrow.

A love affair between the daughter and son of the foundry employer rings truer of an effort at sincerity.

In the daily change and neighborhood houses "The Devil's Trademark" will get by.

Its story holds a glint of something that is being talked over by scientists—the criminal taint in the progeny of the criminal. More of that might have drawn better attention; but, at that, maybe it wouldn't have held popular appeal. Still there may be a story for someone, making it underworld, of course, and tracing back in it to bring out that heredity will prevail, though it jumps a generation.

The House of Scandal

Tiffany-Stahl production and release. King Baggot, director Featured, Dorothy Sebastian, Pat O'Malley, Harry Murray, Gino Corrado, Lee Shumway. Story by E. Morton Hough. Continuity by Frances Hyland. Photography, Barney McGill. Titles, Viola Brothers Shore. At Loew's New York, one day, May 11, as half double bill. Running time, around 60 minutes.

Anne Rourke	Dorothy Sebastian
Pat Regan	Pat O'Malley
Danny Regan	Harry Murray
Morgan	Gino Corrado
Mrs. Chatterton	Ida Darling
Butler	Lee Shumway
Man About Town	Jack Singleton
Mrs. Rourke	Lydia Knott

Just missed. "The House of Scandal" was going along very nicely when it blew up. That leaves it for the usual trade for this kind of a picture, excepting where there is an Irish neighborhood. This is then a cinch.

The story got one of the best starts in a comedy way for a long while and had sufficient dramatic interest intermingled to hold on top of that. But either the time limit or something mixed in, with the story fading away faster than it started, winding up with with a most illogical conclusion, leaving but little besides explained.

It's the tale of Irish policeman in New York meeting his immigrant brother. The immigrant admires his brother's copper uniform. While the cop is sleeping he tries on the uniform and helmet. While wearing it a taxi accident happens below his **window, and he rushes into the street, forgetful of the uniform.**

As a police officer he is given charge of the case, a young girl with a bruised ankle, whom he takes to her home, a private house uptown. Falling for the girl, he calls again the next evening, and, to make it good, again wears his sleeping brother's uniform. But the second evening the gang of crooks in the private house, and with the girl a member, turns off a jeweler for a necklace. When the jeweler discovered his loss he squawked, this calling down the boy with the uniform from an upstairs room, and the jeweler demanded he arrest the thieves.

Instead he arrested the jeweler at the girl's request, but tried to let him go when on the street, realizing he was not the official his suit said he was. The jeweler wouldn't run away, but the cop did, the gem man tearing a button off his coat and mentally taking the number of his shield.

Through these headquarters became aware of the identity of the real cop, who attempted to shield **his brother. The latter, to square himself and brother, sought the girl, finding her, but he was shot by one of the gang.**

In between the real cop brother arrives, arrests the girl, and she is given a stretch.

From that point a jump to the finish. When the girl's term is up she walks out of the prison to find her boy lover now a regular cop waiting to marry her. No reason given why she was with the gang or for anything else..

That was the nuts.

A fine chance muffed.

A MILLION FOR LOVE

Sterling production released by Hollywood Pictures. Story by Peggy Gaddis with Robert Hill directing. Cast: Reed Howes, Mary Carr, Josephine Dunn, Lee Shumway. At Loew's New York as half of double bill, one day, May 25. Running time, 58 mins.

Run off in less than an hour but slow despite the curtailed footage. Main reason is an overlength cut back as the daughter of the district attorney explains why the boy on trial for his life is innocent. About where it belongs on a double bill.

Starts off in a courtroom with young Reed Howes up for the murder of a gang leader. The d. a.'s child has befriended the boy's family on her charity rounds until she has fallen in love with the senior son of the aged but sweet mother for whom the director has made every day Mother's Day.

Boy won't say a word in his defense but the girl finally takes the bit in her teeth and reveals all.

Forbidden by her father, who has an eye on the governorship, to mingle with the socially undesirable Eagans, the girl has followed Denny to a joint where he has gone to tell the mob ruler he's through doing "jobs." Getting into the room where the two-man conference is going on, the girl watches the two struggle with Denny escorting her to an exit as his opponent lies unconscious.

It's brought out that a gang member puts on the finishing touch by knife, for just what reason nobody ever finds out.

Hill, directing, has spent nearly a thousand feet showing the father refusing to allow the daughter to attend Howe's family birthday party the night of the murder. This passage is so slow as to kill off interest in the story, and force walkouts or put 'em to sleep. Otherwise, Hill has done fairly with the material.

Howes and Miss Dunn make a suitable team for this type and Miss Carr again doing her sympathy-catching mother. Lee Shumway is the light comedy younger brother.

A few grins here and there, but the picture is not above standing alone, except in the very small houses, and should have program support at 25c or over. *Sid.*

HEARTS OF MEN

Morris Schlanck production, released through Anchor Film Distributors. Directed by James P. Hogan from screen story based on James Oliver Curwood novel. Robert Cline, cameraman. In cast: Mildred Harris, Thelma Hill, Cornelius Keefe. At Loew's Circle, one day, May 14, one-half of double bill. Running time, 60 minutes.

As an indie meller "Hearts of Men" is okay. It has all of the ingredients necessary for success in the houses frequented by the night workers. The poor lad thwarts his rich competitor, knocking over barriers of a killing and a burglary, to win the girl.

Director Hogan trots his continuity **along at a good gait so that at no time is there any obvious lagging. The leads, however, are not so heavy. They have a marked tendency to overact. Cornelius Keefe is especially studied and artificial in this one.**

Rinty of the Desert

Warner Bros. production and release. Directed by D. Ross Lederman from story arranged by Harvey Gates. Frank Keson, cameraman. Titles by James A. Starr. "Rin Tin Tin" starred. In cast: Audrey Ferris, Carrol Nye and Otto Hoffman. At Tivoli, New York, one day, May 25, one half double bill. Running time, 60 minutes.

"Rinty of the Desert" is very similar to several other productions with desert locales in which this dog has been starred. Very little story and most improbable situations, but will entertain majority who like that stuff.

Dog's activity with basket of puppies will get the laughs and interest. Dog takes some of biggest leaps of the screen in getting help to master at bottom of a pit.

Picture could stand elimination of reel of meaningless bedroom scenes and shots of country streets.

BROADWAY DADDIES

Columbia production and release. Featuring Jacqueline Logan, Alec B. Francis and Rex Lease. From story by Victoria Moore, scenario by Anthony Coldeway. Directed by Fred Windernere. Cast includes Phillips Smalley, Clarissa Selwynne, De Sacia Mooers, Betty Francisco. At Stanley, New York, one day, May 23. Running time 62 mins.

A light-meller with love interest predominating Construction of production and ability of cast overcome lack of action. Can stand up alone where double features are usually booked.

On appearances Rex Lease, youthful lead, stands out as a boy with possibilities given an opportunity. Screens remarkably well, seems able to wear clothes and has the faculty of putting his business across nicely.

Story is of the night club chorus girl who turns down propositions from one of the owners of the joint in favor of the poor boy who turns out to be a millionaire in disguise.

Miss Logan is attractive enough to forget the colorless settings and Alec B. Francis delivers capably as the boy's father. *Mori.*

QUEEN OF CHORUS

Capitol (made) production, released through Anchor Film Distributors. Charles J. Hunt, director. Robert Cline, cameraman. Story arranged by Adele Buffington. In cast: Rex Lease, Virginia Brown Faire, Betty Francisco, Lloyd Whitlock. At Loew's New York one day, May 22, one-half double bill. Running time, about 60 minutes.

Very little backstage stuff but "Queen of Chorus" should prove generally satisfactory.

Story runs along hack lines. Lloyd Whitlock over-acts heavy role adding burlesque touch to parts ordered serious by script. Virginia Brown Faire as "Queen" and Rex Lease, as the boy friend, entertain in light way.

Regular screen type of battle when boy finds his employer tried to gyp him of his girl by showing her bills and getting her to compromise herself as sacrifice to save youth from bars.

INSPIRATION

Excellent (made) production, released through Commonwealth. Starring George Walsh. Directed by Bernard McEverty from story arranged by Arthur Hoerl. Marcel Le Picard, cameraman. In cast: Gladys Frazin and Earle Larrimore. At Loew's New York May 22, one day, one-half double bill. Running time, 75 minutes.

For second run houses in not too particular neighborhoods "Inspiration" will be better than the average screen fare. Cutting out 20 minutes in running time of drawing room and dance hall scenes would help audience interest and also bolster the suspense which is weak enough, due to the plot going off in several tangents.

Title is meaningless. Even somethink like "Who's Baby Am I?" would give better inkling of action which hinges on identity of the father of an illegitimate child.

George Walsh is too abrupt in his movements to be convincing. Action laid in Port Said and New York. Native dancer and New York girl provide inspiration for Walsh, as son unjustly accused by father as child's parent. Conventional finis.

RIDING FOR FAME

Universal production and release. Starring Hoot Gibson. Directed by Reeves Eason, who also gets story credit. Harry Neumann, cameraman. In cast: Ethelyn Claire, Slim Summerville, Charles K. French, Allan Forrest. At Loew's New York one day, May 29, one-half double bill. Running time, 60 minutes.

Gibson does some of his best bronco bustin' in "Riding for Fame." The story is better than his average, and Gibson fans will find the action well sustained.

Use of Slim Summerville in a clowning role works in some good laughs' which well supplant exaggeration of western hokum usually found in these.

Old flivver gag on desert introduces Gibson, girls on ranch and the heavy, who hoodwinks the old man and frames the hero.

Fight in shack, with star beating up three hukies, helped, along with Summerville's bantering.

BRANDED MAN

Trem Carr production, released by Rayart. Directed by Scott Pembroke. Story by Todd Robins. June Marlowe featured. In cast, Charles Delaney, Erin LaBissoniere, Gordon Griffith, Lucy Beaumont. At Loew's New York, one day, May 18, as one half double bill. Running time, 70 minutes.

A weak sister on any bill mainly because of a highly improbable story that drags along and cries out loudly for shears.

Story deals with the familiar triangle situation, with Fred "Deacon" Colgate as the central figure. Colgate (Delaney), studious youth, inherits a row of tenements and falls in love with the daughter of one of his tenants.

Married to her and settled in Larchmont, he soon discovers she is one of the hot and bothered type, continually on the make. When discovering her in a compromising situation with a pal he blows to Texas. There he is the victim of a stickup, the gunman being bumped off by a truck immediately after the job.

The crook is mistaken for Colgate and the latter permits it to become known that he is dead. On the bum he drifts to Juarez and is pushed into the fight racket, soon becoming champ of his division. A college pal discovers his identity by a brand on his arm and brings him back to his sister, Louise.

Not satisfied to end the flicker here the producers drag it out to show that Colgate's wife has married his pal, and the latter, finding her in the arms of another, murdered his wife and her lover.

There isn't a sympathetic character in the film and the slap at the beautiful but under-privileged tenement dame won't help this one in the neighborhoods. With some judicious cutting this might slide by as half of a double bill in some of the grinds.

PRINCE JEAN

(FRENCH-MADE)

Paris, May 11.

Adopted from Charles Mere's melodrama created by Andre Brule at the Renaissance three years ago, "Le Prince Jean" is a good picture we shall not hear much about. It is sure to attract in the provinces.

Rene Hervil has made the most of the scenario and has done his duty to Cineromans. Some fine views of Belgium, action is thrilling (with a pathetic phone scene), and the title alone, for those who know Mere's melo, will help to attract.

Claire is fond of Count Jean, inveterate gambler. He soon ruins himself on the race course and decides to disappear.

After waiting three years Claire accepts the marriage offer of a banker, Arnheim, but puts off the ceremony a little longer. Of course the rich banker is a crook and he was responsible for Count Jean's ruin because he wanted Claire.

Jean, known as the Prince because he is so elegant. reveals the true situation, appropriates Claire's love letters, which had been stolen by Arnheim, and carries off his sweetheart.

The couple abandon their former ties in Belgium and start life again in another country.

Renee Heribel is sweet and pretty in the delightful role of Claire. Dalsace is the Prince, while the other parts are held by Andre Dubosc (aristocratic uncle), Simone Montalet and Nino Costantini.

Kendrew.

Case of Jonathan Drew

(BRITISH MADE)

Produced by the Piccadilly Pictures of England. Directed by Alfred Hitchcock with Ivor Novello and June as principals. At the Fifth Avenue Playhouse, New York ("art" sure-seater), June 10. Running time, 75 minutes.

Here's a story idea that, adequately carried out, would have knocked the "art" fans for a row of ecstatic exclamations. But the English producers couldn't make the grade. They took a smashing theme, gummed it up with cheap and shoddy catering to the lowest taste of what they supposed to be their public, and then further smeared it with acting and photography that belongs to the American studio of 10 years ago. It's a sorry affair. Germ of an epic story in this scenario of a near-tragedy growing out of piling up circumstantial evidence against an entirely innocent man while the newspaper reading mob is inflamed by a series of atrocious crimes. Blundering police arrest well intentioned man and when he escapes with the bloodthirsty mob at his heels, they learn he is innocent.

Problem is to catch up with him before the hunt-frenzied peasants tear him to pieces. The Germans might have made a fine, bitter social satire out of the material for supercillious high brows to rave over. Here it has been turned into a trashy commercial film worthless for the "art" audiences and for the generality of American fans alike.

Picture is full of unbelievably stilted acting by Novello, endless simpering closeups of June, the English ingenue and super-blonde heroine, and vast quantities of very terrible acting by the rest of the cast.

Mike Mindlin has written a special leader for the feature, setting forth that Alfred Hitchcock is the best director the English industry has, which would make a dandy music cue for the British national anthem.

Picture has trick shots borrowed from the German technique and little slants of sex kick lifted from the American studio with that brutal crassness that only the Briton is capable of in his most earnest moments. A Frenchman can assimilate alien moods and make them Gallic, but when an Englishman goes foreign, the result is very melancholy.

Here, for instance, we have a sequence of a lot of English dress models glimpsed in their dressing rooms off the gown salon, disporting in intimate lingerie and it is marvelous to behold. In another case are sprightly peeks at June impersonating a daughter of Albion taking a bath. Now what subtle detail do you suppose they stress to deliver the intimate effect of this last episode? Believe it or not, they screen close-ups of her robust calf from the knee down and the wriggling toes of a No. 3½ D foot, as disclosed through the limpid water of a rooming house bath tub.

Some of the details are equally grotesque. Ivor Novello's love-making, for instance. The heroine's blonde wig is another grating item. George Monroe's thatch was a triumph of realism in comparison. Trick atmosphere shots were rather more successful. But the labored effort to create these effects wastes instead of saves time.

Specifically:

A mysterious criminal has slain a blonde girl on the London embankment on each of seven Tuesday nights. It is desired to picture the inflamed state of public tension over the crimes. The film uses up exactly seven minutes in shots at street mobs crowding around the scene of the newest horror; policemen taking notes on the spot; reporters rushing to their newspapers with harrowing details; telegraphers pounding out the messages, the newspapers being printed; the newspapers being trucked through the streets. How the crowd on the street corners received the news; how they read the reports in the public bars; how they talked about it in chorus girls' dressing rooms (more sex appeal here in half naked chorus girls).

And at length how the news came to the principals concerned in the story. For this last essential they reproduced the newspaper headlines; which, after all, were all necessary in the first place with the elaborate remainder waste footage.

The best thing about the picture is that despite its outrageous crudities, it somehow does manage to suggest that in its script form it probably had literary and dramatic excellence. And the worst thing about it is that the studio was not equal to developing its artistic merit on the screen. *Rush.*

CERTAIN YOUNG MAN

M-G-M production and release. Starring Ramon Novarro. Directed by Hobart Henley. Story by Doris Burcell. Titles by Marion Ainslee. Cameraman Merritt B. Gerstat. At Capitol, New York, week of June 9. Running time, 58 minutes.

Lord Gerald Brinsley......Ramon Novarro
Phyllis....................Marceline Day
Henrietta...................Renee Adoree
Mrs. Crutchley.............Carmel Myers
Mr. Crutchley..............Bert Roach
Mr. Hammond............Huntley Gordon
Hubert....................Ernest Wood

This picture was made and shelved by M-G-M in 1926. Seemingly there have been numerous retakes and a new job of cutting and editing performed. The result is not bad, although plenty of details give a hint of what a palooka it probably was when first turned out. In the original, as recalled by reports at the time, Novarro was a gray-at-the-temple roue. They've wiped away the powder in the new version and made the character more plausible, although Novarro is too boyish in type, stature and personality to make much of an impression attempting a Menjou. Picture is an in-betweener. Novarro at this date may carry it for moderate rating.

It is probably figured by M-G-M that Novarro is strong enough to hold up the picture, where two years ago he needed nursing and could not stand a weakling film.

Picture tells a typically movie history of a man of many loves who in the end finds true happiness with a sweet unworldly girl. Renee Adoree and Carmel Myers stud Novarro's early career and Marceline Day gets the chaste kiss at the fade-out.

Willard Louis (who died in 1926) plays a small role. Carmel Myers and Bert Roach are no longer with M-G-M's stock company. Huntley Gordon also has been an infrequent player on the major screens of late.

One of the worst details in the picture is Lord Brinsley (Novarro), having a valet married to a chic milliner who lives in an extremely swanky apartment and has her own French maid. Numerous other careless moments detract from production. An effort to pep things up by giving pseudo-British subtitles to a fop Englishman, played by Ernest Woods, manages to get laughs. Here's a specimen: "Whither away are you jogging, old thing?" *Land.*

SHOOTING STARS

(ENGLISH MADE)

Original story by Anthony Asquith. Scenario by John Orton. Produced by British Instructional Films, Ltd. Directed by A. V. Bramble. Distributed by New Era Films, Ltd. Lighting by Karl Fischer. Cameraman, Stanley Rodwell and H. Harris. American edited and titled by Merritt Crawford. At Cameo, New York, week June 9. Running time, 70 minutes.

Mae Feather.............Annette Benson
Julian Gordon.............Brian Aherne
Andy Wilks...............Donald Calthrop

In the Feb. 28, 1928, issue of Variety were two reviews of this English made "Shooting Stars." Each was written by a member of Variety's London staff. And both disagreed and both were wrong. The English born reviewer for Variety frankly disliked the picture, while the American in the London office, writing the notice, thought he saw something that isn't there.

This picture is a disgrace to the film industry of any country. If there is no better judgment displayed otherwise in British Instructional Films, only Heaven can help its stockholders.

"Shooting Stars" revoltingly degrades the very profession it represents—acting. It presents Annette Benson as Mae Feather, a picture star who has lust in her body and murder in her heart, besides being a double crosser and a schemer, without being a very good actress.

If English producers prefer to pillory their picture players in that manner, taking in Donald Calthrop's character of Andy Wilks, then it must be accepted that either the English public or the English picture makers have a very low regard for their film players or the picture business they are in.

No American distributor or exhibitor should entertain this picture, for sale or exhibition. It's inexplicable how there could be dumbbells who still breathe, to produce it.

The picture business, the standing hope for scandals by the newspapers and magazines, the source of more harmful reports and comment than any other industry, the fountain of suspicion and innuendo and then this damn fool producer, British Instructional, comes along to okay and verify everything, right from its own studio and on the picture screen.

Anthony Asquith, son of England's former premier, has written quite a good story of its kind, and of course he could have written but of that kind for this picture. Don't blame Asquith; his youth (if he's young) or inexperience, perhaps, or maybe he turned out a book story, for a book story it is, and some fool put it into celluloid.

It won't draw rental anywhere, even at the Cameo with not 100 people there Monday night at 9. There's nothing but a rather involved story well worked out until its finish. The finish goes to pieces with either the author having tired at that time or he thought also he had something that isn't there. There is but one thing out of the ordinary in the entire 70 minutes. That is at that same finish when Brian Aherne believes he sees something familiar in the vanishing form of Miss Benson, and he splendidly suggests it. She is then, years after, a forlorn extra.

"Shooting Stars" as a title means nothing. The picture has quite a lot of sex. At first one is inclined to think it is a satirical effort or a travestied by-play that will explode shortly. Before long the picture has gotten too far to be anything but what it is, a stamp of infamy on all picture players and all picture business.

Two companies are at work on two different sets. In one is Mae Feather, heavily billed film star, supported by her husband, Julian Gordon. On the other is a poor imitator of Charlie Chaplin making a conventional hoke comedy with its star Andy Wilks.

The two stars have an affair with everyone on the lot but the husband wise to it. The Feather girl makes an open play for the comedian. When he invites her out to a show with a party she blows the show and party to remain in his apartment, this all being shown, besides the raw and rough work the girl is made to do to "make" him.

When the comedian receives an offer for pictures in America, the girl is in a frenzy. She wants to go with him and frames a contract for herself over here. But her husband says he'll go too.

In the film drama of western atmosphere apparently the married couple are working. On the set is a shack scene, with the heavy supposed to shoot the girl's sweetie as he bursts through the door to save her. Sweetie is her husband. A prop rifle is placed on a rack in the cabin for the heavy to pick up for the shot.

The wife, seeing a chance as she hears the director tell the heavy what to do, slips a ball cartridge into the rifle, but it's a double-barrelled gun and the other barrel is fired. The remaining barrel, however, with the loaded bullet, through the twists in the story, kills the comedian on his set as he is swinging on a chandelier. That scene also had a shooting bit, and they borrowed the rifle from the drama group.

Studio scenes fairly well done. As a rule there is enough of them to excite curiosity on this side. Minor roles nicely played. Probably Aherne does well enough as the slapsticker, if that's his regular job, and better if it's not. Miss Benson is uneven in work and looks. In different scenes on different days she looked differently and never for the better. She is best in the early portion. Calthrop is a walk througher here. He has looks without personality, and there's no personality in the picture, although Calthrop as the director at the finish looked well enough to stick to the grey sides.

No one who prefers to promote the picture business rather than pull it down in any division can play this film. And if they played it in England they should start the native picture business all over again, the same as should British Instructional.

Sime.

FOOLS FOR LUCK

Paramount production and release. Co-starring W. C. Fields and Chester Conklin. Sally Blane and Jack Luden underlined. Directed by C. F. Reisner from Harry Fried's story. Adaptation by Sam Mintz and J. W. Ruben. George Marion, Jr., titling. Wm. Marshall, cameraman. Paramount, New York, week June 9. Running time, 59 minuttes.

Richard Whitehead..............W. C. Fields
Samuel Hunter..............Chester Conklin
Louise Hunter..................Sally Blane
Ray Caldwell....................Jack Luden
Mrs. Hunter.....................Mary Alden
Charles Grogan.............Arthur Housman

Indifferent male team comedy which doesn't move too fast and has a tough time making 59 minutes seem less than an hour. Plenty of water in the milk on which this one was studio fed, and doubtful if it will be able to keep big house ledgers from turning crimson. Fields' pool table bit, familiar to the trade, is the comedy standout, although a hoke scene with both men in bed, Conkling believing the covered Fields is his wife, has its moments for the laity.

Featherweight yarn has Fields a phoney promoter haboring an idea to sell oil. Invading a village where Conklin is the kingpin, Fields opens up by gyping Conklin, the town champ, out of a dinner check by beating him at pool. Invited into Conklin's home by the women of the family, the feud between the two men continues until the phoney oil stock the latter has hold the villagers starts an uprising when word gets around there isn't an oil can within miles of the well. Oil finally does start to spout, and that's the finish.

Meanwhile there is some sort of a love story. Neither Sally Blane, Jack Luden or the roles mean anything.

Reisner, the director, hasn't done much with the subject. Picture looks as if Fields insisted on putting in all his pool table gags, and rightly. Whatever else is present has evidently sprung from the combined memories of Reisner, Fields and Conklin while trying to hang on to the story. Marion's titles occasionally add momentum, but aren't strong enough to throw off the blanket.

Always difficult to frame stories to catch interest for characters such as Fields and Conklin play, especially when they are the central figures, and "Fools for Luck" isn't the solution. Production and camera work are average, without calling for unusual attention.

Mediocre release which has the male team bug-bear to fight and is on the short end of the betting. Can stand all the stage or help from talking shorts it can get.

Sid.

THE PHYSICIAN

(ENGLISH MADE)

London, May 20.

Produced by Gaumont Co. Adapted by Edwin Greenwood from Henry Arthur Jones' play of the same name. Directed by Georg Jacoby. Photographed by Baron Ventimiglia. Censors' Certificate "A." Preview at the London Hippodrome, May 15. Running time, 100 mins.

Walter Amphiel..............Miles Mander
Edana Hinde......................Elga Brink
Doctor Carey......................Ian Hunter
Jessie Gurdon.....................Lissa Arna
Jessie's Son..................Johnny Ashby
Rev. Peregrine Hindle........Henry Vibart
Lady Valerie......................Julie Suedo

Sir Charles Wyndham first produced this as a play at the London Criterion 21 years ago. He played the Doctor's part, with Mary Moore as "Edana" and Marion Terry as "Lady Valerie." The part of "Jessie Gurdon" did not exist except as a stage reference.

As a film it is fairly strong and could have been stronger if the German director had used fewer closeups to get over captions where he might have used action. With Miles Mander as a dipsomaniac, it calls for comparison with "The Fake," especially as that film was also directed by Jacoby. "The Physician" is a less unpleasant presentation of a man's degradation, and loses nothing by that. It has a more coherent story and the end does not leave a nasty taste. But it lacks the force of "The Fake," and also drags. Some of the situations have been made for this market. Especially the one in which Walter stays with Jessie when due to go with his fiancee to a reception. Doubtless the Continental shots were a little more tense. However, except for the occasional draginess, which editing can snap up, it is a better than average picture, finely directed, well acted and with good camera work and sets.

Walter Amphiel is a temperance reformer and a secret drunkard. After a lecture he is due at a reception with his fiancee, Edana, but gets a note from Jessie Gurdon, whom he had seduced years before. In fear he sees her, and ends up in a drinking bout from which he escapes and tries to go to the reception. Thrown out unrecognized, he is picked up by Doctor Carey who has just been jilted by Lady Valerie because he is going on a mission to India. Carey does not know Amphiel, and when later he is called in to attend to him (Edana believing it is a heart attack) tries to make Amphiel reform. But Walter goes from bad to worse and, after clearing out in fear of Jessie's father, who has sworn to kill his daughter's betrayer, dies in a drunken frenzy while it looks as if Edana will console herself with the doctor.

Direction is of the Ufa school, with many dissolves of a semi-symbolic type to create atmosphere. Miles Mander is developing into one of the best character actors on the screen, if needing a change from these degenerate parts.

Best performance, after Mander's, is from Lissa Arna, a brunette with a strong sense of drama. Elga Brink lacks expression and her profile is too square. Johnny Ashby is an easy acting youngster.

A good picture for its home market, and possibly better for the Continent. A fair one day feature for America if well edited and retitled.

Frat.

CHICKEN A LA KING

Fox production and release. Produced by Henry Lehrman. Screen story from play by Harry Wagstaff Gribble, "Mr. Romeo." Titles by John Schall; scenario by J. Zola Forrester and Mann Page. At Roxy, New York, week June 9. Running time, 60 minutes.

Maisie DeVoe..................Nancy Carroll
Buck Taylor...................George Meeker
Oscar Barrows..................Arthur Stone
Horace Trundle.................Ford Sterling
Effie Trundle................Carol Holloway
Babe Lorraine....................Frances Lee

"Chicken a la King," at the Roxy this week, is a film dish that can be digested without bicarbonate of soda. It's light in theme but fairly heavy in entertainment value. It can go into any first run house.

The high lights are the excellence of the cast, the intelligent supervision of William Conselman, fine direction of Henry Lehrman and lavish production.

The performance of Ford Sterling and Arthur Stone could not have been improved upon. The frails include the eye soothing Nancy Carroll, who is coming along like a prairie fire; Frances Lee and Carol Holloway, the frau who frames with the chorus girls to teach her wandering husband a needed lesson.

Stone plays a brother-in-law with a wine glass full of lavender in him, in a fashion that would get shrieks in Child's 59th street after midnight. He is the reason for his sober going brother-in-law getting mixed up with a couple of gold excavators. Brother Sterling is panicked when discovering that Stone, whom he has been providing for, intends marrying a chorus girl.

Visions of another one in on a rain check drive him back stage to win the girl. He is pegged as a sap by the two dames and goes for the works. His wife tumbles to the lay of the land and like a sensible woman puts in with the girls.

Some of the gags are a trifle far fetched but got laughs. One was a flock of moths flying out of a collar of a raccoon coat that Stone was wearing; another, Sterling registering amazement by falling backward out of a window and saving himself, hanging to the sill.

Stone's predilection for telling the truth, every time he had a dizzy spell, was also milked. He went into the swoons a la Paul Swan, in itself a riot for the peasants.

The credits didn't show who did the screen adaptation from Henry Wagstaff Gribble's "Mr. Romeo," a play that had a cup of coffee on Broadway.

Con.

WALKING BACK

Pathe release of Bertram Millhauser production for DeMille. Directed by Rupert Julian. Adapted by Monte Katterjohn from G. K. Turner's story. Features Sue Carol, Richard Walling and Robert Edeson. Cast includes Jack Keckley, Arthur Rankin and J. Bradbury, Jr. At Hippodrome, N. Y., week June 11. Running time, 54 mins.

Additional exaggeration by the camera in again dealing with the younger generation but holding one novelty and comedy sequence that should squeeze it into the split weeks. Hipp's outside posters carry a strong plug for Sue Carol although main screen title gives Richard Walling and Robert Edeson equal prominence.

Indications are that either Pathe or Millhauser can nurse Miss Carol into the "it" class with some studio headwork. "Walking Back" doesn't mean much to her other than a start and a promising hint of development.

Picture's best asset is an auto duel between two youths over who is going to take the girl home. Youngsters start bumping and chasing each other around the yard until both cars are practically demolished.

The boy who has swiped the family chariot is in a fine pickle and a garage when three holdup men offer him enough dough to resurrect the machine if he'll drive them where they want to go. The cub innocently acquiesces, the crooks place the girl beside him for a blind and they start off.

First stop is at the bank where the boy's father works and where the yeggmen blow the safe. As they're about to drive away the father emerges and a gun shot from the back seat lays him low. With orders to slow up so a motorcycle cop won't pick them up, the kid starts driving like mad, knowing that if the men behind shoot him they're gone too. He keeps on going until he blasts through the door of a police station.

Rupert Julian has steered clear of the frantic petting, drinking, etc., but suggests this usual routine. Film opens symbolizing a jazz mad world and finally narrows down to the boy who has flunked various studies so that Pop won't let him have the machine to keep his date. Meanwhile, the girl attends the dance with a rival suitor as the deficient student goes to the mat with his father. The boy finally walks out to steal the car and go anyway. Here the two boys start the argument which culminates in the gasoline joust outside.

Crazy driving with mobs of kids in cars, girls shaking all over a dance floor and smart crack titles, some brought back, are this release's means of typifying the modern adolescents with Julian's most natural or modern bit that of having the main youth enfolded in a soft shirt under a tuxedo.

Edeson plays the conventional father and Walling makes a more convincing joy seeking kid than the script did.

Not extraordinary material nor expensively made, but of enough voltage to let it click in the smaller towns and sites. *Sid.*

STREETS OF ALGIERS

(GERMAN MADE)

Ufa production, directed by W. H. Harnish. Cast includes Camilla Horn and Warwick Ward, the former featured. At Loew's New York as half of double bill, one day, May 25. Running time, 72 mins.

One of the inferior Ufas, holding little other than the genuine locale to recommend it. Its dramatics drew a couple of laughs from a New York Roof mob. A $15 rental might make house and distributor all square.

Some of these Ufa directors must have cheering sections behind them imploring the cast to "Cry for Ufa, sob for Ufa, emote for Ufa."

And how they do it—with buried chins and heaving shoulders. The anguish a mother goes through in this one is a big argument for birth control.

Through circumstances she is a partner in the proprietorship of an Algerian dive with a back room which serves girls inasmuch as there's no club rule against ginger ale and ice out front. Her partner (Warwick Ward) is known as the "Wolf of the Street," whose happy pastime is stalking innocent femmes.

And as far as the director is concerned Algeria has no cops, except at a film hero's beck and call, and no vice squad. When wanting to clean up the joints they send to France for a young government commissioner who meets the convent daughter (Camilla Horn) on board ship and eventually traces the mother down as the veiled Madame.

The "Wolf" is eased out by a sailor whose sister has become a victim of the underworld routine.

Anybody is going to have trouble identifying Miss Horn for the first two reels. She's as much unlike her Princess Tamara in "The Tempest" as is the difference between Maria Corda in "Helen of Troy" and "The Modern DuBarry" or "Moon of Israel." The Teutons probably won't believe it's either Miss Corda or Miss Horn when they see "Helen" and "The Tempest."

Picture is nothing more than 72 minutes spent in Algiers with a worried mama who's afraid her daughter is going to find out. Atrocious directing offsets whatever merit this product may have and it'll need a posse to trace the assets down over here.

It's likely that somebody dug "Streets of Algiers" up after "The Tempest" opened. Miss Horn certainly won't brag of the effort. It would be interesting to know if this film got any money in Germany, and if so why? Maybe because of Ward, who is known there though he's English. Or perhaps Miss Horn or both. *Sid.*

MONKEYNUTS

(FRENCH MADE)

London, May 24.

Produced and directed by Louis Mercanton. Distributed in the U. K. by the Inter-Cine Corp. Censor's certificate "U." Running time, 90 minutes. Preview and run, London Palladium, opening Monday, May 21.

Monkeynuts.................Betty Balfour
Bob.......................Walter Butler
Pa Morton................Nicholas Koline

Made some time ago in France, before Betty Balfour started on "A Little Bit of Fluff." The fact this film is shown same week as "Fluff" might have been taken as an advance tip as to its quality. And the tip would not have been far out. Story is as familiar as your old man: girl selling candy in a circus rises to be great trapeze artist despite jealous machinations of dark-haired wench also in same circus. Our nurse used to read one of those a week, and that's old-timing.

Circus stuff is good and colorful, but it has been done so, oh! so very many times recently, even in Hollywood, where they get a big-top on the job even for a small picture.

Lots of padding, principally Nice carnival stuff. That's no novelty either. Every director who could frame a vacation in the disguise of work at Nice has shot the carnival to pieces, and they all think they have done something novel.

Miss Balfour's trouping is fair to middling good. She was ill most of the time this film was being made—not a publicity disease, but playing for pneumonia; and she got it before the film was all shot. So there's some room for allowances.

Direction is slow and draggy. Mercanton is always long-winded, but this time worse than usual, stopping the story for most a reel while he shows carnival stuff.

Fair here for the dumbells and the 100 per cent Balfour fans. For others, and for America, no. *Frat.*

Midnight Adventure

Rayart release, produced by Duke Worne. From the story by Arthur Hoerl. Directed by Duke Worne. None featured. Cast includes Cullen Landis, Edna Murphy, Ernest Hilliard and Jack Richardson. At Broadway, New York, week June 4. Running time, 50 mins.

While it is not by itself sufficiently strong as week's film supply in a regular first run theatre, this independently produced picture stands up as a favorable programmer for the smaller theatres out of town. At this house the film fare in addition to "Midnight Adventure" included a 45-minute fight special entitled "Kings of the Ring" in support of a six-act stage lineup.

Production shows intelligent direction and fairly clever editing. The slowing up process which usually characterizes independently made pictures is not in evidence here. Story and action move along at an even pace.

Mystery meller of the action variety. Comedy toward the end in the form of a flat-headed sleuth who turns out to be the murderer.

Action takes place within three or four interiors, opening in the hallway of the country mansion where a man is found mysteriously murdered at midnight. Suspicion rests on four or five women and about as many men, including the district attorney, all house guests over the week end. The murdered man is a blackmailer with the goods on a few women with whom he had had more or less intimate acquaintance prior to their marriage.

Casting is bad as far as the women players are concerned, none standing up successfully under the camera. Male players register favorably. *Mori.*

Chinatown Charlie

First National release, produced by C. C. Burr. Directed by Charles Hines from the story by Owen Davis. Titles by Paul Perez. Photography by Wm. J. Miller and Al Wilson. Featuring Johnny Hines. Cast including Harry Gribbon, Louise Lorraine, Fred Kohler, Sojin, Scooter Towry, Anna May Wong and George Kuwa. At Loew's American, New York, June 7, for four days. Running time, 72 minutes.

For fully 30 minutes nothing happens. Characters are introduced but not built up. No story unless a trip to Chinatown on a sight-seeing bus is a plot. Instead of planting a story the first half hour is **used in silly attempts at well known gags which have long outlived their usefulness.**

The misadventures of the bus on its way downtown include puncture, the introduction of a cop, a tough, and a well-meaning dip.

Finally the mysterious ring comes up. It's one of those rings, with a strange inscription, commanding the complete subjugation of all Chinamen who believe in it. A gang decides to get the ring for evil purposes. The gal, to whom the unfortunate ring belongs, gives it to Charlie, but is captured and sold to a mandarin right around the corner, who, in turn, prepares to sell her to a white slaver.

The dip tells the police of the gang's activities but doesn't get a nibble. He is obliged to bring the force down by the tried and simple expedient of punching policemen and having them run after him.

Everybody worth saving is saved, excepting the producers of the picture.

Fred Kohler has a minor part as the gang leader. Sojin makes a ferocious mandarin, Johnny Hines does as well as possible under the circumstances, and Louise Lorraine supplies ineffective support, photographing badly in addition. Harry Gribbon is responsible for a few laughs.

Screen adaptation and comedy business extremely poor and direction of a low grade, this combination overbalancing Johnny Hines' abilities and screen value. As reproduced in this picture the story did not hold any strong possibilities for filming. Running time of 72 minutes far too long. *Mori.*

THE SCARLET DOVE

Tiffany-Stahl production and release. Adapted and directed by Arthur Greagor. All-star cast billed. Continuity by John Francis Natteford. Photographer, Ernest Miller. At Loew's New York, one half double bill, one day, June 1. Running time, around 60 minutes.

Col. Ivan Petroff.............Lowell Sherman
Eve...................Margaret Livingston
Lieut. Alex Orloff...........Robert Frazer
Anna Andreyna............Josephine Borio
Olga......................Shirley Palmer
Aunt.................Julia Swayne Gordon
Gregory....................Carlos Durand

Ordinary small-time picture with the Tiffany stamp, getting nowhere and meaning nothing. Title best thing in it but little in story suggests that tale was other than built up after title had been selected. Probably good enough for double bills, one day neighborhoods or such stands as can use them cheap.

Rambling theme merely holding an actionless story together. Phony duel isn't much better than the Russian scenery and at times the snow looks to have been painted on the cornices.

Young girl from convent assigned to marry a Russian army officer she has never seen. He has a consort in waiting and who is agreeable to the marriage, since he will gain coin from it and through that, her "position" as his mistress may be maintained.

Enter a lower ranking officer who first meets the girl. Of course he eventually kills his commanding officer in the duel, and marries, or should, the girl.

Tiffany has advanced above such stuff as this. Pictures of "The Scarlet Dove" kind are for the state righters.

Other than a couple of the principals with Lowell Sherman featured, there's nothing here.

The boys could have made this one by long distance phone.

A Gentleman Preferred

Mayfair production, released through First Division. Directed by Arthur Hotaling from story credited to L. Jefferson. Titles by Al Martin. In cast: Gaston Glass, Jimmy Aubrey, Kathleen Meyers, J. L Gasse. At Stanley, New York, one day, June 2. Running time, 45 minutes.

A Gentleman Preferred" is poorer in entertainment than the average indie which the smaller grinds one-day.

Cast is mechanical and performance giving impression of trying to go one better than director. Story is bit of forced writing, and brought to screen in flat, colorless way, evidencing no suspense.

Titles so bromidic provide laugh here and there.

Gaston Glass in cowboy outfit mops up five bad men, who fall like dummies before blow is landed. This, with expressionless girl grabbing gun from bandit, turn serious meller efforts into such burlesque that patrons go into gale of laughter.

THERESE RAQUIN

(FRANCO-GERMAN MADE)

Paris, June 2.

Jacques Feyder, producer of "Atlantide," has realized a triste screen version of Emile Zola's famous novel, "Therese Raquin." It has not attracted the attention anticipated.

A gloomy subject, and the colored verbosity of Zola is lacking in the picture. Feyder has accomplished a praiseworthy feat in adapting this book for popular consumption. In any event, the success of the production has been greater in Germany than in France.

Story modernized by the introduction of automobiles and modern dress, not described by Zola. Scenery is a reproduction of the Pas**sage du Pont-Neuf 50 years ago (the street no longer exists in Paris).**

Therese, a girl of energy and willpower, married to the insipid Raquin, soon begins to detest her plain-looking, simple-minded husband, and rebels at their modest surroundings.

Inevitable love intrigue with a friend of the family and then the lovers scheme how they can be rid of the embarrassing husband. They arrange to make him fall overboard while boating.

Then they marry, but the memory of the murdered man is always between them.

Mother of Raquin learns the secret but is struck speechless by the fright. This living witness also exasperates the guilty couple and their existence is a perfect hell, particularly when the paralyzed woman looks at them with reproach, to such an extent they both commit suicide. "Therese Raquin" was published half a century ago but is still modern.

The role of Raquin, the first husband, is soberly played. Marie Laurent is Therese, and Gina Manes the mother.

The book probably will be preferred to the picture. *Kendrew.*

AVENGING SHADOW

Pathe release, produced by Fred J. McConnell. "Klondike," alleged new dog, starred. Margaret Morris featured. Directed by Ray Taylor; assistant director, Bob Kelly. Adapted by Bennett Cohen. Photography, Harry Cooper and David Smith. At Loew's New York, one-half double bill, one day, June 1. Running time, around 45 minutes.

James Hamilton................Ray Hallor
Worthington................Wilbur Mack
Sheriff Apling..............Clark Comstock
Tom Sommers..............Howard Davies
Marie, daughter...........Margaret Morris
George Brooks, deputy........LeRoy Mason
Gray Boy..........................Klondike

A Pathe dog picture and as a dog picture probably as good as any other. It's a police dog here. As all police dogs look alike on the screen, anyone you may believe this one to be is okay, with the dog anyway.

Mainly about a bank teller who got held up, but was sent to prison for a year. In prison somehow the warden's daughter sensed he was innocent and later the dog proved it.

In between happens what you must expect.

Strictly for the nuts who believe in the dog films.

NO BABIES WANTED

Plaza production (W. E. Shallenbarger), released through Irwin Exchanges. Directed by John Harvey. William O'Connell, cameraman. Priscilla Moran starred. In cast: William V. Mong, Dorothy Devore, Emily Fitzroy. At Stanley, New York, one day, June 7. Running time about 60 minutes.

Downtown grinds and houses catering to stage will find this too tame and the title misleading to their customers. "No Babies Wanted" may find a welcome in the better neighborhood houses, especially at matinees frequented by mothers and their kiddies. The picture should be carefully billed and special attention paid the advertising copy by exhibs in small cities and towns.

Priscilla Moran, as the little baby-loving waif, gives a worthy performance, always sincere although not always convincing for exertions physically impossible for her which the script calls for.

Keeping an abandoned babe from the hands of a hard-boiled landlady and the orphanage results in an amusing chase with little Priscilla carrying the infant over roofs and down fire escapes.

A baby show is also worked in with advantage.

BERLIN

(GERMAN MADE)

Produced by Karl Freund and Walther Ruttman. Based on an idea from Carl Mayer. Special musical accompaniment by Edmund Meisel. At the Fifth Avenue Playhouse, New York, week May 13. Running time, 60 mins.

All the boys who are good at interpreting should immediately write, wire or long distance Mike Mindlin for information leading to the acquisition of the latest cinematic marvel from abroad. Preferably, the picture should first be shown to the most distant relatives. Positively one of the finest opportunities to get even with pass hounds, bill collectors and so on.

Its other name is "The Symphony of a Big City." Very simple to interpret. Ten lessons in German, guide book featuring a map of Berlin and a professor of mechanics lecturing on the platform with a baton would do nicely.

This film purports to be "an impersonal record of the life and rhythm of a huge, modern metropolis." It opens with an intriguing shot of muddy water flowing listlessly from nowhere to no place in particular. The next incident is a photographic study of shadows—vague, sinister, implying some deep, hidden meaning which the smart New Yorkers pretend to understand but know as little about as the average chump movie fan.

Then comes the first intelligible sign of life and activity. Its a train, subjected to every conceivable camera shot, moving slowly, rushing along as if carrying life and death dispatches. Follow shots of the engine, brakes, windows, tracks, wires. It shoots past drowsy hamlets and across waste lands. Finally it reaches Berlin.

From this point the picture takes a leap into the most unprecedented series of action sequences ever witnessed in a picture and this takes in everything including the foreign mades. There is a sudden shot of an empty street at 5 a. m. The customers sit up distractedly. Following is a fat, sleek cat walking along the side of a house. Workmen begin to appear, shades are pulled up, street cars begin to run, factories go into action. It's daytime!

And so this colorful story of the heart throbs of a mighty nation continues, activities of shop girls, stenogs, steam shovels, beggars, bankers and a stray bag swinger until darkness steals over the town once again.

Not satisfied with taking their audience through Berlin in the day time the producers have even ventured into a view of the night life. In this part of the picture are included hitherto unbelievable phases of nocturnal divertissement. Phases which have hardly ever been discussed above a whisper even by the most daring of cosmopolitan scandalmongers. It's an amazing expose of true conditions abroad, showing liquor of every variety being sold openly and two or three couples in one of the dance resorts necking quite unreservedly. Beer seemed to have the edge on everything for sales. Further revelations of Berlin night life included scenes back stage in one of the vaudeville houses. Only hot dogs were missing.

Tom Mix in the lights near the Berlin Pallast drew a little applause and a brief view of Charlie Chaplin's stems in one of the picture houses along Berlin's main ginway resulted in a storm of whispered consultations.

Photography is excellent and makes the picture an ace for the sure-seaters. In German communities, though, seating will not be so sure. Playing to capacity audiences at this house mostly on account of the national draw but will get business from the regular sure-seat trade in addition.

No subtitles, an item which, in itself, stamps this effort a highly meritorious work of art for certain classes.

The whole thing, according to program billing, comes from an idea born in the receptive mind of one Carl Mayer. Ideas in the picture business are okay but a 60-minute version of a 15-minute newsreel in the form of a full length feature attraction is too extensive an allowance. Cut down to around 15 minutes the picture may be used to fill in regular houses as an educational on account of interesting photography and geographical value.

Mori.

Breed of the Sunset

FBO production and release. Story by S. E. V. Taylor, directed by Wallace Fox. Bob Steele featured. In cast Dorothy Kitchen, George Bunny, Leo White, Hank Scully. At Columbus, New York, one day, June 7, as half double bill. Running time, 60 minutes.

Stock western plot No. 444 is used as the basis of this flicker, but it's surefire on any double bill, mainly because of a couple of comedy titles for which Randolph Bartlett is credited. Bob Steele's wholesome appearance and Miss Kitchen's general good looks deserve mention.

Steele, Oklahoma rodeo champ, wants to see California in the worst way. That means via freight, steps on a ranch and wins an outlaw horse by his clever broncho busting. Traveling on he rescues Maria Dominguez from a runaway carriage—and love at a glance.

A practical joker decides to stage a fake hold-up. His foreman double crosses him and makes off with the loot. Steele brings the stuff back after kayoing the foreman and his accomplice and gets the job as boss of the ranch.

As all the action is pictured as taking place in one day and Steele forced to knock the same two crooks cold three times for practically the same reason, the audience may be inclined to giggle in the wrong place, but Bartlett saves the situation with a subtitle reading: "This is getting to be a nuisance." Neighborhood houses can't go wrong with this one.

HUSBAND BY PROXY

(SWEDISH MADE)

Produced by Swedish-Biograph in Paris. No American distributor named. Starring Gosta Ekman with cast unnamed. Directed by Wilhem Bryle. At the 55th Street Playhouse week of June 9. Running time, 105 mins.

Sophisticates will laugh when they see the action which follows the long sub-title prefacing "A Husband by Proxy." According to the introduction the story is supposed to be a highly subtle burlesque on the so-called American title hunting mother.

Picture drags drearily through nearly two hours. Almost any part of it could be cut since only story part is based on the "stepping out of character" gag when one resemblance represents another so that the marquis can get his marriage dowry from the leather tanner's wife because of the cowhand's face.

Gosta Ekman, known here through Murnau's "Faust," flits about like the daughter of a new-rich mother should according to the foreign version. But the foreigners give her far too much drawing room knowledge and hold back the old lady's fat arm when, according to normal American Hoyle of this kind, it would swing into action.

Club room atmosphere, palatial home and a farm scene are worthwhile, but all have been and are being constantly duplicated. Stiff titles and stiffer acting provide laughs. "I am only a farmer" is followed by outstretched arms and a weird expression, at a moment that Europe apparently intended to be extremely dramatic.

Kings of the Ring

(ASSEMBLY)

Produced and distributed by Leon Britton. Titled and edited by Paul Gallico, sporting editor of the New York "Daily News." Photographed by Jack Reiger. At Broadway, New York, week June 4. Running time, 45 minutes.

This picture is a compilation of the most exciting rounds of the most important ring battles of the century, brilliantly titled by Paul Gallico, sporting editor of the New York "Daily News," and suffering a little from bad film editing.

As a 45-minute special attraction, added to a regular picture bill, it should draw. It's a strong offering not only for sporting attention, but as a stimulant for the usual picture trade. Not a slow moment after the first few introductory shots.

The Dempsey-Firpo fight, reproduced in full, carries enough thrills to put over a feature length picture. Photography clear and graphic almost all the way through, including the filming of fights at a time when interior lighting for picture reproduction was not so good.

The seventh round of the second Dempsey-Tunney fight, where the referee is shown conferring with Dempsey about something for fully 10 seconds instead of counting Tunney out, created a storm of protest from the gallery in this house.

Shown on the same bill with "Midnight Adventure" (Rayart), independent production, in addition to a six-act lineup. *Mori.*

LA GRANDE EPREUVE

("The Big Trial")

(FRENCH-MADE)

Paris, May 10.

This patriotic picture was released under most favorable conditions, both in Paris and London. "La Grande Epreuve" ("The Big Trial") as billed in France is entitled "The Soul of France" in Great Britain. Distributed by Paramount, a gala was offered for the premiere.

Picture has been realized for Jacques Halk by A. Duges and A. Ryder, with a reconstruction of battle scenes by Joe Hamman. Interrupting the series of battle views, trench life and exploding shells, is a brief scenario of a French family composed of five (father, mother and three sons). One boy has committed a crime, not recorded, and is in Algeria when the war breaks out with his old mother fretting about him.

Another son is at the officer's college of St. Cyr, while the third is a raw youth. The two elder boys are in the midst of the fight unknown to each other; the young officer is wounded and brought into safety by his brother, a private soldier. The former dies without having recognized the man who rescues him. The other is chosen to get behind the enemy lines to cut some electric wire before a German mine is exploded. He succeeds, but is wounded, being nursed by a girl he had previously met in a field hospital.

At this time the Armistice is announced, and the family is united, thanks to the girl.

There are some excellent episodes of the terrible war, reconstituting historical phases of the attack and defense of the French army.

If a fault is to be found, it is in the length of the battle scenes. The suffering of the people in the villages bombarded is eloquently set forth.

M. Desjardins (actor of the Comedie Francaise) does the stern father; much praise is given to Mme. Jalabert for her pathetic rendering of the mother. Jean Murat and G. Charlia play with some dramatic force the two brothers.

"La Grande Epreuve" is a splendid French picture for local consumption. There is perhaps too much war atmosphere for foreign distribution, notwithstanding the producers' claim the film is intended as propaganda against war. For that purpose it may make a deep impression on the masses—but it is not the masses who are responsible for a conflict of this nature.

Nevertheless, this picture can be classed as a noble effort and worthy of wide distribution. *Kendrew.*

THIEF IN THE DARK

Fox production and release. Directed by Albert Ray. Story by Andrew Bennis. Cameraman, Arthur Edeson. Supervised by Kenneth Hawks. Titles by William Kernel. Cast includes George Meeker, Marjorie Beebe, Michael Vivitch, Gwen Lee, Noah Young. At Academy of Music, New York, three days, June 11-13. Running time, 54 mins.

Neighborhood stuff. Hokey, silly and exaggerated, but possessing enough of the familiar hidden panel and secret passage stuff to have some interest for the non-fastidious audiences.

Nobody in the cast except Gwen Lee (in a bit) who seems even half-way familiar. That handicaps the box office. Albert Ray's direction is jerky, but production has a degree of class. Possibly the big sets were standing for or from a more important Fox film.

Traveling troupe of fake spiritualists with a carnival are crooks on the side. The professor knocks off a rich old bunny, while the innocent young man accomplice falls for the daughter. Plot is better than the picture. *Land.*

Little Bit of Heaven

Excellent (made) production released through Commonwealth. Directed by Cliff Wheeler. Scenario by Elsie Werner. In cast: Lucy Beaumont, Otto Lederer, Jacqueline Gadson, Bryant Washburn, Martha Mattox. At Stanley, New York, one day, June 11. Running time about 60 minutes.

The story of the babe that brings together chorus-queen wife and pampered-son husband is retold in "Little Bit of Heaven."

Gadson okay, but Washburn so insipid as to impress audience of being self-conscious of his prettiness.

Entertainment light throughout, with only suggestion of suspense.

Production well mounted and of society drama type. No rough stuff and theatrical atmosphere confined to star's dressing room and line of chorines.

LION AND THE MOUSE

(DIALOG SEQUENCES)

(2d Review)

This picture previously reviewed by Variety on the coast. A comparison between that report and the New York premiere evidences better synchronization and amplification in New York. Opening at Warner's Friday night, the picture was well received, if not enthusiastically, with the first night skeptics again in and waiting for a chance to snicker at the dialog. They both got their chance and laughed. As a picture it doesn't appear as if "Lion and the Mouse" will mean anything without its Vitaphone accompaniment of dialog.

Running 69 minutes here, 28 minutes of the film are given over to dialog—eight minutes at the opening of the picture, with the final 20 minutes solid talk, except for the shift from scene to scene and a few odd silent feet for a comedy valet. That gives the feature a central stretch of 38 minutes of silent white and black, with the usual film titles.

For the most part the dialog is overly stiff, formal and old-fashioned. Delivered abnormally slow only emphasizes the weakness of the "sides." Especially does this stand out with May McAvoy, whose voice is high, thin and out of all proportion to the bass register of Lionel Barrymore, Buster Collier and Alec Francis.

The retarded delivery is probably due to present methods of recording with heavy concentration to pick up everything. The film would have been better off minus Miss McAvoy's voice, or a double, if possible, for her.

On the other hand, there's a talking sequence in this one that's to the brim with dramatic power and strongly portends just what can and will be accomplished with sound. It's a scene between Barrymore and Collier for four and a half minutes which couldn't have sounded any better on a stage. Both play it well, particularly Barrymore, with the dialog picking up pace and well written. It's Collier, as the son, walking out on his father, Barrymore, as the former berates his parent for his ruthless financial methods and telling him he's going to marry the daughter of the man he (the father) has ruined, regardless of the older man's wishes. Barrymore sarcastically chides the boy during his verbal rampage, so that there are laughs amidst the dramatics. Neat work and the high point of this release.

A sidelight on this talker is that during the final talk passages the characters speak against a musical background, the orchestra muffling to permit the voices to dominate. Good effect and well handled.

Actual dialog is on the following schedule: Two minutes after the flash of the main title Barrymore starts to talk to plant the story. He's pictured in his office at a desk talking to his secretary, a yes man with heavily stressed s-s-s-s. A one-minute silent interlude as Judge Rossmore (Francis) entrances, with Barrymore picking up the dialog again in telling the judge, who has rendered a decision against his company, that he's not angry and to invest in Pacific Oil.

Barrymore enunciates slowly through this, perhaps to emphasize the conniving nature of the character. But Francis' fast "no thanks" to an offer of a cigar is like a fresh breeze on a humid day. Both men register well with their voices, the sequence ending as Francis departs and Barrymore says, "and that's the end of Judge Rossmore."

Music again picks up and carries on through the next 38 minutes until the voices come back to stay until the finish. Barrymore discovers Collier rifling his home desk in search of the letter which will clear the judge by showing he bought the oil stock and did not accept it as a bribe. Music stops and Barrymore opens up abruptly, scoffing at his son.

Following a rather awkwardly worded argument, Collier exits and Miss McAvoy emerges from behind a curtain. It's the first time for her voice, and the initial high pitched tones are a shock. Having little or no tonal shading, it's a tough spot for the girl up against Barrymore. Besides which, particularly bad dialog at this point is against her. It may be from the original script of the play. Anyway, it leads to a two-minute telephone seance during which Barrymore sends a telegram. Excellently done by an actor who could make a telephone dramatic on a raft.

Scene switches to Barrymore and Collier in the aforementioned bit, which is the standout. Against music Miss McAvoy next is heard, telling Collier to go away and that she doesn't love him, all to keep a promise made Barrymore if he'll clear her father. As Collier reaches the steps Barrymore drives up and tells him to go back in, where occurs the grand reunion—all by conversation.

Finish has Barrymore and Francis in an adjoining room to the youngsters patching up their differences. As they open the door to go out they see the lovers in each other's arms—so Francis suggests his friend can't get away and Barrymore asks if his host has anything in the sideboard. Both move off ostensibly to have a drink together. This may be the first point the rigid censors will have to play with in a talker.

Little question that Barrymore's voice holds this one up, although Francis is very good and Collier okay. There's a difference between Collier's voice the first time and the second, the latter being much lower and remaining that way throughout the remainder of the film.

"Lion and the Mouse" about definitely demonstrates just how much is to be done before talkers are perfected. It's some time away yet. Audience reaction was a distinct murmur at the first sound of voices on both ends of the film, and attentive interest throughout. Picture doesn't figure for the big houses minus Vitaphone. However, it's the most extensive talker to date and, with the novelty yet to wear off, is certain to attract in houses already wired. *Sid.*

LADIES OF THE MOB

Paramount production and release starring Clara Bow. Directed by William Wellman. Cameraman, Henry Gerrard. Adapted to screen from Ernest Booth's magazine story by Oliver Garrett and John Farrow. Editorial supervisor, Lloyd Sheldon. Titles by George Marion, Jr. At the Paramount, N. Y., week of June 16. Running time, 66 mins.

Yvonne	Clara Bow
"Red"	Richard Arlen
Marie	Helen Lynch
"Soft Annie"	Mary Alden
Joe	Carl Gerard
The Mother	Bodil Rosing
Little Yvonne	Lorraine Rivero
The Officer	James Pierce

This is not Clara Bow stuff, although Paramount has tried to jazz it up. Story as told originally in "The American Mercury" by Ernest Booth, a life termer at Folsum Prison, Cal., was harsh, sombre and tragic. In attempting to soften a theme that required tense realism Paramount has lost most of the story's dramatic possibilities and emerges with a so-so film about a crook whose sweetheart wanted him to reform.

If it is not typical or good Clara Bow material, neither is it typical or good modern crook melodrama. This despite a final sequence in which cops with rifles surround a house and trap the crook. It has a trite, dishwatery finish. The crook and his moll are both slated for long stretches for bank robbery, aggravated by the pair having resisted arrest and fired upon the police. With years behind the bars awaiting them the moll suddenly goes Pollyanna, sees the bright side of the situation and tells the guy that it is nothing at all. They will pay their debt to society and emerge, middle aged, but free.

There are a couple of action sequences and some spitfire stuff for Bow when another dame tries to cop her guy, but the picture as a whole is sluggish in tempo. Opening passage has been grafted onto Booth's story. It's the electrocution of a criminal while his wife waits in the care of a matron. All done symbolically. When the switch is pulled on the electric chair the light in the matron's office goes dim. The woman screams realizing it is the death current. She grabs frantically for her child and shrieks at the warden and others that she will bring the kid up to get even on society. The kid is supposed to be Clara Bow, but the revenge idea is not developed. Indeed, the kid, grown up, is apostle-in-chief for the "you can't win" campaign.

Booth's story was not fiction. It was a series of incidents, illustrating the wretchedness of the women who love yeggmen. The film does not ring true at any point because of the conventional changes that have been made. However, fidelity to fact, possibility, plausibility or truth, has never been an essential requirement to moving pictures making money. "Ladies of the Mob" is an okay programmer that has exploitation possibilities and the Bow name. The author being a convict is a point.

Fans who come to see Clara do her usual flip flapper will be disappointed, but the unusual seriousness will probably constitute an interesting contrast. *Land.*

THE STATION MASTER

(RUSSIAN MADE)

Sovkino production, released by Amkino. Starring Ivan Moskvin. Directed by U. A. Gelabuzsky and Ivan Moskvin from story by Pushkin. At Cameo, New York, week June 17. Running time, 75 mins.

Station master	I. M. Moskvin
Dunia	V. S. Malinovskya
Capt. Minsky	B. T. Tamarin
The general	N. F. Kostromskoy
The doctor	N. G. Alexandrov
The orderly	V. D. Tikhomirov

Under the untutored directorial guidance of Ulysses A. Gelabuzsky, Pushkin's famous narrative loses all semblance of reality. To add to the confusion are various attempts at comedy characterization during which no one laughs, while general outbursts greeted pathetic scenes intended to convey desolation and sadness.

The poster billing bears a legend to the effect that Ivan Moskvin, star of the Moscow Art Players, is appearing in a light travesty or comedy. This seems to be someone's idea of a gag.

The story treats of the seduction of a station master's daughter by an army officer.

This may be Russia's idea of comedy, but how can an American audience be expected to break into uncontrollable spasms of laughter when the poor girl is thrown into an attic when she attempts to see her aged father who tramps through the heavy snows from a small country village to the great city of St. Petersburg. The old man finally becomes half-demented. He dies after rushing out, bareheaded, in the night to welcome back the shadow of his daughter who, he believes, has returned to him.

It is a story of futility, the drab, dreary life of a station master and his inability to even attempt to cope with the disaster which befalls his daughter. Moskvin flashes sparks of great acting whenever he is called upon to be dramatic. But the calls are so rare they are hardly noticeable.

No special credit is given for the screen adaptation and, to judge from the uneven continuity, the picture may have been produced from the original story without a scenario writer employed.

Among the other players Miss V. S. Malinovskya, as the station master's daughter, screens attractively in one or two poses, but, in the main, keeps running around in circles, pouring tea. A very busy gal, according to this picture, and it doesn't help her a bit.

Photography (no screen or program billing) is poor, titles barely intelligible and scenic backgrounds, exteriors and interiors, in bad taste in addition to being cheap.

For the sure-seaters it can stand up a full week with a chance of holding over. It's a sad picture with a sad beginning, a sad middle and a sad ending. Anything that ends unsatisfactorily seems to hit the sure-seat trade right. *Mori.*

How to Handle Women

Universal Jewel directed by William J. Craft. Glenn Tryon starred. Story supervision Joseph F. Poland. Cameraman Albert Demond. Titles by Arthur Todd. Running time 60 mins. At Roxy, New York, week June 16.

Leonard Higgins..............Glenn Tryon
Beatrice Fairbanks..........Marian Nixon
Prince Hendryx............Raymond Keane
Editor......................Robert T. Hains
The Turk.....................Bull Montana
Tony.........................Cesare Gravina
E. H. Herriman...........E. H. Herriman
Secretary...........................Leo White
Count Olaff....................Mario Carillo
Stenographer.............Violet La Plante

An utterly tiresome comedy that couldn't interest or amuse any audience of intelligence. Not genuinely funny yard of film in its whole length except the titles, almost as humorous without the film action. Effort represents the net result of an author, director and cast getting together and resolving, so help them, to be funny.

It is seldom a comedy is turned out with so little to recommend it. Picture hasn't a spontaneous moment in its entire length; even its knockabout comedy isn't laughable, and when a screen comedian can't get a giggle with a neck fall, the situation is dire indeed.

A few of the titles are smart in text and neatly placed for a quick turn of wit but they are effective on their own account and not because of the sceen action to which they apply. And some of the titles even are laborious and infantile.

To start with story is addressed to the feeble minded. Prince of Volgaria comes to America to negotiate a loan and gets a cold reception. Low comedian propounds the idea that since Volgaria raises a huge crop of peanuts, the trick is to exploit the goober by modern methods and sell the peanut concession.

To that end comedian impersonates the Prince and deals with the American bankers after the manner of a Keystone cop. One of his coups is to give an elaborate peanut dinner which is turned into a sort of bathing-beauty-cabaret sequence. It is during this hilarious episode that the following bit occurs:

Hero-comic is putting salt on his peanut.

"Why do you salt your peanut?" inquires his neighbor.

"That's to kill it. If you are bitten by a peanut, distemper results," wittily returns our hero.

That's a sample of the humor and the whole thing is about of the same grade. The poverty of comedy resource is remarkable in the American studio where the comedy technique is highly developed.

To weigh the acting would be absurd, for there is nothing for the players to work with. Glenn Tryon gets no help from his situations and merely walks through an impossible series of flat pantomime. Marian Nixon, graceful and charming young actress, is as hopelessly at sea. Large cast of minor characters seem to stand about looking on in pained boredom.

Why this inane affair is at the Cathedral is the surprise gag of the entire incident. *Rush.*

HAPPINESS AHEAD

First National production and release. Starring Colleen Moore and featuring Edmund Lowe. Scenario by Benjamin Glazer from Edmund Goulding's story. Directed by Wm. A. Seiter. At Strand, New York, week June 16. Running time, 72 minutes.

Mary Randall...................Colleen Moore
Lionel "Babe" Stewart......Edmund Lowe
Kay Sears.......................Lilyan Tashman
Ma Randall..................Edythe Chapman
Pa Randall.......................Charles Sellon
The Detective...................Robert Elliott
Mary's Chum........................Diane Ellis

Plenty of laughs, a tear and a corking story. A program gem anywhere from the de luxe houses to the sure seaters because no type of audience can or will muff it. It's the best one Miss Moore has had in an age and worthy of the Rivoli or Rialto on Broadway for a try at a grind run.

Edmund Goulding did the story. Benjamin Glazer the scenario, W. A. Seiter directed and Miss Moore and Edmund Lowe troupe in it, and how! That's a lineup that impresses on sight and one that has more than equalled its potential paper strength in celluloid.

Picture has a little bit of everything and never stands still. Seiter has put this film together right, without wasting a foot. And it never turns you loose. Starts out fast, gets funny, then serious, and ends by bringing a lump to the throat—and nobody dies.

It looks like Seiter's answer to Vidor's "The Crowd." The pictures are not unlike each other with the general entertainment advantage in this one's favor. Looking at "The Crowd" was like reading Dreiser, powerful, ponderous, slow and too true. If you like it you're for it 100 per cent; if you don't you're fed up within 100 pages or two reels. There's no in between. "Happiness Ahead" is in a lighter vein, but studded with character and situation shadings and played to the hilt by Miss Moore and Lowe.

No one in pictures can look at a girl like Lowe and roll what he means, his entire mental makeup and character, into one glance. And he gets many an opportunity here as a card table specialist who has been taking the moneyed boys with a show girl (Lilyan Tashman) as the apartment come-on. A spat with the dame, culminating in her telling the victim he's been cheated, forces Lowe to a hideaway in a small town where he starts eyeing the high school girls. Picking out Miss Moore, daughter of the hardware store proprietor, Lowe has the village's younger set in a furore whence Miss Moore's innocence finally forces him into a declaration of marriage to her family.

Not caring particularly for Miss Moore, other than that she's something he can't quite get, and whose naivete is unconsciously disarming him, Lowe goes through with the church wedding under hit and run intentions and is impressed by his first real look at the maid of honor on the way out. Back to New York and in a flat, Mary's love and happiness in her home starts to get under Lowe's skin. He goes to work in a brokerage office. Whence, up pops his former mistress who threatens to put his former victim on his trail again if he doesn't come back to her, and she does.

In the midst of celebrating his birthday with Mary at home, in walks a detective with a warrant. Lowe frames with the cop not to let Mary know, both say it's business and friends bail him out. But when it comes time for him to do six months, Lowe writes a number of letters for a pal to mail who is going to Buenos Aires, and exits on that pretense.

It's strange but plausible to the girl until the detective thinks she should be tipped off and returns to tell her while her parents are visiting in Lowe's absence. A visit to the prisoner shows Mary the former chorister asking for Lowe as "Mrs. Stewart," the two conversing through the wired gate. She returns home without talking to her husband and remains silent, with the letters still coming in from South America.

The day Lowe gets out, he brings back a shawl and a Spanish comb for his bride, tells her all about the country and Mary gets a returned picture of him from the vindictive Kay which Lowe discovers. Realizing that Mary must know where he's been, Lowe starts to insist on telling her the truth as she frantically tries to stop him, finally showing him a small stocking as the reason. That's the finish.

Cast is air tight from Miss Moore to Diane Ellis who plays the former's chum and is the maid of honor. Lowe gives a performance that ranks with his "Dressed to Kill" and Miss Moore gets a chance to do a little bit of everything from her familiar adolescent comedy kid to pathos. This girl has always been able to act, and given a story that means something after a pretty long wait, has leaped at the chance to more than make good. Miss Tashman looks and does well as the gal who won't lay off Lowe, while Edythe Chapman and Charles Sellon make their minor roles as Mary's parents mean something. Robert Elliott's bit as the detective is also in tune.

Entire production splendid with an occasional rich interior dotting the course. Photography is also of high grade and the titles are excellent.

"Happiness Ahead" is a sweet feature for any time of year. Turned loose when the major companies are short of good program product, it stands out like a hole in one. It's still a corking picture, even if watching it with Rose Pelswick gabbing behind you from start to finish. *Sid.*

DOMESTIC TROUBLE

Warner Bros. production and release, with Vitaphone. Directed by Ray Enright from story by C. G. Baker. Titles by Joseph Jackson. Features Louise Fazenda and Clyde Cook. Betty Blythe, Jean Laverty and Arthur Rankin only cast members given screen mention. At Academy of Music, N. Y., June 18. Running time, 60 mins.

With a blonde of Jean Laverty's attractiveness, a capable trouper such as Betty Blythe, smart direction, good photography, extremely intelligent titling and smooth continuity giving the story a sexy twist, this should have been a standout box office success. But with Clyde Cook miscast in the most prominent role it just makes the grade for the minor houses.

Louise Fazenda fades into the background after the first few opening sequences and hardly appears in the balance of the picture. This is very healthy for the picture, since Miss Fazenda's attempt to portray a vamp meets with disaster.

Cook, playing a double role as a fast rounder whose twin brother is a staid reformer, is inefficient in both parts. The comedy, while getting laughs from the extras on the sets in the picture, doesn't register out front. As a snappy first-nighter, the heavy drinker and night club patron, the desired of the women, Cook looks like the other half of a bad No. 2 dance team.

Miss Laverty, as the sly wife of the reformer, was impressive enough to send sections of the house into heavy sighs every time she moved. A big girl but dressed so that everything counts and screens well from all angles.

Action starts when one of the boys is arrested for speeding. He sends his timid brother to take his place at home to prevent a jam with a straight-laced wife. The reformer then has the difficult job of keeping his brother's wife out of the bedroom. To make it harder his own wife appears and recognizes him when, in a forgetful moment, he puts on his spectacles. Bedroom scenes intriguing and comical.

Sound accompaniment with Vitaphone in this picture is used with good results in two or three spots. *Mori.*

HELL SHIP BRONSON

Gotham release of Sam Sax production, directed by J. E. Hennebery. Adapted from N. S. Parker's story. Features Mrs. Wallace Reid and Noah Beery. Cast includes Helen Foster, James Bradbury, Jr., and Jack Anthony. At Hippodrome, New York, week June 18. Running time, 70 mins.

Good enough picture of its kind and just what the title implies. Hardboiled temperaments on the high seas, with the father taking a poke at his son, but going aloft to save the boy during a storm and falling to his death after the rescue. Not for the full week stands, but sufficient to take its place in any house a rung or two under that classification.

Names of Noah Beery and Mrs. Wallace Reid won't hurt any, although the latter is a negligible factor among the acting personnel. Picture belongs to Beery as the heavily muscled and cynical captain. Having snatched his boy and himself away from home and remained away for 15 years, the trouble starts all over when the sailing vessel reaches Frisco again.

Mrs. Bronson traces her men to a waterfront saloon, but can't make any headway against her husband. She's finally forced to become a stowaway on his ship and is joined by a girl (Helen Foster) who thinks she has killed the dive's proprietor with a bottle after answering a phoney ad for a stenographer.

Bronson and his son (Reed Howes) are in on the girl's getaway through a rough-and-tumble, so that when the ship pulls out there are two women on board.

Bronson tries to make his offspring believe the elder woman is just with him for the trip, having brought the youth up to hate his mother; and the kid starts to get fresh with the girl. It winds up by the mother telling the youngster who she really is and the men of the family going to the mat because of the information holdout and the captain finishing one up on his boy.

Realizing he has lost his son, Bronson orders the ship through a storm under full canvass, and finishes by sending the kid up to fix a top sail. A previous cut-back explains the early walkout on the wife as jealousy because of a cousin who has given the Bronson tot a new suit.

Mixed up is the usual amount of slugging, hard drinking and a couple of attempts at comedy through a shanghaied cafe hoofer (James Bradbury, Jr.). Only one laugh, and that late. Beery makes the captain a legitimate figure, despite he has developed a MacLaglen or a Bancroft laugh, and Howes helps with his definition of the two-fisted son.

That about winds up all the acting. Mrs. Reid walks through while Miss Foster is a milk-and-water heroine whom the camera turns against after first flashing her favorably.

Production looks to be well within reason. Ship scenes, however, are authentic, plus several good-looking white-capped backgrounds to the immediate action. Storm isn't much more than a rain-and-wind effect, while the earlier cafe set is normal. Hennebery, directing, has kept the familiar story moving fairly well, but 10 minutes less, or about 1,000 feet lopped off, wouldn't do any harm. Picture is conventionally titled and cameraed. *Sid.*

THE THREAT

(FRENCH MADE)

Paris, May 24.

Adapted and not adopted from a story of Pierre Frondaie, "La Menace," which Jean Bertin has adroitly produced, is a good French picture for the fans of the Aubert circuit. Of true melodramatic atmosphere it contains all the fat that constitutes the popular novel of the present generation.

Compelled to put up at a country inn, owing to an accident to her automobile, Francoise Lefort there meets Paul Gaine and the couple strike up a friendship.

Francoise is a sort of merry widow, in business for herself as a publisher and as free as the wind. Paul makes himself so agreeable during the meal that the widow is a bit gone on the young fellow. When a storm breaks she does not hesitate to take shelter in his room, where she passes the night.

Next morning she feels a bit ashamed and begs Paul to forget their amorous adventure, even writing him a letter to that effect.

Soon after detectives call at the hotel, where they have traced Paul, who is a noted crook.

Years pass. Francoise meanwhile married a rich merchant, LeMorel, living in happiness.

Paul, having paid his debt in prison, has opened a library at Lugano, where he is discreetly paying court to a girl, who happens to be a sister of LeMorel. When she leaves Switzerland to see her brother in France, Paul follows and thus again meets Francoise.

Armed with the compromising letter she wrote him after their night in the hotel, Paul attempts to compel Francoise in adding him to marry her sister-in-law.

But Francoise confesses the past to her husband, who throws the black-mailer out of the house and takes his wife into his arms.

This romantic scenario is well acted by Jacqueline Forzane (wife), Chakatouny (husband), and Leon Bary (crook).

Jean Bertin has done his work well, and "La Menace" can be listed as a good French picture. *Kendrew.*

TILLIE'S PUNCTURED ROMANCE

Al Christie presents this remake of a Chaplin 1915 picture of same name. Released by Paramount. Directed by Ed Sutherland. Featured, W. C. Fields, Chester Conklin, Mack Swain and Louise Fazenda. New story by Monte Brice. Walter Graham production manager. Running time 70 mins. At Loew's Lincoln, Square (second run), June 18.

The Sennett version was adapted from "Tillie's Nightmare," musical farce starring Louise Dresser, who also played in the film version. That picture bore almost no resemblance to the stage performance. The new version has nothing to do with either the first film or its antecedent play. Nothing but the title survives.

It is really a feature length comedy and just misses rating the week stands, because it hasn't quite robust enough knockabout or gags, lacks sufficient speed and a smashing climax of roughhouse which seems to be essential to the big money laughies. In a two-reel version it would have been a scream; but it spreads out over, too much time. Seventy minutes of comedy demands a masterpiece.

Original had in its cast Charley Chaplin, Mack Sennett, Mabel Normand and the same Swain. This reviewer doesn't remember the Sennett Keystone, but the names speak for themselves. On thing against the new film may be that Chaplin himself took off the edge by using the circus tent locale only recently, and the newcomer doesn't measure up to "The Circus."

Picture starts out as rube comedy with farm girl running away to join a circus run by Conklin, with Fields the ring master who is plotting to get the boss into the lion cage to meet his finish, so he (Fields) can grab the circus. Then the war breaks out and we get a military travesty.

The circus goes "over there" as a camp show outfit and in France the action runs into Keystone technique. The producer must have expected the picture to hit important houses, for there has beeen impressive expenditure for mob and war effects, with very large numbers of soldiers brought into the action. It must have cost money. Best test that picture was deemed of less than week stand caliber is the fact that it went into the split weeks as a starter, and seems destined for the daily changes.

Fields has some characteristic comedy moments and the partnership with Conklin brings sophisticated laughs. Titling is well done and the comedy method is generally effective. But despite all these merits, the film somehow doesn't quite land with full score, due probably to the frequent let downs which are fatal in so long a comedy feature, which are measured by high speed and meaty two-reelers of the same style.

An element of weakness also is that story has no outstanding comedy character. Interest and laughs are divided among four principals—Fields, Conklin, Swain and Miss Fazenda and the effect is dissipated attention.

Feature comedy is strictly a single star racket. Four characters can't be built up for the strong haw-haw. *Rush.*

THE SPY

(GERMAN MADE)

London, June 10.

Original story by Thea von Harbou. Directed by Fritz Lang. Photography by Fritz Arno Wagner. Censors' certificate "U." Previewed at the Palace theatre, London, May 31. United Kingdom distribution, W. & F. Film Company. Running time, 130 mins.

Max Haghi	Rudolph Klein-Rogge
Sonia Barranikowa	Gerda Maurus
Miles Jason	Craighall Sherry
No. 326	Willy Fritsch
Dr. Matsumoto	Lupu Pick
Colonel Jellusic	Fritz Rasp

Nothing of the former type of Fritz Lang's work, as in "Metropolis," shown in this film. Intention was to make this a popular melodrama, and it may have succeeded according to the tastes of Continental audiences. As shown here, it is more like a cut-down crime serial.

Characterization is good, especially in the cases of Lupu Pick's representation of a Japanese diplomat who falls for a hard luck story told by a girl, loses the draft of the secret treaty as a result, and commits hari-kari.

Fritz Rasp, who ran away with "Lusts of the Flesh" recently, is outstanding, and Klein-Rogge makes an unbelievable master crook almost credible. Story is so confused it is difficult to tell what it's all about. There is a banker who is the head of a gang of international crooks, and a secret service couple. Stolen treaties, abducted miadens, mysterious murders, etc.

Direction is good, and many of the shots and sets are both novel and attractive. One sequence has a boxing ring in the center of a cabaret floor and staging a fight between each dance.

Too Continental and discursive for this country and it won't mean much in America. *Frat.*

Suicide of Hollyw'd Extra

FBO production and release. Directed by Robert Florey and S. Virkapitch. Runs about 1,200 feet. Among shorts on Cameo's picture bill week June 17. Not billed other than on program. Running time, 12 minutes.

Extra No. 9413	Jules Raucourt
Female Extra	Voya Georges
Star	(Not billed)

A suspicion this is an unannounced foreign made short. Everything looks foreign about it. Program says it is an FBO production. And the program further says:

"A remarkable experiment in film making; made at the astounding cost of $97.50."

A sub-title on a slide announces "The Life and Death of 9413. A Hollywood Extra."

As a 12-minute short it's a fantastic sort of picture, perhaps conceived as a moral to the picture fan or symbolic of the film studios.

It dwells heavily on a sign, "No Casting Today," in English. The short goes through its way without a caption. None is required. Story easily conveyed by an artist sent to a studio with a letter of introduction addressed to "Mr. Almighty." That might mean almost any production head, although likely intended for an indie producer.

As an extra the man is branded across the temple with the figures 9413. About all 9413 thereafter sees around the studios is "No Casting Today." "No Casting Today" gets into his dreams, among other things. Among the other dream things are what he would like to be, A Star. A Star is designated through being branded on the forehead with a star.

The extra sees the masks the star uses. He dreams masks, many of them, but it's only his dreams. In them, though, he also sees "SUCCESS" in electrics. It's a vision, as are the stairs leading to it, nice marble steps that the extra falls over and about but can never reach the top.

So he goes to Heaven riding a funny bike. In Heaven he smiles again, as some unknown rubs the branded 9413 from his temple.

Heaven, according to this picture, is a silent machine shop.

One girl for a brief instant appears.

Many little twists of photography that look like an assembly by clips from many of the German mades. Interesting enough for 12 minutes for the sure seaters or among those audiences with members having had their own picture heroing dreams. Could fit in anywhere, if that $97.50 bunk is worth something outside a theatre.

If so it should be ballyhooed, to teach the community that some picture actors or extras must work for nothing, that celluloid isn't charged for by Eastman, and that the high cost of picture making must be the hooey, for here's 12 minutes of something with three actors or extras costing $97.50. Consequently 60 minutes of the same thing couldn't cost over $477.50.

Page Mr. Mayer!

TONI

(BRITISH MADE)

London, May 25.

Produced by British International. Distributed in the U. K. by Wardour Film Company, and in America through United Motion Picture Productions. Directed by Arthur Maude. From an original by Douglas Furber. Photography by George Pocknell. Running time, 72 minutes. Preview London Hippodrome, May 21. Censor's certificate: "U".

Toni Marini	Jack Buchanan
Princess Eugenie	Dorothy Boyd
Watts	Forrester Harvey
Delavine	Hayford Hobbs
Gardo	Henry Vibart
International Crooks	Moore Marriott Lawson Butt Frank Goldsmith

This is the only film Arthur Maude did for British International. They let him out and kept several directors who have since done other pictures. But this one is better than several British International have thought a lot more of. And it isn't good at that. The story is punk melo. Maude seems to have realized it was so impossible he just went out and, with the aid of Jack Buchanan, gagged it into a comedy which sometimes becomes farce.

Roughly it is the story of an idle rich young man who is the double of a famous detective and changes places with the detective so as to get some excitement. Mixed up in an attempt to rob an exiled Princess of her jewels, he saves her and the jewels, and she abdicates the throne so they can wed.

Most of it is idiotic, some of it creates laughter and little of it is necessary. Buchanan is too stagey, his gags are stock stuff, his actions are in the wrong tempo, but he gets a few good laughs despite these defects.

The rest of the cast is capable of much better work than it puts over in this film, though Dorothy Boyd, hailed as a new British star, needs a powerful telescope to reveal her stellar qualities. *Frat.*

NO OTHER WOMAN

Fox production and release. Starring Dolores Del Rio. Directed by Lou Tellegen. Story by Polan Banks, adapted by Jessie Burns. Cameraman, Paul Ivano. Don Alvarado, Paulette Duval, Ben Bard in cast. At Broadway, New York, week June 19. Running time, 62 mins.

Lou Tellegen, the actor, emerges with this film as a director, and not a bad one. The picture is fairly good in telling one of those basically wrong stories in which the heroine marries the wrong man in mid-picture and needs the unromantic legalism of a divorce to remedy her mistake for the final fade-out with the hero.

Might be taken as significant that Fox did not spot this Del Rio picture at the Roxy. Miss Del Rio, with the exception of "Loves of Carmen," has not shown to the best advantage in Fox program pictures. "Gateway of the Moon," which played the Roxy, was rated very low. Miss Del Rio seems essentially a big production player meaning little in the ordinary feature. Possibly one reason why she does not "star" easily is that she doesn't wear drawing room clothes with any real effect.

In as far as acting honors exist in "No Other Woman" they go to Ben Bard, the one time vaude straight man. He is developing a neat technique of villainy and manages to be thoroughly disagreeable in front of a camera.

The trouble with "No Other Woman" is the trouble with most pictures, trite, unimaginative stories. But this picture has that inestimable something known as "production."

Tellegen has really acquitted himself very well. His directorial method is simple, straightforward and not loose-endish. *Land.*

MODERN MOTHERS

Columbia production and release. Directed by Philip Rosen, from story by Peter Milne. In cast: Douglas Fairbanks, Jr.; Helene Chadwick, Barbara Kent. At Loew's New York, one day, June 12, one-half of double bill. Running time, 60 minutes.

Peter Milne's idea of the sex appeal of a mother would be laughable were it not that Columbia went to the other extreme and selected a flapper type for the role, Helene Chadwick, who looks just as young if not younger than her screen daughter, Barbara Kent. The apparent closeness of their ages kills considerable interest which might otherwise have been aroused for the neighborhood houses in "Modern Mothers."

The actress-mother, who unwittingly falls in love with her daughter's boy friend, essayed with much vim by Doug Fairbanks, Jr., winds up in the conventional way, with the mother making the "great" sacrifice. The dame, however, never discloses to her daughter that she is the mother, and the story terminates with Fairbanks and Miss Kent together, but with a lot of action unexplained to the fans.

The Whirl of Paris

(FRENCH MADE)

Paris, May 25.

The Film d'Art has turned out an excellent picture, thanks to the producer, J. Duvivier, with "Le Tourbillon de Paris," adapted from "La Sarrazine" of Germaine Acremant. It is not exactly the plot which constitutes the success, but the artistic manner in which it has been handled.

The story is mediocre. Lady Abenston, albeit happy at home, left her husband for further fame as an opera singer. She was of Saracen extraction, brought up as a peasant. Pretty, with natural talent, she went on the stage when young and soon reached a lofty position, which she relinquished to marry an English lord.

Call of the stage was too great and she could not resist. Owing to a love intrigue, Lady Abenston soon threw up her engagement and hid herself in a small village in the Alps, where her mother lived. Both her husband and Chalustre (her best friend at the theatre) found her there and prevailed on her to return to her home.

The eccentric lad- started off for Scotland with her husband, but passing through Paris the attraction of the city was again too great for her, and once more she went on the stage. Chalustre loved her so sincerely that he engaged a group of playgoers to give her the bird. What he anticipated happened, for the actress become so disgusted with the theatre that she went back to her noble lord, a sad but wiser woman. As for Chalustre, the man who sacrificed himself on several occasions for her sake, he was left alone in the world.

Lil Dagover, a very good-looking woman, is the lead and proves herself also a capable actress. Leon Bary is the tolerant English lord. Gaston Jacquet is better as the constant lover. Some lovely views of the Alps, with scenes laid in the usual dancing resort, and a theatrical performance realistically reconstituted. All modern films seem to have a terpsichorean spasm, as injecting variety into the scenario.

Photographic work is a feature. On the whole this picture is worthy of praise and can be classed as another good French feature.

Kendrew.

UPLAND RIDER

Charles Rogers production, released through First National. Starring Ken Maynard. Albert Rogell, director. Story by Marion Jackson. Ted McCord, cameraman. In cast: Marion Douglas, Lafe McKee, Sidney Jarvis. At Loew's Circle one day, June 14. Running time, 60 minutes.

"Upland Rider" is every bit of the sure-fire Western. It's got all of the old hoke and some exceptional shots in addition to action well steamed throughout that comes to a regular blow-up of fast riding, falling horses, cliff jumpers and the hero winning the relay by a horse's length.

The story in plot far surpasses most of the rough riders that have been turned out during the past six months. The suspense is started around a test between the old broncs of the plains and thoroughbreds, with the climax reached in the race deciding which breeder will cash in on a large government order.

Before the safety of the oldtimer's ranch is assured audience interest is aroused in the dirty work which the thoroughbred owner must pull off. Clever work on the part of rival horses; fake fire; pony dressed in chaps; some good barroom brawls—all these precede the relay race, which is a corker in "Upland Rider" and would be a magnet for any Western following.

The Girl He Didn't Buy

Peerless (made) production released through Capitol. Dallas Fitzgerald, director. Story and continuity by Gladys Gordon and Ada McQuillan. Pauline Garon starred. In cast: Allan Simpson, William Eugene, Gladden James. At Loew's New York one day, June 15, one-half of double bill. Running time, 55 minutes.

Because the girl he has promised to star doesn't go below deck immediately after he has agreed to finance the show, the angel pouts like a school boy. So "The Girl He Didn't Buy" carries on in its expose of Broadway. This will entertain the sticks and a lot of people in New York, providing they know nothing about the workings of the theatre. Okay indie with plenty of merit for those who book it.

The story, although foppishly implausible, has some back-stage stuff far better than some of the more pretentious cinemas in this category. Fitzgerald uses his chorines to advantage for male attendance. The tights are tight and the moral is held up by the star who plays goody-goody role, marries the right man and shows she is one dame wicked Broadway can't raise to stardom off the straight and narrow.

HER SUMMER HERO

FBO production and release. Story and continuity by Gertrude Orr. Directed by James Dugan. Cast includes: Sally Blaine, Hugh Trevor, Duane Thompson, Harold Goodwin, James Pierce and Cleve Moore. On double feature program at Tivoli, N. Y., June 13. Running time, 49 minutes.

Lightweight stuff for doubleheaders and short engagements in the neighbors and grinds. Direction, photography and production below par, but theme of picture will help.

It's one of those youth affairs with a college background. The importance of winning a swimming race for Alma Mater and not being seen talking to any but the one and only girl is the basis of the plot.

A lot of good looking young men and girls and there's beach stuff appropriate to the warm weather, plus a general breeziness. It's one of the lesser FBO's, but can squeeze by in the classifications mentioned.

Land.

HELLO CHEYENNE!

Fox production and release, starring Tom Mix. Directed by Gene Forde from story by Harry Sinclair Drago. Scenario by Fred Myton. Cast includes: Caryl Lincoln, Jack Naston, Joseph Girard, Al St. John, Martin Faust and William Caress. At Loew's New York, June 11. Running time, about 50 minutes.

One of Mix's typical westerns. Caryl Lincoln supports a gal who looks good and gets away from the dumbness of the usual plains heroines. Al St. John does not register so well for comedy, principally because of lack of material.

One punch scene is where Mix hooks under a wagon and rides down a hill to evade a gang of gunmen trying to stop him from making a telephone connection. The stunt, whether trick or actually done, gets over strongly.

Story is of rival telephone companies trying to be the first to complete a line between Cheyenne and Rawhide. Gal's father heading one of the companies, acquires the services of Tom and his funny pardner.

Mori.

DANGER PATROL

W. Ray Johnson production, released by Rayart. Story by H. H. Van Loan. Screen play by Arthur Hoerl. Directed by Duke Worne. William Russell, Virginia Browne Faire and Napoleon, the dog, featured. At Loew's Circle, N. Y., June 11, as half of double bill. Running time, 60 minutes.

Mildly entertaining Canadian Northwest film in which the Mountie doing his sleuthing on snowshoes gets his man and wins the girl. At the Circle they had this one doubled up with a re-issue of "The Last Laugh." With strong program support this one will slide by in the neighborhoods.

Story centers around Celeste Claveau (Miss Faire) who is forced into a marriage of convenience by a grasping mother. On her bridal night she scrams out and starts mushing back to her father's trading post. Caught in a snow slide she is rescued by Sergeant Daley (Russell) who has her father, accused of murder, in tow. Daley is a victim of snow blindness, Celeste's father thereby getting an opportunity to escape. The girl stays on and nurses the copper back to normalcy and he falls in love with her. A couple of killings clear Celeste's father and reveal her husband as a no good guy, leaving the way open for the inevitable clinch.

A comedy Englishman is worked in to offset the three shootings.

THE UNSLEEPING EYE

(BRITISH MADE)

London, May 17.

Produced by Seven Seas Productions Co. Distributed by British Screen Productions, Ltd. Directed by Alexander Macdonald, F. R. G. S. Photographed and written by Walter B. Sully. Censor's certificate "U." Running time, 70 minutes. Preview, New Gallery, London, May 16.

Claimed to be a "pioneering tale of New Guinea, the most savage island in the world," this is a poor specimen of a travelog and no better an example of a photoplay. All the actors are amateurs, and the natives, who certainly screen with less camera consciousness than the whites, are only too obviously obeying orders.

Thread of a story, of a white ma: who has a big pull with the headhunters, but drinks. He finds gold, brings a partner along, hits the bottle again, goes home for a while, returns with a wife, finds the natives hostile, and apparently is killed fighting the head man for supremacy.

Years after wife and small child return in search of his grave, and fall into a tribal fight. They are saved by the head-hunters, whose chief is killed just as he has given them safe conduct home. The dying chief turns out to be the supposed dead husband, and wife forgives him as he dies.

Most of the stuff is just natives running about, exchanging conversations or dancing. It might have been taken in any tropical spot. Despite interminable captions before the film begins, telling how inaccessible the locations are and how dangerous the film was to make, there is nothing in the picture to show there was any danger or hardship. The natives seem not only friendly but very willing to help and quite amused at the proceedings.

Poor story, no thrills, mediocre camera work and average tropical scenery are all this mess of footage contains.

Frat.

AT EDGE OF WORLD

(GERMAN-MADE)

London, May 16.

Ufa production. Directed by Karl Grune. Distributed in the U. K. by Gaumont-British Company. Preview at the Capitol theatre, London, May 7. Running time, 90 minutes.

A curious mess. The idea seems to be a mill which is on the edge of the world, on the border of two countries, symbolizing the eternal triumph of peace and industry over war. A man from over the border comes to work at the mill, really to act as a spy and operate a telephone line from the cellar when war breaks out. The enemy comes over the border and seizes the mill, and will shoot the miller's little son if the miller's little daughter does not submit. A kind-hearted lieutenant helps the boy to escape because he loves the girl and the old miller at the finish, is posed over the childbed of another daughter, visualizing the building up of a new mill.

In an attempt to avoid giving the troops any nationality the director has made them look like nothing on earth. The uniforms must be seen to be believed. They wear spoutless tin kettles for helmets, and have some kind of radiators over the muzzles of their rifles.

And that would pass if the sets were not so very studio, long shots of the mill looking like cardboard models. Albert Steinruck, Brigette Helm and Jean Bradin are the principals, but except Steinruck they are so badly handled they get small chance.

All around, it has all the faults of what is implied in the term "a Continental picture" when used as a criticism.

And the story is as muddled as it is incredible.

THE MALTESE HOUSE

(FRENCH MADE)

Paris, June 10.

Henri Fescourt is the technical producer of this screen version of Jean Vignaud's novel "Le Maison du Maltais." It has met with a good reception at the pop houses here.

Favorable features about this picture which appeal to the average fan, with plenty of local color of Oriental customs, as well as a peep behind the counter of Parisian diamond merchants. It is the biography of Matteo, living in the Isle of Malta. He is the son of a Catholic father and an Arabian mother, having been reared by the latter in accordance with the precepts of the Koran. All offences call for revenge. Matteo falls in love with Sofia, a native dancer of his mother's tribe, which inspires him to greater work that he may earn more money. His diligence becomes the talk of Sfax. However, his riches are not honestly acquired, for he secretly robs even his own father. In spite of this mark of devotion, Sofia elopes with a stranger to Paris, where Matteo finally traces her.

The dancer, having likewise grown tired of a life of pleasure, is ready to return to Sfax with her former wealthy lover who is secretly planning a terrible vengeance. Matteo entices her to his Oriental house, intending to sequest her forever, but his father appears and counsels pardon.

Scenario is a bit erratic but lends itself to several interesting scenes. Silvio de Pedrelli is quite at ease in the role of the elegant Maltese, while Tina Meller will please with her terpsichorean ability notwithstanding she appears somewhat older than the supposed age of the Bedouin dancer.

Kendrew.

The Hands of Orlac

(GERMAN MADE)

Pan-Film A. G. production distributed by Awyon Films. Directed by Dr. Robert Weine from screen adaptation of novel by Maurice Renard. In cast: Conrad Veidt, Alexandra Sorina, Fritz Strassny, Paul Askenas, Carmen Cartellieri, Frits Kortner. At Greenwich Village week June 2. Running time, 80 mins.

Were it not for Veidt's masterly characterization, "The Hands of Orlac" would be an absurd fantasy in the old-time mystery-thriller class. As the musician who learns that the hands he lost in a train wreck have been supplanted by those from a man guillotined for a murder, Veidt keeps his audience highly tensed in spots. Drab photography and over-footage devoted to long gloomy hallways make for repetition that will render the production monotonous to the average patron of a high-class house.

Poorly titled, the picture is so edited an audience is distracted in its effort to fathom out supporting characterizations, hopelessly complicated until the latter half of the last reel. Not until then is it discovered that a character assumed to be an apparition of the murderer has framed the man who was executed and has perpetrated the second killing, which he endeavored to place on the musician with the dead man's hands.

In the 80 minutes devoted to projection not one evidence of a struggle was screened. The salvaging of a train wreck by torchlight is one of the production's most vivid sequences; the last few feet being so fast moving as to have the effect of an alarm clock upon the audience, leaving the house by this time and still not satisfied as to what it is all about.

VIOLETTE IMPERIALE

(FRENCH-MADE)

French production released in America by Aywon. Stars Raquel Meller. No other credits. At Fifth Ave. Playhouse, N. Y., week of June 16. Running time, 63 mins.

Strictly for the sure seaters. It's a long-winded story of the reign of Napoleon III. Plot, intrigue, and 1870 costumes makes it reasonably interesting art theatre stuff, but entirely non-commercial for general American purposes.

Meller has an unusual screen personality and other types (unprogrammed) are out of the ordinary. Lighting and makeup characteristically French, viz not so good. Direction rather slow and continuity not too smooth. Some dramatic movement but in general it drags.

Doesn't rate important or extended consideration. *Land.*

THE RED DANCE

Fox production and release. Directed by Raoul Walsh from story by H. L. Gates and Eleanor Browne, with scenario by James Creelman. Dolores Del Rio starred, with Charles Farrell and Ivan Linow featured. Movietone sound attachment. Synchronized score by S. L. Rothafel and Erno Rapee. At Globe, New York, on run, June 25, $2 top. Running time, about 90 mins.

Tasia	Dolores Del Rio
The Grandduke Eugen	Charles Farrell
Ivan Petroff	Ivan Linow
An Agitator	Boris Charsky
The Princess Varvara	Dorothy Revier
General Tanaroff	Andre Segurola
Rasputin	Dimitri Alexis

A picture house picture of the new Fox brand, finish and polish, that will even run better in the regular houses when its 90 minutes have been clipped to the pop price size. At $2 in the Globe "The Red Dance" will be mostly held up by the Movietone short of George Bernard Shaw.

Nothing outstanding in this latest Fox special, excepting its production, Ivan Linow, and how Raoul Walsh celluloid-told of the outbreak of the Bolshevik revolution in St. Petersburg, Moscow, or pick your spot.

It's that kind of the now familiar Russian story used by many of the foreign-mades, but here utilized in a way the Soviet Russian reign should appreciate. It seeks to or does give justification, if needed, for the Czar's overthrow. Interesting in a way is the peasant life as exhibited; how the thinkers get life and their women get ruined; what the Cossacks meant in their Ku-Klux raids, and other things, down to Dolores Del Rio's sorrowfulness all of the time and her legs as a dancer otherwise.

Besides Mr. Shaw you must go over to get a load, too, of Ivan Linow. Linow's work here got him featuring besides a five-year Fox contract. He's a Russian, too, on the level, a big gawky Russian some years ago, and a bum wrestler, professional, so much so he had to clown his way through the frames to even stay in. Linow in "The Red Dance" repeatedly says he has brains, a favorite peasant expression evidently in the Russian days when, if they knew enough to stop talking, they saved their necks.

With his brains and probably a short b. r., Ivan went to Hollywood. He may have thought at that time it was a stopoff on the way home, but it was Hollywood, and at least he had six feet four to attract notice with. The over six-footers on the coast are types, so Ivan worked his way filming until now he evolutes from a bum wrestler into a corking actor, a comedian in his way and partly in this role; made heroic by the scenario and a life-saver at the finish, until as Ivan in the other days didn't know whether he had won or lost the fall, now didn't know whether he stood for royalty or his peasant pals.

Which is another way of saying that Ivan Linow runs away with a picture Charles Farrell, the juv, should have sewn up. But it didn't just so happen. Probably the Fox bunch when they saw the speed with which Ivan was sailing along spread it out for him.

Of all of the Russian and German mades which have attempted to suggest the scenes of the Russian uprising, none at home or abroad has succeeded as well as Mr. Walsh. Otherwise there wasn't much to direct in this story except to keep it going, making a couple of hot scenes hotter as a b. o. foundation, but not even hot enough for $2. Nowadays in the films one must know what they want for $2.

In cutting this down to 70 minutes it will be just about right, and the exhibs can ring another of the Fox's in "The Red Dance."

WARMING UP

Paramount production and release. Original by Sam Mintz. Adaptation by Ray Harris. Supervision, J. C. Bachman. Directed by Fred Newmeyer. Titles by George Marion, Jr. Previewed at Strand, Yonkers, N. Y. Running time, 60 mins.

Bert Tulliver	Richard Dix
Mary Post	Jean Arthur
Mr. Post	Claude King
McRae	Philo McCollough
Doyle	Wade Boteler
Edsel	Billy Kent Schaefer
Hippo	Roscoe Karns
Brill	James Dugan
The Veteran	Mike Donlin

Richard Dix's pitching, George Marion's titling, June Arthur's beauty and personality, and the Victor record sound effects, a la Vitaphone, pulled a tough game out of the fire for Paramount, with "Warming Up," a paluka baseball picture.

Despite an incredible, weak, formula story, loaded with implausible gags, every foot betraying lack of knowledge of his subject by the author, and indifferent casting in several of the principal roles, Dix and Miss Arthur enlist the sympathies and interest of their audience from beginning to end, and aided by sound effects, almost make the weakling stand up.

Edward Cronjager, the camera man, also gets an assist. His trick shots of Dix's delivery in the world's series, and other shots where Dix is pitching, gave a necessary touch of authenticity to a picture that needed every slight support it could elicit, to bolster up the story.

The latter concerns the trials and tribulations of Bee Line Tolliver (Mr. Dix), a rube pitcher, who wanders onto the ball grounds where the Yanks are training in Florida. McRae, the slugger of the Yanks, supposed to be a prototype of Babe Ruth, and whose only resemblance to the immortal Bamb is under the arms, decides to trick the rube with the "iodine" bit. This is a goofy invention of the author whereby the rooky is tricked into thinking he has beaned the batter. The latter takes a prop fall and the players sneak a dab of iodine on his forehead.

It couldn't happen, and starts the picture off on the wrong foot with everybody in the audience who has the slightest knowledge of baseball. However, it's vital to the story, so in it went.

The rube, induced to pitch to the hitters during batting practise, is scared to death and sorrowfully leaves the field. He can't understand it. He has pitched in the bushes and was noted for his control. He got his monicker "Bee Line" for his marvelous motorman.

Passing a baby doll rack, after leaving the park, he tries out his control by pegging baseballs at the colored baby dolls. He knocks down the entire rack, winning a doll and a job from the concessionaire.

The daughter of the owner of the Yanks witnesses his exhibition of skill and decides she has discovered a big league pitcher. A kid brother with her pries into the busher's suitcase, and he and the girl become acquainted as a result. Tolliver gets the idea she is a governess for the kid and she lets it stand that way by giving him a phoney name when she makes a date with him. The heights of creative dizziness are reached here. Her name is Minnie Zilch.

The owner's daughter promptly tells the manager of the Yanks that she has a prospect for him. From here on any tabloid reader can finish the story. Of course, Tolliver turns out to be a find. The heavy, McRae, and he are both hot after the jane, of course. McRae being on the Yanks, who have acquired him from Pittsburgh in the National League—how, no one ever finds out—must be transferred to the other league, so that the World's Series, with which every Hollywood baseball picture must end, will find the hero and the heavy on opposing clubs. It is done by ringing in that good old friend of indigent writers, the insert. A telegram is received at the conclusion of the training season to the effect that the Pittsburgh Club has discovered that it still has an option on McRae, and is exercising it. That will chase ball players and fans who know right field from left to the showers.

At any rate after George Marion has dismissed an entire season in a title, we have the Yanks and Pittsburgh hooked up in the "serious." Tolliver, after falling for the iodine gag at the training camp, did actually bean McRae a few days later. This is assumed by the author to be proper motivation for the premise that every time Tolliver pitches against McRae he will be so nervous because of his previous loss of control.

Tolliver does exactly that, in the first game of the World's Series, walking McRae with the bases full, and getting himself taken out when he forces in a run. For that he sits on the bench accumulating splinters until the series is tied and the last game is being played. And he's the star pitcher of the club, mind you.

On the eve of the last game Tolliver decides to visit the girl. He arrives in time to see McRae ostensibly slipping a ring on her finger. The idea is that she's just admiring it and returns it with thanks a moment later. Tolliver, however, has turned away before it's returned and is fooled into thinking she was seriously entertaining McRae's proposal. So was every one else, including the audience, who should have known better.

Next day it becomes necessary to put Tolliver in, after the second string pitcher has weakened, and complained of a sore arm. He is injected into the pastime with the bases loaded and not a soul out. He makes the first two hitters beat all the air out of the park, waving at his hook and fast one. Now comes McRae, handling his war club like a Vassar alumna, and glowering revenge. The tieing run is on third base. In a field box sits the girl. She's still Minnie Zilch to our hero, although a season has passed since their meeting. However, we can cover that in a title, so let's go.

The catcher, who is Bee Line's buddy, is chatting with the girl. He tells her about Minnie Zilch having Bee Line out on a limb, and about the ring episode. The girl is hep instantly. How to give Bee Line the office that he's still tops with her, and that he misunderstood the whole affair. The McRae jinx must be exorcised somehow—but how?

Here's how. When Tolliver first met the girl he had just won a doll for his dexterity in heaving the apple at the nigger babies. The doll was a tall, nondescript, figure, but at its base was printed in large letters, "I'm yours forever."

Don't forget that inscription, for it's very important in view of what's coming. The doll is also carried by Tolliver to the girl's kitchen, where he has his rendevous with Minnie Zilch. Here it is firmly planted in the minds of the audience, when it is broken accidentally.

Why the doll—and why the silly meaningless inscription? Just wait! The doll when wound up does a funny sort of a bow and salute. Now the story conference is over and we can get back to Tolliver facing McRae, and the girl frantically trying to encourage him in the box. Ah! An inspiration. Standing up in the box she catches Tolliver's eye. He looks. She bows and salutes and every lip reader in the house can see her saying, "I'm yours forever."

Comes the dawn, or at least McRae thinks so, by the breeze from the rejuvenated Tolliver's fast one. The heavy doesn't even foul one and the game ends with the crowd carrying Tolliver off the field to the shouts of the Victor record's big league shouters.

The best gag in the picture and the most improbable, occurred when the manager catches Tolliver sneaking in after hours. Entering his room he finds him in bed. He exits, and as Tolliver jumps up to disrobe, returns and catches him. The pitcher explains that he's superstitious and on the eve of a hard game always sleeps in his clothes. This apparently suffices and once more the mgr. blows. Again Tolliver is caught out of bed. He puts on a sweater and retires, as the manager bows out. Once more he gets up and once more he's nailed. This time he puts on an overcoat and jumps back into the kip. Hokey but they yelled at it.

Without the sound effects, which projected the yells of the crowd in the stands, remarks of players at the training camp, etc., the picture is one of the worst duds to ever come out of the Hollywood factory. While the sound record doesn't synchronize with lip movement, it lifts the thing unbelievably. The excitement of the crowd is in some measure transferred to the audience, making the ridiculous story almost plausible at the end, and helping the World's Series sequence build up to a dramatic climax. It was made after the negative had been shipped east and was a real happy thought on someone's part.

The picture itself is as full of flaws as an e flat diamond. The story is responsible for this in a large measure. It's crude, shows lack of technical knowledge, and contains cumbersome gags dragged in for formula motivation purposes. The effort to use the same formula that made "The Quarterback" a box office success, fails miserably.

Dix and June Arthur are splendid in spite of wretched material. Fred Newmeyer's direction was all that the script would allow it to be. Mike Donlin, seen in a few shots, helped as a technical adviser. It's ten to one Mike was never consulted about that telegram insert transferring McRae to Pittsburgh. The "iodine" gag is the tip off on the creative limitations of all concerned. Iodine is brown, and Tolliver is expected to mistake it for blood. Red paint wouldn't suffice—or ketsup.

The doll gag should be enshrined in the Hollywood Hall of Fame, as the most asinine concoction ever trotted out for the edification of that mythical 12-year-old audience the boys have invented. *Con.*

THE COSSACKS

Metro-Goldwyn-Mayer production and release. John Gilbert starred. Ernest Torrence and Renee Adoree featured. George Hill, director. Adapted from Tolstoi's novel by Miss Wilson. Titled by John Colton. At the Capitol, N. Y., week of June 23. Running time, 75 mins.

Lukashka....................John Gilbert
Maryana....................Renee Adoree
Ivan....................Ernest Torrence
Ulitka....................Dale Fuller
Lukashka's Mother............Mary Alden
Stepka....................Josephine Borio
Olenin....................Neil Neely
Uncle Eroshka............Yorke Sherwood
Turk Spy....................Joseph Mari
Zarka....................Paul Hurst

The flaps, who want to see John Gilbert mauling some dame in hot love scenes may not fancy this M-G-M as much as some of his former releases, but picture lovers and adults will find plenty of entertainment in the beautiful photography, production and story.

The yarn concerns a Cossack village. The creed of the men is let the women work while they fight. The Turks are the opposition and until a Cossack has bumped off 10 or more Turks, he's considered a busher by the big leaguers.

Lukashka (Mr. Gilbert) is the son of Ivan the Ataman (Ernest Torrence), head man in this league. He doesn't crave fighting and would rather loll under a shady tree with a copy of the "American Merc" in his duke. This pegs him as a physical coward with the rest of the Turk annihilaters. They become so infuriated they dress him as a dame and throw grapes at him.

That's the pay off. Lukashka goes berserk, kicks the devil out of his old man and as several Turks escape from the local can, Lukashka gives them a tail and croaks several of them.

He had been spurned by Maryana (Adoree) for his non-combative ideas, but after this outburst she declares her love. He meets it with indifference, thinking to punish her.

The village finally rides out on a foray against their natural enemies. Lukashka fattens up his batting average by knocking off several more Turks and returns in triumph. He has also collected a wound on the kisser, considered the last word in warrior embellishments.

Meanwhile Prince Olenin (Neil Neely), messenger of the Czar, is creating a furore in the village among the fems. The Prince is a looker and changes his smocks and vodka every 20 minutes. He has made a strong play for Maryana, but isn't doing so well, when the battlers arrive home. Lukaska is still playing the chill for his skirt, not knowing he has royal opposition. They quarrel and she accepts a proposal of marriage which the Prince had made just before the men returned.

The betrothal party is pulled, Lukashka is present with his mob. Nothing happens. The finale finds Lukashka kidnapping his woman, despite her being penciled in with royalty. She is on her way to the capital when the abduction occurs. A gang of marauding Turks bump off the Prince and everything is copesetty.

The Cossack village is a faithful reproduction of the real thing. Superb horsemanship. The riders are mostly real Russians who came to this country to work in this picture and stopped en route to Hollywood to pull the most gigantic flop that Madison Square Garden has yet housed. The survivors of the fiasco finally reached the coast and are present in this film.

Gilbert is doubled cleverly in some of the stunt stuff on horseback, as are many of the other principals. He gives a splendid performance as does Ernest Torrence who shaved his dome for this one. Mary Alden as the mother also rings the bell. Miss Adoree is winsome and sweet as the little reason for it all and Neil Neely ought to boost the tourist travel of school teachers into the land of the Soviet.

Gilbert will lose none of his following with this in spite of the absence of his usual allotment of huddles. It is also commendable that M-G-M is mixing them up for Gilbert and not giving him the same formula, picture after picture.

Will stand up anywhere in the first runs. *Con.*

The Magnificent Flirt

Paramount production and release. Starring Florence Vidor. Directed by Harry d'Arrast. Jean de Limur and d'Arrast adapted from "Maman." Photography by Henry Gerard. H. J. Mankiewicz titling. At Paramount, New York, week June 23. Running time, 74 mins.

Madame Florence Laverne..Florence Vidor
Count D'Estranges ....Albert Conti
Denise Laverne ....Loretta Young
Hubert ....Matty Kemp
Fifi ....Marietta Millner
Tim ....Ned Sparks

Ordinary program leader that has nothing to recommend it for big league showing other than some impressionistic photography by Gerard, good looking interiors, a few gowns and Albert Conti's performance. Florence Vidor has had previous boxoffice difficulty and "The Magnificent Flirt" is not the remedy with which she'll cure the ailment.

Supposedly unveiling a cross section of Paris' smart set in action, it takes 74 minutes to start and stop. When it's all over the film has simply gone around the block. In many a spot it becomes an outright bore, revealing Miss Vidor as a flip widow who has a daughter as the central figure. No anxiety aroused when the young daughter (Loretta Young) is apt to lose her sweetheart, the nephew of the Count who thinks he knows enough about Mrs. Laverne not to marry her, and does. By the time all this comes around nobody cares as it's taken too long to get there.

Miss Vidor, not too adept at shedding warmth from a screen, has an unsympathetic role to boot. The assignment is unfortunate as her name is over the title on this picture. Gerard's camera work is multiple lens, silhouette and trick stuff torn from a page scribbled on by those boys who work with Murnau. Excellently done it's the top note of this release.

Conti does exceptionally well by his Menjou characterization with Miss Young impressing on youth as the maiden daughter. Matty Kemp, playing the nephew, is a good looking youngster lacking force. Ned Sparks unfolds a drunk and makes it okay but can't be blamed because d'Arrast has seen fit to give him too much footage.

Those who see it will like Conti and Miss Young but that's not enough to erase the story faults. It should increase Gerard's reputation as a cameraman, but that was never the studio objective. Could be called a well dressed filler.

Script lacks a definite spoke upon which to hang interest and screens that way. It will mean nothing to Miss Vidor or the theatres than to increase the public curiosity on talkers. *Sid.*

FOREIGN LEGION

Universal production and release. Directed by Edward Sloman. Norman Kerry and Lewis Stone featured. Feminine lead played by Mary Nolan, the former Imogene Wilson of the stage. Adapted from the novel, "The Red Mirage" by I. A. R. Wylie. Titles by Walter Anthony. Jackson Ross, cameraman. At Roxy, New York, week June 23. Running time, 68 minutes.

Richard....................Norman Kerry
Col. Destinn....................Lewis Stone
Capt. Arnaud................Crauford Kent
Corporal Gotz....................Walter Perry
Gabrielle....................June Marlowe
Sylvia....................Mary Nolan

Of the vogue for Foreign Legion stories, extremely well made from a technical angle. Production has fine scenic and pictorial shots, good military mob scene and high class production handling. It is in the story it falls down. Cast has good names and offers plenty of opportunity for exploitation. Building up Mary Nolan as the much publicized Imogene Wilson, if managed indirectly, could be made to count.

But sophisticated fans will scoff at some of the dramatic sequences, which couldn't be made plausible even by acting of able cast and direction. A smoothly made continuity could have bridged some of the glaring inconsistencies.

These hypersentimental romances call for delicate treatment, for heavy romance can easily stumble into burlesque. This hero is made to act the sap, which is fatal. Here an English army officer confesses he tried to steal plans of an English fort to sell, presumably to a foreign country, all for no other reason than the French spy who was really guilty had married the girl who had just jilted him. No adequate motive established, a matter of right planting of the situation.

All through this hero is doing the most unexpected things. Once he is apparently dying in a hospital, and in almost the next instant, comes upon the scene briskly and in perfect health. When he is in solitary confinement, just casually drops unconscious and one wonders why. They ought to explain these things.

Mary Nolan plays a selfish, gold-digging blonde and does it very well. She is the type of impersonal, characterless beauty and within a narrow range of characterization should prosper on the screen. Here she was distinctly an asset on merit and without reference to her publicity possibilities. Norman Kerry gives his usual suave performance, but went astray due to the illogical things called upon to do. Lewis Stone almost succeeded in not looking foolish, something of a triumph under the circumstances.

Production admirable. Desert scenes splendid. A sequence of a sandstorm swooping down upon a detachment of Legionnaires on the march was nicely handled and numerous settings of barracks, prison corridors and society interiors were worthy of the best modern technique.

All of which is wasted for run houses where the story condemns the work. *Rush.*

THE HAWK'S NEST

First National production and release. Directed by Benjamin Christensen from story by Wid Gunning. Milton Sills starred; Doris Kenyon featured. No slide billing except for director. Previous credits from program. Additional credits from First National press sheet. Adaptation and continuity by James T. O'Donohoe. Photographer, Sol Polita. Film editor, Frank Ware. Art director, Max Parker. At Strand, New York, week June 23. Running time around 70 minutes.

The Hawk / John Finchley }....................Milton Sills
Dan Daugherty................Montagu Love
James Kent....................Mitchell Lewis
Madelon Arden................Doris Kenyon
Barney McGuire..............Stuart Holmes
Sojin.............................. Sojin

Pretty light weight First National programmer. Runs to underworld stuff but draggy and mostly actionless, without tenseness and no holding interest. Story looks as though possessing more opportunities than were taken advantage of. Picture dependent upon its names, Milton Sills and Doris Kenyon. Where they can't draw, this film won't.

Tale set in Chinatown, New York, of a couple of nite dive keepers. One wants to put the other out of business. Localed in Chinatown, the Chinks commence to appear early but not in their usual mysterious ways. One dump operator, wanting to put his rival out of business, starts the works. It winds up in a murder.

A henchman of the Hawk (Mr. Sills) is convicted of the murder. The Hawk frees him just as he is about to be-led to the chair, but the Hawk took a desperate chance waiting until the fatal day before starting to do things.

Before starting at all the Hawk had to have his face beautified. He had been marred in the war and kept away from the day or night light. That gave Sills a chance to make up in character at the opening, but when his distorted nose and cheeks were straightened out, his dual role commenced.

Miss Kenyon as one of the dive's entertainers but a gude gurl had to plod along, with Montagu Love as the political boss dive operator doing the most work. Mitchell Lewis, the convicted one, kept looking out between the cell bars. It must be terrible on those jailbirds of the screen. Why can't they take but one picture of the bars and keep flashing it?

Stuart Holmes was the one bumped off. He looked very knowing when living, nodding while dancing around to the ward boss he was wise, and then asking him what it was about. Maybe that's why the boss himself did the bumping instead of Love.

Lots of monkey business when in a large chamber with a Chinese board of trade in session. When they told Love he would have to confess or be thrown to the Chinks, he confessed. Tough guys, those Chinks.

VAMPING VENUS

First National production and release. Directed by Edward Cline. Original story by Howard Green. Eph Asher supervision. Starring Charley Murray; Thelma Todd featured. At Proctor's Fifth Avenue, week June 25. Running time, 60 mins.
Cassidy....................Charley Murray
Venus..........................Thelma Todd
Mercury.....................Spec O'Donnel

Some genius on the First National lot thought of doing this one so as to utilize the massive sets and props used in "Helen of Troy." It was intended to be another wow travesty on the Greek mythology, which vaudeville used and discarded when James and Sadie Leonard quit doing such skits as "When Caesar Sees Her" 20 years ago.

It has turned out to be one of the dreariest and unfunniest film comedies ever to find its way out of the colony.

Charley Murray almost fractures his chin trying to mug some comedy into it and Thelma Todd's beauty and scant wardrobe revealing a streamline chassis, help a lot but not enough.

The story concerns one Mike Cassidy who has a shrewish frau. He gets out of the house by tricking her in a blind man buff game and wanders to the Silver Spoon Cafe to meet fellow politicians. Michael is later revealed as a political power but living in a dump.

At the cabaret he becomes enamoured of the girl playing Venus (Miss Todd). She has been told to make a play for him. Wandering back into her dressing room he is discovered by her lover, a strong man who plays Hercules in the cabaret show. The strong guy crowns him with a bottle.

He dreams the rest of the story, a hodge podge in which all of the people are ancient Greeks. His wife reappears as Circe (Louise Fazenda). He has a wild affair with Venus but is hailed before Jupiter and on pain of death ordered to make him, laugh. He fails and is thrown to the lions.

In this sequence occurs the baldest steal of stage material yet seen coming out of Jesse Jamesville: the Clark and McCullough lion bit which they did originally in "Peek-a-Boo" burlesque show, and later in the Music Box. It's almost duplicated even to using Clark's line "You even smell like a lion" as a title.

After wading through acres of similar stuff Murray finally wakes back in the dressing room. His wife has heard him making a speech from the joint over her radio. She enters and straightens him out with a little socking around.

The titling rolled up a perfect score of eggs. Samples are: "A man never realizes how happy he is until he's married—then it's too late." Another: "Mike was the light of her life but went out too much."

No credits appeared for the titles at this house but this writer will take a chance on his reputation as a handicapper and bet that they were debated into the picture.

"Vamping Venus" wouldn't entertain in a nursery. *Con.*

STORMY WATERS

Tiffany-Stahl production and release. Directed by Edgar Lewis. Adapted from a Jack London story. Cast includes Eve Southern, Malcolm MacGregor, Roy Stewart and Shirley Palmer. At Broadway, New York, week June 25. Running time, over an hour.

The big water again, this time swirling around two brothers, the elder of whom eventually takes the slap from the kid because of a woman. Can't have a sea without a storm, so that's in, too, although no one gets lost nor do nerves snap. Like looking at a map. You know what's coming, but aren't quite sure where it is. They're apt to enjoy retracing old trails in the splits, two and one day stands, but "Stormy Waters" hasn't the punch to make it a contender above that class.

Its principal item is Eve Southern doing a hit-and-run dame. Plenty hard-boiled in this picture, giving Davey a run-around while making a play for everyone from a prizefighter to her brother-in-law and the ship's crew.

Meantime there's a young girl waiting for Dave back in the home port. Supposition is that he'll retrieve her as the film winds up as Lola is put overboard in a lifeboat, rows to shore and returns to the South American dive in which David found her.

Miss Southern gets enough sensuousness into the role to make it stand up in a loose-hipped characterization under the world's longest eyelashes, which demonstrates how the femmes turn on the s. a. for better or worse. And this being a drama, she's out for no good.

Dave recoups fast enough from a siege of fever through an elastic continuity, to immediately go to the mat with his brother and later the burly second mate, who has been promised things by Lola. It's after the boy has crowned the husk with something other than a fist that he decides maybe he's wrong about Lola, his brother is right, it's hot, it was a tough fight, they're only a mile from shore—so. Just a bad gal.

Lewis has neither attempted or attained the unusual in direction, with titles and camera work simply in the accustomed manner. Roy Stewart, as the captain and older brother, gives valuable support, and MacGregor's performance is factory-made. There are only three major roles.

Figures to kill an hour passably, but can't claim it will be remembered, unless for the round-eyed Miss Southern gone deck-walker. *Sid.*

Good Morning, Judge

Universal production and release. Directed by William A. Seiter from story by Harry O. Hoyt. No credits for photography or titling. Starring Reginald Denny. In cast: Mary Nolan, Otis Harlan, Dorothy Gulliver, Bull Montana. At Hippodrome, week of June 25. Running time, 60 mins.

William Seiter uncorks the bottle of old story tricks, tried through his long association with Reginald Denny, in a way that makes "Good Morning, Judge" screen as one of best of that star's latest efforts. Mary Nolan, the former Imogene Wilson, should get applause for her work. It is not only sincere and convincing but registers her as possessing all of the camera and lighting appreciation of an old timer.

Although only cast in a bit part, Otis Harlan stands out. The comedy support he renders is one of the chief box office assets of this production.

A snappy start at a prize fight with Harlan as the gate crasher slows down for about a reel. When the old stuff of the rich son masquerading as a crook so as to be reformed by the pretty missionary mistress is reached the action peps up for the remainder of the footage. The lad's sister entertaining the crooks ,and the card tricks in lifting pulled on the dance floor, work the audience into a good suspense.

LAW OF THE RANGE

Metro-Goldwyn-Mayer production and release. Starring Tim McCoy, Joan Crawford featured. Directed by William Nigh.

Story by Norman Houston. Screen play by Richard Shayer. In cast Tenen Holtz, Bodil Rossing. At Loew's Circle, New York, one day, June 23. Running time, 60 minutes.

Fast moving Texas range flicker with a "You can't win" plot. Packs enough thrills to satisfy the most rabid followers of westerns. Among the high spots are a couple of holdups, runaway stage coach, gambling house stickup and forest fire, in addition to a brother against brother theme through the picture.

A sentimental bit is added by the woman playing the mother role, who figures her son never had a chance due to his associations, following his kidnapping by a band of renegades while still a youngster.

Can stand alone in the daily changers.

WHAT NEXT?

(BRITISH-MADE)
London, June 15.

Archibold production. Directed by Walter Forde. Photography by Geoffrey Faithfull. U. K. distribution: Butcher's Film Co. Colonial and foreign: F. Alfred. Censors' certificate: "U." Running time, 75 minutes. Pre-viewed at Palace, London, June 14.
Walter.......................Walter Forde
Violet.....................Pauline Johnson
Nick Winterbottom........Charles Dormer
Father...................Frank Stanmore
Cornelius Vandergilt........Douglas Payne

A lot that is good in this full length comedy. And a lot bad. Good parts are a coherent yet funny story, and a good cast, especially the girl, Pauline Johnson, who looks good, screens well and is no bad trouper.

Mistake to let Walter Forde act and direct. The latter appears to be his forte, that and being his own gag-man. As a comedian, almost any other comedian would have been better.

With a first rate pantomimist and knockabout this might have been a really good film. As it is, it just gets over.

The photography is weak in parts, and in some verges on poor. For this there is no excuse except inefficient studio lighting.

Story concerns a salesman at an exhibition who falls in love with the daughter of an antique dealer. Ancient and valuable candlestick is sought after by a millionaire, whose mad brother is also searching for it. Bought from the antique dealer by the hero, the candlestick is the center of the rest of the story.

Some unusually funny sequences in a museum, finishing with the lunatic, who thinks he is Napoleon, trying to guillotine the hero.

For neighborhood houses here, moderately good three-day offer.

For America, far too slow and poorly set. *Frat.*

WHEEL OF CHANCE

First National production and release. Directed by Alfred Santell. Richard Barthelmess starred. Story by Fannie Hurst. No other credits on lead slides or program. Press sheet supplies data. Scenario by Gerald C. Duffy. At Strand, New York, week June 30. Running time, 73 minutes.
Nickolai...................Richard Barthelmess
Schmulka...............Richard Barthelmess
Sara Turkeltaub............Bodil Rosing
Mosher Turkeltaub.........Warner Oland
Hanscha Talinef............Ann Schaeffer
Ada Berkowitz..............Lina Basquette
Josie Drew..........Margaret Livingston
Pa Berkowitz.............Sidney Franklin
Ma Berkowitz.............Martha Franklin

Two angles give this picture good value. First is the excellent handling of a dual role by Richard Barthelmess, and second is a certain O. Henry quality in the story of twin brothers, separated by chance in Russia during childhood and coming together years later in New York, each the product of the mystic chances of life. One is the district attorney and the other the waif of mischance he has to prosecute on a murder charge.

Theme is fairly well worked out, through the use of symbolic views recurring at intervals when it is desired to indicate the circumstances that worked upon first one and then the other of the brothers. Story has as its background a sympathetic treatment of Jewish family life, value of which is perhaps questionable in a screen play of this sort. The "Abie's Irish Rose" vogue gives the Jewish motif a comedy complexion and how the generality of fans will regard it as the atmosphere of a serious drama is a question.

The symbolic shots show a spinning roulette wheel through which bits of action are dimly visualized, the idea being to picture the accidents of life that took two men so far astray from the same beginning. This makes an engaging bit of trick dramatic effect.

Picture has many bits of fine suggestion and Barthelmess plays the dual role of the brothers well, achieving striking effects in contrasts while making both portraits convincing with acting at once authentic and legitimate. Bodil Rosing in this picture takes a high place among the film actresses playing mother roles. Hers is a performance of splendid unaffected naturalness with a world of human appeal. Story has something of a sex kick in certain spicy passages involving Margaret Livingston as the scarlet woman, and there are underworld bits that hold interest.

Dramatic passages are skillfully managed in a vein of quiet emphasis and the cast never over-emphasizes. Technical production is first rate. In summary film makes a satisfactory play for the exploitation of this popular screen star, which spells box office value. *Rush.*

THE BIG KILLING

Paramount production and release. Co-starring Wallace Beery and Raymond Hatton. Directed by F. Richard Jones. Story by Grover Jones, adapted by author and Gilbert Pratt. Cameraman, Alfred Gilks. Supervised by Benny Zeidman. Herman Mankiewicz, titler. At Paramount, New York, week June 30. Running time, 60 mins.
Powder-Horn Pete..........Wallace Beery
Dead-Eye Dan..........Raymond Hatton
Old Man Beagle.........Anders Randolph
Beagle's Daughter..............Mary Brian
Jim Hicks...................Gardner James
George Hicks...............Lane Chandler
Old Man Hicks.............Paul McAllister
Beagle Son No. 1..........James Mason
Beagle Son No. 2..........Ralph Yearsley
Beagle Son No. 3..........Ethan Laidlaw
Beagle Son No. 4..............Leo Willis
Beagle Son No. 5..........Buck Moulton
Beagle Son No. 6........Robert Kortman
Sheriff.................Walter James
Barker.................Roscoe Ward

Better than some of the Beery-Hattons and not as good as others "The Big Killing" looks like moderate pay-box stuff. Coincidental with that prediction the opinion may be vouchsafed that it is well the comedy team is being separated by

Paramount. An association that seemed riotous at its inception now tends to pall.

The spectator with a memory watching the rather silly didoes of the recent Beery-Hattons, including this one, will go back to before "Behind the Front" to the days when Hatton and Beery were two of the screen's outstanding character actors, not slapstick comics interpreting a couple of zero-minded morons.

"The Big Killing" has more story and less gags than previous Beery-Hattons and is that much of an improvement. Also directed with more legitimate attention to reasonableness.

Story is reminiscent of an old Buster Keaton feature. Beery and Hatton as a pair of dubs unwittingly get caught in the midst of a mountain feud. They are everybody's enemy and escape being murdered by dumb luck.

Gardner James, who some seasons ago was the recipient of one of those Hollywood ballyhoos, has his first major assignment in some time. James wears his hair too long for romantic leads and seems facially limited to a pain and agony registry, so his specialty has been, and is, weaklings.

The cycle of weakling heroes has passed. Gareth Hughes is in vaudeville, Jack Pickford retired, Barthelmess is doing prize fighters, George Hackathorne is in eclipse. And with the snappy boys on the ascendency it's a pipe the love interest in "The Big Killing" will be a wash out for all sides. The dames won't care, for it's extremely minor in the picture, and the boys won't admire a hero who does nothing except take it on the jaw and over the head throughout the picture. *Land.*

THE MICHIGAN KID

Universal (Jewel) production and release. Based on Rex Beach's novel. Directed by Irvin Willat with J. G. Alexander adapting. At Roxy, New York, week June 30. Running time, 58 mins.

The Michigan Kid	Conrad Nagel
Rose Morris	Renee Adoree
Frank Hayward	Lloyd Whitlock

Fair material for the big houses during the hot months with the Nagel and Adoree names to help. Putting it all together it's just a picture following a familiar Alaskan trail and winding up in a forest fire. Lightweight for the de luxe theatres but will take on poundage as the admission tap drops.

Story has a dance hall background with the Michigan Kid the best known gambler in the north. Couldn't have cost U much to turn it out although the miniature forest fire and rapids, down which the principals escape by double exposure, may have given the cost sheet a little personality. Yarn is conventional but Nagel gives a good performance and is the main cast balancing to please.

Midway flashback takes the main trio to school to show Rose an argumentative point between Jimmy Rowan and Frank Hayward. Years later both boys are in Alaska with Jimmy running the big joint and Frank gambling to recoup a lost bankroll. A jam sends Frank's watch into Jim for a cash advance and Rose's photo, inside, is the first intimation to him on the former's identity. As Rose is due to arrive shortly to wed Frank, Jimmy takes it upon himself to meet her, Frank having to get back to camp to square a stalling wire sent the girl.

Closeted away in a halfway cabin during a windstorm, Rose finally learns Jimmy is her childhood sweetheart and Frank shows up to try and gum the works. A forest fire brings on the climax of the heavy knocking Jimmy unconscious as he sleeps, trussing him up and leaving him hidden. He then awakens Rose for the runout. The girl, however, finds Jim and the boys battle all over the place as the flames leap toward the cabin. A canoe finally gets them on their way with the ride down the rapids picturesque enough despite the faking. Wild paddling ends as the craft goes over a falls.

Cameraman's double work is smoothly done and this meller has its points, mainly Nagel. Whitlock makes his villainy impress, while Miss Adoree is passive with most of her value for the picture in whatever magnetic quality her name may possess. Willat has smartly kept the film under an hour so that it moves along at a good pace.

Better adapted and strong for the intermediates but good enough for the big capacities in a pinch. *Sid.*

Sally of the Scandals

FBO production and release. Featuring Bessie Love. Story by Enid Hibbard. Directed by Lynn Shores. At Hippodrome, New York, week July 2. Running time, about 54 mins.

The ambitious but virtuous chorus girl is once more glorified in a picture that, like the numerous prints taken from the same stencil, will probably interest, and possibly fascinate, the hinterland.

Remoteness to reality in these back stage yarns makes it difficult for anyone connected with the trade to get a reliable slant on the average non-critical lay reaction.

Bessie Love doing the black bottom in a manner that would get her canned from any Broadway chorus is represented in the picture as a show-wower. Out in Ashtabula, O., they may agree with the scenario writer. But almost anywhere they will probably give Miss Love several points on duckiness, u. s. a. and sweetness. It's her B. B. that's weak.

The story is sweet simplicity itself. A. is a cute little chorus girl who supports B. her crippled little sister, and is courted by C. a rogue, jealous of D. the big producer who in spite of his millions and the women who thrust themselves at him is kindly, domestic and Santa Clausish. Then there is E, the nasty prima donna who tries to frame a little chorus gal.

The title will possibly mean a lot where the expresses don't stop. Production fair. *Land.*

The Wonderful Day
(FRENCH MADE)

Paris, June 25.

This release of the Cineromans has been adapted by Rene Barberis from the farce of Yves Mirande and Gustave Quinson, played a couple of years ago under the title of "La Merveilleuse Journee."

It is a good comic production, excellently acted and while entirely taken from a stage play is not in the least "theatrical." The picture is amusing screen comedy, for an easy going, not over critical public.

Pelloux, archi-milliardair, is fed up with life. It no longer offers him novelty, having everything money can buy. He has been consulting a quack doctor and a druggist at Cassidagne, where he has put in on board his yacht, but acting on the advice of his pretty young nurse, Gladys, he suddenly orders the charlatans ashore and steams for Cannes.

However, the druggist's apprentice, Blaise, was forgotten and when the yacht is on the high sea the youth appears on deck. He had been asleep and now wants to be landed. Pelloux finds the youth so diverting that he engages him as a sort of secretary.

The wonderful days commence when the party arrives in Cannes. Blaise is served like a prince in the hotel, going through all the degree of toilet to make him the elegant companion of the millionaire. He falls in love with a lady in the hotel, but she fights shy of his advances. In the evening, at the casino, the provincial druggist's apprentice is found gambling, winning big stakes by following the lead of Pelloux, rather amused at the situation.

Noticing the lady from the hotel, Blaise gives an order to a jeweler present in the casino for a pearl necklace to be sent to her. A "decaves" offer to sell his villa to pay his gambling debt; Blaize buys it and offers it to the lady.

So occupied with love making the youth forgets his position in the game and when his employer suddenly goes "Banco" he finds himself ruined. He goes home to weep, where his pretty neighbor visits him to return the pearl necklace and the villa.

There is a mutual explanation: they are both of modest circumstances, having a good time for just one day.

Blaise indignantly declines to take back the presents he made. The nurse, Gladys, had also visited the casino, having discarded her service robe for an evening dress.

As might be suspected, Pelloux is so struck by her beauty he is now crazy about her. But the girl wants to leave, having other things in view. Or is it the feminine manner of angling a rich husband?

The vision of being alone, miserable and laid up with his millions without the soothing Gladys to nurse him prompts Pelloux to beg her to marry him. The tantalizing girl accepts, but on condition he returns the money he won from his own secretary.

This enables Blaize to wed the lady of his dreams, who turns out to be a piano teacher.

Dolly Davis is seen to advantage as the delicious nurse; Andre Roanne does Blaise in amusing, "timid" style, and is the star of the picture, which is snappy and diverting. *Kendrew.*

Wild West Romance

Fox production and release. Rex Bell, star. Directed by R. Lee Hough from story by John Stone. Sol Halprin, cameraman. Titles by Delos Sutherland. In cast: Caryl Lincoln, Billy Walters. At Loew's New York, one day, June 26, one-half double bill. Running time, 55 minutes.

Competition between a good cowboy, who wears all the fittings, and a bad lad in an office suit for the smile of the cleric's daughter is the incentive for "Wild West Romance." Rex Bell, Buck Jones' successor on the Fox lot, follows in his master's footsteps. A much younger man with a much broader smile, Bell should be popular with the kids.

Picture ambles along at the start with slow moving stuff of the would-be cowboy ne'er-do-well playing with the youngsters. Minister's daughter also introduces the heavy and his gang.

After that, usual hard riding, stage coach robbing and planting on the innocent man.

Bell, as the good broncho bum, beats up his competitor's gang and lathers his horse in chasing his enemy over the desert.

A scrap on top of the train is good stuff, the kind that will get patrons of westerns at the end of their seats.

A kid pal of Bell's, roping one of the gangsters and generally playing the young hero, will also find school support.

GOLF WIDOWS

Columbia production and release. Directed by Erle C. Kenton from story by W. Scott Darling. Arthur Todd, cameraman. In cast: Vera Reynolds, Harrison Ford, John Patrick, Sally Rand, Kathleen Key, Vernon Dent, Will Stanton. At Loew's New York, one day, June 29, half double feature bill. Running time, about 60 minutes.

Why the extra four reels is the cause for wonderment. "Golf Widows" would still be poor as a two-reeler.

Cluttered with weary gags, the story as brought to the screen would make a sophisticate out of a moron.

Husbands who play golf cause wives to stroll to a Hollywood joint, drink tea, pick up a couple of lads and wind up most harmlessly in Tia Juana.

The cast names are the only help since the captions are as futile in their attempt as the story.

LOVE IS A LIE
(GERMAN MADE)

Aneiko production. Distributor not named. Directed by Eric Waschneck. Author not credited. Featuring Harry Leidtke and Lee Parry. Several other players deserving screen credit not billed. At the Fifth Avenue Playhouse, New York, week June 25. Running time, about 70 mins.

Everything that hitherto has been hurled at foreign production methods and foreign pictures in the way of condemnation seems like complimentary comment in view of this latest importation.

Titles are barely intelligible but at no time intelligent. Direction, scenic construction, camera work and general effect reminiscent of the early pictures turned out 10 or 15 years ago.

One shot stamps this creation of modern vintage. It's a flash of the gigantic presses grinding out a newspaper. Four out of every five foreign pictures nowadays feature from six to a dozen shots of machinery of some kind. It's considered symbolic, a symbol of the crude, old-fashioned ideas still in vogue in Continental pictures.

The story tells of a famous engineer who marries a servant girl. The wife goes wild and the husband leaves her, but he returns in time to save the girl from committing suicide.

Simple? Very.

Interwoven with this pathetic theme is the story of the girl's brother who murders his father for some money the girl had sent him.

Were you ever in Europe? *Mori.*

HUSBANDS FOR RENT

Warner Bros. production and release. Directed by Henry Lehrman. Story by Edwin Justin Mayer. Screen play by Graham Baker. Featuring Owen Moore and Helene Costello. In cast: John Miljan, Kathryn Perry, Claude Gillingwater, Arthur Hoyt. At Tivoli, New York, on double bill, June 28-29. Running time 60 minutes.

Mediocre serio-comic flicker that holds a few laughs mainly through the efforts of Gillingwater as a ritzy Englishman and Hoyt as a snooping society scandal sheet reporter. Lots of monocled men, couple of Rolls Royces and a comedy maid are rung in for atmosphere in a story about English domestic difficulties. Title is purely b.o.

Plot has Owen Moore playing a stupid dude part, engaged to Kathryn Perry. Helene Costello makes him break it. Another marriage. After a short term the quartet are cheating but again the comedy English father patches things up and the scandal seeking scribe is out-witted.

Not much but the comedy bits will hold it in the grinds if the supporting bill is adequate.

LIGHTS OF NEW YORK

(TALKER)

Warner Brothers production on the Vitaphone and release. No cast member starred or featured on program or press sheet. Story and scenario by Hugh Herbert and Murray Roth. Directed by Bryan Foy. Photographed by E. B. Dupar. Opening midnight, July 6, at special performance, $1.50 top, at Strand, New York, continuing thereafter at regular house scale for week July 7. Running time, 57 minutes.

Kitty Lewis	Helène Costello
Eddie Morgan	Cullen Landis
Molly Thompson	Gladys Brockwell
Mrs. Morgan	Mary Carr
Hawk Miller	Wheeler Oakman
Gene	Eugene Pallette
Detective Crosby	Robert Elliott
Sam	Tom Dugan
Collins	Tom McGuire
Tommy	Guy D'Ennery
Mr. Jackson	Walter Percival
Mr. Dickson	Jere Delaney

"Lights of New York," noisy or still, to the sophisticates is applesauce in every way, but as a talker can be pronounced a money-getter for the exhib, even downtown in key cities. This is not solely througn the talking novelty that will hang about for some time to come, but because this picture is getting pretty billing in Warners describing it as "The first 100 per cent. all-talking picture."

The Warners have made it all talking, with every character speaking, more or less. Some exhibs who see this and upon having their houses wired may choose "Lights of New York" for the first talker, but that might be avoided. The all-talking here could militate somewhat against the Warners earlier talkers with broken-up dialog. It might be preferred to lead up to this one as the Warners have done.

It's not an expensively made picture in appearance, either in sets or cast, and its running time, 57 minutes, along with the rest of the hokumed junk likely decided the Warners it would never do for a $2 try at Warner's on Broadway. So the Strand got a first-run out of a Vitaphone full length, the first theatre outside of a Warner's to secure that to date.

As a picture this is an open-face story with roll-your-own dialog. It's underworld, starting in a small town and moving to a nite club on the Giddy Wild Way. There are bootleggers and gunmen, cops and muggs, the latter a couple of simps falling for con men back home in a hotel about twice the size of the town—from the looks of the set.

In the nite club are the chorus, the boss legger, who also runs the joint, and the gal number leader.

Then comes the murder of the boss legger as he is about to kill one of the goofs he had failed to frame. As the legger starts to shoot the simp, a hand comes through the folded curtains and he's shot. It's a self-exposer—the boss' mistress he walked out after about 20 years. She got fussed up when he termed her an old hen. This same "mystery murder" gag is a two-reeler expedient.

It's that kind of a sappy mixture, the kind that recalls the mellers of the ten-twent-thirt of ages ago. As *Sid* said about a talking dramatic sketch a few weeks ago at the Strand: "It's a novelty now, but in six months will be a chaser." In a year from now everyone concerned in "Lights of New York" will run for the river before looking at it again.

Yet the Broadway twist, the double-crossing, the crooks, the "take him for a ride," the dame and the dames, the mush stuff and the terrible voices will still interest nowadays when the terrific quantity of universal publicity being given the talkers before they are actually known keeps curiosity pepped up for something different on the screen.

In work in this talker, casting aside its plotting by its plotters, Hugh Herbert and Murray Roth, and the cast of nearly all vaudeville actors who talk the best they may, in lieu of legits or picture actors who can't talk, it has a standout firstly in Gladys Brockwell as the mistress. Miss Brockwell, evidencing stage training somewhere, ran ahead and far, with Robert Elliott as the detective second. Elliott played the detective exactly as he had done the same role in the Pacific Coast stage company of "Broadway."

Bryan Foy directed. It's his first full length talker and there's some credit in that for him, considering there's no class to story or picture.

Helenè Costello, in the fem lead, a total loss. For talkers she had better go to school right away. Cullen Landis opposite, if a juv even in the indies, will never make anyone believe it in this one. He seemed to talk with much effort. Nervousness might be claimed by all excepting the stage trained. Wheeler Oakman as the legger got through fairly, burdened with much of the bad dialog. Mary Carr in a bit as the mother gave an illustration of what may be accomplished by timed talk from experience.

Bits were well done in a way by Jere Delaney and Walter Percival as the con men, while Tommy Dugan slipped in some semblance of comedy to his delivery and expressions as one of the gangsters. Tom McGuire nicely played and looked a police chief, with hardly anything to say.

Photographed very well and the nite club set tastefully good-looking.

"Lights of New York" may be **called a pioneer in the real sense as an all-talker. Though this 100 per cent. talking picture is 100 per cent. crude, so much so it's conventionalism is tiresome. There are 1,000 holes in it alongside of what it should have, from standards adopted or about to be adopted, by the Warners themselves in other talkers, among others—but still this talker will have pulling power, and the Warners should get credit for nerve even if they didn't do it with a polish.**

Yet "Lights of New York," besides being a pioneer, which excuses so much, stands out as the beacon that there can be no chances taken in casting a talker.

THE RACKET

Caddo production, presented by Howard Hughes. Paramount release. From stage play of same name by Bartlett Cormack. Adaptation by Barlett Cormack. Continuity by De Andrews. Titles by Tom Miranda. Stars Thomas Meighan, with Louis Wolheim and Marie Prevost featured. Lewis Milestone directed. Running time, 70 mins. At Paramount, New York, week July 7.

Captain McQuigg	Thomas Meighan
Helen Hayes, an entertainer	Marie Prevost
Nick Scarsi, bootleg king	Louis Wolheim
Joe Scarsi, Nick's brother	George Stone
Ames, a cub reporter	John Darrow
Miller, a reporter	"Skeets" Gallagher
Pratt, a reporter	Lee Moran
Chick, a gangster	Lucian Prival
Chick's chauffeur	Tony Marlo
Corcan, a bootlegger	Henry Sedley
District torney	Sam De Grasse
"The Old Man"	Burr McIntosh
Johnson, a patrolman	C. Pat Collins

A good story, plus good direction, plus a great cast and minus dumb supervision, is responsible for another great under-world film.

Thomas Meighan has his best role in years as Captain McQuigg, and Louis Wolheim as Nick Scarsi, adds to a screen rep that has already labeled him the best character heavy, the one-eyed monster has ever peeked at.

In transferring "The Racket" from stage to screen, Milestone has sacrificed nothing. By intelligently capitalizing the wider scope of the camera he has added an inch or two to its original stature as an entertainment. Cormack did his own adaptation, keeping the script out of the hands of the enemy, and was given as much license as pictorial requirements would allow. The result is as nearly perfect a slice of screen entertainment as has run the gauntlet in months. It has all the ear-marks of a special, and may move from the Paramount to a more permanent abode at a higher box office tap.

Howard Hughes, the young oil magnate producer, who took over Meighan's contract from Paramount, after he had nearly been obliterated with junk stories, has a few chuckles coming. He has brought Meighan back with a vengeance and by releasing but two or three operas a year, has a male box office magnet, second to none. Wolheim will also pay heavy dividends while in the Hughes stable.

"The Racket," like all great pictures, started with a great yarn and a director alive to its possibilities. It grips your interest from the first shot to the last, and never drags for a second. It's another tale of the underworld, a battle of wills and cunning between an honest copper and a gorilla who has the town in his lap.

Nick Scarsi (Wolheim) is the bootleg king and gang leader who has been getting away with everything on the calendar, until Captain McQuigg (Meighan) decides that he is going to get Nick.

Nick tries to make McQuigg, in the usual ways, but the copper won't turn. Scarsi's political connections are of the strongest through his control of votes and repeaters. He has the captain transferred to a precinct where the goats are the only traffic problems. Two district men on a daily, looking for news, complicate matters here by ribbing McQuade about Scarsi. The Cap tells them he was switched, not because he was afraid of Scarsi, but because Scarsi was afraid of him. He tells them to tell that to Nick. They proceed to do just that, finding Nick attending the funeral of a rival he has croaked. A touch of humor here is Scarsi's objections to a street caliope profaning the obsequies.

Scarsi's brother is picked up by one of McQuigg's men (C. Pat Collins), as a hit and run driver. The kid brother has a yen for Helen Hayes (Marie Prevost) an entertainer. She's poison to Nick, as are all broads. Nick has incurred her enmity at a birthday party he gave the kid brother. At the party Helen, doing a Helen Morgan on top of a piano, is cooing to the kid brother at Scarsi's table, when the gorilla kicks the piano across the room. The gal flies back at him and bawls him plenty. Then she determines to make a play for the kid, just to burn Nick up. They are out in the kid's roadster, prior to the pinch. She leaves him flat when he develops hand trouble, and a police auto passing, stops as she steps out of the car. The kid screws, with the copper chasing. During the flight a spectator is hit but Joe continues stepping on it until he runs the car into a fence, and is nailed.

Joe is booked under a phoney name. He refuses to talk until he is slugged. Helen tips his real **moniker to a sap cub reporter, and is held as a material witness.**

How Nick avenges his kid brother and how McQuigg finally wins out when the district attorney double-crosses Nick and has him shot as he attempts to escape, complete the thrilling yarn.

The cast was one hundred per cent. Skeets Gallagher, with a bottle in one pocket and "American-merk" in the other, made a reporter's role roll over and beg. Lee Moran as another legger also clicked. George Stone as Nick's kid brother made one believe in heredity; G. Pat Collins as Johnson the copper whom Nick kills, probably kissed himself into pictures permanently with his portrayal; Henry Sedley as Spike Corcoran was plenty tough, and Lucian Prival as "Chick" doomed himself to this type of role for ever and ever amen. Sam de Grasse also landed in brackets as the d. a., and Burr McIntosh got the back of his head into the opus, in one flash, as the "Old Man" who **"sprung" the boys when they got jammed up.**

Tom Miranda was given wide latitude with slang and gun chatter and the result is the most authentic set of titles that have graced an underworld picture to date. The gorillas talk as they should and not as some lame-brained obstructionist thinks they should. They don't go to jail—they go to the can—and without those diagrams the average super wants with any title in vernacular.

And shades of Beverly Hills, there's no love interest! Imagine a hero who doesn't cop a moll in the last ten feet.

Boy, page the millenium! ***Con.***

THE ACTRESS

Metro-Goldwyn-Mayer production and release. Directed by Sidney Franklin. Based on "Trelawney of the Wells." Continuity and adaptation by Albert Lewis and Richard Schayer. Titles by Joe Farnham. Starring Norma Shearer. Ralph Forbes featured. Owen Moore featured on program only. At Capitol, New York, week July 7. Running time, 67 mins.

Rose Trelawney	Norma Shearer
Arthur Gower	Ralph Forbes
Tom Wrench	Owen Moore
Sir William Gower	O. P. Heggie
Avonia	Gwen Lee
Colpoys	Lee Moran
Gadd	Roy D'Arcy
Mrs. Telfer	Virginia Pearson
Mr. Telfer	William Humphreys
Mrs. Mossop	Effie Ellssler
Clara Defoenix	Andree Tourneur
Captain Defoenix	Cyril Chadwick
Trafalgar Gower	Margaret Seddon

Though Pinero's brilliant stage production contains a large supply of dramatic and humorous situations transferable to the screen for all of their value, the directorial head of this screen effort has not realized on the possibilities to the fullest extent. As a result, with Norma Shearer unattractive in the early parts of the picture owing to the strange makeup and camera treatment which sharpens and ages her features, the picture cannot be rated a strong draw generally, despite the prominence of the star though it should do moderate business in most cases.

In New York, at the Capitol, the picture stands a good chance. Also in other good show towns where the picture theatre public will be able to appreciate the comedy. It is to be feared, however, that in a majority of instances the comedy will not register because it is too well done, too finely drawn, for the average movie fan. Nor will the dramatic situations register except in the first class houses only. That is because the story has not been overdrawn and the problems are settled naturally but too easily.

In this house Miss Shearer's efforts as a comedienne met with light but noticeable returns. It is doubtful if all other audiences will respond even to that extent. Cyril Chadwick, as Captain Defoenix, is a success in what is practically the outstanding piece of comedy business in the film. With a set of long, bushy side whiskers the captain's horsey, stupid mug, coupled with an inexplicable indecision as to whether he should sit or stand, gets attention from the start and builds up for a strong punch laugh in the final scene.

Ralph Forbes, opposite Miss Shearer, photographs well and delivers a fine performance. Owen Moore has a minor role with only two or three short scenes of any consequence.

Story is of the actress whom love leads into the arms of a man who had never attended the theatre and whose family disapproved of it. The grandfather, Sir Gower, learning of the match, asks the girl to spend the intervening time until the marriage at the family home. Clashes follow and the girl is obliged to leave when, finally, her friends are ordered out because of their drunken condition. Works round to a happy ending, the old man forgiving her and backing a new play to save her from starvation.

"Trelawney of the Wells" should be played up in exploitation copy in equal proportion to the title of the picture for possible attention from those who have seen it on the stage. *Mori.*

HIT OF THE SHOW

FBO production and release. Directed by Ralph Ince. Joe E. Brown featured. Adapted from a short story, "Notices" by Viola Brothers Shore. Adapter not mentioned. Titles by Jack Conway. At Roxy, New York, week July 7. Running time around 60 minutes.

"Twisty"	Joe E. Brown
Kathlyn Carson	Gertrude Olmstead
Tremaine	William Norton Bailey
Trece	Gertrude Astor
Goldenstein	Ole M. Ness
Greening	Lee Shumway
Teague	William Francis Dugan
Charlotte Van	Ione Holmes
Woody	LeRoy Mason
Barnes	Frank Mills
The Slavey	Daphne Pollard
Mr. Carson	Cosmo Kyrle Bellew

"Hit of the Show" is okay for the hinterland. Title tells the locale, actors' boarding house and back stage. Hinterland will like the stage stuff and perhaps the show girls, even if missing action and not finding much of a story.

FBO for the summertime got the Roxy for this one. In July, though a cooled house, the Roxy may have been looking for a flat rental.

Well enough produced for its kind, that means mostly stage scenes, of a rehearsal and later the first night of a musical. If Ralph Ince doesn't know more about a musical than some of the liberties indulged in here might suggest, he should have consulted his wife. Otherwise the direction did what could be done for what was there.

Probably the biggest angle here is the debut of Joe E. Brown, the musical comedy comedian in this picture and featured. Brown has a semi-comic role. When permitted to slightly mugg, he got laughs and when not, not. Another stage comedienne, Daphne Pollard as a slavey, was in much the same fix. Between the two though and the only sources of comedy in what was intended as a light story and film, the laughs are pretty scarce.

Once in a while a neat bit shoved in, but no standout, and the tale trips along. It holds a bit of miscasting in Gertrude Olmstead as the young society girl. She looks altogether too sophisticated for the role. And besides, the important juvenile who should have been present and opposite her, was absent entirely, this due also to the story. Leaving a left handed sort of affair, a low comedian in looks and work against what should have been a frail, highly-bred girl.

The plot starts when the social person walked out on the day of her wedding. A switchback afterward revealed she did so because the night before when sneaking into his bachelor dinner dressed as a boy, she saw a short skirted girl seated on the knees of all of her fiance's male friends, including the fiance's.

The girl looking for a theatrical job runs into Brown in an agency. He's a hoofer out of work and owing the landlady for eight weeks. She has no place to go. He steers her to the rooming house where she pays the landlady $30 for two weeks in advance and is set for life. After that it's the hoofer looking for a job and Broadway, finally finding one in "Jake Hubert's" show.

He got the girl a job also, and between rehearsals taught her to do a comedy Apache dance in his room. She was to have been the dance partner of an Apache dancer who looked like a floorwalker. At the premiere, Brown knocked out the dancer on the impulse of the moment and his chin, taking his place with the girl to do their comedy Apache instead, and making the hit of the show.

After getting the hit, Brown's heart gave out and he died the same night in the managers' office. Probably they didn't know what else to do with him or how to end the picture.

During the picture's unreeling the orchestra played "Laugh, Clown, Laugh." It's a good song and melody but was never intended for the theme song of a comedy play. If the picture is cued for that number, it had better be altered.

Jack Conway's captions are aptly worded to blend with scenes drawing laughs according to situations.

No one other than those mentioned warrants special mention except Gertrude Astor as the landlady. She did quite nicely. Rest were fillers, with each owning dress clothes. A couple of mob scenes were employed. No special setting but the star dressing room seemed to run the length of the studio.

Mr. Brown might be better fitted the next time. He has a homely but attractive face. As his business is making fun, that might be the main line of his next story, including permission for him to mugg all over the lot if it's laughs that are wanted.

GRIP OF THE YUKON

Universal release and production. Directed by Ernst Laemmle from the story by Chas. A. Logue. Continuity by Chas. A. Logue. Title writer not credited. Featuring Francis X. Bushman and Neil Hamilton. Cast includes June Marlowe, Otis Harlin, Burr McIntosh and James Farley. At Keith's Hippodrome, New York, week July 9. Running time, over 70 mins.

Only a filler for the split week and daily change houses, better in the summer since it has plenty of shots of snow, ice and the usual weather indications of the north.

Story of the conventional type, hardly deviating from the typical northern production, even by a situation. The old miner is accidentally killed and his daughter, coming north, is cared for and protected by the two men who did it.

Bushman stands out in a particularly unconvincing role, while Neil Hamilton hasn't many opportunities to do anything but stand still and gape.

Heavily padded with unnecessary footage in many spots and an attempt at comedy, unsuited for the sequence, too long drawn out and without proper material, got laughs only from the screen players. Several of the important scenes are overdrawn for length and, coupled with numerous other slow shots, results in a tiring, unentertaining spectacle. *Mori.*

DIAMOND HANDCUFFS

Metro-Goldwyn-Mayer release produced by Cosmopolitan. Directed by John P. McCarthy. Adapted by Carey Wilson from "Pin Money" by Henry C. Vance. Continuity by Bradley King, adaptation by Willis Goldbeck. Titles by Joe Farnham. Conrad Nagel, Eleanor Boardman and Lawrence Gray featured. Cast includes John Roche, Gwen Lee, Sam Hardy, Lena Malena and Charles Stevens. At Loew's American, N. Y., last half starting July 5. Running time, about 60 mins.

One of the best program pictures of the year produced on an elaborate and even lavish scale, with a keen and intelligent attention to detail. It's a picture likely to appeal not only to the cash customers but to the critics. If someone had dared to book it into a Broadway theatre it stood a chance of getting a million dollars worth of favorable attention.

It is believed that the picture didn't get a first run showing in New York for one of two reasons which have no bearing on its box office potentialities. The bold sex treatment throughout, especially in the first part, might have raised censorship trouble if the film had been conspicuous on Broadway while in this house it is comparatively out of the way. The second reason, it seems, is that because the story doesn't treat of one of the usual themes it was evidently feared the public wouldn't take to it.

The graphic treatment of this powerful story, with various ingredients of a surefire though conventional audience appeal, easily overbalances any possible drawbacks.

About the only discordant note in the production is Eleanor Boardman whose abilities have been so consistently restricted it is no longer surprising to find her miscast again. She is relegated to a comparatively insignificant part. Cast, however, is quite strong, capable and convincing.

Story hinges on the strange vicissitudes of a magnificent diamond called "The Shah." Picture is presented in the form of a play, in three acts, each of the acts being noted on the screen billing with the cast in each act given separately.

First act takes place in the African diamond mines. The negro girl vamp (Lena Malena) tells her lover, who works in the mines, that unless he gets her a diamond he cannot have her. Girl is shown scantily clad and some of the love scenes are intensely hot. To satisfy the girl the boy throws a pick into his leg while at work the next day and hides a diamond in the wound. He is shot while making monikee to a sap cub reporter, and is held as a material witness.

How Nick avenges his kid brother and how McQuigg finally wins out when the district attorney double-crosses Nick and has him shot as he attempts to escape, complete the thrilling yarn.

The cast was one hundred per cent. Skeets Gallagher, with a bottle in one pocket and "American-merk" in the other, made a reporter's role roll over and beg. Lee Moran as another legger also clicked. George Stone as Nick's kid brother made one believe in heredity; G. Pat Collins as Johnson the copper whom Nick kills, probably kissed himself into pictures permanently with his portrayal; Henry Sedley as Spike Corcoran was plenty tough, and Lucian Prival as "Chick" doomed himself to this type of role for ever and ever amen. Sam de Grasse also landed in brackets as the d. a., and Burr McIntosh got the back of his head into the opus, in one flash, as the "Old Man" who "sprung" the boys when they got jammed up.

Tom Miranda was given wide latitude with slang and gun chatter and the result is the most authentic set of titles that have graced an underworld picture to date. The gorillas talk as they should and not as some lame-brained obstructionist thinks they should. They don't go to jail—they go to the can—and without those diagrams the average super wants with any title in vernacular.

And shades of Beverly Hills, there's no love interest! Imagine a hero who doesn't cop a moll in the last ten feet.

Boy, page the millenium! *Con.*

Q-SHIPS

(BRITISH MADE)

London, July 2.

Produced by New Era-National Pictures Co. Directed by Geoffrey Barkas and Michael Barringer. Photography, Sydney Blythe. Produced with the sanction and co-operation of the Admiralty. Previewed at the Marble Arch Pavilion, June 25. Running time, 92 mins.

No cast is given for this film save that Lieut.-Commander Harold Auten, V. C., commander of a Q-ship during the war, and technical adviser on the production, appears in a number of scenes. No known film artist on the screen except Johnny Butt and Roy Travers. Admiral Jellicoe also appears in a few sequences.

It is, of course, more war stuff, but from a hitherto unused angle: that of the exploits of the mystery ships sent out to beat the U-boats. Most of them were old tubs and barges, almost unfit for the sea. Disguised, and manned by a scratch crew of reckless seaport men and a couple of navy gunners, they sank more U-boats than all the rest of the devices put together, and were in the main the outcome of a conference between Admiral Jellicoe and Admiral Sims of the U. S. Navy. This conference is shown on the screen, with Jellicoe playing opposite an actor made up as Sims. Very well done and furnishes an American angle, together with an episode of the stopping of the S. S. Juliana (an American boat) by a German submarine and the earful given by the steamer's captain to the U-boat commander.

There is another American twist in the shots of the first landing of officers and men of the U. S. Navy in this country at Queenstown Harbor, and the welcome of Commander Joseph Taussig of the U. S. S. Wadsworth by Vice-Admiral Sir Lewis Bayley. These shots, of almost studio clarity, were loaned by the Imperial War Museum Trustees.

Apart from this, however, there is not so much to the film. Despite the excellence of the direction and the fact there is no tank stuff or other faking, the film is too monotonous as entertainment for the general picture house. Over footage is given to distant steamers and to submarines rising and submerging, and far too little is seen of the subject matter of the film, the Q-ships themselves.

Only two examples of these are seen. Round one of them, after disabling it with a torpedo, a German U-boat circles for ages until it gets into a position in which the Q-ship can drop its guncovers and get into action. There seemed no earthly reason why the U-boat should not have slipped in another torpedo and settled any doubt as to whether the steamer was a Q-ship or not, and many of the pre-view audience said so audibly.

Interiors of submarines, especially when sinking, are very well done, and as a whole the film is a good and an efficient piece of production. It's probably a novelty for specialized theatres. *Frat.*

Code of the Scarlet

Charles Rogers production, released through First National. Ken Maynard starred. Directed by Harry J. Brown from story credited to Bennett Cohen. Ted McCord cameraman. In cast: Ed Brady, Gladys McConnell, J. P. McGowan, Dot Farley. At Loew's New York one day, July 3, one half double bill. Running time 60 minutes..

Well sustained entertainment is provided by this custom built meller with mounted cops doing just what audiences of second runs expect them to do on the screen. A little slow in gaining story impetus but that starts to bunch out in the third reel. Plenty of one-sided fistic encounters before the conventional finis.

A little less of the open and shut

mystery, characteristic of these Northwest themes, makes this above the average and will increase Ken Maynard's following. Less love-making and more battling with the gang leader responsible for the brother getting a stretch gives Maynard lots of action in his course of proving to the sister that the hard boiled, and not her also potted the brother.

Mounties on horse and in canoe with an attractive wooded locale surrounded by mountains work in some nice camera opportunities.

SOULS AFLAME

First Division release, produced by James Ormont. Directed by Raymond Wells and written by Mr. Wells. Titled by Jack Kelly. Cast includes Raymond Wells, Gardner James, Gael Kelton and Grace Lord. At Stanley, New York, one day, July 12. Running time 60 minutes.

A natural life picture, well written, well produced and well played. The sure-seat operators must be suffering from the heat or are too busy clipping stock and bond coupons to have passed this one up. Playing at the Stanley, 25-cent top daily change grind on 7th avenue, for carfare to Hoboken and it's the easiest holdover the sure-seaters ever knew.

Having writhed in agony through more foreign productions, passing under a bologna art label, than one reviewer should be subjected to in a lifetime, a picture is finally discovered for which no "artistic" claims are made, which exceeds in beauty and entertainment value all except the most outstanding foreign pictures ever shown.

The smooth, even continuity which characterizes this film is surprising in an independently made picture. Considering, also, that the story is simple and straightforward, the climax to which it builds up unwaveringly, holding interest all the way through, points to a directorial ability which has somehow been overlooked in the shuffle by the major producing companies.

This picture is much like "Stark Love," a film accepted for release by Paramount over a year ago, in its construction and natural simplicity. It is as well made, as intelligently directed and as convincing as the former. "Souls Aflame," had it been handled by a larger distributor, would have been entitled to a Broadway showing on merit.

In addition to the sure-seaters where it should find a ready market, the picture has a chance in the regular houses, large or small, and in key cities throughout the country, providing it is given smart exploitation.

For better class audiences, who can appreciate acting and direction of this type, it is unbeatable.

The theme is limited but well handled. It concerns two Southern families and a feud engendered through the disgrace of the daughter of the Lillys by a son of the Bucks.

Action takes place after the Civil War. Following a few introductory remarks and shots of the weary but undaunted Southerners returning home to the tune of "Dixie," the story turns to the Lillys. The girl and her baby are called before a family court. The stern-looking father, as the judge, the rugged mountaineer brothers and several stiff females in outlandish clothes, all stand by and the feud is declared.

Throughout there is a convincing picturization of a half-civilized, semi-barbarous folk which in itself is bound to grip the attention of the average audience of the average first class theatre. The stolid, purposeful faces of the people shown here, their ways of living, their hatred and intolerance of the church, the leering condescension toward those with "book learning" hardly seem like the characterizations of a group of Hollywood actors but more akin to the intensely human emotions of a living, breathing race.

It is said in the foreword that part of the picture was filmed in the Ozarks and that some of the people living in that part of the country were used in the picture. In addition, Wells has made the

balance of the cast act as the others did.

The Bucks are introduced as the bad boys. There are five and they had just killed the father of the boy preacher, the husband of Caroline Lilly. After a trial, during which the Bucks are freed, the foreman of the jury tells the judge that he figured the Buck on trial was a "kin" of his and that the boys thought it would make the judge happier to have him released without much fuss.

The arrival of a young girl Buck, cousin, in the home of the five roughnecks and her treatment carry laughs and plenty of interest. First the boys sniff suspiciously and about five seconds after the spokesman introduces her there is a chorus of outbursts to the effect that no loafing females are wanted and "Tell her to prepare some vittles."

The boy preacher is later beaten up on the charge of "enticing" the girl to church. His mother, no longer able to stand the persecution, drives off to the hills to summon her kinsmen to wipe out the Bucks. The boy preacher pleads for tolerance, arguing that it is time the 60-year-old feud was dropped, but the clan decides to wipe out the Bucks and they descend, en masse, on the little log cabin, leading up to a stirring battle scene.

The boy preacher, the girl, the boy's mother and the leader of the Bucks register as performers of a high order in their characterizations here.   *Mori.*

TELLING THE WORLD

Metro-Goldwyn-Mayer production and release. Starring Wm. Haines. From original by D. V. Every. Sam Wood directing. Titles by Joe Farnham. Wm. Daniels cameraman. At Capitol, New York, week of July 14. Running time, 72 minutes.
Don Davis...............William Haines
Crystal ....Anita Page
Mazie ....Eileen Percy
Don's Father.............Frank Currier
Landlady ....Polly Moran
Lane ....Bert Roach
City Editor.............William V. Mong
The Killer.................Mathew Betz

Bill Haines, America's most assured young man who generally turns the other cheek in time to become a well chastened but better hero for his public, is again displaying his Swaffer attitude in this spool opera which bids fair to make 'em laugh anywhere. The comedy pace for its first 35 minutes is terrific. Laughs stumble over each other. While there isn't a distinct howl, yet they're all solid. Feature drew unqualified approval from an over capacity audience here on its opening afternoon.

Wood's direction, Farnham's titles and Haines' familiar conception of male ego, spiced by a couple of new mannerisms, can plead guilty to queries on why this is a good picture. Add to that the presence of Anita Page, whom the boys are going to give heavy attention, and "Telling the World" is a pretty fair piece of all around program work.

Yarn carries a newspaper theme lightly stressing the technical side and doesn't start to dwindle until it begins to concern itself with the plot. The last half of the footage has Haines pursuing the girl to China where she gets mixed up in a revolution. The navy has to turn loose a couple of aviators and the marines to save the situation. Despite that, it's still a good picture.

Production isn't particularly heavy. Daniels' best camera work crops up in a series of dissolves which following the news of the girl's coming execution from a wireless key to head lines. Story starts with Haines disowned by a wealthy dad and telling a city editor he's about to engage the world's best reporter.

Assigned to interview his father on why he kicked him out, Haines gets the story and then is instru-

mental in quickly unraveling a cafe murder after being framed by a fake phone call from other members of the paper's staff.

It's here that he meets the orphaned Crystal (Miss Page) and carries on a flirtation of ulterior motives until the youngster says that she loves him, and he goes into reverse on this hit and run campaign.

A flash at Don's background, as displayed by a row of photographs on his apartment mantlepiece, frightens Crissle into sailing for the Orient with a show troupe. When Don gets back with flowers and a ring it's too late and he also has to take a boat ride to catch up.

The speed given it by Wood in the by-play between Haines and the secondary characters as the scenes unfold is the foundation upon which Farnham's titles build. Offhand it looks like the latter's best captioning effort for this male star. There's nothing the matter with Haines' performance. Miss Page both looks good and every so often gets a chance to do a little trouping. M-G-M is understood to have fair sized expectations about this girl and with this as evidence, seems to have a good chance of having its prophecy fulfilled.

Mathew Betz and Polly Moran lend substantial support and Eileen Percy is successful in making a small part stand out. Bert Roach, not a bad comic himself, is held to doing straight for Haines.

If they've had too much of Haines as a fresh youngster the country, at large, may be a bit backward about coming into see him, but there was no evidence of this at the Capitol on this damp Saturday afternoon. And whoever drops in will be satisfied, the early pace being sufficient to allow the film to coast in when its gas line starts to become clogged with plot.

Were "Telling the World" a half-miler, it could be said that the picture does a fast 440.   *Sid.*

A Daughter of Destiny
(GERMAN MADE)

Producer not stated—probably Ufa subsidiary. From "Alraune," by H. H. Ewers. Directed by Henrik Galen. U.K. distribution by British International Film Distributors, Ltd., Censors' Certificate "A." Running time, 95 mins. Preview, Astoria theatre, July 4.
Evelyn ....Brigitte Helm
Doctor Strong............Paul Wegener
Dick Westfield ....John Loder
Lionel Hope................Ivan Petrovitch

Cast principals are a strong card. Brigitte Helm was the star of "Metropolis." Wegener is one of Ufa's best bets. John Loder is Jesse Lasky's answer to Sam Golwyn, and Petrovitch has been Alice Terry's boy friend in Ingram productions.

Atmosphere, a fresh method of treatment, and a strong theme are all here, but it is not an audience picture. It lacks polish, and does not sustain entertainment value. Brigitte Helm is apt to be repellent to Anglo-Saxon audiences. Her appeal is rather to the morbid and slightly unhealthy; she is eerie and at times almost unnatural. Slow and involved, the film's main appeal, this side or in America, is to the sureseat art theatres.

Opens with a plethora of captions, wordy and involved. Someone has tried to be intellectual. These are cut through a sequence of a doctor lecturing to students. For about four reels the film grips and is capably directed. Convent and circus sequences are well done and the dramatic value is kept up. Then it wanders, loses itself and goes all to pieces to end incoherently. Possibly due to bad editing.

Chief weaknesses are the vague motive of the characters and failure to provide a logical or even a satisfactory climax. A girl (Evelyn) is brought up without knowledge of her criminal parentage by a doctor who has theories on heredity. She breaks out of a convent, induces a youth to steal for her, elopes with him, leaves him for a circus owner, tames lions, takes another lover, discovers what her parentage was, undergoes a soul transformation, the doctor tries to kill her, and she finally falls into the arms of a good young man, apparently regenerated. Central idea, that only evil can come out of evil, is badly worked out.

Brigitte Helm's acting does not convince in the later part of the film; her sinister and even vicious expression is not affected by the presumed inner change. Paul Wegener is impressive and nothing more; John Loder is undistinguished and Petrovitch has almost been edited out. May do well in high class theatres, but not likely to be a success anywhere as a general release. *Frat.*

Bachelors' Paradise

Tiffany-Stahl production and release. Directed by George Archainbaud, from story by Curtis Benton. Sally O'Neill starred. Chester Lyons, cameraman. In cast: Ralph Graves, Eddie Gribbon, Jimmy Finlayson. At Loew's New York one day, July 11, half double bill. Running time, about 60 minutes.

The scrapper who makes good because of the girl theme is handled in a roundabout way in "Bachelors' Paradise." The production is exceptionally good in spots, ring stuff and street brawls. As a whole the story is fragile being allowed to drag in several reels. A worth-while cast bolsters this up to the fair program entertainment class.

Bowery atmosphere throughout, with too much footage devoted to back tenement house incidents. Sally O'Neill effective as disappointed bride after scrapper she has nursed to health gives her go-by. Winning battle and getting into money, fighter (Ralph Graves) snaps into it.

Fast pie-throwing battle brings couple together.

LITTLE MATCH GIRL
(FRENCH MADE)

Listed as a production of P. Braunberger for the Sofar Film Company, sympathetic fairy story of Hans Christian Anderson has been favorably translated by Jean Renoir.

Released in Paris under the local title of "La Petite Marchande d'Allumettes," it has Karen, little girl in destitute condition, selling matches. Nearly all refuse to buy.

New Year's night in a northern city (somewhere in Scandinavia) and she takes shelter from the snow within the light of a fashionable cake shop, where she is noticed by an aristocratic youth.

But the shopkeeper has Karen driven away and she stumbles with fatigue some distance off, where a well disposed person sends her some cake which his dainty dog has just declined to eat.

Fearing to return home emptyhanded the wretched little creature remains on the street, trying to keep her hands warm by striking her own matches. She falls asleep in the snow and dreams of the kingdom of toys, where the good looking young man she had previously attracted in the cake shop is waiting to meet her. He carries her into the sky, but the youth is killed by a dragon while protecting her.

This shock awakens the dreamer and she finds the rich young man bending over her in real life. Out of pity he picks up Karen and takes her to his own mansion nearby. Simple, poetical, charitable yarn which the name of Hans Anderson will aid much is appealing to the movie fans. Catherine Hessling, now a European star, holds the role of the Little Match Seller and this adds to the attraction. Jan Storm, Norwegian actor, is the nice young man. The scene in the clouds is well done and there are some excellent effects in the toy land. Renoir has produced this picture with good taste. It should find a ready market for houses where the youngsters congregate although it is a production on the advanced school lines. *Kendrew.*

The Fighting Red Head

FBO production and release. Starring Buzz Barton. Directed by Louis King from screen story by Frank Howard Clark. Roy Eslick, cameraman. In cast: Bob Fleming, Duane Thompson, Edward Hearn. At Stanley, one day, June 5. Running time, 60 minutes.

One unnecessarily weak sequence right in the middle of the footage breaks the story back of "The Fighting Red Head." Aside from an innocent blacksmith turning shamefaced when the sheriff arrives shortly after he finds the body of a deputy who has been shot by the bad man, there is the usual hokum. Audience gets restless when the blacksmith takes the blame for no reason other than apparent self-consciousness.

Aside from an unusually weak and disintegrated story, Buzz is the same as usual, doing the same pranks, climbing chimneys, discovering the money and saving the girl from train, hooking the bad man. The only thing deprived him is exonerating the blacksmith. The deputy comes to long enough to do that.

POWER
(GERMAN MADE)

Produced presumably by UFA, although no screen credit given producer or distributor. Titles and editing by Joseph Fleisler. Directed by Robert Wiene. In cast Emil Jannings and Hannah Ralph. At 55th Street Playhouse week July 14. Running time about 50 mins.

An antique from foreign shelves when Emil Jannings was not so good, lighting effects were worse, and the old-fashion elements of so-called drama prevailed on the screen. Better for "Power" had it remained in hiding.

In its arty form, "Power" is stretched into a dream of what a laborer could do if he did what Edison did—only keeping the secret in his own hat.

Nothing dramatic of awe-inspiring. Flat describes it, despite the efforts of the title writer to have his work provide the continuity.

GREASED LIGHTNING

Ted Wells (Rough Rider Series) production, released through Universal. Directed by Ray Taylor, from story by William Lester. In cast: Robert Milasch, Myrtis Crinley, Walter Shumway. At Loew's New York one day, July 11, half double bill. Running time, 45 minutes.

Any western could be titled "Greased Lightning" for all that it means to this production.

A lot of forced comedy which could be cut out and released under another title drags this one into feature length.

New girl, ranch boss, crooked lawyer-cattle-rustler and the theme that cowboy fans know in their sleep is projected. A little poorer than in the old way.

Okay as a filler in the grinds.

PARDONED
(FRENCH MADE)

Paris, June 22.

Nicea Corporation is responsible for this romantic picture. Technical work is perfect with some fine photographic effects by Bayard. Scenario is a bit rocky and the production from that point of view is not O. K.

It is of the novelet order, about a young engineer courting a seamstress, the latter considering she is not getting sufficient attention from the youth absorbed by his daily labors. She runs off with her employer who abandons the girl when she becomes a mother.

Then the young engineer, having made a fortune, locates his former sweetheart, goes to the rescue and marries her, now being assured he himself is the father of the baby which has caused all the trouble. Thus, as from the title, all is forgiven.

Jacquet is the sympathetic lover, ably supported by Simone Vaudry, as the girl-mother undergoing all sorts of hardships for the false step. Playing is by no means a feature of this somewhat indifferent production. Nevertheless, there may be a number of fans on the small time circuit who will find pleasure in sitting out this dramatic "East Lynn" on modern lines. *Kendrew.*

QUICK TRIGGERS

Independent western, designated "Range Rider Series," bearing brand of Universal Thrill Co. Directed by Ray Taylor. Story by Basil Dickey, adapted by Al Pivar. Cameraman, Al Jones; titles by Gardner Bradford. Starring Fred Humes. Derelys Perdue leading woman. Wilbur Mack, heavy. Half of double bill, New York theatre, one day, July 6. Running time 53 minutes.

Brisk action western with strong low comedy incidentals and sure fire on both counts for the juveniles. Made on the familiar formula of land shark who uses gang of cattle rustlers to break the rancher so he can grab his land. Total, just half of double bill as at Loew's New York.

Here the familiar routine is somewhat varied, by making the heroine the daughter of one of the rustlers, which creates some confusion in telling the story due to the necessity of justifying the ethics of such a situation. Involves labored explanation that heroine's father was compelled to obey the land shark in whose power he found himself.

Explanation is vague and unsatisfactory and device illustrates uselessness of departing from the old hoke.

However, the comedy of western types, including a fat boy who rides a mule and some incidental shots of a parrot and a goose who get mixed up in a general fight, good for laughs. Climax of the film is fist fight between hero and heavy which runs into a lot of footage and is well worked up in background and situation, even if the two principals do fake their exchange of blows pretty crudely. *Rush.*

Mademoiselle from Armentierres
(BRITISH MADE)

Produced by Gaumont (England) and released through Metro-Goldwyn-Mayer. Directed by Maurice Elvey from story credited to Victor Fabille. Titles by Ralph Spence. In cast: Estelle Brody, John Stuart. At Loew's Lincoln Square, New York, June 30-July 4. Running time 55 minutes.

This British version of the war song and its 500 naughty verses makes Mademoiselle shine forth from the screen as an up-stager, who serves only beer, lets only one lad kiss her and then marries him right after.

Newsreel cut-ins interspersed in about two reels of war stuff add realism but also distract by the contrast between their hazy photography and the brilliance of the story print.

Newsreel cut-ins interspersed in about two reels of war stuff add realism but also distract by the contrast between their hazy photography and the brilliance of the story print.

An outstanding shot in "Mademoiselle from Armentierres," flanked with 1915 material, is the boys going over the top in a way that eclipses any one moment of such action in "The Big Parade" or "What Price Glory."

Over half of the production convinces the average audience, especially one of war vets, that the thing is a burlesque on the scrap. It is nothing but one round of crap shooting and beer drinking, with the keep-your-distance from the buxom dame, played quite well by Estelle Brody. Taken over for distribution by M-G-M the original print, apparently, was well chopped down and Ralph Spence's pepping up treatment applied. Spence shows a remarkable tendency to give the British the break, in titles at least, for winning the war.

This may be "The Big Parade" for England but it will never get beyond some of the poorer second runs in America, unless deliberate advantage is taken of its excellent title.

Man in the Rough

FBO production and release. Starring Bob Steele. Directed by Wallace Fox. At Columbus, New York, one day, July 7, one half of double bill. Running time, about 60 minutes.

Mechanical adherence to the most conventional of the western story ruts fits "Man in the Rough" for little more than some of the fastest grinds.

Bob Steele spends his time getting bounced on the head in a mine cabin, and again in the no-good assayer's office. The galloping game of tag along country roads thus prevails.

Steele's greased curley hair and saccharine smile, always on the map when the crippled miner's daughter is present, do not contribute one iota toward exploiting the title. Anything but the title's rough baby. A couple of scraps are as stereotyped as the rest of the production.

DISCORD
(SWEDISH MADE)

Swedish-Biograph Company production, released in America by Pathe. Directed by Gustav Molander from story by Paul Merzback. Lil Dagover and Gosta Ekmann featured. At 55th Street Playhouse, New York, week of July 7. Running time 60 minutes.

A picture in what, for Europe, is the "lighter mood." It concerns the marriage of a society girl from London to a big brawny son of the Swedish log country. She is restless in her northern home and returns, at her husband's thoughtful suggestion, to visit with her own kind in London.

There she is engulfed in a round of society doings, forgets to write, and is in the act of posing as Lady Godiva in a charity show when the impulsive brute from Sweden shows up. In his shocked condition he forbids her participation in the show. Husband and wife quarrel and she declares that he is and always will be a peasant.

Lil Dagover, fairly well known on this side, notably among the pseudo-art devotees, is the London wife. Gosta Ekmann suggests a combination of Tom Santschi and Thomas Meighan. Gliva Berg playing the big boy's kindly aunt is a great type for sentimental old ladies.

Production is pretty fair and the picture holds interest better than many of the imported opuses. It is neither arty nor novel except in background, and it apes the Hollywood technique very openly. *Land.*

JAZZ MAD

Universal production and release. Starring Jean Hersholt. Directed by Harmon Weight from an original story by Svend Gade. In cast: Marion Nixon, George Lewis, Alfred Hertz, Charles Clary. At Loew's Circle, New York, one day, July 6. Running time, 58 mins.

Dealing with a proud musician who composes a symphony while supporting himself by leading a burlesque orchestra in a sawdust night club, this story is interesting as a plot idea away from the commonplace and with strong "natural" opportunities for synchronization. Universal did not give it the production it deserves. It has been handled without inspiration in a dead monotone and will be simply another movie.

Alfred Hertz and the San Francisco Symphony Orchestra are brought into the action. The musician, humiliated and discouraged, has sunk into a state of mental torpor and despair. The doctors believe that if he can hear his symphony played it will revive his zest for living. Friends arrange with the symphony director and the piece is played, with the desired effect resulting.

The performance of Jean Hersholt is splendid and arouses anew the pity that this fine actor is so consistently buried under third-rate productions. No one else in the cast is called upon to do anything. It isn't a bad picture by any means, but neither is it distinguished.

Title "Jazz Mad" has no connection, however roundabout, with the story. *Land.*

APACHES OF PARIS
(FRENCH MADE)

Ufa production directed by Malikoff from the novel by Francois Carco. Foreign cast unknown in America. At Broadway, New York, week July 9. Running time 63 minutes.

Although screen-labeled Ufa (Germany) this is advertised by the house as a French melodrama. Background, types, makeup, technique, etc., corroborate the French origin. For a straight program release it is easily one of the best French films here in a long while and is good enough to get into the better houses, although not de luxe. It might easily, with bright exploitation, prove a money proposition.

The title ought to help and the picture should be interesting to American audiences because of its Parisian locale, the Moulin Rouge, back alleys and whatnot. Big city stuff generally clicks in the small town box offices.

Photography good and while the cutting is a trifle jerky now and then, it's a pretty smooth job in toto. The customary French fetich for blue eyelids, stenciled lips, etc., has been happily toned down. The picture is of a very fair production level throughout. The director is billed simply as Malikoff and he is apparently also the leading man, although the credit title loaded with foreign and multi-syllable names was confusing.

Malikoff (if he is the hero) is a good looking chap of pronounced Continental appearance. A certain masculine mental vigor saves him from the suggestion of effeminacy that his almost-too-good looks bring up. The leading lady is a pip blonde and new to this side. The picture is characterized by interesting types.

Throughout the picture there is an effort to kid American wowsers and prohibition. An amusing technical flaw typically French is the American girl who goes to Paris with the investigators. She blithely lights a cigarette in a cabaret after the matron of the party has vigorously ordered mineral water instead of wine. The French evidently are unaware that the real bona fide Yankee crusader regards the insidious coffin nail as only one step behind Demon Rum.

The leading man is the classy quick-thinking leader of a gang of Apaches. Their mental superior he is at constant odds with his cronies and they fall out over the question of the American girl's jewels.

"Apaches of Paris" is better than fair. *Land.*

When the Law Rides

FBO production and release. Tom Tyler, star. Directed by Robert Delacy from story by Oliver Drake. In cast: Jane Reid, Frankie Darrow, Joshua Thurston. At Stanley, N. Y., one day. Running time, about 55 minutes.

Good Arizona desert stuff, with poison water and mirages, opens "When the Law Rides." Generous amount of story interest, including a couple of good scraps, makes this a worthwhile second-runner.

Tom Tyler finds being hard boiled a little too easy. His boldness borders in spots on what the average audience may interpret as personal conceit.

The minister's daughter also figures in this one, but the main interest is in the much worn angle of the bad man, who really is the guardian of the law just enjoying a little diversion at the bartender-boss' expense.

SACRIFICE
(GERMAN MADE)

Produced by Fellner & Somlo. Released in U. K. by W. & F. Co. Directed by Carmine Gallone. Story by Norman Falk. U. K. release, April 22, 1929. Censors' Certificate A. Previewed at Marble Arch Pavilion, July 2. Running time, 102 mins.

Anna Suminski	Olga Tschekowa
Paul, her son	S. Szuberla
Gaston Lereau	Hans Stuwe
Fedor Kornilow	Henri Baudin

A curious production. In parts it seems affected by the Ufa complex; in other places by the French and Italian school of five or more years back.

Some good sequences of a snow chase, and others of fighting in similar locations between cavalry. A wild Paris cabaret sequence is also well done in the sense that it is sexy and leggy. Otherwise, the story is feeble and the direction old-fashioned. Gallone can evidently do crowd stuff much better than he can handle individuals. He gets nothing like as much out of Tschekowa as did Dupont in "Moulin Rouge."

Fedor Kornilow, captain in the Imperial Russian guard, is snubbed by Anna, prima ballerina, and, being a Russian screen villain, vows revenge. During the Revolution he becomes an officer of the Reds and has Anna's husband shot. Escaping with her child, she is caught between the two armies, her sleigh falls into a shell hole and she loses her child, subsequently found by Kornilow. Anna haunts a Polish town seeking news of the lost boy, hears he is in Paris, goes there and finds it is another child and tries to commit suicide in the Seine. Her rescuer, Gaston, falls in love with her and she lives with him till meeting Kornilow at a cabaret and finding he knows the location of her son. She is forced to go away with him as the price for her child. Gaston discovers what is to happen, holds up Kornilow, gets the address of the child and goes there with Anna. Finds child has already been taken by Kornilow, and there follows a race for the Russian frontier to save the boy. Kornilow is drowned trying to cross a frozen lake and Gaston saves the child from the broken ice.

Comedy touches are inane, and exteriors are better than the interiors. Will do fairly well here but would be better trimmed down to 80 minutes or less. For America, will need fixing to avoid the censors. *Frat.*

HOT NEWS

Paramount production and release. Directed by Clarence Badger. Bebe Daniels starred and Neil Hamilton featured. Adapted by Lloyd Corrigan and Grover Jones from original story by Monte Brice and Harlan Thompson. Screen play by Florence Ryerson. Titles by George Marion, Jr. At Paramount, New York, week July 21. Running time 66 minutes.

"Pat" Clancy	Bebe Daniels
"Scoop" Morgan	Neil Hamilton
James Clayton	Paul Lucas
Michael Clancy	Alfred Allen
"Spec"	"Spec" O'Donnell
Benny, the camera boy	Ben Hall
The Maharajah	Mario Carillo
Mrs. Van Vleck	Maude Turner Gordon

A lively story of the news reel, with enough action and quite some comedy, both in situations and titles, makes this a good picture for Bebe Daniels and a better than average Paramount programmer. Its drawing power is confined to the Daniels name.

In the key sections this picture on merit may attract more than it will do at the Paramount. Analyzed, there is much of action and creation, with a smooth running tale exceptionally balanced to give the news reel slant plausible realism.

Everyone connected with the film appears to have caught the spirit of it. That may have been because of the news reel and cameraman angle. Miss Daniels seemingly liked to turn the crank even if using blanks, and Neil Hamilton must have relished posing in the cameraman's outfit. He did it well. The story contains plenty of tricks, particularly in and around the Statue of Liberty, and there are some thrills in this.

It's Harlan Thompson's first film story. He's the dramatist who got the Mankie works and went west. This tells why Paramount wanted to sew him up. George Marion, Jr., is no little fun contributor with his always there captions. Clarence Badger, the director, made everyone work and gave them plenty to do. He wound up with the two principals aboard a bad man's yacht and the coast guard saving them at the last minute without a flag flying, while it was here also that Mr. Pommeroy did some more work with the smoke screen, but it's all okay without any of it akay. Absence of a say in picture stories is worth almost anything.

Besides which, Miss Daniels as the newspaper owner's daughter is the only woman in the cast or picture. She does nicely with the role, better than usual for her. She looks the part, a pert girl who sets out to reduce the head of one Scoop Morgan, the star cameraman of two dailies, "Sun" and "Mercury." Each is operating a news reel. Scoop has been sending "The Sun's" so far ahead, he's being nursed along by Clancy, owner of the paper.

Scoop blows though when told by Clancy he will have to break in his daughter as a cameraman. Scoop says there's no skirt who can do his work and walks, going to "The Mercury," immediately leaving "The Sun's" service standing still.

The daughter with an earful of Scoop's self opinions tells Dad she will go after it alone and becomes the pest of Scoop's newsreeling life, beating him out in any and all things. Her first meeting with Scoop on the road as both are headed to take a wrecked boat off the coast is quite humorous. Later the Liberty business to catch an ocean-crossing blimp and the Harold Lloyd stuff around there, while later both slip into an estate to get exclusive pictures of an Indian rajah, with Miss Daniels and Hamilton made up as adagio dancers, doing their Apache on the stage, nicely adapted also from many another version. Complications here lead into the yacht kidnapping that should make Columbia burn, and then the coast guard without the flag.

Whoever dug up the gag of using the unconscious crook with Hamilton putting his own arms through for deception, landed a familiar bit of business for a long and loud laugh, nicely worked in and out.

FORBIDDEN HOURS

Metro-Goldwyn-Mayer production and release starring Ramon Novarro and featuring Renee Adoree. Adapted from A. P. Younger's original with Harry Beaumont directing. Titles by John Colton and M. G. Gerstad cameraman. At the Capitol, N. Y., week of July 21. Running time, 49 minutes.

His Majesty, Michael IV	Ramon Novarro
Marie Mancini	Renee Adoree
Queen Alexia	Dorothy Cumming
Prime Minister	Edward Connelly
Nina	Alberta Vaughn
Duke de Krassnoff	Roy D'Arcy

Light, frothy and inconsequential piece of work which Novarro's excellent light comedy playing will never be able to hold up for more than mediocre grosses. Tough break for the star that he had to waste such corking frivolous moments on such a yarn. Women will think he's just too cute and the men will not be unaware of his boyish appeal here, but it's one of those 49 minute features disintegrating throughout the final 1,500 feet. One of the shortest screen leaders the house has held in months, with probably plenty cut out.

Entertainment highlights are all concentrated on the flirtation between Miss Adoree and Novarro as the young ruler of a small kingdom on his yearly night out with his officers. The girl turns out to be the niece of the prime minister, the boy abdicates so that he can marry her and the uncle and a cousin (D'Arcy) scheme to show their king the girl in a compromising situation to quell his wild fervor. Persuading the girl to let herself be caught in a room with the cousin, who has no objections, in walks Michael to become disillusioned and to finish the sequence by tossing her among his enlisted men. Subsequent return of the king to rescue her from the common military leads to the weak ending of a flight to the border where the officer in command informs the chauffeur the people want both their king and his sweetheart back.

Little or no interest in the story after the first reel despite the sexy angle. The fresh flirtatious antics of Novarro and Miss Adoree's reactions, as Beaumont has handled them, knit the film together up to this point. Even so, the director has dragged out a couple of love passages. Support cast is competent in limited roles and a fair amount of production value forms the background. Among the dissenting notes is that Miss Adoree doesn't look so good opposite Novarro.

Apparently one of those weaklings M-G is glad to get off the shelf in July. It's major point is that it won't hurt Novarro, personally, while fully demonstrating that he's no minor issue as a light comedian, flashes of which he has shown in previous pictures. *Sid.*

Ladies of Night Club

Tiffany-Stahl production and release. Directed by George Archainbaud. Author, adapter and editor not credited on main title. Ricardo Cortez, Barbara Leonard, Lee Moran, Douglas Gerrard featured in billing. At New York Hippodrome week July 16. Running time, 75 minutes.

Backstage story suggesting more than a little inspiration from "Excess Baggage" and "Broadway." In the main, picture holds skillful treatment in sympathetic vein of the self-satisfied hick hoofer. In this character the film is a duplicate of Joe Lane of "Broadway," while atmosphere is replica of "Baggage."

Here the denouement is differently worked out, with a sort of "Laugh,

Clown, Laugh," finale. Subject-matter is surefire, while the success of the two other plays is fresh in the public mind, and the picture is fairly well made.

Lee Moran as the hoofer walks away with the production. Barbara Leonard is rather an insipid heroine, while Douglas Gerrard and Cissie FitzGerald, only others of any consequence, are terribly stilted and artificial. Ricardo Cortez gives his usual suave performance in the straight lead role.

Picture has abundance of legs, undressed night club chorus girls, deftly exploited for the s. a. punch. Several subtle, under-the-surface angles for the insider and a wealth of the flip argot of vaudeville backstage for good comedy effect in the titles. A sample is the stage manager's suggestion to the flop act on arrival for Monday rehearsal, "Better not send the laundry out till after the first show." Wasted on the Hip mob. Good comedy values throughout, and titles are sparkling.

Picture starts well with graphic character sketches of backstage types and incidents. Raggs and Revere, mixed team of hoofers, open, and register 100 per cent flop, getting canceled on the first show. Night club director impressed with girl of act and offers her a job as a single. Hick man partner crashes on job, thanks to making good impression on woman club owner (character is made a Tex Guinan, of course).

Girl is a riot in the floor show and brassy partner rides along on his nerve and because he knows he's good in spite of all the evidence. Throughout it is evident that team are not married, although they dress together. Millionaire night club spender falls for the girl. As this romance develops, hoofer comes gradually to drift away from his big brother attitude and figure on marriage, although the girl does not understand this.

Hoofer characteristically figures that all he has to do is to get the ring and make the announcement. He gets the ring, but before he springs the proposal other man has proposed and been accepted. All leading to an emotional finale to musical accompaniment of "Laugh, Clown, Laugh." This scene is heavily over-played, but because of its intrinsic strength gets over in the picture.

Despite defects in smooth treatment, material works out into a good program picture, and probably will do especially well with neighborhood clienteles. *Rush.*

THE LOVE PIRATE

(GERMAN MADE)

Ufa production. No American release connection mentioned. Made in Germany. Directed by Dr. Arthur Robinson. Programmed as in cast, Paul Richter, Rudolph Kleine-Rogge and Egode Nisson. At 55th Street Playhouse (sure seater), New York, week July 21. Running time around 65 minutes.

"The Love Pirate" as a foreign made has little for over here besides its title. Designed for the box office, that title has been used on American mades, either comedies or dramatics and probably both. It leaves this Ufa feature as fit for the sure seaters or for double feature bills, playing one or two days and one preferred.

In the days of the ancient Corsairs, says the 55th St. Playhouse program. That may have been in the 16th Century when the swashbucklers fought with knives and one hand free. In the fight here, the pirate captain slipped a little poison on his knife to cinch his lieutenant. It needed a skirt to urge on the lieutenant to kill his best friend, even in battle, but the lieutenant did, as the Spanish Main came in through the pirates' castle in droves, all in brand new uniforms.

Not much in the way of direction, less in photography and often examples of bad cutting. The girl looked well when the camera permitted, the mob of pirates and their women seemed staged to represent old masterpieces of after the banquet or the dirty dogs or one of those things. Mostly one of those things.

The Corsair pirates were a gallant crew of bunglers. They needed a Jesse James as leader, but the gang thought they had picked a nance for captain when they couldn't tear him away from a dame he had kidnapped from the mainland. Even the lieutenant told him to grab her by man power only and get through with that. But this captain said he would win her or else. It was or else for the captain died from knifing in the last 200 feet. The picture had died in the first 200 so that may have made it evenly balanced otherwise.

At the opening the captain, wounded, is taken in by a Spanish doctor and nursed by the daughter. When able to blow, the captain takes the girl with him, not leaving an address or thanks for the doc. The girl didn't appear to mind it much either, for she never mentioned papa again nor did pop reappear. Those were the good old days.

Back in the castle where the pirates hung out, they had a party every evening. Booze and wimmin, with nothing extra looking about the wimmin. One tough guy dragged a dame around by the hair to show her the men were boss and all of the others applauded. It looked like a nite club, 300 years ago.

When the captain returned with his kidnapped sweetie, the mob asked him to get down to pirating, that evidently being the German idea of roughhouse when there's no excuse for another Russian revolution picture. The captain stalled; the girl didn't like him, he whined; she liked Peter, his lieutenant, and Pete did look pretty good. Peter told the captain to take the girl and go to sea or any other place and he (Pete) would remain behind, with the wimmin. It looked great on Peter's part until recalling he would be the only man there among the wimmin.

Cap did go but the girl rushed him back. She wanted to be with Peter, she said; she had lied to the captain, and the captain said that meant fight to him, with Peter, who had called Salvatore, the cap, a coward, because he had struck a woman. It seemed a new system of chivalry among the Corsairs, as most of the scenes of the stew parties showed the men beating up the wimmin to keep in practice.

However, the Spanish Main put everything on the bum, but Peter and his fair one who was able to stand off an entire bunch of pirates with her charm of something that didn't come out on the screen, escaped from the castle by a secret passage to the desert. And the finish was both of them on a nice looking front yard, some one having forgotten all about the desert.

It's the German way.

DETECTIVES

Metro-Goldwyn-Mayer production and release directed by C. M. Franklin. Story and continuity by Robert Lord and Chester Dane. Marceline Day featured. Cast includes Tenen Holtz and Polly Moran. At Loew's New York one day, July 14. Running time, 70 mins.

Spotting in this daily change house reflects the quality of the production and indicates its possibilities. The Dane-Arthur combo flops in this latest effort mainly because of bad direction. The story, as well as the players, has not been properly handled. Many situations muffed with insipid titling and comedy business.

Starring team's work indicates they are only suited for certain type roles. They register for light laughs, but only infrequently and the running time of 70 minutes demands something stronger.

Story is interesting, but slows up. The boob hotel detective suffers the usual humiliations conceived by an over-smart bellhop. Latter finally cops the jewel thieves, the reward and the girl.

Marceline Day registers nicely, but has a minor assignment. Polly Moran delivers a strong comedy characterization in two brief scenes with the hotel sleuth and is then relegated to the background. Tenen Holtz assumes the role of the heavy. *Mori.*

U. S. SMITH

Sam Saxe (Gotham) production, distributed by Lumas. Directed by Joseph Henabery. Story by Louis Stevens. Photographed by Ray June. Titles by Casey Robinson. Supervision of Harold Shumate. Production manager, Don Diggins. Eli Dunn, assistant director. Eddie Gribbon heads cast; no star. At New York Hippodrome week July 23. Running time, 73 minutes.

Sergeant Steve Riley	Eddie Gribbon
Molly Malone	Lila Lee
U. S. Smith	Mickey Bennett
Corporal Jim Sharkey	Kenneth Harlan
Danny	Earle Marsh

A bully program picture, best thing the Gotham outfit has turned out this long time. Appeal from a number of angles. Eddie Gribbon, who has done some extremely good things, here has a high-class comedy character creation, a role that carries the picture on merit.

Besides the genuine laughs, the story has capital sentimental values, a wealth of grand old flag stuff and a melodramatic kick in a first-rate prize fight scene, which also carries a laughing finish that rounds out a highly amusing bit of screen entertainment. For good measure there are a number of rich sequences involving a dandy kid actor in Mickey Bennett.

Number of splendidly built-up comedy passages makes a running fire of sparkling episodes. Such a bit is the sequence where the kid, who needs $40 for a scheme of his own, lures the champion pug of the marine corps into a burlesque house where a bruiser is meeting all comers for $50 to the survivor. Kid gives the bruiser the raspberry when he appears, and so jockeys the situation that a wrangle develops and the marine boxer is drawn into a fight, knocking the bruiser cold and drawing down the needed jack.

Whole picture is interlarded with good gags, some hoke and some of good character stuff growing out of the people themselves and gaited to real humor.

The relationship between the hard-hitting top sergeant of marines and the kid whom he adopts and makes mascot of the outfit gives rise to good sentimental scenes. Marine dresses the youngster up in a spruce marine uniform and trains him in the code of the leathernecks. Drills him to stand stiff at attention for the striking of the colors at sunset, and coaches him in the oath of allegiance. Here are excellent opportunities for redfire stuff for the fans. At the Hip they went for it hard.

Marine and army ring champs are matched, and, as it turns out, the same pair are rivals for the girl. This builds up for a corking climax in the prize fight, another angle to the building up being an effort to buy the marine to lay down. Stage is set for the battle, which is a kick exhibition of fisticuffs in its own right and rich in comedy incidentals. Gribbon, of course, gets the decision, knocking out his man at the very instant when he is himself out on his feet.

Gribbon, staggering around the ring, goofy from the hammering he has received and wearing an expression of idiotic ecstasy, is a comedy epic. Brief sentimental bit for the fadeout has the girl falling into the arms of the doughby rival, leaving the marine a pathetic outsider except his love for the kid.

Some of the hoke is laid on a little thick, but that does no harm before the clientele it is aimed at. *Rush.*

HOUP-LA

(BRITISH MADE)

Produced by British Screen Productions, Ltd. Original story by Arthur Phillips. Directed by Frank Miller. Photography by John Miller. Quota film. U. K. release April 29, 1929. Censors' certificate U. Pre-view, Palace theatre, London, June 29. Running time, 82 mins.

Noah Swinley	George Bellamy
Lion Tamer	James Knight
Clown	Frank Stanmore
Circus Proprietor	Charles Garry
His Daughter	Peggy Carlisle

Circus stories have become so bromide in American films it is hard to review this first production of a recently floated company without drawing harsh comparisons. Story is credible and holds fair interest, but the direction lacks any sort of technique or inspiration, and misses many opportunities.

Despite much of the action centering round a circus, nothing is shown under the top. Photography and acting are competent, but nothing more. Better exterior sets than usual, some village streets into which lions escape being well done, and doubling for the hero in the cages is well handled.

Noah Swinley is a zoologist and a former college boy athlete. He sees a couple of men beating another fellow and goes to the rescue. Rescued man bundles Swinley into a car and takes him to his flat. Next morning Swinley finds himself alone, and on his way home learns from a newspaper he has helped a gangster against a couple of men servants who had caught him making a getaway with the family jewels. So Swinley, thinking he may be arrested, joins a touring circus after driving to their cage three lions which have escaped into a village.

He falls in love with the circus owner's daughter, on whom the regular lion-tamer has an eye, and after frequent fights the tamer is found stabbed and dying. Swinley is charged with attempted murder; the daughter swears she was with him all night, so he couldn't have done it. Then the clown bursts into court and says he did it because the tamer was always hazing him and was around with a razor to kill Swinley and the girl.

Thoroughly British in settings and appeal. Good average routine release here. For America, out. *Frat.*

HUSBANDS FOR RENT

Warner Bros. production and release. Directed by Henry Lehrman from the story by Edwin J. Mayer. Screen adaptation by C. Graham Baker. Titles by Joseph Jackson and Jimmy Starr. Cast including Helene Costello, Owen Moore, Claude Gillingwater, Kathryn Perry, Arthur Hoyt and John Miljan. At Fox's Academy of Music, New York, July 23-25. Running time, over 60 minutes.

Spicy title deceptive, inasmuch as the story does not live up to expectations. Film okey as a filler in the split weeks and down. Helene Costello and Owen Moore, featured, do not figure as box-office attractions of any strength.

Miss Costello as a blonde vamp fails to impress in one of the major roles. Kathryn Perry photographs becomingly and registers well excepting in instances when camera shots of her face are too close, creating an angular outline, which spoils appearance.

John Miljan, Arthur Hoyt and Claude Gillingwater, the latter especially, score nicely in supporting roles. Miljan plays the menace, while the two other boys essay interesting comedy roles.

Stories of this type, which are being put into production consistently, never carry. Use of material of this kind often raises conjecture regarding the mental balance of the supervisor, director or producer responsible for the choice. Without merit of any kind, timeworn, and lacking a single incident or combination of sequences productive of a laugh or even getting attention, this story could have been taken from any one of 50,000 magazine stories which have appeared in print in the past 20 years. There is no particular idea to the story and very little comedy.

Concerns a somewhat aristocratic couple whose emotional affairs become complicated. An engagement is broken. The girl thinks she loves another man who claims to love her. The boy thinks he wants another woman who thinks she loves him. For no particular reason the other pair elope, and the engagement is on, again followed by a marriage. After the marriage the same condition arises, and a divorce is framed when the boy backs out, insisting he loves his wife. *Mori.*

The Crystal Submarine

(FRENCH MADE)

Paris, July 15.

This comic picture has the advantage of the presence of Tramel, a popular French vaudeville star, in the leading role. On the other hand, it will not be of much advantage to the comedian. Tramel is now a sort of household word as a low comedian. The scenario is more of a series of funny episodes, arranged by Marcel Vandal, for the Aubert circuit. It is about a messenger who finds the manuscript of a play entitled by its unknown author "Le Sous-Marin de Cristal," leading to ridiculous situations when the humble porter is credited with the creation of the literary work.

Tramel is quite at home as the messenger, but the picture cannot be classed o.k. Even the technical department is not to be taken as an example of excellency. Andre Dubosc and Rene Lefebvre do their level best to bolster up their friend Tramel in indifferent situations.

Popular comic is not sufficient to make a picture. Other elements are necessary. *Kendrew.*

ROAD HOUSE

Fox production and release. Directed by Richard Rosson. Lionel Barrymore featured, together with Maria Alba and Warren Burke. Story by Philip Hurn, scenario by John Stone. At Audubon, New York, July 19-22. Running time, 54 minutes.

Sally Carroll....................Maria Alba
Larry Grayson...............Warren Burke
Henry Grayson...........Lionel Barrymore
Mrs. Henry Grayson..Julia Swayne Gordon
Grandma Grayson............Tempe Pigott
Helen Grayson..............Florence Allen
Jim, Larry Grayson's Pal...Eddie Clayton
Sam.............................Jack Oakie
Maid..........................Jane Keckley
Joe Brown.......................Joe Brown
Mary, Larry Grayson's Girl Friend
Kay Bryant

Picture of spotty interest. Story deals with life among the gilded youth of an average American town. So far as it treats of their jazz and necking activities it holds attention by audacious sex stuff involving wild petting and flask parties. And a good title for its class of story.

There are also some punchy angles of underworld life into which a sap son of a millionaire adventures. So far the production has strong appeal, but it falls down at the finish because of its pretense of having a serious moral purpose.

Fairly torrid necking sequences and the episode of the underworld girl vamping the gilded youth, together with shots of the activities at a country roadhouse where the elders of the town gather to gamble, even while they hypocritically preach civic virtues in public, all pack a kick, but the whole tale as such is weakened when the story is brusquely switched to point a moral. However, the previous matter stands that off as far as the younger set, who may go for this, is concerned.

Moral purpose seemed to have been an afterthought, designed perhaps to alibi the torrid passages. Point of the story is that a too-indulgent father, also a genial sinner in his private life, is responsible when his son is led into evil.

Father heads the Good Government party in his town, but on the quiet is a hip-flask toter and a poker fan. Because of his easy-going code, he permits the boy to "have his fling," which means joy riding and wild parties with the boys and girls. Even these pretty liberal young people get too quiet for the boy. He goes to a roadhouse to seek even more highly seasoned entertainment.

There he becomes involved with an underworld gang, through their vamping girl hanger-on. He falls in love with her. When the old man finds it out, there is an explosion. Boy leaves home and throws his fortunes with the gang, which is using the sap for its own purposes. The thugs ring the kid into a hold-up, and when there is a killing they throw the blame upon him.

So far the picture moves fast and has been absorbing. Boy is put on trial and convicted in a minor degree and the film ends in a maze of titles when the judge throws blame for the whole affair upon the easy-going indulgence of the parents.

Production is splendidly made and satisfyingly acted by the three principals, Barrymore as the father, Burke as the boy and Maria Alba as the vamp. As a blueprint of the wild life in the younger set it delivers and as a picture of the jazzed up younger generation it has plenty of force and sex kick for the fans. But the safety first "moral" finish leaves a flat final impression. *Rush.*

Prowlers of the Sea

Tiffany-Stahl production and release. Based on a Jack London story. Directed by J. G. Adolfi. Titles by Lesley Mason with E. Miller cameraman. Cast features Ricardo Cortez and Carmel Myers. George Fawcet among players. At Loew's New York, as half of double bill, one day, July 20. Running time, 56 mins.

May have been based on a Jack London yarn, but it screens like a rewrite of "Carmen," smugglers and all. That doesn't necessarily stampede the point that "Prowlers" ought to keep 'em awake for one or two days. Besides which it has the Cortez and Carmel Myers names to push it a little. Both do well, although there are times when the camera hasn't been overly kind to Miss Myers. It would have been better had the cameraman softened her up a bit.

Story is back in the late '90s and Cuba is having its troubles with revolutionists smuggling in arms. It's become a surefire habit until the general (Fawcett) assigns Cortez to command of the coast guard. The gen's fren is behind the hide and seek contest and induces a captain of a runner to persuade his sister (Miss Myers) to turn on the personality for Cortez. It evolves into mutual admiration, but Cortez is off post long enough with the girl to let someone else discover the latest attempt at running and he's placed under arrest.

The girl offers herself to the general as hostage if he'll let the boy go, and the commander probably figuring there'll be a revolution the last half anyway, sends both of them out to get married on condition the bride revises her sympathies and becomes a patriot.

Adolfi, directing, has carried it along at a decent pace without having any particular high points to reach and thereby suffering for a climax. Finish is weak, but the film gets a finger hold on audience interest, despite spending some prolonged moments on the Cortez-Myers amour. Continuity is also slightly loose in permitting the general's friend, the head gun runner, to slip from sight and stay there.

Just ambles along and figures to satisfy the clientele in those houses for which it has been pointed. *Sid.*

FLEETWING

Fox production and release. Directed by Lambert Hillyer from Elizabeth Packet's story. Frank Good, photographer. Cast includes Barry Norton, Dorothy Janis and Ben Bard. At Loew's New York, half of double bill, one day, July 20. Running time, under hour.

One of those desert shootie-ups revolving about the title of the picture, the name of a horse, and a machine gun. It's a Fox paperweight which fitted here on a double-header and seems fair enough solo amusement for the intermediates on a one-day basis.

A New York roof night audience accepted it as just another picture, which it is. Barry Norton, who was killed in "What Price Glory" and "Legion of the Condemned," plays the son of the tribe's leader who captures, releases and then steals the wild stallion and later rescues the maiden (Dorothy Janis) from a slave market with the animal's aid.

But it's not a romp for the youngsters, as the boy isn't a full warrior in the eyes of his people and must divide his spoils. So the father, deeming the horse more safe than the girl, gives the miss to one of his lieutenants. Meanwhile, Zeki (Ben Bard) would exterminate Ami's clan, having a double grouch against the boy who stole his horse and fair one, the latter and a machine gun offered in exchange for Fleetwing.

Zeki is eventually driven off when Ami (Norton) turns the machine gun on its owners, but there's still the old man and his sweetheart's husband to be straightened out, so the house can get a turn over. Caught with the girl, the father rules that both men have violated the code of the tribe and the dispute can only be settled by mortal combat. That washes up the husband.

Norton is hard to recognize in his flowing robes, but meets requirements; Miss Janis is appropriately frail and scared. Bard does pretty well outside of being rather broad in some of his gestures. He apparently screens well, but his Klan outfit prevents a good flash at him.

Mostly exteriors and photographically there's some nice looking sand dune stuff. The horse is a solid white, is given plenty of footage and takes all the theatrical license there is in converting itself to domestic needs.

For the small houses where they like pounding hoofs, a terror stricken maid and retribution. *Sid.*

ON TO RENO

Pathe release, produced and directed by James Cruze. Starring Marie Prevost. Adapted by Walter Woods from story by Joseph Jackson. Ernest Miller, camerman. Cast: Cullen Landin, Ned Sparks, Ethel Wales. At the Tivoli, N. Y., one day, July 23, on double bill. Running time, about 60 minutes.

Cruze's first attempt in the program field since shooting at road shows should register fairly in the better second runs.

With the name of the director to ballyhoo and with Marie Prevost in something better than her recent average, "On to Reno" figures to draw.

The comedy is built around Reno, and is usual in its complications. Laughs are not particularly numerous, but are worthwhile when they arrive. Action, centering in a palatial home, drags for over a reel because of repetition of chaser gags.

Punch is in a swimming pool, where the wife keeps two husbands apart. Clever direction lets audience in on the fact that one hubby is minus bathing trunks, and alimony club, confined to women, uncorks good cackle when Landis is floored by husky Amazons.

Into No Man's Land

Excellent (maker) production, distributed through Commonwealth. Directed by Cliff Wheeler from adaptation claimed to have been made from story "You're in the Army Now." Arthur Guy Empey, technical director. In cast: Tom Santschi, Betty Blythe, Josephine Norman, Mary McAllister, Craufurd Kent. At Loew's New York, one day, July 17, one-half double bill. Running time, 65 minutes.

Fans who shop for quantity will get a couple of loads full in "Into No Man's Land." It is glutted with gangsters, imposters and district attorneys for a couple of reels. These pull a holdup and murder. Then quite suddenly the action shifts to overseas battle fronts, and the war, with plenty of newsreel shots, is carefully reviewed.

Santschi does a fine piece of work as the gang leader who seeks solace in the war because the young d. a. flops for his daughter. Excluding the government film, there are some worthwhile skirmishes worked up on Hollywood sets.

The hodge podge of action is implausibly entertaining until the last reel. Here a weakness that will leave the audience with a bad taste is brought about by poor acting, except by Santschi, and by direction suddenly aware of too rich a mixture and overfootage. The failure of an affectionate daughter to recognize her old man because of war scars is ill timed with his immediate identification by his district attorney son-in-law.

NAME THE WOMAN

Columbia production and release. Directed by Earle C. Kenton. Continuity by Peter Milne from novel "Bridge." Titles by Mort Blumenstock. Photography by Ben Reynolds. In cast: Anita Stewart, Huntley Gordon, Gaston Glass, Jed Prouty, Julanne Johnson. At Stanley, New York, one day, July 17. Running time, 60 minutes.

"Name the Woman" is fair entertainment of the indie kind with a cast of old timers. They do their best in rambling through a story that starts with the court trial of a murder suspect, unfolding details from the witness box.

The mystery woman stuff, much over-played, is carried to the extreme in this case; the woman even coming into the courtroom with her false face on.

Trifling incidents and draggy moments, with the revelation that a greaser did the killing long before the trial is over, rob the story of everything but the mildest suspense. This is realized when the average audience's guess that the masked baby was the district attorney's wife turns out correct.

SAADA, THE GYPSY

(EGYPTIAN MADE)

Cairo, July 15.

Produced by Le Film d'Art Egyptien. Direction of Amadeo Puccini and Jack Schultz. Cast includes Fardous Hassan, Amina Rizk, Gubran Nahum, Abdel Aziz Khalil, Mahmud El Tuny, Fuad Selim, Hussein Ibrahim, Mohamed Kamal, Abdel Halim El Kalaouy, Ahmed Sabet, Zakia Ibrahim and Sha Fika Hosny. At the Metropole Cinema, Cairo, Egypt.

The first Egyptian film made by this new company and extremely successful at the Metropole Cinema in Cairo. It marks the first time any cast member has been before the camera, the troupe being recruited from the Egyptian theatres.

Story attempts to describe the true life of the Bedouins, and to this end is satisfactory. A previous picture, called "Laila," emphasized the love between an American girl and a Bedouin, but wasn't so well received here. This feature adheres closely to home customs.

Allowing for everything, "Saada" is a worthy piece of work. Photography is good and the locales are excellent. These include the Museum of Bonaparte, districts of Sayeda Zeinab, Tombs of the Khalifs, Palaces of Shubra and Zamalek, on the Nile.

Whether this picture will ever mean anything outside of this country, of course, is extremely unlikely, but it should do well here.

Puccini and Schultz, the producers, deserve a lot of credit for breasting severe handicaps and turning out a picture for which no one need feel ashamed. *. Asswad.*

Lost in the Arctic

Fox release of H. A. and Sidney Snow's production. Movietone prolog, five minutes, by Vilhjalmur Stefanson. Edited by K. N. Hawks, with M. S. Boylan titling. Cameraman, Sidney Snow. At Gaiety, New York, for twice-daily run, starting July 25. Running time, 64 minutes.

The Snows, father and son, made "Hunting Big Game in Africa," which showed a few years ago at the Lyric for $2 and had a profitable 12 weeks on that site. The family then went north, and this is the result. Understanding is that Fox decided to bring it in when news of the unfortunate Nobile expedition began to come through.

It's of the traveler type plus the harpooning of a whlae and the capturing alive of a polar bear to give it spice. If the big grind houses use it at all it will probably be in condensed form, but it's okay intact for the sure-seaters (art) and those split-week houses in districts where they're more or less indifferent to heavy lovers.

Film was due at the Gaiety July 15, but synchronization of sound and score made it 10 days late. Musically it's good enough, and one effect, for flocks of sea gulls, is convincing, but the technicians have fallen down in the mechanical mimicking of the baying, or barking, of the seal and walrus. Allowing that the duplication of animal sounds is the most difficult to record or imitate on stage or screen and that the Fox bunch had but 10 days in which to put this together, the total results aren't bad. But the public is unlikely to be interested in that phase.

Picture's kick is in the chase of the bear over ice floes and his final capture by lassooing and a net. Snow's camera work here is excellent, with some telephoto shots of the animal plowing through the water, clumsily galloping across the ice to as awkwardly plunge again into the water. The whale sequence rates second, with a flash of three or four of the aquatic giants spouting as the opening shot.

Men put out in a small boat to harpoon one of the mammals by hand. It's a neat tussle, although much of the action at the throw is muddled, and there are a couple of shots which look tricky.

Creeping up on a herd of walrus marks the third highlight, the antics of the water beasts in bobbing up and down to see what's going on not being without comedy, and the men finally opening up on the herd by rifle. Despite the first salvo and then intermittent fire only one walrus is shown as the result of all the shooting.

Continuity is strung together through Stefanson's command of a Canadian expedition to the north some years ago in which one boat was crushed in the ice and four men were lost. The unraveling of the mystery surrounding these men is the film's explanation and screen excuse.

Footage eventually brings the Snows to Herald Island, where what remains of a camp and human bones are found. A document dated 1924 is cause to believe this film was taken during that year.

Sid Snow and his camera seem to have been fighting the sun or, rather, a lack of it, throughout. Yet on the whole the lens work is good. Shots of Alaska, tremendous ice floes, big Alaskan glacier, some imposing views of the sea kicking up in a gale and various species of animal and birds with young are all included and serve to keep the action moving along. It makes the picture a cinch for the schools, with the bear thing alone good enough for any regular film house. The big theatres can extract an entertaining, moving and highly interesting two or three thousand feet from this subject. More chance of causing plenty of word-of-mouth with a cut but full to the brim version than in this somewhat padded 64 minutes.

Stefanson's opening explanatory monolog of five minutes is brisk and to the point, heralding the valor of all polar explorers.

A Movietone news and magazine, the latter repeating three old newsreel clips, open the "short" program, followed by Clark and McCullough, Kentucky Jubilee Singers, Will Mahoney and Robert Benchley. All this took 52 minutes, including a two-minute natural colored Movietone of a red-headed girl playing a violin, uninteresting despite what technical promise it may hold. It's the weakest selection of shorts Movietone has released in a group. The Clark and McCullough, Mahoney and Benchley subjects are new. *Sid.*

Loves of an Actress

Paramount production and release. Directed by Rowland V. Lee, starring Pola Negri. From story by Ernest Vajda, screen play by Lee and titles by Julien Johnson. Runs 80 minutes at the Paramount, New York, week July 28. This is Par's second sound feature with mechanically synchronized score.

Rachel	Pola Negri
Raoul Duval	Nils Asther
Lisette	Mary McAlister
Baron Hartman	Richard Tucker
Count Vereski	Philip Strange
Dr. Durande	Paul Lukas
Samson	Nigel de Brulier
Count Morency	Robert Fischer
Marie	Helen Giere

An overlong feature, possessed of a good box office title and featuring enough of the flaming French femme's clinch business, "Loves of an Actress" with Pola Negri, is an indifferent picture as a flicker entertainment but a cinch money getter in North America and for the foreign market. With or without the synchronous musical accompaniment, the back-stage stuff dealing with a gutter entertainer suddenly elevated to stardom in the Theatre Francaise has its undeniable box office appeal.

Pola Negri always has been an as-you-like-her star. Even the Negri fans, however, will look askance at the stellar assignment in a role which automatically suggests a Swanson or a Talmadge rather than the severer brunet personality of the Polish star.

The role calls for a certain amount of exoticism which Miss Negri does not quite attain.

The story itself is pretty familiar stuff and coming from the typewriter of a shrewd Continental scrivener like Vajda it is not alone disappointing but surprising in its near banality.

One sees through it like a drunk senses a speakeasy hostess's shallowness, but the manner in which Lee has directed it and offset it with fancy tinsel and the behind-the-scenes' glamor makes it almost acceptable as a general thing.

One knows, of course, that with Rachel's (Negri) general ennui toward masculine attention of the caliber she has been receiving, The Big Love has yet to come into her existence and that she must get That Way by the third reel about some personable vis-a-vis such as Nils Asther, her leading man. In due time, after some strenuous and, at times, hectic onslaughts by an amorous trio, she does get That Way about Raoul—although, truth to tell, hardly with as much conviction as when she was amorously sparring with and stalling the aggressive Count Vareski (Philip Strange turned in a good piece of work in that one scene)—and is kept from a happy if passive ending because one of her benefactors, the newspaper publisher, gets in his dirty work.

One of Julian Johnson's opening captions betokened promisingly in its commentary that this yesteryear idol of Paris, Rachel Something-or-other (the Semitic trimmings throughout cannot help but suggest a reference to the divine Sarah Bernhardt), was the subject of sundry shameless if romantic amours a century ago. Then, with more than a legal amount of deference to the censor boards, Rowland V. Lee produces a considerably denatured continuity which does not definitely establish whether or not Pola went in for the love stuff on the up-and-up, in exchange for the favors which, the titles would have us believe, were instrumental in paving the way to her present histrionic distinction.

The synchronized score, a rather good job on the whole, seems to have been patterned with an eye to universal appeal. The "bravos," with an occasional intermingling of English, should make this recorded score (it's obviously a Victor record process a la Vitaphone, and not Movietoned) appeal to the foreign market as well as locally.

The Continental atmosphere looked authentic and Variety's demon gagster and New Orleans' correspondent, O. M. Samuel, who wrecks homes in N. O. when not globe-trotting, avers the local color is more than Hollywoodishly impressive, pointing to a tiered Theatre Francaise interior, heavy candelabra trimmings and other fine French architecture as proof thereof.

With or without the synchronized score, "Loves of an Actress" will make money. It is not an expensive production and when cut down from 80 minutes to nearer an hour flat it will shape up much better. *Abel.*

BEAU BROADWAY

Metro-Goldwyn-Mayer production and release. Starring Lew Cody and Aileen Pringle, with Sue Carol featured. Directed by Malcolm St. Clair. Original story by F. Hugh Herbert; continuity by George O'Hara. Titles by Ralph Spence. At Capitol, New York, week July 28. Running time, 62 mins.

Jim Lambert	Lew Cody
Yvonne	Aileen Pringle
Killer Gordon	Hugh Trevor
Dejuha	Heinie Conklin
Professor Griswold	Kit Guard
Dr. Monahan	Jack Herrick
Gunner O'Brien	James J. Jefferies

A Cody-Pringle that is all Cody, with Sue Carol added, leaving Aileen Pringle in the outer circle mostly. This proves to be one of the best that Cody has been in for many a moon. It is not expensive, either, and should as a program offering to show unusual returns for a picture presenting this starring combination.

This one might cause the curious to ask why co-star Miss Pringle, when the sweet bimbo from the windy city steals the honors throughout, with folks out front wondering just what Miss Pringle is supposed to do. The Carol girl, who has had a number of good ones, might prove a great running mate for Cody if they were to continue the policy at the studio of presenting stories along this line with the combination. If not, the gal is a great fem lead for any of the male stars. She has that sparkling youth and vivacity that this generation of film fans likes and will encourage at the box office.

Story is that of a fight promoter and gambler (Mr. Cody) showing at the outset he has a heart, though he may be tough with the boys who earn their livelihood in the squared arena. There is an old time pug, Gunner O'Brien (James J. Jeffries) who is putting up his last fight in a camp in the Adirondacks. He goes to visit him and the latter requests that as his time is short on earth he wants the "Chief" to look out for his granddaughter Mona (Miss Carol), whom he does not want to know that he had been a pug.

The old boy passes out. Just before the girl arrives at the home of the chief, the latter calls a wise moll, Vyonne (Miss Pringle), whom he has taken away from one of his stable and makes a date for the evening. He figures that the kid to become his ward is a youngster and has a room fixed up for her that resembles an up-to-date nursery layout. The Kid, a young woman, arrives. He is flabbergasted, turns over his room to her and himself takes possession of the room with its dwarfed furnishings.

Then he turns from a Broadway roue into a home loving daddy. Takes the youngster to church, stops drinking and chasing.

Meantime, the moll, when she finds herself through, begins to squawk and says she will get even.

Along comes the Chief's birthday and he wants to spend it alone with the girl. His pugs and the dame decide to pay a surprise visit. One of the fighters, Killer Gordon (Hugh Trevor), has a yen for the gal and she for him. They dance, spoon, etc., with Cody and Pringle getting in a corner.

A fight manager blows in with a new pug, whom he wants a match for. Cody figures that it is time Gordon gets his and makes the match. He goes alone, with the girl ignorant of what his business is. Pringle hops in and invites her out.

To Madison Square Garden they go, planted in a box and the youngster is surprised to see that the boy friend is a pug. Then comes the bout. Body-to-body blows with the boy friend going down several times for the count and the kid each time shouting to him not to quit. Finally, he accomplishes his job with a k. o. punch.

Party is given the winner. He and the kid dance around. Cody figures that they are to hook and makes a proposal to Yvonne. She says she and Gordon are already engaged. He says no, the boy is going to marry his ward. The girl overhears it. She rushes to her room and turns on the tears. The fighter tells Cody. He goes up to find out why, thinking the boy has turned her cold. She then says no, that it is someone else she loves. Cody asks who and she tells him to open a door; he will see the man. He looks into a mirror.

The Cody-Carol performances are outstanding, with Miss Pringle not measuring up in photography or acting as she usually does. As the blackened up sympathetic servant, Heinie Conklin is perfect. Trevor does not measure up so great as a lothario. As the comedy pugs, Kit Guard and Jack Herrick make much of their situations and get timely laughs. Jim Jeffries is flashed on and off for one scene.

Malcolm St. Clair has done a corking directorial job. Many of his subtle situations are heart throbbers with his comedy touches falling in in good time. Spence had little trouble in titling this one. It lent itself to smart cracks and he probably did not have to dig far to get them.

This one can go anywhere and where Cody has a following, it will be an especially good box office tonic. *Ung.*

AT YALE

Pathe release of DeMille production starring Rod LaRocque. Adapted from play of Owen Davis and directed by E. H. Griffith. No program or screen credit for anybody other than director. At the Strand, New York, week July 28. Running time, 72 minutes.

Jaime Alvarado Montez....Rod La Rocque
Helen........................Jeanette Loff
Professor..................Joseph Cawthorn
Detective....................Tom Kennedy
Valet.........................Jerry Mandy

Rod LaRocque has reached that stage where he needs a pip picture. "At Yale," formerly titled "Hold 'Em Yale," doesn't mean a thing either to the producer or star. Following the broadside of college stuff the past season this release looks a bit foolish. As regards the campus and football it has cut itself a piece of all the theatrical license there is and where it's going to get any b. o. dough is a problem. It projects as light undergraduate stuff for the splits.

One or two flashes of the campus, New Haven, and newsreel shots of the Bowl, comprise the Yale atmosphere after Jaime has migrated from South America to become a college man, and having accidentally met the daughter of one of the faculty. If it weren't for Tom Kennedy, playing a comedy detective, "At Yale" would have nothing to recommend it. Jaime gets mixed up with the dick and Kennedy trails him through the story. Which Owen Davis play this script is based on isn't known. It's better so.

LaRocque does a fresh freshman, gets knocked out by a Harvard heavyweight in the ring and returns for his sophomore year and a fling at football. Meanwhile, Helen has given him air since the Crimson k. o. The night before the Princeton game, Jaime has to go into a cafe to dissuade Helen's brother from marrying a dame and finishes in the hospital as a result of a taxi accident. The game's almost over by the time they find Jaimie and rush him to the Bowl, but the coach puts him in and he runs back a punt for the winning touchdown.

LaRocque is actually doing a mild Haines. Not so fresh and not as good. But he's not a total loss as a light comic. As a matter of fact the star personally does pretty well with what has been handed him. With heavy assistance from Kennedy and a few titles this triumverate manages to explode two or three laughs and a few snickers. However, there's going to be many a spot where there'll be more laughs at than with.

Jeanette Loff looks like Mary Eaton's double everywhere except from the knees down. Her work is 50-50 but she can't stand long shots. Kennedy is excellent and Joseph Cawthorn, formerly of Julia, Donald and Joe, has given up dancing with everybody but his wife to register his conception of a college prof and the girl's father. Light and okay.

For the serious minded on campus and football technique the omissions and commissions here are so glaring as to make the picture ridiculous. Jaime gets plenty of sport page space as Yale's great end and when he finally gets into the game it's at No. 3 in the backfield on the offense and safety on defense. Game flashes are mostly newsreel and the rehearsal plays don't convince. If the studio had wanted to take the trouble, and as long as Jaime was supposed to be an end, it could have inserted the Hoben to Fishwick pass which actually broke up the real game, giving LaRocque the same number Fishwick wore—as M-G-M did with Haines and "Light Horse" Harry Wilson in "West Point."

This is one picture that's bound to play Princeton, N. J. It'd be worth the trip just to hear what the boys would do to it. They may show it in New Haven, too, but there'll probably be no theatre left. All college towns will raise hob with it and the public at large has seen enough screen football and undergraduate life to remain unimpressed by this effort.

"At Yale" is actually a dumb detective chasing a kid he thinks is among those wanted. *Sid.*

Port of Missing Girls

Columbia release of a Brenda Pictures Corp., film featuring Barbara Bedford and Malcolm McGregor. Directed by Irving Cummings. Cast includes Natalie Kingston, Hedda Hopper, Rosemary Theby and Wyndham Standing. At the Hippodrome, New York, week July 30. Running time, 75 minutes.

"Port of Missing Girls" is any large city, and the moral is that when any miss leaves home it's the fault of the parents. Add to that a young bootlegger who takes advantage of the district attorney's daughter and then finally leads the cops to the dastardly but wealthy theatrical manager's office for the rescue, and that's this feature in a much-padded nutshell. Summation is that the smaller the town the better they'll like "Port." It has the usual inconsistencies and surplus footage to give it that rating.

Picture carries a cast as long as your No. 1 iron with a moderately imposing array of fairly known names. Most do bits, with a character named Ann the best looking gal in the troupe. Otherwise Miss Bedford has sufficient presence to make her erring Ruth stand up, although she goes from school books to young womanhood rather abruptly. Hedda Hopper contributes her usual good-looking young mother role, but Malcolm McGregor has a tough time being a hero after doing wrong by Ruth.

Irving Cummings, the director, has made his principal mistake in not drastically cutting this screen opera. It currently unwinds as if every inch of film shot is still there. Around 1,500 feet could be chopped. He has tried symbolizing quite frequently, with more or less success, but the story hardly convinces at any time.

At that point where the liquor deliverer informs the distrait parent he knows where his daughter is and confesses his relationship, the Hip audience found cause to snicker.

It's not far away from a sex educational toned down. Productionally there are some solid looking interiors, and the photography is average. The script's best point is that it may help tip off to a believing public the instability of sending its daughters to unrecognized dancing and acting schools. But why the studio should make the femme chaser a theatrical manager is just one of those things. The theatre has enough social troubles without the studios adding these unnecessary incentives to an eager imagination. Maybe the talkers will bring these two closer together — or farther apart.

One report is that this picture has been sold on a states right basis in four or five states, with Columbia handling the rest of the territory. It will never receive consideration from the big houses, but those changing twice weekly and more can look it over. Where the young 'uns yearn for the big town and expensive parties this one is apt to catch lukewarm approval. *Sid.*

The Bear's Wedding

(RUSSIAN MADE)

Produced by Sovkino (Soviet Russia) and released through Amkino (same). Directed by K. V. Eggert, also starred. Vera Malanovskaya featured. At Fifth Ave. Playhouse week beginning July 28. Running time, 70 minutes.

Admittedly a legend, but ballyhooed as a warning of the horrors of adverse pre-natal influence, "The Bear's Wedding" is a bear with the cat's wail describing one of the bummest bits of film junk shoved on these shores.

Je:ty, it is horrible only from the standpoint of its meaninglessness. If this were intended to carry a lesson to prospective American mothers, it would be better for the reaction were the advertising efforts stressed toward drawing in the great American crossword puzzle strugglers.

There are a couple of shots that are crude and one that is crass enough to be repugnant. The rest is a lot of blah which, in its attempt to be highly dramatic, gets laughter from the audience in the sure-seat theatre—incidentally the only place where it has a chance of getting by. Then they will okay it on demerit.

The shot that does win a few blasts, even from among the would-be sophisticates, is where the son of the bear-bitten mother nearly bites off the breast of his bride on their wedding night.

So sincere is the director-star, whose part calls for him to do the masticating, that he shows a close-up of the nipped wife. Not satisfied with one, it is flashed back several times. How this shot got by the censors is open for conjecture. Possibly the veil pulled over the gnawed part had something to do with it.

Tunney-Heeney Fight

Special Independent. Official picture of the Gene Tunney-Tom Heeney world's heavyweight championship boxing bout held at Yankee Stadium July 26 under auspices of George L. "Tex" Rickard. Presented and made by the Gold-Hawk Pictures Corp.; at the Eltinge, New York, starting July 27, $1 top. Running time, 31 minutes.

Great chance for the Gold-Hawk people to have ensured the popularity of the Tunney-Heeney fight picture if they could have made it as a talker. Had the cheers of the crowd and the comment at ringside been recorded it would have placed on record and canned the authoritative atmosphere of a world's prizefight championship for the first time. An idea of what could have been done in that directiontion was Paramount's release "Warming Up," with the chatter confined to baseball rooters. The sound accompaniment in that case was made after the picture but it supplied a most interesting element.

As it is the Tunney-Heeney fight picture is just fair. Its makers probably depended on the public's interest in an orthodox pictorial report of the event or some unexpected development. The gate at the Eltinge is 50c and $1. Business the first day of grinding grossed $1,800 and the next two days only got as much more, for a three-day gross of $3,600. Not so hot for a grind from noon to 11 p. m. right on top of the fight.

Photography okay considering the fight was shot at a distance on the usual raised platform, with half a dozen machines grinding. It is believed the vibration of the platform caused a flicker and that is the reason given for showing the entire picture in 31 minutes Monday night. At that time a light crowd was in the house. The program was filled out by short "Screen Snap Shots," making the show's total running time about 45 minutes.

Had the picture run normally the 11 rounds it would have consumed 33 minutes alone, with titles, slow motion and introductions not counted. It was stated the film was speeded to eliminate a flicker and it looked as though each reel was run in about 10 minutes. The result of speeding robbed the picture of any kick it has.

The slow motion portion not particularly effective. Heeney is shown being knocked cold and saved by the bell in the 10th round. The knock-down punch came from Tunney striking Heeney on the chin. The eighth round should have been shown in slow motion. It was then that Tunney closed Heeney's left eye with a right sock. Tom held his hand to the damaged optic not shown in the picture. Champion Tunney withheld further punishment to the eye although he could have done so. Gene was given much credit for his sportsmanship in so acting.

It is assumed the makers of the picture didn't care to favor the champ. That may bear out the report that Tunney objected to the same people making the picture as in Chicago. Gene claimed they doctored the 7th round out there and put him in a bad light. However, the same bunch formed another corporation and got the film rights anyway.

By speeding the film Heeney is not shown to be as wozzy as he really was when the referee stopped the battle eight seconds before the end of the 11th. One thing is noticeable and that is Tunney's backing away from the burly New Zealander, but at the same time it does indicate the speed of the champ's footwork. There is also shown the superiority of Tunney's boxing.

The Tunney-Heeney film is just a fight picture. Any trace of excitement that inspired those in the ball park or might have been dished up to the radio listeners-in, failed to be caught by the cameras.

If Tunney made a bid for popularity by showing himself to be a knocker-out, that should be reflected in attendance at the Eltinge where the picture started showing the day after the match. They stayed away from the fight and Rickard lost a bundle. Likewise there is no rush to see the picture. That may be blamed partly at least on the picture itself. There is a repeat at the finish of a late round, showing the men walking to their corners twice. No reason for that in the third day of showing, nor a misspelled word in a caption. *Ibee.*

LIGHTS OF PARIS

(FRENCH MADE?)

Superlative Pictures production; made and released abroad by ABA Corporation (in America by Hi Mark Productions). Adapted from a story by H. B. Wright. Other data including director not caught on slide—if given. Doris Costello featured on billing. Among others in cast, Henry Krauss, Dolly Davies, Robert Coleman, Jack Denton, Rudolph Maron. At Stanley, New York, one day, July 30. Running time about 65 minutes.

Taking a chance to call this a French made although made abroad. Names of cast indicate nothing French about it excepting locale, Paris, and an attempt to impersonate French people. It's a cheaply made picture for this side in this day. Its cabaret and theatre scenes may have given it some weight on the other side. But for the nite life-back stage circles of theatres over here in the one day or double bill class, this should do, for the rental is probably light or should be. Now in the summer time was the time to get this out and the summer time will excuse its playing even in a little better grade of houses.

Nothing of marked merit in the entire picture. A couple of raw bits are set forth, one especially of a Lesbian scene, but so well disguised evidently it got past the New York censors which may be to their honor for innocence or just because they weren't watching at that moment. The other is a woman stepping into her bathing pool, back to the audience, but at that as a protection perhaps for the same censors, she looked to have on trunks. In any event, not important.

Very few in the picture houses this film will play can or will get the Lesbian bit, and just as well. Between the heavy and the other woman, the heroine ran out of the nite club, through the rain, bareheaded, back to mother. She had quit mother and home to go on the stage. After the first night's performance she was cured. Just because those two persons leered at her when all were drinking wine.

Nothing in direction. Something tried for in the thrill way in a scaffold scene, with the hero hanging by his finger tips, finally falling. Self exposer and flat.

Nor anything in the playing, other than Henry Krauss as the heavy. Photography very poor at times and never good. Doris Costello fa': looker and not sylph-like. Some of the extra girls looked better.

A portion of this picture suggests that if the European native homes, people and customs were shown over here, they might be acceptable for interest, if nothing else, much as the Americans first attracted attention abroad.

"Lights of Paris" might be played for a day or so against "The Lights of New York," the Warner talker, during the remainder of the summer, just to get the backwash of the similar titles. Might advertise "See New York first; then come over to Paris."

"Lights of Paris" played one day (July 30) at the Stanley, New York, 25c grind.

LIFE'S MOCKERY

Chadwick production and release. Directed by Robert F. Hill from story credited to I. Bernstein. Betty Compson starred. In cast: Theodore Von Eltz, Alec B. Francis, Dorothy Cummings, Russell Simpson. At Loew's New York, one day, July 25, one half double bill. Running time about 60 minutes.

Whether crime is a matter of heredity or environment is the heavy subject Chadwick handles in a generally entertaining but light and somewhat slow way in "Life's Mockery."

The case of extremes prevails to the point of being ludicrous with an understanding audience.

The old gang leader, with the gun, and a hammer for cats is too emotional in being unable to stand up while a thorn is being withdrawn from a rabbit's foot at the end when he turns farmer.

His girl forgets slang to back up the old judge who conducted the experiment with this tribe just to show that crime is due to environment.

SKIRTS

(BRITISH MADE)

British International production, distributed in the U. S. by Metro-Goldwyn-Mayer. Directed by Wheeler Dryden and Jesse Robbins. Adapted by Dryden from the show or story "A Little Bit of Fluff" by Walter W. Ellis. Sydney Chaplin starred, with Betty Balfour in support. American titles by Ralph Spence. Running time 57 minutes. At Loew's American, New York, July 26-29.

A slapstick farce, written and played with a good deal of ingenuity in trick and device and limitless resource in knockabout gags. It falls down because nobody has yet been able to sustain stuffed club comedy for a full hour.

That's all this picture has. They build up and exploit such things as kicking a lady from the rear, subjecting a respectable man to the embarrassment of having his pants slip down when he's out in company, and for one long elaborate, but lamentable episode knocking all the ladies and gentlemen cuckoo with an Indian club.

Chaplin is an especially heavy handed comedian and in a story like this, built on bludgeoning out its laughs, his technique is rather overpowering. Between story and cast the auditor gets to feel that he is being bullied into merriment.

Picture is full of such hoke as a poisonous mother-in-law who browbeats young bride and groom; young husband who goes off on a spree and gets tangled up with night club girls; friend who impersonates a burglar to carry out a plot and then gets confused with a real burglar. Whole business is a medley of timeworn hoke, made a bit better by its headlong playing and fast pace. Picture has almost no element of surprise. They seem to go out deliberately to tip off each development ahead of time, so they'll be sure the dumbbells will understand.

Picture is beautifully made as to its technical production. Some of the night club scenes are fine bits of film stage management. Backgrounds are engaging always and the photography is of the best modern quality, as good as the best Hollywood.

Farce so grossly overdone that it limits its appeal almost to the feeble minded. On the American Roof they walked out on it the minute the announcer gave the news Thursday night that Heeney had lost on a technical knockout. The film still had six minutes to run. And the American crowd always receives rough comedy with great gusto.

M-G-M distributing this English made over here may have thought to help the subject matter by inserting Ralph Spence titles. Nothing could help or save it from what it was intended for and what it is—an overdose of hoke. *Rush.*

LILAC TIME

(SOUND)

First National production and release. Produced by John McCormick, directed by George Fitzmaurice. Colleen Moore starred with Gary Cooper featured. Scenario by Carey Wilson from adaptation by Willis Goldbeck of the stage play, same title, by Jane Cowl and Jane Murfin. Titles by George Marion, Jr. Photography by Sidney Hickok; aerial photography by Alvin Knechtel. Film editor, Al Hall; art director, Horace Jackson; asst. director, Cullen R. Tate. Additional credits through picture's subject matter—Research by Cullen Tate; technical flight commander, Lieut. Richard Grace, Royal Flying Corps; technical expert, Capt. L. J. S. Scott. French military expert, Capt. Robert de Couedic (26th Blue Devils). Ordinance expert, Harry Redmond. At Central, New York, on $2 run, opening Aug. 3. Running time, 100 minutes.

Jeannine Berthelot..........Colleen Moore
Captain Philip Blythe........Gary Cooper
General Blythe..............Burr McIntosh
Mechanic's Helper.........George Cooper
Captain Russell..............Cleve Moore
Lady Iris Rankin........Kathryn McGuire
Madame Berthelot........Eugenie Besserer
Burgomaster of Berle Les Bois,
Emile Chautard
The Infant.....................Jack Stone
Mike, Mechanic.............Edward Dillon
Aviator........................Dick Grace
Aviator.......................Stuart Knox
Aviator......................Harlan Hilton
Aviator.....................Richard Jarvis
Aviator......................Jack Ponder
Aviator.......................Dan Dowling

"Lilac Time" is sure fire for the regular houses, and even the pop price run houses before them, the latter if with sound. If with sound at the Central this latest First National special might have more closely resembled $2 than it did. Prepared sound effects were absent and manufactured effects employed instead.

As an admixture of war, planes and romance, "Lilac Time" has several sound moments. The manufactured back stage effects essayed the best of them, explosions as airplanes crashed to the ground. The back stage effect was obtained by a heavy explosion, such as is used in stage plays to denote a lightning bolt. Though the bombing noise at the Central was terrific, it's probably not the effect the same explosion would give in the prepared recorder, which must or should be tremendous. It's the sort of an unexpected detonation that at the first hearing might bring the auditor out of his seat.

Effects for the whirring engines of the flock of planes could not be obtained without the record. Latter not present through union or other labor troubles. A vocal trio or quartet did brief singing of the theme song, in person.

The manufactured effects suggest the possibilities of this First National, which in story (from play) has elements recalling "Wings" in the air and "Seventh Heaven" in the closing scenes of the romantic portion. The romance is laid on thick, at times too thick. There is plenty of slack to take up to cut down this picture for the picture house time.

At the Central it ran in two sections, 60 minutes in the first and 40 in the second. The first period had no battle air work and that left much expectancy. It built up nicely and the air forces went into action at the opening of the second part. This held up the second section that commenced to slide with its heavy loving.

Worked into the air battle is the Red Ace of Germany, a famous flier of the war. He is shown in his machine, brightly red. He gets Capt. Blythe, who falls badly hurt, but a later scene shows the Red Ace also down within the French lines, seemingly gotten in turn by Blythe.

This picture will be liked in England. It has for the Allies portion the boys of the British Royal Flying Corps and the picture advances them as a dandy set of fellows. There are a few heart tugs here as the fliers are ordered out at dawn and told by their commander not to come back while an enemy plane remains aloft. They solemnly take a farewell drink with one another, each of the seven breaking his glass and placing it with the row of others on a shelf, every broken glass telling of a life gone in the service. None expected to return. Two did.

It's a picture that while giving unmeasured opportunity for Colleen Moore, and in which she never misses on the light or heavy side, nevertheless throws too much work on the girl.

While her tribulations or those of the fliers and her Captain lover never raise a lump, they are enough to send Miss Moore over with as big a bang as any sound the recorder for this picture will bring out. For Miss Moore, it's a great picture.

Some slight comedy is handled in the early part, when Miss Moore particularly is kicked in the rear by the flying captain as he lands, he believing her to be a boy. But the only real laughs are those of the George Marion, Jr., captions. Here Mr. Marion got a chance to prove his range as a writer. He had to give Miss Moore as the French girl an English accent and make it funny. Marion did.

Gary Cooper readily fell into the role as the flying captain who also fell for Jeannie. His physical build helped him to naturally look the part. Other roles minor but mostly manly, since there are but three women in the cast. George Cooper got a laugh or two with mugging, as did Edward Dillon, and Dan Dowling played the youngest flier, full of thought for the girl back home, very well.

Air battles and machine guns, with destruction of a town through dropping shells much as have been previously done, and still as effective as ever. If eternal peace ever does come to the universe, moving pictures may well be given the credit. War pictures should never grow old for that reason alone. For every one is another reason against war.

First National had the misfortune of opening "Lilac Time" on the hottest night New York had known for almost 50 years. Central is not a cooled house.

As a film production the special looks quite expensive.

While a certainty without sound, insertion of sound may make it a bigger picture. Another review should be asked of the dailies by F. N. when it is properly sounded.

A short, preceding the feature, was of the opening of "Lilac Time" at the Carthay Circle, Los Angeles. It included all of the celebs of the film industry on the Coast, execs as well as talent. The short (silent) is good enough to send out for regular showing at a price.

"Lilac Time" derives its title from the Lilac Farm, where the fliers were billeted, with Jeannie, the daughter of the household, providing them with food and lodging.

The picture's theme song, "Jeannie, I Dream of Lilac Time," is catchy. It was written by L. Wolfe Gilbert (lyric) and Nathaniel Shilkret (music).

POWDER MY BACK

Warner Bros. production directed by Roy Del Ruth. Based on story by Jerome Kingston, adapted by Joseph Jackson from the screen play by Robert Lord. Starring Irene Rich, with cast including Audrey Ferris, Andre Beranger, Anders Randolph and Carroll Nye. At Keith's Hippodrome, New York, week Aug. 6. Running time over 60 minutes.

Picture serves here but does not display any of the usual box office pulling characteristics. Story is too well known to arouse interest while the slight love element involves two elderly people, neither particularly attractive, too old to appeal for audience sympathy.

Tells of the actress in a risque musical who is stopped in the middle of her performance by the town reform candidate for mayor who denounces women of her type and that kind of entertainment. The girl determines to frame the politician and gets into his home after pretending to be seriously injured in an auto accident.

The candidate's son falls for the actress, as an additional complication, but she sends him back to his girl and marries the old boy instead. *Mori.*

WHITE SHADOWS

(In the South Seas)
(SOUND)

Metro-Goldwyn-Mayer release of Cosmopolitan production with synchronized score based on Frederick O'Brien's book. Features Monte Blue and Raquel Torres. Robert Anderson only other studio player in cast. Directed by W. S. Van Dyke with photography by Clyde De Vinna, George Nogle and Bob Roberts. John Colton titled, Ray Doyle adapted, and Jack Cunningham, continuity. Edited by Ben Lewis. At Astor, New York, on twice daily run, starting July 31. Running time, 86 mins.

Glorifying the South Seas by some superb camera work and with a story strong enough to send this picture into the program houses to get money. Demonstrating that the white man can and has physically and morally undermined the native tribes in this sector, "White Shadows" carries an early punch by its insight on the dangers of pearl diving, more than sufficient to hold attention in the hopes that possibly another kick will be forthcoming. That the looked for wallop doesn't put in an appearance is what will keep the picture from being a smash and a profitable $2 proposition for key centers.

Story surrounds a drink demoralized white doctor (Monte Blue) who defends the natives against the greedy store keeper, Sebastian, until the latter finally frames to get the disturbing physician out of the way. Lashed to the steering wheel of a boat rampant with plague, a typhoon finally releases the white man as the ship breaks to pieces, and he is washed ashore. Finding a native and virgin tribe, Lloyd, the doctor, is treated as a white god, and is about to wed the chief's daughter when Sebastian and his boatload of thugs drop anchor off shore. Lloyd pleads with the natives to send the boat away, but their curiosity is too strong. While Lloyd is fighting Sebastian one of the boat crew shoots the doctor. Finish has Lloyd dead, Fayaway (Raquel Torres) in cotton homespun and Sebastian having set up a trading store to gyp the innocent tribe with liquor, tobacco and ridiculous trades for what the natives call "oyster beads."

All three principals, Blue; Miss Torres and Anderson, have turned in legitimate performances with Van Dyke, directing, weaving a closely knit story. Against the background of native customs and scenery the story unfolds logically with side light situations lending color to the subject. At one point Lloyd successfully struggles to save the young son of the chief, who has apparently drowned and at another starts to collect pearls with the ultimate intention of hailing a ship and returning to civilization to enjoy his wealth, the natives discarding the pearls as worthless, but keeping the shells from which they make fish hooks. The first which Lloyd lights atop a hill at night, in the midst of his material hysteria, is the beacon which attracts Sebastian, cruising in the vicinity.

Picture starts off with a rush, delving into under water stuff as a giant clam closes on the foot of a pearl diver, another whose lungs collapse and showing the physical torture of these men as they came to the surface and blood vessels burst with the sudden change from the terrific pressure. Little doubt that the first 25 minutes are vibrant with interest, after which the film settles down to story and its photography.

The panchromatic work in this feature is outstanding. It's so good it very likely makes these Marquesas Islands look better than they really are. And neither is Miss Torres hard on the eyes.

Picture is synchronized and evidently on a disk as the screen image is normal. A weak theme song will never mean anything to the feature and some of the effects seem out of place. Notably, the moaning of the father of a drowned pearl diver This is repeated when the chief's son is endangered. A native banquet and its attendant dances have also been given the effects of pounding drums and clapping hands. The storm which releases Lloyd from the ship is tank and slow motion grinding.

For those who liked "Nanook," "Moana," "Chang," etc., "White Shadows" is sure. For regular picture house audiences its opening wallop and the consistently high grade photography, plus the native customs, figure to make it a worth while transgression from the stereotyped clinch finish. Picture is at the Astor, but would be better suited to the Embassy, a smaller house, and at a $1.50 scale. It may have its $2 troubles.

Ahead of the main feature is being shown 32 minutes of Movietone shorts, including Movietone newsreel, Chic Sale, Miller and Farrell and Richard Bonelli. No intermission.

At the end of the opening week the New York Hearst papers were splurging six-column ads for this Hearst's Cosmopolitan production. *Sid.*

THE PERFECT CRIME

(DIALOG)

FBO production and release. Dialog and musical synchronization by R. C. A. Photophone. Adapted by William LeBaron from the Israel Zangwill story, "The Big Bow Mystery." Directed by Bert Glennon. Clive Brook and Irene Rich featured. At U. A. (Publix) Rivoli, New York, on run, $1 top, starting Aug. 4. Running time, inclusive of dialog, prolog and epilog, 83 minutes. Without prolog and epilog, around 70 minutes. As silent picture, neither prolog nor epilog would or could be used. Neither is required.

Benson	Clive Brook
Stella	Irene Rich
Mrs. Frisbie	Ethel Wales
Trevor	Carroll Nye
Mrs. Trevor	Gladys McConnell
Wilmot	Edmund Breese
Jones	James Farley
Butler	Phil Gastrock
Frisbie	Tully Marshall
Trevor Baby	Jane LaVerne

FBO has turned out in "The Perfect Crime" the first talking dialog picture produced to be easily denuded of its dialog and still stand up as a silent feature. That is because of the film's formation and that the story is a strong interesting one of a detective, the police and crime without the atmosphere of the underworld in or surrounding it.

That the picture was first made as a silent and later sounded and dialoged accounts for this particular case.

It's the story here. Though this is a R. C. A. synchronized recorded picture of sound and dialog, the imperfection of the disc dialog (if that) are overlooked by the audience's tenseness secured by the tale. As a dialog picture this should do business in the wired houses, to rank with novelty and draw almost with the other dialog talkers now out, and as a silent feature it can play the first runs through its unusual trend.

Minus a few and badly sounded noises, such as a phone or door bell and storm, the big dialog punch here is in a court trial. A young man is on trial for murder. The district attorney questions him, in dialog, and he answers likewise; also the widow of the murdered man, while the wife of the accused breaks forth in exclamations, and the judge is heard starting his summation, while the foreman of the jury verbally pronounces the verdict as guilty of murder in the first degree.

Even the baby of the accused man, holding a doll (in the court room), said in dialog to her mother:

"Why doesn't papa look at my dolly?"

The baby wasn't any worse than the mother, however, in voice.

But the trial scene did not come as a surprise, and lost its punch through dialog having been used in the prolog. The picture carries two title slides, the first announcing the R. C. A. Photophone synchronization and the prolog, while the second is of the usual opening slide announcement, with the data following on other slides. That leaves "The Perfect Crime" susceptible of having the prolog cut off, going directly into the subject matter as a silent picture. The same with the epilog, with the climax of the picture proper becoming an anti-climax now because of the talking epilog.

It's like, for the best illustration, a regular feature with a talking sequence of a foreign nature at either end, leaving the body between of the regular picture entirely complete.

The prolog here, joined with the epilog, and with little cutting could almost be sent out as a comedy talking short. It's of newlyweds in their apartment listening to the radio (playing) and the wife in the next room, when the husband answers the phone. He carries on a conversation with Dolly, whom he had met the night before. She had given him her address, 221 Riverside drive. He told her he had memorized the address, tearing up her slip, and he would be right over.

The wife walks in on the phone talk. She has found the slip in his pocket and is wise to the phone. He stalls by saying Dolly is a horse and it's a tip, with the 221 meaning the odds are 2-2-1. Squaring this by singing a theme song, the radio is abruptly broken off and announcements are made. One is to the effect that the breakage in the program is due to Dr. Benson having solved the Foy murder mystery, with accompanying shots of the night extras. A police inspector then speaks through the mike (all seen and heard on the screen), stating that Dr. Benson will talk on "The Perfect Crime," with Dr. Benson disbelieving there is such a thing. The picture has a plug throughout for "You Can't Win" for the crooks, and makes it even stronger at the finale.

As the fadeout arrives for the prolog, with "The Perfect Crime" picture starting, Dr. Benson has handed in his resignation to the chief of police. The chief and his staff are in a quandary. Dr. Benson has unraveled so many mysterious crimes they are in fear of losing him, and also want it believed they can detect without Benson, a somewhat Sherlock Holmes for this picture, with Clive Brook making up as nearly as he could for the Conan Doyle myth.

Benson, who lost his fiancee when he refused to forsake the detective work, is in his study as the chief arrives to persuade him to reconsider his resignation. The Dr. refuses. An aid of the chief mentions there never has been a perfect crime, meaning guaranteed against detection, with the officer adding if there could be, Dr. Benson might commit it.

Later, as the Dr. said in one of these extremely well-worded captions, he was a madman at the time, brooding over the loss of his love. That perfect crime remark stuck with him.

Across the street lived the Frisbies, tenants of Benson's. A hard-working, bullying husband, Frisbie, while suffering with a toothache, struck his wife when she asked him for the rent. He gave her some money and she went over to the doctor's, carrying a black eye, to pay him on account. Benson commiserated with her. She said her husband would be over in the evening with the remainder.

When Frisbie arrived he paid the rent and spoke of his toothache seeing a bottle of booze on the table. The Dr. invited him to have a drink, then told Frisbie he would ease the ache. Giving him some pills, the Dr. instructed Frisbie to go to his single room, take two pills when entering the house and another pair just before going to bed, to lock his door and close all windows, and he would be all right when his wife called him at five in the morning.

At five in the morning the wife couldn't arouse Frisbie nor could she open the door. Returning to the doctor's, who was still walking about his study, she told him of her fears. He accompanied her across the street, first taking a razor out of his drawer. Breaking in the door, the doctor entered, with the wife remaining in the hall. When he came out, the Dr. informed the wife her husband had cut his throat.

The Frisbie murder became a local mystery. Police, puzzled, finally fastened the crime upon a young man. There is a suggestion the cops framed, but it's subtle. That leads to the courtroom scene and conviction.

While awaiting execution, the condemned man's wife concludes to see Dr. Benson as the only possible person who could solve the Frisbie murder. By this time Benson's love, Stella, had appeared. He promises her never to go detective again, and their engagement is renewed.

As the wife is appealing to Benson to aid her, Stella hears it and Benson's refusal. She assures the wife Benson will untangle the murder and free her husband, Stella making the request of Benson that he do so.

Benson calls for the police chief, confesses to him and the young man is freed, he and his wife calling at the Benson home to thank the doctor and Stella. The doctor had been given a 30-minute respite to report at headquarters, the chief refusing to handcuff or place him under arrest, a nice touch.

Here the picture goes into a dissolve of the doctor again at his desk, reading a book on murder, with the solution of whether a dream or vision left to the auditor, and the doctor saying:

"I must go to see Stella tomorrow."

Following is the epilog, the same couple as in the prolog, commenting upon the radio lecture, to a clinch finish.

A certain suspense is upheld continuously; Dr. Benson does not create feeling against himself by the presumed murder, since Frisbie can obtain no sympathy as a wife beater. Its peculiar angles, neatly worked out and up, are holding, and the story becomes superior to the talker as a novelty or otherwise, though without the additional draw dialog at present must give.

Bert Glennon deserves unlimited credit for his handling of the direction. He and William LeBaron, the FBO production head and who adapted the scenario from Zangwill's "Big Bow Mystery," can go 50-50 on putting this one over. While the title writer must again be mentioned for judgment and phrasing, straightaway.

Sterling actors, nearly all, and played their roles. No outstander.

The judge spoke well, as did the district attorney, and Trevor, the young man convicted (Carroll Nye) also has a talker voice. Neither of the leads spoke. Their sides were told in the captions. Nor did anyone of the main principals, excepting Mrs. Frisbie, talk. The young woman of the prolog was no better than the other women, vocally, while Lynn Overman, the light comedian of the prolog, had the same disadvantage as the others on this sounder, that the voice did not come out of his mouth. It sounded throughout, except in rare instances, like any other disc record. In the prolog there was a whirr, while lisps were often evident.

The court scene could be reduced to silence with brief eliminations and without harming its value. Or even captions might cover that entire proceeding that perhaps ran for four minutes.

As a synchronized picture FBO has shown the trade something in this one. It's also a pioneer, in so far as doubling a talker with a silent, and able to separate without a retake in the making, and without leaving doubt with the exhib if a talker, silent, would be the same story in continuity and action. "The Perfect Crime" is.

MYSTERIOUS LADY

Metro-Goldwyn-Mayer production and release. Starring Greta Garbo and featuring Conrad Nagel. Based on Ludwig Wolff's novel, "War in the Dark." Directed by Fred Niblo. Treatment by Bess Meredyth with Wm. Daniels cameraman. At Capitol, New York, week Aug. 4. Running time, 83 minutes.

Tania	Greta Garbo
Karl	Conrad Nagel
General Alexandroff	Gustav von Seyffertitz
Col. Von Raden	Edward Connelly
General's Aide	Richard Alexander

Secret service story involving a Russian feminine spy and an Austrian officer which demands all the drawing power of the Garbo name and whatever impetus that of Nagel can add. Just average program stuff and wide open to heavy cutting.

Using up 83 minutes to unload this yarn is ridiculous. Most of the padding is in the first 2,500 feet. After that it becomes a matter of the number of closeups desired. Reducing the close shots of the principal pair and the early superfluous script footage would have left room for Stan Laurel. The house should have taken care of that.

Productionally this is very nice. Court balls, hundreds of uniforms, big interiors and beneath the surface much intrigue. Tania has engineered her way into the heart of Karl but he turns on her when his uncle says she's a spy.

For that Tania grabs some Austrian plans and Karl is court martialed and stripped of his uniform, much like "The Tempest."

The secret service unc extracts him from prison so he can trail Tania to Warsaw. Posing as a musician, Karl finally finds his former sweetheart who gives evidence that he's still aces with her by returning the plans a fellow Austrian officer has slipped Gen. Alexandroff (Von Seyffertitz), in pursuit of Tania for years. The general becomes so wise that Tania shoots him. At the dramatic high point she fools the Russian military and gets across the border with Karl by auto. Final presumption is that the couple will be at home in Vienna.

Inasmuch as the opening title includes that familiar phrase, "Vienna before the war," little else need be said. Miss Garbo, personally, has done and is capable of better work. Niblo in directing has seen fit to send her scampering through a woods on a spring afternoon closely pursued by her lover. That's one trouble with the picture. It's all very tried and if true just as tiresome. Allowing that other theatres will cut it, and plenty, "The Mysterious Lady" shapes as a moderate feature for the simple minded femmes. Miss Garbo rates and needs story material with more punch. Whatever kick this one held in print, Niblo has diluted with excess footage. It may develop matinee appeal.

Nagel has had his hair waved for the event and gives a capable if quiet performance. Von Seyffertitz does his customary heavy.

Other cast members do not figure importantly. *Sid.*

FORGOTTEN FACES

Paramount production and release. Supervised by David O. Selznick. Directed by Victor Schertzinger. Featuring Clive Brook, Mary Brian, William Powell and Baclanova. From story by Richard Washburn Child. Adaptation by Oliver H. P. Garrett. Scenario by Howard Estabrook. Titles by Julian Johnson. Runs 75 mins. At Paramount, New York. Week Aug. 4.

THE CAST

"Heliotrope Harry" Harlow	Clive Brook
Alice Dean	Mary Brian
Lilly Harlow	Baclanova
"Froggy"	William Powell
No. 1309	Fred Kohler
Tom	Jack Luden

Latest underworld opus to be released by Paramount, goes back to the "Raffles" characterization and has Clive Brook in impeccable evening attire throughout, except for a brief sequence in which Brook as "Heliotrope Harry" Harlow, is in the brig and of course in prison uniform.

Oliver H. P. Garrett who did the adaptation, Howard Estabrook who wrote the scenario and Julian Johnson who titled, managed to make a fairly interesting picture out of a top heavy yarn.

At times Johnson was called upon to alibi those lapses and to dispose of beau coupe footage with his titles, in a manner that would have taxed the ingenuity of a night club lawyer. He hurdled all of the obstacles and saved the opus from banality on several occasions.

The story concerns the father love of Heliotrope Harry, who returns from sticking up a gambling house to find his wife is making cheatie with a wicked looking gent. Harry after fondling his squalling infant left in her crib by his big hearted rib, opens her boudoir door and a puff of smoke rising from below the focus of the shot, informs the peasants that Harry has rubbed out his opposition.

The pair had counted upon privacy, as the wife had thoughtfully notified the coppers just what minute Harry and his pal, Froggy (William Powell) were going to frisk the gambling joint. By getting out a few minutes ahead of schedule, the men had missed the police.

Incidentally the stick up was accomplished without the aid of masks, tear gas or other impedimenta. Just a good old fashioned shake by a couple of hustlers who weren't worrying about their liberty.

After plugging his unseen rival Harry takes the kid and via Johnson's titles tells his frau that if she ever lays her filthy hands on the youngster again she will be given her celestial ukelele and an eternal trip on the rumble seat of some cloud.

Harry and Froggy pick out a nice home on the set and after planting the child on the doorstep, step behind some trees to watch. The bell is answered by two of Hollywood's kindliest mother and father types, and we're hep immediately that it's going to be pretty soft for the kid.

To digress a moment. It has been "established," thanks to Mr. Johnson, that Harry's nickname comes from his addiction to heliotrope in any form from perfume to flowers. The baby has a sprig of it in her hands, when she's fondled. Don't forget that, children. It's important.

Harry evidently calculates his wife will lose no time in notifying the gendarmes of his marksmanship, for he elicits a promise from Froggy that he will go straight and watch over the kid. Picking out a copper who has a wife and kids and needs promotion badly, Harry gives himself up, and we find him next doing life, or doing it all as the boys in stir colorfully peg it.

A clever bit of direction is used here to duck the ordinary time lapse. Brook is shown looking at pictures of his daughter. He is out of the shot after she is shown as an infant. The camera is focused over his shoulder and as the pictures, sent him by Froggy, shows her development into girlhood, a la Mary Brian, we see the father again with gray hair and the marks of his sentence showing plainly in his face.

The girl's mother has been seeking her all these years but hasn't been able to locate her, thanks to Froggy. She hasn't regenerated any and her motives are selfish.

Meanwhile the daughter has become engaged to a young society chap and preparations are being made for the wedding.

Froggy has the clipping from the newspapers with pictures of the couple, etc. The mother frames a phoney accident in front of Froggy's rooms and is carried in by confederates, supposedly dying. She tells Froggy her dying wish is to see her baby. Will he tell her where she is? He won't. One of the confederates then speaks a title about showing her a picture of the girl. "It might help her." Froggy hands him the clipping. Don't you love that?

From then on things happen. The mother visits the jail and taunts Harry with her knowledge of the girl's whereabouts. He goes berserk and is dragged to his cell. He pleads with the head screw to spring him but no chance. Another convict is reported missing. Harry manages to mangle his hand and is carried to the hospital where the other con finally keeps a rendezvous with a trusty in on the crush. Harry is to escape with him. They tie up the trusty, who is in on the frame.

The warden enters as No. 1309 is about to screw via window. They tie him up, but with 1309 out of ear shot the warden reminds Harry he gave him his word of honor he wouldn't try and escape, when he made him a trusty. Harry relents and is untying him when 1309 discovers the cross and tries to knife both of them.

After considerable whoopee the guards arrive. Harry is paroled, but has to give the warden his word he won't croak his wife. Inspired by a passage in the Bible, Harry decides to outwit her and punish her that way. He gets into his daughter's home as the butler, by framing the real butler and frightening him out of town. Then he lays a trail of heliotrope for the wife and frightens her out of several attempts to meet the girl. He intercepts letters written to himself under her foster father's name, plants sprigs of the plant where she'll find them and finally sends her an automatic with a sprig of heliotrope in the box.

On her last attempt to see the girl, he admits her in his character of the butler and leads her to the top of the house. She follows him into a darkened room and he lights up his face with a flashlight. She shoots him.

Froggy darts out from somewhere and is about to give chase when the title, "Let her go! I've arranged everything. The fake cop. The window—the ladder." And if you think he hadn't you're crazy.

The fake copper starts up stairs as she sees the open window with a ladder conveniently placed. She darts to the window, starts to descend and the ladder breaks, crashing her to her just deserts, as Harry makes a graceful exit from this world of angles and close ups. Surrounded by his daughter, her foster father, Froggy and several others, Harry titles that he is sorry he is leaving her service-so soon! But it wasn't unanimous.

Baclanova, as the loose moraled

---

mother, and Brook, as Harry, did what they could with the roles. Powell was swamped under his incredible assignment. Miss Brian was sweet, girlish and charming as the grown up daughter of the crook and Fred Kohler has a few teeth gnashing moments as the escaping convict.

Even sound couldn't have helped this one much. *Con.*

SHACKELTON
(ENGLISH MADE)

Described as an official account of the expedition to the South Pole during which Sir Ernest Shackelton lost his life. No screen credits given. At the 5th Ave. Playhouse, N. Y., week Aug. 4. Running time, 60 mins.

Good entertainment for high class audiences. Majority of shots are in polar regions, duplicated in greater detail in films dealing with other expeditions.

Rough sea of ice and proximity of ship to bergs most thrilling incidents in picture. Intimate study of birds is better than average travelog stuff, and provides laughs. Majority of footage is ordinary of its kind with too much attention paid to the civilized and inhabited locations on the ship's course.

JUST MARRIED

Paramount production and release. James Hall and Ruth Taylor featured. Adapted from Anne Nichols' play, by Frank Butler and Gilbert Pratt. Directed by Frank Strayer. Titles by George Marion, Jr. Cameraman Al Cronjager. At the Paramount, N. Y., week of Aug. 11. Running time, 63 minutes.

Bob Adams....................James Hall
Roberta Adams..................Ruth Taylor
Jack Stanley.................Harrison Ford
Percy Jones................William Austin
Mrs. Jack Stanley..............Ivy Harris
Makepeace Witter............Tom Ricketts
Mrs. Witter..........Maude Turner Gordon
Victoire........................Lila Lee
Steward.....................Arthur Hoyt
Purser......................Wade Boteler
Magnoir.....................Mario Carillo

Farce heavily laden with all the old and reliable gags. The sort of picture that will annoy the fastidious but will be liked by the average person for the laughs it contains. Many of those laughs have been written in by George Marion, Jr., who renders first aid to the doubtful.

William Austin has been supplied with a set of titles that help along his standing as a silly ass comedian. Drunk bits between James Hall and Harrison Ford are also funny. And of course a man in his B. V. D.'s is always comical in the United States.

Action transpires aboard a trans-Atlantic liner and is a typical farce complication of newlyweds, lies, deceptions and frantic antics to avoid the truth. The plot is both complex and transparent and always frivolous.

Cast is lengthy and from a fan standpoint interesting. Lila Lee, in a totally new kind of role, and her first job for Paramount in years, will be news for the regulars. Harrison Ford is also quite a stranger in the larger hamlets.

Outstanding performance is by Hall, who is quite a light comedian as well as a looker. He suggests Wallace Reid but is a better actor than the late favorite.

"Just Married" is just a picture but as programmers go it's okay. Not too silly in its farce and there are some genuinely funny moments. Add to this the production standards and the result spells moderately pleasing and fair grosses.

Land.

HAROLD TEEN

First National release of a Robert Kane production. Directed by Mervyn LeRoy. Adapted from Carl Ed's cartoon strip. Features Alice Lake, Mary Brian and Arthur Lake. Cast includes Lucien Littlefield, Jack Duffy, Jack Egan and Ben Hall. At Hippodrome, New York, week Aug. 13. Running time, 78 mins. Released outside New York some weeks ago.

Class B house material sprinkled with a fair share of names, flavored with hoke amateur movie making and kid stuff so that it pours as a fair comedy which ought to make the grade if it doesn't step out of its class. For the Keith Hip (vaudfilm) it constitutes a break and the picture shouldn't have much trouble going three days and a full week in the smaller-bigger cinemas.

Not having followed a strip since Mutt and Jeff and the Katzenjammers it can't be said how well the characters follow the Ed creation. Reaction of the audience indicated the general idea was close enough and the titles and hoke seemed to supply their share of merriment.

Arthur Lake makes an appealing sappy youngster of Harold, while there are times when Mary Brian gets away from her habitual baby stare. Alice Lake cuts herself a slice as a soda fountain vamp to make the role stand out, and Jack Duffy scores on his own as a chin whiskered grandpop. Lesser characters also impressing as satisfactory.

Main comedy sequence is in a western made by the students and flashed on the high school auditorium screen. It allows for broad travesty and Mervyn LeRoy has taken full advantage in directing.

Action concludes with a semi-serious football game in which Harold does the honors after the young lady has signalled her favor from the stands. Prior to these two passages continuity and business are incidental and not overweight for laughs. It's the main cause for the picture not classifying as top flight celluloid.

Picture has the production necessities and competently photographed without any lens highlights. A miniature dam burst is a thrill moment and the punch laugh is a razzberry in the "Glory" manner.

"Harold" is hardly important but he's light and entertaining in his juvenile way. It looks like a small town picture.

Sid.

BANTAM COWBOY

FBO production and release. Starring Buzz Barton. Directed by Louis King from the story by Robert North Bradbury. Supervised by Robert N. Bradbury. Screen adaptation by Frank H. Clark; titles by Frank J. Daugherty. Cast includes Tim Lingham, Nancy Drexel, Sam Nelson, Frank Rice, Robert Fleming, William Patton. At Stanley, New York, one day, Aug. 13. Running time 55 minutes.

The appeal of a picture of this kind, regardless of construction, story or acting, is necessarily limited. Choice of a juvenue star, perhaps older but looking about 12 or 14 years of age in the picture, makes it impossible to hit except for children.

Perhaps the sole purpose was an appeal to children only, since the balance of the cast as well as the story plays second.

For general purposes it is not good entertainment even as a western. Love interest is ruined. Heroic sheriff is a half-wit, according to some of the sequences here while the girl, Nancy Drexel, who photographs well and might be able to handle an adequate assignment, is confined to the role which calls for more running than anything else.

The funniest sequence is a fight between the pint-sized hero and the menace, heavily-armed, four times the boy's weight and at least twice his size. Here the boy trips the heavy four or five times and gets away with the girl just as help arrives. A laughable situation which can't hold water with anyone but six year olds.

Type story, without a spark of originality and uninteresting. Better stories have been lifted from cheap magazines.

Mori.

MIDNIGHT MADNESS

Pathe release and P. D. C.-DeMille production. Supervised by Hector Turnbull. Adapted from the play by Daniel Rubin, "The Lion Trap." Directed by F. H. Wreight. Titles by Edwin Justus Mayer. Featuring Jacqueline Logan, Clive Brook and Walter McGrail. No other players given screen credit. At Tivoli, New York, Aug. 13, one day, half of double bill. Running time 55 minutes.

With the possible exception of the closing subtitle, "So you kept me in that little shack just to teach me a lesson," unnecessary and a trifle stupid considering that the story had already been completely told, the picture betrays marks of clever handling. A satisfactory programmer for the split weeks.

In addition to the smart performances of Jacqueline Logan and Clive Brook, there is a strong, likeable story, interesting though dealing with a married couple.

The theme on which the story is based is not new but it is not outworn and with a new twist registers. Titles well written. There is no doubt picture gains its strength from the excellent manner in which the featured players put over their assignments.

Story concerns a stenog whose home is the rear end of a shooting gallery. She lives there because of a perpetually soused father. Falling for her youthful employer, who had taken a liking to her, the girl gets a throwback when she discovers his intentions do not conform to her way. She marries the African diamond king for his money and the latter hears her saying it by the true and tried expedient of the open door.

Instead of traveling the usual way he takes his bride to Africa second class and then to a dismal cabin near a diamond claim. The girl rebels when led into thinking her husband is not wealthy and cables the location of his mine to her employer and lover in New York, also asking him to come and get her.

The climax, wherein the husband is almost killed by the drunken overseer and left to the mercy of a lion, brings the girl back to his rescue with a shotgun.

Mori.

OBEY YOUR HUSBAND

Crescent production, released through Anchor Distributing Corp. Story credited to Arthur Hoerl. Direction by Charles Hunt. Robert Cline, cameraman. In cast: Gaston Glass, Dorothy Dwan, Alice Lake, Henry Sedley, Robert Homans. At Loew's New York, one day, Aug. 7; one-half of double bill. Running time, 60 minutes.

"Obey Your Husband" is good material from an indie producer. Arthur Hoerl's story stuff gets by, even though it is full of the usual implausibilities.

The cast's performance is okay and the entertainment, based on the wife who takes matrimony lightly, according to the titles, but who really doesn't have many weaknesses except for cards, according to the action, will hit well in the seconds and grinds.

The yarn is decidedly simple but its hour running time is so well accounted for in excellent handling by Director Hunt that hack incidents and exaggerated conditions of the way a district attorney conducts himself in an examination before trial will all get by with the average payee.

While everything is cut and dried from the start, so far as prophecy by the experienced fan is concerned, suspense lilts along.

Husband and wife all innocent of the murder of the card sharp, who is rightfully bumped off by his discarded paramour.

RANSOM

Columbia production and release. From story credited George Seitz. Joe Walker, cameraman. Titles by Mort Blumenstock. In cast: Lois Wilson, William V. Mong, Edmund Burns. At Loew's Circle, one day, Aug. 3. Running time, about 60 minutes.

"Ransome" is the secret gas a chemist uses to bump off a gang of avaricious Chinamen in return for the kidnapped youngster of his widowed sweetheart.

It's a lot of the hoke stuff familiar to every fan, but there is plenty of quick motion that will key up and satisfy grind audiences.

THE PATRIOT

(SOUND)

Paramount production and release. Historical drama, starring Emil Jannings. Directed by Ernst Lubitsch. Adapted by Hans Kraley from the German stage play by Alfred Neumann. Publix musical synchronization. Score played by Paramount Symphony orchestra under direction of Nathaniel Finston. Special score by Domenico Savino and Gerard Carbonaro. Cameraman, Bert Glennon. Titles by Julian Johnson. At the Rialto, New York, Aug. 17 on daily run, $1 top. Running time, 1 hour 48 mins.

Czar Paul...................Emil Jannings
Count Pahlen....................Lewis Stone
Countess Ostermann.........Florence Vidor
Crown Prince Alexander.....Neil Hamilton
Stehpan.....................Harry Cording
Mlle. Lapoukhine............Vera Voronina

Many elements combine to give "The Patriot" a valid claim to greatness, much as that word has been abused in cinemania. The magnificent performance of Emil Jannings as the mad Czar Paul alone will insure box-office returns appropriate to the high quality of the picture, adding vastly to the already commanding prestige of this star. Jannings' mad monarch as a forceful and artistic creation marks a new support to his position as the leading interpreter of dramatic roles.

If Jannings were unknown instead of an international screen figure this picture would make him overnight. Under the circumstances it will probably make "The Patriot" the most talked about picture of the early season. Certainly with it Paramount gets off on the new theatre season under most favorable auspices.

Besides Jannings the production has a whole array of valuable assets. Story value is excellent, cast is almost flawless and the physical production is rich in beauty and fine graphic background. Story is a moving recital told in a highly flavored and often frankly theatrical manner, but always fascinating in its unfolding. It goes with mounting tension, though a series of episodes that are often remarkably absorbing to a finely wrought climax, craftily staged for heightened effect.

Although the picture is in the mode of what is called period costume play, it has clear character drawing and human motive in its people.

Time is the late 18th century, and locale the righly picturesque atmosphere of the Russian court under Czar Paul, the insane emperor of all the Russias, idiot-monster of Nero-like proportions. Surrounded by murderous plots, the only creature the madman trusts is his minister of war, Count Pahlen (Lewis Stone).

It is out of the conflict in Pahlen—the desire to protect the mad king who is his friend and benefactor, and the horror at his acts that moves him as patriot to remove him from the throne—that the drama evolves to the denouement where Pahlen maneuvers the Emperor's assassination and then gallantly bows out of life himself, his sacrifice to his beloved Russia.

The role of Pahlen is really the star part, and it is only Jannings' genius in grotesquely heroic roles that holds up the character of the Czar. Mr. Stone gives a balanced and polished performance. Pahlen is pictured as a suave man of the world rather than the paragon of virtue as legendary heroes are usually presented. Character comes on the screen without heroics. Until the end you are left to guess whether his motives are noble or selfish. His task is to free his country from an insane tyrant, and when he has to sacrifice even his mistress to the great mission, he does it with imperturbable determination.

A legendary hero innocent of heroics is a screen novelty, and the shrewd handling of this character gives a hint of the sophisticated treatment given to the whole work. Authenticity runs throughout the play.

The dramatic highlight is the scene where Pahlen has tricked his own mistress into a rendezvous with the crazy king in order to keep him in the palace within reach of the conspirators. Here the clash between the leering monarch and the woman delivers a high-powered kick. Florence Vidor plays the heroine with the grace and sufficiency that are always hers.

Pictorially the production is full of magnificent bits. One of the sets is the vast palace courtyard and long shots of soldiers moving through its intricate vistas, columns of foot soldiers with galloping horsemen weaving around dim corners and streaking across the snow-covered spaces, are stunning effects. Sleighs dashing through the snow-covered streets; a lone horseman streaking across the palace yard in the moonlight, vague shots of the mad emperor's soldiery committing pillage on oppressed villages, and a hundred other deft suggestions go to build fine atmosphere.

In the final passage, where the Emperor flees through ghostly palace corridors and up and down enormous staircases, the picture compositions have been remarkably well done. So also is the climax itself, where the madman is brought to bay on his own throne by the courtiers.

Sound effects are managed inconspicuously. There is no dialog. In one sequence the Emperor awakes from a nightmare to call in frightened frenzy for his Pahlen, and his cries for "Pahlen" are recorded, but they supplement the titles. While the cry is heard, the screen also carries the word "Pahlen" done in letters that shiver on the screen.

In other sequences the sound merely supplements the action. In the sequence where the conspirators are awaiting 1 o'clock as the time to strike, screen shows a man striking a huge bell with a hammer. The strokes sounds, but the meaning would be quite as plain without the audible effect. Jubilant cries of the mob before the palace when they receive news that the dreaded tyrant is no more also are conveyed by sound, but camera flashes of the huge crowd expresses the meaning amply.

Musical accompaniment throughout is splendid, merging into the picture so that the auditor forgets it is a mechanical effect and not a functioning orchestra.

Julian Johnson's titles are notable for brevity and artistic restraint. Here for once is a title writer who has the strength of mind and the soundness of taste to make the printed word strictly serve the story rather than the title writer's reputation. *Rush.*

THE TERROR

(DIALOG)

Warner Bros. production and release. Directed by Roy Del Ruth from the play (English) by Edgar Wallace. Scenario by Harvey Gates. Titles not credited in program billing but Joseph Jackson announced by screen talker as responsible and also wrote dialog in collaboration with someone. Photographed by Barney McGill. Featuring May McAvoy. At Warners theatre, New York, Aug. 15, on twice daily run, $2 top. Running time 80 minutes.

Olga Redmayne..............May McAvoy
Mrs. Elvery..................Louise Fazenda
Ferdinand Fane....Edward Everett Horton
Dr. Redmayne..................Alec Francis
Joe Connors...................Matthew Betz
Goodman......................Holmes Herbert
Alfred Katman..................John Miljan
Soapy Marks....................Otto Hoffman
Supt. Hallick...................Joseph Girard
Cotton.........................Frank Austin

"The Terror" is in for a run at $2. It should stay at the Warners four or five months.

The second all-talking picture to be produced ("Lights of New York," first), is more than a novelty; it is bona fide picture entertainment worth $2 of anybody's money. What weaknesses there are in this presentation are more logically attributable to the construction of the play upon which the picture is based than to studio limitations or sound difficulties.

The improvement between the first and the second all-talking picture to be presented by Warner Bros. is surprising. There are, in this picture, many glaring technical errors which may loom large in the eyes of the discerning critic, but few, if any, which could leave a bad impression with any audience.

It is of especial significance that this production shows the tremendous value of talking pictures in making a successful film out of a flop play. As far as can be ascertained, "The Terror," which has had a two-year run in London as a stage play, was never produced in America. While it is evident that the picture is surefire, appealing from many angles to picture patrons, it is just as obvious that the same words, the very same actions, the same plot, wouldn't hold up on a Broadway stage more than four weeks in the form of a play.

Through the medium of the talking pictures it is here shown possible to lend greater power to the simplest dialog and the most inconspicuous action. Situations which would fail to hold on the stage are full of tense, eager interest on the screen.

Every piece of business is over-acted, merely another way of saying that it clicks heavily on all counts.

This is a mystery thriller on a par with anything of the kind ever produced but far more effective than any silent picture owing to the sound. Every member of the cast contributes a necessary and interesting characterization. Even the butler, Frank Austin, scores strongly though limited to only three or four speaking lines. His intonation as he says merely, "I am the butler," sounds as pretentious and as awe-inspiring as a confession of murder would in a silent subtitle.

John Miljan, as Alfred Katman, is another weird personage in the group at the old tavern. His punch line, "This reminds me of a murder," registers for a laugh continuously. Delivers capably throughout in a voice well suited for dialog pictures.

Story concerns a murderous, maniacal criminal known as "The Terror" and also as "Shea," whose identity is unknown until the end. The old tavern, scene of the mystery, is subject to strange, mysterious organ recitals at odd hours of the night. A black, hooded figure is prowling around the house, frightening the girl into hysterics every once in awhile.

Two men released from prison, Soapy Marks and Joe Conners, plan to repay the Terror for framing them for a 10-year jail term and keeping the entire proceeds of a bank robbery.

Action is laid almost entirely in the old house. Louise Fazenda, as Mrs. Elvery, provides a few laughs with a weird giggle resembling the whinny of a horse. She plays the part of a nut spiritualist, trying to summon the good spirits to disperse the gloom.

During a heavy rainstorm the nut comedian, Edward Everett Horton, arrives. He handles a very light line of comedy for good returns and, in the leading role, establishes himself as a valuable player for talkers. Horton plays the nut who later turns out to be the chief of the detectives, the script allowing the audience to guess this as soon as he appears.

The Terror is finally captured just as he is about to murder the girl, May McAvoy.

The heavy veil of mystery is constantly relieved by laughs registering through comedy lines but mainly on the strength of delivery by Miss Fazenda, Horton and John Miljan.

Alec Francis and Holmes Herbert, both with considerable legit stage experience, play with easy assurance. Matthew Betz does nicely in one of the minor roles while Otto Hoffman puts over a strong impression of the sneak type of dangerous criminal. Joseph Girard has a straight assignment as the Scotland Yard super. *Mori.*

THE SCARLET LADY

Columbia production and release. Featuring Lya De Putti, Don Alvarado and Warner Oland. Directed by Alan Crosland from Bess Meredyth's story. Cameraman, J. Van Trees. At the Embassy, New York, on twice daily run at $1.50, starting Aug. 14. Running time, 78 mins.

Lya............................Lya De Putti
Prince Karloff.................Don Alvarado
Zaneriff.......................Warner Oland
Valet..........................Otto Matiesen
A Captain......................John Peters

Columbia, which deals in titles first and then makes pictures, presumably hooked on to "The Scarlet Lady" as a name and transferred it to Russia's familiar revolutions. In script it's not far away from the other program releases which have unfolded their own versions on the inside politics and romance of the historic uprising, but in production it's a lot different from many previous Columbia releases. The background is sufficient to send it into the big program houses for a week where indications are that results would be moderate. For the indie houses it holds class.

The firm has spent some dough and deserves a break for the effort. That it's at the Embassy, M-G-M's diminutive run house, is not so much due to actual merit as that the big operator is shy of suitable pictures for this site and the house was going dark to be wired. So if Columbia wanted it for four weeks, why not?

At $1.50 the picture will be light on the 46th street corner, but the office heads undoubtedly figure prestige on the theory that a Broadway showing increases rentals and rep, pro or con. Discussions on this subject are as prevalent as ever.

Lya De Putti is the main name with Don Alvarado and Warner Oland, hero and heavy, respectively, in support. How much this trio means on exterior billing the exhibs will figure for themselves. It doesn't sound bad.

Alan Crosland and the story have made of the German girl a coy young thing, handicapping her right away. But she gets a chance to display a couple of vamp gowns and indicate s. a. intentions, and the sex motive is the film's main program point.

Miss De Putti entrances as a cross between Sadie Thompson and Lulu Bell, but a title states she's "unspoiled." Despite the conflicting appearance she stays that way until stopping over late enough with the Prince to have breakfast with him the next morning. Inasmuch as she's a Red the theme boils when the Prince is told she's the comeon for his murder and he interrupts her coffee by a curt dismissal.

Also having a string on the revolution's leader, Lya is cleaning up on royalty captures, but isn't satisfied because she hasn't been able to find the Prince and retaliate. This finally happens. After humiliating him as much as footage will permit it looks like curtains for His Highness when Zaneriff decides to bump off a sextet in which the Prince is on the end of the line. Handing Lya his gun for the supreme revenge, she gives Zaneriff both barrels and the two escape over the border in a double-cowl Renault that still looks snappy despite the number of pictures it has graced.

Scenario conforms to the American supposition that all revolutionists are bums, cutthroats and bloodthirsty with blue bloods able to teach 'em how to live and die, as a title explains. Miss De Putti has her troubles being cute but has a couple of spots where she's all animal and the better for it. The camera hasn't been unkind to her although lighting in a few shots is hardly flattering. Oland plays his usual competent heavy and Alvarado conforms to studio standards on what a Prince should be. Otto Matiesen makes his vindictive valet stand out and John Peters convinces as an army captain.

Castle sets, interior and exterior, are solid and lavish plus a few flashes of minor mob stuff. The picture has been well made even though it has passed through a liberal cutting room.

It's a good release for Columbia which will increase its entertainment value as admission scales become lower. It's as strong as some of the weaker films the big companies turn out, and better than some. *Sid.*

FOUR WALLS

Metro-Goldwyn-Mayer production and release. Adapted from stage play by Dana Burnet and George Abbott. Adaptation by Alice D. G. Miller. Titled by Joe Farnhum. Directed by William Nigh. Starring John Gilbert, with Joan Crawford featured. At Capitol, New York, week August 18. Running time, over 60 minutes.

Benny ....John Gilbert
Frieda ....Joan Crawford
Mrs. Horowitz...................Vera Gordon
Bertha ....Carmel Myers
Sullivan ....Robert Emmet O'Connor
Monk ....Louis Natheaux
Roma ....Jack Byron

Another underworlder, well done, and with John Gilbert, Joan Crawford and Robert Emmet O'Connor in three great roles, surrounded by a 100 per cent. cast.

Gilbert as Benny Horowitz, gangster, product of an east side environment, plays with repression and conviction. Miss Crawford as his round heeled frail is splendid, and O'Connor, plain clothes copper, minus the usual nickel owl and iron hat (thanks to Tommy Jackson in "Broadway"), is a natural dick anyone can believe.

The story, adapted from the stage play, lends itself to an interesting film version of the gangster who is regenerated while doing his bit. Benny is the leader of a neighborhood gang and Frieda is his girl. They are enjoying themselves in an east side cabaret when Roma (Jack Byron), a rival gang leader, invades the place. A dead line had been established. Benny chases the jane to safety and orders Roma to screw. His two companions are covered by one of Benny's lieutenants.

Roma walks out followed by Benny. At the head of the stairs Roma goes for his gat and Benny pops him. Benny makes a getaway and tries to establish his alibi by heading for a garage where he's employed. He is driving a coupe borrowed from the garage. Returning he opens the hood to give it an impression of being worked on.

Sullivan, plain clothes cop, arrives at the garage. The engine is hot. Benny explains they have been working on the car. "You forgot to alibi the hot tires," says Sullivan, as he makes the collar.

Benny is settled and while in the can realizes that he's been playing a brace game. He plants seeds in the prison farm and sees things grow for the first time. He says of a plant, "That's the first thing I ever touched that went straight."

Discharged at the expiration of his sentence he returns to his mother's flat determined to go straight. His mother (Vera Gordon) has been befriended by Bertha (Carmel Myers). Bertha, plain, unattractive girl, is in love with Benny, but has smothered her feelings.

The gang calls to sound Benny out. Monk, his right hand man before the pinch, has assumed leadership and Benny's girl. He announces that he won't relinquish either. Benny tells him he's off the old racket and wishes him well with both inheritances.

Frieda invades the Horowitz domain and is given the chill by Benny. She still loves him and wants him back. He won't turn for it. She doesn't love Monk. Benny is cold.

Frieda leaves, but a few days later after Benny has his old job back she entices him into her apartment to have a good old fashioned talk. Benny refuses her advances, although it's plain the old attraction is strong. They quarrel and Benny tells her just what he thinks of her. She's rotten, etc.

Benny goes home and proposes marriage to Bertha. She is overjoyed but suspecting he doesn't love her, questions him and his evasions fail to satisfy her.

She refuses him.

Benny, with thoughts of Frieda, feels the old need for excitement. His home is next door to the cabaret where the gang hang out. He knows Monk is throwing a party and decides to attend. He enters the joint via roof of his tenement. Old friends greet him as he makes his way to the bar. He is invited to drink but refuses.

Frieda, to fan his jealousy, pretends an exaggerated love for Monk. They announce they are engaged to be married. Frieda shows a large ring. As they dance Benny begins drinking.

The Dock Gang is discovered descending upon the joint. Word is passed. The gun molls get the rods out and pass them to the gang. Battle is prepared for. Benny instinctively assumes leadership and is giving orders when Monk protests. Benny leaves via roof, sweeping up Frieda in his arms as the rival gangsters begin to blaze away.

Monk follows them to the roof and overhears Benny confessing his love. They clash and Monk drops his gun. Frieda gets between them and in his efforts to free himself Monk slips on a cornice and falls off the roof.

Benny arrives home. Bertha hears him. He tells her that if anyone arrives to question her, he has been in bed since 10.

Sully arrives. He has been keeping a tail on Benny since he got out of stir. Benny is summoned and appears in pajamas and dressing gown. He recites his alibied speech and Bertha seconds it. Sully asks her how she knows that Benny didn't get up and dress and go out after 10. She answers "Because I was with him."

Frieda appears and complicates matters. Sully makes the others leave the room while he questions her. He tricks her by saying Benny confessed. She doesn't fall for the ruse. Sully finally leaves but listens outside the door. Frieda and Benny suspect him and engage in conversation that will absolve Benny of blame. As Sully listens a tenant in the house passes him and goes down stairs. Frieda and Benny think it's Sully's footsteps and they discuss the roof tragedy as it really happened. Frieda says they'll never believe Benny didn't kill Monk, and the best policy is denial all around.

Sully, now convinced Benny is innocent, re-enters the room and tells them everything will be okay. He leaves with the tag line to Benny, "The next time you go to bed at 10 take off your socks."

A good program picture and comparable with most of the real good underworlds.

Nigh's direction deserves commendation for its reality, restraint and knowledge of his elements.

Con.

OUT OF THE RUINS

First National production and release. Directed by John Francis Dillon. Richard Barthelmess starred; Marian Nixon featured. From story by Sir Philip Gibbs. No other program credits. At Strand, New York, week Aug. 18. Running time, 65 minutes.

Lt. Pierre Dumont	Richard Barthelmess
Sergt. Paul Gilbert	Robert Frazer
Yvonne Gilbert	Marian Nixon
Pere Gilbert	Emile Chautard
Mere Gilbert	Bodil Rosing
Volange	Eugene Pallette
Mere Gourdain	Rose Dione

Not much of a feature for Richard Barthelmess. It lacks the guts of the stories Barthelmess has had of late. Though of war, women and weeps, there's little in it for men and Barthelmess, even for his strongest admirers. But the women may like it for Marian Nixon goes wrong for her soldier boy, when they discover that as a deserter he can't marry her. Making Miss Nixon as a wholesome girl with vampish ideas, ready and wanting to fall for the man she loves may get the women. That's the safest bet for the exhibs, for this much dirt is plainly brought out. It needed something like that.

As a lieutenant in the Blue Devils, France's crack regiment, and as a deserter, rushing to Paris to save his girl from marrying another, Barthelmess could be forgiven and had the sympathy. But when he dallied with his lady love in a nicely furnished apartment for days while his regiment was cut to pieces by the enemy that wasn't so fancy. Neither could that situation be sweetened up nor captions save it.

Though the lieutenant was saved when ordered shot by a court martial, he was shot but not killed, as he himself later explained in a caption: "They were my comrades and didn't shoot straight."

Also another line rung in was "Go now, but don't look back." That must be kept set up in type in Hollywood.

Even as a part war picture not much action. Played languidly. In fact, the tempo is irritating. All of the principals seemed trained for the same pace. As, for instance, Miss Nixon and Robert Frazer as the sergeant, brother and sister in the story, doing almost the exact movements in the precise way under similar situations.

War stuff means nothing; Paris stuff less. Best of the latter a flop air raid scene with the scene only showing the people in the cafe running to the cellar. Best bit of the film is when Barthelmess meets Miss Nixon in the Paris restaurant. Some neat comedy in that. Otherwise blah.

Miss Nixon steals the acting end. Looks very nice and does her vamping with taste.

John Francis Dillon's direction, except for the tempo, okay. Nothing much to do with this story he missed, handling the people equally well under all circumstances. F. N. not giving sufficient credits, even in gross sheet. Title writer deserved it here. Some very capable and intelligent captions.

At the Strand some manufactured back stage sounds tried for with but little effect.

Picture won't do Barthelmess any good but one miss in a row of hits can't hurt him now.

THE FIRST KISS

Paramount production and release. Starring Gary Cooper and Fay Wray. Directed by Rowland V. Lee from the story "Four Brothers." Titled by Julian Johnson, with Alfred Gilks cameraman. At Paramount, New York, week of Aug. 18. Running time, 61 mins.

Anna Lee	Fay Wray
Mulligan Talbot	Gary Cooper
William Talbot	Lane Chandler
Carol Talbot	Leslie Fenton
Ezra Talbot	Paul Fix
"Pap"	Malcolm Williams
Other Suitor	Monroe Owsley

Not a punch but a nice program picture. It particularly ought to mean something to Gary Cooper, as between his performance here and with "Lilac Time" showing around, it looks as if this boy is making his move on the rail and is on his way as concerns popularity.

Picture hasn't any comedy to speak of and is light drama until a finishing courtroom scene, where the action tightens up. Some sequences are pretty well fogged for plausibility and the continuity has a tendency to jump around, but Cooper's uneducated, determined and repressed lover characterization will carry it through to satisfy the girls if not so much their escorts. Fay Wray successfully records a certain winsomeness as the wealthy heroine, and Lane Chandler make a ne'er-do-well brother prominent.

Localed on the eastern shore of Maryland among the oyster fishermen, there's no heavy production involved, but Gilks' camera work gives the exteriors a break and the script calls for shoddy surroundings.

Cooper plays Mulligan, second son of the degenerated Talbot family, who takes charge of his three brothers when their drunken father dies, and beats them into undertaking an education after the girl has scoffed at his social standing. Discovering a supposed wealthy grandfather has been dead a year, Mulligan starts committing robberies to keep his kin in college. He finally sells his and Anna Lee's dream boat, which he has built, to repay the forced "borrowed" amounts.

The refund leading to Mulligan's arrest, the girl sends for the brothers, who, upon learning of the means which has kept them in school, go into court to declare themselves as receivers of the stolen goods, pleading that their brother has taken three derelicts and made men of them. Anna has also been on the stand, but the court finds him guilty, passes a 10-year sentence and then suspends it with Mulligan paroled in the custody of the girl.

Simple but made interesting, with only one love scene leading to a clinch, and good because of it, but a bit prolonged in a few instances. However, the women seemed to like the idea. Cooper extracts a lot from his role and there's no question that it's his picture. Malcolm Williams also sends through a few feet as the liquor-sodden father which count.

Title doesn't imply the exact nature of the story and the picture is hardly dynamic, but for 61 minutes the Paramount crowd didn't find it hard to take. Similar reaction may be expected elsewhere.

Sid.

A SOUTH SEA BUBBLE

(BRITISH MADE)

London, July 27.

Produced by Gainesborough Pictures. Directed by T. Hayes Hunter. From the "Satevpost" story by Roland Pertwee. Scenario by Angus McPhail and Alma Reville. Titles by Roland Pertwee. Photography: Walter Blakely and James Wilson. U. K. distribution: W. & F., Ltd. Foreign rights: Gainesborough Pictures (1928) Ltd. Censors' Certificate: U. Preview at the London Hippodrome, July 23. Running time 100 minutes.

Vernon Winslowe	Ivor Novello
Averil Rochester	Benita Hume
Mr. Isinglass	Ben Field
Lydia la Rue	Annette Benson
William Carpenter	Sydney Seaward
Henry Julius	Robert Holmes
Mary Ottery	Alma Taylor
Olive Banbury	Mary Dibley

A fifty-fifty picture. If you like it you will; if you don't you won't. Old-fashioned technique, confused story and too much footage to tell it in are its chief faults. It is very much like the sort of factory feature Paramount used to turn out years ago, probably for $35,000 or so a throw.

But it has two outstanding merits—team work by the cast and a fine performance by Ben Field, who is known in New York as a stage actor. Field plays an eccentric millionaire who unravels tangles for the purpose of making folks happy with the same childish delight as he lets free a cage full of thrushes in a bird-seller's shop.

Novello begins as a light comedian, but develops into the usual movie hero. Someone wrote that Novello has ambitions to be a second Harold Lloyd, and that he'd beat Lloyd to it. Oh, dear!

Benita Hume, who has been "elevated to stardom" on account of playing a bit very well in "Easy Virtue," is sadly miscast. As a newspaper reporter nosing out a story of hidden treasure she neither gets into the role nor looks like it. With more experience Miss Hume may do better, but she doesn't screen so well even then.

Broke, Vernon Winslowe digs out a chart left by an ancestor, fakes it to show where treasure is buried, and advertises for come-ons. His idea is to get their money and exit. But the arrival at a dinner of the selected victims of a cranky old man, who offers his yacht, organizes the expedition and takes care of the cash Vernon has collected. A girl reporter who has slipped in as a servant to get the story trades it for a share in the expedition, which includes in the party a nurse, consumptive youth in search of health, Jewish financier, vamp, mail office clerk and a down-trodden lady's companion.

They all gain a new outlook, health or some other benefit on the trip, in spite of the effort of a former friend of Winslowe to break up the party by telling them it's a ramp.

On the island the old millionaire plants a treasure so no one shall be disappointed, but the folk dig at the wrong spot and find the pirate ancestor's hoard. The bad lad of the party, who has become drink crazy, steals the stuff and abducts the girl reporter. She is rescued by Winslowe, and they and the rest of the party pair off.

Locations in Colombo and the Algerian coast reasonably good, but the direction lacks snap and characterization. The picture never convinces and seldom grips.

For this side acceptable to Novello fans mainly, and they exist aplenty. For America just a daily change picture with no names they know.

Frat.

FORTUNE'S FOOL

(GERMAN MADE)

Name of foreign producer or distributor not mentioned. Distributor for America, Sam Saxe. Starring Emil Jannings, with the leading lady (name not caught) featured. Story by Hans Kraly, directed by Reinhold Schunzel. Photographers, A. Hansen and L. Lippert. American credits: Titles by John W. (Jack) Conway; edited by Elmer McGovern. At Cameo, New York, week Aug. 11. Running time, 65 minutes.

A most ordinary full length German made feature, with nothing or anybody in it excepting Emil Jannings. Where Jannings has established an American popularity strong enough to stand anything, this could be used for a limited stay or to double the bill, or it might be put in by a grind opposite another and more modern Jannings American made, such as the Broadway, New York, is doing this week, with Jannings' "Patriot" (Par) at the Rialto, nearby.

This picture was made some years ago, but since the war. Jannings' performance in it does not suggest what he has since proven himself to be as a picture actor. Jannings in his playing here resembled Harry Holman of the vaud business. Story is of the formula kind, war-made millionaire widower with only son, who falls in love with young daughter of a poverty-stricken aristocratic family.

Many gags rung in, mostly unnecessarily. One especially is an attempted comedy duel scene such as might be expected in a burlesque show. Entirely extraneous to the action. Limited comedy mostly from Jack Conway's captions. Best thing next to Jannings is the direction with several mobs of extras, it all winding up in a fixed auto race and a murder trial scene.

In Germany the title of the picture is said to have been "The Age of Lust." Hardly any matter in the story to justify that name.

Leading woman, supposed to be ingenue, too elderly in appearance for role. Heroic juvenile just as bad as an actor. Couple of minor roles well enough played.

Just Jannings and best in German communities.

For general playing, the one dayers and double bills.

The Vanishing Pioneer

Paramount production and release. Adapted from the Zane Grey novel by John Goodrich and Ray Harris. Directed by John Waters. Titles by J. Johnson. In cast: Jack Holt, Jack Holt, Jr., Fred Kohler, William Powell. At Loew's New York, one day, Aug. 7, one-half of double bill. Running time 60 minutes.

A covered wagon sequence opens and closes "The Vanishing Pioneer." The irrigation gag and its complications, with a little cold love sequence thrown in, moves along pleasantly enough to send home the average audience, partial to westerns, partially satisfied.

When a nearby city decides that it needs the town's water supply a thug member of the common council gets the assignment to look after the dickering. He finds the town sheriff to be one of the old boys and they work along lines accordingly.

Jack Holt plays a double part, that of the papa who steers the plains commuters right to the fodder land, and later as the son who balks the gyps by either filling them with lead or sending them to the gallows. Everybody shakes hands when Holt holds up his mother's apron. This is taken as the signal for the pioneers' sons to abscond.

Taken altogether, this will not be considered half bad by those who know nothing about westerners.

BEWARE OF BLONDES

(From press sheet.) Directed by George B. Seitz with asst. Joe Nadel. Cameraman, Joe Walker. Film editor, James Mckay. No author, adapter or titler writer named. Columbia production and release. Matt Moore, Roy D'Arcy, and Dorothy Revier featured. Credit data if on slides not caught. At Keith's Hippodrome, New York, week Aug. 20. Running time, 73 minutes.

Mary....................Dorothy Revier
Jeffrey....................Matt Moore
Harry....................Roy D'Arcy
Costigan....................Robert Edeson
Tex....................Walter P. Lewis
Blonde, Mary....................Hazel Howell
Portugee Joe....................Harry Semels

Columbia hit upon a good title here and with enough of substance in film to bear it up, although the matter is not what the common impression of that title will be. This is a detective story, rather good for a Columbia regular. While short on action it's long on interest, and as detective stories seem quite strongly in general favor at present, this one should do nicely where they are wanted.

It's of a secretary in a jewelry house, preventing a robbery of his firm, and given a vacation to Honolulu as a reward. On the trip he must deliver a valuable emerald in that city. He is warned against thieves who are after the gem. The emerald is hidden on the inside of an ordinary cigaret lighter. Especially is he warned against "Blonde Mary," and told to lay off any blonde he may meet, as Mary is a slicker.

On board he meets a blonde and falls for her, with she for him, although he believes her to be Mary and is chary. But she relieves his suspicion when he finds his blonde is a private detective for the Jewelers' Protective Association. A crook on board thinks she is Blonde Mary passing as a detect, and agrees to split with her if either of them gets the jewel from the sec.

Story runs along in this way aboard the ship, with the blonde detect stalling off the crook. To save her sweetie from getting bumped off, she gives him knockout drops in a glass of wine the night before the ship docks, taking the emerald from him to show the crooks.

The sec, frantic, hangs around Manila until locating the girl and as he supposes her crook companion, despite that the sec and blonde became engaged aboard. The girl, however, is merely staying over to bag the gang, which she does, having made the delivery of the original emerald and foisted upon the crooks a phoney.

When the police broke into the den in Manila where they all met, the Hip audience applauded slightly. Enough to display their interest had been held.

Good direction but not always good photography. Ever so many too many long shots. It made the photography at the start rather dim, though some nice directorial business worked in at the start.

Dorothy Revier was the genuine blonde, and okay in works and looks. Matt Moore had an easy role as the sec, as did Roy D'Arcy as the heavy, with another heavy in a light part, Robert Edeson.

GAY ADVENTURER
(GERMAN MADE)

ABA Film Corp. (states rights) release. Presented by A. P. Alexrud with Charles Alden as star. No credits on screen or in press sheet for author, director, etc. On double feature bill at Columbus, New York, one day, Aug. 17. Running time, 55 mins.

This is the German equivalent of a Richard Talmadge or Al Wilson American thriller. Charles Alden, whose name is probably something quite different in Germany, is a big muscle guy strong on acrobatics. "The Gay Adventurer" is one of a series of pictures releasing by ABA starring him. Nobody else is mentioned by name except Axelrud, evidently the American importer or German exporter, as the case may be.

The story is laid in Alaska. It concerns a wild harum-scarum youth who innocently becomes entangled in the murder of another man. Victim's sister is the heroine.

Complications include a more or less hand-to-hand fight with a pack of wolves. Plenty of action and in the state right division film passable, although photography and production detail far from warm.

Land.

LINGERIE

Tiffany-Stahl production and release. Directed by George Melford from the story by J. F. Natteford. Continuity by J. F. Natteford. Featuring Alice White, Malcolm MacGregor and Mildred Harris. Cast includes Armand Kaliz and Kit Guard. At Tivoli, New York, Aug. 20, one day. Running time, 55 mins.

Interesting version of a somewhat familiar story, framed in attractive settings, and showing polished continuity and direction should carry this production in the split weeks nicely.

Practically all of the important scenes indicate smart directorial ability and supervision. Clever photographic effects help in putting the illusion over. Sets look expensive and story runs smoothly despite the frequent changes of locale.

Opens with a wedding ceremony. The husband is disillusioned a few minutes later in the darkened library when his newly acquired wife mistakes him for her lover. Action switches to France where the boy finds a French girl. Wounded and paralyzed, later, he is taken back home. The French girl follows as his wife's maid. Recovery for the finish.

Comedy and gags used ineffective, including the gag from "What Price Glory?" which all the independents have been helping themselves to. With incapable delivery giving the M. P. the razz isn't funny and doesn't even register.

Miss White photographs attractively and displays ability which should carry her into the first runs.

Mori.

UNDERGROUND
(BRITISH MADE)

London, July 27.

Produced by British Instructional Films. Story and direction by Anthony Asquith. Photography, S. Rodwell. Distribution for all countries, Pro Patria Films. Censors' certificate U. Previewed at the Plaza, July 25. Running time, 84 minutes.

Nell, shopgirl....................Elissa Landi
Bill, underground porter......Brian Aherne
Kate, sewing girl....................Nora Baring
Bert, electrician....................Cyril McLaglan

Anthony Asquith has succeeded this time far more than he did with "Shooting Stars," probably because he directed this one himself. One thing it evidences is he is a better director than he is a story-writer. He wrote the story for "Shooting Stars," and it was awful. He wrote the story for "Underground," and it isn't so much. But he has directed it into a good enough movie, even if it is not in the super class. The main reason it isn't is the slowness of the tempo and the long-drawn-out and trite ending to the story.

But the film shows a facet of life that is new to the screen. It is melodrama, and, up to a point, logical and reasonably possible. But it ends in an almost slapstick roof chase and the butting in of people at a main power house to a point which becomes almost ludicrous.

The acting, both of the main parts and of the bits, is really excellent, and the types have been chosen with the same intelligent accuracy that marks the selection and dressing of sets and locations. The whole effect is a dramatized slice of real human life until, as has already been said, the climax, which becomes routine at first and then confused. But on the whole it has the great merit of looking as if it really did happen instead of being made for a movie. It deals with a class and with locations which will be utterly novel to the screen, as much here as in America.

The story opens in an underground (subway) train. Bert is trying to get fresh with a girl in a crowded compartment, and follows here to the escalator. Bill sees him and trips him on the stairway to look like an accident. The girl (Nell) drops her gloves; Bill picks them up, and they fall for each other. But Bert finds Nell at the department store where she works, and continues to pursue her. He has another girl in the rooming house where he lives, but is about to turn her down when, after a rebuff from Nell, he gets the idea of using his girl (Kate) to frame Bill. Kate throws a fake faint on the station, and as Nell comes by screams and accuses Bill, who has taken her off the platform, thinking she is ill, of molesting her.

Previously the two men have had a scrap when Bill has found Bert slinging Nell's name around a saloon.

Nell doesn't believe Bill would have molested the strange girl, but he is in danger of getting fired unless he can prove he didn't. To the store comes Kate to buy some finery, and when she gives her address for delivery Nell notices it is the same as Bert's, from whom she has just had a letter asking her to marry him. She goes to Kate, who believes Bert is about to marry her, and when Kate finds she has been double-crossed by her lover and Bill comes asking her to own up, she goes with him to the power house to do so.

While Bill is with the foreman telling him what has happened, Kate slips into the switch room and confronts Bert, who loses his head and pushes her against an open switch and kills her. Lights go out; the service is at a standstill, and Bert goes loco. He escapes across the roof, Bill after him. They fall into the subway and mount a train. The fight continues in an elevator. Nell, who has seen them from the platform, rushes up in another elevator, and when the doors are opened where the fight is going on there is Bert out on the floor and Bill all safe.

In a closing shot she refuses a fresh old man's offer of a seat on a crowded train because she is with her husband, now a conductor on the underground.

Some very fine shots through tunnels, on escalators and in subways, often from novel and attractive angles. The direction is always good if sometimes a trifle slow and occasionally pernickety; as, for example, where Kate discovers she has really been thrown down and goes around aimlessly fingering objects in her room. This is overdone and spoils its purpose. Half as much footage would have registered the workings of the girl's mind more effectively.

As a whole it is a worthwhile picture and gives promise of at least one efficient and possibly outstanding director emerging from the present boom in British picture making. It is not perfect, but it is a lot better than the average, particularly as it never attempts to ape Hollywood. Lots of our directors do make this attempt and make a monkey of themselves by their aping.

Even the character names are chosen with an accuracy which makes them typify their class and characters to an amazing degree. Acting by Brian Aherne and Cyril McLaglen is good enough to create a series partnership for them. The latter is a brother of Victor McLaglen and has been in vaudeville here for some time.

It will be a big success here and deserves to be. Cut a bit, and certainly retitled, it has no mean possibilities for America as something that is different without being difficult.

The picture has a tie-up with a song, "Arms of Love," published in New York by Waterson, Berlin & Snyder, composed by Pete Wendling, with banjulele additions by Alvin D. Keech.

Frat.

LURE OF THE WEST

Chesterfield release, produced by H. T. Henderson. Directed by Alvin J. Neitz. Story by Alvin J. Neitz. Starring Eileen Sedgwick. Cast includes Les Bates, Ray Childs, D. Maley, Alfred Hewston, Elsie Bower, Carlos Silvers. At Stanley, N. Y., one day, Aug. 20. Running time, 55 mins.

An old-fashioned western made long ago and now being released in this territory. Slower than the usual western and without gun play or horsemanship in sufficient quantity to recommend it.

Action confined mainly to subtitles. Added to poor photography which gives the star the worst of it the picture is spotted just about right in the daily changes or in whatever houses they can stand it.

Story is woven round a quack selling bottled cures in a small western town. The saloon owner buys the services of the quack's daughter as an entertainer and, soon after sending the old boy and the sick daughter away to the city, sets to work pawing the gal and emoting vile thoughts.

The hero has no particular status, remaining the mysterious stranger to the bitter end.

Only one fist fight and not well done.

Mori.

SUZY SAXOPHONE
(FRANCO-GERMAN MADE)

Paris, July 25.

This international picture is more remarked for cast than anything else. It is released as a prize packet of the Films Artistiques Sofar, and got a fair reception at the French trade show when held at the Empire music hall (Paris).

Anny has decided in her own little energetic mind that despite the opposition of her noble sire, she will be a vaudeville star. Having been placed in a boarding school near London she changes names with Suzy, her friend, who takes her place.

Under the pseudonym of Suzy she meets a rich young English lord and is taken by him to a cabaret. Suzy dances so well that she is booked as the captain of a troupe of girls going for a revue in Berlin.

Meanwhile the substitution of names and identity has been discovered and the real Suzy sent home. Herbert follows Anny to Germany, assists in a number of adventures, pleads with Suzy's parents for their daughter's hand, which leads to more complications.

There are features which will interest, such as scenes at a dancing academy, in the cabaret, and at Anny's home.

"Suzy Saxophone" may amuse the boys on the outer circle. It is by no means a feature issue for big time. Anny Ondra as the false Suzy, heroine of the story, is a splendid dancer with a quantity of pep. Malcolm Tood is the elegant English Lord for Germanic consumption, while Gaston Jacquet gets a favorable notice as a sympathetic old beau. Mary Parker and Olga Limbourg are likewise remarked as assets for this comedy.

It should please the American "provinces," having some instructive views of Europe. *Kendrew.*

THE WRIGHT IDEA

First National release; produced by C. C. Burr. Starring Johnny Hines. Directed by Charles Hines, from story by Jack Townly. Cast includes Louise Lorraine, Edmund Breese, Walter James, Fred Kelcey, Henry Barrows, Henry Herbert, Charles Giblyn, Jack McHugh, J. Barney Shea, Charles Girard, Betty Eagan, Blanche Craig and Richard Maitland. At Loew's American, New York, Aug. 16-19. Running time, over 60 mins.

Johnny Hines, with a screen personality and ability as a comedian several notches above the average, is doomed to the split-week stands and the daily change houses as long as he appears in pictures of this type, lacking novelty and originality in construction and direction. Basically impossible on account of a barren, uninteresting, stupid kind of a story, the selection of which is inexcusable.

The picture fails because of its direction, the continuity and the story head who sanctioned the selection of the script. Gagging is ancient and unappealing. Hines tries hard, but wastes his efforts.

It's the story of a boy with a luminous, blotterless ink, looking for backing. Near the climax, on board a yacht harboring a gang of bootleggers instead of the usual crew, the girl sends in an actor to bid for the ink patents against the only buyer. A real buyer comes before the actor and the latter spoils everything on appearance.

A lot of chasing episodes in between and the rescue by the coast guard for a tame finish. Love interest light. *Mori.*

TWO BROTHERS
(GERMAN MADE)

Ufa German-made production and release. Directed by Karl Grune. Conrad Veidt featured with Lil Dagover heading support. At Cameo, New York, week of Aug. 18. Running time, 80 minutes.
Raucheisen ....Harry De Vries
Ester, his daughter..........Lil Dagover
Michael Schellenberg.........Conrad Veidt
Wenzel Schellenberg.........Conrad Veidt
Mary Floaan...................Liane Haid
Her mother.................Frida Richard
George Weidenbach........Werner Futterer
Gaston Leroy...............Paul Morgan

A pretty terrible sample of how bad a picture can be. Evidently grade of ouput in the post-war period when Germany was striving to assemble its studio facilities. In settings, costuming and other incidentals picture must have been an ambitious effort. These things are elaborate, but the acting, directing and story are unbelievably crude.

With flash American made titles it could be turned into a howling burlesque; as a serious story it is unintentionably absurd. Lil Dagover, who usually plays exotic vamp types capably, does a rich travesty on the Theda Bara tradition. Conrad Veidt plays a dual role of two brothers, one an avaricious business man and the other a sappy philanthropist. The story develops a maudlin sentimental theme.

A stagey, sirupy story turned out deliberately to please dumbbells.

Virtuous brother wears a pointed blonde beard and slouchy clothes, so you know he's a good boy. Avaricious brother sports a long tailed coat and is well barbered, from which you suspect early in the business he will come to no good end.

Lil the vamp is a gag. Almost at her introduction to the audience she smokes a cigaret in a long holder. You can't go wrong when you suspect she presently is going to have a scandalous affair. The dame has a giglo in Paris to whom she gives money.

It required no acuteness to anticipate that the avaricious brother and the vamp would presently get tangled. They do. Avaricious brother falls madly in love with the dame with the long ciggie holder. She doesn't love him a mite and right from the bridal night she keeps him out of her bedroom on one pretext or another, until he goes raving mad and kills her in the middle of the shinyest ballroom floor on the screen.

So you can see what kind of a film it is from these things, but you have to sit through it to appreciate how darkly capable actors can do under certain circumstances. Also you can sit and speculate upon the probable reasons for foreign studios using make up like a clay face pack. Otherwise a dead loss. *Rush.*

Duggan of the Dugouts

Crescent production, released by Anchor Distributing Corp. Direction by Robert Roy, who also gets story credit. Robert Cline, cameraman. Titles by Al Martin. In cast: Pauline Garon, Danny O'Shea, Sid Smith. At Stanley, New York, one day, July 31. Running time 53 minutes.

Another war theme graduates from the school popular a couple of years ago, with a percentage which the grinds will chalk as just passing. "Duggan of the Dugouts" is one of those things which ridicules army life by attempting serious portrayal.

Al Martin sticks in a couple of titles that get laughs out of some of the action. This centers around the usual dance hall lad who gets into the uniform because his dame likes the setup of a sergeant. This petty officer, with his private office rates "sir," salutes and a regiment according to the director's version of army ratings.

The sergeant turns out a spy and the mick hero is roped in by the enemy with his girl, as well, who affords the Red Cross angle.

Laughing gas not only comes to the rescue of the couple but also gets the enemy into such a hilarious mood that the Yanks have to carry them off to the brig.

The World Unarmed
(FRANCO-GERMAN MADE)

Paris, Aug. 4.
Trade shown here under the title of "Le Monde sans Arms," this Synchro-Cine release is a dramatic picture of high photographic excellence and an anti-war evangelist story, produced by J. C. Bernard and G. B. Stieber.

The story develops the doctrine that it is not by super-arming a nation that war can be suppressed but by educating the people to a higher sense of humanity.

There is a section dealing with aviation, most attractive, and from all sides it is an interesting international film.

That it is of French and German origin makes it all the more attractive at this time.

In the cast are Paul Wegener as an engineer, Charles Avel, Albert Paulig, Robert Garrison, Aruth Wartan, Marguerite Schoen as the heroine, Annie Reintwald, Nien Soen Ling, also two well known fliers, Lucien Bossoutrot and Raymond Villechanoux.

While more Teutonic than Gallic this output can be listed with the good French pictures for universal small time consumption. *Kendrew.*

SAWDUST PARADISE
(SOUND)

Paramount production and release. Esther Ralston starred, with Herbert Bosworth featured. Directed by Luther Reed from story and adaptation by George Manker Watters. Screen play by Louise Long. At Paramount, New York, week Aug. 25. Running time, 62 minutes.
Hallie....................Esther Ralston
Butch.....................Reed Howes
Isaiah.....................Hobart Bosworth
Danny......................Tom Maguire
Tanner....................George French
Ward......................Alan Roscoe
Mother....................Mary Alden
District Attorney........John W. Johnston
Sheriff...................Frank Brownlee
Organist....................Helen Hunt

A sappy sort of a story of the carnival and evangeling tents, but its sappiness may mean little to many. A sixth months old baby is the biggest standout of this ordinary Paramount programmer.

The baby becomes the star, despite Esther Ralston. Caught in several caressing poses, the kidlet must have had a flood of shots with those shown impossible of coming from coaching. That baby will save the picture for the women in any town. Otherwise "Sawdust Paradise" is one of those celluloid things, illogical and impossible with its moral problematical.

Its sound record has been badly done. Likely attached after the picture had been finished, to make it stronger. It fails to help. Noises are of the carnival lot, terribly noisy, jarring and not helpful to the action. It's a continual blur of noises, as though all of the high and low wheezes of Coney Island had been pushed into one horn and volume.

Neither does the synchronized music for the silent portions of the picture aid them. Music is kept at too high a pitch when the film is quiet in action. Concentration is diverted from the story by it. And the hulabaloo in general may be too much of a nerve wrack for many.

No dialog but some vocalizing that means nothing and organ playing that is an effect. The organ is seen as a substitute for a steam caliope in a street bally for the evangelist.

This carnival is a wagon show, although the outfit looks too large for that. It parks on a lot opposite the tent where an evangelist is doing a slim business, in attendance and coin. Seeing the carnival drawing away from him the evangelist hollers copper, taking a couple of officials around the lot to see what's working wide open.

The story reads as an original. It was probably this phase that hit as an idea, the setting of godliness on one side of the street against ungodliness on the other. Little beyond the idea gets in and that's not enough for more than casual thought.

No carnival or evangelism followers will care for the story. It pans both. Takes the starving evangelist and permits broad "showman" methods of the grifting lot to put him on his feet and the evangelistic thing converts a couple of the best operators of the grift show. While the evangelist knew when the gaff was on the roll down and tipped off the sheriff, who arrested the girl operating it.

That dame was sent away for 90 days, but remanded to the custody of the evangelist who interceded for her. The dame thereupon interjected the "showmanship" into the ministerial tent, pulled in trade and made it come across, either of which the evangelist had been unable to do.

She was the girl who besides running a gyp, lead the coochers on the outside bally. Still she was discovered by the dying mother of the babe as a good girl, and the baby entrusted to her care. No one denied that she was a good girl and her 3-shell sweetheart even said he intended to marry her.

For the action peak a carnival was wrecked on its lot by another proprietor who considered it an interpolator on his "territory." That wrecking business should have been called a comedy or travesty by a title.

It was a caption that got the biggest laugh other than those the innocent kidlet forced. The snickering caption was of the babe, when the dame after having had the kid wished upon her by the mother as the latter passed out, observed to the evangelist she would have to find out whether the babe when grown up would go to West Point or Vassar.

Another bit aimed for low comedy and very low, was when the baby's weight on a scales moved up while drinking a bottle of milk, to immediately sink back, and the dame starting to arrange a diaper. The diaper-for-a-laugh was supposed to have croaked when the Western burlesque wheel blew up over 20 years ago through pulling that kind of stuff.

Miss Ralston is the dame who started the evangelist going after his racket like a showman.

No acting or direction to bring forth notice or comment. This film is always missing. It may fool the saps but not to any alarming extent, for the noisy sound record will stand that off, though the baby will get 'em all.

Best of the technical end are the captions.

OH KAY

First National production and release. Starring Colleen Moore. Adapted from the musical comedy of the same name by Elsie Janis with Carey Wilson doing the scenario. Directed by Mervyn LeRoy. At Strand, New York, week Aug. 25. Running time, 63 mins.

Lady Kay Rutfield	Colleen Moore
Jimmy Winter	Lawrence Gray
Jansen	Alan Hale
Shorty McGee	Ford Sterling
Judge Appleton	Claude Gillingwater
Constance Appleton	Julanne Johnston

A mild comedy for Colleen Moore which nevertheless should stand up for program purposes on her name and a fairly generous supply of giggles. No howls but enough snickers to see it through.

For a picture it follows the show very closely as the organist peals off the tunes from the musical. Most of Miss Moore's support comes from Ford Sterling, with Lawrence Gray the juvenile and filling in capably. Claude Gillingwater is held down to practically nothing but Alan Hale makes something of his hi-jacker-posing-as-a-detective in doing straight for the antics of the lead trio. Production carries some good looking interiors and gives Miss Moore a chance to hoke up a maid passage and also display some good looking clothes.

She is Lady Rutfield doomed to wed a bore of a Lord. Taking a sail boat jaunt to think it over, she is swamped in a storm and picked up by a rum runner on its way to the States. Anchored off Long Island, McGee takes a load to shore and Kay follows. Hiding the liquor in a cellar the house turns out to belong to Jimmy Winter and in which he's to be married on the morrow.

Slapping Jansen with an oar upon her arrival on the beach, Kay takes refuge in the house and plays Jimmy's wife when Jansen shows up posing as a dick. Later, when Jimmy's fiancee arrives, she becomes McGee's wife and a maid, McGee having made Jimmy believe he's the new butler in order to keep secret the liquor downstairs.

Kay's and McGee's antics to break up the wedding follow with Kay finally telling the agreeably frustrated bridegroom who she is.

Strictly musical comedy plot which the studio has made move fast enough to keep it from drowning. Difference of opinion will be with those who like and dislike Miss Moore's work. Nothing much in it to win over the doubtful, but it may seem particularly weak in view of the preceding "Happiness Ahead."

This one ought to do business without threatening house records. It gives Miss Moore a chance to romp and abetted by Sterling the results are lightly satisfying.

Sid.

Romance of a Rogue

Quality (firm's name) release. A. Carlos, producer. Starring H. B. Warner, with Anita Stewart featured. Directed by King Baggot. Based on the novel by Ruby M. Ayres, with continuity by Adrian Johnson. Titles by Tom Miranda. Cast includes Al Fisher, Charles Gerrard, Fred Esmelton and Billy Franey. At Keith's Broadway, New York, week Aug. 27. Running time, over 60 minutes.

Slow-moving 60 minutes, handicapped by the leaden, unexpressive characterizations of H. B. Warner and Anita Stewart. Playing for the week in this house, perhaps on account of the possible drawing power of Warner's name in the outdoor billing, the picture is not suited outside of the double feature and daily change houses.

Starts well, especially so in the titling. A prison scene, with the released man pledged to vengeance on the man whose lies sent him to jail on the eve of his wedding. But, unlike Monte Cristo, this story assumes a familiar and weary tone in its unfolding.

Direction is responsible for the numerous draggy sequences where all that is shown are a couple of people talking, without titles to tell what they are saying. After the first five minutes titles are used mainly in describing the story.

Power of the heavy in this picture is practically negligible since he is shown paralyzed, unable to get around except in a wheel chair.

Mori.

BUTTER, EGG MAN

First National production and release. Directed by Richard Wallace. Jack Mulhall starred. From the stage play of same name by George S. Kaufman. Main title credits to cameraman and title writer lacking. Cast includes Greta Nissen, Sam Hardy, Gertrude Astor, Luch Beaumont, Sam Hardy, Bert Woodruff. At New York Hippodrome, week Aug. 27. Running time, 75 minutes.

They have merely photographed a stage performance, supplying titles where they are necessary to illuminate the action and occasionally inspire a laugh. Latter isn't often successful. Result is a mechanical film that tires by its labored comedy effort.

Here is a typical bit of business. Couple of tin horn stage producers are trying to hook a sucker to bankroll their turkey production, then in rehearsal.

Boob says he wants to read the script. Instead they act out for him the powerful dramatic climaxes. Sam Hardy impersonates the weeping heroine and the outraged husband in a scene of travesty melodrama. His partner does the same thing, and together the two exhaust the whole repertoire of a cheap hoke burlesque.

Just to show the poverty of resource in the direction, it takes nearly 15 minutes to get this single sequence and there isn't the effective building up of a single screen gag or a real laugh in the whole business.

Only one passage fitted for good screen action. That comes at the finish, where the young sap, after being saddled with the flop production, turns it into a Broadway hit and then sells it back at a profit to the con men just in time for them to get hooked in piracy suits that promise to ruin them.

Even this was played so slowly and unfolded so painstakingly it lost its kick. Seventy-five minutes of flickers to bring forth a merely fair climax is wasted effort.

Young Mulhall, among the most likeable of the juveniles, gives a performance that would save a picture less hopelessly mired. Hardy defeats its comedy purpose by overemphasis in the wrong places. Miss Nissen is merely a pale and quiet straight femme lead.

Sets are first rate and other technical appurtenances worthy of better screen product. Just a dull picture that hasn't even the merit of crude low comedy or highly seasoned action that would recommend it to the neighborhood crowds. Half a double bill at a bargain seems its destiny.

Rush

Yacht of the 7 Sins

(GERMAN MADE)

Berlin, Aug. 14.

When one reads Brigitte Helm's name as the star of a picture there is a certain expectation. For this girl who started so auspiciously in "Metropolis" is on the road to become Germany's strongest picture actress.

But the directors, J. and L. Fleck, have left her sadly in the lurch. What started as an interesting idea dwindles to nothing.

Who has murdered Stephen Martini, owner of a steamboat line? Is it his mistress, Marfa, or Kilian Gurlitt, whose fiancee, Leonie, he has tried to seduce, or his assistant, the menacing Roberts?

This latter individual gets them all on the yacht which is making a trip around the world. It looks as though something interesting might occur, but the boat is stopped by police launches and a harmless dumbbell, who turns out to be a detective, has Roberts arrested as an escaped convict and Marfa as the murderess because she used to do a knife throwing act in vaudeville.

Kilian and Leonie, evidently supposed to be sympathetic, go free.

Brigitte Helm is Marfa and is only allowed to copy her former work. John Stuart, as Kilian, shows that he might be sympathetic if well directed, but is here forced to overact. Kurt Gerron and Kurt Vespermann are amusing in minor roles.

DEVIL DOGS

Crescent Production, released by Anchor Film Distributing Corporation. Produced by Morris R. Schlank. Directed by Fred Windermere. Author not credited. Continuity by Maxine Alton, adapted by Adele Buffington. Featuring Alexander Alton and Stuart Holmes. Cast includes Pauline Curley, Ernest Hilliard and J. P. McGowan. No other players given screen credit. At Stanley, New York, one day, Aug. 23. Running time, 55 minutes.

A clumsy attempt at producing the most difficult of all types of entertainment, a farce, with the added handicap of a military background which has been repeated so often and done so much better within recent months there is no room for pictures of this type to follow.

It's a quickie without even the slightest disguise to give it a better appearance. Badly directed, a story which has been strung together from odd bits seen in other pictures, gags which have been used previously and are still unproductive of results, is not worth spotting even in the shooting galleries.

The picture runs for approximately 55 minutes. It could be cut to 30 without weakening.

Story is of two boys who join the army and go to the front. Both after the same girl. One of the boys has a mustache. The other gets into jams with the captain and is sent to jail. He comes out of jail.

And so on, incoherently, to the finish.

Mori.

THE YELLOW PASS

(RUSSIAN MADE)

Berlin, Aug. 14.

No connection with the American melodrama, "The Yellow Ticket," but a Russian film of great depth and power.

Anna Sten proves herself a dramatic actress of moving simplicity.

The director, F. A. Ozep, has branded a piece of Russian reality onto his screen. A young peasant wife is taken away from her husband to serve as wetnurse for the newly married daughter of a rich man. The husband, whom she hopes to help by this, goes from bad to worse. Finally the girl is no longer of use and is turned out. Wandering through the streets late at night she is arrested by the police as a prostitute and is given the famous yellow pass. Not being able to get any other work she finally ends up in a disreputable house.

Particularly these scenes are marvelously handled by the director who photographs a part of them in a cracked mirror hanging on the wall. Later a young man from her home town brings her news of how badly things are going with her husband who is just recovering from a serious illness. She returns home to a comparatively happy ending.

PAY AS YOU ENTER

Warner Bros. production and release. Directed by Lloyd Bacon from the story by Gregory Rogers. Screen adaptation by Fred Stanley. Titles by Joseph Jackson. Featuring Clyde Cook and Louise Fazenda. Cast includes William Demarest and Myrna Loy. No other players given screen or program credit. At Tivoli, New York, one day, Aug. 22. Running time, 50 minutes.

Beneath the tremendous weight of innumerable superficialities which stamp this a Grade C production, are to be found ideas which could easily result in the best farce of the season, in the hands of a smart director aided by a cast better suited for this type of work.

At least five sequences were meant to get continuous laughter, while the repetition of one action, even crudely done as it is here, gets a slight response. Badly directed, the value of the gags lost in the method of supervision, it barely makes the smaller houses where the use of a picture does not indicate any great merit.

Titles are unproductive of laughs or interest and just about fill the lapses between scenes.

The featured combination, Clyde Cook and Louise Fazenda, miss by a mile in their attempts at comedy. Even the audience in this house, ready to laugh at a fall or a funny expression, remained unmoved.

Story is weak, really an idea rather than a finished work. Continuity and titling should have strengthened instead of weakening it.

Built around a couple of street car conductors and a girl running their restaurant. William Demarest, as the supporting and lighter comedian, turns heavy for the finish.

One of the gags plants Demarest as a punch-crazy conductor, once a prize fighter, who starts punching every time the street car gong rings twice, stopping when it rings once. The ballroom scene has Cook in underclothes far too large for him, with comical results, while the dancing contest also contains a few interesting ideas.

Spotted about right in a daily change house.

Mori.

BOLIBAR

(BRITISH MADE)

London, July 27.

Produced by British International Films, Ltd. Adapted from Leo Perutz's novel, "The Marquis of Bolibar." Directed by Walter Summers. Photography, Jack Parker. Previewed at the Plaza, July 26. Censors' certificate U. Running time, 84 minutes.

Marquis of Bolibar......Jerrold Robertshaw
Col. Bellay...................Hubert Carter
Francoise-Marie................Elissa Landi
La Monita....................Elissa Landi

Whether the British board of censors is particularly simple-minded or whether it's the heat, they have done an amazing thing in passing this picture "for universal exhibition."

For the story is almost entirely concerned with the antics of half a dozen officers who have the minds and habits of barn door roosters and the mentality and behavior of cads. That is doing the theme more mercy than justice.

Additionally, the direction is slow and careless, acting crude and the photography none too good. In cases where effective shots might have been obtained in what appear to be rural Spanish exteriors, the picture has been taken against the sun, making the action which takes place in the foreground obscure by turning the actors into silhouettes which cannot be distinguished one from another.

The action is laid in the middle Napoleonic era, yet such anachronisms as a grand piano (they even show the action at work) and street crowds in the Spanish peninsular with some of the men wearing cloth caps of modern cut and make, occur not infrequently.

It is hard to understand why this film was made. It lacks almost every essential of a motion picture. The story is unsuitable for the screen, and has not the superficial merit of being well known; the cast is not particularly distinguished as to picture audience value, and suffers in production from the direction, which is banal and in spots inefficient; the photography is uneven and never brilliant, and the titles are stilted in diction and heavy in lettering.

Spain in 1811. The town of Bolibar is held by the French and Hessian mercenaries, and is besieged by Spanish and British troops.

The Hessian garrison finds life dull, and the officers bewail former days when they deceived their colonel with his wife. One, on patrol, hears a plan by the Marquis of Bolibar to enter the town in disguise and give the besiegers three signals, so that they may assault the town and regain for him his estate. The marquis comes in as a peasant carrying the baggage of a newly joined officer, and, waiting in the officers' quarters, hears them boasting of the amours with their colonel's wife. This is despite the fact she is dead, the colonel still adores her memory, and they are supposed to be "officers and gentlemen."

Realizing the peasant has heard them and fearing their babble may get back to the colonel, they have him shot as a spy, and then discover he is Bolibar.

The colonel has found a girl who so much resembles his dead wife he marries again, and the same business starts among the officers. In a rage at being favored less than another, one of them sets fire to the roof of the colonel's house to upset an assignation, and thus sends unwittingly the first signal which should have come from the shot marquis.

Later three officers who have been given a simultaneous assignation, enraged to find the lady is with her husband instead, play the organ in the house chapel to disturb them, and so send the second signal.

In an attack another is badly hit, and babbles of his own and his fellows' affairs with the late wife, in the colonel's hearing. The colonel think the references are to his new wife, and throws her off. Fearing she may tell the colonel more than he

already knows, one of the officers, at the request of the others, takes her across to the enemy lines in a boat, telling her he is going to hand her over to the troops. She stabs herself with a dagger which was found on the marquis and was to be delivered as the third sign. Whereon the town is attacked, and apparently all the officers and their colonel are killed.

A bright and sweet story of wholesale lechery, in which few details are spared. One officer is shown in a flashback waiting under the window while another is with the colonel's wife. Incidents and suggestions of this degree of decency abound, while the implication that the liaisons are about to be relived with the second woman because she so closely resembles the dead wife is so nasty that one can only hope the sponsors of the film are too ignorant of such an implication to know it exists.

How it will book here it is difficult to say. Strange things happen in this business.   *Frat.*

HOUSE OF SHAME

Chesterfield production and release. Directed by Burton King under supervision of Lon Young. From story by Lee Authmar. Adaptation and continuity by Arthur Hoerl. Photographed by M. A. Andersen. Cast includes Creighton Hale, Virginia Brown Faire, Lloyd Whitlock, Florence Dudley, Fred Walton and Carlton J. King. Previewed in projection room, New York, Aug. 22. Running time over 50 minutes.

Considering the speed with which Burton King can turn out pictures, the result here may be considered meritorious, since it brings a finer product into the states right field than has been available previously. While production costs have been kept down to a predetermined level, the picture has been handled in a manner which betrays no trace of cheapness in scenic effect.

Scenic settings and backgrounds are okay, while the cast is capable for a picture of this type. Florence Dudley shows big league possibilities in a limited but effective characterization.

Direction not any too good. Miss Faire, who photographs well and looks snappy in certain poses, has been subjected to more and longer closeups than suitable. Girl looks good but can't stand a close camera for long, difficult facial contortions.

Story deals with a husband who steals money for fem No. 2. To get out of a jam he gets his wife to plead for him with his employer. The latter agrees to go easy but wants certain things, starting with a friendship with the wife which he expects to blossom into something else.

Climax when the husband finds his wife in his employer's apartment at night and agrees to lay off for a certain amount. Affair framed by the employer to show the wife, whom he has begun to love, what kind of a man her husband is.

Fairly smooth continuity resulting in a picture which moves along at good speed. Should go well in the minor stands, split weeks and daily changes. A couple of the sequences with strong sexy twists.

Title should prove a business getter in some localities. The National Board of Review has placed its okay on the picture without a cut, while the New York State Censorship Bureau made but one elimination showing an actual theft of bonds, giving as their reason for the elimination "Inciting to Crime." *Mori.*

The Passing of Mr. Quinn

(BRITISH MADE)

London, Aug. 2.

Produced by the Strand Film Co. Directed by Leslie Hiscott. Adapted from Agatha Christie's novel. Photography, Horace Wheddon. Censors' certificate A. Previewed at London Hippodrome July 31. Running time, 100 minutes.

Prof. Appleby..........Clifford Heatherley

Mrs. Appleby.................Trilby Clark
Dr. Alec Portal..............Stewart Rome
Derek Capal..................Vivian Baron
Housemaid....................Ursula Jeans

A poor picture. Whatever may have been the merits of Mrs. Christie's novel, they have almost entirely disappeared in the film. Its only point of merit is a rather novel presentation of a murder trial, cross-examination and people on the witness stand being shown in double exposure with the accused woman and members of the public.

As told on the screen, story is nonsensical. Great amount of latitude is to be allowed for melodrama, which this is. But here it is so disjointed and unconvincing, as well as badly motivated, that it fails to hold interest.

Possibly Hiscott, who has been assistant director to T. Hayes Hunter, George Fitzmaurice and others, may do better. Possibly also he was handicapped by the script and by finance. But there are faults in the film which neither of these things excuse.

Three people — his wife, Derek Capel and the housemaid—had opportunities to poison Professor Appleby. Capel was in love with Mrs. Appleby; the professor was horribly cruel to her, and the housemaid was going to have a baby of the professor's. So the three had a motive. Mrs. Appleby is tried and acquitted.

Dr. Portal, who has been in love with her, grows more and more so. He goes to the convent where she has taken refuge and persuades her to marry him. On their first day at home he finds her reading a letter she had long ago written to Capel, which seems to prove her guilt. At least, to suit the weakness of the story, he accepts this as evidence without further question and calls her a murderess.

Comes then to the village Mr. Quinn, a brokendown man who needs the doctor. This man later turns up at the doctor's house during a party, and in one of the most unconvincing scenes ever watched in any film tells the guests how the murder was committed by Capel, and why. Owning up, as he dies from poison, that he is Capel, and his conscience had driven him into African wilds till a fever-wracked wreck, he had come home to confess and die. Everybody save the folk on the screen recognized Quinn at once as Capel, so where there was any mystery and what it was still needs figuring out.

Acting by Clifford Heatherley is very good. Trilby Clark, an Australian, is not too well served by her part, and the rest of the roles are too indefinitely characterized to be noticeable. This is not so much due to the artists as to the failure of the director to make either the characters or the story convincing, to the excessive use of close-ups and to the inordinate length to which many sequences are drawn out.

This picture is a striking example of one of the greatest defects of picture-making in this country—the inability to realize that films need making almost in their entirety before a foot is shot. Few of our native units seem to have the kind of organization which can prepare a film and directors and staffs who can visualize it before it is made. They give the impression of just rushing ahead with an idea and sorting everything out as they go along.

Production management is almost unknown. The fact that we have some "production managers" proves that. Scenario and continuity writing are—well, the less said about it the better.   *Frat.*

Murderer Left No Clue

(GERMAN MADE)

Berlin, Aug. 15.

Just another one of those Ufa program pictures, cheap enough to

get their cost and a small profit back out of Central Europe alone. But apparently the Germans never catch on how to make a real crook picture.

The story is taken from the archives of police headquarters in Berlin and with police officials as advisers. That's the trouble with it, real crooks are not interesting for they are too stupid. Anyone sees the trick of the story long before it is cleared up.

The owner of an amusement park is found dead, but as a big propeller is revolving at the same time it is quite evident that he has been hit on the head by it.

Of the four suspects only one could possibly have done it.

A competent performance was given by Kurt Gerron as the tough crook that bumped the proprietor off by mistake. Juvenile simply excruciatingly affected in the worst Continental fashion. Not much to be said for the heroine or the rest of the cast.

Konstantin J. David directed.

SUBMARINE

Columbia production featuring Jack Holt. Directed by Frank R. Capra. Supervised by Irvin Willat. Story by Norman Springer. Adapted by Winifred Dunn. Continuity by Dorothy Howell. Film editor, Arthur Roberts. Cameraman, Joe Walker. Harrison Wiley, art director. Buddy Coleman, assistant director. At Embassy, New York, for run at $1.50, starting Aug. 30. Running time, one hour 43 mins.

Jack Dorgan....................Jack Holt
Bob Mason....................Ralph Graves
Commander................Clarence Burton
The Boy....................Arthur Rankin
Snuggles....................Dorothy Revier

Columbia and the United States navy got together in a big way on this one, with the result that Columbia obtained at small cost a good box-office picture and the navy got across some valuable propaganda for itself.

The picture refers specifically to the ill-fated S-44, rammed and sunk by a cruiser during battle maneuvers a few years ago in California waters. Another submarine disaster occurred later on the Atlantic coast, and between the east and west the navy was on the receiving end of much criticism. The newspapers of the country devoted considerable editorial energy to lambasting high naval officials.

Without entering the controversial aspects of the tragedies, "Submarine" presents to the public the navy's side. Use of the S-44 was not entirely good judgment, either as story-telling or as propaganda. The S-44 did not end happily and heroically in real life, as in the film. The story could have used a mythical submarine, accomplished its dramatic and other purposes as well, and not left loopholes for cynical comment. That, however, is nothing for showmen to worry about.

"Submarine" is a strong and stirring picture. It is playing at the Embassy at $1.50 and not a bad entertainment buy at that figure. For general release it should be an outstander. It's Columbia's second straight picture on Broadway and it will add lustre to the company's standing nationally.

Man's fight with the forces of nature is always dramatic and the frantic efforts of the navy to get an air line down to the slowly-asphyxiating crew of the S-44 makes natural drama. The under-sea photography is excellent with no suggestion of laboratory faking to break the thread of illusion. "Submarine" has novelty, suspense and the imprint, valid or not, of authenticity.

It shows, sympathetically, the terrific odds against rescue work. The intent is plainly to demonstrate that the navy quickly and intelligently does every thing that can possible be done in such emergencies. The film dramatizes the fight against nature, little homo pitting his brain, his daring and his will against the crushing weight and pressure of 400 feet of ocean depth. Down in the trapped submarine the argonizing crew is commanded by an officer of heroic moral measurements. This part is acted with a wealth of sincerity and conviction by Clarence Burton. If the dreadnaught boys have been peeved against the film industry in the past for "Convoy" and other pictures dealing with the navy Burton squares everything. He is all an officer should be.

The hero of the proceedings is a deep sea diver impersonated by Jack Holt (who has recently returned to Paramount to play gentleman cowboys). Holt's early cinematic career tended toward high hats and drawing rooms and it seems bizarre to have him chewing tobacco. However, he does make it plausible.

Ralph Graves is the diver's buddy and unwittingly the boy friend of the latter's round-heeled wife. The diver has married in San Diego while his friend is on submarine duty. The friend, returning to port in the diver's absence, has a hot week-end affair with the frail lady. In the blow-up the diver accepts his wife's alibi and the friends part bitterly.

There is no love interest, as such, in the picture but Dorothy Revier gives it sex appeal in the early sequences. Miss Revier is a fetching damsel and seems too classy to be a dance hall pick-up. But why be technical? Columbia has a dramatic and box office clicker. *Land.*

State Street Sadie

(SOUND-DIALOG)

Warner Bros. underworld drama designated a Vitagraph special. Directed by Archie Mayo. Musical score by Louis Silvers. Photography by Barney McGill. Conrad Nagel, Myrna Loy and William Russell featured in cast. At the New York Strand Sept. 1. Running time, 75 minutes.

Ralph Blake....................Conrad Nagel
Slinkey....................Myrna Loy
The Bat....................William Russell
Isobel....................Georgie Stone
Hawkins....................Pat Hartigan

Another mediocre picture made into a good entertainment seller on the strength of its dialog talking sequences. Audible passages are two in number, both of them brief, perhaps four or five minutes long, but they put the fan clincher on the whole production.

This sound and dialog treatment is especially interesting from the technical production angle. Aside from the story incidents where the dialog is employed, the story is told with the aid of printed titles and these screen explanatory flashes in the pre-Vita manner make up by far the larger footage. But it is the dialog bits that make the film.

Underworld theme involves an unusually elaborate "planting" of circumstance and antecedent story, and this is covered in remarkably brief time with the audible talk. Tom Blake, employed in a bank, has somehow become involved with a band of gunmen. They rob the bank, killing a policeman during the job, and fasten the murder upon Tom. The police are on Tom's heels at the opening, and the introduction is his suicide by gas, an especially good bit of suggestive filming. Action is conveyed without actually showing the deed, through the medium of trick photography. At the moment of Tom's passing, his twin brother, Ralph, comes upon the scene, learns the situation from a letter in the dead man's effects, and resolves to avenge his framed brother.

He hides the body just as a member of the gang arrives and mistakes Ralph for Tom. Here is a fine dialog passage between the hero and the gangster in the persons of Conrad Nagel and George Stone. Step by step as hero and gunman exchange cautious chat, the underlying situation grows up. Voice reproduction is astonishingly natural, and both men have excellent voices and fine command of diction.

Essence of the whole situation is that the criminal band is supposed to be controlled by a mysterious master mind called "The Chief," while his orders are carried out by "The Bat" (played by William Russell), and it is against this hidden criminal that the hero directs his campaign.

Ralph has to flee when the police are hot on his trail, and takes refuge in a strange apartment, which turns out (a hard to take coincidence) to be the home of the daughter of the policeman slain in the bank robbery. They join forces and therein comes the romantic side of the plot, the pair, pretending to be criminals themselves, go into the night club hangout of the outlaw band.

Even the gangsters do not know the identity of the "Chief." The second straight dialog passage, which serves to build up the sinister atmosphere, is between "The Bat" and one of his lieutenants. **A tricky handling of this is that the gangster's efforts to find "The Chief's" identity and "Bat'" maneuvering to outwit him, is done entirely in a surface vein of comedy while underneath there is a feeling of sinister cruelty.**

Story from there builds up by titles and fast action on the pursuit of hero after "Chief" culminating when "Bat" himself is revealed as the master mind and has the hero in his power. Just at the moment the motorcycle squad of police bandit chasers comes dashing up in battle formation, with much shrieking of sirens and popping of guns, and finale is a roof top battle, medley of thrilling noises as wicked spitting of machine guns, bark of .45 and crash of glass. Sound adds vastly to effect of this climax, giving it a melodramatic kick that would be absent in a silent screening. It is these details of sound effect that saves a story in spite of itself. For the story thread, mechanical and unconvincing in itself, is a pretty weak sister.

Nagel is an asset for the talkers. So is William Russell. This was to be expected. The "find" is in Georgie Stone, hitherto player of underworld bits, but here displaying a capital knack of nice delivery of a complete talking role. Myrna Loy, with her exotic style, doesn't suggest the daughter of a policeman, and certainly not the type that could successfully vamp a tough gunman. Her audible contribution is practically nil.

Effective melodrama picture that will meet all needs of the talking program. At the Strand they were packed in uncomfortably on the evening shows of the opening day. The "sound" billing apparently brought 'em to the "home of the talkers," and the picture obviously satisfied them. *Rush.*

THE AIR CIRCUS

(SOUND-DIALOG)

Fox production and release, with 15 mins. of Movietone dialogue. Louise Dresser, Arthur Lake, Sue Carroll and David Rollins featured. Story by Graham Baker and Andrew Bennison. Directed by Howard Hawks and Lew Seiler. Dialogue staged by Charles Judels. Titles by William Kernell. Film editor, Ralph Dixon. Cameraman, Dan Clark. At Gaiety, New York, opening Sept. 1 at $2 top. Running time, 88 mins.

Mrs. Blake....................Louise Dresser
Buddy Blake....................David Rollins
Speed Doolittle....................Arthur Lake
Sue Manning....................Sue Carol
Charles Manning....................Charles Delaney
Jerry McSwiggin....................Heinie Conklin
Lieut. Blake....................Earl Robinson

With or without the talking sequence this is just a program picture about two 16-year-old high school kids who take a course in aviation. Expert direction has managed to make a fairly interesting lightweight number out of a script that holds nothing but background and a plot that doesn't exist. There is no love interest and the sole and only drama in the entire hour and a half is when one of the two kids develops a case of fright and has to fight it out with himself.

The talking sequence runs about 15 minutes. The boy's mother arrives from Ypsilanti, Michigan, to visit the Pacific School of Aviation. The boy is in his room sobbing into a pillow. Downstairs the students of less nervous disposition are making whoopee with their girl friends. Mother and son have a sentimental session, with tears splashing every way. This scene probably will grip the women. It reduces the hero of the film to the status of a big baby.

Comedy is worked in prior to the mother's arrival between Arthur Lake and Sue Carroll. Lake is the comedian of the picture, and a very good one. He stands out also in the dialogue. Miss Carroll does nicely and is at all times an attractive figure, despite her negative position in the story. Louise Dresser, veteran stage and screen actress, had no trouble with the microphone, and the blah-blah of David Rollins was okay.

However, interpolating a talking short in the midst of a programmer doesn't make it $2. "Air Circus" is a fill-in booking for Fox. It plays one week at the Gaiety and moves over to the Globe to finish Fox's lease there expiring Oct. 8. For Broadway with Movietone support that will probably be just about right.

One circumstance sticks out in "Air Circus." Throughout the film the name "Pacific School of Aviation" appears. It's on the hangars, the planes, the overalls and the stationary. With the story glorifying professional aviation this film is a prospectus for the school and will mean dough to them when the picture starts to circulate in the small towns. "Wings," which contained no plug of any sort and was sombre and tragic rather than a week-end picnic, increased the business in the aviation schools all over the country.

"Air Circus" has advantages that offset its faults. The aviation stuff, some of it faintly technical, is excellent, with special reference to Dan Clark's photography. There is some reliable comedy by Lake and Heinie Conklin. It totals a moderate.

Land.

CARDBOARD LOVER

Metro-Goldwyn-Mayer release of Marion Davies' production, starring Miss Davies. Jetta Goudal and Nils Asther underlined. Adapted from the play of the same name by Carey Wilson. Directed by R. Z. Leonard with Lucile Newmark titling and John Arnold cameraman. At the Capitol, New York, week of Sept. 1. Running time, 71 mins.

Sally....................Marion Davies
Simone....................Jetta Goudal
Andre....................Nils Asther
Signor Torino....................Andres de Segurola
Algine....................Tenen Holtz
Peppy....................Pepi Lederer

Evidently encouraged by her success as a comedienne, Marion Davies has left farce for low comedy. And they yell. About the only thing she doesn't do in this one is to heave a pie. She's gone beyond her imitations. Now she mugs, in and out of closeups, and the balcony bunch love it. The howl at the Capitol Saturday night was Miss Davies placing a piping hot water bottle on Nils Asther's tummie. For program purposes deliberation deems it a nice comedy, of good background with no particular high spot. Its reception at the performance viewed rates it close to a wow.

Regardless of what the play did or was, as a picture "Cardboard Lover" unwinds in a series of sequences, each having its hoped for comedy climax and running off much like short stories, almost blackouts, concerning the same people. Some of these passages are necessarily better than others with the less interesting prone to be rather quiet. As a balance there are a couple of spots where they screamed. It's spotty composition that possibly isn't as important as it might be because of the transparent story which telegraphs its itinerary in the first reel and which the pieces of business smother.

Miss Davies, as Sally, is an autograph hound touring the continent with a group of schoolmates. One look at Andre, France's tennis champ, and he's her supreme objective. An edict permitting the students to be on their own for five hours nightly supposedly allows the time for Sally to follow the athlete into his home to keep him from the vamping Simone. Sally has intentionally made herself the third party of the triangle after discovering Simone isn't on the level with her all-believing lover. Andre strikes a bargain with Sally to keep him away from Simone and that's the basis of all following situations.

Miss Davies romps, flirts, smirks and is happy as the good little devil intent on getting her man. She takes falls, uncorks an excellent imitation of Miss Goudal, does considerable polite mugging and gives herself a buck tooth front during a scene after she has changed clothes with a bellboy. And Leonard, taking no chances, first shows the bellhop sneaking out in long underwear and then fleeing in the girl's clothes. They howled at this, too, which makes the director right as far as this house is concerned.

Nothing subtle about this release. Just broad hoke within rich interiors and sold on Miss Davies' appearance, willingness and ability to forget her dignity. Miss Goudal does her undulating and scheming siren, continuously annoyed by the antics of the American girl, in eccentric clothes, while Asther makes a good looking and personable chap of the boy torn by his infatuation for the sophisticated coquette and regretting his bargain with the naive Sally, whom he eventually elects to take as wife. Other cast considerations are strictly secondary.

Censors in certain sections are apt to play with these reels in that spot where Sally dons pajamas to convince the visiting Simone that she's moved in and flaunts a bit of crepe de chine as the convincer. But it's of harmless intent with Miss Davies clowning the bit.

Picture seems strong enough to give Miss Davies some additional r.p.m. for her comedy career, but how long they'll accept her in such broad technique is open to discussion. Possibly Leonard saw the script as hopeless without dipping into the old hokum bucket, and thereby saved a chestnut. But the idea remains that Miss Davies' droll efficiency deserves more script consideration where it isn't necessary for her to straddle and sprawl.

Sid.

THE WATER HOLE

Paramount release of F. Richard Jones production co-featuring Jack Holt and Nancy Carroll in Zane Grey's story. Runs 66 minutes at Paramount, New York, week of Sept. 1.

Philip Randolph	Jack Holt
Judith Endicott	Nancy Carroll
Bert Durland	John Boles
Mr. Endicott	Montague Shaw
Dolores	Ann Christy
"Ma" Bennett	Lydia Yeamans Titus
Ray	Jack Perrin
Mojave	Jack Mower
Diego	Paul Ralli
Shorty	Tex Young
Joe	Bob Miles
Indian	Greg Whitespear

They have Jack Holt back in westerns, doing a glorified he-man of Arizona role, in contrast to the effete east wherefrom the spoiled and capricious Nancy Carroll as the heroine hails. The action switches from the metropolis to an Arizonian reclamation tract when Holt, in partnership with the heroine's father, goes west for the project.

Miss Carroll who had successfully wagered she would make Holt propose to her within a week back east follows him to Arizona in retaliation for a fancied slight.

The story is one of those present-day taming-of-the-shrew affairs with the flapper heroine quite conscious of the leading man's plans and intentions, even unto being a willing captor in a "kidnapping" scene, until the climatic lost-in-the-desert sequences.

There is the menace also in the form of an evil cowpuncher who, for some unexplained reason, is retained in Holt's employ despite his avowedly frank threat to "get" the hero.

The not-to-be-analyzed scenes and the generally familiar continuity are offset by the leading pair's intelligent playing, particularly that of Miss Carroll, who makes her hoyden a living, breathing character. Holt, as dapper in dinner jacket as he is manly in chaps and sombrero, is perfectly cast for the Zane Grey hero.

For all of its general lightweightedness, "The Water Hole" will please the fans and will, of course, make money for the producer and exhibitor alike. It's an inexpensive production, chiefly outdoors, with more than two reels transpiring on supposedly Arizona wasteland, leading into the mirage stuff when the near-victims search for the water hole as a result of a horse-thieving Indian guide having stolen their mounts.

The interiors are few, the most pretentious flash being a few shots of a ballroom dance. As a result, considering the production and the personnel, this one won't impoverish anyone, and it will please even the skeptical western fans. Feature has enough of the "society" in it to click with the femmes.

There is some natural color protography included in the prolog in the Adam and Eve allegorical byplay and in one mid-section golf scene. It is disclosed that Miss Carroll is a flaming Titian, unless the celluloid is artificially tinted, the black-on-white otherwise showing her off as a blonde. Whether a red-head or not, Miss Carroll is a cutie and a comedienne of surprising resourcefulness and depth.

Abel.

FORGOTTEN

(FRENCH MADE)

Paris, Aug. 20.

Another French film, adapted from a novel "L'Oublie" by the prolific Pierre Benoit. The subject is full of adventures in foreign lands, with an eccentric beautiful lady as exotic heroine.

"L'Oublie" has been produced by Mme. Germaine Dulac with care. It is by no means the best release of this talented lady. Made by Alex Nalpas for L. Aubert Distribution, it carries a couple of known dancers, Mlle. Edmonde Guy and her partner, Van Duren, as principals, supported by Mona Goya, Sylvie Mai, Yvonne Legeai, Valenti Kolino, Paul Lorbert and Jacques Arnna.

The story has been somewhat changed for this picture version, with the book preferable this time.

Pindere is a smart, handsome young man, seeking adventures. He joins a party visiting the ancient sites of Mingrelia, is made prisoner and to receive good treatment Pindere poses as a diplomat.

He is brought into touch with the governing classes of the region and also meets a French dancer, Lily de Thorigny, with whom he falls in love. One day Pindere is invited to visit the oligarche ruling the city, and to his astonishment finds himself in front of Mandane, a beautiful Princess, who constitutes the monarch all on her own. The couple are mutually infatuated. The lady is anxious to shoot the moon, and Pindere assists her in appropriating the court jewelry. Nevertheless, he is gentleman enough to think of Lily. They cross the frontier and are then safe from pursuit, where the two women abandoned their devoted, amorous slave.

Then he woke up; it was a dream. "L'Oublie" is a romantic sort of reel for short-run houses.

Kendrew.

A SHIP COMES IN

Pathe production and release. Directed by W. K. Howard. Original story and adaptation by Julien Josephson. Rudolph Schildkraut, Louise Dresser and Robert Edeson featured. In cast, Milton Holmes, Linda Landi, Fritz Feld and Lucien Littlefield. At the Hippodrome, New York, week of Sept. 3. Running time, 75 minutes.

A story of immigrant life which packs plenty of sentiment but still manages to keep from going overboard on sob stuff. Fine work by Rudolph Schildkraut and Louise Dresser, together with discreet direction by Howard, makes this a worth while screen offering.

Story concerns the trials and tribulations of Peter Pleznik (Schildkraut), a Hungarian immigrant. Peter becomes a patriot almost as soon as he and his family set foot on their adopted land despite the grumblings of an anarchistic countryman. Obtaining a job as a mopper in a federal building he looks forward to the day when he will have citizenship conferred upon him and sees nothing but happiness ahead for his family.

When he is finally naturalized, Peter, to show his appreciation, plans to present the judge with a cake that Mrs. Pleznik (Miss Dresser) has baked. The disgruntled anarchist removes the cake and places a bomb in the box that Peter brings to the judge's office. The infernal machine explodes, the judge who has befriended Peter is seriously injured, his secretary is bumped off and Peter is jailed, convicted of radical tendencies. To add to his misfortunes Peter's son, who has enlisted in the army, is killed in action. Despite all this, his patriotism never wavers and in the end all is cleared up and Peter goes back to his mops and brooms happy.

Lacking a final clinch or box office title the flicker nevertheless should find an appreciative audience in the neighborhoods, especially those drawing from a foreign element.

THE VORTEX

(ENGLISH MADE)

Produced by Gainsborough and released in America through Ameranglo. Few credits. Adaptation of Noel Coward play of same name. Cast: Ivor Novello, Willette Kershaw. At Fifth Ave. Playhouse, week of August 25. Running time, 65 minutes.

The only salvation for "The Vortex" in the American market will be the "arty" houses. At that fans will have to be pretty arty not to laugh at this melodrama, with its ludicrously heavy titles and its belated climax.

Stiff, starchy and absurdly artificial are the members of the cast. The Coward play is there in outline but the substance is so handled as to be mistaken for burlesque by any cluster of American ticket buyers.

Stuff of the mother playing kitten; the athletic boy who could out talk a speakie crowd, the gigolo sequences, the newspaper girl who is an actress of scanty screen experience—all these angles and many more make the picture a poor subject for screen audiences of all grades.

THE BODY PUNCH

Universal production and release starring Jack Daugherty with Virginia Browne Faire underlined. Directed by Leigh Jason from H. O. Hoyt's story. Titles by Gardner Bradford. Cast includes George Kotsonaros, Monte Montague and Wilbur Mack. At Loew's New York as half of double bill Aug. 24. Running time, 55 minutes.

Favorable action episode for the intermediates. It presents the sport controversy of boxer versus wrestler with the ultimate decision in favor of a straight left, the contest going to a finish in a boarding house room. Daugherty is the glove exponent and Kotsonaros the catch-as-catch-can artist.

Love interest flits in when Daugherty saves Miss Faire in an underworld cafe brawl. Her social parasite companion eventually tries to get away with a necklace, Daugherty is blamed and this leads to the private four wall struggle with the wrestler, the latter having taken the trinket from the actual snatcher. Interested in welfare work, Miss Faire stages a charity bazaar, the main attraction to be the boxer and wrestler in a ring. The missing bracelet abruptly calls off the contest and postpones the decision until the two men meet privately.

Sport angle should catch the interest of male patronage and there's enough activity in the cafe scrap, which continues on a roof, to fill in between the start and finish which are 55 minutes apart.

Daugherty screens as no beauty but looks wholesomely athletic and seems able to lead and feint without falling down. Miss Faire merely plays straight and Kotsonaros is the appropriate heavily muscled menace. Comedy touch is derived from a couple of kids continuously giving the uncouth wrestler the bird. Moderate production called for and U evidently had no objections. Camera and title work average and minus high spots.

Novelty sport touch plus Daugherty's two fights to let it stand alone in the daily changes if necessary.

Sid.

Moscow as It Laughs

(RUSSIAN MADE)

Berlin, Aug. 20.

The Russians are leaping ahead in film production. This is their comedy and it is splendid. B. Barnett, who directed for the Sovkino, rushes right up into the Lubitsch class.

What the Hollywood comedies so greatly lack in freshness of viewpoint and vitality is here to be found in abundance. That it sometimes flows over a bit is excusable and hardly disturbs.

A little modiste is registered by her employers as living in their apartment, so that they may be allowed by the police to have an extra room (great shortage of living quarters in Moscow). She has sympathy with a young student who has no place to live, and marrying him, takes him to the apartment and demands her room.

Her employers are furious but are forced to give it to her. They, however, remove all furniture. The two spend their wedding night sleeping on the hard wooden floor—all, of course, in complete childish innocence.

In the end the girl wins a prize in a lottery and after some exciting rough house comedy, the two are really united.

Charming is the work of Anna Sten and Koval Samborsky in the leads.

RIDERS OF THE DARK

M-G-M production and release. Tim McCoy starred. Directed by Nick Grinde with George Nogle at camera. Story by W. S. Van Dyke. In cast: Dorothy Dwan, Roy D'Arcy, Dick Sutherland. At Stanley, New York, one day. Running time 60 minutes.

Tim McCoy may be able to knock over five or six of filmdom's bad boys of the plains and get away with it, but it will take a real fan with moronistic tendencies to assimilate Tim's blase accomplishment of a half regiment or more in his "Riders of the Dark."

How come the dark is another matter for discussion. The sun beams out brightly except when Tim leaves Rex Lease and Dorothy Dwan to defend the prison, while he summons the troops to wipe out Bad Guy Eagan's horde.

Plenty of physical combat in this film baby; in fact, more than pioneers in the racket would ever have attempted.

This is Tim's most glorious contribution to what one man can do to several score or more—on the screen.

CHAMPAGNE

(BRITISH MADE)

Produced by British International Pictures, Ltd. Directed by Alfred Hitchcock. Distributed in the U. K. by Wardour Films, Ltd.; in America by the World Wide Fi m Corp. through Educational Exchanges. Story by Walter Mycroft and Alfred Hitchcock. Scenario by Elliot Stannard. Photography by Jack Cox. Censors' certificate "U." Previewed at the London Hippodrome Aug. 29. Running time, 84 minutes.

Betty, daughter of a Champagne King.. Betty Balfour
The Champagne King.......Gordon Harker
The Boy.......................Jean Bradin
The Cosmopolitan.....Ferdinand von Alten

If J. D. Williams is going to release British pictures in America he will have to get some better than this. The story is of the weakest, an excuse for covering 7,000 feet of harmless celluloid with legs and close-ups.

Be a female star ever so good—and Betty Balfour is not seen here at her best—no audience is going to stand for nine-tenths of a film being devoted to her doing nothing in particular. That's what happens here, with no other woman in the cast, and three men who are indeterminate in character and badly directed.

Two versions of the story are given—one in the press book and another in a v. p. folder. Neither has much resemblance to the story on the screen, which is really an advantage to the literature.

Gordon Harker is supposed to be a "Champagne King," whatever that is, but the film shows him, both in action and captions, as a caricature of Hollywood's idea of a successful New York business man. His daughter wants to marry a boulevard cake-eater, and poppa disagrees. The lover sails on the Aquitania (spelled throughout with a "c"), and Betty follows in a plane, which she crashes in the path of the liner. At this point the film commences on the screen.

The boy friend gets sore at Betty taking a high hand just because poppa has dough, and she gets sore at him for getting sore, throws him down, and plays around with a nasty-looking middle-ager. In Paris she gives wild parties. Then father tells her he's broke, so they go to live in a hovel while she gets work in a cabaret to keep the home fires burning. Boy friend finds her there and goes to fetch poppa. Meantime, fed up with the life, she asks the bad man of the boat, who has turned up again, to take her to America. When she finds he has booked a double berth on the liner she gets cold feet, but boy friend arrives to rescue her, and they both find bad man is a friend of father's who has been framed by him to teach her a lesson.

Technically — settings, photography and lighting—it's as good as they come. But the story, the direction and the acting are dire. Betty Balfour has a thankless role and far too many close-ups. As a New York business man Gordon Harker is a wild burlesque of a Sinclair Lewis complex. Von Alten looks good and plays quietly and well, but has a silly part.

As champagne, it's the kind of wine they sell to boobs in Soho.
Frat.

THE DEVIL'S CAGE

Chadwick production and release. Pauline Garon starred. Directed by Wilfred Noy from screen story prepared by Isadore Bernstein. In cast: Donald Keith, Ruth Stonehouse, Lincoln Stedman, Armand Kaliz. At the Stanley, N. Y., Sept. 3. Running time, 60 minutes.

Straining a hacked theme of artist and dancer-model with the hope of shaping up some original situations ranks "The Devil's Cage" as just an average indie.

Old stuff of the dancer out of work, a storm, and her contact with the wealthy American artist in a Parisian sub-cellar is the opener. Keith's extreme stolidness for a young man and his unexplained suppression up to the last few feet, rob the yarn of even a semblance of romance. Although it must be said that Miss Garon, while doing the vamp thing nicely, wins the sympathy of grind house audiences in her attempts to bring the boy friend around. Story follows the stereotyped course to the letter, with Kaliz, as the cabaret maestro, going in for some superfluous acting.

A couple of scraps, in which Keith is a participant, are conventional and the attempted shooting of the artist, after the dancer has deserted her boss, gets little reaction.

Midnight, Place Pigalle

(FRENCH MADE)

Paris, Aug. 24.

"Minuit, Place Pigalle," (the title under which this L. Aubert production is released here) is a squint at the nocturnal life of the capital and constitutes an excellent picture. It will perhaps figure among the best of the year, much being due to the playing of Nicolas Rimsky.

Plot: Prosper is head waiter at the Flamant Rose, and fulfills his functions calmly, uninfluenced by the gaiety around him until he saves enough to retire on a small farm. After years of struggle, his devoted wife dies. The loss is a terrible blow. Prosper loses his head and allows some former customers to lead him back to the old haunts. But now he returns as a reveller, and quickly spends his little fortune. Prosper is glad even to take a job as dish washer in the Flamant Rose.

He has bitter reflections on the life around him. He pines to be back on the little farm. One night he sees in the cabaret a pure young girl he knew as a child. He saves her from dishonor and in reward she establishes the good old waiter in a little cafe in a Riviera village far from Place Pigalle and its false revelry.

This scenario has been well handled by Rene Hervil, and adroitly executed by Rimsky, Renee Heribel (Suzy), Francois Rozet (the girl's companion) and Suzy Pierson, Fernand Fabre and Andre Nicolle.
Kendrew.

THE BLACK ACE

Leo Maloney production released through Pathe. Don Coleman starred. Leo Maloney, director. Edward Kull, cameraman. In cast: Jeanette Loff, Billy Barton, J. P. McGowan. At Loew's New York, Aug. 28, half double bill. Running time, 60 minutes.

"The Black Ace" is okay. Good story, well cast, excellent workup to suspense. Way above the average western of the present day. First runs in some towns can use it to advantage and seconds all over. All classes can't make a mistake by signing it.

Picturesque locale and adherence to continuity with many old gags handled in clever way, get audience interest after first reel. Bandit, double-crossed by pal, raises kid who later becomes ranger. At same time foster-father turns over page. Double-crosser's return and threat over old man keeps detective son guessing. Father role played sympathetically, and best in cast. Lad, Don Coleman, with assistant ranger, unearths truth vindicating foster-parent, despite his alias, after stage coach holdup, hut fight. Main theme throughout is lad hunting double-crosser, who murdered his father. Teeth marks on wrist keep fans intent on story development.

PALAIS DE DANSE

(BRITISH MADE)

London, Aug. 2.

Gaumont production. Directed by Maurice Elvey. Story by Mrs. John Longden. Censors' certificate A. Photography, Percy Strong. Pre-viewed at London Hippodrome, July 27. Running time, 94 minutes.

No. 16.......................Mabel Poulton
No. 2..........................Chili Boucher
Lady King....................Hilda Moore
Tony King....................Robin Irvine
Sir William King......Jerrold Robertshaw
No. 1..........................John Longden

Program melodrama, efficiently done. Full of reasonably good characterizations and well set, but not more than a program picture on American standards. Maurice Elvey can do this sort of stuff quite well and make it pay Gaumonts here, as the films do not cost overmuch and book pretty well. Their appeal is purely local, however, and they have little value outside the British market and the Colonies.

Lady King is arranging a Cinderella tableau at a Palais de Danse. The name character has dropped out, so her son Tony persuades the daughter of a night watchman to take the part. She makes a success and catches the eye of No. 1, professional dancer who is also having an affair with Lady King, who thinks he is a man of title.

The girl becomes No. 16 on the list of the Palais' professional staff, and Tony falls in love with her. His mother disapproves, and goes to see the girl to stop Tony's acquaintance, and meets No. 1 to discover his identity. Turned down now he is discovered not to be a "gentleman." No. 1 tries a little blackmail over a photograph and No. 16 attempts to steal the picture from the sheik's room to help the mother of the boy she loves. Lady King is on the same errand, and both are discovered in No. 1's room by Tony who, prompted by his mother out of fear for what she calls her reputation, believes the worst and hands the girl off.

The girl tries again, steals the photograph, is caught by the sheik in the act, Tony buts in, discovers all, there is a fight and the villain falls through the roof to the floor of the Palais de Danse.

Mabel Poulton realizes her original promise and troups well. Formerly she has appeared to suffer from awkwardness, now gone. Robin Irvins is too "nice" to make a film-fan's he-man. He would do better to cut loose a bit more in his work. At present he appears priggish. The rest of the cast is efficient but not brilliant.

Good bookers here, and may get by Continentally as a program release. For America, as useful as imported chewing gum.
Frat.

Manhattan Knights

Excellent production released through Commonwealth. Story credited L. Leitzbach. Barbara Bedford starred. Eddie Kull, cameraman. In cast Walter Miller, Betty Worth, Ray Hallor, Crauford Kent, Maude Traux. At Loew's New York, one day, August 31, one half of double bill. Running time 60 minutes.

Another melodrama of the gangster and blackmailers-always-lose class. "Manhattan Knights," although conventional, is well directed and nicely acted. Considerable efforts for thrills include a couple of shootings, fire apparatus pulling through streets. Fire stuff, whole frankly theatrical, provides rescue material okay with not too particular audience.

Barbara Bedford does good work, making strong appeal in efforts to rescue lad from gangsters and save family name.

Gentleman befriending girl misinterprets her character until skyline brightens when story breaks. Too much footage to fire in loft. Soft pedaling kills what could have been big punch stuff. Slowness here wises up crowd as to weakness of prop flames, almost to point of breaking into comedy.

The Girl from the Revue

(GERMAN MADE)

Berlin, Aug. 20.

An average Eichberg Ufa product. They seem to go well in Germany and it is even rumored that Eichberg sells them to some unprotected South American countries. But nobody has been so foolish as to try one of them on New York.

The scenario by Hans Sturm is not only worn out in idea but hasn't a single novel twist. It concerns a count who marries a Tiller girl and then becomes annoyed when the rest of the ballet appear at the wedding. On his wedding night he goes to a fancy dress ball and is brought home by his wife who is masked and whom he does not recognize!

It is really a pity that Dina Gralla, of real talent, should be condemned to make her debut as a star in this picture. She is a comedienne of charm, but if she does not get away from Eichberg she will be killed internationally.

Hound of Silver Creek

Universal production and release. Directed by Stuart Paton from the story by Paul Bryan. Starring Dynamite, the Wonder Dog. Edmund Cobb and Gloria Grey featured. Titles by G. Bradford. Cast including Gladden James, Frank Clarke, Billy Jones and Frank Rice. No other players given screen credit. At Columbus, New York, one day as half of double feature bill. Running time, 45 minutes.

Short outdoor picture, neatly handled and running smoothly without slowing up. Locale not necessarily western.

"Dynamite" is a fine-looking, intelligent dog.

Story is confined to action in which the animal can be played up.

In support, Edmund Cobb and Gloria Grey are a good combination, photographing well and kept from overacting. Billy Jones, juvenile, not very strong, but may appeal to the youthful element in the houses where this picture can be shown.

"Dynamite's" job in this picture is to help capture a murderer; in doing so regaining a large and valuable property for the juve whose father was shot after being swindled.

NONE BUT THE BRAVE

Fox production and release. Directed by Albert Ray. Story by James Gruen and Fred Stanley. Scenario by Dwight Cummins and Frances Agnew. Cast includes Charles Morton, Sally Phipps, Farrel McDonald and Tyler Brooke. At Circle, New York, one day. Running time, 66 mins.

Some laughs in "None But the Brave" and a motor boat race was effective. Yet the outstanding shots were those of the high diving and here the picture deserves a palm. But at best a neighborhooder and best on double bills.

Little to the plot, owing to the desire to adhere all the way to the farcical idea. A beauty pageant wasn't badly arranged yet an effort to make it something more than commonplace came through inserting it in colors. This color effect stood up for a stage spectacle, but on the principals made them look too painted and artificial.

Sally Phipps hasn't a lot to do. Farrell McDonald and Clive Brook dominate the male principals.

There were some things that were not explained but in the scrambling of the farcical idea perhaps they need never be. Opening slow and even the farcical play was at low ebb here with the destruction of an empty motor car by a railway train devoid of laughs anticipated.

The picture has some tense minutes between the boy and the hero he worshiped until his ideal was shattered, but as a whole falls short.   *Mark.*

NOT QUITE A LADY
(BRITISH MADE)

London, July 27.
Produced by British International Pictures. Directed by Thomas Bentley. Adapted from St. John Hankin's stage play "The Cassilis Engagement." Censors' Certificate A. Pre-view at the London Pavilion, July 25. Running time 87 minutes.
Ethel Borridge..............Mabel Poulton
Her Mother..................Barbara Gott
Geoffrey Cassilis..........Maurice Braddell

A comedy of manners on the familiar theme of a youth who gets entangled with a girl of the lower classes, and the successful efforts of his mother to demonstrate the girl is "not quite a lady."

Possibly no other country could, at this era of democracy, produce convincingly a story which reveals all the snobbish gentility and yet all the English aptitude for tradition and correct manner that still characterizes the upper middle class of Britain.

The fetish of "good form," no longer existent in aristocratic society, where gate-crashing is a sport and phoney finance a habit, is still the god of the suburbs and the county families. Though it has disappeared from Cambridge and Oxford it is still taught at Eton and Harrow.

Which makes this film one that may have some appeal to America, at least as a comedy of a type of folly unknown to Babbitry and the masses.

The girl is a cabaret dancer, and has no society manners. She drops her "aitches" and slices her putt, eats with a knife and is bored in a drawing room. Worst of all, and unforgivable in those dear old families where father grows side-whiskers and they have family prayers for the servants every morning, she cannot ride to hounds.

So her engagement to the very well bred and perfectly "correct" near-society lover is broken off. And a jolly good thing, too . . . for the girl.

Thomas Bentley has made a workmanlike job of a thin story by rather delightful characterizations. The social lapses of the girl's mother, very well played by Barbara Gott, are quite a joy, and Mabel Poulton does abandon herself to the part of the fun-loving and pomp-hating cabaret girl who is really a good scout.

Maurice Braddell is stiffer than need be as the lover who prefers good form to good forms.

Well dressed, good settings and locations, it will do pretty good business here but without creating any sensation. For America its appeal is in its difference, and then as a program picture.   *Frat.*

HEART TO HEART

First National production and release. Mary Astor, Louise Fazenda and Lloyd Hughes featured. Directed by William Beaudine from story by Juliet W. Tompkins. Supervised by Wid Gunning. Cameraman, Sol Bonito. At the Paramount, N. Y., week of Sept. 9. Running time, 63 minutes.
Princess Delatorre.............Mary Astor
Phil Lennox................Lloyd Hughes
Aunt Katie.................Louise Fazenda
Uncle Joe..................Lucien Littlefield
Aunt Meta...................Eileen Manning

First National has made a festival of hokum out of a story of some novelty. Absence of artistic restraint does not, however, interfere with the picture getting laughs and lots of them. This advantage, plus crackerjack performances by Louise Fazenda, Lucien Littlefield and Mary Astor, will put the film across.

"Heart to Heart" is especially good for outside the de luxes. It is spotted at the Paramount on the bill with Jackie Coogan's personal appearance and subordinated thereto in advertising. Much of the humor is based on the doubtful premise that stumbling into or over any object is highly comic.

Louise Fazenda, who has at last given up those slapstick domestics, does a splendid piece of acting as a warm hearted small town housewife completely bewildered and mentally paralyzed by learning that her husband is supposedly carrying on with another woman. In several recent pictures Miss Fazenda has contributed genuine characterizations cleverly embroidered with a wealth of naturalism.

Lucien Littlefield, always the dependable character man, has to do most of the stumbling into and over things. His performance is also carefully detailed for humanness. Mary Astor stands out on beauty and charm.

Story concerns an American girl who marries an Italian prince and, being widowed, decides to revisit Millertown, Ohio, after an absence of 14 years. Arriving on an early train and dressed simply, nobody recognizes her although the town is festooned with signs and banners, "Welcome Home, Princess."

At the home of her near-sighted aunt she is mistaken for a seamstress and put to work. Only her uncle and her boyhood sweetheart, now a window washer, recognize her.

Developments establish comedy.   *Land.*

HOME, JAMES

Universal production and release. Directed by William Beaudine. Story by Gladys Johnson. No other credits given on billing or main title. Laura LaPlante starred. Charles Delaney leading man. Comedy old man played by George Pearce. At the Hippodrome, N. Y., week of Sept. 10. Running time, 72 mins.

A light comedy romantic subject modeled after the O. Henry manner, but badly made. Only virtue is a certain ingenuity in winding up hoke comedy situations for a laugh. All story logic is subordinated to this end. They drag in most unconvincing things for a comedy twist. You resist the impossible situations but you do get a mild sort of comedy effect. Titles contribute much to the light treatment and titler entitled to credit.

Director has been at much pains to build up such comedy scenes as a shop girl crawling on hands and knees through a crowded department store in order to escape the eye of a nagging floor walker. Another gag worked up elaborately is girl climbing on high step ladder to get article from high place, with swaying perch and ultimate fall. All labored devices like that. They get their laughs from the pop mob, but they're scarcely worth while.

Story is pretty implausible. Son of millionaire falls in love at sight with shop girl and to save her from embarrassment poses as a chauffeur,

brings her to his home in the supposed absence of his boss and then gets her involved in all sorts of complications. In this case hero's father, returning unexpectedly, has girl arrested and the misunderstandings are all smoothed out when he causes her to be arraigned before the judge, supposedly to be sentenced, but as it turns out to have the judge marry the pair on the theory that any woman who could make that hair brained boy work even for a day gave promise of accomplishing something with him.

Miss La Plante does not make a happy hoyden. She overdoes the cute stuff disgracefully, but she is good in downright gag comedy. Here she got laughs with too energetic methods, but lost out completely on the sympathetic romantic side. Young Delaney is an agreeable juvenile with an easy style about him and a likeable slow smile. Pearce's old man is fairly well balanced, and two rather good character sketches of a couple of small town vixens were well enough done in the familiar manner by two type actresses. Sissified bully floor walker was a gem of film gag comedy.

Strictly for the neighborhood daily changes.   *Rush.*

KREUTZER SONATA
(GERMAN MADE)

M. S. Films (German) production, made in Berlin from Count Leo Tolstoy's novel, directed by J. Machaty and featuring Eva Byron and Jans Petrovich. Presented in America under auspices of the Russian Student Clubs of American Universities in celebration of Tolstoy Centennial Week this week, current at the Fifth Ave. Playhouse, New York. Runs 45 minutes.

Made by a Russian-German cast in Berlin, the Tolstoy novelization is a dreary cinematic transmutation of the great Russian novelist's study of matrimonial jealousy. As a flicker feature, its appeal is principally limited to contrasting picture values with contemporaneous American standards. Which is another way of stating it will not please the masses, although the Russian derivation may be utilized to twofold exhibitor advantage both in the arty sure-seaters like the Fifth Ave. Playhouse and for ghetto neighborhoods with a Jewish following.

Whoever titled and edited the American version did some yeoman chopping to speed things. The short 45-minute feature evidences his radical cutting, some of the scenes projecting jerkingly and falteringly. Eva Byron, the flirtatious wife, is Pola Negri-ish in makeup and suggestion but safe from Hollywood annexation. At times she is quite effective, but a tell-tale double chin nullifies her celluloid future on this side. Like most foreign thespians, she overacts, contrasting the more to Jans Petrovich's reserved characterization as the victim of the green-eyed monster. The violin virtuoso who completes the triangle is unidentified, doing little but appear oilily menacing.

Production cost a herring and rental fee should be ditto. In celebration of Tolstoy Centennial Week, the Russian clubs of American Universities are sponsoring this importation in America.   *Abel.*

Good Men and True

FBO reissuing old timer made by P. A. Powers. Story credited Eugene M. Rhodes. Harry Carey starred. In cast: Noah Beery, Thomas Jefferson, Tully Marshall, Vola Vale, William Steele. At Stanley, New York, one day, Sept. 10. Running time, 70 minutes.

In the pre-war days "Good Men and True" would have been a hummer, but today, with its poor lighting, obvious acting, yellow titles, and ancient wardrobe, this re-issue got razzed even at the Stanley, 25c. grind.

Only chance is in houses that will pull antique day or in arty centers where they might like to get a line

on old timers in their youth. It's too long to get by as second half on ordinary bill and too musty to be featured unless public is advised of its age.

Noah Beery, as the cigar chewing scum politician, scowls with true villainy and changes caps and coats as occasion demands. Vola Vale goes pop-eyed over Harry Carey, who wins the election after kicking a string of waiters in the belt and being framed for a couple of murders.

Tully Marshall as the henpecked pa overhears the plot in an elaborate chink joint in a crude western village, and thus it rolls on. Audiences in an agreeable frame of mind will get a lot of laughs over the dusty directorial technique, but those fans who pay, expecting to find something modern—too bad.

TIRE AU FLANC
(FRENCH MADE)

Paris, Sept. 1.
This is a very amusing picture of French military life in peaceful days before the war, adopted from the successful farce of Mouezy-Eon and Sylvane, which held the stage at the Dejazet for 1,000 performances. The original talking show is better than the screen edition, notwithstanding the excellent efforts of the producer, Jean Renoir, for the Neo-Film (P. Braunberger).

The picture version, distributed by the Armor concern, is brought up to date. Action is sure to delight the French fans, nearly every man having been through it in the barracks, and he will appreciate the adventures of Dubois, the spoilt child, feeling the pinch when he reaches the regiment. "Tire au Flanc" is a sort of local idiom for "passing the buck," but chiefly employed in the army.

Michel Simon is diverting in the part of the valet Joseph; Michael Pomies is the young nobleman, and Jeanne Helbling (Georgette), Esther Kiss, Kinny Dorlay, Fridette Fatton, Mm. Felix Oudart (the colonel), Jean Storm, Zellas, Manuel Ralby hold the other roles. Amusing French picture, for exportation purposes doubtful.   *Kendrew.*

5 and 10 Cent Annie

Warner Bros. production and release. Directed by Roy Del Ruth. Story by Leon Zurade. Screen play by Charles Condon. Louise Fazenda, Clyde Cook and William Demarest featured. Cast: Gertrude Astor, Tom Ricketts, Douglas Gerrard, Andre Beranger, Flora Finch, Bill Franey, Eddie Haffner. At the Tivoli, New York, one day, Sept. 6. Running time, 50 mins.

Mildly diverting comedy that will acceptably round out a double feature program. Heavy dramatics should be its running mate.

Story based on the romance between Annie (Miss Fazenda), clerk in the five and ten, and Elmer Peck (Cook), a street cleaner, is strictly slapstick. When the meek little White Wing inherits a million and a valet from his eccentric uncle his troubles begin. One provision of the old man's will is that in the event his nephew dies unmarried the money goes to the valet in recognition for faithful service. Briggs (Demarest), the valet, shanghies his new master in order to prevent him from acquiring Annie as a ball and chain. Annie, however, slips aboard ship dressed as a seaman and rescues her lover from his captors with the aid of a revenue cutter.

Silly but good enough as a comedy filler in the neighborhoods.

TESHA

(BRITISH-MADE)

British International Pictures' production. Directed by Victor Saville. Adapted from the novel of the same title by Baroness Barcynska. Photography, Werner Brandes. Censors' Certificate "A." Distributed in the U. K. by Wardour Films, Ltd., and in America by Wide World Film Corp., Inc. Running time, 95 minutes. Pre-viewed at the London Hippodrome, August 24.

Tesha	Maria Corda
Dobree	Jameson Thomas
Lenane	Paul Cavanagh

If censors pass this film it will create a much more favorable impression towards British pictures than any that have yet been seen.

A delicate theme has been handled with delicacy, yet with a robustness of direction which makes it 100 per cent entertainment. That it should be only the second film of the director, Victor Saville, is something approaching a wonder. But that it should have been made by the man who directed that awful atrocity, "The Arcadians," is nearer to a miracle.

There is nothing of lighting, sets, locations, camera work or acting (with one exception) that is below the best American standards. In the first three reels there is rather too much footage, and the action becomes draggy. But that is easily remedied with scissors.

It is a problem story, worked out to a logical end. But it will offend the mid-brows, as it will please the low and high.

Tesha is a premiere danseuse. As a child all her natural instincts have been thwarted in the process of turning her into a dancer. She is taken from her dolls. And having a maternal instinct, she finds compensation in sculpturing figures of her dream children.

Then she meets Dobree. He is rich and still nearly young; more than anything he desires a son to carry on the family traditions and business. He and Tesha fall in love, for she is willing to abandon her profession for a home and children.

But several years pass and no children come. In spite of themselves they are becoming estranged. Tesha discovers from the family doctor that it is the fault of shell-shock. In a moment of despair, seeking any end to keep her husband's love, she "gives herself" to a momentary acquaintance. The next time she meets him is in her own home, to discover he is her husband's oldest friend, and he to find his love-light is his friend's wife.

Much of the credit for this, the best British picture yet made under the Quota, should go to Jameson Thomas, who carries most of the film away. Maria Corda is not too well cast. She lacks emotion; sometimes she seems almost listless. To have got the best out of so difficult a part would have needed a director who could take someone like Lya de Putti and impose on her primitive passion a thick layer of the eternal maternal.

But where the film raises a doubt is not in its direction or its acting. It is in the choice of subject. Unusual though the theme is, and delicately as it has been handled, it is one which may be banned by even the fairly broadminded. What will happen to it in Puritan places is a complete black-out. *Frat.*

MIDNIGHT LIFE

Gotham production, featuring Francis X. Bushman, Gertrude Olmstead and Eddie Buzzell. Directed by Scott Dunlap from a story by Reginald Wright Kaufmann. Titles by Delos Sutherland. Nobert Bradin cameraman. Cast includes Monte Carter, Carlton King and Cosmo Kyrle Bellew. At Loew's New York, on double feature bill, Sept. 7. Running time, 57 mins.

Again the influence of "Broadway" in the films. Bad men in a night club, the curtain's parting for the talent to go on and off, the stairway up to the dressing rooms. All reminiscent of the play.

And Francis X. Bushman as a lieutenant of detectives who sucks a toothpick and is very quiet and menacing. Eddie Buzzell as a dumb hoofer and Gertrude Olmstead as the partner are the love interest. Monte Carter is the cafe man with side rackets who riffles silver dollars between his hands a la Colisemo. The movie touch is in changing the racket from bootlegging to silk warehouse pilfering and in having the man higher up none other than the most eminently respectable citizen in town.

"Midnight Life" is understood to have been made in six days and is accordingly lax and wanting in detail. It is good melodrama for the most part appraised by Class C standards. There is action, suspense and colorful background. Story resemblence won't worry them in Idaho.

Picture marks the appearance of Eddie Buzzell, musical comedy comic. Cast as a dumbbell cabaret dancer, that six-day shooting schedule must have made it doubly tough for one not acquainted with camera technique. Buzzell photographs well, but in the absence of good direction wandered rather aimlessly through the picture. Miss Olmstead makes an easy looking heroine in a soubret costume of form-fitting black satin. *Land.*

Troublesome Wives

(BRITISH MADE)

London, Aug. 31.

Produced by Archibald Nettlefold Productions. Directed by Harry Hughes. Adapted from "Summer Lightning." Censor's Certificate "U." Pre-viewed at the Palace, London, August 21. Running time, 70 minutes.

Tony Paget	Eric Bransby Williams
Betty Paget	Mabel Poulton
Norah Cameron	Lilian Oldland
Alec Cameron	Roy Russell
Maxwell	Reginald Fox

Don't seem to have been able to have made up their minds whether they were making a melo or a comedy. But it's so poor it doesn't matter anyway. Sure it's fast action, but that doesn't make a film, which after all has got to have something more than motion. The star—Mabel Poulton—has nothing to do but rush about.

Everything in the picture is so obvious. The foreign spy called Maxwell couldn't be mistaken by the dumbest fan for anything else when first seen.

As a stage play "Summer Lightning" was nothing to rave about. As a motion picture, at least as it's here made, it's something to rave at.

The story is of stolen aeroplane plans, a wife who flirts, and a grass widow who aids and abets her. Pursuit, recovery of 'plane model, domestic peace restored.

A second feature for the sticks here. One of those things that will get a laugh at the idea of us making movies if it gets into any other place.

The whole thing is incredibly silly. *Frat.*

Beautiful But Dumb

Tiffany-Stahl production and release. Directed by Elmer Clifton from story credited John Natteford. Titles by Frederick and Fanny Hatton. Jackson Rose, cameraman. In the cast: Patsy Ruth Miller, Charles Byer, G. Yoltz, George E. Stone. At Loew's New York, one day, Sept. 4, one-half of double bill. Running time, 70 minutes.

With a story amounting to less than an outline, and that old, "Beautiful, but Dumb" cannot attribute its slowness to direction and cast. Where a little meat in the script would have eased it over as a good program offering, its present story status makes a production, otherwise completely worth while, one of those things.

Patsy Ruth Miller does her best and Director Clifton tries to pep up things by working in a cabaret scene, but the staid dame who spruces up to make her boss and, of course, makes him, takes a terrifically long and uneventful 70 minutes to unreel.

THE RINGER

(BRITISH MADE)

Produced by British Lion Film Company. Adapted from the Edgar Wallace play by Mary Murillo. Directed by Arthur Maude. Censors' Certificate "A." Pre-viewed at the London Hippodrome, August 28. Distributed by Ideal Films Co. Running time, 86 minutes.

CAST

Dr. Lomond	Leslie Faber
Cora Ann Milton	Annette Benson
Inspector Wembury	Nigel Barrie
Inspector Bliss	Hayford Hobbs
Maurice Meister	Lawson Butt
Johnny Lenley	John Hamilton

"The Ringer" was a big stage hit here. It is running in 200 theatres in Germany, it has been translated into most languages, and it is being produced in New York this fall "under the personal attention of Edgar Wallace."

Successful as the film version will be here, it is not likely to get the same amount of international distribution as the stage play. Maybe it will get a good break in Germany, where some other Wallace stories have been produced as films. But it is just one of those movies; not so bad and not so good. A program picture that will get them in on the title, won't let them down too badly, but adds nothing to the history or the advancement of British picture-making.

The prologue, showing Meister's earlier connection with the Ringer's sister, confuses the issue somewhat, especially as two girls playing in it are so much alike as to be almost undistinguishable.

Suspense and guessing as to the identity of the Ringer is not as sustained as in the play, though Leslie Faber, in the chief part, gives as good a performance as he did on the stage. Lawson Butt's Meister is overdrawn, but the rest of the cast is adequate, with Annette Benson outstanding.

Arthur Maude has made a workmanlike job of the direction, and the script has followed the stage version very closely.

While it will book the limit here on the vogue and on its absence of Ufa complexes and whirling machinery and doubled-crossed street symbolism, it is merely the sort of stuff that Universal used to turn out and sometimes still does, by the machine process. *Frat.*

THE THUNDER GOD

Crescent production (state rights). Directed by Charles J. Hunt from a story by James Oliver Curwood. Lila Lee featured. Cast includes Cornelius Keefe, Walter Long. On double bill at Loew's New York Sept. 7. Running time, 50 mins.

Typical movie yarn about log camp and the efforts of the villain to prevent heroine getting her logs down the river in time. It's one of Hollywood's oldest plot stencils.

Designed and made for the daily change and small town trade, it has enough action to satisfy accordingly. James Oliver Curwood name may mean something. So-so production. *Land.*

MOTHER KNOWS BEST

(DIALOG)

William Fox production and release. Adapted by Marion Orth from the Edna Ferber novel of similar name. Directed by John Blystone, with theatre and stage portions supervised by Charles Judels and Dave Stamper. Theme song by William Kernell, with Mr. Kernel and Edith Bristol writers of the titles. Musical score by Roxy and Erno Rapee. Madge Bellamy, Louise Dresser and Barry Norton featured. At Globe (wired), New York, on $2 run, opening Saturday mat. Sept. 15. Running time around 110 minutes.

Sally Quail	Madge Bellamy
Ma Quail	Louise Dresser
The Boy	Barry Norton
Sam Kingston	Albert Gran
Bessie	Annette De Kirby
Ben	Ivor De Kirby
Pa Quail	Lucien Littlefield

Tears are the biggest thing in "Mother Knows Best." They may be depended upon to make this Fox special dialog picture a sure fire in the regular houses.

Other than the tears there is little in the story or picture to bring much attention, except Louise Dresser as the mother who thinks she knows best. For the rest it is just so so, with too much given to the love angle, although it is from this that the very draggy closing section catches the tears of the women. Most of this sob stuff will bounce off the men, but even the chill-hearted women of the opening audience, with many of them Broadway show regulars, went to the linen when the water turned on.

Stage mothers may get a different standing after this picture is seen. Though it is an actual matter of record that more stage mothers harm their daughters' show careers than help them. Stage mothers who insist upon accompanying their daughters everywhere, in quest of engagements, into agents' and managers' offices, become general nuisances. They won't believe that of course and won't believe anything but a striking career stands in front of "my wonderfully talented daughter."

Here the stage mother is shown from the outset, when her kidlet of eight was doing sidewalk impersonations, and the mother robbing her husband's drug store till to give the child advantages. From then on Mrs. Quail is a stern, uncompromising parent, losing her husband, but sending the girl along, standing between her and the world, hocking her wedding ring even for carfare back to Broadway from a stranded troupe, to finally see her child have a theatre named after her.

That was when the tears started, when the mimic bawled Ma for that "mother knows best" thing, going to bed and Ma hearing from the Doc a lot of dialog written by Eugene Walter. And about the best phrased dialog yet coming from the screen. That Doctor must have been a legit, for he spoke it well, far beyond any of the others, but is unprogrammed.

The Doc told mother there had been too much interference in the Quail family; that she had better let the girl do as she pleased, and the mother prayed that the boy she had driven away from her girl come back. He did. That was all set from the time Sally started to squawk for the first time in her life.

The picture ran some time before the first talking period. It occurred in a dressing room as Sally was making changes for her turn in a small second rate vaude houses. She had gone bugs over a small time piano player, so it may be left to the show business whether Mother knew best about that. No one else will haggle.

Miss Dresser knows the back stage ma as well as anyone, and she made this one perfect. Probably has met all in the wings at one time or another. But Miss Dresser's screen speaking voice will never get her anywhere in the talkers unless they can do better with it, or her acting makes her presence necessary.

Madge Bellamy's voice isn't much better. Her screen imitations of Lauder, Jolson and Anna Held were fair enough in a way, but not any too well vocally synchronized. Her voice in the songs always appeared to be behind her. Ma in the dressing room said to Sally, as she was blacking up for the Jolson bit: "Dear, don't forget to get down on your knees for 'Mammy.'"

When Edna Ferber wrote "Mother Knows Best" as a novel it was claimed she had Elsie Janis in mind. That was likely through the imitations and Ma Janis' well known show rep. But here it could have been Ina Claire, who also did imitations, and started in the show business on the small time with a mother and exactly as Miss Janis. The only difference between Elsie and Ina in rating and rank up to date has been that Ina did leave her mother to get married, and Elsie did not.

But this stage mother and child could be any of the hundreds in and out of the business for years. In "Mother Knows Best" Sally is first shown getting the bird at an amateur night, then going to an act, always with mother around.

Then an A. E. F. entertainer, then back to her own theatre on Broadway. This story up to the time Sally left for Europe does not show her as beyond a small time mimic. That leaves a lapse why she should have had the theatre named after her, but if that were filled in it would only make the pad stand out more strongly.

Miss Bellamy somewhat resembles Elsie Janis. She played better than she spoke. Scenes between her and Barry Norton were rather catchy in the early section, although both went in for long-distance kissing. Norton is a good looking boy on the screen and gave his role quite some spirit.

The theme song is "Sally of My Dreams," written by William Kernell, and it is plugged to a fare-thee-well in this picture. If talking pictures have reinvigorated the popular music publishing business, as they have, and as talkers rejuvenated the picture business, then perhaps the reason for both may be seen in "Mother Knows Best." Assuredly that is so for "Sally of My Dreams" and a good number besides.

Program mentions Charles Judels and Dave Stamper as taking care of the stage or theatrical end of this dialog talker, with John Blystone doing his proper share in the film's direction. Messrs. Judels and Stamper likely staged the amateur and small time performances in the picture.

This is Fox's first real dialog picture, a most worthy and class effort regardless of that. The dialog idea as expounded through the retention of Mr. Walter substantiates that the dialog pictures must have a high grade of verbal expression to make the dialog stand up, besides a capable deliverer.

DOCKS OF NEW YORK

Paramount production and release. George Bancroft starred. Betty Compson and Baclanova featured Screen play by Jules Furthman from John Monk Saunders' "The Dock Walloper" Direction by Joseph von Sternberg J. G. Bachman, associate producer. Titles by Julian Johnson. Running time, over 60 minutes. At Paramount, New York, week Sept. 15.

Bill Roberts	George Bancroft
Sadie	Betty Compson
Lou	Baclanova
Sugar Steve	Clyde Cook
Third Engineer	Mitchell Lewis
Hymn Book Harry	Gustav von Seyffertitz
The Crimp	Guy Oliver
Mrs. Crimp	May Foster
Steve's Girl	Lillian Worth

"The Docks of New York" is not Joseph von Sternberg's greatest, as advance dope from the west coast indicated. But it's a corking program picture, thanks to George Bancroft, a good story and Julian Johnson's titles. That makes it an okay Paramount regular

Von Sternberg's direction is excellent, but it is in the casting that the picture falls short of special classification Betty Compson as an elliptical-heeled frail, who is punch drunk from life and attempts suicide, only to be rescued by Bancroft, a roughneck stoker, fails to get underneath the characterization. Her assignment is none too soft. To make it acceptable the audience must believe that a beautiful derelict has never been married because no one would have her. In real life she would probably have four husbands in the rack and be chalking up for the fifth.

Bancroft as Bill Roberts, the husky, hard-drinking, two-fisted stoker, has a role that he can make roll over. Roberts, on his one night ashore, saves the girl, and in a spirit of bravado marries her in a water front dive operated by a crimp (Guy Oliver).

Next morning Roberts again is ready for sea. The girl resignedly watches him go, but when she realizes the marriage meant nothing to the coal heaver she turns on him and snarls her resentment.

He is on his way to a ship when a crowd and the arrival of the police arouse his curiosity He returns to find the girl about to be arrested for shooting the third engineer of the crew (Mitchell Lewis), who had entered her room and tried to force his attentions on her Roberts had beaten him up the night before for the same reason The engineer's wife confesses she did the shooting and Roberts leaves once again

Acting upon impulse, after the ship is under way he swims ashore to find his wife has been arrested for possession of stolen clothing. He had taken the stuff to a pawnshop after unsuccessfully trying to arouse the pawnbroker.

Roberts walks into Night Court and explains the situation to the judge. The latter discharges the woman and sentences Roberts to 60 days. The picture ends with the girl telling Bill she'll wait forever.

This story concerns itself with sordid underworld characters, the only love interest resting with Bancroft and Compson. Baclanova as the wife of the third engineer has her best role to date and plays it sympathetically. Lewis as the swaggering third failed to indicate menace and let the picture down considerably. The sense of conflict which existed in "Underworld" and "The Drag Net" is absent here, due to Lewis' mild opposition.

The rest of the cast was adequate with Clyde Cook standing out as "Sugar Steve," Roberts' woman hating pal.

The scenario by Jules Furthman was adapted from the John Monk Saunders original, "Dock Walloper." Exquisite photography helps a lot. Foggy mystic water shots gave the waterfront the same quality of "Street Angel." Inserts of the massive machinery of the freighter were spotted effectively and the dive was a faithful replica of the barrel houses that used to dot the water front.

"Docks of New York" is a good entertaining picture that misses greatness by a whisker. *Con.*

THE CAMERAMAN

M-G-M production and release, starring Buster Keaton. Story by Clyde Bruckman; adapted by Richard Schayer. Directed by Edward Sedgwick. Cameraman, Elgin Lessley. At Capitol, New York, week of Sept. 15. Running time, 68 mins.

Luke	Buster Keaton
Sally	Marceline Day
Stagg	Harold Goodwin
Editor	Sidney Bracy
Cop	Harry Gribbon

Good laugh picture with Buster Keaton. The same old stencil about a boob that does everything wrong and cashes in finally through sheer accident. The familiar pattern has been dressed up with some bright gags and several sequences where the laughs come thick and fast. **All** in all, it will probably deliver general satisfaction.

Apparently some attempt **has** been made to inject more romance into the yarn than customary **in** Buster Keaton films. Keaton **is a** problem on love interest. **In the** present case his cow-like adoration of the heroine (Marceline Day) **is** used to build up sympathy as **a** counterirritant to his abyssmal stupidity in most respects.

In trying to land a job with M-G-M News, Keaton as a tintype **photographer suddenly turned cinematic, goes through a series of hoke adventures. There is the comedy. One of the smartest bits is when setting up his camera to shoot an admiral leaving a hotel—Keaton mistakes the gorgeously uniformed hotel doorman for the admiral. Another clever bit is when swimming in a public tank with women all about Keaton loses his over-size bathing suit. The big punch is when he photographs a Chinese tong war from the center of the melee.**

Miss Day is appealing as the femme. Harold Goodwin has the only other part of consequence, as a newsreel cameraman also soft on the gal. Harry Gribbon appears in the action intermittently as a cop with a growing dislike for the goofish Keaton.

Production, direction and photography all first rate. *Land.*

THE WHIP

(SOUND)

First National Production and release: Directed by Charles J. Brabin. Dorothy Mackaill, Ralph Forbes, Anna Q. Nilsson and Lowell Sherman featured. At Strand, New York, week Sept. 15. Running time around 65 minutes.

Lady Diana	Dorothy Mackaill
Lord Brancaster	Ralph Forbes
Iris d'Aquila	Anna Q. Nilsson
Greville Sartoris	Lowell Sherman
Sam Kelley	Albert Gran
Lord Beverly	Marc McDermott
Lambert	Lou Payne
Richard Haslam	Arthur Clayton

A race track story, with the only changes from the conventional "Kentucky Derby" thing as so well known over here on the states rights screens, the absence of a mortgage or a Kentucky colonel. In their places, if they mean anything nowadays, are English nobility, scene of the Ascot race course, fox hunt, gala ball, and instead of poison to wreck the expected winner of the derby, new stuff on a train. Even with all of these nothing unusual about "The Whip" and that takes in the sound attachment. (No dialog.)

For sound, meagrely employed, the best is the noise of trains toward the end of the film, as the fast expresses rush through the countryside at night. It was here that the heavy let loose the box car carrying "The Whip" to Ascot in the hope that the shortly following London Express would smash it on the same track. The express would have, but Lord Chump threw in the monkey wrench by doing his picture stuff just in time, and having the horse walk out of the box car, seemingly making the five foot step to the ground, without hurting a tendon. That was the only time Lord Chump was anything else.

For about 3,000 feet there are too many captions. The titles make the picture flicker right along. And nothing in them of any account other than the flicker.

Looks like an expensive production. Direction nothing to gloat over. Especially when the racing fox to be so often seen in the fox hunt. If an illusion were ever bumped off in a jiffy, that's it.

"The Whip" was one of Drury Lane's biggest melos and successes in London of years ago.

Dorothy Mackaill as Lady Diana not so hot in her riding costume, but looked nice when in women's wear. Anna Q. Nilsson did the dirty among the women, and well as usual. Lowell Sherman plays the heavies soft and makes them soft for himself, while Ralph Forbes had to do the Lord Brancaster role, making it the chump the Lord appeared to be for women.

MAN-MADE WOMEN

Cecil B. DeMille production, released by Pathe. Produced by Ralph Block. Directed by Paul L. Stein. Featuring Leatrice Joy. Cast given screen credit includes H. B. Warner, John Boler and Seena Owen. At Keith's Hippodrome, New York, week Sept. 17. Running time over 60 mins.

A weak, slow-moving picture destined to play the independent houses or circuits bound to accept it by contract. Not very likely to create favorable comment, it is not suitable except with a strong stage show in a big house. At the Hip this week is an eight-act line-up of vaudeville in the Keith New Era Week ballyhoo.

Action is light and story almost flickers out several times. Story neither interesting nor convincing, and acting stilted.

Concerns a young married woman with a yen for leaving her attractive husband, whom she is supposed to love, for the delights of wild parties staged by an old, funny-looking gent, described as handsome in the subtitles and holding some mysterious allure for pretty gals. According to his appearance this Romeo's billing is badly padded.

The gal finally leaves her husband and later stages a return in an effort to restore her position as his wife.

Tears, complications, subtitles and so on are used in a more or less indiscriminate mixture with a view to making it all look reasonable, but it isn't. *Mori.*

RIVER PIRATE

Fox production and release. Directed by William K. Howard. Adapted from the novel of the same name by Charles Francis Coe (published in Saturday Evening Post, although screen or program silent on point). Victor McLaglen starred and Lois Moran featured. Titles by Malcolm Stuart Boylan. Cameraman, Lucien Andriot. Running time 67 minutes. At the Roxy, New York, Sept. 16.

Sailor Frinz	Victor McLaglen
Marjorie Cullen	Lois Moran
Sandy	Nick Stuart
Shark	Earle Foxe
Caxton	Donald Crisp
Gerber	Robert Perry

Picture of many engaging points. Fine human interest treatment of the under dog theme, splendidly played by Victor McLaglen and a good cast. Produced with intelligence and judgment. Shrewd directorship has succeeded in getting over the straightaway sincerity of the written work without attempting to make it over, a real achievement in translating material from page to screen.

Picture has appeal for all classes of fan; fundamentally because of its theme and secondly because of the capital playing, notable being the simple and natural work of Nick Stuart as the reform school waif. In the nature of things it doesn't lend itself to ballyhoo pull, but should be a builder for week stands. Class program output of the kind that reflects credit upon producer and promotes prestige of players. Not an outstanding box office film and not a repeat.

Subject is utterly without hoke. Deals in sympathetic way with urchin of the waterfront, who, for no fault of his own, finds himself in the reformatory. Becomes friends with notorious waterfront pirate (convict detailed from prison to teach kids sailmaker's trade). The two become pals. Convict gets parole and goes back to robbing warehouses. Helps kid to break jail and join him in craft.

Kid falls in love with casual girl who wants him to go straight. Essence of the story is his struggle to keep faith with the girl's good influence and still remain loyal to Sailor Frinz, the wharf pilferer.

The fascinating thing about the picture is the entirely impersonal way this bazarre history is presented. No preachment against the injustice of shipping petty juvenile delinquents to the reformatory. They don't glorify the dock thief, or point a moral of his trade. No bunk or ennobling a picturesque crook and then pointing out that evildoers can't win.

The only real action in the footage is a chase of the pirate launch by a police boat, a picturesque bit of night photography on a busy river. Chase is ended when Frinz lets the police launch get close enough to smash its searchlight with a missle and then slip away in the maze of shipping.

The love interest is minor and is kept in the background. It isn't especially convincing anyway. Good judgment here in direction and story building. No chance for a title writer to splurge, but Boylan's lines are trim, convey a sense of natural idiom and are brief and crisp.

A novelty finish weakens the story in the artistic sense, although it probably will strengthen it at the box office. The story proper finishes with the two young lovers in the clinch. There is a quick switch to figure of kindly old man reading in his library. He closes his book and addresses the audience from screen with philosophical observations on the novel he has just finished, which of course is "The River Pirate," relating that Sailor Frinz really got out of jail in time to be best man at the boy's wedding.

It's a sort of spoken epilog. It's all anti-climax and a literary defect. On the other hand, it introduces the "sound" element into the production, giving advertising value to the film for commercial purposes.

Rush.

THE SINGING FOOL
(DIALOG)

Warner Brothers-Vitaphone production and release. Al Jolson starred. Directed by Lloyd Bacon. Adapted by C. Graham Baker from story by Leslie S. Barrows. Joseph Jackson, writer of screen dialog and titles. Cameraman, Byron Haskin. At Winter Garden, New York, Sept. 19, on run. $2 top. Running time, 105 minutes.

Al	Al Jolson
Grace	Betty Bronson
Molly	Josephine Dunn
John Perry	Reed Howes
Marcus	Edward Martindel
Blackie Joe	Arthur Housman
Sonny Boy	David Lee
Cafe Manager	Robert Emmett O'Connor

To say that here are Al Jolson and his songs on the screen, is to say that "The Singing Fool" will do what Jolson's "Jazz Singer" did—make gold.

There are seven songs sung by Jolson, four seemingly new, with one, "Sonny Boy," plugged as the theme number, sung by Jolson at three different points. Others are "Keep Smiling at Trouble," "Golden Gate," "Rainbow Round My Shoulder," "Spaniard Who Blighted My Life," "Sitting on Top of the World" and "It All Depends on You."

Besides these, and these would be enough without anything but Jolson, there are tears. You've gotta cry at this one. The cards are stacked against you on the weep.

So after all, what does the thin story mean? It's just a thread for Jolson to walk along by, and to black up in the final reel for the first time, to do his turn and again sing "Sonny Boy," shortly after he had seen his three-year-old son pass out on a hospital cot. But the show had to go on, with that tradition giving "Laugh, Clown, Laugh," another instrumental plug on the synchronized Vita music arranged by Louis Silvers.

Jolson made 'em cry when going in heavy for acting. Once when he met his boy in the park, following a long separation, and again at the death scene.

Al meets two women in the picture and talks to both of them. Both talk back. Josephine Dunn didn't talk so well, and she looked pretty steely-hearted, even for a blonde. Betty Bronson talked a little better, but Joe Jackson's dialog is no smash. There is too much deliberation in the talking roles, excepting by that three and one-half-year-old Sonny.

This little David Lee playing the Jolsons' kid is a perfect wonder. He plays sick, dead, happy, asleep, affectionate and sad, and talks, in his wee voice that gets over without a blemish. His superb coaching expressed itself although it does appear impossible to coach a child of that age so thoroughly.

The story opens in a side street slab called Blackie Joe's, where Jolson is a singing waiter and Miss Dunn the soubret. Jolson goes for the blonde, but she tells him she's off any waiter, even after he had written a song for her that she wouldn't read. So he sang it to her on the floor. It was "It All Depends on You." Marcus, the Broadway producer, was in the joint.

That's it. Al went to Broadway, and Molly went with him, but Molly went wrong after four years, blowing Al and taking herself and the babe to Paris.

Al bumped around, just escaped becoming a bum, and finally wound up again at the slab. There was still the same cigaret girl who always wanted Al, so she slipped him some encouragement. He again made Broadway, and was in his star-marked dressing room, making up with cork after returning from the hospital where the lad had died He had sung "Sonny Boy" to him there and had to sing it again on the stage before the screen audience, at the stage manager's direction.

Back to the Winter Garden, on the screen, and after the unreeling in person on the stage for a short speech, Al Jolson was again home, both ways. The first night audience applauded as heartily as did the audiences in the screen cabaret or theatre, and the $11 first night tickets were at a premium before the doors opened.

What "The Jazz Singer" did for the picture business and Warners can't be forgotten when this "Singing Fool" is seen. And "The Singing Fool" has the "Jazz Singer" popularity for its further drawing field. While the fact that Al Jolson accepted his first Warner picture payment, $75,000, in stock of the Warner company may be another cause of amazement, when it comes time to analyze this whole talking picture business.

BEGGARS OF LIFE
(SOUND)

Paramount production and release. Directed by W. A. Wellman from Jim Tully's story. Features Wallace Beery, Richard Arlen and Louise Brooks. Adapted and supervised by Benjamin Glazer. At the Paramount, New York, week of Sept. 22. Running time, 80 mins.

Oklahoma Red	Wallace Beery
Nancy	Louise Brooks
Jim	Richard Arlen
Mose	Edgar Blue Washington
Skinny	H. A. Morgan
Skelly	Andy Clark
Bill	Mike Donlin
Hopper	Roscoe Karns
Arkansas Snake	Robert Perry
Rubin	Johnnie Morris
Baldy	George Kotsonaros
Ukie	Jacques Chapin
Blind Sims	Robert Brower
Farmer	Frank Brownlee

Not an exceptionally good picture. Title and some plugging should just about get it by. It misses because the story doesn't mean a thing. Whether it could have received better directorial and continuity treatment is questionable. Basically the life of a bunch of hoboes woven round a girl wanted for murdering the man who tried to ruin her isn't the kind of thing that sends people home talking. Nor draw women.

There is little action. Opening is very slow, giving over 20 minutes to a couple of meaningless incidents, the runaway couple being chased and then thrown off a moving train.

First real incident doesn't happen until about the third reel, with the arrival of the champ hobo, Wallace Beery. After this a few laughs and Beery is responsible for whatever merit there is in the audience reaction angle.

Miss Brooks looks attractive, even in men's clothes, and scores in the two or three scenes where she is placed on defensive against male attackers. Yarn mainly concerns the adventures of the girl and the tramp who befriends her. Falling into a group of hoboes bossed by "Red" (Beery) the girl is in danger from two sources, the bo's and the detectives on her trail. She is saved, finally, by "Red," who dies.

Beery has a couple of speaking lines in the picture, hitting several ways for returns. He is also supposed to sing a novelty number. Actually, this is little more than a recitation and it doesn't get the laughs intended. Picture is synchronized with a suitable score which ran smoothly here.

Mori.

EXCESS BAGGAGE

Metro-Goldwyn-Mayer production and release. Starring William Haines and featuring Josephine Dunn and Ricardo Cortez. Adapted from Jack McGowan's stage play of the same name by Frances Marion. Directed by James Cruze. Ralph Spence titling, and Ira Morgan cameraman. At Capitol, New York, week of Sept. 22. Running time, 72 minutes.

Eddie Kane	William Haines
Elsa McCoy	Josephine Dunn
Val Derrico	Ricardo Cortez
Jimmy Dunn	Neely Edwards
Mabel Ford	Kathleen Clifford
Betty Ford	Greta Grandstedt
Cranmon	Cyril Chadwick

Jack McGowan probably had many a headache while this one was going through the usual studio conversion of from stage to screen. If you can't blame him, neither can you blame the gang on the lot. As finally unreeling "Excess Baggage" is good program, short of being able to burn up box offices, but capable of holding theatres to their average level, exceeding here and dipping there.

Haines' name won't hurt and he's not doing his fresh kid, except spasmodically. The routine is so new to him that may be the explanation why this is Josephine Dunn's picture.

M-G-M could have made this a smart inside picture great for Broadway and racketeers, but a mystery and perhaps coinless in Cedar Rapids. In playing safe, it has been much toned down from the show, Spence making but one or two attempts to step out in the titles and a few of these used intact from the original script. So while it's a weak transposition for the mob who dote on the show, business acumen must stamp the undermining as the only recourse because of the difference in circulation between a stage play and a picture.

James Cruze, in taking the proverbial liberties, has about reduced the character of Jimmy Dunn, the small time hoofer in pursuit of the daughter of the sister act, to an inanity. Likewise, most of the punch by-play between Jimmy and the mother has been passed up. Concentration is on Haines and Miss Dunn's marital troubles when she enters pictures.

Result is the film hasn't always got the speed or the laughs it should have. Cruze's idea of comedy has gone one way in the smacking or kicking of about every one's posterior. Haines continuously and playfully flicks Miss Dunn from behind as she makes her stage entrances. Jimmy's debut at the Palace with the Ford Sisters is marked by Kathleen Clifford, as the mother, repeatedly kicking him during dance routines and bows.

That's reducing it down plenty for the sticks, but even they'll lose their taste for so often repeated and familiar a bit. Besides which the public isn't crazy about having a hero take liberties with a heroine. One playful slap on no man's land is apt to convince various sectors.

If you want to be technical there's not a performance in the picture which ranks with the cast that played the show in New York. Haines doesn't always convince as the vaudeville husband, chafing because of his wife's success and his own lack of financial independence. He is best in the early footage as a juggler making a play for Miss Dunn in the girl act on the same bill. It's a throw back to his characterization of male ego and still his high spot.

Miss Dunn's principal asset is appearance, plus ability to get the desired pathos into the story. At that point where she and her husband go to the mat for a row, Miss Dunn's loss is Haines' gain.

Ricardo Cortez is a much curtailed person here with a switch in script specifying he take it on the chin as Haines walks out. Kathleen Clifford does nicely as the ever vigilant mother aided by a couple of titles. Other characters are unimportant, Neely Edwards' either completely missing or being held down to muff the value in the Jimmy Dunn role. Haines' fall from the rope over the audience after his wife leaves him and his comeback at the Palace, where she rushes on the stage to wait for him as he is about to make the slide from the top tier. Having used this bit in "Laugh, Clown, Laugh" for Chaney, M-G-M hasn't left much of a kick in it for "Baggage," yet the instances of Haines on the rope are well staged.

Production and photography parallel the usual standard, although there's a noticeable change in lighting half way through the film.

It's a change of pace for Haines and that's possibly the picture's best point from M-G's angle. Simply another case of writing down, less of sleep by an author and a moderate program release. *Sid.*

PLASTERED IN PARIS

(SOUND)

William Fox sound production and release. Featuring Sammy Cohen. Story by Harry Brand and Andy Rice. Titles by Malcolm Stuart Boylan. Ben Stoloff, director. At Roxy, New York, week Sept. 22. Running time, 61 minutes.

Sammy	Sammy Cohen
Bud Swenson	Jack Pennick
Marcelle	Lola Salvi
Sergeant Cou Cou	Ivan Linow
Hugh	Hugh Allen
Mimi	Marion Byron
French General	Michael Visaroff
Abou Ben Abed	Albert Conti
Doctor	August Tollaire

There's everything in this but the kitchen stove. As a comedy it is funny only through the presence of Sammy Cohen. All other joviality depends on numerous situations, and each has been used, seen and embalmed before. Picture will sell itself where nonsensical hokum is digestible.

Starts off like "The Big Parade," becomes "Legionaires in Paris" for a time, goes into a comedy version of "Beau Geste" and winds up like any two-reeler made by any screen comedian.

Cohen is a kleptomaniac all the way through. Goes into fits and cops things. Film starts off in the trenches, and Sammy gets that way after a rock falls on his head. Previous to that he is gassed when his famous nose interferes with donning a gas mask.

Jack Pennick is Sammy's buddy at the front, and is still with him at the Legion convention in Paris.

A scene at the bar is the only drinking bit in the picture, and at no time do any of the characters appear intoxicated. Hence a question as to why the title?

At the cafe the boys get into an argument and one rips off the other's necktie. The victim retaliates. The headwaiter arrives to stop the fuss, only to have his scarf removed. Follows an epidemic of tie-tearing, involving everyone in the cafe. With everybody grabbing at everybody else's tie, they even sneak around pillars to do it, until finally the population is tie-less. That's funny for quite a while, but overly long.

Next best laugh is in the kleptomania specialist's office in Paris, to whom Sammy is dragged by Pennick for treatment. After having a tough enough time with Sammy on the table, during which the doctor and Sammy discover their respective sweethearts are one and the same when Sammy steals a picture of the gal out of the doc's pocket, the doc enters his reception room to find the rest of his afflicted patients have walked out with the furniture.

Cohen gets one giggle by returning the French general's kiss. A new version of a standby.

Lack of love interest other than a tiny contribution by the general's daughter (Lola Salvi) and Hugh Allen, juvenile. Miss Salvi and Marion Byron have very little to do.

Malcolm Boylan's titles are snappy at times, but far below the set provided for "Legionaires in Paris," similar type of film and a better one.

Exploitation of the title may get something for "Plastered in Paris." *Bige.*

KIT CARSON

Fred Thomson production, Paramount release. Story by F. N. Clifton. Directed by Lloyd Ingraham. At Loew's New York one day (April 19). Running time, 84 minutes.

Just an ordinary western, in spite of possible drawing ability through the title and the star, Fred Thomson.

Runs overly long, especially for this type of film, but offers more than a sufficient number of opportunities for pruning.

The opening subtitle reveals it is not the whole story of Kit Carson, but an incident in the hectic life of the famous Indian scout. In truth, it's just a screen story by F. N. Clifton, fitted out for the Carson character or, rather, the Carson name.

Clifton has Carson on the staff of the government as peacemaker between warring red tribes and the whites. Kit is assigned to step in on the Blackfeet question, currently on the warpath. He is in love with a Spanish dancing gal in one of those western booze joints. That may or may not have been so, likely not.

The villain, a member of Carson's Indian squawk-squaring outfit, tries to make the gal on the eve of departure and is tossed out of the room by Kit. He threatens revenge, but Carson takes him along, anyway.

Near meeting the Blackfeet, Carson runs into the chief's daughter, who is about to be attacked by a bear. His gun clogs, so he grapples and wins. It looked like a tough fight, but Kit came out with only a torn sleeve and a scratched arm.

The rescue makes it a pipe for Carson to win the Blackfeet boss's confidence. While accepting the tribe's hospitality, the villain again makes a futile play for one of Carson's admirers, this time stabbing at the chief's daughter and out in the open. Carson again goes to her rescue. He beats the bad one to the draw, plugging him in the gun hand. Apparently fed up by now, though he should have been long before, Kit tells the troublemaker to hit the trail.

The next morning Carson leaves for home, meanwhile having turned down the squaw, who believes she belongs to the man who saved her life.

Homeward bound and at the end of the first day's travel, Carson finds the Indian girl secreted in a basket tied to the horse. That basket must have been made for her. It's a long way back to the Indian camp, so they hit the hay.

Girl wakes up early and takes a stroll. Runs into the arms of the villain in ambush. Falls off a cliff to evade his second try. Carson and the chief, who has his tribe out looking for the girl, see the tragedy. Kit swears to deliver the murderer, dead or alive, mostly dead. He does later on, and neatly, tossing the villain over another cliff right into the center of a "death circle" formed by the revengeful Blackfeet. The hand-to-hand fight between Carson and the villain just before the deciding toss is a thriller.

In both story and action "Carson" will appeal to the mob it was made for. Needs to be shortened.

Direction okay and photography excellent.

Thomson's phiz looks rather sat upon with those comic sideburns, but he is still the best looking westerner on the screen. *Bige.*

ALBANY NIGHT BOAT

Tiffany-Stahl production and release. Featuring four of the five cast members. Directed by Al Raboch, from story and continuity by Wellyn Totman. Edited by Bryon Robinson. Ernest Miller, camera. Titles by Al Martin (press sheet), although opening slide credits captions to the Hattons. At Loew's New York, one day, Sept. 14, half of double bill. Running time, around 60 minutes.

Georgie	Olive Borden
Ken	Ralph Emerson
Steve	Duke Martin
Mother Crary	Nellie Bryden
The Blonde	Helen Marlowe

Pretty mild sort of a meller, with more of Coney Island than the Albany night boat in it. Picture does not lift itself above the one-day rating.

All of the night boat racket are a couple of shots, mostly of the spotlight picking up neckers on the deck. Each night boat scene is utilized, however, for Ralph Emerson to go overboard into the Hudson drink to save a gal. The first time he saved her for himself and the next he saved her from his pal.

Neither the writers nor the title maker took the trouble to denote any time lapse. That left the main burden of the picture as Emerson and Olive Borden meeting each other for the first time in their boarding house Sunday morning, becoming engaged Sunday evening after the Coney trip, married Monday, taking a furnished apartment the same day, and then the gal-saving ep in the evening.

The second gal saving brought on a parlor - break - all - the - furniture scrap between the two men.

Duke Martin is the rough and heavy tender of the searchlight, with Emerson his sub. Miss Borden was twice attacked in the film; once on the after-deck of a yacht, but Emerson saw her go into the water to escape the man, for he then had the searchlight on that yacht. He went over after her. Again he saw Steve try to assault his wife as the boat passed their Palisades apartment and the spot picked out the silhouette shade. Again the kid went overboard, making his apartment just in time to apparently be left in doubt as to how far Steve had gotten with his idea.

Direction poor. Film unmercifully padded in building up. One passage, where the newlyweds rent a furnished apartment and with Steve conniving to get back alone to the flat, must have run for 1,500 feet, merely up to that conventional fight.

"The Night Boat" is a good name for any story under it that would keep to the suggestion. Here it may draw in some, but they will be far from raving when it's over.

The Hattons may debate with T-S and Al Martin, who wrote the titles. There needn't be another fight over that. As a matter of fact, no one should claim them.

THE HEAD MAN

First National production and release. Starring Charlie Murray, with Loretta Young, Larry Kent and Lucien Littlefield featured. Story by Harry Leon Wilson. Eddie Cline, director. At Loew's New York, one day, Sept. 12. Runs 65 minutes.

This very good program comedy is quite similar to and not far behind another recent First National release, "Heart to Heart," both dealing with small town people, politics and gossip. While "Heart" played the Paramount and "Head Man" shows at the lesser New York, the contrast does not properly gauge their respective values. Former, however, has the edge, though not that much.

Also, "Head Man" may be Charlie Murray's first starring picture. Although the payoff in a series of screen comedies he is not known to have been mentioned above the title before this one. In starring he is not without a battle for comedy honors from Lucien Littlefield, who clicks again as he did in "Heart to Heart." Viewing Littlefield's performance, it is wondered why he is billed below both Larry Kent and Loretta Young.

"The Head Man" falls back on its story for impressiveness, and too often. That must have been the fault of Eddie Cline. Neither his handling of the plot nor the characters equals the tale itself.

All about a small town lawyer, once state senator and supreme leader of his political party, but now only a lawyer without clients. And in his lowly—comparatively—position, he is one of the town's staunchest anti-prohibitionists, in practice as well as belief. He has a printer as his friend and drinking partner.

A flashback shows the lawyer in his former powerful position, refusing to join a crooked deal. The boys threaten to break him and apparently they did.

The same boys now control the party and are about to install a new mayor in the lawyer's office. But the hasbeen knows plenty and still has a following. With the aid of the ladies' auxiliary, they induce him to move to another town, advancing him expenses and supplying him with flattering letters of recommendation.

Instead of getting to the train in time he steps in for "one last drink" with his pal and comes home that way. His daughter's editor-boy friend spots the doped up letters, prints them in his paper and enters his prospective father-in-law in the morrow's mayoralty race. The lawyer, still inebriated, sleeps it off and the next a. m. is still unaware that he is to be the next mayor, though he later finds out he's in the running from posters plastered all over the town. Result of the election is a sure thing with the audience, but the story itself manages to maintain suspense until the finish. *Bige.*

MY CHAUFFEUR

(BELGIAN MADE)

Paris, Sept. 7.

"Monsieur mon Chauffeur" was produced in Belgium by Gaston Schakens, and is listed as a Belgian picture. It is not often a film hails from that gallant little country, and this is a most creditable output.

The plot is good comedy, gaily chronicled, and played with plenty of pep by Esther Delteure, Mlle. Andree Meunier, Geo. Hamlin and Georges Gersan.

Villers, having inherited a fortune, gives his time to football. By a clause in his uncle's will, Villers must marry within the year, and in the event of a divorce all the money goes to charity. He advertises for a wife. Among the letters received is one from a girl of a well known family, Andree Valois, who has without reflecting answered the advertisement for the fun of the thing.

Villers picks her out and the maiden is quite astonished to get a reply. To square the matter she persuades her aunt, Esther, to attend the rendezvous in her stead.

Villers, not being quite sure of the situation, delegates his elderly friend, Robert, to replace him. Robert falls violently in love with Esther, and when Villers is shown a photograph of Andree he likewise is smitten with the real applicant. He calls at Andree's home, offering his services as chauffeur, and is engaged. One day he saves her life when she falls into the sea.

Villers has been on the point of confessing the truth, but is called by his football team, of which he is captain, for an international match at Antwerp and quits his livery without revealing his identity.

Andree is vexed at her chauffeur's disappearance and astounded to see his picture in the papers as the captain of the Belgian team. She attends the football match. There is a pathetic explanation afterward and the couple embrace, but minus the glue-like kiss customary in such romantic sequels.

This Belgian production is going to be okayed by the international cinema fans. *Kendrew.*

SHADOWS OF NIGHT

M-G-M production and release. Lawrence Gray, Lillian Lorraine and "Flash" (dog) featured. Story by Ted Shane. Directed by D. Ross Lederman. Cameraman Max Fabian. Titles by Robert Hopkins. Cast includes Tom Dugan, Warner Richmond, Polly Moran. At Loew's American New York, Sept. 13-15. Running time, 57 mins.

Good canine melodrama. Not intended for de luxes. Geared for action from start with characterization and plausibility entirely incidental to the tempo.

Differing from the conventional dog picture, this one is not laid in the open spaces, but in the close quarters of a big city. The dog does not have to pull the switch to (1) save the train (2), shut the flood gates or (3) stop the advancing buzz saw. The exploits here of "Flash" are quite modest. He tears the license plate off the fleeing automobile of a gunman and thereby makes possible the identification of the murderers of Policeman Barnes.

Lawrence Gray is the young reporter who combines detective work with news gathering. Lillian Loraine, less familiar, is featured leading lady. Polly Moran has a mere bit. Warner Richmond is his usual nasty self as the tougher than that gang leader. The gang stuff is reminiscent of the present cycle of high voltage underworld melos.

Pretty good production all told with a novel twist for the finale when the cop-killer tries to get away as the occupant of a coffin in a trumped-up funeral. *Land.*

FEAR

(GERMAN MADE)

London, Sept. 7.

Messtro-Orplid production. Directed by Hans Steinhof. Adapted from a story by Stephen Zweig. Photographed by Carl Puth. Censors' Certificate "A." Released by British & Foreign Films, Ltd. Running time, 100 minutes. Previewed at the London Hippodrome, September 4.

Henry Godfrey	Henry Edwards
Elsa Godfrey	Elga Brink
Jean Francard	Gustav Frolich
Mrs. Reynard	Vivian Gibson
Francis Bond	Bruno Kastner
Claire Bond	Margit Manstad

If somebody could tell us why the story was written and why the film was made we'd be obliged. We can't figure it out any way. It is slow, dull, muddled and without interest. The acting is wooden, the direction fast asleep. As a cure for persistent insomnia, admirable. As a movie we never succeeded in finding it at all.

Henry is an attorney. He prefers his business to his wife, but doesn't really mean to neglect her. She wants to be l-o-o-oved, and how! He offers to take her to Cannes, but can't make it at the last moment owing to an important case.

Elsa gets kissed during a storm by an artist when she takes shelter in a cottage, and this seems so wicked to her she is afraid to tell her husband. He suspects something, finds out what it is, puts a woman on to blackmail her so she will be forced to tell him, and, when she does, after trying to commit suicide, he tells her he knows all about it and never doubted her "in his heart."

There's some other bit of a story of two other folk who are going to get a divorce, and change their minds, but, save to find an excuse for some suggestive stuff, it does not seem to belong.

This is the first offer in this market by a company floated on the Quota boom, and making Anglo-Continental pictures. They have at least got a suitable title for this film. *Frat.*

THE ADVENTURER

M.G.M. production and release. Directed by V. Tourjansky. Screen arrangement by Jack Cunningham from story by Leon Abrams. Tim McCoy starred. Cyde De Vinna, cameraman. Titles by Ruth Cummings. Cast: Charley Delaney, George Cowl, Dorothy Sebastion. At Loew's New York, one day, Sept. 18, as half double bill. Running time, 50 minutes.

Tim McCoy dips into gaucho land for "The Adventurer." In rescuing the mine president's daughter from marauders and restoring the stolen property, Tim wears several colorful costumes and sticks to old lines of never licking under six big bruisers at one encounter. McCoy theatres know what to expect.

Too much bravado and too many extras who topple over like props every time McCoy tightens mit rob Tim of chance of rising to real meller heights. The fighting stuff is so exaggerated at every McCoy climax that "The Adventurer" and other recent releases are practically identical. They get laughs where the fans are supposed to be slightly excited.

Leader of the upstarts and his assistant overact to a sickeing extent.

Spanish sweeties well done by Dorothy Sebastian.

PARADISE

(BRITISH MADE)

London, Sept. 14.

British International Pictures production. U. K. distribution, Wardour Film Company; American, Wide World Pictures. Directed by Denison Clift. Adapted by V. E. Powell from Sir Phillip Gibbs' story, "The Crossword Puzzle." Photography, Rene Guissart. Censors' certificate "U." Pre-viewed at the London Hippodrome, Sept. 10. Running time, 87 minutes.

Kitty Cranston	Betty Balfour
Doctor Halliday	Joseph Striker
Spiridoff	Alexandre D'Arcy
Reverend Cranston	Winter Hall

An excuse to take a vacation on the Riviera. That's all there is to this. In every way it is on the level of an average American program picture. Sometimes not that. Riviera hotels, the bay from a balcony, the dance floor—all the stuff that has been shot to pieces.

So slow and draggy some of the pre-viewers went to sleep despite the orchestra. 7,000 feet, mainly scenery, is about its description.

Clift's direction is competent but uninspired and slow. Perhaps the story was the cause. Or the cast, which, except D'Arcy, is as flat as the film itself.

Betty Balfour doesn't need many more like this to back her way down —not with the critics; they give everything a hand. But with the fans. This is one of those pictures they'll walk out on unless they're rabid for the star.

Kitty Cranston is a parson's daughter, and craves action. She turns down an offer of marriage from a young doctor. After winning a large piece of change in a crossword competition (that's the kind of girl she is), takes a holiday at Nice because she wants to experience that joie de vivre.

She falls for Spiridoff, gigolo, and the doctor boy friend comes to her rescue.

Outstanding is the acting and screen appeal of D'Arcy, newcomer, cross between Novarro and Valentino. Good appearance, fine trouper, plenty of It. As a juvenile lead Striker—who is said to have come out of the De Mille stable—is badly cast. He is a young character heavy, maybe. But as a juvenile lead—so's your grandmother's false hair.

Photography is patchy. So are sets. And an episode in which after apparently a week or more the doctor looks out of a window and it is still raining got a titter even from a nice, kind, pre-view audience.

This film has all the faults under which British pictures are handicapped at present.

Will probably book well here on Betty Balfour's name and D'Arcy's press, but will not add anything to public enthusiasm for home-made films. For America, it may get by in the daily change grind houses if they run it fast. *Frat.*

FREEDOM OF PRESS

Universal production and release. Starring Lewis Stone in newspaper story by Peter B. Kyne, directed by George Melford; continuity by J. Grubb Alexander; titles by Walter Anthony. In cast: Malcolm McGregor, Henry B. Walthall, Marceline Day and Hayden Stevenson. New York premiere at Broadway, New York, week of Sept. 17. Runs 62 minutes.

Whether an original or a published yarn, Peter B. Kyne has obviously and almost admittedly taken his plot cue from the Don Mellett murder of the Canton, O., newspaper publisher and the attempted wreck of his plant. One title, in a warning threat by the underworld element, makes mention of Mellett. It all sums up as an average society-underworld yarn, merely transplanting the usual hooey formerly wished on the shoulders of some insurgent assistant district attorney, onto those of a doughty newspaper publisher and his son who is forced into his sire's shoes when the political pirates wreak vengeance on the campaigning editor. Okay one dayer.

As the title indicates, it's a conflict for the preservation of the freedom of the local "Free Press." The **opening shots are almost identical to those in William Haines' "Telling the World" (M-G-M), also a newspaper yarn, with its scenes of speeding railroads, airplanes, telegraph wires and other means of communication, all hastening to interpret themselves into printer's ink.**

Story, in entirety, is pretty familiar stuff, of a pattern often encountered before, but lent a somewhat timely touch in this particular season of newspaper plays.

Stone who is starred does not merit the distinction excepting for name value, his performance not being consistent with the honor, not because of inability but plot limitations. What he does, he does, in his usual impressively restrained manner.

Miss Day did not quite click as the femme lead and that went double for Malcolm McGregor in a role that seemed beyond him.

The punch is the bombing of the newspaper plant. *Abel.*

"Q" SHIPS

(ENGLISH MADE)

Made by New Era with the co-operation of the British Admiralty and released through Film Arts Guild. Directed by Geoffrey Barkas and Michael Barringer. Photography, other than official war scenes which are from archives of Imperial War Museum, by Sydney Blythe. Technical advisers: Lieut. Commander Harold Auten, for English, and Commander H. Rohne for German. At Cameo, New York, week Sept. 15. Running time, 60 minutes.

"'Q' Ships" is one of the finest pictures that England has tumbled our way. It is largely composed of picked sea war material with some of the greatest submarine and merchant craft action yet worked into a production. The government film is so skillfully pieced into the artificial that a story crammed with suspense and action dims to a vague outline episodic tendencies so apparent in other productions that have delved into governmental galleries.

No exhibitor need hesitate over booking this foreign made. It will draw if properly publicized in theatres of all classes.

An outstanding feature of "'Q' Ships" is that the editing is near perfect. This state is aided by the texture of the war shots from the Imperial War Museum; so well preserved that an expert would have a difficult time discerning any difference in their color from that of the recent production additions which round out the story. Blazing merchant ships and sinking hulls from the Museum archives fit into a continuity getting its start and constantly referring to recent shots of studio sets and submarine interiors.

The studio work is equally excellent. Lap dissolves from war stuff to action within the submersible when it is struck by depth bombs or when it is crashed by a projectile from a phoney merchant ship, called "'Q'," are almost as convincing as the original.

The production is largely a study of the success and defeat of German undersea warfare in 1917; success until American destroyers were brought into play. And this is one English production that gives the home gobs a certain amount of credit.

The "Q" boats, or merchant ships, secreting guns, deliberately laying themselves open to get a sock at the U craft, come in toward the last half of the production. One such ship and the suspense, with a touch of comedy thrown in, which it builds up is alone worth the admission price. Long after a torpedo has battered it and after a part of its crew have manned small boats to decoy the sub commander within range, the gunners remain aboard, eagerly awaiting the word to let go.

THE APACHE RIDER

Pathe western starring Leo Maloney. Story by Ford I. Beebe. Cameraman, Edward Kull. Directed by star. Cast includes Eugenia Gilbert, Don Coleman, Tom London, Walter Shumway and Fred Dana. At Tivoli, New York, one day, Sept. 15, double feature bill. Running time, 59 mins.

Another telling of the venerable fable about the man who was innocent but nobody except the girl believed him. Everything from murder to cattle rustling is charged against Apache Bob Morgan, and, as the smarter pupils will guess, the real culprit is none other than Dawson, the mustached respectable citizen. And yet, despite the so well known plot, "The Apache Rider" makes a good, rip-snorting prairie melodrama.

Leo Maloney, who is director and star of a series of cowboy operas releasing through Pathe, has developed his technique to a high level of proficiency. He puts in everything including the mob breaking into the town jail to lynch the innocent outlaw. Eight or 10 men are murdered at various points in the unreeling. The bullets fly from every direction, but mostly from the rear, and horses gallop madly through somber canyons.

All the parts are bits, but some of the acting is pretty good and Maloney himself is much better than the average cowboy star. Simple matter to find inconsistencies in the continuity and holes in the production, but it's a pipe the western fans won't notice or, if noticing, won't mind. *Land.*

Germany's Side of War

ASSEMBLED

Mike Mindlin production, no other credit. At the Fifth Avenue Playhouse week Sept. 15. Running time about 40 minutes.

Not a very good argument for Germany. It does not attempt to explain or give a reason for that country's part in what the billing calls "the great misunderstanding."

If Mike Mindlin took the credit for its making from somebody else, that somebody else shouldn't mind.

"Germany's Side of the War" does not approach what the title implies. It follows closely several made on this side or for this side, particularly that one pieced together some time ago by the American Legion (for propaganda). This is a loosely connected series of war shots, some good but mostly uninspiring, together with some news reel items and a lot of dupe film.

Titles not credited but in spots follow a style set by "The Big Parade." At all other times, very formal.

A few dead bodies pictured are not near enough and may be overlooked, however gruesome.

Probably the best shot, and one that will go down in history, shows the Kaiser at the front, personally directing the troops.

Large part of the audience was German when the picture was caught. Applause only for Hindenburg, a couple of hisses for the Kaiser, and dead silence for the Kaiser's little boy.

Only for Mindlin and Germans, if there are enough chump Germans.

The only suggestion of the true attitude of the German people is the scene of the anti-war demonstration at Munich. *Bige.*

THE DIVINE SINNER

Trem Carr production, distributed by Rayart. Vera Reynolds starred. Directed by Scott Pembroke. From story by Robert Anthony Dillon. Hap Depew, camera. At Loew's New York, one day, Sept. 14, half double bill. Running time around 60 minutes.

Lillia Ludwig	Vera Reynolds
Minister of Police	Nigel DeBruller
Johann Ludwig	Bernard Seigel
Prince Josef Miguel	Ernest Hilliard
Luque Bernstorff	John Peters
Millie Claudert	Carol Lombard
Ambassador D'Ray	Harry Northrup
Heinrich	James Ford
Paul Coudert	Alphonse Martel

If this Rayart picture were not a quickie in the making it was in the writing. Such a sloppy vague story is seldom found even in a states righter. This leaves "The Devine Sinner" about what Loew's New York gave it, half a double bill. Suitable for the cheap-looking rentals.

Best point of production, other than a carnival scene, is that the foreign atmosphere demanded has been somehow secured from the characters. The carnival scene looked to have cost more than the remainder of the film, for it could not have been an insert here. Nothing marked in cast, perhaps all one day people, other than Vera Reynolds. Press sheet credits DeMille for the courtesy of loaning Miss Reynolds. That's all the credit anyone deserves in this film.

Production fair in appearance with photography evidencing rapid work. Story is of an Austrian girl after the war going to Paris, to secure work to aid her destitute family and blind brother. In Paris she becomes a designer with a fashion show parade at this juncture for exploitation perhaps. That's about all it is good for.

The girl falls in with a forger, becomes his aid and both are finally arrested by the police. The couple are given their liberty on the girl's pledge to involve Prince Josef Miguel, heir to some unnamed throne.

It takes the girl two weeks to mix up with the Prince, after she had protestingly accepted the job. Then both are in love and then the Prince's father dies. He is apprised of his succession by the diplomats, but renounces the throne with his lady love. The latter seemingly remained pure throughout the entire period, although she didn't mind confessing to forgery.

With titles written perhaps by the office boy.

If pictures like these are built for dumbbells, the dumbs can have 'em.

CHICK

(BRITISH MADE)

London, Sept. 8.
Produced by British Lion Film Company. Directed by A. V. Bramble. Adapted from an Edgar Wallace story. Released by Ideal Films Co. Censors' Certificate "U." Running time, 90 minutes. Previewed at the London Hippodrome, Aug. 31.

Chick	Bramwell Fletcher
Gwenda Maynard	Trilby Clark
Jarviss	John Cromer
Minnie Jarvis	Chili Boucher
Mr. Leither	Edward O'Neill
Marquis of Mansar	Rex Maurice

A curious contradiction, this film. Cheap and on the whole poorly dressed, not too well lit, and old fashioned in technique, it still succeeds in being more entertaining than the average British production.

Its only box office angle is Edgar Wallace. None of the cast matters even in the home market. The male lead has never been in a picture before. The director means nothing to the public. Yet, again, it is a film which will do a lot better after it is released than many of the strongly plugged ones.

And let's say here the Bramwell Fletcher boy is a sure bet for anyone who grabs him quick. He is very young, good looking, twists the fems' heart strings good and plenty and can act like he had been born in front of a camera. He is not unlike Charles Ray, but has more charm, better looks and much more s. a. He'll be passed up here, because they go for names and haven't yet learned to find them unknown and boost them. But if an American producer wants a real find here's one that's okay.

Only American angle on this one is the House of Lords scenes. Here the process of a lord taking his seat in the upper house for the first time is shown in full, but worked well into the story and made full of drama and laughs. The sets are as near as anyone could get without shooting in the House, and must have cost real money.

This stuff should be interesting to American audiences, but the film itself is just a one-day program picture otherwise.

Chick is a clerk, lives in back street lodgings, is shy. He wallops a fellow lodger for annoying a young widow, and minds her baby while she is out. Then his uncle proves his claim to a peerage and dies at the same time. Chick is heir to the title, and takes his seat. He is kidded to go on the board of a bogus oil company, the daughter of the promoter (Chili Boucher) vamping him. At a board meeting he spills the beans and blows the company up. At his first visit to the House of Lords he loses his nerve and makes a sudden speech which saves the government. At his rooming house he gets rid of a brother-in-law who is blackmailing the young widow, and finds he loves her.

The story sounds thin, but it is full of incident. A scene in which Chick is interviewed by a dozen reporters is quite funny, and one in which he exposes a frame-up at the card table in a swell party and saves his friend Lord Mansar $100,000 is well handled for suspense. Altogether, it is one of those just a picture which is unexpectedly entertaining. *Frat.*

JEALOUSY

(GERMAN MADE)

UFA production, released over here by Brill Distributing Co. Directed by Karl Grune. Lya de Putti, Werner Krauss and George Alexander featured. No other credit. At Tivoli, New York, one day, Sept. 19, as half double bill. Running time, 50 minutes.

Variety's files list two other pictures with titles similar, and Al Woods is bringing a stage play into New York shortly with the same moniker.

Story gets going with one of those abrupt scenes showing a jealous husband choking his wife to death in a stage play when discovering her cheating. This melodramatic sequence brought cheers from the males at the Tivoli.

A happily married couple, friends of the playwright, witnessing the show, invite him to their home following the premiere. They argue with him that in this day an intelligent man would not give his wife the works in such a fashion for a breach of her marriage vows.

The playwright sets out to prove his theories regarding jealousy. By framing a letter he makes the heretofore happy wife believe her hus-

band is a bigamist, while the husband gets the impression that his wife has been deceiving him. As the husband is giving his wife the choking business, the playwright-friend walks in and says it's a gag.

Okay screen mellow, with comedy touches supplied by Krauss as the fiendishly jealous husband.

DANGER STREET

FBO production and release. Ralph Ince, producer and director. From story by Harold MacGrath entitled "The Beautiful Ballet." Adapted by Enid Hibbard. Cast includes Warner Baxter, Martha Sleeper, Duke Martin, Hank Mills and "Stec" O'Donnell. At Keith's New York Hippodrome, week Sept. 24. Running time, over 60 mins.

For the amount of money spent on this Ince production the result is slightly above the passing mark. It's a picture that can be played on the tail end of a vaude bill, but not strong enough for the de luxe picture houses. Field mainly in the neighborhoods and grinds.

The title implies another crook melodrama, which it is. Molded along lines figured to meet with the popular demand of the moment, the production weaknesses are in casting and in development of love interest.

The story is of the type which depends quite a lot on characterization. None of the players delivers decisively in this respect, perhaps on account of direction or continuity, despite the abundant opportunities offered.

Warner Baxter moves too heavily for the kind of a young man who goes slightly cuckoo when his girl marries another guy, and falls too easily for a cash girl in a gang district.

The picture opens well, showing the start of a gang war. The introduction of the leading character is also done nicely. The attempt to introduce the love interest and the eccentricities of the leading player is a flop and the picture sags on that account almost to the end, when another shooting takes place, with the exception of two or three sequences.

Story has a man seeking death getting two gangs on his trail purposely. Falling for another girl he changes his mind about dying.

Support weak. *Mort.*

SMASHING THROUGH

(BRITISH MADE)

London, Sept. 15.
Produced by Gaumont-British Company. Directed by Will P. Kellino. Story by William Leas and John Hunter. Photography, Baron G. di Ventimiglia. Censors' certificate, "U." Pre-viewed at the London Hippodrome, Sept. 12. Running time, 85 minutes.

Richard Bristol	John Stuart
Kitty Masters	Eve Gray
James Masters	Hayford Hobbs
Miss Duprez	Julie Suedo

Just an average local program picture. Story of the ancient and venerable vintage. Pretty good programer here, okay for Continent, but U. S.—out.

It works up for a thrill towards the end with an auto-racing smash, but this has been done better scores of times in American program pictures. Neither the technique nor the editing get as much out of the race and the smash as could have been done, and the long-shot of a racing car running off the road to crash is not very convincing.

Acting and direction call for no particular comment. Comedy bits, played by Gladys Hamer, Alf Goddard (retired pug), and Mike Johnson, brighten it up a bit, but as a whole it is tame and rather slow.

One high spot is a skid on a hill to avoid a child during a trial. Well done and a good thrill. As a whole the story is thin and the direction inclined to wobble. No outstanding acting, though the cast is good. Eve Grey was starred in "Moulin Rouge"

and John Stuart is supposed to be fancied by Mary Pickford for a future juvenile opposite her. Neither has a part in this film giving any chance. *Frat.*

GRAIN OF DUST

Tiffany-Stahl production and release. Directed by George Archainbaud from screen story based on novel of same title by David Graham Phillips. Ernest Miller cameraman. Windsor, Alma Bennett, Richard Tucker, John St. Pouls. At Loew's New York one day, Sept. 13. Running time about 65 minutes.

For pure sensuality, Alma Bennett flashes in a couple of spots in "Grain of Dust" enough to set the two Gretas back in the shade. Ricorda Cortez flops for her and ruins the business, so that the story, along custom-built lines, bolstered by good names, furnishes a production slightly above par, for fair second runs.

Alma twirls the big boss around her neck with too much ease to make action wholly convincing. While hot stuff is hot, movements are essentially suggestive but not too literally.

For a gum chewing stenog, Alma displays unreal sophistication, but gets male payees to point they lose continuity in awaiting her camera activities.

No particular suspense, theme conventionally handled mixture of business man, dame and liquor.

Bad boy broke gets back regular girl friend, slightly more than bit part played capably by Claire Windsor.

DANCE FEVER

(GERMAN MADE)

Ufa production, distributed through east by David Brill. Directed by Alex Korda, featuring Marie Corda and Wally Fritsch. No other credits given. At Tivoli, New York, one day, Sept. 12. Running time, 60 minutes.

When they razz 'em on 8th avenue, they must be pretty terrible.

This one started getting the bird shortly after the fourth reel. It's the kind of a flicker that keeps the audience anxiously waiting for the wind-up and wins some scattering applause because as one lady expressed it "everybody's glad it's over." Cinch chaser for the daily changers.

Silly story about a dance mad dame who tosses over her husband and takes up with a gigolo and also plays around with her husband's best friend. Finally with the assistance of the two cabaret hounds she is reconciled with her mate when he decides to be her dancing partner thereafter.

Not a redeeming feature in the film; the photography is of the shimmering eye-straining variety and Miss Corda mugs, squints, makes faces and acts foolishly coy before the camera. The film, evidently edited over here with a box office title slapped on, is badly handled. A flock of innocuous titles explains every bit of action, but doesn't help otherwise.

BITTER SWEET

Peerless (film) production, released through Capitol (states right).
Directed by Charles Hutchison from original story credited John C. Brownell. Titles by C. Daugherty. Cast: Barbara Bedford, Ralph Graves, Crawford Kent. At Loew's New York, one day, Sept. 18, half double bill. Running time about 60 minutes.

While story implausibilities are numerous, good direction and cast save "Bitter Sweet" and make it okay for a states righter.

Entrusting the mission of getting back love notes from a blackmailer to a strange dame who qualified, only by answering an ad, is the first snag in construction. When the girl shoots the letter-holder during a wild part and then ignores the thing she is after, it becomes apparent that the oversight is the excuse for the remaining five reels.

The action thereafter is fast and suspenseful. A good meller finish is provided.

ADAM'S APPLE

(BRITISH MADE)

London, Sept. 7.

Produced by British International Pictures. Released in the U. S. by Wardour Films Co., in America by World Wide Pictures (apparently under the title of "See America First"). Directed by Tim Whelan. Story by Monty Banks and Tim Whelan. Photographed by Rene Guissart and George Pocknall. Censors' Certificate "U." Running time, 85 minutes. Previewed at the London Hippodrome, Sept. 3.

Monty .... Monty Banks
Kitty .... Gillian Dean
Mother .... Lena Halliday
Vamp .... Judy Kelly
Vamp's Husband .... Collin Kenny

This British picture is 100 per cent. American. Just like Hollywood made them for and with Monty Banks. All the same stuff: auto chases, stunts on skyscrapers, slipping pants, and all the hoke there is to this type. It is fast and funny, but there's nothing new from beginning to end. Just fifty-fifty; a second feature for the first-run houses.

Monty has saved up for 10 years to get married, and then the girl's mother announces she is coming with them on their honeymoon. On the boat to Europe Monty gets the once-over from a vamp, which brings her husband after his blood. First in Paris and then in London, the rest is concerned with attempts to get rid of mother and dodge the jealous husband. Ends with the girl being kidnapped in error by a gang Monty hires to frisk the old lady, and the attempts to rescue her. After which they return to America, mother agreeing to leave them alone.

Shots in Paris show all the usual features—Eiffel Tower, Louvre and so on. Angle is rapid driving of Paris taxi showing them around. Of course there's the usual cabaret sequences without which no film made in this country is complete.

London stuff of sight-seeing by horse cab well done, with fog getting thicker till they can see nothing. Also parapet and window-swinging stuff up to American average, with not much doubling.

Monty Banks pulls all his stuff and works fast. The girl, Gillian Dean, isn't so good. Not over-beautiful on the screen and no pep.

The picture is stolen by Lena Halliday as the mother. She gets as many laughs as Banks and is, actually, a better actor. Sequences in which she tastes champagne for the first time and gets lit and gay are as good of their kind as anything can be.

Where there are Banks fans and where they like comedy of this type it will go well over. But it is not a contribution to picture-making, either here or in America. *Frat.*

CLEARING THE TRAIL

Universal production and release directed by Charles Maigne from the story by Reaves Easton. Starring Hoot Gibson. Dorothy Gulliver featured. At Loew's New York on double feature program, Sept. 21. Running time, over 50 mins.

Usual western. Plenty of horses, the typical bar, ranch house, comedy cook and a girl.

Story is of the boy who comes back to the possession of his father's ranch, seized by a pair of naughty men in high boots who killed the old man. Boy has grown up to be a terror with rep as considerable fighter. He enters the camp as an assistant cook and then rounds up his boys for the final gun battle.

Not bad and Gibson is reputed to have quite a following with the kids in certain sections.

Mori.

THE OLYMPIC HERO

James P. Lyons production featuring Charley Paddock. Released by Corn Exchange, state's rights. Story written and directed by R. W. Neill. Titles by Walter Weems. Photography by Foxon Dean. In cast: Julanne Johnston, Dan Stuart, Harvey Clark, Crawford Kent and Jack Selwyn. At the Stanley, N. Y., for one day, Sept. 22. Running time, 60 mins.

This quickie was shown in some of the larger houses in the key cities with Charley Paddock, the sprinter, making personal appearances. With the Olympics over plus Paddock's bad showing in the games it means little alone but might serve to round out a fair double bill.

Little or no story, and the comedy sequences, used to pad, are of the old Sennett vintage. Paddock is no comedian.

Like most film stories with a college background this one is badly handled. Newsreel shots of the 1924 Olympics are about the best thing in the flicker. Weems' titles leave much to be desired, and a belching bit, employed by a comedy assistant coach, just doesn't belong.

Within Prison Walls

B. E. Stearns production. Released by Oxford Film Exchange, state's rights. Directed by Sidney Olcott. Screen story by Basil Dickey, adapted from story "The Right Way," by Thomas Mott Osborne. Tammany Young only known player in cast. At Columbus, New York, one day, Sept. 13, as half double bill. Running time, 60 mins.

Thomas Mott Osborne's theories of prison reform serve as the basis of this flicker, the screen adapter taking few liberties with the original yarn by the former warden of Sing Sing. As such it might be classified as an educational, and a fairly good one.

Story traces the crime history of a son of the slums who serves several stretches and encounters the old-time brutal prison methods, returning each time to his old ways when released. The Mutual Welfare League finally brings about his reformation.

Tammany Young as a snow bird gunman has the fattest role he has ever had, and handles it neatly.

Film will pass muster in the daily changers on double bill, especially if accompanying picture is not too serious in nature.

THE FLEET'S IN

(SOUND)

Paramount sound production and release. Starring Clara Bow; James Hall featured. Directed by Malcolm St. Clair. Story and scenario by Monte Brice and J. Walter Ruben. Titles by George Marion. At Paramount, New York, week Sept. 29. Running time, 75 minutes.

Trixie Deane .... Clara Bow
Eddie Briggs .... James Hall
Searchlight Doyle .... Jack Oakie
Al Pearce .... Eddie Dunn
Betty .... Jean Laverty
Double-Duty Duffy .... Dan Wolheim
Mrs. Deane .... Bodil Rosing
Judge Hartley .... Richard Carle
Commandant .... Joseph Girard

As a picture for downtown de luxe houses with other entertainment, very good. Plus Clara Bow, a bright set of titles and Malcolm St. Clair's intelligent direction. With a so-so story to work on and Miss Bow to work with, St. Clair contributed that which the picture will be most noted for—speed.

James Hall is relegated by script to a half-way William Haines as a wise-cracking, fast-working guy. Also, "Fleet's In" follows the theme of most Haines pictures, that of the egotistical flip who tries to make the questionable but hard-to-get flap; repulsed, sore, repents, explains "didn't know what kind of a girl you were," reforms, and proposes.

Gob or marine or variations, but it's all the same.

As a gob Hall shows more than probably ever before. He looks the part and, above all, looks good, which won't be overlooked by women.

Miss Bow again plays a warm but virginal flapper. The way this modern type of lass can take 'em, fake 'em and shake 'em and still retain her standing is quite nifty, even for the screen's stories.

Clara is a "hostess," a Frisco "taxi" dance hall. She lives on dancing—10c per. It's clear she's a nice girl, crystallizing clear. No job in the daytime, either. All nice girls in ballrooms hold jobs during the day and strut their creep joint stuff at night for pin money.

Clara is known as "Peachy" to almost the entire navy. She is seen welcoming the boys as they arrive on furlough. All the boys brought her presents and she's carrying them home when Eddie (Hall) tries to make by offering assistance. He is advised to scram several times and finally does, later meeting Peachy again at the dance hall. As the lights go out for a moment they accidentally become partners. And they finish by winning the championship cup, unaware they are in the contest.

Still suffering from lack of attention, Eddie frames with a sailor friend via coin to insult Peachy, so he can step in and rescue. Works, and Eddie takes her home, where the usual insult occurs. The way Peachy obviously led him on, he couldn't well be blamed, considering he's a sailor. Both fall in love, Peachy that night in spite of the insult and Eddie the next morning while repenting.

In an anti-climax Eddie gets into a free-for-all protecting Peachy, this time legit, and lands in the police court. He is convicted, but Peachy jumps on the stand and saves him.

Canned musical score suitable and tuneful. *Bige.*

WIN THAT GIRL

(SOUND)

Fox production and release featuring David Rollins and Sue Carol. Directed by David Butler. Adapted by John Stone from a story by James Hopper. Cameraman Glen MacWilliams. At the Roxy, N. Y., week of Sept. 29. Running time, 59 minutes.

Johnny Norton, 3rd .... David Rollins
Gloria Havens .... Sue Carol
Larry Brawn, 3rd .... Tom Elliott
Johnny Norton, 2nd .... Roscoe Karns
Larry Brawn, 2nd .... Olin Francis
Johnny Norton, 1st .... Mack Fluker
Larry Brawn, 1st .... Sidney Bracey
Clara Gentle .... Janet MacLeod
1880 Girl .... Maxine Shelly
1905 Girl .... Betty Recklaw

Extremely weak for the Roxy although a fair program picture for smaller communities where the high school is an important factor in the social life. It belongs to the cycle of Fox pictures which glorifies the American 16-year-old. "High School Hero" and "Air Circus" are examples of the same general type although possessing more merit than this release.

Picture has been sounded and revolves about football, two favorable and timely factors that will have influence upon whatever box office success an essentially ordinary film achieves. Story is wildly impossible with occasional touches of slapstick. Football pictures have always been conspicuous abusers of dramatic license but this one extends the privilege to new lengths.

David Rollins, a good looking but puny youth, and Sue Carol, a pretty child, are the leads and a portion of the fans may be able to take a love affair between them seriously. It's the Booth Tarkington idea lacking this author's wit and pathos. Easily pleased folk will also find nothing difficult about a plot that represents three generations of two different families devoting all their time to producing football players for the sole purpose of defeating the other.

Opening caption states that Americans settled down after the Civil War to enjoy a period of peace but shortly thereafter football was invented. Football of the 80's, the game in 1905, and finally in 1928 is the blueprint of the narrative. Gags fill in the footage.

Synchronization adds little although the Roxy is a difficult test. Production is okay except for photography which seemed foggy at times. This might be due to amperage or projection causes but seems inherent in film. "Win That Girl" is a moderate among the moderate. *Land.*

Three Ring Marriage

Produced and released by First National. Directed by Marshal Neilan. Titles by Garrett Graham. Adapted by Harvey Thew from story by Dixie Wilson. In cast: Mary Astor, Lloyd Hughes, Howard Truesdale, Alice White. At Loew's Circle, one day, Sept. 21. Running time, about 65 minutes.

With a lot of stock circus shots, led off by ranch atmosphere to give it western classification, "Three Ring Marriage" has a society drama finis. Cowboy wins his cowgirl and socks the go-between circus manager in an elaborate hotel suite. Weak story, with good names miscast. Okay on double feature or alone in houses of don't care policy.

Picture has earmarks of being made when Alice White was a bit player, and while Mickey Neilan and Mary Astor were in between their regular work.

Mary too delicate type to be convincing in saddle role. Alice okay as roughneck circus performer doing her vamp stuff.

THE NIGHT BIRD

Universal production and release. Starring Reginald Denny. Directed by Fred Newmeyer. In cast: Betsey Lee, Sam Hardy, Harvey Clark, Corliss Palmer. No other screen credits. At Keith's Hippodrome, New York, week Sept. 30. Running time, 70 minutes.

While this is light matter-of-little-fact entertainment, based upon but a dim story outline; there are some conventional situations which will rate applause in the grinds and laughs in the others.

Reginald Denny has an a la Tunney role, highbrow, disliker of night life and the prize ring. When the promoter decides color is necessary for the championship battle, he lugs his battler into a spacious apartment and night clubs. Fleeing this, the battler comes upon a pretty, but bruised foreign dame in the park. That is the excuse for a romance even peculiar for the screen and rather a flat one, despite the "originality."

When the battler discovers he really loves the no-spika English lady, she pops back to her old man and the horse whip.

On the night of the big battle and while the champ is taking a part of the count because of the absence of his loved one, she is resisting papa and getting a sound trouncing. The audience's mentality will decide whether tears or laughs will be the order of the evening at this point.

A half-grown bambino manages to squirm through the cops and get to the ropes in time to whisper the word to the disheartened champ. Then action. The challenger is put away in the twinkling of an eye and the champ, in his fighting togs —not even the bathrobe—jumps a cab with the kid, socks right and left until the avaricous papa takes a physical roll and strong arms clamp the little darling forever.

Denny has done much better, when handed better stories.

GALLANT HUSSAR
(ANGLO-HUNGARIAN MADE)

Produced by Gainsborough Pictures. Distributed in the U. K. by W. & F. Films. Directed by Georg M. Bolvary. Photography by Eduard Hoesch and Bruno Timm. Adapted from original story by Margarete Langen and Arthur Bardos. Censors' Certificate "U." Pre-viewed at London Hippodrome, Sept. 18. Running time, 80 minutes.

Lieut. Stephen Alrik.........Ivor Novello
Mary Wentworth.............Evelyn Holt
Bubenyik....................Ernst Verebes
Katy.........................Ibolya Szekely
Mr. Ocks...............Julius Von Szoreght

Film is rather like the cast list, of mixed nationality.

Padded beyond all need. Would cut easily to 5,500 feet, and be a better picture. It has some elements of novelty in Hungarian street and country locations, and the Katy and Bubenyik roles are in the hands of a couple of passably good comedy troupers, even if their humor is a bit too bucolic.

Some good sequences of a Hungarian country fair do not strain the continuity. But the story is thin, and Ivor Novello does little but look a good looking fellow.

An attempt to make an American angle has been gotten in by making the heroine return to her native country with poppa, who has made a pile in some nebulous works at Detroit. But Evelyn Holt does not pass muster either as an American girl or as a screen hope.

The Hungarian studio ideas of hotels and restaurants, while they maye be locally correct, look cheap and tawdry without being novel or atmospheric.

In the editing and titling (always one of the worst features in British films) there are some funny breaks. The hero is said to be interested only in two things, "uniform and good form." And he is shown behaving in a restaurant in a way in which no educated European would dream of behaving, even if lit. Much less an "officer and a gentleman."

Then, when suspended from the army, he goes to a farm where, per caption, he finds salvation in "the way salvation is usually found.... hard work." Followed by shots showing him leaning against a post with his hands in his pants' pockets while someone else rustles all the work.

What story there is concerns a young officer who ruins dames and money lenders with equal ease. All the money he borrows he drinks and gambles away, till, forging the colonel's name to a bill, he is "sent on leave" pending being cashiered. He meets a girl with whom he falls in love. His last dollar goes in paying the restaurant band to play under her window. She, being American, thinks this is awfully sweet. Or so the director seemed to think.

Being also an officer and a gentleman, he borrows money from his sister's prospective husband—or rather persuades his father to do it for him when brother-in-law is asking pop's permission to wed the sister. Then goes to brother-in-law's farm to work.

Meets the girl again, and goes with a couple of farm hands to a fair with her, knowing who she is although she is disguised as a farm hand. Makes love, reciprocated, but gets the bird when the girl (who wants to be loved for herself alone) finds he knows she has money.

Called back and forgiven by the colonel, he sends the same band to play the same tune outside the girl's window, whereon she ceases packing her grip to return to Detroit, and falls in his arms.

Better in some ways than it sounds, this film will just about get by here with the Novello fans. Others will find it long and in parts unconsciously funny. Its reactions are also too Continental for this market, where standards of conduct are not quite so lax at any rate in theory. And our audiences do love to be supposed to believe they run true to tradition and theory.

For America—out. *Frat.*

SWEET SIXTEEN

Trem Carr production released through Rayart. Directed by Scott Pembroke from story by Phyllis Duganne. Continuity by Arthur Hoerl. In cast: Helen Foster, Gertrude Olmstead, W. H. Tooker, Gladden James. At Loew's New York, one day, Sept. 11, on double bill. Running time, 65 minutes.

Little sister's first sowing of the oats; how it is repeatedly interrupted with much repentance and then started all over again, is the theme of "Sweet Sixteen." Nice program but too weak to feature except in smallies.

Helen Foster cops the picture. Ideal for role, sweet and demure. Holds throughout.

Roadhouse, swimming pool, very little battling, with customary complications but less than usual quantity of necking.

4 DEVILS
(SOUND)

William Fox production and release. Directed by F. W. Murnau from Berthold Viertel's adaptation of the novel by Herman Bang. Janet Gaynor and Mary Duncan featured; sub-featured, Charles Morton, Barry Norton, Nancy Drexel, Farrell Macdonald. Fox Movietone. Synchronized musical score by S. L. Rothafel. Theme song, "Marion," by Erno Rapee and Lew Pollack. At Gaiety, New York, Oct. 3 on run. $2 top. Running time, 120 minutes.

FIRST SEQUENCE

The Clown..............Farrell Macdonald
Cecchi ....Anders Randolf
Woman ....Claire McDowell
Charles, as a Boy.....................Jack Parker
Adolf, as a Boy..............Philippe DeLacy
Marion, as a Girl.................Dawn O'Day
Louise, as a Girl...............Anita Fremault
Poodle Dog ....Himself
Old Clown.........................Wesley Lake

SECOND SEQUENCE

Marion ....Janet Gaynor
Charles ....Charles Morton
Louise ....Nancy Drexel
Adolf ....Barry Norton
The Lady............................Mary Duncan
Circus Director.................Michael Visaroff
Mean Clown.........................George Davis
Old Roue ....Andre Cheron

"4 Devils" turns out to be an elegantly produced, photographed and directed picture by Fox, of high value regular release quality, and missing the super height class only because it is missing any one big kick.

The picture tells its interesting story picturesquely and graphically, with the vivid circus atmosphere a big item. But after that it's a smart handsome vamp who landed a hicky acrobat and broke another little acrobat's heart to give the snapper. And the snapper seemed to be the acrobat went back to his troupe, blew out on the vamp because she sneered at "acrobats," while his little girl partner and financee of the "4 Devils," unaware of the blow off, let herself drop to the ring in the final high double leap of the casting act.

It isn't such an exciting story to take the two hours it does. In fact, more touching and human is the opening, when a clown rescues a pair, two little sisters and brothers, not related, from the brutal clutches of the circus owner. He intended to train the waifs to be acrobats. The clown beat him up for his roughness to the children, then took them away in his donkey cart, becoming their father and mother until developing the quartet as the 4 Devils, the star turn of an indoor circus in Paris.

Mary Duncan is the vamp. All you see or think of in the picture is Mary Duncan. As a vamp she's gorgeous. Her methods of grabbing men may not be the most modern even in pictures, but as a vamp, Mary's right there. It's her first picture assignment. Miss Duncan is from the legit, making her biggest dent on Broadway in "Shanghai Gesture." Still Miss Duncan is co-featured here with Janet Gaynor and entitled to it.

F. W. Marnau has turned out a commercial proposition in this expensive production. It's going to hold attention, with the sound adjunct other than the catchy theme song, "Marion," not important. Marnau's indoor circus is superb; his entire circus arrangement never falters and no circus on the screen under canvass or roof has approached the semblance of bigness Marnau has given here.

The bit of the vamp seated in the same box nightly, out to make the acrobat of fine figure swinging just over her head in the casting act, is a fine piece of suggestion, if not planting, though the vamp's stew bit all over the parlor of her home may not please as well. There may be exaggeration here and there in the vamp's work, but she's a vamp and working at it.

A pleasing picture is the four kids grown up in their acrobatic costumes, while Murnau has given them a ring entrance that will set every acrobat in the world on fire when seeing it. In flowing devilish wraps, they ride into the ring, each on a white horse, with the clowns preceding them. Their trapezes are lowered. As each of the quartet rides under it, they are taken aloft, their wraps falling off on the way up to the aerial pedestals of the casting turn.

The casting scenes in their way are not unlike those of "Variety." It is much better done here and made more important, though it was important enough for and in "Variety." And Murnau's "Cirque" of Paris pales Dupont's "Wintergarten" of Berlin.

Doubling on the casting, of course, with much if not all of the circus talent from the Ringling-Barnum circus. Animals possibly from the Barnes circus on the coast or from a zoo out there.

Miss Gaynor is one of the sisters, the girl who thought her sweetheart had fallen for that woman, with that women eventually becoming the eyesore of the entire circus while in her box seat nightly. Miss Gaynor has nothing and does nothing to stand out here; she and the others are completely submerged by Miss Duncan. If ever there were a one-person picture, this is it.

Charles Morton is the hick caster the vamp goes after. He plays the booby fellow quite well and certainly looks it; in fact, the figures of the four young people in their tights are most attractive. Nancy Drexel and Barry Norton are the other mixed couple and half of the Devils. Mr. Norton does very well in his role, and Miss Drexel looks nice. They also become engaged during the running of the story.

Best among the men is Farrell Macdonald as the old clown (or it may have been Wesley Lake). Anders Randolf is the tough drinking circus owner, with but a few moments in the prolog. He made the brute pretty tough and rough. Another clown opens and closes the picture with announcements (slides).

A cameo-like picture, the photography cannot be overlooked. While "Four Devils" as a whole is another decided mark of the excellence of the Fox production department.

Murnau made "Sunrise" and it was not box-office in the sense a picture of its production cost should have been. Murnau, German, in the common way would have been thought too artistic for another try with an expensive big picture. Perhaps Winnie Sheehan did the unusual then and followed his belief Murnau could be made box-office. Mr. Sheehan assigned him to "The Four Devils" and Murnau has come through. Winnie appears to be right. It looks as though there is a big picture in Murnau. Maybe it will be his next, and if one, then more. For he classes among the big directors.

LONESOME
(SOUND)

Universal's first talker, co-starring Glenn Tryon and Barbara Kent in Paul Fejos' production, from story by Mann Page, adapted by Edward J. Lowe, Jr. Directed by Edward J. Montagne and supervised by Carl Laemmle, Jr. Runs little over 60 minutes. At Colony, New York, opening Sept. 30 on grind to 75c top.

Mary...............................Barbara Kent
Jim.....................................Glenn Tryon
Overdressed Woman.........Fay Holderness
Romantic Gentleman........Gustav Parthos
The Sport.........................Eddie Phillips

Universal ballyhooed "Lonesome" to a fare-thee-well, its first full-length talker, boldly alleging it to be "the talking wonder picture." It is nothing of the kind. Save for two or three dialog sequences—on the beach between the leading pair, and in the magistrate's court with Jim sassing the court clerk—it's just an ordinary sound picture, average in story and badly synchronized.

The score sounds like a plugfest for one music publisher's catalog. This may be explained by a "Lonesome" theme song published by this firm and a certainty to be a secret to the hit ranks. The score is undistinguished, tin-panny and not particularly fitting from any viewpoint.

The direction and everything about "Lonesome" are tritely familiar. The lonesome premise, sound enough thesis for a screen epic under other conditions, principally backed up by a sturdier story—here is a travelog of Coney Island. It looks like a celluloid ad for Luna Park.

Action takes the Boy and Girl on their Saturday half-holiday to the beach amusement place into a flirtatious mating. The director, through the camera medium of a restless focus, has endeavored to impress the lonesome spirit of two individuals amidst a sea of humans. It is this lonesomeness which prompts a nice boy and a nice girl to engage in unconventional familiarity for the conventional happy ending.

Some of the photography and the basic appeal of the theme saves it for a time, but for the main "Lonesome" drags and ultimately peters out.

U should have saved this one and done something about a stronger opener for the new policy. "Show Boat" and "Broadway" are in the works for later release, which should raise the average considerably.

Abel.

MATING CALL

Paramount release of Caddo production. Directed by James Cruze and starring Thomas Meighan. Walter Woods adapted from the novel by Rex. Beach. Photography by Jos. Morgan. Running time, 72 mins. At the Paramount, N. Y., week of Oct. 6.

Leslie Hatton	Thomas Meighan
Rose Henderson	Evelyn Brent
Catherine	Renee Adoree
Lon Henderson	Alan Roscoe
Marvin Swallow	Gardner James
Jessie	Helen Foster
Judge Peebles	Luke Cosgrove
Anderson	Cyril Chadwick

"Mating Call" has been long heralded. It is revealed as a sincere piece of work and will please the fans. Has drawing power in the names of its players and is good quality output without being an epochal achievement in production.

Picture's best assets is a first rate sympathetic role for Renee Adoree. Another is the presence of some pretty high powered sex sequences and a third, although value of this may be doubtful, is topical interest of Klan activity. Star part fits Meighan's casual style of hero and technical production is in the best mode, with evidences of careful preparation.

Flaw of the release on the audience interest side is the looseness of the story, a fault almost inseparable from pictures made from novels. Action does not build smoothly and there are faults in the development of character and incident, probably representing problems in translation from printed page to screen.

Picture will help Meighan in his comeback that began with "The Racket," but the picture really belongs to Miss Adoree. This young actress here reveals a talent for sympathetic comedy roles of the highest distinction. Her Catherine, immigrant girl, rushed into a marriage of convenience and gradually learning to love her husband, is a delicately shaded bit of acting. It takes on added daintiness in contrast to the boisterously played society vamp of Evelyn Brent.

High light is the passage where Catherine slips out of her husband's farmhouse at night to take a solitary swim in the nearby brook where she is discovered au natural by the anxious mate, who then and there decides that she will be his wife in truth, instead of his farm assistant. Miss Adoree in a filmy chemise—and wet at that—being carried home from the brook, is sex appeal personified. It is a tribute to the fine and sincere playing of both the actress and Meighan that there was no giggling audience reaction to this situation and it was devoid of any taint of forced spicy import. This because it's a legitimate dramatic situation and is handled with taste and discretion.

Sequences having to do with klan activities in a small American town are lacking in punch. Subject of the K. K. K. is pretty blah for dramatic purposes at this late date, anyhow.

Gist of story is that Leslie Hatton marries the town belle and then goes off over there. He is returning after peace to find that the girl's rich parents have had the marriage annuled and she has wed a rich townsman, leader of the klan (called here "The Order"). She has become a hard, worldly woman, meantime, and is determined to throw herself into an affair with the returned soldier, even to the extent of forcing herself half undressed into his bedroom. Here the husband finds them, but nothing much comes of the scene except that the hero, disgusted at doll faced women, goes to Ellis Island for a real woman for his wife. Story interest then takes on speed as the immigrant girl, first insisting upon the position of servant, gradually answers the mating call.

A mechanical sub-plot deals with a klan leader who drives a girl to suicide and then turns suspicion upon the hero. It never creates much suspense, serving principally to furnish a background for the romance of the immigration girl and the heart-hungry farmer.

Rush.

TENTH AVENUE

William C. DeMille production and Pathe release. Directed by DeMille. Adapted from stage play by John McGowan and Lloyd Griscom. At Hippodrome, New York, week Oct. 7. Running time, 65 minutes.

Lyla	Phyllis Haver
Joe	Joseph Schildkraut
Guy	Victor Varconi
Detective	Robert Edeson

In film form the formula in the McGowan-Griscom play of the same title is followed closely, with only the realism of the stage lacking in the screen version. That absence of personal warmth which braced the so-so story on the boards is the difference between the show, fairly successful, and the picture, which is fair.

In picturized "Tenth Avenue" the young woman keeper of a rooming house for thieves, both active and reformed, is made more angelic and given a sick mother.

Phyllis Haver is not at home in the young landlady role. She found herself in "Chicago," and though both of the underworld, the moods are as different as day and night. Joseph Schildkraut is also an uneasy player in his backboneless Joe characterization. He looks and acts less like a dip than the detective.

Victor Varconi's smooth performance leads the cast. "Tenth Avenue" can play the vaudfilms and please. It shouldn't be taken straight in class company.

Bige.

THE NIGHT WATCH

(SOUND)

First National production and release. Directed by Alexander Korda under the supervision of Ned Harin. Continuity by Lajos Biro. Author not credited on screen or program. Starring Billie Dove with Donald Reed featured. At Strand, New York, week Oct. 6. Running time, 72 minutes.

Yvonne	Billie Dove
Captain Corlaix	Paul Lukas
D'Artelle	Donald Reed
Brambourg	Nicholas Soussanin
Ann	Anita Garvine
Dagorne	Gustav Partos
Admiral Mobraye	William Tooker
Fargasson	George Periolat
DeDuc	Nicholas Bela

On account of its sex angle and the appearance, drawing power and ability shown here by Billie Dove the picture should do well in the first runs providing there is a suitable stage program to back it up. It is not strong enough to stand by itself, rating among the seconds for box office possibilities.

The opening is slow and clumsy under Alex Korda's direction and the picture drags for over 30 minutes before going into stride.

The story is not convincing, with sequences leading up to the mystery boring and of the conventional type.

The courageous French captain who had just returned from a victory over the enemy is accused of killing a fellow officer. Gun and other circumstantial evidence seem to be conclusive evidence. It leads into a court room scene for a military trial with the wife getting up at the last minute to say "He did not kill that man—" etc.

From that point onward the action and picturization are handled neatly. A tale of the indiscretions of a beautiful young wife is always appealing from several angles. According to this tale the young wife, Yvonne, remains on board ship against her husband's orders. She stays in the cabin of a former lover, expecting to surprise her husband, Captain Corlaix, later on in the evening.

War is declared and the ship sets out to sea. Brambourg discovers the girl in D'Artelle's cabin and demands concessions in the way of a close relationship. The girl refuses and he threatens to tell her husband. Hubby won't listen and as she is called on deck D'Artelle enters the cabin and shoots the menace with the Captain's gun.

The court room scene is dull and unimpressive. Action on board ship registers. Picture is synchronized but has no dialog.

Mori.

Our Dancing Daughters

(SOUND)

Metro-Goldwyn-Mayer release of Cosmopolitan production featuring Joan Crawford. Directed by Harry Beaumont from Josephine Lovett's story running serially in Hearst dailies. Titled by Marion Ainslee and Ruth Cummings. At the Capitol, N. Y., week of Oct. 6. Running time, 86 minutes.

Diana	Joan Crawford
Ben Blain	John Mack Brown
Beatrice	Dorothy Sebastian
Anne	Anita Page
Anne's Mother	Kathlyn Williams
Norman	Nils Asther
Freddie	Edward Nugent

Booked in here for two weeks "Daughters" may be able to go three. The picture did around $40,000 on the week end, had a big Monday matinee and that night at 9:30 they were five deep behind the last row with standees to the doors on one side of the lobby. As a program leader it's been doing heavy business around the country. After taking a look—in fact two looks—there's reasons.

This jazz epic follows the title, a pip b. o. name in itself, is sumptuously mounted, gets plenty of playing from three girls and is sufficiently physically teasing in undress to do the trick.

Add to that headwork in direction which doesn't show the younger generation doing impossible things, except in one instance, and a story that marries off the juvenile to the scheming flapper before he gets back to the frank and daring but honest heroine. They've got to kill off the unworthy young wife to make the clinch windup but despite that this is 86 minutes away from the lead title, the picture never lost a customer at this performance.

It's mainly because of Joan Crawford and Anita Page who see-saw for cast honors although someone ought to tip the camera boys to stop shooting Anita in profile on closeups or mediums.

And after you wash this all up the story is running serially in the Hearst dailies with that string's customary plug for a Cosmopolitan picture. It's the unusual example of a film substantiating the ballyhoo.

Somewhere in the whole thing is a moral. Evidently that the modern girl is wild but dead on the level like old Sal.

The boyishly figured Miss Crawford has seldom looked better than in this one. She's both heavy and light on clothes and strictly for the camera either way. Other than the appearance thing there are numerous spots where she troupes, and well.

Miss Page is given her major spot down next to closing in a lengthy drunk sequence to which she gives abundant authenticity and which ends in her death after a fall down a flight of stairs. Earlier much of her time is taken up arguing with her money chasing mother while displaying undies and much stocking, Beaumont evidently desiring to make sure that no one would leave this effort early.

Miss Sebastian is close behind as the wronged girl with the fiery husband. She especially registers in scenes opposite Asther and has a couple of spots with Miss Crawford which aren't hard to watch. Both Asther and Johnny Mack Brown are strictly the types the latter, perhaps, lacking fire but getting across because right now he isn't too much the actor. Kathlyn Williams fits as the angling mother.

Allowing that the New York censors didn't touch "Daughters," the showing at the Stanley, Philadelphia, wasn't much different. The Penn scissor brigade drew the line on the closeup of Miss Crawford's undergarments on duty, the peeling off of her skirt while Charlestoning for her crowd (the exaggerated instance) and a rather heavy love scene along the shore line. Otherwise both runs are about parallel on footage with the main difference in synchronization.

The Stanley used the records alternately for about two reels and then switched to its big pit crew, which made it pretty bad because the theatre musicians made a bum out of the canned score. And the musical arrangement is spotty. Theme song isn't bad but when they dip back into "All Alone" and "Broken Hearted" in following Miss Crawford's love affair it's harking back to the shooting galleries and the guy at the piano.

At the Capitol the picture is running solid on recorded score, the disk switch being noticeable on titles and because of the difference in amplification as the change is made—louder on one machine than the other. Why sound effects must include knocks on doors, horses' hoofs and even the tap of a ping-pong ball on a table is beyond the pale.

The public isn't that sound crazy and the Stanley's combination of pit crew and record is quite apt to make the Quakers start wondering why synchronized scores are necessary in the big houses which boast of good orchestras. The Capitol has been smart enough to lay off its musicians for this hour and a half. It's better that way than half and half although it's about time somebody started using their head on where and where not to use these minor effects.

"Dancing Daughters" is a picture.

Sid.

SHIRAZ

(INDIAN MADE.)

London, Sept. 25.

Produced by British Instructional Films Ltd. Directed by Franz Osten. Story by Niranjan Pal. Photography by H. Harris and Ernst Schunemann. U. K. Release, Pro Patria Films Ltd. Running time, 84 minutes. Preview at London Hippodrome, Sept. 21.

Shiraz .... Himansu Rai
Shah Jehan .... Charu Roy
Dalia .... Seeta Devi
Selima (Mumtaz Mahal) ..... Enakshi Rama Rau

Some three years ago the German firm, Emelka, sent a director, Franz Osten, to India to make a picture of "The Light of Asia." They were sold this idea by Niranjan Pal and Himansu Rai, and claimed to have spent a great deal of money on the film. The result contained not a little beauty and some imagination, but amateurish in technique and acting, and failed signally. Then the same two Indians put up the idea of using the Taj Mahal story for screen purposes. After many refusals to deal, finally sold the idea to British Instructional. Its active head, Bruce Woolf, has a penchant for educational subjects. There was a release and partial finance from Germany as a consideration, and local assistance was obtained from the Maharajah of Jaipur for the making of the film. It has been hailed here by the press as a thing of great beauty, and in some respects scenically it is. But it has also been praised as a great picture, which it is not. Direction is lacking in almost every sense of drama; opportunities, locations, immense masses of people and strings of elephants, soldiery, camels, and other normalities of India are used without any conception of how to handle them for effect. Many of the Italian directors of a decade ago could give Osten a score of points in these matters.

There is a crowd stated to contain 60,000 present at an execution. All the use made of it is for a few mid and long shots. The situation is one in which Shiraz is to die by the Death of the Elephant's Foot the huge crowd is watching the approach of the elephant to tread out the life of the condemned man. Here is an obvious chance to create suspense which every Hollywood director has used time and again. Nothing of the kind is done. Shots of the elephant approaching, long-shots of the whole scene, and close-ups of the man on the ground, the one dramatic note being struck by a shot of the elephant's foot about to descend on the man.

The absence of studio work and the non-use of lights are claimed as an asset, but in many cases the photography would have been much improved even if they had used reflectors. As it is, there are many cases in which it is flat and thin. Titling and editing, too, are bad to the point of atrociousness in some cases, a foot-soldier being made to talk 'to a fellow trooper about "within these precincts," and (inexcusable in an Indian film) the list of players is alluded to as the "Caste."

As a semi-amateur effort made by people working under natural conditions the film is not without interest. As an essay in native production it has some merit. But it has reduced a rather sublime legend of the building of the Taj Mahal to something rather petty and personal, and its directors have failed signally to put anything into the picture beyond what the beauty of locations and buildings could give them.

Ruthlessly cut, it will attract some attention in art theatres. But, however much one would like to see it happen, especially as its producers are so sincere in their belief that it is a master-piece, it will fail as a general release. As a piece of entertainment merchandise it offers no possibilities from any angle.

Frat.

DOG LAW

FBO production and release, starring Ranger. Directed by Jerome Storm from story by S. Taylor. Robert DeGrasse, cameraman. In cast: Robert Sweeney, Jules Cowles, Walter Maly and Mary Mabery. At the Stanley, New York, one day, Oct. 8, on double bill. Running time, about 60 mins.

"Dog Law" is okay for the kids and passable in the grinds. It's a typical quickie.

There's practically a story within a story. Granger has his love affair and brings together his collegiate master and a maid of the log rolling country. One villain shoots another and the lad is blamed. By help of the dog and girl he is saved, and all that.

Dog is good. Dulls his teeth cutting ropes and takes a ko twice from a bar room stick. A puppy scene is cute, but the rest is third rate stuff, which drags.

LOVE'S OPTION

(BRITISH MADE.)

London, Sept. 27.

Produced by Welsh-Pearson-Elder Co. U. K. release through Paramount for Quota purposes. Story by W. Douglas Newton and George Pearson. Directed by George Pearson. Photographed by George Pocknall. Censors' Certificate "U." Running time, 70 minutes. Pre-viewed at Plaza, Sept. 25.

John Dacre .... Pat Aherne
Lucian Wake .... Henry Vibart
His Niece .... Dorothy Boyd
Kelly .... Scotch Kelly

If American houses are seeking alibis when they have to tell the Board of Trade they have not been able to book their requisite percentage on the Quota, some are going the right way about it. This film makes a promising start, jibs after the first two reels, and finally goes all to pieces.

The story is trite, not to say tripe. Wicked old man wants to gyp hero out of the copper market. Employs toughs to dynamite South American mine, and then to abduct attorney who is prospecting in Spain on an option. Niece, whose money the wicked old uncle is embezzling to carry out his nefarious schemes, believes hero is the bad one, till she learns otherwise from some cables which he drops in a fight after having stolen them from the old uncle's house. Finally she assists the hero to get his option made valid at the last moment, after a hectic fight with a gang of Spanish toughs hired by uncle, one of whom incidentally tries to rape her.

Some pretty Spanish shots compensate for directional and story defects, but one hacienda does not make a movie. Dorothy Boyd lacks experience, and Pat Aherne has not the face for a hero of this type. He should be cast for saturnine roles. Some comedy of the hoke vaude type is supplied by Scotch Kelly, sometime vaudevillian with all the familiar tricks, gestures and falls.

May fill a gap for Par's Quota here, but if they release it in America they'll have to let it out on parole.

Frat.

The Lost Expedition

(GERMAN MADE.)

Ufa production, released by Brill Distributing Co. Edited and titled by Joseph R. Fliesler. No other credits listed. At 55th St. Playhouse, New York, week Oct 6. Running time, about 60 minutes.

This one billed as the re-creation of a great polar tragedy is short on entertainment value, but will probably please the intelligentsia in the sure-seaters because of its fine snow country photography. Slim story concerns the hardships encountered by those who invade the Arctic waste in the name of science. Film may be similar in theme to recent Fox release "Lost in the Arctic."

Joe Fliesler's titles written in the first person plural have the effect of making one feel he is a member of the party that has set out from one of the northern European countries to rescue a lost expedition. The rescuers are divided in two groups, those who go by boat and those traveling over the snow country with dog teams, with Robbin Bay in the Arctic as the destination. The latter party encounters all the tough breaks and is finally reduced to one man and one dog.

Dog finally assists in the rescue of the man, who is himself a would-be rescuer. Rescuing party then returns home when it is learned that scientists they have been searching for in vain are safe.

Some fine shots of Eskimo home life, with a guide named Milak, figuring. Other outstanding photography includes the breaking up of an icy mountain and the rescue of men and dog teams that have taken a header into deep crevices.

Just a lengthy educational suitable strictly for the so-called art film houses.

HEART TROUBLE

First National production and release. Harry Langdon, star and director. Story by Arthur Ripley. Gordon Bradford, titles. In cast: Doris Dawson, Lionel Belmore, Madge Hunt. At Loew's New York one day, Oct. 2, on double bill. Running time, 58 minutes.

Probably because it is his last for First National, "Harry Langdon's "Heart Trouble" comes into Manhattan unsung. Yet it is one of the best of the few he has made during the past two years. It can stand up without a supporting feature for a short run in any house.

The comic does less of the emoting he gave way to in his last two. He abandons to a great extent his ambition to be the complex of a tradegienne and a comedian. "Heart Trouble" is more compact and the story is more actionful.

That he is directing himself is less obvious.

A novel angle on conscription during the war, with a small-town locale and with Langdon in one of his regular moron roles, is used. Failing to get into the army after pestering a recruiting colonel, Harry, through a coincidence, saves that officer's life and blows up an enemy ammunition depot.

Doris Dawson shapes up physically as a comely leading lady, more sex appeal than a lot of the peaches Harry has picked in the past. The gags are not so numerous, but the ones used are good.

Charge of Gauchos

Julian Adjuria production (independent), released through FBO. Story by producer. Albert Kelley, director. Titles by Garrett Graham. In cast: Francis X. Bushman, Jacqueline Logan. At Loew's New York, one day, Sept. 25, one-half double bill. Running time, about 65 minutes.

Julian Adjuria a year ago landed in Hollywood with a bank roll. From Argentina he came, fired to make a picture on Belgrano, his country's emancipator. After a long time his work was completed and he returned, sad but the wiser. This picture, minus its pep 'em up title, reflects his experiences. It's okay for any theatre as a filler or a substitute when the can man is late with the regular. Otherwise, cold.

"Charges of the Gauchos" is most amateurish. Even an old-timer like Francis X. Bushman seems to have been forced into over-acting by the brilliant artificiality of the sets and atmosphere. The whole thing impresses like Mexican rookies lined up with West Point seniors.

The producer wrote the story, which may or may not have been the cause for this mess. It gets to the screen in the most hokoy form.

WEDDING MARCH

(SOUND)

Paramount release of Pat Powers' production featuring Eric Von Stroheim and Fay Wray. Directed by Von Stroheim from his story in conjunction with Harry Carr. Score by J. S. Zamecink. At Rivoli, New York, on grind run starting Oct. 12. Running time, 115 mins. $1 top.

Prince von Wildeliebe-Rauffenburg, ... George Fawcett
Princess von Wildeliebe-Rauffenburg, ... Maude George
Prince Nicki, their son..Eric Von Stroheim
Fortunat Schweisser........George Nichols
Cecelia Schweisser..............ZaSu Pitts
Anton Eberle ....Hughie Mack
"Schani" Eberle..............Mathew Betz
Martin Schrammell........Cesare Gravina
Mrs. Schrammell................Dale Fuller
Mitzi Schrammell...............Fay Wray
Navaratil ....Syd Bracey

Left of all the footage on "Wedding March" are the present 10 reels with the finish where intermission would have been had the picture come in for $2 with the rest of it. Also remaining is a ponderous slow moving production and some beautiful photography telling a very familiar story, the tip off on which is the lead title, "Vienna 1914." It's fair but hardly brilliant program material which the boys have salvaged from a regiment of reels.

Scissors to the right and left, leaving most of the picture still in cans, has cut the story to the well known blue blooded Austrian army officer having his fling with the country maiden and then wedding a limping heiress as the seduced rural miss promises marriage to pacify the brow beating butcher who has threatened the life of the hit and run lieutenant.

If that synopsis implies von Stroheim for once is the white-washed hero forced into financial wedlock, such is not the case. The director as Prince Nicki continues to be his sinister and very military self, still on the make as concerns the girls. Marrying for money is his father's idea, sowed by the heiress' male parent who is willing to pay heavy for a title, a proposition to which Nicki accedes without much objection.

A caption has him asking his father whether he has ever considered the possibility of two people actually falling in love, evidently an attempt to whitewash Nicki to some extent with the fans but a false note in the general characterization. Picture is climaxed in the symbolism of the innocent Mitzi seeing a vision of the Iron Man of the Danube around whom the peasantry has woven a legend of impending tragedy. The unseen second half presumably takes up the consequences of her misstep with Nicki.

In its present state "Wedding March" can be divided into three locales—the supposed interior of St. Stephen's in Vienna, an orchard and a brothel. The meeting between Mitzi and Nicki comes about through the latter's rearing horse injuring the girl as the natives line the street to watch the Corpus Christi procession, a Viennese religious and military celebration to which Fox's Movietone newsreel beat von Stroheim as far as public screening is concerned. However, this is the big production flash with von Stroheim indulging his penchant for natural color for a few hundred feet.

Almost the entire first half of the footage is given over to this Corpus Christi holiday, the secondary characters of the late Franz Joseph's court being planted as they whisper to each other in church while Nicki carries on a much prolonged flirtation outside with Mitzi. Room for wholesale slicing here in those houses dubious of a 10-reel leader.

Scenes in the brothel are reported heavily cut, one tip being that there's enough out to make a couple of stag dinner reels. It's in the usual champagne guzzling von Stroheim manner with various nationalities of women all over the place. During the whole debauch the prince and the millionaire merchant decide upon the title-money exchange as they drunkenly sprawl upon the floor.

Soft focused cameras dominate much of the footage. Pretty work that lends much to the implied mood of Mitzi as she succumbs to Nicki's spell in the orchard courtship. The wedding at the finish has been lavishly staged so that there's no reason to doubt the reports that burn-it-up Eric upheld his reputation.

Personal performances uniformly good in this limited version. Miss Wray appeals and convinces as the shy, pretty faced and innocent victim, while Von Stroheim's scoundrel is again interesting, despite the half-hearted attempt to soften the character. George Fawcett and George Nichols make conventional fathers. Maude George will startle the peasants with her cigar-smoking mother of Nicki. ZaSu Pitts is the crippled princess, giving the role legitimate interpretation, not too easy because of her comedy inference to the fans who audibly snickered for no apparent cause at one point while she was on view. Betz has been instructed to spit his way through his uncouth butcher, a touch which has lost its novelty and significance since the "Parade," "Glory," etc., and which becomes distasteful through constant repetition. Otherwise Betz meets all demands.

The trials and tribulations of getting "Wedding March" to a screen are unique in an unique industry. It has taken something like two years and over a million. If these ten reels are all Paramount, Powers and Von Stroheim are to realize upon, it rates as the most costly and overly studio handled program picture ever made. Considering its title, production and sex the film would likely have met with fair success for twice daily $2 showings in key centers, allowing that the unwitnessed nine reels could have stood up in completing this "Strange Interlude" celluloid subject.

In its curtailed form the aforementioned three requisites figure to send it across as moderate de luxe house material despite the Viennese-Mary Philbin-Norman Kerry reminiscences. With the less rigid censorship abroad it should reap heavily on the Continent.

Main defect is that deletion has not added pace. Root of the evil is the time given the Corpus Christi event from which the succeeding action never recovers, being none too swift in itself.

Synchronized score is excellent and shows judgment in the use of minor effects. *Sid.*

BATTLE OF SEXES

(SOUND)

United Artists' production and release. Directed by D. W. Griffith from story by Daniel Carson Goodman, adapted by Gerrit J. Lloyd. Featuring Jean Hersholt and Phyllis Haver Photography by Karl Struss and Billy Bitzer. Victor non-synchronous. Synchronized musical score by R. Schildkret. At Rialto, New York, week Oct. 12. Running time, 90 minutes.

Judson....................Jean Hersholt
Marie Skinner..............Phyllis Haver
Mrs. Judson................Belle Bennett
"Babe" Winsor..............Don Alvarado
Ruth Judson................Sally O'Neil
Billy Judson............William Bakewell
Friend of Judsons.............John Batten

Patrons lured to this one by the Griffith bulbs are slated for disappointment, almost a shock. The Griffith hand is seen in the shortest sequence, where the wife contemplates suicide and the camera is focussed downward from the roof of a high building. Otherwise any Harry could have done as well with this conventional theme, "The Battle of the Sexes." It is slow to the point where the editing room could shelve 40 minutes more of the running time and improve this picture At its best it will never rate more than fair program in better class houses.

The subtle touch for which Griffith has piled up considerable of his fame is substituted in this one by suggestiveness too obvious for the sophisticated. Flesh flashes far above the knee by the able Phyllis Haver will not win mother's approval for the small town daughter, nor will her stomach squirmings on a cushioned floor for the edification of her fish, the otherwise perfect father-husband, played by Jean Hersholt, register big except with those who like their sex a la West.

Belle Bennett, as the trusting and simple wife, is inclined to be monotonous in her simplicity early in the story. Consistent emoting of a more boring sort is okayed by Griffith thereafter, when she stumbles into hubby with his sugar in a night club. Little Sally O'Neil almost peps her up on the roof during the near-suicide sequence, but a few feet later she is again in her oatmeal style.

Efforts to play the sentimental angles following the break do not get far. Mother is too blah and father enjoys himself to the extent of getting his audience into that frame of mind where having a bit of blonde entertainment on the side is not so naughty, after all.

Hersholt's efforts to get his rotund form into competition with the sleek build of Don Alvarado, who plays the giglio, gets a number of laughs. The women should enjoy these bedroom antics almost as much as the male patrons and should get a startler out of Miss Haver's prowess along these lines.

The musical synchronization okay with the exception of a song by Miss Haver, several bars behind the movement of her lips. Club applause and horn honking are the only other contributions as sound effects.

Moran of the Marines

Paramount production and release. Starring Richard Dix. Directed by Frank Strayer. Story by Linton Wells. Adapted by Sam Mintz and Ray Harris. Continuity by Agnes Brand Leahy. Ruth Elder featured. Titles by George Marion. At Paramount, New York, week of Oct. 13. Running time, 63 minutes.

Michael Moran................Richard Dix
Vivian Marshall................Ruth Elder
"Swatty"......................Roscoe Karns
Basil Worth..............Brooks Benedict
General Marshall......Capt. E. H. Calvert
The Sergeant.................Duke Martin
Sun Yat......................Tetsu Komai

Only a few pictures ago Richard Dix was cleaning up several Chinese junks filled with river pirates. In that film he was revealed ultimately as an attache of the U. S. Navy. In "Moran of the Marines" the background is still China, the girl is Ruth Elder instead of Mary Brian; but outside of that this latest flicker is a rubber stamp. The popularity of the star is presumably supposed to excuse almost anything.

Miss Elder as an actress here may make it unlikely she will get any repeats. Nervous and awkward, photographs indifferently and fails to create romantic appeal. She comes close to comedy when registering coyness at a couple of points. As to her "name" value to the picture, that remains to be demonstrated. It will be watched, no doubt; but Ruth Elder trying to act will probably ruin that, even if it is there.

The titles of George Marion, Jr., are the real aid. The darb is Marion's crack about marines being sent to China to keep peace in Nicaragua. Editing and cutting seem sloppy, the action jumps badly at times, and general tone of production, a reflection of a too hasty production schedule and a too typical program picture for a popular star.

Dix gets into the marines with a taxi cab driver, following a 10-day bit on the rock pile for brawling in a cafe. He applesauces the general's daughter while in mufti, is exposed as a simple private and later is courtmartialed for kissing the girl. That scheme also by Barrymore in "Tempest."

In China Dix outwits Yung Sat, the Chinese bandit, saves the girl single handed and is simultaneously taken to heart by the girl, his rich uncle and the Marine Corps.

There are laughs and action and Dix, so "Moran of the Marines," although not hot, or even warm, will probably get by. Multiplied by any large digit, this type of film can ruin any star at the box office, and more so if he must carry a "name" novice on her film debut like Miss Elder. *Land.*

The Young Whirlwind

FBO release of William LeBaron production starring Buzz Barton. Directed by Louis King. Cast includes Edmund Cobb, Eddie Chandler, William Patton At the Stanley, N. Y., Oct. 15. Running time, 62 minutes.

Purpose seems to be to make a junior Tom Mix out of freckled-faced Buzz Barton. The lad can ride.

Story is one of those highly improbable affairs centering about a robbery of an airplane. Action depends on Barton's riding and the way he outwits four tough lookin' guys. He slingshots two of them into a fight, kayos another with another shot, and then whams the fourth over the head with a piece of heavy rope and recovers the stolen mail pouch. There is a love story, but it doesn't matter. A little bit here and there for comedy, but it is of the usual stripe.

Good camera work caught a spill by one of the bandits. Seemed too quick, hard and dangerous to have been arranged, but decidedly realistic either way. *Mark.*

The Melody of Love

(DIALOG)

San Francisco, Oct. 10.

Universal (Movietone) sound production and release. Story and direction by A. B. Heath. At Pantages, San Francisco, week Oct. 6. Running time, 83 minutes.

Jack Clark..................Walter Pidgeon
Madelon......................Mildred Harris
Flo Thompson...................Jane Winton
Lefty..........................Tommy Dugan
Music Publisher...........Jack Richardson
The Gawk........................Victor Potel

Universal's first all-sound feature length picture, and incidentally the first 100 per cent all-talking Movietone production, is excellent in some spots and dull in others.

Most of the talking sequences are brutal. But the synchronization is above the average, with some of the musical interpolations unusually well done.

Universal put over a fast one in making this all-talker. A movietone recording outfit was borrowed from the Fox lot in Hollywood, ostensibly to make tests. As there were no written specifications as to the use of the outfit, U hurriedly got together a cast, called on A. B. Heath, who heretofore has directed only shorts, whipped a war story into shape and within six weeks, at a cost of not over $40,000, turned out "The Melody of Love."

Story is very weak. It's woven around a New York song writer, his sweetheart, Flo Thompson, a talented vaude singer; Lefty, his "buddy," and Madelon, French singing waitress, whom the boys meet in France.

Miss Harris is of the vaude and speaking stage, but her talking sequences do not register. She clicks only, so far as sound is concerned, in her song interpolations. In a blonde wig she is a demure, sympathetic picture, and, aside from possibly a little over-acting, is acceptable.

Walter Pidgeon's voice is more or less metallic, excepting when he sings. His piano playing registers, and he plays the lead role with more or less conviction. Outstanding character is that of Lefty, admirably done by Tommy Dugan. As the crap-shooting Nemesis of the American Army in France Dugan provides plenty of comedy. He has no trouble putting his stuff across. Here, too, however, the talking voice is of the metallic sort.

Pidgeon is attempting to write a war song when Dugan busts in the publisher's office with the news he has just enlisted. Soon they are on the side lines and then right in the middle of hostilities overseas. The early part of the picture and the finish are a continual series of double exposures, with the usual marching soldiers, cannonading and customary war stuff.

Throughout the unfolding of the story frequent recourse is had to one-time pop war melodies. Stirring airs are freely used in the score. Then back to Broadway.

Where they are educated to all-sound pictures this one will hardly prove suitable. In the houses where dialog is still more or less of a novelty there are some redeeming features which may help it along.

It's nothing to get unduly excited over. *Edwards.*

Women They Talk About

(DIALOG)

Warner Brothers production and release, featuring Irene Rich, William Collier, Jr., Claude Gillingwater and Audrey Ferris. Directed by Lloyd Bacon. Joseph Jackson titled, and Frank Kesson, cameraman. At the Strand, New York, week Oct. 13. Running time, 60 mins.

Mother..........................Irene Rich
Daughter.....................Audrey Ferris
Son...................William Collier, Jr.
Grandfather..........Claude Gillingwater
Mayor........................Anders Randolf
Frame-Up Man................Jack Santoro
Politician......................John Miljan

Very much of a talking quickie, nothing saving it but Claude Gillingwater doing his well-known grouch and in rare form. Veteran of stage and screen, Gillingwater will push this one through for program purposes. Just 14 minutes of dialog, four and 10-minute sequences, with the audience only wanting to hear the crabbing grandfather—and that's Gillingwater.

Weak-kneed plot is colorlessly played. The dialog handled by Miss Rich and Anders Randolf is in the flat, slow, uninteresting manner from which only occasionally the talkers have been free. But they yell at Gillingwater silent or when talking. In the latter instance the Strand mob chirped loud enough to smother follow-up lines.

It simply proves that comedy is still a dialog picture's best bet and that Gillingwater is surefire and strong enough to become a draw if slipped a couple of more similar roles, and soon.

It's a comedy of two families. The girl's side can point to a family crest while the boy's father has worked himself up from the grandfather's office boy to mayor.

Love affair between the youngsters is opposed by the old man and the town head, previously in love with the girl's mother. He is a widower and she a widow. They, too, get together at the finish after the mother has threatened to run for office against her prospective son-in-law's dad.

Relation of the title to that theme is a bit obscure, but the suspense creeps in when one of the mayor's followers frames the daughter into a compromising flashlight, to stop the mother's campaign, and the son dashes to the rescue. Neither young Collier nor Miss Ferris is heard in the picture, while Miss Rich and Randolf are undistinguished when speaking. A few of Miss Rich's "sides" are almost maudlin.

A synchronized score accompanies minus superfluous minor effects disrupting the attention. Music has been well selected and is a smooth piece of work. Production, photography and titles are average. But nothing counts other than Gillingwater. Not even Audrey Ferris, ingenue of the yarn, who has put on more clothes than she used to wear in sex educationals, but still is a little plump.

The 10-minute dialog passage closes the picture. Previously a four-minute seance didn't mean anything. In both instances the grumpy grandpop saves the inserts from being ridiculous. *Sid.*

RED LIPS

Universal production and release. Co-featuring Buddy Rogers and Marion Nixon. Directed by Melville Brown. No other screen credits. Cast includes Stanley Taylor, Hugh Trevor, Hayden Stevenson. At Hippodrome, New York. Week Oct. 14. Running time, 58 Mins.

College as even low brows know it ain't.

The campus toast loves the freshie because he is different from the hip flaskers she knows. For his own good she gives him ozone. Ascribed reason: He is too inexperienced.

Of course he goes to the dogs, poisons his fine young body with hootch and disgraces himself as a members of dear old Whoopee's track team.

Smart pupils will anticipate Buddy's snapping out of it, renouncing his evil ways, and winning the all-important field meet for Whoopee. Even the duller ones will feel confident that Buddy and Marian will patch up their misunderstandings.

Buddy Rogers was reported last spring as the lucky possessor of a growing fan mail. Paramount which had him under contract has done nothing about it, so Universal may cash in on that fan following if it exists. Rogers is a personable youth of a type now fancied. Miss Nixon co-featured is a contract player to Universal and well known where Universals play.

"Red Lips" is strictly stencil but fair entertainment for those who don't insist on being fastidious. In college towns is ought to qualify as a chuckle-inducer for the mob. *Land.*

Kriemhild's Revenge

(GERMAN MADE)

UFA production with all-German cast. Fritz Lang, director. Photography by Carl Hoffman and Gunther Rittau. At 55th St. Playhouse, New York, week Oct. 13. Running time about 90 minutes.

This sequel to "Siegfried," also German-made and shown in this country in 1925, probably will stand as an artistic success and b.o. zero. "Siegfried" made no money and "Kriemhild" is not even as good a picture.

The former was based on the Nibelungenlied, the ancient German folk legend of how young Siegfried, son of Siegmund, the Wise, won the beautiful Kriemhild, and was then murdered at the wish of the designing Brunhilde. "Kreimhild's Revenge" is a partial rehash and follow-up.

In the latter the formerly beautiful Kriemhild is not so comely, physically as well as mentally overcome with the desire for vengeance. To advance her purpose Kriemhild weds the distorted Attila, King of the Huns. As queen of that domain she avenges the death of her beloved Siegfried, but not without herself meeting death in the end.

Another reason why Kriemhild is not so nice to look at as previously is that she is played by another and not so pretty a blond-wigged lady. The Kriemhild of "Kriemhild's Revenge" is appallingly masculine and not at all the beautiful maiden of the Siegfried picture.

In this film there is little or no action until Kriemhild departs for the land of the Huns. Opening sequences are the closing portions of "Siegfried," from the death scene in that film on. Out of all that comes nothing but a remembrance of much mugging, and all the same kind of mugging.

In the later battle scene there are more men slain than, perhaps, in any motion picture ever produced.

The typical fantastic settings are notable and look like a lot of money. If getting over on this side, it will be a miracle, but if the picture does, all credit should go to the scenery.

A rather bothersome contribution by its U. S. importers is the double set of titles, English and German. Both occupy the screen at once, one on top of the other with a line dividing. Where the titles are lengthy the two translations are flashed individually, German first. Little reason for this at the 55th St., but where shown to Germans exclusively the picture may sell itself with German titles only.

Running time of an hour and a half would make necessary cutting "Kriemhild" in about half for average program use. With its present overabundance of slow motion and overly written sub-titles it would be a better picture than now if cut to 15 or 20 minutes. The battle stuff, in short subject form, would make it playable.

Nothing in it for exhibitors in its present shape. *Bige.*

The Glorious Trail

Charles Rogers production, released through First National. Ken Maynard, starred. Directed by Al Rogell from story by Marion Jackson. Titles, Don Ryan. In cast: Gladys McConnell, Frank Hagney, James Bradbury, Jr. At Loew's New York, one day, Oct. 9, on double bill. Running time 65 minutes.

The job of wiring the continent is undertaken along covered wagon continuity by Charles Rogers in "The Glorious Trail." There is no continued suspense and a great story opportunity is muffed by directorial laxity. In its present state numerous situations are far overshot making the theme drag. Better editing, and certainly clipping, will be necessary before this can be labelled as something worthy of the better second runs.

Covered wagon stuff is the opener with the telegraph and Indians.

Ken Maynard goes through the gyrations of whipping the barroom mob and later bumping off an Indian with every shot when a wagon train is attacked. This is probably the longest exchange of Hollywood hail ever recorded.

DON QUICHOTTE

(DANISH MADE)

Paris, Sept. 22.

"Don Quichotte" of Miguel Cervantes is too well known to presume to speak of the scenario of the picture issued by the Palladium Film Co. of Copenhagen, recently trade shown in Paris under satisfactory conditions by P. J. De Venloo.

This film features the Scandinavian comedians, Carl Schenstrom and Harold Madsen, now famous in European picture circles as Doublepatte and Patachon. They hold the roles of the thin knight with the sad face and his devoted stubby Man Friday, famous in literary history as Sancho Panzo. They interpret the inseparable characters of Cervantes with delightful reality.

Naturally all the principal phases of the Spanish classic have been incorporated by Lau Lauritzen, the producer. His work made a most favorable impression on the trade critics in Paris, and it goes without saying the appearance on the screen of the diverting Schenstrom and Madsen will be hailed by the cinema fans, already acquainted with the quaint antics of these comedians.

A good picture on a well-known subject, but the attraction lies in the two lead actors. *Kendrew.*

THE BABY CYCLONE

M-G-M production and release, co-starring Lew Cody and Aileen Pringle. Gween Lee and Robert Armstrong subfeatured. Directed by Eddie Sutherland. Based on George M. Cohan's play. Adapted by F. Hugh Herbert. Cameraman, Andre Bartalier. Titles by Robert Hopkins. Wade Boteller, Polly Moran, Clarissa Selwyn and Nora Cecil in cast. At Loew's American, New York, Sept. 27-29. Running time 57 minutes.

One of the best stage farces of recent seasons is a very so-so moving picture. Loew's sent it direct to the American for three days, without a first Broadway showing. Eddie Sutherland, former Paramount slapstick specialist, appears lost in attempting ot capture the human characterizations that made George M. Cohan's play delightful.

The adaptation is mechanical and undistinguished. Responsibility can probably be tossed between Sutherland, F. Hugh Herbert and the supervisor. While considering the flaws, first and thoroughly it may be mentioned that there is a sickish pallor to most of the sub-titles supplied by Robert Hopkins.

The good points are its cast and the arresting modernistic settings. Never such a home as Aileen Pringle's. It is a carnival of bizarre effects, cock-eyed angles, cubistic nightmares and startling effects. It alone should attract attention to the production.

Miss Pringle looks good in an evening gown and later in a night gown. Gwen Lee also shows well. The plot has completely omitted the third act complications from the play, so that the roles played on Broadway by William Morris and Georgia Hale are mere bits.

The whole picture is a collection of bits. Bits of acting, bits of interior decorating, and bits of custard pie. *Land.*

3 Comrades and One Invention

(RUSSIAN MADE)

Amkino release of Sovkino production. Directed by Alexis Popoff from his own story; A. D. Grinberg, cameraman. In cast: Serge Iablokov, Serge Iavrentiev, Olga Tretiakova, A. Nirov. At the Cameo, N. Y., week of Oct. 13. Running time, 60 minutes.

Hailed as the first Soviet comedy, "Three Comrades and One Invention" should get a break in the arties if for no other reason than for its being the first one. Some of the higher class second runs might like it because of the same reason. For grinds and other places, thumbs down.

While the Cameo bills this as the premiere of Soviet comedies, the Russian laugh market must crack a grin only when meller stuff is laid on thick. A crack on the jaw or some heavy rough and tumble stuff is obviously intended for the laughs. With a plot a yard and a half long about two brothers inventing a box-making machine and the troubles they have in patenting it, because of a villainous rival of the old school, the production has every indication of having been worked out on the cuff as the director went along.

A dame who loves yokels and who has a city beau, covers all kinds of ground in an inestimable length of time. And this baby never laughs, even when the situations are supposed to be most funny. She just shows her buck teeth when one of her boy friends falls overboard and then reappears to prove that he is a good swimmer.

The farm and woodland scenes, as they must be in Russia, are the best. The rest of the attempts are stiff and forced, even the passengers jumping into the water and helping to push a paddle wheeler off a sandbar. Situation appealed to the director as so original that he inserted a few stanzas of "The Volga Boatsman" hymn to make sure the peasants would get the reason.

Russia better stick to mellers or die laughing at home.

CROSSROAD OF LOVE

Superlative (firm) Pictures' production, released by Hi-Mark. Adapted by F. I. Reinhardt from play, "The Woman Who Squandered Men." Directed by Carmine Gallone. Cast includes Soava Gallone, Jose Davert, Bobby Andrews, Leon Mathot and Marcya Capri. At Stanley, New York, one day, Oct. 11. Running time, 70 minutes.

This pretentious fling at the production of a picture bears the unmistakable imprint of a foreign studio even though presented by Superlative Pictures and distributed by an American concern. There have been, are and probably will be many bad pictures made in America, but there is nothing quite bad enough to compare with a third-rate continental effort such as this is.

There is no official seal of a British, French, German or Russian maker, but the mannish, masculine appearance of the women in the picture, the ill-fitting clothes, the broad, pleated trousers of the men's dress suits, the dull expressions, bordering on stupidity, represent a combination met with only in foreign pictures.

Direction is clumsy, minimizing every possible effect from the opening scene, that of a man pointing a pistol to his head. Meant to be startling, it is only insipid.

The story is intended to deal with the ravages of a beautiful but unscrupulous woman of the British nobility, wealthy and domineering in her attitude toward her many lovers, whom she discards as soon as the novelty wears off. All would be well with a personage of this type except that the appearance of the lady does not measure up within transatlantic phone distance to the picture painted for her by the crudely written titles. *Mori.*

ODDS ON

(AUSTRALIAN MADE)

Sydney, Sept. 15.

Main fault of this picture, trade screened at the Prince Edward, is the story. From this angle it's another weak sister.

Plot deals with the old tale of the racetrack. Phyllis Gibbs, recently in America, is the featured player. She has looks and certainly shows possibilities, but she cannot shoulder a weak story and a weak cast too.

It has been produced and photographed by Arthur Higgins who proves himself a good photographer. Film will do here for the smaller weekly change houses.

For England, maybe, but for America, no. *Gorrick.*

TERROR MOUNTAIN

FBO production and release, starring Tom Tyler. Directed by Louis King from story by Wyndham Gittens. Screen play by Frank Howard Clark. In cast: Frankie Darro, Jane Reid, Al Ferguson. At Stanley, New York, one day, Oct. 12. Running time, 60 minutes.

First rate western that can't miss in the daily changers, and might even be held over for an extra day or two in some houses.

Tom Tyler has been given a story

that holds, and the final sequence, without a fade-out clinch, will please peasants and sophisticates. In addition to Tyler, young Frankie Darro and Jane Reid stand out, and Director King also deserves a bouquet or two.

Story centers around Lucille and Buddy Roberts, who live in a dilapidated ranch house and are harassed by no good guys who know there is considerable money hidden about the premises. Buddie (Frankie Darro) gets the idea of writing his favorite moving picture star (Tom Tyler), enclosing photo of his sister (Jane Reid) and asking him to come to their assistance.

Tyler plays himself in this film. Having completed his latest western in Hollywood, he is about to set out for a month's vacation when he gets the kid's letter. Attracted by the picture and his interest aroused by the pleading letter, the movie star sets out for the Roberts ranch.

Comedy is injected when Tyler leaves his car and slides down the snow-covered mountain side to the ranch after a flock of pratt falls while trying to learn how to handle himself on a pair of skis.

The wind-up has Tyler bidding good-bye to Buddy and his sister in a perfectly natural manner, minus the usual mush, but with the idea solidly planted that the movie star and one of his admirers are that way about each other.

THE MYSTIC MIRROR
(GERMAN MADE)

Ufa production and release. Carl Hoffman credited direction and photography. In cast: Fritz Rasp, Felicitas Malten, Rina de Kigoure. At 55th St. Playhouse week Sept. 29. Running time, 67 minutes.

The first Ufa mystery melodrama, as the 55th Street programs it, establishes a precedent in the meller field which it will be well for the Germans not to follow. "The Mystic Mirror," as the meller is called, is storyless, absurd, overacted and leaves an audience yarning.

Long gaps in the footage are filled with zealous titles, pasture-lands and castle sets. A bad bird from the city buys the castle and to show that he is wicked the director introduces him by having him drive aimlessly through a fence and maiming an innocent little lamb.

A mirror in the castle is supposed to look into the future of any individual who may take a peep while the moon is shining. The villain, while chasing a native dame, abandoning his city woman to her wine, takes such a peep and sees himself strangled. Thereafter an old skull comes in for a lot of duplication while the bad lad with the long mouth and bum teeth seeks the strangler.

Nothing mysterious about the mirror and the direction let the cat out of the bag before the end of the first reel.

Man From Headquarters

Trem Carr production distributed by Rayart. Directed by Duke Worne from the novel, "The Black Book," by G. B. Howard. Features Cornelius Keefe and Edith Roberts. At Loew's New York, Sept. 23, as half of double feature bill. Running time, over 60 mins.

After an unusually strong opening of international intrigue involving a small European country and America, this picture does a nose dive in the last 35 or 40 minutes. Still, it's an interesting story of the mystery type and a good bet for the smaller houses.

Regardless of what the director made of his script, this Howard novel has furnished a fine basis. After the unusual introduction the picture merely evolves into a series of chases which give the picture the grind house stamp.

There are really only two players in the picture, Cornelius Keefe and Edith Roberts. Balance of the cast are mainly extras for group scenes when not engaged in chasing the brilliant secret service man from Washington.

Story opens with the murder of a Duke Albert on board a train by three mysterious ruffians. It's all about a secret document. The trio get away with half of the papers and the Washington sleuth, arriving later, gets the other half. The woman is one of the foreign group seeking the missing half of the document. She does it to save the starving population of Exemia, or Athemia, or something like that. But though it's a case of mutual admiration at first, second and third sight the sleuth finds it his duty to trap the conspirators and regain possession of whatever it was he wanted to gain possession of. The detective is a miracle man. Shot down two or three times, he still manages to rise and laugh idiotically at his enemies. The girl cries dutifully every time the handsome boy is shot, just to impress that she means well despite all. *Mori.*

Making the Varsity

Excellent (firm) production, released through Commonwealth. Directed by Cliff Wheeler. Titles by Lee Anthony. In cast: Rex Lease, Arthur Rankin, Gladys Hulette, James Laddo. Times Square one day, Sept. 20. One-half double bill. Running time, about 60 minutes.

Not much excuse for "Making the Varsity." Even for an independent. Story of the hoke school brought out by a sluggish cast which gets its pep from what seems to be a few newsreel inserts on a football game.

Rex Lease, featured, is studied and artificial, painfully. He bows his head to denote suffering on the least occasion. The bows are over the childish moves of a younger brother who has to be kicked below the belt to prevent him from throwing the big game.

Hardly a tense moment in the entire production.

HUNTED PEOPLE
(GERMAN MADE)

ABA production, released by A. P. Axelrud. Screen play by Kurt T. Brown. Directed by Nuncie Mallasomma. Charles Alden featured. In cast: Vivian Gibson, Inge Lalken. At Stanley, New York, one day, Oct. 10. Running time, 60 minutes.

Continental flicker tailor made to show the prowess of Alden, an Italian actor. He is one of those athletic young men whose forte seems to be an ability to hurdle furniture.

A hand-to-hand struggle with the menace on an aerial ferry close to the finish is the kick that this one holds for the grind house customers. Otherwise moderate screen stuff.

Alden is a detective assigned by an agency to kidnap a child from its mother and deliver the girl to the father, who has obtained a divorce through trickery. He obtains employment as the good woman's chauffeur and, falling in love for her, is torn between love and duty.

As things are beginning to break right for the lovers, a rival detective frames the hero and makes off with the kid.

After considerable fence jumping, jail breaking and the like, Alden sets things right.

A slim story and will just about get by on a twin bill in the sticks.

BLACK BUTTERFLIES

A. Carlos production, released by Quality Distributing Corp. James W. Horne, director. From novel by Elizabeth Jordan. On double bill at Loew's New York, one day (Oct. 5). Running time, 63 minutes.

Dorinda Maxwell..........Jobyna Ralston
Kitty Perkins.................Mae Busch
David Goddard.............Robert Frazer
Norma Davis...............Lila Lee
Judge Davis................Cosmo Bellew
Jimmy.....................Robert Ober
Chad......................Ray Hallor
Hatch.....................George Periolat

Badly played, directed and botched piece of film production that will barely hold up its end of a bargain program, as was the case at Loew's New York.

"Black Butterflies" plays on one's cheaper emotions, emotions that every chump is supposed to reveal when encountered by an expose on the silver sheet, but doesn't. Thrice it reaches a logical ending, and thrice it keeps right on going, to an inevitable clinch finish that, however formal, is the most exciting moment in the picture.

Previous to that an unreasonable "for convenience" marriage is contracted; the hero goes blind in an auto accident and miraculously recovers; a fast living lady passes to the great beyond, or below, in payment; a bunch of dodoes at a stew party suddenly get sentimental over a girl's piano playing, and a gang of flaming youths flame a lot.

Robert Frazer mugs through a principal male part that fails to gain an ounce of sympathy for him until going blind. While three women who have made their own reps ere now are freakishly made-up. Dressing of face and figure by each of the trio is atrocious. *Bige.*

CAPTAIN CARELESS

FBO production and release. Directed by Jerome Strong from story by Robert Steele and Perry Murdock. Featuring Bob Steele. Cast includes Perry Murdock, Mary Mabery, Jack Donovan and Wilfrid North. At the Tivoli, New York, one day, Oct. 3. Running time, about 60 minutes.

A small-time production for the small, low-priced neighborhoods. A picture of the kind made five years ago and still being produced for a certain market. No box-office value. Can't draw a dime, but on double-feature programs, for customers still cheer and applaud when the navy, army and air forces invade the South Sea islands to save the white girl from the cannibals.

This cannibal stuff, it has been thought, has long gone out of style, excepting for comedy purposes. In this grind house it went over in fine shape as straight drama relieved by faint touches of humor suitable for the pliable tastes of Tivoli audiences.

The story, credited to Perry Murdock and Bob Steele, who also have two main character roles, is more like a series of incidents linked in a chain. Hardly any plot.

Comedy, tried for frequently, registered often in this house, while the action is kept going at a fair rate.

It's a tale of the gal who becomes engaged to the wrong guy, not knowing the other boy's secret affection. She goes on a boat trip, with the lucky one as guest on board. The ship founders at sea and the pair are lost on an island inhabited by blacks. The boy back home hears of the disasters and flies to the rescue.

Once on the island, it is mainly continuous chasing episodes for laughs. *Mori.*

Singapore Mutiny

FBO production and release. Directed by Ralph Ince. In cast: Estelle Taylor, Ralph Ince, Gardner James, Martha Mattox, James Mason. At Broadway, N. Y., Oct. 15. Running time, 60 minutes.

"Rain" and "The Hairy Ape" and flashes from other plays and stories are recalled by the "Singapore Mutiny," better than the average

FBO. The picture should rate good program.

Estelle Taylor as Broadway jade seeking refuge on Pacific isle is only dame on oil tanker on which entire action transpires. Her taste for men varies from traveling man to stokers until she falls for a stowaway, weakly portrayed by Gardner James. Ince, who directs himself as blustering firehold boss, gives a fairly good performance, although facial expressions, in attempt to depict ferocity, often overdone.

Good wreck and rescue shots in fog. The three principals drifting in lifeboat not convincing in their sacrifices. Dramatic attempts to save stowaway's life overdone almost to point of comedy.

While the City Sleeps

(SOUND)

Metro-Goldwyn-Mayer production and release. Directed by Jack Conway from original story by A. P. Younger. Lon Chaney starred. Photography by Henry Sharp; titles by Joe Farnham. Synchronized version here. Running time, 70 mins. At Capitol, New York, week Oct. 20.

Dan ....Lon Chaney
Myrtle ....Anita Page
Marty ....Carroll Nye
Skeeter ....Wheeler Oakman
Bessie ....Mae Busch
Mrs. McGinnis..................Polly Moran
Mrs. Sullivan.........Lydia Yeamans Titus

To begin with, Lon Chaney doesn't do at all in a semi-heroic role. You can't disassociate him from something monstrous and all the bizarre characters he has ever played come up to confront the spectator. Good judgment ought to have barred Chaney from the role in the first place. Therefore, a misplaced star turns what might have been a stirring meller into second grade quality program output, wholly dependent on Chaney's name.

The spectacle of a middle aged cop with fallen arches and uncouth manners, even if he has the heart of a lion, getting himself into a sentimental love affair with a flighty flapper, is dreadfully hard to take. It would be hard to take if Herbert Rawlinson, say, essayed it, or Milton Sills. They've both done things quite as exaggerated and gotten by with it because of the romantic aura that by grace of screen tradition envelopes them. But Lon Chaney—Help!

Picture is a strange medley of frenzied gang war on one hand and plodding, everyday characters on the other. These two elements do not blend plausibly. There is the veteran plain clothes detective Dan Callahan, chronically nursing feet battered by years of pavement pounding. There is his landlady, relict of a dead cop, with a widow's cap set for Dan (Polly Moran plays her with her unfailing flair for such types).

On the other side is the glamorous master crook, young, handsome, audacious.

Say what you like about the moral aspect of the case, it's laborious to build and hold sympathy for the agent of law and order when the two forces clash for the girl. The girl herself didn't help much, being a flabby minded kind of jazz addict over whose ultimate fate you couldn't get really excited. She is wildly in love with one of the gangsters, but remained innocent, a type the pictures have made familiar since the gangster vogue.

She learns too much about the master gunman. When he threatens to bump her off, she runs to Dan for protection. While living in his rooming house for safety, Dan falls for her, despite the fallen arches and hard boiled disposition.

Out of gratitude she agrees to marry Dan, and thus builds the climax of Dan vs. gang leaders. As you might surmise this leads up to a grand gun battle and housetop pursuit. As far as dramatic mechanics are concerned, that's dandy sequence. Gang war pictures have disclosed no better incident than this running fight of police against criminals, ending with a tear bomb attack and a revolver duel on the roofs.

In the end Dan, of course, learns that the girl really doesn't love him for himself alone. He brings the two young lovers together, resuming his defensive maneuvers with the artful widow.

The comedy twist almost saves the story at the end, but not quite.

Rush.

ME, GANGSTER

(SOUND)

Fox production and release. From Satevepost story by Charles Francis Coe, adapted by the author. Directed by Raoul Walsh, and titled by William Kernell. At Roxy week Oct. 20. Running time, 70 minutes.

Mary Regan...................June Collyer
Jimmy Williams.................Don Terry
Russ Williams............Anders Randolf
Lizzie Williams...............Stella Adams
Danny..................................Al Hill
Bill Lane, Boss.............Burr McIntosh
Police Capt. Dodds.........Walter James
Factory Owner......Gustav Von Seyffertitz
Sucker.....................Herbert Ashton
Philly Kid......................Harry Cattle
Joe Brown......................Joe Brown
Dan the Dude..................Arthur Stone
Danish Louie..............Nigel De Brulier
Blonde Rosie................Carol Lombard
Tuxedo George..................Bob Perry

The full introductory screen title is "The Diary of Me, Gangster," although the last two words formed the title of Coe's original Satevepost serial. Coe himself adapted his novel, said to have been founded on fact, for Fox filmization. Under the guise of a moral preachment, a rather obvious and banal point is stressed for an equally obvious purpose of circumventing the scissors of the censors. It's a wired crook program feature having the advantage of a Satevepost serialization.

There is some rough stuff, detailing the conception and completion of crime, both of which are among the paramount taboos of the censor bodies. Raoul Walsh had full opportunities for a crook epic, but whether it's the fault of the director or Coe's own screen transmutation, the yarn read better than it screens.

In diary fashion, adhering to the style of the prose serial, excerpts from the story form the titles in recounting the evolution of a sympathetically shiftless criminal, his arrest, conviction, reformation, and final rehabilitation. The film concludes with another hand script title, in diary fashion, to the effect that the anonymous Me, Gangster, hopes his screen autobiography will serve some good purpose in teaching the errant that you can't beat the law.

Don Terry, as the incipient criminal, is traced from babyhood, through adolescense as a street-corner loafer, into young manhood, where his gangland cronies lead him in and out of a couple of hold-ups and a murder, only to be trapped when playing a lone wolf in a $50,000 haul.

With his mind warped by the thought that since he's paying for his booty with a two-year term, there is no reason for returning his plunder, his mother's tragic death and the good influence of Mary Regan decide him to return the money upon his parole.

With this effected, the final punch is a hijacking attempt by his former gangster pals, who seek to intercept Danny's return of the $50,000.

"Me, Gangster" isn't wanting for action, but after a repetition or two of the same formula of dodging the gendarmes, planning and executing a larceny or stick-up the routine becomes tiresome and the impression is negative.

Walsh has striven hard to inject little niceties. A couple of his defter touches still evidence a master hand. One such is the prison visiting room with a fellow-inmate deterred from passing a chocolate bar to his baby, brought in by the convict's wife, because of a placarded warning against the exchange of articles between visitors and prisoners. The guard comes over when signalled, and from the direction of the prisoner, passes the harmless confection to the baby, creating one of the all too few heart-throb moments which a frank morality theme such as that in "Me, Gangster" should possess.

Thrills, too, are few. The crimes committed are machine-made, efficiently expedited affairs. Only real thrill is in the finale, with the paroled Danny attempting to fight off the hijacking gangsters. Here, Walsh exercised restraint in the scenes where June Collyer is manhandled by her attacker, while Terry is held captive in the next room. But it is this very restraint and deliberation of action which makes for the gripping moments.

Although the titular player, Don Terry, an engaging new comer, was overshadowed by Anders Randolf, the only other prominent male assignment, who played his father, a vigorous, forceful character. Randolf stood out individually. Burr McIntosh in the small bit he had as the political boss also made his appearance ultra-impressive. Miss Collyer, in a light role, handled it nicely. Stella Adams as the mother was as passive as her character called for. The rest of the cast were bits.

"Me, Gangster" has a synchronized score. Without or without sound, it makes no difference, none of its values being enhanced or detracted either way.

Abel.

WATERFRONT

(Sound)

First National release of William A. Seiter production, made by Ned Marin, with Dorothy Mackaill and Jack Mulhall co-starred. Story by Will Chappell and Gertrude Orr; titles by Gene Towne and Casey Robinson. At Mark Strand, New York, week of Oct. 20. Running time, 65 minutes.

Sadie Seastrom..........Dorothy Mackaill
Breezy O'Connor..............Jack Mulhall
Uncle Pete...........James Bradbury, Sr.
Captain Seastrom...........Knute Erickson
Oilcan Oleson..........Ben Hendricks, Jr.
Slip Mullins............Wm. Norton Bailey
An Oiler.....................Pat Harmon

"Waterfront," as the title implies, comes under the current cycle of nautical flickers. This F. N. has to do with a San Francisco dock romance. Miss Mackaill as the hoyden with the seagoing yen, and Mulhall as the gob, both do well as the featured pair, although in toto it's just a good program feature, saved by the players, the titles and the good musical synchronization. "Waterfront" is a sounder but no talker, having solely a synchronized score.

Of light texture, the featured pair make the most of none too ambitious assignments. It's the usual dockyard flirtation, romance, dance hall brawl and mild "menace" formula, bolstered by Miss Mackaill's unusual impression in sailor's uniform. It shows off her boyish blond bob to personable advantage and wins audible remarks from the femmes that she looks "cute."

Mulhall makes himself winsomely sympathetic, yessing himself in with her old man by aspiring to a little farm. Sadie Seastrom, with a nautical heritage from her father, Capt. Seastrom, differs from the latter in retaining her love for the sea, while the old boy hates everything about it, particularly sailors.

After frowning on Mulhall because of his occupation, the farm yen puts them on a common footing. Both conspire to dishearten Sadie of the idea through a phony shanghaiing, fake mutiny, etc. It works out well, although the planned details go awry. The 65 minutes are made merry with some effective comedy by-play.

Along with the stellar duo, Knute Erickson as the captain was capital, and James Bradbury, Sr., in a character part also registered. Ben Hendricks, Jr., as Mulhall's screen buddy, was the comedy relief. For want of a more convincing villain, William Norton Bailey became the light menace, despite no real dramatic conflict being in evidence.

Like most of the Mulhall-Mackaill releases, "Waterfront" is innocuous stuff, held up by the incidental hokum. The musical synchronization, through intelligent scoring, served its purpose well. Such pop ditties as "Jealous" and "What Can I Say After I Say I'm Sorry?" and kindred familiar Tin Pan Alley ballads fitted in well to further color some particular emotional interpretation. Considering the general batting average of the histrionics, the implied lyric motifs of the songs employed did more to get the idea across than the actual screen dramatics.

Some of the titles, credited to Gene Towne and Casey Robinson, were wows. The captions did much to sustain the comedy tempo, the production proving a credit both to the editor and title writers. One particular guffaw was in the dance hall with Oilcan Oleson, among the others, patronizing a lung-testing machine. Oilcan exhales and the colored liquid barometer rises only halfway. Oilcan then exclaims, "Now I'll use both my lungs," and on exhaling once again causes the liquid container to burst.

A couple of huch nifties punctuate the picture, but for the main, while innocently diverting, "Waterfront" lacks punch and leaves no decided impression either way.

Abel.

TAKE ME HOME

Paramount production and release. Starring Bebe Daniels and featuring Neil Hamilton. Directed by Marshall Neilan from Harlan Thompson and Grover Jones' story. Screen play by Ethel Doherty with J. Roy Hunt at the camera and H. J. Mankiewicz titling. At Paramount, New York, week Oct. 20. Running time, 60 Mins.

Peggy Lane.....................Bebe Daniels
David North...................Neil Hamilton
Derelys Devore............Lilyan Tashman
Alice Moore......................Doris Hill
Bunny ....Joe E. Brown

Lightly seasoned backstage picture void of a definite punch but stimulated by Mankiewicz titles. Strictly a comedy effort plus an inserted touch of pathos for the chorus girl who guides a country boy into the line and then stands by as the star develops a liking for apples, knows her orchard and extends invitations to the youngster to move in. Shouldn't have much trouble pulling moderately where they like Bebe Daniels but doesn't indicate drawing strength where they're indifferent to this girl's name. Just a program picture.

Harlan Thompson knows his backstage well enough not to have written in the weird happenings similarly located films have held. Marshall Neilan, directing, has also refrained from piling it on and only goes to extremes for a laugh sequence in which the chorister and the star hit the mat over the boy in the latter's dressing room as the show is on. Climax of this has Peggy chasing the No. 1 dressing room inhabitant onto the stage and threatening her from the wings as she works.

Picture is notable for the performance turned in by Lilyan Tashman as the upstate luminary and the burying of Joe Brown in a minor role. Miss Tashman, formerly a chorister herself, comes pretty close to stealing this one.

For Miss Daniels it's just a romp from an effort standpoint but possibly not too happy a gambol as her chorus assignment prevents any splash on clothes. No denying that she doesn't look so well here despite that J. Roy Hunt is again in charge of the angles. Miss Daniels generally needs smart costuming and she long ago proved that she can wear gowns. The obvious thing is to dress her up if the action lacks pace and is inclined to be short winded.

Neil Hamilton foils nicely as the light juvenile, opposite the star, and will impress the flaps as the simple rural representative. The girls invariably go for this boy's appearance and he's still a pretty clean and wholesome looking youngster. This leading cast trio comprise an asset to the film despite that Miss Daniels isn't as strong as she occasionally and previously has been.

Other items in "Take Me Home's" favor list some laugh probing through a hiccough bit and the Mankiewicz titles.

Production is standard in running the usual gamut of backstage, rehearsal, opening night, boarding house and lavish apartment home shots. None of the players leaves a mark beyond the named principals and Brown, who could have stood building for added strength.

Neilan, or somebody, has cut it to an even hour on running time and it helps. If weak it at least keeps moving even though it never fully develops its tendencies to frolic. *Sid.*

Stocks and Blondes

F.B.O. release of William LeBaron production. Titles by Jack Conway. Story and direction by Dudley Murphy. At the Hippodrome, N. Y., week of Oct. 21. Running time, 60 mins.:
Tom Greene....Richard "Skeets"Gallagher
Patsy.....................Jacqueline Logan
Goldie.....................Gertrude Astor
Powers.....................Albert Conti

This picture should go down in history. Not as a picture, but as a sample of what a supervisor, or a flock of supervisors, can do to a set of subtitles.

Jack Conway titled "Stocks and Blondes." The job must have been a pushover for Jack. The story was in his lap and it was a pipe for Jack to word the mouths of the characters. But those supers wrote and rewrote, and blue penciled until only a spotty set of titles is left. Some are typically Conway and the rest are decidedly foreign to Conway's sense of comedy. It's a libel on Jack.

In describing Goldie, a femme character, Jack said she could "make Helen of Troy move to Albany." Funny and the essence of brief description. Later on Goldie, in advising her kid sister, cracks, "You've had enough trouble with your feet; why marry a pain in the neck?" An entertaining character, the only one in the picture, and Conway made this wise-cracking dame the kick of the production. The supers would have her talk like a grandmother.

Film itself is lightweight. With the exception of Gertrude Astor there's not a real performance in the film. "Skeets" Gallagher looks okay and troupes in an acceptable manner, but as a supposed smart aleck kid he's as sober as Coolidge.

The picture had laughs, but the supervisors wouldn't believe it. *Bige.*

STOOL PIGEON

Columbia production and release. Olive Borden and Charles Delaney featured. At Broadway, New York, week Oct. 21. Running time, 62 minutes.

Gang stuff of the machine gun era. A young chap gets involved with the racket boys and is in over his head before realizing. His desire to provide his mother with a nice home is his excuse.

Story won't stand close inspection on plausibility but director has keyed up the action to a nervous, semi-staccato tempo that will grip ordinary audiences. Production does not warrant de luxe bookings but apart from that, picture can play anywhere.

Olive Borden gets almost no opportunity to troupe or display her celebrated lingerie. Charles Delaney is the pivot character with two other male characters, Butch, the chief gunner, and Shields, the fly cop, much in the camera eye.

The customary cinematic magic gets the hero off in the finale when the cop turns softie and the boy, girl and mother pack off to California, sunshine and a new deal. *Land.*

Guardians of the West

Universal western featuring Jack Perrin and Rex (horse), with cast including

"Starlight," Ethlyne Clair, Al Ferguson and Robert Homans. Story by Basil Dickey. Henry MacRand, director. On double bill at Loew's New York one day (Oct. 5). Running time, one hour.

For those who fancy horses, this one has two performing, and both very smart. On top of that, "Guardians" is manufactured of ingredients that the public this type of film is aimed at always enjoys.

Saving of the old homestead as well as a forest fire for an added kick. The usual gun battle somewhat unexpectedly, but there nevertheless.

On two occasions Rex saves the gal by racing to the guy and causing him to follow. Perrin's personal pony, "Starlight," nods yes or no when queried. Lucky the picture doesn't talk so the boys couldn't hear the questions. Both horses are magnificent, with one pure white and the other ebony.

No one in the cast has a chance at anything notable. *Bige.*

POWER OF SILENCE

Tiffany-Stahl production and release. Featuring Belle Bennett. Story by Frances Hyland. Directed by Wallace Worsley. In cast, John Westwood, Marion Douglas, Anders Randolf, John St. Polis, Raymond Keane, Jack Singleton. Titles by Frederic and Fanny Hatton. At Loew's New York, one day, Oct. 16. Half double bill. Running time, 65 minutes.

Strong story of mother love with neatly handled murder trial tossed in makes this first grade screen stuff for the grinds. Slight cutting of the running time would make it acceptable for the better class houses. Several of the flashback scenes during the murder trial sequence are unimportant.

Plot centers about Mamie Stone, a dame who knows enough to keep her face closed in order to assure her son's marital happiness. To do this she has to go through the tortures of a murder trial, although she knows that actual killer of the man who was her common-law husband was her daughter-in-law. She refuses to take the stand in her own defense, but when her diary is introduced as evidence she is acquitted of the crime. Frequent flashback sequences as her lawyer is reading the events in the life of his client, make the story ring true.

Following the acquittal, the son brings his mother to his home. A mother vs. wife battle ensues. When the wife insists that an in-law take air the blow-off comes. The mother getting the tough daughter-in-law alone, tells her that she (the wife) was responsible for the death of the wealthy man who had invited the dame up to his apartment to protect her honor.

Filled with admiration for the woman who had suffered in silence for love of her offspring, the mother and wife get together and decide to forget the past, in order to save the boy they both love from further remorse.

Director Worsley has turned out a smooth, interesting story, aided considerably by the Hattons' titles.

THE TOILERS
(SOUND)

Tiffany-Stahl's first sound feature, synchronized by R. C. A. Photophone, with special score by Dr. Hugo Riesenfeld. Joseph Littau, musical conductor. Reginald Barker's production from original story by L. G. Rigby. Titles by Harry Braxton. At Mark Strand, Brooklyn, N. Y., week Oct. 27. Running time, 78 minutes.
Steve.................Douglas Fairbanks, Jr.
Mary.....................Jobyna Ralston
Joe.....................Harvey Clark
Toby.....................Wade Boteler
Butch.....................Robert Ryan

Tiffany-Stahl's first Tiffany-Tone or sound film feature, debuting at the Brooklyn (N. Y.) Strand, is a strong program feature. It is vigorously forceful, growingly impressive and possesses a somewhat seasonal advantage because of its Xmas theme, which would make it about ripe for the bulk of the booking dates. The holiday period, however, is just as incidental for general purposes, as it is significant for immediate timeliness, paradoxical as that may sound.

Starting a bit slowly, and this can readily be corrected with the cutting down of those 78 minutes of running time, "The Toilers" grows on one, grips the interest with the realism of the three buddies' existence in a coal mining town, packs a tear in the simple earnestness of the grateful orphan waif (Jobyna Ralston), who sacrificially endeavors to signify her gratitude to her savior of the storm, and builds up into an epochal wow finish in that battle against time to rescue the entombed miners.

If nothing else, the finish makes the picture. Here Reginald Barker has extended himself in many forceful yet subtle niceties to build up the suspense and get across the grim realism of it all.

A cul de sac in the mine is barricaded in a desperate effort to halt the flames, which have taken serious human toll already, and the dozen men who are trapped within finally tap out a Morse code S O S, attracting the rescuing crew above, who for 36 hours fight against time in drilling their way into the lower level of the coal mine.

Douglas Fairbanks, Jr., as Steve, is the amanuensis of the unfortunate group, leaving behind memos of the number of men, date and hour, who are forced to retreat into the mine. Building barricade after barricade to check the flames, they are finally trapped at the blind end of the passageway. In lieu of titles his memos, with great impressiveness and undeniable drama, detail the fate of himself and his buddies, with occasional tragic notes punctuating the biography, such as one man dying in the flames, another from asphyxiation, etc.

Outside the mine, at the helm of the rescuing crew, is Toby (Wade Boteler), while his two particular buddies, played by young Fairbanks and Harvey Clark (in an excellent dour role), are among the 12 trapped miners. This very day was to have been Steve's wedding day to the orphan of the storm, whom he had literally rescued out of a snow drift earlier in the film. With this poignantly dramatic premise as a basic background, Barker builds up the human interest significance of the rescue in masterful fashion.

"The Toilers," as a title, is derived from the celluloid saga of three men who toil below the earth for the benefit of humankind in general, which gives little thought to them and their labors.

Under the R. C. A. Photophone process, with the sound waves on a celluloid sound track adjacent to the film, cutting is an easy problem, thus simultaneously eliminating film action and coincidental synchronized music with a snip of the shears. Under the Western Electric system of phonograph records

this cannot be done without damage to the synchronization, particularly where there is dialog.

"The Toilers" is devoid of dialog, but introduces three choruses of a miner's doggerel. There are two other brief snatches of pop song choruses for comedy purposes. The sound effects are limited, but well done, such as a motor car rumbling across a wooden bridge, usual door knockings, gongs, chimes. The big punches are the whirring grind of electric drillers eating into the earth's vitals as the rescue crew is at work, and the shrill siren whistles of distress.

When the air compressor goes awry the effect is walloped across as the trapped miners below bemoan their fate and conclude the rescuers have given up the attempt. As the air compressor becomes efficient again the synchronized whirring effect, coupled with the physical animation of the entombed miners as they react anew to the drilling, is an undeniable effect.

At the Mark Strand, Brooklyn, the Photophone synchronization is projected over the W. E. equipment. Dr. Hugo Riesenfeld's score is excellent and well mated to the theme of the picture.

Tiffany-Stahl has a winner in "The Toilers." It rates a Broadway first run if booking exigencies don't count against that. The Stanley Co. forced this one in at the Brooklyn Strand, thus setting that theatre's feature schedule back a week behind the Manhattan Strand, which was the former routine, although lately both Strands, across the bridge from one another, have been playing the same pictures, day and date, only varying a week apart on the talking shorts. *Abel.*

THE HOME TOWNERS
(DIALOG)

Warner Brothers production and release. Featuring Richard Bennett and Doris Kenyon. Adapted from George Cohan's play of same name and directed by Bryan Foy. Scenarists, Addison Burkhart and Murray Roth. Cameraman, Barney McGill. At Warners, New York, for twice daily run starting Oct. 23, $2 top. Running time, 94 minutes.
Vic Arnold...............Richard Bennett
Beth Calhoun..............Doris Kenyon
P. H. Bancroft............Robert McWade
Mr. Calhoun...............Robert Edeson
Lottie Bancroft..........Gladys Brockwell
Joe Roberts...............John Miljan
Mrs. Calhoun..............Vera Lewis
Wally Calhoun............Stanley Taylor
Casey.....................James T. Mack
Maid.....................Patricia Caron

George Cohan's comedy won't have much, if any, trouble entertaining the proletariat. It's one instance, possibly the first, where the dialog is minus constant heroics and where an effort has been made for tempo, a drastic fault most of the preceding talkers have unfurled. The dialog evidently has been taken intact from the play with Robert McWade, who does the trailer on this one, in his original part and running away with the picture.

It may be an all-legit cast. Yet McWade and Gladys Brockwell are the standouts because they've a majority of the answers, while Richard Bennett and Doris Kenyon are limited to carrying the story and playing straight. Both perform and screen well with Miss Kenyon's voice a bit too high in pitch to sound natural.

Principal error is the 94 minutes, when 80, or even 70, would have been sufficient. A bit slow and too talky in spots. That's something many a stage comedy has suffered from. If the situation is duplicated here it shows how close this talker is running to the in person version. Studio will and can take a bow for itself when its work necessitates such comparison, as that's what the coast has been aiming at ever since it started on sound.

Sooner or later Warners must go outside. Phoney exteriors or outdoor shots with studio made effects cannot and do not impress. These immediately remind that it's a sound picture to dispel whatever illusion has been woven by the interior work, no matter how excellent that may be. This, of course, is looking toward that time when the talkers will be 100 per cent efficient as well as dialog, and when sound films have probed their complete field. It may not make so much difference at present as the novelty angle remains prominent although tapering off in many spots.

"Home Towners" revolves around a man in his late 40's about to wed a girl 25 years his junior with best man coming on from South Bend just to confirm his suspicions that the prospective bride is after his pal's coin. Bennett is the bridegroom and McWade the well meaning friend.

McWade gums up the entire situation to the extent Bennett gets back his ring. McWade, finally convinced that he's wrong, has to bring the would-be honeymooners together again.

Moral of the piece is in the author's indictment of the suspicious small town mind. It is unreeled that the girl and her family are not chasing money but either Bryan Foy, director, or the author have omitted to build up any sympathy for the bride or her kin.

Interest centers on McWade, the jam he [illegible] and the **comedy grouch he develops. Pace and strength taper off during the build up for the grand reunion. Foy might have done better had he not prolonged the trip to the climax. Story is slow in starting. The side arguments continuously going on between McWade and his missus (Miss Brockwell) hold many a chuckle, outright laughs and one or two double entendre replies.**

Miss Brockwell is excellent all the way. She's in talkers permanently and belongs there. With [illegible] rounds out [illegible] working team perfectly cast. McWade has long been known for his stage grouches and hasn't forgotten any of the tricks. **It's likely Foy allowed McWade to direct himself during his supposed unruly moments. Robert Edeson has very little to do and after the main quartet Stanley Taylor is best among the support.**

Picture will do business because **it has merit, besides being a talker with the Cohan, Bennett and Kenyon names. Opening night at Warners, amplification was exceedingly good. Interior sets rather obviously reveal where the microphones are masked with the players' voices becoming indistinct when turning away from these mouthpieces.**

Another conclusion to be drawn from this performance was that no Broadway picture ever received worse projection at a premiere. The booth was possibly concentrating on the records and forgetting that focussing does help. *Sid.*

THE MIDNIGHT TAXI

(DIALOG)

Warner Bros. production and release. Directed by John G. Arnold. No other program credits, other than featured players: Antonio Moreno, Helen Costello, Myrna Loy and William Russell. Titles by Joseph Jackson. At Strand, New York, week Oct. 27. Running time, 62 minutes.

"Taxi" Driscoll............Antonio Moreno
Nan Parker..............Helen Costello
"Mile-Away" Morgan.......Tommy Dugan
Joe Brant.............William Russell
Mrs. Joe Brant................Myrna Loy
Jack Madison..............Bobbie Agnew
Detective Blake.............Pat Hartigan
Lefty.........................Jack Santoro
Squint.....................William Hauber
Dutch.........................Paul Kreuger
Rastus.......................Spencer Bell

As a dialog talkie meller, good enough, on the dialog end mostly after saying that Tommy Dugan steals the picture, for work, voice and comedy. Can go into any wired house for a week.

Story's conventionality no help. About cheating cheaters, rum runners and plain crooks. Its title, "Midnight Taxi," taken from a fleet of taxicabs carrying booze.

Then there are stolen bonds and **the young clerk convicted, a tough kid, too, tougher than the crooks and made a bit too tough for this background, because he looks, talks and acts like a giglio, with boy's sweetheart doing some detect stuff to get his release.**

After that the cheating cheaters frame, an exchange of fur coats on a train, pinch, beating the train by plane, and once more the detached car, rushing backwards.

Ingredients all familiars, but action snapped up, and Dugan does the rest. In this billing, Dugan could have easily stood featuring with the others. It's about time the Warners gave that comedian some billing; he looks the best they have with his natural vocal adaptability for added value. Here he is a stuttering simp crook, a hanger-on, and his dialog contains more laughs than the printed captions.

Dialog is not continuous. There is a long stretch of silence at one period. It hurts, for there is nothing to meet the expectancy meantime.

Antonio Moreno does fairly with dialog; much better in acting. Helene Costello is carefully proficient, having been given much protection, it appears, on the dialog thing. She needed more on her looks here. William Russell runs about second when talking. Bobbie Agnew and Pat Hartigan in their minor roles suggest talking voices with more opportunities.

One of those talking melodramas that Warners seem to do so well at no extravagant cost.

VARSITY

(DIALOG)

Paramount production and release starring Buddy Rogers and featuring Mary Brian and Chester Conklin. Directed by Frank Tuttle from Wells Root's story. Titles by George Marion, Jr., with R. J. Stout cameraman. At the Paramount, N. Y., week of Oct. 27. Running time, 67 Mins.

Jimmy Duffy..............Charles Rogers
Fay..........................Mary Brian
"Pop" Conlan..............Chester Conklin
Middlebrook..............Philips R. Holmes

College story minus a football game and with dialog. It's the yarn for which Yale refused its campus and so the author, a New Haven alumnus, had his prayers answered by Princeton. It's a prettier school anyway. "Varsity," as a picture, doesn't go very far out its way to prove anything but it figures as moderate program material with three dialog passages to help.

Not that the conversation is particularly pert or well played. Understanding is that the dialog scenes were inserted after the picture was completed on the Coast, cast principals **coming east to do it. Only three of these talk—Rogers, Miss Brian and Conklin of whom the latter is best and the girl, as usual, is not heard to advantage. Holmes also says a few minor words. Rogers is vocally colorless. Of the 13 minutes of dialog 10 come at the climax.**

The earlier three-minute insertion and a couple of youngsters singing just go for the "talker" on the outside billing. No laughs in the "sides," Marion's titles getting all the worded merriment.

The Tiger in its lair looks good and the atmosphere is excellent. Synchronized score, of course, aids by playing a good many of the Nassau tunes and even a couple of the cheers have been recorded, four or five voices not yet being able to duplicate the roar of a cheering section, although as this is a snatch of a baseball game it's the right effect. Love story is rather silly and meaningless, young Duffy falling for a carnival girl he meets in Trenton and eventually wedding her after a title has skipped two years and graduation. Suspense hinges on Duffy thinking himself an orphan with his father (Conklin) the janitor of his dormitory and trying to break the boy's inheritance of a lust for drink. Builds up until a couple of carnival men frame Duffy into getting well stewed so they can grab the bankroll the sophomore class has contributed to a drive.

If this is the first one Rogers has been starred in it's not strong as a sendoff. Conklin romps in for personal honors as neither of the juvenile team is sufficiently vivacious or capable of outshining the other. It's a bad camera match, both needing a more powerful personality opposite to strengthen.

Location scenes at Princeton have been better handled than the story. Or maybe it's the impression that it's just another college picture and there's not much to ponder over in the yarn. Picture needs its dialog, no matter what the faults, for b.o. attractiveness and it not especially robust at that. *Sid.*

THE RED MARK

James Cruze production for Pathe release. Nena Quartero starred. Gaston Glass featured. Others are Gustav Von Seyffertitz and Rose Dione. Continuity by Julian Josephson from story by John Russell. Screen gives no credit for photography or titles. At New York Hippodrome week of Oct. 27. Running time, 64 minutes.

What can be said of a film story with the drab background of a penal colony on a Pacific Ocean island, with the romance involving a girl waif and a French pickpocket? What more can be said of the possibilities of such a picture without a single name that means anything?

Depressing is right. In this atmosphere it is difficult to work up interest in the romance. Cruel governor desires the girl waif and so does the pickpocket. The minute a title hints that governor has a long lost son distinguished by a red mark on his throat you know that the pickpocket is the son.

Picture hasn't an excuse; never should have been made; but being made, it ought to have been put on the highest shelf indefinitely. A dandy subject for any exhibitor's opposition. *Rush.*

Legend of Gosta Berling

(SWEDISH MADE)

Swedish production. Distributor in America unnamed. Founded on novel by Selma Lagerlof. Adapted and directed by Maurice Stiller. Greta Garbo and Lars Hanson featured. At 5th Avenue, New York, week of Oct. 27. Running time, 66 minutes.

About pars the average Swedish picture in costume. Interest lies chiefly in the background, foreign locales unfamiliar to this side. Also interesting is the appearance of Greta Garbo, totally unlike the sleeky dame M-G-M's experts made **of her. Still a picture only for the sure-seat circle.**

Story based on what is described as a Nobel Prize novel. Must be another case of a great literary effort lost between the scenario and the cutting room.

Just what is missing in the film story is hard to determine accurately. Too much plot at times and it is frequently difficult to understand the motivation of the characters.

Many foreign films suffer in attempting too much coverage with the result that the lead characters are never developed to their full importance. Despite its faults the American star system has a big advantage over this Swedish scattering of fire.

Photography is never good, a very general commentary on Swedish film product. Story concerns the intrigues, woes and social attitudes of the landed gentry of the late 17th Century in Sweden, with Lars Hanson, an expelled minister, the central character. Clergyman Angle led to the 5th Avenue Playhouse billing the picture as the doings of a "Glorified Elmer Gantry."

"Sure seaters" only. *Land.*

STREET OF ILLUSION

Columbia production, released through Quality and Hollywood, according to screen credits. Directed by Erle C. Kenton. Based on the story by Channing Pollock and adapted by Harvey Thew. Features Virginia Valli. Cast includes Ian Keith, Kenneth Thompson and Harry Meyers. At the Academy of Music, N. Y., week of Oct. 29. Running time, over 70 mins.

If Channing Pollock's literary offspring ever possessed any distinguished or meritorious traits everything possible has been done by the producers to conceal it from a public eager for stories dealing with the inside of Broadway and the show business. It is not conceivable that the painful triteness of this picture was sponsored through the author's original script.

Reduced to simple terms this is the story of a ham actor jealous of another's merited success. Disappointed in himself, but still cherishing dim hopes of thespian greatness, he is too dull in mentality and character to appeal to the popular imagination.

Action and interest have been carefully weeded out. Long, boring rehearsal scenes have been allowed to run without hindrance. For a climax the old expedient of a death on the stage, where the heroic character is supposed to be shot, takes place. There are a few incoherent philosophical titles inserted at odd intervals.

Used in this house to back up a strong, well balanced eight-act vaudeville lineup, the picture impressed as mainly of the grind and not suitable for the better type of neighborhoods. *Mori.*

THE WEST

(FRENCH MADE)

Paris, Oct. 21.

Adopted by Henri Fescourt from the melodrama of Henri Kristemaeckers' "L'Occident," this was carefully produced under the patronage of Cineromans to feature Claudia Victrix (Mme. Jean Sapene). It has met with local success. **Let us add that the Cineromans star has been judged on her merits in this picture, and not entirely on her influence. She has made good and plays the part of an Oriental engaged to a French officer, Lucien Dalsace.**

Story is of Hassina, daughter of the Caid (an Arab governor), captured by brigands. While in captivity she saves Lieut. Cadieres, of the French Navy, and escapes with him to France. Meanwhile, the brigands have also taken away Hassina's younger sister, Fathima, and their chief, Taiebe, follows Cadiere to Toulon, where he accuses the French officer of being responsible for the girl's death. Hassina **first believes this to be true and is on the point of going away with Arnaud, another naval admirer, when Fathima's whereabouts is discovered by Cadiere's servant, and all ends happily.**

Technical work is good while revealing certain flaws in construction. Some interesting battle episodes, and the scenes in Toulon, with sailors' resorts and officers' quarters are faithfully portrayed.

Supporting Claudia Victrix are Jaque Catelain, H. de Bagratide, Paul Guide, Raymond Guerin, R. Lievin, Labry, Mmes. Renee Veller, Andree Rolane, Jane Mea. Without being perfect, this is a good French picture for local consumption. *Kendrew.*

TWO OUTLAWS

Universal (Western) production and release. Jack Perrin and Rex, the horse, starred. Henry MacRae, director. Virgil Miller, cameraman. In cast: Kathleen Collins and J. P. MacGowan. At Loew's New York, one day, Oct. 23, one half of double bill. Running time, 50 minutes.

Based on a stock yarn of the secret utility man posing as outlaw with the additional angle of wild horses and their leader, "Two Outlaws" fills the bill for regular nondescript houses. In fact, it's a little fairer than the average Universal western.

"Rex" had a tough time in this one. Every time he walked on the set or stepped before the camera, a wind machine blew plains dust into his nostrils. A few times he headed a pack of Hollywood nags in front of the lens.

After that his job was to step on bad boys who would pop off the good outlaw.

Girl Perrin saves from herd starts love interest. Always with the black rag on his jowels, girl never identifies him until he arrests her guardian as the real fourflusher.

AUTUMN LOVE

(GERMAN MADE)

Affiliated through European Producers. No credited producer. Lya DePutti and Eugene Klopfer featured. No further screen credits given. At Stanley one day, Oct. 26. Running time about 60 minutes.

When Lya DePutti had long, bristly hair and was not so good and when the World War was not such a memory, some German company turned out "Autumn Love." In its form here it has been cut and titled in such a way as to provide a continuity better than staccato. It is little short of an imposition to ask any semi-intelligent audience to sit through it.

Everything is old-fashioned. The story of the metropolitan star, who picks out a girl from an itinerant company, makes her a star, gets the turndown for a young count and then realizes December is too near to carry through, is—just that.

The acting is in exact accord with the story. Altogether, just one of those things to pass by. Even if the rental may only be a couple of bucks it may prove a costly economy when the audience reaction sets in.

NAUGHTY DUCHESS

Tiffany-Stahl production and release. Directed by Tom Terris. Featuring H. B. Warner and Eve Southern. Chester Lyons, cameraman. Story based on novel, "The Indiscretion of the Duchess." In cast: Gertrude Astor, Martha Mattox, Duncan Reynolds. At Loew's New York one day, Oct. 23, one half double feature. Running time, 60 minutes.

"The Naughty Duchess" may read well, but on the screen it is 100 per cent drawing room. Straight society, with lightest of continuities. High calibre of leads saves it and will get it by in small houses of the upper strata.

Only suspense is built around outcome of meeting on train and a duke posing as husband to save strange dame from dicks. This carried on to chateau and ultimately marriage. Practically no interference.

COURT MARTIAL

Columbia production and release. Directed by George B. Seitz from story by Elmer Harris. Jack Holt featured. In cast, Betty Compson, Doris Hill, Pat Harmon. At Stanley, New York, one day, Oct. 22. Running time, 75 minutes.

Long drawn out Civil War yarn. It depends upon shots of Lincoln and the Stars and Stripes for approval. Photography, production, direction and cast makes it just a so-so release for the daily grinds. Fewer titles and discreet slicing might help.

Jack Holt is commissioned by President Lincoln to bring in Betty Compson, leader of a guerilla band operating on the western frontier, dead or alive. Joining her band under disguise, the Yankee spy wins his way into her confidence. Torn between love and duty sequence then follows for considerable footage with the spy saving the girl's life during a cavalry attack and she returning the favor when her gang discovering his identity is about to do a little neck stretching.

Failing to deliver his prisoner at the fort as he had promised, Holt is accused of allowing her to escape. Court martialed, he is sentenced to be shot at sunrise. But the girl gang leader gives herself up in time to save her lover's life at the expense of her own. She was mortally wounded on her way to the fort by one of her own men, who had attempted to prevent her self-sacrifice.

POWER OF DARKNESS

(FOREIGN MADE)

Gourland release. Producer not credited. Directed by Robert Wiene. Based on story by Tolstoi. Continuity and adaptation not credited. Cast of the Moscow Art Theatre Players, including Peter Sharov, Pavel Pavlov, Vera Pavlova, Vera Orlova, George Serov and Sergie Gosserov. At Stanley, New York, one day, Oct. 25. Running time, 72 mins.

This picture bears the distinction of being among the few foreign productions for which no definite bid for everlasting greatness is made. Merely a simple claim, in the foreword, that the film is far above the average. And another, also in the introduction, that if it is not as good as it could be the censorial shears should be blamed.

Little doubt censors erred on the side of leniency. A few more cuts toward the ending, eliminations in the middle, and a reduction of footage in the beginning, leaving only the introduction to speak for itself, would have made the grind houses this picture may be shown in happier and better.

Nothing more than a grotesque burlesque, crude, primitive, unfinished mockery of a picture. Thrown together by hands untutored in, possibly unaware of, the first principles of picture production. No continuity and it looks also as if no adaptation has been made. It is like a literal translation of Tolstoi's book, meaningless and incoherent.

Story is of a country yokel, strangely endowed with some power over women, glorified beyond all belief. Repentance finally comes, accompanied by the Russian police.

Mori.

PARIS AT MIDNIGHT

Metropolitan Pictures Corp. production, released by P. D. C. (Pathe). Directed by E. Mason Hopper. Screen story by Frances Marion from novel, "Pere Goriot," by Honore Balzac. Jetta Goudel, Lionel Barrymore, Mary Brian, Edmund Burns featured. At Columbus, New York, one day, Oct. 5, as half double bill. Running time about 60 minutes.

Little entertainment value to this one, all about life in a boarding house in the Latin quarter of Paris and a bad man with a heart of gold, who is a sort of Robin Hood, robbing the rich and righting the wrongs of the oppressed.

It gives Lionel Barrymore a chance to strut his Jekyl-Hyde stuff once again. Flicker has everything in it but the kitchen sink, the pay-off being a couple of Parisian tarts who ride in limousines and find it frequently necessary to shake their poor old father, living at the cheap flop house, for a handful of change.

Death of the old man, while the daughters are making whoopee at the Art Students' Ball, run excessively long and grow boresome.

Titles are of the inane variety, overboard with explanations.

Director Hopper has caught the spirit of gaiety in Paris in only one place and that too has been done often and better. Thin love story that shows infrequently in the footage is dragged in for the wind-up with the boarding house lovers reconciled through the kind aid of the Robin Hood of Paris.

Just a lot of wasted film. Probably old P. D. C. anyway.

THE BURNING WIND

Universal production and release. Directed by Henry McRae and Herbert Blache from story by W. M. Raine. Adaptation by Raymond Schrock and George Plympton. Starring Hoot Gibson. Cast includes Virginia Brown Faire and Cesare Gravina. At Loew's, New York, Oct. 26, one-half of double bill. Running time, approximately 50 Mins.

The boys who directed this one know how. It's neat and fast. Another western with a series of stock situations, but it holds because of speed, action and Hoot Gibson's horse and gun manipulation.

At the opening it swings back to another generation for the purpose of injecting a fight sequence. Serves for immediate interest.

The two old friends then lay out a plan to test the son of the American who is cutting loose in New York. The boy is brought out on the pretext that his father is in danger of losing his lands to a neighbor, Valdes. The latter's daughter is left in charge for her father. The crooked foreman is used to promote an element of reality, trying to grab everything, including the gal for himself.

Mori.

City of Purple Dreams

Trem Carr production, released through Rayart. Directed by Duke Worne. Walter Griffin, cameraman. In cast: Barbara Bedford, Robert Frazer, David Torrence, Josephine Gadson. At Loew's New York, one day, Sept. 25, one-half double bill. Running time 60 minutes.

One of the old fairy tales revived. Sandwich man makes up his mind to rise to the occasion. He sweeps everything before him, even to the point of robbing the wheat king of his crown and daughter. Hoke personified, but good suspense if the story isn't taken seriously. Slip it in as second half or feature it in grinds on off day.

Cast good, although Barbara Bedford a little too wild-eyed in spots.

Theme mechanical.

NOAH'S ARK

(SOUND)

Warner Bros. production and release. Starring Dolores Costello and George O'Brien. Directed by Michael Curtiz. Story by D. F. Zanuck. Adapated by Anthony Goldeway. Titles by De Leon Anthony. Miniature effects by Fred Jackman. Photography, Hal. Mohr and Barney McGill. Musical score and Vitaphone Symphony Orchestra conducted by Louis Silvers. World premier at Grauman's Chinese, Hollywood, Nov. 1. Running time, 135 minutes.

Modern.		Biblical.
Mary	Dolores Costello	Miriam
Travis	George O'Brien	Japhet
Nickoloff	Noah Beery	King Nephilim
Hilda	Louise Fazenda	
Al	Guinn Williams	Ham
Minister	Paul McAllister	Noah
Soldier	Nigel De Brulier	High Priest
German	Anders Randolf	Leader Soldiers
Frenchman	Armand Kaliz	King's Guard
Dancer—	Myrna Loy	Slave Girl
Innkeeper	William V. Mong	Guard
Balkan	Malcolm Waite	Shem

Warner Brothers have turned out in "Noah's Ark" more spectacle and thrill than any producer has ever achieved in 14,000 feet of film or less dealing with a subject applicable to this type of production. They have in it touches reminiscent of "Ten Commandments," "King of Kings," "Wings," "The Big Parade" and quite a few other screen epics that have been leaders and money getters in their class.

Better than $1,500,000 is reported to have been spent on this film, and from what is shown on the screen, looks as though the Jack Warner staff did not do any cheating.

They show everything conceivable under the sun—mobs, mobs and mobs; Niagaras of water, train wreck, war aplenty, crashes, deluges and everything that goes to give the picture fan a thrill.

They have turned out the biggest and best edited — that is, from the standpoint of cramming in instances and stressing on them plentifully—picture of the industry. Nothing was missed from 'way back when folks thought that praying to the real God instead of Jehovah was the right thing until Noah got the message from above that it was not. Then they show war, pillage, wreckage, deluge, loss of life, animals, etc.

The story opens with scenes showing what is left of the world after the big deluge. It then drifts into the age where folks have worshipped the Golden Calf and their lust for gold. It flashes modern to the extent of bringing to the fore the selfish motive of man. A flash is shown of the Stock Exchange in New York on a panicky day. A guy gets bumped off.

Then they hop to Europe. The scene is the Oriental express from Constantinople to Paris just as the World War is in the air. There are folks of every nationality on the train. War is the topic. Comes the question of the belief in God. A Russian says there is none; if there were one He would act. A ministerial gent said He would. Thunder, lightning, etc., hit a bridge. The train goes through into the river. Lives are lost. But no deaths among those who are to become the principal actors in the war and biblical sequences to follow. Plenty of attention is paid to touches of detail before the war stuff really starts.

The picture story is told in manifold form., It is far too long and padded in present form, running 135 minutes. It can be cut without stinting, at least 30 minutes of the time, and story told adequately and just as forcefully.

D. F. Zanuck is credited with story. He got all of the so-called sure fire audience material together, original or otherwise, and supervised the production. With what Coldeway had to work for adaptation and continuity assemblage he performed a herculean task.

However, the laurels for production should go to Michael Curtiz, who handled the megaphone. He got the human touches and inspiration into the picture and interpreted the high lights excellently. The war detail, however, was not according to U. S. Army regulations.

Talk did not enter into the picture until after the first 35 minutes. It started with love scene between O'Brien and Miss Costello and then brought in talk by Beery, McAllister and Williams. The talk really can be left out of this one. The Costello voice is just not for the talkers and hurts the impression made by her silent acting. Her silent acting great. O'Brien is surprising on the talk. He has pleasing voice, clear diction and enunciation. Part is possibly his best so far as acting is concerned.

Beery great as the Russian spy and as the King. McAllister, old stage trouper, had hard job with biblical quotations which were overdone. Voice okay but talk just a bit too much. Williams got a great break with comedy part. Looks as though boy is sure fire in the big money class. However, on talking not as good as acting. Louise Fazenda had "slavey" part in early sequences, working with Williams, and hit with every move, twitch and mannerism. Malcolm Waite showed up fine with his double duties, as did Myrna Loy, Wm. V. Mong, Armand Kaliz and Nigel de Brulier.

This is an out and out spectacle and should be sold as such. It is one instance where talk is a detriment instead of an asset and could be taken out.

The Vitaphone musical synchronization provided by Louis Silvers is most fitting and well played by the symphony orchestra. Sound effects, not too numerous, are spotted okay. A few more might be put in and would be quite beneficial, especially for the miniature shots showing destruction.

This one undoubtedly will cover the nut, or more, but Jolson "mammy" pictures are still sure fire and build up bank accounts very fast and keep production accounts very low. *Ung.*

THE WIND

(SOUND)

Metro-Goldwyn-Mayer production and release. Directed by Victor Seastrom. Based on novel by Dorothy Scarborough. Adapted by Frances Marion. Starring Lillian Gish, with Lars Hansen. Featured. At Capitol, New York, week Nov. 30. Running time 70 minutes.

Letty............................Lillian Gish
Lige............................Lars Hansen
Roddy..........................Montague Love
Cora .... Dorothy
Beverly.........................Edward Earle
Sourdough...................William Orlamond
Cora's children........(Laon Ramon
(Carmencita Johnson
(Billy Kent Schaefer

Some stories are just naturally poison for screen purposes and Miss Scarborough's novel here shows itself a conspicuous example. Everything a high pressure, lavishly equipped studio, expert director and reputable star could contribute has been showered on this production. Everything about the picture breathes quality. Yet it flops dismally.

It is a sad, heartrending duty to report, also, that Miss Gish, in some of her most dramatic moments, drew laughter instead of tears from a Sunday afternoon audience composed mainly of New Yorkers. But Miss Gish was not at fault since the sequences did not impress as calling for the fervor which the story evidently provided.

Tragedy on the high winds, on the desolate desert prairies, unrelieved by that sparkling touch of life that spells human interest, is what this picture has to offer. It may be a true picturization of life on the prairie but it still remains lifeless and unentertaining. It may have been spotted in the Capitol on the chance of drawing favorable attention from the critics because of its faithful portraiture of natural life but word-of-mouth comment would offset any such gain.

The story opens with an unknown girl, Letty, from Virginia, trainbound for her cousin's ranch, which she describes as beautiful to the stranger, Roddy, who has made her acquaintance informally.

Roaring, blinding wind and sandstorms immediately frighten the girl. She remains in a semi-conscious state of fright throughout, excepting at the close of the picture.

At Beverly's ranch the girl becomes too popular with Cora's children. Cora grows jealous of her husband and Beverly's friendly liking for the girl. Letty is forced to leave the ranch. She decides to accept Roddy's implied invitation to become his wife. But it seems his intentions were not of the best, being married to one woman.

The girl then accepts a proposal from Lige, whom she had laughed at the night before. He brings her to his home and then discovers that he is repulsive to the girl he married. He decides to get enough money to send her away.

During a round-up of wild horses, brought down by a fierce northern gale, Roddy forces his way into Lige's home and stays there for the night with Letty. He urges the girl to go away with him in the morning. She refuses, shoots him when he becomes too insistent, and hurls the body into the sand where it is buried.

The story is too morbid, the background too dreary in picture form for popular approval.

Synchronization is not voluminous enough in this large house, but should be suitable in smaller house. Sound effects such as the roaring of the wind are effective. But a dog barking sounds like an asthmatic rumble. *Mori.*

THE CAVALIER

(SOUND)

Tiffany-Stahl production and release, directed by Irvin Willat. Adapted by Victor Irvin from the novel, "The Black Rider," by Max Brand. Titles by Walter Anthony. Photographed by John Stevens and Harry Cooper. Recorded by RCA Photophone. Musical score by Hugo Riesenfeld. Recording orchestra under direction of Joseph Littau. At the Embassy, N. Y., Oct. 30, 10 days at $1.50 top. Running time, 69 minutes.

El Caballero............Richard Talmadge
Lucia D'Arquista.........Barbara Bedford
Her Aunt.........................Nora Cecil
Ramond Torreno............David Torrence
Carlos Torreno.................David Mir
Sergeant Juan Dinero.......Stuart Holmes
Pierre Gaston.............Christian Frank
The Padre...............:.Oliver Eckhardt

Seemed rather ill advised for Tiffany-Stahl to present a production of this nature in a special run Broadway house at $1.50, where it was bound to be conspicuously out of place. At best it is a western in Spanish costume and locale. It belongs in the neighborhoods, where it should prove acceptable. Sound accompaniment is not so good.

Story is a bold repetition of the well-known formula concerning the mysterious masked rider who is the **saviour, hero and protector of the poor.**

Of charm, love interest or intrigue of the clever type it has none, making it taboo for the first runs. But it has plenty of speed and action, though ridiculed by a first-night audience because of the absurdity of the leading man's actions. This should give it a good rating in its proper sphere.

Richard Talmadge hasn't a high polish or much personality, but as long as he keeps moving he's as good as the next one. Some of the acrobatics, pure strength and horse stunts are crudely done. In one instance **the Cabellero is fighting a mob of over 100 vassals of the** mighty Torreno. He shoves one **very slightly, and the entire crew tumbles as if shot. Another idea that doesn't quite get over because of its mode of presentation is the quick change gag, whereby the Cabellero becomes Taki, the Aztec servant. The changes lack skillful handling. In the close-ups Talmadge photographs badly, resulting** in uninteresting love sequences.

Synchronization is okay as far as Hugo Riesenfeld's score **is concerned, but the souuding of a vocal number with guitar accompaniment is very faulty. Talmadge's lip movements are out of gear with the record. Several times when Talmadge stops singing the disk voice keeps on.**

Plot tells of a Spanish girl of noble but impoverished family being forced to marry a son of wealth in New Spain. She changes her mind, but is then in the clutches of the boy's powerful father, who insists on the ceremony going through. Meanwhile the girl falls for the masked adventurer.

Final title is a howl for the premier audience. Chased by Torreno's men, the heroic couple arrive at a precipice. The boy queries if she'll take the chance and make the horse jump the gap. She promptly answers, "Death . . . with you."
Mori.

Woman From Moscow

Paramount production and release starring Pola Negri. Directed by Ludvig Gerger. Screen version of Sardou's "Fedora" by John Farrow. Photographer, Victor Milne. At the Paramount, N. Y., week of Nov. 3. Running time, 72 minutes.

Princess Fedora....................Pola Negri
Loris Ipanoff..................Norman Kerry
Vladimir.........................Paul Lukas
Gretch Milner................Otto Matiesen
The General.................Lawrence Grant
Olga Andreavitshka..........Maude George
Nadia............................Bodil Rosing
Ipanoff's brother..................Jack Luden
Ipanoff's mother..........Martha Franklin
Ipanoff's sister..................Mirra Rayo
Groom..........................Tetsu Komai

Any way you look at it, Pola Negri in more than an hour of an old fashioned melodrama made into a modern society play, and with an unhappy ending at that, is not stimulating. Pictorially it's a marvelously artistic production; on its entertainment side for modern screen purposes it just won't do.

Long sequences of Princess Fedora (Miss Negri) at a Paris salon, interminable love passages between the star and Norman Kerry, while the characters and the story languish together, are dramatic static. Action creeps along, and the fact that its settings are of ravishing beauty doesn't help much. Picture is worth just the drawing value of the star in the lobby. Showmen will weigh that for themselves.

Camera work and technical details are as flawless as the story material is unsuited to screen purposes. Some of the interior settings are noteworthy even in this day of artistry in backgrounds. And the costuming is gorgeous. Indeed, everything has been done to enhance the star and story, but that doesn't make a great play written for Sarah Bernhardt in 1882 a good picture for Pola Negri in 1928.

Film has minor sound effects but they remain extremely secondary. Chorus of Cossacks is heard in distance during introductory episodes and again when heroine calls the wild soldier-musicians to furnish entertainment to a sedate social function. Once more a pretext to bill the picture as synchronized for lobby purposes. The few effects, however, are smoothly fitted in.

It's all such heavy, somber stuff, this business of Russian nobles, Nihilist plots, Paris haute monde and stilted, pompous sentiment of 40 years ago. Miss Negri is never Princess Fedora, but just a flicker actress, and the shallow pretense of lofty emotion reacts upon itself. The producer seemed to feel something of the whole thing's out-of-dateness, for he has taxicabs mingling with horse drawn coaches in his Paris streets of 1880, and his costuming blends modern modes to take some of the ugliness off the dress of that period.

If something of the same sort had been done with the literary material, which is quite as outmoded as the bustle, a picture might have been made. But the present day screen has not much patience with languishing heroines, stilted histrionics or hifalutin poses that passed for drama in the last century. Pale and melancholy ladies whose love affairs go wrong don't quaff the hemlock any more. It isn't done. Or if it is, it's material for the tabloids instead of the screen which concerns with lighter matters.
Rush.

DRY MARTINI

(SOUND)

Fox production and release directed by Harry D'Arrast Adapted from John Thomas' story, with D. Doty titling. Synchronized score by Rothafel and Rapee. At the Roxy, N. Y., week of Nov. 3. Running time, 77 mins.

Elisabeth Quimby..............Mary Astor
Freddie Fletcher..............Matt Moore
Lina ....Jocelyn Lee
Lucille Grosvenor..............Sally Eilers
Willoughby Quimby............Albert Grau
Paul De Launay..............Albert Conti
Joseph ....Tom Ricketts
Bobbie Gordon................Hugh Trevor
Frank........................John T. Dillon
Mrs. Koenig................Marcelle Corday

A comedy supposedly taking place in Paris. But there's also a **Paris, Ky. It'll probably figure as smart fare in the latter spot, with or without sound. When these sophisticated tries miss they're quite apt to be a little silly. "Dry Martini" misses.**

For 77 minutes the boys either bend elbows in parlors or stand up against an American bar. Meanwhile, Albert Gran waddles about as the white-haired roue at his wits' end because his grown-up daughter is in town and he supposes that he's got to reform. But the child is so modern she runs off to try companionate marriage with an artist, and father and young friend have to dash to the rescue. Best twist in the picture is that he who would protect the girl's honor finally comes flying through the door after an unseen set-to with the supposed heavy, who isn't so dastardly, inasmuch as the girl asked for the elopement. Finishes with the beaten hero and daughter sailing for home and leaving Papa to his cocktails and mistress.

Gran and Matt Moore divide the picture between them, Moore doing a quiet stew indifferent to everything but his liquor. Actually, Gran stands out. Albert Conti makes it count while he's in front of the lens, but he hasn't enough footage to outscore the first named duo. The women are negligible. And if somebody doesn't watch those hats Mary Astor is wearing **she'll be out of any picture calling for a locale in a town over 15,000.** Picture might well be called "The Girl With the Iron Hat." **And when the men start noticing the headgear it's tough on film ingenues. No reason for it as Miss Astor flings plenty of appearance around, but nothing could be sophisticated where those chapeaux are concerned.**

Sally Eilers and Joselyn Lee both hint at possessing more screen power than they're unleashing in this picture. That's the trouble. The feature never keeps its promise. And the 77 minutes are entirely unnecessary. Shapes as one of those light 60-minute comedies Fox turns out every so often and which never quite make the grade. This one has got a nice production behind it, but no sustaining power and no featured player.

Its best point is its synchronized accompaniment, even if over scored, including the playing of a phonograph. Perhaps the first time the new picture wrinkle has picked up another mechanical. Orchestration at times is so good its out of proportionto the action. Where the

music is so strong that it implies a nation hangs upon the next move, a rotund father is but spluttering protestingly about his daughter and can't make up his mind as to whether he actually means it.

It will have a joyless trip around the big houses regardless of the canned score. There is no dialog.

Sid.

BONDAGE

(GERMAN MADE)
(SOUND)

Ufa production and release, with sound accompaniment. Directed by Rudolph Eichberg. Heinrich George, Mona Maris and Harry Halm in cast. At the 55th Street Playhouse, New York, week Nov. 3. Running time, 70 minutes.

Little in this for the average American exhibitor. But probably soft pickings for the high-hat huts. And it might stand up under billing in the remote stands as an epic of bleeding Russia of the 1850's.

Not till the finish is there a suggestion of what might have been done with the same story by any U. S. producer. The charge of the peasantry on the cruel Countess' mansion and their battle with a squad of Cossacks would have been elaborated into something big, for it involved suspense and action. Previously the Countess resorted to trickery to prevent her son's marriage to a serf girl, but the son refused to marry the reigning Prince's daughter and hit the Prince over the head with an unopened champagne bottle. For that he was tossed out of the army, though the bottle didn't break.

It looked like a pipe for him to get the girl of his heart, but the Prince refused to sign a paper that would have severed her forced marriage to one of the serfs and contrived with the Countess to banish the lowly pair to Siberia. But the uprising queered that and caused the death of the girl's me-no-touch husband, so the Prince's signature was unnecessary to the future happiness of the poor peasant girl and the Countess' son.

That tale would have been right in the lap of Barrymore and Costello or Gilbert and Garbo.

All performing honors in "Bondage" are copped by Heinrich George as the philosopher-drunkard who kindly weds the Countess' son's gal "to save her for him." He looks to have evil attention on that wedding night, but all he does is to say good-night and sleep outside by the fireplace. The girl later squares it with the Countess' son by explaining "We lived as brother and sister, and Heaven is my judge." Heaven didn't show in the film.

Titles stilted and badly written.

Majority of settings are exteriors, a money-saving device that luckily does not seem out of place in this picture.

Several shots of toilers plowing are from the ground up, with the characters outlined by the sky and seemingly working on a ridge. That is recalled as first prominently used in "The Big Parade," but still a good shot and a pretty one.

The sound accompaniment for "Shadows" at the 55th Street is Ultratone. It's on the disk principal with everything apparently handled backstage. It was amplified excellently here and interpreted the moods of the film with song, but it didn't make the picture. The fact that the film was sounded possibly held greater significance for the audience than the sound itself.

Bige.

SHADOWS OF FEAR

(GERMAN MADE)

Defu production distributed in America by First National. Screen adaptation of Emile Zola's "Therese Raquin," by F. Carlson and Willy Haas. Directed by Jacques Feyder. Photography by Frederick Euggang and Hans Scheib. Assistant director, Rudolph Strobl. At the Cameo, N. Y., week of Nov. 4. Running time, 90 minutes.

Therese Raquin	Gina Manes
Mrs. Raquin	J. Marie-Laurent
Laurent	H. A. Schlettow
Michaud	Charles Barrois
Camille	Wolfgang Zilzer
Grivet	Paul Henckels
Susanne, his daughter	La Jana

Out for this country except as a last resort for the art houses. Enough to indicate its character is to relate that it is Emile Zola, the man who wrote "Drink" in his most drab and depressing mood.

Spirit of the story has been reproduced with utmost fidelity. Add an uncompromising German realist director to the greatest of French pessimists and what shows on the screen is dispiriting to the last extreme.

Nobody but a German producer would think of filming an epic of dull, mean people involved in morbid tragedy and then gilding the lily of depression by dwelling persistently upon the bleakest details. The explanation of its ever reaching an American screen probably may be found in the quota system.

Therese, penniless orphan, marries Camille, humble clerk and a puny invalid. She spends her wedding night measuring out his medicine. Life of petty routine wears upon her and, as it is presented by this cast, it also wears upon the audience.

Therese falls a conquest to the robust good-for-nothing Laurent, and connives in her husband's murder by her lover. It is the shadows of remorse and fear that prompt them first to wed and then to hate each other to the point of mutual murder impulses. Ultimately they both take poison.

All that is dreary and morbid in this narrative has been played up by the director. It would be a terrifying work except that its actors are so bad they never drive the story home. No such collection of frumpy women players and no such group of stuff-shirted males have been assembled since the beginnings of flickers. A picture that might have delivered a morbid shock, under this treatment accomplishes nothing but deadly boredom.

Film has some good German trick camera work and some of the backgrounds convey a good deal of sombre atmosphere, but the wretched acting and the drab story put these technical merits at nought. Absolute zero as a commercial in America.

Rush.

TEN DAYS

That Shook the World
(RUSSIAN MADE)

Amkino production and release. Directed by S. M. Eisenstein. Photography by Tiffi. No other credits given. At Little Carnegie Playhouse, New York. Week Nov. 2. Running time, 75 minutes.

This Russian film aroused protest last summer when Arthur Hammerstein tried to book it into his Broadway theatre following "The Fall of St. Petersburg." At that time it was labelled as Soviet Russia propaganda and the censors refused to allow it to be shown.

Mike Mindlin was able to get it past the reviewing board for its American premiere at his new ritzy sure seater. In present form it can harm no one and is likely to prove okay in the art film houses.

Eisenstein, the young Russian director, with all the resources of the Soviet placed at his command to film the events of the 10 historical October days which preceded the overthrow of the Kerensky government in Russia, soon after the Czar had been deposed, has fallen far short in his efforts to create an outstanding screen record. Using no scenario or story for guidance, he has merely strung together a series of news reel shots of various committees in the Russian uprising.

To one not familiar with Russian events immediately prior to the formation of the Soviet government this flicker won't help much. Here and there Eisenstein has hit what he was after. Several of his sequences of rushing troops and rioting peasants are capably handled. His skill in picking types to play the parts of Kerensky, Trotsky and Lenin as well as minor figures also worthy.

Photography by Tiffi (Russians haven't much use for a front moniker) nothing exceptional, most of the shots being recorded with statues in the foreground.

For the average moving picture patron "Ten Days" will be nine days too long.

SHOW GIRL

(SOUND)

First National production and release. Synchronized music score by Western Electris disk system. Directed by Al Santel, with screen story based on J. P. McEvoy novel. Alice White featured. Sol Polito, cameraman. At Strand, N. Y., week Nov. 3. Running time, 61 mins.

Dixie Dugan	Alice White
Alvarez Romano	Donald Reed
Denny	Lee Moran
Jimmy	Charles Delaney
Milton	Richard Tucker
Nita Dugan	Gwen Lee
Mr. Dugan	Jimmie Finlayson
Mrs. Dugan	Kate Price

In "Show Girl" the titles come first. There's a laugh in every other one that's a real laugh. Alice White is a close second since she handles the role well, socking home at the same time plenty of that s.a. that gets the boys.

Then the yarn, a bit of expose on how the tabloids are supposed to spend money for their circulations, comes in. Either version, sound or silent, spell well for First National's boxoffice.

The family and the pretty blonde daughters of the fat mama and the scrawny dad, put over well by Kate Price and Jimmie Finlayson, start out in the usual way at the supper table. There the characters are introduced by pert titling. Alice's intro as the dame who "looks hot but keeps cool," starts off the comedy.

Another sub gets a roar. This describes location: "Brooklyn. Like an elephant's rear end. Big, but unimposing."

Charles Delaney as the tabloid cub who takes advantage of a jealous spick dancer and a sugar daddy to give his baby a play and the paper an exclusive serial, rates close to Alice in honors. From then on how some well known publishers used to okay swindle sheets regardless of the facts and figures, finishes the yarn.

Applause, a couple of night club solos, and some chorus work comprise the only sound exclusive of the music score. Synchronization okay.

Waly.

MONIQUE'S FAULT

(FRENCH MADE)

Paris, Oct. 21.

This comedy drama is good in parts. Maurice Gleize, producer. It is taken from a former best seller by Trilby, a lady novelist now deceased, and constitutes a worthy first half. What is the fault of Monique? Divulging state secrets once more.

Mauriac, before going on a foreign mission, confides some secret military plans to his wife, Monique, for safe keeping. During the night their child, Jacques, is taken ill and is attended by a foreign doctor, who consents to save the boy on condition Monique permits him to examine the plans. She does so, and naturally regrets when it is too late. Suspicion falls on Maurica holding a high position with the government contractors, and to save her husband's honor she confesses her own treachery. Friends go for the real criminal, who shoots himself. Picture should find a market in small houses. Sandra Milowanoff is charming and simple as the erring wife. Victor Vina plays the husband and Rudoff Klein impersonates the doctor.

Kendrew.

LAW OF THE RANGE

Metro-Goldwyn-Mayer production and release directed by William Nigh. From story by Norman Houston. Screen adaptation by Richard Schayer. Starring Col. Tim McCoy, Joan Crawford featured. Titles by Robert Hopkins. Cast includes Rex Lease, Bodil Rosing and Tenen Holtz. At the Columbus, N. Y., Nov. 5, as one half of double feature program. Running time, 45 minutes.

Exhibs and others thirsting for a knowledge of range law will likely be disappointed in this picture as an exposition of that phase of life. But as 45 minutes of western atmosphere, riding, shooting and fighting, it holds its own.

From the practical or financial point of view it seems almost too expensive to make mere westerns on this scale considering the depleted market awaiting product of this type. It harbors a strong, highly satisfactory cast with Tim McCoy, Joan Crawford and Rex Lease in the principal assignments. The added value in the Crawford name at present should help.

Lease tops the cast for appearance, photography and deportment in a limited and familiar role. He looks good and strong enough for better things.

Story is that of two brothers separated in their youth following an attack on the family wagon by a mixed Indian and renegade party. Each of the boys has a star tattooed on his chest. One of the boys becomes a fearless ranger while the other grows up to be a notorious bandit. Both make a play for the same girl, unnaturally coy and too girlish for anything but a western, the Solitaire Kid finally meeting death in the flames of a raging forest fire.

Forest fire is an excellent sequence, while the struggle preceding it is also a realistic piece of work.

Mori.

LIGHTNING SPEED

FBO production and release. Robert North Bradbury, director. Bob Steele starred. Cameraman, DeGrasse. Cast: Will Welch, Mary Maberry, Perry Murdock. At Stanley, New York, one day, Oct. 30. Running time, about 60 minutes.

Reporters who sport high-powered cars and play around the Governor's daughter and are acrobats as well, seem a little far-fetched, even on the screen. But "Lightning Speed" has 'em, as well as a poor cast and a story that is meant to hum, but achieves monotony even for the grinds.

The Governor, who wouldn't shape up so well as a good butler, figures a reporter, Bob Steele, nonsmoker and drinker, as an excellent bet for his daughter. Bob goes to work in light knickers and his city editor has the set-up of a corner in a fashionable woman's club.

The bad man has a brother who is slated for the chair, so he gets a job in the Governor's garden. The reporter naturally knows what it's all about and turns gangster.

When the climax of the bad guy trying to cop the girl in a balloon arrives, with Bob right on the tail rope, even the sleepy Stanley audience, where a negro porter has to keep the boys awake, show their tensity in loud cackles.

DO YOUR DUTY

First National production and release. Story by Julian Josephson. Photography by Mike Joyce. Charles Murray star. In cast: Lucien Littlefield, Charles Delaney, Aggie Herring, Doris Dawson. Directed by William Beaudine. At Stanley, New York one day, Nov. 2. Running time, about 60 minutes.

Of all the films on the home life of the cop, "Do Your Duty" rates the highest. First National has a sure-fire in this one, in the way that Charlie Murray lives the role. Bits of comedy and sentimentality as part of the life of the big city cop with a still larger family are literally perfected by Murray as a cop who makes the lieut's grade. Good for all houses. As far as the grinds are concerned, it will be the best cast and most sincere screen yarn they have screened in more than a long time.

A better cop for the screen than Murray has not been found. The touches of comedy he injects as the ordinary patrolman studying for his lieutenant's papers, with his own kids and wife as the interference, and then again as the commissioned officer with a frame-up and consideration for the family again on the horizon, Murray goes on the books as the 100 per cent screen copper.

In addition to the comedy is what many audiences will detect as a thrill in Murray, as the de-badged and framed lieutenant, getting those who have given him the ride. His Scotch friend and tailor, who slips him the word which wins reinstatement is none other than Lucien Littlefield.

A mighty good melocomedy.
Waly.

COUSIN BETTY
(FRENCH MADE)
Paris, Oct. 23.

It took some responsibility on the part of Max de Rieux to adopt the well known story of Honore de Balzac, "La Cousine Bette," for screen purposes. The author portrayed the innermost feelings of a character with the art of a master psychologist, and it is difficult to convert some philosophical books to ordinary moving pictures for this very reason. Therefore the producer revealed audacity in tackling this book of Balzac, and repeating it in images without literature.

Max de Rieux has done better than expected.

Hutot, an officer in the French Imperial army in 1810, is billeted in a village. He meets in the house two pretty girls, Adeline and her cousin Bette. Hutot falls in love with the former and eventually marries her.

That is the first phase of the other maiden's disappointment, and she secretly thinks of revenge. Twenty years later Hutot has been made a Baron and in a high position in the Royalist party. He has sadly neglected his wife, having other amorous adventures with the wife of a subordinate (among other intrigues), who is an extravagant creature and leads to his financial ruin.

Cousin Bette is behind this and gives a hand in dragging down the Baron in his official career. This jealous lady is living alone, a deluded woman, but is generously helping a young aristocrat in whom she has taken a deep interest. When the spinster learns her protege is to marry the Baron's daughter her rage is sullen but complete.

Fired by a wicked jealousy she schemes to complete the ruin of Hutot and his family, hoping to prevent the marriage. She almost succeeds, but the Baron's downfall is the commencement of a new and happier career.

The famous author in this literary analysis of the soul benevolently depicts good for evil, as it should be but ain't. However, it is not an occasion to prelect on Balzac. The cast is appropriate. Alice Tissot is supported by Suzy Pierson, Andree Brabant, Germaine Rouer, Charles Lamy, Henri Baudin (as the Baron) Francois Rozet and Mansuelle. "La Cousine Bette" is a choice offering for literary folk. *Kendrew.*

THE LOOKOUT GIRL

Quality (firm) release produced by A. Carlos. Directed by Dallas Fitzgerald from the story by Alice Ross Colver. Continuity by Adrian Johnson; titles by Tom Miranda. Featuring Jacqueline Logan. Cast includes Ian Keith, William Tooker, Broderick O'Farrell, Lee Moran, Jimmy Aubrey, Gladden James, Henry Herbert, Jean Huntley, Geraldine Leslie. At Loew's New York, Oct. 19; one-half of double bill. Running time, 70 minutes.

The ancient melodrama of the girl with a past who marries on condition that her husband should never ask questions is here subjected to the longest and most unsuitable form of treatment. On a double feature bill for a day it practically fulfills its greatest expectations.

There seems to be no specific or warranted excuse for the length of the picture. The very same material could easily be handled in 50 minutes.

The most important hindrance to the effective production is the story, in which there is no trace of originality. Picture indicates, also, week direction. Cast is fairly reliable, with Miss Logan photographing well and registering generally.

The plot opens with the attempted suicide of a girl, the lookout for a gang of yeggs, running from the scene of a crime. She is saved by a physician, whom she marries. Her husband's best friend, a secret service man, spots her, and the result is a round up of the gang, in which the girl helps the police.
Mori.

THE COP

Pathe production and release. Starring William Boyd. Alan Hale, Jacqueline Logan and Robert Armstrong sub-featured. Story by Elliott Clawson, adapted by Tay Garnett. Directed by Donald Crisp. Supervision of Ralph Block. Cast includes Tom Kennedy, Louis Natheaux, Dan Wolheim, Phillip Sleeman. At Hippodrome, New York, week Nov. 4. Running time, 64 minutes.

The lowly patrolman comes in for a share of glory in this Pathe melodrama. Picture fairly interesting despite its conventional pattern and a very obvious lack of production co-operation between writers, director, supervisor and editor.

The finished product holds incidents of no particular relevancy, and rather completely fails to take care of the love interest, never adequately explaining the heroine (Jacquiline Logan), her relationship to a gang of yeggs or her character or attitude. Stray ends indicate that Miss Logan may have had a definite characterization when the shooting started in Culver City, but the man with the scissors ruined it. Additionally, Miss Logan gets third billing, although formerly and until recently rating as a Pathe star.

Story is usual. A beloved police sergeant is killed, and his pal, the cop (William Boyd) swears vengeance on Scarface Marcus, the dirty so-and-so, who did the shooting. Robert Armstrong is very disagreeable as the guy with the scarred mugg, his performance being the individual outstander.

Boyd, as always, is pleasant and breezy. He seems like good material being uniformly wasted on stories in which he plays an honest son of toil. Steel worker, switchman, engineer, bridge watchman.

cop, Boyd has been them all, and it is questionable whether the majority of film fans really relish heroes with such prosaic and overallish roles.

"The Cop" is a pretty fair production for outside the de luxe realm. With production care it might have been more of a humdinger. *Land.*

RUNAWAY GIRLS

Columbia production and release. Directed by Mark Sandrich from story by L. Howard. Supervised by Harry Cohn. Starring Shirley Mason. Cast includes Hedda Hopper, Alice Lake and Arthur Rankin. At Loew's New York, one day, Oct. 25, half double bill. Running time, over 60 minutes.

This production first seems to resolve mainly on finding the answer to a vastly intriguing problem, "Why do girls leave home?" Director Sandrich dug deeply into the mysterious causes which prove so fearfully destructive to the home and amassed a wealth of detail served in the form of a vapid, slow-moving rehash of an unrelated series of familiar incidents. Still holds a kick and okay for the neighborhoods.

Just so long as it tries to moralize the picture is wearisome. The continuity has some of the worst tripe ever allowed to remain in a picture. It's the kind of stuff that galls even upon the so-called moronic element in the average audience. It sums up as a set of uninteresting titles for this length of time.

Half way through the girl who wouldn't stand for a mother who took a drink once in a while and a father who liked his women becomes involved in a white slave ring. Action runs up to fever pitch from that point on and finishes with a gun battle.

Last part tailored for b.o. and it hits. Sequences with the girl trapped in the apartment of the evil one, whom she battles vainly, carry a kick. Love interest is slight and deficient. *Mori.*

THE CRASH

First National production and release starring Milton Sills. Thelma Todd featured. Directed by Edward Cline. Story by Frank L. Packard, adapted by Charles Kenyon. Cameraman, T. D. McCord. Cast includes Wade Boteller, William Demarest, DeWitt Jennings and Sylvia Ashton. At Loew's American, Nov. 1-3. Running time, 59 mins.

Prof. Sills' w.k. he-man impersonation is getting pretty stale. "See how a double fisted boss of the wrecking crew is softened by the love of a chorus cutie," says the press sheet and that tells the plot and gives the lowdown on the picture which failed to make Broadway and will fail to be any more than a conventional filler for Main Street.

On a night out Milton and his rough and ready pals attend a traveling burley-cue. Leading lady is a snappy jane and Milt dates her up. While hopping about in a local one step joint it is discovered that Milton is carrying in his pocket a pair of ladies' garters and is not thinking about his Sunday school lessons. He asks her to go rowing on the lake. She says, sure. Milt goes for the boat. Just as he returns cutie is seen slapping a smart aleck. Caption: "The realization that he had almost made a serious mistake."

Milton's illicit intentions become honorable, the cutie becomes his lawful bride and they settle in the small town. The gossips get in their deadly work of prejudicing Milt against his show girl wife, they quarrel, separate, the big train wreck, etc., etc. Dull and foolish.
Land.

WOMAN DISPUTED
(SOUND)

United Artists production and release. Directed by Henry King and Sam Taylor. Based on the play by Denison Clift, adaptation and scenario by C. Gardner Sullivan. Starring Norma Talmadge, Gilbert Roland featured. Photographed by Oliver Marsh. At the Rivoli, New York, Nov. 9, for run on grind $1 top. Running time, 87 mins.

Mary Ann Wagner	Norma Talmadge
Paul Hartman	Gilbert Roland
Nika Turgenov	Arnold Kent
The Passer-by	Boris de Fas
Father Roche	Michael Vavitch
Otto Kreuger	Gustav Von Seyffertiz
The Countess	Gladys Rockwell

In its transition to the screen, Denison Clift's stage play has obviously lost some of its sophistication and a great deal of its charm. The directors, Henry King and Sam Taylor, with the aid of the continuity, have not done as well as a clever motif of this nature provides for. But there is little doubt as to its possibilities in the de luxe picture houses for a week's run and in the bookings following.

There are just enough of those qualities retained which are indisputably recognized in the trade as of sufficient interest to draw considerable attention to any box office. Especially so where the picture is allowed to run as shown in New York without further cuts.

The story opens and continues with a fallen woman as its major subject. The treatment is such as will practically insure matinee business.

Following the opening sequences, which include a suicide in the girl's room, action slows until the introduction of the war theme, running concurrently with the story of the sacrifice a woman of loose morals was prevailed to make on behalf of her nation.

The picture tells of this girl being adopted by two young officers of the Austrian and Russian armies, lifted out of the slime of street life and given some covering of respectability through their friendship. Each falls in love with the girl and wishes to marry her. She chooses Hartman (Roland) and as a result the latter incurs the hatred of Nika Arnold (Kent).

The supreme sacrifice comes when the Russian army is shown invading Lemberg under the leadership of Nika. Austrians are forbidden to leave the city. A priest, Father Roche, and three prominent citizens of the town are caught trying to get away. They are sentenced to be shot for disobeying military orders. Unconcerned about her own welfare, Mary Wagner refuses to accede to Nika's proposal that she come to him willingly and he would release all of those concerned. The priest, Austrian spy, reveals his identity to the girl, impresses her with her duty to her nation, shows her how his freedom and a chance to escape would give the Austrian army victory, and she goes to Nika.

Paul arrives the next morning at the head of the victorious Austrian army. He finds Mary in church, praying. Nika is dying, but conscious and still imbued with a strong hatred which impels him to give Paul an idea of what occurred. Paul leaves the girl, but hears of her objective in her connection with Nika from the commanding officer.

In molding the character of the bag swinger the directors have worked skillfully. She is changed firmly and unhurriedly into a brave, wholesome, likeable person. Her relations with the two young men, on a basis of friendship only, despite their knowledge of her previous life, seems logical. But here, during this process, the picture is not very interesting. It is as the frightened, ill-mannered, foul creature of the night and then, later, as the changed woman that the story rouses interest. Too much has been allowed for the changing process. All the arts of photography fail to protect Miss Talmadge in many of the sequences. Hard lines and faulty posing from different angles detract from her performance.

Kent, as the menace, does well until his final appearance in his death sequence. It is too heavily overdrawn, out of proportion to the smooth, even direction which characterizes the general tone of the picture. Roland serves as the lead.

Mori.

SHOW PEOPLE
(SOUND)

M-G-M production co-starring Marion Davies and William Haines. Directed by King Vidor. Original story by Agnes Christine Johnston and Laurence Stallings. Adapted by Wanda Tuchow. Titles by Ralph Spence. At Capitol, New York, week Nov. 10. Running time, 63 mins.

Peggy Pepper	Marion Davies
Billy Boone	William Haines
Colonel Pepper	Dell Henderson
Andre	Paul Ralli
Casting Director	Tenen Holtz
Comedy Director	Harry Gribbon
Dramatic Director	Sidney Bracy
The Maid	Polly Moran

Periodically Hollywood crashes through with a screen story about itself, thereby branding as insincere its own frequently stressed propaganda for restless femmes to stay away.

"Show People" is enough to discount all the stories the Hays office can send out in a year's time. There never was a girl who got into the movies so easily as this heroine. Her career is a series of lucky breaks. She is a green hick in one reel, comedy wow in the next and dramatic actress 800 feet later. It is all immensely colored, glamorous beyond reality, and calculated to sell plenty of one-way tickets going west.

As an entertainment "Show People" is a good number. It has laughs, studio atmosphere galore, intimate glimpses of various stars, considerable Hollywood geography, and just enough sense and plausibility to hold it together.

As a document of Hollywood it presents some peculiar angles. When Peggy Pepper (Marion Davies) gets the w. k. swell head she is seen to be the complacent girl friend of her leading man, an insufferably conceited stuffed shirt. The odd part of this leading man character is that he (Paul Ralli) looks, dresses and acts like John Gilbert, star of the company which produced the picture. The satire seems pretty sharply pointed at times.

Miss Davies is obviously mimicking the peculiar pucker of the lips identified with Mae Murray, former M-G-M star. This is broad burlesque. However, at other times the story suggests the career of Gloria Swanson, particularly with emphasis upon the custard pie gal becoming an emotional actress. Bebe Daniels is also suggested.

The authors have probably drawn upon their knowledge of Hollywood personalities and have made Peggy Pepper a composite etching, half-clowning, half-sarcastic. It is not a pretty picture of human nature that is drawn, and despite the recurring slapstick, even in the serious parts, Peggy Pepper's distended ego has a familiar quality about it. Audiences are more apt to believe in her going ritz than in her eventual return to perspective.

William Haines was reported as squawking when assigned to co-star with Miss Davies. His fears were well founded. He is nicely submerged in "Show People" with the story revolving about the feminine character.

Luncheon time at a studio club is utilized to get in a flock of celebs.

Marriage by Contract
(SOUND)

Tiffany-Stahl production and release. Produced by John M. Stahl. Original. Directed by James Flood. Patsy Ruth Miller, Lawrence Grey, Robert Edeson, Ralph Emerson featured by Edward Clark. Adapted by Frances Hyland. Ernest Miller, photography. Program bills, captions as by Paul Perez but opening slides mention The Hattons as title writers. At Embassy, New York, on $2 run, opening Nov. 9. Running time, around 70 minutes.
Theme song, "When the Right One Comes Along," by L. Wolg Gilbert (lyric) and Mabel Wayne (music); published by Feist's. R.C.A. Photophone recording.

Margaret	Patsy Ruth Miller
Don	Lawrence Gray
Winters	Robert Edeson
Arthur	Ralph Emerson
Molly	Shirley Palmer
Father	John St. Polis
Mother	Claire McDowell
Grandma	Ruby Lafayette
Dirke	Duke Martin
Drury	Raymond Keane

To the Ladies
Better leave marriage alone. You have never found anything to improve it.

This quotation is the finale caption on the Tiffany-Stahl special picture, "Marriage by Contract," now at the Embassy (M-G-M) on Broadway, at the regular scale of that house, $2. It can play any theatre for the usual time to the usual gross, for it has everything a picture under that title should have.

It's a good picture without being a big one, but the big thing about it is that "Marriage by Contract" is susceptible of high power exploitations. According to the local exploitation will depend whether this T-S special shall exceed the average gross. That's strictly a matter up to the theatre.

"Marriage by Contract" is in with the women and the girls before it gets into town. What's left is to get them in to see it. And the theatre that doesn't make them come in has something wrong with it.

Chains playing this T-S might use the rubber stamp to have the home office exploitation experts lay out a similar campaign for each town it plays on the chain. If the local staff can improve upon it, that's okay, too.

That opening quotation coming right at the end of the picture tells the possibilities of the exploitation end. Women can't resist this film if they are sold right on it, and they will drag in the men. In particular it will start many an argument between husbands and wives. The big subject of trial marriage is here not handled in a big way. Perhaps it's too big a story for seven reels, if properly told. But Edward Clark, maybe under wraps through limitations, brings out his points in a blunt manner, possibly a bit too swiftly at times, but the moral is so certainly set against the trial marriage foolishness there is no answer.

Patsy Ruth Miller runs away with the picture in the playing, and easily. This is quite a picture for Miss Miller. In her make up alone, simulating the different age periods of a girl of 19 to a grey haired woman, she conveyed the proper age at all times, while the acting kept step.

At 19 she married a boy near her age and she declared for a marriage by contract, permitting either to dissolve it at any time for any reason. Three weeks later her husband came home stewed, and said he had been out with another girl. It was 4 in the morning. She remonstrated and questioned. He answered but in defense pleaded the contract, which she thereupon tore up and went home to her mother. It was then 4. Flinging herself upon the bed, the young wife cried herself to sleep.

A jump in time. She has secured a divorce and a newspaper printed the ex-hubby was to again marry to the girl he had taken out.

So Miss Miller got herself another husband, but not the one she wanted. The one she wanted, in her set, all of whom had joked

about the marriage trial, was willing to make but not marry her. He took the girl he had told he would marry when freed from her trial husband, to a private dining room in a joint. The girl got the idea even before she entered, as another girl was just escaping from another room.

So she had to take the next best, a hulking hick, who thought two years long enough for a trial lady and kept his word. At the end of two years, he walked. Then another, and this time older, much, but with dough. He wanted her on the level and she wanted the coin.

Married, the young wife of the elderly chump picked up a giglio, with the A. K. onto it, but letting it ride. Another divorce at the solicitation of the giglio and the wife with $250,000 cash in hand from the settlement. She married the gig.

He wanted his much older wife to buy him speed roadsters and slip him change. And then her checks came bouncing back. She told him they were broke. He answered like a true gig, she was broke, and why should he be tied up with an old dame without coin.

Packing his grips and starting to leave, the giglio saw his wife with her back to the door, holding a gun. Not for him, she said, but for herself if he tried to leave. He tried, a tussle for the gun, explosion, and the gig was out.

Cops come in, see the dead man on the floor and the wife with the gun in her hand. One of the policemen approaches to place her under arrest. She's terrified when a dissolve brings her back in bed, struggling out of her nightmare. The folks rush in to learn the trouble. It's morning and also comes along the original husband, then the plea of the wife for them to be again married, this time in church, and the screen's injunction for the women not to monkey with the only protection they will ever get.

R.C.A. Photophone Recorded

Sound is slight, but has an odd thing in the musical synchronization. The music, inclusive of the theme song, has been adjusted to the picture's situations to bring a smile or laugh here and there. It's the music fitted to the story's moods and very good. The theme song, "When the Right One Comes Along," by L. Wolfe Gilbert and Mabel Wayne (Feist's), sure fire as seller. A couple of vocal choruses sung during the action, off stage (screen) but in the record. One is sung while the action continues and with a caption coming out in the centre of it. Funny.

The Ernest Miller direction stands up, although the cutting room does appear to have speeded up the running but without injury, and there can be no complaint for that.

Well produced picture, mostly interiors. TS can take a bow on it. No one of especial distinction other than Miss Miller in cast, except Robert Edeson as the elderly husband.

Most of the screen folk were stupid when trying to improvise "action" as the camera eye slowly progressed down the table. Gilbert and Miss Murray were among the lunchers.

Picture was synchronized at M-G-M's new Manhattan sound studio and is a good job, although two opinions will exist on the point of having a tenor singing the theme song while silent sub-titles are on the screen.

General quality of production, photography, etc., is good. Picture obviously aimed for quick popularity succeds in its purpose.

Land.

MATA HARI
(The Red Dancer)
(GERMAN-RUSSIAN MADE)

Briskin company production, in association with another foreign producer, name not caught quickly enough on slide. Released over here by National Big Three, an exchange in New York handling foreign film product. Directed by Frederick Feher. Three principals programmed, with none starred or featured. At Cameo, New York, small class grind on 42d street. Running time, 73 minutes.

Mata Hari	Magda Sonia
Count Rakovski	Fritz Kortner
Archduke of Austria	Wolfgang Zilzer

This episodic picturization of Mata Hari and her death will only interest such localities or audiences as may be aware of this alleged spy who was a professional Continental dancer and met death through court martial.

It looks like a whitewash for the dead girl. The story is made confusing, if a historical record. At the finish one can't decide if Mata was in the Russian or Austrian secret service.

Nothing to indicate the girl had done any spying, up to the period commencing early in the picture during which the allegation that Mata was framed is easily made to stand out on the screen. That may be the whitewash. Or the cutter may have taken out too much or the wrong stuff, even with the picture running 73 minutes.

Romance is shoved in through Mata falling in love with a boob farmer boy, with this Mata (Magda Sonia) seemingly so much older than he she would have fallen in love with him or anyone else with much difficulty.

A Grand Duke of Russia, importantly cast, is not programmed. His agent in the Mata matter is Count Rakovski, Russian attache at Vienna. Rakovski has most of the dirty work to do and is always around, even at the execution. Latter is in shadow for Mata at the finale, but with the shooting squad of soldiers in view. This may not be unlike the scene in "Dawn," the story of Edith Cavell, accused and shot by the Germans as a spy.

Mata Hari as a figure in the World War was quite a figure. Many stories have been printed of and about her. Known professionally, the international show business was interested during the time of her trouble and up to her death —and after.

Here at first she is a dancer on a Vienna stage, with the Archduke a bit wild over her, while the Count Rakovski, acting for the Grand Duke, has authority sufficient apparently in Vienna, it seems, to order her arrest and return to Russia. The Grand Duke is anxious to again see her.

An inside is given here of a Russian wild party of nobles and officers and how they handle their women. This scene, however, is not big enough for box office, nor is there any one distinctive thing abstractedly linked with the story itself that could be depended upon to draw.

Mata doesn't like the wild stuff. She has too much trouble holding off the Grand Duke. So skips from the party, takes a sleigh, is stuck in a snow drift and rescued by the farming boy, with a mustache.

That starts the love affair, and in this picture starts the first intimation why Mata Hari was shot as a spy.

To secure the release from prison of her farmer boy lover, she agreed with the Count to get the plans of Lemberg (Austria) from the Archduke. Her boy friend had been imprisoned by the Grand Duke's instructions in jealous revenge.

She saw the Archduke in Lemberg, where he had gone. He refused the plans, but agreed with her suggestion that he give her a false set. A Russian war council had decided to invade Austria; the plans of Lemberg were an urgent necessity. (This sounded like before the war, in action and captions).

A Russian spy disguised as a porter in that particular hotel that never had anyone but the film's principals in the hallways, overheard Mata's conversation with the Archduke, who had called at her rooms. The spy listened outside the door, not taking the time to place his ear at the keyhole.

When Mata returned with the Lemberg plans and secured the release of the boy, the porter-spy shortly followed to expose her to the Russian council. That is a part of the confusing portion, and brought out in this way possibly to denote to what extent Mata was framed to force her to act the spy, although here again her Grand Duke seemed unconcerned as to Mata, spying or fate, for he faded away.

Following the exposure and again through the arrest of the boy, Mata was coerced into signing a confession, to prevent the guards continuing to beat the prisoner. This was made a sound portion, along with others, by funny effects by the Cameo's drummer or back stage. If sound has hit 42d street that hard, the Cameo really should be wired. It's a small Keith house.

After the confession came the court-martial, then the execution, with the farmer boy, released, going home, probably starting off again there with his accordion, the one he could amuse Mata with. That was a chance for thankfulness for non-wiring. Imagine accordion playing in a wired house! The ferry boats would lose all of their orchestras in the summer time!

"Mata Hari" over here may do for the sure seaters, with the probability that audience will recall the case. Otherwise nothing to attract. Neither acting nor production will do that unless the soldier fraternity is interested enough to attend the picturization, which didn't happen with the "Nurse Cavell" picture on this side.

Perhaps "Mata Hari" with more fidelity would have been a much bigger story and picture.

GOOD-BYE KISS

Mack Sennett comedy-drama, distributed by First National, directed by Mack Sennett. Johnny Burke featured. Photographer John W. Boyle. Titles by Tom Miranda. Running time, 80 minutes. At Colony, week Nov. 11.

Johnny.........................Johnny Burke
Sally.............................Sally Eilers
Bill Williams....................Matty Kemp
Serg. Hoffman..............Wheeler Oakman
Mlle. Nannette...........Carmelita Geraghty
"Toots"..........................Alma Bennett

Much better picture than you'd expect from the scheme of blending slapstick Sennett comedy and straight dramatic interest. Sums up as good program material for split weeks with that about its highest aim. Absence of names takes it out of the de luxe category. Other things work against the film for important spotting.

Sennett's forte is the snappy comedy two-reeler and he doesn't quite achieve the sustained effort necessary for a full length feature, either in the comedy or in the story interest. Finally war pictures are for the present in eclipse.

Picture never registers solidly either as a dramatic or a comedy. They could scarcely switch back and forth from downright clowning to tense war drama, so the laugh element is toned down to conform and the result is never entirely right. Dramatic story itself does not stand up by itself.

Burke plays a patsy soldier of the A. E. F. with quiet humor drawing chuckles and hee-hees, but never a hearty haw-haw, while Matty Kemp misses rather sadly with a muddled role of a doughboy from civil life who is terrified beyond control at his first experience in the front line and quits cold. His sweetheart, a Salvation Army girl, sticks to him and tries to save him from disgrace. In an air raid on Paris she forcibly restrains him from craven flight and in the end he overcomes his weakness and turns hero.

The "war stuff" is convincingly handled throughout and there is an extremely lively passage having to do with the spicy exhibition in a Paris cabaret frequented by soldiers on furlough. Some of this is out for a number of the 49 states of the union, although it is amusing. The factor against the story is the rather sorry hero.

However, his rehabilitation is a spirited sequence, working up to an excellent dramatic climax. Hero, who has by now overcome his weakness, accidentally secretes himself in an automobile and when it is stolen by a spy to return to the enemy lines, he sticks, arriving among the enemy just in time to save his own unit from being blown up in a mining operation. Passage is skillfully nursed along as hero creeps through terrific bombardment to engage heavy in hand to hand combat as he is about to explode the mine.

Sally Eilers as the Salvation Army lassie and Alma Bennett do only fairly well with dramatic roles obviously out of their range.

Picture is synchronized with musical accompaniment and has sound effects, those of the Paris air raid, the highlight of the picture, particularly impressive. *Rush.*

HIS PRIVATE LIFE

Paramount production and release. Directed by Frank Tuttle from story by Ernest Vajda and Keene Thompson. Adolphe Menjou starred. Titles by George Marion, Jr. Henry Gerrard, cameraman. At Paramount, New York, week of Nov. 11. Running time, 52 minutes.

Georges St. Germain.......Adolphe Menjou
Eleanor Trent.................Kathryn Carver
Yvette Bergere................Eugene Pallette
Henri Bergere........Margaret Livingstone

Adolphe Menjou has had films far surpassing "His Private Life." The title is practically meaningless, with the story of an extremely light and sketchy variety, about the whims and wherefores of a blase lady-killer.

Picture exceptionally well mounted, and residential Parisian atmosphere is appealing. Players excellently cast and comedy sequences abetted by worthy sub-titles. Production should realize fair draw at all better class houses, along with the names, including Mrs. Menjou (Kathryn Carver), also in cast.

Menjou's matter-of-factness concerning female conquests more extreme than usual. Audience gradually simulates his boredom. His ability to bribe, although illogical, provides humor, especially in sequence where he has engaged a section of the restaurant to provide romantic atmosphere for the unsuspecting female of his final chase.

Girl of his choice well done by Kathryn Carver. With Margaret Livingstone as her friend and Eugene Pallette as Miss Livingstone's suspicious but dumb hubby, complicated domestic situations, old in film production, are somewhat interestingly regarnished by the persistency and ability to elude petty climaxes which Menjou injects into his role. *Waly.*

THE AIR LEGION

FBO production and release featuring Martha Sleeper, Antonio Moreno and Ben Lyon. Story by James Ashmore Creelman. At Hippodrome, New York, week Nov. 11. Running time, 58 mins.

FBO's additioin to the cycle of aviation-glorifying pictures whose epic was "Wings" and whose followers included "Air Circus" and "Lilac Time" besides some indies. Because of the interest in aviation this one may show strength. It represents a very small production investment including exteriors almost entirely. Pipe that it'll mean dough to FBO. Only commercial query would be in exhibs' direction.

Antonio Moreno and Ben Lyon, former favs with the gals, are co-featured with Martha Sleeper, FBO's contract ingenue. Moreno loses the girl to Ben. Theme of "The Air Legion" is the show must go on. The show in this case is Uncle Sam's mail.

Wisp of a story. Ben, young stunt flyer, goes to work for the air mail under the sponsorship of his dead father's wartime buddy (Moreno). On his first job he goes into a panic in an electric storm, wrecks his plane and falls into disgrace with everyone. Later he is the beaming boy in a tight pinch.

Nothing to get excited about and with direction sloppy at points, "The Air Legion" will have to frankly depend on the previous and better pictures on the same subject. *Land.*

ARMORED VAULT

(GERMAN MADE)

(Sound)

UFA production and release. Directed by Lupu Pick. Ernst Reicher, Imogene Robertson, Heinrich George and Johannes Rieman in cast. Presented with Ultratone (disk) accompaniment at 55th St. Playhouse, New York, week Nov. 10. Running time, 68 minutes.

While this fails to equal the aver-artistry and camera work, it possesses wider sales appeal for America through a simple story. It possibly can hold up under double bill spotting in the smaller grinds.

That's more than can be said for most of the alien pictures panned off as high art in the funny film galleries.

"Armored Vault" is a detective story. It is frail in construction and sags in the middle, but contains sufficient action at either end to feint at entertainment.

Principal character, tagged Stuart Webbs, is the Dutch counterpart of Britain's big disguise and magnifying glass man, Sherlock. The difference between Stuart and Sherlock is that Stuart utilizes nothing but his head. He's just as good a copper as Holmsey, too, and gets himself out of as many jams.

Stuart's job in this one is to round up a gang of master counterfeiters. Prior to tossing them out at the plate, Stew is offered a huge sum to blow town for a while so they can operate. But Stew isn't working for the city. He's a private dick and makes more by being honest, he says.

But why any mob that can hook banks for the McCoy without being caught should bother with manufacturing tin dough is unanswered, and that's why this picture is often ridiculous.

Heinrich George, as Webbs, makes plenty of muggey. There's little else to do. Another character, but with an unimportant part, is Imogene Robertson (Wilson). Now emoting for M-G-M as Mary Nolan, Imogene must appreciate the superiority of American lighting when it comes to beautifying dames. She looks much better over here, but still owes a lot to the German picture people.

Heinrich George, as head penman, again top honors in this one as in other recent German releases.

Ultratone (disk) accompaniment at the 55th Street was projected with clarity, but sounded no better than a well-timed phonograph. *Bige.*

SINNERS PARADE

Columbia production and release. Directed by John G. Adolfi. Story by David Lewis with continuity by Beatrice Van. James Van Trees, cameraman. In cast: Dorothy Revier, Victor Varconi, John Patrick, Edna Marion. At Loew's New York, one day, Nov. 9. Half of double feature. Running time, about 60 minutes.

One of those illogical mellers, but works up suspense and conventional climax that will satisfy where house policy not too exacting.

Novel start with scantily clad night club performer as school teacher by day. Follow up regular stuff easily surmised by fans. Action is plentiful enough without having its present surplus captions, which are in majority too obvious.

Honest map of club owner and wise cracks of son of vice-crusader, with latter's wild daughter in dancer's school, give dopesters easy job.

Son turning out bootleg king and using teacher to bait club owner, turned squealer to protect girl, spurred into bright finis by dancer's wayward sister suddenly reforming and introducing coppers. *Waly.*

GARDEN OF ALLAH

(FRANCO-AMERICAN-BRITISH)

Paris, Nov. 2.

Released here under the title of "Le Jardin d'Allah," latest production of Rex Ingram cameraed in North Africa and Nice, is projected at the fashionable Loew-Metro house on the Boulevards, the Cinema de la Madeleine, prior to a general release.

The scenario may not please the masses, the ending being trite.

Boris Androvski, rich novice, has embraced a religious career and become a monk in the Trappist monastery of Staouely, Southern Algeria, under the name of Father Adrien. He is still young and finds the regime too severe, after kissed by a girl he saved while felling a tree. He is tormented to regain his liberty; quits the monastery, becoming an elegant but melancholy man of the world.

While traveling in the Biskta region he is instrumental in saving an English lady, Dominique, from being robbed in a native dance hall which she visits as a tourist. The couple become friendly and finally marry.

Dominique is an orphan of noble birth, extremely religious, and somewhat eccentric as she insists on passing the honeymoon in the desert. During a sandstorm, after recognized by a visitor, Boris confesses his former calling to his wife, and his dislike of modern civilization.

Dominique realizes her husband is not shaped for society and consents to his return to Holy orders. She accompanies him back to the door of the monastery which Boris enters for the rest of his life.

The "widow" then lives alone, in Algeria, somewhat consoled in her solitude by a child, the fruit of her restricted marriage with the monk.

Photographic work of this religious reel is excellent, with a realistic sand storm somewhat lengthy.

Alice Terry (Mrs. Rex Ingram) holds the lead, well supported by Petrovich as the young monk. *Kendrew.*

LOOPING THE LOOP

(GERMAN-MADE)

Berlin, Nov. 1.

Unquestionably the best film Ufa has turned out this season. If it were not for certain weaknesses in the story it would have chances of duplicating "Variety's" international success.

A little girl is left flat by a circus acrobat and a clown in the same circus falls for her. Afraid that no woman can ever take him seriously knowing that he is a clown, he lets her think him a business man. She meets the acrobat again and he persuades her to go to London with him as his partner in a looping-the-loop stunt.

The clown follows to protect her and is starred on the same bill with her. On the opening night the stunt doesn't work and the acrobat falls.

The clown is forced to disclose his identity and finds to his surprise that the girl is proud of his fame.

What isn't convincing is the looping-the-loop trick, which never thrills. Also the character of the acrobat is extravagantly drawn too much so for acceptance.

Fine, however, is the performance of Werner Krauss as the clown. This is one of the greatest impersonations ever flashed on a screen and may be sufficient to put the picture over in America. Karl Hoffmann's photography was full of ideas and Arthur Robison's direction adequate. *Trask.*

BLONDE FOR A NIGHT

DeMille production and Pathe release. Marie Prevost starred. Directed by F. Mason Hopper. Titles by John Krafft. Dewey Wrigley, cameraman. In cast: Harrison Ford, Franklin Pangborn, Lucien Littlefield, T. Roy Barnes. At Arena, New York, one day, Nov. 10. One-half double bill. Running time, 65 minutes.

This is 90 per cent fashion show. Marie and her boy friends change their attire so often in this, or throw material about, that, exclusive of a few funny capers by Franklyn Pangborn in a nance role, the reaction is like that of having looked at a lot of goods and furniture.

The players in "A Blonde for the Night" are secondary. Women will like this if for nothing more than the wraps. Outside of Marie Provost, who flashes her limbs only once, there is little attraction for the he-fan.

The title is worked in for an evening—not a night. Miss Prevost, as the new bride, burns up over a conversation between her husband and a friend on blonde conquests.

Pangborn, as the modiste, gives her the idea of masquerade in a wig. The story has the husband being utterly deceived by this change and makes him compete with the friend for honors.

Pangborn's popping on and off the few sets, all indoors, flopping into a tub and putting on silk pajamas get the grins, but the suggestion of a story that this is, is too insincere to register as good comedy. *Waly.*

SONG
(GERMAN-MADE)

Berlin, Oct. 29.
Richard Eichberg's first film for British International Pictures. Sure fire for Germany and from the trade show reports would seem to be set for England.

The scenario, taken from a story by Volmoeller, called "Dirty Money," seemed inconsistent. It concerned a little Malayan girl who fell in love with a brutal painter, earning his living throwing knives in a cheap cabaret because he was wanted for murder.

The dancer for whose sake the painter murdered comes to the city and he again falls for her. To get money to hold the dancer's favor he joins a hold-up band and in trying to escape the police is blinded by the steam of a locomotive. So that he may be happy, the little Malayan girl impersonates the dancer for the blind man, even stealing money that he might be operated on to regain his eyesight.

Anna May Wong is charming, but Heinrich George as the painter has a type of coarse brutality which no American audience would ever stomach in a would-be sympathetic role. Eichberg's direction is better than usual. *Trask.*

THE SKY RANGER

Educational (firm) production and release. Starring Reed Howes. Adapted from Russ Farrell flying stories in American Boy magazine by Thomson Burtis. Directed by Harry I. Brown. Cast includes Marjorie Daw, Roy Stewart, Henry Barrows, Tom Santchi, Bobby Dunn. At New York theatre, New York; one half double bill, one day, Nov. 10. Running time, 32 minutes.

Educational is running a series of flying pictures, with the main figure, Russ Farrell, of the U. .S. air patrol along the Mex border, played by Reed Howes. With an army background, the Educational has a good excuse for keeping its hero up in the air. And by keeping him up in the air makes it pretty difficult to keep its meller theme at high tension, altitudinously speaking.

Here's a short picture in screening. It has a love streak, but so tame it runs barely secondary to the aviation plot. The one high spot is where Farrell rescues his sweetie's dad from the Chinese smugglers.

Howes, regarded as a stunt man, is stunting it in the air, although a double could even appear with audiences none the wiser.

Director Brown has done fairly well with a scenario that afforded little scope. Barring a spot or two, it is ordinary filming. Photography as a whole is splendid; ether scenes, whether phoney or real, required some expert camera acrobatics.

The men predominate. Film calls for border outlawry and hazardous flying and relegates the gals. And any "western" or aviation story without a plentiful dash of romantic paprika suffers. And this one suffers.

At best, a rider for the double-feature days. *Mark.*

Mysteries of the Orient
(GERMAN-MADE)

Berlin, Oct. 28.
This Ufa special cost a lot of money and tooted highly before its premiere. Disappointment.

An imitation of "The Thief of Bagdad" but without the story, direction, cast or production. The Russian director, Alexander Wollkoff, again proves himself only of second rank. His star, Nicolai Kolin, a serviceable player in supporting character roles, disclosed that he is unable to carry a film alone. His comedy is lacking in sponteneity and he is always the intelligent player, never losing himself in the role.

Ivan Petrovitch and Marcella Albani, featured, have no chance to show any qualities. Scenically the film was also disappointing as well as ridiculously overornate. Story is just another one of those Arabian nights. *Trask.*

TRACKED

FBO production and release. Directed by Jerome Storm from story by John Stuart Twist. Supervision of Robert North Bradbury. Starring Ranger, dog. Cast includes Sam Nelson, Albert J. Smith, Clark Comstock and Carol Lincoln. At Stanley, New York, Nov. 12, one day. Running time, 55 minutes.

A touching drama about a dog falsely accused of killing sheep. Where they like dogs and sheep the picture is on a par with anything else turned out along those lines. Where they want westerns it's only a pain in the neck.

Ranger may be a good dog, and the production runs like a boost in general for all dogdom. It should appeal to dog lovers and children, mainly the latter.

The menace, Albert J. Smith, is just a mean person on the screen, but he likes sheep.

Carol Lincoln is the coy young maiden saved from death by "Ranger," and Sam Nelson is the brave lad who fixes the dainty ankle.

A flash of the villain gnashing his teeth makes it dog-gone perfect. *Mori.*

HOME COMING
(GERMAN-MADE)

Berlin, Nov. 1.
Joe May was one of the first well known German directors. Up to five years ago he held a position almost neck to neck with Lubitsch. Then suddenly he disappeared.

This is an attempt at a comeback under Erich Pommer's supervision.

May has unquestionably kept his eyes open, and the film is a competent one. It might have been exceptional and, for this type of tragic story, it would have to be to get over in the States.

The plot is old: two German prisoners in Russia; one escapes and the other is apparently lost. The fugitive returns to the wife of the other and falls in love with her.

Husband reappears and, realizing the love of the two, walks out. Husband splendidly played by Lars Hanson, but Gustav Froehlich was too sweet as the lover, and Dita Parlo not emotionally ripe enough for the role of the wife. *Trask.*

FARMER'S DAUGHTER

Fox production and release. Directed by Arthur Rosson from story credited Harry Brand and Harry Johnson. Titles by Garrett Graham. In cast: Marjorie Beebee, Arthur Stone, Warren Burke, Jimmy Adams, Lincoln Stedman. At Loew's New York, one day, Nov. 9, half of double bill. Running time, about 60 minutes.

A rube story sticking close to conventional lines is handled in the same way. A smart caption here and there and an old gag garnished with plenty of slapstick will get "The Farmer's Daughter" by in some of the lesser second runs and grinds.

On the whole the action drags badly and film could have been snapped into better entertainment had it been released as a short.

The city slicker and the small town inventor, the swain and the farmer's daughter, all together but get unraveled with a happy ending when an accomplice identifies himself as the son of a worthy cheese maker who will pay for the invention.

Marjorie Beebee, as the daughter, magnifies the stiffness of a girl of the hay. Her rough and tumble antics in her handling of the men folk pull spot laughs. *Waly.*

THE AVENGING RIDER

FBO production and release. Directed by Wallace Fox from original story credited to Adele Buffington. Tom Tyler starred. In cast: Florence Allen, Frankie Darro, Al Ferguson, Bob Flemming. At Stanley, New York, one day, Nov. 6. Running time, about 60 minutes.

One of the Woolworth plots of the plains. Story padded in way so unusual as to be obvious to grind audiences; the only one who will sit through "The Avenging Rider."

Director apparently had bunch of female extras on pay roll. Used them with ridiculous comparison to cut-in and drag along customary ranch murder case. Dames in dusty country and bearded men flitted around barn in classic veils or high cut bathing outfits.

Tom Tyler forces rough expres-

sion and grabs the close-ups, which make it more monotonous. Thing is generally nonsensical and abnormally hacked. *Waly.*

ROUGH RIDING RED

FBO production and release. Directed by Louis King from the story by F. H. Clark. Supervised by R. North Bradbury. Starring Buzz Barton. Cast: James Welch, Betty Welsh, Ethan Laidlaw, Frank Rice, Bert Moorhouse. At Stanley, New York, Nov 8, one day. Running time, 55 minutes.

A western with lowest appeal, minimum of action, and a misdirected sense of comedy. The most exaggerated pretensions would not allow more than thirty minutes of this picture anywhere, and then as filler only.

The story is the simplest, completely denuded every conceivable angle which might possibly lend it attractiveness.

It is different from the usual western in that it lacks the conventional though popular riding, shooting and fighting sequences which form the well known but essential backgrounds for every production of this type.

In addition to the continuity it seems that its juvenile star, Buzz Barton, is a drawback. A boy star in westerns may be appealing to a certain element, but that would be extremely limited. The boy evidently can't be used for a more interesting story calling for stronger action on account of his obvious inability to handle anything but a cinch role.

Frank Rice is a type excellently suited for westerns. But here he is too prominently miscast and directed in a manner which detracts from his usefulness. Properly employed he would be valuable.

Miss Welsh is a vivid feminine lead, surmounting the drabness of her role with smart appearance. *Mori.*

Berlin Premieres

Berlin, Nov. 2.
"Zuflucht" ("Refuge".) Henny Porten again tries to play a type of role for which her age makes her unsuited. Her future is evidently in knockabout comedy. Only mark to this film's credit was the discovery of Franz Lederer, promising juvenile lead.

"Der Freche Husar" ("The Bold Dragoon"). One of those primitive Hungarian films still being turned out. But in the title role Ivor Novello shows he has charm.

"The Village of Sin." Not one of the best films which the Russians have utrned out, but interesting because of the splendidly played village types. While the son is in the war his father rapes the son's wife. When the soldier returns she commits suicide rather than tell him. Delicate.

"Ein Besserer Herr" ("A Gentleman's Gentleman"). Walter Hasenclever's amusing stage play here treated a bit roughly by the Bavarian Emelka Co. But at least a worthier product than this firm usually turns out. Good performances by Leo Peukert, Fritz Kampers and Willi Forst.

"Abwege" ("Byways"). Very worst film ever sponsored by G. W. Pabst, who made the classic "Secrets of a Soul." Conventional story about the misunderstood wife and the overworked husband. Brigitte Helm has not yet freed herself from her overplaying of vampire days. Couple of scenes suggest the possibility of truly great and natural acting.

"Unter der Laterne" ("Under the Lantern"). Poor little prostitute, simply forced by horrid men into taking the easiest way. Laid in a shabby Berlin milieu, nothing at all to recommend it.

"Die Dame mit der Maske" ("The Lady With the Mask"). Again a film built around a revue. Nothing new except the performance of the French girl, Arlette Marechal. She is not beautiful in that sense, but has a quiet dignity and simplicity, charming and moving.

"Revolutionshochzeit" ("Revolutionary Wedding"). Successful old melodrama by Sophus Michaelis does not fit at all accurately into the requirements of the screen. One felt the scenery flapping. Direction and cast competent and Fritz Kortner in secondary role more than that. Along with Werner Krauss, the great character actor of the German screen.

"Ritter der Nacht" ("Knights of the Night"). Extraordinary how well Schiller's classical play, "The Robbers," suits itself to modern treatment. Well directed film with plenty of suspense. Two new actors, Kowal Samborski and George Charlia, add new faces to the screen, and Wilhelm Dieterle and Edith Meinhardt do their best work.

Of American films which have come out this season in Berlin, few have been real successes. Buster Keaton in his steamboat film, Menjou in "A Gentleman of Paris" and Dolores del Rio in "Ramona" (this partially due to the success of the song and her presence in Berlin) got over nicely.

Al Jolson in "The Jazz Singer" and John Barrymore in "Don Juan" only moderate. Surprisingly enough Jannings in his "Last Command" did not raise much dust.

Flops were Lubitsch's "Old Heidelberg," Corinne Griffith in "The Garden Eden" and Pola Negri in "The Second Life."

INTERFERENCE

(DIALOG)

Paramount's first all-talking production and release. Directed by Roy J. Pomeroy and based on a silent version directed by Lothar Mendes, made on the west coast. Dialog arranged by Ernest Pascal. Screen play by Hope Loring. Original stage play by Roland Pertwee and Harold Dearden. Cameraman, J. Roy Hunt. Supervised by John G. Bachmann. At Criterion, New York, opening Nov. 16 at $2. Running time, 90 mins.

Deborah Kane	Evelyn Brent
Philip Voaze	William Powell
Sir John Marlay	Clive Brook
Faith Marlay	Doris Kenyon
Inspector Haynes	Brandon Hurst
Childers	Louis Payne
Dr. Gray	Wilfred Noy
Freddie	Donald Stuart
Reporter	Raymond Lawrence

First dialog film to be done in the drawing room manner shares with pioneer efforts generally the weaknesses of uncertainty. "Interference" is the finest talking production as a production yet turned out in dialog. It possesses all the elegance of gowning, suavity and gorgeous setting that distinguished Paramount's swanky dramas during the silent era. Yet with all these favorable points "Interference" is indifferent screen entertainment.

Essentially the fault seems to be a question of story development. Treatment, approach, motivation, these are the weak links in the chain. And these factors tend to stress the future dependence of talking films upon good writing even more than upon skillful directing. As a play and a Broadway success, "Interference" was a tense, tight, sophisticated melodrama, ingeniously contrived and characterized by sprightly wit. In adapting it as a talking film only the bare outline of the plot was preserved.

Plots as plots seldom mean much. It is the padding and the performance that count. The picture version testifies to this truism. The smart lines, the natural situations and the incessant tempo have gotten lost somewhere between the scenario department and the production office. What has come forth is a sumptuously upholstered picture, the characters in which talk with precise diction and achieve very little realism.

The picture is slow, generally lagging behind its audience instead of setting the pace for its absorption. Beginning is particularly faulty. The necessity because of time restrictions of condensing scenes and omitting a great deal of the original has resulted in an inadequate establishment at the start of who the characters are and why. This is particularly noticeable when Deborah Kane (Evelyn Brent) makes her first blackmail tap against Lady Marlay (Doris Kenyon). Deborah enters and says: "I have letters written by you which if published in the Morning Bugle will ruin your husband's standing as a physician." Lady Marlay consents to the shake with little or no clarifaction of why she is so fearful of the letters.

The point in the play was that Lady Marley was legally married to another man, thought dead. This bigamy angle is never brought out as the dominant motivation for the film. In a review this criticism may seem trivial or captious. But in the following of the story it has a far-reaching importance. The failure to establish Lady Marley renders much that follows hard to accept sympathetically.

Miss Brent gets first billing as Deborah Kane. Her showing is remarkable considering her total lack of experience on the speaking stage. She should avoid pajama costumes; they do not become her.

Clive Brook and William Powell know their stuff thoroughly, reading lines with the easy naturalism of stage-trained Thespians. Doris Kenyon is handsomely unbelieveable.

In cutting "Interference" down from its present length the draggy endings of various scenes can be omitted to the probable improvement of the picture. It is running 90 minutes. During the third quarter it is fairly interesting, moving forward with something approaching speed as Sir John Marley goes about removing the signs of the murder he believes his wife has committed.

"Interference" was started as a silent picture with Lothar Mendes directing. It was a later decision to have Roy J. Pomeroy re-shoot it as a talker. Pomeroy is Paramount's inventor-director. A combination of art and mechanics is revolutionary in itself. No fault to find with the directing as such. Individual sequences are well handled. Closer editing and cutting in the transitions would have helped. But mostly the burden falls on the script and the prodigality of Hollywood in throwing away successful dialog to substitute a dull and entirely business-like line of conversation almost devoid of a single relieving giggle.

Earlier in the epoch of dialog pictures "Interference" would easily have been a clean-up at the b. o. Now it's dubious with the indications that it will be little better than average. Picture is booked for eight weeks at the Criterion. That ought to be ample for the reserved seat engagement locally. Exploitation will hardly be able to entirely overcome the tendency to drag in the present length. *Land.*

JIMMY VALENTINE

(DIALOG)

Metro-Goldwyn-Mayer dialog feature production and release. Directed by Jack Conway. Adapted by A. P. Younger from Paul Armstrong play. Titles by Joe Farnham. Photographed by W. B. Glaslad. Running time, 82 minutes. At Astor, New York ($2), on run, Nov. 15.

Jimmy Valentine	William Haines
Doyle	Lionel Barrymore
Rose	Leila Hyams
Swede	Karl Dane
Avery	Tully Marshall
Mr. Lane	Howard Hickman
Bobby	Billy Butts
Little Sister	Evelyn Mills

M-G-M's first ambitious dialog sounder and a highly rated box office attraction on merit. High lights are value of cast names, especially William Haines, rich human interest translation to the screen of the successful play, and, of course, its appeal to the vogue for dialog pictures.

Notable about the talk feature here is skillful handling. Picture is thoroughly "planted" without talk but by means of titles right up to the moment when it goes into the sequence that provides the final punch. Then it turns to dialog and continues to the end. The effect of this treatment is that the preparation is accomplished swiftly, characters are drawn, preliminary circumstances are established and all the atmosphere is provided, all in broad strokes.

Then when it is desired to build up the climax explanatory matter is out of the way and the dialog goes to enrich the action and character relations.

Dialog sequences are spotty. Lionel Barrymore is better here than in his silent scenes, but Haines and Leila Hyams slip a little from the splendid pace they have kept up in the earlier and silent footage. Nevertheless it is a gripping passage, particularly the verbal fencing between the reformed crook determined to fight for the chance to go straight, and the hard-boiled detective equally determined to bring him to justice for old crimes.

It's a tricky stage scene, pretty far-fetched in its implausibility, but tremendously appealing on the sentimental side. Barrymore plays it to the last inch. Haines is inclined to overdo at this point, but his charming, youthful personality carries him through, helped vastly by the sentimental strength of the underlying situation.

Picture has strong values in its human appeal, admirably set off by a shrewd undercurrent of suave comedy. It is perhaps this element of often tender humor that makes one of the production's most valuable assets. Picture is full of surprise in amusing twists, the light touch running through the entire action like a golden thread, in swift flashes of wit and against a sentimental background. Joe Farnham has contributed to this with the fine quality of his titles, terse, bright and never gaggy.

There is the incident where the small town kid, fresh from raids on an apple orchard, confronts the crook, on his way from a bank cracking expedition. The young yegg in whose mind is working the seed of desire for reform delivers a lecture on the evil of larceny. There is a hilarious scene where the three crooks are maneuvered into church. Dipsy (dandy bit by Tully Marshall), scarcely can be restrained from frisking the devout worshippers. Another laugh when the parson opens his sermon with the quotation, "Saith the Lord, a thief hath entered My house." There is a wealth of comedy also in the dumb Swede (Karl Dane in a rich role) mixed with sentimental appeal in his dog-like loyalty to Jimmy. Capital touch of pathos is the death of Dipsy, breaking away from the trio, trying to do a job on his own and getting shot.

Never for an instant does the fine mood of any situation get away. The whole picture is paced and toned to just the right casual blandness. Quality of humor and texture of sentiment are evenly spontaneous. And it is this very guileless artlessness that saves the sometimes far-fetched situations.

This is Leila Hyams' first important talker assignment and she does herself credit. Her girlish charm fits perfectly, and she plays with an altogether captivating artlessness that goes perfectly with her young beauty.

Sound is admirably employed in many earlier scenes before the beginning of dialog. The opening has Jimmy cracking an express office safe, with the Swede and Dipsy acting as lookouts. Signals are passed in the form of whistled tunes, the relay being reproduced. Nicely woven into the action, and also used for good comedy point, when police emergency wagon clangs past and the lookout's are so paralyzed for the moment their whistling technique is badly crippled. Again singing of the choir and of the congregation is part of the scene in church. Theme song is "Love Dreams" in waltz tempo and a fascinating melody.

For the love scenes a musical background is provided in the solo singing of the theme song, reprised vocally and by orchestral accompaniment as a setting for all the romantic passages, after the style of the theatre of a few years ago, when musical accompaniment suggested the mood of the stage scene. Highly effective here. Altogether as successful use of the new sound technique as has come out. Picture ought to do better than merely last its exploitation term at the $2 scale. It scarcely measures up to a road show cleanup, but it has promise of attracting profit at the $2 scale besides setting itself for general release. That is to say it is better than a program picture forced forward for advertising purposes, but still not in the $2 big lead road staying class. *Rush.*

ON TRIAL

(DIALOG)

Warner Bros. production and release. Vitaphone all-talker based on stage play of same title by Elmer Rice. Directed by Archie Mayo. Byron Haskins, cameraman. Pauline Frederick, Bert Lytell and Lois Wilson featured. Opened Nov. 15 at Warner's, New York, indefinite run at $2 top. Running time, 91 minutes.

Joan Trask	Pauline Frederick
Robert Strickland	Bert Lytell
May Strickland	Lois Wilson
Gerald Trask	Holmes Herbert

Prosecuting Attorney	Richard Tucker
Defense Attorney	Jason Robards
Stanley Glover	Johnny Arthur
Doris Strickland	Vondell Darr
Turnbull	Franklyn Pangborn
Clerk	Fred Kelsey
Judge	Edmund Breese
Dr. Morgan	Edward Martindel

Exhibitors with Western Electric equipment will do well with "On Trial." For them, despite certain marked defects in recording, this production can be classed as a semi-special. It is not a $2 topper. If a silent version is forthcoming theatre owners cannot expect it to be, at its best, better than a fair program picture, and this will require drastic changes in the talker version, which adheres very closely to the stage play.

More than any other exhibition of Warner dialog, "On Trial" proves that talkers, to an amazing degree, are a dry-cleaning medium for older Hollywood material. In this respect Bert Lytell, especially, comes out like a new piece of goods. Voice lends him a personality even greater than his silent heyday. Richard Tucker, Jason Robards, Lois Wilson are others who are contrastingly more convincing and salable in sound.

The antithesis of these is Pauline Frederick. Recording can hardly be blamed because in the same positions on the various sets the majority of the cast enunciated throughout the greater footage in a way that made practically every word distinct and apart to those in the farthest rows. Miss Frederick was so throaty and her talking efforts were so obvious that seldom more than muffled sounds, almost indistinct in their entirety, emitted with the movement of her lips. Careful observers also detected that these sounds were imperfectly synchronized with the movement of her lips, especially the recording shots made while she was conspicuously placed on the witness stand. Miss Frederick is far from meriting featured billing, which she gets at the Warner theatre. Essayed as it is, her role is the least convincing in the cast and relegates to minor importance on the screen the part which was of stellar prominence in the original stage show.

Ground noise, or the scratching of records, is decidedly audible, even to the point of experts in the Warner home office admitting that the recording job in many instances does not shape up to previous releases. But—

Irrespective of recording and Miss Frederick's imperfect speaking performance, the stuff that pulls in the masses is in the story, which lets those masses in on the inside of a murder case. And the bulk of the cast is as close to being 100 per cent as the production is titleless.

While, like in the play, considerable courtroom activities are used, yet well-spoken parts, mannerisms and sidelines sustain interest each time until the flash-back to the scene of occurrence in the testimony. Comedy relief is injected in the court scenes, without impairment to predominating melodramatic qualities, by the brusqueness of Edmund Breese, as the judge; more, however, by Fred Kelsey, who, as the pugnacious clerk, and by using the same tonality every time he swears in a witness, works up laughs from a cackle to a roar. Richard Tucker, as the sarcastic district attorney, exacts some mirth in his handling of legal machinery with the enthusiastic and inexperienced defense counsel, Jason Robards.

The performances of tiny Vondell Darr, as the sweet but precocious daughter of the man on trial, and that of Lois Wilson, wife of the accused, are outstanding. Little Miss Darr's voice rings with an appealing quality, so childishly sincere that, with her silent talent, emotionalism 's at its peak during her testimony,

which changes the tide for her father.

Miss Wilson's recital of how she was transgressed by the man whom her husband was accused of slaying is one of the several anti-climax in the production. Missing since her husband disappeared and dramatically introduced in the courtroom on the final day of the trial, she controls her voice with such perfection that the audience is so concentrated in its tensity that the flash-back to the hotel scene where she was betrayed is barely apparent.

The shooting of Gerald Trask, played rather coldly by Holmes Herbert, as revealed in his widow's (Miss Frederick) testimony, is chilling until the revolver is exploded. The explosion is so recorded that it sounds like snapping a peanut.

Johnny Arthur does a good piece of work when recalled by the defense to give further testimony concerning the tearing of the card bearing the Trask safe combination. The audience knows that the doctor has just testified that the card could not be torn by Robert Strickland, the accused, because of a maimed hand, but Trask's secretary, out of the room at the time, joyfully reiterates his testimony. Arthur's ability to turn from comedian to tragedian when he finds he is tricked adds the final dramatic touch with his confession of stealing the money, which swings the jury for a complete exoneration of Strickland.

In the courtroom scenes only dialog prevails. The flash-backs provide conversations with a low and pleasing orchestral accompaniment. *Waly.*

GANG WAR
(Sound Plus Talking Prolog)

FBO production synchronized by RCA Photophone. Story by James Ashmore Creelman, adapted by Fred Myton. Titles by Randolph Bartlett. Cameraman, Virgil Miller. Silent version and talking prolog directed by Bert Glennon. Prolog written by Edgar Allan Wolff.
Cast in prolog, Lorin Raker, Jack McKee, Mabel Albertson and David Hartman. Cast in story, Olive Borden, Jack Pickford, Walter Long and Eddie Gribbon. At Colony, New York, week Nov. 18. Running time, 70 minutes.

This talking prolog has it all over interpolated dialog. Both as a means of building up a sales assist and strengthening a story the prolog has definite possibilities. "Gang War" without its prolog is pretty fair melodrama. With the conversational preface it makes the good rating.

Prolog is planted in newspaper office with city ed. giving two of his reporters the fireworks for their failure to get dope on the gang wars then raging in the city. Boys head for the underworld with a do or die determination. They have spotted a cafe singer as being chummy with girl friend of big bootlegger. One of the reporters trying to sheik the cafe singer gets himself thrown out. The other reporter, cute shrimp, uses persuasion. As the singer starts to tell the lowdown the fade in picks up the story proper.

Several good laughs in the talking part with the two reporters, Lorin Raker and Jack McKee, looking like a team that could be signed up safely for development. Miss Albertson is also nifty and peddles a couple of songs in bang up fashion. Edgar Allan Wolff authored the prolog.

"Gang War" is Jack Pickford's first screen appearance in a season or two. He is co-featured with Olive Borden. Story holds strong sequences, a Chinese New Year celebration in San Francisco, several machine gun episodes between rival beer runners, and some dance hall stuff. Heroine is a taxi dancer in a twinkletoe emporium

where young Pickford toots the sax. They love, but are menaced by Blackjack Connell (Eddie Gribbon) who loves the gal and doesn't fool when peeved.

Blackjack turns out to be okay. Apart from shooting a half dozen mugs, he has a heart of gold. He marries the gal, but before consumating walks into the rival mob, plugs the dirty dog (Walter Long), saves the sax player, and gets plugged himself.

Synchronization by RCA Photophone is very good. Sound and dialog both made in FBO's New York studio. Bright, lively music, not stressed, but pleasant and helpful. The RCA method appears to have the edge previously reported but not heretofore demonstrated. In the talk its elasticity seemed especially prominent. The talk never was slow or "timed" as with other talkers but adhered to an approximation of normal conversational tempo. It is a great help to the nerves.

"Gang War" will be liked and particularly in wired houses.
Land.

HOMECOMING
(GERMAN MADE)

Ufa production released by Paramount. Directed by Joe May, under supervision of Eric Pommer. Based on novel by Leonhard Frank. Screen adaptation by Fred Majo and Dr. F. Wendhausen. Featuring Dita Parlo and Lars Hansen. At Paramount, New York, week Nov. 17. Running time, over 30 minutes.

Richard	Lars Hansen
Anna	Dita Parlo
Karl	Gustav Froelich

Domestic tragedies of this nature, with the morbid, dismal quirk peculiar to German made productions, are not wanted in pictures. They have proved a failure so often that repetition should be needless, but still they continue to come and to be shown, and under a Paramount release of all things.

It is no longer considered artistic for a wife to betray her husband and the theme is certainly too old-fashioned to bear reconstruction in picture houses.

Especially when the story concerns a woman who is neither old nor young, not pretty and not ugly, not fascinating or charming or alluring or interesting in any way, then is the drama so completely devoid of entertaining qualities as to be boring.

This picture does not belong in the Paramount or in any other first run theatre. At best it is tolerable in second run neighborhoods.

There are only three players of any consequence in the cast. Of these, only one, Lars Hansen, displays any ability. The girl, Miss Parlo, photographs wretchedly in most instances, while Froelich is another whose characterization is entirely unconvincing.

It is not the kind of a theme which would interest even a small part of the American film public. It opens amid snows, mountains and war prison camps. The story starts with two friends in a war prison and, after lingering overlong in the introductory sequences, flows into some slight action.

Richard tries to escape from his Russian prison to go back to his wife, Anna. He is caught but Karl gets away and goes home to Anna. A strong friendship grows up. The girl goes for Karl but he refuses to take advantage of his pal's absence. Finally Richard returns to his home. He finds a man's clothes there. Then, waiting, he sees Karl kissing Anna.

When Richard is finally convinced in part that his wife's relations with Karl have not passed the bounds of conventionality he half-heartedly wants to accept her. But Anna no longer wants him, and he sails away. *Mori.*

SINNERS IN LOVE

FBO production featuring Olive Borden and Huntley Gordon. Others include Seena Owen and Daphne Pollard. Directed by George Melford. Adapted from "True Story" magazine yarn, New York, week Nov. 18. Running time, 57 minutes.

Any poetry written about this picture could rhyme phoney, baloney, hooey, blooey and fooly. It is taken bodily from "True Story" magazine and asks a land with public schools to accept as gospel truth a fake world with fake sinners, fake morals and a murder fading into a dream-world happiness for the good little sap that committed the murder. Just so many feet of wasted celluloid.

The minute the character played by Ernest Wood was introduced it was apparent that his sole reason for being on the screen was to make a felonious attack on Olive Borden. At one point the virtuous proprietor of a fixed roulette game tells Ernest:

"You dirty dope fiend, can't you tell a good girl when you see one?"

The picture abuses Hollywood's privileged manhandling of reality. It is a type of bilge that may appeal to molls with sawdust for brains, but will meet merited disdain from everyone grading higher than lowest.
Land.

MASKS OF THE DEVIL

(SOUND)

M-G-M production starring John Gilbert. Directed by Victor Seastrom. Based on story by Jacob Wasserman. Adapted by Svend Gade and Frances Marion. Cameraman, Oliver Marsh. Alma Rubens featured. At Capitol, New York, week Nov. 24. Running time, 68 mins.

Baron Reiner	John Gilbert
Countess Zellner	Alma Rubens
Count Palester	Theodore Roberts
Count Zellner	Frank Reicher
Virginia	Eva Von Berne
Manfred	Ralph Forbes
Virginia's Mother	Ethel Wales
Dancer	Polly Ann Young

A variation of the Dorian Gray theme of the sinner whose innocent face was a mask for a turpitudinous soul. It is composed of psuedo-metaphysics, deep-breathing passion and a lot of everyday nonsense. The result is a fairly warm John Gilbert attraction.

Picture bears the scars of production and editorial uncertainty and indecision. It leaves audience in a state of unenlightened suspense as to whether Gilbert has been shot, and if so, how seriously.

Up until the final passages of the flicker Gilbert is a charming and unscrupulous libertine on the make for an innocent school girl engaged to his best pal. To win the gal, he finances a scientific expedition to Borneo thereby getting rid of her fiance.

His campaign also includes subsidizing the girl's aunt, all in Hollywood's most prodigious manner.

Sub plot includes a countess (Alma Rubens) madly in love with the handsome, but sinister baron. She throws herself in front of an automobile, is reported seriously injured (in a caption) and thereafter drops from the story. Her husband is shot when wrestling with the baron for a pistol.

As the baron progresses in wickedness he keeps looking into a mirror and seeing himself as the devil. Of course, in the end true love trickles through his vicious habits and achieves what the movies generally call redemption.

Victor Seastrom has injected symbolism rather freely. Intermittently the "Strange Interlude" aside is introduced. Gilbert is seen registering one sentiment and thinking (in a dissolve) something quite different.

Cast holds names and possesses publicity value beyond Gilbert's own pulling powers. Eva Von Berne is introduced to America as the ingenue. Eva's haircut is her weakness now, and her sponsors must solve that problem pronto. She is in toto an appealing figure, photographing well and showing some ability and intelligence as an actress. She has a form that strikes masculine eyes as extremely nifty, although dames, with their phobia for boyish lines have been heard suggesting lamb chops and pineapple.

Theodore Roberts returns to films in a role of limited opportunities. The veteran character actor managed to sneak in a couple of his old time sure-fire tricks.

Alma Rubens, although featured in billing, has a role of no length or importance and entirely subordinate to Miss Von Berne, who obviously had the cards stacked for her. Ralph Forbes is also an on-and-offer, represented in the early sequences as a dull and negative personality. This may have been deliberate so as to obviate creation of too much sympathy when Gilbert systematically sets about to snatch his sweetie.

Ethel Wales hoking up the subsidized aunt provided occasional comedy. Only other part that got enough footage to be recognized was Frank Reicher ably impersonating the hapless count.

It is perhaps unfair to judge the synchronization on a basis of the performance covered. During the first quarter of the picture a series of things went wrong, with the sound blooey. Finally adjusted it was okay thereafter but seemed rather so-so as a score with the music not sufficiently subordinated to the picture.

"Masks of the Devil" will hardly be a wow but it should have enough feminine appeal to hold up generally. It brings Gilbert back in the type of romantic hoke the dames like.

Land.

OUTCAST

First National adaptation of the stage play of same name, directed by William Seiter. Starring Corinne Griffith. Billed as a "sound picture," although has nothing but synchronized music and minor effects. Photography by John Seitz. Titles by Forrest Halsey and Gene Towne. Running time 69 minutes. At Strand, New York, week Nov. 24.

Miriam	Corinne Griffith
Tony	James Ford
Geoffrey	Edmund Lowe
Hugh	Huntley Gordon
Valentine	Kathryn Carver
Mabel	Louise Fazenda
Moreland	Claude King
Mrs. O'Brien	Patsy O'Byrne
Fred	Sam Hardy
Joie	Lee Moran

Stage piece translated to the screen with such admirable directorial judgment and acting excellence that its sentimental appeal is vastly enhanced. Has a world of fine points in production, whale of a cast that justifies itself throughout and a persuasive sincerity in its unfolding that gives its sentimental baloney sure and irresistible heart tug.

In the silent picture era it would have been a box office cleanup. It **has the front of the audible thing in its billing, but the synchronization is distinctly disappointing. Minor effects have been added to the complete negative and often they don't belong. If the effects had been woven in during the making they might have enriched the picture a great deal, for opportunities are many.**

As it unreels there are only a few sound accessories besides the musical accompaniment. These come in the choir singing during the elaborate wedding scene and certain whoopee effects from the flat upstairs when Miriam, heroine of the title, goes back to her humble sphere after tasting of the joys of luxury and romance. Sound incidentals also are worked in in a couple of comedy bits neatly (Miriam's solitary New Year's Eve party is one), and naturally the chiming of midnight at the New Year's Eve cabaret party. All these could have been achieved by a trap drummer as well.

But even as a silent subject it is a dainty piece of work. Settings are beautiful without spilling over on the side of studio splurge, and the atmosphere is craftily created and maintained. Miss Griffith as the street walker who welcomes a better life and strives with all her native courage and honesty to hold it, does a good show.

Players and director have gone so far in restraint that some fans may call the action slow, sometimes the price of avoiding cheap cinema tricks. Discriminating fans will find much in the picture to admire and enjoy and it certainly adds to the prestige of this producer for a capital class output.

Two elaborate scenes are handled in a broad gauged way. The church wedding is splendidly carried out. General effects have spectacular proportions, but the director never once lets mere display take charge. Always he has concentrated upon the human story element and the environment is still a background. Again in the New Year's Eve cabaret scene the same holds true. Ordinarily this passage would serve as an excuse for half dressed floor show girls enough to overshadow the whole drama. But not here. Seiter gets everything he wants of spectacle and hilarious revel, and turns it all to the account of the pure story interest.

Picture has high promise as a silent box office feature, for it has the premier requisite, sentimental pull for women. It gets its hardest test at the Strand where the clientele has been educated to the real thing in sound and dialog pictures. But as a general release it looks like a winner, first on its cast names and its acting excellence and then on its basic story appeal.

Rush.

Manhattan Cocktail

(SOUND)

Paramount production and release. Two vocal numbers, no dialog. Directed by Dorothy Arzner. Scenario by Ethel Doherty from original by Ernest Vajda. George Marion's titles. At the Paramount, New York, week of Nov. 24. Running time, 72 mins.

Babs	Nancy Carroll
Fred	Richard Arlen
Bob	Danny O'Shea
Renov	Paul Lukas
Mrs. Renov	Lilyan Tashman

Reliable program feature with an expensive symbolical prolog meaning nothing but looking good and two vocal selections by Nancy Carroll. Songs are placed at about the quarter and three-quarter poles. Synchronized score and effects, but no dialog.

It's the first time Miss Carroll has been known as a vocalist, although she's a former chorister. Not bad singing, either, though not sufficient to cause Nancy to quit the screen for light opera. However, it establishes Nancy as more than just a silent puppet if she really did the singing. If she didn't, this picture contains the most perfect bit of sound and sight synchronization yet produced.

The short prolog, set in ancient Greece, looks like more coin than the picture proper. It spins the ancient fable of Ariadne and Theseus, but follows the tale only as far as convenience allows. Theseus, beloved of Ariadne, the daughter of the King of Crete, enlists as one of the 14 Greek maidens and youths periodically demanded by the Minotaur, in order to slay the monster. He proceeds with a sword and a ball of silken thread with which to mark his trail back to Ariadne. He slays the beast and returns to flee with his beloved. The second half of the fable, wherein Theseus deserts Ariadne on the Isle of Naxos, where she later weds another, is not included in "Manhattan Cocktail's" prolog, because when Fred and Babs flee from New York, the modern Minotaur, it's expected they will live happily ever after.

Story proper is of two youths and a girl, all graduates of an upstate college and all ambitious for careers that only Broadway offers. They meet ill fate at the hands of Renov, an overly cruel theatrical producer, but only two return to the sticks. Bob winds up his career with a crazy leap from the proscenium arch to the stage. As another tip off on backstage life, it's just another one **of those things. The machinations of the merciless Renov indicate that such a tactless gent wouldn't last 10 minutes in any racket. When this picture establishes him as the theatre's foremost producer, it's ridiculous. At other times the films is credulous and sweet.**

To many the youth of the ambitious trio will predominate. They look and act well, particularly Richard Arlen, Paramount's leading juvenile at the present moment.

One or two samples of Renov's system are actuated by comedy situations. His blonde and high stepping wife is forever discovering talented young men and recommending them to hubby for his shows. The only way he can exterminate the boys is to give them jobs and then air. Without jobs, they'd continue being discovered by the missus.

Despite the slight sympathy of the role, Paul Lukas is likeable as Renov because of a flashy performance. Lilyan Tashman, as the wife, also gives an excellent account of herself. They rate with the youthful trio throughout, **at times even higher. Sheet music of the two songs is on sale in the Paramount lobby.**

Bige.

Napoleon's Barber

(DIALOG)

Napoleon	Otto Matieson
Empress Josephine	Natalie Golitzin
Napoleon's Barber	Frank Reicher
Barber's Wife	Helen Ware
Barber's Son	Philippe de Lacy

This is the playlet which took Arthur Ceaser across the pond to meet Bernard Shaw, at which time the Irish wit greeted Ceasar with: "Do you mind walking around the garden till I get used to your face?"

Shaw used "Napoleon's Barber" for a prolog to one of his plays. The Roxy is using it as the feature on its innovation of a bill comprising two talking shorts, newsreel and a stage show. The Fox Coast studio has taken the Ceasar script so seriously that it's doubtful if the average film audience is going to catch the intended satire. On the other hand, as a serious effort it satisfies, and plus the novelty in the thought of a barber holding the fate of nations in his hands (from which angle most of the picture fans will see it), it's a strong and satisfying feature short. Production and the performance of Otto Matieson, as Napoleon, stand out.

Film audiences aren't going to revel in the subtlety of this writing. It's too subtle as played here. John Ford, directing, has masked it so that it unwinds much as a straightaway incident which might have come out of Ludwig's biography on the French Emperor.

It should be broad where they pay 50 cents for seats. No one knows that better than the studios, and it goes for the talkers as well as the silent features. The only basic comedy point is in the punch line when Napoleon walks out of the shop declaring he can stand for a bad barber and a revolutionist, but can't tolerate bad poetry.

For the three reels it screens and **talks like a straight dramatic sketch, with Matieson the focal point of the attention. Frank Reicher plays the anarchistic barber possessing an anti-prose complex and continually bragging of what he'll do to Napoleon if he ever were to sit in his chair. Plays it well, too, but overshadowed by Matieson. As screened, the interest is in Napoleon, not the barber.**

This may be the first instance of exterior dialog with a Fox feature. There are two such sequences—Napoleon conversing with his officers and also the barber's young son. Good recording and novel. Productionally this three-reeler is splendid. Entrance and departure of Napoleon into and from the village are impressive, as well as the sidelight of a traitor being shot outside the barber's home.

The idea, by itself, will see this one through for public acceptance. High point is that it is interesting throughout and well cast.

Ceasar can drop in at Sardi's and argue just how subtle and satirical is his brainchild. Enough that it's a worthy short. Ben Holmes did the continuity.

While presumably this is a talking short since it's under the usual feature length, by the same token it's over the talking short's usual length. Difficult to accept a 32-minute runner, in three reels, as a short picture. At the Roxy it is headlining the all-talking screen bill for this week, and is here reviewed as

a full-length program dialog picture rather than as a talking short. *Sid.*

POWER

Non-sounded Pathe production and release. Starring William Boyd. Directed by Howard Higgins. Jacqueline Logan and Alan Hale featured. At Hippodrome, New York, week Nov. 25. Running time, 60 minutes.

After the fashion of Captain Flagg and Sergeant Quirt, William Boyd and Alan Hale are pals until the next dame rumbles along. Then it's every man for himself.

Quirt and Flagg really fall in love. Boyd and Hale do, too, and also for the same frail, but theirs is just a gold-digging dame, so the love interest works only half-way.

The gal made the boys by feigning fatigue and requesting help to her hotel. The boys were just returning from work, both in he-man working clothes. She promises to wed the lads, tells them both the same dying mother story, takes them both for the $4,500 between them and blows them both in the a. m.

They say never again, and shake on it, but they both sprint after the next set of gams in sight.

It's supposed to be a comedy.

William Boyd is too good a boy to palm off in this sort of stuff. Alan Hale, always a villain, mostly German, until now, is still a threat as a comic.

Jacqueline Logan, who leaves off where the others begin, retains her mugging championship herein.

The title tacked on this Pathe feature must have been selected in an elimination contest run by another company for a third company's production. That's the only plausible explanation for its presence. *Bige.*

SISTERS OF EVE

Rayart production and independent release. Directed by Scott Pembroke. Screen story based on E. Phillips Oppenheim novel, "The Tempting of Tavernake." Hays Depew, cameraman. In cast: Anita Stewart, Betty Blythe, Creighton Hale. At Loew's New York, one day, Nov. 23, half double bill. Running time, 61 minutes.

Trying to bring an Oppenheim thriller to the screen would be a tough job, even with a lot of dough. Rayart doesn't make such a bad job of it in the last half of the footage. "Sisters of Eve," as it is called, would be far better entertainment for the grinds and the lesser second runs were it made less ridiculous by titles. These are little more than quotations from the book. Slow moving and flowery, they give the production the manifestation of having been originally in many thousands of feet. The cut-to-the-bone reaction is not so good.

The bad but beautiful wife who cokes up her wealthy husband and gets a giant keeper to squeeze out the checks has too many in-laws. Creighton Hale as Tavernake is too immune to feminine susceptibilities to be real. He gives the boys a laugh.

But when hubby finally thrashes his keeper and holds the knife to his wife just as Tavernake is about to fall from virtue, the crowd gets a momentary kick. This is rapidly undone when Tavernake gets more ministerial than ever and his real love follows him to a far away isle in the typical Oppenheim manner. The finis meets with Hays' complete approval. *Waly.*

Eva and Grasshopper

(GERMAN MADE)

Ufa production and release. Directed by Dr. George Asagaroff. In cast, Camilla Horn, Warwick Ward, Gustav Froelich. Insects created and maneuvered by Starevitsch. Titled and edited by Joseph R. Fliesler. At 55th Street Playhouse, New York, week Nov. 17. Running time, 80 minutes.

Weak attraction even for the sure-seaters.

Only redeeming feature are the mechanical insects that do most of the things humans do and also talk in sub-titles. That brings in the fairy tale element and the moral angle. Boring after the first reel.

Evidently a serious effort, but gets onyl snickers after 80 minutes. Joe Fliesler's obvious titles don't help.

HONEYMOON FLATS

Universal production and release. Directed by Millard Webb from story by Earl Derr Biggers. Screen adaptation by Mort Blumenstock. Ross Fisher, cameraman. Cast: George Lewis, Dorothy Gulliver, Bryant Washburn, Kathlyn Williams, Ward Crane. At Loew's New York, one day, Nov. 16, one half of double bill. Running time, 65 minutes.

Honest wage earning lad breaking into harness the slightly pampered daughter of a rich daddy and snooty mah.

Flat life with young wives waving hankies to commuting hubbies biggest laugh in "Honeymoon Flats," newlywed comedy of fair program rating.

Bedroom scenes warmer than expected in this kind but okayed by ring in first reel. Attempts for drama occasionally don't hook. Acting too obvious by leads. *Waly*

THE CLOUD DODGER

Universal production and release. Directed by Bruce Mitchell from story by William Lester. Starring Al Wilson. Cast includes Gloria Grey, Pewee Holmes, Julia Griffith, J. Pat O'Brien, Jim Chandler. At Tivoli, New York, Nov. 14, one-third of triple bill. Running time, 45 minutes.

It's neither here nor hither in entertainment. Occasionally bright flashes of interest through the confusing maze of conflicting action but too infrequent and insignificant to help much. As a filler in a daily change grind this film just about carries its usefulness to the limit.

Story is of the thinnest variety. It concerns a speed demon arrested just as he is eloping with the gal and put behind bars for 30 days. While her lover is in prison the girl yields to her aunt's entreaties to marry a son of wealth and the ceremony is under way when the speedster is released. He arrives by airplane in time to grab the gal.

The fight scenes on board the plane are not convincing. Injection of a throwback to Indian war days, with the principals in the modern drama spotted in period surroundings, is unnecessary and obviously used mainly for the purpose of stretching the picture out into a full length production. *Mori.*

THE VIKING

(In Color)

Herbert T. Kalmus production in Technicolor; released by Metro-Goldwyn Mayer. Adapted by Jack Cunningham from the novel "Leif the Lucky." Directed by R. William Neill. Pauline Starke, Donald Crisp, LeRoy Mason featured. At Embassy, New York, opening Nov. 29, on run at $2 top. Running time, about 100 minutes.

Leif Ericsson	Donald Crisp
Helga	Pauline Starke
Alwin	LeRoy Mason
Erle the Red	Anders Randolph
Signard	Richard Alexander
Egil	Henry Lewis Woots
Kark	Albert MacQuarrie
King Olaf	Roy Stewart
Odd	Torben Meyer
Lady Editha	Claire MacDowell
Thorhild	Julia Swayne Gordon

"The Viking" is a story for students of American history and adults. It starts at Norway and ends at Newport, R. I., all 500 years or so ago. Add 500 years after the bootleggers also found Newport a great landing place. Flaps and flips won't go dizzy over this strip, even though in natural colors. The natural color thing is forgotten after awhile, excepting it does show how many different ways make up on Pauline Starke may look.

It's a long heavy historical tale without relief. Students may find plenty of matter to argue over and they will find it interesting in a way.

Romance has been shoved in, with Miss Starke as Helga having three admirers always hanging around her. And when Lief's father, Eric, the Red, threw a broadaxe at his son because Lief had gone Christian, that was exciting during the throw—but Erie missed.

This novel writing historian, Ottilie A. Liljencrantz, if he poses as a historian of the Vikings, might inquire if the director or adapter of this film story monkeyed with Lief as a Christian. For if Lief did go Christian, his men still acted like barbarians. They grabbed off maidens and Englishmen, making them slaves, and at the same time a caption said "Lief, the Just." Just what the title writer might have added.

It's pretty tough and rough to write history and make a dame predominant to it as Helga here is. It started to look like a mutiny on the primitive sail row boat that started to discover land west of Greenland, in the third thousand feet, but the mutiny never came off. It got a start, however. More important on this trip with the rowing slaves mumbling about "Turning Back" was Helga's proposed marriage to Lief, aboard ship, in the Viking way. The Viking way is for both parties to drink from the same cup, after the second moon. Simple, excepting the wait for the second moon.

Alwin, the captured English boy, who became a Viking slave, had developed into advisor to Lief and was the main issue with Helga. He was about the only one in the picture that didn't go wholly Vikish on costuming and whiskers. Maybe Helga fell for his smooth and pale face.

Too much costuming, too much battling that never got over, and too much whiskering for a holding picture that tried to record history with a jazz love story stuck in. All ~~the flaps can get out of this for~~ their own enjoyment is a couple of kissing scenes, 4,000 feet apart between Helga and Alwin. It would have been better for popular appeal if they had set the locale in Central Park.

No sound record at the Embassy opening. Sound may be of emphasis aid to this picture, but not much else. It isn't there for the regular picture houses, even with 30 minutes out if that length may be cut.

Rather good performances and the best in pantomime by one of the unnamed ungainly crew. He looked sullen, was sullen and acted sullen. That man should have frightened the blonde Helga into a brunet, but didn't. Hel continued to blithely skip along the decks, looking for her Alwin. And Alwin was always waiting for her, gazing into the water. Sad looking guy, Alwin, and not such a fancy actor either. He had a couple of sword fights and doused one fellow in a vat of beer.

Miss Starke looked fine at times and at other times——! Donald Crisp plays Lief, the strong willed who defied his Pop. Anders Rudolph as Eric, the Pop, some roughneck. He cut one of the neighbors in two for wearing a cross. That's 500 years ago, though, and nowadays maybe the best pictures are those that can show 500 years hence. Meanwhile the pictures of today appear to get the most money.

"The Viking" may be called a fine effort. Sure seaters can play it with safety, without cutting.

SOMEONE TO LOVE

Paramount production and release. Featuring Charles Rogers and Mary Brian. Directed by F. Richard Jones. Based on a story by Alice Duer Miller. Adapted by Ray Harris, Keene Thompson and Monte Brice. Titles by George Marion, Jr. Cameraman, Allen Seigler. At Paramount, New York, week Dec. 1. Running time, 58 mins.

William Shelby	Charles (Buddy) Rogers
Joan Kendricks	Mary Brian
Aubrey Weems	William Austin
Michael Casey	Jack Oakie
Mr. Kendricks	James Kirkwood
Harriet Newton	Mary Alden
Simmons	Frank Reicher

Second Paramount picture rotating around Buddy Rogers, clean-looking youth with pretty eyes and wavy tresses. With few statistics on hand to corroborate the publicity department's claims about Rogers being a great favorite with the dames, it is difficult to estimate the commercial aspects of such a picture as "Someone to Love."

It's pretty flyweight in toto, but with some humor and a load of romance that can't fail to help, it will be okay for Paramount. The question is how it will be for exhibs.

It's farfetched fiction from the business-like Alice Duer Miller, Satevepost writer, who formularizes and standardizes her situations, to use over and over. At the same time it's a type of sugar-coated hokum that gets across with the majority of the voters.

Rogers doesn't irritate with his good looks, and if keeping his hat size, is conceivably a bet. It may be a pushover for him.

To George Marion, Jr.'s titles are due most of the picture's laughs. William Austin again functions as a comic Harvard graduate. Austin has been established as a screen funny man entirely on a basis of the sub-titles that have been put into his mouth by Marion. It's already a stencil. "Jaberwocky, a Bulgarian word meaning beat it"; "Omnia Vincit, a Latin expression signifying raspberries." They laugh every time.

Cast includes James Kirkwood, an infrequent screen player of late. Mary Brian is her usual sweetly flapperish self. Others parts just bits.

In a nutshell the plot hinges upon circumstantial evidence indicating a poor but honest sheet music salesman is a calculating and deliberate fortune hunter. Subsequently he puts a languishing girls' boarding school back on its feet, established his personal integrity and marries 20 million.

Typical Paramount quality in production, which glosses over the improbabilities. *Land.*

Caught in the Fog

(DIALOG)

Warner Bros. production and release. Starring Conrad nagel and May McAvoy. Directed by Howard Bretherton from Jerome Kingston's story. Titles by Joe Jackson. Byron Haskim, cameraman. At Strand, New York, week Dec. 1. Running time, 68 minutes.

Jane Regan .... May McAvoy
Bob .... Conrad Nagel
Detective Krausschmidt .... Mack Swain
"Silk Shirt Harry" .... Charles Gerrard
Mrs. Boisin .... Ruth Cherrington
Doctor Boisin .... Emil Chautard
Detective MacDonald .... Hugh Herbert

Ridiculous and badly put together comedy capable of being termed a talker because of four spasmodic verbal passages, no audible sequence of which runs more than five or six minutes. Picture is a set-up for Warners and must have cost all of a nickel because of the adoption of the Jed Harris idea—one set.

Warners will find out this film isn't there when the grosses start to come in from those towns where they're fast becoming sound-wise. Looks plenty cheap. Has a couple of harbor miniatures and numerous subtitles to pad out the synchronized score.

Story is one of those family jewel things in which the young heir (Nagel) surprises a crook and his girl friend in the act, is in turn taken unawares by further arrivals and the initial threesome fake a front by saying they are the newly hired servants—the son allowing the real thief and girl to think as they will.

Elderly phoney guests, supposed to be friends of the houseboat's owners, are also after the gems and later come the two comedy detectives with the heir folding the girl crook (May McAvoy) in his arms at the finish. How she became tangled up with "Silk Shirt Harry" is never explained. Audience has to take her verbal and title word for it that it's her first job and that she's "going straight" hereafter. Tie that for a love story, and who cares?

Dialog is a throw-back to the first talkers and never threatens to become smart or get much on delivery despite the presence of Hugh Herbert who had much to do with Vitaphone shorts. Cast work is just ordinary, as are the settings and photography—the rush for dialog having so far dropped back the cameraman a couple of grades so that they're again in grammar school.

And nothing seems able to square Miss McAvoy's voice. Not even Conrad Nagel's resonant bass. Picture opens with the crook and his femme partner whispering as they approach the parlor safe. She's afraid but that can't offset how silly this stage whispering sounds as a starter, plus all the resultant s's. Dialog films shouldn't whisper, not for a while anyway. Nor should they directly address the audience at the finish. Fox did it with "The River Pirate" and they laughed and razzed it at the Empire, in Syracuse, N. Y. No one thought it was particularly cute at the Strand Sunday when Nagel told the house, "Well, folks, that's all there is." It ruins every illusion and the picture is simply taking the best means by which to defeat its own purpose. "Fog" has enough trouble without adding anything.

Given normal silent speed, technique and camera work, "Caught in the Fog" might have made a fair program picture. Slowed up to allow for dialog it just won't do. In this instance a Jackson title occasionally catches a snicker and the bit of Mack Swain insisting upon telling of one of his captures is killed off by repetition instead of building after a good enough start. A burlesque fight between Nagel and Gerrard, on an awning over a roof, to make the struggle impress as a trampoline act, has its moment.

Warners will get their money back on "Fog" because they haven't got much in it and because the wired houses will play it. But the theatres aren't going to be happy with it and will soon start dodging any more than threaten a resemblance.

The dialog pushover period can't and won't last forever. *Sid.*

RILEY THE COP

(SOUND)

Fox production and release. Directed by John Ford. Story and adaptation by James Gruen and Fred Stanley. Supervised by James K. McGuiness. Photography by Charles Clark. At Roxy, New York, Dec. 1. Running time, 60 mins.

James Riley............Farrell MacDonald
Lena Krausmeyer..........Louise Fazenda
Mary Coronelli..............Nancy Drexel
Joe Smith... ....David Rollins
Hans Krausmeyer...........Harry Schultz
Caroline....................Mildred Boyd
Julius Kuchendorf
Ferdinand Shumann-Heink
Judge Coronelli.............Del Henderson
Crook.......................Mike Donlin
Mr. Kuchendorf.............Russell Powell
Sergeant.....................Tom Wilson
Munich Cabman..............Otto H. Fries
Paris Cabman..................Billy Bevan

Mildly amusing comedy about a cop on the force for 20 years in a big town, without making a single arrest. He is the hero of the kids on his beat and the friend of all those he comes in contact with. Synchronized score and minor effects but no dialog. Film should prove a fair program feature on any screen. Picture is overboard with titles, mostly of the obvious variety. As a few of them hold hearty laughs title writer deserved a break in the credit list.

Farrell MacDonald as Riley, after long service and in line for a pension, is sent to Germany to bring back one of the neighborhood boys accused of embezzlement. In a Munich beer garden he meets up with Louise Fazenda and falls for her, hook, line and sinker, only to discover later that she is the sister of Krausmeyer, the cop on the adjoining beat and his friendly enemy.

Minor love interest has David Rollins wrongfully accused of lifting his employer's dough, that way about Nancy Drexel.

Miss Fazenda is an excellent comedy foil for MacDonald, who looks the part of an Irish cop at home and abroad and plays it nicely.

John Ford's direction and the photography are all that the lightweight script merited.

Behind the German Lines

(GERMAN MADE)

(Sound)

Ufa production, released by Paramount. "Compiled by Ufa through the courtesy of the German authorities." Director not credited. Title writer and film editor not credited. At Rivoli, New York, on run, grind policy, Dec. 1. Running time, 90 minutes.

For distribution through the United States this picture is worthless. Exhibition will not bring any results excepting moderately in New York and one or two other centers with a large German element.

This is the second impossible Ufa production Paramount has undertaken to distribute within the past two weeks. The other was "Homecoming."

With no love interest and newsreel reporting despite its dramatic intent, the picture is incapable of creating any interest with the women, has no matinee possibilities and is generally unsuited for the majority of American theatres. Sound effects ridiculously insufficient in volume and entirely out of proportion where used. Scoring of average caliber.

This is not an official war picture in the sense that it was ordered, supervised or directed by the German Government. It is merely a compilation, gruesome and forbidding in its dismal picturization of scenes behind the German front, repelling in its intense, blood-drenched reality, yet grimly fascinating and elevating in its great lesson to humanity.

This is the kind of picture everyone should see, yet comparatively very few will want to see it. It is the type of picture which best serves as mighty and most effective propaganda against militarism. In it stands revealed war in its actual ghastliness, stripped of the madness of patriotism, wild flag-waving and bombastic oratory. It is war in its complete regalia of living horrors, a far more convincing and awesome spectacle than the most diabolical brutality conceivable by any directors of fictionized war pictures. The sight of arms, legs, faces, bodies; torn by shell and fire, too obviously real camera records to be questionable. They form a story no continuity could tell.

Scenes shot behind the lines were evidently taken at the firing front. The pictures in these instances are natural, the action too strong and too swift to allow for posing. War scenes showing actual conflict are limited. Picture has been built up with maps to fill the want of film of what actually happened, padded with newsreel shots of armies being mobilized and marching, while the entire production is immeasurably strengthened by a set of powerful, expertly written titles. They carry the burden of telling a coherent story without too much verbiage, and help gloss over the slim skeleton of actual war footage.

"The courtesy of the German authorities," to which attention is called in the screen billing, seems to consist mainly of data from the records and abstracts from official military sources and reproductions of orders and notes made by the German war lords during the conflict.

To the actual war scenes are also added studio sequences. These are noticeable through the protography, long, careful shots which are not usual in newsreels, and the overdrawn, though brief, characterizations of the few people used for this purpose. *Mori.*

CRAIG'S WIFE

Pathe production and release. Featuring Irene Rich and Warner Baxter. Based on George Kelly's play. Directed by William C. DeMille. Cast includes Virginia Bradford, Carroll Nye, Ethel Wales, Lilyan Tashman, George Irving, Raida Rae, Charles Hickman, Jane Keckley. At Hippdrome, New York, week Dec. 2. Running time, 62 minutes.

George Kelly's drama of the woman who cared only for her house and her physical possessions has been brought to the screen with an intelligence and faithfulness to the original that is unusual in Hollywood.

"Graig's Wife" is well adapted for the better grade cinemas, more so, indeed, than to the sub-strata of second runs and grinds. It is a class production backed up by a challenging human situation fairly familiar to all Americans. The reputation of the play, combined with the theme, offers smart exploitation ammunition for the house p. a. that knows his Mencken.

Irene Rich is Mrs. Craig to the tips of her fastidiously manicured fingers. She is vivid in her exasperating efficiency, an insufferable, egocentric super-woman with a chunk of ice for a heart and a phobia against ashes on the rug. Miss Rich, ordinarily an appealing figure, has succeeded in being thoroughly disagreeable and annoying. She impersonates a type of woman that drives a guy cuckoo.

The story is simple, hardly more than a character sketch, with a climaxing incident that impels Craig to finally realize that he has been the victim of a woman with an incurable superiority complex. The story remains faithful to the original. No attempt to make Mrs. Craig see the light. She remains consistently blind, incapable of a healthy perspective or a really sympathetic attitude toward another person.

Problem plays are not new to films. They commonly have been phonies, cheap devices to drag in sensationalism, sex stuff, and to point bogus morals. The writers, directors and producers were insincere, and all but the very low grade audience accepted the flickers for what they were worth, which wasn't much.

"Craig's Wife" is a sterling example of a clean, pulsating, cerebral drama making no concessions to bunk and adhering to worthy standards. It is one of the best pictures William C DeMille has turned out in years. While it may not be a sensational grosser, it's a picture that rates commendation. *Land.*

CARRY ON SERGEANT

(CANADIAN MADE)

Toronto, Nov. 18.

First production of Canadian International Films, Ltd. Released by same company. Written and directed by Capt. Bruce Bairnsfather. Photographed at studio of Ontario government, Trenton, by Bert Cann. In cast: Nancy Anne Hargreaves, Louise Cardi, Jimmy Savo, Niles Welch, Hugh Buckler. At Regent, Toronto, Nov. 19. Running time, 1 hour 57 minutes.

They spent a half million dollars and used a year to make this first Canadian picture. It is not worth that, but it is no flop. If the story was there it would be a picture, but as it stands they have to depend on quotas, patriotic ballyhoo, curiosity and that sort of thing to put it over.

Opens with factory scenes in locomotive plant. Pair of firemen (Hugh Buckler and Jimmy Savo) hard at work on boilers. Enter the spy. Business of examining secret papers of plant. Then comes the war and the two firemen enlist in a Canadian highland regiment. Buckler marries Nancy Hargreaves in uniform, and sails. Usual training period shots fair on comedy, then troops go up line. Plenty of trench stuff, with action cutting back frequently to estaminet behind line.

Here flash dame (Louise Cardi) tries to make Buckler, who has risen to top sergeant. He gives her the air, but months later, in midst of air raid, falls, and much film is used up showing them going up to the girl's room—and coming down again. Sergeant thinks of wife at home, goes up the line in remorse and gets killed. There is also a spy hunt that is alien to the story proper, and some explanation as to the effect American troops are going to have when they swing into action.

The photography is technically smart; in many cases beautiful. The trench scenes are true to life and the gas attack in the first battle of Ypres, in which the French Algerian troops fell back, is a great bit of picture.

Bairnsfather brings to the direction an intimate knowledge of the war as it was, and had he thrown out the preliminary bunk and taken his sergeant through more he-man stuff would have had a natural. Buckler, who plays the sergeant, is good in his first effort. He also has a good voice and may have a future in talkers. Jimmy Savo was a good comedian in vaudeville, but he seems camera shy and forced. Nancy Hargreaves, who plays the sad wife, is pretty, and that lets her out. Louise Cardi makes a sensuous lure. Would appeal to any sergeant that ever wore a kilt—and this writer was one who did.

Bairnsfather has had plenty of trouble with this thing and he probably hasn't heard the end of it yet, but give the boy credit for trying hard. For Canada the answer on this one is yes. For the British Empire a yes not so emphatic. For U. S. A. not much of a chance. *Sinclair.*

Power of the Press

Columbia production and release. Featuring Jobyna Ralston and Douglas Fairbanks, Jr. Directed by Frank Capra. Story by Fred C. Thompson. Cameraman, Ted Tetzloff. Cast includes Robert Edeson, Mildred Harris, Philo McCullough, Dell Henderson, Wheeler Oakman. At Broadway, New York, week Nov. 25. Running time, 62 mins.

Exciting and insistently engaging melodrama with a light touch that lifts it out of the stencil class.

While theatricalizing to an extent the newspaper atmosphere is exceptionally restrained and reasonable for Hollywood.

Douglas Fairbanks, Jr., is a cub reporter a newspaperman might believe in. Robert Edeson, as a city editor, is more than a caricature of journalistic enterprise. It is a moving picture newspaper refreshingly plausible if not 100 percent authentic.

Story hinges about a mayoralty election in which the candidate of the w. k. party of intelligence and morality is maneuvered into a disastrous political position by the candidate of vice and corruption. Having by his story ruined the virtuous candidate and disgraced the daughter, the young reporter, upon meeting the daughter socially, goes after the hidden aspects of the scandal and ends by exposing the whole kaboodle.

Audiences in general should like this yarn. It is told simply with no lagging moments for yawning. The production is good, cast excellent, and Frank Capra's directorial job above average.

Young Fairbanks improves rapidly as a light comedian. In ease and confidence he already belies his age and takes after his famous pop, never an introvert in the matter of self-assurance. Miss Ralston is attractive as the girl. A very suave and cold-blooded henchman of corruption is ably played by Wheeler Oakman. Mildred Harris was done dirt in a couple of shots by the camera but looked good in general as the n. g. candidate's dame.

"Power Of The Press" is one of Columbia's best and okay for a lot of the full week stands. *Land.*

BATTLE OF SOMME
(BRITISH MADE)

New Era (British) Co. production and release. Directed by M. A. Wetherell. Based on historic records of famous battle. Literary adviser, Boyd Cable. Re-edited for American presentation by Capt. Austen. Cameraman, Sydney Blythe. Week Nov. 24 at Cameo, New York. Running time, 77 minutes.

New Era, British film concern, at the Cameo, used the byline: "The British 'Big Parade'." That's a pretty strong tag as the "Big Parade" was a robust romance while there isn't a single phase of a love story in "The Battle of Somme." And not a woman principal. A war picture and as such must be considered.

Grim warfare, modern in every phase; on water, by air and on land. Sordid, even ghastly aspects there. All the methods used in the late massacre. Daring rescues by English and Canadian war heroes reproduced in colorful and exciting screen arrangement.

Picture interesting as a huge war document.

Some of the captions are typically English; others Americanized; dash of humor here and there despite the hellish environment.

"The Battle of the Somme" is worth seeing. Its photography pins a big rose on one Sydney Blythe. This Somme battle film seems a try at reality from war records and therefore doesn't qualify for comparison with American-made war pictures that drive continuity along with a pretty girl, athletic hero and a war background to bring out phony boloney heroism. However, that's film license. *Mark.*

Son of the Golden West

FBO production and release. Starring Tom Mix. Directed by Eugene Ford from story by George Pyper. In cast: Lee Shumway, Fritzi Ridgeway, Sharon Lynn, Duke Lee. At Loew's New York one day, Nov. 13, half double bill. Running time, 65 minutes.

"Son of the Golden West" has a theme composed of others that have been ground out hundreds of times. But Tom Mix is in it, does his shooting and riding and careful love making in the Mix way, so that this is a safe bet for Mix audiences.

Single handed, Mix shoots away a tribe of redskins at the opening. Just before the closing, with only a bit of cactus to shield him, he pops over man after man who not only outnumber him 15 to one, but who have the additional odds of a shack to safeguard them.

Long stretches of film are used to show Mix galloping along long stretches of prairie. A bunkhouse singer not only flats vocally, according to the titles, but bores as a long distance filler in the footage.

Sharon Lynn, Mix's leading lady, has little that will appeal. Personality registers mostly negative in this one.

The usual bad men overact in this to show their wickedness. Lassoing a house in which they have hidden themselves, troopers, called by the daring telegraph wirer (Mix) manage to pull it over. This is a fitting climax to what has gone before. *Waly.*

Triumph of Scarlet Pimpernel
(BRITISH MADE)

London, Nov. 9.

Produced by British & Dominions Company. Directed by T. Hayes Hunter. Distributed in the U. K. by W. & F. Company; U. S. and Canada by Wide World Film Corp. Censors' certificate "U." Running time, 94 minutes. Pre-view at the Marble Arch Pavilion, Nov. 5.

Sir Percy Blakeney (Scarlet Pimpernel)	Matheson Lang
Lady Blakeney	Marjorie Hume
Robespierre	Nelson Keyes
Tallien	Haddon Mason
Theresia Cabbarus	Juliet Compton

Another French Revolution film, with angles of the popularity of the authoress's novels and of Matheson Lang here. But direction and acting are only fair, with the crowd scenes well handled but at times rather badly grouped.

A weakness is Matheson Lang's disguises never do, and the suspense falls in consequence. Nelson Keys makes Robespierre a shade too stagy. He is inclined to mug and stride overmuch.

Story is a thread, concerned with Robespierre's attempts to get rid of Blakeney, responsible for saving a number of folk from the guillotine. Action is mainly devoted to Blakeney's maneuvers to outwit him and to save Lady Blakeney after Robespierre has had her abducted.

Very weak, this spot, as the lady is kidnapped and rushed over to France almost in a caption. She appears in Robespierre's house with several changes of gown and plenty of jewels.

Nothing outstanding but still fairly fast-moving and colorful melo with good sales angles for this side. Its value except as a one-day program picture in America is problematical, as its cast is not known and the subject has been done aplenty already. *Frat.*

THE OLD CODE

Crescent production, released by Anchor Film Distributing Co. Presented by Morris R. Schlank. Directed by Benjamin Franklin Wilson from the story by James Oliver Curwood. Adaptation by E. C. Maxwell. Featuring Lillian Rich and Walter McGrail. Cast includes Cliff Lyons, Melbourne McDowell, J. P. McGowan, Neva Gerber, Erwin Renard, Mary Gordon, Rhody Hathaway. At Stanley, New York, one day, Nov. 14. Running time, 65 minutes.

Concerns neither the old code nor the new. The producers never heard of codes, rules or principles, to judge from this production.

This is the kind of a picture that proves the absence of brain matter. The story could be told in three sticks of 12-point type, with blanks and dashes as the major means of expression.

It is one of the slowest, dreariest state righters ever seen.

The frozen north, also dismal and unromantic, is again the uninspiring background. A white girl, an orphan, in love with a trapper who is later beaten up twice by the villainous half-breed, disproving the contention in the subtitles relative to the heroic one's bravery.

Anywhere from three to six anti-climaxes.

Action consists mainly of lengthy subtitles, shots of people talking or gesticulating, and a couple of weakly staged fight sequences. *Mori.*

HARA-KARI
(FRENCH MADE)

Paris, Nov. 15.

"Hara-Kari," scenario by Pierre Lestringuez, produced by Marie Louise Iribe, who plays lead, sponsored by Artistes Reunis and distributed by Jean de Merly, is to be classed among the good local pictures released this season.

Scenario is perhaps a bit off color. The technical work has been carefully nursed, the redeeming point, but the story is too slow, with scenes often repeated.

It would seem Mme. Iribe was trying to catch all the sunlights, with more concern about her role than the run of the picture, an argument against a producer playing first roles.

All the same, she and Maurice Forster, as one of the producers of "Hara-Kari," have done justice to the book furnished, while Constant Remy, Liao-Szi-Jen, Labusquiere, Toshi Komou, Michaud, Andre Berley and Wurlu worked hard to put some kick into it.

A European woman, Nicole, married a cultured Asiatic, Professor Daomi, specialist in religious rites of the extreme Orient, and soon leaves her husband to join a lover, Prince Fujiwum. Daomi, learning of her intention in time, tries in vain to retain her, to warn her of such a fatal step with a man far above her in rank.

But the lovers go to a winter resort in the Alps, where the Prince is killed while mountain climbing. The Japanese ambassador receives instruction to have the Prince's body buried according to the rites of the Shinto religion. No one in Europe can do this excepting Professor Daomi. He is called in and accepts, despite his deep hatred for the deceased.

Daomi thus again meets his wife in the death chamber, and orders her out. Nicole seizes a knife and tries to commit suicide. Her former husband prevents her.

After his departure she is haunted with the idea of Hara-Kari as the means of crossing the Styx, but jibs when it comes to the plunge. Finaly she goes outside with a revolver and kills herself under more modern methods.

Daomi returns, looks with sorrow on the corpse, and pardons his ex-wife for her conjugal infidelity.

Marie Iribe reveals much talent in her impersonation of the rather un-sympathetic part of the guilty spouse, while the camera manipulation is first class. Pruning is much needed in "Hara-Kari." Kendrew.

Phyllis of the Follies

Universal production and release. Directed by Ernest Laemmle. In cast: Alice Day, Matt Moore, Edmund Burns, Lilyan Tashman. At Loew's Circle, one day, Nov. 19, half double feature. Shown with non-synchronized disk accompaniment. Running time, 65 minutes.

Highly moral and strictly conventional. Thread of story and overacted with just enough flash of backstage to work follies into title. Generally cheap production safe in the grinds but precarious for better second runs and others.

The rich bach, who meets married dame on the make, painfully exaggerated by Edmund Burns. Palming off young friend, Alice Day, as wife, Lilyan Tashman masquerades single. Little twist in situation byt story open book in first reel with accomplice falling.

Husband, Matt Moore, returning from phoney trip and unravelling of identities to bachelor seen thousands of times.

Titles, on same order. Laughs in spots with right audiences. Waly.

DOMESTIC MEDDLERS

Tiffany-Stahl production and release. Directed by James Flood from the story by Wellyn Totman. Continuity by Wellyn Totman, titles by Frederic and Fanny Hatton. Photography by Ernest Miller. Featuring Claire Windsor. Lawrence Gray and Roy D'Arcy. At Loew's New York, one day, Nov. 30. One-half of double bill. Running time, over 60 mins.

Claire	Claire Windsor
Walter	Lawrence Gray
Lew	Roy D'Arcy
Jonesy	Jed Prouty

Split week material in the neighborhoods. Plot light, direction lighter, but studio work, suitable.

Scenic settings and ability of Claire Windsor are assets.

D'Arcy and Gray behave like a couple of comedians, registering very much like a team doing a broad burlesque of heavies in the '90's.

D'Arcy, as the entirely too debonair sales manager, begins to covet the credit man's wife, early. He has Walter and Claire in his apartment for dinner. Walter passes out after a couple of drinks and the evil one lures the beautiful young wife up to a roof garden for a dance.

The whisper of scandal soon after reaches the young husband's ears with the usual suspicions arising. Did his wife and his friend do anything wrong, or no, wonders young Walter. In the end he learns of his wife's pure, sterling character and, like Sir Jos. Ginsberg, denounces the menace in loud, angry voice issuing from a distorted mouth.

Ends fittingly with a severe horsewhipping for the covetous one who, after all, couldn't be blamed, considering the nifty appearance of the pulse-quickener. *Mori.*

SILKS AND SADDLES

Universal production and release. Marion Nixon and Richard Walling featured. Directed by Robert F. Hill from story by Gerald Beaumont. Joseph Brotherton, cameraman. In cast: Mary Nolan, Otis Harlan, Claire McDowell, Sam deGrasse. At Loew's New York, one day, Nov. 27, half double bill. Running time, about 60 minutes.

Good race track entertainment along the usual lines. Scenes at the track with the young jockey double-crossing his owners for a blonde decoy have their suspense.

For a jockey Richard Walling stands in a little too high with his old Virginia employers. But this is in tone with the theme.

A safe bet for general bookings. *Waly.*

THE BARKER

(Dialog)

First National production and release. Featuring Milton Sills and Dorothy Mackaill. Adapted from Kenyon Nicholson's play of same name. Directed by George Fitzmaurice, with dialog credited to Joe Jackson. Titles by H. J. Mankiewicz; scored by Louis Silvers. Photographed by Lee Garmes. At Central, New York, twice daily, run starting Dec. 5. Running time, 86 mins. Disk (W. E.) recording.

Nifty Miller.................Milton Sills
Lou.....................Dorothy Mackaill
Carrie.....................Betty Compson
Chris Miller........Douglas Fairbanks, Jr.
Ma Benson...................Sylvia Ashton
Hap Spissel.................George Cooper
Colonel Gowdy.................S. S. Simon

Excellent picture and a good talker. For program purposes it will waltz home to a merry jingle and ought to slice itself a fair-sized chunk of weeks at the Central. Optimistic outlook is because the story is basically there. Cast plays it well. Fitzmaurice's direction doesn't let it slow up, and the four dialog sequences carry weight instead of being but added starters.

Paralleling it with the play, the picture unfolds a wider scope in that it flashes the inside of a carnival train and a free-for-all battle on the lot. Opposing this is the stage's concentrated action. Kenyon's powerful writing and the performances of Walter Houston and Claudette Colbert. Enough to give the stage version an edge, but that doesn't mean that this isn't plenty of picture.

The hanging sword of state censorship has considerably toned down the language of the lot to the point where Sills continuously turns on the mob and his woman with the one expletive, "Rat," until it loses its force. Yet, the restrictions may be said to have been offset in that scene where Sills plunges raging into the tent yelling "Carrie" after finding that she has staked Lou to vamp his boy and that the kid has married the outfit's most careless dame.

A script deletion is that Lou is Col. Gowdy's gal, but Fitzmaurice has made the Nifty-Carrie association vivid by having Sills remove a nightgown and other trinkets from his sleeper when young Chris, his son, drops in from school to spend his vacation.

Picture is well supplied with "it" in Dorothy Mackaill and Betty Compson, who flash plenty of hosiery and are occasionally in various stages of undress. It is also obvious that some of this stuff has already been cut. Pennsylvania and a few other states yet to be heard from. For honors between these two women there is no choice. If the studios featured players on merit Miss Compson's name would be on the same line as those of Sills and Miss Mackaill. In the early reels she runs ahead of her co-worker both on playing and appearance, Miss Mackaill staging a half-way and late rally in building the love story.

Sills dominates and is not only seconded but ably abetted by young Fairbanks turning in one of the best things this youngster has done. Fairbanks obtains much from the guileless boy who wants to know about things and finds out from Lou. Scenes, silent and in dialog, between the two men are uniformly good, although the conversation stiffens to become unnatural now and then. Fairbanks makes neither a silly or hardboiled kid of his Chris, catching and registering the character to convince and make understandable the reason for Lou falling prey to her own game.

All voices record well with Sills trouping as called for when he finds his boy slipping from him. His "barking" outside the tent is very much cut and dried in script. There seems to be some voice doubling as the camera pans across the lot and the voice of the barker is distantly heard. Sills, himself a former and excellently rated legit actor, has no worries on the sound thing. Climax shot of the picture has him barking again after leaving the troupe on a drunk following his son's marriage.

The four talking sequences run about three, nine, 11 and 15 minutes, respectively, close to the final 1,500 feet being all dialog, and strong. Opening is also verbal to plant the story quickly of the father wanting to make his boy a lawyer and keep him away from the lot. The action highlight is the battle in a mill town, which young Chris starts when a mill hand gets fresh with Lou. Resultant cries of "Hey, Rube" being passed down the line (a tradition with which the public is fairly familiar) and the carnival boys turning out for the struggle carries a thrill and some natural comedy which Fitzmaurice has spoiled by inserting the heaving of a pie. Interior of the carnival train stuff is new and novel regardless of how authentic.

Mankiewicz has got at least one corking laugh title in the running and Garmes' camera work is first grade. However, the main laughs in the picture revolve around Tom Dugan, who steps in for Nifty and tries to bark despite his stuttering. A cinch piece of business that builds and builds until it's almost a yell every time the house hears his voice, even though the camera may be trained on something else. This is Dugan's second stuttering role. George Cooper also has a few comedy moments which count.

Technically this feature is very good in unfolding various degrees of volume in the voices as desired. Some of it seems unusually intricate. Louis Silver's score has no theme song and is a nice fit.

There's nothing the matter with "The Barker." It runs 86 minutes and there'll be no objections.

Sid.

REVENGE

(SOUND)

Edwin Carewe production, released through United Artists. Directed by Carewe from Finis Fox's adaptation of Konrad Bercovici's "Bear Tamer's Daughter." Dolores Del Rio starred. Orchestral synchronization and occasional sound via Western Electric process. Photography by Robert Kurrle and Al Green. At Rivoli, New York, week Dec. 8. Running time, 72 minutes.

Rascha...................Dolores Del Rio
Costa......................James Marcus
Binka.......................Sophia Ortiga
Jorga........................Leroy Mason
Tina..........................Rita Carewe
Stefan........................Jose Crespo
Janeu............................Sam Appel
Leana.........................Marta Golden
Lt. De Jorga....................Jesse Cavin

Were it not for the excellent photography, colorful sets and parchment mounted titles which valiantly but vainly attempt to bolster up a suspense not there, "Revenge," also excluding its star's name, could pass for a foreign importation of the average sort. The title and star will save it from mediocrity at the box office for the first few days of a booking. Just fair is its best rating.

While excuses can be made for illogical happenings in fairy tale screen themes, few can be offered when they are not needed. "Revenge" is so written around its star and the title is so often used uselessly in the explanatory lettering that the reaction is little more than that Dolores was a spoiled child who liked her own way, got it and didn't want it.

Flashing a whip and making bears and humans cringe is the frail star's delight in her gypsy role as daughter of the animal tamer, a bloated but mild sort of character. But when they are tamed, she doesn't like them and so:

Nearly half the footage has to be taken up by a bewildered audience wondering when the conquering male will appear. And then comes a laugh, for, without changing his sweet foreign expression, after the titles vividly announce he is coming to kill her father for stabbing his old man (out of camera range), the c. h. takes a whipping. It is not until she weakens herself with the brawny whip and resorts to the milder sport of face slapping that he suddenly waxes irate and cuts off her braids.

This bold bandit, as the titles describe him, later sets his gang to barbering the heads of gyp dames who have given their haughty contemporary the long stare and ridicule for losing her own. The shearing takes place at what the lettering says is a wild gypsy revelry, but the action is nothing more than a lot of costumes and respectable tilting of bottles or tapping of kegs.

After that the bandit amuses himself by sleeping in the bed of the shorn Rascha, while she is out mountaineering to knife him. In fact, after the cutting, the titles make her gloat over a hoped-for anti-climax in that she now has an aim in life—revenge.

As for the sound end, the whip snaps out in the theatre loud enough to nearly drown huge bears' growls. Orchestra work is regular.

"Revenge" opens in card introductory of characters. This part is very effective in color.

Waly.

SHOW FOLKS

(DIALOG)

Pathe production (Ralph Block) and release. RCA synchronization and effects. Directed by Paul L. Stein. From Phillip Dunning's story. John Kraft's titles. At Colony, New York, week Dec. 9. Running time, 70 minutes.

Eddie..........................Eddie Quillan
Rita...........................Lina Basquette
Owens......................Robert Armstrong
McNary.........................Crauford Kent
Kitty........................Bessie Barriscale

The 10 minutes or thereabouts of dialog at the finish doesn't cover "Show Folks'" earlier failings as a picture, but probably will go a long way with the exhibitor and fairly far with the consumer.

It's another column of inside stuff on what may or may not be show business. It's sloppy, mushy and sobby. If not for the fine comedy performance of little Eddie Quillan and the infrequently laughable titles, there would be little to the film.

Phil Dunning's story of a mixed dancing team in love with each other must have been manhandled in the transfer to the screen. It isn't original and it isn't authentic.

The cry finish is reminiscent of "Excess Baggage," extremely so. Boy and gal hoofer have split. The gal has signed to star in a big Broadway revue (producer has a yen for her). Boy can't work without the gal. He gets another partner and a date at Keith's—theatre not mentioned, but he's happy to have landed on the "Big Time"—but the new dame walks out after the opening show flop. The only gal after all scrams from a revue rehearsal in costume and rejoins Eddie at Keith's. They do the old act and stop the show.

Eddie and Rita teamed up when Eddie found her behind a counter in a theatrical prop store. She tried to sell him a trick duck, and he sold her half of his act—the "and Partner" half—"Eddie Quillan and Partner."

They split while playing the floor in a class supper club over a meaningless little argument.

From the film it appeared Quillan did his booking direct. McNary, owner of the theatre where he breaks in his two-act, books small time dancing acts across the dinner table. He must own more than one theatre, because he drove up in a liveried wagon. Unless he doubles in the box office. His pal is Bob Owens, the big revue producer, and Owens falls on his ear for Rita backstage at the break-in slide.

After the split with Eddie, Rita signs a body-and-soul contract with Owens after accidentally seeing a story in Variety, one of those rumor things about Eddie reported marrying his new partner. It was on page one. News must have been scarce that week.

Rita, half of a straight dancing act, is described several times in the titles as Eddie's "feeder." Feeders in a dance act and straight men in sister teams.

At last a pair of picture dancers can dance. Miss Basquette should, because that's what she used to do. Quillan, in his first feature after a two-reel comedy past, is a surprise, both as dancer and all-around performer. Lina is best when dancing.

Some shots from the wings are excellent. Their show-stopping performance at Keith's closing the film, is in sound and realistically recorded, though they took a dozen bows without giving an encore.

Quillan, Basquette, Armstrong and Bessie Barriscale, latter in a small part, all get in on the closing dialog in Eddie's dressing room.

Build-up for the talk thusly: Eddie has flopped at the matinee. He is downcast and alone in his dressing room. 'Knock-knock at the door. In comes Rita. She lies to Eddie, telling him she's been fired from the revue and wants to do the old two-act. Previously Rita had been tipped to Eddie's flop and his new partner's walkout while rehearsing for Owens' revue.

Owens, who has followed Rita from his own theatre to Keith's, spills it when asking Rita why she walked. Eddie refuses to permit her to go on with him when the call buzzer rings, but she escapes from Owens' grasp and on with Eddie.

After the click, Rita returns to Eddie's dressing room to square herself with Owens. He proposes marriage, but she says she loves Eddie. Good boy, Owens says, okay, accepts defeat like a gent and agrees to cancel her revue contract. Meanwhile, while Rita and Eddie are stopping the show, Owens is convinced that he's out by a sob speech from Kitty (Bessie Barriscale).

Fadeout shows Eddie and Rita taking their final bow, with Rita called back to the stage after her confidential dressing room talk with Owens. During the Owens-Rita dialog, lasting about five minutes, the audience apparently continued applauding.

What an audience! And at Keith's!

Too much revealment of backstage life in the past for "Show Folks" to get by on that alone. The dialog might shove it over, though the dialog doesn't rate very high itself.

Long shot week-stander. *Bige.*

THREE WEEK ENDS

Paramount production and release. Starring Clara Bow. Story by Elinor Glyn, with Clarence Badger directing. Neil Hamilton featured. Titled by H. J. Mankiewicz. Harold Rosson, cameraman. Adapted by John Farrow. At the Paramount, New York, week Dec. 8. Running time, 62 mins.

Gladys O'Brien.....................Clara Bow
James Gordon..................Neil Hamilton
Turner.......................Harrison Ford
Miss Witherspoon.....Julia Swayne Gordon
Turner's Secretary...........Jack Raymond

A typical Bow and silent because the boys evidently figure Clara is strong enough to stand without a sound crutch. Nothing great about this one. Just frothy light and in showing wild youth cooped up in the tenement district.

Classifies as good program fare because of the Bow name and frivolous viewpoint. It also has a solid production, the star in a bathing suit and if that flops there is the usual display of lingerie.

That it's a big chunk off the old block can be gleaned from the cabaret scenes, indoor swimming pool house party and the theme of the poor girl seeking a dough better half.

Angle here is that the ultimate husband (Neil Hamilton) is an insurance salesman whom Clara first sees driving away in a Hispano. He's still got the car at the second flash, cinching the girl's impression. What she doesn't know is that he was on an errand for the boss and had been loaned the car for the build-up to a big policy sale.

Sale objective is a young millionaire (Harrison Ford), who has developed a promiscuous yen for Clara after viewing her in action on the cafe floor. It's on the way to this boy's party for the troupe that the principals meet. Hiding Clara's clothes during the aquatic festival is wealth's conception of a great thought until the salesman discovers the hiding place, smacks his prospective on the nose and escorts the stranded girl home.

Later comedy sequence is in the home of the scion, into which Miss Bow forces her way for complications as the mother and fiance are present. But she's only there to help her boy sell the policy, having discovered the phoney front, and when he calls to apologize it's another sock as he discovers his gal in the sumptuous boudoir. Thence the misunderstanding between the lovers and ultimate chasing of the boy by the star down the street in her cabaret costume. Finish points the moral of love willing to take a flat in the same tenement, despite the money disillusionment.

Miss Bow is her own self ably underscored by the work of Hamilton and Ford. Lesser roles are capably cast with the farce pace helped along by the titles of Mankiewicz'. Badger has whipped this froth into some sort of a frosting, and that it at least keeps moving is its chief asset. Camera work strictly okay.

It's just about what the Bow name implies. *Sid.*

UNEASY MONEY

(GERMAN MADE)

Described as a Fox-Europa picture. Made in Germany by Ufa, under direction of Karl Freund, assisted by Berthold Viertel. Story by Karl Freund. In cast are Mary Nolan (formerly Imogene Wilson), Werner Fuetterer, Oskar Homolka and Vladimir Sokoloff. Running time, one hour. At Carnegie Playhouse, New York (sure seater), at $1 top Saturdays and Sundays.

A little better than the average recent Continental, but still a long way from screen material suitable for general American release.

This one tells a fairly straight romantic story, and how it must have pained the German director to deal with love's young dream in any but a tragic manner!

However, he did his best to give it a sombre turn during the entire footage and then grudgingly touched off a dandy comedy incident near the finish and ended it happily. It is the happy ending and that single comedy touch that give it its principal merit for American exhibition.

One good idea is a sort of trick method of unfolding a story. All the incidents here are held together by the adventures of a ten-mark note. Plan is strictly literary and would serve better for a series of short stories than as the thread of a screen narrative. But it is a touch of originality.

Picture's chief merit is the remarkably good acting of Mary Nolan. Not that she's any cinema Bernhardt, but she does extremely well for the simple purposes of this tale. Rest of the cast also good. Men in continental pictures usually are all right; it's the foreign women who are the headache on this side, particularly the polite society actresses.

Anna has just started to work in a mill and as her first wages gets the ten-mark note. Aged mother hides it in the bible and blackguard son steals it. He buys a knife with the money; it goes to a patron in change and presently it leads to the murder of the customer by the blackguard son, who is then headed for the gallows.

Anna's mother tries suicide by gas as a result. Anna, roaming the streets in stunned distress, gets into the hands of the white slavers. Anna escapes, still pure, and her mother recovers, Anna goes back to her first lover and all's serene.

Meanwhile the further journeyings of the bank note are faithfully recorded—too faithfully, for the elaboration of detail here wastes a staggering amount of film—until it flutters back to Anna herself in time to go back into the family bible for the closing clinch.

The solitary gag comes when Anna rushes away from the arms of a too insistent wooer in one of those houses and starts for the river. Rich wooer, terrified, pursues. Reaching the river bank a woman is floating away in the water. He offers his whole bank roll to a rescuer. When a bystander brings the would-be suicide up, it's a bedraggled street waif. Anna turned the first corner and was on her way home.

For the sure seaters oke; for general release, out. *Rush.*

AVALANCHE

Paramount production and release. Story by Zane Grey, adapted for screen by J. Walter Ruben and Sam Mintz. Otto Brower, director. At Broadway, New York, week Dec. 2. Running time, 60 minutes.

Jack Dunton....................................Jack Holt
Jack (at 12)....................Richard Winslow
Grace...................................... Baclanova
Kitty...Doris Hill
Verde...................................John Darrow

A western, but superior to the average. It tells an intelligent story in an interesting manner and has a pair of corking leads in Jack Holt and Baclanova.

The foreign purveyor of pash runs away with her role, gaining sympathy in her meanest moments and having but a few brief chances to vent that Baclanova fury. She's not for this picture, yet the picture can thank her for a share of its value.

Holt wades through in a stolid manner, head back and chin up, but with no alternative. He plays an honest gambler whose purpose in life is to care for the boy he has reared since childhood, like a father. He cheats at cards so the boy can go to mining school and lives in sin with a dance hall gal, but still he's quite an honorable guy.

That's the sort of role they used to reserve for Harry Carey.

Only one gun play, short and snappy.

Photography high grade; direction apparently good.

A rock slide (hence title) well staged.

Doris Hill and John Darow, juvenile leads, good looking kids and therefore competent in this picture. Miss Hill bears a resemblance to Fay Wray. Whether she can troupe as well as Fay isn't known.

There's enough of everything in "Avalanche" to enable it to sell itself to women as well as men. In addition, considerably better than many of the parlor dramas played for a week in the presentation houses.

For exhibs willing to chance a western—but a good western—for a change of pace, here it is. *Bige.*

MECHANICS OF BRAIN

(RUSSIAN MADE)

Laboratory experiments recorded by Sovkino at Moscow for distribution as a popular science subject. Sovkino operated by Soviet government. Directed by Prof. Ivan Pavlov, assisted by group of Russian scientific authorities. Running time, 63 minutes. At 5th Avenue playhouse week Nov. 17.

Mike Mindlin pulled this one several weeks ago at special morning performances at $2. Now its at so-called popular prices, which means 75¢ as a rule and one buck Sundays.

Casting no stones at the scientific standing of Prof. Pavlov or the other aproned guys with trick names that nobody can grab from the title sheet in a dark theatre, this is Mindlin's private gag. In the privacy of his own home, Mindlin must have many a giggle about this art film thing. If anybody fell over the $2 tax on the picture, it must have been a deep bellow.

Film reminds one of elementary textbooks on hygiene once used in the schools to scare the kids off cigarettes and booze. Scientifically it's kindergarten stuff, dressed up in ponderous scientific patter.

Opens with five minutes of library shots in a zoo showing all Noah's ark being fed. After that another 10 minutes of pen and ink charts illuminating intimate details of the nervous system of a frog. Original Russian explanatory matter is retained, with an occasional translation to make it intelligible, English having been added on top of the Russian.

After that they experiment on dogs to show that if you feed a pup often enough within sound of a ticking metronome, the pup will presently associate dog biscuits and the measured taps of the machine. The answer to which is, What of it.

Picture has some rather shoking episodes. One shows a dog paralyzed on one side after a lobe of its brain has been removed by an operation. Another pitiful spectacle along similar lines shows a monkey crippled by removal of a part of the brain.

Numbered in the chamber of horrors is the spectacle of a 22-year-old idiot eating untidily, spattering soup, purpose being to show that his reactions to food are identical with a child of 2. Still another sequence is an intimate stydy of aparetic victim in the act of smearing bread and milk all over his bed, the idea being that paresis does the motor centers no good.

And so on to the accompaniment of such scientific catch words as "sensitory stimuli," "investigatory impulse," "unconditioned reflexes."

It is scarcely conceivable that even the film art bugs will fall for this stuff. If it is an educational subject, Dr. Kahn's medical museum on the Bowery (authorities closed it years ago) was an art gallery. Rush.

FLOATING COLLEGE

Tiffany-Stahl production and release. Directed by George Crone from the story by Stuart Anthony. Continuity by Stuart Anthony. Titles by Paul Perez. Photography by Harry Jackson. Featuring Sally O'Neil and William Collier, Jr. At Loew's New York, one day, Nov. 30. One-half of double bill. Running time, over 60 mins.

Pat Boxby..Sally O'Neil
George Dewey...........................William Collier, Jr.
Frances Boxby...................................Georgie Hale
The Dean..Harvey Clark
Snug...Georgie Harris
Nathan Boxby..E.J. Ratcliffe
Miss Cobbs..Virginia Sale

Light, frothy flap picture, partly dealing with school life on board a floating college. Should appeal to the second run and neighborhood theatres. Plenty of slow spots, but not enough to hurt the speed. A few strong laughs spotted smartly during the middle of the picture help considerably.

Sally O'Neil, photographing excellently, plays the precocious young girl, romantically inclined, with a swimming instructor as her specific prey. The older sister, Frances, desiring the young lad for her own, influences her father to an extent where he sends Sally away on an ocean trip to keep her out of trouble.

Scenes on board ship include a bedroom scene. It ought to take well on the strength of the older sister leading the young man, slightly seasick, into her own state room for the night in an endeavor to attain marrigae on the pretext of being compromised.

Younger sister, Pat, takes all the tricks and winds up as the lawfully wedded wife of the young gallant. William Collier, Jr., isn't allowed to do much except be fought over by the girls. He doesn't photograph well and unimpressive here in delivery. *Mori.*

BOHEMIAN DANCER

(GERMAN MADE)

(Sound)

Ufa production, billed as the first German sounded film. Synchronization called Bell-O-Phone. Main title doesn't mention Ufa, but gives sponsor as Bell Pictures, Inc. Director, Frederick Zelnik. Lya Mara and Harry Leidtke leads. Running time, 65 minutes. At Fifth Avenue Playhouse, week Dec. 1.

Typical second class Continental picture. Stars to American eyes are frumpy and awkward, action is dull and slow, direction silly, and story infantile. Which sums up close to zero.

This is a particularly bad example of the German output, because story is light romance with chance for dainty comedy by leading woman. They give a role that would be meat for a Clara Bow to Lya Mará, who would be none the worse for dieting and has no comedy knack whatever. A big woman in a hoyden character is probably the American fan's pet abomination. In this case it's particularly flagrant.

Director puts the coy spear carrier through endless sentimental scenes. They are meant to drip honey but really turn comic on an American screen. The German idea of tricky effect is to plant a romantic pair before each other and keep them there for a flood of flat titles. The atmosphere is provided by taking the shot back of the heroine's left ear, showing her earring and snappy angle of a German bob. Use such devices endlessly here.

The photography is sometimes good, but occasionally it has that flat, blurred look you get in Russian news reels. The titles are the last word in clumsiness and baldness.

Some of the sentimental passages are gems. For instance, the heroine meets the Grand Duke in one of those graceful naive bits, but you can't get over the startling fact that the Grand Duke himself is a ringer for Chester Conklin.

Synchronization pretty bad. Apparently an equipment delivered complete with the film and consisting of library disks and a phonograph to run them on. Musical setting doesn't keep pace with the action with any success. One passage has to do with an Austrian fox hunt and the hunt dinner. While they are holding the pack of dogs in before the start, the musical accompaniment is a galloping number appropriate for the finish of a close horse race. Change-overs of disks (assuming it is a disk system) do not keep pace with the action. Musical quality is tinny and much too loud for this house.

Just another imported makeshift for the sure-seaters, no better and no worse than the average. Sound doesn't help it at all. *Rush.*

The Isle of Lost Men

Rayart production and release. Directed by Duke Worne from story arrangement by George Pyper. Hap Depew, cameraman. In cast: Tom Santschi, Sailor Sharkey Allen Connors. At Loew's New York, one day, Dec. 4, half double bill. Running time, 62 minutes.

This is a great indie meller. Built on a theme of incorporating all of the villainy of the high seas and low life islands it moves fast and furious and would keep even an intelligent audience in suspense. No question about it for the grinds.

"The Isle of Lost Men," had it been carefully directed, would be 100 per cent for the better second runs. But rough edges overlooked by the megaphoner have also been passed up by the cutting room. The chance now is for a little retitling here and there to smooth over such sequences as an oarless lifeboat beating a barkentine under full sail to the island.

With all of its faults from the standpoint of logical continuity, this meller has ship color and island tang seldom reached by the boys who make more earnest efforts to spend dough. In many respects it is something that Ray Johnson and Rayart may be proud of. Another one like it with a little more consideration for detail should bring this producing company to the attention of box offices outside its present realm. *Waly.*

DOLLY
(FRENCH MADE)

Paris, Dec. 1.

Comedy reel evidently turned to feature Dolly Davis, local star, under the direction of Jean de Merly.

"Dolly" is sentimental to the extreme, with a scenario not particularly brilliant and moth-eaten on novelty.

Action laid on the French Riviera. While flying from Paris to Cannes a smart young man meets Dolly with her juvenile-like step-mother. Mixing up the relationship, he pays court to the latter, whereas the step-daughter loves Robert. Dolly accepts the flirtation with Robert as if intended for her, and even keeps a rendezvous intended for her step-mother.

While this has the effect of hoodwinking her father, so far as his young wife is concerned, it irritates him to find his daughter indulging in an amorous adventure with the elegant stranger. When he discovers Dolly with Robert he insists on their engagement, much to the girl's delight and the youth's disgust. Then Robert confesses to Dolly he cannot marry her because he is in love with her mother. The girl is vexed, and out of spite becomes coquetish, stylish and ultra-modern, which captivates Robert's heart.

This frail story will please for the reason Pierre Colombier has produced an excellent picture for the flappers. Cast suitable, with Dolly Davis and Andre Roanne as the lovers. Others who ran are Paul Ollivier, Jacques Floury and Mlle. Addy Cresso. No alterations are necessary, for the producer has extracted all the juice from the scenario, which in the first instance was the weak element in this emotional love stunt. *Kendrew.*

JEALOUSY
(GERMAN MADE)

Ufa production. Lya de Putti starred. Directed by Karl Grune. In cast Werner Kraus and George Alexander. Running time, 58 minutes. At 55th Street Playhouse, sure seater, week Dec. 1.

Feature length film made out of about enough material to support a short sketch. Same story has been used score of times for just that purpose—and never fascinating sketch at that. Done in the typical Continental manner, which means heavy, with slow action and sombre background.

Lya De Putti has been in this country for two years, so picture must be of far back date. It looks it.

Miss de Putti even in pictures made in the States for American audiences hasn't made much progress. In a revived foreign production she is pretty terrible, stagey to the last extreme in an artificial and theatrical part.

Direction is only fair and costuming almost grotesque. Picture's chief merit is rather good handling of crowds and some striking settings. Not much in the title. Generally another emergency booking for sure seaters lacking a better novelty.

Story has arresting start in what seems to be the murder of a woman by her husband but which turns out to be a scene in a play. With camera panning the sequence is disclosed as the climax of a stage play with audience applauding the curtain. Author makes a speech and friends in a box applaud. At after theatre supper friend tells author he is all wrong in his play theme—husbands don't get jealous in real life and bump off the sweet woman. Then and there playwright plants seed of suspicion in minds of husband and wife and the rest of the hour is devoted to showing growing discord in the family to prove playwright's case.

Whole thing phoney and audience fully aware of pretty much all that will happen at least a reel or so ahead. You could nap at intervals and still finish even with the narrative. *Rush.*

CELEBRITY

Ralph Block production and Pathe release. From play of same name by Willard Keefe. Tay Garnett, director. Cast including Robert Armstrong, Lina Basquette, Clyde Cook. At Tivoli, New York, one day (Dec. 1). Running time, 65 minutes.

As an inexpensively produced film Willard Keefe's saga of a pug doesn't rate with the previous stage presentation. But what a talker it might have made.

In sound could have been the classic of the ring. It oozes with opportunities for the new technique, yet in silent form it's little more than just another pugilistic drama.

Keefe's tale of the beefy pug, tossed onto the heights by his smart little manager because the pilot thought of publicizing his slugger as a literary light only to have the Kid give a competent ghost writer the air to write his own poems, is adhered to the letter in the picture, though lacking the details of the original.

Three excellent performances by Robert Armstrong, the pug; Clyde Cook, manager, and Lina Basquette, gal snatched from a vaude smallie to pose as "the Kid's "fee-ancy." If they can talk as well as act, they, too, missed a bet.

In silence "Celebrity" can't play beyond the grinds. *Bige.*

WEEK-END WIVES
(BRITISH MADE)

London, Dec. 1.

British International Pictures production. Released in United Kingdom by Wardour Film Co.; in America by Wide World Pictures Corp. Directed by Harry Lachman from an original by Victor Kendal and Rex Taylor. Photography by ack Cox. Censors' certificate "A." Previewed at the London Hippodrome Nov. 27. Running time, 100 mins.

Gaby Flaron-Le Grand	Estelle Brody
Max Ammon	Monty Banks
Helene Monard	Annette Benson
Henri Monard	Jameson Thomas
M. Le Grand	George Gee

Pretty good. Nicely directed, has pace, well cast, dressed and set. Just about the standard of first-class American parlor comedies on all points and actually looks as if it were made in Hollywood.

It shows that regular pictures can be made here. Titling is better than usual, some of the wording being smart.

If there were doubts whether Estelle Brody could do anything but low comedy, this film eliminates them. She does a French actress, not above cheating on friend husband, and handles it expertly. Monty Banks is the better for being out of slapstick for once. As a chaser scared of husbands he is seen to better advantage than in his other films made here to date.

Jameson Thomas plays a marriage-tired husband nearly caught cheating. A new role for him, as he usually is condemned to heavies. Does it nicely.

Credit Harry Lachman, formerly with M.-G.-M. on the Ingram outfit, with direction. There is a refreshing absence of the defect common on this side of telegraphing laughs 50 feet ahead. Exteriors in Paris and Deauville work in naturally. This one has been made for the Continent as well as for here, and it's just about sassy enough to go there, too.

Story concerns Monard, an attorney, who is visited by Gaby Flaron actress, married to Le Grand. Latter is away from home late and doesn't understand her. Neither does Monard's wife, so the two play around till it comes to arranging a week-end at Deauville.

Both married couples frame a Deauville trip, and through Gaby losing a dog and Ammon and Mrs. Monard finding it, the women meet. Gaby thinks Mrs. Monard and Ammon, the latter's boy friend, are married. When she hears they are for Deauville she says to make it a joint trip. Follows the usual mix-up.

Good enough to get universal release without drawing any "foreign picture" criticism. *Frat.*

Tyrant of Red Gulch

FBO production and release. Directed by Robert De Lacy from story by Oliver Drake. Continuity by Oliver Drake; titles by Randolph Bartlett. Starring Tom Tyler, with Frankie Darro featured. Cast includes Barney Furey, Harry Woods, M. Serge and Josephine Borio. At the Stanley, N. Y., Dec. 1. Running time, 50 mins.

Substantial western, typical in plot, characters, surroundings, and undoubtedly produced in the best interests of that elusive patronage in uncharted parts of the country.

In addition to the stalwart, slick-haired hero, Tyler, there is the tiny Frankie Darro, juvenile featured player, who screens remarkably well and plays more convincingly than most of the more mature cast members. Boy is at a disadvantage, however, in an unbecoming role.

Action is laid amid the mountains encircling a Mystery Valley, where prospectors have become lost in their search for a lost mine. The entrance to the valley is spied upon by somebody who turns out to be the ringleader of a gang working the mine with the lost prospectors as prisoners.

Girl is an orphan whose tyrannical uncle is none other than the menace. *Mori.*

DRIFTWOOD

Columbia production and release. Directed by Christy Cabanne. Screen play adapted from story by Richard Harding Davis. Don Elvarado and Marcelline Day featured. In cast: Alan Roscoe and Fritzi Brunette. Titles by Morton Blumenstock. At Stanley, New York, one day, November 30. Running time, 70 minutes.

South Sea island story with main characters a prideful prostie and a rum-soaked derelict. This one looks as if someone has taken Richard Harding Davis' yarn and merged it with "Rain" and "White Cargo," holding the best of all three. Average flicker for houses where adult trade predominates, but best passed up by those catering to the kiddies.

Plot has Marcelline Day giving her boy friend the slip when his yacht touches the Island of Luva on its way to Sydney. Barlow, the yachtsman, owns the greater part of the island, and when the girl gives his superintendent, Alan Roscoe, the chill the latter threatens to have her deported by the consul for being an unmarried women without visible means of support. To put one over on Roscoe Miss Day marries Don Alvarado, the derelict, staking him to $10 for the privilege of sharing his bed and board.

Story as a whole follows the plot of "Rain" without the marines or Rev. Davidson.

THE DANGER RIDER

Universal production and release. Starring Hoot Gibson. Directed by Henry MacRae from story by W. James and Arthur Statter. Harold Neumann, cameraman. In cast: Eugenia Gilbert and R. Reeve Eason. At Loew's New York one day, Nov. 27, half double bill. Running time, 60 minutes.

Revival in westerns would be assured were they all as good as "The Danger Rider." Gibson in this one gets a chance to get out of the old story rut. There are some fairly novel angles and a yarn, close knit for a western, that moves at a fast tempo. Great for Gibson houses and a good second on any big double-feature bill.

"The Danger Rider" has a different locale and less of the dizzy hard riding that strains audiences' eyes when too consistent.

A story with a reform farm captained by a pretty dame and Gibson as the fun-loving son of the warden who masquerades as a notorious convict, give the fans a dressing they will enjoy. *Waly.*

BEYOND THE SIERRAS

Metro-Goldwyn-Mayer production and release. Directed by Nick Grinde from story by Jack Neville. Continuity by Jack Neville. Starring Tim McCoy. Cast has Sylvia Beecher, Roy D'Arcy and Polly Moran. At Loew's New York, one-half of double bill, one day, Dec. 7. Running time, 63 mins.

One of the best of the Tim McCoy pictures yet seen. It has strong action, interesting, quick-moving continuity, plausible situations and a deal of irresistible comedy contributed by Polly Moran. It should prove a worthwhile attraction for the western inclined houses.

Miss Moran's mugging brings consistent returns. The leads, Tim McCoy and Sylvia Beecher, despite inane facial contortions during some of the love sequences, do well because of photography and make-up lending attractive appearance.

Story of a well-known type, including the masked avenger, claim jumpers, banditry, duels, pistol battles, horse riding, fist fights and so on. Pretty scenic decorations. *Mori.*

CRIMSON CANYON

Universal production and release. Directed by Ray Taylor from story by Hugh Nagron. Ted Wells starred. In cast: Lotus Thompson, Henri de Velois, Wilbur Mack. At Columbus, one day, Dec. 7, half double bill. Running time, about 60 minutes.

"The Crimson Canyon" is just one of those things with a running wild yarn and camera copping cast. Even the grinds should consider their patients on this one.

A lot of irrelevant stuff gets to the screen in a monotonous way.

Mine, old father and actress daughter, delightful stranger, couple of sham fisticuffs, etc.

Ted Wells licks 'em all and ropes the gal.

Some Sennett antics get reaction in hollower heads. *Waly.*

THE HAUNTED HOUSE

(SOUND)

Richard A. Rowland (First National) production, released by First National, with synchronization (no dialog) probably by Victor Talking Machine Co. at Camden, N. J. Directed by Benjamin Christenson; supervised by Wid Gunning. From Owen Davis' play of same title. At Paramount, New York, week Dec. 15. Running time, 65 minutes.

Mr. Rackham	Chester Conklin
Mrs. Rackham	Flora Finch
Uncle Herbert	Edmund Breese
Billy	Larry Kent
Nancy	Barbara Bedford
Nurse	Thelma Todd
Caretaker	Wm. V. Mong
Mad Doctor	Montague Love
Somnambulist	Eve Southern
Tully	Sidney Bracy
Chauffeur	Johnnie Gough

When they picked the script and cast for this one it probably seemed as though the topnotch program production of the year would be born. More standard film names in "The Haunted House" than in any two pictures around in months, and Owen Davis' play of the same title had a run on Broadway in 1924.

But, with few exceptions, the players were not the happiest of choices, and the Davis manuscript has been altered and rewritten to hold little to resemble the original.

In the play, Davis attempted to satirize "The Cat and Canary," "The Bat" and the other mystery shows around at that time and before. He succeeded in writing a very funny piece of burlesque, and as such it was accepted. In this picture the departure from his original intention as well as from his basic story is complete.

The picture is played legitimately and with no attempt to get a tongue-in-the-cheek laugh. It holds every form of sliding panel and rainstorm mystery material, as did the play, but holds it all with deadly seriousness.

Chester Conklin and Flora Finch, as easily frightened relatives, give gem performances. The rest are in, perhaps, because there wasn't anything else to do around the lot.

"The Haunted House" should get some shrieks and laughs, though it isn't as good a film as another recent boogy-man thriller, "The Terror." The latter had an added kick in its dialog. Nothing vocal to "Haunted House" outside of two songs by the sleep-walking girl, both post - production insertions. Synchronization of the song stuff was badly handled, with the player and the sound always out of kilter and neither starting nor finishing together. Either Eve Southern, as the girl, just moved her lips or sang another number than the one recorded. *Bige.*

THE CIRCUS KID

(Sound-Talking Prolog)

FBO production featuring Helene Costello, Joe E. Brown and Frankie Darro (boy). Directed by George B. Seitz from story by James Ashmore Creelman. Cameraman Philip Tannara. Titles by Randolph Bartlett. Talking prolog with George LeMaire and Co. as "Sure Shot Dick." Synchronized by RCA Photophone under direction of Josiah Zuro. At Colony, New York week Dec. 14. Running time, 65 minutes.

FBO has discovered a cute trick for making brass look like gold. Taking features intrinsically rating so-so, it rigs up comedy prologs with sure-fire laughs, give the feature itself a snappy musical synchronization, and presto! entertainment quite out of proportion to the quality that went into the can for delivery to the sound factory.

With "Gang War," which was pretty good, the yeomen service performed by Prof. Josiah Zuro and associates brought forth excellent film fare for wired houses. With "Taxi 13," rather sour dish, a laugh prolog in dialog and spirited scoring made the stew palpable.

Now, with "The Circus Kid," the acousticians have again come to the rescue and managed to convert what would otherwise be a fair daily change programmer into a passable number for more important stands.

This is the new magic of showmanship, and it is an FBO-RCA discovery. If it were possible to compute mathematically the ratio of enhancement sound has contributed to the three features mentioned it would be 20 per cent at least. That margin of enhancement can slip many a weakling in on a rain check.

The prolog with "The Circus Kid" is called "Sure Shot Dick." It is a revamp on a well-known standard routine long familiar to vaudeville, a sharpshooter who is not so accurate and his nervous jigaboo living target. It is packed solid with laughs under the skillful performance of George LeMaire, William LeMaire and William Haynes.

As a plot "The Circus Kid" is trite, imitative in theme and treatment, and working up to the now pretty thoroughly mawkish "Laugh, Clown, Laugh," situation. It's a story done over and over in the movies and squeezed dry of whatever dramatic juices may have been originally possessed.

The plot is particularly stereotyped in FBO's case, as it was used by the company once before in "Hit of the Show." The parallel extends to Joe E. Brown, the twisted-mouth tragedian, who suffered and died for unrequited love in both pictures.

Helene Costello is featured, more on her name than her performance. The Poodles Hannaford Family crack comedy riding act is used in a number of sequences, and Poodles himself, sans make-up and photographing very well, is represented as adopting Frankie Darro, the little Lord Fauntleroy of the lot and title of the picture.

One of those charming Hollywood touches has young Darro spending the night in a circus wagon wrapped comfortably and innocently in the arms of a ten-foot gorilla.

A young man answering to the prosaic name of Sam Nelson stands out as a leading man worthy of larger responsibilities. He has physique and masculinity on top of a fancy mug, and contrasts favorably with the epidemic of gentle heroes now in the ascendency.

"The Circus Kid" would never be on Broadway without that prolog and the spiritual support of those rhythmic saxes and symphonic xylophones. Incidentally the xylophone is a dandy instrument for scoring where breezy tempo plus melody is desired. *Land.*

LOVE OVER NIGHT

Pathe production and release. Starring Rod La Rocque. Directed by Edward H. Griffith. Story and adaptation by George Drumgold and Sanford Hewitt. In cast: Tom Kennedy, Mary Carr, Jeanette Loff. Photography by Joseph Mccall. Titles by John Krafft. At Times, New York, one day, Dec. 15. Running time, about 60 minutes.

Well handled comedy romance sure of a warm welcome in the grinds and the second run houses, where the patrons still care for a good story even if it isn't sounded. Tom Kennedy as the comedy detective comes close to stealing the picture, but gags given to Rod La Rocque toward the windup make things about even. Jeannette Loff is a blonde looker who rates more stories on a par with this one, and Jack Krafft's titles, on the whole not outstanding, easily top the usual set of subs tacked on this type of picture.

Plot concerns a money changer who is that way about a dame picked up at Columbus Circle. Complications lead him to believe she was an accomplice in a subway stick-up in which he was the victim.

Determined to learn the truth he follows to her Long Island estate and breaking in, is himself mistaken for a crook with a subway detective close on his trail.

Girl helps him give the low comedy dick the slip. Later he busts in on a wedding ceremony into which the girl is being forced, kidnaps her willingly and marries her himself.

La Rocque has a bit where he imitates a pair of neat gams using his hands and arms back of a screen to stall the detective. All in all the flicker packs situations that are laugh producers for the peasants.

THE YELLOW PASS

(RUSSIAN MADE)

Amkino production by Mejrabpomfilm, released by Sovkino (abroad). Directed by F. Ozep. No players featured on slides, but with Anna Sten specially mentioned on Cameo's house outside billing. At Cameo, New York, week Dec. 8 and held over. Caught Dec. 15. Running time, about 65 minutes.

Marie	Anna Sten
Peter, Her Husband	I. I. Koval Samborski
Belsky, The Landowner	M. Marokoff
His Daughter	Annel Sudakevich
The Sin-in-Law	V. P. Fogel
Katharina	S. Yakovleva
The Doorman	D. Baksheev

Over here "The Yellow Pass" is apt to draw on its title from the foreign tongue element or neighborhoods. The yellow pass or ticket is the permit issued in Russia to prosties. It's famous or infamous in Europe. There is hardly anything of interest in the Amkino-Sovkino picture, other than the possibilities the title suggests, which are not there. For other than the sure-seaters and the foreign neighborhoods, nothing.

In the running of the picture it appears that considerable of the dirt has been scissored, probably by the censors. This may be in the portion where Marie inadvertently was given a yellow ticket by the police. After another mishap or two, she is in bed with a young man met in the adjoining "dance hall," both fully clothed and apparently only intent on conversation.

Otherwise, this is the picturization of peasantry of the Russian fields, with that country as flat as Indiana. Waving stalks, ridges, ploughs and farm hands continually repeat on the screen. This Russian director, F. Ozep, is the kind of a meg guy who stops the troup because he sees a creek through the trees. He must have that shot. Mostly it is all shots. Scenery, this, that or the other. And no action. It runs 65 minutes and could be boiled to 40. Then it would still be worthless.

May be liked by the Russians on both sides as a clip from their home life and villages, but not an educational in that respect for over here.

Story terribly draggy in the opening 3,000 feet, trying to plant the tale. Minute detail and those shots. Ozep should be told not to try to make a scenic out of dirt. While the Russian scheme of film acting under his direction is a full-eyed close-up stare or glare, especially by the women. It starts away back and walks into the camera. At staring, Anna Sten is the Russian ace wide-eyeder.

Peter came home after the war. Probably an excellent soldier, but a rotten farmer. Peter's family, wife and baby, pretty poor. Wife told to go to city to nurse daughter of master. Master gave them a rocky farm and the rent ruined them. So wife blew.

In the city everyone wanted to make Marie. When the daughter's husband got in the going, Marie blew again, and got caught, innocently, in a police raid on non-ticketless dames. When given the yellow ticket by the police, Marie thought it was a reference card. And so she became a bum, according to the story, seen in the dance hall where everyone said she didn't belong, but still Marie went to bed fully clothed with the stranger, because the caption writer said she thought he was so friendly.

If the Russian peasants are really that way, they shouldn't blame 20 centuries of czars.

And then Marie went back home, to another farm, as poverty stricken as the other. All Russian peasantry is poverty stricken from this picture. As it is Sovkino released, and Sovkino is Russian-Soviet subsidized, perhaps the Soviet government will conclude that its pictures if shown over here, should run a little bit in propaganda more for Russian — not disgust. There's enough misery in America.

So Peter kissed his wife, the baby brightened up and everyone could thank heaven that was over.

TAXI 13

(SOUND)

FBO production and release directed by Marshall Neilan. Story by Scott Darling. Cameraman Phillip Tauman. Synchronized by RCA Photophone under direction of Josiah Zuro at sound studio in New York. Cast includes Chester Conklin, Martha Sleeper, Ethel Wales, Lee Moran. Special talking short prolog, "Joy Riding" with LeMaire and Phillips runs about 12 minutes. At 5th Ave., New York, Dec. 16-19. Total running time, about 70 minutes.

Pretty poor. Gets considerable support from its synchronization but hardly enough to lift it out of the class of stencil hokum.

There are laughs for the easy gigglers and enough action for the kids, but that's the total. Otherwise it's a very ordinary programmer with Chester Conklin as unsympathetic as he is unbelievable.

Lest this smack of petty faultfinding, Conklin is not singled out save as Exhibit A. He is no more unreal or kindergartenish than the picture in toto.

Picture is preceded by "Joy Riding," a comedy talking short with LeMaire and Phillips. This was added in New York and will be of benefit. It is funny stuff although having next to nothing in common with the picture. For wired houses it will help get "Taxi 13" by, and the feature needs it. *Land.*

HERO OF THE CIRCUS

(ITALIAN MADE)

Pittaluga production, released by Universal. Starring Maciste, Italian strong man. Screen story written and directed by Guy Brignone. In cast: Miny Dovia, Helen Sangro, Albert Collo, Victor Bianchi, Teranz Sala, Humbert Guarracina. Film edited by Sydney Singerman. Titles by Paul Gulick. Photography by A. Brizzi and M. Terzano. At Arena, New York, one day, Dec. 12, as half double bill. Running time, about 60 minutes.

Foreign made thriller that packs a wallop in a scene showing lions turned loose in a crowded house playing an indoor circus. Maciste, Italian strong man and screen stunt artist, is in the title role. As circus stories are now having some fling on the screen, this one rates a place in its class.

Plot concerns the backstage loves and hates of the Pommer circus Sarah, the equestrienne star of the troupe, is undermining the morale by making a play for the weakling son of the owner in order that her secret lover, the manager, can gain control.

Maciste, strong man and lion tamer, returned from a lion hunting expedition in Africa and starts to set things right. Physical combats follow with the manager and boss canvasman of the show. In order to get even the latter turns loose an untamable lion in the arena during Maciste's lion act causing a panic in the audience. This gives the strong man his chance to grapple with the lion in the auditorium, capture him and save the circus from ruin.

Story while weak in love interest is sufficient to show off Maciste's feats of strength. Photography is

good and in some sequences outstanding.

Sydney Singerman, Universal executive, edited the film and Paul
Gulick, publicity man, titled it, getting the most out of what they had
to work with.

HEAD OF THE FAMILY

Gotham production and release. Directed
by Joseph C. Boyle, from story by George
Randolph Chester. Screen adaptation by
Peter Milne. Cast including Virginia Lee
Corbin, William Russell, Mickey Bennett,
Richard Walling and Aggie Herring. At
Loew's New York, Dec. 14, one-half of
double bill. Running time, over 60 mins.

Bright, nicely-presented program
material, backed by satisfactory
scenic effects and smart studio work,
this picture should do well in the
split-week field. A pair of good
leads in Virginia Lee Corbin and
William Russell contribute to the
value of the production, overshadowing weaknesses in direction with
interesting appearance.

For an independently produced
picture the casting is exceptional.
Each player delivers in a snappy,
sophisticated style which cannot but
please in the particular territory
this production is aimed at.

Film is based on a story by the
late George Randolph Chester concerning a newly rich, much hen-
pecked plumber whose wife would
have him forget his calling and act
upstage.

A couple of plumbers in his employ offer a solution. The husband
appoints his help head of his family. He gives them power of attorney of all of his possessions. The
boys reform the weak son, correct
the flapper daughter and close up
the talkative mother.   *Mori.*

LIFE'S CROSSROADS

Excellent Pictures production released by
First Division, Gladys Hulette and Mahlon
Hamilton featured. Story and screen play
by Eloise Macie Lewis, directed by Edgar
Lewis. Cast includes Conklin and Wm.
Humphrey. At Loew's New York Dec. 11
as half double bill. Running time, 60
mins.

A love story with a jungle background. While it never really grips,
it will nevertheless stand up on
double feature bills because the old
triangle is given a novel twist.

Man and a woman, tossed upon
the coast of Africa, are the sole survivors of a shipwreck. Cordially
disliking each other, they are forced
to co-operate in order to make their
way back to the nearest point of
civilization. Things look bad when
the couple are rescued by a white
man, a fugitive from justice, who
has a ranch on the fringe of the
jungle. This man, under pretense
of being the Good Samaritan, is
after the woman and plots the death
of her companion. As he is about to
murder the man in his sick bed,
the girl shoots her pursuer.
From then on the survivors find
their hate has dwindled until the
usual clinch conclusion.

Picture is overboard on subtitles,
especially in the early reels. Shipwreck stuff is poorly constructed
and photographed.

PATHETIC SYMPHONY
(FRENCH MADE)
Paris, Dec. 9.

This release of Luna Film, produced by Nalpas and Etievant to
star Georges Carpentier, is a mixture between a drama of adventure,
a symbolic story and a sentimental
comedy.

Roland, officer in the French
spahis cavalry, Algeria, is engaged
to Zezia, daughter of the Caid, but
she is kidnapped before the marriage. Roland then returns to
France, where he weds Beatrice despite the efforts of a merry widow,

Mrs. Harwood, to net him. Latter
is vexed at the supposed rebuff and
swears to be avenged. Soon after,
Zezia sends Roland a letter appealing for help. Officer takes an airplane for Algeria, leaving his wife,
and going to the rescue of the Arab
girl he still loves. He succeeds in
freeing Zezia and accompanies her
to New York, then to Paris. Here
Mrs. Harwood learns the secret and
tells the Arab girl all about his
marriage. Shock kills Zezia, who
dies in Roland's arms while a musician is playing the Symphonie Pa-
thetique. Roland's uncle takes him
back to the wife, who is ready to
pardon and forget for the sake of
the child.

Melodramatic concoction intended
for international consumption is
good French film for the small
houses here. Appearance of Georges
Carpentier, of course, the feature.
Others in cast are Henry Krauss,
Olga Day, Regina Dalthy and Michele Verly.

Scenes shot by the Centrale Cire-
matographique, outside the studio,
in Algeria, and on the French
Riviera.   *Kendrew.*

CODE OF THE AIR

Bischoff production and release. Directed
by James P. Hogan from the story by
Barry Barrenger. Cast including Kenneth
Harlan, Arthur Rankin, June Marlowe, Wil-
liam V. Mong, Paul Weigel, James Brad-
bury, Jr., and "Silverstreak." At Loew's
New York, Dec. 14, one-half of double bill.
Running time, over 60 mins.

A states righter all the way up, or
down. As suitable as anything else
of this kind for the daily change
theatre and points south.

Starts out slowly, drags unevenly
through an uninteresting 30 minutes
or so, and finally goes into its routine consisting of the mysterious
professor-gangster, airplane attack
by the lawful avenger, rescue of the
girl plus the aged father and the
usual finish.

Picture, and audience, suffers from
extremely bad direction which
has, among many other oversights,
allowed enough superfluous footage
to intervene between actual sequences to make another states
righter.

The story further trades upon
credulity through use of a powerful
machine, held by the desert bandits,
which brings down planes by means
of a death ray. And the aged druggist is shown trading a prosperous
store for another which he had not
seen.

Love interest handled by June
Marlowe and Kenneth Harlan not
very stirring.

"Silverstreak," animal star, useful
addition.   *Mori.*

THE GATE CRASHER

Universal production and release, star-
ring Glenn Tryon and Patsy Ruth Miller.
Directed by William James Craft from
story by Jack Foley. Adapted by Vin
Moore. Cast: T. Roy Barnes, Beth Harol,
Fred Malatesta. At Loew's New York
Dec. 11 as half double bill. Running time,
about 60 mins.

Mildly amusing comedy romance
in which an amateur small town detective and an actress are the principals. Tryon is Dick Henshaw,
correspondence school sleuth, who
follows Mara Di Leon (Miss Miller)
to New York and saves her from
being robbed by her crooked publicity man.

One comedy sequence takes place
in a New York theatre on an opening night when Tryon, on the trail
of the stolen jewels, gets caught on
the stage and puts on a burlesque
performance of the show in order
to elude pursuers. Later, he outwits a gang of blackmailers in a
night club, this scene being mostly
slapstick with the action fast and
furious and, in the main, carrying
laughs.

Film rates spotting on a double
bill in the neighborhood houses due
to Tryon's all around good work.

MY MAN
(DIALOG)

Warner Brothers production and release.
Starring Fannie Brice. Directed by Archie
Mayo from Mark Canfield's story. Frank
Kesson, cameraman. Scenario by Robert
Lord. Dialog by Joe Jackson and James
Storr. At Warners, New York, for twice
daily $2 run starting Dec. 21. Running
time, 99 mins.
Fannie Brand.................Fannie Brice
Joe Halsey.................Guinn Williams
Edna Brand.................Edna Murphy
Landau.................Andre de Segurola
Waldo.................Richard Tucker
Sammy.................Billy Seay
Thorne.................Arthur Hoyt
Mrs. Schultz.................Ann Brody
Forelady.................Clarissa Selwynne

"My Man" is about the same as
watching a recital by Fannie Brice
in all the best things she has ever
done. It ought to be good and is,
but it doesn't lessen the fact that
Miss Brice looks like a one-picture
star. Film will pay for itself and
then some, but it fails to indicate
smash qualifications because it
doesn't hold outside of the star's
songs.

Miss Brice is doing seven numbers
and her "Mrs. Cohan at the Beach."
All click because she is America's
Beatrice Lillie, even if slightly Jewish. Both these two women are
subject to the same handicap,
enough is enough. That's why each
is more at home in a revue where
they can come and go with their
specialties than when playing a
book. They have both tried plot,
not too happily.

Miss Brice is not entirely at her
best when carrying this story, and
37 minutes of these 99 are silent.
But when leading up to a gag line
or delivering a number her showmanship hits.

Actual script is a succession of
thin links to give Miss Brice recurring excuses for her well known
songs. These are familiar to the
trade and cosmopolitan audiences.
There seems to be some question as
to just how well known Miss Brice
is in those spots where this picture
will be screened. If certain localities are apt to chill on the star's
distinct Hebrew clowning, it's also
true that other sectors should rejoice in it. With Miss Brice an outstanding comedienne it doesn't seem
as if "My Man" will have much
trouble in doing national and good
business.

Picture is actually running 'way
over on time, but that's because they
have crowded all of Miss Brice's explosive material into the one screening. All her pet numbers are here
and in the following sequence:
"Florodora Baby," "I'm an Indian,"
"Mrs. Cohen at the Beach," "Second-
Hand Rose," "I'd Rather Be Blue"
(new), "My Man," in comedy and
serious veins, "In the Spring," and
"If You Want the Rainbow" (new),
the latter the plug number and finale
of the feature. Star delivers both
of the new numbers straight and
well. Each is easy to the ear and
ought to become popular, which
won't hurt anything.

Film holds five dialog sequences
opening with 18 minutes of conversation and then skipping 11 to pick
up another dialog 18, 6, 3, and 17
in that order. In between are the
silent but synchronized score and
effect passages, runing anywhere
from 11 to five minutes. Miss Brice's
burlesque ballet bit is next to closing, reached by a producer giving
her a chance in his revue after
picking her out of a costume shop.
Script takes a faulty license here,
after a reasonable explanation for
the engagement, by flashing the
theatre exterior on opening night
and showing "Fanny Brand" starred
in her first show. Looked for a
minute as if Mayo, the director,
were going to establish a record by
letting the heroine make good without billing—but the studio couldn't
stand the realistic innovation and
weakened. Too bad. Entire house
is also seen applauding. Which still
leaves it up to some studio to duplicate a New York opening as is.

Theme has Miss Brice as Fannie

Brand, the clown of a theatrical costume shop, supporting a flaming youth sister (Edna Murphy) and a kid brother. Cross plot is the sister getting mixed up with the big revue man and the love interest is rather crudely dragged in through Fannie making eyes at a physical culture demonstrator and saving him from being pinched for sleeping in the park.

Pathos ingredient is the sister returning home, after being dropped by the producer, and snaring Joe away from Fannie on the eve of the wedding Fannie has practically forced on the boy. Finish has Miss Brice singing "Rainbow" on the stage as Joe leaves Edna flat in the balcony to go backstage and make amends, these two having skipped the ring. Frustrated wedding gives Miss Brice her chance to do "My Man" with a tear, but using a bridal veil instead of a lamp-post.

Dialog lags in spots, but is also studded by gags the star evidently inserted herself. Guinn (Big Boy) Williams does exceedingly well as the awkward physical specimen under obligation to Fannie and permitting himself to be coerced into marriage. He looks like one former football player who can talk and will stick in pictures. Miss Murphy has enough ability and s. a. to get the selfish sister across, while Ann Brody does a good straight for Miss Brice, cast as a tenant with a motherly interest in the star.

Technically, the picture is good and also smart. One sequence has Miss Brice singing "My Man" on the beach during a shop outing, the camera being either far away or shooting from behind Miss Brice so as to mask the synchronization of action and voice. Vitaphone can't go outdoors.

A couple of other long distance shots of Miss Brice vocalizing proves the contention of those who insist that if the lens gets too far away from the talking figure the audience can't tell who is speaking. Camera work is standard and there are times when the sound fades with the picture.

Good picture for Warners and Miss Brice, although it doesn't figure to enhance her future vaude value if she's going to cling to these old favorites. And having used up the dynamite it's going to be tough to parallel this concentration of material in another Brice picture. This one unfolds everything she can do and has done. If it has taken her all of these years to gather the material she has, how long will it take Fannie to get as much and as good stuff again? Yars and Yars. *Sid.*

THE RIVER

(SOUND)

Fox production and release. Charles Farrell and Mary Duncan featured. Directed by Frank Borzage. Based on Tristram Tupper's novel. Adapted by Philip Klein and Dwight Cummins. Cameraman Ernest Palmer. Movietone score by Maurice Baron, directed by Erno Rapee. At Gaiety, New York, opening Dec. 22 on $2 run. Running time, 84 mins.

Allen John Pender	Charles Farrell
Rosalee	Mary Duncan
Sam Thompson	Ivan Linow
Marsdon	Afredo Sabato
Widow Thompson	Margaret Mann
The Miller	Bert Woodruff

Frank Borzage has made quite a lot out of very little. The love affair of a woman of the world and a young, innocent giant of the wilderness with nothing but the vagrancies of mood, the surge and ebb of sex, for "action," is not good or easy material for moving pictures. Under the circumstances that "The River" moves at all is due to the deft handling of its sluggish material by Borzage, although Philip Klein and Dwight Cummins, script men, have probably gotten as much cinematic voltage out of Tristram Tupper's novel as could be squeezed and should be granted recognition for helpfulness.

"The River" is least effective in its attempt to use the flowing waters as a parallel symbolism for the cleansing powers of love. This does not seem important or valid, either as poetry or a background for the flimsiest of stories and a moral never clear, revelant or necessary.

"The River" is from the same well springs that brought forth "Seventh Heaven" and "Street Angel." It has less substance than either and will probably fall short of the commercial success of the others. Having so little action, it is prone to drag and having so much smouldering sexiness, it is occasionally liable to laughter.

They laughed at the Gaiety, although the laughter was not entirely clear in motive. Coming from the women mostly there may have been a factor of overflowing tension expressing itself in tittering. While the situation did border on what New York sophisticates consider imperative giggle material, it can be safely assumed that outside of a few locations the objective attitude will not be conspicuous.

However, there is a legitimate source of ridicule that should promptly be eliminated. That is the theme song sung as a movietone prolog by a 250-pound tenor and an extremely hefty soprano. When he sings to her that he found happiness when he found her, the result is absurd.

Charles Farrell adds another fine performance to his series. His following among the women will be an important asset in carrying this picture while the men will enjoy Mary Duncan. She was perfectly cast, successfully accomplishing the various moods. All other parts mere bits.

Borzage has a talent for these whipped cream fluffs of whimsy. Essentially its unreality achieving illusion. "The River" will probably interest those who see it, although afterward it may be that, thinking it over, patrons will wonder what it was all about.

It does not seem to have cost a great deal, so will easily make dough for Fox, and ought to be okay, though hardly sensational, for exhibs. *Land*

DREAM OF LOVE

(SOUND)

M-G-M production and release. Co-starring Joan Crawford and Nils Asther. Directed by Fred Niblo. Based on "Adrienne Lecouvreur." Scenario by Dorothy Farnum. Titles by Marian Ainslee. Cameraman, Oliver Marsh. At Capitol, New York, week Dec. 22. Running time, 65 mins.

Adrienne	Joan Crawford
Mauritz	Nils Asther
Duchess	Aileen Pringle
Duke	Warner Oland
Countess	Carmel Myers
Count	Harry Reinhardt
Baron	Harry Myers
Michonet	Alphonse Martell
Ivan	Fletcher Norton

Another load of romantic slush from the sugar commissary of M-G-M. This picture is intended not only to enthrall the flaps but to put Nils Asther on the map as the big thing among the newer crop of sheiks Asther is systematically thrust forward and given every advantage of getting across, as he seems to be doing with ease and momentum, judging by dame comment in the Capitol Saturday afternoon.

One remark heard was: "Isn't he adorable looking?" And at another point when, to strike up a conversation with the heroine (Joan Crawford), Asther is represented as resorting to the usual blarney an obviously emotional feminine voice was heard declaring: "Oh, he's a devil!"

Asther is a new type, but falling into the boyish man, or manly boy, group that seems to be the materialization of the maiden's dreams. There seems no question that he is on the commencement end of a feminine landslide of endorsement.

"Dream of Love" is no great shakes as a story. Fred Niblo has succeeded in lacquering the production with a thin but shiny lustre. He has softened the sex stuff and made a rather matter of fact overnight party between Crawford and Asther seem quite innocent.

There is similarity in situation with "The Command to Love," dramatic success of last season, in that, for diplomatic reasons, a handsome young man undertakes to make love to the rich wife of an influential man. Aileen Pringle impersonates the lady thus loved, while the young prince's heart really goes out to the gypsy who became a great emotional actress.

Miss Crawford is considerably less than convincing in the later scenes when she is supposed to be a stage celebrity. Her close-cropped bob was inappropriate, for one thing, and she never suggested the part, for another. She is out of the picture more than she is in it, however, and quite plainly was subordinated to the task of giving Asther everything.

Small parts are played with neat competence by Warner Oland, Carmel Myers and Harry Myers, the latter getting in several laughs.

"Dream of Love," because of its probable dame appeal, should be a good program attraction, despite its familiar plot elements and hopelessly unreal persons. It looks like a fair-sized coin investment. *Land.*

PREP AND PEP

(SOUND)

Fox production and release. Featuring David Rollins and Nancy Drexel. Directed by David Butler from his own and Wm. Conselman's story. Edited by M. S. Boylan. S. Wagner and J. Valentine, photographers. Scored by Rapee and Rothafel. At Roxy, New York, week Dec. 22. Running time, 59 minutes.

Cyrile Reade	David Rollins
Dorothy Marsh	Nancy Drexel
Flash Wells	John Darrow
Col. Marsh	E. H. Calvert
Bunk Hill	Frank Albertson

Another of Fox's adolescent tales, this time having a Culver Military Academy setting and light program material possessing enough comedy-action to make it brisk, clean, and good. It's really one more in the series which Fox has adopted on Universal's "Collegians" idea, except that these haven't taken their college boards yet. This military school stuff generally burns up the boy scouts. But the R. O. T. C. youths snicker at the jack knife wielders, too, so it's all square there.

Shots of Culver are interesting. With the exception of one school, Culver has been recognized by the Government as a distinguished institution (from a military standpoint) more times than any other like academic seat in the country, always excluding West Point. The exception is the Manlius School, just outside of Syracuse, N. Y., and which has been honored by the Government for 25 consecutive years. Of these two institutions Culver has double the enrollment and is one of the most heavily endowed secondary schools in the country. It's plant is magnificent.

That much this picture demonstrates while Butler, the director, has flavored his one layer cake of a script with enough realistic atmosphere to carry across the morale and spirit of the undergraduate body. As a whole "Prep and Pep" is a corking break for Culver on publicity and shapes as a complete Fox reverse from the lingerie displays of the Madges and Olives.

One of these kid pictures is not unlike a glass of cold water in the midst of some bad Scotch. Subject has got to move fast and hold laughs, for the basic interest isn't there, but as this one can check on both those requirements it figures as diverting and especially timely during the holidays, undoubtedly why it's at the Roxy at this date.

As regards the playing personnel, no one does as much to hold this feature up as Frank Albertson, cast as Bunk Hill, a fresh kid with a grouch against the school's top athlete who carries on his feud by managing the weak kneed hero into a triumph over the self-confident Flash Wells. Albertson plays this role of comedy vengeance all the way from the opening gun and gets more than average foiling from John Darrow, as Flash, a good looking youngster who does the juvenile bully and makes him real through not overplaying or having been given impossible things to do.

Butler has taken his share of theatrical license but hasn't gone out of bounds too far or too often. The picture really belongs to Albertson and Darrow. More so than to Rollins and Miss Drexel who are featured. Rollins gives a genuine characterization of the boy who finds his father's athletic record at the school a terrific handicap, but Miss Drexel is just the femme angle minus the poignana love interest the supposed ages of the principals prohibit.

Story winds up by young Reade finally starting to overhaul his Dad's reputation through saving the girl and Flash from a fire and the three boys pledging themselves to a union at graduation. Meanwhile, Reade has taken the worst of it from Flash in a grudge boxing bout arranged by Bunk and a relay race. Bunk (Albertson) also scissors Flash's full dress uniform so that it rips apart on him during a formal guard mount, the laugh wallop of the picture and plenty funny.

Young Reade's comeback starts as he breaks a horse to make the Black Horse Troop, a famed Culver body whose mounts and riding hall were completely destroyed in a fire a few years ago. Young Reade then finds Flash taking Bunk to task for the guard mount humiliation, pitches in and the enemies are hard at it when the call comes to turn the troop out for the village fire. It is here Reade saves Flash and the girl and wins his father's nickname of "Tiger."

Not a frame of football in any of the spools, the closest approach to this being a flash of Bob Peck as track coach, Peck probably having captained from center the greatest Pittsburgh team to ever make a first down—the club of '16.

Yarn for this picture holds water because it turns up the angle of how hard it is for a youngster to follow an illustrious parent in school, especially if he isn't particularly athletic. There's a lot of that around in many a college or prep school.

No dialog but film has its synchronized score and effects, the latter well handled and showing judgment in not trying to catch everything. E. H. Calvert makes a human commandant of cadets with the flashes of this Indiana school always sightly. Picture will likely bring in many inquiries for catalogs (Culver's objective) and show a neat profit, Fox's desired reaction. Camera work and titling first class. *Sid.*

WHAT A NIGHT

Paramount production and release. Directed by Edward Sutherland from story by Lloyd Corrigan and Grover Jones. Screen adaptation by Louise Long. Starring Bebe Daniels; Neil Hamilton and William Austin featured. Titles by Herman J. Mancklewcz. At Paramount, New York, week Dec. 22. Running time, 60 mins.

Dorothy Winston	Bebe Daniels
Joe Madison	Neil Hamilton
Percy Penfield	William Austin
Mike Corney	Wheeler Oakman
Editor Madison	Charles Sellon
Patterson	Charles Hill Mailes
Snarky	Ernie Adams

Another newspaper yarn built around breezy atmosphere and a lot of gags. It's not real, natural or particularly enthralling as a newspaper story but it is mildly entertaining picture material which should round out satisfactorily on a weekly basis.

Comedy is forced all the way and fails to create as much response as the same efforts would have resulted in through natural humor. Holds a pretty good average of laughs. Sprightly continuity in story and action helps greatly in getting attention.

It is in the attempts at broad farce that the production fails to make the full weight. The heroine is pictured as a half-witted society gal, not only bitten by the reporting bug but also possessed of the conventional poodle and a habit of dropping things for the weary hero to pick up. From boredom and disgust Neil Hamilton does a complete about face for the finale by declaring amorous intentions of which there previously had been no trace.

One of the important sequences is drawn out to an absurd length, rendered more so through the absence of the comedy which was attempted and vitally lacking. The girl reporter, with the society editor, are shown trying to get a photograph of the crooked civic official in company with a gang leader (Wheeler Oakman). First she drops the flashlight power, then she gets her finger stuck in a hose pipe, and finally endangers the proceedings by an oncoming sneeze which she works hard to control.

In her escape Bebe Daniels figures in a funny piece of business, dropping from the wall of the building on to a pyramid of barrels which her two helpers had piled up. She falls right through the six or seven barrels and emerges on the ground.

Oakman, as the highly polished gangster leader, de vers the best acting. Without too frequent flashes of gats and minus the rough stuff, Oakman does it in exceptionally good style. He has developed that characterization ever since "Lights of New York," through several pictures and now has it where it can stand but little improvement. The gunman, threatening to squeal on his boss, is another strong and realistic character interpreter. Hamilton handles his reportorial assignment with ease.

Plot is about a newspaper engaged in unveiling the underworld as ruling the city through the crooked mayor. *Mori.*

ABIE'S IRISH ROSE

(SOUND)
(2d Review)

Sound version of the once silent Paramount screening of the Anne Nichols stage play. Theme songs, "Rosemary" and "Little Irish Rose," by J. S. Zamecnik. At the Rialto, N. Y., Dec. 22. Running time, 80 minutes.

Use of added sound makes "Abie" a different matter. Most of the serious religious material has been eliminated and the story treatment has been greatly lightened..

Accompanying score has been skillfully done, a facile accompaniment that holds to the action in its varying moods and introduces a certain humor of suggestion with its switch from Irish to Jewish theme melody, military idea in the war scenes and the like.

Vocal sequences appear in three main parts. One is the birth of Abie, where Solomon calls down to the trumpeting beddler to lay off the horn blowing, for a light laugh. In the child bed scene, where Abie's mother is found dead, Solomon builds up his grief to the extent of reciting the prayer for the dead, a touching bit of sentiment here, and planting a later dramatic passage. School yard scene has been retained in its old form, except that in the new version the children all recite the pledge to the flag and march into the school house, the camera being trained on Abie for this passage. Device used in the first version is retained, that of having the parade of the World War soldiers marching down Fifth avenue directly upon the end of the school yard scene, effective in the first picture and doubly effective here.

The sequence where Abie plays in the entertainment hut over there for a gang of soldiers is splendidly built up in the love passage for the hero and heroine (latter has had stage experience and shows it), and also with side shots at the assembled doughboys, the latter for comedy effect. Whistles blow, calling the soldiers into action. And the following passages have to do with the sentimental relations between friendly priest and rabbi working in the trenches, irrespective of creed

Back to America and into the Irish-Jewish love story proceeds without dialog, although the mechanical accompaniment goes right on. Dialog comes in again after the wedding, when both fathers have cast off the two young lovers, Levy making it a strong dramatic passage by a twin recital of the prayer for the dead, a highlight of pathos in both instances.

Sound is again to the front at the comedy finish, where the rival fathers are under the mistaken belief the grandchild is a boy or a girl Much more effective business for comedy than the silent comedy was before.

Generally speaking sound has heightened the effect of the picture. Also the footage has been cut 49 minutes and the story moves much faster. On both counts the picture is greatly improved. Indeed, to the point where it looks like a run prospect at the Rialto instead of an utter flop for $2. *Rush.*

CAPTAIN SWAGGER

(SOUND)

Pathe production and release. Sound (no dialog) by RCA Photophone. Edward H. Griffiths, director. Story by Leonard Praskins. Rod La Rocque starred. At Strand, New York, week Dec. 22. Running time, 70 minutes.

Hugh Drummong	Rod La Rocque
Sue	Sue Carol
Poole	Richard Tucker
Jean	Victor Potel
Von Stahl	Ulric Haupt

Only the added novelty and kick in screen dialog would have made this a reliable feature for week-run in a straight film bill. At the Strand, without talk and in that kind of a show, it misses Broadway classification by several miles.

The highly incredible story of "Captain Swagger" was given little relief in the screen treatment. Well acted, but the chances for acting are few and slight, and seemingly competently directed. But the script made it tough all around.

Rod La Rocque as Captain Swagger is first an American dare-devil in the French aviation service during the war. He is assigned to bring down Von Stahl, this picture's version of Germany's war ace, of which there have been many. He does, but in German territory. He lands to rescue Von Stahl from the burning plane. In gratitude the opposition flyer covers his getaway from a Hun patrol after making the Yank a present of his engraved gat.

That happened, according to title, in 1917. In 1928 Swagger is a New York boulevardier, living by his wits but with the b. r. down to a deuce. Picks up Stahl's automatic and hunts for someone to stick up. First car that comes along (Rolls roadster) holds a gal just about to walk home. That's the begining of the big romance, with the dame leaving her all-hands host flat to trail along with the amateur bandit.

Later on Swagger and the girl are a Russian dance team in a class night club. The place is held up by a band of mugs headed by none other than Von Stahl, now very Americanized. Because Von Stahl once saved his life, Swagger helps him out of the jam through several ridiculous moves and brings about the return of the jewels to the club's guests.

And about midway Swagger, in want of food, asks $10 on the Von Stahl pistol. The unk carries it to the rear for valuation, where Von Stahl again shows just in the nick of time. Von Stahl is fencing there, and when spotting his own gun and then his old pal Swagger through the peep hole, ordered unk to give the lad $200 on the gun, not $10. And Swag didn't ask why. If he had, and had received an answer, it would have resulted in a different story and picture. If Pathe would take a chance on another "Swagger" there's the spot to drift into a second story.

Cafe shots are of the usual film type but well done herein. Especially good are the doublers for the principals in the dance numbers, while in closeup La Rocque impresses fairly well with a few hocks and knee-drops.

Outside of La Rocque and Miss Carol, cast is unimportant. Victor Potel, who used to be the screen's champ imbecile character man, has the part of Swagger's loyal flunkey, calling for little more than sly lifting of the eyebrows whenever a woman enters the case.

In the early (war) portion, La Rocque makes his entrance in a French taxicap, presumably returning from furlough. The arm and leg dame routine, with no face visible, is included in the cab stuff. When assigned to go after Von Stahl, Swagger is so intoxicated he cannot stand on his feet, yet he sails his ship and brings down the terror of the war while still drunk. *Bige.*

MOTHER OF MINE

(FRENCH MADE)

Zerovich production released by Zakoro. Directed by Jacques Feyder. Author not credited on screen or program. At Cameo, New York, week Dec. 22. Running time, 65 minutes.

The Mother	Rachel Devrys
The Father	Victor Vina
The Priest	Henry Duval
Pierette	Pierette Honyez
Arlette Dertiois	Arlette Peyron
Jean Amsler	Jean Forrest

This astounding idea is paralyzing in its novelty and in the mightiness of its conceptions. Great thoughts, cradled in the mind of this French producer, fostered reverently amid the snowclad mountains of Switzerland, evidently brought on this orgy of celluloid consumption.

The ingenuity in plotting in construction as exhibited here is amazing—amazingly stupid. It is presented as if it were a masterpiece. It is intended to affect the audience as a startling scrutiny of child psychology.

A little boy is left without his mother. He is deeply affected. He cries. He doesn't like his stepmother. He hates his foster-sister. So much so that he splashes her with water on one occasion and throws her favorite doll away on another. Tragic? Yes or no?

There's a priest in it. Meant to be clever because shown playing chess and toying thoughtfully with a pipe. He is a well-meaning, kindly person, but his prominence is inexplicable. He is the unofficial adviser. He tells the boy's father to marry again and tells the boy he must like it.

There are shots of the dead mother's grave, flashes of mountain peaks, pictures of horses walking, trotting and sitting, men, women, children, clothes, snow, a house, and the little boy getting nuttier with every passing sequence.

What the producers have here is the story of a particularly unpleasant child, precocious and obnoxious, a terrible infant always in trouble and troubling others. That his mother died fails to make him interesting.

No acting, no meaning. Blank faces registering at the behest of the blank heads who directed. No story, merely a series of incidents, shots of things and beings, without significance.

It's one of those things that shouldn't have been mentioned in the first place. *Mori.*

LUCRECIA BORGIA

(ITALIAN MADE)

Produced and directed by Richard Oswald. Released here through Unusual Photoplays, Inc. Edited and titled by J. W. McConaughy. In cast: Conrad Veidt, Lina Hals, Paul Wegener. At Little Carnegie Playhouse beginning Dec. 21. Running time, about 75 mins.

Italy's most notorious lady is here revised into a handsome stout who goes into wedlock and sticks. In this picture version her brother, Cesare, is the bad egg. Imposing sets and realistic locales, with a flash of dramatic merit here and there, will get it by in the arty houses.

Story is weak with no sustained suspense and overacting is a conspicuous distraction. Precarious for general bookings.

Anti-Catholic propagandists will probably take to the way the wicked Cesare, who is always having some one killed for no particular reason, winds the Pope around his finger in this yarn.

Excepting the color in the settings, weird lighting and an attack on a castle, little remains to impress. Mixture of intrigues by Veidt, as Cesare, are so exaggerated as to be without meaning. His attitude toward his sister, Lucretia, would be repugnant were the part not played so artificially by Lina Haid. *Waly.*

SALLY'S SHOULDERS

FBO production and release, directed b Lynn Shores, from novel by Beatrice Burton. In cast: Lois Wilson, Huntley Gordon, George Hackathorne. At Loew's New York, one day, Dec. 18, as half double bill. Running time, 65 minutes.

Good domestic drama with a box office title that will win approval in the neighborhood houses on a double bill. Flicker could have stood alone in some of the better class houses, being modern except for a few sequences that call for an elastic imagination.

Plot has Lois Wilson, formerly of the elite, running a restaurant and at the same time trying to keep her giddy sister and bad boy brother out of trouble. Latter, employed in a bank, gets in a jam in a night club which has a game room attached. Under obligation to the gambling house operator he becomes involved in raid on his sister's restaurant, where the night club operators have secreted a load of booze. Her means of a livlihood shut off by an immediate padlock, Sally is forced to become a hostess in the gambling roadhouse that has paved the way for her brother's and sister's downfall.

Sequences that follow parallel

some of the scenes from the current stage play, "Night Hostess."

Title refers to Sally's brave shoulders in managing things and will not disappoint those who pay in expecting something else.

NEW MEN

(FRENCH MADE)

Paris, Dec. 10.

The successful comedy, "Les Nouveaux Messieurs," of F. de Croisset and the late Robert de Flers, created at the Theatre des Varieties a few years ago, forms the scenario under the same title of perhaps the most successful picture produced by Jacques Feyder.

A trade show was held the day he sailed for New York to join the M-G-M at Hollywood.

This political satire in its screen version, made here by the Albatross and Sequana Films concerns, has caused a rumpus in political circles. French censors bluntly refused to issue a visa for "Les Nouveaux Messieurs" (as cabled). Whether the officials will consent to its release after careful purging remains to be seen. Authorities could not stop the comedy for the reason there is no theatrical censor in France. Only the police can interfere if a play is likely to cause a scandal. With a picture it is another thing—the board of film examiners has full control, and that power has been exercised in this instance.

As a consequence, this latest French picture of Feyder is destined for a greater international success than the original play, if it can eventually obtain the necessary visa from the French censors for its release and does not cause diplomatic intervention in foreign countries.

After all, it is but an amusing skit, without cruelty, of local parliamentary procedure.

Gaillac, humble but ambitious electrician, is employed by the Opera. He falls in love with Suzanne, ballet dancer, who is richly supported by a prominent politician and wealthy box holder, Count Montoire.

During a labor strike Gaillac is named secretary of his group, during which he proves himself so proficient and noisy as a leader that at the next parliamentary election he is elected a member of the Chamber of Deputies (local Congress, which really governs in France) by the Radical party. After sundry intrigues, cleverly done, he is given a seat in the Cabinet as Secretary of Labor.

Suzanne, meanwhile, has faithfully divided her dear little self between her two powerful political protectors, but makes no secret of her preference for the boy of her own station of life, the former electrician. The two men are thus rivals in love and politics.

Gaby Morlay, excellent comedienne, does Suzanne with charm and pep. Albert Prejean is the successful union leader and Henry Roussell the crafty aristocrat. Other roles well handled.

"Les Nouveux Messieurs" contains several worthy, interesting episodes, such as a turbulent session of the Chamber of Deputies (faithfully reproduced), inauguration by a Socialist deputy of workingmen's dwellings, up-to-date political meeting, behind the scenes at the Opera and other phases of the popular story.

It is a good French production for feature showing. *Kendrew.*

THE SPEED CLASSIC

Excellent (film) production, released by First Division. Directed by Bruce Mitchell from adaptation of story, "They're Off," writer not credited. Edited by Bertha Montalgen. In cast: Rex Lease, Milred Harris, Mitchell Lewis, James Mason, Helen Jerome Eddy, Otis Harlan. At Arena, New York, one day, Dec. 22, half double bill. Running time, 50 minutes.

Mildly entertaining comedy drama of the auto race tracks, rating classification as the lesser of a twin screen bill. Race track shots are mostly newsreel stuff, and as automobile races carry even less thrill than bicycle races because of the remote action and general uncertainty of what its all about, this one won't pull 'em out of their seats in the grinds.

Story concerns Rex Lease, wealthy youth who has a mania for fast cars, and his fiancee, Mildred Harris, who objects to his competing in the speed classic against professional drivers. When she breaks the engagement Jerry goes on a whoopee, making expedition to Tia Juana, gets in a jam in the gambling rooms below the lines and is thrown in the cooler by the Mex gendarmes.

Old stuff, but good for the neighborhood kids.

The Love Commandment

(GERMAN-MADE)

Produced by Eichberg and released by Ufa. Directed by Victor Janson. In cast: Lilian Harvey, Werner Fuetterer, Dina Gralla, Bruno Kastner. At 55th St. Playhouse week Dec. 22. Running time, 70 minutes.

One of those continentals which has succumbed to the Reg Denny-Priscilla Dean-Rin-Tin-Tin lines. "The Love Commandment" tries to combine the three in one. It achieves the longest 70 minutes on record at the 55th street. They probably calculated that if the American triumvirate were so popular in Germany they certainly would storm American box offices if emulated by Fatherland specialists.

A tall, good-looking blonde lad pulls the Denny but he takes himself too seriously. When the director yelled comedy he registered, but fans here won't laugh or cry. Lilian Harvey busts into his bachelor quarters a la Dean in male burg regalia. She is too kittenish and too obviously anxious to please to be the Priscilla of old housetop days. Then she either gets shaked or suspected all the rest of the way except at the end when she forces a kiss through tears of reformation.

Little black dog does the Warner beast of silent recollection on small scale. Not as "intelligent" as titles would make him.

Old hoke of the crooked dame living with the virile but virtuous young man until she is forced to dip back into the trade long enough to get his sister out of jam with come-on man.

All in all great specimen of the steerage stuff that gets overlooked at the Island. *Waly.*

KING COWBOY

FBO production and release, directed by Robert DeLacey from story by S. E. V. Taylor. Scenario by F. H. Clark. Stars Tom Mix. Cast: Frank Leigh, Sally Blane, Barney Furey, Lew Meehan, W. Mace and Robert Fleming. At Loew's New York, as half of double feature Dec. 21. Running time, over 65 mins.

One of the best westerns seen recently and above the average Mix quality. A natural for any house that can stand westerns and strong enough to fill in on the split weeks.

Conventional but appealing story of a band of cowboys on an expedition in Africa in search of their missing boss. Daughter of the missing man accompanies the outfit. Plans show the layout for oil fields involved and are responsible for the capture of the American by the African Amir. Resultant harem scenes carry a few laughs.

Captured by the Amir and deprived of all firearms, the cowboys are virtually at the mercy of the African despot until they stage a midnight raid on the arsenal to recover their guns, and start a war following a rodeo given for the Amir's pleasure.

Sally Blane is attractive as the heroine. Good support all around for Mix and scenic settings are lavish. *Mori.*

COCKTAILS

(BRITISH MADE)

Produced by British International Pictures Co. Directed by Monty Banks. Original story and continuity by Scott Sydney and Rex Taylor. Scenario by Val Valentine. Photography by Walter Blakeley and James Rogers. Produced in conjunction with Palladium Co., Copenhagen. Censors' Certificate U. Previewed at the London Hippodrome Dec. 4. Running time, 100 mins.

Gin	Pat
It	Patachon
Betty	Enid Stamp-Taylor
Jerry	Tony Wylde
Giles	Nigel Barrie
Bosco	Harry Terry

This is the film which Scott Sydney came over to direct, but he died suddenly and the scenario went over to the two Danish comedians whom it exploits. It was in turn given to Monty Banks, and comes out pretty much as eight reels of slapstick with a dash of meller.

Story just a thread. Two stowaways get mixed up with a dope smuggling gang, one of the latter trying to frame Jerry so he himself can get away with his ward, Betty, who has money. Rest is mostly chase stuff, story coming in a bit with Jerry arrested for smuggling dope and being proved innocent by the stowaways, one of whom develops to be Betty's father with a long lost memory.

Starts fairly well, but runs very thin in the middle and drags so that it almost loses out. Would stand cutting and be better for it. Speeds up nicely later and makes a fast finish with the two Danes hopping a steam truck and coming into court in the middle of Jerry's trial by wall crashing.

Full of hoke and trick stuff and fine for a double program, especially if the other feature is heavy. Nigel Barrie comes out better in the character heavy class than in recent attempts to play as a juvenile, and Tony Wylde looks like he might be a find. He is a recruit from the ranks of jazz drummers and troups well.

The two Danish comedians are average, and too much addicted to Continental vaude and circus ideas of comedy, especially of the taking a mouthful and squirting it sort. Will do fairly well here, and may slip in on your side. Technically, it is okay. *Frat.*

Land of the Silver Fox

Warner Bros. production and release. Starring Rin Tin Tin. In cast: Leila Hyams, John Miljan, Carroll Nye, Tom Santschi. Directed by Ray Enright from story by Charles Condon, and screen play by Edward Smith. Titles by Joe Jackson. At Loew's, New York, one day, Dec. 18; half double bill. Running time, 60 minutes.

In this one the dog star comes to the aid of his benefactor two or three times, backed up with a convincing story of the Canadian Northwest and capable performances by Leila Hyams and Carroll Nye, as the love interest. John Miljan and Tom Santschi as the twin menaces. It can't miss with the kids in the neighborhoods where Rinty brings 'em in.

Plot deals with the love affair of a romantic trapper of silver fox furs and the orphan girl owner of a trading post of which Miljan is the manager.

81ST ST.

(Vaudfilm)

The neighbors sure turn out Sunday night at this house. Capacity before theatre time, plenty of standees paid to stand out the show since the reserved seat policy forestalls any possibility of inheriting a vacant perch.

The show was paced by Ed Stanley as m. c., later doing his own act with Ginger. Stanley has improved immeasurably in a year when last caught at a Loew stand, having discarded the eccentric get-up and working more legit. The titian Ginger is a hot number and a cutie. She pulled the same "riddles with syrup" gag that Sid Silvers slips Phil Baker and otherwise their stuff is plenty oke.

Opening was a so-so seven-piece tab, "Along Broadway," holding six specialty gals and a juvenile, the latter weak. Act is slip-shod and open to plenty of editing. That Spanish danseuse might also give her tight gown a little personal attention. It's too tight and doesn't flatter the lines. Margaret Keir, prima, is featured.

Kitty O'Connor (New Acts) scored solidly in the deuce, after Stanley had contributed a couple of laughs. Joe Keno and Rosie Green also registered, the act begging off with a speechlet and announcing that the Sunday laws prohibit their daughter, Mitzi, dcing her impressions. The youngster is now part of the act and a talented kidlet.

Stanley and Ginger and the Bernie Cummins Hotel Biltmore Orchestra (New Acts) closed well in sequence. "Outcast" (Corinne Griffith), feature. *Abel.*

HIPPODROME

(Vaudfilm)

Moderation seems a virtue little respected by whoever does the planning for those nationality concerts at the Hip. Basically a good idea the concerts are being bolixed by too great length and too little sagacity.

Currently there is the horse and donkey teaming of Russian and Jewish music. What the tunes of the Volga have in common with the chants of Asia Minor is not easy to discern, and when a travelog jumps without even a warning caption from just east of the Suez Canal to the Main Street of Petrograd, an impression of careless assembly is inevitable.

The abrupt appearances of first a Jewish cantor and later a Russian basso and with the whole affair running well nigh half an hour made the concert rather hit or miss.

The two singers preceded Walter McNally, an Irish tenor, in the deuce. McNally was reviewed at the Hip as a new act early in 1925. At that time it was remarked that his soup and fish seemed to have been made in Ireland. McNally seems to still have the same tailor. The overlapping effect might be due to an unusual chest expansion, in which case a cutaway would provide equal dignity with less obvious starch.

All standards in the vaude end cut to five acts because of two features, Clara Bow in "Three Week Ends" (Par), and a revival of the same producer's "Peter Pan" for Christmas week. With the long concert, show was overflowing the three-hour mark.

Agee's Horses and his trained bull, the latter a creature of considerable scientific fascination, opened the show, a great act for the Hip any week and especially apt for kiddie week.

Dainty Marie, still a classy trapezist, was next to closing. The centre position was bulwarked by Jack Benny, whose routine ought by now to be fairly well memorized by most of the Variety staff.

Alexander and Olesen, closing the divertissements, are comedians who labor and fret not but manage to make the pushovers laugh quite heartily with their lazy rehash of senile puns, bits and slapstick. They are the ne plus ultra of any old thing. Probably ideal for kiddie week. *Land.*

1929

LUCKY BOY

(DIALOG AND SONGS)

Tiffany-Stahl production and release. Two prints, in sound and silent. George Jessel starred, with dialog and captions by Mr. Jessel. Adapted from a story by Viola Brothers Shore. Directed by Norman Taurog and Charles C. Wilson. Sound portion supervised by Rudolph Flothow. Harry Jackson and Frank Zukor, cameramen. R. C. A. Photophone sounded and synchronized. Scored by Dr. Hugo Riesenfeld. Theme song, "My Mother's Eyes," written by L. Wolfe Gilbert, Abel Baer, Lewis Young and Axt. Song's publisher, Feist's. Invitation pre-view at Embassy theatre, New York, Jan. 4. Running time, around 100 minutes. Release date not announced. Understood this talker goes direct to regular picture houses.

Georgie Jessel	George Jessel
Momma Jessel	Rosa Rosanova
Poppa Jessel	William K. Strauss
Eleanor	Margaret Quimby
Mrs. Ellis	Gwen Lee
Mr. Ellis	Richard Tucker
Mr. Trent	Gayne Whitman
Becky	Mary Doran

"Lucky Boy" is a very good talking picture with songs, and with George Jessel who sings the songs, five of them. It is backed up by a logical, likable story bearing on the stage and having a boy's love for his mother as the main motif, although a romance is worked in. It also has a theme song, "My Mother's Eyes," that rings like a bullseye among the theme numbers so popular now. Beside these, "Lucky Boy" holds comedy, mostly in the dialog and captions, both written by Mr. Jessel. So this picture can go where the Jolsons already have gone. If the house men care to, though the picture easily stands up by itself, they should make an exploitation play to bring the Jolson fans back for comparisons. Advance work along that line might prove helpful for the b. o.

Of course, admitting no person in the world today can sing a ballad or a pop like Al Jolson, don't doubt but that George Jessel can sing. On top of that Jessel is a finished actor, on the stage or screen. He has a personality and a naturalness here of performance, whether acting, singing or talking, that sends itself over. This talker squares Jessel for any of his other and easier ones, including shorts.

With the R. C. A. Photophone process for the dialog, singing and sounds. If you want to accept this Photophone sounding, heard for the first time by this reviewer in a theatre (previously heard in the projection room of Photophone), then Photophone for sounding seems to have it considerably over the others. Clear, without a blur or whirr, you must hear Jessel talk and sing to know how far ahead Photophone appears to be as a sound reproducer. In one number, "My Real Sweetheart," Jessel sings, he is supposed to be on the rear end of an observation car on a transcontinental train. It's the actual sameness as though Jessel were singing himself in "one," near the apron.

Nearly everyone of the principals speak. About the lightest voiced is Margaret Quimby, the ingenue, who looks sweetly nice. It appears as though by voice control at the studio (R. C. A. Photophone in New York), whatever imperfections may have been in her natural tones were deleted through holding it down to a quite low register.

There is a quartet (people) drawing room scene with the four bridge players all talking. It is clear. A comedy situation and the best laugh situation in the picture, though Jessel has picked some of his best gags and cross fire for other laughs, besides his captions.

Ample direction all of the way, with the continuity making no slips. Dialog particularly well staged.

It's the story of a Bronx boy of Jewish parents, his father a jeweler and he the store's clerk. But he wants to be an actor. Rejected by agents and managers, the boy accepts his mother's earings to pawn, to rent a dark theatre in his neighborhood for one night to display his talent. Neighbors flock to see Georgie, but he falls down on all of the rent ($500) for the one night, and the house is darkened with the crowd turned away.

Determined to make good, the boy works his way to San Francisco, goes on at an amateur night (finely handled in a directorial way) and through that lands in a class Frisco nite club as its sole entertainer. That's where the romance starts.

Back home, the old folks are listening in one evening and by good fortune get San Francisco. They hear their Georgie announced and singing. In the club he sang "Bouquet of Memories" and the theme song, "Mother's Eyes," having earlier in the picture started the singing with "My Blackbirds Are Bluebirds Now."

A message from home says his mother is ill. He returns, and the picture closes with Jessel the new star of "Lucky Boy" under the management of what seemed to be intended for Flo Ziegfeld, the first manager to turn him down when he had tried to break in in the east.

The mother stuff here is stronger than the romantic matter. There is a very bright sequence of the bridge party in a society home.

Entertainment in this picture, fairly evenly balanced, for Jessel is admittedly a showman besides a splendid actor and one of great promise. Any number of the girls will go for Jessel in pictures—he looks that good. **Enough strength in the story and the mother and romance section for the silent version to get over, though naturally the songs greatly strengthen up the dialog print, as Jolson's songs added to his talkers.**

"Lucky Boy" as first outlined had Jessel as a singing waiter. With Jolson's "Singing Fool" and Jolson in that character, Jessel quite ethically declined to appear as a singing waiter. Probably the opening of this picture was changed to correspond with his wishes. In that way the opening section may have been made a bit long. It takes over three reels to get the boy out of the Bronx bound for the coast. Picture now running in 8,500 feet.

Some of the bigger producers might have chanced this "Lucky Boy" as a Broadway $2 special first. It doesn't get that rating. T-S sensibly intends to send it direct to the picture houses.

"Lucky Boy" should get Tiffany-Stahl plenty of money. It's the T-S highlight to date, and this a young producing firm. An extreme credit to T-S to turn out such a thoroughly all around well made talking pictures as this so early—and when other and more strongly entrenched picture producers are still struggling with the talking problems.

Sime.

THE AWAKENING

(SOUND)

United Artists' release of a Samuel Goldwyn production. Starring Vilma Banky. Louis Wolheim and Walter Byron featured. Directed by Victor Fleming. Cameraman, George Barnes. Titles by Katherine Hilliker. Story by Frances Marion, adapted by Carey Wilson. Theme song, "Marie," by Irving Berlin. At Rivoli, New York, for extended engagement, starting Dec. 29. Running time, 105 minutes.

Marie Ducrot	Vilma Banky
Lieut. Count Karl von Hagen	Walter Byron
Le Bete	Louis Wolheim
The Orderly	George Davis
Grandfather Ducrot	William A. Orlamond
Sub-Lieut. Franz Gever	Carl von Hartmann

Same old complaint: Why won't they devote as much time, intelligence and professional competence to the script as they devote, for instance, to the matter of photography? Samuel Goldwyn has spent coin liberally. He has done the thing up shipshape so far as elegance of production is concerned. Yet with all the fusing of technical talent, fine acting and the rest, it is not a good, though it is a passable, moving picture. The explanation is story.

The story is a mulligan stew. There's a pinch of "The White Sister," a seasoning of "Scarlet Letter," a large chunk of all the war pictures since 1918, and several slices of small-time baloney. It's a fake tragedy in essence aggravated by last-minute uncertainty whether to make a bum or a hero out of Louis Wolheim, who shows up in a French uniform, while the hero is, shades of the Liberty Loan, a German.

The Germans after 10 years are starting to get a break from Hollywood. In "The Awakening" they are represented throughout as rather amiable and decidedly handsome fellows. However, Walter Byron, an Englishman, plays the German hero, so that may mollify the four-minute men of the late conflict.

Byron debuts to pictures in "The Awakening." He is an upstanding chappie, sleek thatched and regular of features. Whether his eyes are soft enough or his manner sufficiently debonaire for the exacting American flapper time will have to demonstrate. Meanwhile his performance, while not threatening Barrymore, is good enough.

Miss Banky, somewhat more vivacious in her new responsibility of individual stardom, is always attractive, although so gorgeous a creature should not be wasted as a peasant girl and then a novice nun, all in one picture.

George Barnes' photography is particularly distinguished for clearness, beauty and imagination, although there is no attempt, either by cameraman or director, to take any but a straightforward system of carrying forward the narrative. Without tricks, hocus-pocus or striving for mere effect, the production stands out as first rate. This angle is important in any reckoning of "The Awakening" commercially.

The great fault of the picture is the dragginess and familiarity of the story. Any pruning of the running time, notably in the middle parts, will be an enhancement. Nearly two hours as previewed at the Rivoli was too much for the kindergarten plot to sustain.

"The Awakening" will be moderate at the b. o., but is not the type of picture that will build Vilma Banky as a star.

Land.

SHOPWORN ANGEL

(DIALOG)

Paramount production and release. Directed by Richard Wallace from story by Dana Burnet. Screen adaptation by Howard Estabrook and Albert Shelby LeVino. Featuring Nancy Carroll and Gary Cooper. At Paramount, New York, week Dec. 29. Running time 80 mins.

Daisy Heath	Nancy Carroll
William Tyler	Gary Cooper
Bailey	Paul Lukas

Once in a long while the formula picture factories in Hollywood turn out a glamorous gem such as this, stirring, finely drawn and so beautifully presented that the critical faculties declare a holiday. It happens rarely. **Here is a story sublime in its simplicity, overwhelming in its natural appeal, a girl that holds with her looks and a great little trouper as well, and with it all one of the best popular personifications of a show girl yet attempted in the mad cycle of show pictures produced during the past season.**

Like a great many underworld pictures whose box office value lessened because following earlier films of that type, this picture suffers because of the war theme running through. But for that it should have turned out to be one of the commercial successes of the season. As it is there is every probability that it will clean up wherever it may be shown, regardless of class of audience, because it is a story that grips universally.

Nancy Carroll and Gary Cooper contribute excellent work. Both seem natural and lifelike.

When the lonely doughboy tells the chorus queen of his barren life without a home or a family, and she replies that she had never heard of anything so sad since the "Two Orphans," it gets a laugh without detracting from the piquant sadness the boy inspires. And similarly in all important situations, the girl carries them off in superb style.

As the show girl living with the worldly sophisticate, with nothing to worry over except booze headaches and bawling the dance director when asked to come to rehearsals on time, Miss Carroll never strays from type. She's hard, smart and strong-willed, flashing an armful of diamond trinkets and saying: "That's what good little girls get for doing what their mammas told them not to."

The soldier boy is from Texas where he never saw a show girl or a skyscraper first hand. He bumps into Daisy accidentally, is driven to camp in her limousine, and then brags to the gang. He has to make good and does because the girl has an odd moment in which she weakens enough to get the soldier out of the mess.

In spite of herself the girl begins to fall. But when he asks her to marry him, just before sailing for France, she breaks down. There is a scene with her "guardian" after which she goes through for the boy. He is arrested for being A. W. O. L. halfway through the marriage ceremony and the girl goes back to the chorus, the dance director who had suffered her eccentricities giving her a spot in the second row of the chorus just to get even.

The clincher in the closing scene is a pip, in sound. The girl is doing a song and dance chorus number, singing a love ballad. She sees the boy plunging through the lines in a charge, then shot dead. She wants to scream but the director tells her to snap into it or else.

Only two dialog sequences in the picture, both highly effective, enhancing its value dramatically as well as commercially. First is the marriage ceremony, the minister going through the regular routine, and the girl, knowing she had done wrong, passing out just before she gets the ring. Gary Cooper has a few brief lines. In the second dialog sequence the dance director is putting the chorus through the paces. Miss Carroll has a few lines here and also sings. The girl's voice records surprisingly well, in both efforts.

Paul Lukas, as the girl's man, adds prestige as the menace. Lukas, an Hungarian importation imported by Paramount over a year ago, is a smooth, most nonchalant and likeable heavy. They'll like him even while they hate him.

A smart set picture, with best results evidently in the big towns. Still it is smart enough to click as strongly all the way down the line.

Mori.

WEST OF ZANZIBAR

(SOUND)

Metro-Goldwyn-Mayer production and release. Directed by Tod Browning from original story by Chester Devonde and Kilbourn Gordon. Lon Chaney starred. Synchronized musical score and sound effects, Western Electric. At Capitol, New York, week Dec. 29. Running time about 70 minutes.

Flint	Lon Chaney
Crane	Lionel Barrymore
Doc	Warner Baxter
Maizie	Mary Nolan
Anna	Jane Daly
Tiny	Roscoe Ward
Babe	Kalla Pasha
Bumba	Curtis Nero

Weird atmospheric effects will get this by as a straight one or two-day program attraction. Lon Chaney's name must do the rest. An excellent basis for a story is sacrificed apparently for background and the theme gets to the screen in jumbled episodic way that reduces continuity to shreds.

"West of Zanzibar" indicates an over-worked Chaney. The star is there, but the rush of getting his quota on the release schedule is taking its toll in the most important phase of production—preparation. In this respect Chaney's latest impresses as having exhausted the property men and the casting director and allowing Tod Browning to follow religiously one of those cuff scripts.

Smacking strongly of "Congai," although the thing is called an original, "West of Zanzibar" will satisfy Chaney fans who like their color regardless of the way in which it is daubed.

Lionel Barrymore has little more than a bit. He captures the magician's bride, just after Chaney has sub-titled his affection for her. The latter part is dully played and given scant meaning. She passes out of the picture too soon thereafter for the magician to believe that the competition is the kid's dad.

Then, for no particular reason, the action is transferred to another world. Chaney, too hurriedly, is shown as an ivory robber and just as mysteriously Barrymore suddenly develops to have quit the stage and become a white trader in Africa.

With the same unexplainable rapidity, Chaney is revealed to have started his revenge by training the babe in the ways of tropical fleshpots. Incidentally, Chaney takes advantage of an earlier wallop to go back to Notre Dame days. He drags himself through the major footage with a pair of dead pins. While this deformity is effective, its strength is minimized by the jerkiness of the plot.

Mary Nolan as the grown daughter does not make the matriculation of a prostitute any too vivid. Rather a blonde saint in Chaney's eerie jungle den is the reaction.

Revenge comes when Barrymore is bumped off, but not until after he has proven to the magician that he was partly wet and that the girl is his own daughter. Thereupon breaks the regular cheap meller climax, with Chaney sacrificing his life to the savages so that Mary and Warner Baxter, a broken down doc, whose presence is a mystery, slip off together for an amended existence.

Jungle scenes with crocodiles oozing through slime and a score or so of vaselined black extras doing their dances and attending to their funeral pyres are what will get this by.

Musical score (Western Electric) is regular. Attempts at sound effects are worse, the chanting of savages reproducing like a college boy chorus. *Waly.*

SCARLET SEAS

(SOUND)

First National production and release. Starring Richard Barthelmess; featuring Betty Compson and Loretta Young. Directed by John F. Dillon, from story by F. Scott Darling. Titled by Louis Stevens. Sol Polito, cameraman. At the Strand, New York, week Dec. 29. Running time, 67 minutes.

Steve Donkin............Richard Barthelmess
Rose McRay..................Betty Compson
Margaret Barbour..............Loretta Young
Johnson..................James Bradbury, Sr.
Toomey..............................Jack Curtis
Capt. Barbour..................Knute Erickson

One of those pictures which keeps promising more than it ever attains. It also has been over-sounded. Outside of these two faults, with the aid of the Barthelmess name, it shouldn't do much box-office harm and will likely gross moderately.

Strand audience gave full evidence of this feature's failure to meet its obligation at that point where Barthelmess rushes into the stateroom to save the girl, the next flash showing the men half-way through a half-hearted struggle. Dillon built up this sequence well enough to make balconites applaud just prior to the anticipated battle, but the obvious bad cutting and unconvincing action let the house down with a bump from which neither the film nor customers quite recovered.

Story is Singapore, long since Hollywood's persistent conception of the port of all evil, having Barthelmess as Steve, the rough and tough skipper, in love with the not necessarily pure dance hall girl, Rose (Miss Compson), whom he shanghaies. Fire casts the two adrift on a sea which can't even boast of a ground swell, and they eventually come upon a schooner aboard which mutiny has placed the crew in control.

Inasmuch as both have sworn to revise their codes if answered for their prayers, Steve finds the captain and pledges himself to deliver the boat to port. Rose also turns heroine until the revolt leader tips that her boy friend is after the cap's daughter (Miss Young), whence she reverts to type and tells the crew she'll help grab the shipment of pearls and make Steve roll over.

Resultant battle is between Toomey and Steve, the latter going overboard, and the crew, with their leader gone, going back to work on a pledge of clemency by the captain. Rose also becomes convinced that Steve really means it after having taken a sock from the cudgel meant for Steve.

Picture gets away fast on the uproar of the abduction from the waterfront dive and the blaze at sea. After that it slows down. A deal of aquatic faking is a hindrance, as also the superfluous footage alloted some of the scenes. Less 500 feet the film would be just as good, probably better.

When the pace starts to ease off nothing holds it together but the work of the star and Miss Compson. This girl is on her way back and isn't making any bones about it. She is featured here, and deservedly with Miss Young also underlined for a very small role but looking as angelic as ever. Barthelmess is appropriately dirty and hardboiled in getting across the impression of a diminutive package of power, and Knute Erickson meets the mental vision of a veteran captain. Jack Curtis scowls through his dastardly Toomey.

Synchronization has gone out after everything, the score being superior to the effects. Latter parallel each other during the brawl in he joint and the abandoning of ship, one nullifying the other, and especially in this case, because they come close together. It'll make many a patron wish for the silent version, where a little headwork would have made the sound fit and consistent instead of overemphasizing. Door knocks are particularly ridiculous, listening as sledge-hammer blows as Barthelmess starts searching what seem to be deserted cabins. A crude interruption of suspense for which there is no excuse.

According to report "Scarlet Seas" is the picture this F. N. unit was going to Central America to make last summer. Prospective trip was called off and the presumed revision in script and production is evident. Its best bets are a good share of action, Barthelmess and Miss Compson. The sound can be ignored, the advantage being that without it the footage can be cut and the atmosphere unbroken. Story is familiar, although in this instance the femme half of the love interest is directed to demonstrate that she's done and has been a lot of things the normal screen heroine supposedly knows nothing about. *Sid.*

SYNTHETIC SIN

(SOUND)

First National production and release. Starring Colleen Moore. Directed by William Seiter. Based on play by Frederic and Fanny Hatton, adapted by Tom J. Geraghty. Titles by Tom Reed. Cameraman, Sidney Hickok. Antonio Moreno featured. At Paramount, New York, week Jan. 5. Running time, 66 mins.

Betty.........................Colleen Moore
Donald......................Antonio Moreno
Mrs. Fairfax...............Edythe Chapman
Margary.....................Kathryn McGuire
Sheila.........................Gertrude Astor
Brandy......................Montague Love
Frank....................Ben Hendricks, Jr.

Laughs in this one. Continued, torso-vibrating, infectious laughs. Start to finish it's mostly giggles, sure box office pleaser, a great Colleen Moore feature, and a triumph in comedy technique by William Seiter, the director.

"Synthetic Sin" was a play a couple of years ago. First National bought the screen rights before the play was produced at the Morosco theatre, Los Angeles, early in 1927. For various reasons its production has been postponed several times. It could hardly come more opportunely with the edge off the talkers and First National not overly-stocked with b. o. stuff at present.

There is a lot more to the picture than to the Hatton play. Tom J. Geraghty has tacked on a whole new facade. Where the play opened in the dressing room after the heroine has just done a floppo as an actress, the picture starts in a small southern town and builds up the stage-struck girl who finally runs off to New York to sin and suffer so she can become an emotional actress.

While the plot is novel and gave star, scenarist and director a lot to bite their teeth into, the result is primarily due to an inspired performance and production. Among features for everyday use "Synthetic Sin" stands out like a good fire. There are a hundred delightful touches. The whole thing is warm, human and skillfully compounded. Miss Moore's imitations should be as popular with the fans as Marion Davies' have been, although entirely different in type.

The cast is good but everyone merely surrounds and mirrors the star. The production is first class in every respect with a passing laurel for Tom Reed whose captions fitted the occasions with uniform aptness.

Vitaphone (disk) musical accompaniment not so hot. Several points where the orchestration doesn't lap evenly with the action. The attempts to interpret changing moods by musical emphasis was rather a frost and at a couple of points the overloading of tone produced horrible noises. An organ would have been better.

Otherwise the score on "Synthetic Sin" was 100 per cent. *Land.*

GIVE AND TAKE

(DIALOG)

Universal production and release. Directed by William Beaudine. Adapted from play by Aaron Hoffman. Titles by Alfred DeMond. Dialog directed by A. B. Heath. Synchronized musical score over Western Electric device by Joseph Cherniavsky. In cast: Jean Hersholt, George Sidney, George Lewis, Sharon Lynn, Charles Miller, Sam Hardy. At Colony, New York, commencing Dec. 25. Running time 81 minutes.

"Give and Take" is just mediocre in the program class. Story poorer than the average job on the cuff. Cast saves it from complete flop.

Excepting the clowning of the able Sidney and Hersholt, the dialog is without merit. Wisecracks as old as the pyramids that they keep talking about are given them to recite. Tonality and mannerisms get the laughs but not the lines.

George Lewis as the college lad with big industrial perspective for father's canning factory is better seen. He records like a schoolboy before the village board.

To call the theme a story is erroneous, much less to think of comparing it in sparkle to the play of the same title. This is one of those plays which can't afford the augmentation the screen permits.

A lot of village band playing with intermissions by cast which are as flat as the notes recorded from the instruments.

Pardoning Hersholt and Sidney, the whole thing just registers negatively. *Waly.*

THE LAST WARNING

(DIALOG)

Universal production and release. Starring Laura LaPlante. Adapted from T. F Fall's play of the same name based on W Camp's novel. Directed by Paul Leni. Dialog and titles by Tom Reed. Cast include Montague Love, Mack Swain, Roy D'Arcy, Tom O'Brien, Burr McIntosh, Bert Roach, John Boles, Margaret Livingston, Carrie Daumery, Slim Summerville and others. At Colony, New York, week Jan. 5. Running time, 87 minutes.

Much in the manner of U's "Phantom of the Opera," unto probably the same theatre set, with the exception that this one talks for 25 minutes of its full 87. Plenty of hoke and a wild imagination, but probably okay for moderate grosses, because there are enough screams to stimulate the average film mob into sticking through it plus the La Plante name to draw in those localities where she's strong.

Leni, the director, has 'way overdone it in footage. It takes three minutes shy of an hour and a half to tell this yarn, prolonged, no doubt, by the footage necessary when the characters speak. The resultant slow action while the dialog is on also helps to heighten the impression that the picture is taking a long time getting anywhere.

Particularly is this true during the opening 12 minutes, which is all talk. Not only is most of the conversation dull during this passage, in trying to emphasize a semi-comic detective, but there is no semblance of pace to the vocalizing. Feature starts and finishes talking, the closing sequence running nine minutes. In between is a four-minute interlude of "sides." Remaining time is given over to Joseph Cherniavsky's score, which is superior to the dialog.

Sound effects are multiple, continuous and in detail to the extent of reproducing a kiss. Absurd. Music has many good points, including the reproduction of the theme strain for Roy D'Arcy, which followed him through "The Merry Widow."

No reason for Miss La Plante being in the picture other than her name. She does little or nothing except look frightened and scream every so often, the May McAvoy scheme of "The Terror." Same applies to the rest of the cast with the exception of Montague Love as the man determined to unravel the mystery.

Leni's best work is at that point where the problem starts to unravel when, on signal, a stage crew completely and simultaneously strikes an interior stage set during a performance. Motive is to find the backstage marauder who has been terrorizing the theatre. Basic tragedy is the death of an actor on stage as he reaches behind him to a mantelpiece for a candlestick during a tense piece of business in the play House is closed five years, with the mystery unsolved, until Love leases the theatre to reopen it with the same play and cast.

Suspicion jumps from character to character, object of this being Miss La Plante, but Leni has failed in connecting these links to convince. Finish marks the stage manager, who wears a hideous mask to help along the general morale, after a chase through the flies. His excuse is the owners wanting to frighten stockholders out of the company.

Picture has spots where it grips and misses, but no doubt of there being too much of it. Swain and Summerville have been cast to relieve the tension, but don't do anything with it, while John Boles has been permitted to overact in the love interest, which is never really to the fore. Love's performance stands out in the long cast, with Carrie Daumery right behind as a much frightened and elder member of the troupe.

Leni should learn that dialog must have pace. He probably won't make the same error again, but it's a glaring fault here. Story moves along to better advantage when merely accompanied by the score. Its production and camera work should count, with numerous trick lens effects mostly used at the opening and close. Love's voice reproduces the best.

A thrill picture running too long to attain its full effect, and not a good talker in the final analysis. On the other hand, it is a talker, has its thrill moments and an imposingly photographed production behind it, plus a big cast. Figures to do all right minus unusual grosses one way or the other. Recording is painfully distinct, with a constant undertone of the scratch of the sound track throughout the dialog passages. *Sid.*

Romance of Underworld

Fox production and release. Directed by Irving Cummings. Story based on the stage play by Paul Armstrong, thriller of 20 years ago on the boards. Adaptation by Conrad Wells; cameraman, Frank Hanlon. Titles by Garrett Gregg. At Roxy, New York, week Jan. 5. Running time, about 60 minutes.

Judith Andrews................Mary Astor
Derby Dan Manning...............Ben Bard
Edwin Burke................Robert Elliott
Stephen Ransome................John Boles
Champagne Joe................Oscar Apfel
Blondy Nell................Helen Lynch

Works out as mild screen material, worthy program output, but far from a picture that will inspire fan agitation or notable box office marks. The nature of the subject makes this inevitable. For several years now the public has been fed underworld stories, a number of them of highly flavored type, with thrills in abundance and a world of action.

Comes then a story written for the stage and designed to be played in a subdued key. The great kick of the stage play was the odd trick of surface calm while the forces of violence fight their battle to the death just out of sight and hearing. On the stage it was effective technique. On the screen it is only half way so, because the picture lacks the essential of visible action.

The screen version is probably a pretty free rendering of the original, but the faults of a quiet drama are inherent in the material and even the modern twists don't quite mend its flaws.

The Mary Astor role has little meat in it, but this actress has the beauty that disregards parts. Here she is a white slave in a dance hall dive (that they call her hostess in a night club, doesn't conceal the old-fashioned locale), who goes straight, becomes the wife of her employer and is happy until her past threatens to undo her.

John Boles is a most formal hero, doing a thankless character gracefully. Thus the fat of the picture goes to Robert Elliott, just such a tight lipped and undemonstrative detective as the one in "Broadway." It is he who pulls the wires, without seeming to take much pains to do so, that solves all the problems of the heroine. Then he goes back to the bosom of his family of five, a humdrum citizen, as unromatic as a letter carrier in his hours of leisure. To tell the truth, the part plays itself and gets no special help from the actor, who has not the knack of suggesting the vigor and force that are masked behind his calm exterior.

Technical production is fine with admirable discretion in indicating atmosphere. Even the night club isn't overdone. It's meant to be a cheap joint and that's what it looks like. Whole picture in its settings has this feeling for restrained adequacy. The playing also is subdued. It couldn't be otherwise with this material, so it was inevitable that it would be a quiet, even if absorbing picture. *Rush.*

RECKLESS YOUTH

Columbia production and release. Directed by Christy Cabanne. Story by Cosmo Hamilton. Marceline Day featured. Running time, 56 minutes. New York Hippodrome week Dec. 29.

Dixie Calhoun................Marceline Day
Bruce Neil................Ralph Forbes
John Neil................Norman Trevor
Robert Haines................Robert Ellis
Susan................Mary Mabery
George Baxter................Gordon Elliott
Office Boy................Coy Watson

Program product of medium grade, but below the recent Columbia average. Savorless story treatment of jazzy modern youth, done without a spark of humor and in stilted style. Co-ed campus sequences insipid, according to current screen tastes.

Hottest episode in early footage is flaming youth one-stepping heroine into alcove off ballroom, where she coyly permits herself to be kissed. Mild stuff to a public which looks for rowdy necking in its co-ed stories.

Co-ed is lured to supposed midnight party in college town hotel, and unexpectedly finds herself at bay in a three-room suite with the menace in the form of a campus sheik. Nothing happens. Sheik falls asleep and girl walks out.

Plot thickens here when girl unintentionally kills an intruder and on her trial for murder all the innocent indiscretions of her college days are brought up by a district attorney, who sought to break off a match between the girl and his son. The son steps into the trial as counsel for the heroine at the last minute. He wins her acquittal by pointing out to the judge that the father, the prosecutor, is hounding the girl because of opposition to having her in the family.

It is barely possible that a judge would permit such a situation to arise in the conduct of a capital case, but even if he would it makes a hard-to-take theatrical situation.

Beautiful production. Marceline Day does splendidly as a particularly artificial heroine. Here is a leading woman with character and feminine appeal, lost in a blah role. Ralph Forbes is too perfect in manners and grooming, and under Cabanne, inclined to posing. Otherwise, a nice quiet handling of a formula polite male lead. Coy Watson as a comedy office boy does nicely, but isn't played much for comedy.

Timid handling of story material deletes the kick and marks down the picture's possibilities at the box office. *Rush.*

WHEN DUTY CALLS
(GERMAN MADE)

Ufa production and release. Directed by Eric Washneck. Story by C. J. Broun and H. Brault. Cast includes Rudolf Rittner, Olga Tschechova, Helga Thomas and Henry Stuart. At the 55th St. Cinema, N. Y., Jan. 4. Running time, 65 mins.

Herr Director Washneck and the writing combination of Broun and Brault (it took two people to be so dull) have finally brought to the attention of the American public a noteworthy example of cinematic endeavor when it touches bottom. This Ufa presentation concerns itself with the trials and tribulations of a pensioned fireman.

It seems that after 20 years in the service the old boy sprained a leg and was asked to accept office duty or take a pension. He took the pension, but retained embers of hatred against the younger fire officials, which later break into raging torrents of flame.

Time passes, especially slow in this one, and the fireman's gal, a pretty wench with a pair of eyes that won't stay put, makes the fire inspector. As a special favor to her he brings the old fireman into his office for an intelligence test. The old boy is given a couple of puzzles to work out (this is on the level). He fails to make a square and put rubber balls into holes fast enough, and therefore doesn't get the job.

By this time everybody, including the cast, is ready to break down and weep. But a fire breaks out. The old fireman arrives in time to save his daughter and the fire inspector, and would have taken the safe with him, too, only the walls were too hot. That cleans everything up for a happy reconciliation, while the menace gets a smack on the chin from the old boy on general principles. Strictly the utsnay. *Mori.*

RUSSIA
(GERMAN MADE)

Affiliated European production and release. Directed by Mario Bonnard. Author not credited. Cast includes Marcella Albani, Wladimir Gaidarow and Wilhelm Dieterle. At the 55th St. Playhouse, New York, Jan. 5. Running time, 70 mins.

Purporting to lay bare the inside of nihilistic circles wherein were bred the revolutionary principles which finally resulted in the overthrow of the Czarist regime, this independently made foreign flicker exhibits none of the sensationalism or intrigue prevalent at that time. It is an extremely dull expose of the home life of Russian nobility in 1908, with the basis of the picture a story of a count who lived with a peasant girl and then wanted to marry her.

In most of its exposition it bears a striking resemblance to the "Resurrection" of Tolstoi, but has none of the ingenuity or the greatness of the Russian masterpiece.

What is here shown under a title which is deluding in its scope is merely an oft-repeated theme planted in a Russian locale.

The director evidently worked straight from a story without any special screen adaptation, a method much in vogue among foreign producers unable to afford expert scenarists. It has its ruinous effect upon the picture.

Scenes with splendid possibilities for tense interest are numerous, situations of sufficient strength to carry the picture are in, but none have been capitalized. The principals are absurd in their violent mugging to register emotion. The leading woman is of tylcal Slav cast of features and deportment. *Mori.*

THE BIG HOP

Produced by Buck Jones Productions and states righted. Directed by James Horne. Buck Jones starred. In cast:—Jobyna Ralston, Ernest Hilliard, Edward Hearn. At Loew's New York one day, Dec. 27. Running time over 60 minutes.

This is Buck Jones' first on his own. It's hopeless. Even in the grinds they laugh at what Buck and Murray Garsson figured would go over as a high meller.

Buck does his level best out of the saddle, but as a ballroom artist, garden swain and aviator he isn't there in this one.

The cowboy hero turned flyer isn't half as bad as Jobyna Ralston. The less said about her the better, because a couple of more like this and she's through, except as atmosphere.

Director James Horne should be called on the carpet for "The Big Hop." The general unnaturalness of his characters, their camera hogging and amateur gesticulating and general pre-war technique points to the megaphone—unless Buck tried a Harry Langdon. *Waly.*

A LIGHT WOMAN
(BRITISH MADE)

Produced by Gainsborough Pictures Co. Directed by Adrian Brunel. Distributed in the United Kingdom by Ideal Films Co. Original story by Dale Laurence. Censors' Certificate A. Previewed at the London Hippodrome Dec. 6. Running time, 100 mins.

Dolores................Benita Hume
Don Luis................C. M. Hallard
Don Andres................Gerald Ames
Ramiro................Donald McArdle

A good piece of photography, otherwise not so much. An incredible story, casting spotty and thin direction. Has the merit of a series of fine Spanish locations, but puts nothing into them.

Benita Hume looks Spanish, but is not beautiful, and Donald McArdle is unfortunately blessed with anything but a sympathetic face. Best acting comes from C. M. Hallard, as a father who cheats even on his own sweetie, and Gerald Ames as a Spanish explorer, though this latter role betrays a confusion in either the author's or the director's mind as to what should have been done with the character.

Dolores is expelled from convent school for scandalous behavior and gets a liberal education in being gay from one of her father's mistresses. Ramiro, an exploring partner of Don Andres, is in love with her, and while he is away on an expedition plays around with anybody. Andres pretends to love her, and when she falls for him, throws her over to save Ramiro and to teach her a lesson.

She goes wilder than ever, is found lit by her father in a hideaway, and discovers she really loves Ramiro, whom she dashes to save when he has gone to climb an inaccessible mountain in compensation for losing her.

As lined out by the story, most of the characters haven't any. The film has no particular name appeal here either on cast or story, and is far too weak to stand up as a solo feature and too long for a second feature. Maybe cutting it would get it by as the latter. Means nothing for America. *Frat.*

THE GUN RUNNER

Tiffany-Stahl production and release. Directed by Edgar Lewis. Screen play adapted from Arthur Stringer's novel of same name. Ricardo Cortez featured. In cast: Nora Lane, Gino Corrado, John St. Polis. At Loew's New York as half double bill, one day, Dec. 28. Running time, about 80 minutes.

Mild comedy about one of those mythical Latin-American republics with a comic opera president, cabinet and army that will just about make the grade in the cheaper grinds.

Plot concerns Julio (Cortez), a smart captain who makes a monkey out of his country's chief executive time and again, and makes him like it. Sent to apprehend Garcia, rebel leader, who is plotting a revolution, he falls in love with that guy's sister. When getting his man he faces the familiar choice between love and duty. He decides on love and frees his captive in order to win the smiles of the fair senorita.

Sentenced to be shot, he squirms out of a tight spot, gives the comedy president the finger once more and blows with the love-at-first-sight heart interest.

Will get giggles, snickers and possibly a laugh or two in those houses that play it.

THE GREEN PARROT

(FRENCH-MADE)

Paris, Dec. 22.

"The Green Parrot," from an excellent story by Princess Bibesco, forms a very creditable production for the local market and should also meet with approval beyond the frontier.

The title refers to the constant but unfulfilled wish of Natacha, daughter of a wealthy family in some Balkan state, to possess a green parrot. It is a symbol of her life, made up of disappointments and grief.

Natacha's brother, for whom she had a deep affection, is probably the origin of the malediction. Her father is a political leader and fostering a revolution. His chief associate is a young lieutenant, Felix Solikoff, whom enemies try to assassinate. Instead of which they kill the leader.

Natacha weeps alone over the loss of her father, but Solikoff watches over her. The young couple fall in love.

A short time before the marriage the girl learns Solikoff is her brother, but not by the same mother. Their union impossible, Natacha enters a convent. Thus, like her wish for a green parrot, never realized, she likewise never grasps happiness.

Jean Milva, producer, has created a mystic, thrilling, dramatic picture from Princess Bibesco's scenario. Edith Jehanne is highly emotional as Natacha. She is well supported by Pierre Batcheff and Maxudian. A bouquet can be handed to all concerned. ***Light.***

ON THE DIVIDE

El Dorado production released by First Division. Starring Bob Custer. Directed by J. P. McGowan. In cast: Peggy Montgomery, Lafe McKee, Bud Osborne. At Arena, New York, one day, Dec., 24, as half double bill. Running time, 50 minutes.

Cut to pattern westerner that will pass on a twin bill in the grind houses. In the daily changers where the kids make up the greater part of the audience it can't miss.

Plot has Jim Carson (Custer) arriving in Lariat County in time to upset the plans of an organized band of range grabbers. His particular attention is centered on Sally Martin (Peggy Montgomery) whose father's farm is about to be foreclosed. Carson postpones his own ranch purchasing plans in order to aid the Martins but still has the band of yeggs to contend with, they also being robbers and murderers. After smacking down a half dozen bad guys, Carson recovers the stolen mortgage money and finally identifies the leader of the ranch grabbing gang as a murderer, this being accomplished when he pulls out a watch with its back missing, the sheriff and Jim being on the lookout for a man with a busted watch case. The terrorists on the divide being eliminated the way is left open for Jim and Sally to settle down on the Martin ranch.

Lots of riding, fighting and complications that will satisfy youthful adventure-lovers despite their familiarity with the various sequences in the flicker.

THE RESCUE

(SOUND)

United Artists release, produced by Samuel Goldwyn. Directed by Herbert Brenon. Based on the story of Joseph Conrad, scenario by Elizabeth Meehan. Titles by Katherine Hilliker and H. H Caldwell. Ronald Colman starred; Lily Damita featured. At the Rialto, New York, Jan. 14, for run, grind policy. Running time approximately 96 mins.

Tom Lingard	Ronald Travers
Lady Edith Travers	Lily Demita
Mr. Travers	Alfred Hickman
Carter	Theodore Von Eltz
Hassim	John Davidson
D'Alcacer	Philip Strange
Jorgensen	Bernard Siegel
Daman	Sojin
Belarab	Harry Cording
Immada	Laska Winters
Jaffir	Duke Kahanamoku
Shaw	Louis Morrison
Wasub	George Rigas
Tenga	Christopher Martin

This is a story of mighty conflict between passion and honor. Passion, or box office, wins.

Joseph Conrad's great heart-gripping novel furnishes the base upon which Herbert Brenon has erected a pictorial construction radiating almost every known variety of human emotion with a burning force which satisfies every desire in motion picture entertainment. In the full week big town stands it should be a box office record breaker.

The genius of Conrad's literary creation in its warm, completely enveloping hold on audiences of all types, the intensity of the leading characters and the clever performances contributed to these impressions by Ronald Colman and Lily Damita, the careful attention given to detail in portraiture of minor characters, all build up to a dazzling momentum which carries off an unhappy ending satisfactorily.

Here a married woman, with her husband, on a yacht stranded somewhere near Java, in danger from hostile savages, falls completely and unreasoningly in love with another man, a gunrunner by circumstance, an adventurer from choice. The love of the woman for this man is purely platonic. She, the designing and beautiful female, would have it otherwise but the stern man of the outdoors is bound by honor, crude, entirely of his own making, but strong and immovable nevertheless.

They glide on the waters through the velvety darkness together, this man and this woman, the whole night long, he to save her husband from death by the savages. She tries to make him forget his rigid resolutions but the boy is merely friendly though his eyes betray feelings which send shivers through every brassiere in the audience. What the woman looks like in these scenes, how her head droops, breast heaving, shoulders moving, and hands wandering, no typewriter can adequately convey.

The relationship between the woman and King Tom continues on the same status until near the finish. Daman, the pirate savage, enemy of King Tom's pal Belarab, has seized Immada and Wasub. King Tom's two royal friends for whom he had brought arms to regain their kindom, Woja. The girl is alone on the hulk of a boat in which the ammunitions are hidden. Her husband has been deliverd to the savages because a couple of the blacks had been accidentally killed. **She gets a ring which she is to give to King Tom in order to save Immada and Wasub. She braves the darkness across a stretch of land held by Daman's renegades. She gets to King Tom, wants to** tell him of the ring, but succumbs to desires which he is ready to reciprocate.

So honor, love and everything else go overboard as a result. Immada, Jaffir, the faithful black, Wasub, Jorgensen, the mate who blew himself up with a shipload of gunpowder so that Daman should not win against King Tom, all perish. At Jaffir's grave King Tom parts with the girl who says she is ready to do anything he may wish. She tells him of the ring she failed to deliver and he tells her he knows and that his is the blame because he would have done the same regardless.

Film runs over 95 minutes, too long for regular program showings, and should be cut to speed action. Sound effects limited to one or two vocal chorus numbers during spectacular scenes. Score by Hugo Riesenfeld is effective.

With Ronald Colman added looks like a setup. *Mori.*

ADORATION

(SOUND)

First National production and release. Starring Billie Dove. Directed by Frank Lloyd. Story by Lajos Biro, adapted by Winifred Dunn. Supervised by Ned Marin. Cameraman John Seitz. Titles by Garrett Graham. With synchronized Vitaphone score. At Strand, New York, week Jan. 12. Running time, 73 minutes.

Elena, Princess Orloff	Billie Dove
Serge,, Prince Orloff	Antonio Moreno
Ninette	Lucy Doraine
Count Zubov Vladimir	Nicholas Soussanin
Ivan	Nicholas Bela
Baroness Razumov	Winifred Bryson
Baron Razumov	Lucien Prival
General Count Alexis Muratov	Emil Chautard

Billie Dove features, taking them 12 to the dozen, deviate from form less than the proverbial .005 per cent. This one is not as good as some; not as bad, for instance, as "Heart of a Follies Girl" and just as close to the whole series as it is possible for a drill press to follow pattern.

It is utterly blah as a story, pretty flat and dreary in the telling, and escapes turkey classification because of its production which represents and looks like money. It is nothing but an opportunity for Miss Dove to wear a flock of expensive clothes and flutter her big camera-proof orbs in innumerable closeups. By this time any one with any pretense to being a movie fan knows that this is exactly what they will see and get when patronizing a Dove opera.

So it may safely be assumed that all who buy and enter the parlors exhibiting "Adoration" will feel adequately rewarded since they will choose it as entertainment with their eyes open and their noodles padlocked.

Not to embellish the primitive simplicity of it overmuch this picture concerns the eternal triangle, collapse in Imperial Russia dumping the well-dressed trio in Paris as penniless emigres.

Lucy Doraine, Nicholas Bela and Nicholas Soussanin, newcomers to films, contribute interesting performances in auxiliary parts while Antonio Moreno who has been getting some good parts again after a siege with the indies is all that is needed from the part of Prince Serge Alexandrovitch Orloff.

The production values and the popularity of Billie Dove suggest a prosperous career for "Adoration." *Land.*

Case of Lena Smith

Paramount production and release. Directed by Josef von Sternberg. Esther Ralston featured, James Hall in support. Adapted by Jules Furthman from story by Samuel Ornitz. Harold Rossoel, cameraman. Titles by Julian Johnson. Running time, 68 minutes. At Paramount, New York, week Jan. 13.

Lena Smith	Esther Ralston
Franz Hofrat	James Hall
Herr Hofrat	Gustav von Seyffertitz
Frau Hofrat	Emily Fitzroy
Stefan	Fred Kohler
Stefan's Sister	Betty Aho
Commissioner	Lawrence Grant
Pepi	Leone Lane
Poldi	Kay DesLys
Janitor	Alex Woloshin
Janitor's Wife	Ann Brody
Franz (age 3)	Wally Albright, Jr.
Franz (age 18)	Warner Klinger

Every once in a while the producers who know their box office onions deliberately turn out a picture that departs from all commercial lines. This is one. The story is fine, theme full of meaning, acting and production are of the best. But it holds nothing to captivate the frivolous fan mass.

Story is a bitter arraignment of the ruling class in Austria back around 1895, before the war had taught its lesson. It goes without saying that such a topic in serious vein and treatment often depressing in its realism is pretty remote from the light tastes of movie goers. Its romance is sombre, costuming as ugly as costuming of the period always seems to modern eyes, and it hasn't an atom of humor.

As a literary and artistic product it is admirable. The viciousness of a self-righteous ruling class (military tyranny supported by bourgeoise selfishness) is developed with biting vividness, in the history of a simple village maiden who makes a holiday in Vienna, falls in love with a student-officer and marries him, is slowly crushed by the ponderous machinery of caste prejudice.

The picture hasn't a spark of light to relieve its shadow.

Powerful story taking a fresh angle on the war in analyzing social injustice that existed before the great struggle, and suggesting that out of the devastation 1914 wrought in the old world, there came reforms that were sorely needed. *Rush.*

A LADY OF CHANCE

(SOUND)

Metro-Goldwyn-Mayer production and release. Starring Norma Shearer. Directed by R. Z. Leonard and adapted from story, "Little Angel." Titled by Ralph Spence, with Peverly Marly cameraman. At Capitol, New York, week Jan. 12. Running time, 80 minutes.

Dolly	Norma Shearer
Bradley	Lowell Sherman
Gwen	Gwen Lee
Steve Crandall	John Mack Brown
Mrs. Crandall	Eugenia Besserer
Hank	Buddie Messinger

A good example of a picture that can fool many in a projection room. Looking at it cold, it's got nothing but the Shearer name. Little if any entertainment in its dragged-out story of a racket gal redeemed through love of a country youth. And they loved it.

At least a near-capacity matinee audience went for Miss Shearer and her double-meaning pantomime as she peeks over the stalwart shoulder of him who thinks she's on the level. The matinee girls giggled and gurgled. It rolled off the loge section's knife, but the verdict of those Flossies in the cheaper tier is too strong to name this one as a box-office cluck. In celluloid rhetoric, it's just that. Rather awful, in fact, and much below other films in which both Robert Leonard, the director, and the star have been concerned. But if the Annies like it here, the chances are that Dubuque's Judie O'Gradys will approve, but don't count on the colonel's lady. So that predicts fair grosses around the country.

You can stand on your head trying to figure what they like about "A Lady of Chance." It must be the idea of the angelic looking blackmailing gal getting away with it until Mr. Right comes along, whence she resumes those schoolgirl ideas and complexion of her childhood.

There's no sympathy for Dolly (Miss Shearer) until she turns herself over to the cops to save her husband from one of those "you can't win" deals. She's strictly on the make all the time. The marriage, she believes, is the route to the bank.

Opening footage has Dolly pursued by a mixed team of contemporaries, Lowell Sherman and Gwen Lee, who want to make it a trio in tapping for sap. Having played bait for one $10,000 check, Dolly sneaks the full total upon discovering Bradley (Sherman) is trying to hold out. It's at a cement convention she frames Steve (Johnny Mack Brown). Her supposed southern mansion turns out to be a shanty, and she leaves the boy flat, only to reverse the field and pop up behind a door in the morning.

Meanwhile Brad and his femme have trailed her in pursuit of their missing 10 grand, knowing Dolly's got a nose for dough. They're paid off by the bride, but not before Steve announces his formula for a new cement means $100,000. Whence Brad sticks around on the threat to tell all. Finish has the quartet in New York, with Brad framing Steve into a proposition until Dolly decides to reveal her secret and phones for the gendarmes. Being out on parole, the dick makes a quick trip to call, and climax is Steve securing another parole for Dolly, this time in his custody. Gary Cooper got out of the same kind of jam the same way.

Picture hasn't any action, but extracts some spasmodic good moments from Miss Shearer, who is backed by the smooth-working Sherman in a role which is a pushover for him. Brown fits on appearance, wearing a gold football for those who remember, but isn't a heavyweight on histrionics here. Trying to see it from the balcony angle there's not much doubt that Miss Shearer, backed by Sherman, solely holds this release together. Dolly may be the girl the Flossies like to think they are. If it's anything else, supply your own six-letter word.

Spence has made his titles as crisp as possible, but Marly, cameraman, or somebody, has been daring in permitting so many full-length shots of Miss Shearer. Not much doubt that "A Lady of Chance" is going to bore plenty, but there'll be enough to counterbalance this attitude to class it as moderate program stuff with the Shearer moniker to send it along.

Film has a theme song which doesn't listen tuneful enough to be important. Synchronized score has been well handled.   *Sid.*

Sajenko—The Soviet
(GERMAN MADE)

Ufa production and release. Directed by Erich Waschneck. Starring Michael Bohnen, cast including Suzy Vernon, Henry Stuart and Walter Rilla. At the 55th St. Playhouse, N. Y., Jan. 12. Running time, 90 minutes.

In this characteristic foreign flicker Hollywood production methods are mirrored for but one brief instant—in the opening scene. It then reverts to type, and drags on lamely to a dull, insipid finish.

The picture begins with the blare of fiery revolution. Within two short minutes the Russian duke has been slain and his squealing, black-eyed daughter mauled and ravaged by a wild, unkempt, powerful rebel. The young princess then manages to escape with the aid of a retainer, and the 55 minutes following are spent in an unnamed German capital, where the Russian nobility have taken refuge.

Directorial mismanagement and continuity, in which no attempt has been made towards coherent action, are then responsible for what follows. The princess, involved in a love tangle with a wealthy German industrialist, should have been sufficiently interesting material for the balance of the story. Russian majors, counts, generals and dukes are dragged in, however, complicating the easy movement of the story, detracting from the love interest and adding little of any consequence to the story requirements.

Sajenko, the girl's attacker, is brought back into the story as a Soviet secret service agent, leading into another wrestling scene, with the girl underneath. She makes him sign over some government funds to her and uses the check as a means by which he is captured by the Russian authorities.

Sajenko, the title role, is played by Michael Bohnen, billed as a bass-baritone with the Metropolitan Opera Co. Aside from the scenes which stand little chance of being allowed in regular theatres, Bohnen is largely devoted to interpretations as ludicrous and unconvincing as continental film actors in domestic pictures habitually are.

In directing the expressions and movements of his cast Herr Waschneck has retained to a remarkable degree the faculty for laughable abruptness. Scarcely a piece of business that doesn't impress because of its unnatural, unbelievable quality. The players move like machines, or drilled soldiers on parade, with the facial expressions keeping time.   *Mori.*

FORBIDDEN LOVE
(ENGLISH MADE)

Produced by Gainsborough Pictures of England, directed by Graham Cutts with Lili Damita starred. Screen story adapted from the Noel Coward play, "The Queen Was in the Parlor." No other credits on main titles. Distributed in the United States by Pathe. Running time, 74 minutes. At Cameo, New York, week Jan. 12.
Princess Nadya..............Lili Damita
Sabien Paschal............Paul Richter
Zana, a maid.............Rosa Richards
General Krish..............Klein Rogge
Prince Keri of Zalgar......Harry Leidtke
Grand Duchess..........Trude Hesterberg

Atrocious screen trash. A sloppy version of the "Zenda" stencil, played by a group of stuffed shirt actors and directed by somebody with instant command of all the cheap tricks of ten years ago that Hollywood has happily forgotten.

This includes the cute device of having the buxom heroine take a bath in a glass tub in full sight of the audience. Rest of the picture is as crude as that, or cruder. Sentiment is laid on thick until it slips into travesty.

Here's an incident: The hamiest of leading men has come to supper in the boudoir of the melancholy queen, who was his sweetheart in Paris yeahs and yeahs ago. They sit down to sup, lover registering conflict of passion and gentle sadness at once. Passion gets the upper hand while he is about to go into the hors d'oeuvres opening. Believe it or not he is overcome by emotion at the exact instant he is raising a dainty fork of caviar to his mouth. It was too much for somebody in the Cameo audience who didn't care for caviar. Whole rows of customers broke down at once.

Well after that the evening was ruined too. You couldn't get much of a kick out of the naughty inference of the queen's slippers and her dress lying in confusion right next to the lover's Chesterfield and crush hat near the curtains of the Queen's bedroom. You can't fool American fans with so crude an imitation of Elinor Glyn. Mrs. Glyn can't do it herself any more.

Lili Damita is a handsome woman made absurd by unspeakably bad handling. Her clothes are a fright, her makeup must have been put on with a trowel and a pitiless photographer just turned the unrelenting crank in full, hard lights.

The scenic backgrounds taken in Europe are a delight, particularly authentic shots of Paris and the real thing in Switzerland winter scenery. Also there are some French interiors that are beyond all art for beauty and realism.

And the tragedy of the whole business is that before these exquisite settings there is some of the worst acting ever done in or out of American quickie westerns.   *Rush.*

PHANTOM CITY

Charles R. Rogers' production for First National, directed by Albert Rogell and starring Ken Maynard. Supervision of Harry J. Brown. Story by Adele Buffington. Titles by Fred Allen. Ted McCord photographer. Running time, 65 minutes. At Loew's New York, New York, Jan. 11. One-half double bill, one day.

Western drama done in the manner of a serial chapter, and very badly done. Picture has scarcely a merit, unless it is a hard riding finish culminating when horseman leaps from a cliff into fugitive automobile speeding down a twisting mountain road. It ends when the cowboy hero knocks two men in auto cold and the machine goes over a dizzy precipice.

Even this episode is made absurd. While hero and lone bandit are battling in the tonneau, there's no one at the wheel and the trained car keeps to the road, only poking its bonnet over the cliff.

Story is really a long juggling act. Everybody pulls a gun on everybody on all sorts of occasions, but never a shot is fired. Story has mystery stuff about an abandoned man and spectre frightens all the characters at one time or another.

The dumbest of dumb western hoke. Eugenia Gilbert is an unusually pretty and graceful leading woman for this sort of trash. Fit for daily changes Saturday afternoon.   *Rush.*

---

3 NAKED FLAPPERS
(FRENCH MADE)

Paris, Jan. 2.
The above title is a personal translation, without a claim to copyright. It is the film version by Robert Boudrioz of "Trois Jeunes Filles Nues," an operetta revived at the Marigny last summer, after produced at the Bouffes the year before.

The plot is lengthy but trivial, following the rather weak musical comedy as closely as possible. Three young maidens, nieces of a naval officer, are being raised by their maiden aunt. Three midshipmen fall in love with the girls. They are surprised to meet the flirts later, in scanty attire, on the stage of a music hall.

By a theatrical coincidence the uncle is also present, tied up with the star of the revue, and he is equally astonished to find his nieces there. They were conducted by a sanctimonious tutor who somehow got on the wrong track. This fellow is secretly paying court to another niece.

The midshipmen imagine they have to deal with chorus girls and their attitude changes. They are still more astounded to see the flappers on board their ship which is under the command of the uncle. The story terminates with a series of weddings.

The picture seemed to meet with the exhibitors' approval attending the trade show. It is being distributed by Maurice Rouhier who may get his own back in the provinces where the reputation of a Bouffes Parisiens operetta should attract.

The various roles are handled by Francois Rozet, Rene Ferte, Pierre Labry, Andre Marnay, J. Marie Laurent, Jeanne Brindeau, Helbling, Jenny Luxeuil and a bevy of supers.   *Kendrew.*

NOTHING TO WEAR

Columbia production, released by Hollywood. Directed by Erle C. Kenton. Story and continuity by Peter Milne. Featuring Jacqueline Logan, with cast including Theodore Von Eltz, Jane Winton and Bryant Washburn. At Loew's Circle, New York, Jan. 7. Running time, 60 mins.

Mild farce, moving at a good speed and holding a highly competent cast, actors and lookers. An easy bet for the split weeks, with strong matinee business likely in the neighborhoods and a play from both sexes evenings.

Jacqueline Logan, moving through the early reels in entrancing undies, incidentally displaying a pair of stems bound to start life-long controversies, is almost good enough on appearance here to put it over by herself.

Farcical situations confusing and but lightly amusing, lacking the smashing qualities necessary to put this type of picture over in the first runs. The slow-witted flatfoot is used to good effect, the broad shadowing satire producing marked response.

Plot brings the entire group into a police station. Husband sent his wife an expensive fur coat with a dotty note. Wife thought it was from a lover and sent it back with a note in like vein. Husband arriving doesn't see coat and starts investigation through detective.

Jane Winton, excellent as the goofy dame, affianced of the bachelor involved in the case. Displays an undeveloped comedy vein, which should prove reliable.   *Mori.*

THE WARE CASE
(ENGLISH MADE)

Manning Haynes production, released over here through First National. Directed by Haynes from adaptation by Lydia Hayward. In cast: Stewart Rome, Betty Carter, Pat Ludlow. At Loew's New York, one day, Dec. 26. Running time, 72 minutes.

"The Ware Case" shapes up as a total loss at any American box office. It is one of the most obvious and painfully ambling affairs the British have wished this way.

Glutted with legal moves, dry even when perused on a high court record by a member of the bar, the disentanglement is motivated by a theme so unreasonable as to cause the what-is-it-all-about unrest.

Sir So-and-So was a peculiar living sort of duck who liked his murder stories. That's about all the audience has to grasp. While bailiffs rush around and crowds gather, juries are deliberating, the attorney for defense is having some kind of an eye affair with the accused's wife, and the accused is wringing his hands trying to look hysterical.

It's one of those court things where the story is unfolded on the stand. Witness is irised from the box to the locale and back again.   *Waly.*

FREE LIPS

James Ormont production, released by First Division. June Marlowe featured. Directed by Wallace McDonald. Screen play by Raymond Wells. In cast: Jane Novak, Frank Hagney, Olin Francis, Ernie Shields. At Loew's New York as half double bill, one day, Dec. 28. Running time, about 60 minutes.

Title of this one is the name of a night club, following the current craze in the flickers for freaky names for the hotsy-totsy spots. Aimed for the grinds, it will pass muster on a twin bill mainly because of neat performances turned in by Jane Novak as a hard-boiled hostess, June Marlowe as a girl from the country and Frank Hagney as the owner of tough take-em joint. Miss Marlowe is the pure girl from Indiana who wins the heart of the strong-arm night club operator because she reminds him of his mother, who came from there. Murder in the night club of an old roue involves the girl and the hard guy with the heart of gold.

Blow-off has him flagging the night club racket, giving the smart dames on his list the go-by, deciding to go straight and getting hitched to the innocent kid from good old Indiana.

Murder trial stuff, although stereotyped, is well done, and peasants who patronize the neighborhood shooting galleries will be sold by that b. o. gag title.

SUNSHINE
(FRENCH MADE)
Paris, Dec. 31.

"Un Rayon de Soleil, by Jean Gourguet, who has produced his own scenario for J. P. de Venloo, is more documentary than anything else. It aptly depicts the divers amusements of Parisians during the summer season, particularly on a Sunday afternoon.

Local views of trips on the River Seine, feeding and dancing at countryside inns, driving and motorcycling, with a diverting dash of flirtation.

To inject interest Gourget has imagined a vague yarn in which the scenes of modern French distractions are incorporated. A girl is taken by her best boy for an automobile ride in the country, causing another fellow likewise seeking to win her favor to pursue them in an ordinary taxicab. They visit the various places around Paris well known to excursionists.

This short film is quite amusing and suitable for all programs. Photo work is correct, and the acting natural by Monna Goya (the girl), Georges Peclet (first flirt), Jean Vilette (the rival), and Vallery as a gay dog about town. _Light._

A SINGLE MAN

Metro-Goldwyn-Mayer production and release. Directed by Harry Beaumont from an adaptation of the stage play by Hubert Henry Davies. Scenarists, Hugh Herbert and George O'Hara. Lew Cody and Aileen Pringle co-starred. Titles by Joe Farnham and Lucille Newmark. Cameraman, Ben Lewis. At New York, one day, Jan. 12. Running time, 60 minutes.

Robin Worthington	Lew Cody
Mary Hazeltine	Aileen Pringle
Maggie	Marceline Day
Dickie	Edward Nugent
Mrs. Cottrell	Kathlyn Williams
Mrs. Farley	Eileen Manning

Everything but the custard pie and even that could have been used in this attempt to make Lew Cody a much bedraggled figure in his efforts to show that his advanced age still possessed flaming youth. Lew takes his mauling and his messing like the familiar screen comic who has been taking it fore and aft all these celluloid days. It is all screened for comedy by-play, and while it zooms along familiar channels that make a monkey out of Cody, it serves its purpose twofold. A love story; pretty secretary of the rich bacheloric author finally showing the matured playboy a flapper is not the kind of a gal he should have for a wife. Cody plays the bachelor and well. Miss Pringle is the sec and gets all there is out of such an inanimate part.

The gayest of the fems is Marceline Day. As the flapperiest flapper that ever flapped a flap she's some flap. As the modernized gal she steps on all cylinders.

For once here is a clean-cut theme wherein neither gal nor man shoots up a town, goes wrong or is ruined. A lot of apparent horseplay in putting Lew through a lot of exercise and high school play, but

left out would minimize the preachment that a man growing old isn't as young as he used to be.

Perhaps the most outstanding feature is the photography. That crank turner, Ben Lewis, did a yeoman job; his shots clear and timed to the dot.

This kind of a picture leaves a good impression if nothing else. _Mark._

THE GIRL IN TUXEDO
(AUSTRIAN MADE)
Paris, Jan. 2.

Trade shown in Paris by Superfilm, this comedy reel featuring Harry Liedtke and Maria Paudler met with a good reception. The original Vienna title is not indicated, the picture being released here as "La Girl en Smoking," neither German nor French. It is about a handsome young officer in the Austrian army, loaded with debts, inheriting a profitable dry goods store. The business is directed by a charming damsel named Gisele, favorite of all the males in town.

However, the manageress is dismissed by the Lieutenant on the urgent instigation of a jealous mistress, a dancer. The former counter jumperess, assumes male attire, hence the title of a very amusing production, short and sweet. The antics or adventures of Gisela, the manner in which she freezes off undesired admirers and prompts her new employer to propose marriage constitute the basis of this farcical film. _Kendrew._

FOOLISH MAIDEN
(FRENCH MADE)
Paris, Dec. 17.

Screen version of Henry Bataille's play, "La Vierge Folle," made by Luitz Morat, local producer of decided talent, on behalf of the S.i.c. Eclair, to be universally distributed through Paramount.

Many theatrical folks may remember the Bataille story of the virgin. The "sunlights" do not mar the obscurity of her infatuation. Diane (played by Suzy Vernon), society maiden, daughter of the Duke of Clarence (Maurice Schutz), is madly in love with a married man, Armaury (Jean Angelo), wealthy attorney, several years her senior. The parents by chance learn of their daughter's misadventure and want to put her in a convent.

The brother, Gaston (small role held by Fresney, late of the Comedie Francaise), is determined to get even with the scoundrel, and resolves to avenge what he calls the honor of the family by killing Armaury.

Lovers elope to London, pursued by Gaston, who in turn is followed by Armaury's wife (Emmy Lynn, remarkable in the pathetic role). The latter still adores her unfaithful husband wishes to protect him.

A dramatic scene in a smart London hotel (climax of the stage version) between the four—the outraged brother and the guilty married man as antagonists, the latter protected by both women.

Finally the "foolish maiden," realizing the hopelessness of her passion, shoots herself with the revolver she has wrenched from her brother's hand.

Acting splendid and homogeneous, while the technical side is good.

Henry Bataille's psychological drama is not exactly adaptable for average movie fans. _Light._

STOLEN LOVE

FBO production and release. Directed by Lynn Shores from the story by Hazel Livingston. Featuring Owen Moore and Marceline Day. At Loew's New York, one day, Jan. 4. One-half of double feature bill. Running time, 65 mins.

Joan Hastings	Marceline Day
Bill	Rex Lease
Curtis Barstow	Owen Moore
Ruth	Helen Lynch
Aunt Evvie	Blanche Frederici
Aunt Babe	Joy Winthrop
Modiste	Betty Blythe

"Stolen Love" is not as hot as its title, but it's a moderately interesting program filler, with the added value of having been serialized in all of the Hearst newspapers.

With that title and implication, it should lend itself to profitable exploitation, especially in the neighborhoods.

Picture starts out at a nice pace in its opening love sequences, dealing with a 17-year-old girl who has never had a boy friend, owing to strict surveillance by a couple of spinster aunts.

She falls for a young garage mechanic with the invention bug, but the aunts queer it and the girl runs off to Frisco to become a model under the sponsorship of Barstow (Moore), the menace. Barstow plays the game carefully and then tries to take the girl at the wrong moment, after getting her alone in his mountain cabin. The boy mechanic rushes in for the last minute fist battle.

The runaway sequences and the girl's life as a model too long drawn and slow up picture perceptibly. _Mori._

DEVIL'S TWIN

Pathe Western starring and directed by Leo D. Maloney. Ford L. Beebe, author and supervisor. On one-day, Jan. 11, double bill, Columbus, New York. Running time, 59 minutes.

Saving the old homestead is just a working background for Leo Maloney's cowboy stunt stuff. That partially makes up for some disgraceful cutting and the film's one-man attitude.

Photography is good throughout, although looking injured at times because of the jerky slicing.

One-man western for one-day bills. _Bige._

IN OLD ARIZONA
(DIALOG)

Fox production and release. Featuring Edmund Lowe, Warner Baxter and Dorothy Burgess. Adapted from an O. Henry story by Tom Barry, who also wrote dialog. Directed by Irving Cummings, with Raoul Walsh sharing credit. Hansen, camera; Edeson, sound. At the Roxy, New York, week Jan. 19. Running time, 94 minutes.

Sergt. Mickey Dunn	Edmund Lowe
Tonia Maria	Dorothy Burgess
The Cisco Kid	Warner Baxter
Tad	Farrell Macdonald
Piano Player	Fred Warren
Barber	Henry Armetta
Cowpunchers	Frank Campeau Tom Santschi Pat Hartigan
Commandant	Roy Stewart
Soldier	James Bradbury, Jr.
Second Soldier	John Dillon
Cook	Soledad Jiminez

A long time ago Winnie Sheehan said Fox would never turn loose a full length talker until the studio was convinced the picture was right. "In Old Arizona" is it and that it's right for box office is unquestioned at this time. It's the first outdoor talker and a western, with a climax twist to make the story stand out from the usual hill and dale thesis. In fact the yarn is minus a chase. It's outdoors, it talks and it has a great screen performance by Warner Baxter. That it's long and that it moves slowly is also true, but the exterior sound revives the novelty angle again.

Not much doubt but that "Arizona" could have waltzed into the Gaiety, Fox's $2 Broadway site, and stayed for several weeks. On the other hand, the exhibs have been audibly wondering what has happened to Fox's proposed talkers. General release of this picture is the answer and it's a pretty fair retort.

A third of this picture is indoors. Scene is just a shack but for 34 minutes Baxter waxes amorously over Dorothy Burgess and it's slow going until the action gets outdoors again. Miss Burgess has played stock, in light comedies and assumed the role of ingenue in a Broadway musical. This is her first picture. With the customary broken English dialect and brown makeup she's not unlike another edition of Del Rio.

Miss Burgess is cast as a Mexican vixen who plays the boys across the boards and finally gets in a jam between the Cisco Kid (Baxter) and the army sergeant who is pursuing the bandit. Story takes its change in direction when the Kid frames Tonia so that the sergeant shoots her instead of him as he rides away, her scream ending the film except for a few feet of added scenic footage to soften the blow. It would have more punch in the raw.

Film has no musical accompaniment but holds a theme song which crops out every so often but not by the usual unseen tenor. Melody's biggest plug comes during the prolog the Roxy has arranged for the feature. This is a Brown, De Sylva and Henderson composition which will need a lot of help to make it a national factor. Picture also demonstrates some nice camera work for scenic beauty plus dissolves and fades without the sound dimming in conjunction, just as effective.

Tom Barry's adaptation of the story and dialog has been well done and includes comedy lines wherever possible. Warner's reading of his character is excellent enough to stamp him as having turned in the top talker performance to date. Lowe, again playing a hardboiled sergeant, is also good but suffers from dialog material softened out of respect to the censor boards. Barry has also gone so far back as to dig up the gag on "that's why "they put rubbers on pencils" for him.

Technically the reproduction is excellent with one exception. This is the switch in lighting and vocal tones as Baxter says his final goodbye to the faithless Tonia, an inserted closeup marking the distinct change and breaking the illusion. Balancing this is some excellent work with the mike including an outdoor gun fight between the Cisco Kid and three punchers who are after his dough and the driving of a herd of cattle by the bandit. The effective bit of Movietone News' meadow lark chirping during a horse race clip is also reproduced here although this time it's a rooster crowing in the distance as Baxter rides away from a corral. Effective enough to cause a murmur to run through the house.

Picture gets away jumpily in planting the atmosphere for the story but soon settles down to the principal trio. Miss Burgess gives a legitimate display of the coin and man-crazy lass but may be unconvincing to some as to s. a. power because of the sole ragged costume worn.

Raoul Walsh is given screen and program credit for having co-directed this film, as he actually started it and was intent on finishing and playing the Cisco Kid in it. His unfortunate accident made this impossible, hence Cummings' assignment.

"In Old Arizona" is a corking piece of work but despite its exterior locale demonstrates that dialog inevitably slows up action as far as the screen is concerned. Allowing that it is elementary, almost experimental, it nevertheless has been hitting and will reach high gross receipts on the novelty of its genuine outdoor sound and Baxter's performance. In elementals, one camera shot goes back to the bandit gazing down from a cliff to a pass along which the stage coach is expected. The holdup follows.

Fox spent a barrel of dough in the New York dailies to blaze a trail for this one, the campaign lasting a week. The results were obvious at Saturday's second show with standees behind the loge section, an inside lobby wait at four p. m., and Roxy getting ready to spend two weeks in Miami. *Sid.*

WOMAN OF AFFAIRS
(SOUND)

Metro-Goldwyn-Mayer production and release from Michael Arlen's story, "The Green Hat." Directed by Clarence Brown. John Gilbert and Greta Garbo co-starred. Synchronized score and effects. Continuity by Beth Meredyth. Cameraman, William Daniels. Titles by Hugh Wynn. Special theme song, "Love's First Kiss" (Robbins). At the Capitol, N. Y., week of Jan. 19. Running time, 90 minutes.

Diana	Greta Garbo
Neville	John Gilbert
Hugh	Lewis Stone
David	John Mack Brown
Geoffrey	Douglas Fairbanks, Jr.
Sir Montague	Hobart Bosworth
Constance	Dorothy Sebastian

A sensational array of screen names and the intriguing nature of the story ("The Green Hat") from which it was made. together with some magnificent acting by Greta Garbo, by long odds the best thing she has ever done, will carry through this vague and sterilized version of Michael Arlen's erotic play. Superb technical production and admirable photography count in its favor.

But the kick is out of the material, and, worse yet, John Gilbert, idol of the flapper fans, has an utterly blah role. Most of the footage he merely stands around, rather sheepishly, in fact, while others shape the events. At this performance (the second of the Saturday opening) whole groups of young women customers audibly expressed their discontent with the proceedings.

Entire picture is full of subterfuges and tactful evasions, due to the understanding that producers shall not exploit stage plays that have aroused controversy on moral grounds, at least by name, and shall not emphasize story material regarded as indelicate. So here is a woman who, disappointed in her first love, plunges into an orgy of amorous adventures from Calais to Cairo. Screen story gets over this sequence by having a newspaper editor look over his reference files which include poses of the heroine with her various boy friends. Flicker addicts accustomed to literal facts quite reasonably remain cold.

Miss Garbo saves an unfortunate situation throughout by a subtle something in her playing that suggests just the erotic note that is essential to the whole theme and story. Without her eloquent acting the picture would go to pieces.

Production is noteworthy for its beauty of setting and atmosphere. There is a series of views of Diana (it was "Iris" on the stage) hurrying home through the evening mists that is full of loveliness. There is a sequence of views down white corridors in a French nursing home, with placid nuns gliding about, that have stunning pictorial effect. Bits of the varsity boat races on the Thames are colorful and the interior of English country houses are fine beyond description. It is during the boat races that the sound effects are used, the cheering crowds along the course heightening the effect.

Lewis Stone plays a wise and kindly old counsellor of the madcap heroine that was made to order for his suave and sophisticated style of playing. Hobart Bosworth plays the unsympathetic part of the meddling Sir Montague, and Dorothy Sebastian manages to register real personality as the wife.

Theme song has a pretty sentimental melody. It is not actually incorporated in the action, but is introduced as an accompaniment to one of the love scenes between Gilbert and Miss Garbo in the form of a tenor solo by an unseen singer Just an effect that has no reference to the scene itself. *Rush.*

THE LITTLE WILDCAT
(DIALOG)

Warner production and release. Dialog and sound in Vitaphone. Directed by Ray Enright from story by Gene Wright. Ben Reynolds, cameraman. In cast: George Fawcett, Robert Edeson, Doris Dawson, Audrey Ferris, Hallem Cooley, James Murray. At Colony, New York, week Jan. 19. Running time, 63 minutes.

Very frail story. Entertaining in light comedy vein. Little action and few situations make lags apparent. Excellent characterizations by George Fawcett and Robert Edeson, whose picture it is essentially. Laughs and interest enough for "The Little Wild Cat," 100 per cent. uncensorable, to please for maximum of two days. Especially worthwhile for houses having high-class residential trade.

The title is meaningless unless meant for Fawcett as the ranting old grandpa. Guessing contest on this or who it best fits in the action might spur buys in stick towns.

Dialog through about half of footage generally good and centered mostly on chatter and gibes between two old men.

Some thrill shots from aeroplane only diversion from comedy. Girls and their boy friends in slow moving canter when away from the old timers. *Waly.*

MARQUIS PREFERRED

Paramount production and release starring Adolphe Menjou. Directed by Frank Tuttle from story by Ernest Vadja based on another by Frederic Arnold Kummer. Cameraman, Harry Fishbeck. Titles by Herman Manckiewicz. At the Paramount, N. Y., week of Jan. 19. Running time, 59 minutes.

Marquis d'Argenville	Adolphe Menjou
Peggy Winton	Nora Lane
Mr. Gruger	Chester Conklin
Mrs. Gruger	Dot Farley
Gwendolyn Gruger	Lucille Powers
Albert	Mischa Auer
Floret	Alex Melesh
Jacques	Michael Visaroff

Having all the unreality of farce and never getting under the epidermis so far as its characters are concerned, "Marquis Preferred" must depend for its fan appeal upon the glamor of life as led by an elegant but financially distressed French nobleman. Menjou wears clothes galore, exquisitely tailored, drives about in swanky Isottas, is serviced by a battalion of uniformed flunkies and through this vale of flamboyant colorfulness and dainty indolence, he moves with his customary grace and suavity, ever the well bred gent.

Certainly the gals, and possibly many of the boys, and without doubt those who read romantic novels of high society, will be inclined to like "Marquis Preferred." It will give them an opportunity to day dream while watching the debonair Adolphe rescue his genteel soul from a mercenary marriage with an American sausage manufacturer's daughter.

It is one of the lightest of Menjou features but because of the deft work of director Frank Tuttle it avoids some of the more obvious flaws that have characterized recent Menjou pictures. It seems, from trade indications, that Menjou is still enough of a favorite around the country for this one to get by, as the others have, simply for what they are supposed to be, amusing trifles to demonstrate Menjou's ability to act the way a lot of people would like to be able to.

Nora Lane, playing the sympathetic lead, and Lucille Powers, doing the blonde ingenue, both are newcomers to the screen and nifty lasses on face and form. Neither is allowed any emotional latitude. The chap playing Menjou's valet (not readily identified from credits) is also new and an interesting personality. Chester Conklin, a little less the bricklayer than usual, was almost convincing as an American millionaire. *Land.*

NAPOLEON
(FRENCH MADE)

Gaumont-Metro-Goldwyn production: released over here by Metro-Goldwyn-Mayer. "A General Society of Film Productions" one slide lists. Directed by Al Gance. All French cast, with no names caught off screen. At Loew's New York one day, Jan. 19. Running time, around 70 minutes.

"Napoleon" was made by the French for the French. In Paris, where it played at the Gaumont-Palace, and it was claimed to have been shown on extended screens, the picture must have been liked. Over here it's only for the sure-seaters, but sure in them.

The French can't glorify Napoleon; it's just the other way around. And there's no picture producer who can picture Nap in 70 minutes.

Therefore when the Josephine-Napoleon romance is stuck in for the box-office side, this "Napoleon" is but sketchily outlined. Really it is one big mob scene of Napoleon and his armies. Napoleon taking Touron from the English and Italy from the Italians, all hazily sketched but with plenty of extras in men and horses.

If there is one appealing scene to those that Napoleon doesn't appeal in type or on screen as the most interesting character in history, it is of Rouget DeLisle first singing "The Marseillaise" and having it adopted as the national anthem of France by the Revolutionists. He wrote it. It's in a great hall, and Danton is there. Nap is then a first lieut. Robespierre is present as well.

Three historical women are later seen, Mlle. Recamier among them. They strutted like Broadway showgils. Napoleon became a captain of artillery. He went to Corsica, in the picture, trying to switch his native land to France, and got chased out of the country. Probably all historical, and much in the film too much. Especially the chase and the boat ride that followed. Most of this resembled an American western.

"Napoleon" doesn't mean anything to the great horde of picture house goers over here. Nap wasn't good looking enough and they didn't put in the right scenes for the flaps over here. And Josephine didn't always look so well. Her eyes were blurry when right into the camera

Al Gance gets the most credit. He directed. Whoever impersonated Napoleon looked more like Hearst.

A patriotic picture for France and its friendly foreign allies. Likely sent over here on a chance and may do what states righters will do, unless the sure-seaters can importantly swell the gross. Sending it into Loew's New York as its first metropolitan showing place sorta tells what M-G-M thinks of it. *Sime.*

RASPUTIN
(GERMAN MADE)

Worldart Films producer named in main title. Director, Max Neufeld, who also plays the title role of Russia's "Mad Monk." Cast is made up of Russian actors in Germany, including Renati Renee, leading woman; Eugene Neufeld, Robert Valbar, Victor Kutchere, Grigory Batumkin, Ivon Golovin and Ivan Bedny. At the Fifth Avenue Playhouse, Jan. 13. Running time, 54 mins.

One can't get even an approximation of real value from this version, which apparently has been unmercifully cut. As it stands, the picture is almost worthless. Clarity of story is almost entirely lost. and it's just a chaotic series of episodes picked for their spectacle effect and without relation to the complete whole.

"Rasputin, the Holy Sinner," is the unabridged title and the picture is merely a jumble of scenes in which the sinister power behind the Russian throne is exhibited either in his private orgies, his political intrigues or finally in his sensational murder by the Czar's counsellors, whose influence he had undermined.

Scenes of orgies are clumsily done, dance spectacles resembling the cabaret shots without which no American feature was complete not long ago. High light is the final sequence where Rasputin is lured to a rendezvous by a woman secret service agent and there murdered by military agents.

Notable in the film are the ponderous palace interior settings, characteristic of the German technique. Groupings are bad. Picture has a great many characters. most of them Russian officials and all dressed alike in much gold braid and medals. You can't tell who is who most of the time. Director has further confused the personalities by having them always surrounded by identical figures. Czar Nicholas figures in many groups, but only film fans who knew Nick personally could pick him from the mob.

Renati Renee is an impressive leading woman, both on beauty and a suaveness of acting that is notable in continental actresses. Even in some of the foolish episodes she has here, she manages to maintain some dignity. Men of the cast have the common European fault of being artificial and stilted. *Rush.*

THE PRESIDENT
(GERMAN MADE)

Producer's name does not appear in billing or screen main title. Distributed by the Edward L. Klein Corp. Directed by Gennaro Righelli. Ivan Morjoukine starred. Other players: Suzy Vernon, Nikolai Malikoff, Heinrich Schroth and Luigi Servanti. Running time, 55 minutes. At 55th Street Playhouse, New York, week of Jan. 19.

A Russian star, an apparently Italian director and a flavoring of German names, together with the Teutonic origin, makes a medley of races calculated to puzzle anybody. One guess is that some of the names are phoney.

Character and quality of the picture are equally confusing. It purports to be a broad farcical treatment of politics in a new European republic. There are also hints that it may be a satire directed to Mussolini's address.

After about two reels of political harlequinade, it turns into a romantic comedy. At the end it leaves the sure-seater fan gasping at its clumsiness and stupid chaos. The saving grace is one excellent comedy sequence, in which a country yokel in a hired dress suit crashes a political convention, and getting the floor by accident makes a speech of dumb bromides.

One of the Royalist leaders figures a guy who can talk so much and say so little would make a priceless campaigner in the election and accordingly hires him as a spell binder. Instead of which another dumb break gets the peasant the nomination and he is elected.

Then the romance begins and audience interest stops. The farmer-president marries the daughter of a Royalist, but refuses to betray the people in a Royalist plot. They try to assassinate him, but he outwits them with shrewd peasant devices.

Outside of the gag episode of the convention the whole business is goshawful. Acting is terrible, direction bad even for a Continental studio and the entertainment value nil. Musical comedy plot done as straight comedy and tripping over its own feet.

Suzy Vernon is a looker, of the spiritual Italian type, but can't troup or isn't allowed to here. Men haven't an excuse.

Another one of those foreign things.   *Rush.*

THE LOST EMPIRE

Travel picture No. 2 of a series produced and presented by Edward A. Salisbury. Cameraman, Ernest Schoedsack. At 5th Ave. Playhouse, New York, week of Jan. 20. Running time about 70 mins., with lecture.

Travel stuff has at least the advantage of human interest and novelty. When combined with halfway decent photography it beats the usual screen fare of the sure seaters.

Man-killing pygmies are far more interesting than tenement dramas from Berlin and the royal family of Abyssinia is more intriguing than French Thespians with too much mascaro.

That's roundabout praise for Captain Salisbury's camera jaunts through the South Seas, Ceylon, Arabia and other strange and far-away lands where the ideas on elegant deportment are peculiar to occidental eyes.

The Salisburyites were six years sailing and exploring from 1921 to 1927. All told they took something like 300,000 feet of film. From that mass of celluloid a series of travelog, running an hour each, are being cut and edited. The result is necessarily rather choppy as to continuity.

Neither in organization of material or presentation does "The Lost Empire" compare with such pictures as "Chang," "Nanook," "Grass" or the classic travel records brought back regularly by Martin Johnson and Burton Holmes.

It is good sure seater entertainment and great for non-theatrical uses. While covering many different peoples this release takes title from the hidden kingdom of Abyssinia, Christian negroes in the heart of Africa.   *Land.*

Beauty and Bullets

Universal production and release. Directed by Ray Taylor from story by Karl Krusada. Ted Wells and Duane Thompson featured. Joseph Brotherton, cameraman. At Columbus, New York, one day, Jan. 18, half of double bill. Running time, 45 mins.

In houses like the Columbus, on 8th avenue, they intersperse the unraveling of such westerns as "Beauty and Bullets" with noisy approval. Every time the posse comes up over the hill in pursuit of the stage coach hold-uppers, they let 'em have the hands. Okay for the grinds, and at that better than the average of Universals' western thrill series.

The story is based on the tried and proven recipe that calls for a weak brother, a valiant sister and a two-fisted knock-'em-all-over lover. Lot of rough riding. Plot of the kind that provides some with nice snooze and rabid dopesters with plenty of satisfaction.   *Waly.*

WEARY RIVER
(DIALOG)

First National production and release. Starring Richard Barthelmess. Betty Compson featured. Directed by Frank Lloyd. Story by Courtney Ryley Cooper, adapted for screen by Bradley King. Photographed by Ernie Haller. Art director John J. Hughes. Costume director, Max Ree. Film editor Ed Schoeder. With Vitaphone synchronized score. Theme song, "Weary River" by Louis Silver with words by Grant Clarke. At Central, New York, opening Jan. 24 at $2 top. Running time about 90 minutes.

Jerry Larrabee	Richard Barthelmess
Alice	Betty Compson
Warden	William Holden
Sapdoni	Louis Natheaux
Blackie	George Stone
Elevator Boy	Raymond Turner
Manager	Gladden James

Measured from any angle "Weary River" is a money picture for First National and a credit to Richard Barthelmess, Frank Lloyd, Betty Compson, and almost every artist associated in bringing it to the screen. A catalog of its merits includes a revealment by Barthelmess of a melodious, vibrant tenor with which he sings the song "Weary River," if he sings it, and which, take odds, will cause heavy chattering among the femme sighs.

Barthelmess emerges as possibly the first of the veteran film stars to register a clean-cut wow in the articulate cinema. His voice has a human warmth and he uses it with an unexpected range of effect. Always he is natural, sincere, nicely repressed, conveying by deft suggestion the shades of meaning which speak to the sympathies. His singing is not only a climax to his performance but a new and interesting phase in his career.

The story of "Weary River" is of a gangster who discovers within penitentiary walls a talent for musical composition. Singing over the radio he achieves fame, ultimately winning a governor's pardon. This has a parallel in real life in the case of Harry Snodgrass, pianist, who played in mid-western vaudeville after becoming a "name" by his broadcasting from the Missouri lockup.

The story fits dialog and sound like the proverbial glove. Director Frank Lyold proves, too, that the 50-50 method of sandwiching talk between periods of silent relaxation is the best way of circumventing the nervous exhaustion which some of the all-talkers have occasioned. "Weary River" captures again that much-bandied "visual flow," allegedly assassinated by conversation. It moves with well-lubricated serenity, technically okay.

The theme song by Louis Silver and Grant Clarke listens like big royalties which will help the picture as the picture will make the song.

The advantage of "Weary River" considered from the cold cash attitude is that it is artistic without bein' hard to "get." Its problem is definite, simple; its telling intelligently aimed at those old heart strings and that sentimental barometer, the adam's apple.

The morality angle with its "lesson" in straight living coupled with some good, solid romance between Barthelmess and Betty Compso will hit Americans where they bruise easiest. Miss Compson incidentally is almost as much of a revelation in talkers as the star. There is a feminine cuteness about her voice although she never descends to baby t. She looks great t' ughout and gets her full share of closeups, a type of photography to which Mr. Lloyd is strongly and justifiably devoted. Besides which, Miss Compson's playing is commendable.

Of the remaining players all are, in minor roles, excellent with a number of neat touches, viz., elevator bit by a colored thespian named Raymond Turner who gets

screen credit although in hardly 50 feet of film. William Holden was a believable warden of the human Lawes type. Gladden James, infrequent player for the past several years, has a small speaking part as a vaudeville promoter.

"Weary River" is one of the thoroughly fine films of the current season.

But a better title wouldn't have hurt, although titles seldom affect either way, much.   *Land.*

THE BELLAMY TRIAL
(DIALOG)

M-G-M production and release. Directed by Monta Bell, from adaptation of Frances Noyes Hart's novel. Leatrice Joy and Betty Bronson featured. Joe Farnham, captions. At Embassy, New York, opening Jan. 23 on run. $2 top. Running time, 95 minutes.

Sue Ives	Leatrice Joy
Girl Reporter	Betty Bronson
Boy Reporter	Edward Nugent
Pat Ives	George Barraud
Mimi Bellamy	Margaret Livingston
Stephen Bellamy	Kenneth Thomson
Mother Ives	Margaret Seddon
District Attorney	Charles B. Middleton
Defense Attorney	Charles Hill Mailes

All right as a regular program release to those wanting mystery and seeing it on display.

"The Bellamy Trial" has a couple of novelties. It's one long court scene, with interruptions by switch backs.

Opening is through series of M-G-M news clip leading up the court house and start of the trial. Informative slides follow ending of picture.

Whatever the picture does, and in spots it is going to do very well, even if not at the Embassy at $2, for it's nowhere near a $2 picture, the credit should go to Monta Bell, its director. His direction, aided by skilful cutting, seems to be the entire picture, other than the vague value of the dialog.

Dialog is so placed here, toward the end of the court scene, that the picture, held tense by the direction until that time and continued, could also continue under the same tension, silent. That's quite a feat. It must bounce back upon the director, as so must his faculty of holding an audience despite what looks to be an ordinary court room trial.

A prolog, following the acquittal of the two defendants on trial for murder, reveals the actual murderer, in a confession made after the trial to the presiding justice. A sentimental bit is pushed in here, but if the entire prolog had been left off, this picture might have started the discussion Metro appeared to want: who did kill Mimi Bellamy? A slide note at the finish requests the audience not to divulge the identity of the murderer, who is entirely foreign to everyone's minds while the trial is proceeding.

As the judge is summing up, a new character, unnamed, walks into the picture and the witness chair. He almost steals the entire thing for himself in his few moments. He's a married high school teacher who been taking a chance with one of his pupils the night the murder was committed. She insisted he tell all, and the witness corroborates both defendants, aiding in their acquittal.

Story based on a triangle, with rather a gruesome touch when a model of the murdered woman's bust is displayed in court and a knife thrust into the open wound as in the body when found. Not a pleasing sight for the matinee goers or children. Yet the censors passed it: those obliging censors—at times. They always seem nearsighted somehow in preferred spots.

Quite a deal of dialog, once commencing. Outstanding of the verbal readers is Charles B. Middleton, an old-time vaude sketch player. He did the prosecuting attorney and did it pretty. Leatrice Joy as one of the defendants, Sue Ives, carries rather a good film voice and did nicely on the stand.

There were no exclamations, no highly tensioned dialog to cap a situation, and the only vocal explosion was from that flirtatious high schooler. Sound incidentals, but without notable effect.

Kenneth Thomson did a nice bit in talk and work as Stephen Bellamy. Betty Bronson as a journalistic school reporter and Edward Nugent opposite, were used for slight comedy purposes. Some of their court room whispering was new to the talkers. Margaret Seddon, as the mother, and the unprogrammed judge were distinct in pleasant voice in their special scene. Some other and good comedy is secured from captions by Joe Farnham. But when will Farnham and the others out there allow that eraser on the lead pencil to lie still in its grave?

Reproduction had its ins and outs. Sometimes wholly clear, at others, blurred; and again, unplaced. But on the whole, rather well.

Cutting throughout the court room scene of decided help to action, with the imagination left to grasp a few things.

With no punch or kick other than the trial scene itself, "The Bellamy Trial" stands up, and when that occurs, as it seldom does, there must have been some one person responsible: either the author of the tale or the director of the picture. Here it looks like the director. *Sime.*

WOLF OF WALL ST.

(DIALOG)

Paramount production and release. All-talker by Western Electric Movietone system. George Bancroft starred. Story, screen play and dialog credited to Doris Anderson. Directed by Rowland V. Lee. Victor Milner, cameraman. In cast: Baclanova, Nancy Carroll, Paul Lukas, Arthur Rankin. At the Rialto, N. Y., beginning Jan. 26. Running time, about 74 mins.

Undoubtedly George Bancroft's greatest job for the screen. While the theme is essentially an old one it is handled from the lowdown angle. Some sparkling dialog and tense sex situations make it a sure bet for the sophisticates and higher class first runs.

An unusually convincing cast for the theme, which easily could have been overdone and relegated to the meller class, makes a perfect background for Bancroft. Picture rates the heavy applause a usually not too soft Rialto audience gave it on the first matinee.

Probably a lot in this production that the sticks will not get. But if properly exploited in such parts as an expose of what is supposed to go on behind the Wall Street curtain they should like the wising. Old story is of pushing up a stock, taking off the cream and then driving it down for a second killing. Calls for tickers, stock paraphernalia and a glimpse of the market. In the meantime the major action prevails behind the scene in the pool operator's office and his wife's bedroom.

Sold on his strength and ability never to fall, Bancroft, as the wolf, convincingly juggles stock. His blond wife, with social aspirations, although of Russian steerage antecedents, deceives him for a playboy in his own office. While the audience is let in on the deception, Bancroft's complete ignorance until the last reel gives it a good climax.

As the wife, Baclanova is given great latitude and makes good. Nancy Carroll, as the maid who approaches the "wolf" when her boy friend falls for her boss' manipulation, does some trouping, too. Intonation of her voice and its changes, as she notices the effect her domestic expose is having upon the operator, are stirring.

Bancroft's registration of mind working against impulse when he enters the room, after giving the couple time to regain their composure, is one of the situations that make the picture. Action also has comedy.

Dialog as a whole is okay except for a few whisperings which are blurred and an occasional lapse into a foreign tongue by Baclanova, meaningless for the first few feet. *Waly.*

SINS OF THE FATHERS

(SOUND)

Paramount production and release. Starring Emil Jannings. Directed by Ludwig Berger. Story by Norman Burnstine, adapted by E. Lloyd Sheldon. Cameraman, Victor Milner. Titles by Julian Johnson. At Rivoli, New York, opening Jan. 26 on grind run. Running time, 73 mins.

Wilhelm Spengler..............Emil Jannings
Mama Spengler....................Zazu Pitts
Mary Spengler...................Jean Arthur
Tom Spengler...................Barry Norton
Oscar..............................Jack Luden
Greta........................Ruth Chatterton
Bartender.......................Mathew Betz

Good program feature with the important name and constantly interesting performance of Emil Jannings to sustain it commercially. At several points it comes close to the human heart and greatness.

Many moist eyes during a touching sequence just before the final fade-out. Elsewhere tender and poignant scenes struck body blows at the sympathies. The tall timber and the minor metropolises of the provinces will probably endorse the note of sermonizing that robs the production of some of its artistic sincerity by converting the story and bending the moral to vindicate everything the bluenoses stand for on the subject of booze, poisoned alcohol saloons, hip flasks and bootleggers.

The gist of the irony here is that the beloved son of an ex-saloon keeper goes blind through drinking poison hootch manufactured by his father. In general the story is familiar beer garden atmosphere with a genial but blundering German making pretty much of a mess of his life. Jannings' characterization belongs to his gallery of slow-thinking old Teutons, of which "The Last Laugh" remains the classic example.

Ruth Chatterton takes second honors as an east side trollop, who insinuates herself into the dignity of the second Mrs. Spengler. As such she queens over a pre-Volstead grog shop and later a bootlegger's gaudy mansion. Miss Chatterton registered a wealth of conviction, perfectly assuming the free-and-easy mannerisms of a readily identified type of female.

Barry Norton extremely young-looking juvenile acting like a full-sized leading man left something to be desired as the ex-waiter's son. Jack Luden stood out in a small role and the always insidious Mathew Betz sneered contemptiously in the background. He remarks to the newly married Greta: "He (Jannings) is so dumb we don't even have to be careful."

While qualifying as a good programmer "Sins of the Fathers" represents mediocre stuff for the giant reputation of Emil Jannings. It is an uneugenic union between the German film methods of the heydey of Ufa and the venerable stencils of Hollywood. The result inspires regret that the production does not achieve equality with the star.

Picture is synchronized but without dialog. During one sequence Jannings is supposed to be singing German opera. Photographed from a semi-long shot this impressed as being ghost sung. *Land.*

REDSKIN

(SOUND)

Paramount production and release. Starring Richard Dix. Directed by Victor Schertzinger from Elizabeth Pickett's story. Color photography by R. Rannahan and E. Estebrook. Regular camera work, E. Cronjager. Titled by Julian Johnson and scored by J. Zamecnik. Western Electric disk synchronization. At the Criterion, New York, for limited run, starting Jan. 26, at $2. Running time, 81 mins.

Wing Foot.......................Richard Dix
Corn Blossom.................Gladys Belmont
Judy.............................Jane Novak
John Walton....................Larry Steers
Navajo Jim....................Tully Marshall
Chahi.........................Bernard Siegel
Chief Notani....................George Rigas
Yina........................Augustine Lopez
Pueblo Jim.....................Noble Johnson
Commissioner.............Joseph W. Girard
Wing Foot (Age 9)..........Philip Anderson
Corn Blossom (Age 6).........Loraine Rivero
Pueblo Jib (Age 13).........George Walker

Natural color picture, with the color saving it for the picture houses. Story is ordinary and lightweight. So much so it's doubtful if the film would make the first runs without its various hues; and, despite the Dix name, as it stands, it's a beautiful piece of camera work. Won't mean anything for $2 at the Criterion, but the cinemas should gather between the eye-filling print and Richard.

Presentation here is using Paramount's Magnascope (big screen) to help it along on its final six minutes. Picture needs it and wouldn't be bad to go to the wide angle lens earlier in the climax sequence. Finish is a double race, one angle being Dix's marathon to file an oil claim, and the other his Pueblo sweetheart fleeing from her tribe, both, unknowingly, making for the same settlement.

Yarn is of a Navajo boy forced into an Indian school and thence to college, where he gains prominence as a runner, but learns his social standing upon being snubbed at a dance. Lincoln Stedman and Pauline Garon are prominent in this passage, though neither is given program notation. Unnecessary rebuke sends Dix back to his tribe, where his father, the chief, refuses to except him because of his clothes. With the change back to native apparel, it's Dix's turn to refute, scorning to become medicine man because he can't accept his people's superstitions. Meanwhile his boyhood sweetheart, Pueblo girl, who has followed him to college as a stenographer, has been tricked into returning to cliff dwelling and is slated to marry the menace.

Becoming an outcast, after trying to steal away with the girl, Dix stumbles on oil at about the same time the Indian maid is preparing for hed wedding. Double-crossed by claim jumpers, Dix starts running to beat them to the filing office, while the girl also makes her escape and is picked up in an auto by an Indian agent and her former school teacher. Finale is the shooting of the heavy, the wedding of Dix and the girl, despite tribal differences, and Dix splitting the oil between his own and his wife's people.

Early footage uncovers a couple of corking kids playing Dix and the girl as youngsters. Girl is a particularly cute youngster and the boy troupes exceedingly well. Secondary love theme is unnecessary and ridiculous in having the school teacher and agent split because the latter whips the boy. Years later they are shown reconciling, because the agent has finally apologized to Dix. Got a well-deserved snicker from this audience and will repeat from others.

Picture is at least 80 per cent. color, the Indian school footage being normal, with these frames tinted solidly. Mountains, mesas, sky, clouds and shades in the Indian regalia are impressively picturesque, which this is what will sell the picture. Dix is okay in again playing an Indian. Performance highlight comes from the woman cast as the star's grandmother. Tully Marshall does what he can to relieve in a comedy vein.

Film isn't overboard with action, has not been especially well held together, and there's not much suspense after Dix discovers oil. But it's an unusually good looking picture, serving to cover up a lot of faults. Has been nicely scored, plus a theme song portending no great demand. *Sid.*

SAL OF SINGAPORE

(DIALOG)

Pathe production and release, synchronized by RCA. Featuring Phyllis Haver with Allan Hale and Fred Kohler underlined. Directed by Howard Higgins from E. C. Classon's story. Titles by E. J. Mayer. J. J. Mescall, photographer. Scored by J. Zuro. At the Colony, New York, week of Jan. 26. Running time, 70 minutes.

Good program picture which may not jump receipts to records but should send totals somewhere above average. They may not rave but they won't squawk.

Story doesn't make any pretense to become what it's not in telling of a waterfront dive queen shanghaied by a rough and tough skipper to mind a baby he finds in one of his life boats. Yarn is in the same channel as Barthelmess's "Scarlet Seas," but Hollywood has long been peeking across the aisle to see what the other fellow's doing.

This feature doesn't start talking until its final 18 minutes, at which time it opens up in spurts of one and two minutes and then is almost vocally solid throughout the final 10. No screen credit for the dialog but it's okay if for nothing else than when Sal starts to converse she doesn't talk as if in a drawing room. There's a couple of "aints" and a "lousy" mixed up in the wording.

Action doesn't get around much for three quarters of the way. Finish is a modern version of a ship to ship boarding for a free-for-all, Hale chasing Fred Kohler's ship to bring back Sal to take care of the kid.

Previously, Higgins, the director, has slipped in some nice pathos as Hale and Sal (Miss Haver) watch over the ailing child. Miss Haver does some good work, ably assisted by intelligent [illegible]oring. Orchestration stands up all the way and is surprisingly free from ground noises. Not so the dialog passages which are all heralded by a distinct scratch. Last two reels are pock marked with synchronized sound and dialog sections which constantly exchange places.

Film is sustained until the late footage by Hale and his reactions to the fiery Sal, who goes for the tot 100 per cent and starts chasing the rough and tough cap around for safety pins, etc. Undercurrent is a lustful first mate whom Hale heaves overboard by title to protect the girl.

Picture is free from mush and clinches between the main couple, the story being carried through to a logical climax in Sal figuring that Hale is at least giving her an even break; she'd rather trail with him and the kid than go back to the joints. Finale is introduced by Sal deeming the baby better off with the captain, whence she leaves the boat in 'Frisco to join Kohler on his tramp. Chase and boarding of the latter vessel follows with Hale ordering Kohler to marry him to Sal as the finish.

Higgins has done a worth while job in making this tale believable while dotting it with a few snickers and a tear. It also speaks well for Miss Haver that she can arouse this sympathy despite a role which is basically thick with river front veneer. Also noticeable is that the pathos hits before the dialog although Sal later talks to the babe.

Hale doesn't look like a hard swinging mariner but rates a vote for overcoming the handicap. Kohler ably plays his limited assignment as the rival captain, speaking naturally and fast when called upon. Dialog has been especially well directed in the case of Kohler and Hale's reading of the letter Sal left behind her.

Due to the way this effort has been handled, without trying to give it any unnecessary frills, "Sal" can play 'em big and small, silent or wired, and mean something. It's first run material, and for Pathe a pip. *Sid.*

CAPT. LASH

Fox production and release starring Victor McLaglen. Directed by John Blystone. Story by Daniel Tomlinson and Laura Hase. Titles by M. E. Boylan. Cameraman, Conrad Wells. At the Roxy, N. Y., week of Feb. 2. Running time, 60 mins.
Captain Lash...............Victor McLaglen
Cora Nevins.................Claire Windsor
Gentleman Eddie.............Arthur Stone
Alex Condax..................Albert Conti
Cocky.......................Clyde Cook
Queenie.....................Jean Laverty
Bull Hawks..................Frank Hagney
Condax's Servant............Boris Charsky
Babe........................Jane Winton

Picture takes a lot of figuring. It has an interesting and convincing story; it has McLaglen in a roughneck part that fits him to the life, a wealth of spicy episodes and a line of deeply chucklesome titles. Doubtful element is how will the femme fans react to a gorilla hero who loves 'em and leaves 'em and gets away with it indefinitely?

Probably the comedy of the story will take the poison out of that aspect making everything o. k. Assuming that state of affairs the picture looks like a strong b. o. attraction. They'll talk about McLaglen's playing anyhow. They always do. Against the spicy adventures of the boss ship's stoker, there is a gem of a comedy performance by Clyde Cook as the pigmy pal of the giant.

Picture is full of waterfront women, waterfront dives, casual sailor love affairs, dancehall dames and society crooks. It has action that never ceases for an instant and dramatic tricks that keep one guessing. Good shots in the stoke hole of a big liner bound for Singapore and excellent Oriental atmosphere, a score of interesting angles. But primary interest is cleverly centered on "Capt." Lash, the super-stoker, his breathless adventures ashore and afloat, his lady loves and his pal Cocky, who trails him always trying to keep him from entanglements with casual dames. Cocky carries a concertina and every time the giant falls for a new petticoat, Cocky makes it register a disgusted razzberry, faithfully reproduced in sound.

Sound effects are sparingly used, and then only for effects, such as the rasp of coal shovels, ring of iron furnace doors and crash of pitched coal in the stoke hole scene or the whistles of a departing liner or the music of a dancehall orchestra. Full score is provided by the mechanical arrangement credited to Roxy.

Backgrounds aboard ship are excellent and the dancehall sets are very well done. Photography is flawless. Skillfully managed story builds in alternate drama and comedy, drama always casual and unforced. Several nifties in titles. "I know your gal in Singapore don't wear no wings, but she'll be waiting for you on the quay with what she's got," is a sample.

Fighting or wooing McLaglen is a joy. This player is runner up to Wolheim for capitalizing a homely pan. The radiant smile that can break through that ugly map is a drama in itself. Women's reception of the picture is a gamble. This will mark the difference between moderate box office and exceptional business. *Rush.*

DOCTOR'S SECRET

(DIALOG)

Paramount production and release. Featuring Ruth Chatterton, H. B. Warner and Robert Edeson. Directed by Wm. DeMille and based on James Barrie's play, "Half an Hour." Synchronized on film (W. E.), with J. Roy Hunt cameraman. At Paramount, New York, week of Feb. 2. Running time, 61 mins.
Lillian Garson.............Ruth Chatterton
Richard Garson.............H. B. Warner
Hugh Paton.................John Loder
Dr. Brodie................Robert Edeson
Mr. Redding...............Wilfred Noy
Mrs. Redding..............Ethel Wales

Susie......................Nancy Price
Wethers....................Frank Finch-Smiles

This Barrie work acted as a curtain raiser at the Lyceum and was played by Grace George. As a picture Will DeMille passed up a corking chance of turning out a great talking two-reeler. Even though this picture only runs 61 minutes, it's still overboard on length. Technically it's an hour of closeups and medium shots within parlor sets, with the story failing to tighten until the final 1,500 feet, when it looks as though the wife is in a jam Whalen couldn't unravel. For program purposes it's a talker, indicating moderate grosses at best.

Ruth Chatterton spends these minutes holding up this picture with a good performance. Backed by H. B. Warner and Robert Edeson, all impressive legit names and troupers, the cast clings in face of the slow motion. Warner, in a despicable role of a suspicious husband with an inferiority caste complex and bullying his way out, has been given most of his footage for sinister chuckles, prone to resemble the Century leaving Albany when the amplification is blaring. Likewise the mike is unkind to Miss Chatterton's repressed sobs. Wires do strange things to subdued but audible emotion. Any such attempt has yet to convince. So that leaves Edeson, as the doctor who knows all but saves the wife, capably handling a role clear of heavy histrionics.

Yarn is of a contract marriage for money and position, the wife finally fleeing to a former suitor who still cares and is Egypt bound. Stepping out to call a cab, the lover is run over and killed by a truck. Edeson is the passing doctor.

Unable to help the woman in the case, he goes on to dinner at Garson's (Warner), where he is formally introduced to Lillian (Miss Chatterton) as Mrs. Garson. Having previously related his experience to the dinner party before Mrs. Garson appears, the guests are in a furore of curiosity about the involved woman and circumstances develop to make it look as if Mrs. Garson were the woman. Garson freezes with suspicion, making accusations, but the wife saves herself by retrieving the letter she has left in his desk drawer. Doctor denies ever having seen Mrs. Garson, the husband is apologetic and the wife finally goes in to dinner on the arm of the physician.

Minor parts are well assigned, with John Loder playing the unfortunate second man. Terms of endearment between him and Miss Chatterton in a prolonged love scene do not hold on the screen, be it Barrie's or anyone else's dialog. Miss Chatterton is legitimate throughout, with Loder inclined to overplay.

It's a lethargic drawing room picture holding questionable assets for the second and third-run houses and those first runs in secondary towns. Can't educate a picture clientele overnight, and it's a close follow-up on "Interference," in method and release date. Films minus action provoke restlessness, and this program leader spends a lot of time edging its way to the punch.

Play title implies the time in which it should have been told, and under those circumstances it would certainly have been a much better picture. It is also a questionable start for Warner in talkers. He has not an abundance of lines, and then always as the cad. Photography and production standard, with Miss Chatterton wearing but two dresses. Little or no comedy and wholly void of a change of pace.

DeMille has completely muffed the thrill in picturing the accident. More effective had they given the first intimation of tragedy by carrying the boy back into the house and explained what had happened by dia-

log. Only audience stir, at this house, was the appearance of the same doctor for cocktails. It will be that way within other walls.

Slow and so formal. The idea of talking pictures and Miss Chatterton, her first talker, at least, must send this feature through for whatever success it will achieve. Indications are for a varied career. Useless for the unwired houses. *Sid.*

NAUGHTY BABY

(SOUND)

First National production and release with synchronized score and effects. No theme song. Alice White and Jack Mulhall featured. Mervyn Leroy, director. Story by Charles Beehan and Garrett Fort. At the Strand, N. Y., week of Feb. 2. Running time, 70 mins.
Rosie McGill...............Alice White
Terry Bolton...............Jack Mulhall
"Me Too" Grayson...........Jay Eaton
Bonnie Le Verne............Thelma Todd
Polly O'Toole..............Doris Dawson
Dugan......................Fred Kelsey
Madame Fleurette...........Rose Dione
Max Cohen..................Benny Rubin
Jimmy Malone...............Andy Devine
Tony Bonelli...............Georgie Stone

Full of women, and most of them pips. That should suffice for the masculine trade. Otherwise it's a woman's picture, particularly the young ones.

Story, improbable, far-fetched and full of holes, is a reproduction, with variations, of any flapper's dream. Little Cinderella, slaving as a hat snatcher in a hotel check room, decides to land a rich young guest. Boy is hitting it high and wide and about to be taken by a tall blonde who needs only a table and a couvert charge to be a perfect night club hostess. He's finally landed, but by Cinderella.

Improbabilities are not in a serious mood and all are forgivable. The picture's lightness, brevity and speed make it.

Very much in that class are the three boys who make love to Rosie as a trio, are ever at her beck and call, who match coins to determine which should be the possessor of Rosie's arm, who steal that Rosie may be properly garbed, and who otherwise are strictly for Rosie. But without a chance to create the spark of another sort of love in Rosie's flapperish heart. Rosie is set on the rich young lad from Boston and her three musketeers are mere helpmates. But the three boys are helpful in another way, as comics. If Benny Rubin, a prominent Hebe comic from vaude, just offers a sample of what he can do as a laugh maker in his first feature, he should be in pictures the rest of his life. And Benny can talk, though no chance for talking in this production.

Alice White is in another typical White role and fills it nicely. She looks rather badly when on the verge of crying, but never falls into out and out ears. In the future Alice should be restrained from registering even near-sorrow.

Jack Mulhall's assignment is a cinch, mainly getting in and out of snappy duds. Thelma Todd, as the would-be taker of Jack and his jack, doesn't look so bad herself. When Rosie (Alice White) loses her bathing suit while swimming, she contributes the film's large slice of spice, but Rosie is a good girl throughout. Losing the bathing suit is an accident, and she squawks at being rescued in this bare state.

It's apparent Mervyn Leroy has turned out just what was expected—an enjoyable lightweight for lightweights, whose coin is as good as any other coin. For others "Naughty Baby" won't kiss and won't kill. It should capably fill a program bill from a day to a week. *Bige.*

RED HOT SPEED

(DIALOG)

Universal sound film with dialog sequences. Starring Reginald Denny in story by Gladys Lehman. Directed by Joseph E. Henaberry. Titles by Albert De Monde. Other screen credits incomplete, through being caught off screen. Principal players' names recalled: Alice Day, Charles Byer and Fritzi Ridgeway. At Colony, New York, week Feb. 2. Running time, 60 minutes.

Conclusion is that "Red Hot Speed" is nothing like the title. It is neither cinematically torrid nor speedy in action. Derived from the situation of a traffic violation for speeding, the title is otherwise a misnomer.

Other than that, this Universal sound film is only distinguished by Reginald Denny making his debut as a talking celluloid mime and acquitting himself creditably. In addition there is the highly favorable impression of Alice Day, opposite, and Fritzi Ridgeway in a dialect comedy bit, as a slavey, which should carry this actress far, assuming that her bit in this feature comes to proper attention. It merits her enlisting of an exploitation man just to demonstrate this, for it is the best sales argument Miss Ridgeway would want.

The Gladys Lehman story, adapted by the authoress and another (name not caught), is a silly continuity, and only the yeoman histrionics of the players (but only in spots) was capable of offsetting the innocuous story. As an assistant district attorney, Darrow (get the name!), played by Denny, acts as unprofessional in court and as preposterously unreal as has any pseudo-barrister before him in the halcyon days of Irish Justice travesties.

The heroine (Miss Day) is paroled in his care for 90 days for speeding. Rest of the story is an attempt by the earnest young ass't d. a. to take his parole charge as seriously as possible and at the same time keep "Mary Jones," alias the daughter of Col. Long, free from the criticism of her staid old pater, who is fanatically opposed to all speeders.

Dull, tedious direction. Synchronization spotty and mostly poor with few exceptions. Dialog sequences were best, but these were in spots, as in the traffic tirade, where the faint honking of horns alone helped toward the illusion. Verbal exclamations here, as well as more spontaneous sound effects, could have been utilized to great advantage.

The comedy attempt at bright dialog was punningly painful, such as a one-arm driver with his "other arm going to waste (waist)," strictly a campus weekly wheeze, as was the play on "It'll be a brief case," with the business of elevating a brief case portfolio. Sickly.

Synchronization otherwise awry. No theme song, but a recurrent theme strain over-plugged, suggesting it may become a lyric theme if there is any excuse for it whatsoever. But otherwise the musical motifs were all wrong. In a court scene, where a dramatic situation would have been apropos, they gave out "Ragging the Scale," etc.

Reproduction was raspy and replete with overtones and muddy sounds. Yet some of the other sound effects, such as the radio receiver and the shut-off thereof, were effective, as were the business of the buzzing doorbell, droping of the electric bulb in simulation of pistol shots in another bit, crackle of paper, and others.

Denny all right in his talking assignments, and with better stuff will register even better. Miss Day is a strong contender for distinction in the talkers, as is Miss Ridgeway.

"Red Hot Speed" is a daily changer in calibre for the neighborhood programs; only at Universal's own Colony could this U feature stay a week. Unless Denny's strength and curiosity to hear him talk will hold up the film. U may have banked on that angle. *Abel.*

ANNAPOLIS

Pathe production and release, featuring Johnny Mack Brown and Jeanette Loff. Directed by Christy Cabanne. Cast: Hugh Allen, Hobart Bosworth, William Bakewell, Charlotte Walker, Fred Appleby and Maurice Ryan. At the Hippodrome, N. Y., week of Feb. 3. Running time, 63 mins.

Interesting background helps but does not make a picture. With midshipmen, Chesapeake Bay and the co-operation of the navy to work with, Christy Cabanne has turned out a pretty dull picture, for the simple reason that even the Naval Academy needs to be dramatized. An industrial film company commissioned to grind on Annapolis would probably turn out a more interesting job.

Weakness of the story is not the only flaw. Johnny Mack Brown, the hero, and Hugh Allen, playing the no-good guy, both look alike, or enough so to be confusing. This circumstance is intensified by Cabanne's strange aversion to close-ups, which he seldom uses as a narrative technique, and what few are included are not sharply outlined to build characterization.

Tip-off on story and production is the last-reel conversion of Allen previously a nice fellow, into a dirty so-and-so, and the absurdly flat and machine-made climax. None of the people in the plot are human or real Only reality appears to be the buildings and equipment.

Commercially, probably having been made at small cost, "Annapolis," on the romance of its title and locale, should be okay for Pathe and perhaps a passable everyday programer for the movie parlors. *Land.*

TWO DAYS

(RUSSIAN MADE)

Wufku production released by Amkino. Directed by George Stabojvoy. Story and scenario by S. M. Lazurin. Photographed by Demutski. At the Film Guild Cinema, New York, Feb. 1. Running time, over 65 mins.

Old Servant	I. E. Samchykovski
His son	C. A. Minin
The Young Master	B. Z. Gakebush

Wufko and Sam Gould are modest production and exhibiting beings. Wufku made "Two Days" 65 minutes of misery, and Gould says that Samchykovski, who plays the role of the old retainer, is comparable to Jannings in "The Last Laugh" only that this Russian is superior. "Two Days" is among the most uninspired and exasperating foreign bolognas under the label of art. It's the last gasp in brutal acting, directing and story. It moves laboriously, just like its central character. It is revolting in some spots, merely trite in others. Samchykovski is billed as a Merited Artist of the Soviet Republic and of the three is the worst.

For the first 45 minutes there is no action. Everything is at a standstill while the old servant buries a dog, the family silver and moons over a picture of his wife. Among the opening sequences is one where a puppy is killed by a heavy valise. That dead pup is kept in the foreground at every opportunity. It's buried and dug up again. Repulsive every time it is flashed.

Aside from its vulgarities, its stupidities, its absolute unfitness for showing in a theatre, this production is nothing but outright propaganda for the Soviet government. Opening the new Film Guild Cinema, "Two Days" tops some of the most conspicuous foreign flops of the year.

Story centers around the revolution. The old servant is a staunch supporter of the old regime, faithful to his master to the end. His son is a Soviet commissar. They quarrel when the son and his rebels invade the town and take possession of the house. The old man is hiding his master's son in his room. Finally the Whites gain the town and the old servant's boy is killed through information given the officers by the boy whom the old man had hidden. The old servant then sees the evil of the Czarist reign and sets fire to the building. *Mori.*

BEHIND THE ALTAR

(GERMAN MADE)

Affiliated European release here of unnamed German production, filmed in Italy. Directed by Wilhelm Dieterle, starred. Marcella Albani only other named. Said to have been released abroad as "The Secret of Abbe X." At 55th St. Playhouse, New York, beginning Jan. 26. Running time, 65 minutes. Sure seater.

Even to an arty audience it is an imposition to show this. One of the most absurd, utterly disjointed and lifeless exhibitions that couldn't do a home movie maker credit. Best place for this is back in the can.

Hailed as a mystery thriller it will probably be marketed here under its European title, since the 55th St. likes to jazz up trade by originating its own title for things like this.

Situations too absurd and amateurishly handled to waste space.

Just blotto. *Waly.*

ESCAPED FROM HELL

(Russo-German Made)

Melodrama produced by Derussa, Russo-German film group, and presented in U. S. by Affiliated European Producers, Inc. Directed by Georg Asagaroff. Principal players, Jean Murat, French, and Countess Esterhazy, Hungarian. Supporting cast, European. Running time, 70 minutes. At Carnegie Playhouse, New York, Jan. 27.

First sure-seater release in a long time that has approached the average quality of American program product. This one has its good points. It deals with a sort of Jean Valjean theme, a Frenchman unjustly sentenced to Devil's Island, the French penal colony, from which he escapes, regaining his position in society by heroic action in a mine disaster upon his return to his native land.

Picture has been done in a big way as regards production scope. Sequences having to do with society scenes are splendidly set, although the minor people look very stagey and badly dressed to American eyes. The scenes dealing with the mine disaster are graphically done, most of them night shots of the frenzied mob around the mine entrance when a score of men are entombed below. Rough faces of men, agonized expressions of women terrified for their men in peril, all standing out of surrounding blackness in the flare of torches, are effective.

Best for melodramatic purposes are the scenes in the convict camp, famed the world over as the abode of living horror. These shots give an excellent foundation for the melodrama, with glimpses of broken men toiling in a barren land, brutal prison guards, cynical toward the sufferings of their charges and the desolation of the locale.

The Continental producers have not yet caught the trick of speed and economy of detail that marks the American product. Here it takes about 20 minutes of running time to get the story planted. There is glaring waste of footage in nonessentials. They say the same thing at least twice in order that nobody shall miss the point. Maybe they have to cater to a less alert fan public.

Society scenes have convincing settings, but the people never truly reflect the society manner, working too hard at the haute monde air. American pictures suffered from the same complaint up to and during the Theda Bara epoch, but have outgrown the malady.

Countess Esterhazy looks like a prospect, especially for grande dame types. Even under the handicap of Continental handling and costuming she gives a convincing performance here. Handsome brunette type, with fine eyes, an expressive face and a suave manner before the camera. The others are strictly Continental actors, particularly Murat, whose style is altogether too artificial for American tastes.

Picture also has the great merit of bringing new faces and new locales to the American screen, and for that reason alone is an asset to the sure seaters. *Rush.*

THREE WAX MEN

(GERMAN MADE)

German film presented here by Edwin Miles Fadman as a Viking Production. Directed by Paul Leni. Starring Emil Jannings, Conrad Veidt and Werner Krauss. At Little Carnegie Playhouse, week of Jan. 19. Running time, 65 mins.

Long ago before Veidt, Jannings and Leni were considered worthy enough to be imported here, they all got together and turned out 65 minutes of conglomerous fantasy over there. Here it is being released without credit to the German producer as "Three Wax Men." Great stuff for the arties, queer houses and non-theatricals. Very doubtful for standard policies and exhibs but those who may be interested can demand a pre-view.

Title should be taken literally. Three stories in one are hitched together by the writer called in by wax figure maker to gag statues of Ivan the Terrible (Veidt), Jack the Ripper (Krauss) and Bagdad Caliph (Jannings). Of the three Jannings is the best. With pouchy Jannings assisted by Krauss, as the baker, many wise cracking titles disport the Bagdad noble and his dealings with the baker's wife. Palace scenes as fantastic as story and a suggestion of Fairbanks' "Thief of Bagdad."

Ivan the Terrible is largely a costume affair with gripping scene of Czar torturing victims in Kremlin. Veidt's characterization is there. Jack the Ripper not so good. Studio street stuff with lighting effects make it hard to follow.

Much triple exposure work which made German photography the Hollywood rage for a time. All sets are freakish. *Waly.*

Beware of Bachelors

Warner Bros.' production and release. Directed by Roy Del Ruth from the story by Mark Canfield. Scenario by Robert Lord. Titles by Joseph Jackson. Audrey Ferris and William Collier, Jr., featured, cast including Andre Beranger, Tom Ricketts, Clyde Cook and Margaret Livingston. At Loew's New York, one-half of double bill. Running time over 60 minutes.

Merely a filler. No box-office value and worth spotting only in the daily change grinds.

Story light, action tepid, characterizations weak and uninteresting. Plenty of holes in continuity, resulting in draggy sequences throughout.

Audrey Ferris serves as a highly accomplished and interesting feminine lead, photographing very attractively in face and person. William Collier, Jr., in support, not so hot, while Andre Beranger, as a perfume salesman, provides a few moderate laughs in a type role hardly as effective as it could be under more inspired direction and story provision.

The young couple stand to get 50 grand if still married by the end of the first year. The evil cousin conspires with a woman to break up the home.

No laughs, no dramatic interest, no love interest, no story. *Mori.*

HOMESICK

Fox production and release. Comedy, directed by Henry Lehrman. Featuring Sammy Cohen. Captions, William Kernell. At Loew's New York, one day, Jan. 25, one-half double bill. Running time, around 55 minutes.

A full length slapstick comedy, meaning little except for neighborhoods drawing matinee trade mostly of children. Sammy Cohen, featured, doesn't show very well in this film. If there's any celluloid comedy in him, he failed to bring it out, including his mugging.

Barring a laugh here and there, but little occurred until toward the finish when everyone fell into a soft wedding cake. When they didn't fall into it, the dough was thrown around generally. That made it a vintage comedy picture of a bike race across the continent, with Cohen riding and his male opposite going on there on a Ford, following the riders.

Story nil and sil. Also the object, to marry a servant girl who had written both through a matrimonial medium. *Sime.*

SMOKE BELLEW

Big Four Productions (probably state righter). Adapted from a Jack London story. Conway Tearle and Barbara Bedford starred. Directed by Scott Dunlap. Supervised by David Thomas. At Loew's New York, one day, Jan. 25, half double bill. Running time, around 60 minutes.

As deadly dull as the Alaskan locale it's set in.

All snow or salt, but so much snow would have been too expensive as salt for this picture.

A gold rush and a gold strike; prospectors struggling through snow; always snow and more snow. Ran around 60 minutes and seemed a month.

Conway Tearle in title role, and not always to advantage, in situation or acting. Barbara Bedford the same. Only the snow seemed realistic.

If a state righter, that's it. *Sime.*

THE APACHE

Columbia production and release, directed by Phil Rosen. Cast: Margaret Livingston, Warner Richmond, Don Alvarado and Philo McCullough. Cameraman, Ted Tetzlaff. At Loew's New York, as half of double bill, Feb. 1. Running time, 65 mins.

Second grade program material but rates better than on a double bill in daily change houses. Workmanlike production and fair mystery story. Acting satisfactory for neighborhood purposes. Defect of story is that the outcome may easily be anticipated, although the means of bringing it about is a surprise.

Locale is the Apache dens of Paris, always interesting setting for a melo. Heroine is a girl in a cafe in Marseilles frequented by thieves. A police official befriends and rescues her from that life, but then tries to make her. Same official has her stage partner in knife throwing act sent to jail as a crook. She falls in love with an Apache dancer in Paris and works with him, meanwhile holding her persecutor at a distance. When the menace is mysteriously killed the action tries to make it look like the lover's work,

but anybody can tell it's the old partner, now freed from prison. However, lover is condemned and about to be sent to Davil's Island for life when girl discovers guilty man is the old partner. She forces herself upon him to do the old knife throwing act, and while she has him strapped to the board on the stage wrings a confession from him, freeing the lover for a happy ending.

Climax is not well done and isn't convincing. Implausibility kills the story and probably accounts for its presence in double bill. *Rush.*

KISS ME
(FRENCH MADE)

Paris, Jan. 13.

Under its original title "Embrassez-moi" Alex Naplas has released a screen version of the successful Palais Royal farce by Y. Mirande, Tristan Bernard and G. Quinson, adopted to the screen by Max des Rieux and produced by Robert Peguy. It is a ruling fashion at present, but now on the decline, to take a popular play or operetta for the scenario of a picture.

Chief attraction of "Embrassez-moi" lies in its place of birth, as a rollicking farce of the Palais Royal, and the appearance of the comedian Prince, particularly well known to cinema fans of an earlier generation as Rigadin. Plot is supposed to be founded on a tradition in the Anjou province of France. Whenever a bargain is struck the contracting parties are supposed to seal it by a kiss.

Count Champavert is ruined and threatened with the selling of his ancestral mansion in Anjou. His son Gaston has likewise lost heavily. Latter meets Jules, a former mate of the trenches, a man of humble birth, who has made a fortune. Sympathetic fellow helps his aristocratic chum and Gaston takes him home. The Count receives his son's friend cordially but his maiden aunt, the Marquise, is horrified at such a vulgar man mixing with the family. Jules quickly learns particulars of the mortgage, and to prevent his friend's people being ejected he purchases the mansion. He then claims the customary kiss from the Marquise, but ultimately withdraws from that part of the bargain, making over the property to his younger friend Gaston. Marquise discovers the former workman has a noble heart and the illassorted couple finish by exchanging the traditional kiss and the story terminates with the announcement of their marriage.

All this nonsense is quite merry. While it lacks the sparkling dialog of the spoken farce it still constitutes a good French picture, with views of French country life, suitable for the second half of the show. Besides Prince as the prosperous wine merchant, Suzanne Bianchetti is in the role of the haughty Marquise. Others in the cast are Jacques Arnna, Felix Barre, E. Verne, B. Ibanez, Helene Hallier, Genevieve Cargese. Eliane Tavar. *Light.*

THE BUSHRANGER

Metro-Goldwyn-Mayer production and release. Directed by Chester Withey from story by Madeleine Ruthven. Continuity by George C. Hull. Titles by Paul Perez. Starring Tim McCoy. Cast includes Marian Douglas, Russell Simpson and Arthur Lubin. At Loew's New York Jan. 18, one-half of double bill. Running time, 60 minutes.

In trying to get away from the conventional western while still retaining the outdoor atmosphere, these Tim McCoy productions have been more or less successful in introducing a varying degree of change which should prove interesting and of greater value wherever outdoor pictures can be used.

This picture is superior to the usual western, more valuable to exhibitors since it should create greater audience satisfaction. It is far from inexpensive in production, but it is questionable whether the limited field now available for outdoor pictures warrants the cost.

Regardless of the cost, it is evident that in this and other McCoy westerns, there is a marked attempt to produce good outdoor pictures, and in that effort the producers are successful.

There is a fairly coherent story, not unusual, but of stronger appeal than in most. It is ancient melodrama, suffering from long, conventional use and abuse, acted and told a la stock in the early '90's. Yet it should hold in the field it is intended for, despite its absurdities.

Story opens in England in the last century. The dastardly brother of the hero kisses the wife of his father's friend near a set of French windows. The horrified husband rushes in to demand vengeance, and the heroic brother takes the blame. A duel results, the foolhardy husband dies and the brave brother is sent to jail for life.

Then pass 12 years, the convict has escaped and become a notorious Australian bandit. His father arrives in Australia as the new High Commissioner, and complications result, in which the ward is captured by an opposition gang of robbers and saved by the boy. *Mori.*

WEDDING MARCH
(FRENCH MADE)

Paris, Jan. 15.

The French filial of Paramount made quite a success of the trade show of the screen version of the late Henry Bataille's Comedie Francaise drama, "La Marche Nuptiale." Adaptation of this well-known melodramatic work for the picture was made by Jean Toulout, and it has been adroitly realized by Andre Hugon.

The story is about the amorous daughter of a magistrate in a provincial town. Grace is smitten with Claud Maurillot, her piano teacher and professor at the local college. Grace loves the young fellow, extremely timid and modest, because of these qualities. She has a sort of irresistible wish to mother him and does not disguise her maternal infatuation.

Grace's father looks for a wealthy or influential husband for his pretty eccentric daughter. When learning the meek professor has appropriated his daughter's heart, the furious sire causes a scandal, leading to the music master's dismissal from the school.

Claud has no other recourse than to migrate to Paris, and Grace quits her family to accompany him. They marry and have a mediocre existence.

Grace's best school friend lives in the capital also, married to Lachatelier, big manufacturer. By the intercession of the women folk he finds a subordinate job for the ex-professor. Taking pity on her modest situation, Mme. Lachatellier invites Grace for a few weeks at her country mansion. Here Lachatellier is much attracted by the charm and sadness of his guest, and one evening during a garden party he tells Grace of his passion.

The wife happens to overhear the declaration and has the matter out with her friend. Grace proves her innocence and, further, promises she will never rob her friend of her flighty husband. Avoiding her persecutor, she returns to Claud in Paris, but Lachatellier continues to see her and be so nice that gradually she perceives she also loves the wealthy merchant, and now prefers him to Claud.

Remembering her promise, she beseeches Lachatellier to leave her, dismissing him after bestowing a

locket as a souvenir. Then at home she asks her husband to play her favorite piece of music, "The Wedding March." While he is at the piano she kills herself in the next room with a revolver.

This tragic end does not constitute a thrilling picture, although it is well produced. Bataille was not a writer for the movies. Convincing acting by Louise Lagrange and Pierre Blanchar. The former is emotional and even pathetic as Grace, but Blanchar, e'egant and romantic, is hardly at home as Claud. Paul Guide is natural as the wealthy manufacturer, while Olga Day is his splendid wife. *Light.*

BROADWAY MELODY

(DIALOG)

Metro-Goldwyn-Mayer production and release, featuring Bessie Love, Anita Page and Charlie King. Written as an original by Edmund Goulding. Directed by Harry Beaumont. Music and lyrics by N. H. Brown and Arthur Freed. Sarah Mason, continuity. Dialog, James Gleason and Norman Houston. John Arnold, cameraman. Douglas Shearer, recording engineer. W. E., sound track. Sound men, W. C. Miller, Louis Kolb, O. O. Ceccarini, G. A. Burns. Ensemble number staged by George Cunningham. At Astor, New York, for twice daily run, starting Feb. 8. Run-

Queenie .... Anita Page
Hank .... Bessie Love
Eddie .... Charles King
Uncle Jed .... Jed Prouty
Jock .... Kenneth Thompson
Stage Manager .... Edward Dillon
Blonde .... Mary Doran
Zanfield .... Eddie Kane
Babe Hatrick .... J. E. Beck
Stew .... Marshall Ruth
Turpe .... Drew Demarest

If "Broadway Melody" had a tune there wouldn't be anything to stop it from being another cinema "Fool." As is, there isn't very much that's going to impede it from being a big box-office picture either for $2 in the keys or on a grind. It's the first flash New York has had as to how the studios are going after musical comedy numbers and there's no question of the potent threat to the stage producers. The boys had better lift the body over to this 45th street corner and take a peek at the latest Hollywood menace.

Paradoxically enough, "Broadway Melody," the initial screen musical, is basically going to draw on its story, the performances of its two lead girls and simply the novelty rather than the quality of the interpolated numbers. In the sticks the three-minute inclusion of a natural color first act finale, camaraed through a proscenium arch, may bowl them over. But New York first saw this jazz dancing wedding idea as far back as '14 in "Watch Your Step," maybe before that. They can't startle Manhattan by moving the camera up on a couple of mediocre adagio teams and a tap toe dancer.

The possibilities are what jolt the imagination. This particular interlude classes as just a hint at what's coming. If the talker studios can top the production efforts of the stage and get the camera close enough to make the ensemble seem to be in the same theatre, what's going to happen in Boston between a musical comedy stage at $4.40 and screen at 75c.

This picture was written by Edmund Goulding and directed by Harry Beaumont, with the chances that Goulding was in the next chair to Beaumont all the way. Goulding was the first man in pictures to write an intelligent article on sound, his predictions since coming true. Story appeared in Variety of June 13, '28. Between them and the Houston-Gleason dialog it's the fastest moving talker that has come in to date, especially in its first half and despite it being all interior Last half could stand some cutting. Dialog is fast, crisp and marked by a steady stream of laughs. Its technique is strictly a punch formula, in generally ending dramatic situations with a giggle. Arnold has moved his camera all over the place constantly ranging from closeups, to mediums, to full length. It's pretty near a classic in how to take a talker and then cut it to keep it moving. One cut, from an exit of Charlie King and Anita Page to their return as newlyweds looked like hundreds of feet had been thrown out. It didn't hurt the continuity, simply making it abrupt.

In atmosphere it distinctly smacks of Jack McGowan's "Excess Baggage" (stage), and yet its theme is entirely free from that association. It tells of a vaudeville sister team coming in from the middle west, with the older girl engaged to a song-and-dance boy in a Broadway revue. Latter goes for the kid sister, now grown up, who starts playing with one of the show's backers to stand off the boy and spare the blow to her sister, despite that she, too, is in love with her prospective brother-in-law.

In between are the troubles of the femme team making the revue grade, with the younger girl finally pulling them through on her looks without the older one being wise.

Corking climax is a dressing-room battle between the trio, the youngster rushing out to the house warming the money John has arranged for her new flat, after the boy has unwittingly exploded to the extent that the older girl realizes he's in love with the sister she has mothered. In a cold frenzy the elder girl scornfully berates the boy into following and saving the kid by telling him that she, herself, has just been using him as a means of breaking into the revue.

Both girls, Bessie Love as the elder sister and Anita Page as the youngster, are great in their respective climaxes. Especially Miss Love, who has a short session before her makeup table that had some of the women in the house still crying when they left the theatre. And when the women cry, that's box office.

Not long ago Miss Love came into the local Strand in a Vitaphone short of the late Eddie Foy's last vaude act and established herself as the best femme principal this isle had seen in talkers. Her performance here just about clinches that rating. They call her a trouper in the picture and that's what she is, and a sweetheart for the talkers.

Miss Page is also apt to bowl the trade over with a contribution that's natural all the way, plus her percentage on appearance. Under a handicap during the two instances of the sister team in a tryout and then in leading a number, because she can't dance, the remainder of her performance is easily sufficient to make this impediment distinctly negligible.

A break for Charlie King, who still sings a neat song and can't shout as he was prone to do on a stage. King looks as good as he plays and plants comedy lines as they should be delivered, that also going for Miss Love. Other cast support is up to the mark with the exception of Kenneth Thomson, as the chaser, who plays too slow and doesn't convince amidst the pyrotechnic display going on about him. Jed Prouty is doing a stutter role, as Tom Dugan did in "Lights of New York" and "The Barker," always for a laugh.

Book carries some satirical flings at show business smacking of Gleason and Goulding, the former briefly flashed in the opening sequence in the professional department of a music publishing office, and pie for a first night picture mob which didn't expect it. First of the three melodies is launched almost immediately in this scene, King trying it out for the surrounding mob. Note combination isn't there, the picture's major lapse, and it might have been better had it been interchanged with "You Were Meant for Me," which also doesn't particularly tickle the ear, but is a better bet than the title ditty. "Wedding of the Painted Doll" is the proscenium epic in color with everybody on stage slowly disappearing through trap doors as the curtain drops. No principals involved, it simply being an ensemble number with an off screen voice warbling the lyric to the action. Good looking, but only outstanding from a novelty angle and what it implies for the future. Instance of King singing the love song to Miss Page in an apartment is marked by the theatrical license of bringing in an unseen orchestra for accompaniment, not out of proportion. Chorus numbers are mostly given to time step taps with the color footage also holding ensemble male singing, evidently from an upstage quartet as being about all the volume the microphone could comfortably stand.

Excellent bits of sound workmanship are that of camera and mike following Miss Page and the heavy along a dance floor to pick up their conversation as they glide and a tap routine floating in during dialog in rehearsals. Chorus dance stuff has been aided by dressing the girls in black and white to make them stand in relief. Studio's trouble here is to overcome the miniature size of the individual images when the camera moves back to cover the full stage. Understanding is that the present theory is to overcome this by shooting from the side boxes, or wings, or with the aid of special wide angle lenses. Perhaps the big screen, used for "Trail of '98," might ease this difficulty. It ought to be an effect worth trying as the Astor screen can enlarge and diminish to normal at will.

Somebody has done something with this theatre's wiring since "Valentine" departed. Amplification at this performance was extraordinarily good and delightfully free from ground noises, either during the dialog or instrumental numbers. Also noticeable is the lack of special effort in the picture to make all minor sound register.

"Broadway Melody" has everything a silent picture should have outside of its dialog. A basic story with some sense to it, action, excellent direction, laughs, a tear, a couple of great performances and plenty of sex. It's the fastest moving talker that's come in, regardless of an anti-climax, with some of the stuff so flip and quick that when the capacity gets over 2,000 they may not catch everything. It's perfectly set at the Astor. And will it get dough around the country. Plenty. *Sid.*

THE FLYING FLEET

(SOUND)

M-G-M production and release. Starring Ramon Novarro. Directed by George Hill. Based on an original story by Lt. Commander Frank Wead, U. S. N., and Byron Morgan. Adapted by Richard Schayer. Titles by Joe Farnam. Cameraman, Ira Morgan with special air photography by Charles A. Marshall. At Capitol, New York, week of February 9. Running time, 72 mins.

Tommy .... Ramon Novarro
Steve .... Ralph Graves
Anita .... Anita Page
Dizzy .... Edward Nugent
Tex .... Carrcll Nye
Kewpie .... Sumner Getchell
Specs .... Gardner James
Admiral .... Alfred Allen

Latest of an extensive series of features made by various producers with the co-operation of the U. S. Navy and dealing with various aspects of life in the service. Just last week Pathe's "Annapolis" was first runned on Broadway and now "The Flying Fleet," with scenes at Annapolis. In many ways M-G-M's opus has serious claims to the distinction of being the most successful, technically and dramatically, of all the navy pictures. Its superior credentials on the score of authenticity may perhaps be attributed to the collaboration on the story of Lt. Commander Frank Wead, active participant in admiralty affairs.

It is primarily a glorification of navy pluck and aircraftsmanship. Romance is given in thimble doses at various points in the script. Also moments of horseplay for comedy. These are interludes of relaxation in the drama of roaring motors. It's the old Byron Morgan-Wally Reid racing car formula brought up to date for aeroplanes and given an official setting.

Ramon Novarro is a likeable, natural and clean-cut, but at the same time an unheroic hero. In fact, "The Flying Fleet" is hardly a starring picture at all in the ordinary sense of the term. No posing for effects or sex appeal in the regulation Hollywood fashion.

Six young men have reached the eve of graduation from Annapolis. They intend to train for the Navy Air Corps. As the story progresses the six sworn buddies are diminished in number to two, Novarro and Ralph Graves. One boy is dismissed for intoxication, another can't make the aviation health regulations because of his eyesight, third flunks out on his pilot's test, fourth is killed in a crash.

Anita Page, whose popularity is increasing in leaps and bounds as pictures in which she has appeared get into circulation, is the damsel on the sidelines waiting to be grabbed for the final clinch by Novarro.

Special mention should be accorded Ira Morgan, chief cameraman, and Charles A. Marshall, screen-credited for the aeroplane photography. Director George Hill has performed expertly and deftly his appointed task of wresting entertainment out of what must have been far from fool-proof raw materials.

"The Flying Fleet" will not be sensational, but it should be a steady if moderate grosser. It is a first class program attraction. *Land.*

TRUE HEAVEN

(SOUND)

Fox production and release. Produced and directed by James Tinling. Story by C. E. Montague with scenario by Dwight Cummins. Featuring George O'Brien and Lois Moran. At Roxy, New York, week Feb. 9. Running time, 53 mins.

Philip Gresson .... George O'Brien
Judith .... Lois Moran
Colonel Mannon .... Phillips Smalley
German General .... Oscar Apfel
Sergeant Major .... Duke Martin
British Spy .... Andre Cheron
British Colonel .... Donald MacKenzie
Mme. Grenot .... Hedwig Reicher
Chauffeur .... Will Stanton

Small money picture for the small houses, little chance in the big theatres. One of the usual programers and doesn't mean much.

Another war picture, unrelieved by any new twist or combination of circumstances. Based principally on the love interest but suffers from the war surroundings and doesn't figure for any matinee business.

Sound effects seem to have been attached after the picture was made and mostly ineffective, with the exception of the synchronized score.

O'Brien and Lois Moran, kept to the foreground throughout, photograph well in most scenes, with but one or two exceptions, and work as interestingly as possible under the circumstances without overcoming any of the deficiencies in construction and direction which drag down the production.

Aside from the unwanted war theme, story is neither strong, novel nor suitable. It concerns two spies, man and woman. The girl is first introduced in the bar room of a Belgian town distributing caresses freely to miscellaneous officers. It's supposed to be part of her job but it doesn't go well with the innocent baby stuff handed to this girl later.

In an effort to get the plans, the girl makes a play for the English soldier. Later she falls for him, saves him from death by cauterizing a wound and soon after vanishes upon orders from her superiors. The English soldier soon after goes spying into German territory in a Hun uniform. Torn between duty her country and love for the Englishman, the girl finally has him arrested after spending the night with him. Its unconvincing because the leading feminine player doesn't look like that kind of a girl. Officer is saved at the last second by the signing of the armistice.

Cut to 55 minutes it moves swiftly, but expert cutting couldn't overcome so many handicaps. *Mort.*

CONQUEST
(DIALOG)

Warner all-talking production, starring Monte Blue. Directed by Roy Del Ruth from a story by Mary Imlay Taylor. Adapted by C. Graham Baker. Cameraman, Barney Vale. At Strand, New York, week Feb. 9. Running time, 63 mins.

Donald Overton	Monte Blue
James Farnham	H. B. Warner
Diane Holden	Lois Wilson
Doctor Gerry	Tully Marshall
Mr. Holden	Edmund Breese

Without dialog this would rate with the quickies. It never achieves any real tension, although on this point the inclination is to absolve the director and blame the story, one of those "Well, what of it?" plots. Monte Blue has a following, and that, plus the all-talker label, may carry the picture for nominal box-office results. As entertainment it's a washout.

A year or so ago First National imported and exhibited a German picture called "The Strange Case of Capt. Ramper," telling the story of a polar explorer whose airship was wrecked in the land of chilblains. That central situation or idea is used in "Conquest," although the development is different and there is no further resemblance. "Conquest" is a dime novel exposition on the subject of broken faith between comrades, whereas "Ramper" was, after the German fashion, a dramatized lecture in psychology.

"Conquest" refers to the discovery of the south pole, with its early passages strongly reminiscent of the preliminary preparations, including radio publicity, used by the Byrd expedition now down at the foot of the world. Incidentally, imaginative exhibitors might work up some sort of a tie-up between the present Byrd expedition and this picture.

Cast is competent, dialog straightaway, businesslike, but minus brilliance, sparkle or other antidotes to accumulating dulness. H. B. Warner is a thoroughgoing scoundrel whose catalog of misdemeanors lists desertion of a wounded and helpless comrade, acceptance of honors not rightfully his, marrying his pal's girl under false pretenses, and finally attempted murder with a hammer.

It all seems endlessly prolonged and bogusly dramatic. There can be no permanent place or toleration of such cinematic blah. *Land.*

LOOPING THE LOOP
(GERMAN MADE)

UFA production. Paramount release over here. Direction, story, titles, etc., not credited. Werner Krauss, Warwick Ward and Jenny Jugo featured. No other billing. At Hippodrome, New York, week of Feb. 10. Running time, 70 minutes.

Botto	Werner Krauss
Andre	Warwick Ward
Blanche	Jenny Jugo

This is not a story of Chicago's loop, nor a geographical study of that "L"-surrounded section below the stock yards.

It's a German-made tale of circus life. In Germany and German circuses, a Loop is an apparatus for "death slides." In this film the Loop and the looping are secondary. The story is that of a Pagliacci, with slight variations.

Bitto, clown, as played by UFA's Werner Krauss, contends that no woman loves a clown—all they want is a laugh—and starts out to prove it. He doesn't, as there arrives a gal who doesn't laugh but loves.

And a happy ending for this Pagli, which may be new.

One large hole in the narrative about ruins all other stabs at realism. It isn't very easily understood how Bitto can conceal his identity from the girl from one end of the picture to the other, meanwhile keeping her plenty classy in furs and duds. To her he was "Mr. Bernard, electrical engineer," and she didn't even seem shocked when Bitto told her he was Bitto. Krauss is 'way off form in "Looping the Loop." Role probably too soft. If wishing to succeed Jannings over there, this one won't help him at all.

By far the best performance is Warwick Ward's. This Englishman plays the carefree romanticist throughout, going the limit at the finish by winking at the pretty nurse while apparently dying of a broken neck after a spill from the Loop.

Jenny Jugo is best in profile or when looking up. She's better looking than acting, but a good looking ingenue who possibly would amount to something on this side.

No credit to the director, photographer or author. Either they asked to be out or were forgotten in translation.

Trick shots and dissolves are in abundance, though little new German technique.

Before the sound vogue on Broadway, this foreign made might have chanced a week on that street. But it's silent and not strong enough in silence to now stand the big street gaff, and that tells its story. *Bige.*

The Lash of the Czar
(RUSSIAN MADE)

Mejrabpomfilm released in U. S. through Amkino. Directed by I. A. Protozanov. Scenario by director and Olga Leonidoff from Andreyv's "The Governor." At Cameo, New York, week Feb. 9. Running time, 75 minutes.

Governor	V. I. Kachalov
High Governing Official	V. E. Meyerhold
Chief of Police	A. P. Petrovsky
Police Spy	Ivan Chuvelev
Governess	Anna Stenn

This is far from another "Czar Ivan, the Terrible," although its title, "The Lash of the Czar," would make it appeared outside as greater sensation for morbid fans. Picture has none of the vividness or pace of its Sovkino sister. It makes the effort but drags. Too much of the story action has been left by the director for inside gesture and facial expression. It is devoid of the staying qualities necessary for Broadway or the bigger first runs. At the most in general bookings probably not a safe bet after a single day.

Considerable footage interestingly expended on statues, steeples, bells and portraits, apparently in St. Petersburg. Flashbacks several times abet the generally slow pace and should be clipped.

Only action centered on Governor in opening and close. Weakening to pressure by Czar's friend causes him to order massacre of strikers. Even in this situation, the only one nearing bigness in the entire 75 minutes, director sacrifices dispersing crowd for close-up study of Governor. The same study tires and lessens Kachalov's role, because of repetition.

Finale value diminished by protracted art gallery perusal of camera before spy, spurned by police after identification by workers, shoots the Governor.

Only reference to Czar is picture of his hand. This takes up lot of time in close-ups of pens and writing materials which wearies.

Major reelage devoted to drawing and playroom sets with no other movement than lot of lip moving, frowning and backslapping. *Waly.*

Man Who Cheated Life
(GERMAN MADE)

Produced by Sokal G. M. B. H. Released by Affiliated European Producers, Inc. Directed by Henrik Galeen. Based on the story by Edgar Allan Poe, with scenario by Hans Heinz Ewers. Featuring Conrad Veidt and Werner Krauss. At Little Carnegie Playhouse, New York, week Feb. 9. Running time over 60 mins.

Even his best friends failed him. He was the most popular young man in Prague early in the '90's, to judge from the costumes; the best fencer in the country; quite a dashing blade with the women, all the normal signs of a promising and prosperous future. But there was something wrong with Baldy, the hero of this legend. A moodiness besieged him that was inexplicable.

To the breathlessly expectant exhibitors of America the secret will be unfolded early in the story. Baldy, the young rascal, had sold his shadow to the devil for the goodly sum of a million in gold stage money.

Blithely he took the money, unsuspecting of the evil the dirty Devil had in mind. The devil, Werner Krauss, intended as a terrifying individual, appeared in the guise of Count Scapennelli and created quite a furor among the art worshipers, causing many to laugh till modesty forbade further demonstrations.

Scappy had a mean way of sneaking up behind Baldy that was just one scream after another. When it was supposed to be unearthly and spooky, too. Every time Scappy appeared in his three-gallon undertaker's hat and the pawn shop Prince Albert, embellished with a velvet collar, every one felt that he was supposed to look mean and conniving, but they only laughed louder. That kind of killed off suspense and such things. They can't make a sucker out of a menace with impunity.

Later there was a duel on between Baldy and the Baron. The former didn't want to do any killing, but while he was hastening to the scene to call off the duel the devil used his shadow to kill the Baron, while old Baldy got the blame. One thing led to another, and finally Baldy started climbing down the scale. He played cards, drank good German ale and lager, and showed all of the other well-known film indications of a fallen and dissolute person.

As a last resort he called on his beloved, hoping to find peace in her love. She was ready to forgive and forget, but the lad was silly enough to tell her he had sold his shadow. He stood before a mirror, no reflection showing, and the countess passed right out.

For the finish the unlucky crittur shot his shadow straight through the heart, but woke to find he had shot himself.

Foreign critics hailed it as the height of something or other. American critics may pat its artistic shoulder and ease its suffering with words of kindness; yet it still belongs and won't get any further than behind the bars as a circus freak, the Little Carnegie taking the place of the circus. *Mori.*

RA-MU

Produced by Capt. Edward A. Salisbury. No distributor credited. Travelog of South Sea Isles.' At Fifth Ave. playhouse, beginning Feb. 9. Running time, 58 minutes.

A 10-minute lecture and sub-titles describe this one as a study into an almost extinct race on Islands in the Southern Pacific. Ordinary travelog stuff and very minor study of natives. Production several reels too long for material it has to offer. Good for non-theatrical and highest class community houses.

Picture takes in trip of Wisdom II, Salisbury's schooner. Stopoffs at several islands, including Pago Pago, Tahiti, and the Marquesas. Titles play up Polynesians as dying race reduced from about 80,000 to 2,500 in 15 years because of white diseases and cloth-bearing missionaries.

Most of the film shows crew tasting fruit, natives cooking, dancing and swimming. Hip swinging of heavy breasted native women could have provided sex bet, which cameraman muffed through apparent fear of close-ups. *Waly.*

ADORABLE OUTCAST
(AUSTRALIAN MADE)

Sydney, Dec. 29.

Australian Films, Ltd., imported Norman Dawn from America to produce this picture. Dawn brought with him Edith Roberts, Edmund Burns and Walter Long. What a waste of transportation money. Picture is taken from a story by Beatrice Grimshaw "Con of the Coral Seas." Titles by Gayne Dexter are undoubtedly the best thing in this one.

Story is trivial, the entire picture being only of fair merit with very little appeal. It is only one of many dealing with life in the tropics. Photography is good and was handled by Arthur Higgins and Billy Therise.

Cast is weak including Compton Coutts, Katherine Dawn, Arthur McLaglan, Jack Garvin, Arthur Touchert and Jessica Harcourt. This was the last picture made by Australian Films.

It will probably make some money in this country, being handled here by a great bunch of publicity hounds for Union Theatres. They may also like it in England. In America it can hope for nothing better than a daily change house, if that. *Gorrick.*

HARVEST OF HATE

Universal production and release featuring Rex, the horse. Directed by Henry McRae. Cast includes Jack Perrin and Helen Foster. At the Tivoli, New York, on double feature program Jan. 30. Running time, 50 mins.

Picture has been traipsing around screens since last April, but so far has escaped Variety's files. Main actors are two horses, Rex (the wild horse) and Starlight, Jack Perrin's mount. Rex goes through his usual performance of kicking up his heels, charging madly o'er hill and dale, and finally driving his heels toward the cornered villain.

Story plenty thin and skids along to a finale that's easily guessed. Lot of villainy from the opening. Jack Perrin is a daring rider, but is not so hot in his love scenes. Heroine is Miss Foster as a traveling carnival queen, and the poorest dressed queen shown on the screen in many a day. Paprika for this western has Miss Foster strip down to undies in the cowboy's one-room bungalow.

Rex and another horse, other than Starlight, exchange dialog via captions. Principal men have several hand-to-hand scuffles.

Photographically above average and some of the climaxes are well staged and directed. But the story is so bad. *Mark.*

BROKEN BARRIERS

Excellent firm production and independent release. Adapted by I. Bernstein from C. Hayward's story. In cast: Gaston Glass, Helene Costello. At Loew's New York one day, Jan. 29, half of double bill. Running time, 70 mins.

If the audience is sufficiently illiterate to believe that a publisher would tear up a graft scandal yarn and cover up technical murder evidence, all because his star reporter falls for the bad guy's daughter, then they'll go big for "Broken Barriers." Even as one of those story things it's in a lone class.

Gaston Glass is a strictly screen newspaperman who inspires the college break-ins that publishers are chummier than mothers. He doesn't give his boss the chance to tear up the silencing check. He rips and then goes out to scoop the world. While he does get the scoop, even to the point of finding that the phoney candidate was dead after he left the ring boss' house and before a lieutenant rolled him over a cliff—that doesn't matter.

With all of its unbelievably absurd story taste, "Broken Barriers" moves along fast in its own way. A little more script though and it would have been a good grind stepper. *Waly.*

MONEY

(FRENCH MADE)

Paris, Jan. 20.

It is about 40 years since Emile Zola wrote "L'Argent." This story is the history of a crooked banker exploiting the public savings by dishonest combinations.

Zola's novel remains modern, although it was not the pricking of the Madame Hanau bubble which prompted a screen edition just released by Cine-Romans.

Marcel L'Herbier, one of the best French producers, was inspired by the book for the realization of a thrilling picture which he has laid in our post-war days, bearing the original title of "L'Argent." Thus we find the use of the aeroplane amply propounded in L'Herbier's scenario, quite unknown in Zola's days.

Nicolas Soccard, the banker, is almost ruined by gambling on the local Wall Street in Caledonian Eagle Petroleum stock. Alphonse Gunderman, another magnate of international finance, is determined for spiteful reasons to ruin his rival, Soccard. In this maneuver he is encouraged and assisted by Countess Sandorf, former mistress of the broker who is almost broke.

An aviator, Hamelin, former war ace, during a visit to the Pacific Islands discovered a petroleum field and was smart enough to clinch an option. Soccard became aware of it and persuaded Hamelin to accept a position with the Eagle corporation. Credulous public is informed of the favorable outlook of the Eagle options on the Pacific oil fields. The news sends the Eagle stock sky-high. Usual manipulation on the Bourse ensues.

The good news is ultimately contradicted. A Japanese ship reports Hamelin has been seen to fall into the sea. Panic, with stockholders trying to unload. Meanwhile Soccard gets a cipher cable from his secretary announcing a safe landing, and buys in the stock, which rises once more when an official report of the raid is issued. Then comes the next move, to compromise Hamelin. A slump sets in, increasing when Gunterman sells the holdings he has secretly acquired and causing Soccard's complete ruin. Soccard is arrested, judged and sentenced to a term in prison. Gunterman, now having full control of the Caledonian Eagle, takes Hamelin into his service.

Marcel L'Herbier knows his job, and has told an excellent yarn, albeit somewhat lengthy.

Picture is suitable for all publics and the acting is worthy. Alcover, heavy actor, heads cast as the shady banker. He is perfectly natural, powerful and brutal. Brigitte Helm, revealed to the French fans in "Metropolis," is convincing as Countess Sandorf, while Marie Glory is just as charming as Line. Alfred Abel makes good as Gunderman, and Henry Victor is a proficient aviator and enamoured husband.

Cine-Romans Films de France has a success with "L'Argent," which should cross the seas. *Light.*

Confessions of a Wife

Samuel Zierler production, released by First Division. Helene Chadwick featured. Directed by Albert Kelly. Supervisor, Burton King. From the stage play by Owen Davis. Photographed by M. A. An-

derson and Louis Dengel. At Columbus, New York, one day, Feb. 1. Running time, 70 minutes.

Marion Atwell............Helene Chadwick
Paul Atwell...............Arthur Clayton
Mrs. Livingston..........Ethel Gray Terry
Henri Duval...............Walter McGrail
Handsome Harry............Carl Gerard
Mrs. Jonathan............Clarissa Selwynne

The name of Owen Davis can't save this one. Long sweeps of dull interior scenes between the principals that go snail-like to the climaxes don't tend to hold the tension one generally looks forward to in a Davis story. Whoever did the scenario framed it in a manner decidedly laborious and amateurish. What little interest was maintained at times was given a body blow by the captions.

Helene Chadwick as the wife who lied to her husband to gamble did the best she could with a thankless padded role.

The cast may be high in the film register, but it didn't look so forte when assembled.

Some good shots and some that didn't look so good. The picture appeared to have run through wear and tear as it was not in any too good shape, especially for a Broadway house presentment.

Picture will do well to hold its own on double feature assignment. Overdrawn and interminably padded. *Mark.*

ON THE DIVIDE

Eldorado production, distributed by Syndicate Pictures. Directed by J. P. McGowan, who plays the heavy. Bob Custer starred. Peggy Montgomery leading woman. Story by Sally Winters. Cameraman, Paul Allen. No other credits, except supervision by J. C. Davis, 2d. At Loew's New York, as half of double bill, Feb. 1. Running time, 55 mins.

Average western quickie. Formula story with a neat and workmanlike finale. Plenty of feverish action and hard riding. Whole thing takes place in the open air and didn't cost much. Good material at a price where they like this sort of stuff, for it is excellent of its kind and for its grade. McGowan knows this racket and makes no false moves. Point in picture's favor is a very pretty leading woman in Peggy Montgomery, who acts just enough.

Starts with a murder by range grabbers of a bank messenger. Principal killer drops part of his watch which hero finds. Then into the usual story of land sharks trying to seize ranch of old settler to the distress of his beautiful daughter. Hero frustrates plotters by arriving just after sheriff has foreclosed on the ranch at noon. Hero says it isn't noon yet and flashes his own watch to prove it. Menace produces his watch to show it is 12.10. Watch has no back cover for a tip off that menace is the assassin, and that settles a lot of things.

Who cares if a menace carries around a watch with the works exposed and still has it keep perfect time? C'est la guerre. *Rush.*

OUTLAWED

FBO production and release. Starring Tom Mix. Directed by Eugene Ford. N. Dovel, cameraman. In cast: Sally Blane, Frank Clark, Albert J. Smith. At Loew's New York one day Jan. 29, half of double feature. Running time, 70 mins.

Cut down to 50 minutes this would be a fair Tom Mix offering. In present editing "Outlawed" painfully slow in first half. Then the other extreme is in so much effort for cramming action that the story is whirlwind of much used drug store rough stuff.

Mix and Sally Blane are both poor on the love end. Galloping horsemen that might have been lifted from any old indie western take up considerable footage. In this, however, the kids will get enough flashes of Mix to be happy.

When Mix goes after the villains who would have swung the bank robbery and murder upon him is when the expected mix-up starts. After the dust clears and the bad lads have gotten theirs, Mix gets his—Miss Blane. She, incidentally, is a very blase little creature. *Waly.*

Trail of Horse Thieves

FBO (Radio) production and release. Directed by Robert de Lacey from story "Desert Madness" by W. E. Wing. In cast: Tom Tyler, Sharon Lynn, Frankie Darro. Nick Mesursca, cameraman. At Tivoli, two days, 31-1, half of double bill. Running time, about 60 minutes.

This western takes the usual tack where the hero is believed in the wrong by ingenuous friends. It is just one of those which are gradually dying, even in the grinds.

Tom Tyler overacts to a painful degree, and little Frankie seems to be aping him. Cave effects and quicksand substitute as the applause point the flat lands and the noose. Change is somewhat of a relief. *Waly.*

THE REDEEMING SIN

(DIALOG)

Warner Brothers production and release. Starring Dolores Costello. Featuring Conrad Nagel. Direction by Howard Bretherton, from L. V. Jefferson's story. Titles and dialog by Joseph Jackson. B. Haskin, cameraman. Harvey Gates credited with scenario. Louis Silvers the score. W. E. Vitaphone synchronization on disk. At Warners, New York, for twice daily $2 run, starting Feb. 15. Running time, 75 minutes.

Fleurette..................Dolores Costello
Dr. Duboise................Conrad Nagel
Sewer Rat..................Georgie Stone
Petite....................Phillipe DeLacy
Father Colomb.............Lionel Belmore
Lupine...............Warner Richmond
Mitzi....................Nina Quartaro

A picture for a town's first earful of sound so as to build from this point. Otherwise it's the substantiation of the reverse English on the new era that no picture is as bad as a bad talker. "Redeeming Sin" is a throwback to the early talkers which won't nail the money those films did because the novelty is off in the cities where its predecessors romped, due to the new screen combination. "Sin" is a bad, very bad, talker.

Stands a better chance silent for moderate rating with at least 1,000 feet out and completely retitled, the Costello and Nagel names figuring to then help. Only chance as a talker is in those spots which have yet to experience hear and see celluloid.

Slow and so melodramatic as to try the patience of a first night audience which honestly tried to restrain itself until it could stand the tragic hoke no longer, roaring at the dialog and titles. If it stays three weeks in New York at this time for $2 it can stake a claim to being unique.

Neither Miss Costello nor Nagel can pull this one out from the ridiculous depths which it plumbs in dialog and titling although the star continues to flash a corking appearance. Phillipe DeLacy, youngster, is given lines out of all proportion to his years in a short "side," while the big dramatic situation is Lionel Belmore reciting the Lord's Prayer in full as Miss Costello weeps in repentance before him.

Locale is Paris' underworld with Miss Costello the flower thereof, who eventually falls in love with the young doctor whom she hates, due to a belief that his neglect has allowed her young brother to die. That she never seems interested in finding out who shot the boy is just something Bretherton, directing, has omitted on this slow motion journey. It's not even evident that she knows he was shot. Action eventually reaches the sewers beneath Paris where it looked like a great spot for "Muddy Water," which the score passed up.

These 32 minutes of dialog are split into seven sequences, some as short as one minute and the longest nine, of which there are two. Picture's better points are Haskin's photography and Silvers' score. Former has done a nice piece of work in following a two- or three-story backward fall of the star so as to make the house almost feel the bump.

Chris Morley's mint in Hoboken has screen opposition. *Sid.*

STRANGE CARGO

Pathe (dialog) production and release. Written and directed by Benjamin Glazer. Adapted by Horace Jackson. Cameraman, Arthur Miller. Synchronized by RCA Photophone. At Paramount, New York, week Feb. 16. Running time, 75 mins.

Sir Richard.................Kyrle Bellew
Ship Captain...............Claude King
Tony.......................Andre Beranger
Stoker..................Warner Richmond
Yogi.......................Otto Matiesen
Mrs. Berseau...........Josephine Browne
Diane......................Lee Patrick

Betty	June Nash
Dr. Gans	Frank Reicher
First Officer	Ned Sparks
Boatswain	Charles Hamilton
Steward	Harry Allen
Jack	Russell Gleason
Bertram	George Barraud

Pathe's first all-talker is commendable entertainment of the mystery genre. It compares favorably with any of the spook dramas produced since the flickers decided to talk, and is okay for de luxe houses anywhere. It's not a holdover picture; there have been too many murders in the chattering cinemas for it to be considered very novel or original, but among the regular programmers for wired houses it will be distinctly serviceable.

Nobody of note or moment. Fourteen in the line-up and sold by Pathe as an "all star legit cast." That is the only feasible exploitation angle for exhibitors in circumventing the absence of star appeal. A number of the players, Andre Beranger, Otto Matiesen, Ned Sparks, Frank Reicher and Warner Richmond are at least familiar faces on the screen.

Narrative follows logical rather than hysterical pattern. This is an advantage for class rating, as it eliminates the senseless hokum identified with goosepimple farce. A man is murdered and his body spirited away aboard a private yacht.

Story follows the investigation of the various clues by the ship captain. Several sets of circumstances variously implicating different individuals.

While necessarily reminiscent, the plot has been developed plausibly and moves with enough speed to sustain interest. A number of laughs and deft touches brighten the way.

Various performances uniformly good. It would be slighting the rest to mention any one. "Strange Cargo" is essentially plot rather than characterization which retarded any personal brilliance in the larger service to the production.

Benjamin Glazer directed and authored. Dialog is smooth, although without punches. Same applies to the various sequences.

Considered as the maiden dialog feature of Pathe "Strange Cargo" is conspicuously successful. Appraised by cold cash box office, it is above the average of the program features in dialog.

Land.

Ned McCobb's Daughter

(SOUND)

Pathe screening of the famous stage play, directed by Wm. J. Cowen. Irene Rich, Theodore Roberts, Robert Armstrong, George Barraud and Carol Lombard in cast. Titles by Edw. Justus Mayer. Cameraman, David Abel. RCA Photophone recording, in charge of Josiah Zuro. Running time, 71 minutes. At Colony, New York, week Feb. 16.

A fine play transcribed to the screen with notable judgment, a product in the very best mode and a candidate for box office honors. Outstanding merit of the picture is the resourcefulness of the director in getting not only the sentimental values of the play across, but putting an essentially screen punch into the climax episodes as well.

Production has in it a passage of suspense equal in grip to anything the screen has done in many a day, paced perfectly for maximum effectiveness. Whole work has excellent tone of naturalness.

Passage in point is the scene where the heroine's husband has killed a revenue officer and hidden the body in a bin of apples. Government agents come to search the place for whisky and time and again are on the trembling brink of disclosure. All high voltage kick.

Picture has several unusual angles. One delicately developed is the situation that the wife of a worthless rat finds herself drawn toward his brother, a rough fellow, bootlegger and a racketeer, but a man of high physical courage and a certain rugged primitive honor, virtues which she herself inherits in different surface form from a long line of God-fearing New England mariners.

Point of the celluloid telling of the story is that these things are never deliberately expressed, but develop in the action. On the surface man and woman are hostile in a friendly way, but the real state of affairs is deftly conveyed.

Story goes to a first rate climax for picture purposes. Heavy is dispatched in a bootlegger's motor truck in which is concealed the body of the revenue man he has killed. To avert suspicion he carries the two children of the heroine with him. It is disclosed that revenue men are waiting at the distant drawbridge, ready to shoot any driver who tries to crash through.

Hero and heroine give pursuit in another motor truck and when the heavy's machine gets out of control down a mountain road, hero has to race alongside and catch the children as they jump. Effective melodrama, both from the action itself, and from the situation that underlies the whole thing.

Picture has no dialog and sound effects are sparingly used, confined to such items as roar of racing motor trucks. Musical accompaniment is so unobtrusive one almost forgets it.

Irene Rich is entirely satisfying. A sophisticated audience perhaps would find her playing a bit saccharine, for Carrie McCobb was a pretty strong-minded rather than the rather silken personality here on view. Going to a generality of film fans, however, it's only fair to suppose the character was modified by design. Robert Armstrong draws a convincing portrait of a very human blending of good and evil, also sugar coated for a wide public.

Perhaps the best thing the Pathe studios have turned out under the new regime.

Rush.

THE ENSLAVED

(DANISH MADE)

Paris, Feb. 7.

Elite Films Corp. released an interesting reel from Denmark at a recent trade show, ear-marked as "Les Asservis" for the local market. It may be classed as a patriotic output, dealing with the Prussian annexation of the Danish provinces of Schleswig and Holstein in 1867, and their eventual return to Denmark. On this territory, near the Danish frontier, lives the family of Nills Steffen, a farmer. His youngest son, Eric, is engaged to marry Karen, neighbor's daughter. She is a dainty pre-war maiden. In August, 1914, war breaks out and the effects are soon felt all over Europe.

Eric, being German, due to the annexation, is called for military service. He refuses to serve, his heart being that of a Dane, and he runs away. Old Steffen and his elder son are arrested; there is an arbitrary sort of trial and the homestead is sold. The farmer seeks shelter at the local public hospital, where Karen is a nurse.

Eric cannot resist the temptation of returning to the village to visit his father and sweetheart. On his departure, when almost safe near the frontier, he is wounded by a sentinel. The lad is arrested and sentenced to death as a deserter. At this point, while awaiting execution, the news is brought that the war is over. Germany has asked for an armistice and the empire is overthrown. The sentence of death is not carried out.

Schnedler Soerensen, producer, has made an excellent Scandinavian picture. He has utilized with profit the cold light of the northern countries, obtaining some fine exterior effects. Some scenes are quite emotive. Acting is sincere, with Charles Jorgensen, Randi Michelsen, Peter Malberg, Alex Suhr, Mmes. Clara Shonfeldt, Elith Reumert and Grete Bendix.

"The Enslaved," referring to the people of the annexed provinces of Denmark after the Prussian conquest in 1867, is historical in a way and will please the majority of audiences.

Light.

THE SIDESHOW

Columbia production and release. Directed by Erle C. Kenton. Story by Howard Green. Featuring Marie Prevost, Ralph Graves and Little Billy. Cast includes Alan Roscoe, Pat Harmon, Martha McGruder, Texas Madison, Chester Morgan, Janet Ford, Paul Bismuth, Bert Price and Jacques Page. At Loew's New York one day, Feb. 14. Running time over 65 minutes.

Nothing in it for anything excepting the semi-weekly and daily change houses, and for these as suitable as anything else in the way of fillers. It's not badly done and the old circus stuff somehow holds together for a story. Never bright or snappy, with the atmosphere gloomed up.

It has a midget as a circus boss and trying to make a hero out of a freak is one of the impossibilities in films. The rugged-faced or positively ugly types of characters have a chance to get by in these stories. Freaks never.

Regardless of what this midget does as the circus boss, his goodheartedness, his broad-mindedness, every flash of him repudiates the whole impression. There's no interest when he falls for the shapely girl acrobat. It is hopeless, but not pathetic, only impossible.

A midget giving serious orders to groups of huskies, any one of whom could put him in a side pocket, never registers. His attempt to be impressive is all wrong. Direction or supervision responsible and, primarily, the choice of a story.

Story is of two circuses on the same route. The villainous group offers to buy the midget out, but nothing doing. After that accidents happen.

Marie Prevost and Ralph Graves in wrong through dull photography and feeble as the two lovers. Central character, the midget, never clicks.

Mori.

THE MANXMAN

(BRITISH MADE)

Produced by British International Pictures Co. Released in U. K. by Wardour Co.; in America by World Wide Pictures. Directed by Alfred Hitchcock. Photography: Jack J. Cox. Censor's certificate "A." Preview at the London Hippodrome Jan. 21. Running time, 98 mins.

Pete Quillian	Carl Brisson
Philip Christian	Malcolm Keen
Kate Creegan	Anny Ondra
Caesar Creegan	Randle Ayrton
Granny Creegan	Clare Greet

The Hall Caine novel from which this film has been adapted is a weak one, but the director has done his best with it. All there is to the story is Pete, a fisherman, having Philip, an attorney, for a buddy; Pete being in love with Kate; getting the cold mitt from her father because he is poor, and going abroad to make money, leaving Kate in care of Philip.

Inevitable results—or there would be no story at all—and Pete is said to be dead. Then he turns up and Philip, who is to be deemster of Manx, persuades Kate her duty is to marry Pete. She has a baby which Pete thinks is his, but she swings back to Philip and when she finds he doesn't want her, tries to take the suicide route but is rescued and comes before Philip, now deemster, for trial.

Philip admits it is all his fault, and they fade out together with Pete left fishing.

Two decades ago Hall Caine was reckoned very daring. But now he is milk for infants, and the film suffers from the dating of the story.

More has actually been got out of it by direction and sharply-defined characterization than there is in the story. A fair amount of suspense got into scenes between Pete and Kate arising out of the concealed parentage of the baby and its final revelation.

It suffers from an obvious attempt to save both Philip and Kate from losing sympathy, and the character of the girl occasionally becomes sketchy in consequence.

Minor parts are well cast, especially fisher-folk and women of the island, locations are fresh and at times picturesque. Acting comes best from Malcolmn Keen, who makes Philip credible and vivid. Carl Brisson falls down on dramatic moments, much better suited in roles where physique and a smile are all that matter. There ought to be some future for Anny Ondra who played in one of First National's British films without being very noticeable, but who here shows she has looks and trouping ability. Small blonde with plenty of s. a., at present rather suppressed.

With its semi-tragic ending and its unconvincing story, the film will do better on the continent than here. It will need a lot of clever editing to make it possible for America, where its value rests mainly on the picturesque locations than on the story value.

Frat.

BLINDFOLD

Fox production and release. Directed by C. Klein from story by George Francis Coe. Lucien Andriot, cameraman. In cast: George O'Brien, Lois Moran, Earle Fox, Don Terry, Maria Alba. At Loew's New York, one day, Jan. 17. Running time, about 65 minutes.

Long stretches of inactivity in one of those regulation amnesia and ridiculously improbable crime cop and girl stories relegate "Blindold" to the ordinary grade of grind production.

Starting off with a cop needlessly getting himself bumped off gives another cop the incentive to go after a gang of high-grade crooks, including a handful of men versed in numerous professions and trades.

As the flatfoot out for blood George O'Brien makes the best of things. When the yarn is nose diving, his girl, Lois Moran, loses her mind long enough to become a member of the gang. It is only when O'Brien discovers her and shocks her back into shape that she aids in calling other coppers and convincing the captain that the boy friend had not pulled a boner in original arrests for which he was given the air.

Waly.

CARNIVAL KING

(FRENCH MADE)

Paris, Jan. 17.

"Le Roi de Carnaval," comedy-drama, released by the Elite Film Co. here, is not listed as a French picture, but classed as international.

The scenario is a bit mossy, with adventures over love letters on the Riviera, with the ultimate defeat of the villain. Some excellent scenes of Nice and the carnival season.

Lady Rowson is at the rather mixed resort, and becomes the victim of an adventurer, Dorlini, who attempts to blackmail the distracted woman. He holds letters from her, written when she was young, to a man she did not marry.

Jacques is on the spot. He is paying suit to Gill, Lady Rowson's sister. He is aware of Lady Rowson's troubles and is so concerned in hiding the wicked manipulations of the scoundrel Dorlini that Gill imagines him to be a confederate.

Dorlini reveals the compromising documents to Lord Rowson. To save his sister, Gill assumes the responsibility of the billets doux and agrees to marry Dorlini to keep him still.

Jacques is again on the spot. After divers adventures he recovers the letters, accuses Dorlini of forgery and has him arrested. The two sisters are then able to live in peace with the gentlemen they love.

Gabriel Gabrio is Lord Rowson, with Renee Heribel and Elga Brink as the two ladies.

Interesting views of the Riviera and a quantity of pretty girls as supers.

"Roi de Carnaval" is for the first half in manufacturing towns.

Kendrew.

TROPICAL NIGHTS

Tiffany-Stahl production and release. Directed by Elmer Clifton. Story suggested by Jack London piece, "A Raid on the Oyster Pirates." Patsy Ruth Miller starred. In support: Malcolm MacGregor, Wallace MacDonald, Ray Hallor and Russell Simpson. Cameraman, Harry Carr. Film editor, Frank Sullivan. Running time 67 minutes. At the Times (daily change grind), New York, one day, Feb. 13, half double bill.

One of those things that can happen in the best regulated producing plants. Story material promising, but in the filming necessity of placating censor spoiled everything. Result is one of those sappy affairs where action deals with a stranded actress who takes refuge in a South Seas dive but still remains a good girl.

Foreign audiences ought to get as rich a giggle out of this as American hihats get out of Continental pictures.

Action is very slow. It winds through yards and yards of planting in order to get to the climax, which is over in a minute. Kick comes in a novel under water sequence. Two pearl fishers are at work in deep water, one actually the murderer of the other's brother, a crime which the heroine is charged with. The guilty man is on the bottom while the other is in the boat above, watching. Murderer is caught when his foot is seized by a giant sea monster, and when the other goes to his assistance, he also is attacked by a slimy creature of the deep. Resulting fight under water is well recorded on the screen, convincing and a thrill.

Laborious planting of the story nullifies any merit it may have. Nothing happens for more than 40 minutes, at least nothing in terms of screen action. Shots in the dive where the stranded actress is forced to work are particularly insipid. It might as well be an Epworth League headquarters, except for one mild hula by a couple of native girls, and the passing around of grog among sailors and traders.

The bad features so far outweigh the good that the picture is condemned to the daily changes as here where it was the better half of a double bill.

Rush.

PEACH SKIN
(FRENCH MADE)

Paris, Feb. 2.

"Peau de Peche" is listed as a Louis Aubert production, recently trade showed under favorable conditions. It is screen version of a book by Gabriel Mauriere, but the story in itself is hardly suitable for a picture, more of a psychological analysis.

It demonstrates the advantages of healthy country life compared with the tiresome existence so many lead in the melting pot of a big city. Adaptation is good and will demand a following.

Charlot is a Parisian urchin. His companions have nicknamed him "Peau de Peche" ("Peach Skin"), because he is always blushing. One day at a church door Charlot watches a fashionable wedding party leave. The bride looses a brooch. By chance Charlot picks it up and, running after the bridal party, restores the jewel.

The bride, Mme. Desflouves, wants to reward Charlot for his honesty. Charlot declines. Mme. Desflouves, taking a fancy to the lad, causes inquiries to be made for his future welfare.

Soon after the event Charlot is run over by an automobile. When fit to be moved he is taken by distant relatives, farmer's family named Crocs, into the country. The farmer has a daughter named Lucie. In the village Charlot becomes chummy with a youth known as La Ficelle (bit of string). They grow up together. Our hero is in love with Lucie and hopes soon to make her his wife. But he sacrifices his secret love in favor of a chum, and returns to Paris.

Arriving in the capital he dares to call on his benefactress, Mme. Desflouves, a widow now. He confesses his deep sorrow, and the woman soothes him by taking him back to the village, where he is united to Lucie.

The picture has been well produced by Jean Benoit Levy and Marie Epstein, the producers. Nice scenery and interesting phases. The renters seemed much interested, despite the lack of any sort of thrill. The reel is highly moral.

Cast includes Denise Lorys, Simonne Mareuil and Mme. Beaume The male roles are held by Maurice Touze, Pierre Lecomte, with a juvenile, Petit Jimmy, impersonating the title role.

Light.

THE SKY SKIDDER

Universal production and release. Directed by Bruce Mitchell, featuring Al Wilson, stunt aviator. Helen Foster opposite. Wilbur Mack and Pee Wee Holmes in support. William Adams, cameraman. Running time, 57 minutes, at Times, New York (30-cent grind) as half double bill, one day, Feb. 13.

Couple of minutes of thrilling air stuff and long sequences of straight flying stand out. Otherwise particularly flagrant example of bad writing, worse acting and indifferent direction. Half double bill in daily change neighborhood about fixes its status.

Thrill comes when hero goes up to test his invention of super-fuel (called Economo and will drive a plane 1,000 miles on a pint). As the heavy had framed him with ordinary gasoline, his engine goes dead in mid-air and he has to make a parachute jump during a tail spin. This bit is remarkably well done.

Another stunt bit, spoiled by pretty transparent faking, was hero changing from plane to plane in flight to battle the menace and still another when hero, hanging from ladder below his plane, picked heroine out of a runaway automobile.

Wilson is a good looking hero but his acting is not impressive, and the simpering heroine of Miss Foster doesn't help the situation. Holmes has good comedy moments for neighborhood audiences, for whom film seems designed and who will enjoy it.

Rush.

THE VAGABOND CUB

Radio (FBO) production and release, starring Buzz Barton. Directed by Louis King from original credited Oliver Drake. In cast: Sam Nelson, Ione Holmes, Frank Rice. At Stanley, New York, one day, Feb. 18. Running time, 60 minutes.

Too bad FBO didn't make some more like this before it became Radio and sold its trotters. Action in this every other minute. Houses that have ever used this brand will find "The Vagabond Cub" a straight flush.

Little Barton buzzes in between and ahead of the powerful stallions, which start their racing when the youngster's seedy pal, Frank Rice, gets entangled in a murder he didn't commit.

Vengeance angle of son who does some wild shooting but comes out able to marry the sheriff's daughter, operate his dad's gold mine and watch the law hang the true culprit. Good old hoke.

Waly.

TAKING A CHANCE

Fox production and release. Starring Rex Bell. Featuring Lola Todd. Directed by Norman McLeod. Scenario by A. H. Halprin from story, "Saint of Calamity Gulch," by Richard Bret Harte, Cameraman, Sol Halprin. At Arena, New York, one day, Feb. 6, half double bill. Running time, 70 minutes.

Joe Courtney	Rex Bell
Jessie Smith	Lola Todd
Dan Carson	Richard Carlyle
Billy	Billy Watson
Pete	Jeff Byron
Luke	Morton Kingsley
Jake	Jack Henderson

Judging from the way Fox booms young Rex Bell in this one it may be feeling out the exhibs as to Bell some day filling the Fox niche formerly occupied by Tom Mix. Comparison on this with any of Mix's fast westerns gives Bell the worst of it. Story doesn't stand up any too well, and the work called upon didn't give Bell a chance to show much beyond some riding. It needs more than a zippety hog-dog rodeo buster to stand up as a picture star nowadays.

Bell has plenty of physical wherewithal to wear the chaps and draw a bead on villainous birds. He's young and will no doubt improve if the picture stories come a lot better than this one.

Lola Todd was a sort of fem bandit who outwitted everybody but the dashing young rider. Little romancing, although Bell and Miss Todd make an attractive pair of screen leads.

The picture not as exciting as indicated by the atmosphere; a few near dramatic climaxes, but all so palpably thin thrills were lukewarm. Photography at times seem marred and picture seemed boothworn.

Even on a double feature card but fair western at best.

Mark.

GO AND GET IT

Radio (FBO) Pictures production and release. Bob Steele starred. Directed by Wallace H. Fox from story credited Frank H. Clark. Virgil Miller, cameraman. In cast: Betty Welsh, Jim Quinn, J. Marley. At Tivoli one day, Feb. 13, half double bill. Running time, about 60 minutes.

"Go and Get It," comedy-murder-prize ring mongrel with little continuity. Every film story ever written for Poverty Row has a piece in it. But there's plenty of hit and miss action that makes it a sure bet for cowhands, factory workers and some others.

Technically, excepting the sock-ing match in the last reel, the thing is a mess. Odd and ridiculous situation of neighbors involved in a murder with the wife of the man awaiting to be hanged wearing deep black and with the dead man's wife using her brightest wardrobe. Then the convicted man's son, played along comedian and juggler lines by Steele, and the victim's daughter, listlessly done by Betty Welsh.

As the discharged sailor with a Chinese statue, Steele gets the thing off to no particular start. A Chink and bad man on the pier want his sea bag. Fans are kept guessing until late in the story when their mission develops to be one for pearls hidden in the image.

After the father's murder, things are roughed along until the Chink, double-crossed, agrees to spill for dough. Steele, training and framing, wins the kale. He keeps it because the Chink, after fessing up, is plugged. Then Steele goes to work on the bad guy.

Waly.

SUNSET PASS

Paramount production and release. Directed by Otto Brower. Adapted by J. W. Rubin and Ray Harris from Zane Grey novel. Roy Clark, cameraman. In cast: Jack Holt, Nora Lane, Jack Loder, Chester Conklin. At Loew's New York, one day, Feb. 9. Running time, 67 minutes.

Plenty of human interest in "Sunset Pass." Exceptionally well turned out western, so far above the average it will draw in some of the better second runs and a few of the firsts. Grind audiences find in it a treat and applaud it at finis. Strong enough to buck alone.

Jack Holt as secret copper has crowd guessing while serving time. Quickly snaps into good role when plot reveals he was just stooling. Working in with rustler's gang, intimacy springs up between him and leader. Latter is unusual type for such role, which helps box office. Attractive sister, Nora Lane, provides love interest and complications.

Unraveling comes with Holt identifying himself, but leader, forced to finish job, has to take bullet from detective pal. Tough finis satisfactorily handled with Holt telling girl her brother died aiding him.

Chester Conklin in minor role of bar wiper shoots over good comedy situations.

Waly.

BROADWAY FEVER

Tiffany-Stahl production and release. Directed by Edward Cline from story by Viola B. Shaw. Titles by Frederic and Fanny Hatton. John Boyle, cameraman. In cast: Sally O'Neill, Roland Drew, Corliss Palmer, Calvert Carter. At Loew's, New York, one day, Feb. 8, one-half double bill. Running time, 62 mins.

This should be called the precocious servant girl. The acting of Sally O'Neill in that role is in keeping with the suggestion. "Broadway Fever" is another Tiffany-Stahl success in the waste of production dough and good interior sets. The Shaw story, as it has been adapted and brought to the screen would drag even in a one-reeler.

The entire cast, rendered helpless by an actionless script, make projection more monotonous by over-acting. Nothing but walk ins and outs of lavish parlor and bedroom sets with but a comparative flash of a show in rehearsal—the only situation hooking with the title and that toward the last reel—get even a grind audience squirming.

The story is supposed to be about an actress out of work. That's in the sub-titles. The dumb obvious follows in most dry fashion.

Waly.

UNTAMED JUSTICE

Biltmore production, released through Capitol (state rights). Directed by Harry Webb from story by John Francis Natteford. In cast: Virginia Brown Faire, Gaston Glass, David Torrence, Philo McCullough, Sheldon Lewis. At Loew's New York one day, Jan. 22, half of double bill. Running time, 50 minutes.

One of the regulars in the fast projection, one day, assistant feature stands. "Untamed Justice" lets everything go by the board for action. From the see-and-run patron's viewpoint, with all thought for logic and tailoring over the side, it'll get by.

Virginia opens as steno for hard boiled broker, succumbs to threats of hold-up men first night on job and skips with the blame.

After that the atmosphere is all western. Real crooks are shown up after Virginia on ranch meets the airmail flyer.

Lot of animal naturals used as filler.

Waly.

MORGAN'S LAST RAID

M-G-M production and release. Starring Tim McCoy. Directed by Nick Grinde, from continuity prepared by Bradley King. Arthur Reed, cameraman. In cast: Dorothy Sebastian and Wheeler Oakman. At Loew's New York, one day, Feb. 6, half of double bill. Running time, 60 minutes.

A good second-run meller attraction along the regular Tim McCoy lines.

Dramatically, generally unconvincing because of crude shove-ins at inappropriate moments of slapstick stuff. Audience doesn't get chance for near tensity until last few reels when our hero detects the spy. Even this has its laughs for those who pay attention because fire does not ignite powder until Mac has his chance for Fairbanks tree bending stunts. Then the villain, Oakman, goes boom-boom into the air.

Morgan's men in this one come in for activities suggesting the "Maryland" melodrama, especially the McCoy-Sebastian parts.

But the hard riding in the new western form and the all-powerful and infallible McCoy keep "Morgan's Last Raid" in the rut that the masses seem willing to pay for. Picture will do better on double bill in larger houses.

Waly.

THE MAN IN HOBBLES

Tiffany-Stahl production and release. Directed by George Archainbaud. Screen arrangement by John Natteford, said to have been inspired by Peter B. Kyne's book of same title. Harry Jackson, camera. In cast: Lila Lee, Johnnie Harron, Lucien Littlefield, Sunshine Hart. At Stanley, New York, one day, Feb. 5. Running time, 70 minutes.

Of the consistently poor story material John Natteford has turned out for Tiffany-Stahl the most negative is "The Man in Hobbles." Good cast and sincere direction clipped from the start by a script of so many words. Transferred it has wasted so many reels in a monotonous, actionless, pointless movement.

Exactly 45 minutes are taken to get somewhere near what was apparently intended to be the story. Then the young photographer with a small-town studio fitted up like a Rockefeller hunting lodge proposes to a girl he has seen a couple of times. The family moving in after a lot of stock shots of Niagara have been used for the honeymoon. It could have been amusing if the story had permitted.

They just domesticate in an inane way, and young Harron, with his Fairbanks mustachio, adds to the monotony with meekness.

Grind fans will probably sit through it, if for nothing more than their silver's worth of the chair.

Waly.

WOLVES OF THE CITY

Universal production and release. Directed by Leigh Jason from the story by Val Cleveland and Vin Moore. Continuity by the authors. Titles by Val Cleveland. Featuring Bill Cody and Sally Blane, with cast including Al Ferguson, Monte Montague, Louise Carver and Charles Clary. At Times, New York, one day, Feb. 18. Running time, 45 minutes.

A thriller with a ready-made welcome in the small houses, mostly from the children. Time length limits it to filling possibilities only if the manifestly grind caliber of the picture doesn't previously give it that rating.

Construction of plot and action sequences all molded after type which has been repeated times beyond number in small town action pictures and in serials. This one hasn't a chance in the split-week neighborhoods.

No attempt at acting made, the picture depending almost entirely on the stunts framed with Bill Cody. Fight stuff faked too openly to register, except in grinds, and story is never plausible.

Concerns the theft of a curio for which the bandits demand $50,000 ransom. The collector is attacked in daylight, the possessor of the priceless gem shown without any help whatsoever. The girl is captured and held in a dive and the boy goes to the rescue with bare fists against a mob of over 20 roughnecks. He wins.

Evidently they still use this stuff in the grinds, but it's five years behind the times elsewhere.

Mori.

THE SPIELER

(DIALOG)

Pathe production and release. Sound and dialog (RCA Photophone). Directed by Tay Garnett. Original story by Hal Conklin. Cameraman, Arthur Miller. Titles by John Krafft. At Roxy, New York, week Feb. 23. Running time, 62 mins.

Flash	Alan Hale
Cleo	Renee Adoree
Luke	Clyde Cook
Red Moon	Fred Kohler
The Barker	Fred Warren
The Rabbit	Jimmy Quinn
Butch	Kewpie Morgan

Robust, virile, sinewy melodrama. High tension situations adroitly maneuvered by director Tay Garnett ring the bell with a resounding whack. It's a story of the carnival lot from the angle of the grifters, those sewer rats of the show business.

A picture like this will educate plenty of chumps when it gets into circulation in the carnival territories. This should be easy for local exploitation, through newspaper stories, "Spieler" is propaganda and an expose of the grift carnival. None of the sentimentalizing or soft pink tints of "The Barker," written from the angle of the performer, not the pickpocket. Some may quarrel with "The Spieler" on the grounds it overdraws the grift angle. Exaggerated or not it has the atmosphere, the guttiness and the tang of authenticity. This Pathe feature looks very good, like box office.

The production is plus on all counts. Neat continuity to start with. Sequences dovetail beautifully once the story is under way. There is a unity of parts unusual in pictures. Tempo constantly accellerates, working up to gripping climax when the spieler has to fight his way out of a "hey, rube" mob attack.

Dialog is introduced late and is important commercially only for its ballyhoo value. Talk is okay but not really needed. Excellent synchronization was added in New York by Josiah Zuro, the Pathe Damrosch.

Three classy performances by Alan Hale, Renee Adoree and Fred Kohler, with honorable mention for Clyde Cook. Both Hale and Kohler are of gorilla-like physical proportions, fitting the tough mug roles perfectly. Hale is an interesting type of leading man, good-looking in a huge, well-fed way and knowing how to troupe beaucoup. Miss Adoree looks unusually attractive in this picture and handles herself with her customary easy grace.

Picture opens with a close-up of Billboard story about a girl carnival owner trying to run her show free from grift. Assuming The Billboard would print such a story, if reported, which it would not, this may be accepted as starting at the beginning. Two dips reading The Billboard decide that a carnival presumely on the up and up is an easy locale for their operations. They join up with the troupe, discovering that while the owner may fancy she is running an honest carnival it is really honeycombed with gimmick workers, artful dodgers, and other fungi. These shady gents are captained by Red Moon (Fred Kohler), an all-around soandso, whose repertory includes homicide.

Picture is replete with inside tricks of the hot stuff boys. The quiet, sinister mob assaults in the midst of a milling midway are pregnant with melodrama. Hale when cornered grabs a tent stake and goes on a skull-busting rampage, exciting enough to draw applause at the Roxy.

Only runs about an hour. Distinctly absorbing the whole distance.

Land.

THE IRON MASK

(SOUND)

United Artists release starring Douglas Fairbanks. Written by Elton Thomas, based on Dumas' "Three Musketeers" and "The Man in the Iron Mask." Directed by Allan Dwan. Henry Sharp, photographer. Score by Dr. Hugo Riesenfeld. Lotta Woods, scenario editor. Synchronized by W. E. on disks. Production supervised by Maurice Leloir. At Rivoli, New York, for grind run, opening with reserved seat performance Feb. 21. Running time, 95 mins.

Queen Mother	Belle Bennett
Constance	Marguerite de la Motte
Milady de Winter	Dorothy Revier
Mme. Peronne	Vera Lewis
Louis XIII	Rolfe Sedan
Louis XIV (and twin)	William Bakewell
Cardinal Richelieu	Nigel de Brulier
De Rochefort	Ulrich Haupt
Father Joseph	Lon Poff
Planchet	Charles Stevens
King's Valet	Henry Otto
Athos	Leon Barry
Porthos	Stanley Sandford
Aramis	Gino Corrado
D'Artagnan	Douglas Fairbanks

Typical romantic Fairbanks picture with the usual Fairbanks enthusiasm for this sort of thing. Rollicking and excellent boxoffice fare, Billing will state that the star talks, but not how much. His direct vocal address is in the form of minute and a half appendages as prologs to the first and second halves, into which the picture was divided for this reserved seat premiere. There is no dialog at any time in the direct action but the film is replete with sound effects and a well proportioned score by Dr. Hugo Riesenfeld. It carries a strain of a theme for the return of the screen's "Musketeers."

Eight years later this is the sequel to Fairbanks' "Three Musketeers," which opened at the Lyric, New York, Aug. 28, '21. As sequels go it's a corking effort as a follow up on the original and smart in not trying for $2. It belongs just where it is, not for $2 but above an ordinary program release for a start. Looks good for six weeks at this house unless dialog has so swept the natives out of all reasoning that nothing else in pictures counts right now. But Fairbanks makes 'em clean, there's a decided lilt and verve to his D'Artagnan, and they're quite apt to leave the theatre feeling better for having seen both it and him again as the Gastony daredevil. This despite that the picture takes the bit in its teeth in killing off the heroine before the half way mark and building to its climax by the individual supreme sacrifice of the four men who have sworn "all for one and one for all."

It's so much of a sequel that, besides Fairbanks, Nigel de Brulier and Lon Poff are again together as Cardinal Richelieu and his aid, Father Joseph; Marguerite de la Motte revives her Constance, and Leon Barry has been recast as Athos. On the technical end Lotta Woods repeats in having edited, and Paul Burns is found to have served both productions in charge of wardrobe and properties.

In the original work Adolphe Menjou was Louis XIII, now played by Rolfe Sedan, while the late George Seigman enjoyed one of his few respites from being the menace in doing Porthos. Fred Niblo directed "The Three Musketeers," with Arthur Edeson cameraman.

Current story provides the twist of D'Artagnan going over to the Cardinal's side. It is to protect the young heir apparent who has a twin brother whom Richelieu whisks into hiding at birth to protect the throne, and around whom De Rochefort later constructs his conspiracy to substitute the second heir.

Dwan, directing, has kept the story moving for the full hour and a half and it almost classes as a novelty to again see a mob scene. This is screened as the populace's welcome to the infant heir. Comedy sidelights slip in and out, but Fairbanks and the romantic friendship of the four men hold the picture together. Photography and titling is top grade.

The brief verbal passages ask the audience to come back with the star to the days of chivalry and so forth. Simply a gesture forced by the times, although done well enough for the purpose, opening bit having his three companions grouped beside him. Second vocal interlude is alone but as brief and in the same vein. Finish of the picture has D'Artagnan stabbed by the exposed brother, prone upon a lawn in front of a mammoth horizon back drop upon which the double-exposed Athos, Porthos and Aramis urge him to join them and all walk into the distance, arm in arm, as the king and his court gather around D'Artagnan's lifeless form. An unseen voice then repeats one of the Fairbanks messages.

Picture, of course, is mostly Fairbanks in a role which he has made fit him like a glove. On performance, however, he is closely pursued by Ulrich Haupt as the heavy, and Nigel de Brulier in his first half character of the Cardinal. William Bakewell, in the dual roles of the twin brothers, appears to have done better with the king than as the scheming second son, an assignment in which he has been permitted to exaggerate. The women are not important, held down on footage and situation. Belle Bennett, as the Queen Mother, is a late entry.

When caught by Variety in '21, Samuel (New Orleans) said of Fairbanks and "The Three Musketeers" that the "character provides the star with what will probably go down in film lore as his best effort." Between wrecking homes, pictures and race tracks that's about as close to being right as O. M. has ever been. Fairbanks shouldn't have any trouble getting money with "The Iron Mask." It's enjoyable screen material that the censors don't even have to look at, unless they want to be entertained. *Sid.*

GHOST TALKS

(DIALOG)

Fox production and release. Talker, directed by Lew Seller. Story by Max Marcin and Edward Hammond. Dialog by Frederick H. Brennon and Herbert Thompson. Cameraman, George Meehan. Running time, 61 minutes. At the Roxy, New York, week Feb. 16.

Miriam Holt..............Helen Twelvetrees
Franklyn Green..............Charles Eaton
Marie Haley..............Carmel Myers
Helmie Heimrath..............Earle Foxe
Joe Talles..............Henry Sedley
Peter Accardi..............Joe Brown
John Keegan..............Clifford Dempsey
Christopher C. Lee..............Stepin Fetchit
Isobel Lee..............Baby Mack
Julius Bowser..............Arnold Lucy
Sylvia..............Bess Flowers
Miss Eva..............Dorothy McGowan
Bellboy..............Mickey Bennett

First all-talk full-length featuring the junior Fox team of Helen Twelvetrees and Charles Eaton. It's a crook-spook melodrama treated in a comedy vein to the extent that the melodrama is altogether subordinated and the chief element is comedy. Heralded as a potential box-office smash, early reception left that in doubt. On audience reaction looked to be a satisfactory program product but not much more. Much talk slows action and speed, essential to films farce, suffers.

Another thing that suggests mild fan support is that story attempts to blend romance with comedy. Hero is a sappy youth who blunders into a nest of crooks as a correspondence school detective and comes out on top only through the dumbest of dumb luck. Literary trick is retelling of "Babes in the Woods," and it ought to be fool proof, just as the Cinderella theme is. But somehow it doesn't come out that way. Grotesque stupidity of the boy robs him of sympathy. Comedy at times comes perilously near to gagging, and the sympathetic quality of the leading characters is never quite satisfactorily established.

Mechanically the talking episodes are flawless. Both young leads handle dialog well, and that also goes for the rest of the cast. Especially good was the negro dialect talk of Stepin Fetchit and Baby Mack, dark honeymooners, who supply the low comedy as a bride and bridegroom, wished into the haunted house for their wedding night and terrified by the ghostly manifestations devised by crooks.

Picture has no titles except the introductory main title and cast. Dialog is almost continuous. Talk interferes with swift building of situation and development to climax. Even the gags are robbed of surprise by laborious building. The best gag was without talk. This had to do with the colored comic being chased from the haunted house by a dog and his flight through the streets with more dogs joining the chase at every leap. Laugh is sprung unexpectedly. In like manner terror of the colored pair, only sequences that drew audible laughs, were independent of talk.

Trouble with the picture is that it makes all-dialog a definite object, instead of making it only serve the purpose of action that in itself is intrinsically funny or dramatic. *Rush.*

WOLF SONG

(SOUND)

Paramount sound feature production and release. Co-featuring Gary Cooper, Lupe Velez and Louis Wolheim in story by Harvey Fergusson. Screen play by John Farrow and Keene Thompson. Victor Fleming, director. Western Electric recording, with musical synchronization by Irvin Talbot, recorded under supervision of Mex Terr. Theme song, "Yo Te Amo Means I Love You," by Alfred Bryan (lyric) and Richard Whiting (music). At Embassy, New York, opening Feb. 23. $2 top. Running time, 93 minutes.

Sam Lash..............Gary Cooper
Lola Salazar..............Lupe Velez
Guillon..............Louis Wolheim
Rube Thatcher.......Constantine Romanoff
Don Solomon Salazer.......Michael Vavitch
Duenna..............Ann Brody
Ambrosia Guiterrez........Russell Columbo
Louisa..............Augustina Lopez
Black Wolf..............George Rigas

Labeled the "first musical film romance," this Paramount sound feature is a sluggish western of undistinguished caliber, on Broadway at $2 primarily for its showcase display value. For the box office the pleasant vocalizing, the stellar twain's personal romantic equation, and the song theme are exploitation assets for the regular program houses. Passive feature, but punchless. It's draw wholly depends upon the strength of the names of its feature people.

Presumably primed as another "Ramona," "Wolf Song" has only a fair theme song, which Lupe Velez plugs to a fare thee well. One might captiously comment that this over-exploitation of the theme song made the feature a great trailer for the number. If ever a theme was plugged, this one is. Probably the songwriters' delight, it's unfortunate the number lacks the wow punch which might have contributed as much toward carrying the film as "Ramona" (not a theme song) did for the Del Rio film.

Seemingly it's an old Spanish custom for the characters to sing at each other to guitar accompaniment at the slightest provocation. The vocalization and the heavy romance between Gary Cooper and his bride, Miss Velez, is but incidental relief to what the "Wolf Song" really is—just a western designed for more than the usual masculine appeal.

As one of a trio of hardy fur trappers and incipient wanderers, Cooper's role is that of a roving swain who loves 'em and leaves 'em until, meeting up with Miss Velez, whom he knocks for a Lupe. The titular "Wolf Song" is the pagan call of the wanderlust when, after a period of domesticity, Cooper is moved to desert his bride. Despite her repetitious serenadings of "Yo Te Amo Means I Love You," the hybrid Spanish-American song is blotted out by the refrain of the "Wolf Song," only to have the situation reversed when he reverses his trek for a return home. He is ambushed by a couple of Injuns—period is 1840—and encounters a couple of other mild complications until the final clinch.

Running too long, those 93 minutes could stand paring by fully 20.

Louis Wolheim, sharing third featuring with Cooper-Velez, does a sympathetic backwoodsman role excepting for the one strong rough-and-tumble fight with Cooper, almost literally dragged in for a little action, as was the Injun ambush business.

Picture cried for a real punch which never happened.

Constantine Romanoff was the third of the dougty trio. Rest of the cast tritely "adequate" if undistinguished, and notable for the majority of foreign film names in the personnel. Cooper does his strong silent man role conventionally, and Miss Velez overacts in the emotional scenes, particularly with those ludicrous chest-heavings, as much the fault of direction. As a heaver Lupe's a champ. *Abel.*

THE CARNATION KID

(DIALOG)

Al Christie production; Paramount release; Douglas MacLean starred; E. Mason Hopper, director. Dialog by A. Leslie Pierce. From original story by Alfred A. Cohen. Recorded by W. E. At Paramount, New York, week Feb. 23. Running time, 76 minutes.

Clarence Kendall.........Douglas MacLean
Doris Whitely..............Frances Lee
Blythe..............William B. Davidson
Lucille..............Lorraine Eddy
Crawford Whitely......Charles Hill Mailes
Carnation Kid..........Francis McDonald
Tony..............Maurice Black
Blinkey..............Bert Swor, Jr.
Deacon..............Carl Stockdale

Chicago gunman theme, by now a familiar screen pattern, handled in a light comedy manner. With the addition of dialog. Although it remains a question whether the dialog hurts or helps, "Carnation Kid." The recording or projection wasn't first rate. The dialog is also on and off too often, breaking up the interest by suddenly sneaking in and releasing the film's firm grip just as often. On the other hand, the presence of dialog may mean to this picture the difference between full-week and one-day classification; if dialog in a picture still carries that much weight.

What it doesn't do for the picture itself the talk does for Douglas MacLean. Formerely a fairly popular juvenile, with a fascinating smile and short of stature, MacLean now appears to be a corking light comedian with a voice. If 100 per cent before talking, MacLean is now 200 per cent, because they've heard his voice and it's a good one.

About the best point to Alfred Cohen's story is its pace, although that credit might be due the director. Anyway, it is speedily unconvincing.

The Carnation Kid is a Chicago guy who specializes in bumping people off. Quite a rep for clean-cut work. Always wears a white carnation, and is known by no other name. Has invented a silent machine gun that has no superior in the kid's racket.

Political trouble in the town of Chatham. The righteous D. A. is running for office on a clean-town platform. He's after the burg's vice lord, Blythe. So what does Blythe do but import the Carnation Kid from Chi to give Mr. D. A. a lead massage. On the train en route to Chatham, the Kid is spotted and chased. He forces a fellow passenger to change clothes and dives out the window. And who else could the clothes-changing victim be but MacLean?

Unaware of his attacker's identity, the nice MacLean boy thinks nothing more of it and finally reaches Chatham. He represents a typewriter company that manufactures a machine that's just as fast and just as silent as the Carnation Kid's machine gun.

Mistaken identity in Chatham and finally the re-election of the good D. A. and the routing of the bad vice lord. Also, the D. A.'s daughter for love interest.

MacLean is highly impressive throughout, more so when talking. In the dialog sequences he is rivaled only by Lorraine Eddy, slim blonde in a moll role. Her make scene with MacLean is spicy and well handled. Looks, talks and acts better than Frances Lee, the D. A.'s daughter.

One prolonged double exposure sequence throws a shadow over the general photography. It was a very bad piece of technical work, appearing amateurish, and as poor as anything on the screen in a long while. Boy and girl riding in a roadster down the town's main street. The background seemed to be Times Square. The car was moving, but up and down. The street was moving as it should move. Blending terrible.

Considerable license taken with the crook stuff. People on the street say "There's the Carnation Kid" when the innocent MacLean walks by with a bud in his lapel. No one else in Chatham, perhaps, wears a carnation. One mug on the corner wanted to take a shot at MacLean after he had passed and had been falsely identified. He didn't shoot because his friend advised him of the Kid's own speed with the trigger. Shooting a man down because he wears a carnation! Like referring to every man with a scar as Scarface Al Capone.

If Chicago's police commissioner is looking for an easy way out, here it is. Send every gunman in town a ticket for "The Carnation Kid." They'll laugh themselves to death. *Bige.*

GIRL ON THE BARGE

(DIALOG)

Universal production and release. Version of story and play of same name by Rupert Hughes. Edward Sloman director. Jean Hersholt, Sally O'Neill and Malcom McGregor featured. Titles by Tom Reed; Jackson Rose, cameraman. Dialog credited to Charles Henry Smith. Theme song is "When You're in Love With No One But Me." Running time, 80 minutes. At Colony, New York, Feb. 23.

Dandy human interest story and nice work by Sally O'Neill and Jean Hersholt. Then they spoil the whole picture by ending it with a typical movie punch scene, crude melodrama clumsily faked. Earlier scenes qualify for important dates, but finish condemns film to the neighborhoods.

Miss O'Neill as "Erie," Cinderella of an Erie canal boat, has a role of sure sympathetic appeal, and plays it for all it's worth. She has one scene with extraordinary heart grip, passage where the waif has been separated from her sweetheart by a dour Scotch father, and sends up a childish prayer between sobs.

Locale of a canal boat is a novelty and opens the opportunity for some smashing pictorial effects, opportunities the cameraman has used to the utmost. Scenic backgrounds are a feature.

Hersholt creates a remarkable portrait of the bargeman-father, brutal giant who backs up his cruelties with the authority of biblical texts.

Dialog is skillfully handled. No spoken word for the first half hour during which story is planted and atmosphere developed. It is when the young deck hand of the tugboat that tows the barge persuades Erie to come to his pilot house that the dialog is introduced to promote sentimental comedy effect. Boy is teaching the girl to read against her father's strict rule. Dialog here runs for probably 12 minutes, and has to do with the boy and girl falling in love as they do book exercises out of the advertising signs on the banks of the canal as they drift past.

Boy and girl run away to the fair near Troy. Old man furiously beats his daughter and then nearly kills the youth on the bank, leaving him half dead as the barge creeps off. So much of the story is excellent sentimental comedy with much charm and a good deal of beauty.

Scene shifts to the New York waterfront, where the barge is tied up for the winter. It breaks away in a storm, and is about to be dashed to bits on the rocks of Hell Gate when the boy goes to the rescue in a tug. He is knocked unconscious just as he reaches the foundering barge. The girl drags herself along a tow line amid the raging water, while the father, suddenly brought to a realization of the girl's courage, prays for her safety.

Girl makes the tug, saves the day, and scene suddenly shifts to a happy ending with boy and girl on a barge of their own, with a baby prattling about the old man's knee. Storm stuff in a tank and all the devices of the studio fail to give it reality. Just synthetic melodrama. Picture is a good deal too long for a sentimental comedy, but neatly devised sequences make it seem to move with fair briskness. *Rush.*

KRASSIN

(RUSSIAN MADE)

Amkino production and release. Editorial supervision by Vilhjalmur Stefansson; titles by Shelley Hamilton. Photographed by Wilhelm Bluvstein, cameraman on the "Krassin"; Ignati Valentey, cameraman on the "Malyghin," Eugene Bogorov, cameraman on the "Perseus." At Carnegie Hall, New York, Feb. 19, $2 top. Booked to follow at Film Guild Cinema for a run. Running time, over 85 minutes.

Belated film version of the rescue of the ill-fated airship "Italia" in the frozen north by the Russian ice-breaker, "Krassin," resolved itself into a free-for-all at Carnegie Hall when shown here for the first time at $2 top. Hall was jammed to the doors with reds and Italian anti-everythings. They razzed the preliminary speaker, Stefansson, Polar explorer; held open arguments as various incidents on the screen appeared; they yelled, screamed and stamped from 8:30 to 11 p. m. without a halt.

Picture was incidental. It isn't much of a picture anyway. Supposed to show the rescue of lost members of the crew of the "Italia," there are no motion picture shots of the rescue, a couple of stills being worked in towards the finish with an attempt to cover that purpose.

Most of the footage is devoted to scenic material without any actual bearing on the cruise or the rescue. It starts way back with some stuff about Amundsen and runs for 85 minutes, just about 75 too long. Could do very nicely if cut to a couple of clips for a newsreel but will undoubtedly get a strong play from the Russians and Italians when shown in those neighborhoods in its present form.

The reason for its strong drawing power is simply the appearance of Russian and Italian ships and men. Every time an Italian appeared on the screen the antis in the balconies cheered for long minutes, while the appearance of a Soviet ship or official brought the same result from the Reds.

Russian angle is overplayed from the beginning, so that after a while it becomes purely Soviet propaganda. Sure-seaters, if playing this picture, should get it free and be paid for running it. It isn't above the average sure-seat picture, excepting that it will draw additional business from the two elements mentioned.

Nobile, leader of the "Italia" expedition, was the cause of the display of temperament by the antis at Carnegie. Half of the Italians razzed him and the other half stood up for him. Nobile is under a cloud, as explained by Stefansson, because of alleged blunders he had made on the trip which had caused the death of several of the crew.

An interesting and somewhat lighter touch was added to the proceedings when Stefansson pointed out that the charges made that two of the crew of the "Italia" had eaten the third member, Malmgren, while on an ice floe in the Arctic waiting to be rescued, were not without foundation. Stefansson said it shouldn't be held against the Italians because cannibalism among whites had occurred before during Polar expeditions.

Film is characterized by a series of outstanding titles, such as "On the morning of July 7, at 6 a. m.," followed by a shot of three men carrying a log of wood or having breakfast. Every momentous occasion foretold in the titles by exact date and timing is followed by some inane shots of snow, men walking, talking or eating. Once an aviator is seen taking off from the ice, built up in titles as the beginning of a dangerous flight, all resulting in nothing.

Stefansson, the explorer, speaker of the evening, made a long, dry speech, but not uninteresting. Unintelligible to the gallery, however, they began to stamp and howl for his dismissal long before he was through. The lower floor was partly filled with customers drawn by Stefansson's name as an authority on Polar exploration. *Mori.*

AT THE SOUTH POLE

Pictures claimed to have been taken during Robert Scott's British Antarctic Expedition and handled by Pole Pictures Corp. Revised and titled by Vilhjalmur Stefansson, with photography credited Herbert G. Penting, F. R. G. S., of the expedition. Opening at Lyric, New York, Dec. 20, on special showing. Running time, 75 minutes.

For the first camera work on a polar expedition, as this is represented to be, "At the South Pole" is not only a remarkably well preserved print, but one displaying a cinematographic technique far ahead of that prevailing over a score of years back. The theme is not unlike numbers of its kind which have covered every box office in the country. Its value is considerably enhanced by good newspaper workmanship in the subtitles. These, with a few stock shots, endeavor to tie it up with the Byrd expedition. Ballyhoo along these lines should draw big until Byrd returns with his own footage. Looks especially good for non-theatrical bookings before class audiences, with personal appearance touch and talk by Stefansson. Otherwise, for general bookings, fair now, but dangerous too for distant showings.

On the opening night Stefansson's talk was largely a resume of facts and figures incorporated in the titling. Noteworthy to the trade was **his statement that the picture bears the indorsement of the museums of natural history in Britain and America and the American Geographic Society.** The exploitation angle that a percentage of the proceeds go to the British Antarctic expedition will also help biz in high-class trade.

Flashes of the expedition's vessel in a storm are better than average, as is a study of icebergs and snow-mounds. The outstanding sequence woven together by clever and humorous subtitles is a tenement observation of the lives of penguins. This one sequence can be cut out any time and released as a novelty two-reeler that would create a sensation. It pulled big laughs, even in its serious and frozen surroundings, from an unusually high-brow audience.

Shots of vast ice wastes over which explorers drag their own sledges, after horses and dogs have succumbed, have been almost facsimilied in predecessors to this offering.

Music score on Columbia sound and recording equipment is generally exceptionally poor. Intrusion of shaky male voice deploring Amundsen's scoop on the pole after Scott's mighty efforts would turn tragic climax into hilarious peak with any undignified audience. *Waly.*

MARIE ANTOINETTE

(FRENCH MADE)

Produced by I.F.A., G.m. b. h., distributor not credited. Directed by Rudolphe Meinert. Author not credited. Cast headed by Diana Karenne, others not programmed. At Little Carnegie Playhouse, New York, week Feb. 23. Running time, 65 mins.

One of those compact little foreign flickers which offer, in seven limited reels, to tell of the amorous inclinations of a queen, the ruin of a king, the downfall of a regal household, the reign of terror during the French Revolutions, and a few sundry morals built round the old fable that the ways of transgressors are tough.

Through it all there is one outstanding, dominant personality, the woman behind the throne. Her beauty and power have been the subject of a thousand romances. The charming lady entrusted with the precarious duty of impersonating the magnificent Marie Antoinette is nothing but a tawdry, tarnished caricature of that famous personage. At best she achieves the cheap sparkle of tinsel.

Diana Karenne, reputed to be a French "stage figure," is a study in moroseness. The life of Marie Antoinette was indeed dull and worthless if this were it.

When reproached by the king for leaving their sick child to hold forth, or more, at a ball she registered for a frown. When the king got hot and planted an impassioned kiss on the regal forehead she was still chill and so on to the last reeling foot.

Conditions came and went, revolutions revolved, people starved and stormed the castle gates, directorial ingenuity launched untold schemes **and combinations for a little action, but the queen still frowned.**

Entire production is built around the title role and the amazing incapability of the leading actress marks it among the least stirring of the sure-seat pictures seen in recent times. *Mori.*

UNDERGROUND

(BRITISH MADE)

Produced by Anthony Asquith, distributor not named. Written and directed by Mr. Asquith. Cast includes Elissa Landi, Nora Baring, Brian Aherne and Cyril McLaglen. At Fifth Avenue playhouse, New York, week Feb. 23. Running time, over 60 mins.

Anthony Asquith has another picture, with the dual responsibility of having written and directed. Perhaps the name power of its sponsor may be figured on for some commercial strength in exhibition circles in England, but in America the appeal, box office and human, can be correctly gauged from the assumption that the picture is as good as the class of theatre it first plays in, in this sure seater.

Asquith, from the screen announcement which probably preceded the picture abroad also, is credited with having studied American production methods in Hollywood, also having worked with Charlie Chaplin and Douglas Fairbanks. None of it shows in this film.

Primarily, casting is grievously bad. Asquith has assembled a group of four people, none of whom can do anything except clumsily. They are cast among London's poorer class, but that is no excuse for the way they are dressed. In addition to the unsuitability of any of the players for picture work, photography from the wrong angles exaggerates the faults in their physical appearance.

The love sequences and action scenes are mostly ragged and unnatural, while the continuity is far from smooth. The director has succeeded, however, in getting a few odd shots of interesting characters, appearing but briefly and entirely too inconsequential as atmosphere.

The result is a pretty dull 60 minutes and not worth spotting outside of the sureseaters. Story planted in the tubes of London, mostly. Concerns two boys, one good and the other not so hot, both wanting the same shopgirl. The menace frames the other in a charge of trying to neck with a strange female, the boy standing to lose his job in the tubes and his affianced through it. *Mori.*

Beautiful Blue Danube

(GERMAN MADE)

Pesina (German) production, released here by Aywon. Story claimed to have been based on the Strauss waltz. Directed by Frederic Zelnick. At 55th St. Playhouse week Feb. 23, half of double feature. Running time 58 minutes.

Archduke	Hans Junkermann
Count Zirsky	Julius Falkenstein
Oscar	Harry Liedke
Rudi	Ernst Verebes
Mizzi	Lya Mara

Registers negatively. Story one of those things of the cabaret girl hooking nobility. Only hook-up with song is that she uses it for a dance accompaniment. The river comes in for flash. Poor make-up of leads and rainy print. This sure-seater using it as a second on a double bill. Enough? Regulars, if they consider it at all, should regard it as program filler.

Close-ups of Lya Mara, dancer, could better be out. Her pan from long shot okay. Careless application of grease chief reason.

Rudi clowns in annoying feministic way.

Story done in English way with sub-titles that sock intelligence of average arty crowd, even to point of wringing moan out of some. Performances generally insincere. *Waly.*

HEARTS IN DIXIE

(DIALOG)

Fox production and release. All-Negro picture. Story and dialog by Walter Weems, with Paul Sloane directing. Glenn MacWilliams, cameraman; Howard Jackson, sound. Dances staged by Fanchon and Marco. Gaiety for $2, twice-daily run, starting Feb. 26. Running time, 71 minutes.
Nappus....................Clarence Muse
Chinquapin................Eugene Jackson
Gummy.....................Stepin Fetchit
Chloe.....................Barnice Pilot
Rammey....................Clifford Ingram
Trailia...................Mildred Washington
Deacon....................Zach Williams
Emmy......................Gertrude Howard
Melia.....................Dorothy Morrison
Violet....................Vivian Smith
Voodoo Woman..............A. C. H. Billbrew
White Doctor..............Richard Carlysle

A type picture that would be perfect for the art theatres if these sure-seaters were wired. More apt to appeal to the sympathies of the intelligensia than the mob at large, the main reason it's going to have to fight for whatever it gets. Indications are that the coin pace will be spotty, with everybody satisfied if it holds to normal figures or a little better.

"Hearts in Dixie" is a novelty film that classes as a celluloid "Porgy." It resembles the Guild play in that it unrolls as a series of sketches on the American Negro in different moods. It's more carefree than the stage piece, because it doesn't harp on the tragic, gets away from spiritual dirges and mainly carries through in the lighter veins in being strung together by a thin linked story. That it is well made isn't going to particularly interest that clientele which wants its vital catch-as-catch-can stuff either in battle or on a couch. The worry of whether any house playing it will thereby work up a strong Negro patronage isn't pregnant, as the picture isn't that strong. It will undoubtedly draw members of the race for that full week, split or day that it plays, but no reason to figure beyond that—a sidelight which cropped up before the picture came in.

Popularly, the entertainment appeal rests in Stepin Fetchit, a funny buy, who was the redeeming figure of Fox's "Ghost Talks," as also a couple of silent features. Basically, the Billbrew Chorus of 60 is the background. This group's principal work is confined to a plantation party striving for atmosphere and into which someone has injected a vaudeville quartet doing a comedy cat fight.

Film has pathos in the love of an old slave for his grandson, whom he sends north to school, the picture concluding on the youngster's departure by river boat. Sloane, the director, has intimated rather than shown any love interest, there being no personal contact, except in a comedy way, other than the holding of hands by the grandson and his first sweetheart.

With the program mentioning dances and ensembles staged by Fanchon and Marco, a deduction was that the youngster was going to go north and join a hot colored revue. Not in keeping with the period of the stern wheelers, of course, and it didn't happen. Just what F. and M. did do in the staging is not otherwise discernible.

Story centers on Grandpap Nappus, his daughter Chloe, who dies; her young son and shiftless husband, Gummy. It's to make sure the boy doesn't turn out like his father, plus deliverance from the limitations of a superstitious mentality, that the grandfather sacrifices the only association he cares about in sending the boy away.

Performances by each member of this supposed family is highly creditable, although Muse, as Nappus, may impress as a bit too well spoken for an uneducated Negro. He is the replacement for Charles Gilpin, originally slated. Fetchit is the lazy, careless, indifferent, middle-aged idler to the life, making everything count and having some funny dialog with which to work, no mean help.

Massed singing is uniformly good and interesting, although there is no telling the names of the songs, except in extremely familiar cases such as "Swanee River," as capably rendered as anything in the picture. The Brown, DeSylva and Henderson songs, credited on the lead title, are entirely obscured from public discovery, and unimportant if present.

Film is not a pulse quickener in any sense. In fact, it is slowly paced and is simply a southern Negro study. It is not $2 fare, and if grind audiences do not loose patience with it, more than half the battle will be won. But the ability of the picture house mentality to stick it is the point upon which this one will ride or fall, and the reason for stating the sure-seaters, if wired, would go for it in a big way. Favorable feminine audience reaction will be particularly important in this case, and doubtful.

In workmanship it's far more significant than many of those clucks which have come out of Russia. Technically the picture is a treat in sound as reproduced in this house. It is also easy to look at pictorially, while intimating the production overhead in materials couldn't have been particularly important. That it's different should be a favorable point, but that it can force itself into the important money class is doubtful. A crude and unnecessary two-minute prolog speech really asks compassion for the subject. It should be thrown out, as Negroes are apt to resent it and balconies are quite likely to razz it. *Sid.*

THE DUMMY

(DIALOG)

Paramount all-talking production featuring Ruth Chatterton, John Cromwell and Frederic March. Directed by Robert Milton. Based on play by Harvey O'Higgins and Harriet Ford. Adaptation and dialog by Herman Manckiewicz. Cameraman J. Roy Hunt. Supervised by Hector Turnbull. At Paramount, New York, week March 2. Running time, 70 minutes.
Agnes Meredith............Ruth Chatterton
Trumbell Meredith.........Frederic March
Walter Babbing............John Cromwell
Joe Cooper................Fred Kohler
Barney Cook...............Mickey Bennett
Peggy Meredith............Vondell Darr
Dopey Hart................Jack Oakie
Rose Gleason..............ZaSu Pitts
Blackie Baker.............Ruchard Tucker
Madison...................Eugene Pallette

Fair program entertainment, including quite a few giggles, but apt to leave audiences cold. No love story and Ruth Chatterton, number one in the billing, has what amounts simply to a bit. Frederic March is among the three names billed on the main title although he has even less to do than Miss Chatterton, doesn't get a single closeup and remains a zero throughout.

Picture revolves around the character of a 12-year-old boy played by Mickey Bennett, entitled on merit to receive special mention among the credits. This same story was done by Paramount once before, in 1917. Jack Pickford had the lead at that time. With young Bennett now doing the dummy the inevitable changes in the script are probably the explanation for the absence of romance.

Herman Manckiewicz is responsible for the present adaptation and the dialog. Talk is good but treatment is leaky at the seams. The failure of the picture to get under the epidermis is in great measure due to the concentration on the vocal phase with the accompanying neglect of good old fashioned picture technique.

Robert Milton, stage director from legit, must shoulder the responsibility for the failure to establish characterization, the absence of closeups and certain other structural weaknesses. But the poor lighting and often indifferent photography, not to mention a couple of bad spots in the dialog should have been caught by Hector Turnbull, the supervisor.

Story is melodrama against a kidnapping motif. A detective plants a smart youngster in the midst of a gang of crooks. Youngster signals to the outside with rescue following.

Number of known players in cast but no particular box office strength, unless Miss Chatterton is better known at the present time than her brief film career would indicate. Cannot be exploited too strenuously as picture is unable to meet extravagant expectations. By fall this type of detective and crook hokum will seem as old fashioned as the Perils of Pauline. *Land.*

SONNY BOY

(DIALOG)

Warner Bros. production and release, starring Davey Lee, child player, with Al Jolson in "The Singing Fool." Directed by Archie Mayo. Cast: Betty Bronson, Edward Everett Horton, Gertrude Olmstead. Scenario by C. Graham Baker. Titles by J. A. Starr. Cameraman, Ben Reynolds. Musical score arranged by Louis Silvers. At the opening of the new Mastbaum Memorial theatre, Philadelphia, Feb. 27. Running time, 70 mins.

A picture that is bound to clean up on the strength of a remarkable performance by the Lee baby, and in addition because of the prestige of Jolson and "The Singing Fool" and the sentimental background of the song hit, "Sonny Boy." Easy to forecast a box office sensation comparable to the experience of Jackie Coogan's early features, following his leap to eminence with Chaplin.

Picture itself is light and at times trivial and some of the dialog passages are dull, but the whole thing is shrewdly framed to lead up to a climax in which the youngster sings a verse and a chorus of "Sonny Boy," after which the returns are all in and there's nothing to it.

This climatic episode will make 'em rave. It had an invited audience of 5,000 at the premiere cooing with the fascinating kid and quite carried away. It will be the reaction everywhere. For the feminine contingent it's perfect, and nothing could be sweeter on the box office side.

Inconsequential comedy story furnishes the framework upon which to exploit the little chap. His father and mother, involved in a foolish family row, determine to part. Mother begs her sister to kidnap the child to prevent the father from taking him abroad. Complications pile up swiftly when the kidnaping sister (Aunt Winnie, charmingly played by Betty Bronson) takes refuge in the apartment of a lawyer representing the boy's father in the divorce case. Instead of leaving town as he intended the lawyer returns to the flat just as his parents arrive unexpectedly, and as a result Aunt Winnie has to pose as the lawyer's wife.

Farcical entanglements build dizzily from this point. Davey has been left sleeping peacefully after a delightful scene of being tucked into bed by Aunt Winnie. Awakened and whisked into his clothes when Aunty decides on flight, a new whirlwind of complications leaves him abandoned for the moment, and he determines to venture on an expedition of his own, attracted by the electric sign on a theatre visible from the bedroom window announcing "The Singing Fool." The fire escape provides the escape, and there is more turmoil while everybody searches for the missing baby.

He ambles in presently by the fire escape window and boasting of his solo adventures, offers to sing the "Sonny Boy" song he has just heard.

Picture is mostly dialog, but the talk runs according to no discernible pattern, shifting from spoken word to printed title at intervals.

Talk is best in the comedy passages, as, for instance, the scene where Aunt Winnie flirts with a detective in order to escape with the baby. Where dialog is used to advance story progress it slows action

Technical production is excellent as to settings and conversation is splendidly handled, particularly by Edward Everett Horton and Miss Bronson. *Rush.*

SPIES

(GERMAN MADE)

Ufa production, released here through M-G-M. Directed by Fritz Lang from story by Thea von Harbou with her own adaptation. At 55th Street Playhouse week of March 2. Running time, 90 minutes.
Haghi.....................Rudolph Klein-Rogge
Sonia.....................Gerda Maurus
Kitty.....................Lien Deyers
Morrier...................Louis Ralph
Jason.....................Craighall Sherry
Donald Tremaine...........Willy Fritsch
Dr. Matsumato.............Lupu Pick
Ivan Stefanov.............Fritz Rasp

Technically, "Spies" projects like "Perils of Pauline" or any other old mystery serial. The difference is "Spies" is whole at one sitting. No money has been spared on props. But "Spies" hasn't even the thread of the story "Perils" exhibited. It just unreels like a feature made up of trailers on every meller shown in America.

It's a hopeless hodge podge of unrelated complications. It will get by in houses where they don't know any better. In the big houses strictly a gamble.

Haghi, as the spy maestro is called, has everything with him until one of his females turns state's evidence for the boy friend. Then poison gas, train wrecks, shootings and poisonings all fail.

Before the end of a picture so crammed with bewildering action that even a few much needed subtitles are abandoned, Haghi gives many impressions. First he is like a city editor, so busy are stenos copying down reports from dictaphones planted in spy-victim rooms and rushing copy as for a deadline Then he confuses as the cripple, during which he relaxes for a while and goes in for close-ups.

But, after the fan is sold on the dope that old Haghi's legs are shot, a clown, singing and skipping around, pulls the opera angle and governments rejoice the villain is no more. *Waly.*

GERALDINE

(DIALOG)

Pathe production and release. Produced by Paul Bern, directed by Melville Brown. From the story by Booth Tarkington, adapted by Carey Wilson. Scenario by George Dromgold and Peggy Prior. Cast includes Marion Nixon, Eddie Quillan, Albert Gran and Gaston Glass. At the Colony, March 2. Running time, 80 mins.

Nothing in this picture that hasn't been done to death. It's strictly a type and doesn't figure as a money-getting attraction.

Marian Nixon, the only name with any box office, and that spotty, and the title sufficient to keep plenty of people away. It's too soft or mushy

Picture is with synchronized orchestra music all of the way and dialog only on for the finishing reel or two.

From the production standpoint it is a nice piece of work, cleverly directed and well knit. Miss Nixon is kept looking always at her best, following the remodelling process. A night club raid scene, incidental, and one of those intervals of brightness too infrequent to help the picture, has been well done. Another sequence, at the police court following the raid, with the smart, hard dames making snappy comebacks to the police sergeant, very good too. Nothing startling could be done with the story this director was given.

"Geraldine" is a story of a goody-goody girl, owned by a wealthy father, who can't have the man she loves because she hasn't sex appeal. The father hires a young man to teach her how to win over her desired. The girl is deprived of spectacles, shown how to dress her hair, wear clothes and hoof. Then, when she has her man going, she falls for her nice-looking instructor.

Mori.

Lone Wolf's Daughter
(DIALOG)

Columbia production and release, starring Bert Lytell. Directed by A. S. Rogell. Dialog by Harry Revier. W. E. synchronization. At the Roxy, New York, week of March 2. Running time, 72 minutes.

Michael Lanyard	Bert Lytell
Helen Fairchild	Gertrude Olmstead
Count Polinac	Charles Gerrard
Velma	Lilyan Tashman
Bobby Crenshaw	Donald Keith
Adrienne	Florence Allen
Ethier	Robert Elliott
Mrs. Crenshaw	Ruth Cherrington

Old fashioned film fare with a talking opening but silent the rest of the way. Not a week run picture for the keys.

Educated crook stuff is passe on the screen as well as in life. Both in films and in Chicago the smart boys now direct their brains to the liquor racket. It's far more lucrative and modern. "Lone Wolf's Daughter" seems to have caught the Roxy in a weak moment. Otherwise, no reason for a week stand on Broadway. House is probably holding back for its anniversary splurge.

As the Lone Wolf again, Bert Lytell plays a familiar role. The dialog opening, crossfire between Lytell and the cross examining police inspector, does considerable harm to his vocal reputation. Lytell can talk. It's no secret. They're billing him at the Roxy this week as the star of "Brothers," a legit meller now in New York. But you can't prove it by this picture. A case of poor recording. That the balance of the film is silent, after 10 minutes of talk is a relief.

Here the Wolf, now reformed, journeys to America to visit his adopted daughter. On this side he cleverly foils a jewel robbery, aids in the capture of a couple wanted by the Yard, and gets himself hooked by a nice girl. He's a plenty reformed Lone Wolf, and not so lonely at the finish if a clinch fadeout still means marriage. Before embarking for the U. S. he has been picked up by the English police for questioning and possible detention. He talks himself out of the station house. This is the dialog sequence.

No one but Lytell means a thing. It's his picture, if he wants it.

Bige.

Films in Berlin

Berlin, Feb. 18.

"Somnambul"—Not So Hot

"Somnambul" ("Somnambulist") at the Tauentzien Palast. Censor twice prohibited this film, but it at last got through with numerous cuts and change of title. Objection was made to the serious treatment of a medium and mental suggestion to influence a man to commit a crime. What is now left over is not so hot—in fact, often unclear and always a bore. Such good players as Erna Morena, Fritz Kortner, Julius Falkenstein and Fritz Kampers were wasted. Adolph Trotz directed.

"Buechse der Pandora"—Too Heavy

"Buechse der Pandora". ("Pandora's Box") at the Gloria Palast. Louise Brooks, especially imported for the title role, did not pan out, due to no fault of hers. She is quite unsuited to the vamp type which was called for by the play from which the picture was made.

Grave mistake to try to make a film of a Wedekind play. Heavy vamp stuff which he wrote is already dated—we take our sex more as a matter of course today. On the stage dialog is still of sufficient interest to hold, but the mere plot outline is trivial and overdone.

G. W. Pabst, director, in an attempt to keep the whole natural and easy, succeeded merely in making it superficial and lacking in suspense or thrill. Germany's newly discovered juvenile find, Franz Lederer (engaged for United Artist—Lillian Gish film) didn't have a chance to show much, nor could Fritz Kortner get anything out of the heavy.

"Der Mann"—Okay

"Der Mann Mit Dem Laubfrosch" ("The Man With the Frog") at the Ufa Palast. Without ambitions to creat "art," Gustav Lamprecht has here put together an effective detective film. No particular originality is shown, but it is competent workmanship, which ought to do well on the Continent. Heinrich George as an apparently harmless burger turns out to be the detective played with humor and force. Excellent work also by Hans Junkermann, Karl Hannemann, Harry Nestor and Olga Limburg. Just a possibility as a fill-in in the States.

"Nachgestal-Ten"—Light

"Nachgestal-Ten" ("Shadows of the Night") at the Atrium. This film is not so effective as the Lamprecht opus, because it is evident from the beginning who the murderer is. Competently directed by Hans Steinhoff and corkingly played by the Englishmen Cliff McLaglen and Jack Trevor. Feminine lead, Mabel Poulton, looks like a discovery.

"Die Vierte Von Rechts"—Silly

"Die Vierte Von Rechts" ("The Fourth From the Right") at the U. T. Kurfurstendamm. Ridiculous scenario. Chorus girl takes her sister's place and married a lord, who does not discover her real identity until after the ceremony. Ossi Oswalda, star, passe, just keeps going on her name. The director, Conrad Wiene, sticks to the old school of mug and grimace. They would hoot it even in the sure seaters.

"Die Siegerin"—Flop

"Die Siegerin" ("The Winner") at the Capitol. Taken from a novel about tennis playing by Robert Hitchins, the story proved to be silly and entirely lacking in tension. Heinrich Galeen, the director, has done better work, and it was a crime to throw away such a splendid player as Olga Tschechowa.

"Liebfraumilch"—Good Weak Sister

"Liebfraumilch," at the Primus Palast. A steal from the ever-popular "Froehliche Weinberg," but not a particularly happy one. Milieu of harvest time on the Rhein when the wines are brewed and drunk is an ever popular one here and will put this weak sister across.

Henry Porten, the star, still remains a favorite—justifiably so when she plays roles that verge on drastic comedy. Willi Forst also seems to have the makings of an eccentric comedian.

"Confession of Three"—Weak

"Das Gestandnis der Drei" ("The Confession of the Three") at the Alhambra. Weak detective film. Not even the acting or the direction gave it the slightest excuse for existing. This habit of detective films, four in one week, is one that the German industry should take a Keely cure to break.

"Der Adjutant"—Tiresome

"Der Adjutant des Zaren" ("The Adjutant of the Czar") at the Universum. Iwan Mosjukin has a John Barrymore popularity here and anything he stars in goes over. Unfortunately, this is one of his minor efforts—the modern Russian films have made us lose interest in pseudo films of pre-war czaristic circles. It is all very elaborate, luxurious and a trifle tiresome.

Mosjukin's best film still remains his "Casanova."

"Storm Over Asia"

"Storm Over Asia," at the Marmorhaus. Here Pudowkin again proves that he is one of the great directors of our time. Whether or not you may agree with the propaganda which this Russian film drives home, there is no getting away from the power of the picture. Its originality of milieu alone set it apart. It plays in Mongolia with types of occidental fascination.

A trapper brings a valuable pointed fox to the fur market, and he is paid only a portion of the true price by a swindling American fur trader who is backed by the authority of the white army. He has to flee because he attacks the fur trader, and becomes a rebel outlaw. He is captured, shot and, after being left for dead, is brought back to life by a complicated operation.

Believing him a prince, the white general wants to use him as a cloak for his plans of usurpation. The trapper, not realizing what is happening, lets them dress him up in royal regalia, but comes to himself when he sees one of his countrymen brutally shot. He breaks out of the palace and starts the revolution which annihilates the white army.

Nothing short of phenomenal is the way in which Pudowkin has gotten these Mongolian types to act with absolute naturalness and simplicity.

Sure fire for the sure seaters and should also appeal to a sufficiently large public in the big cities.

Lady of the Pavements
(SOUND)

United Artists release of D. W. Griffith production. William Boyd, Jetta Goudal, Lupe Velez featured with George Fawcett and Albert Conti sub-featured. An original story by Karl Volmoeller adapted for the screen by Sam Taylor. At Rialto, New York, opening March 9 for extended engagement. Running time 90 mins.

Nanon del Rayon	Lupe Velez
Count Arnim	William Boyd
Countess des Granges	Jetta Goudal
Baron Finot	Albert Conti
Baron Haussmann	George Fawcett
Papa Pierre	Henry Armetta
Dancing Master	Franklin Pangborn

Good, but not great, entertainment dominated by Lupe Velez, Joseph M. Schenck's new and interesting personality of Mexican extraction. D. W. Griffith has manipulated his story and people in something less than "the master's" best style, but with an eye for newfashioned sex appeal that will increase the jingle of mazuma at the b. o. "Lady of the Pavements" is apt to be the most successful money picture for Griffith in several years. He adds nothing thereby to his artistic prestige, but possibly he will square much at the pay box.

Karl Volmoeller, the German playwright, wrote the story. Upon discovering the infidelity of his high-born fiancee (Jetta Goudal), a young nobleman (William Boyd), attached to the Prussian Embassy in Paris, 1868, expresses a contemptuous preference for a woman of the streets. The proud dame thereupon schemes to maneuver him into a literal fulfillment of his statement about marrying a woman of the streets. In the Winking Dog Cabaret, a low life rendezvous of Paris, the countess finds her accomplice in the person of a bad-mannered soubrette (Lupe Velez). Of course real love develops between the young Prussian and the soubrette, whose vivacity it appears is wrongly interpreted as moral laxity.

Lupe Velez gets everything in the picture, nine-tenths of the close-ups are hers although she is third in the billing. Quite obviously and with good reason United Artists is developing Lupe by the spotlight method, the quickest of them all. "Lady of the Pavements" is only her third or fourth major picture, but it should definitely establish her. Of a whole flock of Spanish, Mexican and Latin senoritas she and Del Rio are practically alone in clicking importantly.

Sam Taylor was originally slated to direct "Lady of the Pavements" and had the adaptation all set when switched to another picture, with Griffith stepping in and shooting from Taylor's script. Story is compact, neatly dovetailed, and reasonably rapid in tempo. Running time of 90 minutes is a bit overboard, but about average on a special representing production pretentions such as this.

Theme song, by Berlin, runs through the picture, frequently refrained by Miss Velez. It means little, although Miss Velez isn't much of a songster and doesn't bolster the puny melody with distinguished delivery. No dialog except for the intermittent vocalizing. Picture synchronized on coast by Hugo Riesenfeld.

William Boyd, very boyish and good looking in Prussian military turnout, has little opportunity, a complaint peculiar to the entire cast excepting Lupe. Albert Conti, who is a specialist in such roles, suavely impersonates Napoleon III's chamberlain. Conti seems to have the same utility status in Hollywood held by Adolphe Menjou prior to "A Woman of Paris" which lifted Menjou into the star class. In those days they sent for Menjou. Now they seem to be sending for Conti. Miss Goudal's quaint coiffure and tiny features are strikingly "different" as always while that sterling character actor, George Fawcett, is the very model of a Prussian diplomat. Fawcett remains the best known of the older character men whose ranks have been thinned noticeably in the last year, including Theodore Roberts and Frank Keenan.

Photography, production detail, etc., all Grade A. Laughs include a slapstick fight between an effeminate professor of ettiquette (Franklin Panghorn) and the soubrette with many other hokum touches throughout for giggles. "Lady of the Pavements" should find a cordial reception. *Land.*

THE LETTER

(DIALOG)

Paramount production and release directed by Jean De Limur. Starrs Jeanne Eagels. Made from play of same name by Somerset Maugham with adaptation and continuity by Garret Fort. Monta Bell producer. Cameraman, George Folsey. W. E. synchronization on disk. At the Criterion, New York, for twice daily run starting March 7. Running time, 62 mins.

Leslie Crosbie..................Jeanne Eagels
Joyce..........................O. P. Heggie
Robert Crosbie..............Reginald Owen
Geoffry Hammond........Herbert Marshall
Mrs. Joyce.......................Irene Brown
Li-Ti..........................Lady Tsen Mei
Ong Chi Sing...........Tamaki Yoshiwara

First full length feature made at the Long Island studio of Paramount, and a gripping drama. Distinctive among dialog productions to date in that it creates tension at the outset and holds it until a magnificant emotional climax. It will fare better in the de luxe houses than within lesser walls.

Any summary of the picture must record that the merits of the screen production belong to the original play, written for and played on the stage, and the filming has contributed only atmospheric details. That is to say the production is entirely a transcription of a stage work and the cinema version does little to make the subject matter its own.

It is true that certain pictorial shots and camera angles go to the embellishment of the story, but there is a certain formality about the whole affair that has the stage quality. The same effect is intensified by the fact that progress comes out of the spoken word instead of from essential action, which is strictly an attribute of the stage.

Even if it is a straight canning of a play, however, the result is tense drama. If the process adds little to the original, it does retain all the original's intrinsic force. It is entirely probable that for the screen educated fans, it is a little fine. Elemental tastes like to have their heroines and their heroes unmistakably heroic. They like to know which characters to admire and which to dislike. The gallery gets a kick out of hissing the villain.

Maugham has a literary trick of drawing his people in half lights composites of good and bad. Leslie Joyce wasn't a "bad woman," just a victim of circumstances playing on a weak creature. Under the spur of impending doom she took on a certain boldness, but she was generally a drifting, indefinite sort of person. Her husband was a well intentioned dumbbell. Even the Chinese woman had admirable traits of loyalty and a sense of justice. There isn't a character in the play you can really admire or actively hate. This is all very confusing to the gallery clients who want to hiss the villain.

It is an actingf triumph for Miss Eagels. She is called upon for unusual shading of mood. Trial scene is capital. The woman who had murdered her faithless lover brings all h[illegible] feminine arts to play in creating the impression she wants on the jury. Dainty handling of this passage. The climax is immense in its power, certainly the peak of emotional intensity so far recorded on the articulate screen.

Dialog sequences are uniformly excellent in voice recording, Miss Eagels' dicting reproducing particularly well. Several passages in which two native characters speak in their own tongue also are first-rate atmosphere. Scenes of the crowded, narrow Shanghai streets in weird shadow effects, eerie corridors full of Oriental mystic atmosphere, and the boiling crowds of the Chinese dives—all these angles are graphic and live, made more so by shrewd sound incidentals.

One item is questionable. During the scene in a Chinese dive where the white woman confronts her yellow rival, the crowd out in the assembly place are gathered around a table upon which there is supposed to be a fight between a hooded cobra and a mongoose. Here the producer has spliced in sections from the Ufa short subject which has been shown all over the country. The crowd at the film's premiere identified it instantly and the effect on the spectators was distinctly bad, introducing as it did a brutal jolt to the whole illusion.

If they're absorbed in what is taking place in a baudy house in Shanghai, and suddenly the snake fight makes them recall that they saw the same thing in the same or another theatre a month ago, the illusion is killed.

Atmosphere of these dive scenes is remarkably well developed in other directions. There is a native dance for the edification of the riff raff crowd, done by three native girls and the last word in sexy display, but discreetly handled and innocent of offense. Whole picture has been governed by sound dramatic judgment and fine taste.

In short, it is a production that will contribute to the prestige of its maker and of the screen and will prosper in the de luxe houses, but probably fare just moderately in general release. *Rush.*

Canary Murder Case

(DIALOG)

Paramount production and release, 100 per cent talk. Malcolm St. Clair, director. William Powell featured. Adapted by Florence Ryerson and Albert Shelby from S. S. Van Dine's detective story of same title. Sound on film. At the Paramount, New York, week March 9. Running time, 80 minutes.

Philo Vance .... William Powell
Jimmy Spotswood .... James Hall
Margaret Odell .... Louise Brooks
Alys .... Jean Arthur
Dr. Lindquist ..... Gustav Von Seyffertitz
Charles Spotswood .... Charles Lane
Heath .... Eugene Pallette
Cleaver .... Lawrence Grant
Tony .... Ned Sparks
Mannix .... Louis John Bartels
Markham .... E. H. Calvert

A perfect program picture, for entertainment and grosses. Mostly a man's picture because murder is accentuated over romance, but the women will go for William Powell as an actor if not a romantic figure.

It's a picture wherein the principal character, Philo Vance (Powell), detective, doesn't look at a dame without a professional motive. He's strictly a crime solver, but he troups so well that no one, man or woman, will escape being fascinated.

"Canary Murder Case" is Paramount's best since "Interference," which it resembles in structure. Some are going to prefer "Canary," though it's not a $2 two-a-dayer since "Interference" landed priority and the edge.

Also another personal smash for Powell, right now a number one name in the talker field and perhaps the best straight dramatic player on the sound screen so far. Two such performances should lift him into the starring class, all this in a year, and a year ago Powell was the meanest and most treacherous villain in films. And now a player of respectable roles. Though he may still be a great heavy, with a greater range in the talkers.

S. S. Van Dine's original narrative, from which the scenario was adopted, was a best seller among detective novels. It was another adventure of Philo Vance, Van Dine's own Sherlock Holmes.

The "Canary" is Margaret O'Dell (Louise Brooks) musical comedy star. She is a merciless little blackmailer off stage, having three prominent and wealthy men in her power for coin and young Jimmy Spotswood for social climbing. Jimmy borrowed some samples from a bank to satisfy the Canary's whims and, though his father squared the theft, the Canary mentioned marriage or publicity.

On the night she was murdered. Just before the murder, she had called up the three rich suckers, informing them she would shortly marry Jimmy and advising them to deliver some hefty wedding gifts that evening in person. That these three helpless boys, all trying to keep their affair with the Canary under cover, visited her as ordered on the night of the murder added to the mystery.

Vance solves it cleverly after Jimmy had been arrested and had falsely confessed to save his own father, who was the murderer.

Jimmy's father visited the Canary to persuade her to change her mind about the boy. Jimmy is in love with another girl, Spotswood explained, and marriage to the Canary would ruin his life.

Intricacies of the motive, crime and detection have been intelligently directed by Malcolm St. Clair. Next to Powell in the trouping section comes Eugene Pallette as a thick headed detective sergeant. His "looks like you and I have guessed right" to Vance after Vance did the thinking, served as the chief comedy relief.

Vance stages a poker game with suspects to psychologically identify the murderer by his conduct in the game. He lands right on the button as a result. All others in the cast have speaking lines. On performance, they are down excellent. Slight love strain kept aflame by James Hall as Jimmy and Jean Arthur, as a good girl. *Bige.*

SPEAKEASY

(DIALOG)

Fox production and release on W. E. film track. Features Paul Page, Lola Lane and Sharon Lynn. Adapted from Edward Knoblock's and George Rosener's play of the same name. Directed by Benjamin Stoloff. E. Burke, dialog; Lindsey, sound; Valentine, camera. At the Roxy, New York, week of March 9. Running time, 62 mins.

Martin..............................Paul Page
Alice Woods.......................Lola Lane
Fuzzy.................Henry B. Walthall
Min..............................Helen Ware
Cannon Delmont..............Warren Hymer
Cy Williams....................Stuart Erwin
Mazie.........................Sharon Lynn
City Editor..................Erville Alderson

"Speakeasy" really amounts to a Movietone newsreel given continuity by an indifferent story staked out with unknown featured players who do not improve with path to the objective. And plunging through both theme and cast are the Movietone trucks which have gathered snatches of New York's sporting world into about 6,000 feet of film so authentically as to make disk users knash their teeth. Picture is going to get some money just on these Movietone wagons and because the important sets didn't have to be made by Fox. There they are, they're genuine and so is the sound. Only thing the gang missed was the fire department.

It ought to be a tidy morsel out of New York for it's all about the big village, its roar and the boys about town can tell everybody within five throws their memories as the landmarks flash and resound while the women can cluck their tongues over the wickedness of a backroom joint. This is a fight picture which the title cleverly disguises. Previous pictures concerning the ring, good and bad, having proved themselves poison to women this is a point.

As a picture "Speakeasy" has got about everything in it every fight show on Broadway has had for the past three years. Dialog is uneven, sometimes awkward, but directorial or cutting instinct has done much to smooth these spots by quips of the now familiar well stewed reporter or from outside personalities not concerned with the direct theme. Studio has copped the fight bit by radio as a bar room mob hangs about a mike with the victorious return match of the hero an excuse for some pip shots of Madison Square Garden in the flesh and in action during a glove battle. The camera and sound boys who climbed to the top balcony or rafters to get a couple of shots of a real match deserve credit for the best ring angle ever cameraed.

Scenario is a prize fight-newspaper routine, the college boy turned pro being surrounded by his gyp manager and companions while the girl is the reporter who takes a fancy and steers the kid back to his crown. Climax is the old gag of the vacant ringside seat with the boy taking a pasting until the girl shows up, whence he turns on the screen's fastest come-back. One look at the girl is sufficient to throw off rounds of punishment, a strictly theatric recovery, and a sock that immediately floors the opponent. Bound to draw a laugh from the men, as it did here.

But the scheming manager, his yen for the gal, the regaining of the championship and the clinch don't count. It's the Garden, Times Square at night, the subway, Grand Central station, Empire track, and newspaper press room which convince. Anyone who has seen enough of the 'Tone" newsreels will remain untouched by the sound of the galloping goats, but others will like it. So "Speakeasy" is a technical staff picture. It's got the first real double exposure footage of actual sound emitting from one of the dual subjects.

Histrionically, none of the featured trio stands out. Lola Lane, the heroine, looks as though she ought to develop for the screen, but Warren Hymer isn't especially heavy as the menace and it appears a case of miscasting in picking Paul Page as the collegiate boxer, who has forsaken his A. A. U. standing. For actual trouping Henry B. Walthall is still pretty good, and balanced by Helen Ware as a No. 2 Guinan, the older couple give the kids something to worry about. Sharon Lynn does a fickle, cafe singer, being allowed an insert to warble a full chorus of a pop number. Stuart Erwin does well with his half-bunned reporter. Film is full of such interruptions which don't hurt the sound assets, but constantly prevents a story which was none too well at the start from getting better.

On construction the cost sheet must have been a laugh to the studio. An editorial room, a dressing room and a cheap cafe practically winding up the carpenters. Fox's sound newsreel outfit in New York may have, and certainly could have, taken care of the rest of it, the studio simply adding the close-up ring action with Page and Miss Lane cast to get in on a few clips.

Other than the sound from the first hand locations Stoloff has at least kept it moving, and has held it to two minutes over the hour with sufficient humor decorating the structure to offset the shortcomings for the mob at large. Literally a good sound picture *Sid.*

Queen of the Night Clubs

(DIALOG)

Warner Bros. production and release starring Texas Guinan. Story by Murray Roth and Addison Burkhard. Directed by Bryan Foy with Freddie Fox assisting; Ed Du Par, cameraman. At Strand, New York. week of March 16. Running time, 60 mins.

Tex Malone....................Texas Guinan
Eddie Parr....................Eddie Foy, Jr.
Bee Walters....................Lila Lee
Phil Parr.. ....Jack Norworth
Don Holland....................John Davidson
Lawyer Grant....................John Miljan
Andy Quinlan....................Arthur Housman
Ass't District Attorney..William Davidson
Girl....................Charlotte Merriam
Nick....................Jimmie Phillips
Crandall....................Lee Shumway
Judge....................James T. Mack
Flapper....................Agnes Traney
Boy....................Joe Depew

With Texas Guinan as the star, plus that title, "Queen of the Night Clubs" and almost discounting its celluloid contents, this 100 per cent Vitaphone talker is a natural. That it isn't so worse as a feature, although subject to considerable captious comment, makes it that much easier. Warner Brothers should sapolio at the gate with this one.

Tex hasn't much to do, but does what she has pretty well. She's her natural self at all times, fly and flip, pacing the Tex Malone nite club in characteristic manner, and is bound to the romantic interest through Eddie Parr (Eddie Foy, Jr.) being her son, a sort of family skeleton about which neither the boy nor the public knows. She lies to Walter and Mark, the intermittently appearing newspapermen, about the reported relationship. In several other sequences she addresses one as "Winchell." (Both of the scribes, of course, bear no authentic resemblance to either Walter Winchell or Mark Hellinger, all this being strictly local and Tex's idea of reciprocating to the tab nite life addicts for past favors.)

After the locale and the attendant trimmings are set, the story evolves into one of those murder mysteries with a court room trial scene in an effort to clear young Parr of the charge. As the jealous suitor of Bee Walters, his vaudeville partner, everything points to Eddie when Don Holland, Tex's nite club backer, is murdered. Holland and Miss Walters (Lila Lee) seemed attentive to each other.

Bryan Foy has fotten loads of local color into "Queen of the Night Clubs" with Tex's hand showing not a little in it throughout. That report to the query, "Do you understand English?" when she admits: "Yes, but I'm more familiar with Scotch," sounds like a Guinan. Similarly, she agrees that she knows her way downtown to the police inspector's office—"blindfolded."

Tex sings one number, "It's Tough to Be Hostess on Broadway," presumably as some sort of hooey alibi for the hinterland patronage, no doubt, but it's a cinch she doesn't mean it, despite lots of things that have happened on 54th or 58th streets.

Nite club scene introduces George Raft, the hot stepper, as the m. c. and band leader, being brought down for one of his rip-snorting hoofing specialties. Plenty of anti-Volsteadian atmosphere and props throughout the nite club shots, leading one to wonder how the backwoods' censors will cotton to this flagrant refutation of a national amendment. No telling what the Pennsy and Ohio boards might deem too rough for the peasantry.

One crack, antiquated by an act of God, should be eliminated. Tex chides a customer that "the Tex you want is at Madison Square Garden." Considering the sports' promoter's demise, this is not only a false note, ethically, but doesn't ring true otherwise, considering the contemporaneous realism and ultra-modernism of the rest of the atmosphere.

Continuity evidences considerable cutting, hence some jerky transitions and sequences.

Talking throughout is okay. Lila Lee's impression vocally commends her anew for dialog pictures. Eddie Foy, Jr., as the spirited juvenile is likewise effective. Jack Norworth is cast as his father. Tex, of course, always knew how to control her tonsils and John Davidson as Holland, in the unsympathetic assignment, made himself thoroughly disliked.

Court room stuff, while generally familiar, was expedited with staccato precision as to dialog, examinations, etc., highlighting each character sufficiently unto the purpose thereof without any extraneous details.

Texas Guinan and "Queen of the Night Clubs" is a double-barreled come-on at the gate. The ballyhoo potentialities are limitless. Peasants will go for it like unexpurgated literature. *Abel.*

Younger Generation

(DIALOG)

Jack Cohn production for Columbia distribution, directed by Frank Capra. From story by Fanny Hurst. Jean Hersholt featured, Lina Basquette and Ricardo Cortez sub-featured. Rosa Rosanova and Rex Lease in cast. Dialog by Howard J. Green. Cameraman, Ted Tetzloff. Western Electric disk recording. At the Colony, New York, week of March 9. Running time, 75 minutes.

Special appeal to Jewish public and with many angles for exploitation in that direction, principal of which are Fanny Hurst original, Jean Hersholt's name and that of Rosa Rosanova, both of whom have built among their race. For general release, especially out of the big towns, value is questionable.

Sentimental oil has been spread on thick and often spills over. Miss Hurst usually makes her stories more generally interesting than this picture turns out. Sentimental side probably has been over emphasized in adaptation and filming. It's pretty hard to take the Jewish father's discontent when his son's energy and business success move him from a push cart to a Fifth avenue mansion. It's equally hard to take the modern flapper sister who also seems to resent the change of locale.

Fact that girl remains loyal to boyhood sweetheart who is a weak kneed piano player in a club, or something like that, declining to join the up-and-doing brother in his social ambitions, is implausible. It isn't modern.

Worst of all the film has a particularly morbid finish. The daughter has married her sweetheart on the eve of his going to jail as an accomplice to a holdup, his guilt or innocence of which is foggy. Anyhow, they have a baby and through the maneuvers of the patriarch the whole family is brought together in more or less happy reunion, during which the old man dies—probably the most literal and graphic decease ever screened in a light dramatic release.

Whole thing is a particularly inept bit of adapting. One particularly obnoxious scene (as done on the screen) is where the father and mother come home from a visit to the ghetto while the son is entertaining wealthy friends. Their appearance and conduct shame him and he tries to make it appear they are his servants. Altogether unnecessary, but having been introduced, it came as a jolt that the proud old man and his wife continued to live with their son. Circumstance that the old man fell ill was inadequate.

Sound reproduction at this performance was as bad as it could be. Sound and action were 'way out of step. Lips and machine were 10 words apart and dramatic lines inspired only laughs. First 20 minutes of picture are silent, then it goes into dialog and continues so to the end with brief intervals and occasional titles. Quality of tone production is excellent, and all five principal characters sound well, the authentic dialect of Hersholt and Miss Rosanova being effective.

Another insincere attempt to sell sympathetic syrup to the Jewish public, and no more promising in returns than the others with the notable exception of [illegible].

COHENS AND KELLYS

(In Atlantic City)

(DIALOG)

Universal production featuring George Sidney, Mack Swain, Kate Price and Vera Gordon. Directed by William J. Craft. Story by Jack Townley. Nora Lane, Tom Kennedy and Cornelius Keefe also in cast. With synchronized score and incidental dialog. At Colony, New York, week of March 16. Running time, 70 mins.

Sequel to U's former Cohen and Kelly slapstick, this one badly "dated." The date is 1927, not 1929. With cycle definitely departed, Jewish-Irish hoke when as low grade as this can hardly mean much. Picture has number of exploitable angles via the bathing beauty hook-up, but could be over-ballyhooed.

Made in Atlantic City last summer picture gives tantalizing glimpses of an interesting background, but never really capitalizes a pictorially effective setting. Pathe did a similar flop recently when shooting a picture at the Naval Academy in Annapolis.

During most of the boardwalk exteriors the actors and camera are followed by a horde of curiosity-seekers. Needless to record these neck-craners wrecked whatever illusion of reality the sequences possessed. Throughout the picture the general public got into the camera eye and made a newsreel out of scene after scene.

Adagio dancers and hoofers are used in the bathing beauty promenades, further detracting from the possible appeal of shapely lasses in tights. So far as the beauts go the stills and newspaper mats are a lot hotter than the picture. Many a mugg will be exasperated by the abrupt editing.

That many will laugh at the complications of the plot is certain. Colony crowd giggled moderately. But picture is outside the pale of sophistication measured by the thimble full. Nothing rings true and the tempo is so draggey that reasonable license of farce becomes an abuse.

Usual middle-aged business man with old-fashioned ideas about their commodity, in this case bathing suits. Son of one of the partners and daughter of the other proceed to put the company on map. Plot is suspended in the middle to pick up a sub-plot of George Sidney handcuffed to an escaping murderer. This may have sounded excruciating on paper but it was pretty silly on the screen.

Introduction of dialog at a couple of points serves only to retard the tempo already moving with leaden feet. George Sidney handles most of the talk and very ably, but it means nothing because neither lines nor situations have an ounce of real humor or sparkle.

The winner of Cohen and Kelly's $10,000 bathing beauty prize is none other than Cohan's daughter. This is possibly the one touch of sophisticated humor, not to mention practical realism, in the picture.

Only one that meant anything outside of Sidney was Nora Lane as his daughter, a class looker. Mack Swain was padded in stomach and in role. Vera Gordon failed to achieve anything but negation in her conversational opportunities.

Picture is a very moderate moderate. *Land.*

A Woman in the Night

(BRITISH MADE)

British International Production released through Worldwide. Directed by Victor Saville from the novel by Countess Barcynska. Werner Brandes, cameraman. At the Little Carnegie commencing March 9. Running time, 85 minutes.

Tesha....................Maria Corda
Dobree....................Jameson Thomas
Lenane....................Paul Cavanagh

Majority of American fans will never have the chance to see this. Not a pretty theme or story. Satuary and trademarks are used to symbolize the desire for children.

Despite the warning of his family physician, given with many rollings of the head, that the war has rendered him sterile, Dobree, well portrayed by Jameson Thomas, marries the dancer.

Despair at the non-appearance of progeny after five years of marriage, the husband's reference to the unoccupied nursery, as well as an intimate consultation with the wife and doctor on the subject, finally develop into more titles of the "will do anything" kind.

Wife meets a man at a hotel and flashing from his grasp to a closeup of her face the next morning, the action swings back to the home with the hotel gentleman as her husband's pal and guest.

Progress of her condition and the elation of her husband are not allowed to be even suggested. Her gyrations make the situation obvious to the most unsophisticated.

Pal's return and the wife's faint give the husband an inkling. He takes his service revolver, declaring that one or the other must be out of the way but the pal recalls war days. Then clips on war stuff.

Follows the announcement that the child is born. The husband is at first reluctant to accept it from the nurse but finally does, and the audience is left gasping. *Waly.*

BATTLE OF MONS

(BRITISH-MADE)

New Ere production directed by Walter Summers. Produced with official sanction and with co-operation of the British Army Council. Cameramen, Horace Wheddon and Stanley Rodwell. Edited and titled by Harold Auten. Running time, 60 minutes. American premiere at the Cameo, New York, March 16.

Hardly entertainment, certainly not on this side, is this convincing record of the epic of the British stubborn retreat of August, 1914, which began in Belgium and ended only when the invader's thrust at Paris was turned back.

An hour of massed troops in battle, be it ever so magnificently presented, becomes monotonous when it is unenlightened by romance, character, humor or theatre situation. No question of the epic quality of the screen record.

It is illuminated with incident—a Scotch Geordie rescues a comrade and brings him back on the long trail in a wheelbarrow, refusing to surrender his burden. Incident of a surprise upon a British battery when all but one gun is disabled before it can get into action, and the three survivors working the lone piece putting twelve enemy guns hors de combat just as relief dashes up.

Another fugitive Scot hides in a French windmill and holds a horde of enemies at bay in another dramatic episode. Picture has much of such footage which has punch, but the greater part is of large bodies of troops in field action, splendidly screened and graphic in its realism. A program note says official war scenes are exhibited by permission of the Imperial War Museum.

Effect is impersonal war record. Not a thing to give it human sympathy. A case where truth is not nearly so strange and engaging as fiction. Classes as an "educational" and entertainment value is small. All this takes nothing away from the fact that it is a fine, sincere bit of film production. Point it is not commercial product at all. Only

American field is in the sure seaters.

Picture has a set of titles that could serve as models of dignified literary style and brevity. *Rush.*

ONE MAN DOG

Radio production and release. Directed by Leon D'Usseau from story credited to Frank H. Clark. Robert de Grasse, cameraman. In cast: Harry O'Connor, Virginia Bradford, William Patton, Edward Hearne, Sam Nelson. Ranger (dog) starred. At Stanley one day, Feb. 11. Running time, 55 minutes.

Even grind audiences feel the padding in this one. Ranger's most heroic attempts, where he worsts villain, gun et al., gets laughs instead of gasps. Poor direction is to blame. Picture far too weak to stand alone, but can be wedged in in programs of lesser double feature houses.

Groping around for story thread so apparent as to flatten action. Old hoke hacked out too carelessly. Dog tail never stops wagging, and he is always aware of the camera.

Virginia Bradford in tom-girl role. Bad man suddenly decides to run amuck and take it out on her when dough for furs is slow in coming through. Instead, he kills her old man. Trooper and pal happen to be in offing, but dog goes after unworthy gent. Subtitles have him traveling weeks before capture. Even when villain is safely lodged in camp with nippers snapped on in fracas with dog, another padding is his escape and a resume. *Waly.*

That Murder in Berlin

(GERMAN MADE)

Big 3 production and release. Directed by Frederick Feber from the story by Max Brod. Edited and titled by Donald W. Bartlett. Featuring Magda Sonja. At the Cameo, New York, week of March 9. Running time, 72 minutes.

The Husband	Carl Gotz
The Wife	Magda Sonja
The Friend	Anton Pointner
The Butler	Gustav Diesel
The Attorney	Karl Ettlinger
The Prosecutor	Gustav Rickelt

Another listless contribution to the German inertia which has been appearing in the sure-seaters. It is so patently a crude, unknowing, untrained effort as to render attention from either theatre bookers or newspaper reviewers as an absurdity.

Direction, acting, story, photography strictly of the elementary grade. No trace of imagination and no attempt at giving the action any semblance of probability.

It's a mystery murder which is never convincing and finally winds up without being solved. That is, no satisfactory explanation of the murder of an old, wealthy artist is shown in the picture. The suspected woman, the murdered man's wife, is absolved by the jury on the plea of her attorney. Major part of the picture is told in subtitles, action taking place in a courtroom with flash backs.

Girl is charged with murdering her husband for his money and a chance to go to her lover. The prosecutor paints her as a shrewish, designing murderess. Defending lawyer claims the girl was a high-salaried actress; that her lover had more money than her husband, and that the latter commited suicide because he loved his wife and wanted her to be happy.

An argument between two lawyers. *Mori.*

HEY, RUBE

Radio production and release. Directed by George Seitz. Story by Wyndham Gittens and continuity shared by L. A. Sarecky. Cast: Hugh Trevor, Gertrude Olmstead, Ethlyne Clair, Bert Moorhouse, Walter McGrail, James Eagle. At Loew's New York, Feb. 5, as half of double feature. Running time, about 65 minutes.

Were "Hey, Rube" even partly dialoged its supreme situations would eclipse the general entertainment value of a special on the same order. In its silent version it is far above the average program attraction.

Possesses some intense and vivid sequences which are in themselves worthy of the admission. Of these the big punch centers on a high diver's ladder burning while the diver, Ethlyne Clair, is pointing to dizzy depths (remarkably well effected by camera angles) into which she threatens to precipitate her rival, Gertrude Olmstead. Below is the crowd mulling around in a fight over a gyp wheel run by Hugh Trevor, the diver's boy friend.

The diver plunging through the smoke and Trevor rescuing Olmstead by means of a rope from a ferris wheel provide gasps for the most hardboiled audience.

Straightening out Trevor's character is neatly done by the girl. Story is well knit and the chump gag is not overstressed. *Waly.*

SHIRAZ

(INDIA MADE)

Producing and releasing company not credited. Directed by Franz Osten and V. Peers. Story based on popular legend. An all-Hindu cast. At the 55th St. Playhouse, New York, March 16. Running time, 80 minutes.

Shiraz	Himansu Rai
Prince Khurram	Charu Roy
Dalia	Seeta Devi
Selima	Enakshi Rama Rau

This is a love story concerning the Taj Mahal, the tomb which is one of the architectural wonders of the world. This picture is one of the wonders, too.

It starts off with the discovery of a lost baby girl found sitting on a rock in the Indian jungle by a fakir. Meanwhile a soothsayer is predicting for the son of the finder, love, sorrow and great fame.

The little girl is called Selima and the boy Shiraz. When they grow up a couple of slave traffickers kidnap and ride off with the gal to the slave market.

Shiraz pursues the villains right into their home territory. He doesn't do much except look on while his gal is sold as a slave to Prince Khurram.

The prince tumbles hard for the gal, but she says nix.

The princeling gets so heated up his beard curls with excitement. But he must marry royalty.

For no reason at all Shiraz decides to rescue Selima, and enters the women's quarters of the Prince, where he is discovered and sentenced to die by the foot of an elephant. Just as the elephant's foot is raised over Shiraz's nose the Prince learns he has made a mistake, and calls everything off.

Selima makes it clear to Shiraz she desires to remain with the Prince.

When the Prince finds out Selima is the long lost daughter of a princess of the royal household and marries her, who stands by the front gate with a broken heart? None other than Shiraz.

For 18 bitter years thereafter Shiraz stands at the palace gates watching his loved one feeding birds and so on. Then Mamtaz Mahal (the gal's nickname) dies, and who falls in a faint beside the palace gate, blind and worn out with the sadness of the ages? Right! Shiraz again.

After the girl dies the Prince had a contest, offering a prize for a design for a monument to his love for his wife. The blind Shiraz wins with his model. As a reward the emperor orders that his eyes be put out, but they lay off when they find he is already blind.

And so it ends, except that the Emperor wore a white muslin dress over his pants and everybody saluted everybody else for 60 of the 70 minutes. *Mori.*

LIFE OF BEETHOVEN

(AUSTRIAN MADE)

Allianz production and release. Directed by Hans Otto. Based on a biography of the life of Beethoven. Author and scenario writer not credited. At the 55th St. Playhouse, New York, March 9. Running time, 70 minutes.

Beethoven	Fritz Kortner
Joseph Haydn	Ernst Baumeister
Countess Guiccardi	Lilian Gray
Riess	Heinz Altringen
Prinz Lichnowsky	Willy Schmeider

No box office possibilities. Producers have seized upon some of the most commonplace and uninteresting details in the great musician's life, reproducing Beethoven at his dullest. Story fails to give anything but a brief glimpse of the life of the man.

With 70 minutes of celluloid to play around with, it should have been possible to render a far more intimate and convincing study than this. In a series of two reelers produced in America the composing geniuses have been given much cleaner, more expressive and far more entertaining treatment.

Picture runs far too long, overdrawn shots showing Beethoven's impersonator walking around with his hands clenched tightly behind his back. When not walking the principal character is at the piano composing. A commendable labor but it doesn't screen well.

According to the story Beethoven was a chump in love with a woman who loved him. But something kept him from saying the right thing so she married the other guy. Disappointment embittered the composer for the rest of his life. He finally dies from footage—and no kiddin'. Poor photography among other things.

Play it and weep. *Mori.*

JAZZLAND

A. Carlos production, distributed through Quality. Directed by Dallas Fitzgerald. Faxon Bean, cameraman. Titles by Tom Miranda. In cast: Vera Reynolds, Bryant Washburn, Carroll Nye. At Loew's New York, half of double feature one day. Running time, about 60 minutes.

"Jazzland" is a gem in the indie feature class. Its excellent handling, cast and smoothly moving, convincing and actionful continuity, stand it on its own. The picture is a safe bet for the better second runs. It is a sure wow for the usuals.

Seemingly inspired by the assassination of a mid-western small town newspaper editor, the story depicts a newspaperman similarly murdered through his efforts to defeat night club invasion in a small New England town.

The unraveling of the story is accomplished with a logic and consistency rarely found in indie mellers. The cards down stuff is out in this one. Audience suspense is doubled by uncertainty that head of village trustees is backing the bad spot.

Younger sister's story in last reel affords a real climax.

Comparisons of sophistication of sister who stepped to city and the girl who stayed at home add important touch and comprise convincing filler. None of the irrelevant footage, so common in indies, stretched to the regular six reels.

In justice to "Jazzland," hardboiled and sophisticated fans will find themselves thoroughly entertained and unable to hand out at its close a single piece of justifiable adverse criticism. *Waly.*

Daughter of Two Fathers

(JAPANESE MADE)

No screen credit given producer or distributor. Japanese locale, cast, story and direction. Omitsu, Japanese actress, starred. Directed by H. Gosho from story by H. Tamura, with scenario by Kobo Noda. Cast: Masso Inouye and Hideo Fujino. At the Fifth Avenue Playhouse week beginning March 9. Running time, 65 mins.

As a three-reel novelty attraction this Japanese offering would be worthy of reception in the finest key houses. In its present length repetition is apparent and, other than as a curiosity in the arties, it is not sufficiently self-sustaining to be suitable for general bookings.

Picture is probably the finest exhibition of modern camera work and story handling that has yet come out of Japan. Although the yarn is written along Hollywood lines, with a foundling girl, a big-hearted fisherman and the real father finally locating his daughter, the portrayals are strictly in accord with the Orient. As such they are sincere and convincing and undergo the acid test of numerous close-ups during which facial depictions and sufficiently strong to retain the interest and appreciation of an intelligent audience.

In its present length, however, the masses will find too much footage devoted to meal scenes. While the first is interesting, showing the mat and rice custom, the almost constant iris in to the eating floor gets monotonous even to the most reasonable patrons.

Little Omitsu, unusually attractive to an American audience, is a star in every sense of the word. Her very naturalness and feeling exhibited for her fisherman guardian hold. The father is a real actor who would go far on the American screen. He has an uncanny ability to arouse sympathy and grasp an audience.

Attractive exterior shots of river fronts and wooded stretches in Japan are in keeping. Too long but an excellent novelty three reeler. *Waly.*

FANCY BAGGAGE

(DIALOG)

WB production and release. Directed by John Adolfi from story by Jerome Kingston. Adapted by C. Graham Baker. Dialog by James A. Starr and musical score by Louis Silvers. At Loew's New York, one day, March 14. Running time, 70 mins.

Naomi Iverson	Audrey Ferris
Cora	Myrna Loy
Iverson	George Fawcett
Harden	Edmund Breese
Austin	Burr McIntosh
Dickie	Hallam Cooley
Ernest	Wallace McDonald
Steve	Eddie Gribbon
Miss Hickey	Virginia Sales

A very light comedy along must-get-the-papers lines. Dialog, not much of it, partly unintelligible here at opening between McIntosh, as attorney, and Fawcett as the Wall Street wolf licked by rival. "Fancy Baggage" just shapes as program feature of satisfying kind where they aren't too fussy.

Ovearhearing dad's story that he has accepted a million for her and given to a rival a confession for stock manipulation he didn't promote, Audrey Ferris, as the athletic and expensive Naomi Iverson, lifts check from Iverson and sets out to retrieve the papers. Hack stuff of doubling for secretary to Hardin, who has the papers, includes routine of robbing girl, Miss Hickey, of her outfit and boarding the yacht in masquerade. Taxi ride to pier has some laugh situations promoted by Hallam Cooley. Young Harden is essayed by Wallace McDonald.

On board ship the story is an open book with Naomi falling for young Harden. For padding bootleggers boat, pursued by coppers, comes alongside and the two old men are set adrift. Slapstick stuff on yacht follows with Eddie Gribbon using the mits.

Naomi's plunge into water with papers followed by Ernest brings love on the beach and a reconciliation among the dads in jail, having been nabbed for the liquor pullers. *Waly.*

BLACK RIDINGHOOD
(FRENCH MADE)
Paris, Feb. 12.

Drama justly attributed to the Films Celebres corporation. Of a historical tendency, "Les Capes Noires" has been produced by Gennaro Dini for the Esa Film concern, and is quoted as a good French output. Technical work first class; control of the crowds is excellent, with interesting views of the city of Caimbre.

The scenario is laid in Portugal in 1840, and is a slice from the history of that lively little nation. The Black Ridinghoods are the students of the local university who revolt for the freedom of their country, with a love intrigue and plenty of hatred.

"Les Capes Noires" is thrilling and nicely played by Regine Bouet as the peasant girl and Nilda Duplessy as Dona Luisa. The role of Don Diego de Alburque is held by the producer himself, supported by Jorge Infante and Charles Sov. Exteriors taken in Portugal and interesting. The storming of the prison by the students and peasants is a creditable bit of direction. *Light.*

Object—Matrimony

Columbia production and release. Produced by Jack Cohn. Directed by Scott R. Dunlap from the story by Elmer Harris. Adaptation by Sig Herzig, with scenario by Peter B. Milne. Photographed by Jos. Walker. Featuring Lois Wilson. At Loew's Circle, New York, March 11, as one-half of a double-feature program. Running time 65 minutes.

Ruth Butler....................Lois Wilson
Jimmy Rutledge................Hugh Allen
Mrs. Carrie Rutledge......Ethel Grey Terry
Renaud Graham............Douglas Gilmore
Al Bryant......................Roscoe Karns
Mabel....................Carmelita Geraghty
Jimmy Rutledge, Jr..........Dickey Moore
Boarding House Owner........Jane Keckley
Philip Stone................,.Thomas Curran

Neat though unpretentious little drama that holds enough of the various ingredients to entitle its acceptance for split week dates, double feature bills, etc. Under Jack Cohn's supervision they have turned out a feature that looks expensive, with several very impressive interiors, and plenty of smart, clear, photography.

The most important feature in the production of this film is the exceptionally high average of likeable, intelligent players cast. Hugh Allen, the young leading man, photographs well and knows how to behave in front of the camera. Douglas Gilmore, the menace, also personable though weak due to role and partly to direction, while Miss Wilson is always kept looking and playing at her best. Even the juvenile actor, Dickey Moore, is an excellent selection.

Story, however, drags the picture down among the lower grades. It's about a scheming, selfish mother who poisons her son's mind against his wife because the girl didn't belong. The young wife is framed, her husband leaves her, and she has her child alone. Later she is rescued by an enterprising though unrealistic writer who sees a novel in her life. It's a success, and then they write a play together. That's a tremendous success, too. If Mr. Cohn could only give the producers along Broadway a couple of those smashes this season.

The usual finish. *Mori.*

CAPT. FRACASSE
(FRENCH MADE)
Paris, Feb. 25.

Theophile Gautier's well-known book of adventure, "Le Capitaine Fracasse," has been screened by A. Cavalcanti and converted into a good French picture for P. J. de Venloo and the Lutece Corporation. This is the production Maurice Tourneur was to have adopted for pictures.

Story is fairly well known and has been adroitly shaped for the screen. Young Baron de Solignac belongs to a noble but ruined family, following the long series of civil and religious wars. He lives alone in his old castle in Gascony, writing verse and helping the villagers in adversity. His melancholy existence is interrupted by a troupe of players. They are allowed shelter in the castle and the owner falls in love with Isabella, a member of the mummers. He follows the comedians, becoming Captain Fracasse, rescues Isabella from the Duke of Vallombreuse and is accepted as her lover after having deputized for a dead actor.

Picture constitutes a creditable release for native fans liking adventure of the middle ages. Pierre Blanchar is the hero, and a fine actor, if a bit out of place here. Lien Deyers, blonde heroine, makes a delicious comedienne, but her Isabella is not her best effort. On the other hand, Charles Boyer is at home, as is Daniel Mendaille, Vargy, Numes, Mme. Moreno and Pola, Illery. *Light.*

CHEYENNE

Chas. Rogers production; released through First National. Ken Maynard starred. Directed by Al Rogell from story by Bennett Cohen. Frank Good, cameraman. In cast: Gladys McConnell, James Bradbury, Jr., and William Franey. At Loew's New York, one day, as half of double bill. Running time, 65 minutes.

Fans missing the first reel of this one will figure that Mack Sennett has Ken Maynard working in slapstick. It's supposed to be a western meller, but attempts at comedy take up 90 per cent. of the footage. Only in the last reel, when villains and cops are thwarted, does the hero win one of the longest rodeo shows on the screen—and the girl. Strictly a lesser run picture.

Maynard shoots up a town in a laugh-getting way which is near original. He ropes all of the Fords in an effort to locate a hootched judge who has proof that he is riding in the show for the wrong party. All public departments are called out and his capture in a square, taken as a long shot, is one of the best sequences. Courtroom scenes and activities in a bug house raise a few laughs.

Rodeo stuff is like a circus, even with Bradbury clowning through serious moments with a couple of cops trailing his pal.

Had a little more time been spent on the development of situations and continuity, this might have been a bit of well-threaded entertainment. *Waly.*

THE TOURNAMENT
(FRENCH MADE)
Paris, Feb. 14.

"Le Tournoi dans la Cite" is running draw at the Salle Marivaux. It is a well constituted release of the Middle Ages, with realistic exteriors shot at Carcasson. Henri Dupuy Mazuel is responsible for the scenario, which Jean Renoir has adroitly produced with the aid of military cadets, and the output is distributed by Jean de Merly and the Societe des Films Historiques. The plot is gripping, with duels and cavalry movements, not overlooking the reconstitution of a tournament which merits the title of this glimpse into the misty past.

In 1565 Catherine de Medicis undertakes a tour through the southern provinces of her kingdom to present her son, King Charles IX, to his subjects, at the same time scheming to iron out the differences which existed between the Roman Catholics and Protestants. The feud had led to civil war in France, and the situation was serious.

A maiden of the royal escort, Isabelle Ginori reciprocates the love of a young knight, Henri de Rogier. The couple plight their troth. But the Queen-mother, for state reasons, and hoping thereby to unite the opposing factions, orders Isabelle to marry Francois de Baynes, the leader of the Protestant party of the district, and a sort of profligate.

Henri is mad with rage, particularly when he learns his rival has enticed the innocent maiden to attend an orgy. He would fain slay the debaucher in his own castle, but is prevented. As a matter of fact, Francois is a better swordsman. But the tournament, soon to be given in honor of the royal visitors, will enable him to seek revenge. The antagonists swear to meet in a sporting encounter to a finish. God will spare the man he intends for Isabelle's husband. The combat begins, but again Henri is not the stronger.

At that phase milicians on the castle ground discover Francois recently killed Isabelle's brother, Count Ginori, a prominent Catholic, contrary to a royal decree prohibiting duels.

This fight, in an early reel, is one of the big items. Catherine is informed of the circumstances, and she orders the tournament stopped. The guilty Protestant leader must be taken dead or alive. He refuses to surrender and alone against 20 soldiers fights until he is slaughtered by brute force. This episode is another notable feature.

Some scenes are splendid; cavalry evolutions are dexterously handled by the young French officers in appropriate costumes of the period. Cast is starred by Jackie Monnier as the charming Isabelle, and Aldo Nadi as Francois. The latter, a newcomer for the movies, is an Italian fencer. Suzanne Despres, popular French actress, is Francois' sedate mother. Blanche Bernis is correct in the short impersonation of Catherine De Medicis, while Henrique Rivero is the enamoured if weak-wristed knight.

"Le Tornoi" is suitable for all classes, as the week's attraction in leading palaces. It should please the average fan wanting a historical emotion with a happy end. *Light.*

The Million Dollar Collar

Warner production and release. Directed by D. Ross Lederman from story by Robert Lord. Nelson Laraby, cameraman. Rin-Tin-Tin starred. In cast: Tom Dugan, Matty Kemp, Philo McCollough. At Loew's New York, one day, half double bill. Running time, 57 minutes.

Planting the stolen necklace in the dog's collar automatically forces a story which in the same manner provides another stellar vehicle for Rin-Tin-Tin. "The Million Dollar Collar," rough rubbed as the continuity is, gives the bow-wow something different than dashing over the plains. Stupid spots and generally illogical movement. It will get by in houses that give a lot of change for the dollar.

Humans in cast, excepting McCollough, inferior in performance. Love interest of lad who hooks crook's clothes and noble sister of twisted brother have the gyrations without the heat.

Dog is improving. *Waly.*

SOWING THE WIND
(FRENCH MADE)
Paris, March 12.

Taken from a novel by Lucie Delarue Mardrus. "Graine au Vent" becomes quite an ordinary picture. As a matter of fact the producer had not much to work upon from the start, and perhaps Maurice Keroul is not to blame for the weakness of the screen version, any more than his assistant, Guido Pedroli. Yet there are some good scenes of country life in this hackneyed story, and the output is clean.

Plot: Bruno Horpin has ruined himself by gambling. He is a sculptor by profession, and lazy. For the sake of economy he has retired to the country with his wife and daughter, Alexandra. The wife does her level best to keep the home fires burning, while the other selfish two loll about. The poor woman finally dies giving birth to a second daughter. Bruno hates the sight of this child and has it reared by strangers. Alexandra at first does not realize the loss of her mother, not having a deep affection for anybody, but she feels the loss when father takes a scheming peasant girl, Fernande, as housekeeper and falls a victim to her charms. The mother appears to her daughter in a dream and advises her to save her father and sister from the evil influence of Fernande.

Thus Alexandra, previously a naughty little girl, becomes the guiding angel of the family. Fernande is accidently killed. This dull tale, described as a dramatic comedy, is partly saved by its protagonists, Claudie Lombard (a newcomer), as the nefarious servant girl; Celine James as Alexandra, who is fine; Henri Baudin, the indolent sculptor, and several others. Distributed by the Elite Film company. It might attract in provincial theatres, the name of the authoress constituting some sort of a draw. *Kendrew.*

FUGITIVES
(SOUND)

Fox production and release. Directed by William Beaudine. Adapted by John Stone from Richard Harding Davis' "Exiles." Titles by Malcolm Stuart Boylan. Roxy musical score directed by Erno Rapee on Western Electric film track equipment. Chester Lyons, cameraman. At Academy of Music first half of week of March 10. Running time, 57 minutes.

Alice Carroll................Madge Bellamy
Dick Starr.......................Don Terry
Jimmy...\......................Arthur Stone
Barrow...........................Earle Fox
Earl Rand......................Martin Betz
Uncle Knapp.................Lumsden Hare
Scal the Rat....................Hap Ward
Mrs. Carroll..................Edith Yorke

In story and performance "Fugitives" is worked out in a mechanical, routine manner. The sound score is good, but that it was an afterthought is revealed by off-timing on two songs, the only vocal manifestations throughout. Even Fox's crack titlist goes a bit bromidic. Fairest rating does not justify "Fugitives" for anything but ordinary program in better theatres.

Either cutting room or direction has showed sustained suspense by skeletonizing continuity to the point where only the highlights are projected. This completely sacrifices character building and analysis, an essential element in such a theme. "Fugitives" formally adheres to the rut. Effort for story speed makes players routine in their performances.

Early in the picture the gat which a gangster has used to bump off a squealing night club owner, a bit part played by Earle Fox, is tossed into the dressing room of Alice Carroll. The latter role is essayed pleasingly by Madge Bellamy. Of course, another chorine backstage has heard Barrow, the owner, proposition Alice. Her threat then that she would kill him rather than surrender satisfies the young and alert assistant district attorney, played with no great finesse by Don Terry, that she did the job. That there can be no mistake, this conclusion is apparently substantiated by Alice's being found holding the smoking gun over Barrow's body.

The plot thickens when Jimmy, the best job in the production, essayed by Arthur Stone, spirits her away from Sing Sing to one of those refuges of crookdom.

Martin Betz as a dive owner does well. The d. a. is attacked by the gang, but Alice saves him and opens way for romantic finale. *Waly.*

APPASSIONATA

(FRENCH MADE)

Paris, March 12.

Screen version of Pierre Fronday's novel by the same name, released by Franco Film. The story is not entirely suitable for the movies, being of classical, quiet romance, more at home on the stage. Nevertheless it has been carefully filmed by Leon Mathot and Andre Liabel, and may command a following.

Plot: Charlotte, wife of Langer, painter, is of a highly strung romantic disposition. She is in love with a poet, Stifani, who is leading a gay life with his mistress, Bianca. Stifani also writes plays, and Bianca is the vehicle for launching them. Langer and his wife are introduced to theatrical couple on the Riviera. Bianca, woman like, is tired of her poet lover and drops him. Stifani is in despair, and Charlotte assumes the task of consoling him. She quits her husband to remain with the poet, until the latter grows weary of her solicitudes and leaves. Stifani meets Bianca again, and they renew their former "union libre" when he hears her play Beethoven's "Appassionata." Charlotte is heart-broken. She has sacrificed her home. After a stormy interview with her callous lover she flees during a storm. Exhausted, she is carried to a hospital, where her husband, informed of her dying condition, hastens to clasp her in his arms.

Langer, after his wife's demise, swears vengeance. He speeds to the poet's villa and arrives during a party given by Stifani in honor of his mistress, Bianca. The distracted husband informs the former lover of poor Charlotte's death.

"That does not concern me" is the cynical retort. And the painter, mad with rage, kills the poet.

There are some good views of the Riviera, as usual. A symbolical scene of the muses emerging from a piano, when Bianca plays "Appassionata," is less successful. Cast on the whole good. Leon Mathot stars himself as Langer, with Renee Heribel as Charlotte. They are natural, sympathetic and modern. Ruth Weyer, a German actress, holds the role of the tantalizing Bianca with excellent results. Fernand Fabre is less fortunate as the poet. *Kendrew.*

DEVIL'S APPLE TREE

Tiffany-Stahl production and release. Directed by Elmer Clifton from the story by Lilian Ducey. Continuity by the author. Photographed by Ernest Miller. Featuring Dorothy Sebastian and Larry Kent. At Loew's New York, March 15, one-half of a double feature program. Running time, 70 minutes.

Dorothy Ryan	Dorothy Sebastian
John Rice	Larry Kent
Col. Rice	Edward Martindel
Jane Norris	Ruth Clifford
Cooper	George Cooper
The Roue	C. K. Bellew

Slow-moving story constructed with primitive crudeness. Plenty of time and celluloid waste during the first 45 or 50 minutes.

It opens with the heroine aboard ship on her way to be married to a man she had never seen. She wanted to get married and had accepted the boy through a matrimonial paper. That situation sufficient to dispel romantic appeal of the girl from the beginning.

Later the girl plays up to a gray-haired chicken chaser traveling via the upper deck while she is in the steerage.

Finally she steals the name of a woman on board ship who is stricken with fever and likely to die, and on arriving at her destination spurns the poor bum she came out to marry and walks off with the Rices, owners of the rubber plantation.

If the director had been intent on making a heavy out of the gal he couldn't have done better. And in several spots camera work gives Miss Sebastian poor appearance.

Near the finish they have introduced an uprising of the savages of Penango, who get the girl and are on the point of burning her alive as a form of sacrifice to their gods. Fairly intriguing but comes too late to help much.

Fulfills its destiny in the grinds. *Mori.*

PASSION SONG

Excellent production and release. Story and direction by Harry O. Hoyt. Adaptation by Elizabeth Hayter. Andre Barlatier, cameraman. At Loew's New York half of double feature, one day, March 12. Running time, about 60 minutes.

Elaine Van Rynn	Gertrude Olmstead
John Van Rynn	Noah Beery
Keith Brooke	Gordon Elliot
Chief Ulamba	Blue Washington

Mounted like a big line feature, "Passion Song" could have been made into an excellent bet for Sam Zierler had the story not been spoiled by economical treatment. Too weak for anything but the grinds, or on a double feature bill.

Supposedly inspired by Beethoven's "Appassionata," the number rendered on an organ by Gordon Elliot as Keith Brooke makes little Gertrude Olmstead forget that she is married to a Boer. But Brooke, all the way through, is faithful to his pal, Van Rynn, excellently portrayed, by Beery, in the narrowed field he is allowed. Even after Noah has ordered him strangled by the shrinking rawhide in a manner described by the subtitles as existent in South Africa, Elliot's role still calls for allegiance. It is not until the Boer is slain by a native chieftain, whom he horsewhipped in England, that the gallant Englishman marries the girl.

Earlier in the footage the action is slow. This is emphasized by many long shots on huge interior sets made more barren by inadequate detail. *Waly.*

SISTER OF MERCY

(FRENCH MADE)

Paris, March 3.

There seems to be something lacking in "La Petite Soeur des Pauvres," comedy-drama by Marcel Priollet, produced by Georges Pallu distributed through the firm of Georges Petit. It is full of good intention, but like a stew without flavor. Indeed the action is laid in the middle provinces of France, with a few shots in Paris.

Pauline is of a very religious turn of mind, whereas her sister Christiane prefers a mild flirtation with Daniel, their neighbor, and is rather gone on him. Daniel prefers the gentle Pauline, and the girls' cousin Roger also has the same sentiments. Roger is snubbed by Pauline, who would certainly smile on Daniel if she were not in a manner betrothed to the church. The cousin realizes this and plots to give his rival a letdown in the sweet maiden's esteem. Daniel by accident becomes involved with a servant girl, thanks to the treachery of Roger, and when Pauline reveals her contempt, declining to investigate the truth, the handsome young fellow marries Christiane out of spite.

Pauline enters a convent. The bride is soon led to believe Daniel no longer cares for her, and Roger loses no opportunity to inject salt in the wound, telling Christiane of her husband's supposed love adventure with the servant girl which caused Pauline to take the veil.

The wife, furious, writes to the Mother Superior of the Convent, declaring Pauline became a Sister of Mercy because of unrequited love. The nun falls ill when told of her sister's perfidy, and Christiane fails to learn of this. When she finally hears of her sister's serious illness a great remorse strikes her and she rushes to Pauline. When the latter is out of danger she arranges to bring the loving couple together, and she in turn swears to devote her life to charity.

Desdemona Mazza is a pretty bride, but her acting somewhat too tragical. Ducette Martell is the sweet Pauline, while De Saint Andre and George Melchoir the men of the story. *Kendrew.*

MUST WE MARRY?

Trinity Pictures production and release. Pauline Garon starred. Directed by Frank Mattison. Cast includes Vivian Rich, Bud Shaw, Edward Brownell, Louise Carver and Lorraine Eason. At Tivoli, New York, one-half double bill, one day. Running time, 50 minutes.

Not a single lobby card of any kind outside the Tivoli for this one. Tip the Consolidated's celluloid picker grabbed it from the bargain counter. Old Tom Mix western other half of bill. Front of the theatre had up Pauline Garon's name. Polly sure was picking up easy mon. Once she earned her dough. That was the flop she took in a mud puddle. Just wasted celluloid.

The picture was full of prismatic spots, the kind that makes a picture seem full of black specimens of the insect kingdom—static condition, as it were, from film wear.

As one sat vamping this wishy-washy picture he tried to figure the year it was shot. The women had bobbed hair, so it didn't go back to the Seven Sutherland age.

A picture with no story and little for the cast. *Mark.*

THE DRIFTER

Radio production and release, starring Tom Mix. Directed by Robert DeLacy from an original by him and Oliver Drake. Continuity by George Pyper. Norman DeVol, cameraman. Titles by Randolph Bartlett. At Loew's New York, Feb. 8, half of double feature. Running time, 68 mins.

Tom McCall	Tom Mix
Ruth Martin	Dorothy Dwan
Happy Hogan	Barney Furey
Pete Lawson	Albert Smith
Uncle Abe	Ernest Wilson
Seth Martin	Frank Austin

Tom Mix co-stars with a white mule here. A mystery angle about the value of the mule partly bores and arouses curiosity because it is not until half the footage has been projected that the animal's ability to lead to a gold mine is revealed. Last half, however, is crammed with action original for Mix and a battle in the air capitalizes some real thrills. A safe bet in the average house and especially good for the grinds since it is above par both in story and action.

As the two-fisted government agent on the trail of dope smugglers Mix and his pal, Barney Furey, open with bugle practice. Action could be snapped up at the start were less footage devoted to landscapes.

Al Smith, as the aviator dope runner and mystery man, is introduced attacking the daughter of a man who has been murdered, according to subtitles, after discovering a mine. The former role is played by Dorothy Dwan in the regular way.

Key to the mine and the murderer is supposed to be vested in the mule which Mix has bought for 10 bucks. Interest is aroused when Mix socks the aviator and sky-high bidding is commenced by him for the animal.

Going to work on the girl's ranch Mix and his pal experience the usual foul play when bad man goes in for shooting after failing to get the mule. In the rush to get the animal headed for the mine gang double crosses each other. Highlight, particularly well done, is Mix's rush to take his claim in the same plane with rival aviator. Series of loops and double exposures more effective in pilot's effort to loose Mix out of the plane than usual hand-to-hand encounter on a wing.

Story well knit and performances of cast average. *Waly.*

GUN LAW

FBO (Radio) production and release. Directed by John E. Burch from the story by Oliver Drake. Scenario by Oliver Drake. Titles by Helen Gregg. Starring Tom Tyler; Frankie Darro featured, with cast including Barney Furey, Ethlyn Claire, Harry Woods and Lou Meehan. At the Stanley, New York, for one day. Running time, 55 minutes.

A typical western, with the usual possibilities in daily change grinds, conspicuous for the clumsiness with which it has been handled. Cheaply made, badly constructed, it doesn't hold even the usual amount of tenseness to be found in the western of average quality.

Story light, with enough useless footage for unnecessary introductory sequences to make another western. It's a case of an unwanted lover making good by discovering a plot against the gal to deprive her of a piece of property with valuable marble deposits. At the last minute it resolves itself into a race for the registration office to get ownership. Everybody, including heroine's male relatives, throws the girl over but the boy files the claim in her name. *Mori.*

RED WINE

(SOUND)

Fox production and release. Directed by Raymond Cannon. Features June Collyer, Conrad Nagel and Arthur Stone. Story by Raymond Cannon. Scenario by A. W. Bennison. Cameraman, Daniel Clark. Sound on film. At the Tivoli, N. Y., March 13. Running time, 55 minutes.

Alice Cook	June Collyer
Charles H. Cook	Conrad Nagel
Jack Brown	Arthur Stone
Miss Scott	Sharon Lynn
Jack's Friends	E. Alyn Warren Ernest Hilliard Marshall Ruth
Stenog	Dixie Gay
Spanish Girl	Margaret LaMarr

Even sound effects are not sufficient to raise this one very high. The story itself is familiar material. A young married man tastes the hotsy totsy life unknown to the frau and gets into a jam when she drags him into the same night club where he had taken on board a beautiful jag and had been the victime of a practical joke.

The main action depends upon Conrad Nagel as the young man. Considerable footage on the stew stuff and it is all well camaraed and well done, especially Nagel's impersonation of the souse. A lot of padding doesn't help the picture. Some of the night club show is pretty tame and unnecessary.

A light and frivolous story, for a moment it almost jumped the traces, but got back into the farcical stride intended. A good two-reeler spread out thin into feature length. *Mark.*

HIS LAST HAUL

Radio (FBO) production and release. Directed by Marshall Neilan. Story by Louis Sarecky. Continuity by F. Scott Darling. Phillip Tannura, cameraman. In cast: Tom Moore, Seena Owen. At Loew's New York one day, Feb. 12, half of double feature. Running time, 66 minutes.

Kids will go for this at the matinees. Story is too sugary and adolescent for average adult attendance, with production as a whole passing as average program.

Neilan gets a couple of good situation twists showing Seena Owen, as Salvation Army lass, a reformed crook still wanted. Miss Owen, before her screen identity is disclosed, has chance to straighten Tom Moore, a rough neck.

Most of the footage centers on

nild Salvation Army meeting and Christmas hand-outs, with Tom as Santa. Latter situation only real bit of suspense for adults, since it shows Tom eluding cops and doubling in rich home for "Santa," who disappeared with the Xmas liquor.

THE BLACK PEARL

Trem-Carr production released through Rayart. Directed by Scott Pembroke from tory by Mrs. Wilson Woodrow. At Loew's New York Feb. 8 as half of double feature. Running time, 62 minutes.

Eugenie Bromley....................Lila Lee
Robert Lathrop....................Ray Hallor
Ethelbert...................Carlton Stockdale
Silas Lathrop.............Thomas Curran
Stephen Runyan...........George French
Dr. Drake............Howard Lorenz
Miss Sheen....................Sybil Grove
Wiggenbottom..............Baldy Belmont
Sarah Runyan.................Adele Watson
Eugene Bromley.................Lew Short
Claude Lathrop..........Arthur Rowlands

Just a hopeless mixture without rhyme or reason. A cast so confusedly spread over sets that even the director must have found bringing this monotonous and motiveless thing to the camera a tough job to keep identities in mind. Even the lowliest of the grinds will rear up at this one.

Although titles constantly refer to her, Lila Lee's presence on the screen is shorter than the average bit.

Who is who and what's what are still a mystery. Through the entire picture, with time lapses denoting over 20 years, is one terrific storm. Bad men from India look in the windows every time lightning flashes. A bunch of murders supposedly start after a black pearl a quickly killed off relative has brought back from India. Jewel is inherited by Silas Lathrop. Thomas Curran, in this role, has dark hair and a sweet disposition in one flash and in another is gray and a suspicious demon. Attempts are made to work in situations from some of the ancient Broadway mystery hits, but floppo.

Old man is constantly getting death threats pinned by daggers until he calls in the relatives and reads his will. After a few of the relatives are choked the old gentleman, refusing to relinquish the pearl and willing it to two of his relatives, is bumped off.

In the last reel an effort is made to make the story plausible and only climaxes the mess. The butler suddenly becomes a great criminologist, snapping wristlets on with an avidity never before screened. Where all the bracelets and daggers come from is not explained. Oh, boy!
Waly.

LITTLE WILD GIRL

Hercules production and release. Starring Lila Lee. From magazine story by Putnam Hoover. Directed by Frank S. Mattison. Jules Cronjager, cameraman. Gordon Kahem, titles. In cast: Cullen Landis, Arthur Hotaling, Frank Merrill, Bud Shaw, Boris Karloff, Sheldon Lewis, Jimmy Aubrey and "Cyclone," police dog. At Arena, New York, one day. Running time, 67 minutes.

A minor grind production with major interest for kids by virtue of excellent story and fair direction. Lila Lee makes this silent release the more valuable. Realism aplenty in a very probable yarn. The old forest fire, police dog and Royal Northwestern Mounted Police officer with Indian guide tossed in excite the young.

Canadian setting further enlivened by a Broadway angle, lending all possible to be expected from an economical film.

The Wild Girl is Miss Lee, with whom a vacationing playwright and a songwriter fall in love. They bring her to New York, when her father and sweetheart are believed to have been killed during a forest fire. Father died, but sweetheart

and Indian guide escaped, with sweetie crippled and the guide blinded. Both go into the forest to be forgotten, not wishing the world to know, of infirmities.

Wild dame becomes reigning Broadway star. Her "angels" fight over her, one dying in a fist fight. Girl is driven from White Lights by implication in murder, the murderer escaping, later caught in northwest.

Sweetheart inherits huge fortune, and girl returns home. Townsfolk order her to leave, but the stricken sweetie shows up. To make it more perfect, sweetie regains use of legs.

Kids will love the dog and heroine.

GRIT WINS

Universal production and release, starring Ted Wells. Directed by Joseph Levigard from story credited to George Plympton. Among cast: Kathleen Williams and Al Ferguson. At the Arena, N. Y., one day, as half of double bill. Running time, 42 mins.

Typical western quickie. Grind audiences will be a reel ahead of the story all the time but will like it on account of its speed.

Usual stagecoach, riding, shooting, framing, saloon. Fight in flaming gin mill with unconscious uncle and hysterical girl goes on until the whole building, except the room, falls apart.
Waly.

HARDBOILED

Radio (FBO) production and release. Directed by Ralph Ince from Arthur Somers Roche story. In cast: Sally O'Neill, Lilyan Tashman, Robert Sinclair, Donald Reed. At Loew's New York, one day, half of double bill. Running time, about 65 minutes.

Very slow and monotonous with few staying qualities in present footage for any type of audience.

"Hardboiled" attempts reverse of average backstage girlie-playboy situation. Sally hooks her millionaire for the ring. Wealthy pop objects and hubby goes to work over a gambling machine.

Lots of stock situations in home life as well as old man's attempt to buy off. Hoke tearing of check, real love and dad's welcome home finish tepidly.
Waly.

SPIRIT OF YOUTH

Tiffany-Stahl production and release. Directed by Walter Lang. From story and continuity by Eve Unsell and Elmer Harris. Titles by Fred and Fanny Hatton. John Boyle, cameraman. Cast: Dorothy Sebastian, Larry Kent, Betty Francisco, Maurice Murphy, Nita Fremault. At Loew's New York, Feb. 5, as half of double feature. Running time, 67 minutes.

Ready-made story, with conventional situations, pleasingly brought to the screen. Well mounted and with attractive sets characteristic of this company even in its poorest themes.

Aspiring champ gob meeting a gal in a little village opens and closes this one. In the interim the gob discards uniform and story goes along Tunney lines when he gets title. Unlike the real champ, Larry Kent doesn't get the rich girl because his sparring partner double-crosses him at an exhibition. Poor girl (Miss Sebastian), in his corner at defeat, draws the ring when he pulls the Alger.
Waly.

THE SILENT TRAIL

El Dorado production and independent release. Story credited Brysis Coleman. Directed by J. P. McGowan. Paul Allen, cameraman. In cast: Mack V. Lee, Nancy Lee, J. P. McGowan, Peggy Montgomery, John Lowell. At Ideal, half of double feature, one day, March 18. Running time, about 60 minutes.

Even in the dime houses this gets

the snorts. Not even a cuff story. The performers are like the theme, with McGowan credited for the direction and figuring in most of the close-ups.

The thing starts when a tough guy decides he wants a dance and ropes the girl's boy friend. Lot of wild horse riding on "rainy" print when another dame topples over cliff in auto. She forgets everything long enough to have nice stranger, Bob Custer, marry her to save her from the heavy. Then judge-papa, played by John Lowell, ex-writer, recovers his daughter, etc. The projection unravels the theme with even less continuity than that.
Waly.

Films in Berlin

Deutsches Theatre.—"The Merry Wives of Windsor," by Shakespeare. The dialog has been modernized by Hans Rothe and the whole played in costumes suggesting the bustles of 1850. An amusing idea, but just why it should be better than the original is hard to see. Also, the figure of Falstaff is treated with a trifle too much sentimentality—evidently for Werner Krauss, who likes to stress this angle. Otherwise a brilliant performance with Krauss at his humorous best.

Capitol.—"The Living Corpse" ("Redemption"), Prometheus Film, taken from the play by Tolstoi. Although transplanted to Berlin, the Russians lose none of their cunning as film producers and actors. Fejdor Ozep, the 22-year-old producer who directed "The Yellow Ticket," again proves that he is a master in spite of his youth. And Pudowkin, director of "The End of St. Petersburg" and "Storm Over Asia," shows that as an actor he is his own equal as director. In the role which John Barrymore first introduced into America and in which Moissi is now trouping, he creates a character portrait of simplicity and moving truth. Without making a cheap appeal to the emotions, he grabs the sympathy and holds it throughout. The twisting of the story into an indictment of judges and the whole judicial system will annoy some good burghers. Ozep was not able to do much with his non-Russian talent. Picture will make big money in Europe only.

Beba-Atrium.—"Kisses That Cannot Be Forgotten," Orplid Film. Georg Jacoby, director, and Friedrich Stein, scenario writer, refused to accept responsibility for the film in its present form, sending notices to the papers after the premiere, asking to have their names omitted. According to their complaint the film was cut from 2,500 meters to 1,800 without their consent. The story concerns a Viennese girl and a young grand duke who love each other but cannot marry. Years of war bring about the needed change. She is now a famous dancer, he a chauffeur. Direction hardly above the level of the scenario; 700 meters more or less cannot have changed much. Kowal Samborski, whose individual performances in his native Russian brought him deserved praise, is being swamped with unsuitable roles since his coming here.

Primus Palast.—"Lust," British Gaumont. Here Georg Jacoby was in better form and had a better scenario than in "Kisses That Cannot Be Forgotten." Photography and direction are straightforward and underline the climaxes of the story. "Lust" is here the mad desire for drink. It ruins a wealthy man, who

drags down with him the two women who love him and are trying to save him. Miles Manders, well known on the English stage, gives an interesting study of the gradual disintegration of a drunkard. Elga Brink as the passive blonde remains colorless; Lissi Arna is competent in the part of a street girl. With its anti-alcoholic tendency it looks as though this film were sponsored by the English league for prohibition, with an eye on its bigger brother, America.

Beba-Atrium.—"Adventure Limited," directed by Fred Sauer, scenario by Jane Bess and Fred Sauer. This detective film gives Carlo Aldini, the strong man, plenty of chance to show that he possesses not only strength and agility, but a very sympathetic personality, not without humor. One of those breathtaking detective stories with innumerable threads to disentangle, tastefully done and entertaining. Next to the acting of Carlo Aldini stands that of Hans Mierendorff as the brains of crook gang. A popular success.

Kammer Lichtspiele. — "Pat and Patachon." This film of the two Danish comedians is directed by Lau Lauritzen, who has helped these two naive knockabouts to their success. Here they rise from newsboys to private detectives, engaged to watch over the marital happiness of two young people who won a prize for being the happiest couple. Pat and Patachon's humor dates back to the clowns of circus days—putty noses and false mustaches. The penetrating light of the film shows up their artificiality. They never arouse sympathy.

THE DIVINE LADY

(SOUND)

First National production starring Corinne Griffith. Directed by Frank Lloyd. Adapted by Forrest Halsey and Agnes Christine Johnston from E. Barrington's novel. John B. Sietz, cameraman. Horace Jackson, art director. Titles by Harry Carr and Edwin Justus Mayer. Film editor, Hugh Bennett. Costume supervision by Max Ree. Presented by Richard A. Rowland with Walter Morosco billed as associate producer. Synchronized by Vitaphone. At Warner's, New York, opening March 22 for $2 run. Running time, 105 minutes.

Lady Hamilton............Corinne Griffith
Lord Nelson................Victor Varconi
Lord Hamilton..............H. B. Warner
Charles Greville..................Ian Keith
Mrs. Cadogan...............Marie Dressler
Queen of Naples........Dorothy Cummings
George Romney............William Conklin
Capt. Hardy...................Montagu Love
Duchess of Argyle....Julia Swayne Gordon
King Ferdinand...........Michael Vavitch

Everything but a persuasive story. Sumptuous production, good direction, splendid acting, beautiful sets, costumes and photography, but still just moderate entertainment. Only in production investment and in outward trappings is "The Divine Lady" $2. Limited engagements in a limited number of the bigger towns at that figure.

Story is spasmodic, episodic and anemic. It never develops its most interesting phase, the snubbing by the royal court of Lady Hamilton, girl friend without benefit of clergy to Lord Nelson, England's great naval hero of the Napoleonic wars. Both the historical facts of this celebrated amour and the circumstances of the present fiction version are in conflict with censorship. Lady Hamilton and Lord Nelson each have legal spouses and no amount of skillful gliding over the thin ice of what must never be treated frankly can quite make "The Divine Lady" gripping or convincing.

Literary staff must have acquired furrows trying to strike a balance between history on one hand and squeamish morality on the other. Also a factor may have been a wish or command to avoid anything possibly offensive to British hero-worship of their great admiral. All in all Halsey, Johnston, et al., were compelled to take their pens in hand without removing their mittens.

Frank Lloyd, who has had a wealth of experience on ship stuff, "The Sea Hawk" being to his credit, was an ideal choice for handling a story largely told upon frigates. Unfortunately the battle of the Nile in this picture looks exactly like the battle of Trafalgar with the suspicion of one battle and two subtitles. That detracts from the spectacle element that might otherwise have been a big sock.

Technically the battle scenes are great in effect with little likelihood of laymen figuring they were faked in miniature. Looks like plenty of research on the British naval organization of 1805.

H. B. Warner, Victor Varconi and Ian Keith, featured in the order named, are the men in Lady Hamilton's life. Warner marries her but gets the worst break. Varconi is the gallant admiral who does a hideaway in a cottage with his light o'love after the scandal in London. Ian Keith "discovered" Lady Hamilton as the daughter of a cook in a small English village. Emma loves him devotedly and is heart broken when he deserts her in Naples, Italy. Stress on this opening incident is evidently to show Emma in a sympathetic guise despite her naive ideas on sex.

Miss Griffith occasionally comes through with a flash of brilliance, even suggesting a sense of humor. In general she is simply the insistently beautiful willowy creature born to drive men cuckoo.

"The Divine Lady" on its swank cast and pictorial values will be good program fare. It has a theme song with Miss Griffiths the screen singer. Even a layman can sense that the singing in an otherwise inaudible picture was dragged in bodily for the plug. Otherwise, it will receive respectful consideration. *Land.*

THE GREAT POWER

(DIALOG)

M-G-M release of Franklin Warner (independent) (all-talker, made at Bristolphone factory, Waterbury, Conn. Directed by Joe Rock. Story and dialog by Myron Fagan. Minna Gombell featured. At the Capitol, N. Y., opening March 23. Running time, 83 mins.

John Power.....................Hirshel Mayall
John Wray.....................Minna Gombell
Bruce Power............Alan Birmingham
Frank Forrest.......................Nelan Jaap
Judge Ben Forrest.......G. Davison Clark
Senator Dick Wray...........John Anthony
Peggy Wray..............Helene Shipman
Graves...................................Jack Leslie
Senator Charles Davis.......Walter Walker
Rev. Dr. Elliott.........Conway Wingfield
District Attorney Crane....Alfred Swenson
Jordan.........................Walter F. Scott
Maid...........................Eleanor Martin

This is the picture made at the Bristolphone factory in Waterbury, Conn., by Franklin Warner (no relation to Warner Bros.). Originally the entire stage cast of Myron Fagan's melodrama, a Broadway flop, was taken to Waterbury, along with the flat scenery of the actual stage production, the legit stage hands and the whole kaboddle. It had to be done twice, by report, with some regular studio technicians and Joe Rock, the film director, called in for the second take. Acceptance of the picture by M-G-M came as a surprise to the trade, and stresses the declarations of several big league officials that their companies will take any independent talker.

Possibly angles and percentages on this film which won't come out. Entire production is pseudo-moralistic, the sort of stuff William Hodge has been doing on the road for years. Redemption of a human soul by revelation to it of impending judgment.

While some of the players have standing in legit, none are known generally to the public of Times Square, and certainly not to the public of the provinces. Minna Gombell, featured, will mean about as much in South Chicago as Sadie Zilch. It is also safe to predict, without disparagement to the histrionic talents of the cast, that, with the possible exception of Hirshel Mayall, none of them will be seen again on a major screen. They are, one and all, conspicuously lacking in screen personalities, sex appeal or sartorial swank.

Novelty in the sequence where the multi-millionaire has a scene with his soul. Called to produce a witness to testify in his behalf, a series of personages figuring in his life all appear and denounce him. The clergyman whose charities he supported, the senator whose career he made possible, both supposed friends, testify that he was cold, hard, cruel and miserly, and they had no real respect for him. These testimonials are done against a background of clouds, with only the heads of the figures appearing and speaking.

It is not always clear what the plot is about, notably in the early passages. Long arm of coincidence, the hand of Jehovah, the healing power of love—these are the motifs against a web of financial trickery, crooked stock brokers, two-shots-fired-at-same-time murder, family feuds, senate investigations, oil scandals, innocent senator wrongfully accused, etc.

Pretty bad but might pass in sticks. *Land.*

SPITE MARRIAGE

(SOUND)

M-G-M presentation starring Buster Keaton in his own production. Directed by Edward Sedgwick, from an original story b Lew Lipton, adaptation by Ernest Pagano, titles by Robert Hopkins. At the Capitol, New York, week of March 25. Running time, 74 minutes

Elmer ....Buster Keaton
Trilby Drew...............Dorothy Sebastian
Lionel Benmore...............Edward Earle
Ethyl Norcrosse..................Leila Hyams
Nussbaum ....William Bechtel
Scarzi ....John Byron

Bright, nonsensical farce stuff, replete with belly laffs, especially in the backstage hokum, and packing punch later on. When it appears that everything is sacrificed for the sake of the comedy, and a pardonable sacrifice it would be too, considering the laugh returns, the direction manages to pick the story thread right up again and continue it to a plausible if not particularly probable conclusion.

M-G-M slipped "Spite Marriage" into the Capitol on Monday after their scheduled entry, "The Great Power," played six performances to disastrous results. "Spite" proved a life-saver for the house and should more than offset the weekend's negative impressions.

Lipton has fashioned a corking original for screen farce purposes with which Sedgwick, the director, did tricks, and which a highly intelligent synchronizer further embellished with just the proper musical settings. Here's a corking sample of how much a good score can do for a flicker, not alone to sustain it and fit it with a suitably tempoed background, but actually to bolster it for wow returns.

Whoever did the job, presumably the Axt-Mendoza standbys for M-G-M, rates a bow. Their exaggerated wah-wah muted brasses for the clowning, the broad melancholic themes for the sentimental slosh, plus appropriately intermittent laugh and other mechanical effects, lent an arresting realism to it all.

Title is the crux of a tiff between Dorothy Sebastian, cast an operetta prima donna, and her lady-killing leading man, Lionel Benmore (Edward Earle), who falls for a society blonde (Leila Hyams). Keaton is the muchly smitten pants presser who makes a flash in impeccable formal attire which he "borrows" from his cleaning and pressing establishment for his nightly jaunts. He has seen the same show 35 times and his aisle centre location has identified him backstage.

In answer to a yearn to play a bit in the musical because of its osculatory opportunities, Keaton has it thrust on him when a Pinkerton shows up for the real player. Keaton's grotesque crepe make-up as a Union soldier, his mishandling of his bayonet, the upsetting and destruction of the stage set and props, and the usual backstage hoke, had the Capitol's audience in about the same degree of hysterics as the prop screen audience reacted to Keaton's antics. The synchronization of the screen audience's mirthful reaction and that of the actual attendance was, if anything, exceeded by the cash customers.

From that, Keaton is shanghaied on a yacht, in itself a laughing and, not a little, exciting episode, ultimately proving a hero in single-handedly besting a rum-running crew of sea pirates. The "spite marriage" between the uppish stage prima and her husband for convenience, of course, ultimately becomes a more healthy screen romance.

Miss Sebastian distinguished herself in the nite club souse scene and the return-to-the-hotel aftermath when, as a limply inebriated automaton, Keaton manhandles her in an effort to get her seated, into bed, undressed, etc. Being married, if only in spite, at this stage, the physical intimacies (and there's actually nothing for any blue-noses to frown upon) will be okay. There is one bit with the chair-seating biz that won a salvo from the Capitolites, unusual for a Broadway audience to do in acknowledgment of a piece of celluloid business.

"Spite Marriage" will please generally and get plenty pennies at the gate, and for the producers. It's chiefly bit and business mechanized comedy. Skillfully meshed, plus the players' own histrionic contributions, it represents a moderate investment. Two most substantial sets are the yacht and the backstage hokum, although quite a few extras are involved for the audience stuff.

It's an enjoyable low comedy glorified slapsticker. *Abel.*

THE SHADY LADY

(DIALOG)

Paul Block production and Pathe release, with dialog and synchronization by RCA Photophone. Edward H. Griffith, director. Story by Jack Jungmeyer; Garet Graham's titles. At Colony, New York, week of March 23. Running time, 60 minutes.

Lola...........................Phyllis Haver
Blake.....................Robert Armstrong
Prof. Holbrook..............Louis Wolheim
Haley ....Russell Gleason

Even the inclusion of dialog in the final 10 minutes of "Shady Lady" fails to dispel bad impression. In fact, way the dialog sounds and the players look while speaking out of kilter suggests film might have been better off in complete silence.

There is little good trouping, because little is called for, and most of that by Louis Wolheim, with Wolheim also the single convincer while talking.

Scene is Havana. A wagon loaded with half a dozen hard looking guys and something else is easing down a narrow and darkened street. A portion of the cargo slips to the pavement, the crate breaking and revealing a load of rifles. Gun runners. The boys jump down to retrieve the fallen articles, but are routed and scram, leaving their wagon and guns behind. Gats mysteriously barking from dark corners. Hi-jackers.

Two men are vying for the gun-running trade in Havana, both in on big coin through shipping ammunition to the revolutionary Central American countries. They're not only vying, but fighting. Blake (Robert Armstrong) is getting the best of his biz rival, "Professor" Holbrook (Wolheim), besides interrupting the Prof's big deliveries and copping his goods.

A knockout blonde called Lola, in reality an alleged murderess and fugitive from justice, is cajoled into giving Blake the works, by Holbrook who threatens to notify the cops of her identity. She goes to work on Blake, but falls in love with him instead. It's all very obvious, the love part and that she'll finally tip him to the frame.

At the finish the wicked Prof is foiled and Lola is cleared of the indictment when another woman confesses. She's clinching with Blake at the finale and they're planning a honeymoon to New York, but there's no justification for Blake's illegal business connections. He is to be accepted as a good boy in the wrong job.

A youthful newspaper correspondent, in Havana on the gun-running assignment for his N. Y. paper, is ridiculously drawn. Besides the gun yarn, he identifies Lola, an escaped murderess, which is much better tale, but he agrees to forget the latter when Lola sheds real tears, asking him how he would feel if it were his own sister. When she touches his arm and says "You're such a nice kid," it looked as though Blake might get the air for a cub reporter.

And if the New York dailies are sending Haleys down to Havana on gun-running stories, there will be no gun running stories from Havana for the dailies.

An off-screen duo (male) harmonizes a theme song during the more passionate portions, and it seemed as though, in the production, the song and title came first and the scenario next.

Moderate money in the intermediate stands should be about the limit. *Bige.*

WHIRL OF LIFE
(GERMAN MADE)

World Wide release. Directed by Richard Eichberg from the novel by the same title. Cast includes Heinrich George, Louis Lerch and Greta Reinwald. At the Little Carnegie Playhouse, N. Y., March 23. Running time, 72 minutes.

Unnecessarily long, considering the scanty story, and would still be draggy if cut down because of the amount of footage devoted to an explanatory preface without which it would be impossible to understand the story.

Opens in East Prussia with the heroine working in an immigrant aid society. She kills her stepfather when he invites her to take a beating, and is next found in London using a dead girl's name.

All this serves as a sort of preliminary only, merely leading into the much-used clown angle. A kindly, well-known stage comedian lifts the girl and her boy friend to stardom and then finds she has loved the other from the beginning.

Usual finish, the clown bowing to the plaudits of the multitude, hiding a broken heart beneath the smiling face. Not well done in this picture, however.

Interiors mostly of the quickie type. Photography includes shots made in both Berlin and London. None of the players given screen credit. *Mori.*

GREYHOUND LTD.
(DIALOG)

Warner production and release. Directed by Howard Bretherton from story by A. Howson. Joseph Jackson, titles. Louis Silver music score on Western Electric Vitaphone system. At Academy of Music for three days, beginning March 24. Running time, 68 minutes.

Monte Jones	Monte Blue
Bill Williams	Grant Withers
Edna	Edna Murphy
Mrs. Williams	Lucy Beaumont

Monte Blue has posed as a railroad engineer for the Warners a number of times in the past. "Greyhound Limited" is his first for the brothers where the bells ring and the engine wheezes. The story is of the conventional school of railroad melodramas. It is brought to the screen with a zest fan reaction clearly underwritten.

"Greyhound Limited" is a trifle slow in getting under way. All kinds of bells clang for the first ten minutes during which Blue and Withers dialogue in closeup from the window of the caboose. Their lines are clear in reproduction. Blue is the better recorded. The talk serves well as a preface to the yarn that the engineer is the clear-headed kind while his fireman is inclined to be girl crazy.

The railroad locale is abandoned during the major footage for interiors in a lunchroom, and the home of the fireman where the engineer is a boarder. Edna Murphy, as the snappy counter girl who has eyes for Blue and uses Withers as the chump, makes the best of her part.

The interference angle is the meat of the plot. It provides the fireman with a chance to hit the booze and be condemned for the murder of a speak proprietor. Thereafter action of the thriller kind, exceptionally well executed here, fills the remaining reel and a half.

Edna, a few hours before Bill is to be hanged, overhears gangsters telling their story. This enables a neck and neck auto race followed by another sprint alongside freight cars which have been started down an incline to wreck Monte's train. The customary flashback to the condemned man's cell, the clock denoting just another hour, while Blue is uncoupling the passenger cars and leaping over an incline to roll near Edna's auto.

Of note is the performance of Miss Beaumont. As Bill's mother her acting, in a brief trial scene and in a brief act in sequence has superlative effectiveness. *Waly.*

THE SIN SISTER

William Fox production and release. Directed by Charles Klein from story by Frederick H. Brennan. Continuity by Harry Behn. At Loew's New York, one day, March 19, half of double feature. Running time, about 70 minutes.

Pearl	Nancy Carroll
Peter Van Dykeman	Lawrence Gray
Ethelyn Horn	Josephine Dunn
Sister Burton	Myrtle Stedman
Joseph Horn	Anders Randolf
Bob Newton	Richard Alexander

Worst European production has a lot in common with "The Sin Sister." From the title up this thing is a freak. One minute its slapstick, then there is a serious interlude. All the way through subtitles are strained. Attempt to breed comedy and drama and the offspring is burlesque of hybrid variety. Hopelessly boring even to grind audiences.

Early in lengthy footage the characters get out of directorial control. What starts out to be a deep drama of the north with whistling winds and snows and shots of vessel cutting through ice, strongly suggestive of clips from Fox's "Lost in the Arctic," is given cheap comedy turn by rich papa suffering from wanderlust. Anders Randolf in this role contributes largely with his exaggerated interpretation to throw theme off track. Josephine Dunn, as the daughter, Ethelyn, plays him a close hand. She goes in for hysteria while others are treating blizzard like a summer's day.

After paying a couple of grand to fur traders to get him and pals from ice bound ship the party is deserted in desolate hut. Here cheap gags and gaudy hokum prevail until Eskimo suddenly appears and shoots secretary. Fur trader demands as his price for aid little Pearl, vaude dancer of the North Pole circuit. Lawrence Gray is secretary and Nancy Carroll does her best, although obviously bewildered, to interpret the title role.

At trader's cabin things rage along hot meller lines until Pearl pulls trigger and orders food and medicine to the crowd. Just when the end seems a half hour off secretary suddenly recovers, grabs Pearl and off they go in sleds. Arty ending. *Waly.*

SHIPS OF THE NIGHT

Rayart Production and release. Directed by Duke Worne. Adapted by Arthur Hoerl from Fred Nebel's story. Hap Depew, cameraman. At Loew's New York one day, March 22, half of double bill. Running time, 63 minutes.

Johanna Hearne	Jacqueline Logan
Yutson	Sojin
Dan Meloy	Jack Mower
Alec	Andy Clyd
Donald Hearne	Arthur Rankin
Cransey	Glen Cavender
Chief of Police	Thomas A. Curran
Moja	Frank Lanning
Motilla	J. P. McGowan
First Mate	Frank Moran

Derelict islands are always great locale in quickieland, but Rayart's effort to cram in punch-holding battles every few feet skeletonizes the story to a bare structure and makes a good cast seem only ordinary. Had less efforts been made to outfight old dime novels, "Ships of the Night" would be entitled to a better rating than just one-day grind.

Even Sojin, usually sincere portrayer of Oriental roles, goes flat because of the exaggerated artificiality of a cuff script. More so is this true of Miss Logan. She freezes to a smile under circumstances that are always threatening but mild in their materialization.

Miss Logan's search for a brother gone fugitive after winging a man, later murdered, in a drinking bout, is the signal for silk-shirted pirates, a Chinaman with a harem and criminals as slaves, and the rest of whatnots. The desert island stuff is worked in when the Christian captain of the ship headed for the island takes to a lifeboat with her for some unknown reason. Here love interest is established. Then the pirates, among whom is the murderer, a bit part played by Arthur Rankin.

A huge but mild pirate chief is J. P. McGowan. As Motilla he is Miss Logan's foil for the Chinese terror when Derelict Isle and its muddle of pie-throwing antics is reached.

Jack Mower as Dan Meloy, the Christian captain, gets pretty badly manhandled. In the end he rescues everyone and cops himself a bride. *Waly.*

Trial of Mary Dugan
(DIALOG)

Metro-Goldwyn-Mayer production and release, featuring Norma Shearer, H. B. Warner, Lewis Stone and Raymond Hackett. Adapted from Bayard Veiller's play of the same name and directed by Veiller. Synchronized by W. E. disk process with Douglas Shearer recording engineer. Photographer, William Daniels. At the Embassy, N. Y., for twice daily run at $2 starting March 28. Running time, 113 mins.

Mary Dugan	Norma Shearer
Edward West	Lewis Stone
District Attorney	H. B. Warner
Jimmy Dugan	Raymond Hackett
Dagmar Lorne	Lilyan Tashman
Mrs. Edgar Rice	Olive Tel
Marie Decrot	Adrienne D'Ambricourt
Ferne Arthur	Mary Doran
Inspector Hunt	Dewitt Jennings
Judge Nash	Wilfred North
Dr. Welcome	Landers Stevens
May Harris	Myra Hampton
Police Capt. Price	Westcott Clarke
James Madison	Charles Moore
Henry Plaisted	Claud Allister

A moving picture because it comes in cans and unwinds through a projector to reach the screen. Otherwise it's a verbatim celluloid and disk report of the play. Eliminate the intermissions which were in the show and there's hardly any difference in the running time. But "Mary Dugan" is an excellent talker and will do heavy business for the program houses. It's the best subject the Embassy has housed in some time.

Plenty of angles to this one commencing with what's going to happen to it in Pennsylvania and Ohio? After that it makes a trite example for the legit producers to glance over and thereby get an idea of how the studios are going to handle their dramatic plays when the author also directs. "Mary Dugan" will now go on the road, it's former amount of patronage in and out of New York being a drop in the film bucket. Those who didn't see the play are very apt to be delighted with this genuine copy. Those who witnessed the stage version are likely to be disappointed in the exact similarity.

Screen has neither enlarged upon or lessened the original script. That may be because of Veiller who both authored and directed. Hence, what Veiller didn't do is possibly more important than what he has done. To give the screen its due the author-director would have had to cut heavily into his dialog—and what writer likes to dismember his brain child? Result is the questionable sacrifice the studios are repeatedly making to the talking era —much dialog and no action. "Mary Dugan" might not have been such a consistent talker had the expected screen license been taken for movement. It also might have been a better picture had it realized upon its full scope.

A twist is that where Norma Shearer's name normally appears above that of the picture, because this is a talker they'll look beneath the title to find out who's in it. And it's a strong cast. Lobby comment was heavily in favor of Miss Shearer, who doesn't look as well as usual, and allowing that it's her first joust with the microphone there's no doubt her performance is highly creditable. She does particularly well when on the stand under cross examination by the district attorney, although it's an open question how the big house audiences are going to accept her whimpering hysterics in a prolog shot which is one bit of license Veiller has taken, the other being Mary being called from her cell. Neither of these scenes were in the show.

It can almost be said that this is H. B. Warner's picture. As the district attorney Warner is as strong here as he was at a disadvantage in a previous talker for another company. Lewis Stone is also up front with a nice piece of work, it being a cute studio trick to foist the generally heroic or martyred Lewis on an unsuspecting film public as the dastard in the case. And it's tragic that the late Rex Cherryman didn't live to play "Jimmy Dugan" in this picture. A youngster with plenty of ability, appearance and a flair for this role which set him in legit, he would unquestionably have repeated in pictures had he survived to receive the chance.

Raymond Hackett, assigned this character, does exceedingly well with it, and women will probably go for his dimple regardless if he convinces or not all the way. As a pair and opposite one another both Miss Shearer and Hackett, as her brother, seem to occasionally lean heavily upon Warner and Stone for support. That that support is there is as good for the picture as it is for them.

Important witness stand bits are contributed by Lilyan Tashman and Adrienne D'Armbricourt, the latter as the comedy French maid. Miss Tashman, handicapped by a badly scratched print for her footage, plays the dizzy show girl called to testify with a portion of sparkling dialog to unfold in the sombre surroundings. She delivers as also does Miss D'Ambricourt, the purpose of each inclusion being the same let-up in tension.

That this picture may aggravate blue nose censors is not beyond the bounds of possibility in that both Mary's brother and the district attorney probe deeply into her past life on the witness stand, and that examination into character unfolds four men who have proved the means of supplying the innocent Jimmy with his education. The murder of the last of these providers is the reason for the trial.

As with all other mystery films this effort will suffer in the eyes of those who walk in at the climax or half way through in the grind houses. That it is talky and long is obvious but that it never seriously loses its grip is also true. Veiller has taken the edge off his punch, the revelating scream of the widow, by preceding it with another feminine screech as a dummy figure of the murdered man is unveiled in court. Latter inclusion is gruesome enough without the misplaced scream which might better have been held back to permit the following shriek full emphasis.

Picture is about as much of a one-set effort as any film can be, there being but snatch flashes into the corridor crowds for atmosphere and long pause views of the spectators during the booth changeovers now that the titles are gone.

Being on disk "Mary" can't very well stand curtailment and 113 minutes is long program time. Yet, here is a first rate talker possessing a strong story as its foundation which should do much to get Miss Shearer off on the right foot early in the dialog cycle. Recording is exceptionally good. *Sid.*

THE GODLESS GIRL

(PART DIALOG)

Cecil B. DeMille production distributed by Pathe. An original story by Jeannie MacPherson. At Cameo, New York, opening March 30 for extended engagement. Running time, 90 mins.

Judy........................Lina Basquette
Mamie........................Marie Prevost
Bob........................George Duryea
The Kid........................Eddie Quillan
Warden........................Noah Beery

Cecil B. DeMille had his tongue in his cheek when he directed this hack yarn with religious undercurrents. He was ogling for favor in the same direction as "King of Kings," and possibly at the start contemplated a pretentious production. Long delay in bringing the picture into New York indicates weaknesses were appreciated with the hold-out for the purposes of adding dialog. Talk may help the ballyhoo. It does not enhance the entertainment and is so palpably unnecessary that laymen are apt to sense this even if lacking the trade knowledge to define the flaws.

"Godless Girl" is formula preachment of obvious sort. It may jibe with the sentiments of the fundamentalists in the more remote localities, but many intelligent churchmen will resent its bogus moralizing. Homiletics are especially insincere as the sub-titles frequently do not dove-tail with the situations.

Story is not only haphazardly conceived but lacks the careful knitting of incident that constitutes expert narrative. It is nothing but a series of horrible examples in a reformatory school. Noah Beery resembles a Von Stroheim villain as the head guard. He does everything but eat the apple during an execution. His credo as top sergeant of a bunch of adolescent lawbreakers is "brutality for its own sake." He has a truly oriental cunning in devising unique forms of torture for trivial infractions of discipline.

Caption announces that picture reveals conditions actually existing in many reformatories, "although most of them are conducted decently and humanely."

Despite its plentitude of agony "Godless Girl" rates low on the score of realism. Insistent interpolation of Pollyanna twaddle blunts the sharp lines of the attempted photograph of conditions. Reform school stuff has been done much better before.

Direction, editing and production all are below DeMille standards. In fact, it's hard to believe the maker of a long list of snappy pictures could have turned out such a disjointed, listless, length of celluloid.

Acting undistinguished throughout. Lina Basquette and Marie Prevost, the two nifties in burlap, are as human as their parts permit. Prevost is notably confusing as a character. She is for the Bible, but in a smart-cracking, tough egg sort of a way that is incongruous, to express it politely.

Eddie Quillan is the comedy relief. Mack Sennett comedy. George Duryea, the male lead, okay as the gent on the receiving end of Noah Beery's best ideas of deviltry. Still used in Cameo lobby is about as frank a nude study of a picture actress ever publicized. It's Lina Basquette sporting in ye old swimming hole.

"Godless Girl" is a disappointment. It may get in on a DeMille rain check—but it cannot deliver much. *Land.*

CHRISTINA

(SOUND)

Fox production and release starring Janet Gaynor. Directed by William K. Howard. Story by Tristam Tupper. Titles by Katherine Hilliker and H. H. Caldwell. Cameraman, Lucien Andriot. Roxy orchestra supplies musical score. Theme song, "Christina," by Conrad, Mitchell and Gottler. At the Gaiety, N. Y., for twice daily run, starting March 30 at $2. Running time, 75 mins.

Christina........................Janet Gaynor
Jan........................Charles Morton
Niklass........................Rudolph Schildkraut
Dirk Torpe........................Harry Cording
Madame Bosman........................Lucy Dorraine

Syrupy romance likely to be voted downright dull by a fan public that leans to highly flavored action. Like offering Elsie books to Havelock Ellis readers or bread and butter to caviar appetites. Picture has a vast amount of pictorial beauty in the quaint settings of Holland and some acting of the first order, but the net effect is lukewarm, due to a placid story. One of those pictures the White List people recommend, but nobody goes to see and nobody talks about. No dialog and little sound effect.

Film's best assets are its beautiful backgrounds and the playing of Janet Gaynor and Rudolph Schildkraut. Some of the sentimental passages are effective and some of them are maudlin. Of action the subject has none that really delivers a punch. Story is light weight. Christina is a Dutch lass who passes up the rugged local swains and dreams of a hero-wooer on a white horse. First thing that seems to measure up to her ideal is Jan the Hollandaise equivalent of a circus barker.

The two fall promptly in love. Woman circus proprietor is in love with Jan and it is her scheming to keep the youngsters apart that furnishes the feeble plot. A plot that has to be whipped up cruelly to keep moving. Much crude theatre in devices such as the circus woman shooting the boy and posing in his embrace while he's unconscious to make the girl think he is false.

Rudolph Schildkraut has some sentimentally telling scenes as the indulgent old father of the heroine and manages to make the early sequences interesting by his suave humor. But when they make him go blind while his beloved daughter is trying on her wedding dress, it's a little too heavy to really bite.

Words cannot overstate the charm of the settings nor the captivating picture of Miss Gaynor as a wide-eyed and wide-skirted Dutch maid. Backgrounds express the desirable quaint atmosphere, but the storied episodes never are content with just reasonable quaintness. They make the action too quaint to be possible.

Laboring through an hour or so of preparation they managed to create one moment of fair suspense toward the end. This was the episode where Christina accepts a substitute suitor to keep from her father the truth that she believes herself jilted by Jan. At the moment she and the counterfeit wooer were in betrothal ceremony, Jan himself was recovering from a pistol shot and unaware of what was happening. Betrothal ceremony consisted of the pair sitting before a candle until it burned out. If its flame died the betrothal didn't go.

Suspense consists of a question whether Jan will arrive in time. He does, and you knew he would, so it isn't much of a situation to wait an hour for. Besides the capable playing of Miss Gaynor and Schildkraut Charles Morton reveals himself as an admirable young leading man who will one of these days step into a part and become a screen personage over night. Harry Cording is a new type of heavy, likewise of promise.

Picture is without dialog and employs sound effects sparingly. Musical accompaniment is agreeable and theme song has possibilities as a ballad plug, being pure musical hoke, but sounding better than it really is in constant reprise by a soulful tenor. *Rush.*

THE WILD PARTY

(DIALOG)

Paramount production and release, starring Clara Bow. Directed by Dorothy Arzner. All talker on disks. From Warner Fabian's story. Dialog by E. Lloyd Sheldon. At the Rialto, N. Y., for grind run starting March 30. Running time, 77 mins.

Stella Ames........................Clara Bow
Gil Gilmore........................Frederick March
Helen Owens........................Shirley O'Hara
Faith Morgan........................Marceline Day
Eva Tutt........................Joyce Compton
Babs........................Adrienne Dore
Tess........................Virginia Thomas
Ann........................Jean Lorraine
Thelma........................Kay Bryant
Maisie........................Alice Adair
Janice........................Renee Whitney
Jean........................Amo Ingram
Gwen........................Marguerite Cramer
Al........................Jack Oakie
Phil........................Phillips R. Holmes
Ed........................Ben Hendricks, Jr.
George........................Jack Luden
Balaam........................Jack Raymond

Box office picture with a b. o. title, a box office star, and, more box office than ever, Clara contributes her voice. Laughing, crying or condemning, that Bow voice won't command as much attention as the Bow this and that, yet it's a voice. Enough of a voice to insure a general belief that Clara can speak, as well as look—not as well, but enough. Warner Fabian's story fits the redhead like a wet bathing suit.

It's impossible, though. So full of all the things that everybody knows. But take or leave it, there's still Clara.

Champ necker and flame of the campus falls in love with a young and good looking professor. He in turn makes it mutual. That's reasonable, but who wants sense? Sense is seldom box office. When Clara flashes a gam, all senses are deadened. And when she flashes a pair of 'em.

Talking of gams, there are more in one bit in this film than in half a dozen "Follies" choruses. Young professor of anthropology, entering his class room for the first time, is greeted by a forest of lower limbs. All shapely limbs. Anyone bothering to look at the faces will see the most comely all-girl class ever assembled. If it were possible to rope together such a student body as this it would be more of an asset to a school than the best fotoball team in history. And this young Professor Gilmore, teaching anthropology, which is the study of man, was teaching it to a class room full of gals who knew more about them and what it takes than any prof. in anthry.

A valiant thing for Clara to do when she pulled an "I'll take the blame" upon discovery of her innocent room mate's love letters. Letters mentioned "that night on the beach" and Clara hopped a rattler homeward. Who should knock on the drawing room door, but young Gilmore. He chucked the teaching job and is joining a jungle expedition. Clara makes it double.

E. Lloyd Sheldon's dialog is as flip and broad as permissible, much of it forced humor, and most of it to be taken seriously by the flaps.

Performance of Frederic March as the prof. is the picture's best. Vocally, he reigns supreme. Blonde girl whose name cannot be correctly selected from the line-up contributed another very good one, personally hurdling an unsympathetic role of a tattling, catty dame through properly playing it. After that they are down the line, none prominently.

Feminine list of players reads like next year's eligibility line-up for the Wampas duke.

The girls' four years at school are described by the young prof., who also preaches to young girls, as one wild party. An off-screen vocal combination sings a light theme song at intervals. Title is "My Wild Party Gal." *Bige.*

WILD ORCHIDS

(SOUND)

M-G-M production starring Greta Garbo with Lewis Stone and Nils Asther featured. Directed by Sidney Franklin. Original story by John Colton. Adaptation by Hans Graly and Willis Goldbeck. Cameraman, William Daniels. Titles by Marion Ainslee. At Capitol, New York, week of March 30. Running time 90 mins.

Lillie Sterling........................Greta Garbo
John Sterling........................Lewis Stone
Prince de Gace........................Nils Asther

Appraised in its totality this one is good entertainment and probable box office. It will not matter importantly that the picture is too long and often a bit sluggish in tempo. Exotic background sustains the plot over the thin periods. Definitely plus, too, is the swanky production and adroit direction of Sidney Franklin.

Greta Garbo's repressed mode fits perfectly the role of a wife, very romantic and sentimental, who is married to a preoccupied Americano and who utterly refuses to be jealous until the last reel. Lewis Stone, that reliable and gifted Thespian, is topnotch as the chap who forgot to be gallant to his wife. Nils Asther, more robust than usual, impersonates a sleek Javanese prince.

Women in general will probably appreciate the absent-minded husband, the one time lover now just a sleepy guy. They will feel with Miss Garbo the sense of exasperation at hubby's lack of energy and suspicion. And they (the dames) will probably feel that having their marital fidelity tested and tempted by so natty a sheik as Asther is a possible source of pleasurable tremors.

"Wild Orchids" is fundamentally a woman's picture. It's a feminineized plot all the way. Sex is the meat and marrow of its drama, the protagonist of its characters. Miss Garbo gives, with satisfying feminine charm, a continuous closeup of everyday wifely reactions to the problem of the indolent spouse and the fascinating iceman.

Very interesting and skillfully contrived is the atmospheric stuff of Java. It will be awe-inducing for the local stops. Especially novel is the group of oriental dancers, to which considerable footage is wisely devoted. Whether authentic Javanese or not they constitute an exploitable angle for alert house managers. Stills on this one item of "Wild Orchids" will help fasten an association of ideas in the public mind.

Three actors only in cast, but each a favorite. Asther is a comer, or more exactly a new arrival, with the gals. Miss Garbo's vogue needs no emphasis while the always-refreshing Lewis Stone may be regarded as holding unto himself the admiring regard of the upper strata of film-goers.

"Wild Orchids" is strong program fare. *Land.*

STRONG BOY

(SOUND)

Fox production starring Victor McLaglen with Leatrice Joy featured. Directed by John Ford. Story by Frederick H. Brennan. Continuity by John McLain. Titles by Malcolm Stuart Boylan. At Roxy, New York, week of March '30. Running time 78 minutes.

"Strong Boy"	Victor McLaglen
Mary MacGregor	Leatrice Joy
Angus McGregor	Farrell MacDonald
Pete	Clyde Cook
Wilbur Watkins	Kent Sanderson
Wobby	Douglas Scott
Slim	Slim Somerville
Baggage Master	Tom Wilson
Baggageman	Jack Pennick
Baggageman	Robert Ryan
Queen of Louisonia	Eulalie Jensen
President	David Torrence
Prima Donna	Dolores Johnson

John Ford, who has directed many fine pictures, was given a flock of hoke bits and told to make a picture starring Victor McLaglen. Bearing in mind the asinine story, Ford's finished product demands tolerance, especially in a trade sense, leaving the artistic out of the equation. He has in fact demonstrated that a director of finesse and imagination can, if the producers insist on wasting him, take unadulterated hokum and knead it into some sort of form approaching downright merit.

"Strong Boy" has to be approached objectively. Showmen are not apt to like a picture of its type personally, but they must, and will, concede a possible audience that reacts happily to such undiluted blah. For such audiences (with doubt expressed that the Roxy is one) the fact that Director Ford has sneaked in a little, not too much, class is therefore a favorable factor.

Victor McLaglen is presumed to have a following with the extent as yet unfixed in boundaries. His breezy, virile personality and genuine capacity for pantomine comedy is squandered in "Strong Boy" as is the directorial skill of Mr. Ford. Also wasted, and for her fans it must be sad indeed, is Leatrice Joy doing a mere bit as the keeper of a depot news stand.

"Strong Boy" is minus on the romantic element and zero on gorgeous clothes, trim females, and the other ingredients commonly presumed neccessary to the box office It offers as its hero a muscular dumbbell who lugs trunks hither and yon in a railroad terminal. His adventures are uncommonly puny and silly, climaxing with his besting a gang of crooks out to steal the royal jewels of the visiting Queen of Graustark.

Story and cast all founded on bits Consequently acting is unimportant Production detail okay although editing toward end of spool is pretty poor. Picture leans entirely upon McLaglen's popularity and a few giggles of the slapstick school.

In toto, very moderate. *Land.*

CHINATOWN NIGHTS

(DIALOG)

Paramount production and release. W. E. recording. Wallace Beery, with Florence Vidor, featured. W. A. Wellman directed from Samuel Ornitz's story, "Tong War." Adapted by Oliver H. P Garrett, scenarized by Ben Grauman Kohn with dialog sequences by William B Jutto. At the Paramount. N Y. week of March 30. Running time, 88 mins.

Chuck Riley	Wallace Beery
Joan Fry	Florence Vidor
Boston Charley	Warner Oland
The Shadow	Jack McHugh
The Reporter	Jack Oakie
Woo Chung	Tetsu Komai
The Gambler	Frank Chew
The Maid	Mrs. Wing
The Bartender	Peter Morrison
Gerald	Freeman Wood

"Chinatown Nights," heralded as an all-talker, actually has about 60 per cent dialog, with the rest in captions. It's an in-and-out flicker, spotty in its impressions, and altogether missing fire as a satisfying synchronous feature. It marks Wallace Beery's debut in the talkers, although he essayed a hobo song and a snatch of dialog in a previous Paramount release. It also introduces Florence Vidor in dialog.

So many glaring deficiencies in "Chinatown Nights" that a captious critic could devote paragraphs to itemize them. For one thing, the manner of introducing the title with its equal division of titular display to "Chinatown Nights" and its captioning as being taken from "Tong War," lends the impression the producers themselves were uncertain anent the aptitude of either title. Style of billing permits exhibs to make their own choice; possibly, too, there are two sets of paper available.

Paper starts and finishes with a rubberneck wagon ballyhoo, the means for the thrill-seeking Joan Fry (Miss Vidor) being introduced to Chinatown (presumably San Francisco's celestial sector), where she meets Chuck Riley, the Caucasian leader of one tong. Wallace Beery plays Chuck Riley. Warner Oland is Boston Charley, chieftain of the rival tong.

Against this sordid background a colorful enough auro for melodramatics, comes a series of incongruities that does anything but flatter the average intelligence. If the Paramount authoring staff had to get ten-twenty-thirt with their hectic hokum, it seems that a cinema-literary combination of Ornitz, Garrett, Kohn and Jutto, not to mention Wellman, the director, could have done it a bit more glibly and with greater plausibility.

Miss Vidor, as the hit-and-run thrill-seeker, accused by Beery to have the head of "uptown" and a Barbary Coast body, decides to cast her lot with Chuck and stay in the downtown Chinese sector. She becomes rather indirectly involved in the tong warfare as the amour of the Irish-American leader of a wild bunch of Orientals; ultimately, after a series of tribulations, she finally influences Riley to go her way—"uptown" and away from the viciousness of Chinatown.

As a general thing, the picture is a celluloid libel on a harmless group of laundrymen and restaurant waiters. As a contemporary picture of any Chinatown on the North American continent—and there's none actually tougher than that in Montreal—this is somewhat antiquated.

From the players' viewpoint Beery, unfortunately, has not been given a choice assignment. He has a powerful screen personality, akin to that of Bancroft's, with the same up-and-manly stentorian keynote in his address and deserves special script attention. It's the first time in a long spell that Beery has been given a sympathetic dramatic assignment, although as the kindly tramp in "Beggargs of Life," he was not the menace of yore.

Miss Vidor's dialog impressions are puzzling. It is patent that in some sequences another voice is doubling for her since little subterfuge is necessary in these portions. There are other shots where Miss Vidor is unquestionably speaking. These, however, are either brief or minor addresses.

Of the most consistent performances, that seasoned menace of pioneer days in the deaf-and-dumb racket, Walter Oland, does exceedingly well. His screen accomplishments are fortified anew with a decisive speaking voice. For the rest, it matters little either way.

On blanket bookings, plus the key city exhibitions in the Publix houses. Par will exceed in economic benefits the artistic and entertainment values that "Chinatown Nights" possesses. But as a picture it's nothing to brag about. *Abel.*

Children of the Ritz

(SOUND)

First National Vitaphone production, directed by John Francis Dillon. Dorothy Mackaill and Jack Mulhall featured. From Cornell Woolrich's serial that appeared in College Humor. Titles by Paul Perez. At the Strand, N. Y., week of March 30. Running time, 71 minutes.

Angela Pennington	Dorothy Mackaill
Dewey Haines	Jack Mulhall
Gil Pennington	James Ford
Mr. Pennington	Richard Carlyle
Mrs. Pennington	Evelyn Hall
Lyle Pennington	Kathryn McGuire
The Butler	Frank Crayne
Gerald Wilder	Eddie Burns
Margie Haines	Doris Dawson
Mrs. Haines	Aggie Herring
Gaffney	Lee Moran

Angela Pennington (Dorothy Mackaill) explains that she is extravagant because her father is rich. She falls in love with the Penningtons' young chauffeur (Jack Mulhall), doing most of the advancing herself. Angela Pennington's pa goes broke. The young chauffeur wins $50,000 on a horse race.

Mackaill and Mulhall wed. Girl continues extravagant, wading through the boy's 50 g's in a couple of weeks. He reverts to former form and drives a cab. She repents, finds him and states she will willingly go to work to help him, even "make my own dresses." That's the end.

Miss Mackaill looks nice and wears a lot of pretty clothes. Mulhall, the screen's recognized best dressed lead, gets by fairly well in chauffeur's uniforms until the last quarter, and then slides home with a double breasted tux and some more swell mufti. Co-featured, their performances are equally good.

No dialog. Effective synchronization and sound effects.

John Francis Dillon worked uneventfully but capably with this scenario, which is a French farce photographed mostly outdoors and often on the driver's seat of an automobile.

"Children of the Ritz" should see moderate returns. Alternative will be less. Absence of talk at this moment dispels chance for anything better. *Bige.*

THIS IS HEAVEN

(SOUND)

Samuel Goldwyn production. Starring Vilma Banky. United Artists release. Directed by Alfred Santell. Story by Arthur Mantell, adapted by Hope Loring. Titles by George Marion, Jr. Cameraman, George Barnes. Musical score by Hugo Reisenfeld. At "trade showing," New York Roof, March 28. Running time 90 minutes.

Eva	Vilma Banky
Jimmy	James Hall
Mamie	Fritzi Ridgeway
Uncle Frank	Lucien Littlefield
Rounder	Richard Tucker

Vilma Banky as the flapjack queen of Childs' Fifth avenue, Goldwyn's Hungarian star brought up to date and to America, without period fripperies or sword-toting lovers. And in line with the note of modernity, occasionally bursting into dialog rather cutely tinged with foreign accent. Always a dainty, appealing, feminine creature and adding, with each picture, something to her effectiveness as a trouper. "This Is Heaven" is not a great picture nor, perhaps, by the United Artists' standards of a few years ago, a picture up to the expectations of the releasing name, but it is a good programmer. Of the type Paramount makes.

Story minus novelty or sock, but carried by the romantic element. It's the love affair of an immigrant girl who thinks her sweetie is a chauffeur, whereas he is really a millionaire. This is the sort of fable that will give the dames a big kick. It's the stuff continued stories in the tabs are made of.

Love's young sweet dream as expressed in plans for the financial future, furniture, home-building, etc., will find a responsive chord among the lads and lasses who hold hands in the dark. There may also be a sentimental tug for many naturalized citizens in the scenes at Ellis Island. In short, "This Is Heaven," while generating no great amount of tension, does concern itself with things which will interest the great body of fans. That the yarn is both trite and reminiscent does not matter importantly from the showmanly angle.

Small cast and nothing elaborate on the production end. As with all the Goldwyn productions, photography is splendid. Alfred Santell tells the story simply and humanly, accomplishing with quiet competence the transition of Miss Banky from a lady of royalty to a batter-mixer of Childs. James Hall is attractively breezy in the male lead.

Picture was exhibited at a "trade showing" for exhibs, trade press and relatives. Not due in New York for couple months. About 15 per cent dialog out of 90 minutes' running time. One big conversational laugh for Vilma suggests possibility of Goldwyn doing an all-talker with her garbled English as the source of drollery. This could be accomplished without loss of dignity and with probable increase of popularity. Grooming Miss Banky for permanency as a star is going to tax Goldwyn's smartness. "This Is Heaven" is much better stuff toward that end than "The Awakening," with which Miss Banky was launched, without the partnership of Ronald Colman. But lack of beautiful gowning is a detriment. Fans expect their goddesses to be attired as such. *Land.*

CLEAR THE DECKS

(DIALOG)

Universal production and release, starring Reginald Denny. Directed by Joseph Hennaberry from E. J. Rath's story, "When the Devil Was Sick." Western Electric Movietone sychronized score and dialog. At the Colony, New York, March 30. Running time 70 minutes.

Jack Armitage	Reginald Denny
Miss Bronson	Olive Hasbrouck
Pussyfoot	Otis Harlan
Plinge	Lucien Littlefield
Blondie	Collette Marten
Mate	Robert Anderson
Aunt	Elenor Leslie
Trumbull	Brooks Benedict

Romantic comedy with the action mostly aboard ship. Dash of slapstick added to a series of incidents dealing with mistaken identity makes this an amusing flicker that should get moderate money in the better neighborhood houses. Three dialog sequences, of eight minutes each, are a welcome relief from a flock of subtitles that are of the old school and the weakest thing in the picture.

Story centers around Jack Armitage, (Denny), who gets a yen for a passing female and follows her on an ocean voyage, having first obtained the passage ticket and assuming the name of a friend, who has been ordered to take the trip for his health by a wealthy aunt on penalty of being disinherited.

On the liner he is taken in charge by a male nurse who mistakes him for the sick man and insists that he remain in bed and subsist on a diet of goat's milk. A couple of crooks aboard the ship working with a member of the ship's crew are also worried about Armitage's real identity. They are planning to cop a necklace belonging to the girl who unknowingly is the object of hero's affection.

Despite handicaps, Armitage gives the slip on several occasions and finally manages to make the acquaintance of the girl. But just as he is making some romantic progress, he is re-captured by the nurse and several husky members of the crew and the girl is made to believe that he is more or less goofy, his explanations of his actual identity carrying no weight with anyone.

Blow off has the man making his escape from the cabin and unwittingly assisting in the capture of the jewel thieves and setting himself right with the girl, the male nurse and everyone else, aboard.

Denny and Lucien Littlefield provide most of the laugh situations the latter as the male nurse, with a dash of lavender in his make-up getting the most out of their parts Otis Harlan and Collette Merton playing the crook parts, also stand out, especially in the conversational sections of the picture. Joseph Henaberry did a good directing job with this one and those who like Denny's comedy will not be disappointed. Star is okay in the talking sequences.

Filming of Golden Eagle

(BRITISH MADE)

Group of motion pictures and stills assembled by Captain C. W. R. Knight. Special engagement at Fifth Ave. Playhouse, N. Y., beginning March 30. Running time, about 83 minutes.

Strictly for non-theatrical bookings. A jerky nature study of birds, the eagle figures only incidentally. Unless accompanied by a lecturer the screen presentation in its present state is meaningless.

Captain Knight is personally appearing at this house. Decided cockney accent makes him difficult to follow at first. As he warms up to the subject arty audiences, characteristically imaginative, are able to conjure up a lot of action and continuity that are not on the screen. Colored slides are numerous, composing no small part of the running time. A lot of footage is wasted in badly photographed camp scenes and waving trees. Here, however, Knight is able to dwell on the constant vigilance necessary to catch the eagle on the roost.

After a lot of slides in color showing the eagle's nest, moving pictures of the same are introduced. The mother feeding its young is casually interesting. A pecking match between a baby male and female who photograph like a couple of light chicks, is graphically amplified by the lecturer who tells of the aggressiveness and strength of femmes in eagleville.

A happier family, however, is dwelt upon. There the brother and sister, already dark feathered when identified, are shown peacefully gobbling food, with intermissions devoted to wing practicing, until they are able to fly. A tamed owl, wild rabbits, insects and falcons are used as fillers.

Just after the picture terminates with the restoring to freedom of a tamed eagle, Knight produces a live bird of the species and carries it through the aisles. The formal presentation of the bird creates quite a stir among the sure-seat audiences, especially for those devotees who are not frequenters to the local zoo. *Waly.*

LINDA

(SOUND)

Gotham release of Mrs. Wallace Reid production. Directed by Mrs. Reid from story by Margaret Prescott Montague. Screen play by Wilfred Ney. Synchronized score and sound effects by Vitaphone. In cast, Warner Baxter, Helen Foster, Noah Beery, Mitchell Lewis, Kate Price. Theme song "Linda." At Lincoln Square, N. Y., first half of week April 1. Running time, 70 minutes.

Nicely put together backwoods story that should get money in the split week and daily changes despite the fact that the flicker has all the evidences of being a quickie. About 12 choruses of the theme song are sung by an off-screen voice.

Story concerns Linda Stillwater (Helen Foster), a dreamy sort of girl who is hungry for better things but is forced by a brutal father to marry an elderly lumberman, Decker (Noah Beery). Though he treats her with kindness, Linda's heart is Dr. Paul Randall's (Warner Baxter).

Faithful to her husband, Linda is in the early stages of motherhood when a scheming woman steps in and breaks up her home. With her baby in good hands, Linda sets out for the city where her former school teacher, now in the money, befriends her. She clicks with her benefactor's friends and is seen stepping in the best circles. Brother of the girl also goes for Linda in a big way but is given the chill. Meeting Dr. Randall, Linda resumes her romance with him. Just as the doc is about to propose Linda tells him all about her marriage and the blow-off. Summoned back to the sticks by a letter from her husband, she returns to nurse him back to health following an accident. Back home she learns that the woman who accused her husband of bigamy lied and Linda sticks until he passes out.

Just all right and while the tune is no hit it's ample for a picture of this type.

THE LAWLESS LEGION

First National production and release, starring Ken Maynard. Directed by Harry J. Brown from story by Bennett Cohen. Adapted by Fred Allen. Photography by Frank Good. At Loew's New York one day, March 29, half of double bill. Running time, 70 minutes.

Bob Stanley..........Ken Maynard
Mary Keiver..........Nora Lane
Ramirez..........Paul Hurst
Flapjack..........Frank Rice
Sheriff Keiver..........Howard Truesdell
Matson..........J. P. McGowan
Tarzan..........Himself

Typical cow country story that has been cut to pattern for Maynard's plain and fancy riding. Tarzan, his horse, gets a chance to display his expert training. Western fans will like it.

Maynard, in love with the sheriff's daughter, is entrusted with the job of driving a huge herd of cattle from a drought-stricken section of Texas to a watering spot near the border. Cattle represents the combined wealth of the community.

An organized band of border cattle rustlers, who have one of their leaders planted in the council of the cattlemen, steal the herd soon after Maynard and his men hit the trail.

Disgraced and spurned by his sweetheart for his apparent neglect of duty, he sets out to recover the cattle. Breaking jail, he makes his way alone into the cattle thieves' domain, learns the secrets of the crooks and finally succeeds in driving the herd back across the border and setting himself right with his girl friend as well as the cattlemen.

Director Brown has packed plenty of action into the screen story, his handling of the sequences in which thousands of head of cattle appear being especially good. Nora Lane as the love interest and Paul Hurst and J. P. McGowan as the menaces are well cast and give creditable performances. Picture is mostly Maynard and Tarzan, and can't miss pleasing in the grind houses.

Livingstone in Africa

(BRITISH MADE)

Produced and written by M. A. Wetherall, with credits also to Butchers Film Service, Ltd., and Hero Film Service, Ltd. Wetherall in title role of Livingstone. At Fifth Ave. Playhouse week beginning March 23. Running time, 60 minutes.

David Livingstone..........M. A. Wetherall
Stanley..........Henry Walton
Mrs. Livingstone..........Molly Rogers
Gordon Bennett..........Reginald Fox

Actionless, drab and draggy, this attempt to bring the biography of Britain's South African explorer to the screen is a decided flop.

Poor lighting prevails throughout a story that depends upon subtitles for climactic points. Roughest kind of editing jumps the thing as if it were a series of post cards in a lantern slide.

Scenes allegedly African have been done so many times before that their occasional repetition here is not only routine, but inferior to predecessors.

With the flock of real animal shots and jungle tramps on the market, this shapes up like a Hollywood indie, and hasn't a chance. Tying this up with Livingstone is an insult to that great explorer's memory. *Waly.*

The Overland Telegraph

M-G-M production and release. Tim McCoy, starred. Adapted by Edward Meagher from story by Ward Wing. Directed by John Waters, Arthur Reed, cameraman. At Loew's New York, one-half double feature, one day, March 19. Running time, 55 minutes.

Captain Allen..........Tim McCoy
Dorothy..........Dorothy Janis
Easy..........Frank Rice
Briggs..........Lawford Davidson
Major Hammond..........Clarence Geldert
Medicine Man..........Chief Big Tree

Regular kintergarten routine of aimless shooting, socking and bumping around in this one. Like in many of its predecessors everything is written around McCoy resulting in little sustained interest, and action in clumps.

McCoy is definitely out on the sex appeal stuff. Tying him up with a pretty girl doesn't go because of the regular mill way in which it is handled. Tim first arrests her and then toward the end of the show her reappearance for the gag of being married via telegraph. Tough gentleman stuff has been used by McCoy many times, except in this one less than usual is seen of the girl, Dorothy Janis.

While the theme offered worthwhile material, obvious script and directorical carelessness reduced it to one of those things. *Waly.*

FIGARO

(FRENCH MADE)

Franco Film, directed by Robert Hurel, under the title of "Figaro," a picture adapted from Beaumarchais' trilogy, "The Barber of Seville," "The Marriage of Figaro" and "The Culprit Wife."

Production supervised by Gaston Ravel, who arranged the scenario. Figaro, a barber in Seville, popular for his superior common sense and strategy as a man of the people, saves the aristocratic Rosine from her guardian, Dr. Barthelo, an avaricious old chap, who wants to wed his ward in order to get hold of her fortune. Figaro, on the contrary, arranges Rosine's marriage with the proud, handsome Count Almaviva, whom she loves. The artful barber then enters their service, and also marries Suzanne, the pretty, cute soubret performing the function of Rosine's chambermaid. Holding such a position in the servants' hall, Figaro is able to watch over both women, and particularly to check his master from being too gallant with Suzanne, as he was wont.

During a long sojourn in Mexico with her husband, Rosine has an amorous adventure with Don Cherubin, her page (another noted character, familiar to literary folks). The idyll terminates with the birth of a child. Ultimately Figaro, assisted by Suzanne, has to save the guilty wife from an adventurer who tries to blackmail her by the possession of a billet doux from her lover Cherubin, now dead, killed at war. Nevertheless Count Almaviva gets wind of the family secret. But having strayed from the straight path of conjugal duty himself many a time, he readily forgives his still charming spouse. Thus we have the three elongated yarns of the early 18th century, classics today, rolled into one for the convenience of the present generation. And it all reads like an up-to-date "best seller."

Acting is creditable. Van Duren, vaudeville dancer, now also in a local revue, plays Figaro. His partner on this occasion is Marie Bell, of the Comedie Francaise. She is cute and dainty as Suzanne. Arlette Marchall as Rosine is refined and patrician; Tony d'Alger correct as Count Almaviva. Entire production is, in fact, satisfactory. Photo work a bit too conventional. "Figaro" is an expensive production. *Light.*

HONEYMOON

M-G-M production and release. Directed by Robert A. Golden from story by Lew Lipton, adapted by E. Richard Shayer. Continuity by George O'Hara. At Loew's New York, one day, March 29, half of double bill. Running time, 50 minutes.

Polly..........Polly Moran
Harry..........Harry Gribbon
Bert..........Bert Roach
Flash..........Himself

Diverting comedy with plenty of slapstick that will amuse the kids and draw its quota of hearty laughs from the grownups who frequent the grind houses. Simple story has Polly (Polly Moran) presented with a police dog (Flash) on her wedding day by Bert (Bert Roach), a disappointed but nonetheless bighearted suitor. Dog is instructed never to let a man lay his hand on his mistress and carries out the order to the limit.

Taken on the honeymoon by the newly married couple he is the cause of all sorts of trouble for the bridegroom, interrupting comedy love making and figuring prominently in the slapstick situations.

Plenty of chases in the story, with the release of a flock of hounds from a dog catcher's wagon and Flash's dash after a snow white cat standing out for laugh getting results in the sequences. Dog succeeds in busting up the honeymoon completely and has the married pair barking at each other on their bridal night. Fade-out has dog in clinch pose with the cat.

Polly Moran and Harry Gribbon handle their comedy characterization, calling for plenty of mugging, in satisfactory style. Robert Hopkin's titles are mainly of the released gag variety.

German Pics

Berlin, March 20.

Primus Palast: "Fraeulein Faehnrich" ("Miss Midshipman"). Young naval cadet looking for amusement is sent by a jocular friend to a girls' school under the impression that he is going to a maison de joie. He falls hard for one of the girls and, in a desire to reform her, takes her to a house of correction from which she, of course, runs away. Later he learns the real truth of the matter and she comes to his ship to prevent his committing suicide. In the leading roles: Mary Parker, Fritz Schulz and Johannes Roth. Average German feature, only possible for the Reich.

Tauentzien Palast: "Verirrte Jugend" ("Misled Youth"). An attempt to follow up the successful series of films about younger generation which have done good business in Germany of late. This is the least interesting and most hoked of the lot. The emotions of the children are very grown up in motivation. Only one type stands out, a little mulatto girl played by El Dura. This young actress has every possibility of developing into a second Anna May Wong if rightly handled. She has plenty of "it" if you like it light brown. Nice easy performances were also turned in by **Rolph von Goth, Martin Herzberg, Dolly Davis and Otto Reinwaldt.**

Capitol: "S. O. S." Carmine Gallone here proves himself a director of a quality not often found in Germany today. He knows how to build up suspense and how to keep tempo always at the bubbling point. Too bad that his scenario breaks up towards the end. Beginning is a splendidly achieved collision at sea with a big liner going down. A husband, newly married, on his honeymoon, meets an old flame and falls for her again. When the ship sinks he and his wife are rescued but each believes the other dead. He is now in Africa and definitely in the net of the vamp. His wife takes a position as clown in a circus and he doesn't recognize her. An insurrection breaks out. He is wounded and the wife saves him. Comes the dawn. Liane Haid as the wife is as flatly pretty as ever, and Alfons Fryland as the husband is also beautiful and little more. Gina Manes is the vamp and with what elegant insistence she winds herself through the canvas. This happens to be a great film actress, even if America is somnolent enough not to recognize it.

Lubitsch's "Patriot," with Emil Jannings, had a splendid reception at its premiere at the Gloria Palast and promises to be one of the biggest, if not the biggest, box office picture of the season. The publicity is being splendidly handled by Parufamet. On the other hand, the Universal feature, "The Man Who Laughed," in spite of its German director, Paul Leni, and German star, Conrad Veldt, had a very lukewarm reception at the Universum. The applause at the premiere was entirely directed at the newly returned Veidt. Bad reports have also come in from out-of-town showings.

"Piccadilly," E. A. Dupont's English-made, also came in for a terrible panning. Arnold Bennett's scenario is slated as one of the worst of the season and Gilda Gray in the lead is roasted to a crisp. Only Anna May Wong and Jameson Thomas get off with credit.

THE DESERT SONG
(MUSICAL-DIALOG)
(Light Opera)
Los Angeles, April 9.

Warner Brothers present the first Vitaphone light opera from music by Sig. Romberg; book by Otto Harbach, Laurence Schwab, Frank Mandel and Oscar Hammerstein 2d; directed by Roy Del Ruth. Scenario adaptation by Harvey Gates. Cameraman, Bernard McGill. Film editor, Ralph Dawson. World premiere at Warner Brothers' theatre, Hollywood, April 8. Running time, 125 minutes.

The Red Shadow	John Boles
Margot	Carlotta King
Susan	Louise Fazenda
Benny Kid	Johnny Arthur
General Bierbeau	Edward Martindale
Pasha	Jack Pratt
Sid El Kar	Robert E. Guzman
Hasse	Otto Hoffman
Clementine	Marie Wells
Paul Fontaine	John Miljan
Eebel	Del Elliott
Azura	Myrna Loy

Singing chorus of 100.

Taking another step forward in the talking field by doing an operetta, following the story in detail and getting in the entire musical score and compositions, Warner Brothers have another box office winner. With the tuneful melodies being warbled throughout the screen version there is little doubt that the music may be more entrancing and seductive from the box office angle than the acting, the stage show did repeat after repeat on account of the tunes. Now, with the excellent synchronization of the tunes and the splendid voices of John Boles and Carlotta King carrying the major melodies, it is not unlikely that repeats will come in on the screen version too.

The story follows the stage script religiously. It is not what might have been accomplished had picture license been taken, to which it would lend itself easily. The only departures from the actual stage scenes are for those scenes narrated in dialog, such as the riding of the Riffs and desert perspectives.

Story started off rather slowly with the unfolding of the identity of the red shadow by himself to his two faithful followers. A bit complicated in the unfolding of the love angles of Pierre as the shadow was known to his family, but straightened itself out after the picture had run for an hour. From then it ran along smoothly and with suspense, displaying a number of gorgeous scenes in which chanting was the principal ingredient.

Through it all there is little of the romantic on the screen as the principal players were chosen more for their voices than for ability to act screen roles. Nevertheless, they carried the story through credibly and got in a few dramatic moments. The most dramatic scene with Martindal and Miss Loy feeling their parts is the general sending the troops to capture his son. Again with the return of Pierre and the lifting of sadness from the father's heart to the "I Love You" song, sung by Boles to Miss King for the finale.

Mr. Boles and Miss King do exceptionally well on the screen and though they may be more convincing on the stage, their conceptions of the film characters are sincere and not flavoring of saccharine. Arthur as Benny Kid exceptional. Aided by Miss Fazenda he supplies the lighter moments. Jack Pratt as the pasha most convincing as well as disclosing a useful baritone voice for the screen. Marie Wells as Clementine, the Harem vamp, did a nifty bit with Guzman and Hoffman also doing okay.

Picture cost nearly $600,000 and though the opening last night had $5 top, looks with starting on second day of grind to be sure fire at the box office.

Work of Del Ruth shows deftness and tact in holding down situations and still telling a coherent and comprehensive story. Recording and photography excellent with color shots, though few, well chosen, especially the one of Boles leading the Riffts across the desert and chanting the love song.

With this new departure in the films looks as though the way has been paved for more of the operettas which can always meet favor in the key centers and the provinces.

"The Desert Song" should be a box office mop up. *Ung.*

ALIBI
(DIALOG)

Roland West production. Distributed by United Artists. Story and dialog by Mr. West and C. Gardner Sullivan, based on play, "Nightstick," by John Wray, J. C. Nugent and Elaine Sterne Carrington. Cameraman, Ray June. Musical score by Hugo Riesenfeld. No featured players. Opening April 8 at 44th Street, New York, at $2 top. Running time, 90 minutes.

No. 1065 (Chick Williams)	Chester Morris
Buck Bachman	Harry Stubbs
Daisy Thomas	Mae Busch
Joan Manning	Eleanor Griffith
Toots	Irma Harrison
Danny McGann	Regis Toomey
Brown	Al Hill
Blake	James Bradbury, Jr.
Soft Malone	Elmer Ballard
Trask	Kiernan Cripps
Pete Manning	Purnell B. Pratt
Tommy Glennon	Pat O'Malley
O'Brien	DeWitt Jennings
Geo. Stanislaus David	Edward Jennings
Singers in Theatre	
	Virginia Flohri, Edward Jardon

Jolt-packed crook melodrama in dialog. Lots of reliable excitement, de luxe production values and general audience satisfaction. Can probably check respectable $2 runs in a few spots, and when arriving in the regular change parlors ought to pile up the kind of grosses other smash melodrams have achieved in last couple of seasons. This is a hit.

From the human interest standpoint picture belongs to Chester Morris, virile stage juvenile. He comes as a welcome variance from the pretty boys. And he can troupe like the old days. In this picture he is a cruel, cold-blooded gangster, quick to let 'em have the works. When he starts to play more sympathetic roles he should develop as a general fav.

"Alibi" starts out to give the cops the losing end of an expository tract on brutality. It winds up by hinting that the gendarmes have to be tough. Morris impersonates a clever young rodent with the instincts of a Chinese brigand. Quick to shoot when his adversary's back is turned, he is a sniveling, groveling, contemptible coward when cornered himself. Without stressing the moral, picture is dedicated to the proposition that the man with a gun is a dirty name to start with —and was born that way.

There are loose ends and desultory passages in "Alibi," but in general it has the tempo of a Missouri breeze and is punched with some gripping sequences. Third degree stuff is pregnant with melodrama. Police atmosphere and detail have realism and the ring of authenticity. Strong climax illustrating the spineless character of the gangster. Cop fires blank cartridges, with the gangster fainting, although untouched and uninjured.

Acting is generally good, with another newcomer, Regis Toomey, attracting attention as a young detective. He is suggestive of James Murray, the ex-usher who for a time was under contract to M-G-M, but Toomey is a far better actor, having been in the legit.

Eleanor Griffith, a blonde, is also a recruit from the speaking stage. Her performance is okay but not distinguished. Her face in animation photographs well, but in repose not as strong as might be.

Pat O'Malley as a quiet-spoken sergeant of detectives, and Purnell B. Pratt both stand out as preferential talent for talkers. Elmer Ballard as a hophead gangster did a fine bit of character work. Irma Harrison was cute in a bit as a cafe entertainer.

Roland West, who finances, produces and directs his own pictures, is the only entirely independent producer releasing through United Artists. He can sleep in peace in the security that his investment is safe and his picture there. *Land.*

HIS CAPTIVE WOMAN

(HALF DIALOG)

First National production and release. Starring Milton Sills with Dorothy Mackaill. Disk recording. Directed by George Fitzmaurice. Story by Donn Byrne, adapted by Carey Wilson. Cameraman, Lee Garmes. At the Central, N. Y., for twice daily run at $2, starting April 2. Running time, 92 minutes.

Officer McCarthy	Milton Sills
Anna Bergen	Dorothy Mackaill
Alstair deVries	Gladden James
Lavoris Smythe	Gertrude Howard
Bobby	Marion Byron
District Attorney	Frank Reicher
Lawyer	George Fawcett
Judge	William Holden
Governor	August Tollaire

Originally this may have been an interesting story, but in the operation of grafting dialog into and onto it First National has so strained, twisted, pummeled and otherwise mistreated plausibility that the resultant product is pretty silly. And the now thoroughly familiar courtroom scene will not qualify as so hot. It's just fair program.

Milton Sills does not enter until the unspooling has been continuous for 30 minutes. Dorothy Mackaill seated mute and dumb in the prisoner's box has been triple damned by a series of witnesses. She is described as a common boulevard promenader who murdered in a jealous rage the wealthy man who had picked her up and for a time fondled her in luxury. Things look bad for her. Then into the picture and onto the witness stand comes trusty Milton. Does he prove by testimony that Dorothy did not kill Reginald Moneybags? He does not. He tells in his own simple way the immaterial and irrelevant story of how he arrested the prisoner. He wrings the jury's heart and makes a dribbling Pollyanna out of a hard-boiled New York judge by explaining step by step the spiritual transformation that took place in the spotty character of the murderess as he and she lived together happily, shipwrecked for several years upon a deserted island in the south Pacific.

Things happened to Dorothy's soul on that island. This is made very definite. Her wanton ways slip from her and she becomes as a lamb. In the course of time Milton takes to wife the reformed killer at whose trial he is now testifying.

And what does the New York judge do but snap his fingers at the law and the bar association, lay himself open to impeachment, and tell the murderess to go free and murder no more, peacefully happy on her island with her policeman.

Action alternates between dialog in the courtroom and silent passages explaining and amplifying the testimony. Scenes in the south seas are good, both as to photography—unusually effective—and drama. Donn Byrne, recently deceased Irish writer, was a much better craftsman than superficial judgment of his story as brought to the screen would indicate. There is elemental and dramatic conflict between the personalities of the hard-to-get woman avoiding policeman sent to arrest the dame that always got her man. She plays a hundred tricks, including disrobing before him and swimming in the nude. Her wiles avail nothing. He's made of tougher fiber than she is. Time and the quiet beauty of her surroundings wear down her flippancy. She becomes soul sick, doubtful, filled with fears. All this is human, reasonable and well-told narrative.

Miss Mackaill does good work, but in the courtroom is made to seem pretty stupid in being the only character who fails to speak. She does gurgle a few hallelujahs at her exoneration, but it's too late to remove the impression that she's silent because she has to be.

Sills talks well enough, even with a 10th avenue brogue. His trouping in silent portions also strong. Looked a little peaked.

Banality of the dialog parts messes what might have been something. Skillful handling by George Fitzmaurice saves some of the more transparent absurdities, and general production is of high type, with exceptions noted. Many people will be in the proper frame of mind to pronounce "His Captive Woman," from soup to toothpicks, delicious. Which is intended to convey the picture's rating: Moderate with reservations. *Land.*

THE SHAKEDOWN

(HALF DIALOG)

Universal production and release. James Murray and Barbara Kent featured. William Wyler production, directed by Mr. Wyler, from story by Charles A. Logue. Adapted by Clarence Marks. Titles by Albert De Mond. Joseph Cherniavsky did the musical synchronization and C. Roy Hunter is credited for recording supervision. Balance of cast includes George Kotsanoras, Wheeler Oakman, Jack Hanlon and Harry Gribbon. Ran 70 minutes, U's Colony, New York, week April 6.

A not bad 50 per cent. talker—the rest sound synchronized, musically and effects—with a tough little Irish youngster, Jack Handlon, as the unofficial star. If he handles the dialog as apparently he genuinely does he'll be plenty in demand for kid parts. James Murray, once touted as a good Paramount bet, is also destined for renewed importance because of his linguistic accomplishments. Barbara Kent, the heart interest, just looks nice and says little. It's a good release and merits some good bookings.

But this one looks like a quickie among talkers although there's no palpable cheating because it's that kind of a he-man story that calls for little production investiture. The femme interest revolves about the salvation of the street urchin whom Murray as a fake pugilist adopts as a prop for public sympathy purposes in order to heighten neighborly interest in his forthcoming fracas with a pug, subtly labeled Kid Roff.

George Kotsanaros plays the vain Greek battler well. Wheeler Oakman as manager of the outfit is sleek in his assignment of building up pseudo-battles between the planted local talent (Murray) and the barnstorming Kid Roff who offers $1,000 prize to any contender who stays four rounds with him.

Oakman, as the manager, has it primed for a grand killing in the oil boom town of Boonton when Murray is spotted as a driller. The inevitable complications with the heroine and the inspiration to go straight leads to the grand fisticuffs for the finale. Instead of the Shero rushing down to ringside and morally bolstering waning courage and unwilling flesh, the kid is the heart-stuff appeal, and it's done rather plausibly.

There will be some captiousness concerning the untrained battler besting the behemoth Kid Roff. A bit of plausibility could have been injected at the expense of the blonde doll who's part of the Kid's scenery. An inserted title that because of the continuous set-ups and the assured frame the pug was as below par as the hero was physically handicapped might have lent a somewhat realistic touch to it. However, as one would expect, he manages to kayo the Greek leather-pusher and thus saves his honor, his fellow townmen's dough, his gal, his country and his Yale. Of course, until the telling kayo, our hero is shown taking more falls than a cataract, but somehow comes up smiling where Kid Ruff keels over almost at the first healthy clip.

The fight scene is the big punch. There's a prelim fight staged in the second reel to illustrate the racket, the meeting later on, the count-up and the pay-off.

The juvenile attachment between the street urchin and the phoney hero who proves a real hero in a railroad track rescue is pretty well developed. A good touch is injected when Murray looks around and regrets no one viewed his heroism, he counting on the local sentiment as part of the build-up.

Universal has a good partial talker in "The Shakedown." The vigorous title is a bit misleading in its import for the "shakedown" in the argot is by no means synonymous with a "frame-up," which is what this racket actually is. *Abel.*

COQUETTE

(ALL DIALOG)

United Artists production and release. Starring Mary Pickford. Sounded by W. E. system on disks. Adapted by John Grey and Allen McNeil from the stage play of the same name. Directed by Sam Taylor, with additional dialog also credited to him. Assistant dramatic director, Earle Browne, with Karl Struss, photographer. At the Rivoli, New York, for grind run, starting April 6, after reserved seat premiere previous night. Running time, 75 minutes.

Norma Besant	Mary Pickford
Michael Jeffery	Johnny Mack Brown
Stanley Wentworth	Matt Moore
Dr. John Besant	John Sainpolis
Jimmy Besant	William Janney
Jasper Carter	Henry Kolker
Robert Wentworth	George Irving
Julia	Louise Beavers

"Coquette" ought to get plenty in the program houses. It's Mary; she talks and she looks different with the new bob. Film is down to program length, 75 minutes, and that's just what it is, a good program picture. Not great, because the kick is out to satisfy the censors.

Father kills himself in this version after being satisfied that his girl is still pure. Picture seems just strong enough to arouse femme witnessers to the verge of tears, but is without the pathos strength to make the emotions spill over. And that's "Coquette" as a picture.

But at least it is a picture. Sam Taylor, directing, has taken his screen license to insert plenty of scenes which were impossible in the show. The difference, however, isn't sufficient to give it equal rating with the play on a dramatic basis. It neither grasps nor holds the imagination as did the play for three pretty fair reasons—cast, change in story and a repeated tendency to become too talkie and motionless. On the other hand, it has a '29 Miss Pickford who is strictly okay for dialog, and a theme song which is not in the film but may help on the outside. Between the two there isn't much that's going to stop "Coquette" from enjoying solid weeks. Whether it can stand up on holdover tries rest with how strong they go for Mary, not the picture.

Feature got a terrible opening night break when a fuse blew. After a two-minute start it had to be shut off for a second beginning. And even then the amplification didn't sound right.

Advance reports, not from U. A., heralded the recording of this picture and Miss Pickford's voice as outstanding. In lieu of the trouble between booth and horns, there's no true telling on this showing. So it's only fair to give the picture the best of it, and there's no doubt that the disks demonstrated spasmodic instances of fine recording. On the other hand, certain passages had the male voices normal and Miss Pickford's very weak, implying a lapse in monitor room control.

If further showings fail to substantiate the early sound reports, it simply emphasizes the wide difference between projection room and auditorium showings plus the fallacy of building up a picture too big by word-of-mouth before it opens. Many a stage show has suffered from the same overenthusiasm. There isn't a smart Broadway producer who wouldn't rather have skeptical hearsay precede his opera into town.

Miss Pickford gives an excellent performance of the little southern flirt who throws her home into a turmoil which ends in tragedy. If it lacks the depth and understanding which Helen Hayes gave the role on the stage, it is no less sincere, while the difference may possibly be explained by direction and a limitation in story for this medium. So those who contend that the screen is unlimited have forgotten the censors. But Miss Pickford is an ideal screen "Coquette," both playing and looking the role for full screen worth.

Not so with others in the cast. Johnny Mack Brown lacks the maturity, power and unction which Michael, the low-born town ne'er-do-well, needs but has that necessary screen asset, appearance. For New York he's wrong. For Des Moines he may be right. There's a chasm between the average legit and film patron, a factor the studios know all about. And so they've "written down" this play—rightly for the box-office and the censors—because they must write down in pictures. And in this case they've also "cast down."

John Sainpolis, with legit experience behind him, runs next to Miss Pickford for mention as the honor-defending father who shoots Michael in defense of the family name. Remainder of the support is but average at best, with Matt Moore woefully out of place.

Additional scenes which were not in the stage script are noteworthy for an even trend in dialog, regardless of what may be thought of the absence of soft-spoken southern drawls by support characters. Miss Pickford's high spot appears to be her solo work at the cot of Michael before and after he dies. The scene where Norma and Michael become so absorbed in dual parlor conversation that they forget to turn on the lights when it grows dark, is repeated in the picture minus a hint of the cause for the dimming. Those who have seen the play will immediately recall the inference, but there were many in this audience who thought there was something the matter with the projection machine as the studio lights slowly faded. Taylor could have made this more explicit, as it remains a pretty scene.

Not much comedy in the picture, the character of the silly girl whom Norma wishes on Stanley, to get rid of him, being eliminated here. Hence the laugh responsibilities fall upon the younger brother, played by William Janney, who in no way approaches the portrayal of young Andrew Lawlor on the stage. Taylor's best handling of Janney is in a country club sequence where the kids cut in and closely duplicate the dancing of a prep school and college contingent.

Miss Pickford's performance and name will carry "Coquette," the inadequacies in support simply stressing the star's work. One woman's exiting lobby comment was: "Well, after spending an entire night with a man in a cabin, Mary Pickford is still America's sweetheart."

A notice on Mary Pickford in her first talker would not be complete without a personal comment. Miss Pickford's screen career stands without parallel, in any way, in every way. For longevity, for stardom, for cleanliness and for the promotion of the American film industry. What Jolson did for the talkers, Miss Pickford did for the pioneer silents.

And now and with the years, and after Miss Pickford has had her hair cut, and after she has professionally lived almost triple the logical years one girl screen star could or has lived, here she is all over again, in dialog and a play calling for more maturity of character than Miss Pickford has been associated with in the past.

Mary Pickford is not new to dialog or stage training. For there was, if nothing else, her "A Good Little Devil," a Belasco '13 production, after which Miss Pickford hopped from the stage to keep early picture patrons asking, "When is that little girl with the curls coming back?" *Sid.*

SYNCOPATION

(DIALOG)

Radio Pictures (R-K-O) production and release. Recorded by RCA Photophone; 100 per cent dialog, on sound tract (film). Starring Fred Waring's Pennsylvanians (band). Bert Glennon, director. Story and dialog by Gene Markey, adapted by Frances Agnew from Markey's "Stepping High." Bert Harrison, dialog director; Tommy Cummings, sound director. At Hippodrome (presentations), New York (grind), beginning week April 6. Running time, 83 minutes.

Flo........................Barbara Bennett
Benny........................Bobby Watson
Lew........................Morton Downey
Winston........................Ian Hunter
Peggy........................Dorothy Lee
Hummel........................Osgood Perkins
Rita........................Verree Teasdale
Henry........................McKenzie Ward

This is a box office picture, simply because it has a name to exploit in Fred Waring's Pennsylvanians. In the picture there is little else besides the 100 per cent talk classification that would stand exploitation, except the songs and flip remarks, mostly done by Morton Downey.

As a story picture it isn't so good, as the tale is the usual one nowadays of the film musical comedies.

Waring's Pennsylvanians are starred in "Syncopation," with their name above that of the film. Yet they do not enter into the story for a moment and have not been made any too prominent on the musical end. The band is seen twice, both times as the dance band in a nite club and for perhaps 20 minutes all told. And unless they are playing the score throughout while unseen, which is plausible, the two cafe shots, involving seven band numbers, are the extent of the Warings' performance.

The star of the picture, were performance naming the star, is Downey. It's his first picture. In "Syncopation" Downey, as a tin pan alleyite, is singing most of the time, and singing has been Morton's trade for a long time. A good singer here is generally a good singer there, and because he has plenty of opportunity to sing in a picture, besides the wise cracks, he is the picture's natural standout.

Bobby Watson and Barbara Bennett as the principals were miscast, Miss Bennett more so than Watson.

Watson, off the screen, is a Shubert juvenile in musical shows. In "Syncopation" he is the male half of a ballroom adagio team. Watson looks as much like a leaper and lifter as a villain, and he doesn't look like either.

Osgood Perkins, the best actor, for acting, in the cast and possessing the single legit reputation, is blanketed under an exaggerated character of a vaude agent. Ian Hunter plays the polite threat with restraint, never less than gentlemanly in his advances toward the other guy's wife.

Perkins supplies part of the comedy relief. More is contributed by McKenzie Ward as a nance interior decorator, partner of the stately and comely Verree Teasdale, while Downey kicks in with still more through cracks to a dumbdora sweetheart (Dorothy Lee). When Downey finally marries the gal at the finish he concludes the picture with "Now I can stop worrying about house detectives," which can't miss as a laugh or a blush, probably the latter. Laughs are plentiful throughout.

Story is a slight departure from "Excess Baggage," retelling the trials of a mixed smalley turn. As in "Baggage," the feminine portion of Sloane and Darrell grows tired of the grind and falls for society, also the guy who steers her into society; so she blows her husband partner for the villain, and he can't work without her or she without him, so they're back in a clinch and ready to open on the morrow—together. If not "Baggage," then "Show Folks."

Recording job average, though the tone and clarity might depend as much on the theatre, and probably that's it here. Hippodrome, with its many echoes, carried it fairly well.

This is RKO's first musical talker, started some time ago when talking was even younger than now. So that much more credit goes to those mostly concerned, Robert Kane, who cast and supervised, and Bert Glennon, the director.

It's drawing at the Hip, doing capacity all day Saturday, and holding up Sunday despite the heat. As a musical talker it should draw all over, not only because of the Warings, but because it is an enjoyable picture. *Bige.*

Passion of Joan of Arc

(FRENCH MADE)

Produced by the Societe Generale des Films, distributed by M. J. Gourland. Directed by Carl T. Dreyer from the scenario by Carl Dreyer and Joseph Delteil. Photography by Rudolph Mate and Kotula. At the Little Carnegie Playhouse, New York, (sure seater) week March 30. Running time, 85 minutes. Held over week April 6.

Joan of Arc........................Falconetti
L'Eveque Cauchon........................Silvain
Coysleur........................M. Schutz
Jean Besupere........................Ravet
Jean d'Estivet........................Andre Berly
Massieu........................Antonin Artaud

This "Passion of Joan of Arc" isn't worth a dollar to any commercial regular picture theatre in the U. S. Unless the theatre is willing to rely upon the deceptive "Passion" of the title which is meaningless on the screen. If there is a field for this over here other than in some of the sure seaters, it is in the French Canadian districts or the French colonies in large cities of the U. S. The only French colony of any account is right in New York. Perhaps that is why "Jean" was held over a second week at the Little Carnegie Playhouse, or it may have been the rental inducement.

Extracts of reviews of this French made film, reprinted in the Carnegie program, are so utterly extravagant in phrasing, presuming the critics on the New York dailies write for the information of their readers, that it seems a pity picture critics in an endeavor to pose as art reviewers of the screen should have gone so far. If nothing else!

Here is a deadly tiresome picture made for the country where its idol is still a legend, merely making an attempt to historically screen narrate without sound or dialog an allegedly written recorded trial in the 15th or 16th century of Joan of Arc for witchery, this leading to her condemnation and burning at the stake.

One grows terribly weary of seeing her judges reappear, of the long series of captioned questions and answers, of Joan double crossed and of Joan doing a long distance burning sequence, with the French mobs in glimpses as inserts. Totally a cheaply economical film as a product.

In offsets there is some photographic value through the continuous allure of whole screen front closeups, of faces only, and in the exquisite makeups, mostly of the hard visaged elderly men in cloistered costumes. They look like stone images brought to life.

But they are always the same and ever in view, with the saving grace in appearance Joan, at all times immobile in countenance and always staring into the camera when she isn't washing tears off her face. Joan has quite a scheme in tear making; it's much better than glycerine.

Through the raves by the daily picture critics of New York or some of them, two Variety reporters have seen this film at Carnegie. Both agree in this opinion; that it has no value of any account whatsoever for the picture houses of the States. *Sime.*

GERMAN FILMS

Berlin, March 24.

"Hotel Mysteries"

Primus Palast.—"Hotelgeheimnisse" ("Hotel Mysteries") (Derussa Film). One of the best German films of season. Has suspense and humor. A young girl, companion of a countess, is wrongly sentenced to prison for stealing jewels. Released she becomes a thief in reality and, posing as royalty, gets away with a big swag of jewels. District attorney, instrumental in sending her up, has fallen in love with her even though he recognizes her real identity and this time he saves her from conviction.

Discreetly directed by Friedrich Feher. Magda Sonya in the lead is not much to look at but can act. Rest of a well handled cast included Gertrud Eysoldt, Wolfgang Zilzer and Livio Pavanelli.

"Diary of a Cocotte"

Kurfuerstendamm Theater.—"Tagebuch einer Kokette" ("Diary of a Cocotte"). Ridiculous old story about a girl who has the usual bad luck to be "forced" into the oldest profession. A young man who seduces her must leave hurriedly for America and requests his uncle, rich business man, to take care of the girl. He does nothing for her. She goes to him to demand an explanation and is about to bean him when he thoughtfully dies of heart failure.

So it all comes out in court what kind of a girl she is. She tries to commit suicide but is saved by a doctor who insists upon marrying her. Not too badly directed by Constantin J. David with minor roles well taken by L. Stahl Nachbaur, Mary Kid and Matthias Wiemann. Fee Malten and Fred Doederlein in the leads have nothing individual to offer but may develop. Will get by here on its title but all wet for America.

"Miss Else"

Capitol Theater.—"Fräulein Else" ("Miss Else") (Poetic Film). Anything that Elisabeth Bergner plays in is sure to do business in Germany. Outside of her salary this picture can't have cost much and will turn in a nice profit. This actress's quality which gets over so superbly on the stage has not yet been captured for the screen. Too bad, for the scenario in itself has possibilities for distribution in the States. It is taken from a masterly short story by Arthur Schnitzler. An innocent young girl vacationing in Switzerland is wired by her parents that they are on the verge of bankruptcy and she must borrow money from a rich banker staying at the same hotel with her. He demands that she come to his bedroom that night.

Unable to stand the idea of giving herself to him she takes a deadly dose of veronal before going and when she at last finds him is on the verge of death.

These last moments are among the strongest seen in a German film for some time and help one to forget many of the long drawn-out and padded scenes of the beginning. These were the result of a mistaken effort to allow nobody else any part in the picture. Only the lately deceased Albert Steinruck has some moments as the brutal banker.

Interesting for the sure seaters but doubtful for general distribution in the States.

"The Circus Princess"

Primus-Palast.—"Die Zirkus Prinzessin" ("The Circus Princess") (Agfa). Taken from the story of Kalmann's operetta, it is little suited to pictures. It was old-fashioned as a stage plot and is twice as musty when viewed on the screen. One would suppose that the public would at last get tired of these ridiculous concoctions about bogus royalty. But the personal popularity of Harry Liedtke in the lead will undoubtedly make it a business proposition. **He could even play Hamlet and get away with it. Direction of Victor Janson is routine and nothing else.**

"Melody of the World"

(Sound)

Terra Theater.—"Melodie der Welt" ("Melody of the World") (Tobis). Announced as the first German feature length sound film. Expectations were raised high—the disappointment was all the greater. It is really nothing but a travelog with a few sound effects. Ruttmann, who was responsible for the effective "Berlin" picture, flopped badly here. Hamburg-American Line, which evidently paid him to crank the film as an advertisement, will not get much return from its investment. "Berlin" viewpoint is merely repeated without any new angles. On the whole a boring evening. A pity to waste the splendid Russian actor Kowal Samborski and Renee Stobrawa on the puppet roles of a sailor and his sweetheart. If this is really the best that the Tobis can turn out in the way of sound it had better take a year off for experiments. At this rate, the talker will be killed in Germany before it gets started.

"The Midnight-Taxi"

Kammer-Lichtspiele.—"Die Mitternachtstaxi" ("The Midnight Taxi") (D. L. S.), Harry Piel, first of the stunt performers in Germany, has at last decided to take the black make-up off his eye and get somebody human to write a story for him. He is just beginning to realize that the days of the "Perils of Pauline" are over.

Judged from an international angle his work is not so hot, but his name still carries enough weight to get the film by. It contains one amusing idea: A student, in order to earn his way through college, drives at midnight an old wreck of a taxi which no one would think of engaging at any other time of day. He gets mixed up in the usual exciting adventures and finally is set to marry the heroine, charmingly played by Betty Bird, who is on the upgrade.

"Money, Money, Money"

Universum.—"Geld Geld, Geld" ("Money, Money, Money") (Cineromans). Although taken in France, two of the leading roles are played by Germans and the financing was on a joint basis. It looks like a good financial proposition for the continent and might do something in America if rightly handled.

It is founded on Emil Zola's famous novel, "L'Argent," and presses the story into a usable, not overloaded scenario.

Saccard, a get-rich-quick who has made a fortune on the exchange, is beaten by his aristocratic an subtler rival, Gundermann, who at length gets him put in jail.

Charming love between Hamelin and his wife Liane, who are mixed up in Saccard's transactions, but in the end escape.

Marcel L'Herbier again proves that he is one of the best directors on the Continent, indeed a master who needs fear no comparison with any of the boys in Hollywood today. That this picture is not up to his splendid "Therese Raquin" is chiefly the fault of the subject-matter.

Superb performance is turned in by Pierre Alcover as Saccard, and Alfred Abel makes every use of his opportunity as his protagonist. Brigitte Helm develops the usual amount of "it" in a vamp part, and Mary Glory and Henry Victor are satisfactory as the lovers.

"The Virgin Cocotte"

Marmorhaus.—"Die keusche Kokotte" ("The Virgin Cocotte") (Bayerische-Emelka). The second film this week that has the brilliant idea of using the word "cocotte" in its title to draw them in. This time entirely without justification, as it is a silly little story about a business man who, in order to stop his wife from flirting, engages a manicure girl to travel with him to Switzerland as his supposed mistress. Wife falls for the bait and soon appears on the scene, developing the usual jealousy.

Competently enough played under the direction of Franz Seitz, but Otto Gebuehr, who acts the business man, will never be able to forget the years when he as Frederick the Great was the most popular German film actor.

"Pori"

Ufa Pavillon.—"Pori" (Ufa). Germany loves these kind of camouflaged travelogs, and the film will undoubtedly do splendid business all through central Europe. There are some extremely interesting shots of scenery and animals, and the sultry atmosphere of the Sudan in South Africa is caught. For instance: the killing of a zebra by a lion; he goes off after having eaten his fill, and the rest of the carcass is immediately cleaned by a swarm of vultures.

Attempt to put a story was unsuccessful, as either the native actors chosen had no talent or the director had no ability to bring it out. The expedition was led by von Gontard and Herbert Kluge.

"Asphalt"

Ufa Palast am Zoo.—"Asphalt" (Erich Pommer Production for Ufa). Title has little to do with the story. it is merely to illustrate the introduction of the young traffic policeman, Holkk. Off duty, he is called upon to take to the police station a young girl who has been caught stealing jewels. She gets him to take her home instead, and spends the night there. But he is caught there by the girl's lover, whom he kills in self-defense.

Things look black for him until the girl confesses that her keeper was a well-known crook and that the boy had killed him in self-defense. To do this she had to expose her share in the crook's dealings and goes to prison.

Policeman is played by Gustav Froehlich, well enough suited to this type of role, but grimaces too much. Betty Amman, who played the girl, is a newcomer with good looks and figure but no individuality as yet. Pommer will have to do better to keep up his reputation.

Trask.

MOTHER'S BOY

(ALL DIALOG)

New London, Conn., April 16.

Pathe production and release. Produced by Robert Kane. Directed by Bradley Barker. Story and dialog by Gene Markey. Dialog staged by James Semour. Cameramen, Phillip Tannura, Harry Stradling and Walter Strenge. Recorder, V. S. Ashdown. Sets by Clark Robinson. R.C.A. Photophone. At Garden theatre, New London, Conn., April 15. Running time, 82 mins.

Pa O'Day....................John T. Doyle
Ma O'Day....................Beryl Mercer
Tommy O'Day....................Morton Downey
Harry O'Day....................Brian Donlevy
Rose....................Helen Chandler
Press Agent....................Lorin Raker
Cafe Manager....................Robert Gleckler
Debutante....................Barbara Bennett
Professor....................Osgood Perkins

Minimum of story and maximum of Irish-American song and sentiment. Net result, good audience picture. Might sneak by at $2 in a couple of the big stands, but essentially for the programmers, with special rating in that class.

Production fundamentals, sound recording, lighting, photography and development of narrative all represent nice work. Plenty and good close-ups, clear and sustained volume.

"Mother's Boy" is Morton Downey's picture in more ways than one. He not only has the lithographs all to himself, but the story, most of the footage and all of the highlights. No matinee idol ever dominated a production more than he does. Yet, with it all, he looks, acts and sings great. If he keeps that natural boyish way, those Irish dimples and cute tricks of personality, he may easily become the Chauncey Olcott of the talking screen.

Plot is simple yet manages to avoid triteness. An Irish lad leaves home accused by his father of stealing money from the family sugar bowl. He becomes famous as a singer in a night club. On the evening he is to open in a $6.60 stage show, he walks out because his mother is ill. He thinks he has ruined his career, his manager having said if he blows the premiere he will never get another job on Broadway. Clever press agent turns incident into an asset through playing up sentimental devoted son angle. As a result mother's boy finds his salary doubled over night.

Downey sings early and often. He starts his caroling in the kitchen (conveniently provided with a piano), warbles as he rushes groceries for the neighborhood delicatessen, vibrates the thorax in a Bowery mission, does his stuff for the swanky social work, and when the picture ends he is still singing.

Bud Green and Sammy Stept composed some tunes to fit the script. They do not impress as hit numbers although pleasant and agreeable and carrying out the shamrock idea.

Night club show presented at length while plot is forgotten, has Ruth Hunt, radio singer, Ruthie Mahon, jazz dancer, and an Argentine tango duo of ultra quality (reviewer muffed name verbally announced by Downey acting as m.c.). Sound effects and authentic cafe atmosphere should pack a thrill for Main Street.

For human interest, too, should be mentioned scene in Bowery mission with genuine types hired from the streets by Pathe. Also a grin is the Third Ward smoker when all the good, fat Tammanyites foregather in honor of Alderman McGillicutty. This suggests Harrigan and Hart stuff may yet be revived for talkers.

Beryl Mercer, no stranger to films although new to talkers, plays the mother, as sentimentalized as a florist's advertisement. Barbara Bennett appears late and transiently as a society debbie who patronizes the Irish lad. She photographed and sounded much better than in "Syncopation."

Helen Chandler, legit ingenue, is a pretty and plausible tenement sweetheart. She doesn't show so well in some shots but in others, notably in profile, registers excellently. The dialog confirms her dramatic experience.

Sets are fairly numerous and look good. Dialog is natural throughout with everyday conversational tempo maintained, thereby avoiding audience strain where players are over-punctilious.

"Mother's Boy" is compounded from sure-fire sentimental hokum. Should appeal to average American audience and with double strength for the Kellys and Callahans.

Land.

THE DUKE STEPS OUT

(SOUND)

Metro-Goldwyn-Mayer production and release Starring William Haines, featuring Joan Crawford and underlining Karl Dane. Synchronized score and effects on film. Directed by James Cruze and adapted from a Lucian Cary story. Titles by Joe Farnham, with Ira Morgan cameraman. At the Capitol, N. Y., week of April 13. Running time, 62 mins.

Duke....................William Haines
Susie....................Joan Crawford
Barney....................Karl Dane
Jake....................Tenen Holtz
Tommy Wells....................Eddie Nugent
Poison Kerrigan....................Jack Roper
Bossy Edwards....................Delmer Daves
Professor Widdicomb....................Luke Cosgrave
Mr. Corbin....................Herbert Prior

Nice program fare, with the name combo of Haines and Crawford figuring sufficient added inducement to shove this film a little past average grosses in the big houses. It's a college prize fight yarn, Haines being the under cover student-pug. Holds some excellent ring sound effects transposed from the sound news roar of football mobs.

Opening shot is of a football game, but brief and simply to plant the locale of the wealthy young fighter, out to convince his dad he can make good. Haines, as Duke, on board a train gets mixed up in the victory celebration, and after one look at the prize co-ed (Miss Crawford) decides to go back to school. Following action is the star's familiar fresh comedy courtship, with a frosh dance and a barroom slugfest thrown in to help it along. Finish is the championship fight showing Haines much spattered by gore and almost out, but finally reaching the button to win. Descriptive radio announcement is inserted to view the collegians and the girl listening in with the news story on Duke being a wealthy undergraduate breaking via the ether. Just a light laugh picture having a hit and run story and a throw back to the old days in that Farnham's crisp titles draw giggles and as an important aid.

For Haines it's his usual routine and there's not much doubt he's the screen's top disciple of juvenile egotism. However, what this picture will do for Miss Crawford is questionable, because she has nothing to do but walk through. Following "Dancing Daughters," this girl looked to be well on her way, and the impetus of that one is what makes the dual names of Haines and Crawford for this feature so strong. But the sidewalk Don Juans and kitchen Cleos are going to be disappointed with their Joan. She doesn't even get much chance to predominate on looks, which isn't going to do her any good when they expect and don't find. It's a reverse step for Miss Crawford, and she'll have to make up on the next one if she's going anywhere in a fast moving field that's now moving faster.

Dane and Tenen Holtz are cast as Haines' prize ring handlers, the latter doing the manager distraught because of his gentleman battler's love affairs. Jack Roper is the ring opponent and other members are minor.

Cruze evidently sailed through in directing and has got it down so there's no superfluous footage. It gets over the ground by means of enough laughs to make it an entertaining hour, while the title, as in other cases, disguises the fight angle so that it won't hurt matinees too much. Settings and camera work are standard, Morgan getting an especially fine fake on a long shot of the ring in the crowded arena. Accompanying music carries a snatch of a lyric that doesn't mean much, and at this house the picture opened and closed showing Mendoza leading the Capitol orchestra through the score for the film, not sychronized in either case. Fair enough for the orchestra's home site but meaningless away, unless they want to show 'em big orchestras are scoring their screen playlets. *Sid.*

HOLE IN THE WALL

(ALL DIALOG)

Paramount 100 per cent talker, featuring Claudette Colbert and Edward B. Robinson in Fred Jackson's play. Adapted by Pierre Collings. Directed by Robert Florey. Titles by Morton Blumenstock. Produced by Monta Bell at the Long Island studios. Runs 65 minutes at the Paramount, New York, week of April 13.

Jean Oliver....................Claudette Colbert
The Fox....................Edward G. Robinson
Mme. Mystera....................Nelly Savage
Goofy....................Donald Meek
Jim....................Alan Brooks
Mrs. Ramsay....................Louise Closser Hale
Marcia....................Marcia Kagno
Dogface....................Barry Macollum
Inspector....................George McQuarrie
Mrs. Lyons....................Helen Crane

A good mystery meller, okay as a program release and insured as to its 100 per cent qualifications as a 100 per cent talker through a 100 per cent legit cast. Not only the principals, such as Claudette Colbert, Edward G. Robinson (now the star of "The Kibitzer") and Louise Closser Hale, but the balance of the support is virtually a dramatic troupe transplanted to the screen. No going wrong that way as far as the dramatics are concerned.

Almost nine years ago to the day this Fred Jackson play was produced at the Punch and Judy theatre in New York, and while the then chief shortcoming was that the reporter-hero was pretty much of an impossible character, the intervening years has seen the elimination of that type of role to such a degree that his reintroduction becomes almost plausible. Furthermore, direction has taken care of that detail.

Direction and adaptation also has cleverly dwelt on the chicanery and double-dealing of the spiritualism racket to stress its fake and take, although the climax introduces what is represented as a legitimate spiritualistic message when, through the femme medium, a man's voice materializes with instructions where to find the kidnapped child, who is imperiled at the docks from a fast-rising tide. This should be enough to square it for the crystal addicts, besides which it is the real dramatic punch of the picture.

The gimmick, with the electrically worked coded transmissions, and the rest of the props and the layout, is a good inside on the racket, broadly sweeping the situation and yet with enough detail and thoroughness for the necessary authenticity.

The compromise, with the climaxing introduction of a real spirit communication from a dead man, may be dismissed, at its worst, as theatrical license. Anyway, it serves the excellent purpose of saving the sympathetic girl-child, Marcia, and effecting the clinch between the wrong Jean Oliver (Miss Colbert) and the reporter (for some strange reason not programed).

Miss Colbert experiences the same difficulty which has confronted her in her stage career, lack of a sufficiently sturdy vehicle. She is difficult to write for, not having had a good stage assignment since "The Barker." Hence here she is but passably satisfying, although doing her average assignment quite well. Edward G. Robinson as the sinister "Fox" gives better account through shading his "master mind crook" with a thoroughly sympathetic touch.

Even the concluding heroics, when he extracts two conditions from the inspector, are plausible. He holds out for the girl's freedom and forces a confession from the dowager who had originally framed her on a grand larceny charge which resulted in a four years' stretch. He makes no bid for self-immunity. For once the player's own sense of proportions and the director's judgment governed them aright in toning all this down and allowing average intelligence to grasp whatever import the Fox's self-assured statement had when he casually remarked that they had nothing on him.

"The Hole in the Wall" refers to the layout of Mme. Mystera. Usual spook stuff, sliding panels, mysteriously reflecting mirrors and the like are part of the props.

Plenty of action throughout—physical effects and dramatic. Big punch right off is the elevated train wreck. Most of it thereafter is in the spiritualistic stronghold, switching back and forth to the inspector's office. A gruesome flash of the morgue, with a corpse tilted forward for identification, is a realistic touch if nothing else.

Paramount has a good program release in this 100 per cent talker. They'll like it on the whole, balancing its mystery and melodramatic elements with enough romance and not a little heart stuff (via the kidnapped kidlet) to appeal generally.

Abel.

Thru Different Eyes

(ALL DIALOG)

Fox production and release. Directed by John Blystone. From the play by Milton E. Gropper and Edna Sherry. Mary Duncan, Warner Baxter and Edmund Lowe featured. Cameraman, Ernest Palmer. Dialog credited to Tom Barry and Gropper. At the Roxy, N. Y., week of April 13. Running time, 67 minutes.

Viola Manning	Mary Duncan
Harvey Manning	Edmund Lowe
Jack Winfield	Warner Baxter
Frances Thornton	Natalie Moorhead
Howard Thornton	Earle Foxe
Spencer	Donald Gallaher
Myrtle	Florence Lake
Valerie Briand	Sylvia Sidney
District Attorney	Purnell Pratt
Defense Attorney	Felmer Jackson
Anna	Dolores Johnson
Maynard	Nigel de Brulier
Maid	Lola Salvi
Janitor	Stepin Fetchit
Paducah	DeWitt Jennings
Crane	Arthur Stone
Traynor	George Lamont
Aline Craig	Natalie Warfield
First Reporter	Jack Jordan
Second Reporter	Marian Spitzer
Third Reporter	Stan Blystone
Fourth Reporter	Stuart Erwin

A gripping bit of hoke drama that nails attention early and never lets it go. An almost perfect example of terse, economical sound screen exposition. Several spicy episodes that ought to cause talk but still censor proof. A better than average box-office release and among the best of the all-dialog pictures in the quality of the talk registering and reproductions.

Like practically all the dialog films so far, this one follows the play in detail. Its force comes from a dramatic trick of setting up a sequence of facts and then reviewing them from opposite viewpoints. The story unfolds during a murder trial. As the defense presents its case one version of the crime develops. Then the prosecution fabricates an entirely different story out of the same essential circumstances. In the end the real murderer comes forward with a confession, and the real facts are different from both manufactured versions.

There is some delicate literary fencing during these maneuvers and shrewd direction in dialog and pantomime has made the most of them. Indeed, a guess is that the stage material has been bettered in translation to the screen. In speed of development and in drastic editing down of footage the picture is a model. There isn't a superfluous word or a superfluous gesture in more than an hour. And at that Blystone has given the story atmosphere, incident, touches of comedy and some good character etchings, all items that are usually spendthrift in footage in inept hands.

Story develops action in the form of flashbacks from the trial scene. It is during the summation for the state that the spicy episodes take place, a sequence that might have been taken from a French novel. State's contention is that the evening of the crime began in a cocktail party. The wife maneuvered her husband out of the house and then arranged a rendezvous with the man whose conquest she seeks. Arrayed in the scantiest of negligees she starts vamping, and the returning husband finds her clinging to the other man. There is a struggle, the lamp crashes and two shots sound in the dark. It is on this basis that the jury convicts.

Case of the defense is that the other man, an artist, was madly and hopelessly in love with a loyal wife; that he was in despair at his repulse, and committed suicide. This version is also enacted during the summing up of the defense. With the jury's verdict a woman screams in the courtroom, demands a hearing, and reveals that she herself is the slayer, because the other man deserted her and her child.

All this is almost formula of the dramatic stage following a couple of years of courtroom plays. But here the handling is so suave, the acting so plausible and the presentation so smooth that the artificiality of the material is effectively masked.

Warner Baxter as the other man stands out not only in this capital cast, but also among the personages that have been brought forward by the articular screen. In the even naturalness of a particularly difficult role he earns distinction, repeating in a striking performance the high laurels he gained in "In Old Arizona."

Edmund Lowe does well with a part calling for no more than drawing room manners. Mary Duncan is best in quiet passages. Her playing of the vamp was pitched rather too high, although it well may be a matter of judgment. Perhaps overemphasis was better than error toward the other extreme. Her best moment was the one in which she caroled a zippy jazz song during an angry upbraiding by her husband. Anyhow, this trio make a house forget that the dialog is just a mechanical device.

Courtroom sequences are splendid. Blystone goes even to the length of building tension toward the climax by sequences in the reporters' room, with Marian Spitzer, woman in real fact in one scene, and Jack Jordan, veteran New York reporter now working for Fox on the coast, in another. Picture is great in details. There is little or no comedy, but for one brief bit DeWitt Jennings gets the assignment of a puzzle negro porter.

A particularly well-made picture on the technical side, and one with a wealth of popular appeal. *Rush.*

THE CHARLATAN

(¼ DIALOG)

Universal production and release. Adapted from play of the same name. Directed by Harold Watterson. George Melford, Radcliffe Fellows and Margaret Livingston featured. Others are Craufurd Kent, Philo McCullough and Anita Garvin. Titles by Tom Reed. Dialog by Jacques Rollen. Cameraman, George Robinson. Adaptation by B. W. Burton and Robert Jahns. Running time, 60 mins., of which 45 are silent and 15 continuous dialog. At the Colony, New York, week of April 13.

Mystery drama of the era when they took 'em straight and playwrights hadn't spiced 'em with travesty. Hence old style and for the most unsophisticated of audiences, if there are any left. For any clientele at all show-wise it would be a pretty complete bust. It has all the old hoke bag of tricks. So complete a catalog hasn't been screened for a long time. Included are the good old raging storm outside, screams off stage, off stage shots, sinister Oriental figures that flit, the murdered woman and the grand old finger of suspicion that panoramas the whole cast.

Nowadays it inspires the heigh-ho instead of the nervous tremor. Too much mental effort even to try to outguess the scenario as it unfolds. Direction is only so-so, summing up as hack work from a stagey and artificial original.

Technique is the one now pretty familiar, of using silent screen with titles to get over the planting of story with all possible speed, and then going articulate when the climax approaches and holding dialog to the finish. It works out well enough here. The elaborate explanation required for the story would have been cumbersome in talk. It's heavy enough silent.

Clown in a circus is deserted by his wife, an aerial performer who runs away with a rich lover, taking their baby. Fifteen years later wife is living in luxury with old lover, but preparing to elope with a new **boy friend. Prof. Merlin, crystal gazer, appears in the town and becomes society vogue. Of course, he's the deserted husband. On the night of the planned elopement he is entertaining at a party in his former wife's mansion. He confronts her with a demand for possession of the child, now grown to young womanhood.**

During a cabinet trick the wife becomes the subject. She disappears in the cabinet, and when it is opened falls out dead, victim of a poisoned needle fixed in the cabinet wall.

District attorney, a guest at the party, orders arrest of the seer, but before this is accomplished, Merlin makes the district attorney prisoner and impersonates him in an inquiry into the crime. Step by step everybody is made to seem the criminal, until in the end it is revealed that the man who stole the wife from the circus clown really killed her to balk her second elopement.

Some of the theatrical tricks are ingenious. The real slayer is successfully concealed until the last minute, but the thing never really grips, principally because the stage device has been outmoded and nobody really is concerned with the outcome, assured by experience it will all come out right.

Dialog is uneven, ranging from adequate to pretty terrible. Dramatic dialog has to be extremely good or it turns to travesty, and talk in a sequence of melodrama has to be flawless to support suspense and illusion. This is far from perfect and suffers accordingly. *Rush.*

NEW YEAR'S EVE

(SOUND)

William Fox production and release. Synchronized score by S. L. Rothapfel (Roxy). Story by Richard Connell. Harry Lehrman, director. William Kernell's titles. Mary Astor, Charles Morton and Earle Foxe in cast. At the Fox, Brooklyn, week April 8. Running time, 80 minutes.

A dreary, depressing picture, spinning a sad story in a sad manner. Not a moment of brightness 'till the finish.

Mary Astor's performance is the film's one commendable point. While the direction is apparently good, its hands are tied by the script.

Charles Morton and Earle Foxe are not identified individually.

Two-dayer. *Bige.*

TRIAL MARRIAGE

(SOUND)

Columbia production and release. Produced by Harry Cohn. Directed by Erle C. Kenton from the story by Sonya Levien. Photographed by Joseph Walker. At Loew's New York, April 6, one day. Running time, 70 minutes.

Oliver Mowbray	Norman Kerry
Constance Bannister	Sally Eilers
Thorvald Ware	Jason Robards
Grace	Thelma Todd
George Bannister	Charles Clary
Mrs. Geo. Bannister, 1st	Naomi Childers
Mrs. Geo. Bannister, 4th	Rosemary Theby
Prudence	Gertrude Short

An uninteresting story given a trite, long-winded, complicated treatment, with no redeeming features in the picturization. Not much chance outside the grinds unless the title can be depended upon for draw.

It's sounded, with a bright, snappy, well-synchronized score. In a house like the New York the superiority of the synchronized accompaniment over the usual orchestra is striking.

Casting very bad, players in the principal parts not photographing interestingly and killing appeal from the beginning. Sally Eilers as the modern flap Cleopatra, with a dozen men around her neck, doesn't look it. She may have that certain thing, but it doesn't photograph.

Jason Robards as the quiet young physician is meant to be impressive. He merely succeeds in looking dull.

Thelma Todd is the choicest addition to the picture. The girl looks like big time and has leaped plenty since this flicker was made. Here she walks away with all the honors easy, because she is about the only member of the cast who can stand the camera from any angle and give odds.

The story opens with Oliver Mowbray engaged to Constance Bannister. He's her 13th fiance. She throws him for Thorvald Ware, whom she marries. The conniving society gal, Grace, who wanted Thor for herself, finally gets Connie in wrong, and there's a divorce. Grace gets Thorn and Connie marries Oliver. Years later they meet and all are unhappy, so the divorce grind goes through again.

There's a kid in it, too. Thor finds out at the last minute that he's the father. *Mori.*

THE WITCH WOMAN

(SWEDISH MADE)

(Silent)

Svensk Biograph production and release. Directed by Carl Th. Dreyer, from the story by C. Janson. Cast includes Einar Rod, Greta Almroth and Hildur Carlberg. At Fifth Avenue Playhouse, New York, week April 6. Running time, 60 mins.

In Norway was once a quaint old custom that a newly elected parson had to take over the widow of the deceased spiritual leader before he could step into control of the parsonage.

Under these circumstances, upon which the story is based, there is little opportunity for heroism, love, action or any of the elements which a liberty loving motion picture public gives up cash to see or hear.

The hero of this pictorial gag does the best he can, even though appearances are against. They've got him dressed up like a disreputable old bum most of the time. He wears a Pilgrim's Progress hat, with suit and buttons to match, and long white stockings over his lower limbs.

Thus equipped, he seems likely to be elected parson when his two competitors stage a feed for the judges in the hotel. When the ferocious looking widow appears the competitors flee. She is credited with witchery and looks it, but the boy takes a chance.

In her home he takes a drink of something and then proposes to the old woman without thinking of the girl he has promised to marry. After about 30 minutes or so of unnecessary incident the old woman dies, and the parson marries the girl.

Should appeal to the sure-seat customers. *Mori.*

PRISONERS OF SEA

(RUSSIAN MADE)

(Silent)

Apparently produced by Sovkino, although no credit given, and released here through Amkino. Directed by M. Werner. No major credits presented. At the Fifth Ave. Playhouse, beginning April 13. Running time, 70 minutes.

A story thread so thin as to be almost untraceable in the major reelage makes "Prisoners of the Sea" at its best a shuffle of travelog shots. Most of these center on boats and ships in the Russian navy. Only a few sequences attempt to tie these together, and fail. Not a commercial feature release, in fact.

Russian producers seem to have gone through their film libraries, sheared blindly, and pieced the clippings together, if the editing of this is any criterion.

The one sequence that outstands in the entire hodge podge is that of a submarine. The interiors are convincing, and its submerged state is realistic. An exterior shot of the ship striking the bottom suggests strongly a model in a tank.

Men in the sealed ship awaiting rescue give a good performance, but one not half so good as similar scenes in American product which have the added advantage of a well-knit story.

The best imagination can conjure up as the story idea hoped to be put over here is of a Russian sailor, betrayed by an officer comrade, who later rises to the captaincy of the ill-fated submarine. But even the usual Russian ending is abandoned because the double-crosser is the lone diver who effects the rescue of the ship.

Efforts to go any further in doping out a story for "Prisoners of the Sea" would only add to the confusion. *Waly.*

THE JAZZ AGE

(1% DIALOG)

Radio Pictures production and release. Directed by Lynn Shores from story by Paul Gangelin. Ted Pahle, cameraman. Music score by Joseph Zuro on RCA photophone system. At Loew's New York one day, Mar. 28, half of double feature. Running time, 62 minutes.

Steve Maxwell	Douglas Fairbanks, Jr.
Sue Randall	Marceline Day
Mr. Maxwell	Henry B. Walthall
Mrs. Maxwell	Myrtle Steadman
Marjorie	Gertrude Messinger
Todd Sayles	Joel McCrea

"The Jazz Age" is far superior to program productions made by FBO before it changed its name to Radio. Introduction of sound and a few lines of dialogue may be responsible for greater all-round effort in the workshop which this clearly evidences. Title tells the story which has a well worn but worthily handled mellar angle. Big school' fan draw assured. Adults will find it fair entertainment.

Ginning, necking, crap throwing and auto racing youngsters provide the atmosphere. But the story thread of wild American youth meeting emergencies with sterling qualities constitutes the finish.

Fairbanks is excellently cast as the youth with the puritanic eye for his young sister, portrayed with even perkiness by Gertrude Messinger. His role brings him into night life of the younger set where partying is emphasized.

The customary trend of the poor son of the honest city official in love with the jazz mad daughter of the wealthy but dishonest contractor, affords the adult angle. These are well interwoven, except for superfluous subtitling in the opening.

A race between an auto and a trolley car in which the children of both parents man the car creates a situation from which a nicely graduated suspense is worked. Walthall, as the boy's father, is thus trumped on his move to expose his enemy before the Common Council. Old meller stuff is worked in with success when young Fairbanks exposes the reason for his father's hold-out. Marceline Day, as the girl, helps the climax with the revelation that her father will also have to send her to jail if he prosecutes the young hero. *Waly.*

L'ARPETE

(FRENCH MADE)

Paris, March 25.

Franco's screen version of the farce of G. Quinson and Y. Mirande, entitled "L'Arpete," done at the Paris Scala a couple of years ago. Word, in modern vernacular, signifies a smart little errand girl in a dressmaking establishment. Thus Jacqueline works at Pommier's (all self-respecting French firms now bear the apostrophe), although carrying on with a young painter, Jules. Indeed, they are so far advanc-d in matrimonial intentions that they have discounted the parson's blessing and are living together up Montmartre way.

In order to bluff an elderly American buyer Pommier's attires his clever seamstress, or rather arpete, in the supposed latest models. He makes believe Jacqueline is a client of the aristocracy, and the girl is able to impersonate the role. American buyer is inclined to commence a mild flirtation, and without realizing it has soon given orders for dresses he does not need.

Plot becomes complicated when it is discovered he happens to be Jules' father. Of course the boy feels sore when he detects Papa out with Jacqueline, and imagines his sweetheart is unfaithful and goes back to America, bemoaning feminine infidelity. Later he returns to France, unable to keep away from his darling Jacqueline. Jules is told the girl has left the old lodging and is now a great desssmaker herself, making piles of money. She is most happy to see Jules again and the lovers embrace tenderly.

This diverting scenario does not constitute a real snappy picture. Scenes in the dressmaking industry might have proved interesting but are not. Many phases are exaggerated. Donatien, producer, nevertheless, has done good work, while the technical side and photo results are O. K. Cuts have since been made by the Franco Film people which have not met with the approval of Donatien and may lead to litigation. However, the pruning, if judicious, could only tend to the betterment of the production. Lucienne Legrand stars in the title part, with Gurein a suitable "jeune premier." His Jules is sympathetic. The several other smaller roles are in worthy hands. Thus "L'Arpete" as a popular French comedy should suit the local small time second half. *Light.*

MARKED MONEY

(SILENT)

Pathe production and release. Directed by Spencer Bennet. Adapted by George Dromgold and Sanford Hewitt from original story by Howard J. Green. In cast: Junior Coghlan, George Duryea, Tom Kennedy, Virginia Bradford. At Columbus, New York, one day, April 6, as half double bill. Running time, 60 minutes.

Mildest sort of romantic comedy that will just about make the grade in the grinds as the lesser portion of a double feature bill.

Flimsy story concerns events in the life of an orphan boy (Junior Coghlan), whose dying father left him together with a strong box containing a large sum of money in the care of a retired sea captain. Crooks are after the dough with the smart cracking kid upsetting all their plans. Subordinate plot has the love interest wound about niece of the captain and an aviator with the old salt objecting to the romance.

When the aviator proves his worthiness by assisting in the capture of the band of crooks, the old captain sanctions the usual events leading up to the aeroplane honeymoon.

A lot of fake air stuff is rung in to supply some thrills for the grind house patronage, most of it familiar and shop-worn. Titles of the obvious variety don't help this flicker a bit.

YELLOWBACK

(SILENT)

Radio production and release. Directed by Jerome Storm. Story by James Oliver Curwood. Adapted by John Twist. Titles by Randolph Bartlett. At Loew's New York one day, April 12, half of double feature. Running time, 66 minutes.

O'Mara	Tom Moore
Elise	Irma Harrison
Jules	Tom Santschi
Poleon	William Martin
McDougal	Lionel Belmore

Productions of the type of "Yellowback" are the surest means of converting fans to sound features. It is slipshod in every phase of production. Choppy editing of a hack story, with futile attempts to hold it together by clumsy titling, and no more to blame than the performers. Even Tom Moore is influenced by a dominating quickie atmosphere. It is hard to recall another picture in which he has given a worse account of himself.

The let's-get-it-over impression sets an early start when Elise is warned by her aged father to end association with one Jules. A scurvy looking half-breed, Poleon, made an attack on Elise, and Jules, the bad man, hurls Poleon the length of the barroom.

Irma Harrison as the girl who loves Jules until, for no particular reason, he murders her dad, performs like an elementary student.

Tom Moore as O'Mara, northwest mountie without the horse but with a reputation in the colony for cowardice, is dispatched to get the murderer. O'Mara and Elise work hand in hand even to the point of sleeping together in the woods with a log between them. The nap is interrupted by Poleon, who turns out to be Jules' man Friday. Like in 1915 production days, he gloats over a knife before he creeps over to the sleeping mountie. In the hand-to-hand encounter which follows, little Elise does the actual saving.

After binding the prisoner Elise releases him, with instructions to inform Jules that she will meet him at Dead Man's something. This turns out to be the barroom again, and the little girl's motive is shown to be no other than to test the courage of her mountie hero.

Tom strips off his coat and challenges Santschi to a finish fight. Although three bottles are broken over O'Mara's head in the course of the damaging of props which would look cheap in a river boat show, the mountie subdues his prisoner. *Waly.*

SMILIN' GUNS

(SILENT)

Universal production and release, starring Hoot Gibson. Directed by Henry MacRae from story by Shannon Fife, with continuity by George Morgan. Harold Tarshis, titles. Harry Neumann, cameraman. At Loew's New York one day, Mar. 26, half of double feature. Running time, 60 minutes.

Jack Purvin	Hoot Gibson
Helen Van Smythe	Blanche Mehaffy
Mrs. Van Smythe	Virginia Pearson
Durkin	Robert Graves
Count Baretti	Leo White
Ranch Foreman	Walter Brennan
Professor	Jack Wise
Barber	James Bradbury, Jr.
Station Master	Dad Gibson

Universal has spent some money on Hoot Gibson in "Smilin' Guns." It is one of the best dressed productions he has ever made. But the story is without reason and projects like a series of unrelated episodes. With all of its rambling and unreasonableness it clocks quite a few laughs and these, with some shooting and wild riding rushed into a Mix ending, will get it by in the Gibson houses.

As the poor cowboy with only a dog and a horse, Hoot unwillingly halts a train robbery by plugging a vicious man who had winged his dog. He picks up a newspaper and notes the picture of a beauty, westward bound, whose bent is culture and refinement. Hoot, of course, stumbles through weeds, presently to see the pretty damsel, Blanche Mehaffy, seated on the observation car of the train.

There follows the transition of the cowboy into a society beau of parts. And he is just as young when he arrives at the Van Smythe ranch to drill culture into the hands.

The little black mongrel does a Rinty when he detects a blahblah guest as the gent who once shot him. His teeth untie many knots effected by the villain before the ranch is robbed and the girl stolen. Before success, a great cowboy fight is staged, with many an extra getting a real bruising. *Waly.*

SLIM FINGERS

(SILENT)

Universal production and release. Bill Cody starred. Directed by Josef Levigard from story by William Lester. Charles Stumar, cameraman. At Times Square two days beginning March 28, half of double bill. Running time, 47 minutes.

Al Welsley	Bill Cody
Kathryn Graham	Duane Thompson
Detective Riley	Arthur Morrison
Dan Donovan	Wilbur Mack

Even 10-20-30 audiences find flaws in this one. They can't swallow Bill Cody's jump from a high roof, landing on his neck, and bounding up like a rubber ball and similar absurdities.

Production exceptionally poor even for houses with the cheapest policies.

All for nought, so far as U's ambition to make this a thriller, is the tumbling of a prop auto over a cliff and a couple of Cody-versus-the-mob contests. Cody battles in a way that even the fans can visualize the director's bawling to extras to flop as soon as the hero swings. *Waly.*

Circumstantial Evidence

(SILENT)

Chesterfield production and states' rights release. Sotry and direction by Wilfred Noy. M. A. Anderson, cameraman. At Loew's New York one day, April 2, half of double feature. Running time, 65 minutes.

Jean Benton	Helen Foster
Arthur Rowland	Cornelius Keefe
Henry Lord	Charles Gerrard
Lucy Bishop	Alice Lake
Tony Benton	Ray Hallor
Judge	Fred Walton

"Circumstantial Evidence" is made along big company lines. It possesses an expensive atmosphere and a nifty in double-exposure at a trial scene where the audience sees the enactment of a shooting with a thin close-up of the witness' face as the foreground. The story is conventional, and subtitles occasionally fail to account for time lapses. General interest, however, is sustained and the production is far

above the average for exhibitors not too exacting in their bookings.

Charles Gerrard plays the roue boss to perfection. He lets his regular, overplayed by Alice Lake, get Ray Hallor, as the weak brother, to **forge a check for the races while he concentrates on the sister, well** interpreted by Helen Foster. **Incidentally that little blonde exhibits an s. a. in this which should get her** into bigger dough if the voice is half as good as her discreet but commanding gyrations.

Cornelius Keefe, the accused in the last reel, almost spoils the picture. His abrupt movements and general unnaturalness impress as more personal than directorial.

The camera work in the courtroom scene is commendable. It retains the trial atmosphere without resorting to titles or flashbacks, but simply doubling on Miss Foster's close-up, the shooting of Gerrard by the discarded mistress. *Waly.*

When Dreams Come True

(SILENT)

Rayart production and release. Directed by Duke Worne. Story by Victor Rosseau, with adaptation by Arthur Hoerl. Hap Depew, cameraman. At Loew's New York one day, April 12, half of double feature. Running time, 67 minutes.

Caroline Swayne............Helene Costello
Ben Shelby......................Rex Lease
Martha Shelby............Claire McDowell
Jim Leeson..................Ernest Hilliard
Judge Clayburn...............Emmett King
Robert Swayne.............George Periolat
Jack Boyle.......................Johnny Hoy

"When Dreams Come True" takes its place with Rayart's regulars. There is plenty of action, most of it unconvincing because of the antiquated meller trend of the story. The poor boy marrying the rich girl in the southern racetrack locale, with the mysterious parent and murder angle, all provide proven ingredients for mediocre box office.

Rex Lease is the blacksmith lad by whose forge is frequently found Caroline Swayne, essayed with little color by Miss Costello. The complications are provided by the objections of her father. These are unraveled all at once when Swayne, **played by George Periolat, is attacked by the smith when he accuses him of being fatherless. This is followed by Swaynes break with his partner in horse breeding, Jim Leeson, with the heavy role handled in Ernest Hilliard's usual manner.**

Presently the smith's mother is revealed as the daughter-in-law of the town's leading citizen. The angle of the mother keeping her marriage a secret and bringing shame upon her children because of her great love for her socially prominent husband (not accounted for) is the weakest note in the production, and yet is the basis for the plot.

The mother meets a timely death almost at the same moment as the murder of Swayne. Here Miss Costello is especially flat and unsympathetic in her sorrow.

The old hoke proceeds to the end at full blast. The hero escapes from prison in time to hear the heavy framing a horse race with the Swaynes' pet jockey. A bright youngster who plays the hero's brother climbs into the saddle. Although defeated, the Swaynes win out because of fouling detected by the judges. The smith in the meantime has choked a confession out of the heavy's accomplice, and Caroline is set right on the identity of Ben's father. ***Waly.***

BROTHERS

(SILENT)

Rayart production and release. Directed by Scott Pembroke from story by Ford Beebee and Arthur Hoerl. Hap Depew, cameraman. At Loew's N. Y. one day, April 9, on double feature program. Running time, 65 minutes.

Tom Conroy..............Cornelius Keefe
Bob Conroy.................Arthur Rankin
Doris La Rue.............Barbara Bedford
Thomas Blackwood.........Richard Caryle
Randy......................George Cheseboro
Norman.......................Paddy O'Flynn

"Brothers" is oke for the daily and maybe three-day houses. Story has some highly illogical twists, in an effort to break away from conventional meller lines, but they abet the action and should be a decided relief from the average cut-and-dried grind fare.

A couple of clever youngsters, Jim Kain and Edward Anderson, open as the brothers Tom and Bob. Orphaned by the death of their mother, the story realizes a good start by one escaping from officers and the other being taken to an asylum.

In the adult roles, which are featured, Cornelius Keefe and Arthur Rankin are the brothers, who never meet until both are invloved in a murder and series of hold-ups. Although far-fetched, since Tom Conroy, by revenue from crime, has staked Bob through college and has able opportunity to identify him, the angle proves a seller. Delaying the identification enables Tom to take Brother Bob in on a confidence gag. With the revelation, Bob quickly drops collegiate manners even to a subtitle command of the roughest lingo. Hhe develops expert detective qualities, which save Tom from the chair and show Barbara Bedford and George Cheseboro, double-crossing members of Tom's gang, as the murderers. *Waly.*

Seven Footprints to Satan

(SOUND)

First National production and release. Thelma Todd and Creighton Hale featured. J. Christenson production. Direction from story by A. Merrit. Photography by Wid Gunning. Sol Polito recording supervision. Balance of cast includes: Sheldon Lewis, Wm. V. Mong, DeWitt Jennings, Laska Winters, Wm. J. Mong, Cissy Fitzgerald and Joan Christy, et al. Running time, 60 mins. One day at New York theatre.

Another of those fright producers, wholly baffling from start to finish. An utterly moronic sound film appealing to all the passions. Elucidation of mystery which encompasses **the production reveals the salacious scenes a frame-up, which doubtless accounts for its not being censored. Patrons grew tense in their seats at the apparently real wickedness. One scene depicts scores of men and women in evening clothes, lying on the floor. This is unquestionably one of the hottest exhibitions of iniquity done in a long while. Denouement, of course, explains everything as wholesomely innocent but leaves audience nevertheless keyed up to highest pitch of profligacy.**

Story is of a wealthy young man with adventure complex. Won't marry the dame he loves until he has explored Africa. His uncle does all possible to halt his squandering fortune seeking oldest civilization in the bowels of the dark continent. Creighton Hale as the intractable wears tortoise rimmed glasses and is ready to leave for Africa when uncle and his sweetheart, Thelma Todd, frame him, determining to give him his fill of adventure. Lure him into trick house, with disappearing walls, trap doors, phony bookcases and all the usual scare impedimenta of a ghost house.

A midget, a gorilla and a demon in the guise of Satan, who is operating a secret society, comprise some of the terrors into which the young man is thrown. He and dame see women whipped. See them shot to death. Hear terrifying moans, groans and other indications of the reign of murder and immorality which prevails in the house run by Satan. All hokum.

Windup a big banquet at which everything is explained and adventure kicked out of Hale.

No picture for kids.

PLUNGING HOOFS

(SILENT)

Universal production and release. Directed by Henry MacRae. Story by Basil Dickey and William Lord Wright, adapted by George Morgan. Rex, wild horse, featured. In cast: Jack Perrin, Barbara Worth, J. P. McGowan, David Dunbar, Starlight (horse). At Arena, New York, one day, April 10, as half double bill. Running time, 50 minutes.

Mild thriller with Rex, Universal's balky horse, supplying most of the synthetic action and going through a series of riderless chases that will likely please the kids in the neighborhood grinds, but will leave those over 14 cold.

Romantic plot has Parson Jed Campbell (Jack Perrin) in love with Nanette (Barbara Worth), a dance-hall dame. James Wales, Nanette's guardian as well as her employer, has designs on the girl himself, but Rex continually interferes with his plans. Out to get the wild horse from the mountains who is his Nemesis in his romantic schemes. Wales soon learns that the parson, who has befriended the horse, is his rival for Nanette's hand. **In a saloon brawl the parson knocks Wales cold, a left to the chin sending him through the swinging doors, where Rex, summoned by Starlight, an**other horse, tramples the bad man to death. Usual clinch finish for the parson and the dame.

The short footage is crammed full of obvious titles, many of them having the horses holding a conversation in fairy style. Not much to recommend in this flicker, with all things pointing plainly that good old Rex is about ready to retire.

SHOW BOAT

(50% DIALOG, Including Songs)

Universal production and release. From Edna Ferber novel, with original music from Flo Ziegfeld's stage production of same story and title. Western Electric sounded under Fox-Case Movietone process. Directed by Harry Pollard. Laura La Plante, Otis Harlan and Joseph Schildkraut featured. Dialog arranged by Pollard and Tom Reed. Captions by Reed. Photographer, Gilbert Warrenton. Synchronization and score by Joseph Cherniavsky. C. Roy Hunter in charge of recording. At Globe, New York, opening April 17, two-a-day at $2 top. Running time, 130 minutes.

All sound prolog, running 18 minutes, probably becoming part of picture. Holds Helen Morgan, Aunt Jemima and Jules Bledsoe singing their original Jerome Kern numbers from the stage "Show Boat." Prolog, at opening, also held Carl Laemmle and Flo Ziegfeld, each uttering inconsequential remarks, with those two probably cut out in the time revision of this picture for regular house showings.

Magnolia..................Laura La Plante
Gaylord Ravenal........Joseph Schildkraut
Parthenia Ann Hawks.......Emily Fitzroy
Capt. Andy Hawks.............Otis Harlan
Elly............................Elise Bartlett
Julie..........................Alma Rubens
Windy........................Jack McDonald
Child Magnolia }
Kim }............Jane La Verne
Schultzy.....................Neely Edwards
Frank........................Theodore Lorch
Joe...........................Stepin Fechit
Queenie...................Gertrude Howard

PROLOG

Master of Ceremonies..........Otis Harlan
Helen Morgan.......................Herself
Jules Bledsoe.......................Himself
Aunt Jemima........................Herself
Plantation Singers from stage play.

Despite the execrable cutting for the Broadway display of Universal's special, "Show Boat," dialog, songs and sounds, the picture is there, as a special for the larger cities, possibly four in all, at $1.50 or $2, and for a run film in any key city. This should make it a holdover in the regular houses of the larger towns. Any exhibitor can take advantage of the vast opportunities for exploitation, the rebound from the widely read Ferber book, the sureness the Ziegfeld show will never play those places, and the stage featured names of the prolog from the original stage production, besides the "Show Boat" song hits. And whatever glory the strongly ballyhooed name of Ziegfeld may yet hold after its bouncing up and down in lay and trade film circles. On top of this the exhib is safe in saying "Show Boat" by itself is an excellent picture when 25 minutes shall have been cut out, reducing the running time, including the cut down prolog, to not over 105 or 100 minutes.

There can be no alibi for the cutting for Universal's best effort on the screen. While the critics of the dailies refused to note the cutting is the picture's only fault, and their notices hurt the business at the Globe for the rest of the week, the fact remains that it is merely a matter of re-cutting to develop the full strength of this splendidly made picture of the Mississippi River and its shambling show boats.

U not only had this film in its Universal City cutting room, but it was pre-shown in Florida and before opening in New York had been played in some spots in the regular picture houses. So it must have been a stubborn resistance to the necessary cutting that held back this most essential need. Whoever may be to blame took a desperate chance on a large investment, for the dragginess of this film through prolonged scenes would have annoyed the inmates of a deaf, dumb and blind asylum.

"Show Boat" opens with snap and **ginger that any director would like to secure. It's noisy and it's fast; the show boat, "The Cotton Palace," pushed down the Mississippi, with calliope blaring the approach to the landing, and then the villagers swarming to the dock, the parade with band playing and Captain Andy leading. An excellent sequence and lively every second, with that broad expanse of water, the boat, the background and the action. You're on the Mississippi.**

But after that the drama, and with drama an overdose of each and every scene, excepting the one single bit of comedy of the entire film. That occurs in the first part. It's the only dialog section there, running 12 minutes. Quite a long stretch from the opening until the first dialog, but the comedy atoned. It came from the show boat's rep company playing one of those things, this time a drama, and like the show boat drama Harry Reichenbach wished upon New York at the Belmont a few months ago, as a plug for this U picture.

The story follows the book as it pleases, but the film scenario is complete. It brings the small time gambler back to his Magnolia at the finale, and that finale is one of the best bits. As the picture draws to its close, a negro is heard (and seen) singing "Lonely Road," spiritual (interpolated) as Magnolia stands on the top deck of her departed mother's show boat, lonely and alone, with Ravenal coming around, now that he's again certain of a home.

They drown Capt. Andy early, a small loss here, for he's unimportant. Nor is there too much spiritual or jubilee singing. Most of the song hits of Zieggy's "Show Boat" are there. In the prolog, Jules Bledsoe sings "Old Man River" in perfect reproduction. Otherwise the prolog, made in New York, not so nifty in sounding or photography.

A report following the premiere that another error had occurred; the wrong or poorer print was used, may well be believed, but it had no dampening effect upon the total impression, whatever that may have been.

Plenty of little tricks by Harry Pollard in direction. He's entitled to a lot more credit than given him either by the critics or the picture bunch. Many little side sounds have been picked up. One pretty scene, another of those "Sunrises," is where the elopers leave the big craft in a row boat.

In the second part (intermission 10 minutes), are 56 minutes of dialog and song, making 68 minutes of talk or lyrics out of 130. It is in the second part also where one of the best dramatic scenes, held up by Laura La Plante, was ruined through the bad cutting. Joseph Schildkraut, as the gambler, did a laughing souse there and, of course, overdid it, since the cutter failed to save it.

Miss La Plante's average is high, but she's an in and outer here withal. Schildkraut quite all right when protected by cutting. He well did the dandified river man. Miss La Plante sang a couple of "Show Boat's" song hits, and if she did, then perhaps the river was the Mississippi. Otis Harlan as Andy held down after the start. Alma Rubens had a short soft role as Julie, mostly helped by Miss La Plante, playing straight to the latter's nice bit of recognition of "Julie," years later.

A standout piece of playing is by Emily Fitzroy, as Parthenia, the hard-boiled river woman, who knew the river and the people on her boat. The only decent woman to her is her daughter, Magnolia, and she shows it in her face. Stern visaged, Miss Fitzroy made up like an Indian and acted like one. She's a fine picture in her character here. Neely Edwards had but a bit as a stage manager in the booze joint, where Magnolia made good on amateur night, but Edwards put much feeling and one strong laugh into his moment.

Production on interiors so-so, not calling for anything else. Exteriors are so sweeping they become enough. Pollard did a nice trick in indicating the passing of time, also in changing the baby's sleeping room, with the child awakening each time to note the difference in apartments. That was while Schildkraut was in Chicago, gambling away his wife's money and going broke twice daily. Also a flash at some inside dirty driving in a trotting race is the first time this phase of sport has been used outside of a newsreel.

At the Globe premiere Paul Whiteman's band played in person. Their first was the "Rhapsody," followed by a tango medley. The way Whiteman's did his anthem should have assured the U officials present that if they can reproduce it the way Whiteman can play it U's "Jazz King" is over before it starts.

Simc.

RAINBOW MAN

(ALL DIALOG)

Sono-Art production. No release yet announced. Starring Eddie Dowling, sounded by Western Electric system on film. Directed by Fred Newmeyer from original story by Mr. Dowling. Music and lyrics by Mr. Dowling and James F. Hanley. Continuity and adaptation, Frances Agnew. Editorial supervision by G. J. Crone; production manager, J. R. Crone. Production supervisors, G. W. Weeks and O. E. Goebel. No credits for photography or dialog. At Selwyn, New York, for twice daily $2 run, starting April 16. Running time, 96 mins.

Rainbow Ryan....................Eddie Dowling
Mary Lane....................Marian Nixon
Billy Ryan....................Frankie Darro
Doc Hardy....................Sam Hardy
Col. Lane....................Lloyd Ingraham
Bill....................George Hayes
Rounders Quintet.

Well made independent talker which rates program leadership in the deluxe grinds for week stands. Doesn't look like a holdover picture, leave alone a $2 possibility in the key cities.

It's a naive effort of utter simplicity and broad sentimentality, much in the mold of the Eddie Dowling stage musicals which have catered to the $4 audience on Broadway. With the propaganda Dowling will put behind it the feature may do eight weeks at the Selwyn. That it can profitably stay beyond that, or as long, is extremely doubtful, for it lacks a definite punch and a genuine tear.

Dowling is starting out on his picture career under the premise of rigidly clean stories barren of anything to spoil the taste of the apples he will place upon the censors' desks. That's one angle on Dowling's views of showmanship, emphasized by him in an opening night speech and also made a promise by the firm in a program summary.

If he insists upon becoming filmdom's morality standard-bearer, its obvious this musical comedy boy is going to need a wealth of talent around him to make his future pictures stand up sans inherent script power. That or devote the rest of his life to national campaigning before clubs and societies. Should he make no compromise with this principle Dowling can develop into a mother's delight, a vacation treat for school children, perhaps a matinee draw, and finish by making the sound version of "Peter Pan." Women's clubs will adopt him as their favorite example of what screen entertainment should be, but the flaps and their flips will classify him as the fourth Rover boy and expect a halo to be double exposed over his head during the final sanitary kiss. Dowling shouldn't stress this questionable commercial point to the extent he is left minus an out, for a recent example is that they're now serving on the "Leviathan." And Dowling knows too much about show business and is too good a showman not to know how to handle any material.

As a picture "Rainbow Man" consists of manufactured pathos, the first slice of which is cut before the film has been on 20 minutes in the stage death of the acrobat who leaves his six-year-old boy in Dowling's charge. Either the studio or the star has been smart enough to give this youngster (Frankie Darro) all the answers to the future laughs, Dowling depending upon his singing and the telling of a couple of interpolated Irish stories as personal added strength.

Musically the feature holds three tunes, the best melody of which, "Little Pal," is the least heard. ("Little Pal" is the title, at present, of the new Jolson-Warner film). "Sleepy Valley," the plug waltz ballad, is a cross section of half the notes you've ever heard, while "Rainbow Man," the theme, is ordinary at best. Both of these latter named numbers will need heavy concentration to get anywhere, while a revision of either lyric to fit the "Little Pal" melody would have made it easier.

Public will draw the inevitable comparison between this effort and "The Singing Fool," due to both being based on a "Laugh, Clown, Laugh," thesis and the child involved in each case. Young Darro is too much the typical stage child in self confidence and facial sophistication to win direct sympathy on personality, but is a sufficiently clever performer to make all comedy points register. This is another example of how difficult it is to time laughs in a studio, the punch lines of the boy bringing enough response to blot out the follow-up dialog.

How well an actor knows his sure laughs is typified in one of the star's Irish stories, Dowling perfectly synchronizing the wait on it from experience. But that's a gag outside the script. However, if the child has the comedy highlights Dowling comes closest to arousing a real tear in a phone booth bit when telling the stern grandparent he is sending the boy and the girl back to him, the small town maid having followed the minstrel pair to New York.

A strictly theatric climax is worked up in Dowling's minstrel show returning to play a town close to the one in which he met the girl and where both she and the boy have returned since he started the chill because he thought it best for them. Youngster runs away to see his pal again and the girl follows in search of her newly found nephew. Handed a ticket by the manager to see the show, she goes in and is spotted by Dowling in the midst of "Sleepy Valley." Abruptly ceasing to sing, Dowling comes down the runway opposite the girl to plead for a reconciliation in front of a capacity audience and telling them that this situation is not in the book. That's too much theatrical license unsquared by the girl admitting it's a terrible place to bring up the subject. Undertone titters swept through this first night gathering on it. Unconvincing finish and a decided fault.

Dowling has an agreeable screen personality. He fits this type of picture because he sells a song, knows comedy values and gives full evidence of not being selfish about laughs.

This effort will set Marian Nixon in talkers. She not only looks good but unfolds a wealth of charm in voice and manner. No direct evidence if she can bear up under heavy histrionic responsibilities, but as placed here she's a quiet, unassuming foil, easy on eye and ear.

Production is not heavy. What flash sets there are simply unfold minstrel stage stuff, and these are normal. Recording its sound on film there are a few exteriors one of which, a train, listens as an attempt at a sound dissolve into the roar of Broadway as the camera guides the scene change. Fred Newmeyer is credited with the direction, which lacks the unusual and carries its strong points in generally finishing off a sequence on a laugh line from the child. Picture is running too long, 96 minutes, but with the sound on film that simplifies cutting.

If Dowling and Sono-Art can reconcile themselves to sending this one into the picture houses immediately, release channels should not be hard to find, they'll be doing both the picture and themselves more good than if trying to stretch it into $2 runs in the keys. "Rainbow Man" is a nice first run talker and particularly worthy for Dowling and his firm in that it's their first effort. And as a first inde, so much more credit. The boys may not know what they're getting into on the $2 thing.

Initial performance here was a satisfying and smooth running affair having Dave Bernie's band on stage to play the assembling audience to their seats. Screen schedule included a Pathe sound news, "The Great Train Robbery," brought back for comparison and a verbal screen introduction by ex-Governor Smith. Both recording and amplification on the feature excellent, booth holding it too low for the first reel but stepping-up until it was right. No credits given for the recording.

Sid.

NOTHING BUT TRUTH

(ALL DIALOG)

Paramount production and release, starring Richard Dix. Made at eastern studio with Western Electric recording on disk. Features Helen Kane and Louis J. Bartels. Adapted from John McGowan's story and James Montgomery's play of the same name. William Collier, Sr., director of dialog; Victor Schertzinger, picture director. E. Cronjager, cameraman. At the Paramount, N. Y., week of April 20. Running time, 78 mins.

Robert Bennett....................Richard Dix
E. M. Burke....................Berton Churchill
Frank Connelly....................Louis J. Bartels
Clarence Van Dyke....................Ned Sparks
Mabel Riley....................Helen Kane
Sabel Riley....................Wynne Gibson
Gwen Burke....................Dorothy Hall
Mrs. Burke....................Madeline Gray
Ethel Clark....................Nancy Ryan

Frothy piece of work, the important points of which are that Dix is set for talkers, at least for the light comedy type, and that this picture is going to do more business than other recent entries from the Dix string. After that it's a matter of a good cast well directed in dialog with either Collier or Schertzinger to blame for permitting the footage to run so far past the hour. And as it's on disk, that's not easy to rectify.

Plenty of legit people in this release, Helen Kane being an insert and featured to help push via whatever draw her phonograph record rep may inspire. Miss Kane should particularly be a help here, as it was on this stage she first drew important attention. Cabaret sequence permits her to sing a comedy lyric into the ear of a staid business man. Just all right and short of a solid kick. Playing dumb in a dumb part, Miss Kane is at ease while shedding a nice enough personality which fits. Her appearance is in jeopardy for both camera and stage in that there's too much of her.

As much scared by a microphone as any film star has ever been, Dix has waged a winning battle against the invader. He can do light comedy, always could, and with the smartness of the veteran Collier to coach him his initial dialog effort is assuredly in his favor. Maybe he should carry Collier with him. Anyway Dix now has nothing but his former worry, i.e., stories.

In this instance he is capably aided by a male threesome, the trio who bet him $10,000 he can't tell the truth for 24 hours. Dix's dough being charity money his fiancee has turned over to him to double, because her father has promised to duplicate any amount over that figure she raises. Inasmuch as the father has a third of the bet the complications aren't long in developing. Churchill, Bartels and Sparks, the latter making his frozen face pessimism fit the mike, are excellent support.

Bartels plays quietly and straight other than having an off screen entrancing laugh planted in the hope that someone will remember they heard it in "The Showoff," doubtful in 99 percent of the spots this film will play. Churchill pries much from the fuming father, who reaches the boiling point after the cabaret instance which ends in a raid, with the sister team therefrom sleeping in his garage all night to catch him the next morning on a promise to back their show. Wife puts Dix on a spot by hopping questions at him and because of the bet he makes it worse and worse for the old man, besides getting in wrong with the daughter.

Running time is overboard mainly on the studio supposition that Miss Kane should get heavy footage. Situations involving her which might have been bright are heavily padded and lose their lustre. Wynne Gibson is paired with the songstress and foils neatly while hurting the latter on appearance. Of the remaining feminine members, Dorothy Hall, currently in "The Love Duel," gets as much as possible from the limited Gwen both on voice and looks. Camera deportment is not new to this girl, she having made a series with George Walsh, and plus a definite vocal appeal indications are that she can handle bigger material. Madeline Gray, now in a Broadway mus'cal, gives Mrs. Burke plenty of class while Nancy Ryan is agreeable in what amounts to a bit.

Schertzinger has found a means of moving his camera around and Cronjager, at the lens, has taken about every advantage possible of this all-interior picture. Continuity is smooth, except in a bad, awkward and sudden switch from Miss Kane to Miss Hall. Production end is worthy on sight, a factor the Long Island studio is striving for even in its shorts.

Less 1,000 feet this feature could rate at the top of the full length light talking comedies of which there haven't been many to date. It fits Dix and Dix fits it—which ought to mean a sigh of relief all around. A far more than capacity audience gave repeated proof of its approval to the extent it appeared as if the studio didn't think there was a laugh in the picture, mostly because of the failure to anticipate where the laughs might be and to provide appropriate waits. Many of the laughs carried a distinct Collier label. Excellent recording job and an unusually good presentation on amplification at this showing, the only slips a booth tendency to be overeager on the changeovers in order to get them to first base in time. *Sid.*

GIRLS GONE WILD

(SOUND)

Fox production directed by Lew Seller. Sue Carol and Nick Stuart featured. Titles by Malcolm Stuart Boylan. At Roxy, New York, week of April 20. Running time, 57 minutes.

Babs Holworthy....................Sue Carol
Buck Brown....................Nick Stuart
Dan Brown....................William Russell
Tony Morelli....................Roy D'Arcy
Mrs. Holworthy....................Hedda Hopper
Speed Wade....................John Darrow
Augie Sten....................Matthew Betz
Judge Elliott....................Edmund Breese
Grandma....................Minna Ferry
Dilly....................Louis Natheaux
Tom Holworthy....................Lumsden Hare

Another of the 18-year-old comedy melodramas Fox and others have been turning out for last couple of years. Persistence of this type of offering predicates commercial value for them. They are trifling and unimportant but entertaining enough in the unreeling. Probably appeal in the generality of film houses because of the conceded importance of the younger generation.

"Girls Gone Wild" proceeds on the premise that the adolescent high school crowd and their doings are just about the most vital happenings in the world. It thus belongs to what the literary world calls and denounces as juvenilism, the glorification of immaturity.

Older persons are apt to be a little impatient with this Fox cycle, but the youngsters and the romantics, the predominant movie audience type, will think them cute and interesting.

Plot is of a young daughter of wealth who runs wild and gets tangled up in a bootleggers' feud with consequent unpleasantness resulting in a disposition for reform and a more modest pace. Hero (Nick Stuart) is a son of a motorcycle cop (William Russell) which brings in a little moralizing about influential citizens thinking themselves above law.

Picture has been neatly directed and put together. Production values are Grade A and general quality sufficient to get it by. Acting is okay without any individual rating special mention. Several laughs in Malcolm Stuart Boylan's captions.

Film devoid of dialog. That reduces its availability. Rates as a moderate. *Land.*

SCANDAL

(1/3 DIALOG)

Universal production and release. Produced and directed by Wesley Ruggles. Starring Laura La Plante. Based on the story by Adele Rogers St. John, continuity by Paul Schofield. Titles by Walter Anthony. Cast includes John Boles, Huntly Gordon, Jane Winton, Nancy Dover, Eddie Phillips and Julia Swayne Gordon. No other players given screen credit. At the Colony, New York, Saturday, April 20. Running time, 70 minutes.

Not worth spotting in house with a reliable draw. Weak melodrama with an indifferent cast, rarely effective, mostly due to uninspired direction.

The story, molded along lines similar to hundreds of others used in pictures, has received an abrupt, familiar treatment. Only about 22 minutes of dialog, presumably added after the picture had been made, so that is discounted.

Synchronization is mechanically off while the musical arrangement is the same as that used with "Lonesome," one of the first Universal pictures with dialog.

Story concerns the bootleg loves of married couples. The heroine, after many years, is again beset by the love of a man whom she had once cared for. She repulses him but tongues wag as tongues will. The man's wife is killed, he is suspected of murder, but won't tell where he was the night of the killing. It's to protect the honor of the woman he was with.

The girl finally comes through, at the risk of losing her husband's love, to save the accused from the death penalty.

Attempts to make the various sequences convincing don't click. The garden scenes, where the woman repulses her lover after submitting to his embraces, may provoke laughs with wise audiences.

Huntley Gordon's voice registers clearly and strongly in some instances, but doesn't get over elsewhere, the difference probably due to the mechanical reproduction. He photographs well and plays excellently in this type of role, calling for the characterization of a young millionaire sportsman.

Laura La Plante has a speaking voice which should improve. *Mori.*

THE LEATHERNECK

(10% DIALOG)

Pathe production and release. RCA Photophone recording. Produced by Ralph Block, and directed by Howard Higgin. William Boyd starred. Story by Elliott Clawson. Photographer, John Mescall. At the Cameo (Keith's), New York, week of April 20. Running time, 76 mins.

William Calhoun....................William Boyd
Otto Schmidt....................Alan Hale
Joseph Hanlon....................Robert Armstrong
Heckla....................Fred Kohler
Tanya....................Diane Ellis
Tanya's Brother....................James Aldine
Petrovitch....................Paul Weigel
Cook....................Jules Cowles
Gunnery Sergeant....................Wade Boteler
Judge Advocate....................Philo McCullough
Colonel....................Joe Girard
Captain Brand....................Michell Lewis

Officers of the Court Martial
Joseph Girard, Richard Neill, Lloyd Whitlock, Lee Shumway, Jack Richardson and Philo McCullough

No particular kick to this Pathe talker other than it is another "trial" picture. This time a court martial. That's about the only portions where there is dialog, during the snatches of the court scene, with William Boyd talking in them. It must rest with Boyd's popularity or the "trial" end. Picture itself has nothing to pull although some publicity should be gotten out of the names of the two legits in the cast, Alan Hale and Robert Armstrong.

It is a film of cut backs. Picture opens with three buddies in the Marines being accounted for, after charged with desertion. One is dead, the other insane, while the remaining member is charged with the murder of his buddy. On trial for that and desertion William Calhoun testifies. Reciting the adventures of the three men after they accidentally got into a booze scrape, the picture cuts back continuously.

Their travels take them to several foreign countries, with fights and by-play, also a search for the Russian girl Calhoun had married in Russia. Calhoun is the one who locates the other two and also the menace who is dead by that time. As the court martial ends and Calhoun is pronounced guilty on both charges, Tanya, his wife, shows, with the trial reopened, and you know.

Boyd looks pretty good in uniform, with Hale and Armstrong playing competently. Diane Ellis looks to be in a constant pose. You get her from every angle.

Dialog during the court martial, especially when delivered by Joe Girard as the colonel, is excellent in reproduction. Sound process also helps Boyd's delivery.

Seems an attempt has been made in this picture to do a dissolve while the voice still speaks. This happens a few times in the cut backs. But there is no voice dissolve, that of one voice fading out and another coming up. The present dissolve is no more than if the music continued with the screen scene shifting. However, aids realism to a limited extent.

A theme song runs throughout the picture, most of the time by unseen singers. Latter of no apparent benefit and distracting at times. May have been voted differently with a more melodious song. *Sime.*

Adventures of Maya

(SILENT)

Produced and distributed by Edward L. Klein. Written, adapted and directed by Waldemar Bonsel. At the Fifty-fifth Street Playhouse beginning April 20. Running time, 50 minutes.

An unusual popular science study, centering on bees, is represented in "The Adventures of Maya." Good subtitling contributes a continuity rarely found in film efforts of this class while a number of situations denote excellent accomplishments by patience, knowledge of the subject and sound camera judgment.

The picture, however, is not suitable for the average film audience. High class community theatres and non-theatricals, especially schools, where biology is taught, will rate this adaptation of the Bonsel novel, by the author a subject worthy of every consideration.

Interior shots of a beehive and hornets' nest compare with little exertion of the average imagination to castle and dungeon sets. Woodland, flowerbed, night and early morning scenes would make this ideal for coloring.

Following the book upon which he bases the picture story, Bonsel focuses his camera on the travels and experiences of a bee. The birth scene in the comb and activities in the hive with the introduction of a new queen bee at the same time are followed by Maya, as the star insect is called, flitting out into the world.

Close-ups of insects, magnified many times, add to interest and realism. Grasshoppers, and rabbits, as well as snakes popping out of eggs are incidental to the network of a regular story which starts when Maya, after witnessing a frog gulp a bottle fly and a dragon fly clamly chew off the head of another insect, becomes friendly with a rose beetle.

A spider weaving his web so that each thread is discernible on the screen, entraps Maya. The beetle is shown cutting her from the meshwork. Then a hornet captures the little star and takes it to its dreary nest. There, after hearing plans for an attack on the queen bee and her hordes, so the sub-titles go, little Maya effects another escape to sound the warning.

The climax, a battle royal between the bees and the hornets, is staged inside the hive. Close-ups show the insects actually grappling.

Children in the audience with their parents go wild at this point and the production ends with plenty of applause. *Waly.*

KING OF THE CAMPUS

(95% DIALOG)

Universal production and release in "Collegian" series. Directed by Nat Ross. Written by Carl Laemmle, Jr. Dialog by Harry Fraser. Starring George Lewis. At the Colony, New York, April 20. Running time, over 25 mins.

Ed Benson....................George Lewis
June Maxwell....................Dorothy Gulliver
Don Trent....................Eddie Phillips
Coach Jones....................Hayden Stevenson
"Doc" Webster....................Churchill Ross
Collette....................Collette Merton

This is the first of the Collegians series of two-reel Universal comedies to be released with dialog, according to home office report. Same cast and director are used in each picture. This is the beginning of the fourth series.

For filling out an all-talking program this two-reeler can serve as a first-class comedy feature. Almost all dialog, excepting a few titles, it has been skillfully assembled and neatly directed.

Plenty of action, a lot of laughs, and more than enough plot. Practically all principals have good speaking voices, Dorothy Gulliver excepted.

Churchill Ross, as "Doc" Webster, a minor character, has been allowed too much liberty with comedy lines, but the same material read well in screen titles. Laugh situations built up interestingly enough to overcome any minor holes in production.

Carl Laemmle, Jr., is credited with authoring and supervising. First dialog attempt with this series should prove generally pleasing, with others also standing the same chance if given the same attention. *Mori.*

THE RED SWORD

(SILENT)

Radio (FBO) production and release. Directed by Robert Vignola. Original story credited F. E. V. Taylor, with continuity by Wyndham Gittens. Nick Musuraca, cameraman. At Loew's New York, one day, April 16, one half double feature. Running time, 65 minutes.

Paul....................William Collier, Jr.
Vera....................Marian Nixon
Catherine / A Russian Actress....................Carmel Meyers
Veronoff....................Demetrios Alexis
Litvoski....................Allan Roscoe
Foveless....................Charles Darvas
A Cook....................Barbara Bozoky

Were sound and dialog applied, "The Red Sword" would be a safe bet for a week's run in one of the better Broadway emporiums. As a silent it is one of the real life savers of the season for unwired houses of all classes, particularly first runs. Theatres with installations which use an occasional silent as a divertissement can book this one without hesitation.

Story, cast, sets, camera work are all big time. Directorial finesse of Vignola is manifested, and to this

director undoubtedly goes major credit for turning out one of the most complete audience pictures of silent class from the old FBO lot in a long time.

As a rapacious Russian officer, Litvoski is made the target for peasant revenge early in the footage when he blinds an innkeeper after raping his wife. The suspense is built around him. Allan Roscoe handles the heavy lead with surprising merit. The force and sincerity of his acting, especially the struggle with Carmel Meyers as Catherine in the bedroom scene, demands audience concentration at the start.

Charles Darvas, as the blind man inculcating the spirit of vengeance into the illegitimate offspring of his dead wife, plays stirringly. His clinching of the whip, which deprived him of his sight, on the day that a fortune teller has informed Litvoski he will be murdered by a woman, features in the suspense structure.

Even the illogical situation of revenge being abetted by the powerful Litvoski having a relative in love with his illegitimate child is so handled by Vignola as to unfold without disappointment to even a sophisticated audience. These roles. Paul and Vera, played by William Collier, Jr., and Marian Nixon, have a skillfulness which allows only a favorable reaction.

A well-timed mystery angle is what woman will assassinate Litvoski when he returns to the inn.

Waly.

BORDER WILDCAT

(SILENT)

Universal production and release. Directed by Ray Taylor from the story by Karl Kusaba and Van Moore. Continuity by the authors. Featuring Ted Wells and Kathryn McGuire. Cast includes Tom London and William Malon. No other players given screen credit. At Arena, New York, one day, April 17, half of double program. Running time, 48 mins.

Another western. A series of chasing episodes and one free-for-all, staged with the usual saloon backdrop.

Running time slightly under 50 minutes, it is practically limited to filling on double feature programs. Possibilities are slim.

At the Arena, an 8th avenue dime grind, this picture was shown in conjunction with "Interference," Paramount all-talker, at the usual admission price. Has practically no drawing power, children perhaps excepted.

Kathryn McGuire doesn't photograph well, though registering attractively in other westerns. Ted Wells walks through. None of the players show much coaching from director.

Mori.

Anny of Montparnasse

(Franco-German Made)

(SILENT)

Paris, April 11.

The energetic Sofar Film Corp. has launched this picture, meeting with local success. Exteriors made in Paris and studio work in Berlin.

Scenario is fixed in Paris, in the art students' quarter known as Montparnasse. Nothing particular about the story, in fact a bit moth eaten, but diverting.

Anny is a popular character of the district, snappy and attractive. She is dubbed a "regular sport." Poses as an artist's model for a profession, and still makes good.

One evening she meets Jacques Servieres, wealthy young painter, and agrees to pose. Jacques' sweetheart is jealous of the newcomer and schemes to turn her out of the studio while the lessee is not on the job.

When Jacques learns of this he hunts through Montparnasse for his model and even goes to her former address. He enters the girl's room and there finds a baby. The discovery rather upsets his equilibrium, so he takes leave.

That night he sees Anny at a students' ball, and his thoughts fly back to the poor little kiddie left alone in its cradle. He follows his thoughts; goes to the girl's room which he is able to enter without trouble (no safety locks in this film), and takes the baby to Anny. Then he discovers the mistake. It is not a case of "Bottle's Baby," nor "Baby Mine," but was simply being cared for by the kind girl during the mother's absence. It belongs to another tenant. Jacques is delighted at the maternal sentiments of his pretty model and marries her.

"Anny, de Montparnasse," is quite amusing, rather American in style, and contains some excellent gags. Anny Ondra plays her name-sake. She is a live wire. Andre Roanne impersonates in refined style the youthful millionaire art student. The picture has been produced by Charles Lamac, and looks like a winner, from the commercial side.

Light.

Great Diamond Robbery

(SILENT)

Radio Pictures production and release. Directed by Eugene Forde from Frank Howard Clark's story adapted by John Stuart Twist. Titles by Randolph Bartlett. Norman Devol, cameraman. At Loew's New York, one day, April 16, half double feature. Running time, 65 minutes.

Tom Markham	Tom Mix
Ellen Brooks	Kathryn McGuire
George Brooks	Frank Beal
Aunt Effie	Martha Mattox
Rodney Stevens	Ernest Hilliard
Barney McGill	Barney Furey

"The Great Diamond Robbery" could be edited into three short subjects. The production is so brought to the screen that, except for the titles and a few very thin directorial threads, the first two reels provide an old-fashioned comedy; the second pair a fast society meller of the quickie school, while the last duet constitute a cowboy comedy-drama. A little realism just before the close as meller tonic.

More has never been demanded of Tom Mix in any other picture. He is society man, ranch foreman, detective, bouncer and whatnot.

While fans usually have the utmost cordiality for Tom, the guffaws of a grind audience are unmistakable when Tom leaped a street width from roof to roof. They were silent when, single-handed, he outwitted a gang of thugs who had stolen the jewels and laughed again when Tom, in a dark shot, hurled his lasso from the ground over a chimney perched three stories up.

In this one, incidentally, autos beat trains and horses out-sprinted autos. It's that way all through, with no regard for plausibility.

Tom has to lean out of a taxi and pull a girl off her horse. Many film feet later on Tom's cab, breaking down, again halts the girl, this time in a car ducking the traffic cops.

Were it not for the heavy's sly expression the picture could end there. But this bridges a gap to a night scene, burglars and a jewel robbery. Mix awakes and goes in for his first roof-jumping sequence. After trailing them to their den he overpowers the guy with the jewel and uses the bad man's chewing gum to secret it beneath a table. Mix delivers the stone to the girl on an outbound train, inviting the taxi driver to the country.

But the audience doesn't leave here. Following the train fade-out the bad men decide to take a short cut to the ranch and get back the jewel.

The picture goes into a cowboy burlesque, the idea being to give the boss' daughter an idea of the old west. The outlaw gang arrives. Tom allows them to be received as guests, and more rough and tumble ensues.

Waly.

VOICE OF THE STORM

(SILENT)

FBO production and release. Starring Karl Dane. Directed by Lynne Shores. From the story by Walter Bard. Photographed by Robert Martin. Titles by Randolph Bartlett. Cast includes: Martha Sleeper, Warner Richmond and Theodore Van Eltz, et al. Running time, 55 minutes. One day, April 19, at New York theatre.

Smallie with all the melodramatic hokum of pioneer pictures, comprising such situations as reaching the governor's cabin in the woods to save the innocent fellow who is standing on the gallows. Trees fall across path of dashing auto. Bridge washed away as car crosses. Wicked butler; scientific formula which can destroy the world; storms, and all the abracadabra of the old school.

Karl Dane is trouble shooter for telephone company. His pal in love with a dame whose father, a scientist, expects her to marry another gent, who shares his secret formula which can destroy the world.

Father murdered by butler, seeking the formula for band of foreigners. Dane's pal blamed.

Dane, the tobacco-chewing blunderer, loads the film with laughs He essays to be detective, working in the house. Father's friend, though one would believe him to be in with the butler, is in reality a hero and uncovers the plot.

Big moment of the picture is when Dane and the girl with her father's friend attempt to reach the governor, when Butler confesses on deathbed. Get to governor but storm causes break in telephone wires. Boy being led to gallows while friends drive frantically to his aid, the gov. promising to keep calling every five minutes on telephone hopeful wire will be fixed. Car can't make it. Dane finds break in wires and lifting telephone pole on his shoulders attempts to join broken wire. Wire too short. Won't meet. so he uses watch chain for contact holding pole up until telephone company wagon arrives. Learns the governor's call got in and saved his pal.

Dane then decides to be detective, producing laugh finish.

S. O. S.

(ITALIAN-FRENCH MADE)

(SILENT)

Paris, April 10.

This Latin union thriller is an Erda Sofar production. "S. O. S." is the classical melodrama for popular publics. Author of the scenario is Carmine Gallone, who has produced it himself. No complaint.

Mario Monti, Italian army officer, is called for duty in the colonies (Tripolitain), and leaves with his wife, Sylvia Monti, who was an actress in Rome.

Crossing the Mediterranean, Monti sees his former "best girl," Rita. The ship is wrecked on the voyage and goes down. Call for help, hence title.

Monti is separated from the others and believes them drowned. Rita was saved, and she later meets a mysterious man, Mohamed, by whom she is taken in tow. She becomes his mistress, not an event in her checkered career.

Mohamed is a rebel chief, whose tribe is to be chastised by the Italian troops, commanded by Monti. Rita becomes the accomplice of her native over and undertakes spy work particularly as knowing a lot about Monti. She is able to get the military plans for the forthcoming Italian attack on the natives, who have declined to pay taxes, etc.

But, unfortunately for the honor of the family, Sylvia was also saved from a watery grave and is on hand in the nick of time to save her husband. She shoots the wicked Rita, while Monti pursues Mohamed in the desert, recovers the document, and the campaign is a success.

Monti is wounded in the battle, but finds a devoted nurse in the person of his devoted wife.

The cast for this mixed romance well selected. Liane Haid is the affectionate Sylvia, with Gina Manes as the vamp Rita. The latter has an important role and was remarked. Of the male parts Aphons Fryland (Monti), Harry Nestor (Mohamed), Andre Nox (in a restricted role), and Raimondo van Riel as a young officer devoted to his chief and friend, Monti.

Light.

IDAHO RED

(SOUND)

FBO production and release. Starring Tom Tyler. Featuring Frankie Darro. Directed by Robert DeLacey. Photographed by Nick Musuraca. Cast includes Patricia Caron, Lew Meehan, et al. Fifty mins. One day at Stanley, N. Y.

Inferior cowboy stuff with counterfeiting outfit attached to hero's ranch. Photography O. K. Story simple.

Story about fellow returning from France, meeting dame in city whom he doesn't know is sister of his buddy killed in France. In picking up girl's purse, he accidentally kicks it into gutter getting it all wet. Girl sore from then on. Fellow takes train home with little boy he adopts. Played by Frankie Darro.

Meets same girl on the train Takes auto to home. Girl obliged to use same car. Wreck. Arrives home, the foreman of the ranch being a villain who makes counterfeit money in cellar of owner's house. Hero finds he and girl both own the house, insomuch as hero and his buddy owned it together and when buddy was killed he willed it to sister. Tyler and girl now own house and ranch. Girl takes beautiful close-ups but not so good at distance.

Fake dough being passed in country store. Sheriff calls and Tyler is blamed. Shooting affray in the night in which Tyler wings a man in the dark. Proves to be counterfeiting outfit making getaway.

Windup with Frankie Darro on pony getting to Tyler in sheriff's office to tell where the hidden staircase is leading to counterfeit plant

Tyler gets to scene and is bound and tied, acid (used in counterfeiting) turning over and nearly suffocating him. Frankie is on hand Auto and horse chase in which Tyler licks the mob with fists and turns 'em over to sheriff. Uninteresting picture, except for possibility of holding kids by virtue of Frankie's pony.

THE QUITTER

(SILENT)

Columbia production and release. Starring Ben Lyon. Directed by Joseph E. Henebery. Titles by Harry Corn. From the story, "The Spice of Life," by Dorothy Howell. Photographed by Joseph Walker. Cast includes Dorothy Renier, Fred Kohler and Clare McDowell among others. Running time, 60 minutes. One day, April 19, at New York theatre.

Splendid continuity and a highly plausible story to which Ben Lyon does more than his usual justice. Bristling with action. Irrespective of its economical phase, the picture is entertaining from the start to finish and a bet for any silent house. Pretty girl lends it added enchantment. Played by Dorothy Renier. An ideal cast generally.

Ben is a stableboy for cafe owner and his amazing knowledge of medicine gets him in strong with the boss, played by the hard-boiled Fred

Kohler. Brings sick horse around, winning the big race.

Cafe owner playing dancing girl in his night club. She treats Ben to chill. When he gets credit for winning the race, she tells him she likes him. He tells her how little her opinion matters. Dame burnt up. That night at club, Ben amazes everyone by his ability to play the piano and finds the girl strong for him, cafe owner playing second fiddle.

Boy and girl obviously in love and cafe owner's henchmen tip him off. Girl gets Ben to tell her his past. Flashback reveals that he was young surgeon, Ben at hospital being congratulated b" his father, a noted brain specialist. on his first operation. Ben's mother is nearly killed in auto crash. Operation necessary immediately. Ben takes her to nearest house. Operates in kitchen but faints. Father arrives. Mother dies. Father says: "Just when mother needed you most you failed." Ben goes to dogs.

Back to scene. Kohler and Lyons fight over girl, Ben nearly being killed. Makes tryst with gal. They intend to flee. Kohler with revolver stands in window to knock off Ben. Gal shoots him from transom. Ben operates, saving man who would kill him. Happy windup.

Behind Closed Doors

(SILENT)

Columbia production and release. Directed by R. William Neill. In the cast: Virginia Valli, Gaston Glass, Otto Mathieson, Andre De Segurola. At Loew's Circle, April 22, half double feature. Running time, 63 minutes.

A rather dull, nicely mounted production, with story about nothing at all, makes "Behind Closed Doors" worthy of consideration by the lesser houses only when the silent famine becomes more severe.

The absence of a plot outline results in complications more slow, however, than intriguing Royalists see the re-enthronement of their king if they deliver certain papers to an American woman of great wealth. At the same time Republicans know that the document is to be delivered. Thus it starts.

Virginia Valli poses as an admirer of the rich woman until the latter's identity as aunt to the ambassador is about to be disclosed. Then Miss Valli reveals herself as a secret service operative and surrenders the Royalists' plans. The aunt dies and the yarn is back where it started from.

During the interval Gaston Glass, as the young man sent to America to see that the papers are not delivered, is as confused about Miss Valli's intentions as the average fan in a grind audience. When two gentlemen are shot in cold blood just before identifying the mysterious representative, there is no concern expressed and the audience gets a matter-of-fact reaction. Who did the shooting is left to the imagination.

Greatly inferior to Columbia standard. *Waly.*

German Pics

Berlin, April 12.

Capitol—"The Crimson Circle" (Defina). Friedrich Zelnik has here taken one of Edgar Wallace's best novels but not been successful in getting much of its suspense onto the screen. A blackmailing organization sends a crimson circle to those who refuse to accede to its demands and a short time afterward the recipients are mysteriously murdered. Sweet heroine is always present at these tragedies, so she gets suspected by the hard hearted police. But not by the audience and that's why there isn't any suspense. Lya Mara is still liked in Germany and looks passable through gauze. Should go in England where Wallace is more popular than the king but hasn't any chances in the States.

Terra—"The Gypsy Violinist" (Aco) based on the Kalman operetta "Sari." Another of those pictures taken from operettas—a grave error before the arrival of sound. Operetta plots are nonsensical enough when accompanied with music; on the screen they become utterly ridiculous. This is all about a gypsy violinist who retires at the height of his fame and plans to marry his charming young niece. But the girl falls for the son, whom the father has disowned because he plays from notes, not in the old gypsy fashion, extempore.

Father refuses to come and play for the king and the son takes his place. As he has a tremendous success, the father forgives him and also lets him have the girl. Karl Wilhelm, who directed, is the oldest German megaphone wielder, having even discovered Lubitsch as an actor for the film. This picture is pretty primitive technically but as it is said to have cost only $10,000 it should easily get this sum back from the German provinces where it will be liked.

Kammerlichtspiele—"The Hero of All Girls' Dreams" (Deutsches Lichtspiel Syndikat). There is a demand for a certain number of Harry Liedtke films yearly and this one supplies the unquenchable longing better than the average. Robert Land is a director of qualities well above the German average. The story concerns an elegant French count who is really poor and merely puts up a bluff of wealth.

He wins away a dancer from his rival, a marquis, and then lets her drop. Out of revenge the marquis bets that he will grab the count's next flame. The latter falls for a little seamstress and takes a position in the country as a horse trainer in order to earn enough money to marry the girl. Under a false pretext the marquis gets the girl to his apartment and then has the count notified so that he will discover them together. Broken hearted he goes back to his old night-rounding but the plot is disclosed to him and a good middle class marriage looms. From a Continental viewpoint Liedtke has a lot of charm and is even developing some talents as a comedian.

Atrium—"Furnished Rooms" (Strauss). A ridiculous scenario that wanders around without the slightest motivation. The hero lavishes his affections on most of the female members of the cast and the heroine is also very big-hearted. Fred Sauer, the director, hokes it in the style of 1910 and his lead is followed with enthusiasm by Fritz Schulz and Margot Landa. Nothing short of a crime.

Primus Palast—"You Are the Woman That Everyone Loves" (Deutsche Universal). Henny Porten goes on forever and ever. It would seem that in the dark regions of the provinces she is still the ideal type. She should stop trying to be cute. What a beautifully trained staff of yes-men she must have about the studio!

Here she plays a little (?) shopgirl who is so awfully, awfully talented but daren't go on the stage because her husband-to-be looks on that sort of thing with disgust and disapproval But then, just by mistake, she happens to be out alone on the middle of a stage when the curtain goes up, and, of course, just has to become a star overnight. Then her fiance, who is even dumber than usual, falls in love with her as an actress, never having recognized her at all, so finally she tells him the truth and he believes it. Karl Froehlich used to be a director before he followed the call of the filthy lucre and started tacking this sort of junk together.

Bavaria Lichtspiele—"What a Girl Dreams About in Spring" (Arthur Ziem). Well, in Germany they dream that they win a prize contest and get a trip to the Riviera. There they pretend to be a countess and fall for a film star who is shooting exteriors. It even goes so far as allowing them to step in at the last moment and take the film star's role in said exterior.

But it all comes out about their not being a countess, and Ramon spurns them. So they return to Berlin and their cloak and suit fiance. But it seems that those scenes were just too wonderful, and so they become a film star, anyhow. In America they would suggest that the scenario writer change his restaurant. Director's name is Kurt Blachnitzky and the star Colette Brettl.

Primus Palast—"People of the Soil" (Germania). Set among a season of good features, this would look like mere competent mediocrity—old-fashioned peasant drama. But this spring Jensen and Lang deserve credit for bringing out anything even as competent as this. Particularly so, as it gave Albert Steinrueck a chance to play brilliantly the role of an old farmer and Hermann Valentine could wallow lustily in villainy.

It's about the good son who is away as a sailor and whose letters are kept back by his bad brother, to whom everything is then willed. The father finds out the truth, but is done away by heart failure before he can get to the notary. But the good brother returns and manages to kick the naughty boy out, anyhow. They will eat it up in darkest Bavaria. *Trask.*

MADAME X

(ALL DIALOG)

Metro-Goldwyn-Mayer production and release. Adapted from the French stage play of Alexandre Bisson's. Directed by Lionel Barrymore. Ruth Chatterton, Lewis Stone and Raymond Hackett featured. Sounded by Western Electric Movietone (Fox-Case) process. Dialog by Willard Mack. Photographer, Arthur Reed. Recording engineer, Douglas Shearer. At the Harris, New York, April 17, for twice daily, $2 run. Running time (no intermission), 95 minutes.

Jacqueline	Ruth Chatterton
Floriot	Lewis Stone
Raymond	Raymond Hackett
Noel	Holmes Herbert
Rose	Eugenie Besserer
Doctor	John P. Edington
Colonel Hanby	Mitchell Lewis
Laroque	Ulric Haupt
Merivel	Sidney Toler
Perissard	Richard Carle
Darrell	Carroll Nye
Valmorin	Claud King
Judge	Chappell Dossett

An advanced piece of dialog picturization that takes rank in its dramatic field with "The Broadway Melody" of talking musical comedy and "The Desert Song" for the operetta or light opera end. But without the urge among the masses of the picture house patrons just now for the heavily dramatic as against the lighter musical entertainment. So that while "Madame X" is all as a talking picture the critics will claim for it, there still remains the question if it will draw from the masses as did and do the musicals.

For this reason "Madame X" should show other than in the metropolises and the keys before it is determined by the film buyers if there is mass appeal in it. The younger element nowadays doesn't want this kind of sex, for the sex angle here is of the sordid sort, the thoroughbred woman going down the line to become an absinthe wretch.

"The Letter" (Par) with a trial scene, another class talker drama, couldn't do big b. o. things in the sticks; "Interference" (Par), also class, had to have the Eddie Cantor short carried with it for additional strength, while "On Trial" (Warner's) showed a surprising pull in those very same rural sections.

It is to be considered that at present the talking screen is flooded with two kinds of full lengths; the trial picture for the drama and back stage or Broadway for the musicals. Either one or both must shortly wash up the scheme.

Today in talking pictures it's the story. The story has become the emancipator of the producer. His star is no longer his boss. In the selection of "Madame X" for the dialog film, this is made more forcibly evident. Next to the story is the casting. And again "Madame X" brings out what casting means to a talker as it does to the legit stage play. So in view of these two and previously unnoticed items, wouldn't it be in fairness to mention on the program who selected the story as well as the name of the caster?

This is Lionel Barrymore's first full length directorial effort on a talker. Taking "X" as an actor-proof meller and conceding its author, the Frenchman, Alexandre Bisson, knew emotion well enough to make it do somersaults in this tale, Barrymore had no difficult job with this story and cast. There was nothing he could do for Ruth Chatterton, for she is as smart a showwoman actress as Barrymore is an actor, or Lewis Stone, stage and screen wise. But Barrymore did excel in the minor bits and roles. These were all made important and stood out. That above par park scene, with the kiddies watching a Punch and Judy show, that immensely human bit in the hotel's corridor with the landlord wanting his room rent from the besotted Jacqueline, or that almost unbelievably superb scene wholly dominated by the doctor (John P. Edington), who appeared but there. Mr. Edington's brief performance may well stand as a model for playing, talking, makeup and diction.

No less again in the early section with the small noises picked up for reproduction to an annoying extent, such as footsteps, the gurgling of poured water, etc., but all required to plant a bit for the plot; the awakening of Floriot through the click of a door's closing, to find his wayward wife in the room with him.

The two big moments are Jacqueline killing her small time blackmailing companion to prevent her son discovering what a horror his mother has become; the other the famous trial scene, the grand finale which made "Madame X" on the stage.

In Variety of October 1, 1920, appeared a review of the Goldwyn silent film of "Madame X," directed by Frank Lloyd, with Pauline Frederick starred. Of the trial scene that nine-year-old review said:

"Even such an emotional adept as Pauline Frederick cannot sit in the witness box through many minutes of footage and writhe and convulse the features convincingly enough to supersede that concrete something so essential to picture success and so absolutely necessary to sustain interest-'action.'"

Substitute "dialog" for "action" in the above paragraph and you have the secret of "Madaxe X" on the talking screen. Perhaps of all dramas on the same sheet.

A great drama for the screamer, but mayhaps it is leaping too far, too fast to make great dramas before the great public has had time to absorb the beginning of talkers. From "Lights of New York" to "The Letter" within a year. Isn't that pressing it? For this is drama without singing and dancing or music.

In production and reproduction not one word against "Madame X." Its reproduction is immensely aided by the trained stage voices, but the Movietone process employed carried all sound off perfectly. And the picture came in letter-perfect. It was set before it opened. Nice thing about the talkers; at least in dialog they are always letter-perfect at the premiere.

During the picture's running, Miss Chatterton in her character is twice knocked down, each time by a different brute. And each time she "takes the slap," as it is called in stage parlance; warding off the blow by her open hand at the point it is struck. In this film the slaps are taken so obviously by her they will bring a smile. To the lays they are invisible.

Reviewers will rave over Miss Chatterton and well they may. This girl from the legit is showing the screen way. Not a flaw in her performance or make up. She sacrificed everything for the role, even to looks at the finish. In the same notice of Miss Frederick's performance as partially quoted above, it was mentioned that Miss Frederick appeared more youthful in the court scene than she had at the opening of the story.

Next to Miss Chatterton and Mr. Edington comes Raymond Hackett as the son. He showed little in the going until the court scene and then he let loose. Ulric Haupt will draw attention as Laroque, the last paramour of Jacqueline. Court scene is finely done with all that it includes, which takes in the death of Madame X before the verdict of the jury is turned in.

Pictures of this calibre and their makers are entitled to untold commendation, whether too early or no, in lending to the screen a quality that the screen needs. Pictures like "Madame X" confound the reformers, elevate the name of pictures and tell the world that there is an art in film making.

Sime.

INNOCENTS OF PARIS

(ALL DIALOG)

Paramount production and release. Starring Maurice Chevalier. Dialog by Ernest Vajda, with Ethel Doherty adapting from C. E. Andrews' story. Directed by Richard Wallace. Cameraman, Charles Lang. Recorded by W. E. system on film. At Criterion, New York, twice daily, $2 top, starting April 26. Running time, 73 mins.

Maurice Marny............Maurice Chevalier
Louise Leval...............Sylvia Beecher
Emile Leval...............Russell Simpson
Mons. Marny...............George Fawcett
Mme. Marny.........Mrs. George Fawcett
Mons. Renard...................John Miljan
Mme. Renard..........Margaret Livingston
Jo-Jo.........................David Durand
Musician....................Johnnie Morris

Another naive back-stage story uninterestingly told with a French male star for whom it is difficult to figure in a successful American screen career from this start. In a native French talker, when they eventually make them over there, Chevalier will probably be perfect, as he's the biggest musical comedy juvenile France has known in years. He came up there from the music halls. Here he's simply a young Frenchman with a nice personality in a bad picture. That it can stick at the Criterion for six weeks is doubtful. The same apprehension clouds its future as to bettering normal deluxe house figures, and that due to dialog plus a campaign.

Minus sound Chevalier wouldn't be over here for pictures. With it he's still not a sufficiently deft pantomimist to completely explain his interpolated French ditties. And if the women don't care, this release hasn't much chance. The feminine proposition is the one upon which the Paramount publicity staff has been working for this star, the danger thereby being in a too strong build up. It's a cinch the male populace outside the profession isn't going to be particularly interested in this boy, so if the women also snub it, the final and sole resort is Leo Robin and Dick Whiting's tune, "Louise." It's the best melody any picture has uncorked in recent months. The number will assuredly get a strong radio, dance floor and record plug which may prove the raft upon which this production will float home. "Habit of Mine" also may have a chance to step out.

It's a skimpy little tale with Chevalier joining the ever-growing list of male stars who must be seconded by sonny boys. In this instance its David Durand as the youngster, made much too wise for his years in dialog. After an appealing start the kid tapers off due to that fault. Studio workmanship also early develops and retains a deplorable habit of ending almost every scene silently, the sequence building to a climax, reaching it, and then a few soundless feet for an exit or a fade. Result is an in and out film journey which doesn't satisfy.

Taking a lowly junk man and making a revue star of him over night permits the girl stage flash with Chevalier leading a number. Chevalier can't dance, if this film is full evidence, and his voice is unimpressive when warbling in English, which leaves the number a matter of sight values. The star is at his best in native and fast comedy lyrics with the film as a whole, Chevalier, and the boy all reaching their peak soon after the opening when the older man sings the youngster out of tears by a rollicking song.

The ditties which Chevalier brought over with him are pattern duplicates of those which are looked for in the light, snappy French style of pop music. That ought to make it good for Quebec and New Orleans, but there are other sides to the Mississippi. Also when Chevalier sings in French which you cannot understand, no good, and when he sings in accented English, no good also, over here, for he can't sing U. S. songs in English.

Production and camera work are standard, the main discrepancies being in the loosely pieced story and Vajda's dialog which never arouses emotion. Sylvia Beecher is the girl. Easy to look at and occasionally smooth as to voice but not always a convincing actress. Other cast members are minor with the exception of Margaret Livingston, who does well enough as a semi-vamp, and Russell Simpson as a grim grandpap delivering Hoboken speeches.

Direct comparison between these reels and the Eddie Dowling film. Both have the hard-hearted grandfather, the grandson, the daughter and the song and dance vagabond. But the real parallel is in the finales of the two love stories, each of which straightens out in front of a theatre audience as both juveniles bring their sweethearts onto the stage. Not as broadly done in this instance as at the Selwyn.

"Innocents" is an ordinary talker and unfortunate for Chevalier. It needs more than the certain charm Chevalier owns to make this feature a stand-out. Possibly the Frenchman can bite into something more substantial.

If it become an assured fact that the femmes over here are going for this French boy, whose billing, "The Idol of Paris," is literally true, and the chances the girls will do it are in Chevalier's favor, then he must be fitted much better the next try, for in "Innocents" it looks up to "Louise."

Sid.

CLOSE HARMONY

(ALL DIALOG)

Paramount production and release. Featuring Nancy Carroll and Buddy Rogers. Directed by John Cromwell and A. E. Sutherland from original story by Elsie Janis and Gene Markey. Dialog interpreted by J. V. A. Weaver. J. Roy Hunt, cameraman. Songs and lyrics by Leo Rubin and Dick Whiting. Percy Heath, adapter. Sounded by Western Electric system on film. At Rialto, New York, for grind run, starting April 27. Running time, 66 mins.

Al West........................Charles Rogers
Marjorie.........................Nancy Carroll
Max Mindel.......................Harry Green
Ben Barney.........................Jack Oakie
Johnny Bray...............Skeets Gallagher
Mrs. Prosser.......................Ricca Allen
Sybil..............................Baby Mack

Out of the west, where it's been cleaning up and displaying a big reason for the heavy grosses. Just a pip program picture which doesn't take itself seriously, holds plenty of laughs, has a good cast, at least one sweet dance-floor tune, and gets where it's going quickly. Another in the back-stage chain, but a good one.

It's about the best thing Charles Rogers has done since his fan mail jumped as "Wings" began to circulate. Still doing his shy, modest, clean-cut American boy, but it fits for this one and he's human. Singing a hot tune, if not, then animating it, the result is better for screen consumption over here than the Chevalier method across the street. One cause is that "All a-Twitter" has a definite dance-floor lilt while Rogers mouths it as if he meant it.

Behind the love story of the featured players is Harry Green's comedy house manager and the bristling crossfire of Oakie and Gallagher as a radio team who are delving into the picture palaces and split by the girl who undertakes to break up the new stage headliners so that West (Rogers) and his stage band won't be thrown out.

Punch finale is Marjorie (Miss Carroll) goading the boy friend into showing some stuff, whereupon he goes out on the stage and is so steamed up he gets sore at his boys and plays about every instrument in the band as a personal demonstration of what he wants. The unsuspected versatility wows the screen-stage house and he's on the verge of being able to write m.c. after his name and sign a $1,000 contract as the film closes.

Meanwhile, Green goals in a rather lengthy but never-tiring sequence, during which West turns down his bid of $300, then $500, and finally $750, at the instigation of the girl. Hebe comedy vet from vaudeville is a cinch in this role, scoring all the way and every way. Green hasn't left out a thing. Having been around so long, plus the camera and mike's proximity to catch all details, he hasn't missed a trick to almost dominate the screen each time he's on it.

Oakie and Gallagher are the follow-up on Green, entrancing late but clicking immediately on a full display of egotism and fast chatter which keeps getting faster as the men start making a play for Marjorie. The latter, incidentally, is installed at the house as permanent leader of the house chorus, which gives Miss Carroll a chance to lead a number. Item isn't particularly flashy but interesting, because this girl needs no double, having leaped from the line herself. Girl has a nice voice, minus the range to variate a melody in the modern pop style. She could have been helped by a special lead sheet arrangement, something she should insist upon if the occasion again arises. Miss Carroll also dances a little, throwing in a series of pirouettes which are neat, if lacking in pace. But, more important, Miss Carroll troupes in this instance with a sense of humor to give an unusually natural• impression of the self-respecting stage girl. An excellent all-'round performance, with her appearance, as always, taking care of itself.

No little credit to Cromwell and Sutherland for the dual direction. Picture always moves and to the extent Al and Marjorie are in their first clinch at the 19-minute mark. Entire story is planted within two reels. If there's no early sock, it is likewise true that it never stops after the scene between Green and Rogers starts. Oakie and Gallagher also know most of the tricks, and in a natural assignment the directors have been smart enough to crisply clip their scenes on punch lines which mean something.

Band of about 13 pieces accompanying Rogers is not given program or screen credit, but it's a good dance combination making up instrumentally what it lacks in appearance. Not many medium shots of the gang and they look good in natty naval attire from far away, the scheme of the stage setting. Climax works up proportionately and not without a touch of excitement, until Rogers does a belated handspring from the piano top to slide into a knee-bent bow with arm extended, which ought to be titled "Give!" About the only apparent muff in direction, and that it takes place after an after-beat, the incident is emphasized as unnecessary.

They were licking their chops over it at this house, standees laughing with the rest practically all Monday afternoon. Sweet piece of work for all concerned, including those Robin and Whiting tunes, one of which should reach smash proportions and gain important ears for the other numbers

Both recording and photography more than merely good, and the booth evidently was told to take no chances of anything being missed by anemic amplification. Lots of volume here, but the fast dialog demands it.

Sid.

Saturday's Children

(60% DIALOG)

Walter Morosco production, distributed by First National. Directed by Gregory La Cava. Starring Corinne Griffith in her first talker. Scenario from Pulitzer Prize Play of same name. Cameraman John Seitz. Titles by Paul Perez. Running time, 90 minutes. At Strand, New York, April 27.

Bobby Halvey..................Corinne Griffith
Jim O'Neill.......................Grant Withers
Mr. Mengle.........................Albert Conti
Florrie...............................Alma Tell

Willie.....................Lucien Littlefield
Mr. Halvey...................Chas. Lane
Mrs. Halvey.................Ann Schaeffer
Mrs. Gorlick................Marcia Harris

A tender little human comedy revealing Corinne Griffith anew as an actress of persuasive beauty and captivating charm, a perfect choice for this exquisite role. Picture has a fascinating sentimental quality about it and perhaps would have made a better choice for Warner's theatre than the same actress's "Divine Lady" now current and breaking no records there.

Director LaCava has done a capital job in embroidering the artless story of youth and romance with shrewd touches that enhance its appeal, brief but sure, like the bold strokes of a sketch. Expert handling of comedy here, too, in side incidents that go to build a delicate fabric of human interest.

Arrangement of dialog is unusual. Starts with 20 minutes of titles and minor incidental sounds. Then into 25 minutes of dialog. Another 20 minutes of titles and then 25 of dialog again to the finish. Titles fill in the intervals adequately. Perez has caught the spirit perfectly. His lines are pithy and have the appropriate quality of bland humor. "If all the interfering relatives were laid end to end—wouldn't it be great!" serves as a sample.

Production is complete, unobtrusively adequate and settings perfectly in tune. In short a fine play has been turned into a captivating picture, mild perhaps for the gum-chewing flap but a sure pull for adult patronage. For the women the combination of play and star should be invincible.

Amid so many excellencies it is difficult to apportion honors. Perhaps weight of credits should go to Miss Griffith. This actress achieves eminence among feminine screen stars for her dainty playing of what might be called grown up ingenue roles, and here finds a part peculiarly appropriate for her knack in that direction. Her performance is a great bit of high comedy.

There is the incident of the dinner with the rich philanderer, where the dinner check amounts to exactly $27, the amount she split with Jim when the young couple separated and divided their cash on the collapse, as they thought of their marriage. There was the snooping landlady in the terribly respectable rooming house, who crashed on men visitors to her roomers and insisted upon having the door open.

There were the delightful courtship scenes, when the kids went to the Park band concerts and were interrupted by fat men and their rank cigars, or by the soda pop boy who wanted bottles passed; there was the wide brimmed hat that made snuggling a problem, and a score of other trivial but graphic details. One dandy bit was the blowing of autumn leaves around the lovers' feet on the eve of their expected separation.

Whole picture is a delight of illuminating trifles, insignificant in themselves, but all contributing to the sentimental romance that has in it so much of shrewd wisdom, masked behind a grin that is at once sympathetic and sophisticated.

Grant Withers gets just the tone to his role of the dominant male dumbbell in love, a nice balance for the square shooting girl who scorned to employ the feminine wiles at her command to get her man, but in the end found she had to do just that. Marcia Harris the snooping landlady accomplished a triumph in smooth playing of a role that invited low comedy, and Charles Lane made the small part of the heroine's father count.

Miss Griffith discloses a speaking voice that escapes classification. It isn't a cultured voice or an elo-

cutionist's voice, but it has a distinctly feminine quality that fits her personality, or at least does so in this role. Young Withers does well by the mike. Voice is full and clear without anything of the stagey tone. Lane has one of the best voices heard so far in dialog. *Rush.*

LOVES OF CASANOVA
(FRENCH MADE)
(Accompanying Score)
(Film Silent)

Cinroman (French) production. Released in U. S. by Metro-Goldwyn-Mayer. Adapted from the Casanova tales. English captions by Edwin Justus Mayer. Scenario by Norbert Falk and Ivan Mosjoukine. M. Mosjoukine featured. Directed by Alexander Volkoff. At Little Carnegie Playhouse, New York (sure seater), $1 top, week April 27. Running time, 86 minutes.
Casanova...................Ivan Mosjoukine
Catherine II...............Suzanne Bianchetti
Maria, Duchesse de Lardi...Diana Karenne
Carlotta...................Jenny Jugo
Corticelli.................Rina de Liguoro
Countess Vorontzoff........Nina Koshetz
(Accompanying music score includes adaptations from the works of Paginini, Puccini, Mascagni, Giordano, Verdi and Wolf-Ferrari).

Much more interesting, perhaps, than this doubtful French-made "Loves of Casanova" will be over here is the inside story connected with the feature's release on this side by Metro-Goldwyn-Mayer (Loew's). That dates back some two years or more, when Jean Sapene sent two representatives to New York to sell this picture, or else.

That may have started what later became the French four-flushing idea of selling America what America didn't want in the French film way. It's still going on with the Americans but lately making up their mind the French had done enough four-flushing for a foreign nation that has never sent to this country over $1,000,000 net in any one year for the rentals of U. S. pictures in France. Will Hays knew that much when he went over to Paris the first time. Yet the example of what France had gotten away with American films started the quota rage all over Europe, after Mr. Hays had returned home. Recently the American picture makers have taken a more firm position in their relations with the French, happily backed up by the State Department at Washington.

Jeane Sapene occupies the relative niche in France that William R. Hearst does over here. Where Hearst is stronger as a publisher here than Sapene is in France, Sapene is stronger in pictures over there. Hearst has his film-newspaper counterpart in other countries, like Beaverbrook in England and Huenneger in Germany. They are merely counterparts, however, of the American in general outline. Where Hearst will laugh off a year's picture loss of $3,000,000 or more, as he did before Marcus Loew induced him to become a business gross getter for Cosmopolitan by joining Metro, the Sapenes want their money back, and more. According to Sapene, the more had to come from the United States.

Sapene's two representatives stopped at the Waldorf-Astoria in New York. One was Sapene's right hand. A Variety reporter called upon them, hearing about the "or else" ultimatum. They had nothing to say, but if the gentleman from the Variety would call again in a week they would have plenty to say, they expected. They would then tell the gentleman from the Variety what Mr. Sapene thought of the American picture distributors and what he intended to do about it—plenty, yes, plenty.

The week ran out and the Variety reporter called again at the hotel. The Frenchman had sailed the day before—the day after they had received $150,000 from Marcus Loew for "The Loves of Casanova." No other bid or offer had been received

from any other distributor during the Frenchmen's stay in New York. Previously Marcus Loew had been voluntarily selected, without his knowledge, for the French Legionnaire decoration. When receiving it Mr. Loew made no promises nor had he made any before accepting the high honor. But he did inform the French Embassy at Washington through its message bearer that if France made a picture suitable for American release, he would see that it got circulation; that if France wanted American picture talent to improve its native product, Metro would furnish it with such talent, and that if France wished to send its picture makers to Hollywood for a schooling, they would be graciously received and schooled at the Metro studios.

No request was made by the French, and "Casanova" was the first French-made submitted in New York for release, after the Loew decorative ceremonials. Whether Mr. Loew permitted sentiment to enter into his purchase of this Sapene picture never came out but he paid a very big price for a very ordinary film. There is also a 35 per cent distribution cost to be figured in this French-made that had to find an opening in New York at a sure-seater—Carnegie Little Playhouse—whereas Loew's could have placed it, if warranted, in its own Embassy, also a small house, with a $2 top.

After holding the negative here for quite a while, it was decided to send "Casanova" back to France to be colored. This period costume film must have needed something. Perhaps it was coloring. According to the picture there is but one youthful good looking girl in pictures—in France. The other women Casanova went nuts over or they went nuts over him look middle age, of no attractiveness, and you don't have to be a Casanova to land hundreds like those in any country.

Best thing about the film, of course, is the title. "Loves of Casanova" augurs for romantic chasing on the screen. There is lots of chasing, but unromantic. More like the westerns.

After Cas got jammed up in Paris he blew to Russia, stealing from a dressmaker on the way and trying to make Catherine when reaching there. Chased again for that, and back to Venice. That city seemed his stamping ground in carnival season, when you can pick 'em at will with their masks on and trust to luck.

All of this runs slowly, broken up by titles given as the thoughts of Casanova, in the first person. An unusually ungallant braggart, these titles seem to take up almost an equal footage with the picturized scenes. As the film progresses the titles, Casanova and his women grow terribly dull, a monotonous repetition of a chaser with a single routine and not much variation in expression.

Nor is Casanova himself any fetish for women to fall over or for. He and the women in black and white with their colonial make-ups must have looked pretty dreadful. They don't come out to much better appearance under the coloring. Diana Karenne as the Duchess is the young and pretty girl, the only one. The elderly looks of the cast otherwise would kill this picture under its title and story if nothing else did, and everything else does.

Direction fairly good, with production so-so. Most dependence on latter is the Venice scenes. No comedy other than the sorry attempts in the titling, often repulsive in the brutal admissions of Casanova with his affairs, such as this one:

"I have successfully won over 137 lean husbands, why should a fat one worry me?"

In France "Casanova" no doubt would be liked, for over there perhaps the Casanova way is looked

upon as subtle. Over here Cas would be termed a crude worker.

Picture all right for the sure seaters. May also do in some neighborhoods or the smallest towns when anything that is as broad on the make as this broad maker might be a relished novelty. There's little dirt in it, but heaps of suggestion. Plenty probably left out of original for showing over here.

Not for the first runs, for this cannot stand billing; it won't stand up.

Particularly in this day of talkers. Only sound is a synchronized score that fits in with the type and tempo of story. *Sime.*

DONOVAN AFFAIR
(ALL DIALOG)

Columbia production of Owen Davis' play. Jack Holt and Dorothy Revier featured. Directed by Frank Capra. Dialog by Howard Green. Continuity by Dorothy Howell. Cameraman, Ted Tetzloff. At Roxy, New York, week of April 27. Running time, 83 mins.
Inspector Killian..........Jack Holt
Jean Rankin................Dorothy Revier
Cornish....................William Collier, Jr.
Jack Donovan...............John Roche
Carney.....................Fred Kelsey
Lydia Rankin...............Agnes Ayres
Dr. Lindsey................Hank Mann
Porter.....................Wheeler Oakman
Mary Mills.................Virginia Brown Faire
Captain Peter Rankin.......Alphonse Ethier
Nelson.....................Edward Hearn
Mrs. Lindsey...............Ethel Wales
Dobbs......................John Wallace

Columbia has a strong dialog feature here that can stand the de luxe test anywhere. In addition to a well-conceived and neatly developed cock robin yarn there are laughs liberally sprinkled along the way, obtained through by-play and with a minimum of mugging.

Of the two types of crime story now prevalent in the talkers, namely, the court room technique on one hand and the scene-of-the-crime unravelment on the other, the latter has been used less and escapes the arbitrary limitations and ceremonial trimmings of the legal chamber. "Donovan Affair" is of the inspector-has-arrived school.

Suspense is built through the inspector in charge of case putting characters in same places as when murder was committed in dark. With conditions exactly duplicated another murder is committed. A third try for the denouement tricks the guilty party into a betrayal of his crimes.

Story in play form was a moderate success on Broadway a couple of seasons ago and easily adapts for talkers. Capra has manipulated his story and people with restraint and intelligence. As with the majority of talkers, story comes first, players dropping into the puzzle where they fit with no over-stressing of personalities. Accordingly there is little to be reported individually on the cast, although the tout ensemble gets a bouquet.

Jack Holt gets top billing as the inspector and does some good trouping. He is a somewhat perplexed copper with his share of dumbness, but a scientist by comparison with his assistant (Fred Kelsey). Dorothy Revier, second feature, is putting on flesh as is Agnes Tyres, both of whom appear to be debuting in this picture to talkers. Their voices are okay. Ethel Wales, as the mother of twins, and Hank Mann, as the responsibility therefore, get most of the giggles.

Recording and technical details all nicely taken care of. Production looks good. In short, Columbia has rung the bell. *Land.*

VOICE OF THE CITY
(ALL DIALOG)

Cosmopolitan production released by Metro-Goldwyn-Mayer. Directed and written by Willard Mack. Featuring Willard Mack, Robert Ames and Sylvia Field. Sound supervisor, Douglas Shearer. At the

Capitol. New York, April 27. Running
time, 32 minutes.
Doyle....................Robert Ames
Biff....................Willard Mack
Beebe....................Sylvia Field
Wilmot....................James Farley
Wilkes....................John Miljan
Johnny....................Clark Marshall
Mary....................Duane Thompson
Kelly....................Tom McGuire
Martha....................Alice Moe
Betsy....................Beatrice Banyard

Willard Mack's first talking production fits right into the picture at
the present time, with the vogue for
detective mellers evidently un-
dimmed and steadily growing
toward a peak.

It's not a smashing success, lacking hit potentialities, but it's a picture that will easily get its share of
the money on the regular weekly
runs. In the neighborhoods it
should be slightly stronger.

The title is not inviting, the casting in the lead roles is acutely unfavorable, and there are a couple of
spots where action slows and becomes draggy. But these latter instances are infrequent and the general high-powered tempo of the picture, with an undercurrent of taut-
ness that breeds suspense and holds
interest, puts it over for a healthy
week's business here and elsewhere.

Willard Mack himself is the outstander as the tough, square-minded
sleuth who won't be bribed, cajoled
or frightened away from his duty
of capturing an escaped murderer.
Mack shows them all up now, all
those picture detectives of this type
that have appeared in talkers to
date. Not only as an actor with the
easy, practiced form of expression
of the finished stage performer, but
also with the most effective screen
voice heard to date.

Mack is over for talkers in this
picture as a performer if not quite
there as a director. He lives up to
all the possibilities indicated in his
overpowering delivery in a bit part
in "Madame X," which opened last
week.

Sylvia Field and Robert Ames, as
the leads, are never appealing,
either from the vocal or photographic angle. The girl screens
very harshly, with angular lines.
Equally lost when subjected either
to closeups or long shots. Ames is
slightly better in talking, but photographs unsympathetically.

Next to Mack, John Miljan, first
known through the flickers, scores
most strongly. It's when Mack and
Miljan are together that the story
seems most alive and stirring. Both
girls—the other is Duane Thompson
—are negative screen personalities.
The servant girl, Beatrice Banyard,
fed some of the best lines in the
show, does excellent work, sending
them across for strong laughs.

The overlong love scenes are
mainly responsible for the slow
spots. Regardless of any other angles, this picture is mainly a crook
thriller, and anything tending to
slow it up hurts. It doesn't gain
anything in liking for the leads
here, since both miss for attractiveness, to have them sugaring each
other.

The story is interesting, dialog
speeches brief, funny in spots, and
carry the story forward instead of
holding it back. It's good dialog
except for the love sequences. After
having written a couple of dozen
plays or thereabouts Mack unquestionably knows how.

One of the early laughs is at police station quarters. Wilkes, the
Dapper Dan gang leader, is trying
to buy the cops off. He's fresh, and
Biff, the sleuth, doesn't like it. Winds
up with Wilkes stamping his cigaret
out on the perfectly clean floor.

There is a Salvation Army street
scene, incidental but effective, and
a third degree sequence which is
not as strong as that in "Alibi," but
still okay.

Action opens with a prison break.
Doyle, up for 20 years for a killing,
escapes. His pal Johnny, a hophead, arranged the break and hides
him in an attic over his own room.
Doyle, telling his girl he is inno-

cent, hopes to find out who framed
him and who actually did the shooting. "Dapper Don," his alleged pal,
is finally discovered as the criminal.

The last few minutes are hot and
heavy. The police have been tipped
off by Wilkes, and they go for Doyle
in the attic. They find the figure of
the boy hanging from a hope. They
later look again and he has escaped.

Doyle discovers Wilkes' treachery
and threatens to wash him up.
Wilkes pulls a gun and offers to
shoot first. As he does so, Johnny,
hiding in a lounge, fires and gets his
man. The police pour in from every
room in the building, but a note
from a dying member of Wilkes'
gang clears everything.. *Mori.*

BULLDOG DRUMMOND
(ALL DIALOG)

Samuel Goldwyn production, released by
United Artists. Adapted by Wallace Smith
from stage play of same title. Ronald Col-
man starred. Directed by F. Richard Jones.
Photography by George Barnes and Gregg
Toland. No other important credits pro-
gramed. At Apollo (legit), New York, open-
ing May 2, twice daily, $2 top. Running
time, 80 minutes.
Bulldog Drummond........Ronald Colman
Phyllis....................Joan Bennett
Erma....................Lilyan Tashman
Peterson....................Montagu Love
Lakington....................Lawrence Grant
Danny....................Wilson Benge
Algy....................Claude Allister
Marcovitch....................Adolph Milar
Travers....................Charles Sellon
Chong....................Tetsu Momai

Entertaining picture of the highly
charged thriller meller kind, but another misfit for any $2 showing.
"Bulldog Drummond" should get a
nice week's business in the regular
houses and this mostly because of
the even likeable performance of
Ronald Colman in his first screamer.

As a picture it's intense with
the suspense often and sharply
broken into for a laugh by a fop
Englishman of the very common
stage type. Many laughed at the
interruptions and the Englishman
the opening night at the Apollo.

But that same evening several
young girls in the front orchestra
seats made monkeys of themselves
when Colman appeared in an upper
box. It was a supreme exhibition of
idolatry and idiocy. While Colman
nonchalantly waved his hands to his
admiring public as though meaning
gratitude or aw nuts.

Adapted from the English stage
play, many scenes were on the
screen that could not have been set
upon a stage. These were the scenes
when Bulldog Drummond did his
stuff and easily, so much so that
when the muffled camera work was
over, Drummond was safe, presumably having all alone whipped another army of insane asylum attendants. This became the ridiculous
part, but holding nevertheless.

Drummond was an idler looking
for excitement. He got it by saving
the grandfather of a strange young
woman from the asylum's crooks.

A little bit brought exclamations
from the women, to indicate the
tenseness at times. Drummond in
disguise was being carried to the
asylum in an auto. He wore a rain-
coat with a gun in one of its pockets. Getting out of the car the gun,
unnoticed, jumped out of the pocket
into the mud. Ahs of despair were
heard from the lady muggs in the
audience.

Play appears to have been pretty
faithfully followed. This seems the
best way, in an all-dialog. Many
sounds picked up, mostly the engines with the cut-outs open, of a
couple of machines. Reproduction
worked nicely other than an often-
heard whirr.

Samuel Goldwyn gave the story a
good production in all ways, with F.
Richard Jones expertly handling the
direction.

Figuring Colman's first talker, his
surprisingly good performance and
easily the best of the film, his drawing power taking the lady muggs as
the criterion for many such, "Bulldog Drummond" looks safe enough,
without at any time being anything
to send over a rave about.

Lilyan Tashman was the she-devil
and it. She took her whisky
straight without water. Lawrence
Grant played the fiendish doctor and
well enough, although Mr. Grant
might decide he cannot keep on impersonating Kaiser Bill forever.

Joan Bennett, the new lead, is oke
on the looks side. She seemed held
down here, probably through inexperience. What she did do, though,
she did well, like Anita Page, and
after Anita Page, what is acting?

A new trick for the screen is called
"The Circus Gag." It's a bunch of
roughnecks uniformed as cops walking in to rescue their leader. It's
not known as "the circus gag,"

though that is a sufficient name for
it. That gag mostly has been employed by the Mann Act blackmailers. It fitted in here. *Bime.*

BETRAYAL
(NO DIALOG)
(Synchronized Score)

Paramount production and release. Di-
rected by Lewis Milestone. Written by
Victor Schertzinger and Nicholas Souseanin.
Titles by Julian Johnson. Screen adapta-
tion by Hans Kraly. Starring Emil Jan-
nings with Esther Ralston and Gary Cooper
featured. At the Paramount, New York,
May 4. Running time, 73 mins.
Poldi Moser....................Emil Jannings
Vroni....................Esther Ralston
Andre Frey....................Gary Cooper
Hans....................Jada Weller
Peter....................Douglas Haig
Andre's mother....................Bodil Rosing

Probably the most uninteresting
picture Emil Jannings has appeared
in for Paramount in America. Would
not have been great in the silent
era, and without any dialog and
only an indifferent sounded score,
has small chance to hold up where
talkers are being shown.

The story is lengthy, bitter tragedy. It should do reasonably well
abroad, considering Jannings' prestige, if that is any comfort to the
distributors, but in America, for
American audiences, not a chance.
In this house it is being backed
up by the tremendously powerful
drawing strength of Rudy Vallee.

Responsibility for this dismal
subject is primarily to be laid at the
door of the authors. Lewis Milestone, director, after getting an assignment of this nature could do
nothing but turn out a weak box
office picture. No material in the
script for anything else.

Story opens with a gaunt, dreary-
looking hero (Cooper), who has
somehow wooed and won a pretty,
but simple country maid without
benefit of clergy. He promises to return in a little while, but when he
does, much later, the girl is being
married.

With Vroni (Ether Ralston) happily married to the burgomaster
years later Andre, the former lover,
is not satisfied. He threatens her
with visits, on the strength of a
friendship with her husband. Vroni
has two children at this period, but
it doesn't seem to make much difference to Andre.

Poldi (Jannings) finally learns
that his wife has been unfaithful
and that one of her two children
was by Andre. But Varoni is dead
and Andre dying. In a frenzy Poldi
almost murders the child that Andre had said was illegitimate.

It isn't nice reading, and it is
much worse pictorially. Photographic treatment continually
throws everything into shadows, as
though the story was not already
sombre enough.

Won't stand up in the full weeks
unless very heavily upholstered with
stage material. Even where Jannings ordinarily draws, on this side,
results are doubtful. *Mori.*

NOT QUITE DECENT
(25% DIALOG)

Fox production and release. Directed by
Irving Cummings from story by Wallace
Smith. Titles by Malcolm Stewart Boylan.
Dialog by Edwin Burke. Musical score by
S. L. Rothafel on Western Electric system.
Charles Clarke cameraman. At the Roxy
May 4. Running time, 58 minutes.
Linda Cunningham....................June Collyer
Mame Jarrow....................Louise Dresser
Jerry Connor....................Allan Lane
Canfield....................Oscar Apfel
Al Bergon....................Paul Nicholson
A Crook....................Ben Hewlett
Another Crook....................Jan Kenney

The human interest Louise
Dresser injects into her role of
mammy-hollerer and night club
dame compels forgetfulness that the
theme is pretty old. Her performance magnifies the threadbare story,
with its modern but, ultra simple
dressing, until the audience is sold

on "Not Quite Decent" being above the average Roxy offering in entertainment. It is not until the last 17 minutes, when the dialog and Miss Dresser's song, "Empty Arms," are introduced, that this decision is reached.

It is not only Miss Dresser's picture from the critical viewpoint, but literally as well, since her few absences from sight are limited to a bare minute or so in the total running time.

As Mame, Miss Dresser is introduced as a night club duchess. The mother angle is introduced in her interest in a young girl whom she meets en route for her first stage appearance in the big city.

The girl, Linda, is played with a sympathetic understanding and subserviency to Miss Dresser by June Collyer. Her appearance at Mame's night club with her "angel" Al Bergon, played by Paul Nichsolson, provides a slant on double-door speaks which will register in the sticks. Mame has to okay Bergon. Then a snapshot is introduced showing him as one of her early playboys.

Staging her act in darkface, although the theme song is not sung until a repeat in the final sequence on the same set, Mame gets a further line on Linda. She later confides in her dressing room to her associate, Canfield, played by Oscar Apfel, that Linda is the daughter who was taken from her by relatives after the death of her husband years back.

The ruses used by an old timer to keep her innocent daughter out of the roue's net provide Miss Dresser with splendid opportunities. Never revealing her own identity, she wires to the girl's home-town boy friend, Jerry Connor, played by Allan Lane, when she sees that her own efforts are failing.

As the sacrifice, which bars her from making known her relationship, Mame discloses her relations with Bergon when he brings her daughter to the speak a second time. An excellent directorial flash as well as general performance comes when Bergon socks Mame and she laughs off an infuriated crowd. Miss Collyer here does a nice piece of acting. Her understanding of Bergon's attentions after her flop in his show is also aided by Bergon's terse explanation. The finis forces the toughest heart strings to twang. It's not the old stuff of the boy and girl going home, but the way in which Miss Dresser expresses the sentimental situation the climax in her song. *Waly.*

WHY BE GOOD?

(SOUND)

(No Dialog)

First National production and release. Starring Colleen Moore. No dialog. Vitaphone sound score (on disk). Directed by William A. Seiter. Carey Wilson's story. Presented by John McCormick. Titles by Paul Perez. At Cameo (straight pictures), New York, week May 4. Running time, 80 minutes.

Pert	Colleen Moore
Peabody, Jr.	Neil Hamilton
Ma Kelly	Bodil Rosing
Pa Kelly	John Sainpolis
Peabody, Sr.	Ed. Martindel
Tom	Eddie Clayton
Jerry	Lincoln Stedman
Jimmy	Louis Natheaux

After the first mild three-quarters of an hour, "Why Be Good?" becomes a series of questions, back and forth, as to whether the flaming Pert is a "good girl." At the finish, when Pert and Peabody, Jr., both in pajamas, inform Peabody, Sr., that they have wed, the boy assures his father that, yes, she is a "good girl."

He took her to a roadhouse and showed her a bedroom to find out whether she really was. The way she acted, she must have been. So that proved his original contention, which, unfortunately, was not shared by papa.

Previously, after Pert had stayed out till 3 in the morning with her sweetheart, her mother asked, "Is everything all right?"

Story of poor but pure department store girl who falls for the wealthy boss' son, and vice versa. Usual complications and windup.

Without Colleen Moore and an average Moore performance, film rates slight attention. No dialog, and that's against it from any possible exploitation.

The flaming youth theme, the basic content in this tale, is becoming well worn in the manner used, and all are using it in the same manner.

Louis Natheaux, through his playing of an unsympathetic and typical dance-hall lizard, should have the featured male billing that is now allotted to Neil Hamilton. *Bige.*

THREE PASSIONS

(ENGLISH MADE)

(No Dialog, but Sounded and Synchronized Score)

Presented by Alastair Mackintosh, with St. George's Productions, producer. Distributed over here by United Artists. Adapted from the Cosmo Hamilton story by Rex Ingram. Mr. Ingram produced and directed. Alice Terry, Ivan Petrovitch and Shayle Gardner featured. Cameraman, L. H. Burel. Technical director, John Birkel. At Loew's New York Theatre, New York, one day, May 4. Running time, about 70 minutes.

Lady Victoria	Alice Terry
Hon. Philip Wrexham	Ivan Petrovitch
Viscount Bellamont	Shayle Gardner
Lady Bellamont	Claire Eames
Father Aloysius	Leslie Faber
"Bobbie"	Gerald Fielding
Hairless Man	Andrews Engleman

"A strike at the mill, boys; get out the pineapples,' 'with Rex Ingram so long ago away from home he doesn't know the old mill thing has run dry. This hokey-pokey wouldn't have meant anything before the talkers and that tells what it's worth now. United Artists sent it into the New York for one day after opening it last week at Loew's Metropolitan, Brooklyn, as the regular feature. The Met's gross last week should be a headache for Loew's.

Of course the title! That's oke on the billboards, but on the screen Three Passions appear to be breakfast, dinner and supper. At supper in England where this was made, they toss lemon in your tea.

As a pash picture, it wouldn't press the blood pressure either way. It has Alice Terry as Lady Victoria, daughter of the Duke of Devon, trying to prevent young Wrexenham from entering the priesthood. Young Wrex (Ivan Petrovitch) walked out on his old man, Lord Bellamont, because Pop's machinery at the mill ground up a workman. That and as he grew tired of carting Victoria around to the joints until 8:30 in the morning, just to see a strip tap dancer unfold at that hour.

Lord Belly gave the kid a check for $2,500 and told him to let them know who he was or is. Young Wrex had been going around with the vision of the killed man's widow before him, but he didn't slip her the $2,500. It was an unexpected disappointment.

Instead he went back to Oxford. Oxford in England is a college; over here it's a bad cigaret. In college a priest was telling the boys his mission needed waiters. A caption explained that Oxford is the seat of British learning where "England trains her athletes and lets them educate themselves."

Young Wrex fell for the mission stuff. Meanwhile the old man was fuming because the workmen were growing testy and his wife carried a mob of gigolos on his charge accounts. And Wrex wouldn't come into the mill to help him.

Vic told Pop she could fix that; a young man goes for Love when everything else fails, but Wrex didn't go so strong for Vic when she also became a waitress in the mission.

Meantime, the strike discontent grew apace at the Old Mill.

One evening they cleaned out the Mission so that only Vic and a guy homely enough to be the understander in an acrobatic act were left there. This guy started to make Vic by the rough method. He had her in the office, trying to kiss her on the right side of the neck when Wrex came strolling along. Did they fight, Wrex and the bum, but not a bum fight. It ended when the homely one took a fall from the balustrade.

Meantime the strike was on at the old mill.

"Where's that boy of mine now that I need him?" bawled Lord Belly in a caption. It might have sounded better sounded.

And the boy came in as Pop started to die, the second death in the picture. First was the ground up workman, the Rex Ingram scheme of making both ends pleasant.

So young Wrex stopped the strike, let his father die, and kissed Vic. Probably blew the priesthood, too.

Not a bad picture 20 years ago.

No dialog, with the film sounded apparently after it got here. Very crudely. The noon whistle blew without steam. Dr. Hugo Riesenfeld socked on the musical synchronization, but neither that nor the sounds can save it.

Lord Belly is a pretty good apopletic actor and died gracefully. Miss Terry might have made up younger to grab such a young man as Petrovitch. They both acted well enough in the silent way. Ivan is right in depending more on his looks, though that is the very reverse for Alice.

It costs 50 cents to sit in the dark at the New York. For 50 cents nowadays you can get a load of pictures in a lot of places. *Sime.*

DESERT NIGHTS

(NO DIALOG)

M-G-M release starring John Gilbert. Directed by William Nigh. Story by John Thomas Neville and Dale Van Enery. Cameraman James Howe. Titles by Marion Ainslee. At Capitol, New York, week of May 4. Running time, 72 minutes.

Rand	John Gilbert
Steve	Ernest Torrence
Diana	Mary Nolan

Without benefit of dialog "Desert Nights" leans heavily upon its star and cast. Story is interesting but only in a minor key. Production detail up to M-G-M standards with the probability that picture will deliver general satisfaction without creating any box office records.

Torrence and Mary Nolan head a band of clever diamond robbers who escape from a diamond mine with half a million in gems, taking along as hostage the manager (John Gilbert) of the company. In the desert, with no water following a series of misfortunes, they finally appeal to their captive for help. The girl reforms and makes the final clinch while the old bunny who remains remorseless is presumably destined for that institution where rocks doesn't mean diamonds.

Miss Nolan does better work than usual in this picture. A good teammate for Gilbert.

Capitol, New York, made a synchronized score and a shot of the boys in action under David Mendoza which is inserted preceding and following the picture. This may be helpful on the sound angle. Apparently the first instance of its kind.

"Desert Nights" is an okay feature but only a one week John Gilbert booking. Title will help. *Land.*

RED MAJESTY

(SILENT)

Filmed and presented by Harold Noice, the explorer, who leaped into fame through his heroic rescue work on Wrangle Island in 1924. This film is the record of a journey into the jungles in the Northwestern border of Brazil, where the Tariano Indians, communists from time immemorial, dwell in a wilderness Utopia. Running time, 60 mins. Week of May 4 at Fifth Avenue Playhouse.

Appearing four times a day in person, Harold Noice lectures ten minutes on the interesting subject of the Tariano tribes. Talks ten minutes between halves of the picture. Noice is breaking himself in as a lecturer again, having been off the platform a long time and wishing to regain his stride.

Noice, who has made ethnological studies in the Arctic and expeditions into many uncivilized countries, is an engaging young man, who speaks with some show of authority. His camera work, however, is superior to his lecturing.

He has made 6,000 feet of absorbing interest, showing these Tariano Indians shooting rapids, hunting, bathing children, making bread and beer, weaving nets and making pottery. Work is well done and shots e entertaining captions.

Amazing camera studies are to be seen in "Red Majesty" of herons, cranes and other gorgeous tropic creatures of the air. He shows the natives in their community dwellings, living fifteen families under one roof. He paints them a very moral tribe.

Native boys at play, old men weaving, stalwart tribesmen hunting and mothers bathing babes in rapids are far more interesting than the recital can be. There is much artistry in the close-ups of strange animals, such as the tapir, kinkajous, macaws, tancans and scores of others. Picturesque treatment and novelty of spbject give film measure of interest beyond usual travel subject and it qualifies as a good freak for the sure seaters.

When Dreams Come True

(SILENT)

Rayart production, released by First Division. Directed by Duke Worne, featuring Helene Costello and Rex Lease. Story by Victor Rousseau, screen adaptation by Arthur Hoerl. Photography by Hap Depew. In cast: Claire McDowell, Ernest Hilliard, Emmett King, George Periolet, Danny Hoy, Buddy Brown. At Times, New York, two days, May 2-3, as half double feature bill. Running time, 75 minutes.

Romantic screen play with a Dixie breeding farm and race track for background. Plenty of action, the high spot an exciting race in which the jockey riding the pony on which the heroine has bet the works is given a rough ride. Fine photography in this sequence. Film will be liked in the grinds on a twin bill and a little cutting might ease it into the better houses for split weeks.

Story centers about Ben Shelby (Rex Lease), a blacksmith who cares for Caroline Swayne (Helene Costello) in a big way. Her father, a wealthy breeder and race horse owner, objects to the romance on the grounds that Ben's parentage is doubtful. When Swayne is found murdered and robbed in his barn Ben is accused of the crime because he had been overheard threatening when Swayne had brought up the subject of illegitimacy in regard to his birth.

Too many breaks for the hero are crammed into the final reel and the bit where the stewards of the track call up the jock at home to tell him about the disqualification is the nuts. Picture is well cast with Lease and Buddy Brown turning in capable performances.

IT CAN BE DONE

(10% DIALOG)

Universal production and release. Starring Glen Tryon. Featuring Sue Carol. Story by Mann Page and Edward Montagne. Titles and dialog by Albert DeMond. Ross Fisher, cameraman. Running time, 60 mins. One day at Tivoli, May 4. Cast includes Richard Carle, Richard Carlyle, Jack Egan and Tom O'Brien.

Glen Tryon again has a banquet table for his comedy frame. This is an entertaining picture despite notably poor photography and a great deal too much of Mr. Tryon. Sue Carol has little to do and nothing to say.

Story is of young man who is getting nowhere in his business. He is clerk in large book publisher's house. Of a naturally retiring nature, he decides he must get ahead. Another fellow in same office who has forged ahead comes down an hour late. Tryon observes his perfect attire. The fellow allows Tryon to put on his hat and coat and carry his walking stick.

Tryon in glad rags looks hot. Fellow tells him that's the way to succeed. Wear clothes! Meanwhile the boss, having observed the wearer of the fine clothes to have been an hour tardy, catches Tryon posing and fires the lad. Boy still wears the coat, hat and cane.

As he goes out, a pretty girl hands him a manuscript, mistaking him for the boss. Dumbfounded he takes Mss., a work called "It Can Be Done," and the life work of the girl's father.

Most of the dialog has Tryon reading excerpts from success axioms in the book. He does this very well. His change of being under the guidance of the book is especially well balanced.

He winds up addressing a convention of book publishers. Speech is in dialog. Consists mostly of sneezes and remarks about Washington, Lincoln, Napoleon and Lindbergh having followed the phrase, "It can be done." Publishers go wild about idea and order fabulous numbers of the tome.

Finale with the boss taking Tryon in as junior partner. Girl and father elated. Tryon asks girl to take wire. She jots down a message, "will you marry me?" Picture ends with her inquiring to whom it is addressed. He says, "You."

Her reply is, "It can be done."

CALIFORNIA MAIL

(SILENT)

First National production and release. Directed by Al Rogell from the story by Marion Jackson. Ken Maynard starred. Cast includes Dorothy Dwan, Paul Hurst, Lance McKee, B. E. Anderson, Fred Burns. At Loew's, New York, one day, April 30, half of double feature. Running time, 60 minutes.

Western truly describes "California Mail." A horse is not overlooked in any single foot of film. Three stage coaches are used, each drawn by six ponies. A gang of cowboys earn their 10 bucks per day in supporting Ken Maynard. Picture is undoubtedly the most virile turned out by this cowboy star. All houses excepting first runs can book it as a safe bet.

Story is laid in coach days on the plains, when competition was keen among independents for approval of their stage routes by the Government. Ken, as a government agent, drives in such a contest. Three coaches are used, and their wild dash over winding roads in an obvious Arizona locale is exciting.

Then the double-cross of Ken to the gang by surrendering a chest of iron instead of gold, followed by a series of single-handed captures that would be ludicrous if not so well acted. Paul Hurst, as a gangster who goes good, aids Ken overcome the outlaws at several points where they have planned to waylay him. Maynard does most of the work, chiefly lassoing mobs of gangsters and letting them hang over cliffs, tied up in gunny sacks, roped to trees.

Dorothy Dwan's work is incidental, solely for the usual angle, which could be overlooked here without hurting.

Waly.

STOLEN KISSES

(50% DIALOG)

Warner Bros.' production and release. Directed by Ray Enright from the story by Franz Suppe. Scenario by Edmund T. Lowe, Jr. Titles and dialog by James A. Starr. Starring May McAvoy, with cast including Claude Gillingwater, Hallam Cooley, Edna Murphy and Reed Howes. No other players given screen credit. At Loew's New York, May 3, one-half of double feature program. Running time, over 70 mins.

Entrusting precarious farce material of this nature to indifferent direction and continuity treatment results in a semi-interesting domestic comedy that never quite registers strongly. With its dialog and Claude Gillingwater's distinguished performance it has a good chance in the split weeks regardless of crudities in construction.

Picture is all Gillingwater. He gets laugh with or without material.

Next is the character actor, not credited, who plays as his secretary. Miss McAvoy photographs more convincingly than ever before, but is lost in speaking lines. Hallam Cooley and Reed Howes manage well with dialog, while Edna Murphy is also in difficulties when talking.

James A. Starr, who titled and dialoged is to be credited for the dialog laughs, mostly spotted in spots and help to revive action when most necessary.

Gillingwater plays the irate editor-publisher papa, who wants his son to be more manly and also produce a few children instead of allowing the wife to shower so much affection on a poodle.

The young man responds to treatment in the form of a frame, in Paris, while on a second honeymoon with his wife. The old man is crossed on the deal by the mixed team he hired to vamp his son. It ends up in a divorce court.

A last-minute reconciliation before the judge pronounced judgment, the young wife refusing to go through with it and the husband about ready to give in also. The framing sequences are not convincing.

Mori.

LOVE IN THE DESERT

(10% DIALOG)

Produced and released by Radio Pictures. Directed by George Melford from the story by Harvey Thew. Dialog and title writers not credited in press sheets. Featuring Olive Borden and Noah Beery. At Loew's New York, May 3, one-half of a double feature program. Running time, 68 mins.

Zarah..........................Olive Borden
Abdullah..........................Noah Beery
Bow Winslow..........................Hugh Trevor
Harim..........................Frank Leigh
Hassan..........................Charles Brinley
Fatima..........................Pearl Varvell
Mr. Winslow..........................Wm. H. Tooker
Mrs. Winslow..........................Ida Darling
Sears..........................Gordon Magee
Houdish..........................Alan Roscoe
Briggs..........................Fatty Carr

A sheik story with conventional penny thriller situations. Outside of the grinds there isn't a chance for picture material of this type to get play dates. About 10 minutes of dialog, opening sequence in talk serving as a kind of prolog and closing scene in the form of an epilog, both probably added on silent.

Plenty of sand but not much excitement. Lapses are too long. Still, if worth very little as a production, this effort at least merits recognition in the trade for showing what can be done for a girl like Olive Borden with her mouth closed.

As long as Miss Borden was photographed with her mouth open in her previous efforts she killed every possible appeal. It is obvious that Miss Borden is under a strain here in controlling her lips, but she does, and photographs very attractively. She has a chance to talk, too, very briefly, but enough to indicate a good chance in talkers providing she controls that upper lip.

Hugh Trevor, male lead, good-looking, impressive juvenile. He speaks well and needs only a smart director.

Story is the usual desert stuff. The young American sap, sent to Arabia to keep away from the girls, is kidnapped. He is saved by Zarah, Arabian chieftain's daughter. That promotes a war. Abdullah, vicious turbaned gangster, is bumped.

Preliminaries, introductions, overdrawn scenes and character delineations slow everything. And the hero never gets a chance to work at his job of fighting or saving anyone.

Mori.

ORIENT

(FRENCH-GERMAN MADE)

(SILENT)

Paris, April 20.

This is another Sofar-Stark production, recently trade showed. It is a thriller suitable for all classes, except, perhaps, the highbrows. G. Richelli is the producer, and he has made good. He was assisted by an excellent cast, headed by Dolly Davis, the French star. Resume:

A romantic American lass, Ellinor, travels in Africa with her companion, Daisy Young, and a fiance, Bobby Black. Ellinor dreams of desert adventures, and, to please his betrothed, Bobby secretly organizes one, with the assistance of a stray friend. Alfred is the name of the latter, and he is a sort of explorer. There is to be a quasi holdup, with Bobby to the rescue. By an unfortunate coincidence real bandits get mixed up with the attack, Ellinor being taken prisoner. Alfred pursues the brigands and saves the girl. Consequently she eschews Bobby, falls in love with Alfred and vows to marry the brave fellow.

On the other hand, Bobby has discovered, meantime, that Daisy is more suited to his taste, so it is a case of all's well that ends well. There are some diverting scenes between Bobby and Daisy. Claire Rommer holds the part of the quixotic Ellinor, coupled with Georges Charlia as the amusing Bobby. W. Gaidaroff and Aruth Wartan respectively play Alfred and the bandit chieftain. "Orient" will suit the local loops.

Light.

WOMAN I LOVE

(SILENT)

Radio production and release. Directed by George Melford. Story by Gordon Rigby. Titles by Randolph Bartlett. In cast: Norman Kerry, Margaret Morris, Robert Frazer, Emmett King. At Loew's New York, one day, April 26, half of double feature. Running time, 68 minutes.

Routine domestic story. It has a quartet instead of the triangle. The court room scene is there with the customary exoneration of the husband as the killer and the wife as unfaithful, with discarded girl friend taking all the blame for shooting the home wrecker. "The Woman I Love" on the whole is better than the average in this class.

Margaret Morris good as nice wife, little disgruntled over hubby's failure to get raise, who innocently starts the rumpus by doing a little superficial experimenting under influence of wise dame neighbor. Later's boy friend, played by Norman Kerry with a finesse that gives production better tone than usual run of this stuff, makes bold play for the wife.

Situation where hubby, getting promotion to traveling job, finds wife's photo in Kerry's suit case, is well handled. Instead of usual mauling scene on train Director Melford lets husband return home and check missing picture before gun is introduced.

Shooting scene, however, is unconvincing. Anticipation that dead man's mistress will confess something is there but decidedly weak when it comes. Audience reaction is that it was naturally tacked on for the happy ending.

Waly.

THE BETRAYAL

(BRITISH-MADE)

(SILENT)

British-made feature distributed in America by States Rights. Directed by Walter Summers from a story by Leo Perutz. Cast includes Elissa Landi, Jerrold Robertshaw, Gerald Peing and Charles Emmerald. At 5th Avenue Playhuose, New York, week of April 27. Running time, 72 minutes.

Foreign picture of no general utility for America. Rather well made with fair photography and production detail, but makes what is for America the fatal mistake of sacrficing personality to story. Characters remain throughout puppets blindly worked by fate.

As a plot it resembles "The Bridge of San Luis Rey" in classification although not similar in situations or events. Adapted from a novel "The Marquis of Bolibar," it tells the story of a French army marooned in Spain during the Napoleonic wars. A French officer overhears the marquis plot with the English and Spanish troops a plan whereby the captured city can be won back and the French expelled. There is a series of three signals to be given at intervals.

Story is fatalistic. Although knowing in advance of the enemies' plans and although the marquis is executed as a spy, everything eventually transpires as the marquis decreed. This is accomplished through the blind passion of four officers for the Spanish mistress of their colonel. In their personal campaign for her favor the officers one by one betray their army unwittingly.

Picture is on the whole interesting from the restricted sure-seat viewpoint. It's not commercial for over here, however.

Land.

MAKING THE GRADE

(10% DIALOG)

Fox production and release. Adapted by Harry Brand and Edward Kauffman from George Ade's short story of same title. Directed by A. Green. William O'Connell, cameraman. At Loew's New York, one day, April 23, half double feature. Running time, 63 minutes. Fox-Case film track. Musical score by Erno Rapee.

Herbert Dodsworth..........Edmund Lowe
Lettie Ewing..........Lois Moran
Lawyer..........Albert Hart
Silas Cooper..........Lucien Littlefield
Budd Davidson..........Jim Ford
Art Burdette..........Sherman Ross
Egbert Williamson..........John Alden
Frank Dinwiddle..........Gino Conti

The most is made of situations in a story superlatively trite in screen material, and these earn a place for "Making the Grade" which qualifies as fair for the average house program.

As the youngster who comes back to the town which his people control, and the efforts he makes to be recognized as a he-man and win the girl, Edmund Lowe is depended upon for romantic story interest. He carries off a polite hero role to such good purpose that the grind fans find plenty of genuine entertainment. Two talking sequences are short but snappy. The first, where Lowe attempts to address the Royal Order of Woodchucks, is full of laughs. The angle where the girl and his polished rival are listening in on the radio gets over because of its naturalness.

A deep sea fishing sequence in which Lowe aspires for honors in the Tuna Club is fast moving and realistic. Dragged overboard after wrestling with a hooked monster, Lowe is again made ludicrous when he, and not the fish, is hauled up in the net.

The final situation in which the hero snaps into the fighting traditions of his family, is shrewdly designed for suspense.

Lois Moran as the heroine has a small but appealing role. Lucien Littlefield, who does a little of the talking, as funny as his characterization, registers as usual. *Waly.*

LATIN QUARTER

(FRENCH MADE)

(Silent)

Paris, April 20.

The scenario of "Qaurtier Latin," produced by Augusto Genina was specially written for Sofar Film Corp. by Maurice Dekobra, the popular French novelist. Picture at the Salle Marivaux catalogued as a good French production, suitable for all publics.

Ralph, a wealthy youth, obtains by luck an invitation card to a masquerade ball held by the Students' Association in the famous Bullier (which still exists). At this rollicking function he meets Louise, an impecunious girl student. It is a case of love at first sight for both of them. He pretends to be a painter, and, to suit the circumstances, makes believe he is poor, like the majority of the brotherhood. The couple become intimate, Louise having full confidence in her lover.

Soon after Ralph becomes acquainted with an amateur vamp. She takes a fancy to the youth, giving him the glad eye, and suggesting a trip to Italy, the former land of honeymoons. The newcomer even has a sleeper on the train booked for her new sheik.

Louise gets wind of the proposed elopement. Louise, in despair, rushes to the depot to see Ralph and prevent his departure. She searches in vain, and when the train for Italy starts she is badly injured. Ralph was not in the Rome express, having recanted at the last moment. He goes, meanwhile, to the room Louise occupied, where he encounters mutual friends. There he learns that the girl has gone to seek him at the station. They all set out to look for Louise, and after an all-night search find her in the hospital.

Of course, Louise recovers and the wedding bells are tolled.

The scenario is so-so, extremely melodramatic, intended to appeal to romantic fans. Still, "Quartier Latin" possesses many redeeming points. The acting is noteworthy. Carmen Boni is emotional and natural in the part of Louise, full of youth. Gina Manes fascinates as the vamp; Ivan Petrovitch elegant and sympathetic in the role of Ralph. Other minor characters are all correctly played, making a good cast throughout. On the whole, this realization of the Sofar company is above the average in France. *Light.*

ARIZONA DAYS

(SILENT)

El Dorado production, released by First Division. Bob Custer featured. Directed by J. P. McGowan from story by Brysis Coleman adapted by Mack W. Wright. In cast: Peggy Montgomery, John Lowell Russell, J. P. McGowan, Mack V. Wright, Jack Ponder. At the Ideal, New York, one day, April 24, as half double bill. Running time, 50 minutes.

Good western that will be a sure pleaser for the kids in the grinds. Older class of cowboy flicker fans will also find it to their liking, the fighting, riding and romantic sequences all crammed with action.

Story revolves about Chuck Drexel (Bob Custer), a detective sent into the cattle country to round up an organized band of rustlers. In his efforts to drive the crooks out of the country that has suffered most because of their presence he crosses the path of Dolly Martin (Peggy Montgomery), who believes he belongs to the band. When Chuck with the aid of another representative of the Cattlemen's Association finally succeeds in arresting the leader of the band and several of his lieutenants, Dolly falls for him.

McGowan and Wright, as the duo of menaces, provide capable characterizations especially in the rough and tumble fight sequences with Custer who is always on hand when the girl or her father is in danger.

McGowan has handled the script in workmanlike style, surrounding the star with an excellent supporting cast. Jack Ponder as a comedy detective doing bits, gives a neat performance.

Okay for any of the daily changers on a twin bill.

LOVE MASCARADE

(FRENCH MADE)

(Silent)

Paris, April 21.

A sweet little flapper, Paulette, secretly loves Pierre Delmas, well-known novelist. However, the creator of "best sellers" has other fish to fry. He is taken up with a mistress named Dolly, and pays little attention to Paulette. The infatuated maiden dons masculine attire. She poses as an elegant young aristocrat and woos Dolly. The latter takes a fancy to the pseudo boy and is ready to fall into his arms. Delmas learns of this flirtation and becomes angry. He is determined to have the matter out with this intruder into his amorous affairs, and goes after his rival.

Thus he learns the truth of the story, and is so attracted by the charms of Paulette that he asks her hand in marriage.

Such is the scenario of "Mascarade d'Amour," by Augusto Genina, who has produced other pictures recently sampled to the exhibitors at a private show in Paris. This one looks all right, notwithstanding a childish impression which prevails. But the fans will like it, for the production is excellent while Carmen Boni is cute and dainty as Dolly. This seems to be a favorite name at present on the local screen. Jack Trevor is correct as the novelist, but is somewhat too stiff and cool for the role. Carmen Boni wears evening dress with elegance —much better than many a man seen in society. "Mascarade d' Amour should find a ready market in the equivalent of big town neighborhood theatres. *Light.*

ONE STOLEN NIGHT

60% DIALOG)

Warner Bros. Vitaphone production, part dialog (on disk). Betty Bronson and William Collier, Jr., featured. Directed by Scott R. Dunlap from D. D. Calhoun's story. E. T. Lowe, Jr., scenarist. Frank Kesson, camera. Theme song, "My Cairo Love," published by Sam Fox Publishing Co. At Fox's Academy, New York, week April 29. Running time, 58 minutes.

Jeanne	Betty Bronson
Bob	William Collier, Jr.
M'sieu Blossom	Mitchell Lewis
Chyra	Nina Quartero
Madame Blossom	Rose Dione
Balzar	Harry Todd
Abou-ibn-Adam	Otto Lederer
Dwarf	Angelo Rossitto
Brandon	Jack Santora
Sheik	Harry Shults
Daoud	Charles Hill Mailes

On the performances of two or three of its players and its scenic beauty at times, not a bad picture. For story and treatment, a secondrater.

It's one instance of dialog's failure to lift a frail film into prominence.

The talk in "One Stolen Night" totals around 50 per cent. It is spotted at odd and brief moments throughout the running, in such a manner as to seem more than it really is. That is a slight departure from the usual, with the general procedure until now to toss in the dialog in large chunks at either end.

Title is significant of nothing, is not explained at all by the subject and no more than a box office gesture. While they were picking something so foreign to the story, they might have picked something hotter.

Plot is ridiculous and never sublime. Some of the situations arising out of it are the old hokum, generously poured in. Villainy enters from four different sources, and the four-ply menace stuff, bothersome to the featured couple for 50 odd minutes, is dealt with with a single stroke at the finish.

Of Jeanne (Betty Bronson) they have made another street angel, though this time not so convincingly. Jeanne, "a flower from the gutter," is the maiden of the traveling troupe of M'sieu and Madame Blossom. The Madame is a wild tempered tigress and professionally a whip cracker. M'sieu is a rotter. The show also includes a native girl who targets for the Madame, a rum soaked juggler, a props (Buster Collier) and a dwarf.

Collier is one of those mysterious strangers who "dropped in from nowhere." He falls for Jeanne and vice versa. In flash back he tells his past. He shouldered his brother's blame in a theft charge and deserted from an English fort in the Sudan.

Before the finish Jeanne is sold to a nearby sheik, but saved when it is discovered she is white. The Madame had stained her skin.

Vindication for the boy and love for the girl, fading out together under desert skies to accompaniment of off-screen singing of the theme song. The song receives four or five plugs, always off-screen.

Role of Rose Dione as the tempestuous Madame is the performance of the picture. Miss Bronson, Collier and Mitchell Lewis, especially the latter in character, are not far behind.

Recording excellent and photography good in spots. The flashbacks of a desert fort are bad. *Bige.*

THE LARIAT KID

(SILENT)

Universal production and release. Adapted by Jacques Jaccard and Sylvia Seid from novel of same title of Buckleigh Fritz Oxford. Directed by Reaves Eason. Harry Neumann, cameraman. Titles by H. Tarshis. At Loew's New York, one day, April 22, half double feature. Running time, 62 minutes.

Tom Richards	Hoot Gibson
Mary Lou	Ann Christy
Scar Hagerty	Cap Anderson
Aunt Bella	Mary Foy
Cal Gregg	Francis Ford
Pat O'Shea	Walter Brenan
George Carson	Andy Waldron
Trigger Finger	Bert Osborne
Pecos Kid	Joe Bennett
Jackknife	Jim Corey

Hoot Gibson pulls real revival propaganda for westerns in "The Lariat Kid." The interest is bonafide and the story is meaty. Some novel gags are introduced and the suspense never wanes. Good bet for any silent house.

Gibson starts as the marshal, out to avenge his murdered dad. Girl interest introduced in the first few feet when Hoot runs into Mary Lou, played by Ann Christy, escaping from a scheming aunt and burly escort, member of a bad town gang.

Into the village where all forces of law and order, including his father, have been vanquished, Hoot boldly strides. With a crazy street cleaner as an ally Hoot rounds up the whole mob. Using the water wagon as a jail he gets the crowd laughing. And Hoot does his business logically because he takes 'em one at a time in backyard challenges.

His girl spirited away by the heavy, played by Francis Ford with characteristic effectiveness, provides against story monotony. Hoot shows some great hard riding. *Waly.*

FALSE FATHERS

(SILENT)

Eldorado production. Noah Beery starred. Directed by Horace B. Carpenter. Photographed by Harry Newman. Cast includes Horace B. Carpenter, the director; Francis Pomerantz and E. A. Martin. At Arena, one day, April 28, half of double bill. Running time, 60 mins.

"False Fathers" may best be characterized as an attempt to break the hearts of the 10-20-30 audiences. The high-hatters inundating the sure-seaters would consider this a masterpiece for laughs.

If its incoherence may be called a story, it is the tale of two gold prospectors who for about 40 minutes are depicted in their hut taking care of a baby saved from Indians who shoot up a covered wagon. Their quarreling leads to fist fights, the baby, of course, providing the medium which saves them from slaughtering each other. Beery as the parson appears only for a few moments.

A mining town is shown; then a covered wagon; then the Injuns. The two prospectors, returning from another town, observe the massacre. They dynamite the redskins. A dog leads them to baby. One of the prospectors is a man hunted by the law for murder he is innocent of. He is always dreaming of his garden of roses and the gal who believes him innocent.

The baby takes his mind off his dreams. The two men fashion such intimate garments as babies need, for laughs. They learn to love the babe.

The law reaches out to the West for the accused murderer. A storm nearly kills detective. Accused saves him from wildcat. Man is told by dick that real murderer has confessed; also informs him that he was after the covered wagon with band of crooks who kidnapped the baby. Turns out that the kid belongs to one of the prospectors. Law takes baby from men, but they learn their rights from Beery, the parson, who tells them the child must be returned to father. That's the story. Child returned for the joyous ending. Rank hokum which was too sad for Eighth avenue patrons.

German Pics

"THE STRANGE LIE"

Berlin, April 24.

Ufa Palast — "Die wunderbare Luege der Nina Petrowna" ("The Strange Lie of Nine Petrowna) (Ufa). Undoubtedly the best German picture of the season. A certain section of the press anti-Ufa because it is owned by Hugenberg jumped on the scenario and there is no doubt that it is full of holes. But it seemed if not brilliantly original.

at least competent film stuff. Hokum as they like it even in the big cities.

It concerns the mistress of a rich general in prewar Russia. She falls for a young officer just mustered into service and out of pique against the general gives him the key to her apartment.

He calls there the same night but, being naive in the best film tradition, spends the night curled up in a chair.

Next morning the general finds them together. When she tells him that she has fallen for the boy, he turns her out.

The youth has been warned against her and only after he realizes that she has given up everything for his sake does he finally give in to her.

They live together in a shabby little apartment and have great difficulty in making ends meet. To earn money for her the boy gets into a poker game in which the general is playing. The latter discovers him trying to cheat and with the boy's confession goes to the girl. If she will return to him he will tear up the paper, otherwise the boy's only way out is suicide. She acquiesces and makes the boy believe that she is returning to the general because she wants more luxury. He leaves her disgusted.

The general returns to his apartment to find her dead—she has poisoned herself.

There is no doubt that under Pommer's supervision the film has been put across in the most velvety of fashions. Hans Schwartz seldom allows the actors to step over the line of unreality and with the aid of the cameraman Karl Hoffmann gives the whole mood and atmosphere. And never has Brigitte Helm been half so good as here in the title role. Franz Lederer again proves himself one of the best of juvenile leading men. Even Warwick Ward as the general gives a completely satisfactory performance in the restrained English society tradition.

"PAINTED YOUTH"

Titania Palast — "Geschminkte Jugend" ("Painted Youth") (Boese). Inspired by the sensational Hilde Scheller process, it is, nevertheless, a worthy product. German version of the American "Flaming Youth" story but, as the Germans are more outright in matters of sex, it does not treat the problem so superficially.

Here a young girl, the daughter of a flighty widow who is making the most of her time, gets mixed up with Arthur, a boy who goes to the same school with her.

On a party with several others of their age they are forced to spend the night in a village inn when their auto breaks down. Arthur comes into her bedroom, but she turns him out.

The escapade becoming known at the school next day she is expelled. She goes to Arthur's room to ask his help in justifying her, but he only uses the opportunity to again try to seduce her.

Walter, a quieter decent friend, arrives at the crucial moment. In the struggle which follows Arthur is shot with his own revolver.

At the trial it is made evident that the girl is a victim of her mother's lack of interest in her upbringing and her engagement to Walter is suggested.

Karl Boese has directed with discretion and his youthful players act naturally and with comparatively little sophistication.

Good work is turned in by Kurt von Wolowski and Wolfgang Zilzer as the boys and Georgia Lind and Ruth Albu in secondary school girl parts.

A discovery for the German industry is Tony van Eyck in the female lead—and one that America is not liable to bid for. She is undoubtedly a corking little actress, but far from beautiful and has something over-ripe about her. Perhaps a possibility when graduating into mature roles for the girl certainly can troupe.

"CAGLIOSTRO"

Capitol—"Cagliostro" (Deutsches Lichtspiel Syndikat). Richard Oswald always gets somebody to invest money again in his productions and always turns out about the same sort of product. A lot of pomp, scenery and costumes and nothing that grips in the acting line. Here he handles the story of Cagliostro and leaves Continental audiences as cold as he would American ones.

It has nothing to do with the interesting figure of the historical swindler, but is merely a good looking young man who falls for Lorenza, an Italian small town beauty. Because he is going to be arrested, the girl follows him to Versailles.

Wishing to get him free from this swindling type of life, Lorenza discloses the affair to the king, and they both are forced to leave the court.

Back in Italy, the two are captured and about to be beheaded. He believes it is to be a mock execution, but at the last moment realizes its earnestness and, freeing himself, escapes with the girl.

A pity to waste so handsome and forceful a player as Hans Stuewe on the title role, but he will surely find work more worthy of his type. Renee Heribel as Lorenza is attractive, but didn't deliver much emotionally.

"MASCOTTCHEN"

Kurfuerstendamm—"Mascottchen" (Aafa). Kathe von Nagy, young Hungarian star, is being pushed strongly. From here it looks like a false alarm. The girl is undoubtedly talented and has a nice little figure, but is now clowning so mercilessly difficult to tell whether she has any possibilities of development.

Fritz Basch, director, does not know even the a b c of his trade, and the cameraman delivers muddy photography that would have been a disgrace 10 years ago.

The story is taken from the Bromme operetta of the same name, and the next company that decides to make a silent out of an operetta deserves all the tortures.

This is a lot of hooey about a little salesgirl who becomes a revue star, just like that, and drags up her fiance, a bum actor, into the leading role.

"CITY BUTTERFLY"

Universum — "Grosstadt Schmetterling" ("City Butterfly") (Suedfilm). Richard Eichberg's last film with Anna May Wong, "Song," was a good money maker. This time he has not caught her personality and her exotic charm half as completely.

It's just a conventional film story which could have been played by any girl of any race. There is something to be made of Anna May Wong in the silent film, although her stage appearance in London proved that her voice is unsuitable for the talkers.

Here she plays a little sideshow dancer who flees the attractions of a brutal clown. She takes refuge with a young painter, who makes money selling portraits of her. The clown finds her again and steals money from her which she has gotten for the painter.

To save his life, which is threatened by the clown, she lies about the affair and he turns her out, believing her a thief. On the Riviera she meets him again, and, getting the money back from the clown, who has become a successful gambler, clears herself. The painter, however, now loves another, and she goes out of his life.

Alexander Granach brings the brutal clown to life, and Tilla Garden, in a minor role, seems a comer.

"MARITAL HAPPINESS"

Kurfuerstendamm — "Ein kleiner Vorschuss auf die Seligweit" ("A Little Advance on Marital Happiness") (Suedfilm). Dina Gralla remains as the best youthful comedienne of the German screen. She is grotesque when necessary, but always with discretion, and her contours are good to gaze upon.

Present film nothing to rave about —just an excuse to hang on broad farce situation.

Two opposing perfume manufacturers are bringing out a new perfume, and both naming it for Ninette, the revue star. Dolly, a little salesgirl of one of them, Nuddlich, has fallen for the head of the other firm, Victor. She discovers him having a love scene with Ninette, and decides to be revenged.

Hearing that Victor's cousin, a young boy at Eton, is coming for a vacation, she impersonates the youth, and always gets in the way between Victor and Ninette. When her identity is finally disclosed, Victor discovers he has been strong for her all along.

Jaaps Speyer's direction is somewhat above competent, and the film is sure fire for these parts.

"THE LIEUTENANT"

Beba Atrium — "Der Leutnant Ihrer Majestaet" ("The Lieutenant of His Majesty") (Hegewald). Fleck and his wife have here turned out the best film of their record. Not that this proves much, but at least it is well photographed and directed.

In Lillian Ellis the German screen seems to have found a new face worthy of further photographing.

The Czarina discovers that her husband is being unfaithful to her, and falls for an attractive young lieutenant. A young countess has also fallen in love with him, and, in escaping from a tete-a-tete with the Czarina, the lieutenant is found in the bedroom of this countess by the Czar, and is forced to marry her.

Ferdinand Hart gives a powerful characterization as the Czar, Agnes Esterhazcy lends somber beauty to the Czarina, Ivan Petrovitch has little chance to do more than look well as the lieutenant, and Lillian Ellis, mentioned above, is the countess.

"FOOLISH HAPPINESS"

Primus Palast — "Das narrische Gluck" ("Foolish Happiness" (Aafa). One of those childish products that can't be shown in a first-class German theatre. A humorless and inconsequent scenario about a little factory girl—the third this week. Maria Paudler in the lead looks occasionally like Laura La Plante; but that's where the resemblance ends, for it is always a Laura La Plante who looks as if she had been on a wild party for a month.

Johannes Guter, the director, doesn't even know where the sun comes up.

"HAMBURG AT 12:30"

Schauberg—"Auf der Reeperbahn Nachts um Halb Eins") ("In the Coney Island of Hamburg at 12:30") (Deutsche Universal). Just what is the German branch of the Universal's idea in bringing out Eddy Polo in Germany at this day and age? He is nothing but a straight stunt man, with no qualities to recommend him as a lead.

On top of that is a scenario as ridiculous as this. They brought the picture out at a slum house; but, no matter where it plays, from now on it can be nothing but second on a bad double feature bill.

"WHAT PRICE LOVE"

Beba Atrium—"Was kostet Liebe" ("What Price Love" Strauss). Nothing above the middle line, but the young director, Emo, proves himself a hope. Igo Sym and Helen Steels, in the leads, both play simply and charmingly, and Hans Thimig and Leopold Kramer are exceptionally good in minor roles.

A rich lonely old millionaire adopts his poor nephew under the condition that he have nothing to do with his former friends.

A girl with whom he has been in love reads that he is to be married to a young society girl, and tries to commit suicide. The uncle hears of this, and, realizing that he was wrong, unites the two—the young man having already regretted his engagement to the other girl.

Trask.

THE BLACK WATCH

(ALL DIALOG)

Los Angeles, May 10.

Fox production and release. Featuring Victor McLaglen. Directed by John Ford from Talbot Mundy's story. Dialog by J. K. McGuinness, with John Stone scenarist. Cameraman, J. A. August; film editor, A. Troffey; chief soundman, W. W. Lindsey. Western Electric system, sound on film. At the Carthay Circle, Los Angeles, for twice daily run at $1.50, starting May 8. Running time, 91 minutes.

Capt. Donald King	Victor McLaglen
Yasmini	Myrna Loy
Lieut. Malcolm King	David Rollins
Colonel	Lumsden Hare
Rewa Ghunga	Roy D'Arcy
Mohammed Khan	Mitchell Lewis
Major Twynes	Cyril Chadwick
General (India)	Claude King
Major MacGregor	Francis Ford
Harrim Bey	Walter Long
Field Marshal	David Torrence

A talker with too many ifs to make it smash program material, but should sail for a normal swing around the de luxe sites. The boys will go for it despite that at times it distinctly reads like a dime novel, or maybe because of that fact.

Story is loose jointed and far from well knit, the audience being asked to take plenty for granted. Opposed to this are the strong points of some excellent pictorial work plus sufficient action to hold suspense. This feature, at least, keeps that promise.

It's a sound and action picture. Dialog is distinctly secondary and in one or two spots drips with melodramatic hoke, besides almost becoming maudlin in a love scene between McLaglen and Myrna Loy, the latter the only femme principal. The unfortunate choice of the name of Yasmini for Miss Loy, which the "mike" translated as "Yes, Mini," brought laughs the opening night; but this was immediately cut. Necessity of scissoring, however, leaves an awkward sequence spasmodically gasping for relief. Report is that these scenes were added after Ford completed the picture. Doesn't make for smooth going, but as the picture reveals a tendency to jump around, anyway, the distortion in pace is not too flagrant.

Mundy's tale is that of the Scottish Captain King, who is ordered to India to prevent a native uprising on the eve his regiment is leaving for France. He leaves without explanation and to an eyebrow-raising chorus from his brother officers. He further apparently besmirches his standing upon arriving in the East by getting into a drunken brawl, during which he supposedly kills a fellow service man, the ruse being an escape among the pack of fanatics planning to overthrow British rule.

The natives worship a woman as their goddess, who, in turn, succumbs to the brawn of King. Too much the gentleman to carry his deceit that far, he quells the rebellion in a machine gun slaughter after the natives have shot their goddess, following her appeal to them to lay down their arms.

Just how King manages to get about a dozen British soldiers among the hordes, who, at a signal, throw off their robes to reveal khaki, is not explained. That they have seeped their way into the clan under orders is something patrons will have to figure for themselves. Also unexplained is the presence of Mohammed Khan (Mitchell Lewis) in the secret cave, a native but loyal officer to His Majesty and friend of King. Only reason for not blowing up the much coveted ammunition dump seems to be that the "mike" wouldn't stand the strain.

Ford's best work, and sufficient to hold this one up for A house consumption, is the opening of a Scottish officers' dinner on the eve of war, with bagpipes wailing. In addition there is a long but holding passage as the Black Watch regiment entrains, an excellent piece of work minutely recorded by lens and wire. Later thrills are the pipes playing the boys into action in France, a cut back as McLaglen gazes into a crystal, and the wholesale mowing down of the natives as they attack up a steep incline within a mountain cave.

August's camera work is superb in both these instances, the Scots being silhouetted against a strong hidden light as they come down a road through a wood. Intervening footage is given over to ponderous dialog carrying a mediocrely pieced story. A slow journey with occasional high lights.

"Black Watch" is a peculiar example of a picture which wouldn't mean much silently, for the thrill in those pipes is potent and doesn't rate importantly with dialog. Minus the talk but with the sound effects, and less the constant pauses for verbal passages to permit swift continuity, it might easily have been a corking release.

Fox has been sending slow paced films into the Gaiety, New York, minus dialog. Here was one promising heavy action which sound effects alone would have mightily enhanced. So, with the detracting elementary dialog, the total rating is not much above the others, even though it should have an improved Gaiety chance because of Broadway's masculine drop-ins.

McLaglen's performance is just normal. He's much toned down since a microphone has been placed on the set. Doing a strong, silent British soldier, the role has been taken literally, with his talking no more than necessary. Miss Loy sheds an attractive appearance under, at times, outstanding lighting, aided by long robes. Roy D'Arcy and Walter Long are the dual menace personalities, both permitted to overact, especially Long, and D'Arcy adhering to the ultra slow articulation generally associated with a scheming Hindu.

Of comedy there is little or none, Mr. Lewis handling the majority of a meagre quantity in continuously asking Allah's forgiveness for his sins and then pushing some one off a cliff or running a saber clean through. Lewis could have stood more footage, as, with a splendid voice and his burly personality, he fits with McLaglen, and the picture needs all the vocal high lights it can secure. A not-so-polite "raspberry," offered a London street singing trio, failed to register for a laugh here.

Weird notes of the pipes, Ford's handling of his mob stuff and August's method of recording his director's direction of mass are the foundation of this release. It will probably take much cajoling to induce McLaglen to play another love scene (house giggled at it), and they'd better give this boy some virile conversation if he's going to retain his popularity.

A program picture which might have been a pip. *Sid.*

THE SQUALL

(ALL DIALOG)

First National production and release. Directed by Alexander Korda, based on Bradley King's arrangement of the Jean Bart play. Recorded on Western Electric disc system, with musical score credited Leo Forbstein. At Central May 9, twice daily, $2 top. Running time, 104 minutes.

Nubi	Myrna Loy
Josef Lajos	Richard Tucker
Maria, his wife	Alice Joyce
Paul	Carroll Nye
Irma	Loretta Young
Peter	Harry Cording
Lena	Za-Su Pitts
El Moro	Nicholas Soussanin
Uncle Dani	Knute Erickson
Niki	George Hackathorne

"The Squall," on screen especially if not on stage could have been written around Harry Rosenthal's privately distributed little song, "When I Lay in the Hay." As a picture this First National will get its quota of money in the regular houses for it's full of make and hay. Otherwise it's too muchly padded and it's not $2. Of course not $2, so few are.

The hay thing is suggested by Myrna Loy as Nubi, the gypsy girl who blew the troupe, landing in a farm house, seemingly knowing every haystack in the territory. That's where she made her dates, on the sunnyside of a stack. And on the make she did a cleanup in the farmhouse, from the hired man to the son and his father. The only one Nubi muffed was the grandfather, and, from what the girl did do the old man would have been a pushover for her.

At the Central the picture ran past its logical ending. That should have been when Nubi had to go back to the gypsies and the horsewhip. She didn't bust up the home, after all, but she put several bad dents into it. For Nubi as a gypsy was a gyp out for jewelry, etc., probably the queen of the dirty-skinned gold diggers.

Miss Loy's overconfidence in her gypsy sex prowess is doubtless the fault of the script. It is sadly apparent after the first 15 minutes what is going to happen in the remaining hour. This in itself blunts the edge for suspense. Bromides and dead pan performances by several in the cast provide an unexpected amusement at times.

Had the camera shunned close-upping Alice Joyce during her talking moments, Miss Joyce's mother who knows all but keeps mum would have been meritorious. As it is, this actress' endeavor to articulate within a few feet of the lens, coupled with a voice of monotone register, impresses as sound conscious. Her manifestations become marked, as does the audience inclinations to giggle, as she discovers the gypsy's wrecking tactics. Miss Joyce's "Oh, My God!" or "Go to your room," which she delivers numerous times to Nubi and her son Paul, become more hacked and amusing, since the same tonality is there.

Perhaps the most natural performance is rendered by Za-Su Pitts as Lena, the house servant, whose boy friend, Peter, is the first to fall. The big Harry Cording, with a ferocious expression but light voice and select English, essays Peter excellently when he is not talking.

Loretta Young as the innocent Irma, betrothed to Paul, played by Carroll Nye, is a beautiful screen subject. Her voice, however, is identical with commencement exercises in a grammar school. Nye gives a stereotyped juvenile performance.

The inconsistent father, Josef Lajos, is played by Richard Tucker. Here, also, Tucker shows flashes of an ability cramped by directorial command.

Like the opening and closing of some theatrical shows of yore, a gang of geese and some oxen indicate the beginning and ending of each day by being paraded out of the barnyard in the morning and returned in the evening. The first few times their passing is interesting, but after that the blare of sound quacks and scientific renditions of chicks klucking become irritating. *Waly.*

GENTLEMEN OF PRESS

(ALL DIALOG)

Paramount production and release. Directed by Millard Webb. Based on the play by Ward Morehouse. Screen adaptation by Bartlett Cormack. Dialog directed by John Meehan. Photographed by George Folsey. Walter Huston featured. At the Paramount, New York, Saturday, May 11. Running time, 75 minutes.

Wickland Snell	Walter Huston
Myra May	Katherine Francis
Charlie Haven	Charles Ruggles
Dorothy Snell	Betty Lawford
Ted Hanley	Norman Foster
Mr. Higginbottom	Duncan Penwarden
"Red"	Lawrence Leslie

Fair enough for the single week stands, this talking picture version of the slightly anemic stage play will create no tumult, though it is practically assured of moderate business as gauged from the new talker level.

There is drama in this story, but it never quite clicked in the stage play, and there was no reason to suspect it would be otherwise in the picture. The values of the production depend largely on characterization, and in the group sequences the picture is lifelike and vivid, moving swiftly and humorously.

Then come spots where there is an undercurrent of determination to be grimly dramatic, but nothing that Walter Huston could do injected any sense of reality into the proceedings at those times.

There are several opportunities for stirring dramatic action and here direction is cold. After flopping with these sequences the story reels back unevenly to a dull level, somewhat disconnected.

Action is held up several times, making it draggy where clever propping should have been used to bolster.

Story is of a newspaperman who is away from home when his baby girl is born, not with her when she is married, and too busy getting out a special edition of his paper when she dies in childbirth. As he sits at his desk, stunned, a Yale college boy with ink on his nose and hero worship in his eyes humbly asks the great Mr. Snell (Huston) for some advice on the newspaper business, and is told to get out of it before it poisons him.

It is a strong climax, yet it never gets over. The death scene of the young woman at the hospital, with her father away, doesn't hold, either.

Comedy, lines and delivery, about the only things that register with regularity. But no steady stream of punch laughs. Charles Ruggles, as the stew reporter, is the biggest asset to the picture. He has the most effective part in the story, the strongest laugh lines, the best delivery and displays exceptional ability. He scores the heaviest returns with the invitation he hands out to Snell's secretary, "Come up to my apartment some time and fight for your honor."

Huston is supported by a fine cast of players, the two girls both looking and speaking well. With Katherine Francis as the seductive siren and Betty Lawford as the daughter photographing well and also recording, the major difficulty in casting this talker was over.

Next in importance to Huston, who plays a straight, natural type without any fireworks, is Ruggles, who cops the honors. Huston isn't at his best in this kind of an assignment. It doesn't call for much except stolid, even delivery. Ruggles has all or most of the color and the lines.

In general the picture serves up a sombre, if accurate, portrait of newspaper life. Accuracy in most aspects is natural, considering that Ward Morehouse of the New York Sun, aided and abetted by five or more co-authoring scribes on other local dailies, is responsible for the script. *Mori.*

ETERNAL LOVE

(SOUND)

United Artist's release of Ernst Lubitsch production starring John Barrymore, with Camilla Horn featured, in Hans Kraly's adaptation of story by Jacob Chistoph Heer; titles by Katherine Hillikr and H. H. Caldwell; musical syncaronization and score by Dr. Hugo Riesenfeld. Runs 60 minutes at the Rivoli. New York, week of May 11.

Marcus Paltram	John Barrymore
Ciglia	Camillia Horn
Lorenz Gruber	Victor Varconi
Rev. Tass	Robert Bosworth
Housekeeper	Dodil Rosing

Pia .... Mona Rico
Pia's Mother .... Evelyn Selbie

With a peach of a box-office title and a great star, "Eternal Love" is a disappointer as a Barrymore. It will get by as a program release but will not hold up for the few weeks it is spotted into the Rivoli, regardless of the fact it's primarily a showcase Broadway exhibition.

It's a straight love story, but generally familiar, although with the Barrymore artistry and distinction and the satisfying Lubitsch production, the theme takes on a measure of special significance.

As a picture it's almost a cheater considering the outdoors stuff, but everything was done with a view to realism and does not call for any heavy "nut." Action is laid in the Tyrolean Alps, time around 1812 in the midst of the Franco-Austrian warfare, which made the neutral Switzerland a geographical connecting link between both nations.

Compromised by a scheming village gal, Barrymore is forced to go through a marital ceremony with her, leaving Camilla Horn bereft and forced into marrying the character personated by Victor Varconi.

Circumstantial evidence points to Barrymore as the murderer of Varconi and with the escape of the pair to the Alpine heights, they find their "eternal love" in the afterlife as they walk to meet their doom amidst a glacial avalanche; this, as an alternative to the enraged village posse which is pressing on their heels.

The tragic ending, for all its sentimenality, is not the least of the flicker's shortcomings, although as a general commercial proposition it will ring the cash register, thanks to that title and the John Barrymore name value.

Sound synchronization (there is no dialog) is excellently carried out by Dr. Hugo Riesenfeld's score. There is no theme song. Sound effects are limited to the rifle shots, sounding of the door gong, door knocking, etc. The village revel in the town hall to celebrate the French emancipation was the occasion for considerable atmospheric color, native dance music, masque effects, etc., but that was the sole important production effect; rest was mostly outdoors.

Lubitsch has some fine touches to indicate the sex stuff in Barrymore's relations with Camilla Horn and Mona Rica, the hoyden whom he seduces in a drunken aftermath of the masquerade whoopee. For the main, however, it's innocuous romance stuff, a bit thick, but on the whole mildly pleasing.

Casting generally is satisfactory, as is the play. *Abel.*

THE VALIANT

(ALL DIALOG)

Fox production featuring Paul Muni. Based on play of same name by Robert Middlemass and Holworthy Hall. Adaptation and dialog by Tom Barry and James Hunter Booth. Directed by William K. Howard. Cameraman, Lucien Andriot. At Roxy, New York, week of May 11. Running time 66 mins.

James Dyke .... Paul Muni
Mary Douglas .... Marguerite Churchill
Warden .... De Witt Jennings
Judge .... Henry Kolker
Mrs. Douglas .... Edith Yorke
Chaplain .... Richard Carlyle
Robert Ward .... John Mack Brown
Police Lieutenant .... Clifford Dempsey
Dr. Edmondson .... George Pearce
Policeman .... Don Terry

Despite its fine recording and acting the impression is inescapable that this one might better never have been produced as its theme and story is essentially too drab, agonizing and grim to appeal to the average American moviegoer as entertainment.

It's the story of a drifter who commits a murder and valiantly fights to keep his family from learning of his guilt. It matters very little under the circumstances that Director William K. Howard has done his job well and that the dialog is as natural and intelligent as any heard to date. No amount of technical competence could have redeemed such material from bleakness. It is not sufficiently epic to be powerful tragedy and it is too fatalistic and sorrowful to be other than depressing.

At no point is there any doubt that in the end the valiant will go to the electric chair. Nor are the cause, motive and circumstances of the murder made clear. The audience never sees the murdered man. An off-set shot at the start symbolizes the crime. All this tends to increase the agony-for-agony's-sake effect.

The scene between the valiant and his sister in a room at the penitentiary is strong and perhaps there will be tears from sentimental folks. On the other hand the thinness of the story, the lack of action or incident, and the debatable plausibility of the valiant's trick of hiding his shame from his sister and at the same time creating an honorable alibi for the mother's peace of soul makes the sum total of the picture pretty slight.

Paul Muni, the former Muni Wisenfreund of the Yiddish stage, brings to his role a wealth of humanity. He registers splendidly with utter naturalness and while he will be difficult to cast he should find an important niche in the talkers. His voice is rich and pleasant, his personality strong and virile, and if he is not pretty, neither is Lon Chaney or Emil Jannings, and Muni has what those fellows have not, dialog utility.

It's going to require much smart showmanship to exploit this young Yiddish-American actor, but directed and handled intelligently, he looks like one of the legits who will survive in the talkers.

Marguerite Churchill also gives a finely shaded and strong performance. She is an ingenue representative of the home girl type of American womanhood, but without any spilling over of the sugar bowl.

With mention of the able performance of the veteran screen actor, DeWitt Jennings, there is little else to report on the cast. The production is first class, although not expensive (appraising what shows in the finished product).

It doesn't appear from a showmanly standpoint that "The Valiant" will do more than get by. It's dubio diversion for the generality. *Land.*

THE PAGAN

(NO DIALOG)
(Song Sequences)

M-G-M production and release; directed by W. S. Van Dyke. Ramon Novarro starred. Adapted from the short story by John Russell. On film tract Movietone. Titles by J. H. Jasson. Cameraman Clyde de Vinna. Running time, 80 minutes. At Capitol, New York, week May 11.

Henry Shoesmith, Jr. .... Ramon Novarro
Madge .... Renee Adoree
Tito .... Dorothy Janis
Joranson .... Donald Crisp

"Pagan Love Song," sure fire formula sentimental ballad, together with the billing possibilities of Ramon Novarro singing it, is enough to do the trick for the release. Picture has plenty of assets, among them the always effective tropic love element, smashing photography and a fine production. Particular interest to the fem fan, and word of mouth should make it a builder for week dates.

Novarro does a capital bit of acting, the only weakness being a dull fight climax, which injures an otherwise effective performance. Weakness here probably is inherent in the story rather than a lapse of either player or director.

Point of the whole narrative is a contrast between the simplicity and kindliness of the South Seas half-caste and the hypocritical cruelty of the white trader. When these two characters come to grips at the finale, it might injure the literary point to have the docile native turn tiger. Delicate ethnic question here, but for screen purposes the present treatment is disappointingly mild.

Story has in it a quality resembling "Sadie Thompson," although it is dealt with in an incidental way. Even then it contributes to interest.

Van Dyke also directed "White Shadows," which had its day on Broadway. In "The Pagan," the same director, working in the same locale, has achieved notable beauty of settings for his romantic tale. Sky and sea shots are stunning. Tricky camera angles of the hero swimming out to an off-shore vessel are examples of fine dramatic and pictorial sense.

Theme song, one of those slow, lilting chansons, is skillfully woven into the action, reprised time and again always in a manner appropriate to the situation and taking effectiveness from that fact. Here, on tropic beach, sings to moonlit sea, and heroine, captive on trader's ship, replies. Again, when the lovers have for the moment triumphed and are together in a mountain retreat, hero sings a phrase, and the girl, idling in the house, makes musical reply.

Novarro and Dorothy Janis have nice voices in this reproduction, and the sentimental motif of the song touches the romantic situation with a good deal of color, no matter who is singing.

Picture is entirely without dialog, although sound effects of many kinds. Church bells ring, birds carol around the couple's retreat and other incidental bits, but the title method of exposition is used throughout. Title writer has done a good job, titles being colored with just the right shade of humor. For instance, on the introduction of the vicious white trader, line is "When East meets West the result is six barrooms and one bank," neatly expressing the picture man's idea that influence of civilization is to corrupt idealistic life of the simple native.

Renee Adoree has an entirely secondary role, as a sort of Sadie Thompson, and plays it for all it is worth. Donald Crisp is the white trader, handling the heavy role with commendable judgment and restraint. Miss Janis is new to leading roles, picked here perhaps for her voice and because she fitted the role of native girl by her brunet coloring. She does handsomely by the casting direction, playing a passive role with a good deal of naive charm, eloquent in spite of its quietness.

Picture on a certified box office subject, neatly handled and sure fire for the family and neighborhood trade, as well as for the de luxes. *Rush.*

HOT STUFF

(30% DIALOG)

First National production and release. Alice White starred. Directed by Mervyn Le Roy from story by Robert Carr. Musical score on Western Electric disk system by Louis Silvers. At the Cameo, New York, week May 11. Running time, 73 minutes.

Barbara (Babe) Allen .... Alice White
Aunt Kate .... Louise Fazenda
Mack Moran .... William Bakewell
Thelma .... Doris Dawson
Sandy McNab .... Ben Hall
Wiggam .... Charles Sellon
Tuffy .... Buddy Messinger

A slow and padded tag on the cycle of collegiate themes that will afford very little excitement even to the adolescent minds to which it cates, about sum up "Hot Stuff."

Except in smaller towns Alice White's latest vehicle hasn't the sustaining powers, unless the adults are misled by the title, to pull for over two days. The picture just hasn't the snap and sparkle of even some of its independent predecessors.

Dialog in the opening sequence for about 15 minutes, again in the middle for about five, and in the close for several, is spotted so as to impress as covering more of the running time. The opening session with Alice White and Louise Fazenda discoursing on the subject of the wherewithal for a college career is blurred and has to be followed closely, otherwise some of it is unintelligible.

The theme has not much action. College boys driving up to Aunt Kate's (Louise Fazenda) gas station afford an exchange of a few lines between Kate and the postman on the difference in times. The letter is opened and, in cut-and-dried fashion, Auntie has an order for 10 grand, covering damages in an accident years back.

At the campus, where Auntie is shown as chaperone for Babs, the heroine is sized up as a hot number and the school don tries his stuff. William Bakewell as Mack Moran makes a good job of this role.

The rest of the story is given over to Babs showing Mack that she can gather just as many hearts. It's all done in a very conventional way. One sequence, the nearest to being "hot," is where Babs and Mack take refuge in a hut during a storm. An undress sequence is introduced, each gesture indicating that the move is for clothes drying. Other students drive up. Apparently as an afterthought one of them gets socked by Mack after a series of innocent remarks.

A solo dance by Babs at a party where many glasses are lifted is also quickly tailored to Hays' requirements. Mack takes the little girl home and feeds her stuff out of a flask. Then the truth comes out. The pretended vamp admits that she is just a country girl, while the sheik reveals his honest nature. As for the flask, Mack confesses it contained only cold tea and Babs really never had a drink.

One of the most amusing sequences has to do with Miss Fazenda's activities in a skating rink. Her falls and jams will get laughs out of any type of fan. *Waly.*

THE KID'S CLEVER

(SILENT)

Universal production and release. Starring Glenn Tryon. Directed by William J. Craft. From story by Vincent Moore. Cameraman, Al Johns. Titles by Albert DeMond. Production supervision, Harry L. Decker. Cast includes Katherine Crawford, featured; Russell Simpson, Joan Stanley, Florence Turner, George Chandler, Lloyd Whitlock. Two days, May 8 and 9 at Times theatre. Running time, 50 mins.

More hyperbole for Glenn Tryon. This time he's in one of those chase-me pictures, driving frantically in and out traffic demonstrating a freak automotive contraption which runs on land and sea, deriving its power from the air. He is the inventor and falls for the daughter of a motor magnate, who becomes interested in his invention.

Picture opens with Tryon as "Bugs" Raymond, inventor, tire salesman and soda fountain proprietor. He has inventions for everything. Chums with girls from seminary, who are running a Colonial dance. Meets the motor magnate's daughter among them when they have spill in old time hansom, in which they are publicizing their hop.

Tryon's assistant double crosses him when the test is made of his freak motorboat-automobile. Home town turns out for the celebration and Tryon is on the spot with a big speech. Test of motor nearly kills magnate. Helper bribed by other motor interests.

Girl sticks to him despite trouble. Tryon's assistant breaks down and confesses the double cross. Boy and girl then approach father. Says it's too late, he has signed contract for other motor. Tryon takes the old man in his car and pursues the villain with the paper. Captures him and winds up in girl's arms.

Photography poor. Picture a replica of all the traffic chase cinemas seen before. Only novelty is the freak boat, which has been done in short comedies. Good for small time audiences.

THE DEVIL'S TOWER

(SILENT)

Rayart production and release. Directed by J. P. McGowan from the story by Victor Rousseau. Photographed by Ernest Depew. At the Ideal, New York, May 10. Running time, 60 minutes.

James Murdock	Buddy Roosevelt
Tom Murdock	Frank Earl
George Stilwell	J. P. McGowan
Doris Stilwell	Thelma Parr
Phillip Wayne	Art Rowland
Dutch Haynes	Tommy Bay

Playing at the Ideal, an 8th Avenue grind, with a 10-cent admission price, is in itself a classification of this production. With the grinds in some parts of the country beginning to suffer from a shortage of silent pictures everything goes to fill and quality doesn't figure.

This picture now stands a better chance on general bookings in the daily grinds than it did before, owing to the cut in production.

It is an outdoor picture with the story of the opposition to the new dam. The villain looks like a good-natured, harmless soul excepting that he needs a shave. A couple of scars would have helped for realistic villainy.

Dutch Haynes, the criminal master mind, demands money and threatens to blow up the dam. The heroic James Murdock stops him. In between, little things such as kidnaping, highway robbery, extortion and general connivery take place.

With the increasing number of grind house closings continuing, this type of picture will pass out with them. *Mori.*

DANGEROUS WOMAN

(ALL DIALOG)

Paramount production and release. Recording (on film) by W. E. Baclanova, Clive Brook, Neil Hamilton featured. Directed by Rowland V. Lee. Margery Lawrence's story. Adaptation and dialog by John Farrow and Edward Paramore, Jr. Harry Fischbeck, photographer. At Paramount, New York, week May 18. Running time, 80 minutes.

Tania Gregory	Baclanova
Frank Gregory	Clive Brook
Bobby Gregory	Neil Hamilton
Tubbs	Clyde Cook
Peter Allerton	Leslie Fenton
Chief Macheria	Snitz Edwards

"A Dangerous Woman" should better average money in the key combination stands, for it has the essentials of good program material. It continuously harps on the "the jungle will get you if you don't watch out" theory, and bases its action on that familar piece of belief. Yet that gag hasn't failed to attract and convince so far, and no reason why it should not as handled in this release.

The acting in "Dangerous Woman" is first rate, photography is commendable and the sound record excellent. One technical fault stands out, but not due to mechanical slip. It is always raining in the stinking African hole where the narrative is laid. Rain drops are a symphony in the quarters of the English district commissioner. The perennial hissing denotes rain fall. But a second or so before each character reads a line the rain chorus is shut off. So unhandily has this clearing of the mike been done that it seems the rain itself stops falling to permit a human being to speak.

The dangerous woman is fiery Baclanova, as Tania, Russian-born frau of Commissioner Gregory. Tania must have her outside attention. When not forthcoming, she goes out and creates. First to fall for the tropical spell and the blond Tania is Peter Allerton, upstanding English youth and Gregory's assistant. His finish is a self-inflicted bullet through the head. Gregory's own kid brother steps in to take poor Allerton's job, and it looks like the same finish for Bobby. But Tania dies (not naturally) before too late, and Gregory and the clean kid return to England.

Tania kicks off in a mystifying manner. Upon learning she has worked her wicked wiles on the kid, Gregory slips a mickeyfinn in Tania's orange juice. Tubbs, his faithful flunkey, sees him. In the morning Tubbs screams that the mistress of the house is dead in her bed from snake bite. There's a dead reptile near the body. Gregory thought he had committed the crime, but was dumbfounded when convinced otherwise by Tubbs.

Truth was Tania did drink the poisoned orange juice and died from it. Tubbs and the local medicine man worked up the snake gag to cover Gregory, without letting Greg in on it. And Tubbs refilled the glass to clinch the conviction for Gregory.

Baclanova gets in her usual Russian folk songs. At one point it goes vocally during a solo at the piano. Throughout this sound shot, during which the voice reaches impossible heights for Baclanova, the subject's back is always to the camera. Otherwise Bac does her own singing, maybe.

Clive Brook's strong-willed Englishman is a quiet study of worth, while Hamilton and Fenton, particularly the latter, make the most of their two chances at dramatics. Clyde Cook as Tubbs, typically limey, bears the comedy.

One scene registers 100 degrees heat without containing as much as a kiss. Tania and Bobby were out to see an African tribal dance. Tania went on the make on the way home and the pulsating boom-boom of the drums gave her background. She did her best, but the kid resisted. But audiences will not be half as strong as the kid. *Bige.*

THE VILLAGE OF SIN

(RUSSIAN-MADE)

(Silent)

Sovkino production, released through Amkino. Directed by Olga Preobrezhenskaya. K. A. Kuznetsov, cameraman. At Little Carnegie Playhouse week May 18. Running time, 68 minutes.

Vassili Shironin	A. Yastrebitzky
Anna	R. Puzhnaya
Vasilissa	E. Cessarskaya
Ivan	G. Babynin
The Blacksmith	M. Savelieff
Lukeria	E. Maksimova
Matveyevna	C. Narbekova

Faulty direction, allowing great gaps of irrelevant atmospheric shots to constantly submerge the story thread, kills off the chances this had to become one of Russia's outstanding film dramatics. Thin story that prevails is segregated in lumps throughout the reelage. Even these, however, are so well done as to carry on over the intervening jargon of action. The latter is like bits of a film magazine, but colorful with some exceptionally fine exteriors. Theatres with arty policies can safely book it for a week. It is too jumbled and strictly foreign for the average American audience, though.

The title, "The Village of Sin," libels a small town locale, because only a hypocritical parent is the offender. His viewpoint drives a daughter to a common law life with the blacksmith. Later the father, responsible for his son's marriage, attacks his daughter-in-law. He refuses to acknowledge the illicit child until after the mother's suicide and his boy's return from the war.

Well over half of the production is devoted to scenes in the field and home, of no particular bearing. Wheat cutting, spinning wheels, celebrating, and several long shots of winding roads and hills are entertaining for a time, but distracting in the way they are cut into the story. The editor seems to have dozed off. What there is of the continuity, as the result, is slapped at an audience according to the moods of the cutter.

Unusually few subtitles for a foreign production are used. *Waly.*

KIF TEBBI

(ITALIAN MADE)

(Silent)

Produced and released by Aida. Based on the story by Luciano Zuccolli. Directed by Antonio Barreara. Cast includes Marcello Spada, Donatella Neri, Gini Vioti and Ugo Graccio. At Fifth Avenue Playhouse, New York, week May 18. Running time, 60 mins.

Aida is a subsidy of the Italian government. The program announcement advises that with this epic masterpiece Italy hopes to recover the position in the film industry it held prior to the war. May be better for Italy and reviewers if Aida would now settle down and try to make pictures.

Kif Tebbi is an almost endless series of long shots of people. No trace or any attempt of interesting narrative. Episodes, meaningless in themselves, have been strung together under a title.

The Italian actors in this picture walk away with the booby prize, previously held by the Russians.

Plenty of saluting. The Turks salute the Arabs, the desert Arabs salute the big time Arabs, enemies salute each other as well as friends.

The story is pathetically barren, though complicated. There are more anti-climaxes than can be counted on an adding machine. No sooner does one plot end than other blossoms almost right next to it. Incidents are left uncompleted, action is confused, and relations generally are at no time intelligible. Which may be blamed on the cutting, maybe.

It seems, according to one of the plots, that a young Arab with an American college education saves a young Arab desert girl from nothing in particular. Later an Arab called Rassim makes a play for her and is killed in a duel by the heroic college Arab.

To add interest there is a war between Turkey and Italy, and the young college Arab leads his troop. The menace having been disposed of comparatively early in the picture, little to hold interest to the finish.

While the war is being arranged a faithful servant of the young college Arab is ordered to disappear because he was a witness to the duelling. And other such dramatic events presented in so colorless and cheerless a manner that it will probably chill the sure-seaters among others. *Mori.*

Geo. Washington Cohen

(SILENT)

Tiffany-Stahl production and release. George Jessell starred. Directed by George Archainbaud. Adapted by Isidore Bernstein from Aaron Hoffman's play, "The Cherry Tree." Harry Jackson, cameraman. At Loew's New York one day, May 14, one-half of double feature. Running time, 62 minutes.

George Washington Cohen	George Jessel
Mr. Gorman	Robert Edeson
Mrs. Gorman	Corliss Palmer
Mr. Connelly	Lawford Davidson
Marian	Florence Allen
The Child	Jane La Verne

While adults will find laughs in "George Washington Cohen" and at the same time brand it mediocre, parents with children taught truth is virtue will decide the theme has the emphatic twang of an unhelpful reactionary. The story is 100 per cent home-wrecking truth, and wreaks upon its vendor, played in this by George Jessel, all sorts of injustices. The finis is a preachment on the white lie as a guarantee for happiness.

A directorial muff on audience psychology is also found in the opening. Over-detail in Jewish christening rites establishes an intimacy bordering closely on the offensive. Several long subtitles in Hebraic script register negatively with the average audience.

Jessel, living up to the surname of the country's father, finds a pocketbook and gets a 10 grand a year job on the sole qualification of his tenacity to truthfulness. The latter impresses more, in Jessel's handling of the part, as pure brass and ignorance than any dominating innuence of a virtue.

Robert Edeson as Mr. Gorman proves an over-patient and short-sighted gent as a big business boss. He provides the production opportunity for a series of cut-ins while listening to Jessel recount his tales of woe. Some of these are amusing, especially truth-telling mania, causing the star's arrest as a material witness and getting a worse mauling than the murderer.

A long courtroom sequence follows Cohen's disclosure to Gorman that the latter's wife is guilty of indiscretions with one Connelly. As the wife, Corliss Palmer does little but photographs very well.

Cohen's telling the defense attorney that even the jury looks dumb gets a long laugh out of the audience. When the divorce decree is awarded a serious trend is attempted. Florence Allen as Marian, the female ingenue, rebukes George, and he tells his first lie. After that it is one lie after another, but release from jail for "perjury," marriage and money for the renegade George. *Waly.*

11 WHO WERE LOYAL!

(GERMAN MADE)

(Silent)

UFA A.G., production and release. Directed by Rudolf Meinert. Photographed by Ludwig Lippert. Settings by Gustav Kannert. Based on the novel by Max Jungke. At the 55th St. Playhouse, New York, week May 18. Running time, 60 mins.

Mary Von Wedel.......................Mary Nolan
Fritz Von Wedel.............Ernst Rueckert
Queen Luise...................Grete Reinwald
King Wilhelm III............Gustav Semmler
Major Von Schill............Rudolph Meinert
French Commander.......Albert Steinrueck
Herr Von Malwitz.................Fritz Alberti

Even in the sure-seaters this picture is worth next to nothing. This house in particular, on 55th street, would probably do much better with third and subsequent run American pictures than with these foreign productions.

This is just another of the unentertaining importations. It is lustreless, unimaginative, and badly constructed. Direction terrible. Mary Nolan photographs well but isn't worthy of any further attention on anything she does in this picture.

People are badly costumed, action is draggy, and limiting the use of extras in the war scenes has merely robbed the production of any slight interest it might have had.

Story concerns an uprising in Prussia against Napoleon in 1808, led by a Major Schill against the wishes and orders of the King of Prussia.

Love story has been dragged in with a force that is apparent. It has no place in the action, as presented here, and slows the picture considerably.

Towards the end the girl is about to have a baby, the father having been called away to war before a marriage ceremony could be performed.

Another one of those pictures with several plots, two or three little stories, and an unintelligible general tale, all rolled into one. *Mori.*

EAST SIDE SADIE

(Silent)

Worldart Film Co. production, released independently. Story and direction by Sidney Goldin. Frank Zuker, cameraman. In cast: Bertina Goldin, Jack Ellis, Boris Rosenthal, Lucia Segar, Abe Sinkoff, Jack Halliday. At Stanley, one day, May 20. Running time, about 65 minutes.

With a 98 per cent "Cohen" cast and story slant the remaining two per cent "Kelly" in "East Side Sadie" comes out only in a fist fight and family squabble. Production is a very crude piece of workmanship. With a rainy print thrown in, it all smacks of something that was done before the war and with considerable haste then. Neighborhood houses with large Jewish draw and some of the grind houses should be able to find a place for it if for nothing more than folklore and conventional sentimentalism.

The action is as matter of fact and humdrum as a constantly repeated close-up of a sweatshop showing the sacrifice made by a girl to send her boy friend through college.

The lad is a sickly would-be double for Valentino, made more uninteresting by a weak-kneed role. The couple for half the reel is centered by the camera going through slow posey necking. This starts in Europe and winds up on a tenement roof where the lad, played by Jack Ellis, gets his yen for education.

The Irish taxi-driving son of a Jewish step-father puts over the wallop on the wedding night. Even the beating fails to animate the collegian and the picture just closes with him going back to the delirious seamstress after learning that she paid for his days with the books. *Waly.*

ETERNAL WOMAN

(SILENT)

Columbia production and release. Directed by John P. McCarthy. Olive Borden, Ralph Graves and John Miljan featured. Screen play by Wellyn Totman, adapted from story, "The Wildcat." Synchronized musical score. At Tivoli, New York, two days, May 20-21, as half double bill. Running time, 65 minutes.

Good romantic story with the settings spotted in the Argentinian hills, at sea in the midst of a storm and eventual shipwreck, and finally in a swell American suburban home. Action aplenty from the start, and the plot one of those rare ones that will make even sophisticates remark, "It can happen." This silent one can play split weeks with satisfactory results assured.

Story moves about Anita (Olive Borden), proud daughter of an innkeeper in the hills back of Buenos Aires, who returns home from the South American metropolis to find her sister has been wronged and her father murdered by an American guest at the small hotel. She swears vengeance on the man who has disrupted her home, having only a memory picture of the woman she believes to be his wife to guide her in her purpose.

This woman was cheating and Anita is chasing the wrong man, having followed the woman aboard a ship bound for America as a stowaway. Man is bound for America to give his wife air for double-crossing with she trying to square it.

Storm at sea wrecks the ship. Only Anita and Hartley Forbes (Ralph Graves) are saved, the latter being the husband of the woman indirectly the cause of the murder.

From there on the story moves rapidly with Anita and Ralph all set for the altar when the girl discovers a picture of the woman and is all ready to shoot her fiance. Tragedy is averted.

Slight cutting might improve this flicker. If with sound and dialog it would qualify for the better class week-stand palaces.

THE CHINA SLAVER

(SILENT)

Trinity production and release. Directed by Frank Mattison. Author not given program or poster billing. Starring Sojin, with cast including Albertino Valentino, Jim Aubrey, Bud Shaw and Opal Baker. At the Stanley, New York, May 10. Running time, 65 minutes.

Seems to be an independently produced film for states' right distribution. Mostly likely made by Sojin, the Oriental star, for foreign distribution, with especial reference to the Orient.

Sojin is the menace, and story is laid out with the Chinese actors carrying the important detail of the production.

In its intended field the picture should result in a profit both for distributors and exhibitors. Much like the old-fashioned thriller type of serial of 10 or 15 years ago, it should hold in the states' right field, locally also.

Story deals with the Chinese boss of an island which serves as a base for traffic in narcotics and white slavery. The Corba, as the menace, is designated, is the almighty ruler until a humble Chinese stowaway appears to upset everything. The little stowaway turns out to be a Chinese Secret Service agent.

Mori.

DELIA'S SECRET

(FRENCH MADE)

(Silent)

Paris, May 5.

"Le Secret de Delia," just trade showed by Franco Film, is a thriller, and is evidently intended for export. It should find no difficulty in crossing the sea or frontier.

The realization is really smart. A girl baptized Delia Fitzbury has been mixed up in a scandal in which the death of a man is the pivot. The fellow passed away in Bombay. Delia comes to Paris under the name of Marion Something. She meets a low down son who was also implicated, more than the innocent Delia, in the Bombay tragedy. He attempts to blackmail her.

But John Fitzbury, Delia's brother, assisted by the amorous Olivier, save her from the crook.

Sounds a bit ordinary, but it is the manner in which the picture has been developed. Some scenes are realistically excellent, such as a gambling club and an apache ball in Paris. Nothing new about that but this one tickles the fancy.

The producer is a newcomer named Menessier. He has been for years an appreciated studio decorator. "Delia's Secret" is his debut and he has turned out his first picture in a style that will please all publics.

Cast has Jean Murat, Maurice de Canonge, Gerald Fielding, Werner Fuelter, Marcelle Albani and Florence Grey. *Light.*

SHANGHAI ROSE

(SILENT)

Rayart production and release. Directed by Scott Pembroke from an original story credited Arthur Hoerl. Hap Depew, cameraman. Irene Rich starred. In cast: William Conklin, Richard Walling, Ruth Hiatt, Sid Saylor, Robert Dudley. At Loew's New York one day, May 7, one-half double feature. Running time, 71 minutes.

"Shanghai Rose" is hopeless cop of almost anything distasteful, with all of its hodgepodge of "Mary Dugan."

The direction is as poor as the story, which rambles to the point of being jarring.

Most glaring is the miscasting of Irene Rich. Protracted trial scene explanation fails to relieve fans of the shock of witnessing Miss Rich empty quarts of hooch at a sitting. Worse, still, is the relegating of an actress whose reputation is founded on clean-cut roles to a prostie house mistress. A long siege in the cutting room—or, far better for Miss Rich and her following—the shelf.

Atmosphere in the "house" is crassly handled. To show that it sells more than liquor, Director Pembroke has couples wise-eying while they enter rooms or else dames chasing men out into hallways.

Nothing else left after her acquittal, Rose seeks the nearest river. Someone should do the same thing with the prints of "Shanghai Rose." *Waly.*

SIOUX BLOOD

(SILENT)

Metro-Goldwyn-Mayer production and release, starring Tim McCoy. Directed by John Waters from story credited Harry Sinclair Drago. Arthur Reed, cameraman. In cast: Marian Douglas, Robert Frazer, Chief Big Tree, Sidney Bracey. At Loew's New York, one day, April 26, half of double feature. Running time, 60 minutes.

Although Tim McCoy's stock in trade is limited to the same facial expressions and gestures in every production, "Sioux Blood" has a better story angle than usual. The regulars will enjoy a consistent story in this one and find less need to use their imagination when unexplained things happen.

A couple of young brothers hold the interest at the opening. The Indians carry away one of them to raise in their own way and another is brought up by the whites. A title indicates time lapse. Then Tim is the avowed killer of the Injuns, a mighty man who cracks 'em off like clay ducks. Robert Frazer is the other brother into whom the anti-white spirit has been so inculcated by a venomous medicine man that he never lets his associates wash off the war paint.

Suspense is centered along the definite lines when the brothers identify each other. This comes after the appearance of the conventional stage coach, the beautiful girl and the surrender of Tim and the maid as hostages for her captured father. The father is revealed as murdered by the savages, but it is too late and Tim gets tied to a stake preparatory to a burning while the girl (Marian Douglas), holds off the savages with a knife to her heart. During an interim the medicine man tips Tim about the chief being a white man. During a battle the chief hears the story for the first time and recalls, between punches on the mid-section, that he really had a father and mother as well as a brother.

Some gags that get plenty of laughs are introduced by Tim during his escape. Pursued by half the tribe to a river a swimming contest ensues. In an under-water battle Tim borrows the headgear and stone walloper of a weak redskin and comes up to tap off the whole mob. A comic and a horse, that flops on his side every time an attempt is made to ride him, also please the fans. *Waly.*

JUST OFF BROADWAY

(SILENT)

Chesterfield production (State rights). Directed by Frank O'Connor. Supervised by Lon Young and presented by George R. Batcheller. Story by Fanny D'Morgal, adapted by Arthur Hoerl. Cameraman M. A. Andersen. Ann Christy and Donald Keith featured with cast including Lawrence Steers, DeSacia Moors, Syd Saylor, Jack Tanner, Beryl Roberts and Albert Dresden. At Loew's New York, one day, May 10, on double bill. Running time, 56 mins.

Another stencil from the world of night clubs and bootleggers with villainy in the form of hi-jacking and murder. Title is calculated to provide marques glamour for Main Street and story's triteness will not seriously matter in the places where picture is apt to play.

Bathcheller and Young have formularized their productions along with their state right mathematics so it may safely be assumed that these Chesterfields will make money for all concerned. They have at least the advantage of good photography and prints and a general tone of newness and even brightness. There are some giggles tucked away in "Just Off Broadway" which will season the drama. *Land.*

The Manhattan Cowboy

(SILENT)

El Dorado production and Syndicate (state right) release. Directed by J. P. McGowan from story by Sally Winters. Bob Custer starred. Paul Stern, cameraman. In cast: Lafe McKee, Mary Mayberry, Charles Whittaker, John Lowell. At Loew's New York one day, May 7, one-half of double feature. Running time, about 55 minutes.

For a western in the strictly quickie class "The Manhattan Cowboy" is slightly above average.

Following the new trend effected by shoot 'em ups in their efforts for a last stand, this one has the society start. Bob Custer as the playboy of a wealthy dad gives a new twist by first stealing a taxi starter's coat and being shipped to his father's ranch for reformation.

After that it's the regular stuff. The lad, naturally, proves to be the best rider and gunman on the plains. Mary Mayberry, the ranch boss' daughter, falls for the hero before he is off the train. Something about a family heirloom, worked in the story awkwardly at its best, brings out the bad hombres. One of them wants the girl as well, so Bob has plenty of work keeping the grind fans amused. *Waly.*

THE PEACOCK FAN

(SILENT)

Chesterfield Production (State rights). Directed by Phil Rosen from a story by Arthur Hoerl. Produced by Lon Young and presented by George R. Bathcheller. Cameraman, M. A. Andersen. Titles by Lee Authmar. On double feature program at Loew's New York, one day, May 10. Running time, 57 mins.

Lucien Prival	Dorothy Dwan
Rosemary Theby	Tom O'Brien
Gladden James	Spencer Bell
David Findlay	Carlton King

Fairly interesting melodrama of the who-killed-Reginald-Moneybags school. Dr. Chang Dorfman, a mysterious fellow of Chinese aspect, walks in on the scene of the crime and asks a few penetrating questions, quickly cuts through the confusion and names the murderer in time for the bulldog editions.

Lucien Prival who specializes on characterizations requiring a monocle and a sneer, impersonates the canny Dorfman with much slow motion and a countenance that remains consistently impenetrable. He wears a morning suit and his only weapon is a cool, precise, super-logical cerebellum. Its unmitigated hooey, but apt to pass for thrilling drama in the silo country.

Nobody particularly notable in the picture except Prival and Dorothy Dwan, who looks extremely pretty. Carlton King is the murderer.

Many elements favor "The Peacock Fan" as a first rate state righter in the silent division. Direction and production, barring some sloughing of detail, is meritorious. *Land.*

BAD MAN'S MONEY

(SILENT)

J. Charles Davis production and release. Story, direction and a performance by J. P. McGowan. Yakima Canutt starred. George K. Hollister, cameraman. In cast: Peggy Montgomery, Bud Osborne, Charles Whittaker, John Lowell. At Ideal, one day, May 17, one half of double bill. Running time, 50 minutes.

J. P. McGowan tripples in brass again and the result is the same. In "Bad Man's Money," when J. P. should be writing the story he's acting. When he's close-upping any moron in the ten-centers, where it's even an imposition to take up their time and dimes with this, can tell he should be megaphoning.

The thing's that way all the way through. Impossible to follow because McGowan, himself, couldn't. A lot of dead pans, something about a check, aimless riding from a ranchhouse to a small town until the audience is dizzy. Some fights are thrown in. Then Yakima almost throws out his arm before he scores a knockdown. They all get up—happy. And so J. P. ploughs on.

The only "tense" angle is when Yakima lassoes a dame from a horse. She takes such a pratt fall that audience indignation would be high were it not for the coldly dignified manner in which she arises and the lacing she gives the big cowboy.

Incidentally, this young woman, Peggy Montgomery, hurls two men out of her house as if they were egg plants. *Waly.*

GIRLS WHO DARE

(SILENT)

Trinity Pictures Corp. production and release. Rex Lease and Priscilla Bonner co-featured. Cast includes Rosemary Theby. At Stanley, New York (grind) May 11. Running time, 60 minutes.

Story is stencil and a rather sickly attempt to meller it up with a canoe upset and later an auto crash didn't help much. The picture just mooned itself to an untimely end.

Long stretches of uninteresting shots were the actors mope. Girls trapping rich men for their money seems to be the point aimed at.

At first the story looked as though it was going to involve a Tex Guinan type. It had a night club atmosphere of a sort with the hostess (Miss Theby) calling for a lil' hand for the gals, and so forth. But that was as far as the Guinan thing went. The hostess was living in a swell elegant apartment place paid for by "Uncle John," who turns out to be the daddy of a boy (Rex Lease) who falls in love with one of the "club" gang, played by Miss Bonner. There was a nice looking cop in love with the girl, but he passed out in an auto accident and made it easy for the hero to marry the night club kid.

Most of the story pictured indoors with drawnout scenes that inspired only boredom. Picture didn't show much expenditure. Acting of the rich boy's parents spoiled any chances the picture might have had.

Picture of service on double feature days were silents are still in demand. *Mark.*

THE DIVINE CRUISE

(FRENCH MADE)
(Silent)

Paris, May 10.

The successors of the late G. Petit (his sons Robert and Henri), trading under the firm of Etablissements Petits fils, prove they are well on the move by the release of another good picture, "La Divine Croisiere," modern legend composed and produced by Julien Duvivier. This picture may be cataloged as highly moral, intended for Catholic spheres, but will suit all audiences.

A sailing vessel, "Cordillere," is sent to sea by its greedy owner in a pretty dilapidated condition. It is understood a revolt occurs on board. No news is received, and it is taken for granted that the ship has gone down.

Simone, daughter of the owner, loved Jacques de Saint-Evremont (captain of the "Cordillere"), and is broken hearted.

One night, after her prayers, Simone has a vision. The Holy Virgin tells her the crew is still living. Through the influence of the village priest the girl obtains a sailing ship, "Maris Stella," and sails to the rescue of Jacques.

After several months cruise, under the command of Simone, the entire crew of the "Cordiliere" is discovered on a Pacific island.

"La Divine Croisiere" is a worthy production. Some shots are real bull's eyes. Acting is correct, Jean Murat and Suzanne Christy starring as the captain and his rescuer. Others are Henry Krauss, excellent actor; Tommy Bourdelle and Mme. Barbier Krauss. *Light.*

DEVIL'S CHAPLAIN

(SILENT)

Rayart production and release. Directed by Duke Worne from story by George Bronson Howard, adapted by Arthur Hoerl. Photographed by Hap Depew. At New York, New York, one day, May 17 as half double bill. Running time, 60 minutes.

The King	Josef Swickard
Princess Therese	Virginia Brown Faire
Yorke Norray	Cornelius Keefe
Nicholay	Wheeler Oakman
The Prince	George MacIntosh
Boris	Boris Karloff
Ivan	Leland Carr

Flimsy story of a revolution in a mythical Balkan state. Princess Therese, betrothed to the heir to the throne, pretends to be a leader of the mob storming the palace to save the life of her sweetheart. Story limps badly but crammed full of action, mainly international intrigue, with an operative of the U. S. Secret Service thrown in for love interest. It is apt to pass muster on a twin bill in the daily grinds.

This picture earns its chance for bookings in the daily changers owing to general reduction in the quality and quantity of silent flicker stuff aimed for the shooting gallery trade.

Following the opening sequence the scene shifts to Washington where the fugitive heir to the foreign kingdom has taken refuge and is under the wing of the ace operator of the secret service, Yorke Norray. After saving her fiance's life any number of times and seeing him restored to his throne the girl finally decides to give him air and hook up with the clever dick.

Miss Faire and Keefe handle the leads acceptably and Duke Worne's direction is all that the story deserved.

BLOCKADE

(10% DIALOG)

FBO (RKO) production, released by Radio Pictures. Directed by George B. Seitz from story by Louis Sarecky and John Twist, adapted by Harvey Thew. Sound and dialog recording by RCA Photophone. Musical score by Jos. Zuro. Titled by Randolph Bartlett. Photographed by Robert Martin. At Loew's New York one day, May 17, as half double bill. Running time, 70 mins.

Bess	Anna Q. Nilsson
Vincent	Wallace MacDonald
Gwynn	James Bradbury, Sr.
Hayden	Walter McGrail

Badly handled yarn, about rum running, hi-jacking and lawlessness growing out of the prohibition, spotted on the lowest coast of Florida and the numerous islands that lie east of the southern liquor frontier.

Highly illogical story has Bess Maitland, hi-jacker; Mona Van Slyke, society girl, and Revenue Agent Canavan, all played by Anna Q. Nilsson. She, with the aid of the army and navy, the U. S. Marines and the flying corps finally land the ring leaders of the rum ring.

Those who know the Florida winter hideaways will snicker plenty at this one. Even the peasant patrons of the cheaper neighborhood houses, where this film stands chance for screening, will laugh at the attempt to glorify the dry snoopers by ringing in a lady agent.

Two dialog sequences used are inconsequential.

Insipid love story has Vincent Goddard, New Yorker, looking for a fishing camp location on the Florida coast, getting tangled up in the activities of the rum runners, but winning the clean up girl.

Strictly for the few wired daily changers and can hardly stand alone there.

Daughters of Desire

(SILENT)

Excellent (producer) production and release. Directed by Burton King from story by Janet Vale. Irene Rich starred. In cast: Richard Tucker, Julius Molnar. At Loew's New York one day, May 14, one-half of double feature. Running time, 66 minutes.

A little serious attention to several twists in the story and some cutting would have made "Daughters of Desire" an exceptionally fine independent picture. Well cast and dressed, direction failed to take into consideration an absurd climax in the continuity where an obviously meaningless sacrifice is made. This affords the bridge into some more tedious courtroom stuff and falsifies efforts for what could have been sound melodrama.

Although the action is slow in the first reel or so, interest is kept alive and building by the threat made by a bootlegger after a lawyer has refused to defend him, and by the growing affection between the widower attorney and his secretary. The roles are played by Julius Molnar, Richard Tucker and Irene Rich.

Ultimately the couple is married, to the joy of a couple of boys, who are close-upped too frequently, since they rarely change register, and the sorrow of a blonde daughter. Heavy necking affairs among the young people in bathing regalia show the girl's defiance to her stepmother. The bootlegger naturally provides the liquor, leads the girl to a night club, parks on the way home and is accidentally shot in a struggle with her.

Miss Rich's appearance in another car just after the shooting is too timely. But her ordering the girl to drive away while she remains to take the blame, without any attempt to secure an explanation, hits the most gullible in an audience.

The courtroom scene stuff is insipid, as is the wife's refusal to see her husband, while she takes a great interest in scrubbing jail floors.

No accounting for time lapses, but that is of little concern, since the interest has been sacrified. Subtitles try to explain that the stepmother did her bit because she figured it would be a greater blow to her husband were he to know that his daughter was involved.

All so much flub-dub. *Waly.*

THE DREAM MELODY

(SILENT)

Produced by Samuel Zwierler and distributed by Excellent Pictures Corp. Directed by Burton King. Story by Leon Gray. Adapter for screen by I. Bernstein. Cameramen, William J. Miller and Walter Haas. Cast includes John Roche, Mabel Julienne Scott, Eleanore Leslie, Robert Walker, Rosemary Theby. At Ideal, New York, one-half double feature day, May 15. Running time, 57 minutes.

A dull story that never gets started. Little interest over a man continually thumping away at a piano to grind out his "dream melody."

Cheaply-constructed picture. Cast given nothing to do and most of entire grinding devoted to the boarding house room interior with the melody maker.

Silent picture, silent in every way. *Mark.*

Bridge of San Luis Rey

(25 PER CENT DIALOG)

M-G-M production and release. Directed by Charles Brabin. Four players co-featured—Lily Damita, Ernest Torrence, Raquel Torres and Don Alvarado. Adapted from Thornton Wilder's novel, Pulitzer prize winner. Screen version by Alice D. G. Mille. Photographer, M. B. Glesiud. Running time, 86 minutes (about 60 minutes non-dialog). At the Capitol, New York, week May 18.

Camile	Lily Damita
Uncle Pio	Ernest Torrence
Pepita	Raquel Torres
Manuel	Don Alvarado
Esteban	Duncan Rinaldo
Father Juniper	Henry B. Walthall
Viceroy	Mikhail Vavitch
Marquesa	Emily Fitzroy
Dona Clara	Jane Winton
Jaime	Gordon Thorpe
Captain Alvarado	Mitchell Lewis
Don Vicente	Paul Ellis
Nun	Eugenie Besserer
Townsman	Tully Marshal

A profoundly religious story, magnificantly screened picture, but not box office.

In the scope of its production and in its pictorial quality the subject has the quality of a $2 product. It may have been aimed at that goal. When it was withdrawn and sent out as program material, probably good commercial judgment was employed.

Story is of a sombreness often painful, the ending is supremely tragic and the lesson of religious resignation, admirable as it may be doesn't help much in appeal to light spirited people paying for entertainment. Very minus capacity at this Saturday afternoon show, but not a fair test against glorious outdoor afternoon in May.

It makes no difference either way, but perhaps it would have been a good idea for Metro to put the picture out as a special with the deliberate purpose of taking a loss, for what the screen might gain in a perfect answer to critics who harp on the dumbbell pictures that come from Hollywood. If the fan public won't support a picture of this high quality, that's that, and the industry's case for the "Wild Party" box office smashes is complete.

Scene is Lima, Peru, in 1714. It is feast day of Saint Louis, patron saint of the ancient bridge into the town, symbol of the eternity of the church. While the faithful trudge into the Spanish town the bridge gives' way and five-persons are dashed to death.

Simple parishioners flock to the church in terror lest this be a sign of calamity. Has the patron saint deserted them? Will a scourge follow in punishment of their wickedness? Here is a great dialog passage between Tully Marshall, frightened townsman, and Father Juniper (Henry B. Walthall), the priest, a work of art for literary power and a splendid bit of screen dialog in a mechanical and acting sense.

It's a typical tragic story. Lily Damita is a Spanish colonial dancer and a vixenish little courtesan who schemes for power with the viceroy and breaks hearts all around.

She does some very good emotional acting, while Walthall, with the simplicity of his acting, adds a splendid chapter.

Dialog sequences are confined to the opening and closing of the film —10 minutes at the end and probably 14 or 15 at the beginning. Rest is conveyed in action and titles.

Production is of the highest type, reaching its climax in the church sequences described.

Cast is notably even and of high quality. Special excellence in the playing of Torrence, Raquel Torres, as a Madonna-like noviate, Emily Fitzroy, who plays this particular austere old woman as no other screen actress could do it, and Don Alvarado and Duncan Rinaldo as twin brothers.   *Bush.*

GERMAN PICTURES

Berlin, May 12.
"Woman Longed For"
"Die Frau nach der man sich sehnt" (The Woman—One Longs For) (Terra). Discovery of a female star is something for a German film to accomplish. Here Marlene Dietrich shows herself as a strong contender for international honors. At the moment she is imitating Greta Garbo's half closed eyes and langorous eroticism, but there is enough individuality in her work to show that the girl is there. She has the right face and figure and she can troupe.

The script by Ladislaus Vajda is competent film material. It is simple and holds for just that reason. A young Frenchman marries a girl whom he does not really love to save his firm from bankruptcy. On his wedding trip he meets a fascinating woman accompanied by a sinister foreigner. The two fall for each other and the girl, who seems terrified of her escort, begs the youth, whom she has introduced as her cousin, to save her.

He leaves his bride on the train and follows the pair to a hotel. At a masked ball that night the two are planning to flee from the foreigner but are prevented by him. Then it comes out that girl's brutal husband has been murdered by the foreigner with the girl's knowledge. The police capture both and the foreigner shoots the girl at her request.

Kurt Bernhard directs the performance with subtlety and a feeling for mood. What under another director might have been draggy he keeps alive with tension. In the roles of the youth and murderer Uno Henning and Fritz Kortner deliver.

"Marriage"
"Die Ehe" (Marriage) (Laender). Based on the book sensation of the season, "The Perfect Marriage" by Van der Velde, this film is sure of doing business. It has been elegantly hoked and probably would go well even without this advantage.

The original was a very frank treatment of sex in marriage and even went into technical details which formerly were only obtainable in Arabian erotic literature. Of course, they couldn't put that in the film but it is surprising how much the censor let by. Little episodes showing how marriages should and shouldn't be, among other things. The unhappy marriage of the faithful husband. The business man who takes his secretary as his mistress because he works with her. The jealous wife who shoots her husband because he is unfaithful to her.

And finally the ideal marriage illustrated by Emperor Franz Josef of Austria and Maria Theresa who were made happy by the sane advice of a doctor.

Among the cast are such good performers as Lil Dagover, Maria Solveg, Livio Pavanelli and Gustav Diessl.

If it could get by the censor in America, a gold mine.

"Merry Widower"
"Der lustige Witwer" (The Merry Widower) (Deutsches Lichtspiel Syndikat). Harry Liedtke, darling of the provinces, has of late been first-run in Berlin in the suburbs. But now he is back again in the Ufa's biggest house. With justice, for the present film is a big advance over his last efforts.

The director, Robert Land, has handled a really amusing scenario with tact and humor. It concerns a middle class married couple who, getting on each other's nerves, go to separate resorts for their vacation.

The husband lands in a Riviera hotel with prices far beyond his pocketbook. To pay off he proposes that he pose as a wealthy marriageable widower and thus help fill the house which is doing badly.

The wife, tired of her loneliness, arrives to find him flirting with a countess, and casts the glad eye on a millionaire in revenge. Finally both get jugged and are bailed out by the wife's generous admirer.

"Inherited Passions"
"Vererbte Triebe" ("Inherited Passions") (Hom). This picture takes itself earnestly and bluffs the serious section of the Berlin press into taking it earnestly, too. Its theme is the bunk, but it is, nevertheless, an effective piece of picture gruesomeness. Nothing for the average American taste.

The young director, Gustav Ucicky, here rates himself a comer, and Walther Rilla delivers in the lead.

All about a poor young leading man who is ever so sympathetic but, when he has had a shot of liquor, up and murders the dame whom he has taken out.

First he croaks a prostitute and is about to finish off the charming young second wife of his supposed father, a lawyer, when the police arrive. At the trial he is defended by his adoptive father, who admits the lad is the son of a famous murderer who did his victims in the same fashion. The attorney's final plea is for the sexual sterilization of such criminals. The boy is to be turned over to a lunatic asylum, but hangs himself in his cell beforehand.

Pretty bedtime story.

"Perjury"
"Meineid" ("Perjury"). Another picture that bluffs its way into serious consideration by pretending to advocate reform. Vaudeville manager is unfaithful to his wife, but their daughter, eight, shows talent as a dancer.

Father wants to clean up by exploiting the kid, but the mother doesn't want it robbed of its youth in this fashion. She therefore has the child kidnaped and swears in court that she doesn't know where it is. The truth comes out and the mother gets a year in prison and loses her child besides.

This is the best picture that the director, Georg Jacoby, who turns out his eight or 10 a year, has been responsible for ages.

Leads are well taken by Alice Roberte, Franz Lederer and Miles Manders. Inge Landgut, the child player, is a find.

"Call at Midnight"
"Anschluss um Mitternacht" ("A Call at Midnight") (Maxim). Jaques Natanson's amusing comedy, "Coeur Bube," had a long run here last season, but the scenario turned out mild fare. The charm of the original was its dialog, and they tried to make up for this by gratuitous clowning.

Although such comedians as Curt Bois and Ralph Arthur Roberts did their stuff with elan, it was not organic enough to help the picture much.

It is impossible to tell the story in concentrated form, as it merely concerns a series of intrigues around a charming demi-mondaine and her former, present and future lover.

In the lead, Marcella Albani is voluptuous in the style of the last decade, and Jean Bradin, as number three, is his usual engaging self.

"Labyrinth of Passion"
"Irrwege dere Leidenschaft" ("A Labyrinth of Passion") (Derussa). One of the few mediocre Russian films here of late. Director and leading player, Konstantin Eggert, exaggerates in both capacities. No sign of the simplicity and naturalness that characterizes the work of Pudowkin.

Taken from a novel by Tolstoi, it tells about a Russian nobleman who goes around seducing women with brutal callousness. But he pays for it, ends in the gutter and meets his death at the hands of the sister of one of his victims.

The "comrades" of Soviet Russia are here shown what naughty, horried people the former nobility were.

A pleasing young girl, Vera Malinowskaja, is a ray of light.

"Diana"
"Diana" (Tschechowa Film). Olga Tschechowa, the easy-to-gaze-upon Russian with the historic name, lept up close to stardom in Dupont's London-made "Moulin Rouge." She has returned to Berlin and started her own film company. This is its first product. Better luck next time. Scenario is exceptionally atrocious. Laid during Napoleon's advance into Russia, it concerns the wife of a French officer, whom most of the staff of the Russian army try to put to bed. They almost get her down on the couch when something historical intervenes.

At the end she goes wandering off into one of those handy snowstorms.

Pity to waste Pierre Blanchard, Boris de Fas and von Schlettow on this Keystone bungle.

"White Roses"
"Die weissen Rosen von Ravensberg" ("The White Roses of Ravensberg") (Derussa). This title is stolen from one of those sentimental pop ballads dear to the hearts of the biddies and the solid provincial. It has nothing to do with the scenario, but it may drag a few guileless ones into the emporiums trying to sell it on a double feature bill.

How it ever got into one of the Ufa first-run houses is a mystery which will never be explained. And who cares, anyhow?

BROADWAY

ALL DIALOG

(With Songs)

Universal production and release. Adapted from the Phil Dunning and George Abbott stage smash by Edward T. Lowe, Jr., and Charles Furthman, with the entire Phil Dunning dialog transferred to screen. Directed by Paul Fejos; Carl Laemmle, Jr., associate. Glenn Tryon, Merna Kennedy, Evelyn Brent and Otis Harlan featured. Players from original cast of stage play in this picture; Thomas E. Jackson and Paul Porcash. Sounded on Western Electric process (Fox-Case Movietone). Technicolor in final scene. Music by Con Conrad, Archie Goettler and Sidney Mitchell. Published by DeSylva, Henderson & Brown. Synchronization and score by Howard Jackson. Dance numbers staged for screen by Maurice L. Kusell, Gus Arnheim and Cocoanut Grove orchestra, Los Angeles, in cabaret scenes. Opened at Globe (legit), New York, May 27, at $2.50 top; twice daily on run. Running time, 105 minutes.

Roy Lane..........................Glen Tryon
Pearl..............................Evelyn Brent
Billie Moore...................Merna Kennedy
Dan McCorn.............Thomas E. Jackson
Steve Crandall....................Robert Ellis
"Porky" Thompson...............Otis Harlan
Nick Verdis......................Paul Porcash
Lil Rice..........................Marion Lord
Mose Leavett.......................Fritz Feld
"Scar" Edwards................Leslie Fenton
Dolph.........................Arthur Hausman
Joe..................................George Davis
Mazie...........................Betty Francisco
Ruby..............................Edythe Flynn
Ann...........................Florence Dudley
Grace.............................Ruby McCoy

Universal may be thankful there is but one "Broadway." That saves and makes this unusually good production, opening Monday at the Globe on the legit scale, twice daily. It will do business there and do plenty in the regular picture houses, giving Universal a score of two in a row for the pop price palaces. Other is U's "Show Boat." At present in many towns it is equalling or bettering the record run of Warners' "Singing Fool."

Phil Dunning wrote material for a dozen pictures when he wrote "Broadway." "Broadway" was Dunning's show. George Abbott got credit and royalty for some construction work upon it. If Dunning was paid royalty for the pictures preceding "Broadway," with base ideas stolen from it, he might have enough money to become a picture producer himself, since U paid $200,000 for the screen rights to his smash.

Despite the lifts and with a couple or more pictures almost direct copies in some ways, "Broadway" on the film will get over because it has a thrill tenseness about it, runs nicely and without padding, speeds up as it goes along, holds comedy from dialog mostly and some from situation, and, besides, though closely following the original, has been made in the picture way.

No sobbing over "Broadway"; you laugh, worth much more, despite the belief of the sobbing reviewing sisters. When the intermission sign at the Globe flashed it seemed as though that slide brought the audience out of their suspense, for suspense was hanging heavy right there.

Whether "Broadway" was seen as a play will not enter here; it must be as good and better as a picture, judged by this guy, who did not see the stage show. As a melodrama with music the screen play expands 'way beyond the stage production in the musical end, and likely also in the melodramatic portion with its street scenes. Finest of these is a duplicate of Broadway at Times Square, from a miniature. Through Broadway strides a big bronze Demon Rum, and the picture starts right out of this scene, starting before the slide details arrive. That same scene is often thrown upon the sheet during the hour and three-quarters the picture takes.

Excellent casting, with two creators of the stage roles, especially Thomas E. Jackson, who became so marked in the play and will be as much so here.

U's own film players hold the leads, with Glenn Tyron as the hick hoofer. Tryon does nobly, discounting the singing and dancing suspicion. Evelyn Brent will probably be first choice for good acting, with Merna Kennedy doing her little bit mildly as the hoofer's partner. Robert Ellis as the heavy runs alongside Jackson for realism. Paul Porcash, the other original, also was as wisely chosen for the hard role of the cafe proprietor.

Paul Fejos directed, with much judgment, if little novelty. His work and the cutting, however, do much to make this film.

A magnificent set, interior of a nite club, made on a lavish and extended scale, holds most of the action. Numbers nicely staged in workmanship shape, considering all long shots, with dressing room scenes, besides a couple of hair-pulling fights between choristers.

Picture's ballad, "The Song of Love," sounds very good among the five songs and a likely seller, while "Broadway" is a fast number that should get over.

The final scene of a carnival night in the cabaret was done in Technicolor, giving a corking finish to a corking picture. *Sime.*

THE COCOANUTS

(ALL DIALOG)

(With Songs)

Paramount production and release. Starring Four Marx Brothers, with Mary Eaton and Oscar Shaw. Screen adapted by Morris Ryskind from the musical production of same title; book written by George Kaufman. Special songs for film by Irving Berlin. Made at the Paramount Long Island studios; produced (directed) by Monta Bell with James R. Cowan assoc. prod. Numbers directed by Joseph Santley and Robert Florey as film director. Cameraman, George Folsey. Opening on grind run at Rialto, New York, May 24. Running time, 90 minutes.

Hammer..........................Groucho Marx
Harpo................................Harpo Marx
Chico.................................Chico Marx
Jamison.............................Zeppo Marx
Polly................................Mary Eaton
Bob.................................Oscar Shaw
Penelope....................Katherine Francis
Mrs. Potter..................Margaret Dumont
Yates................................Cyril Ring
Hennessy........................Basil Ruysdael
Bell Captain.......................Sylvan Lee
Dancers.....................Gamby-Hale Girls, Allan K. Foster Girls

"The Cocoanuts" is a comedy hit for the regular picture houses. That's all it has—comedy—but that's enough. This picture may be gone for heavily as a laugh, for it is that, with the Marx Brothers the laugh and the picture.

Here is a musical talker with the musical background, music, songs and girls, taken from the Sam H. Harris Broadway stage success with the Marxes also starred in that. Everything is there but nothing comes out, excepting the four Marx comedians.

Comedy plenty, low comedy, too, perhaps the best thing the screen can sell today besides s. a. And laughs from dialog, laughs from the brothers, so many laughs someone forgot to time them for overdraught. Groucho is always talking right into his laughs, killing the immediate ensuing dialog which might also hold another giggle. If Julius isn't talking too fast for the sticks, this may be more manifest there. But if his talk isn't too fast and overflip for the yokes, then the countryside is in for a good time when "Cocoanuts" comes to town.

Mary Eaton and Oscar Shaw as the juves mean nothing. Miss Eaton was badly dealt with on profile with plenty of the side views. She's no look panic here full face either. Mr. Shaw has little and does it but fairly. And the others don't matter, except those brothers.

Groucho (Julius) always around and talking as he did in the stage show. Arthur (Harpo) that adorable pantomimist, does his work with craftmanship, also making it again apparent that the harp is the most faithfully reproduced instrument the sounder has yet discovered. Chico (Leo) likewise has his own score and more of the comedy end than usually falls to this foil. While his piano bit displayed that Chico was the only one of the brothers who thought to time his applause by a bow, first fishing for it with a wide smile and look toward the front. Smart kid. Zeppo had to be straight here all of the while.

In production and technically, up again is the matter of ensembles. Forty-eight girls, divided between Foster's and Gamby-Hale's, worked very well but couldn't be placed properly in the focus. When the full 48 were at work only 40 could be seen and those behind the first line could be seen but dimly. In one scene of six abreast on a close-up but four and one-half were in sight. While to get a larger revealment long shots had to be utilized, ruining those scenes, leaving the physical illusion a total blank. An eight-group of girl bellhops did nicely, always in close-ups.

Only effect of near-novelty was an above shot on the ballet girls, thrown head on toward the audience. This was much liked by the house.

Sound reproduction okay as the rule with a bit of muffling now and then. Miss Eaton's poor vocal recording might be blamed by several on the equipment, but Miss Eaton's canned voice is at fault.

Only Berlin song of merit is the theme number, "When Our Dreams Come True," good enough musically to gain a sale but as trite in idea as the title suggests.

"Cocoanuts" is set in a Florida development hotel barren of guests. Groucho is the fast thinking and talking boniface. A couple of slickers, girls, bathing beach, etc., some undressing but no s. a.

This is a picture where the comedy must make it stand up. It will. *Sime.*

Fox Movietone Follies

(OF 1929)

(ALL DIALOG)

Fox production and release. Words and music by Conrad, Mitchell and Gottler. Dialog by William K. Wells. Directed by David Butler and Marcel Silver. Cameraman, Charles Van Enger. Numbers staged by Fanchon and Marco. At Roxy, New York, week May 25. Running time, 80 mins.

George Shelby....................John Breeden
Lila Beaumont............................Lola Lane
Jay Darrell................De Witt Jennings
Ann Foster........................Sharon Lynn
Al Leaton........................Arthur Stone
Swifty............................Stepin Fetchit
Martin...........................Warren Hymer
Stage Manager................Archie Gottler
Orchestra Leader..................Arthur Kay
Le Maire.......................Mario Dominici

SONG AND DANCE NUMBERS

Sue Carol	David Percy
Lola Lane	David Rollins
Sharon Lynn	Bobby Burns
Dixie Lee	Frank Richardson
Melva Cornell	Henry M. Mollandin
Paula Langlen	Frank La Mont
Carolynne Snowden	Stepin Fetchit

Jeanette Dancey

Considered as a pioneer effort, Fox "Movietone Follies" is a success, although Fox wisely elected not to try a $2 run. It's good entertainment all the way and occasionally arresting in its implications of the possibilities to come. Within the necessary limitations of a two-dimension medium the numbers, specialties and song and dance stuff comes through very well. This, too, with none of the principals trained musical comedy personalities.

Photography seems dead, but here it must be remembered that a cameraman these days is pretty thoroughly handcuffed. One bit done in technicolor offers a variant from the black and white but achieves little itself. Sound and dialog recording is clear, and the production has the advantage of imaginatively conceived sets, costuming and ensemble.

Fox in casting followed its traditional custom of sticking to the home lot. Sue Carol, David Rollins, Stepin Fetchit, Sharon Lynn, Carolynne Snowden, Dixie Lee, Arthur Stone and Warren Hymer are members of the Fox stock company, with some others of the cast probably under term contracts also. Absence of names or reputations among the players seems remarkable for a first try in a new direction, as it gives the production no auxiliary drawing power.

It requires little divination to forsee that the Fox "Follies" is going to have its greatest appeal in the smaller communities.

"The Breakaway" and "Walkin' with Susie" are the big numbers. Former is a dance-song along the lines of "Kinkajou" and "Varsity Drag." "Susie" is a minstrel number along stage band lines with cakewalk, strut, etc.

Touch of Fanchon and Marco is apparent throughout production. Numbers represent carefully planned and rehearsed work nicely balanced to the requirements of the camera and microphone.

Wisp of a story. A young Virginian sells his plantation and comes north to marry his sweetie. She is in the chorus of a new show about to open and refuses to quit the theatre to settle down as a wife.

Chagrined by her refusal to chuck everything and go to the parson's, young man buys the controlling interest in the show and fires her. She refuses to quit and says he cannot fire her.

"Why not?" he demands.

"Because Equity won't let you," she retorts.

"Who's he?" demands the hick.

Most of the action and the "Follies" part of the picture represents the opening night of the revue. Scenes backstage for color, by-play, comedy and intermittent resumption of the Virginia romance. Most of the stuff is photographed from the audience sector.

Couple of brief blackouts in the revue. Daniel Boone gag about the shotgun marriage is used. Principally "The Follies" consists entirely of song and dance with a little pageantry. This throws the burden on personality.

Sue Carol takes first honors, her performance being the more notable as she has no stage experience. Needs dancing lessons if to continue as a musical ingenue, as faking will not suffice indefinitely.

Warner Hymer makes a stage manager pretty rough, tough and nasty.

Stepin Fetchit, colored comic and hoofer, rates number two for notice. His sleepy characterization earned many laughs. David Rollins mama's boy lisp seemed attractive to the women.

Experimental costs charged against this one not apparent in the finished product, although it looks like a substantial outlay. Moderate salaries but lots of them. Doubtful as a record-smasher, Fox "Movietone Follies of 1929" should nevertheless earn ample tallies. *Land.*

THE KNIFE

(ALL DIALOG)

Fox production and release. Under Fox-Case system, starring Lionel Atwell. Directed by T. B. Chalmers. From playlet by Henry Arthur Jones. Cameraman, George W. Lamare. Running time, 31 minutes. At the Cameo, New York, week May 20.

Dr. Ridgeway....................Lionel Atwell
Lady Ridgeway.................Violet Heming

Faithful transcript of the play, typical of the work of Henry Arthur Jones, which is to say it served the dramatic tastes of 20 years ago. Here it is brought to the screen with no changes except perhaps exaggerated brevity. Whole story is told in oue setting, that of a surgeon's waiting room, with a perspective in the cold, hard whiteness of an operating room beyond.

People stand still and talk. Never a raised voice or a spirited gesture.

One of those plays where the essence of suspense lies in the surface appearance of calm while emotions surge below. It doesn't make good screen drama.

Story briefly is that an eminent London surgeon has agreed to perform a dangerous operation upon a young man friend. His wife unexpectedly appears from their country estate. Trifles give the husband the suspicion that youth is his wife's lover. Bit by bit the evidence piles up until she confesses her guilt. Surgeon goes into the operating room, leaving the issue open.

Close ups and fade outs are used to convey the anguish of the woman while the operation is going on. To this end a capital trick is employed. View of the waiting room fades out from time to time and Tower of House of Parliament is shown, with the clock striking the hour.

In the end surgeon walks out, bids his wife farewell, assuring her that her lover will recover and he (the surgeon) is leaving her free by taking a government mission to some far place.

Lionel Atwell catches precisely the right tone. In his repressed playing is a sense of power behind the quiet needed to make the necessary point. This is not true of Violet Heming, who gives a performance of singular flatness, both in reserve and where the situation calls for emotional intensity.

Dialog is a model of terse economy. Every word tells, but the whole thing is too delicately woven to hold on the screen, which calls for more robust material, even for half an hour. *Rush.*

THE MAN I LOVE

(ALL DIALOG)

Paramount production and release. Directed by William A. Wellman. Story and dialog by Herman Manklewicz. H. Gerard, cameraman. In cast: Richard Arlen, Mary Brian, Baclanova, Leslie Fenton, Pat O'Malley. At Paramount, New York, week May 25. Running time, 70 minutes.

While the prize ring plays went floppo on Broadway during the past season, a picture containing nearly all of their ingredients and some additional hoke, called by Paramount "The Man I Love," got many feminine hands vigorously applauding at the close of its opening matinee at the Paramount house here.

Even with Richard Arlen substituting for Dempsey, it's one of the best fight pictures yet released. Herman Manklewicz has worked into his theme and dialog a woman angle that the legits treated lightly or else were unable to inject as convincingly. Mary Brian handles this phase to perfection while Baclanova affords the feminine menace situation.

The ring is constantly used. As the promising welter in California, Arlen puts on a slugging match in his home town before seeking laurels in Manhattan. Arlen is allowed only a few raps at the sandbag and words with his Cohen manager before little Mary, as the music store girl, comes in.

Love interest is snappy, but not too obvious. The angle of her first fight, when he heads the card, and giving her the impression it is his brother who is the scrapper, goes well with an audience.

A transcontinental trip with a horse car used as the bridal suite provides novel comedy.

Activities in a New York gym are conventional. The hero stuff here is over-played for a sophisticated audience, when the green guy whips the champ in an exhibition staged by a fight promoter for visitors.

The usual follows with Arlen falling for the hot countess, Baclanova.

Shots of Madison Square Garden, especially one above the ring lights, used in title fight sequence. Regular screen fight with contender in bum shape and depressed by domestic troubles being saved from count by bell in first round. Then manager reveals wifie is listening in on set. Hubby peps up to knock down the champ so many times audience starts to guffaw.

New champ pulls a Tunney to get back with wife. *Waly.*

WHERE EAST IS EAST

(SILENT)

M-G-M production, starring Lon Chaney with Lupe Velez and Estelle Taylor featured. Story by Tod Browning and Harry Sinclair Drago. Adaptation by Waldemar Young. Directed by Tod Browning. At Capitol, New York, week of May 25. Running time 70 mins.

Tiger	Lon Chaney
Toyo	Lupe Velez
Bobby	Lloyd Hughes
Padre	Louis Stern
Ming	Mrs. Wong Wing

Lon Chaney pictures might be described as romantic adventure yarns written and directed by Tod Browning with the hero scarred, crippled, or at least horribly embittered, and the background as exotic as a diligent search of the Atlas can discover. Most of the Chaneys make money, some, of course, being better than others. "Where East Is East," despite its trite title confusingly like many others from the Chaney factory, is one of the better efforts. But you must like Chaney to like his pictures. This one is silent, besides.

Central idea holds a stronger dramatic germ than usual in these stories of the far corners of Asia. A Chinese siren who has deserted her American husband (Lon Chaney) and child (Lupe Velez) returns years later, still vamping, and out to snatch for her own sinister purposes the idealistic, but impressionable young lover (Lloyd Hughes) of her daughter. A love duel between mother and daughter for the affections of the daughter's beau is apt to appeal strongly to women as sex realism of the first order. This situation is occasionally reported in the tabloids.

Chaney himself is rather subordinated, with the picture belonging to Estelle Taylor and Lupe Velez as mother and daughter, respectively. Miss Taylor gives an intriguing performance. By some ingenious trick of make-up her eyes are shaped almond Chinese-fashion, giving her a characterization that seems certain to create great discussion among the fans. It is Theda Bara stuff brought up to date.

Theme, rather than any twist of plot, holds the attention. From the instant a close-up and caption calls attention to a captive gorilla, the smart pupils will easily and correctly surmise that it is the plot function of this gorilla to remove the evil woman at the critical moment.

Locale is Indo-China. Chaney catches wild animals for American circuses. His face is marked with tiger scratches and his credo is his daughter's happiness. There are elephants, coolies, rickshaws, jungle, river boats, and Lupe Velez in form-revealing costumes. *Land.*

BERLIN AFTER DARK

(GERMAN MADE)

(Silent)

Ufa production and release. Directed by Constantin J. David. Titled and edited for American release by J. W. McConaughy. At 55th St. Playhouse week May 25. Running time, 75 minutes.

Edith Ramsay	Grita Ley
Harry Homan	Ralph von Groth
Harry Ramsay	Paul Rehkopf
Charles Mills	Fritz Kampers
Fat Frank	Kurt Gerron
Inspector Wesley	Ernst Stahl-Nachbaur

A silent talker in many respects. It will have a chance in America's lesser runs if Ufa takes it back to the cutting room and shears off 30 minutes of camera conversations.

"Berlin After Dark," properly cut, would be a relief from the Hollywood rage of solving the murder in the courtroom. Director David opportunely makes the Berlin cops the heroes. From the time the badly bashed body of a German Coney Island operator is found, police technique prevails.

A lot of moves that fans have memorized from other pictures are supplemented by a few not so familiar to the uninitiated. Witnesses are questioned in the reelage, almost as long as they would be in headquarters. But the case is solved without the insert of a courtroom door.

Ernst Stahl-Nachbaur deserves major credit for sustaining the interest, very thin at times because o the monotony of portions of polic routine. As the police inspector h contributes an interesting, kindl and yet commanding personality.

The type of cop who introduces his wife to crooks between sentences, passes out cigars and never intimates a knowledge of third degree, is this inspector.

The handling of the story, excepting the length, is fair. Excess is found in overstudy of certain characters whose appearance and attire would be sufficient analysis without parading them around until even elementary minds are satiated.

The Elysium in Berlin, given as a playground for crooks and innocents, shows the owners at loggerheads. One works and the other collects, while the worker threatens to throw out the other. But when the worker is found dead near a piece of moving mechanism, the inspector recalls meeting one Fat Frank, a rogue, on the grounds and also Fat's fight over a phoney wheel. Even a third theory, the threat made by a youth when the worker intercepted a necking party in which his daughter was a participant, adds itself to the web. *Waly.*

HOUSE IN THE SUN

(FRENCH MADE)

(Silent)

Paris, May 10.

"La Maison au Soleil" is a post-war story by Raymond Clauzel which Gaston Roudes has turned into a picture, to be released by Franco Film.

There are good and indifferent features in the production, with the acting of Gaston Jacquet as the best.

Some homely views of the sunny South, in the Provence, constituting a good French reel.

Goel, in a small town on the Riviera, meets his former army companion, Pignaire, recorded as killed in action. Pignaire confesses he escaped, but was disfigured, and not wishing to disturb his wife, remarried to his brother when the husband was reported dead, had preferred to live alone.

Goel discreetly investigates, learns Mme. Pignaire remarried for business reasons while still loving her first husband, and has never become the real wife of her second hubby.

Sounds a bit romantic, but enables the veteran to return home and embrace his former wife.

Roudes has closely followed the book, which does not mean much. Cast is not up to this category of romance, excepting Jacquet. They overdo the drama action. *Kendrew.*

WINGED HORSEMAN

(SILENT)

Universal production and release. Starring Hoot Gibson. Directed by Arthur Rosson from story by Raymond L. Schrock. Harry Neuman, cameraman. In cast: Ruth Elder, Charles Schaeffer, Allan Forest. At Loew's New York, one day, May 24, half double feature. Running time, 60 minutes.

Hoot Gibson is back to stay with a lot of new friends if he keeps on turning out pictures like "The Winged Horseman." It introduces a mechanical era in westerns. It is the best ever for Gibson exhibitors and would register as an innovation in some of the biggest first runs were it not for occasional slips of the story into the old routine.

Excellent sky views of rolling western country and aviation stuff realistically effective abound in the production. Aerial tricks, battles and parachute jumping, with the much-publicized Miss Elder at the stick of a dazzling white machine, all to keep the fans agog.

Not satisfied with sky work Hoot substitutes a cream-colored motorcycle with a machine gun perched on the handlebars for his horse. He uses the animal for one sequence to provide the grass touch. If a double does the motoring no one is the wiser, for close-ups of Hoot are constantly irised in before the machine gun mounts a tricky hill and outgyrates ranch equestrians on every move.

Gangsters, after oil property, open by starting a series of mystery fires by dropping bombs from their plane. The owner calls the Texas Rangers. Their ace, Hoot, is assigned the job. Playing dumb, with heavy glasses and golf togs, Gibson affords comedy with the investigation. He first finds that the ranch foreman, in love with the boss' daughter, is a war deserter.

After that things go boom boom. *Waly.*

ONE SPLENDID HOUR

(SILENT)

Excellent (firm) production and release. Story adaptation by Isidore Bernstein. Directed by Burton King. Viola Dana starred. In cast: George Periolet, Allan Simpson, Lucy Beaumont, Lewis Sargent. At Loew's New York one day, May 24, half of double feature. Running time, 67 minutes.

"One Splendid Hour" is just a jazz title for an innocuous blurb. Kind of stuff producers wished on the nickelodeons before the de luxe was discovered.

The cast—stiff, unnatural and dead-panned—reflects the direction. Burton King either followed Isidore Bernstein's adaptation of someone's story or else kept it a closed book in the hands of an assistant.

A Hollywood-conscious gin affair, with some plastered into sleep, tears this open and leaves it hanging until some minutes later a settlement doctor is shown promising a mother he will locate her wayward daughter. *Waly.*

ON WITH THE SHOW

(ALL DIALOG)
(With Songs and Technicolor)

Warner Bros. production and release. Entirely in Technicolor. Directed by Alan Crosland. Dances and numbers staged by Larry Cebellos. Cameraman, Tony Gaudio. Story by Humphrey Pearson; adapted by Robert Lord. Songs by Harry Akst and Grant Clarke. Western Electric (Vitaphone) process. Opening May 28 at Winter Garden, New York, twice daily run at $2 top. Running time 2 hours.

Nita	Betty Compson
Sarah	Louise Fazenda
Kitty	Sally O'Neil
Ike	Joe E. Brown
Sam Bloom	Purnell B. Pratt
Jimmy	William Bakewell
Twins	Fairbanks Twins
Durant	Wheeler Oakman
Jerry	Sam Hardy
Dad	Thomas Jefferson
Pete	Lee Moran
Joe	Harry Gribbon
Harold	Arthur Lake
Harold's Fiancee	Josephine Houston
Father	Henry Fink
Bert	Otto Hoffman
Ethel Waters	Ethel Waters
Harmony 4 Quartette	Harmony Quartette
Four Covans	Four Covans
Angelus Babe	Angelus Babe

Plenty of entertainment and other things in Warners' "On With the Show." Principally of the other things are drama, melodrama and the romance of the story all going on backstage while the picture presents its see and hear sight of a musical comedy on the stage. This leaves the talker as a whole overloaded with each, including a too heavy coloring at times. This too much makes the film too long in running. Whoever tackles the cutting job of reducing its two hours for the regular houses is in for no picnic.

Rating this picture as a cinch for any picture house and probably due for a run at the Winter Garden at its $2 top on the strength of the novel natural coloring alone, that all coloring gives the film its leading topic of notice.

Warners are the first of the talkers. Other credits due are a first also for operetta as with "The Desert Song" and now again another first for its initial all-colored musical "On With the Show." So the Warners continue leading with talking innovations. Another known first remains, that to be the expanded screen for a full length feature.

All color as gauged by this Warner film immediately becomes important. That coloring is dominating for musicals was brought out in the single scene holding it in Metro's "Broadway Melody." Coloring continuously as a rule and any way in the dramatic or straight picture stories, such as were colored in the silents, becomes wearisome, akin to an eye strain. Not so here, however, excepting perhaps for the heavy shading given Louise Fazenda and her red mop. Flesh coloring also at times too prominent, perhaps due to makeup.

Saying that the talkers are young enough to be advanced by experimentation of engineers or directors is true, for here is the coloring, a decided step. Place "On With the Show" with its color on an extended screen and it must be a whale of a picture. That may be visualized by anyone who saw the R. C. A. Photophone's demonstration of the George Spoor huge screen in New York a couple of weeks ago. This picture ideally suitable for the expanded screen, as it is mostly of large ensembles in the stage playing portion.

Spoor's device screen extending across the entire proscenium was of glass. Just how that could be contracted isn't known, if it could be. But the huge screen that may stand expansion or contraction, to take in the groupings or extended for closeups of from one to five persons in their scenes, or in other words adapting an elastically built screen to the story, will give the talkers another impetus.

"On With the Show" would have been a magnificent picturization on the big sheet. It could then have avoided the too numerous rangy shots now existing on the standard size. They keep the stage people at too long a distance on the film and in a picture house where the majority of the patrons are far removed from the screen as it is.

Yet with its drawbacks and its length, the film is impressive, both as an entertainment and as a talker. It was talking a chance to throw into it as much extraneous matter as has been done, the inner story angles backstage. They are continually moving in and out of the picture itself. That is one of the obstacles to the cutting. Were a staged number bit to go out here, it would carry with it a portion of the inner story continuity in dialog, without any spot left where that particular allotment of story dialog could be fitted.

This becomes evident as the mostly melodramatic tale unfolds in the wings or dressing room. It starts with a musical on its break in date and flat. The backer has walked. He was on the make for **the coat room girl, the court room girl and chief usher (boy) being shoved into the plot.**

Intertwined is the hold up of the box office on the only night it held any real money, with everyone suspected by a comedy dick. Thief finally disclosed as the old doorman, whose daughter is the coat room girl, with the entire Broadway house staff of the theatre seemingly traveling to the out of town date in their customary places. Immaterial though to lay audiences.

With another twist the prima donna, unrevealed wife of the backer, refuses to go on in the second act unless her two weeks' $1,500 overdue salary is paid forthwith, an impossible feat on any break in date. With the prima donnaing wife then discovering her husband-angel started everything because the coat room girl turned him.

Meanwhile the stage show is proceeding, the entire action occurring during it, enough to give Chris Morley a couple of more old-fashioned mellers.

The stage portion is mainly numbers. More than customary doses of girls, with several songs and a specialist without part in the plot, Ethel Waters, colored. Miss Waters has two songs, "I'm Blue" and "Birmingham Bertha." Preferred is the "Blue" song for that sounds like a selling hit, though Harry Askt, who wrote in collaboration with Grant Clarke on the lot, prefers "Bertha." These two writers wrote all of the numbers, Warner-Witmark publishing. A couple of the other songs sound quite good, especially what is probably the theme song, and "Two Lips" as sung by Henry Fink is a good general number, with Mr. Fink reputed one of the busiest ghost singers in Hollywood. Here, however, he is singing in person under a character disguise and must do a little bit of acting.

Sally O'Neil has the sympathetic ingenuish part as the coat room girl who won't go wrong, wants to act and is in love with the ushering boy. He wants to marry her when the coat room holds 60 hats more than usual. Miss O'Neil got her chance just as they copped the old man copping the dough. She sang the theme song and her voice didn't sound greatly different than when Betty Compson, the burn up wife also sang the number.

Miss Compson does very well as the prima who knows how to handle a producer. Miss Fazenda gets a laugh now and then, as does Joe E. Brown, with Brown's role and laughs limited by the script. Arthur Lake is the usher, rather good at times when he's Arthur Lake.

Lee Moran as Pete, "Props," is right at the top for work, with Sam Hardy giving a first-class performance as the harried producer.

In the show proper the Fairbanks Twins dance nicely and also have some rough twin stuff back stage with dialog. They talk all right Cast very evenly balanced, a strong factor in the good average performance in front and behind.

Larry Ceballos did a lot with the numbers, though the jumble of the long shots does not bring all of the movements out as they should be. His stair staging ensemble of notice

Alan Crosland has done a class A directorial job. The way he speeded up the action with the inserts carries the many stories in a manner not to hold sight on any one moment too long. Considerable of the front stage matter could have been boiled down though, and cutting would not have injured several back stage scenes. These are the spots likely where the cut will go for the regular house length, with that handicap of how to cut with dialog preserved still entering.

"On With the Show," with its coloring and potentialities for talkers, will give anyone understanding pictures lots to think over *Sime.*

FATHER AND SON

(65% DIALOG)

Columbia production and release. Directed by Erle C. Kenton, starring Jack Holt Sound and dialog on Western Electric disk Story by Elmer Harris; dialog written by Frederic and Fanny Hatton. continuity by Jack Townley; cameraman, Teddy Tetzlaff. Musical score by Constantine Bakaleinikoff. Theme song, "Dear Little Boy of Mine," published by Witmark. Running time, 67 minutes. At the Embassy, New York, June 3, for a two-a-day run. Scale, $1.50.

Frank Fields	Jack Holt
Grace Moore	Dorothy Revier
Jimmy Fields	Mickey McBan
Mary White	Helene Chadwick
Anton Lebau	Wheeler Oakman

Significant picture for a number of reasons. Okay for first runs, easily.

One reason is that it is among the early important contributions to the new sound technique by an independent; another is the distinguished writers who are concerned in its creation. But more than these, the production is the first that comes to mind that could not have been screened without the use of sound—that is to say, the articulate screen is the only medium that could have given this particular story its present treatment.

This circumstance is important. Most of the really effective sound and dialog pictures so far have been taken over bodily from the stage and their screening has been largely a straight transcription of the footlight performance. "Father and Son," on the contrary, appears to have been created from the beginning with the new sight-sound technique in view—written for the talking screen instead of adapted to its uses from a stage source.

All these things give it particular interest and should draw attention. Besides, the story stands up on its merits as admirable picture material, excellent in treatment and admirable in its production quality. It moves rapidly, carries the sentimental appeal of father and son affection in somewhat the same casual and jaunty spirit that gave "Sorrel & Son" its charm, and finally goes to a climax that has a first-rate punch.

It is in this strong ending that the sound element develops its surprise. Situation has been planted this way: Young Jimmy on his birthday receives as his father's gift a recording and reproducing talking machine. Thereafter the father is tricked into a marriage with an adventuress who deals harshly with the boy, so that the father and son are alienated.

Boy seeks to win back the father's affection by making a phonograph record explaining how he feels over the situation. Youngster is interrupted by the wife who drives him from the house. A lover out of the woman's past intrudes at this point and in a violent quarrel she is shot to death.

Boy's father is accused of murder; youngster tries to assume guilt of the crime and to prove he was in the house on the morning in question relates that he was making a phonograph record. Coroner's jury calls for the record, which, of course, reveals who fired the shot and saves the father from peril of his life.

Sounds not so reasonable, but so craftily has the story been dovetailed and so shrewdly has it been developed that whole thing unfolds naturally and smoothly. Narrative has a number of good dramatic surprises. One comes in the tricky disclosure of the woman's character. Another is the gradual realization of the father that his wife has been a notorious woman, a particularly neat bit of dramatic exposition.

Development of character is notably fine, with particular reference to the relations of father and son. Kid calls the older man "Big Boy," and father addresses youngster as "Old Timer." Capital picture of companionable pair, charmingly shaded with humor and sentiment.

Physical production is of the best, and the cast has been selected happily. Jack Holt, who too often is an artificial actor when he's dressed up, here supplies the strong masculine quality which gives the relation to the boy a special charm. The youngster himself is great. He's Mickey McBan, whose homely pan makes him very human. (If the much abused screen has done no other service, it has killed off the Little Lord Fauntleroy horror). Kid has a knack of sentiment that really gets over. There's something inexpressibly touching in his plain, tear stained map.

Dorothy Revier does an unusual heavy woman, first because she's a blonde vamp and second because she doesn't overact in the formula way. Helene Chadwick, very brunette, plays the "good girl" with restraint similarly commendable.

Management of the dialog is unusual. Picture opens with 17 minutes of unbroken dialog; goes silent for 27 minutes and ends with 20 minutes nearly all talk, but with a few titles in lieu of the spoken word. The estimate of 65 per cent dialog is an approximation.

Scarcely an outstanding box office picture perhaps by the nature of its subject matter, but a substantial bit of entertainment and certainly a step forward in the sound screen technique. *Rush.*

THE GLAD RAG DOLL

(ALL DIALOG)

Warner Brothers production and release. Michael Curtiz, director. Asst., Cliff Salm. Dolores Costello starred. Written by Harvey Gates. Adapted by Graham Baker. Cameraman, Byron Haskin. Vitagraph sounded. Musically synchronized. At Strand, New York, week June 1. Running time, 70 minutes.

Annabel Lee	Dolores Costello
John Fairchild	Ralph Graves
Bertha Fairchild	Audrey Ferris
Nathan Fairchild	Albert Grant
Aunt Fairchild	Maude Turner Gordon
Admiral	Tom Ricketts
Sam Underlane	Claude Gillingwater
Jimmy Fairchild	Arthur Rankin
Miss Peabody	Dale Fuller
Butler	Douglas Gerrard
Barry, an actor	Andre Beranger
Press Agent	Lee Moran
Manager Foley	Tom Kennedy
Hannah	Louise Beaver
Chauffeur	Stanley Taylor

Dolores Costello has been well enough fitted with this story, titled after the song selling hit, three months old. Where the Costello draw is rampant any reliance may be placed upon "Glad Rag Doll." Where the Costello name is not so warm at the b. o. this Warners should do an average week's trade.

If this broadly lined farce comedy had been held down to its satirical conception it would have been a finely done bit of picture work, in story and action. But perhaps just as well that it was broadened out. Several laughs at frequent intervals, and ofttimes some giggles from the ready to wear dialog handed Arthur Rankin.

Ager, Yellen & Bornstein publishes "Glad Rag Doll," with Milt Ager and Jack Yellen of that firm its writers. You hear "Glad Rag Doll" sung two or three times by unseen singers during the picture, but you hear it played by the synchronizing orchestra all of the time. When leaving the Strand it may be heard again through a loud speaker in the entrance. If that isn't a plug for a theme song that isn't, then what can be? Whoever eased that song for title and plug into Warners can tip his cap for promotion work.

Another back stage story that moves into an aristocratic Philadelphia home. It makes Miss Costello winsome and smart. She outsmarts the hi-hat clique against her, laughs her way in and out of bedroom jams and wins the tough mugg for a husband, after he had said she couldn't marry his younger brother.

The Fairchilds were it socially in Philly. As dug up by Annabel Lee, the musical comedy queen, after 24 hours in their home, this was the layout:

Uncle John Fairchild had started after the housekeeper; Auntie played a bit with the butler while manifesting kleptomaniacal tendencies; Sis Bertha kept her eye so closely on the chauffeur he married her, and John Fairchild, the grouchy elder brother, fell for the same pretty face his sappy brother had before him.

Going against this layout in a fairly breezy way, Annabel just ambled along, for the script was aimed right, along with Hannah, her colored maid, very well done by Louise Beaver. Miss Beaver sang the only other song, "Some of These Days."

Ralph Graves is Brother John and got the right slant upon the role. Albert Grant as Uncle Nathan responsible for several of the laughs with stereotyped farcical stuff of any vintage.

Good production and elaborate for the Philly mansion sight, John and Annabel taking a long walk up a flight of stairs and down a hall. It looked as if the studio had shoved three sets together.

A pleasant talker with Claude Gillingwater of course as an attorney making himself stand out through excellence of everything, but voice first. It has an extremely pleasant girl too in Dolores Costello. *Rime.*

A MAN'S MAN

(SILENT)

Metro-Goldwyn-Mayer production and release. Directed by James Cruze. Based on the play by Patrick Kearney. Screen adaptation by Forrest Halsey. Titles by Joe Farnham. Featuring William Haines. At Capitol, New York, week June 1. Running time, 76 mins.

Mel.........................William Haines
Peggy.........................Josephine Dunn
Charlie.........................Sam Hardy
Violet.........................Mae Busch

Picture is silent, with the exception of a synchronized musical score. There are two sound effects, both bad. Production is mainly in the second class house rating. Silent, and not particularly strong even in that category, it would be risky in a full week first run unless bolstered heavily with stage talent. Haines is only name to depend upon where he has established a personal draw.

The trouble is with the story. It is a casual recital of an everyday occurrence, dealing with a soda fountain jerker who married one of the million girls who want to break into pictures.

According to this tale it seems that the young woman traded her self-respect or something else for the glib promises of a pool room braggart who said she looked like Greta Garbo and that he would see that she became a star.

In rare moments Haines has an opportunity to display what is recognized as a veritable genius for mimicry. Added to these too infrequent moments are the brief appearances of Joe Farnham's titles.

On these titles Farnham is entitled to more than a few bows. Without them and the little there is of Haines, this wouldn't be more than a 10th rate grind house picture. The titles give it class and comedy.

Josephine Dunn is appealing. Sam Hardy extremely villainous, and Mae Busch essays the hard-faced but kind-hearted little trooper trying to keep a good girl straight.

It's no go, for the story is impossible, despite the thinly veiled dirt angle. *Mori.*

DOCTOR'S WOMEN

(GERMAN MADE)

(Silent)

Ufa production and release. Directed by Gustav Molander from Paul Merzbach's novel. Editing and titling by J. R. Fleisher. At 55th St. Playhouse week June 1. Running time, 66 minutes.

Jeanne Duval.........................Ruth Weyher
Nita Duval.........................Margit Manstadt
Gambetta Duval.........................Alexander Murski
Rose Duval.........................Karin Swanstrom
Dr. Robert Monnier.........................Louis Lerch
Armand de Marny.........................Miles Mander

Title is a complete misnomer. It's just a boring jargon about a doctor who chases and marries the girl friend of a playwright, then finding he loved her sister. Thing is so edited as to have a few machine-gun sequences where courtship, marriage, row and back to the playwright flashes take less than a couple of minutes, while repetitious close-ups of over-emotional pans, some lense conscious and others just pure hoggish, yawn out the hour.

As to subtitling, the job was such a careless one that it didn't get all around, leaving in two places just "Fade Out" and "Fade In" explanations.

The physician, about whom the 55th Street makes so many sexy intimations in its poster work, is at first just a boy running adolescently from one sister to another. The good sister, Jeanne, posed for by Miss Weyher in best wax flower manner, is at first jilted for the knowingly good—even though fat-backed—Margit Manstadt, as Nita.

The guy who really rates female honors in this, although they center on the one Nita, is the playwright, the ever-suave and certain Armand but, in Miles Mander, the only real performer in the production. He just twists things to suit himself, letting his dame marry the doc but effecting the indentation while they are honeymooning. This interlude writer even slips in the bridal compartment on the train and pinches the bride's stanchion.

The pinch is about the most "daring" thing in it. The stage contributor has a joint with chink trappings and every time Nita arrives he feigns sleep on a downy cot near his desk. When he is awakened by the coy German girl, whose back rolls over her stays, the audience always expects that the lowdown is to commence. But it only starts, because Nita is permitted sufficient agility by the director to slip by a broad margin from censor worries.

In apparent desperation to get the shooting angle in, the cutter allows the plump one to play hide and seek with her boy friend until she pumps a little lead into his chest. After that the heavy dramatics blast away with the good sister taking the blame to save her platonic lover, the doc. The physician saves the playwright only to realize his true love by turning over little Nita to the playwright. This time the latter gent takes no companionate risks, and also knocks out another play. *Waly.*

THE BONDMAN

(ENGLISH MADE)

(Silent)

British and Dominion Film Corp. production; distributed by World Wide. Directed by Herbert Wilcox. Screen play by T. A. Ennis, adapted from novel, "The Bondman," by Sir Hall Caine. Photographed by David Kesson. At Stanley, New York, one day, May 21. Running time, 90 minutes.

Jason.........................Norman Kerry
Sicilian Mother.........................Dora Barton
Man Father.........................Edward O'Neil
Michael.........................Donald MacArdle
Greeba.........................Frances Cuyler
Mrs. Fairbrother.........................Florence Vie
Adam Fairbrother.........................Judd Green
Father Ferrati.........................Henry Vibart
Testa.........................H. Saxon Snell
Captain.........................C. Emerald

Dull draggy story of the brother against brother classification, with the locations in Sicily and Isle of Man. Title means a man who replaces another not a bondman as security. Latter would be first suggested in this country.

What little action in this importation revolves about Jason (Norman Kery, American), whose dying mother swears him to a vendetta against his father and brother who had deserted them some 20 years before. About the same time the father on his deathbed has sworn his son Michael (Donald MacArdle) to find his mother and brother and square things.

Journeying from Sicily to the Isle of Man, off the Irish coast, Jason learns that his brother has gone to Sicily and decides to wait for him. Getting his brother's job, Jason falls in love with his brother's girl and is about to marry her when she hears from Michael and gives him air. The girl goes to Sicily to marry Michael, meanwhile becoming the governor, with Jason following. Becoming involved in a plot to kill his brother, Jason is sent to the sulphur mines for life. Soon after the governor is overthrown and is himself sent to the same prison camp by the revolutionists.

There the two brothers, following an uprising, are chained together without knowing that they have found each other, one for vengeance and the other for atonement. In an explosion in the mines Jason saves the life of his brother who has become blinded by sulphur fumes.

The ex-governor is banished to a lonely island while his supporters attempt to re-establish him in power. As a firing squad is about to put an end to Michael's chances in that direction Jason, having escaped from prison, steps in, reconciles Michael and his estranged wife, and becomes the bondman for the brother he had sworn to kill.

Lots of mugging on the part of all the characters. Scenes of harvest time customs on the Isle are repeated with deadly monotony. A sheet of music of a folk song employed by the natives at the festival is screened about a dozen times.

Kerry handles the lead in fairly good style, but the rest contribute little of any value. Cut down considerably, this one might earn a fair rating on a double bill in the daily changers.

CHINA BOUND

(Silent)

M-G-M production and release starring Karl Dane and George K. Arthur, with Josephine Dunn and Polly Moran co-featured. Cast includes Carl Stockdale and Harry Woods. Directed by Charles F. Reisner. Story by Sylvia Thalberg and Frank Butler. Continuity by Peggy Kelly. At New York (double feature) one day, June 1. Running time, 74 minutes.

Much of the intended laughs come through bits. These bits before the camera bear the stamp of the director, Chuck Reisner. It is one of those impossible, incongruous stories that has Dane and Arthur going through ups and downs.

Not much new to the entire story although the makers did drag in a Chinese revolutionary affair to give some dramatic tension. The leads get messed up considerably and some of the bits used caused intermittent laughter at the New York theatre.

Polly Moran pulls her usual facial contortions and roughing things up a bit even to a physical clash with the boat crew. Dane and Arthur do their best to try and pull out a mediocre story.

Some fine photographic results. But picture at best can't hold up alone. *Mark.*

SOME MOTHER'S BOY

(SILENT)

Rayart production, starring Mary Carr. Duke Warne, director. Arthur Hoerl's story. Jobyna Ralston, Jason Robards, William A. Dickson, in cast. At Loew's New York, on double bill, one day (May 31). Running time, 60 minutes.

Just an old-fashioned tintype in motion.

There is nothing in "Some Mother's Boy" to recommend it for anything but splitting with something better on double bills. Action, story and treatment are of the passe sort, minus sound.

Similarity of title to Pathe's "Mother's Boy," all-talker with a Broadway date under its belt, may carry some weight here or there, perhaps much more than the picture itself.

False impersonation is the basis of the story, but done as in the past with righteous intent. Two youths are partners in thievery. They're clipped and one is shot. Other escapes, donning his partner's identity and deciding to see the mother of pard. Mother and son have been separated for 15 years. Goes straight, with help from the usual girl. That the real son, who is a bad boy, shows up, fails to ruin the evening.

Complete lack of physical resemblance in the two men makes the faker's successful impersonation really amazing. It's the only food for thought in the picture.

Mary Carr couldn't do a bad mother part if she had to. Jobyna Ralston is the girl and Jason Robards the good boy, though doubtful that either is bragging about it. *Bige.*

WOMAN IN WHITE

(BRITISH MADE)

(Silent)

Produced by British and Dominions Film Corporation; distributed by World Wide. Produced and directed by Herbert Wilcox, from the story by Wilkie Collins. Scenario by Herbert Wilcox and Robert Cullen. Titles by Wilkie Collins. Photography by David Kesson. Starring Blanche Sweet. At Stanley, New York, one day, May 24. Running time, 70 mins.

Laura Fairlie.........................Blanche Sweet
Walter Hartright.........................Haddon Mason
Marion Halcombe.........................Louise Prussing
Philip Fairlie.........................Jerrold Robert Shaw
Sir Percival Glyde.........................Cecil Humphries
Count Fosco.........................Frank Pefitt
Mme. Fosco.........................Mina Grey
Mrs. Catherick.........................Irene Rooke
Anna Catherick.........................Blanche Sweet

It's one of those horrifying mystery stories, fulfilling its mission in America with one day at the Stanley, 7th avenue grindery, at 25c.

Presumably a heavy sale of mystery fiction in England at the present time, and this figured to hit the public just about right over yonder. Not a chance on this side.

Stolid, stark mystery, unrelieved by comedy, entertainment or lively action. Mostly explained in subtitles. Direction awful. Backs continually kept to the front.

Love interest cold. Opening of

story slow and needlessly long. Story in itself leaky and uninteresting.

It seems, of all things, that the beautiful young heiress promises her dying father that she will marry the positively impossible Sir Percival e'en though her heart has gone to another.

Everyone feels the meany looking Sir Percival is no good and he fulfills everyone's suspicions. He locks his new wife in her room, has her terrified by an evil companion, and finally has her sent to a lunatic asylum, all for the sake of her money.

Villainy of every conceivable type as if there were no law or government in the whole of Great Britain. Impossible actions are never explained, and the mysterious is never enthralling when this is not done.

Blanche Sweet doesn't behave well in front of the camera, hindered also by Wilcox's direction and old-fashioned lights and settings.

This picture may be considered a representative type of current British production but useless over here except in grind houses as a filler.

Mori.

PHANTOM OF NORTH

(SILENT)

Biltmore (independent) production and state rights release. Directed by Harry Webb. Story credited Flora Douglas. In cast: Edith Roberts, Donald Keith. At Loew's New York, one day, May 28, half of double feature. Running time, 48 minutes.

"Phantom of the North" is a quickie that a home movie group wouldn't figure good box office, even for their friends in the parlor. The dime grinds may be able to rush this through, but others will find biz kept away if they chance it.

A bunch of nags and dogs supposed to be wild open it along Pathe's "Rex" lines. Then the mare leading the mob romps with a hound and eats sugar from a dame's hand, dispelling any call for the wild.

Then an asinine shooting and murder charges against an innocent are dragged out with no more effectiveness than filler in a newsreel.

Waly.

LAUGHING AT DEATH

(SILENT)

FBO production and release. Directed by Wallace Fox. Starring Bob Steele. Photographer, Virgil Baron. Cast includes M. Joyce, Hector V. Sorna, Ellan Ludlow and Lou Schmidt. At Tivoli, New York, one day, June 1. Running time, 55 mins.

A small time picture with only the Fairbankian antics of Bob Steele to recommend it. One continuous jaw-socking. Story lifeless. Photography medioc. Setting laughable.

Steele plays dual role, that of crown prince of Libania and stoker working for college money. Saves the prince from assassins, belting their jaws and receiving commendation from the royal one, who on a secret mission to United States notes, as does his prime minister, the amazing resemblance of himself to young stoker. To fulfill his mission he thinks it best to change places with the coal heaver, who agrees, but is warned his life is in danger.

KITTY

(BRITISH MADE)

(20 Per Cent Dialog)

Billed as "first imported talking picture," distributed over here by World Wide. English producer not named. R. C. A. Photophone sounded. Director, Victor X. Savile, who also wrote scenario from similarly named novel by Warwick Deeping. Estelle Brody and John Stuart featured. At Cameo, New York, 400-seater, on 42nd street, 75c. top, week June 8. Running time, 92 minutes.

Kitty Greenwood	Estelle Brody
Alex St. George	John Stuart
Mrs. St. George	Dorothy Cumming
Sarah Greenwood	Marie Ault
Furnival	Winter Hall
Leaper	Olaf Hytten
Reuben	Charles O'Shaughnessy
Dr. Dazely	E. F. Bostwick
Dr. Drake	Rex Maurice
The Artist	Jerrold Robertshaw
The Electrician	Gibb McLaughlin

"Kitty," with or without its dialog, is useless. Dialog first starts in this 92-minute film 65 minutes after it has been running. If it had stopped running before it started at the hideaway Cameo it would have been just as well, for this entire picture is an entire waste of time, from producer to public. But in this day of high rentals for U.S. talkers a low price for this one may recommend it to the starving wired house. That's its only recommendation.

Excepting that the English may like a passive story of this character and that the English are so infantile they relish the Laura Jean Libby junk of 30 years ago.

At the Cameo the billing is quite heavy on Warwick Deeping, who wrote this adapted novel and also authored "Sorrel and Son." The latter goes with the billing. A distinct difference appears to be that Herbert Brenon, American, directed "Sorrel and Son" as a picture, while Victor Saville both adapted and directed "Kitty" as a film. Saville did about an equally bad job in both. Accepting that "Kitty" as a novel must have had some vogue to sell for pictures, whatever kick it may have held between covers has been kicked out of it in the celluloid transition.

The dialog portion appears to have been an after thought during the final 25 minutes. As it is R.C.A. Photophone sounded, whether the dialog was added in England or New York is an open and immaterial question. Called the "first imported talking picture," for the sake of Germany, France and the rest of Europe, all boasting about that should cease. It will be a secret over here, any way.

In this latter day of English picture making "Kitty" is almost as primitive in its making as occurred in the British first days. What was said then, that England doesn't know the first thing about picture making for world distribution remains true, taking "Kitty" as the recent criterion.

Story just stumbles along. No life, no action other than the sound part, an airplane crash with the whirring motor. This becomes a gag in itself, for the flying stuff is the most abominable ever seen on the screen. Roy Pomeroy was over there some time ago. Five minutes with Pomeroy and whoever devised the abortional miniatures in this would have known better.

While the dialog comes after such a tedious lapse with none, that the audience merely resent, they must still sit and suffer.

Action and direction appear to be haphazard. At one moment a woman in a lawyer's office pulled down her veil. No reason whatsoever for the action, but suggesting the instruction had been called from the side line. It looked awkward. Again a taxi driver is seen to delay making change for a woman passenger. No reason for this. It had no bearing upon the story and held no comedy, unless for the English. Other directorial absurdities. Another was two of the principal women seen driving in an open car, for no place as it turned out. The immediate following scene was one of the women in the car walking down a street holding an umbrella in a pouring rain.

While for a comedy touch in the sound, squeaky shoes. Fade outs had to be on a clinch, once two women clinching.

In air stuff it's the poorest of the poor, made so of course by the miniatures. In fact, "Kitty" looks as though it had come out of a foundling asylum.

Dialog came over well enough, without anything to the talk other than stereotyped phrasing to fit the situation. "Do you love me?" said the girl, and the boy answered, "Oh, so much." Like that.

Story is of a boy called to the British air forces and marrying a shop girl before leaving. The patrician mother of the boy, to blast the marriage, writes him a letter his wife has a lover. He reads it when about to go into air battle and takes a dive.

Returned home a cripple with loss of memory. Ma won't let Kitty see her husband. This goes on for weeks and weeks. But finally they meet. You know he is going to walk again or there will be no finish. That's when the dialog starts and it takes him 25 minutes to step.

No one stands out in the playing. Estelle Brody, American ingenue, tries hard, without anything or anyone to aid her. The girl was taken profile too much. She's no profile poser. Make up hardened instead of softening her face. These things keep up until one is impelled to inquire is there no one in England who knows anything at all about making moving pictures?

And isn't Miss Brody normally a **blonde? And if so, doesn't she look ever so much better blondy than in the dark hair worn here? Miss Brody creates quite some sympathy, seems smart enough and probably needs but a story or an American director.**

John Stuart, featured, and the juve, nil. His role didn't allow for much and that little, nothing. Dorothy Cumming did the hard hearted mama rather well, although the director made her stand in an ordinary hotel room watching her daughter-in-law's store through opera glasses. English never heard of private detectives, probably. Charles O'Shaughnessy as Ruben, an old handy man, carried a white-black beard that one expected to see a goat hop out of at any time. E. F. Bostwick spoke very well as the Dr., and Gibb McLaughlin made a likeable grouchy electrician.

If World Wide picked "Kitty" for America, it had better get another picker. Pictures like "Kitty" should be happily kept at home, wherever that home may be. The quickies on this side can do better in one-third of the time and one-fourth of the cost, no matter what either was over there.

Sime.

HONKY TONK

(With Sophie Tucker)

(ALL DIALOG)

(With Songs)

Warner Bros. production and release. Vitaphone sounded. Sophie Tucker starred. Songs by Milton Ager and Jack Yellen. Miss Tucker's special dialog by Mr. Yellen. Directed by Lloyd Bacon. Adapted by V. C. Graham Baker from story by Leslie S. Barrows. At Warners, New York, June 4, twice daily at $2 top. Running time, 68 minutes.

Sophie Leonard	Sophie Tucker
Sophie's Daughter Beth	Lila Lee
Jean Gilmore, Beth's friend	Audrey Ferris
Freddie Gilmore	George Duryea
Jim	Mahlon Hamilton
Cafe Manager	John T. Murray

Sophie Tucker is "Honky Tonk" and because of that with her songs, must draw in the regular picture houses. If Sophie can't, her songs can, and both will. Perhaps not $2 for songs only, as per scale at Warners.

Warners picked Sophie because she can sing songs. It was Harry Warner who did the picking. None of the remainder of the Warner bunch could see Soph in a talker. So Harry is right, made righter through standing firm against the judgment of many.

Not only is Soph okay in this picture but she will be the same in many more where she can sing songs as good as those in "Honky Tonk." Since Milt Ager and Jack Yellen seem able to write songs for Soph as they have in the past, that combination looks due to be on the screen for a long while.

In tackling Soph as a first timer on the sheet, the Warners did not want to load her up. Soph is given a simple, idiotic story, but one she can play, as a first timer. It's better for Soph and the Warners to be simple and idiotic the first time than a flop for all time. Saving Soph here makes her good there. This picture is bad but the judgment and Soph great.

"Honky Tonk" is another nite clubber. Sophie Leonard is the star entertainer. She has a daughter finishing abroad. When the little girl comes back a big girl now, she finishes off her mother. Daughter says Ma shouldn't be doing things like this, meaning singing songs for stews. How daughter happens to know is almost the plot. Rest of the story is Ma getting squared and squaring.

Didn't daughter know Ma was working her head off keeping drunks quiet so baby could get the Continental finish? No. Nobody knew. It was a secret shared only by Mahlon Thompson as the headwaiter in the joint. Jim was pretty strong for Soph and kept that way too, after the grownup daughter hove into sight. Jim must have been wised up.

Jim used to take Soph home at seven in the morning, to her apartment, have a cup of coffee and go to his own house without kissing her. Proper?

Scheme of the story is to whitewash all nite club hostesses, if they need washing. Much of this stuff is mushy in its thick sentiment. But Soph is even protected through those portions by having her own dialog written by the same Jack Yellen. Probably an innovation in **talkers for a special material writer (talk) for one person, but Sophie knows her Jackie.**

Sophie's "Red Hot Mamma," as always, pipe. "Some of These Days" another. Those are Soph's always sure shots. "Good Man to Have Around" ballady hit, for all of these songs are hits—otherwise they wouldn't be on the screen. "Little Bluebird" sounds peachy and for among the best sellers, while "Don't Want to Be Thin" is another snappy comic. "Take Off Your Mask," a number leader required for the story, but "Dying to Love" another Soph sock.

Maybe one or two more songs. You become so absorbed in Soph when she's singing, like Marie when she's dancing, that you forget everything.

As for Soph on the screen for the first time, she'll surprise you. The Madam is there. Her singing voice aces and her speaking voice far beyond expectation. In fact for a first time, Soph is beyond expectation all of the way.

With Lloyd Bacon, the director, doing an awful lot in the way of protecting and presenting Soph. If Mr. Bacon doesn't get the credit he deserves, he still deserves it. The closeups of Soph are elegant. They brought the girl right into your lap and you knew it was Soph; that voice and that face. It seemed to ease up Soph too, even when not singing, for she was at ease. While with the light acting called upon in all but one tense scene with her daughter, it was so handled by the director that Soph had no stretch to grow nervous.

Support, too, very nice in action. All deferred to Soph. No one tried to steal at her expense or inexperience. Looked splendid and worked out well. Mr. Hamilton and Lila Lee were away in the lead in playing. George Duryea had a hard role as the snippy snob, made more so when he had to turn over.

And Wilbur Mack stuttered. He wasn't programmed, but he stuttered. When he stuttered this picture had to go over. The Warners may have discovered the talkers, but Tommy Dugan made the stutterers. Mr. Mack got the best laughs outside of Soph's lyrics, other than when Duryea got a bump on the bean in the joint for calling the star entertainer " a cheap dame."

An interesting picture to the show business as bringing out how a personality may be made to stand out notwithstanding, in the talkers whereas the same personality would have died standing up in the silents.

Sime.

CONSTANT NYMPH

(BRITISH MADE)

(Silent)

Gainsborough (English) production. Distributor over here not named. Adapted by Basil Dean and Margaret Kennedy from Miss Kennedy's novel of same title. Produced by Mr. Dean and directed by Adrian Brunel. Ivor Novello and Mabel Poulton featured. At Little Carnegie Playhouse (sure seater), New York, week June 8. Running time, 80 minutes.

Tessa	Mabel Poulton
Lewis Dodd	Ivor Novello
Sanger	George Heinrich
Pauline	Dorothy Boyd
Florence	Frances Dable

In the lobby of the Carnegie Little Playhouse, one of those freaky sure-seaters on 57th street, where the ping pong and date 'em up room are worth more than the $1 admission, a reproduced poster of an English trade film paper says "The Constant Nymph" was chosen as the prize moving picture made in England last season.

If so, or anywhere near, why do not the English throw up their hands? This one silent hasn't a living chance over here. It would be tedious as one-half of a double bill in a 15c grind on Canal street, New Orleans.

The English are so slow in their picture making. Besides which this is silent. Fne opportunity here for sound as the story revolves around composers, with the juvenile made a famous composer-to-be, conducting his symphonic orchestra on the screen to the music of a three-piece band in the Carnegie's pit. Oh, boy!

But that didn't murder the picture. If anything did, it was the photography. No lighting, no camera work, nothing; just a dull passing through a series of slow scenes. And such scenes! Drawn with a broadness that could only have been aimed for school children intelligence.

It seems almost a pity in New York, viewing these pictures, and since Tilley for some reason unknown here has stopped giving the English slant for reviews in Variety, to believe that if this kind of picture, along with "Kitty," is the best of the British mades, why they should be sent abroad to ruin whatever reputation the English might retain as picture makers if these were kept in England.

That Basil Dean's name is attached to "The Constant Nymph" and Gainsborough as the producing firm, while entitled to consideration, cannot alter the facts.

Story is of a hoydenish group, children of a great composer, who dies in his studio in the Austrian Tyrol. Later his most hoydenish daughter also dies. In between the picture died.

All of the charm of a usual tale of this kind on the screen has been spoiled. No attraction is left. If not the direction, it is the photography, and if neither, then the actors, excepting Ivor Novello. Mabel Poulton as Tessa, the little hoyden, who should look about 15, looks often 25, and again 35. She has a libel action against the cameraman and make-up man. Frances Dable gives an even performance as Florence, but it is wasted in the rabble.

"The Constant Nymph" played on Broadway on the stage and was a success. The stage may have gotten the spirit of the script, but this screen utterly lost that most important factor.

The last reports on stock selling in England said the great British public is holding $93,000,000 in picture stocks. May heaven preserve them! This kind of picture making never can, unless for Britain, only.

Sime.

Studio Murder Mystery

(All Dialogue)

Paramount production and release. Frank Tuttle for story, adaptation, dialog and direction. Victor Milner, cameraman. In cast: Neil Hamilton, Chester Conklin, Warner Oland, Florence Eldridge, Guy Oliver. Western Electric recording. At Paramount week June 8. Running time, 62 minutes.

"Studio Murder Mystery" is the perfect picture hamburger, with odds and ends on the Paramount Hollywood lot cooked, prepared and all but served by the versatile Frank Tuttle.

Few sets had to be built and even electricians were cut low on time by not having to move lamps and paraphernália during shooting. If the company budget figures were revealed they probably would hurt the pride of many an indie economist.

With all the hoke in the story and comedy situations allowed to brew over into things dramatic; with all of the conventional script swerves and a lowly gag writer solving the mystery while conversing to himself over a phone—the thing holds enough interest and suspense specks to get by as a fair programer.

Major credit for holding the thing together goes to Warner Oland. Continental manner, deep voice, dark appearance and real ability are the Oland assets.

A young man rehearsing a murder sequence under Oland's guidance flops at it. Within four minutes' worth of running time, he is threatened with actual killing by the director, the wife, the girl friend and the latter's brother.

A lot of people will like the studio stuff. Camera takes in a couple of sets, some Paramount streets and something that looks like B. P. Schulberg's sanctum.

Chester Conklin, who gets a play in the billing, essays only the bit part of a gateman who writes as many figures on a pad as there are close-ups of clocks and watches in the padding—and there are a lot.

Waly.

SHE GOES TO WAR

(10% DIALOG, WITH SONG)

Inspiration production for United Artists release. Directed by Henry King. Eleanor Boardman starred; John Holland lead. From the Rupert Hughes story, adapted by Mme. Fred De Grasse. Photography by Tonio Gaudio and John Fulton. Titles by John Monk Saunders. Theme song, 'There's a Happy Land," by Harry Akst. Associate producers, Victor and Edward Halperin. Running time, 87 minutes. At Rivoli, New York, week June 8.

Joan	Eleanor Boardman
Tom Pike	John Holland
Reggie	Edmund Burns
Rosie	Alma Rubens
Bill	Al St. John
Katie	Glen Walters
Tom's Mother	Margaret Seddon
Yvette	Yola D'Avril
Joan's Aunt	Evelyn Hall
Joan's Maid	Dina Smirnova
Major	Augustino Borgato
Major's Wife	Yvonne Starke
Matron of Canteen	Eulalie Jensen
Major	Capt. H. M. Zier
Top Sergeant	Edward Chandler
Lady Hostess	Ann Warrington
Knitting Ladies	Gretchen Hartman Florence Wix

A war picture with special reference to the feminine angle in story material and treatment. Topic is probably outmoded but the new twist gets it out of the rut. Splendid cast, excellent sentimental appeal. Qualifies for first run and week stand de luxes on the strength of its names. Will please mildly generally and probably enjoy good word of mouth reports by women.

Well managed battle stuff and some fine sentimental passages involving Alma Rubens and several appealing women character types. What Henry King has done in his production is to strip the glamor from war as it touches women workers at home and in the field. Picture has a certain "literary" quality that helps to make it smooth entertainment, but at the same time robs it of sincerity and strength. Hughes is a prolific and skilled magazine fiction maker. This material is first class magazine stuff, but it's a long way from notable writing. Directorship of high order and fine acting get the full value and a little more out of the matter supplied.

Spoiled daughter of wealth goes to France in search of glory and adventure, and balks at the rough stuff of a canteen worker. He fiance, of the same social order, has a safe berth with the outfit. When they are all ordered up front, he dogs it. In a spirit of hysterical bravado, she slips into his place, learning all about war in a series of serio-comic battle experiences. Net result is that she saves the command by a happy accident, is rescued by a rough-and-ready lieutenant from her home town, and the final clinch is a triumph for American democracy and romance.

A lot of it is hard to take, but the tale as told on the screen has a persuasive thread of good comedy, several well-managed sequences of pathos and a couple of melodramatic thrills. Probably the thing that does most toward holding the film up is the work of Alma Rubens, the last thing that actress did before her collapse.

As the humble Rosie Cohen from Flatbush, doing scullery work around a canteen back of the lines, and trying with her ukulele and her voice to cheer the soldiers, she has a great chance.

Neat dramatic twist is the passage where a dying doughboy is brought in delirious. Lieutenant asks the proud heroine to help him die by pretending to be the mother he calls for. She backs away from the job and the humble Rosie is pressed into service. Bit as done by Miss Rubens gets close to a genuine tear.

There is also a dandy bit by Glen Walters, another humble canteen worker, in her awkward fondling of a soldier-sweetheart, back exhausted from the trenches and too wornout for love-making. This is all the best of human interest. King has stretched it out a little, but wisely, for it is the genuineness of these passages that saves the whole picture from plain popular fiction hackwork. Matter of fact, the Rubens and Walters roles steal the subject away from the star, hampered by an unsympathetic part. Al St. John is a standout as a comedy doughboy, far overshadowing the leading male role.

Battle sequences pack one solid kick. American unit is moving forward unaided, tanks having been delayed. Enemy waits until the attackers reach bottom of steep slope, then roll down and explode casks of liquid fire, which envelops the whole countryside in flames. Boys retreat and when the tanks come up load themselves in the iron wagons and drive on through the blazing field. Some great effects here, with a kick in the success of the attack.

Sound accompaniment always effective. Practically no dialog. Miss Rubens has a song early in the picture, singing the theme number to the soldiers in the canteen, and later has her big moment singing the same number as a sort of lullaby to the dying doughboy. This episode, even if it is somber, is the high spot of the picture. Titles serve in place of dialog throughout.

Rush.

CAREERS

(ALL DIALOG)

First National production and release. Starring Billie Dove. Directed by John Francis Dillon, from play by Alfred Schirokayer and Paul Rosenhayn; adapted by Forrest Halsey. Photographed by John Seitz. Theme song, "I Love You, I Hate You," by George W. Meyer and Al Bryan. Musical synchronization by Vitaphone orchestra. At Strand, New York, week June 8. Running time, 92 minutes.

Helene	Billie Dove
Victor	Antonio Moreno
Hortense	Thelma Todd
The President	Noah Beery
Carouge	Holmes Herbert
The Woman	Carmel Meyers
Lavergne	Robert Frazer
Biwa player	Sojin

Fair programmer that will need plenty of stage support to get real b. o. returns. At the Strand the bill is bolstered up considerably by unusually good shorts, two of the four screened carrying surefire laughs. One of those was awarded more applause than the feature at the second show Saturday.

Story is one of love and intrigue in the French diplomatic corps stationed in a remote section of French Indo-China. It's Billie Dove's first appearance in a talker. A few melodramatic sequences give her opportunity to show that the mike holds no fears as far as she is concerned. Her followers will not be disappointed in that department, while the voice recordings of the supporting cast, especially Noah Beery and Holmes Herbert, are up to par. Antonio Moreno, playing opposite the star, appeared a bit self-conscious at times.

Plot revolves about Helene, wife of a French magistrate in a small town in Cochin-China, anxious to foster her husband's career and eventual promotion to a berth in Paris. When the advancement he thinks he deserves is not forthcoming after four years of service, the husband, Victor, decides to take his case to the governor of the French colony and give him the low-down on the a. k. president of the settlement.

Latter is continually on the make for the beautiful wives of his subordinates, those boys whose wives give in getting the breaks from the old boy. Helene's virtue and lack of amiability to the president is the cause of her husband's failure to carve a career of importance for himself.

Calling on the president to get his slant on the reason less gifted men than her husband have risen in the diplomatic ranks, Helene tips him to her husband's contemplated breach of etiquet in going to the governor. Realizing that she has made things worse, she is about to agree to submit to the president's advances as a squarer when a native hiding in the darkened room, awaiting an opportunity to lift some trinkets, is discovered and in the ensuing scufile the president is killed.

This murder is worked in as a flashback when Helene's husband is appointed by the governor to find the murderer, with he not knowing that his wife is implicated. Trite happy ending has husband and wife reconciled, she convincing him that the murder of the treacherous president prevented any irregular conduct on her part.

Theme song, "I Love You, I Hate You," is sung in the early part of the picture by Carmel Meyers. Holds little value here, not plugged to any extent. Andre de Segurola, from opera, sings a French aria during the course of another sequence for fair results.

Production and direction are fair and the Billie Dove fans will likely vote it that kind of entertainment.

ONE-WOMAN IDEA

(SILENT)

Fox production and release. Featuring Rod La Rocque and Marceline Day. Directed by Berthold Viertel. Story by Alan Williams, adapted by Marion Orth. Supervised by Phillip Klein. At Roxy, New York, week June 8. Running time, 65 mins.

Prince Ahmed............Rod La Rocque
Lady Alicia Douglas and
Alizar, half-caste dancing girl
Marceline Day
Lady passengers on the boat
Shirley Dorman, Sharon Lynn and Sally Phipps.
Hosain....................Ivan Lebedeff
Lord Douglas.............Douglas Gilmore
Bordinas..........................Gino Corrado
Captain of Steamship....Joseph W. Girard
Ali..............................Arnold Lucy
Zuleide..........................Frances Rosay
Captain of the Body Guard.....Guy Trento
Bodyguard....................Jamiel Hasson
Bodyguard....................Tom Tamarez
Buttons..........................Coy Watson

Molasses has more speed than this lumbering, heavy-handed old-fashioned moving picture. Doubtful if there ever was a successful film, either commercially or artistically, in which the villain was the husband of the heroine. It just isn't a good theme for Anglo-Saxon audiences, largely because censorship requirements rigidly curtails the story development on every point and the scenario makeshifts create an inescapable impression of insincerity.

"The One Woman Idea" is of the final few silent features on the Fox program. It will be lucky with its double handicap to get by. Not an attractive entertainment and will lean heavily upon whatever box office appeal the names of Rod La Rocque and Marceline Day possess.

Director Berthold Viertel, unknown, will not step either upward or onward on such fragile underpinnings as this picture. Additionally the photography done in half-tones increases the tedium.

Another of those situations of the Oxford graduate from the orient. Rod LaRocque as a Persian prince is more Episcopalian than the most veritable of the nordics and the English villain. Lord Douglas himself, is as polygamous as orientals used to be before Mrs. E. M. Hull and the late Valentino founded the dynasty of wholesome sheiks. Between the idealistic Persian and the no-good Briton is the colorless, formless and uninteresting figure of English wifehood as interpreted by Marceline Day.

Most of the action and the relationship between the various characters are conveyed by captions. Background may hold a degree of interest for the hoi polloi but seems scarcely adequate to carry the feeble antiquated story. *Land.*

A SCANDAL IN PARIS

(GERMAN MADE)
(Silent)

Felsom-Europa production directed by Robert Weine, who created "Caligari." Starring Lili Damita. Continental cast, including Vladimir Gaidarow, Johannes Reimann, Arthur Pusey, Vivian Gibson and Fritz Kortner. Story adapted from old English society play, "A Butterfly on the Wheel." Running time, 72 minutes. At Fifth Avenue playhouse week June 8.

An intensely British play of the Jones-Pinero school, interpreted by a German director and a polyglot cast, looks pretty mixed. All in all it rates a better than usual foreign made for American uses. Probably because the material is Nordic. Piece has a fine technical production. Thing that hurts it most is the foreign brand of acting. That's plenty to ruin it.

Story is well-knit drama, albeit old-fashioned, and incidents are theatrically effective. But as it unfolds on the screen the men are hopeless and the women frumpy to American eyes. Acting technique is the flamboyant picture style of 15 years ago in the States. The hero doesn't for a minute look like an English M.P. and suggests that character even less.

Lili Damita, who has done some splendid things in Hollywood, and is doing more now, is sadly out of place as a sedate English wife. Picture was made less than a year ago, program note explained, and was the last assignment of Miss Damita before she left for the States.

Silent pictures manufactured out of old plays are back numbers. Sound finished them. But even before sound the British polite society drama didn't make good screen. Here the story and the drama are all in the titles and the acting only supplements the printed word. The German device of trick composite shots is admirably used to suggest the mental state of a woman slowly being crushed while she is on the witness stand in an English divorce court testifying in her own defense. But that is one of the few good dramatic moments in a long feature.

Settings are admirable and photography nearly up to first-rate American standards. Acting altogether alien to us and gives the whole play an artificial tone that no amount of skilful backgrounds can overcome.

Story grows convincingly and naturally. It made an absorbing stage play with its craftily built-up incidents and situations. But it is not screen material, particularly as here treated, and certainly not adapted to the silent technique. As a dialog production it might be another matter.

Strictly for the sure-seaters as here. *Rush.*

FOR THE TERM OF HIS NATURAL LIFE

(AUSTRALIAN-MADE)
(Silent)

Produced and released by Australasian Films. Direction and story adaptation credited Norman Dawn. Foreign cast, excepting Eva Novak, including Arthur McLaglen, George Fisk, Kay Souper, Marian Clark, Dunstan Webb, Susan Dennis. At Stanley, New York, one day, June 4. Running time, 84 minutes.

Made in a real convict locale, this Australian subject is richer in felon colony color than, doubtless, any previous release in the same category. "For the Term of His Natural Life" meets the most morbid illusion of convict ship and settlement book readers. While it is grippingly dark-hued and old worldish from start to finish, a jumbled story along Dumas' "Monte Cristo" lines, and directorial laxity in keeping the threads of the yarn and characters apart, unfortunately cause an otherwise excellent production to fall short of the classification which it would most certainly have rated as the film epic on old penal life.

The picture is a good bet as a novelty in any unwired house. Arty policies should realize their biggest pull in proper publicity. Non-theatricals will find it excellent fodder.

The penal settlement on Van Dieman's Island, Australia, as it existed in 1827 before Queen Victoria decided to keep her bad boys closer at home, is the center of action. Around this is written a hoke yarn about a bastard son of a murdered lord taking the blame in order to save his mother the shame of public identity.

The trip on a convict ship, similar, on a much larger scale, to the rot-gut barge that occasionally takes in the public at a half buck per, is well pictured. Here the attempt to unravel the characters, including two men of like physiques, but opposite inclinations, gets beyond the direction. General conglomeration and hopeless but thrilling meshwork become a mutiny.

High walls of rock, rough water far below, chain gangs at work in the field and in the shop with an occasional outbreak against tyrannous guards, command audience attention.

Worked in between is the story of the commander's daughter in love with the bastard prisoner. The latter situation canters off into a sequence where a flagship to the convict schooner is conquered by the bad man and the hero convict, a worthless captain and the girl are marooned on an island. After cared for by the prisoner, rescue comes but the girl loses her memory and the captain takes all the credit.

Despite marriage, the girl eventually remembers when the prisoner, set free by a conscience-stricken clergyman afraid to name the original killer, escapes with her on another boat. Here a miniature is used effectively of a storm at sea.

Several gruesome but well done incidents include a gorilla-like convict who plots the gang's escape and feeds on his own companions until captured in the swamps. Two boy felons leaping off a cliff to end their careers furnish a suspense gem rarely caught with such sincerity by American cameras. *Waly.*

Hoofbeats of Vengeance

(SILENT)

Universal production and release. Directed by Henry McRae from story by William Lord Wright and George Plympton. Jack Perrin and "Rex" (horse), featured. In cast: Helen Foster, Al Ferguson and "Starlight" (horse). At New York, New York, one day, June 4, as half double bill. Running time, 50 minutes.

Mild thriller, again about the Canadian Northwest mounted cops. The kids in the neighborhood grinds know this formula by heart but on a twin bill it may slide by.

"Rex," the horse, knows the man who killed his master, one of the aces of the royal mounted police, and is out for vengeance. When Sergeant Jack Gordon (Jack Perrin) is sent to trace the slayer "Rex" leads him to Regan (Al Ferguson), head man of a gang of border smugglers, who is guilty.

When the copper gets in a jam with a gang of tough muggs the smart horse brings a troop of mounties to his aid. Hoofbeats of the horse finally force the murderer to confess his crime and the rep of the R. N. W. M. P. is saved. They got another man.

Slight love story has Helen Foster supplying s. a. opposite Perrin. Titles are mostly inane but those in which horses hold conversation are the pay-off.

And whatever did become of Hal Roach's uncanny "Rex?" Is this the same or did the Germans make two?

BLACK CARGOES OF THE SOUTH SEAS

(AUSTRALIAN-MADE)
(Silent)

Australasian production and released here independently through Norman Dawn, director. Distributed abroad under title of "The Adorable Outcast." In cast: Edmund Burns, Edith Roberts, Susan Denis. At Stanley, New York, one day, June 7. Running time 75 minutes.

Except as a scenic of the Fiji Isles and for that it would have to be cut to two reels, "Black Cargoes of the South Seas" hasn't a conscientious look-in here.

A stupid story allowed to paw hopelessly through the reelage by incompetent direction abetted by similar editing, attempts everything from Sennett's oldest ones to serial stuff.

A laugh is afforded when the town grocer's daughter returns from college, enciente. Right after titling about the delivery she is shown holding a black infant which, however, is later revealed not to be the child.

The slave angle is worked in a chunk. The whole picture is like that. Just the kind of a cutting job a kid would make on its father's hair. Comedy is slapped in where drama is supposed to dominate and audience reaction is negative. *Waly.*

THE TIP-OFF

(SILENT)

Universal production and release. Directed by Leigh Jason. Story by Basil Dickey. Bill Cody featured. In cast: George Hackathorne and Duane Thompson. At Times, New York, one day, June 5, as half double bill. Running time, 55 minutes.

Neatly handled crook story, screened in convincing style and a sure pleaser for those who lay it on the line at the neighborhood grind houses on double feature days.

Opening sequence rivets the attention and thereafter action piles up, with a few laughs to lighten the tension. This flicker gives the crook determined to go straight a break and is a rap against stool pigeons, but a plug for fortune tellers.

Start has Jimmy LaMarr (Bill Cody), gentleman crook, plugged by a cop's bullet while making a getaway from a burglary. His pal, "The Shrimp" (Geo. Hackathorne), manages to save him from the jug by secreting him in the home of his girl friend, Crystal Annie (Duane Thompson), whose racket is fortune telling. While being nursed back to health Jimmy wins his pal's gal. Convinced he has been double-crossed, Shrimp nurses a grudge while pretending frie[illegible]ship for both. Seeking to get even, he tips off the cops to his next job and persuades Jimmy to join the mob in a jewelry haul before going straight and hooking up with Annie.

Gazing in her crystal, Annie gets wise to the frame against Jimmy and busts in just as the cops start shooting up the trapped gang of yeggs. When things look bad for the lovers, t[illegible] pigeon repents of his action and while enabling his pal and former sweetheart to get away, gets in front of a bullet himself.

Director Jason did well by this thriller, and Cody, Hackathorne and Miss Thompson all give creditable performances with a much better than average crook picture resulting.

THE IDEAL WOMAN

(FRENCH MADE)

Paris, June 2.

Latest of Franco Film is "La Femme Revee," lifted from a Spanish novel by J. Perez de Razas, and adroitly produced by Jean Durand, who had not much to work upon.

Scenario is rather diluted. As the views are in Paris and Spain there are some excellent views for travel fiends.

Durand probably tried to crowd in as much variety as possible for export purposes. There is a music hall, Casino de Paris, with Harry Pilcer.

A Parisian banker, Coal, falls in love with Mercedes, the niece of Dona Caridad, while he is in Spain. Had an accident on the road, and is offered hospitality in Caridad's country mansion. Coal repays his host by running away with the niece. He makes it a binding match, however, by marrying the girl in Paris.

He has a mistress, of course, called Suzanne, and she feels her nose is out of joint. She schemes for Mercedes to have a love adventure with a dancer, and a fashionable one at that. Coal turns his wife out of doors.

Soon he learns of the wicked maneuvers of his former mistress and realizes Mercedes has been a victim of her jealousy.

Not very novel, this moss covered intrigue. The cast barely recuperates the other short comings. Arlette Marchal, delightful, but fails to be convincing, as a jealous mistress. Harry Pilcer is quite at home as the professional dancer. Alice Roberte pleases as Mercedes, as also Charles Vanel as the Banker Coal. Tony d'Algy and Therese Kolb complete the main cast.

"La Femme Revee" should be able to squeeze into the second part for provincial towns. *Kendrew.*

MONTMARTRE ROSE

Excellent (producer) production and independent release. Directed by Bernard McEvety from Isidore Bernstein's adaptation of story of same title. In cast: Marguerite De La Motte, Paul Ralli, Martha Mattox, Rosemary Theby. At Stanley one day, June 5. Running time, 62 minutes.

Strictly dime attraction and pretty slow for that money. "Montmartre Rose" based on worn-cuff script, or nothing at all. Leading man, Paul Ralli, new from the extra ranks, has much to learn. Lad is allowed to pan too much. Story is one of those wealthy boy falling for the dancer kind. Too bad. There are some people ordinarily good in the cast. Sets and props are better than those used in the average indie. *Waly.*

HIS LATE EXCELLENCY
(GERMAN-MADE)
(Silent)

Ufa production, directed by Ernst Licho and Wilhelm Thiele. From a stage play by Rudolf Presber. Cameraman, Werner Brandes. At 55th Street Playhouse, New York, week June 8. Running time, 72 mins. The cast: Willy Frisch, Ernst Gronau, Max Hansen, Hermine Sterler, Lydia Potechina, Olga Tschehowa, Fritz Kampers, Hans Junkerman, Truus von Aalten, Max Gueckstorf, Julius Falkenstein.

This German comedy from the Ufa factory constitutes an odd mingling of Mack Sennett slapstick with certain lingering refinements that made some of the German pictures of three years ago distinguished. Idea is basically good farce, but for general American consumption the approach and technique employed render unintelligible, or at least uncommercial, the whole effort.

A considerable measure of credit is seemingly due whoever wrote and edited the titles for over here. They help a lot and their viewpoint seems essentially American.

Story is of a baroness (Olga Tschechowa) who finds upon the death of her protector and patron, prime minister, that the bureaucrats and other spiteful officials of the royal court are out to give her the air.

In this exigency she concocts the idea of pretending the prime minister wrote a book of memoirs prior to his death revealing the inside workings, intrigues and private scandals of the government classes.

By sly hints of what the supposed memoirs contain, the baroness throws a scare into her will o' wisp friends, who hypocritically reverse their venomous attitude and start to bull her.

Handsome young grand duke (Willy Frisch) enters the situation and falls in love with the baroness. After farcical complications they clinch.

Some respectable giggles along the way, variety of interesting types and touches, with production, photography, etc., acceptable. For houses accustomed to a German diet this may possibly be one of the year's standouts. *Land.*

PRIDE OF PAWNEE
(SILENT)

Radio production and release. Starring Tom Tyler. Directed by Robert De Lacey, from story by Joseph Kane. Nick Musuraca, cameraman. In cast: Jack Hilliard, Lew Meehan, Ethelyn Claire. At the Stanley one day, June 10. Running time, about 55 minutes.

This was made after Radio Pictures decided westerns were passe and it shows it. Just the old hoke, with all of the tricks and bad enough to sell the public that Radio was right in quitting this kind of stuff.

A gang of truck drivers remember by degrees that they are Indians. By the time "The Pride of Pawnee" is half over, most of them have acquired a studio sunburn.

Tom Tyler, inanimate, is allowed to pan too often. Same for Ethelyn Claire. The good boys find out the bad boys after gats putter for a couple of rounds and the girl hitches up with the great hero and town deliverer. *Waly.*

THE FOUR FEATHERS
(NO DIALOG)
(Sound)

Non-talker produced and directed by Merian C. Cooper and Ernest B. Schoedsack. Paramount release. William Powell, Richard Arlen, Fay Wray, Clive Brook and Noah Beery featured. Screen play by Howard Estabrook from Hope Loring's adaption of novel by A. E. W. Mason. W. E. sounded. Score and effects by William Peters. Opened June 12 at $2, twice daily run at Criterion, New York. Running time, 80 minutes.

Harry Faversham	Richard Arlen
Ethne Eustace	Fay Wray
Lieut. Durrance	Clive Brook
Captain Trench	William Powell
Lieut. Castleton	Theodore von Eltz
Slave Trader	Noah Beery
Idris	Zack Williams
Ahmed	Noble Johnson
Ali	Harold Hightower
Harry (age 10)	Philippe de Lacy
Col. Eustace	Edward J. Radcliffe
Col. Faversham	George Fawcett
Col. Sutch	Augustin Symonds

"Four Feathers" is a good picture, though silent. It is built for the grinds and should get money that way. It is not a $2 special for any other place than Broadway, because it lacks too much, especially dialog.

Not an individual name picture. William Powell is a star today, but a talking picture star. Because of that he's merely one of five featured players. If the women show any great interest in this harsh tale, it will be a surprise.

Merian C. Cooper and Ernest B. Schoedsack were the producers. They made "Chang." It is no secret that "Feathers'" treatment was primarily photographic. The dramatics followed. Cooper and Schoedsack must also have been the directors of the story part, for no one else is credited. Nor is a photographer named.

Ever see a herd of hippo slide down the steep bank of a jungle watering place? Or even one hippopotamus? The sliding here is made important cogs in the narrative.

Ever see a large family of baboons hop from limb to limb, and also into a stream, to escape a forest fire? Just for effect.

Or a huge army of black savages dashing to battle on white camels against a gigantic desert background?

These three items are "Four Feathers."

A man's story.

The white feather is the symbol of cowardice. In the British army, receipt of a white feather by a soldier signifies he has been adjudged yellow by his fellow warriors. It means he must redeem himself and prove that his spine is not of that tint, or blow his brains out to preserve the honor of the army. The principal character and subsequent hero of Mason's story receives four white feathers. So much for the title.

Tale is set late in the last century. Often in action, in theme and in progress, "Four Feathers" is highly reminiscent of "Beau Geste." Pictorially they are much the same. As a narrative, "Geste" was the better, for in its unwinding it held mystery, while this picture's outcome can be easily guessed at any point along the way.

A prolog is played by children, altogether remindful of that other desert military tale.

The grown-up lieutenant is the buddy of lieutenants Durrance, Castleton and Capt. Trench. He is telling them of his approaching marriage. A messenger boy delivers a wire. It's a tip-off from a friend in on the know, and the tip is that there's going to be war. Young Lieut. gulps. Wire advises to slip Trench the same info. Instead, he crumbles it up and tosses it away. As he's getting married, the lieut. informs his brother officers he might as well resign from the army.

Trench finds the discarded wire.

Three white feathers from his three friends.

He confesses to the girl. Enough for her. And the fourth white feather—from her.

His father, the Col., is on his death bed. He asks his son if this vile story is true. His son admits he is afraid. "My legacy to you is in that drawer," says the Col. It's a pistol. And the Col. dies then and there.

The boy's winning back of his honor is the story and the picture from then on. It's not a new story, this redemption stuff.

He becomes a hero to square himself. He rescues, at risk of his own life, the three accusers. At the finish, after the excitement on the desert, he is back in England, back in the army and decorated for bravery, beside the three men whose lives he saved. And then he's back in the good graces of the girl who once told him to go bump himself off.

Richard Arlen's performance is good most of the while, excellent at times. During the build-up period, while under verbal fire for cowardice, Arlen was instructed to do little more than shift his eyes in guilt and hang his head in shame. He could have made more of the moments in England.

Powell is next with the most to do and does it like Powell. Clive Brook was not handed his usual weighty part and isn't impressive because of that, while von Eltz, as the lesser of the four chums, has no opportunity to be more than satisfactory.

Of the other featured players, Noah Beery is in the picture for but five minutes, as a cruel slave trader, and killed off in one of the rescue scenes. Fay Wray only had to look good.

When the story drags, it drags plenty, and nothing that the cast could do would help it. Takes 50 minutes for Faversham to rescue his first comrade and return the first of the four feathers. The picture runs 80.

The hippo, monkey and battle scenes drew appreciative applause. Not likely they'll miss doing the same very often. The Criterion screen was extended to its full width to hold and eccentuate the battle panorama, and provided a thrill not yet topped in a moving picture. *Bige.*

FOUR DEVILS
(25% DIALOG)
(2nd Review)

Fox production and release. Directed by F. W. Murnau from Berthold Viertel's adaptation of the novel by Herman Bay. Janet Gaynor and Mary Duncan featured. Fox Movietone. Synchronization musical score by S. L. Rothafel, directed by Erno Rapee. At the Roxy, New York, week June 15. Running time, 125 minutes.

First Sequence

The Clown	Farrell Macdonald
Cecchi	Anders Randolf
Woman	Claire McDowell
Charles, as a boy	Jack Parker
Adolf, as a boy	Philippe DeLacey
Marion, as a girl	Dawn O'Day
Louise, as a girl	Anita Fremault
Poodle Dog	Himself
Old Clown	Wesley Lake

Second Sequence

Marion	Janet Gaynor
Charles	Charles Morton
Louise	Nancy Drexel
Adolf	Barry Norton
The Lady	Mary Duncan
Circus Director	Michael Visaroff
Mean Clown	George Davis
Old Roue	Andre Cheron

When Fox produced "Four Devils" on Broadway at the Gayety, New York, in October, it had sound effects, but no talker dialog. Before Fox shot it into the popular priced channels via Roxy, starting June 15, the last two reels virtually or 2,000 feet of the picture was given a dialog finish. Picture is 8,800 in complete footage.

The "talking" as done by Janet Gaynor especially where she realizes that her aerialistic sweetheart has fallen for another woman and that her sincere love is hooey, touches a response with an audience; makes all the more stronger the sympathy that the Gaynor part has worked throughout.

Miss Gaynor isn't overly strong with her vocal assignment, but she attempts it under the handicap of heretofore depending on her acting and personality. While Janet Gaynor talking becomes an immediate added attraction for "Four Devils."

Charles Morton, circus lover, also does some talking, but he seems too conscious of what was expected of him. Most of his talk didn't ring natural. With Mary Duncan several phases seemed strident and metallic, a fault that may be overcome in some of Miss Duncan's next pictures. She photographs well; knows how to act and has had sufficient stage experience to tackle any of the speaking roles assigned by the Fox film makers.

Where Miss Gaynor was called upon to shed tears and show decided grief and Miss Duncan was directed to laugh and evidence contempt of the trapeze girl when she visits her apartment, each had the recording seemingly too strong and loud. It may have been the Roxy projection, yet the volume made both sound harsh.

The addition of dialog for the two should add to its impression. General theme of the picture is of the type apparently constructed to unleash the tear ducts and make the sad-eyed sisters pull out their handkerchiefs in unison.

At the Roxy the audience appeared to obtain real satisfaction out of the dialog; the picture whether silent, with sound or otherwise, is one that could not take on real speed at any time. It is just that kind of a story. *Mark.*

AT EDGE OF WORLD

(GERMAN MADE)

(Silent)

UFA production and release. Directed by Karl Grune. German title, "Am Rande Der Welt." Cast: Albert Steinrueck, Wilhelm Dieterle, Imre Raday, Brigitte Helm, Camilla von Hallay, Erwin Faber, Max Schreck, Victor Janson, Jean Bradin. Running time, 71 mins. At 55th St. Playhouse, week June 15.

Intensely juvenile production based on war of the future. German cast composed of immobiled-faced people, incapable of registering emotion. Most notably childish are the sub-titles. One reads such lamentable captions as "Sadness spread o'er the gathering," "War, What for? What for?" etc.

Insipidity of this picture may be grasped in toto by one scene of a street vendor stepping into a roadside to halt four horsemen in hooded gowns, informing them he is government operator. Tells them war is declared; to spread the news and mobilize all towns. The riders go, each taking forked roads to all points.

Story is centered about a family who have owned a mill 300 years. Happiness of peace time indicated by a festival.

A spy is guest of the miller, who has a daughter and two sons. Phone wires are laid by spy. He receives the commission from the street vendor.

War is declared during festival. Scene shows folks with bowed heads at news. Orators shout "Three cheers for our country." Then the folks make merry and one son dances in glee at prospect "of battle." Spy falls in love with girl and tries to release himself from official work. Street vendor declines to allow that.

Scenes show war in progress. Just a few cursory shots of men in strange war habiliment, the enemy wearing black sweaters, spittoon-like helmets and gas-masks. Soldiers sprinting into battle as if in a leg race. Miller's youngest son taken as prisoner when enemy invades mill. Captain gives sister 24 hours to decide whether she will "give herself" to save brother. A subordinate enemy falls in love with the girl and releases brother. Sub-officer unable to explain his presence with girl is commanded to commit suicide, his superior believing him guilty of releasing the boy.

Spy meanwhile has volunteered to betray his soldier companions to save girl's brother. This is the crux of the feeble situation. Girl disdains him for turning traitor. Wind-up with traitor taking blame for all the trouble caused the miller. He is shot as he confesses. Mill burned to ground and lovers clasp each other.

Picture dizzily incoherent.

THE FALL OF EVE

(ALL DIALOG)

Columbia production and release. Dialog by Frederic and Fanny Hatton. Directed by Frank Strayer from adaptation by Gladys Lehman. Teddy Tetzlaff, cameraman. Western Electric sounded. At Embassy, New York, June 17, twice daily; $1.50 top. Running time, 65 minutes.

Eve Grant	Patsy Ruth Miller
Mr. Mack	Ford Sterling
Mrs. Ford	Gertrude Astor
Tom Ford, Jr.	Arthur Rankin
Tom Ford, Sr.	Jed Prouty
Mrs. Mack	Betty Farrington
Cop	Fred Kelsey
Bob White	Hank Mann

Worn comedy situations and antiquated lines in the sterotyped domestic complications long used in farces of playboy husbands compose the greater reason for the story end of Columbia's "The Fall of Eve." The lady, incidentally, is not of the garden, but a simple office steno with the name. Good cast carries the first three-quarters of the footage over to the last fraction, which is a machine gun for laughs and sends audience out satisfied. Picture, while far from a Broadway long termer, is adequate as program material in the average house.

Ford Sterling as Mr. Mack, woolen goods buyer from Chicago, and his wife, the hefty Betty Farrington, do excellent work. They rate major credit for keeping up story interest.

The Hattons atone for borrowing in the dialog by several gag lines just before the finis. One, used when a cop is trying to determine which of two women is Mrs. Ford, wife of the wholesaler whose genial entertaining for the fat contract causes the grief, got the crowd at first night at maximum hilarity. It was after the Fords had been examined and Mack, pointing to his own wife, declared:

"This is a Mack."

Jed Prouty as Tom Ford, Sr., who enlists his stenographer, Eve, played by Patsy Ruth Miller, to entertain the buyer, does a good job. Miss Miller's role, although the center of the complications that start when Mrs. Mack insists on joining the party, is less impressive than those of Sterling, Farrington and Prouty.

The radio brings in the real Mrs. Ford, played nicely by Gertrude Autor, from a week-end, after a night club associates her name with a request number.

Meantime the party returns to the Ford home when the picture's fund of fun gets underway. Mrs. Mack insists upon the Fords retiring. Young Ford (Arthur Rankin) helps things along by first aiding his father by posing as a prohibition agent and then adding to the complications when he thinks the affair with Eve is on the up and up.

Miss Astor lets things warm up before identities are unmasked. Rankin provides the happy ending by copping Eve and explaining the misunderstanding was caused by the night club announcer's failure to tack on "Junior." *Waly.*

THE IDLE RICH

(ALL DIALOG)

M-G-M production and release. Directed by William DeMille. From stage play, "White Collars," by Edith Ellis, adapted by Clara Berenger. Photographed by Leonard Smith At Capitol, New York, week June 15. Running time, 80 minutes.

William Van Luyn	Conrad Nagel
Helen Thayer	Bessie Love
Joan Thayer	Leila Hyams
Henry	Robert Ober
Mr. Thayer	James Neill
Mrs. Thayer	Edythe Chapman
Tom Gibney	Paul Kruger
Frank Thayer	Kenneth Gibson

Spring tonic for ailing box offices. A fine picture all about the great middle classes and their problems. Well cast and intelligently directed, should build steadily on week stands when the office stenogs start passing the word along.

Story hit home solidly. That class conscienceness which seizes the average family of workers when believing they are being patronized by the wealthy class is here presented in all its aspects. Situations created pack plenty of laughs for regular picture fans.

As a stage play this was "White Collars." It ran for over a year in Los Angeles, following that up with eight months on Broadway. Most of the comedy elements of the play are retained on the screen. A small cast and an inexpensive production makes this one a certain money-maker for Metro with no small credit due William de Mille, who directed; Conrad Nagel, Bessie Love and Leila Hyams in the principal roles.

Plot centers about Joan Thayer (Miss Hyams), stenog from a middle class family married to her employer, William VanLuyn (Mr. Nagel), scion of proud New York family and a multi-millionaire. Introduced to his wife's family, Van Luyn soon discovers the snobbishness of the upper is only exceeded by that of the middle and lower classes, when they are in their own environment.

VanLuyn's efforts to lift his bride out of her ordinary existence are met with objections provoked by her boresome cousin's long winded remarks about class equality. Determined to prove he's a regular guy VanLuyn moves in with the in-laws, at his wife's suggestion, suffering all sorts of inconveniences to prove that a happy marriage is on the point of being disrupted by class distinction.

Sequences in which various members of the white collar family bicker and quarrel give Bessie Love and Miss Hyams a few chances to emote convincingly. Nagel is excellent as the husband and Ober makes the most of his role. James Neill and Edythe Chapman as the father and mother give fine characterizations.

That great army of stenogs will go for this screen comedy in a big way, for it's right in their back yard.

THE LAST FLIGHT

(FRENCH MADE)

(Silent)

Maurice Tourneur production from the novel "L'Equipage," by J. Kessels. Continental cast includes Jean Dax, Pierre de Guingand and Claire de Lorez. Film edited and titled by Samuel Detlow. At 5th Avenue Playhouse week June 15. Running time 63 minutes.

Sure seater stuff of the worst sort, likely to prove a chaser in the intimate houses although there's no way of gauging the reaction of the sophisticates who are apt to rate any flicker with a foreign tag as arty.

Fragment of a story has the activities of one of the French flying squadrons as background. Continuity is jumpy and as a result a flock of long winded sappy subtitles have been written in, probably on this side.

Obvious plot concerns an ace pilot on leave in Paris during the World War making a dame who later turns out to be the wife of his best pal. He renounces her and returns to camp in time to take part in a battle.

The ace is coupled up with the man whose wife he has been living with during his week's furlough, handling the machine gun and knocking off the enemy planes, a dozen or more, in rapid succession. Just before killed himself he confesses his indiscretion. On his deathbed the double-crossed husband forgives his wife.

All the action is confined to newsreel and phoney air battle sequences. Jean Dax and Pierre de-Guingand do their roles in the usual Continental style. Miss de Lorez is a statuesque blonde with a dead pan who excels at mugging.

Perhaps the last atrocity of the late lamented war.

HOUSE OF HORROR

(1% DIALOG)

First National production and release. Featuring Louise Fazenda, Chester Conklin and Thelma Todd. Directed by Benjamin Christensen. Titles by Tom Miranda and dialog by William Irish. Western Electric sounded, with score by Louis Silver. In cast: William V. Mong, Dale Fuller, T. Holtz, Yola D'Averlle. At Loew's New York, one day, June 14, one half of double bill. Running time, 65 minutes.

"The House of Horror" is one of the weakest and most boring afterbirths of pseudo mystery-comedy grinds out of Hollywood. The thing actually rants and rambles, with audience of any mental caliber at sea until the last reel when the title writer makes a supreme effort to account with cart before horse angle.

Fans who miss the first three or four minutes will figure theatre has pulled a fast one in billing dialog. It all takes place then between Louise Fazenda, Chester Conklin, as a country store couple, and William V. Mong. The latter always carries an umbrella and essays a charlatan role until just before finis when he is revealed as head of a gang of gem smugglers.

Old gags are strained by Fazenda and Conklin who overwork for the few spotted laughs they clock. Christensen directs as if he had been instructed to consider the players secondary and concentrate on every bit of old property in the Burbank studios. If the thing ever had a script Christensen apparently never knew it, judging strictly from the finished product, and Tom Miranda stayed up nights trying to dope out the hodge-podge of shots turned over to him for sequencial explanation.

Every trick in the moth-eaten bag ripped time and again, first by the legits and then passed on to the picture people, is pushed into "The House of Horrors." Panel doors are used most. Falling crockery and a lot of things boring to grandpa fill in when those that flopped on Broadway are exhausted.

People chased each other around until the audience is dizzy.

Miss Fazenda finally loses all but her drawers and Conklin, tiring of his own woolen undie, exposes his fat tummy for many feet before he suddenly appears a la femme in togs with bustle, etc.

Then Miss Todd flashes a gat and reveals that the rush is all about a blue diamond. Her pal joins the melee and the two are calculated a couple of crooks until the brain-storm breaks and they are titled as just hard working reporters out to solve the mystery before the cops.

Waly.

MOLLY AND ME

(20% DIALOG)

Tiffany-Stahl production and release. Belle Bennett starred. Featured, Joe E. Brown; sub-featured, Alberta Vaughn. Story by Lois Leeson. Directed by Albert Ray. Titles and dialog by Frederick and Fanny Hatton. Synchronization and score by Hugo Riesenfeld. Orchestra conducted by Joseph Littau. Sound supervised by Rudolph Flothow. RCA Photophone sounded. Photographed by Frank Zucker and Ernest Miller. Theme song, "In the Land of Make Believe" by L. Wolfe Gilbert and Abel Baer. At the New York, New York, one day, June 15. Running time, 87 minutes.

Molly Wilson.................Belle Bennett
Jim Wilson.................Joseph E. Brown
Peggy McCoy.................Alberta Vaughn
Dan Kingsley.................Charles Byer

A story of the stage. Credited to Lois Leeson. Although Belle Bennett is starred the work of Joe E. Brown is so prominent and worth-while he should have been co-starred with Miss Bennett. It has laugh producing bits and a touch of nature that will be liked.

When Miss Bennett and Brown are talking and singing they carry the picture right along as the married burlesque troupers, Molly and Jim Wilson. Folks who know their "Burlesque" and similar stories including "Excess Baggage," where the act split to let the woman step ahead, comparisons will be made.

And while one gets a kick out of the rough comedy hoke Brown puts over the theme song is going to get a lot of play. Wolfie Gilbert and Abel Baer in "In the Land of Make Believe" have turned out a natural. Both Miss Bennett and Brown sing it and they wham it over. Miss Bennett's voice isn't a world beater but she knows her stage letters and sells it. Brown has a good voice, and he uses showmanship in singing it from a stage box during a performance of the burlesque show.

Granting this talker will entertain even with its limited dialog, one talking bit seems overplayed.

On the road the "Gay Paree" burlesquers troup along; Jim and Molly are principals; their work stands out while offstage they are happy and take what comes their way with a smile. Then Jim is wanted alone to appear with the "Frolics" in New York. He accepts. His new partner (Alberta Vaughn) seems a most affectionate kid. When Molly goes back on the sticks her hubby and the girl seem to hit it up, at least that is the slant Jim gets and he writes to Molly telling her about his desire to be free. Then Jim is set back when he hears Molly is engaged and he tries to get his letter back.

Jim appears at a show when Molly is broken up over Jim's letter. Jim steps into his old hoke work in the box, going into Molly's song, and the finale brings the old troupers together.

The role was made to order for Brown. Miss Bennett as the burlesque queen makes the character stand out.

Photographically superb. RCA Photophone results are in the picture's favor. All the theatre interiors and especially the scenes and bits calling for the songs and dialog corkingly reproduced.

Mark.

PAWNS OF PASSION

(RUSSIAN-FRENCH MADE)

(Silent)

Wide World production and release. Made on Russian border and in Paris. Story and direction by Carmine Gallone; adapted by Norbert Falk and titled by Harry Chandlee. Olga Chekova starred. At Stanley, New York, one day, June 11. Running time, 91 minutes.

Mother.................Olga Chekova
Son.................Sidney Suberly
Artist.................Hans Stever
Model.................Lola Josane
The Commissar.................Harry Beaudine

A 10c picture in a 25c house. Nothing would have been missed had they kept it at home. Title is suggestive enough to draw the morons, but once inside it won't take them long to realize they are in for a ride.

Where the "Pawns of Passion" comes in is a complete blank. A few scenes where Olga Chekova and Lola Josane walk around half nude or where they wear flimsy gowns with a strong light behind them, but aside from those spots there is little sex and less suggestion.

Photography very poor. Action slow with 40 minutes smelling of newsreel stuff. Carmine cannot slap himself on the back for direction or story. Every comma creaks. Titles are of the "came the dawn" type.

As an actress, Chekova, according to this picture, has a marked resemblance to Pola Negri and nothing else.

The story concerns a member of the Russian Imperial Ballet, who loses her little son while fleeing from the revolution torn country to Poland.

The mother wanders over half of Europe looking for her boy and ends up trying suicide via Seine. Rescued by an artist, she goes to his home, arousing the ire of his model, Lola Josane. The story continues with a good shot of an artists' ball and Chekova's finding there the man who attempted to cop her honor.

The title brought practically a 100 per cent male audience with only three women in the half-filled Stanley. After 30 minutes the discordant organ kept them awake.

HOLLYWOOD REVUE

Metro-Goldwyn-Mayer production and release with all-star cast. Directed by Charles Reisner, dances staged by Sammy Lee. Music and lyrics by N. H. Brown, Arthur Freed, Gus Edwards, Joe Goodwin, Martin Broones, Andy Rice, Fred Fisher, John T. Murray, Louis Alter, Jo Trent, Dave Snell, Raymond Klages, Jesse Greer. Skit by Joe Farnham. Score arrangement, Arthur Lange. Dialog by Al Boasberg and Robert Hopkins. Cameramen—John Arnold, I. G. Ries, Maximilian Fabian. Edited by William Gray. Recording engineer, Douglas Shearer. Western Electric sound track system. Production under personal supervision of Harry Rapf. Cast—John Gilbert, Norma Shearer, Joan Crawford, Bessie Love, Lionel Barrymore, Cliff Edwards, Stan Laurel, Oliver Hardy, Anita Page, Nils Asther, Brox Sisters, Natova Co., Marion Davies, William Haines, Buster Keaton, Marie Dressler, Charles King, Polly Moran, Gus Edwards, Karl Dane, G. K. Arthur, Gwen Lee, Rasch Ballet, The Rounders, Biltmore Quartet. Main mixed dancing ensemble 12 boys and 12 girls and about 60 choristers in all. Conrad Nagel and Jack Benny, masters of ceremony. In two acts, eight scenes and 18 numbers. Two Technicolor sequences. At Grauman's Chinese for twice daily $1.50. Run starting June 20. Running time, exclusive of intermission, 113 mins.

With a cast that reads like a benefit how can this one miss for coin? Besides which it's the top novelty film to be turned out to date. Must be looked at the same as any Broadway revue, for it's that to the letter, plus the knowledge that it's going to play for 50 and 75 cents in spots where they've never seen those ballets which open the second half of any Shubert extravaganza. And they've got one here in the same spot, "Tableau of Jewels." A box office pushover and if they turn it loose in the Roxy instead of the Astor the mint will feel the pressure.

Boys are going to be able to pick flaws because the flaws, as a revue, are there. As a picture in Watertown they won't know and won't care—the difference between half a dollar and $6.60. In front of a smart audience the picture will suffer from that bugbear of all revues, comedy, but that smart coterie is going to be very much in the minority—perhaps a reason for sending it into the Roxy or the Capitol and letting the high-hats hear themselves smothered by the glee of the mob at large.

And all the world's fault finding isn't going to take away an opening number which the yokels will like, but which will make the Stem gasp, a sure hit, maybe smash, tune in "Singin' in the Rain" and the staging of this number, that of "Lon Chaney Will Get You," and the Rasch ballet in color at the finale shot across water to get the reflection of the dancers and then double the lights as the illuminated flower ladders descend.

These are the production highlights, the surprises being the use of but one full stage set throughout the first half and the failure of the big screen to put in an appearance.

But that opening number. It even paralyzed many in this first night mob, strictly a picture and New York gathering. Just a formation tap routine by the ensemble in black and white costume with somebody discovering that running the negative through the projector, with gradual developing to reach a full positive, duplicates the stage's radium effect, only on the screen it's even more striking. Number froze the easterners in their seats because of the immediate thought on how is the stage going to compete with such effects and if this were merely a sample of what was coming during the evening the ship has sailed. A terrific start of definite portentions for the future, but the picture never topped it on the effect end, although the staging of "Singin' in the Rain" will overshadow it in the public eye. First shot following the list of credits is the original of the living billboard, now on Wilshire Blvd.; 16 girls sitting for raised letters spelling the title and reciting the usual opening lyric in unison.

"Rain" is a sweet dance melody delivered by Cliff Edwards and his uke under a side-screen tree as the water pours down into a stage-wide pool. Dancing ensemble is on a floor behind the rain and tank working in supposed oilskins. Lighting eventually silhouettes the figures of the girls through the transparent rubber coats. Double pair of stairs against a wall, or eye, holds these silhouettes for the finale. Placed late in the second half the number is a cinch and can't miss.

Ditty devoted to Chaney has Gus Edwards lyrically warning a dozen bedtime girls with as many boys entrancing wearing hideous masks, picking up the girls and the entire ensemble disappearing below on a big trap door, through which clouds of steam ascend. Finish of this was perfect spot for Chaney to have appeared immaculately dressed to take a bow if nothing more, but report is he refused to appear in the picture. He muffed a great bet.

Hideousness of the masks is lessened by having the two dozen choristers go into a snap dance to a hot tune prior to the finish, probably thinking of the picture house children and plenty smart. Incidentally, this item marks the first instance of the camera shooting directly down on the dancers.

Individually no one stands out like Marie Dressler. Stage veteran has got the one real comedy number of the picture in "For I'm the Queen," is back on her old stamping ground and runs away with the femme trio, rounded out by Bessie Love and Polly Moran, in doing a satire on the old-fashioned girl and then as kids. Girls follow Cliff Edwards, Gus Edwards and Charlie King, laying the foundation of a bad number, which only Miss Dressler holds up. Entire male sequence could be cut and certainly doesn't belong next to closing. Would be better to change position with Miss Dressler's "Queen," a pip number on lyrics excellently taken care of by this performer. Male trio particularly unfunny and could be eliminated for use just in the "Strolling Thru the Park" climax with the women.

Trick camera work is confined to Jack Benny taking Bessie Love out of his pocket, not as well done as might be supposed, and Charlie King's sudden diminutiveness after hearing Conrad Nagel sing "You Were Meant for Me," and King's song in "Broadway Melody" to Anita Page. Bit is approached by King telling Nagel this is where the stage contingent has the picture actor licked. Benny and Nagel are on and off all the time in "one" introducing the following full stage scenes, Nagel drifting out at about the half-way mark to let Benny carry on alone. Both are good, Nagel playing straight and Benny administering in his familiar manner, but not too sharply under these film circumstances.

First of the color sequences is John Gilbert and Norma Shearer's "Romeo and Juliet," the modern version, with Lionel Barrymore briefly flashed directing, being excellent. Brief and to the point with Joe Farnham's opening and tag lines of "Listen, boy friend," and "I'm utsnay about ounay," Romeo's exit, surefire, and they'll love it. Both principals look great and play well, Gilbert appearing a bit nervous on the straight interpretation, but hopping to the slang phrasing and slipping through an inside crack about "Irving." Picture's finale, "Orange Blossom Time," familiar in layout, plus an aroma of oranges drifting the theatre, with this first night audience almost in an uproar trying to figure the girl to whom Charlie King sings. Two scenes, and no waits, the pool being again utilized to enhance the 18 Rasch girls in green ballet skirts and white stockings. Corking effect with camera angles an emphatic aid to the group. Girls on the lighted ladders finish off and everybody on in yellow oil skins singing "Rain" for the extreme finale. Exit march consists of tunes from the picture through which can be heard the taps of choristers. Neat showmanship.

Errors appear to be the similarity between the Bessie Love and Marion Davies specialties. Both are boy numbers, finishing with the lads dragging the girls off stage exhausted. And the second half slows up because of the jewel tableau, theme for which is sung by the regulation tenor, James Burroughs, off screen, and an adagio quartet. Each of these latter numbers has a comedy angle, Buster Keaton doing a burlesque Salome as a pearl dancer descends back to the sea, and Benny gagging a story around the adagio antics. What also hurts is that these related numbers are each in their own half. Camera effect for underwater atmosphere very hard on the eyes while Keaton is on.

Miss Love does especially well with her assignment, 12 boys tossing her around on their locked arms. She looks great all the way. Miss Davies does "Tommy Atkins" with her high point a hard shoe dance on a big drum. Despite the production build-up of 12 mammoth singing guardsmen, topped by those high fur hats, Miss Davies doesn't appear at ease. Might have been better to let her do some of her imitations. Taps are very ordinary, and if it weren't Miss Davies, this nine-minute number wouldn't be in.

But that's the answer to a lot of things in this one. Including Joan Crawford, who has been rightly spotted No. 2. She sings "Gotta Feelin' for You" assisted by a male quartet, but doesn't do much with it. Melody isn't bad either. Another tune which seems to have a chance is "Your Mother and Mine," rendered by Charlie King, who has developed a tendency to over-croon. "Low Down Rhythm" is an insert on that opening number warbled by June Purcell, who is as vocally warm as sightly. Each of these songs has a chance to catch on, with "Rain" always the leader.

Comedy sidelights include William Haines tearing Benny's clothes during the "one big happy family" angle and Nils Asther doing a late straight for a gag by this m. c. Two guys roll a carpet on stage—and it's Dane and Arthur. Also during an introduction the curtains suddenly part and there are Laurel and Hardy getting ready to do sleight-of-hand. A load of low hoke here, smashing of eggs, with Hardy taking the face fall into an oversized cake and then tossing it off stage to catch Benny, the latter announcing the next act while covered with frosting. Not $6.60, but how about Sioux City?

It's a revue from gong to gong with the audience proscenium arch conscious all the way regardless of whether they see the border or not. No semblance of story, and considering cast nobody is going to care. It's a novelty, good, and a great idea as a once yearly production for any of the big lots. The public can walk in on this one at any time and not have to pick up the script, and you can bet they won't walk out. Camera doesn't go near the chorus to pick up appearance, only moving up on the jewel sequence for the costume flash. Being in black and white, it's not particularly impressive.

Harry Rapf gets credit for having put it over, and as a first effort in the strictly film revue direction it's a pip. Sammy Lee's numbers are strong, despite using Seymour Felix's "Whoopee" hat routine, aided by effects no stage director has ever had before. And the score is potent. Cast is undeniably led on ability by the musical comedy stage, contingent, the eastern actor's strong point, but the film players always have that national box office draw to offset everything else.

"Singing in the Rain" was originally used in a local Music Box theatre revue last winter and passed by unnoticed, how, nobody seems to know. At no time in the entire film is the accompanying orchestra on view. With some trimming which has already been attended to and rearrangement in running order the picture should be in excellent shape.

Results figure to justify the grief packed into this undertaking, and as a pioneer it's bound to make everybody do some bedtime mental calisthenics, plus another portion of that at breakfast. If the theatre booths give it an even break, nothing can stop it, and if Howard Dietz and Pete Smith will take a tip—make diplomatic requests that the dailies' dramatic men be assigned to review this picture in all spots.

Sid.

THE VEILED WOMAN

(FRENCH MADE)

(Silent)

Fox production and release. Lia Tora and Paul Vincenti featured. Ernest Flynt, director. Musical score by S. L. Rothafel (Roxy) synchronized by Western Electric system. At New York, New York, one day, June 22. Running time 60 minutes.

Biographical story of a woman's life in Paris, screened almost entirely in flash-back sequences. Lia Tora, in the title role, tells her story to a young girl in a Montmartre dive. The veiled lady steps in to save her from Paris' most notorious rake.

Couple of suggestive episodes makes the film one not suitable for viewing by the kids, but for neighborhood houses with adult patronage, rates unreeling. Fair enough feature for the grinds, where they like it spicy.

Story concerns four men in the life of Nanon (Miss Tora) the first, the seducer she spots pulling the old line on the innocent kid. Second is Pierre (Vicenti) owner of a gambling joint, who gives her a job as a roulette wheel shill and means right by her. Third guy is an Englishman on the make, bumped off by the girl when he attempts to attack her.

Nanon finally marries and blows Paris for the suburbs. On one of his trips to the city her husband learns about her past life from the wagging tongue of the first man and airs her.

On her way out of the joint with the young girl she has rescued, Nanon discovers the taxi driver is Pierre, former gambling casino owner, who sacrificed everything to cover up the shooting she committed.

DRAG

(ALL DIALOG)

First National production and release. Starring Richard Barthelmess. Directed by Frank Lloyd. Adaptation and dialog by Bradley King from a novel by William Dudley Pelley. Cameraman, Ernest Haller. Film editor, Edward Schroeder. Art director, John J. Hughes. Theme song by Al Bryan and George W. Meyer. W. E. (Vitaphone) sounded. At Warners, New York, opening June 20, twice daily, $2 top. Running time, 118 mins.

David Carroll........Richard Barthelmess
Pa Parker..................Lucien Littlefield
Ma Parker.................Katherine Parker
Allie Parker..........................Alice Day
Charlie Parker.....................Tom Dugan
Clara Parker...............Margaret Fielding
Dot.......................................Lila Lee

Another wow Richard Barthelmess picture following on the heels of "Weary River," and making more secure than ever the screen position of this long-reigning young star. "Drag" is human, real, persistently delightful. It possesses that seldom-encountered, intangible thing, an intelligent approach. As an example of what can be done with dialog, it's pursuasive ammunition against skeptics.

It's a feather for Frank Lloyd's bonnet. He has done a sweet job in holding characterizations rigidly within the precincts of plausibility, in punching scene after scene with just the proper twist or touch, and in keeping his narrative rolling on ball bearings.

There's some plumage, too, coming to Bradley King for a thoroughly bright, nicely sensitized adaptation and dialog. This job goes beyond the ordinary scenarist's task. It ranks as dramaturgy of exceptional technical competance.

Basically it's the old fable about the sponging family. From thence comes the title, the most unattractive item of the production. Titles don't mean much either way, but "Drag" seems particularly far-fetched, uninspired and drab. There is, too, for the bigger cities, the double entendre implication, "Drag" being a slang term for orgies among the abnormals.

Story has Barthelmess again as a song writer as in "Weary River," but with unexpected good sense somebody out in Hollywood has realized the danger from this direction, with the result that this angle hardly is mentioned. The theme song, languid tune of slight appeal, is refrained but twice, and briefly in both cases.

An especially natural scene is where Barthelmess suddenly and without the slightest premeditation is jolted into an engagement with a girl he does not love and whom he marries in the dazed hopefulness he is somehow doing a wise thing. The girl (Alice Day) is a chip off the old block and the old block is about as offensive, lazy, no-account and thick-hided a family as ever was etched in fiction.

Miss Day performs with exasperating perfection the wishey-washey young dumb dora. She will annoy anyone who is capable of following a film story with real absorption.

Particularly fine, because not overdone, are the family members played by Lucien Littlefield, Tom Dugan and Katherine Ward. It's the sort of domestic brigandage that arouses spontaneous indignation.

Lila Lee will be on the distinctly available list after "Drag" gets around. This still youthful actress after 12 years in films is again on the upgrade, with "Drag" by all means her best performance and biggest opportunity in years. She handles lines well and looks fine. In the intelligent order prevailing in this picture she is permitted to take the hero away from his legally wedded wife. Dialog is working more wonders than may be immediately discernible.

Most of the action of "Drag" occurs in Paris, Vermont, where the hero is attempting to build up the local newspaper. Later it switches to New York, theatrical offices and such backgrounds. Sound recording is excellent throughout.

A gem for the show mob is the unprogramed actress who plays Miss Blah, the unreceptive reception clerk of the Broadway producer's office. Dozens of her sisters daily inspire maniacal impulses in job-seeking Thespians.

With so many fine points "Drag" is sure to be a heavy dough picture. It's packed with entertainment and fan appeal and is value received, even at $2. When it hits the general releases it will be solid.

On the way out opening night a clever satirical replica of a tabloid newspaper was distributed. *Land.*

THUNDERBOLT

(ALL DIALOG)

Paramount production and release. W. E. recording (on film). George Bancroft starred; Fay Wray and Richard Arlen featured. Josef von Sternberg, director. Story by Charles and Jules Furthman. Herman Mankiewicz, dialog. Open grind run at Rivoli, New York, June 20. Running time, 91 minutes.

"Thunderbolt" Jim Lang..George Bancroft
Ritzy.....................................Fay Wray
Bob Morgan......................Richard Arlen
Warden............................Tully Marshall
Mrs. Morgan..................Eugenie Besserer
"Snapper" O'Shea..........James Spottswood
"Bad Al" Frieberg....................Fred Kohler
Prison Chaplain....................Robert Elliott
District Attorney McKay....E. H. Calvert
Mr. Corwin........................George Irving
Kentucky Sampson..................Mike Donlin
Negro Convict...............S. S. R. S. Stewart
Police Inspector..........William L. Thorne
Dog...King Tut

Another gangster picture that looks like most of the others until about the half-way mark, when the action is transplanted to the death cell of a penitentiary. The narrative and characters remain there until the finish. And some finish; one they won't forget. The door of the execution chamber closes on the broad back of Thunderbolt (George Bancroft), who had laughed his way across the threshold, laughing in the usual Bancroft manner. A good picture all the way and great from the halfway on. Can't miss for the money between the picture and Bancroft.

Star is in a role he has played before, that of a master gunman, police baiter and underworld chieftain. He registered his usual believable and powerful performance.

First half of "Thunderbolt" is unimportant. Second part, in the pen, is the picture. First half draws the characters, plants the motive and sends the tale to jail, taking plenty of time doing it.

Thunderbolt, as Jim Lang was nationally known, landed in the death cell after evading the cops for months, or maybe years. Just before nabbed Thunderbolt learned that his sweetie, Ritzy, had fallen for a straight kid, Bob Morgan, and was attempting to give him (Thunderbolt) the scram. Thunderbolt was on his way to bump off the boy when arrested.

Thunderbolt's cronies later have the Morgan kid framed on a murder charge, pulling a phoney bank robbery and enticing him to the scene to pin it on him. Bob lands in a cell opposite Thunderbolt's.

The death house action is great and looks authentic. The pitiful attempts by the inmates at being cheerful, ragging of each other, their actions under the terrific strain and carryings-on look and sound good enough to be quite true.

The way a new arrival is introduced around, without leaving his own cell and without seeing the fellow prisoners he is talking to, is unique.

When Thunderbolt arrives, the first thing he is asked is whether he can sing tenor. It is explained the boys had a good quartet, "but they took the tenor away." It was his turn, of course. Thunderbolt answers, "I kill tenors." That's the kind of a guy he was.

Bancroft's crook goes to his doom as a relentless gangster should. He first confesses he had the Morgan boy framed, just as the boy and Ritzie were being married, each on the other side of the bars, and right across from Bancroft's cell. This happens four hours before the boy is to go.

Thunderbolt has his own reason and the reason is explained by one of the gang in a flashback, with this member seemingly knowing his Thunderbolt. Latter plans his own revenge on the boy who stole his woman by getting him when saying goodbye, just as he is walking to his own death. It never happens, because Thunderbolt softens with his mitt an inch from Bob's neck.

There are directorial touches every few moments. Von Sternberg has gone symbolic with a vengeance. Clarity is a rarity in picture symbolism.

Canine member of the cast, billed as King Tut, gets in on much of the sentiment. The dog is responsible for Thunderbolt's capture. He takes a fancy to the hardboiled gunman on the street and follows him to Morgan's house. Thunderbolt is trying to get the dog outside and out of his way for the third time when the cops nab him. But Thunderbolt makes the dog his own then and there. "He cost me plenty," he says.

Richard Arlen is Bob Morgan, and Fay Wray, Ritzy, the same team from "The Four Feathers." Both impress, Miss Wray with more of a chance in "Thunderbolt" than in the other film. Arlen is rapidly progressing as a screen juvenile, getting better film by film, and in this one showing he can talk.

Tully Marshall, as the neurotic warden; Eugenie Besserer, Bob's mother; James Spottswood, a Thunderbolt lieutenant, and Ferd Kohler in a death house bit, all land. Robert Elliott, usually a dick, is the prison chaplain here. Latter is continually consoling Thunderbolt but Thunderbolt won't go for religion. But as he is walking to the execution chamber Thunderbolt changes his mind. "Come on, chaplain," he cracks, "I'll give you a break, too." Nifty.

No complaints in the casting. A lot or a little, all is done well. While Herman Mankiewicz's dialog fits, always scores and sometimes whams.

Running 91 minutes at the Rivoli and too long. As much cutting as may be found necessary for the average run should be done before the death house sequence. All of the latter is much too good to drop.

Black and tan cafe scene and the jail quartet and band contribute the music.

Bige.

BROADWAY BABIES

(ALL DIALOG)

First National production and release, starring Alice White. Directed by Mervyn Leroy from Jay Gelzer's story, adapted by Monte Katterjohn. Dialog by Mr. Katterjohn and Humphrey Pearson. Sol Polito cameraman. Musical Score by Leo Forbstein. Western Electric sounded (Vitaphone). Starting at Central June 21, twice daily; $2 top. Running time, 89 minutes.

Delight Foster	Alice White
Billy Buvanny	Charles Delaney
Perc Gessant	Fred Kohler
Navaree King	Sally Ellers
Florine Chanier	Marion Byron
Scotty	Tom Dugan
Durgan	Rodil Rosing
August Brand	Louis Natheaux
Nick the Greek	Maurice Black
Blossom Royale	Jocelyn Lee

While hardly heavy enough to weather Broadway's $2 top, "Broadway Babies" is sufficiently different in several situations of backstage story material to attract in the big key houses. It is a picture that insures First National a good profit margin and the type of stuff warranting option renewals for Alice White's services.

Dressing rooms, night clubs, old fashioned theatrical boarding house, card shark halls and quite a bit of prancing before the lights furnish the interior sets, where 90 percent of the action takes place.

With considerable footage devoted to the blonde Alice and her two chums, handled well with the little they had to do by Sally Eilers and Marion Byron, the production is censor proof. It does not contain a suggestive gesture. Even the camera lense chops off portions of anatomies that predecessors and newsreels have featured with zest.

But Miss White as the cautious chorine and Fred Kohler, as Perc Gessant, the Detroit rum runner who never drinks and lets the audience in from the start that he is wise to the tricks of New York professionals, sustain the interest, nevertheless.

Miss White sings the theme song a couple of times in a voice startlingly good for a non-pro and the synchronization is perfect. Her dancing and acting are typical of the role she plays, and as a whole, one of the best performances the little ex-film cutter has rendered.

Charles Delaney works the poor stage producer's start into a big time handler as convincingly as he is allowed: The stuttering Dom Dugan aids the Delaney tempo with occasional well-timed comedy.

Before Buvanny gets into the money and wins the star he helped make, the card boys are allowed to gape into a rehearsal hall across the street and inspire their ticket from Detroit to protract his dough-dropping.

Gessant finds Delight easy make on dinners because of her boy friend's insincere osculation with a fired chorine, Jocelyn Lee. It goes on that way until the bridal night, when Perc reveals to the smarties he can take them and get away with it, backed by his beer city gang.

On the way to the ceremony Perc gets the necessary bullet in the lungs so that the big turn-over to the boy friend with the winnings as a present in conventionally but satisfactory scene.

Waly.

PARIS GIRLS

(FRENCH MADE)

(Silent)

Paris, June 7.

Dramatic comedy executed by Henri Roussell for Cineromans. Suitable for exportation without fear of being branded a turnip. It is of the spectacular category, slightly overdone, but not marring the **successful effect of this good French picture.**

In "Paris Girls" is a rapid contrast of fashions of pre-war days with the present mode.

Marguerite quits her family to try her luck in America before the war. She joins a troupe of dancers and becomes "Captain" Peggy.

Returning home after the war she marries a cousin, Robert. A former companion in the troupe, jealous of Marguerite's happiness, tries to wreck the home.

On board their yacht Marguerite saves her mother-in-law's honor by pretending to be implicated in an amorous intrigue with an American youth, and leaves her husband, resuming her role of captain of "The Paris Girls." Robert is ultimately convinced of his wife's innocence when his mother confesses her responsibility and begs for pardon. The matrimonial yoke is resumed on a firmer basis after a duel between two girls.

Suzy Vernon and Esther Kiss are the leads of a good cast. Also Fernand Fabre, Cyrille de Ramsay and Danielle Parola. Technical side is fair, with pretty scenes, but photo work not always up to the high-water mark.

Light.

STAIRS OF SAND

(SILENT)

Paramount production and release. Directed by Otto Brower. Story by Zane Grey, adapted by Agnes Brand Leahy, J. Walter Ruben and Sam Mintz. Wallace Beery, Jean Arthur, Chester Conklin featured. In cast: Phillips R. Holmes, Fred Kohler, Guy Oliver, Lillian Worth, Frank Rice. At New York, New York, one day, June 21, as half of double bill. Running time, 45 minutes.

Mild western thriller that might get by in the remote grinds on a double bill mainly on the strength **of the featured players.**

Story concerns folks of the 1880 period in the west. Title means nothing.

Wallace Beery is the bad man with a sympathetic heart who loves Jean Arthur, but steps aside when he finds she is in love with a younger man.

Previously he has warned the youth to keep away from the girl, he having introduced them. When the bad man is wounded after a series of robberies and the youth is ready to sacrifice himself, the kind-hearted tough guy is convinced of his loyalty and scrams.

This one is strictly for the Zane Grey fans.

THE WHEEL OF LIFE

(ALL DIALOG)

Paramount production and release. Starring Richard Dix. Esther Ralston and O. P. Heggie featured. Directed by Victor Schertzinger. Story by James Bernard Fagan. Adaptation by John Farrow and dialog by Julian Johnson. Cameraman, Edward Cronjager. At Paramount, New York, week June 22. Running time, 55 mins.

Capt. Yeullet	Richard Dix
Ruth Dangan	Esther Ralston
Col. Dangan	O. P. Heggie
Faraker	Arthur Hoyt
Mrs. Faraker	Myrtle Steadman
Major	Larry Steers
Buddhist priest	Nigel de Brulier
Boy officer	Regis Toomey

Way below Paramount standards. Dull enough for sleeping, stupid enough for even the good-natured to complain, "Wheel of Life" has only the name of its star to recommend it. It's doubtful if any star, however popular, could carry such a burden. Particularly strong surrounding bill must be provided for this one.

All the faults of dialog production wedded to a story written out of the sappiest page of film history, **the eternal triangle of respectability. A little Theosophy and phoney preaching about transmigration of souls, reincarnation, Nirvana and such highly esotoric and wholly undramatic ideas are tossed in by way of theme.**

They'll be asking one another what it's all about in the sticks. It will confuse the yaps and bore the ever-so-faintly critical.

Richard Dix is an officer in the British Army in India. Discovers the girl he met in England on leave is the young wife of his beloved colonel. He changes his regiment.

A year passes. He is called upon to rescue a party of white people marooned in a Buddhist monastery, menaced by hostile hillmen. The girl is there.

For four minutes they think they are doomed. They prattle of love. An inscrutable priest gives an illustrated lecture with charts on Theosophy.

Reinforcements and the Colonel arrive. He speaks of his consuming passion for the young wife. For that he is killed in the last 50 feet by a stray bullet.

About as tedious 55 minutes as ever packed in one can.

Land.

TWO WEEKS OFF

(25% DIALOGUE)

First National production and release. Featuring Jack Mulhall and Dorothy Mackaill. Directed by William Beaudine. Dialog by Richard Weil and orchestration by Louis Silvers on Western Electric (Vitaphone) system. At Strand, New York, week June 22. Running time, 88 minutes.

Kitty Weaver	Dorothy Mackaill
Dave Pickett	Jack Mulhall
Agnes	Gertrude Astor
Pa Weaver	Jimmie Finlayson
Harry	Jed Prouty
Sid Winters	Eddie Gribbon
Maizie Loomis	Dixie Gay
Tessie McCann	Gertrude Messinger

Director Beaudine went on a shooting rampage in this one. As the result, he got by the cutting room one of the most tiresome and aimless messes of repetitious drivel run in the Strand in quite awhile.

Half of the running time could be cut and still the thing would drag since, while the story idea is a good one, the plot has been so carved as to possess little or no motivation. Houses that go for "Two Weeks Off" for more than the flimsiest kind of a program feature without good support around it may suffer.

The fragile yarn is of a stenog vacationing and finding that her film star is the home town plumber. That is told in subtitling and later repeated in dialog. Titles go in heavy for puns, some pulling laughs. Most of the dialog is the kind that makes the public yearn for the old dumb era.

The climax in the picture's boredom comes when enough footage to make a short is wasted for the silent recitation of the "Shooting of Dan McGrew." This is done with much hair wrestling by Jack Mulhall as Dave Pickett, the plumber, posing as a film actor at a beach resort. Miss Mackaill as Kitty Weaver, the gum-chewing vacationist, adds to the restlessness of the audience by having her piano synchronized in accompaniment with the recitation.

The thing is brought to the screen in the clumsiest fashion. Either the script writer or the director is responsible.

A gag that is funny until overworked is the kid plumber's assistant following the well-tailored Mulhall around the beach with kit. The illogical angle of such a situation, even in the films, is apparent to an audience by its reaction.

Eddie Gribbon as a life-saver provides some of the best laughs with his buckshot rolling on the dance floor while the imposter is performing. Gribbon gets socked in the eye so many times by the plumber that his showing toward the end is nearly crabbed.

The end, incidentally, seems set a half dozen times in the production. But each time the drag asserts itself and the picture is stretched into another sequence. Finally the audience has to listen to the tale of all that has previously happened on the screen when Kitty's aggressive girl friend, Agnes, played by Gertrude Messinger, breaks into talk after the vacation. Then the plumber hoves to and there is one of the longest explanations yet recorded by the talkers.

Waly.

THE JADE CASKET

(FRENCH MADE)

(Silent)

First American showing of a satirical story from "Arabian Nights." Produced by Gaumont, France. Adapted and directed by Leon Poirrer. Story by Pierre Victor. M. Roger Carl, Mille Myge and M. Mandaille in case. Running time, 65 minutes. At Fifth Avenue Playhouse week June 22.

A wholly bizarre offering, appealing to the sensual. Will catch the moronic. The director knows his harems. Photography remarkable in several scenes, particularly the closeups. Characters nicely cast. Story coherent. Altogether, an oddity deserving of praise in its exactitude and adherence to "Arabian Nights" era, but censurable in its rapacious entirety. Captions are masterpieces of literature running to adages and hand-drawn pantomimic art.

Story is of a sage, who drops all work, having fallen for a beauty in **the harem of his neighbor. Spends all his time at a peephole watching the girls bathe and flit about a hot garden. Hunchback servant with parrot on his headdress warns him in classic language to disdain love, reminding him of the thorns. Sage ignores preaching.**

One night the girl of his dreams goes into garden. He breaks open the peephole and as she is about to kiss him her master lashes her with a whip. Then he goes for the Mussulman next door, who pretends he is asleep, his life thus being spared.

Sage broods. A bandit seeks shelter in his menage. Saves the criminal from soldiers. Then he tells bandit a fable. This story is a hint he wants the neighbor knocked off. Bandit crawls into garden and releases hilt of owner's sword, which hangs over a hammock in which he is sleeping with 40 women reclining near. His enemy dead, the sage marries the girl.

Soldiers seek bandit. Judiciary issues warrant that whomsoever is harboring him shall be executed. Bandit returns to sage for shelter. Sage denies him, but bandit threatens. So sage hides him. Bandit then surrounds himself with luxury and takes all the sage's women, wine and wife.

Sage pretends he is dying and shows him a casket with two different powders, one an elixir of life and the other death. Says he won't live long and bequeathes his treasures to wife and bandit. They conspire to kill sage. He turns the tables on them by the poison, which kills the bandit. Sends wife to hard labor and winds up contented to prove you can't win.

VENUS

(FRENCH-MADE)

(Silent)

Paris, June 8.

United Artists released the new Louis Mercanton production "Venus" on this side. Story is by Jean Vignaud. Picture on an unlimited run at Salle Marevaux and can be listed as one of the best French film successes of the season.

Action is laid in Marseilles and Oran, Algerie, with some excellent photography. Scenario and location will interest the fans in any country, but perhaps the big attraction for this reel is the advent of Constance Talmadge in the French made quota. In "Venus" she has another role cut to measure.

The cast is a great asset, Jean Murat, Maxudian, Maurice Schutz, Andre Roanne and Mercanton's little son being among the trumps.

Characters are traced with a sure hand, side-stepping slightly from their prototypes.

Princess Doriani (Miss Talmadge) is president of a steamship corporation. While cruising with friends on her yacht, "Venus," she impersonates the said goddess during an evening swim. Her intended innocent fun is seen by passengers of a passing ship. They talk scandal.

Later Captain Franqueville (Murat), of the Doriani Line, inadvertently knocks a scandal monger overboard. The Princess, unaware of the reason of the accident, signs his revocation.

Thus sacked, the captain earns his living in Oran until the princess, acquainted with the real facts, goes to find him. She takes another name. The couple fall in love.

But Franqueville discovers her identity when he sees her on board her own yacht and joins a sanitary expedition visiting the desert.

Meanwhile a blackmailer (Maxudian) humiliates the princess for a previous snub by threatening to denounce Franqueville if she does not appear as Venus at a nautical gala. She consents but the blackmailer, having gained his end, relieves her of the promise, and she hastens to find the young captain a second time. She is shot by Arabs on the way, but reaches her lover.

Thrilling, sentimental drama, constituting a good feature picture.

Light.

MORGANE

(FRENCH-MADE)

(SILENT)

Franco Films production, brought to this country by the maker and exhibited in house leased for exploitation of Franco product. Directed by Leonce Perret, former director for American companies. Ivan Petrovitch starred. Adaptation of novel, "La Siren," by Charles Le Goffic. Cameraman, C. Vinkniglia. English titles by Jacques Rollens. Running time, 65 minutes. At Craig, New York, week June 22. Scale, 75c. top.

George de Kerduel.........Ivan Petrovitch
Princess de Bangor........Clara de Lorez
Annette............................Josyane
Mme. Lefoulon..............Rachel Devirys
Pierre Lefoulon..................P. Damores

Operating Franco Films' campaign to introduce French product to American picturegoers, the French producer gets off on the wrong foot. Picture is very little improvement on the average foreign productions already shown to the sure-seat audiences. It is a little worse in story material, although Perret's knowledge of American studio acting technique is a vast improvement upon usual Continental methods.

Physical production excellent; interiors beautiful and some of the outdoor locations, particularly marine scenes on the coast of Brittany, smashing bits of photography.

Story is hopeless. It wouldn't qualify in America as second class magazine fiction, say of the Argosy grade. As a dramatic narrative, absurd. Starts out as a society drama, then switches to a fishing village and turns fantastic.

Result is a jumble. It takes 35 minutes to plant the situation that a Paris banker has gone broke, and arrangements for the marriage of his daughter to a rich young man have been declared off. Father drops dead and mother and daughter retire to their country place in Brittany. It is here the story starts and what has gone before is pure waste—35 minutes of footage thrown away.

Recital begins all over again. Lover of the heroine, ditched for the banker's son, returns, and the pair agree to wed. Girl is lost in a storm at sea while out with village fisherman, but is rescued by a mysterious woman who occupies an amazing castle on a nearby island. She lives in the traditional style of a Princess and on the screen is a composite of Hans Anderson, Grimm brothers and Anthony Hope, plus a trace of Ziegfeld and maybe a touch of Elinor Glyn. Anyhow, an amazing person.

To anybody but a 12-year-old school girl, the whole business is a burlesque parading as thrilling romantic drama. Titling is terrible, stilted and provoking laughs where it seeks to be most serious.

Program carries half a dozen quotations from French trade paper reviews, describing the picture in hysterical superlatives. Perhaps over there but it sounds like kidding or advertising. If not, situation of producing pictures for French audiences who liked this one and selling them in America is out of the question.

Rush.

Behind That Curtain

(ALL DIALOG)

Fox production and release. Directed by Irving Cummings from Earl Derr Biggers' novel. Dialog on Western Electric (Movietone) system. At Roxy, week June 29. Running time, 91 minutes.

John Beetham.................Warner Baxter
Eve Mannering....................Lois Moran
Sir Frederic Bruce..........Gilbert Emery
Sir George Mannering.........Claude King
Eric Durand....................Philip Strange
Soudanese Servant............Boris Karloff
Habib Hanna..................Jamiel Hassen
Scotland Yard Inspector..Peter Gawthorne
Alf Potnick.......................John Rogers
Hilary Galt................Montague Shaw
Nunah..................Mercedes De Valasco
Charlie Chan.......................E. L. Park

Why William Fox isn't running "Behind That Curtain" at a $2 top is an enigma. It is big box office from the first iris to the last camera flower. It is on a par with the best Fox has put on Broadway and far superior in meaty earning qualities to many in his recent average.

Although the lines technically subject themselves in a few sequences to adverse criticism, the tendency to be bromidic in these will be overlooked by an audience above even average intelligence. Acutely logical direction, abetted by the sympathetic interpretation of an almost perfect cast, is the reason.

Outstanding are Gilbert Emery's manner and voice as Sir Frederic Bruce, chief of Scotland Yard. A lesser personality would have changed the shading in the entire production. Vested in it are practically all of the story's climactic points. Emery lends each a touch classical in its reserved forcefulness.

While the story deals essentially with the unraveling of a London murder by Sir Frederic, events are not all shunted to one side, as in the customary treatment. The time is always the present. This eliminates flash-backs, does away with confusing reaction and, although the audience is always intimate with the situation before the great detective, there is just enough mystery-lowdown to let the events work up 100 per cent. suspense on their own merit.

A wide locale, including London, India, the desert and San Francisco contribute largely to the color and story divertissement. Some shots of the sandy hills, long and close-up, of winding camel trains and camps, are records of exquisite photography.

Lois Moran shows more promise as a young actress of emotional ability in "Behind That Curtain" than in any picture in which she has yet appeared. Occasionally her voice gets above the scale during a dramatic moment and her introductions are slightly choppy, but her general performance is one of superb sincerity.

Opposite Miss Moran is Warner Baxter as John Beetham, explorer and lecturer. These honors are shared through the greater footage by Philip Strange, playing the heavy. Both men perform consistently well.

The production hasn't a conspicuously dull moment except in one short sequence in which E. L. Park as Charlie Chan, Bruce's Chinese lieutenant, is forced to recite several Sunday comic strip lines.

The main characters are introduced within the first 15 minutes, fast work, because the action is so well knit the average fan will believe it a 45 instead of a 91-minute show.

Claude King, as Sir George Mannering, is allowed only a bit. As Eve's uncle he has ordered an investigation into the habits of Durand, playing for the girl, which results in the murder of the investigator, Hilary Galt, another bit by Montague Shaw. The quick network of complications is augmented by the arrival of Beetham after an argument with Shaw. Then Sir Bruce, with odd Chinese slippers found on the feet of the corpse and owned by Beetham, arrives and the question is recorded.

Eve's elopment with Durand to India and row with her husband over a native woman are followed by the arrival of Beetham and a letter from a night watchman, who says Durand is behind in hush money.

Next, the detective shows up and a plane is chartered to the camel train in the desert conducting Beetham and Mrs. Durant, with her discovery still a secret. Here the romance peak is reached.

The hunt concludes in Frisco with all of the zest of a high class meller. The detective gets all parties into the hall where Beetham is lecturing; Durand does some shooting and is killed by the Chinese lieut.

Then the detective tosses the slipper back to Beetham and Eve pulling together the curtain.

Waly.

FASHIONS IN LOVE

(ALL DIALOG)

Paramount production and release. Starring Adolphe Menjou. Dialog on Western Electric system. Directed by Victor Schertzinger from screen play by L. Long. In cast: Fay Compton, John Miljan, Robert Wayne, Joan Standing, Russell Powell. At Paramount, New York, week June 29. Running time, 70 minutes.

Adolphe Menjou's first talker proves the star has a diction tailored to his silent screen personality. Paramount gives him a couple of talents, one playing a piano and the other singing a theme song. His film is a light, familiar, domestic farce, but entertaining. Sophisticated audiences will find many laughs in the Menjou touches. The actor uses the same treatment in speaking his lines.

As the temperamental musician, the idol of women who gets away with anything but depends upon his wife for everything, Menjou leads the characteristically bored existence for a few reels until he meets another blonde wife.

A little trip to his mountain cabin is planned and executed. While both give the same reason to their affiliations, a jealous secretary, it is revealed in the last reel, sends the word to husband No. 1 who promptly slips it to wife No. 1.

Adolphe's trip up a mountain side in a heavy coat and cracks about his athletic playfriend furnishes one of the amusing sequences. In the cabin while the dame is changing in a room, Menjou is calmly stowing away beer. When she appears properly gowned for his embrace, Schertzinger has the star singing the theme song and later raging over a discordant note in the instrument.

Just as the business is about to start, the better halves appear. Instead of a blow-up the plot takes a neat twist. Arrivals announce they are in love and awaiting court decrees when, they propose, the new ceremonies take place at the same time.

Unraveling himself from the toils of the blonde, who insists upon reporting to his home, the climax is freshened by the maid's disclosure. Then the patent things happen and old vows are renewed.

Waly.

THE HEADWAITER

(GERMAN MADE)

(Silent)

Aafa (German) production. No U. S. release credited. Directed by Ludwig Volger. In cast: Ralph A. Roberts, Jack Trevor, Xenia Desni, Hans Brauswetter. At Fifth Ave. Playhouse, New York, week June 29, half double bill. Running time, 67 minutes.

Excepting for the beauty of natural German scenery and old castles, as well as the performance by Ralph A. Roberts in the title role, "The Headwaiter" might pass for the initial production of a phoney American-Italian picture school. It hasn't a chance in the American market. Even in a Fifth Ave. arty they laugh at it.

Roberts is a mighty fine actor. With everyone against him, technically speaking; with subtitles as blunt and stupid as the general action in the film, this Roberts forces a sympathetic reaction.

It's supposed to be a comedy. Theme has an old man suddenly discovering he has a grown daughter, after posing for a number of years during his vacations as a baron at a little hostelry.

A gawky high school boy furnishes the romance. The girl falls for him, on the street, and they are in arms in the next flash. The shears are probably responsible for that one, but no amount of editorial leniency would make the semblance of an actor out of this Hans Brauswetter. To make things worse the clumsy Hans is a musician.

The early century script style is adhered to. Idea was a good one, as the story incentive for a lot of foreign product quite often is. But the Anderson fairy angle, of the roue getting the headwaiter drunk and then turning over his castle to get the chance to propose to daughter, rings worse than some of the church bells recorded in the talkers. *Waly.*

Schmeling-Uzcudun Fight

(SOUND)

Presented by the Sport Film Exchange (Henry Sonnenshein). Recorded in sound by remote control. Running time, 28 minutes. Distributed by Tiffany-Stahl. Cameo, New York, June 28.

This is the first fight picture recorded with sound. It is a success, for the babble of the fight crowd supplies the true atmosphere of a major boxing contest, something pictures of the kind have not had heretofore. It's just too bad the a. k. law that prohibits interstate transportation of fight films limits this showing to New York state. Hardly enough interest in a non-championship contest such as this was to take chances bootlegging the film outside.

But Europe will doubtless eagerly wait for the sound picture, with Max Schmeling, Germany's contender for the world's heavyweight championship, battling the Spaniard Paulino Uzcudun, even if the remarks at ringside are in English.

The referee can be plainly heard ordering the men to break. Rarely did he have to step in between and separate them—evidence that foreign fighters obey the referee without stalling. The crowd is often heard roaring for the men to come on and battle.

Paulino fights in a crouch, and it is no easy task for an opponent to force him to stand up and box. Frequently the voice of a close-by fight bug yells: "Come on, Max, straighten him up."

The fight was staged in the Yankee Stadium, New York, a baseball park. Many of the spectators were in the stands and remote from the ring itself. They saw the motions and the direction of the blows but could not be sure if they landed. Schmeling protected his jaw with his right hand fending off many a sock. The roar of the crowd can be heard when some of Paulino's blows were deflected by the much cleverer Schmeling, but those far away yelled in excitement, not knowing if they landed or not.

The fight film is no better than the contest itself. Photographically it is ordinary because the faces of the men are hardly if ever clearly seen. Taking fight pictures is still a problem, in that the lights required for clear camera vision would blind the spectators. The sound feature, however, makes this film extraordinary.

In taking the picture, the sound portion of which is recorded on the film itself—Photophone—it is shown that sports events may be made more graphic than the tabloids ever can make them. The Schmeling-Uzcudun film was accomplished with sound by remote control. The noise of the recording device was noticeable now and then but seemed to be swallowed by the constant comment of the crowd. That defect will doubtless be rectified.

The cutting of the picture was intelligently done. Right off the titles stated that only the most interesting portions of the fight would be shown. Portions cut included more than one dreary round with the men head to head, hitting each other inside and nobody seeing what it was all about.

Eight of the 15 rounds shown—the first, third, fifth, seventh, 11th, 13th, 14th and final (15th). Even then the men were often doubled over trying to belt each other about the body.

For some reason the 10th round was not shown. That was the session when Schmeling first made Paulino stand up and battle. Schmeling claimed he hurt his right hand in the fifth round. Pictures give no indication of it. He was using that right lunch-hook plenty from the 10th round on, that portion of the contest that damaged the Spaniard most. Maxie made a mistake in making an alibi later for not knocking Uzie out. He should have been content in knowing that he hurt Uzcudun more than anyone had ever been able to do in the ring.

According to the titles and the press accounts, Paulino was wobbly at the end of the 14th round and that he fought the final round virtually blinded. The pictures do not show that. Paulino was doubtless hurt and it is certain he was cut around the face, but the film shows him stepping around much too lively for a man who can't see or who is on the verge of a knockout.

The fight pictures run 28 minutes. Had the contest been shown in entirety the contest itself would have consumed 45 minutes plus the titles, which would about have taken up the rest period of a minute after each round.

There is no preliminary bunk, as for instance the men in training or the promoters and such.

After seeing and hearing the Schmeling-Uzcudun fight picture, it is going to be tough watching a silent film of a similar event. *Ibee.*

THE JOLLY PEASANT

(GERMAN MADE)

(Silent)

Fery Film production. Directed by Frans Seitz. Werner Krauss featured. Screen story adapted from German operetta of same title by Leo Fall. In cast: Carmen Boni, Mathias Wieman, Andre Nox, Ivy Close, Leo Peukert, Hans Brausewetter. At 55th Street Playhouse, New York, week June 29, as half double bill. Running time, 55 minutes.

Sob story of father love that has little value anywhere outside of the sure-seaters and a lightweight entry in those houses. It is overboard with pointless sentiment. This German operetta, highly rated on stage abroad, has little substance in it on which to build a screen play, but gives Werner Krauss plentiful opportunities to mug in the best Continental style, registering remorse, sorrow and heart-ache with the same expression. Film is otherwise practically devoid of action.

Krauss is Reuther, the jolly peasant father who runs heavily in debt so that his son can go to Berlin to study for the priesthood, following the wishes of his godfather who is financing the boy's education.

In Berlin the boy changes his mind about becoming a priest and decides to become a physician. This decision is a sad blow to the old man as well as the godfather.

Later the father is reconciled to his son's plan and borrows from a money-lender to continue his son in college.

The son meantime is romancing the daughter of the university's most distinguished professor. Upon graduating he marries her, without inviting his father, sister or godfather to the ceremony.

While the son, now a physician, is evidently ashamed of the humble parentage from which he has sprung, his bride is not as ritzy as he had supposed and the old folks are invited to attend the wedding feast. The father is warmly greeted by the swells and everybody decides to settle down to some consistent drinking.

Musical comedy windup has the bridal pair and the wedding guests standing on a balcony while the university students march by in a torch light parade.

MOULIN ROUGE

(BRITISH MADE)
(SILENT)

British International production, directed by E. A. Dupont. Cameraman, Werner Brandes. Titles by Harry Chandlee. Featuring Olga Chekova, and including Eva Gray, Jean Brodeb, George Treville and Marcel Vibert. At Stanley, New York, one day, June 27. Running time, 90 mins.

Well done, but over-long. British picture directed by E. A. Dupont, famous for his "Variety," with Jannings made for Ufa a couple of years ago. Theme of "Moulin Rouge" is Continental rather than Anglo-Saxon, this angle more than any other, limiting the picture's utility for over here. It's a love complication with the young man falling for his fiancee's mother, the leading lady of the Moulin Rouge revue.

Except for occasional shots where the players' eyes are over-shadowed with that persistent habit of the European film makers to ignore the importance of proper make-up, "Moulin Rouge" is photographically good. Its principals are interesting personalities, notably Olga Chekova who resembles Pola Negri, but with more humor. She is a little too heavy for current American styles in physique, but attractive to the masculine eye nevertheless.

Some of the backstage stuff is done exceptionally well, better, in fact, than the usual Hollywood efforts to reproduce convincingly a musical stage show. On this angle alone and on the general richness and novelty of its background "Moulin Rouge" will hold interest for the small towns and other stands still unwired. *Land.*

UNKNOWN DANCER

(FRENCH MADE)
(SILENT)

Paris, June 20.

"Le Danceur Inconnu," comedy turned out by Cineromans, is adapted from a popular stage play. It had a big success.

The story is romantic and fairly well told on the screen, but not the best Rene Barberis has produced. His "La Merveilleuse Journee" (already reviewed in Variety) pleased better.

The fans may find plenty to tickle over by the antics of Andre Roanne as the unknown dancer. Perhaps he over does it.

A youthful draughtsman, out of a job and wearing an evening dress loaned him by a pal, notices a private ball taking place in a mansion. He enters the house and is accepted as one of the guests.

He fox-trots with a beautiful maiden. She seems pleased with him. The fellow ascertains from a friend he meets in the place she is a rich heiress, and the friend then introduces him to the girl as a coming art genius who will soon make a fortune. Naturally they fall in love.

Then the hero, unkown dancer, realizes it is caddish to deceive such a delicious creature and writes the girl an explanation. He disappears from that circle of society, becoming a salesman in a furniture store. The girl's interest is aroused and love prevails. She locates the boy to whom she has given her heart.

Vera Flory, Janet Young, Paul Olivier and Andre Nicolle in the cast. They keep well within bounds and help this picture through the shoals. Andre Roanne gets all the plums. *Light.*

THE WONDERFUL LIE

(GERMAN MADE)
(Silent)

London, June 20.

Ufa production, produced by Erich Pommer. Directed by Hans Schwarz. British Censors' Certificate "A." London Hippodrome for three weeks, opening June 24. Running time, 90 minutes.

Nina Petrovna .... Brigrette Helm
The Colonel .... Warwick Ward
The Lieutenant .... Franz Lederer

Moss Empires is putting this German silent film in for three weeks between "The Five O'Clock Girl" and "Mr. Cinders," partly to fill the gap and partly because of their association with Gaumont, Ufa's distributors here.

Made originally as "The Wonderful Lies of Nina Petrovna," this film has in the cast the people of "Vaudeville" and "Metropolis," but has the box-office value of neither. It is one of those arty productions full of typical German symbolic touches—such as the phallic symbol of a cone of ice cream lit by brandy round the base at the first meeting of hero and heroine.

Well and thoughtfully directed, the film fails as entertainment from the lack of balance in sympathy, its persistent gloom and its suicide climax. Put in to find whether there is a public in the West End of London for silent films during this talker boom, it will not prove anything because it will not be a popular attraction and would not be if synchronized.

It is one of those really fine Continental films suited to little theatres, but with no appeal for the regular picture house audience.

Nina lives with the Colonel, but does not think him so much. She sees the Lieutenant riding by in full regalia and falls for him heavily, throwing him a rose from the balcony and later getting the Colonel to introduce her! She slips the lieutenant the key of her apartment while they are dancing and he goes along the same night, but doesn't know he's being vamped and finally sleeps in another room. Colonel arrives next morning and tells the Lieut. to keep away, but Nina walks out on the Colonel and goes to live with the youth.

They have a tough time. To make the grade the Lieut. cheats at poker in the officers' mess and is caught by the Colonel, who says nothing, but gets a written confession later. With this he forces Nina to go back to him as the price of not squealing on the Lieut. Nina makes a play she doesn't love the boy any more so he won't think she's being forced and follow her. Then she throws him another rose as he rides by with his troop, but it falls on the snow and he doesn't see it. Nina takes the suicide route by poison just as the Colonel arrives to welcome her back.

The three principals give magnificent performances—simple and convincing. But the story is gloomy, the sympathy is with the Colonel, who behaves much better than the other two, and the end is morbid if logically obvious. If a producer could make films to please his own ideas of art, it would be a good picture. But as even a film producer in Europe has to earn money to live, it's another proposition how this helps him do it. *Frat.*

SMILING TERROR

(SILENT)

Universal production and release. Featuring Ted Wells. Directed by Joseph Leviyard. Running time, 50 minutes. One day, June 28, at Ideal, New York.

A 10-20-30 Western.
Nothing new.
Ted Wells, rough rider.
Skillful on peppy nag.
Looks best on the horse.
Derelys Perdue a looker.
Photography lucid.
Story drab.
Continuity passable.
Numerous little episodes.
Wells' skill given play.
First shot race.
First to saloon for the drinks.
Nice and fast.
Old-fashioned melo stuff.
Stage-coach hold-up.
Father buys mine from gang.
Old man goes to work in pit.
Finds gold.
Gyps try to get it back.
Kidnap the daughter.
Villian goes to father.
Wells walks in, drawing gat.
Father says gal being held.
Wells to rescue.
Wells fights them all.
And rescues.
Dizzy captions.

THE LOST TRIBE

(ENGLISH MADE)

(Silent)

Captain Hurley's Expedition into South African jungle lands. No U. S. distributor credited. At Fifth Ave. Playhouse, New York, week June 29, half double bill. Running time, about 35 minutes.

Last half of the four reels, to which "The Lost Tribe" has been cut, is one of the most blood curdling things of its kind in the many headhunting film tales in the cans. Gory titles for once are truthtelling. This reel packs in an entire warehouse of grinning skulls, as well as a couple being processed over a fire.

It's a little bit too strong for some of the fragile, arty women, but great stuff for the robust and mongers of flesh-burning novels.

The three first reels are fairly tame. Poor editing makes a young schooner do incredible antics, even working its way up a stream that, in the last flash, a thin native canoe was finding difficult to ford.

Captain Hurley's putting out from an Australian port with a seaplane is not clearly accounted for, but green and brown effects give the sea some attractive tints. While the trip to the fourth reel is of the conventional explorer type, it does extend the atmosphere of adventure. Had the production been properly cut and titled it would have been a possible road show and a positive non-theatrical bet. *Waly.*

WHIRL OF LIFE

(GERMAN-MADE)
(SILENT)

Worldwide production. Adapted from the novel, "The Confession," by Clara Ratzka. Directed by Richard Eichberg. Featuring Fay Malten, Henry George and Louis Leich. At Columbus (double feature), New York, one day, June 21. Running time, 75 minutes.

Those foreign makers of films especially those making the features in Germany, and most of this one has all the Teutonic earmarks, are still shooting at "Variety."

"The Whirl of Life" nowhere approaches the former. In some respects it forces comparison with "Four Devils" when the clown, working with the two younger performers in their "whirl of death," drops the boy and girl from the air as he (clown) suspends them to a whirling bar held fast by his teeth. Then the clown also falls and is hurt, but goes to the stage for his bows. The clown loves the girl, who in turn loves the boy. That is the story, though long drawn out.

Admitting some splendid photographic shots and allowing for scenes of some of the big foreign cities, including Berlin, the apparent slow upbuilding harmed what otherwise might have been an impressionistic verdict. Of course, it is a silent film, and as such will have to take what booking crumbs are thrown its way.

Once or twice the picture sat on the edges of the kind of risque stuff that has been whamming both the films and stage stories on this side.

Two shots of the heroine taking a bath were shown and they were some shots. That long throw where the girl is making the soapy suds fly was a nifty. No attempt to make it raw other than show how a poor girl can take a bath with lots of foamy suds.

Runs through an apparent interminable channel. Padded so it hurts.

Some of the scenes seem pretentious, although the shots of the audience were not taken when the "whirl" was being made.

The cast did fairly well, the girl, Fay Malten, not a bad looker, holding pace with the other principals. The young man screens splendidly, while the player doing the clown did some creditable work.

Creditable work by the camera on the carnival scene, one of the highlights. Direction an in-and-out. *Mark.*

LUTHER

(GERMAN-MADE)
(SILENT)

Cob-Film production, released by Reformation Films. Directed by Hans Kyser. Photographed by M. Paetz. Eugene Klopfer featured. In cast: Carl Elzer, Bruno Kastner, Jakob Tiedtke, H. K. Mueller, Elsa Wagner. At Little Carnegie Playhouse week June 22. Running time, 90 minutes.

Biographical picture of the life of Martin Luther, German religious leader, typical sure-seater stuff. Film might attract those interested in the Lutheran Church and its founder, but without value for general distribution.

Eugene Klopfer in the title role is a middle-aged German actor who never changes his make-up at any period of Luther's life. He looks 45 when Luther is in college and still 45 when the religious reformer has translated the Bible into German.

Long drawn out and a repetition of religious ceremonies, processions and mob scenes. Titles, also lengthy, are in the main Biblical quotations or excerpts from the writings of Luther.

One of the sequences of interest is that in which a religious group in medieval Germany is shown selling indulgences which guarantee remissions of sins. That was one of the customs that Luther fought against. Branded as a heretic, he finally wins the confidence of the people and sets up a new religion.

One of Luther's quotations used is, "My writings are not for the learned, but for the people." The film is not for the people, but for sure-seaters.

It's Easy to Become Father

(GERMAN MADE)

(Silent)

Ufa production and release. Directed by Erich Schoenfelder, with story idea credited to Ernst von Wolzogen. At 55th St. Playhouse week June 22. Running time, 73 minutes.

Lord Fairfax..............Franz Egenieff
Lady Fairfax..............Mathilde Sussin
Lord Fairfax, Jr..............Harry Halm
Mr. Underberry..............Hans Mierendorf
Harriet..............Lilian Harvey
Saake..............Albert Paulig

Just a lot of boloney this Continental comedy. The performers act up like in American nickolodeon stuff around 1910. One of Ufa's flattest pancakes.

Insinuating title, some more subtitles, injected here in the arty way. "It's Easy to Become a Father" keeps arty audiences thin and even walkouts among the few.

A bunch of people and a camera seem to have been turned loose on a French locale. As long as they kept in shooting range the director obviously didn't care. Once in a while he remembered it was a comedy. Then the travelogue stuff was forgotten for further asininity among the cast.

A wealthy American dame, played by a German actress with a Chaplin-Viola Dana complex, finds a waif in her car. She quits home to follow instructions in a note when dad turns down the brat.

At the same time a stupid young lord is snapping out of adolescency with Decameron's yarns while his mama devours the Good Book. His papa decrees that the time has arrived when he must sow some of the caged oats. Off to Paris the kid lams.

On the way to the train the youth looks over a maiden's shoulder, stur the her reading the want ads and fires her on as his secretary.

On boat the director allows the oy to go to the rail so many times that nausea spreads among the arty payees. Then a dime detective, the most boring thing in the thing, goes through the manual. Thanks to the dick, Ufa was able to drag this picture abortion over six reels.

Every time the director found the story "idea," as the cinema bills it, running into a rough sea he ordered the sunspot turned on an infant. In the last couple of reels the job took another ancient twist rounding the cast on a full stage for the welcomed curtain. *Waly.*

BLACK HILLS

(SILENT)

Dakota Productions, states' rights release. Directed by Norman Dawn. In cast: Susan Denis, George Chandler, George Fisher, Bob Webster. At Ideal, New York, one day, June 20, as half double bill. Running time, 40 minutes.

Comedy drama with the Black Hills of North Dakota as background has slim value even on a double bill. It's a quickie made quicker than that.

Girl has inherited a lumber mill and crooks are trying to steal it.

Bum who gains employment there later proves to be a detective while the Swedish cook he falls in love with is the owner of the property.

Film looks as if it's been cut plenty for no good purpose.

WEEKEND WIVES

(ENGLISH MADE)
(SILENT)
(Disc Orchestration)

British International production. Directed by Harry Lachman. J.J. Cox, cameraman. In cast: Monty Banks, Estelle Brody, and several English Players. At Loew's, New York, one day June 20, as half of double feature. Running time 77 minutes.

Every foot of film exposed in the taking of "Weekend Wives" seems to have gotten by the cutting room, if any. The original American farce about disgruntled couples is threadbare, with an interchange started, but more innocuously innocent than local producers would dare. Thing should be edited before bookings here considered.

Reels are devoted to close-ups of bacon and eggs, dresses, conversations and trunk packing. Too bad the director didn't give as much thought to the story as he did to irrelevant details. Same comparison goes for the sets and exteriors, which are mighty attractive.

Monty Banks' continuous prattfalling got the few laughs registered in the Loew daily grind.

Chopped to about five reels with snappy subtitling, "Weekend Wives," because of cast and mounting, would be better than the average indie attempt at comedy.

Estelle Brody, as a French actress hunting for divorce, starts things with a lawyer. He bawls out the wife and gives her a chance to meet Banks, some kind of a fat, wealthy ne'er-do-well.

Before both couples plan beach week-end, the women meet and become pals. Actress' husband, reminding of old burlesque derby number, unwinds quantities of repetitious movement in the old school way. *Waly.*

TWO SISTERS

(SILENT)

(Disc Orchestration)

Rayart production and release. Directed by Scott Pembroke. Viola Dana, starred. Hap Depew, cameraman. Story by Virginia Water adapted by Arthur Hoerl. In cast: Rex Lease, Claire Du Brey, Boris Karloff. At Loew's New York one day, June 28, half of double bill. Running time 48 minutes.

Rayart deliberately sacrifices the chances it has as a promising indie with the stuff it is wishing on Viola Dana and the way in which it is handling that little player. "Two Sisters" is the poorest of some recent bad ones.

Miss Dana does a dual here and even the cast gets confused over her sudden shifts from the wicked to the good sister. Cheapest grind fare.

Girl bandit space in dailies apparently inspired the writing. Hacked situations, ridiculous coincidences, and the directorial stupidity of letting a machine-like comic clown in a murder sequence compose the stuff called the yarn. *Waly.*

SQUARE SHOULDERS

(20% DIALOG)

Pathe production and release. Directed by E. Mason Hopper. Original story and adaptation by George Dromgold, Houston Branch and Peggy Prior. Junior Coghlan and Louis Wolheim featured. In cast: Philippe de Lacy, Anita Louise, Montague Shaw, Johnny Morris, Kewpie Morgan, Clarence Geldert. Recording by RCA Photophone. At New York, New York, one day, June 21, as half of double bill. Running time, 60 minutes.

Good human interest story, with a military academy locale. It will be liked in the neighborhood houses, despite the lack of love interest outside of kid stuff. Film also has an unhappy wind-up.

Louis Wolheim is cast as Slag, a hero who has turned tramp. Back in his home town he discovers his kid running wild. Without revealing his identity, he determines to give him the benefits of a military school education. To do this he turns crook, gets the money to see the kid through school, and double-crosses his pals. He himself turns straight and gets a job as stableman in order to be near the boy.

Kid makes good at the academy and he and his unknown benefactor and father are sitting pretty until the tramps, who had been given the works, show and complicate matters. In an attempt to save the academy from being robbed by his former pals, Slag is killed, with the kid never realizing that the man he knew as a friend was his father.

Junior Coghlan as the boy handles himself neatly, but falters during the single talking sequence, an emotional bit. Wolheim's voice at times is throaty and indistinct, possibly due to poor reproduction. Philippe de Lacey and Anita Louise, the only girl in the picture, are well cast, supplying comedy relief and kid love stuff in moderation.

FROZEN RIVER
(5% DIALOG)

Warner production and release. Starring "Rin-Tin-Tin." Directed by Harmon Weight from story by John Fowler, adapted by Anthony Coldeway. In cast: Davey Lee, Nina Quartero, Josef Swickart, Raymond McKee. Music score on Western Electric system by Louis Silver. At Loew's New York, one day, June 14, half double bill. Running time, 61 minutes.

Talk in this, and a lot of badly synchronized barking, more scientific than doggy, make it little better than Rinty's usual silents. Tiny dialog is as bromidic as the nursery and only serves to make the story, along regular dog life saving lines, slower in spots.

"Frozen North" should not be worth more in price over the silent versions than the per cent of the dialog it contains.

A jumpy story brings out the regular bad men doing their routine for the gold cached away by the old gent for his daughter. The daughter is camera conscious in this one and shows it in every move.

Rinty does his usual as the beast who is savage until the right people come along. One of these is Davey Lee, who is shown in only a few feet of film. He does not talk or sing but Louis Silver has re-worked "Sonny Boy" into the closing orchestration. *Waly.*

STARK MAD
(ALL DIALOG)

Warners production and release. Featuring H. B. Warner, Louise Fazenda, Jacqueline Logan, Harry B. Walthall, Claude Gillingwater. Directed by Lloyd Bacon. Story by Jerome Kingston, adapted by Harvey Gates. Bernard McGill, cameraman. At Fox's Academy, New York, June 22-25. Running time, 70 mins.

In the present state of dialog development "Stark Mad" will hardly do for important deluxe bookings, but for general release, neighborhoods and small towns, will probably please. It's a stenciled plot but with a good cast and enough speed and action to sustain interest.

Plot opens aboard a yacht at anchor off the Caracas Jungle in South America, on an expedition to learn the fate of the yacht-owner's son. The captain of the yacht is a dangerous criminal unknown, of course, to the party. A deserted temple, chained ape, lunatics, and eerie atmosphere. Some of the comedy, notably the stock in trades of Miss Fazenda, doesn't register because of familiarity.

Love interest is between Jacqueline Logan, little nervous in her lines, and the ever-unctious H. B. Warner, looking particularly virile and dominant. Lionel Belmore, Warner Richmond and Andre Beranger add their mite to the respectable acting score.

Elevated eyebrow gentry will sneer at this sort of entertainment, but the masses may find it diverting. *Land.*

LAW OF MOUNTED
(SILENT)

El Dorado production and release. Starring Bob Custer. Story by Sally Winters. Directed by J. P. McGowan. Adapted by Philip Schuyler. Cameraman, Paul Allen. Cast includes: J. P. McGowan, Sally Winters, Frank Ellis, Cliff Lyons, Mary Maybery and Lynn Sanderson. Running time 50 mins. Loew's, New York, one day, June 25, half double bill.

Author and director appear in this entertaining smallie, devolving on Canadian fur smuggling. No directorial masterpiece, yet the simplicity of the story and splendid characters elevate the silent production.

Bob Custer has a strong chin and fine features. Mary Mayberry takes an exquisite close-up. It is in that department the photography excels. J. P. McGowan, the murderous leader, is an Eric Von Stroheim type, with sweaty face and bald head. His characterization is especially well done.

Two mounted officers are fired upon by three fur thieves, who are on foot, the sergeant orders his buddy to proceed to their shack. Whatever the distance may have been, the men on foot arrive at the cabin several minutes before the officer. It was a detour, as the officers had been there before.

Again, the same officer recovers from a bullet wound in his shoulder simultaneously with the report of a woman who tells them her husband has been murdered and his furs stolen. The murder and theft occurred the same time as the shooting of the officer.

Not so drab as it sounds on paper.

German Pics

Berlin, June 15.
ASIA'S DESERT

"With Sven Hedin Through Asia's Deserts" (Deutsches Lichtspiel-Syndikat). Sven Hedin as explorer and scientist is a big name in Germany. And America knows him through his controversy about Tibet two years ago. Here, with the help of Paul Lieberenz, he has made an interesting travelogue of Mongolia. Photographically there are many excellent shots and he has caught the spirit of the land. But for America it is merely another travelog.

"AMANULLAH'S LAND"

"In Amanullah's Land" (Derussa). This Russian travelog has considerably more general interest as the whole question of Afganistan is very much on the front page at the moment.

These Russians have gone at their work like American star reporters, and when seeing the picture you realize why Amanullah failed. Without underlining we are made to clearly understand the extraordinary contrasts that exist in this strange land. A thriving modern factory beside a primitive worker who does everything by hand.

Should go big as an educational if released in the right spot. Could also be cut into a series of interesting short scenics.

"CHILDREN OF METROPOLIS"

"Grossstadtjugend" (Aafa). Although the Aafa has combined two of its stars, Harry Liedtke and Maria Paudler, result is considerably less satisfactory than the last two Liedtke films which were handled by Robert Land.

Here, it is true, Rudolph Walter-Fein is handicapped by an impossible manuscript, but his work is exaggerated and lacking in nuance.

It begins in a Swiss hotel, where Magda loves the handsome Alex but is too proud to show it. A will discloses that he is not to inherit the money he had expected and he takes a position as 'tutor to Magda's younger brother. Magda is still upstage and is set to marry an Italian count. But Alex unmasks him as a swindler. Alex and Magda marry in his place. Will get back its investment on Liedtke's personality.

"LADY IN BLACK"

"Die Dame in Schwarz" (Deutsche Universal). Liane Haid has been a star in Germany for years and now is finding out how to act. If Liane really learns before she gets too old she might have international qualities, as she is good to gaze upon.

Present picture has a conventional scenario concerning a cabaret dancer who is really a countess. Her papers have been stolen by a female swindler who claims to be real countess and is trying to get the girl's fortune from a bank.

With the aid of a boxer friend and a journalist she exposes the crook and turns her over to the police. Charles Lincoln is fair as the boxer, Kurt Vespermann clowns too excessively as the reporter, and Marcella Albani is her voluptuous self as the fake countess.

"BRANDENBURG ARCH"

"Durchs Brandenburger Tor" (Deutsche Universal). Too bad to waste June Marlowe on such trash. Fritz Kampers also wastes a lot of talent on a leading role.

Not possible for any of the larger cities but might slip by in the provinces.

"SPY OF ODESSA"

"Der Spion von Odessa" (Meschrabpom). Example of the hokum feature as they make it in Russia today. Camouflaged propaganda but entertaining at that.

In Odessa in 1919 the white troops are in control. A communistic spy, Berinski, pretends to be a count and contends with the two leading white generals for the favors of a dancer. At the headquarters of the Reds it is discovered and all except the leader, Lugowetz, are captured. He gives Birinski the funds of the organization but is captured himself as he leaves the hotel. Lugowetz' wife tries to notify Birinski of the capture but finds him in the dancer's room. She believes him a traitor and notifies the communistic comrades. But Birinski trades a night with the dancer for a general's clothes and is able to set Lubowetz free. The comrades then capture him but Lubowetz comes just in time to save him from being shot.

Competently directed and played with telling if melodramatic emphasis. Comarow is splendid as Birinski, and Galmia Kraftschenko is succulent as the dancer.

"CHAMPAGNÉ"

"Champagner" (Sascha). Betty Balfour is a nice little comedienne, perhaps England's best screen actress, but here she does not photograph up to international standard.

As Sparkuhl, who took this picture, is a first-rate operator, one gathers it is due to Betty's physiognomy.

Not exactly a brilliantly original story but it keeps moving. A little kitchen maid is fired because she steals a bottle of champagne to give her friend, the waiter. She does not leave, but hides under a table. At a fancy dress ball that night a rich South American finds her

there and, believing her one of the attractions, makes her dance. She is a big hit. The waiter, seeing that the South American finds her attractive, realizes his love for her.

Gezca von Bolvary directed, and the cast includes Jack Trevor and Marcel Vibert.

"MONTE CHRISTO"

"The Count of Monte Christo" (Louis Nalpas). This story will always be good food for the camera, silent or otherwise, but there is no use attempting it with old-fashioned methods and without a sure-fire star. Jean Angelo, who plays the title role here, has undoubted qualities, but the director, Henri Fescourt, is behind times and only succeeds in making him melodramatically ridiculous.

Such good German players as Lil Dagover and Bernhard Goetzke are also inundated by the stuffy atmosphere.

Has no chances in German capital.

CHARMING SINNERS

(ALL DIALOG)

Paramount production and release. Robert Milton, director. Adaption by Doris Anderson from W. Somerset Maugham's story. Dialog not credited. William Powell, Ruth Chatterton, Clive Brook featured. Dialog and sound on film. At Paramount, New York, week July 6. Running time, 65 minutes.

Kathryn Miles	Ruth Chatterton
Robert Miles	Clive Brook
Anne-Marie Whitley	Mary Nolan
Karl Kraley	William Powell
Mrs. Carr	Laura Hope Crews
Helen Carr	Florence Eldridge
George Whitley	Montague Love
Margaret	Juliette Crosby
Alice	Lorraine Eddy
Gregson	Claude Allister

Light drawing room comedy, with story rooted deeply in the French farce school. Despite the fine cast, all the members of which are far superior to their assignments, one of the frailest of all talkers yet turned out.

All dialog means all dialog in this instance. There's little else to it but talk. Among the missing ingredients is action. It's all from the stage play, "The Constant Wife."

Everything handled in typical stage manner, where this type of story is classed as farce. Neither the manner of handling nor the story itself will land 'em in the hinterlands.

The usual sort of marital mixup: husband errs with his wife's kittenish lady friend; old sweetheart of wifey conveniently drops in from Japan to help the latter make her mate jealous and evens; everything else that goes with it. Just a slightly different ending but that doesn't make a picture.

And the broad British accent.

Two more legitimate names in the cast besides Miss Chatterton—Laura Hope Crews and Florence Eldridge, both in small roles.

Clive Brook went into reverse to play light comedy in "Charming Sinners" and looks good enough under the conditions. Miss Chatterton and Mary Nolan have suitable roles.

Pity to waste William Powell.

Another in a new sort of characterization is Montague Love, as the innocent and apologetic husband of the cheating Anne-Marie.

No dialog credit, leaving the inference the lines were taken as written from Somerset Maugham's story. No title sheet info as to the publication of the story, so possibly a mag yarn or an orig by the English author.

All interior photography, excepting a few feet of news reel stuff on a horse race, sounded to fit.

Bige.

THUNDER

(Sound Effects Only)

M-G-M production and release. Directed by William Nigh. Lon Chaney starred. From original story for the screen by Byron Morgan. Photographer, Harry Sharp. At Capitol, New York, week of July 6. Running time, 85 minutes.

Grumpy Anderson	Lon Chaney
Zella	Phyllis Haver
Tommy	James Murray
Jim	George Duryea
Molly	Frances Morris
Davy	Wally Albright, Jr.

Second Lon Chaney picture lately with that player of bizarre roles doing a straight character old man. Poor stuff from all angles. Film has one effective moment of melodrama, when the heroic engineer (Chaney) speeding to the relief of flood sufferers, drives his train with the track "four feet under water." How they achieved this photographic stunt is a mystery.

Looked like the real thing with alternate shots of the train throwing up clouds of spray, its wheel submerged, and of the engineer in his cab with the water streaming past in deluge.

That sequence took perhaps four minutes leaving 80 minutes or thereabouts of dull picture, confused in action and motivation and of mild entertainment value.

Film was apparently made silent and perfunctory sound effects later added. These consist entirely of the noises made by running locomotive. Job is poorly done. Engine chug-chugs with large self consciousness, but when the noble engineer pulls the whistle cord, you have to take it on faith. There is no dialog and no audible effect except the chug-chug.

Story was probably built around the submerged track idea. They work too hard getting up to it. Takes much footage at the start to plant the idea that grouchy old Anderson runs his train on time no matter what difficulties he encounters. At the opening he's 29 minutes late into Chicago and the tracks are piled with snow drifts. But he makes up the minutes, driving his own son, who is his fireman to exhaustion.

His inexorable determination to keep to schedule in all things ultimately sends another son to death, while his daughter-in-law is driven away and the fireman-son alienated. Old man's stubbornness gets him into a wreck and he is relegated to the railroad machine shop.

Just then the Mississippi floods come, and old Anderson is sent out on a relief train. The son is impressed in the same service on another train. The two meet for the last lap to the stricken area. All the other trains halt at the point where the tracks are under water. Old man says, "Where there are tracks, I can go through," and does just that. Of course, the boy's sweetheart and the daughter-in-law are facing death in the flood area and the arrival of the train saves them.

Phillis Haver is the free and easy actress sweetheart of the fireman boy, a part so badly over-written it obliges her to over-play. James Murray does extremely well in the secondary role of the son.

Chaney fans don't want him as a serio-comic, semi-heroic old man. And fans of all kinds, don't want marathon melodramas leading up to trick mechanical climaxes. Besides in a sound era makeshifts like this are unworthy of a first line producer.

A dull picture used to fill in for a dull summer week.

Rush.

Time, Place and Girl

(ALL DIALOG)

Warner Bros. production and release. Directed by Howard Bretherton. Screen play by Robert Lord, based on musical comedy of the same title, book and lyrics by Frank R. Adams, Joseph E. Howard and Will Hough. Musical score directed by Louis Silvers. Sound synchronization by Western Electric Vitaphone. At Strand, New York, week of July 6. Running time, 70 minutes.

Jim Crane	Grant Withers
Doris Ward	Betty Compson
Mae Ellis	Gertrude Olmsted
Professor	James R. Kirkwood
Mrs. Davis	Vivian Oakland
Mrs. Winters	Gretchen Hartman
Mrs. Parks	Irene Haisman
Ward	John Davidson
Radio Announcer	Gerald King
Butter and Egg Man	Bert Roach

Musical comedy title of some importance about 15 years ago covers a straight screen comedy drama that rates pegging as a fair programer. Theme song, "Honeymoon," old-timer, is resurrected and is rather discreetly sung but once. No chorus or dance numbers employed. Smart, up-to-the-minute, realistic dialog will sell this one to the average picture fan.

Love interest centers about a college football hero and a private secretary and is the second of recent screen plays on Broadway which tends to plug stenogs and secretaries as choice candidates for double harness.

Jim Crane, a college football hero, whose conceit exceeds his newspaper rep, is nevertheless the heart throb of Mae Ellis. He hardly gives her a tumble while they are both at college. When finding employment in the same investment house after graduation, he as a bond salesman and she as private secretary to the head of the firm he begins to take notice.

The swell headed college boy is a total flop as a bond seller. He is about to get the air when the boss notes he has a way with women, especially the married ones, and decides to set him up in a phoney securities racket in which he is to make a play for the coin of his fem admirers.

Unaware that he is being jobbed into jail by his crooked employer, Jim is making great headway with his new line until Mae puts him wise to the frame. Knowing that his boss' wife has a yen for him he gets out of the impending mess by selling her enough bonds to pay off the other women who have bought and blows with the girl, leaving the crook holding the bag.

Withers gives a fine characterization as the swell-headed bond salesman. Betty Compson, as the wife of the broker on the make for the college kid also gets the most out of her sophisticated role. Supporting cast handle themselves neatly before the mike. Bert Roach, as a bond salesman and James R. Kirkwood as a professor have light comedy parts, nicely done.

This picture is one of the first made from an old time musical comedy, one which had a definite plot structure and modernized as it has been, advantageously, should find fair favor, especially with the fems, in the regular week stands.

APPASSIONATA

(FRENCH-MADE)

(Silent)

Franco Film production and release. Starring Leon Mathot. Adapted from the novel by Pierie Frondaie. Directed by Mathot. Cast includes: Rene Heribel, Ruth Weyher, Therese Kolb, Fernand Fabre, et al. Running time, 75 mins, at Cameo, New York, week of July 6.

A foreign monstrosity whose ill photography is only surpassed by the ludicrous direction. Its denouement is weaker than a pallbearer's smile. A phastasmagoria of colorless lips, spasmodic gestures and incongruous characters.

If the novel is famous, the cinema version is unjust. One sees Charlotte Langer and Jean Langer living with Jean's mother. Jean is an artist. Their friends, Spifani and Bianca Banella, the former a playwright and the latter an actress, fall out. Charlotte and Jean visit Spifani to condole with him.

Spifani goes for Charlotte in a big way. She gives up Jean, who bemoans his misfortune, while Spifani and his woman cheat together.

One day Spif looking out the window sees his actress friend return home. He goes to her abode. Charlotte follows. Broken up, she runs away in a storm. Next in a hospital.

Jean, a Napoleonic little fellow with broad shoulders and a brooding phiz, receives a letter that she is very ill. He kisses his mother goodbye and bounds out of the house like a little boy. Looks funny seeing a middle aged guy run out of the house as if going to play ball in the street. Idea is to show he is a peppy fellow. One shudders.

He gets to the hospital and is ushered to Charlotte's room. Unconscious, she clutches the bed clothes in her agony. He touches the clenched hand. Charlotte comes out of the coma, smiles and then expires.

Next scene is a formal dance at Spifani's. A colored band of six pep it up. As a waltz is completed, Spif leads his actress girl through portieres, where he embraces her. During the soul-kiss, she spies Jean on the veranda. He is unshaven and wild. Spif turns, looking very mad. Jean enters and says: "Charlotte is dead. You're a murderer." Spif replies: "You must be crazy. I had nothing to do with Charlotte's death."

Jean rushes as Spif attempts to return to the dance. He clutches the villain by the throat. The actress puts her arm over her eyes as the combatants roll over. Whether Jean kills the fellow or not is left to the imagination.

Stupid is a compliment when applied to this French made film in its entirety.

CARNIVAL OF CRIME

(GERMAN MADE)

(Silent)

PFA production and release. Directed by Dr. Willy Wolff from Ernst Klein's novel "The Woman With the Tigerskin." German title is: "Die Dam mat dem Tigerfell." Cast: Ellen Richter, Bruno Kaster, Henry Schroth, Evi Eva, George Alexander and Alfred Gerasch. Running time 60 mins. Week July 6 at 55th Street Playhouse, New York.

A foreign picture similar to "Carnival of Crime" appeared at this theatre recently, wherein one saw a hotel elevator which while in ascent did not stop at any floor, the passengers hopping off at their respective numbers. Such a sight is wholly amusing to an American audience. It is such shots of strange contraptions and mannerisms which entertain in "Carnival of Crime." Otherwise the picture is a complex medley of juvenile continuity with captions, bizarre and unenlightening. Summed up the picture is three shades lower than awful.

The criminal aspect of this firm, which is best characterized a melo-comedy, would attack the risibles of a native crook. It is difficult to grade the acting of a foreign people whose gestures and facial reactions seem askew.

The story has an immense start when at a rendezvous called the Casino, a tiger-skin coat remains uncalled for. A story in an evening paper concerning a woman with such a coat being the subject of police search in connection with a murder leads the coatroom woman to inform the gendarmes.

They trace the coat to a Lord, who placed the coat in the check-room. He conceals the identity of the woman, whom he escorted. She hides behind a pillar in the lobby of a hotel when the police quiz him in the lounge. When the officers have left the fellow learns the girl has two passports.

"Then you are a criminal," he says to her.

"No, let me explain," she says. Then the story is screened.

The girl, weighty-shouldered brunet with a continuous smile, even when she holds a revolver at the heart of her suspects, trails the criminals, but is held up by another fellow. If the plot of that story can be followed in this review that is more than can be done in the screen version.

BLACK WATERS

(ALL DIALOGUE)

Made in Hollywood by British and Dominion Films, Ltd. Released by World Wide. Directed by Marshall Neilan. Adapted from the stage play, "Fog," by John Willard, featuring James Kirkwood and Mary Brian. At Arena, N. Y., one day, July 8. Running time, 90 minutes.

Everything in this one including the kitchen sink. Too much talk with mellerish action slowed the picture to a wabble.

The talker deserves credit for its

photography; some splendid shots aboard the ship.

Special mention should go to the giant playing the murderous Negro. Just one feminine character.

Whoever wrote all that dialog tried hard at times to be funny. The supposed wisecracks sound untimely and uncanny. A sample is where one of the men remarks that the giant Negro worker aboard the boat would have made a good secretary for Cal.

If Mickey Neilan could have sat in at the Arena presentation of this film at night and heard some of those wise-cracking juvs from 8th avenue almost pull the Bronx cheer at times he would no doubt order a rehashing of a lot of the dialog.

The talkers may be in the infancy, but some of the babies that are coming along are talking out of turn. And this baby is about the gabbiest that has come down the film pike.   *Mark.*

SPARTAKIADA
(Or "The Red Olympiad")
(RUSSIAN MADE)
(Silent)

Sovkino production, released by Amkino. Directed by I. M. Poselsky and P. V. Rotov. At Film Guild Cinema, New York, week July 6. Running time, 60 minutes.

Nothing in this one outside of newsreel stuff stretched out into feature length for the sure-seaters patronized by the nuts.

It's the film record of a set of athletic games held in Moscow about a year ago, serving to prove that the Soviet Republic has made rapid strides since 1923, when a Physical Culture Council was appointed to foster athletics throughout the nation.

If cut down to 10 minutes there might be some excuse for this film having been shown generally shortly after the games were held and the Moscow athletes cleaned up everything in sight.

An hour of athletes doing their stuff on the screen is just about the ultimate in dull entertainment offered by an intimate picture house in New York. For the average picture house patrons, it's about as important and timely as would be the pictures of last year's world series shown on the screen of a Moscow picture house today.

DESERT RIDER
(Silent)

M-G-M production and release. Starring Tim McCoy. Directed by Nick Grinde. Story by Ted Shaine and Milton Brend. Adapted by Oliver Drake. Titles by Sinclair Drago. Cameraman, Arthur Reed. Cast: Raquel Torres, Bert Roach, Ed Connelly, Harry Woods, Jess Cavin. Running time 55 minutes. One day, July 2, at Loew's, New York, half double bill.

Land grant westerner. Smoked-glasses photography. Antique situations. Even a fist fight on a precipice.

Imagine Raquel Torres on desert just in time to save Tim McCoy by popping a deadly snake with her trusty rifle.

McCoy, unhorsed, is delivering letter to Raquel. Chases mirages for miles across the wastes. Big action centers around shipment of gold.

Anne Against the World
(Silent)

Ray-Art production and release. Starring Shirley Mason. Directed by Duke Worne. Photography by Hap Depew. In cast: Jack Mower, James Bradbury, Isabelle Keith, Tom Caron, Bell Stoddard. Running time 60 mins. One day, July 2, at Loew's, New York, half double bill.

Absurd Broadway film. Producer after his star femme. Story infantile. Such inane titles as "I want you to be the happiest person in the world."

Shirley Mason, as the ingenue, pursued by countless men. Nothing but flowers and parties. Producer in dressing room tells her everybody in New York will be talking about her. She's a hit. Asks her to be nice to him. She is flighty and pretends not to understand that language. Takes her to a party. She lamps John Forbes, tall and handsome, rolling in wealth.

Anyway you fill in rest, oke!

BLACKMAIL
(BRITISH MADE)
(All Dialog)
London, July 1.

British International production. United Kingdom release. Wardour Co. Adapted from play by Charles Bennett. Directed by Alfred J. Hitchcock. Dialog by Benn Levy. Camera: Jack Cox. Recorded on RCA Photophone. Running time, two hours. Preview at the Regal, London, June 21.

Alice White.....................Anny Ondra
Mrs. White...................Sara Allgood
Mr. White.....................Charles Paton
Detective Frank Webber.....John Longden
Tracy........................Donald Calthrop
Artist.......................Cyril Ritchard

A piece of craftsmanship which makes the stuff which has come over so far look like nobody's business. Not just a talker, but a motion picture that talks. Alfred J. Hitchcock has solved the problem of making a picture which does not lose any film technique and gains effect from dialog. Silent, it would be an unusually good film; as it is, it comes near to being a landmark. It will have much the same effect on American technique that some of the German films had half a dozen years ago.

As a stage play, with Tallulah Bankhead, "Blackmail" was not a success. Story has been expanded, but still does not stand close analysis, either for logic or sympathy.

This defect disappears before the fast-moving production and the novel uses of sound and dialog. A semi-trick ending, fading on the sound of several policemen laughing aloud at the idea the girl knows anything about the murder, comes almost as the director's cynical epilog to the story itself.

Frank Webber is one of the Flying Squad of Scotland Yard. His girl, Alice, gets sore with him at having to wait till he comes off duty. She tells him no one would ever hear of his Scotland Yard if it weren't for Edgar Wallace, and walks out on him in a tea shop to go off with an artist pick-up.

Goes to his studio to see the decorations, and discovers the artist is interested in other things besides paint. While struggling on the bed she grabs a bread-knife and kills the artist. Walks about all night and goes home to father's cigar store, where all the neighbors drop in to discuss last night's murder.

Her detective sweetheart is on the case and finds a glove. Knows it is hers. He goes to the shop to ask her about it, but is interrupted by Tracy, who has been blackmailing the artist and saw Alice leave, which she also dropped.

Artist's landlady (fine cameo from one Hannah Jones) goes to the police and tells a man had been hanging around. They turn up records and she recognizes Tracy.

Supposing him to be possibly the murderer, as he has a bad dossier, the police send out a hurry call to the Flying Squad, which Frank gets. He proceeds to put the reverse on Tracy, having previously fallen for the blackmail to protect his girl.

Tracy makes a getaway and is chased through London by the Squad, gets into the British Museum and is killed falling off the roof.

Alice, meantime, goes to the Yard to confess and is turned over to Frank by the Chief, who does not know who she is. Frank tells her he knows she did it, but as the police think it was Tracy, let it go at that.

An impossible story, it still gets by on production and acting. Dion Calthrop runs away with the picture, for voice and playing. Anny Ondra looks the dumbbell she is supposed to be, and gets a good voice double in Joan Barry, Anny having a Czecho accent. John Longden well fitted. Small roles exceptionally well cast.

Phyllis Monkman has an effective bit as a gossip who thinks murder is not a nice thing when a knife is used. A good effect is made by cutting away from her in the shop and showing Alice and her parents at breakfast, with Alice trying to cut a loaf while the voice drifts in through the door with ". . . knife . . . blur, blur, blur . . . knife" till she gets hysterical.

Production values good, with some fine shots of Scotland Yard, interior of British Museum and first night exit from a Cochran revue. Hitchcock still cannot get away from the staircase complex he found in "The Lodger." So many of the sobbers raved about his "art" he believes it consists in long, winding staircases!

At this stage of talkers, mighty near the best yet. But with the certainty of quick developments in talking technique, it needs a quick release.   *Frat.*

NO DEFENSE
(50% DIALOG)

Warner Bros. production and release. Directed by Lloyd Bacon. Story by J. Raleigh Davis. Screen play by Robert Lord. Monte Blue and May McAvoy featured. Synchronized musical score directed by Louis Silvers. In cast, William Tooker, William Desmond, Kathryn Carver, Lee Moran. At New York, New York, as half double bill, one day, July 5. Running time, 60 minutes.

Punchless western, dull and draggy from start to finish.

Dialog is all of the blah variety and the love interest equally unconvincing.

Plot centers about an engineering project over western mountains. Boston engineer brings his daughter west to get a load of the bridge his firm is building. She goes for the big he-man in charge of the construction. Her sister-in-law also along with her husband on the trip is also on the make for the bridge foreman, but gets nowhere in her efforts to compromise him.

Talk at no time holds interest, not even a trial or investigation scene. Collapse of a bridge is kickless, showing steel girders being twisted into figure eights.

"West of the Great Divide" is evidently the theme song of this one, played all through and sung several times by an off-screen voice. Picture holds little value even for wired grinds.

MONTE CRISTO
(FRENCH MADE)
(Silent)
Paris, July 1.

Another version of "Monte Cristo" and a local success. It is likely to have the same warm reception in the United States as Verne's "Mathis Sandorf."

Henri Fescourt has turned out almost a perfect picture for Louis Nalpas. This latest edition is artistic, while appealing to popular taste. It is neither junk nor bunk, yet it will appeal to the masses while interesting the high brows.

The scenario follows the book, that thriller that all schoolboys have devoured. It is delightful, if not edifying, to learn history from Dumas.

Get out the book again if you have forgotten the exploits.

Cast is favorable, with Angelo in the title role, Lil Dagover and Mary Glory holding the feminine leads. Others are Modot, Goetzke, Michelle Verly, Pierre Batcheff, Francois Rozet, Tourout and Henri Debain.

The title alone should still be an attraction.   *Kendrew.*

Daughter of Regiment
(GERMAN MADE)
(With BETTY BALFOUR)
(Silent)
Berlin, June 26.

"The Daughter of the Regiment," (Hom. Film), premiere at the Titania Palast. British International Pictures did well to bring its star, Betty Balfour, over to Germany and let a German director handle her. Although still heavy she nevertheless proves herself a competent little comedienne.

The rule for English actors and actresses is evidently: keep as far away from England as possible.

The story from a manuscript by Hans A. Zerlett concerns Marie, a girl who has been adopted by a regiment when found as a baby among the hills. She grows up to be a regular tomboy. Her first experience of pash comes when she falls for a young smuggler whom she helps escape from the guardhouse of the regiment.

A countess is dining with the officers of the regiment and discovers the girl to be her long-lost niece. She takes her with her to Paris and there the girl again meets the youth. It is disclosed that he is an officer in disguise spying on the smugglers.

Hans Behrendt does wonders as a director. Support includes Alexander D'Arcy as the juvenile and Kurt Gerron in a comedy role.   *Trask.*

MELODY LANE

(All Dialog)

Universal production and release. Starring Eddie Leonard. Adaptation from "The Understander"; play by Jo Swerling, directed by Robert F. Hill; adaptation by Hill and J. G. Hawkes (also credited for screen play and dialog). Bert Fiske synchronized; Joseph Brotherton, camera; Maurice Pivar, supervisor; C. Roy Hunter, recording supervisor; Johanna Mathieson, costumes; Western Electric recording; special songs by Eddie Leonard and Jake Stern. Opened twice daily run July 15, at the Globe, New York, at $2 top.

Des Dupree	Eddie Leonard
Dolores Dupree	Josephine Dunn
Juan Rinaldi	Huntly Gordon
Danny Kay	George E. Stone
Constance Dupree	Jane La Verne Rose Coe

At the most would-be sentimental portion of Eddie Leonard's "Melody Lane," where he is singing the over-plugged "Lovable" theme song to his Wonderful (baby girl-child), the picture becomes the most laughable. An all dialog talker with songs, it's perhaps the poorest of the big league production attempts at the backstage stuff. It looks as if Eddie Leonard in person with his Prolog (New Acts) should travel with this one in the theatres.

An almost outdated theme now, what with the talkers developing and progressing in leaps and bounds, the small-time vaudeville yarn is not especially bolstered by Universal treatment.

The story itself is a mess. To begin with—in itself something the film editor might have elided—it is credited that Jo Swerling's play, "The Understander," was the basis for this concoction. Obviously, the original "understander" had to do with an acrobatic theme. Here, Dupree and Dupree (man and wife), with their child, Constance, completing the trio of principal characters, are a small time song and dance team.

Eddie Leonard works chiefly in white face. He only dons the cork for the song specialties. The continuity is replete with blatant discrepancies. The general whole is merely a female "Sonny Boy," even unto Leonard singing his Connie (Sunny Girl) into convalescence in the sick-room.

Why and how Universal yanked "Broadway" out of the Globe, where that picture took a rise in gross last week, and shoved this one is another of the ceaseless film mysteries. And at $2!

And maybe the deadheads didn't smell this one, although in seeming deference to the venerable minstrel man they stuck it out sturdily. Leonard himself wasn't bad, although physically, sans the cork, working chiefly in whiteface in the most dramatic portions, it was a mistake to couple him up with the beauteous Josephine Dunn as his partner-wife. The Dunn gal registered despite the grave shortcomings in general.

Primarily, of course, it was story and direction damage. From the very start inconsistencies asserted themselves, such as spotting a dog act in the body of the vaudeville bill and ringing down the screen for the picture exhibition (in the same theatre set) whereas one has seen the annunciator with two more acts yet to follow Dupree and Dupree. In the kids' party set, with Eddie ingratiating himself onto the premises with an excuse to the hostess that he likes children and would be pleased to amuse them extemporaneously, his songs are picked up by a visible orchestra. Its utter implausibility, of course, is blatant.

The musical background against the dialog sequences is something else again the picture people are currently eliminating in their current productions. Here in the sick-room, Leonard warbles "Beautiful" in a supposedly hushed room, in the midst of a crisis, with an off-screen orchestra doing the accompaniment.

There have been instances, of course, as with Jolson doing it similarly in "The Singing Fool," or Charlie King dueting "You Were Meant For Me" in the hotel room (in "Broadway Melody") but aside from these being somewhat pioneering instances, it was a case where either the personality or the story development so dominated everything else it was pleasurably accepted as theatrical license.

There's plenty more. One never heard a theatrical impresario on this earth as Huntley Gordon plays him when he utters fancy phrases such as being "de trop" and "unspeakable perfidy." That comes up in the Pagliacci stuff when Miss Dunn, as his new star, can't go on because Connie has been hurt in a fall.

There's the "Ivanhoe" parable also which consumes fully two reels, possibly more, of long-winded, negatively accepted footage. It's here that Leonard is visualized by the almost impossibly precocious Constance (baby girl) as her knight out of Sir Walter Scott—which too is kinda tough to take considering the veteran Mr. Leonard.

There are a couple of bright moments, strictly gag stuff, that registered, and only because it was mechanical cross-fire and a click with the wise first-nighters. One had to do with Connie asking her dream-knight's "henchman" if he was going back to the Palace and he replied: "No, I'm playing at the Orpheum this week."

And, of course, the usual "poor old Eddie is getting old" was some more inside stuff. He even pulls that in a song, "I'm On My Way," both in the picture and in the prolog.

"Melody Lane" will have a better chance with Leonard making personal appearances with his prolog. It runs 25 minutes. In the other stands Eddie Leonard's name will likely take care of the draw. He has a strong rep as a minstrel man.

Abel.

TWIN BEDS

(All Dialog)

First National production and release. Western Electric disk system. Credited with being based on play by Salisbury Fields and Margaret May. Directed by Al Santell. At Strand week July 13. Running time: about 70 minutes.

Danny Brown	Jack Mulhall
Elsie Dolan	Patsy Ruth Miller
Monty Solari	Armand Kaliz
Mrs. Solari	Gertrude Astor
Pa Dolan	Knute Erickson
Ma Dolan	Edythe Chapman
Mazie Dolan	Jocelyn Lee
Bobby Dolan	Nita Martan
Tillie	Zasu Pitts
Red Trapp	Eddie Gribbon
Pete Trapp	Ben Hendricks
Jason Treejohn	Carl Levinnes
Mrs. Treejohn	Alice Lake

"Twin Beds" is a mild little thing, way too long, with most of the dialog leaning to the "tell it to the Marines" vintage. The Strand matinee crowd, particularly the women, sprinkled it with laughs. Based on the old legit comedy, the seasoned hubby getting into the groom's bed, calls out all of the old domestic situations. Director Santell doesn't try to change any of them, but just lets things plug along in established slapstick manner without modern veneer. It'll do okay on the average program, especially the daily change.

Jack Mulhall parts company with Dorothy Mackaill in this one for Patsy Ruth Miller. As one of three phone operating sisters who know their out-of-town customers, Miss Miller plays without the Mackaill flash, but with pleasing sexy conservatism.

The rather worn line of ditching a frisky boyfriend, wrenching her ankle in the leap from the taxi and bumping into the office of Danny Brown, songwriter, by mistake is used for the hook-up. Danny's new musical brings in the w. k. backstage and girlies in rehearsal once more.

Armand Kaliz as Monty Solari, leading man, and Zasu Pitts as Tillie, the newlyweds' dumb maid are the chief laugh provokers.

Incidentally the script is so arranged as to overwork the theme song. First Armand sings it in rehearsal and again on a record in his apartment. Then Mulhall renders it in the Dolan home where some good Irish wit is recorded. When the leading man gets drunk and starts the bed business a substitute, not credited in the screen cast, pipes it off again.

Waly.

SCARLET PIMPERNEL

(BRITISH-MADE)

(Silent)

Produced by British and Dominion Film Corp. Distributed by World Pictures. Directed by T. Hayes Hunter. Story from a best seller novel of some years ago by Baroness Orczy. No further credits given. Running time, 76 minutes. At Little Carnegie Playhouse, New York, week July 6.

Sir Percy Blakeney	Matheson Lang
Lady Blakeney	Margaret Hume
Robespierre	Nelson Keys
Tallien	Madden Mason
Theresia	Juliette Compton
Rateau	Douglas Payne
Finville	Harold Huth

An improvement on the general run of British-mades, but still an indifferent picture by American standards. Best passages are the well managed mob effects in the latter footage. Come to think of it, all these pictures made abroad do well with mass effects. They excel in pageantry, but they never seem to manipulate the situation background to get the dramatic punch in the stage picture. Just a sure seater prospect without a chance of general release on this side.

This is a particularly good example. Good direction and stage management nullified by a poor handling of the script. "The Scarlet Pimpernel" as a novel had a world of picture material. Here it is disposed without dramatic judgment.

Early sequences are very dull, moving sluggishly. Planting is laboriously done and multiplicity of characters is confusing. Character of Tallien is a sad bit of miscasting. From the beginning one gets the impression Hadden Mason's Tallien is going to be a semi-comedy role. Instead it develops into the second lead and actually takes the central interest away from the hero toward the end. Robespierre turns out to be a sort of character old man, instead of the sinister demon of history. You never get over the feeling that Matheson Lang, the hero, is going to break out in a tenor solo or something of the kind.

Build-up to the climax is all wrong. They have tried to compass the whole book into the last few minutes. Result is chaos. Hero's wife is a prisoner at Robespierre's mercy and they leave her there while attention is directed at 10 different other angles. When these have been settled they bring you back to her and get her rescued in a perfunctory manner as a sort of afterthought. Probable reason is that they went a bit dizzy in building up of the mob effects, regarding them as a dramatic end in themselves, rather than as elements in support of the underlying dramatic situation.

Acting of the two women is the best detail. Both are beautiful, but they lose effect of contrast. Margaret Hume is lovely in costume of the 18th century revolution period, playing the wife of the hero. Juliette Compton is equally beautiful as the Robespierre spy. But both are delicately modeled brunets and in rapid action not always distinguishable.

Finally it is a costume play and stories of that kind are for the moment out of public favor over here.

Rush.

THE PAUL ST. BOYS

(HUNGARIAN MADE)

(Silent)

Produced by Bela Balogh in Budapest. Story by Ferenc Molnar, with screen adaptation supervised by the noted foreign playwright. In cast Laszlo Gyarfas, Geza Berczy, Erno Verebes, I. Mattyasovsky, Imre Kis and cast of Hungarian boys. At 55th St. Playhouse, New York, week July 15 as half double bill. Running time, 60 minutes.

Inconsequential effort to prove that the kid gangs in Budapest are no different than those in the slum districts of New York or elsewhere. Some of those playing kid parts in this flicker look as if they shave every morning. Inane titling, streaky photography and poor lighting make this one a weak entry even for the sure seaters.

Action is mainly confined to the preparatory efforts of the Paul St. gang to resist the attack on their stronghold of their rivals, the Redshirts.

The Paul streeters dress up for the battle wearing striped shirts and get an elderly man to dig their trenches. The Redshirts wear distinctive caps and look like boy scouts going through maneuvers. The battle in which long wooden spears are used by both sides winds up with nobody hurt.

The kid with a bad cold, and the only member of the Paul St. boys who is a private in the ranks, proved his bravery in the fight. On his deathbed he is proclaimed a hero and made a captain.

All the boys in the film seem private school boys trying to look and act military, and be tough in a nice way. Acting is along the accepted Continental style, overboard with mugging.

PLEASURE CRAZED

(ALL DIALOG)

Fox production and release. Scenario by Douglas Doty from Monckton Hoffe's play, "Scent of Sweet Almonds." Directed by Donald Gallaher. Charles Klein, pictorial director. Clare Kummer's dialog. Marguerite Churchill and Kenneth MacKenna featured. At Roxy, New York, week of July 13. Running time, 60 minutes.

Nora Westby	Marguerite Churchill
Captain Anthony Dean	Kenneth MacKenna
Alma Dean	Dorothy Burgess
Gilbert Ferguson	Campbell Gullan
Nigel Blain	Douglas Gilmore
Colonel Farquar	Henry Kolker
Holland	Frederick Graham
Peters	Rex Bell
Maid	Charlotte Merriam

Box office title on a fair all-talker. Society love quadrangle, involving a cheating wife, a good girl who loves the c. w.'s honest husband, and the c. w.'s fickle lover. Mixed in is a crook story, to make it tough enough for the good girl, who loves the c. w.'s husband.

The good girl is a bad girl in a thieving way, but not of her own free will. She's forced into the lift racket by a couple of mugs who gained her confidence by playing kind. But she can't keep it up and go through with the final job, because she's fallen for the proposed victim.

An auto chase winds it up.

Most important is the joint performance rendered by the erstwhile legit people in the cast. Marguerite Churchill, the good girl who was bad through circumstances for some or another doesn't look as well as she did in "The Valiant."

Kenneth MacKenna. No Adonis, while not really bad looking, has a voice that will make you forget all else. He sings the words in his own way, and it's a dramatic way of talking that sails over forcefully.

Dorothy Burgess, as the two-timey wife, delivers another favorable job, much as she did in "In Old Arizona," and this time in an altogether different sort of role.

Balance of the people generally good. Campbell Gullan rates notice for his Limey con man.

Donald Gallaher is billed as director, though Charles Klein is on the sheet also as "Pictorial Director." That possibly means Gallaher directed the film in its entirety while Klein supervised the picture taking end. Gallaher timed his situations and connecting movements effectively.

One title in the picture, the only one, stands out in this film like Hornsby in the National League. It reads, "One Week Later." The following action doesn't need the explantation. Change of costume and attitude by the characters denotes sufficient flight of time. *Bige.*

DANGEROUS CURVES

(ALL DIALOG)

Paramount picture and release: Starring Clara Bow. Directed by Lothar Mendes. Story by Lester Cohen. Adaptation by Donald Davis and Florence Ryerson. Dialog by Viola Brothers Shore. Running time 78 minutes. At the Paramount, New York, week July 13.

Pat Delaney....................Clara Bow
Larry Lee....................Richard Arlen
Zara Flynn....................Kay Francis
Tony Barretti....................David Nowell
Col. P. P. Brock..........Anders Randolph
"Ma" Spinelli....................May Boley
"Pa" Spinelli................T. Roy Barnes
Jennie Silver..................Joyce Compton
"Spider"....................Chas. D. Brown
First Rotarian....................Stuart Erwin
Second Rotarian....................Jack Luden

New chapter in the Clara Bow career promises well. Fans had begun to tire of this star in the heavily featured flaming sex appeal role as reflected in the returns on her last release, but renewed interest greets this experiment of casting her in a sympathetic character role of a good deal of sentimental force.

Background of the circus is good atmosphere for her character of the big top waif. The story has first rate incidental comedy angles leading up to the finish that has her performing a thrill stunt for the punch finale.

Story gives her a clean cut legitimate characterization to work with, widely different from the hilarious and slightly goofy flapper parts that have been her lot lately. She's a roughneck kid, without elegance or artifice, but with a heart of gold. The rowdy side of the character serves to supply well timed comedy touches that blend effectively as contrast to sentimental bits.

It's all away from screen formula in its jaunty, casual handling of a light romantic theme. A circus story that avoids heavy emphasis on the dramatic side is a novelty. Here the usual glorification of the sawdust world is taken from a slightly satirical angle. Trick of coloring even the sentimental scenes with comedy shadings is used skillfully even to the extent of flavoring the final clinch with a surprise laugh.

It's a picture that grown-ups can sit through and get something out of and that hasn't been uniformly true of the Bow stories so far. Dialog is the best this star has had, partly because the character of the untutored little tomboy of the circus fits neatly into the mannerisms of Miss Bow, who somehow never could quite make herself convincing as a collegiate or most other straight polite personage. On the basis of this production it would seem that she will now pass on from the flippant flap type of jazzy ingenue to a new specialty as sentimental gamine.

Picture is not strong on dramatic force, retain highly colored acting scenes for the star taking the place of that element. Kid wants to become a wire walker and worships the young man who does the high wire act with the show. He is going to pieces through the faithlessness of the woman he loves, his partner in the act. When she deserts him, he goes to the bad, is coaxed back to the show by the girl and gradually without knowing it is encouraged to get on his feet again. All these things she does by artifice without leting the boy know her solicitude and in the end he realizes that she has saved him from ruin and so forth.

Dramatic highlight is rather hard to take for the show wise. Boy is drunk in his dressing room when it is time for him to go on with the act. Girl puts on his clown makeup and costume and takes his place in the daredevil feats aloft, sacrificing thereby her chance to win a feature spot in the show for herself. *Rush.*

BLUE SKIES

(Silent)

Fox production and release. Directed by Alfred Werker from Frederick Brennan's story adapted by John Stone. Helen Twelvetrees and Frank Albertson, featured. Titles by M. S. Boylan. At Lowe's, New York, one day, July 8. Running time, 60 minutes.

"Blue Skies" is Fox's kid version of "Over the Hill." It's about an orphan asylum instead of a poorhouse, with none of the tears the adult orphan picture possessed. Just simple, slow, mildly satisfying entertainment for the average house.

Youngsters occupy a reel with close-ups and ice cream. Hack situations of turning the hose on the matron, the fat boy getting a licking by the little boy for eating the tiny girl's ice cream—they're all in it.

Then of a sudden it's Frank Albertson wearing overalls and Helen Twelvetrees, the girl. The kids around them are still as young as they were in the first reel, excepting one or two.

A rich daddy visits the home and Frank changes his foundling dress for that of the girl's. Off she goes to the wealthy home.

Of course a year later an identification card is found, but Frank satisfies daddy and the girl. Marriage does it.

If the pictures were all like this one censors would be renting wooden legs. *Waly.*

LE BLED

(FRENCH MADE)

(Silent)

Paris, July 6.

"Le Bled" is best translated as a part of the Algerian wilderness. Action is laid in Algeria and the title is excellent for the local audience. Picture has been produced by the Societe des Films Historiques and trade showed last week. It is a dramatic novelette, though some parts are much too long.

Pierre Hofer is a sympathetic young beau, but broke. He goes to visit his uncle, wealthy planter, in Algeria.

On the steamer he meets Claudie Duvernet. Claudie is en route to Algiers to collect a big inheritage from a deceased uncle.

On her arrival the heiress is met on the pier by her cousins, Manuel Duvernet and his sister, Diane. These worthy relatives had organized a scheme to deprive Claudie of her fortune. But Pierre is watching over her. His adventures form the basis of this romantic effusion. Fairly nice reel, with interesting scenery, particularly the hunt in the desert. Mlle Jackie Monier is Claudie, and Henrique Rivero, Pierre. Arquilliere and Diana Hart in the cast.

Popular product for popular publics. *Light.*

FECDUNDITY

(FRENCH MADE)

(Silent)

Paris, July 10.

French film company Mappemonde has a screen version of Emile Zola's book "Fecondite." Story happens to be patriotic and exemplary, inasmuch that it preconizes progeny. Folks who try to keep to one, or even none, point out to others the beauties of large families. In any case this picture is bound to be popular.

A wealthy manufacturer, Beauchamp, is not living on the best of terms with his wife. He is not a faithful husband. They have but one child, son, Maurice. Their cousin, Blaise, has 10, and a very happy family, in their country home.

Blaise's eldest son is an engineer and works in Beauchamp's factory. Maurice, only son and heir, is in delicate health.

On fine night, while whoopeeing in a fashionable Parisian cabaret, he falls into the swimming pool, gets pneumonia and dies. Parents are broken hearted. Too afflicted to attend to business Beauchamp leaves everything to the young engineer (his cousin's son), who however, is killed in an accident.

Having no one to inherit his fortune the manufacturer offers the job in the factory to Blaise's second son, who thus takes the place of his late brother.

Meanwhile Mme. Beauchamp has become insane, and her husband looks for consolation in the slums with girls and drink, in the conventional Zola style.

This deep, but austere plot is trimmed with a love romance between another of the Blaise boys and the daughter of a neighbor. The youngsters get married and have twins the first year. The grief of the family is partly alleviated by this event.

The production is interesting, enhanced by a capable realization signed by Etievant and Evreinoff. Photo work, lighting effects and sets O. K.

In the cast may be specially chronicled Andre Lafayette, Gabriel Gabrio, Albert Prejean, Michele Verly, Ravet and Diana Karene, all appreciated on European screens. *Light.*

COME ACROSS

(10% DIALOG)

Universal production and release. Starring Lina Basquette. Directed by Roy Taylor. Adapted by Peter Milne from story, "The Stolen Lady," by William Dudley Pelley. In cast: Reed Howes, Flora Finch, Crauford Kent. At Loew's New York, one day, July 12, as half double bill. Running time, 60 minutes.

Romantic story of a long Island society girl who passes up a season at Palm Beach to study sociology and falls in love with a playwright who is posing as a crook in order to get local color for his drama. Story requires an elastic imagination but on the whole is fair wired grind double bill material.

Mary Houston (Lina Basquette) walks out on her society suitor and gets a job in a night club as a dancer. Owner of the joint, big time crook, plotting a 20 grand touch, gets Mary to join his mob, she thereby hoping to reform Harry (Reed Howes) one of the boys.

Needing a swell front for the proposed job, the mob takes possession of the Houston home without knowing the house is the girl's regular residence during the summer.

Blowoff comes when Mary gets her suitor to pose as the millionaire who is to be framed. He, disgusted with the whole affair and jealous of Mary's apparent growing affection for the young crook, tips off the cops.

When the gendarmes bust in the real crooks are grabbed and the dicks inform the girl that the man she loves is not a crook but a playwright who continually gets into jams while searching for dramatic material. While somewhat disappointed in not having grabbed herself someone to reform, nevertheless she goes into the necessary clinch.

Plenty of action. Musical score consists mainly of variation on "Girl of My Dream," pop tune of a few years ago.

Six minutes of dialog at the end of the flicker.

From Headquarters

(60% DIALOG)

Warner Bros. production and release. Directed by Howard Bretherton. Story by Samuel Hartridge. Scenario by Harvey Gates. Monte Blue starred. Titles by Joseph Starr. Cameraman, William Rees. Synchronized by Western Electric-Vitaphone. At Loew's Circle, New York, one day, July 12.

Happy Smith....................Monte Blue
Sergeant Wilmer..........Guinn Williams
Mary Dyer..............Gladys Brockwell
Senor Corroles..............Lionel Belmore
Buffalo Ryan............Henry B. Walthall
Private Murphy..............Eddie Gribbon
Innocencia....................Ethlyne Clair
Spike Connelly..............Pat Hartigan
O'Farrell....................John Kelly
Bugs McGuire....................Otto Lederer
Major....................Joseph Girard
Fritz....................William Irving
Hendricks....................Pat Somerset

A heavy wham bang on the old imagination to believe that a tiny infant, a baby girl not long in the hectic world, could be carried through a jungle inferno, survive storms, escape fevers, endure hardships and privations that shuffle off a leatherneck of the U. S. Marines with rebels and bandits lying in ambush—and arrive at headquarters apparently o. k. And at the finish two of the surviving band of marines invading that raging hellhole were staggering and reeling like drunken men, later shown in the hospital as having much to be thankful for in their terrible jungle excursion to rescue a mining party.

Only the baby was left of the party and it was rescued in a manner that took the heart out of the adult rescuers. If the audiences can really stand for that bit of film license then "From Headquarters" is a good picture.

While Monte Blue was immense as the derelict guide, acted well his part and talked himself into screen credit, the work of Guinn Williams as the hardboiled sarge and Joseph Girard as the marine major were highlights.

Of the women only two had anything to do. Miss Brockwell really had a bit but worked hard to make it stand up under talker fire. Miss Claire was the tropical girl who loved Happy Smith despite his drunkenness; not much in the way of big climaxes but withal satisfactory.

Photographically this one was a remarkable specimen of camera work. Apparently not a blemish on the Circle's screen.

Talker carries a dramatic punch barring the terrible stretch of imagination as to the baby. *Mark.*

A SOLDIER'S WIFE
(RUSSIAN MADE)
(Silent)

Berlin, July 1.

"The Wife of a Soldier" (Derussa-Sovkino), premiere at Beba Atrium. Almost everything that the Russians turn out today has some quality that interests. Here Emma Zessarskaja proves herself an actress of real emotional power and she has beauty of a quiet classic sort.

This is a not particularly stimulating story about a peasant girl who marries against her will and never learns to love her husband. His leaving for war awakens no emotion in her.

Later on an Austrian prisoner is commissioned to work her land for her and she is strongly attracted to him. The two live together for several years until the man leaves to become a communistic agitator.

The woman's husband has become an officer in the white, anti-revolutionary troops. He returns one day to the village, raping and mishandling his wife who flees for help to her lover. The latter returns to avenge her, but is shot by the husband.

The direction by Strischack and Posnanskiji, two young Russians, is in the best Soviet tradition and is simple, natural and unforced.

Trask.

German Pics

Berlin, July 15.

"The Last Eagle"

"The Last Eagle" (Ufa), premiere at the Universum. No doubt about it, the Swedish naturalist, Bengt Berg, who made this film is a real personality. His lecture in broken German is full of comedy.

A physical giant of pleasing appearance, he begins his sentences in a deep bass and trails off to a comic falsetto. It is to be supposed that his accent would be just as amusing in English. If this is so, he should get over nicely in the States if well handled. Without him, the present picture is not an evening-filling entertainment. His witty comment is what put it across.

Very few eagles left in the world, as they are robbers of the air and considered fair game for any dumbbell with a musket. Berg defends them in this picture. He has taken infinite pains to photograph them from all angles, even going up into the air with a plane to follow their flight. A novelty are the pictures of the daily life of the young birds in their nest, and these were only acquired by setting up a tree next to that on which the nest was built.

No doubt that the birds, for all their unpleasantness, have majesty and dignity.

"Women My Weakness"

"Women Are My Weakness" (Mondial-Film), premiere at the Titania Palast. Average German comedy helped out by the eccentric humor of Hans Albers. If this player gets the right kind of scenario, he might develop into a draw.

In a banking firm, the son of one partner, Bing, is fired because he can't keep away from S. A. That does not worry him much, for he becomes a film star overnight. Lilly, daughter of the other partner, now falls for him and arranges a rendezvous, pretending she is a maid. He engages her as his chauffeur and she manages to muss up all his dates with fems. Without

learning her identity, he marries her and sets off for America to fulfill a Hollywood contract.

In the female lead Georgia Lind does not develop much, and the rest of the cast is so-so. May just squeezed by in Germany.

"Eroticism"

"Eroticism" (Star Film), premiere in the Capitol.

Undoubtedly this brilliant title will get the film by, although, surprisingly enough, films with sex monakers did not stand up among the first 30 in the list of successes last season. Otherwise it is just a cheaply thrown together bunch of hooey.

The daughter of the station master falls for the elegant traveling salesman, who immediately deserts her. She leaves home and follows in the footsteps of the Margaret Saenger Club. She is rescued by a passing juvenile from an attempted rape by a cab driver. She marries the young man, out of gratitude, but when she meets the traveling salesman later on, again is taken in by his villainous wiles. While visiting him one day, the husband of a married woman he has seduced shoots him and commits suicide himself. The girl realizes the error of her ways and she returns to hubby.

Olaf Fjord is the sexy salesman, but seems to have about as little electricity as any leading man on view for some period. The dames don't go for him. *Trask.*

"Love of Rott Brothers"

"The Love of the Rott Brothers" (Derussa), premiere Marmorhaus. Olga Tschechova's second starring venture on her own has panned out considerably better than her first effort. The direction of Erik Waschneck is well above the present German average and the scenario, if not original, is well put together and builds to an effective climax.

Two peasant families live side by side and Robert, the oldest son of one, is set to marry Theresa, the daughter of the other. But the youth is shy and never gets to the popping point. His younger brother, Wolf, who is a sailor, returns for a short vacation, and the girl soon is attracted by him and promises to wait until he returns again and then marry him. The two fathers do everything in their power to influence her to take Robert, but she is adamant. Then nothing is heard from Wolf for a year and it is rumored that he has been shipwrecked. But the girl still insists upon waiting.

Robert's father, with the aid of a shyster lawyer, gets a faked announcement of Wolf's death. After some months Theresa marries Robert and, although not at first liking him, comes to really love him. Meantime the shyster lawyer has been blackmailing the father. One day, in a moment of rage, he shoots the swindler, and himself falls over a precipice. On returning home, the girl finds that Wolf has returned. She is suspected of the murder but acquitted. Realizing that the girl now loves Robert, Wolf goes back to the sea again.

The star turns in a splendid performance and is well supported by Paul Henckels, Jameson Thomas and Ekkehard Arendt. Sure fire for the provinces.

"When Lilacs Bloom"

"When the Lilacs Bloom Again" (Bayrische Film), premiere at Marmorhaus.

Using the title of one of the most popular of German song hits, this picture seems set for a successful

career in Germany. At least, it is splendidly photographed and has two engaging young people in the leads, Vera Schmitterloew and Walter Grueters.

Film opens with some beautiful shots of spring on the Rhine. Audience often applauded these and they will be liked anywhere.

The story suffices without being anything to throw a rave about. It concerns a young man who photographs a girl looking out of a lilac bush without either he or she realizing it occurred.

When the picture is developed he is enchanted and tries to find her, but without success. Finally he publishes the picture on a poster and offers a reward for information about her.

The girl's father, an old aristocrat, is in financial difficulties and is helped out by a jeweller who wants to marry the girl. Meantime the girl has seen the poster and in order to help a poor old woman allows her to get the reward. The jeweller learns of the love of the two, etc.

DR. FU MANCHU
(ALL DIALOG)

Paramount production and release. Directed by Rowland V. Lee. Neil Hamilton, Jean Arthur, Warner Oland and O. P. Heggie, featured. From story by Sax Rohmer. Screen play and dialog by Florence Ryerson and Lloyd Corrigan, with comedy dialog interpolations by George Marion, Jr. At Rialto, New York, July 20, on daily grind, indef. Running time 80 minutes.

Dr. Fu Manchu..............Warner Oland
Lia Eltham.................Jean Arthur
Dr. Petrie.................Neil Hamilton
Nayland Smith.............O. P. Heggie
Sylvester Wadsworth......William Austin
Sir John Petrie...........Claude King
General Petrie...........Charles Stevenson
Li Po.....................Noble Johnson
Fai Lu.....................Evelyn Selbie
Weymouth.................Charles Giblyn
Trent...................Donald MacKenzie
Clarkson................Lawrence Davidson
Fu Mela....................Lask Winter
Singh....................Charles Stevens
Rev. Mr. Eltham..........Chappel Dosset
Chinese Ambassador........Tully Marshall

A first class mystery story, shrewdly built up with new twists of the familiar devices, rich in surprises and suspense and splendidly acted and produced. It has all the punch the mystery technique tries for but only occasionally obtains as here. Picture has merits from many angles such as interesting bizarre atmosphere, attractive romance and neat touches of contrasting comedy. Certain for b. o., where mystery draws.

Opens fast action, capital example of preparation that stands on its own dramatic feet. At the first go-off, British Legation in Pekin is under assault of Boxer hordes during the rebellion. Good sequence of battle stuff realistically staged on a big scale. One of the officials, anticipating massacre, sends his little daughter to the protection of a friendly Chinese noble, Dr. Fu Manchu. Englishman is killed as soon as his object is accomplished, the child safe with Dr. Fu.

Presently the Allies enter the town. Another chance for flag waving here is used, with views of the American marines moving up to the relief. Rebels take refuge in Fu's garden. In the ensuing attack by English troops, Fu's wife and son are slain. Whereupon the Oriental swears revenge on the white foreign devils.

All this slam-bang action. Years later it is made plain that the same Dr. Fu is on the trail of Sir John, who commanded the English in Pekin, having disposed of all the other white commanders by subtle murder in pursuit of his oath to wipe out the men who robbed him of his family.

Scotland Yard warns Sir John, and his son and seeks to protect them from the yellow peril, as the play traces the insidious schemes of the China master mind to gain his end. He has brought up the white girl left in his charge and by putting her in a trance, has her carry out his designs. He brings about a meeting between the girl and Sir John's son; schemes to have her introduced into Sir John's seashore castle and then begins to close in on his victim.

Usual mysterious passages, ghostly apparitions and grisly happenings of mystery stories occur, but here they always have an air of reality instead of the trick magic. One by one the minor people are killed off by mysterious and horrifying means, as the doom approaches the nobleman's son, who is seeking to save the girl.

It all works up to a pip of a melodramatic climax, the English boy in the Oriental's power and the outlook dark, when a sudden twist brings all right.

Punch of the picture is its speed and sustained suspense. One excellent sequence is laid in the Chinese quarter of Limehouse district, London. Eerie bits in dives and dim water front settings, capitally managed for effect.

Picture discloses a fine cast of

articulate players, notably Neil Hamilton as the young lead, Claude King as Sir John, and Warner Oland, who alone seems to be able to make an Oriental heavy believable.

As an illustration of the care in casting, Tully Marshall plays a straight role as a Chinese diplomat and does it with his unfailing finish. Jean Arthur makes an appealing heroine, a girl who can act and handle lines without overplaying.

Flawless performance all around, with special tribute also to O. P. Heggie, who plays an English detective extremely well by the simple expedient of acting human and natural.

William Austin has one of his effeminate roles, which supplies the comedy in judiciously measured quantities.

Production is as lavish in settings as it is in player names. Oriental interiors are good atmosphere; scenes in and around the ancient castle are novel and striking.

As good a mystery play as Conan Doyle's "Sign of the Four" was a novel. "Dr. Fu," by the way, resembles the Doyle novel strongly in form and substance. *Rush.*

WONDER OF WOMEN

(40% DIALOG)

Metro-Goldwyn-Mayer production and release. Directed by Clarence Brown from Bess Meredyth's adaptation of a Herman Suderman novel. Western Electric sounded. In cast: Lewis Stone, Leila Hyams, Peggy Wood, George Fawcett, Harry Myers, Sarah Padden. At Capitol, New York, week July 20. Running time, 95 minutes.

Paramount made a concert pianist out of Adolph Menjou before they let him go, and Metro has done the first thing with Lewis Stone in "Wonder of Women." The only difference between the pictures is that Menjou's was in the Paramount two weeks ago and didn't try to be serious. The Stone thing is a rambling mess that gets an audience squirming in seats the second of a half dozen times a fitting finis presents itself.

Metro could capitalize on two dramatic sequences. These, however, are strictly Peggy Wood's. Stone has never pretended to be a Menjou, and the shearing of considerable of this stuff would bring him nearer to type and make this less lethargic for every house that projects it.

The story has a German locale with the railroad exterior Metro built for "Old Heidelberg" worked overtime, but interestingly. German street and water scenes, particularly the village where the Tromholts (Stone-Wood) live, are attractive.

As the great player, Stone is allowed to open by Director Brown, surrounded by a bevy of women on a train. A simple one passing in the corridor catches his eye and he hoofs away to dine with her, misses his concert station for the evening and, before the sun has set, sung his theme song, proposed and accepted.

The home scenes are the best, about all the production has to offer. The widow's three kiddies, all bright youngsters with plenty of appeal, will get the women in any theatre.

The theme, an excellent one if compact, runs away. It takes the roundabout route to tell the truism that most folks are always hungering for independence.

Stone may be able to sing, but he will have a tough time in convincing.

Miss Wood sustains what sympathy there is. Her first piece of excellent acting is when she returns home, after finding her husband unfaithful, and sees a crepe on the door. The pianist who had been considering giving her the air, for the first time of numerous times following, is halted by a wire announcing the sudden death of his favorite step-child.

The child is scarcely buried when Dad, although sub-titles indicate a long time lapse, drifts back to his girl friend, played by the pretty Leila Hyams. He is returning home to break with his wife. Her arising from bed, when the doctor, a bit part played by George Fawcett, expects her to die within an hour, arouses more skepticism and dulls the real dramatic edge this situation could have possessed.

In the death scene the wife again weakens the climax by dialoging nearly all that had been related in the sub-titles and the action. *Waly.*

LUCKY STAR

(40% DIALOG)

Fox production and release. Co-featuring Janet Gaynor and Charles Farrell. Frank Borzage directed, from story by Tristram Tupper. Dialog by John Hunter Booth. Titled and edited by Katharine Hilliker and H. H. Caldwell. Adaptation by Sonya Levien; Lew Borzage, assistant director. Sounded by W. E. (Movietone) equipment. Runs 85 minutes at Roxy, New York, week July 20.

Timothy Osborn............Charles Farrell

Mary Tucker.................Janet Gaynor

Ma Tucker................Hedwiga Reicher

Martin Wrenn...Guin "Big Boy" Williams

Joe ....Paul Fix

Flora ....Gloria Grey

Pop Fry....................Hector V. Sarno

Indifferent picture, bound to create a division of opinion as to its merits and box-office strength. It has the same appeal of psychological healing as in "The Miracle Man," without any healer actually figuring. Yet when the climatic physical regeneration of Charles Farrell, as a war-shattered victim, occurs, one portion of the audience is carried way by the dramatics and is applauding, while the majority is tittering unsympathetically.

A prime fault is its length. Yet there are times, despite Frank Borzage's painstaking devotion to detail and character painting, that the sluggish unfolding is barely noticed. These are the picture's strongest moments, of course.

"Lucky Star" is Borzage's first talker production. The director, with Janet Gaynor and Farrell, clicked twice before with "Seventh Heaven" and "Street Angel," both silents, excepting for the synchronized score and the theme songs. Miss Gaynor has not done any dialog but for the added talker sequences to "Four Devils," and, for that reason, many may regard this release as her first dialog production.

The femme lead has a wistfully appealing voice, while her co-star, Farrell, lacks linguistically. His is a strident, high-pitched address, not quite in keeping with his characterization, while Miss Gaynor, cast as Baa-Baa, the black sheep, is too Vassar in her inflections. And, of course, a "Black Sheep" theme song.

The last 25 minutes (about 40 per cent.) of this 85-minute exhibition include dialog and various sound effects, such as the phonograph music, choo-choo train, and attendant noises produced by physical motion, such as when Farrell attempts locomotion on his war-paralyzed legs.

Sundry discrepancies crop ever and anon, forcefully counteracting the several niceties Borzage and his players evidence. A couple of highlights when Farrell falls off his crutches produce realistic shocks to the audience's collective nervous system, in sympathy with the pitiably struggling cripple who feels the handicap of his physical condition and endeavors to steel himself into action. It is this too realistic presentation of apparently hopeless recovery that reacts negatively for the climatic fisticuffs between Farrell and Guin "Big Boy" Williams, who does the light-heavy as a renegade ex-soldier.

There's another scene at the Halloween ball at the local hinterland Fireman's Hall, where dance music is produced by a crack Hollywood synchronizing orchestra which sounds as no Fireman's Hall band ever could.

"Lucky Star" could be helped by some speeding up through cutting, but it's still a poor programmer. *Abel.*

IN OLD SIBERIA

(Kartoga)
(RUSSIAN MADE)
(Silent)

Produced by Gosvojenkino, and released in U. S. by Amkino. Directed by J. Reisman from S. Yermolinsky's scenario. Titles revised for America by Shelley Hamilton. At Cameo week July 20. Running time, 70 minutes.

Chief Overseer, Chernyak.........V. Popoff

Old Warden, Peshehodov.........P. Tomm

Illya Bertz, Political..........A. Zgilinsky

Ostrobeylo, new Warden.........V. Taskin

Political Prisoner..............B. Lifanoff

If Russians ever get wise to story values and treatment, they can literally flood this market and still American box-offices will be open for more. They have the people and the atmosphere to make productions like "In Old Siberia" the most vivid and awe-inspiring. But when they inject a lot of absurd and misplaced comedy in themes supposed to be as dramatic as this one, and when they play the Soviet propaganda to the point where prisoners in the Czar's time can be insolent and get away with it—why, it's just too bad.

The picture gets under way like a winner. Blinding snow beating against prison walls with a number of German camera angles. Then a prisoner escaping; hounds, horses, rough faces and lamps. But there it stops. The inmate disappears, with no clue or answer found in the rest.

The thing resembles a lot of unrelated episodes. A group of gents reading mags, sleeping, and bulldozing the warden, a queer kind of comic. There are the politicals, obviously the ones fostering Sovietism.

Then the new warden, one V. Taskin, with a Napoleonic hand. Truly an eccentric actor as well as prison overseer. He laughs at convicts, orders them to church, and amuses himself playing a guitar when he is not on the make for a fat and slovenly greaseball of a housekeeper.

All the way through the direction and what is left of a story suggestion beat a tattoo that the political prisoners are being treated unjustly, although the action only once shows them picking salt, and then they mutiny. Eventually they are freed after a lot of repetitious camera juggling, during which the director seems to have taken the count. *Waly.*

PICCADILLY

(BRITISH MADE)
(With Gilda Gray)
(3% DIALOG)
(Sound Effects and Synchronized Score)

British International production released by World Wide over here. Gilda Gray starred. Anna May Wong featured. Directed by E. A. Dupont. Screen original by Arnold Bennett. Made at Elstreet studios, England. R. C. A. Photophone sounded. Camerman, Werner Brandes. At Little Carnegie Playhouse (sure seater), New York, week July 13. Running time, 92 minutes.

Mabel Greenfield ....Gilda Gray

Valentine Wilmot ....Jameson Thomas

Shosho ....Anna May Wong

Jim ....King Ho-Chang

Victor Smiles ....Cyril Ritchard

Bessie ....Hannah Jones

A Night Club Hawk ....Charles Laughton

A good picture that in the silent days could have made the deluxe first runs over here with its Gilda Gray name. It is virtually silent despite a useless prolog. It may have been added and contains its only dialog, badly done. Now it is playing on this side in company with the personal apeparance of Miss Gray, starred. The combination has been getting money. In present silent houses "Piccadilly" is okay for a week or a day, this due to Miss Gray's name, the story and Ada May Wong, who outshines the star.

Despite its clasification as a good silent, the finish is badly muddled and will operate against word of mouth publicity for it. If any of this finish was cut for the American showing, it was an error. Nothing but confusion remains. While "Piccadilly" may be the proper title for it in Great Britain and the colonies, a better name could have been slipped on for world wide distribution for this is one British made that can go around the world.

Though a British made, its two women leads are from the U. S. Miss Wong film originated in this country. Whether E. A. Dupont, its director, is German or French is unknown, but he's not English. So while a British made, it is not all English, which leaves the all-British picture making exactly as it has been.

Dupont has done nothing unusual in "Piccadilly." For the information of Americans, Piccadilly Circus, usually from its name to be a place of entertainment, is a lively night section of London, comparable to the Broadway running through Times Square in New York.

This Arnold Bennett story is set in a cabaret in Piccadilly at the time Charlie Cochran's "Year of Grace" smash was playing there. The Cochran revue is billed in the lights flashing out of Piccadilly.

The owner of the class joint digs up a chink dancer from the scullery. It's Miss Wong, a dish washer there whom the proprietor catches dancing for her companions, as he reaches the scullery through the help passing the buck as he investigates the source of a dirty plate given a patron who complained.

From the moment Miss Wong dances in the kitchen's rear, she steals "Piccadilly" from Miss Gray; in fact Miss Wong also steals Gilda's cooch. The Chinese girl inserts a cooch into her dancing while Gilda does not. It must have taken weeks to compromise on this at Elstree.

In the cabaret are a couple of ballroom dancers, with Miss Gray one of them. She's strong for the owner, while her partner is strong for her. The owner commences to go for the dancing girl. He eases out her partner on a pretext.

Business commences to fade and the house staff concludes the male dancer must have been the draw. With trade shot, the proprietor remembers the chink downstairs, calls her up and dresses her up, taking a long chance. She gets over, improves her clothes and rooms, but doesn't leave Limehouse.

Then the owner falls for the chink. She likes the idea, despite her Chinese lover who would correspond to a piano player over here, as he's the chink's uke accompanist.

Miss Gray as the remaining white dancer is so peeved over the entire affair she calls upon the Chinese dancer the same night the owner took the girl home to her new apartment, still in the Limey neighborhood.

The two women meet after the owner leaves. They have words. The audience apparently sees Miss Gray shoot Miss Wong, as the latter unsheathed a dagger. But at the inquest the Chinese lover, who tried to pin the crime on the owner, later shot himself and confessed he had done the killing, although Miss Gray previously on the stand had told the truth as she knew it of the shooting.

A switch back reveals how the chink boy shot his girl friend, after dragging her around the apartment in a jealous rage. It left the audience to decide just who did shoot and kill. It's not a finish that will create talk. No one particularly cares, but it just tosses overboard all of the value of the suspense until that time.

The Limeys and the Limehouse district hold as much attraction in their types for anywhere as any native alien slum characters would hold for the English.

Dialog in the prolog is the reason for the picture. One Englishman starts to tell another why he quit Piccadilly, and the story commences. The story could have started without Photophone, for either the dialog, music or sound. Sounding very poor, such as bell hop whistling, applause and table rattles. Music the usual medley of pop dance stuff, with the cabaret set about the best thing in production. This set is almost as massive and attractive in design as that one in Universal's "Broadway."

Looked a couple of times as though Dupont intended to freak the photography, but he didn't. Camera work on close up excellent, and favored Miss Wong in these more than Miss Gray.

"Blackmail," all English, got quite a boost in a London notice in Variety last week. It's coming over and if it's all English, let's see. But the English might take notice of "Piccadilly" and kinda think over how far a good story will send any picture. *Sime.*

SILENT SENTINEL

(SILENT)

Chesterfield production. Released by Capitol Film Exchange. Starring Gareth Hughes. Directed by Alvin J. Neitz. Cast includes: Josephine Hill, Walter Marley, Lew Meehan, Aline Goodwin and Alfred Hueston. Running time, 60 mins. One day, July 16, at the New York, New York.

Insipid. Dull. By way of indicating the grossest error in each department:

In point of story, a crooked banker would not be likely to make confederates of his butler, maid and chauffeur when he has a band of thieves under his direction. Again he would not execute the jobs himself.

In point of direction dogs have not nine lives, as the police pup in this case did. When a dog is shot, he rarely lies flat for ten minutes and then pursues a fleeing car from midnight until dawn. Again dogs don't answer telephone calls. Even this might have been justified by canine license, but the dog's prompter was in evidence as the pup fumbled.

In point of titling, the word inasmuch is not three words in the best circles. Photography makes picture hard to watch, and continuity is chaotic.

Story is of a banker who robs his own institution, placing the blame on his cashier. Another cashier is serving time for a like offense. A third cashier comes and is warned by the first cashier who escapes from prison. The sister of the hero, the second cashier, visits her boy friend, the third cashier, with Champion, a police dog. Dog and girl hide in bank and observe the bank president robbing the vault. Dog attacks him but is outwitted.

Third cashier gets police and they pursue the banker and his cronies in a police boat, as the thieves twin-screw for South America. Girl's brother released from jail and third cashier winds up in girl's arms. Plenty of cashiers but not much entertainment.

THE OFFICE SCANDAL

(1% DIALOG)

Pathe production and release. Phyllis Haver starred. Directed by Paul Stein. Raymond Hatton and Margaret Livingstone featured. Sound on RCA Photophone. At Arena, New York, July 17-18. Running time, about 70 minutes.

As precocious as the average screen version of life in a newspaper office, but enough suspense and motivation, with the w. k. murder angle to make "The Office Scandal" better than the usual attraction in the daily change house.

Phyllis Haver is a good sob-sister on a mid-western paper. She's got an exceptional "in" with the local judge, able to get a suspect for the killing of a wealthy race track man thrown out on her simple say-so that he's a newspaper man on a souse.

Raymond Hatton, rather a hang-dog character for a newshound gone drunk, gets a job on Phyllis' sheet. After that the city editor, pretty soft for lingo from his men and with a lot of time on his hands, regardless of editions, goes through the morgue and discovers that the reporter was pretty friendly with the wife of the killed, played by Margaret Livingstone with her regular s. a.

Meantime the wife spills the story without names to the sobbie. The c. e. has to get rid of her, figuring she's falling too fast for the alleged bad guy.

But Phyllis, after seeing the whip marks on Hatton's arm, does some of her own calculating. She checks up the widow and finds similar scars on her back. After that it's simple for her to prove her rights to the story and to wring out a confession for the cops.

Some of the sound in this is not so good. The ringing of a phone eclipses the noise inspired by a mighty daily going to press, and quite a bit of the dialog, as reproduced in the Arena, is muffled. *Waly.*

TEMPTATION

(FRENCH MADE)
(SILENT)

Paris, July 14.

"La Tentation," melodrama by Charles Mere, has been hashed into a picture by Cineromans. Reception by the critics was favorable, which does not mean much.

This screen version was commenced by the late Rene Leprince and finished by Jacques de Baroncelli. A fair French production has been the outcome of this posthumous collaboration. But Cineromans has turned out better.

Irene causes a sensation in society circles, frequenting the smart hotels on the Riviera. She is married to Bergue, a fellow she does not respect, and who cares little for her, and even carries on openly with other women. Irene likes Jourdan, attorney and friend of the family. Nevertheless she refuses to run away with him.

The wife is soon relieved of her unfaithful husband when Bergue is found dead on the highway, having met with an accident in Jourdan's automobile.

Irene retires to her villa at Cannes while the attorney returns to Paris. His behavior attracts attention. It is secretly believed he knows more of the accident which killed Bergue than he confesses. Irene receives several offers of marriage, but refuses. She prefers Jourdan and imagines he will propose. While expressing his passion, when next they meet, the lawyer announces his departure for the colonies.

Irene is astounded until a rival confides a secret she has learned. Jourdan killed Bergue to set the unhappy wife free, and his remorse prompts his self-imposed banishment.

Time flies, grief is appeased, and Irene marries another devoted suitor, Brinon. She thinks she has forgotten Jourdan until he returns. She sees him in the presence of her present husband.

The wretched man is able to prove his innocence. He did not kill Bergue but he might have saved his life by quick action. That was the temptation. He let the husband of the woman he loved die from neglect.

Shortly after, during a masque ball, he meets Irene alone and prevails on her to elope. While packing her valise for the journey, Brinon enters her room. The husband grasps the situation but is too fond of his wife to interfere with her plans.

Such sublime sacrifice touches Irene. She decides to remain with the man who prefers her happiness to his own. She lets Jourdan know her resolution and the fellow kills himself under her window. This is a dramatic thrill unfavorable for the film. Some excellent sets, with artistic accessories and the rest, serving as an appropriate frame for the chic of Claudia Victrix as Irene. Elmire Vautier is a scheming rival for the love of poor Jourdan, played by Lucien Dalsace.

The cast also includes Andre Nicolle, Fernand Mailly, Jean Peyriero and several talented performers, but naturally Mme. Victrix gets the most sunlights and close-ups. *Kendrew.*

HEADIN' WESTWARD

(SILENT)

El Dorado production, released by First Division. Directed by J. P. McGowan. Story by Sally Winters, adapted by Philip Schuyler. Bob Custer featured. In cast Mary Mayberry, John Lowell, J. P. McGowan, Charles Whittaker, Dorothy Vernon. At Loew's New York, one day, July 12, as half double bill. Running time, 60 minutes.

Stereotyped western quickie. Typical Bob Custer stuff cut to his measure many times before this one was shot. But loads of action earns it a rating as the fill-in portion of a grind house twin bill.

Oklahoma Adams, drifter, gets a load of Mary Benson (Mary Mayberry) in a stockyard city and follows her to Arizona, where her father has his ranch. The ranch foreman, a crook, is slowly, but surely, sending Mary's dad over the hills to the poorhouse.

Adams puts a stop to that and helps the sheriff round up the gang of cattle crooks, as well as the guy who stole the rodeo box office receipts.

J. P. McGowan, who directed, plays a comedy role opposite Dorothy Vernon, he using a trick sneeze (silent) for laughs and she depending on slapstick stuff.

THE LITTLE SAVAGE

(SILENT)

Radio (RKO) production and release. Story by Frank Howard Clark. Direction by Louis King. Virgil Miller, cameraman. Buzz Barton starred. Sam Nelson, Patricia Palmer and M. Morante in cast. At Stanley one day, July 11. Running time about 60 minutes.

Radio Pictures anxiety to sweep into its much-ballyhooed regime of classics is raising havoc with the odds and ends in the old FBO's schedule. Little Buzz Barton is another made to suffer by glaringly sloppy and quickie story, direction and the other production what-nots in "The Little Savage."

The youngster, clever and capable, despite the present frown on Westerns, is forced through a threadbare routine. Action is so slow that a couple of reels seem to be centered on a few stills. It's silent, of course.

One of those absurd stage hold-ups where a nice lad is forced by hunger to submit to the machinations of a wicked gent is incidental.

Buzz works in his hard-riding when he pulls the familiar lasso, letting his pony stamp out the existence of the heavy.

Dime entertainment. *Waly.*

WOMAN IN WHITE

(SILENT)

Worldwide picture starring Blanche Sweet. Story the old Wilkie Collins novel. Directed by Herbert Wilcox. Produced by British & Dominion Film Corp., Ltd. Distribution by Educational. At the Columbus, N. Y., one day, July 17. Running time, 60 minutes.

Looking at this silent meller done in the old film meller way, it's a cinch that without any kind of sound or dialog it can't go far in these days of picture production. Even the heroic work of the star, Blanche Sweet, fails to lift it; the entire film flounders around and even a bolony fire toward the end doesn't prove much of an asset.

A Wilkie Collins story ought to be standard in a literary way, but as a dynamic, intense melodramatic film theme it stops short at the very outset. Much obvious meller done in the way of pictures of 15 years ago tries in vain to give the story tense moments.

This film was hooked up with a Tom Mix in double bill and one can imagine where that slow-moving, out-moded thriller compared with any part of a Mix western.

The story has a decided English angle and is yet a cumbersome affair at best. Nothing to it but Miss Sweet. *Mark.*

MODERN LOVE

(25% DIALOG)

Universal production and release. Western Electric sounded. Titles and dialog written by A. DeMond. Direction by Arch Heath, from Beatrice Van's story. Jerry Ash, cameraman. In cast: Charlie Chase, Jean Hersholt, Kathryn Crawford, Anita Garvin, Betty Montgomery. At Loew's New York one day, July 19, on double feature bill. Running time, 71 minutes.

Very good program comedy and better than many with more talk that have been given a week on Broadway. The folks in the neighborhood houses will enjoy this clean-cut fun. The Loew New York brood clocked more than they have on a feature there in many weeks.

Charlie Chase is excellent in feature lengths, and Director Arch Heath kept his eye on details that rounded "Modern Love" into its rating.

Simple, but conventional along ultra modern lines, the story gives him the old stuff of the hubby posing as the butler because wifie wants to keep her state a secret until she cleans up dough in her own job.

To do this Chase first gets the smiles when he has to duck back to his own apartment so that the neighbor's won't see a strange man in the morning. The biggest noise comes when, as the butler tipping off the visiting French modiste, a lot of backward table manners are introduced.

After that the audience is geared up for anything. Some pretty old stuff does, such as Anita Garvin sitting on the bed under which is planted Chase and at first mistaking his bare feet for her own. *Waly.*

THE SKY RIDER

(SILENT)

(Disc Orchestration)

George Batcheller production distributed through Chesterfield (independent). Story and direction credited Alfred Neitz. In cast: Garreth Hughes, Josephine Hill, J. Lockney, John Tansey, Lew Meehan, Sheldon Lewis, "Champ," dog. At Loew's New York, one day, July 19, half double bill. Running time, 48 minutes.

Slot machine claptrap, ideally cast, that would have registered about average before houses had organs. Today "The Sky Rider," with some plane touches, is a low average for the dime grinds.

Dog, "Champ," directed to write rings around "Rinty's" intelligence. Knows so much about a plane some of the boys in shirtsleeves hahhahed.

Old yarn, told in indie staccato manner, about disinherited nephew gettin' after the old man, after plan to bump off his favorite adopted son flops.

Doctor's operating table as torture chamber nearest thing to novelty. No one gets hurt and fans get dizzy watching cops repeat tour and then go in for studio tussle. *Waly.*

NOISY NEIGHBORS

(5% DIALOG)

Pathe production and release. Adapted from original story by F. Hugh Herbert. Directed by Paul Bern. Features Eddie Quillan and the Quillan Family. Cast includes Alberta Vaughn and Theodore Roberts. Directed by Charles Reisner. At Arena, New York, one day, July 19, half double bill. Running time, 74 minutes.

A happy mixture of comedy and melodrama here that dovetails into some most amusing climaxes. As the situations pile up one imagines there is going to be a lot of hot action and sure enough, there is. It's that hokey fun and the tense meller that will make this one welcome in any neighborhood.

Hugh Herbert, who knows his vaude, milled a story here that calls for a family of small-time troupers suddenly falling heir to a southern plantation and putting themselves right into the heart of a bitter feud. There is a hard bunch of hill nockers who delight in drilling lead into any of the Vanrevels. As the Monarch Family from the stage is Vanrevel in real life the hill billies were expected to furnish some excitement for the troupers. They did in a way that reflects credit on Director Reisner and Author Herbert.

The talker part is so short it really seemed a pity more wasn't worked in. The late Theodore Roberts used his splendid voice to advantage and the man playing the lead hill billy was immense when speaking. The talking was worked in at almost the close of the picture; seemed an afterthought, but what was used was not overdone.

The Arena crowd seemed tickled pink over this one and it's a cinch that it packed the kind of entertainment the neighborhoods eat up.

As one watched Mr. Roberts show the class of the actor he was and how he made big moments out of little ones, and was imposing and glorious in his climaxes of dramatics, one realized what the picture world lost when that splendid actor passed out. *Mark.*

MASKED EMOTION

(SILENT)

Fox production and release. Directed by Kenneth Hawkes and Dave Butler, from Ben Ames Williams' story. Featuring George O'Brien, with Nora Lane, Farrell MacDonald in cast. At Loew's New York, one day, July 22. Running time, 60 minutes.

Excepting title being a complete misnomer "Masked Emotion" is good program entertainment of the George O'Brien physical culture and hero variety. There's plenty of kick in it all for the O'Brien fans.

Simple story, figuring a few California coast spots, sailboat, schooner and few glimpses of house exterior in locales. For 20 minutes George does nothing but flex his muscles and extend that chest astern the catboat. Then a girl is spotted and the two brothers head for shore.

Action gets underway when younger brother takes out boat to schooner in search of girl. Chink aboard is smuggling some countrymen with aid of local seaman, unknown to girl's old dad, the captain. Lad gets in line for beating and knifing.

George spots "Bargee" pounding shore and carries brother over a subtitled two miles to doctor's.

Back to the schooner he beats up the two bad gents, with fight on deck and in rigging. Then to recuperating pal and the girl following. *Waly.*

The Wild Heart of Africa

(SILENT)

Walker-Arbuthnot African expedition. Released by Oscar Price. At Stanley, New York, one day, July 17. Running time, 68 minutes.

Audience feels it has been bitten by Africa's sleep producing bug long before the Walker-Arbuthnot gang projects one half of its trip through the dark country. "The Wild Heart of Africa" has nothing to hold an audience. It is composed chiefly of landscape and zoo-like shots, seen time and again. Needs a lot of cutting before the grinds (the only houses outside of biological institutes) can possibly find a place for this one.

A lot of footage, that has been worked even in the newsreels as magazine stuff, starts off the expedition with deadly slow camera work on some of the ancient things in Egypt. One of the longest rides down the Nile yet recorded follows.

The animal hunting rarely works in actual bullet pelting. A couple of elephants are shown after the massacre. These will be sickening to women.

Considerable film is taken up with the tribe dances. Some of the femmes are a little more underclothed than have been witnessed in predecessors to this film; but not enough to get a rise out of a smoking crowd.

All in all, just one of those things that could have been shot in the Bronx zoo with a dash of Westchester weeds thrown in for the African swamp effect, or assembled from the 20 others ahead of this one. *Waly.*

GIRLS WHO DARE

(SILENT)

Trinity production. States rights release. Directed by Frank Mattison. Screen play adapted by Seton Burtis-Hall from story, "Cocktails," by Ben Herschfeld. Rex Lease and Priscilla Bonner featured. In cast: Rosemary Theby, Ben Wilson, Eddie Brownell. At Columbus, New York, one day, July 18, as half double bill. Running time, 60 minutes.

Dreary night club story concerning the romance between a wealthy youth and a night dancer. The hostess of the joint is known as "Alabam" Kenyon and the role played by Rosemary Theby is a futile take-off on Tex Guinan. Stereotyped plot and long winded obvious titles make it a weak quickie for the cheapest grinds.

Sally Kelly tosses her cop boy friend for Chet Randolf. The boy's father is playing around with "Alabam."

When the showdown comes he refused to allow his son to marry the night club chorus kid. Sally is about to marry the copper but an auto accident puts a stop to that. In the hospital she is finally hitched to the boy she loves with his parents consenting.

No action, suspense or sympathetic character in this flicker. Direction and photography are a throwback to the nickelodeon product of 10 years ago.

FRECKLED RASCAL

(SILENT)

Radio Pictures production and release. Buzz Barton featured. Directed by Louis King. Story by Frank Howard Clark. Photographed by Nick Musuraca. In cast, Milbourne Morante, Tom Lingham, Lotus Thompson, Pat O'Brien. At Columbus, New York, one day, July 19. Half double bill. Running time 70 minutes.

Lively westerner that gives Buzz Barton, freckle-faced kid, plenty of opportunity to do his heroic cowboy stuff. The kids in the grinds will like his riding and his marksmanship with a stone slingshot. Light love story running through also makes this one okay for any of the small neighborhood houses.

Buzz and his elderly traveling companion come into a desert town threatened with a water famine because the man who owns the reservoir is holding out for more money for his wet stuff. Buzz finally gets the profiteer in a spot where he is slowly dying from thirst and forces him to agree to supply water to the parched town at a reasonable rate.

Plenty of hard riding, shooting and sling-shooting a la David and Goliath.

A little judicious cutting would help this one stand out for speed and action in those stands where they still like westerns.

THE OPPRESSED

(Silent)

(FRENCH MADE)

Although not credited, probably produced in France and presented here by William Elliot. Raquel Meller, starred. Story and direction by Henry Asselin. At the Cameo, New York, week July 13. Running time 85 minutes.

Philip of Horn..............Audre Roanne
Don Zuniga Y. Requesense....Marcel Vibart
The Duke of Alva....................M. Shultz
Don Ruy..........................Albert Bias
Conception.....................Raquel Meller

Wreaking with staginess, "The Oppressed," highly misrepresented as a deep slant on the Spanish inquisitors, has a shallow romance for the working lines of a 15th century over-costumed cast. Playing is uninspired, from Raquel Meller down. Arties can use it, if for nothing more than wardrobe and antiques on sets. It's too big a gamble the red way for the regulars.

Henry Asselin, while selecting for the time a period of Spanish rule in the Belgian lowlands, so wrote his story around Miss Meller. He made an effort to present her in the guise of another Joan of Arc, so that the screen play is little more than a series of feints and over-acting on Miss Meller's part, some poorly handled mob scenes and gestures at beheading on the other.

Subtitles, frowns and occasional gatherings on a courtroom set attempt to show inquisitorial rule, such lurid and vivid material for dramatization if but followed verbatimly from history.

Aude Roanne makes a weak-kneed opposite for Miss Meller. He wastes considerable motion and has a pan that never registers for the sympathy expected from a role as Belgium's prospective deliverer, Philip of Horn.

A jail scene reminiscent of the Dumas' novel, "The Two Dianas," is the leading ante-climatic point, with Conception futility going to the rescue of her mild lover.

In the long run of little more than worthy atmospheric shots of heavily shrouded sets (production's only asset), Philip escapes decapitation by the Spanish king's sudden edict of pax vobiscum for Belgium. Even here the story ridiculously swerves to add to Miss Meller's "glory" and the union of two countries by her marriage to the insipid Philip. *Waly.*

BROTHERS

(SILENT)

Ray-Art production made by Trem Carr. Cast includes James Cain, Barabara Bedford, Cornelius Keefe and Arthur Rankin. Directed by Scott Pembroke. At Arena, N. Y., one day, July 19, half double bill. Running time, 59 minutes.

Another of the celluloid stripe of the sacrificial brother who goes through the purgatory and back to give his younger brother an education. This one has two boys made homeless. The orphanage people come to take them away. The older lad escapes but Bobby goes to the institution. Will hold its own where they play silents on double days.

The bigger brother becomes the head of a band of thieves in which a woman is important. Story is steeped in murder long before it ends.

Some very good scenes and well acted. At times the film wobbles only to hit into a meller stride that saved it from doing a nose dive.

Not a lot of newness or anything out of the stereotyped of underworld plots. Just another screened story that you can't win with crime. *Mark.*

THE BACHELOR GIRL

(25% DIALOG)

Columbia production and release. Directed by Richard Thorpe. William Collier, Jr., and Jacqueline Logan featured. In cast Thelma Todd and Edward Hearn. Story by Jack Townley. At Loew's New York, one day, July 17. Running time, 63 minutes.

Dull story that holds little value for the remote wired spots except possibly on a double bill. Action is lacking and three talking sequences at the start, in the middle and windup are of no great value in helping this one along.

Story concerns Larry Marshall, a swell headed salesman in a mercantile house. When he is fired for incompetence, his girl (Jacqueline Logan), private secretary to the head of the firm, helps him get a better job with a competing concern by lying about his ability. To help him to further success she resigns her position and hooks up as the boy friend's secretary.

Dialog sequences loosely hung together and talk is mainly blah. Miss Logan and Collier are hardly a well matched pair but both make the most of a featherweight story.

AMAZING VAGABOND

(SILENT)

Radio Picture production and release. Directed by Wallace W. Fox, from story by Frank Howard Clark. Cameraman, Virgil Miller. Feminine lead's name not flashed. Running time, 50 minutes. At Columbus, New York, July 19-20, half double bill.

Jimmy Hobbs ....Bob Steele
Gelorge Hobbs........Tom Lingham
Phil Dunning............Lafe McKee
"Haywire"..........Perry Murdock
Bill Wharton............Jay Morley
Myrtle....................Emily Gredes

A hit and run flicker that tickles the imagination of the kids. Okay for double feature or one-day western stands.

With one sweep of his mighty arm "High Gear" (Bob Steele) makes four villains hit the dust.

"High Gear" is the spoiled son of a rich lumber manufacturer and has a weakness for stunt flying which always causes his Dad to chew the ends off four more cigars. Boy meets a nice looking blonde, not knowing she is the daughter of the superintendent of his dad's lumber camp, and goes for her in a big way.

"High's" dad decides to teach sonny boy a lesson and ship him to his camp out west where he instructs the superintendent to make a man of him.

"High" is shanghaied aboard a freight train going to the lumber camp. On the freight he meets a hobo, "Haywire," who cons him into changing clothes with him and then knocks him cold. Lumber men find "Haywire" with "High's" bags and so mistake him for the boss' son and puts him on the daily grind.

High steps off the train, meets the sup's daughter again and decides that's the town for him and goes to work.

High's dad has been threatening to fire the superintendant because of a shortage in the lumber. High goes to work to unravel the mystery, finds that a few men from his camp are selling lumber to another, is caught eavesdropping, and a great free-for-all scrap ensues. Of course High knocks 'em all out.

Meanwhile dad has heard that his boy, whom "Hay Wire" is taken for, is flirting with the cook. Comes out to his camp and denounces the imposition. Sees High chasing the villain in the hand-car and follows with the gal. Villain is overtaken by High knocked into a river and a quite impossible under-water battle ensues with High the must victor.

"I thought you were just a sapling, my boy, but you're big timber." (new caption, first since 1916, on a Western).

Steele plays the part as well as the part demands. Femme has nothing to do but look pretty, which she does now and then. Photography, mostly outdoors, average.

Not a believable sequence in the picture.

SMILING IRISH EYES

(ALL DIALOG)

(With Songs)

First National production and release. Colleen Moore, starred. John McCormick, producer. James Hall featured. William A. Seiter directed from screen play by Tom J. Geraghty. Camera, Sid Hickcox and Henry Freulich; settings, Anthony Grot; edited by Al Hall; costumes, Edward Stevenson; special songs by Ray Perkins, Norman Spencer and Herman Ruby; musical conductor-arranger, Louis Silvers; Irish dances by Walter Wills; number staging by Larry Ceballos and Carl McBride; asst. director, James Dunne. W. E. (Vitaphone) sounded. Opened July 23 at the Central, New York, at $2 top, twice a day; running time, 90 minutes.

Kathleen O'Connor ....Colleen Moore
Rory O'More ....James Hall
Michael O'Connor .....Claude Gillingwater
Shamus O'Connor ....Robert Homans
Granny O'More ....Aggie Herring
Frankie West ....Betty Francisco
Goldie Devore ....Julanne Johnston
Sir Timonthy ...Robert Emmett O'Connor
Ralph Prescott ....Edward Earl
Black Barney ....Tom O'Brien
County Fair Manager ....Fred Kelsey
Fortune Teller ....Madam Bosocki
Taxi Driver ....George Hayes
Landlady ....Ann Schaefer

A weak sister as a picture, it's a personal triumph for Colleen Moore, its star, whose piquant personality of the yester-month's silent cinematic days dovetails charmingly with her talking personality. Miss Moore's drawing power, the story and the title, the latter for or against, as the territory may be, should take care of this one in the regular houses. As a picture production, however, it's pretty poor stuff, thoroughly obvious from the first reel on, and at no stage convincing, even though one permits himself to be carried away by the peppery star who also sings and dances.

"Smiling Irish Eyes" may not be the best idea as a picture title. The racial differentiation, regardless of any inherent merit, may detract from its box office chances in one section or improve in another. Still Miss Moore has her fans in all races. Fox's "Mother Machree" was up against the title thing.

It's the Irish ballad which is the crux of an all too wide open development. If merely a matter of Irish appeal, what more could one ask beyond the coupling of the Colleen and the Moore?

Back home in County Kerry, James Hall, somewhat of a fiddlin' fool, and his colleen, Miss Moore, fashion this "Smiling Irish Eyes" ballad. In a series of unconvincing sequences, Hall is transplanted to America where he clicks as a songwriter and as a song-and-dance man. That songwriting thing is hooey and the backstage stuff goes in spades.

Bill Seiter's directorial lapses are many. Perhaps it's screen license for an unseen orchestral accompaniment to pick up the theme song as Miss Moore reprises it on the lonely wishing well set back in Erin, but after all, such shots as having the heroine walk about without her handbags and then be seen in an immediately ensuing scene carrying them, passed out of date long ago. Even the off-screen musical accompaniment is fast becoming outmoded in these fast progressing synchronization days. Then, too, Hall's palpable fiddle faking could **have been overlooked had the other elements been more arresting.**

Some mildly effective work at the Irish county fair, what with the squealing of the pigs and the other live-stock noises, as well as the greased pig race. In between moments, in a too mechanical Weber and Fields manner, Claude Gillingwater and Robert Homans asserted themselves as the scrapping a. k. Tads. That was carried on right through the picture until the very finale, to the degree it soon became unfunny and too hackneyed a theatrical manifestation, even to the least discerning.

This picture was in production last winter or over a full half year ago. Its calibre becomes somewhat of an interesting biological study to picture people, to evidence how fast-moving have been the strides of talker production standards. If nothing else, that streamer head on Variety (in the theatrical boarding house scene) indicated how far back that issue was current.

Production doesn't look as if there was anything involved to delay release, hence it was a mistake to hold up its general distributing, excepting, of course, for the run of "Jeannine"; yet somehow something should have been done to have released this one.

"Smiling Irish Eyes," of course, isn't $2. But showing, like many other such in a $2 Broadway house, it calls from the lay reviewers a $2 criticism. The theme song won't be much of a help. The songsmiths strove for another "When Irish Eyes Are Smiling," in their original composition and flopped, but at least this has the saving grace of not attempting to evolve a continuity from the theorem that "When Irish Eyes Are Smiling" is the leading character's own composition.

Abel.

SINGLE STANDARD

(SILENT)

(Disc Orchestration)

Metro-Goldwyn-Mayer production and release. Greta Garbo starred. Directed by John S. Robertson. Screen story based on Adela Rogers St. John's theme. Titles by M. Ainslee. Victor records contain musical score with no sound or dialog. At Capitol, New York, week July 27. Running time 73 minutes.

Arden Stuart......................Greta Garbo
Packy Cannon.....................Nils Asther
Tommy Hewlett.........John Mack Brown
Mercedes....................Dorothy Sebastian
Ding Stuart.....................Lane Chandler
Anthony Kendall..............Robert Castle
Mister Glendenning........Mahlon Hamilton
Miss Glendenning..........Kathlyn Williams
Miss Handley..................Zeffie Tilbury

What some girls do today, and a lot more would like to, Greta Garbo does in "The Single Standard." Thus a big pull-in is guaranteed any box office that pushes this Metro silent. This, with all of the quickie material and rough story edges, as well as a much too blase Miss Garbo, the thinking buyers will discover shortly after the production gets under way.

But the thousands of typing girlies and purple-suited office boys will find this made to their order. Titles attempting a sophisticated explanation of the psychology causing a young girl to suddenly seek an affair with the family chauffeur, and, after that, dividing her time between two other men, may please some of the adults.

Although the lettering in the film would set forth Miss Garbo, as Arden Stuart, throwing off the cloak of conventionalism for free plunges claimed so common in spots here and on the Continent, the actress is almost unfeline in her brazen directness. While censors probably expect to leap on this point, when the picture gets to them, they will find no show, except a veiled peep at Arden's garters. The star keeps well wrapped throughout and her intimate postures are so frequent and so matter of fact after the first dozen times that only once, when expectation is aroused with the initial fall, do they come anywhere near getting an actual kick.

Nils Asther, with his black hair and John-like mustache, while doing a good job, does not lend the sailor-artist-boxer role the Gilbertine touch.

The sequences in several instances are tied together choppily. The impulsive rush to the chauffeur, after watching some friendly husbands kiss away their affinities, hits as too quick a stepping out of character and too sudden a drop for a moral aspect that had been fairly high.

The chauffeur deliberately wrecking his boss' car and killing himself immediately after the conquest, is an illogically sincere interpretation by a man, so capable of being seduced, to make of the simple losing of his job.

Greta is sub-titled as letting a couple of months elapse after the tragedy before she is impelled to seek another victim. This time it is the over-gifted Packy Cannon, a regular villager with a Rockefeller fountain of dough, judging from the sets used for his studio, yacht, etc. Asther is Packy.

A few book titles on activities in love are flashed before the first Asther-Garbo clinch. This is followed by a regular film trip through the South Seas with plenty of stretching and necking.

Finally even Packy tires. This permits Miss Garbo and the picture to go in for matrimony with a mild **but virile man who gives her the son that kills off moral turpitude.**

Before the reformation Packy, wearied of a China locale, returns for Arden. With her child on the beach and hubby nearby, she immediately forgets obligations and plans for another expedition. The husband (J. M. Brown) knows all and decides to bump himself off. But the sleeping child provides the medicine and Packy shoves off alone. ***Waly.***

EVANGELINE

(SONGS ONLY)

United Artists production and release. Directed by Edwin Carewe. Starring Dolores Del Rio. Finis Fox story based on Longfellow's poem. Photography by R. B. Kurrhe and Al M. Green. Running time, 87 minutes. At Rivoli, New York, July 27, on grind run.

Evangeline...................Dolores Del Rio
Gabriel.............................Roland Drew
Father Felician.............Alec B. Francis
Baptiste...........................Donald Reed
Benedict Bellefontaine......Paul McAllister
Basil..............................James Marcus
Rene LeBlanc.................George Marion
Michael...........................Bobby Mack
Governor-General..................Lou Payne
Colonel Winslow..............Lee Shumway
Peasants, British soldiers, sailors, provincial officers

Allowing for the great beauty of production, fine quality and appeal of the great American love epic, picture carries with it the handicap of being somewhat "an educational." Picture will pull from the schools, but the fan mob is likely to shy away. Commercially it looks a bit doubtful; artistically it is a credit to everybody concerned. Pictorially it is a smash; romantically it's a rave; but as entertainment it's very mild indeed.

One of those pictures the literary minded will laud and the entertainment seekers pass by. Doubtful if even the special following of Miss Del Rio will go wild about it. The paprika Latin girl has some good emotional sequences, but somehow she doesn't seem to fit with the role of the saint-like maid of Grand Pre.

Directorate of the Rivoli must have had something of the kind in mind, for even at the premiere of the picture the screen gave a good deal of footage to a "coming soon" trailer for "Burlesque," including snappy scenes in color from the "Follies" portion of the picture.

Producer and director may take what comfort they can for a first-rate filming of the Longfellow classic. Whatever shortcomings the picture may disclose at the box office, it isn't due to the production, which is a succession of magnificent pictorial passages. Backgrounds of the Canadian coast and the northern forests are lovely beyond telling.

Attempt to translate the beauty of the poem into terms of silent drama, however, has not been happy. It isn't drama at all, not even pastoral drama for screen purposes. There are action passages to be sure, and here very well handled. Such was the driving of the simple Arcadians into British ships for exile to the distant wilderness. But there never is any tension, no situations to grip or conflicts to thrill. Reason, of course, is that it's a poem and not a film drama, and couldn't be made into one.

Picture has no talk except one brief line at the finish, spoken by the heroine as her long search for her lover ends with his death in her arms. But it has three or four admirable song numbers, two by Miss Del Rio and one by Roland Drew, the hero. Singers are shown in closeups and impression they are actually doing the songs is convincing in all cases. Several good bits of sound effect, in ringing of village bells and crash of the surf on the beach. One song number by Al Jolson and Billy Rose.

Picture has all the accessories of drama—excellent atmosphere, engaging character studies and fine sentiment—but is fatally lacking in drama itself. A high-class literary transcription, but not a release of wide public appeal. *Rush.*

RIVER OF ROMANCE

(ALL DIALOG)

Paramount production and release. Featuring Buddy Rogers and Mary Brian. Adapted from Booth Tarkington's play "Magnolia." Screen play by Ethel Doherty, dialoged by Dan Totheroh and John Weaver. Directed by Richard Wallace. At Paramount, New York, week of July 27. Running time 80 mins.

Tom Rumford ....Buddy Rogers
Gen. Rumford ....Henry B. Walthall
Lucy Jeffers ....Mary Brian
Elvira Jeffers ....June Collyer
Orlando Jackson ....Wallace Beery
Capt. Blackie ....Fred Kohler
Mexico ....Natalie Kingston
Major Patterson ....Walter McGrail
Joe Patterson ....Anderson Lawlor
Madame Rumford ....Mrs. George Fawcett
Rumbo ....George Reed

Once before Paramount brought to the screen this fighting romance of the old Mississippi River ripsnorters. Then as now it was a great yarn and a strong picture. It is thoroughly delightful program entertainment that the fans will dote upon, not only for the intrinsic charm of its rich drama and humor, but for the numerous interesting sidelights on film personalities it reveals.

There is Wallace Beery playing the role done with such unction in the silent version of four or five years ago by Ernest Torrence. Dialog presents the confirmed film-goer with a new and different Wallace Beery- strangely shorn of his familiar tricks but no less interesting in his articulate self.

Mary Brian, formerly merely pretty, now a first class sample of trouping. She has captured to perfection the romantic, sentimental young Lucy Jeffers of Booth Tarkington's etching.

Still another performance to create buzzing, is that of June Collyer's. Heretofore that young woman has gotten few breaks on the screen although attached to Fox's congested payroll for a couple of years. She realizes the coquettish southern belle with a nice shading for the petulance and silly vanity of the type.

To Buddy Rogers falls the difficult role of Tom Rumford, alias the "notorious Colonel" Blake, originally done on the stage by Leo Carrillo. Rogers is a little young for the masterful scenes but discounting this handicap, gives an able performance. He earns some right to be judged as a performer of ability and not merely as a handsome lad the ladies have crowned Apollo.

Comparisons will inevitably be made by the long memories crew between the silent and the conversational versions. In some respects talk has robbed the story of its swift movement but the deliciousness of the boy who doesn't want to fight, learning by accident how to play at being bad is not lost. The original scenario appears to have been followed quite closely in the main with necessary condension because of the time-consuming dialog.

Mechanically and technically, "River of Romance" is one of the best talker specimens produced to date. Detail in particular bespeaks intelligent attention. It has an intimacy not always present in the talkers. This applies especially to the tender episodes between Buddy and Mary. They will go straight to the heart strings of every day dreamer in the 48 states.

It will make money. *Land.*

The Fight for Matterhorn

(GERMAN MADE)
(Silent)

Produced by Hom Fim, Berlin, distributed here by Brill. Directed by Marie Bonnard and Nuntie Malasomma. Scenario credited Dr. Arnold Franck. Cameramen, Sepp Allgeier and Willy Winterstein. In cast: Luis Trenker, Marcella Albani, Alexandra Schmidt, Clifford MacLaglen, Peter Voss, Johanna Evald. At Little Carnegie, week July 27. Running time about 70 minutes.

Mountain climbing pictures haven't been seen in quite a while, the newsreels giving them plenty of coverage. That's all "The Fight for Matterhorn" has to offer, other than a foolish attempt at a story in a little Swiss village, that awkwardly stumbles along.

Nothing interesting about the first climb. The cameramen had the toughest job but were careful to keep their lenses from sheer drop perspectives. Those are taken care of in the long shots so that the question of bonafide altitude arises in the audience's mind. None of the climbers ever impresses as having taken any real risk during the shooting.

One climb deserves another, until the thing is repeated three times, with rock after rock. A story interest has been attempted for the other two, the Swiss who saved the English contender in the first actually taking the Londoner on a "ride" in the second.

A relative has poisoned the guide's mind about the wife. The heavy, Clifford MacLaglen, has a grin like Vic's "What Price Glory" but is in the kintergarten compared to his West Coast namesake.

But church bells dispel the killing motive and a storm, very meagrely shown, brings the boys down.

MacLaglen, as the wicked Giaccomo, stepbrother to the Swiss guide, again works the needle so that the latter gent sets out determined to beat the Englishman to the top. Peter Voss, as a foreigner tries to overtake the Swiss—and so they climb, climb, climb.

Meantime Mac goes for the wife and is repelled by the appearance of an elderly matron. Down comes the Swiss, beaten, and learns the truth. He rushes out to rescue the Englishman, victor but stuck on top of the peak without a rope.

And so the climb or crime ends. *Waly.*

QUO VADIS

(ITALIAN MADE)
(Silent)

Film of Italian origin, having been produced near Rome. Revival or reissue. Released by First National. Starring Emil Jannings. Running time, 100 mins. At Fifth Avenue Playhouse, New York, week June 27.

Plenty of thrill left in this old classic. It is good to see Emil Jannings as a younger man than he is now. His artistry has in no recent productions transcended his role of Nero in "Quo Vadis." Even the extravagance of the sets with their multitudinous statuary and gigantic replicas of the Coliseum and other celebrated memorials of the Roman hey-day is yet staggering.

The picture, done in an era when ancient epics flourished, is a historical panoramic Gibraltar of production, with magnificent mob scenes, dazzling regal quarters and adequate cast, over which Jannings looms as a genius of regal impersonation.

Love theme is weak, commensurate with the prodigiousness of events. More interest is diverted to scenes in the arena, wherein the Christians are herded to be torn by ravenously hungry felines.

The particular scene in which one woman dashes to the wall of the amphitheatre, throwing her cape to the spectators in an attempt to escape the hungry jaws of a half dozen lions, is a thrilling and horrible spectacle. One sees the Romans in the front tiers pulling her up the wall as the lions leap at her, succeeding in snatching her to safety.

Again the Christians tied to chariots which whirl around, dragging the bodies behind. Lygia, the daughter of a vanquished king, held as hostage, is attached to one chariot, but climbs into it, tripping the charioteer from his perch. She is pursued throughout the film by Venicius, Roman leader.

Lygia is next tied to the back of a wild bovine, which is bull-dogged by her servant, Ursulus, strong man of the picture.

Scenes of debaucheries in Nero's palace are moronic splendors. The coy phrases of Petunius, who stuffs his handkerchief in Nero's throat when he would bewail the loss of the infant crown prince, saying, "Let Rome burn, but spare your marvelous voice," are beautifully phrased in the titles.

Jannings' emotion displayed by him in "The Patriot" is in "Quo Vadis" and more. Photography is exquisite.

"Quo Vadis" was and still is an epic film. The burning of Rome and its consequences unto the suicide of Nero to escape Calba's cavalry are unforgettably well executed. The film should and will survive time.

PALS OF THE PRAIRIE

(SILENT)

Radio Pictures production and release. Directed by Louis King from original story credited Oliver Drake. Virgil Miller, cameraman. Buzz Barton starred. In cast: Frank Rice, Natalie Joyce, Duncan Reynolds. At Stanley, New York, one day, July 26. Running time 57 minutes.

In the class with the last three or four the old FBO company ground out for Buzz, "Pals of the Prairie" is just a little slower and less interesting--if that is possible.

With one of those make-shift yarns that would waste time were more than a half hour spent on the typewriter, the thing stumbles along until even dime payees start whistling.

Buzz and his lanky friend in a most obviously stereotyped way bowl over gangs of men after they waste a reel trying to get into trouble.

The decrepit sets on the lot long before the Radio folk knew about Hollywood are pulled within camera range for Buzz to do his stuff. At one point it gets so desperate the otherwise capable kid borrows a girl's locks and is made to play floosey with guys whose hard looks are just thrown away in this one.

But somehow or another the long forgotten inspiration that a Latin mayor's son is ordered kidnapped to prevent matrimony with a cobbler's lowly but pretty daughter (Natalie Joyce) is brought into the final fall.

By that time the average crowd doesn't care whether the ceremony comes off or not, but they must give little Buzz some reason for "glory," so he trips the villain in the presence of the rescuers. *Waly.*

HOMECOMING

(GERMAN MADE)
(Silent)

London, July 17.

A prize parsnip of the Prussians. As dull a feature picture as ever came out of any studio. Lars Hanson doesn't help it.

Just a dumb Enoch Arden yarn of two German prisoners in a Russian camp. One is always talking about his wife and home. Other is the listener. They try to escape. Listener succeeds, but home-lover gets caught and goes back to the mines.

Listener makes for friend's house and then for his femme. Home-lover arrives after peace is declared, sees the layout and leaves as mate on a tramp steamer, leaving his femme to the listener.

How Eric Pommer ever let his name go out on this one can only be explained on the grounds that it's in his contract to take credit whether he wants it or not.

Only redeeming feature is that you can see this show at the Regal at 7 o'clock, order tea, toast, cake and ice cream to be served in your lap, and do it all for about 42 cents.

They tried to save this "Homecoming" with "Two Weeks Off," Mulhall-Mackaill, 25 per cent dialog and 75 per cent tripe, already reviewed unfavorably in Variety. *Scully.*

WOMAN FROM HELL

(SILENT)
(Sound Effects and Score)

Fox production and release. Mary Astor featured. Directed by A. F. Erickson from the play by Jaime Del Rio, George Scarborough and Lois Leeson. Conrad Wells, cameraman. Sounded by Western Electric (Movietone). Half double feature, one day, July 26, at Loew's New York. Running time, 58 minutes.

Dee Renaud.......................Mary Astor
Alf Roslyn...............Robert Armstrong
Jim Coakley......................Dean Jagger
"Slick" Ericks...................Roy D'Arcy
Mother Prince....................May Boley
Pap Coakley............James Bradbury, Sr.

Flicker adaptation of the play "From Hell Came a Lady." Film story is punched full of holes. Picture starts off with a bang but remains that way for five minutes, when it begins to sag, then remains actionless until the last sequence. After the first sequence, the remainder is disappointing. Will need plenty of stage help to stand up alone.

Jim Coakley, lonely in the lighthouse which he tends with his father, goes to a beach resort nearby. He hears Alf Roslyn, barker for the amusement, "The Lady From Hell," telling all to see it for two bits. They will be given the opportunity of chasing "The Lady F. H." and if they catch her they may kiss her.

Jim gets a flash at the "lady," Mary Astor, and goes in. Lost in the cavern he finds Roy D'Arcy, who has caught Dee, trying to overdo the kiss. He knocks him down. D'Arcy gets up, walks away and never reappears in this picture.

After a three-minute acquaintanceship during which time he explained how lonely he was in the lighthouse to Dee, Jim proposes marriage. Dee says she needs time to think it over, but the next morning accepts, with Alf telling her that she'll come back to him; she's not the type for marriage.

Dee goes with Jim to their lighthouse and is introduced to the old man, called Pap, who is sore. He doesn't want a woman around.

At the end of a month the couple decide to celebrate by going to the resort. **While there, Jim catches Alf talking to Dee. He burns but Dee cools him. They take home a duck as a pet from the resort and the old man kills it for dinner. She tells Jim that Alf would have treated her kindlier. Jim decides to settle Alfy and goes to the resort.**

While away a storm comes up. The old man, in a fit of temper, breaks the works that turns the light which direct the boats. Old boy gets boozed up and dozes. Boat sirens for the light. Dee, finding it doesn't turn and the old man's asleep, put a beam in an opening in the bottom of the light and turns it by walking around in a circle, pushing the beam.

Alf walks in on the scene and attempts to make Dee, who grasps a revolver and holds him off, meanwhile turning the light. Her strength fails and she faints. Alf picks her up and lays her on the couch and starts making violent love to her. Trying to repulse him, Dee tells him truthfully she is pregnant.

Alf decides the kid's a square shooter and turns the beam for her.

Meanwhile Jim has heard that a man had gone to the light and tries to get there but can't on account of the storm. Next morning he finds Dee pouring coffee for Alf. Suspecting the worst, he knocks down Alf.

Alf gets up again, holds Jim in a chair and tells him all and off.

Miss Astor as Dee Renaud in a blonde wig looks appealing and puts just the right touch to her work. Dean Jagger, as Jim Coakley, is a newcomer and is entirely too histrionic. Though well built, he holds no appeal and needs polish. Robert Armstrong, as Alf the barker, handles his Jekyll-Hyde role capably.

Direction wobbly in spots. Some good shots of the beach resort, otherwise photography has nothing to recommend it.

The projection at the Stanley in part sounded like a radio full of static. Though having a fine musical accompaniment, something went wrong with the mechanism as it knocked, dragged and bounced over notes. Synchronization and sound effects bolster up this picture.

THE WONDERFUL LIE

(GERMAN MADE)

(Silent)

London, July 16.

They threw this one into the Hippodrome to sink or swim for three weeks. Mouth-to-mouth advertising had it going better at the end than it did the first week. It's as good a Pommer production as "Homecoming" is bad—and that's saying everything.

Brigette Helm, who went over **so** well in "Metropolis," is starred. She's worth it. In this picture playing the pash scenes in a silk robe and no undies. They hopped her up to look like Garbo and they certainly did a swell job.

Story is slender and interest would be better held if a reel were cut out. But where a good symphony orchestra is still intact, this defect can be overcome.

Title comes from early sequence when Brigette as mistress of a regimental colonel (Warwick Ward, English) is caught waving to a young lieutenant. She tells Colonel shavetail is a childhood playmate of hers. Colonel calls kid up and sees they're lying. She gives lieutenant her key and he calls. She explains the mess she's got him in. He plays shy, she the sure mistress. Knowing Prussian officers this ought to bring a laugh, but it's played so well picturegoers take it okay.

He stays the night, using her bed. She sleeps outside the door, reversing the usual treatment of this situation. They breakfast and the colonel catches them in "The Wonderful Lie." She goes to live in a hovel awaiting day the loot can marry her. Before this arrives, the loot gets in a poker game and wins plenty till the colonel joins, tempts the kid into cheating to draw four of a kind and then nails him as a crook for doing it.

Only outlet is for dame to go back to the colonel's swell house. Kid has bought her a pair of new shoes. She uses their ugliness **as a pretense for giving him the air and goes back to the colonel's house where she takes a shot of veronal and passes out. Rolling shot showing her in all her beauty falls out on her feet—dressed, of course, in the patent leather pumps the kid gave her.**

Worth importing, if it hasn't already been. *Scully.*

COME ACROSS

(SILENT)

Universal production and release. Starring Lina Basquette. Directed by Ray Taylor. From William Dudley Pelley's story, "The Stolen Lady." Western Electric recording. Cast includes Reade Howe, Flora Finch and Craufurd Kent. Running time, 65 mins. One day, July 26, at Circle theatre, New York.

"Come Across" has plenty of flaws. About where it belongs, in the one-dayers.

A night club is raided. Lina Basquette as a dancer is trampled in the rush. Two officers are sniped by Pop Hanson, the owner. His confederate picks Lina from the floor, creeps with her out a back door, and brings her unconscious to his apartment in a fast car. When he arrives, Hanson is already there; **has played a hand of solitaire and is resting in an arm chair. The close-up of the hand of cards is the pay-off.**

Indifferent photography; villainous faces; insipid situations, etc.

Lina, as a Long Island heiress, selects dancing in a tough night club as a medium to study sociology. Wants to know people and foregoes a Florida vacation with aunt to dance.

Night club owner eyes her as a decoy for a plot he has in mind, whereby she is to put the touch on a Mr. Billings, from Montana, who is coming east to meet his long, lost brother.

Club owner lays scheme before Miss Basquette. He tells her he has access to a Long Island mansion, from which the occupants have departed for Palm Beach. It is her own shack. She "agrees" to work with him.

Her reason is to put a test to a young man from the cafe for whom she has fallen. Believes him straight as he is against her aiding Hanson. Goes into her own home with the crooks. Calls one of her real admirers to pose as Billings. He arrives and plays part of the Montana millionaire, while the young man acts the long lost brother.

At the showdown the young man backs out on Hanson, saying he'll take none of the $20,000 for which Lina has touched the "brother." Admirer meanwhile believing Lina has gone far enough with act calls in cops.

Wind-up is that the young man is the real Billings, an author, who has connected with Hanson for local color.

THE BLOCKADE

(SILENT)

FBO production and release. Starring Anna Q. Nilsson. Directed by George B. Seitz from story by Harold Thews. Cameraman, Robert Martin. Titled by Randolph Bartlett. Cast includes Walter McGrail, Wallace McDonald and James Bradbury, Jr. Running time, 66 mins. One day, June 27, at Columbus, New York.

Notwithstanding its implausibility, "The Blockade" confers high diversion for the smaller houses. Miss Nillson plays a rugged role of hijacker with much naivette. The less deductive portions of any audience are left in the dark as to the identity of the government operative, Canavan, until the very end of the film, when Miss Nilsson reveals herself. The duplicity is amplified by virtue of her being under two other names in the film, that of Mona Van Slycke, society girl, and **Bess Maitland, intrepid hijacker.**

Photography is on a par with the extravagance of the story of the government attacking rum-runners with cruisers, plane and marine corps.

Government officers on one of the cruisers are treating the rum activity as impossible to thwart. Then a Canavan is assigned to take charge. Orders come from this mysterious party.

One sees a Mr. Gwynn lauded by the people for his charitable works and a tablet erected for his work as a prohibitionist. He is in reality a rum king. Miss Nilsson is bent on determining the master mind of the runners. She hijacks the boats right and left with her cruiser, "The Fury," but is captured. Runner makes a deal with her to split returns on the Christmas shipments. She agrees.

Meanwhile a young man from New York City arrives to go fishing in the vicinity. He brings letters of recommendation to the rum king, Gwynn, who later is led to believe the young man is Canavan, the mysterious federal operative.

He falls for Bess Maitland and later picks her up rowing as she escapes from the rum-runners. Gwynn gives young man a letter to his lieutenant, whose place is supposed to be good for fishing. The epistle is merely a note to take the fellow for a ride.

Bess, who gets back with the runners, pretends the young man has offended her and undertakes to give him the works. Takes him for a boat ride and shoots in the air, telling him to swim for her boat. The runner and the girl then go to unload the Christmas booze.

Crews are switched to prevent double-cross. Opposish crew find young man in hold of boat. Get Bess and say: "We thought you knocked him off." She replies she had a better idea. Then she puts him to work sending messages by radio to government, revolver at his head. Phony messages.

Troops, aeroplanes and cruiser arrive in nick o' time to capture all the rum-runners.

Picture has plenty of punch, despite its hard-to-believe composite.

STREET GIRL

(ALL DIALOG)

(With Songs)

RKO (Radio Pictures) production and release. Under William Le Baron's supervision. Nine reel production of "musical drama," staged by Wesley Ruggles from W. Carey Wonderly's "Viennese Charmer." Betty Compson featured. Dialog by Jane Murfin; three special songs by Oscar Levant (music) and Sidney Clare (lyrics); dances by Pearl Eaton; costumes, Max Ree; camera, L. Tover; musical direction, Victor Barabelle. RCA Photophone sounded. At Globe, New York, July 30, twice daily, $2 top.

Mike........................John Harron
Happy........................Ned Sparks
Joe..........................Jack Oakie
Pete........................Guy Buccola
Freddy....................Betty Compson
Keppel..................Joseph Cawthorn
Prince Nickolaus............Ivan Lebedeff
Club Manager.................Eddie Kane

Doris Eaton and Radio Beauty Chorus.

Raymond Maurel and the Cimini Male Chorus.

Gus Arnheim and his Ambassador Band.

"Street Girl" is a good picture and a money picture. The fans will like it. Had this RKO musical talker come in six months ago it would have rated the $2 it is scaled at. Regardless, at the present standard of things, it will reap a box office harvest in the regular houses. As a picture it has plenty in its favor. There are laughs galore. The comedy alone would have put this one over.

Ned Sparks as the dour jazz fiddler, and Jack Oakie, as the happy-go-lucky clarinetist, comprise half of a little cafe jazz band known as the Four Seasons. John Harron and Guy Buccola complete the quartet, elevated from 100 bucks a week into the heavy dough, at three grand for their act, which is fortified by Fredericka Joyselle (Betty Compson), whom they befriend and whose business acumen is directly responsible for the boys' professional success.

The story, as a faithful cross-section of theatrical life, may be open to captious criticism, but it is quite entertainingly done with not a little conviction. In toto it is more of a tribute to the direction and playing than the fundamental story. Still the yarn possesses plenty of action. It progresses interestingly from the very start when Harron rescues Miss Compson from a street masher, the probable explanation of the hazy but selling title. Our heroine is hungry, she is taken in for the night and permitted to share a corner of the large room the quartet occupies. Not only does she make herself domestically useful, but proves a great little business manager for the jazz boys.

A number of niceties to the production. Cafe stuff is impressively realistic. The consistent manner of having the boys work in a definite unique style, concluding each number with their backs to the audience, **lends an undeniable touch of faithfulness. The characters are real. Sparks never forgets himself as the eternal pessimist. Oakie, with that comedy pan of his, battling with the wop guitarist (Guy Buccola) registers a living character.**

Miss Compson troupes excellently to the degree that she almost overcomes certain not-to-be-slighted physical shortcomings. Some of the photographic shots of her were not quite flattering and the role really called for a younger personality.

Joe Cawthorn turned in a good performance as the Austrian cafe proprietor and Ivan Lebedeff creditably personated Prince Nickolaus, playing the role with admirable restraint.

RCA Photophone's recording is consistently tempoed, the aim for which was probably the cause of the occasional "muddy canning." There is one dialog sequence in the phone booth, which will have to be stepped-up to improve the amplification.

Sidney Clare and Oscar Levant have three good songs in the picture. "Huggable and Sweet" is the plugged hot number, but "My Dream

Melody" is the sympathetic strain which Miss Compson appears to render with so much realism. If she's fiddle-faking, it's one of the most skillful jobs of its kind. "Broken Up Tune," the third number, is led by Doris Eaton in a cafe ensemble set, wherein some trick cinematic staging is essayed with camera effects.

Unfolding of the picture aims to simulate the illusion of a stage presentation, even unto the programing of the players "in the order of their screen appearance."

"Street Girl" is a coin clicker.

Abel.

Hungarian Rhapsody

(GERMAN MADE)

(Sound-Synchronized)

Ufa production, released by Paramount. Producer, Erich Pommer; director, Hanns Schwartz; American adaptor, Julian Johnson; author, Hans Szekely; screen play authors, Fred Majo and Hans Szekely; photographer, Carl Hoffmann. Running time 70 minutes. At Paramount, New York, week Aug. 3.

Camilla	Lil Dagover
Franz	Willy Fritsch
Marika	Dita Parlo
Her Father	Fritz Greiner
Her Mother	Gisella Bathory
General Hoffman	Erich Kaiser-Tietz
Baron Barsody	Leopold Kramer

The first German sound picture and the first foreign production of any kind presented under major American auspices in many months. Looks like a money release on intrinsic merit from all angles, and ought to be a test of the question whether American fan public in the mass will accept meritorious foreign talker product.

World producers may well rest their case on this output. It is in all respects up to the best American standards as to physical character and pictorial beauty and has real freshness in personalities and atmosphere while its backgrounds have a very definite charm in their unfamiliarity.

A cast, in all respects adequate, plays in a persuasive vein of restrained smoothness. There is none of the stilted acting familiar in the bulk of European pictures. Production is impeccably dressed as to its conventional characters and the picturesque dress of the peasants is an asset to the spectacular side.

Story in its elements is rather formula, but treatment has a certain sophisticated European flavor that goes becomingly with its locale in the countryside outside Vienna. For instance the naive worship of caste is illustrated. An impoverished young nobleman in the army is saved from the disgrace he richly deserved by a girl of the middle class who sacrifices her good name in his behalf. Thus when the young man generously agrees to make her his wife, it is accepted all around as the handsome thing to do and everybody, including the girl's father, regards the situation as an altogether happy outcome Sort of bland assumption that boys will be boys and young army officers are that way, too.

Picture has many curiously interestingly alien side lights of this kind, trifles that have a certain piquancy to the American view. And it has one passage of distinctly spicy import, the visit of the gay young officer to the apartment of a philandering Viennese wife in the absence of her elderly husband, full of rather torrid innuendo. Lil Dagover plays the sprightly Viennese in the manner that made her talked about here in vamp roles some time ago, and something she has missed under other directors.

The romance is nicely handled and the settings are beautiful beyond telling, particularly scenes of peasants working in enormous wheat fields; peasants and the gentry in their harvest festivities and the ceremonies of the priests blessing the harvest with all the pageantry of the church.

The feminine lead is Dito Parlo, unfamiliar on this side, but showing possibilities. Here she gets small opportunity, having a passive ingenue role that doesn't set off her acting ability; merely gives a charming setting for her engaging beauty, a beauty something of the Janet Gaynor type. The picture really goes to Miss Dagover for acting scope. Several of the types are excellent, particularly the stern father of Fritz Grainer.

Picture has no dialog and its sound effects are inconsequential—such things as ringing church bells and orchestra playing in a cafe—but its scoring of several haunting Mayar melodies and the weaving in of the "Hungarian Rhapsody" itself give it an admirable musical atmosphere.

Chief merit this reviewer finds in the picture is that it is a sincere effort to screen native European material in a genuine way, instead of the usual second hand copy of Hollywood technique in story and method.

Rush.

MAN AND MOMENT

(40% DIALOG)

First National production and release. Directed by George Fitzmaurice. Sol Polito, cameraman. Film theme credited Elinor Glyn's story. Orchestration by Leo Forbstein. W. E. (Vitaphone) sounded. At Strand, New York, week Aug. 3. Running time, 75 minutes.

Joan	Billie Dove
Michael	Rod LaRocque
Viola	Gwen Lee
Skippy	Robt. Schable
Joan's Guardian	Charles Sellon
Butler	George Bunny

"The Man and the Moment" will pass as light entertainment in the average house. George Fitzmaurice has diluted the Glyn molasses so that the screen version avoids most of the love licorice and dwells on the comedy situations. A little cutting would improve the picture's program assurances.

Only once does the dialog insinuate in a way, boldly subtle and then repeated until even the janitors know it is the sex relation. Most of the lines get by, although a few are so bromidic in their expression of fidelity that the Saturday matinee crowd laughed a little derisively.

A swift novelty of outboard motor polo introduces the chief locale, niche in the West Coast and a yacht. Photography rips the small boats through the water at an unnatural, but audience thrilling speed. The young, reckless and somewhat dumb millionaire provider of the attractions is shown just before he crashes with the seaplane operated by the theme's heroine.

Rod LaRocque and Billie Dove play these roles. Fantastic as Miss Glyn has made them, Fitzmaurice and the principals are unable to eliminate a recitation tonality, characteristic of small town stock voices, that creeps into some of the more stereotyped lines. Both players, however, give a worthwhile performance, especially LaRocque.

There is too much of the comedy, with the exception of a mildly enacted eye and ear kissing sequence, for "The Man and the Moment" to register anything really hot. The audience knows from the subtitling that Miss Dove as Joan, the little girl from Iowa, is out of her class with the boozing yacht crowd and that Mike, the supposed philanderer, has really fallen for pure love, after the second half of the first reel.

To duck her guardian, who hates planes, and to rid himself of a blonde fortune hunter, Joan and Mike go through the ceremony before the girl's clothes are found in Mike's stateroom on the following morning.

Getting in with the blonde, who seeks to ruin her rep, a night club scene provides a highlight. This comes when Mike breaks the glass of a swimming pool revue to gain access to his wife in the arms of another.

Many of the known auto chases occur before Mike, in trying to kiss his fleeing wife in a plane, wrecks the flight a second time. A marooning for the night before they are picked up by the yacht satisfies both, and the fans, that conventionalism is the best way to get out of the theatre.

Waly.

COLLEGE LOVE

(50% DIALOG)

Universal production and release. Directed by Nat Ross and featuring George Lewis, Dorothy Gulliver. Story credited Leonard Fields. George Robinson, cameraman. Starting at Colony, New York, week Aug. 3. Western Electric sounded. Running time, approximately 80 minutes.

A conglomeration of the Collegian Series, inaugurated some time ago by the younger Laemmle, into a feature has been accomplished by Universal in "College Love." While strictly machine-made, the long-length version will be liked even better by those who enjoyed the same stuff during its episodic release.

General recording (or possibly reproduction in the Colony is the fault) is poor. Considerable of the dialog is unintelligible unless good ears are attuned, and a lot of the orchestrating reproduces a raspy and thin quality.

All in all, "College Love" exceeds in box office value a lot of attempts by contemporaries of U to conjure up for screen material their ideas of the playboy side of universities.

The Laemmle organization in its collegian revue holds things together by having a youth sacrifice girl, honor and vengeance so that the unworthy football star may bring glory to dear old Caldwell on the big day in the stadium.

The team, quite apparently, is taking a terrific licking until, just before the deciding quarter is neared, the star reveals that it was he, and not the wholesome ender, who was drunk the night before.

The football stuff is excellent. Magazine shots of a crowded stadium on a bonafide event are worked in "College Love" grid affairs with amazing trueness. Closeups of the various plays are all well made and will hold attention of grid enthusiasts.

College porch choruses, bonfires, dances, yells and senior gags on the freshmen, while a little lengthy in spots, provide the divertissement.

George Lewis, star in the recent series, is the utopia of college spirit in this one. Dorothy Gulliver is the girl who believes he is right.

Waly.

THE FLYING MARINE

(70 PER CENT DIALOG)

Columbia production and release. Directed by Al Rogell from screen play credited John Natteford. In cast: Ben Lyon, Shirley Mason and Jason Robards. Western Electric sounded. At Loew's Circle, New York, one day, Aug. 2. Running time, 60 minutes.

Good grind picture, but nothing more. Little real action, except several flights. Last of these, just before finis, is one of the most vivid yet photographed.

Natteford's stories have been consistently devoid of action, but Jason Robards and Ben Lyon as brothers with Shirley Mason as the girl, help work up an interest.

Reproduction of sound and lines excellent.

"The Flying Marine" has nothing to do with the war or corps, except a stock shot of a V squadron of planes. Lyon in the tile role is a civilian from the start and the flying is from a native field in California.

The girl shifts her attentions upon the appearance of the exsoldier. Hocking the engagement ring for the horses, brings her back to the elder and sacrificing brother, played by Robards.

The first plane crash deafens the marine long enough to learn the state of things and the girl's change in attitude. Taking the plane up on its second and fatal dive some thrilling air stuff is caught. Catching of parachute strap on wing causes soldier brother to lose control in saving his pal.

Too bad that the story called for so much inanimate parlor grinding before action, since this could have been worked into real thriller class.

Waly.

COCK-EYED WORLD

(ALL DIALOG)

Fox production and release. Featuring Victor McLaglen, Edmund Lowe and Lily Damita. Directed by Raoul Walsh. Story by Laurence Stallings and Maxwell Anderson. Dialog by William K. Wells. Cameraman Arthur Edeson. Western Electric (Movietone) sounded. At Roxy, New York, week Aug. 3. Running time 115 minutes.

Top Sergeant Flagg	Victor McLaglen
Sergeant Harry Quirt	Edmund Lowe
Mariana	Lily Damita
Olga	Leila Karnelly
Olson	El Brendel
Connors	Bobby Burns
Fanny	Jean Bary
Brownie	Joe Brown
Buckley	Stuart Erwin
Sanovich	Ivan Linow
Innkeeper	Solidad Jiminez
O'Sullivan	Albert Dresden
Jacobs	Joe Rochay
Katinka	Jeanette Dagna
Scout	Warren Hymer

Those two bawdy Marines from "What Price Glory," Messrs. Flagg and Quirt, are presented in a sequel by the authors, producer, director and stars of the original yarn. "The Cock-Eyed World" picks them up in Vladivostock (Russia) and takes them to Nicaragua, via Coney Island, taking five minutes less than two solid hours to accomplish the unreeling. This picture is going to make tubs full of money for Fox and exhibitors.

Raw, rough and Rabelaisan the Stallings-Anderson story with plenty of risque gags by the vaude writer, William K. Wells, is a gem of healthy vulgarity that is going to make most Americans laugh, although possibly not the rigid and solemn-minded members of some of the censor boards.

United States Marines are represented as virile, gutty, gin-guzzling, dame-chasing devotees of rowdy horseplay. There's no pansies among them and they are on familiar terms with the facts of life and biology. It is refreshingly free from restraint or puritanical taboo. If Fox has made a silent version it should be a big hit across the pond, as it comes closer to the Continental ideas on humor and sex than the average Hollywood picture.

Basically, it's old stuff. Victor McLaglen has been in half a dozen pictures with the same theme besides "What Price Glory." Two hardboiled hombres are continuously at odds over women. Each is vain about his attractions for the opposite sex. Comedy is derived through repetition of the conflict, piling on of complications, first the breaks going to one, then to the other.

McLaglen and Lowe are excellent. McLaglen, making a brief personal appearance after the picture Saturday, received one of the longest receptions a star has ever been given on this coast. His work is truly great, natural, likeable, human, no flossy heroics, just a tough top sergeant. Lowe shares equally in the plaudits although as the good looking one of the rivals, getting less sympathy..

Of the numerous women, but one, Lily Damita, had any prominence. She does not enter until the picture has been showing an hour. She seems rather over-acting although her role, hoydenish Nicarauguan tease and novice trollop, was difficult to make convincing.

Some of the gags are belly laughs. One has El Brendel, as a goof Swede Marine, telling Top Sergeant Flagg he has the lay of the land. This same expression lately used in a mag serial. Scattered throughout the picture are other remarks with unmistakable inference. Safe to say "The Cock-Eyed World" has the broadest stuff yet seen or heard on the screen. Few films of either era have ever been so frank and undisguised in their treatment of sex as a subject of humor.

Little long and tends to dull, particularly when they finally drag in fight scenes late in the picture. Incidentally dialog frequently cracks "big business" as being responsible for wars of aggrandisement, such as the Nicaraguan campaign. This radicalism is a hold-over from the tone of thought in "What Price Glory."

In toto, "The Cock-Eyed World" is rich and racy entertainment and sure-fire box office. *Land.*

SAY IT WITH SONGS
(ALL DIALOG
With Songs)

Warner Brothers production and release. Al Jolson starred. Davey Lee featured. Director, Lloyd Bacon. Scenario adaptation by Joe Jackson from story by Darryl Zanuck (gen. mgr. Warners coast studio) and Harvey Gates. Sounded by Vitaphone (Western Electric). Four songs by De-Sylva, Brown and Henderson; three other songs by Billy Rose and Dave Dryer—all of the numbers credited to Jolson as collaborator. Opened at Warner's, New York, Aug. 6, twice daily, $3 top (loges); $2.50 top orchestra. Running time, 95 minutes.
Joe Lane......................Al Jolson
Little Pal.....................Davey Lee
Katherine Lane.............Marian Nixon
Dr. Robt. Merrill..........Holmes Herbert
Joe's cellmate................Fred Kohler
Surgeon......................John Bowers

Again Al Jolson and songs in a Warner Brothers talker—and money. Jolson and songs are about as staple as the screen can get for the box office. And Jolson can get the songs because he gets the song writers, and getting them he can sing them. Four of these songs rate as hits, probably two going into the best selling lists.

With Jolson, "Say It With Songs" is a marked advancement for him as a screen player. It far overshadows "The Jazz Singer" or "The Singing Fool" in that respect. Perhaps it is but a matter of course that it should, as his third talker in three years. But it's not the advancement in the mechanism that helps Jolson the most here—it's Jolson himself.

He plays more naturally and looks the human Al Jolson on the screen, even in the betterment of his make up, than previously.

Jolson is happily cast as a radio singer. It is in that role which gives the talker its very fast and entertaining start. A radio broadcasting station, highly satirized.

Again the story has Jolson married with a son, the same Davey Lee, that remarkable kidlet. Davey doesn't sing. That's a pity since hearing him do it in "Sonny Boy," but he talks a lot, says "swell" and "grand," and keeps unbelieveably mute for a boy of four when the script calls for it.

Jolson, the kid, and Marian Nixon as the wife and mother, are the picture. The station announcer tries to make Miss Nixon. He is Jolson's best friend on the film. The station announcer tells the wife if she'll be nice her husband will be an ether singing champ.

She wouldn't be nice, not before or after her singing husband forgot dates with her, prefering craps and booze. Besides she told him of the announcer's campaign.

So that night, while driving with the announcer toward the station, the radio singer couldn't resist and let him have it. The blow that did the trick sent the announcer against a stone cornice, and the husband-father got life for manslaughter.

It was here that the tension commenced to burn and never stopped after it. But this picture, unlike Jolson's others, doesn't tear the tears out of you. Enough sobs if you like or have a family of your own. Otherwise you can watch the story run on, although not without appreciating a really fine lyric of the song Jolson sings behind the bars of his cell, "Why Can't You?", a number due for the two best sellers of the score.

Still, jails so far have not been wired. It does look a bit incongruous (if that word's left) to have a prisoner sing to synchronized music. In "Weary River," Dick Barthelmess played a piano accompaniment, at least on the screen. No lift here, however, in the business or idea.

The prisoner was paroled before the film wound up, and Little Pal got hit by an auto. He was following his Daddy. Davey waddling along in his long trousers, not unlike a Chaplin walk, was the laugh hit of the evening. The boy was in bad shape, but saved by a surgeon who also loved the wife, now a nurse, and Davey's lost speech was restored when Daddy again sang "Little Pal" to him as the boy dreamed.

And at the finish Al was back again at the mike, wife and kid home, everything hunky dory, and nothing left to do for the Warners except count up.

Besides "Little Pal" as a certain ballad, there is "I'm In Seventh Heaven," as the pop hit, with "Little Pal" the plug, "Why Can't You?" the peach, and "Used to You" as the big possibility.

Al sings seven songs in all, four by DeSylva, Brown and Henderson, and that trio's the four prospects, whilst the other three were written by Billy Rose and Dave Dryer, Jolson credited with having participated in the writing of the entire seven. Other numbers are "Just One Sweet Kiss," "I'm Ka-ra-zy For You," and "Back In Your Own Back Yard," by Rose Dryer. This "Kiss" number also sounds very good and likely.

Much of the smoothness of the running is due to the direction by Lloyd Bacon. Particularly in the radio station scene did Mr. Bacon's work stamp itself, while in the later scenes he kept the action moving in as brisk a manner as could be expected in sobbing times. With Jolson in between songs and sobs, gagging for laughs.

Miss Nixon looked nice as the young mother, in not a brilliant role. She mostly had to listen to her husband squaring himself by saying "Honey" or "Baby," though Miss Nixon did real well when cast off by her convict-husband, after he had listened to his cellmate relate how wives of convicts forget. That little lesson has its own big moral and is set in here neatly by Mr. Bacon as a very human bit.

Photography excellent and great for Jolson, with reproduction without a mar at Warner's theatre.

There's no need comparing one Jolson picture with the other; it's just songs, for Jolson himself is incomparable as the singer of them.

But maybe the next time Al goes on the screen they will let him remain single, though he must adopt Davey to get the kid again in the same picture. *Sime.*

Greene Murder Case
(ALL DIALOG)

Paramount production and release. S. S. Van Dine's best seller mystery novel directed by Frank Tuttle, with Louise Long adaptation). Bartlett Cormack (dialog), and Richard H. Digges, Jr. (titles), collaborating on the filmization; Henry Gerrard, cameraman. Produced on west coast under B. P. Schulberg's supervision. Runs 68 minutes at the Paramount, New York.
Philo Vance ....William Powell
Sibella Greene ....Florence Eldridge
Dr. Von Blon ....Ullrich Haupt
Ada Greene ....Jean Arthur
Sergeant Heath ....Eugene Pallette
John F. X. Markham ......E. H. Calvert
Mrs. Tobias Greene .....Gertrude Norman
Chester Greene ....Lowell Drew
Rex Greene ....Morgan Farley
Sproot ....Brandon Hurst
Mrs. Mannheim ....Augusta Burmeister
Hemming ....Marcia Harriss
Barton ....Mildred Golden
Nurse ....Mrs. Mildred Buckland
Police Nurse ....Helena Phillips
Medical Examiner ....Shep Camp
Lawyer Canon ....Chas. E. Evans

The second of Paramount's all dialog adaptations of the S. S. Van Dine mystery best-sellers and another box-office clicker, possessing some added niceties and finer improvements over the "Canary Murder Case," as is to be expected with the progress of talker technic. William Powell again impersonates Philo Vance, the gentleman detective creation of Van Dine's. The progression in these productions for public edification is along the lines of bigger and better and more murders, for three of an unsympathetic family of Greenes go to their an-

cestors before Vance finds the solution. The fourth, the least suspected member, goes to her doom before the law takes its toll. Picture should be potent b. o. stuff anywhere.

Tuttle has done a good job of this murder mystery tale. It possesses all the elements of box office appeal plus a few new wrinkles. The casting is convincing and such sidelights as a German-speaking servant, religiously-demented slavey, convincingly bombastic detective sergeant, suave, quiet personation of the psychologist-crime student, Vance, and the rest, all tend to ring the bell.

Powell again turns in a neat performance. A couple of legits, Ullrich Haupt and Morgan Farley, evidence their cinematic "mike" values on a par favorably comparable with their past stage performances. Florence Eldridge's conception of the eldest of the Greene heirs was impressively real, while the testy Gertrude Norman made her crass role equally authentic. *Abel.*

LAST of MRS. CHEYNEY
(ALL DIALOG)

M-G-M production and release. Starring Norma Shearer. Directed by Sidney Franklin. Basil Rathbone, Herbert Bunston and George Barraud, featured. Photography by William Daniels. Adapted from the Frederick Lonsdale play of same name. Running time, 94 minutes. At Capitol, New York, week Aug. 10.
Mrs. Cheyney..............Norma Shearer
Lord Arthur Dilling.........Basil Rathbone
Charles....................George Barraud
Lord Elton..............Herbert Bunston
Lady Marie.................Hedda Hopper
Joan............................Moon Carroll
Mrs. Wynton.............Madeline Seymour
Willie Wynton..............Cyril Chadwick
George.................George K. Arthur
William.....................Finch Smiles
Mrs. Webley................Maude Turner

One of the longest—in point of running time—of the all-dialog pictures to come out so far. Goes for more than one hour and a half without intermission and, except for a badly delayed finish, doesn't lose its grip for an instant. Play is an unusual and very clever kind of sentimental hokum, the sort of thing the fans will go for heavily, and it's a better than ordinary money picture.

Significant angle is that its whole method is more of the stage than of the screen. No visible action, whole development depending upon the spoken word. Tension and suspense lie in the tricky lines rather than in situation expressed in movement.

Fact that here is a picture that holds through its dialog, bodes no good for the regular stage in the further development of that competition between the screen and spoken play in the immediate future.

In other words this canned drama is just as effective as was the stage play from which it is made. It is an almost literal transcription. Looking at the picture one can see the division of scenes the play had. The studio has added little in the retelling, but it has preserved all the merits and tricky persuasiveness of the original.

Whole story is sentimental, a deftly manipulated series of the bunk about the good girl drawn into associations with a band of crooks, getting herself accepted into society so they can prey upon the rich, the girl all the time retaining the chaste and delicate spirit of a nun.

It's bum literature but great theatre, particularly here with a splendid group of players. Norma Shearer does extremely well with the heroine. She most successfully plays the role of elegance and high breeding, the two qualities which are the key to making Mrs. Cheyney plausible. Basil Rathbone falls into a role for his casual, easy stage style, and the character of Lord Elton, composite of stupidity and meanness and the whole trick of the play's sentimental punch, is happily in the hands of

Herbert Bunston, to whom it is pie.

The picture's finish could be made brisker as a concession to screen tradition. It has good comedy and pretty romance, but the fan public has been trained to the snappy finale without artistic trimmings. This audience was a bit impatient at this point, after giving the rest of the picture its complete and riveted attention. *Rush.*

THE WRECKER
(BRITISH MADE)

Gainsborough production (sound effects) released by Tiffany-Stahl over here. Directed by G. M. Bolvary. Carlyle Blackwell and Joseph Striker featured. Screen play by Agnes McPhail, based on stage play by Arnold Didley and Bernard Merivale. Theme song. Sounded by RCA Photophone (in New York). Running time 70 minutes. At Cameo, New York, week Aug. 10.

Ambrose Barney ....Carlyle Blackwell
Mary Shelton ....Benita Hume
Sir Gervaise Bartlett ....Winter Hall
Roger Doyle ....Joseph Striker
Rameses Ratchett ....Leonard Thompson
William ....Gordon Harker
Beryl Matchley ....Pauline Johnson

An old fashioned English melodrama which the American screen public outgrew years ago. Not much above the screen serial type of story. Only merit is that it has some excellent settings.

No dialog and the sound effects, musical scoring and introduction of a theme song ("Are You Really Mine," by Jose H. Santly and Irving Caesar) plainly introduced after it was finished as a silent production. Job of matching up the sound details has been skillfully done, but no skill could conceal that the articulate accessories were an afterthought.

Whole business unreels after the manner of a rather frantic melodrama, with the high lights of action the actual wrecking of no less than three railroad trains. Incidents that have all the dramatic plausibility of the "Blue Jeans" school of thrill. A sample of the action will serve to illustrate the tone of the production.

Hero and heroine have cornered the demon who has been wrecking trains all over England. They even have a phonograph record of his telephoned instructions to cause a collision between an express freight and a fast train carrying hundreds of holiday merry-makers. Thus equipped they invite him to the railroad office to hear the phonograph reproduce the evidence of his crime, neglecting entirely to prevent the starting of the holiday train.

Criminal escapes from the room, there is a chase, and by one of those coincidences they are presently all aboard the very train dashing toward destruction, held at bay by the armed maniac, until the heroine climbs along the running board of the train (one of those English compartment cars, of course) to disarm him just in time to have the two trains stop within eight inches of each other.

American audiences above the age of 12 hoot at the start of things. Playing is about as subtle as episodes like the one described. Carlyle Blackwell, who once was a screen flap idol in America, plays the heavy, a grotesque performance made up of stilted grimaces and mugging to express sinister crime.

Benita Hume is a puppet heroine, husky British type whose strivings to register coy maidenly reserve are pretty hard to take. Pauline Johnson, playing the beautiful tool of the arch criminal in all seriousness, is uproarious comedy and in addition is the frumpiest pretty girl in all international filmdom.

Camera work is a valuable study. Close ups are as hard and uncompromising as a commercial photograph for collar ad illustration. An American camera man could get more human quality into the blue print of a machine shop pattern.

This goes for studio shots where apparently light handling was at fault. In the open the photography is better. Some of the shots at trains rushing through lovely landscapes, are excellent.

One solitary detail was a credit to the production staff. It had a really good designer of sets. Several interiors are capital in composition and lighting. One in particular was the apartment of the arch criminal, capital bit of modern designing and a first class handling of shadows.

Only sequence where talk is employed is the audible reproduction of the incriminating phonograph record, which, of course, could have been synchronized with the action after the picture was completed. Theme song also is dragged in by off stage voices during a love passage near the finish and certainly was added to a completed negative.

As a study of what is the matter with the English studio, this picture is interesting and may contain the answer. As a commercial product for American exhibition, it's pretty impossible. *Rush.*

THE POWER OF EVIL
(ARMENIAN MADE)
(Silent)

Claimed to be the first picture made under supervision of the Armenian Soviet. No American release credited. Directed by M. Goldvani and P. Barkhoudian. Leading feminine role by Barbara Matatian. At 6th Ave. Playhouse, New York, week Aug. 10. Running time 71 minutes.

Devotees of Ibsen and Tolstoi will enjoy the first production credited Soviet Armenia. It is filled with exquisite shadings of tragedy and played by one of the most facially sinister casts ever assembled.

While "The Power of Evil" far surpasses in sustained interest and classic outline more recent importations and while it is ideally suitable for sure seat audiences, the percentage of American fans who would appreciate a production of this kind is too low to warrant the average exhibitor giving it serious consideration. In its native land, may be looked upon as a pippin.

One sequence, amounting to little more than a flash, should be clipped. Its elimination would deprive only the agnostics and aetheists of a chuckle since it blasphemes a religion and is distasteful even to sophisticates. This is where the mother is shown praying for the recovery of her daughter from epilepsy, with a cut to the rear disclosing a clergyman feeding water to a mechanical tear duct in the portrait of a Madonna.

The epileptic daughter is Barbara Matatain, soulful-eyed maiden whose clear complexion and carriage affords a marked contrast to all others in the cast.

Effectively associated with the girl is a demented outcast, who sees in her the image of his own daughter. Early in the story the daughter topples over a cliff in fear of his approach.

Concealment of their daughter's affliction at the time of her marriage into the village's wealthiest family is the first important thread in the story.

Jealousy of the bride leads groom's mother and sister to connive with a charlatan, following the infliction of a child in the family with a malady. Because of the young husband's fidelity they are unable to drive her from the house. After resorting to different practices of witchery, such as the burying of a crow in the garden, decide to strangle her.

The tensity of the sequence culminating with the murder reaches a degree realized by few of the most notable productions in this class. The three women dressed in

black are on a darkly lighted set, refusing to admit callers who, generally arouse the villagers. Then the entrance of the victim her sense of danger, and the sudden precipitation of her head into a smouldering hole beneath a couch-like table.

Suddenly, the crazy man tearing at the witch and crushing the corpse to the hairy form that had shielded a rag doll—the only memory of the tragedy in his own life. *Waly.*

HALF-MARRIAGE
(All Dialog With Song)
Dancing)

Radio Pictures' production and release. Directed by William J. Cowen from George Kibbe Turner's story, adapted by Jane Murfin. William LeBaron producer; Henry Hobar, assistant producer. R.C.A. Photophone sounded. Runs 68 minutes. At Albee, Brooklyn, week Aug. 10.

Judy Page.................Olive Borden
Dick Carroll.................Morgan Farley
Charles Turner.................Ken Murray
Ann Turner.................Ann Greenway
Sally ....Sally Blane
George Page ....Richard Tucker

For purposes of a stage and screen tieup in which Ken Murray, the vaude mime, is featured, he was accorded stellar billing in connection with this Radio Pictures' all talker. Otherwise it's a starless feature but a good little program release, with or without any personality ballyhoo. Actually, for the general run of releases, Olive Borden who, with Morgan Farley, comprises the principal love interest, will probably be accorded marquee distinction by exhibitors. Indie exhibs have a real buy here.

Ken Murray's unit was the stage feature of the Albee's stage vaudeville program, hence the hook-up ballyhooing him as a stage and screen satellite. It's a good stunt for any affiliated Keith house likely to book both Murray and this feature as a joint attraction.

"Half-Marriage" is strictly a young folk's picture which means it will appeal generally. The secret marriage stuff, the post-marriage scenes and the amorous clinches, if a bit overdone, spell box-office for general purposes, and will please on the whole.

Miss Borden is a revelation in dialog. She is as natural a modernistic ingenue in her every action and speech as could be desired. The realism and authenticity of it all impresses from the start and even in the delicate boudoir shots, on the morning following their secret elopement, the intimate stuff is rather willingly accepted for all its palpable audience objective.

Farley is a natural enough, if not particularly strongly characterized juvenile, opposite Miss Borden. Murray and Ann Greenway, another variety alumnus, are cast as the secondary couple.

Murray gets in his innings, as does Miss Greenway, in the introductory studio party scenes. The latter plants the pollyannaish "clouds roll away" theme song and Murray cuts up. In a later set, with a country club dansant as the occasion, he shows to even better effect with a panto bit, a band number scene and nonsense. The band presentation was quite a novelty utilizing a psychologically timely Zeppelin foreground as a staging effect.

The light heavy (billing not caught or programed) did well, as did that comedy-panned zany in the opening clown allegorical nonsense; another not billed.

Romantic interest of "Half-Marriage" holds right through. A melodramatic touch in which the stewed light-heavy suffers a fatal fall brings it to a punchy climax. That excellent screen "father" personator, Richard Tucker, tops everything off to a happy ending, augering well for his son-in-law, who is

also one of his architects in his office. An intelligent official investigation by a homicide squad dick further dovetails nicely into the picture.

"Half-Marriage" is okay program. *Abel.*

NIGHT CLUB
(60% DIALOG)

Paramount production and release. Directed by Robert Florey and claimed to have been inspired by Katherine Brush's novel. Running time, 40 minutes with 12 minutes taken up with prolog talk by Donald Ogden Stewart. Flash appearances of Fannie Brice, Ann Pennington, Tamara Geva, Bobbe Arnst, Minnie Dupree, Pat Rooney and son, Jimmie Carr. At Little Carnegie, week Aug. 10. Western Electric sound system.

"Night Club," in the form Paramount decided to release its first talker feature made in Astoria, L. I., a nonentity. At its best a poor short subject because Donald Ogden Stewart's talk is pasted on. What follows is nothing but a mess of miscellaneous ends of a revue, broken into by shots to ladies' room and coat rack. And another good title ruined.

Cut until 28 minutes is all that remains of what Robert Florey directed for a feature, the thing is without the semblance of a story. The only point the editor overlooked was the applause, as miserably recorded as the voices which make the women in their retiring room cackle like a yard full of perturbed hens. Fully 14 minutes is taken up by handclapping which reproduces as though the extras were using barrel staves.

As an illustration of the exaggerated palm blistering efforts, the Rooneys get a hand never equaled in their stage life. All during their tapping the audience on the screen works its mitts. The same is true for the others. As soon as Jimmie Carr announces the name the applause starts and does not stop until curtain.

To compensate for an offering that permits no further shearing, since regulating the noise would reduce it to less than a reel, Paramount throws in "Pusher-in-the-Face," credited F. Scott Fitzgerald for theme inspiration, to every exhibitor willing to take a chance on costly sweepings that project only as a badly edited trailer.

Shown in New York at the Little Carnegie small sure-seater on 57th street. House usually plays cheap foreign mades, not paying for most of them.
Waly.

MADONNA OF AVE. A
(60% DIALOG)

Warner production and release. Starring Delores Costello. Directed by Michael Curtiz. Byron Haskin, cameraman. Dialog by Francis Powers. Orchestration by Louis Silvers on Vitaphone (Western Electric) system. In cast: Louise Dresser, Grant Withers, William Russell. Running time, 71 minutes. At the Hippodrome, New York, week Aug. 10.

"Madonna of Avenue A" is so parallel to "Not Quite Decent," which Fox released a few months ago, that some of the Louise Dresser cabaret-mother sequences seem to have been lifted in their entirety from that actress' job for Fox. This Warner picture is slightly better than an ordinary programer, but a certain hazard for bookings over two days.

In this Miss Dresser is not given sufficient play to steal the honors. Delores Costello, regardless of production merits, outstays all others before the camera.

A bootlegger, who plays a guitar and sings to himself in the moonlight, is the hero role essayed by Grant Withers. This gent discovers the lonely private school girl on a beach and introduces her to some of the boat's supply.

A timely raid gets the young lady ousted from school and provides her the opportunity to locate the Park avenue domicile she has never seen, but which her mother described during the years of academicia.

Meantime sets change to a lowly Manhattan dive where the mother (Miss Dresser) is taxing around with sailors and what-nots. And to be sure that the audience will keep in touch with the amorous bootlegger, the gent is now one of mama's gang.

More meller than dramatic is the meeting of mother and daughter near the bar. Fans have been too well preened for that event by the unoriginality of the story and the hack way in which it has been allowed to travel along.

The runner turns out to be a good guy and genuine so far as the school miss goes. He marries her and serves a term in jail when the mother frames him, believing that it will give the girl a chance. The mother finally realizes her error and takes poison so that an attorney can get the insurance. *Waly.*

GIRL OVERBOARD

(5% DIALOG)

(With Song Effects and Synchronized Score)

Universal production and release. Directed by Wesley Ruggles. Mary Philbin featured. Western Electric (probably Movietone) sounded. Theme song only for synchronized music, sung also, "Port of Dreams." At Loew's, New York, one day, Aug. 6, one-half double bill. Running time, 65 minutes.

Universal in "Girl Overboard" has provided what might be called a freaky talker, which wired houses trying to dodge a high rental for a day or two can play, while it will also be as useful for the short run silent houses and the hideaways.

It's freaky in its make-up, running silent with a theme song, few effects and a synchronized score, then suddenly bursting into dialog beyond half way and again lapsing into the silent effect thing. At first thought it could be said Universal had gotten this out as a sample of a talker with the real thing to follow next week, but still the picture carries enough in its story to make it stand up for its purpose.

What little dialog is there is mostly an aggravation. For instance, it stars with the two young people, entirely unsuspected as to talk, with the juve saying:

"Mary, will you always love me?"

"Always, Denny."

"Forever, Mary?"

"Forever, Denny."

"Gee, that's great" added Denny as that bit broke off.

Not the exact dialog, but the idea. Later the ship's captain got a laugh out of a bit he did in talk.

Then there's Mary Philbin singing "Port of Dreams," the theme song, also sung by a parrot. Of course if you don't think doubling for a parrot is funny, then this picture was really built for the side street sad sobbers.

But the parrot fits into the plot, also its singing.

"Girl Overboard" not a befitting title, though the girl does go overboard and is saved by Denny. Nor is there sufficient explanation for many incidents.

Story harps upon the rigors of the prison parole system. That bound a young man paroled with eight years to go, with Rule No. 3 saying he must lay off romancing or marrying. But he fell for the same Mary who fell overboard. That's all straightened out. With plenty of asides in doing it, including a court scene, without dialog. Universal is so contrary!

The talking sequence is in the center. It's not on either end and

cannot be ep or prolog. Just a freak among talkers. Perhaps Universal has an idea here for those houses that can't stand the high priced good or bad first run talkers which still charge heavy when over their first runs. A good near-talker like this may do well, not alone for the indies but for the shooting galleries on the chains, with U itself having many of those.

Four characters do very well, Miss Philbin, no matter what you think of her singing (?) or speaking voice, the juve as Denny, the sea captain, Cappy, and the parole commissioner, the latter excellent, in action and voice. *Sime.*

TEXAS TOMMY

(SILENT)

Eldorado production, with Syndicate releasing (Indies). Directed by J. J. McGowan, who also plays a principal role. Bob Custer featured. At Loew's, New York, one day, Aug. 6, half double bill. Running time, 48 minutes.

A western with plenty of riding chasing. Since westerns are fast dying out, this one now looks better than it would have in the days of silents only.

The biggest fault of westerns has survived the biggest fault of pictures, and the biggest fault of pictures was no novelty. Talkers altered that. But one man whipping an army in a western continues, to destroy anything else in it.

A western hero pulling punches and hitting a dozen men around their bodies, finally knocking them all out, is only a hero to his banker. This is Bob Custer's big stuff here. He can whip three or a band at one time. And among the roughnecks of the plains, he's as safe without a gun as with one, for he has his hands and feet.

Some day when Bob shall have quit pictures and become a big business man, he'll probably show some of these westerns to his children. What will they think of their Pop?

But meanwhile where they play westerns because they're cheap, play "Texas Tommy," a title that 17 years ago started the jazz dance craze. And the girl here is oke, for she doesn't fight—just looks good.

And if they can make 'em look any tougher than J. J. McGowan, the director, did as the tough Texas Tommy, a sea tale should be woven around them. *Sime.*

A SCANDAL IN PARIS

(French Made)
(Silent)

Felson production, Fox distribution. Featuring Lily Damita. Directed by Robert Wiens. Foreign cast not credited. At Loew's New York one half double bill, one day, Aug. 9. Running time, 47 mins.

Quota picture that will get its first runs in the third run houses. Yet in its way it represents a much higher production standard than the average importation that has to find its market among the cheaper playdates. Photography and lighting good, characterization interesting, story weak, but neatly spun, and the settings and background attractive and possessing the glamor inherently attaching to foreign locales.

It's a matrimonial misunderstanding with a scheming woman plotting to separate a couple in the hope of capturing the husband for her own. In a court room scene that will be interesting for the foreign detail and customs pictured, this woman is proved to be ambidexterous, having written the poison pen letter with her left hand.

Story is not quite clear at start and it is not a commercial feature in the American sense. Still it can be shown in the non-deluxes without apologies.

Newspapermen will smile at the atmospheric touch of eight court reporters waiting with dignity and perfect manners to get into one phone booth during a recess in the trial. *Land.*

EXALTED FLAPPER

(Disc Orchestration)

Fox production and release. Directed by James Tinling from Walter Irwin's story, adapted by Matt Taylor. Titles by H. Caldwell. In cast: Sue Carroll, Barry Norton, Irene Rich, Albert Conti, Sylvia Field. At Loew's New York one day, Aug. 7. Running time 60 minutes.

Folks in an asylum couldn't go wrong on doping out this yarn after the first 50 feet. The princess is going to marry the prince despite the Irish press agent. "The Exalted Flapper" is one of those unoriginal things that makes good easy entertainment for the average fan.

Newsreel clip of Lindbergh paper tearing crowd used as opener. Sue Carroll as princess quickly sheds petticoat for flapper undies. Pretty gam view here.

Then there's the night club raid, but no publicity, and the Queen's (Irene Rich) negotiations for wealthy hubby.

Picture would only be a two-reeler if closed here. But it must go along so that Barry Norton and Miss Carroll may wrap up in bedroom silks before the jaded parents have the opportunity to announce their betrothal. *Waly.*

LAW OF MOUNTED

(SILENT)

El Dorado production; independent release. Directed by J. P. McGowan, who co-stars with Bob Custer. Paul Allen, cameraman. Sally Winters in cast. At Stanley, New York, one day, Aug. 10. Running time about 65 minutes.

In the dime theatre market "Law of the Mounted" rates average. For J. P. McGowan, unique even on Hollywood's Poverty Row as a director-semi-star, the production is par excellence.

Fans who watch closely, and J.P's face is biggest on the screen most of the time, can almost picture him saying in the best known and most accessible of filmland's Western locales:

"Now you sock me. There! Now when I wallop you, you drop and stay down. Fine!"

And so it goes.

In this one, while they pan frightfully and overwork their jaws for the tough expression, the dime payees will find the nearest thing to sustained suspense in any of McGowan's efforts.

The boys actually do perform like a lot of cowhands, with the exception of Custer, but J. P. is getting on to the serial idea of not telling everything in each sequence. *Waly.*

RIDERS OF STORM

(Silent)

J. Charles Davis production (states rights). Featuring Yakima Canutt. Story and direction by J. P. McGowan. Cameraman Paul Allen. Cast includes Ione Reed, Dorothy Vernon, Bobby Dunn, Charles Whitaker, on double feature bill at Loew, New York, one day, Aug. 9. Running time 48 mins.

Same old western stencil with a couple of flourishes to alter the pattern slightly. Not enough to deceive the naked eye. Suspense is .005, although production, photography and acting fairly good for a cowboy opera.

Strictly for the shooting galleries and nickelodeons with no occasion for detail. It's as familiar as beans in the army.

Title has no connection. *Land.*

FAST LIFE

(ALL DIALOG)

First National production and release. Directed by John Francis Dillon from screen version of play of same title by Samuel Shipman and John B. Hymer. Western Electric (Vitaphone) sounded. Chester Morris, Douglas Fairbanks, Jr., and Loretta Young featured. In cast: William Holden, Ray Hallor, Frank Sheridan, Purnell Pratt. At Central, Aug. 15, twice daily, $2 top. Running time, 80 minutes.

First National brings the stage play practically line for line and set for set to the talker screen. Picture version is better played, but the average audience will rebel against over-mugging, during which long chunks of dialog, that drag to the point of fan restlessness, are released. With a theme, like numerous predecessors concerning youth and the chair, that has little sustained suspense because of over-conversation, "Fast Life" is okay program, but not $2 Broadway.

Where the play allowed the curtain to go up on the couple in bed, the First National version veers to bathrobes and a couch following the whoopee party. The marital tie is just as quickly revealed so there is nothing censorable.

Hysteria is much better for live reproduction if it is to be carried to the extent it exists in this picture. Everyone has a chance to cry and register high voice after the shooting of an admirer who returns unexpectedly and discovers the couple a la negligee. Mechanically, some of the tearful moments, possibly because of vigorous and rapid repetition, give an audience too much time for checking.

Loretta Young, who plays the maiden over whom the shooting occurs and whose husband is condemned to the death house, shows more promise with each production. One of Hollywood's prettiest ingenues, she is also gifted with an excellent speaking voice.

As the joy leader and young hubby, Doug Fairbanks, Jr., does a workmanlike job. Chester Morris is a little out of cast in the role of the Governor's weak-kneed son. Morris' performance is good, but he is directorially driven to too much wailing and feature clinching.

The last few sequences, dealing with the innocent man in the death house and the warden wondering how he will break it to his brother that the official son is the murderer, are attention getters. Some excellent prison interiors, particularly one showing the witnesses through a window in the chair house.

The conventional finale comes with the Governor's son committing suicide and the couple reformed joy makers. *Waly.*

THE DANCE OF LIFE

(ALL DIALOG)
(With Songs and Dances)

Paramount production and release of "Burlesque," retitled from that play by George Manker Watters and Arthur Hopkins. Watters dialog adaptation for dialog; screen play by Benjamin Glazer. John Cromwell (dialog) and A. Edward Sutherland co-directed; J. Roy Hunt, photography. Color sequences in Technicolor; theme song, "True Blue Lou." At Rivoli, New York, Aug. 16, on grind. Running time, 115 minutes.

Bonny Lee King............Nancy Carroll
Ralph "Skid" Johnson..........Hal Skelly
Harvey Howell..............Ralph Theadore
Lefty.....................Charles Brown
Sylvia Marco..............Dorothy Revier
Bozo.........................Al St. John
Gussie.........................May Boley
Jerry........................Oscar Levant
Miss Sherman................Gladys Du Bois
Jimmy......................James T. Quinn
Champ Melvin...............James Farley
Minister...................George Irving

"The Dance of Life," the rechristened talker, "Burlesque," with Hal Skelly and Nancy Carroll, is an intelligent and fairly faithful screen reproduction of Arthur Hopkins' dramatic smash of '27-8. Skelly does equally as well in synchronized dialog as he did in the stage production. Rest of the dramatic values are insured by such stage originals as Ralph Theadore, Charles Brown and Oscar Levant re-creating their roles for Paramount. Nancy Carroll, co-featured with Skelly, does the Barbara Stanwyck creation of Bonnie King, the eternal faithful.

While there may be some inside comment on how a "looker" like Nancy Carroll stuck with a lousy road burlesque turk like the one they open and close with, for general laity acceptance that doesn't figure. After all, the customers want their heroines as attractive as possible, with name value extra, even though in actuality a swell number like Bonnie King (Miss Carroll) would be swiped by a rival musical management if only for her looks.

As a general release, this backstage story will prove great box office fodder. The switch in title from "Burlesque" to the more alluring "Dance of Life" was smart. The play's original title is only known to New York, Chicago and a few key cities; for exhibition purposes "Burlesque" might be a detracting screen monicker.

John Cromwell, handling the dialog staging, and A. Edward Sutherland, in co-directing, have made a good job of it. Perhaps the unfolding is a bit slow, but for true character delineation the length is almost necessary. Still there's no getting away from that two hours (lacking five minutes) of running time. They'll have to chop somewhere.

The petty jealousies, hates, trivial joys over a bottle, loyalty and loves of a third-rate burlesque troupe are excellently mirrored by a capable cast. Skelly's characterization of the pratt-fallin' fool carries conviction. The girls will live with Miss Carroll as the "True Blue Lou" reincarnation of a not particularly pat theme song. That's the title and the words reflect the character of Bonnie King (Miss Carroll), but it was rather incongruously dragged in by Skelly in an olio specialty.

Skelly would have really turned in a reproachless performance had his Ziegfeld "Follies" debut been as sensational as the tempo of the picture would indicate, not to mention the incandescents above the Ziegfeld theatre. Great plug for Zieggy, of course, but Skelly's hoofin' specialty was just so-so. Still the fans won't quibble over that, either, nor about those somewhat hazy Technicolor scenes.

Performances consistently good. Mr. Theadore as the wholesome westerner; Charles Brown as Lefty Miller; Dorothy Revier, the polite femme menace; May Boley (excellent) as the "beef-trust" burlesker; Al St. John and the others all registered.

The heart-throb stuff further cinches "The Dance of Life." Love interest is tense, although it's not a tear-jerker. Talker has all the elements of sturdy box office stuff. *Abel.*

WRATH OF THE SEA

(GERMAN-MADE)
(Silent)

German production, released over here by John M. Kelley (states rights). Edited by Pierre Arnaud. Direction by Namfred Noa. Feautring Nils Asther, Bernard Goetzke and Agnes Esterhazt. At Cameo, New York, week Aug. 17. Running time, 62 mins.

Another foreign war picture synthetically created in the cutting room with the aid of a studio story woven into and around official camera records. As the photography is good, the scenes interesting and invested with a note of authenticity, picture may be regarded and classified as acceptable stuff for houses that can play, or previously have played, this type of film entertainment. Exhibitors and bookers will know from experience whether the Battle of Jutland is apt to be an interesting theme for their patronage. If they played and made money with other foreign pictures of the war, "Wrath of the Sea" will be okay. It is not commercial in the wider American trade sense, but in its war group, pretty good.

It deals with the struggle of the British and German navies. Rival commanders are life-long friends, but must destroy each other in battle. German commander has domestic difficulties with his wife, who considers herself neglected and looks at a subordinate officer of philandering disposition. Wife, widowed, in end marries the English commander, whom she nursed back to health.

Battle stuff is good. *Land.*

SALUTE

Los Angeles, Aug. 15.

Fox production and release, featuring George O'Brien and Helen Chandler. Directed by John Ford from Tristram Tupper and John Stone's story. Dialog credited to J. K. McGuinness with W. W. Lindsay, Jr., sound engineer. J. A. August, cameraman. At Loew's State week starting Aug. 15. Running time, 83 mins.

Cadet John Randall........George O'Brien
Midshipman Paul Randall..William Janney
Midshipman Albert E. Price............
..........................Frank Albertson
Midshipman...................Ward Bond
Nancy Wayne.............Helen Chandler
Marion Wilson..............Joyce Compton
Major General Somers.....Clifford Dempsey
Rear Admiral Randall......Lumsden Hare
Smoke Screen................Stepin Fetchit
Navy Coach...................David Butler

On undergraduate and gridiron atmosphere "Salute" rates with "Brown of Harvard" as the best picture of its kind to date. It will reap for coin because it's a good football yarn for fall release and there hasn't been anything to top it in the film work turned out on either of the Government Academies. It's football, but more important than that—there's laughs, and plenty of 'em, with Frank Albertson outgrossing Step Fetchit for those who care to clock the mirth. Besides which the dialog fits, is delivered all the way and there isn't too much of it. Add a Booth Tarkington angle to the adolescent love interest and you're apt to have quite a picture. It is.

Football stuff is exciting, especially with sound, but it's the sidelights in the build-up which send this picture to the front. Albertson plays the proverbial fresh plebe, but how. Between the dialog given him and the way he handles it this youngster looks "in." He promised in "Prep and Pep" and he's kept it. It's an excellent piece of casting throughout. O'Brien, as John Randall, plays the Pointer and older brother of Paul (William Janney), and is Army's triple threat on a field or a dance floor. Meanwhile, the slighter family member is on his way to sea full of determination if punch drunk from the doe eyed glances of the baby talk Marion, Annapolis' academic impediment.

On the fringe of this circle is Nancy Wayne, a naval daughter living on post, who thinks Paul is a little bit all right and spurs him back to duty when the youngster becomes fed up after being ragged into ridiculing his grandfather by an upper classman. John, having pegged Marion as the ingenue vamp, makes a play for Nancy to show Paul what he's passing up, and Paul's resultant grouch gets him into the Army game with orders to stop his brother on the coach's psychology hunch. Contest ends in a 6-6 tie, both brothers scoring. David Butler, director, does well by the Navy coach.

Step Fetchit rings in as the servant in Paul's household who follows the boy to the Naval school and becomes a rubber for the grid squad. From spots in this picture it listens as if the sound boys will have to be careful with Step. The colored boy is mumbling so freely he can't always be understood. But they laugh when they see him so maybe it doesn't make much difference. Directorial end has pretty nearly taken the edge off the football stuff in a scene of John being spilled out of bounds and upsetting Fetchit on the sidelines. With both lying in the mud there's a conversational exchange. It doesn't chime and should be cut. Technically the game's only weak points are John's play boy spirit, good theatrical license, however, and Paul looking over his shoulder on a way to a touchdown after recovering a blocked punt. Just two periods shown, first and last, with the latter enhanced for the camera by mud, a radio announcer explaining rain in the third period. The announcer, minus program credit, is Lee Tracey behind a moustache, and very good.

Usual newsreel stuff has been inserted on the game, the final celebration of the Middies for their "moral" victory looking like a clip from last fall's Navy-Princeton game over at Franklin Field. Yells of the mob have also been cut in after the plays, somewhat awkwardly in lieu of the quiet while the play is in motion, but that's a minor point. Balancing this are some tackles, seen and heard, that football bugs will almost feel besides cries of the players to "Get that guy," etc.

In that the Fox studio idea appears to be to turn out many pictures minus any particular draw names, but with youthful principals, "Salute" stands off the b. o. handicap of that theory by meeting the added story, general cast calibre, and pictorial requirements which are among the necessities such a policy demands. And, the title is good.

No question that the producing company has turned loose a good looking and well playing group of youngsters in this effort. That goes for William Janney, excellently fitting the central character; Helen Chandler in her first talker, Albertson and Ward Bond, a linesman from U. S. C., playing his first picture role as a light heavy and not a little responsible by his "straight" for making Albertson stand out to such an extent. Bond will probably stick in pictures after this effort. He's not unlike McLaglen. Technically the entire staff must split credit.

Picture is well sprinkled with standout bits. Best one is a lengthy comedy sequence peaking to a stairway entrance, to the tune of "Rosita," by the pip looking sister of the homely plebe the boys have been dodging all evening as he tries to fill her dance program. Among the best entrances ever given a girl in pictures. Another nice piece of work has Paul and Nancy walking together immediately after the boy has been told to turn in his football togs because he's too light, both youngsters sniffling as they dejectedly amble and blaming it on suddenly contracted colds. Three or four titles mark the time advance so that Paul makes the trip to the Polo Grounds with the team the following November as a reward for amassing bruises on the scrubs all fall. Film has no theme song except "Anchors Aweigh," famous Navy pigskin melody, which is used as a duet, jazzed up for dancing, and sung enmasse.

Those Pointers who see it may be inclined to razz a little, but Annapolis and the public at large will certainly like it. It's a sincere enough effort to, perhaps, have some bearing on definitely swinging public sentiment towards the resumption of Army-Navy games.

Every so often a picture comes along that an audience can have a lot of fun watching, and feel just a little refreshed for having sat in. "Salute" is one. *Sid.*

PRISONERS

(10% DIALOG)

First National production and release. Starring Corinne Griffith. Directed by William Seiter. Produced by Walter Morosco. Story by Ferenc Molnar. Adapted by Forrest Halsey. Cameraman, Lee Garmes. Titles by Paul Perez. Shown at New York, N. Y., Aug. 15. Running time, 87 minutes.

Riza Riga	Corinne Griffith
Kessler	James Ford
Brottos	Bela Lugosi
Nicholas Cathy	Ian Keith
Lenke	Julanne Johnston
Aunt Maria	Ann Schaeffer
Kore	Baron Hesse
Sebfi	Otto Matiesen
Prosecuting Attorney	Harry Northrup

The grizzled book wormers know well how Ferenc Molnar stands in the batting files of the literary league, yet in the filming of his novel, "Prisoners," the celluloid fans will be disappointed. Even the charming Corinne Griffith, cast in the role of Riza Riga, working to make the character stand out, fails to prevent the picture from becoming irksome long before its close.

And the film, in failing to eke out just punishment to the gink who shot another down in cold blood with an eye witness to the murder, leaves a sort of dark brown taste in the mouth. The girl starting off to prison to serve a seven months' sentence for stealing at the final fade out isn't so sweet either.

The picture has sound effects, not much, but enough to call the picture sounded and also a bit of dialog at the end. This latter was effective, especially the reproduction of the trial scene.

The story is of Hungarian atmosphere and Miss Griffith is the wistful-eyed waitress who tries to forget her early life of misery and shame and live decently, only to get in another jam when she steals money to buy a pretty dress.

Some nice photographic shots and some of the scenes set a Hungarian background on a Hollywood lot.

Exhibs with this picture must sell Griffith. *Mark.*

LOVE IN THE DESERT

(10% DIALOG)

Radio Pictures production and release. Directed by George Melford. Noah Beery and Olive Borden featured. Hugh Trevor lead. Sounded by RCA Photophone. Story by Louis Serecky, adapted by Paul Percy. Titles by Randolph Bartlett. Running time, 68 minutes. At Arena (grind), New York, one day, Aug. 14.

Sample of salvaging an original silent picture by trick introduction of dialog. As a silent this would have been poor material even for a grind house on daily change. With dialog and chance to build the "see and hear" idea for lobby display it is a good flash for a probable moderate price as dialog product goes. Regardless of literary quality, it is vastly better than mere synchronized material.

Original negative was the usual sheik story, crude in idea and formula in production, with the principal merit of big mob effects when the desert tribes gather to war on the white man. Romantic hooey about the beautiful desert girl captured by cruel native chief and held captive until white hero undertakes rescue. Then hot action battle scenes up to the routine clinch.

They took the poor thing in its entirety, titles and all, and then tacked on a dialog and an epilog. Prolog deals with a Broadway chorus girl who comes to blackmail the rich father of a young man she has ensnared. Old man pays up and then she sends the young man to work on his far east desert irrigation project as discipline. Fair enough comedy introduction. Lasts about five miutes. Then picks up the original silent negative.

When this goes to its anticipated clinch, scene shifts back to New York home of hero's parents. Mother receives word that son is returning with his desert bride and Ma throws a fit at the expectation of a fat and probably black daughter-in-law. Son arrives with bride, preceded by bride's native maid servant. Ma mistakes native girl for son's wife, and there is a comedy bit before the beautiful Olive Borden is disclosed as the Eastern princess in a Paris gown and the last word in new world chic.

Epilog gives the dumb formula of the desert sheik story a bit of comedy twist that takes the curse off the cheap melodrama.

Whole business works out as fair amusement, with the dialog bits as a class flash for such grind establishments as this. *Rush.*

NEW ORLEANS

(20% DIALOG)

Tiffany-Tone production and release. Directed by Reginald Barker from story credited John Natteford. In cast: Ricardo Cortez, Alma Bennett, William Collier, Jr. Musical score by Irvin Talbot. At Loew's Circle, one day, Aug. 14. Running time, 68 minutes.

A couple of pals, a gold digger, and a race track for locale. The action could have happened in any city, except for some shots of the Mardi Gras. But, it's a great little program gem!

Collier and Cortez hook up nicely and it is the effectiveness of their work that largely keeps a mild story out of quickie class.

Alma Bennett is deserving of special attention. As the woman out for love and dough, she does a great job. Miss Bennett's portrayal of passion is of the Garbo type, only far more concentrated. Every muscle in her nicely rounded form, tightened by silks, works sometime or another. If given a real break Alma would corner a lot of the fan trade specializing in screen hot mammas.

The race track stuff is a lot less newsreely than in many of this kind. Collier is close-upped on the horse, and away he goes to win so that the pal who copped his girl will be able to put back in the company's safe the bet money. Dame, however, keeps it and prison term served. Then the lads are pals again. *Waly.*

MY LADY'S PAST

(40% DIALOG)

Tiffany-Stahl production and release. Directed by Albert Ray from the continuity by Frances Hyland. Dialog and titles by Frederic and Fanny Hatton. Hugo Riesenfeld musical score by RCA Photophone sounded. Running time, 34 minutes. At Loew's Circle, New York, one day, August 15.

Mamie Reynolds	Belle Bennett
Sam Young	Joe E. Brown
Typist	Alma Bennett
John Parker	Russell Simpson
Maid	Joan Standing

Too unsophisticated and implausible for the big cities, but in smaller towns it should be devoured. The best moments in this flicker are the talking sequences, mostly and clearly delivered by Joe Brown.

Belle Bennett, it is given to understand, is not meant to be older than 30 but even so at times appears too maternal for the role. She gives what may be called a tender touch for loads of sympathy. Belle Bennett receives the major billing. Marquee at this theatre read: "Hear Belle Bennett." But when it comes to vocal interpretations and in many instances pantomimic, to Joe Brown belongs the spoils. To play a sweetheart and lover with a pan like Joe's and still get away with it deserves some special consideration.

Barely any action, the interest lying in the plot, which at times appears like a good old fashioned meller. The boy and girl are engaged for 10 years and then needing opposition to show him it's about time he slipped a marriage ring on her finger.

One talking sequence for about eight minutes was a drunken soliloquy by Joe Brown. He was talking up enough courage to manhandle the villain. Brown was really fine here, twisting that widemouthed map of his into all manners of facial contortions and applying a proper thickness to his tongue. Over big and the highlight.

At this theatre four-fifths of the synchronization was horrible, almost killing the picture. For three minutes during one sequence the sound went dead entirely and nothing but a faint scratching could be heard. At other times the scratching was predominant.

A song which seemed to be the theme vocaled twice off screen, once by a male and then mixed. The projection of these songs was never clear enough to hear the lyrics.

PRINCE AND DANCER

(AUSTRIAN MADE)

(Silent)

Hugo-Engel foreign production, released by World Wide. Directed by Max Neufeld. Starring Dina Gralla with Albert Paulig, Werner Pittschau and Carmen Cartellieri. Billed as synchronized in Vienna with no device named. At Loew's New York one day Aug. 16, as half double bill. Running time, 77 minutes.

Sending over foreign pictures of this type only prolongs the ridicule with which Americans look forward to foreign pictures.

The acting of the entire troupe was done with as much naturalness as the string-controlled puppets of a punch and Judy show.

No excuse for a story like this even in Austria.

Synchronization cued terribly and spoils some pretty Viennese waltzes. Projected with fair clarity.

On the whole, pretty rotten.

LIGHT FINGERS

(ALL DIALOG)

Columbia production and release. Directed by Joseph Henaberry. Screen play and dialog by Jack Nutteford. Photographed by Ted Tetzlaff. Featuring Ian Keith and Dorothy Revier, supported by Carroll Nye and Ralph Theadore. At Loew's New York, one day, Aug. 16, as half double bill. Running time, 60 mins.

Dialog is everything here. Ian Keith's legit training brings results, with an easy delivery. Dorothy Revier's voice sounds sweet and clear, but she has a pronounced slow delivery in trying for pronounciation.

Story of the crook who reformed because a sweet young thing believed in him, as usual.

Just a fair action crook meller with the dialog the only new twist. Probably all right on the rental end for many wired houses.

THE SOPHOMORE

(ALL DIALOG)

Pathe production and release. Featuring Eddie Quillan. Directed by Leo McCarey. William Counselman, supervisor. From story by Corey Ford and T. H. Wenning. Earl Baldwin and Walter DeLeon's dialog. Joseph Franklin Poland, adapter. At Paramount, New York, week Aug. 23. Running time, 73 minutes.

Joe Collins	Eddie Quillan
Margie Callahan	Sally O'Neil
Tom Weck	Stanley Smith
Barbara	Jeannette Loff
Dutch	Russell Gleason
Mrs. Collins	Sarah Padden
Armstrong	Brooks Benedict
Nephew	Spec O'Donnell
Radio Announcer	Walter O'Keefe

This picture is box office and entertainment. It is youthful, speedy, hokey and full of fun. Compared with others it looks like an inexpensive production job. But so simple that it's easy and nice to watch and listen to.

As the title informs, collegiate. College stuff with a pinch of salt. There is the football game—close finish ending, but handled in a corking comedy way. Through the gagged up radio announcing job, as done by Walter O'Keefe, the football sequence is funny all the way and the picture folds with a laugh. It is a laugh built up like a million. Before sprung they are waiting for it, but they were just waiting to laugh as they knew the answer. And they laughed. The radio bit and Eddie Quillan's performance are much if not most of the picture.

Eddie is Joe Collins, college wise guy. He loses his tuition money ($200) the first day of school via dice. That means back to the soda counter job. Sally O'Neil is the waitress there and the boss is stuck on her. But she likes Joe, so the boss fires him. Joe is about to leave school for want of funds. The dough shows up mysteriously, sent, of course by Margie (Miss O'Neil) who touched the boss for it. Joe thinks his ma mailed it in. He learns the truth before the finish, and that's the big heart throb.

Margie slips into Joe's room in the fraternity house to intercept a giveaway note and save Joe from knowing, but is caught and Joe is canned from the frat and school. The game next day is the squarer.

And the game! Joe gets in with three minutes to go and the score tied. On the first play he lets a punt slip through his fingers and in the ensuing scramble as his side loses the ball, is knocked cold and taken out on a stretcher. Then Joe learns of Margie's sacrifice and runs off the field to catch her at the train.

In the play on the grid one of the home team boys intercepts an opposition pass and starts to run for a touchdown. But he's running the wrong way. If he crosses the goal, it means points for the other side and loss of the game. It looks as though he will, for he has passed all the tacklers. At that moment Joe Collins rushes onto the grid and throws his team mate. Just then the gun is fired.

That's a funny situation, making 12 men on the field for Joe's school, but the radio announcer explains it happily and it is a darb comedy situation.

Although Quillan had been selling comedy from the opening, the big laugh number arrives with the school play. Some very funny business, juvenile kind, but funny.

As a youthful comic Quillan is neat. And Miss O'Neil is sweet. The cast is good looking and finished all the way. Not a flaw.

Quillan is making a personal appearance with the film at the Paramount, getting over on the rostrum as well as he does on the screen. *Bige.*

Hallelujah

(ALL DIALOG—With Songs and Dances)

(Owing to the uncertainty of universal appeal in an all-colored talking picture of the character of "Hallelujah" Variety prints three reviews by different writers. One on its premiere at the Embassy, New York, Aug. 20, at $2, and another on its reception at the Lafayette, all-colored theatre of Harlem, where the film is simultaneously appearing. The third review here is by a girl staff writer, and from the woman's angle.

It is scarcely to be expected a trade paper reviewer could pass a casual opinion as to this universal appeal, which means so much to the producer in the way of a profitable return. Both of Variety's male reviewers pear to think "Hallelujah" will mostly appeal in the sticks. It may be that "Hallelujah" will attract more strongly at $2 than in the pop price houses.

With "Hallelujah" the decision can only arrive with the returns. If the colored race can appeal on the shadowy screen to all, in other than colored comedy, the Negro dramatic and musical comedy actor may find a place in the studios.

Any other all-negro picture of the past is disregarded in favor of "Hallelujah" as the example for general picture fan favor here and abroad.

M-G-M production and release. Story and direction by King Vidor. Scenario by Wanda Tuchock. Treatment by Richard Schayer. Dialog by Ransom Rideout. Cameraman, Gordon Avil. Edited by Hugh Wynn. Western Electric sounded (disk). At Embassy, New York, Aug. 20, twice daily, $2 top. Running time, 109 minutes.

Zeke....................Daniel L. Haynes
Chick....................Nina Mae McKinney
Hot Shot....................William Fountaine
Parson....................Harry Gray
Mammy....................Fannie Belle DeKnight
Spunk....................Everett McGarrity
Missy Rose....................Victoria Spivey
Johnson Kids.................... Milton Dickerson, Robert Couch, Walter Tait
and Dixie Jubilee Singers

In his herculean attempt to take comedy, romance and tragedy and blend them into a big, gripping, all-colored (Negro) talker, King Vidor has turned out an unusual picture from a theme that is almost as ancient as the sun in his "Hallelujah." It is Vidor all over the screen. He wrote the story and directed it. It's 100 to 1 shot that wherever it is shown in the white man's theatres it will hold high tension and reel off whole entertainment. Vidor's strict adherence to realism is so effective at times it is stark and uncanny.

Whites will accept it as a camera reproduction of the typical southland with its wide open cotton spaces, where the good natured, singing negro continues to eke out a bare existence; where he lives untrammeled by city ways unless he invades their riotous precincts; where he has his moments of joy, passion and religion. It brings realistically to the screen how he lives in nondescript surroundings, with continual evidence of illiteracy that even remains unpolished when becoming hysterically religious; how that spiritual emotion sends him into the highest region of outward demonstration of having gone religious; the picturesque river baptismal in the open; with earlier scenes showing his old-styled method of giving vent to grief; of the happier side of plantation life, the carefree, syncopating singing and dancing cotton pickers whose lives run uneventful until death stalks in their midst or sordid tragedy drops into their gayety.

The story is a plain one, the characters not too many and no fancy long drawn out monickers and thus the average screen fan can follow its theme without the slightest difficulty. This is all a big feather in Vidor's hat. Where Vidor has achieved his greatest here is the taking of inexperienced players of both sexes from a race that hasn't had all the progressive chances in the film world to get very far and established them as capable, willing actors, who by voice and action make impressionistic standouts of their respective parts. That is a big, worthwhile accomplishment.

Nina Mae McKinney as the dynamic, vivacious girl of the colored underworld, who lives by her wits and enmeshes the males by her personality, sex appeal and dancing feet, never had a day's work before a picture camera. Yet paying close attention and following instructions minutely she stood out as one of the biggest things in the film. Perhaps the best way of describing Nina Mae is that she comes closest to being the Clara Bow of her race, so far seen on the screen. This girl stepped in on the Metro lot when Honey Brown, originally selected by Vidor for the leading femme role didn't reach expectations. There were times when she displayed a tendency to overact, yet mostly stuck to the directorial knitting and won out on her own.

Daniel L. Haynes as the principal male is the big, rough, lazylike colored boy, happiest when he sings and who loved his women.

In "Hallelujah" his pipes get plenty of action in dialog and in song. Haynes also apparently followed Vidor's direction blindly, and made something of the character.

Victoria Spivey is the "blues" singer who amazed everybody by doing a pretty naturalistic bit of acting as the girl who loved and waited. And it was rather strange that Vidor didn't have her do a crooning, moaning number. She has a rep for piping daylight out of such stuff. She moaned a little but nary a vocal croon or song. Her first screen work.

William Fountaine, who for years managed and sang with the Exposition Four in vaude, became a dominant figure as the heavy, a colored menace who by looks, dress and deportment acquitted himself creditably. Fannie Belle DeKnight was the mother of the film, or to be more explicit, the "mammy" and what a mammy! Years of colored stock experience equipped her for the role. Everett McGarrity oke in a minor role as Zeke's brother.

A characteristic figure was Harry Gray as the white bewhiskered parson and daddy of the Johnson family. This is the same 80-year or more man who, prior to this film job, was a porter in the Amsterdam News (colored newspaper) uptown in New York. He also proved experience isn't necessary to make an action register or a voice effective in talkers.

And last but not least the Johnson kids, played by Masters Fickerson, Couch and Tait. Their playful, gingery kiddish antics were within bounds and held under restraint.

Throughout the film can be heard the harmonious voices of the Dixie Jubilee Singers, who, thanks to Eva Jessaye's skillful offcamera direction, made the vocal embellishment high standard. Especially necessary were their voices in the spirituals. In all the ensembles, evangelistical or otherwise, the jubilee warblers were in all the time.

Highlights might be ascribed to **the cabaret scene where an unprogrammed big negro did a corking shuffle and a bevy of white aproned waiters shuffled forward and back in a syncopating number made hot by Miss McKinney; the gun play climax where Zeke's favorite brother is killed;** the wake, the redemption of Zeke, the prayer meeting and reclamation of colored souls by Zeke who had turned preacher; the baptismal and the hallelujah hurrah in the church where sex appeal as churned by Miss McKinney takes the evangelical spirit (Haynes) right out of the religious melting pot into the outside world where the two proceed to make love unmolested, until the girl's old love, Hot Shot, returns; then to the finale where the girl and her gambling-man lover go to their death, the former in an accident when the ramshackle buggy overturns and the latter in the swampland of Tennessee when the hero overtakes and chokes him to death for causing the girl's death.

Maybe the wake, baptismal and swamp scenes may be considered as overdrawn or extended interminably, yet Vidor's desire to stamp them as complete and realistic may be the reason.

Photographically, Gordon Avil has done something that adds further luster to his crown. Well nigh perfect many of those shots with his swamp photography notably so.

Looking "Hallelujah" over from every angle it should go into the hinterland houses and make money. It has a lot to its credit and is censorproof as to its complete presentment. Time and again Vidor could have resorted to daring, risque or vulgar bits, yet he sidetracked them and touched up his lovemaking scenes with a deft, master hand that left the picture as clean as a hound's tooth.

Apparently in the massed or ensemble groups Vidor had a mighty tough job holding that bunch back, yet he held them under remarkable restraint and still brought out the effects desired.

Two special numbers aside from the spirituals and the combined jubilee vocalizing are done by Haynes and Miss McKinney. Both by Irving Berlin. Haynes' was "The End of the Road," used as the general theme song, and McKinney's "Swanee Shuffle." "Road" came in for the most attention.

Vidor in confining his work to the scuthland remained out of the big city environment as much as possible. Only interiors showing how the country or plantation boy picked up a hot gal, lost his money he had gotten for his cotton by loaded dice and the subsequent tragedy in the dance hall were about all that gave any indication that big city life had any part. A street parade of the evangelistic party headed by the reformed Zeke but it was just a dash.

"Hallelujah" to the whites is a big, entertaining picture. To the negroes it will either be a gigantic sensation or revelation or looked upon as holding up some of the ancient sacred rites of the race to ridicule. Most likely the former.

Mark.

King Vidor's all-negro picture may be regarded as the climax and the popularization of that increasing body of sentiment which in recent years has found expression through such channels as the American Mercury and The Nation. It has tended to glorify the primitive negro life of the south and the emerging race consciousness and intellectual vigor of the colored people.

Upon such a relatively high plane of tolerance and sympathy, Vidor made his picture. Exhibitors, the trade in general, and possibly much of the public, may not wholly be attuned to the implications. That raises the problem, is the story, or narrative value, strong enough to carry through? Will "Hallelujah" have any common denominator for the everyday white person detached from the liberal movement that centers in New York City?

There are clouds in the forecast. "Hallelujah" will not be universal in appeal although it's a distinguished production and a worthy novelty for de luxe houses, with the south an open question for competent showmen to determine for themselves.

And from another source it may tap sympathy. Its revival meetings, baptizing in the river and other scenes may possibly find a response from Methodists and Baptists in smaller communities. On the other hand, although the religious angle is handled with sincerity, it may create antagonism. It has very definite potential reactions from this direction, either pro or anti.

Unquestionably "Hallelujah" is an artistic success. It is an extremely well done effort. Many of the effects, much of the photography, is stirring in its beauty or strength, or both. If toward the end it loses the tempo and pace of the early footage there is no conspicuous letdown.

Natural, convincing and unbelievably good is the verdict on the entire cast. Daniel Haynes, the deep-baritoned hero, and Nina Mae McKinney as the high yellow cutie, stand out on the dominance of their personalities and the importance of their roles.

It is perhaps in the manipulation of masses, the levee cabarets, plantations, holy roller meetings, etc. that Vidor has accomplished his greatest work. No white person enters either the story or the camera eye throughout. It is entirely a story of and with negroes.

Simple emotions, primitive situations of love, lust, jealousy and remorse, a son who falls upon evil, accidentally kills his brother and in an agony of repentance, receives grace and turns preacher. To these credulous children of cotton the devil is a real person, ever-present, and violation of God's edicts brings bad fortune.

Students of Freud will read into the revival shindig a close affinity between religious frenzy and sex impulses. This is intelligently presented when the hot mamma in a fever of sudden repentance for her former sins is, all unconscious to herself, consumed with a desire for the strong, manly preacher.

Vidor has poured himself into this picture, designed as an epic of the negro. He has packed in a lot of glamor and action and humanity. If the picture is limited, its boundaries are inherent to the subject.

It is, in any event, ammunition with which to meet those who contend that they never try anything new in the film industry. *Land.*

By Ruth Morris

"Hallelujah," an all-Negro film at the Embassy, isn't good matinee fare. It is not, in itself, a woman's picture.

There is nothing in it to attract the flappers or superficial lunch-goers who flock to a matinee after a morning's shopping in town. This element, wanting only a box of chocolates and a little light diversion, will be quickly bored by the picture, and take a rather indignant leave, as did several of its number at Monday's crowded matinee.

It is generally believed that if a film cannot be called a "woman's picture," it won't be a hit; this one isn't, yet it should be a smashing success. For many reasons.

One is that it rings true, even when good, old-fashioned hoke is injected. It's a smooth piece of cloth with comedy threads interwoven where they belong.

Only femme dumb-bells will be bored with the fact that it has no hey-hey night club scene, no handsome white hero and no sparkling gowns which usually set the pace for what should not be worn. The thinking woman spectator will realize from the first few sequences that a fine intelligence is in back of the telling of the simple story, that a real feeling for artistic composition is in back of the photography, that the dialog in itself is a musical accompaniment and that a masterpiece is unfolding on the screen.

There may be an angle in the picture's moments of hysteria which may, despite the film's seriousness as a whole, draw in the matinee element. This is in the Greenville cabaret scenes done with "lowdown nigger" flavor. It is Covarrubias at his most modern and blue.

As revolting as a black and tan cabaret it is nevertheless treated with the sincerity and frankness that somehow remove offense. Only a leer would make it nauseating, and King Vidor has removed this possibility by throwing on atmospheric colors with primitive, bold strokes. Human nature being what it is, this sequence, although relatively unimportant, will probably be the most discussed, and the giggling element may drop in, having heard that it was "naughty."

For the women who mind the fact that the little cabaret girl is the very incarnation of evil—gay, unbridled and pathetic—there is her final suffering and death as a recompense. Nina Mae McKinney's performance in this role is flawless.

"Hallelujah" is a saga of the cotton fields. It starts happily with the family at work against a snowy background, rides into disaster with the hero's trip to town to sell his bale, and comes back to happiness with Zeke sitting contentedly on a freight-load of cotton singing the lovely Largo from Dvorak's Symphony. It shows the itinerant preacher of the south and his hysterical parishioners as no picture and few books have done. It mixes the childish superstition and simple grandeur of the colored race. It's a human document.

THE GAMBLERS

(ALL DIALOG)

Warner Bros. Vitaphone production and release. Featuring Lois Wilson, H. B. Warner and Jason Robards in adaptation of Charles Klein's play. Directed by Michael Curtiz; scenario by J. Grubb Alexander. At Strand, New York, week Aug. 23. Running time, 60 minutes.

James Darwin	H. B. Warner
Catherine Darwin	Lois Wilson
Carvel Emerson	Jason Robards
Emerson, Sr.	George Fawcett
George Cowper	Johnny Arthur
Raymond	Frank Campeau
Isabel Emerson	Pauline Garon
Tooker	Charles Sellon

Conventional comedy-drama of the Wall street and society genera. It would have satisfied five or 10 years ago, but a play (from the original of the late Charles Klein) which is just average for talker presentation.

The capable cast includes an imposing roster of proven dialog screensters who manage a fair job in toto.

The sympathy is uncertain and the line of demarcation in the triangle is too vague to satisfy the average fan. That's one thing the picture public will not accept; it wants to be sure of its hero, heroine and menace. The sole exception is the mystery meller and that's only because the "who killed Cock Robin?" element is paramount.

Here, Lois Wilson as H. B. Warner's wife and former amour of Jason Robards presents an indeterminate situation. As the spouse of a relentless prosecutor, there is nothing negative about Warner's characterization to turn audience sympathy to Robards, while the latter is likewise handicapped because the romantic interest is up in the air. That's not especially good direction albeit enough of a contemporary situation to ring true.

Robards becomes involved in a Wall street manipulation which results in his indictment. At the last minute, his prosecutor, Warner, quashes it. The feminine angle to this triangle figures as the reason, but the climatic twist lacks the essential wallop.

Picture will satisfy as a daily change programer; title and standard cast will help a lot. *Abel.*

COLLEGE COQUETTE

(ALL DIALOG)

Columbia product and release. Story by Ralph Graves. Directed by George Archinbaund. At the Little Carnegie Playhouse, New York, week Aug. 24. Running time, 68 minutes.

Betty Forrester	Ruth Taylor
Tom Marion	William Collier, Jr.
Doris Marlowe	Jobyna Ralston
Harvey Porter	John Holland
Ethel Forrester	Adda Gleason
Mrs. Marlowe	Gretchen Hartman
Edna	Frances Lyons
Slim	Edward Piel, Jr.
Ted	Edward Clayton
Jimmy Doolitte	Morris Murphy

Another of the college boy and girl flickers that seems to be running film excursions into New York. They are still polishing up ideas that made old-timers like "The College Widow" and "Brown of Harvard" worth their weight in gold. But makers of present-day celluloid sounders and talkers seem to think that a drunken party of university flaming and thirsty youths is necessary to give it modern color. And "College Coquette" is no exception. And it doesn't make the picture any better for it other than burn up some good money.

"Coquette" is a nice Frenchy word meaning "flirt." That's Ruth Taylor here. She starts off to school alone driving her own new roadster and a girl friend refuses to go along because her mother has an idea that riding with Ruth isn't the best kind of a passport entering a school where boys and girls mix.

Ruth gets a rep for making the boys one at a time. In her conquests is the football coach, who isn't "made" until the last few feet.

Many flaws and little palpable inconsistences throughout. One can surmise how the boys in the college towns, and there are slews of 'em, will say about some of those college scenes.

Mawkish sentiment in the main idea to show how a pure, innocent girl leaves her fireside and goes away from mother, only to fall for hot temptation and then get plastered to stand for private necking that ruined her body and soul. The gal, overhearing her lovey dove say he was only kidding her and didn't love her and rushing out only to fall down an open elevator shaft and dying after she had exacted a promise from the other girl not to tell her mother the real truth of her condition and death.

It may be an expose or a moral.

Dialog ran along uninterestingly with much of it done by Miss Taylor in a rather throaty and guttural manner. She overplayed, perhaps not her fault, but either direction or script. She is a blondy blond; at times attractively pretty and other times the camera didn't do her any favors. Jobyna Ralston showed her stage experience was a handy thing to have around in these hectic talker days. She made an effective character out of the girl who went wrong and met death. Her work toward the end of the picture was a standout. Voice most acceptable.

Collier, Jr., the cad; always a bad boy in college stories. He got away nicely with his dialog exchange. John Holland has an athletic figure enough for the coach. He didn't do so badly with his talk.

A vaporish story at best; overdrawn and inconsistent. Some splendid photography at times and a good reproducing job.

Seemed a pity to waste so much celluloid on such. It didn't stand up under photographic pressure. *Mark.*

FLYING FOOL

(ALL DIALOG)

Pathe production and release. Directed by Taylor Garnett from the original story by Elliott Clawson. Dialog by James Gleason. Photography by Arthur Miller. Featuring William Boyd, Marie Prevost, Russell Gleason and Tom O'Brien. At Loew's New York, one day, Aug. 23, as half double bill. Running time, 73 minutes.

The dialog by that wisenheimer, James Gleason, steals the picture, forcing the plot into second place. About two brothers, one who has mothered and fathered his kid brother falling for the same gal, is appealing. This flicker, if not for its misnomer, which speels small time, should be able to stand by itself in most towns and outlying districts of big cities.

Pig latin and slang all through the picture. Gleason even forgot himself and in a war shot in 1917, as the opening sequence, used a little pig latin. It's a sophisticated big town picture, omitting its flying sequences. But the pig talk helps to brighten it.

Story has Boyd as the "Flying Fool" and his kid brother (the younger Gleason) falling in love with Marie Prevost, a night club gal. These three, plus Tom O'Brien as the pestiferous one to Boyd, characterize their roles with a whole heartedness which can be felt.

The younger Gleason, who feels so pash about Miss Prevost, loses out because he is a kid. His part is secondary in importance only to Boyd. As such, the kid does some very good work. As the connoisseur of women and the two-fisted heman, Boyd feels quite at home, as this is about the 'steenth such parts he's had.

Miss Prevost sings (?) the theme song "If I Had My Way." She looks cute and appeals, but the greatest metamorphosis she is made to undergo is due to the plot. When the kid brother goes out with her at first, she is the hard, calloused woman of the bright lights, but when the older brother goes for her, she becomes the sweet and home-loving daughter.

Some thrilling stunt flying and supposed to be the major feature, but the air specials which have preceded it take off most of the edge.

It's problematical whether Gleason's big town quips and slang will fetch them in the sticks, but in Times Square a big city audience got every gag.

THE VERY IDEA

(ALL DIALOG)

Radio Pictures production and release. Featuring Frank Craven. Directed by William LeBaron and Richard Rosson. Adapted from LeBaron's play of same name. Edited by Ann McKnight and George Marsh. Cast includes Theodore Von Eltz, Doris Eaton, Hugh Trevor, Sally Blaine and Jeanne De Bard. RCA Photophone sounded. At Albee, Brooklyn, week Aug. 24 (premiere). Running time, 65 minutes.

Finishing a lot better than the start indicated, "The Very Idea" comes home an enjoyable farce screen comedy, smartly played and shrewdly directed. The extremely delicate subject forming the plot has been handled carefully all around, and that makes it farcical. Treated any other way the story and situations might have been difficult to screen. Which in all should make it a box office picture.

William LeBaron wrote "The Very Idea" as a play in 1917, produced that year with Ernest Truex in the lead. Since then the world has become wised up to what is meant by eugenic babies, so the edges are not so jagged now. It must have been much harder to get it across 12 years ago.

The perfect child in "The Very Idea" is to be born by the chauffeur and maid of a rich but childless young couple, and then turned over to the latter for a sum of money. The plan is conceived by the young wife's brother, a writer on eugenics.

Couple go away for a year. Chauffeur and maid are married. At the year's end, when the babe is to be delivered, the real parents refuse to give it up, of course. And funny when the disappointed pair try to explain to friends. But the young wife tells her husband something she didn't know whether to tell him or not, so it's accepted that they're going to have one of their own after all.

Snickers for the introductory business can't be evaded. Later on the laughs come often and are wholesome.

Lines are intelligent and the performances unanimously excellent.

Too talky at the first, but that also is forgotten later on. *Bige.*

SECRETS OF NATURE

(GERMAN MADE)

(Silent)

Ufa production of an educational, running 49 minutes. Composite of several short subjects previously released. Week Aug. 24 at 55th St. Playhouse, New York.

Only an arty sure-seater like the 55th St. could get away with this 49-minute educational as the flicker feature of the evening. Not that it isn't meritorious—in fact, much of it is noteworthy—but other than program short material it's valueless for the general releases.

Hence the wisdom of splitting the six or seven subjects into as many shorts as has already been done in the past in previous exhibitions, all under the Ufa trademark. What has been done here either by the 55th St. management or as may have been the original intent, was the assemblage of the various clips.

As feature material it's great library stuff. Yet some of the insect and wild animal warfare waged in the jungles, in ant-hills, on treetops, in shrubbery, possesses considerable dramatic tension. The best by far is that mongoose-cobra death battle which has been seen around and which Paramount thought so much of that it interpolated it as an allegorical clip in "The Letter" (Jeanne Eagels).

The opening Kingdom of the Bees is just educational stuff, rather long and tedious. That attack by the busy little ants on a caterpillar (and besting him), and the snail's successful withstanding of the onslaught through the protective salivary ejection started the insect dramatics.

Some comedy elements, too, with one very ambitious ant hauling what looked like a splinter or a shred of a tough foliage which was fully 10 times the size of the little ant. The insect's idea was to get that long thing-a-jig into his ant-hole, where he was building a nest. How he accomplished it through backing in made one not only marvel at the wonders of nature and the patience of this extraordinary photography, but also conjecture on whether or not they can train ants like they do circus fleas.

Some other great stuff, especially the carnivorous Pirhana fish of the Amazon, no larger than one's hand and yet is shown devouring 120 pounds of pork bait—a pig—in six minutes. This fish's teeth are so sharp the South American natives use them to cut their hair with.

"Secrets of Nature" is a fine educational. The schools could teach more with this release than many a treatise of forest, bird and fish lore.

It's a pip for the sure-seaters, especially if skillfully surrounded by a type program as at the 55th St. Cinema (a corking Chaplin reissue, "The Champion," and "Light of India," dramalet in Technicolor), but for regular consumption the exhibitors can clip almost any of the series, save possibly that bee-hive exposition which is only mild by comparison to the other zippy stuff, and have a half dozen corking shorts to choose from in over as many weeks. *Abel.*

FOURCHAMBAULT

(FRENCH MADE)

(Silent)

Paris, Aug. 12.

The main interest in the picture produced by Georges Monca and Jean Dard for C. G. P. C. under the title of "Les Fourchambault" is that it is an adaptation of the play of Emile Augier, unknown to the present generation.

There must be a lot of works of Augier, Becque, Scribe and even Labiche which have not yet been filmed, albeit some would make a poor showing on the screen unless cunningly manipulated to such an extent as to render them unrecognizable with the original.

In this picture, Mme. Bernard, girl-mother, abandoned by her lover, has carefully reared her son, and the lad becomes a wealthy ship owner. Then the mother confesses the name of his father. He is Fourchambault, who left the betrayed girl to marry a rich woman. Of this latter union there are a son and daughter.

It happens, by stage coincidence, Bernard is doing business with his father. Forgetting the harm done his mother, thereby including himself, he saves Fourchambault from ruin. Moreover, Bernard and his half-brother love the same girl, an orphan, who is compromised but not harmed by young Fourchambault trying to win her.

The action is slow, and perhaps sticks too closely to the XIX century comedy. Nothing particular about it as a picture, preaching honesty, kindness and toleration.

Jeanne Marie Laurent, Simonne Damaury, Charles Vanel, Charles Sov, Henriette Delannoy and other conscientious players do their best to put some ginger into the antiquated story. Picture may please provincial publics as a small time feature. *Kendrew.*

LAST ROUND-UP

(SILENT)

(Disc Accompaniment)

J. P. McGowan Production, released by Syndicate Pictures. Directed by J. P. McGowan. Titles by Sally Winters. Hap Depew, cameraman. Featuring Bob Custer, Hazel Mills and Bob Osborne. At Loew's New York, one day, Aug. 23, as half double bill. Running time, 56 minutes.

One of the last of the silent westerns. A real western goulash. Nothing missed. If you don't like cattle rustlin' they're women stealin' and if you don't like either there's prairie fires, or Bob Custer will wipe up the corral with four men at a time.

Not a western villainy or heroism omitted. Bob as the hero and paragon of virtue wears a spotless and well tailored cowboy outfit. A supposedly captivating schoolmarm is Hazel Mills, but a harsh makeup even scared the bovines.

Dirty villainy abounds galore in the person of Bob Osborne as Dirty Dalton who knows his sneers.

A microscope is necessary to see this flicker from any angle.

Gold Diggers of B'way

(ALL DIALOG)

(ALL COLOR)

(With Songs)

Warner Brothers Vitaphone production and release. Coloring by Technicolor. Featuring Ann Pennington, Conway Tearle, Nancy Welford, Albert Gran, Lilyan Tashman and Nick Lucas. Scenario by Robert Lord from the late Avery Hopwood's stage play (Belasco), "Gold Diggers." Directed by Roy Del Ruth. All original song numbers by Al Dubin and Joe Burke. Western Electric Vita sounded. Dance numbers staged by Larry Ceballos. At Winter Garden, New York, opening Aug. 30 on two-a-day at $2 top. Running time, 105 minutes.

Jerry	Nancy Welford
Stephen Lee	Conway Tearle
Mable	Winnie Lightner
Ann Collins	Ann Pennington
Eleanor	Lilyan Tashman
Wally	William Bakewell
Nick	Nick Lucas
Violet	Helen Foster
Blake	Albert Gran
Topsy	Gertrude Short
Stage Manager	Neely Edwards
Cissy Gray	Julie Swayne Gordon
Dance Director	Lee Moran
Barney Barnett	Armand Kaliz

Lots of color—Technicolor—lots of comedy, girls, songs, music, dancing, production and Winnie Lightner, with Nick Lucas the main warbler in "Gold Diggers of Broadway." That's what's going to send the picture into the money class for the Warners, in the regular houses.

Somebody tossed the picture right into Winnie Lightner's lap, or else she stole it, for when Lucas isn't mandolining for the canning of his voice with at least two sure fire best sellers in songs, it's Winnie Lightner. And since it's Winnie, who's unknown to the picture fans in the sticks, despite her two talking shorts or so with the hot songs, it's best first to tell about Winnie, at last made by some one, this time the Warners.

She's from vaudeville, in what is known in vanishing vaudeville as a standard act, Newton Alexander and the Lightner Sisters. Then Winnie went single turn, picked songs for their lyrics that a single should sing in vaude and then into a production or two; then the shorts and now pictures for most of the rest of her time. The talkers gain another comedienne and they haven't any too many, so Winnie is set, whether she's mugging, talking, singing or slapsticking, for she can do them all and does in this picture.

And then Nick Lucas. Maybe he's singing a bit too much in "Gold Diggers," while the original numbers provided by Al Dubin and Joe Burke run too closely in the same key, tempo and general theme, but there's no voice on the discs like Lucas' for the type of number sung by him. He's a paradox, as on the screen, great and can win with his voice, while on the stage Nick must get over on the strength of the canned rep he has piled so high. The two certain hit songs sung by him among the several others in "The Diggers" are "Tulips" and "Painting the Clouds." Another one or so may edge in. Winnie sings a couple, too.

When they got through with Belasco's **"Gold Diggers," the Warners had the title only left. Around that they built another show, on and off stage. Larry Ceballos attended to the staging of the on stage portion. And well, so well he used 24 chorus boys in walking suits and silk hats for one bit. It must have made the show producers gasp last Friday night at the Winter Garden.** For this lively film with its comedy, songs and numbers at 50c would chill even a Shubert who thinks any stage turkey can get $4.40, and most of them from or on the stage look like turkeys after a picture maker gets through with this or that extravagant production as a talker.

A couple of debuts otherwise from the stage in the celluloid "Gold." Nancy Welford and Ann Pennington. Technicolor has made a real little beauty out of the girl with the feet, who didn't dance so much here or make herself notable. But her name is something. Miss Welford did nicely enough what she had to do. In the stew scene, Miss Welford, at least, surpassed Conway Tearle, for Tearle too often forgot he was soused. He sobered up dreadfully to denounce Nancy, then remembered and staggered out of the door.

Next to Miss Lightner in work was her comedy opposite, Albert Gran, as a grey-haired heavyweight lawyer, whom Winnie landed. Winnie really landed twice. Once when she got him on a yes proposal, but before then when Winnie took a leap from a table, right on to Gran's bread department. It was a howl.

Lilyan Tashman did an upstage show dame rather well, but someone forgot to make her say "ain't" too after squawking over it. Those gag men on the coast are only recalling half the stuff.

Helen Foster and William Bakewell were the kids in a very slim love thread, but Miss Foster looks well enough to be tried out in some of those Anita Page roles.

In the rewritten "Gold Diggers" the love thing is only the alibi. The new story is hung onto it, with just enough of the digging to hold up the title.

Well worked out, with plenty of speed all of the time, and coloring all of the while, whether in the regulation individual scenes or the ensembles. And the director, Roy del Ruth, entitled to equal bows.

Hard shoe dancing or tapping is frequently in use for its sound effect.

While the Warners "Say It With Songs" is also an all-colored talker, somehow here the Technicolor process appears to give greater strength to the picture; a part of it. Technicolor's smoothness in the taking may also cause those many others who believe they have color processes to wonder.

A very good entertainment on the screen. Regardless of how long it runs at the Winter Garden at $2, "The Gold Diggers," splendidly photographed and recorded, is in. *Sime.*

GIRL FROM HAVANA

(ALL DIALOG)

Fox production and release. Directed by Benjamin Stoloff. Story by John Stone. Edwin H. Burke, dialog. Western Electric (Movietone) sounded. At the Roxy, week Aug. 31. Running time, 65 minutes.

Joan Anders	Lola Lane
Allan Grant	Paul Page
William Dane	Kenneth Thomson
Lona Martin	Natalie Moorhead
Spike Howard	Warren Hymer
Dougherty	Joseph Girard
Babe Hanson	Adele Windsor
Sally Green	Marcia Chapman
Toots Nolan	Dorothy Brown
Detective	Juan Sedillo
Joe Barker	Raymond Lopez

A rough house battle between the hero and heavy threat, some scenic stuff on the Panama Canal and Havana, a crook story and a nice little slice of love interest, make "Girl From Havana" a moderate talking picture.

It hasn't the strength for high recognition, and on top of that there isn't a drawing name on the list.

None of the silent blow-off battles of the past, while some may have been rougher, looked more like the real thing than this one between Paul Page and Warren Hymer.

Lola Lane plays a detective, which, offscreen, would be unusual for such a girl. She's assigned to unravel a jewel mystery. The mob is fleeing to Havana.

Paul Page, one of the members, seems too nice to be a common thief, while Miss Lane makes it tougher for herself by falling in love with him. Lack of faith is misplaced, for he's only mixed up with the gang to find the murderer of his father. Simple?

In the closing fisticuffs Page lands the one he was after. It happened to be the wicked Hymer, whose tough guy antics provide the picture's comedy relief. His is the best played role.

Ship's concert on board the Havana-bound steamer provides a chance for more comedy and a plug for a theme song, "Time Will Tell," apparently rendered by Miss Lane.

The crook talk is a bit overdone in the dialog, but most of the time bright enough to avoid being taken too seriously.

Voice explanation of the trip through the Canal is interesting and well planted. An officer of the boat does the explaining to two kids. When he's through they ask each other, "What did he say?" *Bige.*

UNGUARDED GIRLS

(Sex Picture)

(SILENT)

Circle Films, Inc. (Samuel Cummins), road show sex feature with lecturer. Story by Jack Townley. Directed by William Curran. Cast includes Paddy O'Flynn, Jack Hopkins, Tom Gerley, Alphonse Martell, Merle Williams. At Times Square, New York, indefinitely, starting Aug. 31, at 50-75. Running time 80 mins.

• Junior clerks, men who never found out what it's all about, gents with time to kill, visiting firemen who believe everything they read and see on three-sheets—these are the curious peasants who drift into a sex show like "Unguarded Girls." When they slap down their six bits and penetrate the veil of "the truth about white slavery" they may, or may not, feel like umchays, but unless they left school at the fourth grade they probably notice there's a long swim between what the lobby promised and what the screen delivers.

This, of course, has been going on for some little while. Every burlesque house in the country operates on the same principle, putting its best show in the lobby. Time has built up a technique and frequently a very high order of showmanship is represented in the exploitation of sex shows. The law allows managers to arouse curiosity, but does not permit its gratification. So the boys strike a balance. It's an organized business.

"Unguarded Girls" is no more, and no less, than a younger generation sermon and shows far less than a Clara Bow picture. As to quality it's passable, story is a little minus on logic, but involved in details, direction is pretty fair, photography only so-so, and it is very definitely on the side of the fundamentalists. Its theme song would be, if it had a theme song, "Say No, Little Girl, Say No."

As with most sex pictures the spieler does a work-up for his literature, sold in bulk, seven pamphlets for a buck. He alludes to the purpose of the presentation. A stranger might deduce that "Unguarded Girls" is a philanthropic enterprise innocent of commercialism, solely intent upon bringing light and understanding into lives darkened by ignorance of Santa Claus.

Sin struts its flamboyant hips late in the picture. They call it a speakeasy, but there's an older name. At least if there are any speakeasies like this one around Variety's staff would probably do a story on 'em. It'd make page one.

"Unguarded Girls" doesn't turn out a very strong case for virtue, but it artfully subscribes to the requirements of censorship, and will probably find its way into most of the states. *Land.*

THE ARGYLE CASE

(ALL DIALOG)

Warner Bros. Vitaphone production-release, all dialog, starring Thomas Meighan, with H. B. Warner and Lila Lee featured, in picturization of play by Harriet Ford and Harvey J. O'Higgins; directed by Howard Bretherton; scenario by Harvey Thew. At Mark Strand, New York, week of Aug 30. Running time, 85 minutes.

Alexander Kayton......Thomas Meighan
Hurley......................H. B. Warner
Mary Morgan.....................Lila Lee
Bruce Argyle.................John Darrow
Mrs. Wyatt......................ZaSu Pitts
Joe..............................Bert Roach
Sam..........................Wilbur Mack
Finley.....................Douglas Gerrard
Kitty.......................Alona Marlowe
Skidd...............................J. Quinn
Man............................Lew Harvey

"The Argyle Case" is good box-office as a talker. It possesses all the elements of popularly appealing mystery melodramatics, fortified by the added significance of this being Thomas Meighan's first talker. As the star-detective hero of "The Argyle Case," Meighan more than sustains his end, even lending conviction to an occasional banality which the continuity writer wished onto him, such as: "Thanks, sergeant, I'll see that you're promoted for this."

With H. B. Warner and Lila Lee featured in support, plus ZaSu Pitts and Bert Roach in comedy assignments, the casting is handily taken care of. Miss Lee looks and speaks well, now "grown up," and Roach as the slightly dumbbell assistant injects enough of a light touch to maintain a consistent pace as comedy relief to an otherwise ultra-dramatic situation.

Against the background of the murder of the head of the house of Argyle is a sinister sequence of antecedents going back 20 years, which also brings in a strong counterfeiting element. The theatrical hooey with the Secret Service agents, the sliding panels, dictagraph set-ups (this now outmoded theatrical prop is lent new significance in this treatment) and the would-be menacing assailant of the heroine all combine into agreeable audible cinematic tenseness. (Play was originally produced 15 years ago.)

Of course, calling the hero, Alexander Kayton, "A. K." sounds a bit awry for the Broadway bunch, but otherwise that won't mean anything. Roach's observation that "this case is getting more screwy every day" was the big belly laugh.

A new element in the cock-robin exposition of mystery mellers is struck here in that one pretty well suspects who the murderer is but appreciates that the criminologist's primary task is not to apprehend him until the necessary circumstantial evidence is first completed.

The analytical may become curious about the plausibility of certain things like the TNT-loaded cigars, the warning scrap of paper that falls from the ceiling, the gullibility of an otherwise astute gang and other loose ends, but the mystery fans love this bamboozling and realize that much of the extraneous hokum is put in "just to make it harder."

Picture running 85 minutes, maintains interest throughout. "Argyle Case" will not permit the ticket-choppers to fall asleep in the lobbies. *Abel.*

WOMAN TRAP

(ALL DIALOG)

Paramount production and release. Featuring Hal Skelly, Chester Morris and Evelyn Brent. Directed by William Wellman. Story by Edwin Burke. Dialog by Bartlett Cormack. Adaptation by Louise Long. Cameraman Henry Gerard. At Paramount, New York, week Aug. 30. Running time, 82 mins.

Dan Malone.....................Hal Skelly
Ray Malone................Chester Morris
Kitty Evans...................Evelyn Brent
Watts.....................Wm. B. Davidson
Mrs. Malone....................Effie Ellsler
Mr. Evans........................Guy Oliver
Eddie Evans..................Leslie Fenton
Smith........................Charles Giblyn
Reporter..................Joseph Mankiewicz
Detective Captain..........Wilson Hummell

Melodrama of average program quality. Generates enough suspense to pump up the balloon of an hour's engrossment. It's gangster and tough copper hodge-podge, seen before, but holding a primitive punch that will suffice to get it across.

Hal Skelly is the dominant character, an easy-going sergeant in the early footage, developing conscience later and becoming the terror of the scofflaws.

Romance is present to about ½ of 1%.

Originally Edwin Burke's story was a vaudeville act. It was revived around New York a couple of months ago by Robert Gleckler. This episode is incorporated at the finale of the picture, but falls pretty flat, the film ending a bit lamely.

"Woman Trap" remains in the programer classification because of the muddled condition of the script from time to time. This, of course, may be due to editing.

Flaws can be picked, but the tout ensemble passes muster as reasonably tense melodrama. *Land.*

BACHELORS' CLUB

(SILENT)

Oscar Price production. Richard Talmadge, star. Support includes Barbara Worth and Edna Murphy. Independent release. At Loew's, New York (one day), Aug. 30, half double bill. Running time, 64 mins.

It's Dick Talmadge up to his old acrobatic stuff, touched up in a new way, but still the same old display of athletic skill that brought R. T. to the fore when he stopped doubling for Fairbanks. Leaving this picture good for double bills as a silent with acrobatics.

The picture was made before talkers became necessary to the exhibs. It is given some help on the modernistic scheme of things by having a musical accompaniment made since the picture was turned out. Otherwise silent.

This indie sure is story shy. Attempt made to make something out of a president of a bachelors' club going goofy over a girl and then having the club mete out punishment to him for breaking the very rule he established.

Talmadge does those long handsprings and bumpety bump roll-overs for no good reason other than to make Dick look sprightly. The picture, however, gets its best inning on Talmadge's athletic prowess.

All of Talmadge's skyrocketing around lumber yards and aboard steamship.

Photography good. Ship scenes especially well cameraed. *Mark.*

THE LOVE TRAP

(10% DIALOG)

Universal production and release. Starring Laura LaPlante. Directed by William Wyler. Story by E. G. Montagne. Cast includes Neil Hamilton, Norman Trevor and Jocylyn Lee. Western Electric sounded. At New York theatre, one day, Aug. 29. Running time 63 mins.

Much dramatic quality with nice comedy relief. Captions and dialog indisputably good. "The Love Trap" is not merely another chorus girl picture. Numerous unique situations. Recording of Laura La-Plante and Neil Hamilton stands out.

Story gathers momentum from the start, reaching high interest with the voices. Backstage and society life well set forth. Girl fired from chorus, desperate for funds to pay landlady, goes with fast chorus girl friend to party to make half a "C". Attacked, she beats it home to find herself dispossessed. Picked up in street by young man, who offers shelter in his taxicab. Fellow puts furniture in three other cabs, ordering drivers to go "South." Bill runs up into the hundreds. Wind-up married.

Folks of the man belong to upper crust and disdain the chorus girl. Gets the sympathy of the audience throughout.

Dramatic kick when husband slaps his uncle for accusing girl of being mistress of host of original party. Goes with uncle and mother for showdown. Dialog here perfect.

Wife turns the trick by compromising the uncle in her bedroom, when he comes through with check for $50,000 to settle up marriage of his nephew.

Entertaining picture.

CITY OF TEMPTATION

(BRITISH MADE)

(Silent)

M. J. Gourland production. Directed by Walter Niebuhr. Story by Sir Philip Gibbs, adapted by Lucille Squiers. Olga Checkova, Juliane Johnson, Julius Klein featured. In cast Hugh Miller, Malcolm Tod. At 5th Ave. Playhouse, New York, week Aug. 31. Running time, 60 minutes.

Cheap foreign-made quickie of the sort that won't draw a dime in the arty houses or anywhere else, lacking in story development, casting and direction.

Philip Gibbs' novel has either been butchered or never was intended for screen adaptation. Old-fashioned plot has a Turkish roue on the make for a Russian refugee maiden in Constantinople.

SILVER KING

(ENGLISH-MADE)

(Silent)

T. A. Welch presents this adaptation of the old—very old—Henry Arthur Jones melo, described as "A Paramount Foreign Release.", Directed by T. Hayes Hunter. Percy Marmont featured with British cast. Photography by Bernard Knowles. Running time 70 minutes. At Little Carnegie Playhouse, New York, week Aug. 31.

Wilfred Denver.............Percy Marmont
Nellie Denver......................Jean Jay
Capt. Skinner...............Bernard Nedell
Olive..........................Chili Bouchier
Jaikes......................Hugh E. Wright
Geoffrey Ware...................Harold Huth
Corkett.........................Donald Stuart
Coombe..............................Ben Field
Cripps........................Henry Wenman
Selwyn............................Philip Lord
Dicky.........................Raymond Ellis
Cecily Denver....................Pearl Hay
Ned Denver...................Peter Carpenter

An awkward screen adaptation of this ancient melo leaves it hopelessly old-fashioned. Try to wish an underworld story of 30 years ago on this generation of fans educated to the subtle niceity of dramatic crime, and all you get is a derisive giggle.

It's a beautiful technical production and neatly enough acted, for the most part, but the material and tone of the whole thing is absurd. Represents apparently Paramount's purchase of a picture for English quota purposes, film being released for what it will bring, and that won't be much, based on the rental scale the sure-seaters pay. **Something should be salvaged from the purchase price from the daily changes, which is the field for this one.**

"The Silver King" was one of Jones' earlier works, done in collaboration with Martin Herman and probably dates back to the late '80's. It's still in the late '80's and is "Blue Jeans" with a few of the rough edges smoothed out. When it was an American success Harrison was president and horse cars ran across 42d street. Whoever adapted the old boy for the screen couldn't get the musty smell out of it.

All the old hoke is still there, even if they have injected such sprightly modern touches as a vamp type who stands around for a brief scene in up-to-date undies. Chili Bouchier does this role and over-acts painfully. Nevertheless she has possibilities with restrained direction, and is by all odds the best thing in the film, getting over the torrid sex appeal in spite of a silly role crudely acted.

Compared to the modern underworld story dished up with atmosphere and studio slight-of-hand, this stuff is raw Nick Carter against Conan Doyle. They even have the heroine kidnapped by the master crook and held prisoner in a steel lined chamber at the end of an underground tunnel. Underground tunnels aren't good technique any more. They haven't been used for escapes since Chicago gangdom discovered the real blessings of the writ of habeas corpus.

Another detail is the return home years later of the English Monte Cristo in the midst of a heavy stage snowstorm. The comic papers killed off that dramatic device before the films began to cut into the drama's gate, and now it is the exclusive property of the two-reel comedy makers.

The tip-off on what Paramount thought of the film's value, of course, is that the company just dumped it on the market without taking the trouble to give it synchronized score or sound effects. Anyhow, the Carnegie Playhouse is candid about it. They bill it prominently as silent. *Rush.*

Conquest of Holy Land

(FOREIGN MADE)

Producers not named. At 5th Ave Playhouse, New York, week Aug. 31. Running time 30 minutes.

This three-reeler is said to be an authentic record of General Allenby's campaign in Palestine during the World War, and made in that country.

Allenby headed British troops against Turkish uprisings in the Holy Land while the big conflict on the Continent was raging. Several of the scenes seem faked, notably a sequence showing a British captain performing an exceptional act of gallantry for which he received the Victoria Cross. Lengthy titles and troop movements, shown on maps, help to pad it out.

With Palestine daily in the headlines, **on account of the Jewish-Arabian riots, this picture may hold timely interest on a screen program, especially in neighborhoods with a large Jewish population.**

Reconstruction of Palestine

(FOREIGN MADE)

No producer named. At 5th Ave. Playhouse, New York, week Aug. 31. Running time 35 minutes.

Three reels of Palestine newsreel shots released by Hadassah, woman branch of the Zionist organization, without charge to the exhibitor.

Picture most likely has been used previously in Zionist campaign drives in this country. Dug out of the vault because of the current pogroms in Palestine, the film contains many scenes of places where Jewish-Arab race riots are now taking place, but it is propaganda for the Zionist movement, showing what the organization has done with the money it has received.

mainly in this country, for the up-building of a Jewish Homeland in Palestine.

Photography is poor, but as subject is timely the film rates a place on any Jewish neighborhood house program.

BLACK MAGIC

(SILENT)

Fox production and release. Directed by George Seitz. Scenario by Beulah Marie Dix. Josephine Dunn featured. At Loew's New York one day (Aug. 27), half double bill. Running time, 66 minutes.

As nutty a story as a story could be, enough character parts for all the films in Hollywood and a villain for every honorable person in the picture.

A prolog shows how three men were doomed to exile. Henry Walthall performed an operation while stewed, and the knife slipped; Earle Fox seduced a girl; Fritz Feld lost his honor but saved his life by posing as a woman in a shipwreck.

Three dreadful gents.

The three bad guys go so far as to pull phoney death scenes, and even that doesn't get them the polls.

A not too intelligent picture for not too intelligent audiences.

Bige.

Our Modern Maidens

(SILENT)

M-G-M production and release (non-talking), with musical synchronization. Starring Joan Crawford. Jack Conway, director. Story and continuity by Josephine Lovett. Marian Ainslee and Ruth Cummings, titles. At Capitol, New York, week Sept. 6. Running time, 70 minutes.

Billie......................Joan Crawford
Abbott.......................Rod La Rocque
Gil................Douglas Fairbanks. Jr.
Kentucky.......................Anita Page
Reg........................Edward Nugent
Blondie...................Josephine Dunn
B. Bickering Brown...........Albert Gran

Silent sequel to "Our Dancing

BIG TIME

(ALL TALKING)

Fox production directed by Kenneth Hawks. Lee Tracey and Mae Clarke head cast but are not featured in billing here. Credits include: Story by Wallace Smith; dialog by William K. Wells and Sidney Lanfield; staging by A. H. Van Buren; photography by L. William O'Connell. At the Roxy, New York, Sept. 7. Running time 85 minutes.

Eddie Burns.....................Lee Tracey
Lily Clark.....................Mae Clark
Sybil ....Daphne Pollard
Gloria ....Josephine Dunn
Eli ....Stepin Fetchit

The first of the Fox pictures with Lee Tracey, starting on a time contract. Picture's special merit is it's authentic back stage atmosphere handled in a fine spirit of sympathetic comedy. Tracey having a role almost counterpart of his Joe Lane in "Broadway." Back stage stuff is genuine and an element of strength at the box office, where Tracey is likely to count also.

Thin dramatic story as regards tension and action, marking the subject for the better class houses rather than the daily changes where its quiet humor will be at a discount. Story ought to register feminine interest on its sentimental side which is strong.

Nice piece of directing done in a well sustained tone of restrained comedy for the most part, blending neatly into certain sentimental sequences and relieved by the capital low comedy character sketch by the colored actor Stepin Fetchit who has now earned featuring by his distinctive style of handling the dumb darky type.

Running through the picture there is a bright line of wise cracking in the flash vaudeville manner in the making of which Billy K. Wells probably spread himself. Plenty of stage-and-audience shots and Miss Clarke sings the theme agreeable, in one bit. Song itself scarce, likely to go into the leading seller class. Just a machine-made ballad.

"Big Time" follows the technique of both "Broadway" and "Excess Baggage" and like those plays is a penetrating study of the self assured "ham hoofer" actor type, always from the sympathetic side. Eddie Burns is another Joe Lane of "Broadway," a blundering, child-like boob under his sophisticated surface.

He teams up with Lily Clark (Mae Clarke), out of a girl act, and together they go to the heights of "Big Time." They marry and the baby comes. A scheming dame works on Eddie's vanity and eases herself into Lily's place in the act. Lily quits cold. The new act goes from bad to worse and Eddie, broke and beaten drifts as an extra to the Hollywood studio lot.

Lily on her own has become a picture star and when the meeting comes she takes Eddie back. In the telling of this seemingly bare tale, nicety of touch and a sure instinct for the human quality make the people real (doubly real to insiders of the show business) and a certain sparkle of character drawing and wit make an engaging entertainment. It is on this quality that the film will make its bid, probably with satisfactory program returns.

Rush.

Daughters," which was also silent, and along the same lines, in story, star and in general. This is no "Dancing Daughters," nor will it get the attention its predecessor received, but it has most of the elements of box office power with one exception—dialog.

But the lack of talk can't hold "Maidens" down, for its youth, hot stuff and abundant appeal for the flaps should sell it.

Story is juvenile and silly, but the sort of silliness the more youthful fans gobble by the carload. So they won't mind that either.

Joan Crawford is the star and has the meatiest role, but Anita Page, the "Broadway Melody" girl, runs away with the picture. Miss Page is truly a trouper.

In "Our Modern Maidens" she makes the fatal step with Gil (Doug Fairbanks, Jr.) just before he's to marry the modernistic daughter of B. Bickering Brown, motor magnate. The wedding is staged as planned, but just before they're to leave on the honeymoon Billie discovers the love of Anita for Gil, and steps aside. It happens that Billie is in love with another guy, so it's a break for her as well. The other guy is globe trotting, dashing, young member of a South American embassy. She hops to S. A. to join him, and that ends the picture.

The loving quartet was jumbled, and that made the story, but straightened out in time for a nice finish.

Gil and Kentucky's misstep has been planted in the usual way, with the boy and girl embracing after a chase through the woods. Then the suggestive fadeout. That Kentucky was "in trouble" has been planted in another manner. Billie finds a card that Kentucky had been hiding. It tells of an "appointment" that Ken has for the following day. No mention of a doc, but no need to. Another way of tipping them.

It's in the card bit that Miss Page gives a great part of her performance. She makes her hysterics look real.

Plenty of extravagant settings, just one party after another, and lagoon affairs that would tax even the b. r. of a B. Bickering Brown. While each bridesmaid at the wedding received a diamond bracelet from the old boy. The flaps won't go for that—much.

Fairbanks does nicely all the way, hitting the top with some imitations in party scene. He apes John Barrymore, John Gilbert and the elder Fairbanks. Latter the most faithful and Gilbert very funny.

Rod La Rocque eases in as the suave ambassador, overcoming the fact that he always looks more like a sheik than a politician.

Miss Crawford's fans won't be disappointed, even a little bit. She wears her clothes as she always does and gives them the limit in a half-clad dance at one of her own house parties. Her pantomime is far-fetched, but vivid.

Bige.

THE HOTTENTOT

(ALL DIALOG)

Warner production and release. Directed by Roy Del Ruth from theme based on William Collier's stage play of same name. Western Electric disc recording. At Strand beginning Sept. 6. Running time, 79 minutes.

Sam Harrington....Edward Everett Horton
Peggy Fairfax..........Patsey Ruth Miller
Ollie Gilford...........Edmund Breese
Larry Crawford.............Edward Earle
Alec Fairfax...............Stanley Taylor
Swift, butler..............Douglas Gerrard
May Gilford.........Maude Turner Gordon

Edward Everett Horton gives the talker screen version of Collier's play more natural laughs than those clocked in any other Warner attempt at farce for months back.

While "The Hottentot" for some

will get a little too horsey, the average fan will thoroughly enjoy it.

Although the dialog is abundantly hoked, with some male members of the cast exaggerating this by inferior performance, the theme is touched by the whip at the start. It quickly gets from a jog to a smart trot, through pseudo jockey being called to turn. The steeplechase, while a symposium of trick photography, realizes its big moment. The audience by then is in a frame of mind where only the conventional finis of the lovable fake mastering the toughest horse and winning race and girl would be satisfactory.

Next to Horton as laugh maestro comes Swift, the butler, ably played by Douglas Gerrard. Tips make them friends at the start, or after Horton has satisfied his girl and friends that he has bridled the furious steed "Hottentot." The spiriting away to another stable of the favorite he is to ride in the chase also has its semi-thrills and comedy. The high point of mirth is when the horse is discovered, bloated beyond recognition by a meal of apples and water left by the butler.

Miss Miller, as Peggy Fairfax, holds up a large part of the dialog and is an attractive little thing in a riding habit. Edmund Breese has the bit part of a senior overseer. Production is exceptionally well mounted. *Waly.*

STREET CORNERS

(SILENT)

Produced by Russell Birdwell. Released by Film Arts Guild. Directed and written by Mr. Birdwell. Photography by Ernest Lazlo. In cast: Henry B. Walthall, Josef Swickard, Derelys Perdue, Rex Lease, Patsy O'Leary, Royer Cannon, Owen Gorin, Billy Colvin. Franklin Park, Clyde McClary. At Film Guild Cinema, New York, week Aug. 31. Two reels, running time, 12 minutes.

Group of human interest stories centering about real life in the big town make a dandy program filler for the silent spots catering to a sophisticated clientele. On the strength of this picture, Russell Birdwell, former New York dramatic critic, gained quick recognition in Hollywood and was signed as a director by one of the major producing companies.

Plot deals with a hick's visit to the big city to see and snapshot the tall buildings and other points of interest under the guidance of a friend. While so engaged he misses the street corner tragedies going on all about him, as does his materialistic friend.

One incident has a crippled newsboy encouraging a phoney beggar, another deals with a street walker and an armless war veteran, while still another has a crook sticking up a picture house box office. Each of the yarns has an O. Henry twist that has been caught by the camera without wasted motion or film.

As a distinct film novelty it deserves a showing in any of the better class houses and is sure fire for the arty spots.

RICHTHOFEN

(The Red Knight of the Air)
(GERMAN-MADE)
(Silent)

Gemeinschaft Film Co. production, released by Mercury Films. Directed by D. Kortesz and Peter Joseph. Photography by Albert Schattman, Arthur von Schwertfuhrer and Walter Lichtentstein. Settings by Paul Bunger. Aviation photography under supervision of Com. D. Otto Phillipp and Lieut. Karl Osterkamp. Edited and titled by Samuel Marx. At Film Guild Cinema, New York, week Aug. 31. Running time, 65 minutes.

M. de Val...............George Burghardt
Yvonne........................Sybil Morell

Charles........................Arne Molander
Suzanne........................Helga Thomas
Alphonse de Rivera..........Angelo Ferrari
Werner Dewall.............Egon V. Jordan
Baron von Richthofen......Carl W. Meyer

Feeble romantic story of the World War from the German angle, with a French girl's love for a German aviator used as an excuse to ring in a few incidents from the career of Richthofen, ace of the German air fighters.

The aviator, credited with bringing down about 80 of the Allies' planes during the conflict before he was bumped off, figures little in the action, but his name on the film will sell it in German centers on this side.

Using circulars printed in German, the German dailies and covering the German sections of New York City thoroughly, the Film Guild Cinema, arty Greenwich Village house, packed them in solidly at five shows daily last week and the picture is being held over. Thursday night it was estimated that at least 75% of the capacity audience had traveled from remote parts of the greater city to get a load of this flicker.

Air stuff, much of it faked, doesn't rate mention above a whisper in comparison with the aviation sequences in "Wings" and other American-made pictures of that class. Photography is streaky and eye-straining. Direction lacks distinction along the usual Continental style, with the actors mugging at the slightest provocation. Samuel Marx did a good job editing and titling this one, considering the material he had to work with.

Newsreel shots of Richthofen's state funeral in Berlin following the close of the World War are added to pad it out after the weak-kneed story winds up with a happy ending.

Properly exploited, despite its many failings, the film can't miss in the German neighborhood spots.

THE LADY LIES

(ALL DIALOG)

Paramount production and release. Walter Huston and Claudette Colbert featured. Directod by Hobart Henley. Story and dialog by John Meehan. Adapted by Garrett Fort. At Paramount, New York, week Sept. 6. Running time, 75 mins.

Robert Rossiter..............Walter Huston
Joyce Roamer............Claudette Colbert
Charlie Tyler..............Charles Ruggles
Jo Rossiter...............Patricia Deering
Bob Rossiter....................Tom Brown
Hilda Pearson..................Betty Garde
Ann Gardner......................Jean Dixon
Henry Tuttle...........Duncan Penwarden
Amelia Tuttle—..—Virginia True Boardman
Bernice Tuttle..................Verna Deane

Paramount's projection room must have seen a more accelerated version of this picture, judging by what still remains for public consumption. It still has a liberal allotment of "hells" and "damns" surrounded by a complicated tale of free love and sophisticated children. It looks like a box office sure fire.

For the picture going populace, acclimated to more or less spice on the screen, "The Lady Lies" is all of a good and interesting drama, flavored with potent ingredients for young and old.

Walter Huston, from legit, steps out in this for his first feature length attempt. And Huston can thank Paramount for picking Claudette Colbert, long a legit luminary, to play opposite him. While Huston can be put down for some very fine acting, at times predominating, it is Miss Colbert who steals the picture with one of the most winning personalities the talkers now possess. Running a close second, and walking away with all of the needed comedy relief, is Charles Ruggles, also from the stage.

In transcribing to the screen the stage play of the same name, which had a short career last season, little variation was probably done to the original plot. Perhaps because John Meehan, the author, also directed the dialog.

Huston falls in easily as the widowed and wealthy attorney, who, with two modern children on his hands, becomes entangled in a maze of domestic difficulties through a clandestine affair with a woman not in the same social register.

Before this background is woven the social problem of libertine apartment dwellers in New York, in contrast to the man's sedate and pedantic family, who impress upon him the morality clause and the consequential stain.

The kids, brought up to regard their father as a friend and pal, decide to take matters in their own hands. They begin by throwing monkey wrenches into everything. Not until they discover that the "lady does not lie," that she really means and proves her love for their father, do the kids relent and join the pair.

A strong support with splendid performances by Ruggles, Betty Garde, another "lady of leisure," and Patricia Deering and Tom Brown, the juveniles.

Hobart Henley's excellent direction is an important factor.

THE MASQUERADE

(ALL DIALOG)

Fox production and release. Directed by Russell J. Birdwell. Story from the Louis Vance novel. Stage direction by Lumsden Hare. Leila Hyams featured, with Alan Birmingham opposite. Clyde Cook billed. Photography by Charles Clarke. Running time, 65 minutes. At Loew's New York, one day, Sept. 5.

A snappy story so loosely knitted in the screen version it sprawls. Stuffed shirt performance by Alan Birmingham and general crudeness of direction discounted any possibility of Leila Hyams carrying the picture. Best she can do in this is to register youthful charm.

Starts out as a crook story of swift complications with interest centered in rapid surprise developments. Tricky background is laid and then the whole thing goes to pieces in a sea of meaningless dialog. Story pauses on the brink of tense situation while principals go into long exchanges of useless conversation.

A sample is a long sequence of shots that show nothing but the young leads riding along in an auto, nothing visible but their faces, the windshield and a suggestion of an auto wheel. Where they're going has no significance and the episode apparently was introduced to pile on dialog for its own sake.

Story never quite makes up its mind whether it wants to be a crook melo or a Sennett comedy. Valet character of the hero does a comedy relief role that would be appropriate to Ben Turpin, while Clyde Cook's comedy detective did all the hoke business short of the wooden mallet. Effort to blend the two-reel comedy atmosphere with a romantic crook melo doesn't work out.

Just as the audience feels an awakening of interest in the lovers or sets itself for a brisk action, all bets are off while young Birmingham goes into Omaha stock love making or the comedy valet does a pratt fall. *Rush.*

SEEDS OF FREEDOM

(RUSSIAN MADE)

(Disc Orchestration)

Produced by Belgoskino and released here through Amkino. Directed by G. Roshal from scenario by S. Roshal and V. Stroevoy. L. M. Leonidoff starred. In cast: J. Undershlak, T. Adelgeim, A. Sandel, M. Sinelnikova, A. Neshkov, A. Grinfield. American titles by Shelley Hamilton. At the Cameo Sept. 7. Running time, 88 minutes.

"Seeds of Freedom" is designed for special audiences. Dedicated to the Jewish fighter, Hirsch Lekkert, and said to be based on a historical occurrence in the Jewish Ghettos of old Russia, the production scored vast enthusiasm in scattered parts of the Cameo. To those unfamiliar with the incident, however, "Seeds of Freedom" is composed of propaganda and Soviet sequences made familiar to arty goers by numerous other Russian importations.

Like its antecedents, this offering is crowded with local color and odd faces. Although it rambles and slips off the story quite frequently this picture possesses more of a theme and sustains interest better than many foreign-mades.

Poorly titled for general audiences, the action attempts to portray the socialistic tendencies of younger Jews which are frowned upon not only by the czaristic rule but also by a rabbi and wealthy members of the orthodox faith.

Much space is devoted to meetings where little action takes place. The character studies here substitute as interest.

L. M. Leonidoff, masterly star of the Moscow Art Theatre, duals as the arrogant Governor and the stern Rabbi. As the former he is finally murdered by a rebel leader, played by J. Untershlak. Here the picture comes to an abrupt halt with the dust blowing over an unknown grave, but with no hint whether it contains the martyr or the Governor.

By way of feminine interest, an adopted daughter of the Rabbi is disowned and joins the socialists.

The highlight of the production is the scourging of leaders. The actual whippings are not shown, but the director has emphasized the sidelights, such as flies feeding on the bloody block, until the imagination is spurred to vivid understandings. *Waly.*

CAMPUS KNIGHTS

(SILENT)

Chesterfield production. Featuring Raymond McKee. Written and directed by Al Kelly. Cameraman, M. A. Anderson. Cast includes Shirley Palmer, Marie Miller. On double feature bill at Loew's New York, one day, Sept. 6. Running time, 57 mins.

Pretty poor even being charitably disposed towards a cheap states right production not intended for flossy dates. Thrown together, hodge podgy, and extremely bad negative. Looks like the laboratory turned this out without much attention to proper development. Cameraman may share the onus, but it looks like a mediocre job by some lab.

Raymond McKee enacts a sap professor whose twin brother is a high stepper with a yen for chorus girls and a disposition for getting into jams. Plot is obvious; bad brother always making it tough for the academic replica.

Hardly rates serious comment. *Land.*

HONOR

(RUSSIAN MADE—SILENT)

Sovkino production, released by Amkino. Directed by A. Shirvanzada. In cast: H. Appelian Elsie Hasnick, Tatiezan Shahdoodakian, L. Hajinian, Madame Maysoorian. At Fifth Avenue Playhouse, week Sept. 7. Running time 70 minutes.

One of those grim Russian stories which starts with an earthquake with the dead and dying shown in close-up and ends with a murder and suicide. The story deals with customs in a small Russian town and shows husbands beating their wives and fathers horse-whipping their daughters for minor faults. Film holds little value even for the American arty house.

Sousan and Soran are engaged to be married but are forbidden to see each other until their marriage day. When the boy defies this edict and secretly meets the girl, her father is certain that her honor has been sullied and another marriage is arranged for her.

Sousan's husband hearing false gossip affecting his wife and her first lover accuse her of infidelity and kills her. Soran rushes to the funeral and, proclaiming that his sweetheart was innocent, picks a soft spot next to her and stabs himself to death.

Direction and photography are poor. Titles are in Russian and English.

About the only thing of note in this flicker is the finest collection of schnozzolas ever screened in full face and profile. One of the men doing comedy bore a close resemblance to Jimmy Durante, except that he sported a ragged crop of chin whiskers.

BECAUSE I LOVE YOU

(FRENCH-MADE)

(Silent)

Paris, Sept. 2.

"Parce que je t'aime," produced by Grantham Hayes and released by Integral Film and United Distributors, is listed as a dramatic comedy. While a good local picture it is not destined to soar the world. Scenario is at least clear.

Marchal is a professor at the top of his fame. His thoughts turn to love, on his secretary, Jacqueline, who reciprocates. She consents to marry Marchal.

Several months of bliss, then Serge enters the china store. He is the professor's godson and comes to spend a few days with his benefactor. Marchal devotes his evenings to study and is blind to Serge buzzing 'round.

She fights against her inclination, begging Serge to leave. Marchal learns of the situation by a letter. He pretends to have a mistress, to tranqualize his wife, wishing only her happiness. This phase seems to have been done to death.

Jacqueline, disgusted, runs away to join Serge. As expected, the fellow is a cad. Marchal still adores his wife and Jacqueline becomes acquainted with the details of his sacrifice.

Perhaps the main feature is Nicolas Rimsky as the professor. He is supported by Diana Hart, Rene Ferte and Elza Temary, who strive hard to renovate the antiquated yarn. *Kendrew.*

Spy of Mme. Pompadour

(GERMAN-MADE—SILENT)

Amer.-Anglo Corp. releasing Emelka production. Directed by Karl Grune. Story by Max Fliner. A Carnegie Playhouse, New York, week of Sept. 7. Running time, 80 mins.

Marquis d'Eon......................Liane Hald
Mme. Pompadour......Countess Easterhazy
Czar Paul..........................Fritz Korner
Czarina..............................Mona Maris
Louis XV........................Alfred Gerash
Lord Hatfield......................Dene Morel

German production made by Emelka of Munich and parelleling in many respects "The Patriot," made by Paramount. In both cases the chief characterization is the mad, imbecilic Czar Paul and the plot rotates about his court and the events culminating in his assassination. Treatment of the essential details is quite similar, although the embroidery and plot trimmings are entirely different in design.

As a foreign picture it is impressive on the score of splendid photography and clear print of American standard. Production values in general are first rate, sets are numerous, big and munificent. Cast is suave, interesting, handsome and players uniformly give a good accounting of themselves.

It's silent, old-fashioned in theme, and a costume picture. Exhibs and bookers should know from this where it is likely to be accepted. And they can book it for such places in the assurance it's an exceptionally good foreign picture of its type.

Fritz Korner's czar is in its way as fine a piece of pantomime as was Emil Jannings. It is less detailed necessarily through being less prominent, but is replete with touches that tell. In the matter of posture and carriage Korner conveys more about the crazy emperor than did Jannings.

Liane Haid, playing both a girl and a boy, is attractive and competent. Countess Esterhazy as La Pompadour, lends additional beauty.

Land.

PROTECTION

(SILENT)

Fox production and release. Story by Clarkson Miller. Directed by Benjamin Stoloff. Cameraman, H. Valentine. Cast includes Dorothy Burgess, Robert Elliott and Paul Page. One day, Sept. 7, at the Stanley, New York. Running time, 58 mins.

Light bootlegger-newspaperman picture. Amusing for silent neighborhood houses. Hoke portrait of journalism. Small realism also in liquor traffic angle. Wholesome love interest. Fair degree of melodramatic punch. Reporter and girl nicely cast. Bootleggers out of order. Delightful comedy. Continuity fair. Photography passable. Titles merely fitting.

Young newspaper reporter bothered to death by sob sister. Marries her in the end to keep her from cleaning off his desk and placing flowers in his lapel. Bootleggers subsidize the newspaper. Managing editor walks out. Takes over The Register, a down and out rival paper. Publisher of first paper puts reporter in m. e. chair. He walks out to be with original editor. Girl follows him on The Register.

Managing editor starts campaign against king of bootleggers. Uses story the other paper declined to print. Sends reporter sleuthing. Gets pictures of men unloading liquor. They follow him in car. He gets scratched by machine gun bullets as he enters office. Girl doctors him.

Bootleg king's girl and he split. Reporter goes to interview her. She gives him lowdown. Breaks a whale of a story. The king legger comes into m. e.'s office to bump him off, but is checkmated. As he leaves office, he gets the works from a confederate whom he has slapped. Wind-up shows town cleaned up by The Register, the reporter and girl asking for an hour off.

THE TRESPASSER

(ALL DIALOG, With Songs)

Joseph P. Kennedy production; United Artists release. Gloria Swanson starred. Directed by Edmund Goulding from an original story by Mr. Goulding. R. C. A. Photophone sounded. At R. C. A. Photophone's projection room, New York. Running time, 120 minutes.

Marion Donnell..............Gloria Swanson
Jack Merrick..................Robert Ames
Hector Ferguson..............Purnell Pratt
John Merrick, Sr...........William Holden
Fuller.....................Henry B. Walthall
"Jackie"......................Wally Albright
"Flip" Merrick...............Kay Hammond
Miss Potter................Blanche Frederici
Blanche.....................Marcella Corday

Seeing "The Tresspasser" with Gloria Swanson talking and singing along with the picture itself, it's easy to understand the smash it is in London. For it's one of those cinch money picture. A hold over.

Chances are that after the English got a flash at "The Tresspasser" they realized in part at least what their trouble or drawback is as picture producers. For, aside from Miss Swanson and the drawing craze of hearing her voice two ways on the screen, this talker is an elegantly made and finished production.

It has been given superior direction by Edmund Goulding, with Mr. Goulding taking a conventional tale to make it stand up very high by twisting it about. Plenty of emotion in the story and enough tears for the sobbers.

Likely there is no picture on the record with as many anti-climaxes as "The Tresspasser" contains. At least four times the film goes to a finish, as one might suspect, to take another interesting tack. That is one of the novelties of the story. Three others are Miss Swanson, her voice and clothes.

Singing two songs, with "Love" the theme number but not plugged, Gloria Swanson is going to paralyze the picture goers with her singing voice. She sings like a prima. No wonder the Jos. P. Kennedy bunch decided it would be necessary for Miss Swanson's voice to go on the phonograph discs as the convincer, for it's well known no disc maker will stand for a double.

In the parlor scene where Miss Swanson walks in, while singing, first heard off screen, the women of the house are apt to stand up in their seats in amazement. In all of the talkers, all of the controversy about voice and delivery, from stage or screen, there has been no utter surprise like this singing voice of Gloria Swanson's. With her dialog after that, of course, there's no question.

"The Tresspasser" will do so much with Miss Swanson as a talker star that she should be made to repeat with two or three more as quickly as possible. This one will carry far, not solely with voice, but her acting and her clothes! Even a guy who's nuts about red heads could go for her in those gowns.

In the story are throat catches often, about this mother and her baby, left flat by the son of a financier. The boy had married a lawyer's stenographer, but his father convinced him within 24 hours after the elopement that the old man's sugar would be worth more than than the bitter sweet he had stumbled into.

But the girl walked first, fighting her rich father-in-law then as she did at all times when meeting him thereafter, holding tnto the growing son. She becomes the favorite of her former employer, supported by him in luxury even if the story does clean up her on that bit, and then returning to his estate the $500,000 left her by the lawyer at the latter's sudden death.

There's a scene here that will burn some women and tickle others. Upon the lawyer being seized with a fatal stroke, his final wish is that the girl be sent for. She goes to his bedroom and the lawyer's wife who had consented to the visit, walks in. There she stands, the wife, the evident reason why her husband fell, glaring at "that woman." A hard boiled doesn't know whether to laugh or feel sorry for each of them. But the unprogrammed player of the wife role did it peachily.

Many little bits; many big bits. One of the biggest for the throat choke is the second wife the boy married, and who became an invalid following an auto accident, wheeling to the home of the first wife, seeing the child, and telling her husband she wants a divorce so that the boy and his mother may have the father back again.

Of course the second wife died just in time for the finish. About that time also the old man capitulated to the girl with grit. There's another nice bit for the finale and unexpected.

Lot of stuff in this picture. Give Miss Swanson and her companion players all of the acknowledgment they should have, but a huge hunk must go to Goulding, the director and author.

Mr. Kennedy has been pretty liberal on the production that has a great deal of background. The Swanson clothes in the originals could be ballyhooed for a fashion show anywhere, and they had to put her in that well kept apartment to show them off. Just before the girl and the baby had been pushed out for owing too much room rent.

With Swanson—a natural. *Sime.*

FLIGHT

(ALL DIALOG)

Columbia production and release. Produced by Harry Cohn. Directed by Frank R. Capra from original story credited to Ralph Graves, one of the featured principals. Jack Holt and Lila Lee also featured. Cameramen: Elmer Dyer and Joe Novak. Dialog by Mr. Capra.

Panama Williams..................Jack Holt
Elinor................................Lila Lee
Lefty Phelps..................Ralph Graves
Major............................Allan Roscoe
Steve Roberts.............Harold Goodwin
Sandino................Jimmy De La Cruze

Following all of the other air pictures, "Flight" goes to the lead. It's a certain gross maker for the regular houses and at the Cohan with its $2 scale will have a profitable run. This talker breaks in the height of the airplane publicity of every sort. As it is a complete exploitation of the flying the public likes to see, there are any number of angles for local exploitation to fatten the money this picture will naturally draw.

As a talker and a picture, "Flight" is a fine piece of workmanship. Credit for that goes four ways, to Harry Cohn, who has built a niche of his own among contemporary picture producers; to Frank R. Capra, a most skilful and imaginative director and with plenty of guts, it seems, while Jack Holt and Ralph Graves in the lead fit into this film like a rubber band. Graves, who wrote the holding original story, gets in twice.

Capra's guts show in a cremation scene. It's probably the first cremation bit ever put on the screen or stage. Nervy extraordinary, and over. While another all new idea here is to have one fellow in love with a girl act as proxy for another, his pal, in proposing marriage to her for him. Two new ideas in any one picture spell dizziness nowadays. And no theme song.

Critics may hop onto that cremation, but it's not gruesome, the way it is done and Graves does it.

A preliminary slide generously credits the Marine Corps for cooperation, saying "Flight" could not have been made without its aid. This sort of cremation is said to be traditional with the corps. Two of the fliers, with Harold Goodwin the pilot and Graves the observer, go to a drop hunting native gorrillas in Nicaragua. Goodwin tells Graves in a lengthy scene he is washed up and passing out, but "don't let the ants get me, Lefty."

Graves is continually brushing off the climbing ants from Steve's bare chest, as the boy can't move, lying on a wing of the machine. Steve goes west. Graves covers him with a large white cloth, with the next scene a match applied to the sheet. The fire consumes everything burnable in and on the plane. It was a daring thing to try and as much so to let it remain in.

This picture gets an actual running start in the adaptation of that notorious bonehead running the wrong way in a football game last season on the Coast. Here again Graves runs the wrong way, can't stand the kidding and winds up in the Marines, meeting Jack Holt as the hard boiled sergeant. Holt takes the kid under his care, but they almost go to the mat in a dandy bit where Holt, believing Graves had crossed him with the girl, slaps Graves' face twice, without a return, a neat and another bit breaking this off threatened fight.

The girl is Lila Lee, a nurse, who goes for Graves while unconsciously leading on the serg. Her role is lightweight but she looks it.

Flying here for a picture may be said to be near-incomparable. A majority must be on the level and any miniature stuff has been so well handled it is almost beyond detection.

Reproduction in the 1,100-seat Cohan excellent. Dialog over nicely all of the time with amplification perfect.

Dialog given to the men, including the leads, without a mar, written to suit them and every situation they are in. Not so good for Miss Lee, with trite lines handed her.

Graves will be given the best of it for the acting force, but Holt gives a performance calling for just as much. Graves is the juve with a million-dollar smile he knows how to work, and personality plus here. Both handle dialog like veterans. It's an even bet now that Graves with his voice and presence will rank among the leading draws of the screen within a year. If Columbia has him under contract, it should work Graves to the utmost limit, for the faster the better with and for him—and Columbia.

A crackerjack picture for an independent producer. One of those that Columbia turns out every now and then with sublime judgment, apparently, for a super-talker to Columbia or any indie, with its attending heavy investment, means an awful lot.

Sime.

THE GREAT GABBO

(ALL DIALOG)

Independent production with presentation credited Henry D. Meyer and Nat Cordish. Distributed through Sonc-Art World Wide. Directed by James Cruze from the Ben Hecht adaptation of an uncredited story. Continuity and dialog by Hugh Herbert. Original songs, used in Western Electric recording, by Paul Titsworth, Lynn Cowan, Don MCNamee, King Zany. Opening for special Broadway run at the Selwyn Sept. 12, twice daily, $2 top. Running time, 91 minutes.

Great Gabbo ....Erich Von Stroheim
Mary ....Betty Compson
Frank ....Don Douglas
Babe ....Margie (Babe) Kane
Otto Gabbo ....a dummy

All the superlatives in a heavy vocabulary can be expended and yet "The Great Gabbo" will just remain the picture prodigy of the independent ranks and a talker drama, from the standpoints of theme originality and absorbing qualities, above the average show window display of the big companies. It's not a $2 picture, but a cinch for the regular houses.

It is Cruze's first large one for the independents and Erich von Stroheim's first screen release of his voice. With a new Betty Compson, the Hecht story mind and the Herbert lines included, oke.

The story is simplicity itself. Just a pair of show people; one a lovely, considerate girl and the other a ventriloquist with a hyper-egotist complex. The expected break, followed by a rise from the grinds to the individual success of both. Then the too late realization of love by the dummy manipulator.

Von Stroheim, as the eccentric and arrogant performer who reveals a Pagliacci heart through the medium of Otto, the dummy, doubles the enhancement of a dominant screen personality with his lines. It is the voice, frenzied and then modulated to a pianissimo, that is one of the strongest threads compelling audience concentration and carrying the interest over sequences devoted to color and stage show that would be irrelevant gaps in productions less skillfully directed and enacted.

The recording job on "The Great Gabbo" is one of especial note. Voices are more natural and poses are entirely devoid of the constrained and stiff mannerisms so apparent in the average talker. In only a few feet does the mechanical phase become apparent in this production. This is early in the footage in a dressing room scene in a honky tonk house where the lighting also is poor. Again, in part of the colored sequence the print is rainy and the characters blurred. But both of these conditions are too brief to make sufficient impression even to be considered drawbacks.

In the ensemble work, Cruze flashes back to Gabbo often enough and injects little deft touches of the story in the whispers between an adagio team, to keep interest in the theme taut. *Waly.*

THE DRAKE CASE

(ALL DIALOG)

Universal production and release. Edward Laemmle, director. Recorded on Western Electric System. Story by Charles Logue, dialog by Logue and J. G. Hawks. At the Colony, New York, week Sept. 14. Running time, 74 minutes.

Lulu Marks	Gladys Brockwell
District Attorney	Forrest Stanley
Roger Lane	Robert Frazer
Hugo Jepson	James Crane
Mrs. Drake	Doris Lloyd
Georgia	Barbara Leonard
Capt. Condon	Bill Thorne
Edmonds	Eddie Hearn
Bill	Tom Dugan
Judge	Byron Douglas

Very recent and generally superior films of the same category will hold this court room talker out of the smash program class. Interest and suspense that are naturally created and carried along by murder trails on the stage or screen insure "The Drake Case" moderate fan attention. But no name to draw with, no background to exploit and the lack of a really important mystery story, combine to stamp it as no better than moderate.

Returned through "The Drake Case" are several picture personalities of other days, most of them confined to the indies and freelance employment for quite a while. All of that class record vocally as well as they screened silently years ago, and those years of camera training are always apparent.

The court room portion consuming most of the footage, follows the same formula employed in "Mary Dugan," "On Trial" and the others. It differs a bit in the absence of the usual number of explanatory flashbacks, fading out but once for that purpose, and unwinds the mystery in the witness box. Identification of the guilty one is reserved for the last minute, providing a finish highly reminiscent of "Mary Dugan."

The Drake case concerns the murder of the wealthy Mrs. Drake. Lulu Marks, servant in the household, is accused, placed on trial with mountains of circumstantial evidence against her, and then vindicated. First five minutes or so of the film, preceding the actual murder, are used to plant a motive for Lulu's act of violence and complicate the mystery as much as possible.

Though shown to be a servant, Lulu forces her mistress to postpone a trip to Europe by threatening exposure, and it looks like blackmail. A few minutes later, as Lulu is giving Mrs. Drake's adopted daughter, Georgia, a dose of what the daughter believes to taste like poison, the police siren is heard in the street and Lulu threatens to "get even." Mrs. Drake had previously been shown calling up the police and filing the complaint against Lulu.

Then the shots, the finding of Mrs. Drake's body and the trial of Lulu, who won't talk. Brought out, however, that Lulu was the first Mrs. Drake, the real mother of Georgia, and working in the house to protect her daughter, with the daughter not in on the know. The evil Mrs. Drake's scheme was to make a dope fiend of the girl and marry her off to her (Mrs. Drake's) own lover to grab an inheritance.

The "poison" given to the girl by her mother, it is brought out at the trial, was no more than a dose of bromides, a harmless sedative.

The murder finally found is Mrs. Drake's own working partner, Jepson.

No love interest, except that of the accused mother's efforts to protect her daughter, and not a chance in this court room for romance. The Georgia-Jepson affair is busted wide open by the uncovering of Jeppy's guilt. That may be another barrier in the way of "The Drake Case.

Gladys Brockwell does Lulu to perfection, nicely supported by the cast of principals. *Bige.*

WHY LEAVE HOME?

(ALL DIALOG)

Fox production and release. Directed by Raymond Cannon from an adaptation of "The Cradle Snatchers," by Robert S. Carr. Music and lyrics by Conrad, Mitchell, Gottler. Dialog by Walter Catlett. Western Electric recording. At the Hippodrome, commencing Sept. 14. Running time, 70 minutes. Cast includes Sue Carol, Dixie Lee, Jean Bary, Nick Stuart, Richard Keene, David Rollins, Walter Catlett, Jed Frouty, Gordon De Main, I. Chase, Dot Farley, Laura Hamilton.

"Why Leave Home?" the screen version of the farce comedy, "The Cradle Snatchers," is good program entertainment, but hardly anything more. The domestic jumbles that made the play such a hit are too perfectly scrambled in the film. Despite the cut-and-dried series of dove-tailed coincidences, there are enough laughs in the lines and stereotyped mix-ups to keep the average audience from boredom.

The highlight of the picture version is an elaborate night club set and garden, where the three husbands and the boys' girl friends and the three boys and the husbands' wives shuffle around before gradually working into the melee which comes with recognition.

One bull's-eye view of the garden, showing the principals madly scrambling after one another, with a bouncer in the lead giving it a Mack Sennett touch, is immediately followed by a close-up at the fountain.

The requirements of the club that its guests be masked is a good gag for suspense, since it permits hubbies and wives to admire one another, although on a dual cheating basis.

Credits for performances are most impartial, since the nine principals involved all have the same opportunities. Sue Carol, as one of the show girls, and Nick Stuart, as one of the college trio, get a little better break than the others in some special necking sequences. Sue also sings the theme song from her perch on the revolving orchestra pit in the club.

The college lads teaching the wives to blackbottom in the apartment before the trip to the resort is also a laugh-getter. The picture version makes it very emphatic that the boys are just boys and escorting the married femmes simply to get dough to entertain their showgirls. And the theme similarly stresses the girlies need a meal when accepting the invite of the three hubbies after the boys have called off another date. *Waly.*

Chasing Through Europe

(No Dialog—Effects)

Fox production and release. Synchronized with about 5% in sound. Sue Carol, Nick Stuart and Gustav von Seyffertitz are featured. Directed by David Butler and Alfred Werker. Cast includes Gavin Gordon and E. Alyn Warren. At Loew's New York, one day (Sept. 13), half double bill. Running time, 62 minutes.

Mild but worth a place on a double bill. The story is slim but contains a light laugh or two and several thrilly newsreel shots including an interesting double exposure of Il Duce and the Prince of Wales, Mt. Vesuvius in action as background.

Nick plays the part of a newsreel cameraman on a roving assignment. The kind of job every newspaperman and cameraman has wished for since he was crazy enough to take up the work—but never gets.

Stuart is having one glorious time jumping across to Europe and bandying about London when romance overtakes him. Linda Terry (Sue Carol) unhappily promised as wife to a chap she despises gets into a jam with her guardian and would be fiance right under Nick's nose. Naturally Nick interferes. The villains are bigger than Nick but what's that in a picture? Nick bowls both over and elopes—platonically—with the girl. They first go to Paris.

On, in and about the Eiffel Tower the guardian, who by this time has become some kind of a crook in addition to being a bad smelling oyster anyway, tries to have Nick pinched for kidnapping the girl. But French ideas of romance prove superb and the kids escape to Rome. The two villains follow.

In the Italian capital the story gets its happy ending. The villains are arrested and the two kids set off for the States and of course the altar.

MIDSTREAM

(10% Dialog)

Tiffany-Stahl production and release. Ricardo Cortez and Claire Windsor featured. In cast: Montagu Love, Helen Jerome Eddy, Larry Kent. Directed by James Flood. Musical score by Hugo Riesenfeld. Synchronized by RCA Photophone. Story by Bernice Boone. Adapted by Frances Guihan. Titles by Frederic and Fanny Hatton. At Loew's New York one day, Sept. 12. Running time, 85 minutes.

Good feature for the daily changers. With a little editing it would make the grade in the split-week neighborhood houses.

Film has about 20 minutes devoted to scenes and arias from the opera "Faust" interpolated, with the singers of the operatic roles drawn from the concert field. Director Flood, in an attempt to develop his story, which deals with rejuvenation, also the theme of "Faust," allows the opera stuff to run too long, a fault that might easily be remedied by application of the shears.

Jim Blackstone (Ricardo Cortez), Wall street operator who has seen youth and romance pass him by while he has been accumulating wealth, falls in love with his next-door neighbor, Helen Craig (Claire Windsor). To win her he travels abroad, where he submits to a rejuvenation operation. Emerging as a young man, he cables of his own death, and then reappears in New York as a nephew who has inherited everything. The young-old boy wins the girl away from a youth of her own age.

On the eve of their marriage they attend a performance of "Faust." The girl's comments on the performance finally cause the financier to break down, the resultant shock causing the old man to be his age. When the young girl takes a runout on learning that her youthful lover is really a man old enough to be her father, he finally decides to get hitched to his private secretary, who has been faithful to him for a score of years.

Cortez, Miss Windsor and Montagu Love handled the dialog sequence at the finish in neat style, with Miss Eddy also worthy of favorable mention for the manner in which she plays a minor role.

Rejuvenation as a subject for the screen has an element of newness.

Under Greenwood Tree

(BRITISH MADE)

(Some Dialog)

London, Sept. 7.

Produced by British International. Directed by Harry Lachman and adapted from Thomas Hardy's novel of same title. Dialog by Frank Launder. Camera: Claude Friese-Greene. RCA recording. Running time 90 minutes. Pre-viewed at the Regal Theatre, London, Sept. 5.

Fancy	Marguerite Allan
Dick	John Batten
Shinar	Nigel Barrie

A very difficult picture to review. In its favor are the excellent direction, perfect recording and beautiful photography. Set off by a weak story and poorly cast leads. Also some dialog between the juvenile leads which should never have been recorded; affected, unnatural and inept.

Someone with big ideas ought to give Lachman a proper break. He has got so much of beauty and holding power out of a thin thread of story and a company composed almost entirely of extras that with a strong subject and a reasonable cast he should touch the front rank of direction.

In Hardy's novel there is no story; in the adaptation all there is consists of the Squire (Shinar) buying an organ for the parish church and so dispossessing the village choir which has existed for generations. Shinar does this so he can get close to the village school-marm, who is a newcomer and can play an organ. He bribes a fortune-teller to make the girl believe she must marry him, but Fancy discovers this and walks out on him in front of the church.

Opening with preparations for Christmas carols, Lachman, with a choir played by extras who are perfect types, keeps away from the story as much as possible and plays on the theme of the march of progress from the pathetic angle as represented by the forcing out of the instrumentalists composing the choir, whose posts—and instruments—have been handed down through generations.

Choir practices, a rural party with barn-dances and quartet singing (the Gotham Quartet was used here and records exquisitely), all the atmosphere touches building up the forlorn despair of the old gaffers when the choir is displaced, are finely done. Composition is always faultless, and nothing is hoked.

As a contrast to jazz and backstage, it is a sweet piece of work. Whether it will stand up for a public used to snap and hectic sound and movement is another matter. Certainly it is a clean and pretty picture. But this reviewer doubts, because of the story and the weak juveniles, whether it is box office despite the talker shortage on this side. *Frat.*

JEALOUSY
(All Dialog)

Paramount production and release. Starring Jeanne Eagels. Jean de Limur, director. Adapted by Garret Fort from Eugene Walter's stage adaptation of French play by Louis Verneuil. John D. Williams' dialog. At Paramount, New York, week Sept. 13. Running time, 66 minutes.

Yvonne	Jeanne Eagels
Pierre	Frederic March
Rigaud	Halliwell Hobbes
Renee	Blanche Le Clair
Clement	Henry Daniell
Charlotte	Hilda Moore

Notable performance by Jeanne Eagels doesn't go far enough to help "Jealousy" to become 'better entertainment for picture audiences than its story permits it to. One of the most inexpensive (to produce) of last season's dramatic shows, calling for but two characters and a single set, "Jealousy" was similarly economical for screen usage. That might be the best reason for its selection. Otherwise it does little more than sell Miss Eagels as a personality and an actress, although that's doing the same thing over again with Miss Eagels after "The Letter." All of "Jealousy's" drawing will be done by the star.

"Jealousy" as a picture has not greatly changed the original narrative. Film version also ends with the murder by Miss Eagels' husband of her wealthy but lustful ex-keeper. The play had the jealousy-wracked couple residing together before marriage. The picture begins with their marriage.

Will take about five minutes for average audiences to forget how very British the accents are. And then so much longer for this story to get going.

The jobs done by Frederic March as the husband and Halliwell Hobbes as the heavy-holding scoundrel compare well enough with Miss Eagels'.

Bige.

When Moscow Laughs
(RUSSIAN MADE)
(Silent)

Mezhrapom-Russ production. Released by Amkino. Directed by B. Barnet. Photographed by V. Francisson. Original story by V. K. Turkin, V. G. Shershenevitch and B. Barnet. Edited and titled by Shelley Hamilton. Cast includes Anna Stern, V. Mikhailov, W. Fogel, Kowal-Samborski, Mme. S. Birman, and P. Pol. At the Film Guild, New York, Sept. 14. Running time, 60 minutes.

The title is misleading. Amkino realized this. They thus have provided an alternate tag line, "The Girl With the Bandbox," which suits better. Even a district attorney will admit that Moscow is nil in this filmfoto. As for story it's just sarsaparilla. Character describing titles that come after the filmed action makes the yarn all the weaker. But the acting is good. So is the direction.

For exhibition purposes in the States, however, the picture belongs exclusively arty. Its best bet even then being a double feature bill.

For only the arty can sympathize with a peasant girl who marries a farmer whom she has only seen once before and then under a bench in a railroad station just to give the book carrying milkman a place to sleep.

It's a striking example of Russian sentiment—it runs to extremes. When the actors in the picture are serious they are grim. When they attempt humor they are ludicrous. And the comedy in this picture is no exception.

Natasha is a peasant girl. She does homework in millinery. Her output is bought by a big-town mode shop where for some unexplained reason the girl also maintains a sleeping room. The Russian law which demands registration of every citizen's address also demands, according to the picture,

that the registrant inhabit that address. But Natasha did not inhabit so the author caused her to meet with Ilya, a farmer, under a settee in a railroad station.

The great big city of over 1,600,-000 roomers had no vacancy. So Ilya goes to sleep sitting up on a park bench. There Natasha found him the following day. She proposes to him. Like an inexperienced milkman Ilya consents.

But—Natasha's landlords are having a dinner party in the girl's room when the newlyweds arrive and the landlords get sore and complain to the authorities to oust Natasha. The action fails and Natasha now fired from her job demands payment and gets a supposedly worthless lottery bond in lieu of salary.

And—as Mr. Grimm, the greatest fairy reporter of them all once related—the bond proved a winner.

MAN FROM NEVADA
(Silent)

J. P. McGowan production and Bell Pictures Corp. release. Directed by J. P. McGowan. Hap Depew, cameraman. Tom Tyler, starred. In cast: Natalie Joyce, K. Cooper, Godfrey Craig, Al Heuston, Al Ferguson. At Loew's New York one day, Sept. 10, one half double bill. Running time about 55 minutes.

J. P. McGowan is turning out a lot better stuff. This one with Tom Tyler called "The Man from Nevada" has it over anything J. P. has released in months. It's all the old hoke, but it's tied together better. Technically, from the camera and lighting points of view, it's above McGowan's average. The quickest grinds and cheaper third runs will appreciate these improvements.

Tom Tyler, ex-FBOite, just likes to do good. Fortunately for the theme (and McGowan has never been known to think up one without plenty of wild socking) Tom has a chance to bowl over the strong bad gents at hysterical tempo. There is some cold shooting, but minor wounds are the only development. J. P. plays to the kid angle this time, showing a flock of them and a timid papa who finally keeps his land after learning from Tom that a jilt on the chin is better than good penmanship in sticking to a land claim.

There's a girl. Natalie Joyce, in the motherless big sister role. Not much love stuff. J. P. is all for the men. Plenty of hard riding, with the audience not so often forgetting what it is all about. *Waly.*

POINTS WEST
(Silent)

Produced and released by Universal. Featuring Hoot Gibson. Story by B. M. Bower. Directed by Arthur Rosson. Photography by Henry Neumann. At Tivoli, New York, one day, Sept. 16. Running time, 59 minutes.

Rates a good toe hold among westerns. Usual Hoot Gibson stuff. Photography good. Skimpy bit of comedy plenty of scowling faces; raft of horse flesh and a good dose of gun play, thus putting the picture up-to-date in crime and punishment.

Gibson plays Cole Lawson, Jr. He falls heir to a pretty piece of alfalfa when his old man is knocked off by an ex-con who murdered for revenge. The killer's name is McQuade, alias Roper. He's tough; stops at nothing.

Old man Lawson having been secretly informed that his murder was about to take place, left a note wising up his son to get McQuade. So Lawson, Jr., poses as a horse thief and trails up to McQuade's stronghold. He falls in love with the only one of two decent women in the burg—the younger one.

Should a Girl Marry?
(10% Dialog)

Rayart production and release. Directed by Scott Pembroke. Story by Arthur Hoerl. Disc orchestration by the Ben Pollak Park Central orchestra. In cast: Helen Foster, Don Keith, William V. Mong. At Loew's New York, one day, Sept. 10, one half of double bill. Running time about 65 minutes.

"Should a Girl Marry" has most of the dialog after the finis, when the judge expounds on the mistake the little girl in the story made by not telling her boy friend that she had committed murder, even though acquitted of the crime. It's just a program theme of very ordinary appeal at best, with the propaganda stuff obviously tacked on as an after-thought.

Helen Foster, as the girl, does the shooting after a low Lothario has wronged "beyond death's threshold" an innocent, but hooch-loving sister. She is an excellent actress, despite the role.

A courtroom scene, where the summations of counsel and judge's charge compose the other half of the dialog, is satisfactory to the grind payees. *Waly.*

GIRL IN GLASS CAGE
(Silent)

First National production and release. Synchronized with music and featuring Loretta Young, Ralph Lewis and Carroll Nye. Directed by Ralph Dawson. Story by George Kibbe Turner. Cameraman, Ernest Haller. Adaptation by James Gruen. Cast includes Matthew Betz, Lucien Littlefield, Charles Sellon and Julia Swayne Gordon. At Loew's New York, one day (Sept. 13), half double bill. Running time, 75 minutes.

This picture was originally intended for dialog but wound up dumb. The story as screened is nothing to rave about. Direction is ordinary. Photography rates better than average. As half of a double bill, however, the film is well graded.

There is nothing much to the glass cage idea. It merely means a box office.

Locale is a small town. The town's pip movie ticket seller is annoyed by members of the "Deep River Social Club." The chief annoyer is "Doc" Striker. Sheik Smith rates second.

Striker gets socked by Terry Pomfret, the town's biggest highbrow, in a squabble over the dame and the picture gets its excuse for a killing. This happens in the last half hour of the action.

Sheik Smith has followed the girl home. "Doc," however, trying to frame Pomfret for the coffin, has him lured to the girl's house also. Then the "Doc" sends the dame's crab of an uncle to bump off Pomfret. But fate intervened for the picture and the old man shoots Sheik Smith instead.

Everything winds up at the trial. Although the dame is up for the murder she takes hold of the case and miraculously persuades everybody to confess.

LIVING RUSSIA
(RUSSIAN MADE)
(Silent)

Produced by Wufku. Released by Amkino. Conceived and directed by Dziga Vertoff. Photographed by M. Kaufman. At the Film Guild, New York, Sept. 14. Running time, 60 minutes.

If this picture were not intended as propaganda when at first conceived there must be no doubt that its ballyhooing possibilities for the Soviet were distinctly obvious at the film's completion. Thus a substitute title has been provided for the picture, "The Man With the Camera." If anything, the "Living Russia" name is the more appropriate.

Producers' explanation for the

making of the picture is that this filmfoto without titles or actors is intended as an experiment in projecting visual phenomena purely by means of the camera, thereby creating an international and absolute cinema language, completely divorced from the language of the theatre, and literature.

It's a bum alibi, however. For the picture is nothing but a tedious and long-drawn-out series of futuristic news shots taken somewhere in Russia. And until the cameraman begins to get smart after the first half of the picture the shots are good and prove interesting because the brighter side of the Soviet is clearly shown. Many of the shots are repeated, and for the arty that is really interested in entertainment the picture should be cut and thrown in as a short of about two-plus reels.

The picture proves that Russians bathe, swim and even go in for athletics; that there are modern transportation conveyances in the Soviet and that an occasional unfortunate lingers in the bigger cities of Russia—and what may have been only an optical illusion because it flickered for a few seconds only, that both sexes can and do bathe side by side in the nude in dear old Russe. This shot even drew giggles from the artie goers.

KING OF THE HERD
(Silent)

Frank Mattison production, released by Aywon. Directed by Frank Mattison. Photography by Jade Fuqull. Featuring "White Star" (horse). Raymond McKee and Nola Luxford. Running time, 70 minutes. At Columbus one day, Sept. 12, as half double bill.

Well, well, at last a western which variates. Hero takes an awful trouncing from the villain and the eastern society dame is not a hard boiled sophisticated city gal, but loves the lowly man of the pampas.

"White Star," the nag, is the feature and the shots of him are the most interesting. Some very good horse shots here, but not much horse sense in making the picture. It is very choppy.

Titles are amusing in trying for western chatter, with all the he-men expressions used scores of times.

Just a cute little yarn of the cowboy who captures and tames the king of the herd of wild horses and uses him as a polo pony.

Raymond McKee an appealing cow hand, but appears meek, weak and unrobust for the lusty hero. The rest doesn't matter.

These exhibs in Texas who are squawking for the red meat westerns can go for this in a big way.

German Pics

Berlin, Sept. 4.

FOOL OF LOVE

"The Fool of His Love" (Terra United Artists), premiere, Mozart Saal: Olga Tschechowa, Russian actress, who did so nicely in the lead of "Moulin Rouge," takes her first at direction. She has done a very workman-like job. There are moments of delicacy which suggest the feminine touch. If she develops in this field, there should be a distinct place for her work.

The scenario is from the comedy "Poliche," by Henri Bataille. Like most modern French dramas, it is conventional and old fashioned—the French theatre has been dead for 20 years.

Old, old fable about the man who loves but is never taken seriously. When he finally does win the girl through a trick, it is only to lose her shortly afterwards to the sportsman whom she really loves.

Trite as it is, the leading role is a fat one, and the Russian actor Michael Checkoff makes the most of it. He is a player of very exceptional qualities. When learning simplicity and subtlety are the first demands of the screen, he may develop into an international star.

THE LAST FORT

"The Last Fort" (Nationalfilm), premiere, Titania Palast. Four excellent character actors, Heinrich George, Alexander Granach, Fritz Odema and the lately deceased Albert Steinruck, make this film worth looking at. Otherwise, it is way below standard as regards scenario.

Concerns four adventurers fighting against the French in Africa. The Fench major is captured and his daughter arrives to try to free him. All four are interested in the girl, but the lieutenant really falls in love with her, and, freeing her father, goes off with her. But when his comrades are attacked he returns to fight with them, and the girl finds him again, badly wounded in a hospital.

The role of the girl is flat enough, but Maria Paudler makes it even less palatable by her superficial playing. Kurt Behrendt has done much better work than this, and he must regret his name used as director.

"Sinful and Sweet" (Hom Film), premiere, Titania Palast. Anni Ondra is a real little trooper who knows how to be comic without clowning. Also, clothed or unclothed, she measures up to international standards.

Here she plays a Parisian artists' model who applies to a rich American painter looking for a subject. She has already met him and even been brought to his house by his own automobile.

He becomes interested in her, but, going to call on her, finds the baby of a neighbor in her bed. Much depressed by what he believes to be continental immorality, and gives her the American high hat.

That evening he finds her at a ball where she has had a trifle too much champagne and, when he accuses her of loose living, she considers committing suicide.

An old professor, sorry for her, takes her home with him, and she drinks, without knowing what it is, a bottle of his newly discovered youth-bringing serum.

The American has seen the girl disappear and, getting the baby, brings it to the apartment of the professor. But the girl explains that it is not her child.

The professor finds the baby instead of the girl and believes that his serum has been a tremendous success.

The direction of Karl Lamac is well above the German average, and a new French leading man, Andre Roanne, is a double for Jimmy Walker.

Miss Ondra is a possibility for the States.

DICE OF FATE
(British Made)

"The Dice of Fate" (British Instructional), premiere, Universum. In Germany everything connected with India is swallowed whole. They like to play with the idea of Indian philosophy and make themselves believe that they are in sympathy with them, although, of course, this is nonsense. So this rather silly story will do fairly well on account of its atmosphere.

It has a fairy-tale-like quality and concerns two kings, a very good and a very bad one, rivals for the hand of a princess. The naughty king does everything that isn't in Hoyle to win the girl away. His final gag is to win his kingdom with loaded dice.

All the roles are taken by real Indians and very good work is turned in by Himansu Rai as the menace. Seeta Devi as the princess is good to gaze upon.

Audiences who like artistic hokum should be a pushover for this.

BATTLE FOR PARIS
(Russian Made)

premiere Capitol. Not much of a story to this Russian feature, but, for all that, a masterly film.

During the siege of Paris by the Germans in 1830 a little shopgirl meets a soldier in a dance hall. They are planning to marry after the victory which they are expecting daily.

Hopes are dashed by the capitulation of the authorities. Many of the citizens of Paris are not in agreement with this paper defeat, and, forming themselves in communes, attack the civic troops.

The little girl and the soldier are on opposite sides. After weeks of bloody guerilla warfare the communes are at last stamped out. But the last scene of the film is a dying hand writing the words in blood: "Vive la Commune!"—a portent of the coming French Revolution.

Leading roles are well enough played, but it is the extraordinary types in every minor role that give the film its individuality. The two young directors, Kosinziw and Trauberg, prove that they can deliver almost as brilliant work as Eisenstein and Pydowkin. It seems that the Russian actors are so colorful and virile that it is almost impossible to make a bad film with them.

Pie for the sure seaters.

THREE SUCCEED

"Three Succeed" (Engels Film) Premiere Marmorhaus. One of those German comedies that hardly annoys a Teutonic audience at all. They are used to them as every-day diet.

But heaven help the exhibitor who tried to show one in New York! They cost 30 cents and look as though they cost even less.

This one has as its leading figure a young German who leaves a good job in a factory to go to America. There has been trouble made by communistic agitators where he has been employed and, as he is the only one leaving, is suspected and followed by a detective.

On the train he meets a young girl who has gotten on the wrong train. He gives up his American plans and returns to Berlin to ask for her hand. Back in the factory, the boy is responsible for the discovery of a band of crooks who are stealing important documents.

Hans Brausewetter, eternal German juvenile, plays the lead with a good deal of lightness and humor and Renate Muller proves herself a comer.

MEN

"Men Without a Profession" (Deutsches Lichtspielsyndikat), Premiere Ufa Palast am Zoo.

Harry Piel was the first German stunt man and he has stuck tenaciously to his position. Realizing that the old "Perils of Pauline" tripe no longer draws even in the shooting galleries, he removed the nonsensical black makeup from his eyes and engaged himself a scenario writer.

Robert Liebmann is responsible for the present conventional film, but it holds some highlights of comedy. The original idea, that something called the white slave trade really exists, is the motivation. Harry plays the detective who returns from South America disguised as a well-known trader whom he has arrested. He falls for a young girl who is in the net of the gang.

At this rate, Harry should be able to keep going for several years to come, although none of his films are ever likely to get a showing in the States.

SMUGGLER'S BRIDE

"The Smuggler Bride of Mallorca" (Ufa), premiere Ufa Palast am Zoo.

Jenny Jugo has a good following here and should not lose any on account of this film. Its scenario is not brilliantly original, but suffices to present her in her best light. She is always engaging to look upon and their is no deep emotion required.

In a small Spanish town the gay Rosita has two suitors, Pedro and Andrea, fishers by trade. She is also desired by Tolomeo, rich man of the village.

The latter persuades Andrea to take part in a smuggling expedition and Rosita and Pedro go with him. At an inn where the booty is to be delivered Tolomeo has Rosita kidnapped. Trying to rescue her, Andrea is shot but Pedro breaks through the crowd and does it. As Tolomeo is going to shoot him he is arrested by the police.

Hans Behrendt, director, gets all that can be gotten out of this thin theme, making use of the beauty of the Spanish landscape and the local color to its full.

Enrico Benfer and Clifford MacLaglen fill in nicely as the suitors.

"Adieu Mascotte" (Ufa), premiere Universum.

Lilian Harvey is a great favorite here and well liked in London. Deservedly so, for she has a good deal of fragile charm and has learned her comedy oats. One should be careful of photographing her too much in direct profile.

The picture, directed by Wilhelm Thiele, is about up to her average. It concerns Mascotte, usual Parisian artist model, who to aid a sick friend auctions herself off at a ball. She is bought by Jean, a novelist, merely to annoy his wife, Josette, who is flirting outrageously with Gaston, young man of the world.

When Mascotte comes to him next day to keep her promise, he is about to dismiss her but finding a farewell letter of his wife, tells her to remain. She then offers her services to him to go around with him and make everybody believe that they are having an affair. Thus getting the wife jealous.

The scheme succeeds, but meantime, Mascotte and Jean have fallen in love with each other.

Rest of a good cast included Ego Sym, who suggests Conway Tearle; Harry Halm, nice light comedian, and Marietta Millner.

Trask.

Married in Hollywood
(ALL DIALOG, With Songs)

William Fox production and release. Directed by Marcel Silver. J. Harold Murray and Norma Terris featured. Dialog and lyrics by Harlan Thompson. Mr. Thompson's story, adapted from original by Leopold Jacobson and Bruno Hardt-Warden. Music by Oscar Straus. Additional music by Dave Stamper and Arthur Kay. Numbers staged by Edward Royce. At Roxy, New York, week Sept. 21. Running time 110 minutes.

Prince Nicholai	J. Harold Murray
Mitzi Hofman / Mary Lou Hopkins	Norma Terris
Joe Glinter	Walter Catlett
Annushka	Irene Palasty
King Alexander	Lennox Pawle
Mahai	Tom Patricola
Queen Louise	Evelyn Hall
Stage Prince	John Garrick
Adjutant Octavian	Douglas Gilmore
Charlotte	Gloria Grey
Captain Jacobi	Jack Stambaugh
Herr von Herzen	Bert Sprotte
Mrs. von Herzen	Lelia Karnelly
Herr Director	Herman Bing
Namari	Paul Ralli

Either originally intended as a $2 special and fell along the wayside, or started as a first-rate program feature and emerged a near-smash. In any event, they must have thought it over before letting "Married in Hollywood" slip out as a programer. Seemingly, they guessed right, for though it has many spec requisites, this Fox musical talker will look better in the deluxes, where it can't help doing business.

At the Roxy the picture is running 10 minutes less than two hours, fair hint of the original intention. Program pictures aren't made that long ordinarily. While, unles extraordinary, they don't run that long in the turnovers.

"Married in Hollywood" happens to be a honey, no matter if its story is cut from the prince-pauper pattern. As it stands at the Roxy the 110 minutes include few that are not worth while. Cutting may be necessary, of course, for other spots, but when they cut, it's a cinch they won't touch the musical numbers.

The finish in color, bringing the lovers together on a studio set, good enough to make the preceding hour or so worth sitting through.

Two talented, comely and camera-wise leads borrowed from the musical stage, mean a lot to the picture. Very much in the first hour, when something else is needed to kick the w. k. yarn along. Norma Terris and J. Harold Murray are the leads.

"Married in Hollywood" means the sweethearts are reunited and married there, after the prince had fallen in love with the stage girl in Vienna.

Lots to this story. Sidetrack details that don't need recounting. They all fit in and the result is a good production.

Stage numbers, set in the Viennese theatre where Mary Lou is singing, and where the prince sits in a box, are frequent. A ship's concert when Mary Lou returns to America. Her performance on the boat gets her the picture job and Joe Glinter (Walter Catlett) moves her from the third class to the best cabin. Then the final music, plus color, in the studio finish.

Due to the success of her last production, Mary Lou Hopkins, now known to the fans as Mitzi Hofman with the dialect, is permitted to write her own story for the next one. Mary's idea of a yarn is her own sorrowful romance with Nicky. And her idea of a perfect finish is to stab the prince in the back as he walks down the aisle with the princess, who she imagines trimmed her. Catlett wants a happier ending, and when he says, "Don't you think so, boys?" the boys all answer in chorus, "Yes."

Tom Patricola plays Nicky's flunkey without dancing. He scores as a simple comic. High-grade performances all the way and the cast is big.

Miss Terris' voice never slurs. It must be a perfect talker singing voice, else the recording was unusually proficient. She even looks better in this picture than on the stage. Murray swings right in line as a leading man and vocalist.

Score rates extra mention. Melodies are of the low, swaying sort, always remindful of Vienna.

Outstanding program picture.
Bige.

PARIS BOUND

(ALL DIALOG)

Pathe production and release. Starring Ann Harding. Produced by Arthur Hopkins and directed by Edward H. Griffith. Adapted from Phillip Barry's stage play by Horace Jackson with dialog co-directed by Frank Reicher. Music score by Josiah Zuro. At Paramount, New York, week Sept. 20. Running time, 73 minutes.

Mary Hutton	Ann Harding
Jim Hutton	Frederic March
James Hutton, Sr.	George Irving
Richard Parrish	Leslie Fenton
Peter	Hallam Cooley
Nora Cope	Juliette Crosby
Helen White	Charlotte Walker
Noel Farley	Carmelita Geraghty
Fanny Shipman	Ilka Chase

Transcribing Phillip Barry's medium weight stage play to the screen left a lot of loopholes to be plugged, and seemingly, some extraneous shooting that retards most of its naturally slow action anyway. Yet Pathe has a moderate money maker in this talker, mostly because the stage title will get some recognition and again because of that sterling legit actress, Ann Harding.

Miss Harding is reckoned with as something of a big find out Hollywood way. Unfortunately "Paris Bound" does not do full justice and is only a suggestion of Miss Harding's future possibilities in pictures.

No indication anyone in particular erred in picturizing the play. Simply a case where necessary appendages and maintenance of continuity slows up the action throughout the film, running into several particularly tedious scenes. Musical score is just a thin thread coursing through. With the exception of a ballet symphony, splendidly projected by double exposure, it is unimportant.

Narrative is nonetheless diverting, despite its slow moving tempo that taxes one's patience at times. In its theme essence the picture is a faithful reproduction of the play where a marital sermon is preached, harping on the infidelity clause and upholding minor promiscuities as something apart, independent and not necessarily in opposition to real existing love between the man and woman.

Some of the affectionate and vivid embraces executed by Miss Harding and Frederic March, that estimable young lead, seemed a little too much overdone.

Creditable mention also goes to Leslie Fenton, who gives a consistent performance as the composer on the nethermost angle in the usual triangle.

Rest of the cast suitable to roles.

CARELESS AGE

(ALL DIALOG)

First National production and release. Directed by John G. Wray. No star credited; Douglas Fairbanks, Jr., and Loretta Young, featured leads. Adapted from John Van Denten's play, "Diversion," by Harrison Macklyn. W. E. ..Vitaphone recording. Photography by Ben Reynolds; special camera work credited to Alvin Knetchel. Running time, 65 minutes. At Strand, New York, week Sept. 20.

Wyn	Douglas Fairbanks, Jr.
Muriel	Loretta Young
Ray	Carmel Myers
Sir John	Holmes Herbert
Owen	Kenneth Thomson
Le Grande	George Baxter
Lord Durhugh	Wilfred Noy
Mabs	Doris Lloyd
Bunty	Ilka Chase
Tommy	Raymond Lawrence

Smooth, workmanlike bit of direction and producing, excellent in its acting and with some striking spectacular sequences. Good average entertainment of a program grade, and rating a credit mark to the all-around cast, as suave and even a group of players as has appeared anywhere in an all-talker. A graceful but varied program release, deserving artistically but commercially only so-so.

So good is the direction and production it lifts a weak story to strength far beyond its deserts. There are sequences where the persuasive acting and the splendid settings and atmosphere are much more interesting that the intrinsic hold of the story itself. Adequate playing was vital here, for the story is mild.

The narrative of a sappy young English boy for a musical comedy actress isn't particularly hot stuff, except as the audience can be intrigued into so lively a state of sympathy with the boy himself as to become absorbed in his fate. Here's where young Fairbanks enters to turn the trick. His is a truly good performance, of simple artlessness that captivates. Matching him in suavity and ease is Holmes Herbert in a role made notable by its intelligent restraint.

It's one of those father and son stories of no dramatic force whatever and probably limited in fan appeal, by no means a "Sorel and Son" but still a neat handling of the theme. Picture has excellent incidentals. Pleasant theme song in "Melody Divine" nicely woven into the action and another number, "Carless Age," introduced in a heavy bit of spectacular staging, representing the heroine-prima donna leading a stage number and produced on the Ziegfeld scale.

It's a poor part for Carmel Myers, the gold digging prima having no sympathetic appeal to the feminine contingent. The woman interest generally is weak, for the hero is by no means a heroic figure in his stumbling romance. That angle rather limits the picture to the adults, arguing not so well for the box office.

Atmosphere of a cultured English household is admirably reproduced. Detail of the family relations are charmingly pictured and production is full of polite niceties that ingratiate. But all this grace doesn't quite compensate for the absence of dramatic grip in story.

Picture ought to do well in England, for the dialog is carried on in the studied English manner and the whole thing has the repressed British atmosphere. *Rush.*

TONIGHT AT 12

(ALL DIALOG)

Universal production and release. Produced and directed by Harry Pollard from stage play of same name by Owen Davis. Recorded on Western Electric. Continuity by Matt Taylor. Photographer, Jerome Ash. At Colony, New York, week Sept. 21. Running time, 78 minutes.

Jane Eldridge	Madge Bellamy
Tony Keith	George Lewis
Jack Keith (father)	Robert Ellis
Alice Keith (mother)	Madeline Seymour
Nan Stoddard	Margaret Livingston
Tom Stoddard	Dan Douglas
Barbara Warren	Vera Reynolds
Bill Warren	Hallam Cooley
Dora Eldridge (mother)	Josephine Brown
Prof. Eldridge	Norman Trevor
Ellen	Mary Doran

Houdini Owen Davis wrote this one. Every time the yarn shut up it opened again. Hide and seek story. Mr. Davis has written so many plays he's a story magician who loads his character aides along with him so whenever he gets stuck in a situation he eenie-meeny-moes around to tag the answer on one of them. Maybe it's this reason the play didn't last so long on Broadway last season. Herman Shumlin produced it. It opened in November and closed the first week in January. And even if the picture does weary a bit here and there it's pretty good film entertainment and fairly well done.

Actors do swell in tough situations. Lotta pepper suspense; it has cynical humor and some careless comedy and a fair pathos. Exploitation name possibilities are many and the title is worth some mystery thinking. So any house can afford to play the film.

The story is about a lively darling and the play proves that anyone might have a heart.

Being stuck on the only child of a snooty family the gal takes on a job as maid with a neighbor. The boy friend who liked the kid when he was in college, however, now reverts to type and goes for his childhood sweetheart, prof's daughter and lady to the maid.

But the boy's papa hurdles friendship, fatherhood and everything so's he can play around. In one week he already has necked the mother of his son's future mother-in-law who it seems used to be his boyhood sweetie anyway so she wasn't hard to get, and also the newly taken bride of another dear friend. Papa was set for a third killing when his act was crabbed by mama.

The boy's old man had prepared a note for the newest bride to meet him at twelve. Wifie saw the job done. Like a sweet pet she invited the three girl friends of papa to dinner—with their hubbies.

The old gal swiped right into the three gals and everybody gets mad; the boy takes the slap; his rich sweetie reneges, and he busts his own heart by going back to the lively gal.

But everything winds hunky dory.

THE ROYAL SCANDAL

("Die Hose")

(GERMAN MADE)

(Silent)

Produced by Phoebus-Film A. G. Berlin and released here through Moviegraph. Directed by Hans Behrendt from adaptation of Carl Sternheim's comedy. In cast: Werner Krauss and Jenny Jugo. At 55th St. Playhouse week Sept. 21. Running time, 78 minutes.

"The Royal Scandal," Berlin tidbit, has the artiest kind of a ballyhoo for the sure seaters. It is quite original, even though claimed to be Rabelaisianized, since the theme is motivated by a pretty housewife who keeps dropping her panties in public places.

After the heavy cotton teddies or whatnots have been floored a couple of times in the home over which Werner Krauss presides as a contented beer imbibing, bowling, gullible German hubby, the story gets under way in front of a church. It is there that the downward undies catch the eye of a prince, his clown and a barber's assistant.

Thereafter something happens to the lady, or her contact apparel, because the droppings cease. Probably director at last saw a theme or heard about "'Tween Kelly." Rather long in unwinding, but more endurable than most of the arty importations because of nearly sustained interest. And the audience's curiosity is aroused but never satisfied by this American edition.

To bring things to the home set the husband is allowed to rent two rooms. Naturally they are grabbed by the student barber and clown. The wife flops for the prince's jester, and thus tastes good grade liquors and enjoys a night with royalty.
Waly.

SPEEDWAY

(SILENT)

(Disc Orchestration)

M-G-M production and release. Directed by Harry Beaumont from Byron Morgan's story. William Haines starred. In cast Anita Page, Karl Dane, Ernest Torrence, John Miljan. At Capitol week Sept. 21. Running time, about 82 minutes.

William Haines does his small alecky stuff in the regular way, this time largely assisted by the title writer, who packs his laughs in one big parcel. "Speedway" is every bit that, since the fans are whirled around the Indianapolis track until they leave the theatre with eye strain. But they like it, and prints will go back in the can after good program duty.

The picture is about 80% race track. Some obviously stock shots of auto contests where cars take the bumps help the acceleration in a bona fide way, since Haines or the heavy, Miljan, are frequently cut in at wheels. Fifteen or 20 minutes of the track running time could be sheared without accomplishing much more than making the story compact.

Besides the 500-mile grind, all of that in the camera footage, there is a restaurant scene where the title writer probably registers the most consistent wave of hearty laughs ever clocked in any one sequence of a comedy. It's about the food and Haines' efforts to pick up the girl he inevitably marries. The latter is Anita Page, with much girlie appeal.

Miss Page happens to be the daughter of an airplane man, and Bill gets a ride in the ether before business gets down to the track. The air stuff looks good until the prop plane loses a wing.

Ernest Torrence as an old-timer out to win his last race is counting on Bill doing the driving. But Renny, played by John Miljan, gets Bill to tune his own motor before revealing the double cross.

After that it's just the race, with Bill learning his lesson and beating Renny but letting the old man take the car across the line. *Waly.*

ILLUSION

(ALL DIALOG With Songs)

Paramount production and release. Directed by Lothar Mendes. Featuring Buddy Rogers and Nancy Carroll. From story by Arthur Train. Adapted by E. Lloyd Sheldon. At Paramount, New York, week Sept. 27. Running time, 80 minutes.

Carlee Thorpe......Charles (Buddy) Rogers
Claire Jernigan..............Nancy Carroll
Hilda Schmittlap..............June Collyer
Zelda Paxton..................Kay Francis
Eric Schmittlap...............Regis Toomey
Jacob Schmittlap..........Knute Erickson
Queen of Dalmatia...Maude Turner Gordon
Mother Fay..................Emelie Melville
William Austin, Frances Raymond, Katherine Wallace, John E. Nash, Eddie Kane, Michael Visaroff, Paul Lukas, Richard Cramer, Bessie Lyle, Col. G. L. McDonnel and Lillian Roth.

With one box-office nifty already to its credit in "Close Harmony," the Buddy Rogers-Nancy Carroll polite necking combination is presented to enough advantage in "Illusion" to sail nicely along on the tide. Only drawback is that the team is a notably flap and jelly fav, while this picture in spots attempts some class dialog.

Rogers and Carroll do a magic act in a circus, and finally get a chance to crash big-time vaude. But Rogers has been playing around in society, working his way up by entertaining with parlor tricks and making plenty of dough in bridge games. He falls for Hilda Schmittlap, whose old man has made his pile and is doing a social climb for the family.

Miss Carroll is broken hearted when Rogers refuses to take the vaude contract, and splits with him to team up with another magician named Magus, conveniently altered in reproduction to sound like "Maggot." After a fling at the society racket Rogers decides to blow back to Nancy. He and the Schmittlap girl have talked it over and decided they couldn't hit it up together.

Nancy has become morose and changes harmless carbide bullets to real ones in the bit where Magus has gents from the audience shoot at her with rifles. Buddy comes to the theatre just before the shots are fired and is handy to pick the girl up when one out of the five guys shooting happens to hit her in the shoulder. A makeup scene in the hospital ends it.

Featured pair make a very likeable team, with youth, appearance and a talent for naturalness. Supporting characters are good. Regis Toomey, who played the laughing drunk in "Alibi" and made it a specialty, is again seen through the bottom of a glass as the Schmittlap girl's no-good brother who tries to make Nancy. Emelie Melville as a retired trouper has a short bit, but makes it a standout. The rather tough part of Hilda Schmittlap—one of those "like-her-or-not" characters—is handled capably by June Collyer.

Inevitable song, dance and music in a cabaret set and also a little theatre in the Schmittlap castle. Both Rogers and Miss Carroll have song spots.

There's a gag burlesque on Queen Marie's visit to America, with the Queen of Dalmatia visiting the Schmittlaps to arrange a little loan for her country. Lots of comedy, and easily recognized. "Variety" also used, this time with a No. 3 head on what a good act Rogers and Carroll have. That makes two burlesques.

Plenty of pitfalls in this story waiting for Mendes, but he skipped the gutter gracefully. A cleanly handled job. *Bang.*

THREE LIVE GHOSTS

(ALL DIALOG)

Max Marcin production and United Artists release. Directed by Thornton Freeland and based on the stage play of the same title. Robert H. Planck, cameraman. In cast: Robert Montgomery, Claude Allister, Charles McNaughton, Beryl Mercer, Joan Bennett, Tenen Holtz. At the Rivoli Sept. 28. Running time, 81 minutes.

While the talker screen version of the play, "Three Live Ghosts," is a good program comedy, well acted and far above the average in the twists of its theme, the interest threads are slightly frayed by a dragginess apparent almost during its entire projection.

Long conversations, few close-ups and an adherence to three or four interior sets, obviously reminding of the original show, may be accountable for retarding the speed and sparkle of the picture just enough to keep it from rating par excellence.

The Marcin effort is reminiscent of Dickens in more respects than that author's penchant for detail. The characteriztions and sets have the musty, cockneyed atmosphere of London's Cheapside. And Beryl Mercer, excellent as the grog addicted ma of the soldier boy reported "casuality" by the government, is a little too literal at times in the slowness of her movements.

The theme itself comes to the rescue of over-deliberations sanctioned by the director. Together with the dialog, which contains many laugh-provoking lines, situations are sufficiently numerous and original to maintain suspense.

As Jimmy, the son, Charles McNaughton does an efficient job with creditable work also for Claude Allister and Robert Montgomery as "Spoofy" and "Foster the American," respectively.

The government declaration they are officially dead, in compliance with the war department's report, is the biggest of complications, the unraveling of which keys up audience expectancy. Thereafter the action centers in the home of Jimmy's mother. Her desire to secure a reward by turning over Foster to the American authorities and the difficulties which she encounters, first through the objections of her own boy and then by the loss of an address, run through the picture story as in the play.

"Spoofy" brings matters to the climax when he kidnaps an infant after robbing the home of its parents. Scotland Yard's investigation and Ma's loquacity get them all in the hoosegow. Sudden recovery from shellshock realizes one of the biggest mirth moments. Then "Spoofy" recalls his identity and it happens to be the father of the babe he appropriated.

Joan Bennett's role is the minor one of the girl artist friend who supports the American member of the trio. Tannen Holtz has a bit for a few moments as the proprietor of a china store.

At the Rivoli two minutes' worth of a war flash back is being magnified and projected on the wide screen, making an effective bit of showmanship. *Waly.*

HARD TO GET

(100% DIALOG)

First National production and release. Directed by William Beaudine from a theme based on the Edna Ferber story, "Classified." Recording on Western Electric disc. At the Strand, beginning Sept. 27. Running time, 80 minutes.

Bobby Martin..................Dorothy Mackaill
Pa Martin....................Jimmie Finlayson
Ma Martin......................Louise Fazenda
Marty Martin......................Jack Oakie
Dexter Courtland................Edmund Burns
Mrs. Courtland.................Clarissa Selwynne
Jerry Dillon....................Charles Delaney

"Hard To Get" is one of those rare all round comedies so well knit and naturally performed as to hold the interest of any type of audience for every inch of running time.

The injection of the theme song is the only forced part of the production. It is held out until the picture is well underway and then swung in by a member of a typical pick-up orchestra in a cheap night club atmosphere. "Hard To Get" would have been just as modern had the producer stepped out of the theme song rut.

Dialog is excellent and so well handled by the cast as to get the most out of its laugh punctuations.

Mirth centers around Jack Oakie. As Marty, the son in the Martin brood, Oakie's facial expressions contribute largely in getting his gibes at Bobby, the high brow sister in the 10th avenue family, played by Dorothy Mackaill, across with vim.

Louise Fazenda and Jimmie Finlayson play little more than bit parts, as Pa and Ma Martin. Their repeated exits in all-dressed-up-for-Sunday attire when Dexter Courtland, Fift' Avenuite, (Edmund Burns) appears, have a modicum of laughs. Funniest is Finlayson's juggling with a four-inch collar.

Charles Delaney, as the outspoken Jerry Dillon, gives an amusing performance.

Intro of characters aids considerably in smoothness of continuity and reflects excellent directorial judgment on William Beaudine's part.

As the manikin with polloi ideals, Miss Mackaill essays her role in a manner which brings her closer to the audience with each sequence. Picking up Jerry driving a big car on the "avenoo," Bobby gets her first setback. Courtland is also neatly introduced in a barber shop scene, where he poses as her hubby to relieve her of the advances of an elderly Lothario.

Human interest angle well timed with Courtland pitted against Jerry for honors. Though the wind-up is conventional, directorial twists and cast co-operation take off the usual onus.

Residential Fifth avenue is a little antiquated for New York fans but Beaudine's job is good enough to warrant a trip East and refreshment of street recollections before he starts his next one about the Manhattan highway. *Waly.*

SKIN DEEP

(ALL DIALOG)

Warner Bros. production and release. Based on Mark Edmund Jones' magazine story "Lucky Damage;" scenarized by Gordon Rigby and directed by Ray Enright. W. E. Vita recording. At Colony, New York, Sept. 28. Running time, 64 minutes.

Joe Daley.......................Monte Blue
Son of Dist. Atty..............Davey Lee
Sadie Rogers..................Betty Compson
Elsa Langdon......................Alice Day
Blackie Culver.................John Davidson
Dist. Atty. Carlson..........John Bowers
Dippy.........................Georgie Stone
Dr. Bruce Langdon........Tully Marshall
Tim.............................Robert Perry

Hackneyed, time worn and weary underworld opus to be taken with a grain of salt, even in neighborhoods. Neither story nor direction is convincing.

Following so many other good gangster yarns, this one just too bad. Just two femme characters in "Skin Deep," twisted around so that what flimsy thread of love interest exists is not taken seriously.

Considerable negligence evident in lining up an intrinsically fine cast and then throwing it away. Betty Compson is given a joke book role to play, while Monte Blue, heading the cast, is just a plain, dumb mistake as the regenerated gangster carrying a Lon Chaney makeup for three quarters of the picture. Davey Lee, the Jolson kid, is another pulled into the mess for just a flash and minus any background; doubtless to bolster any possible b. o. appeal.

Slip shod continuity and disgressing direction has the action dragging most of the way, until a made-to-order shooting affair puts an end to its misery.

Story about Joe Daley, gangland hombre, who married Sadie the silky, sinful cabaret singer, out to take him, and how! Gold digging gal, while picking Joe for the dough, still waxes hot and bothered about Blackie Culver, rival ping ponger. Daley, suddenly deciding to go straight, throws a scare into Sadie who sees her hold loosening. She goes to Culver and they frame the unwitted Daley for a stretch across the pond. For safety's sake the moll keeps a tearful face and visits the prison regularly. Just before the gangster's time is up he's inveigled to escape, led to believe that the district attorney not only framed him but was after his wife.

He makes a clean getaway, and after copping a motorcycle meets with an accident. Picked up by a plastic surgeon's daughter, Daley is taken to their home, where the doc plants a new mug on him and tells him to go sin no more. Meanwhile there develops a friendship between Daley and the doc's daughter. Out for revenge, Daley averts murdering the district attorney only after he finds out the faithlessness of his moll. Finding his wife and Culver together, he pulls the rod, when the lights go out and Sadie is bumped off in the melee. Completely regenerated by this time the repentant gangster seeks out the doc's daughter for a wistful fadeout.

Alice Day looks pretty as the simple maid, but not much else. John Davidson makes Culver the kind of tough mug found only in story books and these pictures. Georgie Stone has about two seconds and probably calls it a couple of weeks' work.

"Skin Deep" is very much so, and just a flim-flam.

AFGHANISTAN

(RUSSIAN MADE)

(Silent)

Picture made by Sovkino of Moskow (Soviet Russia government) and released by Amkino (American agent). Directed by Vladmir Yerofeyev, in charge of Russian expedition into Asia. American titles by Norman Taurogder. Photographs by V. H. Belyayev. At the Cameo, New York, art theatre, Sept. 28. Runnng time 65 minutes.

Another strictly travel picture, and only a fair one at that, is masquerading as a screen feature entertainment. It isn't. More than an hour of straightway silent scenery and bizarre foreign people is tiresome.

Really the picture is a capital two-reeler ruined by staying too long. In two reels this would be a good program item. Two reels is about the meat of it and the rest is padding.

Titles emphasize that Afghanistan, in the upper right hand corner of India, is one of the places of the world locked away from the Western eye and still living back in the distant ages. The enlightened new ruler, Amanullah, opened the country somewhat to the rest of the world and the Sovkino expedition went in. Amanullah was later deposed by native reactionists who objected to his reforms and the revolution was in the American newspaper spotlight about five months ago. The picture should have been sprung then. Now it's cold.

It has some remarkably fine photographic shots at Himalayas, staggering vistas of overpowering mountains; dizzy mountain pass roads, curious ways of transportation such as a raft supported by inflated animal skins. Peasants at work with ancient implements are interesting. One scene shows methods of threshing grain by having oxen trample it. Picturesque native types and customs invite attention, but there are long stretches of dull matter, scarcely up to the grade of magazine fillers, such as long sequences of a trolley car in some remote village.

Only excuse for picture in this form is that it isn't quite as dull as a third-rate foreign drama and thus is endurable for the sure-seat mob. Impossible outside of that narrow field. Titles are well done, but who cares about the political situation in Afghanistan? *Rush.*

AMERICAN PRISONER

(BRITISH MADE)

(ALL DIALOG)

London, Sept. 20.

Produced at Elstroe by British International. Directed by Thomas Bentley from the novel by Eden Phillpotts. Scenario and dialog by Eliot Stannard. Camer: Rene Guissatt. RCA recording. Previewed at Regal, Marble Arch, Sept. 18. Running time, 70 minutes.

Lieut. Stark .... Carl Brisson
Grace Malherb .... Madeleine Carroll
Squire Malherb .... Bremley Davenport
Peter Norcot .... Cecil Harry

Save for direction, story, dialog, acting, and being a period play, this is a good one.

Recording is exceptionally clear, only the talk is not worth recording. Photography is good on the whole, and the locations and most of the sets are admirable. Crowd scenes, both with troops and with a mixed bunch of prisoners and villagers, are really finely handled.

But the individual acting, except that of Nancy Price as an old hag who helps the prisoners to escape, is poor, mainly on account of what looks on the screen like the inability of the players to believe in their roles. This comes out particularly in dialog. They all seem in the majority of sequences to be very conscious of the sloppy ineptitude of the lines, the artificiality of which is reflected in the stiffness and lack of naturalness the words impose upon the artists.

Madeleine Carroll is good to look at and could obviously do a lot better with good material. She struggles to make her part live, but gets weighed down with it till she just mugs.

Cecil Barry and Bromley Davenport, both experienced troupers, sometimes look and sound as if they will burst out crying or laugh themselves off at the unreality of what they have to say. Nancy Price, with a toothless makeup and some fat moments, breaks through the rut of mediocrity and puts over a good performance, with a witch's laugh that is nerve-racking.

The film's a pity many ways. Looks like a fair amount of money had been spent on it, and all the elements of a good melo are there. But the treatment is so weak and inane it dies, and it's tough enough to put over costume dialog stuff even if it's right.

Carl Brisson has one song, "Will You Remember?" which might have been a hit, but with the picture being costume he is accompanied only on a spinet, which is not heard through his voice and so the song loses out by sounding as if it's sung unaccompanied. And it is not strong enough to stand that.

Story is 100% hoke. Villian loves girl. Her father is in his debt. Much against his will pa has to try to force her to marry the bad man. She has fallen for hero, the American prisoner who has been captured running supplies to the French. Prisoner escapes but is shot and girl nurses him. Back in prison, he escapes again, same time girl flees from the squirarchical homestead rather than marry villian.

Hero is captured while with girl, and at that identical moment news comes the war is over. Hero, free, fights villian with swords, and latter, disarmed, won't fight on and creeps out of picture. Close-up and fade.

It's all a question of treatment. But when they started treating this one they must have thought they were in a Prohibition country. *Frat.*

WAGON MASTER

(60% DIALOG)

Universal production and release. Ken Maynard starred. Directed by Harry J. Brown from story by Marian Jackson. Titles and dialog by Leslie Maselli. Featuring Edith Roberts and Tony Santschi. At Loew's New York, one day, Sept. 19. Running time, 70 minutes.

A pioneer in the field of dialog and sound effects for small time westerns. There has been talk of dialog slowing up action and that especially would it be detrimental to ~~the usually packed full of motion~~ westerns. This small time flicker, to the contrary, has benefited amazingly by the dialog and the effects. Due to that it's high above the usual cow land picture.

Unlike Fox's "In Old Arizona" where, due to the dialog, barely any of the outdoor shots were mob shots, here they consist solely of the boys whooping it up. This is Ken Maynard's first talking role. With a distinct voice and with the intonation one expects from the kind hearted but nevertheless he-man of the wide open, he takes full advantage of the departure. Besides speaking he instrumentalizes on the guitar and violin. Only default is when the rough, sloppy men surrounding him join in the chorus with voices like a well trained choir, instead of the husky cracked tones expected.

Flicker is just packed full of action and interest and plenty of chuckles. A fight scene in an old time beer saloon seemed an excerpt from a burlesque blackout and had them rocking. This, put over without the dialog or effects, would practically be meaningless. It's ludicrous western hokum, such as the saloon gals applauding every time one guy's fist landed flush on the chin of the other, or the pianist **attempting to play tunes befitting the action, or the antics of the three henchmen to Maynard, who carry all the comedy and seem as though clipped from "Three Bad Men."**

Plot is the attempts of the two villains to keep Maynard, as the wagon master, from reaching his destination with the wagon train.

An interesting whip fight between Santschi, as the villain, and Maynard held all eyes with their dextrous manipulations of the whips. Wagon train racing across the desert and open plains provided plenty of red-blooded meller, personified by the shouts of the wagon drivers and the swift thuds of the hoofs of the racing nags.

All in all, an unusually fine species for this type, which, plus its modernization, should prove dessert for the lovers and followers of pictures that tell a story of the times when men were men and shot from the hip.

HIS LUCKY DAY

(30% DIALOG)

Universal production and release. Directed by Eddie Cline. Story by John B. Clymer and Gladys Lehman. Titles by Albert Demond. Photographed by Arthur Todd. Synchronization and score by Joseph Cherniavsky. Sounded by Western Electric. Starring Reginald Denny. The cast includes Otis Harlan, Cissy Fitzgerald, Eddie Phillips, LaRayne DuVal, Tom O'Brien and Harvey Clarke. At Arena, one day, Sept. 27. Running time, 59 minutes.

Reginald Denny's last floppo of the season for Universal. Swell for kiddies up to 15 years of age—especially girls, and for restless housewives. Story is as cock-eyed as ever bounced off a typewriter. But for high and dry grinds where customers still regard pie throwing and stepping into milk bowls as art, it's a wow.

Reproduction is weak in spots and diction is not quite clear in other spots. Synchronization and score, however, are clean and good.

Reggy may not draw any more checks from Universal although it is reported he has still two more filmfotos to make this new season for the Laemmle company. He still has a drawing power among the flapperinos of tender age who sink or swim in their own neighborhoods.

Here Denny is a thick witted real estate salesman in love with a pretty girl whose father has rented a house from Denny with an option to renew the lease some time in the hereafter. The old man, however, decides no, and sticks to no renewal of the lease unless Denny can rent the adjoining property.

In the customary accidental manner new tenant prospects arrive just before the bell. Denny, the hustling realtor idiot, hustles them into a lease contrary to all Fifth Avenue traditions in the suburbs. It is only natural then that the new neighbors of the old man should so expectedly turn out to be a gang of pearl collectors and safe movers. Follows hokum cafe scene and hokum ghost mystery—and all ends happy that begins sappy.

GROWTH OF SOIL

(NORWEGIAN MADE)

(Silent)

Norrone production, released by Film Guild Cinema. Directed by Gunner Sommerfelt. Edited and titled by Benjamin de Casseres. All-Scandinavian cast not named on program or screen, house management explaining data was lost in transmission from Norway. Story and screen adaptation from novel of same title by Knut Hamsun. At Film Guild Cinema, New York, week Sept. 28. Running time, 60 minutes.

Not much value to this one generally, but available for spots located in Scandinavian sections if properly exploited. Knut Hamsun is regarded as Norway's foremost author, one of his novels winning the Nobel prize some years ago. Film, it is claimed, was made under his supervision in the actual locales mentioned in his book.

Film is a series of episodes in the life of a hardy Norwegian who penetrates beyond the established settlements in his native land and conquers the soil through his pioneering spirit and indomitable will. He takes as a wife a comely but harelipped girl, and together they start to build a community. Copper is discovered on the pioneers' property, and the remote colony takes on the proportions of a boom town, with Isak, the first settlers, well on the way to financial independence.

With the coming of civilization to the wild country their follows murder, robbery and rapine. The harelipped wife, Inger, takes a prison rap for murdering her baby daughter, born with a hare-lip. Released from prison some years later she returns to the colony with a prison-born child but minus the facial blemish that has been the bane of her existence, and everything is lovely once more.

Story is unfolded in dull, disjointed style, Ben do Casseres' editing and titling being about the only things that saves it from being so much wasted film. Many sequences are irised in and out, and the casting, direction and photography is of little consequence. Hamsun's name, however, will sell this cheap film in the arty shots.

Romance of Hine Moa

(FOREIGN MADE)

(Silent)

Gustave Pauli production, released by Gaumont. Played by a cast of natives in the Lake Rotorua district of New Zealand, and supposedly based on an old Maori love story. At the 55th St. Playhouse, New York, Sept. 28. Running time, 55 minutes.

Another venture in exploitation of a little known country by means of a native legend enacted by native players. This film is said to have been officially endorsed by Rt. Hon. J. Gordon Coates, premier of New Zealand. Only commercial possibilities are in the art spots, as a strip scene a la good old U. S. A. eliminates its chance to become a generally released educational film. And the nude shots will do much to sell it in the other places.

The story is simple, and hinges on an idea that seems ludicrous to Americans. Tatanekai, son of a chieftain, sets out in search of more fertile fields for the old man's tribe. Bumping into the tribe of Umukarai, he falls in love with Um's daughter. But another guy named Tai also loves the daughter, and frames Tatanekai by blaming him for theft of some of the chief's sacred sweet potatoes. It turns out later that Tai stole the spuds himself, but in the meantime young Tatanekai is cast into a cave, where he must pass through fire, lava and boiling water before escaping.

That sweet potatoes gag seems pretty funny. Then, when it's figured how a columnist squawks when somebody steals a pun, it's not so ridiculous.

The gal, Hine Moa, is about to be married to another chiefain, but swims across a lake to the arms of her lover. She bares herself to the hips from then on, and provides a chance for some good lobby displays. Not bad looking at all. When her old man comes with his tribe to get her and kill the lover, Tai is exposed as the guy who stole the sweet potatoes, and everything's oke. Even a final shot of Hine Moa and her baby, while hubby sits contentedly on a knoll playing his flute.

These natives can't act worth a darn, but anybody can alibi that by saying they act well for natives. Direction sticks out all over the picture, with the players showing response to commands very obviously. Scenery is naturally excellent and the photography is good.

On the strength of that bare stuff this one might be used on a double-feature bill. But it's tuned for the free coffee stands. *Bang.*

HIGH TREASON

(BRITISH MADE)

(ALL DIALOG)

London, Sept. 20.

Gaumont-British production and release. Directed by Maurice Elvey. Adapted from play by Pemberton Billing. British Acoustic sounded. Starring Benita Hume and Jameson Thomas. At Marble Arch Pavilion, London. Running time, 95 minutes.

Evelyn Seymour .... Benita Hume
President of Europe .... Basil Gill
Dr. Seymour .... Humberston Wright
Michael Deane .... Jameson Thomas
President of Atlantic States ... Milton Rosmer
The Judge .... Henry Vibart

Gaumont tossed this one cold into Marble Arch and it's proved a hot hit. American-made and plugged, it would have been a sensation, and it will make a lot of money for Gaumont even with its dumb sense of showmanship.

"High Treason" deals with such boob-bumping scientific items as women's fashions 10 years from now, television phone calls from your sweetie, roofs where helicoptered aeroplanes can land in London, electric newsboards for newspapers, women drafted for war service, English Channel train service by tunnel, and, in fact, everything yellow newspapers give the mob on Sunday.

What every British producer has done to date is to follow the American lead—years later. Not so, Maurice Elvey. When he saw the talker wave coming he stopped production for eight months and then with no sound studio and a lousy untried recording system, set out to make a glorious clean-up or a terrible flop.

He let the other birds play 'em close to the chest, but for himself he tossed out blue chips as if they were cigar bands.

He didn't have a story, but he had a climax. This scene showed a man about to broadcast a declaration of war to the world and being shot down by a peace advocate who sent out a peace message instead. With that as his hop-off, Elvey zoomed into the unknown and landed with the best entertainment that has come out of Europe since "Metropolis."

This, of course, is faint praise, but with some healthy editing, shearing the last half reel or more completely, "High Treason" can be made into acceptable entertainment for any house anywhere. They'll like it or they'll hate it, but they'll all go.

A pip of a cast and Elvey's old stage producing days show in the directing of this all-talker, all-screecher. Chief among the eye-fillers is Benita Hume, humdinger. She's the first femme they've flashed on a British screen who didn't look like a powdered frump. And to show her s. a. is not at all in her eyes, they have her do a strip act behind a frosted glass that's more complete than an old Moulin Rouge number. She skips from her office to a dressing room next door, takes a shower and then nose-dives into what the young girl of 1940 will wear. For dinner dances their clothes don't differ much from today except that instead of silk knickers that only show half the time, the girls wear silver panties that show plenty all the time.

But that's not Elvey's picture. That's merely to get the mob by the door. His real idea is to show that 20,000,000 people can't be wrong. A mob of that size against war could stop an international row whatever the provocation. This one is caused by booze troubles on the frontier (Canada) between the Federated Atlantic States and the United States of Europe. Before you could say Cecil B. DeMille, everybody is burning everybody else and the bombing squad is all set to make New York look like a dumping ground.

The love-interest is pumped up between Miss Hume, who is the daughter of the head of the peace league, and Jameson Thomas, head of the air force. They act well and are awful good to look at, so the fact that the love-interest is dragged in by the ears doesn't matter. Humbertson Wright, looking like a white-robed General Booth entering heaven, gives a swell performance as head of the peace league.

There are lots of ideas the coupon-clippers will think seditious in this picture, but what of it? If Shaw had done as well by the forward-lookers of the world as Elvey has, even Swaff would have been satisfied. It's a rough diamond as productions go, but that's better than a smooth performance about nothing at all.

With anti-war feeling on a rising market, this one's in the bag.

Scully.

PHANTOM RIDER

(SILENT)

Produced by Syndicate. Release by Bell Pictures. Directed by J. P. McGowan. Featuring Tom Tyler. Cast includes J. P. McGowan, Harry Woods and Lotus Thompson. At Loew's New York, one day, Sept. 24, one-half of double bill. Running time, 57 minutes.

Tom Tyler has little to do in this one. J. P. McGowan, who directed the film, copped all the acting space. He's about in every sequence, which doesn't make this firemen's opera any the better. McGowan has used all his stuff in this filmfoto except a fire. He's got the stuttering grass plower, the tough criminal, windblown ranch owner and a purty girl.

But it's a tough tamale of a picture, even for McGowan's sort of stuff. The story runs away from the camera more than a half-dozen times, only to be reined in by the captions, written it seems to tell the customers why something is going to happen.

Besides the title is useless to the film. Customers never see the rider doing his phantoming except once, and then he is off the horse.

WHISPERING WINDS

(65% DIALOG)

Produced and released by Tiffany-Stahl. Directed by James Floor. Story and continuity by Jean Jannette. Dialog by Charles Logue. Photographed by Harry Jackson. Music score by Erno Rappe. Synchronized by RCA Photophone. Patsy Ruth Miller, Malcolm McGregor and Eve Southern featured. In cast, Eugenie Besserer and James Marcus. At Loew's New York, one day, Sept. 24, one-half double bill. Running time, 59 minutes.

Only the grind double bill rates this one. Story is chunky and made stereotype with silent titles. Dialog is reproduced clear but ordinary, and the film bears resemlance to a floppo stage play of the first breed.

Acting is slush and direction so flatfooted it gets tangled up in the shoe strings as the picture staggers on to its end.

"Whenever I Think of You" is the theme song. If it is Eve Southern's voice yodeling she rates a couple of palms, but she should lay off the acting. She's too pretty to flop at that.

Story concerns a young sailor boy up in Maine. He lives with ma and is in love with the village blond, who can sing. But the neighbor's gal also loves the boy and she gets him after he returns from a two-day sea trip to find blondy chasing a stage career.

Two years later blondy returns to find the boy and neighbor-gal parents of a child and comfortably married. So blondy puts on a rotten gal act and leaves the village pair flat on their lot.

WORDS AND MUSIC

(All Dialog)

Fox production and release. Directed by James Tingling. Featured are Lois Moran, Tom Patricola and David Percy. Story by Frederick H. Brennan and Dick McEdwards. Music and lyrics credited to Dave Stamper, Harlan Thompson, Conrad and Mitchell, and William Kernell. Others in cast are Helen Twelvetrees, Frank Albertson and Elizabeth Patterson. Photography by Charles Clarke and Charles Van Emper. Running time, 60 minutes. At Loew's New York Sept. 22, one day.

An elaborate singing and dancing revue framed in the collegiate atmosphere, all done in sumptuous style, unheralded in this daily change house. Hard to guess this one. It's an odd sort of talker. These canned stage spectacles have had no test. It's story, such as it is, means nothing.

Picture is framed in the new style of a singing and dancing production, distancing an important stage production of the same kind in the lavishness of spectacle and personnel, the specialty features being framed in a light, romantic story. Revue staging is spectacular and impressive.

Picture's appeal is entirely on the basis of its theatrical production. Story which backgrounds the show is trivial to the last degree and is a hindrance rather than help. Of comedy the picture has practically none, and its romantic note doesn't register.

It's questionable whether the fans will go for a lavish musical song and dance production only, on the talking screen. In this particular the producer has shot the works.

Co-ed college is putting on its annual amateur revue, offering a prize of $1,500 for the best original number composed and staged by a student. Hero (Tom Patricola) is rehearsing his number and the college heavy is preparing his and both are competing to have Mary (Lois Moran) lead his number, and incidentally are battling for her favor.

Tom wins out in the preliminaries, but Mary gets into one of those college scrapes which mean expulsion and is about to be exposed by another girl who sets as the price of her silence the privilege of leading Tom's number. That much planting being accomplished, the actual revue is staged in three gorgeous numbers, delivering by their very sumptuousness. It is here the picture justifies itself by its pictorial magnificence. The numbers are beautifully done in their spectacular staging and in their musical settings, the finale being Tom's romantic number, "Too Wonderful for Words," sung by Tom, with a world of tricky staging behind him.

This sequence, which takes up probably a third of the footage, is the meat of the production, the last word in prodigal studio effect.

Cast is nicely chosen. Principals all give the cheerful feeling of youth and sprightliness the situation calls for, but the adventures of these collegiate young people are rather tiresome. Director has pepped up the action with generous shots at pretty girls in all-revealing togs. For instance, there is a swimming pool episode with scores of girls in attire rivalling the Columbia's runway. Abundant sex appeal likewise in numerous sequences showing the girls in rehearsal for the college revue, Miss Moran herself being a bountiful eyeful in one-piece bathing suit or rehearsal get-up.

Musical adjuncts are capital. Early scenes are in a music shop near the campus, where a glee club foregathers for harmony sessions. Rehearsal bits make agreeable musical interludes, and the revue performance is likewise a fine musical sequence, besides its sight angles. Theme song, "Too Wonderful," doesn't sound like a best seller, although one never knows what a screen plug by a rich, silky baritone can do for a song. Still, it makes a pleasurable detail of the screen performance.

Rush.

Riders of Rio Grande

(SILENT)

(Disc Accompaniment)

J. P. McGowan production for Syndicate Pictures. Distributed by Bell Pictures, Inc. Directed by J. P. McGowan. Photography by Hap Depew and titles by Sally Winters. Bob Custer featured and supported by Edna Eslin and H. B. Carpenter. At Loew's New York one day, Sept. 27, as half double feature. Running time, 50 minutes.

A quickie western below par and fit only for the double-feature houses. Usual story of the pretty gal o' the plains being kidnapped and held for ransom by the villainous leader of a gang of outlaws and then rescued in the nick of time by the handsome hero. What little suspense this quickie might have held was killed half-way through the flicker when it was shown that our hero was not the villain he pretended to be, but an upright individual bent on avenging the wrongs inflicted on his pardner by the dirty doers.

Almost bereft of action except for the ordinary shots of horses galloping across country or a fistic battle or two.

Custer has made so many of these tiny westerns that he walks through his paces mechanically. Edna Eslin as the leading femme has her make up spread all over her face, as if she were caught in the rain with it. Looks cute, though, and petite in contrast with the stalwart men of the plains. Simply a state-righter dying on its feet.

Greeted by a salvo of yawns at the finish.

THE TRESPASSER

(Second Review—From London)
(ALL DIALOG, With Songs)

("The Tresspasser" was reviewed in Variety last week by one of its New York reporters.

This review is from London, where "The Trespasser" had its world premiere, and reviewed by Frank Tilley, of Variety's London office staff. Mr. Tilley, who conducts a weekly column of comment in Variety on the British picture industry, is considered the leading trade paper writer of Britain.

As the first review Variety has ever received from abroad of an American-made picture, Mr. Tilley's notice is printed, following the first review on the same picture, as giving the English idea on a well made American talker).

London, Sept. 10.

Joseph P. Kennedy production. United Artists release, featuring Gloria Swanson. Sounded by RCA Photophone. Directed by Edmund Goulding from original story by director. Censors' Certificate U. Running time, 100 minutes. World premiere and run, New Gallery Kinema, London, Sept. 9, on run.

Marion Donnell	Gloria Swanson
Jack Merrick	Robert Ames
Fuller	Henry B. Walthall
John Merrick Senr.	William Holden
Miss Potter	Blanche Friderici
Catherine "Flip" Merrick	Kay Hammond

On technical advance and story value, rated about the best talker seen here yet. "Trespasser" shows definite swing away from filmed stage play and develops motion picture technique in sound-film presentation to a point not previously put on screens here. With sobs aplenty and everything figuring like a tragic ending, but swinging into reverse with a rush at end, "Trespasser" should be box-office plus here, especially as it puts Gloria Swanson into the type of part in which she is seen acting, which her last two features have not done. But these latter had not backed her off here. English audiences wait and hope that through a number of weak pictures their favorites will eventually get into something their fans will like, and with this Miss Swanson has done it plenty.

Speaking and singing, she is okay, with a soft and clear diction which does not grate and with a singing voice of the kind audiences fall for. As drama, her acting is better than anything she has done, and she is preferred in this country, at any rate, in "suffering" parts more than she is in flip comedy, especially if the former lets her wear pretty clothes most of the time.

Dialog is good and snappy, and steers well clear of melo, with William Holden having plenty of strong lines.

Robert Ames does not quite get over, being out-trouped and outspoken by Swanson in most all his scenes. After the star and Holden, most-liked work at this showing was from Blance Friderici as Miss Potter, her Cockney accent being just right both for tone and vocabulary, and got many laughs. The kid, Wally Albright, also made a strong appeal to the feminine element and will bring in all the mothers and childless middle-aged spinsters, who form 70% of picture house audiences here outside the West End.

Picture is well planted with emotional climaxes, none of which are overdone. Especially well handled is Marion's parting from her kid, with the boy running off after the nurse and not looking back as he turns the corner. This touch created much audience comment.

Marion Donnell, stenog to Hector Ferguson, elopes with Jack Merrick, rich man's son, and a few days after father Merrick horns in and persuades Jack annulment to be followed by building up of Marion through publicity and remarriage later is socially essential.

Jack agrees, but Marion does not, and walks out on him. Works for her living and to keep baby, aided by Miss Potter in a cheap apartment house. In debt, refuses suggestion she should go to the Merricks for aid on account of the kid, but learning of Jack's subsequent marriage to "Flip" Carson, which Merrick, Sr., had been playing for, goes to him and finds he is leaving for France, where Jack and bride have been damaged in a railroad smash. Near a breakdown, Marion is persuaded by Ferguson to live in the country with the baby, Ferguson being in love with her, but on the level. He has a stroke and sends for her before he dies, telling her he loves her, but Marion brings in his wife and he passes out in her arms, thinking it is Marion.

Newspaper hounds get on the trail, as Ferguson's will names Marion heiress, and she at last calls in Jack to protect the child against newspaper stories. Merrick, Sr., wants to take kid away as family heir because Jack's wife, through the railroad smash injuries, is a cripple.

Framed to carry a sob at the close of every sequence and with a luscious part for Swanson to bring the tears with, "Trespasser" made a terrific hit at the premiere and will play all the houses wired in this country and those still to be wired.
Frat.

German Pics

Berlin, Sept. 21.
"MANOLESCU"
"Manolescu" (Ufa), premiere, Gloria Palast.

Some years ago Richard Oswald made a successful picturization of the life of this famous swindler and the idea of repeating it was not a bad one. But Robert Liebmann, who wrote the scenario, hit everything but the target.

Instead of an amusing and dramatic story in which we see how Manolescu, Hungarian master thief, put across his clever and amusing swindles, we are made acquainted with a sentimental leading man who only steals out of love for a vamp.

Finally one of the dame's former lovers returns after a prison sentence and beans him. Recuperating in a hospital he learns to love an innocent little trained nurse. But the vamp won't let up and when she realizes that it is final, turns him up to the police.

Photography by Karl Hoffmann is superior in beauty and variety but Turgansky's direction is heavy and lacking in subtlety. Iwan Mosjukin, Russian player, starred, gets comparatively little out of his role. He is at his best in romantic parts in which he can wear colorful costumes. Brigitte Helm again delivers one of her erotic studies as vamp—she was better in "Nina Petrowna" with an opportunity to be human. Heinrich George as the former crook-lover delivered the best rounded performance of the picture; rough and brutal without being unsympathetic.

"BOBBY"
"Bobby, the Gasoline Boy" (Defina), premiere, Titania Palast.

It is an error to believe that any attractive kid can be a picture star. True enough, any nice looking child is sure to rouse the female part of

the audience to whoops in a bit, but when they have to endure him all evening they begin to realize that Jackie Coogan really had some acting ability.

Bobby Burns, starred here, is just one of a thousand boys and has not the ability to keep the audience interested or hold up this weak story.

Scenario has really little to do with him. Though he is on the screen most of the time, his part of the plot is really dragged in.

He is apparently the child of the owners of a tanking station, but in reality the illegitimate child of the daughter of a rich painter. A doctor falls in love with the girl but she refuses him because of her misstep. He, however, is not kept back by this discovery but proposes to marry the girl and adopt the child. She does not want to have anything to do with the child and this influences the doctor to withdraw his marriage proposal. The girl comes to realize her fault and takes the child back again. He helps to bring the two together again.

Ruth Weiher and Livio Paranelli do the best they can with the wooden roles.

"HOUND OF BASKERVILLES"
"The Hound of the Baskervilles" (Sudfilm), premiere, Capitol.

A good idea to revive this old thriller, one of the best of the Sherlock Holmes novels. It suits itself excellently to the pictures and should have a big success on the Continent. The name might even put it across for moderate returns in the States. No need to repeat the story which concerns a crook who uses the apparition of a phosphorescent dog to frighten the heirs of the house of Baskerville whose property he wants to get control of.

Richard Oswald has turned in a better piece of work than he has had to his credit for some time; it is workmanlike throughout. The old American favorite, Carlyle Blackwell, does well as Sherlock Holmes. Fritz Rasp, Betty Bird and Alexander Mursky fit into the general scheme.

"COME BACK"
"Come Back, All Is Forgiven" (Sudfilm), premiere, Marmorhaus.

No one can accuse Dina Gralla, star, of being beautiful, but she is well put together and has talent for the droll. German audiences like her slightly exaggerated mugging. There is no saying what she might do with American direction qualities. Here Erich Schonfelder keeps her moving without disturbing her much. The scenario hasn't more than its share of original ideas but seldom stops long enough to let you realize this deficiency.

In the main it concerns itself with a young girl who leaves home because she is being forced to marry a fat youth. On her way she is held up by two crooks who strip her of everything except her chemise. She in turn holds up the leading man who gives her his overcoat and lets her ride behind him on his motor bike. They take shelter in a house prepared for a new doctor and have to take over his practice. Still followed by the fat boy, they make their escape and appear in a side show, the youth as announcer, the girl as the legless lady. To get near them the fat boy takes a position as fat lady.

In the end she gets her parents' permission to marry the thinner youth.

Teddy Bill is acceptable in the Fatty Arbuckle role and Robin Irvine is distinctly amusing as the juvenile.

"THE CONVICT"
"The Convict from Stamboul" (Ufa), premiere, Universum.

Competent feature made interesting by the playing of Heinrich George and the pleasing visibility of Betty Amann.

A crook returns from a prison term to find that his best friend is living with his sweetheart in his apartment. He kicks them both out with some unction, but is, nevertheless, distinctly depressed.

A girl selling vacuum cleaners faints in front of his door, and he takes her in, falls in love with her and later marries her. He was formerly married, but believes his wife dead.

His crook friend, who now bears a grudge against him, finds the wife is still living, and sends her to tell the girl her husband is a bigamist. She immediately commits suicide by turning on the gas, and the crook has another disappointment.

The direction of Gustav Ucicky and the photography of Karl Hasselmann are up to international standard. Should do nicely on the **Continent and might even be chance on a double program in the States.**

"Sensation in Wintergarten"
"Sensation in the Wintergarten" (Deutsches Lichtspiel Syndikat), premiere Beba-Atrium.

Usual attempt to repeat "Variety" and with the usual lack of success. Gennaro Righelli is no Dupont and has no Jannings. Scenario is so much blanc mange.

In his youth Count Mensdorf left home because he didn't like the man his mother married after the death of his father.

Meantime he has become a star trapeze performer. He had lost track of the daughter of the circus manager who took him in as a boy, but finds her again and is able to arrange that she also can appear in a leading position on a Wintergarten (Berlin) bill with him.

The present husband of his mother tries to seduce the girl, and this forces the count, who is believed dead, to disclose his real identity to his mother and inform her of her husband's unfaithfulness.

But the mother is completely under the influence of her husband and refuses to recognize her son. The husband wants to get rid of him for good, and tries to cut the rope which holds his trapeze. He is discovered by a clown and falls to his death instead. Paul Richter, who played Siegfried in the "Nibelungen," has done nothing acceptable since that role, but is, nevertheless, still being given leading parts on the strength of it. From the rest of the cast only Wladimir Sokoloff as the clown delivers anything out of the ordinary.

"I LIVE FOR YOU"
"I Live for You" (Universal), premiere Ufa Pavillon.

Setting of this picture will undoubtedly make it unattractive to a non-German audience, and many Germans will also find it objectionable.

It is laid in Switzerland in a sanitarium for tuberculosis. A blond haired girl comes to be cured and brings happiness to all the patients. She makes the last days happier of a young man and a middle-aged count, and both die peacefully in her arms.

On Christmas Day she gets the news that she has been cured, but meantime has fallen in love with a young man who is incurable. She is set to return to the world, but when she comes to realize that her departure will mean the end of everything to him she decides to stay along.

Here the picture is given commercial possibilities by the acting of the leading role by Wilhelm Die-

terle, who has a matinee following. Lien Deyers is a new if rather emaciated blond type. Hubert von Mayrink makes something exceptional out of a small role.

"THE NIGHT WHISPERS"
"The Night Whispers" (Aafa), premiere Primus Palast.

Hans Stuwe reaches the top of the ladder as German leading man in this picture. He is manly and yet has the regularity of features that intrigues. Lil Dagover delivers one of her best performances here, and that's saying a good deal.

The whole picture is strongly reminiscent of Ufa's "Hungarian Rhapsody," but has an entirely different plot. A young Hungarian officer finds his boyhood sweetheart married to a captain who neglects her and squanders all his money on gambling.

The two fall in love with each other again, and she spends the night in his apartment. Her husband's servant discovers what has occurred and promises silence only on the condition that the wife allow him the same liberties as the lieutenant. Terrified, she agrees, but before the servant can take advantage of her he meets the lieutenant, insults him and is shot by him in self-defense. The lieutenant has to leave the service, but the wife divorces her husband and the two are united.

To the performances of the two leads must be added the brilliant work of Veit Harlan as the servant, who is a pocket edition of Jannings. Could interest a sophisticated audience in the States.

"MY SISTER AND I"
"My Sister and I" (National Warner), premiere Beba-Atrium.

Best work that Mady Christians has turned in for a long time. Her comedy is developing, and she looks delectable.

Under the discreet directorial hands of Manfred Noa, Verneuil's farce has been skillfully adapted for the screen. A princess is supposed to marry a baron, but is only interested in the shy librarian of her father's castle. He is too modest to believe she is making advances to him. He is called away to become professor in a university, and she conceives the scheme of telling him that she has a sister, a black sheep of the family, who is employed in a shoe store in the university city.

In her car she arrives there ahead of him and, by subsidizing a store, is taken on as salesgirl. The young man soon falls in love with her.

Igo Sym seconds well in the male lead, and other well-played roles are by Jack Trevor, Tilla Garden and Karl Huszar.

RIO RITA

(DIALOG AND SONGS)

RKO production and release. Produced by William LeBaron. Directed by Luther Reed and adapted by Mr. Reed from the Flo Ziegfeld stage musical of same title. Bebe Daniels, John Boles, Bert Wheeler, Robert Woolsey and Dorothy Lee featured. Two added songs by original song writers, Harry Tierney and Joe McCarthy. Dances staged by Pearl Eaton. Dialog directed by Russell Mack. R. C. A. Photophone sounded. Opened at Earl Carroll theatre, New York, Sunday evening, Oct. 6, running twice daily, $2.50 top. Running time, 135 minutes.

McGinn.........................Sam Nelson
Wilkins.........................Fred Burns
Cafe Owner.........................Sam Blum
Roberto Ferguson.........................Don Alvarado
Chick Bean.........................Bert Wheeler
Lovett.........................Robert Woolsey
Dolly.........................Dorothy Lee
Captain Jim Stewart.........................John Boles
Rita Ferguson.........................Bebe Daniels
Ravenoff.........................George Renevant
Carmen.........................Eva Rosita
Padrone.........................Nick De Ruis
Davalos.........................Tiny Sandford
Mrs. Bean.........................Helen Kaiser

RKO has a valuable piece of screen property in its talker operetta, "Rio Rita." It's a picture full of entertainment and polish for the masses and the classes, due for a long life as it may be revived or reissued at almost any period. The music alone would carry this film to success anywhere.

Ziegfeld's stage "Rio Rita," from which the screen play has been adapted with close adherence to the original stage story, has a national fame but played comparatively little territory in the legit. By reason of that and the picture itself, "Rio Rita" could be road showed in the keys. It is more advisable however to shift this finished product into the regular picture houses for the benefit of the trade. In those houses "Rio Rita" is quite apt to build up new patronage for the screen.

Opening the Carroll as a special picture theatre Sunday evening, it's scale is $2. "Rio Rita" was heavily pre-plugged by word of mouth and had to overcome that at the premiere. That it did speaks all the better for it.

In production again this talker forces the comment that the screen for the talkers is so far beyond in background the possibilities of the stage that the stage can never commence to catch up. In the stage "Rio Rita" the "Ranger" song was the big number. There the rangers lined up across the footlights and sang it. On the screen they come in from afar, on horseback and at a gallop, to alight and sing. Or the other scenes of this Mexican locale.

The picture with one exception is in black and white on the standard size film and screen. The exception is the ballroom portion, handsomely natural colored by Technicolor. About the only picture dimmer in sight for future re-releases of this ever-catchy music and performance would be the prevailing wide film and screen with color.

In casting, the picture is perfect, with the paralyzer Bebe Daniels. She hogs the talker, although anyone will agree that John Boles as the ranger captain is entitled to a world of credit, both for a splendid canned voice and his playing, the latter not often sent over by a tenor.

In comedy it's Bert Wheeler, first with Robert Woolsey next, while Dorothy Lee, not so long ago in pictures and formerly with Waring's Pennsylvanians, stands second to Miss Daniels. Messrs. Wheeler and Woolsey are the only members of the stage company on the screen.

George Renevant as the heavy General Ravenoff did a good villian and the minor roles were as well taken care of.

In production many dancing girls, neatly staged and plenty of Mex extras besides a troop of the Rangers.

Miss Daniels will receive the most attention from those who are familiar with her picture career and the terrific comeback she does, in acting and in singing. Par her with Bessie Love for that. While Mr. Boles has a peculiar personality voice on the screen that never tires.

Wheeler and Woolsey split up the comedy, from cross fire to slapstick and Wheeler the 80 of the 80-20 with Woolsey on the short end. And the comedy is no light portion of this operetta.

Bringing the operetta to the screen in the manner Luther Reed as director and William LeBaron as general RKO producer have done opens up the field again for the class musical, offset by comedy, high or low. This proves it can be done for "Rio Rita" as a reproduction from the stage is as attractive and entertaining as any original could be, if not more so, for here at least the music was staple before transferred.

Sounded by RCA Photophone and first to run in the newly wired Carroll, the result is very complimentary to the Photophone for the sounded picture and the wiring. Barring a few muffled voices early, a seeming off synchronization of Miss Daniels' singing in a close up and the evident over orchestration of the early section, later corrected, the sounded picture holds no faults. This is rather a high average for a first time out of a legit theatre.

The talker ran 135 minutes the opening night, with an intermission. Not a person walked. A romantic story such as "Rio Rita" is always holding and the elaborate picturization added to its zest. The story is or should be familiar, that of a captain of the Texan Rangers seeking a bandit over the border and falling in love, with the attendant incidents, sometimes melodramatic.

On the program Flo Ziegfeld is liberally credited, more so than the several others who are much more responsible. And RKO is entitled to take several bows for itself.

An expensive picture on looks, but worth it and a big profit maker for the exhib and for RKO. *Sime.*

SUNNY SIDE UP

(ALL DIALOG, with Songs)

Fox production and release. Janet Gaynor and Charles Farrell featured. Directed by David Butler, who adapted the script. Numbers staged by Seymour Felix. Original story, words and music by De Sylva, Henderson and Brown. Ernest Palmer and John Schmitz, cameramen. Western Electric (Movietone) sounded. Musical direction by Howard Jackson and Arthur Kay. At Gaiety, New York, opening Oct. 3 on twice daily run, $2 top. Running time, 80 minutes.

Molly Carr.........................Janet Gaynor
Jack Cromwell.........................Charles Farrell
Eric Swenson.........................El Brendel
Bee Nichols.........................Marjorie White
Eddie Rafferty.........................Frank Richardson
Jane Worth.........................Sharon Lynn
Mrs. Cromwell.........................Mary Forbes
Joe Vitto.........................Joe Brown
Raoul.........................Alan Paull
Lake.........................Peter Gawthorne

If there are enough admirers of Janet Gaynor and Charles Farrell willing to spend $2 to see them in a crackerjack musical talker, William Fox has a $2 picture in "Sunny Side Up." As additional attractions there are a likely group of four song hits, and a musical number produced and staged as no screen or stage has previously known. Which, forgetting the doubtful $2 thing, makes this a holdover talker.

Here is seen the power of youth on the screen. Opening night at the Gaiety a literal mob of little damfool flaps hung around the lobby and outside to see Charlie Farrell in person. He was there. They didn't have $2 or a normal mind, it would seem, but they had their eyesight and a yen. The next night in the lobby of the Gaiety more young flaps flopped in and out. One would say: "There he is! Look!" pointing to a lobby picture of Farrell, while another "I like him best like that," pointing to another.

There are a thousand Farrells in any city, but this one is on the screen. To an aged mugg who can't analyze why the east or the west side can go so completely off its nut over any actor, the facts remain. Farrell looks like an odds-on draw just because he's Charlie Farrell of pictures.

Buddy De Sylva, Lou Brown and Ray Henderson have turned out an average screen film "Cinderella" story for Miss Gaynor, and she plays it. And sings it. David Butler in direction has done so well by Miss Gaynor that you even believe she has a voice. It's the way Butler is continually throwing the girl into the faces of the audience through close-ups, and they are dandy. So is the girl, and Farrel, who has an easy role, with El Brendel never having done as well any place, now minus his breakaway clothes, or Marjorie White, who must establish herself in this talker, besides her side partner worker, Frank Richardson.

Winnie Sheehan can team up Miss White and Mr. Richardson for comedy and keep them teamed for a long while. Not often a producer gets a comedy break in one picture like those two, besides Brendel.

While Bobby Crawford's ace songsters have piled up likeable songs so fast they have to be sung over again in the picture to decide which is the best. And here it's "If I Had a Talking Picture of You." But for delivery Miss Gaynor's "I'm a Dreamer—Aren't We All?" leads. The songwriting trio must have taught her.

While that "Turn On the Heat"—hot! And how!—Seymour Felix has surpassed himself. It was the talk of Broadway immediately. A cooch by 36 gals. And what a cooch! Besides its production. An Esquimaux scene. As the hot dance proceeds the snow melts, trees and palms grow, and all of this while those 36 coochers go the limit. When a couple down front on the screen go beyond the limit, the place catches fire, and it all burns up. If they get this number right in the sticks the natives will arrange to sleep in the theatre. There's a bit of hinted color in this scene.

It's one of those sidewalk of New York tales, but switches on the Cinderella end to Southampton. And there's another number in the Southampton scenes, a garden fete that will compel stage musical producers to concede that they cannot possibly compete with the screen.

While this picture and perhaps many another in the woods at 60c. top against a $5.50 musical! Come, on, boys, it's time to go home. Or close up.

Everything entirely original in the picture, from story to staging.

It's not tense, however. There are no tears. Because there's never any doubt.

Plenty of comedy. Some of it by Joe Brown as an undertaker acting as m. c. for a block party. That's on the east side. Down at Southampton the garden party gives its affair on a stage fronted by a large lake. And the curtain is made a natural one through a rising waterfall. When the Shuberts see that! That will probably be when they will kiss Joe Kennedy for letting the pictures rescue them.

Mr. Richardson has plenty of the comedy, with much of it with Miss White. Miss White is from vaudeville—Marjorie and Thelma White (not the other White Sisters). Mr. Richardson had his knocks coming up, also, through cabarets. While Brendel's enormous training has been vaude and musical comedy, to now become, as he is in this talker, one of the best character comedians on stage or screen. A kidlet of about 4 does a song bit that's a big laugh. He looks like another Davey Lee.

Sharon Lynn seems new in name, but plays a social deb extremely well, and looks it. That girl should be worth netting also.

A clean-up picture.

For it is a musical of a high order of production, always in good taste in every part of it, and always hugely entertaining. *Sime.*

APPLAUSE

(ALL DIALOG)

Paramount production and release. Adapted by Garret Fort from the best seller of similar title by Beth Brown. Produced by Monta Bell. Directed by Rouben Mamoulian. Helen Morgan featured on program, but heavily starred on marquee lights. George Folsey, cameraman. Made at Paramount's Astoria Studio, Long Island. At Criterion, New York, $2 top, twice daily. Running time, 80 minutes. No original songs or music. All of either of the period.

Kitty Darling.........................Helen Morgan
April Darling.........................Joan Peers
Hitch Nelson.........................Fuller Mellish, Jr.
Joe King.........................Jack Cameron
Tony.........................Henry Wadsworth
Mother Superior.........................Dorothy Cumming

This picture as "Applause" would have been a better Arthur Hopkins "Burlesque" than "Dance of Life" is, both made by Paramount. This is the real old burlesque, in its background, people and atmosphere. So was Beth Brown's book, "Applause," and Garret Fort has adapted with sufficient fidelity to hold together the odd story that makes an odd picture. Add to that the tricks in this talker, of direction and photography, and it's a picture for the people, with Helen Morgan a crack draw, by herself.

For the sticks this film is made more engaging by its downtown New York sightseeing — Brooklyn Bridge at what looked like dawn; that ever entrancing skyline at the Battery; a liner going out to sea, with the Statue of Liberty still smiling over Prohibition in the distance.

Rouben Mamoulian, of the Theatre Guild directing stage forces, directed "Applause" according to the program. No doubt Mr. Mamoulian did direct the stage work of the burlesque show and the attendant scenes back-stage, but to ask one to believe that a stage director on his first picture try could turn out this film as it has been turned out is asking one to believe as big a lot as a studio occupies. Monta Bell is the picture's producer.

Helen Morgan is the fading star of burlesque, aging on the stage as her daughter, born in a dressing room, grew up. Miss Morgan will panic those of the picture-goers who see and hear her here under the belief she is a singing cabaret hostess, or a Mississippi Magnolia, but her dramatic work in the stage "Sweet Adeline" is in line, but not as heavy or as strong as the tragedy she is continually going through with in "The Parisian Flirts."

Kitty Darling had to choose between her daughter and her pi, so she chose poison. That is the ending, as the daughter who fell for the first boy she met, a gob, walked with him to still another dressing room to tell Kitty they were going to be married. But Kitty had passed out, after her day had gone. Even Jack Singer, who may have helped in the direction, had told her he had no job for old women.

That sounded all over again like the day Sam Scribner said the old women would have to get off the Columbia burlesque wheel or the wheel would have to go out of business. And the first burlesque queen to suffer by that order was Sam's sister-in-law.

There are plenty of smiles at this burlesque troupe. Larry Weber might believe that the Weber & Rush title of "Parisian Flirts" had been faithfully reproduced in name and people, one of those $700 payroll shows of olden days that depended upon the blonde leader.

Here the blonde is Miss Morgan in a wig, but looking the queen at first from her face down to the **ankles, with everything freely exposed. The chorus girls are of the Beef Trust type and size, beefy all over and 1,000 years old. They're most of the laugh. But the entire burlesque portion in itself and on the stage is a tintype of it of 20 years ago.**

Joan Peers comes to the front toward the finish as the daughter, April. Earlier and in the convent scenes she didn't convince. Nor perhaps or mayhaps everyone will not go so forte for the convent scenes with that prayer, but they were planted for effect against the burlesque surroundings. And had their effect, especially when the pi, now Kitty's husband, tries to make the daughter.

Hitch Nelson as done by Fuller Mellish, Jr., was the pi, a peach of a pi, too. A turkey burlesque chiseler with the women stuff on the side, and always bullyragging his woman. A good performance every minute by Mr. Mellish. Jack Cameron as Joe King sparsely appeared early. Henry Wadsworth was the juv, opposite Miss Peers. He grew and can stand watching.

Plenty of production and the coherent tale make extra attractions. This picture was made at Paramount's Long Island studio.

All kinds of ballyhooing and exploitation possible. That street parade alone of the burlesque show as seen at the opening in any town would have to pack the house. And when exploiting, those cotton tights that wrinkle on the chorus girls should not be overlooked. For who will believe, and especially women nowadays, that chorus girls ever wore cotton tights? Not even Jacobs & Jermon's mill hand choristers from Massachusetts ever did.

Nor will anyone ever see the burlesque show of 1910 again except in "Applause." *Sime.*

WHY BRING THAT UP?

(ALL DIALOG)

Paramount production and release. Starring Moran and Mack; Evelyn Brent and Harry Green with featured billing. Directed by George Abbott. Adapted by Hector Turnbull from Octavus Roy Cohen's story. Premiere showing at Rialto, New York, Oct. 4, at $3 top; thereafter on grind scale. Running time, 80 minutes.

Moran	George Moran
Mack	Charles Mack
Betty	Evelyn Brent
Irving	Harry Green
Bert	Bert Swor
Powell	Freeman S. Wood
Casey	Lawrence Leslie
Marie	Helene Lynch
Eddie	Selmer Jackson
Treasurer	Jack Luden
Skeets	Monte Collins, Jr.
Doorman	George Thompson
Manager	Eddie Kane
Tough	Charles Hall

The nationally known vaude routine of the blackface comedians, Moran and Mack, stretched out on a fragile story frame. Probably the best way of all others to screen the Moran-Mack stage cross-fire without cutting it down to a two-reel short, it amounts to an acceptable program picture that never gets very near to bigness.

"Why Bring That Up?" solely through the team name will get enough box office attention for moderate grosses. Yet regardless of the name, on merits it shouldn't hit the ceiling in very many spots. Not that sort of a picture.

The picture's first recommendation rests with the popularity of the starring team, of course. Moran and Mack are perhaps the most widely known blackface combination of this era of show business. That was gained not only on the stage or the air, but through phonograph disks that reached and are still reaching remote spots, records that penetrated the home. And this picture will also play the hideaways never touched by Moran and Mack in the flesh.

"Early Bird Catches the Worm," "Head Man" and "Let's Not Talk About That" are widely known comedy lines by this time. The fact they are so familiar supports a belief that most everyone knows the answers. This w. k. material is the meat of the dialog in the film. So instead of waiting for something to laugh at, many, many audiences will be waiting to laugh at something they know is due to follow.

There was only one way to transfer the Moran and Mack blackface talk to the talking pictures, and that was by means of a backstage story. This one follows all of the others in much the same way.

George Moran, in whiteface, opens the story by asking a traffic cop the address of the nearest speakeasy. It develops his partner, Casey (Moran and Casey), has gone on a bender over a dame just as they have been fortunate enough to scare up two weeks of work. Casey has his elbows grooved into the bar and won't listen. Exiting from the combination speakeasy-pool room, Moran tries to double his last four bucks in a cue game, is framed, and then helped out of the jam by Charlie Mack, who pours java in a nearby coffee pot. Mack used to be a blackface comedian himself and he has some great ideas, so they make it Moran and Mack.

Then some introductory business in a theatrical boarding house, where the wicked dame (Evelyn Brent), who drove Casey to drink, resides. Among the other residents is Irving Berger (Harry Green), Hebe comic on the local vaude bill. His yen is to be a manager, not an actor, so he turns agent for the boys, giving them his pot on the bill by faking a toothache and canceling at the last moment. Moran and Mack, doing the early bird, Adam and Eve and the boxing bout, are a hit.

Five years later they are producing their own show on Broadway. Re-enters trouble in form of Betty, the boarding house siren. Betty has a swindle idea on with her boy friend and is looking for a job in the show. The boy friend's scheme is to take Moran for the roll. The show goes over, and Betty proceeds to do the taking.

She's almost successful until Mack steps in. Betty frames a story to blacken him in his partner's eyes, and Moran says it's the end. When Mack attempts to stop Betty and her evil partner from taking him out for the final fleecing, the b. f. stops Mack with a vase on the head.

In Betty's lair, Moran repents suddenly and blows back to the theatre. There he finds his buddy was booked into a hospital.

Then the big dramatic scene. Mack lies in a coma. Nothing can bring him out of it. Nothing but Moran, maybe. George steps to the bedside. "Charlie, don't you remember me? It's your pal, George," he cries. But no good. "Charlie, the early bird catches the worm." That does it. Charlie opens his eyes and gives the right answer.

You can't beat that for hokum. Yet it amounts to the biggest punch in the picture—a picture with few real punches.

Unfortunately George Moran's appearance is against him, besides a distinct lack of screen personality. He hasn't a camera face and never lets loose in the acting. Even more unfortunate is the fact that Moran had the sympathy to himself had he wanted it.

Charlie Mack, the original Mack of the stage team, does nicely all the way. Green can hang up another click for himself. While Miss Brent is, as usual, the looker and trouper.

Bert Swor, of another standard blackface team, Swor Bros., steps into the picture to replace Mack as Moran's partner when the former is taken to the hospital, but doesn't get into actual work. In the poolroom scene one of the players looked like Swor without cork.

Another former vaudevillian present is Eddie Kane, with a small part. Earl Lindsey is recognizable as the dance stager, though not programed.

Theme song, title not known, but ending with "I Love You," that sounds likely. *Bige.*

DARK STREETS

(ALL DIALOG)

First National production and release. Directed by Frank Lloyd. Based on story by Richard Connell. Adapted by Bradley King. Photographed by Ernest Haller. Music by Vitaphone Orchestra. Sounded by Western Electric (Vitaphone). Featuring Jack Mulhall and Lila Lee. At Loew's New York, one day, Oct. 3. Running time, 55 minutes.

Talker is all right. The acting isn't the best and the story is kinda blah. But there are some melo spots and a couple of gun fights which, with the help of the two headline names, will send the picture over.

Everybody talks plainly. Synchronization okeh.

Mulhall plays twins; cop and a gunman—both brothers.

One of the twins is a bad egg and both love the same girl. Pat is the cop and Dan is the crook. Dan belongs to a gang of silk house wreckers whom the cops are out to get. The captain of the district, without asking the commissioner, has let out orders to shoot first and kill afterwards. The gang to which Dan belongs does likewise. And the war is on.

Pat warns Dan against showing in the warehouse district—and Dan, like a good crooked brother, tips off Pat to do the same thing. Both are stubborn so both go out.

Dan, without notifying the audience, gets religion and kidnaps his brother, dons his outfit and steps out masquerading as the flatfoot.

He gets bumped off and then the picture shows that he did it all for his brother and the girl they both loved.

BLACKMAIL

(BRITISH MADE)
(ALL DIALOG)
(2d Review)
(In New York)

British International production. Released over here by Sono Art-Wide World. Director, Alfred Hitchcock, only, featured. Adapted by Mr. Hitchcock from the English stage play by Charles Bennett. R. C. A. Photophone sounded. Made at Elstree Studios, London. Dialog by Ben Levy. Cameraman, Jack Cox. Musical score by Campbell & Connolly (English music publishers). Music compiled and arranged by Hubert Bath and Harry Stafford. Played (synchronized) by B. I. Symphony Orchestra, John Reynders, conductor. At Selwyn, New York, $2 top, for twice daily two-week engagement (announced). Running time, 75 minutes.

The Girl	Anny Ondra
Her Mother	Sara Allgood
Her Father	Charles Paton
Detective	John Longden
Blackmailer	Donald Calthrop
Artist	Cyril Ritchard
Landlady	Hannah Jones
Chief Inspector	Harvey Braban
Detective Sergeant	Ex-Detective Sergeant Bishop, late of Scotland Yard

As the admittedly best in England of any all-English all-talker to date, "Blackmail" for America ranks in the class known on this side as a fair program picture. If it makes this country's first run deluxe houses it will have to be on the novelty of a good and first English talker with a detective-mystery story and that it contains a relationship to Scotland Yard. Otherwise it has nothing to depend upon. Against it is the race of the American-made talker, its easy supremacy and just at this moment a remarkable line-up of domestic pictures that ordinarily might keep any foreign-made of an average such as here out of the first runs, until the native supply has been exhausted.

As a picture and talker, the first British speaker coming over, "Blackmail" bespeaks an intense improvement by British International, at least, in picture making. A deduction accordingly is that the dialog picture is forcing a better product, regardless, not only abroad but at home. Or else why the large number of really box office power in America at present, playing or about to be released? It was not that way with the silents on this side, ever.

As a talking picture "Blackmail" is most draggy. It has no speed or pace and very little suspense. Everything's open-face. To sum that up, it may be said that half of the picture is drag and the remainder picture. Points are hammered at, but the English atmosphere does much to atone, besides the English-speaking actors, always superior in diction to our home-made.

Nicely sounded as reproduced at the Selwyn, a legit house gone wire. Legit houses are not always the better of legit or picture for reproduction of sound.

"Blackmail," as a title, holds some pull, but it is thinly associated with the story itself. The blackmailing attempt is but an incident leading to bigger things.

It's a story that has been told in the native silents in different disguises—the story of a girl who killed a man trying to assault her. The murder was committed behind (That) a curtain. The tale is subtitled "The story of a foolish girl" and "A drama of Scotland Yard." Across the street from the Selwyn is a stage play named "Scotland Yard." "Scotland Yard" to the peasants around would mean more in the mystery manner than "Blackmail." For the Scotland Yard of legendary fame to Americans is more intriguing than our own secret service or the state troopers. Also at the Selwyn in the billing are quoted excerpts from Frank Tilley's English review recently in "Variety," on this film.

The foolish girl portion slips in when Anny Ondra left a very lively scene in one of the Lyons feederies after flirting with a stranger and airing her steady, a regular Yard dick, to join the other half of the flirtation. The other half lived near the cigar store of her father, and asked the girl upstairs to see his studio, he being an artist. She foolishly assented, and then followed the jam.

After the artist had passed out, the (her) dick arrived, found her glove and spoke to her about it in the cigar store the next morning. They were interrupted by a crook getting an idea of the thing. He wanted coin, but Scotland Yard had learned the crook also was in the studio when the murder occurred, and he's suspected.

First blackmailing for a little money, the sweetie-dick, on info from the Yard, is about to take his man when the fellow lams it through a window. Then a chase through and up to the steeple's top of the British Museum. An overhead shot of the Musuem likens it to the Congressional hall at Washington. That is and should be quite interesting to those who go to pictures over here who may have heard of the British Museum, if they don't confuse it with Barnum and Bailey's.

With the assumed murderer out of the way, the heavy lover takes his girl by the hand and, telling her to shut up, or something like that, probably marries her, to be ever after watchful of her knife hand.

In performance the standout is Donald Xalthrop as the rat crook. He looks it. Miss Ondra is excellent as the girl with a lot of work thrust upon her. She looks well and talks probably according to direction, with the direction in whole admirable for a British-made, but also due to it, the halting periods, in action, scenes and in speech.

Dialog ordinary but sufficient. Camera work rather well, especially on the Museum and the eating house scenes. A bit of comedy here and there, but not enough to be called relief.

As the sweetie-dick, ex-detective sergeant Bishop is programed as late of Scotland Yard. If he's a detective on the level, merely cast for this picture, no matter what was the Yard's loss when he quit, the English acting force is the gainer. And if Bishop gives up acting to become a private detect, if the Yard doesn't want him back, he's a chump. That's Americanese for dumbbell. For the lad played just as good a copper on the screen as the American copper in "Broadway," who is just an actor without a past.

Cyril Ritchard does the dirty cad, and passed out all too early. He is rather a finished villain. Besides, he plays the piano and sings. Those Britishers on the stage or screen seem very versatile.

"Blackmail" is a creditable English output. A study of it by other British producers should be a lesson in talker making; that is, unless they prefer to see "The Trespasser," "The Letter," "Alibi" or "Madame X" and 20 other American-made talking pictures that now rank as models for the screen over here—besides the musical talkers. *Sime.*

Forest People of Siberia

(RUSSIAN MADE)

(Silent)

Produced by Sovkino. Released by Amkino. Travelog. At Film Guild, New York, Oct. 5. Running time, 65 minutes.

Purely educational and would be worth showing in educational institutions, but, like most everything the Soviets shoot into the States, secretes propaganda. Mostly dumb propaganda, which doesn't reach the people over here aimed at. It's entirely too long for an entertainment house.

The way these Russians try to put over their ballyhoo stuff is almost insulting. In this film they tried to slip in a word for dear old Russe in the last 10 minutes of the picture when they deliberately gave up that celluloid space to proving that even Mongolian illiterates who eat raw fish as a delicacy have finally decided to be Sovietized.

The picture otherwise depicts a tribe of Mongolian Indians who resemble Alaskan Eskimos and who number less than 1,500 and live along the Taiga and Naeocha rivers in Siberia. Interesting and scenery beautiful. There's a piece or two of good hunting action—the shooting down of a wild boar and the spearing of a bear. Also fishing with spears.

YOUNG NOWHERES

(All Dialog)

First National production and release. Richard Barthelmess starred. Directed by Frank Lloyd. Bradley King adaptation of a story by Ida A. R. Wylie. Cameraman, Ernest Haller. At Central, New York, opening Oct. 1 at $2, twice daily. Running time, 65 minutes.

Albert.................Richard Barthelmess
Annie..........................Marion Nixon
Mr. Jesse..........................Bert Roach
Cleaver.......................Anders Randolf
George........................Raymond Turner

Artistic successes have a way of being less than tumultous at the paybox and this picture is a definite attempt at something a little finer and more imaginative than the usual Hollywood hokum. But for $2 it's commercially silly, and far from adding gloss the Broadway engagement probably netted the picture injury through inevitably prejudicing its chances by false pretentions.

Running but 65 minutes, "Young Nowheres" is the cinema equivalent to a short story as distinguished from a full-length many-episoded novel. It deals with a situation rather than a plot and bases appeal entirely on humanity. Dickens and O. Henry, in collaboration, would have turned out something of the sort.

Albert, inarticulate, bewildered, over-worked and underpaid elevator boy in an apartment house, has a romance with Annie, heart-hungry domestic drudge. Miserably poor, they have no privacy, no dignity as individuals, and none of the normal expectations of happiness. On a Christmas Eve they illegally appropriate for their use the luxurious apartment of a wealthy and absent tenant. Discovered, their arrest follows. They tell their story in night court, winning exoneration and an influential friend.

It requires a certain courage, coupled with confidence, to attempt such a fragile and homely story. It is remarkable, too, that a star deliberately chooses to impersonate anyone so deficient in glamor as an elevator boy and so submerges the personality of the actor that the audience sees only the eventlessness of an existence that is a dull ache and a haircomb only a lift engineer would wear.

Barthelmess, since "The Patent Leather Kid," has been identified with a series of interesting and for the most part successful pictures. Probably through his own knowledge of values he manages to get good stories. "Wise guys," Broadway commentators, and other equally unreliable barometers, will be facetious about "Young Nowheres," yet the picture may find the heart of sentimental America far from the over-sophisticated zone. And with Christmas coming on the tear, inducement will be additional.

Marion Nixon does a Lillian Gish without a close-up of nervous fingers. It's a great job of trouping for Miss Nixon, whose eyes have an eloquence not heretofore fully realized. She discharges her lines easily and naturally and without making them seem like dialog.

"Young Nowheres" should do okay as a Barthelmess programmer, winning friends even if others view it with impatience. *Land.*

SALUTE

(100% TALKING)

Fox production and release. Directed by John Ford. Story by Tristram Tupper and John Stone. Dialog by James Kevin McGuinness. Photography by Joseph A. August and sound by W. W. Lindsey. At the Roxy, New York, Oct. 6. Running time, 83 minutes.

Cadet John Randall........George O'Brien
Midshipman Paul Randall..William Janney
Midshipman Albert Edward Price
Frank Albertson
Nancy Wayne.............Helen Chandler
Marion Wilson.............Joyce Compton
Maj.-Gen. Somers, U. S. A.
Clifford Dempsey
Rear Admiral Randall, U. S. N.
Lumsden Hare
Smoke Screen.................Stepin Fetchit
Navy Coach.....................David Butler
Cadet.................................Rex Bell
Midshipman...................John Breeden

No occasion to worry about this one while the annual football fever grips the country. It should be a cleanup between now and Thanksgiving, with the sporting page working for the box office all the time. Outside of that it is a mild story working up to the formula climax of the tieing touchdown in the last 30 seconds of play, with the girl and other elements of happiness for the young people hanging in the balance.

Matter of fact the characters are subordinated in interest to the backgrounds in which they move. There is more intrinsic kick to some of the pictures of the navy cadets in drill on their parade ground, the pictorial splendors of real settings taken in the grounds of the Naval Academy and in the breathless atmosphere of the great American football classic itself, than in any fictitious literary maneuvering of hero and heroine.

This is where the screen has it all over the stage. This picture more than any of the others taken in the same locale gets the illusion of reality from its backgrounds. The trickily angled shots of the cadets on review, dressed in line or marching are really inspiring quite aside from any situation in the story.

There is, for instance, a view of the Middies marching down the viaduct near the Polo Grounds and going upon the football field with their cheers that carries a real punch to anybody that has felt the unique sensation of the game itself between the two arms of the service. Clips of the football crowd and of play probably were spliced in from a newsreel, together with the appropriate sounds that accompany the struggle, sounds which are the essence of drama in themselves.

Picture has good comedy values through the presence of the priceless Stepin Fetchit, most amusing of Negro character clowns.

Rialog is rather sappy, inevitably so with these college campus romances, but it is neatly managed by the principal characters, charming foursome of young people in George O'Brien, William Janney, Helen Chandler and Joyce Compton. Cast and the skill of the director in handling his backgrounds here has made what otherwise would be a mediocre picture stand out as an agreeable bit of light entertainment. The topical football angle does the rest, making a satisfactory total from the customer's and the box office angles, both. *Rush.*

HIS GLORIOUS NIGHT

M-G-M production and release. Directed by Lionel Barrymore from Willard Mack's adaptation of Ferenc Molnar's play, "Olympia." At the Capitol beginning Oct. 4. Running time, 80 minutes.

Capt. Krovacs.......................John Gilbert
Princess Orsolini......Catherine Dale Owen
Eugenie.............................Nance O'Neill
Krehl..................Gustav von Seyffertitz
Mrs. Collingsworth Stratton..Hedda Hopper
Priscilla Stratton.......................Doris Hill
Prince Luigi Caprilli..........Tyrrell Davis
Lord York..........................Gerald Barry
Lady York...................Madeline Seymour
Count Albert......................Richard Carle
Countess Lina......................Eva Dennison

A few more talker productions like this and John Gilbert will be able to change places with Harry Langdon. His prowess at love making, which has held the stenoes breathless, takes on a comedy aspect in "His Glorious Night" that gets the gum chewers tittering at first and then laughing outright at the very false ring of the couple of dozen "I love you" phrases designed to climax, ante and post, the thrill in the Gilbert lines.

The theme is trite at best. And the dialog, while aiming most of the time for irony in the continental manner, is innane.

Evidently hoping to speed up a listless script, made more so by the princess who is icy during the drawing room scenes that compose the center of action and who has little time to thaw out in the arbor and balcony locales where Gilbert recites his "hot" paragraphs, Director Barrymore apparently had a nervous reaction in the cutting room. This is borne out by the way the sequences literally grasshopper into one another. Conversation barely starts in one room when it cuts lightninglike to veranda, steps and back to the bedroom or dinner table.

Miss Owen, for whom "His Glorious Night" also marks a debut in feature dialog, is given a difficult role as the Princess Orsolini. She is reminded by her mother, Eugenie, that princesses are expected to be austere. Her father as well observes she is a cold proposition. The average audience, too, will feel that Miss Owen, herself, is too posey and despite her excellent diction, a trifle stiff in her "readings."

Captain Krovacs for Gilbert means chiefly wearing a wardrobe of uniforms. Always on parade and aware of the attention of women young and old at the continental resort, Gilbert presents a voice passable when it does not have to work into a crescendo. The love lines, about pulsating blood, hearts and dandelions read far better than they sound from under the dainty Gilbertian mustach.

The hauteur of the Princess toward the Captain in the opening reel when occurs the best shot, possibly borrowed from an actual spill in a steeplechase, is as quickly irised into an over-stressed necking party made more pronounced by the dialog.

After that the audience knows that another and still another hugging and talking laugh combo is to go on record before the princess marries our hero.

In the interim, however, the couple is alotted the necessary separation. The captain is an imposter. And Krovacs verifies this and also that he is not of aristocratic blood but the ambitious son of a simple Riga shoemaker.

But it all cuts to the Captain, a creature of noble sentiment, just arranging it with the Vienna police to have him pose as a notorious, shady bird on the wanted list. And he makes the Princess run half way into the woods to get another clinch and the ring.

The title is interpreted in one of the earlier huddles. Orsolina has summoned Krovacs to her bedroom and told him she knows all. The Captain announces he will accept neither bribe nor secret deportation until his wish is granted. Whereupon he carries her away. Next day the sleepy-eyed Priscilla, daughter of a title hunting mother, substantiates suspicions that the destination was Krovac's own room. *Waly.*

BIG NEWS

(ALL DIALOG)

Pathe production and release recorded by RCA system. Directed by Gregory La Cava from George S. Brooks' story adapted by Jack Jungmeyer. Frank Reicher credited dialog. At the Colony beginning Oct. 5. Running time, 75 minutes.

Steve Banks..............Robert Armstrong
Mrs. Banks.......................Carol Lombard
Reno...................................Sam Hardy
Patrolman Ryan..................Tom Kennedy
Hansel.............................Louis Payne
O'Neill..............................Wade Boetler
Editor.............................Charles Sellon

"Big News" will make money wherever it is shown. It is one of the most absorbing mellers filmed in a long time, and, although its theme centers in a newspaper office, it is handled and enacted in such a way that every sequence has a one-two sock.

Pathe's "Big News" is worthy of any rave it gets. And that goes for the superlatives they'll probably use in the press sheet.

The theme picks a news room of the daily in a second class city. Radio recorders never forgot to keep the typewriters clicking into their mikes. The writing tempo never ceases.

It's a case of the star reporter sleeping off a stew in the editor's chair and getting the gate when the advertising manager kicks that the constellation's toughness is causing him to lose a good account. Director LaCava remembers his own daily days sufficiently not to let the editor blow up until the reporter has actually called the turn.

Robert Armstrong, Charles Sellon and Louis Payne couldn't fit the roles of reporter, editor and advertising manager any better.

The romantic interest is skillfully worked in. Not a girl friend, but a wife of two years, trying to get her repoter husband, Steve, away from bar inclinations that are becoming a habit. As Mrs. Banks, sob-sister on a rival paper, Carol Lombard steps before the camera just often enough to provide the necessary touch and not spoil a good job.

Sam Hardy is excellent as a speak prop and coke runner. He plays Reno, the underworld guy who gets Banks fired.

Action gets into a big blaze when Banks, returning with a confession which involves Reno in a murder, is given a raise along with the job. At the same time Reno, across the hall, overhears the conversation and bumps off the editor, using a knife Banks had left in the speak.

The discovery of the dead editor leads to the immediate accusation of Banks. It is here that novel twists are used to advantage. Banks has a dictaphone record of what Reno told the editor before the killing.

Tom Kennedy makes a good Patrolman Ryan. He is just the kind of a cop who would rile the boys in the office of a small daily. *Waly.*

FAST COMPANY

(ALL DIALOG)

Paramount production and release. Featuring Jack Oakie, Evelyn Brent and Skeets Gallagher. Directed by E. A. Sutherland. Adapted from the play, "Elmer the Great," by Ring Lardner and George N. Cohan. Script and dialog by Florence Ryerson, Patrick Kearney, Walton Butterfield and Joe Mankiewicz. Cameraman Edward Cronjager. At Paramount, New York, Oct. 4. Running time, 70 Minutes.

Evelyn Corey	Evelyn Brent
Elmer Kane	Jack Oakie
Bert Wade	Skeets Gallagher
Dave Walker	Sam Hardy
Rosie La Clerq	Gwen Lee
Mrs. Kane	Eugenie Besserer

Perhaps because most persons suffer from inferiority complexes and secretly envy those cocksure fellows commonly described as conceited, there has been a cycle of motion pictures in the last couple of seasons devoted to the impudence and audacity of egocentrics. As interpreted by the character's best known exponent, William Haines, the disciple of self-praise and self-confidence is generally addicted to a very low offensive form of practical joke, great for laughing purposes, but not very close to the core of genuine characterization.

Now comes Jack Oakie as Elmer the Great, a character that carries reality, a blend of sap, boundless naivete, a horse's appetite for food, and a heart that's melon size. And with it all not a trace of smart aleck. It's thoroughly human. Elmer wins the sympathies while remaining Elmer and not going through one of those complete over-night last-minute changes of nature by which Mr. Haines makes himself companionable and lovable in the end.

Ring Lardner and George M. Cohan had a dandy idea when they wrote the play which, unfortunately, couldn't quite get the combination of the box office, but is an attractive program release. Hollywood reverses its critics in this case by improving upon the original. They have stripped the baseball story bare of the rather cumbersome plot mechanics and with an economy of complication keep the pace and interest tightly riveted.

Oakie, it is now no secret, is a comer in a big way. This ex-vaudevillian has followed one fine job with another and is definitely enroute to an important destination. He possesses on top of his trouping ability rugged good looks and a knack for ingratiating himself. His fan mail should be feeling that undercurrent.

"Fast Company" is a program release that will easily carry through for the general gratification of audiences and auditors. It is not belly laugh entertainment, but it is uncommonly agreeable light comedy buttressed by humanity and an idea.

In passing it cannot escape comment that Eddie Sutherland, for reasons not intelligible to proletarian minds, has suddenly gone ritz after all these years and is now billing himself as A. Edward Sutherland. He'll have to grow a vandyke to go with such elegance.

Edward Cronjager, veteran Paramount cameraman, performed his chore with accustomed competence. Evelyn Brent was a little out of character in a role that called for less ice. Skeets Gallagher and Oakie made a laugh-winning battery and Gwen Lee rates a corsage bouquet for doing something with a smaller role.

The scenario department very emphatically is entitled to a bend (not a bender) on "Fast Company." *Land.*

DISRAELI

(ALL DIALOG)

Warner production and release. Starring George Arliss. Directed by Alfred E. Green. Adapted by Julian Josephson from the play by Louis N. Parker. Cameraman, Lee Garmes. Presented at Warners, New York, opening $2 twice-daily engagement Oct. 2. Running time, 90 minutes.

Disraeli	George Arliss
Lady Clarissa Pevensey	Joan Bennett
Lady Beaconsfield	Florence Arliss
Charles—Lord Deeford	Anthony Bushell
Lord Probert	David Torrence
Hugh Myers	Ivan Simpson
Mrs. Travers	Doris Lloyd
Duchess of Glastonbury	Gwendolen Logan
Potter	Charles E. Evans
Mr. Terle	Kyrle Bellew
Bascot	Jack Deery
Count Bosrinov	Michael Visaroff
Foljambe	Norman Cannon
Duke of Glastonbury	Henry Carvill
Dr. Williams	Shayle Gardner
Flookes	Powell York
Queen Victoria	Margaret Mann

Acting and characterization a continuous delight. One of those occasional and memorable treats of vibrant trouping with all the embroidery and clever tricks so agreeable to encounter, is the report on George Arliss and Warners' "Disraeli."

While it is possibly true that some of the peasants won't get the smartness or appreciate the subtle shades of the Arliss technique, not to mention a plot that concerns the diplomatic imperativeness of possessing the Suez Canal, it seems certain that the de luxe audiences will take to "Disraeli" in a big way.

It is difficult to gauge from New York the probabilities of Sheboygan's reactions but as normal keenness for zestful acting seems to be pretty universal there is little reason for being afraid of the superiority of "Disraeli."

By classification "Disraeli" belongs with those older stage pieces known and best described as a "starring vehicle." To think of "Disraeli" without Arliss is to shudder. Everything hinges upon performance here. The professional equipment of the central figure constantly present carrying and dominating both plot and conversation. This is the first instance since dialog pictures of such a piece being done. There will never be many of the same kind for obvious reasons.

When "Disraeli" reaches the smaller communities the response from the literate element should be enthusiastic. They haven't ever tasted such dramatic caviar on the talking film. In the silents Barrymore's "Jeckyll and Hyde" and Jannings' "Last Laugh" are parallels.

Warners have done it right. Production is unstinted, sedate, and colorful, in the style of 1874. Small bits as well as principal roles are equally meritorious. Florence Arliss, wife of the star, plays his wife in the picture and makes the family circle complete by attaching runner-up honors.

Doris Lloyd as a woman spy was interesting and plausible as she wove her little net of intrigue. She provided the "menace" to the plan to purchase the big ditch through Egypt.

Opportunities for publicity are endless. Disraeli was in life novelist, wit, dandy, lover, prime minister of England and the most famous and brilliant Jew of his generation. History books are full of him. He was an amazing person. Arliss has made Disraeli, the statesman, vivid and appealing.

Good taste and general excellence mark this apex picture which should be commercially successful. It deserves to be. *Land*

EVIDENCE

(ALL DIALOG)

Warner Bros. production and release. Starring Pauline Frederick. Directed by John G. Adolfi from stage play, "Divorce Evidence," by J. Du Rocher MacPherson. Screen adaptation and dialog by J. Grubb Alexander. At Mark Strand, New York, Oct. 4. Running time, 79 minutes.

Myra Stanhope	Pauline Frederick
Cyril Wymborne	William Courtenay
Harold Courtenay	Conway Tearle
Norman Pollock	Lowell Sherman
Harbison	Alec B. Francis
Kenyon Wymborne	Freddie Burke Frederick
Mrs. Debenham	Madeline Seymour
Peabody	Ivan Simpson
Native Girl	Myrna Loy
Innkeeper	Lionel Belmore

The sure fire "mother" motif in "Evidence" plus its interpretation by Pauline Frederick and a wholesome supporting cast, cannot miss bringing this one into the money getting class.

Story and direction receives more than usual attention and care, with John Adolfi turning out a fine all-around job in coursing the action, continuity and pace of the story. Warners are understood to have considered tagging this in the special class before eventually deciding to let it go as a programmer. Decision appears for the better. The multitude of picture goers and a good many Frederick fans may have hesitated to pull the purse strings for $2, but will certainly go for this at pop scale. And it's not a special anyway, unless for Miss Frederick, who again demonstrates a tear jerking mother part to its fullest extent, getting some superb emotional acting out of it without becoming balmy or maudlin. Which is another reason why "Evidence" is as convincing as it is.

Consistency of the cast, with but one minor exception, enters as an important factor in building and holding several tightly strung high spots. Seems too bad to put a 20-year-old head on a six-year-old's shoulders. That's just what they did with young Freddie Frederick (not Miss Frederick's son), a cute and promising kid, but extremely mechanical in this picture. They put words in the youngster's mouth that would do credit to a divinity student, at the same time taking away from him all those juvenile attributes the average audience will be disappointed in not finding.

A vivid and human problem is treated here with becoming restraint, and blazing expletives, touching the heart strings all the time. A faithful wife and devoted mother stands unjustly convicted of an indiscretion on circumstantial evidence brought about by a jealousy-crazed rejected suitor. There is a splendid court scene where Miss Frederick rises to heights in renouncing her rights as wife and mother, finding herself the victim of circumstances with no one to believe her. She is forced to give up her child to the father, turning to an emblem of justice in the courtroom and laughing hysterically.

The action jumps six years. Child has been brought up with no knowledge of his mother and the father is contemplating marriage again. A chance meeting in the park brings mother and child together. She comes to see him at home and is discovered by the husband who turns a deaf ear to her pleas and sends her away. The child follows his mother, leaving a suspicion of having been kidnapped. A friend of the family, secretly in love with the woman, remonstrates with the husband and breaks off their friendship. By a twist of conscience the rejector suitor appears on the scene with a signed confession absolving the woman, but will not relinquish it unless she agrees to his bargain. It a fit of remorse and illness he chokes on a glass of liquor and dies just as the vindictive husband and loyal friend arrive.

There is a touching tete-a-tete between the woman and man who fears to speak of his love for her, bowing out gracefully when he understands her unchanged feeling for her husband. With the evidence of her innocence in hand she confronts the man who made her suffer, who asks for and is granted forgiveness with the bond of their child linking them.

William Courtenay expresses the husband with a fine touch, always convincing and never theatrical. An outstanding bit is that of Lowell Sherman on the other end of the triangle. Sherman has two punch spots in the picture at the start and close, bringing both together in a splendid performance. Comparatively and though handling a role of proportionate unimportance, Conway Tearle carries a sympathetic strain, while giving a bang-up account of himself in what little he does. Tearle, long a silent screen luminary, should find a place in the talkers. His previous stage background gives him a distinguished touch.

"Evidence" is a personal triumph for Miss Frederick, but just as much a box office one for its producers.

GIRL IN THE SHOW

(ALL DIALOG)

Metro production and release. **Based on** play by John Kenyon Nicholson and John Golden, "Eva the Fifth." Directed by Edgar Selwyn. Photographed by Arthur Reed. **Featuring** Bessie Love and Raymond Hackett. Sounded by Western Electric. At Loew's Metropolitan, Brooklyn, Oct. 5. Running time, 74 minutes.

Somebody done our little Bessie Love dirt. Because this filmfoto is just bad. Even the Brooklynites who saw this thing on this day could be heard calling the picture names right in the theatre. Believe it, all right, all right, it's sad, when they get together a cast that includes besides Bessie Love, such players as Jed Prouty, Ford Sterling, Mary Doran, Edward Nugent, Lucy Beaumont and several others, and then turns out a piece of boloney.

Of course there was Raymond Hackett, too. But he didn't help the picture much. He's still Mary Duganning. This player, unless he is tipped off, bids fair to become a photomaton. He's still the champion high school orator whose voice catches a sob and lumps up on the right note whenever the director swings his baton. He ought to forget that he ever played a lawyer role.

Just one more crack. The direction was terrible, that is judging from the finished stuff. And the story wasn't so hot either.

It's all about an Uncle Tom's Cabin troupe managed by Ford Sterling. Bessie Love is the Eva character. Hackett does Legree. Jed Prouty is a big undertaker and furniture man in a small Kansas town and the other roles don't matter.

The gang gets stranded when a washout that isn't filmed happens and Sterling trips off alone. Prouty by this time has somersaulted for Bessie. He offers to be chained and balled if Bessie will quit the trouping. Being an honest-to-goodness show girl, Bessie decides to take the vows with Prouty just to save the gang from hunger and provide schooling for her little sister, Oriole, who is traveling with her.

But—a guy in the troupe, played by Hackett, has Bessie's heart and she his'n. So there come some knots in the situation.

Just as the Western Electric is about to record the wedding chimes, the hero, Hackett, crashes with the announcement that the gang can act again. And—well, it's tradition, ain't it, that an actor would rather act than eat? So the nuptials are called no contest and the show goes on that nite—but not with Bessie. It is little sister, Oriole, who plays Little Eva.

This makes Bessie mad, you can guess. Here four of her ancestors have been Little Evas and now she's gotta give up the role. So she feeds her little sister some candy. This makes the kid sick to her tummy and she falls down in the middle of her part. So Bessie goes on and knocks 'em dead—all for pride and love. And Prouty steps out of the picture in favor of Hackett.

THE WEAVERS

(GERMAN-MADE)

(Silent)

Produced independently by Friedrich Zelnick, who also directed it, in Germany. Independent release here. Based on drama of same title by Gerhart Hauptmann. At 55th St. Playhouse beginning Oct. 5. Running time, about 80 minutes.
Dreissiger.....................Paul Wegener
Jager.......................Wilhelm Dieterle
Mrs. Dreissiger...........Valeska Stock
Baumert.....................Herman Picha
Emma Baumert.......Hertha von Walther
Old Hilfe...............Arthur Kraussneck
Louise Hilfe...............Dagney Servaes
Militia Captain.............W. Krussinski

Except for beautiful framing of some of its loom and street sequences, "The Weaver" has little more to recommend it than the host of specials imported for the exclusive benefit of sure-seaters which hardly return the ocean freight charges.

And the pseudo-intellectual so well known to arty cashiers will find this capitalist versus worker story far too ancient for modern entertainment. It's all about German handworkers opposed to machinery and the thing is largely an overworking of closeups, even of hands and feet, while the remainder concentrates on a milling crowd brandishing sticks in the manner of many similar importations.

There is nothing gripping in the entire footage and very little that is impressively dramatic. The biggest sequence is when the mob encounters the militia on a main thoroughfare with a great crucifix only between the antagonists. The soldiers fire upon the crowd and the cross, but after a few stones are exchanged for volleys the crowd disperses and machinery prevails.

Through the production the rioters are permitted to pause in their seemingly endless and victorious rush for the introduction of a character work. This commences when Dressiger, the mill owner, played by Paul Wegener, announces that new mechanisms are perfected and handworkers will have to cut their rate. At that time Jager, the worker, essayed by Wilhelm Dieterle, returns from the army and immediately sets himself at the head of the mob. Thereafter it is a brandishing of sticks, with Dressiger calmly smoking his pipe until forced to evacuate with his family. In this role Wegener has little more to do than to look imperious and open and unlock a money box.

The Jager Dieterle portrays is principally a hymn leader submitting to closeups of his mouth, open or closed for ironic effect.

Of all the weavers, the only one who remains at his loom is Old Hilfe. This worker quotes the Lord as saying ".Vengeance is mine" and adheres to it and his position by a window until he is shot. Hilfe

is played by Arthur Kraussneck in a way that would have registered strongly. Good effect was injured when direction permitted the mob to ramble into the room and shatter the trend of thought. *Waly.*

They Had to See Paris

(ALL DIALOG)

Fox production and release. Starring Will Rogers; directed by Frank Borzage. Adapted from the novel by Homer Croy, with dialog by Owen Davis. At the Roxy, New York, week Oct. 11. Running time, 95 mins.
Pike Peters...................Will Rogers
Mrs. Peters, wife..............Irene Rich
Opal Peters, daughter.Marguerite Churchill
Ross Peters, son..........Owen Davis, Jr.
Claudine.........................Fifi Dorsay
Marquis De Brissac.......Ivan Lebedeff
Marquise De Brissac......Marcelle Corday
Grand Duke Makiall........Theodore Lodi
Clark McCurdy.................Rex Bell
Fleurie...................Christiane Yves
Ed Eggers..................Edgar Kennedy
Tupper.........................Bob Kerr
Miss Mason.................Marcia Manon
Valet.........................Andre Cheron
Prince Ordinsky...............Gregory Gay

Will Rogers in pictures without dialog was as Senator Borah with his tongue cut out. Speaking in "They Had to See Paris," he is completely the man who has made a fortune out of being strictly and ridiculously American. His first talking picture is a certain moneymaker, especially for the great southwest territory, where Rogers and fundamentalism and the "Saturday Evening Post" walk hand in hand. And Rogers gets all the laughs.

Picture has two locales—Claremore, Okla., and Paris, France. When Rogers' land in Oklahoma spouts oil, his wife persuades him to take the family to Paris. Thus results the venerable hoke mine of a simple hick in a classy setting. It was the same idea in Rogers' first feature, "Texas Steer," but that was silent and so was Rogers.

In Claremore the Peters family was content before oil spouted. Rogers had his garage, wife's ambitions were pretty well buried and the son and daughter were easing along to an eventual decent small-town funeral.

Then oil and the trip to Paris. Mrs. Peters buys a chateau and divides her time between trying to get the daughter married to a title and instilling some class in the old man. For Peters it's one long ordeal.

Hoke scenes galore, and all darbs.

A riot of laughs when Rogers looks over his new chateau for the first time. Stands in the center of the massive layout and bellows train calls. In his bedroom he comments it's a drive and two niblick shots from the door to the bed.

More sure laughs whenever Rogers tackles French. His little cafe girl friend is the teacher. She also straights for him in the necking scene, trying to make him, but just making him perspire.

Three singing bits, with Rogers doing a strained barber shop tenor for a gag. Fifi Dorsay, the French kid, does the other two. She's a snappy brunet, with a wealth of personality and a catchy French accent.

Irene Rich as the wife handles a slightly unfavorable part well, impressing most in her transition from an Oklahoma wife to a Parisian chump. Owen Davis, Jr., is the Peters boy. Some tendency to recite lines, but good appearance. Daughter is Marguerite Churchill, who sounds well and looks fair. Others are character types and all good performers.

Loose moments will be eliminated when the 95-minute running time is cut. Direction by Borzage was wise, with nothing spared in the interests of hoke. Photography and recording good.

All Paris shots probably library. Two shots showing the characters on the streets were faked. *Bang.*

VENUS

(FRENCH MADE)

(Silent)

United Artists production and release. Produced in France by Louis Mercanton.

Constance Talmadge starred. Louis Mercanton director. From novel by Jean Vignaud. At Little Carnegie, New York, week Oct. 12. Running time, 80 minutes.
Princesse Beatrice Doriani.............
.......................Constance Talmadge
De Valroy..................Andre Roanne
Capt. Franqueville..........Jean Murat
Zarkis..................Max Maxudian
Captain of "Venus"........Baron Fils
L'Enfant..................Jean Mercanton

Not so hot, but if exploited properly might build up decent business. Title and angle of scenes, with Constance Talmadge supposed to be shot in the nude, lend to campaign and billing that might attract.

A few years ago Miss Talmadge made a picture called "Venus in Venice." Title must have done so well the star wanted it for this picture, where it fits. Part of the plot revolves around the suppression of report she entertained friends on a yachting party off Cyprus by doing a Venus in the moonlight.

The 80 minutes, on the whole, boring, with little genuine action and practically no comedy to lift the picture out of the second or third-rate class. Precisely two laughs in the eight reels, and these aren't noticeable.

In the emotional scenes Miss Talmadge again proves she is not an emotional actress, but in "Venus" she has a bad sort of role. It is neither altogether sympathetic nor convincing.

Opening plants the impression she is haughty and not at all a good fellow as the owner of a fleet of ships. After about the first reel she tries to be the opposite to whip in some love interest. The captain she dismissed because she killed a man to defend her name, played well by Jean Murat, is a far more convincing character.

Direction by Louis Mercanton is far better than by the average Frenchman. Injection of more comedy would have been a wise move. Photography o. k. and titles average.

No sound to "Venus" as shown here (artie), but understood it will be released by U. A. as synchronized product.

HOLD YOUR MAN

(ALL DIALOG)

Universal production and release. Directed by Emmett Flynn from story by Maxine Alton. In cast: Laura La Plante, Scott Kolk, Eugene Bordon, Mildred Van Dorn. At Colony, New York, week Oct. 12. Running time, 60 minutes.

"Hold Your Man" is devoid of day run stuff, let alone ingredients that would hold it up for a week. It's a little slower than what is known as one of those things.

Trite domestic stuff of the business hubby and the artistically inclined wife. Stuff that's been done countless times, with a little action to divert. The Universal version also contributes dialog as antiquated and as unoriginal as the threadbare theme.

Cut to a two-reeler, at least there would be a suggestion of action, although it hasn't enough real body for that length.

Conversation, coffee, etc., take a turn for a Parisian set when Laura La Plante as the wife decides to go abroad for art's sake and because of hubby's indifference. The expected meeting of a model believed to be a member of royalty and revealed as a crook occurs in a single sequence. After that the husband, played dead-pan by Scott Kolk, comes over with the wife's rival, essayed by Mildred Van Dorn. Some more coffee and the wife turning tables on the friend's scheme to wean husband away hold interest for a few feet.

One incident which gets a gasp from the women and an open eye from the men (only rise in the entire production) occurs in a bedroom scene. Miss La Plante, in tight satin pajamas, uses a most vigorous instrument before retiring. She backs into it, turns on the current, and has a certain part of her anatomy shaken in a shameful but exhilarating manner. In vaudeville they'd probably call this a pratt reducer, but, whatever it is, there's not much chance of censors elsewhere okaying it for such public demonstration. *Waly.*

THE UNHOLY NIGHT

(ALL DIALOG)

Metro-Goldwyn-Mayer production and release. Directed by Lionel Barrymore. Story by Ben Hecht with adaptation by Dorothy Farnum. Ira Morgan, cameraman. Western Electric recording. At Capitol, New York, week Oct. 11. Running time, 92 minutes.

Dr. Ballou....................Ernest Torrence
Lord Montague....................Roland Young
Lady Erfra....................Dorothy Sebastian
Lady Vi....................Natalie Moorhead
Butler....................Sydney Jarvis
Maid....................Polly Moran
Orderly....................George Cooper
Mystic.................... Sojin
Abdoul....................Boris Karloff
Sir James Rumsey....................Claude Fleming
Inspector Lewis....................Clarence Geldert
Major Mallory....................John Miljan
Col. Davidson....................Richard Tucker
Capt. Dorchester....................John Loder
Lieut. Williams....................Philip Strange
Lieut. Savor....................John Roche
Major Ebdicott....................Lionel Belmore
Capt. Bradley....................Gerald Barry
Maj. McDougal....................Robert Travers

A hopelessly involved script handled by Lionel Barrymore in a way that would discredit a quickie director. Worse than the worst would-be thrill meller staged on Broadway and impressing as a pointless souffle burlesquing them all. More bell ringing in this than when the talkers were feeling their oats. And the title probably hoped to capitalize on a similar one given a successful Chaney picture. That's all there is about "The Unholy Night." It's an all-talker and a 100% lemon.

The theme suggests a re-write of the vengeance angle in "Dr. Fu Manchu." Some of the interiors, especially the English house sets, are identical with those in the Paramount picture.

Where Fu murdered one by one the officers in a British company which wronged him during a Chinese rebellion until Scotland Yard mustered the survivors in an English home and kept them there until they got the story out of a woman, so it goes with "The Unholy Night."

It takes nearly two hours for the Hecht version to cover a lot of aimless conversation, running around, and performances like a bunch of college amateurs, before the whirligig of complications and drivel are all contradicted in a few long winded speeches by Dr. Ballou and Sir Rumsey of Scotland Yard. Reaction is completely negative because the explanations, rapidly recited, only add to the befuddlement of an audience and its desire to get the fresh air.

This M-G-M thing gets under way in a London fog with members of a company being strangled off until but 10 are left. Lord Montague, played by Roland Young, sells Scotland Yard on the idea of keeping them pent up in his house until the sun comes out.

Something about a disgraced officer dying a billionaire and leaving his dough for the rest of the army to battle over is worked in as the first clue. Then a girl, Lady Erfra, played by Dorothy Sebastian, suddenly weeps into the house. And about that time the scar-faced Major Mallory (John Miljan) is found, choked in another room.

That night the corpse comes to life and is shown strangling all of his brother officers. Close-ups of the dead men here provide an Eden Musee touch.

At this point, Barrymore apparently decided it was time to clean up. So Sojin, in a bit part, calls a seance. The "dead men" all parade in and the girl pulls the revelation. She then bumps off Major Mallory and herself.

The windup is that they are the only two actually dead. When or when not to be alive is all so much blotto by this time. *Waly.*

THE DEVIL'S PIT

(NEW ZEALAND MADE)

(Silent)

Produced by a foreign company in New Zealand with all-native cast. Released here through Universal. Directed by Lew Collins. Titles by Hugh Hoffman. At Fifth Ave. Playhouse, New York, week Oct. 12. Running time, 60 minutes.

Hip wigglers and spear wavers with the men flabbier breasted than the women, dominate this. Called "The Devil's Pit," it is like any other picture having to do with natives, except that the activity does, to a greater extent than in most importations, help authenticate subtitling. Still, peculiarly fit for the sure-seaters, where it will rate average.

Although claimed to have been shot in New Zealand, the exteriors in the release could have been obtained within a few miles from Hollywood. This, unless the volcano wasn't prop. Looked more artificial when it commenced drooling.

The tribesmen did their best acting in a jousting contest. But the performance was as mechanical as the movements in most of the native dances, which majored in the reelage.

According to the title writer the action had to do with two tribes. In these were featured a bad prince and a good prince—and a princess.

In the good or bad old way the bad prince won the princess by double-crossing the good prince in an athletic contest to the altar. And just as conventionally did the princess break her taboo to meet the good prince in a cave until the prospective groom trailed her one night and was precipitated into the volcano for his zeal.

After that came war, separation and a hot mud bath from the angry mountain. When the sun came up the good prince had to call only twice. Then the princess danced from a tree. *Waly.*

Madonna of Sleeping Cars

(RUSSIAN MADE)

(Silent)

Produced abroad by Natan Productions and released in this country by Little Playhouse Film Co. Adapted from novel of same name by Maurice Dekobra. Scenario and direction by Maurice Gleize. Photography by Raymond Angel. Scenic designs by Eugene Carre. All-foreign cast headed by Claude France, Olaf Fjord, Boris De Fast and Mary Serte. At Cameo, New York, for week Oct. 12. Running time, 77 mins.

Most all pictures from Europe are unable to make the grade here. This one is no exception. Even for the arties the picture is a dud, incapable of holding the interest of the sure-seater patrons who go for most anything.

The sordid side of "Madonna of the Sleeping Cars," with prison scenes paralleling those Sovkino likes to do when making pictures of the old Russian regime and its cruelty and intrigue, is hardly the sort of realism that would put this importation over. But the shooting of a woman (by a man) and the scenes on the opening of the fair heroine in her gilded bathroom might get a ripple out of artie-lovers.

Censors, who have stripped American films now and then of bathroom stuff have allowed a couple of shots to get past here that would indicate even they are getting a little more broadminded with the times. In one shot Claude France as Lady Diana Wyndham is served up "au naturel" with only a scrim drop between her and the camera.

She is a wealthy widow who rounds up as her secretary a Prince. He takes the job for the adventure of it and gets aplenty, although no one ever knows what half of the action in the picture is all about. Sequences are strung together without obvious relationship, and the audience must sit to the end without finding out what the incidents covered were all about.

The prince gets on a train for Stamboul apparently to look into plans to retrieve a bunch of oil wells in Russia and lands in a prison. A somebody or other, representing some country (possibly Russia from appearances) is to marry Lady Diana as a part of the oil well deal, and the prince languishes in jail, escaping with the warden, who has a scrap with Mary Serte, also something or other in an intrigue.

Lady Diana moves all over Europe and finally ends in Scotland, in luxury, though supposed to be broke.

One of the worst set of titles ever written on this weakling, making it weaker.

"Madonna of Sleeping Cars" as a novel has been translated into 16 languages. It gets its name from the fact the heroine loves to travel a lot. Only the final shot in the picture shows her on a train but the action moves all around—without much direction.

SOUL OF FRANCE

("La Grande Epreuve")

(FRENCH MADE)

(Silent)

Produced by Jacques Haik. Released by Paramount. Story by G. Le Feure. Directed by A. Dugas and A. Ryder. Cast includes Mme. Jalabert, M. Desjardins, M. Jean Murat and M. Michel Verly. At Film Guild, New York, Oct. 12. Running time, 78 minutes.

France rates a Croix de Guerre and all the palms for this one. And it smacks all over like some film fever has taken root in the land of the lily. Pictorially, photographically, and even from the acting standpoint, this picture stands a couple of heads at least above the stuff that has been shipped over here from Over There in recent months.

But—the picture ain't got merchandise value as entertainment. It's too much war and told too staccato, with the love theme and the theatre stuff getting the old back seat while this film rides thru the projector.

Of course, the battle shots are keen. They ought to be, for they were taken from actual war office film. And in the try to preach the foolishness of powder and gun the directors forgot the flavor of romance, without which the film fan can't exist.

Besides, the title is a misnomer. Very little of the spiritual side of French peasantry is pictured. It's all realistic and practical. And with nearly a half generation of almost continuous war pictures it'll be a tough job to coax customers thru the turnstiles for a proposition like this picture.

It has some value as propaganda, and, in fact, some of the celluloid space toward the finish is deliberately given over to peace argument titles, and as an educational item the film could be used advantageously if the titles can be dressed up to fit the editorial viewpoint.

Acting in the film is rich in restraint, and the keenest piece of emoting is done at the very close by the two old characters in the picture, a man and woman. The man who plays the lead rates high for looks and ought to be a good bet for American producers.

The story concerns a peasant family of two old folks and three sons. One of the boys was self-exiled from home and country because of an army mixup. Another is turned out an officer at the French West Point, St. Cyr, when July, 1914, rolls around. While the old man is a Franco-Prussian war veteran of '71.

The deserter rejoins the army under an alias. He proves a hero and wins the orphan aristocrat of his home village for a sweetheart, after his officer-brother dies from war wounds, and everything ends as nearly completely happy for the surviving bunch as the war permitted.

SHIP OF LOST MEN

(GERMAN MADE)

(Silent)

Berlin, Oct. 3.

"The Ship of Lost Men" (Max Glas), Premiere Ufa Pavilion. Lot of money and effort spent on this first Maurice Tourneur production, but all thrown away on a futile scenario, of which Tourneur admits the authorship.

Action is laid on a smuggling ship on which a young millionaire has landed by mistake in trying to help a wounded sailor.

The captain as an exaggerated "sea wolf" and the crew are the usual collection of lecherous menaces.

A young heiress who is making an ocean flight is forced to land near the ship and is taken on board by the young millionaire unbeknownst to the crew of the ship—who are all looking over the other side. The bad boys almost get her, but signalling with a pocket light brings a ship to their rescue.

Fritz Kortner mugs through as the captain without ever getting a chance to do anything out of the ordinary. Marlene Dietrich is an attractive heroine. Sokoloff has moments of comedy as a cook.

But outside of the picturesque quality of his photography, Tourneur delivers nothing to justify his international reputation. *Trask.*

MIDNIGHT DADDIES

(ALL DIALOG)

Mack Sennett production, released by World Wide. Directed by Mack Sennett. Story by John A. Waldron. RCA Photophone sound. Harry Gribbon, Andy Clyde and Alma Bennett, featured. Addie McPahil, Rosemary Theby, Vernon Dent and Catherine Ward in support. At Loew's New York, one day, Oct. 8, one-half double bill. Running time, 58 minutes.

In spite of some second-rate vaudeville gags and padding in some of the scenes to drag this semi-slapstick comedy into feature length, the picture isn't bad entertainment. Hinterland should go for the situations the master of slapstick acquired for his two leading comics, Harry Gribbon and Andy Clyde.

Sennett allows both every opportunity to pull for laughs, but sometimes they overdo it a trifle. Approximately 90% of the laughs issue from the actions and dialog of this comical pair as they get themselves into a number of tight squeezes.

Opening shots develop the necessity for an Iowa boy, making good in the modiste business, to dig up capital for his shop. His sudden meeting with a hick cousin from the home town, who has retired, starts the farce scenes, with the old bucolic looking over the models and being entertained at a cabaret with them.

Becoming involved in trouble with his wife, who frames him and his shop-owner cousin, the Iowa playboy determines to commit suicide.

Dialog is on a par with that found in two-reel shorts, which this might have been. Scenes in the modiste shop are so padded out that the picture begins to look like a fashion show.

Photography often a little dull but recording satisfactory.

A better cutting job would have

improved this talker, with the sequences in the women's shop and at the dinner following good spots to have done a little of the pruning.

Grinds ought to do all right with Sennett's first talking feature, with the smaller towns possibly getting a bigger kick out of it than cities.

THE SADDLE KING

(SILENT)

Independent production. Starring Cliff Tex Lyon. Distributed by Anchor. Directed by Frank Wilson from Ben Cohen's story. Cast: Al Ferguson, Neva Gerber and Glenn Cook. On double feature bill at Columbus, one day, Oct. 14. Running time, 60 minutes.

One of those machine-made westerns that finally decides to have vengeance for the motive. Not bad for the 10-centers.

Cliff Lyon has the regular Killarney map and dimples. Spends his time hunting the menace, Al Ferguson, and then beating him until the whole cow country turns out to hold him back.

Neva Gerber is resurrected to play the innocent girl burden with child by oily Al. She spills the soup about the sheriff's doctor-brother being bumped off by the heavy and that's all Cliff needs.

Not so much eye-tiring riding in this one and plenty of attention paid to plot.

Lyon can make money on stuff of this kind. His type of fan won't mind. *Waly.*

Thundering Thompson

(SILENT)

Produced by Morris R. Schlank; released by Anchor Film. Story by Robert Dillon. Photography by Robert Cline. Directed by B. Frank Wilson. Featuring Cheyenne Bill. At Columbus, New York, one day, Oct. 8. Running time, 58 minutes.

Genuine Western becoz the titles tell the story and the action is incidental. But it's good as these open air panckers go, much better than the usual stuff as most of the hokum is in the titles.

It's a story about an argument between a homeless sheep herder and his daughter, and a bunch of hay and iron saddle polishers.

But just in the nick of time a colored cowboy lopes over to Cheyenne and settles everything. That's a jump like the cutting.

WELCOME DANGER

(ALL DIALOG)

Harold Lloyd production, released by Paramount. Directed by Clyde Bruckman. Dialog by Paul Gerard Smith. Harold Lloyd star. Barbara Kent featured. Story by Felix Adler, Lex Neal and Clyde Bruckman. John L. Murphy production supervisor. Walter Lunden and Henry L. Kohner, photography. Cecil Bardwell and Lodge Cunningham, sound technicans. Western Electric recording. Running time, 112 minutes. At Rivoli, Oct. 19, pop prices, for grind run.

Harold Bledsoe	Harold Lloyd
Billie Lee	Barbara Kent
Buddy Lee	Douglas Haid
Patrick Clancey	Noah Young
John Thorne	Charles Middleton
Captain Walton	William Walling
Dr. Chang Gow	Jimmy Wang

Harold Lloyd long held out against talkers, but if there is any doubt in the minds of exhibs that his first isn't a good Lloyd picture it should be dispelled immediately. Even talkers haven't stopped the begoggled comedian from digging up a lot of new gags and working up situations for all they can stand. Some of the sequences could have borne more than they show, with cutting evidently having dropped some to go on to the next even if gags had to go out with it.

Picture runs 112 minutes but doesn't seem half that long, this in itself being pretty strong proof it has what a Lloyd comedy is expected to have. As in "Speedy," Lloyd's last silent, a lot of new twists and bits have been woven into the story picked to introduce the star's tongue and a lot of them high-powered laughs.

Lloyd's voice is sometimes prone to weakness and even a consciousness of culture, but luckily for Lloyd and his customers this is mainly in the calmer scenes. When the big comedy sequences begin to build up and he goes hectic with his pantomime and slapstick his voice arises to the occasion and the audience will be likely to forget or overcome any disappointment over it in other spots.

Laughs are well distributed and start where they should, at beginning of picture, when Lloyd, getting off at a way station on the trail to California, allows the train to pull out without him. Stumbling upon the love interest (Barbara Kent) and her busted-down Ford, he mistakes her for a boy and does things he shouldn't to build up the comedy interest.

Later in 'Frisco, where the botany student is to join the police department, the picture gathers more laughs. Scenes having to do here with his going nuts about fingerprinting and those in which he rounds up "The Dragon," Chinese underworld character, packing the biggest punch.

Girl manages to stay in picture with doctor, treating her young brother, kidnapped by "The Dragon" and discovered by devious and divers ways by the lady-fingered hero.

Much of the comedy is derived from the cops thinking Lloyd is a loon and from the adventures he and Patrolman Clancey, a good type played well by Noah Young, have in the underground hangout of the insidious "Dragon." A lot of the old battling stuff of slapstick days is done over with a new and fresh twist.

It is the new touches and cleverness of direction and execution, together with the original material in "Welcome Danger" that makes it a worthwhile comedy talker.

Recording is generally satisfactory, and Miss Kent is an attractive opposite to Lloyd. She photographs nicely and speaks distinctly.

Occasionally the photography isn't as good as might have been desired, but fault not serious. In the sequence in the underworld labyrinth the screen is entirely white in several spots to denote darkness, with characters still talking. This, of course, is as intended, but if a black shot could have been spliced in—blacker at least than the talker has—it would have been far more effective.

Dialog by Paul Gerard Smith not unusual though clever in spots, with gag lines here and there greatly aiding Lloyd.

There should be a big demand for this first talker from the boy with the spectacles in city and hinterland. It may not be quite as funny as "Speedy," but it is not far from it. Exploitation possibilities are as big.

MOST IMMORAL LADY

(ALL DIALOG)

First National production and release. Directed by John Griffith Wray, based on the play of same title by Townsend Martin. At Hippodrome, New York, week Oct. 19. Running time, 77 minutes.

Laura Sargeant	Leatrice Joy
Tony Williams	Walter Pidgeon
Humphrey Sargeant	Sydney Blackmer
John Williams	Montagu Love
Joan Porter	Josephine Dunn
Gradford-Fish	Robert Edeson
Pedro	Donald Reed
Natalie Davis	Florence Oakley
Hoskins	Wilson Benge

Except for a few spots the picture version of "A Most Immoral Lady" is a series of entrances and exits, endless conversations, and repititious close-ups of Leatrice Joy, who seems to sing the theme song every time the director feared the action was gasping. As the result Miss Joy, who gives as good a performance as possible, has to tax the audience with a voice that would pass as sweet parlor if heard once or twice in any production. Feature is made slower by an artificial and starchy atmosphere throughout.

Following the lines of the play, the story attempts to center on a wife who let her husband use her as bait in a campaign to blackmail wealthy men friends. The film script is long in divulging this, considerable footage being wasted in what the audience considers a lot of palaver before vagueness clears.

In Tony Williams, essayed by Walter Pidgeon with a sincerity that would be appreciated in a well-knit production, the wife, Laura Sargeant, meets her match. By that time John Williams, Tony's uncle, has already paid hush money to Humphrey Sargeant and brings about the expose when he learns of Tony's activities. Sargeant and Williams are done by Sydney Blackmer and Montague Love in a routine way.

A Parisian night club set brings Tony and Laura together after Tony has married the blond Joan Porter, played by Josephine Dunn, and has brought her overseas for a divorce; also, following Laura's decree and her song bird job in the club. *Waly.*

SAILORS' HOLIDAY

(ALL DIALOG)

Pathe production and release. Directed by Fred Newmeyer from story by Joseph Franklin Poland. Arthur Miller, cameraman. RCA Photophone sounder. In cast: Allan Hale, Sally Eilers, George Cooper, Mary Carr, Charles Clary. At Colony, New York, week Oct. 19. Running time, 58 minutes.

Pathe is turning out some excellent program productions, and this is another.

Fred Newmeyer, Harold Lloyd's old director, clearly shows his hand in the comedy touches and gags which infest "Sailors' Holiday." The picture, however, isn't just a comedy. It's got a suspense that ever mounts. Laughs are crisp, but efforts to obtain them are never apparent. The theme is the thing that counts.

Starting on board a battleship with the captain summoning the boys aft. Allan Hale and George Cooper are immediately identified as the mischievous gobs who are going to cause the trouble that follows. These and a tough bosun's mate, the Nemesis of the two, scurry through a Pacific amusement park—fights and mix-ups from the time the boys are granted shore leave until they wind up for home cookin' in Mary Carr's establishment.

The story thread that abets the fast tempo is that of a girl, played by Sally Eilers, questioning gobs in an effort to locate her missing brother, Ethelbert. Zest is added this angle by a professional crier pulling the same gag, and the boys, after a tip-off, figuring Sally is another phoney.

Hale carries a parrot throughout, which helps situations. The bird is responsible for a rumpus in a restaurant which causes Sally to be taken for a pickpocket, although the two boys have pulled the pinch, innocently, on the bosun as one of their countless tricks in eluding him.

Taxi is also worked to advantage. Plenty of laughs in its cruising around for Hale and Eilers, while Cooper is watching the meter with no dough in his pocket.

Tough bosun in end is disclosed as the missing brother, so nothing but more laughs gets on the navy docket. *Waly.*

The Return of SHERLOCK HOLMES

(ALL DIALOG)

Paramount production and release. Directed by Basil Deane. Based on the adaptation of two Conan Doyle stories by Deane and Garrett Fort. Clive Brook featured. William Steiner, cameraman. In cast: H. Reeves-Smith, Betty Lawford, Donald Crisp, Harry T. Morey, Arthur Mack, Hubert Bruce. Western Electric recording. At Paramount, New York, week Oct. 18. Running time, 71 minutes.

Doyle readers will find Paramount's Sherlock Holmes too youthful to recite antiquated lines. They may note that detective methods convincing adolescent minds in type are unwound unconvincingly in film. Matter of factness, over-assurance and the like of such ilk make the picture version of "The Return of Sherlock Holmes" a guarantee-to-solve proposition after the first 50 feet. After that it takes on a strictly recitational perspective. But, with the title and some of the situations, it will probably pull fairly well in the key centers, although in actual merit it rates little more than program average.

Clive Brook gives a smooth performance. But the dialog he is forced to elocute obviously intended for an older man and therefore makes this Sherlock register as a decidedly precocious individual. The flat, almost embarrassed execution of H. Reeves-Smith as Dr. Watson at times almost makes the great dick ridiculous. Too many "marvelouses" and "elementaries." And Doc Watson's enforced stupidity is too apparent.

The best casting is that of Donald Crisp as Dr. Moran, poison specialist of the insidious inventor and classical criminal, Moriarty. The role is suited for Crisp. He injects into it a personality far more holding, when the two appear in the various sequences, than that of Brook's.

Harry T. Morey is revived for Moriarty. Faltering in considerable of his dialog mars Morey's performance for the critical. Physically, Morey is excellent.

As the daughter of a retired captain in league with Moriarty until he repents, when he is bumped off by a poisoned cigaret case and the mystery gets under way, Betty Lawford is negative. Strictly a light type with no exhibition of the dramatic prowess which her part demands, this little girl is better for another collegian series.

Practically all of the action takes place aboard ship. A few exteriors of ocean wake and Par's Hollywood liner set gives way to interiors.

Sherlock does some quick changes. First as a member of the orchestra whose tricks for the passengers get back from Moran the confession of the murdered man. Then as a cabin boy, whose cleverness in painting phosphorus on the soles of Moran's shoes leads the way to Moriarty's ship camp and the place where the dead man's son is held captive.

When Sherlock and Moriarty finally get together over a dinner table some adroit conversation transpires. Sherlock knows all about the cigaret case trick but he shams illness to get the criminal on record over a dictaphone extending into the captain's cabin.

Before the bad birds are thrown into the irons the high class criminal conventionally thwarts justice by scratching himself with the poison needle. The wise Sherlock in discussing elementary things at the finale exhibits a steel thumb cover to the startled Watson. The dope, thus, just didn't take with him. *Waly.*

MARIANNE

(All Talking)

M-G-M (Cosmopolitan) production and release. Starring Marion Davies. Directed by Robert Z. Leonard. Story by Dale Van Enery, with dialog by Lawrence Stallings. Songs by Turk and Ahlert. Cameraman, Oliver Marsh. At Capitol, New York, week Oct. 18. Running time, 84 mins.

Marion Davies, Cliff Edwards, Lawrence Grant, Benny Rubin, Scott Kolk, George Baxter.

War yarn with French setting and parley-vous songs, strongly suggestive of "Buddies." It's musical comedy with an ingenue, but no chorus nor dancing. Knit together well and holding much laugh material, the result is a pleasing entertainment okay for general exhibition.

"Marianne" survived six weeks at $1.50 in a Los Angeles legit house. That means very little, as business in the latter weeks hung around $5,000, and in no event can it be taken seriously as a picture rating above regulation exploitation.

There are awkward moments in "Marianne," but by and large Robert Z. Leonard has welded the seams of a commonplace, gagged-up story with commendable neatness. It moves and it has interest if no great persuasiveness.

For its main strength "Marianne" relies upon singing specialties and the agreeable and lilting tunes provided by Turk and Ahlert. Of plot there is but a faint trace. Marianne loves and is loved by an American doughboy, but is betrothed to a French soldier, now blind. For the clinch the French boy enters the priesthood, making Marianne free to follow her Yankee to America for those wedding bells.

Marion Davies never forgets to impersonate someone. This time she mimics Maurice Chevalier and Sarah Bernhardt, both clever although not up to her Lillian Gish and Mae Murray classics. She speaks French with what strikes American ears as a fairly authentic pronunciation. And she handles her lines and herself with lots of poise and ability, again contrasting favorably with Marion Davies, the swell clothes mannikin of years ago. And also she overcomes her slight stutter for the screen's purpose.

Benny Rubin and Cliff Edwards are teamed for comedy, and remain genteel throughout by the new standards of measuring soldier humor since "Cock Eyed World."

Lawrence Gray is his usual serious-eyed, smiling self, bringing vast sincerity, a needed quality where horseplay is the main dish.

'Marianne" should please generally and possibly evoke sentimental response for anyone who remembers the late mess pleasantly. *Land.*

HOUSE OF SECRETS

(ALL DIALOG)

Batchellor Production, released through Chesterfield (independent). Edmund Lawrence, director. Sound system not credited. In cast: Joseph Stryker, Marcia Manning, F Verdi. At Times, New York, one day, Oct. 31. Running about 60 minutes.

This is one of the first 100% talkers indies producing for the dimers have turned out. When the recording is almost good, the lighting is terrible and the print rainy. The dialog is indie awful all the way.

To work in all the cowbells, shrieks, yowls, chink jargon, taxi horns—and other tinny sounds supposed to record well and reproduce better—the Batchellor crowd dusted out the Fort Lee emporium of a decade ago for a mystery thriller.

Even some of the colored gentlemen commingling the sweat of a day's trucking with odors characteristic of joints like the Times, indicated they couldn't comprehend what the theme was all about. But there is some gun waving, blackjacking, gas poisoning, treasure hunting—so the story didn't matter so much; that part where they could hear the dialog occasionally enlightening, but most of the time complicating the junkwagon full of mongrelized hoke of earlier theatre.

The more intelligent the mind, the greater the suffering "House of Secrets" inflicts, not only upon the performers, who wouldn't rate very high in a backwoods revival of Unk Tom's hut, but on the listeners too.

But bigger companies than this one have turned bad on attempts to screen mystery plays that dove none too late. And this one follows the routine of explanation in the last couple of reels in dialog.

The guy who apes Chaney and forgets to keep bent half of the time is a great scientist who murdered his housekeeper in the noble cause of experimentation. His pal, another doctor, got him out of a condemned cell with the aid of an English government official, and thus he was able to live on in the house that belonged to another.

The owner of the house is in love with the pal doc's daughter, so he keeps his American detective friend from calling Scotland Yard.

The real trouble is instigated by a Yankee criminal, who has half of a house map showing where gold is cached. He is so anxious to get its mate he stabs a few folk before apprehension. *Waly.*

DELIGHTFUL ROGUE

(ALL DIALOG)

RKO production and release. Featuring Rod La Rocque. Directed by Leslie Pearce and Lynn Shores. Recorded on RCA Photophone. At Loew's New York one day, Oct. 18. one-half of double bill. Running time, 64 minutes.

Zat wun Castillian villaine—wot a man! Wot a man!

No guns he used, but just his head. And how he bragged and gagged! Money meant nothing to him, and jewels he flung away, just to prove the philosophy of love and win a maiden's hand.

But the directors muffed it.

This picture is hitting the grinds, and for them it's swell fare. But the yarn and the cast possessed potentialities that, with more subtle direction, could have lifted the talker into first-class film realms. It is one of those romantic comedies with a teasing little love song running through the middle. As it flickered on the screen it could be easily seen that the directors tried hard to get that soft comedy into the thing but just missed.

The story is what the kind theatre fans like to chew on. A handsome, tall pirate of Spanish type, brave, philosophical and careless. A pretty dance hall girl who speaks with a cultivated tongue. An educated bounder and a ludicrous constabulary. Here were all the ingredients of one of those light serio-comedies, but it all got lost in the shuffle.

Diction was clear and the cast tried hard, but the continuity and the sequence crashed, making the voices sound as if in recital and the acting a bit too obvious.

Lastro was a bold pirate. He skippered a private yacht and stopped off at Tepete. Like a wise guy, he tried to get off without paying a check at the chief cafe. Partnered by a mixed team.

The male buddy of the proprietors' crew figured on calling the soldier-cops, as he knew there was a reward out for Lastro. Nidra, the singer, however, was hard boiled enough to walk up to the handsome devil and demand the coin. All this time Nidra's boy friend, millionaire bounder, is looking on.

Lastro goes for the skirt. Making a personal appearance before the town's constabulary, Lastro, by sheer personality force, paralyzes the soldiers and he walks off free.

Later he pursues the girl and her boy friend gets sore. The soldiers again are called. Lastro turns the table and takes everybody but the girl prisoner. He proves the bounder to be white livered and wins the girl—on board his yacht.

THE RIVER WOMAN

(Disc Orchestration)

Sonoratone-Gotham-Sam Sax production; independent release. Directed by Joseph Henneberry from story by Adele Buffington. Recording on Bristolphone. In cast: Lionel Barrymore, Jacqueline Logan and Charles Delaney. At Stanley, New York, one day, Oct. 16. Running time about 60 minutes.

When things looked biggest potentially for the Sonora-Bristolphone thing that never merged Sax slipped out to Hollywood and made this one. "The River Woman" hasn't a line of dialog. Only trouble is in the story, a frail tidbit as brought to the screen. It nearly wastes cast, director, and sets unusually excellent for an indie production.

The yarn as reduced is nothing more than about conventional doings of a saloon prop, his chief entertainer and an oiler from a Mississippi backwheeler who quits sailoring for drinks after he meets the dame.

Nothing much happens until the last reel or so. Then the river at flood tide inundates the saloon and town and the oiler quits drinking.

Just a pity. For once an indie spent some money on people and preparation; even went miles away from Hollywood for locations. But the story link in the chain was overlooked. *Waly.*

FROZEN JUSTICE

(ALL DIALOG)

Lenore Ulric starred in this Fox Movietone production and release. Allan Dwan, director. Story and dialog by Owen Davis. At the Roxy, New York, week Oct. 25. Running time, 75 minutes.

Talu	Lenore Ulric
Lanak	Robert Frazer
Duke	Louis Wolheim
Capt. Jones	Ullrich Haupt
Douglamana	Laska Winter
Dancer	Tom Patricola
Little Casino	Alice Lake
Moosehide Kate	Gertrude Astor
Boston School Ma'am	Adele Windsor
Bartender	Warren Heymer
Yukon Lucy	Neyeen Farrell
Swede	El Brendel
Proprietor	Lou Morrison
French Sailor	Charles Judels
Jewish Character	Joe Rochay
Harmony Duo	Meyers Sisters
Singer	George MacFarlane
Mate Moore	Landers Stevens
Medicine Man	Jim Spencer
French Pete	Arthur Stone
English Eddie	Jack Ackroyd
Talu's Mother	Gertrude Chorre

Lenore Ulric plays a swell looking Eskimo gal in her first talking picture. Her blood is a mixture, half white, and she rebels at her secluded life as the wife of a young Eskimo chieftain, running away with a dastardly white sea captain.

Talu gets herself into plenty of hot water in white man's land, finally meeting violent death. Death interrupted her attempt to return to her husband, a return that would have meant a happy ending to this picture. It finishes sadly after the depression all the way through. Either way would amount to about the same, with a happy ending probably no better.

No matter what they started out to make—it begins like an epic of the north—the wind-up is mainly a picture introduction of Lenore Ulric. The picture itself is moderately good and the grosses should be on the same level. When better, Miss Ulric's possible ability to draw in certain localities should be held responsible.

As a debut film for Miss Ulric, "Frozen Justice" and its story seem satisfactory, though impression is that the star might have received a better chance to shove off in a part calling for some clothes and a little parlor activity.

Besides considering that if there were any Eskimos with Miss Ulric's looks, half breeds or not, Zieggy would have been there long ago, there are many unbelievable facts to this story and many far fetched bits of action. All rub the wrong way and count up at the finish.

Member of an Eskimo tribe, wife of the chief and apparently raised with the people—her mother an Esk and father a sailor—Talu speaks pretty fair English to the trading sailors who take her to her doom. That's plausible, because of her white pop and the contact with white traders. But, when six months later as an entertainer in a Nome dive, Talu speaks perfect drawing room English, she doesn't sound or seem real.

Conversations between the Eskimos themselves, in English, of course, is in the stilted style to denote they are really using their own language. That's okay, but not the sudden change in dialect by the girl dialectician. In the first place, no one will believe Talu learned to speak so well in that Alaskan joint.

All desirable women residents of the Eskimo village going to a ship party tossed by the white sailors, while their husbands and male relatives are ceremoniously chasing away the storm devil and not looking, is another believe-it-or-not that accentuates the not. The way these Esk women carry on with the sailor boys, all getting stewed and lovable, without worrying about what their own gents will think, speaks not so well for Eskimo morals.

Talu falls for the sheikish captain of the boat and for his white woman gowns.

To Nome later on with this captain, where she becomes the star singer in a '99 Nome cafe. She rooms with the capt. across the street and the capt. collects the coin.

The Nome of those wild gold rush days is fascinatingly painted in the best set of the picture. The ice field views seem to be miniatures or backdrops for the most part, but always notably realistic.

The cracking glacier sequence, in which Tulu and the captain are killed, is a peach. The girl and the villain fall into the pit when the berg breaks. She is rescued in time by her husband, to die in his arms, but the heavy cannot get out and is crushed when the two huge cakes of ice return to position. At the finish, Lanak, the heart-broken chieftain, is walking across a field of ice with the body of his wayward wife in his arm. Against the sky is the Aurora Borealis, a beautiful piece of lighting.

Robert Frazier is Talak, Ulrich Haupt the captain, and Louis Wolheim, Duke, the captain's mate, a sympathetic villain always fearful of his crony's activities with women. His predictions of doom through a dame come true.

In the joint scene Miss Ulric sings in a talk-sing way, not impressing as a musical vocalist, but as a talker she's always impressive.

Lenore Ulric should be built into an important talking picture name. She has all of the requisites.

Bige.

RETALIATION

(CHINESE-MADE)

(Silent)

To see this picture is to take one back to the old Biograph days, when distinct photography was practically unknown. This particular film was produced by the Great Wall Film Co., of Shanghai (China) and imported for the New Chatham theatre, a Bowery grind—New York's only Chinese film house.

Its story centers on the career of one of China's mythical heroes, Wu Soan.

It is long and tedious, runs for two and a half hours with the plot braiding up continuously until at the close of the picture the averag- mind is more than slightly confused. Made for the Chinese—only the Chinese can grasp it.

Only 13 persons are murdered during the various phases of the picture—and all by the hero.

Acting is done with dignity. Every movement is precise and in American films would be considered slow motion stuff. Humor is unknown, but villainy runs rampant.

Most of the acting is done with the eyes and eyebrows. Faces are expressionless and in keeping with tradition. For talking with their hands these Chinese rival only the French.

In each of the murders the hero passed through three stages of attack. First he kicked his victim in the stomach. This knocked the opponent down. Then he stamped his right foot upon the fallen gent, after which with slow, deliberate motion the hero proceeded to carve a slice out of the dying one's side with a broad scimitar.

All this was done carefully with the adversaries co-operating of course.

The policemen in old China evidently carried scimitars that looked like huge Shriner emblems, or long wooden poles as their badge of office. Ancient Chinese bandits rode on burros while their armies trotted carelessly on foot.

Titles are given in Chinese and English. While to the Chinese the titles are seriously drawn, the Caucasian will find much humor in the literal translation into English.

When an actor is supposed to express terrible surprise, title reads: "Ah!"

When three characters are simultaneously surprised there will be three separate titles, reading in their order, "Ah! Yea! Oh!"

When a tenant is disturbed by a knocking on the door just before retiring, he arises in anger thus:

"Thief, you have come too soon. I am not yet asleep."

There is a tremendous gentility of thought in them, too. As for instance when the policemen and their prisoner stop to eat at an ancient Chinese roadhouse, the cops remove the pillory board from their captive's neck with these words:

"We assume the risk and take off your pillory so that you may consume several cups of liquor."

To complain about food in a Chinese cafe, so far as the picture shows, was cause for murder. In one scene when the hero calls the wine served him "insipid," the maid sends his two cop companions into the "yonder world" by means of wine which she termed "turpid."

Once when the hero asks to see his benefactor "immediately" he gets the reply that the latter will not see him for a few months.

The choicest translation comes when after the picture has had its several big murder scenes the greatness of Wu Soan and the screen flickers this:

"Wu Soan's career was intimately connected with his wine cup"—as his friend says to him:

"Brother, you are intoxicated."

Ah! Yea! Oh!

SWEETIE

(ALL DIALOG, with Songs)

Paramount release and production. Directed by Frank Tuttle. Story and dialog by George Marion, Jr., and Lloyd Corrigan. Music by Richard Whiting, lyrics by Marion, Jr. Alfred Gilks, cameraman. Dance director, Earl Lindsay. At Paramount, New York, week Oct. 25. Running time, 95 minutes.

Barbara Pell....................Nancy Carroll
Helen Fry....................Helen Kane
Biff Bentley....................Stanley Smith
Tap-Tap Thompson..............Jack Oakie
Percy (Pussy) Willow......William Austin
Axel Bronstrup..................Stuart Erwin
Bill Barrington.........Wallace MacDonald
Dr. Oglethorpe..............Charles Sellon
Miss Twill....................Aileen Manning

College life, according to box-office formula, is a delightful mixture of romance and play. Quartets singing under the elms, everybody rehearsing for the school musical comedy, and the big game with Oglethorpe only one day off. "Sweetie" is that way. More than most collegian films, it adheres to the musical comedy idea of capers on the campus; and to overlook its appeal among the high school flaps and toiling Tillies is to overlook the predominant audience type. The picture is set for profit, its cinching draw being Nancy Carroll and Jack Oakie.

From any angle other than the all-important financial, "Sweetie" is a brooch of pearls inlaid in dried spinach. With the wild plot thrown away, several bits remain as classic moldings of comedy. George Marion, Jr., who collaborated on the story and wrote the lyrics, is responsible.

Oakie, as a hoofer who has thrown away his career and entered the school because he likes everybody, is an unforgettable riot in his delivery of "Alma, Mammy," a Broadwayite's idea of a good Alma Mater song. With a nasal Jolson delivery and both knees in, Oakie drew a roar of laughter and applause at the Paramount. Whole-hearted applause is remarkable in this advanced day of sound pictures, and a lesser but still unusual reception tendered Miss Kane in one number is also worth noting.

Both instances resulted from combination of Marion's talents with adept performers. Marion's lyrics in this overshadowed his reputation as a title and dialog writer.

Four songs are spotted about 12 times during the running, with only the theme ditty, "Sweeter Than Sweet," weakening through repetition. It's a sugary ballad, almost forgotten immediately, despite the hammering. Title song, "Sweetie," is sung by Miss Kane to her dumb boy friend, and should have a big play among the personality girls. If "Alma, Mammy," Oakie's classic, doesn't knock the school crowd for a goal they're nuts. Remaining number is "Prep Step,' fair hoofing affair.

Plot has Miss Carroll, musical comedy girl, inheriting a boy's college in North Carolina. The boy friend, Stanley Smith, has just refused to elope because he must play in the football game against Oglethorpe. He happens to be captain of the team at the school she's just inherited. Holding a last-minute English examination, Miss Carroll flunks Smith and makes him ineligible for the big game. She also sells an option on the school to Oglethorpe, head of the rival college. Then, stung by the havoc she has caused, Miss Carroll bets the school against the option she has given Oglethorpe, and reinstates Smith through a re-examination. Next day Smith wins the big game in the last minute of play with a riotous run down the field.

Sometimes it's pretty silly. Students are continually rushing together for a good old song, with dances and orchestra music. Idea of Miss Carroll running a college is nobody's business. And Miss Kane, at an adjacent girls' college, is continually spurring her dumb b. f. on to greater things by shooting him in the pants with an air rifle. Dumbbell as done by Stuart Erwin is very good.

Miss Carroll gets less sympathy in this than her previous roles. Her performance is convincing when possible. Mr. Smith, her vis-a-vis, is fine looking, clean-cut kid with an excellent voice if it's his. Mr. Oakie is the lifesaver, both in comedy performance and his big song. William Austin, head prof at the college, is an intentionally silly ass.

Miss Kane's part is 20 miles from logic, but she'll draw her laughs. Especially when singing.

Tuttle's direction an alternation of sparkle and inanity. Tough story to handle.

Football players will be interested in learning what the Pelham College coach said to the boys after a brutal day's practice:

"Hurry, boys. Remember, you have to rehearse for the school musical comedy."

And the big game only a few days off! *Bang.*

MISSISSIPPI GAMBLER

(ALL DIALOG)

Universal production and release, featur- Joseph Schildkraut. Reginald Barker, director. W. E. recorded. Story by Kane Brown and Leonard Fields. At the Colony, New York, Oct. 26. Running time, 57 minutes.

Jack....................Joseph Schildkraut
Lucy....................Joan Bennett
Blackburne....................Alec B. Francis
Tiny....................Otis Harlan
Suzette....................Carmelita Gerahty

The answer to this one is known before the first five minutes are over. Even your first guess after reading the title will be correct. As the story of a gambler on a Mississippi steamboat, ever one of America's most romantic characters, this one follows most of the others preceding it.

Reads like a Saturday Evening Post short story, reaching the expected climax after an hour and crawling all the way to get there. There's nothing exciting to the tale, not even when the old man who has been fleeced is caught trying to shoot himself by his lovely young daughter.

Dashing Jack, the card sharp, turns gool, as per original pattern, doing it in a game with the lovely daughter — her father's money against her honor—and throws away three aces to permit her to win with three kings. Love conquers all.

He's the kind of a guy, this handsome bad man, who gives his worshipful but jealous decoy-sweetheart plenty of air while going on the offensive make for the sucker's lovely daughter. The steer gal tips his mitt finally, but he wins the other way by going straight.

Coming so soon after "Show Boat," this Universal is reminiscent in many of its water views and the group of darkies singing spirituals at start and finish. They would have looked better if not so stagey.

The looks of the love pair, Schildkraut and Joan Bennett, place the appearance section above the rest of the film. Carmelita Gerahty, the naughty shill, not so bad looking herself. Alec Francis and Otis Harlan are in roles that suit them. Playing very good excepting when Schildkraut overdoes conceit.

"Mississippi Gambler" telegraphs all of its punches. *Bige.*

ISLE OF LOST SHIPS

(ALL DIALOG)

First National production and release. Directed by Irving Willatt from film adaptation of Crittendon Mariott's novel. Theme song, "Ship of My Dreams." At Strand, week Oct. 25. Running time about 75 minutes.

Frank Howard....................Jason Robards
Dorothy Renwick....................Virginia Valli
Aunt Emma....................Clarissa Selwynne
Captain Forbes....................Noah Beery
Jackson....................Robert O'Connor
Gallagher....................Harry Cording
Mrs. Gallagher..........Margaret Fielding
Mother Burke....................Katherine Ward
Mr. Burke....................Robert Homans
Harry....................Jack Acroyd
Sam Baker....................Sam Baker

The talker version of "The Isle of Lost Ships" will clean up in any type of house. A little more attention to dialog, which occasionally slumps into the bromidic, and a more careful directorial eye on the knitting of some of the situations would have unquestionably rounded this into a Broadway topper set for an enviable long term.

In its present release as a program feature it is without a competitor in the current market of thrillers. The originality of the story this time shares honors with the weird effect established by sets and the camera angles at which they are focused.

The maze of derelicts piled into an island in the Sargasso Sea is a technical accomplishment in itself. So great is the variety of wrecked vessels, from palatial liners, to pirate brigs and barkentines that the artistry provided in the carpentry and painting achieves that goal so rare in film or stage. The sets, and atmosphere which they volunteer, keep an audience ever interested and tense. Occasionally the background eclipses the performances of the players. For many fans, in fact, a camera study of the wreckage would suffice.

Pounding of the liner opening the theme in a rough sea and the abandoning of ship are presented with a realism and verve also as seldom shown in film novelizations. There is little suggestive of the use of miniatures except a long shot of a partly submerged vessel.

The rescue of Dorothy Renwick from a capsized lifeboat by Frank Howard is a little stagy; other women struggling about and this one seemingly picked out by the convicted murderer to carry on the story.

Drifting through the seaweed, the liner, with the two and the detectives, Jackson, the sole survivors, eventually sights the island.

A custom requiring a single woman to be married within a day after joining the colony, composed mainly of mariners, is used by the village king, Captain Forbes, as the opener for a series of complications involving Dorothy and her rescuers.

Fights are frequent, but not too numerous, before another melodramatic highlight, escape in a submarine, is seen. It so happens that Howard, the convicted man, is an ex-navy officer and knows all about subs. Again, one of the natives is an engineer whose hobby has been keeping the submersible in perfect mechanical condition.

A last wallop is Howard's being shot through a torpedo tube. Although eight fathoms under the surface with no headgear, he is able to hold his breath sufficiently to sever a thick hauser interfering with the trip and to ride to the top on the ship's deck. The action is quick here and this helps lessen the impossible.

Virginia Valli is rather stiff and over-English. Her lack of warmth is not so apparent, since in the major footage her only competitors for femme honors are two elderly characters.

An excellent Forbes is found in Noah Beery. Such roles are all to Beery's tailoring. Jason Robards is equally as good in the Howard part. Jackson is handled by Robert O'Connor as the filler in the story.

Theme song, "Ship of My Dreams," is undistinguished, but pleasing and not over-worked. Those islanders, possessed of all worldly goods from grog to silks, also had a guitar player. *Waly.*

Why Weep at Parting?

(GERMAN MADE)

(DIALOG, SYNCHRONIZED)

Berlin, Oct. 15.

"Why Weep at Parting?" (Südfilm). Premiere, Universum.

This looks like the beginning and the end of pictures recorded by the Breusing Lignose system, for to judge by this one it must be terrible.

The synchronized musical equipment sounds terrific most of the time. Except for an occasional solo instrument it is tinny, thin and sharp. The dialog, too, has hardly a moment of naturalness and never any bottom to it. This picture was made on the crazy system of first making a silent version and then synchronizing the whole dialog with other actors, most of them unknown bit performers.

Perhaps Lignose should be given another chance to show what it can do on direct recording, but the incompetence of the musical accompaniment seems to prove that this would be merely wasted effort.

The scenario is one of the worst of the century. Dina Gralla, star, plays a private detective who follows the juvenile Harry Halm about under the belief that he is a thief. Halm is an engaging performer but can do nothing with the lemonade which is served to him here. He has to fall back on exaggerated and repititious grimacing. The same is true of Miss Gralla, who is reaching a cross-road. With all possibilities of developing into a good knockabout comedienne of the Florence Moore type she is simply standing still, not having moved for several years.

The German industry should really chip together and stop the showing of this mugging party which will do a lot of harm to the future of the talking picture in Germany. *Trask.*

SEDUCTION

(Erotikon)

(CZECHO-SLOVAKIAN MADE)

(Silent)

Paris, Oct. 16.

Czech film production, made in Prague by Gem-Film, directed by Gustav Machaty. Photography by W. Wich; 78 minutes at Cinema Imperial, Paris (Pathe-Natan house), 3d week.

Ita........................Ita Rina
Georges....................Olaf Fjord
Jean.......................Luigi Servanti
M. Hilpert.................Theodore Pistek
Mme. Hilpert...............Charlotte Suza
Ita's father...............S. Sleichert

This silent flicker features what probably is the Garbo-Gilbert team of Czecho-Slovakia: Ita Rina and Olaf Fjord, the former reminding of the pre-Paramount Pola Negri of her early Ufa days, and Fjord impressing even more favorably for possible American consumption. Miss Rina's profile nullifies her for Anglo-Saxon appeal, although her heavy emoting here would stampede the box offices if the censors dared okay this one.

Eliminate the rough stuff and there's no flicker. It's some pretty hot to punctuate an otherwise drably trite romance wherein Fjord is the heavy lover who has a way with wimmen and those he doesn't slay, he cripples. In the end, an irate husband (well played by Theodore Pistek as the colorlessly stolid spouse) kills the Czech sheik. Opposite Pistek is Charlotte Suza, somewhat Lilyan Tashmanish as a flighty blonde who likewise comported herself well.

But Miss Rina and Fjord are the picture. It opens grippingly with Ita's father providing shelter to the lead who has missed the last train. The old man, quite convincingly, registers his simple joy with an automatic lighter the city slicker presents him with as a means to allay suspicion.

Quite naturally the amorous situation between Fjord and the railroad man's daughter is built up when the old man goes into the stormy night for his nocturnal duties.

All the elements are there for a most plausible development, even unto Georges presenting Ita with a bottle of the Erotikon perfume which accounts for the original title of the picture, "Erotikon." The French transferred it into "Seduction," quite fitting.

Up to now everything evidences some rather shrewd Continental direction and motivation. One begins to wonder what the Czechs have been holding out on us. Photography is noteworthy although Wich's camera-work happened to remain consistently satisfactory throughout. Then for no reason there is a heavy clinch. The close-ups of Ita in the throes of a somewhat unholy amorous struggle, with her face contorted in fierce pleasure, came too soon thereafter.

If a question of censor-cutting—this flicker is supposed to have been French censored!—it looks like they cut out the wrong things or else those scissored clips would make great stag subjects.

This, along with another scene showing the unwed mother in the throes of childbirth, is a sample of the Czech cinema standards, obviously made with no thought to the English market. It's a certainty no English-speaking nation would approve a release of this type for the general public. When not dirty it's nothing.

As many directorial shortcomings as strong highlights. Stolidness of the silhouetted midwife, calmly munching her crust, as Ita registers pre-natal anguish, is a slice of east-European life no doubt.

From the few local pictures seen, with dual English-French titles, let's hope that in the near future, just for the English-speaking clientele alone, of course, the translated titles are not merely literal counterparts of the French. It would well be worth while to import a few crack American title writers who know the idiomatic French and English alike and not commit such garish unconscious faux pas as the title: "I wish I could stay with you forever," following the seduction scene.

What happens, seemingly, especially with these indies, is that a native, with a British university knowledge of English, merely transposes the literal French into literal English without cognizance of Anglo-Saxon idioms, like an American or British caption writer would be prone to fall into unconscious traps if translating literally into French.

In addition to the players mentioned, Luigi Serventi as one of those sympathetic polished players impresses favorably for Hollywood possibilities. He has the front and the histrionic ability.

"Seduction," playing here at the Imperial, on a thrice-daily reserved seat schedule to an 85c top, has been a wow because of the hot stuff.

That's what killed it for America. *Abel.*

WIDECOMBE FAIR

(ENGLISH MADE)

(Silent)

Produced by British International. No American release credited. Directed by Norman Walker, with screen theme based upon the novel by Eden Phillpotts. At the Litt-e Carnegie Oct. 26. Running time, 63 minutes.

Squire.....................Wyndham Standing
Daughter...................Marguerite Allen
Lover......................William Freshman
Uncle Tom Cobleigh.........Moore Marriott
Widow......................Violet Hopson
Bailiff....................Aubrey Fitzgerald

British International's film transcription of the Phillpotts' novel, "Widecombe Fair," is mediocrity. It is an uninspired effort, slow in projection, with no particular attention to casting, except the Squire role Wyndham Standing essays. Entertainment in spots. Notable features are English cow lands and home life.

A conceited, girl-faced cowhand threatens to start things up in the first reel, but this dies down quickly when the squire sees "the love light" in his daughter's eye and approves the marriage. In fact, William Freshman rates the cognomen of "the lover" only for a few feet in the production.

This land owner, a generous fellow, is offered another opportunity to make a story by his debts. But the bailiffs overclown, and Uncle Tom, a farm foreman, as rendered by Moore Marriott, is little more than a punch-muffing, beer-drinking comic who seldom gets across to the American mind.

Again the production threatens to settle down to business of attempting suspense when an interested widow plants her jewels and enrolls the squire's son-in-law to enact the bit of folklore associated with the estate. In true English fashion the jewels are discovered just before the hammer descends, and the squire buys drinks for the town while "the lover," who was inclined to abandon the wreckage, then takes credit for its rejuvenation. *Waly.*

Broadway Scandals

(ALL DIALOG WITH SONGS)

Columbia production and release. Featuring Sally O'Neil, Jack Egan and Carmel Myers. Produced by Harry Cohn, with George Archainbaud directing, from story by Howard Green. Dialog by Norman Houston with Harry Jackson cameraman and John Lividary sound engineer. Stage numbers produced by Rufus LeMaire. At Cohan, New York, for twice daily run at $2, starting Oct. 28. Running time, 73 minutes.

Mary.......................Sally O'Neil
Ted Howard.................Jack Egan
Valeska....................Carmel Myers
Le Claire..................J. Barney Sherry
Pringle....................John Hyams
Jack Lane..................Charles Wilson
Bobby......................Doris Dawson
George Halloway............Gordon Elliott

Not for the $2 Cohan for long, nor will it make many of the first runs. They can't make a hit musical show of an opus which solely depends upon its chorus numbers to get over. At least, they haven't done it yet, and the same tihng goes for other pictures. There's another words and music picture playing around, which is absent from most of the first glimpse chalets, and flapping in those big emporiums where it does gain entrance, for the same reason.

This feature unwinds as if Columbia couldn't make up its mind whether to do a revue or a book musical. Consequently it's overboard on numbers and shy on script.

Plenty of songs and dance numbers, but there doesn't seem to be a real click melody. At one time they throw 'em so fast at the camera there's four in a row without an important cut to the story. As it stands this product will have to pick up its gross outside of the major cities as the musical-revue studio scheme is unfolding too keen competition to permit a lightweight yarn such as this one to get over to any degree.

Carmel Myers and Jack Egan shoulder the cast responsibilities and do valiantly. Miss Myers will likely surprise with her voice and knowledge of delivery. Egan also handles his vocal assignments capably, his final warbling bit, up against a supposed radio mike, being top.

Case of Sally O'Neil shapes as unfortunate two ways, for Miss O'Neil and the picture. Without a chance to wear flash clothes this youngster, as a chorus girl, is buried under plain suits and tams which fall 'way short of helping her appearance. Troupes nicely, but must sing and dance as well. Her high spot, that of burlesquing the prima's (Miss Myers) love ballad to Egan during a "pick out" number, sounds as if Miss Myers had doubled for the imitation and kidded her own voice to secure the desired effect. If Miss O'Neil did do it, so much the better. Anyway, they'll believe the latter, and that's the main point.

But they can't or don't believe that page one streamer on a love duel between the two boys. It's such weaknesses as that which keep undermining the film. Chorus numbers would look better if there weren't so many of 'em. That bow music for Egan and O'Neil the first time flashed as a two-act. That not only sounded familiar, but was familiar.

What story there is to this one Archainbaud gets over capably, although a tough order in any case. Vaude bunch ought to get a laugh out of Johnny Hyams doing a nance. Rufe LeMaire knows production values, and they show. Too, after the great search looking for a Valeska, that Carmel ought to be a valuable girl to have around. Also a wad for Charles Lane as the radio announcer. Very good.

But dust off Belle and get her ready, and remember me to Marie. *Sid.*

SEA FEVER

(FRENCH MADE)

(Silent)

Produced in France by Neofilms and presented here through Moviegraph. Directed by Alberto Cavalcanti. At the Fifty-fifth Street Playhouse, beginning Oct. 26. Running time, 66 minutes.

Boy........................Georges Charlia
Mother.....................Nathalie Lissenko
Girl.......................Catherine Hessling
Longshoreman...............Tommy Bourdel
Idiot......................Philippe Heriat

According to the French idea "Sea Fever" is about a dock barmaid who goes into despair when she can't find a virtuous seaman. More so does it center on the young son of a local laundress, who moons through five reels trying to make up his mind to take a boat trip. Then he eats the hay in his pillow and sticks to sidewalks because he finally lost control of orderly hands and the blighty-eyed beer slinger put him in the class with bo'suns' mates and etc.

It's a sad affair, pictorially. Sure-seaters which use the title prolog the Fifty-fifth is flashing, about what is to come being "an all-too-rare aesthetic delight," may sell the intellectuals that they are really getting a new technique, etc.

The prolog, which has more type lines than the average silent has subbies, is correct in its exclamation that this great French effort suffers its action to get along without titles. In fact, the only titles flashed on the screen are before and after the incidents that a grind moron would grasp.

Using the lyric of that exquisite piece of maritime music, "Sea Fever," is a blasphemy. Yet all verses are worked in at start, middle and close of this production. And nary a change in the sets except a dirty laundry shop and a filthy wharf, plus the gin mill.

The hero yearner for things of the sea, who never gets beyond the coal pile on the dock and who allows the cameraman to grind on departing vessels that have been better studied in news reels, impresses as just a lazy, good-for-nothing son of a hard-working laundry forelady. There is no sympathy aroused for him at any time. He just eats, sleeps and walks around with hands in pockets except for the one near-event with the bar lady.

This boy is allowed to be constantly confused in the thing called theme with an idiot seaman, a totally harmless fellow. When the end comes it would be impossible to tell who pushed out in the little boat to sea and floated back a corpse were it not for the young man being faded in on his down cot, sad about his necking party with the saloon dignitary, but apparently content to sleep it off.

The prolog praised "Sea Fever" for being a daring attempt at originality and etc. The conclusion of the reelage, however, manifests the only daring as on the part of this French producer believing he can force such innocuous stuff as this on anything but that tiny portion of the American industry characterized by the trade as plain stupid.

Waly.

Land Without Women

(GERMAN MADE)

(25% Dialog)

(Called first German made talking picture. Tobis process employed.)

Berlin, Oct. 17.

"The Land Without Women" (Tobis). Premiere, Capitol.

Although only about 25% dialog, this is the first German picture that even suggests a talker. And it gives the first opportunity to judge whether the Germans are in a condition to produce talkers of international character. Judging by this effort they still have a lot to learn but there is no doubt that the Tobis equipment can turn out high-grade results.

The chief trouble in the present picture was that the synchronized musical accompaniment was too loud in contrast to the dialog. Often even a solo violin was so loud in tone as to be unpleasant, especially as the Tobis amplification tends to make the tones shriller.

In the opposite, the dialog passages were natural throughout but often much too quiet. Although in one of the front rows had to strain to catch almost every word and often missed the sense of some of the passages entirely. But these are all merely minor technical difficulties which should be able to be remedied when sufficient experimentation has taken place.

The scenario is unfortunately futile. It starts with an excellent notion, that of the shipping by the British government of 413 women to Australia where they are to be married to gold miners looking for wives. There is a tremendous shortage of women in the country, and the government encourages the production of children.

Dick, telegraph operator, has drawn number 68 but during the trip over one of the women dies and by the drawing of lots he loses his chance. He is a hysterical individual and, finding out about his bad luck, falls in love with the girl he missed who is now the wife of Steve, a miner. The husband goes prospecting and Dick hides in his cabin. It is discovered that a man is with the girl and Dick announces he has been attempting to steal her. He is going to be lynched but is saved at the request of the wife by a young American doctor who announces that he is crazy.

The wife now takes up with the doctor. Meantime the husband has struck gold but the water supply is overturned by his camel. He and his partner immediately break camp in an effort to reach the telegraph line, the severing of which is a signal for help. The telegraphist realizes that it must be Steve who is in need and does not give the order for sending out the rescue expedition. But a rainstorm comes up in time to save Steve's life and he is rescued when another telegraphist comes on duty.

When the doctor realizes that Steve is returning he commits suicide and the wife has to return to her now wealthy husband. The demented telegraphist meets his death by running along a railway track shouting the wife's name until he is run over.

Needless to remark, this muddy plot has no centralization of interest. Nobody is interested in the nutty telegraphist or the sentimental philandering wife. Konrad Veidt turns in one of his usual pathological studies which are getting to be rather a bore but his dialog passages would have been effective had they been a trifle louder. The best work is done by Clifford McLaglen as the husband who scores the high point of the evening when he sings "The Girl I Left Behind Me." His deep, ringing tones show the possibilities of the Tobis Equipment.

But, anyhow, the German talker is started.

Trask.

BARNUM WAS RIGHT

(ALL DIALOG)

Universal production and release. Directed by Del Lord. Story by Hutchinson Ford from the stage play by Phillip Bartholomae and John Meehan. Jerome Ash, photographer. Featuring Glenn Tryon, Myrna Kennedy and Otis Harlan. At Loew's New York, one day, Oct. 23. Running time, 55 minutes.

First they pick 'em up, then they knock 'em down. First they feature Glenn Tryon and Myrna Kennedy in one of their over a million-dollar cost publicized films, give them both a big time rep with a first run following, and then spot them in a flicker like this where they totter along on their reps for awhile, to succumb to the poor material and situations.

"Barnum Was Right" is an unconvincing, ridiculous farce and though it may have been a pioneer in this type of plot when produced on the stage in 1923, now it is simply a re-hash of many more which have been released previously. It's the story of the poor boy lover, who can't marry the gal until he has a few thousand dollars, while her dad wants her to wed the multi-millionaire Englishman.

Tryon supports the whole burden of lifting up the plot and does it in likable fashion. Without him it would be a sleep maker. Miss Kennedy has done and can do much more and better than here, for all her role consists of is pouting and playing up to the boy. Otis Harlan is the Englishman, and as usual speaks in an exaggerated English accent.

Deadwood and won't be able to hold up by itself except in the tiny timers. No reaction at all here except a few yawns.

HURRICANE

(ALL DIALOG)

Columbia production and release. Directed by Ralph Ince, from story by Norman Springer. Dialog by Norman Houston. Western Electric recording. Featuring Hobart Bosworth, Johnny Mack Brown, Leila Hyams, Allan Roscoe and Tom O'Brien. At Tivoli, New York, Oct. 25-26, as half double feature. Running time, 60 minutes.

Blood and thunder all talking sea drama. Starts at a fast clip and holds suspense until half way, when the love interest is suddenly introduced and slows up the action. Story is laid 50 years ago so the sailing schooner, where the story is unfolded, will not seem obsolete. No difference in costumes necessary as sea dogs always appear to be clothed the same way.

No musical synchronization for atmospheric background. Just effects and dialog. Effects clear but talk not always clearly audible, especially when the commands are shouted, as they boom through the house and re-echo, making it entirely indistinguishable. This may have been the fault of the projector in not controlling the volume correctly for this sized house.

Love angle between the youngsters, and the reconciliation of the captain with his wife after 20 years, are submerged in the interest lying in the attempted mutiny of the villainous stranded captain and his sea-going henchmen.

Hobart Bosworth as Hurricane, who isn't afraid to dare the wrath of Neptune at any time, puts over a capable interpretation but looks pretty gray for the vital, tough captain. It calls for a great stretch of imagination to swallow the easy manner in which he manhandles and mauls the villainous official around, though he himself was eventually beaten. Johnny Mack Brown is the paragon of virtue. Nothing much for Brown to do, though, except look handsome and young.

All Leila Hyams adds here is her name. The feminine interest and the Cupid touch runs hither and thither. Tom O'Brien entertaining as the red blooded mate who treats 'em all rough.

Should go nicely where a male audience is in the majority. Femmes won't go for it much.

Strictly small time.

ETERNAL PRAYER

(In Yiddish)

(ALL DIALOG, with Songs)

Produced by Max Cohen at the Metropolitan Studios, New York. Lucy Levine, Anna Appel, Mark Schweid and Lazar Freed of Yiddish Art Theatre, and "Shmelikel," boy cantor, in cast. Directed by Sidney Goldin, Music by Abe Ellestein; lyrics by Dave Meyerovitch. Disc recorded. At Clinton, New York, half of a double bill, for five days, Oct. 25-29. Running time, 36 minutes.

A ritual and liturgical four-reeler in all Yiddish dialog and singing limited in scope and box office appeal away from the Yiddish communities. For exhibs elsewhere won't bring a quarter.

One of the quickest "quickies," produced on a shoe string, with the producer probably leery of his dough when he made it. Under the circumstances, Goldin, director, did about all that anyone could. Some of the scenes show skilful and detailed attention, though very badly dressed from atmospheric and scenic angles.

No story material here of any value. Just a thin skein of plot the majority and average American Jew will not understand and probably doesn't want to. Seemingly, it would have been much better to cut this film down to an average short, retaining only the singing parts and throwing away the rest.

As is, idea is all jumbled up, opening with traditional candle blessing by two women, then fading to a synagogue where "Shmelikel," 12-year-old boy cantor, has a solo spot. Boy highly touted and considered for vaudeville, but unless he can show more than what he does here, it's no use worrying over him. For straight liturgical chanting this boy measures up about on par with a good many others of his type and age.

Last couple of scenes are devoted to even more concentrated chanting and praying, winding up with the eternal prayer of the Jew, the "Kaddish" (memorial). Much too dreary, beatific and solemn for any but the orthodox.

SCANDAL

(RUSSIAN MADE)

(Silent)

Wufka production, released over here through Amkino. Directed by Ivan I. Perestiany from scenario by Leonid Gurevich. Photographed by A. F. Stanky. Cast: Lena Filkovskaya, Ivan Stalenin, S. Gubin, K. Yakovleva, A. Poltavtseva, M. Yesikovsky, N. Lyoneva and B. Borodin. At Film Guild Cinema, New York, week Oct. 26. Running time, 70 minutes.

Primarily a propaganda issue from the Russian Soviet regime, showing topographical features, natural resources and economic life in present Russia first, then the screen story by way of hooking and holding the film together. Most ardent Bolshevik fan will not get excited over "Scandal."

For those over here who still think bearded Muscovites carry bombs under their chins, this flicker, of course, doesn't mean a thing.

Two principals, carrying the love interest, will never be awarded medals for effervescence of youth. If this couple (Lena Filkovskaya and Ivan Stalenin) is Russia's idea of a Gilbert-Garbo, they'd better kept it a secret from the States.

Plot of the story is threadbare. It tends to reveal the conflict between age and youth in Russia today, illustrating the Soviet morality leeway. What the film actually serves to point out will never substantiate this conducive argument of the Bolsheviks, probably through no fault of the producers after American censors got through with it.

Usual foreign aptitude for trick photography is not on view. Rather drab lighting all around, with several indistinct shots noticeable. It seems the film shows only what it is intended it convey, with the rest just trailing for an alibi. No outstanding contributions from the cast. Probably another Soviet idea, not to permit individuals to hog anything too much. After all, the film industry in Russia is like any other economical and industrial institution, with government rules applying to all alike.

"Scandal" is just plain propaganda, not box-office to exhibs over here.

CONDEMNED

(ALL DIALOG)

United Artists release of Sam Goldwyn production. Starring Ronald Colman. Featuring Ann Harding, Louis Wolheim and Dudley Diggs. Directed by Wesley Ruggles from Sidney Howard's adaptation of novel, "Condemned to Devil's Island." Dialog direction by Mr. Diggs. Cameraman, George Barnes and Gregg Toland. Stuart Heisler editing. At Selwyn, New York, for twice daily $2 run, starting Nov. 3. Running time, 93 mins.

Michel........................Ronald Colman
Vidal........................Dudley Diggs
Mme. Vidal........................Ann Harding
Jacques........................Louis Wolheim
Pierre........................William Elmer

Nice program material for box-office purposes with much of this strength to come from the wake of the Ronald Colman click in "Bulldog Drummond" left behind. "Condemned" is neither a b. o. "Drummond" or $2.

Neither has it the fibre to stand the strain of the intermission allotted it at the Selwyn. It takes a strong group of reels to retain audience interest over the theatre's conventional cigaret period, and this latest Goldwyn effort lacks that grip. No intermission and some smart cutting would help this feature and should certainly be attended to for general release. No reason whatsoever for the 93 minutes unfolded here.

But it has Colman, Ann Harding and Dudley Diggs, a trio who figure to see this one through to satisfactory receipts. Those contending Diggs steals the picture will not be without grounds.

For the New York opening "Condemned" had to stand off an atrocious preceding travelog short verbally describing its various Spanish locales. This one reeler's serious intentions drew not only snickers but howls.

Diggs is programed credited with having played overseer to the dialog. It's a cinch he didn't give himself the worst of it. That being true no one's going to get sore due to the excellence of his performance. Both directors, Wesley Ruggles on the camera end, have crammed their adroit touches into the early reels. Lots of stuff in this portion demands and secures steady eye and ear attention. It's nice team work until both men succumb to the story in the second half which goes native by reverting to the melodramatic chase formula.

"Hallelujah's" pursuit through a swamp has its companion here and the bit of Colman, in his escape, drawing unto himself a flat bottomed skiff upon the stern of which rests an outboard motor proved a concoction which the audience just couldn't swallow. And the reaction won't be any different when the 50-centers view it.

The best Howard, the adapter, has been able to do with this situation is toss Colman a line which gives the script a temporary life on a base on balls after the audience has mentally called two strikes. Line is, "I thought this was going to be an escape and it turns into a yacht race." A sure laugh because of its unexpectedness and being a perfect analysis of the patrons' thoughts.

"Condemned" is the well known sexometry triangle set in the French penal colony (South America) with the raffish warden's wife turning to the well mannered thief whom the head of the house has inducted into his home as servant. Michael (Colman) times his escape from solitary confinement to coincide with the wife's departure for France, the latter by request of the now insanely jealous warden. Struggle through the jungle is to reach the next calling port of the ship, where the lovers intend to continue on alone. Capture of Michel on board, the death of the warden at the hands of Jacques (Louis Wolheim), Michel's prison friend, and the troth that the abruptly widowed girl will wait for him close out the picture.

Film has too many false notes to make it a standout effort. Flash of 20 or 30 women peeking over a garden wall to see how the warden's wife and her servant are doing, and so discovered by the husband, is unbelievable and regrettable because of some neat composition previously having reached the same objective. Some neat cutting could still leave Diggs his scene of realization.

Then that boat thing, plus the inevitable and unnecessary tender touches as Colman repeatedly returns for a last caress with pursuers milling all around him. They can't and won't stomach overly sweet love scenes in dialog. The same thing can, has, and will be accomplished by less obvious and awkward means. For it's quite evident that sympathizers become embarrassed for their screen favorites during these sequences in the face **of the resultant laughter and the knowledge, or instinct, that these scenes simply don't belong. And that "Condemned" is going to draw snickers as it approaches its conclusion is as certain as that the cutter is going to stay up nights trying to find a way out.**

But Colman plays well, at times is outstanding in his pantomime and has his already established ability to handle lines. If ever given a chance he will probably scintilate in a light comedy theme. Also, there's not much doubt Ann Harding is in pictures to stay. As true of most of the stage people, she has yet to learn that the camera's imperative demand is to emphasize everything. Miss Harding may have figured she was acting all over the place, still, it's not yet enough for pictures. Nothing the matter with this girl's appearance, either, and letting that blonde flock down isn't going to impede the fan mail.

Camera work, sound, and reproduction at this house, excellent.

Sid.

JAZZ HEAVEN

(ALL DIALOG WITH SONG)

RKO production and release. Directed by Melville Brown. Produced by William Le Barron. Sally O'Neill and Joseph Cawthorn featured. Story original by Dudley Murphy and Pauline Forney, with adaptation and dialog by Cyrus Wood and Walter Ruben. Music and one song ("Someone") by Oscar Levant and Sidney Clare. R. C. A. Photophone sounded. At Globe, New York, twice daily, $2 top, opening Oct. 30. Running time, 80 minutes.

Barry Holmes..............John Mack Brown
Max Langley....................Clyde Cook
Mrs. Langley..............Blanche Frederici
Ruth Morgan....................Sally O'Neill
Herman Kemple..............Joseph Cawthorn
Walter Klucke....................Albert Conti
Tony........................Henry Armetta
Prof. Rowland....................Ole M. Ness
John Parker..............J. Barney Sherry
Miss Dunn....................Adele Watson

If RKO's "Jazz Heaven" makes the first runs, it will have to be on the strength of Joseph Cawthorn and his Hebe comedy. That's quite possible, for the comedy here is very pleasant, entertaining and laughable as Cawthorn does it. Comedy is too valuable on the screen to be ignored, especially when it's low comedy and in the dialog, so "Jazz Heaven" is entitled to a showing where an exhibitor knows his audience likes to laugh. Besides, there's Sally O'Neill, even if only her name here is useful. And Clyde Cook in a role that just fits him as he plays it, with his own way of dumb fun making.

A tangled impossible story that staggers along, relieved only by the two partners in the music publishing business, Kemple and Klucke, funnier than the original Potash and Perlmutter, though one of the m. p. partners plays straight. Cawthorn as Herman Kemple, the wily and elder partner, does it all. The scenes in the publishing offices give the talker its title, only.

Both partners are after their good-looking and flip song demonstrator, Miss O'Neill. She goes bugs over a southern kid, flat broke, with nothing but a melody and a bum piano. He brought both from the south to New York and can't pay his room rent. Miss O'Neill lives in the same rooming place.

The young couple meet each other and the landlady orders both out for being in one room. And she's going to hold the piano for four weeks' rent. Her husband, Mr. Cook, frames with the kids to save the piano. He'll move it across the street while his wife sleeps. Cook is a night watchman in a piano factory.

One of the best comedy scenes of some time here, very low, but very funny, based on the old piano moving gag of vaudeville. Cook gets a wop huckster and they start to roll the piano out and downstairs. Wife gets them, the noise awakening her. The wop is on the downside as the piano is on the stairs. Cook lets it slide, the wop jumps out of the way and the piano goes plumb to ruin, through the front door into the middle of the street.

Of course RKO will cinch Cawthorn after this picture, but how about developing that wop? He got laughs on grunts and facial expressions as he was made the mugg of the moving by Cook. He's probably the Tony of the program, Henry Armetta, and that guy is a character comedian on his own.

Rest is applesauce, interrupted by the two partners scrapping, double crossing and betting over the gal, with the young couple made broadcasters at the finish.

Unendurable without the comedy, although the single song, "Someone," sounds good. As the only song and worked up to by the kid composing it on his planner, the plug can be imagined.

No one does, no one has done, anything for this picture but the comedians of it. It can still be cut if the comedy is left as iz.

Sime.

IS EVERYBODY HAPPY

Warner Bros. production and release starring Ted Lewis. Directed by Archie Mayo; story and dialog by James A. Starr and Joseph Jackson. Special music by Grant Clark and Harry Akst. At Strand, New York, week Nov. 1. Running time, 110 mins.

Tod Todd........................Ted Lewis
Gail Wilson........................Alice Day
Lena Schmidt..............Ann Pennington
Victor McInar..............Lawrence Grant
Mrs. Molnar..........Julia Swayne Gordon
Landlord....................Otto Hoffman
Stage Manager..............Purnol B. Pratt

Ted Lewis has been left at the post by Al Jolson. "Everybody Happy" is so weakly a copy of "Singing Fool" as to border on the criminal neglect of Lewis and his following. Picture will be an in-and-outer, capitalizing on the popularity of its star and then blowing because there is nothing left to draw the customers.

At the Strand all recording was muffled and indistinct from the rear of the orchestra. Photography is ordinary and studio obtained nothing from two mild production numbers.

What might have been accomplished is evident whenever Lewis is in the setting he knows so well—backed by his band and twirling his battered silk hat. Twice he sings "I'm the Medicine Man" and sells it for a pretty penny. "Wouldn't It Be Wonderful?" is another highlight. And, scattered through the picture, unbilled, are numbers that Lewis knows how to handle, including "St. Louis Blues."

Story drags. Lewis' father has been a concert master in Budapest, but there's the war. He centers all his hopes in Lewis, the young fiddler, and takes him to America with mother.

The old man hates jazz. But Lewis can't find a spot doing concert fiddling and hocks the family Strad for a sax and clarinet. Kidded into believing his son is with the New York Symphony, papa buys some balcony seats. Heartbroken, when he finds Lewis isn't there, the father takes mama into a high class Hungarian restaurant for a rest, and there stands the boy, clowning in front of a band. "Never darken my door again!" says pop, but Ted visits mother secretly. Then pop disappears, and Lewis brings the mother into his own flashy apartment.

Two girls are after Lewis. One is the secretary of a producer and the other a dancer from Budapest to whom Lewis was once engaged. Lots of misunderstood doings, but love conquers. Lewis finally plays Carnegie hall—at a benefit. He's the hit of the layout, and standing in the wings is an old janitor—pop. Home to a Christmas dinner, and the Lewis band is even in the dining room for fadeout music.

Lewis, away from his band, would not be incongruous with a decent story and dialog. He doesn't photograph badly. Ann Pennington, as the little snob from Budapest, gets little sympathy. Her hula dance is rung in as a scene in a show. Alice Day, the sweet girl, has little and registers likewise. Stilted character of the Hungarian father becomes ridiculous, although Lawrence Grant tries hard. Lewis fans won't like it.

Bang.

Love, Live and Laugh

(ALL DIALOG)

Fox production and release starring George Jessel. Directed by W. K. Howard. Based on stage play, "Hurdy Gurdy Man," with screen arrangement by LeRoy Clemens and John B. Hymer. Dialog credited to George Jessel and Edwin Burke. Song and lyrics by Wolfe Gilbert and Abel Baer. Western Electric system. At the Roxy, N. Y., week of Nov. 1. Running time, 81 mins.

Luigi........................George Jessel
Margharita........................Lila Lee
Pasquale........................David Rollins
Enrico........................Henry Kolker
Dr. Price..............Kenneth MacKenna
Mario........................John Reinhart
Mike..............Dick Winslow Johnson
Tony........................Henry Armetta
Sylvia........................Marcia Manon
Barber........................Jerry Mandy

Strictly a program picture and nothing above average for such houses except in neighborhoods where they go for Jessel. Picture is dependent upon irrelevant situations that, fortunately, could be sheared in a re-editing. All the cutting, however, will not eliminate the strained and highly artificial atmosphere dominated by Jessel. Not a person in the cast who can handle the Italian lingo much of the dialog calls for. Once in a while Jessel remembers he's an accordion player, and that's that.

As the pal of Luigi, young David Rollins presents a Pasquale that flap fans will probably call "ridiculously cute." He's out of place but maybe the girls will go for him.

A lot of things in the story probably looked like dramatic nuggets in the script. But Howard, directing, has allowed them to be brought to the screen with choppy and bromidic characteristics. In the latter respect Jessel picks on one line more than any theme song was ever over-sung.

"In one little minute anything can happen." Jessel uses it all the time as punctuation for a dramatic incident. It first comes in when he meets Margharita and gets a job in her uncle's music store. Then when he gets the cable about his father's illness. After that you lose track of the line and don't care about the story.

One of the most entertaining sequences is that dealing with kiddies in a day nursery. The youngsters are all natural actors, unconscious of the tragedy in the heart of their head nurse, then the single Margharita. Latter role is played by Lila Lee and her screen personality is as attractive as usual. Song used seems catchy but Jessel, or the manner of recording it, doesn't give the tune the best of it. *Waly.*

LONG, LONG TRAIL
(ALL DIALOG)

Universal production and release, starring Hoot Gibson. Directed by Arthur Rosson. Adapted by Howard Green from Earl W. Bowman's novel, "Ramblin' Kid." Cast includes Sally Eilers, Kathryn McGuire, James Mason, Archie Ricks, Walter Brennan and Howard Truesdale. At Colony, New York, week of Nov. 2. Running time, 5d mins.

Universal still has faith in westerners. As a cowboy chaser this is just another. One redeeming feature here comes in at the finish when a rodeo sweepstakes sweeps across in enlarged screen, house going to the Magnascope for the race and then the blow-off fight between hero and heavies.

Discarding everything else in this horse opera it brings out Hoot Gibson as a talker for the first time, more important to U than the picture. If Gibson can go on talking with the same lucidity and ease of speech as in this one, he won't have to give up westerns.

Gibson is at home, and if they'll give him story lines he can keep on doing verbal westerns. His audible self will likely prove a pleasant surprise to kids and the fans who still like the wide open spaces. Other than that, however, "The Long, Long Trail" is just the conventional framework with no apparent reason for the title.

Typical ranch yarn, has been subdued for the sake of modernism probably. Gibson is the lad who goes galloping through town shooting it up while pretending he's stewed. The villainy crops out when Gibson is doped before the race, but shakes it off on the last lap to win. He then calmly proceeds to give the menace brothers a thrashing without being as much as scratched himself.

Sally Eilers, who has looks, practically wasted in this film as the heroine. Can't convince in the part as it's one of those things. Kathryn McGuire has just a bit, but Walter Brennan counts. Rest of cast fits.

Some of the exterior sound stuff is very good, a background of music being almost continuously played against the dialog and either heralding or fitting the action.

PARADISE
(ENGLISH MADE)
(Silent)

Produced by British International, with no American release credited. Directed by Dennison Clift. In cast: Betty Balfour, Joseph Striker, Alexander D'Arcy. At 5th Ave. Playhouse week Nov. 2. Running time, about 65 minutes.

Wired houses that use an occasional silent for divertisement's sake can book this in without hesitancy. It's a certain pleaser for patrons of all-mut theatres.

Richly mounted, well cast and directed, "Paradise" has a suspense realized by comparatively few English-made in this class.

Substance of the story ropes in an old proverb that there's no place like home and charity. But during the time the minister's daughter leaves home and boy friend to spend her cross-word puzzle prize money on the Riviera suites and gigoloes, a lot of things happen.

Betty Balfour is the girl who is almost but never getting burned on the French sands. A little too perk at first, she warms up until carrying her audience with bonafide interest through the major footage.

This Alexander D'Arcy makes up to an exceptionally handsome and cultured gigolo in "Paradise." The fact that the story doesn't permit

---

him to cull the girl is of decided advantage to the suspense.

Conventional routine of the quiet boy back home grabbing a plane, rescuing the girl from strong liquor and socking the professional lover is never restored to.

But an angle somewhat original is used. The admirer, played by Joseph Striker, steals the girl's prize money when she sticks by the gig, so that she will be forced out of the hotel. At the same time jewels are missing from another boudoir, and the Englishman is held.

Nice touch in the end when the gig reveals he lifted, this time for love. Almost spoiled by a little too much palaver about reform, charities, home, etc. Could snap it up considerably by clipping last 20 or 30 feet. *Waly.*

SECRETS OF NATURE
(GERMAN MADE)
(Silent)

Ufa production and release. Second of series made by same company. At 55th Street Playhouse week Nov. 2. Running time, about 50 minutes.

"Secrets of Nature" presents a regular amateur boxing night card of bouts among insects, fish, lobsters and crabs.

None of the contests as thrilling as that captured by Ufa between the mongoose and the copperhead, an earlier release, chiefly because this feature contains such a variety of buggy and bee things it is remarkable it succeeded in covering the crawling territories it does.

On bookings, the second of Ufa's nature series will naturally rate 100% in schools and theatres catering to students. It will attract nearly as big in any type of house where they can find the spot for 50 minutes' worth of excellent running time.

The get-together between an octopus and a giant lobster is the main event. More of this footage would be appreciated because the tentacles weave in and out and the jaws click while a shot of tentacle ink blurs the head grasp which takes the lobster for the count.

Flyweights on the card are a couple of spindly spider crabs. They go to it for death, also. They're sincere enough, but not convincing.

By way of side entertainment, one shot shows a couple of octopi together. Titles define this as mating time, even explaining that cohabitation is promoted by the femme absorbing one of the boy friend's legs. Titles don't mean much, because shot on screen registers like a huddle of tentacles. Intellectuals gasp, however.

Bees, ants, beetles — almost every insect except the grasshopper—are included in the side show. *Waly.*

LAST PERFORMANCE
(SILENT

Universal production and release. Directed by Paul Fejos under production supervision of Carl Laemmle, Jr. Conrad Veidt and Mary Philbin co-featured. Story and continuity by James A. Creelman. Titles by Walter Anthony. Film editor, Robert Jahns. At Little Carnegie, week Nov. 2.

Erik the Great..............Conrad Veidt
Julie......................Mary Philbin
Buffo.....................Leslie Fenton
Mark Royce...............Fred MacKaye
Theatre Manager..........Gustav Partos
Booking Agent...........Wm. H. Turner
Judge..................Anders Randolph
District Attorney.........Sam De Grasse
Defense Attorney...........George Irving

This is Conrad Veidt and Mary Philbin's swan song for Universal, contracts of neither being renewed. The picture was produced as a part-talker, with dialog in the last reel only, but is released at Little Carnegie (artie) in the silent version, dialog reel apparently not standing up in opinion of U. heads.

"Last Performance" is one of the draggiest pictures ever made, with the photography of the poorest. Apparently, Paul Fejos was up against handicaps at the start, and

---

with a story that is more foreign than domestic in brand, he sought to give it the German touch. Photography, of the subdued type as in "Sunrise" and "Street Angel" (both Fox), was one of the results, another the deliberate manner in which the picture moves.

Besides being very slowly paced there isn't a great deal of action. After a deluge of circus and stage stories in which the villain gums up the works to get even with the hero, picture can't rely on originality, if there is any here. There doesn't seem to be the least.

"Last Performance" opens in Europe and ends in America, but all of it in every way looks like Europe and its picture product.

AROUND THE WORLD
VIA GRAF ZEPPELIN
(SOUND—Inserted)

M-G-M release, presented in association with Hearst newspapers. Combination of ground newsreel shots and record of the trip made by an M-G-M photographer aboard the Zeppelin. At Cameo, New York, week Nov. 2. Running time, 52 mins.

As the first complete pictorial and sound chronicle of an historical "first time," this picture indubitably is of great value, and will be much more so in the future, as an educational record. But as a commercial venture for today, to be shown for its full running time it is best suited to small downtown wired houses to be exploited in the same manner as pictures of other explorations.

There is a market among deluxe houses for the film in shortened version, to be run in conjunction with a regular feature. Interest in the Zeppelin's feat as a current event item has not yet expired.

Trouble with the 52 minutes of film is that quite a portion has been seen in newsreels. Shots from the ground as the Zeppelin passes over various cities, and Dr. Eckener getting the glad hand from native dignitaries, are the only authentic sound records in the picture. For the most part they are ordinary news clips.

Remainder is taken by the M-G-M cameraman from the Zeppelin, showing life aboard the dirigible and panorama views of the countries and seas. These were made on silent film, later converted to sound with an invisible speaker explaining everything in a continuous spiel.

Hum of the Zep's motors has also been faked on the silent shots. Two other phonies are evident: one a victrola playing "Singing in the Rain" in the cabin, and the other a crew member playing accordion.

Thereby through modern fakery does the composition of a couple of Hollywood songwriters go down in history with the miraculous feat of Dr. Hugo Eckener and the sandwich-making attempts of Lady Drummond Hay. *Bang.*

HANDCUFFED
(SYNCHRONIZED)

Rayart production and release. Directed by Duke Worne from story by Arthur Hoerl. In cast: Virginia Brown Faire, Wheeler Oakman, D. Jagger, J. Harrison, George Cheeseboro. At Loew's New York, one day, Oct. 31. Running time, 60 minutes. On disk.

Arthur Hoerl writes nearly all of the themes for Rayart. This one is evidence of brain fag and Duke Worne's megaphoning isn't any better. The mistake should have been recognized and admitted in the cutting room.

Just a slow moving galaxy of bromidic inconsistencies.

Father of a lad commits suicide, charging it to an unfaithful friend. Then the son threatens the friend but another enemy takes advantage of the situation and does the job. The night of the double kill-

---

ing the grown-up children of the dead daddies get together. The girl, Miss Faire, is out to get evidence but falls in love with the man she believes shot her father. The enemy, Wheeler Oakman, has to go on posing as the girl's protector until after the trial, when he marries her.

Things are so balled up by this time that Hoerl starts feeling his way out of the story by having Oakman tip the bottle until he starts talking about the affair. The convicted man has escaped from the death house and hears the confession at the same time. But the enemy just horses along because a wife can't testify against a hubby and a convict's word is no good. Detectives come in. The same muddlers who overlooked simple evidence that would have closed the case in the first reel. One of them knocks the enemy out of a window, so it remains for a housekeeper to introduce herself and get the butler to admit that he was an accomplice and helped plant the evidence in the second killing on the boy.

Waly.

WOMAN TO WOMAN

(ALL DIALOG with Songs)

Tiffany production and release. Directed by Victor Saville. Betty Compson featured. Adapted by Nicholas Fodor from the Michael Morton stage play. RCA Photophone sounded. Two or three songs published by Feist. Writers not named. At Globe, New York, $1.50 twice daily, opening Nov. 11, limited to two weeks. Running time, about 90 minutes.

```
Lola..................Betty Compson
David.................George Barraud
Vesta................Juliette Compton
Florence...........Margaret Chambers
Hal.................Reginald Sharland
Davey.................Georgie Billings
Dr. Gavron..............Winter Hall
```

Betty Compson and tears may carry this Tiffany talker, "Woman to Woman" into the first runs of the keys. There's little besides, other than the sobbing story. But the trouble with the sobs is that they are of the same kind and character that prevail in the Gloria Swanson talker, "The Trespasser." Probably a coincidence, since both were in the making simultaneously and this one adapted from a stage play.

The teary end is strong in its and the Compson way, if Miss Compson can convince you, which she doesn't do to the hardboileds. It's about her son, and that son got the only laugh Monday night at the Globe. No comedy relief whatsoever, but the laugh was there, and hearty. It came about when Miss Compson led her soldier boy sweetie from the old days in Paris during the war into a bedroom, and there he was, little David. It depressed Big David, but amused the audience, which had been led to believe that the little Parisian affair of a couple of days had been purely lovely.

So many people lost their memory in the war, according to the silents. Now they have commenced to do it in the talkers. Early parts of the story singularly familiar, about how David did go to Paris on leave, fell into and for Lola, but had to forthwith rejoin his English regiment at the front without notice to her, after having gone forth for an hour to arrange about their marriage.

And then the front and the trench and the German shell, and Dave forgot it all.

Back in the old boiler room near London Dave was again a business man, remembering he was wealthy but forgetting Lola so completely he had married. No children. And then Lola, a singer in a Paris joint in the days when Dave met her, came to London as a noted music hall star. He saw her, but recognized her not. She sang that same song she had done in the joint, and Dave was hep.

Then the sobs started. He told Lola he had always wanted a boy, and there the boy was. But Mrs. David went up stage. The two women could not agree, and "woman to woman," Lola finally consented to let little Davey go to his foster mother while she did her dance of death and died on the lot. In the Swanson picture the finish is much happier and less painful.

Miss Compson seemingly sings her concert hall songs in French, if you can be convinced by her that she is doing it herself, but she talks straight English, whether in Paris or London, probably figuring any accent is a nuisance to a blonde. Otherwise her performance is middling, but she looks well, although when the two women, wife and near-wife, stood together for their big argument which they never made big, Miss Compson's lips looked like a raspberry ice and Juliette Compton's make-up around the mouth like coffee ice cream. Between the two they seemed to be advertising Schrafft's.

No other performance of note. The kid, maybe, George Billings, ofttime mechanical, though, even for a kidlet. George Barraud had the sappy big David role, with some pretty tough dialog at times to handle. Let's hope the picture always plays the houses without a gallery.

One of the songs, in march time, sounded good.

Reproduction at the Globe first class.

Tiffany has the Globe for two weeks, taking it for this talker at $1.50 top. It won't do Tiffany a bit of harm, although "Woman to Woman" is like most of the others in the $2 sent class—it ain't.

Sime.

SO THIS IS COLLEGE

(ALL DIALOG, with Songs)

Metro-Goldwyn-Mayer production and release. From original story by Al Boasberg and Delmer Daves. Dialog by Joe Farnham and Boasberg. Directed by Sam Wood with Leonard Smith, cameraman. Songs by Martin Broones; edited by Frank Sullivan. At Capitol, New York, week November 8. Running time, 97 mins.

```
Eddie.................Elliott Nugent
Biff.............Robert Armstrong
Windy.................Cliff Edwards
Babs...................Sally Starr
Betty.................Phyllis Crane
Polly.................Polly Moran
Coach.................Lee Shumway
```

There seems to be a lot of good screen football around this fall and this is another one. Peculiar part of the extreme length, 97 minutes on the screen, is that few will object. Picture carries a car load of laughs, Elliott Nugent doing a modified Haines to dialog, and the climax game is a pip.

Metro has invariably turned out smart gridiron matter. Somebody on the lot knows football and lays that part of the script out accordingly. This studio was the first to take its cue from the newsreel grid stuff to give the hero a number which matched the ground gainer in the news shots. Also, if memory serves, this plant was the first to follow the genuine play in that the close-up matter was made to coincide with the team formation shown in the news clip. That is, when the press stand view shows somebody starting around end, or fading back to heave a pass, the prop close-up action picks up the same play half way through to magnify its completion. It's great cutting and well worth the time and trouble it must entail.

In this picture the studio has selected the University of Southern California's campus. It's the '28 Stanford-U. S. C. game in the Los Angeles Coliseum which is used. Actual grid battle was a 10—0 upset in favor of U. S. C., but the studio has it twisted into a 9—7 victory. Coast fans and those who saw Army-Stanford last fall in the east will easily recognize Hoffman, Fleischacker, Sims and the rest of Pop Warner's last year's mob.

On story "College" hardly means a thing. It's the dialog, comedy situations, interpolated tunes, the work of Nugent and Armstrong, and the game which make the picture. Just a tale of a couple of room and teammates who split over a girl until, between halves, they overhear the co-ed telling her real boy friend she's only been kidding them along. Revelation floats through a dressing room window after the non-speaking pals have taken a verbal lacing from the coach. Both being halfbacks, they go out to split things wide open in the second half.

"I Don't Want Your Kisses" listens as having an excellent dance band chance and is the basis of more praise for the cutter. One sequence has Nugent singing this to the girl as he sits at a piano. Nugent can't sing and it's doubtful if he can play piano, but he does both here. Piano angle is a cinch to cover up, but vocally they have cut in another voice between the lyric lines which Nugent talks rather than sings. In other words, those lines demanding that the melody be carried have been given to the double and the voice closely parallels Nugent's register. Whenever this happens Nugent turns his head to help mask it, but when he's

talking the song himself it's a full face shot. Almost a shame to say anything about it, but such a corking piece of work shouldn't go unrecognized. Not one in a thousand fans will ever spot it. For smart voice doubling and really only half doubling this tops to date.

Both Nugent and Armstrong are excellent. Nugent predominates because he has almost all the gag lines as the self-assured senior who admits he's a panic with the girls. That he doesn't quite physically fit as a varsity back can, and will be overlooked in lieu of his performance—an effort that's not far away from the late Gregory's Kelly's "Seventeen" (stage) although in a more aggressive vein.

This is also supposed to be Sally Starr's film debut. Of the Bow-White Carol type, Miss Starr has some appearance slants to cover up if she's going to travel in fast company. In this lightweight role her work is superior to the illusion she presents, so it appears as if M-G will have to tell the camera boys to concentrate if the intention is a build-up.

Other characters involved are all secondary, although two youngsters pry a lot of laughs loose from the business given them to do as freshmen, and the younger fans will like Cliff Edwards' vocal pyrotechnics.

Recording and camera work of the best, and especially during the game. Mikes have evidently picked up the mixture of screams and yells from the U. S. C. side of the L. A. bowl so truly as to make an audience tingle. This part of the sound track has, of course, also been cut in and around the close-up footage on Nugent and Armstrong. Feature also marks one of the few instances of a studio taking the theatrical license to employ an off screen orchestra accompaniment without manufacturing an excuse.

Only that portion of the populace which is rabid against screen college yarns will snub this one.

Sid.

Footlights and Fools

(ALL DIALOG, with Songs)

First National production and release, starring Colleen Moore. Directed by W. A. Seiter from story by Katharine Brush. At the Strand, N. Y., week of Nov. 8. Running time, about 70 mins.

```
Fifi d'Auray...............Colleen Moore
Jimmy Willet.............Raymond Hackett
Gregory Pyne.............Frederick Marsh
Claire Floyd............Virginia Lee Corbin
Call Boy.................Mickey Bennett
Chandler Cunningham...Edward Martindel
Jo...................Adrienne D'Ambricourt
Treasurer.................Frederick Howard
Stage Manager...............Sidney Jarvis
Press Agent..................Cleve Moore
Song Plugger...............Andy Rice, Jr.
Stage Doorman........Ben Hendricks, Jr.
Bud Burke..................Larry Banthim
```

For a materialistic twist to this one, Miss Moore at the finish marries the wrong guy. More, she orders him out of her house, never to return, while the nice gentleman also goes, apparently never to return. With the picture released, there's no need telling what might have been done with that ending.

But it is going to hurt ticket sales. "Footlights" looks like medium money, and Miss Moore will draw it all on personality and past achievements.

Five vocal numbers, three sung by the star, in full stage production settings photographed in Technicolor. Miss Moore, as a revue star and singing with a French accent and dancing slightly, is cute and logical. A minority of the footage is in color.

Another backstage story. Broadway producer has sent Betty Murphy to Paris for French atmosphere and brings her back as Fifi d'Auray, a continental sensation. She clicks, and must fake a dialect and manner except in the strictest privacy. This is the laugh angle, and is handled well. Fifi loves a lazy, racketeering

youngster but won't consider marriage until he gets a job and becomes ambitious. A young millionaire also loves Fifi, but she considers him a John and won't warm up.

To help her the millionaire secretly has the boy employed in his office. Later there is a robbery, and the boy is accused of being an accomplice. He tells the girl he was framed by the millionaire and she believes him. Even to the extent of marrying him. Then she tears into the millionaire. Wealthy one questions the boy and proves before the girl that the kid is a thief.

Still an unkissed bride, the girl orders her husband out of her life forever. And the millionaire also goes. Pathetically alone, the girl dully gives routine instructions to her maid—about having the car ready to take her to the theatre, etc. Fade.

Miss Moore's presentation of the one girl with two names and opposite characteristics is a good bit of acting. She is and always was a beautifully sincere performer. Two male leads, Raymond Hackett as the gambling kid, and Frederic Marsh as the millionaire, have rather difficult assignments but both pull through neatly. Idea is to keep the customer guessing which is the deserving suitor.

Virginia Lee Corbin is adept as a dumb chorine, and Edward Martindel is old reliable as the producer.

Andy Rice, Jr., has a song-plugger bit, singing a boop-boop number to Miss Moore in a dressing room sequence. Clicked in the short workout, mostly by means of Miss Moore's surprised expressions.

Peppy tune which likely will be picked up by dance bands is "You Can't Believe My Eyes." Ballad, "If I Can't Have You," is a mild entrant in a flooded field. Other featured number is "Pilly Pom Pom Plee," reminiscent.

William Seiter directed and must have followed the script religiously.

Bang.

Romance of Rio Grande

(ALL DIALOG with Songs)

Fox production and release. Directed by Alfred Santell from Marion Orth's adaptation of novel "Conquistador," by Katharine Fullerton Gerould. Cameraman, Arthur Edeson. At Roxy, New York, week Nov. 8. Running time, 95 minutes.

```
Pablo Wharton Cameron....Warner Baxter
Carlotta.....................Mary Duncan
Juan....................Antonio Moreno
Manuelita...................Mona Maris
Don Fernando.............Robert Edeson
Vincente..................Agostino Borgato
Padre Miguel...............Albert Roccardi
Catalina...................Mrs. Jiminez
Dorry Wayne...........Major Coleman
Dick Rivers..............Charles Byers
Luca.................Merrill McCormick
```

Taking this one apart to see what makes it tick compels increased admiration for the technical adroitness and skill of the co-ordinated production departments. It isn't anything new. Dolores Del Rio and Lupe Velez, to mention only the more contemporaneous, have been around too long and the devices of cow country villainy have been too thoroughly exploited for the plot, setting or characters to represent novelty or arresting innovation.

It simmers down to the manner rather than the content. Rarely beautiful photography, sound engineering that commands extravagant praise, scrupulous attention to detail in production and story. Excellence in acting and probably inspired editing, all combined, with a splendid film resultant.

Money and lots of it poured into "Romance." It is stamped in every reel with the innumerable touches that find their way only into productions painstakingly executed from a carefully wrought design.

Running 95 minutes and never very melodramatic or otherwise "tense," it still holds interest and packs a little of many things—gunfire, hard riding, singing, coquetry, comedy and a liberal dosage of love's old molasses.

It's the lowdown on the Alvarez family, big nabobs and landowners in Mexico. Grandpa yearns for his estranged grandson, meanwhile finding his presumed heir, nephew, less than the perfect caballero. How the grandson returns unwittingly and the events leading up to the final clinch form more of a chronicle than a plot.

Warner Baxter and Antonio Moreno, the latter the real McCoy in things Spanish, play grandson and nephew, respectively. Baxter is enormously good. He is in all his actions an actor who knows exactly what he is doing and how to do it. Moreno, too, discharges himself well.

Mona Maris, new, has the burden of the feminine participation. Hers is a strange personality, often radiantly animated and attractive; at other times less so and looking terrible in the final fadeout shot. Yet she has a clear-cut claim to a big okay on her performance, replete with what is ticketed by the highbrows as nuances. She can act. That can be emphasized.

Mary Duncan gets another bad break. This former legit arrived in Hollywood before dialog and has been handicapped by her assignments and the manner of handling her generally. She's not easy to cast. Here she does well what there is for her to do, but it's entirely a non-progressive performance and unsympathetic. It is made quite clear that she unconventionally receives gentlemen in her boudoir.

Robert Edeson, as always, splendid.

"Romance of Rio Grande" is a picture of which Fox may boast. Whether or not it has the requisite sock to be a standout grosser is too hazardous a guess. But it should do very well financially for both producer and exhibs. *Land.*

THE LOVE DOCTOR
(ALL DIALOG)

Paramount production and release. Featuring Richard Dix. Directed by Melville Brown from story based on "The Boomerang," by W. Smith and Victor Mapes In cast: June Collyer, Miriam Segar. At Paramount week Nov. 6. Running time, 60 minutes.

Theme so light action occasionally drags, but "The Love Doctor," bolstered by good cast and dialog that fosters numerous spot laughs, will register well in comedy program class.

Richard Dix as the young medical graduate personality pluses through some of the situations that are threadbare of plot. Even in slow moving, repititious office sequence, the Dix voice and manner are entertainment in themselves.

The doctor who prescribes three things to win in love is shown falling for his own prescription shortly after the first reel when June Collyer enrolls as nurse and immediately commences the eye work.

Suspense ends here, since the finale is written on the faces of the leads. In the complications that ensue are some good gags. These are furthered in carrying power by Dix's naturalness.

Spill in lake and incarceration in cabin of doctor and nurse, both of whom are now using the prescription on each other, is one of the baby spots of entertainment value.

Girlie fans, especially, giggle through the sequence in which the doc entertains an aggressive girl friend who has crashed his study while his pants are on another chair. And Dix keeps the lower limbs bvded all through an audience-conscious exchange of innocent dialog audacity. *Waly.*

SHANGHAI LADY
(ALL DIALOG)

Universal production and release. Directed by Harry Pollard. In cast: Mary Nolan, James Murray, Wheeler Oakman. At the Colony, N. Y., week of Nov. 7. Running time, about 60 mins.

Despite a lot of cheap dialog and situation this film will go well with those fans who like their mellers meller. Holds interest throughout in bringing together an escaped convict and a reformed prostie, both out to kid the world that they are on the up-and-up.

Mary Nolan is eventually screen wed to James Murray, the convict. But before that their activities in their separate spheres are chronicled.

Miss Nolan is shown as the white girl getting the air from a Chinese hop joint. Her defiance and utterance is that she will force society to recognize her. Then, Murray, he is the bearded white who confides to a sleek stranger in a Shanghai gin place that he slid over the wall. Revelation that stranger is a Pekin dick. After that his escape, blackjack and rescue by a couple of Chinese maidens who are anxious for white attention. These shave him while he is unconscious and press his suit before the mob gets around to the front door. Then it's just Mary and Jimmie kidding each other throughout the rest of the footage.

A peeved Chinaman, earlier extraed into the footage, is revived to bump off the inevitable annoying detective, and everybody's happy. *Waly.*

PARIS

First National production and release. Starring Irene Bordoni. Adapted by Hope Loring from Martin Brown's play of the same name. Clarence Badger, director. Cameraman, Sol Polito; supervised by Bobby North; dances staged by Larry Ceballos; songs by Al Bryan and Eddie Ward. At Central, New York, twice daily $2 run, Nov. 7. Running time, 97 mins.

Vivienne Rolland............Irene Bordoni
Guy Pennell................Jack Buchanan
Cora Sabbot...........Louise Closser Hale
Andrew Sabbot.............Jason Robards
Brenda Kaley...........Margaret Fielding
Harriet.......................Zasu Pitts

Long program picture promising nothing hysterical in the way of box office beyond those points where Irene Bordoni is a favorite stage daughter.

Of the feature's overboard 97 minutes, 39 are spent in color split into two sequences of 10 and 29 minutes each. Rainbowed moments are for the stage numbers upon which this effort depends to get over. Story is shy both on attack and defense with Louise Closser Hale the script's only buoy. There are slow spots.

Picture's first half hour belongs to Miss Hale alone. This condition has a tendency to repeat itself whenever the action gets away from the theatre angle. Yarn is thin. Neither Miss Bordoni nor Jack Buchanan is apt to intrigue the screen public as love interest.

Stage ensembles have been conceived to fill the eye and Buchanan's "Miss Wonderful" is a tune which stands an excellent chance of reaching popularity proportions. Also a help is Miss Bordoni's specialty down next to closing. As the cutting room has turned it out, the star's personally weak footage is her opening single number. In the later production scenes a chorus of about 40 girls, two-thirds dancing mediums and the remainder show girls, dress the stage. Dance routines suffice minus novelty with a triple scene shift before the camera on one number. The old adage that show girls, the tall mesdames who parade in extravagant costumes, never sing evidently goes for the studio as well as the stage.

Plot is nothing more than a line upon which is hung the various individual performances. Miss Hale's first 30 minutes as a tight-lipped New England mother who goes into a mild Paris brandy bun, makes it plenty tough for Miss Bordoni to catch up. And any way you look at it you can't give the elder woman worse than a draw despite Miss Bordoni's songs and flash costumes. Miss Hale's work is doubly valuable in that she holds the picture together when it has no other means of support. It can even be said that she saves it by holding attention until the film reaches its color and the star's song strength.

Buchanan, Britain's top comedy-juvenile, holds plenty of class, wears clothes in front of the lens as aptly as on a stage, and continues adept at leading numbers. He has too much class to be completely ignored by film audiences, although, at the same time, he lacks that sheikish aspect to which the average femme fan succumbs.

Zasu Pitts plays a dumb, monotone maid and Jason Robards is the Yankee son who breaks far enough away from the apron strings to become engaged to the French actress. Just a part.

As on the stage, Miss Bordoni seems best suited to the revue type of entertainment where she can come and go in specialties to turn loose her full strength. In her own show the French girl can pick her road spots, few as those may now be, but "Paris" in film form is going places where they never heard of her or a $5.50 b. o. tap. Her songs figure to entertain after they come in, but the title, the word-of-mouth on the color ensembles, and additional exploitation must do the national drawing.

Studio has tried to insert a thrill by a backstage fire which is reason for turning loose the chorus from a dressing room in various stages of undress. Audiences won't be oblivious to the angle and it's an asset.

As to script it concerns Buchanan and Miss Hale's ruse to break up the Bordoni-Robards troth by trotting around themselves until the circumspect mother finally bobs her hair and announces her engagement to the actor who is years her junior. Idea is that mom wants her boy to stay in his own circle and the juvenile would like to wed his stage partner. Expose of the scheme is held back until the finale for those who have stayed in line.

Picture figures to do all right because of the stage build-ups for the star, the comedy unloosed by Miss Hale, and the probability that one, maybe two, of its tunes will make an impression. It won't stay at the Central very long, despite Miss Bordoni's personal New York draw, but that isn't so important. *Sid.*

NIGHT PARADE
(ALL DIALOG)

Radio production and release. Directed by Mal St. Clair and based on "Ringside," play by George Abbott, Ted Paramore and Hyatt Daab. Screen play by James Gruen and George O'Hara. William LeBaron, producer. Louis Sarecky, associate producer. Jack Kilchen, photography; Lambert Gay, recorder. Cast includes Hugh Trevor, Lloyd Ingraham, Dorothy Gulliver, Aileen Pringle, Robert Ellis, Lee Shumway, Ann Pennington, and Ann Greenway. RCA Photophone recording. At the Hippodrome, N. Y., week of Nov. 9. Running time, 72 mins.

Ought to stand up satisfactorily everywhere. It's the old prizefight hoke, but done with showmanship written and an idea of what should click with the patron.

Outstanding factor is that the picture maintains its suspense, building from the start to an effective and exciting finish. Fight, alone, in the last reel, compensates for any dull moments the fault-finders will

---

discover. And to make it the more unusual, the producers have staged the battle in a pouring rain. It's at least different.

Title can't be construed as having any direct connection with the story. A few slow moments, but none which make any particular difference.

Sequence in which the gang of crooks, mainly through the wiles of their vamp confederate, snare the young middleweight champ (Ingraham) into willingness to throw the fight for $100,000, is a peach. Into this scene, St. Clair directing, has stuck Ann Greenway and Ann Pennington, latter doing a dance routine. Miss Greenway's assignment mostly is wisecracks. Also strong scene is that between father and son, or manager and champ, in the latter's dressing room just before the big fight when dad disowns his boy in stiff language because he has turned crooked. Fans will rejoice in the lad's last-minute decision to tear up the check and go in to win.

As the siren in the case, Aileen Pringle is seen in a somewhat different role than usual, but plays it with uncommon finesse. Dorothy Gulliver is nice as the heroine. Hugh Trevor is oke as the father-manager, and Robert Ellis and Lee Shumway, in minor roles, round out a good cast. Recording and photography above average and St. Clair's direction studied, careful and effective.

Only music this picture has is in the party sequence, where an unimportant cast member is heard singing a pop number during some dialog in the nearby hall.

It's a prize fight picture, and the title is probably meant to disguise that fact. But once they come in, the picture figures to entertain. Where they like stories about the ring, a cinch.

ARSENAL
(RUSSIAN MADE)
(Silent)

Wufku production releasing through Amkino. Directed by Alexander Dovzhenko from his own scenario. Photographed by D. Demutsky. American titles by Shelley Hamilton. S. Swazhenko featured, with others in cast not credited. At Film Guild, N. Y., for two weeks beginning Nov. 9. Running time, 65 mins.

As long as New York has an outlet for Soviet propaganda, Russia will likely continue to shoot in flickers of this kind. Anywhere outside New York it's doubtful if there's a market for this sort of stuff.

"Arsenal" is not as powerful as the title implies. Out and out revolutionary stuff, hidden behind a maze of pseudo-psychology, symbolism and cinematic imagination. No story value of any kind and even the usual attempt at continuity is missing. Director evidently took his material from historical incidents during the blood days of 1917.

This particular locale is Ukrania. A panoramic view of the southern section of Russia is tensely visualized, together with the sordid and devastated condition it was in at the period depicted. Most of it is quite familiar to those who have seen Russian pictures. Only the action will seem strange as there is a complete absence of story. Characters seem to have no connection with one another.

Everything is symbolic. Horses, for instance, are given spoken titles, while a train wreck is understood to be not literally so, although it is pictured with realistic detail. Supposed to be man's inability to run things he doesn't know how to run. Also the chief character is made bullet proof for the purpose of showing that the spirit of the working classes cannot be killed.

Photography is generally good, in spots unusually so. Not many trick shots. The Ukraine country is known for its beautiful landscapes, quaint villages and quainter inhabitants. All of this is perceptibly gathered into the film giving it the only interest. Battlefield shots and other war sequences appear to have been recruited from stock.

"Arsenal" has revolutionary significance but no general box office appeal.

FANNY HAWTHORN
(ENGLISH MADE)
(Silent)

Produced by Maurice Elvey and released in U. S. through Excellent. Directed by Elvey and Victor Saville from an adaptation of the Stanley Houghton play of same title. At the 55th St. Playhouse, N. Y., beginning Nov. 7. Running time, about 70 mins.

Fanny Hawthorn.............Estelle Brody
Alle Jeffcote.................John Stuart
Kathe Hawthorn..............Marie Ault
Chris Hawthorn......Humberstone Wright
Nate Jeffcote...........Herman McKinnel
Marie Jeffcote.................Irene Roche
Mary Collins................Peggy Carlisle
Beatrice Farrar..........Gladys Jennings
Mayor......................Arthur Chesney

"Fanny Hawthorn" sustains a suspense which would be appreciated by the average American audience. Its main fault is that the ending is too abrupt despite the 70 minutes expended. Too much plot construction omitted by the crude cut-off, leaving Fanny evidently about to become a mother, but turning down the responsible son of the rich man and a bonafide admirer, as well, in the Lancashire cotton mills.

Maybe that's the way it's supposed to end. If so, it's strictly for that handful of fans who believe atmosphere is obtainable only in the barn-like structures which feature odd finales and things unsuited to the box office. If they can piece on a suitable finish, just to get Fanny's status settled one way or the other, "Fanny" could be used by a lot of silent picture houses over here.

In this case it's the story. Estelle Brody is the Fanny who falls for Alle, son of the owner of the mill in which she and her dad work. Fanny and Alle are seen in an auto bound for a hotel. This leads to the father's threat to disinherit his boy unless he legitimatizes the affair. In so doing the lad has to relinquish the Mayor's daughter, readily accomplished when knowledge of the disinheritance is revealed. But Fanny, who counted on a postcard alibi which never materializes because her girl friend drowns before she can buy the stamp, thwarts all by refusing to go through with the ceremony. She has given the rich philanderer a pathetic handclasp and he has presented her with a quizzical glance of growing interest when the shop foreman reminds her that he is standing by and that the "time" is getting close. They then flash "finish" up at the 55th.

Individual performances are satisfactory with Miss Brody showing the way.

Waly..

German Pics

Berlin, Oct. 24.
"WOMAN IN MOON"

"Woman in the Moon" (Ufa), at the Ufa Palast am Zoo.

This is the long awaited production by Fritz Lang, director of "Metropolis," who has been working on it for fully a year. Said to have cost over $500,000, and looks it. Many models are used and are skillfully photographed. From a spectacular angle the film is fine.

Idea is fantastic. It concerns itself with the shooting of a rocket ship to the moon. The ship, in the form of a torpedo, is brought from its hangar and sunk in a pool of water, as it is too light to stand alone. Shot off it goes hurtling through space, the first eight minutes being a terrific strain on the passengers who must adapt themselves to the overpowering air pressure. Inmates are shown fighting for breath, but the crisis is passed. Speed of the vehicle increases and it hits the moon with fearful impact. Passengers do not know whether it is possible to live on the moon so one goes out in a diving suit and an oxygen tank. He lights a match, it burns freely, he throws off his hood, and the conquest of the moon is a fact.

Unfortunately the human beings concerned in these exploits can't compete with the machines. Thea von Harbou, Lang's wife, also responsible for the scenario of "Metropolis," has not created any characters which interest.

The slight story is the main reason, besides which Lang shows he has not kept up to date as a director of actors. Only Willi Fritsch delivers anything in the way of a performance. Fritz Rasp is far too much of an old-fashioned menace. Gustav von Wangenheim overacts, and Gerda Maurus is not seen advantageously.

Picture is sufficiently interesting to be shown in New York as a mechanical oddity, but that's all.

"PARAGRAPH 173"

"Paragraph 173" (Ines Film), at the Beba Atrium.

Interesting picture with a strong theme. German law against incest, paragraph 173 of the penal code, makes a criminal offense of intermarriage between parents and children who are not related by blood. That is to say, as in this film, a father may not marry the daughter of his wife even though she be the offspring of another marriage. In the film the wife dies. The stepdaughter then has a child by the father, but when they go to be married they are informed that marriage is impossible and both are imprisoned. Finish is suicide for the girl and a renewed sentence for the father.

This is one of the better German pictures and is discreetly directed by James Bauer. Walter Rilla is splendid as the father, and Paul Henckel's masterly as the judge. Olga Tschechowa, as the girl, delivers her usual good work but is not too well cast in such youthful parts.

Film could never get into Chicago but would have a good chance in the New York sure-seaters, those "art" theatres.

"FALLEN GIRL"

"Diary of a Fallen Girl" (Hom Film), at the Ufa Kurfürstendamm.

G. W. Pabst is among the best of German directors still working here but has had atrocious luck with his scenarios. This one, taken from a best seller of years ago, is no exception. Its melodramatic treatment of a young girl become a prostitute (Louise Brooks) is ridiculous in its exaggerated theatricalism.

Discretion which Pabst displays in his direction only softens the comic qualities of the story. This time he has also been unfortunate in the choice of his heroine. Louise Brooks (American), is monotonous in the tragedy which she has to present.

"OTHER SIDE"

"On the Other Side of the Street" (Prometheus Film), at the Beba Atrium.

An attempt to translate into German one of those studies of milieu at which the Russians are so masterly. An excellent scenario, which suggests an O. Henry story, has as its leading figures a prostitute, a beggar, and a young fellow out of work.

Beggar picks up a pearl necklace in the street, his action being seen by the prostitute who follows him to his hut, where he lives with the out-of-work boy. In order to get hold of the necklace the girl seduces the idle youth and the two fall in love. He searches for the beggar to steal the necklace from him, but the latter escapes, and, in fleeing, falls into a river. Final shot is a newspaper notice reporting that an unknown man was drowned clutching an imitation string of pearls.

Leo Mittler, who makes his debut as a film director (he had formerly done some work on the stage) only partially succeeds in creating atmosphere. Best work is by Fritz Genschow as the boy. Lissi Arna is starred.

Sure seaters will likely appreciate its sardonic quality.

ATLANTIC
(ALL DIALOG)
(GERMAN MADE)

Berlin, Nov. 7.
Produced by British International; distributed by Sued Film in Germany. Premiere Gloria Palast. Recorded on RCA Photophone.

The first 100 per cent German talker, but made in England, at Elstree, with British capital. The Ufa won't have its first 100-percenters ready before January or February. It is not definite when Tobis will bring out its first product which belongs in this category.

No question this film will do business wherever it can be played. Unfortunately, at present there are not over 20 German wired houses. For this reason British International and the director, Dupont, deserve credit for their pioneer work. But instead of that, almost the whole press jumped on the picture and picked faults.

The picture is far from a perfect product. Its scenario, founded on a deadly play by Ernest Raymond, a flop on the English stage, is practically plotless. It is founded on the "Titanic" catastrophe—in itself an interesting and exciting incident, but essentially undramatic when made the chief focus point of interest.

There is a group of characters so large none arouse any particular interest. They can only be briefly sketched and remain merely puppets. On top of this there is no suspense, as it is known the catastrophe is coming, and there is so much light conversational dialog, even when the ship is actually sinking, that the spectator is encouraged to take the whole affair as lightly as do the leading figures.

On the other hand, the director, E. A. Dupont, responsible for the master film, "Variety," has caught the atmosphere of the ship splendidly and has a brilliant ensemble. At the head is Fritz Kortner, one of Germany's best stage and screen players, who delivers extraordinary work as a lame author of satirical books who proves heroic under the ordeal. Willi Forst is a young lounge lizard. He mixes tragedy neatly with his comedy. In the small role of the writer's valet, Georg John well puts over the humor of his role.

Lucie Mannheim, stage star, miscast as a young wife. She is beyond the ingenue class. Herrmann Valentin's vocal work is still too stagey.

The recording by RCA is satisfactory, but the German Klangfilm wiring often did not give tone enough and, when it was sufficiently loud, it broke. This especially noticeable in the recording of the jazz band, often excruciatingly tinny and impure. Before a reviewer could judge where the fault lay, he would have to hear the picture on Western Electric. It is hard to believe RCA could turn out such faulty recording and, until shown to the contrary, blame must be placed on the Klangfilm wire device.

Whatever its faults, this first German all-talker is considerably better than the first 100-percenter from America, and it should start the dialog ball rolling briskly over here.

Trask.

SEVEN FACES

Fox production and release. Featuring Paul Muni. Based on Richard Connell's "Friend of Napoleon" with dialog by Dana Burnett. Production supervisor, George Middleton. Dual direction—Berthold Viertel, camera; Lester Lonergan, dialog. Cameraman, Joseph August; sound, Donald Flick. Marguerite Churchill, Lester Lonergan, Russell Gleason, underlined. At Roxy, N. Y., week Nov. 15. Running time, 78 mins.

Papa Chibou....................Paul Muni
Helene Berthelot........Marguerite Churchill
Judge Berthelot...........Lester Lonergan
Georges Dufeyel............Russell Gleason
M. Pratouchy......Gustav von Seyffertitz

Another ordinary program picture for a good actor. Its novel aspect of ably executed wax figures, six of whom Muni plays in a dream sequence, will likely keep it alive for average grosses.

And it may better that somewhat in those spots in which Muni is to make personal appearances, Fox sending the featured player around to permit the fans to get a glimpse of him. This week he's spending 30 seconds a de luxe performance orally expressing his gratification and appreciation.

Evidently a tough man to fit, this former Yiddish star. And that he's considerable actor doesn't rest upon the audience's intuition. For pictures he's proved it twice, both times in scripts the art emporium disciples would rave about but around which your tab reading, or picture house, public finds no glamor.

Muni's reported private burn-up is to be compared to Chaney. That's no reflection upon the latter's ability but is simply Muni's reaction to the similarity of parts which the Lon undertakes. Muni is said to have said: "I'm an actor. I'll play any part." Those who doubt that he can do it haven't popped off to date, and, after all, that two-sentence summary covers everything. Basically, your real actor will and can play any assignment. Another Muni angle is that he will not twice play the same type of character. Therefore there can't be so very much wrong with Muni due to ability and ideas. There may, however, be something wrong with the scripts selected for him. It's happened twice now. Nothing particularly out of the way except that neither has been box office.

In "Seven Faces" Muni plays the aged attendant of a Parisian Mme. Tussaud's, a corking performance all the way.

After taking foot after foot to get going, the drama finally arrives when the owner decides to sell and Papa Chibou (Muni) realizes he's to lose all his stationary friends of 25 years, especially the figure of Napoleon for which he feels a fanatical attachment. Subsequent auction sale and his inability to meet the opposing bidder, leads Chibou to steal Napoleon with both finally landing in court. Love twist is that the judge's daughter and Chibou's young lawyer, frowned upon socially by the court, are in love. Having kept trysts in the wax works, with Napoleon the secret cache for notes, all this comes out in court when the final message is discovered in Nap's pocket during the hearing. It ends merrily with Chibou on his way to be gardener at the youngsters' new home.

Picture's best moments are, by far, in the court room, Muni and Lester Lonergan, as the judge, equally share in holding this together. Russell Gleason falls somewhat short in his dramatic appeal to save the old man from the minor charge. **Studio has also layed it on a bit thick by the wild rejoicing of the spectators who break into "Le Marseilles." Touch of irony in the defense enumerating Chibou's** devotion to the former Emperor, France, etc., and the old man later asking the judge if Napoleon had really lived, it being just the wax figure he wants, won't register in all spots.

Film has been so cut that not much more than 1,000 feet are spent on Muni's characterizations of the six dummies. This comes when Chibou is in a dilemma as to how to get the lovers together again after a quarrel, a problem over which he falls asleep. His best impression appears to be that of a Cockney with the camera and sound build-up to the brief Napoleon delineation a splendid illusion. Joseph August, cameraman, is as important as Muni during these transpositions, due to the limited time Muni is given for his six characters in search of a screen story. The double camera work is very good, with the sound track merely made to fit.

Viertel and Lonergan are credited as the directors. The court sequence smacks strongly of stage direction but somebody has been guilty of allowing this yarn to take too long in getting started. Productionally the multiple wax figures are interesting and a ballet, or a wax works revel, has also been introduced during the dream. Not much comedy, and that but snicker provoking. Marguerite Churchill is able and is once flashed in lingerie for no apparent reason. Tom Patricola is interpolated for an unbilled bit. His screen career to date has been nothing else but unbilled.

Nothing the matter with Muni. It's the stories. *Sid.*

SATURDAY NIGHT KID

(ALL DIALOG)

Paramount production and release. Starring Clara Bow. Directed by A. Edward Sutherland from play by George Abbott and John V. A. Weaver. Screen script by Ethel Doherty, adapted by Lloyd Corrigan. Cameraman, Harry Fischbeck. At Paramount, New York, week Nov. 15. Running time, 62 minutes.

Mayme....................Clara Bow
Bill....................James Hall
Janie....................Jean Arthur
Lem Woodruff....................Charles Sellon
Ma Woodruff....................Ethel Wales
Ken....................Frank Ross
Miss Streeter....................Edna May Oliver
Ginsberg....................Hyman Meyer
Jim....................Eddie Dunn
Pearl....................Leone Lane
Hazel....................Jean Harlow

A silent screen adaptation of the stage play, "Love 'Em and Leave 'Em," was made in 1926 by Paramount, under the stage title. Evelyn Brent, Louise Brooks and Lawrence Gray were featured. Clara Bow's latest is an all-talk version of the same story, with an entirely different cast in somewhat revised situations. Showing that stuff, shooting craps and using all the words, dishing a redhot philosophy about free and easy necking, the chemise girl should have no box office troubles with this. It's the Miss Bow her fans want, with plenty of "aint's" and that inevitable bedtime undress peep.

Mayme and her younger sister, Janie, work in Ginsberg's department store. So does Bill. They all live in the same rooming house.

Mayme sacrifices consistently for her younger sister, who's a sneaky little snipe always on the make. When Mayme and Bill are about to be married, Janie balks it by framing her sister and appropriates the boy friend.

Young sister has the gambling craze and eats into the Ginsberg Welfare money entrusted to her. To save her neck she blames sister, who has even been so helpful as to win it all back from the race track bookie in a crap game.

That's the last straw. Mayme tears into the kid, slapping her all over their bedroom while Bill listens in the next room with an understanding look in his eyes. Straight to Mayme he goes for the fadeout.

Part of a sacrificing elder sister is out of the ordinary for Miss Bow in theme but not as she jazzes it up. There's the crap game and the frenzied slapping scene, and pulling the love 'em and leave 'em gag when her heart is busted. Shopgirl lingo rolls off her tongue perfectly. The whinnying role of younger sister is given to Jean Arthur. She fits it in voice and appearance. James Hall as the boy friend rounds a capable trio.

Support good. Especially Edna May Oliver playing the director of personnel at Ginsberg's—sonorous, school-mammy dame.

Two scenes break away from the straight love theme, and provide healthy laugh intervals. One is a pep meeting at Ginsberg's, performed as a satire. Finishes with employees singing glory to Ginsberg to tune of "Hallelujah," but dropping it abruptly when the 9 a. m. bell rings. Ginsberg makes 'em come down early for the pep hokum.

Other good comedy mob bit is the Ginsberg pageant, to be performed as the climax of a Ginsberg social night. Called off at curtain time because Miss Bow is away shooting craps.

Selecting a moderately good program silent release to be remade with dialog is a hazardous venture, but this lines up as entertaining stuff for the big Bow crowd, including those who saw it silent.

A. Edward Sutherland's direction is a cleancut job. *Bang.*

SONG OF LOVE

(ALL DIALOG with Songs)

Columbia's release of Edward Small production starring Belle Baker. Erle C. Kenton, director; supervised by Harry Cohn. Howard Green and Henry McCarthy, story. Dorothy Howell and Norman Houston, dialog. At the Cohan, New York, twice daily for $2, starting Nov. 13. Running time, 76 mins.

Anna Gibson....................Belle Baker
Tom Gibson....................Ralph Graves
Buddy Gibson....................David Durand
Mazie....................Eunice Quedens
Joe....................Arthur Housman

Belle Baker is a pleasant surprise in her first picture. It's mostly Miss Baker, but the picture has other things to recommend it for program use. It's not $2, but looks like certain money in the regular houses.

Finding a yarn for Miss Baker couldn't have been an easy task, but the backstage narrative selected is okay. As a young mother Miss Baker is one-third of the Three Gibsons, one of those family combinations who bring on the kid for a finish. The Gibson kid picks up the final chorus of his mother's song in a stage box, steps on for some gagging with the old man and then makes the curtain speech.

When this youngster reverts to being just a kid, instead of a trouper, and misses a show to play ball in the yard adjoining the theatre, his mother realizes the unfairness of depriving him of his boyhood. So she breaks up the act to give the lad a home and an education. Pop goes off to do a two-act with a blonde, has gone with blondes before, and he likes his likker. Meanwhile, the son has been sent to military school and the mother clicks in a class cabaret as a single singer.

Pop has split with the blonde and now spends most of his time boozing. Mom is on the bill at the Palace for plenty of sugar, having graduated from the cafe, when the kid comes to town for a two-day vacation. Pop is playing solitaire and talking to himself in a nearby speak. A friendly acrobat takes the kid to the joint to straighten out pop, and pop comes to the Palace. They sit in the box, the kid picks up the final chorus of his mother's ballad and there is the reunion.

Youngster is very good. His name is David Durand and he does his own singing. Little of the mechanical in his performance, and when he builds up to a dressing room sob scene with his mother it's acting for a boy.

Ralph Graves does pop with restraint, playing a vaudevillian like a vaudevillian. Contrary to expectations, he looks right opposite Miss Baker. And what a job the studio had picking somebody for this part. Arthur Housman comes through as a Scotch acrobat, always borrowing a handful of cold cream from somebody on the bill. Remaining credited player is Eunice Quedens as the blonde come-between, a cinch part. Unbilled bits by the partner-owners of the cabaret should be billed.

Sob dialog is not too sobby and won't get any undue laughs. The backstage flippancy isn't too bright but relieves the dramatics in the right way.

"Take Everything But You" and "I'll Still Keep Wanting You," both ballads, sound likely. A third by Miss Baker is "White Way Blues," not important as a song but competent dance music. When "showing" for the cabaret job Miss Baker sings two comedy specials, one being "Itless," a standby with her.

Miss Baker is excellent for a first time in talkers. She took off a lot of weight for this effort, and Joe Walker, cameraman, did the rest. She is not singing "Eli, Eli." *Bige.*

THE KISS

(SILENT)

(Disc Orchestration)

Metro-Goldwyn-Mayer production and release. Directed by Jacques Feyder from George Saville's story adapted by Hans Kraley. At Capitol, week Nov. 15. Running time, 62 minutes.

Irene....................Greta Garbo
Andre....................Conrad Nagel
Guarry....................Anders Randolf
Lassale....................Holmes Herbert
Pierre....................Lew Ayres
Durant....................George Davis

Another murder trial, but so different from the rest in performance and setting it is like an original. "The Kiss," with an unusual taste exhibited in casting and direction, is entertainment of the holding kind. And it is one of Miss Garbo's best, without stretching the elastic of kindness. Though this is silent it may be stronger that way than with dialog.

Few actresses could weather the series of close-ups required of Miss Garbo in this one. In each she registers an individual perfection. The series proves her biggest asset is naturalness.

By Miss Garbo in several of the sequences, especially the intro when Irene tells Andre of her love but the impossibility of securing consent for a parting from her husband, Conrad Nagel, registers the manner of an interpreter.

Pierre, the juvenile admirer of Irene who does not know until the last few story feet of her real interest, is essayed superbly by the youthful Lew Ayres.

Getting the theme out of the regular rut by having Durant, detective, employed by the suspicious husband, Guarry, discover Pierre in the innocent company of Irene, veils the clandestine affair in a way that contributes largely to the suspense.

The title is introduced in the climax when Irene is found in the wild embrace of the lad, after submitting in a motherly fashion to his request for a kiss. Anders Randolf does exceptionally fine playing as the infuriated husband returning unexpectedly. His vicious swings at the youth's face have a force that is real to the audience.

Secreting the angle of the husband's death until Irene's trial for murder and the acquittal, another interest builder for the story. Its final unwind is thus with a punch since it remains for Irene to tell her lawyer-lover, Andre, that she shot her husband to prevent him from murdering the innocent kid.

Action is laid in France. During the trial the tedium of courtroom scenes is minimized by camera moving from short semi-closes on Nagel and the Judge to almost a concentration of the study in black presented by Miss Garbo.

Modernistically furnished sets and clever injections of art museums and dog shows as trysting places provide a needed change. *Waly.*

LES TROIS MASQUES

(FRENCH MADE)

(First All-Talker)

Paris, Nov. 8.

Pathe production and release. In French and directed by Andre Hugon from Charles

Mere's novel. Cast features Renee Heribel, Jean Toulout, Francois Rozet and Marcel Vibert. RCA Photophone equipment for production and reproduction. At the Salle Marivaux, Paris.

As a picture production, "Three Masks" is nothing to annoy anybody. Rather mediocre, stiltedly dramatic, slow and uninteresting as a celluloid offering. Yet, this film presents an angle for the American picture field.

As an all-talker in the native language, and France's first, with the locale of Corsica, nothing can stop the picture in this country. The heavy biz it is enjoying indicates the native hunger for the native tongue. Feeling that they are missing something through any titular transition, or dubbing in an American-made talker, is akin to the feeling of seeing a French-made picture with English sub-titles and sensing that the Anglo-Saxon compromise is but a sketchy counterpart of the full and original import of what the French had in mind.

Chevalier's "Innocents of Paris," particularly as concerns his French songs, is an example. The French must have missed something when he warbled "Louise." Hence, with "The Patriot" (Jannings) sounded, at the nearby Paramount, and "Broadway Melody," playing further up the boulevard at the Madeleine-Cinema, the fans have got the idea of what they want and will ultimately accept.

So far "Melody's" advance bookings are reasonable, but that house has a sizeable Anglo-American draw; let that peter out and the rest will tell the story. "The Patriot," with Jannings a continental fav, is only doing fair since the advent of "Les Trois Masques." Perhaps an even greater conception of things is that Franco-Aubert's "Cameo," diagonally across the Boulevard des Italiens, is getting away with murder on "The Queen's Necklace," starring Marcelle Jefferson-Cohn. It's doing biz, despite some local negative reaction through misrepresentation that it is the first French talker, when actually it's merely a sound synchronized flicker —and poor—with songs. No dialog. Theatre has been compelled to change its marquee from "Parlant et Chanson" (talking and singing) to "Sonore et Chanson" (synchronized with songs).

In direct antithesis, the canny Madeleine-Cinema (Metro) is maintaining good will through being frank in stressing in the French ads that "Broadway Melody" is an all-talker in English, with French titles merely superimposed.

"Les Trois Masques" is overly long and drives the biological auditor to distraction, but the natives are buying it for the same reason the pioneer American talkers did boom business at the gate. Outside of French-speaking localities it is meaningless.

Curiously enough, Pathe made this talker in England, not having RCA Photophone equipment available as Pathe-Natan now have. There are two other French talkers due in shortly, one made in Germany and another also outside of France. Adolphe Menjou's first for Pathe, under Jean de Limur's direction, will actually be the first home-made production. Menjou film is using Photophone equipment. *Abel.*

THE INVADERS

(Synchronized)

Syndicate Pictures production released by Big Productions Film Corp. Directed by J. P. McGowan from story by Sally Winters. Adapted by Wm. Sterret; titles by Wm. Stratton. In cast: Bob Steele, featured; Edna Aslin, Thos. Lingham, J. P. McGowan, Celeste Rush, Tom Smith, Bud Osborne and Chief Yolache. At Loew's New York, one day, Nov. 14. Running time, 50 mins. On disk.

Indie flicker comes under the so-so tab in the western catalog. Stock yarn, titles, situations, etc., ages old, but apparently not yet obsolete. McGowan, who has rated better things, projecting himself in the cast doesn't help any, other than probably being an economical gesture.

Plot is just another covered wagon parody, treating of the pioneer days when Custer made his last stand. But even the usual action stuff is missing. Starts with an Indian raid on a lonely caravan, where all but two tots, brother and sister, survive. Girl is picked up by the redskins, while the lad is grabbed by the Col. in charge of the rescue troops. Years elapse and the boy grows up to be a lieutenant under his foster father, in love with his step-sister.

An order to move a tribe of Injuns to a reservation is where the panic begins. Redskins go on the warpath, incited by an inspiring young brave who is also trying to grab the Chief's daughter. Latter makes a play for the young Lieut. and gets him in bad with his sweetie. Tangled in are a couple of menaces. This pair renege on their own people and, naturally, get bumped off at the end. There is the climax of the Indians attacking the fort, the discovery that the young squaw is really the sister of the white boy, and the final clinch between the hero and heroine.

Up to the standard for the one-day stands on a lenient ballot.

BRIDE OF THE DESERT

(ALL DIALOG—Western)

Rayart release, directed by Duke Worne. Story by Arthur Hoerl. In cast, Alice Calhoun, LeRoy Mason, Etham Ludlow and Lum Chan. At Loew's New York one day, Nov. 6. Running time, 50 minutes.

Inexpensively produced western, all dialog, and so reminiscent of "In Old Arizona" as to indicate it was aimed to capitalize on that picture's click. Panned out sufficiently well to merit single feature one-day bookings in the small spots.

One set used—interior of a cabin on the desert. Man has been prospecting for gold three years. His wife driven frantic by the loneliness and hubby's disregard. Dying to meet a boy friend and admits it to her hubby.

When wife is alone in the living room, gent staggers into the cabin—rather good looking but heavily bearded and wounded. He's the Killer, for whom a sheriff and posse are scouring the desert. Wife hides him in the cabin lean-to and does her best to make him.

And on and on. Windup has the husband identified as the Killer who framed the alleged Killer. He's shot just as he starts to bump off his wife for conniving with the other guy.

Direction too involved with plot buildup to give the love stuff more than passing attention. Photography alright and dialog recorded clearly.

Alice Calhoun shy on s. a. in a house apron. LeRoy Mason as the wounded fellow injects a little life but is absent from most of the footage. Etham Ludlow capable as the ornery husband.

Shouldn't be difficult to turn out pictures like this. *Bang.*

SHOW OF SHOWS

(ALL DIALOG, Songs, Dances)
(86% Color)

Warner Brothers production and release. Straight revue with all-star cast. Production supervised by J. L. Warner and Darryl Zanuck. John Adolfi credited as director. Dance ensembles by Jack Haskell and Larry Ceballos. Orchestra under direction of Louis Silvers. Settings, Max Parker; costumes, Earl Luick. Cameraman, Bernard McGill. Music and lyrics by J. K. Brennan, M. K. Jerome, Herman Ruby, Al Dubin, Joe Burke, Ray Perkins, Ned Washington, Herb Magidson, M. H. Cleary, Al Bryan, Eddie Ward, Perry Bradford and Jimmy Johnson. At Winter Garden, New York, for twice daily $2 run starting Nov. 20. Running time, 124 minutes, exclusive of intermission.

Sure box office for regular house display on its ensemble numbers, color, and the cast star names involved. From the $2 angle, or looking at it on the same basis as a stage revue, there are a flock of regrets.

If ever a picture needed the new wide film and screen, this is it. Dance directors have stairwayed the numbers to death and a wide angle projection lens can't overcome the limitations of the normal camera glass. Hence, the spectacle of a mass chorus is limited so that almost half are off the screen too frequently. When they're all on it's a diminutive crowd.

Of the 124 minutes only 21 are without color, a 17-minute stretch in the first part and a four-minute opening of the second half as running here.

For the program houses these 124 minutes can actually be cut at will by reel. Entire spools can go out and not be disastrous to the release as a whole. There's no story, plot or continuity. Being a disk recording it's evident that this will be the only way the grind houses can eliminate.

Reason for the reckless use of footage appears to be the studio's disinclination to hold the chorus numbers down. Practically all are 'way overboard on time, finale of the picture being the worst offender in running at least 1,000 feet and appearing endless. Result is that the numbers build to a point and then linger to taper off.

As to legitimate revue entertainment the two highlights involve Irene Bordoni and John Barrymore, the former against a piano for "Just An Hour of Love," the best melody in the picture but not new with this star, and the latter doing the soliloquy from Henry VI plus a superb presentation behind him.

There can be no question that the picture lacks a comedy sock, regardless of Frank Fay as m. c., and despite the inclusion of Beatrice Lillie. Miss Lillie is mixed up in a satirical recitative quartet, just all right and from a former Lillie show, while Fay is all out of proportion on footage compared to his material. Impression will be that there's too much Fay and there is, but it's mostly because his gags and "business" do not stand up.

With Barrymore, Fay shares the distinction of being given eight minutes alone, the m. c. also hanging on a piano for a snatch of his former act and to do a ballad.

For musical popularity "Singing in the Tub" sounds as having a good chance with the production for this number not up to advance rumors. And Miss Lillie's comedy item with the midgets is out entirely. If it's on a shelf somewhere, and any good at all, the boys ought to take it down and splice it in.

Picture opens thunderously in unraveling a military drill on a tremendous staircase by 192 girls arranged 16 abreast and 12 rows deep. Jack Haskell did it and has evolved some pip formations. A male drum and bugle corps of 45 augments for the finale. Haskell's other contributions of 48 girls on a web behind Georges Carpentier, and a ladder routine for "Chinese Fantasy," are also outstanding. All are allotted the big screen, and are too long. A back stage muff of the cue to spread the borders hurt the Chinese number opening night.

Larry Ceballos' "Black and White" girls (64), also on the stairs, is a corking piece of work in attaining an effect and not guilty of prolongation.

Film could have stood two or three masters of ceremonies. It was noticeable that both Barrymore and Barthelmess evidently declined to kid with or be kidded by Fay. Barthelmess rigidly introduces one number and Barrymore serves as his own trail blazer, though with something of a gag tag line. An inkling as to whether these two stars were smart or not in insisting on preserving their dignity can be had in the "sister" number. It's doubtful if Dolores Costello did herself any good by joining Helene to be one of a string of family "sister acts" leading chorus groups of 12 as representing various countries. An adagio foursome, Williams Dancers, are a click in a pirate set.

Everybody on the WB-FN lots in on this one, some who aren't under contract, although Dorothy Mackaill is among the absentees.

This revue's cost ran to $800,000. With the color it's a great flash and the numbers figure to send it through to get back the production tap and more. But those numbers are also a paradox in that they'll keep this picture from classing as sensational entertainment or box office. A revue, stage or screen, has got to have more than numbers. It's like a fast backfield with a weak strong line or a big stage benefit with too much show. The cry remains—comedy material.

Recording, for which no one is credited, is, at times, excellent. Color camera work is also uniformly good with some laboratory laxity noticeable on the last few feet of some of the sequences. *Sid.*

THE LOVE PARADE

(ALL DIALOG, with Songs)

Paramount production and release. Starring Maurice Chevalier. Jeanette MacDonald, Lupino Lane and Lillian Roth featured. Directed by Ernst Lubitsch. Screen play by Ernst Vajda and Guy Bolton from stage play, "The Prince Consort," by Leon Xanrof and Jules Chancel. Nine songs. Music by Victor Schertzinger, with lyrics by Clifford Grey. "The Love Parade" theme song. Photography by Victor Milner. No credits to recorders. Western Electric system. At Criterion, New York, on $2 run (twice daily), Nov. 19. Running time, 107 minutes.

Count Alfred	Maurice Chevalier
Queen Louise	Jeanette MacDonald
Jacques	Lupino Lane
Lulu	Lillian Roth
Ambassador	E. H. Calvert
Le Mari	Andre Sheron
Paulette	Yola D'Avril
Master of Ceremonies	Edgar Norton
The Prime Minister	Lionel Belmore
The Foreign Minister	Albert Roccardi
The Admiral	Carlton Stockdale
The Minister of War	Eugene Pallette
Afghan Ambassador	Russell Powell
Priest	Winter Hall
Cross-Eyed Lackey	Ben Turpin

In "The Love Parade," 2d starring talker for Maurice Chevalier, "it" man from France, Paramount has its first original screen operetta, production whose story is more than made up in magnificence of sets and costumes, tuneful music, subtlety of direction, comedy and general appeal. It's a fine, near-grand entertainment.

At the outset the Chevalier personality is put to the fore in the manner the Parisian music hall star knows best. He sings "Paris, Stay the Same," with straw hat and all, as he leaves the city of joy to return to Sylvania. In this number perhaps more than any other in the entire picture he is the Chevalier of "Innocents of Paris" in bold relief. Following this light and cheery melody, admirably done, the French star has to go into the stiff military and other costumes that the kingdom of Sylvania demands.

Later, however, he does a number similar in nature, "Nobody's Using It Now," referring in the main to his sex appeal and permitting Chevalier to indulge the tricky flashes that go to make up his ingratiating personality. At other times it is the way in which the French star obviously holds himself in check and frequently tries to be the dramatic actor in too big a way that detracts from a distinct impression, such as he made in "Innocents of Paris." There should never be any attempt at involving the Par "it" man in heavy stuff, as he immediately appears to go entirely out of his meter.

In Jeanette MacDonald, ingenue prima donna from Broadway with "Boom Boom," "Yes, Yes, Yvette" and "Angela" behind her on the legit stage, Chevalier had an actress opposite who all but steals the picture. Her personality, looks and voice make "Love Parade" all the more a charming, intriguing picture for the masses, with the actress' appeal coupled with that of Chevalier's rendering it the surefire qualities essential to its future record as an outstanding talker production of the year.

As Queen Louise, a none-too-haughty ruler of the mythical kingdom that is hers, Miss MacDonald is everything that a queen in the popular (film) conception of the word should be. Ernst Lubitsch, who well knows the value of charm, introduces the new musical talker star in a scene where she is awakening from a lovely dream. In the most gossamar of boudoir raiment, the director gives her her first cue for a number, "My Dream Lover," and then marches her to the bath, where, as only Lubitsch would do it in a case of this kind, some comedy relief is injected.

There is nothing about Miss MacDonald's performance that would indicate the talker is a new medium of expression that she cannot rise to superbly. She photographs beautifully, speaks with a clarity and softness altogether pleasing, and in song numbers is always equal to the occasion. Miss MacDonald has a fine operetta voice, with none of the qualities that make the recording job a difficult one, while her manner of delivery is particularly engaging.

There's not the slighest doubt that the success of "Love Parade" enjoys will be due in a large measure to this new find from the musical comedy stage.

Considering Miss MacDonald's side, Chevalier made an excellent opposite, and especially in view of the story, which says that the philandering Parisian, brought back to Sylvania because of his scandalous affairs as a military attache in France's capital, must, in accepting marriage to the queen, keep his fingers out of all matters of state, come second in consideration about the palace at all times, and not only obey the queen in a husbandly sort of way, but be subject to her commands, even to the point of having to appear in the best of humor when the antithesis is the feeling.

In rebelling at this attitude and condition, Chevalier goes in for the heavy acting. It is unpleasant seeing him try to look tragic. Were it not for the comedy relief about the middle of the picture, when it is inclined to drag a little, this part (a couple of reels) would be tiresome.

The wedding is an extravaganza, with one of the largest sets ever built used for it, but, musically, lacks the punch of other scenes. In scenic splendor and atmosphere Lubitsch has nothing to his credit to match this, and in the actual wedding ceremony, with the queen in the usual Benedict role, even to placing the ring on her wedded's finger, the German director had an opportunity to indulge in the touch of smartness and sophistication for which he is noted.

The sequences in which the to-be-chastised prince meets the queen for the first time and the dinner date that evening also gave Lubitsch ample chance to apply his touch.

But the best sequence in the entire picture from all angles is toward the end, where the queen, convinced her husband is determined on leaving her to return to Paris, becomes the docile, heartbroken, crying creature of human nature and follows the irate prince all around, hoping she can entice him into her bedroom for a reconciliation. She finally succeeds, but only after following him back to his own room.

"The Love Parade" and "Anything to Please the Queen" are the duet numbers. First is the chief number, continuously plugged. It is a hit song that should strike while the other, one of those smart, intimate lyrics, is the melody type that ought to do overtime with the whistlers.

"March of the Grenadiers," a good number of its kind, is used in a military scene about the middle of the picture. Of the numbers done by Lupino Lane and Lillian Roth, the hit of the group is "Let's Be Common," with lyrics putting it over. Another done by the comedy relief is "Gossip," with lackeys in the palace as the chorus. Lane early in the picture has a number to himself, "Champagne," a tricky little tune that serves well.

The Lane and Roth combination provide what comedy isn't otherwise found in various interesting routines, including a dance number of the knockabout style that's a wow. As a comedian Lane is altogether there, and for the laugh stuff Miss Roth is as much there as he is.

Although Ben Turpin is in the cast, he could almost as well have been out of it.

Edgar Norton, Eugene Pallette and Lionel Belmore, as members of the queen's staff and government, are more in prominence than their associates and others of lesser figuring in the supporting cast, but even so have small parts to do. Pallette wears a mustache for the first time and has lines that are intended to be light comedy material.

Guy Bolton, who wrote the libretto for "Love Parade," comes from the legit, while Vajda, who did the story, is the noted Hungarian playwright and author, with several of his stories on the screen.

Victor Schertzinger, who wrote the music, is a Par director, with "Marcheta" the biggest song hit on his record. The lyricist, Grey, English, has written the words for several American musicals.

The director, Lubitsch, does his first operetta in "Love Parade." His job clearly shows that he has been keenly appreciative of the production values a costume talker of this kind must have. In the handling of the many song numbers he has worked them into the action with the least obtrusiveness yet noticed in pictures requiring as much music. The thread of the story is maintained at all times, and as far as it is possible to inject the musical numbers without dropping the illusion of the narrative, just so far has Lubitsch been able to go.

In the shooting of the ballet number in the royal theatre, the Teutonic director has taken his camera to the top of the proscenium and shot the dancers from on high. As a result, he has actually produced the effect of more of a close-up than contemporaries have, with the entire ballet caught in action.

Lubitsch and probably Bolton, have thrown over all the studio inhibitions about off screen musical accompaniments. Camera is never idle during an entire number, and it can be said that this is the first true screen musical. It will educate and reap accordingly.

Char.

THE SACRED FLAME

(ALL DIALOG)

Warner Bros.' production and release. Starring Conrad Nagel and Lila Lee. Pauline Frederick and William Courtenay featured. Directed by Archie L. Mayo. Adapted from W. Somerest Maugham's play of same name. Theme song "The Sacred Flame." At Strand, New York, week Nov. 22. Running time, 65 minutes.

Col. Maurice Taylor..........Conrad Nagel
Stella..............................Lila Lee
Mrs. Taylor.................Pauline Frederick
Major Laconda..........William Courtenay
Colin Taylor......................Walter Byron
Dr. Harvester..... ....Alec B. Francis
Nurse Wayland....................Dale Fuller

Too much talk about a depressing situation withholds this from lively film classification. It's a real talker and some good dramatic performances—good enough, with one exception, to be taken seriously by most audiences, but not the sort that's box office.

W. Somerset Maugham's stage play, imported from England for a short Broadway stay last season, has been boiled to 65 minutes for the screen without much change. But for the wedding scene at the opening and the accident sequence on an air field, no increase in the number of people over the stage company, either. Even the butler in the large household is not seen. When he says "Dinner is served," he says it at long distance, unseen.

A bad item of the picture at the Strand seems to be a bit of ungainly cutting, perhaps enforced by censorship. It arrived a line before the mother completely confesses to the murder of her crippled son. Her fatal words were not spoken, the screen went blank for a second, and when the picture resumed, the dialog (on disc) was in its right place. If a slip in projection of the film, the disc may have run ahead and out of kilter. As it happened, punched a big hole in the finish.

Maugham's story of the young aviator who is crippled in a crack-up on his wedding day, just after the ceremony, keeps Conrad Nagel in a wheel chair until he finally passes out at the hands of his merciful mother toward the end. Unknown to Nagel, his younger brother has replaced him in his pitying young wife's affections. His mother knows it, however, and presumably ends his life so that he may never know.

With some action in place of the solid hour of talk here and there, the flaps would have something to look at. But this way they won't relish the sadness at all.

Nagel does the crippled husband in good style. In his pleasant voice, from the wheel chair, he sings the theme song ("The Sacred Flame"). Number vocalized just that once, but reprised by offscreen orchestra throughout.

Lila Lee is a stunning wife in looks and a good one in acting. All excellent performances by other veterans, with Pauline Frederick's a finished one. The one bad troupling note was that contributed by the sex-starved nurse, as played by Dale Fuller, appeared due to poor direction of this particular player. Miss Fuller over-mugged and over-acted until the audience snickered. A surprise to find her in such a sullen role, for Dale Fuller has a natural comedy pan, having proven it in the past.

Bige.

NIX ON DAMES

(ALL-DIALOG, with Songs)

Fox production and release. Directed by Donald Gallaher. From story by Maude Fulton, with screen play and dialog by Maude Fulton and Frank Gay. Music by Wolfe Gilbert and Abel Baer. Photography by C. G. Clark. H. A. Wilson, sound. Mae Clark, Robert Ames and William Harrigan featured. At Roxy, N. Y., week of Nov. 22. Running time, 67 mins.

Jackie Lee..........................Mae Clarke
Bert Wills.........................Robert Ames
Johnny Brown............William Harrigan
Stella Foster.....................Maude Fulton
Ed Foster................George MacFarlane
Miss Woods.................Camille Rovelle
Bonnie Tucker...............Grace Wallace
Jim Tucker...............Hugh McCormack
Billy...........................Marshall Ruth
Cliff..............................Benny Hall
Hoffman..........................Gilly Colvin
Baring....................Frederick Graham
Magnolia.......................Louise Beaver

Weak for the key first runs with average grosses its top hope. Outside of the title this one is without sufficient quality to prop it up.

Although the story is backstage, and concerns vaude people, it has angles and touches that remove it somewhat from the much trodden path. Dialog is heavy on shop talk and vaude slang, but with so many theatrical talkers lately none of it should slip over anyone's head. Most all of the action is in an actors' boarding house in the roaring 40's. This particular brownstone is a madhouse, with a measure of comedy derived from the sax player and the German with a dog act, both contributing plenty to the bedlam.

No names in the cast to entice the talker shopper, but trio of Mae Clarke, Robert Ames and William Harrigan are adequate in their parts, Ames and Harrigan shaping up nicely as the acrobatic team. Miss Clarke proves less adequate as the dancer coming between the team. Camille Rovelle appears miscast. Others have minor assignments with the story's author, Maude Fulton, doing the boarding house keeper. Louise Beaver, colored, leads a Negro spiritual backed by a chorus.

All the music in the picture is in this sequence with the exception of the first song offered, "Fading Away," sung by Miss Clarke and well handled. "Fading Away" is a pleasant tune, but its chances as a hit are not strong. "One Sweetheart," is not outstanding, "I'm Wingin' Home" (minstrel number) and a part of another ditty rendered by Miss Rovelle makes up the balance of the musical matter.

In directing Donald Gallaher has handled some of the scenes with imagination. A post-card suddenly comes to life, and in another bit, Gallaher has taken one of the characters from one door down a stairs to another, with the camera flashing the stairs so fast in transit you can't distinguish them. Actor is at the other door flight below in a second. Another quick transition is the shaving of a mustache, seven days having elapsed.

Dialog not out of the ordinary, but for a story of this kind it passes. Recording and photography entirely satisfactory.

Char.

Dancer of Barcelona

(FOREIGN MADE)
(Synchronized)

Presented by Richard Currier. Directed by Robert Wiene from story by Solar De Rodrigo. Adapted by Casimiro Gonzalos. Starring Lily Damita. In cast: Don Pedro DeLeon, Carlo DeMendoza and Ramon Gomez. Disk synchronization. At the Cameo, N. Y., beginning Nov. 23. Running time, about 60 mins.

No screen credit given the producer but this film is obviously a foreign production made shortly before Lily Damita's trip to Hollywood. Other than being a show off vehicle for Miss Damita, in which she does little more than twirl on her toes in ballet and bedroom attire, when she is not making eyes at a young man, the picture is nondescript. No draw for general bookings and negative even for the sure-seaters.

Directed by the German, Wiene, written by a Spaniard and with a Spanish support cast a number of the locales are also in Spain. A bullfight, with Miss Damita and Ramon Gomez in the stands, is one of the main scenes. Scrap is taken from distant camera perspective, evidently to meet with censors' pleasure. Sequence is irrelevant, and later in reelage proves to be nothing but a filler to emphasize Miss Damita's toreador dance in home.

Story idea seems to have been an effort to prove that art can be conquered by true domesticity. To get the leads together Miss Damita, as the famous ballet soloist, has to come out of a side door and pick up a young man standing at edge of crowd. Gomez makes a cold admirer, having to be led by the hand to a cafe. When Lily discloses her identity Gomez suddenly works up a tempo which reacts as having been inspired by the name rather than the form. Warwick Ward, who gets a featured credit, has little more than the bit part of the ballet master. *Waly.*

WALL STREET
(ALL-DIALOG)

Columbia production and release. Directed by R. W. Neill, from story by Paul Gangelin and Jack Kirkland. Dialog by Norman Houston. Photography, Ted Tetzlaff. Harrison Wiley, art director. Ray Snyder, editor. Recording by W. E. Aileen Pringle and Ralph Ince co-featured, with Sam De Grasse, Phillip Strange, Ernest Hilliard, Jimmie Finlayson and Freddie Fredericks in support. At the Hippodrome, N. Y., week of Nov. 23. Running time, 68 mins.

With the great financial headache lingering on, this programmer has timeliness and should draw to a certain extent on the strength of the theme and title. Presenting a hardboiled side of the romance that's played down in cow canyon, it should do all right in the intermediate grinds.

In the picture the rough diamond in velvet is again the central role. Ralph Ince plays it to perfection. Ince is almost everything this exhibit has to recommend it outside of the propitious release date.

The brutish Ince is a former steel worker who through sheer grit and cunning has climbed to a soft perch. Girl in the case is a lady and outside of her complex vengeance for Ince, because he broke her husband, she plays the game as squarely but as unmercifully as he does. In choosing Aileen Pringle for the widow role the selection is good. Her performance is only second to Ince, and not by much. Even when she is won over to Ince in spite of herself, after breaking him as he did her husband, there is more of a genuine note in the acting than in most pictures insisting on the happy finish.

Picture has plenty of Wall Street color to satisfy the average patron. A point in its favor is that it moves. No bad dull spots and it has good dialog and some comedy. Sam De Grasse, Phillip Strange, Ernest Hilliard and Jimmie Finlayson turn in favorable performances.

Lends itself to plenty of exploitation stunts. *Char.*

THE TREASURE
(GERMAN MADE)
(Silent)

Only screen credit calls it Royal production and a Film Arts Guild release. Directed by C. W. Pabst from scenario by Oscar Pucin. Edited and titled by John Richards. At the Film Guild theatre, N. Y., beginning Nov. 23. Running time, 55 minutes.
The Bellfounder..........Albert Steinrueck
His Wife....................Ilka Gruening
Their Daughter............Lucie Mannhein
Journeyman Artisan....Hans Brausewetter
Bellfounder's Ass't.........Werner Krauss

Insufficient plot and repetitious character studies make "The Treasure," in its present length, decidedly monotonous. As a two-reeler it would be a sure-seater natural. Pastry architecture for street and house sets, strongly reminiscent of earlier German works, are good atmosphere.

While Krauss, at the outset, has what seems an excellent opportunity for one of those morbid characterizations for which he is noted, he very shortly establishes the halfwit assistant bellfounder as a creature whose chief delight is to walk up and down crooked stairs, drink

wine and make a feeble effort for the hand of his master's daughter.

Krauss' performance is nearly eclipsed by that of young Hans Brausewetter. Latter is almost too worldly-wise for his innocent expression but he charms his girls from the innkeep's sweetheart to the old Bellfounder's dark haired child. Brausewetter, however, makes the journeyman artisan the most real and interesting figure in the cast.

Little of the heavy drama in this offering usually found in so many of its kind from Germany. Lighting is subdued and sets are of the dark and cobwebby kind. But there is a general insincerity; an over-indulgence in wine, so that when the grand stew arrives these qualities are minimized. *Waly.*

FIGARO
(FRENCH MADE)
(Silent)

Produced and released by Franco Film. Directed by Gaston Ravel. Screen story based on operatic versions of Beaumarchais' trilogy. At the Little Carnegie Playhouse, N. Y., beginning Nov. 23. Running time, 76 minutes.
Rosine....................Arlette Marcal
Figaro.....................E. Van Duren
Count Almaviva...............Tony D'Algy
Suzanne...................Marie Bell
Cherubin....................Jean Weber
Begearss.................Genica Missirio

Seldom have celebrated writings been conglomerated into a more hopeless befuddlement for the screen than this inspiration from three of Beaumarchais' works. "Figaro," the picture, is such a maze of intrigues and misplaced loves that even the cast seems bewildered. The director is the real hero of the undertaking.

Hardly does one affair start when another commences. Ends are left hanging in the air, with an effort in the final reel to explain all. More likely it's an adaptation far beyond the capacity of the company's personnel. Cast's performance is generally amateurish. It's strictly a powdered wig and costume offering.

E. Van Duren is a Figaro who starts in a barber shop and abandons it after a few feet. He then intermingles with royalty, more often on than off the same footing. He is only off when the director remembers he's a barber to the Count Almaviva. And he becomes that when he holds the ladder while the count courts and weds Rosine, described as a wealthy orphan who is kept under key by a covetous physician.

Count soon returns to bachelor practices, and it is then that his eye falls on Suzanne, Rosine's servant girl. A lot of footage required before Rosine masquerades as Suzanne and sets the count right on his duties as a husband. It is after Suzanne and Figaro come from the altar that both change from servant's attire to the lace and breast work of their employers. From then on, for several sequences, anyhow, it's up to Rosine, the countess, to do something. She submits to Cherubin, her page, when he informs her that he will welcome death at the front if his love is unrequited.

Big question in the series of other fan interrogations comes when the countess has a child. She's too blah in her interview with the page for the babe to be his, while the regular husband's galavanting places him beyond suspicion. However, the page is the father.

An adventurer gets the story from the lad before he dies, also a letter. Documents gets him a job in the Almaviva household until he spills the contents to the Count, after the Countess has repressed some more amorous advances. And on it goes. Finally, the adventurer falls for the married Suzanne. Figaro lets this

ripen until things are set for a regular American meller down-the-hill embroglio. Then marital vows are renewed, and the finale is finally reached. *Waly.*

TAMING OF SHREW
(ALL DIALOG)

United Artists release of talker production by Douglas Fairbanks and Mary Pickford, co-starred. Directed by Sam Taylor, who is credited with having adapted the Shakespearean comedy. Cameraman, Karl Struss. Mentioned as of production staff: Earle Browne, Lucky Humberstone, Walter Mayo. At Rivoli, New York, opening Nov. 29 on grind. Running time, 65 minutes.
Katherine..................Mary Pickford
Petruchio............Douglas Fairbanks
Baptista...................Edwin Maxwell
Gremio...................Joseph Cawthorn
Grumio.......................Clyde Cook
Hortensio...............Geoffrey Wardwell
Bianca....................Dorothy Jordan

A money picture, easily, for it's worth 75c for anyone to see Mary Pickford and Douglas Fairbanks do this kind of stuff in a vastly extravagant burlesque of Bill Shakespeare's best laugh. The two stars often turn that into a howl. So many ballyhoo and exploitation angles there's not one town where it should fall down.

Of course, Bill will never know what the talkers have done to and maybe for him. This is apt to make the Bard more popular than he has been of late at $2, up. Which gives the Pickford-Fairbanks combo the edge, without royalty.

Nearly everyone has seen "The Taming of the Shrew" without always catching the source. The suggestion must have come to Shakespeare with the older story of the lion tamer after subduing his beast, afraid to go home to the wife. Bill twisted it around. But more gently in his way.

Fairbanks and Pickford, slapstick artists, give it another bang. They go to it knockabout. And Miss Pickford takes the prattfalls. Two and each good. One lands her in a bridal gown while it rains in the mud with the pigs. All for 75c.

The other is you-slap-me-and-I'll-slap-you, the mainstay of all rough comedy hoko mixed teams, and again Miss Pickford goes kerflop, clear across the room to land on a feather bed this time. Maybe the first fall hurt.

Mr. Fairbanks skeletonizes the scheme when first meeting Katherine, the hell raising daughter. He says, "Howdy, Kate." She says, "Katherine to you, mugg," or something near, and the warrior answers, "Kate, d'ya hear, plain Kate." Then to show her it stands, he and Katie roll down a flight of stairs.

Somewhat of a changed opinion of course of what these two veteran and gilded stars of the screen would do in and for their first co-starring picture. While there is plenty of romance and dialog, slapstick and mud, there's no dirt, so that part of Miss Pickford's career remains as clean as ever.

Splendid settings in the Fairbanks massive production manner to more sharply contrast the very low comedy, as low as Shubert common and more common.

And if 65 minutes, perhaps the cutter said stick to the laughs. It sticks. Maybe the rep companies can follow this up with Bill's original stage version without the prattfalls but still at 75c.

As this was built for laughs only and gets them, nothing else matters. For laughs get money, and besides the laughs you have Mary Pickford, with Douglas Fairbanks—and Shakespeare at last!

Had the talkers been of other days, what travesty stars Mabel Fenton and her husband, the late Charles J. Ross (Ross and Fenton), would have been. *Sime.*

VAGABOND LOVER
(ALL DIALOG, with Songs)

Radio Pictures (RKO) production and release. Starring Rudy Vallee. Directed by Marshall Neilan from J. A. Creelman's story. RCA Photophone sound track recording. Leo Tover, cameraman; John Tribby, sound. At Globe, New York, at $2 top, twice daily run starting Nov. 26. Running time, 65 mins.

Rudy Bronson..............Rudy Vallee
Jean..............................Sally Blane
Mrs. Whitehall............Marie Dressler
Officer Tuttle...............Charles Sellon
Sport...........................Eddie Nugent
Mrs. Tod Hunter............Nella Walker
Ted Grant.....................Malcolm Waite
Manager.........................Alan Roscoe

Figures to do all right in the program houses because of Rudy Vallee's songs and Marie Dressler. In those spots where the girls are Vallee bound, the feature stands a chance of beating average figures due to the resultant matinee business. For New York, where the gals, young and old, are nuts over the boy, "Vagabond Lover" may surprise for $2 and hang around a few weeks. Who can figure the feminine tangent? They threw orchids at him at the Riverside. So, upon that deduction, this release classes as an oddity.

It's certainly no great shakes as a picture. For Marshall Neilan, who directed, it unwinds as just a passing fancy. He could have phoned this one in from the golf course.

Story is merely a series of excuses to permit Vallee to sing. Otherwise, the studio has covered up and supported the kid band leader with everything but a new contract. And that's not an impossible eventuality, dependent, of course, upon what degree they go for the songs. If somebody can make Vallee relax in front of the camera, grab on to a half decent yarn and figure cast support as imperative there may be further celluloid coin around for this break kid.

Marie Dressler isn't any more to this picture than its heart. Veteran and fully capable comedienne is all over the screen as a flighty social climber who has her ups and downs, due to mistaking Vallee and his boys as Ted Grant's band, the supposed ace dance outfit of the country. Reasons for the band playing and Vallee singing are screened as a musicale in Miss Dressler's home and a charity benefit.

Meanwhile, Vallee and his mob are threatened by the village cop because Vallee has taken the gag Grant correspondence course and insists that the orchestra mogul hear his outfit. Boys invade the vacant Grant home, on the supposition that he's there, and start playing, which brings on the constable.

Sally Blane is the girl to whom Vallee keeps tossing his vocal efforts. Playing Miss Dressler's niece she's off Rudy on the mistaken identity thing. Eddie Nugent, who reminds strongly of Raymond Hackett, is placed as a dummy band member to lend valuable support as this unit's spokesman throughout the running.

Production is fair enough including a brief but pleasant ballet during the charity affair, which turns "hot" for a climax. Recording is good and excellent on the Vallee songs. One of these numbers sounds new, but the three others are familiar as Vallee standards or from other sources. One or two of the ditties are reprised, so there's plenty of Vallee's voice.

One thing in the film's favor is that it runs only 65 minutes. That may have been smart cutting. The Vallee fans are sure to go for and chortle over it. For the others not so addicted it rates as light but pleasing entertainment indicative of nothing in particular.

Opening night at the Globe Vallee made a brief address preceding the picture, virtually asking the audience not to expect too much of him as an actor and modestly referring to his singing. That was smart, too. To what extent New York femininity goes for this boy was evidenced in the following applause which ran through the lead titles and from the girls of from 13 to 60 in the audience and lobby.

Sid.

UNTAMED

(ALL DIALOG)

Metro-Goldwyn-Mayer production and release. Directed by Jack Conway. Starring Joan Crawford. Story by Charles Scoggins; dialog by Willard Mack. Oliver Marsh, cameraman. Theme songs titled "Chant of the Jungle," "Wonderful." At Capitol week Nov. 29. Running time 85 minutes.

Bingo.............................Joan Crawford
Andy..........................Robert Montgomery
Ben Murchison...............Ernest Torrence
Howard Presley...............Holmes Herbert
Bennock...............................John Miljan
Marjory.................................Gwen Lee
Paul.................................Edward Nugent
Gregg.....................................Don Terry
Mrs. Mason...................Gertrude Astor
Jollop.................................Milton Farney
Dowling...............................Lloyd Ingram
Milly..................................Grace Cunard
Moran.....................................Tom O'Brien
Billcombe...........................Wilson Benge

Hollywood's all-night coffee drinkers never conjured up a more nondescript assortment of writings for any one imaginary story for the screen than the melange contained in "Untamed." This is the picture of inconsistencies; so many sequences designed for the dramatic often get bigger laughs than those intended for comedy. First runs should emphasize this comic aspect in their ballyhoo. Houses where they don't know any better can let it go for a grand old thriller, meller or what-not.

"Untamed" is one of those that starts and ends and starts again. Picture can be cut to six reels with no one the wiser, except less conscious of sitting through all episodes of a serial. As it stands, doesn't seem "Untamed" reached within a mile of the editing room.

It's Joan Crawford's first talker, but Ernest Torrence holds it together. Miss Crawford, as Bingo, opens the reelage singing one of the theme songs, "Chant of the Jungle," in a highly artificial atmosphere supposedly tropic. Although her English is perfect, the dialog of others would have her just a wild dancing daughter of an Englishman battered by heat and booze.

Torrence and Holmes Herbert, as Ben and Howard, in search of Bingo's dad, arrive just after a native has been led into insulting the girl and in time to witness him slash the old man for no particular reason. Death scene is overdone, with Miss Crawford's wails seemingly endless.

Subtitles explain that Miss Crawford has spent the following eight months with her father's friends locating his oil well, and is now a rich girl.

On the ship to New York, Bingo is cultured one moment and a little rough the next. Impresses more as a school girl acting smart than a female from fetid swamplands.

It's Uncle Ben's troubles in locating her that come nearest saving the situations. Monkey playing with bottle of prize hooch, etc.

Andy, first young man Bingo is supposed to have seen, is at first a woman-maker. As soon as Bingo comes along, even popping into his cabin, Andy changes and becomes a regular Horatio Alger character. This role is played in a collegian way by Robert Montgomery. Like others in the cast, due to poor script and direction, he is allowed to drag on until becoming a dime hero.

Theme song is unreeled again on deck. Incidentally, injection of songs is at oddest moments. Andy tries one of them while shaving and the couple, after a row and while dancing, suddenly break into a duet that first startles audience and then gets one of biggest laughs in the footage.

Desperate efforts to keep her wild once she dons evening dresses and opens a New York estate, the direction finally diverges from series of drinking parties to set up a ring on dance floor. Her man must win, and he does after taking the count so many times that the audience has lost track in its accompanying mirth and guffaws. It's just sad attempt at a scrap, even for the screen.

There's other stuff, but it doesn't matter.

Waly.

THE NEW BABYLON

(RUSSIAN MADE)
(Synchronized)

Produced by Sovkino and releasing through Amkino. Directed by G. M. Kozintsov and L. Z. Trauberg. American titles by Shelley Hamilton. A. N. Moskvin, cameraman. Synchronized on disk. At the Cameo, N. Y., beginning Nov. 30. Running time, 110 mins.

Soldier Jean...............Peter Sobolevski
The Soubrette.................Sofie Magarill
Store Owner.......................D. Gutman
Sales Girl.....................Elena Kuzmina
Head Clerk...................A. Kostrichkin
Deputy.................................A. Arnold
Journalist..................Sergei Gerassimov
Shoemaker..............................S. Gusev
Laundress.........................A. Glushkova

A teetotaler will be doubtful of his own sobriety after sitting through "The New Babylon." Its opportunities for dramatic register are fast and fleeting. The whole thing is a whirl of close-ups and triple exposures. No foreign production can compare with it for flagrant excess of trick photography. It leaves an audience dizzy; not from the strain of suspense, but from eyes.

So restless is the direction that this film has only the vestige of continuity. Faces, feet, mud, singers, soldiers, guns. Projected time and again. Babylon is described in the subtitles as the name of a department store. The owner, one D. Gutman, is allowed plenty of footage in which to sip liquor monotonously or adjust his top hat. Then the barrage of miscellaneous things are suddenly flung back at the audience as though the director suddenly realized there ought to be something doin'.

Nearest line to the story is an extemporaneous romance suddenly springing up between the soldier Jean and a sales girl. Between the triple exposures the couple are brought together. The soldier usually looks straight into the camera with one of those far-away expressions. At the crucial period Jean is with the Nationals who, licked by the Prussians, are now dealing with the Commune, the political faction within. Chances for the latter battle possessing the big dramatic punch that it could, with the characters given some opportunity for individualism, are also sacrificed by a burlesque touch. This is provided by flash-backs to what is described as a nearby hill on which the store keeper and others are shown taking in the butchery as Americans would a football game. At the finis Jean and the store girl are again brought together. He is her grave digger and she is one of the targets for the firing squad.

Picture claims it follows episodically events in the Franco-Prussian war and Commune activities in 1871. It doesn't matter. Can't blame it on the cutting room this time. Doubtful if anything could help it.

Waly.

ATLANTIC

(BRITISH MADE)
(All Dialog)

Produced at Elstree by British International Pictures, Ltd. Adapted from Ernest Raymond's play, "The Berg." Directed by E. A. Dupont. Camera: Charles Rosher. RCA recording. Preview at Regal, Marble Arch, Nov. 15. Running time, 100 mins.

Reviewing "Atlantic" presents a number of primary difficulties, whether the film is approached from the purely native angle or from that of world appeal. Over a period of 100 minutes it piles horror on terror, until a normal person feels it were better the ship sank. It will hardly succeed outside Central Europe, when the German version will be shown as the first all talker in that tongue.

Dupont, directing, shows a lack of balance. He translates the ship disaster into the terms of a penny-a-liner's stock description of a cataclysm which he has not witnessed.

Heroic attitudinizing of officers and crew, the singing of hymns as the ship finally settles down, the exchanging of grandiloquent platitudes—all the familiar stock routine of a daily newspaper descriptive writer are here. The native press with one exception (Manchester "Guardian") raves over "Atlantic." No adjective has been left out; no claim to the ultimate perfection is lacking. But . . .

Monty Banks is woefully miscast, sings (off key) Henley's ballad of soul-mastership and captaincy of fate; the captain exhorts everyone to "Be British," and the remaining passengers sing a hymn while the vessel is sinking. It should be said that the evidence given to the American commission during the inquiry into the sinking of the "Titanic," upon which Ernest Raymond's play was based, failed to show any truth in these alleged incidents.

Once, and once only, does Dupont approach realism—when he shows the engine room men standing around and whispers are heard, "Perhaps there's a chance," "It'll soon be over now," and the like. Claiming to be realistic, this is the film's one point of true realism, its real dramatic moment.

Cast seldom become human beings. They are shown as, and they remain, stock figures of melodrama: the young husband with a pregnant wife, the cheating elderly husband with a tearful wife and an angry daughter, the heroic old cripple and his equally I-will-never-leave-you wife, the blase drunk, the lip-chewing calm young officer, the mild and peacefully-calm-amid-dangers parson. All stock types.

"Atlantic" is a fine piece of craftsmanship, but it is untrue to life on the one hand and it is not entertainment on the other. Credible correspondents say it is a great success in Germany. German masses are entertained by vivisected gloom and detailed morbidity. They enjoy the oblique expression of sadism. It is true that "Nibelungen" took more money in Germany than any other German film yet made. But it is also true that in the Anglo-Saxon countries it died overnight.

Rush for the boats is finely staged; the collision with the iceberg is weak and lacks conviction. Engine room scenes, especially the closing of the watertight doors, are splendidly done. Scenes on the bridge are bad. And so much is the thematic action confined to a small group of first class passengers that the audience effect is apt to be antagonistic as an unconscious protest against the implied contempt for the other classes.

Acting is fair, with John Longden outstanding. Franklin Dyall convinces at first, then tails off into a stock figure. John Stuart gives a good performance as a machine-made young husband, and the rest of the cast is negligible.

Frat.

FORWARD PASS

(ALL DIALOG, with Songs)

First National production and release. Featuring Douglas Fairbanks, Jr., and Loretta Young. Directed by Eddie Cline from story by Harvey Gates. Dialog credited to H. E. Rogers. Music and lyrics by Herb Magidson, Ded Washington and M. H. Cleary. Supervised by Ned Marin. At Strand, New York, week Nov. 29. Running time, 73 mins.

Marty Reid.........Douglas Fairbanks, Jr.
Patricia Carlyle..............Loretta Young
Honey Smith..................Guinn Williams
Mazie ...."Peanuts" Byron
Coach Wilson.........................Bert Rome
Assistant Coach..............Lane Chandler
Ed Kirby..............................Allen Lane

More football backed by a quartet of tunes, one of which Loretta Young warbles. Grid stuff is good but short of a big punch. Mainly due to Warners being handcuffed on exterior sound and not taking the trouble to transpose the roar of the crowd from sound track to disk and cut it in all the way on the game as well as just using unimportant newsreel shots, one carelessly. Packs some laughs and should do average business in most program houses. Where they're fed up on the collegiate thing this one will likely have a time making the grade.

Young Fairbanks and Miss Young make a likable screen couple, the latter stepping out to warble in contralto which is not hard on the ear. Seconded by a male quartet in later choruses, Miss Young's debut as a songstress of the "intimate" type is okay. Fairbanks is film cut to stand up to football measurements, and when off the field plays oke, closely pursued for actual performance by Allen Lane as the undergraduate heavy. Comedy angle is tossed to Guinn Williams and four supposed freshmen who find repeated trouble with upper classmen.

Theme is just one of those things in having Fairbanks, regular quarterback, voluntarily resigning from the squad after getting banged up in a mid-season game. Coach sics the campus Cleo on him as the decoy to get him into his togs again. He gives in and just before the big game discovers the frame.

Between that wallop and his rival, who is playing end and stalling on going down under passes, Fairbanks looks bad in the first half and is yanked. Heavy fakes an injury to get out. The two boys then mix hand-to-hand, but make it up in the dressing room before the squad troops in for the rest period.

During the last quarter the girl gets a note to Fairbanks which squares everything. When called upon to go back into the game he asks that the former "menace" also be sent back to end. Between the two they forward pass the other team to defeat in the last five minutes to win.

Photography is generally good, also recording. An interior train sequence is particularly noteworthy for sound in that the chugging of the engine up front, as well as its whistling, has been retained to undertone the dialog throughout this passage. The only time it quits is during Miss Young's song. A swell piece of work which fully attains a realistic effect. Other sound concentration lists particular pains with supposed cheering sections for yells in close-up.

"Hello, Baby," has evidently been selected as the plug tune, reprised any number of times, vocally or instrumentally. Doesn't sound like a "natural" but possibly may get somewhere through forcing. Other numbers suit the purpose without readily threatening to install themselves as spontaneous guests in the average memory. Specialty girl trots out at a sorority house dance to do "Huddlin'."

Nice, average college picture held back a little too long for release, in view of the preceding strong football screen matter which has been around this fall. *Sid.*

HEARTS IN EXILE

(ALL DIALOG, with Songs)

Warner Bros.' production and release. Based on play by John Oxenham. Scenario and dialog by Harvey Gates. Directed by Michael Curtiz. Theme song, "Like a Breath of Springtime." Lyrics by Al Dubin. Music by Joe Burke. Dolores Costello starred. At Colony week Nov. 28. Running time, 82 minutes.

Vera Zvanova.............Dolores Costello
Paul Pavloff...............Grant Withers
Serge Palma..........James R. Kirkwood
Dimitri Ivanova............George Fawcett
Governor...................David Torrence
Anna Rascova......................Olive Tell
Rat Catcher..................William Irving
Soldier..............................Tom Dugan
Maid..................................Rose Dione

As a programmer, not half bad. Holding the interest throughout, with well-knit scenes and action, the suspense always beautifully sustained and a theme song that's better than the average in program talkers.

Along about the second reel the story is slowed up considerably, but quickly regains its pace and drives along to the finish with one situation on top of another redeeming.

Strength lies not only in interest story creates but in surprising turns it takes. Even ending is different, with audience left to decide whether it is a happy or unhappy one.

A lot to the story of "Hearts in Exile," the material available having been plenty sufficient without need of padding. It concerns the love between a fish dealer's daughter and a young medical student who likes his booze better than his studies. While it sometimes lacks logic, faults in this direction are not so glaring as to injure picture's chances with average audience.

Marriage to a baron interrupts the love affair, but it blossoms again in far-off Siberia when both husband and former sweetheart are exiled there to serve terms for various offenses. The hero, sorry for the wife and baby, changes identification with the husband and rival to allow the latter liberty within two years, but the heroine-wife unknown to both has gone to Siberia to be with her husband, the switching thus throwing her with the other.

Neither seems to mind this a great deal until the husband, in effecting an escape, turns up to take the two with him and learns the actual state of affairs, killing himself as a martyr or something.

Part in the escape kills hero and heroine's chances for a likely pardon, everything having been badly bungled up.

More than the usual human interest and appeal here, with the sequences bringing out the horror of Siberia and lot of exiled prisoners, impressive, to say the least.

In direction, Michael Curtiz has turned out a neat job, free from many of the faults that pictures based on similar stories ordinarily have evidenced.

The theme song, "Like a Breath of Springtime," running through the action at appropriate points, is a melody that ought to have a place on everybody's whistle. Song has chances of being a fair hit.

Acting o. k. throughtout, Dolores Costello doing the leading femme role competently. Opposite her, Grant Withers is an excellent type as the hero, while James R. Kirkwood, in spite of his pronounced English accent, cuts an impressive figure as the luckless baron. Although most talkers he has appeared in have not brought out his voice clearly, George Fawcett's here is always distinct and audible. David Torrence's part as the Governor at the Siberian prision is not an important one, but well done. Others are very minor.

Recording and photography good. *Char.*

THE ROYAL RIDER

(SYNCHRONIZED)

First National production and release starring Ken Maynard. Olive Hasbrouck and Phillipe De Lacey in cast. Charles R. Rogers the producer. Directed by Harry J. Brown; story by Nate Gatzert; titles by Leslie Mason. Ted McCord, photography. Cast: Olive Hasbrouck, Phillipe De Lacey, Theodore Larch, Joseph Burke, Harry Semels. At the Columbus, N. Y., as half of double bill, Nov. 26. Running time, 66 mins.

Ken Maynard has been moved from a western locale to a mythical kingdom in Europe as the owner of a wild west show. While there is none of the six-shootin', rip-roarin' action, there is plenty of good comedy to recommend this picture where silents are still used. Pleasing musical score accompanies for the wired houses. There are also a few sound effects, but no dialog or vocal bits.

Phillipe De Lacey is king of Alvania, the palace looking like a fixed up rancho somewhere in the west.

Love interest is Olive Hasbrouck, whose main duty is to look nice at all times. She ensnares Maynard and some of his cowboys to remain at the palace where they upset in slapstick fashion a plot of a scheming prime minister to kidnap the young monarch. Free-for-all in the final reel brings more laughs per minute than a dozen average westerns. This sequence alone makes picture fair entertainment. Some roping stuff worked in for additional laughs.

Picture is slow during its first half and often stilted in its direction. Titles only fair and photography ditto.

Comedy this one's selling point. *Char.*

TANNED LEGS

(ALL DIALOG With Songs)

Radio Pictures production and release. Directed by Marshall Neilan. Musical comedy book by Louis Seracky. Music and lyrics by Oscar Levant and Sidney Clare. RCA sounded. Ann Pennington featured in cast including Arthur Lake, Dorothy Revier, Sally Blane, June Clyde, Albert Gran, Allan Kearns. At Hippodrome, New York, week Nov. 30. Running time, 68 minutes.

A musical comedy on the screen needs a punchier story than this has to get out of the average programer class. "Tanned Legs" has mostly legs and anatomical displays in bathing suits, secondly clothes and society stuff the flaps may go for to an extent. It can be exploited as a musical comedy and hold up better under that billing.

Ann Pennington, featured in the billing but not the lead in the picture, tans more than her legs at the ritzy beach club where the plot is set. Penny wears some awfully summery bathing apparel. Looks like a kid at times, and at other times facially older than the girl she plays. From the chin down, however, always the knockout Pennington, and nothing hidden here.

Mother and father are in their second respective childhoods. She's playing around with a boy and he with a gal. Eldest daughter has fallen for the scoundrel who poses as a millionaire but is the undercover lover and con partner of father's chicken. Youngest daughter loves a boy she won't marry until untying the knots in her parents' heart affairs. Mother's boy friend is the boy friend also of Penny, who isn't really one of the family but is around enough to be.

Musical numbers are tossed in at random in the guise of rehearsals for the charity show. Tunes are sung at each other by the numerous and somewhat mixed up teams of lovers. The reprised theme song is "You're Responsible," not bad, while in back of it musically is "How Lovely Everything Could Be." A couple of comedy songs dependent on their lyrics quicken the pace.

It's down to 68 minutes, which lessens chances of dragging. *Bige.*

GENERAL CRACK

(ALL DIALOG)

Warner Bros. production and release, starring John Barrymore. Story by George Preedy adapted by Walter Anthony and dialoged by J. Grubb Alexander. Directed by Alan Crosland. Cameraman, Tony Gaudio. At Warner's, N. Y., for twice daily $2 run starting Dec. 3. Running time, 97 mins.

Prince Christian, Gen. Crack..........John Barrymore
Leopold II.................Lowell Sherman
Archduchess...................Marian Nixon
Fidelia..................................Armida
Count Hensdorff..........Hobart Bosworth
Countess Carola..........Jacqueline Logan
Colonel Gabor................Otto Mathieson
Colonel Pons..............Andres de Segurola
Lieut. Dennis................Douglas Gerrard
Capt. Schmidt........William von Brincken
Capt. Banning..................Theodore Lodi
Gypsy Chieftain.............Nick Thompson
Court Lady...............Julanne Johnston
Pietro..............................Gus Schacht

John Barrymore's most interesting production since "Beau Brummel." Certain to be an important booking and a money-maker all over.

Beyond argument it's a good action-crammed melodrama with a stellar performance. That it is less than a great picture will not perhaps concern the gentlemen who make, sell, buy and exhibit films.

It is the fortune and also the curse of Barrymore to have fine legs calling for tight pants. Costuming is not objectionable except that it regrettably points the whole direction and tempo of the average Barrymore picture. In "General Crack" insistence upon the physical person is again responsible for the squandering of this actor's talent on bedroom twaddle and stenographer's day dreams. Because of Barrymore's personal performance this synthetic sex is exposed in its complete puniness as the marshmallow of which program entertainments, but not screen epics, are made. "Disraeli" is demonstrating that film audiences can be exhilarated without aphrodisicals.

"General Crack" is historical fiction of some novelty dealing with a condition of former centuries when independent and unaffiliated armies sold their services to the highest bidder. General Crack sells his military tactics and following to the Emperor of Austria who has wars on his hands and wishes to possess the crown of the Holy Roman Empire. Crack has married a gypsy from chivalry rather than any necessity, and is the only one who does not perceive the essential lightness of her moral scruples. Going to the wars and leaving his bride behind in Vienna, the emperor plays iceman while a dishonored officer spies and reports to Crack. Revenge thereafter sets the motivation.

A versatile chap, this Crack. It takes him but a few minutes to clean up the most complicated international situations. He rides half across Europe with 500 cavalrymen and fortunately discovers his Russian adversaries in the midst of a good old-fashioned debauch with nip-ups, cartwheels, legomania, and other manifestations of the cinema party spirit. A few expert thrusts, parries, and side-swipes and the hussars control the country.

A long cast fails to reveal any performance particularly worthy of mention. Armida, a Mexican girl, probably has what Del Rio and Velez have, if some company cares to exploit her. Lowell Sherman is probably second for honors. Marian Nixon is okay but not at her best, and Jacqueline Logan, Julanne Johnston, and others are in but a scene or two.

No credits are screen-given for sound. It is generally a smooth and competent job bringing Barrymore's voice to the screen for the first time and doing it well. Gaudio's photography is first class. Technicolor coronation scene in a cathedral uses the wide screen and is a helpful flash.

"General Crack" is engrossing and exciting. It looks like money both ways, and will satisfy generally. *Land.*

Half Way to Heaven

(ALL DIALOG)

Paramount production and release. Starring Buddy Rogers. Directed and adapted by George Abbott from H. L. Gates' "Here Comes the Band Wagon." Cameraman, Alfred Gilks. W. E. sound track. At Paramount, New York, week Dec. 6. Running time, 66 mins.

Ned Lee..........Charles (Buddy) Rogers
Greta Nelson..........Jean Arthur
Nick..........Paul Lukas
Mme. Elsie..........Helen Ware
Manager..........Oscar Apfel
Mrs. Lee..........Edna West
Eric..........Nestor Aber

If this picture falls short of setting box offices on fire, neither will it burn up the managements of same. Unreels as normal program material with the Rogers name and pull seeing it through for satisfactory receipts.

But Buddy Rogers should take a few minutes off and check up on himself. Well on his way to becoming America's Little Lord Fauntleroy in long trousers. And no fistic battle with the heavy at the finish can offset the impression of some 5,000-odd preceding feet. Too much shy stammering may soon start to slip that femme following elsewhere. A number of male patrons will now only sit in attendance upon him according to the girl in his pictures. If kids can cut the apron strings of mamma's boys in high or prep school, film audiences can eventually do the same thing. So Buddy may as well go on a screen tear and smoke a cigaret or do something. Being the fourth Rover boy has its drawbacks as a career.

George Abbott's direction and Paul Lukas' heavy send this picture across. Lukas will probably set himself on this effort for the future when the studio boys start looking for a menace with an accent. A consistent piece of work under Abbott's guidance. It evidently didn't take long for the latter to find out. Having considerable rep as a stage director, not without reason, Abbott has pieced some neat spots into the telling of this carnival story while making it move all the time. That implies a knowledge of superfluous material and a sure scissors touch.

As a matter of fact, cutting has as much to do with holding this film together as anything else. The way it's been done hints strongly of Abbott, but William Shea, listed as film editor, may also have had a hand in the slicing. Whoever did it turned in an outstanding example of the art.

A simple and ordinary story is on and off in 66 minutes and made to intrigue. Opens on a carnival lot with Jean Arthur as one quarter of a casting act who rather likes the young "flyer." Lukas is the jealous "bearer," ruthlessly letting the kid drop at the next show on the finish of a blind double, the youngster being inside a sack. Act works without a net.

Nobody can prove anything, but the girl knows and to get away from Lukas she hides from the train on the next jump. That brings her to Rogers' homestead. Boy is a "flyer" and has been sent for to fill the vacancy in the girl's troupe. Both are unaware of the other's occupation. Carnival fortune teller and the manager's assistant track the girl down, but she won't go back to the act until accidentally discovering that that's Rogers' destination. Which takes the action to a state fair and Lukas obviously scheming to give the new member the same treatment because of Greta.

Anti-climax is Rogers' outwitting the "bearer" by making a leg catch instead of hand-to-hand at the finish of the blind double somersault, preventing Lukas from dropping him. Soon after the boy and the man go into a rough and tumble to the usual finish.

Casting shots are generally good, though Gilks might have speeded up the camera a little to slow the action so the audience could more easily follow the "flyer." Rogers doesn't look unlike Cordona, the Barnum-Ringling circus's principal "flyer," who had most of the picture femmes doing Mary Duncans the week the big show was in Los Angeles last summer.

Miss Arthur does well by the love interest in the case in a soft, husky voice which isn't hard to take. Good looking girl who, given a chance to slip in a little more s. a., may be going somewhere. Other cast support is able, future audiences undoubtedly picking out Nester Aber, as Rogers' kid brother, because of the lines tossed him and the way he handles them. Rogers, as previously mentioned, is the same sugary Buddy, highly excitable when in combat.

Title selected may have been picked to cover up the carnival angle while having a distant relationship to the story. But houses playing "Half Way to Heaven" won't have much to worry about. It'll do all right.

Sid.

SOUTH SEA ROSE

(ALL DIALOG, with Songs)

Fox production and release, starring Lenore Ulric. Allan Dwan credited as producer and director. From play by Tom Cushing, with dialog by Elliott Lester. Scenario by Sonya Levign. Songs by L. Wolfe Gilbert and Abel Baer. Harold Rosson, photography. W. W. Starr, sound. Settings by W. S. Darling and costumes by Sophie Wachner. At the Roxy, N. Y., week of Dec. 6. Running time, 69 mins.

Rosalie Dumay..........Lenore Ulric
Captain Briggs..........Charles Bickford
Dr. Tom Winston..........Kenneth MacKenna
Hackett..........Farrell MacDonald
Sarah..........Elizabeth Patterson
Willie Gump..........Tom Patricola
Maid..........Ilka Chase
Tavern Keeper..........George MacFarlane
Cabin Boy..........Ben Hall
Mrs. Nott..........Daphne Pollard
Ship's Cook..........Roscoe Ates
Mother Superior..........Charlotte Walker
Rosalie's Uncle..........Emile Chautard

Program feature possessing the elements of wide appeal and word-of-mouth advertising. Last-mentioned fact will likely concern Lenore Ulric's performance.

Comedy and the one song, tuneful, almost put this picture over alone. Production is fair despite a few technical shortcomings and the obvious non-synchronization of the theme song when a South Sea native is photographed doing the number. Only a flash and could advantageously be cut.

Story is suited to Miss Ulric as a French girl in the South Sea islands. When brought to staid New England's shores in the midst of a pack of blue-noses who think her shameful, Miss Ulric again has an opportunity to do her stuff. She does, and how!

Tom Patricola, Ilka Chase, Daphne Pollard, Roscoe Ates and others are also in, but it's always Miss Ulric. Her best scenes are aboard ship when arguing with her newly wedded skipper husband, and when she plays possum for an obliging doctor who treats her ills.

Patricola has one sequence for laughs as a country hick who plays a uke accompaniment to an impromptu dance by the bundle of s. a., and goes nuts when she suddenly quits. Charles Bickford and Kenneth MacKenna as the swashbuckling sea captain and the doctor play satisfactorily. Lighting and make-up in some of the scenes not too good.

Song is a lilting tune called "They Call Me South Sea Rose." Sung several times by Miss Ulric and plugged by other players, natives, ship crew and a special chorus.

Char.

SKINNER STEPS OUT

(ALL DIALOG)

Universal production and release, starring Glenn Tryon. Directed by W. C. Craft from story by Henry I. Dodge. Adapted by Matt Taylor. Dialog by Albert deMond and Taylor. W. E. recording. Synchronization and score by David Broekman. Myrna Kennedy, Lloyd Whitlock, Burr McIntosh and E. J. Radcliffe in cast. At the Colony, N. Y., week of Dec. 6. Running time, 70 mins.

Just a fair program film destined for the outposts. Familiar title, recurring from previous "Skinner" stories, may create some interest, further enhanced by its being the first talker in the series.

Author of this one has written a flock of others around the same character, originally done for the screen in silent days by Bryant Washburn and later, about three years ago, by Reginald Denny. FBO did a silent sequel, titled "Skinner's Big Idea," with Washburn. Net result with Tryon is not as hilarious as some of this boy's other work. What laughs he evokes come from his own personality and natural antics rather than that of the character in the story.

Dialog is a bit spotty, clicking in secluded sequence, but too gabby and listless as a whole. Direction is okay, with but five principal characters in the picture. All of the "Skinner" yarns run along the same lines; idea of ambitious young wife nagging white-collared hubby to do something big. Hubby starts by asking for a raise and gets air. With his last couple of dollars he buys a dress suit, spangles for wifey, and steps out into society at a charity bazaar. Hubby does his stuff and impresses a big business man on the verge of a merger with the young man's erstwhile firm.

Skinner thinks the big b. m. is trying to bluff his boss into a deal, and by interfering comes near spoiling everything. All turns out well, with Skinner promoted to a big job and wifey content.

Myrna Kennedy lends good support, handling lines with clarity and persuasion. Loyd Whitlock, Burr McIntosh and E. J. Radcliffe also contribute solid performances.

Span.

MISTER ANTONIO

(ALL DIALOG)

Tiffany production and release. Directed by James Flood and Frank Reicher from Booth Tarkington's story. Ernest Miller, cameraman. Adaptation by Fanny Hatton. Cast: Leo Carrillo, Garreth Hughes, Frank Reicher, E. Besserer. At Loew's New York, one day, Dec. 6. Running time, 71 mins.

Tiffany's version of Booth Tarkington's "Mr. Antonio" will go great with the kids, but it's hardly a picture for adults. While the latter will enjoy the performance of Leo Carrillo they'll probably find the picture too illogically old-fashioned, and maybe monotonous.

A cultured ward of a hypocritical small town politician falling for an organ grinder may read well, but on the screen, and to dialog, it's hardly entertainment for the normal fan.

Woodland camp, obviously a studio set, is picked as the place for a moron boy to hold up a fleeing maiden plus the grinder guardian speaking words of love, cooking macaroni, and fixing a berth for the girl immediately after her first fright. Virginia Valli lends sympathy to the girl.

Garreth Hughes, as the mind-wandering attache of the organ, plays a stupid role intelligently. Other than some of Carrillo's lingo, Hughes succeeds in copping what laughs this audience could find.

Carrillo has previously saved the small town mayor from disgrace in a Manhattan night club. And when Leo, gypsy enough to drive his instrument and donkey all the way to the mayor's town, gets jailed and then is out again, he knows that the mayor, up for re-election, fears the talk of someone on the inside. So, even though the Mayor succeeds in impressing the organ grinder that another is interested in the maiden, said maiden hitches on to the donkey cart and is there to assure the grinder that he comes before all others.

Waly.

ROSES OF PICARDY

(BRITISH MADE)

(Synchronized)

Produced by Gaumont Co., Ltd., and released by First Division. Directed by Maurice Elvey from the adaptation of R. H. Mottram's novel, "The Spanish Farm." All British cast featuring Lillian Hall Davis, John Stuart and Humbertsome Wright. At Loew's New York, one day, Dec. 8. Running time, 68 mins.

More than 18 months ago Variety reviewed this supposedly English war epic when it was first released in Canada. Then it was given an all around panning, especially for the lengthy running time, two hours. It has been cut practically in half for American consumption. Picture remains just as bad. Only change is that it's over sooner.

What there was of a plot when first released must have been cut out. Adding of sound is just a gesture. For the sure-seaters, and not sure there.

THE FEATHER

(BRITISH MADE)

(Synchronized)

Produced by the Strand Film Co. for United Artists' quota. Directed by Leslie Hiscott. Cast: Jameson Thomas, Vera Florey, Randle Ayrton, Charles Paton. Censor's Certificate "A." Reviewed at London Pavilion Nov. 15. Running time, 100 minutes.

Just another quota picture and 'way too long. Apart from being told in a series of jerky flashbacks, with the heroine singing a badly duped song against a gray backcloth, interlaced with scenes of the same girl perfectly silent in long shots in front of an orchestra, the production's pretty hot.

Directed by Leslie Hiscott, who might have done better if he'd cut 4,000 feet out of it. It gives Jameson Thomas the chance to forget his characterization every five minutes, with the result he's a short sighted insurance agent, very respectable and rather shy, one minute, and a bright young lover with a taste in blondes the next.

Story, told to illustrate a convict's downfall as though read by an old professor who pops in and out of the action every now and then, opens by showing the heroine rejoicing at the death of her husband. Enter the insurance man, all sympathy and rosebuds. The girl sings jazz to a "great master," and is signed as his pupil, the agent raising the money by lifting the safe. On emerging from prison he tells the old professor who promptly goes out and unites the loving couple. Well, well.

Picture promises to finish now and then in the last reels, but keeps letting the audience down. Doesn't end until after the girl has been shot singing high opera, her voice badly duped in the sound track. No dialog.

Okay as quota footage this side, but won't fit anywhere in the States.

PANDORA'S BOX

(GERMAN MADE)

(Silent)

Nero-Film production, releasing through Moviegraphs. Directed by G. W. Pabst from theme claimed to be based on combo of Wedekind dramas. At the 55th St., N. Y., beginning Nov. 30. Running time, about 85 minutes.

Lulu	Louise Brooks
Dr. Schoen	Fritz Kortner
Alva Schoen	Franz Lederer
Countess G.	Alice Roberte
Schigolch	Carl Goetz
Rodrigo Quast	Krafft-Raschig
Casti-Piani	M. von Newlinsky
Doctor's Bride	Daisy D'Ora

Better for Louise Brooks had she contented exhibiting that supple form in two-reel comedies or light Paramount features. "Pandora's Box," a rambling thing that doesn't help her, nevertheless proves that Miss Brooks is not a dramatic lead. Picture has a difficult time keeping up with itself. Will get by in the sure-seaters and some of the unwired indies.

Story unwinds awkwardly. Miss Brooks as Lulu hurls herself at men of all ages and even a possible Lesbian or so. There's a doctor who has some prior rights until he decides to marry. Then Lulu compromises him and has the ring coming her way until the siren's old dancing teacher gets a yearning, followed by a reflection in the prospective groom's own son.

As the doctor Fritz Kortner bows out before the part gets the chance to weary witnesses, as do the others. He commands Lulu to shoot him, providing at the same time opportunity for one of those conventional murder trials. Even the presiding justice, scarred and gray, falls when addressing the jury. Miss Brooks, however, takes the trial, killing, lovers and what-nots all with the simple attitude and reaction of a diner who finds the soup just so-so. In fact, Lulu's first move, when some friends spirit her away from the courtroom by sounding the fire gong, is to enjoy a bath in the dead doctor's house and then to tease his son into taking her to a Parisian gambling joint. In this locale all of her pals suddenly decide to turn her over to the cops unless she provides them with dough. Something has to happen, so the cops come in, anyway. Then Lulu, the doctor's son, and the aged dancing master row across the English channel in a flat-bottom boat. Finis in one of those artificial Limehouse attics.

Management at this house blames the N. Y. censor for having to end everything with Pandora and boy friends joining the Salvation Army.

Waly.

ACQUITTED

(ALL DIALOG)

Columbia production and release. Directed by Frank Strayer. Continuity and dialog by Keene Thompson. Recording by W. E. Cast: Lloyd Hughes, Margaret Livingston, Sam Hardy, Charles West, George Rigas, Charles Wilson and Otto Hoffman. At the Circle, N. Y, for two days, beginning Dec. 3. Running time, 62 mins.

This picture should be on double feature programs. Story is tied like a sailor's knot, tripping whatever opportunity Lloyd Hughes and Sam Hardy have. Margaret Livingston is the same as ever. Photography and recording good.

All about a tough who's chock full of sentiment to such a degree that he frames his girl for stretch just to remain in love with her. He also has a weakness for love songs.

Pet parody is "What'll I Do," and every time his gang hears the tune they drop their guns and give a bum his life back.

Eight years later, when the gal gets out of jail, the hardboiled one is still playing the same tune. He's the guy who bumped off a pal and then framed the girl's prison buddy for the trick. The bud is a doctor, and when the gal shoots hardboiled just before her prison pal, released from the pen, is about to sing to the angels at the bark of the gang's guns, the doctor saves the gunman's life by medical treatment. He finally confesses his earlier murder and frame, and embraces police armlets just to prove he's still fond of ballads.

Favorite of Schonbrunn

(GERMAN MADE)

(Synchronized)

Berlin, Nov. 25.

"Der Günstling von Schönbrunn," Greenbaum Film, first run at the Capitol, Berlin. Directed by Erich Waschneck. Lil Dagover and Ivan Petrovitch featured. Cameraman, Friedl Behn-Grund. Sound recorded on Tobis.

As a silent this picture is sure of a good reception on the Continent, for it fulfills all desires of an average audience. It is laid in a sumptuous romantic atmosphere and its leading figures are good to gaze upon. Particularly the Russian, Ivan Petrovich, shows in this picture that he is a leading man of the Gilbert type, and with, perhaps, some advantages over that player.

Lil Dagover, who may be remembered in America as the sexy wife in "Hungarian Rhapsody," here delivers another sensuous exhibition. If a trifle younger, no saying what could be made of her in the States.

Story is simple and concerns Queen Maria Theresia of Austria and her love for the Hungarian nobleman Trenck, whom she first meets incognito. Later, influenced by the Kaiser's jealousy, she arranges a marriage between Trenck and one of her waiting women. Waschneck has directed with much discretion and if there were more pace it would be a completely satisfactory picture.

Synchronized score, and the few dialog scenes, were made after the picture was completely cut and against the wishes of the director. The dialog, although hardly more than 5%, was so bad that it was cut out after the first show. But the synchronized score, and several songs sung by Petrovich remain. Recording is no advance over the talker, "The Land Without Women," brought out by Tobis some weeks ago. If anything, the music sounded hollower and often, in the fortes, unbearably sharp. How much this is due, if any, to the Tobis theatre equipment, used here, is not known.

Trask.

White Hell of Piz Palu

(GERMAN MADE)

(Silent)

Berlin, Nov. 25.

Sokal Film directed by Dr. A. Fanck and G. W. Papst. First run at Ufa Palast am Zoo, Berlin.

Despite "Singing Fool," this comparatively inexpensive German silent film will probably be the big money-maker of the season over here. It fits the German taste with complete accuracy. In New York it cannot hope to play the big first runs but it will bowl them over in the sure seaters and fill in nicely on a double feature program. Technically, and from the angle of action and direction, it rates well up in the international ranks.

Frank has already produced several films, all of them successful, which played in the same milieu, namely mountain climbing in the Bavarian alps. This is unquestionably his crowning effort. The scenario is more simple and more human, the actors keep real by the sensitive direction of Papst, who handles this end of the megaphone waving.

It is a simple fable concerning a mountain climber who has lost his wife on the Piz Palu, a dangerous Alp, and who since then climbs in the mountains alone. He encounters a young married couple in a shelter and the youth, without cause, becomes jealous. So he decides to go along on a dangerous ascent. But the girl will not be left out and forces her way into the party. An avalanche throws the youth down to the end of his rope and the older man in rescuing him breaks his leg. So the three are trapped half way up an ice wall. After three maddening days, rescue comes but too late to save the older man, who freezes to death as he has given his sweaters to save the other two.

Photography of the mountains is always interesting and often awe-inspiring. Actors deliver a first-class performance from the sporting angle, and Gustav Diessl is undoubtedly a leading man who would appeal in Hollywood. Leni Riefenstahl, formerly a dancer, is a typical German sporting type but too buxom for the average American taste—more on the line of Gertrude Ederle.

Trask.

THE WHITE SHEIK

(ENGLISH MADE)

(Silent)

British International production releasing through World Wide. Directed by H. Knoles from continuity by Violet Powell. Cast: Jameson Thomas, Lillian H. Davis, Warwick Ward, Julia Suedo, G. McLaughlin. At the Little Carnegie, N. Y., beginning Dec. 7. Running time, 62 mins.

Unreels much like the old "Poor Pauline" serial except that the perils are not included. A clumsy piece of work filled with what impresses as old newsreel strips of galloping Arabs. Poor fare even for the mongrel policies.

Little or no continuity. Jameson Thomas is too English for the title role, and Lillian Davis, as the lady who deliberately rides into the danger zone occupied by hostile Riffs, is painfully stiff and formal under all circumstances. Warwick Ward, as the menace, is cast as the sheik's traitorous lieutenant. His grimaces approach out and out mugging.

Waly.

Hunting Tigers in India

(Descriptive Dialog)

Talking Picture Epics, Inc., presentation of Commander George M. Dyott's scenic and wild game film. RCA sounded. Copyrighted by Dyott. Photographed by Dyott in conjunction with A. S. Vernay on Vernay-Faunthorpe Expedition, under auspices of American Museum of Natural History. Descriptive dialog by Dyott. No plot cast. Opened Dec. 9 at Cohan, New York, two-a-day at $1.50. Running time, 81 minutes.

Strictly a scenic and jungle-life educational for schools and the lecture halls. Doesn't rate as theatre after the record of weakness in the regular pop houses of preceding animal films, making this one particularly dubious.

Run as a $1.50 spec at the Cohan may help the distributors sell it as a commercial in the regular stands here and there. Some plugging in the schools and places of instruction may aid, and plenty of it is needed, besides being employed.

After 65 minutes of footage, during which time not a single tiger is produced, the picture reaches a 16-minute climax in form of a tiger hunt. Three of the jungle kings are bagged and not much excitement. The antics of the frightened transport elephants is interesting but not provocative of extra heart beats. It's probable that without the 65 minutes of build-up the tiger hunt would not be as exciting as it is.

Of course, the views of the people and lower animals of India are arresting. For the record the picture is valuable. For the popular theatre box office even the praiseworthy photography holds slight value.

Previous to the tiger hunt, the gun and camera sportsmen seek elephant, rhino and spotted deer. Interesting but not thrilling. More like a natural history exhibit.

Every few feet hold an inserted shot of vultures on the wing or looking for dead flesh. Next-to-closing scene of the picture (fade-out is old-fashioned sunset) flock of vultures on a carcass. Vulture is an ugly creature, almost sickening to look at. Not so pretty and leaves a not-so-nice farewell impression.

Commander George M. Dyott, photographer, first introduced in a drawing room set and proceeds to verbally illustrate the entire picture. The Commander is a pleasant talker, but apparently his memory is not so good. When in view of the camera while talking (all the talk was added) he obviously glances at notes planted behind a silver receptacle.

A well-played score of jungle and oriental music runs through the footage and mingles nicely with the Commander's chatter.

RCA sounding job was impressive at the Cohan, where projection is faultless.

Program announcement by the sponsors of "Hunting Tigers in India" informs that other pictures of the same type will follow. Others should have the semblance of a story if wishing to improve the commercial worth of an educational.

Bige.

LOVE IN CAUCASUS

(RUSSIAN MADE)

(Silent)

Georgkino production. Released by Amkino. Adaptation made from "Eliiso," by Georgian novelist, A. Karbek. All-Caucasian cast. Scenario by Tretyakov and Shengelai. Directed by N. Shengelai. Cameraman, V. Kereselidze. At Film Guild, New York, week Nov. 30. Running time, 67 minutes.

Nix as entertainment. Just another Russian effort at photographing places.

Again the trouble is that many things some folks do in life are uninteresting, even in the theatre, regardless of how realistic the action may be copied. Russians, ever since the Punch and Judy dawn, have been pantomiming, and they haven't yet learned there's much more to the picture art than facial twitches, hand-clapping and legging. This film is nothing more than an analysis of the art of pantomime laid on thick and sober and utterly lacking recreative quality. Though, of course, in Russia, where it should have remained, they may go for it.

Story supposedly based on actual incident among Caucasian tribes in Tersk country and matter of historical record in Russian army archives, period not given.

Some action so goofy that even the artie customers hissed at this house.

Napoleon On St. Helena

Berlin, Nov. 25.

Lupu Pick Film. Directed by Lupu Pick, with Werner Kraus and Albert Bassermann featured. First run at the Ufa Pavillion, Berlin.

Lupu Pick is unquestionably one of the very few topnotch directors still left in Germany. This production is one of the best he has turned out.

Interesting idea to picturize Napoleon's last days, and Werner Kraus is an ideal exponent of the part. After seeing him on the screen, the other portraits of the man seem untrue. He gives the character that combination of sharp intelligence and power which historians have led us to believe belonged to the great Corsican, and at the end, when he is left almost alone, there is distinct pathos.

Albert Bassermann, as the English governor, also delivers an extraordinary performance. Scenes between these two men are as strong as any seen in latter day pictures.

Whether the historical treatment of the last days of Bonaparte will interest the public is a question, but surely there are enough Napoleon fans to give the picture a reasonable run. No denying that it is an outstanding example of continental film art.   *Trask.*

SKY HAWK
(ALL DIALOG)

Fox production and release. Features Helen Chandler, John Garrick and Gilbert Emery. Directed by John Blystone, from a J.lewellyn Hughes magazine story. Adaption and dialog by Hughes and Campbell Gullan, latter also staging. Cameraman, Conrad Wells; sound, W. W. Lindsay. Mechanical effects by Ralph Hammeras. At Gaiety, New York. $2 top, twice daily. Dec. 11. Running time, 75 mins.
Joan Allan ....Helen Chandler
Jack Bardell ....John Garrick
Major Nelson ....Gilbert Emery
Lord Bardell ....Lennox Pawle
Judge Allan ....Lumsden Hare
Tom Berry ....Billy Bevan
Minnie ....Daphne Pollard

"Sky Hawk" will do business on its air battle between a Zeppelin and a lone plane over London. The screen shows all three. This is slightly more than a two-reel sequence reported to have cost the Fox studio not far from $250,000 by itself; worth it because it's the picture. Otherwise, "Sky Hawk" is a Lambs Club delight and due to its very British flavor general trade interest will also center on its reception in England. Picture will particularly please the men, because of the air fight, and few women will walk on it once they're in. A good film which should run up better than average grosses but doesn't suggest general holdover qualifications.

So it looks as if Ralph Hammeras ought to get the credit for this release's financial income. Hammeras staged the air fight with highly geared slow motion cameras and built the London set in a dirigible hangar at Arcadia, Cal. Result is as sweet a piece of miniature work as has ever been turned out. And the accompanying sound track is equally expert, which about makes this release a triumph for the technical staff.

As the story has been melded into celluloid it's distinctly secondary to the mechanical effects. But it would be tough for any yarn to dominate the aerial warfare as here staged for the camera. Much of the London set is smothered by a smoke screen (fog) so that only one or two shots imply its magnitude. Rather surprising in view of the publicity planned on this tremendous miniature. That the set hasn't fully been brought out seems, in a way, a pity.

Perhaps the best thing Blystone, directing, has done with the film is to have had the good sense to hold it down. Final half hour is completely consumed with building up to and then launching the Zep raid followed by the dirigible's destruction. From this point a direct cut is made to the honeymoon getaway of the victorious Royal Flying Corps lieutenant and his Canadian bride for the finish.

It may be that the British have never had such a break in an American picture as they get here. Story is heavily sweetened by John Bull accents, atmosphere and slang expressions as called for by the locale. And the cast's comic comes so close to stealing the picture on performance that there's not much difference. Billy Bevan plays the aeroplane mechanic, servicing young Bardell's ship, who becomes the heir's defender when his valor is smirched by suspicion. This is because of a crash as he returns from an against orders flight to say goodby to Joan. Real British landscape for this flight is credited to a Fox sound news cameraman over there. That Bardell is due to fly to France that afternoon explains the inference that the crack-up was intentional.

Temporarily paralyzed from the waist down, Bardell has a condemned plane slipped over to his father's estate where the loyal sergeant spends his evenings putting it in shape. Meanwhile, the boy has broken off his engagement because of his unwelcome social and military position.

Arrival of the Zep over London causes Bartell to have his bus wheeled out to go up against the dirigible alone, despite his legs, for the happy ending. That no other R. F. C. machine takes off against the invader is a license which the story takes. If the supposition is that there is not another available plane at Croydon (flying field), either the adapter or film cutter has failed to make this clear.

Bevan gives an excellent performance in a sympathetic part added materially by production judgment to make the carefree courage of the English Tommy stand out. In a couple of spots he is capably aided by Daphne Pollard as a pub habitue. The direction has missed with Emery as the middle aged major who is doomed to disappointment in his delicate suit for Joan. Instead of evoking the sympathy evidently figured upon for the character, the way the picture unwinds leaves Emery as not much more than a necessary atmospheric inclusion. A good performer throttled by unforeseen circumstances.

John Garrick leaves a pleasant impression as a symbol of the R. F. C. but, perhaps, without that fire to make it a memory. Helen Chandler may have been permitted to direct herself. Either way, her intonations constantly imply that she's on the verge of tears, a detrimental method of delivery over a period of an evening or a picture. Her appearance is wholesome and more than that toward the end when she wears a white gown. Canadian angle in the story stands off by lack of a consistent broad "a" while all other participants are relegated to bits. First love scene between the principals evoked a noticeable snicker from all portions of the house (not on opening night), for no apparent screen reason other than the strictly British dialog involved.

Directorial background touches include the waves of apprehension which swept London at the air raid signals by poking the camera's nose into flats, pubs, night clubs, underground (subway), and a theatre where the comedian announces the raid, goes on with the performance and nobody leaves the theatre.

But the top sidelight introduces the Zep sequence when a captured R. F. C. captain is brought before the commanding German officer for questioning. Scene is particularly well handled and superbly played by the German involved, unmentioned in the cast credits. Interiors of the Zep's main cabin hold whenever flashed, the German tongue being given full rein, and the stoicism of the crew as the air giant catches fire is also gotten over. There is no disparaging of the enemy at any time and those looking for a preachment against war will find it in a pre-dinner parlor discussion between Joan, her father and the major which almost gave this picture the title of "The World Moves On."

"Sky Hawk's" run at the Gaiety will be no criterion as to its program value. It was abruptly brought in to finish out the Fox tenancy of the house expiring Jan. 1. Due to its normal running time a double newsreel (Hearst and Fox), sound cartoon, Roach two-reeler and a piano short item are preceding it here.   *Sid.*

THE B'WAY HOOFER
(ALL DIALOG, with Songs)

Columbia production and release. Featuring Marie Saxon, Jack Egan and Louise Fazenda. Directed by George Archainbaud; produced by Harry Cohn. Original story, continuity and dialog by Gladys Lehman. Cameraman, Joe Walker. Chief sound engineer, John Livadary. Sound mixing engineer, Harry Blanchard. Asst. director, Dave Selman. Film editor, Maurice Wright.

in projection room, New York. Running time, 63 minutes.
Adele......................Marie Saxon
Bobby.......................Jack Egan
Jane.....................Louise Fazenda
Larry....................Howard Hickman
Morton...................Ernest Hilliard
Anabelle.................Gertrude Short
Dolly......................Eileen Percy
Mazie..................Charlotte Merriam
Billy.....................Fred MacKaye
Baggage Man...............Billy Franey

An entertaining little program talker that establishes Marie Saxon, a feature from the musical comedy stage, for the talking screen. The picture should carry neatly in the three-day or less run houses, and looks like a certain pleaser for the shorter than a week stand neighborhooders.

Besides the most agreeable Miss Saxon there is a boy here, who seems to have a future in films, Jack Egan. About the only picture name of any weight in the cast is Louise Fazenda. Exhibs will have to exploit more on the entertainment end and youth in the picture than anything else in sight, excepting in those towns where Marie Saxon may be known from her stage musicals.

With a back stage story that takes in a burlesque troupe, it opens with a Ziegfeld "Follies" production number. Miss Saxon is in the centre of 24 silk-hatted boys, all dancing, with her dancing as effective on the screen as it always has been on the stage. It's a very fast start, almost too fast for the number side of a turkey trouping burlecue show to follow. The numbers staged by Jack Cunningham, and with the stage part supervised by Rufus Le Maire, the burlesque portion is made to do nicely. This section, however, lacks the rough low comedy that easily could have been inserted and which the entire picture misses as well. Probably no better system ever has been devised than Columbia's to keep the cost down and still get away with it, but sometimes a little more in the overhead, like here, might turn a fair picture into a very good one, especially with the talkers.

In the tale Miss Saxon is a star of Broadway, closing a hard season after a long run. She's going away, for a rest, with only the maid accompanying her knowing her whereabouts. Drifting into a tank town and taking a cottage, Miss Saxon is shoved onto the stage of the local opry house when there is a rush outside by locals looking for the chorus job advertised. She is walking by.

Mr. Egan, the young and goodlooking head of the troupe, from author to manager and taking in the principal juve role, picks Miss Saxon as likely for the line. They mutually notice each other otherwise, and the girl thinks it will be a lark to go along, assuming the name of her maid, Jane Brown. She goes with the troupe, is rapidly advanced and in a short time is cofeatured with Egan.

Meanwhile her Broadway manager is frantic, as his star has not reported for rehearsals. And the maid grows alarmed over the growing attachment of the young couple. She wires the manager, who rushes to Glens Falls to catch the troupe and his star. Along with him goes the star's John flame from Broadway. The latter, sensing the situation, tells Egan his leading woman has been making a monkey of him, although Egan thinks he taught Jane Brown everything she knows. Egan is told she's not Jane Brown but Adele Doray from Broadway.

Egan finally believes it, and the girl admits it. Egan calls the turkey company to witness he is firing the Broadway star from a third-rate burlesque on the spot, which he does, bringing an effective and sob scene for Miss Saxon, who's in love with Egan.

During the rehearsals in New York Miss Saxon is inveigled into a nite club where Egan is making his first eastern appearance. Dancing and no panic, she saves him by going onto the floor, giving him the cue of their former two-act in the burlesque olio, and he's over. So is the picture, for the manager of the musical tells Egan to report also in the morning for rehearsal.

Miss Saxon has considerable light and shade in this film, doing it well, especially to the strictly family group that caught the new talker in the Columbia's projection room. The Old Boy grabbed the chance for the notice, to stand off "The Skirt" who motherly believes Marie is the greatest actress, the greatest dancer, or anything else you want to slip in. As you may conclude, she's nuts over Marie.

Columbia had a light print for the projection room showing. It gave both Miss Saxon's and Egan's singing voices a rasp. Miss Saxon's speaking voice is quite as charming as she is herself when in dance action or playing a role. There are very few girls with charm and class who can do as much in performance as the small group of ingenues who have dominated the Broadway musical stage for a while. If those girls, and this takes in Marie as well, used more judgment in their agent and ran their agent instead of allowing a manager's agent to run them, the majority of the girls would be better off. They might even change their agent and stop the evident juggling he does to and with them.

It's more a matter of personal satisfaction than anything else with this Columbia picture with Marie. She was another of those who were unfortunate enough to go against those New York studio tests of a year or so ago.

Mr. Egan plays very well, and both of these young people display personality in addition to good screen work. Miss Saxon's personality is changed some by the screen, for the better and more forcible, making a very comely girl more so.

Miss Fazenda has but little chance to get a laugh. About the only laughter is when the native girls try out for the burlesque job. The chorus of the burlesque troupe is typically burlesquy. Some of the mechanics back stage are revealed. There may be a giggle in them in the regular houses.

It's not known if the projection room print is the final cutting. If not, a bit more may speed up a few spots, including fade-outs. *Sime.*

DANCE HALL

(ALL DIALOG)

Radio production and release. Directed by Melville Brown from magazine story by Vina Delmar. Supervised by Henry Hobart; scenario and dialog by Jane Murfin and J. Walter Ruben. Jack Mackenzie, cameraman; Ann McKnight, film editor. RCA Photophone sounded. At Globe, New York, on grind. Week Dec. 14. Running time, 65 minutes.

Gracie Nolan	Olive Borden
Tommy Flynn	Arthur Lake
Mrs. Flynn	Margaret Seddon
Ted Smith	Ralph Emerson
Bremmer	Joseph Cawthorn
Bee	Helen Kaiser
Ernie	Lee Moran
Truck Driver	Tom O'Brien

Miscasting hurts an interesting and otherwise fairly well-made picture of the younger generation, snapping it up in a modern "taxi" dance hall. Numerous characters leave so unfavorable an impression it is probable the film will be identified with just ordinary grosses.

Unfortunate, as "Dance Hall" is a box office title and would carry far if backed by good stuff. Vina Delmar, who wrote the short story originally appearing in "Liberty," has a knack of picking 'em catchy.

Olive Borden and Arthur Lake form the incongruous love interest; one obviously a matured young lady, despite a blonde wig and brief skirts, the other a gawky, exaggerratedly boyish kid still suited to high school parts. Third corner to the necessary triangle is played by Ralph Emerson, photographing and impressing negatively.

Joseph Cawthorn, as the ballroom owner, is fortunate comedy relief, and outclasses his surroundings like a skyscraper in Central Park. He has been put in lights at the Globe, and deserves it for distracting attention from other members of the cast in this one.

"Dance Hall" pictures a "taxi" ballroom more graphically than any previous film has done, and has some novelty on this angle. Frowzy little flaps and sleek young jellies are seen tearing into their own ideas of terpsichore, going into goofy acrobatic routines with that "Hey-look-at-us" attitude typical of any pop dance spot. Types are naturals and will naively laugh at themselves in theatres all over the country.

Gracie Nolan is hostess in a flashy looking but quite democratic dance hall. Tommy Flynn, shipping clerk, goes without lunch so he can have money to dance with the girl three nights each week. The pair win loving cups regularly at the ballroom's hoofing contests.

Into the enjoyable monotony comes Ted Smith, an aviator, and Gracie falls easy. Tommy also worships the aviator, and quietly backs out of the picture. Smith gets a chance to substitute for an injured flyer in a cross-country attempt at a record and crashes. The shock sends the dance hostess to bed. She is taken to the home of the young shipping clerk where his mother can care for her.

When Smith recovers from the accident he doesn't visit the grl, but takes an apartment with another hostess. Hearing he has returned and believing the shipping clerk jealously withheld information of her whereabouts from the aviator, Gracie calls the kid a mob of names and tears out for the aviator. She finds him with the other hostess.

Then back to the shipping clerk, who tried to make the aviator visit the girl and got a black eye for his efforts. To cap the reconciliation is an offer of $200 weekly from the dance hall owner for Gracie and Tommy as his featured ballroom team. Doesn't unreel as implausible as it sounds.

Melville Brown in directing achieved life-like atmosphere too effectively at times, but outside of casting there isn't any fault to find with the technical handling. It may have been impossible to restrain the Harold Teen antics of Arthur Lake, so greatly in contrast to the drawing room style of Olive Borden. The kid seems naturally as he acts. Mother played capably by Margaret Geddon.

Recording highly sensitive and clear throughout, with photography good. Cutting slipped up in showing the same dance scenes for two **different nights—made very apparent by a kid without a coat doing a highly freak routine with his gal right in the center of the ballroom.**

Miss Delmar is the author of "Bad Girl" and "Kept Woman," two best seller novels. That's why she's getting unusually prominent billing for having written this. *Bang.*

THE LOST PATROL

(ENGLISH MADE)

(Silent)

Pro Patria production and release. Directed by Walter Summers and photographed by Stanley Rodwell. At Cameo, New York, week Dec. 14. Running time 75 minutes.

Lieut. Hawkins	Arthur Woods
Corporal Bell	Terence Collier
Samuel Abelson	Fred Dyer
Augustus Brown	Andrew McMaster
Matlow Cook	James Watts
William Henry Hale	Charles Emerald
Angus McKay	John Valentine
Mick Morelli	Hamilton Keene
H. G. Sanders	Sam Wilkinson
John Pearson	Frederick Long
The Sergeant	Cyril McLaglen

Unwired and arty houses can book "The Lost Patrol" and satisfy their patrons. The picture, while ideally cast and with a realistic locale, is without consistent suspense, little being made of the theme; therefore a poor bet for any house classes except those mentioned.

Practically all of the action occurs among a few palm trees with a sandy outlook. Company alleges it was made on the Sahara.

Other than time being designated as between 1913-16, patrol of 11 men could be taken for French Legionaires. Production opens with flash character sketches, from woodcutter to fisherman and prize fighter. Meaningless until later in the footage when bunch are together on the desert. Then more character cut-ins are introduced via newspaper clippings and vaude bills.

All these phases serve merely to weaken the theme, and to distract. Real story is in the activities of a soldier detail lost in the desert and without horses. Had latter angle been fully developed, well directed and edited, "The Lost Patrol" could have easily commanded world wide attention.

Cyril McLaglen shows some real stuff and an ability at character work which would bring him close to his Americanized brother, Vic, if given a similar opportunity. As the sergeant in command of the detail, since the lieutenant, Hawkins, is bumped off by Arabs after trees first disappear, McLaglen majors both in role and performance.

The death of the men, one by one, from sniping Arabs who have gathered among the sand hills surrounding the oasis refuge, is well done. It is while the men are reminiscing that the production drags. One especially good sequence is a fist fight between the boxer and fisherman.

Suggestion of a nude body despoiled by the enemy and found near the camp by a religious fanatic is vivid. The sergeant's last stand, and conquering of the marauders after the others have failed him, brings in some trick tripple gun shooting familiar in old American westerns. *Waly.*

DARKENED ROOMS

(ALL DIALOG)

Paramount production and release. Directed by Louis Gasnier. Adaptedby Patrick Konesky and Melville Baker from the story by Philip Gibbs. Dialog by Patrick Kearney. Archie Stout cameraman. At Loew's New York, one day, Dec. 13, half double bill. Running time, 63 minutes.

Ellen	Evelyn Brent
Emory Jago	Neil Hamilton
Joyce Clayton	Doris Hill
Billy	David Newell
Mme. Silvara	Gale Henry
Bert Nelson	Wallace MacDonald
Mrs. Fogarty	Blanche Craig
Mr. Clayton	E.H. Calvert
Sailor	Sammy Bricker

Evelyn Brent's first starring film for Paramount but a weak sister to the previous films which but featured her. Incongruous story with the incidental action holding spotty interest. It mainly deals with the usual film subject of spiritualism. Through that it may be a fair pleaser for the neighborhoods.

Seances with Miss Brent as a partner of Neil Hamilton, playing a medium, and Hamilton a clairvoyant, are the most entertaining. Throughout the subject matter spiritualism is treated as a grafting racket. A few of the more obvious and minor tricks practiced by mediums are exposed.

Miss Brent is still the ultra-sophisticated and hard-boiled miss. A bit too much so for her present interpretation. Otherwise she stands out with her supposedly spiritual delivery during the state of her trance.

It is difficult to take Hamilton as the pseudo-hypnotist and clairvoyant, due to his boyish appearance. Other characters are submerged to the two leads and barely given any footage. except for Gale Henry, as a practiced old timer in the game of clairvoyance, and Doris Hill as Joyce Clayton.

Dialog distinctly audible and well handled.

Will offend no one, except perhaps Conan Doyle. Chump educator and that only angle to exploit. Might be added what Houdini tried to do on stage is here illustrated on screen. And as there are more Conan Doyles over here than any skeptic is aware of, steaming this up might bring on an under cover controversy. If so, let it rage.

LUCKY IN LOVE

(ALL DIALOG, with Songs)

Pathe production and release. Featuring Morton Downey and Betty Lawford. RCA sounded. Directed by Kenneth Webb. Robert Kane, supervisor. Story and dialog by Gene Markey. Music by Bud Green and Sam H. Stept. "Love Is a Dreamer," theme song. At Colony, New York, week Dec. 13. Running time, 76 minutes.

Michael O'More	Morton Downey
Lady Cardigan	Betty Lawford
Capt. Fitzroy	Colin Keith-Johnston
Earl of Balkerry	Halliwell Hobbes
Connors	J. M. Kerrigan
Tim	Edward McNamara
Rafferty	Edward O'Connor
Paddy	Richard Taber
Kate	Mary Murray
Cyril	Mackenzie Ward
Feinberg	Louis Sorin

"Lucky in Love" is 90% Morton Downey and 10% romantic background for the tenor and his songs. The story selected to frame the Downey singing is away from the backstage formula and, while frail, fairy-tailish and unbelievable, serves the program purpose mildly. Not too much confidence for this one.

With all of that in mind, it is a mystery why Morton Downey is not starred in this picture. He is featured along with Betty Lawford, comparatively unknown on stage or screen. Downey certainly means more after his previous film performances than the trite title "Lucky in Love" possibly can. The performance of Downey places him miles above the picture and the title.

Downey is Michael O'More, stable boy on a royal Irish estate. The young mistress of the castle falls for him and his voice. Old mortgage is dragged in after Mike sails for America. Things look rocky for Lady Mary and grandpop.

Mike sailed because the cops were after him for socking Capt. Fitzroy, the on-the-make villain. Abroad, Mike impresses Abe Feinberg, department store magnate, and the latter places him at the music counter. That's more Downey's singing, after all of the singing in Ireland.

"Love Is a Dreamer" is the themer and a fair pop. "For the Likes O' You and Me" and "When They Sing the Wearin' of the Green" are just that.

Kenneth Webb's directing held down the silliness of story that could easily have ruined the picture if given full play. Some eye-filling country scenes for the Erin portion.

Cast is all-Downey, with Miss Lawford, Colin Keith-Johnston, Halliwell Hobbes and Louis Sorin acting as far as the scenario permitted them. Keith-Johnston, as "Lucky in Love's" heavy, may have herein experienced his first film job on this side. He came over as star of the English "Journey's End" (legit) cast.

Downey's voice has been suitably recorded. His constant singing isn't the sort that fatigues. *Bige.*

This Thing Called Love

(ALL DIALOG)

Pathe. Directed by Paul Stein under supervision of Ralph Block. Adapted by Horace Jackson from stage play by Edwin Burke. Cameraman, Norbert Brodine. At Roxy, New York, week Dec. 13. Running time, 72 minutes.

Robert Collings	Edmund Lowe
Ann Marvin	Constance Bennett
Harry Bertrand	Roscoe Karns
Clara Bertrand	Zasu Pitts
Alverez	Carmelita Geraghty
DeWitt	John Roche
Fred	Stuart Erwin
Dolly	Ruth Taylor
Dumary	Wilson Benge
Secretary	Adele Watson

On the stage this script was a fairly profitable short-lifer. Its box office capabilities as a picture are likewise not more than moderately optimistic and there may be censor trouble in some spots.

Co-starred are Edmund Lowe and Constance Bennett, both engaging performers in their parts. But, like many "problem" stories, this one prefers to leave the problem vaguely answered, if at all—and picture audiences won't stand for that sort of dodging.

Scenario follows stage presentation with few deviations. Just returned from Peru, Lowe has plenty of dough and is anxious to settle down. The man who is attempting to have him sign merger papers invites him to the house for a slant of happy married life. Other couples are present, and the affair winds up in a marital free-for-all.

But Lowe is still unconvinced. He asks the business man's sister-in-law to marry him. She consents to a business-like marriage, wherein she is to be put on straight salary for managing a home but doesn't have to sleep with hubby. Both are free to neck whom they please on the outside.

Later each deliberately cuts up on the side to make the other jealous. Things can't continue like that, so they decide to be really married. As soon as they decide, Lowe starts nagging the wife for admitting she was getting amorous with a boy friend. She in turn throws in a few digs about his Spanish girl friend.

This jealousy and husbandly sense of possession are just what the wife didn't like about marriage. She decides to blow, but hubby locks himself in a room with her. She still wants to get out, so he hands her a skeleton key. Smiling enigmatically, she throws the skeleton key away, and the husband cries: "Darling!"

That isn't sophistication; it's the nuts.

Paul Stein, directing, made everything obvious. Many giggles at the Roxy as Lowe tried to fenagle into the bedroom with his $25,000-per-year board but not bed bride. More sex stuff concerning the mistress of Lowe's business friend. This mistress parades before her lover's wife, bragging about who pays for her clothes, and the wife partially pulls the clothes off. Picture is full of unfaithful marriage brocolli.

Whenever Lowe goes into light comedy, interest picks up. Likewise Stein seems at his best when directing the lighter moments.

Constance Bennett is consistently good in performance. A nagging wife as handled by Zasu Pitts is an irritating and therefore successful character. Ruth Taylor has a minor part as a dumb wife and handles it well. Her similarly dumb husband is acted convincingly by Stuart Erwin. Harry Bertrand as the business man with a mistress gets pretty good results in comedy tries.

Dialog recording not always good as projected at the Roxy, which is supposed to have about the best equipment in the country. Photography uniformly good. One three-minute color sequence in a cafe set. *Bang.*

The Marriage Playground

(ALL DIALOG)

Paramount production and release. Co-featuring Mary Brian and Frederic March. Directed by Lothar Mendes. Based on Edith Wharton's novel, "The Children." Adapted by J. Walter Ruben. Cameraman, Victor Merner. At Paramount, New York, week Dec. 13. Running time, 70 mins.

Judy	Mary Brian
Martin	Frederick March
Cliff Weader	Huntley Gordon
Joyce Weader	Lilyan Tashman
Lady Wrench	Kay Francis
Lord Wrench	William Austin
Terry	Phillip de Lacey
Mrs. Seegar	Seena Owen

A peach of a picture well above the satisfaction-giving average of a program release and the kind that leaves a sense of full-hearted, human pleasure behind it. Can be booked in safety and exploited with confidence.

It's packed with children, amusingly impudent, touchingly warm youngsters who will carry a tremenous appeal to the great home-keeping, family-loving American public. In the midst of the children and for this reason, as for others, suggestive of Thomas Meighan, although in no respect similar as to looks, is Frederich March, sharing billing with Mary Brian, and getting a great break. A couple of pictures like this one and March will romp upward pronto.

Miss Brian is splendid. This young performer has had a fine growth. Her work now has sureness and sympathy. It is impossible to think of anyone doing this role better. Without having read the novel it seems she must very nearly approximate Edith Wharton's original of the girl who brought up her young brothers and sisters because the fashionable parents were too busy traipsing about Europe.

In a production characterized by quiet, unostentatious elegance, Paramount has created fullness of narrative and characterizations. None of the puny one-incident plots so prevalent nowadays, but the depth and breadth of a novel plus that good old-fashioned heart tug.

Lothar Mendes has a product here which he can use as a prestige endorsement. He has done a fine directorial job with the valuable co-operation of cameraman, sound man and, not to slight one always important if ofttime ignored, the cutter.

But, fundamentally, the story must get a big chunk of the credit. It is rich in the things that make films glamorous, as well as arousing definite sympathetic responses in the audience. In other words, the spectator is always absorbed. *Land.*

THE MANXMAN

(ENGLISH MADE)
(Silent)

British International production with no American distributor credited. Directed by Alfred Hitchcock. Based on novel of same title by Sir Hall Caine. Jack Cox, cameraman. At the Little Carnegie, New York, week Dec. 14. Running time, 76 minutes.

Pete Quilliam	Carl Brisson
Kate Cregeen	Anny Ondra
Philip Christian	Malcolm Keen
Caesar Cregeen	Randle Ayrton
Granny Gregeen	Clare Greet

Antiquated adaptation of best seller of another day, first error. Lustreless performance by this all-British cast plus usual foreign direction and editing, the second. English locale about the only asset for "The Manxman," a pancake even for the die-hard sure-seaters.

Story is unfolded in a stupid elementary way. Much footage is devoted to Caesar's grog shop where Anny Ondra, pretty but inoffensive blonde, starts the Kate role, off in a barmaid capacity. Of course, there's more—but less. *Waly.*

SALLY

(ALL DIALOG, With Songs)
(Color)

First National production and release. Starring Marilyn Miller, with Alexander Gray, Joe E. Brown and Pert Kelton featured. Adapted from the musical comedy of that name. Jerome Kern's original score. Additional numbers by Al Dubin and Joe Burke. Dance numbers staged by Larry Ceballos. Directed by John Francis Dillon, with Dev Jennings and C. E. Schoenbaum cameramen. Orchestra under direction of Leo Forbenstein. Screen version by Waldemar Young. At the Winter Garden, New York, for $2 twice daily run, Dec. 23. Running time, 100 mins.

Sally	Marilyn Miller
Blair Farrell	Alexander Gray
Connie	Joe E. Brown
Otis Hooper	T. Roy Barnes
Rosie	Pert Kelton
"Pops" Shendorff	Ford Sterling
Mrs. Ten Brock	Maude Turner Gordon
John Farquar	E. J. Ratcliffe
Roue	Jack Duffy
Marcia	Nora Lane

Rasch Ballet

"Sally" will come pretty close to being the convincer to the studio mob that they can throw the adaptations of musical shows in the alley, write their own and turn out better pictures. That's the Warner idea anyway, and maybe "Sally" instigated the thought. It's a good program picture and easily sets Marilyn Miller for future film work, but other than its production background and star, "Sally" is quite a way from being a smash.

Trouble seems to be that the studio took the stage script not only seriously, but literally. Like putting a pony in a corral when it has the whole pasture to romp in. Result is that the opening half hour is so deadly that the film never fully recovers, and the fourth reel lacks speed. By that time it's too late. The situation then solely rests with Miss Miller plus magnitude and taste in the settings behind her. One of these, a sunken garden supposedly attached to one of those Long Island estates, is gasp provoking. In fact, the color combinations and the production constantly impress. They've got to because there's not much action or comedy.

As laid out Pert Kelton is completely throttled. T. Roy Barnes only occasionally flickers, Joe E. Brown isn't exactly the type, and Ford Sterling is the outstanding comic individual.

So, summing it all up, "Sally," as a picture, smacks of being a bit old-fashioned. Enough to prevent becoming a hold-over feature in the regular film houses. For single weeks it won't have any trouble doing business, and will probably get away to a big holiday send-off at the Garden. After that it's something else again, with the last two weeks in January figuring to define its $2 career on Broadway.

Story of "Sally" has been done 18 different ways. It's always "Sally." Which also may be an angle on what's the matter. From the screen's standpoint Colleen Moore's silent version of the same piece equalled this edition because it had action and laughs. That goes despite sound and color.

Alexander Gray here is merely a juvenile with a voice. Amidst various hues he impresses as colorless, possibly the fault of the script—but there it is.

Interpolated tunes added to the original score do not listen as important.

They've shot Miss Miller from gingham to a bridal veil, including some sort of a boudoir arrangement in which she is about the last word. And this girl has been easy on the eyes since stepping on a stage. She's vocally doing the same songs better than when in the show, because her voice has improved, and she hasn't had to worry about new dance routines, for this is a new clientele. They've about let her use her own judgment on numbers, even

"Mecca" is in, and no harm done because all her dances are good.

Perhaps the high point is the conventional boy number which Larry Ceballos, having found out what a camera's for, has given a great exit. This routine is nice work all the way, with that finish topping off. Miss Miller is holding up her dance with Joe Brown alone, and her appearance will get both the women and the men. That's the main thing they were talking about strolling out. Complimentary to the cameramen, too, the photography only spasmodically having that out-of-focus effect. Sound recording is good throughout.

First National hasn't anything to worry about in that it has Miss Miller tied up for the next four years. And you can bet her next picture will be better than this celluloid entree.

The main thing "Sally" lacks as a picture is Leon Errol. *Sid.*

DEVIL MAY CARE

(ALL DIALOG, With Songs)

Metro-Goldwyn-Mayer production and release. Ramon Novarro starred. Dorothy Jordan and Marion Harris featured. Directed by Sidney Franklin. Music by Herbert Stothart and lyrics by Clifford Grey. Dialog by Zelda Sears. Stage direction by Clifford Brooke. Scenario by Hans Kraly from the Richard Schayer adaptation of a French drama, "La Bataille Des Dames." Programed as musical romance. At Astor, New York, Dec. 22 (Sunday) at $2 top on twice daily run. Running time, 110 minutes.

Armand	Ramon Novarro
Leonie	Dorothy Jordan
Louise	Marion Harris
De Grignon	John Miljan
Napoleon	William Humphrey
Groom	George Davis
Gaston	Clifford Bruce

An average good talker in the better class of near-specials now being turned out and a very good product for its star, Ramon Novarro, but not a $2 film for any extended Broadway run, nor is it a hold over prospect in the regular houses. The qualification to the last two is if Novarro can draw $2 anywhere in sufficient numbers to make a decent run, which is doubtful in this picture and if his following is strong enough from the masses to anywhere equal a house record or draw enough to keep the picture for two weeks in one house, also doubted for the same reason.

The extra attraction in "Devil May Care" is the music by Herbert Stothart and a high grade of lyrics by Clifford Grey. Mr. Stothart has composed three of his four numbers for lilting notice anywhere. Especially is the march song melodious, as sung by a soldier mob and again by 50 horsemen while galloping into and out of sight as against the 20 Texan rangers with the "Ranger" song who got off their horses to sing it in "Rio Rita." While the "shoe" song here is attractive for its lyric and again for the smooth manner in which that has been built up for a real "number" in this comedy drama. The love song which may be called the theme song is also catchy.

An actual ensemble number in color is tried for in a brief scene, where the only kick in it has been lifted from Fox's "Sunny Side Up." That is the bit of the girls dancing at the water's edge with their shadows inverted under the water and the fountained curtain for the finish of it. Color here is too briefly shown to be of any value and it is the single time color is employed. Color's maker is not named.

Direction goes in fits and starts but mainly well executed. Particularly does the picture start fast with a well handled crowd of Napoleon's guards singing him fare-well as he departs for Elba. This beginning is too swift for much of the slower mush stuff later between the young couple and others. While the cutting goes along with no visible mar, there could have been quite some more for better speed. This may be accomplished when cuting down for the regular houses. Some of the warlike action recalls the meller-dramas of the old days. A ⁝uelling bit in a bedroom is a painful part of this.

Novarro sings well, with an accent, the only accent of this French-character cast. He is also singing the four numbers. Novarro sang "The Pagan Love Song" only in "The Pagan." He handles the well written dialog nicely, and Zelda Sears has written commendable dialog of a different nature throughout. Though she did supply Marion Harris with an over-supply of the same quality talk, all aimed to let the audience and world know Miss Harris' heart had gone bust, because Ramon loved another gal. That did not surprise the audience as much as it did Miss Harris.

Miss Harris may have been cast for this picture to help work out a contract. She seemed in a strange role for this popular song singer and had but one song which wasn't and won't be popular. Her make up looked odd, although perhaps that was in the Napoleonic period. period.

Casting excellent otherwise, with Dorothy Jordan having a large and playing part. The girl handled it capably, considering that Novarro was always walking into her bedroom either when she was asleep or awake. Nothing developed in the bedroom scene excepting most of the plot and Novarro picking up Miss Jordan in her night clothes. When she ran away after he had taken her out of another bedroom, she still had her bedroom clothes on. The final view was the couple seated alongside a lake late at night, side by side, and the girl still lightly enough dressed to have caught plenty of pneumonia.

John Miljan and Clifford Bruce ﬁt their roles without exertion and if William Humphrey isn't the Napoleon others have been, his Napoleon is just as good.

Comedy is had through situations and dialog, mostly the latter and Novarro's light comedy style in talk and action. One of the best scenes and with a laugh brought about by dialog is Novarro again at the bedroom door, but this time the girl won't let him in. He kissed her that afternoon when they were out riding and she thought him the butler. Miss Jordan got the b[illegible] on this scene. It was a tough one for any girl to juggle.

In story Novarro is a Napoleon follower, condemned to martial death by King Louis for conspiracy against the throne. Escaping when before the firing squad by a ruse, Novarro accidentally runs into Miss Jordan's bedroom, is given up by her to the soldiers because he's for Napoleon, and the devil may care lad becomes the butler or first asst. but in the home of a Countess friend, to which same home the same girl later goes as a guest.

Some nice photography and some better bits here and there without any novelty. Novarro picture all of the way, for a front rank juvenile and actor, whose singing voice is not unlike Maurice Chevalier's. Perhaps it's the accent.

Sime.

THE VIRGINIAN

(ALL DIALOG)

Paramount production and release. Directed by Victor Fleming. From the story by Owen Wister and Kirk La Shelle, adapted by Howard Estabrook. At the Rialto beginning Dec. 20, on grind run. Running time, 92 minutes.

The Virginian	Gary Cooper
Trampas	Walter Huston
Steve	Richard Arlen
Molly Wood	Mary Brian
Uncle Hughey	Chester Conklin
Honey Wiggin	Eugene Pallette
Judge Henry	E. H. Calvert
"Ma" Taylor	Helen Ware
Nebraskey	Victor Potel
Shotty	Tex Young
Pedro	Charles Stevens

"The Virginian" proves that with the right material properly handled sound turns the knell for westerns into one of animation. This Paramount production takes the old play dirt of ancient plains pictures, shuffles it around a bit, and, with the studio mind fully concentrated, makes of the Wister and La Shelle story 92 minutes of projection, superbly combining drama and comedy. It will be an outstanding money maker during 1930. This goes for any theatre that shows it, because "The Virginian" is truly a nugget of rare entertainment.

Victor Fleming has done a great directorial job, preserved in the cutting room. Although there are laughs throughout unanimous in their spontaneity, the audience is never permitted to forget that it is things dramatic which are underlying. The laughs are simply necessary comedy relief from situations so tense that the audience cannot resist that feeling of rigidity.

An ante-climax toward the middle, one of the most harrowing and vivid sequences ever before the lense. It is when the silent and lanky Virginian is forced to give the signal which sends his pal, Steve, along with three other cattle rustlers, galloping to their death in nooses. Close-ups of the adjusting of the ropes are followed by the sudden swishing of tails before the rear hoofs plunge forward.

Trampas, the menace, and proven as such during the first 10 minutes when he is restrained by the Virginian from assaulting the barmaid, is saved from the hanging to bait along the story for the vengeance climax at the picture's close.

That's the theme idea, one that has been used hundreds of times by indies in the silent days for grind consumption.

But the indies slap-banged away while Paramount, as "The Virginian" substantiates, regarded the theme in a serious and thoughtful manner. No all-shooting with some patched-in comedy and the organization didn't pad nothing into less.

The school mam, played by the pretty Mary Brian, didn't fly at the neck of the tall backwoodsman. She teased him, letting him use the old gag of rescuing her from a frightened cow and then promptly bawling him out. This provided Gary Cooper, in a style that is one of the reasons why the entire production is that way, with a chance for a bit of byplay and wise-cracking with Richard Arlen as a sincere but out-for-easy-dough Steve.

And the village folk gathered to fete the new teacher, just as in hundreds of this western's predecessors. But here it is also a christening and the boys had to change the babies so that the Virginian could walk the tutor home.

Even the cowboy bathing gag, as old as Hollywood, got a maximum of laughs; not just the gag itself but the manner in which it was wedged in.

Returning to the old barroom after the Virginian has been shot in the back hunting for Trampas, is recovered, and has the gun oiled once more. Then the menace appears and orders the hero out of town by sunset.

It's all that way. The same old story stuff, but made brand new by Paramount. All the fans know what is going to happen and yet they don't. This goes even when the Virginian, stalking the town for Trampas, is shot at, returns three shots for a perfect target and takes his little teacher farther west.

Waly.

THE KIBITZER

(ALL DIALOG)

Paramount production and release. Featuring Harry Green. From the stage play of the same name by Jo Swerling and Edward G. Robinson; adapted by Sam Mintz and Viola Brothers Shore. Directed by Edward Sloman. Marion Diz, Scenarie. Alfred Gulick, photographer. At Paramount, New York, week Dec. 20. Running time, 77 minutes.

Ike Lazarus (the kibitzer)	Harry Green
Josie Lazarus	Mary Brian
Eddie Brown	Neil Hamilton
Bert	David Newell
Yankel	Lee Kohlmar
Kikspoupolos	Henry Fink
Meyer	Tener Holtz
McGinty	Guy Oliver
James Livingston	Albert Gran
Phillips	Eddie Kane

Should kibitz through the first runs to moderate grosses, on strength of its timely stock market theme, well travestied, and accompanying laughs. Stage angle may mean something; play having done fairly well in New York, Chicago and the Coast.

While the screen treatment of the stage script may have been expected to result in variations from the original, it doesn't happen to be the case here, though considerable liberties were taken in elaborating and drawing out the primary continuity. All of which combines to provide a good many extraneous and ambiguous shots, hardly necessary to the plot, as the scenario sticks pretty close to the play in directing and centering entire action around one character; the kibitzer. Holding on to that was okay, as it probably couldn't have been done otherwise, without hurting the story proper, but injecting a lot of atmospheric sequences that have no bearing actually did squelch the picture a good deal. As a result the 77 minutes it runs is too long, with several dull and draggy moments that might have been eliminated by judicious cutting. No fault of the director, who evidently took pains not to deviate too much from the original script, and yet had screen proportions of the story in mind. In silent version this may have proved acceptable, but not where dialog holds together everything.

For Harry Green, former vaude comic, and who since has contributed some excellent bits and roles on the Paramount lot, this picture will doubtless mean something. Besides projecting him in his first featured work it serves to accentuate not so much what he does with the lead here, but what he could do in specially prepared roles along Yiddish lines in the future. With "The Kibitzer" fitting right into his knapsack, Green walks away with all honors.

Story is of the proverbial annoyer who dishes out advice to others while never participating in anything himself. Through coincidence of mistaken identity in a young man who is after his daughter, Lazarus, the kibitzer, falls heir to a block of stock with free rein to dispose of it at his judgment.

A sudden upheaval in the poor storekeeper's life naturally follows. Installing a ticker in his store he lets business go hang and can think of nothing but anticipated profits.

Daughter is in love with a good but poor boy who loses his life's savings on a horse race through a tip by Lazarus. But the old man alibis himself by saying the boy shouldn't have heeded him. The way he previously dopes the losing nag should be a howl. Every horse, says Lazarus, must win at least one race in his career. This one hasn't come in yet in 59 starts, but is being retired after this particular race, so by the old man's consensus he can't miss. That the nag does, and by a mile, is another story.

Climax is when Lazarus's stock goes into action and from a rise of nine points suddenly drops and wipes everything out. Surrounded by cajoling friends and other kibitzers, Lazarus is suddenly confronted with the millionaire who gave him the stock, who congratulates him on selling to a $39,000 profit before it was too late. Then it's discovered that Lazarus's half wit brother did it by answering a phone call from the broker with "Yes, sure, certainly," the only English he knew.

Rest of the cast is substantial enough with little to do. Mary Brian, whom Paramount has been giving a big play of late, is demure and charming as the daughter. Neil Hamilton also acceptable as her lover.

Eddie Kane (Kane and Herman) has just a whiff of a bit in this, but good. Kane and Henry Fink, both vaudevillains, handle dialog in true fashion and photograph well.

Span.

Girl From Woolworth's

(ALL DIALOG, with Songs)

First National production and release. Alice White featured in screen credit, but starred in Strand's advertising. Charles Delaney underlined. Directed by William Beaudine from Adele Comandini's story. Dialog by Richard Weil and E. Luddy; music and lyrics by Al Bryan and George Meyer. Cameraman, Jackson Rose. Supervised by Ray Rockett. At Strand, New York, week Dec. 20. Running time, 6[illegible] mins.

Pat King	Alice White
Bill Harrigan	Charles Delaney
Lawrence Mayfield	Wheeler Oakman
Tillie Hart	Rita Flynn

Nice program picture with the title and the Alice White name composing the draw. Inside the dialog, Charles Delaney, Rita Flynn, and a melody which sounds as if it had a chance will be found all important.

This picture may turn out to be a working girl's delight, that going for the boys, too. Reason is that the dialog is strictly according to the film's title. Couched in tenement style, the flaps and jellies can't muff it, and as delivered by Miss Flynn and Delaney, it's not only naive, but at times plenty funny. And this Flynn girl: oke on looks with a great sense of delivery for droll comedy. Maybe a future Helen Broderick. Pretty close to being her picture, as Delaney is the only rival in this respect.

Miss White can't take bows on this one. Warbles a couple of songs fairly, but if she's going to continue to lead dance numbers something ought to be done about it. Not much doubt that Miss White is restricted to this type of story, and if that's the case a stitch in time would be constant vocal and terpsichore coaching, mostly the latter in lieu of what the bunch has found out they can do with a microphone.

To have had less well-fitting dialog "Girl from Woolworth's" might easily have become one of those things. An example of taking an ordinary story and building it into something via writers and cast. Not an expensive picture, the flash end being a cabaret set and the usual numbers. Mention of the cabaret added to the film's title tells the whole scenario, even unto the cafe proprietor as the on the make menace.

Feature is constantly on the move, a feather for Beaudine, while the crossfire between Miss Flynn, Delaney and Miss White holds laughs. Opens with Miss White turning on the chill for Delaney at a flat party while her sidekick, Miss Flynn, is ready to give in after one flash at the sax playing subway guard. That Delaney must fall for the Harlem Carmen isn't always going to be the way audiences would have it, due to Miss Flynn's sympathetic assignment and the manner in which she plays it. But that takes the edge off Miss White more than the picture. By the time the latter gets through trying to impress the other half of the love interest with her importance, and he, in turn, has dutifully registered his indifference, they're both well on their way to a license. Girl's acceptance of the cabaret job brings about the threatened split-up.

Ditty which sounds as if it may mean something is "What I Know About Love," sent in by Miss White and not badly, although further tutoring in putting over these pops will help. Wheeler Oakman does excellently by the heavy, but the dialog writers can be designated the outstanding factor; also Beaudine, who probably had a hand in it somewhere. Release is Ray Rockett's supervising swan song to FN.

It's trashy and snappy, a combination which doesn't often miss for business, no matter how the intellectuals shudder. And keep an eye on that Flynn person. *Sid.*

Nosferatu the Vampire

(GERMAN MADE)
(Silent)

Parana production. Film Arts Guild release. Directed by F. W. Murnau. Titles by Benjamin de Casseress. Cast includes Max Schreck, Alexander Granach, Gustave Wagenheim, Greta Schroder, Karl Schnell and Ruth Landshoft. At the Film Guild, New York, week Dec. 14. Running time, 70 minutes.

Skillfully mounted and directed, this symbolical legendary cinema story of reanimated ghosts in a period set about a century or so ago when vampirism was pretty well entrenched in the world's beliefs, is a depressive piece of art made even more incompatible for bourgeoise theatre fare because of misspotted and poor titling. Latter lends the film more than one confusing moment and therefore it is a risky exhibit for the sure seaters too—although the artistic quality of settings and direction command consideration, this and Murnau's work leaving the question open whether this film was made long ago or lately.

Story is claimed to have been inspired by "Dracula." Whether the play or the book not told. Bram Stokes authored the novel more than 20 years ago and the play which was based on it, written by Hamilton Dean and John Balderson, produced on Broadway by Horace Liveright in October, 1927.

Like the play the picture is a shivery melo spilling ghostlike impossibilities from beginning to end. Action details the forages of a nobleman who is dead yet alive, making night time raids on human beings and compelling them to become subservient to him by sucking the blood from their necks, often plaguing them to death. His especial delight is a pretty woman.

Murnau proved his directorial artistry in "Sunrise" for Fox about three years ago, but in this picture he's a master artisan demonstrating not only a knowledge of the subtler side of directing but in photography.

One shot of the sun cracking at dawn is an eye filler. Among others of extremely imaginative beauty is one which takes in a schooner sailing in a rippling stream photographed in such a manner that it has the illusion of color and an enigmatic weirdness that's more perplexing than the ghost action of the players.

His funeral scene in the deserted town street where the bodies of the plague victims are carried in coffins held aloft by straggling pallbearers is unusual to say the least. Empty shattering buildings photographed to suggest the desperate desolation brought on by the vampire is extremely effective symbolism.

Max Schreck as the vampire is an able pantomimist and works clocklike, his makeup suggesting everything that's goose pimply. He did his worst on every occasion—which was good.

OH YEAH!

(ALL DIALOG)

Pathe production and release. From story "No Brakes," by A. W. Somerville. Adapted and directed by Tay Garnett. Dialog by James Gleason. Cameraman, Arthur Miller. James Gleason and Robert Armstrong featured. Music by George Green and George Waggner. "Love Found Me When I Found You," theme song. RCA Photophone sounded. At 55th St., New York, three days, Dec. 18-20. Running time, 74 minutes.

Dude....................Robert Armstrong
Dusty....................James Gleason
Pinkie....................Patricia Caron
The Elk....................Zasu Pitts
Pop Eye....................Bud Fine
Hot Foot....................Frank Hagney
Splinters....................Harry Tyler
Superintendent....................Paul Hurst

"Oh, Yeah!" is now a picture with a series of situations made plausible by dialog. Looks very much like Tay Garnett missed an opportunity to shoot action into this one that would make it cohesive and active. Only dramatic action that filters through is a fist fight or two where the two weaker brethren smack over a couple of bigger and tougher looking hombres in a way that makes a guy feel ashamed he's over six-feet tall. James Gleason wrote the dialog as well as acted in one of the principal roles. To him belongs the credit of saving the film from an altogether negative possibility. His gags provide laughs that make the film fair meat for neighborhood houses.

Couldn't go better for several reasons. Main one is that story is presented too weakly.

"Love Found Me When I Found You," theme song, is pleasant but mild, and Armstrong's singing of it in one sequence is nothing to make it sure fire.

In technique, picture suffers from too many chatter scenes between Gleason and Armstrong. Former shows up well as film actor, although the brown derby should go to ZaSu Pitts for the role of the soft speaking, dumb acting camp waitress. Patricia Caron as the heroine, while new to pictures as Gleason is, tramps off evenly but she must not be confused with Pauline Garon, diminutive blonde.

Photographically the film is well done and has a teasing shot or two that carries the warmth of the outdoors where most of story takes place. Recording is okay except in spots where difficulty is probably more likely due to actors' enunciation than equipment.

Story is tale of two boomer brakemen played by Gleason and Armstrong. They land in one of those interior railroad centres that dot the west and land a job with the super by proving their physical prowess over a guy who tried to hang the crook tag to them.

Pair have been bumming together for years. When Armstrong meets the paymaster, commissary chief and general factotum of the camp, a girl named Pinkie, he reforms and gets set to give up hitting the road. His pal goes likewise for The Elk, the dumb waitress.

Armstrong loses his roll in a crap game and gets jobbed for a theft he didn't commit. It upsets the romance of the pair only to become ironed out when the two bums accidentally hit upon the real crooks on a runaway gondola.

SHANNONS OF B'WAY

(ALL DIALOG—With Songs)

Universal production and release, starring James and Lucile Gleason, who created piece on stage. Directed by Emmett Flynn. Adaptation of stage play by Agnes Johnston. Cameraman, Jerry Ash. At the Colony, N. Y., week of Dec. 20. Running time, 65 mins.

Mickey Shannon....................James Gleason
Emma Shannon....................Lucile Gleason
Swanzey....................Charles Grapewin
Tessie....................Mary Philbin
Chuck....................John Breeden
Bradford....................Tom Santschi
Eddie Allen....................Harry Tyler
Alice Allen....................Gladys Crolius
Minerva....................Helen Mehrmann
Albee....................Robert T. Haines
Newt....................Slim Summerville
Burt....................Tom Kennedy
Hez....................Walter Brennan

"Shannons of Broadway" loses a good deal in its translation to the screen, but even at that it makes first rate entertainment. Production is directed mechanically, and settings are not well done, but even mediocre studio technique does not blur innate humanness of the Gleason play of a vaudeville couple who are hicks on the surface but a loveable pair at heart. Figures to do fair business.

Screen has done nothing to enhance the original while much that carried weight in the play has been lost in the shadow transcription, the result of uninspired direction. The Gleasons in their old parts have none of the flicker tricks, playing the roles as they would before the footlights. Performance in consequence is of rather too fine—in the sense of subdued quiet—a quality.

Story should have been a comedy natural if it had been heightened with Hollywood's usual resourcefulness in gagging and elaboration of settings. As revealed here it is no more than a good program picture, plus the value of the play's Broadway success and the prestige of the Gleasons' name, whatever that may mean in pictures.

Script needed pointing and dressing for the screen. It is without the sprightly background of most back stage stories, depending upon the subdued humor of the character sketches. Job of the adapter and director should have been to translate these elements into screen values as was done with "Broadway," also by Universal, and a much better bit of work.

Lacking the elaborate setting, director has concentrated on the brisk comedy of the characterizations, the punch of surprise gag lines, and the singing, dancing and musical specialty of the vaudeville pair, all of which go to keep it alive for the necessary 65 minutes.

Film has nothing but the principal pair, subordinate characters being extremely subordinate. Mary Philbin is the usual ingenue and plays it trimly as always. Charles Grapewin, likewise does splendidly with a bit, and John Breeden looks the manly juvenile with little to do. Outside of the Gleasons nobody had much of a chance to shine. Cameraman did no better than so-so with his photography, although there was not much to spread on in the main scene of a country hotel lobby.

Finish, with the pair returning to the stage in an elaborate revue act produced out of their real estate winnings, makes a capital finis to the story, the only touch of the splurge that should have been better emphasized all the way. *Rush.*

MYSTERIOUS ISLAND

(COLOR, 90%; DIALOG, 5%)

M-G-M production and release. Adapted and directed by Lucien Hubbard from story of the same title by Jules Verne. Photographed by Percy Hillburn. Musical score (synchronized) by Broones and Lange. In Technicolor, 90%. At the Capitol, New York, Dec. 20. Running time, 95 minutes.

Dakkar....................Lionel Barrymore
Sonia....................Jane Daly
Nikolai....................Lloyd Hughes
Falon....................Montagu Love
Mikhail....................Harry Gribbon
Anton....................Snitz Edwards
Dmitry....................Gibson Gowland
Teresa....................Dolores Brinkman

Based on a story by Jules Verne, who dreamed fantastic and imaginatively described devices later to materialize, this picture, of necessity, is weird and greatly at variance with both logic and history. But its impressiveness and unusualness are unquestioned, and therein rest its box office possibilities. It should draw fair grosses, with the advantage of being suited to revivals and showing in the art theatres after its original field has been exhausted.

There is a steep production cost to overcome. Shot almost completely in Technicolor, with a wealth of special sets, costumes, mechanical devices and elaborate miniatures. Picture is reported to have been two years in the making, probably on the shelf most of that time.

Where foreign distribution is not ruined by politics, there are further gross possibilities. And with only a few minutes of opening dialog, conversion to foreign understanding is easily accomplished.

Aside from the continual novelty of scenes, performance of Lionel Barrymore as the inventive genius is predominant. He never fails to hold tense interest, from the moment he explains his mechanical creations to the time he demands to be buried alive in his one remaining submarine. It is a powerful yet perfectly toned role. Lloyd Hughes and Jane Daly as the love interest supply an attractive background.

Barrymore plays Count Dakkar, who on his island off the mainland supervises construction of two submarines many years before they became historic realities. Falon, also a noble, is anxious to secure the throne by revolution and believes Dakkar's inventive genius will aid him. Failing to secure the inventor's assistance by pleas, he captures Dakka and his island crew while Dakka's assistant is below the sea testing one of the submarines. Men in the submarine later rescue Dakka from torture but cannot find his sister, with whom Falon is in love. As they are preparing to submerge again, Falon's men turn cannons on the submarine, sending it to the bottom helpless though still watertight in certain compartments.

At the bottom, Dakka and his men look out upon an underground city, populated with repulsive creatures somewhat resembling men. By slaying a huge dragon with torpedoes, they win the people's gratitude and prepare for a short period of investigation in diving suits before dying for lack of air.

Dakka's sister, meanwhile, has hidden in a duplicate submarine on the island and is about to flee with a few crew members when Falon and several of his men enter the ship. The girl cripples the submarine by hurling a bomb at its key mechanism, and the ship sinks alongside the other one.

There is a short battle undersea between Falon's and Dakka's men, with Falon killed. Warm blood stirs the undersea people to [illegible]ist. They attempt to kill all the humans by sicing a huge octopus on them. Dakka is fatally crushed, but lives to be brought to the surface by his assistant and the sister, who fix one submarine with a part from the other. Then when his island is recaptured from Falon's remaining men and his sister is safe in the arms of his young assistant, Dakka voluntarily goes down in his submarine to a living burial.

Lucien Hubbard's handling of mob scenes and individual performances is excellent. His finished product would have been greatly benefited by stricter cutting. There are several intervals causing 95 minutes to be obviously too many. Photography by Percy Hilburn is skilled craftsmanship. Shots of mobs, sets and miniatures are always impressive.

Technicolor is used except in underwater sequences. Musical score is synchronized to act throughout as emotional stimulant. Dialog for five minutes to set the story at the start.

Disclosure of the submarine, radio and harnessed electricity as ancient history may gall some sticklers. But blame that on Verne. *Bang.*

MEISTERSINGER

(GERMAN MADE)
(Silent)

Produced by Phoebus Films. Released by Moviegraphs, Inc. Based on Richard Wagner opera of same name. Original film title is "Der Meister von Nurenberg." Directed by Ludwig Berger. Photographed by Carl Puth and A. Graatkjer. Architect, R. Bamberger. Cast includes Rudolf Rittner, Max Guelstorf, Maria Solveg, Gustav Froehlich, Julius Falkenstein, Veit Harlan, Else Wagner and Hans Wassman. At 55th St., New York, week Dec. 14. Running time, 82 minutes.

It's a job to plant an operatic ideal into silent films and still retain dramatic harmony. In this picture though the producers attempted a sincere effort they failed in transposition endeavors to carry over the imaginative qualities of the Wagnerian opera that takes a light, sensitive theme and with music transforms it into a tingling, soulful masterpiece.

The picture is flat even for the sure-seaters. With the music of the opera deleted the story becomes blunt, sombre, humorless and naive.

Cast okay and action is carried out with good directorial effort, but the soul of the drama is missing. It lies in the music.

In present state it's neither spectacle nor worthwhile theatre fare.

Only ray is Maria Solveg, as the girl. She is keen and a good player, and her bright complexion coupled by the fact that she wore a light costume throughout the film, in contrast to the scowling, scheming, black countenances of the rest of the cast in their black outfits.

The villain wore tortoise shell glasses of a 1930 make.

Beyond this it may be said for Director Berger that he produced some fine acting and especially detail with the mob scenes.

COURTIN' WILDCATS

(ALL DIALOG)

Universal production and release. W. E. recorded. Directed by Jerome Storm. Story by William Dudley Pelley. Cast includes Hoot Gibson, Eugenia Gilbert, Harry Todd, Joseph Girard, Monty Montague, John Oscar, Jim Corey, James Farley, Pete Morrison, Joe Bonomo. At Loew's New York, one day, Dec. 17, one half double bill. Running time, 56 minutes.

This is good example of how talker stuff has changed old line westerns, until only thing resembling the silent pancakers ground out in the pre-dialog days are the horses, and if their neighs could be recorded even they might be different. Yet picture must be classed in old style —with talk. And on such basis makes fitting opera for the deserted western fans. It's got several laughs, brief broncho-busting episode, auto race, two-gun heroine and a finish that tickles.

Hoot Gibson is a book worm college boy, son of wealthy foundry owner. Papa wants to put him into foundry to help build him up physically, and son balks. So, with aid of family doctor, boy is farmed to friend owning wild west, and the kid is a howl. He saves the leading lady, who's the toughest hombre in

the outfit, from the police for shooting her father's enemy—and then marries her.

Dialog's okay. Recording good and photography in approved manner.

HIS FIRST COMMAND

(ALL DIALOG)

Pathe production and release. Directed by Gregory LaCava, also credited with dialog. William Boyd, Dorothy Sebastian featured. RCA sound recording. At the Hippodrome, N. Y., week of Dec. 21. Running time, 65 minutes.

Terry Culver...............William Boyd
Judy Gaylord............Dorothy Sebastian
Lieut. Allen................Gavin Gordon
Jane.......................Helen Parrish
Col. Gaylord.............Alphonz Ethier
Major Hall..............Howard Hickman
Sergeant Westbrook...........Paul Hurst
Corporal Jones...............Jules Cowles
Mrs. Pike...................Rose Tapley
Mrs. Sargent..........Mabel Van Buren
Homer.....................Charles Moore

Folks who never were in the army won't be the wiser that anyone acting like Terry Culver would be automatically slapped into the brig. The Hollywood version would end too abruptly if army regulations were known out there. So, young Terry is able to sneer and wisecrack at officers until he gets a commission himself, after which he simply marries the Colonel's daughter. Well enough knit to run smoothly and be considered a good program picture by the masses.

William Boyd is called upon to do a Haines and he accomplishes it with poise. Dorothy Sebastian plays right along with him as Judy, daughter of the Commandant. Paul Hurst does a tough sergeant. As Westbrook he is as good as the script and direction permit him to be. Had this non-com been allowed to take a sock at the wisecracking hero, the picture would have gained far more realism than even the color guard in one colored sequence.

Average audience will find plenty of laughs in the dialog, all inspired by Private Terry's deliberate blundering. Saluting a post as part of his lesson in army etiquette rates the most hilarity.

Steeplechase is given a new twist for a thrill, despite the obviousness of tiny Jane taking a spill just before pounding horses reach the final barrier. Terry, of course, rescues the child to come back with an arm in a sling and a commission.

Off screen scrap between a lieut. and Terry earlier in the footage is well handled for suspense. *Waly.*

CHRISTINA

(20% DIALOG)
(2d Review)

Fox's "Christina" is at the Roxy, New York, this week (Dec. 20) with a 17-minute dialog finish, more than seven months after a $2 run without talk at the Gaiety.

Question of taste as to whether the verbal ending improves the film dramatically, but that it increases "Christina's" sales value to exhibs and audiences is hardly to be doubted. A dialog line in "Christina's" billing is unquestionably better present than absent.

Oddly enough, because of the talk, "Christina" in its pop grind at the Roxy is about eight minutes longer than when a two-a-daying at the Gaiety, where it ran 75 minutes. Little change noted in the action in the switch from silence to talk, but the actual speaking consumes the extra time.

Sudden insertion of talk after more than an hour minus dialog brought the audience up with a start and tittering resulted when picture was caught at the Roxy. Silence is broken without warning when, in the story, Christina returns to her home after being tricked into believing her wounded sweetheart is

drunk. From then on until the unchanged ending, all is chatter.

The talkers are Janet Gaynor, Charles Morton, Rudolph Schildkraut, Harry Cording and an unbilled woman in a landlady role. Miss Gaynor has proved herself vocally before and does as well herein. Schildkraut as an eminent stage player needs no comment as to his voice. It records well. Morton talking is remindful of Charlie Farrell, whom he resembles in other ways. *Bige.*

DARK SKIES

(ALL DIALOG, with Songs)

Biltmore production. Released by Capitol Film Co. Directed by Harry S. Webb. Story by John Francis Nateford. Recorded by Telefilm. In cast: Shirley Mason, Wallace McDonald, William V. Mong, Tom O'Brien, Josef Swickard. At Loew's New York, one day, Dec. 10, one half double bill. Running time, 68 minutes.

Pretty tough on the exhib if he's gotta consider this. In making the producers doped it up plenty. Everything, from hula-hula dancing, rum running, Chinese dancing girls, Mexican greaser, and U. S. Navy—so it's got nothing. Story still hash.

Singing toward close by hero wouldn't fit in Harlem night club but that evidently makes no diff, because next to the exhib the guys who suffer most are the fans.

Opens in smirky California fishing village. Few minutes later same village is fashionable Riviera. Rum running Mexican hero meets girl by knocking her down in a big city where she goes for no good reason. Six months later the two meet again in casual intimacy in the village. Little later picture explains girl is innocent maid but uncle lashes her just the same.

And as choppy as this explanation sounds in print, just as choppy are the sequences in the film.

With Car and Camera Around the World

(Silent)

Travelog produced by Aloha Wanderwell. At 5th Avenue Playhouse week Nov. 14. Running time, 66 minutes.

Purely geographical. Cut down would make an interesting short if sounded, but in present shape doesn't mean a thing for box office. Mrs. Wanderwell, accompanied by her husband and two children, covered more than 100,000 miles over a period of 10 years in filming these scenes.

Apparently the sequences were completed about seven or eight years ago. Starting out from France, Mrs. Wanderwell cameraed the European continent, covering topographical and character features, then proceeded to the Orient. Traversing over every principal city through Japan and China, the expeditionists gathered a lot of unique shots.

From the Orient, Mrs. Wanderwell traveled to Harbin, Manchuria, after photographing the Great Wall of China and flashing a peek at Peking. Harbin is the spot where Russia and China had their latest conflict. San Francisco is the next stop, showing landscape of the American coast town, with Hollywood appendixed in close-ups. From there to Miami during the hurricane there several years ago, getting some nifty clips of land and water. Cuba is next, then the jungles of Africa. Considerable time must have been spent by Mrs. Wanderwell in the wild animal regions, but aside from skimming the deserts and jungles no outstanding camera work of beasts. Last lap is Portu-

gal, wih its quaint customs and people.

Photography as a whole is poor. Here and there some shots display unusual color and effect, but it appears that Mrs. Wanderwell was handicapped a good deal by climatic conditions. *Span.*